WB 105 MAR

WB 105 MAR

ROSEN'S EMERGENCY MEDICINE

Volume 2

ROSEN'S
EMERGENCY MEDICINE
Concepts and Clinical Practice

sixth edition

Editor-in-Chief
John A. Marx, MD, FAAEM, FACEP
Chair and Chief
Department of Emergency Medicine
Carolinas Medical Center
Charlotte, North Carolina
Adjunct Professor
Department of Emergency
  Medicine
University of North Carolina
  School of Medicine
Chapel Hill, North Carolina

Senior Editors
Robert S. Hockberger, MD, FACEP, FAAEM
Chair
Department of Emergency
  Medicine
Harbor–UCLA Medical Center
Torrance, California
Professor of Clinical Medicine
David Geffen School of Medicine
  at UCLA
Westwood, Los Angeles, California

Ron M. Walls, MD, FAAEM, FACEP, FRCPC
Chair
Department of Emergency
  Medicine
Brigham and Women's Hospital
Associate Professor of Medicine
  (Emergency Medicine)
Harvard Medical School
Boston, Massachusetts

Editors
James G. Adams, MD, FACP, FACEP
Chair
Department of Emergency
  Medicine
Northwestern Memorial Hospital
Professor of Medicine
Northwestern University
  Feinberg School of Medicine
Chicago, Illinois

William G. Barsan, MD
Professor and Chair
Department of Emergency
  Medicine
University of Michigan
  Medical School
Ann Arbor, Michigan

Michelle H. Biros, MD, MS, FAAEM, FACEP
Research Director and Faculty
  Physician
Department of Emergency
  Medicine
Hennepin County Medical
  Center
Professor of Emergency Medicine
University of Minnesota
  Medical School
Minneapolis, Minnesota

Daniel F. Danzl, MD
Professor and Chair
Department of Emergency
  Medicine
University of Louisville School
  of Medicine
Louisville, Kentucky

Marianne Gausche-Hill, MD, FACEP, FAAP
Professor of Medicine
David Geffen School of Medicine
  at UCLA
Director of EMS and Pediatric
  Emergency Medicine Fellowship
Department of Emergency Medicine
Harbor–UCLA Medical Center
Torrance, California

Glenn C. Hamilton, MD, MSM
Professor and Chair
Department of Emergency Medicine
Wright State University School of
  Medicine
Dayton, Ohio

Louis J. Ling, MD, FACEP, FACMT
Professor of Emergency Medicine
  and Pharmacy
Associate Dean for Graduate
  Medical Education
University of Minnesota Medical
  School
Associate Medicine Director for
  Medical Education
Hennepin County Medical Center
Senior Associate Medical Director
Hennepin Regional Poison Center
Minneapolis, Minnesota

Edward J. Newton, MD, FACEP
Chair
Department of Emergency Medicine
Los Angeles County and University
  of Southern California Medical
  Center
Professor of Clinical Emergency
  Medicine
University of Southern California
  Keck School of Medicine
Los Angeles, California

MOSBY

ELSEVIER

MOSBY
ELSEVIER

1600 John F. Kennedy Boulevard, Suite 1800
Philadelphia, PA 19103-2899

ROSEN'S EMERGENCY MEDICINE: Concepts and Clinical Practice, 6th Edition
Three-Volume Set   0-323-02845-4
Online Edition   0-323-03686-4
E-dition   0-323-04302-X

Copyright © 2006, 2002, 1998, 1992, 1988, 1983 Mosby, Inc.

NOTICE

Knowledge and best practice in this field are constantly changing. As new research and experience broaden our knowledge, changes in practice, treatment and drug therapy may become necessary or appropriate. Readers are advised to check the most current information provided (i) on procedures featured or (ii) by the manufacturer of each product to be administered, to verify the recommended dose or formula, the method and duration of administration, and contraindications. It is the responsibility of the practitioner, relying on their own experience and knowledge of the patient, to make diagnoses, to determine dosages and the best treatment for each individual patient, and to take all appropriate safey precautions. To the fullest extent of the law, neither the Publisher nor the Editors and Authors assume any liability for any injury and/or damage to persons or property arising out of or related to any use of the material contained in this book.

Library of Congress Cataloging-in-Publication Data

Rosen's emergency medicine : concepts and clinical practice.—6th ed. / editor-in-chief,
    John A. Marx ; senior editors, Robert S. Hockberger, Ron M. Walls ; editors, James Adams . . .
    [et al.]
        p. ; cm.
    Includes bibliographical references and index.
    ISBN-13: 978–0–323–02845–5   ISBN-10: 0–323–02845–4
    1. Emergency medicine. I. Title: Emergency medicine. II. Marx, John A. III.
Hockberger, Robert S. IV. Walls, Ron M. V. Adams, James VI. Rosen, Peter Emergency
medicine.
    [DNLM: 1. Emergencies. 2. Emergency Medicine. WB 105 E555 2006]
    RC86.7.E5784 2006
    616.02'5—dc22   2005041694

ISBN-13: 978–0–323–02845–5
ISBN-10: 0–323–02845–4

Acquisitions Editor: Todd Hummel
Developmental Editor: Kimberly Cox
Publishing Services Manager: Frank Polizzano
Project Manager: Robin E. Hayward
Cover Design Direction: Steven Stave
Text Designer: Jayne Jones
Marketing Manager: Dana Butler

Printed in China

Last digit is the print number: 9   8   7   6   5   4   3   2

Contents

vi

Contents

Contents

PART THREE

Medicine
and Surgery

CHAPTER

69 Oral Medicine

James T. Amsterdam

PERSPECTIVE AND PRINCIPLES OF DISEASE

Anatomy

The stomatognathic system comprises the musculoskeletal unit of the mandible, maxilla, and muscles of mastication; the dental unit (teeth); the attachment apparatus that anchors teeth; and other soft tissues of the oral cavity.

Musculoskeletal Unit

The *mandible* is formed by two rami that divide into a horizontal and an ascending portion. The horizontal portion forms the body of the mandible. The ascending ramus divides into the coronoid process anteriorly and the condylar process posteriorly. The temporomandibular articulation is unique because it consists of a bilateral joint or diarthrosis between the mandibular fossa and articular eminence of the mandible's temporal bone and condyle (Figure 69-1). An intervening layer of fibrous connective tissue separates the articulating surfaces. A fibrous capsule also surrounds the temporomandibular joint (TMJ) and is reinforced by capsular ligaments that help limit mandibular range of motion. Functionally, when the mandible opens, the condyles move inferiorly and anteriorly down the eminence; during closure, the mandible moves posteriorly along the eminence and superiorly into the fossa.[2]

The muscles of mastication are divided into the mandibular elevators (the supramandibular group) and depressors (the inframandibular group). The elevators, or "masseteric sling," consist of the masseters, medial pterygoids, and temporalis. The posterosuperior movement of the condyle during mandibular closure is the result of bilateral, simultaneous movement of this group. The muscles involved in the opening or depression of the mandible include the lateral pterygoid, digastric, geniohyoid, and mylohyoid. Bilateral activity of these muscles results in opening; unilateral contraction causes the mandible to deviate to the opposite side. At rest, the mandible assumes a position in which the mandibular and maxillary teeth are separated by a few millimeters of space. During functional activity, mandibular closure occurs as the action of the elevators predominates.

Teeth

The *pulp* is the tooth's center and serves as its neurovascular supply. The primary purpose of the pulp is to provide sensation and to produce dentin, a microtubular structure that hydrates and cushions the tooth during mastication. The part of the tooth normally visible in the oral cavity is the *coronal portion* covered with enamel, the hardest substance in the body. The part that is not normally visible and anchors the tooth is called the *root*. The root is covered with cementum, which is much softer than enamel and not designed for exposure in the oral cavity (Figure 69-2).[2]

The normal primary or deciduous dentition consists of 10 mandibular and 10 maxillary teeth. The primary dentition is important for mastication, cosmesis, and growth and development and functions as a "physiologic space maintainer." Starting at the midline and moving posteriorly in any quadrant, the normal dentition consists of a central incisor, lateral incisor, canine, and two primary molars. The lower central incisor is the first tooth to erupt, at approximately 6 months of age; all primary teeth should be present by 3 years of age. If not, further investigation for developmental or endocrine abnormalities is warranted. The permanent dentition begins to erupt at approximately 5 to 6 years of age with the appearance of the first molar. Normally, the permanent dentition consists of 32 teeth: the central incisor, lateral incisor, canine, two premolars, and three molars. The third molars are the last to erupt, appearing at approximately 16 to 18 years of age, and are commonly called "wisdom teeth." The primary molars are replaced by the permanent premolars (Figure 69-3).[3]

There are many numbering systems for teeth, but none are universal. Perhaps the most common system for the permanent dentition consists of numbering the teeth from 1 to 32, starting with the upper right third molar (1) to the upper left third molar (16) to the lower left third molar (17) to the lower right third molar (32). Because there may be congenital absence of teeth or additional, supernumerary teeth, it is perhaps best for practitioners to describe anatomically which tooth is involved (e.g., the upper left second premolar or the lower right second molar).[2,4]

Specific terminology is used to describe aspects of dentition. The *labial* or *buccal surface* faces outside the oral cavity; the *oral, palatal,* or *lingual surface* faces the tongue; the *medial surface* is toward the midline; and the *distal surface* is toward the ramus of the mandible. The *interproximal surface* refers to the contacting area of adjacent teeth, and the *occlusal surface* refers to the biting area. Finally, *apical* is in the direction of the root, whereas *coronal* is toward the crown of the tooth.

Periodontium

The periodontium consists of the gingival unit and the attachment apparatus. The *gingiva* is covered with keratinized, stratified, squamous epithelium and invests the tooth and alveolar bone. Apical to the gingiva is the alveolar mucosa, which is covered by nonkeratinized epithelium and is more subject to trauma. In healthy individuals, the gingiva is attached firmly to the tooth by connective tissue fibers inserting into the cementum, extending coronally from the alveolar bone to the cementoenamel junction. A 2- to 3-mm cuff of tissue, the *gingival sulcus,* is bordered by the enamel surface of the tooth, the gingival epithelium, and the junctional epithelium at its base (see Figure 69-2). In a disease state, such as in the presence of the loss of alveolar bone, this cuff increases in depth and is called a "pocket."[2,5,6]

The *attachment apparatus* refers to the cementum on the tooth, the periodontal ligament, and the alveolar bone. The *periodontal ligament* is a fibrous structure that surrounds the root of the tooth. It is the key structure that anchors the tooth because it serves as a double periosteum that lays down cementum on the tooth on one side and alveolar bone on its other side.

Fascial Planes of the Head and Neck

The fascial planes of the head and neck are defined as potential spaces filled with loose areolar tissue that separates the layers of fascia of the head and neck. The deep cervical fascia is most important in a discussion of the extension of oral infection to the head and neck (Figure 69-4). The *deep cervical fascia* consists of the superficial and investing layer, the pretracheal layer, the prevertebral layer, and the carotid sheath. The superficial and investing layer surrounds the entire neck; it splits as it attaches to the inferior border of the internal pterygoid muscles at the mandible's ascending ramus. This split forms the masticator space. This space communicates superiorly above the level of the zygomatic arch with the superficial and deep temporal pouches.[7-9]

Other spaces of importance in the neck to which dental infection may spread include the *lateral pharyngeal* or *parapharyngeal space,* which is lateral to the pharynx and medial to the masticator space; the *retropharyngeal space,* which is between the deep cervical and prevertebral fascia; and the *prevertebral space,* which is posterior to the retropharyngeal space. The pharyngomaxillary space extends from the base of the skull to the hyoid bone and is especially important because it communicates with all deep spaces.

The mandible itself may be divided further. The *mylohyoid muscle* divides the superior sublingual and inferior submaxillary spaces.

Pathophysiology

Nontraumatic Dental Emergencies

Two pathophysiologic processes affect the dental health of most of the population: (1) dental caries and (2) periodontal disease. Variables related in both

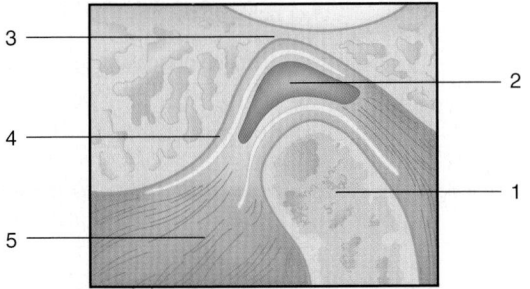

Figure 69-1. Temporomandibular joint structures in sagittal section: *1,* condyle; *2,* disk; *3,* mandibular (temporal-fossa); *4,* eminence; *5,* lateral pterygoid. (Redrawn and modified from Weisgold AS, et al: Dental medicine. In Kaye D, Rose LF [eds]: *Fundamentals of Internal Medicine.* St. Louis, Mosby, 1983.)

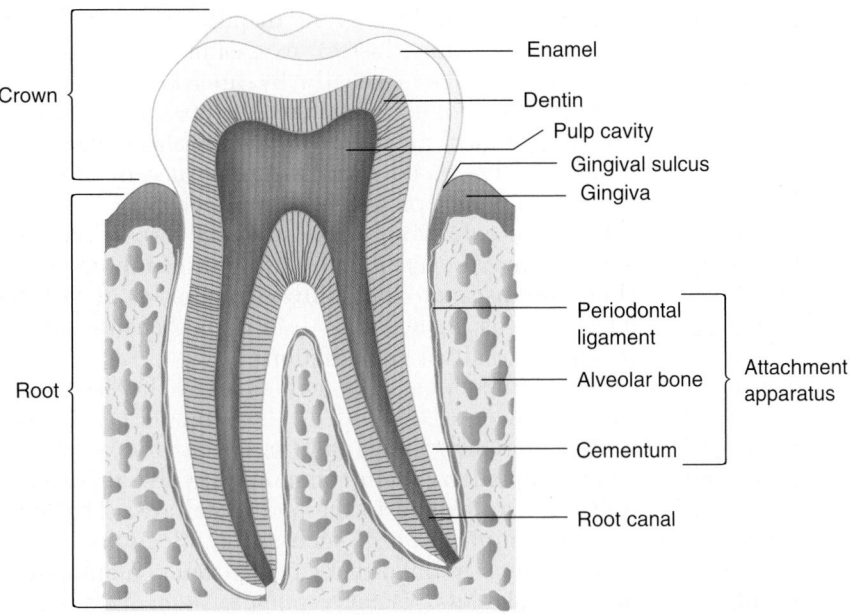

Figure 69-2. The dental anatomic unit and attachment apparatus.

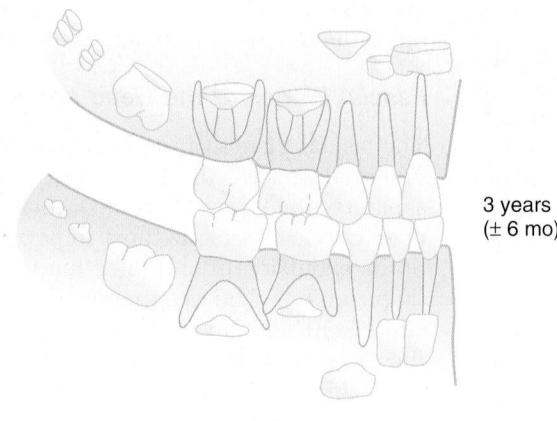

3 years
(± 6 mo)

Deciduous dentition

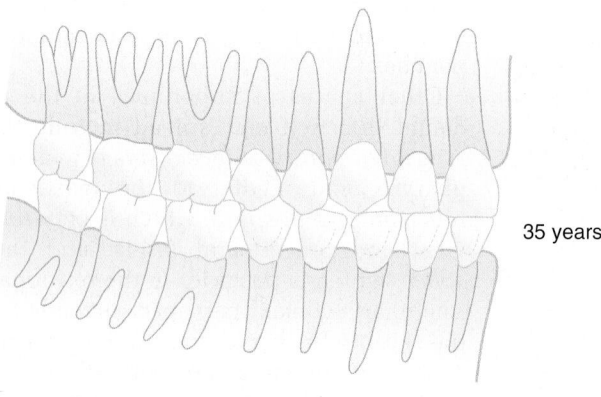

1 Upper right 3rd molar
2 Upper right 2nd molar
3 Upper right 1st molar
4 Upper right 2nd premolar
5 Upper right 1st premolar
6 Upper right canine
7 Lateral incisor
8 Central incisor
25 Lower right central incisor
26 Lower right lateral incisor
27 Lower right canine
28 Lower right 1st premolar
29 Lower right 2nd premolar
30 Lower right 1st molar
31 Lower right 2nd molar
32 Lower right 3rd molar

35 years

A   Permanent dentition

Figure 69-3. A, Numbering and naming of deciduous and permanent dentition on the right side. Tooth numbering is in the more conventional upper right third molar (1) to lower right third molar (32). *Continued*

disease states include the oral environment, consisting of the teeth, attachment apparatus, presence of local factors such as bacterial plaque and oral microflora, and substrate, and host states, including immunocompromised diseases and nutritional status. Factors such as water fluoridation, fluoride supplements, and plaque control techniques (e.g., flossing, brushing, and dental surgical procedures) have decreased significantly the prevalence of dental caries and periodontal disease.[10-12]

Dental Caries

Dental caries is a multifactorial disease involving a susceptible host, cariogenic oral flora, and a substrate. In 1890, it was proposed that caries resulted from the decalcification of enamel by the production of acids from bacteria.[8,9] In the presence of saliva and a carbohydrate, cariogenic oral flora are able to develop a matrix called *dental bacterial plaque*. The bacteria metabolize the carbohydrate to form acids that decalcify the enamel.[10] After the carious process has invaded the enamel, the microporous dentin is able to transmit saliva, byproducts of the bacteria, and the bacteria themselves to the pulp. The pulp initially reacts with a hyperemic response, which continues to an inflam-

matory state, progressing to total degeneration and necrosis.

Pus leaks from the apex of the root and forms an abscess; this is termed a *periapical abscess*. Periapical abscesses are confined within the alveolar bone (Figure 69-5). The abscess may break through the cortical plate of either the mandible or the maxilla and spread subperiosteally. Subperiosteal extensions are generally well confined anatomically by muscle attachments; however, if the muscle attachments are violated either during a surgical procedure or by the natural extension of an infective process, the bacteria can gain access to the fascial planes of the head and neck.[13-17]

Infection extending to the submaxillary, sublingual, and submental spaces with elevation of the tongue is called *Ludwig's angina*. Ludwig's angina is one of the most serious mandibular infections because of its potential for airway obstruction.

Space infections also may involve the face. The canine space is bounded by the orbicularis oris, the levator labii superioris, and the buccinator; abscessed anterior maxillary teeth commonly involve this space. Infection can extend to the periorbital area. The most serious complication of such space infections is cavernous sinus thrombosis resulting from contamination of the (valveless) facial venous system. The buccal

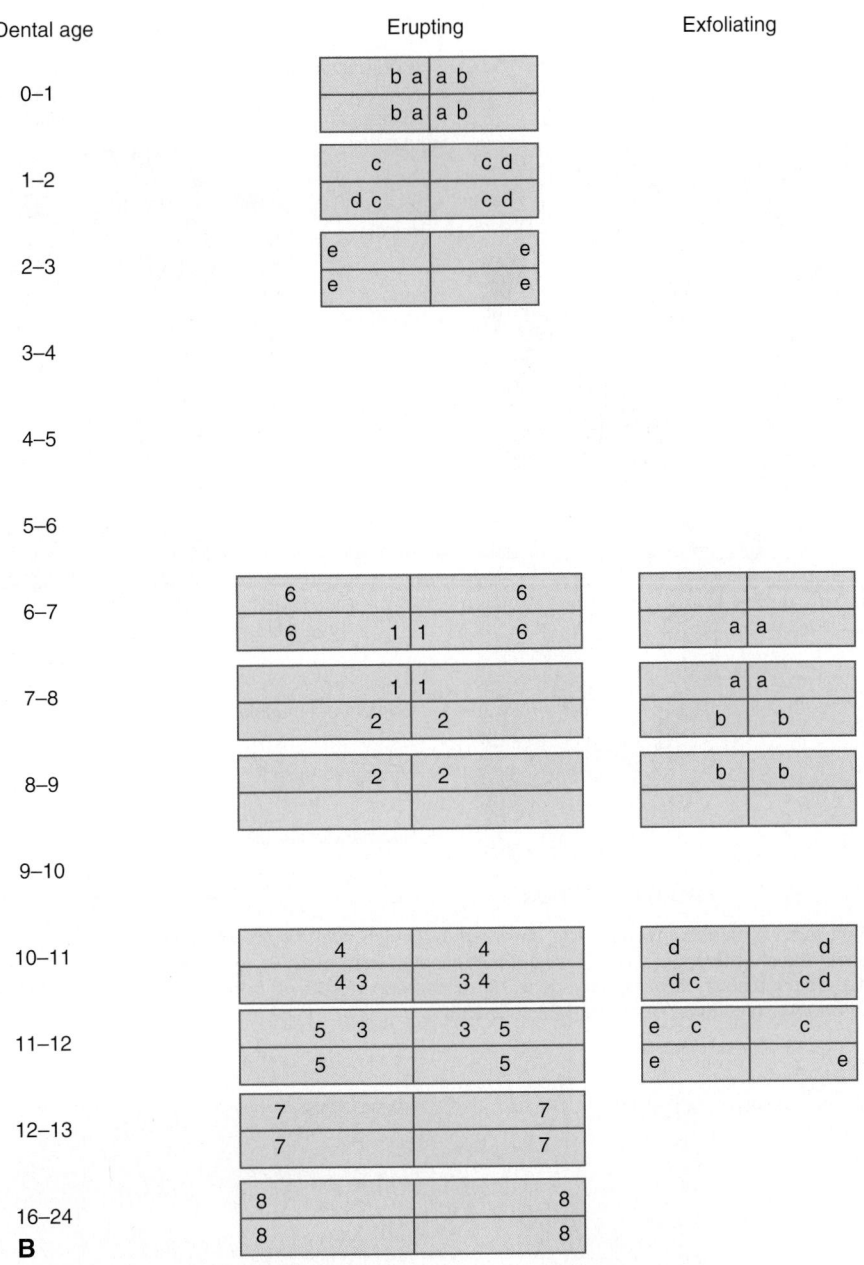

Dental age	Erupting	Exfoliating
0–1	b a a b / b a a b	
1–2	c / d c c d / c d	
2–3	e e / e e	
3–4		
4–5		
5–6		
6–7	6 6 / 6 1 1 6	a a
7–8	1 1 / 2 2	a a / b b
8–9	2 2	b b
9–10		
10–11	4 4 / 4 3 3 4	d d / d c c d
11–12	5 3 3 5 / 5 5	e c c / e e
12–13	7 7 / 7 7	
16–24	8 8 / 8 8	

B

Figure 69-3, cont'd. B, Most common pattern of dental development. *a-e,* Primary teeth; *1-8,* secondary permanent teeth. (**B** redrawn from Belanger GK, Casamassio PS: Dental emergencies. In Barkin R [ed]: *Pediatric Emergencies.* St. Louis, Mosby, 1987.)

space is superficial to the buccinator and limited by the anterior border of the masseter; maxillary molar infection commonly spreads to this space. The mental space is located at the anterior table of the mandible and often is infected by abscessed lower anterior teeth.[17]

CLINICAL FEATURES

Examination of the Oral Cavity

It is recommended that the examiner wear eye protection, a mask, and gloves for universal precautions when examining the oral cavity. Ideally the patient should be placed in a dental/ENT chair or on a cart at a 45-degree angle. Pediatric patients are not likely to cooperate with the examination; the following technique is used by some experienced practitioners. The child first should be placed in the parent's lap facing the parent. The examiner then sits in front of the parent. While the parent gently restrains the child's arms and legs, the emergency physician can lean the child backward and lock the child's head between the physician's legs.

An overhead examination light, headlight, or flashlight can be used for illumination. Other ancillary aids include a tongue depressor, 2 × 2 gauze, and possibly a dental mirror. To prevent the mirror from fogging, it should be warmed under hot water or a flame or moistened with the patient's saliva.

Examination of the oral cavity should be systematic, beginning with the soft tissues, including the tongue. The base of the tongue is examined for lesions, and

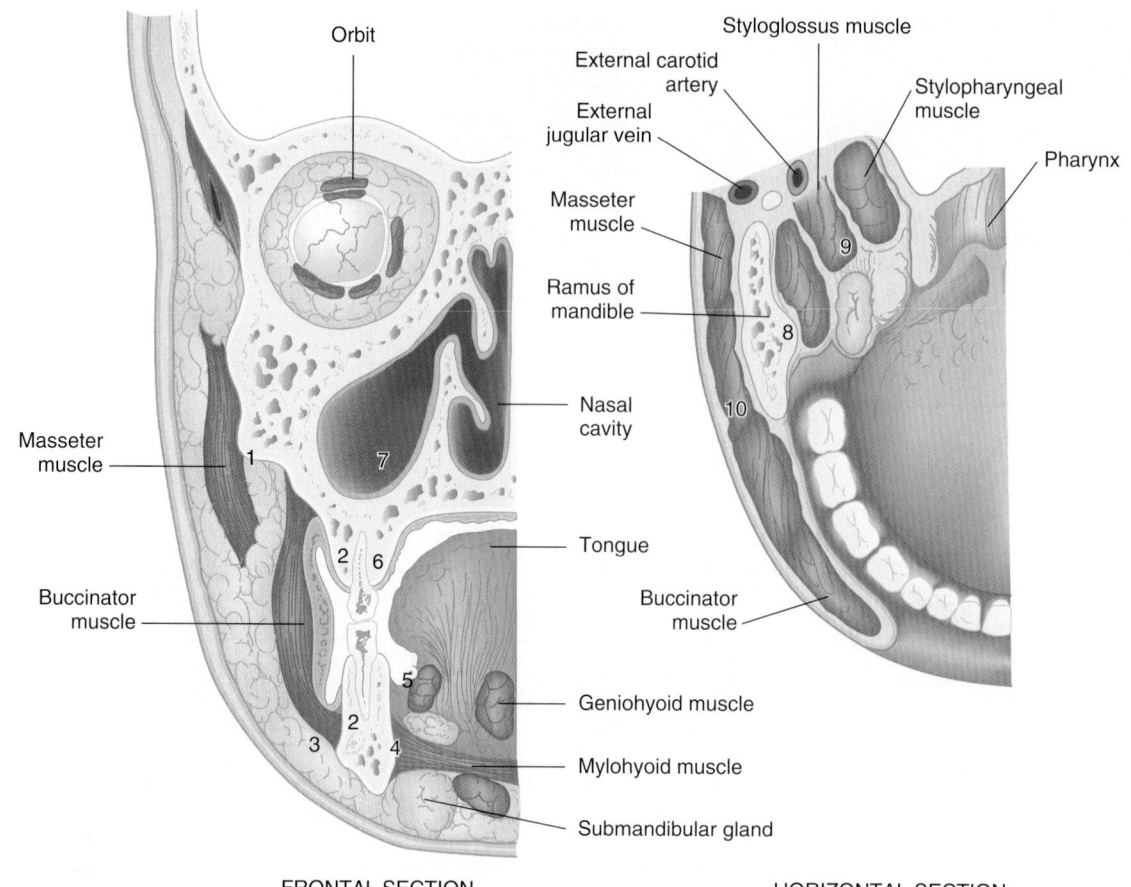

Figure 69-4. Natural progression of dental infection. The pathways by which such infections may travel are: *1,* postzygomatic (from canine fossa in cuspid and bicuspid region; pterygomaxillary fossa communicates from rear); *2,* vestibular; *3,* facial; *4,* submandibular; *5,* sublingual; *6,* palatal; *7,* antral; *8,* pterygomandibular; *9,* parapharyngeal; *10,* masseteric. (Redrawn from Rose LF, Hendler BH, Amsterdam JT: Temporomandibular disorders and odontic infections. *Consultant* 22:125, 1982.)

Figure 69-5. Periapical abscesses *(arrows)* as seen on Panorex film.

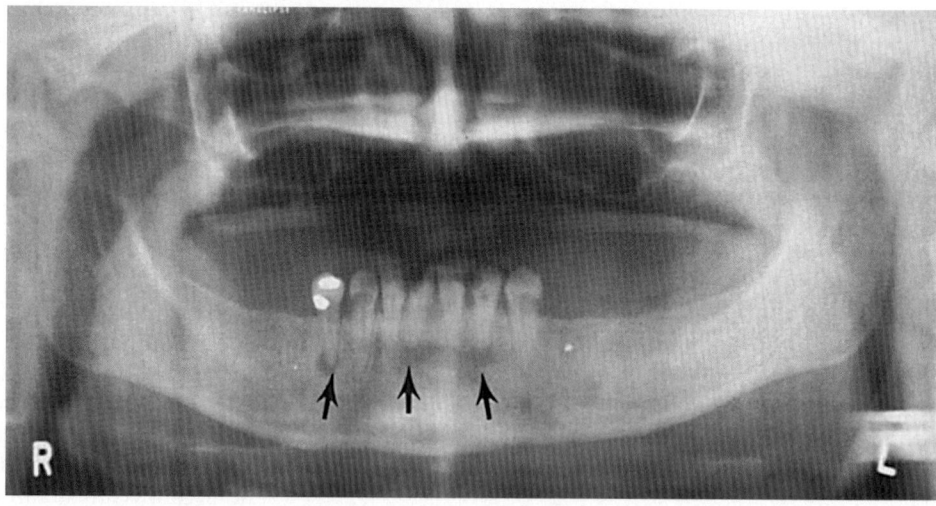

Wharton's duct is milked. Stensen's duct, opposite the maxillary molars, should be examined on each side. The teeth should be examined next. Percussing a tooth with a tongue blade or handle of a mirror is a good way to elicit tenderness.

Radiographic evaluation of teeth is best accomplished using dental (periapical) films. These films are generally not available in the emergency department,

however. A panoramic radiograph is a useful alternative (see Figure 69-5).

Signs and Symptoms

Dental Caries

Dental caries are the most common cause for pain of odontogenic origin. The patient may give a variable

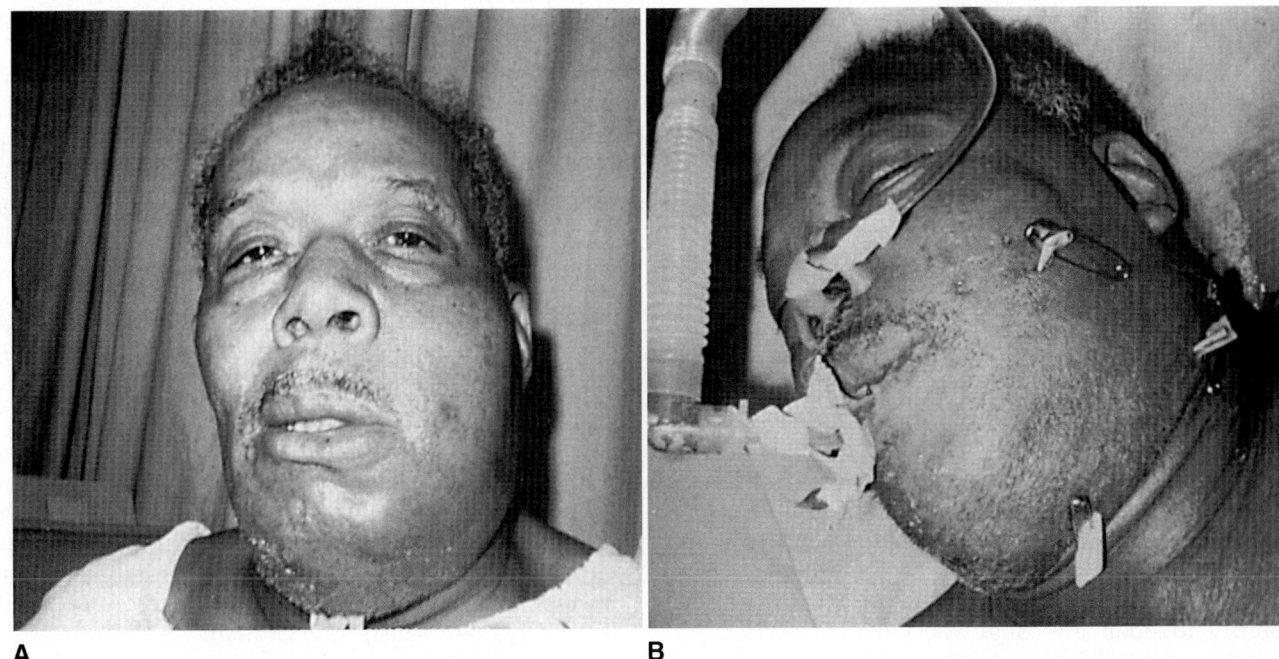

Figure 69-6. Extensive spread of infection of odontogenic origin involving masseteric, sublingual, submental, and submandibular spaces with extension to mediastinum. **A,** Preoperative. **B,** Postoperative. Note drainage from mediastinum. (From Guernsey LH: Practical problem solving in oral surgery. In Cohen DW [ed]: *Continuing Dental Education,* vol 2, suppl 10. Philadelphia, University of Pennsylvania School of Dental Medicine, 1979.)

history of a sudden or gradual onset of a sharp to dull, throbbing pain. In most cases, the patient can indicate the specific tooth involved, but at times the pain may be generalized. An early pulpitis is sensitive to changes in temperature and aggravated by lying down; a more advanced pulpitis is worsened by any stimulus, including air. Pain may be referred to the ear, temple, eye, neck and, rarely, the opposite jaw.

Physical examination may reveal a grossly decayed tooth; however, if the carious process is interproximal or did not result in destruction of the outer table of enamel, the offending tooth may not be obvious. Localization of the involved tooth may be accomplished by percussing the teeth with a tongue blade or by having the patient bite on a piece of a tongue blade. Exquisite pain to percussion suggests an underlying periapical abscess, especially if the tooth is not sensitive to hot or cold. Palliative management is indicated for most odontalgia. Systemic analgesics, such as nonsteroidal anti-inflammatory drugs (NSAIDs) or synthetic opioid agents, are indicated. Although NSAIDs should be sufficient for most pain resulting from carious teeth, a therapeutic dental block also may be helpful. Synthetic opioids also are useful and are indicated in some cases, but should not be used in chronically carious teeth without acute tooth fracture, filling crack or expulsion, or abscess because of their propensity for abuse.[18,19] A dental anesthetic nerve block is helpful.[20,21] A limited quantity of analgesics should be dispensed, which encourages follow-up with a general dentist.

Patients with dental pain should be examined carefully for swelling caused by abscessed teeth. A periapical abscess or a localized swelling of the gingiva adjacent to the apex of the tooth (called a *parulis*) may cause pain from distention of the tissues. More com-monly, fluctuant abscesses are a result of periodontal abscesses and are best treated with an incision and drainage. The gingiva and tooth are anesthetized by apical nerve block, or the gingiva is anesthetized superficially with 2% lidocaine with 1:100,000 epinephrine. A stab incision is made toward the alveolar bone and must extend through the periosteum; blunt dissection is carried out with a mosquito hemostat. In contrast to other abscess drainage, it is unnecessary to open the abscess from end to end—such a large incision exposes too much alveolar bone. In the dental office, a simple curettage between the tooth and the gingiva would establish drainage. For physicians not trained in dental scaling and curettage, the simple stab incision is sufficient. The cavity is irrigated, and assuming there is sufficient space, a Penrose or iodoform drain is placed and secured with a No. 4-0 silk suture.[2]

The patient is started on phenoxymethylpenicillin or erythromycin and warm saline rinses and is referred to an oral maxillofacial surgeon or general dentist. Drains are removed in 24 to 48 hours, and antibiotics are continued for 7 to 10 days.[7]

The presence of cellulitis or swelling in the contiguous spaces of the head and neck indicates the spread of a localized infection. In the early stages of such an infection, the upper half of the face is generally involved, with extension of infection from maxillary teeth; cellulitis from mandibular teeth generally involves extension to the lower half of the face and the neck (Figure 69-6). More advanced infections may extend into any of the fascial planes of the head and neck down to the mediastinum. In the nondebilitated host, untreated dental infections tend to localize and drain spontaneously and extraorally. In the presence of a compromised host or aggressive microorganisms, spread into the fascial planes is more common, with a potential for greater morbidity and mortality. General indications for admission include suspected spread of infection to fascial planes, high fever, toxic appearance, trismus, and an immunocompromised host.[7]

The potential sequelae of sepsis and airway obstruction must be appreciated. Computed tomography of the head and neck can be useful if the diagnosis is in doubt. Airway management should be undertaken when indicated, particularly if signs or symptoms of impending airway obstruction are present or developing (altered voice, drooling, stridor). The intubation should be approached as a difficult airway, as outlined in Chapter 1. An ear, nose, and throat (ENT) specialist or oral maxillofacial surgeon should be consulted for ongoing management of the patient, including determining the site of the initial focus so that pus can be evacuated.

Signs of infection peak in 3 to 5 days. Fever usually is present. Any irritation of the internal pterygoid or masseter muscles results in trismus. Trismus is the inability to open the mouth because of involuntary muscle spasm. Trismus limits visualization of the pharynx and may make diagnosis of lateral or retropharyngeal space involvement difficult. Trismus is muscular in origin, not a result of impaired or augmented neuromuscular transmission, and so is often minimally improved or not improved at all after administration of a neuromuscular blocking agent (e.g., succinylcholine) for intubation. All patients with trismus must be presumed to be difficult intubations. Difficulty swallowing or handling secretions increases the suspicion of retropharyngeal or parapharyngeal infection. Respiratory distress may be apparent, or the airway may occlude rapidly after a period of minimal signs of impending obstruction.[7]

Ludwig's angina is a bilateral, boardlike swelling involving the submandibular, submental, and sublingual spaces with elevation of the tongue. The most serious immediate sequela is airway obstruction. A characteristic brawny induration is present; there is no fluctuance for incision and drainage. Hemolytic streptococcus is most commonly responsible for the infection, although a mixed staphylococcal-streptococcal flora is common, and both may lead to an overgrowth of anaerobic gas-producing organisms, including *Bacteroides fragilis*. Treatment consists of airway management as indicated, followed by admission to a unit capable of observing and managing the airway after airway maintenance. Although oral intubation can be attempted, inability to displace the tongue into the submandibular space with a laryngoscope may make oral intubation impossible; cricothyrotomy may be necessary in these patients for emergent airway control.[9]

High-dose antibiotic therapy, such as 15 to 20 million U of intravenous penicillin daily, is necessary to achieve good tissue penetration. *B. fragilis* infections may be highly resistant, and a second-generation or third-generation cephalosporin, clindamycin, or metronidazole may be required to eradicate them.[8] If antibiotic therapy is not helpful, surgery is performed to eliminate causative factors and to explore for pockets of pus.

In general, the most important therapeutic treatment of orofacial infections is surgical drainage and removal of necrotic tissue. Involved teeth require endodontic therapy if they are restorable or extraction if they are nonrestorable or have lost all alveolar support. Antibiotic therapy is useful for halting the spread of cellulitis and preventing hematogenous dissemination, but it is no substitute for the prompt evacuation of pus.[7]

Penicillin is the antibiotic of choice for treatment of orofacial infections. Minor infections respond to 250 to 500 mg of penicillin V potassium (Penicillin VK) four times a day. More serious infections, such as Ludwig's angina, require 12 million U of penicillin G intravenously a day. Most oral bacteria are sensitive to penicillin, with the exception of some *Bacteroides* species. Second-generation or third-generation cephalosporins are useful in these cases or in penicillin-allergic patients, although care must be exercised for the potential of crossover sensitivity. Clindamycin also is effective when there is a predominance of anaerobes in a penicillin-allergic patient or a patient in whom penicillin or third-generation cephalosporins seem ineffective. Potential side effects should be monitored carefully. Erythromycin is a potential alternative because it is active against most oral bacteria, but it is less active against anaerobic and microaerophilic streptococci, fusobacteria, and anaerobic gram-negative cocci. There is also a problem with long-term intravenous administration because of its irritant effects.[12]

Periodontal Disease

Periodontal disease represents a continuum of pathology. Early periodontal disease is manifested by inflammation of the gingiva, termed *gingivitis*. Gingivitis is generally the result of an inflammatory response to an irritant, such as dental bacterial plaque and calculus. With extension of inflammation, there is ultimately loss of alveolar bone, termed *periodontitis*. A physiologic space from the crest of the alveolar bone to the base of the junctional epithelium is maintained for the insertion of gingival fibers into cementum. In response to a loss of alveolar bone, there is a migration of gingiva down the root of the tooth, termed *gingival resorption*. This is often accompanied by formation of gingival pockets. Advanced periodontitis results from a continuation of this process and causes marked mobility of the teeth and eventual loss as the attachment apparatus is destroyed.[2,5,6]

Space infections of the head and neck occasionally result from periodontal disease. The combination of periodontal lesions and resultant pulpal pathology can create periapical abscesses with the same sequelae as those caused by dental caries alone.

Gingivitis and periodontitis in themselves rarely cause a patient to come to the emergency department, unless there is sudden alarm at seeing blood on a toothbrush or the realization that certain teeth are loose. Occasionally, a patient complains about sensitive teeth.

The patient can be advised to improve home care and see a dentist as soon as possible.

More commonly, a patient presents with pain from a periodontal abscess or swelling of the gingiva when food or pus becomes trapped in a "pocket." In the dental office, a periodontal abscess is treated with curettage to establish drainage. In the emergency department, treatment consists of a small conservative stab incision at the most fluctuant point to establish drainage, saline rinses, and antibiotic coverage. Use of tetracycline in patients older than 8 years of age is preferable because it provides better coverage for the gram-negative and anaerobic organisms found in the gingival pocket. The patient should be referred to the general dentist or periodontist for further treatment.[2,5,6]

Acute Necrotizing Ulcerative Gingivitis

In contrast to gingivitis, in which the gingiva becomes inflamed in response to an irritant such as bacterial plaque but is not invaded by bacteria, acute necrotizing ulcerative gingivitis (ANUG) is a periodontal lesion in which bacteria actually invade non-necrotic tissue. ANUG lesions commonly are accompanied by systemic manifestations of fever, malaise, and regional lymphadenopathy.[2,5,6] ANUG is characterized by painful edematous interdental papillae. The normally pointed interdental papillae are blunted and ulcerated. A gray pseudomembrane covers the tissue and leaves a bleeding surface when removed. The lesions can involve any part of the gingiva but are more common in the anterior incisor and posterior molar regions. The patient complains of pain, a metallic taste, and foul breath (Figure 69-7).

Gingival crevices in ANUG show a predominance of fusobacteria and spirochetes. Electron microscopy reveals a layering pattern showing fusobacteria in superficial layers with spirochetes invading in deeper layers. Other necrotizing ulcerative oral diseases, such as Vincent's angina (extension of ANUG to the fauces and tonsils), cancrum oris (extension of ANUG to the lips and buccal mucosa eroding through the teeth), and some pulmonary abscesses, also are caused by fusospirochetes.[22]

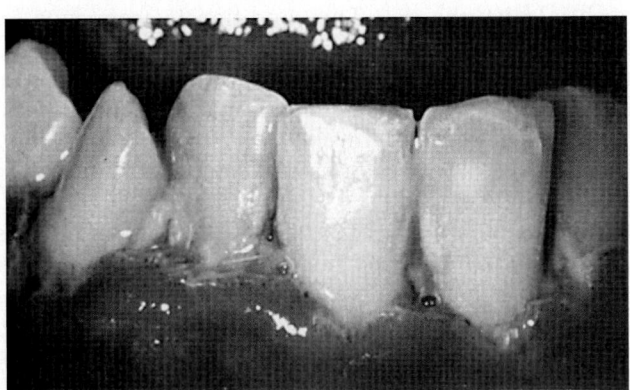

Figure 69-7. Acute necrotizing ulcerative gingivitis involving lower anterior teeth.

Because ANUG results from an overgrowth of bacteria normally present in the gingival crevice, immunologic factors probably contribute to the disease. ANUG has been associated with immunocompromised hosts, fatigue, local trauma, emotional stress, and smoking. ANUG has the name "trench mouth" from its occurrence in large populations living in close quarters under significant stress, such as in the trenches in World War I, military barracks, and college dormitories.[23] Despite this occurrence, there is no evidence that ANUG is communicable.

ANUG treatment consists of prescribing warm saline rinses; systemic analgesics so that the patient can improve oral hygiene; and systemic antibiotics, such as penicillin, erythromycin, or tetracycline. Topical local anesthetics, such as viscous lidocaine, may provide some relief. Antibiotics provide dramatic relief within 24 hours, as do dilute (3%) hydrogen peroxide rinses. Although the patient feels better, he or she should be advised to see a general dentist or periodontist for follow-up (this should be documented on the chart). The soft tissue and alveolar bone destruction from ANUG predisposes the patient to further periodontal disease; corrective procedures are necessary to create an environment conducive to maintaining periodontal health.[5,6]

Oral Pain

Although dental caries is the most common source of oral pain, the following disease entities also may cause oral or facial pain.

Root Canal Pain

Endodontic or root canal therapy involves opening the pulp chamber of the tooth, removing pulp tissue from the chamber and the root portion of the tooth to the apex, irrigating and effectively sterilizing the canal, and sealing the pulp chamber to prevent ingress of saliva and contamination. After surgery, the patient may experience exquisite pain caused by irritation beyond the apex of the tooth from instrumentation or from the buildup of gas from the irrigation solutions. Swelling may cause the tooth to be elevated slightly out of the socket so that premature contact during chewing causes extreme pain. These patients may have no relief with either systemic analgesics or anesthetic nerve blocks, presumably from the sensation of intense pressure. Treatment may consist of opening the canal to allow the gas or fluid to escape and of occlusal adjustment to take the tooth out of contact; the patient's general dentist or endodontist may have to be contacted.[24]

Cracked Tooth and Split Root Syndromes

Patients with cracked teeth or a split root may report having a toothache. Pain occurs primarily with chewing or forced closure. The patient may have had an extensive dental restoration, previous endodontic therapy, or a history of having received an upward blow to the jaw. In the emergency department, the diagnosis is made from history and from having the patient bite on a piece of wood. In the dental office, the diagnosis is made by removing a restoration and inspecting the cavity floor. Management is similar to that for carious teeth, including symptomatic pain medication and referral back to the dentist to consider possible causes.[2]

Maxillary Sinusitis

Dental pain often is referred to the area of the sinuses; similarly, congested or inflamed sinuses in the proximity of the apices of the maxillary teeth may cause apparent odontogenic pain. The patient may complain of throbbing pain unrelated to changes in temperature and aggravated by lying down. On examination, there is no apparent dental cause. There may be tenderness over the maxillary sinuses or periorbital regions. Nasal discharge may be present. The Panorex film can screen for dental and sinus pathology.

Atypical Odontalgia

Atypical odontalgia describes dental pain for which there is no dental cause. The patient may have a history of multiple dental procedures with no relief. The pain is chronic and occurs spontaneously. Percussion may elicit pain, and there may be thermal sensitivity as if a vital tooth were present. If paroxysmal pain of neuropathic origin is excluded, atypical odontalgia can be entertained. Similar to many chronic pain syndromes, treatment with tricyclic antidepressants may be efficacious. Such management is best left to the dentist or pain management consultant who would follow the patient on a long-term basis.

Postextraction Pain

Pain after an extraction (i.e., immediate periosteitis) is common for approximately 24 hours. Systemic analgesics are usually adequate for pain control. Aspirin-containing compounds and NSAIDs are effective analgesics but can contribute to postoperative bleeding and oozing.

A much more painful condition, acute alveolar osteitis or dry socket, may occur approximately 3 to 4 days after an extraction. The patient has a pain-free interval followed by sudden onset of excruciating pain associated with a foul odor. The pathophysiology involves premature loss of the healing blood clot from the socket with a localized infection of the bone.[25]

Treatment of a dry socket consists of an anesthetic nerve block, gentle irrigation of the socket, and packing the socket with iodoform gauze saturated with a medicated dental paste, such as Sed-A-Dent, or barely dampened with eugenol (oil of cloves). The packing affords almost immediate relief. Patients with a dry socket require daily follow-up for pack changes until the condition resolves. Most dentists include oral antibiotic (e.g., penicillin or erythromycin) coverage, analgesics, and NSAIDs with this regimen until the condition resolves. Although the condition is secondary to premature loss of the blood clot from the socket, no attempt should be made to stir up bleeding in the socket to form a new clot because this procedure is associated with a high incidence of osteomyelitis.[25]

Paroxysmal Pain of Neuropathic Origin

Paroxysmal pain of neuropathic origin is most commonly caused by tic douloureux, or trigeminal neuralgia. The diagnosis is made principally on the basis of history. The patient complains of paroxysmal episodes of an excruciating, lancinating pain, also described as recurrent bursts of an electric shock. The pain follows the anatomic distribution of the involved division of the fifth cranial nerve. On physical examination, the pain sometimes can be elicited by tapping specific areas of the face (the so-called trigger zones) in the region of the distribution of the nerve involved.[26]

Medical management for tic douloureux consists of carbamazepine, although some patients may be afforded no relief. Patients who fail medical management and are in significant distress may be candidates for neurosurgical procedures that ablate the nerve. Close follow-up is required if treatment for tic douloureux is initiated in the emergency department. Patients taking carbamazepine require adjustment of the dosage to achieve therapeutic effect and require monitoring for toxicity. Patients in whom the diagnosis is considered need additional evaluation to exclude the presence of multiple sclerosis, cerebellopontine angle tumor, acoustic neuroma, or nasopharyngeal carcinoma. Patients with this condition commonly require a full dental, otolaryngologic, and neurologic evaluation to investigate correctable causes.

Other causes of orofacial pain of the paroxysmal type include headaches (see Chapter 17). Vascular headaches such as migraine and cluster headaches may have facial pain as their principal manifestation. Rheumatologic disorders, such as giant cell arteritis and polymyalgia rheumatica in the elderly, can result in facial pain. Dull pain in the lower jaw is not always of dental origin. Myocardial ischemia may cause isolated jaw pain.

Temporomandibular Myofascial Pain Dysfunction Syndrome

The TMJ is a bilateral joint subject to almost continuous use. It is extremely sensitive to proprioceptive stimuli and can react to interferences in occlusion of only fractions of a millimeter. TMJ syndrome results from anatomic disharmony (see Figure 69-1) and occlusal disturbances. The condition is aggravated by trauma, clenching of the teeth, or bruxism. Patients complain of pain in the region of the TMJ, usually unilateral. The pain is dull, worsens during the course of a day, and in extreme cases may result in trismus with palpable masseter and internal pterygoid spasm.[26-29]

TMJ radiographs are not helpful. Treatment consists of the external application of heat for 15 minutes four to six times per day, soft diet, analgesics including NSAIDs, and a muscle relaxant such as diazepam. Patients should be referred to a dentist specializing in TMJ disorders, such as a periodontist or a periodontal prosthodontist. Treatment at this stage consists of continued physiotherapy, bite appliances that put the musculature at rest, and occlusal adjustment.[30]

Although certain anatomic abnormalities are amenable to surgical correction, most oral maxillofacial surgeons consider surgery only for the most intractable cases.[28]

Pericoronitis

Pain from the eruption of the third molar teeth (i.e., wisdom teeth) in an adult is common. Trapped food and plaque cause the gingiva surrounding crowded, malerupted, or impacted third molar teeth to become inflamed and swollen. This condition is called *pericoronitis* and is extremely painful because of repeated trauma from the opposing third molar biting on tender tissues and from distention of retromolar tissue on opening of the mandible. Pericoronitis is treated locally with warm saline irrigation, with or without hydrogen peroxide rinses. If the condition is severe or if there is a fever, an antibiotic is recommended. If fluctuant pus is present, an incision and drainage should be performed, exercising care not to track the infection posteriorly or to dissect deeply into distorted tissues, possibly encountering the internal carotid artery.[7] Definitive treatment involves removal of the opposing third molar tooth for immediate relief and removal of the involved third molar tooth after the infection is resolved.[2] These patients should be referred to an oral maxillofacial surgeon.

Oral Manifestations of Systemic Disease

Although the oral manifestations of many systemic diseases are nonspecific, several diseases have distinct oral presentations. In certain instances, recognition of the oral signs aids in the specific diagnosis. In other disease states, the oral condition is a contributing factor to the overall pathophysiology.[31]

Diabetes Mellitus

Oral manifestations of diabetes mellitus are associated primarily with periodontal lesions. Diabetic patients seem to be more susceptible to periodontitis. Acute gingival abscess and sessile or pedunculated gingival proliferations have been described as being caused by or intimately associated with diabetes.[31]

Similar to other systemic manifestations of diabetes, the degree of control of diabetes seems to correlate with its effects on the periodontium. Uncontrolled diabetes generally results in greater periodontal disease. Control of diabetes helps decrease periodontal severity, although irreversible damage—such as bone loss—may result.

Although the severity of periodontal disease in diabetic patients is a function of the response to local factors, such as plaque and calculus, there is also evidence to support the role of vascular changes and alterations in the role of polymorphonuclear leukocytes, monocytes, oral microflora, the patient's immune response, and genetic variables. Patients with diabetes who have advanced retinal changes also have been found to have more periodontal manifestations.

Maintenance of a healthy periodontium is important in a diabetic patient. Just as the degree of diabetic

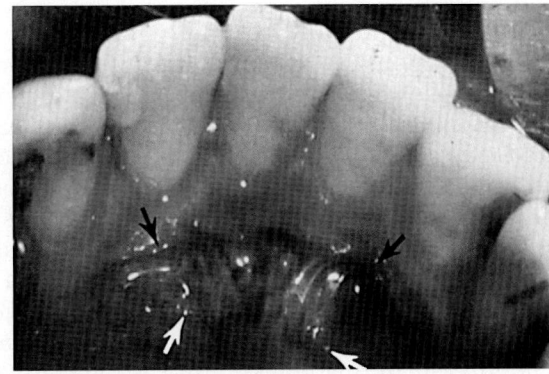

Figure 69-8. Lesion *(arrows)* secondary to systemic lupus erythematosus involving the floor of mouth.

control affects the periodontium, so too does periodontal disease affect the degree of control. Patients with brittle diabetes or subject to repeated episodes of ketoacidosis might be thrown out of control from a simple periodontal abscess. The presence of advanced periodontal disease in a young patient, especially in the absence of local factors, should lead one to exclude the diagnosis of diabetes. A sudden change from a healthy periodontium to a diseased state would lead a physician to suspect a similar diagnosis in an adult. Human immunodeficiency virus infection also should be ruled out.

Collagen Vascular Diseases

Systemic lupus erythematosus is the most common collagen vascular disease to have oral manifestations. Patients commonly have large ulcerated intraoral lesions with necrotic borders. The lesions are usually secondarily infected and painful (Figure 69-8).

Scleroderma usually is recognized by the characteristic facies. The periodontal ligament may appear thickened on dental radiographs. Characteristic microscopic changes can be seen on gingival biopsy specimens. Rare entities, such as the midline lethal granuloma or Wegener's granulomatosis, present with large intraoral ulcerative lesions, usually involving the hard palate.[31]

Granulomatous Diseases

Oral manifestations of granulomatous diseases are fairly rare today, but are still seen. Tuberculosis may give rise to lesions of the tongue or tonsillar area. These lesions are confused most commonly with syphilitic ulcerations or infections caused by actinomycosis. A more common and benign entity is pyogenic granuloma,[6] which is a proliferation of highly vascular connective tissue in response to an irritant. The lesions range from sessile to pedunculated and have a warty texture. Pyogenic granulomas in the oral cavity are usually gingival in origin. They are especially common in pregnancy and are called "pregnancy tumors." Pregnancy tumors generally resolve 2 to 3 months after delivery; tumors that do not resolve require surgical excision.

Blood Dyscrasias

The gingiva may be massively infiltrated by leukemic cells in acute leukemic states, especially acute granulocytic leukemia. The gingiva is edematous and bluish red and may cover the teeth. These gingivae are compromised and may allow for the ingress of bacteria, leading to sepsis. Chronic leukemic states have no specific gingival lesions, and leukemic states in remission are associated with normal gingiva. In addition to sepsis, gingival hemorrhage is a serious sequela. Gingival sequelae are more severe with underlying periodontal disease; during remissions, it is imperative to maintain good periodontal health. Acute hemorrhage is controlled with the application of gauze pressure and hemostatic agents, such as topical thrombin, absorbable gelatin powder, and oxidized regenerated cellulose.[2]

Thrombocytopenic purpura commonly presents with oral manifestations. Spontaneous gingival bleeding from trauma is characteristic. Acute hemorrhage is managed in a fashion similar to that discussed for acute leukemia. Less serious persistent oozing responds to treatment of the underlying state.

Drug-Induced Gingival Hyperplasias

Some degree of gingival hyperplasia is present in 40% of patients receiving long-term phenytoin therapy. Younger patients seem to be affected more often than older patients. The degree of gingival hyperplasia does not seem to be related to dosage. The disease ranges from slight enlargements of the interdental papillae to massive enlargement of the gingiva, which covers the crowns of the teeth and may move the teeth. The hyperplastic tissue is subject to infection. The presence of local irritants seems to make the hyperplasia worse.[32-35] Treatment of the condition includes removal of local irritants and surgical excision of the hyperplastic tissue. If the drug is not discontinued, hyperplasia is likely to recur, although less severely if good oral hygiene is maintained.

Aphthous Stomatitis

Patients may complain of recurrent small oral mucosal ulcers. The ulcers are approximately 2 to 3 mm in size with a white center. The lesions tend to be tender but rarely become infected. Multiple ulcers that have coalesced can create an impressively large lesion. One third of the population may be affected by this condition, which is believed to be related to stress, nutrition, oral trauma, and hormonal etiologies. Treatment is symptomatic (hydrogen peroxide rinse; topical dental preparations such as benzocaine and an emollient gel; 50:50 mixture of diphenhydramine [Benadryl] and Kaopectate or Maalox; or prescription regimens, such as steroid-antibiotic ointment [Kenalog in Orabase] or sucralfate), with oral antibiotics for secondary infection. A new topical agent, Debacterol, available only by prescription, can be applied to the ulcer; Debacterol seals the ulcer and promotes rapid healing. Ulcers that may appear similar to aphthous ulcers are those on the soft palate associated with hand-foot-and-mouth disease or lesions on the gingivae and tongue from herpetic stomatitis.[36,37]

TRAUMATIC DENTAL EMERGENCIES

Fractures of Teeth

The anterior teeth are commonly injured from falls or blows directly to the teeth. Forceful blows to the mandible directed superiorly may result in fractures of the premolars and molars caused by a wedgelike effect of the cusps of the mandibular teeth in the central fossae of the maxillary teeth. Many children have an anterior overbite, which makes this part of the dentition more prone to injury. Blunt trauma to the dentition may result in damage to the neurovascular supply to the tooth, bleeding within the tooth, fractures of the root or crown, loosening of the tooth, or actual expulsion of the tooth from its socket. A long-term sequela of blunt trauma or reimplantation of teeth is resorption of the root.[2,38,39]

Fractures of the anterior teeth are managed based on the type of fracture, its relation to the pulp of the tooth, and the patient's age. The Ellis classification system was used to describe fractures of anterior teeth; however, now it is the accepted practice simply to describe the anatomy involved.[40] Fractures involving enamel; enamel and dentin; and enamel, dentin, and pulp exposure traditionally have been referred to as Ellis classes I, II, and III (Figure 69-9).

The simplest and most common dental fracture involves only the enamel portion of the tooth, leaving

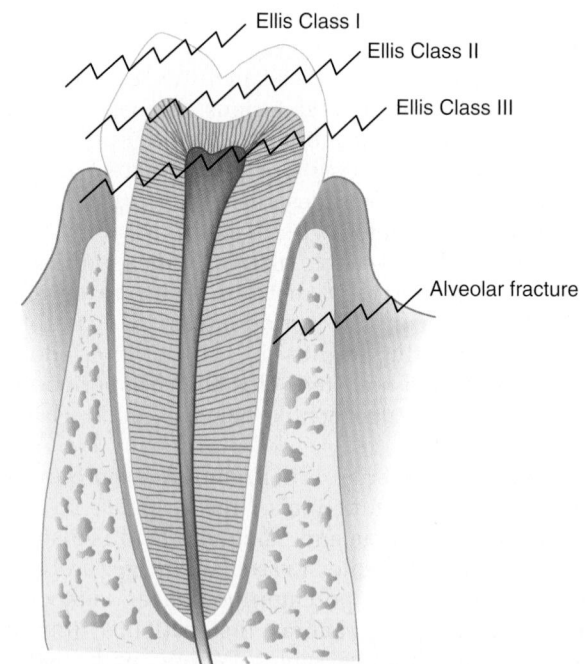

Figure 69-9. Ellis classification for fractures of anterior teeth. (Redrawn from Tintinalli JE, et al: *Emergency Medicine: A Comprehensive Study Guide,* 4th ed. New York, McGraw-Hill, 1996.)

a chalky-white appearance. These injuries are usually minor, unless a sharp portion of the tooth causes soft tissue trauma, in which case the sharp edge may be smoothed with an emery board. The patient or parents usually are concerned about the cosmetic deformity, but they can be reassured that the tooth can be restored to its natural appearance with the use of enamel-bonding plastic materials. Referral to the dentist is necessary but not urgent.

Fractures involving the dentin have an ivory-yellow appearance. The pulp continually lays down dentin throughout the life of the tooth in response to normal and noxious stimuli. In a child, the pulp is relatively large in size, and there is less dentin; the inverse is true in the adult. Because dentin is a microtubular tissue capable of allowing bacteria to percolate into the pulp chamber, fractures involving dentin are more serious in children and adolescents as there is little dentin to protect the pulp after it is exposed to the oral cavity.

In younger patients, the management of dentin fractures involves the immediate placement of a dressing of calcium hydroxide paste over the exposed dentin covered with dry foil, a metal band or, more commonly, an enamel-bonded plastic. Early intervention may prevent contamination of the pulp and the need for subsequent root canal treatment. A pediatric or general dentist should be notified as soon as possible. Exposed dentin may be exquisitely sensitive, so the patient should avoid extremes in temperature. In an adult, who has a greater thickness of dentin compared with pulpal tissue, there is less need for urgent referral to a dentist. A dressing can be placed on the tooth for comfort. Referral should be made to a dentist for the next working day.

Fractures of teeth resulting in pulp exposure are the most serious class of fractures of anterior teeth because the pulp chamber is immediately contaminated. Care should be taken to differentiate dentin exposure from the pulp. The tooth is wiped clean with a piece of gauze and examined for a pink blush or a drop of blood, indicating a pulpal exposure. There may be excruciating pain from exposure of the nerve, or the shock of the trauma may have disrupted the neurovascular supply at the apex of the tooth, eliminating most sensitivity. This injury is often accompanied by serious fractures of the tooth, possibly involving the entire crown or root.[41]

Pulp exposures are true dental emergencies. In the primary dentition, exposure of the pulp can be treated by performing a pulpotomy, in which the pulp in the chamber is removed, the remaining tissue is mummified with formocresol and covered with a layer of calcium hydroxide, and the tooth is restored. In most cases, if there has been minimal contamination, the primary tooth lasts its natural lifetime. In an adult, the pulpotomy is not a successful procedure, and all pulpal tissue from the crown and root must be completely removed. Although management of pulp exposures is more urgent in a child, endodontic therapy is less complicated and more successful in an adult if there is

also a minimum of contamination; in the case of a pulpal exposure from a dental fracture, a general dentist, pedodontist, or endodontist should be notified immediately if possible, or the patient should be instructed to follow up the next working day. If no dentist is available, a piece of moist cotton can be placed over the exposed pulp and covered with a piece of dry foil or sealed with a temporary root canal sealant (e.g., Cavet). Although some authors have advocated removal of the exposed pulpal tissue with a dental endodontic instrument called a barbed broach, this procedure is not recommended because this instrument breaks easily, even in the hands of a skilled endodontist.[41] In cases of extreme pain, a dental anesthetic nerve block might be helpful.

Subluxed and Avulsed Teeth

Teeth that are loosened in their sockets as a result of a force are called *subluxed*. There may or may not be associated fractures. The diagnosis of subluxation can be made by gently tapping a tooth with two tongue blades. Any perceptible mobility is evidence for subluxation. There may be a ring of blood surrounding the gingival crevice. Minimally mobile teeth respond well to a soft diet for several days. Markedly mobile teeth require stabilization as soon as possible for 10 to 14 days. Teeth can be stabilized (generally by a dentist) by means of Erich arch bars, wire ligation, enamel bonding plastics, or a combination of modalities.[3] Most of these techniques require an oral maxillofacial surgeon, hospital dentist, or pedodontist. They should be performed as soon as possible.[41]

As a temporizing measure, the patient can bite gently on a piece of gauze, or the teeth can be stabilized for 24 to 48 hours with the application of a periodontal pack (e.g., Coe-Pak).[42] A resin and catalyst paste are mixed together in equal quantities to a firm consistency and molded over the anterior and posterior aspects of the involved tooth and two or three adjacent teeth on each side. The patient is asked to close the mouth while the mixture hardens (Figure 69-10). The patient is advised to avoid hot liquids that would soften the pack, eat a liquid to soft diet, and see a dentist as soon as possible.

Avulsed teeth are completely torn from the socket and are a true dental emergency. If teeth are unaccounted for, the possibility of aspiration or entrapment in soft tissues should be considered.[43] Management of recovered avulsed teeth depends on the age of the patient and the length of time that the tooth has been absent from the oral cavity.[44] Avulsed primary teeth in a pediatric patient age 6 months to 6 years are not replaced in the socket. Reimplanted primary teeth ankylose or fuse to the bone so that although the dentofacial complex grows downward and forward, the reimplantation site does not. There also may be interference with the eruption of the permanent tooth. Cosmetic deformity results in either case. Such patients should be referred to a pedodontist for consideration of a space maintainer or cosmetic appliance.

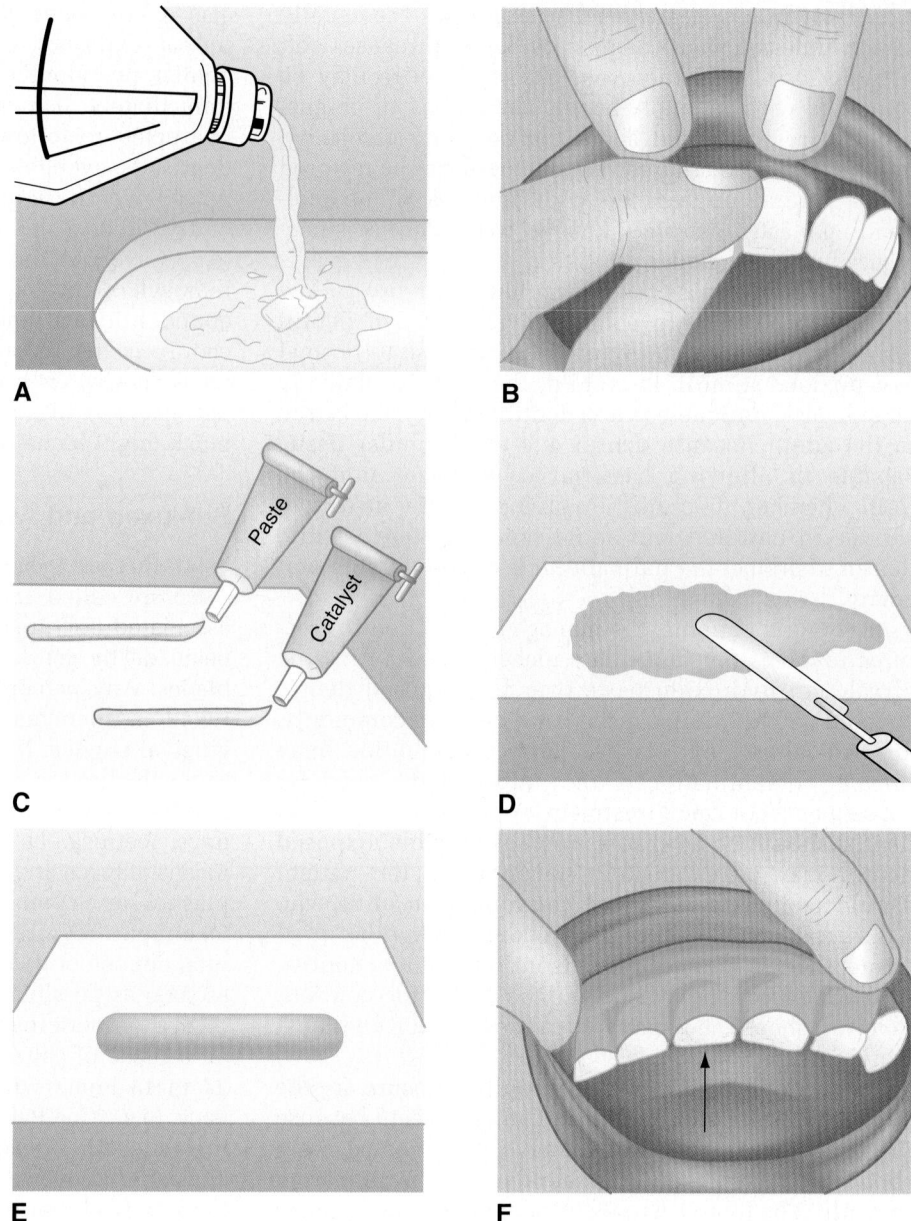

Figure 69-10. Reimplantation and stabilization of an avulsed tooth. **A,** Tooth is rinsed. **B,** Tooth is placed back into socket. **C** and **D,** Periodontal pack is mixed. **E,** Splint material is ready for application. **F,** Packing is molded over reimplanted tooth and two adjacent teeth to either side.

Avulsed permanent teeth require prompt intervention. When a tooth has been avulsed from its socket, the periodontal ligament fibers are torn; fragments remain attached both to the cementum on the root of the tooth and to the alveolar bone in the socket. Ideally, the best environment for an avulsed tooth is its socket, and it has been known since the mid-1960s that an avulsed tooth can be successfully replanted if it is returned to its socket within 30 minutes of the avulsion.[43,45,46] A 1% chance of successful reimplantation is lost for every minute that the tooth is outside of its socket; however, there is often difficulty with immediate reimplantation. On-site personnel (parents, teachers, trainers, paramedics) may be unfamiliar or uncomfortable with tooth reimplantation. The tooth may be soiled, or the patient may be uncooperative. Occasionally, other, more serious life threats may preclude immediate reimplantation. Because of these factors, investigations were undertaken to find the ideal medium for transport and storage of an avulsed tooth.

The worst situation is to allow the tooth to be transported in a dry medium. Storage in plain water is not much better.[47] Although saliva is a reasonable storage medium, milk is preferable because of its osmolarity and essential ion concentration of Ca^{++} and Mg^{++}.[47] The best storage and transport medium is Hank's solution, a balanced pH cell culture medium.[48] This solution is commercially available as the "Save-a-Tooth" system (3M). Hank's solution can maintain the viability of the cells for 12 to 24 hours or more.[49] If the tooth has been avulsed for more than 30 minutes or has been allowed to dry, placement of the tooth in Hank's solution helps restore the periodontal ligament cells.[50,51] With the "Save-a-Tooth" system, the tooth is simply dropped into the basket and the lid replaced (Figure 69-11). For removal, the lid is removed, the basket is lifted out of

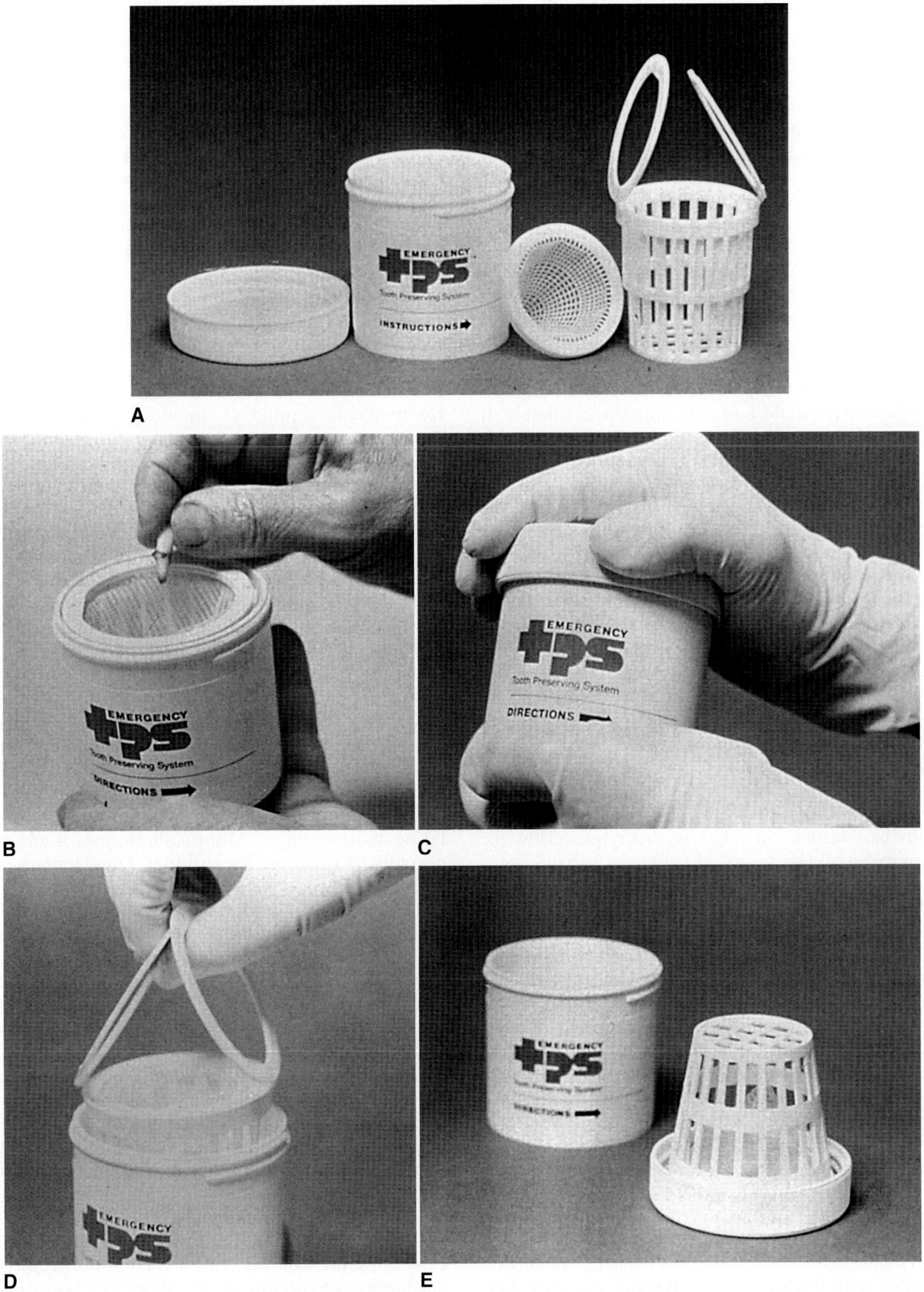

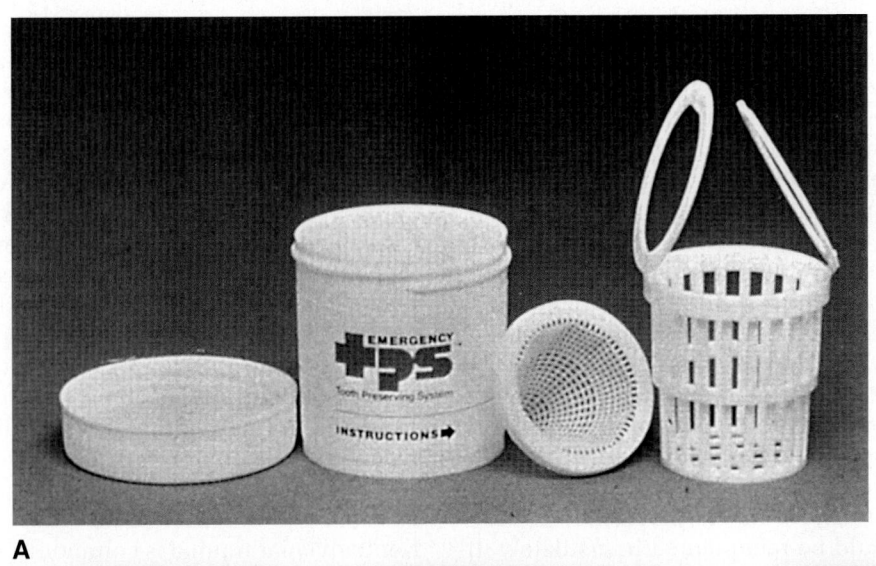

Figure 69-11. A, Tooth Preserving System (TPS). B, Each avulsed tooth is dropped into a separate TPS container of Hank's solution. **C,** Lid is secured tightly. Container can be swirled gently to clean tooth. **D,** Tooth is removed from container by lifting basket. **E,** Tooth is retrieved by turning basket over onto cushioned interior lining of lid. (Courtesy of Paul Krasner, DDS, Save-A-Tooth, Inc., Pottstown, Penn.)

the solution, and the tooth is retrieved by tipping the basket over onto the padded lid.

If a call is received about an avulsed tooth, it first should be determined whether the tooth is permanent. If it is, the caller should be instructed to rinse the tooth off in saline or water and reimplant it immediately into the socket. If this cannot be performed for technical or emotional reasons, the patient should be instructed to place the tooth under his or her tongue or in the buccal pouch so that it is bathed in saliva. If the patient is too young, the tooth can be placed in the parent's mouth. If this is unacceptable to the parent or if there is concern about aspiration or swallowing of the tooth, it should be transported in a cup of milk. If milk is unavailable, saline should be used.[51] Ideally, the tooth should be transported in Hank's solution.

When the patient arrives in the emergency department, the tooth should be reimplanted immediately. If this cannot be done, the tooth can be placed in Hank's solution or a "Save-a-Tooth" system (especially if avulsion has been longer than 30 minutes or if the patient has other life threats that are being managed). If Hank's solution is not available, the tooth is rinsed with saline, the socket is suctioned if necessary, and the tooth is immediately implanted. Local anesthesia may be necessary. The tooth should be manipulated only by the crown, if possible, so that the remaining periodontal ligament fibers are not damaged. Stabilization must be performed immediately, or the tooth will exfoliate. Stabilization is performed as described for markedly subluxated teeth (see Figure 69-10). The status of tetanus immunization should be checked, and the patient should be treated according to the standard for a non–tetanus prone wound (i.e., 10-year immunization update). The patient should be started on phenoxymethylpenicillin or erythromycin.[2,52]

The patient is placed on a liquid diet for several days and advanced to a soft diet for 1 week. Stabilization is maintained for approximately 2 weeks, and the tooth is gradually brought into function to prevent ankylosis. Teeth that have been avulsed for longer than 30 minutes invariably require endodontic therapy.[44] Although there may be concern about the anatomic orientation of the tooth or more confusion about which socket to use when several teeth are avulsed, each tooth should be placed into a socket with the best fit so that the tooth remains in a good physiologic environment. The dentist can make any necessary readjustments before final stabilization.

Alveolar Bone Fractures

Dental fractures and subluxed or avulsed teeth may be associated with fractures of the alveolus. Alveolar fractures may be apparent clinically from exposed pieces of bone or diagnosed radiographically. In massive facial trauma, care should be taken to conserve as much of the alveolar bone as possible, unless there is a tremendous danger of aspiration. Indiscriminate loss of alveolar bone results in tremendous cosmetic deformity that is difficult to restore with prosthetic devices.[53]

An arch bar stabilizes alveolar fractures. An alveolar fracture requires 6 weeks of stabilization for adequate healing; if there is an associated subluxed or avulsed tooth, stabilization is maintained at the expense of possible ankylosis of the tooth. The loss of alveolar bone ultimately results in more cosmetic deformity for the patient. A permanently ankylosed tooth can remain functional for some time, and although it may be difficult for an oral and maxillofacial surgeon to remove, it can be reconstructed more easily than supporting alveolar bone. The dental materials, including local anesthesia supplies and the "Save-A-Tooth" system, are conveniently assembled in a commercial package called "The Dental Box" (Pittsburgh, Penn).

Soft Tissue Injuries

Dentoalveolar trauma is commonly associated with soft tissue injuries of the lips, intraoral mucosa, and tongue. Wounds always should be examined for debris and tooth fragments. As with any surgical wound, debridement and irrigation should be performed. Final closure of soft tissue injuries should await the initial management of fractured teeth or the procedures necessary for stabilizing teeth because manipulation of the soft tissues is required. Carefully placed sutures may be torn and have to be replaced in already compromised tissue if soft tissue closures are performed first.[54]

Gaping intraoral lacerations tend to become ulcerated, secondarily infected, and painful. Fibrotic healing results in a cumbersome scar that is subject to repeated trauma during chewing. A well-prepared mucosal wound is closed with No. 4-0 absorbable or black silk suture. Gingival and tongue lacerations are best closed with No. 4-0 black silk because this material is less irritating to the touch. Absorbable suture, such as 4-0 chromic, is excellent for children. Large tongue lacerations should be well approximated or a cleft will form during healing, necessitating a revision. Anesthesia can be achieved by either direct local injection or lingual block. Small (<1 cm) lacerations are best left alone, especially in children. The management of through-and-through lacerations involving skin and oral mucosa is controversial. With proper preparation, mucosa can be closed as described previously. Subcutaneous sutures (absorbable) are placed to close the subcutaneous tissues from the outside, removing tension from the skin. Skin is closed with No. 6-0 or No. 7-0 synthetic nonabsorbable sutures that are removed in 3 to 4 days, depending on the amount of muscle tension on the wound. Intraoral silk closures are removed in approximately 7 days.[54]

Through-and-through lacerations and other significant intraoral wounds may benefit from prophylactic antibiotics (penicillin is the drug of choice).[52] The patient is advised to maintain oral hygiene, use saline rinses six times a day, place a triple-antibiotic ointment over the skin closure, and watch carefully for infection. These patients should be seen in 48 to 72 hours to check for infection. Normal postoperative soft tissue swelling should not be mistaken for an infected wound.

Temporomandibular Joint Dislocation

The mandibular condyles may dislocate from trauma, but more often dislocation follows extreme opening of the mandible such as occurs after a yawn or laughter. TMJ dislocation occurs when the condyle travels anteriorly along the eminence and becomes locked in the anterosuperior aspect of the eminence. The masseter, internal pterygoid, and temporalis go into spasm attempting to close the mandible; trismus results, and the condyle cannot return to the temporal fossa. Mandibular dislocation is painful and frightening for the patient. Patients prone to mandibular dislocation include individuals with anatomic disharmonies between the fossa and articular eminence, weakness of the capsule and the temporomandibular ligaments, or torn ligaments. Dystonic reaction to drugs may result in mandibular dislocation. Patients who have had one episode of mandibular dislocation are predisposed to further dislocations. If a unilateral dislocation has occurred, the jaw deviates to the opposite side. More commonly, a symmetric dislocation occurs. In cases of traumatic dislocation, a mandibular series, Panorex, or TMJ radiographs should be taken to exclude the possibility of a fracture.[2,7,53-55]

Reduction of a dislocated mandible is straightforward, although often difficult because the strength of the masseter contraction must be overcome. The patient requires procedural analgesia and sedation as for any other dislocation. Either facing the patient or from behind, the emergency physician grasps the mandible with both hands; the thumbs rest on the ridge of the mandible intraorally, posterior to the molars, and the fingers wrap around the outside of the jaw. It is best to have the patient sitting up, with a firm surface behind the head, so that posterior and inferior pressure can be exerted without accompanying movement of the patient's entire head. Some physicians prefer to place the thumbs on the occlusal surfaces of the teeth; in this case, the thumbs must be wrapped with gauze to protect them when reduction is accomplished because the masseter muscles can contract with tremendous force. Downward pressure is applied on the mandible to free the condyles from the anterior aspect of the eminence; the mandible is guided posteriorly and superiorly back into the temporal fossae (Figure 69-12). The patient is advised to avoid extreme opening of the mandible such as occurs during laughing and yawning, to begin a soft diet for 1 week, and to apply warm compresses in the TMJ area. NSAIDs and muscle relaxants

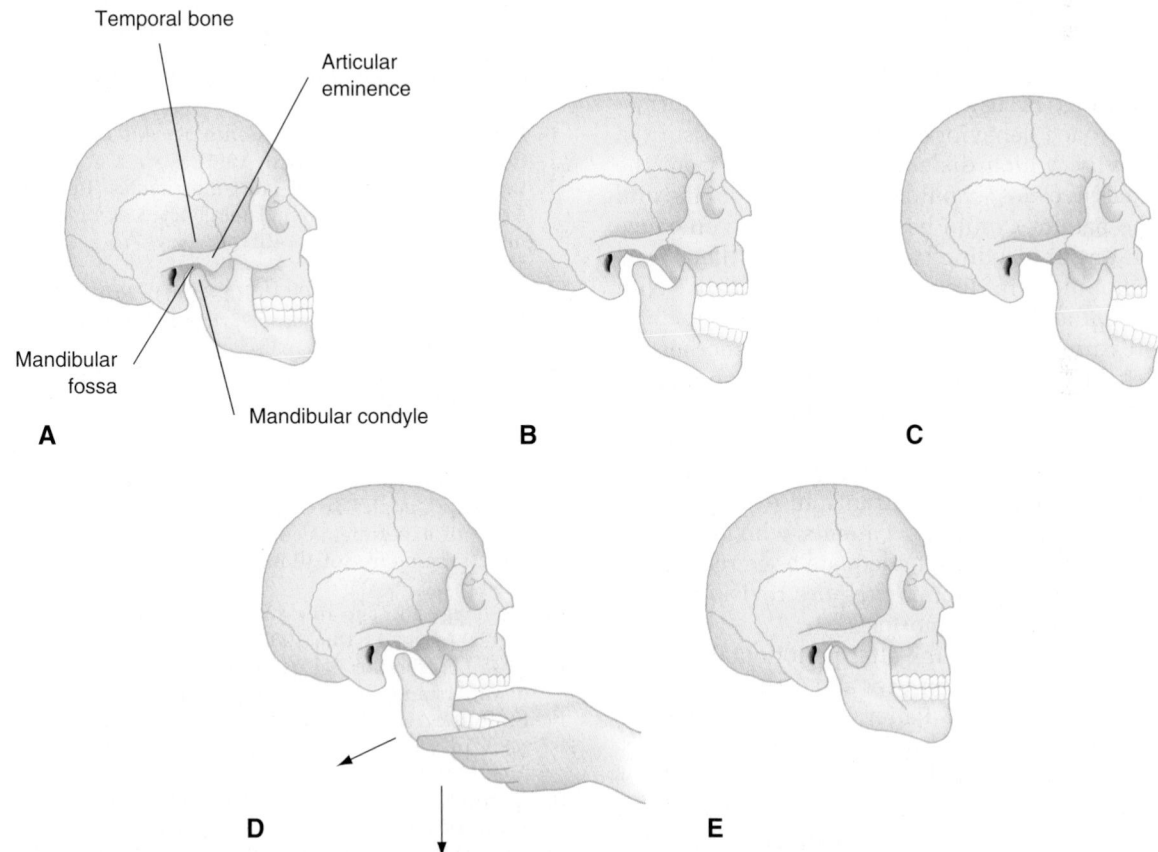

Figure 69-12. Reduction of temporomandibular joint dislocation. The temporomandibular joint is illustrated in normal and dislocated positions. **A,** Closed position, with the mandibular condyle resting in the mandibular fossa behind the articular eminence. **B,** In maximally open position, the mandibular condyle is just under and slightly behind the articular eminence. **C,** In dislocated position, the mandibular condyle moves forward and upward slightly above the articular eminence; muscle spasm then occurs. **D,** To reduce dislocation, the thumbs are placed intraorally and lateral to the lower molars and pressure is applied to the lower molar ridge area near the jaw angle in a downward and backward direction. **E,** When the mandibular condyle has cleared the articular eminence, muscle contraction returns the jaw to a normal closed position. (Redrawn from Rose LF, Hendler BH, Amsterdam JT: Temporomandibular disorders and odontic infections. *Consultant* 22:125, 1982.)

may be helpful. Patients with chronic dislocation may be helped initially with the application of a Barton bandage (elastic fabricated bandage that wraps around the top of the head and mandible). Intermaxillary fixation with wire and elastics may be necessary. Patients who have difficulty reducing themselves or who are plagued by recurrences may require surgical revision of the eminence for relief.[2,7]

Hemorrhage

Oral hemorrhage is a common complication of dental scalings, periodontal surgery, and dental extractions. Hemorrhage is controlled easily with local measures postoperatively. Patients may have sustained or recurrent hemorrhage after these procedures, however, and present to the emergency department. History should be obtained for recent dental procedures, drugs with antiplatelet activity such as aspirin, underlying coagulopathy, or a history of spontaneous bleeding. Spontaneous gingival hemorrhage without an inciting factor warrants a screen for coagulopathy and a complete blood count and differential. Diseases that result in spontaneous gingival hemorrhage are discussed in the section on oral manifestations of systemic disease. Management of coagulopathies from factor deficiencies requires factor replacement and administration of aminocaproic acid if there has been a recent dental extraction or periodontal surgery.[2,7]

Bleeding after extraction is the most common cause for oral hemorrhage. History of cigarette smoking, excessive spitting, or using straws is helpful information because each behavior creates negative pressure in the oral cavity, which dislodges blood clots from the socket. Excessive clots should be removed from the oral cavity. The patient should be allowed to bite on gauze for 20 minutes. If bleeding has not stopped, the extraction site should be infiltrated with 2% lidocaine with 1:100,000 epinephrine so that the tissue blanches. Gauze pressure should be repeated for another 20 minutes. If bleeding continues, the socket should be packed with an absorbable gelatin sponge or oxidized regenerated cellulose and secured with a No. 4-0 silk suture. Gauze pressure is applied again. Failure to respond to these measures warrants an evaluation for an underlying coagulopathy. Patients who have had multiple extractions without adequate bone recontouring and soft tissue closure may require revision of the surgical site to achieve hemostasis.[2]

Patients who have bleeding after periodontal surgery usually respond to local measures and continued application of gauze pressure. Patients who are bleeding excessively after a deep scaling may be helped by injection of local anesthetic with epinephrine or the placement of a periodontal pack. Patients who recently have undergone periodontal surgery involving gingival flaps may have dislodged the periodontal packs that were placed to ensure proper tissue alignment and wound healing. The periodontist should be informed if possible so that the pack can be replaced as soon as possible to ensure appropriate healing.

KEY CONCEPTS

- The most common nontraumatic dental emergencies are pain from dental caries, periodontal abscesses, and spread of infection of dental origin.
- The most important concern of dental infection is any compromise of the airway.
- Fractures of teeth are managed differently depending on which structures are involved—enamel, dentin, or pulp exposure.
- Avulsed teeth must be reimplanted as quickly as possible and are best preserved in Hank's solution.
- Soft tissue injuries, such as lip lacerations, when involved with dental injuries should be managed after the teeth have been stabilized.

REFERENCES

1. Amsterdam JT, Wagner DW, Rose LF: Interdisciplinary training: Hospital dental general practice/emergency medicine. *Ann Emerg Med* 9:310, 1980.
2. Amsterdam JT: Emergency dental procedures. In Roberts JR, Hedges J (eds): *Clinical Procedures in Emergency Medicine*, 4th ed. Philadelphia, WB Saunders, 2003.
3. Amsterdam JT: General dental emergencies. In Tintinalli JE, Krome RL, Ruiz E (eds): *Emergency Medicine: A Comprehensive Study Guide*, 4th ed. New York, McGraw-Hill, 1995.
4. Meford HM: Acute care of avulsed teeth. *Ann Emerg Med* 11:559, 1982.
5. Cohen DW (ed): *Contemporary Periodontics*. St. Louis, Mosby, 2004.
6. Linde J (ed): *Clinical Periodontology and Implant Dentistry*, Copenhagen, Munksgaard, 1997.
7. Peacock WF: Face and jaw emergencies. In Tintinalli JE, Krome RL, Ruiz E (eds): *Emergency Medicine: A Comprehensive Study Guide*, 4th ed. New York, McGraw-Hill, 1995.
8. Mandell GL, Bennett JE, Dolin R (eds): *Principles and Practice of Infectious Disease*, 3rd ed. Edinburgh, Churchill Livingstone, 2000.
9. Iwu CO: Ludwig's angina: A report of 7 cases and review of current concepts of management. *Br J Oral Maxillofac Surg* 28:189, 1990.
10. Amsterdam JT: Dental caries. In Honigman B (ed): *Emerg Index*. Denver, Colo, Emergency Information Center, 1994.
11. Orland FJ, et al: Use of germ free animal techniques in the study of experimental dental caries: I. Basic observations on rats reared free of all microorganisms. *J Dent Res* 11:232, 1954.
12. Holloway PJ: The role of sugar in the etiology of dental caries. *J Dent* 11:189, 1983.
13. Rose LF, Hendler BH, Amsterdam JT: Temporomandibular disorders and odontic infections. *Consultant* 22:110, 1982.
14. Solinitsky U: The fascial compartments of the head and neck in relation to dental infections. *Bull Georgetown U Med Center* 7:86, 1954.
15. Barkin R, Todd JK, Amer J: Periorbital cellulitis in children. *Pediatrics* 62:390, 1978.
16. Dice WH, Pryor GJ, Kilpatrick WR: Facial cellulitis following dental injury in a child. *Ann Emerg Med* 11:541, 1985.
17. Karlin RJ, Robinson WA: Septic cavernous sinus thrombosis. *Ann Emerg Med* 13:449, 1984.
18. Ahmad N, et al: The efficacy of non-opioid analgesics for postoperative dental pain: A meta-analysis. *Anesth Prog* 44:119, 1997.

19. Po AL, Zhang WY: Analgesic efficacy of ibuprofen alone and in combination with codeine or caffeine in postsurgical pain: A meta-analysis. *Eur J Clin Pharmacol* 53:303, 1998.

20. Amsterdam JT: Regional anesthesia of the head and neck. In Roberts JR, Hedges J (eds): *Clinical Procedures in Emergency Medicine,* 3rd ed. Philadelphia, WB Saunders, 1998.

21. Bennett CR: *Monheim's Local Anesthesia and Pain Control in Dental Practice,* 6th ed. St Louis, CV Mosby, 1978.

22. Laskin D: The role of the dentist in the emergency room. *Dent Clin North Am* 19:675, 1975.

23. Schluger S: Necrotizing ulcerative gingivitis in the army: Incidence, communicability, and treatment. *J Am Dent Assoc* 38:174, 1949.

24. Ingle JI: *Endodontics.* Philadelphia, Lea & Febiger, 1974.

25. Colby RC: The general practitioner's perspective of the etiology, prevention, and treatment of dry socket. *Gen Dent* 45:461, 1997.

26. Brightman VJ: Chronic oral sensory disorders—Pain and dysgeusia. In Lynch M (ed): *Burket's Oral Medicine, Diagnosis and Treatment.* Philadelphia, JB Lippincott, 1994.

27. Sicher H: Structural and functional basis for disorders of the temporomandibular articulation. *J Oral Surg* 13:275, 1955.

28. Alderman MM: Disorders of the temporomandibular joint and related structures. In Lynch M (ed): *Burket's Oral Medicine, Diagnosis and Treatment.* Philadelphia, JB Lippincott, 1994.

29. Alderman MM: Disorders of the temporomandibular joint and related structures: Rationale for diagnosis, etiology, and management. *Alpha Omegan* 69:12, 1976.

30. Weisgold AS, Laudenbach KW: Occlusal etiology and management of disorders of the temporomandibular joint and related structures. *Alpha Omegan* 69:12, 1976.

31. Rose LF: General health affecting periodontal disease and therapeutic response. In Goldman HM, Cohen DW (eds): *Periodontal Therapy,* 6th ed. St. Louis, CV Mosby, 1980.

32. Kimball OP: The treatment of epilepsy with sodium diphenylhydantoin. *JAMA* 112:1244, 1939.

33. Lederman D, et al: Gingival hyperplasia associated with nifedipine therapy. *Oral Surg* 57:620, 1984.

34. Ramon Y, et al: Gingival hyperplasia caused by nifedipine—A preliminary report. *Int J Cardiol* 5:195, 1984.

35. Cohen DW: Gingival hyperplasia—A new lesion for the cardiologist? *Int J Cardiol* 5:205, 1984.

36. Alpsoy E, Er H, Durusoy C, Yilmaz E: The use of sucralfate suspension in the treatment of oral and genital ulceration of Behcet disease: A randomized, placebo-controlled, double-blind study. *Arch Dermatol* 135:529, 1999.

37. Vincent SD, Lilly GE: Clinical, historical, therapeutic features of aphthous stomatitis: Literature review and open clinical trials employing steroids. *Oral Surg Oral Med Oral Pathol* 74:79, 1992.

38. Andreason JO: *Traumatic Injuries of the Teeth.* Philadelphia, WB Saunders, 1981.

39. Coccia CT: A clinical investigation of root resorption rates in reimplanted young permanent incisors: A five year study. *J Endodontol* 6:413, 1980.

40. Johnson R: Descriptive classification of trauma: The injuries to the teeth and supporting structures. *J Am Dent Assoc* 102:195, 1981.

41. Medford HM, Curbs JW: Acute care of severe tooth fractures. *Ann Emerg Med* 12:364, 1983.

42. Medford HM: Temporary stabilization of avulsed or luxated teeth. *Ann Emerg Med* 11:490, 1982.

43. Soder PO, et al: Effect of drying on viability of periodontal membrane. *Scand J Dent Res* 85:164, 1977.

44. Grossman LL Ship II: Survival rate of reimplanted teeth. *Oral Surg* 29:899, 1970.

45. Andreasen JO, Hjorting-Hansen E: Replantation of teeth: I. Radiographic and clinical study of 110 human teeth replanted after accidental loss. *Acta Odontol Scand* 24:263, 1966.

46. Andreasen JO, Hjorting-Hansen E: Replantation of teeth: II. Histologic study of replanted anterior teeth in humans. *Acta Odontol Scand* 24:287, 1966.

47. Blomlof L: Milk and saliva as possible storage media for traumatically exarticulated teeth prior to replantation. *Swed Dent J* 8(Suppl):1, 1981.

48. Lindskog S, Blomlof L: Influence of osmolality and composition of some storage media on human periodontal ligament cells. *Acta Odontol Scand* 40:435, 1982.

49. Kristerson L, Soder PO, Otteskog P: Transport and storage of human teeth in vitro for autotransplantation and replantation. *J Oral Surg* 34:13, 1976.

50. Matsson L, et al: Ankylosis of experimentally reimplanted teeth related to extra-alveolar period and storage environment. *Pediatr Dent* 4:327, 1982.

51. Krasner P: Modern treatment of avulsed teeth by emergency physicians. *Am J Emerg Med* 12:241, 1994.

52. Steele MT, et al: Prophylactic penicillin for intraoral wounds. *Ann Emerg Med* 18:847, 1989.

53. Irby WB (ed): *Facial Trauma and Concomitant Problems.* St. Louis, CV Mosby, 1979.

54. Hendler BH, Wagner D: Injury to the lip and oral mucosa: Trauma rounds. *Emerg Med* 6:278, 1974.

55. Myall WT, Sandor GK, Gregory CE: Are you overlooking fractures of the mandibular condyle? *Pediatrics* 79:639, 1987.

CHAPTER

70 Ophthalmology

Douglas D. Brunette

PERSPECTIVE

Background and Epidemiology

Two percent of emergency department patients have eye complaints, ranging from minor problems to vision-threatening crises. The emergency physician requires skill in the evaluation and treatment of primary ophthalmologic pathology, infectious problems, and traumatic injuries. The majority of eye complaints can be treated without ophthalmologic consultation, but a few require ophthalmologist involvement as well as immediate action.[1] Some specific problems such as central retinal artery occlusion and caustic exposure require emergent therapy, even as assessment proceeds. Many other ophthalmologic conditions can be evaluated with a history and examination before treatment by the emergency physician.

Figures 70-1 and 70-2 are provided as brief reviews of normal ocular anatomy and funduscopic appearance.

OCULAR TRAUMA

Perspective

A systematic evaluation of the periorbital and orbital structures aids in the evaluation of patients with ocular trauma. Many extraocular structures are found in close proximity, and concomitant, nonocular injury is common. Penetrating and blunt ocular trauma may involve several eye structures.

Nonpenetrating Trauma

Orbit and Lid

Clinical Features and Management
Contusion. Blunt injury to the orbits and surrounding tissues results in ecchymosis, swelling, and an often dramatic appearance. Related significant injury must be considered. Basilar skull fractures may occur with bilateral ecchymosis (raccoon eyes). Underlying globe injury may be present and complete examination impeded by swelling. The emergency physician should attempt to visualize and examine all structures underlying the eyelids and obtain an accurate visual acuity. This should be done soon after the patient presents, before further swelling occurs. Examining the structures underlying severely swollen eyelids is difficult. A Desmarres retractor may help avoid global pressure.

Treatment of isolated soft tissue injury to the eyelids and surrounding area is symptomatic. Head elevation and cold compresses started in the emergency department should continue for 48 hours and decrease the pain and swelling. Complete resolution takes 2 to 3 weeks. Patients should be instructed to seek follow-up care for any increase in pain or swelling, decreased vision, double vision, or significant flashing lights or "floaters."

Orbital Wall Fractures. When blunt force causes an acute rise in intraorbital pressure, the thin walls of the orbit frequently fracture. Prolapse of orbital soft tissues into the maxillary sinus may result because the orbital floor is generally the weakest point.[2] Entrapment of the inferior rectus and inferior oblique ocular muscles, orbital fat, and connective tissues results in enophthalmos, ptosis, diplopia, anesthesia of the ipsilateral cheek and upper lip, and limitation of upward gaze. Subcutaneous orbital emphysema may be palpable. Associated globe injuries occur in 10% to 25% of patients with orbital floor fractures.[3] Radiographic examination of the face can help but is imperfect. A computed tomography (CT) scan of the orbits is preferred. On x-ray film, the teardrop sign, a bulge extending from the orbit into the maxillary sinus, and an air-fluid level in the maxillary sinus are indirect signs of orbital floor injury (Figure 70-3). If the fracture involves an infected sinus, treatment consists of nasal decongestants, broad-spectrum oral antibiotics, and ice packs to the orbit for 48 hours. Some ophthalmologists use steroids to reduce swelling. Surgical repair is only for persistent diplopia or cosmetic concerns and is generally not performed until swelling subsides in 7 to 10 days.[4,5] Patients can usually be discharged to be reevaluated by an ophthalmologist in 1 to 2 weeks.

Medial orbital wall fractures, through the lamina papyracea of the ethmoid bone, involve entry into the ethmoid sinus. Clinical features include orbital emphysema and epistaxis. Diplopia from medial rectus impingement can occur.[2] The finding of orbital emphysema should prompt a search for associated injury.[6] Rarely is orbital emphysema significant enough to compress the optic nerve and result in acute visual loss.[7,8] In most cases, orbital emphysema is a benign finding that resolves with time. Prophylactic antibiotics are not needed unless the fracture involves an infected sinus.[6] Patients with orbital floor and medial orbital wall fractures should avoid blowing their noses and performing Valsalva's maneuver to limit the extent of emphysema.

Orbital rim fractures are also common. They are a result of direct force.

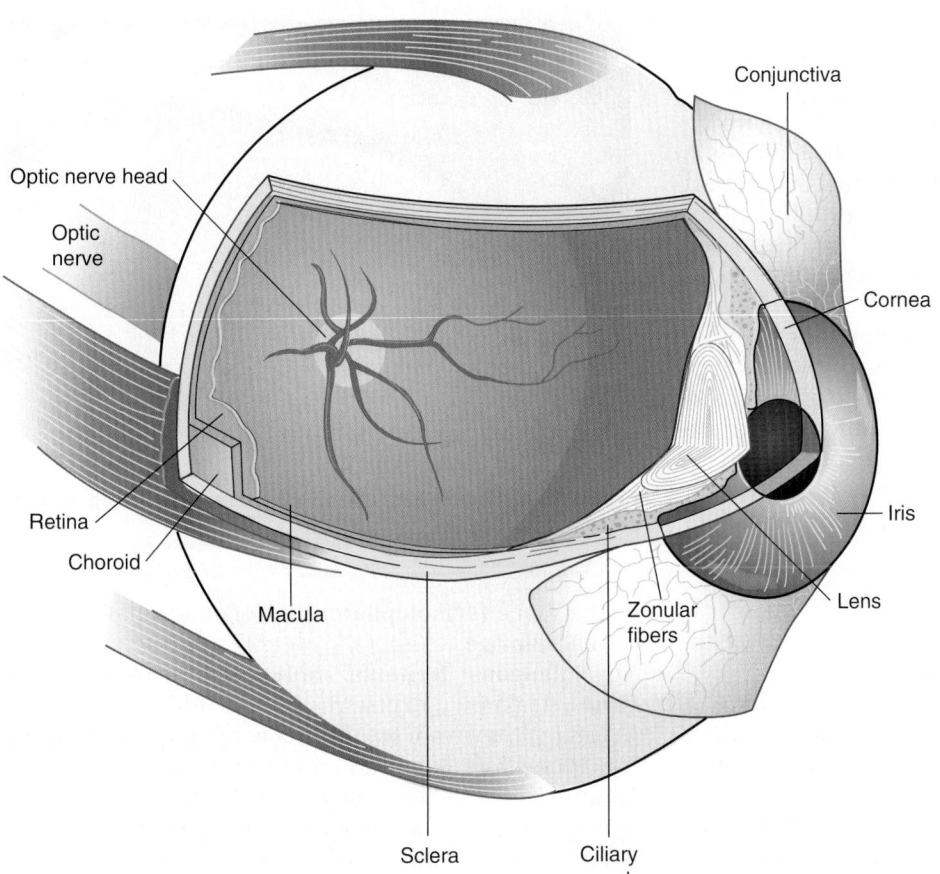

Figure 70-1. Cutaway section of the eye. (From Stein HA, Slatt BJ, Stein RM: *The Ophthalmic Assistant: Fundamentals and Clinical Practice*, 5th ed. St. Louis, Mosby, 1988.)

Conjunctiva

Optic nerve head

Optic nerve

Cornea

Retina

Choroid

Iris

Macula

Lens

Zonular fibers

Sclera

Ciliary muscle

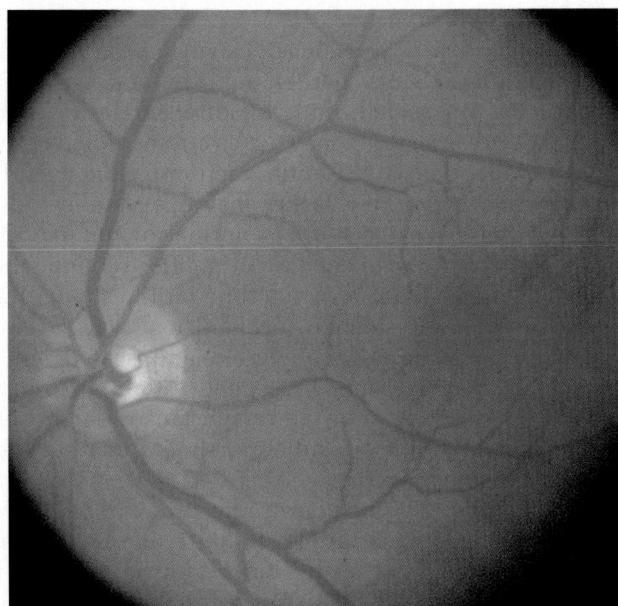

Figure 70-2. Normal fundus.

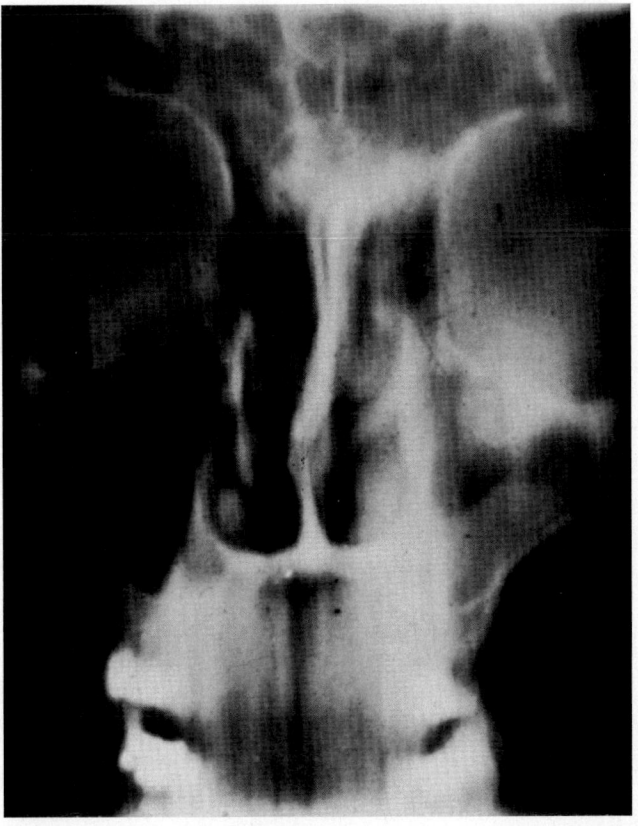

Figure 70-3. Facial radiograph demonstrating teardrop sign in right maxillary sinus from orbital floor fracture.

Retrobulbar Hemorrhage. Orbital hemorrhage in the potential space surrounding the globe may occur after blunt trauma and injury to the orbital vessels. Significant hemorrhage results in an acute rise in intraorbital pressure that is transmitted to the globe and optic nerve. This may result in occlusion of the central retinal artery. Clinical findings include proptosis, limitation of ocular movement, visual loss, and increased intraocular pressure. An orbital CT scan demonstrates a hematoma.

When a retrobulbar hematoma compromises retinal circulation, immediate ophthalmologic consultation for decompression is warranted. Treatment of increased intraocular pressure includes carbonic anhydrase inhibitor, topical β-blocker, and intravenous (IV) mannitol. A lateral canthotomy can be done in the emergency department as a temporizing measure before definitive decompression.[2]

Cornea and Conjunctiva

Clinical Features and Management

Chemical Burns. Exposing the eye to chemicals is a true ocular emergency. Exposure to strong alkaline chemicals, found in drain cleaners, chemical detergents, industrial solvents, and as lime in plaster and concrete, produces a liquefactive necrosis that penetrates and dissolves tissues until the alkaline agent is removed. Acid burns tend to be less devastating than alkali burns because acidic exposure causes coagulation necrosis and the precipitation of tissue proteins limits the depth of the injury.

Treatment should begin at the scene with immediate irrigation using copious amounts of water. Irrigation should continue for at least 30 minutes before any attempt to transport the patient to the hospital. Any particles should be removed from the fornices using a cotton swab.

Upon hospital arrival, irrigation should continue. Topical anesthetics and manual lid retraction may be needed for proper irrigation. Irrigation is needed until the pH of the tear film is neutral as tested by Nitrazine paper dipped into the inferior conjunctival fornix. If the pH tested immediately after irrigation is still alkaline, irrigation should be reinstituted. A normal pH should be checked again 10 minutes after the cessation of irrigation and periodically thereafter. Treatment after irrigation consists of a cycloplegic (avoid phenylephrine), topical antibiotics, treatment of increased intraocular pressure, and pain management.

Ophthalmologic consultation is indicated in all significant chemical exposures. Identification of the substance and its pH value is important. Alkaline substances with a pH less than 12 and acidic substances with a pH greater than 2 are thought not to cause significant injury, although high concentration and prolonged contact time can alter this general rule and may cause injury.[9,10]

Severity can be judged by the degree of corneal cloudiness and scleral whitening (Figure 70-4).[11] Long-term complications include perforation, scarring, and neovascularization of the cornea; adhesions of the lids

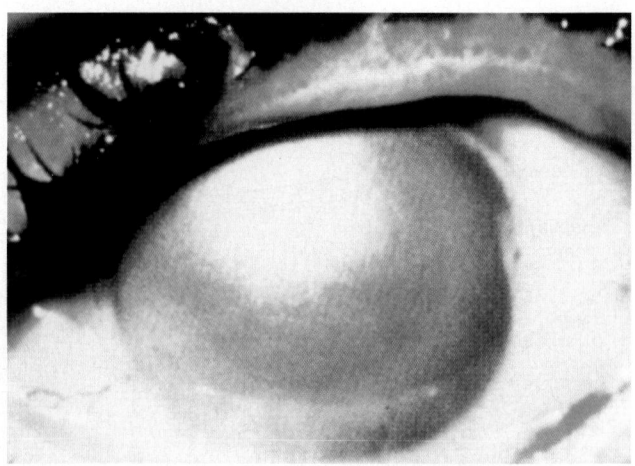

Figure 70-4. Severe alkali burn. Note scleral whitening and the cloudy cornea.

to the globe (symblepharon); glaucoma; cataracts; and retinal damage.

Miscellaneous Irritants, Solvents, Detergents, and Glues. Unknown exposures should initially be treated as though they were an alkali or acid exposure, prompting immediate irrigation. Detergents generally cause conjunctival irritation only. More irritating substances may denude the corneal epithelium and cause anterior chamber inflammation. After copious irrigation, these injuries should be treated as corneal abrasions.

Aerosol exposures are common. Intraocular foreign bodies may result from the propellant. Exposure to the compounds found in personal defense devices (e.g., mace) should be treated in the same manner as other chemical injuries.

Super glue (cyanoacrylate adhesive) exposure is also common. These glues harden rapidly, and typically the eyelids are sealed shut. Misdirected lashes and the hardened super glue may act as a foreign body and cause corneal defects.[12] Gentle traction on the eyelids and separating glued eyelashes may open the eyelids. If the eyelids are sealed shut in a normal anatomic position and cannot be opened with gentle traction, the eye may be left alone, allowing time for the super glue to dissolve by physiologic mechanisms over several days.[13] If the eyelids are inverted and sealed shut, surgical intervention may be needed. Attempts to dissolve the super glue with other substances should be avoided. Ophthalmic consultation should be obtained for super glue exposures.

Thermal Burns. Thermal burns affect the eyelids more than the globe because of reflex blinking and Bell's phenomenon. Superficial eyelid burns can be treated by irrigation and topical antibiotic ophthalmic ointment. Second- or third-degree eyelid burns need ophthalmic consultation. Hot liquid splashes and cigarette ashes to the cornea usually result in a superficial corneal epithelial injury and are treated as corneal abrasions. Molten metals and other hot objects may result in globe perforation.

Radiation Burns (Ultraviolet Keratitis). Ultraviolet light from sun lamps, tanning booths, high-altitude environments, or a welder's arc results in direct corneal

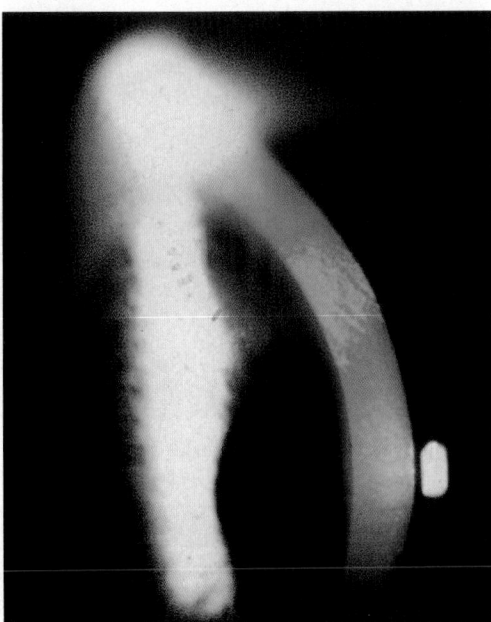

Figure 70-5. Corneal abrasion demonstrated by slit-lamp examination.

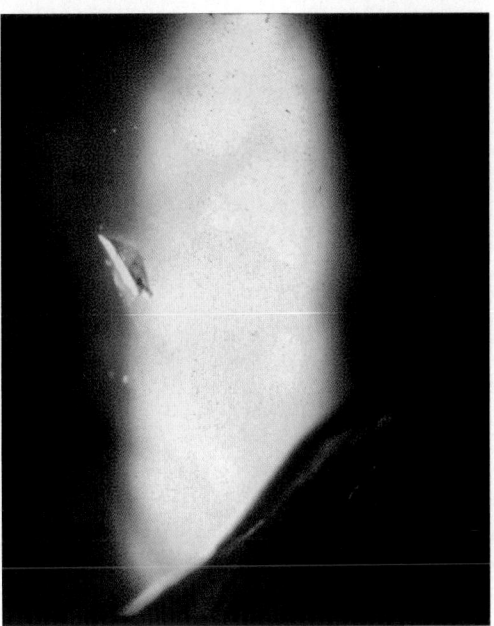

Figure 70-6. Corneal foreign body (glass) seen by slit-lamp examination.

epithelial damage. After a latent period of 6 to 10 hours, patients develop a foreign body sensation, tearing, intense pain, photophobia, and blepharospasm.[14] Topical ophthalmic anesthetics facilitate physical examination. Examination reveals decreased visual acuity, injected conjunctiva, and diffuse punctate corneal lesions, often with a discrete lower border defining the cornea protected by the inferior lid. Treatment consists of a short-acting cycloplegic and a topical broad-spectrum antibiotic ointment. Eye patching may be used for the patient's comfort on the more affected eye. Oral narcotics are commonly needed. Patients should not be prescribed topical anesthetics because frequent use retards healing and can lead to corneal ulcer formation.[15] Patients should have ophthalmologic follow-up in 24 hours.

Mechanical Corneal Abrasions. Patients complain of a foreign body sensation, pain, photophobia, and decrease in visual acuity. The degree of relief afforded by topical anesthesia can differentiate corneal injury from other causes of acute eye pain.[16] Physical examination reveals injected conjunctiva, decreased visual acuity if the defect is large or lies in the visual axis, and demonstration of the epithelial defect with slit-lamp examination using fluorescein (Figure 70-5). Foreign bodies of the lid conjunctiva must be identified. Treatment consists of cycloplegia, topical nonsteroidal anti-inflammatory medications, and topical antibiotics. Patients with contact lenses should be treated with topical antibiotics with antipseudomonal coverage. Eye patching should be avoided, especially in injury involving vegetable matter or contact lens use. Data suggest that eye patching confers no benefit in healing small, uncomplicated corneal abrasions.[17,18] Patients with corneal abrasions should not wear their contact lenses. Oral pain medications may be needed. Patients should have ophthalmologic follow-up in 24 hours.

Corneal Foreign Bodies. Patients with corneal foreign bodies experience pain, foreign body sensation, injected conjunctiva, tearing, and blepharospasm. Administration of a topical ophthalmic anesthetic facilitates physical examination. Diagnosis is made with slit-lamp examination (Figure 70-6). After a topical anesthetic is applied, the initial attempt at removing corneal foreign bodies should be with a stream of sterile saline solution. If this fails, the foreign body should be removed using a commercial eye spud or 25-gauge needle with a 1- to 3-mL syringe as a handle and magnification, generally the slit lamp. The patient must be totally cooperative and the patient's head firmly stabilized within the slit lamp. Alternatively, a short plastic 20-gauge catheter can be placed on a syringe and, with slit-lamp visualization, the foreign body can sometimes be irrigated out of the cornea.

Iron-containing corneal foreign bodies leave a residual rust ring (Figure 70-7). Removal of the rust ring should be left to the ophthalmologist at the 24-hour follow-up visit because the affected cornea gradually softens, and the rust migrates toward the corneal surface, making removal easier.

Ophthalmologic consultation for corneal foreign bodies is recommended if a large area of the visual axis is involved, the object is deeply embedded within the cornea, the risk of perforation is increased for any reason, or there are multiple foreign bodies.

Treatment after foreign body removal is similar to that for corneal abrasion, with ophthalmologic follow-up within 24 hours.

Use of high-speed drills, saws, grinders, and pounding objects or involvement in explosions should alert the emergency physician to the likelihood of an intraocular foreign body with perforation. CT can be used to rule out the diagnosis of an intraocular foreign body.

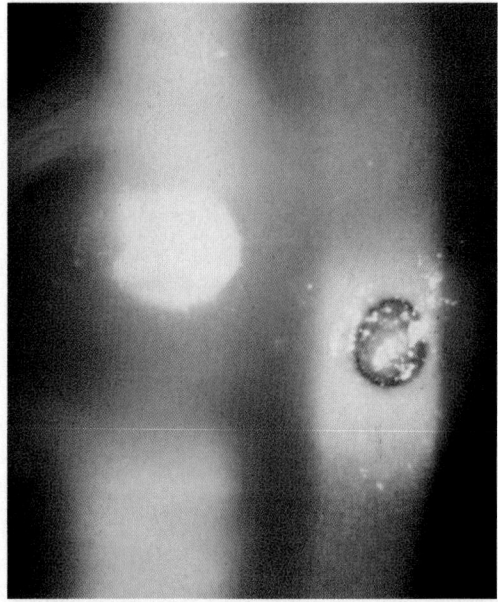

Figure 70-7. Corneal rust ring after removal of iron-containing foreign body demonstrated by slit-lamp examination.

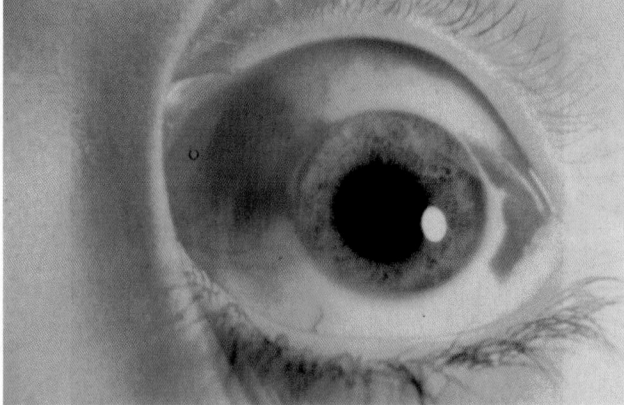

Figure 70-8. Subconjunctival hemorrhage.

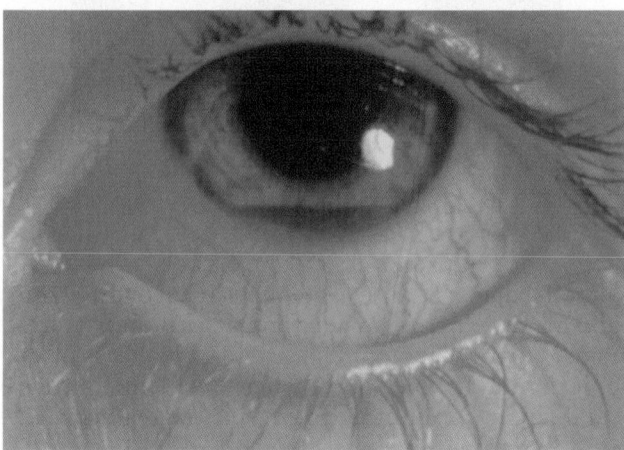

Figure 70-9. Small hyphema layering out in the inferior portion of the anterior chamber.

Conjunctival Foreign Body. Conjunctival foreign bodies can be removed under topical anesthesia with a cotton-tipped applicator or fine forceps. Topical phenylephrine can be used to reduce the conjunctival bleeding.

Subconjunctival Hemorrhage. Rupture of small subconjunctival blood vessels is common and occurs as a result of trauma or Valsalva's maneuver or without apparent cause. Patients complain of its appearance. Pain, diminished visual acuity, or photophobia suggests a more serious pathologic condition. Subconjunctival hemorrhage is flat, bright red, smooth, limited to the bulbar conjunctiva, and sharply demarcated at the limbus (Figure 70-8). Subconjunctival hemorrhage must be distinguished from bloody chemosis, which is indicative of more serious globe pathology. Bilateral or recurrent subconjunctival hemorrhage may require workup for bleeding diathesis. Treatment consists of local cold compresses for 24 hours, with resolution in 2 to 3 weeks.

Anterior Chamber and Iris

Clinical Features and Management

Traumatic Hyphema. Disruption of blood vessels in the iris or ciliary body results in hyphema. If the patient is sitting, the blood often layers and forms a meniscus with the aqueous humor. Hyphemas range from minimal blood seen only with the slit lamp to the "eight ball" or total hyphema with blood that has clotted. Patients complain of pain, photophobia, and decreased visual acuity. The emergency physician sees the blood directly or with the aid of the slit lamp (Figure 70-9). There is generally no afferent pupillary defect present. Intraocular pressure may also rise.

Management of hyphema must be individualized for a given patient. Selected low-grade hyphemas in reliable patients may be managed on an outpatient basis; all other patients should be admitted. General therapy includes elevating the bed 30 to 45 degrees, bed rest, and limiting eye movement such as reading.[11] Analgesics are appropriate, but the patient should avoid taking aspirin and other platelet inhibitors.[19] Antiemetics and sedatives should be used cautiously. Increased intraocular pressure occurs as a result of aqueous flow blockage from the blood present. In patients without sickle cell disease, initial treatment is a topical β-blocker; a topical α-agonist or topical carbonic anhydrase inhibitor is added if needed. Oral acetazolamide or IV mannitol may also be used.

Specific treatment for hyphema with miotics, mydriatics, cycloplegics, steroids, and antifibrinolytics such as aminocaproic acid varies depending on the specific clinical situation and is best left to the ophthalmologist.[11,20-22] Failure of medical therapy to control high intraocular pressure, failure of a large clot to resolve, and corneal blood staining are indications for surgical intervention.[21] There are case reports on the use of anterior chamber thrombolytics in those whose large clot fails to resolve.[19]

The major complication of hyphema is rebleeding, which occurs after 2 to 5 days when the initial clot retracts and loosens.[23] Rebleeding is more common in those with visual acuities of 20/200, initial hyphema covering more than one third of the anterior chamber, medical attention delayed more than 1 day after injury, and elevated intraocular pressure at the initial exami-

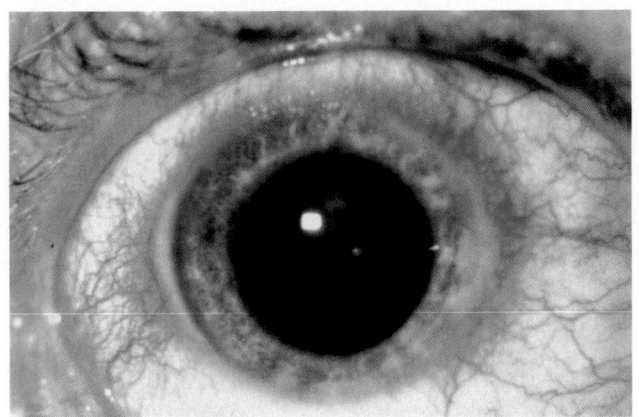

Figure 70-10. Ciliary flush. Note that conjunctival injection is most prominent immediately around the limbus.

nation.[24] Other complications include corneal blood staining, acute or chronic glaucoma, and anterior or posterior synechia formation.

Patients with hemoglobinopathies (e.g., sickle cell disease, thalassemia) are at increased risk for hyphema complications. Red blood cells in the anterior chamber sickle in the relatively acidic and hypoxic environment,[25] which leads to decreased aqueous humor outflow and a rapid rise in intraocular pressure. Increased intraocular pressure in a sickle cell patient with a hyphema should be treated with topical β-blockers. All other antiglaucoma medications should be prescribed by an ophthalmologist. If needed, methazolamide by mouth, and not acetazolamide, may be used.

Traumatic Iridocyclitis. Blunt injury of the globe may contuse and inflame the iris and ciliary body, resulting in ciliary spasm. Patients complain of photophobia and deep, aching eye pain. Examination reveals perilimbal conjunctival injection (ciliary flush), cells and flare in the anterior chamber, and a small, poorly dilating pupil (Figure 70-10). These symptoms indicate white blood cells and protein as a result of the inflammation.

Treatment consists of paralyzing the iris and ciliary body with a long-acting cycloplegic agent, such as homatropine methylbromide 5%, given four times daily for 7 to 10 days.[26] Prednisolone acetate 1% may be given to help relieve the inflammation if there is no improvement after 5 to 7 days but should be avoided in patients with a corneal epithelial defect. Resolution occurs within 1 week.

Traumatic Mydriasis and Miosis. Blunt injury may result in either pupillary dilatation or constriction and may persist for days. For significant head trauma and altered mental status, a cranial nerve palsy must be ruled out before ascribing pupillary mydriasis to local contusion.

Permanent pupillary mydriasis may result from small radial tears in the pupillary sphincter muscle. The pupil margin may look irregular or scalloped. No specific emergency department treatment is warranted.

Iridodialysis. Traumatic iridodialysis is a tearing of the iris root from the ciliary body, leading to the formation of a "secondary pupil." This injury is often the cause of a hyphema. If no associated hyphema is present, no specific emergency department treatment is needed.

Large tears can lead to monocular diplopia and may require surgical correction. Immediate ophthalmologic consultation is warranted when iridodialysis has caused a hyphema or a decrease in visual acuity.

Anterior Chamber Angle Recession. Blunt injury to the ciliary body may cause posterior displacement of the iris and surrounding tissues, deepening the anterior chamber, widening the anterior chamber angle, and causing potential damage to the trabecular meshwork that drains the aqueous humor. Severe damage can cause acute glaucoma.

Scleral and Lens Injuries

Clinical Features and Management

Cataract. If the lens capsule is disrupted by either blunt or penetrating trauma, the relatively dehydrated stroma absorbs fluid, swells, and becomes cloudy. Acute glaucoma may develop from blockage of the aqueous humor flow through the pupil, necessitating surgical intervention. In less severe injury, cataract formation may occur over weeks to months.

Lens Subluxation and Dislocation. Complete disruption of the lens zonule fibers by blunt trauma may result in anterior or posterior dislocation of the lens. Incomplete disruption of the lens zonule fibers results in subluxation of the lens. Lens dislocation may occur with minor trauma in patients with Marfan's syndrome, homocystinuria, tertiary syphilis, and other predisposing conditions. Patients complain of monocular diplopia or visual distortion with subluxation and marked visual blurring with dislocation. Examination reveals decreased visual acuity. The edge of a subluxated lens can be seen when the pupil is dilated. Iridodonesis is a trembling or shimmering of the iris after rapid eye movements and is a helpful sign of lens dislocation. Treatment ranges from observation to surgical removal and is dictated by the location of the dislocated lens and associated eye injury. Immediate ophthalmologic consultation is warranted.

Scleral Rupture. Blunt trauma causes scleral rupture by suddenly elevating intraocular pressure. Ruptures are most common at the insertions of the intraocular muscles or at the limbus, where the sclera is thinnest.[27] The diagnosis of scleral rupture is obvious when intraocular contents are visualized; however, occult global rupture can be difficult to diagnose. Patients complain of eye pain and decreased vision. Examination may reveal a bloody chemosis or severe subconjunctival hemorrhage overlying the scleral rupture site. Uveal prolapse through the scleral wound, appearing as a brownish-black discoloration, can also be seen (Figure 70-11). Although a lower than normal intraocular pressure is a good indication of rupture, tonometry should not be performed in suspected globe rupture. Any maneuvers that increase intraocular pressure need to be avoided. A CT scan, ultrasonography, and indirect ophthalmoscopy all play a role in the diag-nosis of occult globe rupture but may be left to the ophthalmologist.

Treatment in the emergency department for a known globe rupture includes avoidance of further examination or manipulation and the placement of a protective

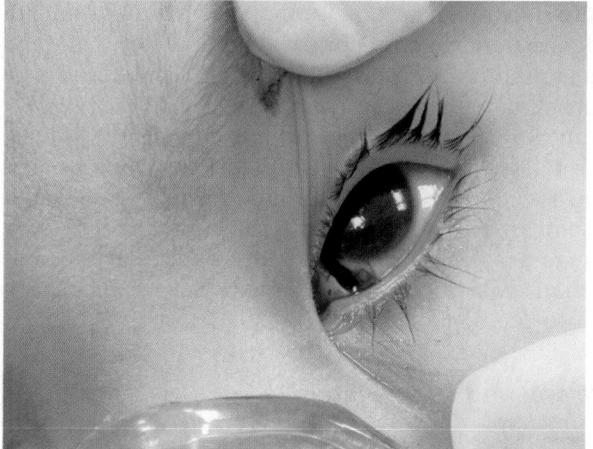

Figure 70-11. Scleral laceration with penetrating globe injury. Note care being taken not to increase intraocular pressure with examiner's fingers.

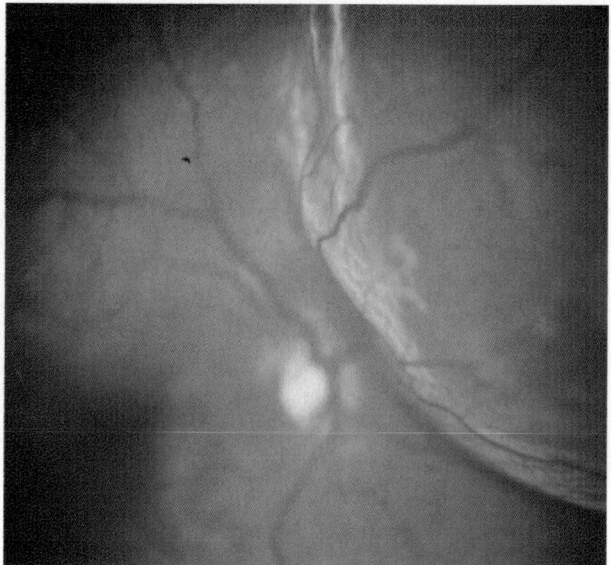

Figure 70-12. Retinal detachment. Note large portion of retinal billowing forward.

metal eye shield to prevent accidental pressure on the globe. The patient should be kept with nothing by mouth and a tetanus injection given as needed. Antiemetics should be given if the patient is nauseated. Broad-spectrum IV antibiotics should be instituted.[28]

Theoretical classical teaching states that the use of succinylcholine is contraindicated in the presence of a penetrating ocular injury because of the rise in intraocular pressure and potential for ocular extrusion. Increased intraocular pressure occurs 1 to 4 minutes after succinylcholine administration, and the pressure returns to baseline after 7 minutes.[29] The literature contains many conflicting studies of the efficacy of pretreatment with various agents including nondepolarizing muscle relaxants, gallamine, *d*-tubocurarine, diazepam, and others that reduce or attenuate the rise in intraocular pressure resulting from succinylcholine use.[29] However, one study reported on the use of succinylcholine after pretreatment with nondepolarizing agents in 100 patients with penetrating eye injury; no adverse events were found.[30] Given the need for rapid airway management in a patient with penetrating ocular injury, rapid sequence intubation with succinylcholine after pretreatment with nondepolarizing and sedative agents is appropriate.

Ophthalmologic consultation is required for all patients with suspected or proven globe rupture.

Posterior Segment Injuries

Clinical Features and Management
Vitreous Hemorrhage. Bleeding into the vitreous may occur from injuries to the retina and uveal tract and their associated vascular structures. Patients complain of decreased visual acuity and floaters. Floaters, described by the patient as dark dots or strands moving in the visual field in the direction of the preceding eye movement, are caused by vitreous blood. There is a diminished red reflex and an inability to visualize the fundus clearly with the direct ophthalmoscope. With vitreous hemorrhage caused by blunt trauma, B-scan ultrasonography is used to search for retinal injury and determine the need for operative repair.[31]

Treatment of vitreous hemorrhage includes elevating the head of the bed to allow settling of the blood and avoiding platelet-inhibiting drugs and Valsalva's maneuver. Vitrectomy is performed for vitreous hemorrhage with an associated retinal detachment. Ophthalmologic consultation is warranted for acute traumatic vitreous hemorrhage.

Retinal Injuries. Blunt injury to the retina may result in hemorrhage, a tear or detachment, or commotio retinae.

Hemorrhage can occur in the preretinal (subhyaloid), superficial retinal, or deep (subretinal) spaces. Preretinal hemorrhage appears boat shaped, superficial retinal hemorrhage flame shaped, and deep retinal hemorrhage as rounded and grape-purple in color.

Tears and detachments from blunt trauma are common. Symptoms include floaters from bleeding, flashing lights from stimulation of retinal neurons, and visual field cuts or decreased visual acuity. Retinal tears or detachments do not cause pain. Examination may reveal the hazy gray membrane of the retina billowing forward (Figure 70-12), but many tears are peripherally located and not seen with direct ophthalmoscopy. Visual acuity may be normal unless the macula is involved. Indirect ophthalmoscopy is warranted if historic clues to the presence of retinal tears are present.

Ophthalmologic consultation is warranted in all cases of suspected or proven retinal detachment. Treatment includes photocoagulation or operative repair; prognosis depends on the condition of the macula.

Commotio retinae occurs after recent ocular trauma. Patients may have decreased visual acuity or be asymptomatic. Examination reveals a cloudy whitening of the involved area that subsides in a few weeks with no specific treatment. Serial follow-up is necessary to ensure that retinal tear or detachment has not occurred.

Optic Nerve Injury. Significant blunt force to the orbital contents may avulse, transect, compress, or contuse the optic nerve. Fractures may extend into the orbital canal and cause optic nerve damage. Patients complain of visual field cuts or decreased visual acuity. Examination reveals an afferent pupillary defect, assorted visual field cuts, a decrease in visual acuity, or total blindness. The optic disk is normal initially, but pallor eventually develops.[2] An orbital CT scan can help define the location and extent of injury. Management of traumatic optic neuropathy is controversial. High-dose methylprednisolone and surgical decompression have been used with varying degrees of success.[2] When edema or bleeding within the optic nerve is visualized, or with significant reduction in visual acuity, high-dose steroids can be used. Surgical decompression should be considered when decreasing visual acuity is occurring from a known orbital canal fracture.

Penetrating Trauma

Lacerations of the Eyelids

Clinical Features and Management
Any laceration involving the eyelids should prompt a search for penetrating globe injury and, if indicated, a thorough search for a foreign body. Soft eye pads should be avoided to prevent increases in intraocular pressure.

Emergency physicians can manage simple horizontal or oblique partial-thickness lid lacerations. These can be closed primarily using 6-0 or 7-0 nylon interrupted sutures. Sutures should be removed in 3 to 5 days.

Several lid lacerations have a high likelihood of cosmetic or functional complications and should be managed by ophthalmologists or plastic surgeons skilled in this area. The following lid lacerations fall into the category of complex lid lacerations and need immediate referral.

1. Lacerations involving the lid margins.
2. Lacerations involving the canalicular system. Injury to the canalicular system should be suspected in any laceration involving the medial lower eyelid area (Figure 70-13).
3. Lacerations involving the levator or canthal tendons.
4. Laceration through the orbital septum. Orbital fat protrudes through septal lacerations into the wound. Because eyelids have no subcutaneous fat, the appearance of fat in a lid laceration confirms this diagnosis. These wounds are associated with a high incidence of globe penetration and intraorbital foreign bodies.
5. Lacerations with tissue loss.

Conjunctival Lacerations

Clinical Features and Management
Lacerations of the bulbar conjunctiva commonly involve intraocular foreign bodies or underlying scleral perforation. Slit-lamp examination can distinguish superficial from deeper lacerations. Small, superficial lacerations require no suturing and heal quickly. Topical prophylactic ophthalmic antibiotics are advisable. Larger (>1 cm) and deeper lacerations may require repair by an ophthalmologist.

Corneal and Scleral Lacerations

Clinical Features and Management
Corneal Lacerations. Signs of corneal perforation (full-thickness corneal lacerations) include loss of anterior

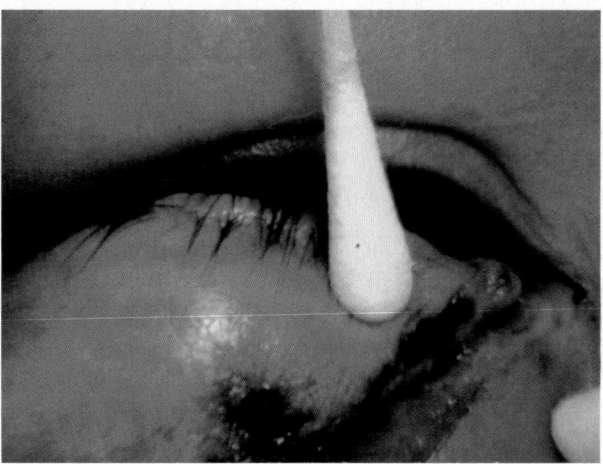

Figure 70-13. Facial laceration near the medial canthus with involvement of the canaliculus.

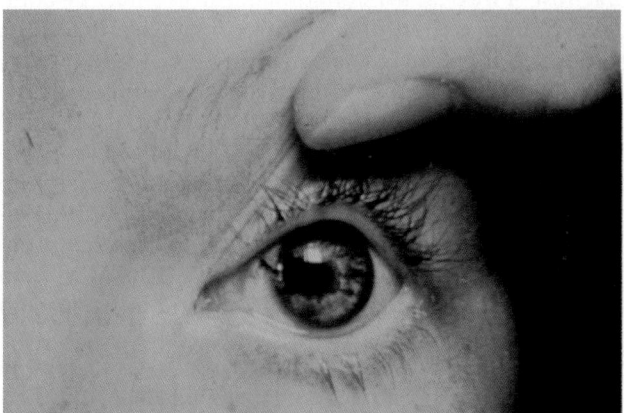

Figure 70-14. Teardrop-shaped pupil demonstrating anterior chamber perforation through corneal laceration.

chamber depth, teardrop-shaped pupil caused by iris prolapse through the corneal laceration, and blood in the anterior chamber (Figure 70-14). Small corneal lacerations can be difficult to diagnose. If aqueous humor is leaking from the corneal wound, it appears as streaming fluorescent dye surrounded by an orange pool of solution on slit-lamp examination (Seidel's test).[32] Full-thickness corneal lacerations are managed as described for blunt traumatic globe rupture.

Superficial partial-thickness corneal lacerations without a widened wound can be treated with a cycloplegic, topical antibiotic, and a pressure patch. Repairs of partial-thickness corneal lacerations requiring suture closure are performed in the operating room.

Scleral Lacerations. Penetrating scleral lacerations occur with the signs and symptoms of blunt globe rupture. Globe perforation may be unrecognized in the absence of significant physical examination findings.

Orbital and Intraocular Foreign Bodies

Clinical Features and Management
Any orbital and intraocular penetration should be approached with the possibility of intracranial injury.

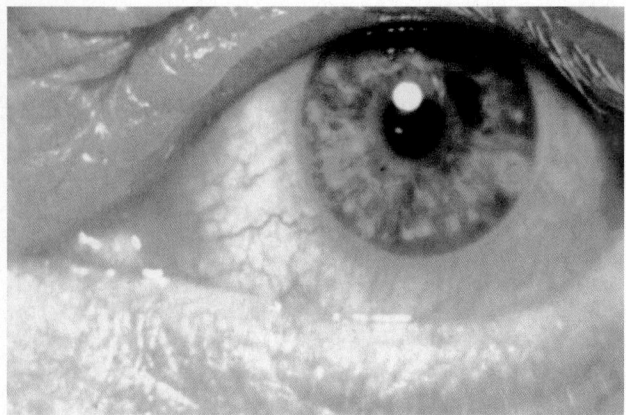

Figure 70-15. Peripherally located corneal ulcer.

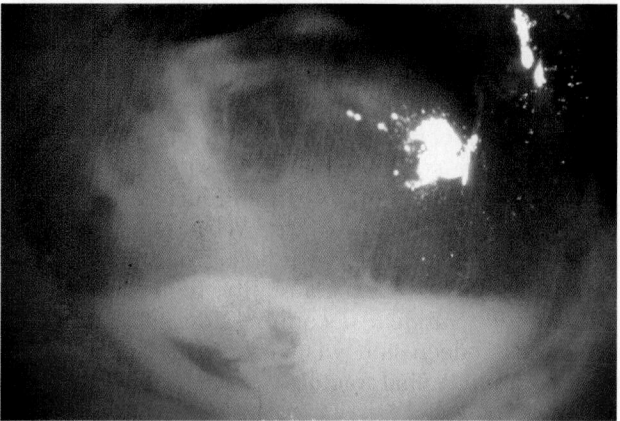

Figure 70-16. Endophthalmitis resulting from globe rupture.

Small intraocular and intraorbital foreign bodies can occur with any perforating injury and be difficult to diagnose. Physical examination of the eye may be completely normal at initial presentation. Occult foreign bodies should be suspected with any penetrating injury associated with mechanical grinding, sanding, drilling, and hammering. Plain orbital films, orbital CT scan, magnetic resonance imaging (MRI) scans, and ultrasonography aid in diagnosis. Although the decision to use one modality over another is dictated by individual clinical circumstances, an orbital CT scan is probably the most useful diagnostic tool. The MRI scan should not be used when an iron-containing foreign body is suspected.

Treatment of intraocular foreign bodies is dictated by clinical circumstances and is left to the ophthalmologist. Patients with acute intraocular foreign bodies should be hospitalized, have nothing by mouth, have a protective shield placed, and given antibiotics. Generally speaking, acute intraocular foreign bodies are surgically removed.[27] Plastic, glass, and many metals are relatively inert, and their nonacute removal is sometimes likely to cause more damage than their permanent presence. Organic foreign bodies are more important to remove because of their propensity for infection. Siderous oxidation of ocular tissues is a late complication of iron-containing intraocular foreign bodies that can lead to visual loss. Chalcosis, a sterile inflammatory reaction to copper-containing compounds, may occur, requiring removal of the offending object.

Complications of Ocular Trauma

Clinical Features and Management

Posttraumatic Corneal Ulcers. Any defect in the corneal epithelium may become infected with bacteria or fungi. Ulcerations are surrounded by a cloudy white or gray appearing cornea (Figure 70-15). A reactive sterile hypopyon may be present in the anterior chamber. Emergent ophthalmologic consultation is needed. Treatment includes cycloplegia, topical antibiotics, and often admission to the hospital. Corneal perforation is a complication.

Endophthalmitis. Endophthalmitis is an infection involving the deep structures of the eye, namely the ante-

rior, posterior, and vitreous chambers. Patients complain of pain and visual loss. Examination reveals decreased visual acuity, chemosis, and hyperemia of the conjunctiva, and the infected chambers are hazy or opaque (Figure 70-16). Endophthalmitis is a complication of blunt globe rupture, penetrating eye injury, foreign bodies, and ocular surgery. Prompt diagnosis and early treatment with intraocular and systemic antibiotics are important in the successful management of posttraumatic endophthalmitis.[33] Common pathogens are *Staphylococcus*, *Streptococcus*, and *Bacillus*.[34] Topical, intravitreal, and systemic antibiotics are all used.

Sympathetic Ophthalmia. This is an inflammation that occurs in the uninjured eye weeks to months after the initial insult to the injured eye. It is thought to be an autoimmune response to the normally sequestered uveal tissues of the injured eye becoming exposed with injury. Patients have pain, photophobia, and decreased visual acuity. Treatment includes steroids and other immunosuppressive agents.[34] Enucleation of the blind injured eye can reduce symptoms even after the sympathetic ophthalmia has developed.

DISEASE OF THE CONJUNCTIVA

Clinical Features and Management

Conjunctivitis

Conjunctivitis is an inflammation of the bulbar and palpebral conjunctiva caused by various viral, bacterial, mechanical, allergic, and toxic agents. When the cornea is also involved, it is known as keratoconjunctivitis. Multiple viral and bacterial pathogens are responsible for acute conjunctivitis. Adenovirus, coxsackievirus, and enteroviruses have been isolated as causes of conjunctivitis. Common bacterial agents include *Streptococcus pneumoniae*, *Haemophilus influenzae*, *Staphylococcus* organisms, *Moraxella catarrhalis*, and *Neisseria gonorrhoeae*. Less common bacterial causes are *Klebsiella* and *Pseudomonas*.

Acute Bacterial Conjunctivitis

Patients complain of pink eye, redness, a foreign body sensation, lid swelling, drainage, and eye crusting in the morning. Photophobia and visual loss are notably absent.

Treatment of acute bacterial conjunctivitis includes warm compresses and topical ophthalmic antibiotics. In uncomplicated acute bacterial conjunctivitis, topical trimethoprim and polymyxin are a good initial selection.[35] Neomycin ophthalmic solutions should be avoided because of the high incidence of hypersensitivity reactions.[35] Medications should be continued for 7 days. Corticosteroids and eye patching should be avoided.

Cultures are indicated when symptoms are severe or when prior treatment has been inadequate or unsuccessful.[35] Complications of acute bacterial conjunctivitis include corneal ulcer formation, keratitis, and corneal perforation. Patients with complicated bacterial conjunctivitis should be referred to an ophthalmologist.

Acute bacterial infection caused by *N. gonorrhoeae* is uncommon but important because of its significant complications. Infection results from direct contact with individuals infected with urethritis or pelvic inflammatory disease. Signs and symptoms are markedly increased, including a copious purulent discharge. Gram's stain may reveal the diagnosis, although cultures are more sensitive.

Treatment is more aggressive than with other causes of bacterial conjunctivitis. Hospital admission for IV antibiotics, saline irrigation, and topical ophthalmic antibiotics is warranted in moderate and severe cases and any patient with corneal involvement. Outpatient management may be used in selected mild cases with ceftriaxone 1 g intramuscularly as a single dose, topical erythromycin ointment, and saline solution irrigation of the conjunctiva.[35] A substantial proportion of patients have concomitant *Chlamydia trachomatis* infection and should be treated with oral doxycycline, tetracycline, or erythromycin (20 mg/kg PO) or a single dose of 1 g of azithromycin.[35]

Viral Conjunctivitis
Viral infection is the most common cause of conjunctivitis. Viral conjunctivitis generally produces more redness, itching, eye irritation, and preauricular lymphadenopathy (Figure 70-17). It commonly occurs in the setting of other viral symptoms (e.g., fever, myalgias, malaise).

Viral conjunctivitis is very contagious for 10 to 12 days after onset and appropriate preventive measures should be taken. Treatment consists of artificial tears and cool compresses. A vasoconstrictor and antihistamine combination can be used if itching is severe.

Ophthalmia Neonatorum
Conjunctivitis that occurs within the first month of life is termed ophthalmia neonatorum and has several causes. A bacterial cause should be investigated with Gram's stain and cultures within the first 2 weeks of life. *N. gonorrhoeae* and *Chlamydia* are both transmitted from mother to infant through the birth canal.[35]

Infection with *N. gonorrhoeae* is manifest within 2 to 4 days after birth. The infant should be carefully

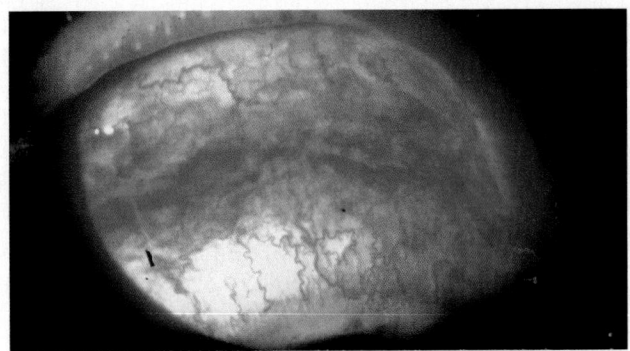

Figure 70-17. Conjunctival injection resulting from viral conjunctivitis.

examined for evidence of systemic gonococcal infection. Hospitalization and blood and cerebrospinal fluid examination may be indicated. Nonsystemically infected neonates can be effectively treated with a single dose of ceftriaxone, 125 mg intramuscularly, topical polymyxin B–bacitracin ointment, and saline washes.[35] These patients should also be treated for ocular chlamydial infection. Close follow-up is needed.

Infants with chlamydial infection develop symptoms between 5 and 13 days after birth. Topical erythromycin ointment and oral erythromycin are the antibiotics used.[36] Treatment is for 14 days.

Chemical conjunctivitis from antibiotic ointment administration immediately after delivery occurs within 1 to 2 days of birth but should not be the diagnosis if the infant has significant symptoms, the time course is inappropriate, or other historic and physical examination parameters are not classical. In such cases, a bacterial cause should be assumed.

In neonates with no information from stains or cultures and in whom an organism is not known or suspected, topical erythromycin ointment and oral erythromycin are utilized.

Miscellaneous Conjunctivitis
Allergic conjunctivitis is common. Allergens include drugs, cosmetics, and environmental agents. Eye itching is generally more pronounced in patients with allergic conjunctivitis and tends to be bilateral. Artificial tears, cool compresses, combination topical ocular decongestants, topical vasoconstrictor-antihistamine combinations, and topical nonsteroidal agents may be used for treatment. Other types of conjunctivitis include toxic conjunctivitis from topical ocular medications (aminoglycosides, antivirals, and preservatives), molluscum contagiosum, and chronic conjunctivitis.

DISEASE OF THE CORNEA

Differential Considerations

Clinical Features and Management

Pterygium and Pinguecula
A pterygium is a wedge-shaped area of conjunctival fibrovascular tissue that extends onto the cornea. A pinguecula is white or yellow, flat to slightly raised

tissue on the conjunctiva, immediately next to but not on the cornea. Patients can be asymptomatic or present with irritation and redness. Treatment includes protection from wind, dust, and sunlight and artificial tears. An inflamed pinguecula can be treated with a short course of a topical nonsteroidal agent. Nonemergent referral to an ophthalmologist is recommended. Surgical removal is possible for selected individuals.

Superficial Punctate Keratitis

Superficial punctate keratitis consists of superficial, multiple, pinpoint corneal epithelial defects. Patients present with pain, photophobia, redness, and a foreign body sensation. Superficial punctate keratitis is a nonspecific finding that is seen in many conditions. The most common precipitating conditions are ultraviolet burns (welders or sunlamps), conjunctivitis, topical eye drug toxicity (neomycin, gentamicin, drugs with preservatives including artificial tears), contact lens disorders, dry eye and exposure keratopathy, blepharitis, mild chemical injury, and minor trauma. Specific treatment is aimed at the underlying offending cause. Nonspecific treatment for a significant non–contact lens–associated superficial punctate keratitis includes nonpreserved artificial tears, topical antibiotics such as trimethoprim-polymyxin drops, and cycloplegia. Patients with a significant contact lens–associated superficial punctate keratitis should stop wearing their contact lenses and be treated with a topical fluoroquinolone or tobramycin drops during the day and ointment at night. Patients should have ophthalmologic follow-up the next day.

Corneal Ulcers and Infiltrate from Infection

Corneal infiltrates arise as a focal white opacity without an epithelial defect. Corneal ulcers have an overlying corneal epithelial defect that stains with fluorescein in addition to the corneal infiltrate. Patients present with pain, redness, photophobia, and decreased vision. The most common cause is bacterial, but fungal and herpes simplex infections are also possible. Patients should be immediately referred to an ophthalmologist for corneal culturing before treatment is initiated.

Herpes Simplex Infections

Infection with herpes simplex may be either primary or reactivation of preexisting disease. Symptoms include foreign body sensation, tearing, photophobia, clear discharge, and decreased visual acuity. Physical examination reveals a red eye and may or may not include the classical herpetic vesicles located on the lids or conjunctiva. Corneal involvement is seen on slit-lamp examination and may appear as a superficial punctate keratitis, ulcer, or the classical dendritic lesions (Figure 70-18). Treatment for epithelial keratitis consists of topical antiviral agents such as trifluridine 1% every 2 hours for 14 to 21 days.[37] Topical prophylactic antibiotics and cycloplegia are also employed. Topical steroids are contraindicated in corneal epithelial disease but have proved to be beneficial in stromal disease.[37] Emergent ophthalmologic consultation is advised.

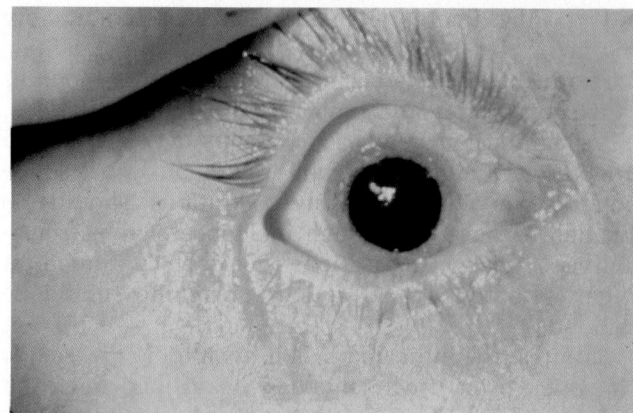

Figure 70-18. Herpes simplex infection. Note typical dendritic pattern on cornea.

Herpes Zoster Infection

Herpes zoster keratoconjunctivitis occurs as a result of activation of the virus along the ophthalmic division of the trigeminal nerve. The rash follows dermatomal patterns, involves the forehead and upper eyelid, and produces significant pain. Involvement of the nasociliary nerve, manifested by zoster lesions on the tip of the nose (Hutchinson's sign), is associated with a 76% risk of ocular involvement versus 34% risk if the nerve is not involved.[38] Ophthalmic zoster mandates emergent ophthalmologic consultation. Treatment is complex and depends upon the type, location, and degree of ocular involvement. Oral and topical antiviral and steroid agents as well as antibiotics are used.[39,40]

Contact Lens Complications

The common complications of contact lens use involving the cornea include mechanical damage such as abrasions, corneal neovascularization, infections producing corneal ulcers, hypersensitivity or toxicity reactions to preservatives in solutions, and contact lens deposits. If no significant signs or symptoms exist that indicate corneal infection, the patient should discontinue contact lens use and follow up with his or her ophthalmologist. When corneal infection is present or suspected, immediate ophthalmologic consultation is indicated.

DISORDERS OF THE LIDS AND OCULAR SOFT TISSUES

Differential Considerations

Clinical Features and Management

Hordeolum and Chalazion

Hordeolums and chalazions are localized, nodular, inflammatory processes of the eyelids. Symptoms and signs include pain, swelling, and redness (Figure 70-19). Spontaneous rupture may occur, and most resolve with warm compresses applied for 15 minutes four to six times each day. Topical antibiotics (erythromycin) may be used. Incision and drainage are indicated for chalazia unresponsive to conservative therapy.[41]

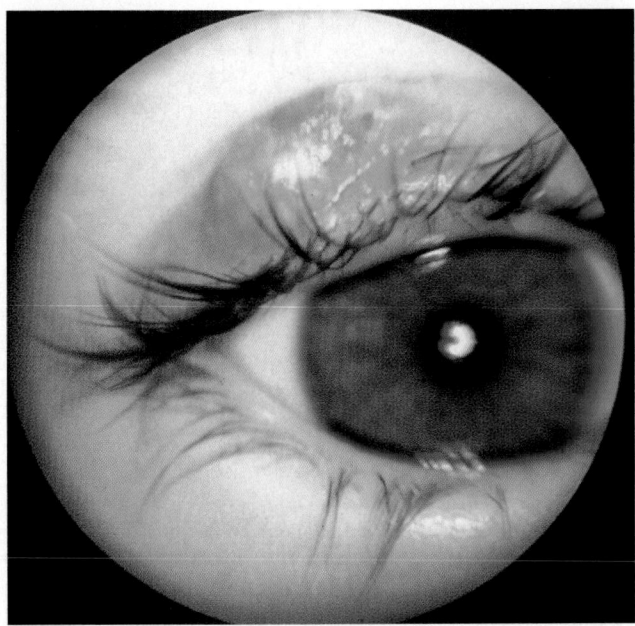

Figure 70-19. Chalazion of the upper eyelid.

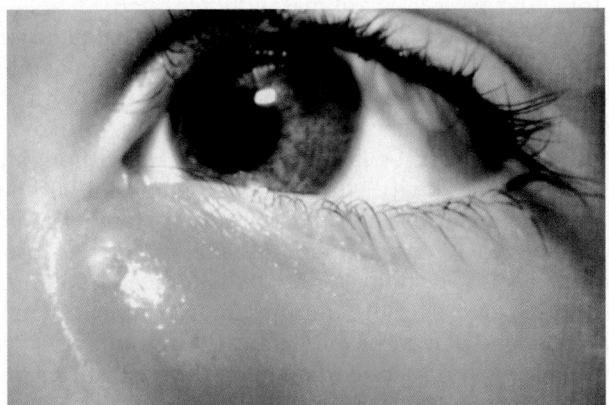

Figure 70-20. Dacryocystitis.

Dacryocystitis

Dacryocystitis is an acute infection of the lacrimal sac from nasolacrimal duct obstruction. The most common organism is *S. aureus*. Symptoms and signs include pain, tenderness, swelling, and erythema over the lacrimal sac (Figure 70-20). Pressure over the sac may express purulent material from the puncta. Treatment includes topical ocular and oral anti-*Staphylococcal* antibiotics and warm compresses. Gentle massage of the area during warm compress application may help decompress purulent material and relieve symptoms. Systemically ill patients should be hospitalized.

Blepharitis

Patients present with thickened, mattered, red eyelid margins with pronounced blood vessels. Patients complain of burning, itching, tearing, foreign body sensation, and morning crusting of the eyelids. Treatment includes rubbing the eyelid margins with a mild shampoo using a cotton-tipped applicator or cloth twice per day, warm compresses, and artificial tears. Severe blepharitis can also be treated with topical antibiotic ointment applied at night.

Preseptal Cellulitis

Patients present with lid erythema and warmth, tenderness, and swelling and may have a low-grade fever. It is important to note the absence of findings associated with orbital (postseptal) cellulitis (i.e., proptosis, restriction of extraocular movements, pain with eye movement, and patient's toxicity). If any of these findings are present, orbital cellulitis or abscess should be suspected and the patient managed more aggressively with imaging studies (CT scan of brain and orbits) and hospitalization. Preseptal cellulitis is characterized by a continuum of disease, and treatment is tailored for the degree of patient's toxicity. Mild disease can be treated on an outpatient basis with oral antibiotics, but hospitalization with IV antibiotics may be needed for moderate to severe disease.

GLAUCOMA

Clinical Features and Management

Aqueous humor is produced by the ciliary processes. In addition to providing structural support to the eye, aqueous humor delivers oxygen and nutrients to the avascular lens and cornea and removes their waste products. This fluid passes from the posterior chamber to the anterior chamber through the pupillary aperture. The aqueous humor is transported into the trabecular meshwork located at the anterior chamber angle formed by the junction of the root of the iris and the peripheral cornea. The trabecular meshwork serves as a one-way valve and filter for the aqueous humor into the canal of Schlemm, which in turn drains into episcleral veins.

Intraocular pressure is determined by the rate of aqueous humor production relative to its outflow and removal. Normal intraocular pressure is between 10 and 20 mm Hg.[42]

Glaucoma is an optic neuropathy caused by increased intraocular pressure. Irreparable optic nerve damage can result. The simplest classification is to divide the glaucomas into primary or secondary and open angle or closed angle. Secondary glaucoma is associated with another ocular or nonocular event, whereas primary glaucoma is not. Closed-angle glaucoma is caused when the anterior chamber angle is narrowed, reducing the outflow and removal of aqueous humor, whereas open-angle glaucoma occurs with a normal anterior chamber angle.

Patients vary in their susceptibility to a given level of intraocular pressure. Some may develop significant optic nerve findings despite a relatively low intraocular pressure (low-tension glaucoma), whereas others may have scant optic nerve changes despite relatively high intraocular pressure (ocular hypertension).[43]

Primary Open-Angle Glaucoma

Primary open-angle glaucoma is the most common form of glaucoma and is a leading cause of blindness in the United States. There is increased resistance to aqueous humor outflow through the trabecular meshwork. Primary open-angle glaucoma is generally insidious, slowly progressive, chronic, bilateral, and painless. Advanced disease occurs before symptoms. Symptoms begin as visual field loss at the periphery that progresses centrally. Signs include an optic cup to optic nerve ratio of greater than 0.6.[44] Other findings include vertically oval, deep, and pale optic cups, with nasal displacement of blood vessels.

The three treatment options are medications, argon laser trabeculoplasty, and guarded filtration surgery. Initial treatment is generally with one or more topical agents. β-Blockers, selective α_2-receptor agonists, carbonic anhydrase inhibitors, prostaglandin agonists, miotics, and sympathomimetics are all used.

Topical ocular medications are absorbed and may produce significant systemic side effects.[45] Topical β-blockers have produced asthma, heart block, congestive heart failure, hypoglycemia, and depression. Adrenergics have produced hypertension and cardiac dysrhythmias, whereas carbonic anhydrase inhibitors have produced renal calculi and hypokalemia. Complications may arise as a result of drug interaction. Prolonged apnea, for example, has resulted when succinylcholine has been given to a patient receiving topical ophthalmologic acetylcholinesterase inhibitors.[46]

Secondary Open-Angle Glaucoma

Secondary open-angle glaucoma can have a number of causes, including lens induced, inflammatory, exfoliative, pigmentary, steroid induced, traumatic, angle recession, and ocular tumor.

Treatment is directed to the offending mechanism and includes the methods used for primary open-angle glaucoma.

Primary Angle Closure Glaucoma

Primary angle closure glaucoma occurs in patients who have anatomically small and shallow anterior chambers. This anatomic variation results in the iris being nearly in contact with the lens, resulting in resistance to aqueous humor flow from the posterior to anterior chamber. This is called pupillary block.[47]

Attacks of primary angle closure glaucoma are precipitated by pupillary dilatation. Dimly lit rooms, emotional upset, and various anticholinergic and sympathomimetic medications are common precipitating events. The dilatation of the pupil increases the degree of pupillary block, leading to an accumulation of aqueous humor in the posterior chamber. The iris bulges forward, obliterating the angle between the cornea and iris, obstructing the trabecular meshwork, decreasing outflow, and leading to a rapid rise in intraocular pressure.[48]

A second, less common mechanism of acute angle closure glaucoma, produced without pupillary block, is caused by a flat or plateau iris. This leads to a narrow angle recess. Dilatation of the pupil causes the iris to fold and bunch over the angle, blocking aqueous humor outflow into the trabecular meshwork.

Symptoms are abrupt in onset and include severe eye pain, blurred vision, headache, nausea, vomiting,

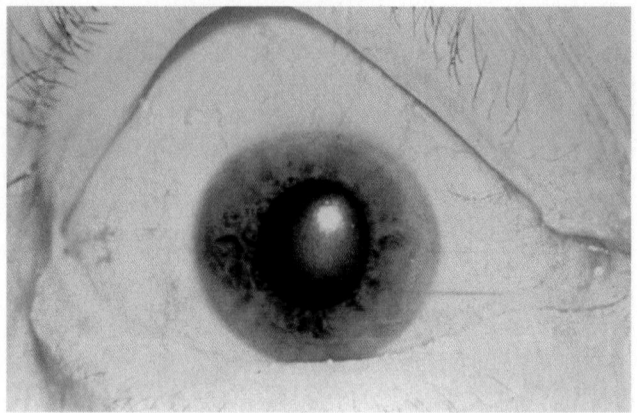

Figure 70-21. Acute narrow-angle glaucoma. Note steamy appearance of cornea with a midpositioned and sluggish pupil.

and occasionally abdominal pain. Patients see a halo around lights. Signs include conjunctival injection and a cloudy (steamy) cornea with a midpositioned to dilated pupil that is sluggish or fixed (Figure 70-21). Visual acuity may be significantly decreased, and intraocular pressures are markedly elevated.

Treatment should begin promptly. If visual acuity is markedly reduced (hand movements or less), a combination of all topical glaucoma medications with IV osmotics and acetazolamide should be utilized.[39] Intraocular pressures less than 50 mm Hg without significant visual acuity change can be managed without the IV medications.[39] Topically administered timolol 0.5% decreases intraocular pressure within 30 to 60 minutes.[49] Pilocarpine 1% to 2% is topically administered, one drop every 15 minutes for two doses, and one drop may be placed prophylactically in the unaffected eye. A topical α_2-agonist (apraclonidine 1.0%) for one dose and topical steroid (prednisolone acetate 1% every 15 minutes for four doses) should be given.[39] In the setting of a severe attack, acetazolamide, a carbonic anhydrase inhibitor, is given in an IV dose of 250 to 500 mg, and mannitol 1 to 2 mg/kg over 45 minutes.[50] Sedatives and antiemetics may be administered as needed. Ophthalmologic consultation is warranted.

The definitive therapy for primary angle closure glaucoma is surgical.

Secondary Angle Closure Glaucoma

Pupillary block may develop from a swollen or dislocated lens or posterior synechia (adhesions between the iris and lens). Secondary angle closure glaucoma, without pupillary block, can be caused by intraocular tumors, central retinal vein occlusion, or postoperatively. Treatment is directed at the offending cause.

ACUTE VISUAL LOSS

Differential Considerations

Acute visual loss, usually in only one eye, occurs over a period ranging from a few seconds to a day or two. The vision is generally reduced to 20/200 or worse. Patients need to be quickly evaluated to determine whether a treatable lesion exists. The differential diagnosis of acute visual loss not related to trauma includes vascular occlusion, retinal detachment, vitreous hemorrhage, macular disorders, neuroophthalmologic disease, and hysteria. Most of these patients need ophthalmic or neurologic referral for a complete workup.

Patients may complain of acute visual loss when they may have neither an acute process nor a visual loss caused by the eye itself. For example, a patient with a visual field cut secondary to a neuroophthalmologic lesion may have an acute visual loss when the patient discovers the field cut. A patient with a hemianopia usually has normal visual acuity even though both eyes are affected. An accurate history of how the patient discovered the visual loss, as well as the timing of that loss, is vital.

Clinical Features and Management

Central Retinal Artery Occlusion
Acute visual loss as a result of vascular occlusion of the central retinal artery is typically painless.

Central retinal artery occlusion causes an ischemic stroke of the retina. It occurs most commonly in those between 50 and 70 years of age, and 45% have carotid artery disease.[51] Risk factors include hypertension, cardiac disease, diabetes, collagen vascular disease, vasculitis, cardiac valvular abnormality, and sickle cell disease. Patients with increased orbital pressure are also at risk, including patients with acute glaucoma, retrobulbar hemorrhage, and endocrine exophthalmos. Patients complain of a severe loss of vision that develops over seconds. Examination reveals a markedly reduced visual acuity with a prominent afferent pupillary defect. On funduscopic examination, the retina is edematous with a pale gray-white appearance, and the fovea appears as a cherry-red spot (Figure 70-22).

Therapy should be instituted immediately and should be directed at dislodging the embolus, dilating the artery to promote forward blood flow, and reducing intraocular pressure to allow an increase in perfusion gradient. Digital global massage should be begun immediately in the emergency department. Global massage is performed by applying direct digital pressure through closed eyelids. The pressure can be applied for 10 to 15 seconds and followed by a sudden release.[52] Increases in carbon dioxide pressure (PCO_2) lead to retinal artery vasodilation and increased retinal blood flow. Increases in PCO_2 are obtained by either rebreathing into a paper bag for 10 minutes each hour or inhaling a 95% oxygen, 5% carbon dioxide mixture (carbogen). Intraocular pressure may be reduced by instilling timolol maleate 0.5% topically. Acetazolamide, 500 mg IV or by mouth, lowers intraocular pressure as well as increases retinal blood flow.[53] Emergent ophthalmologic consultation should be obtained as anterior chamber paracentesis may be attempted. One study, however, failed to find any therapeutic benefit for patients who received anterior chamber paracentesis and inhaled carbogen.[54] Thrombolytic agents have been studied, but no clear guidelines for their use exist.[52] A complete medical evaluation is nec-

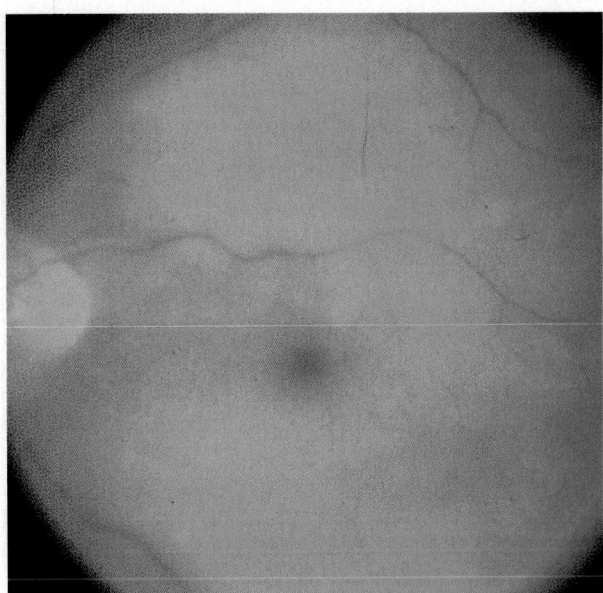

Figure 70-22. Central retinal artery occlusion. Note cherry-red spot (fovea).

essary because central retinal artery occlusion is usually an embolic event.

Central Retinal Vein Occlusion
A painless loss of vision, central retinal vein occlusion leads to edema, hemorrhage, and vascular leakage. The wide spectrum of clinical appearances depends on the degree of venous obstruction present. Loss of vision can range from minimal to recognition of hand motion only. There are two types of central retinal vein occlusion, ischemic and nonischemic. The nonischemic type involves mild fundus changes and does not have an afferent pupillary defect. These patients tend to have less severe visual loss, with two thirds of the patients having 20/40 or better visual acuity without therapy.[55] Patients with ischemic central retinal vein occlusion have a marked decrease in visual acuity and often an afferent pupillary defect. Appearance can vary but classically includes dilated and tortuous veins, retinal hemorrhages, and disk edema (Figure 70-23). Branch retinal vein occlusions occur just distal to an arteriovenous crossing, and hemorrhages occur distal to the site of occlusion. The differential diagnosis of central retinal vein occlusion includes hypertension, diabetes mellitus, hyperviscosity syndromes, and papilledema. All of these are bilateral processes, whereas central retinal vein occlusion is generally unilateral. Neovascular glaucoma is the major complication of ischemic central retinal vein occlusion. Treatment is complex and includes lowering of intraocular pressure, topical steroids, cyclocryotherapy, and photocoagulation.[55,56] Underlying medical disease should be managed as well. The prognosis depends on the degree of obstruction and resultant complications.

Retinal Breaks and Detachment
The retina has two layers, the inner neuronal retina layer and the outer retinal pigment epithelial layer, which can be separated by fluid accumulation.

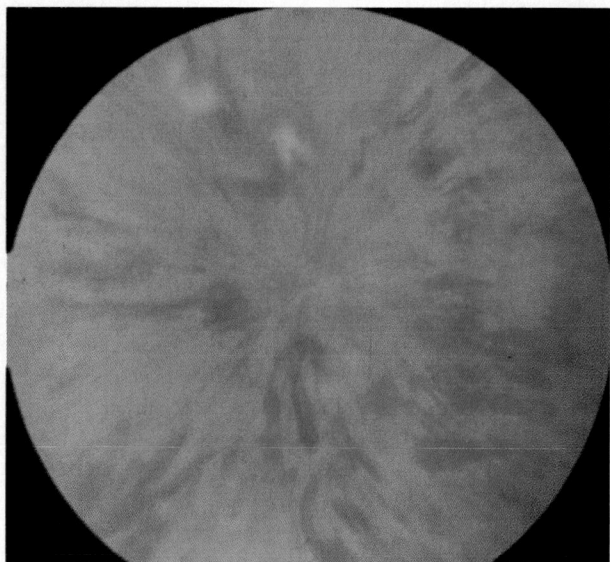

Figure 70-23. Central vein occlusion.

A retinal break is a tear in the retinal membranes and may or may not lead to retinal detachment. Retinal detachments occur by three mechanisms: rhegmatogenous, exudative, and tractional. Rhegmatogenous retinal detachment occurs as a result of a tear or hole in the neuronal layer, causing fluid from the vitreous cavity to leak between and separate the two retinal layers. Rhegmatogenous retinal detachment generally occurs in patients older than 45 years, is more common in men than women, and is associated with degenerative myopia.[57] Trauma may be associated with rhegmatogenous detachment by causing tears in the retina or by causing a disinsertion of the retina from its attachment at the ora serrata anteriorly. Traumatic retinal detachment can occur at any age. There is greater risk with severe myopia.

Exudative retinal detachment occurs as a result of fluid or blood leakage from vessels within the retina. Conditions leading to exudative retinal detachment include hypertension, toxemia of pregnancy, central retinal venous occlusion, glomerulonephritis, papilledema, vasculitis, and choroidal tumor.

Traction retinal detachment is a consequence of fibrous band formation in the vitreous and contraction of these bands. These fibrous bands result from the organization of inflammatory exudates or blood from prior vitreous hemorrhage.

Typically, patients complain of flashes of light related to the traction on the retina, floaters related to vitreal blood or pigmented debris, and visual loss. The visual loss is commonly described as a filmy, cloudy, or curtain-like appearance. Pain is absent. Visual acuity can be minimally changed to severely decreased. Visual field cuts relate to the location of the retinal detachment, and an afferent pupillary defect occurs if the detachment is large enough. When the detachment is visualized by ophthalmoscopy, the retina appears out of focus at the site of the detachment. In large retinal detachments with large fluid accumulation, the bullous detachment, with retinal folds, can easily be seen (see Figure 70-12). Retinal detachment cannot be ruled out by direct funduscopy. Indirect ophthalmoscopy is needed to visualize the more anterior portions of the retina.

Acute rhegmatogenous and tractional detachment that threaten the fovea should be urgently surgically repaired.[39] Acute retinal breaks are surgically repaired within 24 hours. All other acute rhegmatogenous and tractional retinal detachments can be repaired within a few days.[39] Treatment of exudative detachment is aimed at the underlying cause or use of laser photocoagulation. Any patient suspected of having retinal break or detachment requires immediate ophthalmologic consultation.

Posterior Vitreous Detachment

Posterior vitreous detachment is a common occurrence in patients older than 60 years. With aging, the vitreous gel pulls away from the retina, which can lead to symptoms similar to those of retinal break, vitreous hemorrhage, and retinal detachment. No specific treatment is indicated for posterior vitreous detachment unless it is accompanied by a retinal break, vitreous hemorrhage, or retinal detachment.[39] Patients with a new posterior vitreous detachment should have prompt evaluation by an ophthalmologist to rule out these surgically amenable complications.

Vitreous Hemorrhage

Vitreous hemorrhage results from bleeding into the preretinal space or into the vitreous cavity. The most common causes are diabetic retinopathy and retinal tears. Additional causes include neovascularization associated with branch vein occlusion, sickle cell disease, retinal detachment, posterior vitreous detachment, trauma, age-related macular degeneration, retinal artery microaneurysms, trauma, and intraocular tumor. Symptoms begin with floaters or "cobwebs" in the vision and may progress over a few hours to severe visual loss without pain. Direct ophthalmoscopy reveals a reddish haze in mild cases to a black reflex in severe cases. Details of the fundus are usually difficult to visualize. Vitreous hemorrhage by itself does not cause an afferent pupillary defect, which, if present, indicates a retinal detachment behind the vitreous hemorrhage. The hemorrhage may be evenly distributed throughout the vitreous or focal. Long-standing preretinal hemorrhage can become a white mass that may be misdiagnosed as a tumor, exudate, or infection. Initial therapy consists of bed rest with elevation of the head of the bed and avoidance of anticoagulative medications. Definitive therapy is targeted at the underlying cause. Vascular retinopathy is treated with laser photocoagulation or cryotherapy, and retinal tears and detachments are repaired. If the cause of the hemorrhage is unknown, prompt diagnostic workup is indicated to look for surgically correctable lesions. Ultrasonography can be used to determine whether a retinal detachment is present and may also deter-

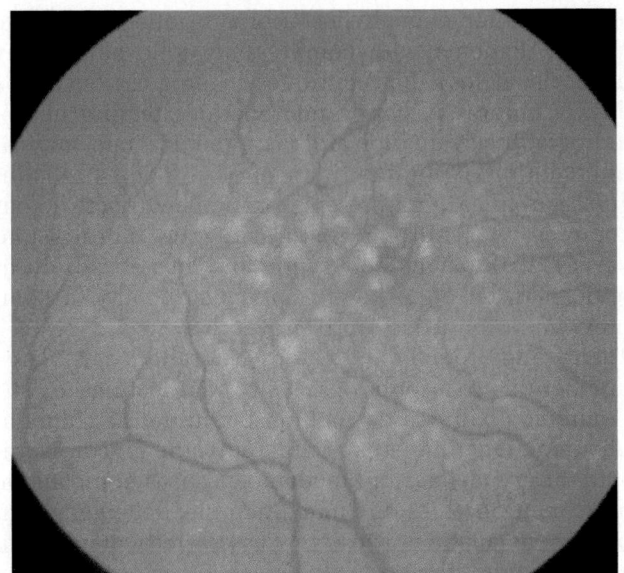

Figure 70-24. Drusen occurring in macular degeneration.

mine the cause.[58] Vitrectomy is indicated in certain patients.

Macular Disorders

Many disease processes cause acute changes in the macula leading to acute visual loss. The role of the emergency physician is to recognize the maculopathy and refer the patient to an ophthalmologist. Keys to the diagnosis of macular dysfunction include loss of central vision with preservation of peripheral vision, complaints of central visual distortion, and anatomic changes in the retina.

Degenerative maculopathies occur as the result of trauma, radiation exposure, inflammatory or infectious disease, vascular disease, toxins, or hereditary disease or may be idiopathic in nature.

The most common form is age-related macular degeneration after the age of 65 years.[59] It is a leading reason for legal blindness in the United States. Patients present with either a gradual or rapid onset of visual loss. Funduscopy reveals scattered drusen. Drusen are small, sharply defined yellow-white masses (Figure 70-24). Some patients with age-related macular degeneration and drusen develop a choroidal (subretinal) neovascular membrane, which appears as a grayish-green membrane beneath the retina. If this membrane is left untreated, hemorrhage, transudation, scar formation, or exudative detachment of the retina can result. If a large hemorrhage occurs from the neovascular membrane, it can cause severe central visual loss and may break through the retina into the vitreous, causing peripheral visual loss. Laser photocoagulation is the treatment for choroidal neovascular membrane formation and should be performed as soon as possible.[59]

Inflammatory processes involving the retina may also cause visual loss, especially if the macula is involved. Bacterial, viral, and protozoal agents have been shown to cause maculopathy. The presenting symptoms and signs vary according to the disease process and severity. Inflammatory debris from exudative processes may fill the vitreous, leading to a cloudy appearance. Infections within the eye are often associated with severe pain, redness, and periocular edema. If the retina and choroid are obliterated, the lesions appear white. Patients suspected of having an inflammatory maculopathy need emergent consultation and thorough medical evaluation.

Neuroophthalmologic Visual Loss

Visual loss not readily explained by an obvious abnormality on physical examination is called neuroophthalmologic visual loss. Patients can be divided into those who complain of decreased vision and have reduced visual acuity and those who complain of visual loss but have normal visual acuity. It is important to conduct careful visual field testing in the latter group.

Neuroophthalmologic visual loss can be further divided into prechiasmal, chiasmal, and postchiasmal anatomic areas.

Prechiasmal Visual Loss. Patients with prechiasmal disease have decreased visual acuity or visual field loss in the eye on the affected side. Prechiasmal disease may be a unilateral or bilateral process. The swinging flashlight test reveals an afferent pupillary defect on the side involved unless the process is bilateral. In such cases, the relative degree of afferent defect determines the results. Visual field testing demonstrates a field defect that does not respect the vertical meridian and is often localized to the center of the visual field. Causes of prechiasmal visual loss include optic neuritis, ischemic optic neuritis, compressive optic neuritis, and toxic and metabolic optic neuritis.

Optic Neuritis. Optic neuritis is an acute monocular loss of vision caused by focal demyelination of the optic nerve. The patients' ages range from 15 to 45 years. Symptoms include a progressive loss of vision over several hours or days and ocular pain with eye movement. Visual acuity can range from minimal loss to no light perception. An afferent pupillary defect is always present, and direct ophthalmoscopic examination reveals a normal or swollen disk.[60] The natural history of optic neuritis is for visual acuity to reach its poorest within 1 week and then slowly improve over the next several weeks. Approximately 30% of patients presenting with acute optic neuritis develop multiple sclerosis within 5 years.[61] In an initial study of patients with acute optic neuritis, treatment with a 3-day course of IV methylprednisolone reduced the rate of development of multiple sclerosis over a 2-year period.[62] However, 5-year follow-up of the same cohort of patients revealed no significant differences among treatment groups in the development of multiple sclerosis.[61] Use of oral steroids for hastening optic neuritis is controversial. The Optic Neuritis Study Group showed an increased risk of optic neuritis recurrences in patients treated with oral prednisone.[61,62] However, a randomized and controlled study of high-dose oral methylprednisolone in acute optic neuritis showed improved recovery from optic neuritis at 1 and 3 weeks but no effect at 8 weeks or on subsequent attack frequency.[63] Long-term visual outcome is no different from that with observation alone.

Ischemic Optic Neuropathy. Ischemic optic neuropathy is the most common optic neuropathy and one of the most common causes of visual loss past middle age. Ischemic optic neuropathy can be giant cell arteritis or idiopathic. Temporal arteritis (giant cell arteritis) is characterized by weight loss, malaise, jaw pain, headache, scalp tenderness, polymyalgia rheumatica, low-grade fever, and severe painless visual loss. It is extremely rare in people younger than 50 years, but the incidence rises with each subsequent decade. A significant proportion of patients sustain visual loss, which can be sudden, severe, and bilateral.[64] Occasionally, visual loss is preceded by episodes of amaurosis fugax. In one series of patients, visual loss was unilateral in 46%, sequential in 37%, and simultaneously bilateral in 17%.[65] There is a large afferent pupillary defect, visual loss, and a visual field defect that may respect the horizontal meridian. The optic disk shows pallor and swelling. The diagnosis can be aided with an elevated erythrocyte sedimentation rate (ESR), but can be seen with normal sedimentation rates.[66] A guide to the upper limit of normal ESR is age/2 for men and (age + 10)/2 for women.[39] The diagnosis is confirmed by temporal artery biopsy, although biopsy has been normal early in the disease. Treatment for temporal arteritis should be instituted when typical signs and symptoms, particularly visual loss, exist. The standard treatment is high-dosage corticosteroids, which should be started as soon as the diagnosis is suspected. Treatment should not wait for biopsy results. Biopsy should be performed within 1 week of diagnosis. Patients treated with oral prednisone were less likely to have visual improvement and more likely to develop fellow eye involvement than those receiving high-dose IV methylprednisolone.[65] Patients with visual loss had a 34% chance of improvement with IV methylprednisolone.[65]

Nonarteritic Ischemic Optic Neuropathy. Nonarteritic ischemic optic neuropathy is much more common than temporal arteritis. These patients lack the classical symptoms of temporal arteritis and do not have an elevated ESR. Most of these patients have systemic vascular disease, diabetes, or hypertension, and they tend to be younger. They have painless visual loss, afferent pupillary defects, disk swelling, and visual field defects that respect the horizontal meridian. The visual loss is less severe than with temporal arteritis, and improvement occurs in one third of patients. Steroids have been advocated, but the results are unclear. If there is doubt about whether a particular patient has temporal arteritis or an idiopathic form of ischemic optic neuropathy, treatment with steroids should be started until a temporal artery biopsy is performed.

Compressive Optic Neuropathy. Compressive optic neuropathy occurs at any age and can be caused by tumor, aneurysm, sphenoid sinusitis or mucocele, blunt trauma, and thyroid disorders. Although defined as a prechiasmal disorder, compression can occasionally occur far enough posteriorly to affect the optic chiasm. Patients with compressive optic neuropathy have visual loss that continues to progress beyond 7 days. Compressive optic neuropathies require neuroradiographic evaluation and rapid medical and surgical intervention. Optic neuritis can be difficult to distinguish from a compressive optic neuropathy, but compressive syndromes tend to involve other cranial nerves. If the signs and symptoms do not closely fit optic neuritis or ischemic optic neuropathy, a compressive lesion exists until proved otherwise.

Toxic and Metabolic Optic Neuropathy. A large number of toxic and metabolic neuropathies exists. Common toxic causes include barbiturates, chloramphenicol, emetine, ethambutol, ethylene glycol, isoniazid, heavy metals, and methanol. Causes of metabolic optic neuropathies include thiamine deficiency and pernicious anemia. These processes are bilateral, progressive, and symmetrical. Visual loss can be severe, and visual field testing reveals central defects. Treatment is aimed at the underlying toxin or metabolite involved.

Chiasmal Visual Loss. Chiasmal disease is the second category of neuroophthalmologic visual loss, most commonly caused by chiasmal compression from pituitary tumors, craniopharyngioma, or meningioma. Visual loss is gradual and progressive. Although formal visual field testing is necessary to stage the condition, the diagnosis can usually be made by confrontation visual field testing. The classical defect is a bitemporal hemianopsia; however, tumors often compress the optic chiasm and optic nerves asymmetrically, resulting in combined central and temporal defects. When a visual field defect respects the vertical meridian from a neuroophthalmologic visual loss, the lesion is out of the globe and must be either chiasmal or postchiasmal.

Postchiasmal Visual Loss. Postchiasmal disease represents the third category of neuroophthalmologic visual loss. The most common causes are infarction, tumor, arteriovenous malformation, and migraine disorders. Patients complain of difficulty in performing a certain task, such as reading. Lesions can be located from the immediate postchiasmal optic tract to the occipital cortex. The classical visual field defect is homonymous hemianopsia. Patients with such lesions have a focal neurologic deficit and need neurologic consultation. Cortical blindness is a special cause of neuroophthalmologic visual loss that is most commonly caused by bilateral occipital infarction. Cortical blindness is often mistaken for functional blindness because patients have both normal funduscopic examinations and intact pupillary reflexes. Anton's syndrome is characterized by bilateral blindness, normal pupillary reflexes, bilateral occipital lesions, and, interestingly, denial of blindness. It is this denial of blindness that may be incorrectly assumed to be evidence for a functional process.

Functional Visual Loss. Patients with functional visual loss fall into two categories: hysterical conversion reactions and malingering. Patients with hysterical conversion reactions have a nondeliberate, imagined visual loss. The patient has a flatter affect than one would expect under the circumstances of acute visual loss. The patient might appear completely unaffected emotionally by the acute visual loss. The malingerer, on the other hand, is a patient who is well aware that no visual loss exists, yet deliberately feigns visual loss for secondary gain. This patient is typically overemotional concerning the visual loss.

Examination of a patient with a suspected functional visual loss should be conducted in the same manner as every other ophthalmologic examination, with particular attention to possible neuroophthalmologic deficits. Normal pupillary reflexes and the absence of an afferent pupillary defect, together with a normal funduscopic examination, point toward functional visual loss. Multiple tests can ascertain whether a visual loss is organic or functional. Patients with feigned visual loss are hesitant to try to appose the index fingers of each hand and often write their names in a disorderly fashion, whereas genuinely blind patients can sign their names without difficulty. One effective test involves placing a large mirror directly in front of the patient's face and asking the patient to look straight ahead. The mirror is then tilted slightly back and forth. Most patients follow the reflection of their eyes in the mirror as it changes position, proving feigned visual loss. Some difficult cases require more sophisticated tests. If the diagnosis of feigned visual loss cannot be definitively made, consultation is required to rule out neuroophthalmologic visual loss.

ANISOCORIA

Clinical Features

Anisocoria in a patient with head trauma or decreased level of consciousness requires immediate and aggressive evaluation and intervention because it may result from increased intracranial pressure. If a patient is awake and alert, has no signs of trauma, and has anisocoria of unknown cause, less urgency exists. The first step is to determine which pupil is abnormal. If one pupil constricts poorly to a light stimulus, it is likely to be the abnormal one. Anisocoria greater in dark suggests that the abnormal pupil is the smaller pupil, whereas anisocoria greater in light suggests that the abnormal pupil is the larger pupil. If anisocoria exists in a patient with a normal afferent visual system, either an innervational or structural defect in the iris sphincter exists. Most structural defects in the iris can be diagnosed by slit-lamp examination. If both pupils react well to light and no iris abnormalities are seen with slit-lamp examination, the next step is to determine whether the anisocoria increases in light or darkness. Adie's tonic pupil, pharmacologic blockade, and third-nerve palsy are associated with anisocoria that increases in light, whereas benign anisocoria and Horner's syndrome are associated with anisocoria that increases in darkness.[39] Comparing pupillary size in a brightly and dimly lit room is the easiest method to evaluate the effect of lighting on anisocoria.

Adie's Tonic Pupil

With Adie's tonic pupil, patients complain of blurred near vision but have normal distant vision. Adie's syndrome is seen in young women 70% of the time and has associated symmetrically reduced deep tendon reflexes. Examination reveals poor accommodation with a very slow constriction to near testing. The pupil redilates slowly when the vision is again made distant. Slit-lamp examination reveals sector palsies of the iris. The diagnosis is confirmed when a weak cholinergic agent (pilocarpine 0.1%) causes an intense pupillary constriction as a result of cholinergic supersensitivity in the affected pupil compared with the normal pupil. These patients need to be referred to an ophthalmologist on a nonemergent basis for cholinergic agent therapy.

Pharmacologic Mydriasis

Pharmacologic mydriasis can be caused by deliberate or inadvertent local administration of both sympathomimetic and parasympatholytic agents. Phenylephrine and cocaine are two sympathomimetic substances commonly used as a nasal premedicant for nasotracheal intubation; careless administration may lead to anisocoria. Parasympatholytic agents, such as atropine and scopolamine, have been implicated in the development of anisocoria. The transdermal scopolamine patches placed for the prevention of motion sickness can cause anisocoria. Pilocarpine 1.0% can be used in special circumstances to help differentiate a third-nerve palsy from pharmacologically mediated mydriasis. The administration of pilocarpine 1.0% rapidly constricts the pupil that is dilated secondary to a third-nerve palsy but does not produce miosis in a pupil dilated from anticholinergic agents.

Third-Nerve Palsy

Patients with anisocoria that increases in light, without evidence of Adie's tonic pupil or pharmacologic medication, should be suspected of having a third-nerve palsy. They almost always have other signs of third-nerve involvement, including ptosis and extraocular muscle dysfunction. Patients complain of diplopia, and the involved eye is turned down and out. Patients may have ptosis and extraocular dysfunction with or without pupil dilatation. Any patient who has a new-onset third-nerve lesion involving the pupil should be admitted to the hospital to rule out aneurysm.

Horner's Syndrome

Horner's syndrome consists of ptosis, miosis, and facial anhidrosis resulting from an interruption of sympathetic innervation. The dilatation lag, a classical finding, results from the Horner's pupil requiring up to 15 seconds to dilate fully. The anisocoria is greater at 3 to 5 seconds of darkness than at 15 seconds of darkness, although the anisocoria is still more pronounced than in light. Topical ophthalmologic cocaine 10% can be used to aid the diagnosis. A Horner's pupil dilates less than the normal pupil in reaction to topical cocaine. Central nervous system strokes and tumors, lung carcinomas, thyroid adenomas, Pancoast's tumors, headache syndrome, carotid dissection, herpes zoster, otitis media, and congenital Horner's syndrome (trauma during delivery) are all causes of Horner's syndrome. Hydroxyamphetamine 1% administered 24 hours after the cocaine test can be used to determine the level of sympathetic interruption and dictate the type of workup indicated. In general, patients with new-onset Horner's syndrome should receive a thorough and immediate workup to determine the etiology.

Physiologic Anisocoria

Twenty percent of the population may have anisocoria of greater than 0.4 mm at any given examination.[67] This anisocoria may be transient or prolonged and may alternate pupils. Although the anisocoria increases in darkness, there is no dilatation lag as seen with Horner's syndrome.

ABNORMAL OPTIC DISK

Clinical Features and Differential Considerations

An important acquired cause of an abnormal optic disk is papilledema. Papilledema refers to the changes in the optic disk from increased intracranial pressure. Causes include intracranial tumor, pseudotumor cerebri, intracranial hematomas from trauma, subarachnoid hemorrhage, brain abscess, and meningitis or encephalitis. There is swelling of the optic disk and blurring of the disk margins, hyperemia, and loss of physiologic cupping. Flame-shaped hemorrhages and yellow exudates appear near the disk margins as the edema progresses. Patients may have significant headaches or be completely asymptomatic. Visual acuity is not affected until the papilledema is long standing. Brief obscurations of vision, enlargement of the physiologic blind spot, and inferior nasal visual field loss are common. Papilledema is a bilateral process but may be asymmetric. A patient with newly diagnosed papilledema should be admitted to the hospital for immediate neuroradiographic evaluation.

Many conditions may mimic papilledema, including central retinal vein occlusion, papillitis, hypertensive retinopathy, ischemic optic neuropathy, optic disk vasculitis, and diabetic papillitis with retinopathy.

NYSTAGMUS

Clinical Features and Differential Considerations

Clinically significant nystagmus is an oscillation of the eyes that occurs within 30 degrees of the midline. Pendular nystagmus is of equal velocity in both directions. With jerk nystagmus, the velocity is faster in one direction. The pathologic component is the slow movement, but the nystagmus is named according to the direction of the fast component. Nystagmus can also be divided into monocular or binocular, conjugate (both eyes moving in the same direction) or disconjugate (eyes moving in opposite directions), and primary gaze position or gaze position nystagmus. Important questions include the presence of tinnitus, nausea, vomiting, oscillopsia, and vertigo.

Congenital nystagmus is noted at birth or within the perinatal period and is usually horizontal, conjugate, bilateral, symmetrical, and pendular. On lateral gaze, this nystagmus may become jerky in nature but remains horizontal despite upward or downward gaze. Congenital nystagmus is damped by convergence, increased with fixation, accentuated by covering one eye, and abolished with sleep. These patients do not have oscillopsia, nor do they have other neurologic complaints. Almost all of these patients have recognized their nystagmus previously, and the diagnosis is generally straightforward.

There are many causes of acquired nystagmus. General categories of disease that result in nystagmus include toxic exposure, defective retinal impulses, diseases of the labyrinths or of the vestibular nuclei, and lesions of the brainstem or cerebellum controlling ocular posture. The workup includes drug and toxic screening and neuroradiologic testing with a CT or MRI scan.

DISORDERS OF EXTRAOCULAR MOVEMENT

Clinical Features and Differential Considerations

Patients complain of diplopia produced or exacerbated by certain eye movements. The first step is to determine whether the diplopia is monocular or binocular. Binocular diplopia disappears with either eye covered. Monocular diplopia is less concerning, caused most commonly by refractive errors, dislocated lens, iridodialysis, and feigned disease.

Binocular diplopia from misalignment of the eyes has a multitude of causes. Local mechanical defects such as hematoma, orbital floor fractures, or abscess and palsy of cranial nerve III, IV, or VI can lead to motility problems. Thyroid disease, progressive ophthalmoplegia, extraocular muscle fibrosis syndrome, multiple sclerosis, and myasthenia gravis can all lead to newly acquired extraocular movement dysfunction.

The most common cause is cranial nerve palsy. Patients with brainstem disease often have involvement of other cranial nerves, disturbances in level of consciousness, and sensorimotor loss. Isolated third-nerve lesions produce a palsy in which the patient develops ptosis, an inability to turn the eye inward or upward, and pupillary mydriasis. The causes of third-nerve palsy are varied and require aggressive and immediate neurologic and radiologic examination.

Isolated fourth-nerve palsy is an easily missed disorder. Patients complain of double vision, which is made worse in downgaze, or gaze away from the paretic side.

These patients typically have a head tilt to the opposite shoulder to compensate for the vertical extorsion and have weakness in downward gaze. Trauma and vascular disease account for most cases of isolated fourth-nerve palsy, but aneurysm, intracranial tumor, and myasthenia gravis have been implicated.

Sixth cranial nerve palsies are the most commonly reported ocular motor palsies. Patients with sixth cranial nerve palsies have an esotropia that is worsened by lateral gaze and often turn their heads laterally toward the paretic side to compensate. Sixth-nerve palsy is caused by a variety of diseases. Wernicke-Korsakoff Syndrome, aneurysm, vascular disease (diabetes, hypertension, atherosclerosis), trauma, neoplasm, multiple sclerosis, meningitis, thyroid eye disease, and increased intracranial pressure may all cause dysfunction. Workup consists of careful neurologic and radiologic examination.

MANAGEMENT

Ophthalmic Drugs

General Considerations

Most ocular medications are administered as drops, which have the advantage of concentrating drug delivery to the anterior segment of the eye and reducing unwanted systemic side effects. Eye drops have the additional advantages of rapid absorption, brief effect, and minimal interference with the visual media.

Unfortunately, the eye retains only a small amount of the drug; the remainder is cleared by the rapid turnover of tears.

To improve absorption, patients who are taking more than one eye drop should ideally wait 10 minutes between drops to prevent the second drop from washing out the first. Patients should apply digital pressure at the medial canthus of the eye to prevent drainage of drug through the nasolacrimal duct and keep their eyes closed for several minutes after instilling their drops to halt the lacrimal pumping mechanisms. Ointments increase the contact time of the medication with the anterior segment of the eye. Ointments blur vision but provide a pleasant lubrication to the eye that has been traumatized and patched and do not seem to interfere with corneal wound healing.

Drug Classification

Box 70-1 provides a listing of the most commonly used agents in each of these categories.

BOX 70-1. Commonly Used Ophthalmologic Medications

Anesthetics
Proparacaine
Tetracaine

Antibiotics
Bacitracin
Ciprofloxacin
Erythromycin
Gentamicin
Neomycin/bacitracin/polymyxin B
Norfloxacin
Ofloxacin
Polymyxin B/bacitracin
Polymyxin B/trimethoprim
Sulfacetamide
Tobramycin

Antivirals
Fomivirsen
Trifluridine
Vidarabine

Corticosteroids
Dexamethasone
Fluorometholone
Loteprednol
Prednisolone
Rimexolone

Decongestants/Antiallergy
Cromolyn Sodium
Levocabastine
Lodoxamide tromethamine
Naphazoline
Naphazoline/pheniramine
Olopatadine

Glaucoma: β-Blockers
Betaxolol
Carteolol
Levobunolol
Timolol

Glaucoma: Carbonic Anhydrase Inhibitors
Acetazolamide
Brinzolamide
Dorzolamide

Glaucoma: Other
Apraclonidine
Brimonidine
Cosopt
Dipivefrin
Echothiophate
Latanoprost
Pilocarpine

Mydriatics/Cycloplegics
Atropine
Cyclopentolate
Homatropine
Phenylephrine
Tropicamide

Nonsteroidal
Diclofenac
Ketorolac

Other Medications
Artificial tears

Local anesthetics block neurotransmission along sensory nerve fibers. Ocular procedures facilitated by topical anesthetics include direct inspection, foreign body removal, irrigation, tonometry, and contact lens removal. Topical anesthetics inhibit wound healing, and severe keratopathy can result from indiscriminate use of topical anesthetics. Local anesthetic drops should not be prescribed as pain medicine for self-administration by patients.

Antibiotics and antiviral agents are commonly prescribed. The choice of antibiotic agent should be guided by culture, Gram's stain, or suspected bacteria or virus. Antiviral agents are generally prescribed after consultation with an ophthalmologist.

Corticosteroids are used by ophthalmologists for many ocular conditions, but their use by emergency physicians should be limited. Corticosteroids can accelerate the activity of herpes simplex virus and should not be given to a patient when the diagnosis is uncertain. Posttraumatic iridocyclitis is one of the few conditions in which an emergency physician might consider prescribing a topical steroid agent, but close follow-up with an ophthalmologist is highly recommended.

Cycloplegics block the muscarinic receptors, producing paralysis of the ciliary muscle, which always causes mydriasis. Cycloplegics are useful in relieving pain and photophobia secondary to ciliary spasm related to corneal abrasion, ocular trauma, and iridocyclitis.[7] Mydriatics dilate the pupil, but not all mydriatics are cycloplegics. Mydriatics are contraindicated in any patient with a history of glaucoma, evidence of increased intraocular pressure, presence of a shallow anterior chamber, suspicion of a ruptured globe, or if a lens implant is present. Atropine has a long duration of action (1 to 2 weeks) and should be prescribed only by an ophthalmologist. Decongestants and antiallergy ocular medications are commonly prescribed and lessen allergic ocular symptoms.

A number of agents are used to treat glaucoma. It is important to know that these are absorbed and can have systemic effects. For example, topical β-blocker agents can result in symptomatic bradycardia or increased bronchospasm.

Nonsteroidal anti-inflammatory agents are useful in alleviating the symptoms of inflammation in a wide variety of ocular conditions.

Artificial tears relieve symptoms related to dry eyes and protect the corneas of unconscious patients as well as patients suffering from Bell's palsy.

KEY CONCEPTS

- *Orbital floor fractures*: Surgical repair is only for persistent diplopia or cosmetic concerns and is generally not performed until swelling subsides in 7 to 10 days.
- *Retrobulbar hematoma*: When a retrobulbar hematoma compromises retinal circulation, immediate treatment of increased intraocular pressure includes carbonic anhydrase inhibitor, topical β-blocker, and IV mannitol. A lateral canthotomy can be done in the emergency department as a temporizing measure before definitive decompression.
- *Corneal abrasions*: Data suggest that eye patching confers no benefit in healing small, uncomplicated corneal abrasions.
- *Globe rupture*: Treatment includes avoidance of further examination or manipulation and placement of a protective metal eye shield to prevent accidental pressure on the globe. Antiemetics should be given if nausea is present. Broad-spectrum IV antibiotics should be instituted.
- *Retinal detachments*: Retinal tears or detachments do not cause pain. Examination may reveal the hazy gray membrane of the retina billowing forward, but many tears are peripherally located and not seen with direct ophthalmoscopy. Visual acuity may be normal unless the macula is involved. Indirect ophthalmoscopy is warranted if historical clues to the presence of retinal tears are present.
- *Bacterial conjunctivitis*: In uncomplicated acute bacterial conjunctivitis, neomycin ophthalmic solutions should be avoided because of the high incidence of hypersensitivity reactions. Corticosteroids and eye patching should be avoided.
- *Glaucoma*: Attacks of primary angle closure glaucoma produce symptoms that are abrupt in onset and include severe eye pain, blurred vision, headache, nausea, vomiting, and occasionally abdominal pain. Signs include conjunctival injection and a cloudy (steamy) cornea with a midpositioned to dilated pupil that is sluggish or fixed. Intraocular pressures are markedly elevated.

REFERENCES

1. Department of Emergency Medicine, Hennepin County Medical Center, Emstat, 1999.
2. Baker SM, Hurwitz JJ: Sports and industrial ophthalmology: Management of orbital and ocular adnexal trauma. *Ophthalmol Clin North Am* 12:435, 1999.
3. O'Hare TH: Blowout fractures: A review. *J Emerg Med* 9:253, 1991.
4. Mathong RH: Management of orbital blowout fractures. *Otolaryngol Clin North Am* 24:79, 1991.
5. Spoor TC, Nesi FA: *Management of Ocular, Orbital, and Adnexal Trauma*. New York, Raven Press, 1988.
6. Birrer RB, Robinson T, Papachristos P: Orbital emphysema: How common, how significant? *Ann Emerg Med* 24:1115, 1994.
7. Dobler AA, et al: A case of orbital emphysema as an ocular emergency. *Retina* 13:166, 1993.
8. Zimmer-Galler IE, Bartley GB: Orbital emphysema: Case reports and review of the literature. *Mayo Clin Proc* 69:115, 1994.
9. Joondeph BC: Blunt ocular trauma. *Emerg Med Clin North Am* 6:147, 1988.
10. Murphy JC, et al: Ocular irritancy responses to various pHs of acids and bases with and without irrigation. *Toxicology* 23:281, 1982.
11. Janda AM: Ocular trauma. *Postgrad Med* 90:51, 1991.

12. Dean BS: Cyanoacrylate and corneal abrasion. *Clin Toxicol* 27:169, 1989.

13. Leahey AB, Gottsch JD, Stark WJ: Clinical experience with *N*-butyl cyanoacrylate (Nexacryl) tissue adhesive. *Ophthalmology* 100:173, 1993.

14. Lubeck D, Greene JS: Corneal injuries. *Emerg Med Clin North Am* 6:73, 1988.

15. Rosenwasser GO, et al: Topical anesthetic abuse. *Ophthalmology* 97:967, 1990.

16. Sklar DP, Lauth JE, Johnson DR: Topical anesthesia of the eye as a diagnostic test. *Ann Emerg Med* 18:1209, 1989.

17. Hulbert MF: Efficacy of eye pad in corneal healing after corneal foreign body removal. *Lancet* 337:643, 1991.

18. Roberts JR: Myths and misconceptions: An eye patch for simple corneal abrasions. *Emerg Med News* February:4, 1995.

19. Hamill MB: Sports and industrial ophthalmology. Current concepts in the treatment of traumatic injury to the anterior segment. *Ophthalmol Clin North Am* 12:457, 1999.

20. Safran MJ: Management of traumatic hyphema. *Hosp Physician* June:20, 1987.

21. Farber MD, Fiscella R, Goldberg MF: Aminocaproic acid versus prednisone for the treatment of traumatic hyphema: A randomized clinical trial. *Ophthalmology* 98:279, 1991.

22. Jackson J: Hyphema. *Optom Clin* 3:27, 1993.

23. Pavan-Langston D: *Manual of Ocular Diagnosis and Therapy,* 3rd ed. Boston, Little, Brown. 1991.

24. Fong LP: Secondary hemorrhage in traumatic hyphema: Predictive factors for selective prophylaxis. *Ophthalmology* 101:1583, 1994.

25. Charache S: Sickle cell disease: Eye disease in sickling disorders. *Hematol Oncol Clin North Am* 10:1357, 1996.

26. Weisman RA, Savino PJ: Management of patients with facial trauma and associated ocular/orbital injuries. *Otolaryngol Clin North Am* 24:37, 1991.

27. Lubeck D: Penetrating ocular injuries. *Emerg Med Clin North Am* 6:127, 1988.

28. Shingleton BJ: Eye injuries. *N Engl J Med* 325:408, 1991.

29. Ferrari LR: Trauma. The injured eye. *Anesthesiol Clin North Am* 14:125, 1996.

30. Libonati MM, Leahy JJ, Ellison N: The use of succinylcholine in open eye surgery. *Anesthesiology* 62:637, 1985.

31. Reppucci VS, Movshovich A: Sports and industrial ophthalmology. Current concepts in the treatment of traumatic injury to the posterior segment. *Ophthalmol Clin North Am* 12:465, 1999.

32. Solley WA, Broocker G: Ocular trauma. In Palay DA, Krachmer JH (eds): *Ophthalmology for the Primary Care Physician.* St. Louis, Mosby, 1997, pp 268-269.

33. Alfaro DV, Roth D, Liggett PE: Posttraumatic endophthalmitis. Causative organisms, treatment, and prevention. *Retina* 14:206, 1994.

34. Linden JA, Renner GS: Trauma to the globe. *Emerg Med Clin North Am* 13:581, 1995.

35. Diamant JI, Hwang DG: Ocular infections: Update on therapy. Therapy for bacterial conjunctivitis. *Ophthalmol Clin North Am* 12:15, 1999.

36. Treatment of sexually transmitted disease. *Med Lett* 32:5, 1990.

37. Barequet IS, O'Brien TP: Ocular infections: Update on therapy. Therapy of herpes simplex viral keratitis. *Ophthalmol Clin North Am* 12:63, 1999.

38. Harding SSP: Management of ophthalmic zoster. *J Med Virol* 1(Suppl):97, 1993.

39. Rhee DJ, Pyfer MF: Conjunctival/scleral/external disease. In Friedberg MA, Rapuano CJ (eds): *The Wills Eye Manual,* 3rd ed. Philadelphia, Lippincott Williams & Wilkins, 1999, pp 86-89.

40. Miedziak AI, O'Brien TP: Ocular infections: Update of therapy. Therapy of varicella-zoster virus ocular infections. *Ophthalmol Clin North Am* 12:51, 1999.

41. Lederman C, Miller M: Hordeola and chalazia. *Pediatr Rev* 20:283, 1999.

42. Pederson JE: Glaucoma: A primer for primary care physicians. *Glaucoma* 90:41, 1991.

43. Shiose Y: Intraocular pressure: New perspectives. *Surv Ophthalmol* 34:413, 1990.

44. Beck AD: Glaucoma. In Palay DA, Krachmer JH (eds): *Ophthalmology for the Primary Care Physician.* St. Louis, Mosby, 1997, p 139.

45. Urtti A, Salminen L: Minimizing systemic absorption of topically administered ophthalmic drugs. *Surv Ophthalmol* 37:435, 1993.

46. Fraunfelder FT: *Drug Induced Ocular Side Effects and Drug Interactions,* 3rd ed. Philadelphia, Lea & Febiger, 1989.

47. Kooner KS, Zimmermann TJ: Management of acute elevated intraocular pressure, I. Diagnosis. *Ann Ophthalmol* 20:46, 1988.

48. Yanofsky NN: The acute painful eye. *Emerg Med Clin North Am* 6:21, 1988.

49. Morgan A, Hemphill RR: The difficult diagnosis: Acute visual change. *Emerg Med Clin North Am* 16:825, 1998.

50. Bertolini J, Pelucio M: The red eye. *Emerg Med Clin North Am* 13:561, 1995.

51. Delaney WV Jr: Ocular vascular disease: In-office primary care diagnosis. *Geriatrics* 48:60, 1993.

52. Sharma S, Brown M, Brown GC: Retinal vascular disorders: Retinal artery occlusions. *Ophthalmol Clin North Am* 11:591, 1998.

53. Rassam SM, Patel V, Kohner EM: The effect of acetazolamide on the retinal circulation. *Eye* 7:697, 1993.

54. Atebara N, Brown GC, Cater J: Efficacy of anterior chamber paracentesis and carbogen in treating nonarteritic central retinal artery occlusion. *Ophthalmology* 102:2029, 1995.

55. Hayreh SS: Retinal vascular disorders: Central retinal vein occlusion. *Ophthalmol Clin North Am* 11:559, 1998.

56. Bolling JP, Hernan DC, Pach JM: Disorders of retina, vitreous, and choroid. In Bartley GB, Liesegang TJ (eds): *Essentials of Ophthalmology.* Philadelphia, JB Lippincott, 1992, pp 136-139.

57. Hardy RA, Crawford JB: Retina. In Vaughan D, Asbury T, Riordan-Eva P (eds): *General Ophthalmology,* 15th ed. New York, Appleton & Lange, 1999, p 188.

58. O'Malley C: Vitreous. In Vaughan D, Asbury T, Riordan-Eva P (eds): *General Ophthalmology,* 15th ed. New Jessey, Appleton & Lange, 1999, pp 167-168.

59. Alexander LJ: Age related macular degeneration: The current understanding of the status of clinicopathology, diagnosis and management. *J Am Optom Assoc* 64:822, 1993.

60. Miller NR: *Walsh and Hoyt's Clinical Neuro-Ophthalmology,* 4th ed. Baltimore, Williams & Wilkins, 1991.

61. Optic Neuritis Study Group: The 5 year risk of MS after optic neuritis: Experience of the optic neuritis treatment trial. *Neurology* 49:1404, 1997.

62. Beck RW, et al: The effect of corticosteroids for acute optic neuritis on the subsequent development of multiple sclerosis. *N Engl J Med* 329:1764, 1993.

63. Sellebjerg F, et al: A randomized, controlled trial of oral high-dose methylprednisolone in acute optic neuritis. *Neurology* 52:1479, 1999.

64. Weinberg DA, et al: Giant cell arteritis: Corticosteroids, temporal artery biopsy, and blindness. *Arch Fam Med* 3:623, 1994.

65. Liu GT, et al: Visual morbidity in giant cell arteritis: Clinical characteristics and prognosis for vision. *Ophthalmology* 101:1779, 1994.

66. Wong RL: Temporal arteritis without an elevated erythrocyte sedimentation rate: Case report and review of the literature. *Am J Med* 80:959, 1986.

67. Lam BL Thompson HS, Corbett JJ: The prevalence of simple anisocoria. *Am J Ophthalmol* 104:69, 1987.

OTITIS MEDIA

Perspective

Background

Otitis media (OM) is the most common diagnosis made by U.S. physicians for children younger than 15 years old.[1] In the greater Boston area, 60% of 877 children were diagnosed at least once with acute otitis media (AOM) by 1 year of age; by 3 years of age, more than 80% had AOM, with 40% having more than three episodes.[2] The financial impact is enormous; one estimate is that $5 billion per year is spent on the evaluation, treatment, and socioeconomic effects of OM.[3]

Epidemiology

Male gender, day care attendance, parental smoking, and a family history of middle ear disease have been implicated to increase risk.[4] Children with anatomic abnormalities, such as cleft palate and Down syndrome, have a higher rate of OM, probably because of eustachian tube abnormalities. Some immunocompromised patients, including patients with human immunodeficiency virus, may have recurrent OM as an initial symptom of their underlying disease. OM and upper respiratory infections occur primarily in the winter. Breast-feeding seems to be protective.[5]

Definitions

Otitis media is broadly defined as inflammation of the inner ear and is a continuum of disease. *Acute otitis media* is defined as the signs and symptoms of an acute infection, with evidence of effusion; this has also been called *acute suppurative* or *purulent* OM. *Otitis media with effusion* (OME) has effusion without signs or symptoms of an acute infection; additional descriptive terms include *serous, mucoid, nonsuppurative,* or *secretory* OM. OME is classified further into acute (<3 weeks), subacute (3 weeks to 3 months), and chronic (>3 months). Chronic OM, or *chronic suppurative otitis media,* refers to chronic discharge from the ear through perforation of an intact membrane. *Recurrent* OM is defined by three or more episodes over 6 months or four episodes in 1 year.

Principles of Disease

Pathophysiology

Eustachian tube dysfunction is the central theme to most theories of AOM pathogenesis. The eustachian tube, between the middle ear cavity and the nasopharynx, ventilates the middle ear to equilibrate pressure, allow for middle ear drainage, and provide protection from nasopharyngeal secretions. In children, it measures approximately 18 mm and is almost horizontal. As individuals age, the eustachian tube widens, doubles in length, becomes more vertically oriented, and stiffens (which may explain the decreased incidence of AOM in adults). Normally, the tube is collapsed, but it opens during yawning, chewing, and swallowing.

The eustachian tube may become either mechanically or functionally obstructed, decreasing middle ear ventilation. Examples of mechanical obstruction include inflammations from an upper respiratory infection, hypertrophied adenoids, and a cleft palate.[6] Functional obstruction from persistent tubal collapse occurs primarily in young children, who have less fibrocartilage support of the medial eustachian tube than older children or adults.[6] It has been postulated that this dysfunction results in negative middle ear cavity pressure, causing a transudate of fluid that combines with the reflux of nasopharyngeal secretions and bacteria.

Etiology

The most common bacterial causes are *Streptococcus pneumoniae, Haemophilus influenzae* (primarily nontypeable), and *Moraxella (Branhamella) catarrhalis. Streptococcus pyogenes, Staphylococcus aureus,* and gram-negative bacteria are much less common.[7] Adult infection involves similar organisms. In OME, there is a greater proportion of *H. influenzae* and a higher percentage of sterile effusions.[8] Viruses also have been found in the middle ear aspirates of children with OM. In one study, viruses were identified in 90% of children with AOM and as the sole source in 5% to 6% of cases.[9] Some authors believe that viral infection is the cause of the inflammatory reaction in most cases and antibiotics are not necessary. Respiratory syncytial virus is the most common virus, followed by rhinovirus, influenzavirus, and adenovirus.[8] These viruses may be responsible for some of the treatment failures seen in AOM, possibly by interfering with eradication of bacterial pathogens.

In young children, it was believed that gram-negative organisms and *S. aureus* were the causative factors. Although these organisms may be the causes in intubated patients or patients in the neonatal intensive care unit, healthy newborns tend to be infected by the same pathogens as healthy older children.[10] A special note should be made about bullous myringitis. Middle ear aspirates in this condition generally grow the usual organisms that cause AOM.[11] *Mycoplasma pneumoniae* is uncommon. Other, less likely, organisms that can cause AOM include *Mycobacterium tuberculosis* (primarily in children) and *Chlamydia trachomatis* (most commonly seen in children younger than 6 months old with pneumonia).[12]

Clinical Features

OM may be manifested by a multitude of symptoms, such as cough, poor appetite, diarrhea, vomiting, fever, and pulling at ears, all of which are nonspecific. Older children may be able to verbalize pain, but otalgia is not universally present. In OM, pain usually precedes otorrhea, in contrast to OME, in which pain accompanies the drainage. Children often have associated upper respiratory tract infections. Fever may be present, but in one large series, a temperature of 38.3°C or greater was present in only 26% of the episodes, with only 4% having a fever of 40°C or greater.[13] Some authorities have modified the definition to include otoscopic findings of acute inflammation regardless of symptoms; with this definition, one third of cases are not accompanied initially by acute symptoms.[14]

The auricle and external canal should be inspected for signs of erythema, discharge, or tenderness. If the canal is occluded with cerumen, an ear curet with direct visualization may be successful in clearing the canal. If not, the placement of 3% hydrogen peroxide or emulsifying drops, followed by gentle irrigation, may cleanse the canal.

The tympanic membrane (TM) may be bulging (as in AOM), neutral, or retracted as seen in chronic OME.[15] The color may be red, pink, yellow, or a normal pearly gray or translucent. The presence of erythema in itself does not indicate infection because crying or fever may cause hyperemia; however, a TM that is distinctly red (defined as *hemorrhagic,* strongly or moderately red) suggests AOM.[15]

Landmarks that should be visible include the pars flaccida, the malleolus, and the light reflex below the umbo.[15] The TM may have air-fluid levels, may have bubbles behind the TM, or may be completely opacified, all of which indicate middle ear effusion. The lack of mobility is one of the most sensitive indicators of middle ear effusion. A TM that is cloudy, bulging, or distinctly immobile indicates AOM.[15] In OME, the TM often is retracted, with the malleolus being particularly prominent. The landmarks all may be obscured in the presence of significant fluid. A comparison examination of the other ear may help in confirming suspected infection.

In neonates, the TM appears thickened and opaque normally in the first few weeks of life, and the TM is in a highly oblique position. With tympanostomy tubes, in the absence of infection, the TM may have decreased mobility, altered landmarks, opacity, or dullness. If the tube is patent, erythema and discharge may indicate infection. If not, erythema, bulging of the TM, and immobility indicate AOM.

Complications

Before the use of antibiotics, there was a 20% incidence of complications from AOM, with mastoiditis and otic meningitis relatively common.[16] Complications generally are considered either intratemporal or intracranial. The development of either complication of OM is thought to occur by one of three mechanisms: (1) direct extension of infection through bone weakened by osteomyelitis or cholesteatoma; (2) retrograde spread of infection by thrombophlebitis; or (3) extension of infection along preformed pathways, such as the round or oval windows or through dehiscences that are the result of congenital malformations.[17]

Intratemporal

Hearing impairment is the most common complication in OM. Almost all children with OM have a temporary conductive hearing loss; sensorineural deficit occurs less commonly, probably as a spread of infection through the round window. This deficit may contribute to the association of OM with decreased or delayed speech, language, or cognitive development.

TM perforation occurs most commonly at the pars tensa and usually resolves spontaneously. It may persist for a longer period, resulting in a chronic perforation, chronic OM, or both.[12] Chronic OM refers to chronic discharge from the ear through perforation of an intact membrane. It can occur spontaneously or through tympanostomy tubes for 2 to 3 months or longer.[17] The organisms involved are usually *Pseudomonas aeruginosa* or *S. aureus*. Treatment begins with oral/topical antibiotics; patients should be referred to an otolaryngologist.

Cholesteatoma is an accumulation of keratin-producing squamous epithelium in the middle ear and may result in erosion of bone within the middle ear cavity. It is seen most often in OME, in which retraction of the TM is a common problem. Treatment is usually surgical.

Labyrinthitis occurs when infection spreads to the cochlear and vestibular apparatus, usually through the round or oval windows. Serous labyrinthitis results when bacteria from the middle ear spread into the labyrinth space, resulting in a mixed conductive/sensorineural hearing loss and vestibular symptoms. Suppurative labyrinthitis is the development of purulence directly into the labyrinth as a result of bacterial invasion through the round window or around the annular ligament of the round window. It generally begins suddenly with mixed hearing loss and vestibular symptoms and is generally more severe than the serous form.[17] Facial nerve paralysis is a rec-ognized complication in children with OM. The facial nerve courses through the middle ear and may be affected by infection.[12] Treatment consists of intravenous antibiotics, myringotomy, and tube placement.

Infectious eczematoid dermatitis may result from the otorrhea of OM, with perforation or tympanostomy tubes infecting the external auditory canal. Treatment involves otic suspension (*not* solution). Although

Table 71-2. Treatment Guidelines for Otitis Media

Temperature ≤ 39° C or Severe Otalgia or Both	At Diagnosis for Patients Being Treated Initially with Antibacterial Agents		Clinically Defined Treatment Failure at 48-72 Hours after Initial Management with Observation Option		Clinically Defined Treatment Failure at 48-72 Hours after Initial Management with Antibacterial Agents	
	Recommended	Alternative for Penicillin Allergy	Recommended	Alternative for Penicillin Allergy	Recommended	Alternative for Penicillin Allergy
No	Amoxicillin (80-90 mg/kg/day)	Non–type I: cefdinir, cefuroxime, cefpodoxime Type I*: azithromycin, clarithromycin	Amoxicillin (80-90 mg/kg/day)	Non–type I: cefdinir, cefuroxime, cefpodoxime Type I*: azithromycin, clarithromycin	Amoxicillin-clavulanate (90 mg/kg/day of amoxicillin with 6.4 mg/kg/day of clavulanate)	Non–type I: ceftriaxone—3 days Type I*: clindamycin
Yes	Amoxicillin-clavulanate (90 mg/kg/day of amoxicillin with 6.4 mg/kg/day of clavulanate)	Ceftriaxone—1 or 3 days	Amoxicillin-clavulanate (90 mg/kg/day of amoxicillin with 6.4 mg/kg/day of clavulanate)	Ceftriaxone—1 or 3 days	Ceftriaxone—3 days	Tympanocentesis—clindamycin

*Type I sensitivity—urticaria or anaphylaxis.
From American Academy of Pediatrics Subcommittee on Management of Acute Otitis Media: Diagnosis and management of acute otitis media. *Pediatrics* 113:1451, 2004.

and tympanostomy tubes may be beneficial in children who have failed medical treatment, have had OME for 4 to 6 months, and have a greater than 20-dB hearing loss.[1] Tonsillectomy is not beneficial, but adenoidectomy may be helpful in older children. Tympanostomy tubes also have been used in recurrent AOM unresponsive to prophylactic antibiotics; complications of AOM, including mastoiditis, meningitis, brain abscess, and facial nerve paralysis; and complications of eustachian tube dysfunction, including TM retraction with hearing loss, ossicular erosions, or retraction pocket formation.[28]

Conjugate pneumococcal vaccine has been effective in markedly reducing invasive disease in young children and decreasing the incidence of OM.[29] It is estimated that its use would decrease the number of visits for OM by 1 million, and the number of children receiving tympanostomy tubes might decrease by 500,000.[30]

Disposition

Children normally are seen in 10 to 14 days for follow-up. This follow-up appointment may not be necessary in children older than age 2 years with resolution of symptoms and no recurrent risk factors.[31] Infants younger than 2 months old with OM should be evaluated with blood, cerebrospinal fluid, and urine cultures.[6] Patients with complications need ear, nose, and throat (ENT) referral. Adults who have persistent OME need ENT referral to rule out nasopharyngeal carcinoma.

OTITIS EXTERNA

Principles of Disease

External otitis is an inflammation of the external auditory canal. The canal is lined with squamous epithelial cells and cerumen glands that provide a protective lipid layer.[32] This protective layer may be disrupted by high humidity, increased temperature, maceration of the skin after prolonged exposure to moisture, and local trauma (e.g., cotton swabs or the use of hearing aids), resulting in the introduction of bacteria.[33] The most common bacterial causes are *P. aeruginosa, S. aureus,* and *S. epidermidis.* Otitis externa occurs most often in the summer and is common in the tropics.

Clinical Features

The canal is initially pruritic and becomes erythematous and increasingly swollen. The diagnosis is made clinically with ear pain, erythema or edema of the canal, and reproduction of the discomfort with pulling on the auricle or tragus. Severe otitis externa is manifested by intense pain, canal occlusion, and conductive hearing loss.[32] Cultures are unnecessary. The disease may progress to a chronic form with itching, eczema, and flaking of the epithelium, which may be from bacterial, fungal, or dermatologic conditions. In children, it is usually secondary to OME.

Differential Considerations

It may be difficult to distinguish otitis externa from OM, particularly in children. The TM may be erythematous in both conditions, and the edema may preclude diagnosis. The discharge may be from otitis externa or a perforated TM, and in equivocal cases it is prudent to treat for both conditions.

Otomycosis or fungal infection can occur as a primary or secondary infection and accounts for 10% of cases of otitis externa.[34] Itching is the prominent symptom, often with minimal pain or otorrhea. Aspergillosis is the cause in most cases. Otomycosis appears most often in individuals in tropical climates, in patients with diabetes, in immunocompromised patients, and in patients on immunosuppressive therapy. Treatment involves cleansing and acidifying and antifungal eardrops, such as thimerosal or gentian violet. Specific antifungal agents, such as clotrimazole and itraconazole, also are effective.[34]

Furunculosis is a small, erythematous, and well-circumscribed infection of the cartilaginous portions of the external canal, usually caused by *S. aureus*.[32] There is usually no drainage, and treatment involves incision, drainage, and an oral antistaphylococcal antibiotic. Cellulitis of the auricle and canal may cause erythema, induration, and other systemic signs. Treatment is with antibiotics directed at the offending organisms. Parenteral antistaphylococcal antibiotics (e.g., nafcillin) may be required in severe infections.

Herpes zoster oticus, also known as the *Ramsay Hunt syndrome*, is a viral manifestation of disease affecting the auricle, with resulting facial paralysis that may involve multiple cranial nerves. It initially causes pain, with erythema, swelling, and vesicles developing approximately 3 to 7 days later.[34] These patients need ENT referral. Treatment consists of analgesia, warm compresses, and acyclovir.

Management

Historically, combination drugs containing neomycin, polymyxin B, and hydrocortisone four times a day have been effective for treatment, although there has been a problem with hypersensitivity. The new fluoroquinolones are less reactive, need to be given only twice a day, and are rapidly becoming the preferred therapy.[35] Initial management may involve cleansing the external canal with a combination of gentle suctioning and irrigation, depending on the amount of obstructing exudate. Cleansing solutions include tap water, sterile saline, 2% acetic acid, and Burow's solution. In severe infections, a wick of cotton, gauze, or compressed hydroxycellulose facilitates medication delivery. The wick is placed 10 to 12 mm into the canal, moistened with antibiotic drops, and left in place for 2 to 3 days. Cephalosporins and ciprofloxacin, among others, may be necessary in infections involving the skin and periauricular areas.[34] Opioid analgesia may be necessary. Patients with severe inflammation (fever, cervical lymphadenopathy, or periauricular nodes) need close follow-up and ENT referral.

NECROTIZING (MALIGNANT) EXTERNAL OTITIS

Previously known as *malignant otitis externa* because of its high mortality, necrotizing external otitis is an extremely aggressive form of otitis externa. It occurs primarily in adults with diabetes mellitus but also has been seen rarely in immunocompromised children. *Pseudomonas* is the predominant pathogen, but *S. aureus, S. epidermidis, Proteus mirabilis, Klebsiella, Aspergillus,* and *Salmonella* all have been described.[36] The infection begins in the external canal and progresses through the periauricular tissue and cartilagi-

nous bony junction of the external auditory meatus. It then spreads into the adjacent tissues along clefts in the floor of the meatus known as the *fissures of Santorini*.[37] It may spread to the base of the skull at the temporal bone, with a resultant skull-base *osteomyelitis*, another term often used to describe this entity. The facial nerve is the first cranial nerve affected, but additional nerves may be involved. The pathogenesis is uncertain but may be related to vascular insufficiency or immune dysfunction.[38]

Clinical symptoms include pain, tenderness, and swelling around the periauricular area, headache, and otorrhea. It may be difficult to distinguish this entity from a severe external otitis, a further reason for close follow-up. Any persistent external otitis in an elderly person with diabetes with associated pain should be considered to be temporal bone osteomyelitis. The clinical finding characteristic for the disease is granulation tissue in the floor of the ear canal at the bony cartilaginous junction. Facial paralysis occurs when there is involvement of the stylomastoid foramen, and further extension can result in cranial nerve IX, X, and XI palsies.[39] Further complications include thrombosis of the sigmoid sinus and meningitis.

Bone scanning (technetium 99m) and gallium are sensitive radiographic tests, but they are not specific for the disease. CT is useful for detecting infratemporal spread of the disease and abscess formation,[37] which further define the extent of the disease.

Treatment includes an aminoglycoside and a semisynthetic penicillin. There has been excellent success with ciprofloxacin, and its oral availability makes it ideal. Although extensive surgical debridement was used previously, its role is now limited. Hyperbaric oxygen has been used as an adjunct therapy.[32] Because of the incidence of external otitis in adults with diabetes, a blood glucose level should be obtained in all patients with severe external otitis.

MASTOIDITIS

The incidence of acute and chronic mastoiditis has decreased significantly since the advent of antibiotics in the United States, but in Denmark, where antibiotic use is restricted, the rate of mastoiditis is twice that of the United States, although still low. Although it is still associated primarily with OM, many patients have not had an episode of OM.[40,41] Mastoiditis also has been described as a complication of leukemia, mononucleosis, sarcoma of the temporal bone, and Kawasaki disease.[42]

Pathophysiology

Acute mastoiditis is a natural extension of middle ear infections because the mastoid air cells are generally inflamed during an episode of AOM. The aditus ad antrum is a narrow connection between the middle ear and mastoid air cells. If this connection becomes blocked, a closed space is formed, with the potential for abscess development and bone destruction. The infection may spread from the mastoid air cells by venous channels, resulting in inflammation of the overlying periosteum. Progression results in the destruction of the mastoid bone trabeculae and coalescence of the cells, resulting in acute mastoid osteitis or coalescent mastoiditis. The resulting pus may track through many routes: (1) through the aditus ad antrum with resultant spontaneous resolution; (2) lateral to the surface of the mastoid process, resulting in a subperiosteal abscess; (3) anteriorly, forming an abscess below the pinna or behind the sternocleidomastoid muscle of the neck, resulting in an abscess (often called a *Bezold abscess*); (4) medial to the petrous air cells of the temporal bone, resulting in a rare condition known as *petrositis*; and (5) posterior to the occipital bone, resulting in osteomyelitis of the calvaria or a Citelli abscess.[40-42]

Chronic mastoiditis is generally a complication of chronic OM. There may be extensive invasion of granulation tissue from the middle ear into the mastoid air cells. Another entity, latent or "masked" mastoiditis, also has been described. It is indolent in nature, with minimal signs and symptoms, little or no fever, and a history of otalgia. The TM may be intact or perforated. Suspicion should be raised in the presence of intracranial complications without an apparent source.[43] Patients at risk for this condition include newborns and immunosuppressed patients (recent chemotherapy, steroids, or diabetic or geriatric patients).

Etiology

S. pneumoniae is the most common organism found in mastoiditis, but other organisms involved do not always mirror those of acute otitis.[40] Mixed cultures of aerobes and anaerobes are common. Common aerobes include group A streptococci, *S. aureus,* and *S. epidermidis.* Chronic mastoiditis also often has mixed cultures, with *P. aeruginosa* as the predominant organism.

Diagnostic Findings

Clinical findings in acute mastoiditis include fever, headache, and erythema. Pain is universally present.[40] Physical findings include postauricular or supraauricular tenderness, with late edema. The TM is similar to AOM (erythema, bulging, and decreased mobility) but may be normal in 10% of cases.[40] Suspicions should be heightened if symptoms of AOM have lasted longer than 2 weeks.[44] In chronic mastoiditis, symptoms include persistent drainage through the perforated TM, redness, edema, and retroauricular sensitivity.[45]

Ancillary Testing

Radiographs of the mastoid area may be negative.[41,44] CT is of greater value, especially when there is abscess formation.[45] Magnetic resonance imaging (MRI) may be more useful, particularly if there is evidence of intracranial complications.

Management

The diagnosis of mastoiditis requires admitting the patient for antibiotic therapy. Traditional antibiotic choices include a semisynthetic penicillin combined with chloramphenicol or, more commonly, a third-generation cephalosporin such as cefuroxime (50 to 150 mg/kg/day) or ceftriaxone (50 to 75 mg/kg/day), usually for 1 week. Surgical procedures may range from myringotomy drainage and tympanostomy tube placement to mastoidectomy and drainage for more extensive disease progression. Mastoidectomy is required in approximately half of mastoiditis cases.[42]

Antibiotic choices for chronic mastoiditis are based on culture of the persistent drainage but often include medication to cover *Pseudomonas,* such as ticarcillin-clavulanate or ticarcillin alone. Local cleansing also is efficacious. Antibiotics may obviate the need for surgery, although mastoidectomy may be required in some cases.[44]

SUDDEN HEARING LOSS

Sudden hearing loss, although uncommon, may be of great concern to the patient. It may be noticed gradually or have a sudden onset. Although there is no accepted definition of sudden hearing loss, it is most often sensorineural in nature and occurs over a brief period, usually about 3 days.[46] Severity ranges from difficulty with conversation to complete hearing loss.

The speed of onset may give clues to the etiology (Box 71-1).[46-48] A sudden onset may be from trauma or a vascular complication; gradual hearing loss suggests a tumor.[47] A history of trauma, medications, illnesses, physical activity at the time of the event, and unilateral or bilateral involvement all are helpful clues. The presence of tinnitus, vertigo, and neurologic symptoms ranging from cranial nerve abnormalities to brainstem or cerebellar dysfunction is helpful. In conductive hearing losses, such as otosclerosis, individuals hear better in noisy environments.[47]

Physical examination should include a thorough inspection of the external canal and TM integrity. Weber's test for hearing and Rinne's test may help in distinguishing conductive versus sensorineural deficits. A comprehensive neurologic examination including cranial nerves and cerebellar testing may localize brainstem involvement. CT may reveal trauma or tumors, and neurologic and chemical screening should be based on the history and physical findings.[48] Sudden sensorineural hearing loss is an otologic emergency.[46] Treatment is directed at the underlying causes.

EPISTAXIS

Perspective

Epidemiology

Epistaxis is a common otolaryngologic problem, with 15 per 10,000 people requiring physician care annually

BOX 71-1. Causes of Sudden Hearing Loss

Infectious
Mumps
Measles
Influenza
Herpes simplex
Herpes zoster
Cytomegalovirus
Mononucleosis
Syphilis

Vascular
Macroglobulinemia
Sickle cell disease
Berger's disease
Leukemia
Polycythemia
Fat emboli
Hypercoagulable states

Metabolic
Diabetes
Pregnancy
Hyperlipoproteinemia

Conductive
Cerumen impaction
Foreign bodies
Otitis media
Otitis externa
Barotrauma
Trauma

Medications
Aminoglycosides (gentamicin, neomycin, vancomycin, kanamycin, streptomycin)
Loop diuretics (furosemide, ethacrynic acid)
Antineoplastics
Salicylates

Neoplasm
Acoustic neuroma

From Shikowitz MJ: *Med Clin North Am* 75:1239, 1991; Lawrence LJ, Brown CG: *Emerg Med Clin North Am* 5:193, 1987; and Nadol JB: *N Engl J Med* 329:1092, 1993.

and 1.6 per 10,000 requiring admission to the hospital.[49] Most cases occur in children younger than age 10 years, and the incidence decreases with age. It is more common in colder seasons and in northern climates because of decreased humidity and subsequent drying of the nasal mucosa. Epistaxis is a frightening condition for patients but is seldom life-threatening. A solid understanding of physiology and treatment allows for prompt and efficient management of the disorder.

Definition

Anterior epistaxis accounts for 90% of all nosebleeds and usually involves Kiesselbach's plexus on the anteroinferior nasal septum.[50] Epistaxis is unilateral and can be controlled with anterior packing. Posterior epistaxis accounts for 10% of nosebleeds and usually arises from a posterior branch of the sphenopalatine artery.[50] It cannot be controlled with a well-placed anterior pack. Posterior bleeding is rare in children.[50]

Principles of Disease

Anatomy

Three arteries with anastomoses between them supply the nasal area. The sphenopalatine artery supplies the turbinates and meatus laterally and the posterior and inferior septum medially. The anterior and posterior ethmoidal arteries from the ophthalmic branch of the internal carotid artery supply the superior mucosa medially and laterally. The superior labial branch of the facial artery provides circulation to the anterior mucosal septum and anterior lateral mucosa (Figure 71-1).

Etiology

There are many reasons for epistaxis, but the most common are upper respiratory infection with con-

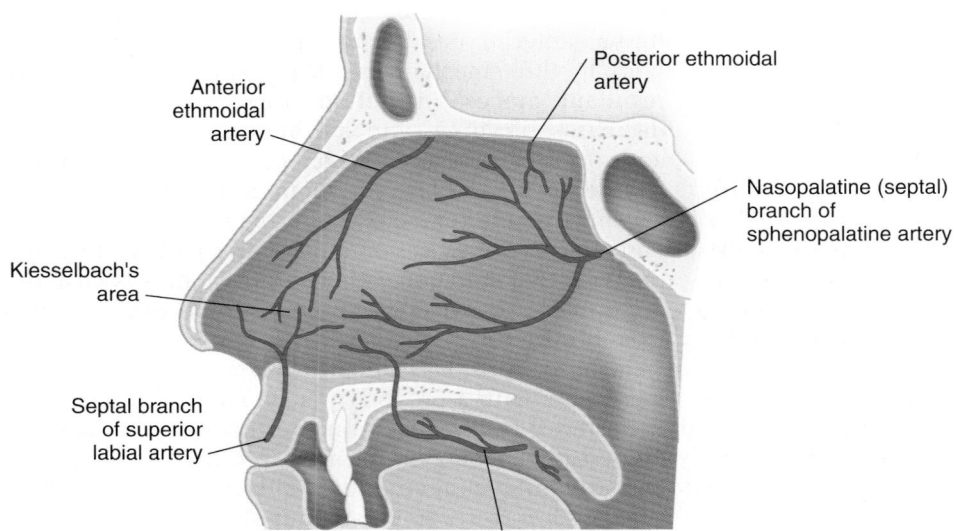

Figure 71-1. Arterial supply to medial wall of nose.

Posterior ethmoidal artery

Anterior ethmoidal artery

Nasopalatine (septal) branch of sphenopalatine artery

Kiesselbach's area

Septal branch of superior labial artery

Greater palatine artery

BOX 71-2. Etiology of Epistaxis

Local
Nasal or facial trauma
Upper respiratory tract infections
Nose picking
Allergies
Low home humidity
Nasal polyps
Foreign body in the nose
Environmental irritants
Nasopharyngeal mucormycosis
Traumatic internal carotid artery aneurysm
Chlamydial rhinitis neonatorum
Postoperative

Idiopathic
Habitual
Familial

Systemic
Atherosclerosis of nasal blood vessels
Hypertension (controversial)
Anticoagulant therapy
Pregnancy
Abrupt changes in barometric pressure
Hereditary hemorrhagic telangiectasia (Rendu-Osler-Weber
    disease)
Blood dyscrasias (e.g., hemophilia, leukemia, lymphoma,
    polycythemia vera, anemias, idiopathic
    thrombocytopenic purpura, granulocytosis, inherited
    platelet disorders, acquired platelet disorders [i.e.,
    aspirin])
Hepatic disease
Rupture of internal carotid artery aneurysm
Diabetes mellitus
Alcoholism
Vitamin K deficiency
Folic acid deficiency
Chronic nephritis
Chemotherapy
Blood transfusion reactions
Migraine headache
Drug-induced thrombocytopenia

From Myers A, Kulig K: *Epistaxis emergindex;* and Wurman LH, et al: *Am J Otolaryngology* 13:193, 1992.

comitant mucosal congestion and vasodilation and trauma, either accidental or iatrogenic (i.e., nose picking) (Box 71-2).

Diagnostic Strategies

Patients initially should have their hemodynamic status evaluated, with resuscitation and laboratory studies performed as needed based on suspicion of possible etiologies mentioned in Box 71-2.[50] Patients often are anxious and hypertensive. Elevated blood pressure is usually from stress and anxiety and resolves with treatment. Hypertension has never been shown to cause epistaxis, although it can worsen the bleeding when present.[50] Sedation with benzodiazepines or narcotics may help these patients.

The key to successful management is identifying the site of nasal bleeding and whether it is anterior or posterior. If the nose is actively bleeding, the patient should clear clots by blowing the nose, then apply bilateral pressure on the nasal septum by compressing the cartilaginous part of the nose for 10 to 15 minutes. This simple maneuver also educates the patient on how to self-manage further episodes. During this time, materials for illumination, suction, visualization, and treatment should be assembled. Discharge without identification and treatment of the bleeding site often results in recurrences. Anterior clots and obstructions may give the appearance of a posterior epistaxis if the blood runs posteriorly. Persistent bleeding should be controlled with pledgets soaked in cocaine, lidocaine-epinephrine, or phenylephrine (Neo-Synephrine) to promote vasoconstriction and anesthesia.

Management

With an identified site of bleeding in anterior epistaxis, several treatments are available. Application of silver nitrate chemically cauterizes the area but is unsuccessful during active bleeding. With 4 to 5 seconds of application, nitric acid is formed and coagulates tissue. Coagulation should never be maintained longer than 15 seconds because septal damage may occur.[50] The area should be cauterized peripherally to centrally and superiorly to inferiorly to avoid blood, which renders the sticks ineffectual. Bilateral application of silver nitrate to the septum is not advised because it may deprive the septum of blood supply and theoretically could lead to necrosis. Cautery should not be done in the face of a coagulopathy.[50] An alternative treatment is the application of topical agents, such as absorbable gelatin sponge (Gelfoam) and absorbable knitted fabric (Surgicel), with light packing, which induces coagulation at the site. Patients are instructed on compression techniques and to keep mucosa moist with antibiotic ointment. They should avoid closed-mouth sneezing, nose picking, coughing, nose blowing, and aspirin. If bleeding persists, anterior tamponade with a commercially available nasal tampon or balloon or a formal anterior nasal pack may be necessary. These work by three mechanisms. Direct pressure is applied, resultant mucosal irritation from the foreign body decreases bleeding, and surrounding clot formation adds further pressure. When placed, anterior packs should be left in place for about 48 hours. Discomfort caused by anterior packs may require sedatives and narcotic pain medication. Bilateral packs usually are required to obtain adequate compression. It is customary to place patients on antibiotics to prevent sinusitis from obstruction.

Posterior epistaxis is identified when posterior bleeding occurs with a properly placed anterior nasal pack. A posterior pack is necessary in this case. A standard Foley catheter may be inserted into the nasopharynx, partially inflated, then pulled anteriorly, creating pressure posteriorly. A small amount of fluid can be added to the balloon, but caution should be exercised to avoid pressure necrosis. Vaseline gauze should be packed around the catheter anteriorly. Commercially available balloons, such as the Nasostat and Epistat, are more comfortable than the posterior pack. The packs are left in for 2 to 5 days, and antibiotics, such as cephalexin and amoxicillin-clavulanate, traditionally are administered. If these techniques do not provide successful control, ENT consultation is necessary. Definitive care may require internal maxillary artery ligation or embolization with Gelfoam or posterior endoscopic cautery.

Patients with posterior nasal packs should be admitted to the hospital and may require sedation and supplemental oxygen. The partial pressure of oxygen (PO_2) may decrease 10 mm Hg, and partial pressure of carbon dioxide (PCO_2) may increase 10 mm Hg after posterior packing. This is thought to be secondary to a postulated nasopulmonary reflex. Dysrhythmias, bradycardia, myocardial infarction, stroke, and aspiration also have been reported after posterior nasal packing.

SIALOLITHIASIS

Stones of the salivary glands occur in 1% of the population.[51] They are found most commonly in people between ages 30 and 50 years, although they are reported rarely in children. The most common gland affected is the submandibular (submaxillary) gland, accounting for 80% to 95% of cases. The patient has pain and swelling of the gland. Differential diagnosis includes infections, inflammation, and granulomatous and neoplastic processes. The most common viral pathogen is mumps. *Staphylococcus, Streptococcus viridans, S. pneumoniae,* and *H. influenzae* predominate in bacterial infections. Stones may be confirmed by palpation or purulent discharge from the glandular duct with massage. Ultrasonography can be helpful, potentially revealing diagnoses other than stones. Treatment consists of antibiotics (covering penicillinase-resistant organisms), moist heat, massage, sialagogues (tart hard candies to promote glandular secretions), and sialolithotomy, if necessary, using probes or endoscopy.[52] Follow-up within 24 hours should be arranged for stones not removed in the emergency department and 4 to 5 days otherwise.

NECK MASSES

Perspective

Neck masses are a relatively common clinical finding and are usually the result of inflammation but may be an indicator of head and neck malignancy as well. An extensive discussion of head and neck cancer is beyond the scope of this chapter, but some basics are discussed. Children and young adults are more likely to have benign disorders, such as inflammatory or developmental abnormalities, including thyroglossal or brachial cleft cysts. Adult neck masses are more likely to be neoplastic. In general, 80% of nonthyroid neck masses in adults are neoplastic, of which 80% are malignant.[53] In children, however, more than 80% of neck masses are benign. This is often referred to as *the rule of 80* or *80% rule.* Risk factors that may predispose patients to ENT malignancies include alcohol and tobacco use, viruses such as herpesvirus, sunlight exposure, genetics, diet, exposure to dust, and inhalation exposures.[54]

Principles of Disease

It is crucial for the clinician to be familiar with some basic anatomy of the neck. Identifying the location of the parotid and submandibular glands and thyroid cartilage and gland can help avoid confusion when evaluating the neck mass. In addition, knowing where the lymph nodes are can help distinguish lymph nodes from other types of masses (Figure 71-2).

Clinical Features

Numerous symptoms should be inquired about in head and neck disease, including dysphagia, odynophagia, otalgia, stridor, speech disorders, and globus phenom-

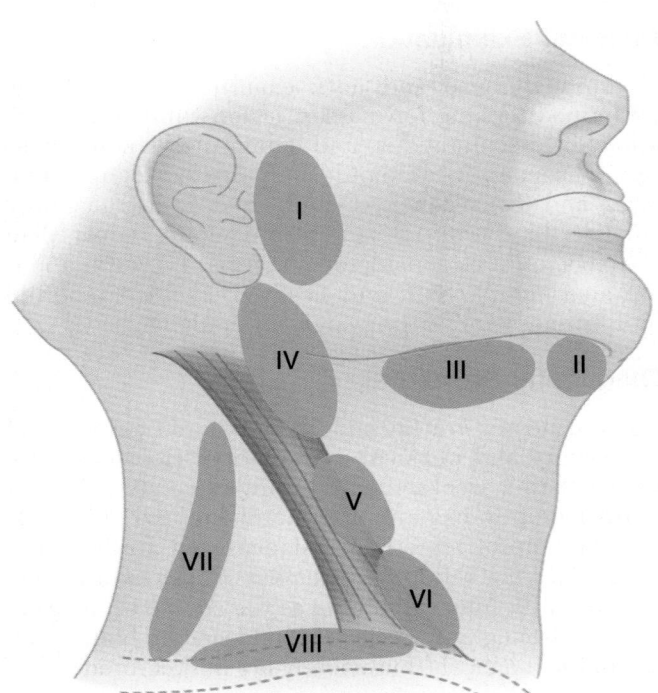

Figure 71-2. Major lymph node groups in the head and neck: *I,* parotid nodes; *II,* submental nodes; *III,* submandibular nodes; *IV,* jugulodigastric nodes (superior jugular nodes); *V,* midjugular nodes; *VI,* lower jugular nodes; *VII,* spinal accessory nodes; *VIII,* subclavian nodes. Groups VI and VII are often termed "scalene nodes." (Redrawn and modified from Moloy PJ: How to (and how not to) manage the patient with lump in the neck. In American Academy of Otolaryngology–Head and Neck Surgery Foundation: *Common Problems of the Head and Neck Region.* Philadelphia, WB Saunders, 1995.)

ena. *Dysphagia* is difficulty swallowing and may be caused by physical obstruction or neurologic disorders. *Odynophagia* is pain on swallowing and can be caused by many entities, such as tonsillitis or carcinoma of the pharynx. *Otalgia* is pain felt in the ear that may be referred from the larynx, pharynx, and cranial nerves V, IX, and X. Referred ear pain is considered an ominous sign in adults and should be presumed to be cancer until proved otherwise.[55] Unilateral OME in older adults should be considered nasopharyngeal carcinoma until proved otherwise. Stridor, specifically inspiratory stridor, is diagnostic of upper airway obstruction. It localizes a lesion to above or at the level of the larynx and, when present in adults with a neck mass, should increase the suspicion for carcinoma. Speech disorders, particularly that of hot potato speech, are suspicious for space-occupying lesions above the oropharynx, a classic example being peritonsillar abscess. The globus symptom is a lump in the throat. It has occurred in almost everyone at one time or another, is localized to the pharynx, and is often a functional complaint.[55] Hoarseness, the final symptom, is a fairly common complaint, with a myriad of etiologies ranging from viral pharyngitis to laryngeal cancer. Also, similar to the term *dizziness,* hoarseness has many descriptions, including breathiness, muffling, harshness, scratchiness, or unnatural deepening of the voice.[56] Hoarseness lasting longer than 2 weeks needs investigation.

Physical Examination

A thorough head and neck examination should be performed looking for masses, lesions, mucosal ulcerations or discolorations, and cranial nerve abnormalities. The mass itself should be palpated for location, size, and consistency. Lymph nodes are generally smaller than 1 to 1.5 cm, so any nodes larger than 1.5 cm should be considered abnormal.[57] Lymph nodes are also mobile, soft, and fleshy. Decreased mobility and firmness are warning signs of malignancy.[57]

Diagnostic Strategies

The diagnostic strategy should be tailored to results of the history and physical examination. Hoarseness for longer than 2 weeks should be investigated, generally with fiberoptic examination. Serologic and skin tests may be helpful in certain instances, but are best performed by the referring specialist. Chest radiography may identify lung carcinoma as the source of metastasis. Ultrasonography, CT, MRI, and needle biopsy can aid in the diagnosis, but usually are not required in the emergency department.

Differential Considerations

Box 71-3 lists common causes in the differential diagnosis of neck masses.[57-59]

Management and Disposition

Most masses in children are inflammatory; it is a reasonable strategy to start the patient on antibiotics with 2-week follow-up. If inflammation is considered in adults, a similar strategy can be used.[58] Adults generally need ENT referral if the mass does not resolve in 2 weeks, the mass is enlarging, the mass is fixed, cervical lymph nodes are matted, or masses are noted in the parotid or thyroid gland.[59]

BOX 71-3. Differential Diagnosis of Neck Masses

Inflammatory
Adenitis
 Bacterial (*Streptococcus, Staphylococcus*)
 Viral (HIV, EBV, HSV)
 Fungal (coccidioidomycosis)
 Parasitic (toxoplasmosis)
Cat-scratch disease
Tularemia
Local cutaneous infections
Sialoadenitis (parotid and submaxillary glands)
Thyroiditis
Mycobacterium avium
Mycobacterium tuberculosis

Congenital/Developmental
Brachial cleft cyst
Thyroglossal duct cyst
Dermoid cyst
Cystic hydromas
Torticollis
Thymic masses
Teratomas
Ranula
Lymphangioma
Laryngocele

Neoplastic

Benign
Mesenchymal tumors (lipoma, fibroma, neural tumor)
Salivary gland masses
Vascular abnormalities (hemangiomas, AVM, lymphangiomas, aneurysm)

Malignant
Primary tumors
 Sarcoma
 Salivary gland tumor
 Thyroid or parathyroid tumors
 Lymphoma

Metastasis
From primary head and neck tumors
From infraclavicular primary tumors (e.g., lung or esophageal cancer)

AVM, arteriovenous malformation; EBV, Epstein-Barr virus; HIV, human immunodeficiency virus; HSV, herpes simplex virus.
From Armstrong WB, Giglio MF: *Postgrad Med* 104:63, 1998; McGuirt WF: *Med Clin North Am* 83:219, 1999; and Brown RL, Azizkhan RG: *Pediatric Clin North Am* 45:889, 1998.

KEY CONCEPTS

- Most cases of acute OM are likely viral. Children older than age 2 years may be observed for 3 days to determine whether antibiotics are required. When indicated, amoxicillin is the initial choice for treatment of AOM at a dose of 80 to 90 mg/kg/day.

- Necrotizing otitis externa should be considered in immunocompromised patients who have a persistent otitis externa.

- Patients with epistaxis with posterior nasal packing should be admitted to the hospital. Antibiotic therapy typically is prescribed.

- All neck masses that do not respond to antibiotics or persist for more than 2 weeks or hoarseness lasting for more than 2 weeks need ENT referral.

REFERENCES

1. Stool SE, et al: *Managing Otitis Media with Effusion in Young Children: Quick Reference Guide for Clinicians* (AHCPR Publication No. 94-0623). Rockville, Md, Agency for Health Care Policy and Research, Public Health Service, U.S. Department of Health and Human Services, 1994.
2. Teele DW, Klein JO, Rosner B: Epidemiology of otitis media during the first seven years of life in children in greater Boston: A prospective cohort study. *J Infect Dis* 160:83, 1989.
3. McCracken GH Jr: Diagnosis and management of acute otitis media in the urgent care setting. *Ann Emerg Med* 39:413, 2002.
4. Daly K: Risk factors for otitis media sequelae and chronicity. *Ann Otol Rhinol Laryngol Suppl* 103:39, 1994.
5. Paradise JL, et al: Otitis media in 2253 Pittsburgh-area infants: Prevalence and risk factors during the first two years of life. *Pediatrics* 99:318, 1997.
6. Bonadio WA: The evaluation and management of acute otitis media in children. *Am J Emerg Med* 12:193, 1994.
7. Hoberman A, Paradise JL: Acute otitis media: Diagnosis and management in the year 2000. *Pediatr Ann* 29:609, 2000.
8. Ruuskanen O, Heikkinen T: Otitis media: Etiology and diagnosis. *Pediatr Infect Dis J* 13:S23, 1994.
9. Heikkinen T: Role of viruses in the pathogenesis of acute otitis media. *Pediatr Infect Dis J* 9:S17, 2000.
10. Burton DM, et al: Neonatal otitis media: An update. *Arch Otolaryngol Head Neck Surg* 119:672, 1993.
11. McCormick DP, et al: Bullous myringitis: A case controlled study. *Pediatrics* 112:982, 2003.
12. Haddad J: Treatment of acute otitis media and its complications. *Otolaryngol Clin North Am* 27:431, 1994.
13. Howie VM, Schwartz RH: Acute otitis media: A year in general practice. *Am J Dis Child* 137:155, 1983.
14. Berman S: Otitis media in children. *N Engl J Med* 332:1560, 1995.
15. Rothman R, Owens T, Simel D: Does this child have acute otitis media? *JAMA* 290:1633, 2003.
16. Giebink GS, et al: Antimicrobial treatment of acute otitis media. *J Pediatr* 119:495, 1991.
17. Wetmore RF: Complications of otitis media. *Pediatr Ann* 29:637, 2000.
18. Roland PS: Clinical ototoxicity of topical antibiotic drops. *Otolaryngol Head Neck Surg* 110:598, 1994.
19. Bluestone CD, Klein JO: Intracranial suppurative complications of otitis media and mastoiditis. In Bluestone CD, Stool SE (eds): *Pediatric Otolaryngology*. Philadelphia, WB Saunders, 1990.
20. Culpepper L, Froom J: Routine antimicrobial treatment of acute otitis media: Is it necessary? *JAMA* 278:1643, 1997.
21. Dowell SF, et al: Acute otitis media: Management and surveillance in an era of pneumococcal resistance—A report from the Drug Resistant *S. pneumoniae* Therapeutic Working Group. *Pediatr Infect Dis J* 18:1, 1999.
22 American Academy of Pediatrics Subcommittee on Management of Acute Otitis Media: Diagnosis and management of acute otitis media. *Pediatrics* 113:1451, 2004.
23. Green SM, Rothrock SG: Single dose intramuscular ceftriaxone for acute otitis media in children. *Pediatrics* 91:23, 1993.
24. Barnett ED: Antibiotic resistance and choice of antimicrobial agents for acute otitis media. *Pediatr Ann* 31:794, 2002.
25. Dowell SF, et al: Otitis media: Principle of judicious use of antimicrobial agents. *Pediatrics* 101:165, 1998.
26. Kozyyrskyj AL, et al: Treatment of acute otitis media with a shortened course of antibiotics: A meta-analysis. *JAMA* 279:1736, 1998.
27. Paradise JL: Short course antimicrobial treatment for acute otitis media: Not best for infants and young children. *JAMA* 278:1640, 1997.
28. Rosenfeld RM: Comprehensive management of otitis media with effusion. *Otolaryngol Clin North Am* 27:443, 1994.
29. Black S, et al: Efficacy, safety and immunogenicity of heptavalent pneumococcal conjugate vaccine in children. *Pediatr Infect Dis J* 19:187, 2000.
30. Black S, Shinefield H: Vaccines and otitis media. *Pediatr Ann* 29:648, 2000.
31. Hathaway TJ, et al: Acute otitis media: Who needs post-treatment follow up? *Pediatrics* 94:143, 1994.
32. Hirsch BE: Infections of the external ear. *Am J Otolaryngol* 13:145, 1992.
33. Roland PS, Stroman DW: The microbiology of acute otitis externa. *Laryngoscope* 112:1166, 2002.
34. Bojrab DI, et al: Otitis externa. *Otolaryngol Clin North Am* 29:761, 1996.
35. Dohar JE: Evolution of management approaches for otitis externa. *Pediatr Infect Dis J* 22:299, 2003.
36. Evans P, Hofman L: Malignant external otitis: A case report and review. *Am Fam Physician* 49:427, 1994.
37. Guy RL, et al: Computed tomography in malignant external otitis. *Clin Radiol* 43:166, 1991.
38. Rubin J, et al: Malignant external otitis in children. *J Pediatr* 113:965, 1988.
39. Slattery WH, Brackman DE: Skull base osteomyelitis: Malignant external otitis. *Otolaryngol Clin North Am* 21:795, 1996.
40. Gliklich RE, et al: A contemporary analysis of acute mastoiditis. *Arch Otolaryngol Head Neck Surg* 122:135, 1996.
41. Hoppe JE, et al: Acute mastoiditis: Relevant once again. *Infection* 22:178, 1994.
42. Nadol JB, Eavery RD: Acute and chronic mastoiditis: Clinical presentation, diagnosis, and management. *Curr Clin Topics Infect Dis* 15:204, 1995.
43. Martin-Hirsch DP, et al: Latent mastoiditis: No room for complacency. *J Laryngol Otol* 102:115, 1991.
44. Ogle JW, Lauer B: Acute mastoiditis: Diagnosis and complications. *Am J Dis Child* 140:1178, 1986.
45. Betar CN, Kluka EA, Steele RW: Mastoiditis in children. *Clin Pediatr* 35:391, 1996.
46. Shikowitz MJ: Sudden sensorineural hearing loss. *Med Clin North Am* 75:1239, 1991.
47. Lawrence LJ, Brown CG: Approach to decreased hearing. *Emerg Med Clin North Am* 5:193, 1987.
48. Nadol JB: Hearing loss. *N Engl J Med* 329:1092, 1993.
49. Josephson GD, et al: Practical management of epistaxis. *Med Clin North Am* 75:1311, 1991.

50. Wurman LH, et al: The management of epistaxis. *Am J Oto-laryngol* 13:193, 1992.
51. Pollack CV, Severance HW: Sialolithiasis: Case studies and review. *J Emerg Med* 8:561, 1990.
52. Nahlieli O, Neder A, Baruchin AM: Salivary gland endoscopy: A new technique for diagnosis and treatment of sialolithiasis. *J Oral Maxillofac Surg* 52:1240, 1994.
53. Alvi A, Johnson JT: The neck mass: A challenging differential diagnosis. *Postgrad Med* 97:87, 1995.
54. Walton F, Masuredis C: The epidemiology of maxillofacial malignancy. *Oral Maxillofac Surg Clin North Am* 5:189, 1993.
55. Moloy PJ: How to (and how not to) manage the patient with lump in the neck. In American Academy of Otolaryngology–Head and Neck Surgery Foundation: *Common Problems of the Head and Neck Region.* Philadelphia, WB Saunders, 1995.
56. Kenna MA: Hoarseness. *Pediatr Rev* 16:69, 1995.
57. Armstrong WB, Giglio MF: Is this lump in the neck anything to worry about? *Postgrad Med* 104:63, 1998.
58. McGuirt WF: The neck mass. *Med Clin North Am* 83:219, 1999.
59. Brown RL, Azizkhan RG: Pediatric head and neck lesions. *Pediatr Clin North Am* 45:889, 1998.

Section II PULMONARY SYSTEM

CHAPTER

72 Asthma

Richard M. Nowak and Glenn Tokarski

PERSPECTIVE

The word *asthma* is derived from the Greek ασυμα, signifying panting, and was used initially as a synonym for "breathlessness." In 1698 Floyer published "A Treatise of the Asthma," in which he attempted to differentiate asthma more clearly from other pulmonary disorders. Subsequent definitions of asthma highlight concepts of airway hyperresponsiveness, bronchospasm, and reversible airway obstruction but fail to encompass the many facets of this disease.

The National Heart, Lung, and Blood Institute summarized our current understanding of asthma as "a chronic inflammatory disorder of the airways in which many cells and cellular elements play a role . . . this inflammation causes recurrent episodes of wheezing, breathlessness, chest tightness, and coughing . . . episodes are usually associated with widespread but variable airflow obstruction that is often reversible either spontaneously or with treatment."[1] Asthma is thus a chronic inflammatory disease, and control of symptoms is ultimately dependent on ameliorating the inflammatory reaction that produces alterations in airway function and structure.

EPIDEMIOLOGY

The United States National Health Interview Survey for 1980 to 1999 reported that 96.6 of 1000 (26.7 million) people have been diagnosed with asthma during their lifetime.[2] In 2001 (Figure 72-1)[3] this number increased to 114 of 1000 (31.3 million); the current prevalence (individuals having asthma at the time of the interview) is 69 of 1000 (14 million) in adults and 87 of 1000 (6.3 million) in children. Asthma attack prevalence (the number of persons who had at least one asthma attack

in the previous year) is 43 of 1000 (12 million) people. Asthma was responsible for more than 1.7 million emergency department visits and nearly 500,000 hospitalizations in 2001.

The estimated financial burden of this disease totaled $12.7 billion in 1998, with almost 60% attributable to direct costs (hospital inpatient, outpatient, emergency department and physician services); it is estimated that less than 20% of asthma patients account for 80% of the direct costs.[4]

Emergency department visits related to asthma in the United States increased from 1992 to 1999 (Figure 72-2).[2] Emergency department visit rates were more than three times greater for non-Hispanic blacks than non-Hispanic whites[5] and highest among children 0 to 4 years old. In 2000 the rate of hospitalization was 220% greater in non-Hispanic blacks than non-Hispanic whites and 25% higher in females than males.

Disturbing increases in mortality related to asthma were reported in the 1980s, with a disproportionate number of deaths occurring in the age range 5 to 34. In the United States, moderation of this trend was noted in the early 1990s and continued throughout the decade. A total of 4487 deaths from asthma were reported in 2000 and decreased to 4269 in 2001. Deaths caused by asthma were infrequent in children (0.3 per 100,000) compared with adults (2.1 per 100,000). Non-Hispanic blacks had an asthma death rate more than 200% greater than that of non-Hispanic whites and 160% higher than that of Hispanic Americans. Females had an asthma death rate 40% higher than that of males.

New Zealand, Australia, Great Britain, and Canada all reported increases in asthma prevalence, hospitalizations, and deaths during the 1980s, with reversal of these trends during the 1990s. Developed nations have higher rates of asthma, which suggests that urbaniza-

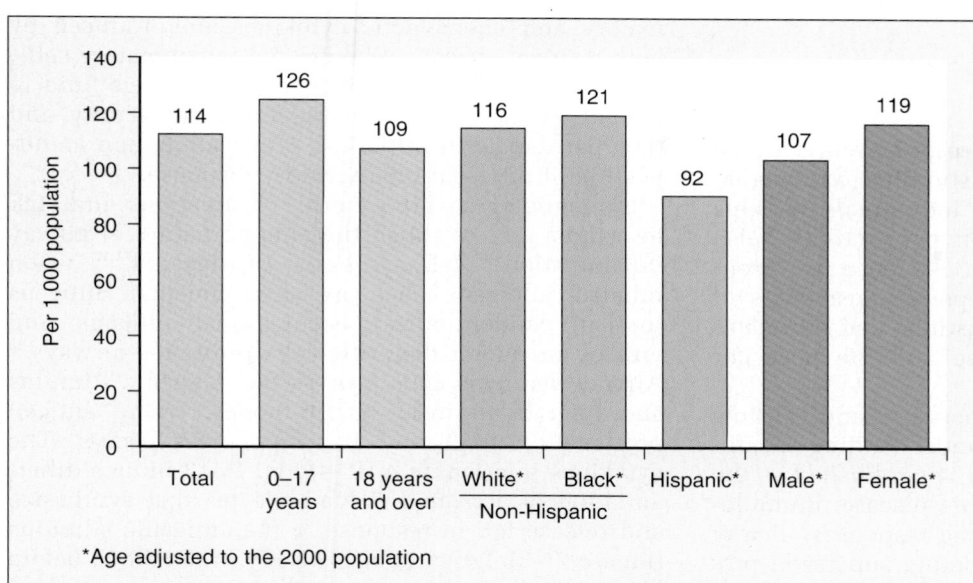

Figure 72-1. Prevalence of lifetime asthma diagnosis, 2001. (National Center for Health Statistics, 2004.)

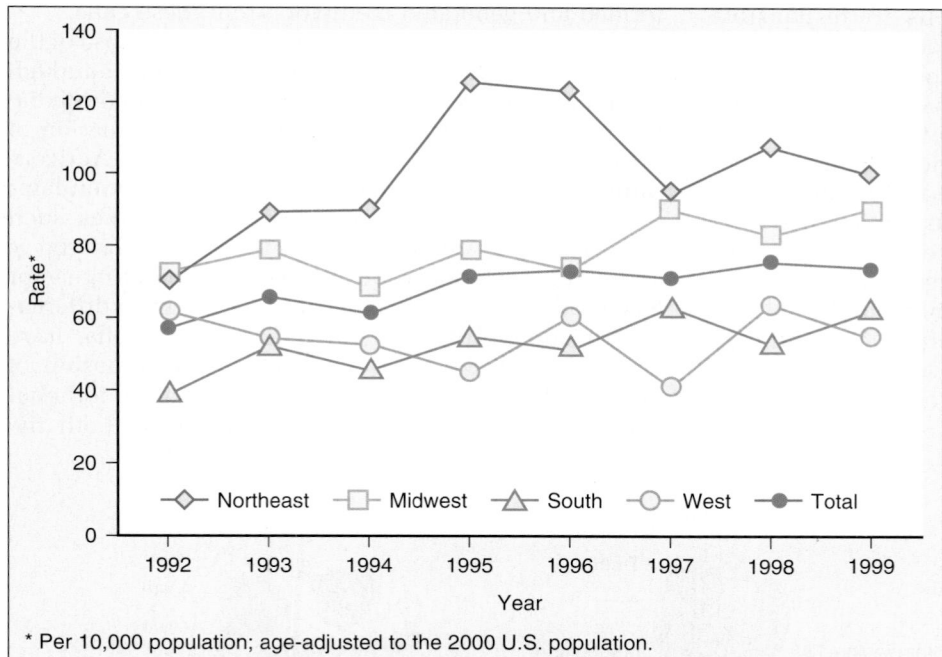

Figure 72-2. Estimated annual rate of emergency department visits for asthma. (From Mannino DM, et al: Surveillance for asthma—United States 1980-1999. *MMWR Surveill Summ* 51[SS01]:1, 2002.)

tion and westernization are correlated with increased asthma prevalence. Interestingly, migrants who move from an area of low asthma prevalence to an area of high asthma prevalence assume an increased asthma prevalence, suggesting that environmental factors play a role. Urban areas in the United States (New York City, Los Angeles, and Chicago) have high mortality rates associated with asthma, indicating that poverty and lack of access to medical care may also be major determinants of asthma complications.

Factors believed to contribute to asthma morbidity and mortality include inadequate patient and physician assessment of an acute episode resulting in undertreatment, overuse of prescribed or over-the-counter medications leading to delays in seeking treatment, failure of physicians to consider previous hospitalizations or life-threatening episodes of asthma, and failure to initiate corticosteroid therapy early in the course of an exacerbation. Socioeconomic factors, environmental influences, and overreliance on emergency facilities for all asthma care are also contributing factors. Initiatives to educate physicians and patients about asthma pathophysiology, monitoring, and therapy may be in part responsible for the moderation of asthma mortality.

PRINCIPLES OF DISEASE

Pathophysiology

Bronchial reactivity refers to the responsiveness of the airways to a bronchoconstricting stimulus (e.g., methacholine). Compared with healthy individuals, patients with asthma show bronchial hyperreactivity (also called hyperresponsiveness) in response to bronchoconstricting stimuli. This hyperresponsiveness of the airways is characteristic of asthma and correlates with the severity of the disease and the need for treatment.

Although bronchial hyperreactivity and airflow obstruction remain basic to our understanding of asthma, allergic airway inflammation is established as the primary pathologic process of this disease. Immunoglobulin E (IgE)–mediated immune responses, airway inflammation, and airway remodeling supersede previous theories of intrinsic and extrinsic triggers, smooth muscle dysfunction, and imbalances in the adrenergic and cholinergic nervous systems. Immune response and inflammatory cells, their messengers and metabolic products, and effector cells are responsible for the clinical manifestations of acute and chronic asthma. Understanding of the various aspects of the allergic and inflammatory processes occurring in the airways is fundamental in directing therapy.

The concept of the role of allergic inflammation in asthma has its basis in the pathologic findings in the airways of asthmatic patients. Intense inflammation is evidenced by infiltration of mast cells, macrophages, eosinophils, neutrophils, and lymphocytes; loss of airway epithelium; basement membrane thickening; and bronchial smooth muscle hyperplasia. Significant inflammatory changes can occur even in mild cases. These changes are found in both the central and peripheral airways and vary with asthma severity.[6-9] Inflammatory and chemotactic cytokines are produced by both resident airway and recruited inflammatory cells. They are identified in bronchoalveolar lavage fluid in patients with various degrees of asthma severity, and they participate in initiation, propagation, and amplification of the local inflammatory response.

Epidemiologic and clinical observations link IgE to asthma and establish the allergic nature of airway inflammation.[10] IgE synthesis is triggered[11,12] when inhaled allergens such as environmental antigens (pollen, dander, mites), occupational antigens, and viruses encounter dendritic cells lining the airways.[13] Airway dendritic cells process the antigenic stimulus and migrate to local lymph nodes, where antigen presentation to T and B lymphocytes occurs. The cytokines interleukin 4 (IL-4) and IL-13 induce differentiation of activated B lymphocytes that synthesize and release IgE in response to the antigenic stimulus (Figure 72-3). IgE circulates briefly in the blood before binding to surface receptors on airway mast cells and peripheral blood basophils, lymphocytes, eosinophils, and macrophages. Further interaction of antigen with membrane-bound IgE activates and then releases preformed and generated mediators from these cells.

Mast cells reside in the mucosa and submucosa of the airways. Cross linking of antigen and surface-bound IgE on the mast cells induces release of preformed mediators such as histamine and initiates the production of prostaglandins (PGs) and leukotrienes (LTs). Antigen-induced IgE cross linking on mast cells also stimulates synthesis and subsequent release of cytokines such as IL-1 to IL-5, tumor necrosis factor α, interferon γ, and granulocyte-macrophage colony-stimulating factor (GM-CSF). These cytokines induce further differentiation and proliferation of inflammatory cells, have chemoattractant properties, and increase adhesion of inflammatory cells to pulmonary vascular endothelial cells.[14] Thus, mast cells may contribute to both the

Figure 72-3. Cellular interactions involved in immunoglobulin E (IgE) and inflammatory reactions in asthma.

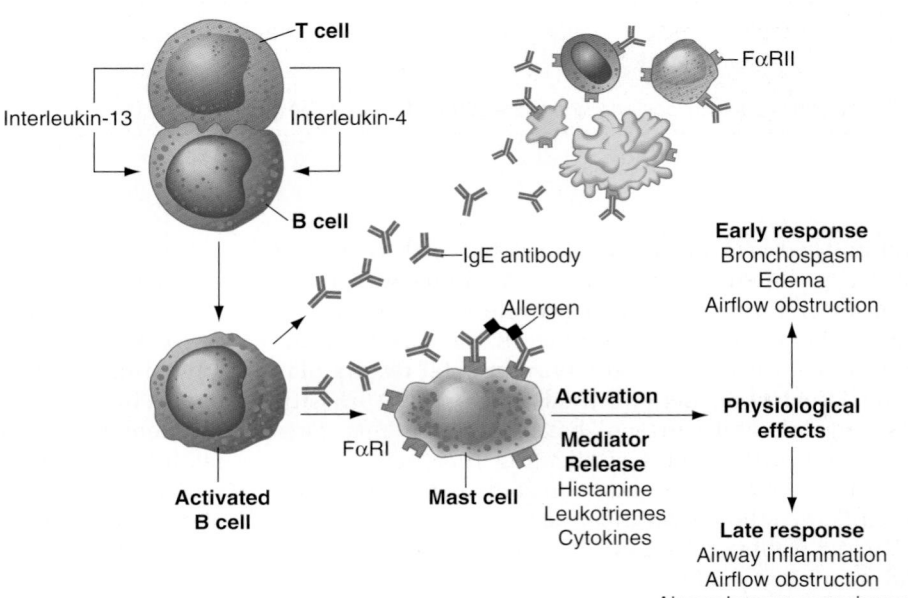

acute and chronic inflammatory reactions occurring in the airways.

Release of preformed histamine from mast cell granules constricts bronchial smooth muscle and causes airway edema, resulting in wheezing and airflow obstruction. This reaction usually resolves within an hour and is referred to as the *early asthmatic response.* Similar clinical manifestations occur 4 to 6 hours later as a result of cytokines generated and released by mast cells and other local and recruited inflammatory cells. The airflow obstruction and bronchospasm may be prolonged and are referred to as the *late asthmatic response.*

Eosinophils are major effector cells in asthma, and their presence is evidence of the allergic nature of this disease. They contain granules that release inflammatory mediators including major basic protein, cationic protein, and LTs. Major basic protein causes constriction of airway smooth muscle and desquamation of the airway epithelium. This effect exposes nerve endings, provides submucosal access for inflammatory cells and mediators, and negates epithelial cell regulation of the inflammatory process. Eosinophil cationic protein increases airway mucus production and can cause histamine release from mast cells. LTs are potent bronchoconstrictors produced by eosinophils that are more potent than methacholine.[15] LTs also promote the secretion of thick viscid mucus, leading to airway plugging, and enhance airway vascular permeability, leading to airway edema. Eosinophil-produced ILs and GM-CSF stimulate eosinophil proliferation and enhance pulmonary vascular endothelial cell adhesion, which locally amplifies the inflammatory process. Platelet-activating factor, superoxides, and free radicals produced by eosinophils also cause bronchospasm and bronchial tissue destruction.[16] The role of the eosinophil as the central effector cell in asthma is challenged by studies that demonstrate that reductions in sputum and blood eosinophilia do not reduce airway hyperresponsiveness.[17,18]

Preformed mediator and cytokine release from other airway inflammatory cells (neutrophils, basophils, macrophages) following the triggering stimulus also contributes to bronchial smooth muscle spasm, edema, and mucus production. Extensive intercellular communication and widespread activation of the immune system occur with the lung and tracheobronchial tree as the target organ.[11] Ongoing synthesis and release of cytokines (e.g., IL-1 to IL-18, GM-CSF), PGs, and LTs (Figure 72-4) are responsible for propagation and intensification of airway inflammation[19] and disruption of the airway epithelial border. Further migration of inflammatory cells from the circulating blood into the airway mucosa and submucosa is influenced by activation of cellular adhesion molecules on pulmonary endothelial cells. The end result of persistent and self-reinforcing inflammation is airway smooth muscle stimulation and structural alterations evidenced by wheezing and airflow obstruction. The inflammatory response may continue because of persistent exposure to triggers, lack of appropriate therapy, and impairment or destruction of cellular reparative processes. This

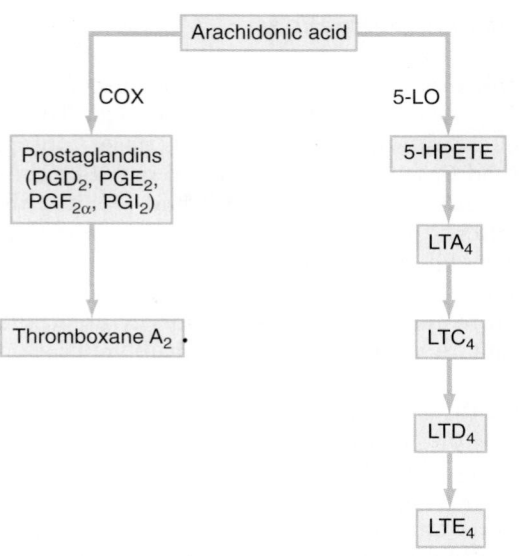

Figure 72-4. Metabolism of arachidonic acid into prostaglandins (PG) and leukotrienes (LT). COX, cyclooxygenase; 5-HPETE, 5-hydroperoxyeicosatetraenoic acid; 5-LO, 5-lipoxygenase.

continuing response leads to prolonged symptoms, worsening obstruction, fatigue, and, ultimately, respiratory failure.

Airway remodeling is distinctive in chronic asthma, and advanced airway remodeling is probably due to the presence of repetitive or chronic airway inflammation. It consists of airway wall thickening, subepithelial fibrosis, mucous gland metaplasia, increases in airway smooth muscle, myofibroblast hyperplasia, and epithelial hypertrophy.[20] Basement membrane thickening may be protective by preventing inflammatory cells and proteins from entering the airway submucosa through a damaged epithelium; simultaneously, this process may be counterproductive by reducing the elasticity of the small airways, leading to severe obstruction from mucosal swelling and smooth muscle contraction. Airway remodeling may explain the resistance to therapy observed in patients with prolonged asthma histories and the decline in pulmonary function noted with age in adults with asthma.[21,22] Finally, if asthma is improperly treated, airway remodeling induced by chronic inflammation may lead to the development of chronic irreversible airflow limitation and a shortened life expectancy.[23]

The clinical implications of the immune and inflammatory nature of the early and late asthmatic responses are crucial because therapy may be directed differently toward each phase. Mast cell stabilizers (e.g., β_2-agonists) are more effective in the early asthmatic response but are of less use later in the course of an exacerbation. Anti-inflammatory therapy (e.g., corticosteroids, LT antagonists) are more effective in the late asthmatic response. Interference or inhibition of cytokine activities, suppression of chronic inflammation, and modulation of airway remodeling are potential therapeutic targets.

Miscellaneous Situations

Aspirin-exacerbated respiratory disease (AERD) was first described more than 100 years ago. The triad of aspirin sensitivity, asthma, and nasal polyps was described in 1922 and popularized in 1968. The prevalence of AERD is 21% in adult and 5% in childhood asthmatics.[24] It occurs more often in women than men. Nonsteroidal anti-inflammatory drugs (NSAIDs) can also precipitate AERD. AERD is a common precipitant of life-threatening asthma—one survey noted that 25% of asthmatics requiring mechanical ventilation have AERD.[25]

Clinically, most patients with AERD develop symptoms in the third decade, frequently after a viral respiratory illness. Over several months, chronic nasal congestion, rhinorrhea, and nasal polyps develop. Bronchial asthma and sensitivity to aspirin (acetylsalicylic acid, ASA) then result. After ingestion of aspirin or a nonsteroidal drug, acute asthma symptoms occur within 3 hours, usually accompanied by profuse rhinorrhea, conjunctival injection, periorbital edema, and occasionally a scarlet flushing of the head and neck.

The pathogenesis of AERD is being elucidated. Metabolically, ASA inhibits cyclooxygenase (COX), of which two isoforms are identified. COX-1 produces PGs that are involved in normal physiologic maintenance of renal function, gastric mucosal integrity and hemostasis, and inflammatory states. COX-2 is not expressed in normal physiologic circumstances but produces PGs only in response to inflammatory stimuli. AERD occurs as a result of ASA inhibition of COX leading to increases in the production of LTs, some of which are potent bronchoconstrictors (see Figure 72-4). An alternative view is that LT production remains at basal levels while there is a decrease in the COX-1–dependent production of PGE_2. This modulates LT production by regulating the activity of 5-lipoxygenase and preventing release of mast cell mediators—a decrease in the amount of PGE_2 removes the modulation of LT synthesis and decreases mast cell stability, resulting in asthma symptoms.

Anti-LT drugs treat AERD. These agents block synthesis of LTs (e.g., zileuton) or block specific LT receptors (e.g., zafirlukast). Most patients with AERD benefit from treatment with these agents.

COX-2 inhibitors have the advantage of inhibiting inflammation without inducing renal, gastrointestinal, or hematologic side effects. AERD is not reported after administration of COX-2 inhibitors. These agents provide a potentially safe alternative for treatment of inflammatory conditions in patients with AERD.[26]

Exercise-induced asthma (EIA) has been recognized since the first Olympic games. It occurs in 40% to 90% of asthmatic patients and 6% to 13% of the general population. Atopy is strongly associated with EIA, and up to 40% of patients with allergic rhinitis have EIA.[27] Clinically, EIA is usually preceded by 3 to 8 minutes of exercise. Peak symptoms usually occur 8 to 15 minutes after exercise is complete and then begin to remit spontaneously; recovery occurs within 60 minutes. Treatment is required only to abort the acute symptoms of bronchial narrowing.

The etiology of EIA remains unclear. In the "osmotic" hypothesis, airway cooling leads to mucosal drying and increased surface osmolality that causes mast cell degranulation and release of inflammatory mediators. The "thermal" hypothesis suggests that airway cooling during exercise followed by rapid rewarming after exercise causes airway vascular congestion and increased permeability resulting in airway edema and obstruction. It is likely that a combination of these events occurs. Prophylaxis with an inhaled β_2-agonist is the therapy of choice. Inhaled cromolyn and LT antagonists are also effective.

Menstruation-associated asthma affects 30% to 40% of asthmatic women; health care for asthma increases in the premenstrual phase. Premenstrual reductions in peak expiratory flow rates of 35% to 80% are reported. Fluctuations in estrogen and progesterone levels are postulated as causal factors.[28] Estradiol inhibits eosinophil degranulation and suppresses LT activity—estrogen withdrawal in the luteal phase may enhance these actions. In animals, estrogen withdrawal down-regulates β-receptors and increases cholinergic induced bronchoconstriction.

Adult women present more often than men to the emergency department and have higher hospitalization rates with longer stays, possibly because of hormonal, biochemical, or weight differences.

Psychological factors may precipitate bronchospasm. Associations between emotional states and asthma are described. Panic disorder and generalized anxiety disorders are more common in asthmatics than the general population. An association between asthma and depression is noted in children. The mechanisms of bronchospasm associated with psychological factors may be related to autonomic nervous system activation or hyperventilation; the influence of immunologic mediators is unknown. Compliance may be adversely affected by psychological factors. Relaxation as a therapy for asthma has inconsistent effects[29]; hypnosis may be beneficial.[30] The actual influence of psychological factors in the induction or continuation of an episode of asthma is unknown but probably varies from patient to patient and episode to episode.

Genetics and Asthma

Identifying the predisposing genes is complex. The lack of absolute qualitative or quantitative criteria for the diagnosis of asthma is problematic; thus, identification of "true" asthmatics to study for genetic inheritance patterns is subjective. Environmental factors undoubtedly influence the phenotypic manifestations of asthma. The extent of exposure to environmental factors is also contributory. In the western world, many environmental factors are ubiquitous, leaving genetic factors to determine individual risk.

The significance of genetic studies in asthma lies not only in knowing the basic molecular defects in asthma but also in developing a diagnostic test for asthma. As a result, if infants at high risk for asthma could be identified, subsequent allergen avoidance might modulate the development or the severity of asthma. The application of pharmacology to genetics has tremendous importance. Some pharmacologic targets of asthma therapy show genetic variability, and knowledge of any treatment response may assist in therapeutic decision making.

Pathology

Airway secretions evaluated by bronchoalveolar lavage in patients with mild to moderate asthma reveal increased numbers of mast cells, eosinophils, lymphocytes, and airway epithelial cells. Their presence supports the concept of chronic inflammation in the airways. Antemortem endobronchial biopsies demonstrate submucosal infiltration with eosinophils and other inflammatory cells along with epithelial cell denudation, increased numbers of goblet cells, mucous gland hyperplasia, and thickening of airway basement membranes. These findings, which are noted in both small and large airways, suggest airway remodeling.[31] In contrast to patients with mild to moderate asthma, patients with acute severe asthma have inflammatory cells in the airways that consist of more neutrophils than eosinophils and elevated levels of IL-8 responsible for neutrophil activation.[32] This difference suggests an alternative pathologic mechanism.

Necropsies of patients with status asthmaticus reveal grossly inflated lungs that may fail to collapse on opening of the pleural cavities. Histologic examination reveals luminal plugs consisting of inflammatory cells, desquamated epithelial cells, and mucus. Marked thickening of the airway basement membrane, submucosal inflammatory cells, increased deposition of connective tissue, mucous gland hyperplasia, and hypertrophy of airway smooth muscle are also observed. Reports of patients experiencing sudden-onset fatal asthma demonstrated less mucus in the airway lumens, suggesting that terminal events in this group may be dominated by bronchoconstriction without excessive luminal plugging.[33] Another investigation disputed this concept[34]; the contribution of mucus production and composition to airway plugging may play a greater role in fatal asthma than previously appreciated.[35]

CLINICAL FEATURES

National and International Guidelines for the Diagnosis and Management of Asthma

In response to the increasing prevalence, morbidity, and mortality of asthma in the industrialized world, many guidelines have improved the detection and treatment of this disease. Some of these, including the U.S. National Institutes of Health (NIH) Expert Panel Report 2 (EPR-2), have specific portions devoted to the management of acute exacerbations of asthma.[36] The NIH EPR-2 has been further condensed as a practical summary for emergency physicians[37] and has been critically analyzed regarding limitations and identifying areas for further study.[38] Although these guidelines initially reflected multidisciplinary expert recommendations, they are now graded evidence based[1,39] and serve as a basis for education. They also provide a common set of recommendations for asthma management through which patients' care can be audited, studied, and subsequently improved.[40]

Emergency practice programs based on the EPR-2 and the 2002 update[1] have improved acute asthma care[41] with effective resource utilization.[42] Many studies have shown suboptimal guideline implementation in chronic asthma management, especially in the use of anti-inflammatory medications, resulting in more frequent emergency department and hospital use.[43,44] The chronic asthma management strategies in EPR-2 and the implementation of anti-inflammatory therapy when appropriate on emergency department discharge can improve care.[45]

Symptoms

Most patients with acute asthma have a constellation of symptoms consisting of cough, dyspnea, and wheezing. Cough often begins early in the attack, may be the sole manifestation of the disease in cough-variant asthma and elderly patients, can be associated with sputum production, and is probably the result of subepithelial vagal stimulation. Nocturnal worsening is common, with most patients reporting cough or wheeze at least once per week. Nighttime mortality is higher than in the general population. Although increased airway resistance, diminished flow rates, and increased bronchial hyperactivity are contributing factors, asthmatic patients who present nocturnally to the emergency department have disease severity similar to that of other asthmatics and are treated in the same way. Up to 40% of asthmatic women suffer from premenstrual worsening of symptoms, which peak 2 to 3 days before menses and are associated with more severe disease.[46] Emergency department visits increase during the preovulatory and perimenstrual intervals.

There are interindividual differences in the dyspnea perceived by asthmatic subjects for the same level of airway narrowing. This difference results in poor correlation of symptoms with airway obstruction as determined by pulmonary function testing (PFT), both chronically and on presentation to the emergency department. Patients with a blunted perception of dyspnea (the "poor perceivers") have more emergency department visits, hospitalizations, and near-fatal and fatal asthma attacks.[47]

The wheezing that develops depends on the air movement velocity and turbulence, and its intensity varies according to the radius of the bronchi. With severe airway obstruction, it decreases or vanishes because there is insufficient air movement velocity to produce sound.

Many asthmatics report symptoms of gastroesophageal reflux that are thought to cause airway narrowing through a vagally mediated pathway or microaspiration. Proton pump inhibitor therapy decreases asthma symptoms in these patients. Approximately

80% of patients with asthma have symptoms of rhinitis. Approximately 5% to 15% of patients with perennial rhinitis have asthma, and control of sinonasal inflammation can lead to asthma improvement.

Lastly, as asthma can appear at any age, including the ninth decade, it is important to realize that the classical picture of wheezing and dyspnea may be ascribed by both patients and physicians to heart failure, bronchitis, chronic obstructive pulmonary disease, occupational lung disease, or poor exercise capacity.

Historic Components

In the past, most asthma deaths appeared to follow a period of poor overall control, with increasing use of noneffective bronchodilator therapy, underestimation of symptom severity, and late arrival for care. It is now clear that a minority of patients suffer a predominantly hyperacute, bronchospastic "sudden asphyxic asthma" that kills within hours. Studies of nonfatal, sudden, severe acute asthma show that these patients have less identifiable triggers but also have rapid recovery.[48]

It is important to obtain a brief asthma history as acute episodes tend to have similar courses, which helps in decision making concerning therapy and disposition. Risk factors for death from asthma are important to determine and are listed in Box 72-1.[1,49,50]

The brief history pertinent to the current exacerbation should include onset and possible triggers, severity of symptoms, and other comorbidities (especially those that may be worsened by systemic corticosteroids such as diabetes, peptic ulcer, hypertension, and psychosis). In addition, one should note all current asthma medications, including times and amounts recently used, and any potential asthma exacerbators such as aspirin or NSAIDs, β-blockers (including topical agents used for glaucoma), and angiotensin-converting enzyme inhibitors.

BOX 72-1. Risk Factors for Death From Asthma

1. Past history of sudden severe exacerbations
2. Prior intubation for asthma
3. Prior asthma admission to an intensive care unit
4. Two or more hospitalizations for asthma in the past year
5. Three or more emergency department care visits for asthma in the past year
6. Hospitalization or an emergency department care visit for asthma within the past month
7. Use of >2 MDI short-acting β2-agonist canisters per month
8. Current use of or recent withdrawal from systemic corticosteroids
9. Difficulty perceiving severity of airflow obstruction
10. Comorbidities such as cardiovascular diseases or other systemic problems
11. Serious psychiatric disease or psychosocial problems
12. Illicit drug use, especially inhaled cocaine and heroin

MDI, metered-dose inhaler.

Physical Assessment

Although alterations in mentation or consciousness indicate severe asthma, restlessness and agitation do not reliably indicate hypoxia or hypercapnia. Patients who are sitting upright have severe airway obstruction; cyanosis is uncommon because of the left shift of the oxyhemoglobin dissociation curve produced by respiratory alkalosis. Diaphoresis can occur secondary to the work of breathing, but profound diaphoresis, usually accompanied by a decreasing level of agitation and interaction with caregivers, may be a preterminal event.

Tachypnea and tachycardia with a heart rate greater than 120 beats/min are associated with severe obstruction, but a lower or normal rate does not rule out severe asthma.[51] The respiratory rate correlates poorly with PFT and indicates severe obstruction only if it is greater than 40 breaths/min.[51]

A pulsus paradoxus or inspiratory fall in systolic blood pressure greater than 10 mm Hg usually signifies severe disease, but its absence does not exclude it. Rarely does measurement of a pulsus paradoxus provide new information when taken in the context of the patient's overall evaluation. When pulsus paradoxus is present, it may disappear with minimal improvement in airflow through larger airways.[51] Similarly, the presence or absence of the use of accessory muscles of respiration (sternocleidomastoid and scalenus muscles) is not prognostic.

Wheezing does not designate the presence, severity, or duration of asthma. It correlates poorly with the degree of functional derangement and may be absent when maximal effort produces minimal airflow. Physical examination may help to identify the complications of asthma such as pneumonia, pneumothorax, or pneumomediastinum that may arise atypically as subcutaneus emphysema or simulate upper airway obstruction.

DIAGNOSTIC STRATEGIES

Pulmonary Function Studies

Because physicians tend to underestimate the degree of airway obstruction in acute asthma, particularly on initial assessment, routine PFT should be part of the emergency department assessment and monitoring of these patients.[52] The forced expiratory volume in 1 second from maximal inspiration (FEV_1) or the peak expiratory flow rate (PEFR) in liters per second starting with fully inflated lungs and sustained for at least 10 milliseconds may be used in the emergency department. Both measurements require the patient's cooperation for maximal effort and are effort dependent. Whenever possible, the best of three consecutive values should be recorded.

Most asthmatic assessments in the emergency department use single-patient-use portable peak flow meters. Although they record valid values, there is wide limit of agreement between different devices, and different portable meters should not be used interchangeably.[53]

Lastly, although generally similar, the FEV_1 and PEFR measurements do not appear to be interchangeable in assessing acute airway obstruction, which is not addressed in all management guidelines.[54]

Although absolute PFT measurements can be used,[55] percentage of predicted performance (% predicted) values are preferable because they account for the individual's age (now to age 85 years), sex, and height. More ideal recordings are the percentage of the patient's personal best effort as this individualizes the assessment and treatment.

Arterial Blood Gas Analysis

Assessment of oxygenation can be done quickly, continuously, and noninvasively in most patients using pulse oximetry, with changes in equilibration of oxygen saturation with supplemental oxygen occurring in 3 to 4 minutes. With initial onset of an asthma attack, stimulated hyperventilation leads to a modest fall in the partial pressure of carbon dioxide in arterial blood ($PaCO_2$). As airway obstruction increases, the $PaCO_2$ becomes normal (PFT 15% to 25% predicted) and then increases (PFT < 15% predicted) with worsening hypoxemia. Because neither pretreatment nor post-treatment arterial blood gases (ABGs) correlate with PFTs or predict clinical outcome, ABG determination is rarely clinically useful in acute asthma exacerbations unless oxygen saturation cannot be obtained reliably using pulse oximetry. ABG determination is of no value in determining the need for tracheal intubation. Clinical evaluation over time, particularly of the patient's stamina, guides the decision. ABG sampling should be limited to a subset of patients with PFTs less than 30% predicted whose clinical course is perplexing. Occasionally, despite improving PFTs with bronchodilator therapy, some patients have a transient fall in the partial pressure of oxygen in arterial gas (PaO_2) secondary to pulmonary vasodilation and worsening ventilation-perfusion mismatch.[56]

Other Blood Testing

Leukocytosis is common in patients with acute asthma exacerbation and has little meaning. A white blood cell count is of marginal discriminatory value in attempting to determine whether patients with fever or purulent sputum have acute superimposed pulmonary infection, and it should not be interpreted in this way. A white cell count over 20,000 should be associated with concern about infection. In addition to the effects of the asthma exacerbation, corticosteroid and epinephrine therapy demarginates polymorphonuclear leukocytes after 1 to 2 hours.

Serum electrolytes are likewise of little value unless the patient is taking corticosteroids or diuretics or has cardiovascular disease and is receiving aggressive β_2-agonist therapy. In theory, frequent albuterol treatments can cause transient hypokalemia, hypomagnesemia, and hypophosphatemia, but this is generally of no clinical significance.

The serum theophylline concentration should be measured in patients receiving chronic theophylline therapy because there are no reliable clinical predictors of these levels.

In the older asthmatic with cardiovascular comorbidities who presents with wheezing, it may be prudent to measure the B-type natriuretic peptide level to determine the contribution of unrecognized congestive heart failure to the clinical picture.

Radiology Studies

A chest radiograph is of little or no value in acute asthma exacerbation, and its use should be restricted to patients suspected of having a complicating cardiopulmonary process such as pneumonia, pneumothorax, pneumomediastinum, or congestive heart failure. Also, patients who do not respond to optimal therapy and who require hospital admission are at risk for radiographically identifiable, unsuspected, clinically significant pulmonary complications (e.g., pneumothorax, pneumomediastinum) of asthma in 15% of cases.[57]

Electrocardiogram and Cardiac Monitoring

The electrocardiogram in patients with severe asthma may show a right ventricular strain pattern that reverses with improvement in airflow. Older patients, especially those with coexistent heart disease or with severe exacerbation, may require continuous cardiac monitoring to detect dysrhythmias. All patients with severe hypoxemia, and those for whom intubation is contemplated, should have continuous cardiac monitoring.

Future Monitoring Strategies

Nasal capnography is a noninvasive and independent method of continuous, real-time monitoring of severity of bronchospasm. This technique requires further study before being routinely used in the emergency department.[58]

Noninvasive monitoring of bronchial inflammation may find a place in the emergency department assessment of acute asthma as a method of customizing care for individual patients. It may include measurement of cytokine profiles in the blood, evaluation of LTE_4 in the urine, and monitoring of exhaled pentane, hydrogen peroxide, nitric oxide, or carbon monoxide levels.

Assessment Summary

The severity of airflow obstruction cannot be accurately judged when relying on patients' symptoms, physical examination, and laboratory tests. Measurements of airflow obstruction (FEV_1 or PEFR) are key components of disease assessment and response to therapy. A more detailed comparison between commonly measured variables and PFTs is shown in Table 72-1.

Table 72-1. Objective Findings in Asthma Assessment

Factor	Severe Asthma (FEV$_1$ <1.0 L)
Pulse rate (beats/min)	≥120, but may be less with equally severe asthma
Respiratory rate (breaths/min)	≥40, but most are >20, therefore nondiscriminating
Pulsus paradoxus (mm Hg)	≥10, but may be absent with equally severe asthma in 50% of cases
Pulse rate ≥120, respiratory rate ≥20, pulsus paradoxus ≥10	If all three abnormal, 90% with severe asthma, but only 40% with FEV$_1$ <1.0 L have all three abnormal
Use of accessory muscles of respiration	If present, may indicate severe asthma; if absent, may have equally severe asthma in 50% of cases
ABG analysis (mm Hg)	PaO$_2$ ≤ 60 or PaCO$_2$ ≥ 42 indicates severe asthma; all other values difficult to interpret unless PEFR or FEV$_1$ known
Pulmonary function studies	PEFR and FEV$_1$ measure directly the degree of airflow obstruction; most useful in assessing severity and guiding treatment decisions

ABG, arterial blood gas; FEV$_1$, forced expiratory volume in 1 second; PaCO$_2$, partial pressure of CO$_2$ in arterial blood; PEFR, peak expiratory flow rate.

DIFFERENTIAL CONSIDERATIONS
(Box 72-2)

MANAGEMENT OF ACUTE EXACERBATIONS

Home Strategies

Ideally, patients should monitor their symptoms and PEFR to recognize early deterioration in their airflow and have a written action plan in the event of an exacerbation. Home management includes early use of oral corticosteroids, increased use of inhaled β$_2$-agonists, and specific instructions on when to seek emergency care.[1]

Management of Acute Asthma in the Emergency Department

The goal in the emergency department is to reverse the acute airflow obstruction safely, and the rapidity of this reversal is predictive of the outcome of the attack.[59] Effective bronchodilation often results in a decreased need for hospitalization with significant cost savings.[60] As outlined in Table 72-2, the severity of attack as measured by PFTs determines the aggressiveness of the therapy.

Oxygen

All patients should receive variable doses of supplemental oxygen to maintain an arterial oxygen saturation greater than 90% (>95% in pregnant women

BOX 72-2. The Differential Diagnosis of Asthma

Cardiac Conditions
Valvular heart disease
Congestive heart failure

COPD Exacerbation

Pulmonary Infection
Pneumonia
Allergic bronchopulmonary aspergillosis
Löffler's syndrome
Chronic eosinophilic pneumonia

Upper Airway Obstruction
Laryngeal edema
Laryngeal neoplasm
Foreign body
Paradoxical vocal cord dysfunction

Endobronchial Disease
Neoplasm
Foreign body
Bronchial stenosis

Pulmonary Embolus

Carcinoid Tumor

Allergic/Anaphylactic Reaction

Miscellaneous Conditions
GERD
Noncardiogenic pulmonary edema
Addison's disease
Invasive worm infection

COPD, chronic obstructive pulmonary disease; GERD, gastroesophageal reflux disease.

and those with coexistent heart disease) rather than using predetermined concentrations or flow rates. Continual oxygen saturation monitoring is essential during the acute phase. Humidification of the inspired air-oxygen mixture is not recommended, although studies suggest that active airway rehydration should be revisited.[61]

Adrenergic Medications

Controversies in Use
Epidemiologic studies report an association between death and near death from asthma and the use of inhaled β$_2$-agonists, with use of more than one canister per month increasing this risk and the risk doubling for each additional monthly canister used.[62] This relationship does not imply causality but may be a marker for more severe disease, particularly if anti-inflammatory treatment is underused. Recommendations for chronic use of inhaled β$_2$-agonists, however, allow limited daily use in a rescue-only mode.[1]

The commonly used form of albuterol is a racemic mixture of equal amounts of R and S isomers. Data from animal and human studies suggest that the S isomer, which contributes no bronchodilator activity, is proinflammatory, spasmogenic, and induces bronchial hyperreactivity, thus possibly explaining the adverse

Table 72-2. Initial Severity Assessments and Therapies in the Emergency Department

	Mild-Moderate	Severe
FEV$_1$ or PEFR %	>50%	Unable or <50%
Oxygen	Maintain SaO$_2$ >90%	Maintain SaO$_2$ >90%
Nebulized albuterol solution		
Levalbuterol (optimal)	1.25 mg q20-30 min × 3 doses	1.25 mg q20-30 min × 3 doses Continuous for 1 hr if severe
Racemic albuterol	2.5 mg q20-30 min × 3 doses	5.0 mg q20-30 min × 3 doses Continuous for 1 hr if severe
MDI with spacer		
Racemic albuterol (90 µg/puff)	6-12 puffs q20 min for up to 4 hr (with supervision)	Same but may be unable to do (with supervision)
Inhaled anticholinergics		
Nebulized ipratropium solution	If known with previous response (same dose as for severe)	0.5 mg q20-30 min × 3 doses (mix with albuterol solution)
Systemic corticosteroids		
Oral (preferred)	40-60 mg prednisone or equivalent	40-60 mg prednisone or equivalent
IV (unable to take PO or absorb)	60-125 mg methylprednisolone (or equivalent)	60-125 mg methylprednisolone (or equivalent)
IV magnesium sulfate (FEV$_1$ <25%)	Not indicated	2-3 g over 20 min (or at rates of up to 1 g/min)

FEV$_1$, forced expiratory volume in 1 second; MDI, metered-dose inhaler; PEFR, peak expiratory flow rate; SaO$_2$, oxygen saturation in arterial blood.

effects of increased morbidity and mortality associated with regular or excessive use of this drug.[63]

Some investigations of the β-adrenergic receptor polymorphisms show differential responsiveness to inhaled albuterol, a possible explanation for the varying responses seen clinically when treating patients with acute disease.

Inhaled β$_2$-Agonist Choice and Dosing Schedule

Racemic albuterol has been the main β$_2$-agonist used in the emergency department for treatment of acute asthma for over 30 years. It is more β$_2$ selective, longer acting, and with fewer side effects than other previously available drugs such as metaproterenol or isoetharine. Other agents such as bitolterol and pirbuterol have not been studied in acute asthma.

Levalbuterol (Sepracor), the R isomer of racemic albuterol, is commercially available as a preservative-free nebulizer solution (unit doses of 0.31, 0.63, or 1.25 mg) for prevention and treatment of bronchospasm. In chronic asthma, levalbuterol seems to provide a better therapeutic index than the standard dose of racemic albuterol, further fueling the debate on the potential adverse effects of the S isomer of β-agonists.[64] Clinical studies in acute disease report that levalbuterol on a milligram for milligram basis is a better bronchodilator than similar amounts of R-albuterol delivered with the S isomer in the racemic mixture.[65,66] This implies that the noninertness of the S isomer of albuterol has problematic clinical implications in acute therapy for asthma.

The amount and frequency of delivery of levalbuterol and racemic albuterol are dependent on the initial severity and response to therapy, as shown in Table 72-2 and Table 72-3. Patients with more severe obstruction on arrival at the emergency department with a poor response to initial therapy should receive higher dosing

Table 72-3. Response to Initial Management Strategies

	Moderate Exacerbation	Severe Exacerbation
FEV$_1$ or PEFR %	50%-80%	<50%
Oxygen	Unnecessary	Maintain SaO$_2$ >90%
Nebulized albuterol solution		
Levalbuterol (optimal)	Reassess as may need less than racemic therapy	Reassess as may need less than racemic therapy
Racemic albuterol	Hourly for 1-3 hr	Hourly or continuous
Inhaled anticholinergics		
Nebulized ipratropium solution	Unnecessary	Every 4-6 hr
Corticosteroids	Every 6-8 hr	Every 6-8 hr

FEV$_1$, forced expiratory volume in 1 second; PEFR, peak expiratory flow rate; SaO$_2$, oxygen saturation in arterial blood.

schedules. When patients are stable but **require non–intensive care unit (ICU) admission, it may be possible to dose nebulized levalbuterol at 1.25 mg every 8 hours as opposed to racemic albuterol at 2.5 mg every 4 to 6 hours.**[67]

Nebulizer versus Metered-Dose Inhaler and Spacer/Holding Chamber

A metered-dose inhaler (MDI) plus spacer/holding chamber, used often and frequently (see Table 72-2), provides similar bronchodilation and side effects, even in severe asthma, when compared with wet nebulization.[68] This therapy requires more supervision because some patients have difficulty firing the canister before inhalation, inhaling slowly, and breath holding for 5 to 10 seconds. Wet nebulization by mouthpiece or mask requires no coordination and minimal cooperation and is less expensive.[69]

Intravenous Use of Adrenergic Agonists

Most international asthma guidelines, with the exception of those in the United States, recommend the use of intravenous β-agonists for very severe and nonresponsive acute asthma. Intravenous (IV) albuterol (not available in the United States) is given as a load of 4 μg/kg for 2 to 5 minutes followed by an infusion of 0.1 to 0.2 μg/kg/min, with close cardiopulmonary monitoring.[36] Likewise, intravenous epinephrine with similar close cardiopulmonary monitoring can be given as a loading dose of 200 μg to 1 mg of a 1 : 10,000 solution over 5 minutes and followed by an infusion of 1 to 20 μg/min if there is improvement with therapy.

Some reviews conclude that evidence is lacking to support the use of IV β-agonists in emergency department patients with severe acute asthma because the potential risks are obvious and that they should be considered only when inhaled therapy is not feasible.[70]

Subcutaneous Adrenergic Agents

Epinephrine has been used in the treatment of asthma for almost 100 years. It has both α and β effects and can produce tachycardia, hypertension, dysrhythmias, and vasoconstriction, especially in older asthmatics with heart disease. Given the potential for increased side effects, it should be given subcutaneously (1 : 1000 solution 0.2 to 0.5 mL every 20 to 30 minutes as needed for three doses) only to asthmatics who are severely bronchospastic and not able to inhale adequate albuterol.

Terbutaline is a longer acting β₂-agonist with bronchodilating properties equivalent to those of epinephrine in acute asthma. It can cause skeletal muscle tremor and tachycardia. A 0.25-mg dose can be given subcutaneously every 20 minutes for three doses and, as with epinephrine, it should be used only in those unable to inhale bronchodilating drugs adequately.

Long-Acting β₂-Agonists and Acute Disease

Salmeterol (Serevent) is a long-acting (12 hours) β₂-agonist that is an effective additional medication for management of daytime and nocturnal symptoms that are not adequately controlled by regular and adequate doses of effective controller medications such as inhaled steroids. It has an onset of action of 20 minutes and thus is not indicated for the treatment of acute attacks. Manufacturer-sponsored studies indicate that regular use of this drug without concomitant use of inhaled steroids results in greater asthma-related deaths; thus, the controversies regarding regular use of short acting β-agonists now extend to the long-acting classes.

Formoterol (Foradil) is another long-acting β₂-agonist that has an onset of action within minutes (similar to albuterol) and maximal effect within 2 hours. This agent could evolve as a rescue medication with extended length of action (12 hours). Patients receiving long-acting β-agonists but with acute asthma attacks are treated in the same way as all other asthmatics.

Corticosteroids

Corticosteroids have been used to treat asthma for approximately 50 years and there is general agreement about their effectiveness. Their main action in the airways is inhibition of recruitment of inflammatory cells and inhibition of release of proinflammatory mediators and cytokines from activated inflammatory and epithelial cells. Corticosteroids activate cytoplasmic glucocorticoid receptors to regulate directly or indirectly the transcription of certain target genes.

Despite the long history of corticosteroid use, the resolution of fundamental acute care issues remains uncertain. These include the types and quantities required to induce a rapid remission, the time needed for drug action, the route of administration, the existence of dose-response effects, and the determination of which populations of patients respond to this therapy.[71]

Systemic Corticosteroids in the Emergency Department

These medications should be given promptly to patients with moderate to severe attacks or those experiencing an incomplete response to initial β-agonist therapy. In addition, early systemic corticosteroids should be considered for patients who are taking oral or inhaled corticosteroids, have relapsed after a recent exacerbation, or have had prolonged symptoms. Steroid effects begin within hours (not minutes) in acute asthma and increase to peak over about 24 hours. Early use of systemic steroids decreases admissions in severe asthma but not in mild to moderate attacks.[71] Some data, however, suggest that the PEFR may improve within 2 hours of steroid therapy in those not responding to initial albuterol inhalation.[72]

Injectable preparations include methylprednisolone and hydrocortisone. The former has five times more anti-inflammatory effects, whereas the latter has marked mineralocorticoid effects resulting in sodium retention (making it unsuitable for some patients). Emergency department initial dosing of intravenous methylprednisolone is 60 to 125 mg for adults and of hydrocortisone is 200 to 500 mg, each given every 6 to 8 hours until improvement, at which time the frequency can be decreased.

Oral steroids used are prednisone or its active form, prednisolone (Medrol). Prednisone is commonly the agent of choice for oral therapy and is given in an adult dose of 40 to 60 mg in the same regimen as the intravenous agents. No study demonstrates the superiority of intravenous corticosteroids over oral preparations. Oral steroid therapy is preferred unless the patient is very ill, is unable to swallow or vomiting, or is suspected of having impaired gastrointestinal transit or absorption.

Side effects of short-term (hours or days) steroid use include reversible increases in glucose (important in diabetics) and decreases in potassium, fluid retention with weight gain, mood alterations including rare psychosis, hypertension, peptic ulcers, aseptic necrosis of the femur, and rare allergic reactions to these agents.

Inhaled Corticosteroids in the Emergency Department

Use of these agents in acute asthma has the potential benefits of reduced systemic side effects, direct delivery to the airway, and greater efficacy in reducing airway reactivity and edema alone or in addition to systemic steroids. Patients treated with inhaled steroids are less likely to be admitted whether they received systemic steroids or not, and no increased cough or bronchospasm is seen with their use.[73] The optimal agent, delivery system, and dosing regimens need to be determined, as well as whether these agents can replace systemic steroids in all or some patients.

Corticosteroids and Discharged Patients

Discharged patients who have received systemic corticosteroids in the emergency department should continue oral therapy for 3 to 10 days to control disease and prevent relapse, and the need for additional steroids should be determined at the patient's follow-up visit. An acceptable regimen is 40 to 60 mg of prednisone (or equivalent) per day in a single or divided dose. Dose tapering to prevent asthma rebound is unnecessary[74] unless the patient was already receiving systemic steroids or a prolonged course of therapy (more than 2 weeks) is deemed necessary. An alternative approach, if compliance is an issue, is to give an equally efficacious single intramuscular 40-mg dose of triamcinolone diacetate before emergency department discharge.[75]

Patients who present to the emergency department for acute exacerbations of asthma may be taking insufficient amounts of chronic controller medications based on their symptoms and excessive use of β_2-agonists.[1] If the patient is not taking oral or inhaled steroids, the addition of inhaled high-dose budesonide (Pulmicort, 400 μg, two puffs twice per day) to the patient's regular asthma medications on emergency department discharge improves symptoms and decreases relapse by approximately 50% in the ensuing 3 weeks.[76] Patients already inhaling steroids at low to medium doses may double the inhalation regimen until seen by their physician. These patients should use a spacer device and be reminded to rinse their mouths after steroid inhalation to decrease the side effects of dysphonia and oral or esophageal candidiasis.

Corticosteroid-Resistant Asthma

Chronic asthma is considered a steroid-responsive disease. A small proportion of asthmatics do not respond to even high doses of oral and inhaled glucocorticoids, which presents considerable management problems. The mechanism of this steroid resistance may be related to abnormalities in the glucocorticoid receptor number or binding properties. These patients present in the emergency department with alternative therapies such as cyclosporine, methotrexate, troleandomycin, hydroxychloroquine, azathioprine, gold, intravenous immune globulin, or (if with severe allergic asthma) maintenance anti-IgE recombinant humanized monoclonal antibody (omalizumab).

Anticholinergic Agents

The atropine-containing botanicals *Datura stramonium* (stinkweed or thorn apple) and *Atropa belladonna* (deadly nightshade) were smoked centuries ago in India for treatment of asthma. In the 19th century smoking leaves of the *Datura* species was common in England, and by the middle of the last century Salter's treatise on asthma listed *D. stramonium* as one of asthma's truly effective remedies. Atropine-containing cigarettes or powders smoked in pipes were available into the 20th century, but their use faded after the introduction of the adrenergic agents.

The anticholinergic drugs available for inhalation therapy include atropine sulfate, atropine methylnitrate, glycopyrrolate, and ipratropium bromide. They are all bronchodilators that override the smooth muscle constrictor and secretory consequences of the parasympathetic nervous system, blocking reflex bronchoconstriction and reversing acute airway obstruction. As atropine use is associated with side effects and glycopyrrolate is not well studied, the discussion is limited to ipratropium bromide (Atrovent), a quaternary derivative of atropine that is poorly absorbed from the mucosal surfaces of the lung, resulting in decreased side effects.

The maximum effect with inhaled ipratropium is in 30 to 120 minutes, with the effect lasting for up to 6 hours. Its bronchodilating potency is lower and onset of action slower than those of the β_2-agonists; hence, it should not be used alone in patients with acute asthma. Reviews of trials assessing the role of this drug in combination therapy with β_2-agonists for acute disease found that ipratropium provides a modest improvement in PFTs and a reduction in hospitalizations.[77,78] This benefit is higher in patients with more severe disease.[79] There is wide interpatient variability in response to anticholinergic therapy, implying that cholinergic mechanisms play a varied role in acute attacks. Accurate prediction of who will respond is not yet established.

Treatment recommendations (see Table 72-2) include adding the inhalation of ipratropium (0.5 mg) with the first three racemic albuterol treatments with severe acute asthma (<50% predicted). This dose should be continued every 4 to 6 hours for those not responding to therapy for up to 36 hours. The equivalent MDI dose is approximately 10 to 20 puffs (18 μg/puff) in the acute setting. Data suggests that less ipratropium might be needed in patients treated with levalbuterol nebulizations. Ipratropium can be given to anyone, both acutely and at discharge, who has documented improvement with its use. There is evidence that ipratropium may be more effective in patients older than 40 years, should be used in reversing bronchospasm secondary to β-blocking agents, and might help in those with psychological factors contributing to their disease.

Magnesium Sulfate

Magnesium relaxes bronchial smooth muscle in vitro and dilates asthmatic airways in vitro. Mechanisms for this direct relaxing effect on bronchial smooth muscle include calcium channel blocking properties, inhibition of cholinergic neuromuscular transmission, stabilization of mast cells and T lymphocytes, and stimulation of nitric oxide and prostacyclin. Intracellular magnesium levels are lower in acute asthma,[80] and the level correlates with airway reactivity in chronic disease.[81]

Magnesium has been reported to cause clinical bronchodilation since 1940, but its role in treating acute disease is being clarified. Aggressive intravenous magnesium therapy for severe attacks can obviate the need for intubation. Clinical trials and meta-analyses show that magnesium adjunctive administration in severe asthma attacks (FEV_1 <25% predicted) improves airflow obstruction and decreases the need for hospital admission.[82,83] The optimal dose and rates of infusion are unclear, but it is reasonable to administer 2 to 3 g of intravenous magnesium sulfate over 20 minutes or at rates of up to 1 g/min while continuing aggressive inhalation therapy.

Uncommon and manageable side effects of magnesium infusion are dose related and include warmth, flushing, sweating, nausea and emesis, muscle weakness and loss of deep tendon reflexes, hypotension, and respiratory depression. Inhalation magnesium in acute asthma may have a role as an isotonic vehicle for nebulized bronchodilator therapy to improve the PFT response[83] or be nebulized alone for bronchodilation.

Methylxanthines

The naturally occurring methylxanthines caffeine and theobromine (in coffee and tea) have been used by asthmatics for hundreds of years to treat wheezing. Currently, theophylline is the main oral methylxanthine used to treat asthma; aminophylline (80% theophylline by weight) is used intravenously (Table 72-4). The mechanism for theophylline's bronchodilatory effects is unclear, and current therapeutic approaches capitalize on its nonspecific arousal properties in chronic obstructive pulmonary disease (increased ventilatory drive) rather than bronchodilation. Theophylline also enhances diuresis, cardiac output, mucociliary clearance, ventilatory drive, and contractility of the diaphragm while inhibiting the release of inflammatory mediators and suppressing microvascular permeability. A number of studies of chronic asthma have demonstrated additional potential anti-inflammatory and immunomodulatory activity of these drugs[84] and may explain the usefulness of theophylline in nocturnal asthma[85] and moderate asthma managed with inhaled corticosteroids.

There is no evidence to support the use of aminophylline in the emergency department, although there is a small subset of ambulatory asthma patients who may benefit from the chronic administration of theophylline, and these patients may also benefit from methylxanthine administration in the hospital, although the evidence for this is weak.[86,87]

Theophylline has a narrow therapeutic window with many significant side effects. These include nervousness or agitation, nausea and vomiting, abdominal discomfort, headache, a variety of dysrhythmias, seizures, confusion, hyperglycemia, hypokalemia, hypophosphatemia, hypomagnesemia, leukocytosis, and respiratory alkalosis or metabolic acidosis.

Leukotriene Modifiers

The cysteinyl leukotrienes (LTC_4, LTD_4, and LTE_4) are highly potent mediators of inflammation thought to play a large role in the pathogenesis of asthma. Zafirlukast (Accolate, 20 mg twice a day) and montelukast (Singulair, 10 mg daily) are rapid-acting, safe, asthma controller drugs, taken orally, that are potent and highly selective antagonists of type 1 cysteinyl LT receptors.

Asthmatics generally produce elevated levels of LTs, and in acute attacks the levels in the urine can be markedly increased. The addition of either 7 or 14 mg of IV montelukast (not available in the United States) to standard therapy for acute asthma causes a 15% non–β_2-mediated increase in FEV_1 over placebo with no increase in side effects.[88] Oral zafirlukast, when given as adjunctive therapy (20 or 160 mg) for acute asthma in the emergency department, improved PFTs and dyspnea but did not decrease admissions to the hospital.[89] The acute non–β-mediated bronchodilating effects of these relatively safe medications will potentially be very useful in managing acute disease.

Other or Future Therapies

In patients without signs of dehydration or hypovolemia, there is no evidence that vigorous administration of fluids aids in clearing airway secretions. Mucolytics may worsen cough or airflow obstruction, and chest physical therapy in general is not beneficial. Sedatives are contraindicated in acute disease because of their respiratory depressant effect.

Bacterial, chlamydial, and mycoplasmal respiratory tract infections infrequently contribute to acute asthma. The decision to administer antibiotics should generally be reserved for patients with fever, purulent sputum, pneumonia, or evidence of bacterial sinusitis (restated in the NIH update on selected topics in 2002).

Future asthma therapies may include the second-generation antihistamines, even though earlier com-

Table 72-4. Intravenous Dosage of Aminophylline

	Dosage
Loading dose (based on actual body weight)	5-6 mg/kg over 20 min, peripheral IV
Maintenance infusion (based on ideal body weight)	
Children to age 18	1.0 mg/kg/hr
Adult smokers under 50	0.9 mg/kg/hr
Adult nonsmokers under 50	0.5 mg/kg/hr
Adults over 50	0.4 mg/kg/hr
COPD, acute viral illness	0.6-0.7 mg/kg/hr
Congestive heart failure	0.35-0.68 mg/kg/hr
Liver dysfunction	0.25-0.45 mg/kg/hr

COPD, chronic obstructive pulmonary disease.

pounds were considered contraindicated in the disease.[90] Neurokinin antagonists, inhaled loop diuretics (furosemide in acute attacks), and lidocaine may help in asthma through inhibition of neurogenic inflammation, and heparin may have a role in the inhibition of mast cell products. Lastly, specific cytokine antagonists, agonists, inhibitors of T-cell function, selective inducible nitric oxide synthetase inhibitors, and possibly gene-directed therapies may become novel treatments.

Pregnancy and Acute Asthma

The maternal and fetal risks of uncontrolled asthma are higher than those of using all typical asthma medications to manage an attack, and acute disease should be maximally treated, with the prevention of maternal and fetal hypoxia as the principal goal. Continuous electronic fetal monitoring should be considered when the fetus is potentially viable. Of note, pregnant asthmatics receive corticosteroid therapy in the emergency department less often than nonpregnant women, resulting in continued exacerbation at 2-week follow-up after discharge.[91] Recommendations for managing asthma during lactation are the same as those for managing the disease during pregnancy.

Acute Severe, Near-Fatal, and Fatal Asthma

Acute severe asthma is characterized by bronchospasm that is refractory to outpatient therapy. *Status asthmaticus* refers to severe bronchospasm that does not respond to aggressive therapies within 30 to 60 minutes.[92] *Near-fatal asthma* is identified by respiratory arrest or evidence of respiratory failure ($PaCO_2$ >50 mm Hg). *Fatal asthma* occurs when patients succumb to asthma.

Two types of fatal asthma are recognized. Slow-onset near-fatal asthma typically reflects a gradual deterioration of asthma symptoms over several days, usually superimposed on chronic poorly controlled asthma. Rapid-onset near-fatal asthma is characterized by symptom onset and progression to life-threatening status in 3 hours or less. Clinically, rapid-onset near-fatal asthma is characterized by greater hypercapnia compared with the slow-onset type. Interestingly, the hypercapnia in rapid-onset near-fatal asthma is rapidly reversible, and these patients require shorter durations of mechanical ventilation. Deaths associated with the slow-onset mechanism are thought to be preventable in many cases because the gradual progression of symptoms allows patients to seek medical evaluation before succumbing.

Risk factors for death from asthma have been identified (see Table 72-1). Although a history of previous endotracheal intubation is identified as a risk for fatal asthma, lack of a history of previous endotracheal intubation better distinguishes fatal from near-fatal asthma (as patients with a history of asthma-related intubation receive prompt attention in most emergency departments).[93] Other risk factors linked to near-fatal and fatal asthma include hospital admission for asthma treatment within the past 12 months, low socioeconomic status (related to increased allergen exposure and less access to health care), environmental exposures (air pollution, cigarette smoking), and psychosocial and emotional problems. Patients with an episode of near-fatal asthma are also likely to depend on emergency departments for asthma crisis management. Patients who succumb to fatal asthma commonly tend to be of African ancestry, live in inner city areas, and are between 15 and 34 years of age. Most deaths occur outside or on the way to the hospital, at night, and within 24 hours of the onset of symptoms.

Clinical Approach to the Critically Ill Asthmatic

The critically ill asthmatic appears agitated (hypoxemic), assumes an upright position, and appears to be in severe respiratory distress. Tachypnea, diaphoresis, and accessory muscle use are evident. Speech is fragmented into single or short bursts of syllables or words. Pulsus paradoxus is present. Absence of wheezing indicates severe expiratory obstruction and minimal air movement. Peak expiratory testing is difficult for the patient to perform but, when possible, indicates severe expiratory obstruction. Alterations in consciousness and bradypnea indicate hypercarbia and impending respiratory arrest.

There are no laboratory markers that identify patients with near-fatal asthma. In critically ill patients, elevated lactic acid levels reflect tissue hypoxemia and anaerobic metabolism; persistent elevations of arterial lactate levels are often associated with a poor prognosis. An elevated lactic acid level is not predictive of respiratory failure in critically ill asthmatics, and blood lactate levels are not helpful.

Noninvasive Strategies

Therapy must be initiated immediately (see Table 72-2) with high concentrations of supplemental oxygen and continuous oximetry. Attempts to abort the episode may be made by administration of high-dose frequent or continuously nebulized β_2- and anticholinergic agents. If parenteral adrenergic therapy is desired, terbutaline is preferred because of its β_2 selectivity. Intravenous use of magnesium sulfate or β_2-agonists (where available) may be of benefit. High-dose intravenous corticosteroids should be administered. The duration of this therapy depends on the patient's response.

Helium is an inert gas with one eighth the density of nitrogen. When 60% to 80% helium is blended with 20% to 40% oxygen, the resulting gas mixture (known as *heliox*) has a threefold reduction in density compared with air. Heliox reduces the resistance associated with gas flow through airways with nonlaminar flow and reduces respiratory muscle work; it also increases the diffusion of carbon dioxide and may improve alveolar ventilation, thus improving gas exchange.[94]

Although heliox is not intrinsically therapeutic, it may theoretically decrease the work of breathing long enough to abort intubation by allowing bronchodilators and anti-inflammatory agents to achieve their effects. There are no data to indicate that heliox reduces the need for intubation or hospital admission, length of hospital stay, or mortality.[95] Heliox is administered by nonrebreather mask and may be an alternative strategy to mechanical ventilation in selected asthmatics. Considerations for heliox include the patient with severe airflow obstruction (PEFR < 30% predicted and a rapid onset of symptoms <24 hours), a history of labile asthma or previous intubation, and inability to be adequately mechanically ventilated.[94] Heliox should be begun as soon as possible and used for at least 1 hour, but it is usually not needed for more than 8 hours. Lack of response to heliox should prompt search for an alternative diagnosis.

Noninvasive positive pressure ventilation may be of benefit in carefully selected patients. Continuous positive airway pressure improves oxygenation and reduces respiratory muscle fatigue by increasing functional residual capacity and lung compliance and supplying some of the inflating pressure required during inspiration. Bilevel positive airway pressure (BiPAP) provides continuous positive airway pressure but delivers higher pressure during inspiration than expiration. One trial suggested that BiPAP improves lung function and may reduce the need for hospitalization,[96] but data demonstrating that BiPAP decreases the need for intubation or mechanical ventilation are lacking.

Ketamine, an intravenous dissociative anesthetic, has bronchodilator effects and may prevent the need for intubation and mechanical ventilation. Adverse effects include increased airway secretions and emergence reactions.

Intubation and Ventilator Strategy

Endotracheal intubation is required in 2% of all asthma exacerbations and 10% to 30% requiring ICU admission.[97-99] With the exception of apnea or coma, there are no absolute indications for intubation in the asthmatic patient, but intubation should occur before the patient develops profound acidemia or hypoxemia. Exhaustion, hypoxemia, and depression of mental status strongly argue for intubation.

The bradypneic, somnolent asthmatic should be administered high concentrations of oxygen while immediate preparations for intubation are made. Time should not be wasted on trials of aerosolized, subcutaneous, or intravenous pharmacologic agents because respiratory arrest is imminent.

The technique of endotracheal intubation is operator dependent. Orotracheal rapid sequence intubation utilizing induction agents and muscle paralysis is preferred.

Ketamine, a dissociative anesthetic with bronchodilating properties, is the preferred agent for induction in rapid sequence intubation. Succinylcholine or a competitive neuromuscular blocking agent, such as rocuronium, can be used for intubation paralysis. Pretreatment with lidocaine, 1.5 mg/kg, given 3 minutes before the succinylcholine and ketamine, may mitigate the exacerbation of bronchospasm by the endotracheal tube. After intubation, additional ketamine may be given and a benzodiazepine should be administered to keep the patient sedated and to prevent a ketamine emergence reaction. Alternatively, propofol offers rapid-onset deep sedation and also possesses bronchodilating properties. Continued deep sedation with propofol or an equivalent agent may avoid the need for muscle paralysis. Opioids should be avoided as adjuncts to intubation in asthmatic patients because of the potential to depress respirations before intubation is accomplished. After intubation, an opioid that does not release histamine, such as fentanyl, can be used to improve the patient's comfort with the ventilator.

Nasotracheal intubation is an alternative approach that may be used in selected patients when the patient's anatomic attributes predict difficult intubation (see Chapter 1) and fiberoptic intubation is not available. Nasotracheal intubation usually requires use of an endotracheal tube with a smaller internal diameter, resulting in greater airway resistance and the potential for difficulty in removing airway secretions.

A ventilator strategy providing adequate oxygenation and ventilation while minimizing high airway pressure, barotrauma, and systemic hypotension must be instituted. The technique of *permissive hypercapnia* (also known as controlled hypoventilation) is common. Oxygenation is maintained by using a high fraction of inspired oxygen (FIO_2); hypercarbia and respiratory acidosis (pH maintained at 7.15 to 7.2 using sodium bicarbonate) are tolerated. Airway pressure is kept low by providing low tidal volumes (6 to 8 mL/kg), thus preventing excessive increases of intrinsic positive end-expiratory pressure, stacking of ventilations, and barotrauma. Low ventilation rates (<10 breaths/min) and high inspiratory flow rates provide prolonged time for expiration. Adjunctive therapies (in-line β_2-agonists and anticholinergics, intravenous corticosteroids, intravenous ketamine, and possibly magnesium) to decrease airway pressure and airway obstruction are delivered simultaneously.

Moderate levels of hypercapnia are well tolerated and have few deleterious effects. Elevated CO_2 levels have vasodilatory effects on cerebral vessels. Cerebral blood flow reaches its maximum at a $PaCO_2$ level of 120 mm Hg, which may increase intracranial pressure. Although there is no consensus on the level of hypercapnia that is safe, $PaCO_2$ levels above 100 mm Hg should be avoided.[98] Hypercapnia can decrease cardiac contractility and produce cardiovascular collapse; thus, permissive hypercapnia should be supplemented by generous repletion of intravascular volume through intravenous fluid administration.

Neuromuscular blockade improves ventilator performance and pulmonary compliance. Use of neuromuscular blocking agents also decreases oxygen consumption and allows resting of the respiratory muscles while bronchospasm is being aggressively treated. Myopathy attributed to the prolonged use of competitive neuromuscular blocking agents occurs in about 30% of asthmatic patients with neuromuscular blockade.[97] Neuromuscular blocking agents are currently recommended only in intubated patients who cannot be controlled by sedation alone.

Intubation and mechanical ventilation may be life-saving in near-fatal asthma attacks. Although hazards of mechanical ventilation (nosocomial infection, barotrauma) may occur, the treatment of critically ill asthmatics with mechanical ventilation is associated with low or zero mortality and few complications. Most asthmatics requiring mechanical ventilation improve rapidly and require short ICU stays.

Complications of mechanical ventilation in the asthmatic patient include hypotension and barotrauma. Hypotension is almost uniformly secondary to increased intrathoracic pressure with a subsequent decrease in venous return and cardiac output. It is best managed by administration of IV fluids and maneuvers to reduce mean airway pressure. Pneumothorax should be suspected whenever sudden clinical deterioration occurs or when hypotension is accompanied by a significant rise in peak inspiratory ventilator pressures and falling oxygen saturation.

Treatment of the Refractory Critically Ill Asthmatic

If the intubated critically ill asthmatic continues to have elevated airway pressures, persistent hypoxemia, and continued bronchospasm after the preceding agents and procedures are employed, general anesthesia should be administered. This generally requires transfer to the operating room, where anesthetic gases and scavenging systems are available. Isoflurane and halothane have similar bronchodilating efficacy, but isoflurane has lower arrhythmogenic and hypotensive properties.[100]

External chest compression may be of assistance when patients cannot exhale. Chest compression is delivered by bilateral squeezing of the lower chest walls immediately after end inspiration occurs. Compression delivered too early (i.e., during inspiration) may increase airway pressure and result in barotrauma. In children, this technique decreases peak airway pressure and $PaCO_2$ and increases pH.[101]

Cardiopulmonary arrest may result from unrecognized barotrauma. Empirical bilateral tube thoracostomy should be performed if unexplained cardiac arrest occurs, especially in the context of dramatic increases in peak inspiratory pressure. IV epinephrine is a logi-cal agent to use in the setting of cardiopulmonary arrest because it has both cardiostimulatory and bronchodilatory properties.[102] Isoproterenol, a pure β-agonist, may increase heart rate and provide bronchodilatation but it decreases coronary perfusion pressure. Cardiopulmonary bypass and extracorporeal lung assist are also used in the treatment of near-fatal asthma.

DISPOSITION

Prediction of Relapse

Asthmatic patients discharged from the emergency department have rates of relapse (usually defined as any urgent treatment for asthma, regardless of location) that vary from 11% over 3 days to 45% at 8 weeks. In a multicenter study, the relapse rate was 17% in the 2 weeks after emergency department discharge with increased risk for relapse in those with numerous asthma-related emergency department visits within the last year, with more outpatient medications, and with longer duration of symptoms before the emergency department visit.[103] Other studies have found similar out-of-control indices predicting relapse but have also included insufficient improvement in PFTs with hospital-based treatment for an attack.[104]

Inpatient versus Observation or Clinical Decision Unit

Patients requiring extended care who are without life-threatening exacerbations, pregnancy, or complications of asthma can generally be managed in a clinical decision unit (CDU) for 12 hours with 8-week outcomes equal to those of patients managed in a hospital ward but with significant cost savings.[105] The ability to predict discharge from the CDU can be assessed by the emergency department PEFR response to the third β2-agonist treatment (PEFR > 40% predicted is often associated with successful CDU discharge).[103] Lastly, patients prefer CDU management of acute attacks over routine inpatient care when satisfaction and problems with care processes are assessed with standardized instrumentation.[106]

Table 72-5 summarizes disposition guidelines for asthmatics on the basis of their response to therapies in the emergency department.

Table 72-5. Emergency Department Disposition Decision-Making Guidelines

	Good Response	Incomplete Response	Poor Response
FEV₁ or PEFR % (predicted/personal best)	>70%	>50% but <70%	<50%
Disposition site			
Home	Yes	Individualized decision (see text)	No, continue therapy
Clinical decision unit	No	Yes, if available	Yes, if available and appropriate
Hospital ward	No	Yes, if no CDU	Yes, if appropriate
Critical care unit	No	No	Yes, if with respiratory insufficiency/failure

CDU, clinical decision unit; FEV₁, forced expiratory volume in 1 second; PEFR, peak expiratory flow rate.

BOX 72-3. Instructions for Metered-Dose Inhaler Use

1. Remove cap from the MDI container.
2. Assemble the MDI and hold it upright.
3. Shake the canister.
4. Place the mouthpiece loosely between the teeth (or hold it 3 to 4 cm in front of the open mouth).
5. Exhale fully (to functional residual capacity).
6. Actuate the inhaler at the beginning of a slow and full inhalation (as if sipping hot soup) lasting 5 or 6 seconds.
7. Hold breath for at least 10 seconds.
8. Wait 1 minute before reuse.

Planning Discharge from the Emergency Department

An asthma exacerbation does not end on emergency department discharge; airway inflammation and peripheral obstruction may take hours to days to resolve. Patients are likely to need continued β_2-agonist rescue therapy during this time, and it is important that they can demonstrate the correct use of their inhalers (Box 72-3). If the patient is having difficulty coordinating the canister activation with inhalation, a breath-activated inhaler (Maxair Autohaler) or spacer device can be prescribed. A patient using a portable, pre-loaded, multidose dry powder inhaler must inhale from the mouthpiece in a rapid and forceful inhalation to total lung capacity.

Patients receiving systemic corticosteroids in the emergency department must continue these orally for 3 to 5 days. Asthma patients treated in the emergency department are more likely to have moderate to severe disease, not receive controller therapy, and be younger, poorer, and less educated. They have reduced asthma management skills and are more likely to miss school or work. If the patient is not using controller medications and is with persistent disease, moderate-dose inhaled steroids or a combination inhaled steroid and long-acting β-agonist (e.g., salmeterol xinafoate–fluticasone propionate [Advair]) should be started. A less preferred option is to prescribe an LT modifier (zafirlukast 20 mg twice a day, montelukast 10 mg daily) to decrease relapse and improve asthma control. Patients should have an outpatient follow-up visit with their physician within the next 3 to 5 days. At this visit it can be decided whether oral steroid therapy needs to be continued and whether any adjustments to the control drug regimen are effective or require further changes, and a comprehensive asthma action plan can be made.

The asthma patient can be provided with limited asthma education through written information about discharge medications, a simple action plan for medication adjustment if the condition is not improving, and a peak flow meter with education on how to use it for daily measurements.

KEY CONCEPTS

- IgE-mediated immune responses, airway inflammation, and airway remodeling are concepts crucial to our current understanding of asthma and are the targets of current and future therapies.
- Steroid medications are effective in controlling airway inflammation and have important roles in management of asthma exacerbations.
- Single-isomer albuterol (levalbuterol [Xopenex]), the result of improving isomer technology is a better bronchodilator in acute asthma than the traditional racemic form.
- Leukotriene antagonists (montelukast, zafirlukast) are agents useful in the therapy of aspirin-induced asthma.
- The emergency department's management of acute asthma is expanding (up to 24 hours) as more noncritically ill asthmatics are managed in the clinical decision unit and discharged home.
- Integration of discharged acute asthmatics into chronic management strategies to prevent relapse requires that asthma patients' physicians be familiar with controlling medications such as inhaled corticosteroids and LT modifiers.

REFERENCES

1. National Institutes of Health, National Heart, Lung, and Blood Institute: Expert Panel Report: Guidelines for the Diagnosis and Management of Asthma Update on Selected Topics 2002 (NIH Publication No. 02-5074). Bethesda, Md, National Institutes of Health, 2003.
2. Mannino DM, et al: Surveillance for asthma—United States 1980-1999. *MMWR Surveill Summ* 51(SS01):1, 2002.
3. National Center for Health Statistics: Asthma Prevalence, Health Care Use and Mortality, 2000-2001. http://www.cdc.gov/nchs/products/pubs/pubd/hestats/asthma/asthma.htm. January 2004.
4. Weiss KB, et al: The health economics of asthma and rhinitis. I. Assessing the economic impact. *J Allergy Clin Immunol* 107:3, 2001.
5. Centers for Disease Control and Prevention: Asthma prevalence and control characteristics by race/ethnicity—United States, 2002. *MMWR Morb Mortal Wkly Rep* 53:145, 2004.
6. Haley KJ, et al: Inflammatory cell distribution within and along asthmatic airways. *Am J Respir Crit Care Med* 158:565, 1998.
7. Kraft M, et al: Alveolar tissue inflammation in asthma. *Am J Respir Crit Care Med* 154:1505, 1996.
8. Hamid QA, et al: Molecular pathology of allergic disease. I. Lower airway disease. *J Allergy Clin Immunol* 105:20, 2000.
9. Vignola AM, et al: Airway inflammation in mild intermittent and in persistent asthma. *Am J Respir Crit Care* Med 157:403, 1998.
10. Burrows B, et al: Association of asthma with serum IgE levels and skin-test reactivity to allergens. *N Engl J Med* 320:271, 1989.
11. Kay AB: Role of T cells in asthma. *Chem Immunol* 71:178, 1998.
12. Wenzel SE: Arachidonic acid metabolites: Mediators of inflammation in asthma. *Pharmacotherapy* 17:3S, 1997.
13. Jahnsen FL, et al: Rapid dendritic cell recruitment to the bronchial mucosa of patients with atopic asthma in response to local allergen challenge. *Thorax* 56:823, 2001.

14. Bradding P, Holgate ST: The mast cell as a source of cytokines in asthma. *Ann NY Acad Sci* 796:272, 1996.

15. O'Byrne PM: Eicosanoids and asthma. *Ann NY Acad Sci* 796:251, 1996

16. Thomas LH, Warner JA: The eosinophil and its role in asthma. *Gen Pharmacol* 27:593, 1996.

17. Leckie MJ, et al: Effects of an interleukin-5 blocking monoclonal antibody on eosinophils, airway hyper-responsiveness, and the late asthmatic response. *Lancet* 356:2144, 2000.

18. Bryan SA, et al: Effects of recombinant human interleukin-12 on eosinophils, airway hyper-responsiveness and the late asthmatic response. *Lancet* 356:2149, 2000.

19. Busse WW, et al: Asthma. *N Engl J Med* 344:350, 2001.

20. Elias JA, et al: Airway remodeling in asthma. *J Clin Invest* 104:1001, 1999.

21. Lange P, et al: A 15-year follow-up study of ventilatory function in adults with asthma. *N Engl J Med* 339:1194, 1998.

22. Redington AE, et al: Airway wall remodeling in asthma. *Thorax* 52:310, 1997.

23. Fabbri LM, et al: Physiologic consequences of long-term inflammation. *Am J Respir Crit Care Med* 157:S195, 1998.

24. Jenkins C, et al: Systematic review of prevalence of aspirin induced asthma and its implications for clinical practice. *BMJ* 328:434, 2004.

25. Marquette CH, et al: Long-term prognosis for near fatal asthma. A 6 year follow-up study of 145 asthmatic patients who underwent mechanical ventilation for near-fatal attack of asthma. *Am Rev Respir Dis* 146:76, 1992.

26. West PM, et al: Safety of COX-2 inhibitors in asthma patients with aspirin hypersensitivity. *Ann Pharmacother* 37:1497, 2003.

27. Tan RA, et al: Exercise-induced asthma: Diagnosis and management. *Ann Allergy Asthma Immunol* 89:226, 2002.

28. Vrieze A, et al: Perimenstrual asthma: A syndrome without known cause or cure. *J Allergy Clin Immunol* 112:271, 2003.

29. Lehrer PM: Emotionally triggered asthma: A review of research literature and some hypotheses for self-regulation therapies. *Appl Psychophysiol Biofeedback* 23:13, 1998.

30. Anbar RD: Hypnosis in pediatrics: Applications at a pediatric pulmonary center. *BMC Pediatr* 2:11, 2002.

31. Roche WR: Inflammatory and structural changes in the small airways in bronchial asthma. *Am J Respir Crit Care Med* 157:S191, 1998.

32. Ordonez CL, et al: Increased neutrophil numbers and IL-8 levels in airway secretions in acute severe asthma: Clinical and biologic significance. *Am J Respir Crit Care Med* 161;1185, 2000.

33. Sur S, et al: Sudden onset fatal asthma. A distinct entity with few eosinophils and relatively more neutrophils in the airway submucosa? *Am Rev Respir Dis* 148:713, 1993.

34. Kuyper LM, et al: Characterization of airway plugging in fatal asthma. *Am J Med* 115:6, 2003.

35. Hays SR, et al: The role of mucus in fatal asthma. *Am J Med* 115:68, 2003.

36. Nowak RM: National and international guidelines for the emergency management of adult asthma. In Brenner BE (ed): *Emergency Asthma.* New York, Marcel Dekker, 1999, pp 289-305.

37. Emond SD, Camargo CA, Nowak RM: 1997 National Asthma Education and Prevention Program guidelines: A practical summary for emergency physicians. *Ann Emerg Med* 31:579, 1998.

38. Emond SD, Camargo CA, Nowak RM: Advances, opportunities, and the new asthma guidelines. *Ann Emerg Med* 31:590, 1998.

39. Boulet LP, et al: Canadian asthma consensus report, 1999. Canadian Asthma Consensus Group. *CMAJ* 161:S1, 1999.

40. Lenhardt R, Malone A, Grant EN, Weiss KB: Trends in emergency department asthma care in metropolitan Chicago. *Chest* 124:1774, 2003.

41. Edmond SD, et al: Effect of an emergency department asthma program on acute asthma care. *Ann Emerg Med* 34:321, 1999.

42. Goldberg R, et al: Critical pathway for the emergency department management of acute asthma: Effect on resource utilization. *Ann Emerg Med* 31:562, 1998.

43. Doerschug KC, Peterson MW, Dayton CS, Kline JN: Asthma guidelines: An assessment of physician understanding and practice. *Am J Respir Crit Care Med* 159:1735, 1999.

44. Akerman MJH, Sinet R: A successful effort to improve asthma care outcome in an inner-city emergency department. *J Asthma* 36:295, 1999.

45. Brenner BE, et al: Circadian differences among 4,096 emergency department patients with acute asthma. *Crit Care Med* 29:1124, 2001.

46. Zimmerman JL, et al: Relation between phase of menstrual cycle and emergency department visits for acute asthma. *Am J Respir Crit Care Med* 162:512, 2000.

47. Magadle R, Berar-Yanny N, Weiner P: The risk of hospitalization and near-fatal and fatal asthma in relation to the perception of dyspnea. *Chest* 121:329, 2002.

48. Woodruff PG, Emond SD, Singh AK, Camargo CA: Sudden-onset severe acute asthma: Clinical features and response to therapy. *Acad Emerg Med* 5:695, 1998.

49. Krantz AJ, et al: Heroin insufflation as a trigger for patients with life-threatening asthma. *Chest* 123:510, 2003.

50. Corbridge T, Cygan J, Greenberger P: Substance abuse and acute asthma. *Intensive Care Med* 26:347, 2000.

51. Carden DL, Nowak RM, Sarkar DD: Vital signs including pulsus paradoxus in the assessment of acute bronchial asthma. *Ann Emerg Med* 12:80, 1983.

52. Emerman CL, Cydulka RK: Effect of pulmonary function testing on the management of acute asthma. *Arch Intern Med* 155:225, 1995.

53. Koyama H, et al: Comparison of four types of portable peak flow meters (Mini-Wright, Assess, Pulmo-graph and Wright Pocket meters). *Respir Med* 92:505, 1998.

54. Giannini D, et al: Comparison between peak expiratory volume in one second (FEV1) during bronchoconstriction induced by different stimuli. *J Asthma* 34:105, 1997.

55. Nowak RM, et al: Comparison of peak expiratory flow and FEV1 admission criteria for acute bronchial asthma. *Ann Emerg Med* 11:64, 1982.

56. Nowak RM, Tomlanovich MC, Sarkar DD: Arterial blood gases and pulmonary function testing in acute bronchial asthma: Predicting patient outcomes. *JAMA* 249:2043, 1983.

57. Pickup CM, Nee PA, Randall PE: Radiographic features in 1016 adults admitted to hospital with acute asthma. *J Accid Emerg Med* 11:234, 1994.

58. Egleston CV, Aslam HB, Lambert MA: Capnography for monitoring non-intubated spontaneously breathing patients in an emergency room setting. *J Accid Emerg Med* 14:222, 1997.

59. Rodrigo G, Rodrigo C: Early prediction of poor response in acute asthma patients in the emergency department. *Chest* 114:1016, 1998.

60. Stanford R, McLaughlin T, Okamoto LJ: The cost of asthma in the emergency department and hospital. *Am J Respir Crit Care Med* 160:211, 1999.

61. Moloney E, et al: Airway dehydration: A therapeutic target in asthma? *Chest* 121:1806, 2002.

62. Spitzer W, et al: The use of beta-agonists and the risk of death and near death from asthma. *N Engl J Med* 326:501, 1993.

63. Nowak RM: Single-isomer levalbuterol: A review of the acute data. *Curr Allergy Asthma Rep* 3:172, 2003.

64. Jenne JW: The debate on S-enantiomers of beta-agonists: Tempest in a teapot or gathering storm? *J Allergy Clin Immunol* 102:893, 1998.

65. Nowak RM, et al: Levalbuterol compared with racemic albuterol in the treatment of acute asthma: Results of a pilot study. *Am J Emerg Med* 22:29, 2004.

66. Carl CC, Myers TR, Kirchner HL, Kercsmar CM: Comparison of racemic albuterol and levalbuterol for treatment of acute asthma. *J Pediatr* 143:731, 2003.

67. Truitt T, Witko J, Halpern M: Levalbuterol compared to racemic albuterol: Efficacy and outcomes in patients hospitalized with COPD or asthma. *Chest* 123:128, 2003.

68. Newman KB, Milne S, Hamilton C, Hall K: A comparison of albuterol administered by metered-dose inhaler and spacer with albuterol by nebulizer in adults presenting to an urban emergency department with acute asthma. *Chest* 121:1036, 2002.

69. Frei SP: Cost comparison of bronchodilator delivery methods in emergency department treatment of asthma. *J Emerg Med* 19:323, 2000.

70. Travers AH, et al: The effectiveness of IV beta-agonists in treating patients with acute asthma in the emergency department: A meta-analysis. *Chest* 122:1200, 2002.

71. Rowe BH, et al: Early emergency department treatment of acute asthma with systemic corticosteroids (Cochrane review). In: *The Cochrane Library*, issue 2. Oxford: Update Software, 2000.

72. Lin RY, et al: Rapid improvement of peak flow in asthmatic patients treated with parenteral methylprednisolone in the emergency department: A randomized controlled study. *Ann Emerg Med* 33:487, 1999.

73. Edmonds ML, Camargo CA, Pollack CV, Rowe BH: Early use of inhaled corticosteroids in the emergency department treatment of acute asthma (Cochrane review). In: *The Cochrane Library*, vol 3. Oxford: Update Software, 2003.

74. Cydulka RK, Emerman CL: A pilot study of steroid therapy after emergency department treatment of acute asthma: Is a taper needed? *J Emerg Med* 16:15, 1998.

75. Schuckman H, et al: Comparison of intramuscular triamcinolone and oral prednisone in the outpatient treatment of acute asthma: A randomized controlled trial. *Ann Emerg Med* 31:333, 1998.

76. Rowe BH, et al: Inhaled budesonide in addition to oral corticosteroids to prevent asthma relapse following discharge from the emergency department: A randomized controlled trial. *JAMA* 281:2119, 1999.

77. Rodrigo G, Rodrigo C, Burschtin O: A meta-analysis of the effects of ipratropium bromide in adults with acute asthma. *Am J Med* 107:363, 1999.

78. Rodrigo GJ, Rodrigo C: The role of anticholinergics in acute asthma treatment: An evidence-based evaluation. *Chest* 121:1977, 2002.

79. Lin RY, et al: Superiority of ipratropium plus albuterol over albuterol alone in the emergency department management of adult asthma: A randomized clinical trial. *Ann Emerg Med* 31:208, 1998.

80. Zervas E, et al: Reduced intracellular Mg concentrations in patients with acute asthma. *Chest* 123:113, 2003.

81. Silverman RA, et al: IV magnesium sulfate in the treatment of acute severe asthma: A multicenter randomized controlled trial. *Chest* 122:489, 2002.

82. Alter HJ, Koepsell TD, Hilty WM: Intravenous magnesium sulfate as an effective adjunct in acute bronchospasm: A meta-analysis. *Acad Emerg Med* 6:521, 1999.

83. Nannini LJ, et al: Magnesium sulfate as a vehicle for nebulized salbutamol in acute asthma. *Am J Med* 108:193, 2000.

84. Spina D, Landells LJ, Page CP: The role of theophylline and phosphodiesterase isoenzyme inhibitors as anti-inflammatory drugs. *Clin Exp Allergy* 28(Suppl 3):24, 1998.

85. Martin RJ: Nocturnal asthma and use of theophylline. *Clin Exp Allergy* 28(Suppl 3):64, 1998.

86. Parameswaran K, Belda J, Rowe BH: Addition of intravenous aminophylline to B2-agonists in adults with acute asthma (Cochrane review). In: *The Cochrane Library*, Issue 2. Oxford, Update Software, 2002.

87. Huang D, et al: Does aminophylline benefit adults admitted to the hospital for an acute exacerbation of asthma? *Ann Intern Med* 289:1155, 1993.

88. Camargo CA, et al: A randomized controlled trial of intravenous montelukast in acute asthma. *Am J Respir Crit Care Med* 167:528, 2003.

89. Silverman RA, et al: Zafirlukast improves emergency department outcomes after an acute asthma episode. *Ann Emerg Med* 35:S10, 2000.

90. Malick A, Grant JA: Antihistamines in the treatment of asthma. *Allergy* 52(Suppl 34):55, 1997.

91. Cydulka RK, et al: Acute asthma among pregnant women presenting to the emergency department. *Am J Respir Crit Care Med* 160:887, 1999.

92. Panacek EA, Pollack CV: Medical management of severe acute asthma. In Brenner BE (ed): *Emergency Asthma*. New York, Marcel Dekker, 1999, pp 395-417.

93. Strunk RC, et al: Fatal and near-fatal asthma questionnaire: Prelude to a national registry. *J Allergy Clin Immunol* 104:763, 1999.

94. Kass JE: Heliox redux. *Chest* 123:673, 2003.

95. Ho AM, et al: Heliox vs air-oxygen mixtures for the treatment of patients with acute asthma: A systematic overview. *Chest* 123:882, 2003.

96. Soroksky A, et al: A pilot prospective randomized, placebo-controlled trial of bilevel positive airway pressure in acute asthma attack. *Chest* 123:1018, 2003.

97. Phipps P, et al: The pulmonary physician in critical care. 12: Acute severe asthma in the intensive care unit. *Thorax* 58:81, 2003.

98. Mutlu GM, et al: Severe status asthmaticus: Management with permissive hypercapnia and inhalation anesthesia. *Crit Care Med* 30:477, 2002.

99. Spyros P, et al: Clinical review: Severe asthma. *Crit Care* 6:30, 2002.

100. DeNicola LK, et al: Inhalation anaesthetics as an adjunct to ventilator management in severe status asthmaticus. *Intensive Care World* 15:126, 1998.

101. Weber JE, et al: Closed lung massage improves ventilation in status asthmaticus. *Acad Emerg Med* 1:A49, 1994.

102. Smith D, et al: Intravenous epinephrine in life-threatening asthma. *Ann Emerg Med* 41:706, 2003.

103. McCarren M, et al: Prediction of relapse within eight weeks after an acute asthma exacerbation in adults. *J Clin Epidemiol* 51:107, 1998.

104. McDermott MF, et al: A comparison between emergency diagnostic and treatment unit and inpatient care in the management of acute asthma. *Arch Intern Med* 157:2055, 1997.

105. McCarren M, Zalenski RJ, McDermott M, Kaur K: Predicting recovery from acute asthma in an emergency diagnostic and treatment unit. *Acad Emerg Med* 7:28, 2000.

106. Rydman RJ, et al: Patient satisfaction with an emergency department asthma observation unit. *Acad Emerg Med* 6:178, 1999.

73 Chronic Obstructive Pulmonary Disease

Stuart P. Swadron and Diku P. Mandavia

PERSPECTIVE

Chronic obstructive pulmonary disease (COPD) is now the fourth leading cause of death worldwide. Although in the United States mortality among men is leveling off, the rate for women is still increasing. Epidemiologists agree that the prevalence of COPD is underreported and that its burden is increasing.[1] Regardless of the success of smoking cessation programs, smoking behavior in the past several decades and the delay to the appearance of symptoms in an aging population virtually guarantee an increase in prevalence. It has been estimated that COPD will be the fifth leading cause of lost disability-adjusted life years worldwide by 2020.[2] The financial burden of COPD is enormous: billions of dollars every year for treatment and lost productivity.[3] Despite its enormous impact, COPD has received less attention from basic medical researchers and clinicians than other diseases. In the past decade, this trend has begun to reverse.[4] Large multinational collaborations such as the National Heart, Lung and Blood Institute/World Health Organization–sponsored Global Initiative for Chronic Obstructive Lung Disease (GOLD) have been designed to help reinvigorate the scientific and medical communities frustrated by the unrelenting progressive nature of COPD and its poor response to existing therapies.[1]

There is no universally accepted definition of COPD; however, the GOLD collaborators define it as "a disease state characterized by airflow limitation that is not fully reversible." Their definition also states that "the airflow limitation is usually both progressive and associated with an abnormal inflammatory response of the lungs to noxious particles or gases." This new definition avoids mention of chronic bronchitis and emphysema, two entities that have been traditionally included in the definition of COPD. The collaborators point out that chronic bronchitis, defined as the presence of cough and sputum production for at least 3 months in each of two consecutive years, can occur *without* airflow limitation and that emphysema, the destruction of alveoli, is a pathologic term, not one that pertains to clinical diagnosis. Unlike many earlier definitions of COPD, the GOLD definition also specifically excludes asthma, which is *reversible* airflow limitation.[1] Whether reversible airflow limitation is considered to be part of COPD itself or due to coexistent asthma is of limited significance to the emergency physician, who continues to make every attempt to identify and reverse airflow limitation, regardless of how it is defined.

As many as 50% of all acute COPD exacerbations are not reported to physicians. In addition, not all reported exacerbations require hospitalization.[5] Nonetheless, in 1998, almost 2% of all hospital admissions in the United States were directly attributed to COPD, and it was considered a contributory factor in another 7%.[3] As the severity of the underlying disease progresses, so does the frequency of exacerbations. Moreover, in a subset of patients, incomplete recovery from acute exacerbations may reflect a contribution of exacerbations to the pathophysiology of relentless disease progression.[6]

PRINCIPLES OF DISEASE

Pathophysiology

In the past two decades, the discovery that chronic airway inflammation plays a central role in the pathophysiology of asthma led to an important change in its management, specifically, the liberal use of corticosteroids for moderate to severe disease. Airway inflammation is also at the center of the pathophysiology of COPD, but the inflammatory process of COPD is different from that found in asthmatics. In COPD, there is a predominance of neutrophils, CD8+ lymphocytes, and macrophages in bronchial washings, whereas in asthma the cellular response is characterized by the presence of eosinophils.[7] The inflammatory mediators differ in COPD, and several mediators, such as tumor necrosis factor, leukotriene B_4, and interleukin 8, are linked to the destruction of parenchyma.[8] These differences in the nature of the inflammatory response in COPD account for its poorer response to current anti-inflammatory treatment compared with asthma.

Pathologically, the abnormalities in COPD are found throughout the lungs. Although certain changes may be more or less prominent in a given patient, most patients have at least some component of the two main pathologic entities: chronic obstructive bronchitis and emphysema. Evidence of airway inflammation is found from the trachea down to the smallest peripheral airways, which become progressively scarred and narrowed. An increase in both the number and size of mucus-secreting goblet cells results in the formation of mucous plugging that further contributes to airflow obstruction. Damage to the endothelium impairs the mucociliary response that clears bacteria and mucus. The lung parenchyma is progressively destroyed over time, usually in a pattern of centrilobular emphysema. This pattern consists of destruction of alveoli, loss of lung elasticity, and the closure of small airways, which rely on the radial support of surrounding connective tissues to maintain their patency during expiration.

The combination of airway obstruction and obliteration of the pulmonary vascular bed results in a failure of gas exchange. Thus, arterial blood gases (ABGs) may reveal both hypoxemia and hypercapnia. As the overall size of the pulmonary vascular bed decreases with time, chronic hypoxia induces a thickening of the vessel walls. Both of these factors contribute to the development of pulmonary hypertension, polycythemia, and, eventually, right-sided heart failure (cor pulmonale).[4,8,9]

The pathophysiology of COPD reflects an apparent imbalance of proteases and antiproteases that favors the destruction of connective tissue in the lungs. A multitude of factors in COPD negatively affect this balance; perhaps the clearest example is α_1-antitrypsin deficiency. In this congenital condition, a lack of α_1-antitrypsin, an enzyme that inhibits neutrophil elastase, leads to the pathology of severe panacinar emphysema.[10] These patients, however, represent a small minority of all patients with COPD. The protease-antiprotease relationship in patients with acquired COPD is still being elucidated.[11,12] Oxidative stress, the imbalance of oxidant and antioxidant activity in favor of oxidants, is another important facet of the pathophysiology of COPD. External oxidants are found in cigarette smoke, whereas the products of the inflammatory process result in intrinsic oxidants. Not only may oxidants cause direct parenchymal damage, but oxidative stress indirectly fuels further inflammation and protease activity.[13]

Cigarette smoking, the most significant risk factor for the development of COPD, exerts its effects at multiple points in the inflammatory cascade of COPD, negatively affecting both the protease-antiprotease and oxidant-antioxidant balances.[8,13,14] Although smoking cessation slows the progression of the disease, it does not end the chronic inflammatory process within the airways, indicating that mechanisms independent of smoking are involved.[8] Moreover, although a majority of COPD patients have a significant smoking history, only a minority of smokers ever develop airflow limitation. This suggests the importance of other factors, both environmental and genetic.[15] Other identified causative factors include heavy occupational exposure to dusts and air pollution from indoor cooking, particularly in the developing world. Outdoor air pollution, passive exposure to tobacco smoke, and early childhood lower respiratory tract infections are also contributory.[1]

Compensatory physiologic responses in COPD vary according to the balance of underlying pathologic derangements seen in individual patients. In a minority of patients, ventilatory drive is increased to maintain a near-normal partial pressure of oxygen (PO_2), preventing any cyanosis. The resultant tachypnea may also cause a slightly low PCO_2. In such patients with relatively normal blood gases, pulmonary hypertension and cor pulmonale may not occur until very late in the course of the disease.

Although the precise mechanisms are ill defined, the pathologic processes of COPD extend beyond the cardiac and pulmonary systems. The effects of circulating inflammatory mediators, oxidative stress, and protease-antiprotease imbalance may be responsible for the weight loss, muscular wasting, metabolic derangements, and depression often seen in the later stages of disease.[14,16,17] These features of COPD are partly responsible for the impact of COPD as a comorbid illness, even when the presenting complaint is nonpulmonary. COPD influences a variety of management decisions in the emergency department, ranging from the choice of agents for procedural sedation and rapid sequence intubation to the appropriate disposition of patients with nonpulmonary diagnoses.

Staging the Severity of Disease

Most classifications of disease severity are based on quantitative measurements of airflow limitation, such as the forced expiratory volume in 1 second (FEV$_1$) and FEV$_1$/forced vital capacity ratio. These indices are measured after any *reversible* airflow limitation is addressed by treatment with bronchodilator medications. The GOLD collaborators define four stages, beginning with an at-risk stage (stage 0), when spirometry is normal, and ending in severe COPD (stage 3), when FEV$_1$ is less than 30% of predicted (Table 73-1). Frequent exacerbations are usually seen when the FEV$_1$ falls below 50% of predicted—leading to the division of stage 2 into two substages.

A classification system that incorporates clinical features of COPD, including the degree of dyspnea, exercise tolerance, and body mass index, has greater prognostic value than the FEV$_1$ alone.[18] This scoring system, however, has not yet been evaluated in the emergency department setting, and an evaluation that focuses on acute parameters, such as the patient's res-

Table 73-1. The GOLD Classification of Severity of Chronic Obstructive Pulmonary Disease

Stage	Characteristics
0: At risk	Chronic symptoms of cough and sputum production Normal spirometry
I: Mild COPD	FEV$_1$/FVC < 70% FEV$_1$ ≥ 80% of predicted With or without chronic symptoms
II: Moderate COPD	FEV$_1$/FVC < 70% With or without chronic symptoms (IIa: 50% ≤ FEV$_1$ < 80% of predicted) (IIb: 30% ≤ FEV$_1$ < 50% of predicted)
III: Severe COPD	FEV$_1$/FVC < 70% FEV$_1$ < 30% of predicted, or the presence of respiratory failure or clinical signs of right-sided heart failure

COPD, chronic obstructive pulmonary disease; FEV$_1$, forced expiratory volume in 1 second; FVC, forced vital capacity.
Adapted from Pauwels RA, et al: Global strategy for the diagnosis, management, and prevention of chronic obstructive pulmonary disease: National Heart, Lung, and Blood Institute and World Health Organization Global Initiative for Chronic Obstructive Lung Disease (GOLD): Executive summary. *Respir Care* 46:798, 2001.

piratory effort, mental status, oxygen saturation, and alteration from baseline function, is likely to be of more value in the emergency department than scoring systems that predict long-term outcomes in outpatient populations.

Acute Exacerbations

Unlike asthma exacerbations, COPD exacerbations are not necessarily associated with major reductions in peak flow and FEV_1 measurements. An acute exacerbation is defined by the presence of one or more of the following: worsening dyspnea, increase in sputum volume, and increase in sputum purulence.

Acute exacerbations are more common in the winter months, which most likely reflects the importance of viral infections in their pathogenesis. As with asthma, viral infection appears to be a frequent inciting agent in COPD exacerbations. Commonly implicated viruses include rhinovirus, respiratory syncytial virus (RSV), coronavirus, and influenza virus.[19-21] Exacerbations associated with a viral etiology are longer and more severe than those without an apparent inciting agent.[21,22]

There is considerable controversy about the role of bacterial pathogens in acute exacerbations of COPD. Almost one half of all exacerbations are associated with negative cultures for the typical respiratory pathogens such as *Haemophilus influenzae*, *Streptococcus pneumoniae*, *Moraxella catarrhalis*, and *Pseudomonas aeruginosa*. In addition, these organisms are recovered from the tracheobronchial tree of patients in their chronic, steady state, suggesting that bacteria may play a more important role in the pathogenesis of chronic COPD than in acute exacerbations.[23,24] Although molecular typing shows that recent colonization with new serotypes of the common pathogens is associated with an exacerbation, there is a possibility that this relationship is not causal.[25-27]

Environmental factors, such as air pollution, are also implicated in COPD exacerbations. Indirect evidence for this relationship is largely derived from hospitalization rates for exacerbations during periods of increased air pollution.[28] Finally, in as many as one third of all COPD exacerbations, no specific cause can be identified.[1]

In addition to acute exacerbations, patients with COPD may present with worsening symptoms related to comorbid conditions such as pneumonia, congestive heart failure (CHF), pneumothorax, pulmonary embolism, lobar atelectasis, pleural effusion, or dysrhythmias. All of these are associated with COPD and may mimic or coexist with an acute exacerbation.

CLINICAL FEATURES

Symptoms and Natural History

COPD patients have a long preclinical course during which decreases in airflow indices can be measured in the absence of symptoms. Early symptoms, such as intermittent cough or shortness of breath on exertion, may be easily misattributed to poor physical condi-

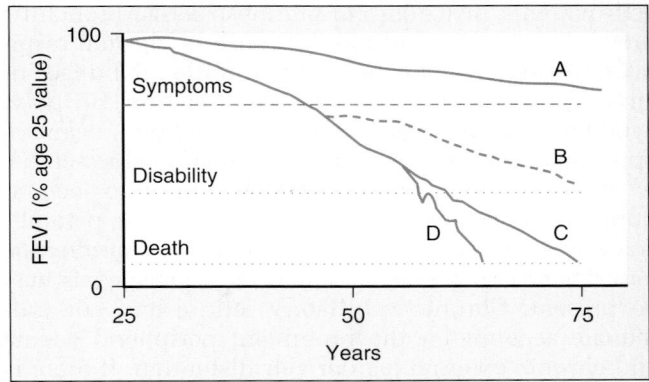

Figure 73-1. Natural history of chronic obstructive pulmonary disease (COPD) as measured by the forced expiratory volume in 1 second (FEV_1) as a percentage of the baseline value at age 25. Normal nonsmoking individuals (**A**) have a progressive loss of FEV_1 but never become symptomatic with airway obstruction. Patients with COPD who quit smoking (**B**) experience an FEV_1 decline that parallels that of a nonsmoking, age-matched person. Patients with progressive COPD (**C**) can develop a loss of FEV_1, which may eventually produce symptoms, disability, and death. Some COPD patients (**D**) have steep declines in lung function during discrete clinical episodes. (From Heffner JE: Chronic obstructive pulmonary disease on an exponential curve of progress. *Respir Care* 47:586, 2002.)

tioning. Moreover, patients may remain asymptomatic for many years by gradually limiting their activities in proportion to their pulmonary reserve. After several years, a daily productive cough frequently develops and periods of dyspnea, the cardinal symptom of airflow limitation, increase. The clinical progression of COPD is slow and insidious with gradual decreases in airflow punctuated by increasingly frequent and debilitating exacerbations. Eventually, the patient becomes truly incapacitated by dyspnea on minimal or no exertion. Profound muscle wasting and weight loss and the emergence of cor pulmonale or chronic ventilatory failure are characteristic of end-stage disease. Figure 73-1 depicts the progression of COPD over time.

Physical Examination

The division of patients with COPD into two phenotypes, the "blue bloater" (for the patient with chronic obstructive bronchitis) and the "pink puffer" (for the patient with emphysema), is outdated because many patients with COPD do not conform to these descriptions. Nonetheless, these classical images do highlight some of the important clinical features that may be encountered in the patient with COPD and have implications for management. Most patients present with some combination of chronic obstructive bronchitis and emphysema and appear with a mixture of the syndromes described subsequently. The precise identification of which process is predominant is less important than individual evaluation of each patient and formulation of a specific treatment plan based on the clinical findings. In particular, the degree of chronic hypoxemia and dependence on home oxygen therapy, the presence of cor pulmonale, and evidence of comorbid illness (especially ischemic heart disease) should be determined.

In patients in whom chronic obstructive bronchitis predominates, the findings are those of chronic respiratory failure and cor pulmonale. Little air hunger or anxiety is present, and the combination of polycythemia and hypoxemia creates a plethoric, cyanotic appearance. Cough, the clinical hallmark of bronchitis, is prominent and, when vigorous, causes expectoration. If acute ventilatory failure is present, the patient's consciousness is clouded. This condition can often be described as "irritable somnolence," and asterixis may be present. Chronic ventilatory failure and cor pulmonale account for the prominent peripheral edema and chronic external jugular vein distention. If there is relatively little emphysema, the thoracic anteroposterior diameter is normal and diaphragms are not abnormally low. The presence of severe bronchopulmonary secretions is evidenced by scattered rhonchi and rales, especially at both lung bases posterolaterally. These patients often have chronic CO_2 retention, requiring close monitoring of O_2 therapy because of their relative dependence on hypoxemic drive for ventilation.

When emphysema predominates, the patient is often thin, anxious, alert and oriented, dyspneic, tachypneic, and utilizing accessory muscles of breathing. The patient often self-administers positive end-expiratory pressure (PEEP) by using a pursed lip exhalation pattern to increase intraluminal bronchial pressure and provide internal support for bronchial walls that have lost their support externally. Such patients usually assume a sedentary existence, chronically hunched forward. Gross lung overinflation occurs, with low immobile diaphragms and an increased anteroposterior diameter of the thorax. Percussion of the chest reveals hyperresonance, and auscultation demonstrates diminished breath sounds with faint end-expiratory rhonchi. Despite air hunger caused by the extensive lung parenchyma destruction, the patient maintains adequate oxygen saturations and often has near-normal ABG levels. The heart is small and hypodynamic, and the blood pressure is usually low.

Cardiac examination in a patient with suspected COPD is crucial to diagnose cor pulmonale and coexisting left ventricular failure. A subxiphoid or retrosternal heave suggests chronic right ventricular hypertrophy, an S_4 suggests decreased left ventricular compliance, an S_3 indicates left ventricular failure, and a holosystolic blowing murmur of tricuspid insufficiency is secondary to right ventricular and tricuspid ring dilation. Accentuation of the pulmonic component of the secondary sound reflects pulmonary hypertension. Chronic visceral congestion causes hepatomegaly, hepatojugular reflux, and sometimes prominent abnormalities of liver function.

DIAGNOSTIC STRATEGIES

Pulse Oximetry and Arterial Blood Gas Analysis

Pulse oximetry is part of the evaluation and monitoring of every patient with a COPD exacerbation. Comparison with prior values, both in crisis and in baseline state, helps to interpret measurements obtained during an acute exacerbation. The change in pulse oximetry from baseline or in response to emergency therapy is generally more important than absolute levels.

The stages of COPD severity correlate with arterial gas tensions. Abnormal ventilation-perfusion relationships of COPD produce only modest decrements in the partial pressure of oxygen in arterial blood (PaO_2) in its early stages (80 to 100 mm Hg). Later in the course of the disease, hypoxemia below 60 mm Hg stimulates respiratory centers, producing hyperventilation (PCO_2 < 35) and acute respiratory alkalosis. As pulmonary dysfunction progresses, the work of hyperventilation becomes cost ineffective; that is, more carbon dioxide is produced by the effort than is cleared by the increased ventilation. Eventually, alveolar hypoventilation impairs gas exchange, leading to CO_2 retention and acute respiratory acidosis. With renal compensation through bicarbonate retention, the pH becomes normal. Finally, when acute ventilatory failure is superimposed at this stage of the disease, an elevated PCO_2, lowered pH, and elevated bicarbonate are found.

ABG measurements, once a mainstay of emergency department evaluation of COPD patients, are of limited value. A direct measurement of ABGs may be considered in patients with severe exacerbations for whom hospitalization is anticipated. The presence of respiratory failure unresponsive to therapy (defined as PaO_2 < 60 mm Hg, $PaCO_2$ > 70 mm Hg, and pH < 7.3) warrants consideration of admission to an intensive care unit, but clinical evaluation is much more important than any particular blood gas values.[1] When baseline blood gas levels are not available, the utility of the ABGs is even more limited, and interpretation should be based on the degree of acidosis present, which probably represents the extent of acute CO_2 retention. ABGs should not be used to determine whether a patient requires intubation or noninvasive ventilatory support (NIVS). These decisions should rather be guided by the overall state of the patient, progression of fatigue, comorbid illness, and response to therapy. Patients with very poor blood gas values may do well without intubation or NIVS, whereas others with mildly disturbed values may require urgent airway intervention. Thus, ABGs should not be performed routinely in the emergency department and should be undertaken only in response to specific circumstances, such as irregular or apparently unreliable pulse oximeter values.

Chest Radiography

In patients who are known to have COPD, the primary role of the chest radiograph is to determine whether there is an acute, treatable cause for clinical deterioration, especially pneumothorax or parenchymal consolidation (atelectasis secondary to mucous plugging, pneumonia, or obstruction by tumor). Otherwise, the chest radiograph is of limited use and may exhibit a range of chronic changes, depending on disease severity and the relative degree of the various pathologic processes. Findings may include hyperinflated lung fields, decreased vascular markings, and a small cardiac silhouette or, in contrast, normal inflation, with increased vascular markings and an enlarged heart.[29] In cor pulmonale, impingement on the retrosternal airspace by the enlarged right ventricle can be seen on the lateral film. Bullae may also be present and resemble or mask a pneumothorax.

In addition, chest radiography may reveal important coexistent pathology including CHF, effusions, and tumors. Routine chest radiography, although challenged, is appropriate in patients with acute exacerbations of COPD.[30-32]

Forced Expiratory Volume and Peak Expiratory Flow Rate

Pulmonary function tests are more useful in asthma, in which there is a significant reversible component of airway obstruction. Moreover, the patient in acute respiratory distress is often unable to cooperate, making testing unreliable. Thus, pulmonary function tests add little to decision making in cases of acute COPD exacerbation.

Sputum Examination

During acute exacerbations of bronchitis, sputum may be thicker and grossly purulent. Although once a routine part of the evaluation of bronchitis, Gram stain examination correlates poorly with cultures.[33] Even if the patient is severely ill, has an infiltrate clinically or on chest radiography, and is being admitted, sputum culture is of very limited value and rarely results in a change in diagnosis or therapy. Nonetheless, if superinfection with a particular etiologic agent, such as *Legionella* spp., *Mycobacterium tuberculosis*, *Pneumocystis carinii*, or a fungus is suspected clinically, sputum evaluation can be diagnostic. Thus, sputum cultures are generally not necessary in patients presenting with an acute COPD exacerbation but may be obtained in specific clinical scenarios.

Electrocardiogram and Cardiac Monitoring

The classical descriptions of P pulmonale (peaked P waves in leads II, III, and aVF), low QRS voltage, clockwise rotation, and poor R wave progression in the precordial leads are interesting correlates of COPD but are both insensitive and nonspecific. The presence of electrocardiographic (ECG) criteria for right ventricular hypertrophy suggests established cor pulmonale. These findings, however, can be easily obscured on the ECG by other processes, and the absence of criteria for right ventricular hypertrophy cannot be relied upon to rule out cor pulmonale.[34]

In severely ill patients or those with concomitant chest pain, continuous ECG monitoring may helpful, at least for the initial phase of the patient's evaluation and treatment. ECG monitoring can detect dysrhythmias associated with COPD exacerbations and changes of rate and rhythm in response to therapy. The most common dysrhythmias associated with COPD are atrial tachydysrhythmias, such as atrial fibrillation and multifocal atrial tachycardia. Although atrial fibrillation may require treatment with rate control or conversion, multifocal atrial tachycardia often resolves with the treatment of the COPD exacerbation itself.[35]

Blood Tests

Routine hematologic evaluation adds little to the management of the patient with COPD and acute exacerbation. A complete blood count may reveal polycythemia associated with chronic hypoxia. An elevated white blood cell count is nonspecific and should not be interpreted as indicative of coexistent infection. Elevations in white blood cell counts in COPD are more often related to the hyperadrenergic state of acute dyspnea. Although its use has declined markedly, if the patient is taking a theophylline preparation, a theophylline level is warranted because many patients take additional medications when their breathing deteriorates and toxicity may be seen. Patients may have symptoms or effects of theophylline toxicity even with a "normal" level because the therapeutic margin of this agent is so narrow.[36]

The measurement of B-type natriuretic peptide (BNP) is a tool to differentiate acute CHF from other disease processes, mainly COPD and asthma, that may present similarly with acute dyspnea. BNP is a naturally occurring peptide that is released by the ventricles in response to volume expansion and stretch. It plays a central role in the neurohormonal response to "unload" the ventricles in CHF through natriuresis, diuresis, vasodilation, and suppression of the renin-angiotensin system. It is a sensitive marker for both acute and chronic CHF and correlates well with the functional class of patients as well as their prognosis.[37,38] Both rapid bedside (whole blood) and plasma assays are available. Using a cutoff value of 100 pg/mL, BNP is significantly more accurate in diagnosing CHF in acutely dyspneic patients than a conventional clinical assessment by general internists and emergency physicians. As the cutoff value is lowered, the assay is more sensitive for detecting CHF but at the expense of overall accuracy.[39] Moreover, the utility of BNP is debated in patients for whom it is most likely to be helpful (e.g., those with equivocal clinical evaluations).[40] Thus, BNP measurements may be helpful in uncovering unsuspected CHF, but its role in the management of acute COPD exacerbations is yet to fully delineated.(see "Differential Considerations")

DIFFERENTIAL CONSIDERATIONS

The differential diagnosis of the acutely dyspneic and hypoxic patient is broad. The condition that is most commonly mistaken for COPD is cardiogenic pulmonary edema, which may present with dyspnea and wheezing ("cardiac asthma"). Other serious cardiac etiologies include myocardial ischemia and pericardial effusion. Important pulmonary diagnoses include pneumothorax, pulmonary embolism, pneumonia, asthma, adult respiratory distress syndrome, bronchiectasis, pulmonary fibrosis, pleural effusions, and tuberculosis. In addition, metabolic acidosis and shock may present with dyspnea and ventilatory failure.

In most cases, differentiation of COPD exacerbation from acute CHF can be made on clinical grounds. Nonetheless, a significant percentage of patients presenting to the emergency department with acute dyspnea and an established diagnosis of COPD are ultimately diagnosed with acute CHF despite having no prior history of heart failure. The addition of a BNP assay to the emergency department evaluation of such patients is likely to identify the majority in whom a new diagnosis of CHF was not suspected by the emergency physician.[41] Although this strategy would potentially result in a greater number of patients being treated in a timely fashion for CHF, because of the limited specificity of BNP measurements, it would also falsely identify a substantial number of patients as having CHF at any cutoff value used.

Conversely, because of the high negative predictive value of a very low BNP (<100 pg/mL), acutely dyspneic patients with very low BNP values despite a moderate degree of clinical suspicion for CHF are more likely to lead the emergency physician to the correct diagnosis of COPD.[42]

Because BNP can be elevated in association with right ventricular stretch, incautious interpretation of an elevated BNP may lead the clinician to favor the diagnosis of acute left-sided CHF and overlook cor pulmonale and pulmonary embolism, both critical considerations in the patient with COPD.[37] Moreover, acute CHF and COPD may coexist, and even severe elevations in BNP do not obviate the identification and treatment of acute pulmonary pathology. Thus, although BNP measurement may be helpful in the evaluation of the acutely dyspneic patient, it cannot be interpreted in isolation.

Acute pneumothorax is a common complication of COPD. This diagnosis should be actively pursued in patients presenting with worsening respiratory status, especially when its onset is abrupt. In older patients with COPD, chest pain is often absent. A small pneumothorax cannot be excluded by physical examination and can be very difficult to detect on inspiratory chest films, especially in patients with bullous emphysema. In cases in which plain films are difficult to interpret, it is appropriate to obtain a chest computed tomography (CT) scan when clinical suspicion of a pneumothorax remains high.

Patients with COPD are often sedentary and consequently at increased risk for venous thromboembolic disease.[43] The patient with cor pulmonale is at even higher risk because of increased blood viscosity, high peripheral venous pressure, and venous stasis. Pulmonary embolus (PE) should be considered when an acute exacerbation is more severe than prior episodes, particularly if deterioration occurs quickly, with no other apparent cause.[44] Unfortunately, because there is significant overlap in their patterns of presentation, differentiating a PE from a COPD exacerbation can be extremely difficult. Prophylactic measures to prevent venous thromboembolic disease are important consid-

erations in the inpatient management of patients with an acute exacerbation of COPD.

Nuclear (ventilation-perfusion) scanning is rarely of use in patients with COPD because of the extensive preexisting lung disease and the likelihood of an indeterminate scan. A negative screening test with a sufficiently sensitive D-dimer assay (enzyme-linked immunosorbent assay or whole-blood agglutination), however, is reassuring in all but high pretest likelihood situations.[45] The determination of pretest probability can be assessed using any one of several structured, validated scoring systems. If either the D-dimer is elevated or the pretest probability for PE is high, CT pulmonary angiography should be performed.[46] This requires multislice CT capability and should include indirect CT venography to evaluate the lower extremities for deep vein thrombosis.[47-51] Alternatively, lower limb duplex ultrasonography can be used if lower limb CT venography is not included in the institutional thromboembolism CT protocol. If advanced CT capability is not available, a combination of lower extremity duplex ultrasonography and nuclear scanning, seeking unmatched segmental or subsegmental perfusion defects, may be the best alternative.[46] A more detailed discussion of the diagnostic evaluation and treatment of PE can be found in Chapter 87.

Lobar atelectasis occurs as a result of mucous plugging of bronchi and can be lethal. Like pneumothorax and PE, it may arise abruptly. The chest film may show linear horizontal streaking or small flare-like shadows; more often, it is normal. A protracted course unresponsive to bronchodilators should prompt consideration of pneumothorax, PE, or atelectasis. If pneumothorax and PE are excluded, such patients often require endotracheal intubation and aggressive interventional pulmonary toilet.

Pneumonia is a common, devastating complication of COPD that leads to mortality in many patients. Its clinical appearance is more muted than that of the classically described lobar pneumonia of young adults. Classical symptoms of cough, fever, and toxicity are seen less often than the more nonspecific and subtle symptoms of malaise, weakness, decreased activity, and anorexia. Leukocytosis may or may not be present, and its presence should not be taken as indicative of infection because of its low specificity. An infiltrate may or may not be seen, and correlation with previous x-ray studies may be necessary.[52]

Rib fractures occur in patients with COPD secondary to trauma, but in patients receiving steroid therapy, they can be due to vigorous cough alone. When rib fractures are identified, secondary pulmonary contusion and pneumothorax must be also be considered. An intercostal nerve block may relieve enough discomfort to restore baseline pulmonary function.

Electrolyte disturbances, such as hypokalemia, hypomagnesemia, hypocalcemia, or hypophosphatemia, may impair the contractility of muscles.

There are other treatable chronic, *nonobstructive* pulmonary diseases. For example, bronchiectasis is an often overlooked cause of purulent expectoration. It

BOX 73-1. Causes of Acute Decompensation in the Patient with COPD

I. Acute exacerbations
  A. Infectious
    1. Viral: rhinovirus, respiratory syncytial virus, coronavirus, influenza virus
    2. Bacterial: *Haemophilus influenzae, Streptococcus pneumoniae, Moraxella catarrhalis, Pseudomonas aeruginosa*
    3. Atypical bacteria: *Chlamydia pneumoniae, Legionella*
  B. Air pollution
    1. NO_2
    2. Ozone
    3. Particulate particles
II. Other critical events
    1. Pneumothorax
    2. Pulmonary embolism
    3. Lobar atelectasis
    4. Congestive heart failure
    5. Pneumonia
    6. Pulmonary compression (e.g., obesity, ascites, gastric distention, pleural effusion)
    7. Trauma (e.g., rib fractures, pulmonary contusion)
    8. Neuromuscular and metabolic disorders
    9. Unrelated treatable chronic pulmonary disease (bronchiectasis, tuberculosis, sarcoidosis
    10. Noncompliance with prescribed treatment regimens
    11. Iatrogenic: inadequate therapy, inappropriate therapy (e.g., deleterious drugs)

BOX 73-2. General Therapeutic Guidelines for Exacerbations of Chronic Obstructive Pulmonary Disease

Life-Threatening
Address ABCs
Bag valve ventilation/preoxygenation
Intubation ± rapid sequence technique
In-line β-agonist/anticholinergic
IV corticosteroid
IV antibiotic
± IV aminophylline/theophylline

Moderate/Severe
Oxygen to maintain O_2 saturation near 90%
Nebulized β-agonist/anticholinergic
Noninvasive ventilation if severe
IV corticosteroid
IV antibiotic

Mild
Oxygen to maintain O_2 saturation near 90%
MDI or nebulized β-agonist/anticholinergic
Consider oral or IV corticosteroid
Consider oral antibiotic on discharge

It is important to consider an inciting or aggravating factor and provide specific therapy as discussed in text.
ABC, airway, breathing, and circulation; MDI, metered-dose inhaler.

may accompany and contribute to COPD exacerbations. Although its pathologic characteristic is dilation, not constriction, of airways, the secretions that accompany it may result in an obstructive component. Active tuberculosis must be considered in patients with infiltrates (not only apical), a chronic wasting course, and risk factors for active disease, such as human immunodeficiency virus (HIV) disease and homelessness. Sarcoidosis, which can arise with chronic cough and constitutional symptoms, usually causes a dry cough and may be suspected on the basis of the chest x-ray appearance.

Finally, iatrogenic causes of acute decompensation in COPD exist. Many agents may directly or indirectly produce bronchospasm, such as β-blockers and cholinergic agents. A second group of potentially deleterious drugs are sedatives. It is important not to confuse hypoxic agitation with anxiety because patients with chronic respiratory failure are abnormally sensitive to the respiratory depressant effect of sedatives and even small doses may significantly worsen hypoventilation. Box 73-1 summarizes the causes of acute decompensation in the patient with COPD.

MANAGEMENT

The only modalities that alter the progression of COPD and reduce mortality are smoking cessation and chronic oxygen therapy for those with severe disease.[53-55]

Vaccines, against both influenza and pneumococcus, are another important aspect of ongoing outpatient care. An overview of the emergency assessment and management of COPD exacerbations is provided in Box 73-2. Successful emergency department management of patients with COPD demands a sophisticated understanding of disordered pulmonary function, an ability to make a rapid and accurate clinical assessment, and skill in definitive airway and ventilation therapy.

Ventilation and Oxygenation

The most important consideration in the emergency care of the COPD patient is the severity and acuity of ventilatory compromise. All COPD patients in acute respiratory distress need continuous ECG and pulse oximetry monitoring. The patient in terminal ventilatory failure is cyanotic, speechless, lethargic, usually confused, and has gasping, ineffective respirations. Such patients require immediate endotracheal intubation and mechanical ventilation. If the patient presents in full cardiopulmonary arrest or is unconscious and unresponsive, intubation may be considered without pharmacologic adjuncts. Because these patients have exhausted all pulmonary reserve, rapid sequence technique should be performed with the goal of rapid paralysis and unconsciousness. For induction and paralysis, a combination of a hemodynamically stable sedative-hypnotic such as etomidate and a rapidly acting paralytic such as succinylcholine is an appropriate regimen.

Initial ventilator settings should include a fraction of inspired oxygen (FIO_2) of 100%, tidal volume in the 6 to 8 mL/kg range, and respiratory rate of 8 to 10 breaths/min in an assist control mode with an inspiratory flow rate of 80 to 100 L/min.[56] Sedation and neuromuscular blockade are indicated to facilitate ventilation. Increased air trapping and resultant high intra-alveolar pressures physiologically induce intrinsic PEEP (iPEEP), which can cause barotrauma. In addition, increased intrathoracic pressure decreases cardiac filling and output; therefore, peak flow pressures and systemic blood pressures must be carefully monitored. ABGs should be obtained after 15 to 20 minutes to ensure that ventilation is appropriate. In some settings, placement of an arterial line is helpful for monitoring of blood pressure and ABG tensions. After intubation, *permissive hypercapnia* is essential to the ventilatory management of these patients, and subsequent normalization of pH and P_{CO_2} should be gradual over many hours. Low volume and rate settings result in hypercapnia and respiratory acidosis, but this approach helps prevent associated barotrauma often seen in managing these patients.[57] Moreover, hyperventilation alkalosis must be scrupulously avoided, particularly because patients may have preexisting chronic metabolic alkalosis. This alkalosis can result in seizures and dysrhythmias, especially with coexisting hypokalemia.[58]

NIVS is an accepted alternative to invasive ventilation in many patients with ventilatory failure (see Chapter 2). NIVS can be highly effective in avoiding intubation, increasing pH, reducing P_{CO_2} and dyspnea in the first 4 hours of treatment, and reducing mortality.[59,60] Selection of patients for NIVS continues to be challenging, however, and there are no accepted guidelines for selection. Patients who are likely to benefit from NIVS are those with moderate to severe ventilatory failure and elevated P_{CO_2} but without marked hypoxemia. NIVS cannot substitute for invasive ventilation in patients who are hemodynamically unstable or in whom respiratory arrest appears inevitable. On the opposite end of the spectrum, it remains unclear whether NIVS should be instituted in patients with mild to moderate exacerbations. Although the Cochrane systematic review authors stress the need for early NIVS therapy to prevent the development of worsening acidosis and need for intubation, there is insufficient evidence to recommend the routine use of NIVS in mild exacerbations.[60,61] Table 73-2 outlines inclusion and exclusion criteria for the use of NIVS.

NIVS can be delivered either by a nasal or a full-face mask. Modes of ventilation include continuous positive airway pressure (CPAP) and bilevel positive airway pressure (BiPAP).[62] Patients with COPD and respiratory distress have significant iPEEP, and this acts as an inspiratory threshold for the patient, increasing the work of breathing.[63] Both modes of NIVS help to counteract iPEEP and thereby decrease the work of breathing. Nasal CPAP is a simple technique, and 5 to 10 cm H_2O pressure is required.[64] When using BiPAP ventilation, expiratory positive airway pressure is usually kept at 2 to 4 cm H_2O and inspiratory positive airway pressure at 8 to 10 cm H_2O.[65]

Table 73-2. Suggested Selection and Exclusion Criteria for the Use of Noninvasive Ventilatory Support

Selection Criteria (One or More May Be Present)	Exclusion Criteria (Any May Be Present)
Moderate to severe dyspnea with use of accessory muscles and paradoxical abdominal motion Moderate to severe acidosis (pH 7.30-7.35) and hypercapnia (P_{CO_2} 45-60 mm Hg) Respiratory rate >25 breaths/min	Respiratory arrest Cardiovascular instability Uncooperative patient (agitated or severely somnolent) Upper airway obstruction High aspiration risk Recent facial or gastroesophageal surgery Craniofacial trauma, fixed nasopharyngeal abnormalities Nonfitting mask

P_{CO_2}, partial pressure of carbon dioxide.
Adapted from Pauwels RA, et al: Global strategy for the diagnosis, management, and prevention of chronic obstructive pulmonary disease: National Heart, Lung, and Blood Institute and World Health Organization Global Initiative for Chronic Obstructive Lung Disease (GOLD): Executive summary. *Respir Care* 46:798, 2001 and Soto FJ, Varkey B: Evidence-based approach to acute exacerbations of COPD. *Curr Opin Pulm Med* 9:117, 2003.

If the patient experiences relief of dyspnea, has stronger respirations, and becomes more alert, intubation may be averted, but diligent observation for deterioration must be maintained. Increasing respiratory rate, lethargy, exhaustion, speechlessness, paradoxical abdominal breathing movements, and falling oxygen saturation despite therapy mandate invasive ventilation.

The most important factor in the decision to intubate is the patient's clinical status, not results of ABG measurements. Even in the presence of a significant rise in P_{CO_2} with oxygen administration, intubation may be unnecessary if the patient's clinical status has stabilized. Similarly, improving ABG values should not overrule the clinical impression of deterioration. Temporary improvement may be followed by exhaustion and respiratory failure. Table 73-3 outlines indications for invasive mechanical ventilation. Several of these criteria, adapted from the GOLD collaborators, are vague and subject to interpretation, underscoring the critical role of clinical judgment in airway management decisions.

An inherent anxiety exists among physicians about using oxygen therapy in patients with COPD because of the fear of inducing apnea by removing the hypoxic drive to breathe.[66,67] Although controversy surrounds the appropriate use of oxygen in exacerbations of COPD, the risks of hypoxemia need to be weighed against the risk of reducing ventilation. A patient should not be subjected to continued, severe hypoxemia, with its attendant risk of myocardial or tissue ischemia, worsening metabolic acidosis, and muscular fatigue, because of fear of reducing hypoxic ventilatory drive. A patient with severe hypoxemia requires intervention, including oxygen therapy, and if intubation is ultimately required, intubation should be undertaken. Although P_{CO_2} rises in response to oxygen therapy,

Table 73-3. Proposed Indications for Mechanical Ventilation

Respiratory arrest
Depressed level of consciousness*
Cardiovascular instability (shock, heart failure)*
Noninvasive ventilatory support failure or exclusion criteria (see Table 73-2)
Severe dyspnea with use of accessory muscles and paradoxical abdominal motion*
Severe tachypnea*
Life-threatening hypoxia
Severe acidosis and hypercapnia*
Other complications (metabolic abnormalities, sepsis, pneumonia, pulmonary embolism, barotraumas, massive pleural effusion)*

*For several of these parameters, criteria are deliberately imprecise—clinical decisions must be individualized in each case.
Adapted from Pauwels RA, et al: Global strategy for the diagnosis, management, and prevention of chronic obstructive pulmonary disease: National Heart, Lung, and Blood Institute and World Health Organization Global Initiative for Chronic Obstructive Lung Disease (GOLD): Executive summary. *Respir Care* 46:798, 2001.

minute ventilation changes little.[68,69] Thus, titrated oxygen therapy to maintain an oxygen saturation close to 90%, while avoiding an unnecessarily high FIO_2, is recommended. This can be done more reliably with the use of Venturi masks than with nasal cannulas.[61] Patients with partial correction of hypoxia, who have mild respiratory acidosis, continue to have a high respiratory drive.[70] It is the patient who is breathing inappropriately *slowly* who is at highest risk for apnea with oxygen therapy.[71]

In more compensated patients, hypoxemia is avoided by hyperventilation. Administering low-flow oxygen by nasal cannulas at 1 to 2 L/min in such patients raises the FIO_2 by a few percent, relieving the sensation of dyspnea. The patient then usually stops hyperventilating, thus reducing the work of breathing and oxygen consumption. This intervention may have significant benefits, especially in the setting of multiple comorbidities, such as myocardial ischemia or sepsis.

General Drug Therapy

Bronchodilators

Although bronchospasm is not the primary inciting event in acute COPD exacerbation, both β-agonists and anticholinergic agents are considered first-line agents. The choice of agent for a given patient may depend on the respective side effect profiles of these two classes of agents.[5,31]

Although many choices are available, inhaled albuterol, which is short acting with selective β_2-receptor action, is the β-agonist of choice. The nebulization dose of albuterol is 2.5 to 5.0 mg (0.5 to 1.0 mL of 0.5% solution). Most patients tolerate two to three rapid successive doses of oxygen-nebulized β-agonist with little difficulty. Therapy occasionally needs to be titrated if the side effects of tremor, tachycardia, or ventricular ectopy are significant. Metaproterenol is a much less commonly used alternative, in a dose of 10 to 15 mg (0.2 to 0.3 mL of 5% solution).[72]

Anticholinergic agents block muscarinic receptors and prevent smooth muscle contraction while decreasing the release of secretions from submucosal glands.[73] Nebulized anticholinergic agents are as effective as β_2-agonists in COPD and can be used alone or in conjunction with β_2-agonists as first-line therapy in acute exacerbations.[74-76] Although evidence regarding the efficacy of their coadministration is controversial, in patients with moderate to severe exacerbations presenting to the emergency department, it is recommended that they be given together for their possible synergistic effects.[1,5,31] Anticholinergics can be administered by nebulization or metered-dose inhaler (MDI) and are also effective for intubated patients. Ipratropium bromide, a quaternary ammonium compound, is extensively studied in COPD. It has few systemic effects and has powerful bronchodilating properties.[77] It is available as a nebulization solution and is prepared in MDI form as well. The nebulization dosage is 0.5 mg every 4 hours.[72]

Long-acting bronchodilator agents such as salmeterol (β2-agonist) and tiotropium (anticholinergic) have been added to treatment recommendations for chronic stable COPD. Although these agents may reduce the frequency of COPD exacerbations, their role in emergency department management of acute exacerbation is not yet known.[78]

The COPD patient with a mild to moderate exacerbation may be able to self-administer bronchodilator agents using an MDI with a spacer device, which is as effective as nebulized treatment.[79] Studies demonstrate the efficacy and cost benefit of MDI therapy over nebulization in acutely hospitalized patients. Because of the smaller dose delivered with single MDI puffs, MDI protocols often involve multiple puffs at each dosing interval. This mode of therapy should be considered only for stable cooperative emergency patients. The intubated patient should receive bronchodilator therapy by in-line nebulization.

Methylxanthines, principally aminophylline, were once prominently used in COPD exacerbations, but they do not appear to improve outcomes, even when combined with β-agonists and anticholinergic agents. Evidence does not support the routine use of methylxanthines for COPD exacerbations. Recommendations that include methylxanthines as a second-line therapy when other modalities have failed are tempered by concerns about toxicity, which may outweigh the theoretical positive effects of these agents.[80] Patients taking methylxanthines on a chronic, ambulatory basis should likewise not receive additional methylxanthines in the course of treatment of acute COPD exacerbation in the emergency department. Continuation of oral therapy, if deemed desirable to stimulate ventilation, can be undertaken on the inpatient service.

Corticosteroids

The anti-inflammatory effects of steroids provide a strong rationale for their use in acutely ill patients with COPD. Although steroids may not alter the immediate emergency department course, evidence points to a modest decrease in the relapse rate of acute exacerbations and improvement of dyspnea.[81,82] For severe exacerbations requiring admission, IV methylprednisolone may be used in a dose of 125 mg every 6 to 8 hours, and a 10-day oral prednisone course with a dose of 40 mg once daily is appropriate for discharged patients.[81,82] Inhaled steroid preparations have significantly less systemic absorption and potential for adverse effects. Although there is some evidence for their role in acute exacerbations, it has yet to be fully delineated.[83]

Antibiotics

In contrast to patients with acute bronchitis in the setting of normal lung function, COPD patients with an acute exacerbation consisting of dyspnea, increased sputum volume, and increased sputum purulence do appear to benefit from antibiotic therapy.[84] In these cases, antibiotic therapy decreases symptoms and improves respiratory function.[85,86] Furthermore, some patients may have clinical pneumonia without radiographic evidence. Because antibiotic therapy is generally benign and potentially beneficial, it should be considered for acute exacerbations in patients presenting to the emergency department.

Most of the randomized controlled trials that have shown a treatment benefit with antibiotics were performed before patterns of widespread resistance of the common bacterial pathogens. Amoxicillin, tetracycline, and trimethoprim-sulfamethoxazole were the most common antibiotics used in these studies. Although antibiotics with broader spectrum coverage such as the fluoroquinolones and third-generation cephalosporins are commonly prescribed, the evidence for the superiority of these newer agents is indirect.[30] The GOLD collaborators recommend using antibiotics that reflect local patterns of antibiotic sensitivity to *S. pneumoniae*, *H. influenzae*, and *M. catarrhalis*.[1] Azithromycin has the added advantage of once-a-day doses for only 5 days.[72] Ampicillin alone is not recommended because of high rates of resistance.[87]

For outpatient therapy of pneumonia in patients with COPD, an advanced macrolide, such as azithromycin or clarithromycin, can be used in patients who have not recently received antibiotic therapy. In patients who have recently received an antibiotic, a respiratory quinolone, such as levofloxacin, gatifloxacin, or moxifloxacin, can be used, or a beta-lactam, such as high-dose amoxicillin or a cephalosporin, can be added to the macrolide. Oral therapy should last for at least 10 days, with longer therapy (2 weeks) if *Mycoplasma* or *Chlamydia pneumoniae* is suspected. For inpatient therapy, no distinction is made for patients with COPD.[88] A more extensive discussion of antibiotic therapy in pneumonia may be found in Chapter 75.

Other Therapeutic Agents

Mucokinetic Medications and Mucus Clearance Strategies

Because mucus production and cough are cardinal symptoms of COPD, a mucokinetic medication should,

in theory, help symptoms. Unfortunately, little objective evidence exists that they are successful, and they are not recommended.[5,30,31] Nebulized water and saline and the oral expectorants guaifenesin and saturated iodide are also of no benefit[89] and chest physiotherapy may be harmful.[31]

Respiratory Stimulants

Several respiratory stimulants have been studied in patients with COPD, including opioid antagonists, progesterone, acetazolamide, doxapram, and almitrine.[90,91] Doxapram and almitrine appear to be the most effective of these agents. Although doxapram can effect small, temporary improvements in blood gas exchange in the first hours of treatment, it is less effective than other techniques, such as NIVS.[92,93] Almitrine, which may have a role in chronic therapy, does not have a role in acute respiratory failure.[94] Respiratory stimulants are therefore not recommended for routine use in the emergency department.

Heliox

Helium-oxygen mixtures decrease the work of breathing and improve airflow by virtue of their low density. Such mixtures, however, have failed to demonstrate a benefit in either ventilated or nonventilated patients with COPD exacerbations.[95]

DISPOSITION

Significant deterioration from baseline is the general guideline for admission of patients with COPD. Important factors in the decision include the presence of coexisting conditions, failed outpatient management for the current exacerbation, and lack of improvement while in the emergency department. The GOLD collaborators have proposed guidelines for admission, and these are adapted in Table 73-4. If the decision is made to discharge the patient, attention should also be directed to the patient's vaccination status, proper technique of inhaler use, evaluation of outpatient support systems, appropriate referrals, and, perhaps most important, smoking cessation.[1,96]

Table 73-4. General Guidelines for Admission of the Patient with Chronic Obstructive Pulmonary Disease

Significant worsening of symptoms from baseline
Inadequate response of symptoms to emergency department management
Significant comorbid condition (e.g., pneumonia, heart failure)
Worsening hypoxia or hypercarbia (from baseline), or both
Inability to cope at home or insufficient home resources

Adapted from Pauwels RA, et al: Global strategy for the diagnosis, management, and prevention of chronic obstructive pulmonary disease: National Heart, Lung, and Blood Institute and World Health Organization Global Initiative for Chronic Obstructive Lung Disease (GOLD): Executive summary. *Respir Care* 46:798, 2001.

KEY CONCEPTS

- COPD is a chronic disease with acute exacerbations. In contrast to asthma, it has slow recovery periods and patients do not usually show dramatic improvement with emergency department therapy.

- β-Agonists, anticholinergics, and corticosteroids are the mainstay of drug therapy of acute COPD exacerbation.

- Therapeutic advances have not matched the severity of the disease.

- Noninvasive ventilatory support is an important therapeutic option in the COPD patient with respiratory failure. It has significant advantages over traditional mechanical ventilation and should be considered when significant dyspnea, acidosis, hypercapnia, and elevated respiratory rate are present.

- Acute complications are common exacerbating factors and need consideration during evaluation. These include pneumonia, pneumothorax, and pulmonary embolism.

REFERENCES

1. Pauwels RA, et al: Global strategy for the diagnosis, management, and prevention of chronic obstructive pulmonary disease: National Heart, Lung, and Blood Institute and World Health Organization Global Initiative for Chronic Obstructive Lung Disease (GOLD): Executive summary. *Respir Care* 46:798, 2001.
2. Lopez AD, Murray CC: The global burden of disease, 1990-2020. *Nat Med* 4:1241, 1998.
3. Mannino DM: COPD: Epidemiology, prevalence, morbidity and mortality, and disease heterogeneity. *Chest* 121:121S, 2002.
4. Heffner JE: Chronic obstructive pulmonary disease: On an exponential curve of progress. *Respir Care* 47:586, 2002.
5. Soto FJ, Varkey B: Evidence-based approach to acute exacerbations of COPD. *Curr Opin Pulm Med* 9:117, 2003.
6. Wedzicha JA: Exacerbations: Etiology and pathophysiologic mechanisms. *Chest* 121:136S, 2002.
7. Barnes PJ: Mechanisms in COPD: Differences from asthma. *Chest* 117:10S, 2000.
8. Barnes PJ: Chronic obstructive pulmonary disease. *N Engl J Med* 343:269, 2000.
9. Rennard SI: Pathogenesis of COPD. *Clin Cornerstone* 5:11, 2003.
10. Blank CA, Brantly M: Clinical features and molecular characteristics of alpha 1-antitrypsin deficiency. *Ann Allergy* 72:105, 1994. Erratum in: *Ann Allergy* 72:305, 1994.
11. Hogg JC, Senior RM: Chronic obstructive pulmonary disease—Part 2: Pathology and biochemistry of emphysema. *Thorax* 57:830, 2002.
12. Turino GM: The origins of a concept: The protease-antiprotease imbalance hypothesis. *Chest* 122:1058, 2002.
13. MacNee W: Oxidants/antioxidants and COPD. *Chest* 117:303S, 2000.
14. Petty TL: COPD in perspective. *Chest* 121:116S, 2002.
15. Siafakas NM, Tzortzaki EG: Few smokers develop COPD. Why? *Respir Med* 96:615, 2002.
16. Wouters EF, Creutzberg EC, Schols AM: Systemic effects in COPD. *Chest* 121:127S, 2002.
17. Wouters EF: Chronic obstructive pulmonary disease. 5: Systemic effects of COPD. *Thorax* 57:1067, 2002.
18. Celli BR, et al: The body-mass index, airflow obstruction, dyspnea, and exercise capacity index in chronic obstructive pulmonary disease. *N Engl J Med* 350:1005, 2004.
19. Seemungal TA, Wedzicha JA: Viral infections in obstructive airway diseases. *Curr Opin Pulm Med* 9:111, 2003.
20. Greenberg SB, Allen M, Wilson J, Atmar RL: Respiratory viral infections in adults with and without chronic obstructive pulmonary disease. *Am J Respir Crit Care Med* 162:167, 2000.
21. Seemungal TA, et al: Detection of rhinovirus in induced sputum at exacerbation of chronic obstructive pulmonary disease. *Eur Respir J* 16:677, 2000.
22. Seemungal TA, et al: Time course and recovery of exacerbations in patients with chronic obstructive pulmonary disease. *Am J Respir Crit Care Med* 161:1608, 2000.
23. Sethi S: Bacterial infection and the pathogenesis of COPD. *Chest* 117:286S, 2000.
24. Hirschmann JV: Do bacteria cause exacerbations of COPD? *Chest* 118:193, 2000.
25. Hirschmann JV: New strains of bacteria and exacerbations of COPD. *N Engl J Med* 347:2077, 2002.
26. Sethi S, Evans N, Grant BJ, Murphy TF: New strains of bacteria and exacerbations of chronic obstructive pulmonary disease. *N Engl J Med* 347:465, 2002.
27. Bresser P, van Alphen L, Lutter R: New strains of bacteria and exacerbations of COPD. *N Engl J Med* 347:2077, 2002.
28. Spix C, et al: Short-term effects of air pollution on hospital admissions of respiratory diseases in Europe: A quantitative summary of APHEA study results. Air Pollution and Health: A European Approach. *Arch Environ Health* 53:54, 1998.
29. Takasugi JE, Godwin JD: Radiology of chronic obstructive pulmonary disease. *Radiol Clin North Am* 36:29, 1998.
30. Snow V, Lascher S, Mottur-Pilson C: Evidence base for management of acute exacerbations of chronic obstructive pulmonary disease. *Ann Intern Med* 134:595, 2001.
31. McCrory DC, Brown C, Gelfand SE, Bach PB: Management of acute exacerbations of COPD: A summary and appraisal of published evidence. *Chest* 119:1190, 2001.
32. Emerman CL, Cydulka RK: Evaluation of high-yield criteria for chest radiography in acute exacerbation of chronic obstructive pulmonary disease. *Ann Emerg Med* 22:680, 1993.
33. Minocha A, Moravec CL Jr: Gram's stain and culture of sputum in the routine management of pulmonary infection. *South Med J* 86:1225, 1993.
34. Harrigan RA, Jones K: ABC of clinical electrocardiography. Conditions affecting the right side of the heart. *BMJ* 324:1201, 2002.
35. McCord J, Borzak S: Multifocal atrial tachycardia. *Chest* 113:203, 1998.
36. Aitken ML, Martin TR: Life-threatening theophylline toxicity is not predictable by serum levels. *Chest* 91:10, 1987.
37. Collins SP, Ronan-Bentle S, Storrow AB: Diagnostic and prognostic usefulness of natriuretic peptides in emergency department patients with dyspnea. *Ann Emerg Med* 41:532, 2003.
38. Wang TJ, et al: Plasma natriuretic peptide levels and the risk of cardiovascular events and death. *N Engl J Med* 350:655, 2004.
39. Maisel AS, et al: Rapid measurement of B-type natriuretic peptide in the emergency diagnosis of heart failure. *N Engl J Med* 347:161, 2002.
40. Hohl CM, Mitelman BY, Wyer P, Lang E: Should emergency physicians use B-type natriuretic peptide testing in patients with unexplained dyspnea? *Can J Emerg Med* 5:162, 2003.
41. McCullough PA, et al: Uncovering heart failure in patients with a history of pulmonary disease: Rationale for the early use of B-type natriuretic peptide in the emergency department. *Acad Emerg Med* 10:198, 2003.
42. Mueller C, et al: Use of B-type natriuretic peptide in the evaluation and management of acute dyspnea. *N Engl J Med* 350:647, 2004.

43. Ambrosetti M, et al: Prevalence and prevention of venous thromboembolism in patients with acute exacerbations of COPD. *Thromb Res* 112:203, 2003.

44. Erelel M, Cuhadaroglu C, Ece T, Arseven O: The frequency of deep venous thrombosis and pulmonary embolus in acute exacerbation of chronic obstructive pulmonary disease. *Respir Med* 96:515, 2002.

45. Frost SD, Brotman DJ, Michota FA: Rational use of D-dimer measurement to exclude acute venous thromboembolic disease. *Mayo Clin Proc* 78:1385, 2003.

46. Fedullo PF, Tapson VF: Clinical practice. The evaluation of suspected pulmonary embolism. *N Engl J Med* 349:1247, 2003.

47. Kavanagh EC, O'Hare A, Hargaden G, Murray JG: Risk of pulmonary embolism after negative MDCT pulmonary angiography findings. *AJR Am J Roentgenol* 182:499, 2004.

48. Goldhaber SZ, Elliott CG: Acute pulmonary embolism: Part I: Epidemiology, pathophysiology, and diagnosis. *Circulation* 108:2726, 2003.

49. Remy-Jardin M, et al: CT angiography of pulmonary embolism in patients with underlying respiratory disease: Impact of multislice CT on image quality and negative predictive value. *Eur Radiol* 12:1971, 2002.

50. Cham MD, et al: Deep venous thrombosis: Detection by using indirect CT venography. The Pulmonary Angiography-Indirect CT Venography Cooperative Group. *Radiology* 216:744, 2000.

51. Ghaye B, Szapiro D, Willems V, Dondelinger RF: Combined CT venography of the lower limbs and spiral CT angiography of pulmonary arteries in acute pulmonary embolism: Preliminary results of a prospective study. *JBR-BTR* 83:271, 2000.

52. Melbye H, et al: Pneumonia—A clinical or radiographic diagnosis? Etiology and clinical features of lower respiratory tract infection in adults in general practice. *Scand J Infect Dis* 24:647, 1992.

53. Anthonisen NR, et al: Effects of smoking intervention and the use of an inhaled anticholinergic bronchodilator on the rate of decline of FEV1. The Lung Health Study. *JAMA* 272:1497, 1994.

54. Tarpy SP, Celli BR: Long-term oxygen therapy. *N Engl J Med* 333:710, 1995.

55. Gorecka D, et al: Effect of long-term oxygen therapy on survival in patients with chronic obstructive pulmonary disease with moderate hypoxaemia. *Thorax* 52:674, 1997.

56. Jain S, Hanania NA, Guntupalli KK: Ventilation of patients with asthma and obstructive lung disease. *Crit Care Clin* 14:685, 1998.

57. Bidani A, Tzouanakis AE, Cardenas VJ Jr, Zwischenberger JB: Permissive hypercapnia in acute respiratory failure. *JAMA* 272:957, 1994.

58. Stogner S, George R: Steps to prevent cardiac arrhythmias in acute respiratory failure. *J Crit Illness* 9:1027, 1991.

59. Peter JV, Moran JL, Phillips-Hughes J, Warn D: Noninvasive ventilation in acute respiratory failure—A meta-analysis update. *Crit Care Med* 30:555, 2002.

60. Lightowler JV, Wedzicha JA, Elliott MW, Ram FS: Noninvasive positive pressure ventilation to treat respiratory failure resulting from exacerbations of chronic obstructive pulmonary disease: Cochrane systematic review and meta-analysis. *BMJ* 326:185, 2003.

61. Keenan SP, Sinuff T, Cook DJ, Hill NS: Which patients with acute exacerbation of chronic obstructive pulmonary disease benefit from noninvasive positive-pressure ventilation? A systematic review of the literature. *Ann Intern Med* 138:861, 2003.

62. International Consensus Conferences in Intensive Care Medicine: Noninvasive positive pressure ventilation in acute respiratory failure. *Am J Respir Crit Care Med* 163:283, 2001.

63. Petrof BJ, et al: Continuous positive airway pressure reduces work of breathing and dyspnea during weaning from mechanical ventilation in severe chronic obstructive pulmonary disease. *Am Rev Respir Dis* 141:281, 1990.

64. Miro AM, Shivaram U, Hertig I: Continuous positive airway pressure in COPD patients in acute hypercapnic respiratory failure. *Chest* 103:266, 1993.

65. Meduri GU: Noninvasive positive-pressure ventilation in patients with acute respiratory failure. *Clin Chest Med* 17:513, 1996.

66. Hoyt JW: Debunking myths of chronic obstructive lung disease [editorial; comment]. *Crit Care Med* 25:1450, 1997.

67. Gomersall CD, et al: Oxygen therapy for hypercapnic patients with chronic obstructive pulmonary disease and acute respiratory failure: A randomized, controlled pilot study. *Crit Care Med* 30:113, 2002.

68. Crossley DJ, McGuire GP, Barrow PM, Houston PL: Influence of inspired oxygen concentration on deadspace, respiratory drive, and PaCO2 in intubated patients with chronic obstructive pulmonary disease. *Crit Care Med* 25:1522, 1997.

69. Dick CR, et al: O$_2$-induced change in ventilation and ventilatory drive in COPD. Am J Respir *Crit Care Med* 155:609, 1997.

70. Erbland ML, Ebert RV, Snow SL: Interaction of hypoxia and hypercapnia on respiratory drive in patients with COPD. *Chest* 97:1289, 1990.

71. Wasserman K: Uses of oxygen in the treatment of acute respiratory failure secondary to obstructive lung disease. *Monaldi Arch Chest Dis* 48:509, 1993.

72. *Physicians Desk Reference*. Montvale, NJ, Medical Economics Data Production, 2004.

73. Rosen RL, Bone RC: Treatment of acute exacerbations in chronic obstructive pulmonary disease. *Med Clin North Am* 74:691, 1990.

74. Cydulka RK, Emerman CL: Effects of combined treatment with glycopyrrolate and albuterol in acute exacerbation of chronic obstructive pulmonary disease. *Ann Emerg Med* 25:470, 1995.

75. Campbell S: For COPD a combination of ipratropium bromide and albuterol sulfate is more effective than albuterol base. *Arch Intern Med* 159:156, 1999.

76. Gross N, et al: Inhalation by nebulization of albuterol-ipratropium combination (Dey combination) is superior to either agent alone in the treatment of chronic obstructive pulmonary disease. Dey Combination Solution Study Group. *Respiration* 65:354, 1998.

77. Cordova FC, Criner GJ: Management of advanced chronic obstructive pulmonary disease. *Compr Ther* 23:413, 1997.

78. Tashkin DP, Cooper CB: The role of long-acting bronchodilators in the management of stable COPD. *Chest* 125:249, 2004.

79. Brocklebank J, Raverty S, Robinson J: Mycobacteriosis in Atlantic salmon farmed in British Columbia. *Can Vet J* 44:486, 2003.

80. Barr RG, Rowe BH, Camargo CA Jr: Methylxanthines for exacerbations of chronic obstructive pulmonary disease: Meta-analysis of randomised trials. *BMJ* 327:643, 2003.

81. Niewoehner DE, et al: Effect of systemic glucocorticoids on exacerbations of chronic obstructive pulmonary disease. Department of Veterans Affairs Cooperative Study Group. *N Engl J Med* 340:1941, 1999.

82. Aaron SD, et al: Outpatient oral prednisone after emergency treatment of chronic obstructive pulmonary disease. *N Engl J Med* 348:2618, 2003.

83. Maltais F, et al: Comparison of nebulized budesonide and oral prednisolone with placebo in the treatment of acute exacerbations of chronic obstructive pulmonary disease: A randomized controlled trial. *Am J Respir Crit Care Med* 165:698, 2002.

84. Murphy TF, Sethi S, Niederman MS: The role of bacteria in exacerbations of COPD. A constructive view. *Chest* 118:204, 2000.
85. Anthonisen NR, et al: Antibiotic therapy in exacerbations of chronic obstructive pulmonary disease. *Ann Intern Med* 106:196, 1987.
86. Saint S, Bent S, Vittinghoff E, Grady D: Antibiotics in chronic obstructive pulmonary disease exacerbations. A meta-analysis. *JAMA* 273:957, 1995.
87. Grossman RF: The value of antibiotics and the outcomes of antibiotic therapy in exacerbations of COPD. *Chest* 113:249S, 1998.
88. Mandell LA, et al: Update of practice guidelines for the management of community-acquired pneumonia in immunocompetent adults. *Clin Infect Dis* 37:1405, 2003.
89. Ferguson GT, Cherniack RM: Management of chronic obstructive pulmonary disease. *N Engl J Med* 328:1017, 1993.
90. Bardsley PA: Chronic respiratory failure in COPD: Is there a place for a respiratory stimulant? [editorial]. *Thorax* 48:781, 1993.
91. Kerr HD: Doxapram in hypercapnic chronic obstructive pulmonary disease with respiratory failure. *J Emerg Med* 15:513, 1997.
92. Greenstone M, Lasserson TJ: Doxapram for ventilatory failure due to exacerbations of chronic obstructive pulmonary disease. Cochrane Database Syst Rev CD000223, 2003.
93. Angus RM, Ahmed AA, Fenwick L, Peacock AJ: Comparison of the acute effects on gas exchange of nasal ventilation and doxapram in exacerbations of chronic obstructive pulmonary disease. *Thorax* 51:1048, 1996.
94. Gorecka D, et al: Effects of almitrine bismesylate on arterial blood gases in patients with chronic obstructive pulmonary disease and moderate hypoxaemia: A multicentre, randomised, double-blind, placebo-controlled study. *Respiration* 70:275, 2003.
95. Rodrigo G, Pollack C, Rodrigo C, Rowe B: Heliox for treatment of exacerbations of chronic obstructive pulmonary disease. Cochrane Database Syst Rev CD003571, 2002.
96. Celli BR: Standards for the optimal management of COPD: A summary. *Chest* 113:283S, 1998.

CHAPTER

74 Upper Respiratory Tract Infections

Frantz R. Melio

PHARYNGITIS (TONSILLOPHARYNGITIS)

Perspective and Principles of Disease

Tonsillopharyngitis (from this point on referred to as pharyngitis) is among the most common reasons for seeking medical attention.

Pharyngitis is an inflammatory syndrome of the oropharynx that is primarily caused by infection. Transmission is mainly through contact with respiratory secretions, but transmission through food and fomite contact is also possible. The infection tends to localize to lymphatic tissue and produces suppuration and swelling of the tonsils, tender cervical adenopathy, and fever. Occlusion of the eustachian tubes may result in secondary otitis media. Although most cases of pharyngitis are uncomplicated, the swelling may be of sufficient extent to threaten airway patency or preclude ingestion of adequate liquids, thereby resulting in dehydration. Chronic pharyngitis differs from the acute infection in that the tonsillar crypts appear to be inflamed and infected rather than the tonsils themselves.

Etiology

Viruses are responsible for most cases of pharyngitis. The etiology of bacterial pharyngitis in adults differs from that in children. Group A beta-hemolytic streptococcus (GABHS) is the most common bacterial cause of pharyngitis in children, with a peak incidence of 30%.[1,2] In adult patients, acute pharyngitis can be caused by beta-hemolytic streptococcus (all groups, 23%), *Mycoplasma pneumoniae* (9%), and *Chlamydia pneumoniae* (8%).[1,3-7]

Cultures obtained in cases of chronic or recurrent pharyngitis often grow mixed aerobic and anaerobic bacteria. Commonly isolated aerobic organisms include streptococcal species, *Staphylococcus aureus*, *Haemophilus influenzae*, and *Moraxella catarrhalis*. The anaerobic bacteria most commonly isolated include *Bacteroides*, anaerobic gram-positive cocci, and *Fusobacterium*. β-Lactamase production is extremely common in bacteria responsible for chronic pharyngitis. Epstein-Barr virus (EBV) and *Actinomyces* are also implicated as causes of chronic or recurrent pharyngitis.[1,3,8] Rare causes of bacterial pharyngitis include *Francisella tularensis* and *Yersinia enterocolitica*.[1,4]

Clinical Features

The most common symptom is pharyngeal pain that is aggravated by swallowing and may radiate to the ears. Examination usually reveals pharyngeal erythema, pharyngeal or tonsillar exudate, tonsillar enlargement, and tender cervical lymphadenopathy (Figure 74-1). Clinical differentiation of the etiologic organisms is virtually impossible.[1,3-6,9]

Viral pharyngitis is usually seen in conjunction with cough, rhinorrhea, myalgia, headache, stomatitis, conjunctivitis, exanthem, and odynophagia. Low-grade

Figure 74-1. Bilateral tonsillopharyngitis.

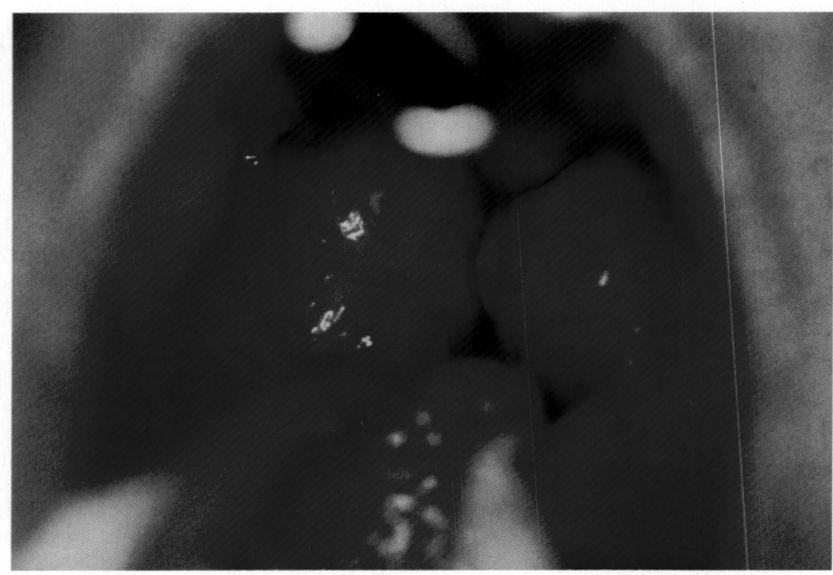

fever and white pharyngeal exudates may be present. Cervical lymphadenopathy is generally absent.[3,9,10] Mild pharyngeal edema and erythema associated with a "scratchy" throat are present in 50% of patients with the common cold. Systemic viral infections, including measles, cytomegalovirus, rubella, and human immunodeficiency virus (HIV), may initially be manifested as mild pharyngitis.[1,3,4,9] HIV pharyngitis may be clinically indistinguishable from infectious mononucleosis.[3]

Influenza occurs in epidemics and is associated with high fever, myalgia, and headache. Whereas 50% to 80% of patients with influenza experience pharyngeal discomfort, pharyngeal exudate and cervical lymphadenopathy are rare. Adenovirus may cause severe pharyngitis similar to streptococcal pharyngitis. Thirty percent to 50% of cases of adenoviral pharyngitis are associated with a follicular, usually unilateral conjunctivitis.[9] Coxsackieviruses are the most frequent cause of hand-foot-and-mouth disease and herpangitis.[3,9]

Pharyngitis is a common manifestation of infectious mononucleosis (caused by EBV) in young adults.[3,4,9,11] A tonsillar exudate or membrane (which is cheesy or creamy white) is often present. Generalized lymphadenopathy (90% to 100%) and splenomegaly (50%) are usually noted, and palatal petechiae may be present. Periorbital edema and rash are rare findings. In up to 90% of patients with mononucleosis who are inadvertently given ampicillin or amoxicillin, a diffuse macular rash develops that may be diagnosed as an allergic reaction.[3,9]

Herpes simplex also causes pharyngitis. These infections typically affect young adults. Herpes pharyngitis is characterized by painful superficial vesicles on an erythematous base. Ulcers may be present on the pharynx, lips, tongue, gums, and buccal mucosa. Pharyngeal erythema and exudate, fever, and tender lymphadenopathy are common for 1 to 2 weeks. In an immunocompromised host, large painful ulcers may be present. Herpes can be due to primary infection or reactivation. Concomitant bacterial superinfection may occur.[3,9-11]

GABHS is primarily a disease of children 5 to 15 years old and, in temperate climates, occurs in winter and early spring.[1,3] It is responsible for less than 15% of cases of pharyngitis in patients older than 15 years and rare in patients younger than 3 years. In epidemics, the incidence may double.[3,10] GABHS pharyngitis is associated with temperatures higher than 38.3° C (101° F), tonsillar exudates, palatal and uvular petechiae, uvular edema and erythema, and tender anterior cervical lymphadenopathy. Headache, nausea, vomiting, and abdominal pain may be present, especially in children. Cough, rhinorrhea, coryza, or other viral symptoms are absent. GABHS pharyngitis associated with a fine sandpaper erythematous rash that subsequently desquamates is termed *scarlet fever*. These findings, however, cannot be used to reliably diagnose or exclude streptococcal pharyngitis. Patients with recent exposure to others at risk for GABHS pharyngitis or in whom it has been diagnosed are more likely to become infected.[1-6]

Diphtheria is a potentially lethal cause of pharyngitis that is uncommon in countries in which adequate vaccinations are administered. U.S. serologic surveys show that a large percentage of adults and adolescents lack immunity to diphtheria toxin.[12] Patients have a sore throat, fever, and dysphagia. Examination early in the disease process may reveal pharyngeal erythema and isolated spots of gray or white exudate that later coalesce to form a pseudomembrane. This gray-green pseudomembrane is usually well demarcated and covers the tonsils, pharyngeal mucosa, and occasionally, the uvula. The membrane may extend to involve the larynx and lead to hoarseness, cough, and stridor. Tender and at times painful cervical lymphadenopathy may be found. Severe inflammation and edema can produce dysphonia and what is described as a "bull neck" appearance. Some strains of *Corynebacterium diphtheriae* produce a systemic toxin that may cause myocarditis, polyneuritis (at first autonomic and then peripheral), vascular collapse, diffuse focal organ necrosis, and death. Asymptomatic carriers may transmit the disease.[3,12]

Arcanobacterium haemolyticum (previously called *Corynebacterium haemolyticum*) typically affects the 10- to 30-year-old age group and can be indistinguishable from streptococcal pharyngitis. Most patients have an associated rash that may be scarlatiniform, urticarial, or erythema multiforme (occasionally skin manifestations may be the only complaint). Patients complain of a moderately severe sore throat and are usually nontoxic and afebrile. *A. haemolyticum* may cause a membranous pharyngitis that strongly mimics diphtheria; it is also associated with chronic tonsillitis.[3,4,9]

Anaerobic pharyngitis, or Vincent's angina, is characterized by superficial ulceration and necrosis that often results in the formation of a pseudomembrane. Foul-smelling breath, odynophagia, submandibular lymphadenopathy, and exudate are often present. Patients typically have poor oral hygiene.[4,8,9]

Gonococcal pharyngitis is a sexually transmitted disease that may occur independently of genital infection. Its severity is variable and it may result in an exudative or nonexudative pharyngitis. These differing manifestations can be explained in part by the lack of symptoms during the latent period of infection. Asymptomatic carriers are described, as is chronic and recurrent pharyngitis. Gonococcal pharyngitis is an important source of gonococcemia.[3,4,9,10] Syphilitic pharyngitis is a manifestation of primary or late (tertiary) syphilis and is seen as painless mucosal lesions.[10]

Tuberculous pharyngitis usually occurs in patients with advanced disease. Symptoms and signs include hoarseness and dysphagia with pharyngeal ulcerations. Candidal pharyngitis is usually found in immunocompromised adults. Patients have dysphagia, odynophagia, and adherent white plaques with focal bleeding points.[10]

Mycoplasma pneumoniae infection usually causes a mild pharyngitis. *Mycoplasma* occurs in epidemics and in crowded conditions and can be responsible for approximately 10% of cases of adult pharyngitis.[3,7,9] Pharyngeal and tonsillar exudates, cervical lymphadenopathy, and hoarseness are common. Lower respiratory tract infection may also be present.[4,7]

Chlamydia pneumoniae pharyngitis resembles *M. pneumoniae* pharyngitis. It also occurs in epidemics or crowded conditions. Severe pharyngitis with laryngitis is suggestive of *C. pneumoniae* infection. Swelling and pain in the deep cervical lymph nodes may be prominent. Lower respiratory tract and concomitant sinusitis occur. The hallmarks of chlamydial pharyngitis are recurrence and persistence.[3,4,13]

In contrast to *C. pneumoniae*, *Chlamydia trachomatis* pharyngitis is a sexually transmitted disease. Similar to gonococcal infection, *C. trachomatis* pharyngitis is associated with orogenital sex. Urogenital culturing is necessary along with treatment of sexual contacts. Patients are usually asymptomatic or may have only mild symptoms.[3,10,13]

Diagnostic Strategies

Monospot tests are positive in up to 95% of adults, 90% of children older than 5 years, 75% of children 2 to 4 years old, and 30% of children 0 to 20 months old with mononucleosis, but such tests may be negative in the first week of illness. IgM antibodies to EBV capsid antigen develop in 100% of cases. EBV nuclear antigens develop within 3 to 6 weeks and are useful if an initial negative test becomes positive at a later date. Peripheral blood smears demonstrate atypical mononuclear cells in 75% of patients, with the peak incidence occurring in the second to third week of illness.[3,9,10] Herpes pharyngitis may be diagnosed by culture, cytopathologic tests on scrapings of lesions, and serologic tests.

Diagnosis of GABHS infection is important to prevent complications, particularly rheumatic fever. Even the most experienced practitioner has difficulty clinically diagnosing streptococcal pharyngitis.[1,3-6,9] Several authors have proposed scoring systems based on clinical findings,[3-6] but the only valid method of determining acute GABHS infection is by acute and convalescent antistreptolysin O titers, which is not practical in the emergency department. A single throat culture has a sensitivity of 90% to 95% in detecting *Streptococcus pyogenes* in the pharynx. Variables that affect the accuracy of throat cultures include collection and culturing technique, as well as the recent use of antibiotics.[1,4-6,9]

Rapid diagnostic tests for GABHS (listed in order of increasing sensitivity) detect streptococcal antigens by latex agglutination, enzyme-linked immunosorbent assay, optical immunoassay, or chemiluminescent DNA probes. Rapid streptococcal tests (RSTs) have a reported specificity of 70% to 100% (with most being >95%) and a sensitivity of 31% to 100% (with most being 60% to 95%). Sensitivity and specificity in actual practice are lower than in controlled trials.[1,9] A positive RST seems to reliably indicate the presence of *S. pyogenes* in the pharynx. Patients with positive cultures or RSTs may actually be carriers who may not need treatment and are at low risk for transmission and complications. The use of RSTs in patients with clinical findings consistent with GABHS may decrease false-positive results. In contrast, RSTs are often negative in the setting of pharyngitis with a low bacterial count (these patients are still at risk for complications, including rheumatic fever). A negative RST in a child must be followed by a confirmatory culture. In adults, because of the lower incidence of GABHS and the extremely low risk for complications, confirmatory cultures of negative RSTs may not be warranted.[4-6] Pharyngitis caused by other treatable organisms must also be considered and is associated with serious complications.[1,3,5,6,9,10,12]

Confirmation of diphtheria requires culturing on the proper media. Toxigenicity testing must also be performed.[3,12] The diagnosis of *A. haemolyticum* infection should be considered if pharyngitis is accompanied by a rash, including erythema multiforme. The diagnosis of Vincent's angina is based on clinical findings and

Gram stain. Suspected gonococcal infection should be plated on Thayer-Martin agar. Tuberculous pharyngitis is diagnosed by acid-fast staining. Syphilitic pharyngitis is diagnosed by darkfield microscopy, direct immunofluorescence, and serologic testing. Candidal pharyngitis is diagnosed by noting yeast on potassium hydroxide preparations of throat swabs or Sabouraud's agar.[3,10] The diagnosis of mycoplasmal pharyngitis can be confirmed serologically or by culture. Rapid antigen tests for *Mycoplasma* are available.[7,9] Chlamydial pharyngitis can be diagnosed by serologic testing, by culture, or by antigen detection tests.[13] Studies on patients with chronic pharyngitis have found that surface cultures do not correlate well with the etiologic pathogens, which are often concealed within the tonsillar crypts.

Differential Considerations

The differential diagnosis of adult pharyngitis includes deep space infections, tumors, foreign bodies, pemphigus, Stevens-Johnson syndrome, drug reactions, allergic reactions, uvulitis, angioneurotic edema, chemical and thermal burns, esophagitis, gastroesophageal reflux disease, cricoarytenoid arthritis, thyroiditis, and epiglottitis.[6,9,10]

Management

Patients with pharyngitis should be treated symptomatically with topical anesthetic rinses or lozenges and with acetaminophen or ibuprofen. Most cases of pharyngitis are self-limited and follow a benign course.[1,2,4-6,9]

Treatment of infectious mononucleosis is supportive. Patients should be advised to avoid contact sports for 6 to 8 weeks to minimize the small risk of splenic rupture. Corticosteroids are indicated for patients with tonsillar hypertrophy that threatens airway patency, severe thrombocytopenia, or hemolytic anemia.[3,9] Acyclovir or famciclovir is indicated in immunocompromised patients with herpetic pharyngitis.[9] The use of acyclovir or famciclovir in acute pharyngitis may be beneficial.[11]

Although many studies focus on GABHS pharyngitis, proper treatment of nonstreptococcal pharyngitis can also avoid serious complications. Because clinical judgment is insufficient and rapid diagnostic tests are not always accurate and diagnose only GABHS, this disease process is often treated empirically. The choice of antibiotic for the empirical treatment of adult pharyngitis has not been fully elucidated. Some authors question whether antibiotics should be given in uncomplicated cases of non-GABHS pharyngitis. Antibiotics may modestly shorten the course of the disease process, but they are also associated with increased recurrence, increased bacterial drug resistance, decreased immune response, and patient expectations for antibiotics with subsequent episodes of pharyngitis.[1,2,4-6]

GABHS pharyngitis must be treated adequately (within 9 days) to prevent rheumatic fever. The incidence of rheumatic fever has markedly diminished with the use of antibiotics; it parallels that of GABHS,

with the peak incidence occurring in children 5 to 15 years old, less common in adults, and rare in children younger than 3 years. Patients with mild cases of GABHS pharyngitis may contract rheumatic fever. Current estimates show that rheumatic fever complicates 0.3% of cases of GABHS pharyngitis, but in epidemics the incidence increases to 3%. More troubling has been an increase in sporadic outbreaks of rheumatic fever.[4-6,9,10] The incidence and course of poststreptococcal glomerulonephritis that is caused by nephridogenic strains are unaffected by antibiotic therapy.[4-6] Antibiotic therapy is extremely effective in eradicating GABHS and its other complications. Untreated, GABHS pharyngitis is a self-limited illness that lasts 3 to 4 days. Early antibiotic treatment of streptococcal pharyngitis leads to a 13% earlier resolution of symptoms and shortens the course of illness by about 1 day. Antibiotic therapy decreases transmission. It is thought that patients no longer transmit GABHS after 24 hours of antibiotic treatment.[1,2,4-6,9,14]

There seems to be a consensus that in children, treatment of GABHS should be based on evidence of infection (positive RST or culture).[1,2,4-6,9] Diagnosis and treatment of GABHS in adults is more controversial and the subject of two expert panel recommendations.[4-6] It is agreed that antibiotics are overused in the treatment of pharyngitis, the use of clinical criteria in conjunction with RSTs improves the accuracy of RSTs, adults with negative RSTs do not require confirmatory cultures, and neither testing nor antibiotic treatment should be used in patients who are clinically at low risk for GABHS infection. Both panels agree that the most useful clinical criteria for GABHS are the Centor criteria (tonsillar exudates, tender anterior lymphadenopathy or lymphadenitis, absence of cough, and history of fever).[4-6]

The position of the Infectious Disease Society of America is that a positive throat culture or RST in addition to clinical signs and symptoms is needed to confirm the diagnosis of GABHS pharyngitis. The society stresses that clinical criteria alone are appropriate to determine which patients do not need testing but are insufficient, without bacterial confirmation, to diagnose GABHS pharyngitis.

Cooper and colleagues argue against the use of throat cultures and place strong emphasis on the Centor criteria.[6] They recommend that patients with no or one Centor criterion not be tested or treated. Patients with two or more criteria could be treated by one of three methods: test all patients and treat only those with positive RSTs; do not test and treat only patients with three or four criteria; or treat patients with four criteria, perform RSTs in patients with two or three criteria, and treat only those who have positive results.[5,6]

These recommendations apply only to immunocompetent patients with no underlying comorbid conditions or a history of rheumatic fever. They do not apply in settings of outbreaks of GABHS infection or rheumatic fever, nor are they appropriate in situations in which the endemic rate of rheumatic fever is higher than that in the United States. It is important to consider local epidemics and be prepared to revise the approach to treatment if evidence of GABHS infection or complications exists. To date, no large prospective study of either set of recommendations has been published.[4-6]

At present, the antibiotic regimen of choice in adults for GABHS pharyngitis is either a single intramuscular injection of 1.2 million U of benzathine penicillin or a 10-day course of penicillin V, 500 mg orally twice a day. Less frequent dosing is less effective in preventing rheumatic fever.[1,4-6] Intramuscular penicillin may be more effective than oral penicillin and ensures compliance, but allergic reactions are more severe as a result of procaine allergy, and treatment is more expensive. Penicillin failure is thought to be due to either noncompliance, reinfection, or the presence of β-lactamase–producing organisms.[2] Erythromycin is recommended for patients who are allergic to penicillin. A 1-g total daily dose must be given for 10 days, but dosing intervals of two, three, and four times a day are equally effective in preventing rheumatic fever. Erythromycin resistance is rare in the United States (<5%), as opposed to 60% in Japan and Finland, areas where erythromycin is used more extensively to treat pharyngitis.[1,2,4,6] Preliminary evidence suggests that once-daily amoxicillin therapy may be effective in children.[4]

Alternative regimens include cephalosporins, clindamycin, and the macrolide antibiotics. Oral cephalosporins may be more effective than penicillin in eradicating GABHS pharyngitis. Cure rates after 5-day therapy with oral cefpodoxime, cefixime, ceftibuten, cefdinir, cefadroxil, or cefuroxime may prove to be higher than after 10 days of penicillin. Azithromycin is safe and effective and requires only 5 days of once-daily therapy. Azithromycin, cefadroxil, cefixime, ceftibuten, cefpodoxime, cefprozil, and cefdinir may be given once daily. Clarithromycin given twice a day for 5 days is as effective as both penicillin and erythromycin and has fewer side effects than erythromycin does. These alternative regimens should be reserved for patients not responding to penicillin or unable to tolerate either penicillin or erythromycin.[1,2,4] Ampicillin, amoxicillin, and penicillinase-resistant penicillins generally offer no advantage in the treatment of uncomplicated streptococcal pharyngitis and are useful only when concomitant infections require additional coverage.[1,4]

Patients whose symptoms return within a few weeks of treatment may have been noncompliant with oral therapy or may have acquired a new infection (at times from asymptomatic close contacts.) Evaluation and treatment should be similar to that of the first episode, with consideration given to treatment with intramuscular penicillin. Further recurrences mandate more extensive evaluation. Pharyngeal cultures should be obtained and consideration given to evaluating and treating close contacts for GABHS infection.[4]

When diphtheria is strongly suspected on the basis of clinical findings, treatment must begin immediately. Airway collapse may occur suddenly and without warning. The mainstay of therapy is antitoxin (a horse serum product), which should be administered immediately on clinical suspicion of diphtheria. The dose of antitoxin varies widely and depends on the site of infection and the duration of symptoms. Consultation with another specialist is usually required. Antibiotics have little effect on the resolution of local infection and systemic toxicity, but they are useful in eradicating C. diphtheriae infection and preventing transmission. The antibiotic of choice is penicillin G for 5 days, followed by penicillin VK for 5 days, or erythromycin, 500 mg four times a day for 10 days. A small percentage of patients require an additional 10-day course of erythromycin for persistent infection. Rifampin, 600 mg/day for 10 days, is also effective in eradicating the carrier state of C. diphtheriae and treating erythromycin-resistant diphtheria.[3,12,15]

A. haemolyticum may be resistant to penicillin. Erythromycin, 250 mg orally four times a day for 10 days, is the treatment of choice.[3] Vincent's angina is treated with penicillin or clindamycin and rinses with an oral oxidizing agent (hydrogen peroxide).[15] Gonococcal pharyngitis is often more difficult to eradicate than genital infections. Treatment is similar to that for gonococcal urethritis and consists of ceftriaxone, 125 mg intramuscularly, or single-dose oral treatment with either ciprofloxacin, 500 mg, ofloxacin, 400 mg, or gatifloxacin, 400 mg. Concomitant treatment of chlamydial infection with a single oral dose of 1 g of azithromycin or doxycycline, 100 mg orally twice a day for 7 days, is also recommended.[3,15] Tuberculous pharyngitis is seen with disseminated disease. Patients should be isolated and treated with a multidrug regimen. Pharyngitis caused by primary syphilis is treated with 2.4 million U of benzathine penicillin (long acting), with 14 days of tetracycline or doxycycline used as an alternative. Candidal pharyngitis is treated with oral fluconazole or itraconazole. Alternative therapy includes nystatin (suspension or tablets) or oral clotrimazole for 14 days. Chronic suppression therapy with ketoconazole, clotrimazole, or fluconazole is usually required for HIV pharyngitis.[15]

M. pneumoniae is treated with erythromycin, tetracycline, or doxycycline for 7 to 14 days.[3] Chlamydial pharyngitis is treated with doxycycline, trimethoprim-sulfamethoxazole, or a macrolide antibiotic. C. pneumoniae pharyngitis should be treated for 7 to 10 days to prevent treatment failure and recurrence. C. trachomatis pharyngitis may require prolonged or repeated courses of antibiotics.[3,13]

Treatment of recurrent or chronic tonsillitis should include β-lactamase–resistant antibiotics active against aerobic and anaerobic organisms. Choices include oral cephalosporins, amoxicillin–clavulanic acid, clindamycin, penicillin, rifampin, and metronidazole with a macrolide antibiotic.[1,3]

Steroids given in conjunction with oral antibiotics in adults with acute pharyngitis may significantly shorten the duration of symptoms and provide a greater degree of pain relief without increasing complications.[16,17]

Disposition

Although most cases of pharyngitis follow a benign course, life-threatening complications can occur.

Complications often require consultation and hospital admission. Airway compromise from tonsillar enlargement, local and distant spread of infection, deep neck abscesses, necrotizing fasciitis, sleep apnea, bacteremia, sepsis, and death have all been reported.[3,4,18]

Infectious mononucleosis may lead to airway obstruction, tonsillar and peritonsillar abscess, lingual tonsillitis, necrotic epiglottitis, airway obstruction, hepatic dysfunction, splenic injury, neurologic disorders, pneumonitis, pericarditis, and hematologic disorders, including thrombocytopenia and hemolytic anemia.[3] Herpetic pharyngitis may lead to necrotizing tonsillitis, epiglottitis, and recurrent disease. Complications of *A. haemolyticum* infection include peritonsillar abscess, sepsis, and airway obstruction.[3,12]

Complications of GABHS pharyngitis can be both suppurative and nonsuppurative. Suppurative complications include peritonsillar abscess, retropharyngeal and other deep space abscesses, suppurative cervical lymphadenitis, otitis media, sinusitis, and mastoiditis. In addition, bacteremia with subsequent sepsis, osteomyelitis, empyema, meningitis, or soft tissue infections are described. Nonsuppurative complications include scarlet fever, rheumatic fever, poststreptococcal glomerulonephritis, nonrheumatic perimyocarditis, erythema nodosum, and streptococcal toxic shock syndrome. In contrast to rheumatic fever, other complications of GABHS pharyngitis have increased in incidence and severity in the last decade. A chronic carrier state of streptococcal infection exists and can persist for several months regardless of whether antibiotics are given. These patients are asymptomatic, at low risk for rheumatic fever, and not considered highly contagious. Non–group A streptococcal pharyngitis may be complicated by the same suppurative complications as group A infections. Scarlet fever and acute glomerulonephritis, but not rheumatic fever, are linked to group C and G pharyngitis.[1-4,6,18]

LINGUAL TONSILLITIS

Lingual tonsillitis is a rarely diagnosed cause of pharyngitis that usually occurs in patients who have had their palatine tonsils removed. The lingual tonsils are a collection of nonencapsulated lymphoid tissue most commonly (size and location are highly variable) located symmetrically on either side of the midline just below the inferior pole of the palatine tonsils and anterior to the vallecula at the base of the tongue. This lymphoid tissue may enlarge after puberty, repeated infection, and tonsillectomy.[19] Patients with lingual tonsillitis have a sore throat that worsens with movement of the tongue (including tongue depression) and phonation. The patient may have a classic "hot potato" voice and complain of feeling a swelling in the throat. Dysphagia, fever, respiratory distress, and stridor may be present. Chronic or recurrent lingual tonsillitis may also cause a chronic cough or sleep apnea. Physical findings are likely to show a normal-appearing pharynx with mild hyperemia. Direct or indirect laryngoscopy

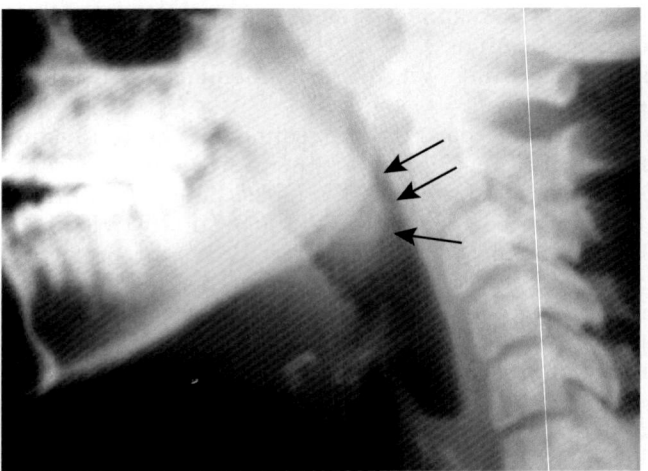

Figure 74-2. Lingual tonsillitis. Notice the "scalloped" appearance of the lingual tonsil on the anterior surface of the vallecula with a normal epiglottis and aryepiglottic fold.

reveals an edematous lingual tonsil covered with a purulent exudate. Diagnosis is aided by lateral soft tissue neck films. These films demonstrate a normal-appearing epiglottis and aryepiglottic folds, with a scalloped appearance on the anterior surface of the vallecula caused by an enlarged lingual tonsil (Figure 74-2).[19]

Management includes maintenance of airway patency, antibiotics (similar to those used in pharyngitis), and supportive therapy. Rarely, acute lingual tonsillitis may be a life-threatening condition. Airway management includes warmed humidified oxygen, hydration, and corticosteroids. Nebulized epinephrine can successfully treat the acute respiratory distress and stridor in this condition. Antibiotics of choice are similar to those used for the treatment of pharyngitis.[19]

LARYNGITIS

Laryngitis is manifested as hoarseness and aphonia. It is usually caused by viral upper respiratory tract infections. In up to 10% of cases, bacteria (including streptococci and diphtheriae) may be responsible. Other infectious causes include tuberculosis, syphilis, leprosy, actinomycosis, and fungal infections.[9] These patients should be evaluated for epiglottitis. Noninfectious causes include tumors, caustic or thermal injuries, trauma, and esophageal reflux disease.[20] Antibiotics are not indicated unless signs of bacterial infection are present.[9] Steroids may aid in decreasing the time to resolution of symptoms.[21]

ADULT EPIGLOTTITIS

Perspective

Adult epiglottitis can lead to rapid, unpredictable airway obstruction. It was first described by LeMierre in 1936. Before the introduction of *H. influenzae* vaccine, epiglottitis was primarily a pediatric disease.

Although the incidence of pediatric epiglottitis has diminished, there has been an increase in adult epiglottitis. Whether the increase is due to increased recognition or prevalence is unknown.[5,22-24]

Principles of Disease

Adult epiglottitis is a localized cellulitis involving the upper airway. There is marked involvement of the supraglottic structures, including the base of the tongue, vallecula, aryepiglottic folds, arytenoid soft tissues, lingual tonsils, and the epiglottis. Inflammation does not extend to the infraglottic regions because the submucosa is so densely adherent to the mucosa below the vocal cords. Some adults have a normal epiglottis in the setting of severe supraglottic involvement. The term *supraglottitis* is a more accurate description of this disease process. Adults with epiglottic involvement are prone to epiglottic abscesses.[22-25]

The most commonly isolated bacterial pathogen causing adult epiglottitis is type b *H. influenzae*. Only a minority of patients, however, have *H. influenzae* isolated from epiglottic or blood cultures. *H. influenzae* infection is associated with a more aggressive disease course. In many cases, no organisms can be cultured from either blood or the supraglottic structures, which suggests that respiratory viruses may play an important etiologic role. The predominant organisms isolated from epiglottic abscesses are *Streptococcus* and *Staphylococcus* species. Adult epiglottitis may also result from thermal injury.[22-24,26]

Clinical Features

Adult epiglottitis seems to have no age or seasonal prevalence. Males and smokers are more commonly affected. Adults with epiglottitis typically experience a prodrome resembling that of a benign upper respiratory tract infection. The duration of the prodrome is usually 1 to 2 days but may be as long as 7 days or as short as several hours. Patients who have a rapid onset of their disease are more likely to require airway interventions.[22-24,27]

Patients typically have dysphagia, odynophagia, and a sore throat. Pharyngeal pain may be severe and is often disproportionate to the clinical findings. Dysphonia and a muffled voice are common. Hoarseness is unusual. Fever is absent in up to 50% of cases and may develop only in the later stages of the disease. Tachycardia disproportionate to fever correlates with severe disease. Tenderness to palpation of the anterior aspect of the neck in the region of the hyoid and when moving the larynx side to side is a reliable finding in epiglottitis. Ear pain may be a manifestation of adult epiglottitis. Concomitant uvulitis, pharyngitis, tonsillitis, Ludwig's angina, peritonsillar abscess, and parotitis can occur; therefore, these findings on pharyngeal examination do not exclude the diagnosis of epiglottitis. The classic symptoms and signs of imminent airway obstruction (respiratory difficulty and stridor) may not appear until immediately before complete obstruction occurs, thus making the earlier signs of drooling and dysphonia much more compelling as

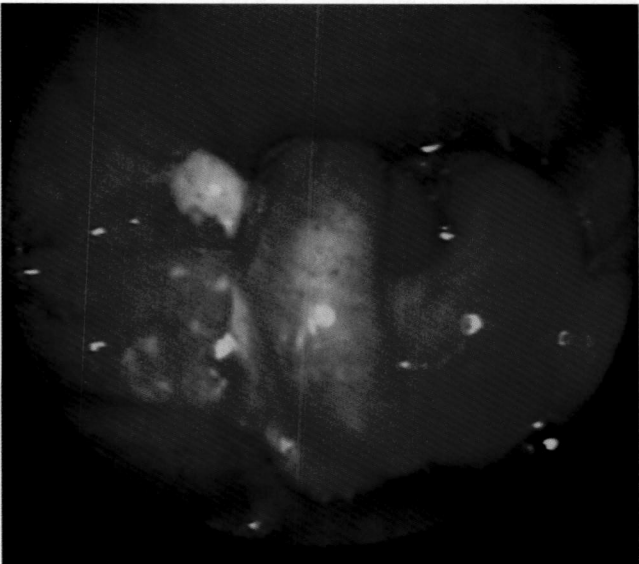

Figure 74-3. Epiglottitis.

indications to manage the airway. Patients who assume a classic sniffing position are at imminent risk for rapid airway obstruction, and immediate action is indicated. These patients should not be laid flat, and immediate preparations must be made to rapidly secure the airway (see Chapter 1).[23-25]

Diagnostic Strategies

Although severe cases of adult epiglottitis are easily recognized, a large number of less severe cases are initially misdiagnosed. In up to a third of adult patients, epiglottitis is present but not diagnosed within 48 hours of admission.[5]

Adult patients without respiratory distress should undergo direct or indirect laryngoscopy, but preparations should include the ability to provide immediate bag/mask ventilation, intubation, or cricothyrotomy because infrequently, laryngospasm and complete obstruction can occur during instrumentation of the inflamed airway. Flexible fiberoptic laryngoscopy provides direct visualization of the airway while serving as a guide for intubation. Laryngoscopy reveals a swollen epiglottis and surrounding structures (Figure 74-3). The epiglottis may appear "cherry red" but is often pale and edematous. In patients with respiratory distress, drooling, aphonia, or stridor, indirect laryngoscopy is contraindicated and direct laryngoscopy should be undertaken only as part of a "double setup" with the ability to proceed immediately to cricothyrotomy.[23-27]

Lateral cervical soft tissue x-ray films have a sensitivity up to 90% when compared with direct laryngoscopy; however, normal soft tissue x-ray films do not exclude adult epiglottitis. Adults with suspected epiglottitis and normal soft tissue x-ray films should undergo laryngoscopy. Radiologic findings include obliteration of the vallecula, swelling of the arytenoids and aryepiglottic folds, edema of the prevertebral

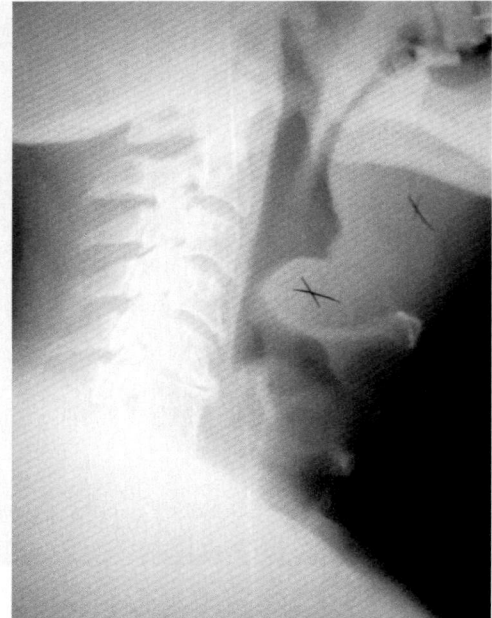

Figure 74-4. Radiograph of epiglottitis.

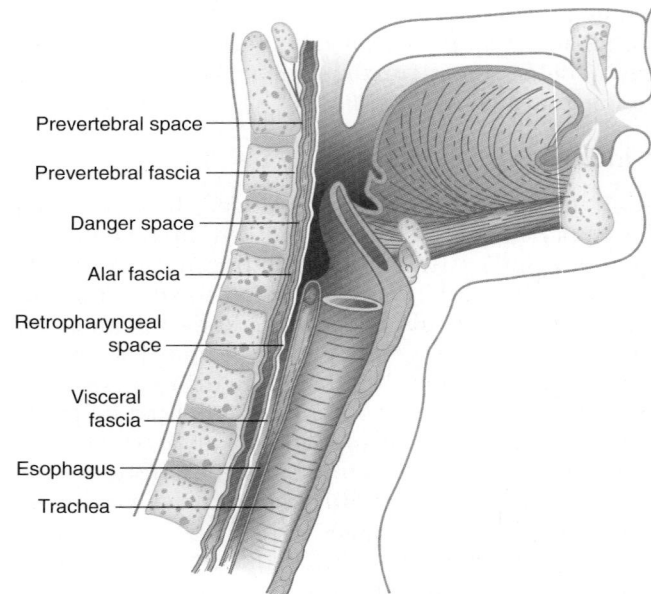

Figure 74-5. Lateral view of the neck showing the relationship of fascia to the prevertebral, "danger," retropharyngeal, and submandibular space.

and retropharyngeal soft tissues, and "ballooning" of the hypopharynx and mesopharynx. The edematous epiglottis appears enlarged and thumb shaped (Figure 74-4). An epiglottic width greater than 8 mm or an aryepiglottic fold width greater than 7 mm is suggestive of epiglottitis.

Differential Considerations

Adult epiglottitis is often misdiagnosed as streptococcal pharyngitis. Other entities that must be considered include mononucleosis, deep space abscesses, lingual tonsillitis, diphtheria, pertussis, and croup. Noninfectious considerations include angioedema, allergic reactions, foreign body aspiration, laryngospasm, tumors, toxic inhalation or aspiration, and laryngeal trauma.

Management

Adults with epiglottitis should be treated with extreme care because of the possibility of unpredictable sudden airway obstruction. Both orotracheal and laryngoscope-guided nasotracheal intubation have been reported to be safe and efficacious.[25-27] Blind nasotracheal intubation can lead to airway obstruction and is contraindicated in the setting of epiglottitis. Endotracheal intubation should always be performed under direct visualization. Intubation can be performed over a fiberoptic laryngoscope with direct visualization of the vocal cords at the time of diagnosis. Be prepared for immediate cricothyrotomy when intubation is attempted. Whenever possible, definitive airway control should be performed in the operating room.

Antibiotics should be initiated against *H. influenzae* and other likely bacterial pathogens. First-line agents pending culture and sensitivity results are cefotaxime and ceftriaxone. Alternative antibiotics include ampicillin-sulbactam and trimethoprim-sulfamethoxa-

zole.[15,16] The role of steroids and racemic epinephrine is unresolved.[23-26]

Disposition

Stable patients without respiratory distress can be safely monitored continuously without intubation. Such patients include those with mild swelling on laryngoscopy and without drooling, stridor, or dyspnea. Care should be taken with patients who have a rapidly progressive course, are immunocompromised or diabetic, or have an epiglottic abscess or significant epiglottic enlargement on x-ray study or laryngoscopy.[22-24]

Extraepiglottic infections are less likely to occur in adults than children. Meningitis, retropharyngeal abscess, pneumothorax, empyema, pneumonia, sepsis, acute respiratory distress syndrome, necrotizing fasciitis, mediastinitis, and pulmonary edema are reported in conjunction with epiglottitis.[25,26] Adults can contract epiglottitis after contact with children who have *H. influenzae* type b meningitis. Mortality in adults is higher than in children, probably because of misdiagnosis and undertreatment.[23,24]

DEEP SPACE INFECTIONS OF THE LOWER PART OF THE FACE AND NECK

Patients with deep space infections of the head and neck (Figure 74-5) are in danger of rapid decompensation. The incidence and complications of deep space infections have decreased dramatically because of improved dental hygiene and the advent of antibiotics.[28] Airway distortion and trismus may complicate intubation attempts. Neuromuscular blockade is generally ill advised, unless as part of a "double setup" with the ability to proceed directly to cricothyrotomy, because both intubation and bag/mask ventilation may be impossible. Awake techniques are preferable. Fiberoptic-guided endoscopic intubation can be useful in this setting.[29-31] Blind nasotracheal intubation can cause abscess rupture and further compromise and is thus contraindicated.[30,31] Cricothyroidotomy is generally the procedure of choice, except in some cases of Ludwig's angina, where anatomic distortion may necessitate tracheostomy.

The submandibular space is formed by the fasciae of the lower part of the face. This space is a conglomerate of two spaces, the sublingual and submaxillary spaces. Clinically, these two spaces function as a single space. The submandibular space is involved in Ludwig's angina.[28,31] Five potential communicating spaces in the neck are clinically relevant: the peritonsillar, parapharyngeal, retropharyngeal, "danger," and prevertebral spaces. The peritonsillar space is not a true space because it is not contained within fascial planes. The parapharyngeal space contains the carotid artery, the jugular vein, the cervical sympathetic chain, and cranial nerves IX through XII. The retropharyngeal space lies in the midline (medial to the parapharyngeal space) and extends from the base of the skull to the superior mediastinum (at about the level of T2). The superior constrictor muscle adheres to the prevertebral fascia and forms a raphe in the medial aspect of the retropharyngeal space. Therefore, retropharyngeal abscesses tend to occur lateral to the midline.

Posterior to the retropharyngeal space lies the "danger space," which extends from the base of the skull to the diaphragm. The prevertebral space extends from the base of the skull to the coccyx. Danger space and prevertebral abscesses are located in the midline. Infections in the retropharyngeal, danger, and prevertebral spaces have easy access to the mediastinum.[28,32,33]

The primary pathologic process of deep space infection is regional cellulitis. The fasciae may confine infections within their boundaries, thereby leading to abscess formation. There is little resistance to spread of infection within the fascial planes and spaces, thus allowing for rapid spread of infection.

PERITONSILLITIS (PERITONSILLAR CELLULITIS AND PERITONSILLAR ABSCESS)

Perspective

Peritonsillar cellulitis and abscess should be regarded as the clinical continuum of peritonsillitis. Peritonsillar abscess, also termed *quinsy*, is the most common deep infection of the head and neck in adults.

Principles of Disease

Peritonsillitis may occur as a result of acute tonsillitis. Infection in either Weber's glands or the tonsillar crypts invades the peritonsillar tissues and thereby leads to cellulitis and abscess formation. Fibrous fascial septa divide the peritonsillar space into compartments and direct the infection anteriorly and superiorly.[34]

Dental infections, chronic tonsillitis, infectious mononucleosis, smoking, chronic lymphocytic leukemia, and tonsilloliths are predisposing factors. Peritonsillar abscess occurs in patients who have undergone complete tonsillectomy and is seen in all age groups. Peritonsillitis recurs in up to 50% of patients, with the incidence of recurrent peritonsillar abscess being approximately 10%. The highest incidence of recurrence is seen in patients younger than 40 years and those with a history of chronic tonsillitis.[35,36]

Most peritonsillar abscesses are polymicrobial, with a mixture of aerobic and anaerobic organisms. The etiologic agents resemble those involved in pharyngitis. The most common aerobes cultured are *S. pyogenes* (GABHS), *Streptococcus milleri*, *H. influenzae*, and *Streptococcus viridans*. The most common anaerobic isolates are *Fusobacterium*, *Bacteroides*, *Peptostreptococcus*, and *Actinomyces* species. In patients receiving antibiotics in whom peritonsillar abscesses develop, fewer aerobic bacteria are found, particularly streptococcal species, and more β-lactamase–producing organisms are isolated.[35,37,38]

Clinical Features

There is often a delay of 2 to 5 days between abscess formation and local and systemic symptoms. Symptoms include odynophagia, dysphagia, drooling, trismus, and referred otalgia. Patients may have a characteristic muffled, "hot potato" voice and rancid breath. Systemic signs include fever, malaise, and dehydration. Patients often relate a history of recurrent tonsillitis with multiple trials of antibiotics but without resolution of symptoms.[34,35]

Examination of the pharynx may be limited by trismus. Physical findings of peritonsillitis include inflamed and erythematous oral mucosa, purulent tonsillar exudates that obscure the tonsil, and tender cervical lymphadenopathy. Peritonsillar cellulitis mimics peritonsillar abscess. Peritonsillar abscess is characterized by a greater frequency of drooling, trismus, and dysphagia, whereas peritonsillar cellulitis is more commonly bilateral. The distinguishing feature of peritonsillar abscess is inferior medial displacement of the infected tonsil (at times involving the soft palate), with contralateral deviation of the uvula (Figure 74-6). The abscess is generally unilateral and located in the superior pole of the tonsil. Bilateral peritonsillar abscesses occur occasionally.[37,39]

Diagnostic Strategies

Aspiration of pus establishes the diagnosis of peritonsillar abscess. Because patients with peritonsillar abscess have a 20% incidence of mononucleosis, laboratory confirmation should be considered.[36,40]

Roentgenographic examination in uncomplicated cases contributes little to the diagnosis. Contrast-enhanced computed tomography (CT) and ultrasonography (both intraoral and transcutaneous) aid in differentiating peritonsillar abscess from cellulitis, especially when patients are unable to cooperate with needle aspiration. These modalities are also useful in

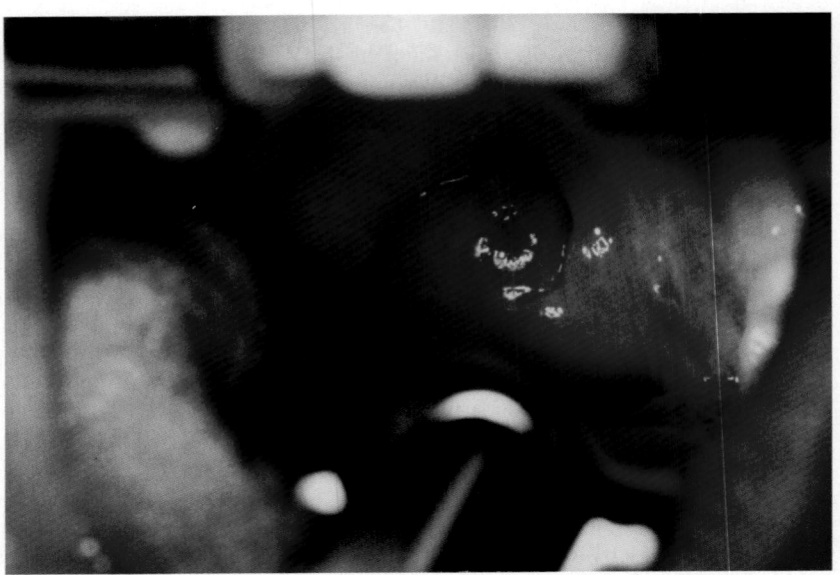

diagnosing posteriorly and inferiorly located abscesses and in guiding needle aspiration.[34,39,41]

Differential Considerations

The differential diagnosis of peritonsillitis includes hypertrophic tonsillitis, infectious mononucleosis, tubercular granuloma, diphtheria, other deep space infections of the neck, cervical adenitis, congenital or traumatic internal carotid artery aneurysms, foreign bodies, and neoplasms.[34]

Management

Emergency abscess aspiration is necessary in cases of complete or impending airway obstruction. Peritonsillar cellulitis may be controlled by intravenous antibiotics alone. Penicillin is the antibiotic of choice, with erythromycin and other macrolides reserved for patients with penicillin allergies.[36,38,40] Other regimens include the addition of metronidazole to penicillin, cefoxitin, amoxicillin–clavulanic acid, clindamycin, and the combination of penicillin and rifampin.[15] β-Lactamase–producing bacteria and poor penetration of antibiotics into the abscess limit the effectiveness of antibiotics. Drainage of the abscess is curative. Patients with peritonsillar abscess who fail to improve with penicillin and proper drainage may benefit from a trial of a penicillinase-resistant antibiotic.[36,38,40]

Classically, surgical treatment (immediate tonsillectomy or incision and drainage) was recommended for the treatment of peritonsillar abscess.[35] Needle aspiration of abscesses by both emergency physicians and otolaryngologists is diagnostic (although false-negative aspirations occur in approximately 10% of cases and another 10% may require repeated aspirations), less painful, and easier to perform, and it immediately relieves symptoms and is more cost-effective than incision and drainage.[35,36,40,41] Intraoral ultrasound-guided needle aspiration is a useful adjunct in the presence of

trismus.[41] Immediate tonsillectomy under general anesthesia may be needed in extremely young or uncooperative patients.[37]

Disposition

Hospital admission is required for patients who have underlying disease; are dehydrated, toxic appearing, unable to tolerate oral fluids, or in severe pain; or have other complications. The most dangerous immediate complication of peritonsillitis is pharyngeal obstruction with upper airway compromise. Other complications include abscess rupture and pulmonary aspiration leading to pneumonia, empyema, and pulmonary abscess formation. Infection can spread contiguously to the parapharyngeal and retropharyngeal spaces. Ludwig's angina, mediastinal involvement (including mediastinitis, pneumonia, empyema, and pericarditis), myocarditis, carotid artery erosion, jugular vein thrombophlebitis, septic embolization, abscess formation, Lemierre's syndrome (postanginal septicemia), and cervicothoracic necrotizing fasciitis can complicate peritonsillitis. Intracranial extension of peritonsillitis may result in meningitis, cavernous sinus thrombosis, and cerebral abscess. Systemic complications also include dehydration and sepsis.[34]

LUDWIG'S ANGINA

Perspective and Principles of Disease

Ludwig's angina is a cellulitis first described in 1836 and a potentially fulminant disease process that can lead to death within hours.[30,31,42]

Ludwig's angina is a progressive cellulitis of the connective tissues of the floor of the mouth and neck that begins in the submandibular space. Dental disease is the most common cause of Ludwig's angina. An infected or recently extracted lower molar is noted in most affected patients.[30,31,42] Dentoalveolar abscesses easily break through the relatively thin cortex of the mandible below the mylohyoid ridge and infect the submandibular space. Other causes of Ludwig's angina include a fractured mandible, foreign body or laceration in the floor of the mouth, tongue piercing, traumatic intubation and bronchoscopy, secondary infections of an oral malignancy, osteomyelitis, otitis media, submandibular sialoadenitis, peritonsillar abscess, a furuncle, infected thyroglossal cyst, and sepsis.[31,42-44]

Ludwig's angina is most commonly a polymicrobial disease of mixed aerobic-anaerobic bacteria of oral origin. The most frequently isolated organisms are streptococci, staphylococci, and *Bacteroides* species. Other organisms include *H. influenzae*, *Pseudomonas aeruginosa*, *Klebsiella* species, and *Candida albicans*.[31,42,43,45]

Clinical Features

Infection of the sublingual and submaxillary spaces leads to edema and soft tissue displacement, which may result in airway obstruction.[30,31,42,43] The most common symptoms in patients with Ludwig's angina include dysphagia, odynophagia, neck swelling, and neck pain.[31,42] Other symptoms include dysphonia, a "hot potato" voice, dysarthria, drooling, tongue swelling, pain in the floor of the mouth, restricted neck movement, and sore throat.[31,42,43] Patients should be questioned regarding recent dental extraction and disease. A foul taste in the patient's mouth, feeling air release at the time of extraction, rapid development of crepitus, and unilateral pharyngitis in patients who have recently undergone tooth extraction may be early clues to the diagnosis of Ludwig's angina.

The most common physical findings in Ludwig's angina are bilateral submandibular swelling and elevation or protrusion of the tongue. Other findings include elevation of the floor of the mouth, posterior displacement of the tongue, and a "woody" consistency of the floor of the mouth. The combination of tense edema and brawny induration of the neck above the hyoid may be present and is described as a "bull neck." Marked tenderness to palpation of the neck and subcutaneous emphysema may be noted. Trismus and fever are usually present, but generally no palpable fluctuance or cervical lymphadenopathy. Tenderness to percussion may be elicited over the involved teeth.[30,42,43]

Diagnostic Strategies

The clinical diagnosis of Ludwig's angina is based on five criteria: cellulitis with little or no pus present in the submandibular space; bilateral cellulitis; gangrene present with serosanguineous, putrid fluid; involvement of connective tissue, fascia, and muscles, but sparing of glandular tissue; and cellulitis spread by continuity and not by lymphatic vessels.[44] Gram stain with culture and sensitivity testing of drained fluid and pus should be performed. Soft tissue x-ray films of the neck may confirm the diagnosis by showing swelling of the affected area and airway narrowing and by identifying gas collections. Panorex and dental films may demonstrate associated periodontal abscess and other disease.[42,43] Chest radiography, CT, and magnetic resonance imaging (MRI) may aid in the diagnosis of mediastinitis and other thoracic complications. Ultrasonography is useful in diagnosing abscesses and edema in the setting of Ludwig's angina.[31,42]

Differential Considerations

The differential diagnosis includes deep cervical node suppuration, peritonsillar and other deep neck space abscess, parotid and submandibular gland abscess, oral carcinoma, angioedema, submandibular hematoma, and laryngeal diphtheria.

Management

Asphyxiation is the most common cause of death in patients with Ludwig's angina.[30,42] Airway impairment may occur suddenly. Stridor, tachypnea, dyspnea, inability to handle secretions, and agitation are all indicative of impending airway compromise. Fiberoptic-guided oral or nasotracheal intubation is the preferred method of airway control. Endotracheal intubation may be difficult because of distortion of the upper airway, trismus, pooled secretions, an inability to displace the tongue into the submandibular space, and a tendency for the development of laryngospasm.[30,42] Cricothyrotomy may be difficult and opens tissue planes that increase the risk of spreading infection into the mediastinum, but it is the procedure of choice if fiberoptic intubation is not available.[29]

Emergent antibiotic regimens include high-dose penicillin with metronidazole, or cefoxitin. Alternately, clindamycin, ticarcillin-clavulanate, piperacillin-tazobactam, or ampicillin-sulbactam may be used.[15,42] The value of corticosteroids in the setting of Ludwig's angina is unclear.[45]

Surgical incision plus drainage was the therapy of choice in the preantibiotic era. With the exception of dental extractions, surgery is reserved for patients who do not respond to medical therapy and those with crepitus and purulent collections.[29-31,42]

Disposition

Mortality caused by Ludwig's angina is less than 10% with early aggressive antibiotic therapy and adequate protection of the airway.[30,31,42,43] Infection can easily spread into other deep spaces of the neck and into the thoracic cavity and cause empyema, mediastinitis, mediastinal abscess, and pericarditis. Aspiration may lead to pneumonia and the formation of lung abscesses. Other reported complications are internal jugular vein thrombosis, carotid artery infection and erosion, bacteremia and sepsis, pneumoperitoneum, subphrenic abscess, cervicothoracic necrotizing fasciitis, and spontaneous pneumothorax.[31,42]

RETROPHARYNGEAL AND PREVERTEBRAL SPACE ABSCESSES

Perspective and Principles of Disease

Retropharyngeal swelling reflects expansion of either the retropharyngeal, danger, or prevertebral spaces. This discussion refers to infections in these spaces collectively as retropharyngeal abscesses.

Retropharyngeal abscess was previously a disease of childhood, with 96% of cases occurring in patients younger than 6 years. Adults are now increasingly affected. Children younger than 4 years have prominent retropharyngeal lymph nodes that may become infected and lead to retropharyngeal cellulitis and abscess formation. The increased use of antibiotics to treat pharyngitis in children has led to a declining incidence of retropharyngeal abscess in this age group. These retropharyngeal nodes atrophy after 4 to 6 years of age, and thus the incidence and pathophysiology of this entity differ in adults.[46-49]

In adult patients, cellulitis develops in the retropharyngeal area.[46] Once the retropharyngeal space is involved, the infection spreads rapidly and an abscess may form. Nasopharyngitis, otitis media, parotitis, tonsillitis, peritonsillar abscess, dental infections and procedures, upper airway instrumentation, endoscopy, lateral pharyngeal space infection, and Ludwig's angina are all implicated in the development of retropharyngeal abscess.[47,48,50] Other causes include blunt and penetrating trauma (usually from foreign bodies, commonly fish bones), ingestion of caustic substances, vertebral fractures, and hematologic spread from distant infection.[47,48,51] Vertebral osteomyelitis and diskitis may lead to infection of the prevertebral space. Danger space infections are caused by extension of infection from either the retropharyngeal or prevertebral spaces. Underlying systemic disorders (e.g., diabetes and depressed immune system) may predispose individuals to retropharyngeal infections.[47,51]

Retropharyngeal abscesses are most commonly polymicrobial with a mixture of aerobes and anaerobes.[47,48] Although tuberculosis was the most frequent cause of retropharyngeal abscess in the past, it is now rarely reported in the United States. *Staphylococcus* is currently the most common cause of pyogenic vertebral osteomyelitis leading to the formation of retropharyngeal abscess.[52] Disseminated coccidioidomycosis may also cause retropharyngeal abscess. The source is usually direct extension of vertebral body osteomyelitis in which the intervertebral disk is spared, unlike tuberculosis.

Clinical Features

Patients typically have a sore throat, dysphagia, odynophagia, drooling, a muffled voice, neck stiffness, neck pain, and fever. Dysphonia is usually present and is described as a duck "quack" *(cri du canard).* Patients may complain of feeling a lump in their throat. Patients with a retropharyngeal abscess may appear quite ill and generally prefer to hold their necks extended and remain in the supine position. This position will keep the swollen posterior pharynx from compressing their upper airway. Forcing the patient to sit may lead to increased dyspnea.[47,49,51]

Physical examination may reveal tender cervical lymphadenopathy, tender cervical musculature, neck swelling, torticollis, and often a high fever. Trismus may be present and make visualization of the pharynx difficult. In cases of retropharyngeal cellulitis, diffuse edema and erythema of the posterior pharynx are present.[46-48,51] Once an abscess develops, palpation of the pharynx may demonstrate a unilateral mass if the retropharyngeal space is affected and a midline mass if the abscess is in the prevertebral or danger space. Palpation of a fluctuant mass is unreliable and carries a risk of inadvertent rupture of the abscess.[46] Tenderness on moving the larynx and trachea side to side (tracheal "rock" sign) is commonly present. A retropharyngeal abscess may also cause pain in the back of the neck or shoulder that is precipitated by swallowing. Cold abscesses (caused by tuberculosis) are characterized by insidious onset, chronicity, constitutional symptoms, and less of a febrile response. Symptoms disproportionate to the findings should prompt further evaluation.[51]

Diagnostic Strategies

Diagnosis rests on the clinical findings and lateral cervical radiographs, CT, and MRI (Figure 74-7). Inspiratory lateral neck films often demonstrate thickening of the retropharyngeal soft tissues with forward displacement of the larynx and esophagus.[33,50] The soft tissue

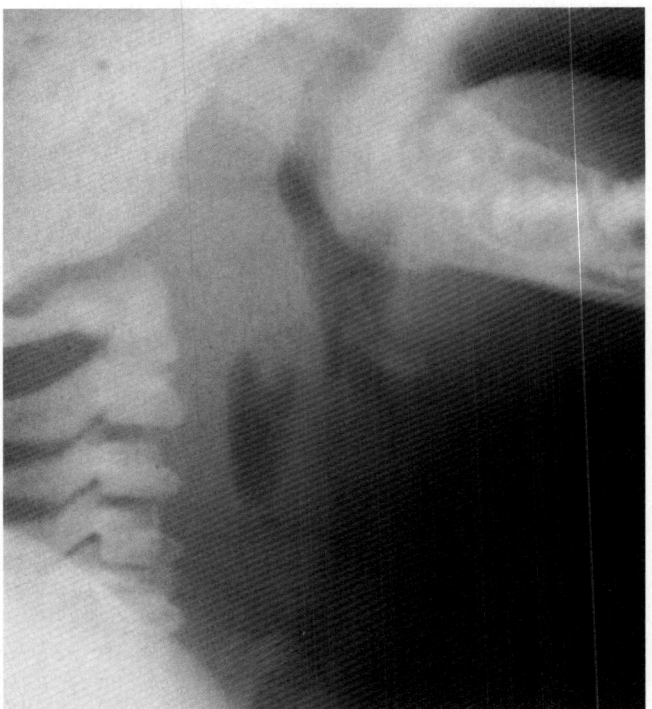

Figure 74-7. Radiograph of a retropharyngeal abscess demonstrating retropharyngeal soft tissue swelling.

swelling may be diffuse in the case of cellulitis or more focal if an abscess cavity is present. A pathologic process should be suspected if the retropharyngeal space on lateral neck films (measured from the anteroinferior aspect of the second vertebral body to the posterior pharyngeal wall) is wider than 7 mm in both children and adults or the retrotracheal space (measured from the anteroinferior aspect of the sixth vertebral body to the posterior pharyngeal wall) is more than 14 mm in children and 22 mm in adults. True lateral films with the neck fully extended during deep inspiration are the most reliable. Other radiographic findings include reversal of the normal lordosis of the cervical spine, air-fluid levels in the abscess cavity, foreign bodies, and vertebral body destruction. Chest radiographs should be obtained to determine whether mediastinal extension has occurred. The retropharyngeal space and complications of retropharyngeal abscess are well illustrated by CT and MRI.[33]

Plain films may not be sufficiently sensitive to diagnose retropharyngeal abscess. CT or MRI should be performed in these instances. These studies will not only aid in the diagnosis and differentiation between cellulitis and abscess but will also determine the extent of the disease process and the presence of complications (Figure 74-8).[33,47,48,50,52] Ultrasonography is useful for differentiating retropharyngeal cellulitis from retropharyngeal abscess.[46]

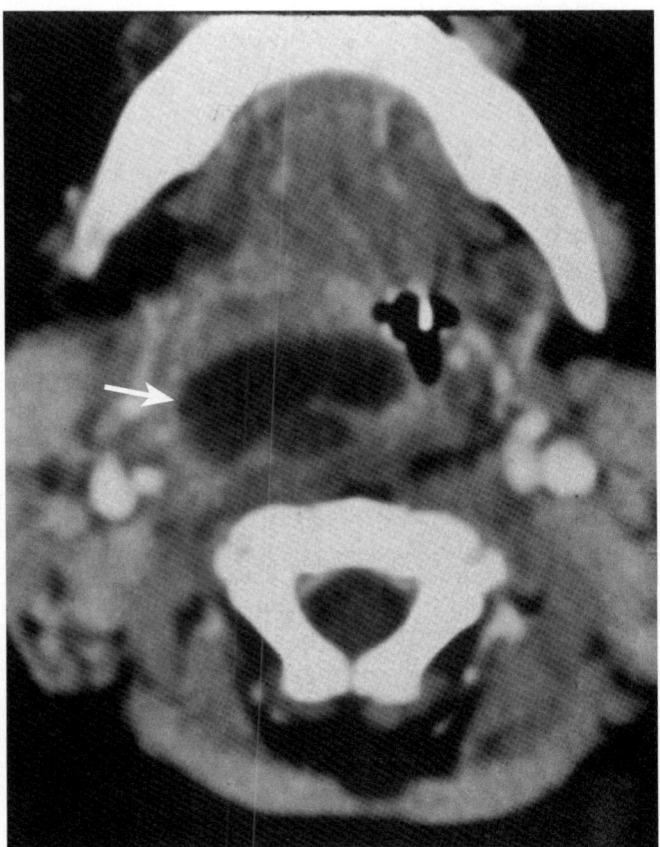

Figure 74-8. Computed tomographic scan demonstrating a right-sided retropharyngeal abscess (*arrow*).

Differential Considerations

The differential diagnosis includes retropharyngeal tumors, foreign bodies, inflammation, hematoma, aneurysms, hemorrhage, lymphadenopathy, and edema. Other considerations include tendinitis of the longus colli muscle and retropharyngeal thyroid tissue.[33]

Management

Patients with retropharyngeal cellulitis are best treated with intravenous antibiotics. Appropriate regimens are similar to those used for Ludwig's angina. Tuberculosis and fungal infections must also be considered. Resolution of retropharyngeal cellulitis is possible without surgical intervention.[46,49,51,53]

Retropharyngeal abscess is generally treated with antibiotics in conjunction with incision and drainage of the abscess by a specialist familiar with the procedure and complications. In selected cases, retropharyngeal abscess can be treated successfully only with antibiotics. Cold abscesses should only be drained extraorally, unless the patient is in acute respiratory distress.[49,53]

Neck immobilization may be necessary in patients with vertebral body destruction caused by osteomyelitis or atlantoaxial separation. These patients need neurosurgical or orthopedic evaluation and may require internal or external fixation.

Disposition

Patients with a retropharyngeal abscess should be admitted to a monitored hospital bed after a thorough airway evaluation or sent directly to the operating suite. Airway compromise can be caused by anterior displacement of the pharyngeal tissues. Pulmonary complications include abscess rupture with aspiration and subsequent pneumonia, empyema, and asphyxiation. Extension of the infection along tissue planes and through other deep spaces may lead to mediastinitis and mediastinal abscess formation, pericarditis, pleuritis, and empyema.[47,51] In addition, abscesses may track into the back of the neck and into the axilla.[52] Vascular complications occur from the extension of the retropharyngeal abscess into the lateral pharyngeal space.[51] Atraumatic atlantoaxial separation is due to damage to the transverse ligament of the atlas by the abscess. These patients may have neurologic symptoms and a widened predental space on plain films. The diagnosis is made radiologically and may include a CT scan and flexion-extension plain films. Acute transverse myelitis and epidural abscesses are also reported, both resulting in quadriplegia. Other complications include erosion into the esophagus and auditory canal, necrotizing fasciitis of the neck, acute respiratory distress syndrome, sepsis, and death.

PARAPHARYNGEAL ABSCESS

Perspective

The parapharyngeal space, also known as the lateral pharyngeal and pharyngomaxillary space, is divided into two compartments by the styloid process. The anterior compartment contains connective tissue, muscle, and lymph nodes. The carotid sheath (which contains the carotid artery, internal jugular vein, vagus nerve, cranial nerves IX through XII, and the cervical sympathetic chain) runs in the posterior compartment.

Principles of Disease

Odontogenic and pharyngotonsillar infections are the most common causes of parapharyngeal space abscesses. Parapharyngeal space infections can also arise from contiguous spread from other surrounding deep neck space infections.[54,55] Other causes include parotitis, sinusitis, spread from infected neck tumors, infected branchial cleft cysts, suppuration of local lymphadenitis, iatrogenic introduction of organisms during a mandibular nerve block or anesthesia for tonsillectomy, nasal intubation, tooth extraction, chronic otitis with cholesteatoma, and mastoiditis.[54,55]

Parapharyngeal abscesses are most often polymicrobial infections. Abscesses of odontogenic origin are caused by organisms similar to those found in Ludwig's angina.[54] Parapharyngeal abscesses originating from pharyngeal infections are caused by mixed flora similar to those responsible for the formation of peritonsillar and retropharyngeal abscesses.[54]

Clinical Findings

Pain and swelling of the neck are the most common complaints. Odynophagia is present in most patients. A history of an antecedent sore throat may be elicited in some patients. Torticollis caused by irritation of the sternocleidomastoid muscle is also reported.[54]

The classic physical findings of infection involving the anterior compartment of the parapharyngeal space are medial tonsillar displacement and posterolateral pharyngeal wall bulging.[54] Other findings include fever, trismus (caused by irritation of the muscles of mastication), edema, and swelling at the angle of the jaw. An erythematous, tender, nonfluctuant swelling at the angle of the mandible is a consistent finding in patients with an anterior parapharyngeal abscess.[54]

Involvement of the posterior space is associated with many of these same signs. If the anterior compartment is spared, however, little or no trismus occurs. Instead, posterior displacement of the tonsillar pillar and retropharyngeal swelling may be present.

Diagnostic Strategies and Differential Considerations

The diagnosis of parapharyngeal abscess is suggested by the presence of a severe sore throat with the characteristic physical findings just described. Blood cultures are usually sterile unless jugular vein thrombophlebitis is complicating the parapharyngeal space infection. Lateral radiographs may show upper prevertebral soft tissue swelling but are often not helpful.[54] Ultrasonography, CT, and MRI are more useful in diagnosing parapharyngeal abscess and its complications

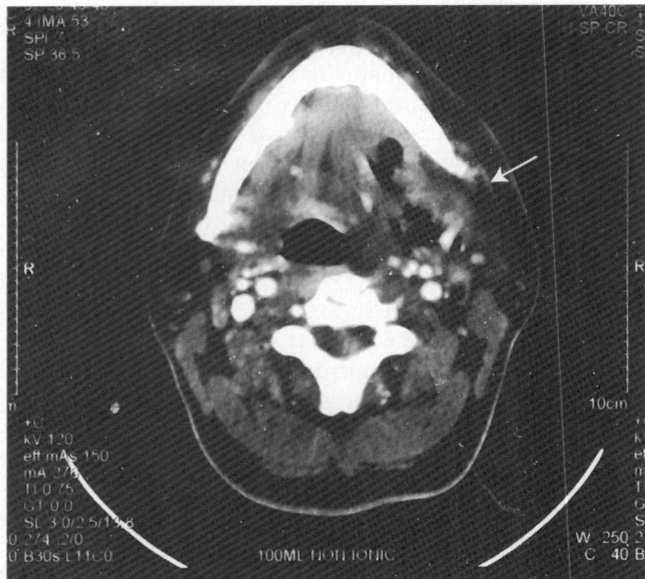

Figure 74-9. Computed tomographic scan demonstrating a left parapharyngeal abscess (*arrow*).

(Figure 74-9).[54,55] Angiography, Doppler flow studies, and magnetic resonance angiography may also be helpful in evaluating vascular complications.[55]

The differential diagnosis includes infections in other deep spaces of the neck, tumors and metastatic lymph nodes, thyroiditis, branchial cleft cyst, and carotid artery aneurysms.

Management

Treatment must be aggressive and usually consists of intravenous antibiotics and referral to an otolaryngologist for surgical drainage of the abscess cavity. Appropriate antibiotic regimens are discussed in the treatment of Ludwig's angina. Intravenous antibiotics alone will cure parapharyngeal space infections in selected patients and should be started on an emergency basis.[53,54,56] Successful resolution is reported with high-dose intravenous antibiotics and repeated CT-guided aspiration, although hospitalization is significantly prolonged when compared with treatment by early surgical incision and drainage.[54]

Disposition

Complications of a parapharyngeal abscess can be fatal. Local complications include airway obstruction and abscess rupture with subsequent aspiration, pneumonia, and empyema. Infection can spread to surrounding spaces and into the mediastinum and pericardium. Such spread may lead to mediastinitis, mediastinal abscess, pericarditis, myocardial abscess, and empyema. Other complications include osteomyelitis of the mandible, cervicothoracic necrotizing fasciitis, parotid abscess, cavernous sinus thrombosis, and meningitis.[8]

Posterior parapharyngeal space infections are particularly dangerous. These infections may affect the cervical sympathetic chain, carotid artery, or internal jugular vein. Ipsilateral Horner's syndrome and neuropathies of cranial nerves IX through XII may occur. Carotid artery erosion may lead to hemorrhage and the formation of aneurysms. Oral, nasal, and aural warning bleeding is common with carotid artery erosion, with aural bleeding being particularly ominous. Any unexplained bleeding associated with parapharyngeal or other deep neck space infection should be investigated thoroughly. Persistent peritonsillar swelling despite resolution of the parapharyngeal abscess or a tender unilateral pulsatile mass may indicate an arterial aneurysm. Aspiration or incision of a carotid artery aneurysm thought to be a parapharyngeal abscess may have disastrous complications.[55]

Involvement of the internal jugular vein may lead to septic thrombosis and Lemierre's syndrome.[57] This entity, also called postanginal septicemia, affects primarily young healthy patients and is easily confused with right-sided endocarditis or aspiration pneumonia. The manifestation is one of a pharyngitis that initially improves but is then followed by severe sepsis. It is thought that the pharyngeal infection spreads to the parapharyngeal space and causes septic thrombophlebitis of the jugular vein. Patients are usually ill appearing and febrile. Metastatic infections involve primarily the lung and are manifested by bilateral nodular infiltrates, pleural effusion, and pneumothorax. Septic arthritis, osteomyelitis, soft tissue cellulitis and abscesses, meningitis, and a vesiculopustular rash are also reported as a result of septic embolization. Leukocytosis and elevated bilirubin and liver function test values, with and without hepatomegaly and jaundice, are often present. Albuminuria, hematuria, and elevations in serum creatinine and blood urea nitrogen are reported. Septic shock rarely develops, although acute respiratory distress syndrome, transient coagulopathies, and hypotension commonly occur. The most frequent cause of this entity is *Fusobacterium* (primarily *Fusobacterium necrophorum*), although *S. aureus* is the most common pathogen in intravenous drug users. Treatment consists of parenteral antibiotics. Jugular vein ligation and resection are necessary in patients with uncontrolled sepsis and respiratory failure caused by repeated septic pulmonary emboli. The value of anticoagulation is unknown.[55,57]

SINUSITIS

Perspective and Principles of Disease

Sinusitis ranks as one of the most common afflictions of Americans. It is estimated that 0.5% to 2% of viral upper respiratory tract infections are complicated by sinusitis.[58]

The paranasal sinuses (frontal, maxillary, ethmoid, and sphenoid) are named for the facial bones with which they are associated. Pneumatization may involve other bones but represents extension from the main sinus.[59] The maxillary sinus is triangular, with its base being the lateral nasal wall and its apex extending into the zygoma. The ethmoid sinus, commonly divided into anterior and posterior portions, is composed of between two and eight anterior air cells and one to eight posterior cells. The blood supply to the ethmoid cells directly connects with the ophthalmic vessels and cavernous sinus. Infectious processes in this sinus are dangerous because of their ability to spread to the orbit or central nervous system.[59]

The frontal sinus has quite variable pneumatization ranging from extensive to totally aplastic. The left and right frontal sinuses are separated by a bony septum. The paired sphenoid sinuses are also separated by a bony septum. The optic nerve and carotid artery occupy the lateral walls of the sphenoid sinus.[59] The maxillary, anterior ethmoid, and frontal sinuses drain into the medial meatus, located between the inferior and middle nasal turbinates. This area is named the ostiomeatal complex and is the focal point of sinus disease. The posterior ethmoid sinus drains into the superior meatus and the sphenoid sinus just above the superior turbinate.[60]

A healthy sinus depends on a patent ostium with free air exchange and mucus drainage. A healthy sinus is sterile and does not accumulate mucus. Viral upper respiratory tract infections and allergic rhinitis are the most common causes of ostial obstruction with resultant sinusitis. Ciliary abnormality or immobility inhibits drainage and is another important cause of sinusitis. Ciliary dysfunction can be temporary (e.g., upper respiratory infection) or permanent (e.g., syndromes associated with cilial structural abnormalities). Infection leads to increased mucus viscosity, thus further impeding drainage. Once drainage is compromised, resorption of air within the sinus lowers oxygen tension, and increased metabolism lowers the pH. Bacteria are introduced into the sinus by coughing and nose blowing. These processes lead to increased inflammation and bacterial overgrowth. Other factors predisposing to sinusitis include immunocompromised status, nasal septal deviation and other structural abnormalities, nasal polyps, nasal tumors, trauma and fractures, rhinitis medicamentosa, rhinitis secondary to toxic mucosal exposure, barotrauma, foreign bodies, nasal cocaine abuse, and instrumentation (including nasogastric and nasotracheal intubation).[58]

It is important to distinguish infectious from allergic sinusitis. Allergic sinusitis is associated with sneezing, itchy eyes, allergen exposure, and previous episodes.[61] Approximately 90% of patients with colds have an element of viral sinusitis. Viral infection does play a role in acute sinusitis.[58] *S. pneumoniae*, nontypable *H. influenzae*, and *M. catarrhalis* are the primary pathogens responsible for acute bacterial sinusitis. Anaerobic bacteria, streptococcal species, and *S. aureus* are more prominent causes of chronic sinusitis.[62,63] Fungi also have a role in chronic sinusitis.[64,65] *P. aeruginosa* is associated with sinusitis in the setting of HIV infection and cystic fibrosis. *Rhizopus*, *Aspergillus*, *Candida*, *Histoplasma*, *Blastomyces*, *Coccidioides*, and *Cryptococcus* species, as well as other fungi, may cause sinusitis, primarily in immunocompromised hosts.[58,66]

Clinical Features

Acute sinusitis typically progresses over a period of 7 to 10 days. During the first 5 to 7 days of illness, it may be difficult to differentiate viral from bacterial sinusitis. Bacterial disease is suggested by worsening symptoms after 5 days, persistent symptoms after 10 days, or "double sickening," which refers to patients with a cold who improve initially, only to have worsening sinus congestion and discomfort.[60,67] Patients may experience a variety of symptoms, including nasal congestion, mucopurulent nasal discharge, nasal obstruction, postnasal drip (which may lead to coughing), pressure over the involved sinus, malaise, and fever.[68] Patients usually have facial pain or headache over the involved sinus. The exception is sphenoid sinusitis, which may cause vague headaches and focal points almost anywhere in the head. Maxillary sinusitis may be seen with pain over the zygoma, in the canine or bicuspid teeth, or periorbitally. Ethmoid sinusitis can cause medial canthal pain and periorbital or temporal headaches.[67,68]

Purulent nasal discharge, maxillary tooth or facial pain (especially when unilateral), unilateral maxillary sinus tenderness, and "double sickening" are good indicators of bacterial disease.[67] Chronic sinusitis is slow in onset, prolonged in duration (greater than 12 weeks), and recurrent in frequency. Symptoms may be similar to those of acute disease, but they may also include chronic cough, fetid breath, laryngitis, bronchitis, and worsening asthma.[60,61,67,69]

Physical examination is best performed after the application of a topical decongestant. Mucosal erythema and edema are usually present. Purulent discharge from the nasal meatus may be observed if the sinus ostia are not completely obstructed. Head positioning may be useful in differentiating the sinus involved. Pain caused by ethmoid, sphenoid, and frontal sinusitis is exacerbated by placing the patient supine and relieved by positioning the patient's head in an upright position. The reverse is generally seen in cases of maxillary sinusitis.

Invasive fungal sinusitis (mucormycosis) is an aggressive opportunistic rhinocerebral infection that affects immunocompromised hosts. Mucormycosis *(Rhizopus)* is generally associated with fever, localized nasal pain, and cloudy rhinorrhea. On examination, the affected tissue (usually the turbinates) appears gray, friable, anesthetic, and nonbleeding because of infarction caused by mucormycotic angioinvasion. In advanced cases the affected tissues are necrotic and black, and the infection spreads beyond the sinus.[62]

Diagnostic Strategies

Both nasal and nasopharyngeal cultures correlate poorly with cultures of sinus aspirates and cultures obtained at the time of open antrostomy.[58,61,67] Culture and biopsy are indicated for chronic bacterial and fungal sinusitis. Radiographic examination should be limited to questionable diagnoses, to unresponsive disease, or to investigation of complications. The accuracy of plain films is much higher for maxillary sinusi-

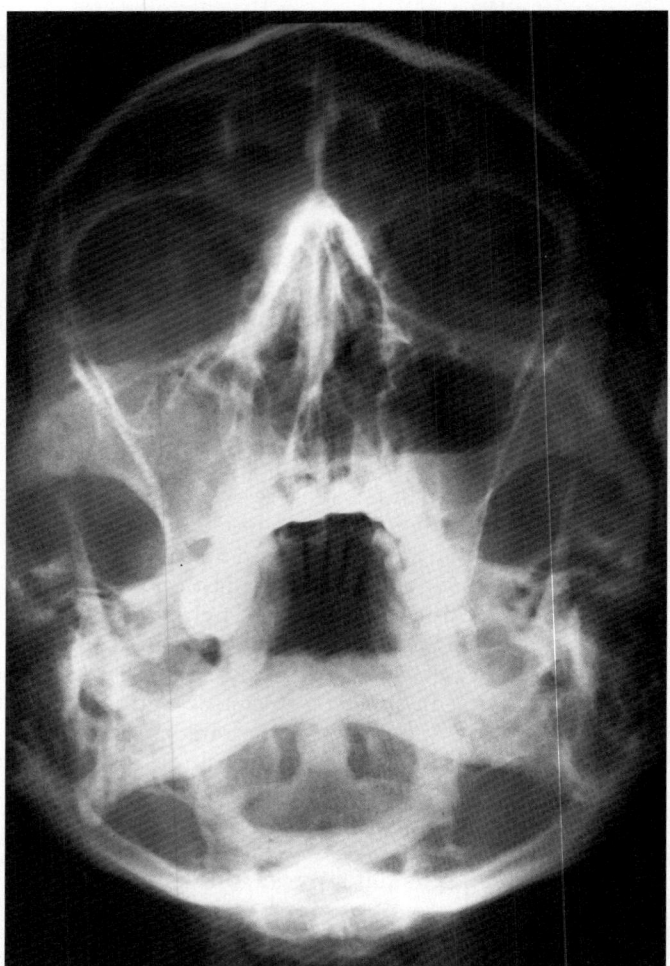

Figure 74-10. Radiograph showing right maxillary sinus opacification and a left maxillary sinus air-fluid level.

tis than for the other sinuses. A Waters view alone can evaluate the maxillary sinus but may miss pathologic conditions in other sinuses (Figure 74-10). Positive findings on plain films include sinus opacity, an air-fluid level, or mucosal thickening of 6 mm or more. The diagnostic accuracy of plain films is limited because opacity may represent other processes, including tumor. The gold standard of sinus imaging is axial and coronal CT scans. CT findings suggestive of sinusitis include air-fluid levels, sinus opacification, sinus wall displacement, and 4 mm or greater of mucosal thickening (Figure 74-11). Intravenous contrast may be required to evaluate central nervous system or orbital complications. In some centers, CT scanning with a limited number of cuts is used in place of plain films, with little difference in cost or radiation exposure. CT is sensitive, though not specific. Incidental sinus mucosal thickening is seen in about 40% of asymptomatic patients, and abnormal CT findings can also be noted in just half of patients with seasonal allergies. MRI is also helpful in distinguishing sinus disease and its complications. Sinus endoscopy is useful for specialist evaluation of sinus pathology.[58,62,67,70]

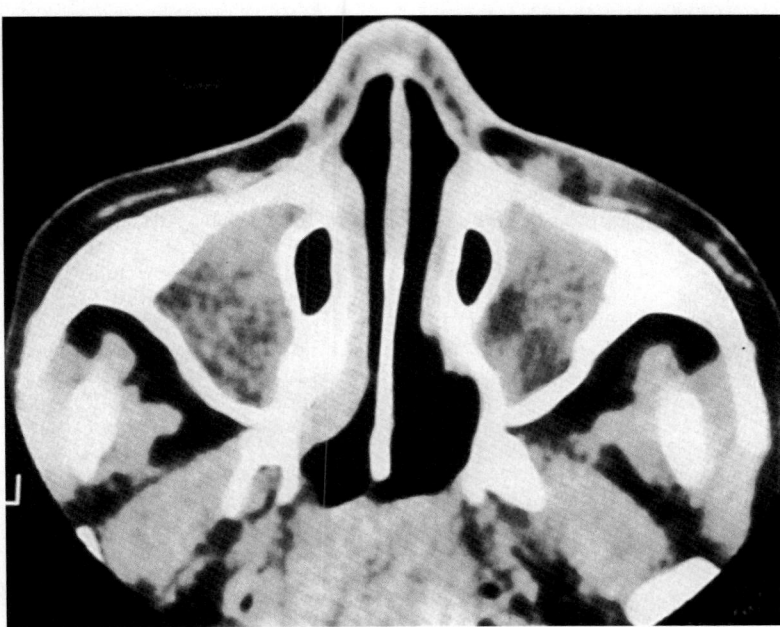

Figure 74-11. Computed tomographic scan showing bilateral maxillary sinus opacification.

CHAPTER 74 Upper Respiratory Tract Infections

Differential Considerations

Rhinitis can be differentiated from sinusitis by the increased response of nasal obstruction to treatment, clear nasal discharge, and absence of pain. Rhinitis does not lead to ostial obstruction, and thus patients do not complain of facial pain. Tension headaches, vascular headaches, foreign bodies, dental disease, brain abscesses, epidural abscesses, meningitis, and subdural empyema may also occur in a manner similar to sinusitis.

Management

A large proportion of cases of viral and bacterial sinusitis resolve spontaneously.[60,66,67,71] For this reason, the role of antibiotics in the treatment of uncomplicated sinusitis is questioned. Antibiotics should be reserved for patients with signs and symptoms of sinusitis who are not improving after 7 days or for patients with moderate to severe symptoms strongly suggestive of sinusitis, regardless of the duration of symptoms.[67,71] The choice of antibiotics must consider β-lactamase production and multidrug-resistant pneumococci. Amoxicillin administered for 7 to 10 days is still the first-line agent, but benefits are limited and treatment failures occur in areas with a high percentage of β-lactamase–producing bacteria.[65,67] Penicillin-allergic patients may be treated with trimethoprim-sulfamethoxazole. A 3-day course of trimethoprim-sulfamethoxazole or azithromycin and decongestants may be as effective as the standard 10-day antibiotic course.[72] Failure of symptoms to resolve after 7 days of therapy necessitates a change to a broader-spectrum antibiotic. Appropriate management include a 10- to 14-day course of amoxicillin-clavulanate, cefuroxime axetil, other second- or third-generation cephalosporins, clindamycin alone or in combination with ciprofloxacin, sulfamethoxazole, azithromycin, clar-

ithromycin, or one of the fluoroquinolones. Metronidazole may be added to any of these regimens to increase activity against anaerobic organisms. Antibiotics for chronic sinusitis should be effective against anaerobic and β-lactamase–producing bacteria. Treatment of life-threatening complications requires consultation and high-dose intravenous antibiotics, including cefuroxime, ceftriaxone, or ampicillin-sulbactam.[15,60,62,63] Antifungals may be beneficial in the treatment of chronic sinusitis.[64,65]

The goal of decongestant therapy is to reduce tissue edema, facilitate drainage, and maintain patency of the sinus ostia. Although they are routinely recommended, there is no good scientific evidence that decongestants are effective. Decongestants are available in topical and systemic preparations, both of which should be used simultaneously in conjunction with appropriate antibiotics.[73] Local agents include 0.5% phenylephrine hydrochloride and 0.05% oxymetazoline hydrochloride. Topical agents should be used for only 3 to 5 days. Extended use results in rebound vasodilation and nasal obstruction, a condition termed *rhinitis medicamentosa*. Systemic oral adrenergic agonists (e.g., phenylpropanolamine or pseudoephedrine) reduce nasal blood flow and congestion. These medications should be used cautiously in patients taking tricyclic antidepressants, monoamine oxidase inhibitors, and nonselective β-adrenergic blockers.[58,62,67,72] Antihistamines should be reserved for the treatment of allergic sinusitis because these agents may impede sinus drainage. Topical steroids are indicated for chronic and allergic sinusitis.[58,62,64]

Complications

Most cases of uncomplicated acute bacterial sinusitis can be treated on an outpatient basis with systemic decongestants, topical decongestants, and oral antibiotics. Failure of definitive antibiotic therapy suggests that the patient's sinusitis has extended to the chronic stage and necessitates referral to an otolaryngologist. Treatment of chronic sinusitis requires a prolonged (3 to 6 week) course of antibiotics.

Frontal or sphenoid sinusitis with air-fluid levels may require hospitalization. A previously healthy, non-toxic patient with good home support can be treated as an outpatient but should return immediately for any signs or symptoms of complications, including severe headache, neurologic changes, or visual changes. Patients who are toxic, have a compromised immune system, or have poor home resources require hospital admission and intravenous antibiotics.[66]

Sinusitis is associated with an increased incidence of bronchitis and asthma. Complications of sinusitis can be fulminant. Sinusitis may extend to involve the bones and soft tissues of the face and orbit. Facial and peri-orbital cellulitis, periorbital abscess, optic neuritis, blindness, and orbital abscess may develop (see Figure 74-10). Patients with orbital complications may have marked swelling, decreased ocular motility, and decreased visual acuity. Sinusitis may also lead to intracranial complications. Meningitis, cavernous sinus thrombosis, epidural or subdural empyema, and brain abscess are reported. Intracranial involvement may result in headache, decreased sensorium, or focal neurologic deficits and has a rapidly progressive course. Acute fulminant fungal sinusitis requires emergency consultation and admission for intravenous antifungal therapy and aggressive surgical debridement.[58,62,67,68] Complications of mucormycosis are directly related to delay in diagnosis and treatment. This opportunistic fungal infection rapidly progresses to involve the central nervous system and is associated with high morbidity and mortality.[58,62]

KEY CONCEPTS

- A severe sore throat with surprisingly minimal findings on examination of the oropharynx suggests serious soft tissue infection such as epiglottitis, retropharyngeal abscess, or peritonsillar abscess.
- Adult epiglottitis often has symptoms disproportionate to the clinical findings.
- Peritonsillar cellulitis is difficult to differentiate from peritonsillar abscess and may require needle aspiration.
- If a retropharyngeal abscess is present, the mass is unilateral; in contrast, a midline mass suggests a prevertebral or danger space abscess.
- Posterior parapharyngeal abscess may involve the cervical sympathetic chain, carotid artery, or internal jugular vein.
- Aspiration and incision of a carotid artery aneurysm thought to be a parapharyngeal abscess may be disastrous.

REFERENCES

1. Bisno AL, et al: Diagnosis and management of group A streptococcal pharyngitis: A practice guideline. *Clin Infect Dis* 25:574, 1997.
2. Pichichero ME, Cohen R: Shortened course of antibiotic therapy for acute otitis media, sinusitis, and tonsillopharyngitis. *Pediatr Infect Dis J* 16:680, 1997.
3. Bisno AL: Acute pharyngitis. *N Engl J Med* 344:205, 2001.
4. Bisno AL, et al: Practice guidelines for the diagnosis and management of group A streptococcal pharyngitis. *Clin Infect Dis* 35:113, 2002.
5. Snow V, et al: Principles of appropriate antibiotic use for acute pharyngitis in adults. *Ann Intern Med* 134:506, 2001.
6. Cooper RJ, et al: Principles of appropriate antibiotic use for acute pharyngitis in adults: Background. *Ann Intern Med* 134:509, 2001.
7. Williams WC, Williamson HA, LeFevre ML: The prevalence of *Mycoplasma pneumoniae* in ambulatory patients with nonstreptococcal sore throat. *Fam Med* 23:117, 1991.
8. Finegold SM: Role of anaerobic bacteria in infections of the tonsils and adenoids. *Ann Otol Rhinol Laryngol Suppl* 154:30, 1991.
9. Middleton DB: Pharyngitis. *Primary Care* 23:719, 1996.
10. Vukmir RB: Adult and pediatric pharyngitis: A review. *J Emerg Med* 10:607, 1992.
11. McMillan JA, et al: Pharyngitis associated with herpes simplex virus in college students. *Pediatr Infect Dis J* 12:280, 1993.
12. Farizo KM, et al: Fatal respiratory disease due to *Corynebacterium diphtheriae*: Case report and review of guidelines for management, investigation, and control. *Clin Infect Dis* 16:59, 1993.
13. Ogawa H, Hashiguchi K, Kazuyama Y: Prolonged and recurrent tonsillitis associated with sexually transmitted *Chlamydia trachomatis*. *J Laryngol Otol* 107:27, 1993.
14. Del Mar CB, Glasziou PP, Spinks AB: Antibiotics for sore throat. *Cochrane Database Syst Rev* 4:CD000023, 2000.
15. Gilbert DN, Moellering RC, Sande MA: *The Sanford Guide to Antimicrobial Therapy*, 33rd ed. Hyde Park, Vt, Antimicrobial Therapy, 2003.
16. Marvez-Valls EG, Stuckey A, Ernst AA: A randomized clinical trial of oral versus intramuscular delivery of steroids in acute exudative pharyngitis. *Acad Emerg Med* 9:9, 2002.
17. Bulloch B, Kabani A, Tenenbein M: Oral dexamethasone for the treatment of pain in children with acute pharyngitis: A randomized, double-blind, placebo-controlled trial. *Ann Emerg Med* 41:601, 2003.
18. Shulman ST: Complications of streptococcal pharyngitis. *Pediatr Infect Dis J* 13(Suppl):S70, 1994.
19. Allen DM, Hall KN, Barkman HW: Lingual tonsillitis: An uncommon cause of airway compromise responsive to epinephrine [letter]. *Am J Emerg Med* 9:622, 1991.
20. Napierkowski J, Wong RK: Extraesophageal manifestations of GERD. *Am J Med Sci* 326:285, 2003.
21. Colton RH, Casper JK (eds): *Understanding Voice Problems. A Physiological Perspective for Diagnosis and Treatment*, 2nd ed. Baltimore, Williams & Wilkins, 1996.
22. Berger G, et al: The rising incidence of adult acute epiglottitis and epiglottic abscess. *Am J Otolaryngol* 24:374, 2003.
23. Mayo Smith MF, et al: Acute epiglottitis: An 18 year experience in Rhode Island. *Chest* 108:1640, 1995.
24. Hebert PC, et al: Adult epiglottitis in a Canadian setting. *Laryngoscope* 108:64, 1998.
25. Frantz TM, Rasgon BM, Quesenberry CP: Acute epiglottitis in adults: Analysis of 129 cases. *JAMA* 272:1358, 1994.
26. Dort JC, Frohlich AM, Tate RB: Acute epiglottitis in adults: Diagnosis and treatment in 43 patients. *J Otolaryngol* 23:281, 1994.

27. Andreassen UK, et al: Acute epiglottitis: 25 year experience with nasotracheal intubation, current management policy and future trends. *J Laryngol Otol* 106:1072, 1992.

28. Levitt GW: Cervical fascia and deep neck infections. *Laryngoscope* 80:409, 1970.

29. Dreyer AF, de Kock SE, Rantloane JL: Ludwig's angina: A case report and review. *J Dent Assoc S Afr* 45:397, 1990.

30. Shockley WW: Ludwig angina: A review of current airway management. *Arch Otolaryngol Head Neck Surg* 125:600, 1999.

31. Bansal A, Miskoff J, Lis RJ: Otolaryngologic critical care. *Crit Care Clin* 19:55, 2003.

32. Marra S, Hotaling AJ: Deep neck infections. *Am J Otolaryngol* 17:287, 1996.

33. Chong VF, Fan YF: Radiology of the retropharyngeal space. *Clin Radiol* 55:740, 2000.

34. Petruzzelli GJ, Johnson JT: Peritonsillar abscess: Why aggressive management is appropriate. *Postgrad Med* 88:99, 1990.

35. Savolainen S, et al: Peritonsillar abscess: Clinical and microbiological aspects and treatment regimens. *Arch Otolaryngol Head Neck Surg* 119:521, 1993.

36. Herzon FS: Peritonsillar abscess: Incidence, current management practices, and a proposal for treatment guidelines. *Laryngoscope* 105:1, 1995.

37. Friedman NR, et al: Peritonsillar abscess in early childhood. *Arch Otolaryngol Head Neck Surg* 123:630, 1997.

38. Kieff DA, et al: Selection of antibiotics after incision and drainage of peritonsillar abscess. *Otolaryngol Head Neck Surg* 120:57, 1999.

39. Scott PM, et al: Diagnosis of peritonsillar infections: A prospective study of ultrasound, computerized tomography and clinical diagnosis. *J Laryngol Otol* 113:229, 1999.

40. Herzon FS, Nicklaus P: Pediatric peritonsillar abscess: Management guidelines. *Curr Probl Pediatr* 26:270, 1996.

41. Blaivas M, Theodoro D, Duggal S: Ultrasound-guided drainage of peritonsillar abscess by the emergency phsysician. *Am J Emerg Med* 21:155, 2003.

42. Barakate MS, et al: Ludwig's angina: Report of a case and review of management issues. *Ann Otol Rhinol Laryngol* 110:453, 2001.

43. Finch RG, Snider GE, Sprinkle PM: Ludwig's angina. *JAMA* 243:1171, 1980.

44. Spitalnic SJ, Sucov A: Ludwig's angina: Case report and review. *J Emerg Med* 13:499, 1995.

45. Freund B, Timon C: Ludwig's angina: A place for steroid therapy in its management? *Oral Health* 82:23, 1992.

46. Ben-ami T, Yousefzadeh DK, Aramburo MJ: Pre-suppurative phase of retropharyngeal infection: Contribution of ultrasonography in the diagnosis and treatment. *Pediatr Radiol* 21:23, 1990.

47. Sharma HS, Kurl DN, Hamzah M: Retropharyngeal abscess: Recent trends. *Auris Nasus Larynx* 25:403, 1998.

48. Goldenberg D, Golz A, Joachims HZ: Retropharyngeal abscess: A clinical review. *J Laryngol Otol* 111:546, 1997.

49. Craig FW, Schunk JE: Retropharyngeal abscess in children: Clinical presentation, utility of imaging, and current management. *Pediatrics* 111:1394, 2003.

50. Boucher C, Dorion D, Fisch C: Retropharyngeal abscesses: A clinical and radiologic correlation. *J Otolaryngol* 28:134, 1999.

51. Tannebaum RD: Adult retropharyngeal abscess: A case report and review of the literature. *J Emerg Med* 14:147, 1996.

52. Bhargava SK, Gupta S: Large retropharyngeal cold abscess in an adult with respiratory distress. *J Laryngol Otol* 104:157, 1990.

53. McClay JE, Murray AD, Booth T: Intravenous antibiotic therapy for deep neck abscesses defined by computed tomography. *Arch Otolaryngol Head Neck Surg* 129:1207, 2003.

54. Sethi DS, Stanley RE: Parapharyngeal abscess. *J Laryngol Otol* 105:1025, 1991.

55. Gidley PW, Ghorayeb BY, Stiernberg CM: Contemporary management of deep neck space infections. *Otolaryngol Head Neck Surg* 116:16, 1997.

56. Sichel JY, et al: Nonsurgical management of parapharyngeal space infections: A prospective study. *Laryngoscope* 112:906, 2002.

57. Weesner CL, Cisek JE: Lemierre syndrome: The forgotten disease. *Ann Emerg Med* 22:256, 1993.

58. Gwaltney JM: Acute community-acquired sinusitis. *Clin Infect Dis* 23:1209, 1996.

59. Wagenmann M, Naclerio RM: Anatomic and physiologic considerations in sinusitis. *J Allergy Clin Immunol* 90:419, 1992.

60. Poole MD: A focus on acute sinusitis in adults: Changes in disease management. *Am J Med* 106:38S, 1999.

61. Josephson GD, Gross CW: Diagnosis and management of acute and chronic sinusitis. *Compr Ther* 23:708, 1997.

62. Kennedy DW, Gwaltney JM, Jones JG: Medical management of sinusitis: Educational goals and management guidelines. *Ann Otolaryngol Rhinol Laryngol* 167:22, 1995.

63. Brook I, et al: Microbiology and management of chronic maxillary sinusitis. *Arch Otolaryngol Head Neck Surg* 120:1317, 1994.

64. Ponikau JU, et al: Intranasal antifungal treatment in 51 patients with chronic rhinosinusitis. *J Allergy Clin Immunol* 110:862, 2002.

65. Thrasher RD, Kingdom TT: Fungal infections of the head and neck: An update. *Otolaryngol Clin North Am* 36:577, 2003.

66. Rubin JS, Honigberg R: Sinusitis in patients with the acquired immunodeficiency syndrome. *Ear Nose Throat J* 69:460, 1990.

67. Hickner JM, et al: Principles of appropriate antibiotic use for acute rhinosinusitis in adults: Background. *Ann Intern Med* 134:498, 2001.

68. Williams JW, Simel DL: Does this patient have sinusitis? *JAMA* 270:1242, 1993.

69. Low DE, et al: A practical guide for the diagnosis and treatment of acute sinusitis. *Can Med Assoc J* 156:S1, 1997.

70. Zinreich SJ: Imaging of chronic sinusitis in adults: X-rays, computed tomography, and magnetic resonance imaging. *J Allergy Clin Immunol* 90:445, 1992.

71. Snow V, et al: Principles of appropriate antibiotic use for acute sinusitis in adults. *Ann Intern Med* 134:495, 2001.

72. Williams JW, et al: Randomized controlled trial of 3 vs 10 days of trimethoprim/sulfamethoxazole for acute maxillary sinusitis. *JAMA* 273:1015, 1995.

73. Inanli S, et al: The effects of topical agents of fluticasone propionate, oxymetazoline, and 3% and 0.9% sodium chloride solutions on mucociliary clearance in the therapy of acute bacterial rhinosinusitis in vivo. *Laryngoscope* 112:320, 2002.

CHAPTER

75 Pneumonia

Gregory J. Moran and David A. Talan

PERSPECTIVE

Pneumonia is the sixth leading cause of death and the leading cause of death from infectious disease in the United States.[1] The annual incidence of community-acquired pneumonia in the United States ranges from 2 to 4 million, resulting in approximately 500,000 hospital admissions. Most cases of community-acquired pneumonia are managed in the outpatient setting, and the mortality is low (<1%), but pneumonia requiring hospitalization is associated with a much higher mortality rate (approximately 15%). Most deaths occur in elderly or immunosuppressed patients. Pneumonia remains challenging because of numerous constantly changing factors, including an expanding spectrum of pathogens, changing antibiotic resistance patterns, the availability of newer antimicrobial agents, and increasing emphasis on cost-effectiveness and outpatient management.

The epidemiology of community-acquired pneumonia is changing. As the percentage of the population older than age 65 continues to increase, the incidence of pneumonia is expected to increase. An increasing number of patients are taking immunosuppressive drugs related to treatment of malignancy, transplantation, or autoimmune disease, resulting in more cases of pneumonia due to other opportunistic pathogens. Patients with acquired immunodeficiency syndrome (AIDS) are at increased risk of infection with *Streptococcus pneumoniae, Mycobacterium tuberculosis,* or *Pneumocystis carinii.* Antibiotic resistance is more common among *S. pneumoniae* and other pathogens. In addition, the threat exists of respiratory infections due to biologic terrorism or newly recognized pathogens that have the potential to spread quickly through international travel.

Although the morbidity and mortality of pneumonia may be significant, the outcome can be improved by prompt diagnosis and initiation of appropriate therapy.[2] Identification of a specific etiology of pneumonia is extremely difficult within the time frame of an emergency department visit. Even after a thorough inpatient evaluation, many patients with pneumonia never have a specific pathogen identified. When pneumonia is diagnosed, the priorities in the emergency department are to initiate appropriate empiric antibiotic therapy based on the most likely pathogens, provide appropriate respiratory support, assess the severity of disease, and recognize indications for hospitalization.

PRINCIPLES OF DISEASE

Despite the constant presence of potential pathogens in the respiratory tract, the lungs are remarkably resistant to infection. The alveolar surface of the lungs covers an area of approximately 140 m^2. Approximately 10,000 L of air passes through the respiratory tract each day, and typical ambient air can contain hundreds to thousands of microorganisms per cubic meter. Numerous potential respiratory tract pathogens may colonize the oropharynx and upper airways. Although the cough and laryngeal reflexes keep most large particulate matter out of the lower respiratory tract, aspiration of oropharyngeal contents may be a common occurrence during normal sleep. Despite these hazards, the body is usually able to maintain a virtually sterile environment in healthy lungs.

The development of clinical pneumonia requires a defect in host defenses, the presence of a particularly virulent organism, or the introduction of a large inoculum of organisms. If the challenge of invading organisms overwhelms host defenses, microbial proliferation leads to inflammation, an immune response, and clinical pneumonia. If host defenses are weak, a minimal challenge may lead to the development of pneumonia.

The mouth normally contains numerous microorganisms. Saliva contains approximately 10^8 bacteria/mL, with anaerobic organisms predominating. *Bacteroides* and *Fusobacterium* spp. are the most common anaerobic organisms. Streptococci are the most common aerobic organisms, but staphylococci, *Haemophilus* sp., *Moraxella catarrhalis,* and *Neisseria* sp. also are found. The presence of these bacteria and their adherence to oral epithelium is important in maintaining the normal balance of oral flora. Various substances are present in mucus and saliva that control colonizing organisms, and many organisms that normally colonize the oropharynx produce products that inhibit the growth of other organisms. Anything that upsets the balance of normal oral flora may permit the growth of more virulent organisms. Systemic illness may alter epithelial binding of oral flora, leading to increased colonization with aerobic gram-negative bacilli. Antimicrobial therapy also can adversely alter normal oral flora.

The anatomy of the upper respiratory tract filters larger particles before reaching the alveoli. The gag reflex and closure of the epiglottis during normal swallowing protect against aspiration. Coughing is an effective means of expelling material from the larynx and central airways. Airflow in the trachea of about 250 m/sec during a cough creates a strong shear force to expel mucus and trapped particles. The sharp angles at which the central airways branch cause particles to impact on the mucosal surface, where they are entrapped and removed by mucociliary clearance. Only small particles less than 5 μm may reach the alveoli. At the alveoli, a variety of substances, such as immunoglobulin G (IgG), complement, lysozyme, free fatty acids, and alveolar macrophages, provide defense against infection.

Host defenses can be impaired in many ways. An altered level of consciousness (e.g., intoxication, stroke, seizures, anesthesia) can suppress protective airway reflexes and lead to aspiration of oropharyngeal contents into the lower respiratory tract. Interventions that bypass the usual defenses of the upper airways, such as endotracheal intubation, nasogastric intubation, and respiratory therapy devices, predispose to infection. Cigarette smoking damages mucociliary function and macrophage activity. Viral infections of the respiratory tract may destroy respiratory epithelium and predispose to bacterial infection. Increased risk of bacterial pneumonia after influenza or other viral respiratory infections is well described. The elderly seem to be at increased risk of pneumonia secondary to decline of mucociliary clearance, elastic recoil of the lungs, and humoral and cellular immunity. Human immunodeficiency virus (HIV) infection can impair humoral and cellular immunity.

If an infectious organism is able to reach the alveoli and begin replicating, a series of host immune responses occurs that ultimately may lead to the development of clinical pneumonia. As antigens of the infecting organism are identified by the host, cytokines, such as interleukin-1, interleukin-8, and tumor necrosis factor, are produced that mediate the inflammatory response. Transudation of plasma fluids into the lung tissue allows entry of IgM and IgG for bacterial opsonization, complement activation, agglutination, and neutralization. Neutrophils are recruited into the lung to ingest and kill the infecting organisms. Cell-mediated immunity plays an important role in defense against certain pathogens, such as viruses and intracellular organisms such as *Mycobacterium* and *Legionella* spp. As fluids and inflammatory cells enter the alveolar spaces to combat the infection, the patient develops the clinical and radiographic signs of pneumonia.

Etiologic Agents

The challenge with pneumonia generally lies in identifying the etiologic agent rather than in diagnosis of pneumonia itself. It is extremely difficult to determine with a high degree of certainty the specific organism responsible for pneumonia, especially within the time frame of an emergency department evaluation. Empiric therapy must be chosen that has activity against the spectrum of likely pathogens based on the overall clinical picture.

Difficulty in determining the specific etiology of pneumonia exists, even with advanced microbiologic

and serologic testing that is not generally available during an emergency department evaluation. In community-acquired pneumonia, a microbial etiology cannot be determined in one third to one half of cases, even after thorough investigation. In hospitalized adults with community-acquired pneumonia, traditional pathogens such as *S. pneumoniae* and *Haemophilus influenzae* account for about one fourth of cases. *Legionella, Mycoplasma,* and *Chlamydia* spp. together account for 15%.[3] Serologic testing for common viral agents reveals a viral etiology in about 17% of cases, with influenza and parainfluenza viruses being most common.[4] Adults who require intensive care unit admission have *S. pneumoniae* as the most common pathogen, with prevalence of 38%, and 50% or more of fatal cases. *Legionella* sp., *Staphylococcus aureus,* and aerobic gram-negative bacilli also appear to be relatively more common among adults with severe community-acquired pneumonia.[5,6] Atypical organisms such as *Mycoplasma* sp. or viruses seem to account for a relatively higher proportion of pneumonias in patients who have milder illness that is amenable to outpatient therapy.[7] Although the prevalence of various organisms can vary considerably in different settings, the frequency with which atypical organisms are identified should influence therapy decisions, even in patients with severe illness requiring hospitalization. Coinfection, such as with *Chlamydia pneumoniae* and *S. pneumoniae,* also is well recognized.

S. pneumoniae is a gram-positive coccus that is the most common etiology of community-acquired pneumonia among adults. It is found in the nasopharynx of about 40% of healthy adults. Although this organism can cause pneumonia in healthy persons, patients with a history of diabetes, cardiovascular disease, alcoholism, sickle cell disease, splenectomy, and malignancy or other immunosuppressive illness are at increased risk. A vaccine containing the 23 capsular polysaccharides of pneumococcal types most commonly associated with pneumonia reduces the likelihood of serious pneumococcal infection. It is recommended for persons at increased risk because of underlying illness or age older than 65.[8] Many emergency department patients have not received pneumococcal vaccine, and vaccinating eligible patients in this setting seems to be feasible and effective.[9] A heptavalent protein-conjugate pneumococcal vaccine effectively reduces invasive pneumococcal disease in infants and young children, including pneumonia.[10]

H. influenzae is a common pathogen in adults with chronic obstructive pulmonary disease (COPD), alcoholism, malnutrition, malignancy, or diabetes. The organism is a pleomorphic gram-negative rod that can be encapsulated and identified as serotypes a through f, with type b most commonly leading to serious illness with bacteremia. *H. influenzae* is the second most frequently isolated organism in community-acquired pneumonia among adults. Nontypeable strains of *H. influenzae* that previously were thought to be benign now are recognized as a frequent cause of lower respiratory tract infection in patients with chronic lung disease.

Intravenous drug users may develop hematogenous spread of *S. aureus* that involves both lungs as multiple small infiltrates or abscesses (e.g., tricuspid endocarditis resulting in septic pulmonary emboli). *S. aureus* also may cause a primary bacterial pneumonia that may be clinically indistinguishable from other bacterial pneumonias, although organisms such as *S. pneumoniae* and *H. influenzae* are much more common. Staphylococcal pneumonias are often necrotizing, with cavitation and pneumatocele formation. An increased incidence of staphylococcal pneumonia is noted during epidemics of influenza. Community-associated methicillin-resistant *S. aureus* (MRSA) infections seem to be increasing in the United States.

Other pyogenic bacterial etiologies include *Moraxella (Branhamella) catarrhalis,* a gram-negative diplococcus that can be associated with lower respiratory tract infections in patients with COPD. *Klebsiella pneumoniae* is a gram-negative rod that rarely causes disease in a normal host and accounts for a small percentage of community-acquired pneumonias, but it may cause severe pneumonia in debilitated patients with alcoholism, diabetes, or other chronic illness. Because the organism is often hospital acquired, there is a high incidence of antibiotic resistance.

Mycoplasma pneumoniae is one of the most common causes of community-acquired pneumonia in previously healthy patients younger than age 40. Another important organism in community-acquired pneumonia is *C. pneumoniae,* an intracellular parasite that is transmitted between humans by respiratory secretions or aerosols. Seroprevalence studies show that virtually everyone is infected with *C. pneumoniae* at some time and that reinfection is common. *C. pneumoniae* is a relatively common etiology of community-acquired pneumonia, especially in older adults, accounting for at least 8% of cases, although this is likely an underestimate owing to difficulty in diagnosing infection with this organism.

At least 30 species of *Legionella* have been isolated since the 1976 outbreak in Philadelphia from which the organism derives its name, and at least 19 are known to be human pathogens. *Legionella* is an intracellular organism that lives in aquatic environments. There is no person-to-person transmission. Although it has often been implicated in point outbreaks related to cooling towers and similar aquatic sources, the organism also lives in ordinary tap water and probably has been underdiagnosed as an etiology of community-acquired pneumonia. *Legionella* may account for 19% of community-acquired pneumonia cases, although the prevalence seems to vary greatly by region.[11]

Lower respiratory infections due to anaerobic organisms generally result from the aspiration of oropharyngeal contents with large amounts of bacteria. These infections are typically polymicrobial, including *Peptostreptococcus, Bacteroides, Fusobacterium,* and *Prevotella* spp.[12] Presentation is often subacute or chronic and may be difficult to distinguish clinically from other etiologies of pneumonia. Clinical factors that would suggest an anaerobic infection include risk factors for aspiration, such as central nervous system depression or swallowing dysfunction; severe periodontal disease; fetid sputum; and presence of a pulmonary abscess or empyema.

Viral pneumonias are common in infants and young children and are being recognized as an important cause of pneumonia in adults. Respiratory syncytial virus and parainfluenza viruses are the most common causes of pneumonia in infants and small children, occurring mostly during autumn and winter. Influenza viruses are the most common cause of viral pneumonia in adults. Winter influenza outbreaks, usually due to influenza type A, may cause 40,000 deaths yearly in the United States, more than 90% of which occur in people age 65 or older.[13] Metapneumovirus is a more recently described paramyxovirus that seems to be an important cause of viral pneumonia in children and adults.[14] Cytomegalovirus (CMV) primarily causes pneumonia in immunosuppressed patients, such as transplant recipients. Varicella-zoster virus (or chickenpox) may cause pneumonia that seems to be more common and more severe in adults and is predisposed to by factors such as smoking or pregnancy. Severe acute respiratory syndrome is a respiratory illness due to a coronavirus identified in Southeast Asia. Severe acute respiratory syndrome is associated with a high case-fatality rate (approximately 10% to 15% overall), which is even greater in the elderly.

Fungal infections due to organisms such as *Histoplasma capsulatum, Blastomyces dermatitides,* and *Coccidioides immitis* commonly present as pulmonary disease. These organisms are present in the soil in various geographic areas of the United States: *H. capsulatum* in the Mississippi and Ohio River valleys, *C. immitis* in desert areas of the southwest, and *B. dermatitides* in a poorly defined area extending beyond that of *H. capsulatum.* These infections should be considered in persons in appropriate geographic areas, especially in persons who are near activities that disturb the soil, such as construction or dirt bike riding. Clinical presentation varies from an acute or chronic pneumonia to asymptomatic granulomas and hilar adenopathy found on a chest radiograph.

P. carinii pneumonia (PCP) occurs in compromised hosts, principally persons with AIDS or malignancy. Although *P. carinii* often has been classified as a protozoan, biochemical evidence indicates that it is probably more closely related to fungi. PCP is one of the most common presentations leading to a diagnosis of HIV infection and AIDS. Patients with pulmonary complaints should be questioned about HIV risk factors, and clinicians should search for signs of HIV-related immunosuppression, such as weight loss, lymphadenopathy, and oral thrush. PCP typically presents subacutely with fatigue, exertional dyspnea, nonproductive cough, pleuritic chest pain, and fever.

M. tuberculosis is a slow-growing bacterium transmitted between persons by droplet nuclei produced from coughing and sneezing. *M. tuberculosis* survives within macrophages as a facultative intracellular parasite and may remain dormant in the body for many years. Active tuberculosis (TB) develops within 2 years of infection in about 5% of patients, and another 5%

develop reactivation disease at some later point. Reactivation is more likely to occur in persons with impaired cell-mediated immunity, such as patients with diabetes, renal failure, immunosuppressive therapy, malnutrition, or AIDS. The risk of developing active TB in HIV-infected persons with a positive tuberculin skin test is estimated to be 8% per year.[15]

Approximately one third of the world's population is infected with *M. tuberculosis*. Approximately 8 million new cases of active disease develop annually, resulting in 3 million deaths worldwide. An estimated 10 to 15 million persons in the United States (4% to 6% of the population) are infected with TB. Multidrug-resistant strains of *M. tuberculosis* are found in increasing numbers, especially among immigrants from South East Asia and AIDS patients.

Unusual Causes of Pneumonia

Q fever is an acute febrile illness caused by the rickettsial organism *Coxiella burnetii*. It is most common in persons with occupational exposure to cattle or sheep or parturient animals, including cats. Fever is present in all patients, and a severe headache occurs in approximately 75% of cases. This infection is rarely fatal. Other zoonotic pulmonary infections include *Rhodococcus equi* associated with exposure to horses and *Bordetella bronchiseptica* associated with exposure to ill dogs ("kennel cough").

Plague, caused by *Yersinia pestis,* is endemic in many parts of the world. It occurs in the southwestern states of the United States in persons bitten by fleas from infected rodents or carnivores. Hematogenous spread may lead to pneumonia that is highly contagious and has a high mortality. It typically presents with cough and chest pain with purulent sputum and hemoptysis associated with fever and adenopathy (i.e., a bubo).

Hantaviruses are associated with a syndrome of severe respiratory distress and shock in several areas of the United States. Infection seems to occur from inhalation of aerosols of material contaminated with rodent urine and feces. Patients are typically healthy adults presenting with a prodrome of fever, myalgia, and malaise followed in several days by the onset of respiratory distress. Hypoxia may progress rapidly, requiring ventilatory support. Characteristic laboratory findings include thrombocytopenia, hemoconcentration, and leukocytosis with atypical lymphocytes. Chest radiographs show bilateral interstitial lung infiltrates that are more pronounced in dependent areas. Death typically occurs from depressed cardiac output and eventual cardiovascular collapse.[16]

Tularemia is a febrile illness caused by the bacterium *Francisella tularensis,* which is spread by contact with body fluids of an infected mammal (especially rabbits) or the bite of an infected arthropod. Illness usually begins with an ulcerated skin lesion and painful regional lymphadenopathy. Some patients have a typhoidal form with only fever, malaise, and weight loss. Pneumonia may occur with either form, presenting as a nonproductive cough and patchy infiltrates on a chest radiograph.

Psittacosis can be spread to humans from birds infected with *Chlamydia psittaci*. It may occur in owners of pet birds, pet shop employees, workers in poultry processing plants, or others exposed to birds. Illness often begins rapidly with chills, high fever, myalgias, and malaise. Severe headache is often the major complaint. Cough is usually nonproductive. Splenomegaly is often present. Radiographic findings are variable, but patchy perihilar or lower lung field infiltrates are most common.

CLINICAL FEATURES

The emergency department evaluation should focus on establishing the diagnosis of pneumonia and determining the presence of epidemiologic and clinical features that would influence decisions regarding the need for hospitalization and choice of antibiotics. Key elements of the patient history include the character and pattern of symptoms, the setting in which the pneumonia is acquired, geographic or animal exposures, and host factors that predispose to certain types of infections and are associated with patient outcome.

Pneumonia generally presents as a cough productive of purulent sputum, shortness of breath, and fever. In most healthy older children and adults, the diagnosis can be reasonably excluded on the basis of history and physical examination, with suspected cases confirmed by chest radiography. Absence of any abnormalities in vital signs or chest auscultation substantially reduces the likelihood of pneumonia. No single clinical finding is highly reliable, however, in establishing or excluding a diagnosis of pneumonia.[17]

Elderly or debilitated patients with pneumonia often present with nonspecific complaints and may not show the classic symptoms. Pneumonia commonly presents in the elderly as acute confusion or a deterioration of baseline function. Elderly patients are more likely to have advanced illness at the time of presentation and may present with sepsis in the absence of a previous syndrome suggestive of pneumonia. Rarely, patients with lower lobe pneumonias present with a complaint of abdominal or back pain. The diagnosis of pneumonia may be more difficult in infants and small children who are unable to give an adequate history. Pneumonia may present in infants as a fever associated with irritability, tachypnea, tachycardia, intercostal retractions, nasal flaring, or grunting. Cough may be minimal or absent.

Pneumonia is often divided into "typical" pneumonia caused by pyogenic bacteria, such as *S. pneumoniae* or *H. influenzae*, and "atypical" pneumonia caused by organisms such as *Mycoplasma* and *Chlamydia* spp. This division is artificial, and a clear differentiation between these two types of pneumonia on clinical grounds alone is impossible. Certain clinical factors are often said to be suggestive of atypical organisms. Factors studied prospectively and found *not* to be more frequent with atypical pneumonias than with pyogenic bacterial etiologies include gradual onset, viral prodrome, absence of rigors, nonproductive cough, lower degree of fever, absence of pleurisy, absence of consolidation, low leukocyte count, and an ill-defined infiltrate on a chest radiograph.[3] Although it is impossible to determine with a high degree of certainty the specific etiology of pneumonia without results of microbiologic or serologic tests, certain clinical factors may suggest that a specific pathogen should be considered.

The classic presentation of pneumococcal pneumonia is the abrupt onset of a single shaking chill followed by fever, cough productive of rust-colored sputum, and pleuritic chest pain, but many patients do not exhibit the classic pattern. Patients often have a preceding upper respiratory illness, and the onset of pneumonia may be insidious, especially in the elderly or patients with underlying lung disease. Patients with a history of asplenia, sickle cell disease, AIDS, multiple myeloma, or agammaglobulinemia are at increased risk of pneumococcal bacteremia and sepsis with high mortality rates. Extrapulmonary complications (e.g., meningitis, endocarditis, or arthritis) may rarely be present. Tachypnea and tachycardia are usually present. Examination of the chest may reveal signs of consolidation. Adults with chronic lung disease who develop pneumonia due to H. influenzae typically present with an insidious worsening of baseline cough and sputum production, and bacteremia is rare.[18] K. pneumoniae may cause severe pneumonia in elderly or debilitated patients. Sputum is often described as "currant jelly" because of the necrotizing, hemorrhagic nature of the infection. Abscess formation, empyema, and bacteremia are common with this organism, and mortality is high.

Atypical pneumonia is caused by organisms such as M. pneumoniae, C. pneumoniae, viruses, Legionella sp., or rickettsiae such as C. burnetii. Mycoplasmal infection usually begins as a flulike illness with headache, malaise, and fever. Cough is usually nonproductive, but may sometimes produce clear or purulent sputum. Skin lesions, including maculopapular, vesicular, urticarial, or erythema multiforme–type rashes are common, especially in younger patients. Although bullous myringitis sometimes is described as a classic finding, it is not specific for mycoplasmal infection and is present in only a few cases. Common physical findings include pharyngeal erythema, cervical adenopathy, and scattered rales and rhonchi. Rare extrapulmonary manifestations include pericarditis, glomerulonephritis, aseptic meningitis, and Guillain-Barré syndrome.

Patients generally do not appear toxic, and most can be treated as outpatients. Although mucopurulent sputum generally indicates the presence of pyogenic bacterial pneumonia or bronchitis, it also may be present with mycoplasmal or viral pneumonia. Viral pneumonia in adults often is preceded by symptoms of upper respiratory infection, such as rhinitis or sore throat. The onset of pneumonia may be insidious. Cough is usually nonproductive, and pleuritic chest pain is less common than with bacterial pneumonia. Chest examination often reveals scattered rhonchi or rales. Signs of consolidation are less common.

Most C. pneumoniae infections in young adults cause a minor, self-limited upper respiratory illness that is subacute in onset. This organism also is associated with bronchitis, wheezing, sinusitis, pharyngitis, and atherosclerosis.[19,20] Development of radiographically evident pneumonia is more common in the elderly, in contrast to the common perception that atypical pneumonias occur in the young.[21]

Some patients with Legionella infection have a mild, self-limited atypical pneumonia presentation. Older patients, smokers, and patients with chronic disease or immunosuppression are more prone to develop the more acute and severe manifestations of legionnaires' disease. This infection presents as a severe systemic illness with malaise, lethargy, and high fever. Dry cough is usually present, accompanied by pleuritic chest pain in 25% to 30% of cases. Purulent sputum often develops later. Gastrointestinal symptoms, such as diarrhea and abdominal cramping, are sometimes prominent. Patients may appear toxic with high fever and altered mental status.

In addition to age, presence of underlying illness, and presenting symptoms, the setting of acquisition of pneumonia may provide clues to likely etiologies. Community-acquired pneumonia that occurs in otherwise healthy individuals is likely to be due to viruses, Mycoplasma sp., or S. pneumoniae. Nonimmunized patients in a nursing home setting are prone to influenza during outbreaks, and this may be complicated later with pneumonia due to S. aureus. Hospitalized patients may develop pneumonia due to agents that are uncommon in community-acquired pneumonia, such as Enterobacteriaceae, Pseudomonas aeruginosa, and S. aureus. Healthy patients in an institutional setting, such as a dormitory or military barracks, are likely to have pneumonia due to Mycoplasma sp. or viruses.

Patients with underlying lung disease, especially COPD, constitute an important group likely to develop pneumonia. The lower respiratory tract of these patients is commonly colonized with organisms such as S. pneumoniae, H. influenzae, and M. catarrhalis. Cystic fibrosis patients are prone to pneumonia due to P. aeruginosa or S. aureus. Defective mucociliary clearance in both of these groups make them highly susceptible to repeated episodes of pneumonia.

Patients with immunosuppression due to hematologic malignancy, patients receiving chemotherapy for malignancy, and transplant recipients are prone to pulmonary infections with a wide variety of organisms. In addition to the usual pathogens, these patients may develop pneumonia secondary to viruses such as CMV, varicella, or herpes simplex virus. They also are more likely to develop pneumonia due to aerobic gram-negative bacilli, fungi such as Candida sp. or H. capsulatum, and P. carinii.

DIAGNOSTIC STRATEGIES

The chest radiograph is generally the most important test. Although many chest radiographs are obtained

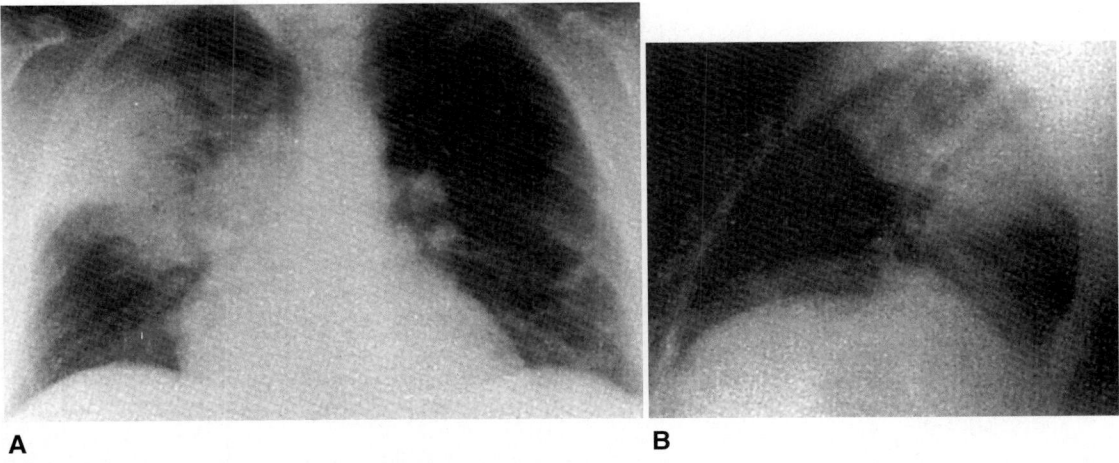

A   B

Figure 75-1. Posteroanterior (**A**) and lateral (**B**) chest radiographs reveal a right upper lobe pneumonia and a patchy left lower lobe infiltrate. A variety of organisms can produce this pattern, including *S. pneumoniae, H. influenzae, Legionella* sp., *Chlamydia pneumoniae*, gram-negative bacilli, *Mycoplasma*, and viruses.

unnecessarily for patients with upper respiratory tract infections or bronchitis, it is difficult to identify a set of specific criteria to direct test ordering that is better than the clinical judgment of an experienced physician.[22] A routine chest radiograph for all patients who present with cough is not necessary; chest radiography may be reserved for patients without a history of asthma who have other suggestive findings (e.g., fever, tachycardia, oxygen desaturation, or an abnormal lung examination).[23] Among patients suspected to have pneumonia, these clinical findings are prospectively validated and are better predictors of a radiographic infiltrate than physician judgment.[24] Patients with serious underlying disease, patients with severe sepsis or shock, and patients in whom hospitalization is considered should have chest radiography performed. Computed tomography (CT) of the chest seems to be more sensitive than plain radiography for detecting the presence of pulmonary consolidation, although the natural history of CT-positive, plain radiograph–negative pneumonia is not clear.[25] Young healthy adults with a presumptive diagnosis of pneumonia, who will be treated as outpatients, may have a chest radiograph deferred, unless there is a suspicion of immunocompromise or other unusual features of disease. A chest radiograph should be obtained subsequently if there is a poor initial response to treatment. Routine performance of chest radiography for patients with exacerbation of chronic bronchitis or COPD is of low yield and may be limited to patients with other signs of infection or congestive heart failure.[26] Studies of infants with fever show that a routine chest radiograph is of low yield in the absence of other symptoms or signs of lower respiratory tract infection (e.g., cough, rales, or elevated respiratory rate).[27,28]

Although the causative agent cannot be determined solely by the results of chest radiography, certain radiographic patterns may suggest the possibility of specific pathogens. In pyogenic bacterial pneumonias, radiographs usually show an area of segmental or subsegmental infiltration and air bronchograms (Figure 75-1).

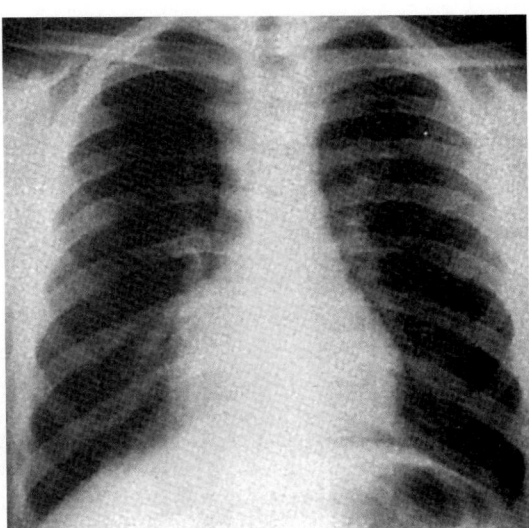

Figure 75-2. Posteroanterior chest radiograph reveals a diffuse interstitial infiltrate. Viruses and *Mycoplasma* are the most likely etiologies in an otherwise healthy patient, but many bacterial organisms also may produce this pattern.

Lobar consolidation is present in a few cases of bacterial pneumonia, often due to pneumococcus or *Klebsiella*. A dense lobar infiltrate with a bulging fissure appearance on a chest radiograph is often described with pneumonia due to *Klebsiella*, but this finding is nonspecific, and most cases present as a more subtle bronchopneumonia. Pneumonia resulting from spread of infection along the intralobular airway results in fluffy or patchy infiltrates in the involved areas of the lung. A wide variety of bacteria and agents such as *Chlamydia* sp., *Mycoplasma* sp., *Legionella* sp., viruses, and fungi may cause this pattern.

An interstitial pattern on a chest radiograph (Figure 75-2) typically is caused by *Mycoplasma* sp., viruses, or *P. carinii*. Tiny nodules disseminated throughout both lungs represent a miliary pattern typical of granulomatous pneumonias, such as TB or fungal disease.

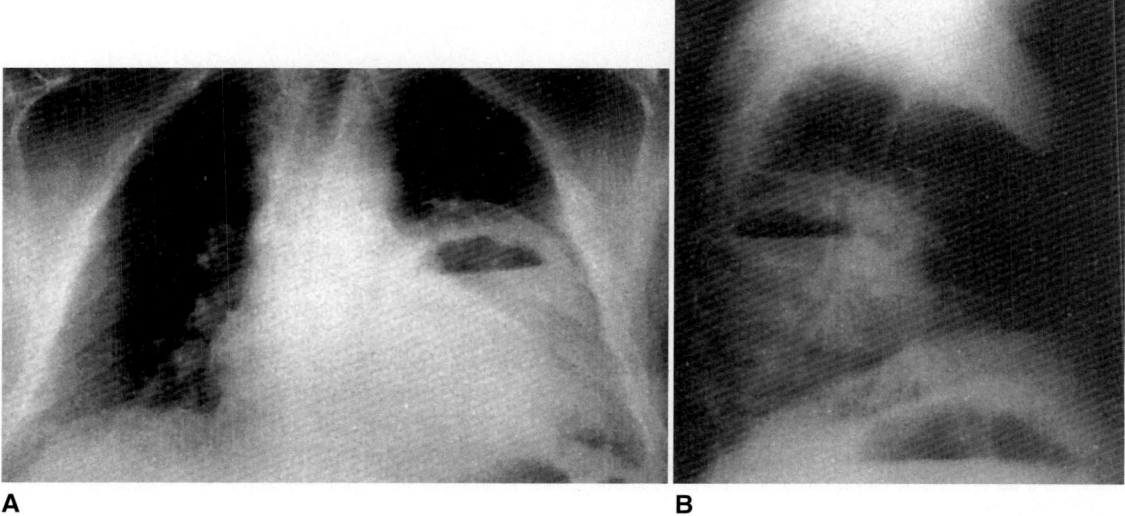

Figure 75-3. Posteroanterior (**A**) and lateral (**B**) chest radiographs reveal a lung abscess in the left lower lobe with a distinct air-fluid level.

The location of infiltrates also may give a clue to the etiology. Aspiration pneumonia occurs in dependent areas of the lung, most commonly the superior segments of the lower lobes or posterior segments of the upper lobes. Pneumonias produced by hematogenous spread (e.g., *S. aureus*) tend to be peripheral. Apical infiltrates suggest TB.

The presence of additional radiographic features in association with infiltrates may suggest a specific etiology. An infiltrate associated with hilar or mediastinal adenopathy suggests the presence of TB or fungal disease or may indicate pneumonia associated with a neoplasm. Bacteria most likely to be associated with cavitation (Figure 75-3) are anaerobes, aerobic gram-negative bacilli, and *S. aureus*. Cavitation also may be present in fungal disease or TB and with noninfectious processes (e.g., malignancy and pulmonary vascular disease). Pneumatoceles or spontaneous pneumothorax may be seen in AIDS patients with PCP. Pleural effusions can be seen with a wide variety of organisms, including many types of pyogenic bacterial pneumonias, *Chlamydia* sp., *Legionella* sp., and TB. Anaerobic infections associated with an effusion are especially prone to development of empyema. The diagnosis and aspiration of pleural effusions can be aided by use of emergency department bedside ultrasonography.

Radiographic findings are nonspecific for predicting a particular infectious etiology. *Mycoplasma* pneumonia may present as a dense infiltrate, or pneumococcal pneumonia may present as a diffuse interstitial infiltrate. Immunocompromised patients are particularly prone to having atypical radiographic appearances. Rarely, patients with a clinical picture strongly suggestive of pneumonia have a normal chest radiograph, and some are found to have an infiltrate within the next 24 to 48 hours. The absence of findings on a chest radiograph should not preclude the use of antimicrobial therapy in appropriate patients with a clinical diagnosis of pneumonia.[29] Whether the state of hydration can affect the radiographic appearance of pneumonia is controversial. Although severe dehydration theoretically could result in a diminished exudative response by decreasing blood volume and hydrostatic pressure, this has not been shown experimentally.[30,31]

Laboratory studies also are nonspecific for identifying the etiology of pneumonia. Although the finding of a white blood cell count (WBC) greater than 15,000/mm³ increases the probability of the patient having a pyogenic bacterial etiology rather than a viral or atypical etiology, this finding depends on the stage of the illness and is neither sensitive nor specific enough to aid decisions regarding therapy in an individual patient. A WBC may be helpful if it yields evidence of immunosuppression, such as neutropenia, or if it reveals lymphopenia that may indicate immunosuppression from AIDS. Serum chemistry studies may be helpful in identifying patients with renal or hepatic dysfunction or metabolic acidosis associated with sepsis. These findings may assist in predicting a complicated course and influence decisions regarding disposition, choice of antimicrobial agents, and dosages.

Assessment of respiratory function with pulse oximetry is important in the evaluation of patients with pneumonia. Because clinical assessment of oxygenation can be inaccurate,[32] a pulse oximetry reading should be obtained in any patient suspected to have pneumonia in the emergency department. Respiratory failure due to pneumonia is common in elderly patients and may require intubation and mechanical ventilation.

Sputum Gram stain is often recommended as a means to determine the presence of a bacterial pathogen, allowing more specific antimicrobial therapy, but rarely results in a change in therapy or outcome. Community-acquired pneumonia guidelines from the American Thoracic Society and the Infectious Diseases Society of America (IDSA) vary in their recommendations regarding the use of this test. IDSA guidelines recommend more aggressive attempts at etiologic diagnosis to provide pathogen-specific therapy, but do not provide solid evidence to support this approach.[1] American Thoracic Society guidelines recommend a more empiric approach to therapy, reserving more aggressive diagnostic testing for patients with more severe illness or patients who fail to respond to therapy.[33] If sputum Gram stain and culture are considered, they should be reserved for the small subset of patients with more serious illness (e.g., admitted to the intensive care unit), in whom the bacteriologic diagnosis is highly uncertain, and for whom it is thought that the outcome may be most dependent on optimal antimicrobial therapy. Even in such cases, it is unlikely that this analysis would yield information that would change therapy or alter outcome.

The use of sputum Gram stain as a basis for empiric therapy in the emergency department can be problematic for several reasons. Many patients are unable to provide an adequate sputum specimen. Induction of sputum without adequate isolation facilities can put patients and staff at risk if sputum is induced from persons with unrecognized TB. Correlation between identification of pneumococcus on Gram stain and sputum culture results is poor, even when commonly used criteria for an adequate sputum specimen (<5 squamous epithelial cells and >25 WBC/high-power field) are applied. Gram stains are even less likely to show gram-negative pathogens, such as H. influenzae, and should not be relied on to rule out a gram-negative etiology. Sputum Gram stains are less accurate when done by less experienced physicians outside of the microbiology laboratory and may lead to erroneous conclusions regarding which pathogens are present.[34] Recommendations regarding sputum analysis arose in the era of narrow-spectrum antibiotics and have been slow to incorporate the therapeutic advantages of modern, broad-spectrum agents. Empiric antimicrobial agents are usually highly clinically effective if chosen based on clinical information without sputum analysis.

Blood cultures are also controversial and have shown mixed results in terms of improved diagnostic accuracy or ability to guide therapy. Blood cultures should be obtained in seriously ill patients and, if drawn, should be obtained before the initiation of antibiotics (although antibiotics should not be delayed for this reason). When positive, blood cultures reflect the etiologic agent more accurately than sputum cultures, but still only uncommonly lead to a rational change in antimicrobial therapy. Bacteremia occurs in approximately 25% to 30% of hospitalized pneumococcal pneumonia cases, but the diagnosis and therapy are usually well established before blood culture results are available. Although IDSA guidelines recommend blood cultures for all admitted pneumonia patients,[1] the cost-effectiveness and utility of this practice are highly questionable in patients without risk factors, such as immunosuppression, recent antimicrobial failure, recent hospitalization, or suspected endovascular infection.[35] Patients with a pleural effusion should have a diagnostic thoracentesis performed with fluid sent for cell count, differential, pH (pH < 7.2 is predictive of a need for chest tube), Gram stain, and

culture. Serologic tests are available for the diagnosis of many organisms, including C. pneumoniae, Legionella sp., and fungi. The use of serologic tests to determine the etiology of pneumonia may be helpful retrospectively, but they usually require acute and convalescent serum titers and are of little use at the time therapeutic decisions must be made. Mycoplasma pneumonia is associated with the presence of serum cold hemagglutinins in 60% of cases, but they also may be present in many viral infections. Diagnosis of the exact etiology of viral pneumonia is made difficult by the nonspecificity of presentation and the lack of widely available rapid tests. Rapid diagnostic tests for viral antigens are available for several viruses, including respiratory syncytial virus, influenza, and CMV. Rapid testing for influenza A and B is available. Although the specificity of these tests appears to exceed 90%, sensitivity is lower, making it difficult to exclude this infection on the basis of a negative result in a high-risk patient.[36] These tests may be most useful to document the existence of an influenza outbreak in a community at the beginning of an epidemic. Also, testing of admitted pneumonia patients during an influenza outbreak may be a reasonable indication for early adjunctive antiviral therapy. Developments in rapid testing using technology such as urine antigen tests or polymerase chain reaction may provide emergency physicians with a reliable method to determine the specific etiology of pneumonia.

Pneumonia Associated with Human Immunodeficiency Virus Infection

The AIDS epidemic has greatly changed the spectrum of pulmonary infections seen in many communities. The approach to an HIV-infected patient with pulmonary complaints must consider the likelihood of opportunistic lung infections. Although the use of highly active antiretroviral therapy (HAART) is decreasing the incidence of opportunistic infections among HIV-infected patients, individuals who are not under regular care often present to emergency departments. In the setting of a patient with risk factors for HIV but an unknown serologic status, a decision must be made as to the likelihood of AIDS and the need to search aggressively for opportunistic pathogens.

Respiratory infections are the most common type of opportunistic infection in AIDS patients. In addition to P. carinii, there is also an increased incidence of pneumonia due to M. tuberculosis and common bacterial pathogens such as S. pneumoniae and H. influenzae. The incidence of pneumococcal pneumonia is 7 to 10 times higher in HIV-infected persons, and the incidence of H. influenzae pneumonia is about 100 times higher than in non–HIV-infected individuals.[37,38] Other less important causes of pneumonia in HIV-infected patients include Mycobacterium avium complex, CMV, aerobic gram-negative bacilli, Cryptococcus neoformans, and Rhodococcus equi.

Before antimicrobial prophylaxis for PCP became widespread in AIDS patients, PCP was the initial opportunistic infection in more than 70% of patients

Figure 75-4. Posteroanterior (**A**) and lateral (**B**) chest radiographs of an HIV-infected patient reveal interstitial disease mixed with patchy alveolar infiltrates. *P. carinii* is the most common etiology, but bacterial pathogens and tuberculosis also must be considered.

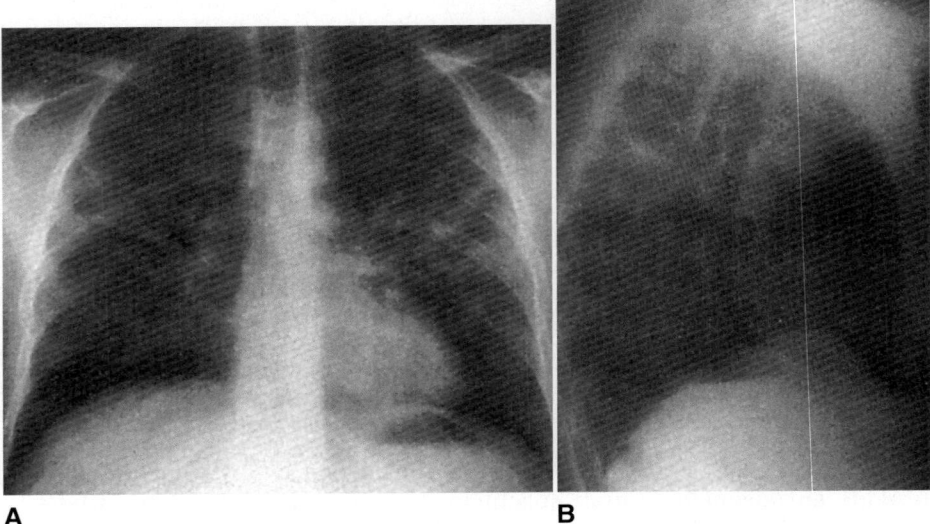

A   B

with AIDS reported to the Centers for Disease Control and Prevention.[39] The incidence of AIDS in general and PCP in AIDS patients specifically has decreased due to HAART and routine PCP prophylaxis.

Although some patients have known HIV infection or AIDS, many patients are unaware of their HIV status, and many are reluctant to volunteer that they may have risk factors for HIV. The first crucial step in the diagnosis of PCP is the recognition that a patient may be at risk. If the possibility of HIV infection is established, the likelihood of immunosuppression must be determined. The potential for opportunistic pulmonary infection can be predicted by a recent absolute CD4 lymphocyte count less than 200/mm^3. This count is often known by patients with recognized HIV infection or may be surmised by a peripheral total lymphocyte count less than 1000/mm^3.[40] In patients who do not know their HIV status, the presence of findings such as weight loss, hairy leukoplakia, and oral candidiasis strongly suggests immunosuppression.

Although patients with PCP may present with typical features of subacute onset of nonproductive cough, fever, shortness of breath, diffuse interstitial infiltrates on chest radiography, and arterial hypoxemia, 10% to 20% of patients subsequently proven to have PCP lack these findings. PCP usually has a subacute presentation characterized by nonproductive cough, exertional dyspnea, and weight loss. Tachypnea and tachycardia are usually present.

The classic radiographic findings in PCP are bilateral interstitial infiltrates that begin in the perihilar region. Radiographic manifestations of PCP can vary considerably, however, ranging from a normal appearance to dense consolidation. Lobar infiltrates, pleural effusions, hilar adenopathy, parenchymal nodules, and cavitary disease also are described. Apical infiltrates, spontaneous pneumothoraces, and extrapulmonary PCP are more common in patients receiving inhaled aerosolized pentamidine for PCP prophylaxis. Hypoxemia, hypocapnia, and an increased arterial-alveolar oxygenation gradient are usually present. Serum lactate dehydrogenase is significantly elevated in AIDS patients with PCP compared with patients with non-PCP pneumonia.[41,42] The demonstration of oxygen desaturation with mild exercise may be helpful in patients with more subtle presentations.[43] Confirmation of the diagnosis of PCP requires sputum induction and staining and, in some cases, further invasive procedures, such as bronchoscopy with bronchoalveolar lavage or biopsy. In most settings, patients suspected to have PCP are admitted to the hospital and given presumptive therapy against PCP.

AIDS patients also are predisposed to developing life-threatening bacterial pneumonias that may mimic or coexist with PCP. The bacterial pathogens most commonly responsible for pneumonia in these patients are the pathogens most frequently encountered in immunocompetent individuals with community-acquired pneumonia.[44] Typical pyogenic pneumonia may have an atypical radiographic presentation in these abnormal hosts. In studies of AIDS patients with pneumonia due to pathogens such as *S. pneumoniae* and *H. influenzae,* more than half have diffuse infiltrates.[44]

There is a broad differential diagnosis for pulmonary infiltrates in AIDS patients (Figure 75-4). Because AIDS patients with pulmonary TB cannot be distinguished reliably from AIDS patients with other pulmonary infections at presentation, it is important to consider TB in all HIV-infected patients with respiratory complaints and initiate respiratory isolation. AIDS patients also are at risk for pneumonia due to other mycobacterial species (e.g., *M. avium* complex), although the finding of acid-fast bacilli in the sputum should prompt empiric therapy against *M. tuberculosis* unless another mycobacterial species is definitively identified. AIDS patients also are at increased risk for pneumonia due to *Cryptococcus neoformans* or other fungi associated with geographic exposure. Viral pneumonia due to CMV usually presents as a systemic illness and often coexists with PCP in end-stage AIDS patients. Kaposi's sarcoma also may present with pulmonary infiltrates.

DIFFERENTIAL DIAGNOSIS CONSIDERATIONS

At times, the differentiation between upper and lower respiratory tract infections may be difficult. A chest radiograph is helpful to differentiate between upper respiratory tract infection or bronchitis and pneumonia, but is probably not necessary for all patients with cough and sputum production unless other factors are present that would suggest the possibility of pneumonia or would obscure its clinical diagnosis (e.g., toxic appearance, extremes of age, underlying illness, abnormal chest examination).

Many noninfectious etiologies may result in inflammatory lung processes, including exposure to mineral dusts (e.g., silicosis), chemical fumes (e.g., chlorine, ammonia), toxic drugs (e.g., bleomycin), radiation, thermal injury, or oxygen toxicity. Immunologic diseases (e.g., sarcoidosis, Goodpasture's syndrome, collagen vascular disease), or hypersensitivity to environmental agents (e.g., farmer's lung disease) also may result in pneumonia. Tumors may be confused with pneumonia radiographically or may present initially as a postobstructive infection or adenopathy with peripheral infiltrates. Lymphangitic spread of lung malignancy may resemble interstitial pneumonia.

Aspiration

It is important to recognize the distinction between the acute aspiration of gastric contents or other liquids and bacterial pneumonia that may develop later as a complication of aspiration. Aspiration of liquids into the lung disrupts surfactant and causes an inflammatory response that may lead to hypoxia and respiratory failure. Aspiration of acidic gastric contents is particularly damaging to lungs and is common in patients who are unconscious from intoxication or anesthesia or who have neurologic deficits. Patients may present initially with coughing or shortness of breath or may appear well initially and then develop respiratory dysfunction over the next several hours. Patients who aspirate while unconscious are sometimes unrecognized until respiratory insufficiency develops.

Acute aspiration of acidic fluid into the lungs may produce fever, leukocytosis, purulent sputum, and radiographic infiltrates that mimic bacterial pneumonia. Although many of these patients go on to develop bacterial pneumonia, prophylactic administration of antibiotics is controversial. Some studies indicate that prophylactic antibiotics do not seem to be beneficial and may select for resistant organisms.[45] Antibiotics should be initiated if the patient develops signs of bacterial pneumonia, including new fever, expanding infiltrate appearing more than 36 hours after aspiration, or unexplained deterioration. Systemic corticosteroids for acute aspiration are of no benefit and are not indicated.

MANAGEMENT

Patients with underlying asthma or COPD who present with wheezing may benefit from bronchodilator therapy and corticosteroids. Seriously ill patients who present with volume depletion or septic shock require fluid resuscitation and vasopressors.[46]

The possibility of communicable disease must be considered early and isolation initiated when appropriate. Patients suspected to have pulmonary TB because of a history of TB exposure, suggestive symptoms (e.g., persistent cough, weight loss, night sweats, hemoptysis), or belonging to a group at high risk for TB (e.g., homeless, intravenous drug user, alcoholic, HIV risk, immigrant from high-risk area) should be placed immediately into respiratory isolation before evaluation, including chest radiography.[47] Emergency departments that frequently care for patients at risk for TB should consider triage protocols to identify these individuals rapidly before patients, visitors, or staff are unnecessarily exposed.[48]

Because timely antimicrobial treatment for community-acquired pneumonia is associated with improved patient outcomes for patients requiring hospital admission,[2] empiric therapy should be started in the emergency department, unless treatment protocols provide for prompt administration on arrival to the inpatient setting. The antibiotics chosen must cover the likely etiologies based on clinical, laboratory, radiologic, and epidemiologic information.

The prevalence of drug-resistant S. pneumoniae (DRSP) is increasing steadily. In the United States, among outpatient pneumococcal sputum isolates collected between 1998 and 2002, approximately 18% had high-level resistance to penicillin.[49] Isolates that are resistant to penicillin are usually resistant to other β-lactams, macrolides, tetracyclines, and trimethoprim-sulfamethoxazole (TMP-SMX). Many extended-spectrum or "respiratory" fluoroquinolones are available, such as levofloxacin, moxifloxacin, gatifloxacin, and gemifloxacin. These agents have activity against DRSP and other typical and atypical pneumonia pathogens. Because oral bioavailability of fluoroquinolones is high, oral therapy provides serum and tissue levels essentially equivalent to parenteral therapy. These fluoroquinolones are recommended instead of vancomycin if DRSP is a concern. It is not clear, however, whether in vitro resistance—and what level of resistance—is related to adverse clinical outcome to treatment drugs given at conventional doses. In one study, patients infected with resistant pneumococcal isolates (mostly intermediate level) had no greater mortality than patients with susceptible organisms, even when treated with antibiotics to which the organism was resistant.[50] Other studies suggest that high-level resistance may be associated with increased mortality.[51]

Appropriate agents for outpatient treatment of adults with community-acquired pneumonia include macrolides, doxycycline, and fluoroquinolones with enhanced activity against S. pneumoniae (Table 75-1).[1,33] In patients properly identified at low risk for complications and who are evaluated for careful outpatient follow-up, use of a macrolide or doxycycline is reasonable. Respiratory fluoroquinolones should be considered for patients with a higher likelihood of DRSP (e.g., patients with more severe illness, underly-

DISPOSITION

The decision to hospitalize a patient with pneumonia is not a commitment to prolonged inpatient care. Observation for 12 to 24 hours in the emergency department or hospital ward may allow the early discharge of certain moderate-risk patients. Inpatient treatment of pneumonia is 15 to 20 times more expensive per patient than outpatient treatment, and most patients are more comfortable in a home environment.

Although no firm guidelines exist regarding hospital admission, there are many well-recognized risk factors associated with an increased risk of death or a complicated clinical course.[33,59,60] A prospectively validated predictive rule for mortality among immunocompetent adults with community-acquired pneumonia suggests a two-step approach to assess risk.[61] Patients in the lowest risk class who are recommended for outpatient management are patients younger than age 50, without significant comorbid conditions (neoplasm, congestive heart failure, cerebrovascular disease, renal disease, liver disease, and HIV), and without the following findings on physical examination: altered mental status, pulse 125 beats/min or greater, respiratory rate 30 breaths/min or greater, systolic blood pressure less than 90 mm Hg, or temperature less than 35° C or 40° C or greater. Patients who do not fit the lowest risk category are classified into categories based on a scoring system that accounts for age, comorbid illness, physical examination findings, and laboratory abnormalities (Table 75-3). Hospitalization is recommended for patients with a score greater than 91, and brief admission or observation may be considered for patients with a score of 71 to 90. Although this method of assessing the likelihood of successful outpatient management is helpful in establishing general guidelines, it can be cumbersome to use, has not been modeled to predict acute life-threatening events, does not take into account dynamic evaluation over time, and has many important exceptions (e.g., an otherwise low-risk patient with severe hypoxia would be discharged by strict interpretation of this rule). Good clinical judgment should supersede a strict interpretation of this scoring system. A study in which physicians were educated and provided the patient's risk score revealed a significantly lower overall admission rate, cost savings, and similar quality-of-life scores, however, compared with patients conventionally managed by their physicians.[62] Additional discharge criteria could include improving and stable vital signs over a several-hour observation period, ability to take oral medications, an ambulatory pulse oximetry greater than 90%, home support, and ability to follow up.

The disposition of HIV-infected patients with possible PCP is dictated by the likelihood of progression to severe disease and by the feasibility of close outpatient follow-up. Factors associated with decreased survival in AIDS patients with PCP include history of prior PCP, an elevated respiratory rate, an abnormal chest examination, WBC count greater than 10,300/mm^3, elevated lactate dehydrogenase, hypoxemia, hypoalbuminemia, and an abnormal chest radiograph.[55] Patients without multiple poor prognostic factors may be discharged from the emergency department with close outpatient follow-up, ideally within 2 to 3 days. Because of the potential toxicity of TMP-SMX, empiric treatment with this agent for well-appearing patients with a low probability of disease is generally not recommended. An empiric trial of a macrolide may be indicated for treatment of bronchitis or mild community-acquired pneumonia in a patient at low risk for PCP (e.g., recent CD4 count > 350/mm^3). Any deterioration on outpatient oral antibiotics should prompt admission for a more extensive evaluation. Some clinicians initiate oral outpatient therapy with TMP-SMX or an alternate drug for patients with a high probability of PCP and favorable clinical parameters, but this should be done only if the patient can be followed closely for continued diagnostic workup and observation for toxicity.

Most patients with community-acquired pneumonia do not need respiratory isolation. Patients who are suspected to have an etiology of pneumonia that could pose a threat of transmission to other patients (e.g., influenza, varicella, TB, plague) should be isolated. Neutropenic patients generally are placed in reverse isolation. HIV-infected patients who present with pneumonia ideally should be isolated until TB can be evaluated by sputum acid-fast bacilli smears; this is particularly true for patients with other risk factors for TB. The chest radiograph cannot be relied on to exclude TB in AIDS patients because it often does not have the typical appearance of TB. Isolation should be strongly considered for others at high risk for TB, such

Table 75-3. Scoring System for Pneumonia Mortality Prediction

Patient Characteristics	Points
Demographic factor	
Age	
Male	No. years of age
Female	No. years of age − 10
Nursing home resident	10
Comorbid illness	
Neoplastic disease	30
Liver disease	20
Congestive heart failure	10
Cerebrovascular disease	10
Renal disease	10
Physical examination finding	
Altered mental status	20
Respiratory rate > 30	20
Systolic blood pressure < 90 mm Hg	20
Temperature < 35° C or > 40° C	15
Pulse > 125 beats/min	10
Laboratory or radiographic finding	
Arterial pH < 7.35	30
Blood urea nitrogen > 30 mg/dL	20
Sodium < 130 mEq/L	20
Glucose > 250 mg/dL	10
Hematocrit < 30%	10
Arterial PO$_2$ < 60 mm Hg	10
Pleural effusion	10

Adapted from Mandell LA, et al. Update of practice guidelines for the management of community-acquired pneumonia in immunocompetent adults. *Clin Infect Dis* 37:1405, 2003.

as inner city homeless persons or intravenous drug users.

ACUTE RESPIRATORY DISTRESS SYNDROME

Acute respiratory distress syndrome (ARDS) is a form of noncardiogenic pulmonary edema that is a result of the nonspecific response of the lung to a variety of insults. ARDS is defined as respiratory failure indicated by a requirement for mechanical ventilation and PaO_2/fraction of inspired oxygen ratio 200 or less in the appropriate clinical setting with one or more recognized risk factors. This presentation is accompanied by new, bilateral, diffuse, patchy or homogeneous pulmonary infiltrates on the chest radiograph, with no clinical evidence of heart failure, fluid overload, or chronic lung disease (pulmonary artery occlusion pressure ≤ 18 mm Hg).[63]

Respiratory failure results from damage to the region of alveolar-capillary oxygen exchange with increased permeability to plasma fluid and protein. ARDS can be caused by a direct injury to the lungs (e.g., aspiration of liquids or inhaled toxins) or may result from circulating inflammatory mediators associated with multisystem trauma, sepsis, or drugs such as aspirin or opioids (Box 75-1). A variety of mediators are impli-

---

BOX 75-1. Conditions Associated with Acute Respiratory Distress Syndrome

Sepsis
Shock
Toxic gas or smoke inhalation
Aspiration
   Gastric contents
   Near-drowning
   Hydrocarbons/solvents
Pneumonia
Drug reaction
   Salicylates
   Opiates
   Tricyclic antidepressants
   Cyclosporine
   Amiodarone
   Cancer chemotherapeutic agents (e.g., bleomycin)
   Hydrochlorothiazide
   Many others
Trauma
Burns
Transfusion reaction
Radiation injury
Pancreatitis
Thromboembolism
Fat embolism
Air embolism
Amniotic fluid embolism
Eclampsia
Neurogenic (e.g., subarachnoid hemorrhage, head trauma)
Disseminated intravascular coagulation
High-altitude exposure
Oxygen toxicity
Cardiopulmonary bypass

---

cated in the development of ARDS, including neutrophil production of proteases and oxygen radicals, interleukins and other cytokines, tumor necrosis factor, and complement factors.[64] This syndrome most often develops in patients already seriously ill in the hospital.

Treatment of ARDS is primarily supportive. High inspiratory pressures and positive end-expiratory pressure often are required to maintain oxygenation, so it is difficult to avoid barotrauma. Peak airway pressures should be kept at less than 35 cm H_2O if possible. Outcome is improved with use of reduced tidal volumes, allowing arterial partial pressure of carbon dioxide ($PaCO_2$) to increase.[65] Inverse-ratio ventilation with prolonged inspiratory time also may be beneficial. Fluid balance must be managed carefully to avoid increased pulmonary capillary pressure while maintaining organ perfusion. Prone positioning during ventilation may improve distribution of perfusion to ventilated lung regions, but improvement in oxygenation is variable. Drugs such as inhaled nitric oxide, N-acetylcysteine, prostaglandin E_1, ketoconazole, and nonsteroidal anti-inflammatory drugs have been studied for ARDS, but results have been variable.[66,67] Corticosteroids do not reduce mortality in early ARDS, but may have benefit in the late fibroproliferative phase. Although mortality is high in ARDS, most survivors recover normal or near-normal lung function. Research is focusing on preventive measures for ARDS that may be used in the emergency department for patients at risk. Agents being studied include aerosolized surfactant, free radical scavengers, prostaglandin inhibitors, and agents that can modify interleukins and other inflammatory mediators.

 KEY CONCEPTS

- Empiric antimicrobial therapy should be started in the emergency department for patients admitted with pneumonia. Empiric therapy should treat the most likely pathogens, including *S. pneumoniae, H. influenzae, M. pneumoniae,* and *C. pneumoniae.*
- HIV or other immunosuppressive conditions should be considered in all patients in whom pneumonia is suspected.
- Respiratory function should be assessed in pneumonia patients using pulse oximetry or other means.
- TB should be considered and respiratory isolation initiated for patients with HIV or other risk factors for TB.
- The disposition of patients with pneumonia is dictated by the patient's underlying medical conditions, the severity of illness and likelihood of clinical deterioration, and the feasibility of home care and outpatient follow-up.

REFERENCES

1. Mandell LA, et al: Update of practice guidelines for the management of community-acquired pneumonia in immunocompetent adults. *Clin Infect Dis* 37:1405, 2003.
2. Meehan TP, et al: Quality of care, process, and outcomes in elderly patients with pneumonia. *JAMA* 278:2080, 1997.

3. Fang GD, et al: New and emerging etiologies for community-acquired pneumonia with implications for therapy: A prospective multicenter study of 359 cases. *Medicine* 69:307, 1990.

4. Marrie TJ, Durant H, Yates L: Community-acquired pneumonia requiring hospitalization: 5-year prospective study. *Rev Infect Dis* 11:586, 1989.

5. Potgieter PD, Hammond JM: Etiology and diagnosis of pneumonia requiring ICU admission. *Chest* 101:199, 1992.

6. Rello J, et al: Microbiological testing and outcome of patients with severe community-acquired pneumonia. *Chest* 123:174, 2003.

7. Beovic B, et al: Aetiology and clinical presentation of mild community-acquired bacterial pneumonia. *Eur J Clin Microbiol Infect Dis* 22:584, 2003.

8. Centers for Disease Control and Prevention: Prevention of pneumococcal disease: Recommendations of the Advisory Committee on Immunization Practices (ACIP). *MMWR Morb Mortal Wkly Rep* 46(No. RR-8):1, 1997.

9. Stack SJ, Martin DR, Plouffe JF: An emergency department-based pneumococcal vaccination program could save money and lives. *Ann Emerg Med* 33:299, 1999.

10. Centers for Disease Control and Prevention: Preventing pneumococcal disease among infants and young children: Recommendations of the Advisory Committee on Immunization Practices (ACIP). *MMWR Morb Mortal Wkly Rep* 49(No. RR-9):1, 2000.

11. Bates JH, et al: Microbial etiology of acute pneumonia in hospitalized patients. *Chest* 101:1005, 1992.

12. Bartlett JG: Anaerobic bacterial infections of the lung and pleural space. *Clin Infect Dis* 16(Suppl 4):S248, 1993.

13. Centers for Disease Control and Prevention: Prevention and control of influenza: Recommendations of the Immunization Practices Advisory Committee (ACIP). *MMWR Morb Mortal Wkly Rep* 52(RR-8):1, 2003.

14. Stockton J, Stephenson I, Flenming D, Zambon M: Human metapneumovirus as a cause of community-acquired respiratory illness. *Emerg Infect Dis* 8:897, 2002.

15. Centers for Disease Control and Prevention: Prevention and treatment of tuberculosis among patients infected with human immunodeficiency virus: Principles of therapy and revised recommendations. *MMWR Morb Mortal Wkly Rep* 47(RR-20):1, 1998.

16. Butler JC, Peters CJ: Hantaviruses and hantavirus pulmonary syndrome. *Clin Infect Dis* 19:387, 1994.

17. Metlay JP, Kapoor WN, Fine MJ: Does this patient have community-acquired pneumonia? *JAMA* 278:1440, 1997.

18. Griffith DE: Pneumonia in chronic obstructive lung disease. *Infect Dis Clin North Am* 5:467, 1991.

19. Hahn DL, Dodge RW, Golubjatnikov R: Association of *Chlamydia pneumoniae* (strain TWAR) infection with wheezing, asthmatic bronchitis, and adult-onset asthma. *JAMA* 266:225, 1991.

20. Grayston JT: Background and current knowledge of *Chlamydia pneumoniae* and atherosclerosis. *J Infect Dis* 181(Suppl 3):S402, 2000.

21. Grayston JT: Infections caused by *Chlamydia pneumoniae* strain TWAR. *Clin Infect Dis* 15:757, 1992.

22. Singal BM, Hedges JR, Radack KL: Decision rules and clinical prediction of pneumonia: Evaluation of low yield criteria. *Ann Emerg Med* 18:13, 1989.

23. Heckerling PS, et al: Clinical prediction rule for pulmonary infiltrates. *Ann Intern Med* 113:664, 1990.

24. Emerman CL, et al: Comparison of physician judgment and decision aids for ordering chest radiographs for pneumonia in outpatients. *Ann Emerg Med* 20:1215, 1991.

25. Syrjala H, et al: High-resolution computed tomography for the diagnosis of community-acquired pneumonia. *Clin Infect Dis* 27:358, 1998.

26. Sherman S, Skoney JA, Ravikrishnan KP: Routine chest radiographs in exacerbations of chronic obstructive pulmonary disease: Diagnostic value. *Arch Intern Med* 149:2493, 1989.

27. Bramson RT, et al: The futility of the chest radiograph in the febrile infant without respiratory symptoms. *Pediatrics* 92:524, 1993.

28. Baraff LJ: Management of fever without source in infants and children. *Ann Emerg Med* 36:602, 2000.

29. Melbye H, et al: Pneumonia—A clinical or radiographic diagnosis? *Scand J Infect Dis* 24:647, 1992.

30. Hall FM, Simon M: Occult pneumonia associated with dehydration: Myth or reality? *Am J Radiol* 148:853, 1987.

31. Caldwell A, et al: The effects of dehydration on the radiologic and pathologic appearance of experimental canine segmental pneumonia. *Am Rev Respir Dis* 112:651, 1975.

32. Mower WR, et al: A comparison of pulse oximetry and respiratory rate in patient screening. *Respir Med* 90:593, 1996.

33. Niederman MS, et al: Guidelines for the initial management of adults with community-acquired pneumonia: Diagnosis, assessment of severity, and initial antimicrobial therapy, and prevention. American Thoracic Society. *Am J Respir Crit Care Med* 163:1730, 2001.

34. Fine MJ, et al: Evaluation of housestaff physicians' preparation and interpretation of sputum gram stains for community-acquired pneumonia. *J Gen Intern Med* 6:189, 1991.

35. Campbell SG, et al: The contribution of blood cultures to the clinical management of adult patients admitted to the hospital with community-acquired pneumonia: A prospective observational study. *Chest* 123:1142, 2003.

36. Landry ML, Cohen S, Ferguson D: Impact of sample type on rapid detection of influenza virus A by cytospin-enhanced immunofluorescence and membrane-linked immunosorbent assay. *J Clin Microbiol* 38:429, 2000.

37. García-Leoni ME, et al. Pneumococcal pneumonia: Adult hospitalized patients infected with the human immunodeficiency virus. *Arch Intern Med* 152:1808, 1992.

38. Steinhart R, et al: Invasive *Haemophilus influenzae* infection in men with HIV infection. *JAMA* 268:3350, 1992.

39. Bartlett JG: Pneumonia in the patient with HIV infection. *Infect Dis Clin North Am* 12:807, 1998.

40. Blatt SP, et al: Total lymphocyte count as a predictor of absolute CD4+ count and CD4+ percentage in HIV-infected persons. *JAMA* 269:622, 1993.

41. Kagawa FT, et al: Serum lactate dehydrogenase activity in patients with AIDS and *Pneumocystis carinii* pneumonia: An adjunct to diagnosis. *Chest* 94:1031, 1988.

42. Katz MH, Baron RB, Grady DB: Risk stratification of ambulatory patients suspected of *Pneumocystis* pneumonia. *Arch Intern Med* 151:105, 1991.

43. Smith DE: Diagnosis of *Pneumocystis carinii* pneumonia in HIV antibody positive patients by simple outpatient assessments. *Thorax* 47:1005, 1992.

44. Magnenat JL, Nicod LP, Auckenthaler R, Junod AF: Mode of presentation and diagnosis of bacterial pneumonia in human immunodeficiency virus-infected patients. *Am Rev Respir Dis* 144:917, 1991.

45. Marik PE: Aspiration pneumonitis and aspiration pneumonia. *N Engl J Med* 344:665, 2001.

46. Rivers E, et al: Early goal-directed therapy in the treatment of severe sepsis and septic shock. *N Engl J Med* 345:1368, 2001.

47. Centers for Disease Control and Prevention: Guidelines for preventing the transmission of *Mycobacterium tuberculosis* in health-care facilities, 1994. *MMWR Morb Mortal Wkly Rep* 43(RR-13):1, 1994.

48. Moran GJ, McCabe F, Morgan MT, Talan DA: Delayed recognition and infection control for tuberculosis patients in the emergency department. *Ann Emerg Med* 26:290, 1995.

49. Karlowsky JA, et al: Factors associated with relative rates of antimicrobial resistance among *Streptococcus pneumoniae* in the United States: Results from the TRUST Sur-

veillance Program (1998-2002). *Clin Infect Dis* 36:963, 2003.

50. Pallares R, et al: Resistance to penicillin and cephalosporin and mortality from severe pneumococcal pneumonia in Barcelona, Spain. *N Engl J Med* 333:474, 1995.

51. Feikin DR, et al: Mortality from invasive pneumococcal pneumonia in the era of antibiotic resistance, 1995-1997. *Am J Public Health* 90:223, 2000.

52. Heffelfinger JD, et al: Management of community-acquired pneumonia in the era of pneumococcal resistance. *Arch Intern Med* 160:1399, 2000.

53. Gleason PP, et al: Associations between initial antimicrobial therapy and medical outcomes for hospitalized elderly patients with pneumonia. *Arch Intern Med* 159: 2562, 1999.

54. Waterer GW, Somes GW, Wunderink RG: Monotherapy may be suboptimal for severe bacteremic pneumococcal pneumonia. *Arch Intern Med* 161:1837, 2001.

55. Masur H: Prevention and treatment of *Pneumocystis* pneumonia. *N Engl J Med* 327:1853, 1992.

56. Consensus statement on the use of corticosteroids as adjunctive therapy for pneumocystis pneumonia in the acquired immunodeficiency syndrome. The National Institutes of Health-University of California Expert Panel for Corticosteroids as Adjunctive Therapy for Pneumocystis pneumonia. *N Engl J Med* 323:1500, 1990.

57. Dunbar LM, et al: High-dose, short-course levofloxacin for community-acquired pneumonia: A new treatment paradigm. *Clin Infect Dis* 37:752, 2003.

58. Centers for Disease Control and Prevention: Prevention and control of influenza: Recommendations of the Immunization Practices Advisory Committee (ACIP). *MMWR Morb Mortal Wkly Rep* 52(RR-8):1, 2003.

59. Fine MJ, Smith DN, Singer DE: Hospitalization decision in patients with community-acquired pneumonia: A prospective cohort study. *Am J Med* 89:713, 1990.

60. Black ER, et al: Predicting the need for hospitalization of ambulatory patients with pneumonia. *J Gen Intern Med* 6:394, 1991.

61. Fine MJ, et al: A prediction rule to identify low-risk patients with community-acquired pneumonia. *N Engl J Med* 336:243, 1997.

62. Marrie TJ, et al: A controlled trial of a critical pathway for treatment of community-acquired pneumonia. *JAMA* 283:749, 2000.

63. Ware LB, Matthay MA: The acute respiratory distress syndrome. *N Engl J Med* 342:1334, 2000.

64. Martin TR: Lung cytokines and ARDS. *Chest* 116:2S, 1999.

65. The Acute Respiratory Distress Syndrome Network: Ventilation with lower tidal volumes as compared with traditional tidal volumes for acute lung injury and the acute respiratory distress syndrome. *N Engl J Med* 342:1301, 2000.

66. Sokol J, Jacobs SE, Bohn D: Inhaled nitric oxide for acute hypoxemic respiratory failure in children and adults. *Cochrane Database Syst Rev* (1):CD002787, 2003.

67. Wyncoll DLA, Evans TW: Acute respiratory distress syndrome. *Lancet* 354:497, 1999.

CHAPTER

76 Pleural Disease

Joshua M. Kosowsky

Pleural disease is commonly encountered in the emergency department. Presentations range in severity from asymptomatic pleural effusion to tension pneumothorax. This chapter reviews the two most common nontraumatic pleural problems seen in the emergency department: spontaneous pneumothorax and pleural inflammation and effusion. Pleural space problems associated with trauma are discussed in Chapter 42. See Chapter 19 for the approach to a patient presenting with pleuritic chest pain.

SPONTANEOUS PNEUMOTHORAX

Perspective

Under normal conditions, the visceral and parietal pleura lie in close apposition, with only a potential space between them. *Pneumothorax* is defined as the presence of free air in the intrapleural space. A *spontaneous pneumothorax* occurs in the absence of any external precipitating factor, either traumatic or iatrogenic. *Primary spontaneous pneumothorax* occurs in individuals without clinically apparent lung disease.

Secondary spontaneous pneumothorax arises in the context of an underlying pulmonary disease process.

The incidence of primary spontaneous pneumothorax is estimated at approximately 15 cases per 100,000 population per year among men and 5 cases per 100,000 population per year among women. Primary spontaneous pneumothorax typically occurs in healthy young men of taller than average height. Factors associated with primary spontaneous pneumothorax include cigarette smoking and changes in ambient atmospheric pressure. Physical exertion does not seem to be a precipitating factor. Familial patterns suggest an inherited propensity in some cases of primary spontaneous pneumothorax. Mitral valve prolapse and Marfan's syndrome are associated with spontaneous pneumothorax in the absence of clinically apparent lung disease.

Approximately one third of spontaneous pneumothoraces occur in the context of underlying pulmonary disease (Box 76-1). The incidence of secondary spontaneous pneumothorax is three times higher in men. The most common condition associated with secondary spontaneous pneumothorax is chronic obstructive pulmonary disease (COPD). Patients with severe COPD (e.g., with forced expiratory volume in 1 second <1 L) are at highest risk. The incidence of spontaneous pneumothorax among patients hospitalized for emphysema is 0.8% and for asthma 0.3%.

Spontaneous pneumothorax occurs in approximately 2% of patients with acquired immunodeficiency syndrome, almost always in the setting of *Pneumocystis carinii* pneumonia.[1] Bilateral pneumothoraces are common with *P. carinii* pneumonia, as are problems with delayed re-expansion and recurrences. Mortality in these patients is high.[2]

Malignancy is another common etiology of secondary spontaneous pneumothorax. The occurrence of spontaneous pneumothorax in a patient with known malignancy should prompt a search for lung metastases. In developing countries, tuberculosis and lung abscess remain leading causes of secondary spontaneous pneumothorax.

BOX 76-1. Causes of Secondary Spontaneous Pneumothorax

Airway Disease
- Chronic obstructive pulmonary disease
- Asthma
- Cystic fibrosis

Infections
- Necrotizing bacterial pneumonia/lung abscess
- *Pneumocystis carinii* pneumonia
- Tuberculosis

Interstitial Lung Disease
- Sarcoidosis
- Idiopathic pulmonary fibrosis
- Lymphangiomyomatosis
- Tuberous sclerosis
- Pneumoconioses

Neoplasms
- Primary lung cancers
- Pulmonary/pleural metastases

Miscellaneous
- Connective tissue diseases
- Pulmonary infarction
- Endometriosis/catamenial pneumothorax

Catamenial pneumothorax is a rare condition in which recurrent spontaneous pneumothorax occurs in association with menses (typically within 72 hours of onset).[3] Although it has been termed *thoracic endometriosis syndrome* and often responds to ovulation-suppressing medications, the exact etiology of catamenial pneumothorax is uncertain.

Spontaneous pneumothorax is rare in childhood. The principles of diagnosis, imaging, treatment, and surgical management for pediatric primary spontaneous pneumothorax are similar to those for adult pneumothorax.[4]

Pathophysiologic Principles

Normally, intrapleural pressure is negative (less than atmospheric), fluctuating from −10 mm Hg to −12 mm Hg during inspiration to approximately −4 mm Hg during expiration. Intrabronchial and intra-alveolar pressures are negative during inspiration (−1 to −3 mm Hg) and positive during expiration (+1 to +3 mm Hg). The alveolar walls and visceral pleura form a barrier that separates the intrapleural and intra-alveolar spaces and maintains the pressure gradient. If a defect occurs in this barrier, air enters the pleural space until either the pressures equalize or the communication seals.

With the loss of negative intrapleural pressure in one hemithorax, the ipsilateral lung collapses. A large pneumothorax results in restrictive ventilation impairment, with reduced vital capacity, functional residual capacity, and total lung capacity. Shunting of blood through nonventilated lung tissue may result in acute hypoxemia, although over time this effect is mitigated by compensatory vasoconstriction in the collapsed lung. In tension pneumothorax, the alveolar-pleural defect acts as a one-way valve, allowing air to pass into the pleural space during inspiration and trapping it there during expiration (Figure 76-1). This trapping leads to progressive accumulation of intrapleural air and increasingly positive intrapleural pressure causing compression of the contralateral lung with asphyxia and worsening hypoxia. Intrapleural pressure exceeding 15 to 20 mm Hg impairs venous return to the heart. If allowed to progress, cardiovascular collapse and death ensue.

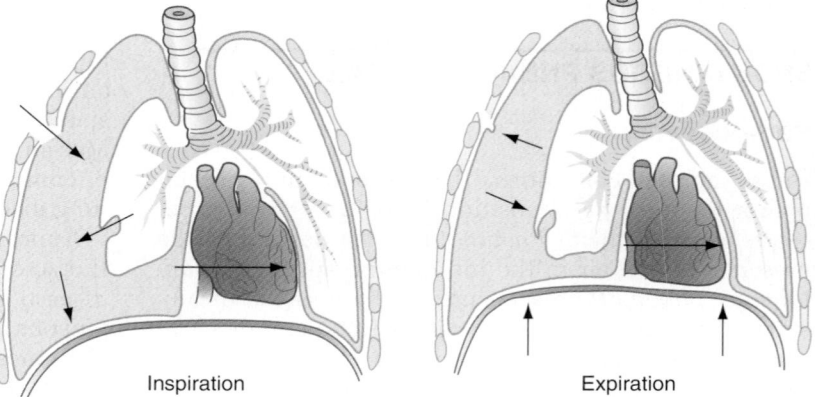

Figure 76-1. Tension pneumothorax with total collapse of the right lung and shift of mediastinal structures to the left. Air is forced into the pleural space during expiration and cannot escape during inspiration.

Inspiration

Expiration

In primary spontaneous pneumothorax, disruption of the alveolar-pleural barrier is thought to occur when a subpleural bulla (or bleb), typically located at the lung apex, ruptures into the pleural space. Subpleural bullae are found in almost all patients who undergo surgical treatment for primary spontaneous pneumothorax and can be identified on computed tomography (CT) of the chest in 90% of cases.[5] The etiology of these bullae is unclear, but is thought to be related to degradation of elastic fibers within the lung and an imbalance in the protease-antiprotease and oxidant-antioxidant systems.[6]

In the case of secondary spontaneous pneumothorax, the underlying lung disease weakens the alveolar-pleural barrier. In patients with *P. carinii* pneumonia, the cytotoxic effects of repeated episodes of inflammation lead to bullous and cystic changes. In patients with COPD, chronic exposure to cigarette smoke results in the development of large, thin-walled bullae that are at an increased risk of rupture. Other factors, including increased intrabronchial and intra-alveolar pressures generated by bronchospasm and coughing, probably also play a role.

Clinical Features

Symptoms of primary spontaneous pneumothorax typically begin suddenly while at rest. Ipsilateral chest pain and dyspnea are the most common symptoms. At the outset, the pain is typically "pleuritic" in nature (i.e., often described as sharp and made worse with deep inspiration), but it often evolves over time into a dull, steady ache. Although patients frequently describe shortness of breath, extreme dyspnea is uncommon in the absence of underlying lung disease or tension pneumothorax. Cough is present in a few individuals. Occasionally, patients are asymptomatic or have only nonspecific complaints. Patients may wait several days before they seek medical attention, and a significant number delay presentation for 1 week or more. Without treatment, symptoms often resolve spontaneously within 24 to 72 hours, although the pneumothorax is still present.

Physical findings tend to correlate with the degree of symptoms. A mild sinus tachycardia is the most common physical finding. With a large pneumothorax, decreased or absent breath sounds with hyperresonance to percussion may be present. Other classic signs include unilateral enlargement of the hemithorax, decreased excursion with respirations, absent tactile fremitus, and inferior displacement of the liver or spleen. Absence of any or all of these findings does not exclude pneumothorax, however, and a chest radiograph should be obtained when pneumothorax is suspected.

With tension pneumothorax, signs of asphyxia and decreased cardiac output develop. Tachycardia (often >120 beats/min) and hypoxia are common. Hypotension is a late and ominous finding. Distention of the jugular veins is common, but may be difficult to detect. Displacement of the trachea to the contralateral side is classically described, but is a rare finding, occurring only in the immediately preterminal phase of the pneumothorax, if at all. Its absence should not be considered evidence that a tension phenomenon is not present.

In patients with significant underlying lung disease, pneumothorax presents differently. Because of poor pulmonary reserve, dyspnea is nearly universal, even when the pneumothorax is small, and symptoms tend not to resolve on their own. Physical findings, such as hyperexpansion and distant breath sounds, often overlap considerably with the underlying lung disease, making the clinical diagnosis difficult. For this reason, the diagnosis of pneumothorax should be considered whenever a patient with COPD presents with an exacerbation of dyspnea.

Although suggested by the patient's history and physical examination, the diagnosis of pneumothorax is generally made with the chest radiograph. The classic radiographic appearance is that of a thin, visceral pleural line lying parallel to the chest wall, separated by a radiolucent band devoid of lung markings. The average width of this band can be used to estimate the size of the pneumothorax with a fair degree of accuracy (Figure 76-2), but in general, it is more reasonable simply to characterize the pneumothorax as small, moderate, large, or total. The estimated size of the pneumothorax and the patient's clinical status can be useful in guiding management decisions.

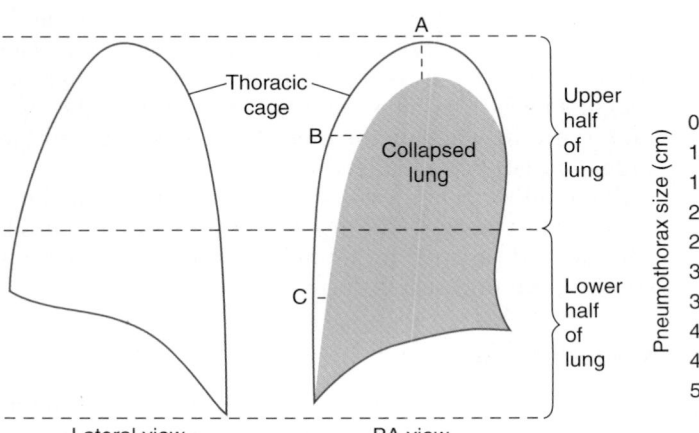

Figure 76-2. Determining the size of a pneumothorax. Calculation of average interpleural distance to predict pneumothorax size. PA, posteroanterior.

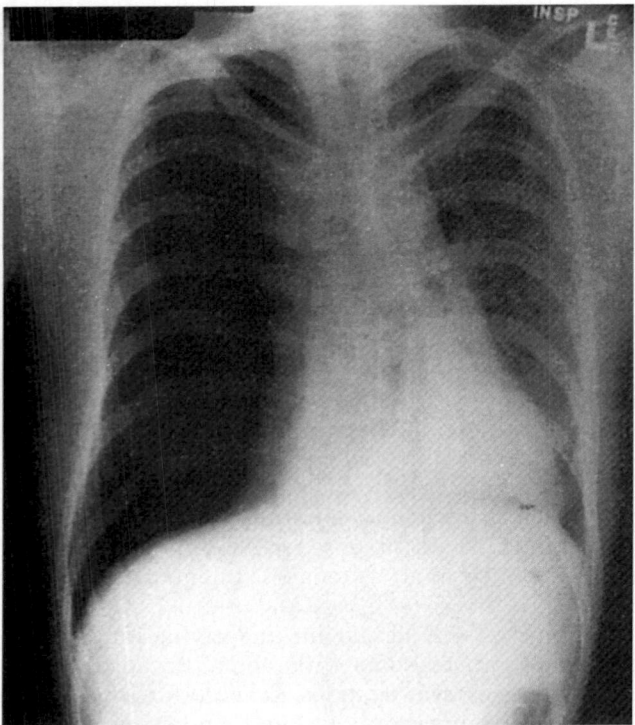

Figure 76-3. Radiograph of tension pneumothorax with mediastinal shift to left.

Tension pneumothorax is a clinical diagnosis, and delaying treatment to obtain radiographic confirmation is inadvisable. When the diagnosis of tension pneumothorax is not apparent clinically, and a chest radiograph is obtained, the classic appearance is one of complete lung collapse with gross distention of the thoracic cavity on the affected side and shift of mediastinal structures across the midline (Figure 76-3). In patients with underlying pulmonary disease, however, pleural adhesions and lack of lung elasticity may mask the fact that a pneumothorax is under significant positive pressure.

When pneumothorax is suspected but not seen on a standard chest radiograph, an expiratory film may be obtained. Theoretically, the volumes of the lungs and the chest cavity are reduced during expiration so that the relative size of the pneumothorax is enhanced. Although occasionally helpful in identifying a small apical pneumothorax, routine use of expiratory films does not improve diagnostic yield.[7] In some cases, a lateral decubitus film (with the suspected hemithorax up) allows visualization of a small amount of intrapleural air along the lateral chest wall. In critically ill patients for whom only a supine chest radiograph can be obtained, the finding of a "deep sulcus" (i.e., a deep lateral costophrenic angle) can suggest the presence of pneumothorax on that side (see Figure 76-3).

Special care should be taken when viewing the chest radiographs of patients with underlying lung disease. In patients with COPD, the relative paucity of lung markings makes pneumothorax more difficult to detect. At the same time, giant bullae may simulate the radiographic appearance of pneumothorax. A clue to differentiating a pneumothorax from a giant bulla is that the former tends to run parallel to the chest wall, whereas the latter tends to have a more concave appearance. When the diagnosis is unclear, a radiograph obtained in a different position (e.g., decubitus) or CT can be used to differentiate between the two entities.[8] Thoracic ultrasound may diagnose pneumothorax rapidly when radiographs are unobtainable; however, data on the accuracy of ultrasound come almost exclusively from studies of traumatic pneumothorax.[9]

The differential diagnosis of pneumothorax includes numerous conditions associated with chest pain and dyspnea. The most important of these is acute pulmonary embolism, which may present in identical fashion but without confirmatory radiographic findings of pneumothorax. Acute or chronic pulmonary embolism especially should be considered in patients with COPD exacerbation that is not typical for them. Pleural irritation caused by inflammation also may mimic pneumothorax. Often the pain of the pleural irritation creates a sensation of shortness of breath, even when true dyspnea and hypoxemia are absent. Most pleural-based processes (pneumonia, embolism, tumor) have corresponding findings on chest radiograph.

Pneumothorax can mimic an acute myocardial infarction with electrocardiogram changes simulating an acute injury pattern.[10] Electrocardiogram changes, including axis deviation, decreased QRS voltage, and T wave inversions, may occur as a consequence of mechanical displacement of the heart, increased intrathoracic air, acute right ventricular overload, or hypoxia resulting in myocardial ischemia.

Spontaneous pneumomediastinum is a closely related clinical entity, diagnosed by presence of subcutaneous emphysema and the finding of mediastinal air on chest radiograph. In contrast to spontaneous pneumothorax, spontaneous pneumomediastinum typically occurs during exertion, particularly after a strenuous Valsalva maneuver. Most cases of spontaneous pneumomediastinum occur in the absence of known underlying disease and have a benign course. Secondary causes of pneumomediastinum (e.g., Boerhaave's syndrome) are more serious, and treatment is aimed at the underlying disorder.

Spontaneous hemopneumothorax is a rare but potentially serious condition that occurs when collapse of the lung is associated with rupture of a vessel in a parietopleural adhesion. The clinical presentation is similar to that of spontaneous pneumothorax, but may be accompanied by symptoms and signs of hemorrhagic shock. Treatment entails large-caliber tube thoracostomy, to evacuate the pleural space, re-expand the lung, and tamponade bleeding.

Pneumothorax has a readily available, highly reliable confirmatory diagnostic test (i.e., chest radiography). Absence of a pneumothorax on chest radiograph should prompt a search for an alternate diagnosis.

Management

Whether in the field or in the emergency department, if the clinical circumstances suggest tension pneumothorax, treatment should not be delayed awaiting further cardiovascular compromise or definitive diagnosis by chest radiograph. As soon as tension pneumothorax is suspected, the pleural space should be decompressed. This decompression may be accomplished by insertion of an intravenous catheter or by immediate tube thoracostomy, depending on the availability of equipment and the expertise of the providers. The diagnosis is confirmed by the hiss of air escaping under positive pressure as the needle or chest tube enters the pleural space. Needle decompression is only a temporizing procedure, and definitive management requires prompt tube thoracostomy.

The management of spontaneous pneumothorax has two goals: (1) to evacuate air from the pleural space, and (2) to prevent recurrence. Pursuit of the latter goal extends well beyond the realm of the emergency department, but often influences the initial strategy as well. Therapeutic approaches to pneumothorax range from simple observation or aspiration with a catheter to video-assisted thoracoscopic surgery or thoracotomy. Decisions must be individualized and consider several factors, including size of the pneumothorax, severity of signs, presence of underlying pulmonary disease, other comorbidities, history of previous pneumothoraces, patient reliability, degree and persistence of the air leak, and available follow-up monitoring.

For otherwise healthy, young patients with a small primary spontaneous pneumothorax (i.e., <20% of the hemithorax), observation alone may be appropriate. The intrinsic reabsorption rate ranges from 1% to 2% per day, a rate that is accelerated by a factor of 4 with the administration of 100% oxygen.[11] By lowering the alveolar partial pressure of nitrogen, supplemental oxygen increases the rate at which air diffuses across the pleural-alveolar barrier. The disposition of patients managed noninterventionally for a small pneumothorax varies by institution. Most physicians admit these patients for at least 6 hours of observation, often in an emergency department–based observation unit. A repeat chest radiograph can be obtained before discharge to document that there is no increase in the size of the pneumothorax. Discharged patients must be able to obtain emergency medical services quickly and should have definitive follow-up evaluation in 24 hours. Air travel and underwater diving must be avoided until the pneumothorax has completely resolved. Unreliable patients are not candidates for this approach.

For primary spontaneous pneumothoraces that are larger in size (i.e., ≥20% of the hemithorax), aspiration with an intravenous catheter may be attempted. If the chest radiograph 6 hours after aspiration shows no reaccumulation of the pneumothorax, the catheter is removed, and the patient can be discharged home, with the same caveats that apply to patients managed with observation alone.

Although there is not universal agreement on the optimal treatment of patients presenting with a first episode of primary spontaneous pneumothorax, pilot study data suggest that manual aspiration is equally effective as chest tube drainage.[12] Advantages of simple aspiration include low morbidity, lack of invasiveness, and overall cost savings.[13] Reported rates of successful outcome range from 45% to 71%.[14-17] Success is less likely when the patient is older than age 50 or the volume of air aspirated exceeds 2.5 L, suggesting a continuing air leak. If aspiration fails to re-expand the lung fully, the catheter can be attached to a water-seal device or to a one-way Heimlich valve and managed like a small-caliber chest tube.

Although the trend is toward less invasive approaches, tube thoracostomy remains widely used and is the treatment of choice in many clinical circumstances. Most secondary spontaneous pneumothoraces should be managed with tube thoracostomy because less invasive approaches (i.e., observation or simple aspiration) are associated with significantly lower success rates.[17] Patients who present with respiratory distress, have tension pneumothorax, or are likely to require mechanical ventilation should undergo tube thoracostomy to re-expand the lung definitively. If there is detectable pleural fluid (hemothorax or hydrothorax), tube thoracostomy also is required. Finally, tube thoracostomy may be considered in uncomplicated cases of primary spontaneous pneumothorax either as a first-line intervention or after a less invasive approach (i.e., observation or simple aspiration) has failed.

For most primary spontaneous pneumothoraces, placement of a small-caliber (7F to 14F) tube is generally sufficient because air leakage tends to be minimal.[18,19] Small-caliber tubes are easy to insert, are well tolerated by patients, and leave only a small scar after removal. Potential problems with small-caliber tubes include kinking, malposition, inadvertent removal, occlusion by pleural fluid or clotted blood, and large persistent air leaks. For secondary spontaneous pneumothorax, a standard size (20F to 28F) thoracostomy tube is recommended. When there is detectable pleural fluid or an anticipated need for mechanical ventilation, a larger tube size (≥28F) is required.

After insertion, the tube is attached to a water-seal device and left in place until the lung has re-expanded fully and the air leak has ceased. A Heimlich valve, which consists of a one-way flutter valve covered in transparent plastic, can be used in place of a water-seal device and allows for unhindered ambulation. Specific complications associated with the use of a Heimlich valve include accidental disconnection and occlusion by fluid.

Routine application of suction neither increases the rate at which the lung re-expands nor improves patient outcome and is no longer recommended after standard tube thoracostomy.[20] The use of suction (with a pressure of 20 cm H_2O) is reserved for situations in which the lung fails to re-expand after drainage through a water-seal device or Heimlich valve for 24 to 48 hours.

In most cases, chest tube management requires hospital admission, although outpatient management of spontaneous pneumothorax with a small-caliber tube and Heimlich device is described.[21] Common complications of chest tube placement include incorrect placement, pleural infection, and prolonged pain.

Re-expansion pulmonary edema and re-expansion hypotension are rare occurrences after rapid evacuation of large pneumothoraces.[22,23]

Outcome

Most spontaneous pneumothoraces resolve within 7 days of tube thoracostomy. Air leaks that persist for longer than 2 days are less likely to resolve on their own. If an air leak persists beyond 4 to 7 days, tube thoracostomy is considered to have failed, and surgical intervention generally is recommended.

Failure of tube thoracostomy is more common with secondary spontaneous pneumothoraces because these tend to be associated with larger and more persistent air leaks. In the setting of COPD, healing of the alveolar-pleural barrier may be impaired by chronic inflammatory changes and loss of vascularity in pulmonary tissue. The success rate also decreases substantially with recurrent episodes of pneumothorax, declining from 91% for treatment of a first pneumothorax to 52% for treatment of a first recurrence and to 15% for treatment of a second recurrence.[24]

Recurrences of spontaneous pneumothorax are common. The risk of recurrence after a primary spontaneous pneumothorax is approximately 1 in 3, with studies reporting rates between 16% and 50%.[25] Younger age, lower weight-to-height ratio, and history of smoking are associated with an increased rate of recurrence. Recurrence rates after a secondary spontaneous pneumothorax are slightly higher (39% to 47%).[6]

Because recurrences may be life-threatening for patients with serious underlying lung disease, intervention is advocated to prevent recurrence as part of the initial approach to secondary spontaneous pneumothorax. In contrast, for patients with primary spontaneous pneumothorax, interventions typically are not considered until after a second ipsilateral pneumothorax. Preventive treatment also is recommended for patients who plan to continue activities such as flying or diving that increase the risk of serious complications if a pneumothorax recurs. CT can be used in primary spontaneous pneumothorax to detect emphysematous changes, predict the likelihood of recurrence, and guide decisions with respect to intervention.[26]

A variety of operative and nonoperative interventions prevent recurrences. One strategy promotes adherence of parietal and visceral pleura, which obliterates the pleural space. Pleurodesis can be accomplished by mechanical pleural abrasion or by instillation of sclerosing agents. Another strategy involves resection of apical bullae or other lesions at risk for causing recurrences. Often the two strategies are combined. Minimally invasive procedures, such as video-assisted thoracoscopic surgery, allow for resection of bullae and pleurodesis.[27] Patients with extensive bullae may require thoracotomy for wider visualization of lesions. Success rates are generally good, ranging from 86% to 100%.

PLEURAL INFLAMMATION AND EFFUSION

Perspective

Under normal circumstances, a thin layer of fluid lies between the visceral and the parietal pleura. Pleural effusion implies the presence of an abnormally large amount of fluid in the pleural space. Pleural effusions are relatively common.[28] The most common cause of pleural effusions in Western countries is congestive heart failure, followed by malignancy, bacterial pneumonia, and pulmonary embolism.[28] In other countries, tuberculosis is the leading cause of pleural effusions. Other conditions commonly associated with pleural effusions include viral infections of the lung parenchyma or pleura, uremia, myxedema, cirrhosis, nephrotic syndrome, ovarian hyperstimulation syndrome, collagen vascular diseases (e.g., systemic lupus erythematosus, rheumatoid arthritis), and intra-abdominal processes (e.g., acute pancreatitis, subphrenic abscess, ascites). Esophageal perforation is a rare but uniquely morbid cause of a pleural effusion.

Pleuritis (also referred to as *pleurisy*) is a nonspecific term denoting inflammation of the pleura. Pleuritis can occur with or without significant exudation of fluid into the pleural space. Pleuritis is a common presentation for a range of disease processes, from self-limited viral syndromes to more serious acute conditions, such as pneumonia and pulmonary embolism, to chronic illnesses, such as systemic lupus erythematosus and other connective tissue diseases.

A pleural effusion associated with bacterial pneumonia, bronchiectasis, or lung abscess is called a *parapneumonic effusion*. The term *complicated parapneumonic effusion* refers to parapneumonic effusions that require tube thoracostomy for their resolution. Empyema (or pus in the pleural space) requires the presence of bacteria on Gram stain of the pleural fluid.

Fluid anatomically confined and not freely flowing in the pleural space is termed a *loculated effusion*. Loculated effusions occur when there are adhesions between the visceral and the parietal pleura. Hemothorax and chylothorax (i.e., from rupture of the thoracic duct) are special instances of pleural effusion that are approached separately.

Pathophysiologic Principles

Pleural fluid is produced from systemic capillaries at the parietal pleural surface and absorbed into pulmonary capillaries at the visceral pleural surface. Lymphatics also play an important role in removing pleural fluid. Movement of fluid across the pleural surfaces is governed by Starling's law so that under normal circumstances the direction of pleural fluid flow is largely governed by the difference in hydrostatic pressure between the systemic and the pulmonary circulations (Figure 76-4). Pleural fluid exists in a dynamic equilibrium in which influx equals efflux, with approxi-

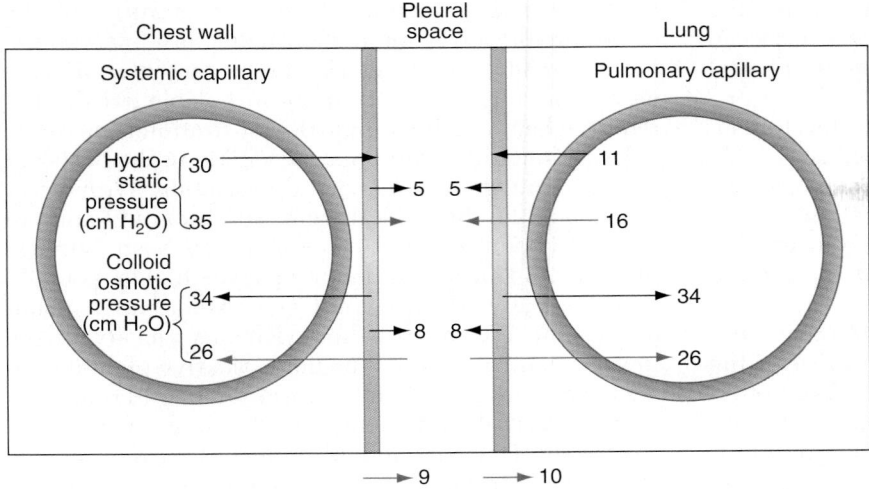

Figure 76-4. Diagram representing pressures involved in formation and absorption of pleural fluid. (Modified from Fraser RG, et al: *Diagnosis of Diseases of the Chest*, 3rd ed. Philadelphia, WB Saunders, 1988.)

mately 1 L of fluid traversing the pleural space in 24 hours. Under normal conditions, the amount of fluid that remains in the pleural space is small (approximately 0.1 to 0.2 mL/kg body weight) and undetectable either clinically or radiographically. Pleural effusion develops whenever influx of fluid into the pleural space exceeds efflux. Numerous disorders can lead to formation of a pleural effusion. Pleural effusions classically are divided into two groups—*transudates* and *exudates*—according to the composition of the pleural fluid (Box 76-2).

Transudates are essentially ultrafiltrates of plasma, containing very little protein. A *transudative effusion* develops when there is an increase in the hydrostatic pressure or decrease in the oncotic pressure within pleural microvessels. The primary cause of increased hydrostatic pressure is congestive heart failure, which is responsible for about 90% of transudative effusions. In hepatic cirrhosis and nephrotic syndrome, increased hydrostatic pressure is combined with loss of plasma oncotic pressure because of significant decreases in serum albumin. Patients with severe malnutrition may develop transudative effusions resulting from severe isolated hypoalbuminemia.

Exudates contain relatively high amounts of protein, reflecting an abnormality of the pleura itself. An *exudative effusion* is the result of increased membrane permeability or defective lymphatic drainage. Any pulmonary or pleural process associated with inflammation can result in an exudative effusion. In the absence of clinically apparent effusion, pleuritic symptoms may still be present. The most common form of exudative effusion is a parapneumonic effusion, in which infection of the adjacent lung elicits an intense inflammatory response in pleura, disrupting normal membrane permeability. Malignant effusions are the second most common form of exudative effusion and often reflect alterations in pleural permeability and problems with lymphatic drainage. Exudative effusions also may arise in response to inflammatory abdominal processes, such as pancreatitis or subphrenic abscess,

BOX 76-2. Causes of Pleural Effusion

Transudates
- Congestive heart failure
- Cirrhosis with ascites
- Nephrotic syndrome
- Hypoalbuminemia
- Myxedema
- Peritoneal dialysis
- Glomerulonephritis
- Superior vena cava obstruction
- Pulmonary embolism

Exudates
Infections
- Bacterial pneumonia
- Bronchiectasis
- Lung abscess
- Tuberculosis
- Viral illness
- Neoplasms
- Primary lung cancer
- Mesothelioma
- Pulmonary/pleural metastases
- Lymphoma

Connective Tissue Disease
- Rheumatoid arthritis
- Systemic lupus erythematosus

Abdominal/Gastrointestinal Disorders
- Pancreatitis
- Subphrenic abscess
- Esophageal rupture
- Abdominal surgery

Miscellaneous
- Pulmonary infarction
- Uremia
- Drug reactions
- Postpartum
- Chylothorax

presumably owing to altered permeability of the diaphragm itself. Exudative effusions may be reabsorbed or organize into fibrous tissue, resulting in pleural adhesions.

Some pleural effusions can present as either transudates or exudates or may have characteristics of both. In the case of pulmonary embolism, the pathogenesis of pleural effusion is often multifactorial, reflecting increased pulmonary vascular pressure (a transudative process) and ischemia and breakdown of the pleural membrane (an exudative process).

Massive effusions (>1.5 to 2 L) are most commonly associated with malignancy, but also can arise in the setting of congestive heart failure, cirrhosis, and other conditions. Massive effusions may restrict respiratory movement, compress the lungs, and result in intrapulmonary shunting. In extremely rare cases, tension hydrothorax can develop, with mediastinal shift and circulatory embarrassment.

Clinical Features

The patient's history often helps to establish the diagnosis for pleural effusion or pleural inflammation. A history of congestive heart failure, liver disease, uremia, or malignancy directs subsequent evaluation of an effusion. The pain of viral pleuritis usually is preceded by several days of a typical viral prodrome, with low-grade fever, sore throat, and other upper respiratory or constitutional symptoms. In the absence of such prodromal symptoms, an alternate etiology for pleuritis must be sought; in particular, the possibility of acute pulmonary embolism should not be overlooked. Symptoms associated with pleural effusion are most often due to the underlying disease process and not the effusion itself. Small pleural effusions can be entirely asymptomatic. A new pleural effusion may be heralded by localized pain or pain referred to the shoulder. Viral pleuritis and pulmonary infarction commonly are associated with pleuritic chest pain. When the volume of pleural fluid reaches 500 mL, dyspnea on exertion or at rest may occur as a result of compromised pulmonary function.

Physical findings depend on the size of the effusion, but are often either dominated or obscured by the underlying disease process. Classic physical signs of pleural effusion include diminished breath sounds, dullness to percussion, decreased tactile fremitus, and occasionally a localized pleural friction rub. The simple technique of auscultatory percussion (i.e., percussing the chest while listening for a dullness with the stethoscope) may be even more sensitive and specific for the physical diagnosis of pleural effusion. Egophony and enhanced breath sounds can often be appreciated at the superior border of the effusion because of underlying atelectatic lung tissue. In the setting of pleuritis, a pleural friction rub may be appreciated. With massive effusions, signs of mediastinal shift may be present.

Chest radiography confirms the clinical suspicion of pleural effusion and occasionally reveals a pleural effusion as an incidental finding. The classic radiographic appearance of a pleural effusion is blunting of the costophrenic angle on the upright chest radiograph. On a frontal (anteroposterior or posteroanterior) projection, a volume of 250 to 500 mL of pleural fluid is required before radiographic demonstration is possible. A lesser amount of fluid may be visible in the posterior costophrenic gutter on a lateral projection. With larger effusions, the hemidiaphragm is obscured, and an upwardly concave meniscus may be seen because pleural fluid has a tendency to layer higher laterally than centrally. Pleural fluid can extend up a major fissure and appear as a homogeneous density in the lower two thirds of the lung field. Massive pleural effusion can appear as a totally opacified hemithorax.

In the recumbent patient, free pleural fluid gravitates superiorly, laterally, and posteriorly and may not be clearly discernible on a supine radiograph. If the effusion is large enough, diffuse haziness or partial opacification of a hemithorax may be seen. Other findings on the supine radiograph may include apical capping, obliteration of the hemidiaphragm, and a widened minor fissure. A cross-table lateral radiograph obtained in the supine position can be used to show posterior layering of a pleural effusion, but a lateral decubitus radiograph (with the involved side down) is better for detection of small amounts of fluid. When combined with slight Trendelenburg positioning, the lateral decubitus view can detect 5 to 15 mL of pleural fluid.[29] A lateral decubitus film also can be used to confirm the layering nature of free pleural fluid. On an upright chest radiograph, pleural thickening may blunt the costophrenic angle and simulate a small pleural effusion. On the lateral decubitus radiograph, thickened pleura does not change in configuration as does free pleural fluid, however, which seeks a new position. Likewise, a loculated pleural effusion does not freely layer on a lateral decubitus film. Ipsilateral and contralateral decubitus views also may allow visualization of the underlying lung and show the underlying cause of the effusion.

The radiographic appearance of pleural effusions can be confusing. Subpulmonic effusions (fluid collections between the lung base and the diaphragm) can be difficult to diagnose, often simulating an elevated hemidiaphragm. Clues to the presence of a subpulmonic effusion include shifting of the apparent dome of the diaphragm toward the lateral chest wall and, when located on the left side, an increase in the distance between the gastric bubble and aerated lung. Fluid that loculates in a fissure may take on a fusiform appearance and can simulate a mass (Figure 76-5). Such "fluid pseudotumors" are common in patients with congestive heart failure.

Other imaging techniques, such as ultrasound, CT, and magnetic resonance imaging may be helpful in localizing effusions, distinguishing transudates from exudates, and characterizing underlying lung processes.[30] Ultrasound also can be used to guide thoracentesis and decrease the risk of complications, particularly in the case of small or loculated effusions.[31]

Pulmonary embolism is the most commonly overlooked disorder in the workup of patients with pleural

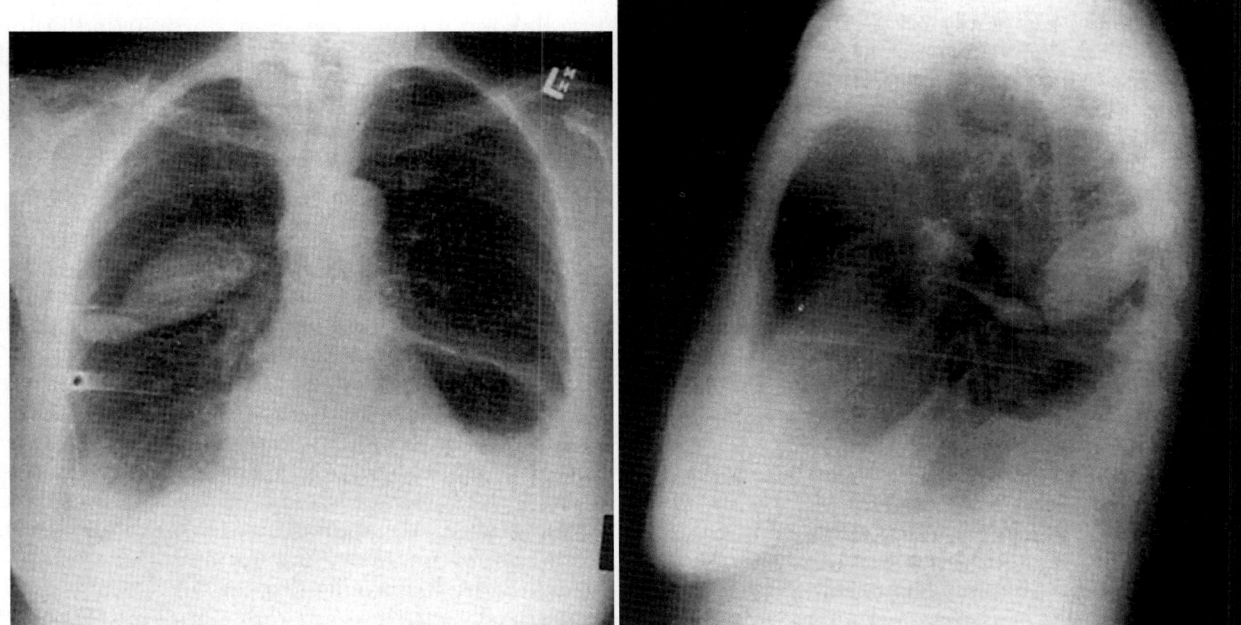

Figure 76-5. Radiographs of pleural effusion along major and minor fissures.

effusions. Pulmonary embolism is the most common cause of pleuritic chest pain and pleural effusion in patients younger than 40 years old, and any patient with an undiagnosed pleural effusion should be evaluated for possible pulmonary embolism.[32] Pleural effusion resulting from pulmonary embolism usually occupies less than one third of the hemithorax, but dyspnea is frequently out of proportion to the size of the effusion. Laboratory studies, such as serum lactate dehydrogenase, can be used to help determine the characteristics of obtained pleural fluid (see later). Serum electrolytes may confirm uremia. Complete blood counts and specifically leukocyte counts are too insensitive and nonspecific to be of discriminatory diagnostic value.

Management

The emergency department management of pleural effusion centers on the underlying disease process. Treatment of serious conditions, such as pulmonary edema or pneumonia, should be initiated without delay.

Pain relief is an important consideration in the management of patients with pleuritis, which may have a significant inflammatory component. Nonsteroidal anti-inflammatory drugs are relatively successful in treating pleural pain.[33] Opioid analgesia is safe and effective, but care should be exercised in debilitated patients or patients with severe lung disease because of potential respiratory depression.

The decision to proceed with thoracentesis in the emergency department, for either diagnostic or therapeutic purposes, must be individualized. Unless thoracentesis is necessary for stabilization of the patient's respiratory or circulatory status, it is appropriately deferred until the patient is admitted. Relatively asymptomatic pleural effusions of clear etiology may not require any further attention. In general, any unexplained pleural effusion requires investigation.

Diagnostic thoracentesis in the emergency department is indicated with potential life-threatening conditions, such as empyema or esophageal rupture in a toxic patient. Thoracentesis should be considered in the emergency department for patients with known, recurrent malignant effusion, in whom the symptomatic relief obtained may permit discharge. In most other cases, if thoracentesis is performed in the emergency department, hospital admission is required to treat the underlying illness and to observe for any complications.

Patients with pneumonia and significant pleural effusion on chest radiograph (i.e., >10mm wide on a lateral decubitus radiograph) should undergo thoracentesis to diagnose empyema or complicated parapneumonic effusion. Patients with pleural effusions that seem to be due to congestive heart failure should undergo thoracentesis if fever or pleuritic chest pain is present or if the effusion is unilateral (particularly if left-sided) or grossly unequal in size.

Relative contraindications to thoracentesis include coagulopathy and other bleeding disorders. Thoracentesis may be safe with a prolonged prothrombin time in the absence of active bleeding.[34] Pleural adhesions, suggested by a prior history of empyema, represent a relative contraindication to thoracentesis because of the high risk of pneumothorax associated with blind needle insertion.

After thoracentesis is completed, a chest radiograph should be obtained to rule out iatrogenic pneumotho-

BOX 76-3. Light's Criteria for Differentiating Transudates from Exudates

Pleural fluid is considered an exudate if one or more of the following hold true:

1. $\dfrac{\text{Pleural fluid protein level}}{\text{Serum protein level}} > 0.5$

2. $\dfrac{\text{Pleural fluid LDH level}}{\text{Serum LDH level}} > 0.6$

3. Pleural fluid LDH level $> \frac{2}{3} \times$ (upper limit of normal for serum LDH level)

LDH, lactate dehydrogenase.
From Light RW, et al: Pleural effusions: The diagnostic separation of transudates and exudates. *Ann Intern Med* 77:507, 1972.

rax. Other potential complications of thoracentesis include hemothorax, lung laceration, shearing of the catheter tip, and infection. Transient hypoxia caused by ventilation-perfusion mismatching often occurs, whereas unilateral, postexpansion pulmonary edema is rare except when large volumes (>1500 mL) are drained in one session. Hypotension also can occur after removal of a large volume of fluid, particularly in patients who are already intravascularly volume depleted.

The primary goal of pleural fluid analysis is to distinguish between transudative and exudative effusions. The presence of a transudate directs attention toward treatment of the underlying process (e.g., congestive heart failure, nephrotic syndrome), whereas the presence of an exudate indicates the need for a more extensive diagnostic evaluation. Although numerous alternative measurements are proposed, Light's criteria still remain a widely accepted means of differentiating transudates and exudates (Box 76-3).[35]

Light's criteria have high sensitivity (98%) for the diagnosis of an exudative effusion, but occasionally misclassify a transudative process as exudative.[36] Some investigators recommend the serum-effusion albumin gradient in such cases. If the serum albumin minus the pleural fluid albumin is greater than 1.2 g/dL, the patient in all probability has a transudative effusion, and Light's criteria can be ignored.[36]

In the presence of an exudative effusion, additional pleural fluid analyses further classify the effusion for diagnostic and therapeutic purposes. The visual appearance and odor of an exudative effusion may or may not be diagnostic of empyema. Regardless, pleural fluid from any patient with an undiagnosed exudative pleural effusion should undergo Gram stain and culture for bacteria (aerobic and anaerobic), mycobacteria, and fungi. (Routine staining for mycobacteria and fungi has a low yield.)

The presence of empyema on the basis of either visual appearance or Gram staining mandates insertion of a chest tube to drain the pleural space adequately and prevent the development of loculations. Tube tho-

racostomy should be performed expeditiously, before a free-flowing effusion develops fibrinous adhesions. If an effusion is already loculated, streptokinase or urokinase can be injected by a thoracic surgeon, pulmonologist, or interventional radiologist into the pleural space in an attempt to dissolve adhesions and allow fluid to drain freely.

Pleural fluid acidosis is a marker of severe pleural inflammation. A pleural fluid pH of less than 7.3 is associated with parapneumonic effusions, malignancies, rheumatoid effusions, tuberculosis, and systemic acidosis. A pH of less than 7.0 strongly suggests empyema (or esophageal rupture). Similar to low pH, high lactate dehydrogenase levels and low glucose levels also reflect an active inflammatory process. On this basis, various combinations of low pH, high lactate dehydrogenase, and low glucose have been used to define which parapneumonic effusions require chest tube drainage. Although there is no absolute consensus of opinion, a pH less than 7.0 and glucose less than 50 mg/dL are reasonable indications for tube thoracostomy in the setting of a parapneumonic effusion.[36]

If the effusion appears bloody, a hematocrit should be obtained on the pleural fluid. In the absence of a traumatic tap, bloody fluid suggests trauma, neoplasm, or pulmonary infarction.[36] If the hematocrit of the pleural fluid is more than 50% that of the peripheral blood, the effusion is, by definition, a hemothorax. A traumatic hemothorax is relatively rare, but can occur with spontaneous rupture of a tumor or blood vessel (e.g., ruptured aortic aneurysm). Hemothorax should be treated with tube thoracostomy to evacuate the pleural space, quantify bleeding, and allow apposition of the two pleural surfaces to tamponade hemorrhage. If bleeding exceeds 200 mL/hr, thoracotomy should be considered.

A pleural fluid cell count may be helpful. Normal pleural fluid contains less than 1000 white blood cells/mm^3; exudative pleural fluid may contain 10,000 white blood cells/mm^3 or more. Although the absolute cell count has limited diagnostic value, the differential cell count can be helpful. A predominance of neutrophils suggests an acute process, such as pneumonia, pulmonary embolus, or acute tuberculous pleuritis. A predominance of monocytes or lymphocytes suggests a more chronic process, such as malignancy or established tuberculosis.

Additional pleural fluid analyses may be indicated depending on the clinical circumstances. An elevated pleural fluid amylase is highly sensitive for effusions caused by pancreatic disease or esophageal rupture. Pleural fluid amylase level also is elevated in approximately 10% of malignant effusions. Bacterial antigen testing may provide for rapid identification of the pathogen responsible for a parapneumonic effusion. A pleural fluid adenosine deaminase level greater than 45 IU/L or an interferon-γ level greater than 3.7 U/mL is strongly suggestive of a tuberculous effusion.[37,38]

If the diagnosis of a malignant pleural effusion is being considered, pleural fluid should be submitted for cytologic examination. Contrary to popular conception, the sensitivity for diagnosis of pleural malignancy does not depend on the volume of pleural fluid extracted during thoracentesis.[39] Cytologic analysis provides the diagnosis of cancer in 40% to 87% of malignant effusions.[36]

Outcome

Some pleural effusions carry little or no clinical significance. Pleural effusions are a common finding in the postpartum state.[40] Small pleural effusions also are common after abdominal surgery, most resolving spontaneously within a few days. Effusions associated with viral pleuritis are generally self-limited and resolve without specific treatment.

For patients with congestive heart failure, pleural effusions generally respond well to diuretic therapy. If an effusion persists despite several days of aggressive diuresis, a diagnostic thoracentesis should be considered to search for an alternative diagnosis.

Pleural effusions associated with malignancy carry a poor prognosis and are a significant cause of morbidity in patients with advanced cancer. The presence of a malignant effusion indicates disseminated disease, and most of the malignancies that cause pleural effusions— mainly lung or breast carcinoma and lymphoma—are not curable by this stage. Therapeutic thoracentesis can relieve dyspnea in the short-term, but malignant effusions tend to be recurrent, often rapidly so. Management strategies include chemical or mechanical pleurodesis to obliterate the pleural space or placement of a pleuroperitoneal shunt to provide continual drainage. Control of pleural effusions can reduce morbidity and improve quality of life in these patients.[41]

Parapneumonic effusions contribute significantly to the morbidity and mortality of pneumonia.[42] The presence of a parapneumonic effusion has an impact on the decision to hospitalize a patient with community-acquired pneumonia.[43] Empyema can be expected in 5% to 10% of patients with a parapneumonic effusion.[42] In most cases, empyema can be treated adequately with parenteral antibiotics and pleural drainage. When a loculated empyema cannot be drained, surgical or thoracoscopic decortication may be required. Aggressive early surgical drainage results in shorter hospital stays and may be more cost-effective than conservative management.[44] Pulmonary embolism with associated pleural effusion is treated no differently than pulmonary embolism without pleural effusion. Typically the pleural effusion resolves within a few days after instituting anticoagulation therapy.

In nearly 20% of pleural effusions, no definitive diagnosis can be established even after extensive investigation. A sizable percentage of these effusions may be due to viral infections, and most resolve spontaneously without sequelae.

KEY CONCEPTS

- For healthy, young patients with a small (<20%) primary spontaneous pneumothorax, observation alone (with administration of 100% oxygen) is an appropriate treatment option; for larger symptomatic pneumothoraces, simple aspiration with an intravenous catheter is often successful.

- In most cases of secondary spontaneous pneumothorax, tube thoracostomy should be considered because less invasive approaches are associated with lower rates of success.

- Application of suction after routine tube thoracostomy is no longer recommended and does not accelerate lung re-expansion.

- The most common cause of pleural effusions in Western countries is congestive heart failure, followed by malignancy and bacterial pneumonia; however, the diagnosis of pulmonary embolism should not be overlooked with a pleural effusion of uncertain etiology.

- Therapeutic thoracentesis is indicated for the relief of acute respiratory or cardiovascular compromise.

- The clearest indication for diagnostic thoracentesis in the emergency department is to diagnose immediately life-threatening conditions, such as empyema or esophageal rupture in a toxic patient; in most other cases, diagnostic thoracentesis to distinguish between transudative and exudative processes can be deferred to the inpatient unit.

REFERENCES

1. McClellan MD, et al: Pneumothorax with *Pneumocystis carinii* pneumonia in AIDS: Incidence and clinical characteristics. *Chest* 100:1224, 1991.
2. Ingram RJ, et al: Management and outcome of pneumothoraces in patients infected with human immunodeficiency virus. *Clin Infect Dis* 23:624, 1996.
3. Carter EJ, Ettensohn DB: Catamenial pneumothorax. *Chest* 98:713, 1990.
4. Shaw KS, et al: Pediatric spontaneous pneumothorax. *Semin Pediatr Surg* 12:55, 2003.
5. Mitlehner W, Friedrich M, Dissmann W: Value of computer tomography in the detection of bullae and blebs in patients with primary spontaneous pneumothorax. *Respiration* 59:221, 1992.
6. Sahn SA, Heffner JE: Spontaneous pneumothorax. *N Engl J Med* 342:868, 2000.
7. Seow A, et al: Comparison of upright inspiratory and expiratory chest radiographs for detecting pneumothoraces. *AJR Am J Roentgenol* 166:313, 1996.
8. Bourgouin P, et al: Computed tomography used to exclude pneumothorax in bullous lung disease. *J Can Assoc Radiol* 36:341, 1985.
9. Dulchavsky SA, et al: Prospective evaluation of thoracic ultrasound in the detection of pneumothorax. *J Trauma* 50:201, 2001.
10. Werne CS, Sands MJ: Left tension pneumothorax masquerading as anterior myocardial infarction. *Ann Emerg Med* 14:164, 1985.
11. Northfield TC: Oxygen therapy for spontaneous pneumothorax. *BMJ* 4:86, 1971.
12. Noppen M, et al: Manual aspiration versus chest tube drainage in first episodes of primary spontaneous pneumothorax: A multicenter, prospective, randomized pilot study. *Am J Respir Crit Care Med* 165:1240, 2002.

13. Packham S, Jaiswal P: Spontaneous pneumothorax: Use of aspiration and outcomes of management by respiratory and general physicians. *Postgrad Med J* 79:345, 2003.
14. Delius RE, et al: Catheter aspiration for simple pneumothorax. *Arch Surg* 124:833, 1989.
15. Talbot-Stern J, et al: Catheter aspiration for simple pneumothorax. *J Emerg Med* 4:437, 1986.
16. Vallee P, et al: Sequential treatment of a simple pneumothorax. *Ann Emerg Med* 5:45, 1988.
17. Soulsby T: British Thoracic Society guidelines for the management of spontaneous pneumothorax: Do we comply with them and do they work? *J Accid Emerg Med* 15:317, 1998.
18. Martin T, et al: Use of pleural catheter for the management of simple pneumothorax. *Chest* 110:1169, 1996.
19. Conces DJ Jr, et al: Treatment of pneumothoraces utilizing small caliber chest tubes. *Chest* 94:55, 1988.
20. So SY, Yu DYC: Catheter drainage of spontaneous pneumothorax: Suction or no suction, early or late removal? *Thorax* 37:46, 1982.
21. Campisi P, Voitk AJ: Outpatient treatment of spontaneous pneumothorax in a community hospital using a Heimlich flutter valve: A case series. *J Emerg Med* 15:115, 1997.
22. Pavlin DJ, et al: Reexpansion hypotension: A complication of rapid evacuation of prolonged pneumothorax. *Chest* 89:70, 1986.
23. Rozenman J, et al: Re-expansion pulmonary edema following spontaneous pneumothorax. *Respir Med* 90:235, 1996.
24. Jain SK, Al-Kattan KM, Hamdy MG: Spontaneous pneumothorax: Determinants of surgical intervention. *J Cardiovasc Surg (Torino)* 39:107, 1998.
25. Schramel FM, Postmus PE, Vanderschueren RG: Current aspects of spontaneous pneumothorax. *Eur Respir J* 10:1372, 1997.
26. Warner BW, Bailey WW, Shipley RT: Value of computed tomography of the lung in the management of primary spontaneous pneumothorax. *Am J Surg* 162:39, 1991.
27. Massard G, Thomas P, Wihlm JM: Minimally invasive management for first and recurrent pneumothorax. *Ann Thorac Surg* 66:592, 1998.
28. Marel M, et al: The incidence of pleural effusion in a well-defined region: Epidemiologic study in central Bohemia. *Chest* 104:1486, 1993.
29. Henschke CI, et al: Pleural effusions: Pathogenesis, radiologic evaluation, and therapy. *J Thorac Imaging* 4:49, 1989.
30. McCloud TC, Fowler CD: Imaging the pleura: Sonography, CT, MR imaging. *AJR Am J Roentgenol* 156:145, 1991.
31. Yu CJ, et al: Diagnostic and therapeutic uses of chest sonography: Value in critically ill patients. *AJR Am J Roentgenol* 159:695, 1992.
32. Light RW: Pleural effusion due to pulmonary emboli. *Curr Opin Pulm Med* 7:198, 2001.
33. Klein RC: Effects of indomethacin on pleural pain. *South Med J* 77:1253, 1984.
34. McVay PA, Toy PT: Lack of increased bleeding after paracentesis and thoracentesis in patients with mild coagulation abnormalities. *Transfusion* 31:164, 1991.
35. Light RW, et al: Pleural effusions: The diagnostic separation of transudates and exudates. *Ann Intern Med* 77:507, 1972.
36. Light RW: Useful tests on the pleural fluid in the management of patients with pleural effusions. *Curr Opin Pulm Med* 6:245, 1999.
37. Valdes L, et al: Tuberculous pleurisy: A study of 254 patients. *Arch Intern Med* 158:2017, 1998.
38. Villena V, et al: Interferon-gamma in 388 immunocompromised and immunocompetent patients for diagnosing pleural tuberculosis. *Eur Respir J* 9:2635, 1996.
39. Sallach SM, et al: Volume of pleural fluid required for diagnosis of pleural malignancy. *Chest* 122:1913, 2002.
40. Gourgoulianis KI, et al: Benign postpartum pleural effusion. *Eur Respir J* 8:1748, 1995.
41. Ruckdeschel JC: Management of malignant pleural effusion: An overview. *Semin Oncol* 15:24, 1988.
42. Teixeira LR, Villarino MA: Antibiotic treatment of patients with pneumonia and pleural effusion. *Curr Opin Pulm Med* 4:230, 1998.
43. Fine MJ, et al: A prediction rule to identify low-risk patients with community-acquired pneumonia. *N Engl J Med* 336:243, 1997.
44. Lim TK: Management of parapneumonic pleural effusion. *Curr Opin Pulm Med* 7:193, 2001.

Section III **CARDIAC SYSTEM**

CHAPTER

77 Acute Coronary Syndromes

William J. Brady, Richard A. Harrigan, and Theodore Chan

Acute coronary syndrome (ACS) refers to the constellation of clinical diseases occurring as a result of acute myocardial ischemia. ACS includes a spectrum of clinical presentations ranging from unstable angina to non-ST segment elevation myocardial infarction (NSTEMI) and ST segment elevation myocardial infarction (STEMI). ACS and in particular acute myocardial infarction (AMI) remain the leading cause of death in the United States and much of the developed world. Tremendous progress, however, has been made in the last two decades in the diagnosis and management of ACS.

HISTORICAL PERSPECTIVE

Several advances in the mid-1900s drastically changed the approach to acute coronary care. The development of external defibrillators and cardiac pacemakers, as well as new pharmacologic agents, provided physicians with an effective approach for treating life-threatening dysrhythmias—the most feared acute complication of ischemic heart disease. The introduction of selective coronary arteriography by Sones in 1959 revolutionized the evaluation and management of patients with coronary artery disease (CAD). In 1960, Kouwenhoven and colleagues published their method of external cardiac massage, which inaugurated the era of cardiopulmonary resuscitation (CPR).

These developments led to the recognition that the time between onset of symptoms and the initiation of therapy was critical. Day was the first to organize a cardiac arrest team in 1960 and established the first coronary care unit 2 years later, reducing AMI mortality by half. In the 1980s, DeWood and colleagues performed coronary angiography early in the course of AMI and demonstrated coronary occlusion in the infarct-related artery. The early experience of Rentrop with the intracoronary administration of streptokinase in AMI ushered in the era of thrombolysis, now termed fibrinolytic therapy.

Recognition that the majority of sudden deaths from ischemic heart disease occurred outside the hospital led to numerous advances for prehospital ACS care specifically and for Emergency Medical Service (EMS) generally. In 1969, advanced prehospital cardiac care was initiated in Belfast with the use of Pantridge's mobile cardiac care units (CCUs). In 1970, Nagel and coworkers reported the successful use and benefits of prehospital telemetry, providing the technologic basis for field advanced cardiac life support in patients experiencing dysrhythmias or sudden cardiac death. In the 1980s, portable prehospital 12-lead electrocardiograms (ECGs) were introduced, making field diagnosis of ACS possible.

Although much information in the diagnostic evaluation of ACS is still contained within the ECG, computer-assisted and artificial intelligence algorithms improve the diagnostic accuracy of the clinician. More sensitive and specific serum markers for myocyte injury now play a central role in the diagnosis and risk stratification for ACS. Diagnostic tools such as echocardiography, stress testing, nuclear imaging, and the chest pain center (CPC) continue to be studied for their utility in evaluating the chest pain patient with possible ACS in the emergent setting.

Fibrinolytic therapy and interventional, catheter-based techniques revolutionized the treatment of patients with STEMI during the 1980s. Combination therapies with antiplatelet, antithrombotic, and fibrinolytic agents continue to be studied for STEMI patients. Interventional success has improved with the use of newer stenting devices and glycoprotein platelet inhibitors. Efforts aimed at timely, appropriate care for more AMI patients have focused on the establishment of regional cardiac centers as well as expansion of interventional capabilities to smaller hospitals. This revolution in acute reperfusion therapy has made early diagnosis, as well as rapid treatment, a substantial challenge for the emergency clinician.

EPIDEMIOLOGY

Ischemic heart disease and CAD continue to be the leading causes of death among adults in the United States and many developed countries. Ischemic heart disease accounts for nearly 1 million deaths in the United States annually, of which approximately 160,000 occur in persons 65 years of age or younger. More than half of all deaths from cardiovascular disease occur in women, and CAD remains a major cause of morbidity and mortality in women beyond their middle to late fifties.

A significant reduction in age-adjusted mortality from CAD has occurred in the United States over the past four decades.[1,2] In large part, the decline has been accompanied by diminished mortality from AMI. This fall in mortality appears to be due to a reduction in the incidence of AMI by 25% and a sharp drop in the case-fatality rate when a myocardial infarction (MI) has occurred. The reasons for this decline are multiple. Reduction in cigarette smoking, management of lipids, and improved management of hypertension and diabetes mellitus have undoubtedly played a role, along with significant advances in medical treatment, including resuscitation, hospital cardiac care, and the advent of reperfusion and other therapies.

Despite these advances, there is still much room for progress. Annually, nearly 6 million patients are evaluated for chest pain or related complaints in the emergency department in the United States, of whom approximately 2 million are diagnosed with an ACS.[3-5] In addition, approximately 2% of patients with ACS are discharged to home from the emergency department. In the United States, approximately 900,000 persons suffer an AMI, of whom 20% die before reaching the hospital and 30% die within 30 days.[6,7] The majority of fatalities from CAD occur outside the hospital, usually from an ACS-related dysrhythmia within 2 hours of onset of symptoms, suggesting that a number of these deaths could be prevented by improving rapid access to medical care. For many patients who suffer a nonfatal AMI, their lives are limited by an impaired functional status, anginal symptoms, and a diminished quality of life. The economic cost for the evaluation and care of patients with an ACS is estimated to be $100 to $120 billion annually.[8]

SPECTRUM OF DISEASE

ACS includes the spectrum of clinical presentations resulting from the common pathophysiology of myocardial ischemia and necrosis. There is a continuum of disease from asymptomatic CAD and stable angina to unstable angina, AMI, and sudden cardiac death.

Stable Angina

Stable angina pectoris is defined as transient, episodic chest discomfort resulting from myocardial ischemia. This discomfort is typically predictable and reproducible, with the frequency of attacks constant over time. Physical or psychological stress (physical exertion, emotional stress, anemia, dysrhythmias, environmental exposures) may provoke an attack of angina that resolves over a constant, predictable period of time spontaneously, with rest or nitroglycerin (NTG).

The Canadian Cardiovascular Society classification for angina is defined as follows: class I, no angina with ordinary physical activity; class II, slight limitation of normal activity as angina occurs with walking, climbing stairs, or emotional stress; class III, severe limitation of ordinary physical activity as angina occurs on walking one or two blocks on a level surface or climbing one flight of stairs in normal conditions; and class IV, inability to carry on any physical activity without discomfort as anginal symptoms occur at rest.

Unstable Angina

Unstable angina is broadly defined as angina occurring with minimal exertion or at rest, new-onset angina, or a worsening change in a previously stable anginal syndrome in terms of frequency or duration of attacks, resistance to previously effective medications, or provocation with decreasing levels of exertion or stress. Rest angina is defined as angina occurring at rest, lasting longer than 20 minutes, and occurring within 1 week of presentation. New-onset angina is angina of at least class II severity with onset within the last 2 months. Increasing or progressive angina is diagnosed when a previously known angina becomes more frequent, longer in duration, or increased by one class within the last 2 months of at least class III severity. Symptoms that last longer than 20 minutes despite cessation of activity are consistent with angina at rest and indicate the diagnosis of unstable angina.

Unstable angina is often referred to as preinfarction angina, accelerating or crescendo angina, intermediate coronary syndrome, and preocclusive syndrome, underscoring its difference from stable angina. Unstable angina should be considered a possible harbinger of AMI and hence should be treated aggressively. If a patient with a diagnosis of angina comes to the emergency department, the presumption of unstable angina should be made until a thorough clinical evaluation reliably determines otherwise.

Unstable angina can also be defined from a pathophysiologic perspective, irrespective of the temporal course. From this perspective, plaque rupture accompanied by thrombus formation and vasospasm illustrate the intracoronary events of unstable angina; this presentation is characterized frequently by electrocardiographic abnormality, including T wave abnormality and ST segment changes.

Variant angina—also known as Prinzmetal's angina—is caused by coronary artery vasospasm at rest with minimal fixed coronary artery lesions; it may be relieved by exercise or NTG. The ECG reveals ST segment elevation that is impossible to discern from AMI electrocardiographically and, at times, clinically.

Acute Myocardial Infarction

AMI is defined as myocardial cell death and necrosis of the myocardium. The four-decade-old World Health Organization (WHO) definition for AMI has been replaced by new clinical criteria developed jointly by the European Society for Cardiology and American College of Cardiology (ACC) that focus on defining infarction as any evidence of myocardial necrosis. The new clinical definition for an acute, evolving, or recent MI requires a typical rise and fall of the creatinine phosphokinase MB fraction (CK-MB) or troponin biochemical marker for myocardial necrosis with clinical symptoms, ECG changes, or coronary artery abnormality based upon intervention data.[9] The actual definition[9] includes the following; either one of these criteria satisfies the diagnosis for an acute, evolving, or recent MI:

1. Typical rise and gradual fall (troponin) or more rapid rise and fall (CK-MB) of biochemical markers of myocardial necrosis with at least one of the following:
   a. Ischemic symptoms
   b. Development of pathologic Q waves on the ECG
   c. ECG changes indicative of ischemia (ST segment elevation or depression)
   d. Coronary artery intervention (e.g., coronary angioplasty)
2. Pathologic findings of an acute MI

Any one of the following criteria satisfies the diagnosis for established MI:

1. Development of new pathologic Q waves on serial ECGs. The patient may or may not remember previous symptoms. Biochemical markers of myocardial necrosis may have become normal, depending on the length of time that has passed since the infarct developed.
2. Pathologic findings of a healed or healing MI.

In the past, AMI was often classified as transmural or nontransmural on the basis of the presumed pathologic involvement of myocardial tissue. Similarly, the terms *Q wave* and *non-Q wave infarction* were used on the basis of the ECG findings purportedly associated with this pathologic involvement. The former was thought to involve a transmural process that arose with ST segment elevation and resulted in significant myocardial necrosis if unchecked. The latter was defined as a nontransmural, or subendocardial, process that manifested with electrocardiographic changes other than ST segment elevation and resulted in smaller portions of infarcted myocardium. Research suggests that the descriptors *transmural* and *Q wave* are misnomers in that they fail to describe adequately the coronary event and its related pathophysiology, electrocardiographic presentation, and pathologic outcome. The terms *ST segment elevation* (STEMI) and *non-ST segment elevation* (NSTEMI) AMI are preferable.

PATHOPHYSIOLOGY

The underlying pathophysiology of ACS is myocardial ischemia as a result of inadequate perfusion to meet myocardial oxygen demand. Myocardial oxygen consumption is determined by heart rate, afterload, contractility, and wall tension. Inadequate perfusion most commonly results from coronary arterial vessel stenosis as a result of atherosclerotic CAD. Usually, the reduction of coronary blood flow does not cause ischemic symptoms at rest until the vessel stenosis exceeds 95%. Myocardial ischemia, however, may occur with exercise and increased myocardial oxygen consumption when there is as little as 60% vessel stenosis.[4]

CAD is characterized by thickening and obstruction of the coronary vessel arterial lumen by atherosclerotic plaques. Although atherosclerosis is usually diffuse and multifocal, individual plaques vary greatly in composition. Fibrous plaques are considered stable but can produce anginal symptoms with exercise and increased myocardial oxygen consumption because of the reduction in coronary artery blood flow through the fixed, stenotic lesions. Vulnerable or unstable fibrolipid plaques consist of a lipid-rich core separated from the arterial lumen by a fibromuscular cap. These lesions are likely to rupture, resulting in a cascade of inflammatory events, thrombus formation, and platelet aggregation that can cause acute obstruction of the arterial lumen and myocardial necrosis.[10]

Thrombus formation is considered an integral factor in ACS, including unstable angina, NSTEMI, and STEMI. All of these syndromes are initiated by endothelial damage and atherosclerotic plaque disruption, which leads to platelet activation and thrombus formation. Platelets play a major role in the thrombotic response to rupture of coronary artery plaque and subsequent ACS. Platelet-rich thrombi are also more resistant to fibrinolysis than fibrin- and erythrocyte-rich thrombi. The resulting thrombus can occlude the vessel lumen, leading to myocardial ischemia, hypoxia, acidosis, and eventually infarction. The consequences of the occlusion depend on the extent of the thrombotic process, the characteristics of the preexisting plaque, the extent of the vessel obstruction, and the availability of collateral circulation.

In the setting of unstable angina, acute stenosis of the vessel is noted; complete obstruction, however, is encountered in only 20% of cases. In these cases, it is likely that extensive collateral vessel circulation prevents total cessation of blood flow, averting frank infarction.[4,11] With AMI, the occlusive fibrin-rich thrombus is fixed and persistent, resulting in myonecrosis of the cardiac tissue supplied by the affected artery. Angiographic studies demonstrate that the preceding coronary plaque lesion is often less than 50% stenotic, indicating that the most important factors in the infarction are the acute events of plaque rupture, platelet activation, and thrombus formation rather than the severity of the underlying coronary artery stenosis. The wide variety of clinical presentations of patients with complete coronary artery occlusion suggests marked differences in the rate of development of total occlusion, the amount of collateral circulation, or both.

Another important aspect of ACS is vasospasm. After significant coronary vessel occlusion, local mediators and vasoactive substances are released, inducing vasospasm, which further compromises blood flow. Central and sympathetic nervous system input increase within minutes of the occlusion, resulting in vasomotor hyperreactivity and coronary vasospasm. Sympathetic stimulation by endogenous hormones such as epinephrine and serotonin may also result in increased platelet aggregation and neutrophil-mediated vasoconstriction. Approximately 10% of MIs occur as a result of coronary artery spasm and subsequent thrombus formation without significant underlying CAD. This mechanism may be more prevalent during unstable angina and other coronary syndromes that do not result in infarction.

Further myocardial injury occurs at the cellular level as inflammatory, thrombotic, and other debris from the occlusive plaque lesion are released and embolize into the distal vessel. Such embolization can result in obstruction at the microvasculature resulting in hypoperfusion and ischemia of the distal myocardial tissue, even after reopening of the more proximal, initial, obstructing lesion. In particular, the introduction of calcium, oxygen, and cellular elements into ischemic myocardium can lead to irreversible myocardial damage that causes reperfusion injury, prolonged ventricular dysfunction (known as myocardial stunning), or reperfusion dysrhythmias. Neutrophils probably play an important role in reperfusion injury, occluding capillary lumens, decreasing blood flow, accelerating the inflammatory response, and resulting in the production of chemoattractants, proteolytic enzymes, and reactive oxygen species.

CLINICAL FEATURES

Prehospital Evaluation

Appropriate pharmacotherapy for persistent anginal chest pain in the prehospital setting includes sublingual NTG, oral aspirin (acetylsalicylic acid, ASA), and intravenous morphine sulfate. Establishment of the diagnosis of ACS in this setting is difficult, however, as chest pain is a poor predictor of the diagnosis and adjunctive tools for evaluation of the patient are limited.[12] Prehospital 12-lead electrocardiography offers high specificity (99%) and positive predictive value (93%) for AMI in patients with atraumatic chest pain while increasing the paramedic scene time by an average of only 3 minutes. This approach offers the advantages of earlier detection of ST segment elevation AMI as well as more rapid application of reperfusion therapy.[13,14] Prehospital 12-lead electrocardiography would be necessary in the limited populations in whom prehospital fibrinolytic therapy might be applicable, such as those with prolonged out-of-hospital times (greater than 90 to 120 minutes).[13,14]

Emergency Department Evaluation
The History

If there is chest discomfort, the character of the discomfort as well as the onset, location, radiation, duration, and any exacerbating or alleviating factors should be sought. It may be helpful to inquire whether the patient recognizes the sensation or has had it before. Associated symptoms, especially of a cardiac, pulmonary, gastrointestinal, and neurologic nature, should be elicited. Results from prior cardiac testing (e.g., ECGs, echocardiograms, stress tests, cardiac catheterizations) should be obtained.

Traditionally, a history of risk factors for CAD is sought; these include male gender, age, tobacco smoking, hypertension, diabetes mellitus, hyperlipidemia, family history of ischemic heart disease, artificial or early menopause, and cocaine use. Indeed, approximately 80 of a population of more than 122,000 patients with known CAD were found to have at least one of the four conventional risk factors (diabetes mellitus, cigarette smoking, hypertension, or hyperlipidemia).[15] Such risk factors are more relevant to research than to clinical diagnosis, however. Bayesian analysis tells us that risk factors are a populational phenomenon and have no ability to increase or decrease the likelihood of any condition in any one patient. Thus, the presence of an individual risk factor, or a collection of risk factors, is far less important in diagnosing acute cardiac ischemia in the emergency department setting than the history of presenting illness, the presence of ST segment or T wave changes on the ECG, or serum marker abnormalities.[16]

The Classical History

The term angina means "tightening," not pain, per se. Thus, the chest pain of classical angina pectoris may not be pain at all but rather a "discomfort," with a "squeezing," "pressure," "tightness," "fullness," "heaviness," or "burning" sensation. Classically, it is substernal or precordial in location and may radiate to the neck, jaw, shoulders, or arms. If the discomfort does extend down the arm, it classically involves the ulnar aspect. Discomfort in the left chest and radiation to left-sided structures is typical, but location and radiation to both sides or to only the right side may be consistent with angina. Further, classical features of angina pectoris include exacerbation with exertion, a heavy meal, stress, or cold and alleviation by rest. The onset of pain at rest in no way excludes the diagnosis of angina. Anginal discomfort characteristically lasts from 2 to 5 minutes up to 20 minutes, and it is very rare for it to last only a few seconds or to endure for hours or incessantly, "all day." Table 77-1 shows the clinical characteristics of classical anginal chest discomfort.

Symptoms characteristically associated with angina pectoris, or other entities of ACS, include the following: dyspnea, nausea, vomiting, diaphoresis, weakness, dizziness, excessive fatigue, or anxiety. If these symptoms arise, either alone or in combination, as a presenting pattern of known ischemic coronary disease, they are termed anginal equivalent symptoms. Recognition that coronary ischemia may arise with an anginal equivalent, rather than a classical, symptom is the key to understanding the atypical presentation of ACS.

Table 77-1. Clinical Characteristics of Classic Anginal Chest Discomfort

Characteristic	More Likely to Be Angina	Less Likely to Be Angina
Type of pain	Dull, pressure	Sharp, stabbing
Duration	2 to 5 min, always <15-20 min	Seconds or hours
Onset	Gradual	Rapid
Location	Substernal	Lateral chest wall, back
Reproducible	With exertion	With inspiration
Associated symptoms	Present	Absent
Palpation of chest wall	Not painful	Painful, exactly reproduces pain complaint

Modified from Zink BJ: Angina and unstable angina. In Gibler WB, Aufderheide TP (eds): *Emergency Cardiac Care.* St. Louis, Mosby, 1994.

Complaints of "gas," "indigestion," or "heartburn" in the absence of a known history of gastroesophageal reflux disease or reproducible pain upon abdominal palpation should raise suspicion of ACS, and similarly if the heartburn is different from the patient's usual gastroesophageal reflux. Angina pectoris is considered stable or unstable, as already defined.

The Atypical History

A description of typical symptoms (crushing, retrosternal chest pain or pressure) is often lacking in patients with ACS; this lack may be due to atypical features of the pain (e.g., character, location, duration, exacerbating and alleviating factors) or the presence of anginal equivalent symptoms (e.g., dyspnea, nausea, vomiting, diaphoresis, indigestion, syncope). Patients with an ultimate diagnosis of AMI or unstable angina can have pain that is pleuritic, positional, or reproduced by palpation.[17] Some patients describe their pain as burning or indigestion, sharp, or stabbing.[18]

A large study highlights the atypical nature of this disease. Of nearly 435,000 patients ultimately diagnosed with AMI, one third did not have chest pain on presentation.[19] Multiple studies have identified risk factors for atypical presentation of ACS: diabetes mellitus, older age, female gender, nonwhite ethnicity, dementia, no prior history of MI or hypercholesteremia, no family history of coronary disease, and previous history of congestive heart failure or stroke.[19-24] In patients with AMI or unstable angina, atypical presenting complaints include dyspnea, nausea, diaphoresis, syncope, or pain in the arms, epigastrium, shoulder, or neck.

Atypical features of ACS are present with increasing frequency in sequentially older populations; before age 85, chest pain is found in the majority of patients with acute MI, although stroke, weakness, and altered mental status are notably present as atypical presenting symptoms. In those older than 85, however, atypical symptoms are more common than chest pain, with 60% to 70% of patients older than 85 presenting with an anginal equivalent complaint.[21-24]

Table 77-2. Symptoms of Acute Myocardial Infarction: Typical and Atypical

Symptom	Bayer et al[*,†]	Tinker[‡]	Uretsky et al[§]	Pathy[‖]
Typical				
Chest pain	515	51	75	75
Atypical				
Dyspnea	118	19	14	77
Syncope	72	4	1	27
Confusion	46	1		51
Stroke	32	6		26
Fatigue	36	2	4	10
Nausea or emesis	28		1	10
Sudden death				31
Giddiness	18	3		22
Diaphoresis	18			2
Arterial embolus	3			19
Palpitation	4			14
Renal failure				11
Pulmonary embolus				8
Restlessness				4
Abdominal pain			5	
Arm pain only			1	
Cough			1	
Silent				
No symptoms	17	1		
Total	**777***	**87[¶]**	**102****	**387[¶]**

*Patients able to report multiple symptoms; therefore, total exceeds 777.
†Bayer AJ, et al: *J Am Geriatr Soc* 34:263, 1986.
‡Tinker GM: *Age Ageing* 10:237, 1981.
§Uretsky BE, et al: *Am J Cardiol* 40:498, 1977.
‖Pathy MS: *Br Heart J* 29:190, 1967.
¶Patients classified by principal symptom, although all patients with complaint of chest or epigastric discomfort were placed in typical group.
**Same as ¶ except patients with epigastric complaints were placed in atypical group.
Modified from Scott PA, Gibler WB, Dronen SC: Acute myocardial infarction presenting as flank pain and tenderness: Report of a case. *Am J Emerg Med* 9:547, 1991.

Patients with *diabetes mellitus* are at heightened risk for ACS as well as an atypical presentation. Medically unrecognized AMI can occur in 40% of patients with diabetes mellitus compared with 25% of a nondiabetic population, and autopsy data demonstrate that myocardial scar unaccompanied by antemortem diagnosis of MI is three times more likely in diabetics than in their nondiabetic counterparts.[26] Atypical symptoms such as dyspnea, nausea or vomiting, confusion, and fatigue are found commonly in diabetics with AMI.[25,26]

As with age and diabetes, female gender is an important risk factor for MI without chest pain.[24] In some series, less than 60% of women reported chest discomfort at the time of their MI, with others reporting dyspnea, indigestion, or vague symptoms such as weakness, unusual fatigue, cold sweats, sleep disturbance, anxiety, or dizziness.[27,28]

Finally, nonwhite *racial and ethnic populations* may be likely to have atypical symptoms in ACS.[19] There are compelling data demonstrating a disparity in treatment approach related to race in patients with acute manifestations of coronary heart disease[29]; how or whether this is related to the atypical nature of presenting symptoms in different racial groups is not clear.

Symptoms of AMI, both typical and atypical, are shown in Table 77-2; much of these data were derived

Table 77-3. Key Entities in the Differential Diagnosis of Chest Pain

Acute myocardial infarction	Unstable angina
Stable angina	Prinzmetal's angina
Pericarditis	Myocardial or pulmonary contusion
Pneumonia	Pulmonary embolism
Pneumothorax	Pulmonary hypertension
Pleurisy	Aortic dissection
Boerhaave's syndrome	Gastroesophageal reflux
Peptic ulcer disease	Gastritis or esophagitis
Esophageal spasm	Mallory-Weiss syndrome
Cholecystitis or biliary colic	Pancreatitis
Herpes zoster	Musculoskeletal pain

from an elderly population. Risk stratification to identify patients at risk for atypical presentation of ACS cannot be applied to individual patients in the emergency department, and all patients with a history, even atypical, suggestive of ACS warrant consideration of myocardial ischemia as the cause of their presentation.

The Physical Examination

Special attention should be devoted to the pulse for signs of dysrhythmia, respiratory rate for signs of cardiopulmonary failure, and blood pressure for evidence of shock or hypoperfusion. The physician should focus on the cardiac, pulmonary, abdominal, and neurologic examinations, looking for signs of severe illness in patients with symptoms of ACS as well as in an attempt to explore other entities in the differential diagnosis of chest pain and the anginal equivalent syndromes (Table 77-3). Altered mental status, diaphoresis, and signs of congestive heart failure (e.g., rales, a third heart sound, jugular venous distention, hepatojugular reflux, peripheral edema) are all ominous findings in patients presenting with symptoms consistent with ACS. Historical studies using untrained physicians have identified chest wall tenderness or "reproducible" chest wall tenderness in up to 15% of patients ultimately diagnosed with AMI, but these data are highly suspect, and the real incidence of truly reproducible chest wall tenderness (i.e., when the patient reliably identifies to the examiner that the pain produced on palpation is identical to the pain causing the patient's presentation) in ACS is probably vanishingly small.

Outcomes in Atypical Presentations

Not surprisingly, atypical presentation of patients with ACS is linked to delay in diagnosis and poorer outcomes.[30] In the Second National Registry of Myocardial Infarction (NRMI-2) study, patients with MI presenting without chest pain were significantly more likely to die in the hospital (23% versus 9% for patients with chest pain) and were more likely to experience stroke, hypotension, or heart failure that required intervention, possibly reflecting the older age and greater comorbidity in this group.[19] Patients presenting atypically present to medical care later and are less likely to receive aspirin, β-adrenergic blockers, heparin, thrombolysis, and primary angioplasty.[19]

Missed Diagnosis of Acute Coronary Syndrome

Approximately 2% to 8% of patients with acute MI who present to the emergency department are discharged without the condition being identified.[31] The highest mean payments for emergency physician medical malpractice claims are related to this population of patients. Atypical presenting symptoms are an obvious causative consideration. Patients with undiagnosed ACS discharged from the emergency department are significantly younger, more likely to be women or nonwhite, more likely to have atypical complaints, and less likely to have ECG evidence of acute ischemia.[32-34] Among all patients with cardiac ischemia, women younger than 55 years seem to be at highest risk for inappropriate discharge. With respect to ECG findings, 53% of patients with missed AMI and 62% of patients with missed unstable angina had normal or nondiagnostic ECGs, yet for 11% of the MI patients, the emergency department physician failed to detect ST segment elevations of 1 to 2 mm. Finally, the risk-adjusted mortality ratio for all patients with acute cardiac ischemia was 1.9 times higher among nonhospitalized patients as among hospitalized patients.[31] Factors identified with misdiagnosis of ACS in medical malpractice closed claims analysis include physicians with less emergency department experience who had a tendency to document histories less clearly, admitted fewer patients to the hospital, and had difficulty in ECG interpretation.

Early Complications of Acute Myocardial Infarction

Bradydysrhythmia and atrioventricular (AV) conduction block are reported to occur in 25% to 30% of patients with AMI; sinus bradycardia is most commonly seen in this group.[35,36] Patients with AV block in the setting of anterior AMI tend to respond poorly to therapy and have a poor prognosis. Tachydysrhythmias are quite common in the setting of AMI and may be atrial in origin (e.g., sinus tachycardia, atrial fibrillation) or ventricular (e.g., ventricular tachycardia and fibrillation). Not all need to be treated, such as a compensatory sinus tachycardia in patients with AMI complicated by congestive heart failure. Primary ventricular fibrillation occurs in an estimated 4% to 5% of patients with AMI, with 60% of those cases occurring in the first 4 hours and 80% within 12 hours.

Cardiogenic shock can be defined as hypotension with end-organ hypoperfusion resulting from decreased cardiac output that is unresponsive to restoration of adequate preload. Patients at risk include those with large infarcts, prior MI, low ejection fraction on presentation (<35%), older age, and diabetes mellitus. Although some entities in the differential diagnosis can usually be reasonably excluded (e.g., sepsis, anaphylaxis, adrenal crisis, and hypovolemic or hemorrhagic states), other causes of shock with similar presentations should be considered, such as aortic dissection, pulmonary embolism, pericardial tamponade, and ventricular free wall rupture accompanying acute

MI. Adjunctive diagnostic measures include bedside echocardiography and invasive hemodynamic monitoring, with the latter demonstrating systemic hypotension, low cardiac output, elevated filling pressures, and increased systemic vascular resistance. Therapeutic measures include vasopressor and inotropic support, intra-aortic balloon counterpulsation, and early revascularization; fibrinolytic therapy does not appear to decrease mortality when the patient is in cardiogenic shock (see Chapter 80).

Left ventricular free wall rupture occurs in the first 24 hours in one third of cases, and the remainder occur 3 to 5 days after transmural MI. Clinically, free wall rupture may occur with sudden death, pulseless electrical activity, or precipitous decline in the presence of AMI. Subacute presentations include agitation, chest discomfort, and repetitive vomiting. Signs of pericardial effusion on the ECG or echocardiogram are suggestive of the diagnosis in the setting of acute or recent MI. Free wall rupture is almost universally fatal, although prompt diagnosis followed by emergent surgical intervention may rarely be lifesaving; pericardiocentesis is indicated as an immediate temporizing intervention. Rupture of the interventricular septum may also occur; it may arise similarly to cardiogenic shock and free wall rupture of the ventricle. The clue to this diagnosis on physical examination is the development of a new, harsh, loud holosystolic murmur heard best at the left lower sternal border. The diagnosis can be confirmed by echocardiography with color flow Doppler imaging, but the presentation of acute, catastrophic deterioration with a new, harsh systolic murmur should prompt cardiac surgery consultation for repair of a septal defect or ruptured papillary muscle of the mitral valve, both of which are acute surgical emergencies.

Medical therapy including vasopressor and inotropic support, as well as intra-aortic balloon counterpulsation, is an important bridge to the definitive surgical treatments of valve repair or replacement.

Pericarditis, when associated with AMI, can occur early or in a delayed fashion; the former is termed infarct pericarditis, and the latter is known as post-MI syndrome or Dressler's syndrome. *Infarct pericarditis* is associated with transmural insult and thus principally involves the pinnacle of the infarct zone near the epicardium. Although the characteristic ST segment changes may be obscured by ST segment abnormalities related to the infarction itself, if they are evident, they are logically quite localized. Infarct pericarditis is a common cause of new chest pain in the first week after MI; this pain is characteristically pleuritic and worse in the supine position. Embolic complications are more common in patients with infarct pericarditis; linked to this is the higher rate of ventricular aneurysm development in this population.

Dressler's syndrome, unlike infarct pericarditis, does not require transmural involvement. It is a relatively uncommon, late complication occurring from 1 week to several months after the MI. Clinical features include fever, malaise, pleuropericardial pain, and at times the presence of a rub on cardiac auscultation. Laboratory findings are highly nonspecific and include an elevated sedimentation rate and leukocyte count. The ECG may show ST segment–T wave findings of pericarditis, although as with infarct pericarditis, these changes may be overshadowed by the evolving changes of the recent MI. PR segment depression is a telltale clue. Pericardial or pleural effusions may be evident and can be serous or bloody. Echocardiography assesses pericardial fluid and risk for tamponade. The pericardial reaction is believed to be immune mediated, and treatment centers on the use of anti-inflammatory agents.

Stroke may also complicate AMI. The most common type of stroke after MI is the ischemic, thromboembolic variety. The major predisposing mechanisms for such strokes in the milieu of recent MI are embolization from left ventricular mural thrombus with decreased ejection fraction, embolization from the atrial appendage with atrial fibrillation, and hypercoagulability with concomitant carotid arterial disease. A case-control study found the rate of stroke to be higher in the setting of MI (0.9% tapering to 0.1% at day 28 after MI) than in control subjects (0.014%).[37]

Hemorrhagic stroke is an obvious concern in the patient receiving fibrinolytic therapy. The rate of hemorrhagic stroke across several studies with varying fibrinolytic agents is under 1%, although the rate climbs in older patients. Percutaneous coronary intervention lowers the overall risk of stroke compared with fibrinolytic therapy. Analysis of only fibrinolytic-eligible patients from the NRMI-2 database yielded more than 24,000 patients treated with alteplase and more than 4000 who received primary angioplasty; the difference in stroke rate is highly significant (1.6% in the fibrinolytic group versus 0.7% in the angioplasty group). Considering hemorrhagic strokes, the difference is again dramatic (1.0% in the fibrinolytic group versus 0.1% in the angioplasty group).[38]

DIAGNOSTIC INVESTIGATIONS

Electrocardiography

In patients with ACS, the ECG assesses the evolution of the syndrome and the response to treatment delivered in the emergency department. It also assists in within-hospital disposition and helps predict risk of cardiac complications and mortality. The ECG is analyzed for signs of ST segment elevation AMI, evidence of cardiac ischemia, determination of cardiac rhythm, and possible evidence of a noncardiac cause of the chief complaint (e.g., in pulmonary embolism, pericarditis).

The ECG in ACS may manifest a variety of dynamic changes. Morphologic changes may occur in the T wave, the ST segment, the QRS complex, and even in the PR segment (e.g., ST segment depression in atrial infarction or infarct-related pericarditis). A variety of rhythm disturbances are also possible. Notably, the ECG may be normal or nonspecifically abnormal in the presence of ACS, including AMI. Thus, a single ECG must be evaluated in context; although it is a quick, easy, noninvasive test, it is neither 100% sensitive nor 100% specific for AMI, and it is representative of only a single point in time. In addition, it has been shown that overreliance on a normal or nonspecifically abnormal ECG in a patient with anginal chest pain who is currently sensation free—because of either spontaneous resolution or medical therapy—should be avoided. Patients with an initially nondiagnostic ECG who later develop AMI during that hospitalization more often are sensation free or minimally uncomfortable on presentation; these patients frequently also lack a past history of ischemic heart disease. Further, the total elapsed time from chest pain onset in patients with normal ECGs does not assist in ruling out the possibility of AMI in patients with chest pain with a single electrocardiographic observation. Although the negative predictive value is quite high, it is not 100%, even up to 12 hours after the onset of the patient's chest symptoms.[39] The patient's history of the event—and the physician's interpretation of the history—is the most important diagnostic study; the ECG is interpreted within the context of this interpreted history.

Electrocardiographic Abnormalities in Acute Coronary Syndromes

The earliest electrocardiographic finding in AMI is the *hyperacute T wave*. The hyperacute T wave in acute coronary occlusion maintains its vector but becomes tall and peaked within minutes of the interruption of blood flow. It is usually broad based and slightly asymmetric. The hyperacute T wave progresses to ST segment elevation in classic MI. This hyperacuity may be missed on the initial ECG. The differential diagnosis of the tall T wave includes hyperacute T waves of ischemia, hyperkalemia, benign early repolarization (BER), left ventricular hypertrophy (LVH), left bundle branch block (LBBB), and pericarditis (Figure 77-1).

As the AMI progresses, *ST segment elevation* may become evident. Morphologic variations of ST segment elevation can be seen by scrutinizing the part of the waveform from the J (or junction) point at the end of the QRS complex to the apex of the T wave. This upsloping portion of the ST segment usually progresses as it elevates from flat to convex or domed; if flat, it is characteristically horizontally or obliquely so. At times, the ST segment may be concave or scooped in its elevation with AMI; this morphology may progress to a convex shape or may stay the same throughout the infarction. The concave morphology, if noted in all elevated ST segments, is atypical for AMI and more commonly seen with other ST segment elevation syndromes (Table 77-4 and Figure 77-2).[40]

ST segment elevation is measured in millimeters; one block on the ECG tracing is equivalent to 1 mm in height. The baseline is usually considered to be the TP segment, although some advocate using the terminal point of the PR segment. In general, the most definable, constant baseline evident on the ECG should be used.

ST segment elevation, both benign and pathologic, is common (see Table 77-4). Most normal ECGs, especially those of men, may have some degree of ST segment elevation—indeed, upward of 90%. This ele-

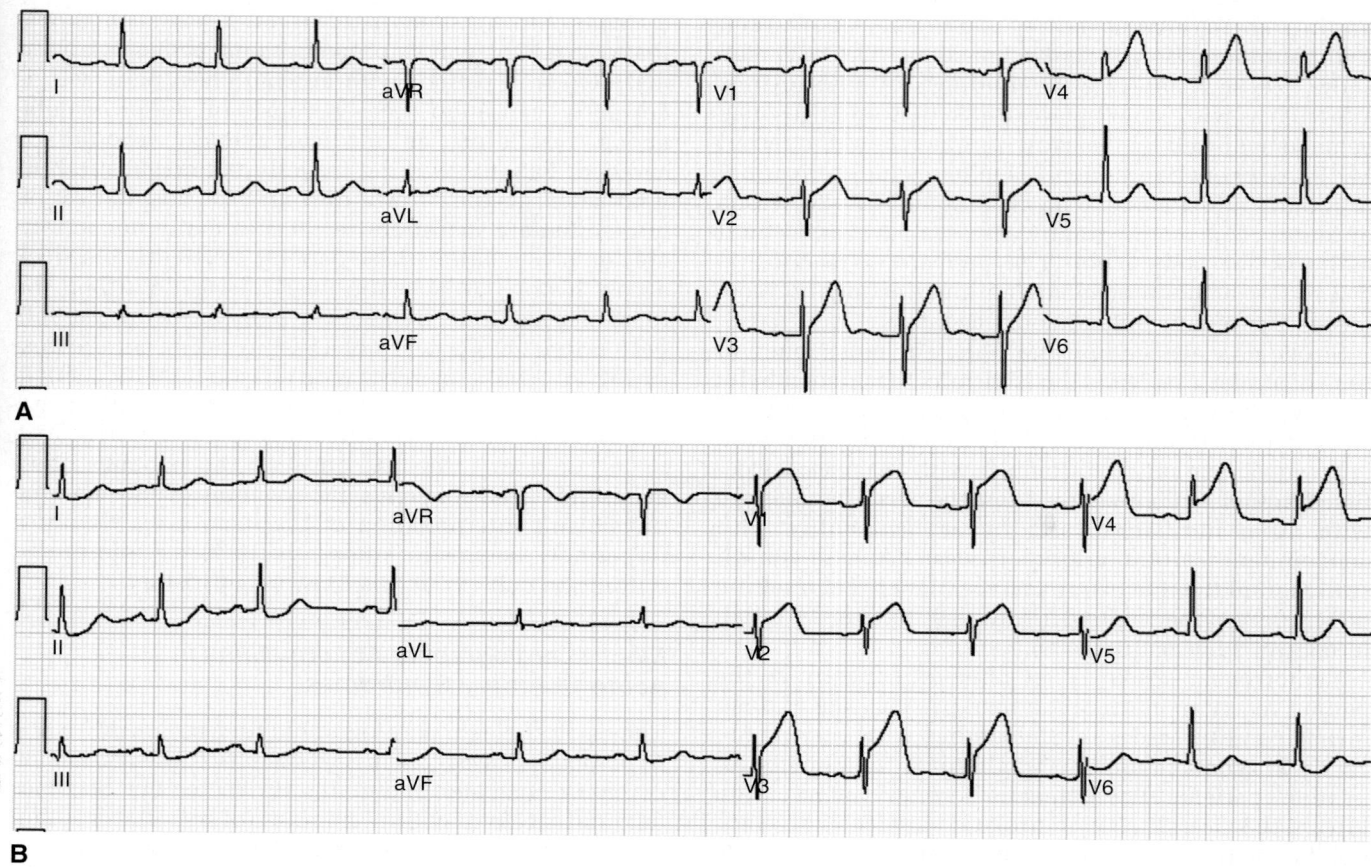

Figure 77-1. Hyperacute T wave of acute myocardial infarction. **A,** Note the broad, tall T waves in leads V_3 and V_4 *(arrows)* in this patient with chest pain and diaphoresis. These are the hyperacute T waves of early ST segment elevation myocardial infarction. The ST segment is just beginning to rise in leads V_3 and V_4; leads V_1 and V_2 are also suspicious. **B,** This tracing is from the same patient, roughly 30 minutes after the electrocardiogram in A. Note the prominent ST segment elevation in leads V_1 to V_4.

Table 77-4. Differential Diagnosis of ST Segment Elevation on the ECG

Acute myocardial infarction	Acute pericarditis
Left ventricular hypertrophy	Left ventricular aneurysm
Ventricular paced rhythm	Benign early repolarization
Normal variant	Osborn wave of hypothermia
Hyperkalemia	Brugada's syndrome
Pulmonary embolism	Acute cerebral hemorrhage
Prinzmetal's angina	Postelectrical cardioversion

vation is seen in the precordial leads and it is usually 1 mm or more in men and 1 mm or less in women. The ST segment elevation is concave and is more prominent the deeper the corresponding S wave. Because of the common occurrence of this finding, it is not a normal variant but rather a normal finding.[41] A helpful point in differentiating normal ST segment elevation from the pathologic ST segment elevation of AMI is that the latter is a dynamic phenomenon; ECGs recorded sequentially over time with waxing and waning symptoms should demonstrate some fluctuation in the degree of ST segment deviation in the presence of ACS.

ST segment depression is generally considered to represent subendocardial or noninfarction ischemia. In addition, ST segment depression in ACS (1) may be seen in non-ST segment elevation AMI, (2) may precede ST segment elevation in ST segment elevation AMI, (3) may reflect a "mirror image" of ST segment elevation from posterior MI when found in the right-sided precordial leads (i.e., ST segment depression in V_1 to V_3 in posterior MI), and (4) may represent reciprocal ST segment depression seen with ST segment elevation AMI. With *reciprocal ST segment depression*, such changes are seen in leads on the "opposite" side of the heart from simultaneous ST segment elevation. Inferior MI with ST segment elevation more frequently manifests reciprocal ST segment depression than does its anterior counterpart. The reciprocal ST segment depression in inferior MI is best seen in lead aVL, which is 150 degrees removed from lead III when considering the positive poles of these leads in the frontal plane. Anterior ST segment elevation AMI may feature reciprocal ST segment depression in at least one of the inferior leads (II, III, or aVF). The ST segment depression seen in leads V_1 to V_3 with posterior MI is actually a reciprocal change from the ST segment elevation that would be recorded in posterior leads V_8 and V_9, were they to be employed. Reciprocal changes in the setting of STEMI increase the likelihood of a poorer outcome; they also increase the specificity and positive predictive value of the ECG in AMI.[42,43]

Ischemic ST segment depression is typically horizontal or downsloping; an upsloping contour may be seen but is less frequently associated with ischemia.

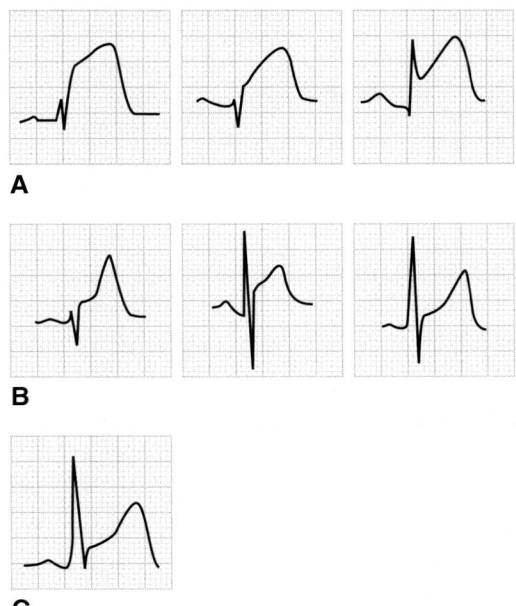

A

B

C

Figure 77-2. Analysis of ST segment–T wave morphology in acute myocardial infarction (AMI), benign early repolarization (BER), and acute pericarditis. An analysis of the ST segment–T wave morphology (from the beginning at the J point to the end at the apex of the T wave) may be particularly helpful in distinguishing among the various causes of ST segment elevation (STE) and identifying the AMI case. **A,** The initial upsloping portion of the ST segment is usually either flat (horizontally or obliquely) or convex in the patient with AMI. This morphologic observation, however, should be used only as a guideline; it is not infallible. **B,** Non-AMI causes of STE are seen here with concavity of the ST segment–T wave (left BER, middle pericarditis, right BER). **C,** Patients with STE related to AMI may demonstrate concavity of this portion of the waveform.

Subendocardial ischemic ST segment depression may be diffuse, spanning anterior and inferior leads. The differential diagnosis of ST segment depression includes myocardial ischemia or infarction, repolarization abnormality of ventricular hypertrophy (the "strain" pattern), bundle branch block, ventricular paced rhythm, digoxin effect, hyperkalemia, hypokalemia, pulmonary embolism, intracranial hemorrhage, myocarditis, rate-related ST segment depression, postcardioversion of tachydysrhythmias, and pneumothorax (Figure 77-3).

T wave inversions, although extremely nonspecific, should suggest possible myocardial ischemia. Normally, the T wave is upright in the left-sided leads I, II, and V_3 to V_6 and inverted in the right-sided lead aVR. T wave vectors are variable in leads III, aVL, and aVF. They are usually normally inverted in V_1 and are occasionally normally inverted in lead V_2. The T wave inversions of ACS are classically narrow and symmetrically inverted; that is, the downsloping portion mirrors the upsloping portion. The preceding ST segment is typically isoelectric and may be bowed slightly upward or concave. Associated ST segment depression may occur. T wave inversions are best viewed in comparison with the most recent prior ECG, given the multitude of normal variations regarding T wave vectors and the nonspecific nature of these changes (Figure 77-4).

A notable subgroup of ischemic T wave inversions are associated with *Wellen's syndrome,* which classically manifests either deep symmetrical T wave inversions or biphasic T wave changes in the anterior precordial leads; the presence of biphasic T waves is suggestive of ischemic heart disease. Other electrocardiographic features include isoelectric or minimally elevated (<1 mm) ST segments and no precordial Q waves. This finding may manifest in the anginal or pain-free state, may or may not be accompanied by cardiac enzyme elevations, and is indicative of a lesion of the left anterior descending artery.

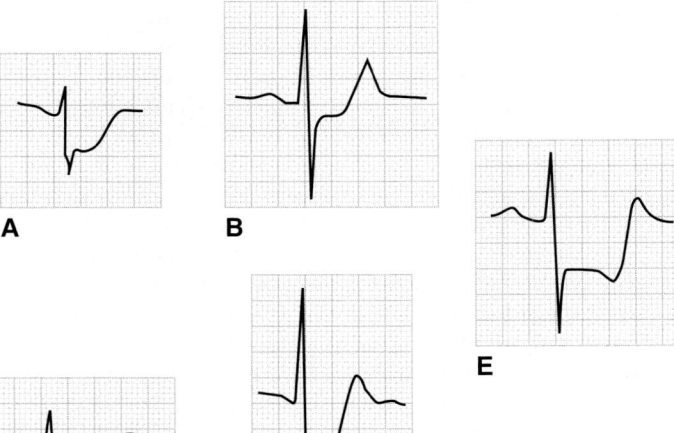

A   **B**

C   **D**   **E**

Figure 77-3. ST segment depression (STD) in ACS. **A,** Horizontal STD unstable angina pectoris (USAP). **B,** Horizontal STD (non-STE acute myocardial infarction). **C,** Downsloping STD (USAP). **D,** Upsloping STD (USAP). **E,** Horizontal STD as seen in lead III in a patient with anterior wall acute myocardial infarction, an example of reciprocal STD, also known as *reciprocal change.* STE, ST segment elevation.

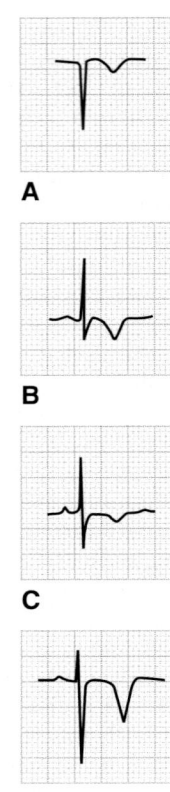

A

B

C

D

Figure 77-4. T wave inversions of ACS. **A** and **B**, T wave inversions in patients with AICS. **C**, T wave inversion in a patient with non-STE acute myocardial infarction. **D**, Deeply inverted T waves in a patient with proximal left anterior descending artery stenosis, Wellen's syndrome. STE, ST segment elevation.

Although T wave inversion is sought as a harbinger of ACS, it can also occur as an evolutionary change after MI. In MI without culprit artery reperfusion, as the ST segments return to baseline, the T waves may invert, although not particularly deeply. In hearts that have been reperfused, T wave inversion may follow ST segment elevation, in either a biphasic or deeply inverted morphology, appearing much like the T wave changes of Wellen's syndrome.[44,45]

The clinician must also consider pseudonormalization of the T wave as a potential electrocardiographic indicator of ACS. Pseudonormalization occurs with an apparently normal-appearing T wave on the ECG at presentation; a comparison with previous ECGs reveals that the T wave in that distribution had been inverted. The T wave has assumed a normal appearance and may indicate ACS at this presentation.

The differential diagnosis of T wave inversion is broad and includes ACS, ventricular hypertrophy, bundle branch block, ventricular paced rhythm, myocarditis, pericarditis, pulmonary embolism, pneumothorax, Wolff-Parkinson-White syndrome, cerebrovascular accident, hypokalemia, gastrointestinal disorders, hyperventilation, persistent juvenile T wave pattern, and normal variants.

Q waves are generally representative of irreversible myocardial necrosis but are rarely the sole manifestation of AMI. Pathologic Q waves may emerge

Table 77-5. Regional ST Segment Changes in Acute Myocardial Infarction

Location	Leads	ST segment
Anterior wall MI	V_1 through V_4	Elevation
Lateral wall MI	I, aVL, V_5, and V_6	Elevation
Inferior wall MI	II, III, and aVF	Elevation
Right ventricular wall MI	V_4R	Elevation
Posterior wall MI	V_8 and V_9	Elevation
	V_1 through V_3	Depression

MI, myocardial infarction.
Modified from Aufderheide TP, Brady WJ: Electrocardiography in the patient with myocardial ischemia or infarction. In Gibler WB, Aufderheide TP (eds): *Emergency Cardiac Care.* St. Louis, Mosby, 1994.

within the first hour of infarction, but most commonly develop 8 to 12 hours into the infarction. It follows that ST segment elevation with concomitant Q waves does not preclude consideration of emergent reperfusion therapy. Q waves may persist after MI as enduring markers of previous infarction on the ECG; in some cases, however, Q waves disappear with time regardless of whether the infarcted territory was reperfused.

Anatomic Location of Acute Myocardial Infarction

The regional distribution of an AMI can be derived from noting the pattern of the various morphologic changes that have been described. Awareness of the region and extent of the infarction has prognostic and therapeutic implications. Therefore, the true extent of any given MI may not be clearly confined to a given set of regional electrodes (Table 77-5).

Anterior infarctions are primarily evidenced by changes in the precordial leads V_1 to V_4 (Figure 77-5). Septal involvement is reflected by changes in V_1 and V_2. Extension to the lateral wall (i.e., anterolateral MI) is evident if the pathologic changes extend beyond leads V_1 to V_4 to include leads V_5, V_6, I, and aVL. In anterior ST segment elevation AMI, reciprocal ST segment depression may occur in leads III and aVF. The anterior wall is served by the left anterior descending artery. The first diagonal branch of the left anterior descending artery is likely to be involved when the ST segment elevation extends to leads I and aVL.

Lateral infarctions are frequently seen in concert with anterior infarction (anterolateral), inferior infarctions (inferolateral), or inferior infarctions with posterior extension (inferoposterolateral). This association is due to the fact that the lateral wall of the heart is variably served by the left anterior descending, right coronary, and left circumflex coronary arteries. Thus, lateral involvement is manifested by changes in some or all of the lateral leads I, aVL, V_5, and V_6. So-called high lateral infarctions are restricted to leads I, aVL, V_5, and V_6 (Figure 77-6) and are suggestive of occlusion of the left circumflex coronary artery; ST segment elevation in these leads may be accompanied by reciprocal ST segment depression in leads III, aVF, and V_1.

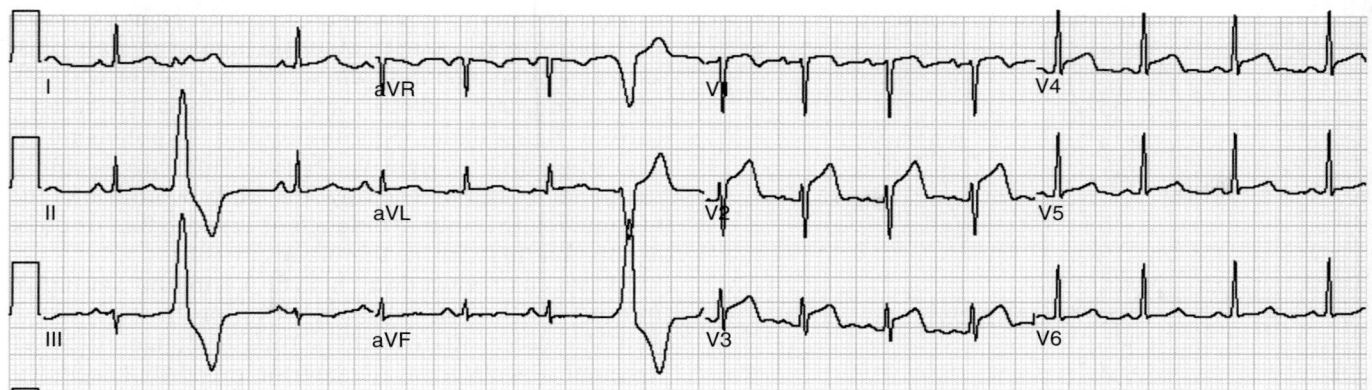

Figure 77-5. Anterior wall acute myocardial infarction (AMI). ST segment elevation is evident in leads V_1 to V_4. The morphology seems obliquely straight. Emergency cardiac catheterization revealed a 90% stenotic lesion in the left anterior descending artery; the patient did well after placement of a coronary stent but showed serum marker evidence of AMI.

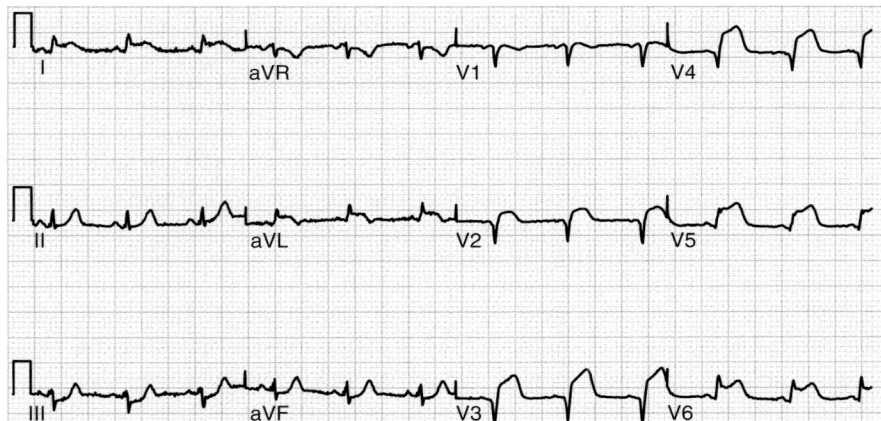

Figure 77-6. Anterolateral acute myocardial infarction. ST segment elevation is seen in leads I, aVL, V_5, and V_6. A proximal left anterior descending artery lesion with thrombus was noted at emergent percutaneous coronary intervention.

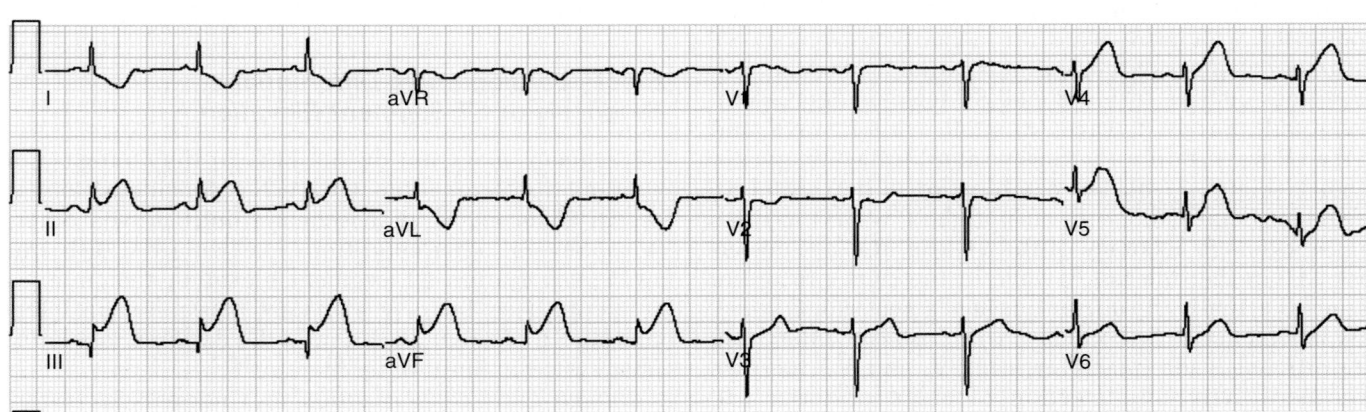

Figure 77-7. Inferior acute myocardial infarction with reciprocal changes. Marked ST segment elevation is seen inferiorly (leads II, III, and aVF). Classic reciprocal ST segment depression is evident in leads I and aVL.

Inferior infarctions are characterized by morphologic changes in limb leads II, III, and aVF. The inferior wall of the heart and the AV node are served by the right coronary artery in roughly 90% of cases (right dominant); in the remainder, the left circumflex artery serves that function (left dominant). An inferior ST segment elevation AMI is present if two or more contiguous inferior leads (III, aVF, II) are involved; reciprocal ST segment depression is frequently seen in lead aVL, lead I, or both (Figure 77-7) and perhaps in the anterior precordial leads: V_1 less than V_2 and V_3. ST segment depression in leads V_1 to V_3 in the presence of inferior MI can be due to reciprocal change, to posterior extension, or to simultaneous anterior ischemia during inferior infarction. ST segment elevation in lead V_1 in the presence of an ST segment elevation inferior MI suggests concomitant right ventricular infarction. Coexistent reciprocal change with inferior STEMI is associated with larger infarct size and increased mortality.

RIGHT PRECORDIAL LEADS

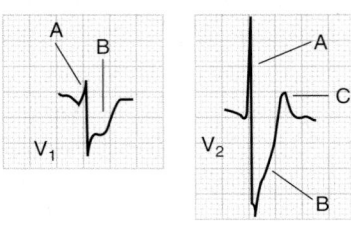

POSTERIOR LEADS

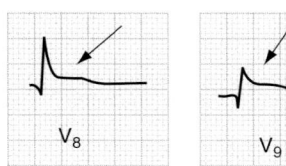

Figure 77-8. Isolated posterior wall acute myocardial infarction (PMI); complexes from right precordial leads and posterior leads. The right precordial leads V_1 and V_2 reveal typical findings of PMI with prominent R wave (A), STD (B), and upright T wave (C). The posterior leads V_8 and V_9 in the same case demonstrate STE *(arrows)*, confirming isolated PMI. STD, ST segment depression; STE, ST segment elevation.

Posterior infarctions as isolated infarctions are rare but are estimated to contribute to 15% to 20% of all AMIs and are usually seen along with inferior or inferolateral infarctions. The culprit lesion may be in the right coronary artery, its posterior descending branch, or the left circumflex artery. In that the 12-lead ECG features no electrodes placed directly over the posterior wall of the heart, one must infer acute STEMI of the posterior wall from what are actually reciprocal ST segment changes in the right precordial leads (V_1 to V_3). Findings include (1) horizontal ST segment depression; (2) a tall, upright T wave; (3) a tall, wide R wave; and (4) an R wave amplitude/S wave amplitude ratio greater than 1 (Figure 77-8). The combination of horizontal ST segment depression with an upright T wave increases the diagnostic accuracy of the 12-lead ECG for posterior MI. In that the tall R wave in the right precordial leads is actually the mirror image of a posterior Q wave, its emergence may be delayed in posterior infarction. Additional leads (posterior leads V_8 and V_9) increase the sensitivity for detection of acute posterior MI. Patients with inferior MI who have either ST segment depression in leads V_1 to V_3 or ST segment elevation in the posterior leads V_8 and V_9 generally have larger infarction zones, lower resultant ejection fractions, and higher cardiovascular morbidity and mortality than patients with isolated inferior MI.[46]

Right ventricular infarctions rarely occur in isolation and are usually associated with inferior or inferoposterior MI, although only about one third of inferior infarctions have associated infarction of the right ventricle. At times, an anterior MI involves some (but less than half) of the right ventricular wall. It follows that occlusion in any of the major coronary arteries may lead to right ventricular infarction, although the right coronary

is most commonly involved. Clinically, right ventricular infarction arises with elevated jugular venous pressure and hypotension in the setting of inferior wall MI. These findings, however, are also suggestive of pericardial tamponade. Nitrate-induced hypotension is also suggestive of right ventricular infarction—and of tamponade. Initial therapy for both would include volume loading and avoidance of vasodilators or other agents that may lower the blood pressure.

ST segment elevation in lead V_1 in the setting of inferior MI (i.e., ST segment elevation in leads II, III, and aVF rather than in the setting of concomitant ST segment elevation in all anterior precordial leads) is suggestive of right ventricular infarction; this is not surprising in that lead V_1 is the most rightward of the precordial leads. These changes occasionally extend into lead V_2 with right ventricular infarction. ST segment elevation is usually greater in lead III than in lead II when right ventricular infarction coexists with inferior AMI.[47] This logically follows in that (in the frontal plane) the positive vector of lead III is more rightward than that of lead II. Application of "right-sided" precordial leads is the best means to diagnose right ventricular infarction with the ECG. These leads, as a mirror image of the left precordial leads, demonstrate ST segment elevation with right ventricular infarction in leads V_3R to V_6R, with V_4R having the highest sensitivity. ECG changes in the right-sided precordial leads with right ventricular infarction may be subtle owing to the smaller muscle mass of the right ventricle and the resulting diminution in QRS size (Figure 77-9). Patients with inferior MI with concomitant right ventricular infarction have larger infarcts and experience more in-hospital complications and higher mortality rates.[48]

Electrocardiographic Differential Diagnosis of ST Segment Elevation

ST segment elevation on the ECG in the context of a presentation compatible with ACS is considered to represent acute myocardial ischemia until proved otherwise. Several other conditions, particularly LBBB and LVH, also feature ST segment elevation that mimics infarction (see Table 77-4).[49] Care is required in interpreting ST segment elevation in the decision to administer systemic fibrinolytic therapy.[50]

Benign early repolarization is a normal electrocardiographic variant that does not imply, or exclude, CAD. BER includes the following electrocardiographic characteristics: (1) ST segment elevation; (2) upward concavity of the initial portion of the ST segment; (3) notching of the terminal portion of the QRS complex at the J point (i.e., junction of the QRS complex with the ST segment); (4) symmetrical, concordant T waves of large amplitude; (5) diffuse ST segment elevation on the ECG; and (6) relative temporal stability over the short term, although these changes may regress with old age. J point elevation is usually less than 3.5 mm, and the concave ST segment is usually elevated less than 2 mm (although it may be elevated as much as 5 mm in some cases) in the precordial leads and 0.5 mm

PART THREE MEDICINE AND SURGERY • Section III Cardiac System

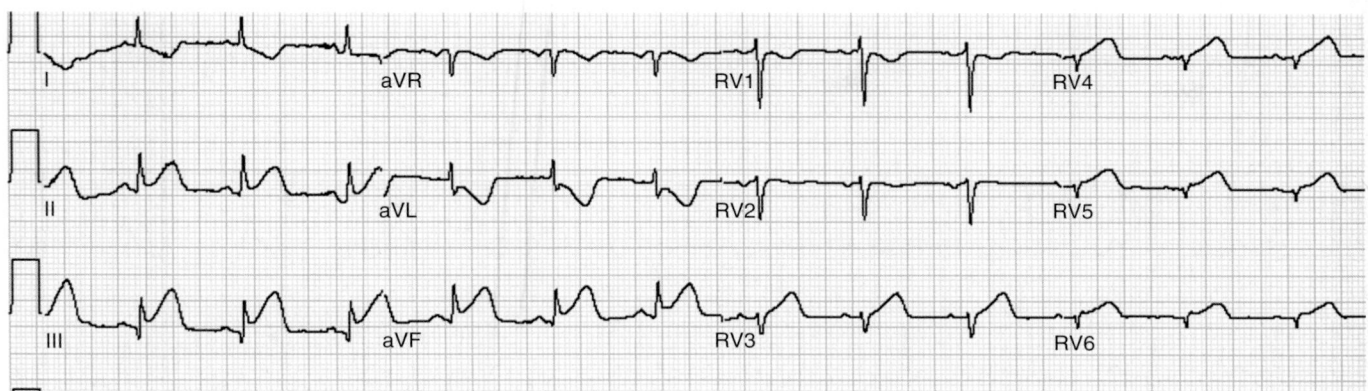

Figure 77-9. Right ventricular infarction demonstrated with right-sided precordial leads (RV₁ to RV₆). This tracing is taken from the same patient as in Figure 77-7. The ST segment elevation of inferior acute myocardial infarction is still present, as is the reciprocal ST segment depression in leads I and aVL. The precordial leads are right-sided chest leads, as might be inferred from the relatively low voltage. ST segment elevation is noted in leads V_3R to V_6R, consistent with right ventricular infarction.

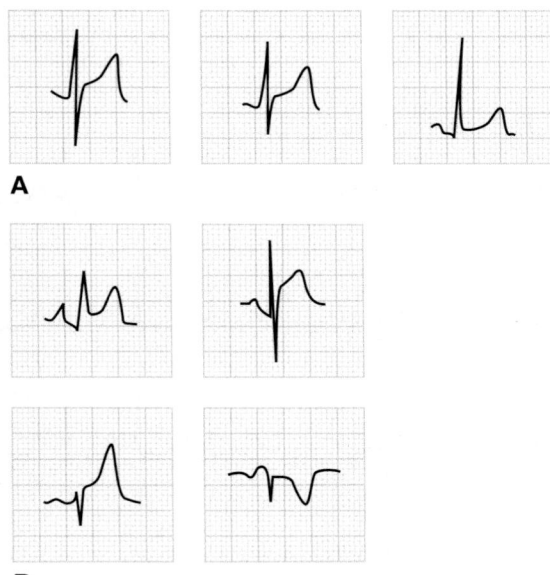

A

B

Figure 77-10. Noninfarctional ST segment elevation (STE). **A,** Benign early repolarization (BER) with concave STE. **B,** Acute pericarditis with concave STE and PR segment depression (*upper two examples*); concave STE without PR segment abnormalities (*lower left example*); and "reciprocal" STD and PR segment elevation in lead aVR (*lower right example*).

in the limb leads. Maximal ST segment elevation in BER is typically seen in leads V_2 to V_5. Isolated BER in the limb leads is quite rare and should prompt reconsideration of AMI (Figures 77-10A and 77-11).

Pericarditis, in the acute phase, features diffuse ST segment elevation as well. In pericarditis, the ST segments are concave with an initial upsloping contour and are usually less than 5 mm in height. Occasionally, the initial contour is obliquely flat, but convex or domed ST segment morphology is suggestive of AMI. The ST segment elevation is usually seen in all leads with the exception of aVR (where it is depressed); V_1 is variable. Focal pericardial inflammation is manifest as a more accentuated change in the leads reflecting the

affected region. PR segment depression is an insensitive yet specific associated electrocardiographic finding in pericarditis, which is typically best seen in the inferior leads and in lead V_6; correspondingly, PR segment elevation may be evident in lead aVR (Figure 77-12; see Figure 77-10B).

Left ventricular aneurysm (LVA), wherein a focal area of myocardium paradoxically bulges outward during systole, has characteristic electrocardiographic changes that can be difficult to differentiate from those of AMI. Considerable overlap exists between populations of patients with potential for AMI and LVA, and the electrocardiographic changes of LVA tend to be regional rather than diffuse.[51] Anatomically, LVA is most commonly found anteriorly, and changes are most often seen in leads V_1 to V_6 as well as leads I and aVL. ST segment elevation may be of any morphology (e.g., convex or concave), and Q waves may be present (Figure 77-13). The calculation of the ratio of the amplitude of the T wave to the QRS complex may help distinguish acute anterior MI from LVA. If the ratio of the amplitude of the T wave to the QRS complex exceeds 0.36 in any single lead, the ECG probably reflects acute MI. If the ratio is less than 0.36 in all leads, however, the findings are probably due to ventricular aneurysm.[52]

Left bundle branch block (LBBB) is a confounding pattern that reduces the ECG's ability to detect ACS. A new, or *presumably new*, LBBB is strongly suggestive of ACS when noted in the appropriate clinical presentation. Preexisting LBBB, however, shares many ECG similarities to various electrocardiographic findings of ACS. In the right-sided precordial leads, ST segment elevation and tall, vaulted, upright T waves mimic those seen in acute anterior MI. The QS pattern of LBBB in these leads resembles the Q waves seen in infarction. Depressed ST segments with T wave inversions are seen in some or all of the lateral leads (V_5, V_6, I, and aVL) in LBBB; both of these resemble ischemic changes seen in ACS. Yet, these findings in LBBB are merely expressions of the "rule of appropriate discordance." The ST segment and T wave vectors are expectedly

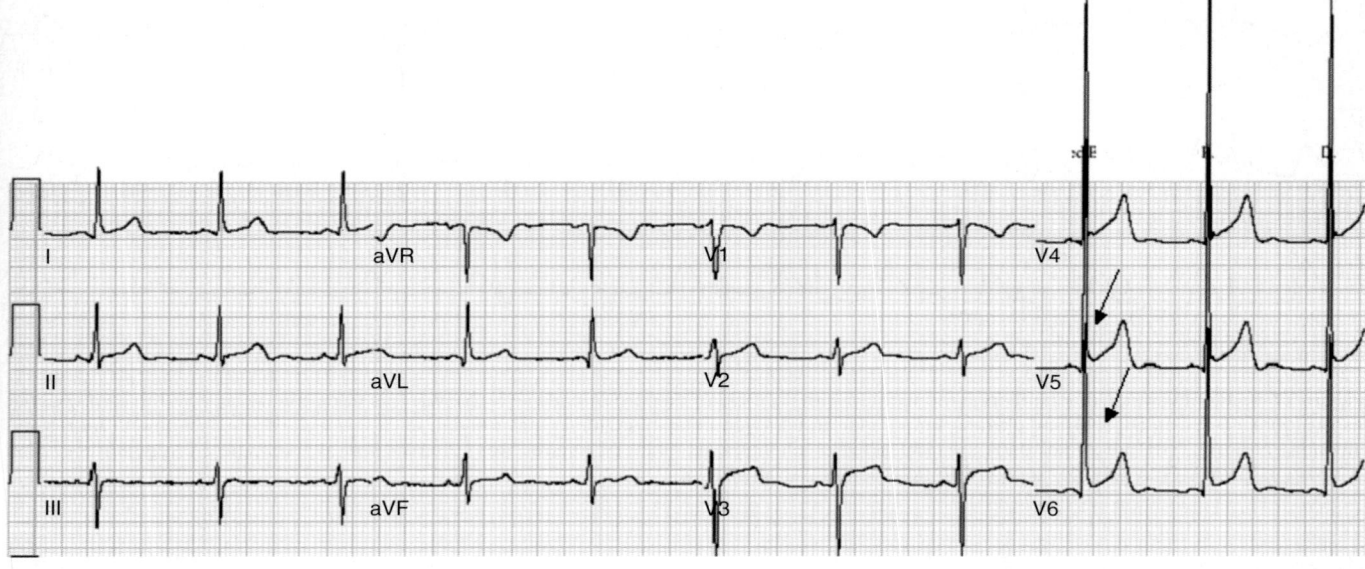

Figure 77-11. Benign early repolarization. Note the upwardly concave ST segment elevation, best seen in leads V_4 to V_6. The T waves are relatively large in the same leads. Subtle notching is also seen at the J point in leads V_4 and V_5. Prior electrocardiograms of this patient were unchanged.

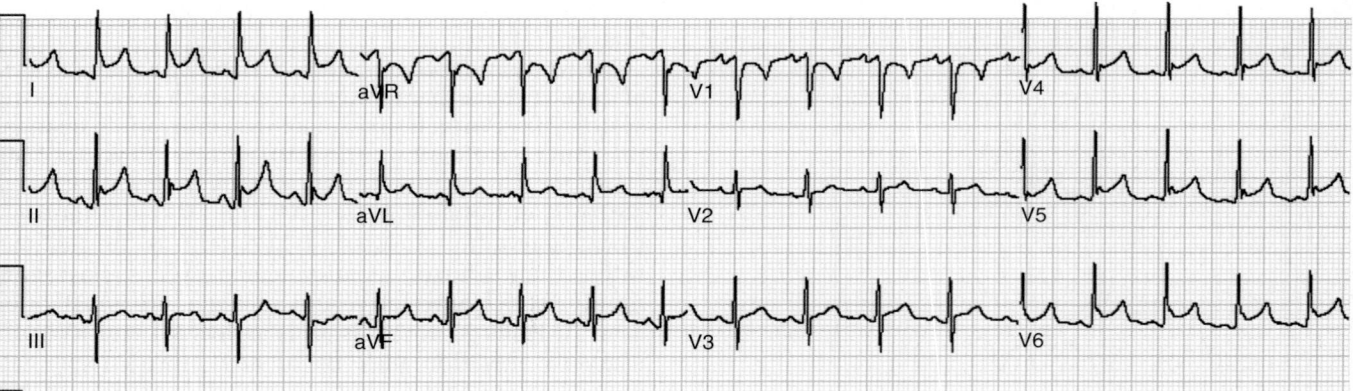

Figure 77-12. Pericarditis. This tracing demonstrates several classic signs of pericarditis: (1) sinus tachycardia; (2) diffuse, concave upward ST segment elevation; (3) PR segment depression, best seen in lead II; and (4) PR segment elevation in lead aVR.

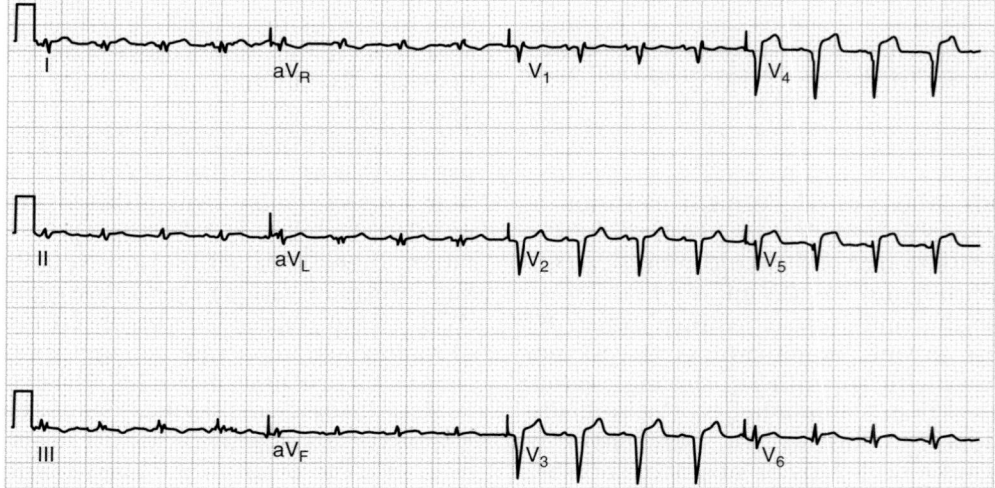

Figure 77-13. Left ventricular aneurysm: representative example of 12-lead electrocardiogram from patient with anterior left ventricular aneurysm. Note well-developed, completed Q waves in leads V_2 through V_5 and absence of reciprocal changes in contralateral leads. (Modified from Aufderheide TP, Brady WJ: Electrocardiography in the patient with myocardial ischemia or infarction. In Gibler WB, Aufderheide TP [eds]: *Emergency Cardiac Care.* St. Louis, Mosby, 1994.)

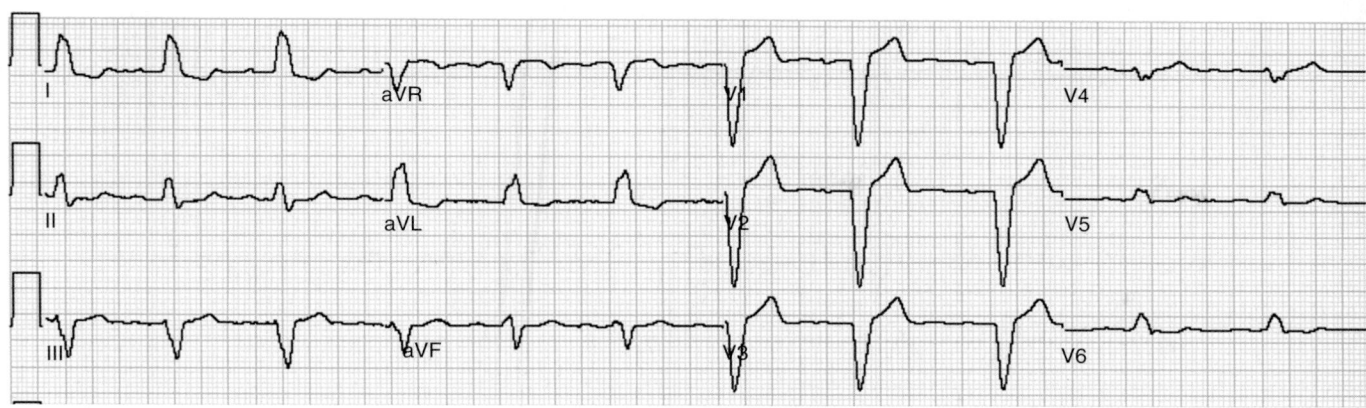

Figure 77-14. Left bundle branch block (LBBB) (normal). This tracing demonstrates the classic findings of LBBB: (1) QRS complex width greater than 0.12 second; (2) absence of Q wave in lead V_6; (3) broad monophasic R wave in leads V_5, V_6, I, and aVL; (4) discordant ST segment–T wave changes in leads V_1 to V_3 (simulating acute myocardial infarction), I, and aVL. A first-degree atrioventricular block is also apparent.

discordant, or opposite in direction, to the major vector of the QRS complex in those leads. Since LBBB is a frequent finding on the ECG of a patient at risk for CAD, the normal findings in LBBB (Figure 77-14), and the presentation of ST segment AMI in a patient with LBBB must be distinguished.

Sgarbossa and colleagues[53] reported using the Global Use of Streptokinase and t-PA for occluded coronary arteries (GUSTO-I) trial database to obtain a population of patients with LBBB and enzymatic evidence of AMI. Three independent electrocardiographic predictors of MI in the presence of LBBB were identified: (1) ST segment elevation of at least 1 mm that is concordant with the QRS complex; (2) ST segment depression of at least 1 mm in lead V_1, V_2, or V_3; and (3) ST segment elevation of at least 5 mm that is discordant with the QRS complex. These findings were assigned weighted scores of 5, 3, and 2, respectively. For accuracy in diagnosis, a specificity of 90% requires a score of at least 3. Thus, if an ECG features only discordant ST segment elevation of 5 mm or more but neither of the other two criteria, further testing is recommended before concluding that the ECG is indicative of AMI[53] (Figure 77-15). Subsequent literature yields mixed reviews of the Sgarbossa criteria[53] for diagnosis of AMI in the presence of LBBB.[54] Ultimately, the approach to the patient with LBBB and possible MI remains complicated; diagnostic adjuncts to the history and physical examination (e.g., serial ECGs, comparison with prior ECGs, echocardiography, serum cardiac marker measurement) should be liberally employed when the ECG does not show obvious evidence of AMI as noted by the Sgarbossa criteria.[53] A new LBBB together with a clinical impression of AMI remains an indication for fibrinolytic therapy.

Ventricular paced rhythms (VPRs) can mimic and mask the manifestations of AMI. VPRs originating in the right ventricular apex create a wide QRS complex, with a pseudo-LBBB pattern. As with LBBB, the right precordial leads in VPR typically feature predominantly negative QRS complexes with discordant ST segments and T waves that are elevated and tall or vaulted, respectively. Unlike LBBB, however, VPR orig-

inating in the right ventricular apex often yields a predominantly negative QRS complex in lead V_6 as well (which is oriented leftward and slightly downward, whereas the impulse generated from the pacemaker wire is oriented superiorly). Furthermore, small vertical pacemaker spikes immediately preceding the QRS complex should be a clue to VPR, although these deflections are at times hard to detect on the 12-lead ECG.

Limited data exist to guide the clinician in interpretation of the 12-lead ECG in this setting. As with the LBBB scenario, the VPR pattern represents a significant confounding variable in the evaluation of the patient with chest pain suspected of having ACS. Sgarbossa and associates advanced criteria for detection of AMI in the presence of VPR[55] that are similar to those for LBBB.[53] These, too, are derived from the GUSTO-I database, but from a smaller group of patients. The criteria are essentially the same as the LBBB criteria: (1) ST segment elevation of at least 5 mm that is discordant with the QRS complex; (2) ST segment elevation of at least 1 mm that is concordant with the QRS complex; and (3) ST segment depression of at least 1 mm in lead V_1, V_2, or V_3. Sensitivities of these findings for AMI were 53%, 18%, and 29%, respectively, and specificities of these criteria for AMI were 88%, 94%, and 82%, respectively (Figure 77-16).[55]

Left ventricular hypertrophy may mimic or obscure ACS on the ECG. LVH may feature prominent left-sided forces, manifesting as large rS or QS complexes in the right precordial leads—yet these changes seldom extend beyond V_1 and V_2 in the case of LVH. Consistent with the rule of appropriate discordance, the leads demonstrating such a pattern feature discordant ST segment elevation and tall, vaulted T waves, paralleling the changes of AMI. The initial portion of the elevated ST segment in LVH is generally concave, as opposed to the obliquely straight or convex pattern that usually (but not always) is seen with ST segment elevation in AMI. In LVH, the left precordial leads (and at times leads I and aVL) may show evidence of repolarization abnormality (or strain pattern), with ST segment depression and asymmetrically inverted T waves. The

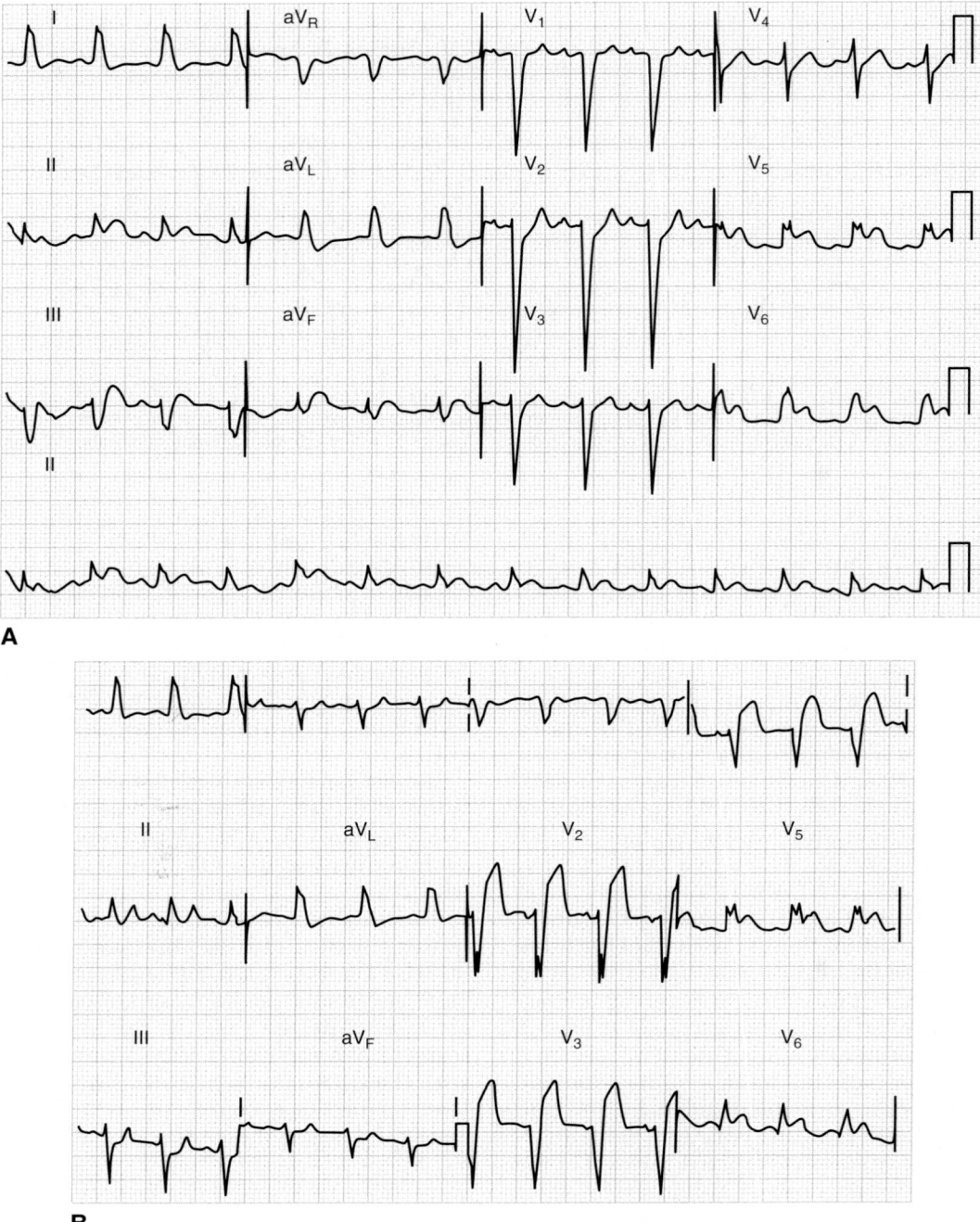

Figure 77-15. Acute myocardial infarction (AMI) in left bundle branch block (LBBB). **A,** Using the Sgarbossa criteria,[53] there is strong evidence of AMI because of the concordant ST segment elevation greater than 1 mm in leads II, V₅, and V₆; also suggestive is the ST segment depression seen in V₂. **B,** Again, applying the Sgarbossa criteria[53] to this tracing with underlying LBBB, AMI is strongly suggested. There is concordant ST segment elevation in leads V₅ and V₆ that appears to exceed 1 mm; furthermore, there is excessively discordant ST segment elevation in leads V₂ and V₃, probably greater than 5 mm.

presence of this strain pattern in the left precordial leads is reassuring when attributing ST segment elevation and tall T waves in the right precordial leads to LVH rather than to AMI because one is essentially the mirror image of the other. Once again, as with the other patterns described in this section that bear resemblance to the ST segment elevation of AMI, the changes in LVH should be static over time (Figure 77-17).

Non-ST Segment Elevation Acute Myocardial Infarction

This terminology supplants "non-Q wave MI," which in turn replaced "subendocardial infarction." Precision in terminology is difficult because Q waves may disappear with time and criteria for significant Q waves vary. Moreover, ST segment elevation may have existed

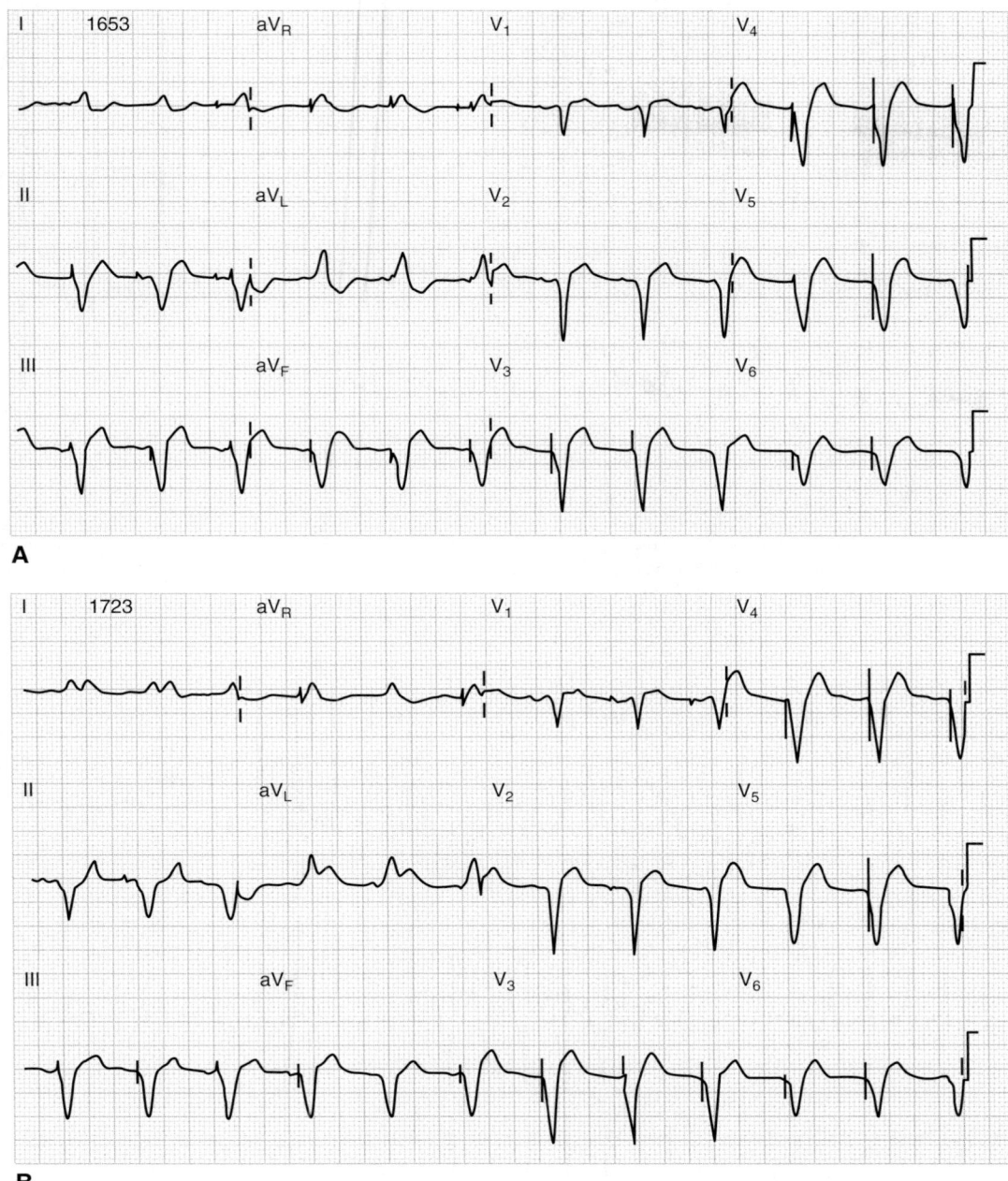

Figure 77-16. Permanent right ventricular paced pattern with acute myocardial infarction (AMI); ventricular paced rhythm. **A,** Appropriate ST segment–T wave findings in the patient with a paced rhythm. **B,** Serial electrocardiogram from the patient in A, revealing evolution of changes worrisome for AMI, including concordant ST segment elevation in leads I and aVL consistent with lateral wall AMI.

and simply been missed electrocardiographically. Nonetheless, it seems useful to have a term that describes the entity wherein there is serum marker evidence of MI in the appropriate clinical scenario but ST segment elevation was not captured on the ECG. Pathophysiologically, total occlusion of the diseased artery may not have occurred, or the infarct zone may have been partially spared by collateral circulation or therapeutic intervention. Electrocardiographic manifestations of non-ST segment AMI include ST segment depression and T wave inversion; the T wave inversions may be deep and symmetrical. ST segment depression may herald true posterior infarction on the 12-lead ECG; posterior lead placement (i.e., leads V_8 and V_9) yields evidence of a posterior STEMI if it is present.

Electrocardiographic Adjuncts in the Diagnosis of Acute Coronary Syndrome

Additional lead ECGs can increase sensitivity for AMI by evaluating regions of the heart prone to electrical silence on the 12-lead tracing. Most commonly, additional lead ECGs use posterior (leads V_8 and V_9) and right ventricular (RV_4) electrodes, thus constituting the 15-lead ECG (Figure 77-18). Posterior leads V_8 and V_9

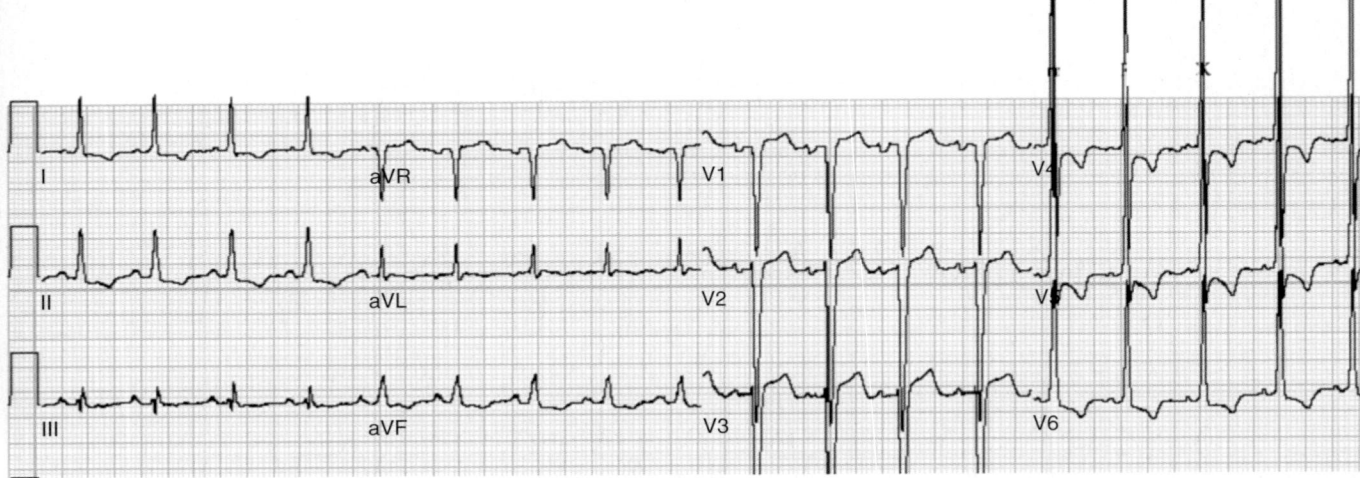

Figure 77-17. Left ventricular hypertrophy (LVH) with repolarization abnormality. This tracing demonstrates classic repolarization abnormality, with ST segment depression in the left-sided precordial leads following large-amplitude R waves. The T waves in these leads are asymmetrically inverted. The right precordial leads (V_1 and V_2) show a mirror image of the changes seen in V_3 to V_6, with slight ST segment elevation (contour initially concave) and asymmetric tall T waves. See Figure 77-20B for evidence of evolving acute myocardial infarction in a patient with LVH and repolarization abnormality.

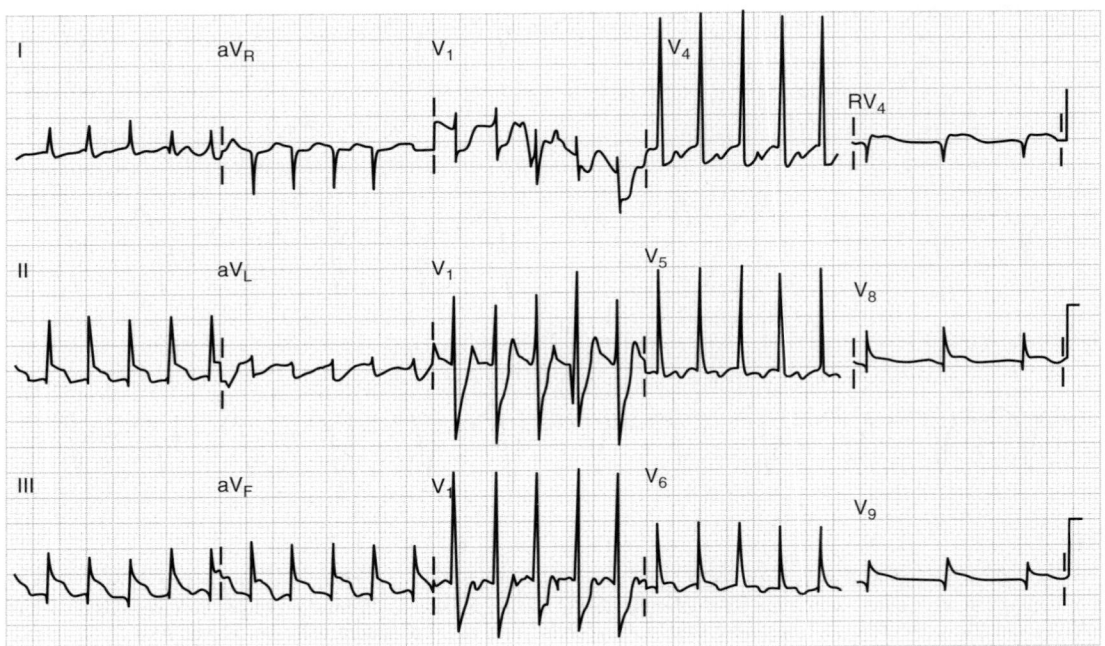

Figure 77-18. Fifteen-lead electrocardiogram (ECG) with inferior, lateral, posterior, and right ventricular acute myocardial infarction (AMI). The standard 12-lead ECG reveals the typical ST segment elevation (STE) in the inferior and lateral leads as well as ST segment depression (STD) with prominent R wave in the right precordial leads. Posterior AMI is indicated by both the right precordial STD with prominent R wave and the STE in posterior leads V_8 and V_9. Note that the degree of STE is less pronounced than that seen in the inferior leads because of a relatively longer distance from the posterior epicardium to surface leads. The right ventricular infarction is noted in this case using the simplified approach with only RV_4, which demonstrates STE of relatively small magnitude.

are placed under the tip of the left scapula and at the left paraspinal area, at the same level as leads V_4 to V_6. Morphologic changes in the posterior leads may be subtle, principally because of the increased distance between these electrodes and the posterior wall of the heart (Figure 77-19). Electrocardiographic imaging of the right ventricle is enhanced with the use of the right-sided chest leads V_1R to V_6R (also termed RV_1 to RV_6). These are placed in mirror image fashion across the right precordium, using the same landmarks for electrode placement that are employed for the left precordial leads. Of the right precordial leads, V_4R has the highest sensitivity for right ventricular infarction and hence is the lead of choice to include in the 15-lead tracing. Morphologically, less pronounced changes can be expected in the right-sided chest leads because of the relatively thinner wall of the right ventricle.

Use of the 15-lead ECG may improve diagnostic precision in ACS but does not appear to affect the rate of AMI diagnosis, use of reperfusion therapy, disposition, or outcome in patients with chest pain evaluated for ACS.[56] In the subset of emergency department patients identified as candidates for admission to the CCU (i.e., high-risk patients), the use of the 15-lead ECG increased the sensitivity of ACS detection by 12%.[57] Possible applications for additional lead ECGs include the following: (1) ST segment changes (depression or elevation) in leads V_1 to V_3, either in an isolated lead or in more than one; (2) equivocal ST segment elevation in the inferior (II, III, aVF) or lateral (I, aVL) limb leads, or both; (3) all inferior STEMI; and (4) hypotension in the setting of ACS.

Serial ECGs and ST segment trend monitoring are means to overcome the limitations of the snapshot 12-lead ECG. Intuitively, acquiring more electrocardiographic data should increase the chances of detecting symptomatic or asymptomatic ischemia. The use of increased electrocardiographic surveillance has demonstrated diagnostic benefit in patients with recurrent or continuous chest pain and an initially normal ECG, a nondiagnostic ECG, an ECG with possible ST segment mimicking syndrome (i.e., ST segment elevation potentially resulting from BER), or a confounding ECG. Fesmire and colleagues[58] examined ST segment trends (measured every 20 seconds for at least the first hour) and automated serial ECGs (at least every 20 minutes) in 1000 emergency department patients with chest pain. Such monitoring significantly increased the sensitivity and specificity for detection of AMI and ACS compared with that of the initial ECG (Figure 77-20). Serial 12-lead ECG monitoring discovered an additional 16% of AMI patients compared with the initial ECG. These findings had implications for level of care, intervention, morbidity, and mortality as the group

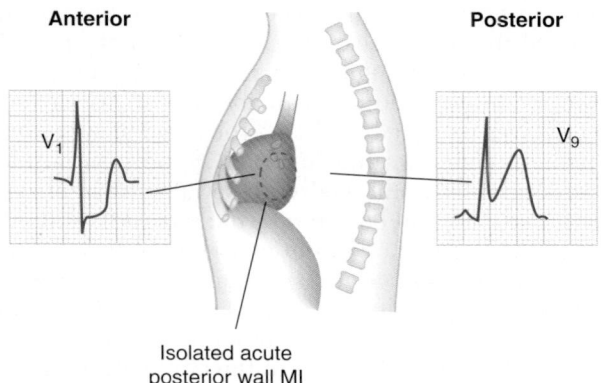

Figure 77-19. Schematic of thorax depicting single anterior and posterior complexes in posterior wall acute myocardial infarction (AMI). The standard electrocardiographic precordial (anterior) leads image the posterior wall of the left ventricle from the anterior perspective of the thorax. Acute infarction of this region manifests electrocardiographic changes that are frequently the reverse of the typical abnormalities of AMI. In this schematic example, lead V_1 reveals ST segment depression with an upright T wave and prominent R wave. Use of the posterior lead V_9 demonstrates ST segment elevation, consistent with AMI.

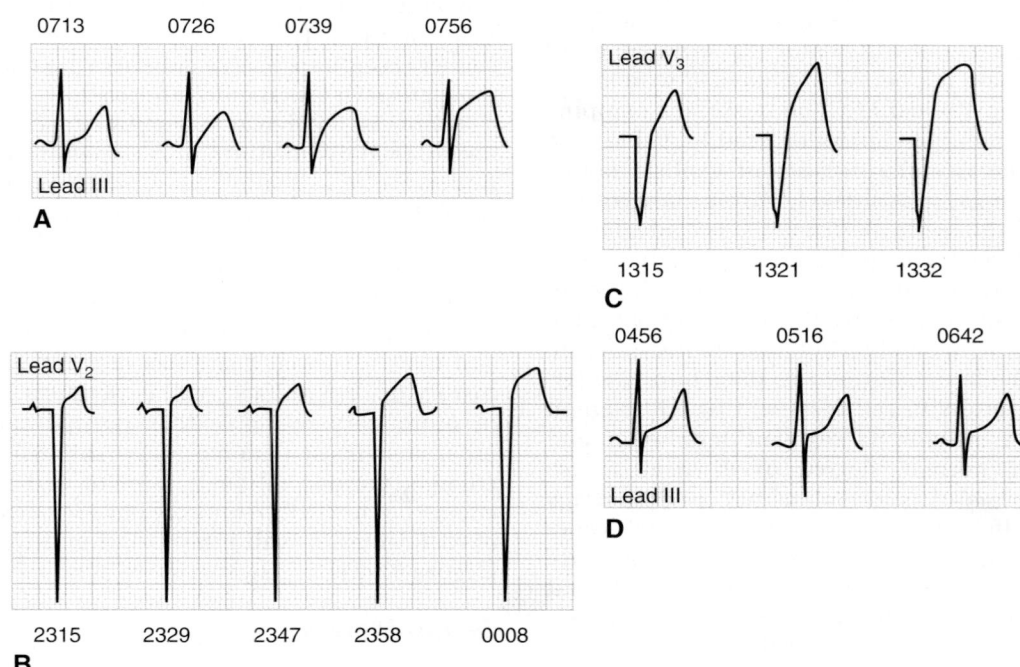

Figure 77-20. Serial electrocardiography. **A,** Representative example of lead III in a patient with chest pain and an initially nondiagnostic electrocardiogram depicting the evolution of ST segment elevation acute myocardial infarction (STE AMI). **B,** Representative example of lead V_2 in a patient with the left ventricular hypertrophy pattern. Serial sampling of this patient with ongoing chest pain and a confounding electrocardiographic pattern reveals the progression to STE AMI. **C,** Representative example of lead V_3 in a patient with left bundle branch block and evolving AMI. **D,** Representative examples of lead III in a patient with chest pain and noninfarctional STE; note the lack of change (degree of elevation as well as morphology of elevation) over time in this patient with benign early repolarization.

featuring changes on serial monitoring proved to be at greater risk for MI and death.[58] In more than 600 patients admitted with nondiagnostic initial ECGs and symptoms consistent with ACS, 12 hours of continuous 12-lead ECG monitoring in a coronary care unit setting revealed that only serum cardiac marker elevation and presence of ST segment episodes (defined as ST segment elevation or depression more than 1 mm different from baseline that endured for at least 1 minute) predicted cardiac death or MI.[59] The cost-effectiveness of this strategy for emergency department patients with suspected ACS is unknown, especially because the absence of pathology on ST segment trend monitoring does not definitively exclude the diagnosis of significant underlying CAD.

QT dispersion is the calculated difference between the longest and shortest QT intervals on a 12-lead ECG. Because ischemic myocardium has a prolonged repolarization time compared with normal myocardium and the QT interval measures time from ventricular depolarization to repolarization, increased variability in measured QT intervals on an ECG translates to greater QT dispersion, reflecting underlying regional ischemia. Comparing patients ultimately found to have ACS or AMI with those found to be free of such disease reveals a difference between populations in QT dispersion values. Difficulties may be encountered in either the manual or computerized measurement of QT intervals because of a variety of factors, including varied T wave shape, U waves, artifacts, dysrhythmias, and inter-rater reliability. Future applications include risk stratification, assessment of therapeutic success, and monitoring of ongoing pharmacotherapy.

Body surface mapping increases the amount of electrocardiographic data for processing and decision making. Whereas serial ECGs and ST segment trend monitoring increase the period of time over which data are collected on a 12-lead ECG, body surface mapping increases the number of electrodes used to gather data and thereby increases the number of vantage points from which the heart is evaluated. Various devices use between 40 and 120 leads. With an 80-electrode device, 64 chest and 16 back electrodes are applied in a vest-like fashion with self-adhering strips. Recording from all electrodes simultaneously, the body surface map puts data on ST segment elevation and depression into a computer, which transforms the data into a color-coded torso image. With red representing ST segment elevation, blue signifying ST segment depression, and green reflecting normal, degree of disease is also expressed in terms of color intensity.[60] Body surface mapping may offer increased sensitivity for MI, especially in areas of the heart that are relatively electrically silent on the 12-lead ECG (e.g., posterior and lateral walls of the left ventricle and the right ventricle) as well as in patients with underlying LBBB.[61]

Limitations of Electrocardiography in Acute Coronary Syndrome

Although estimates vary, the sensitivity and specificity of a single ECG for AMI are approximately 60% and 90%, respectively; repeated use of the ECG in the setting of continued or recurrent pain increases the diagnostic utility of this technology.[62] The initial ECG is nondiagnostic in approximately half of the patients presenting to the emergency department who are ultimately diagnosed with AMI. Moreover, nondiagnostic and even normal ECGs do not exclude the diagnosis of ACS—or even AMI—in that 20% of patients ultimately diagnosed with AMI have demonstrated these electrocardiographic findings earlier in their course. As time elapses from symptom onset to ECG recording, the ability of the ECG to exclude AMI does not markedly increase.[39] Thus, a single normal or nondiagnostic ECG cannot be interpreted to mean absence of ACS, even if the ECG was recorded well after the onset of symptoms. In patients being evaluated for ACS, only serial electrocardiography, combined with serial cardiac enzyme determinations, can be used to rule out AMI, and even then unstable angina without actual myocardial necrosis may be present. These statements, of course, are made assuming that the clinician has a reasonable clinical suspicion of ACS; in other words, the clinical history guides the physician in the application of diagnostic testing in the emergency department.

Chest Radiography

In the setting of suspected ACS, the chest radiograph (CXR) is usually normal or unchanged but can provide important information concerning the appropriate application of therapies (i.e., an evaluation of mediastinal width in the consideration of fibrinolytic agent use and the determination of pulmonary congestion in the consideration of acute parenteral β-adrenergic blocking therapy). Further, the presence of congestive heart failure (CHF) on the CXR places the patient in a higher risk group of AMI patients who may benefit from an aggressive therapeutic approach.

There is evidence of pulmonary congestion in approximately one third of AMI patients. Radiographic findings often parallel the clinical examination. AMI patients who develop CHF have increased mortality, as reported by the Killip classification; the CXR provides prognostic data. The chronicity of the CHF syndrome may also be suggested by the heart size. Patients who present with AMI complicated by pulmonary edema and have a normal heart size most often have no past history of CHF. In fact, AMI is the most frequent cause of pulmonary edema with a normal cardiac size. In other instances, patients with AMI who manifest an enlarged cardiac silhouette with or without pulmonary edema on the CXR frequently have a preexisting history of CHF, anterior wall infarct, and multiple-vessel CAD (Figure 77-21).

Serum Markers

Biochemical markers play a pivotal role in the diagnosis, risk stratification, and guidance of treatment with ACS. Historically, the elevation of CK-MB in the serum over several days of hospitalization was the standard method for diagnosing AMI. The European Society of Cardiology and ACC redefined the criteria for AMI

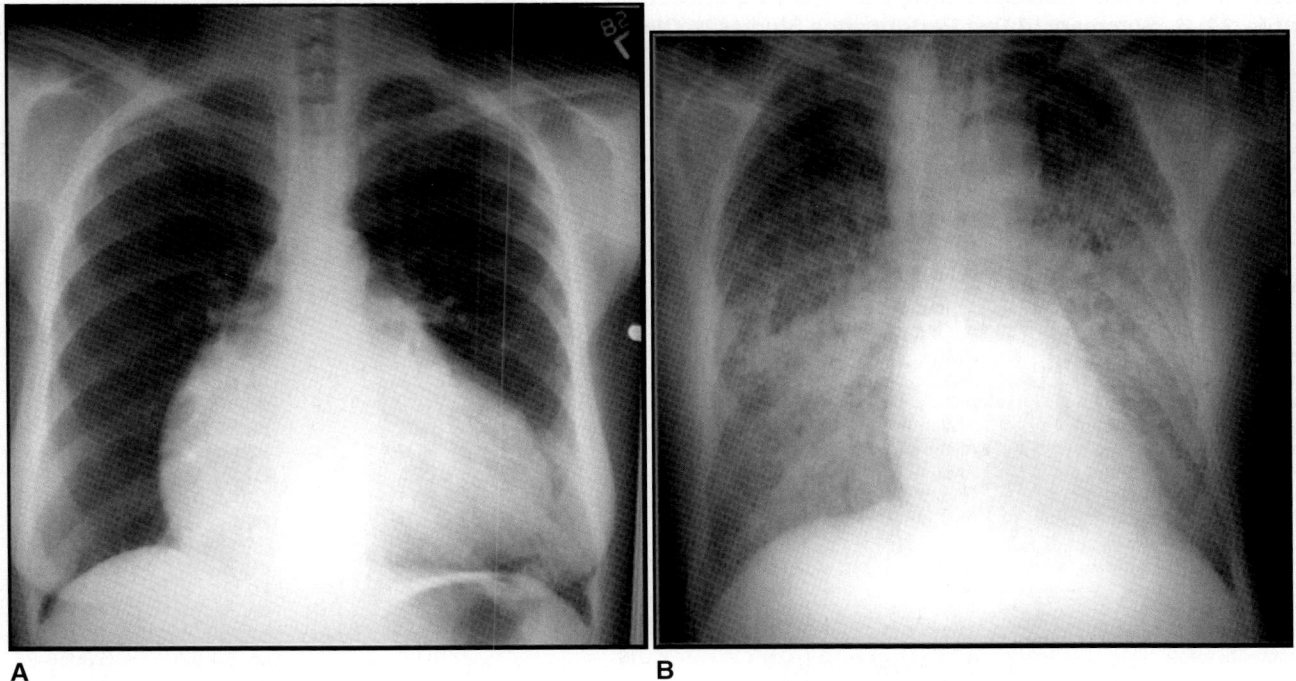

Figure 77-21. Chest radiographs in patients with acute coronary syndrome. **A,** Cardiomegaly. **B,** Borderline cardiomegaly with pulmonary edema.

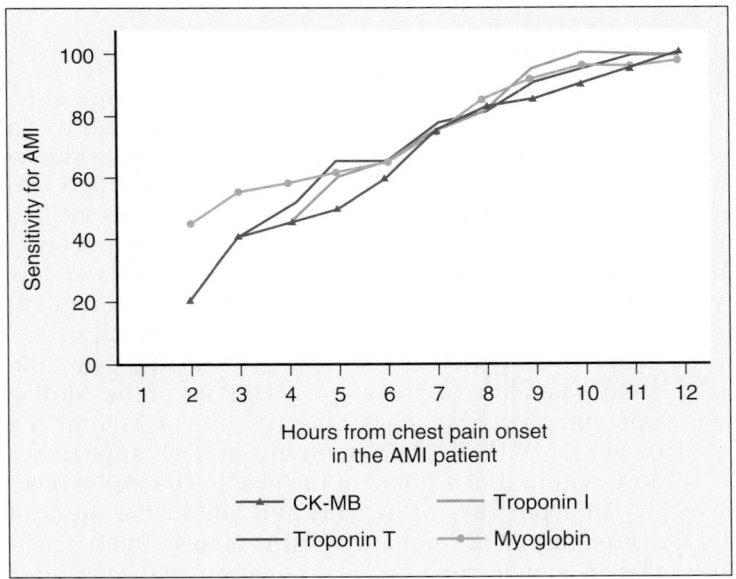

Figure 77-22. Serum marker sensitivity relative to the time of onset of chest pain in the patient with acute myocardial infarction. Data obtained from the medical literature. AMI, acute myocardial infarction; CK-MB, creatine phosphokinase MB fraction.

diagnosis on biochemical grounds in recognition that specific markers, particularly the troponins, indicate irreversible cell damage.[9] In the past, detection of AMI by characteristic enzyme elevations over 48 to 72 hours was sufficient to establish the diagnosis of AMI because there was essentially no specific therapy to reverse or prevent the developing myocardial necrosis. The evolution of fibrinolytic therapy and acute intervention has created significant pressure to identify patients with AMI as early as possible and by any available means to facilitate timely intervention.

For patients with a nondiagnostic ECG, early serum markers of myocardial necrosis, when positive, can alter the diagnostic course, treatment plans, and disposition location. Caution is advised, however, when interpreting the results of single serum marker determinations. The patient's history remains the most vital portion of the diagnostic evaluation of the patient with chest pain with potential ACS. Serial testing over time substantially improves the sensitivity of these tests. Moreover, cardiac enzymes are insensitive for the evaluation of unstable angina, as opposed to AMI (Table 77-6 and Figure 77-22).[63]

Table 77-6. Summary of Test Performance Studies of Diagnostic Technologies for Acute Coronary Syndrome in the Emergency Department

Technology	Disease Studied	No. of Studies (Subjects)	Population Category of Studies*	Studies Prevalence Range, %	Disease Sensitivity,[†] % (95% CI)	Disease Specificity,[†] % (95% CI)
Creatine kinase (single)	AMI	12 (3,195)	I/II/III/IV	7-41	37 (31-44)	87 (80-91)
Creatine kinase (serial)	AMI	2 (786)	I	26-43	69-99	68-84
CK-MB (presentation)	ACS	1 (1,042)	III	20	23	96
	AMI	19 (6,425)	I/II/III/IV	6-42	42 (36-48)	97 (95-98)
CK-MB (serial)	ACS	1 (1,042)	III	20	31	95
	AMI	14 (11,625)	I/II/III/IV	1-43	79 (71-86)	96 (95-97)
Myoglobin (presentation)	AMI	18 (4,172)	I/II/IV	6-62	49 (43-55)	91 (87-94)
Myoglobin (serial)	AMI	10 (1,277)	I/II/IV	11-41	89 (80-94)	87 (80-92)
Troponin I (presentation)	AMI	4 (1,149)	II/III/IV	6-39	39 (10-78)	93 (88-97)
Troponin I (serial)	AMI	2 (1,393)	III/IV	6-9	90-100	83-96
Troponin T (presentation)	AMI	6 (1,348)	II/III/IV	6-78	39 (26-53)	93 (90-96)
Troponin T (serial)	AMI	3 (904)	I/III/IV	5-78	93 (85-97)	85 (76-91)
CK-MB and myoglobin combination (presentation)	AMI	3 (2,283)	II/IV	9-28	83 (51-96)	82 (68-90)
CK-MB and myoglobin combination (serial)	AMI	2 (291)	IV	11-20	100	75-91
Exercise stress ECG	ACS	2 (312)	III	6-10	70-100	82-93
Rest echocardiography	ACS	2 (228)	III	3-30	70 (43-88)	87 (72-94)
	AMI	3 (397)	I/III	3-30	93 (81-91)	66 (43-83)
Stress echocardiography	AMI	1 (139)	III	4	90	89
Sestamibi (rest)	ACS	3 (702)	III	9-17	81 (74-87)	73 (56-85)
	AMI	3 (702)		2-12	92 (78-98)	67 (52-79)

*Results from meta-analysis of several studies, with random effects calculations unless otherwise indicated.
[†]Point estimate from a single study or a range of reported values; meta-analysis not performed.
ACS, acute coronary syndrome; AMI, acute myocardial infarction; CI, confidence interval; CK-MB, creatine phosphokinase MB fraction; ECG, electrocardiogram.
Modified from Pope JH, Selker HP: Diagnosis of acute cardiac ischemia. *Emerg Med Clin North Am* 21:27, 2003.

Troponins

Because of their superior sensitivity and specificity compared with CK-MB, cardiac troponins are the best markers for myocardial cell injury. Two myocardium-specific proteins—myocardial troponin T (TnT) and troponin I (TnI)—slightly precede the release of CK-MB into the serum. The cardiac troponins are genetically distinct from troponin forms found in other muscle tissue, rendering them highly cardiac-specific markers. Monoclonal antibodies have little cross-reactivity with troponins from skeletal muscle. Unlike CK-MB, the cardiac troponins are not found in the serum of healthy individuals.

The biokinetics of troponin release are related to the location of the protein within the cell. Normally, small quantities of troponins are free in the cytosol and the majority is entwined in the muscle fiber. After injury, a biphasic rise in serum troponins corresponds to early release of the free cytoplasmic proteins, followed by a slower and greatly prolonged rise with breakdown of the actual muscle fiber. The slow destruction of the myocardial cell contractile proteins provides a sustained release of the troponins for 5 to 7 days. Serum troponin concentrations begin to rise measurably in the serum at about the same time as CK-MB elevations become detectable, as early as 3 hours after onset, but troponin levels remain elevated for 7 days or more.

The cardiac-specific troponins, determined serially, are highly sensitive for the early detection of myocardial injury. A positive test is associated with significant risk and repeated negative studies (i.e., serial tro-

ponins) predict low risk.[64] A single troponin measurement on presentation, however, has limited utility in excluding AMI and no ability to detect unstable angina without infarction because cell injury is required and because of the time delay in the rise in levels (which may not be detected until 10 hours after symptom onset in some AMI patients). Sensitivities vary from as low as 4% to as high as 100%, depending on timing and attributes of the patient.[63] Serial measurements, particularly when performed at least 6 hours after symptom onset, markedly improve the sensitivity of the cardiac troponins for AMI. Regarding the use of TnT in the diagnosis of AMI, the sensitivity of TnT approaches 50% within 3 to 4 hours of the event. The test is positive in about 75% of patients at 6 hours after onset of symptoms; at 12 hours, the test is almost 100% sensitive. A single troponin determination, however, may have utility in evaluating patients who present several days into the possible ACS event. The time course of the event with respect to the kinetics of troponin allows its use in these situations to exclude recently past AMI. Furthermore, a single serum troponin value may also have utility in elderly patients with nonspecific presentations for AMI, such as weakness, confusion, or altered mentation. As with other diagnostic studies in the ACS patient, the appropriate use and interpretation of these tests must be made by the clinician at the bedside of the individual patient.

There is less evidence for the utility of cardiac troponins in the diagnosis of ACS in the absence of AMI. In a number of studies, up to 33% of patients diagnosed with unstable angina with normal CK-MB levels had elevated troponin levels, indicating the markers' improved sensitivity for myocardial cell injury.[66] The fact that the risk of these patients for cardiac events and mortality is similar to that of the patients diagnosed with AMI by traditional WHO criteria led to the redefinition of AMI on the basis of biochemical markers. On the basis of data from the Thrombolysis in Myocardial Infarction-IIIB study, there is almost a linear correlation between increasing troponin levels and risk for cardiac events and mortality, even in patients with a nondiagnostic ECG and normal CK-MB levels.[66,67] Small elevations of troponin may be used as an objective measure of "preinfarcts" that characterize unstable angina and are associated with increased risk for infarction in the near-term, whereas marked elevations in troponin consistent with AMI represent further progression along the continuum of ACS toward "traditional" AMI.[68]

In addition to their diagnostic and prognostic value, cardiac troponins may provide guidance on treatment strategies for ACS patients. Data from studies such as the Treat Angina with Aggrastat and Determine Cost of Therapy with an Invasive or Conservative Strategy–Thrombolysis in Myocardial Infarction (TACTICS-TIMI 18) trial suggest that patients with elevated troponin who are treated with an early invasive interventional strategy within 48 hours have a marked improvement in recurrent ischemia, infarction, and mortality both in the short term and at 6 months. These studies include patients without major ECG criteria for immediate interventional reperfusion strategies.[69,70] The use of glycoprotein IIb/IIIa inhibitors in patients with elevated troponins may prevent early complications in patients with ACS. It is likely that the improved sensitivity of troponin has captured a high-risk ACS population not previously diagnosed or treated. Elevated troponin values appear to be excellent indicators of risk of death and acute cardiovascular complications in all ACS patients—even those who do not meet traditional criteria for AMI.[71]

Troponins I and T are very similar in their diagnostic and prognostic utility as well as their serum kinetics and rates of rise and fall associated with myocardial ischemia, infarction, and ACS. TnT, a 37,000-dalton protein, is, however, found in the serum of individuals with skeletal muscle disease and renal failure. In the setting of renal failure, and in particular diabetic patients receiving dialysis, TnT levels can be markedly elevated. The pathophysiology as well as clinical significance of this finding remains unclear, and it may still represent evidence of subclinical myocardial damage.[72] Alternatively, TnI, a 21,000-dalton protein, is found only in the serum of patients with significant ACS and is not found in the presence of renal failure. As a result, TnI may be the preferred cardiac marker given its improved cardiac specificity.

Creatinine Phosphokinase

CK is an enzyme found in large quantities in cardiac and skeletal muscle. After AMI, increases in serum CK are detectable within 3 to 8 hours with a peak at 20 to 24 hours after injury; assuming a single, one-time event, the levels become normal within 3 to 4 days. Total CK values obtained at the time of emergency department presentation show a sensitivity of 37% and a specificity of 87% for the diagnosis of AMI; measurements taken as late as 12 hours after the onset of chest pain have a marginally improved sensitivity approaching 50%.

Total CK is found not only in cardiac muscle but also in skeletal muscle, brain, kidney, lung, and gastrointestinal tract and is of little value in the assessment of patients with suspected ACS. These various areas of the body have CK subtypes; the myocardium has the CK-MB subtype of creatinine kinase. In fact, myocardial cells are by far the most abundant potential sources of CK-MB; thus, the appearance of CK-MB in the serum is highly suggestive of MI. Unfortunately, skeletal muscle does contain small amounts of CK-MB, particularly the pelvic musculature. Abnormal CK-MB elevations may be seen in trauma, muscular dystrophies, myositis, rhabdomyolysis, and after extremely vigorous exercise. In the setting of AMI, CK-MB is released and is detectable in the serum as early as 3 hours after onset of the necrosis. CK-MB characteristically peaks at 20 to 24 hours and becomes normal within 2 to 3 days after injury. Elevated CK-MB values identify a patient at considerable risk for a poor outcome but do not correlate well with infarct size.

The CK-MB fraction remains the best alternative to the troponins as a cardiac marker. The sensitivity of a single CK-MB determination in diagnosing AMI is dependent upon the elapsed time from chest pain onset. Values obtained within 3 hours of onset are poor diagnostic tools, with a sensitivity of only 25% to 50%. CK-MB determinations obtained beyond this 3-hour time period have increasing sensitivities for the diagnosis of AMI, ranging from 40% to nearly 100%, particularly when obtained 12 to 16 hours after onset.[5,63] Diagnostic utility is improved by requiring that the CK-MB value not only be elevated but also be at least 5% of the total CK value. False-positive elevations can occur with noncoronary conditions such as pericarditis, myocarditis, skeletal muscle disease, rhabdomyolysis, trauma, and exercise.

The use of single determinations of CK-MB is of no value in excluding ACS. Serial sampling, even over relatively short time periods (12 hours), increases sensitivity considerably, particularly when considered with serial electrocardiography and repeated assessments of the patient. CK-MB values rise quickly after an AMI, typically doubling within 3 to 6 hours of the event. Although serial CK-MB measurements increase the diagnostic accuracy, this approach still has the potential to miss a significant number of AMIs. Moreover, serial CK-MB sampling cannot exclude the diagnosis of unstable angina.

High-voltage electrophoresis can rapidly identify patients with AMI by detecting CK-MM (skeletal muscle) and CK-MB (brain) isoforms or subforms. Serum enzymatic cleavage of terminal amino acids from the subforms released by infarcted myocardial cells occurs within several hours after onset, providing a "fingerprint" for determining the time of AMI onset.

Puleo and colleagues demonstrated 92% sensitivity for detecting AMI using CK-MB isoforms within 4 to 6 hours after symptom onset and 100% sensitivity within 6 to 8 hours after symptom onset.[73] In a similar fashion to immunochemical testing for CK-MB, such isoform analysis can provide the clinician with valuable information for diagnosis, treatment, and disposition of the patient with AMI who has a nondiagnostic ECG.

A positive CK-MB in the appropriate patient strongly suggests AMI; such patients should be admitted to the CCU. A negative test, in the form of either a single determination or serial measurement, does not reliably exclude AMI or ACS. A single negative result in the patient suspected of ACS only suggests that a non-CCU admission disposition is appropriate. A single CK-MB determination should not be used to support a decision to discharge the patient home from the emergency department.

Myoglobin

Myoglobin, a small protein (17,000 daltons) found in muscle tissue, is rapidly released into the circulation after cellular injury. In cases of myocardial injury, myoglobin rises in the initial 1 to 2 hours, peaks at 5 to 7 hours, and returns to baseline by 24 hours. Because of its rapid rise, myoglobin is attractive as an early indicator of myocardial injury. Myocardial myoglobin, however, is not currently distinguishable immunologically from skeletal muscle myoglobin. Myoglobin is elevated in patients with renal failure because of reduced clearance. It is also elevated in any clinical situation involving the skeletal muscle, such as trauma, exercise, and significant systemic illness.

The sensitivity of an initial myoglobin at presentation for AMI varies from as low as 21% to as high as 100%.[63] Serial testing at 2 to 4 hours after presentation significantly improves the assay's diagnostic power. A doubling of the level as soon as 1 to 2 hours after the initial measurement greatly increases the sensitivity for the diagnosis of AMI, but this approach is very non-specific, because many non-AMI patients demonstrate such a pattern of results.[5] The value of myoglobin may be in its excellent negative predictive power for AMI and its early rise kinetics compared with other markers. The evidence suggests that a normal myoglobin value 2 hours after presentation may be used safely to rule out active AMI; however, a normal myoglobin cannot be used to rule out active ACS.[5] Myoglobin levels are elevated in the serum within 1 to 2 hours after symptom onset, peaking 4 to 5 hours after AMI in patients coming to the emergency department with AMI.[5] Sensitivity improves from 62% on emergency department presentation to 100% 3 hours later, compared with 50% and 95%, respectively, for immuno-chemical CK-MB analyses. Myoglobin has a 100% negative predictive value for AMI—*not ACS*. Myoglobin can also be used for rapid triage of patients with low clinical likelihood of AMI. Myoglobin's rapid renal clearance, however, limits its value to the time window of 4 to 6 hours after symptom onset, making early phlebotomy imperative for detection.[59] More important, this negative predictive power applies to the detection of AMI—*not ACS*.

Other Cardiac Markers

Biochemical assays for potential new cardiac markers are being developed in the hope of finding ones with improved sensitivity for ischemia as well as significant risk determination capability and prognostic power. The Food and Drug Administration has approved an assay for the amino terminus of albumin (so-called cardiac albumin) that reportedly detects early myocardial ischemia as opposed to the later myocyte necrosis, and may have even earlier elevation than myoglobin. Elevated plasma levels of myeloperoxidase, an abundant leukocyte enzyme found in vulnerable coronary plaques that have ruptured, are reported to predict short-term risk for adverse cardiac events and death in patients presenting to the emergency department with chest pain. This association was even seen in patients with negative cardiac troponin and no evidence of myocardial necrosis on presentation.[74]

Similarly, B-type natriuretic peptide (BNP), most commonly used as a marker for CHF, has good predictive power for recurrent ACS events and cardiac-related deaths, as well as CHF exacerbations, in patients with AMI.[75] A number of markers are being studied as measures of CAD and risk for cardiac events in patients with and without evidence of ACS. Chief among these is the inflammatory marker C-reactive protein (CRP) and high-sensitivity CRP (hsCRP), which have long-term prognostic value for cardiac events in healthy individuals as well as potential short-term prognostic value when combined with other markers such as cardiac troponins in patients with ACS.

Multiple Marker Strategies

All of the available biochemical cardiac markers have their limitations. Diagnostic, risk stratification, and prognostic accuracy might be enhanced by the utilization of multiple markers with their varying characteristics in terms of pathogenesis, sensitivity for AMI and ACS, cardiac specificity, and time frame for detection.[76] Studies suggest that the combination of CK-MB and myoglobin measurement has a sensitivity from 62% to 100% and specificity from 72% to 89% for AMI on presentation. Serial measurements of these markers significantly improve the performance of this combined marker approach.[63] McCord and colleagues reported on the utility of a multimarker strategy using the early but noncardiac-specific marker myoglobin with the more specific and prognostic marker TnI. In their study of 817 patients evaluated for ACS in the emergency department, the combined marker approach had a sensitivity of 96.9% and negative predictive value of 99.6% for AMI when applied at presentation and at 90 minutes.[77] Similarly, Ng and coworkers studied the utility of a three-marker approach (CK-MB, TnI, and myoglobin) in an accelerated critical pathway, reporting 100% sensitivity and 100% negative predictive power for AMI in 1285 patients assessed for ACS.[78] Other multimarker strategies include combining measurement of a conventional marker for myocardial necrosis (troponin) with a marker for inflammation (CRP) and a marker for a short-term cardiac adverse event (BNP) that can assist with the rapid diagnosis and risk stratification of patients being evaluated for ACS.

Echocardiography

Two-dimensional echocardiography is an effective tool for detecting regional wall motion abnormality associated with ACS. Impaired myocardial contractility can be observed echocardiographically in patients with ACS, often following a progressive course from hypokinesis to akinesis. Impaired myocardial relaxation during diastole results in decreased ventricular distensibility. After AMI, paradoxical wall motion observed during systole indicates the subsequent loss of muscle tone from necrosis. Decreased ejection fraction may result from these ventricular wall motion abnormalities.

Regional wall motion abnormality occurs in association with ACS, assisting in the diagnostic process particularly in individuals with nondiagnostic ECGs. The presence of regional systolic wall motion abnormalities in a patient without known CAD is a moderately accurate indicator of an increased likelihood of acute myocardial ischemia or infarction, with a positive predictive accuracy of about 50%.[79] The age of wall motion abnormalities, however, often cannot be determined because these findings can also be associated with old infarction and myocardial scarring. Accordingly, the ability to compare findings with prior echocardiograms significantly improves the diagnostic accuracy of this imaging modality.

The absence of segmental abnormalities (presence of either normal wall motion or diffuse abnormalities) has a significant high negative predictive value, as high as 98% for cases of suspected MI.[79] Moreover, segmental wall motion abnormalities can be seen not only in the zone of acute infarction but also in regions of ischemic stunning of viable myocardium. Resting echocardiography provides an assessment of global and regional function, an important predictor of complications and mortality in patients with ACS. Data from the ACC/AHA task force indicated that patients with mild and localized as opposed to extensive wall motion abnormalities had a low risk of ACS complications.[79] In addition, echocardiography can help evaluate other causes of clinical presentations mimicking ACS, including valvular heart disease, aortic dissection, pericarditis, mitral valve prolapse, and pulmonary embolus. Finally, echocardiography is an important tool to assess for various complications of AMI including acute mitral regurgitation, pericardial effusion, ventricular septal and free wall rupture, and intracardiac thrombus formation.

Technical limitations restrict the use of echocardiography in the emergent diagnosis of AMI and myocardial ischemia. These limitations include the quality of the study, which is proportional to the experience of the operator, and the expertise of the reader interpreting the study at the patient's bedside. Injury involving more than 20% of the myocardial wall is required before segmental wall motion abnormalities can be detected echocardiographically.[9] In addition, the inability of the two-dimensional echocardiogram to distinguish between ischemia, AMI, or old infarction and the potential absence of wall motion abnormality in nontransmural infarctions can further limit the usefulness of two-dimensional echocardiography. Echocardiography is typically less expensive than radionuclide ventriculography, however, and offers more anatomic detail while avoiding the use of radionuclides.

Stress echocardiography, as opposed to resting echocardiography, can detect CAD as well as assess cardiac function early after an AMI. Stress echocardiography can be performed with graded increases in cardiac workload, either by standardized exercise or pharmacologic adrenergic stimulating agents such as dobutamine. In addition, vasodilating agents, such as dipyridamole and adenosine, induce heterogeneous myocardial perfusion and reveal functional myocardial ischemia in susceptible patients. Stress echocardiography is superior to conventional treadmill testing for CAD in women. Graded dobutamine stress echocardiography has utility in assessing myocardial viability and ventricular function within the first few days after an AMI.

The utility of stress echocardiography in the diagnostic evaluation for ACS in the emergent setting is unclear. Trippi and colleagues[80] reported a sensitivity and specificity of 89% each for the diagnosis of AMI or CAD in patients with a nondiagnostic ECG, negative markers, and negative rest echocardiography. This study, however, was limited in its scope and the numbers of subjects.[80] Other approaches under investigation include the use of ultrasonography contrast agents and measurement of acoustic signal variability to identify ischemic myocardial tissue. The clinical utility of stress echocardiography in the evaluation of ACS in the emergent setting remains to be determined.

Myocardial Scintigraphy

Radionuclide tracer injection and scanning or scintigraphy, such as with single-photon emission CT (SPECT), allows real-time assessment of myocardial perfusion and function. Technetium-99, a lipophilic monovalent cation that relies on the negatively charged mitochondrial membrane for uptake, provides important information regarding myocardial perfusion at the time of injection. Technetium-99 sestamibi has a slow redistribution to ischemic myocardium. This property allows immediate injection and imaging, which detects altered distribution consistent with some form of ischemic heart disease, followed by subsequent scanning, which provides more definitive data regarding the particular subtype of ACS. In patients with a normal initial study, the likelihood of ACS is extremely low. In patients with an initial study revealing abnormal distribution (i.e., reduced uptake) of the tracer, some form of ischemic heart disease is likely. Subsequent imaging then reveals one of two patterns: normal redistribution (normal uptake) or continued reduced uptake. The redistribution pattern is consistent with active coronary ischemia and the continued reduced uptake is found in patients with MI, either remote or recent. Myocardial scintigraphy has promising positive and negative predictive values for cardiac events with high sensitivity and a good specificity for CAD.[81,82]

Immediate myocardial scintigraphy is useful in detecting ACS and risk for cardiac events in selected patients presenting at the emergency department with atypical chest pain, nondiagnostic ECGs, and low to moderate risk for AMI. Multiple studies have found a relatively high incidence of cardiac events, presence of AMI, and need for revascularization in patients with a positive nuclear scan. The probability of a cardiac event is 10-fold higher in patients with abnormal scans than in patients with a normal scan. The incidence of cardiac events with a normal scan was 1% or less per year. Myocardial scintigraphy has also shown some promise in reducing the number of patients admitted from the emergency department with chest pain who are ultimately determined not to have ACS without reducing appropriate admissions for patients with ACS.[83]

Myocardial scintigraphy studies for emergency department patients have significant pragmatic limitations. The studies are difficult to perform in the very early time period after the patient's presentation to the emergency department. Radioisotopes and the personnel to administer them may not be immediately available; furthermore, in most centers, physician interpretation experience and availability are quite variable. Images may be equivocal in terms of diagnosing ACS in the setting of previous MI or myocardial dysfunction. Finally, studies of emergency department utility of perfusion imaging have focused on immediate resting studies. Few data are available on the clinical utility of more provocative stress (exercise or pharmacologically induced) perfusion studies in this setting. Certainly, such imaging is of value when employed by experienced clinicians in conjunction with other diagnostic studies such as the history and examination, ECG, and serum markers.

Graded Exercise Testing

Evaluation of clinical, hemodynamic, and electrocardiographic responses to graded exercise testing has a sensitivity of 70% for identifying patients with inducible ischemia and underlying CAD in the general population.

The use of exercise stress testing for emergency department patients has been investigated in a number of studies evaluating its safety, utility, and cost-effectiveness. Gibler and coauthors[84] reported on 1010 *low-risk* patients with chest pain who underwent exercise testing after negative serial markers and 9 hours of ECG monitoring in the emergency department. In this population with an *approximately 5% rate of CAD*, stress testing had a negative predictive value of 98.7% for the diagnosis of ACS or cardiac event within 30 days. Mikhail and colleagues[85] employed an abbrevi-

ated emergency department–based "rule out MI" protocol followed by mandatory stress testing in 477 emergency department patients; 67 patients (13%) were admitted to the hospital, of whom 44 (66%) had a final diagnosis of CAD or ischemic heart disease. Twenty-four patients with such diagnoses were identified only with stress testing. Four hundred ten patients (86%) were discharged home from the emergency department after a negative evaluation; all of these patients were alive and well at 5 months without AMI. Exercise stress testing appears to be an effective diagnostic method for the detection of symptomatic CAD in low- to moderate-risk patients.

ACC/AHA guidelines on exercise testing state that such testing can be performed when patients have been free of active ischemic or heart failure symptoms for a minimum of 8 to 12 hours.[86] Immediate stress testing (i.e., without the rule out MI evaluation), however, may be safe and cost effective in low-risk patients suspected of ACS. Amsterdam and coworkers[87] attempted to determine the safety and utility of immediate exercise testing in the evaluation of low-risk patients presenting to the emergency department with chest pain. A total of 1000 low-risk patients underwent immediate exercise testing with no adverse effects. One hundred twenty-five patients (13%) had positive results on exercise ECGs, with 33 of these individuals demonstrating abnormalities strongly suggestive of CAD on subsequent evaluation. At 30-day follow-up, 4 had suffered an AMI and 12 had undergone revascularization. Six hundred forty patients (64%) had negative exercise test results, all of whom were discharged home from the emergency department. At 30-day follow-up, one patient had suffered an AMI and another had been diagnosed with CAD by nuclear imaging. Two hundred thirty-five patients (24%) had nondiagnostic tests, of whom 25 were diagnosed subsequently with CAD and 7 underwent revascularization within 30 days. In general, the rate of CAD diagnosis or cardiac event within 30 days was 29% for the positive stress group, 13% for the nondiagnostic group, and 0.3% for the negative stress group. In total, 30-day follow-up was achieved in 888 (89%) patients and revealed no mortality in any of the three groups.

Graded exercise testing in the emergency department has its limitations. At most institutions, testing resources and personnel are not available 7 days a week, 24 hours a day. The mortality rate is extremely low (1 in 2500), but absolute contraindications include recent AMI (within 2 days), high-risk unstable angina, uncontrolled cardiac dysrhythmias causing symptoms or hemodynamic compromise, symptomatic severe aortic stenosis, uncontrolled symptomatic heart failure, acute pulmonary embolus or infarction, acute myocarditis or pericarditis, and acute aortic dissection.[86]

As with any diagnostic test, the pretest probability of disease in the population studied must be considered; patients with a high pretest probability of CAD have a significant rate of false-negative results, and patients with a low pretest probability have a significant rate of false-positive stress tests. The specificity of the test is decreased in the presence of underlying electrocardiographic abnormalities secondary to medications, electrolyte abnormalities, LVH, or artifact. A false-positive test may result from aortic stenosis or insufficiency, hypertrophic cardiomyopathy, hypertension, arteriovenous fistula, anemia, hemoglobinopathies, low cardiac output states, chronic obstructive pulmonary disease, digitalis toxic states, LVH, hyperventilation, mitral valve prolapse, and bundle branch blocks. An increase in the rate of false-positive test results in women tends to decrease the usefulness of graded exercise testing in this population.

CHEST PAIN CENTERS: SPECIALIZED EMERGENCY DEPARTMENT–BASED EVALUATION AND TREATMENT UNITS

Initially developed to address the urgent treatment of patients with AMI, the CPC has evolved to focus on the rapid diagnosis of ACS in the lower risk population of patients. These specialized units have grown remarkably in the past decade and now are utilized in some form in 30% of the emergency departments in the United States. The goal of the CPC is to provide an integrated approach to patients with chest pain or potential ACS that includes early identification, rapid triage, and treatment of high-risk AMI or ACS patients and risk stratification for low-risk patients. Guidelines and critical pathways play an essential role in the CPC process. Staff, resources, and space are often dedicated for a CPC, but the unit can be part of an emergency department observation unit or a "virtual" unit located near or within the emergency department itself.

The care of patients with chest pain and possible ACS can be approached in a pathway-driven fashion in a CPC, where urgent evaluation and treatment may occur as well as prolonged observation with abbreviated rule out MI programs. A CPC protocol should rapidly direct patients with possible ACS into a high-level treatment area where an ECG and clinical examination can be obtained within the first 10 minutes. Patients with STEMI requiring immediate reperfusion therapy or patients having clinical syndromes consistent with unstable angina in need of further intervention can be identified quickly. This goal can be combined with an efficient emergency department evaluation of patients with low to moderate risk for ACS. The greatest medical benefit from the CPC is likely to be the early identification and treatment of patients with AMI and unstable angina; the most significant financial impact will be related to its potential for reducing the number of inappropriate hospital admissions.

The National Heart Attack Alert Program (NHAAP) of the National Heart, Lung, and Blood Institute (NHLBI) has challenged clinicians to provide care for emergency department patients with clear symptoms and signs of AMI within 30 minutes of arrival. The NHAAP recommends (1) a specific area of the emergency department equipped for assessing and monitoring patients potentially having ischemia, including standing orders for initial diagnostic and therapeutic actions; (2) a standing protocol with inclusion and exclusion criteria for reperfusion therapies, including language authorizing the physician to administer fibrinolytic therapy or to mobilize the catheterization laboratory for prespecified cases; (3) a clear demarcation of responsibilities for all members of the reperfusion team; and (4) policies and procedures for the treatment and possible transfer of patients with ST segment elevation AMI who are ineligible for fibrinolytic therapy.

These recommendations highlight the advantages of the CPC concept. CPCs can have staff, protocols, and established procedures for the rapid identification of patients with AMI and unstable angina as well as procedures to achieve a target "door-to-drug" time of 30 minutes (or less) or a door-to-balloon-inflation (where percutaneous transluminal coronary angioplasty [PTCA] is available) time of 90 minutes (or less) for patients with typical presentations of AMI with ST segment elevation. For example, the CPC can have assigned nursing personnel who rapidly evaluate the patient with chest pain with a 12-lead ECG, as well as screening vital signs and cardiac monitoring, and deliver the ECG directly to a clinician capable of making a decision about activation of the catheterization laboratory or administration of fibrinolytic therapy.

The CPC may also be used as an observation and evaluation unit where patients with chest pain and low to intermediate clinical likelihood of ACS can be monitored with electrocardiography, ST segment trending, serial 12-lead ECGs, and sequential serum markers; these tools compose the rule out MI or accelerated diagnostic protocol. The development of any life threat, including sudden cardiac death, is rapidly identified and aggressively managed. In addition, many CPCs now employ further ACS evaluation with stress testing, echocardiography, or myocardial scintigraphy before disposition. Evaluation of such protocols has proved medically effective and safe in short-term follow-up. Significant cost savings occur, with typical charges and actual costs ranging from 20% to 50% of the costs for the usual inpatient approach.

The Chest Pain Evaluation in the Emergency Room (CHEER) investigators performed a prospective, randomized trial of a chest pain unit compared with the traditional hospital admission for rule out MI in patients with chest pain.[88] Over a 16-month period, patients with chest pain determined to be at intermediate ACS risk on the basis of history, examination and ECG were randomly assigned to either CPC or hospital admission for additional evaluation. CPC patients then underwent serial serum marker and ECG determinations over a minimum of 6 hours. If investigations were negative and the course was uncomplicated, patients underwent further evaluation with an exercise stress test, nuclear stress test, or stress echocardiography. If this evaluation was positive, the patient was admitted; if negative, the patient was discharged with cardiology follow-up within 72 hours. In the CPC group, all events occurred among those with a positive stress test; no cardiac events occurred in the negative stress test group after emergency department discharge. In the 6-month period after discharge, cardiac investigations and therapies were greater among patients in the admitted group. Admissions to the hospital were reduced by 45.8%.

Gibler and colleagues[84] performed a comprehensive diagnostic 9-hour evaluation (Heart ER Program) for 1010 patients with possible ACS over 32 months. Patients underwent serial testing with the following: CK-MB at presentation, 3, 6, and 9 hours; continuous 12-lead ECGs; and serial ST segment trend monitoring. Two-dimensional echocardiography and graded exercise testing were performed in the emergency department after the 9-hour evaluation. Such a program provided an effective method for evaluating low- to moderate-risk patients with possible ACS in the emergency department setting.

As seen in the preceding two investigations, a chest pain accelerated diagnostic protocol approach to low- to intermediate-risk patients can be feasible, safe, and effective in medical terms and financial costs. Studies indicate that approximately 80% of patients with chest pain can be safely and effectively evaluated in the emergency department with ultimate discharge to home. The resources required for a successful CPC-based operation in which these patients undergo rapid exclusion of ACS through serial testing, continuous monitoring, and immediate provocative stress testing are considerable. In addition, although studies suggest that CPCs decrease the number of admissions, they also increase the number of patients who undergo rule out MI protocols, suggesting that physicians may overuse the CPC accelerated diagnostic protocol approach in patients whom they would otherwise have discharged from the emergency department.

Issues to consider before developing such a unit include entry criteria for patients; the resources, abilities, and desires of the emergency department; the availability of cardiac diagnostic testing; support from local cardiology groups; and the impact on primary care physicians. Appropriate patients—low to intermediate risk—must be chosen for such an evaluation. The emergency department must also have a dedicated area for continuous cardiac monitoring with dedicated nursing staff and resources, timely return of serum markers, and knowledgeable, motivated physicians. Support from cardiologists is vital in the form of availability of cardiac diagnostic testing as well as timely outpatient follow-up. Primary care physicians must also be considered in this process, in terms of both financial issues and referral and resource utilization concerns.

MANAGEMENT OF ACUTE CORONARY SYNDROME

The pathophysiology of an acute coronary event involves numerous steps, including (1) endothelial damage through plaque disruption, irregular luminal lesions, and shear injury; (2) platelet aggregation; (3) thrombus formation causing partial or total lumen occlusion; (4) coronary artery vasospasm; and (5) reperfusion injury caused by oxygen free radicals, calcium, and neutrophils. In patients with noninfarction ACS, spontaneous fibrinolysis of the thrombus occurs rapidly, minimizing ischemic insult; persistence of the occlusive thrombus, however, results in MI. Treatment of patients with ACS addresses five basic issues: (1) increase myocardial oxygen supply through supplemental oxygen and restoration of coronary blood flow; (2) use β-adrenergic blockade to decrease the force of myocardial contraction and therefore oxygen demand; (3) increase metabolic substrate availability to the myocardium through NTG, morphine, fibrinolytic agents, and angioplasty; (4) protect injured myocardial cell function by decreasing inflammation or toxic injury through anti-inflammatory drugs and perfluorochemicals; and (5) prevent reocclusion of the coronary artery through inhibition of platelet aggregation and thrombus formation by use of antiplatelet and anticoagulant agents.

Relationship of Time to Treatment with Outcome

The beneficial effect of reperfusion is a function of the length of time between AMI onset and treatment. In the late 1970s, the wave front phenomenon of ischemic cell death was described. In this model, myocardial necrosis progresses from the subendocardium to the epicardium after coronary occlusion; subsequent release of the occlusion after various times demonstrated that earlier release produces a smaller infarct characterized by less transmural progression of the necrosis. In human clinical studies, the 40% to 50% reduction in mortality observed in patients treated in the first hour and the overall 25% to 30% mortality reduction seen in randomized clinical trials also support this hypothesis (Figure 77-23).

Early patency resulting in myocardial salvage is the key benefit of emergent revascularization therapy using either fibrinolysis or primary angioplasty. Treatment within the first hours after symptom onset may result in substantial myocardial salvage. Treatment delivered at a later time, from 2 to 12 hours after AMI onset, may result in a modest yet significant benefit; this benefit results from the opening of the occluded artery with less adverse ventricular modeling, reduced occurrence of ventricular aneurysm, increased blood flow to myocardium still in jeopardy, and improved electrophysiologic stability. In the angiographic substudy of GUSTO, preserved left ventricular function and mortality at both the 24-hour and the 30-day end points were related to angiographic patency at 90 minutes.[89] Fibrinolytic therapy of patients with AMI has significantly greater benefit for those treated within the first 1 or 2 hours compared with those treated later. In the Myocardial Infarction Triage and Intervention (MITI) trial, the mortality rate among patients treated within 70 minutes was 1.3% compared with 8.7% in those treated later.[90]

Substantial delays often occur between symptom onset and hospital-based initiation of fibrinolytic

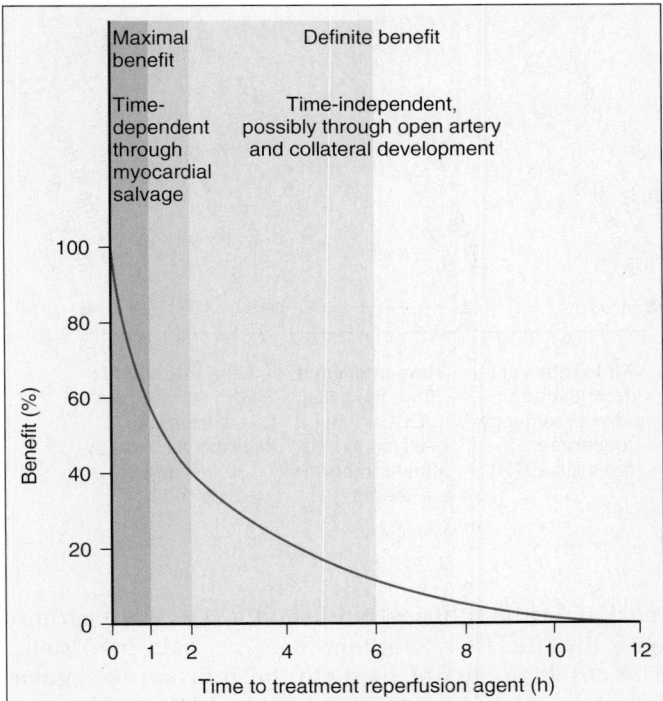

Figure 77-23. Relationship between time to reperfusion and benefit in ST segment elevation acute myocardial infarction. This figure depicts combined human and animal data and represents the time-dependent benefit anticipated, depending on the length of the interval between coronary artery occlusion and reperfusion. (Modified from Tiefenbrunn AJ, Sobel BE: Timing of coronary recanalization. Paradigms, paradoxes, and pertinence. *Circulation* 85:2311, 1992; © 1992 American Heart Association. Reproduced from U.S. Department of Health and Human Services, Public Health Service, National Institutes of Health, National Heart, Lung, and Blood Institute (NIH Publication No. 93-3278), September 1993, p 8.)

therapy in AMI patients. In 1991, the NHLBI launched the NHAAP to promote the rapid identification and treatment of AMI. The factors responsible for delay in the care of AMI patients are grouped by the NHAAP into three phases: patient-bystander, prehospital, and hospital. Patient-bystander factors are those that keep the patient from seeking immediate medical care through the EMS system. Median delays range from 2 to 6.5 hours; in fact, 26% to 44% of AMI patients delay more than 4 hours before seeking medical care. In all major studies evaluating patients' delay, the median time of arrival at hospital is delayed well beyond the critical first hour during the time period in which half of AMI deaths occur. Self-treatment is a significant component of patients' delay, occurring in approximately one third of patients with AMI and sudden death.

Prehospital delay factors are those that occur from the time the patient decides to seek medical attention until the patient arrives at the emergency department. It is not uncommon for patients to call their primary care physician; such a phone call, although laudable, has the potential to delay definitive care significantly.

Only half of patients with suspected AMI call the EMS system. Many transport themselves or wait for someone other than EMS personnel to take them to the hospital. Other patients far removed from an emergency facility spend considerable time being transported to a hospital. Further complicating prehospital issues include wide variations in the availability and quality of emergency medical systems throughout the United States.

Further delays can occur between the time a patient arrives in the hospital and the initiation of acute revascularization therapy. Overall, the average time to fibrinolysis ranges from 45 to 90 minutes, although shorter times have been reported. The GUSTO trial demonstrated a median time from hospital arrival to treatment with fibrinolytic therapy of 70 minutes.[89] The AHA recommends that all patients with heart attack who are to receive fibrinolytic therapy receive the treatment within 30 to 60 minutes of arrival in the emergency department. It is encouraged that AMI patients who undergo primary PTCA have therapy initiated no later than 90 minutes after arrival.

AMI patients who receive hospital-based reperfusion therapies (fibrinolytic agent or primary PTCA) progress through a sequence of steps that can be used to define process time points (Figure 77-24). Within each interval, various barriers and impediments to timely care can occur. Reducing delay times is applicable to all time points in the emergency department by addressing the four Ds: door (events prior to arrival at the ED), data (obtaining the ECG), decision (arriving at the AMI diagnosis and deciding upon therapy), and "drug" (administering the fibrinolytic agent or passing the angioplasty catheter across the culprit lesion for PTCA candidates).

Prehospital care providers may alert the emergency department to the impending arrival of a patient with a suspected AMI. A 12-lead ECG acquired in the field may assist the emergency department in diagnosis and decrease the time to administration of appropriate therapy. Self-transported patients with possible ACS should be evaluated by the triage nurse immediately. A nurse's identification of a potential heart attack should be immediately communicated to the emergency physician, with rapid performance of a protocol-driven 12-lead ECG; furthermore, the emergency department nurses should be trained to recognize electrocardiographic changes indicative of AMI.

Development of hospital-based protocols and system response plans for identifying and rapidly treating patients reduces the amount of time to treatment. When using fibrinolysis in uncomplicated cases, the emergency physician should activate the hospital-based system for reperfusion. Checklists of inclusion and exclusion criteria for fibrinolytic therapy should be available. Fibrinolytic agents should be stored in the emergency department to avoid delays. Treatment should be administered in the emergency department and not delayed by transporting the patient to another area of the hospital. Communication prior to administration of the agent with family physicians, internists, or cardiologists may result in unnecessary delays. Consultative discussions during administration of therapy

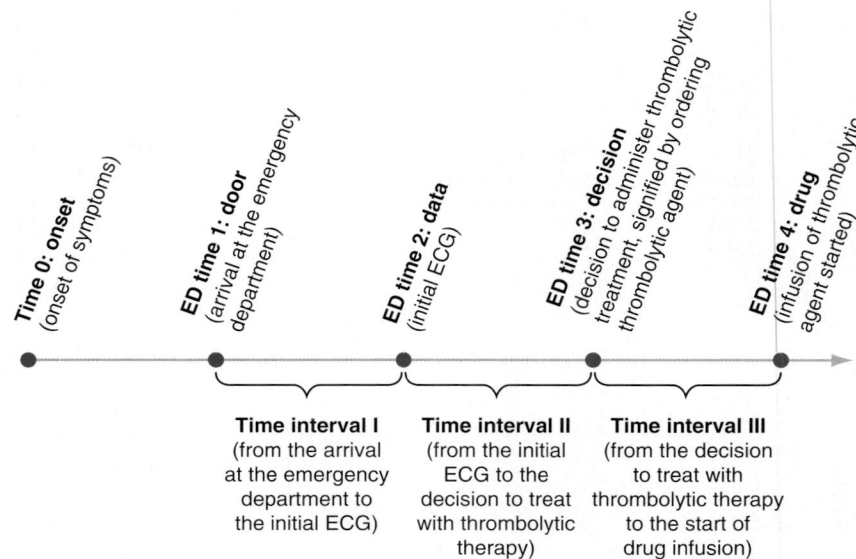

Figure 77-24. The four Ds of emergency department (ED)–based diagnosis and management of the patient with acute myocardial infarction (AMI). Shown are the process time points and intervals through which the patient with AMI passes until treatment in the emergency department. ECG, electrocardiogram. (From U.S. Department of Health and Human Services, Public Health Service, National Institutes of Health, National Heart, Lung, and Blood Institute (NIH Publication No. 93-3278), September 1993, p 10.)

are warranted. In situations involving a complicated AMI presentation, rapid consultation is appropriate.

If the hospital offers primary percutaneous coronary intervention (PCI), immediate consultation with the cardiologist should be obtained. Many hospitals have developed "STEMI alert" responses to the AMI patient with ST segment elevation. In such a response, which is analogous to the trauma alert, the cardiologist and catheterization laboratory personnel are immediately mobilized when the system is activated by the emergency physician,. Interhospital transfer of AMI patients for PCI, when they are also candidates for fibrinolysis, should be discouraged if definitive therapy (i.e., catheter placement across the culprit lesion) is likely to be delayed beyond 3 hours.[91]

PHARMACOLOGIC INTERVENTION

Nitroglycerin

Nitrates provide substantial benefit to patients with ACS by decreasing myocardial preload and, to a lesser extent, afterload. Nitrates increase venous capacitance, inducing venous pooling, which decreases preload and myocardial oxygen demand. Direct vasodilation of coronary arteries may increase collateral blood flow to ischemic myocardium. Most studies of intravenous NTG in the setting of AMI are from the prefibrinolytic era. A meta-analysis of multiple small trials noted a 35% mortality reduction with intravenous NTG.[92]

In the emergency setting, patients with possible ACS and a systolic blood pressure greater than 90 mm Hg should receive a sublingual NTG tablet (0.4 mg or 400 µg) on presentation. If symptoms are not fully relieved with three sublingual tablets, the patient may be started on intravenous NTG. Care must be exercised in patients with bradycardia, hypotension, inferior wall AMI, and right ventricular infarction when administering NTG because a sudden decrease in preload associated with NTG use can result in profound hypo-

tension. Initial infusion rates should start at 10 µg/min with titration to a symptom-free (i.e., pain-free) state. The clinician should increase the infusion at regular intervals, allowing a 10% reduction in the mean arterial pressure if normotensive and a 20% to 30% reduction if hypertensive. Sublingual bolus therapy, the use of additional sublingual NTG in the setting of intravenous NTG infusions, more rapidly increases the serum level of the medication with delivery of 400-µg boluses. Maximal benefit is probably achieved at 200 µg/min, although certain patients may receive additional benefit at higher infusion rates.

Morphine

The use of morphine sulfate for the treatment of unstable angina has not been evaluated in large, randomized trials. Morphine is a potent opioid analgesic with weak sympathetic blocking activity, systemic histamine release, and anxiolytic effects, each of which can be beneficial in the treatment of patients with ACS. If a patient with possible ACS is unresponsive to NTG or has recurrent symptoms despite maximal anti-ischemic therapy, administration of morphine sulfate is appropriate. The relief of pain and anxiety decreases oxygen consumption and myocardial work. Some vasodilatory effects are also noted with preload reduction. Standard doses of morphine sulfate are 2 to 5 mg delivered intravenously, repeated every 5 to 30 minutes as necessary. In addition to allergic reactions, the most significant adverse effect of morphine sulfate administration is hypotension, which is managed with intravenous fluid in bolus fashion.

β-Adrenergic Blockers

β-Adrenergic blocking agents are effective in ameliorating catecholamine-induced tachycardia, increased contractility, and myocardial oxygen demand. β₁-Receptors, located in the myocardium, also increase sinoatrial node rate and AV nodal conduction velocity when stimulated. β_2-Receptors are located primarily in vascular smooth muscle and the lungs. β Blockade has been demonstrated to be effective in decreasing mortality for patients with AMI. Although the impact of β-adrenergic blockade in treating unstable angina is less well studied, a meta-analysis showed a 13% reduction in the risk of subsequent AMI.

Intravenous metoprolol can be given in 5-mg increments by slow infusion over 1 to 2 minutes with repeat doses of 5 mg given at 5-minute intervals, for a total of 15 mg. Alternatively, atenolol, esmolol, or propranolol can be administered. Atenolol is the longest acting agent. Esmolol is an ultrashort-acting β-blocker that may be given to patients who potentially would not tolerate β-adrenergic antagonism, such as patients with mild CHF or chronic obstructive pulmonary disease; caution is advised in these situations. Contraindications to β-adrenergic blockade include pulmonary edema or other manifestations of acute CHF, chronic obstructive pulmonary disease and asthma, AV nodal blockade, bradycardia, and systemic hypotension.

Despite the potentially beneficial effects of this treatment in the early phase of management in the AMI patient, clinicians appear to use this medication less often than is possible. A large review of the inpatient care of AMI patients revealed a low rate of β-adrenergic blockade in eligible patients; only 60% to 75% of eligible patients received this treatment.[93] Physicians should consider the use of β-adrenergic blockade in all such AMI patients lacking contraindications.

Angiotensin-Converting Enzyme Inhibitors

Angiotensin-converting enzyme (ACE) inhibitor agents have long been known to benefit patients with CHF of various causes. It has also been suggested that ACE inhibitors may reduce morbidity and mortality after AMI. In particular, patients treated with ACE inhibitors experience a reduction in cardiovascular mortality, decreased rates of significant CHF development, and fewer recurrent AMIs. These benefits are noted to increase when ACE inhibitors are used in conjunction with other agents such as aspirin and fibrinolytics. The mechanism of action regarding a reduction in recurrent AMI is unknown but may involve a reduction in plaque rupture related to decreased intracoronary shear force or neurohumoral influences.

Captopril, enalapril, lisinopril, or ramipril may be used in this setting. The ultimate doses used should be maximized, but care must be exercised with these potent agents such that initial doses should be low and applied cautiously in order to avoid hypotension. Therapy should be initiated early in the post-AMI course, preferably within the first 24 hours; their use in the emergency department, however, is usually not indicated unless the patient has a prolonged emergency department stay. In patients with asymptomatic left ventricular dysfunction, therapy should be applied for a minimum of 2 to 4 months; in patients with symptomatic CHF, ACE inhibitors should be administered indefinitely. Contraindications to ACE inhibitor therapy include hypotension; relative contraindications include volume depletion and borderline perfusion. Renal function must be monitored closely during therapy.

Calcium Channel Blockers

As with β blockade, the primary benefit of calcium channel blockers appears to be with symptom resolution. Unfortunately, these agents may be accompanied by a significant vasodilatory effect resulting in hypotension and therefore potentiation of the coronary ischemic process. Like β-blocking agents, calcium channel blockers have a substantial negative inotropic effect, further affecting perfusion. AV nodal blockade is also a significant side effect that may be exacerbated in patients previously treated with β-blockers or with ischemia-related conduction disturbance. Unless specifically used for rate control of supraventricular dysrhythmia in a patient who cannot tolerate β blockade, calcium channel blocker agents are not recommended as therapy for ACS.

Antiplatelet Therapy

In non-AMI ACS patients, dramatic reductions in the progression to acute infarction have been noted with aggressive antiplatelet therapy; furthermore, patients in the acute phase of AMI also experience significant benefit with antiplatelet therapy with mortality reductions ranging from 25% to 50%. Thus, there is a sound scientific basis for recommending administration of antiplatelet therapy, particularly aspirin, in the emergency department for virtually all ACS patients.

Aspirin

Aspirin, the standard antiplatelet agent, represents the most cost-effective treatment available for patients with ACS; it should be administered early to all patients suspected of having ACS without contraindication. It irreversibly acetylates platelet cyclooxygenase, thereby removing all cyclooxygenase activity for the life span of the platelet (8 to 10 days). Thus, aspirin stops the production of proaggregatory thromboxane A_2 and is an indirect antithrombotic agent. Aspirin also has important nonplatelet effects because it inactivates cyclooxygenase in the vascular endothelium, thereby diminishing formation of antiaggregatory prostacyclin.

The Second International Study of Infarct Survival (ISIS-2) trial provides the strongest evidence that aspirin independently reduces the mortality of patients with AMI without fibrinolytic therapy (overall 23% reduction) and is synergistic when used with fibrinolytic therapy (42% reduction in mortality).[94] The usual dose is 325 mg of non–enteric-coated aspirin, chewed and swallowed. Administration of aspirin in the emergency department is strongly recommended immediately upon identification of any patient with suspected ACS, either AMI or unstable angina; it should be administered to all such patients unless significant allergy contraindicates its use.

Glycoprotein IIb/IIIa Receptor Inhibitors

The glycoprotein IIb/IIIa receptor inhibitors (GPIs) represent a relatively recent addition to the therapeutic armamentarium employed in AMI. This class of medication has provided the clinician with potent antiplatelet therapy; the GPI, however, has demonstrated clinical utility in only a subset of ACS patients—those undergoing PCI. Therefore, the primary indication regarding GPI administration for the emergency physician is planned mechanical coronary intervention; this therapy may also be administered by the cardiologist immediately prior to intervention, removing the urgent need for this agent from the emergency physician's area of concern.

During platelet stimulation, surface receptors are activated, particularly the membrane glycoprotein IIb/IIIa receptors. These receptors represent the final common pathway for platelet activation and ultimate aggregation. Once activated, the glycoprotein IIb/IIIa receptors allow the various circulating factors, von Willebrand factor and fibrinogen, to link into a chain-like arrangement; this linked-chain formation ultimately results in platelet adhesion and clot.

Three agents in this class currently enjoy widespread clinical use: abciximab, eptifibatide, and tirofiban. Abciximab was the first such GPI to have undergone large clinical trials. As a monoclonal antibody specific for the glycoprotein IIb/IIIa receptor, it provides prolonged inhibition of platelet aggregation, even after cessation of drug infusion. Eptifibatide, a synthetic peptide, prevents binding of fibrinogen to the glycoprotein IIb/IIIa receptor; this antagonism blocks platelet aggregation and subsequent thrombus formation. Tirofiban is a synthetic, nonpeptide, shorter acting GPI with a mechanism of action similar to that of eptifibatide.

Numerous trials have demonstrated the effectiveness of these agents in ACS patients, yet only a subset of these patients actually derives benefit from their application—those who are managed with PCI with or without an intracoronary stent. The Evaluation of 7E3 for the Prevention of Ischemic Complications (EPIC) trial[95] investigated the effect of abciximab in ACS patients (high-risk unstable angina and AMI) scheduled for PCI and demonstrated a 35% reduction in mortality rate, recurrent MI, and need for unplanned rescue therapies balanced by an increase in hemorrhagic complications. The Evaluation of PTCA to Improve Long-term Outcome with abciximab GPIIb/IIIa Receptor Blockade (EPILOG) trial[96] further evaluated the effect of abciximab in those with ACS presentations, including AMI patients, who underwent invasive coronary interventions; these investigators noted a 68% reduction in death or nonfatal AMI with a lower incidence of major bleeding episodes than in the EPIC study. In the GRAPE study, which investigated the use of a GPI in patients scheduled for urgent PCI,[97] increased rates of TIMI grade 3 flow were noted in the abciximab group. In the Integrilin to Minimize Platelet Aggregation and Coronary Thrombosis-II (IMPACT-II) trial,[98] ACS patients treated with eptifibatide who were bound for PCI

demonstrated a modest reduction in the rate of emergent revascularization, AMI, or death at 30 days that was lost at 6 months.

A meta-analysis of GPI use in ACS patients reinforces this finding—that patients who undergo PCI benefit markedly from glycoprotein inhibitor administration.[99] In ACS patients who are managed medically without mechanical revascularization, consistent benefit with GPI therapy is not found, using either direct outcome measures (death, recurrent ACS, or need for urgent revascularization) or secondary markers of successful reperfusion (TIMI flow grades and serum marker elevation). The GUSTO IV trial revealed that abciximab did not alter the rate of death or recurrent MI at 1 month in patients with ACS and hemorrhagic complications occurred more often in the active treatment groups.[100] A meta-analysis of GPI use in ACS patients revealed that individuals managed without PCI did not derive significant benefit from its application.[99] The PRISM and Platelet Receptor Inhibition in Ischemic Syndrome Management in Patients Limited by Unstable Signs and Symptoms (PRISM-PLUS) trial[101] investigators did not demonstrate significant benefit in ACS patients managed with tirofiban. The Integrilin to Manage Platelet Aggregation to Combat Thrombus in Acute Myocardial Infarction (IMPACT-AMI) investigators[102] reported the results in AMI patients receiving fibrinolytic agents and varying doses of eptifibatide (i.e., nonmechanical means of reperfusion); they noted similar rates of death, recurrent MI, and the need for revascularization procedures but observed an increase in TIMI grade 3 flow at 90 minutes. Furthermore, using troponin values as an estimate of infarct size, investigators did not demonstrate benefit in eptifibatide-treated patients with non-ST elevation ACS presentations.[103]

The glycoprotein IIb/IIIa receptor inhibitors have consistently demonstrated benefit in ACS patients treated with urgent mechanical revascularization; other groups of ACS patients, such as medically managed, combination fibrinolytic agent, or transferred patients, have not established an invariable positive affect. Consequently, the ACC/AHA has provided the following guidelines for GPI use in ACS patients: (1) GPIs should be given, in addition to ASA and heparin, to ACS patients in whom PCI is planned (a class I indication; that is, evidence is found supporting that treatment is effective); (2) GPIs should be given to patients already receiving heparin, ASA, and clopidogrel in whom PCI is planned (a class IIa indication; that is, conflicting evidence is found regarding effectiveness); and (3) eptifibatide or tirofiban, in addition to ASA and heparin, may be given to patients without continuing ACS who have no other high-risk features and in whom PCI is not planned (a class IIb indication; that is, efficacy is less well established by evidence).[104]

Other Antiplatelet Agents

The thienopyridines ticlopidine and clopidogrel are potent platelet inhibitors; in fact, these agents inhibit platelet function to a greater extent than aspirin. The thienopyridines inhibit the transformation of the glycoprotein IIb/IIIa receptor into its high-affinity ligand-binding state, irreversibly inhibiting platelet aggregation for the duration of the life of the platelet. Ticlopidine has nonlinear kinetics and, after repeated dosing, reaches a maximal effect after 8 to 11 days of dosage. Clopidogrel, a ticlopidine analogue, has the advantages of a rapid onset of action and an intravenous route of administration. Clopidogrel is currently the preferred agent because of its more rapid onset of action and also because of its safety profile; ticlopidine is associated with a risk of neutropenia and agranulocytosis that is not encountered with clopidogrel. Maximal platelet inhibition occurs after 3 to 5 days of clopidogrel therapy (75 mg daily); an earlier onset of platelet inhibition is seen when a higher loading dose is used (300 to 600 mg). In the ACS patient, clopidogrel in combination with aspirin is more effective than ASA alone in reducing cardiovascular death, MI, and stroke for 9 months after the index visit. These patients also have a greater incidence of bleeding; in the individuals undergoing coronary bypass grafting within 5 days of therapy, an increased risk of major hemorrhage requiring transfusion and reoperation was noted.[105] Clopidogrel, 300 to 600 mg by mouth or intravenously, should be considered in the ACS patient in whom emergency coronary artery bypass grafting is not anticipated. Many of these therapies should be considered in the emergency department for several reasons aside from their efficacy: (1) there is a tendency for omission if not administered in the emergency department, (2) many ACS patients now have prolonged stays in the emergency department, and (3) these agents are safe and easily given with demonstrated efficacy; their use, however, should be considered only with consultation.

Antithrombins

As with antiplatelet therapies in ACS patients, significant reductions in the progression to acute infarction, recurrent infarction, extensive infarction, and death have been noted in individuals treated with aggressive antithrombin therapy. The antithrombins include unfractionated heparin, low-molecular-weight (fractionated) heparin (LMW heparin), and the direct thrombin inhibitors (hirudin and bivalirudin). Antithrombotic therapy is indicated in a portion of emergency department ACS patients without contraindication, including patients with the following characteristics: recurrent anginal pain, AMI (non-ST segment elevation and ST segment elevation), positive serum marker, and a dynamic 12-lead ECG.

Heparins

The term *heparin* refers not to a single structure but rather to a family of mucopolysaccharide chains of varying lengths and composition—hence, unfractionated—with pronounced antithrombotic properties. Unfractionated heparin is composed of a mixture of polysaccharide chains with varying molecular weights.

At standard doses, unfractionated heparin binds to antithrombin III, forming a complex that is able to inactivate factor II (thrombin) and activated factor X. This effect prevents the conversion of fibrinogen to fibrin, thus preventing clot formation. Heparin by itself has no anticoagulant property. This indirect effect on thrombin inhibits clot propagation; it prevents heparin, however, from having any effect on bound thrombin in a thrombus. Unfractionated heparin also assists in the inactivation of factors XIa and IXa through antithrombin and interacts with platelets.

LMW heparins constitute approximately one third of the molecular weight of heparin and are less heterogeneous in size. The LMW heparins inhibit the coagulation system in a fashion similar to that of unfractionated heparin. Approximately one third of the heparin molecules bind to both antithrombin III and thrombin. The remaining molecules bind only to factor Xa. The variable efficacy that has been found among the LMW heparins has been attributed to different ratios of antifactor Xa to antifactor IIa. High-ratio preparations appear to demonstrate a clear advantage over standard heparin; enoxaparin has the highest ratio of the currently available LMW heparins. LMW heparin was designed on the basis of the hypothesis that inhibition of earlier steps in the blood coagulation system would be associated with a more potent antithrombotic effect than inhibition of subsequent steps. This effect is thought to result from the amplification process inherent in the coagulation cascade; that is, a single factor Xa molecule can lead to the generation of multiple thrombin molecules.

Unfractionated heparin has been shown to have a profound synergistic effect with aspirin in preventing death, AMI, and refractory angina in ACS patients, particularly those with AMI and, to a lesser extent, high-risk unstable angina. Unfractionated heparin should be administered early in patients with the following ACS features: recurrent or persistent chest pain, AMI, positive serum marker, and dynamic ECG. In patients undergoing PCI, bleeding and mortality were higher in TIMI 14 in patients receiving an 80-U/kg bolus and 18-U/kg infusion than in patients receiving a 60-U/kg bolus and 16-U/kg infusion. Therefore, the initial recommended dose is 60-U/kg by intravenous bolus, followed by a maintenance infusion of 16-U/kg/hr. The activated partial thromboplastin time (aPTT) should be titrated to 1.5 to 2.5 times the control value using the maintenance infusion. Contraindications to heparin therapy include allergy to the medication, active ongoing life-threatening hemorrhage, and predisposition to such hemorrhage.

The Fast Revascularisation during InStability in Coronary artery disease (FRISC) trial[106] established that the combination of aspirin, β-blocker, and LMW heparin (dalteparin) significantly decreased the rate of nonfatal AMI or death at 1 week of therapy compared with a less pronounced effect at 40 to 150 days and an increased number of minor bleeding episodes. In the Efficacy and Safety of Subcutaneous Enoxaparin in Non-Q-Wave Coronary Events (ESSENCE) study,[107] a benefit was found with LMW heparin over unfractionated heparin at 30 days; the risk of minor bleeding was higher. Conversely, the Fragmin in Unstable Coronary Artery Disease (FRIC) study[108] investigated the use of LMW (dalteparin) compared with unfractionated heparin in patients with unstable coronary disease (unstable angina and non-ST segment elevation AMI). The rates of death, recurrent angina, and AMI and the need for revascularization procedures were similar at 1 week and at 45 days. In this study, both forms of heparin provided similar benefit in these patients with unstable coronary disease. In general, it appears that the LMW heparin, particularly enoxaparin with its favorable antifactor Xa/antifactor IIa ratio, offers a short-term therapeutic benefit in the unstable coronary patient that decreases significantly beyond the first week of treatment. It may be administered in a twice-daily regimen subcutaneously at a dose of 1 mg/kg; doses should be reduced for patients with pronounced renal insufficiency.

Other advantages of LMW heparin over unfractionated heparin include greater bioavailability, more consistent therapeutic response among patients, longer serum half-life producing a more manageable dosing schedule, and reduced rates of adverse bleeding episodes. LMW heparin inactivates factor Xa, which is resistant to inactivation by unfractionated heparin. LMW heparins have lesser binding to coagulation factors such as platelet factor 4, other plasma proteins, and endothelial cells, resulting in higher bioavailability. LMW heparin has a longer half-life and less individual variability of the anticoagulant response compared with unfractionated heparin. It has lower affinity for von Willebrand factor, increased vascular permeability, and a weak effect on platelet function. These differences could explain why LMW heparin produces less bleeding than unfractionated heparin with equivalent or higher antithrombotic effects. The long half-life of LMW heparins and their predictable anticoagulant response to weight-adjusted doses allow once-daily subcutaneous administration without laboratory monitoring. LMW heparin is markedly more costly than treatment with unfractionated heparin; this cost difference, however, is probably less if one considers nursing, hospital, and laboratory costs related to unfractionated heparin's more complicated use.

Certainly, the vast majority of patients with AMI require therapy with heparin, whether it is fractionated or unfractionated. Non-AMI ACS, however, is an entirely different issue. To state the obvious, not all unstable angina cases are the same. For example, the stable patient with a classical description of new-onset angina who is sensation free with a negative serum marker and a normal ECG is still correctly diagnosed with unstable angina. In contrast, the case of an individual who presents with ongoing pain, either intermittent or constant, with a dynamic ECG clearly represents an active, unstable coronary event. The latter patient, who is at high risk, benefits from heparin therapy more than the former. Heparin therapy is not without risk. It has been reported to be a major contributor to morbidity and mortality among hospitalized patients, and it has been estimated that major bleeding

develops in 1 of every 90 patients treated and that 1 in 34 develop heparin-induced thrombocytopenia. LMW heparin has been found to be as effective as unfractionated heparin in patients with ACS and does not greatly increase the bleeding risk while decreasing the risk of thrombocytopenia. Heparin therapy is not indicated in all patients with ACS, specifically patients with low-risk presentations.[109]

Direct Thrombin Inhibitors

The direct thrombin inhibitors hirudin and bivalirudin (formerly known as hirulog) are potent antithrombin anticoagulants providing significant theoretical advantages compared with heparin. Hirudin is a peptide derived from the leech salivary gland but is also synthesized as recombinant hirudin. It binds directly with high affinity to thrombin and can inactivate thrombin already bound to fibrin (clot-bound thrombin), which unfractionated heparin cannot do as effectively. Hirudin does not require endogenous cofactors such as antithrombin III for its activity. Also, unlike heparin, hirudin can inhibit thrombin-induced platelet aggregation. Bivalirudin is a bifunctional 20–amino acid peptide designed on the basis of the structure of hirudin. It has properties similar to those of hirudin but in addition interacts with the catalytic site of thrombin. Hirudin and bivalirudin have not been associated with drug-induced thrombocytopenia in contrast to the heparins.

In the Organisation to Assess Strategies for Ischemic Syndromes (OASIS-2) trial,[110] patients with unstable angina or suspected non-STE AMI were randomly assigned to intravenous heparin or hirudin; the primary outcome measure was cardiovascular death or recurrent AMI in 1 week. Patients in both groups experienced the same rate of death and recurrent AMI, yet symptomatic angina was noted less often in the hirudin group. Of concern, patients in the hirudin group more often experienced major bleeding requiring transfusion. The Hirudin for Improvement of Thrombolysis (HIT-4) trial[111] investigated the use of hirudin as an adjunct to fibrinolysis in AMI patients. No significant difference was noted between groups regarding coronary flow but ST segment elevation resolution occurred more rapidly in the hirudin segment. No major differences were noted in other outcome parameters including death, recurrent acute coronary ischemia, major bleeding, and stroke. In the Hirulog Early Reperfusion/Occlusion (HERO) trial,[112] AMI patients treated with streptokinase and aspirin were randomly assigned to receive either heparin or bivalirudin with a primary outcome measurement of achieving TIMI grade 3 flow at 90 to 120 minutes. In a later trial of similar design (HERO-2), no significant difference in mortality was found in bivalirudin-treated patients who received stroptokinase.[113] Therefore, the direct thrombin inhibitors do not offer any benefit over heparin as adjunctive therapy in the ACS patient; it is anticipated that these agents would be employed only for heparin-ineligible patients, such as individuals with heparin-related thrombocytopenia.

REPERFUSION THERAPIES

Reestablishing perfusion in the infarct-related coronary artery with the use of fibrinolytic therapy or PCI, in essence reopening the infarct-related artery, increases the opportunity for salvage of the ischemic myocardium and reduces morbidity and mortality. Pharmacologic and mechanical methods of reperfusion are both effective under specific clinical conditions. Considering both methods, prompt initiation of reperfusion therapy is still the most critical determinant of outcome. The importance of early coronary artery patency was affirmed by the GUSTO investigators in their angiographic substudy when they demonstrated that 90-minute patency predicted rates of survival and preserved left ventricular function were superior to those of patients not achieving normal coronary flow.[89]

Fibrinolytic therapy unequivocally improves survival in patients presenting with ST segment elevation AMI. Although fibrinolysis has widespread availability and a proven ability to improve coronary flow, limit infarct size, and improve survival in AMI patients, many individuals with acute infarction are not considered suitable candidates for such treatment. Patients with absolute contraindications to fibrinolytic therapy, certain relative contraindications, cardiogenic shock, and unstable angina may be ineligible to receive fibrinolytic therapy. The requirement of administering prompt reperfusion therapy to these patients, as well as the other limitations of fibrinolytic therapy, has led many clinicians to advocate PTCA with or without intracoronary stent placement, also known as PCI, as the primary therapy and treatment of choice for AMI. In fact, investigations have demonstrated that rapidly performed PCI is the treatment of choice in the AMI patient; such therapy, to provide the most significant benefit, must be performed as soon as possible after the initial presentation.

Fibrinolytic Therapy

Fibrinolytic Agent Selection

Three megatrials comparing tissue-type plasminogen activator (t-PA) with streptokinase have been published. The Gruppo Italiano per lo Studio della Streptochinasi nell'Infarto Miocardico (GISSI-2) trial[114] and the closely related International Study[115] compared a 100-mg infusion of t-PA over 3 hours with streptokinase with or without heparin. The GISSI-2 study was the first large-scale mortality trial directly comparing t-PA and streptokinase in patients with AMI. The investigators found no difference in mortality between the two treatment groups. More strokes were reported with t-PA than with streptokinase (1.3% versus 1%) in the International Study, yet the frequency of confirmed hemorrhagic stroke was similar for both agents. Similar results were found in the ISIS-3 trial,[116] the next fibrinolytic megatrial, which compared t-PA, streptokinase, and anisoylated plasminogen-streptokinase activator complex in approximately 40,000 patients. In marked contrast to current practice, the inclusion criteria

allowed entry up to 24 hours after symptom onset and did not require diagnostic electrocardiographic change. All patients received adjunctive aspirin therapy and approximately half of the patients were given delayed, unmonitored subcutaneous heparin. A significant difference in both 35-day mortality and intracranial hemorrhage was not found. The results of the ISIS-3 study[116] proved controversial because of the unmonitored, delayed subcutaneous heparin protocol, particularly with studies now proving improved infarct artery patency using early therapeutic intravenous doses of heparin.

Current fibrinolytic practice was highly affected by the results of the GUSTO-I trial.[89] The purpose of the GUSTO-I trial was to test the hypothesis that early and sustained infarct vessel patency was associated with better survival rates in patients with AMI.[89] More than 41,000 patients were randomly assigned to four different fibrinolytic strategies: accelerated t-PA given over 90 minutes plus intravenous heparin, a combination of streptokinase plus a reduced dose of t-PA along with intravenous heparin, and two control groups (streptokinase plus subcutaneous heparin and streptokinase plus intravenous heparin). Unlike the approach in previous trials, t-PA was given in a more aggressive, front-loaded 90-minute infusion (referred to as accelerated t-PA). In addition to a primary end point of 30-day mortality, the GUSTO investigators explored coronary artery patency and degree of normalization of flow in the angiographic substudy; this portion of the larger trial was designed to determine the relationship between early coronary artery patency and outcome. In this trial, accelerated t-PA, administered with intravenous heparin, was shown to reduce 30-day mortality significantly by 15% compared with streptokinase with either form of heparin or the combination of t-PA and streptokinase with intravenous heparin. The benefit was highly consistent across virtually all subgroups, including elderly patients, location of AMI, and time from symptom onset. These differences remained significant at 1 year of follow-up.

The angiographic substudy demonstrated a strong relationship between TIMI flow and outcome. Patients with strong forward flow (i.e., TIMI grade 3 flow) at 90 minutes had significantly lower mortality rates than patients with little to no flow. The mechanism for this benefit was found to be earlier, more complete infarct vessel patency with accelerated t-PA; this early t-PA patency advantage over other agents was lost by 180 minutes after symptom onset. As would be expected, the patients with the higher risk derived the most substantial benefit with accelerated t-PA compared with streptokinase in this large study. Patients who received accelerated t-PA did suffer more hemorrhagic strokes than those who received streptokinase, but the combined end point of death and disabling stroke still favored the accelerated t-PA regimen.

Another important addition to the fibrinolytic agent literature base includes the GUSTO-III investigation.[117] This study compared accelerated t-PA with r-PA; r-PA is a mutant form of t-PA that can be administered in a fixed double bolus dose with no adjustment required for weight, which simplifies administration. In this very large trial, r-PA was found to be equivalent to accelerated t-PA, and the overall results were nearly identical for the two drugs. The one exception is that of patients who present more than 4 hours after onset of symptoms—a significant number of patients in many institutions. In this group of patients, accelerated t-PA may be superior to r-PA because of its greater fibrin specificity.[117]

The Assessment of the Safety and Efficacy of a New Thrombolytic Agent (ASSENT-2) trial investigated the use of TNK, another mutant of wild-type t-PA. TNK has several interesting characteristics and associated potential benefits: (1) its longer half-life allows it to be administered as a single bolus, (2) it is 14 times more fibrin specific than t-PA and even more so than r-PA, and (3) it is 80 times more resistant to plasminogen activator inhibitor type 1 than t-PA. The ASSENT-2 trial[118] randomly assigned approximately 17,000 patients with AMI to single-bolus TNK (30 to 50 mg on the basis of body weight) or accelerated t-PA (100 mg total infusion); the primary outcome variable was 30-day all-cause mortality. The investigators found no differences in mortality or ICH.[118] In a subgroup analysis, however, significantly lower 30-day mortality was noted among patients who presented more than 4 hours after onset of symptoms in those treated with TNK; furthermore, fewer nonintracranial major bleeding episodes were encountered in the TNK group. On the basis of these results, it was concluded that TNK was equally or minimally more effective, particularly in late presenters. Concerning adverse reactions, TNK also appeared to be modestly safer than accelerated t-PA. Lastly, because of its single-bolus administration, TNK is markedly easier to use in the emergency department as well as in other settings, such as the air and ground prehospital environments.

Eligibility Criteria for Fibrinolytic Agent Therapy

The 12-Lead Electrocardiogram

Combined with the patient's history and physical examination, the 12-lead ECG is the key determinant of eligibility for fibrinolysis. The electrocardiographic findings include two basic issues: (1) ST segment elevation of 1 mm or more in two or more anatomically contiguous *standard limb* leads and elevation of 2 mm or more in two or more contiguous *precordial* leads, and (2) new or presumed new LBBB. No evidence of benefit from fibrinolytic therapy is found in patients with ischemic chest pain who lack either appropriate ST segment elevation or the new development of LBBB.

Patients with LBBB and AMI are at an increased risk for a poor outcome; these patients should be rapidly managed in the emergency department with appropriate reperfusion therapies. This observation was noted before the introduction of fibrinolytic agents and continues to be true today. The new development of LBBB in the setting of AMI suggests proximal occlusion of the left anterior descending artery; such an obstruction places a significant portion of the left ventricle in ischemic jeopardy. Despite this increased risk for a poor outcome, patients with LBBB receive fibrinolytic agents less often. The same patients show significant benefit when treated with fibrinolytic therapy.

Patients with AMI in anterior, inferior, or lateral anatomic locations benefit from administration of fibrinolytic therapy. The relatively favorable prognosis associated with inferior infarction without fibrinolytic therapy requires larger sample sizes to detect a significant survival benefit. The ISIS-2 trial[94] demonstrated a statistically significant mortality benefit for fibrinolytic therapy in patients with inferior AMI; the mortality at 5 weeks was 6.5% for streptokinase plus aspirin versus 10.2% for placebo. Patients with inferior AMI with coexisting right ventricular infarctions, as detected by additional lead ECGs, are likely to benefit because of the large amount of jeopardized myocardium. Acute, isolated posterior wall MI, diagnosed by posterior leads, may represent yet another electrocardiographic indication for fibrinolysis. Although it has not been proved in large fibrinolytic agent trials, patients with isolated posterior AMI may be considered for possible candidacy for such reperfusion therapy.

The current evidence strongly indicates that fibrinolytic therapy should not be used routinely in patients with ST segment depression only on the 12-lead ECG. The mortality rate may actually be increased by administration of fibrinolytics in this subgroup of patients. The TIMI-3 trial[119] demonstrated a significant difference in outcome in fibrinolytic-treated patients with only ST segment depression—7.4% incidence of death compared with 4.9% in the placebo group. These findings are further supported in the Fibrinolytic Therapy Trialists' (FTT) meta-analysis, which demonstrated that the mortality rate among patients with ST segment depression who received fibrinolytic therapy was 15.2% compared with 13.8% among control subjects.[120]

Patient's Age

Past trials do not provide evidence to support withholding fibrinolytic therapy or choosing one particular agent over another on the basis of the patient's age. In fact, the FTT Collaborative Group[120] concluded that "clearly, age alone should no longer be considered a contraindication to fibrinolytic therapy." Patients older than 75 years do have a higher incidence of hemorrhagic stroke than younger patients.

Time from Symptom Onset

The generally accepted therapeutic time window for administration of a fibrinolytic agent after the onset of ST segment elevation AMI is 12 hours. Certainly, the earlier the treatment is initiated, the greater likelihood that the patient will experience a good outcome. Such is the case in patients managed within the first 6 hours of AMI. Later administrations, from 6 to 12 hours after AMI onset, also confer benefit, although of a lesser magnitude. The Late Assessment of Fibrinolytic Efficiency (LATE) trial, which compared fibrinolytic therapy with placebo, found a significant 26% decrease in 35-day mortality in patients treated with t-PA, heparin, and aspirin 6 to 12 hours after the onset of symptoms.[121]

There was no significant decrease in mortality among patients treated 12 to 24 hours after symptom onset.

These studies clearly establish benefit from 0 to 12 hours in patients who are otherwise appropriate candidates for fibrinolytic therapy. Treatment beyond that time is not supported by the literature. The single exception may be a patient with a "stuttering" nature of chest pain between 12 to 24 hours after symptom onset—once again emphasizing the importance of an adequate history. With evidence of marked ST segment elevation on the 12-lead ECG, the patient should be considered as a potential fibrinolytic candidate.

Blood Pressure Extremes

Current evidence indicates that patients with a history of chronic hypertension should not be excluded from fibrinolytic therapy if their blood pressure is under control at the time of presentation or can be lowered to acceptable levels using standard therapy for ischemic chest pain. The admission blood pressure is also an important indicator of risk of intracerebral hemorrhage. The FTT meta-analysis[120] demonstrated that the risk of cerebral hemorrhage increases with systolic blood pressure greater than 150 mm Hg on admission and further increases when systolic blood pressure is 175 mm Hg or higher. Despite an increased mortality rate during days 0 and 1, the FTT meta-analysis demonstrates an overall long-term benefit of 15 lives saved per 1000 for patients with systolic blood pressures greater than 150 mm Hg and 11 lives saved per 1000 for patients with systolic blood pressures of 175 mm Hg or greater.[120] Although the FTT meta-analysis appears to indicate an acceptable risk-benefit ratio for patients with substantially increased systolic blood pressure, a persistently elevated blood pressure greater than 200/120 mm Hg is generally considered to be an absolute contraindication to fibrinolytic therapy.

The benefit of fibrinolytic therapy in patients with hypotension remains controversial. The GISSI-1 and GISSI-2 trials showed no apparent reduction of mortality rate with fibrinolytic therapy among patients classified in Killip class III or IV.[114] These findings have led to the suggestion that primary angioplasty, not fibrinolytic therapy, be used in patients with cardiogenic shock. The FTT meta-analysis, however, does not support this hypothesis.[120] In this meta-analysis, patients with an initial systolic blood pressure less than 100 mm Hg who were not treated with fibrinolytic therapy had a very high risk of death (35.1%), and those who were treated with fibrinolytic therapy had the largest absolute benefit (60 lives saved per 1000 patients).[120] On the basis of this evidence, the FTT Collaborative Group suggested that hypotension, heart failure, and perhaps even shock should not be contraindications to fibrinolytic therapy.[120] These data support immediate treatment followed by diagnostic angiography and further intervention as indicated.

Retinopathy

Active diabetic hemorrhagic retinopathy is a strong *relative* contraindication to fibrinolytic therapy because of the potential for permanent blindness caused by intraocular bleeding. Current data, however, indicate that there is no reason to withhold the use of a fibrinolytic agent in a diabetic patient with evidence of simple background retinopathy. Patients with diabetes mellitus who sustain an AMI have an almost doubled incidence of mortality.

Cardiopulmonary Resuscitation

CPR is not a contraindication to fibrinolytic therapy unless CPR has been prolonged—more than 10 minutes—or extensive chest trauma from manual compression is evident. Although the in-hospital mortality rate is higher in AMI patients who experience cardiac arrest and then receive fibrinolytic agents in the emergency department, no difference is found in the rates of bleeding complications. Hemothorax and cardiac tamponade were not diagnosed in those receiving fibrinolytics who survived to admission.

Previous Stroke or Transient Ischemic Attack

A history of previous stroke or transient ischemic attack is a major risk factor for hemorrhagic stroke after treatment with fibrinolytic therapy. A history of previous ischemic stroke should remain a strong relative contraindication to fibrinolytic therapy. A history of previous hemorrhagic stroke should remain an absolute contraindication.

Previous Myocardial Infarction or Past Coronary Artery Bypass Graft

In the setting of AMI, a previous MI should not preclude consideration for treatment with fibrinolytic agents. Without treatment, there is a potential for greater loss of function in the newly infarcting region of the myocardium. Although the GISSI-1 trial showed no treatment benefits for patients with previous MIs, the ISIS-2 trial demonstrated a 26% relative mortality rate reduction for patients with previous MIs treated with fibrinolytic therapy.[94] The FTT meta-analysis further demonstrated that patients with a history of past MI who receive fibrinolytic therapy for recurrent acute infarction have a mortality rate of 12.5% compared with 14.1% among control patients.[120]

Many studies reported successful fibrinolysis in AMI patients with a prior coronary artery bypass graft (CABG). Complete thrombotic occlusion of the bypass graft is the cause of AMI in approximately 75% of cases as opposed to native vessel occlusion. It has been suggested that because of the large mass of thrombus and absent flow in the graft, conventional fibrinolytic therapy may be inadequate to restore flow. Because patients who have undergone coronary artery bypass grafting may be relatively resistant to fibrinolytic therapy, they should be considered for direct angioplasty or combined fibrinolysis and rescue angioplasty.

Recent Surgery or Trauma

Recent surgery or trauma is considered a relative contraindication to fibrinolytic therapy. The term *recent* has been variably interpreted, however, in fibrinolytic therapy trials. In the GISSI-1 trial,[122] patients were

BOX 77-1. Fibrinolysis in Acute Myocardial Infarction: Absolute and Relative Contraindications

- Recent (within 10 days) major surgery (e.g., coronary artery bypass graft, obstetric delivery, organ biopsy, previous puncture of noncompressible vessels)
- Cerebrovascular disease
- Recent gastrointestinal or genitourinary bleeding (within 10 days)
- Recent trauma (within 10 days)
- Hypertension: systolic BP ≥ 180 mm Hg or diastolic BP ≤ 110 mm Hg
- High likelihood of left heart thrombus (e.g., mitral stenosis with atrial fibrillation)
- Acute pericarditis
- Subacute bacterial endocarditis
- Hemostatic defects, including those secondary to severe hepatic or renal disease
- Significant liver dysfunction
- Diabetic hemorrhagic retinopathy or other hemorrhagic ophthalmic condition
- Septic thrombophlebitis or occluded AV cannula at seriously infected site
- Advanced age (older than 75 years)
- Patients currently receiving oral anticoagulants (e.g., warfarin sodium)
- Any other condition in which bleeding constitutes a significant hazard or would be particularly difficult to manage because of its location

AV, atrioventricular; BP, blood pressure.
Modified from *Physicians' Desk Reference,* 50th ed. Montvale, NJ, Medical Economics, 1996.

excluded if they had surgery or trauma within the previous 10 days. In the Anglo-Scandinavian Study of Early Thrombolysis (ASSET) trial, patients were excluded for surgery or trauma within the previous 6 weeks.[123] Other fibrinolytic therapy trials have not defined "recent surgery or trauma." It is prudent to consider alternative interventions such as angioplasty—if available—in patients with AMI within 10 days of surgery or significant trauma.

Menstruating Women

There has been concern regarding whether menstruating women with AMI should be considered candidates for fibrinolytic therapy. Because natural estrogen is cardioprotective, there has been little experience with fibrinolysis among premenopausal women. Significant adverse effects, however, have not been reported in such patients. Gynecologists indicate that any excessive vaginal bleeding that may occur after receiving fibrinolytic therapy should be readily controllable by vaginal packing and therefore can be considered as a compressible site of bleeding.

Contraindications

A list of absolute and relative contraindications is shown in Box 77-1.

Primary Percutaneous Coronary Intervention

Although fibrinolysis has widespread availability and a proven ability to improve coronary flow, limit infarct size, and improve survival in AMI patients, many individuals with acute infarction are not considered suitable candidates for such treatment. Patients with absolute contraindications to fibrinolytic therapy, certain relative contraindications, cardiogenic shock, and unstable angina may be ineligible to receive fibrinolytic therapy. The requirement of administering prompt reperfusion therapy to these patients, as well as the other limitations of fibrinolytic therapy, have led many clinicians to advocate PTCA, also known as PCI, as the primary therapy and treatment of choice for AMI. Primary PTCA has many theoretical advantages over fibrinolysis, including an increased number of eligible patients, a lower risk of intracranial bleeding, a significantly higher initial reperfusion rate, an earlier definition of coronary with rapid triage to surgical intervention, and risk stratification allowing safe, early hospital discharge. Potential disadvantages include operator expertise, local and regional availability, and time to application of the therapy.

Several trials of varying sizes comparing primary PTCA with fibrinolysis have been reported. Interventions in the early trials were performed using PTCA, prior to the current widespread use of coronary stents or GPI. Despite a clear and consistent benefit of PCI in restoring patency of the infarct-related artery, differences in mortality in the individual trials were difficult to evaluate because of the smaller sample sizes in the studies. The Primary Angioplasty in Myocardial Infarction (PAMI) trial[124] enrolled 395 patients who were randomly assigned to undergo primary PTCA or to receive t-PA. Compared with standard-dose t-PA, primary PTCA reduced the combined occurrence of nonfatal reinfarction or death, was associated with a lower rate of intracranial hemorrhage, and resulted in a similar left ventricular function. The results of the Netherlands trial indicate that primary angioplasty was associated with a higher rate of patency of the infarct-related artery, a less severe residual stenotic lesion, better left ventricular function, and less recurrent myocardial ischemia and infarction than in patients receiving streptokinase.[125]

In a substudy of the GUSTO IIb trial,[126] the authors randomly assigned 1138 patients with AMI to either primary PTCA or accelerated t-PA. The composite end point of the study included death, nonfatal reinfarction, and nonfatal disabling stroke, all occurring within 30 days of the AMI. Of the patients assigned to primary PTCA therapy, 83% were candidates for such treatment and underwent angioplasty 1.9 hours after emergency department arrival for a total elapsed time from chest pain onset to therapy of 3.8 hours. Ninety-eight percent of the patients assigned to fibrinolytic therapy received t-PA 1.2 hours after hospital arrival. The occurrence of the composite end point was encountered significantly less often in the PTCA group (9.6%) than in the t-PA group (13.7%) at 30 days. When the individual components of the composite end point at 30 days were considered separately, the incidence of death (5.7% versus 7%), infarction (4.5% versus 6.5%), and stroke (0.2% versus 0.9%) occurred at statistically similar rates for both treatment groups, PTCA and t-PA, respectively. A meta-analysis[127] reviewed 10 major studies comparing fibrinolysis with primary PTCA in more than 2600 patients. The 30-day mortality was found to be significantly lower in the PTCA group, 4.4% versus 6.5% in the patients treated with fibrinolytics. Primary PTCA was also associated with a significant reduction in total stroke and hemorrhagic strokes.

The most recent comprehensive investigation of the PCI strategy is the second Danish acute myocardial infarction (DANAMI-2) trial.[91] Conducted in Denmark on a large proportion of the population, investigators randomly assigned AMI patients to receive either PCI or accelerated treatment with alteplase (t-PA). Patients presented to hospitals without invasive capabilities (totaling 24) or to hospitals with angioplasty capability (totaling 5); patients received either fibrinolysis or angioplasty. Stents and GPI were available and used at the discretion of the treating physicians. For angioplasty-managed patients presenting to noninvasive centers, transfer to PCI-capable institutions had to occur within a 3-hour time period. Significant differences were observed in a composite end point of death, reinfarction, or disabling stroke at 30 days between the groups with rates of 8.5% in the PCI group versus 14.2% in the fibrinolytic group. Transfer for PCI occurred within 2 hours in 96% of patients. These additional studies agree with the findings of the DANAMI-2 trial[91] and support the contention that PCI, if performed within a specific time period after presentation, offers a more effective management strategy to the AMI patient.[124-127]

The longer term results with primary PTCA, however, are less clear. The GUSTO IIb study[126] showed no overall mortality advantage of primary PTCA at 6 months; conversely, 2-year follow-up from the PAMI trial[124] found a significant reduction in hospital readmission, recurrent ischemia, target vessel revascularization, and reinfarction, with a trend toward a reduction in mortality in the PTCA group compared with treatment with fibrinolysis. Much of the literature comparing the acute reperfusion therapies in AMI does not include the use of coronary stenting during PTCA. The introduction of intracoronary stenting is likely to alter favorably the outcomes of AMI patients, making PTCA with stent placement a superior method of management.

Rescue Angioplasty

Current information suggests that rescue angioplasty may be advantageous in patients whose infarct-related arteries fail to reperfuse after fibrinolytic therapy.[128] Some centers routinely catheterize patients after fibrinolytic therapy to determine whether successful reperfusion has occurred and to perform angioplasty if necessary and anatomically feasible. Other centers catheterize patients after fibrinolytic therapy only if there is clinical evidence that the infarct-related artery has failed to open, such as continued chest pain or persistent ST segment elevation.

Choice of Reperfusion Therapy Method

It is widely accepted that the early restoration of perfusion in the AMI patient limits myocardial damage, preserves left ventricular function, and reduces mortality; such restoration may be accomplished by administration of a fibrinolytic agent, performance of PCI or, in the rare case, emergent coronary artery bypass grafting. Rapid application of reperfusion therapy is important in the patient with ST segment elevation AMI. Many factors must be considered by clinicians regarding the early reperfusion treatment decisions when managing the AMI patient. Although PCI may offer an improved outcome over fibrinolysis, catheter-based techniques must be applied early without prolonged delay.

Should catheterization laboratory activation delay be anticipated or actually occur, the treating physician must proceed with fibrinolysis, assuming that the patient is an appropriate candidate. Prior agreement between the emergency department and the cardiovascular physicians at institutions with angioplasty capability must be obtained so that PCI consideration does not introduce further delays in fibrinolytic drug administration; such cooperation has been shown to limit additional delays in the administration of fibrinolytic agents in patients who are considered for PCI in AMI. A cooperative effort between emergency medicine and cardiology as well as among the emergency department, the catheterization laboratory, and the CCU has the potential to reduce markedly the door-to-therapy time in AMI patients. A "STEMI alert" system, analogous to the trauma alert approach, mobilizes hospital-based resources, optimizing the approach to the AMI patient. This system, whether activated by data gathered in the emergency department or prehospital-based information, has the potential to offer time-sensitive therapies in a rapid fashion to these ill patients.

If applied without time delay in experienced hands, PCI provides improved outcome in the AMI patient. It must be stressed that although PCI is thought to be superior in the treatment of AMI, it must be initiated within 1.5 to 3 hours of arrival at the initial hospital emergency department.[13,94] As noted in the DANAMI-2 study,[94] PCI initiated within 3 hours of initial hospital arrival was superior to fibrinolysis. The latest ACC/AHA guidelines advocate PCI as an alternative to fibrinolytic therapy in patients with STEMI "who can undergo angioplasty of the infarct-related artery within 12 hours of onset of symptoms or greater than 12 hours if symptoms persist, if performed in a timely fashion by persons skilled in the procedure, and supported by experienced personnel in an appropriate laboratory environment." These guidelines further recommend primary PCI in candidates for reperfusion therapy for whom fibrinolytic therapy is contraindicated or who are within the first 18 hours of cardiogenic shock related to STEMI.[13] If the time required to mobilize staff and arrange for PCI is prolonged or delays in transfer are anticipated, fibrinolysis may be the preferred method. Anticipated delays beyond this time period are unacceptable if the patient was originally a fibrinolytic candidate. These various time periods are suggestions; individual patient- and system-related issues must be considered in the treatment decisions.

Several related issues must be considered by the clinician. The literature base to answer this question is somewhat heterogeneous in construction (e.g., different therapies, study sites, outcome measures), making absolute, all-encompassing recommendations impossible and thus providing fuel for further debate. The question of technical expertise should be considered. In the GUSTO-IIb trial,[126] the vast majority of physicians performed at least 75 procedures a year; these results may not generalize to smaller volume centers with less experienced operators (i.e., less than 50 cases per year). Another system issue regarding time to arrival in the catheterization laboratory must be considered. In certain centers, PCI may not be available, necessitating rapid transfer to another facility; alternatively, in centers with PCI capability, the catheterization laboratory may not be in operation at the time of the patient's arrival, particularly a consideration at night and during weekends.

Reperfusion Therapy in Cardiogenic Shock

Patients with AMI who present with cardiogenic shock, which occurs in up to 10% of cases, demand special consideration because of a mortality rate approaching 80%. Fibrinolysis is not effective in these ill AMI patients, probably because of a significantly lower coronary perfusion pressure; in the shock state, it is thought that the occlusive thrombus is not exposed to the fibrinolytic agent, resulting in clinical failure of the drug. In large fibrinolytic trials such as GISSI-1[122] and ISIS-2,[94] AMI patients presenting in cardiogenic shock did not benefit from fibrinolysis. Conversely, primary PTCA has been investigated in more than 600 patients in several small studies; a cumulative analysis of the data revealed a significantly lower mortality rate (45%) compared with placebo or historical controls.[129] The SHOCK trial[130] compared the outcomes of AMI patients presenting in cardiogenic shock; patients were randomly assigned to emergency revascularization (primary PTCA or emergent CABG) or initial medical stabilization, including fibrinolysis. The primary end point was mortality from all causes at 30 days; 6-month survival was the secondary end point. Overall mortality at 30 days did not differ significantly between the revascularization and medical therapy groups (46.7% versus 56%, respectively). Six-month mortality was lower in the revascularization group than in the medical therapy group. The authors concluded that in AMI patients with cardiogenic shock, emergency revas-

cularization did not significantly reduce overall mortality at 30 days. After 6 months, however, there was a significant survival benefit. The prespecified subgroup analysis of patients younger than 75 years showed an absolute reduction of 15.4% in 30-day mortality and 21.4% in 6-month mortality in the revascularization group. Thus, when catheterization facilities are not available, fibrinolytic therapy should be given to eligible patients, and urgent transfer to an interventional facility should be strongly considered.[130]

Combination Therapies in the Reperfusion-Treated Patient

Reperfusion with PCI has been improved with the use of glycoprotein IIb/IIIa inhibitors. The use of GPIs with intracoronary stenting in AMI has been studied in the ReoPro and Primary PTCA Organization and Randomized Trial (RAPPORT),[131] ADMIRAL,[132] and CADILLAC[133] trials. In the RAPPORT trial,[131] a significant reduction in the combined end point of death, MI, and urgent need for revascularization was noted at 30 days; no significant differences, however, were seen at 6 months. An increase in major bleeding episodes and a need for transfusions were encountered in the abciximab group, probably because of high-dose heparin therapy. The ADMIRAL trial[132] reported a significantly lower rate of occurrence of the combined end point of death, recurrent MI, and target vessel revascularization at 30 days in the treatment group. In addition, lower doses of heparin were given to patients in the abciximab group, and no increase in major bleeding was observed. The CADILLAC trial[133] randomly assigned primary PTCA patients with AMI to stenting and abciximab versus placebo. Results suggest that the abciximab-treated patients had a modest reduction in acute events. The use of glycoprotein inhibitors in the setting of AMI treated with primary angioplasty with or without intracoronary stenting appears to benefit the patient. The clinician should consider their use in the AMI patient bound for the catheterization laboratory.

For the clinician, perhaps the most interesting area of the combination therapy approach to the AMI patient involves the use of a fibrinolytic agent and glycoprotein inhibitor; unfortunately, the use of a GPI in this setting does not significantly alter outcome in these non-PCI patients. For example, the IMPACT-AMI study[102] examined patients with AMI and randomly assigned them to receive either eptifibatide or placebo. In addition, patients received aspirin, heparin, and t-PA. Thus, this study looked at the role of a GPI in conjunction with a fibrinolytic agent in AMI—a departure from studies of unstable angina with or without catheter-mediated revascularization. The highest dose of eptifibatide studied achieved higher 90-minute patency rates than placebo but similar rates of in-hospital death, stroke, reinfarction, vascular procedures, and new heart failure.

The ASSENT-3 study group has reported the superiority of a combined treatment regimen of either tenecteplase plus enoxaparin or reduced-dose tenecteplase plus abciximab over tenecteplase plus unfractionated heparin in terms of efficacy and safety at 30 days. Considering the excellent clinical outcomes, the ease of administration (bolus therapy for both agents), and lower comparative cost, the tenecteplase-enoxaparin regimen appears to be the most attractive fibrinolytic option at this time.[134]

The use of a reduced-dose fibrinolytic agent in the AMI patient who is a candidate for primary PTCA has also been explored. The Plasminogen-activator Angioplasty Compatibility Trial (PACT) trial[135] randomly assigned patients in the emergency department to either reduced-dose t-PA (50 mg) or placebo in preparation for primary angioplasty. Fibrinolytic-managed patients demonstrated higher rates of infarct vessel patency and TIMI grade 3 flow with similar rates of adverse effects, suggesting that reperfusion can be enhanced prior to immediate PTCA. This approach, called facilitated percutaneous coronary intervention, suggests that early reperfusion therapy before catheterization is not only safe but also effective.

A significant development in the use of PTCA in the treatment of AMI involves coronary stents. Early use of stenting in the AMI patient was considered problematic because of the real possibility of stent thrombosis. With the introduction of aggressive antiplatelet therapy using aspirin, GPI, and ticlopidine or clopidogrel, the rates of stent thrombosis have significantly decreased. Exploring early stent placement in the AMI patient, the PAMI stent trial[136] compared urgent treatment with PTCA with or without stenting in 900 patients. Stenting significantly reduced both stenosis and reocclusion at 6 months. No difference in death, reinfarction, or stroke at 6 months, however, was noted. Thus, it appears that in selected patients with AMI, primary stenting can be applied safely and effectively, resulting in a lower incidence of recurrent infarction and a significant reduction in the need for subsequent target vessel revascularization compared with balloon angioplasty.

TRANSFER OF A PATIENT WITH ACUTE CORONARY SYNDROME

Indications for transfer of a patient with ACS to a regional tertiary care facility with angioplasty and cardiovascular surgery capability include patients with fibrinolytic therapy contraindications who may benefit from PCI or CABG, persistent hemodynamic instability, persistent ventricular dysrhythmias, or postinfarction or postreperfusion ischemia. Hospital transfer for PCI is required in patients with fibrinolytic agent contraindications. The urgent transfer of a fibrinolytic-eligible AMI patient for PCI to another institution is not recommended until fibrinolytic therapy is initiated if a delay in PCI application is anticipated beyond that, as noted in the DANAMI-2 study.[91] If delays in PCI performance are anticipated and the patient is an acceptable candidate for fibrinolysis, the fibrinolytic agent should be started before or during transport to the receiving hospital. Many areas of the country, by virtue of geography and hospital coverage, do not have immediate access to a regional tertiary care facility, necessitating management at the local institution level. The availability of emergent transfer and weather conditions can further complicate the issue and affect individual management decisions.

Potential Pharmacologic Management Approach

The emergency physician has a broad range of medications at his or her disposal in the management of the ACS patient. A reasonable approach is outlined. This suggested approach is a guide to care only and in no way a reflection on all patients with chest pain suspected of having or diagnosed with ACS. Issues related to the individual patient, physician, and institution must be considered in the real-time application of these medications. Particular consideration must be given to patients' allergies, comorbid states, and current clinical presentation—in fact, numerous factors may provide a contraindication to one or more of the modalities.

The patient with stable chest pain who presents with a normal to minimally abnormal ECG and negative serum marker is best initially managed with NTG sublingually or topically in combination with aspirin. Resolution of the discomfort with continued stability probably does not warrant further emergency department pharmacologic management. Continued or recurrent pain in the emergency department may be treated with parenteral morphine sulfate and β-adrenergic blockade; continued pain may ultimately require intravenous NTG and heparinization with unfractionated or LMW heparin. The patient with "stable" unstable angina (i.e., new-onset or altered pattern but now symptom free and lacking abnormal serum markers and ECG) does not require heparin therapy in most cases.

The ACS patient with an abnormal ECG, particularly ST segment and T wave abnormalities, or elevated serum marker may warrant numerous therapies, including ASA, heparin and β-adrenergic blockade; NTG may be administered by the topical or intravenous route. The patient with recurrent angina may also benefit from such an approach. Heparin therapy is generally indicated in this instance.

The AMI patient without ST segment elevation requires aspirin, NTG, and heparin; morphine sulfate and β-adrenergic blockade may also be applied. Depending on hospital protocols, clopidogrel is given in the emergency department or in the coronary care area. The patient with ST segment elevation AMI is treated with the preceding medications as well as considered for urgent revascularization, achieved by either fibrinolytic agents, PCI, or, in the rare case, coronary bypass grafting. Patients who are to undergo acute PCI should receive GPI therapy, either in the emergency department or in the catheterization laboratory, depending on the local protocol.

1. Hunink MGM, et al: The recent decline in mortality from coronary heart disease, 1980-1990. The effect of secular trends in risk factors and treatment. *JAMA* 227:535, 1997.

2. Rosamond WD, et al: Trends in the incidence of myocardial infarction and in mortality due to coronary heart disease, 1987 to 1994. *N Engl J Med* 339:861, 1998.

3. McCaig LF, Burt CW: National Hospital Ambulatory Medical Care Survey: 2001 Emergency Department Summary. Advance Data from Vital and Health Statistics, Publication No. 335. Hyattsville, Md, National Center for Health Statistics, 2003.

4. Diop D, Aghababian RV: Definition, classification, and pathophysiology of acute coronary ischemic syndromes. *Emerg Med Clin North Am* 19:259, 2001.

5. Pope JH, Selker HP: Diagnosis of acute cardiac ischemia. *Emerg Med Clinic North Am* 21:27, 2003.

6. Ryan TJ, Melduni RM: Highlights of latest American College of Cardiology and American Heart Association guidelines for management of patients with acute myocardial infarction. *Cardiol Rev* 10:35, 2002.

7. Spertus JA, et al: Challenges and opportunities in quantifying the quality of care for acute myocardial infarction. *J Am Coll Cardiol* 41:1653, 2003.

8. Weinstein MD, Stason WB: Cost-effectiveness of interventions to prevent or treat coronary heart disease. *Annu Rev Public Health* 6:41, 1985.

9. The Joint European Society of Cardiology/American College of Cardiology Committee: Myocardial infarction redefined—A consensus document of the joint European Society of Cardiology/American College of Cardiology Committee for the redefinition of myocardial infarction. *J Am Coll Cardiol* 36:959, 2000.

10. Badimon L, et al: Pathogenesis of the acute coronary syndromes and therapeutic implications. *Pathophysiol Haemost Thromb* 32:225, 2002.

11. Theroux P, Fuster V: Acute coronary syndromes: Unstable angina and non-Q-wave myocardial infarction. *Circulation* 97:1195, 1998.

12. Hargarten KM, et al: Limitations of prehospital predictors of acute myocardial infarction and unstable angina. *Ann Emerg Med* 16:1325, 1987.

13. Ryan TJ, et al: 1999 update: ACC/AHA Guidelines for the Management of Patients with a Myocardial Infarction. *Circulation* 100:1016, 1999.

14. Aufderheide TP, et al: Acute coronary syndromes. *Ann Emerg Med* 37:S163, 2001.

15. Khot UN, et al: Prevalence of conventional risk factors in patients with coronary heart disease. *JAMA* 290:898, 2003.

16. Jayes RL, et al: Do patients' coronary risk factor reports predict acute cardiac ischemia in the emergency department? A multicenter study. *J Clin Epidemiol* 45:621, 1992.

17. Lee TH, et al: Acute chest pain in the emergency room. Identification and examination of low-risk patients. *Ann Intern Med* 145:65, 1985.

18. Tierney WM, et al: Physicians' estimates of the probability of myocardial infarction in emergency room patients with chest pain. *Med Decis Making* 6:12, 1986.

19. Canto JG, et al: Prevalence, clinical characteristics, and mortality among patients with myocardial infarction without chest pain. *JAMA* 283:3223, 2000.

20. Canto JG, et al: Atypical presentations among Medicare beneficiaries with unstable angina pectoris. *Am J Cardiol* 90:248, 2002.

21. Lusiani L, et al: Prevalence, clinical features, and acute course of atypical myocardial infarction. *Angiology* 45:49, 1994.

22. Grossman SA, et al: Predictors of delay in presentation to the ED in patients with suspected acute coronary syndromes. *Am J Emerg Med* 21:425, 2003.

23. Bayer AJ, et al: Changing presentation of myocardial infarction with increasing age. *J Am Geriatr Soc* 34:263, 1986.

24. Maynard C, et al: Gender differences in the treatment and outcome of acute myocardial infarction: Results from the Myocardial Infarction Triage and Intervention Registry. *Arch Intern Med* 152:972, 1992.

25. Jacoby RM, Nesto RW: Acute myocardial infarction in the diabetic patient: Pathophysiology, clinical course, and prognosis. *J Am Coll Cardiol* 20:736, 1992.

26. Zheng ZJ, et al: Sudden cardiac death in the United States, 1989-1998. *Circulation* 104:2158, 2001.

27. Shlipak MG, et al: The incidence of unrecognized myocardial infarction in women with coronary heart disease. *Ann Intern Med* 134:1043, 2001.

28. McSweeney JC, et al: Women's early warning symptoms of acute myocardial infarction. *Circulation* 108:2619, 2003.

29. Venkat A, et al: The impact of race on the acute management of chest pain. *Acad Emerg Med* 10:1199, 2002.

30. Uretski B, et al: Symptomatic myocardial infarction without chest pain: Prevalence and clinical course. *Am J Cardiol* 40:498, 1977.

31. Pope JH, et al: Missed diagnosis of acute cardiac ischemia in the emergency department. *N Engl J Med* 342:1163, 2000.

32. Lee TH, et al: Clinical characteristics and natural history of patients with acute myocardial infarction sent home from the emergency room. *Am J Cardiol* 60:219, 1987.

33. McCarthy BD, et al: Missed diagnoses of acute myocardial infarction in the emergency department: Results from a multicenter study. *Ann Emerg Med* 22:579, 1993.

34. Brady WJ, Perron A: Acute cardiovascular complications in ED patients with AMI. *Ann Emerg Med* 36:S33, 2000.

35. Brady WJ, et al: The efficacy of atropine in the treatment of hemodynamically unstable bradycardia and atrioventricular block: Prehospital and emergency department considerations. *Resuscitation* 41:47:1999.

36. Swart G, et al: Acute myocardial infarction complicated by hemodynamically unstable bradyarrhythmia: Prehospital and emergency department treatment with atropine. *Am J Emerg Med* 17:647, 1999.

37. Mooe T, et al: Ischemic stroke after acute myocardial infarction. A population-based study. *Stroke* 28:672, 1997.

38. Tiefenbrunn AJ, et al: Clinical experience with primary percutaneous transluminal coronary angioplasty compared with alteplase (recombinant tissue-type plasminogen activator) in patients with acute myocardial infarction: A report from the Second National Registry of Myocardial Infarction (NRMI-2). *J Am Coll Cardiol* 31:1240, 1998.

39. Singer AJ, et al: Effect of duration from symptom onset on the negative predictive value of a normal ECG for exclusion of acute myocardial infarction. *Ann Emerg Med* 29:575, 1997.

40. Smith SW: Upwardly concave ST segment morphology is common in acute left anterior descending coronary artery occlusion. *Acad Emerg Med* 10:516, 2003.

41. Wang K, et al: ST-segment elevation in conditions other than acute myocardial infarction. *N Engl J Med* 349:2128, 2003.

42. Otto LA, Aufderheide TP: Evaluation of ST segment elevation criteria for the prehospital electrocardiographic diagnosis of acute myocardial infarction. *Ann Emerg Med* 23:17, 1994.

43. Brady WJ, et al: Reciprocal ST segment depression: Impact on the electrocardiographic diagnosis of ST segment elevation acute myocardial infarction. *Am J Emerg Med* 20:35, 2002.

44. Doevendans PA, et al: Electrocardiographic diagnosis of reperfusion during fibrinolytic therapy in acute myocardial infarction. *Am J Cardiol* 75:1206, 1995.

45. Wehrens XH, et al: A comparison of electrocardiographic changes during reperfusion of acute myocardial infarction by thrombolysis or percutaneous transluminal coronary angioplasty. *Am Heart J* 139:430, 2000.

46. Matetzky S, et al: Significance of ST segment elevations in posterior chest leads (V7 to V9) in patients with acute inferior myocardial infarction: Application for fibrinolytic therapy. *J Am Coll Cardiol* 31:506, 1998.

47. Saw J, et al: Value of ST elevation in lead III greater than lead II in inferior wall acute myocardial infarction for predicting in-hospital mortality and diagnosing right ventricular infarction. *Am J Cardiol* 87:448, 2001.

48. Zehmer U, et al: Effects of fibrinolytic therapy in acute myocardial infarction with or without right ventricular involvement. *J Am Coll Cardiol* 2:876, 1998.

49. Brady WJ, et al: Electrocardiographic ST segment elevation in emergency department chest pain center patients: Etiology responsible for the ST segment abnormality. *Am J Emerg Med* 19:25, 2001.

50. Sharkey SW, et al: Impact of the electrocardiogram on the delivery of fibrinolytic therapy for acute myocardial infarction. *Am J Cardiol* 73:550, 1994.

51. Brady WJ, et al: Electrocardiographic ST-segment elevation: Correct identification of acute myocardial infarction (AMI) and non-AMI syndromes by emergency physicians. *Acad Emerg Med* 8:349, 2001.

52. Smith S, Nolan M: Ratio of T amplitude to QRS amplitude best distinguishes acute anterior MI from anterior left ventricular aneurysm. *Acad Emerg Med* 10:516, 2003.

53. Sgarbossa EB, et al: Electrocardiographic diagnosis of evolving acute myocardial infarction in the presence of left bundle-branch block. *N Engl J Med* 334:481, 1996.

54. Edhouse JA, et al: Suspected myocardial infarction and left bundle branch block: Electrocardiographic indicators of acute ischemia. *J Accid Emerg Med* 16:331, 1999.

55. Sgarbossa EB, et al: Early electrocardiographic diagnosis of acute myocardial infarction in the presence of ventricular paced rhythm. *Am J Cardiol* 77:423, 1996.

56. Brady WJ, et al: A comparison of the 12-lead ECG to the 15-lead ECG in emergency department chest pain patients: Impact on diagnosis, therapy, and disposition. *Am J Emerg Med* 18:239, 2000.

57. Zalenski RJ, et al: Assessing the diagnostic value of an ECG containing leads V4R, V8, and V9: The 15-lead ECG. *Ann Emerg Med* 22:786, 1993.

58. Fesmire FM, et al: Usefulness of automated serial 12-lead ECG monitoring during the initial emergency department evaluation of patients with chest pain. *Ann Emerg Med* 31:3, 1998.

59. Jernberg T, et al: ST-segment monitoring with continuous 12-lead ECG improves early risk stratification in patients with chest pain and ECG nondiagnostic of acute myocardial infarction. *J Am Coll Cardiol* 34:1413, 1999.

60. Ornato J: Electrocardiographic body surface mapping. In Chan TC, et al (eds): The ECG in Emergency Medicine and Acute Care. Philadelphia, Elsevier, 2004.

61. Ornato JP, et al: 80-lead body map detects acute ST-elevation myocardial infarction missed by standard 12-lead electrocardiography. *J Am Coll Cardiol* 39:L332A, 2002.

62. Menown IB, et al: Optimizing the initial 12-lead electrocardiographic diagnosis of acute myocardial infarction. *Eur Heart J* 21:275, 2000.

63. Balk EM, et al: Accuracy of biomarkers to diagnose acute cardiac ischemia in the emergency department. *Ann Emerg Med* 37:478, 2001.

64. Hamm CW, et al: Emergency room triage of patients with acute chest pain by means of rapid testing for cardiac troponin T or troponin I. *N Engl J Med* 337:1648, 1997.

65. Malasky BR, Alpert JS: Diagnosis of myocardial injury by biochemical markers: Problems and promises. *Cardiol Rev* 10:307, 2002.

66. Antman EM, et al: Cardiac-specific troponin I levels to predict the risk of mortality in patients with acute coronary syndromes. *N Engl J Med* 335:134, 1996.

67. Ohman EM, et al: Cardiac troponin T levels for risk stratification in acute myocardial ischemia. *N Engl J Med* 335:1333, 1996.

68. Apple FS, Wu AHB: Myocardial infarction redefined: Role of cardiac troponin testing. *Clin Chem* 47:377, 2001.

69. Morrow DA, et al: Ability of minor elevations of troponins I and T to predict benefit from an early invasive strategy in patients with unstable angina and non-ST elevation myocardial infarction: Results from a randomized trial. *JAMA* 286:3405, 2001.

70. Quinn MJ, Moliterno DJ: Troponins in acute coronary syndromes: More TACTICS for an early invasive strategy. *JAMA* 286:2461, 2001.

71. Ottani F, et al: Elevated cardiac troponin levels predict the risk of adverse outcome in patients with acute coronary syndromes. *Am Heart J* 140:917, 2000.

72. Freda BJ, et al: Cardiac troponins in renal insufficiency. *J Am Coll Cardiol* 40:2065, 2002.

73. Puleo PR, et al: Early diagnosis of acute myocardial infarction based on assay for subforms of creatine kinase-MB. *Circulation* 82:759, 1990.

74. Brennan ML, et al: Prognostic value of myeloperoxidase in patients with chest pain. *N Engl J Med* 349:1595, 2003.

75. Omland T, et al: Prognostic value of N-terminal pro-atrial and pro-brain natriuretic peptide in patients with acute coronary syndromes. *Am J Cardiol* 89:463, 2002.

76. Morrow DA, Braunwald E: Future of biomarkers in acute coronary syndromes: Moving toward a multimarker strategy. *Circulation* 108:250, 2002.

77. McCord J, et al: Ninety-minute exclusion of acute myocardial infarction by use of quantitative point-of-care testing of myoglobin and troponin I. *Circulation* 104:1483, 2001.

78. Ng SM, et al: Ninety-minute accelerated critical pathway for chest pain evaluation. *Am J Cardiol* 88:403, 2001.

79. Cheitlin MD, et al: ACC/AHA/ASE 2003 guideline update for the clinical application of echocardiography: A report of the American College of Cardiology/American Heart Association Task Force on Practice Guidelines (ACC/AHA//ASE Committee to Update the 1997 Guidelines for the Clinical Application of Echocardiography), 2003. Available at: http://www.americanheart.org.

80. Trippi JA, et al: Dobutamine stress tele-echocardiography for evaluation of emergency department patients with chest pain. *J Am Coll Cardiol* 30:627, 1997.

81. Hilton TC, et al: Technetium-99m sestamibi myocardial perfusion imaging in the emergency room evaluation of chest pain. *J Am Coll Cardiol* 23:1016, 1994.

82. Kontos MC, et al: Value of acute rest sestamibi perfusion imaging for evaluation of patients admitted to the emergency department with chest pain. *J Am Coll Cardiol* 30:976, 1997.

83. Udelson JE, Beshansky JR, Ballin DS: Myocardial perfusion imaging for evaluation and triage of patients with suspected acute cardiac ischemia. A randomized controlled trial.. *JAMA* 288:2693, 2002.

84. Gibler WB, et al: A rapid diagnostic and treatment center for patients with chest pain in the emergency department. *Ann Emerg Med* 25:1, 1995.

85. Mikhail MG, et al: Cost-effectiveness of mandatory stress testing in chest pain center patients. *Ann Emerg Med* 29:88, 1997.

86. Gibbons RJ, et al: ACC/AHA 2002 guideline update for exercise testing: A report of the American College of Cardiology/American Heart Association Task Force on

Practice Guidelines (Committee on Exercise Testing), 2002. Available at www.acc.org/clinical/guidelines/exercise/dirIndex.htm

87. Amsterdam EA, et al: Immediate exercise testing to evaluate low-risk patients presenting to the emergency department with chest pain. *J Am Coll Cardiol* 40:251, 2002.

88. Farkouh ME, et al: A clinical trial of a chest-pain observation unit for patients with unstable angina. Chest Pain Evaluation in the Emergency Room (CHEER) Investigators. *N Engl J Med* 339:1882, 1998.

89. The GUSTO Angiographic Investigators: The effects of tissue plasminogen activator, streptokinase, or both on coronary-artery patency, ventricular function, and survival after acute myocardial infarction. *N Engl J Med* 329:1615, 1993.

90. Weaver WD, et al: Prehospital-initiated vs hospital-initiated thrombolytic therapy: The Myocardial Infarction Triage and Intervention Trial. *JAMA* 270:1211, 1993.

91. Andersen HR, et al: A comparison of coronary angioplasty with fibrinolytic therapy in acute myocardial infarction. *N Engl J Med* 349:733, 2003.

92. Yusuf S, et al: Effect of intravenous nitrates on mortality in acute myocardial infarction: An overview of the randomized trials. *Lancet* 1:1088, 1988.

93. Chen J, et al: Do "America's best hospitals" perform better for acute myocardial infarction? *N Engl J Med* 340:286, 1999.

94. Randomised trial of intravenous streptokinase, oral aspirin, both, or neither among 17,187 cases of suspected acute myocardial infarction: ISIS-2. ISIS-2 (Second International Study of Infarct Survival) Collaborative Group. *Lancet* 2:349, 1988.

95. Use of a monoclonal antibody directed against the platelet glycoprotein IIb/IIIa receptor in high-risk coronary angioplasty. The EPIC Investigation. *N Engl J Med* 330:956, 1994.

96. Platelet glycoprotein IIb/IIIa receptor blockade and low-dose heparin during percutaneous coronary revascularization. The EPILOG Investigators. *N Engl J Med* 336:1689, 1997.

97. Lambert F, et al: Abciximab in the treatment of acute myocardial infarction eligible for primary percutaneous transluminal coronary angioplasty. *J Am Coll Cardiol* 33:1528, 1999.

98. Randomised placebo-controlled trial of effect of eptifibatide on complications of percutaneous coronary intervention: IMPACT II. Integrilin to Minimize Platelet Aggregation and Coronary Thrombosis-II. *Lancet* 349:1422, 1997.

99. Boersman E, et al: Platelet glycoprotein IIb/IIIa inhibitors in acute coronary syndromes: A meta-analysis of all major randomised clinical trials. *Lancet* 359:189, 2002.

100. Simoons ML, GUSTO IV-ACS Investigators: Effect of glycoprotein IIb/IIIa receptor blocker abciximab on outcome in patients with acute coronary syndromes without early coronary revascularisation: The GUSTO IV-ACS randomised trial. *Lancet* 357:1915, 2001.

101. Zhao XQ, Theroux P, Snapinn SM, Sax FL: Intracoronary thrombus and platelet glycoprotein IIb/IIIa receptor blockade with tirofiban in unstable angina or non-Q-wave myocardial infarction. Angiographic results from the PRISM-PLUS trial (Platelet receptor inhibition for ischemic syndrome management in patients limited by unstable signs and symptoms). PRISM-PLUS Investigators. *Circulation* 100:1609, 1999.

102. Ohman EM, et al: Combined accelerated tissue-plasminogen activator and platelet glycoprotein IIb/IIIa integrin receptor blockade with Integrilin in acute myocardial infarction. Results of a randomized, placebo-controlled, dose-ranging trial. IMPACT-AMI Investigators. *Circulation* 95:846, 1997.

103. Roe MT, et al: A randomized, placebo-controlled trial of early eptifibatide for non-ST-segment elevation acute coronary syndromes. *Am Heart J* 146:993, 2003.

104. Braunwald E, et al: ACC/AHA guideline update for the management of patients with unstable angina and non-ST-segment elevation myocardial infarction—2002: Summary article: A report of the American College of Cardiology/American Heart Association Task Force on Practice Guidelines (Committee on the Management of Patients With Unstable Angina). *Circulation* 106:1893, 2002.

105. The Clopidogrel in Unstable Angina to Prevent Recurrent Events Trial Investigators: Effects of clopidogrel in addition to aspirin in patients with acute coronary syndromes without ST-segment elevation. *N Engl J Med* 345:494, 2001 [errata, *N Engl J Med* 345:1506, 1716, 2001].

106. Low-molecular-weight heparin during instability in coronary artery disease, Fragmin during Instability in Coronary Artery Disease (FRISC) study group. *Lancet* 347:561, 1996.

107. Cohen M, et al: A comparison of low-molecular-weight heparin with unfractionated heparin for unstable coronary artery disease. Efficacy and Safety of Subcutaneous Enoxaparin in Non-Q-Wave Coronary Events Study Group. *N Engl J Med* 337:447, 1997.

108. Klein W, et al: Comparison of low-molecular-weight heparin with unfractionated heparin acutely and with placebo for 6 weeks in the management of unstable coronary artery disease. Fragmin in unstable coronary artery disease study (FRIC). *Circulation* 96:61, 1997.

109. Brewster GS, Herbert ME: Medical myth: Heparin should be administered to every patient admitted to the hospital with possible unstable angina. *West J Med* 173:138, 2000.

110. Effects of recombinant hirudin (lepirudin) compared with heparin on death, myocardial infarction, refractory angina, and revascularisation procedures in patients with acute myocardial ischaemia without ST elevation: A randomised trial. Organisation to Assess Strategies for Ischemic Syndromes (OASIS-2) Investigators. *Lancet* 353:429, 1999.

111. Neuhaus KL, et al: Recombinant hirudin (lepirudin) for the improvement of thrombolysis with streptokinase in patients with acute myocardial infarction: Results of the HIT-4 trial. *J Am Coll Cardiol* 32:876, 1998.

112. White HD, et al: Randomized, double-blind comparison of hirulog versus heparin in patients receiving streptokinase and aspirin for acute myocardial infarction (HERO). Hirulog Early Reperfusion/Occlusion (HERO) Trial Investigators. *Circulation* 96:2155, 1997.

113. White H, Hirulog and Early Reperfusion or Occlusion (HERO)-2 Trial Investigators: Thrombin-specific anticoagulation with bivalirudin versus heparin in patients receiving fibrinolytic therapy for acute myocardial infarction: The HERO-2 randomised trial. *Lancet* 358:1855, 2001.

114. GISSI-2: A factorial randomised trial of alteplase versus streptokinase and heparin versus no heparin among 12,490 patients with acute myocardial infarction. Gruppo Italiano per lo Studio della Sopravvivenza nell'Infarto Miocardico. *Lancet* 336:65, 1990.

115. In-hospital mortality and clinical course of 20,891 patients with suspected acute myocardial infarction randomized between alteplase and streptokinase with or without heparin. The International Study Group. *Lancet* 336:71, 1990.

116. ISIS-3: A randomised comparison of streptokinase vs tissue plasminogen activator vs anistreplase and or aspirin plus heparin vs aspirin alone among 41,299 cases of suspected acute myocardial infarction. ISIS-3 (Third International Study of Infarct Survival) Collaborative Group. *Lancet* 339:753, 1992.

117. A comparison of reteplase with alteplase for acute myocardial infarction. The Global Use of Strategies to

Open Occluded Coronary Arteries (GUSTO III) Investigators. *N Engl J Med* 337:1118, 1997.

118. Single-bolus tenecteplase compared with front-loaded alteplase in acute myocardial infarction: The ASSENT-2 double-blind randomised trial. Assessment of the Safety and Efficacy of a New Thrombolytic Investigators. *Lancet* 354:716, 1999.

119. The TIMI-IIIB Investigators: Effects of tissue plasminogen activator and a comparison of early invasive and conservative strategies in unstable angina and non-Q-wave myocardial infarction: Results of the TIMI-IIIB trial. *Circulation* 89:1545, 1994.

120. Indications for fibrinolytic therapy in suspected acute myocardial infarction: Collaborative overview of early mortality and major morbidity results form all randomised trials of more than 1000 patients. Fibrinolytic Therapy Trialists' (FTT) Collaborative Group. *Lancet* 343:311, 1994.

121. Late Assessment of Thrombolytic Efficacy (LATE) study with alteplase 6-24 hours after onset of acute myocardial infarction. *Lancet* 342:759, 1993.

122. Gruppo Italiano per lo Studio della Streptochinasi nel-l'Infarto Miocardico (GISSI): Effectiveness of intravenous thrombolytic treatment in acute myocardial infarction. *Lancet* 1:397, 1986.

123. Wilcox RG, et al: Trial of tissue plasminogen activator for mortality reduction in acute myocardial infarction. Anglo-Scandinavian Study of Early Thrombolysis (ASSET). *Lancet* 2:525, 1988.

124. Grines CL, et al: A comparison of immediate angioplasty with thrombolytic therapy for acute myocardial infarction. The Primary Angioplasty in Myocardial Infarction Study Group. *N Engl J Med* 328:673, 1993.

125. Zijlstra F, et al: A comparison of immediate coronary angioplasty with intravenous streptokinase in acute myocardial infarction. *N Engl J Med* 328:680, 1993.

126. A clinical trial comparing primary coronary angioplasty with tissue plasminogen activator for acute myocardial infarction. The Global Use of Strategies to Open Occluded Coronary Arteries in Acute Coronary Syndromes (GUSTO IIb) Angioplasty Substudy Investigators. *N Engl J Med* 336:1621, 1997.

127. Weaver WD, et al: Comparison of primary coronary angioplasty and intravenous thrombolytic therapy for acute myocardial infarction: A quantitative review. *JAMA* 278:2093, 1997.

128. Califf RM, et al: Evaluation of combination thrombolytic therapy and timing of cardiac catheterization in acute myocardial infarction: Results of thrombolysis and angioplasty in myocardial infarction phase 5 randomized trial. *Circulation* 83:1543, 1991.

129. Goldberg RJ, et al: Cardiogenic shock after acute myocardial infarction: Incidence and mortality from a community-wide perspective, 1975 to 1988. *N Engl J Med* 325:1117, 1991.

130. Hochman JS, et al: Early revascularization in acute myocardial infarction complicated by cardiogenic shock. *N Engl J Med* 341:625, 1999.

131. Brener SJ, et al: Randomized, placebo-controlled trial of platelet glycoprotein IIb/IIIa blockade with primary angioplasty for acute myocardial infarction. ReoPro and Primary PTCA Organization and Randomized Trial (RAPPORT) Investigators. *Circulation* 98:734, 1998.

132. Montalescot G, et al: Abciximab associated with primary angioplasty and stenting in acute myocardial infarction: The ADMIRAL study, 30 day final results. *Circulation* 100:I87, 1999.

133. CADILLAC TRIAL

134. Assessment of the Safety and Efficacy of a New Thrombolytic Regimen (ASSENT)-3 Investigators: Efficacy and safety of tenecteplase in combination with enoxaparin, abciximab, or unfractionated heparin: The ASSENT-3 randomised trial in acute myocardial infarction. *Lancet* 358:605, 2001.

135. Ross AM, et al: A randomized trial comparing primary angioplasty with a strategy of short-acting thrombolysis and immediate planned rescue angioplasty in acute myocardial infarction: The PACT trial. *J Am Coll Cardiol* 34:1954, 1999.

136. Suryapranata H, et al: Randomized comparison of coronary stenting with balloon angioplasty in selected patients with acute myocardial infarction. *Circulation* 97:2502, 1998.

CHAPTER

78 Dysrhythmias

Donald M. Yealy and Theodore R. Delbridge

Although controversy over nomenclature exists, the term *dysrhythmia* (as opposed to arrhythmia) denotes any abnormality in cardiac rhythm. This chapter reviews common and potentially lethal dysrhythmias, with the exception of cardiac arrest and the rhythms associated with specific toxidromes. To facilitate dysrhythmia recognition and treatment, an understanding of the physiology of normal and abnormal cardiac impulse formation and conduction is essential. Diagnostic tools include the history, the physical examination, and the surface electrocardiogram (ECG). Therapeutic options in the prehospital and emergency department treatment of each dysrhythmia are presented.

CARDIAC CELLULAR ELECTROPHYSIOLOGY

The function of individual cells in the conductive and contractile tissues of the heart depends on an intact resting membrane potential. Na^+, K^+, and Ca^{++} ions have a primary role in creating the membrane potential and regulating conduction and contraction. The membrane

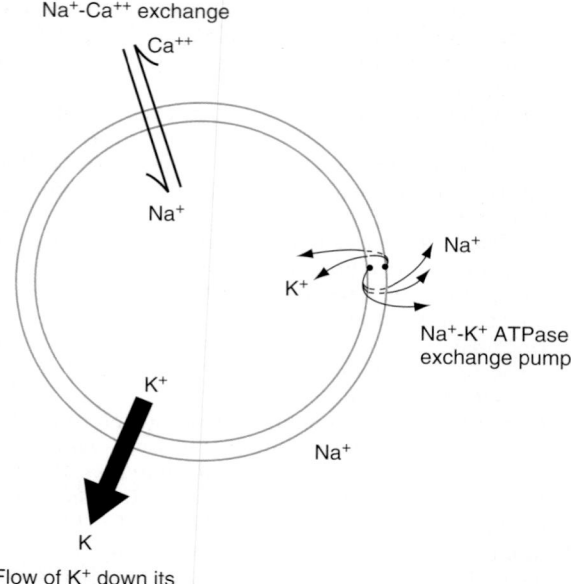

Figure 78-1. Flow of various ions across the myocardial cell membrane. Na^+-K^+ pump exchanges three Na^+ ions for each two K^+ ions, generating a net negative flow of 10 mV. The flow of K^+ down the concentration gradient *(dark arrow)* generates another 80 mV of current. The Na^+-Ca^{++} exchange adds little to the resting potential. ATPase, adenosine triphosphatase. (From Marriott HJL, Conover MB: *Advanced Concepts in Arrhythmias*, 2nd ed. St. Louis, Mosby, 1989.)

Na⁺-Ca⁺⁺ exchange
Ca⁺⁺
Na⁺
Na⁺
K⁺
Na⁺-K⁺ ATPase
exchange pump
K⁺
Na⁺
K

Flow of K^+ down its
concentration gradient

potential is the result of a differential concentration of Na^+ and K^+ on each side of the cell membrane; the potential measures approximately 90 mV in normal resting nonpacemaker cells, with a relative net negative charge in the intracellular area (Figure 78-1). This electrical gradient is created and maintained mainly by the sodium-potassium exchange pump and by the natural concentration-dependent flow of K^+ out of the cell. An Na^+-Ca^{++} exchange also exists, regulating the intracellular concentration of Ca^{++}. Although the latter exchange mechanism contributes little to the resting membrane potential, it does influence myofibril contractility.

The sodium-potassium pump depends on adenosine triphosphate (ATP) for energy to transport Na^+ out to the extracellular fluid. The energy generation process for this pump requires adenosine triphosphatase (ATPase) and Mg^{++}. During normal pump function, three Na^+ ions are transported out of the cell in exchange for two K^+ ions, generating a 10-mV potential across the membrane (see Figure 78-1). This process creates an osmotic gradient, allowing Ca^{++} to be exchanged for Na^+ without energy expenditure. Disturbances in intracellular and extracellular ion concentrations from ischemia, electrolyte and metabolic derangements, or drugs can alter the membrane potential and produce abnormalities of impulse generation, conduction, and myofibril contraction.

The remaining 90 mV of the resting membrane potential is generated from the flow of K^+ down a concentration gradient toward the extracellular fluid (see Figure 78-1). The cell membrane is far more permeable to

potassium ions than sodium ions, resulting in a greater loss of intracellular positive charge. Abnormalities in the K^+ gradient can interfere with normal impulse formation and conduction.

In normal nonpacemaker cells, the application of an electrical stimulus causes the membrane potential to become less negative, termed *depolarization*. When the membrane potential reaches −70 mV, specialized channels for Na^+ entry open, causing a rapid influx of positive charge into the cell. This "fast" channel activity further decreases the membrane potential and is augmented at approximately −30 to −40 mV by a second "slow" channel that allows Ca^{++} influx. When channels close, the resting potential is restored by the sodium-potassium pump and the K^+ concentration gradient, an event known as *repolarization*.

The electrical activity of a myocardial cell membrane can be traced with a microelectrode and is called the *action potential* (Figure 78-2). Phase 4 represents electrical diastole, with the normal cell membrane at a resting potential of −90 mV. Nonpacemaker cells maintain this potential until an electrical stimulus arrives. When a stimulus arrives, abrupt membrane depolarization occurs (phase 0). Phase 1 is a short period of membrane repolarization, caused by the closure of the fast Na^+ channels and transient K^+ efflux from the cell. Phase 2 is the plateau phase of the action potential, in which the slow Ca^{++} channels remain open, maintaining a near balance between ion influx and efflux. During this phase, an increase in the cytosol Ca^{++} concentration occurs as both the extracellular and intracellular (within the sarcoplasmic reticulum) stores are mobilized. This increase in intracellular Ca^{++} concentration facilitates mechanical coupling and myofibril contraction. Phase 3 represents the rapid membrane repolarization period as the slow channels close and K^+ flows down the concentration gradient. The ATP-driven pump exchanges Na^+ and K^+ until the phase 4 resting potential is reached.

In nonpacemaker cells, additional depolarization from a second electrical stimulus is not possible when the membrane potential is more positive than −60 mV (initially achieved during phase 0 and maintained until phase 3) irrespective of impulse strength. This period is termed the *effective refractory period* (Figure 78-3). At a membrane potential of −60 to −70 mV, a strong impulse can cause a response that is likely to be propagated, although abnormally; this response represents the *relative refractory period* (see Figure 78-3). At a membrane potential of −70 mV or less, virtually all fast channels are ready for activity if properly stimulated.

Pacemaker cells differ from non–impulse-generating cells in two ways: their resting membrane potential is less negative, and they can exhibit spontaneous depolarization during phase 4 (see Figure 78-2). Pacemaker cells are found within the sinoatrial (SA) and atrioventricular (AV) nodes as well as on the atrial surfaces of the AV valves and within the His-Purkinje system. The spontaneous depolarization is the result of slow Na^+ influx. When the membrane threshold is reached, further depolarization in pacemaker cells occurs largely from activation of the slow Ca^{++} channels. Non-

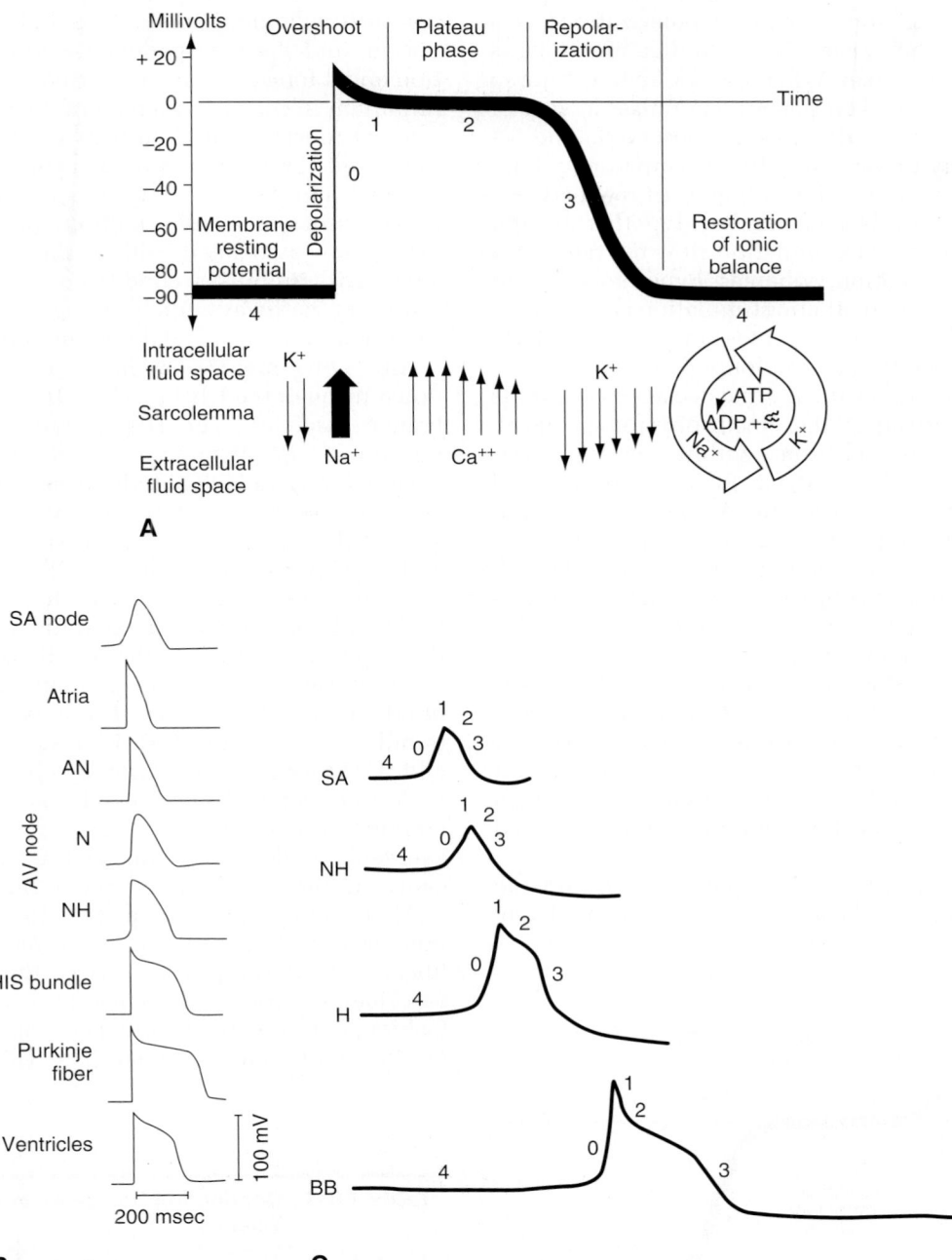

Figure 78-2. A, Action potential of a myocardial cell and its relation to ion flow. B, Action potentials of various myocardial tissues. C, Action potentials of various pacemaker cells. Note that phase 4 becomes flatter as location becomes more distal. AN, atria-nodal; AV, atrioventricular; BB, bundle branch fascicles; H, His bundle; NH nodal-His; SA, sinoatrial. (A and B, From Calcium in Cardiac Metabolism. Whippany, NJ, Knoll Pharmaceutical Co., 1980; C, from Conover M: Understanding Electrocardiography, 5th ed. St. Louis, Mosby, 1988.)

pacemaker cells may develop altered resting potentials and undergo spontaneous depolarization under pathologic conditions, especially during ischemia.

Afterdepolarizations are fluctuations in membrane potential that occur as the resting potential is approached; these fluctuations may precipitate another depolarization (Figure 78-4). Afterdepolarizations can occur just before full resting potential (early afterdepolarizations) or after full resting potential (delayed afterdepolarizations) is reached. Delayed afterdepolarizations are associated with ischemia, pump failure, catecholamine excess, and electrolyte disturbances (especially K^+, Mg^{++}, and Ca^{++}) and are enhanced by faster heart rates. Early afterdepolarizations are associated with high resting membrane potentials and are enhanced by slower heart rates.

ANATOMY AND CONDUCTION

The SA node is located at the junction of the right atrium and the superior vena cava. It is supplied by the right coronary artery (RCA) in 55% and the left circumflex artery (LCA) in 45% of subjects. The normal

SA node produces spontaneous depolarizations at a faster rate than other pacemakers and thus functions as the dominant pacemaker. When the SA node is injured or when other pacemakers generate impulses at a faster rate, nonsinus cardiac rhythms are observed. The SA node is normally under a slight parasympathetic dominance, which maintains the resting heart rate between 60 and 90 beats/min in most adults. Hypothermia and increased relative vagal stimulation slow the rate of SA node impulse formation, whereas hyperthermia and increased relative sympathetic stimulation can increase the rate. Other pacemaker sites may be similarly affected by temperature and autonomic tone.

Figure 78-5 correlates the normal surface ECG events with those occurring at the electrophysiologic level. The impulse generated from within the SA node, imperceptible on the surface ECG, is propagated through the atrial tissue to the AV node. The atrial depolarization wave is characterized by the P wave on the surface ECG. The AV node is supplied by a branch of the RCA in 90% of subjects (termed right-dominant circulation) and by the LCA in the remaining 10% of patients (left-dominant circulation). Transport of the impulse within the AV node is slower than other areas of the conducting system (Table 78-1) because of the dependence on slow-channel ion influx to depolarize the cell membranes. This delay limits the ventricular rate and allows complete atrial emptying, providing a greater ventricular diastolic volume and increased stroke volume.

The two functionally distinct pathways within the AV node are termed alpha and beta. The alpha pathway has relatively slow conduction and a short refractory period, and the beta pathway exhibits faster conduction and a longer refractory period. These paths can be important in sustaining a reentrant tachycardia. The PR interval (normally 0.10 to 0.20 second) represents the time needed for conduction of a sinus impulse through the atria and AV node. Impulses originating in the low atrial tissues, the AV junction, or other infranodal tissues are associated with a shortened PR interval, along with impulses conducted to the ventricles by accessory pathways. PR prolongation usually results from nodal or supranodal conduction system disease.

After entry into the AV node, the impulse is carried down through the His bundle to the three main bundle branch fascicles. The His bundle is the distalmost portion of the AV node and derives its blood supply from the RCA and left anterior descending (LAD) artery. The bundle branch fascicles beyond the His area supply the right (RBB), left anterior-superior (LASB), and left posterior-inferior (LPIB) ventricular myocardium. Before separating into the three fascicles, His bundle fibers assume a topographic distribution. Thus, the appearance of a specific bundle branch pattern on the ECG can be the result of injury within a specific bundle branch fascicle or a lesion within the main His bundle. The RBB and LASB are supplied by the LAD, and the LPIB can be supplied by either the RCA or the LCA. Occlusion of these vessels can cause a variety of conduction abnormalities; commonly, RCA occlusion causes AV node block, whereas LAD occlusion usually causes infranodal (bundle branch) block.

After conduction down the three main bundle branches, each impulse is delivered to the Purkinje fibers. The Purkinje fibers carry the impulse to the ventricular myocardial tissues in a rapid and orderly fashion, and the final result is contraction and ejection of the ventricular contents. The QRS complex (the

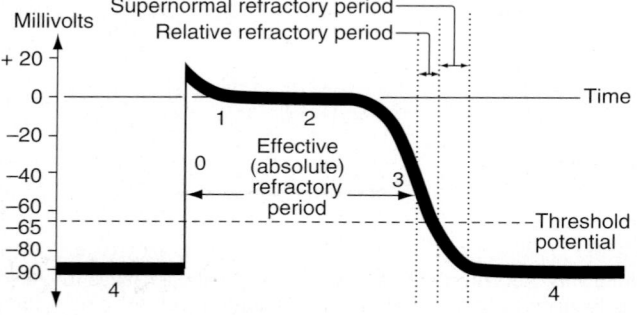

Figure 78-3. Action potential showing various refractory periods. (From *Calcium in Cardiac Metabolism*. Whippany, NJ, Knoll Pharmaceutical Co., 1980.)

Table 78-1. Conduction Velocities in Various Heart Tissues

Tissue	Velocity (m/sec)
Atrium	1000
Atrioventricular node	200
His-Purkinje system	4000
Ventricles	400

Figure 78-4. Early afterdepolarizations *(left)* compared with delayed afterdepolarizations *(right)*. (From Marriott HJL, Conover MB: *Advanced Concepts in Arrhythmias*, 2nd ed. St. Louis, Mosby, 1989.)

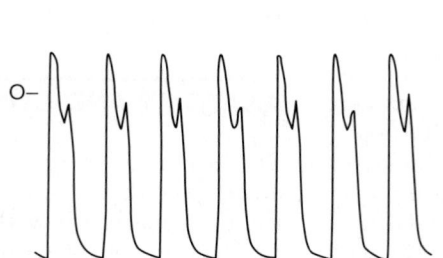

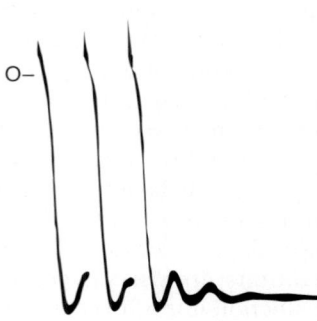

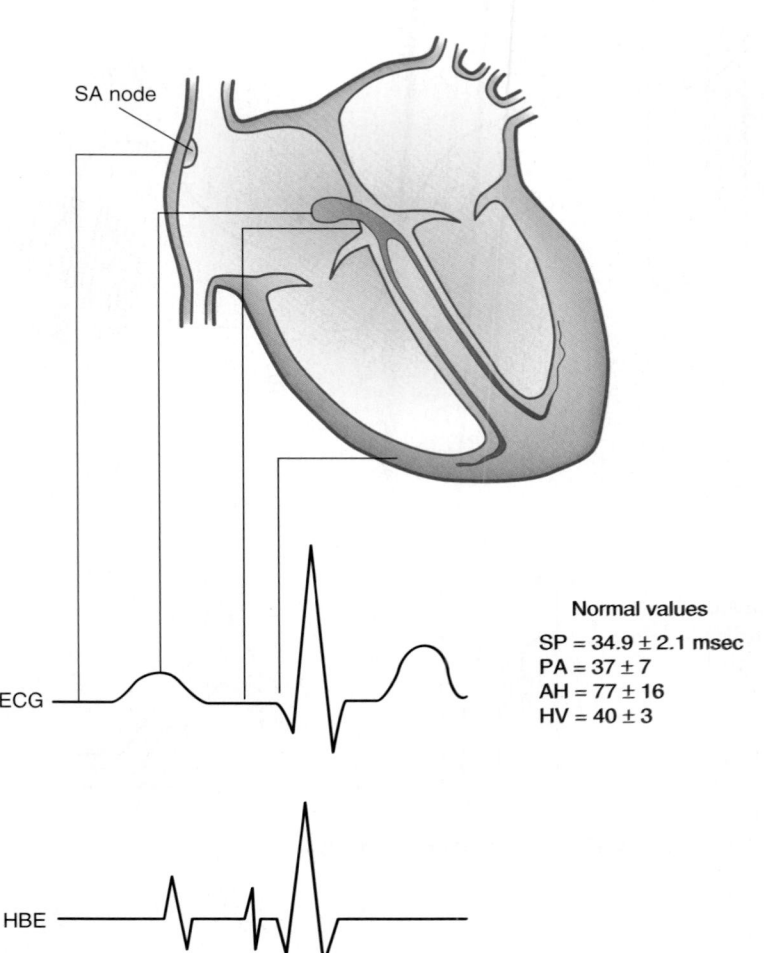

Figure 78-5. Electrical events in heart related to surface electrocardiogram (ECG) and His bundle electrogram (HBE). Approximate relationship of sinus node discharge is also related to surface ECG. AH, atrioventricular nodal conduction time; HV, His-Purkinje conduction; PA, intraatrial conduction time; SA, sinoatrial; SP, SA conduction time. (From Marriott HJL, Conover MB: *Advanced Concepts in Arrhythmias*, 2nd ed. St. Louis, Mosby, 1989.)

Normal values

SP = 34.9 ± 2.1 msec
PA = 37 ± 7
AH = 77 ± 16
HV = 40 ± 3

normal duration is less than 0.09 second) represents ventricular depolarization, and the T wave reflects repolarization. The total time of ventricular depolarization and repolarization is represented by the QT interval; the normal duration of the QT interval is debated and must be corrected for age, sex, and heart rate.

The time required for complete conduction system repolarization is a function of the preceding cardiac cycle length. Shorter cycle lengths, represented as shorter preceding RR intervals (i.e., faster heart rates), beget a shorter repolarization time. Conversely, longer cardiac cycles (slower heart rates) are associated with longer repolarization times. If an underlying slow sinus rhythm is present and an ectopic atrial impulse arrives between sinus impulses, the ectopic impulse may be conducted aberrantly (if bundles are relatively refractory), or they may be blocked (if the bundles are completely refractory). The preceding cycle is called the setup cycle because it dictates the refractory time of the infranodal conducting tissues.

The *Ashman phenomenon* refers to aberrant ventricular conduction of an atrial extrasystole after a long setup cycle, occurring in any irregular atrial dysrhythmia. Classically, the Ashman phenomenon is seen in atrial fibrillation, in which long-short cycle sequences are often seen as a result of the chaotic rhythm. In normal subjects the right bundle branch is the last part of the infranodal system to repolarize completely. Thus, aberrantly conducted impulses in the Ashman phenomenon usually assume a right bundle branch block appearance on the ECG.

Normally, the AV node is the preferred path for impulse delivery to the infranodal conducting system. In some patients, pathologic accessory pathways connecting atrial, infranodal conducting, and ventricular myocardial cells may exist. These accessory pathways do not share the normal conduction delay of the AV node and may allow a rapid ventricular response rate and subsequent reduced cardiac output when supplanting the normal conduction system. *Preexcitation* refers to the early depolarization of ventricular myocardium when accessory paths are employed instead of the normal conduction system.

The AV node may serve as a subsidiary pacemaker in the absence of normal SA node activity; this node has an intrinsic impulse formation rate of 45 to 60 beats/min. Infranodal pacemakers, found within His bundle, bundle branches, and the Purkinje system, usually function at a rate of 30 to 45 beats/min. These rates may vary widely based on the underlying pathologic process present. In addition, as a result of ischemia or drug effect, atrial and ventricular nonpacemaker myocardial cells may become pacemakers.

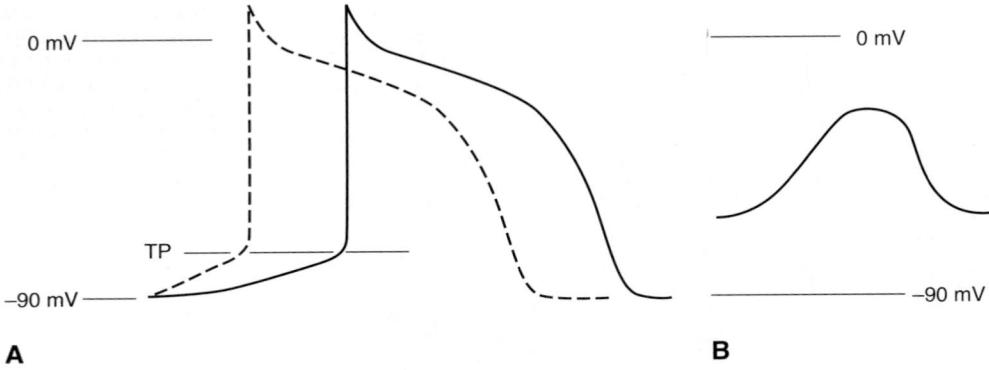

Figure 78-6. A, Enhanced normal automaticity *(dashed line)*. TP, threshold point. **B,** Abnormal automaticity. (From Marriott HJL, Conover MB: *Advanced Concepts in Arrhythmias*, 2nd ed. St. Louis, Mosby, 1989.)

MECHANISMS FOR DYSRHYTHMIA FORMATION

The three theories of dysrhythmia formation are based on the electrophysiologic cause: altered automaticity, reentry, and triggered mechanisms. The history and surface ECG can help distinguish between these mechanisms.

Altered automaticity can result from spontaneous phase 4 depolarization in nonpacemaker cells ("abnormal automaticity") or an increase in the slope of depolarization in cells that normally undergo phase 4 depolarization ("enhanced automaticity") (Figure 78-6). Both types of altered automaticity can occur in the setting of ischemia, electrolyte disturbances, and drug therapy.

Dysrhythmias caused by altered automaticity usually require a "warm-up" period; clinically, a patient may report a gradual increase in palpitations as opposed to an abrupt onset. A similar gradual increase in abnormal impulses should accompany these symptoms on the ECG. These dysrhythmias also tend to terminate in a gradual fashion. Atrial or ventricular nonpacemaker cells that display abnormal automaticity usually have resting membrane potentials between −30 and −60 mV and display decreased or absent fast Na^+ channel activity. Ventricular tachycardia within the first 24 hours after myocardial infarction is often the result of abnormal automaticity.

Enhanced automaticity occurs when catecholamine excess stimulates a non-SA nodal pacemaker source to become the dominant pacemaker. A typical enhanced automatic dysrhythmia is an idioventricular rhythm (from increased depolarization of the Purkinje fiber) after myocardial infarction. Another enhanced automatic dysrhythmia is atrial or junctional tachycardia with digitalis toxicity. In this setting, digitalis interferes with SA node impulse conduction and increases phase 4 depolarization in other myocardial cells, resulting in this dysrhythmia.

Reentry mechanisms are a common cause of narrow-complex (QRS duration less than 0.10 second) tachy-dysrhythmias, accounting for 50% to 80% of these rhythms. For reentry to occur, three conditions must exist: two paths (or a circuit) must be available for a given impulse to travel through, unequal responsive-

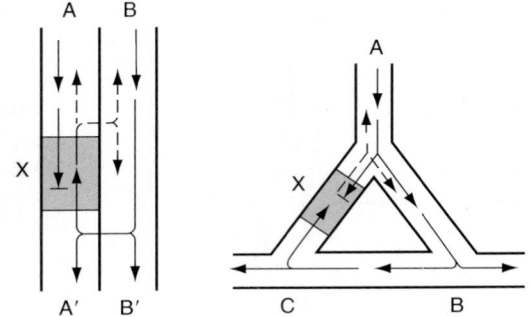

Figure 78-7. Mechanism of reentry.

ness of each limb of the circuit must be present, and slowed conduction must exist in one limb. Thus, reentry dysrhythmias are the result of abnormal conduction, as opposed to the abnormal impulse formation that occurs with altered automatic dysrhythmias (Figure 78-7).

In a reentrant dysrhythmia, an impulse reaching a circuit finds one of the two limbs refractory. The impulse is conducted down the nonrefractory limb to the distal tissues. If the initial refractory limb has recovered during the time required for the impulse to traverse the other limb, however, the impulse can then enter the distal end of the latter limb and travel in a retrograde direction. Thus, the unequal responsiveness of the limbs creates a functional unidirectional block of one. When the impulse exits the second (retrograde conducting) limb, it may then reenter the first limb. Each cycle can be repeated, creating a self-sustaining, or "circus movement," tachycardia. These cycles can be ordered or disordered (i.e., fibrillatory) and are termed *microreentry* when larger circuits are employed. In the AV node the *alpha* pathway usually serves as the anterograde limb and the *beta* pathway as the retrograde limb during a junctional reentrant tachycardia, although the converse can be seen in 10% of cases.

Reentry mechanisms are responsible for most regular narrow-complex tachycardias, some atrial and ventricular bigeminal and trigeminal rhythms, and ventricular tachycardias. Clinically, these dysrhythmias start and terminate abruptly, without a warm-up period.

Treatment is based on altering the refractoriness of the involved circuit by slowing or speeding conduction in one limb.

Triggered dysrhythmias are the result of afterdepolarizations and are highly dependent on heart rate for propagation. Triggered dysrhythmias secondary to delayed afterdepolarizations are associated with an intracellular Ca^{++} overload and can occur during reperfusion therapy in myocardial infarction and with digitalis toxicity. Ectopic atrial and junctional rhythms are often the result of this mechanism, along with some forms of ventricular tachycardia and bigeminy. These dysrhythmias are enhanced by faster heart rates and are inhibited by drugs that slow the heart rate or interfere with calcium entry into the cell.

In contrast, triggered dysrhythmias from early afterdepolarizations are enhanced by slower heart rates. The classical dysrhythmia associated with this mechanism is a specific form of acquired polymorphic ventricular tachycardia called torsades de pointes. Increasing the heart rate by overdrive pacing or drug administration (especially isoproterenol) can terminate triggered dysrhythmias from early afterdepolarizations.

CLASSIFICATION OF DRUGS FOR DYSRHYTHMIA TREATMENT

On the basis of their effect on the action potential and on impulse conduction in myocardial tissue, the drugs used to treat dysrhythmias can be classified into four major categories (Box 78-1).

Class I agents are further subdivided into three categories (A to C). Some agents exhibit properties of more than one class; for simplicity, these agents are grouped according to their major effect. Other agents fall outside this classification system and are discussed separately.

Class I agents exert their major effect on the fast Na^+ channels, resulting in slowed conduction and membrane stabilization. The subclasses are based on specific effects on action potential duration and conduction. Class IA agents moderately slow depolarization, prolong repolarization and action potential duration, and slow conduction. Class IB agents cause minimal slowing of depolarization and conduction and shorten repolarization and action potential duration. Class IC agents markedly slow depolarization and conduction and prolong repolarization and action potential duration.

Class II agents are the ß-adrenergic antagonists (blockers); these agents slow the SA node rate and AV node conduction. ß-Blockers also prolong the action potential and can depress conduction in ischemic myocardial tissues, although the normal His-Purkinje system is unaffected.

Class III agents prolong the action potential and refractory period duration, thus exhibiting a clinical antifibrillatory effect.

Class IV agents are the slow Ca^{++} channel entry antagonists, causing a depression of anterograde conduction through the AV node and suppression of other calcium-dependent dysrhythmias. Miscellaneous agents impor-

BOX 78-1. Classification of Antidysrhythmic Drugs

Class I
Sodium (fast) channel blockers. Slow depolarization with varying effects on repolarization. Called "membrane-stabilizing" drugs and have prominent antiectopic effects.

IA
Moderate slowing of depolarization and conduction. Prolong repolarization and action potential duration.
Quinidine
Procainamide
Disopyramide

IB
Minimally slow depolarization and conduction. Shorten repolarization and action potential duration.
Lidocaine
Phenytoin
Tocainide
Mexiletine
Moricizine*
Aprindine

IC
Markedly slow depolarization and conduction. Prolong repolarization and action potential duration.
Flecainide
Encainide
Lorcainide
Propafenone*

Class II
ß-Adrenergic blockers.
Propranolol
Esmolol
Acebutolol
Nadolol
Metoprolol

Class III
Antifibrillatory agents. Prolong action potential duration and refractory period duration with antifibrillatory properties.
Bretylium
Amiodarone
Dofetilide
Ibutilide[†]
Sotalol[†]
Dronedarone
Azimilide

Class IV
Calcium (slow) channel blockers.
Verapamil
Diltiazem

Miscellaneous
Digitalis
Magnesium sulfate
Adenosine

---

*Shares effects with class IA agents.
[†]Shares activity with class II agents.

tant in the emergency treatment of dysrhythmias include magnesium sulfate, digitalis, and adenosine.

Although these drugs are used as antidysrhythmics, they are also associated with "prodysrhythmic" effects.[1,2] The term refers to the exacerbation of an underlying dysrhythmia or to the provocation of a new dysrhythmia after institution of drug therapy. The class I and III agents cause prodysrhythmic effects in up to 15% of patients, including ventricular tachycardia. In general, the class IB agents are associated with the least (less than 2% incidence) and the class IC agents the most prominent (5% to 15% incidence) prodysrhythmic effects. For the class II and IV agents, the prodysrhythmic effects are primarily an extension of the electrophysiologic actions and usually are manifested as bradycardia and increasing AV nodal block.

Class IA Agents

All class IA agents slow conduction through the atria, AV node, and His-Purkinje system directly and decrease conduction in accessory pathways.[3-5] Class IA agents also exhibit anticholinergic and negative inotropic effects, with disopyramide displaying the most prominent and procainamide the least effect on contractility. Both procainamide and quinidine have peripheral vasodilatory actions, as a result of α-adrenergic blockage, which contributes to hypotension after administration. Disopyramide has vasoconstrictor properties, which together with its marked negative inotropic effects limits its use for acute dysrhythmia treatment.

Each class IA agent has high oral bioavailability; this route may be useful in the emergency treatment of certain dysrhythmias when symptoms are minimal. This subclass of drugs, particularly quinidine and procainamide, is associated with prolonged ventricular repolarization and a lengthened QT interval on the surface ECG.[6] These changes mirror an increased risk of acquired polymorphic ventricular tachycardia in some patients treated with these agents.[5,6] The aggregate incidence of prodysrhythmic effects appears to be approximately 5% in this class.

Procainamide

Procainamide is the most commonly used class IA agent in the emergency treatment of selected ventricular and supraventricular dysrhythmias.[7,8]

Intravenous procainamide is administered at a rate of 20 to 30 mg/min until the dysrhythmia is terminated, hypotension occurs (defined as a drop in the mean blood pressure of 15% or greater of the pretreatment value, or to a systolic pressure below 90 mm Hg), the QRS complex widens (to greater than 50% of the pretreatment width), or a total dose of 18 to 20 mg/kg is administered (or 12 mg/kg if congestive heart failure is present). The arbitrary limiting of the total dose to 1 g may limit the success of this agent. Intravenous procainamide can cause a transient increase in heart rate when used to treat a supraventricular dysrhythmia as a result of its anticholinergic properties. A decrease in heart rate from its direct effect on AV nodal conduction and depolarization, however, may also occur and force the termination of its use because of bradycardia. If successful, intravenous maintenance therapy is at a rate of 1 to 4 mg/min, with the lower rate suggested for elderly, congestive heart failure, and renal failure patients. Oral

therapy can be started at 2 g daily in divided doses (depending on the preparation) and titrated to effects and serum levels of procainamide and N-acetylprocainamide (an active metabolite). In addition to prodysrhythmia, other complications that can occur are heart block, orthostasis, abnormal liver function tests, and a lupus-like autoimmune syndrome (which clear on cessation).

Quinidine and Disopyramide

Quinidine and disopyramide can emergently control rhythm but are better suited for long-term oral therapy.[1,9] If used intravenously (IV), quinidine gluconate is given at a rate of 0.4 mg/kg/min and adjusted downward if side effects are noted. Termination of quinidine therapy is based on the appearance of side effects (similar to procainamide) or after a total dose of 10 mg/kg is infused without successful control of the dysrhythmia. Because of its anticholinergic properties, quinidine can also transiently increase the ventricular response rate when used to treat a supraventricular dysrhythmia.

Oral quinidine is well absorbed and is eliminated primarily by hepatic metabolism (50% to 80%), with some renal excretion. The initial daily oral dose for adults is 150 to 300 mg every 6 hours, with therapeutic serum levels of 3 to 8 μg/mL.[10] Oral quinidine can also be used in the pharmacologic conversion of atrial fibrillation but requires extended (2 to 6 hours) observation (see Box 78-1). Sustained-release preparations are best used after successful titration with short-acting preparations.

Intravenous disopyramide is not approved for use in the United States. Oral doses are well absorbed (80% to 95%) by the gastrointestinal tract and are eliminated by hepatic metabolism (50%) and renal excretion. Treatment begins with 400 to 800 mg/day in four divided doses, and the therapeutic serum level during long-term use is 2 to 4 μg/mL. Approximately 15% to 20% of patients treated with disopyramide develop new or increased clinical signs of congestive heart failure, limiting its long-term use.

Class IB Agents

Of all the class I agents, class IB agents slow conduction and depolarization the least, and they shorten repolarization and action potential duration instead of the prolongation seen with the class IA and IC agents.[3,4] These agents have little effect on accessory pathway conduction. The two class IB agents most commonly administered in the emergency department are phenytoin and lidocaine, with the latter used as the drug of choice in the initial emergent treatment of most ventricular dysrhythmias.

Lidocaine

Lidocaine is the most commonly used membrane-active drug for the treatment of ventricular tachycardia and fibrillation. It is rapidly absorbed by the gastrointestinal tract but largely inactivated by first-pass hepatic metabolism, limiting oral utility. Lidocaine can suppress dysrhythmias secondary to enhanced automaticity, although it has little effect on abnormal automatic rhythms. When used for ventricular dysrhythmias, lidocaine successfully terminates 60% to 90%, depending on the specific rhythm encountered and the dose used.[2] Lidocaine can also depress SA and AV node conduction and slow the ventricular rate, usually in the presence of myocardial ischemia. In atrial fibrillation or flutter, lidocaine may cause a transient increase in conduction and heart rate; otherwise, it is usually devoid of effects on autonomic and vascular tone, myocardial contractility, and the surface ECG in therapeutic doses.

Phenytoin

Phenytoin is used for the treatment of generalized seizures, but it also has antidysrhythmic properties[11] and has a limited role in the emergency treatment of dysrhythmias.

Phenytoin is 70% to 90% protein bound and is eliminated primarily by hepatic metabolism, with only 5% excreted by the kidneys. Often during long-term outpatient use, the daily dose must be lowered as metabolism slows. Many drugs increase or decrease phenytoin levels through their effects on protein binding and metabolism (Box 78-2).

Intravenous phenytoin should be started at a rate no greater than 50 mg/min (25 mg/min in those with heart failure); this dose can be given by intermittent bolus or by continuous infusion in a non–dextrose-containing solution (usually normal saline) with ECG monitoring. In therapeutic doses phenytoin has little effect on the ECG aside from mild shortening of the PR and QT intervals. Intravenous loading should be discontinued if the dysrhythmia is controlled, hypotension or conduction delays develop, or after a total dose of 18 mg/kg

---

BOX 78-2. Drugs Affecting Phenytoin Levels

Increase Level
Sulfonamides
Cimetidine
Trazodone
Isoniazid
Warfarin (Coumadin)
Chloramphenicol
Halothane
Disulfiram
Ethanol (acute)
Salicylates

Increase or Decrease Level (By Effects on Hepatic Metabolism)
Phenobarbital
Valproic acid/sodium valproate

Decrease Level
Ethanol (long term)
Calcium-containing preparation (especially antacids)
Carbamazepine
Reserpine

---

is administered. Although serum phenytoin levels between 10 and 20 µg/mL are considered therapeutic for seizure prophylaxis, lower serum levels may be optimal for rhythm control in some patients. Intramuscular injection of phenytoin should not be performed because of the pain, erratic absorption, and high risk of sterile abscess formation. Fosphenytoin allows intramuscular or more rapid intravenous administration, however, its role in rhythm management is unclear.

Other Class IB Agents

Mexiletine and tocainide are not used in the emergency department and are rarely indicated in the outpatient treatment of ventricular dysrhythmias[12,13] but are more commonly used in neuropathic pain syndromes. These two agents are approved for oral use only in the United States. A positive response to intravenous lidocaine predicts successful dysrhythmia control with either of these agents.

With cardiologic consultation, treatment with mexiletine is begun with 400 to 600 mg/day in three to four doses. Tocainide is usually given as an initial 800-mg dose in adults, followed by 1200 to 1800 mg/day in two or three doses. Their side effects are similar to those seen with lidocaine, although the incidence of dizziness and paresthesia is slightly greater. Neither agent has a significant effect on the ECG in therapeutic doses. There is an additive side effect risk when lidocaine is used in patients maintained with either of these two agents.[14]

Moricizine hydrochloride is a phenothiazine derivative that shares activity with class IA, IB, and IC agents. The usual dosage is 200 mg orally every 8 hours initially. Moricizine currently has no role in the initial management of ventricular dysrhythmias.

Class IC Agents

The class IC agents profoundly slow depolarization and conduction and are associated with significant antidysrhythmic properties.[3,6,15] The true incidence of prodysrhythmic effects in this class is unclear because these agents are used primarily in patients refractory to more conventional therapies, creating a potential magnification of the effect. Up to 15% of patients treated with class IC experience new or increased ventricular dysrhythmias, with up to 5% developing polymorphic or sustained monomorphic ventricular tachycardia. The incidence of prodysrhythmia, especially polymorphic ventricular tachycardia, is highest when IC agents are used in patients with a persistent ventricular tachycardia or decreased ejection fraction.[4] The total morbidity and mortality associated with any cardiac-related event (including dysrhythmias and shock) is also relatively high when these agents are used in the long term, even in patients being treated for mildly symptomatic cases of ventricular dysrhythmias.[15]

Class IC agents are approved for oral use in the United States and thus have a limited role in the initial management of dysrhythmias. In Europe, these agents are employed for emergent intravenous dysrhythmia treatment. Each can cause an increase in the PR, QRS, and QT intervals on the surface ECG, although this does not reliably predict the risk of polymorphic ventricular tachycardia.

Flecainide

Flecainide, in addition to the electrophysiologic effects shared with all class IC agents, increases the refractory period in most accessory pathways.

It has a mild negative inotropic effect, with up to 4% of treated patients experiencing increased heart failure. Flecainide is well absorbed from the gastrointestinal tract, with 30% excreted unchanged in the urine and 70% metabolized by the liver. The mean serum half-life is 14 hours, although this time may vary widely in a given patient.

Flecainide controls 60% to 90% of all ventricular dysrhythmias and between 40% and 100% of supraventricular dysrhythmias. Side effects may occur in up to 40% of treated patients but are usually minor. These include visual disturbances, dizziness, paresthesia, headache, and nausea; they are treated by decreasing the dose. An increase in ventricular rate may occur in 10% and hypotension in another 10% of patients in addition to the previously mentioned risk of heart failure. Because of the latter risks and the risk of prodysrhythmic effects, oral therapy is usually initiated in hospital with continuous monitoring for both QRS and QT prolongation.

Encainide

Encainide has an electrophysiologic profile similar to that of flecainide, with the advantage of a less negative inotropic effect.[3,16] It is well absorbed from the gastrointestinal tract, with extensive hepatic metabolism forming two active metabolites. The serum half-life of all active forms is 3 to 12 hours. Treatment is usually begun with 75 mg/day in three dosages and increased every 3 to 5 days on the basis of response and side effects to a maximal daily dose of 300 mg. Although it is not approved for intravenous use, research using a dosage of 0.6 to 1 mg/kg over 15 minutes showed that it can be effective in treating ventricular and supraventricular dysrhythmias. The side effects and success rates are similar to those seen with flecainide.

Propafenone

This agent shares properties with IA and IC agents, with effects intermediary with respect to sodium channels.[17] It also possesses some ß-adrenergic and calcium channel blocking properties. It is not available for intravenous use but is available for the oral treatment of ventricular dysrhythmias. Although not approved for supraventricular dysrhythmia management, propafenone is effective in converting and maintaining sinus rhythm in 40% to 60% of patients with atrial fibrillation and flutter. Compared with other class IC agents, propafenone has a lower observed prodysrhythmic rate in therapeutic doses. Its side effects are usually related to conduction disturbances on the ECG, dizziness, taste alteration, or blurred vision.

Class II Agents

In general, class II agents (ß-blockers) are better suited to control ventricular response rates and break a reentrant circuit in a supraventricular dysrhythmia than to treat a ventricular dysrhythmia. In the setting of acute myocardial infarction, however, ventricular dysrhythmia and reinfarction prophylaxis are important indications for ß-blockers, especially metoprolol.

All ß-blockers are active at both β_1 and β_2 receptors (Table 78-2) but to varying degrees; those with more prominent β_1 effects are termed *cardioselective*. Through their effects on β_1 receptors, all class II agents slow SA node impulse formation and depress myocardial contractility to varying degrees. β_1 selectivity is desirable because a lowered incidence of bronchospasm is observed with therapeutic antidysrhythmic doses. The usual effect of class II agents on the ECG is slowing of the heart rate and PR prolongation, with no effect on QRS and QT duration.

Relative contraindications for ß-blockers include asthma or chronic obstructive lung disease, congestive heart failure, and third-trimester pregnancy. Long-term use of ß-blockers in patients with diabetes mellitus is not recommended, although their use to terminate a dysrhythmia is acceptable. ß-Blockers should not be used in patients with bradycardia or greater than first-degree heart block. Although often used together during long-term oral therapy, intravenous ß-blockers should be given with great caution after recent intravenous calcium channel antagonist (class IV) use because of the increased risk of hemodynamic side effects. Acute side effects of ß-blockers include bronchospasm, heart failure, excessive bradycardia, hypotension, and vasospasm (especially if the Raynaud syndrome is present).

Table 78-2. Cardiac and Respiratory β-Adrenergic Receptors and Responses to Pharmacologic Manipulation

Receptors	Location	Response to	
		Stimulation	*Antagonism*
β_1	Heart	Increased heart rate and ectopy Increased contractility	Decreased heart rate and ectopy Decreased contractility
β_2	Airway (smooth muscle) Peripheral vasculature	Decreased tone (relaxation) Decreased tone (relaxation)	Increased tone (contraction) Increased tone (contraction)

Propranolol

Propranolol is nonselective and well absorbed by the gastrointestinal tract. It undergoes extensive first-pass liver metabolism after oral intake, requiring a much higher dose by this route than an equipotent intravenous dose. The serum half-life is 3 to 6 hours, requiring a four times daily dosing regimen. Therapy is usually monitored by rhythm control and side effects, not serum levels. Oral dosages begin at 80 mg/day of a short-acting preparation in divided doses. Oral propranolol is better suited for maintenance therapy than for acute dysrhythmia treatment. Intravenous propranolol is given in 0.5- to 1-mg dosages over 60 to 120 seconds every 15 minutes until a therapeutic effect is seen, side effects occur, or a total dose of 0.2 mg/kg has been given.[10,18]

Propranolol is effective in terminating 30% to 80% of reentrant supraventricular tachycardias, depending on the pathway, especially if the rhythm is catecholamine induced. Because of its relatively long effect, it is not commonly employed in emergent settings. Its use in other rhythms is associated with a lower success rate and increased side effects when compared with class I agents.

Esmolol

Esmolol is an attractive ß-blocker in the emergency treatment of supraventricular tachydysrhythmias. It is $ß_1$ selective with a rapid onset of action and a 5- to 10-minute duration of effect.[19-20] The brief clinical effect is the result of its short elimination half-life (9½ minutes) because of metabolism by plasma cholinesterase. Esmolol is given as an intravenous bolus of 500 µg/kg, followed by a continuous infusion starting at 50 µg/kg/min; if side effects are seen, stopping the infusion results in a rapid decrease in therapeutic and toxic effects. If the dysrhythmia persists after the initial bolus and infusion, a repeated loading dose should be given and the infusion rate increased in increments of 50 µg/kg/min. Usually an infusion rate of 200 µg/kg/min or less is effective, and the maximal recommended rate is 300 µg/kg/min.

Metoprolol

Another $ß_1$ selective agent, metoprolol, is available in oral and intravenous preparations. Although not approved for initial dysrhythmia treatment in the United States, metoprolol (5 to 10 mg IV every 10 to 15 minutes) is effective in the treatment of narrow-complex tachycardias, with response patterns similar to that seen with verapamil.

Nadolol and Acebutolol

Nadolol and acebutolol are used for oral dysrhythmia treatment but are not approved for intravenous use. The effectiveness and side effect profiles are similar to those of propranolol and metoprolol, aside from a lowered risk of bronchospasm with acebutolol, which has an intrinsic sympathomimetic effect.

Class III Agents

This class is called the *antifibrillatory* group, for the treatment of atrial and ventricular fibrillation. All class III agents prolong the refractory period and action potential duration but have variable effects on the QT interval.[21] In general, class III agents are alternative drugs to the class I agents for the treatment of many ventricular and atrial dysrhythmias.

Bretylium

Bretylium was previously the most commonly used class III agent.[22] Because of its profound hemodynamic effects and the emergence of newer class III drugs, it is unavailable in the United States.

Amiodarone

Amiodarone is approved for the treatment of both ventricular and supraventricular dysrhythmias, including atrial fibrillation or flutter and accessory pathway syndromes.[21,23-25] In addition to features of all class III agents, amiodarone prolongs the action potential duration and refractory period, slows automaticity in pacemaker cells, and slows conduction in the AV node. It also displays a noncompetitive blockade of adrenergic receptors and causes smooth muscle relaxation. When given IV, amiodarone may cause a mild drop in blood pressure and heart rate along with a slight decrease in contractility.

After an oral dose, absorption is slow and erratic, varying widely among subjects. The serum half-life is about 50 days during long-term oral use and approximately 25 hours after a single intravenous dose. Because of the unusual pharmacokinetics, oral dosing regimens vary widely, starting at 600 to 1000 mg/day initially for up to 7 days followed by 400 to 800 mg/day for a maintenance dosage. The recommended intravenous dose is 5 mg/kg over 10 to 15 minutes.[23-25]

The acute side effects of amiodarone are primarily limited to hypotension, bradycardia, and heart failure (Box 78-3). Between 1% and 3% of patients experience prodysrhythmia with long-term use, often without QT prolongation. Torsades is rare (less than 1% with long-term use and much less with acute use). Long-term use is associated with significant side effects, including prominent extracardiac issues, forcing many patients to discontinue treatment after 1 to 2 years.[23] Because of the risk of pulmonary toxicity and fibrosis, this agent should be used with caution for maintenance therapy in patients with underlying pulmonary disease. Amiodarone also causes an increase in the serum level of many agents, especially digoxin and warfarin. It can cause an additive risk of bradycardia and hypotension when used in conjunction with calcium channel or ß-adrenergic blockers.

Ibutilide

This agent is approved in the United States only for intravenous use. When it is given in a dose of 0.015 to 0.02 mg/kg, approximately 5% to 65% of patients

BOX 78-3. Adverse Effects of Amiodarone

Acute
Hypotension
Slowing of heart rate
Decreased contractility

Long-Term

Common
Corneal deposits
Photosensitivity
Gastrointestinal intolerance

Less Common
Hyperthyroidism
Heart failure
Pulmonary toxicity
Hypothyroidism
Bradycardia
Prodysrhythmic effect

Drug Interactions

Increases levels
Quinidine
Phenytoin
Procainamide
Warfarin
Digoxin
Flecainide

convert from atrial fibrillation or flutter to a sinus rhythm, usually within 20 minutes.[26] Prolongation of the QT interval and prodysrhythmia, especially torsades, are more common than with amiodarone when used chronically (but similarly rare in acute use) with few other side effects. This drug is an alternative to intravenous procainamide for pharmacologic conversion of atrial fibrillation and flutter in the emergency department, with easier use and a good safety profile offset by higher cost.

Sotalol and Other Agents

Sotalol (a mixed class III–adrenergic blocking agent) has a limited emergency department role and is associated with a higher incidence of prodysrhythmia (especially polymorphic ventricular tachycardia) than other class III agents. It has been used IV for conversion of atrial fibrillation but offers limited advantages over other regimens.[24,27] Dofetilide, dronedarone, and azimilide are investigational class III agents that possess other properties.

Class IV Agents

Class IV agents block the slow calcium channels in both myocardial and vascular smooth muscle cells.[3,4] Each agent exhibits activity at both the myocardial and peripheral vascular levels, with specificity for particular areas within the group. Verapamil and diltiazem exhibit the most potent effects on myocardial cell calcium entry and hence conduction and contractility; verapamil has the least effect on peripheral vascular tone, and diltiazem has an effect intermediary between those of verapamil and nifedipine.

Verapamil

Verapamil is used to treat narrow-complex tachycardia and rapid atrial flutter or fibrillation, terminating or controlling the ventricular response rate in 80% to 90% of cases.[28-29] Verapamil has little direct effect on accessory pathways and is used in these syndromes only when anterograde conduction through the AV node exists.

Verapamil slows conduction within the AV node (primarily at the atrial-His level) more than it does within the SA node. These actions are only partially reversed by atropine. In diseased ventricular tissues, particularly during acute ischemia, verapamil can diminish the conduction of reentrant impulses, but conduction within the normal His-Purkinje system is unaffected. After an intravenous dose of verapamil, the ECG is usually unchanged aside from a slower heart rate and prolonged PR interval. Because of its effects on conduction, intravenous verapamil should not be used in patients with second- or third-degree AV block and should be used with close monitoring in those with first-degree block.

Verapamil has negative inotropic and mild peripheral vasodilatory properties. Reflex increases in sympathetic tone usually maintain cardiac output and blood pressure, but elderly patients and those using adrenergic blocking or other negative inotropic drugs may be susceptible to heart failure or significant hypotension. In particular, intravenous verapamil should be used with great caution after intravenous administration of any class II agent (aside from esmolol and after an appropriate washout period). Most evidence suggests that in the absence of hypovolemia, heart block, hypotension, or left ventricular dysfunction, verapamil can be used safely in infants.[30,31]

Intravenous verapamil is given at a dosage of 0.1 mg/kg over 1 to 2 minutes; for the average healthy adult, this translates to a dose of 5 to 10 mg. Hypotension seen as a direct effect of the excessive ventricular rate is usually not worsened and is often reversed when verapamil is used in these doses. In elderly patients or those with preexisting borderline hypotension (systolic blood pressure of 90 to 110 mm Hg), a smaller dose (0.05 mg/kg, or 2.5-mg increments) should be employed. Repeated doses (either the same or larger, up to twice the initial dose if there is no response in younger patients with cardiovascular stability aside from tachycardia) should be given every 10 minutes on the basis of response; use of a longer dosing interval, especially if over 30 minutes, may interfere with successful treatment of a dysrhythmia because of redistribution. Another dosing regimen, using 25 mg of verapamil in 50 mL of crystalloid infused at a rate of 1 mg/min (120 mL/hr), successfully treats more than 80% of patients with a narrow-complex tachycardia.

Calcium chloride, 500 to 1000 mg (5 to 10 mL of a 10% solution), can reverse or prevent verapamil-induced hypotension.[32-33] Calcium salts attenuate the peripheral vasodilatory actions without altering the chronotropic (antidysrhythmic) effects of verapamil. If verapamil-induced hypotension persists after calcium administration and intravenous fluids, a direct-acting vasopressor agent should be instituted. Aside from AV block, hypotension, and congestive heart failure, verapamil can cause other side effects, including nausea, vomiting, constipation, dizziness, nervousness, and pruritus.

Verapamil is rapidly absorbed from the gastrointestinal tract but undergoes such extensive first-pass liver metabolism that only 25% to 30% of an oral dose is biologically available. As with propranolol, this low availability results in a much larger oral dosing requirement compared with an equipotent intravenous dose. The drug is 90% protein bound and is eliminated primarily by renal excretion. After an oral dose, the duration of effect is 4 to 6 hours, with a total elimination half-life of 3 to 12 hours. Daily maintenance with 120 to 720 mg of a short-acting preparation in four divided doses is recommended for prophylaxis from recurrent dysrhythmias. A long-acting preparation of verapamil is available, but it is not approved for the treatment of dysrhythmias.

Diltiazem

Like verapamil, diltiazem prolongs AV conduction. Oral doses are rapidly absorbed, although a significant first-pass effect is seen. Intravenous diltiazem (0.25 mg/kg over 2 minutes, followed by 0.35 mg/kg 15 minutes later if the first dosage is unsuccessful but tolerated) controls the ventricular response rate in up to 93% of patients with atrial fibrillation and atrial flutter and is associated with minimal hypotension.[34] If the intravenous bolus is successful, a continuous infusion (5 to 15 mg/hr) or an oral dose (60 to 90 mg initially) can be titrated on the basis of the response. Although laboratory data suggest that diltiazem causes less diminution in myocardial contractility than verapamil, clinical experience suggests that the relative difference in induced hypotension or heart failure is modest. Thus, in the absence of known or suspected left ventricular dysfunction, either is a reasonable choice for rate control.

Miscellaneous Agents

Digitalis

Digoxin is the main form of digitalis used in the emergent treatment of cardiac dysrhythmias. In addition to their positive inotropic effects, digitalis compounds have variable electrophysiologic effects on myocardial cells (Table 78-3). These effects can be divided into excitant and depressant actions. Digitalis excitant effects are manifested as an increase in altered automatic and triggered ectopic impulses, particularly when it is given in toxic doses. Digitalis also depresses conduction and lengthens refractoriness in the AV node in therapeutic doses. Although the therapeutic effects are primarily the result of the depressive actions, toxic dysrhythmias may be the result of either or both of these mechanisms.

Digitalis inhibits the membrane-bound enzyme ATPase, impairing the active transport of Na^+ out of and

Table 78-3. Effects of Digitalis on Heart Tissues

Tissue and Property	Direct Therapeutic Effect*	Direct Toxic Effect	Indirect Effect†
Sinoatrial node automaticity	0	D	D
Atrial conduction	0	I	D
Atrial refractoriness	I (small)	I	D
Atrioventricular node refractoriness and conduction	I (small)	I	I
Purkinje fibers			
Automaticity and conduction	I (small)	I	0
Refractoriness	I (small)	D	0
Conduction	0	I	I
Refractoriness	I (small)	D	0

*D, decreases; I, increases; 0, minimal effect.
†Indirect autonomic effects (vagotonic and sympatholytic).

K^+ into the cell. Aside from increasing intracellular Na^+ concentration and decreasing intracellular K^+ concentration, the disruption of the pump indirectly causes a mild increase in intracellular Ca^{++} concentration, which accounts for the positive inotropic effects of digitalis. In therapeutic doses, many of the observed clinical effects of digitalis are a result of indirect effects upon the autonomic nervous system (see Table 78-3). On the surface ECG, digitalis usually slows the heart rate and decreases the QT interval slightly in therapeutic doses. Also, characteristic ST segment depression and shortening and T wave inversion are seen during digoxin therapy.

Digoxin is often used as a positive inotropic agent in congestive heart failure, with therapeutic serum levels considered to be between 0.8 and 2 ng/mL. When it is used as an antidysrhythmic, higher levels may be necessary in a given patient. Digitalis controls the ventricular rate in narrow-complex tachycardias, including atrial fibrillation, atrial flutter, and paroxysmal supraventricular tachycardia. Because of its relatively slow onset of action and narrow therapeutic window, digitalis is less often used as a first-line agent for emergency therapy today but is a good choice in the outpatient management of these rhythms, particularly when underlying heart failure is present.

Digoxin is given in an initial intravenous dose of 0.5 mg in adults. A clinical effect may be seen within 30 minutes, but the peak effect does not occur until 1½ to 2 hours. Because of this, repeated dosages are given every 1 to 2 hours when used for rate control and every 4 to 6 hours when used for inotropic effect. These repeated dosages are administered in 0.25-mg increments until the rate is controlled or the dysrhythmia terminated, side effects occur, or the total dose reaches 1.5 mg. The latter ceiling is arbitrary because some patients may require a higher dose to control rate but risk increased side effects.

Digoxin is excreted 50% to 75% unchanged in the urine and is 25% protein bound with a large volume of distribution. The serum half-life is 24 to 48 hours, allowing a daily or every other day maintenance regimen. Side effects of digoxin are listed in Box 78-4

BOX 78-4. Adverse Effects of Digitalis

Common

Gastrointestinal intolerance (nausea, vomiting, abdominal pain, diarrhea, anorexia)
Fatigue
Drowsiness
Visual disturbances
Headache
Depression
Apathy

Less Common

Psychosis
Cardiac symptoms
Heart block
Increased ectopy
Combined block and ectopy (multifocal atrial tachycardia with block or complete atrioventricular block with accelerated junctional rhythm)
Ventricular tachycardia

and are enhanced by hypokalemia, hypercalcemia, hypomagnesemia, increased catecholamines, and severe acid-base disturbances. The concomitant use of quinidine can increase the serum levels of digoxin by interfering with renal and nonrenal elimination.

Two misconceptions about digoxin persist. Often it is used in atrial fibrillation because of a belief that conversion to a sinus rhythm is more likely than after the use of other rate-controlling agents. Structured observations do not confirm this perception.[24,35] Furthermore, ß-adrenergic and calcium channel blockers are often better tolerated than digoxin when attempting to control the ventricular rate in the absence of ventricular dysfunction. Another concern is the safety of cardioversion during digoxin therapy and the possible development of ventricular dysrhythmias. If no clinical or laboratory evidence of toxicity is present, cardioversion of atrial fibrillation or flutter is safe, with little added risk of precipitating ventricular dysrhythmias compared with patients not receiving digoxin.[36]

Magnesium

Magnesium has been used for 40 years as an antidysrhythmic but is often the forgotten electrolyte. It may control the ventricular response rate in a variety of narrow-complex tachycardias, including atrial fibrillation, multifocal atrial tachycardia, and reentrant supraventricular tachycardia.[37] Magnesium (2 to 4 g as a slow IV bolus) can terminate ventricular tachycardia, including digoxin-induced and polymorphic ventricular tachycardia (especially torsades de pointes). Aside from the latter rhythm, magnesium is generally a second- or third-line agent.

Adenosine

Adenosine is a naturally occurring purine nucleoside used for the intravenous treatment of narrow-complex tachydysrhythmias. It causes a concentration-dependent slowing of AV conduction and a slowing of conduction in both anterograde and retrograde paths of a reentrant circuit.[38] This agent shortens the action potential duration and is devoid of effects on ventricular contractility. Adenosine hyperpolarizes atrial myocardial cells and can cause a decrease in atrial contractility. It also reduces cyclic AMP levels and attenuates presynaptic norepinephrine release. In extremely low doses, adenosine causes selective coronary vasodilation; as the dose is increased to the level needed for a maximal antidysrhythmic effect, peripheral vasodilation occurs.[39]

After an intravenous dose, adenosine has an onset of action of 5 to 20 seconds with a duration of effect of 30 to 40 seconds.[38-44] It is eliminated primarily by deamination in endothelial and blood cells, with a 10-second serum half-life. Aside from a decreasing heart rate and an increasing AV block, adenosine has little effect on the ECG. Except in rare cases of catecholamine-induced ventricular dysrhythmias, adenosine has little effect on infranodal conduction. This fact, coupled with clinical data, prompted some to recommend adenosine as a diagnostic agent in the wide-complex tachycardias.[39]

An initial dose of 6 mg as a rapid bolus for adults weighing 50 kg or greater is recommended. If no response is seen within 1 to 2 minutes, the dose is doubled (12 mg) and repeated. If no effect is seen after a third 12-mg dose, the rhythm should be reassessed and another agent employed. Pediatric doses of 0.05 mg/kg initially are suggested at similar intervals up to a total dose of 0.25 mg/kg.[41]

Side effects coincide with the onset of clinical effects and occur in up to a third of patients but are usually minor. These include flushing, dyspnea, chest pressure, nausea, headache, dizziness, transient bradycardia or heart block, and hypotension (seen rarely, from the vasodilatory properties). All resolve rapidly without treatment, although many patients are intensely uncomfortable for a short period. Other rhythms rarely seen after adenosine use include atrial fibrillation and ventricular tachycardia. Aminophylline and methylxanthines antagonize the effects of adenosine, and dipyridamole potentiates its effects. Digitalis, calcium channel blockers, and benzodiazepines can all augment the activity of adenosine.

In comparative studies of patients with narrow-complex tachydysrhythmias, adenosine has response rates equivalent to those of verapamil (85% to 90%) with fewer serious side effects.[42-43] Because of its short duration of action, recurrence of the tachycardia occurs in 10% to 58% (mean of approximately 25%) of patients.[42-44] For this reason, adenosine is not a definitive therapeutic agent for atrial fibrillation or flutter and nonreentrant rhythms, although its effects on conduction can help unmask these rhythms when not apparent on the initial ECG. Similarly, adenosine should not replace a careful search for a ventricular source or the rare but potentially lethal combination of atrial fibrillation with an accessory pathway. The use of *any* drug that depresses the AV node primarily in these settings (including adenosine and calcium channel or ß-blockers) can result in precipitous hemodynamic collapse.[45] Finally, adenosine often fails in practice because it is used for the wrong reason, especially unrecognized atrial fibrillation or ventricular tachycardia.

APPROACH TO DYSRHYTHMIA RECOGNITION AND MANAGEMENT

Dysrhythmias can be classified according to their electrophysiologic origin, ECG appearance, and the underlying ventricular rate. The following five categories are presented, although overlap does exist between categories:

- Bradycardias, sinus and atrial rhythms, SA and AV block
- Extrasystoles and parasystoles
- Narrow-complex (QRS less than 0.12 second) tachycardias
- Preexcitation and accessory pathway syndromes
- Wide-complex (QRS 0.12 second or greater) tachycardias

The treatment of specific dysrhythmias can also be divided into two broad categories on the basis of clinical stability, which is a continuum. Unstable patients are defined as those with evidence of end-organ hypoperfusion as a direct result of the dysrhythmia. The specific symptoms and signs of unstable rhythms follow:

- Hypotension
- Chest pain suggestive of myocardial ischemia
- Dyspnea or pulmonary edema
- Altered sensorium (from mild changes to coma)

The latter three are more specific because absolute blood pressure values may vary widely. For example, a patient with chronic hypertension who has a blood pressure of 110/60 and crushing chest pain with a wide-complex tachycardia at a rate of 180 beats/min is "more unstable" than a young woman with a similar rhythm and a blood pressure of 88/50 without other symptoms. Patients with an unstable rhythm deserve rapid pharmacologic or electrical therapy after a focused assessment, whereas stable patients can be treated after a more thorough evaluation to identify the exact cause. In general, rapid unstable dysrhythmias aside from sinus tachycardia require sedation and cardioversion, especially when more than one symptom or sign of instability is present. Slow unstable dysrhythmias require temporary pacing, although atropine can be used while preparing for pacing.

The Initial Assessment of Stable Patients

The approach to the patient with a stable dysrhythmia attempts to gather subjective and objective data concerning the underlying rhythm. The following steps are followed:

- Directed history
- Physical examination
- 12-lead ECG and rhythm strip
- Diagnostic and therapeutic interventions

When the patient is without symptoms or signs of an unstable dysrhythmia, this information should be gath-

ered before treatment. This approach helps ensure that the treatment is correct and provides ample documentation of the conditions surrounding the dysrhythmia should treatment fail. These steps are often taken concurrently (e.g., history taking during the initial physical examination and combined ECG monitoring with certain physical examination techniques) to facilitate a rapid assessment and improve data collection. In the presence of clear instability, the ECG is assessed while preparing for pacing or cardioversion.

In stable patients, the exact subjective nature of any symptoms and the timing and velocity (gradual or abrupt) of symptom onset must be elicited. A history of palpitations, dizziness, chest pain, dyspnea, or syncope should be sought specifically. The previous history, especially of heart disease or dysrhythmias, and current medications are important because both may offer a clue about the underlying rhythm. For example, a 22-year-old man treated with propranolol for "palpitations" who seeks treatment for abrupt onset of a regular tachycardia with a QRS duration of 0.12 second at a rate of 200 beats/min is more likely to have a reentrant supraventricular tachycardia with aberrant conduction than ventricular tachycardia. Conversely, a 55-year-old man with a history of a previous myocardial infarction and "extra heart beats" who takes nitroglycerin and procainamide and has palpitations and chest pain and a similar wide-complex regular tachycardia is more likely by history to have ventricular tachycardia. Occasionally, the family history can be helpful. The combination of deafness with paroxysmal palpitations, syncope, and a family history of sudden death strongly suggests a specific form of torsades de pointes.

On physical examination, evidence of end-organ hypoperfusion should be sought. Alteration in cognitive function (from mild excitation to depressed consciousness), as well as clammy or dusky skin, suggests hypoperfusion. Cannon waves in the neck and variation in the intensity of the first heart sound or arterial pulse suggest AV dissociation, which may help distinguish supraventricular from ventricular rhythms. Close auscultation of the heart sounds may detect valvular disorders. Certain clinical toxidromes, such as organophosphate, anticholinergic, and cyclic antidepressant ingestion, have prominent physical findings.

The most important ECG observations are listed in Box 78-5; diagnosis using a single lead is often successful, but in many cases multiple leads are needed to define the dysrhythmia accurately. Although lead II is usually chosen, at least two other leads should be examined. Occasionally, an apparently narrow-complex rhythm is discovered to be a wide-complex rhythm when a different lead is examined. The paddles from a defibrillator and monitor unit can be helpful for short periods because a modified chest lead can be created to optimize the appearance of the P wave and QRS complexes. Long-term monitoring using paddles is impractical; often leads V_1 or V_2 can be substituted to provide data that lead II does not. Finally, the most useful information about paroxysmal dysrhythmias occurs at the onset and termination of the rhythm.

BOX 78-5. Basic Electrocardiographic Observations
During Dysrhythmia Analysis

1. Ventricular rate: Fast (>100 beats/min), slow (<60 beats/ min), or normal (60 to 100 beats/min).
2. Rhythm: Regular, completely irregular (chaotic), regular with occasional irregularities, or grouped impulses. Calipers and long strips are recommended to detect subtle irregularities.
3. QRS width: Prolonged (>0.12 sec), borderline (0.09 to 0.12 sec), or normal. If done without electrocardiogram physically present (e.g., prehospital radio medical command), ask for QRS duration in number of small boxes from printed rhythm strip (each box equals 0.04 sec) to ensure accuracy.
4. P wave presence and relationship to QRS complexes may require mapping of P waves with calipers to detect those falling within QRS complex or T wave.
5. Rhythm changes: Examine these areas closely for clues.
6. Multiple leads, especially chest leads or esophageal lead if difficulties with no. 4.
7. Compare with previous tracing (if available).

A long rhythm strip (up to a minute) may be needed to define a dysrhythmia. Other adjuncts to standard ECG monitoring include increasing the paper speed and the use of esophageal electrodes. Normally, a paper speed of 25 mm/sec is used; when it is increased to 50 to 100 mm/sec, the relationship of the P wave to the QRS complex may be better defined (Figure 78-8). Esophageal leads can also help better define the P-QRS relationship (Figure 78-9). A pill electrode is available for virtually painless recording of esophageal tracings and can be helpful in determining the source of a dysrhythmia.[46]

The use of certain maneuvers in combination with ECG monitoring can help uncover the cause of dysrhythmias. Carotid sinus massage and the Valsalva maneuver increase vagal (parasympathetic) tone. Vagal maneuvers transiently slow AV conduction, which may help terminate or uncover the primary rhythm disturbance.[47,48] The use of ice packs or cold-water head dunking (with care to avoid aspiration) has similar effects, especially in children, through the diving

Figure 78-8. Note the P waves before the QRS complexes in lead aVF.

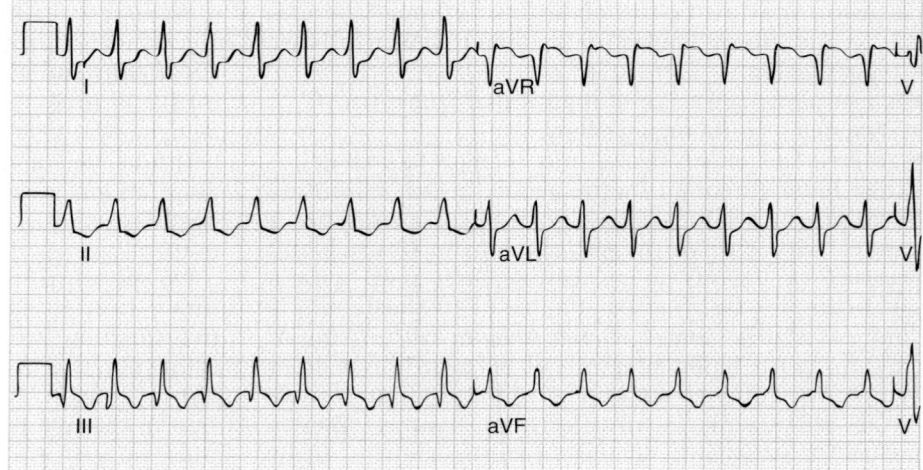

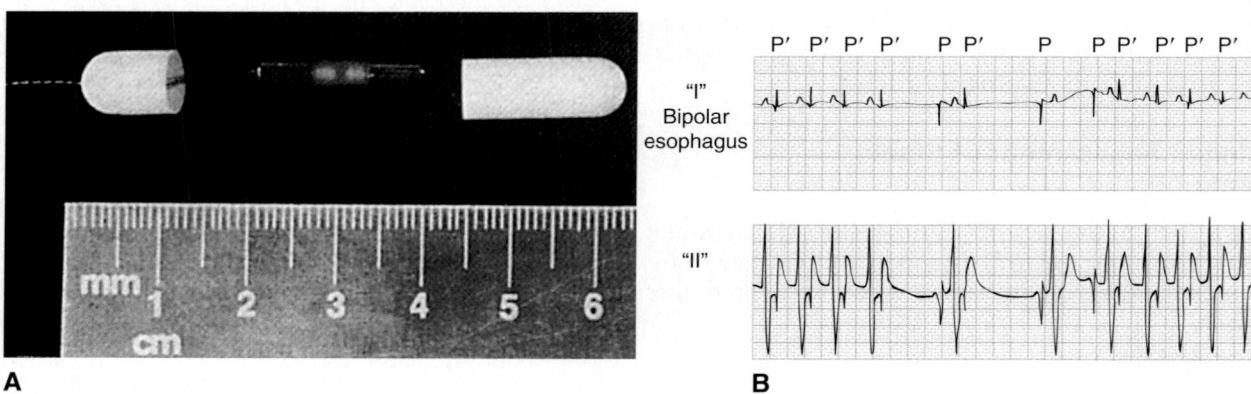

A　　　　　　　　　　**B**

Figure 78-9. An esophageal pill electrode (**A**) and a representative tracing of a reentrant tachycardia with retrograde (P′) depolarization not appreciated on the simultaneously recorded lead II strip (**B**). (From Hammill SC, Pritchett ELC: In Campbell R, Murray A [eds]: *Dynamic Electrocardiography*. Edinburgh, Churchill Livingstone, 1985.)

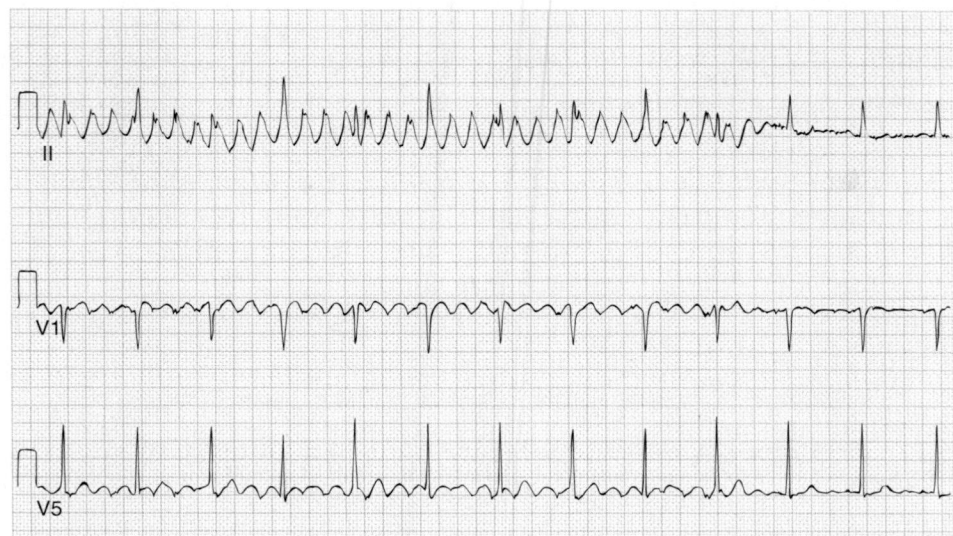

reflex. Carotid sinus massage is best avoided in elderly patients because of the risk of embolic phenomena. Auscultation of the neck for bruits should be performed before carotid sinus massage is attempted. Ocular massage, rectal massage,[49] or inflation of MAST trousers is not recommended.

The effectiveness of any maneuver alone or in various combinations compared with pharmacologic treatment is unclear. Generally, reentrant dysrhythmias abruptly terminate or continue with little change in rate, whereas atrial fibrillation and tachycardia slow temporarily. Vagal maneuvers usually fail to terminate supraventricular dysrhythmias but rarely cause deterioration. This failure may result from poor technique (carotid massage should not be performed upright) or a selection bias because those who respond to vagal maneuvers often do so before arrival (whether the result of planned or inadvertent maneuvers).[47]

Pseudodysrhythmias

Occasionally, an artifact on the ECG produces an apparent dysrhythmia. Muscle contraction or movement (especially shivering), loose leads, and stray external signals from other electrical equipment and monitoring devices can produce these artifacts, called *pseudodysrhythmias*. (Figure 78-10) These findings may often be mistaken for serious ventricular dysrhythmias, including ventricular fibrillation. Pseudodysrhythmias illustrate the need to avoid treating the ECG.

Specific Dysrhythmias

Bradycardia, Sinoatrial and Atrioventricular Block

Bradycardia, variably defined as a heart rate of less than 50 to 60 beats/min, can be normal in well-conditioned subjects or the result of two basic disturbances. Depression of the dominant pacemaker, usually the sinus node, causes bradycardia. Another cause is conduction system block, in which the normal sinus node impulses are incompletely carried to the AV node and ventricular tissues. In both situations, a subsidiary pacemaker may assume the dominant role, with heart rates of 30 to 60 beats/min. The rhythms seen with subsidiary pacemakers during SA and AV nodal block are called *escape* rhythms because they provide a physiologic escape from no impulse generation (asystole).

The treatment of bradydysrhythmias is based on the underlying cause and symptoms. The two options are intravenous atropine (0.5 to 1 mg for adults) and temporary pacing, either transcutaneous or transvenous. Isoproterenol, a nonselective ß-agonist, can also increase the heart rate but may cause hypotension (from vasodilation) and ventricular dysrhythmias. Because of these undesirable effects and the wide availability of transcutaneous pacemakers, isoproterenol has fallen from favor as a treatment of bradydysrhythmias. These rhythms require emergent treatment only when the rate is less than 50 beats/min with evidence of hypoperfusion or if the rhythm carries a high risk of progression to complete block. A transcutaneous pacemaker should be readily available.

Sinus Bradycardia

Sinus bradycardia appears on the surface ECG as a regular rhythm at a rate below 60 beats/min, with a normal consistent P wave morphology and PR interval duration (Figure 78-11). This pattern may be found in healthy adults or during sleep and periods of fright. Other causes include hypothermia, excessive parasympathetic or diminished sympathetic stimulation (often from drug therapy, especially β-adrenergic and calcium channel blockers), and carotid sinus hypersensitivity. The last is sometimes seen in men with bradycardia or syncope while wearing a tight shirt collar. Sinus bradycardia may be seen in the early stages of an acute inferior wall myocardial infarction, resulting from parasympathetic stimulation. Generally, sinus bradycardia is a benign dysrhythmia and requires no specific treatment aside from that required for any underlying

Figure 78-11. Sinus bradycardia.

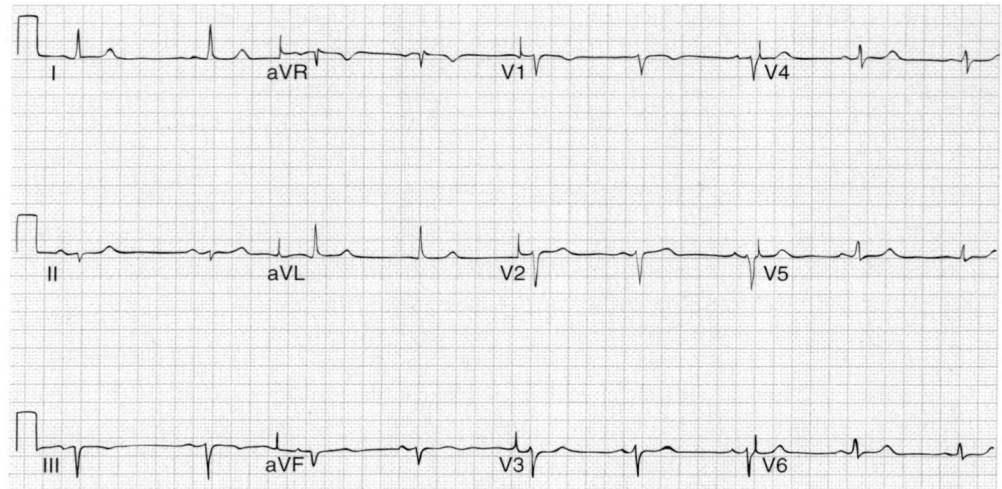

Figure 78-12. Sinus dysrhythmia (note slight irregularity).

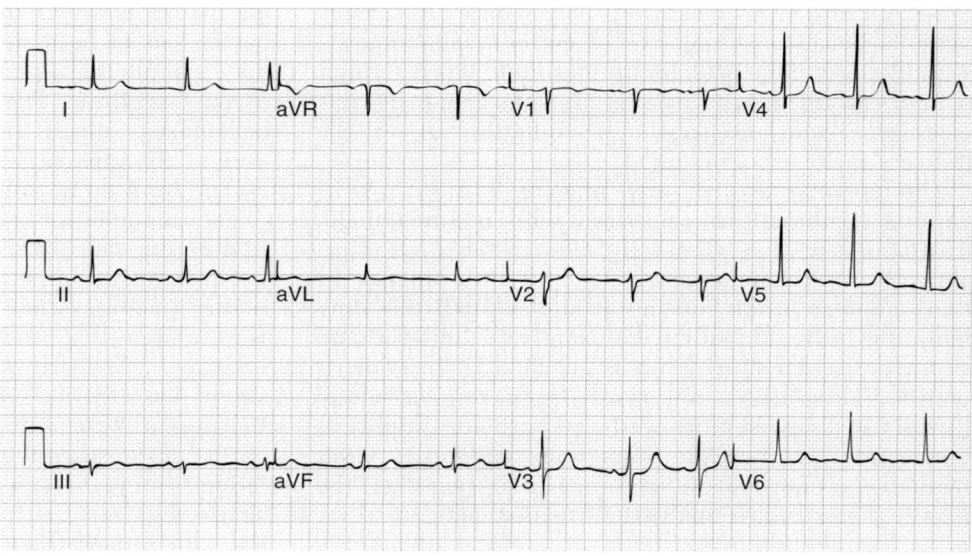

condition such as hypothermia or acute myocardial ischemia.

Sinus and Atrial Dysrhythmias

Sinus dysrhythmia is seen at variable rates in the normal ranges. The ECG features are similar to those of sinus bradycardia, aside from the varying and normal ventricular rate (Figure 78-12). Atrial dysrhythmias have ECG features similar to those of sinus dysrhythmias, except that an atrial source other than the sinus node serves as the pacemaker, producing P′ waves that are consistent in structure yet different from the sinus P waves. The P′R interval may also vary from the normal sinus PR interval, which distinguishes these rhythms. Both dysrhythmias may be normal variants, with sinus dysrhythmias often resulting from respiratory variation. Neither has clinical significance except that they may be confused with other dysrhythmias. No treatment is required for these rhythms.

Sinoatrial Block and Escape Rhythms

The underlying feature of SA block is absent atrial depolarization, characterized by missing P waves. This lack of atrial depolarization occurs for three reasons: (1) failure of the sinus node to generate an impulse, (2) failure of impulse conduction out of the SA node, or (3) failure of the impulse to activate the atria, from either inability of the atria to depolarize or an inadequate stimulus intensity. SA block can be the result of ischemia, hyperkalemia, increased vagal tone, or drug therapy including ß-blockers, calcium channel blockers, and digitalis.

Incomplete SA block is diagnosed when an occasional P wave is dropped from the normal P-QRS-T sequence on the ECG. There are no P waves on the ECG (Figure 78-13) in complete SA block (sinus arrest). Usually, a lower pacemaker emerges in complete SA block; if this pacemaker is within the AV node, the QRS complex is narrow and results in an "idiojunctional"

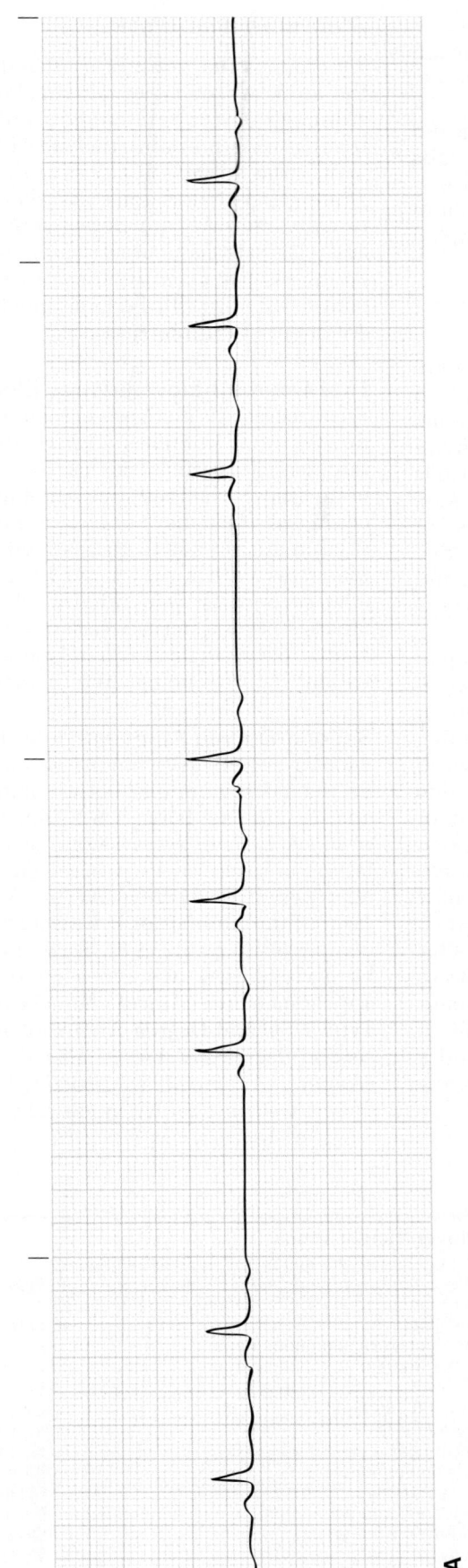

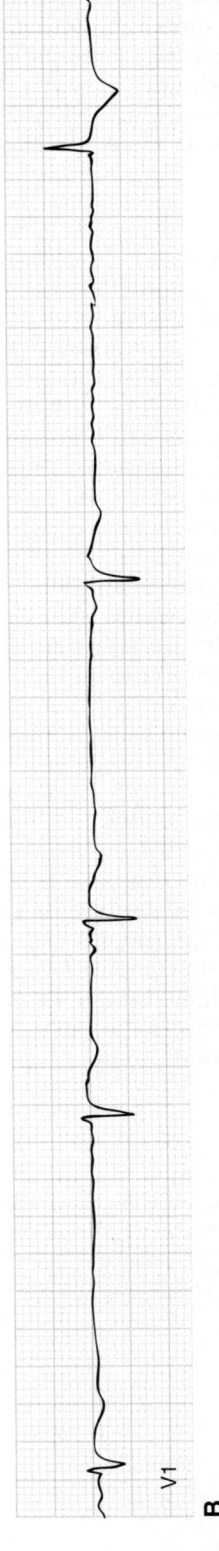

Figure 78-13. A, Incomplete sinus block. **B,** Complete sinus block (sinus arrest) with ventricular escape rhythm.

escape rhythm at a rate of 45 to 60 beats/min. Pacemakers within the His-Purkinje system usually result in a wide-complex "idioventricular" escape rhythm at a rate of 30 to 45 beats/min.

The treatment of SA block is based on symptoms and includes atropine (aside from the setting of digitalis toxicity) and temporary pacing. Patients without evidence of hypoperfusion should be observed without treatment. Type I antidysrhythmics should be avoided because they may extinguish an escape rhythm.

Sinus Node Dysfunction (Sick Sinus Syndrome)

This syndrome refers to a myriad of overlapping pathologic states ranging from frequent sinus pauses and bradycardia to the tachycardia-bradycardia syndrome. The latter represents bursts of an atrial tachydysrhythmia, usually atrial fibrillation, alternating with periods of sinus or atrial bradycardia. The tachycardia-bradycardia syndrome usually occurs in elderly persons but is also associated with ischemia, inflammatory diseases, cardiomyopathy, connective tissue diseases, and drug therapy (especially ß-blockers, calcium channel blockers, digitalis, and quinidine).

The diagnosis is made when symptoms, such as palpitations or syncope, are correlated with the bradycardia or tachycardia, usually through outpatient Holter monitoring. The ECG manifestations vary, depending on the rhythm at presentation. Treatment consists of rate stimulation (with atropine or a pacemaker) or rate control (with calcium channel blockers, ß-blockers, or digitalis) when symptoms of hypoperfusion coexist. Either modality should be attempted with caution because excessive bradycardia or tachycardia may result, although generally the response is blunted (i.e., the heart rate increases to 90 beats/min or less after atropine). Recognition and referral are the mainstays of emergency department management. Long-term management is often accomplished by a combination of an antidysrhythmic to suppress the tachycardia and a demand pacemaker (to provide a "floor" against excessive bradycardia).

Atrioventricular Block

AV block is the result of impaired conduction through the atria, AV node, or proximal His-Purkinje system. Although electrophysiologic studies using His bundle tracings can pinpoint the area of conduction disturbance, the surface ECG can provide information and guide clinical decisions. AV block has been conventionally divided into three grades, based on the ECG and clinical characteristics. First- and second-degree AV blocks represent an incomplete conduction disturbance, whereas third-degree block indicates complete AV conduction interruption.

First-Degree Atrioventricular Block

First-degree AV block is defined as prolonged conduction of atrial impulses without the loss of any single impulse. This can occur at the level of the atria, AV node (most common), or His-Purkinje system (least common). On the ECG, a regular narrow-complex rhythm at slow (40 to 60 beats/min) to normal ventricular rates with a prolonged PR interval (greater than 0.20 second) is seen (Figure 78-14). First-degree AV block is often a normal variant without clinical significance, occurring in 1.6% of healthy young adults. This variant requires no specific treatment.[50]

Second-Degree Atrioventricular Block

Second-degree AV block is an intermediate step between every impulse being conducted (albeit slowly) and no impulses being conducted. On the ECG this type of block is manifested as one or more sinus impulses failing to reach the ventricles. The *conduction ratio* in all types of incomplete AV block is described as the ratio of the number of P waves to the number of QRS complexes (e.g., 3:2, 4:3). Second-degree AV block can be divided into two types on the basis of the ECG appearance and clinical characteristics (Table 78-4).

Type I Second-Degree Atrioventricular Block. Type I second-degree AV block, also called *Wenckebach* or *Mobitz I AV block*, is associated with a conduction deficit within the AV node. On the surface ECG, a

Table 78-4. Characteristics of Second-Degree Atrioventricular Block

Feature	Type I	Type II
Clinical	Usually acute	Often chronic
	Inferior myocardial infarction	Anteroseptal
	Rheumatic fever	Lenègre disease
		Lev disease
	Digitalis or β-blockers	Cardiomyopathy
Anatomic	Usually AV node	Infranodal
Electrophysiology	Increased relative refractory period	No relative refractory period
	Decremental conduction	All-or-none conduction
ECG features	RP/PR reciprocity	PR interval stable
	Prolonged PR interval	PR interval usually normal
	QRS duration normal	QRS duration prolonged
Response to atropine and exercise	Improves	Worsens
Response to carotid massage	Worsens	Improves*

*Primarily refers to conduction ratio.
AV, atrioventricular; ECG, electrocardiographic.

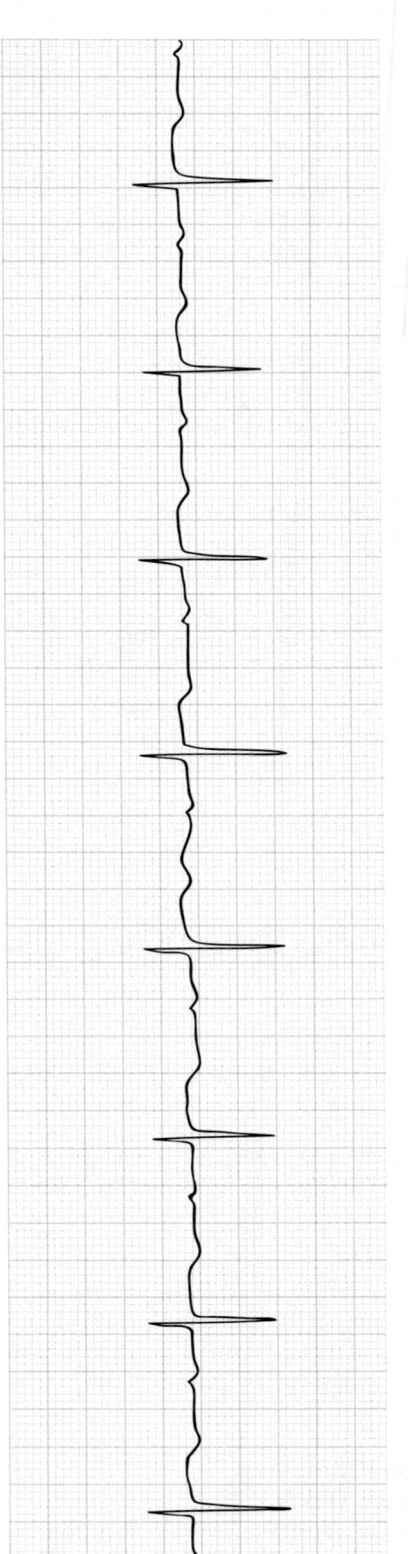

Figure 78-14. First-degree atrioventricular block.

narrow-complex rhythm with the following three basic characteristics is seen (Figure 78-15):

- Grouped beating (especially pairs or trios, but occasionally larger groups).
- Progressive lengthening of the PR interval until an impulse is not conducted ("dropped beat").
- The longest cycle (of the dropped beat) is less than twice the length of the shortest (usually the impulse after the dropped beat).

The progressive lengthening of the PR interval gives the appearance of successive P waves retreating into the preceding QRS complexes. This highlights another feature of type I block, the concept of *RP/PR reciprocity*. This means that as the interval between the preceding R wave and the next P wave becomes shorter, the PR interval of the next cycle becomes longer until an impulse is dropped.

Type I second-degree AV block occurs in a variety of acute and chronic conditions (see Table 78-4) and usually requires no treatment. In the setting of acute myocardial infarction, this type of AV block is associated with inferior wall ischemia and a good outcome. Children with asymptomatic type I second-degree AV block may eventually develop complete heart block but usually remain asymptomatic because of adequate subsidiary pacemaker function. Carotid massage and increased vagal tone worsen type I block, whereas atropine and isoproterenol improve conduction.

The Wenckebach phenomenon can occur in other conduction disturbances, including SA block, producing grouped impulses. Grouped impulses should always raise the question, "Is a Wenckebach mechanism present?" Not all grouped impulses are caused by this phenomenon (Box 78-6).

Type II Second-Degree Atrioventricular Block. Type II second-degree AV block, or *Mobitz II block*, is never a normal variant and implies a conduction block below the level of the AV node, usually in the His-Purkinje system. On the ECG, intermittent conduction of atrial impulses occurs without changes in the PR interval (Figure 78-16). The QRS complex of conducted beats is often narrow, but wide-complex beats may result if infranodal conduction disturbances (e.g., bundle branch block) or escape impulses are present. Type II second-degree AV block is associated with a variety of acute and chronic diseases (see Table 78-4). Compared with type I second-degree AV block, type II block carries a worse prognosis. In acute myocardial infarction, type II AV block is associated with anterior wall ischemia and often progresses to complete AV block.

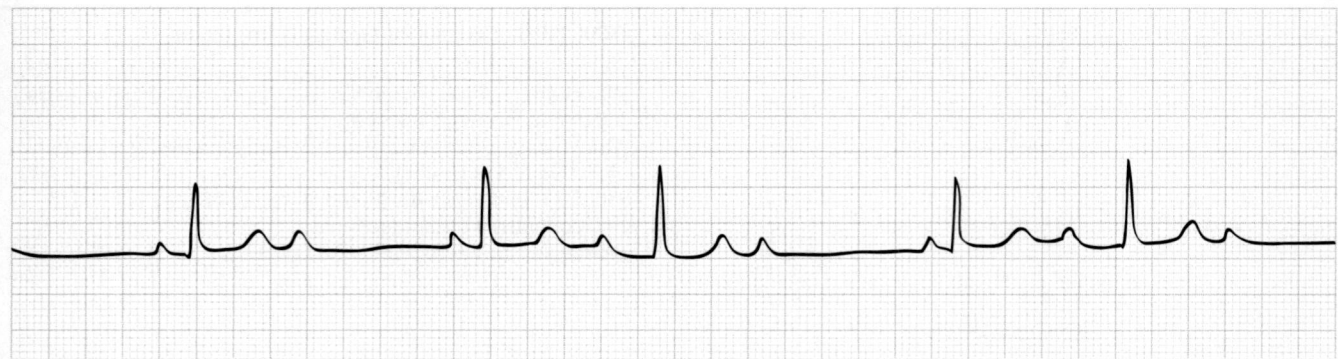

Figure 78-15. Second-degree atrioventricular block, type I (Wenckebach). Note the prolongation of the PR interval between the second and third beats followed by a nonconducted atrial impulse.

Mobitz type II second-degree AV block

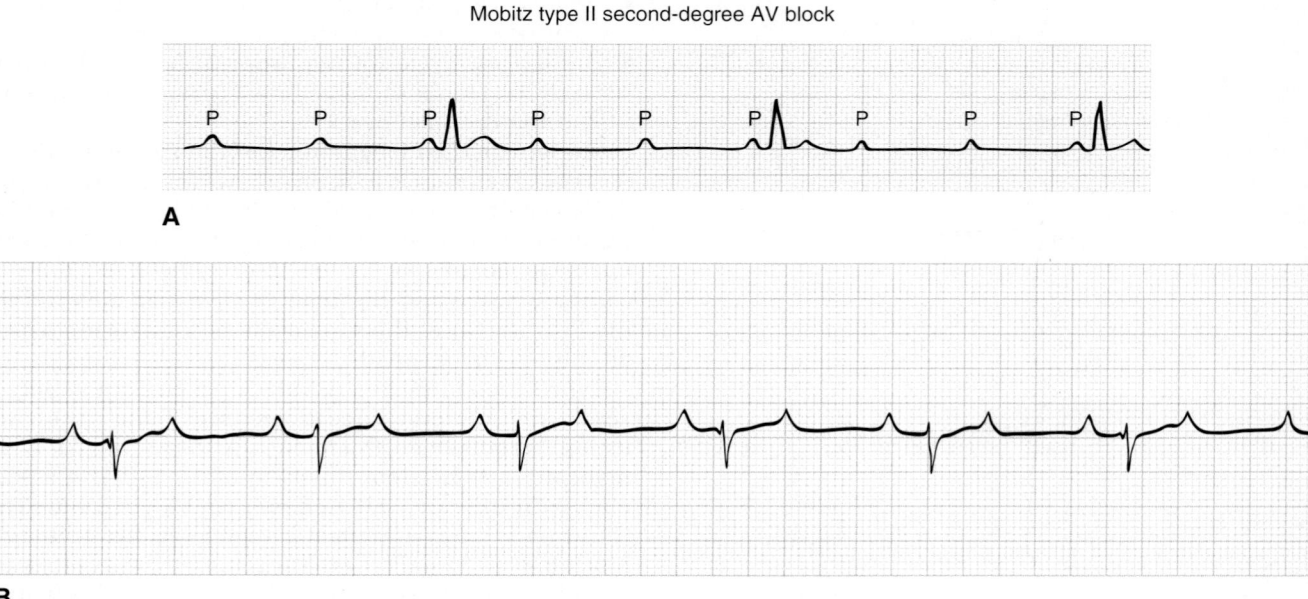

A

B

Figure 78-16. A, Second-degree atrioventricular (AV) block, type II. In this example, 3:1 conduction is seen. **B,** Second-degree AV block with 2:1 conduction. From the rhythm strip alone, it is difficult to categorize this as type I or II block. (**A,** From Goldberger AL, Goldberger E: *Clinical Electrocardiography*, 2nd ed. St. Louis, Mosby, 1981.)

This variety of block is further complicated by poor subsidiary pacemaker function and mandates that temporary pacing be readily available.

When the conduction ratio is 2:1, it may be impossible to distinguish type I from type II AV block on the ECG. The response to autonomic manipulation, however, can aid in this task. Atropine usually has no effect on the His-Purkinje system[51] and may worsen the conduction ratio in type II AV block by increasing the number of atrial impulses without improving conduction (although clinical deterioration is not likely). Carotid sinus massage may transiently improve the conduction ratio (but not the overall condition) in type II AV block by slowing the conduction in the proximal AV node, allowing the lower conductive tissues to recover and be less refractory.

Pharmacologic treatment of type II AV block is not indicated. In the prehospital setting, symptomatic type II second-degree AV block should be treated with transcutaneous pacing; in the emergency department,

transcutaneous or transvenous pacing can be used. Emergent cardiology consultation should be sought for all patients, and none should be discharged to home unless the condition is chronic and without new symptoms.

Third-Degree (Complete) Atrioventricular Block

Third-degree, or *complete*, AV block is characterized by absent conduction of all atrial impulses (Figure 78-17) resulting in complete electrical and mechanical AV dissociation. Not all AV dissociation is complete heart block; for complete heart block to exist, the underlying supraventricular or junctional rhythm must be of a rate sufficient to overcome the action of any subsidiary infranodal pacemakers. For example, an accelerated junctional focus at 80 beats/min (as a result of enhanced automaticity from catecholamine excess) may usurp the sinus node and become the dominant pacemaker. In this situation, the underlying sinus

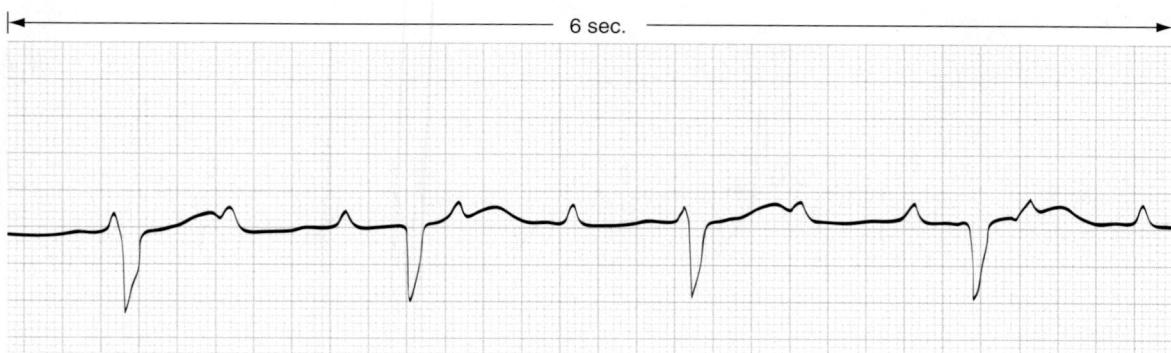

Figure 78-17. Complete (third-degree) atrioventricular block. Note that there is no constant relationship of P waves to QRS complexes even though some are noted in close proximity.

rhythm of less than 80 beats/min would be manifest as regular P waves unrelated to the source of ventricular depolarization, the junctional rhythm. This junctional rhythm is not complete heart block because no underlying AV nodal conduction disorder is present. In a similar fashion, complete SA block coupled with a junctional or ventricular escape rhythm can be misidentified as complete AV block (see Figure 78-13).

During complete heart block, the P waves and QRS complexes are present but are unrelated and occur at different rates. When the atrial and escape rates are similar, *isorhythmic AV dissociation* exists; this can be difficult to appreciate unless a long rhythm strip is examined and the P waves and QRS complexes are closely tracked. The duration of the QRS complex depends on the site of the escape rhythm pacemaker; pacemakers above the His bundle produce a narrow complex, whereas pacemakers at or below the His bundle produce a wide-complex rhythm. The narrow-complex rhythms usually operate at a faster rate (45 to 60 beats/min) and respond to atropine and isoproterenol; the wide-complex escape rhythms are slower (30 to 45 beats/min) and are unaffected by autonomic drugs. When atrial P or fibrillatory waves are coupled with a slow and regular ventricular response, atrial tachycardia or fibrillation with third-degree heart block and a junctional rhythm should be suspected; this combination is commonly the result of digitalis toxicity.

Third-degree AV block can be congenital or acquired. In general, congenital third-degree AV block is associated with a narrow-complex escape rhythm and fewer symptoms. The fixed rate of the subsidiary pacemaker limits the ability to increase cardiac output, with exercise intolerance of varying degrees resulting. Acquired third-degree block is often associated with a wide-complex escape rhythm and symptoms of hypoperfusion at rest or with minimal exertion.

In the field, the treatment of patients with third-degree AV block depends on the symptoms. Patients with clinical evidence of hypoperfusion can receive atropine but are best treated with transcutaneous pacing. A concern regarding atropine in third-degree heart block is that worse conduction rates can occur, but in practice, clinical deterioration (and improvement) is rare. Asymptomatic patients should be rapidly

transported with the preceding therapies readily available and care taken to avoid maneuvers that increase vagal tone (e.g., Valsalva maneuver, painful stimuli).

In the emergency department, the treatment includes close assessment of the patient's hemodynamic status. The patient should be admitted to an appropriate monitoring unit if acquired or symptomatic third-degree AV block is diagnosed. A transvenous temporary pacemaker is usually indicated but can be placed electively if the transcutaneous pacemaker is functioning well. Isoproterenol should be used only after failure of atropine when pacing is unavailable. Type I antidysrhythmics should be avoided because they may extinguish the escape rhythm.

This classification scheme has shortcomings. The conduction ratio depends on the atrial rate and the presence of underlying nodal pathology. A 2:1 conduction ratio does not necessarily imply more conduction system disease than a 3:2 ratio, and not all 2:1 conduction is pathologic. The following two examples of 2:1 AV conduction help illustrate the latter point. An atrial impulse rate of 300 beats/min (as seen in atrial flutter) presented to the AV node usually results in conduction of half the impulses, producing a ventricular rate of 150 beats/min; this conduction ratio does not represent significant AV block because the AV node is responding normally and preventing excessive ventricular stimulation. Conversely, a sinus rhythm at a rate of 70 beats/min paired with a similar conduction ratio produces a ventricular rate of 35 beats/min; this ratio clearly represents significant second-degree AV block. The term "high-grade second-degree block" should be applied to conduction disturbances that prevent physiologic ventricular response rates and not solely to higher conduction ratios.

Extrasystoles and Parasystole

Extrasystoles, defined as ectopic impulses that occur in addition to the underlying normal sinus rhythm, are present in most individuals when closely monitored. Certain specific extrasystoles may help identify patients with a poor prognosis when coupled with symptoms. Not all extra impulses are translated into mechanical contractions; even without associated con-

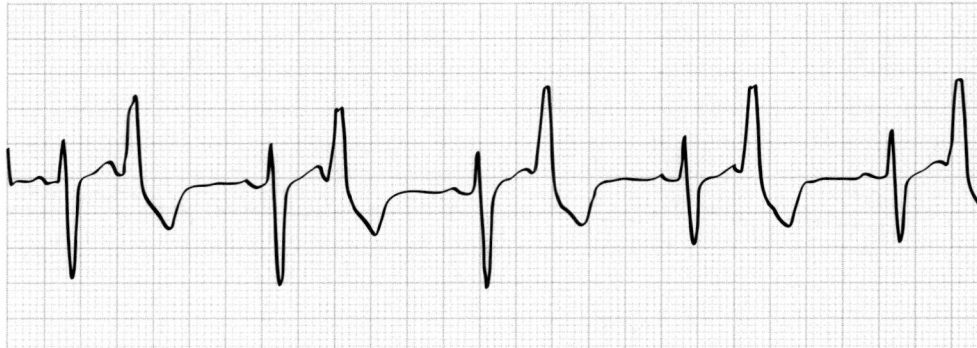

Figure 78-18. Ventricular bigeminy.

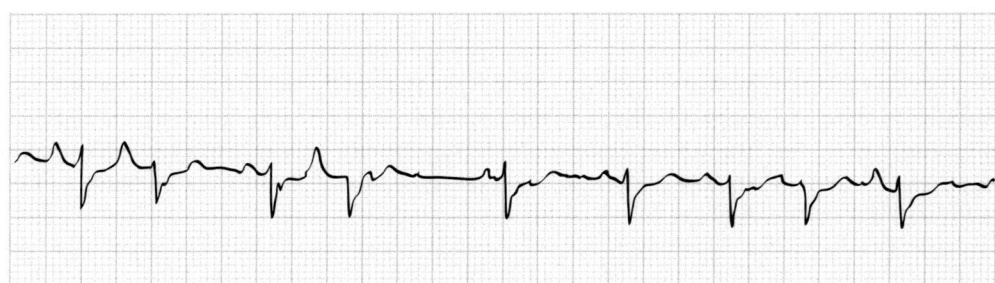

Figure 78-19. Premature atrial contractions.

tractions nonconducted impulses can trigger a secondary irregularity of the pulse by interfering with conduction. In fact, the most common cause of a pause on the ECG is a nonconducted atrial extrasystole that resets the SA node.

The mechanism responsible for most extrasystoles is abnormal automaticity, although some can result from reentry or triggered automaticity. In general, ectopic impulses occur earlier in a cardiac cycle than the normal sinus impulse and are termed *premature*. By convention, the term *contraction* is applied to these extra impulses, although a true mechanical contraction may not always occur. The source of these ectopic impulses can be the atria, AV node, His-Purkinje system, or ventricles. *Bigeminy* occurs when an extrasystole follows every sinus beat, and *trigeminy* occurs when every third beat is extrasystolic (Figure 78-18). These forms can occur with any of the three sources (atria, junction, or ventricles) and are usually benign rhythms.

The extrasystole and its preceding beat are referred to as the *couplet*, and the *coupling interval* refers to the period between these two beats. When the coupling interval in a given rhythm is constant (or "fixed"), a single focus is believed to be responsible for the extrasystoles. Although previously considered to be solely the result of reentry, fixed coupling does not reliably define the mechanism of ectopic impulse formation. There are three basic extrasystolic foci, along with a specific form of abnormal impulse generation and propagation called *parasystole*.

Premature Atrial Contractions

Premature atrial contractions (PACs) are often the precipitating event for a variety of dysrhythmias, including atrial fibrillation, atrial flutter, and supraventricular tachycardia. Abnormal automaticity and atrial or AV nodal reentry are the most common causes of PACs. The diagnosis of PACs is made from the ECG, where an abnormal P′ wave is seen early within a cardiac cycle (Figure 78-19). The P′ wave may be difficult to see if it is buried within the preceding T wave, although increasing the paper speed and use of an esophageal lead can help. Inverted P′ waves suggest an atrial source near the AV junction, where nearly normal P′ waves imply a focus near the SA node. If the P′ waves, P′R intervals, and coupling intervals are constant, a single focus is likely. Variations in these three characteristics are consistent with multiple foci. Either the left or right atrium can be the source of PACs.

Most PACs depolarize the sinus node, which resets the intrinsic sinus node rate. On the ECG, the PP interval after a conducted PAC is equal to the PP interval of the cycle preceding the PAC. Because of this adjustment of the sinus cycle, the RR interval surrounding the ectopic beat is less than twice the intrinsic RR cycle length (see Figure 78-19). This is referred to as a *noncompensatory pause*, a hallmark of PACs. Occasionally, PACs do not depolarize the sinus node, and a compensatory pause may result. Fully compensatory pauses are more commonly seen with premature ventricular contractions (PVCs). Table 78-5 lists ECG features to help distinguish PACs from PVCs.

If it is conducted to the ventricles, a PAC results in a QRS complex occurring earlier than the expected sinus QRS complex. The QRS complex from a PAC is narrow and identical to the sinus rhythm complex unless aberrant conduction occurs (Figure 78-20). Aberrancy is likely to occur if a PAC arrives early within the cardiac cycle, with a right bundle branch block pattern commonly seen on the ECG. In a similar fashion, a PAC that follows a long cardiac cycle (reflected as a preceding long RR interval) may also be aberrantly conducted because the bundles require more time to repolarize. In the latter setting, aberrant conduction occurs because of the relatively early arrival of the PAC for the given cycle length. This aberrant conduction is called the Ashman phenomenon and can occur with any irregular atrial rhythm, including PACs and atrial fibrillation.

A PAC is the most common cause of a pause on the ECG. Although the source of this type of pause is obvious when a PAC is conducted, nonconducted PACs are frequently responsible for pauses. In this situation, the sinus node is depolarized by the PAC, causing an interruption and resetting of the regular rate. If the same extrasystolic impulse reaches the AV node or infranodal conducting system during the refractory period, no ventricular depolarization is possible. This combined sinus node reset with a nonconducted atrial extrasystole creates the pause seen on the ECG. Often the PAC responsible for a pause falls within the previous T wave and is not visible on the ECG.

On rare occasions an extremely late PAC can cause atrial depolarization in combination with the sinus node impulse. The P′ waves in these cases represent a *fusion complex* and have qualities of both impulses.

The management of PACs is based on recognition, with no need for specific therapy. Underlying causes, such as catecholamine excess, hypoxia, myocardial ischemia, congestive heart failure, or acid-base and electrolyte imbalance, should be treated if symptomatic or frequent PACs occur. If caused by a reentrant mechanism, frequent PACs can be terminated with a calcium channel blocker, a ß-adrenergic blocker, or magnesium; however, this treatment is rarely needed.

Premature Junctional Contractions

Premature junctional contractions (PJCs) are the result of either altered automaticity or nodal microreentry. On the ECG, a P′ wave from retrograde atrial depolarization is buried within the QRS complex, and the extrasystole appears as a lone additional QRS complex (from a high nodal focus) that may be seen as a result of retrograde conduction to the atria. If seen, the P′ waves from PJCs are usually inverted because of the opposite direction of the depolarization wave compared with the normal sinus impulses and can be difficult to distinguish from PACs emanating from a low atrial source. If a high nodal focus is involved, the QRS complex is narrow; wide QRS complexes imply a lower His source or abnormal infranodal conduction (bundle branch block).

Table 78-5. **Features to Distinguish Premature Atrial Contractions with Abnormal Conduction from Premature Ventricular Contractions**

Premature Atrial Contractions	Premature Ventricular Contractions
No compensatory pause	Fully compensatory pause (unless interpolated)
Preceding P wave (different from sinus P wave; occasionally buried in T wave)	No preceding P waves (although retrograde atrial conduction can cause inverted P wave after QRS)
Usually classical right bundle branch block pattern (especially if long-short cycle sequence appears)	Left bundle branch block, right bundle branch block, or hybrid pattern
Initial QRS deflection identical to sinus QRS	Bizarre QRS structure
QRS axis normal or near normal	Frequently bizarre QRS axis
QRS rarely > 0.14 sec	QRS often > 1.14 sec

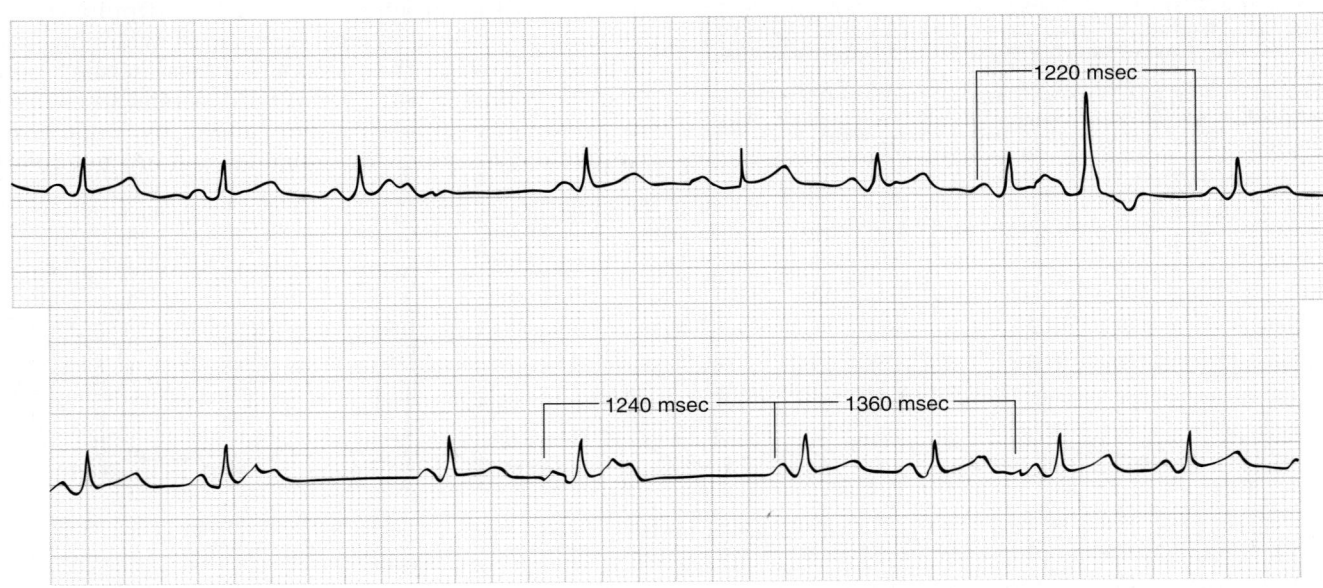

Figure 78-20. Premature atrial contractions (PACs) with noncompensatory pauses and one aberrantly conducted impulse *(upper strip)*. Note that both conducted and nonconducted PACs reset the sinus node, with the latter creating a pause.

Fully compensatory pauses and aberrant conduction occur more often with PJCs than with PACs. The causes and treatment of PJCs are the same as those of PACs.

Premature Ventricular Contractions

PVCs can occur in a variety of pathologic and non-pathologic states. Their major importance is related to the clinical scenario accompanying their presence and the risk of more serious ventricular dysrhythmias (i.e., ventricular tachycardia and fibrillation).[52] Extrasystoles that occur during ventricular repolarization (the "R-on-T phenomenon") are believed to carry a higher risk of precipitating ventricular tachycardia, although the magnitude of this effect is debated. Other data suggest that PVCs occurring during the next atrial depolarization (the "R-on-P phenomenon") carry as high or a higher risk of precipitating serious ventricular dysrhythmias as R-on-T PVCs.[53]

BOX 78-7. Causes of Premature Ventricular Contractions and Ventricular Tachycardia

Acute myocardial infarction
Hypokalemia
Hypoxemia
Ischemic heart disease
Valvular disease
Catecholamine excess*
Other drug intoxications
Idiopathic causes†
Digitalis toxicity
Hypomagnesemia
Hypercapnia
Type I agents
Alcohol
Myocardial contusion (especially cyclic antidepressants)
Cardiomyopathy
Acidosis
Alkalosis
Methylxanthine toxicity

---

*Relative increase in sympathetic tone from drugs (direct or indirect) or conditions that augment catecholamine release or decrease parasympathetic tone.
†Isolated PVCs can occur in up to 50% of young subjects without obvious cardiac or noncardiac disease; however, multiform and repetitive PVCs and ventricular tachycardia are rarely seen in this population.

PVCs can be caused by varying mechanisms (Box 78-7), including reentry, abnormal automaticity, and triggered afterdepolarizations. Classically, PVCs appear on the ECG as wide QRS complex extrasystoles (greater than 0.12 second) unassociated with a preceding P wave (Figure 78-21). In a single lead a PVC may appear as a narrow QRS complex. This narrow complex occurs if the wave of depolarization is traveling directly perpendicular to the ECG lead and underscores the need to examine multiple leads to identify PVCs accurately. Although P waves from nonconducted sinus impulses may be seen on the ECG, these should have no consistent relationship with the QRS complexes from the PVCs. Rarely, retrograde conduction of PVCs can produce an inverted P′ wave after each QRS complex. PVCs usually cause a fully compensatory pause, with the resulting RR interval encompassing the PVC equal to twice the intrinsic RR interval length (see Figure 78-21). Rarely, noncompensatory or subcompensatory pauses can be seen with PVCs and are associated with retrograde conduction and sinus node depolarization. *Interpolated PVCs* refer to another rare instance when the underlying sinus rhythm is unaffected by a PVC (Figure 78-22).

The structure of the QRS complexes depends on the origin of the impulse. PVCs with a left bundle branch appearance result from a wave of depolarization beginning in a right ventricular source and vice versa. Multiform (or "multifocal") PVCs refer to ventricular extrasystoles from more than one source and appear as varying QRS complex structures. When a PVC depolarizes the ventricles at a similar time as a conducted atrial beat, a *fusion QRS complex* is seen (Figure 78-23). Identification of fusion QRS beats indicates the presence of PVCs.

PVCs produce abnormal repolarization as a direct result of the abnormal depolarization of the ventricles. *Secondary T wave abnormalities* refer to the repolarization changes seen as a result of pathologic depolarization and are seen with PVCs along with bundle branch blocks and left ventricular hypertrophy. These secondary T wave changes consist of widening and deflection opposite the main QRS deflection (see Figure 78-21). *Primary T wave abnormalities* refer to changes in ventricular repolarization caused by underlying cardiac disease (such as ischemia) and are not solely

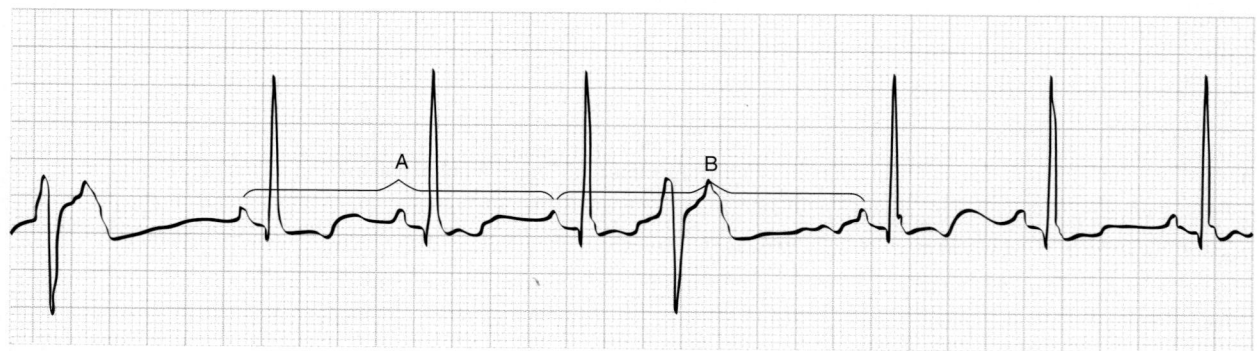

Figure 78-21. Premature ventricular contractions with compensatory pause. Note that a sinus P wave can be seen in the T wave of the extrasystolic beat. Also note the secondary T wave changes in beats 1 and 4 (T wave is opposite the main deflection of the QRS complex).

the result of depolarization abnormalities. Primary T wave changes often consist of T wave deflection in the same direction as the main QRS vector.

The pattern of PVCs is commonly classified by the Lown criteria (Table 78-6). In general, these criteria are intended to distinguish benign PVCs from those likely to degenerate into ventricular tachycardia and ventricular fibrillation. After myocardial infarction, PVCs in Lown classes 3 to 5 carry a high risk for these malignant ventricular dysrhythmias and sudden death, with class 4 having the highest risk. The use of this classification system in other patients with PVCs does not predict the risk of morbidity and mortality. PVCs are found in healthy young patients and their frequency generally increases with age.

Therapy for PVCs is directed toward correcting the underlying cause, especially if ischemia, electrolyte imbalance, or drug overdose is evident. Often, PVCs are not symptomatic aside from a sensation of palpitations; when antidysrhythmics are given, they are intended as prophylaxis against ventricular fibrillation and ventricular tachycardia. In the absence of ischemia, asymptomatic PVCs alone rarely require antidysrhythmic therapy. Although lidocaine can lessen or abolish PVCs in the setting of acute myocardial infarction, it is recommended only when PVCs in Lown classes 3 to 5 are present or close monitoring and rapid defibrillation capabilities are not readily available.

The difficulty of delivery limits the use of all class I agents except lidocaine in the prehospital setting, but treatment of PVCs is rarely, if ever, indicated there. In the emergency department, alternative agents such as amiodarone and procainamide are options for the few cases in need, although lidocaine remains the primary agent used. In selected cases, ß-blockers (e.g., for catecholamine-induced PVCs and those occurring after myocardial infarction) and calcium channel blockers (after reperfusion therapy) can diminish PVC frequency and decrease the risk of ventricular fibrillation and ventricular tachycardia. Magnesium sulfate (2 to 4 g IV over 10 to 20 minutes) can also diminish the frequency of PVCs, particularly in the setting of acute myocardial ischemia.

Patients with syncope, presyncope, dyspnea, chest pain, or frequent palpitations associated with PVCs should be monitored. This can be done on either an inpatient basis (if the symptoms noted are reported) or an outpatient basis (with a Holter monitor if otherwise asymptomatic in the emergency department) after an evaluation to eliminate the causes listed in Box 78-7.

Parasystole

Parasystole occurs when two separate pacemakers compete to produce ventricular depolarization in the absence of structural conduction disease.[54] The latter distinguishes parasystole from high-grade incomplete

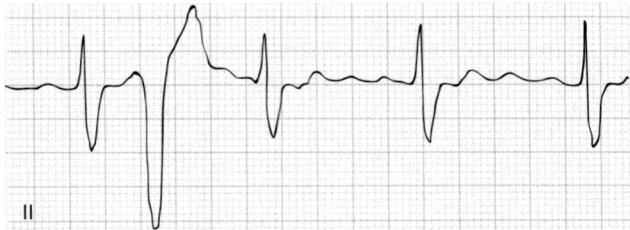

Figure 78-22. Interpolated premature ventricular contraction.

Table 78-6. Lown Classification of Premature Ventricular Contractions

Class	Description
0	None
1	<30/hr
2	30 or more/hr
3	Multiform (or multifocal)
4A	Two consecutive
4B	Three or more consecutive
5	R on T phenomenon

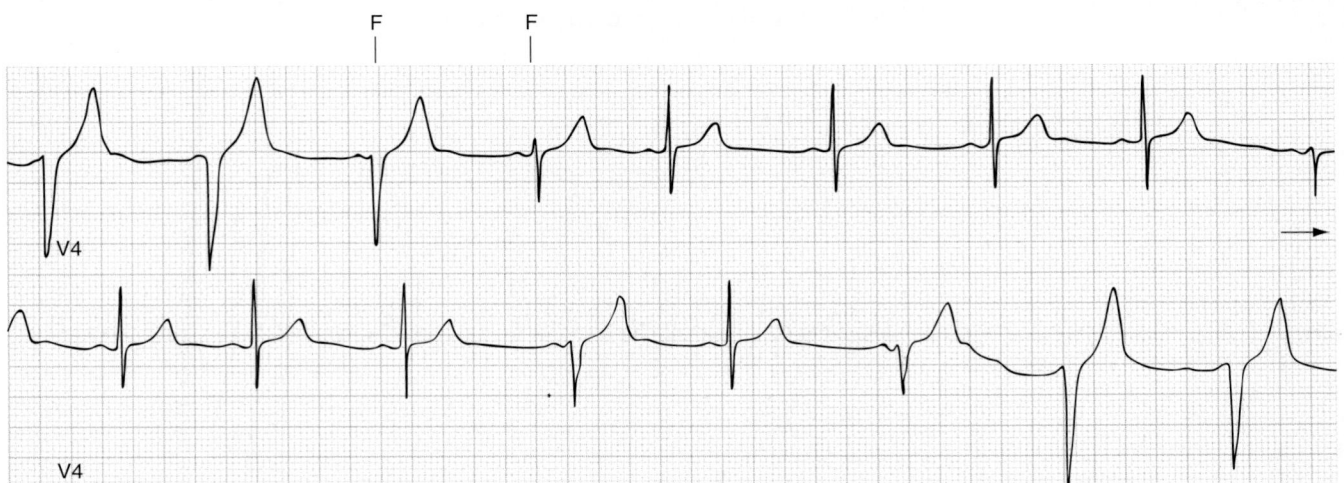

Figure 78-23. Sinus rhythm with run of accelerated idioventricular rhythm. Note fusion beats (F) displaying hybrid appearance of both morphologies.

or complete AV block. In addition to the sinus node, the usual source of the second pacemaker is the ventricular conductive or contractile tissues, although atrial and junctional pacemakers can also cause parasystole. The key point in identifying the competing pacemaker is that it functions like an artificial fixed-rate pacemaker, producing impulses irrespective of the sinus node activity. The second pacemaker displays an entrance block, which prevents any outside impulse from depolarizing the area and resetting the rhythm.

Ventricular parasystole has five characteristics on the ECG in addition to its wide QRS extrasystolic complexes and fixed rate[54] (Box 78-8) (Figure 78-24). One hallmark of parasystole is a fixed interectopic interval. In this, the R'R' intervals are the same throughout a rhythm strip or follow a similar denominator. This is a direct result of the protected parasystolic focus; if all impulses exiting this focus find the conducting system nonrefractory, a fixed interectopic interval is observed. If the conducting tissues are refractory (usually from recent conduction of a sinus impulse), no ventricular depolarization is seen on the ECG, yet the protected parasystolic focus continues to fire at the same rate. If the next impulse from the parasystolic focus finds nonrefractory conducting tissues, the interectopic interval is equal to two times the basic cycle length; if the first and second parasystolic impulses are not conducted but the third in a series finds nonrefractory tissues, the interectopic interval is three times the basic cycle length. For example, based on a 1-second interval, ven-tricular parasystole may have R'R' intervals in multiples of this interval (e.g., impulses seen 1, 2, or 3 seconds apart at various times).

Ventricular parasystole is usually the result of an altered automatic mechanism and does not have the serious implications that frequent PVCs have even when an R-on-T phenomenon is seen. Ventricular parasystole may be difficult to distinguish from frequent PVCs in the field because it requires close observation of a prolonged rhythm strip with multiple leads. Fusion QRS complexes may be seen but are not essential to the diagnosis. Ventricular parasystole is usually a benign rhythm, with treatment similar to that of non–ischemia-related PVCs.

Atrial and junctional parasystoles are rare and are more difficult to diagnose.[55] They can be identified when P' waves or junctional impulses are seen throughout an underlying sinus rhythm with a fixed interectopic interval. As with ventricular parasystole, the P'-P' intervals or junctional RR intervals should be the same or in multiples of a common interval. Atrial and junctional parasystoles are usually benign and require no specific emergency therapy.

Narrow-Complex Tachycardia

Narrow-complex tachycardias are defined as rhythms with a QRS complex duration of less than 0.12 second and a ventricular rate of greater than 100 beats/min.[56,57] Although virtually all narrow-complex tachydysrhythmias originate from a focus above the ventricles (with the rare exception of a very high His bundle rhythm), the term *supraventricular tachycardia* is conventionally used to denote the rhythms aside from sinus tachycardia, atrial tachycardia, atrial fibrillation, and atrial flutter. The atrial depolarization waves may be difficult to appreciate on the ECG, especially if the ventricular response rate is over 150 beats/min. The use of multiple-surface leads, increased paper speed, an esophageal lead, or vagal maneuvers can help identify the atrial depolarization waves and diagnose the source of the dysrhythmia. Also, atrial or junctional parasystole can create a narrow-complex tachycardia, termed *pseudo-tachycardia* because neither focus has a rate greater than 100 beats/min.

BOX 78-8. Electrocardiographic Features of Ventricular Parasystole

Protected pacemaker—fixed discharge rate (although all impulses may not be evident on ECG)
Wide QRS complexes
Interectopic intervals fixed or in multiples of shortest interval
Fusion beats if simultaneous to conducted sinus impulse (not mandatory for diagnosis)
Variable coupling intervals

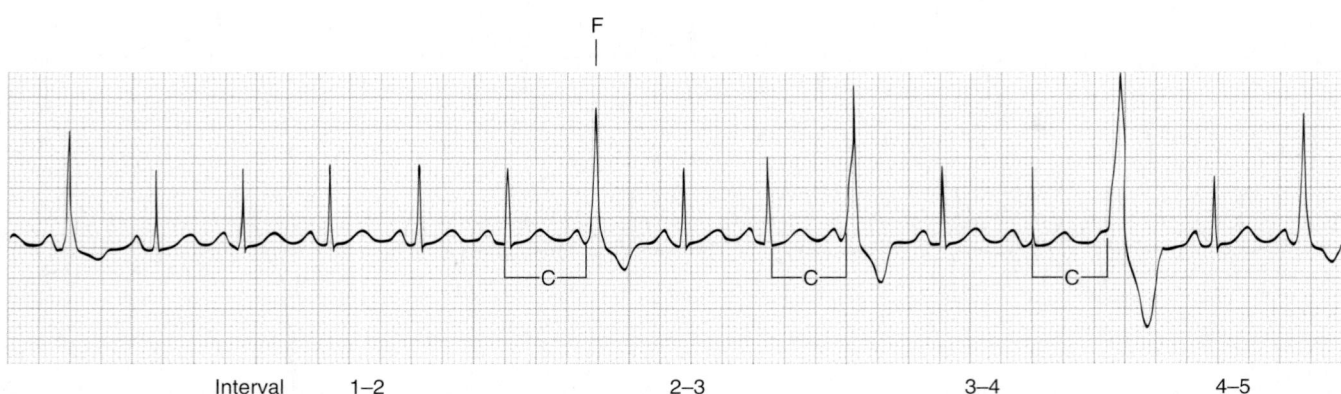

| Interval | 1–2 | 2–3 | 3–4 | 4–5 |

Figure 78-24. Ventricular parasystole. Fusion (F) beats are seen, and coupling intervals (C) vary. Interectopic intervals are all based on a common denominator (0.4 second).

One ECG feature that can help distinguish the source of a tachydysrhythmia is the location of the P waves and the regularity of the QRS complexes. If nearly normal appearing atrial depolarization waves precede each QRS complex and the underlying pattern is regular, a sinus rhythm, atrial flutter, or single-focus atrial tachycardia is commonly present. If a completely irregular (or chaotic) pattern of QRS complexes is seen, atrial fibrillation, multifocal atrial tachycardia, or one of the rhythms with varying conduction is possible (Box 78-9). The identification of atrial depolarization waves and the appearance of irregularity or regularity can be deceiving within any short rhythm strip.

The treatment of each narrow-complex tachycardia is based on the specific rhythm and symptoms. In general, class II and IV agents are used to slow AV nodal conduction, although these agents may terminate certain dysrhythmias (especially nodal reentry). Adenosine transiently slows AV nodal conduction and can help diagnose or treat certain rhythms. Class IA and IC agents are useful in converting other narrow-complex tachycardias (e.g., atrial flutter and fibrillation) to a sinus rhythm. Finally, cholinesterase inhibitors such as edrophonium or neostigmine slow AV conduction, but they are associated with frequent side effects such as nausea, vomiting, and bronchospasm. These agents have no role in the treatment of narrow-complex tachycardias.

BOX 78-9. Causes of Completely Irregular (Chaotic) Rhythms

Atrial fibrillation
Atrial tachycardia or flutter with varying conduction
Multifocal atrial tachycardia
Multiple extrasystoles
Wandering pacemaker (usually atrial)
Parasystole

After identifying the specific dysrhythmia during an episode, the underlying cause of the tachycardia should be sought. Hypovolemia should always be considered as a possible cause of a narrow-complex tachycardia, especially in the young. Fever, anemia, hypoxemia or impaired oxygen delivery (including abnormal hemoglobin states), relative sympathetic excess, drug intoxication, endocrinologic disease (especially thyroid), metabolic derangements, ischemia, infections, and inflammatory causes (including myocarditis and pericarditis) should also be considered.

Sinus Tachycardia

Sinus tachycardia is characterized by a narrow-complex regular rhythm at a rate of greater than 100 beats/min. The P waves are upright in all leads but aVR and the appearance of each is consistent (Figure 78-25). The PR and PP intervals are usually constant, but both may shorten as the rate increases. Increasing vagal or decreasing sympathetic tone decreases the rate of impulse formation and conduction in a graded continuous manner. Conversely, sinus tachycardia can result from increased catecholamine tone or decreased vagal stimulation.

Functionally, sinus tachycardia is a response to physiologic stress and is intended to increase cardiac output. This response can be compensatory for a relative lack of perfusion or oxygen delivery (e.g., congestive heart failure, pulmonary embolism, hypovolemia, anemia, or sepsis) or can occur in nonhypoperfusion states when a relative sympathetic excess exists. Treatment is based on the recognition and treatment of the underlying cause. Although anxiety or pain can cause sinus tachycardia in patients, this is a diagnosis of exclusion after a careful search for evidence of the aforementioned physiologic causes of tachycardia.

Sinus tachycardia can be easily mistaken for other causes of a regular narrow-complex tachycardia, especially in young patients, and the converse can occur (e.g., regular atrial flutter at a rate of 150/min mistaken

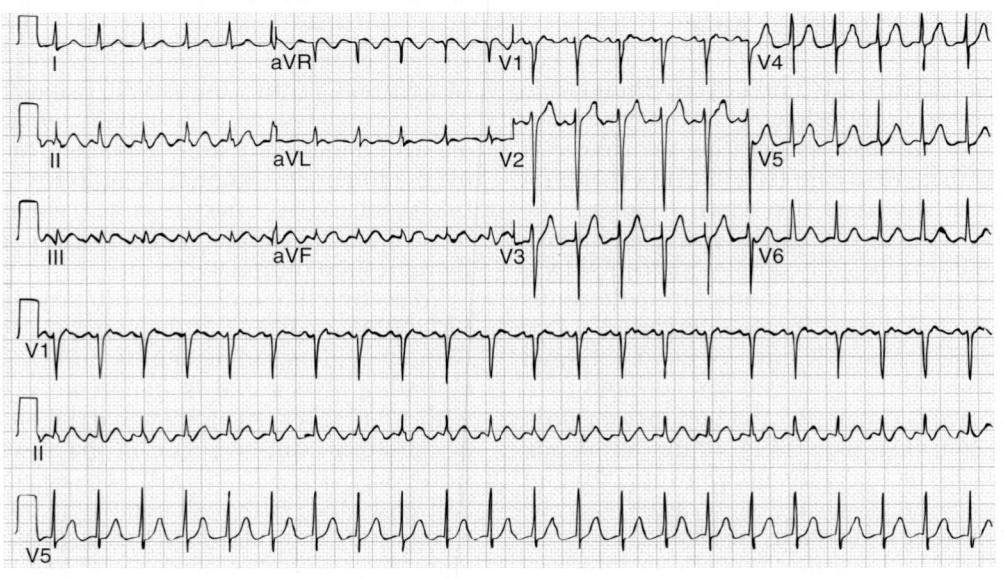

Figure 78-25. Sinus tachycardia.

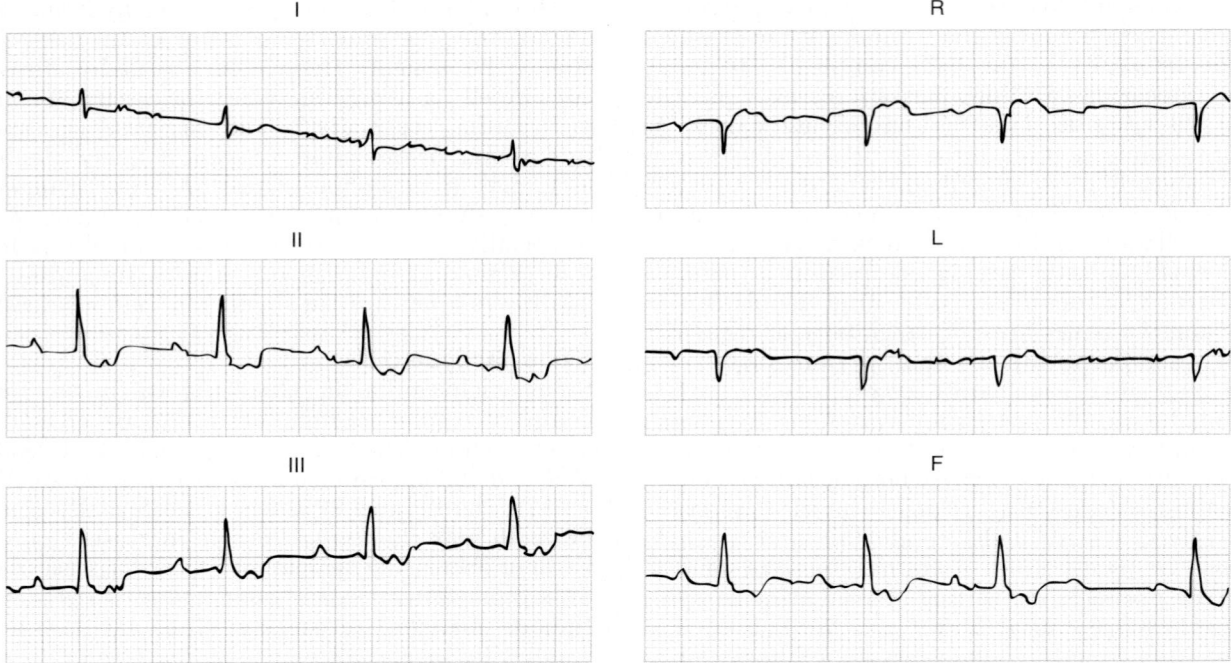

Figure 78-26. Atrial tachycardia (with 2:1 conduction) in a patient with digitalis toxicity. (From Marriott HJL, Conover MB: *Advanced Concepts in Arrhythmias*, 2nd ed. St. Louis, Mosby, 1989.)

for sinus tachycardia). Infants and young children can easily attain ventricular rates of 170 to 225 beats/min with an episode of hypovolemia-induced sinus tachycardia; this may be mistaken for a paroxysmal atrial or junctional tachycardia,[58] with disastrous consequences if a rate-controlling drug is given. Adults do not often reach a rate above 150 to 170/min because of the braking properties of the AV node.

Specific antidysrhythmic therapy for sinus tachycardia is almost never indicated. If the patient is symptomatic or if the risk of precipitating myocardial ischemia is high, the use of a ß-blocker is warranted only after all possible primary causes are treated or eliminated from consideration.

Atrial Tachycardia and Multifocal Atrial Tachycardia

Atrial tachycardia refers to any rapid dysrhythmia from a nonsinus focus above the AV node. Atrial tachycardia can be gradual in onset (suggesting an abnormal automatic mechanism) or abrupt (suggesting a reentrant mechanism). The hallmark of this dysrhythmia on the ECG is a narrow-complex tachycardia at a rate above 100 beats/min, with each QRS complex preceded by a P′ wave that is morphologically different from the sinus P wave (Figure 78-26). If the P′ wave is inverted, a low atrial source is likely. The P′R interval can be normal or abnormal and is usually constant unless more than one focus is involved. Generally, the conduction ratio is 1:1, but this can vary, especially as the atrial rate increases. If no ECG tracing of the normal sinus rhythm is available, single-focus atrial tachycardia can be indistinguishable from sinus tachycardia.

Paroxysmal atrial tachycardia (PAT) is an intermittent dysrhythmia with an abrupt onset and termination,

often seen in children and young adults without concomitant SA node disease. PAT is usually reentrant in origin, as opposed to nonparoxysmal (sustained) atrial tachycardia (NPAT),which is often automatic in nature. PAT can be precipitated by a PAC, or rarely by a PVC, and often originates and terminates abruptly. Other causes of PAT and NPAT include electrolyte and acid-base disturbances, drug toxicity, fever, and hypoxemia. NPAT with varying or complete AV block is classically seen in digitalis toxicity.

Multifocal atrial tachycardia (MAT) is a subset of atrial tachycardia, with more than two foci of impulse formation.[59] On the ECG, at least three distinctly different P waves with varying P′R, RR, and P′P′ intervals are seen (Figure 78-27). Strictly defined, MAT requires three or more nonsinus foci, but distinguishing the sinus P wave from nonsinus P′ waves can be difficult. In addition to the causes just listed for PAT, MAT is often associated with pulmonary disease and hypoxemia, either directly from these conditions or as a result of ß-adrenergic agonist or chronic methylxanthine treatment. MAT often resolves when hypoxemia is resolved with supplemental therapy and when other therapies are optimized.

Correcting the underlying primary disturbance treats PAT, NPAT, and MAT. If the patient is symptomatic and without evidence of instability or if concerns about precipitating myocardial ischemia are present, treatment with a ß-blocker or calcium channel blocker (verapamil or diltiazem) can be begun in the absence of hypotension. Magnesium (2 to 4 g IV) is a second-line agent for PAT and MAT. Although adenosine may slow the ventricular rate or occasionally extinguish atrial tachycardias, these rhythms often recur because of the short therapeutic effect of this drug. Procainamide and digi-

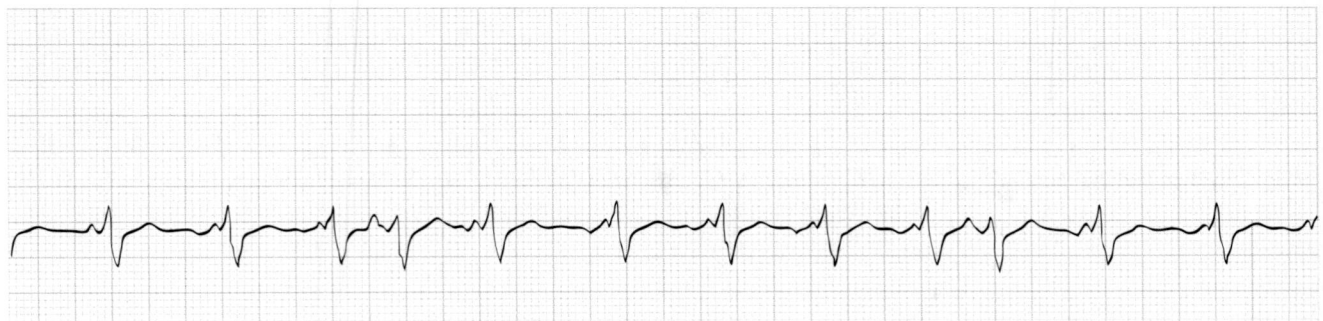

Figure 78-27. Multifocal atrial tachycardia. Note that although the rhythm is irregular, at least three distinct P wave morphologies are present.

talis are used as second-line agents or for outpatient maintenance therapy. Overdrive transvenous atrial pacing can be used if a reentrant mechanism is suspected and drug treatment fails.

In general, electrical treatment is rarely needed in PAT and MAT. If hypotension or other manifestations of instability exist, synchronized cardioversion with sedation at 50 to 100 J can be performed. Cardioversion is not useful in refractory cases of MAT because the dysrhythmia is likely to recur if no other treatment is employed. When the result of digitalis toxicity, PAT and MAT should be treated by correcting hypokalemia if it exists followed by administration of magnesium and digitalis antibody fragments. Emergency cardioversion should be avoided if possible in this setting.

Atrial Flutter

The most accepted characteristics of atrial flutter are the following[60] (Figure 78-28):

- A regular atrial depolarization rate of 250 to 350 beats/min with a rate of 300 beats/min considered classical, although commonly this is not present.
- Distinct ECG manifestations of abnormal atrial depolarizations in a "sawtooth" appearance. These are referred to as *flutter waves* and are best seen in leads II, III, aVF, and V_{1-2}.
- Frequent occurrence of a 2:1 or 4:1 AV conduction ratio, although any ratio may be seen. The 2:1 ratio with an atrial rate of 300/min accounts for the classical (although not exclusive) ECG appearance of atrial flutter as a narrow-complex tachycardia with a regular ventricular rate of 150 beats/min (often mistaken for sinus tachycardia).

Most experimental data suggest a reentrant mechanism for atrial flutter, although some patients may display an abnormal automatic mechanism. In the emergency department, it is easy to mistake atrial flutter for sinus tachycardia, especially if the flutter waves resemble normal P waves or a nonclassical ventricular rate is present.

Atrial flutter is often associated with underlying heart disease, congestive heart failure, valvular dysfunction (especially mitral), or metabolic derangements. The clinical importance of atrial flutter is primarily the result of symptoms caused by the ventricular response rate, including palpitations, syncope, presyncope, hypotension, chest pain, and heart failure. Varying AV conduction and the presence of a Wenckebach mechanism can produce an irregular ventricular response rate. Rarely, high-grade AV conduction block can result in a slow response rate and clinical bradycardia.

In stable patients, ventricular response rates can be controlled with a calcium channel blocker (verapamil or diltiazem) or a ß-adrenergic blocker.[48] Diltiazem may be a better choice in atrial flutter and fibrillation because laboratory and limited clinical data suggest less evidence of negative inotropic effect and resultant hypotension; in practice, there is little difference in the effects and complication rates between equipotent doses of verapamil and diltiazem in patients without overt ventricular failure. Digitalis can be used as a second-line agent or in those with mild tachycardia and preexisting congestive heart failure. Magnesium (2 to 4 g IV) can be employed as an adjunctive or second-line therapy to control the ventricular response rate. The major value of adenosine may be in unmasking flutter waves in a narrow-complex tachydysrhythmia, helping to identify the underlying rhythm correctly.

All AV nodal conduction slowing agents, including calcium channel blockers, ß-adrenergic blockers, adenosine, and digitalis, should be avoided in patients with atrial flutter and a suspected accessory pathway because these agents primarily block AV nodal conduction and may enhance anterograde conduction in the accessory path. Rapid ventricular response rates (especially over 200 beats/min) are a tip to the possibility of an accessory pathway because normal AV nodal tissues rarely allow a ventricular response rate of more than 150 to 165 beats/min. The use of any predominantly AV nodal blocking agent in the presence of an accessory pathway and atrial flutter or fibrillation may allow unbridled rapid ventricular response rates and precipitate ventricular fibrillation.

Type IA agents (especially procainamide or quinidine) can be used to convert atrial flutter if the previously mentioned drugs fail, or they may be used to prevent recurrence in an outpatient setting. The type III agents amiodarone and ibutilide are alternative primary converting agents.[23-24,26] Finally, synchronized electrical cardioversion with sedation, beginning at 25 to 50 J, is effective in terminating atrial flutter in refractory or unstable patients. If electrical therapy is successful but atrial flutter recurs, a type IA agent should

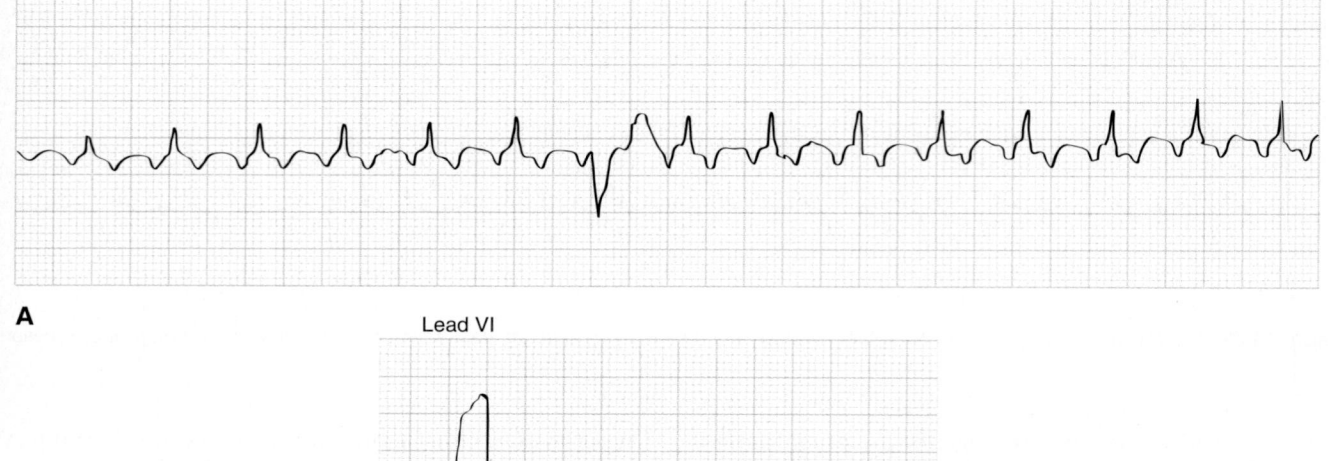

A

Lead VI

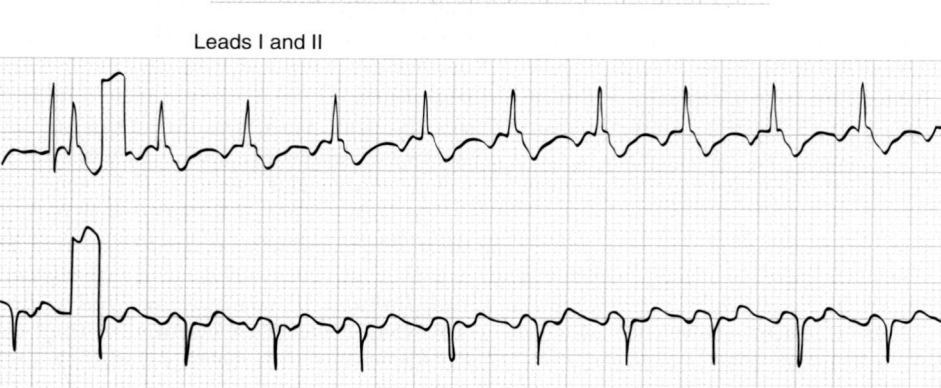

Leads I and II

B

Figure 78-28. A, Atrial flutter with 2:1 conduction and isolated premature ventricular contraction. **B,** Atrial flutter with 2:1 conduction. In lead VI, diagnosis is unclear, but examination of other leads, especially lead II, helps identify characteristic flutter waves.

be used before repeated electrical cardioversion to help prevent this from occurring again.

Atrial Fibrillation

Atrial fibrillation is the result of chaotic depolarization of atrial tissues. This chaotic activity can lead to reduced cardiac output from a loss of coordinated atrial contractions and a rapid ventricular rate, both of which may limit the diastolic filling and stroke volume of the ventricles. Atrial fibrillation may be paroxysmal or chronic; the paroxysms may last for minutes to days. On the ECG, fibrillatory waves are seen and accompanied by an irregular QRS pattern (Figure 78-29). These fibrillatory waves are best seen in the inferior leads or lead V_1 and are described as fine to coarse on the basis of their amplitude. Atrial fibrillation is the result of multiple microreentry circuits, creating 300 to 600 impulses/min.

The QRS complexes are usually narrow unless an underlying bundle branch block is present. The Ashman phenomenon can cause isolated or repeated

aberrant ventricular conduction, usually in a right bundle branch block pattern (Figure 78-30). These Ashman beats can be mistaken for PVCs if the long-short cycle sequence is not recognized. The ventricular response rate depends on the conduction path and ratio, with the normal AV node maximal response rate being no greater than 150 to 170 beats/min. As noted with atrial flutter, the presence of a chaotic rhythm (irrespective of the QRS duration) at a rate of more than 200 beats/min strongly suggests atrial fibrillation coupled with conduction down an accessory pathway. This rhythm is prone to deteriorating to ventricular fibrillation, especially if the rate reaches 250/min or greater or an AV nodal blocking agent is administered.

Atrial fibrillation often occurs in an otherwise normal heart (*lone atrial fibrillation*) but is also associated with a variety of underlying diseases (Box 78-10). One etiology of new-onset atrial fibrillation is the "holiday heart" syndrome.[61] This can occur after an ethanol binge, producing atrial fibrillation, atrial flutter,

Lead III

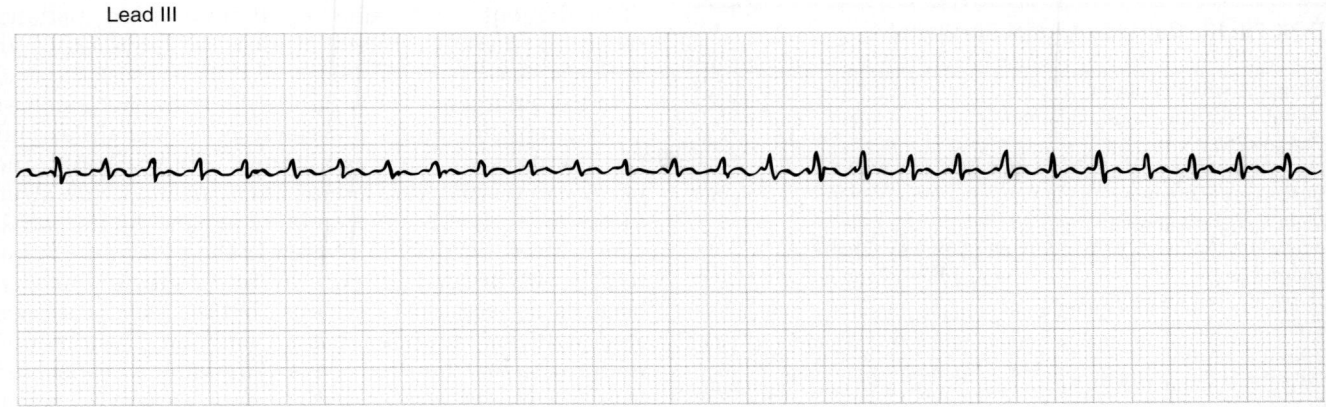

Lead II

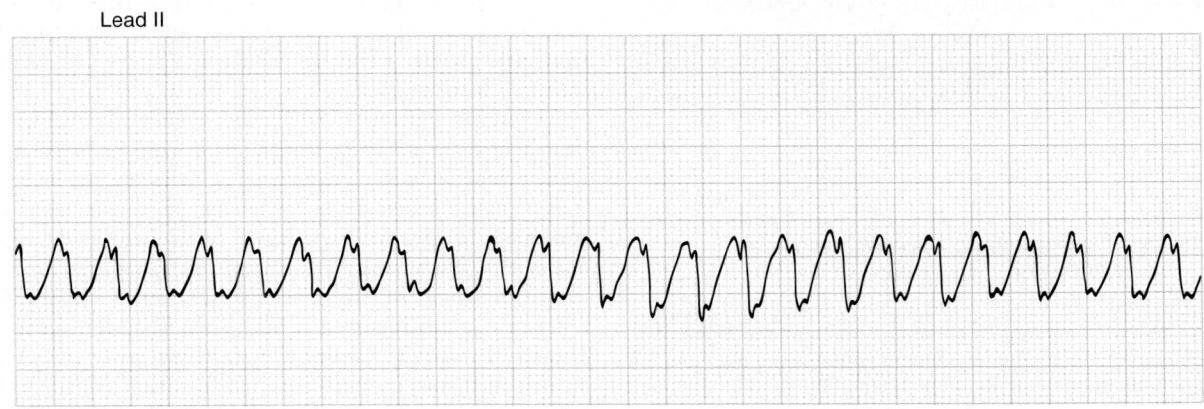

C

Figure 78-28, cont'd C, Atrial flutter with 1:1 conduction. This is rare and can be mistaken for ventricular tachycardia (lead II).

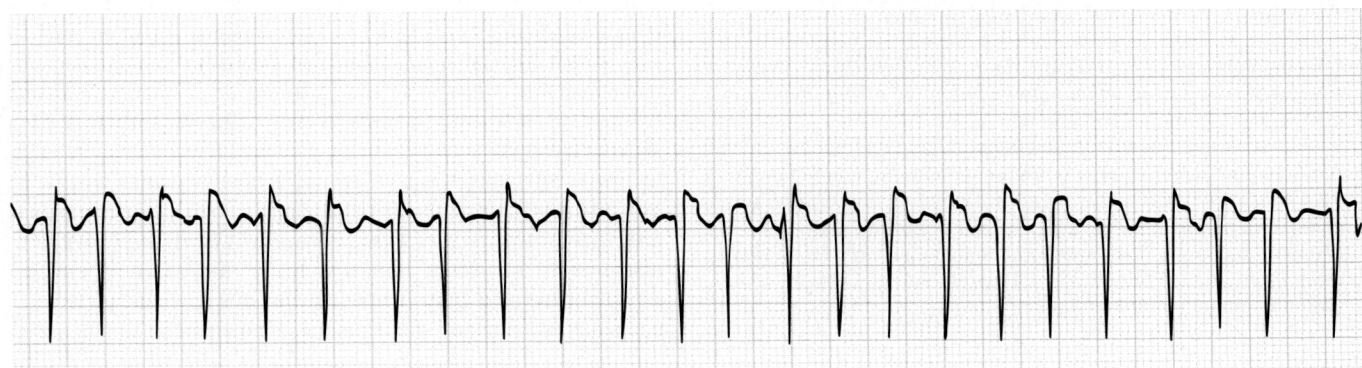

Figure 78-29. Atrial fibrillation with rapid ventricular response.

or atrial tachycardia. These rhythms usually revert spontaneously to a sinus rhythm after 24 to 48 hours.

Atrial fibrillation may also result from the degeneration of atrial flutter, irrespective of the cause. In this case, an intermediary condition called *atrial fibrillation-flutter* shows characteristics of both rhythms on ECG. It may be manifested as fine fibrillatory waves with irregular QRS complexes intermixed with flutter waves and a stretch of regular QRS complexes. Rapid atrial fibrillation followed by sinus bradycardia in an elderly patient suggests the aforementioned *bradycardia-tachycardia syndrome*. Finally, irregular atrial fibrillatory waves coupled with regular narrow or

wide QRS complexes may represent atrial fibrillation coupled with complete heart block and an accelerated junctional or ventricular rhythm; this syndrome strongly suggests digitalis toxicity.

The treatment of atrial fibrillation is based on distinguishing it from other chaotic rhythms (Box 78-11) and the recognition of any underlying causes and symptoms. Asymptomatic atrial fibrillation at a rate of 120 beats/min or less requires no specific emergency therapy. Patients who are unstable from acute rapid atrial fibrillation should receive sedation and synchronized cardioversion starting at 50 to 100 J. Electrical cardioversion is not associated with an increased risk

BOX 78-10. Causes of Atrial Fibrillation

Ischemic heart disease*
Valvular disease (especially mitral)*
Pericarditis
Hyperthyroidism
Sick sinus syndrome
Myocardial contusion
Acute ethanol intoxication (holiday heart syndrome)
Idiopathic
Hypertensive heart disease*
Cardiomyopathy*
Cardiac surgery
Catecholamine excess
Pulmonary embolism
Congestive heart failure*[†]
Accessory pathway (Wolff-Parkinson-White) syndrome[‡]

---

*Related to increased left atrial size.
[†]Can also be a result of atrial fibrillation.
[‡]Especially in patients with a ventricular response rate >200 beats/min.

BOX 78-11. Pharmacologic Approach to Atrial Fibrillation Conversion

Intravenous procainamide, 50 mg/min, up to a total dose of 18 to 20 mg/kg (12 mg/kg in patients with congestive heart failure) or until conversion or side effects occur
or
Ibutilide, 0.015-0.02 mg/kg IV, over 10-15 minutes (conversion usually occurs within 20 minutes if successful)
or
Amiodarone, 5 mg/kg IV, over 15-20 minutes
or
Oral quinidine sulfate, 200-300 mg initially, then 200-300 mg every hour until conversion, side effects, or a total dose of 1000 mg has been administered
If needed:
A calcium channel blocker (verapamil, 40 to 80 mg PO or 5-10 mg IV, or diltiazem, 60 to 120 PO or 20-25 mg IV) can be given before the type IA agent (if no contraindications are present) to lower the ventricular response rate to <120 beats/min and to attenuate further tachycardia from the vagolytic effects of these agents

of malignant ventricular dysrhythmias in patients receiving digitalis unless clinical or laboratory evidence of toxicity coexists.

In the emergency department, the therapeutic course chosen depends on the aforementioned principles plus the duration of the dysrhythmia. Both chronic and paroxysmal atrial fibrillations are associated with atrial thrombus formation and embolic events. Acute paroxysmal atrial fibrillation of greater than 72 hours duration is best treated initially by rate control if needed because conversion to a sinus rhythm may be associated with an increased risk of embolic phenomenon within the first hours to days. The latter is especially true the longer atrial fibrillation is present or when underlying valvular disease or chamber enlargement is present. Long-term attempts to return or maintain a sinus rhythm may not offer a clear benefit to many patients with atrial fibrillation compared with rate control strategies.

In stable patients with new-onset atrial fibrillation for 72 hours or less, ventricular rate control and cardioversion can be attempted.[8] Patients with atrial fibrillation of more than 72 hours duration should have therapy tailored, beginning with rate control. After carefully assessing the functional implications (seeking evidence of myocardial ischemia, heart failure, syncope, or other symptoms directly attributed to the dysrhythmia), a decision regarding conversion versus continued rate control must be made together with any other long-term care provider. If a decision to convert is made, a search for atrial clot (using echocardiography) coupled with systemic anticoagulation is often done, usually on an inpatient basis. Longer durations of fibrillation predispose to conversion failures and to atrial clot formation. Atrial clot can develop during fibrillation and also for days after conversion, the latter related to stunned myocardium after restoration of a sinus rhythm.

The control of rapid ventricular response rates in symptomatic atrial fibrillation is with intravenous calcium channel blockers (verapamil or diltiazem) or ß-adrenergic blockers because both decrease AV nodal conduction and may interrupt the microreentry circuits responsible for the dysrhythmia. As noted with atrial

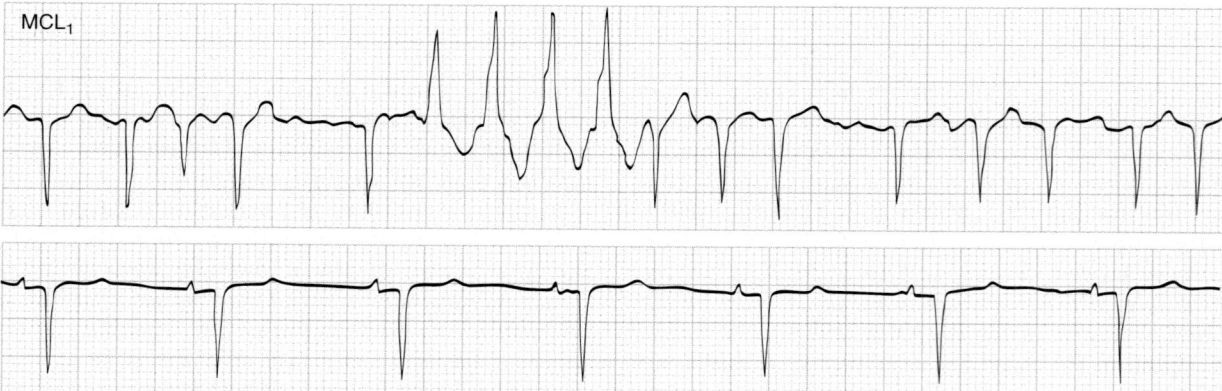

MCL₁

Figure 78-30. Atrial fibrillation with classical Ashman phenomenon series of beats. Note long-short cycle before aberrantly conducted impulses. (From Marriott HJL, Conover MB: *Advanced Concepts in Arrhythmias*, 2nd ed. St. Louis, Mosby, 1989.)

flutter, the relative effectiveness and complication rates in clinical practice between verapamil and diltiazem are similar in the absence of overt heart failure; careful titration of either agent is appropriate.

ß-Adrenergic blockers are particularly effective in atrial fibrillation secondary to hyperthyroidism or catecholamine excess. Digitalis is a second-line agent for ventricular rate control because of its relatively slow onset of action. Calcium channel and ß-adrenergic blockers, adenosine, and digitalis should not be administered in patients with atrial fibrillation and an accessory pathway because of the risk of precipitating ventricular fibrillation.[45,62,63]

Intravenous magnesium sulfate (2 g over 2 minutes) can serve as an adjunctive or second-line therapy to decrease the ventricular response rate. As with its use in atrial flutter, adenosine is not indicated as a primary therapy because of its short duration of effect. For outpatient rate control, calcium channel and ß-adrenergic blockers are preferred over digitalis in patients without contraindications.

Pharmacologic cardioversion of atrial fibrillation is best accomplished with procainamide, amiodarone, or ibutilide. If attempted, a calcium channel blocker or ß-adrenergic blocker should be given before a type IA agent to control the ventricular rate, with a target of 100 to 120 beats/min before administering the type IA agent (see Box 78-11). This approach may also prevent or attenuate any increase in the ventricular rate from the type IA agent. Irrespective of the route and specific agents chosen, pharmacologic cardioversion requires close monitoring and observation after conversion. If a class IA or III agent fails, it is best not to switch to agents of another class in the ensuing minutes to hours to avoid complications.

Type IC agents are not available for intravenous use in the United States (but are used in Europe for this indication) and therefore not currently indicated in the emergency management of atrial fibrillation. Electrical cardioversion (with 50 to 100 J) may be indicated if the previously described measures fail to convert symptomatic atrial fibrillation or in unstable patients; although a synchronized countershock is recommended, the irregularity may require delivery of an unsynchronized countershock.

Admission criteria for a patient with atrial fibrillation include symptoms of instability or myocardial ischemia, worsened heart failure, symptomatic recurrence in the emergency department, or the need to cardiovert electrically. Traditionally, all patients with new-onset atrial fibrillation were admitted to "rule out" causes such as myocardial ischemia or infarction and pulmonary embolism. These diagnoses are rarely occult, however, and selective discharge of patients in the absence of clinical evidence of acute coronary ischemia, new valve dysfunction, acute lung illness (including pulmonary embolism), or thyroid disease may be acceptable after emergency department observation and with close follow-up.[64,65] If conversion is successful, no comorbid illnesses requiring admission are present, and the postconversion observation is uneventful, discharge with follow-up and initial maintenance therapy is a reasonable option. Short-term outpatient anticoagulation with newer heparinoids and warfarin can be used to limit the embolic risk for those being treated as outpatients, particularly if the duration was greater than 72 hours.[66]

Junctional (Atrioventricular Nodal) Tachycardia

The identification of paroxysmal junctional tachycardia (PJT) on the ECG is based on the presence of a narrow-complex regular tachycardia without preceding atrial depolarization waves (Figure 78-31). PJTs often produce retrograde atrial depolarization and a P′ wave, but these P′ waves are usually buried within the QRS complex. P′ waves may be located anywhere in relation to the QRS complex and assume either a normal or abnormal structure. The location of the P′ waves can be useful in defining the electrophysiologic source of a PJT and help distinguish it from other causes of a regular narrow-complex tachycardia (Figure 78-32).

Among all patients with a regular paroxysmal supraventricular tachycardia, reentrant PJT (also termed *AV nodal reentry*) is the most common cause. The alpha pathway within the AV node is used for anterograde conduction in 90% of cases of sustained PJT and accounts for the common finding of P waves buried within the QRS complexes (see Figure 78-32). Clinically, patients experience the abrupt onset of a regular tachycardia at a rate of 120 to 200 beats/min. A PJC or PAC often initiates PJT; termination is also abrupt, from increased vagal tone, drug therapy, or spontaneous conversion. PJTs at a rate more than

EC - 48

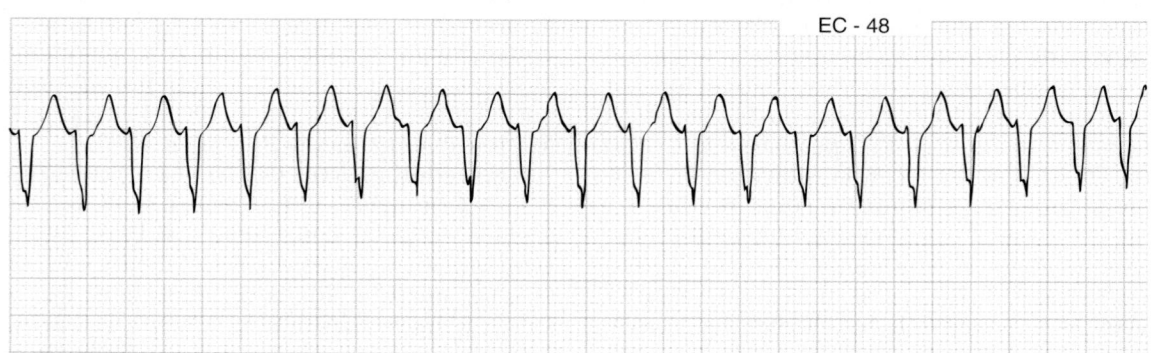

Figure 78-31. Paroxysmal supraventricular tachycardia. Note the narrow, regular QRS complexes.

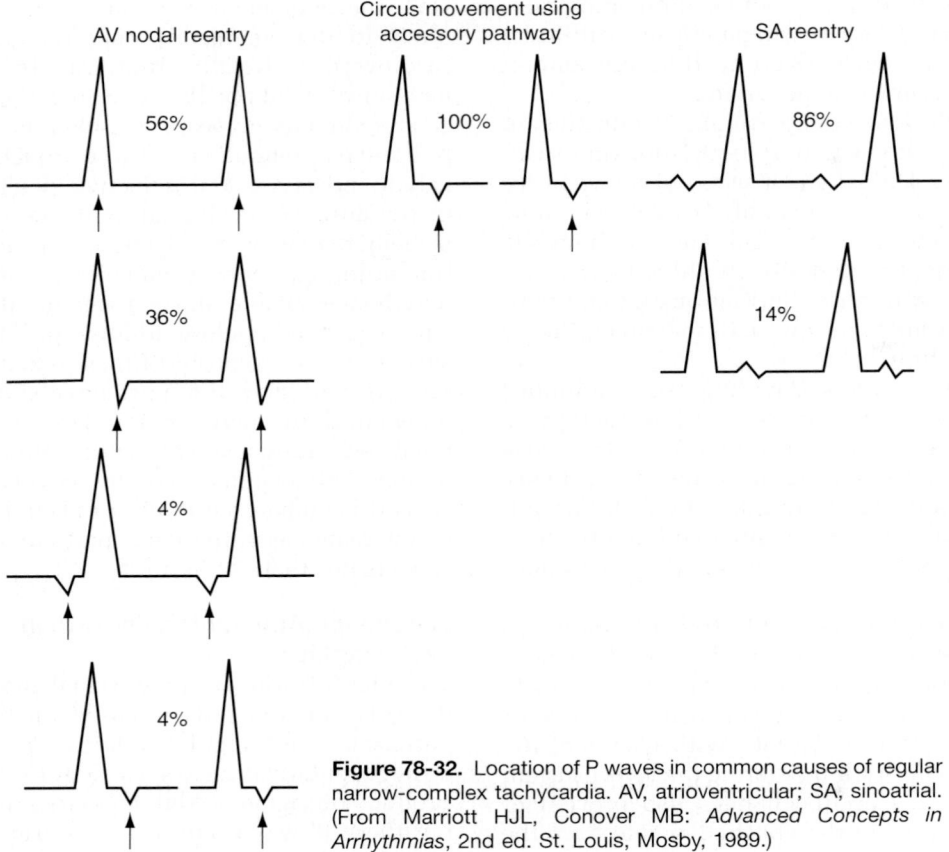

Figure 78-32. Location of P waves in common causes of regular narrow-complex tachycardia. AV, atrioventricular; SA, sinoatrial. (From Marriott HJL, Conover MB: *Advanced Concepts in Arrhythmias*, 2nd ed. St. Louis, Mosby, 1989.)

200 beats/min are rare and, when seen, suggest an accessory pathway syndrome. All "regular" narrow-complex tachycardias (QRS duration less than 0.10 second) are treated in the same way, whether a PJT or accessory pathway syndrome is responsible. As noted previously, sinus tachycardia may be mistaken for supraventricular tachycardia or PJT in infants and young children.[31,59]

Nonparoxysmal (or sustained) junctional tachycardia (NPJT) is usually the result of an automatic mechanism, with gradual onset and termination. NPJT rarely exceeds a rate of 130 beats/min. Compared with PJT, NPJT is more often associated with underlying heart disease, electrolyte imbalance, or excess catecholamine states.

Asymptomatic junctional tachycardia at a rate less than 120 beats/min does not require specific therapy aside from correcting any underlying abnormalities. Stable symptomatic patients can be successfully treated in 85% to 90% of cases with a calcium channel blocker or a ß-adrenergic blocker (see previous dosing regimens in pharmacology section) if PJT persists after vagal maneuvers. Often, the tachycardia slows with treatment before abrupt conversion to a sinus rhythm[28,67]; this slowing is the result of increasing block within the reentrant circuit. Adenosine is another first-line option for emergent therapy, giving initial success rates similar to those seen with verapamil but higher recurrence rates because of the short therapeutic effect. Calcium channel blockers and adenosine are both considered

safe and effective in prehospital treatment of PJTs, with strong medical control.[67,68]

With the success of the preceding regimens, other techniques of treating PJT are rarely needed. Vasoconstrictors (methoxamine or phenylephrine, 0.5 to 1 mg IV over 2 to 3 minutes, or metaraminol, 200 mg in 500 mL of water, begun at 1 to 2 mL/min) can terminate a PJT through reflex vagal stimulation and may be useful in hypotensive patients without other signs of instability. Blood pressure must be monitored closely, however, to avoid excessive hypertension, making electrical cardioversion a better choice in these selected patients. Digitalis can be used to control the ventricular rate in mildly symptomatic patients in the absence of digitalis toxicity. Magnesium sulfate is effective in slowing the response rate in PJTs and is useful as an adjunctive therapy. Type IA and IC agents may be used to prevent the recurrence of PJT, particularly in individuals who cannot tolerate calcium channel or ß-blockers. Cardioversion (synchronized preferred but not mandatory) with 50 to 100 J is the best treatment for unstable patients with PJT or NPJT.

Many adult patients can be discharged to home if the PJT is terminated. Oral therapy with a class II or IV agent should be considered for those with frequent symptomatic episodes of PJT. Patients with underlying serious medical illnesses, recurrent symptoms, or any evidence of instability should be admitted. Most patients requiring electrical cardioversion should be admitted, although an otherwise healthy patient who is easily cardioverted without recurrence may be considered for discharge with close outpatient follow-up. Referral for ambulatory Holter monitoring and electrophysiology studies or interventions should be considered for anyone discharged to home who has not previously been evaluated, particularly if the problem is recurrent or associated with profound symptoms.

Preexcitation and Accessory Pathway Syndromes

Preexcitation refers to depolarization of the ventricular myocardium earlier than would occur by conduction of an impulse through the AV node. This implies the existence of a pathway from the atria to the ventricular myocardium in addition to the AV node, hence the term *accessory pathway*. These terms are related but not interchangeable because not all accessory paths are used to activate the ventricles early. The Wolff-Parkinson-White (WPW) syndrome is the most common accessory pathway syndrome, although it probably represents a group of pathologic conditions.[69,70] The clinical hallmark of this syndrome is paroxysmal tachycardia at a rate of 150 to 300 beats/min, the direct result of the loss of the normal AV node conduction restraint. Any tachycardia in an adult at a rate greater than 200 beats/min should raise the suspicion of an accessory pathway syndrome.

The classical WPW syndrome consists of tachycardia with the following three features (Figure 78-33):
- A short PR interval (less than 0.12 second)
- QRS duration greater than 0.10 second
- A slurred upstroke to the QRS complex, referred to as a *delta wave*

The short PR interval is the result of the absent AV node conduction delay, and the delta wave occurs because of early activation of the ventricular myocardium. Although the WPW syndrome typically has a prolonged QRS duration as a result of the delta wave, the QRS duration commonly varies with the location and conduction direction of the accessory pathway. Pathways inserting into infranodal conducting tissues can produce a near-normal QRS complex, whereas those inserting in the nonconductive tissues produce a wide QRS complex with an abnormal structure. If this classical triad is present, secondary T wave changes (a deflection opposite the main QRS vector) are seen.

Multiple possible connections between the atria and ventricles can create an accessory path in the WPW syndrome (Figure 78-34), with up to 13% of patients having more than one anomalous AV path. The Kent fibers are the single most common accessory pathway. Historically, the WPW syndrome was divided into left-sided (QRS mostly positive in V_1, type A) and right-sided (QRS mostly negative in V_1, type B) paths, with the latter being more accessible to surgical ablation. With the advent of catheter radiofrequency ablation, this classification is no longer relevant.

The accessory path or paths can participate in a reentry circuit that produces or sustains the tachycardia. The AV node often constitutes one limb of these circuits. When the QRS complex is narrow and a delta

BOX 78-12. Diseases Associated with Wolff-Parkinson-White Syndrome

Idiopathic*
Cardiomyopathy (especially hypertrophic)
Transposition of great vessels
Endocardial fibroelastosis
Mitral valve prolapse
Tricuspid atresia
Ebstein's disease

*Most common.

wave absent, the AV node is being used for anterograde conduction to the ventricles and the accessory path is used for retrograde conduction; this is termed an *orthodromic tachycardia*. Conversely, if the QRS complex is wide and a delta wave is present, the accessory pathway is being used as the anterograde limb and the AV node the retrograde limb of the reentry circuit; this is termed an *antidromic tachycardia*. The majority of symptomatic patients with the WPW syndrome have a regular orthodromic tachycardia (making detection of the syndrome difficult in the emergency department). Conversely, asymptomatic WPW syndrome is usually discovered when a delta wave or waves and wider QRS complex of antidromic WPW are seen on the ECG.

Patients with the WPW syndrome often have one or more of the classical features missing on the surface ECG, especially if a sinus rhythm is present at the time of evaluation. In these times, the presence of the pathway is concealed, and the normal sinus impulse is carried to the ventricles through the AV node. A PAC, PJC, or PVC can serve to initiate a tachycardia. The WPW syndrome is present in 0.1% to 0.3% of the population, with men affected twice as often as women. On the basis of this prevalence, it is estimated that only 25% to 50% of patients with the WPW syndrome become symptomatic. The WPW syndrome is associated with a variety of conditions, although up to 70% of patients have no underlying heart disease (Box 78-12). In those without underlying heart disease, especially if the WPW syndrome is discovered in the absence of symptoms, the prognosis is excellent with an extremely low risk of sudden death.

The presenting rhythm in symptomatic patients with the WPW syndrome is usually a reentrant tachycardia (70% to 80%), although atrial fibrillation can be seen in 10% to 30% of patients. Emergency treatment depends on the following three observations:
- Symptoms of instability
- QRS duration or delta wave presence
- QRS regularity or irregularity

Unstable patients, irrespective of the QRS duration or regularity, should be cardioverted (synchronized preferred) with 50 to 100 J (0.5 to 2 J/kg for children) after sedation if time permits.

A regular orthodromic (narrow QRS complex) tachycardia is the single most common presentation of the WPW syndrome (and often not recognized) and is treated in the same way as PJT. Calcium channel

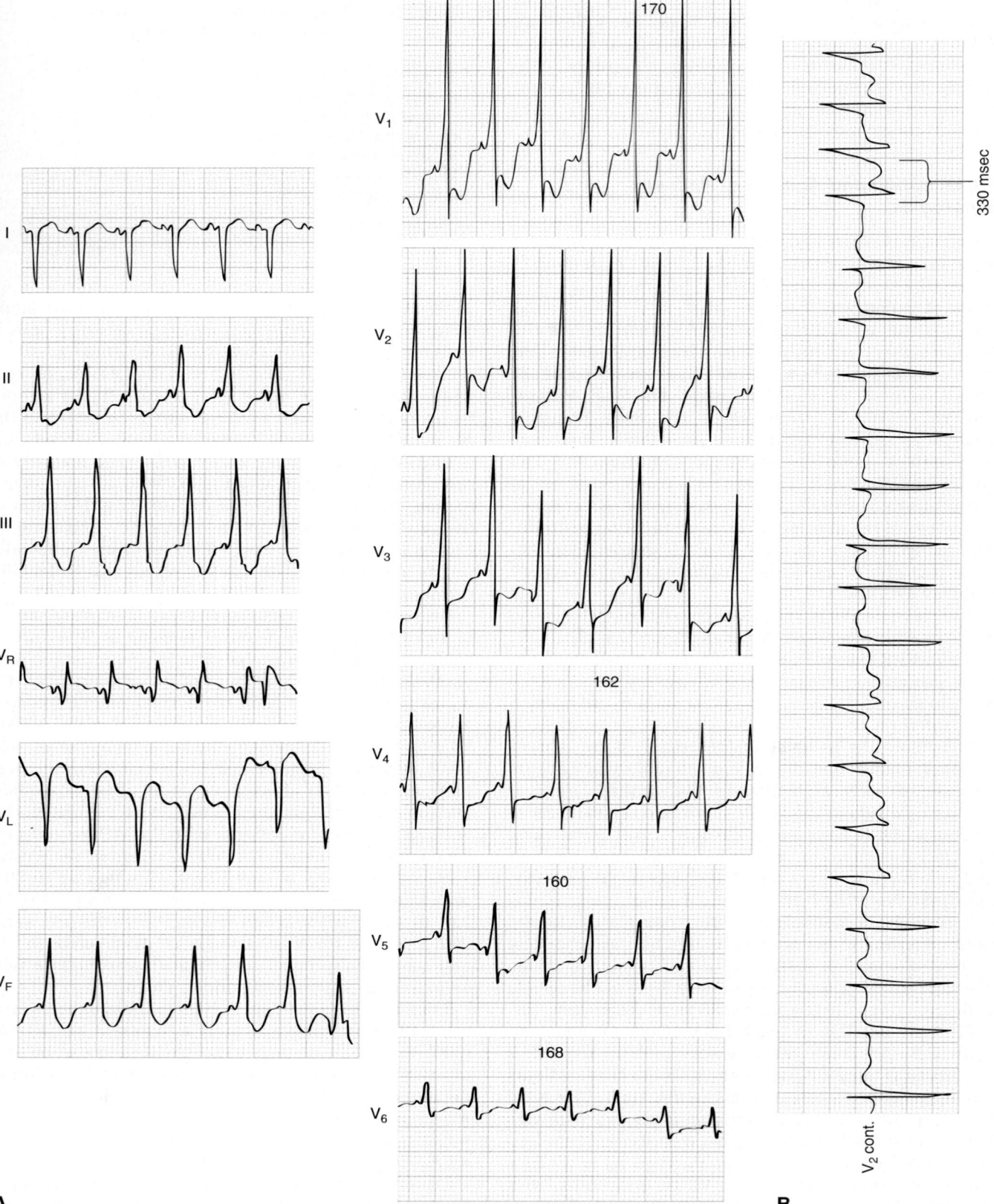

Figure 78-33. A, Wolff-Parkinson-White (WPW) syndrome. **B,** WPW syndrome with atrial fibrillation. Note short refractory period (330 msec). (**A,** From Watanabe Y, Dreifus LS: *Cardiac Arrhythmias*. New York, Grune & Stratton, 1977.)

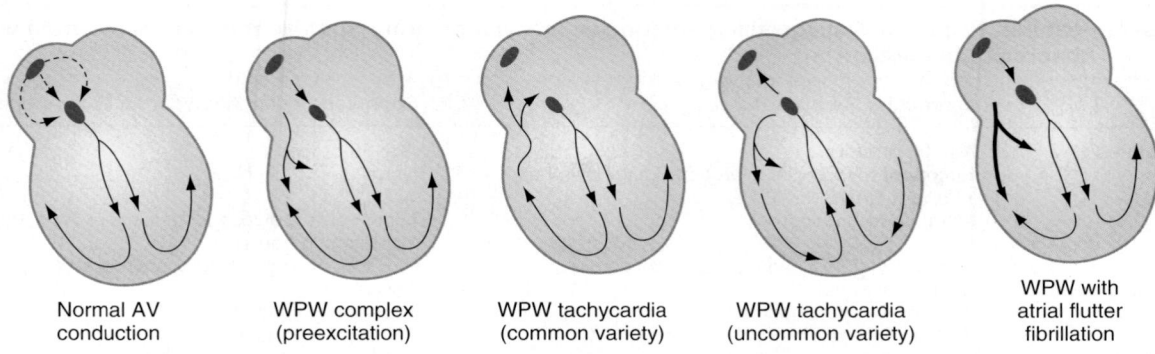

Figure 78-34. Wolff-Parkinson-White (WPW) paths and associated rhythms. AV, atrioventricular. (From Watanabe Y, Dreifus LS: *Cardiac Arrhythmias*. New York, Grune & Stratton, 1977.)

blockers, ß-adrenergic blockers, procainamide, and adenosine are all suitable for first-line therapy if vagal maneuvers fail. Procainamide may be preferable as the primary therapy for all stable patients with the WPW syndrome and tachycardia because of its efficacy and safety irrespective of the conduction pathway. Digitalis, amiodarone, or class IC agents are alternative therapies for orthodromic regular tachycardias. All of these drugs except adenosine are suitable for outpatient prophylaxis after termination of the tachycardia. Lidocaine is unlikely to have any effect on orthodromic WPW-related tachycardia,[71] and magnesium is not well studied in this syndrome.

Symptomatic patients with an antidromic (wide QRS complex) regular tachycardia or any irregular tachycardia (irrespective of QRS duration) have a more serious prognosis because of the high risk of ventricular fibrillation, especially when the RR interval is less than 0.20 second. In these situations, *all AV nodal blocking drugs (especially calcium channel and ß-adrenergic blockers, but also digoxin and adenosine) are contraindicated.* These agents may create a faster ventricular response rate from unopposed and potentially enhanced conduction through the accessory path. The rapid rates are associated with a high risk of degeneration into ventricular fibrillation. It is important to emphasize that irregularity can be difficult to detect at extremely fast rates and must be carefully sought. A wide-complex irregular tachycardia at a rate of 250 beats/min or greater is highly suggestive of atrial fibrillation and the WPW syndrome.

Procainamide is the drug of choice in all antidromic or irregular WPW-related tachycardias.[72] Electrical cardioversion should be considered any time the ventricular rate is 250 beats/min or greater, drug therapy fails, or instability or clinical deterioration occurs. Amiodarone is also an alternative to procainamide. Lidocaine has unclear utility in antidromic or irregular accessory pathway syndromes; it usually has little effect on conduction, although isolated reports of both decreased and enhanced conduction through the accessory pathway exist.[73] For these reasons, lidocaine is not recommended for antidromic or irregular accessory pathway syndromes.

All patients requiring electrical cardioversion should be admitted to the hospital, as should patients who ex-perience recurrence in the emergency department and those with underlying complicating diseases or symptoms (e.g., chest pain, congestive heart failure, electrolyte imbalance). Those without the aforementioned features in whom tachycardia is easily terminated can be discharged and be referred for electrophysiologic studies to map the location of the pathway and potential radiofrequency ablation of the tract.

The Lown-Ganong-Levine syndrome is a rare accessory pathway syndrome associated with paroxysmal tachycardia, a short PR interval, and a normal QRS complex without a delta wave. The syndrome is often the result of an intranodal bypass tract termed the fibers of Mahaim. Patients usually have a paroxysmal reentrant narrow-complex tachycardia, but occasionally ventricular tachycardia is seen. The treatment parallels that for the WPW syndrome.

Wide-Complex Tachycardias

Wide-complex tachycardia refers to dysrhythmias greater than 100 beats/min associated with a QRS duration of 0.12 second or more.[74,75] Wide-complex tachycardia can be divided into two broad categories, depending on whether the initiating focus is supraventricular or ventricular. Supraventricular foci can produce a wide-complex tachycardia if a conduction abnormality exists. The widened QRS can occur with a preexisting bundle branch block, acquired bundle branch block (often related to fast or irregular heart rates and ischemia), or conduction through an accessory pathway. A focus below the level of the AV node results in ventricular tachycardia. The treatment of wide-complex tachycardia is based on the ability to distinguish ventricular tachycardia from supraventricular tachycardia with abnormal conduction.

The approach to the differential diagnosis of a wide-complex tachycardia is based on systemic evaluation of evidence gained from a focused history, physical examination, and ECG tracing. The classical Wellens criteria (Table 78-7)[74-76] use multiple, unordered clinical data points to help estimate the likelihood of a ventricular or supraventricular source. As an improvement, the Brugada criteria[76-79] use the ECG principles encased in the Wellens approach, surrounded in a four-step decision tree approach (Figure 78-35).

Table 78-7. Features Helpful in Distinguishing Ventricular Tachycardia from Supraventricular Tachycardia with Abnormal Conduction

	Ventricular Tachycardia	Supraventricular Tachycardia Plus Aberrancy
Clinical features	Age 50 or older	Age 35 or less
	History of myocardial infarction, congestive heart failure, CABG, or ASHD	None
	Mitral valve prolapse	Mitral valve prolapse (especially in Wolff-Parkinson-White syndrome)
	Previous history of ventricular tachycardia	Previous history of supraventricular tachycardia
Physical examination	Cannon A waves	Absent
	Variation in arterial pulse	Absence of variability
	Variable first heart sound	Absence of variability
Electrocardiogram	Fusion beats	None
	AV dissociation	Preceding P waves with QRS complexes
	QRS > 0.14 sec	QRS usually < 0.14 sec
	Extreme LAD (<−30 degrees)	Axis normal or slightly abnormal
	No response to vagal maneuvers	Slow or terminate with vagal maneuvers
Specific QRS patterns	V_1: R, qR, or RS	V_1: rsR′
	V_6: S, rS, or qR	V_6: qRs
	Identical to previous ventricular tachycardia tracing*	Identical to previous supraventricular tachycardia tracing*
	Concordance of positivity or negativity[†]	

*If proven by electrophysiologic studies or by a preponderance of evidence.
[†]Main deflection of QRS complex either positive or negative in every precordial lead.
ASHD, arteriosclerotic heart disease; CABG, coronary artery bypass graft; LAD, left anterior descending artery.

No one criterion or system that helps distinguish a supraventricular from a ventricular source is infallible. A careful collection of multiple data points usually leads to the correct diagnosis. The treating physician should always initially assume that any new-onset symptomatic wide-complex tachycardia is ventricular tachycardia until proved otherwise (which often can be done by history, examination, and evaluating the ECG).

Patients with a history of a previous myocardial infarction are more likely to have ventricular tachycardia than supraventricular tachycardia with abnormal conduction.[78-80] This historical point, coupled with the onset of a dysrhythmia after the infarction, strongly suggests the diagnosis of ventricular tachycardia. Other features more frequently associated with ventricular tachycardia are an age of 50 years or older, known ischemic or structural heart disease, congestive heart failure, and a previous history of ventricular dysrhythmias. Conversely, younger patients (younger than 35 years) and those with a history of supraventricular tachycardia are more likely to have a supraventricular source with abnormal conduction.

During the physical examination, clues about the source of a wide-complex tachycardia can be gleaned from careful inspection, auscultation, and specific maneuvers. Evidence of AV dissociation (variation in the first heart sound or in the systolic blood pressure beat to beat or cannon jugular waves) suggests a ventricular origin. The absence of these findings, however, does not imply a supraventricular source. Slowing or termination of a wide-complex tachycardia in response to carotid sinus massage, Valsalva's maneuvers, or other techniques of increasing vagal tone suggest a supraventricular source.[80-82]

One common error in the differential diagnosis of wide-complex tachycardia is the belief that the blood pressure and level of consciousness can be used to distinguish ventricular tachycardia from supraventricular tachycardia with abnormal conduction. Although ventricular tachycardia is more often associated with reduced cardiac output, hypotension, and a depressed sensorium, the absolute blood pressure and level of consciousness are not useful in discriminating ventricular tachycardia from supraventricular tachycardia with abnormal conduction. Many patients with ventricular tachycardia tolerate the dysrhythmia well, with few subjective complaints.

ECG clues to the origin of a wide-complex tachycardia can be distilled into a few simple rules (see Table 78-7 and Figure 78-35). Again, *evidence of AV dissociation strongly suggests a ventricular source for a wide-complex tachycardia.* Retrograde conduction to the atria during ventricular tachycardia can, however, occasionally produce a consistent P′ wave after the QRS complex, creating the appearance of AV association (though the P waves should look abnormal). Another strong indicator that ventricular tachycardia is present is fusion beats, occurring when an atrial impulse reaches the AV node and infranodal conduction system at the same time as the ventricular impulse, creating a hybrid QRS complex. This hybrid fusion QRS complex is often intermediate in duration and structure between the narrow atrial impulse and the wide ventricular impulse.

The appearance of specific QRS patterns in the precordial leads, especially leads V_1 and V_6, can also help identify the origin of a wide-complex tachycardia (see Table 78-7). A QRS duration of greater than 0.14 second is more commonly associated with ventricular tachycardia, especially when coupled with a history of previous myocardial infarction. A bizarre QRS axis, manifested as an extreme left-axis deviation, also suggests ventricular tachycardia. Finally, a previous ECG tracing can be helpful; QRS complexes that are identical to those seen on an old ECG strongly suggest the same source. If the QRS morphology during a wide-

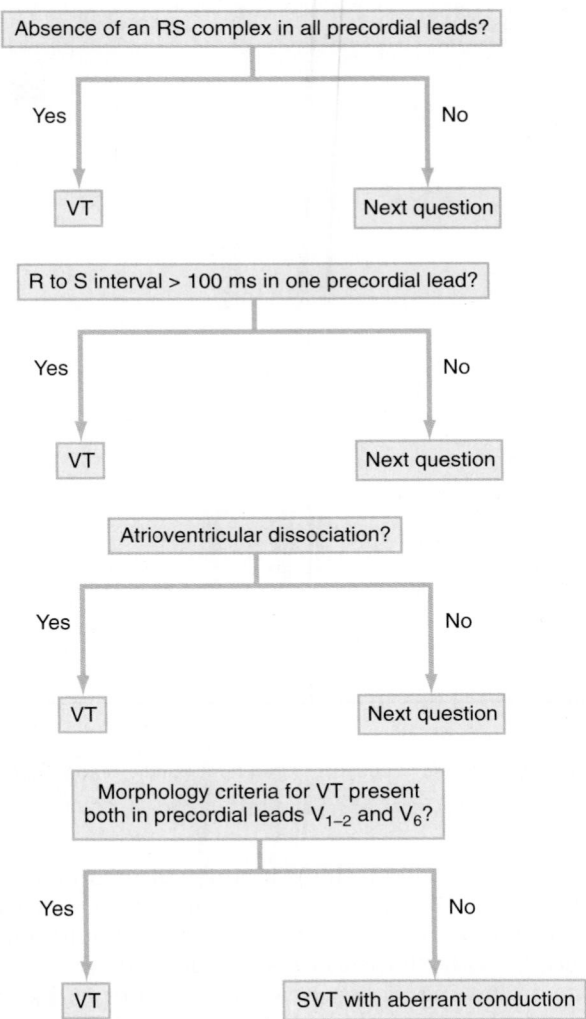

Absence of an RS complex in all precordial leads?

- Yes → VT
- No → Next question

R to S interval > 100 ms in one precordial lead?

- Yes → VT
- No → Next question

Atrioventricular dissociation?

- Yes → VT
- No → Next question

Morphology criteria for VT present both in precordial leads V$_{1-2}$ and V$_6$?

- Yes → VT
- No → SVT with aberrant conduction

Figure 78-35. Four-step approach for differentiating ventricular tachycardia (VT) and wide-QRS supraventricular tachycardia. Only when a negative response to all four questions occurs is a supraventricular rhythm with abnormal conduction diagnosed. As soon as a single "yes" answer is noted, ventricular tachycardia is diagnosed. (From Brugada P, et al: A new approach to the differential diagnosis of a regular tachycardia with a wide QRS complex. *Circulation* 83:1649, 1991.)

complex tachycardia is the same as the morphology of sinus rhythm with bundle branch block, it is more likely that the wide-complex tachycardia is supraventricular with aberration rather than ventricular tachycardia. This indicator is not without pitfalls; subtle changes in QRS morphology or duration can be difficult to see, yet may be important clues in separating ventricular tachycardia from supraventricular tachycardia with abnormal conduction.

The Brugada ECG-based criteria search for four pieces of evidence of VT from among those listed previously[76]; as soon as one is found, the diagnosis is made. *The rhythm must be regular for these to be employed* (chaos suggests atrial fibrillation with altered conduction). The sequential criteria are (see Figure 78-35):

- Absence of any RS complexes in the chest leads
- RS duration (measured from beginning of R to deepest part of S wave) greater than 100 msec

- AV dissociation (often present but overlooked—look at inferior limb leads and V$_{1-2}$)
- Specific VT morphologic criteria (Figure 78-36)

Only when none of the criteria are present is a supraventricular etiology diagnosed. Although the original authors found excellent sensitivity (98.7%) and specificity (96.5%) in detecting VT, follow-up investigations have not duplicated this level of accuracy in emergency department patients, with nonagreement between emergency physicians seen in 22% of cases. In patients receiving class I agents, these criteria are less reliable.[76,77]

The regularity of the QRS complexes can be helpful in distinguishing ventricular tachycardia from supraventricular tachycardia with abnormal conduction and in guiding treatment. Most episodes of ventricular tachycardia and supraventricular tachycardia with abnormal conduction are completely or predominantly regular, although some irregularity can be seen with both. Nevertheless, *a wide-complex tachycardia with an underlying chaotic rhythm (irregularly irregular) should raise the suspicion of atrial fibrillation with abnormal conduction*. The conduction abnormality can result from a preexisting bundle branch block, an acquired bundle branch block (often in a right bundle branch block appearance), or an accessory pathway syndrome. The latter should be suspected whenever a chaotic rhythm at a rate of 200 beats/min or greater is seen, irrespective of the QRS duration. Atrial fibrillation with an accessory pathway syndrome, whether associated with a wide or narrow QRS complex, should not be treated with calcium channel blockers or digoxin because of the risk of precipitating ventricular fibrillation. Cardioversion, procainamide, or amiodarone should be used as outlined in the previous section on accessory pathway syndromes.

Unstable patients with a wide-complex tachycardia should be treated as if ventricular tachycardia is present. Patients with pulseless wide-complex tachycardia should be treated as outlined previously in the discussion on pulseless ventricular tachycardia and fibrillation. For unstable patients with a wide-complex tachycardia and a palpable pulse, cardioversion with 50 to 100 J initially (after sedation if time permits) is recommended. If the initial countershock is unsuccessful, repeated attempts with increased doses in 50 to 100 J increments (up to a maximum of 360 to 400 J) should be administered. Although a synchronized countershock is preferred, unsynchronized countershock of ventricular tachycardia is acceptable and is not associated with an increased risk of postcardioversion ventricular fibrillation (occurring at an incidence of 5% with both methods).

If the patient is "borderline unstable" (only one nonextreme sign or symptom present) or if the patient is stable yet the source of the wide-complex tachycardia is unclear, treatment should proceed assuming that ventricular tachycardia is present. Pharmacologic agents, such as lidocaine, procainamide, or amiodarone, can be employed. The advantages of lidocaine are that it can be given rapidly and terminates most cases of ventricular tachycardia. Lidocaine is unlikely to have an appreciable effect on a supraventricular

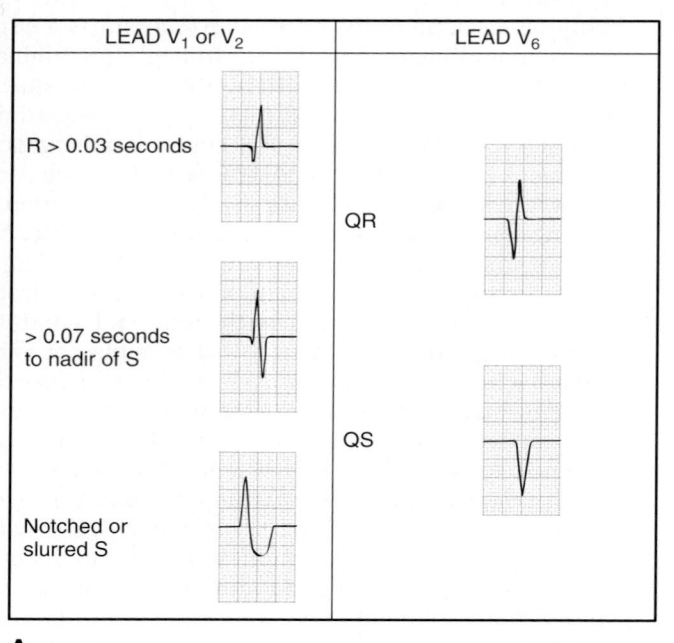

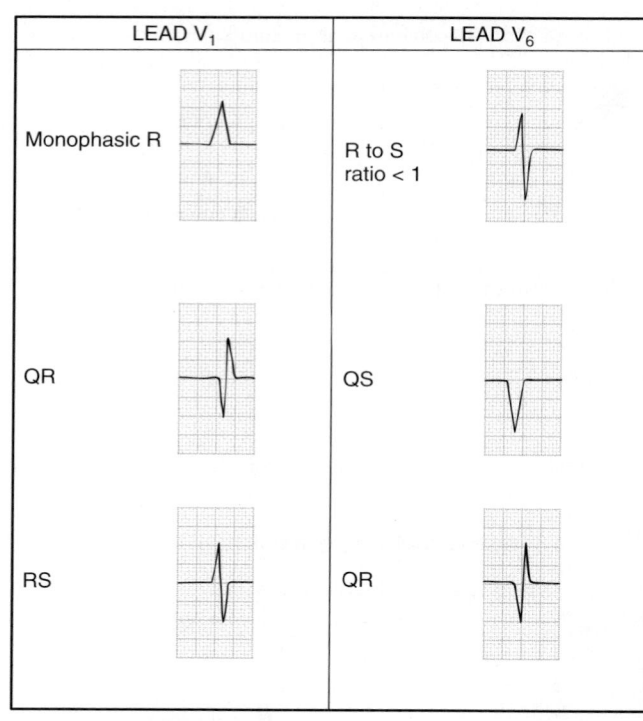

Figure 78-36. The morphology associated with the fourth criterion in the Brugada system. **A,** In patients with a right bundle branch–appearing complex. **B,** In patients with a left bundle branch–appearing complex.

tachycardia with abnormal conduction, but is also likely to cause no harm. Procainamide may be preferable as the initial agent in patients with a wide-complex tachycardia of uncertain origin because it can convert both supraventricular tachycardia (including those associated with accessory pathways) and ventricular tachycardia. Amiodarone is another option. If procainamide or amiodarone is used, the infusion rate should be much slower than that of lidocaine to help lessen any prodysrhythmia or hypotension. Electrical cardioversion remains an option in stable patients if pharmacologic treatment fails.

Because ventricular tachycardia does not usually respond to adenosine (only 5% to 10% of ventricular tachycardia cases terminate with this agent) and most supraventricular tachycardias are terminated or temporarily slowed, this agent can help in the differential diagnosis of wide-complex tachycardia. Overall, this approach is relatively safe, although case reports of poorly defined hemodynamic collapse after adenosine administration in wide-complex tachycardia exist, tempering the widespread enthusiasm associated with this approach.[45] This parallels (albeit to a lesser magnitude) the experience with calcium channel blockers, which were previously believed to be useful as a diagnostic measure for similar reasons. It is now clear that calcium channel blockers are contraindicated in the initial treatment of wide-complex tachycardia.[81] Although calcium channel blockers have little direct effect on most forms of ventricular tachycardia, many patients with this rhythm experience immediate cardiovascular collapse from the vasodilatory effects of these drugs. When a supraventricular source for a wide-complex tachycar-

dia has been verified, the principles of treatment parallel those outlined for narrow-complex tachycardia. The evaluation of clinical and ECG data should not be replaced with indiscriminate adenosine, calcium channel blocking, or any other AV nodal drug therapy.

Ventricular sources of wide-complex tachycardia can be divided into three categories: ventricular fibrillation and flutter, paced ventricular rhythms, and ventricular tachycardia.

Ventricular Tachycardia

Ventricular tachycardia is the result of a dysrhythmia originating within or below the termination of the His bundle.[82] On the ECG, a minimum of three consecutive wide QRS complex beats is necessary to diagnose ventricular tachycardia. *Nonsustained* refers to short episodes (seconds) that revert spontaneously, whereas *sustained ventricular tachycardia* refers to more prolonged episodes. Reentry mechanisms are the most common cause of ventricular tachycardia, although automatic and triggered mechanisms also occur. Ventricular tachycardia can be precipitated by any extrasystole, with PVCs the most common inciting stimulus. Extrasystole that occurs during ventricular repolarization (the R-on-T phenomenon) may carry a risk of precipitating ventricular tachycardia, although the magnitude of this risk is debated. Most patients with ventricular tachycardia have underlying heart disease, although other conditions can be responsible.

Several groups of ventricular tachycardia can be identified on the basis of the ECG pattern and history. *Monomorphic ventricular tachycardia* can occur in the presence or absence of ischemic heart disease and

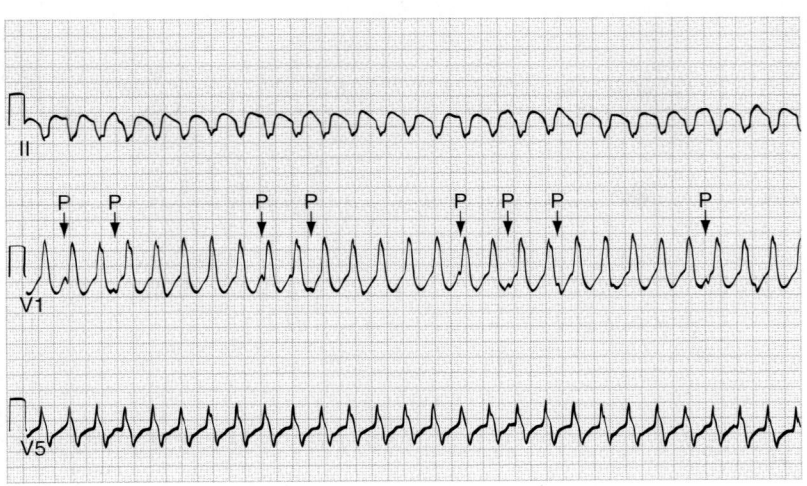

A

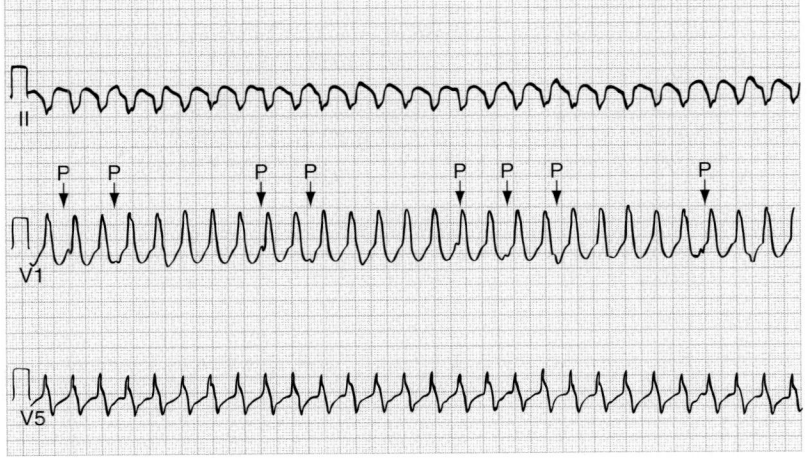

B

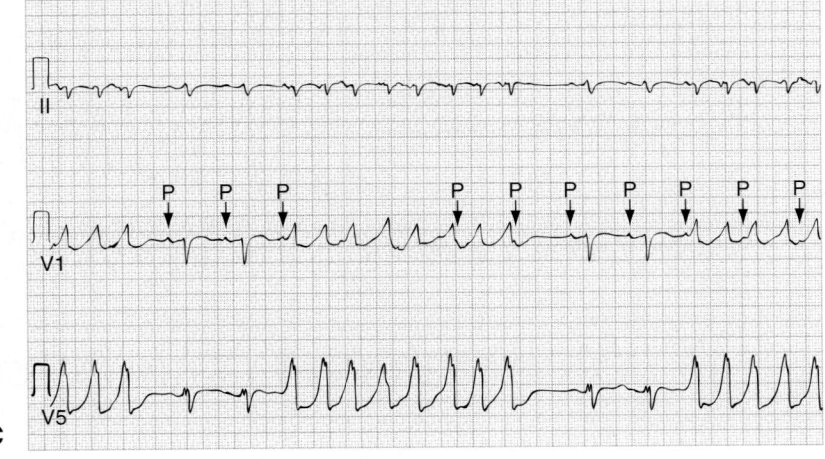

C

appears as morphologically consistent QRS complexes, usually in a regular pattern and at a rate of 150 to 200 beats/min (Figures 78-37 and 78-38). An irregular rhythm and a rate greater than 200 beats/min or less than 150 beats/min may be seen. Monomorphic ventricular tachycardia associated with chronic coronary artery disease is the single most common form of ventricular tachycardia.

Polymorphic ventricular tachycardia is manifested as QRS complexes that vary in structure or duration and is associated with more severe underlying disease[6,82] (Figures 78-39 and 78-40). *Torsades de pointes* is a specific form of polymorphic ventricular tachycardia. *Bidirectional* (or *alternating*) *ventricular tachycardia* occurs most frequently in digitalis intoxication and appears as a ventricular tachycardia with a QRS structure and axis that change periodically (see Figure 78-39). During all forms of ventricular tachycardia, the main vectors of the ST segment and T wave are usually in an opposite direction from the terminal

Figure 78-38. Ventricular tachycardia. **A,** RS complexes are present in chest leads, but RS duration is greater than 100 msec. Although Brugada criteria indicate that no further analysis is necessary, atrioventricular dissociation is also evident and QRS morphology (R:S ratio <1 in lead V_6) is consistent with ventricular tachycardia. **B,** Some RS complexes are present, RS duration is not greater than 100 msec, and atrioventricular dissociation is difficult to appreciate; morphologic criteria for ventricular tachycardia are fulfilled because S is notched in V_1 and QR is present in V_6. **C,** Diagnosis is based on morphologic criteria because S is notched in V_1 and V_2 and QS is present in V_6. (Courtesy of Edward Curtis, MD.)

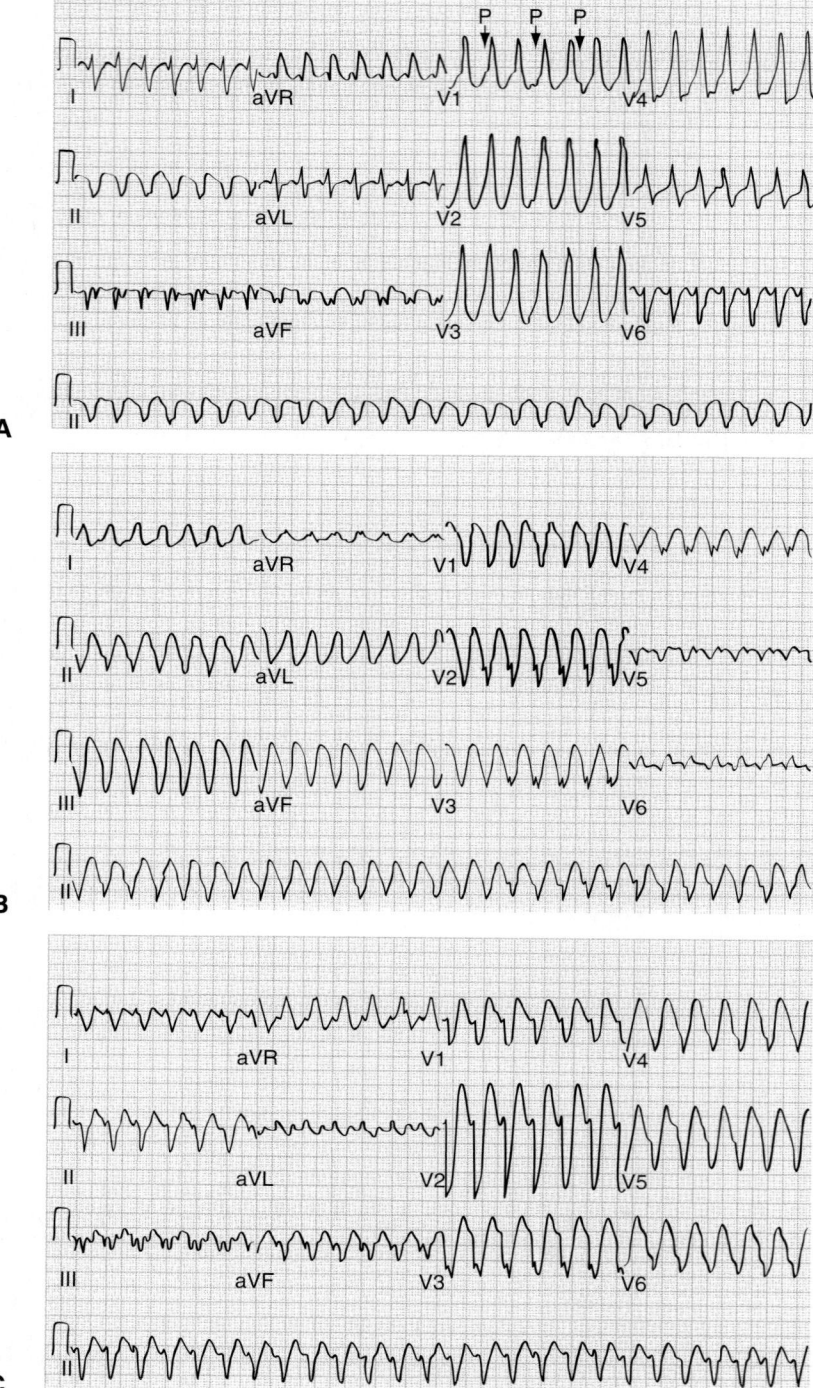

portion of the QRS complex; this phenomenon is termed a *secondary repolarization abnormality*.

Treatment of stable monomorphic ventricular tachycardia is based on correcting any underlying cause (especially electrolyte imbalance, hypoxemia or hypercapnia, and myocardial ischemia) and intervening pharmacologically to terminate the dysrhythmia. Lidocaine (1.0 to 1.5 mg/kg bolus, up to 3 mg/kg maximum) remains the drug of choice initially, with up to 90% of episodes successfully terminated.[82,83] If ventricular tachycardia is refractory to lidocaine, amiodarone or

procainamide can be used as a second-line agent. Magnesium sulfate (2 to 4 g IV as a slow bolus) can augment or serve as a third-line agent in the treatment of ventricular tachycardia, especially in the setting of ischemia. Unstable patients or those refractory to drug therapy should be cardioverted with 50 to 100 J initially, with maximal doses of 360 J in 50 to 100 J increments.

In the rare cases of ventricular tachycardia caused solely by catecholamine excess, ß-adrenergic blockers may be useful in the primary treatment; otherwise,

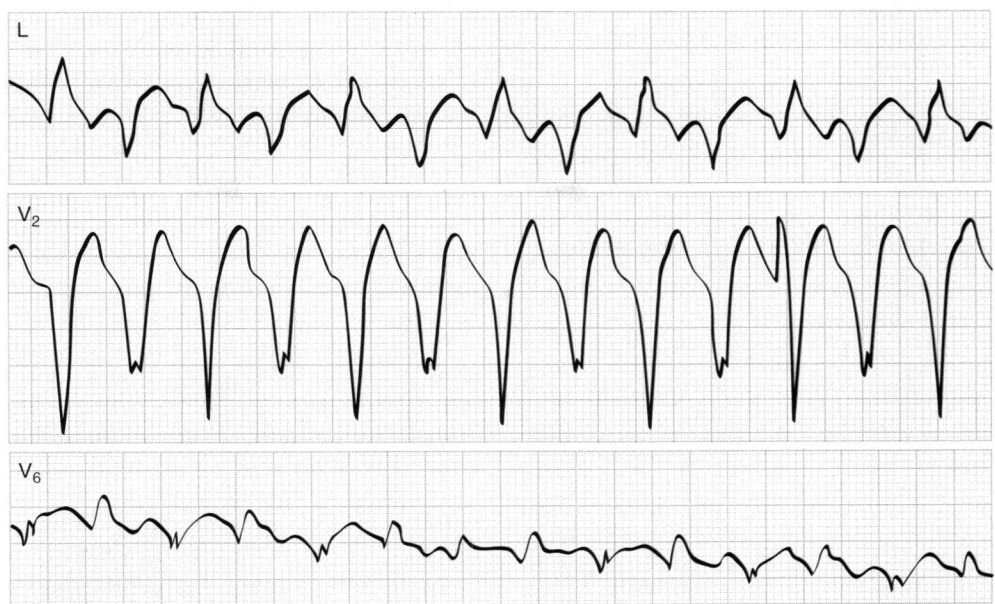

Figure 78-39. Bidirectional ventricular tachycardia in a patient with digitalis toxicity. (From Marriott HJL, Conover MB: *Advanced Concepts in Arrhythmias*, 2nd ed. St. Louis, Mosby, 1989.)

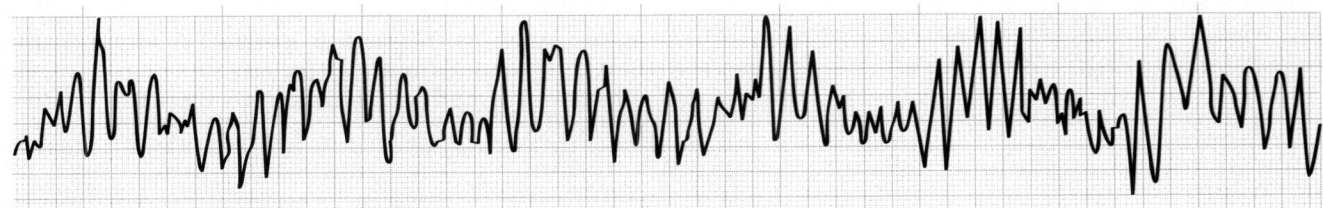

Figure 78-40. Torsades de pointes with classical spiraling of QRS complexes around baseline.

these agents are best suited for prophylaxis. Calcium channel blockers may prevent ventricular tachycardia associated with reperfusion but are not indicated for the treatment of ventricular tachycardia. These two classes of agents are also useful in young patients without underlying structural heart disease who have monomorphic ventricular tachycardia and a classical right bundle branch block (calcium channel blockers) or left bundle branch block (ß-blockers) pattern. Lidocaine remains the first-line drug even in these cases because of its effectiveness and the difficulty of making the diagnosis of "no heart disease" with certainty in the emergency department.

All patients with symptomatic ventricular tachycardia, new-onset ventricular tachycardia, or ventricular tachycardia requiring electrical therapy should be admitted. The only patients eligible for discharge are those with chronic ventricular tachycardia who have no change in symptoms or acute ischemia. These patients should be released after consultation and given immediate close outpatient follow-up. Many patients with ventricular tachycardia are candidates for an implantable defibrillator; data suggest that this (along with use after ventricular fibrillation and in certain patients at high risk for sudden death related to ven-

tricular dysrhythmia) may improve outcomes. The prognosis for patients with ventricular tachycardia depends on the symptoms and the presence of underlying heart disease. Those with structural heart disease and syncope have a poor prognosis.

Polymorphic Ventricular Tachycardia and Torsades de Pointes

Polymorphic ventricular tachycardia implies more severe underlying cardiac disease and is usually treated in the same way as monomorphic ventricular tachycardia.[6,82,84] One specific form of polymorphic ventricular tachycardia requires recognition and specific therapy. Torsades de pointes, literally translated as "twisting of the points," is a paroxysmal form of ventricular tachycardia that meets the following clinical criteria (see Figure 78-40):

1. Ventricular rate is greater than 200 beats/min.
2. QRS structure displays an undulating axis, with the polarity of the complexes appearing to shift about the baseline.
3. Occurrences are often in short episodes of less than 90 seconds, although sustained runs can be seen.

Torsades often occurs in the setting of a prolonged QT interval during sinus rhythm, which is a reflection

BOX 78-13. Classification and Causes of Prolonged QT Syndromes

Pause Dependent (Acquired)

Drug induced: 1A and 1C antidysrhythmics, phenothiazines, cyclic antidepressants, organophosphates, antihistamines.

Electrolyte abnormalities: hypokalemia, hypomagnesemia, hypocalcemia (rarely)

Diet related: starvation, low protein

Severe bradycardia or atrioventricular block

Hypothyroidism

Contrast injection

Cerebrovascular accident (especially intraparenchymal)

Myocardial ischemia

Adrenergic Dependent

Congenital

Jervell and Lange-Nielsen syndrome (deafness, autosomal recessive)

Romano-Ward syndrome (normal hearing, autosomal dominant)

Sporadic (normal hearing, no familial tendency)

Mitral valve prolapse.

Acquired

Cerebrovascular disease (especially subarachnoid hemorrhage)

Autonomic surgery: radical neck dissection, carotid endarterectomy, truncal vagotomy

---

of abnormal ventricular repolarization. The true normal ranges for QT duration are debated and must be corrected for age, sex, and heart rate; however, a QT interval of 500 msec or longer is clearly indicative of an increased risk of torsades. This repolarization abnormality can be congenital or acquired, with the latter being more common. Female sex is independently associated with a greater risk of QT prolongation and torsades.[6]

Acquired QT prolongation and torsades are often the result of multiple interactions, especially drug therapy and electrolyte disturbances (hypokalemia and hypomagnesemia). With respect to drug triggers, either high concentrations or abrupt infusion can increase the risk of QT prolongation and torsades, although either can be seen at any time after starting or altering drug therapy. Delayed episodes (months after treatment is begun or altered) are often the result of an additive effect on ventricular repolarization, such as electrolyte imbalance, clearance issues (e.g., renal or liver failure), or addition of another drug implicated in this syndrome.

The majority of adult cases of torsades are acquired and *pause dependent* and are associated with an acquired QT prolongation (Box 78-13). These episodes of torsades are precipitated by a slow heart rate. Treatment of intermittent torsades in stable patients is based on correcting any underlying metabolic or electrolyte abnormalities and increasing the heart rate to shorten ventricular repolarization. The latter can be done with

isoproterenol or overdrive pacing (external or transvenous) to a ventricular rate of 100 to 120 beats/min. Intravenous magnesium sulfate is also effective in treating paroxysmal torsades.[85] Class IA and IC agents are contraindicated because they may worsen the dysrhythmia by further prolonging repolarization. The class IB agents (including lidocaine and phenytoin) shorten repolarization, but their overall success rate is low in these cases.[82,86] Amiodarone is an alternative therapy, even though it can rarely precipitate this rhythm.

Patients who are unstable or in sustained torsades should be treated with cardioversion. As with ventricular tachycardia, unsynchronized countershocks (50 to 100 J initially up to a maximal dose of 360 J) are usually needed because of the varying R wave structures.

In contrast, torsades de pointes associated with a congenital QT prolongation syndrome is rare and usually arises in childhood or early adulthood. This form is precipitated by catecholamine excess (e.g., exercise or medications) and termed *tachycardia dependent*. Similarly, torsades after neck surgery and cerebrovascular accidents may be precipitated by catecholamine excess. Treatment of all forms of catecholamine-induced torsades is based on slowing the heart rate, usually with ß-adrenergic blockers. Other agents, such as magnesium sulfate, calcium channel blockers, amiodarone, or phenytoin, have varying effectiveness and are second-line therapies in these patients.

REFERENCES

1. Coplen SE, et al: Efficacy and safety of quinidine therapy for maintenance of sinus rhythm after cardioversion. *Circulation* 82:1106, 1990.
2. Wyman MG, et al: Multiple bolus technique for lidocaine administration in acute ischemic heart disease. Treatment of refractory ventricular arrhythmias and the pharmacokinetic significance of severe left heart failure. *J Am Coll Cardiol* 2:764, 1983.
3. Vaughan Williams EM: A classification of antiarrhythmic actions reassessed after a decade of experience. *J Clin Pharmacol* 24:129, 1984.
4. Somberg JC: Antiarrhythmic drugs: Making sense of the deluge. *Am Heart J* 113:408, 1987.
5. Nygaard TW, et al: Adverse reactions to antiarrhythmic drugs during therapy for ventricular arrhythmias. *JAMA* 256:55, 1986.
6. Roden DM: Drug-induced prolongation of the QT interval. *J Emerg Med* 350:1013, 2004.
7. de Haas DD, Taliaferro EH, Amin NM: Intravenous procainamide for the conversion of new onset atrial fibrillation in the emergency department setting. *J Emerg Med* 6:185, 1988.
8. Michael JA, Stiell IG, Agarwal S, Mandavia DP: Cardioversion of paroxysmal atrial fibrillation in the emergency department. *Ann Emerg Med* 33:379, 1999.
9. Morady F, Scheinman MM, Desai J: Disopyramide. *Ann Intern Med* 96:337, 1982.
10. Venditti FJ, Garan H, Ruskin JN: Electrophysiologic effects of beta blockers in ventricular arrhythmias. *Am J Cardiol* 60:3D, 1987.
11. Cranford RE, et al: Intravenous phenytoin: Clinical and pharmacokinetic aspects. *Neurology* 28:874, 1978.

12. Campbell RWF: Drug therapy: Mexiletine. *N Engl J Med* 316:29, 1987.

13. Roden DM, Woosley RL: Drug therapy: Tocainide. *N Engl J Med* 315:41, 1986.

14. Shuster MR, et al: Effect on seizure threshold in dogs of tocainide/lidocaine administration. *Ann Emerg Med* 16:749, 1987.

15. Echt DS, et al: Mortality and morbidity in patients receiving encainide, flecainide, or placebo. The Cardiac Arrhythmia Suppression Trial. *N Engl J Med* 324:781, 1991.

16. Horowitz LN: Encainide in lethal ventricular arrhythmias evaluated by electrophysiologic tests and decrease in symptoms. *Am J Cardiol* 58:83C, 1986.

17. Funck-Brentano C, Kroemer H, Lee JT, Rosen DM: Propafenone. *N Engl J Med* 322:518, 1990.

18. Abrams J, et al: Efficacy and safety of esmolol vs propranolol in the treatment of supraventricular tachyarrhythmias: A multicenter double blind trial. *Am Heart J* 110:913, 1985.

19. Esmolol Research Group: Intravenous esmolol for the treatment of supraventricular tachyarrhythmias: Results of a multicenter baseline controlled safety and efficacy study in 160 patients. *Am Heart J* 112:498, 1986.

20. Anderson S, et al: Comparison of the efficacy and safety of esmolol, a short acting beta blocker, with placebo in the treatment of supraventricular tachycardias. *Am Heart J* 111:42, 1986.

21. Brendorp B, et al: A benefit-risk assessment of class III antiarrhythmic agents. *Drug Saf* 25:847, 2002.

22. Koch-Weser J: Drug therapy: Bretylium. *N Engl J Med* 300:473, 1979.

23. Mason JW: Drug therapy: Amiodarone. *N Engl J Med* 316:455, 1987.

24. Joseph AP, Ward MR: A prospective, randomized controlled trial comparing the efficacy and safety of sotalol, amiodarone, and digoxin for the reversion of new-onset atrial fibrillation. *Ann Emerg Med* 36:1, 2000.

25. Ochi RP, et al: Intravenous amiodarone for the rapid treatment of life-threatening ventricular arrhythmias in critically ill patients with coronary artery disease. *Am J Cardiol* 64:599, 1989.

26. Ellenbogen KA, et al: Efficacy of intravenous ibutilide for rapid termination of atrial fibrillation and atrial flutter: A dose-response study. *J Am Coll Cardiol* 28:130, 1996.

27. Hohnloser SH, Woosley RL: Sotalol. *N Engl J Med* 331:31, 1994.

28. Waxman HL, et al: Verapamil for control of ventricular rate in paroxysmal supraventricular tachycardia and atrial fibrillation or flutter. *Ann Intern Med* 94:1, 1981.

29. Tommaso C, et al: Atrial fibrillation and flutter: Immediate control and conversion with intravenously administered verapamil. *Arch Intern Med* 143:877, 1983.

30. Porter CJ, Garson A, Gillette PC: Verapamil: An effective calcium blocking agent for pediatric patients. *Pediatrics* 71:748, 1983.

31. Epstein ML, Kiel EA, Victoria BE: Cardiac decompensation following verapamil therapy in infants with supraventricular tachycardia. *Pediatrics* 75:737, 1985.

32. Salerno DM, et al: Intravenous verapamil for treatment of multifocal atrial tachycardia with and without calcium pretreatment. *Ann Intern Med* 107:623, 1987.

33. Haft JI, Habbab MA: Treatment of atrial arrhythmias: Effectiveness of verapamil when preceded by calcium infusion. *Arch Intern Med* 146:1085, 1986.

34. Schreck DM, Rivera AR, Tricarico VJ: Emergency management of atrial fibrillation and flutter: Intravenous diltiazem versus intravenous digoxin. *Ann Emerg Med* 29:135, 1997.

35. Falk RH, et al: Digoxin for converting recent-onset atrial fibrillation to sinus rhythm: A randomized double-blinded trial. *Ann Intern Med* 106:503, 1987.

36. Mann DL, Maisel AS, Atwood JE: Absence of cardioversion-induced ventricular arrhythmias in patients with therapeutic digoxin levels. *J Am Coll Cardiol* 5:822, 1985.

37. Iseri LT, Chung P, Tobis J: Magnesium therapy for intractable ventricular tachyarrhythmias in normomagnesemic patients. *West J Med* 138:832, 1983.

38. Belardinelli L, Linden J, Berne RM: The cardiac effects of adenosine. *Prog Cardiovasc Dis* 32:73, 1989.

39. Wilson RF, et al: Effects of adenosine on human coronary arterial circulation. *Circulation* 82:1595, 1990.

40. Rankin AC, et al: Value and limitations of adenosine in the diagnosis and treatment of narrow and broad complex tachycardia. *Br Heart J* 62:195, 1989.

41. Clarke B, et al: Rapid and safe termination of spontaneous supraventricular tachycardia in children by adenosine. *Lancet* 1:299, 1987.

42. Garratt C, et al: Comparison of adenosine and verapamil for termination of paroxysmal tachycardia. *Am J Cardiol* 64:1310, 1989.

43. DiMarco JP, et al: Adenosine for paroxysmal supraventricular tachycardia: Dose ranging and comparison with verapamil. *Ann Intern Med* 113:104, 1990.

44. Cairns CB, Niemann JT: IV adenosine for the emergency department management of PSVT: Just a pharmacologic vagal maneuver? *Ann Emerg Med* 19:957, 1990.

45. Pelleg A, Pennock RS, Kutalek SP: Proarrhythmic effects of adenosine: One decade of clinical data. *Am J Ther* 9:141, 2002.

46. Shaw M, et al: Esophageal electrocardiography in acute cardiac care: Efficacy and diagnostic value of a new technique. *Am J Med* 82:689, 1987.

47. Taylor DM, Auble TE, Yealy DM: First line management of paroxysmal supraventricular tachycardia. *Am J Emerg Med* 17:214, 1999.

48. Waxman MB, et al: Vagal techniques for termination of paroxysmal supraventricular tachycardia. *Am J Cardiol* 46:655, 1980.

49. Munter DW, Stoner R: Ventricular fibrillation during rectal examination. *Am J Emerg Med* 7:57, 1989.

50. Mymin D, et al: The natural history of primary first-degree atrioventricular block. *N Engl J Med* 315:1183, 1986.

51. Schweitzer P, Mark H: The effect of atropine in cardiac arrhythmias and conduction, parts 1 and 2. *Am Heart J* 100:119, 255, 1980.

52. Horan MJ, Kennedy HL: Ventricular ectopy. History, epidemiology, and clinical implications. *JAMA* 251:380, 1984.

53. Tye K, et al: R-on-T or R-on-P phenomenon? Relation to the genesis of ventricular tachycardia. *Am J Cardiol* 44:632, 1979.

54. Lanza GA, et al: Ventricular parasystole: A chronobiologic study. *Pacing Clin Electrophysiol* 9:860, 1986.

55. Glass L, Goldberger AL, Belair J: Dynamics of pure parasystole. *Am J Physiol* 251:H481, 1986.

56. Bar FW, et al: Differential diagnosis of tachycardia with narrow QRS complex (shorter than 0.12 second). *Am J Cardiol* 54:555, 1984.

57. Klein GJ, et al: Classification of supraventricular tachycardias. *Am J Cardiol* 60:27D, 1987.

58. Binder LS, Beoche R, Atkinson D: Evaluation and management of supraventricular tachycardia in children. *Ann Emerg Med* 20:51, 1991.

59. Kastor JA: Multifocal atrial tachycardia. *N Engl J Med* 322:1713, 1990.

60. Boineau JP: Atrial flutter: A synthesis of concepts. *Circulation* 72:249, 1985.

61. Ettinger PO: Holiday heart arrhythmias. *Int J Cardiol* 5:540, 1984.

62. McGovern B, Garan H, Ruskin JN: Precipitation of cardiac arrest by verapamil in patients with Wolff-Parkinson-White syndrome. *Ann Intern Med* 104:791, 1986.

63. Garratt C, et al: Misuse of verapamil in pre-excited atrial fibrillation. *Lancet* 1:367, 1989.
64. Shlofmitz RA, Hirsch BE, Meyer BR: New onset atrial fibrillation: Is there a need for emergent hospitalization? *J Gen Intern Med* 1:139, 1986.
65. Michael JA, Stiell IG, Agarwal S, Mandavia DP: Cardioversion of paroxysmal atrial fibrillation in the emergency department. *Ann Emerg Med* 34:687, 1999.
66. Kim MH, et al: A prospective, randomized controlled trial of an emergency department-based atrial fibrillation treatment strategy with low-molecular weight heparin. *Ann Emerg Med* 40:187, 2002.
67. Wang HE, et al: The use of diltiazem for treating rapid atrial fibrillation in the out-of-hospital setting. Ann Emerg Med 37:38, 2001.
68. McCabe JL, et al: Intravenous adenosine in the prehospital treatment of supraventricular tachycardia. *Ann Emerg Med* 20:445, 1991.
69. Milstein S, Sharma AD, Kline GJ: Electrophysiologic profiles of asymptomatic Wolff-Parkinson-White pattern. *Am J Cardiol* 57:1097, 1986.
70. Wellens HJ, Brugada P, Penn OC: The management of pre-excitation syndromes. *JAMA* 57:2325, 1987.
71. Akhtar M, Gilbert CJ, Shenasa M: Effect of lidocaine on atrioventricular response via the accessory pathway in patients with Wolff-Parkinson-White syndrome. *Circulation* 63:435, 1981.
72. Mandel WJ, et al: The Wolff-Parkinson-White syndrome: Pharmacologic effects of procainamide. *Am Heart J* 90:744, 1975.
73. Ferrer MI: Preexcitation. *Am J Med* 62:715, 1977.
74. Wellens HJ, Bar FW, Lie KI: The value of the electrocardiogram in the differential diagnosis of a tachycardia with a widened QRS complex. *Am J Med* 64:27, 1978.
75. Wellens HJ: The wide QRS tachycardia [editorial]. *Ann Intern Med* 104:879, 1986.
76. Brugada P, et al: A new approach to the differential diagnosis of a regular tachycardia with a wide QRS complex. *Circulation* 83:1649, 1991.
77. Herbert ME, et al: Failure to agree on the electrocardiographic diagnosis of ventricular tachycardia. *Ann Emerg Med* 27:35, 1996.
78. Tchou P, et al: Useful clinical criteria for the diagnosis of ventricular tachycardia. *Am J Med* 84:53, 1988.
79. Baerman JM, et al: Differentiation of ventricular tachycardia from supraventricular tachycardia with aberration: Value of the clinical history. *Ann Emerg Med* 16:40, 1987.
80. Halperin BD, et al: Misdiagnosing ventricular tachycardia in patients with underlying conduction disease and similar sinus and tachycardia morphologies. *West J Med* 152:677, 1990.
81. Stewart RB, Bardy GH, Greene HL: Wide complex tachycardia: Misdiagnosis and outcome after emergent therapy. *Ann Intern Med* 104:766, 1986.
82. Akhtar M: Clinical spectrum of ventricular tachycardia. *Circulation* 82:1561, 1990.
83. Reiter MJ, Easley AR, Mann DE: Efficacy of class IB antiarrhythmic agents for prevention of sustained ventricular tachycardia secondary to coronary artery disease. *Am J Cardiol* 59:1319, 1987.
84. Smith WM, Gallagher JD: "Les torsades de pointes": An unusual ventricular arrhythmia. Ann Intern Med 93:578, 1980.
85. Perticone F, Adinolfi L, Bonaduce D: Efficacy of magnesium sulfate in the treatment of torsades de pointes. *Am Heart J* 112:847, 1986.
86. Vukmir RB, Stein KL: Torsades de pointes therapy with phenytoin. *Ann Emerg Med* 20:198, 1991.

CHAPTER

79 Implantable Cardiac Devices

James T. Niemann

PERSPECTIVE

Electrical cardiac pacing for the management of brady-arrhythmias was first described in 1952, and permanent transvenous pacing devices were introduced into clinical practice in the early 1960s.[1] The first devices for endocardial defibrillation were implanted in surviving victims of sudden cardiac death in 1980.[2] Currently implanted electrical devices for the management of cardiac dysrhythmias have changed rapidly over the years with both increasing complexity and miniaturization. In 1991, it was estimated that 1 million patients in the United States had permanent pacemakers, and survey data from 1989 indicated that about 425 new pacemakers per million population were implanted annually in the United States.[3,4] New indications for the use of permanent pacemakers in the management of congenital and acquired heart disease include cardiac resynchronization therapy for heart failure.[5,6]

As of 2000, the number of implanted endocardial defibrillation devices was approximately 100,000.[2] A number of large clinical trials comparing implantable cardioverter-defibrillators (ICDs) with antiarrhythmic drugs for the prevention of sudden cardiac death resulting from ventricular dysrhythmias indicate that ICDs significantly improve survival.[7,8] Hence, the number of ICDs currently in use has continued to increase. The widespread use of these devices ensures that the emergency physician frequently encounters such patients, often with symptoms that may be related to malfunction of the pacemaker or ICD.

INDICATIONS FOR PERMANENT PACEMAKERS AND ANTIARRHYTHMIA DEVICES

Guidelines for the implantation of these devices have been developed by a joint task force of the American

BOX 79-1. Class I Indications for Permanent Pacing in Adults

1. Third-degree AV block at any anatomic level associated with any of the following:
   - Symptomatic bradycardia presumed secondary to AV block
   - Symptomatic bradycardia secondary to drugs required for dysrhythmia management or other medical condition
   - Documented periods of asystole lasting more than 3 seconds or an escape rate of less than 40 beats/min in an awake, asymptomatic patient
   - After catheter ablation of the AV node
   - Postoperative AV block that is not expected to resolve
   - Neuromuscular disease with AV block (e.g., the muscular dystrophies)
2. Symptomatic bradycardia resulting from second-degree AV block regardless of type or site of block.
3. Chronic bifascicular or trifascicular block with intermittent third-degree AV block or type II second-degree AV block
4. After acute myocardial infarction with any of the following conditions:
   - Persistent second-degree AV block at the His-Purkinje level with bilateral bundle branch block or third-degree AV block at the level of or below the His-Purkinje system
   - Transient second- or third-degree infranodal AV block and associated bundle branch block
   - Symptomatic, persistent second- or third-degree AV block
5. Sinus node dysfunction with symptomatic bradycardia (including sinus pauses) or chronotropic incompetence
6. Recurrent syncope caused by carotid sinus stimulation

AV, atrioventricular.

BOX 79-2. Class I Indications for Implantable Cardioverter-Defibrillator Therapy

1. Cardiac arrest resulting from VF or VT not caused by a transient or reversible event
2. Spontaneous sustained VT
3. Syncope of undetermined origin with clinically relevant, hemodynamically significant sustained VT or VF induced at electrophysiologic study when drug therapy is ineffective, not tolerated, or not preferred
4. Nonsustained VT with coronary artery disease, prior myocardial infarction, left ventricular dysfunction, and inducible VF or sustained VT at electrophysiologic study that is not suppressible by a class I antiarrhythmic drug

VT, ventricular tachycardia; VF, ventricular fibrillation.

Heart Association and the American College of Cardiology (AHA/ACC) and are periodically updated.[9] Using an evidence-based approach, recommendations are categorized as class I, II, or III. Class I includes conditions for which there is general agreement that a device should be implanted. A class II recommendation includes conditions for which these devices are frequently used but for which there is disagreement about their need or benefit. Class III is reserved for conditions for which there is general agreement that a device is not needed.

In the case of pacemaker therapy, additional factors are considered when selecting the mode of pacing and include, but are not limited to, overall health, lifestyle, and occupation of the patient. Class I indications for a permanent pacemaker or ICD are listed in Boxes 79-1 and 79-2. In general, pacing is recommended for patients with symptomatic heart block, symptomatic sinus bradycardia, and atrial fibrillation with a symptomatic bradycardia (low ventricular response rate) in the absence of medications that affect atrioventricular (AV) conduction. Controversial indications include pacing in patients with syncope, heart block, or fatigue in the presence of some conduction disease or bradycardia. The likelihood of a patient's improvement after pacing can be assumed only if the symptoms can be closely correlated with inadequate rate.

Pacemaker Terminology

A letter code, initially established in 1974 and since revised as technology has advanced, standardizes nomenclature for pacemakers.[10] Table 79-1 includes an explanation of the five-letter code scheme and the standard abbreviations in each category. The first three code letters are used most commonly. Using this table, one should be able to understand the features of any pacing mode. For example, a VDD pacemaker is capable of pacing only the ventricle, sensing both atrial and ventricular intrinsic depolarization, and responding by dual inhibition of both atrial ventricular pacing if intrinsic ventricular depolarization occurs and triggering a paced ventricular beat in response to a sensed intrinsic atrial depolarization. The codes of a permanent pacemaker that are used most frequently and the indications, advantages, and disadvantages of each are listed in Table 79-2. Detailed algorithms for matching a patient with a pacemaker have been developed.[11] The majority of permanent pacemakers are now dual chamber and often rate adaptive.[12]

Pacemaker Components

All pacemaker systems have three basic components: the pulse generator, which houses the power source (battery); the electronic circuitry; and the lead system, which connects the pulse generator to the endocardium.[12]

Nearly all implanted pacemakers are lithium powered. Lithium-powered pulse generators function normally for 4 to 10 or more years, depending on the pacemaker features such as single versus dual chamber, pacing threshold, and rate adaptiveness. This long "battery life" and the fact that the output voltage of the lithium-iodine cell decreases gradually rather than abruptly, as occurred with the early mercury-zinc cell, make sudden pulse generator failure an unlikely cause of pacemaker malfunction.[1]

Permanent pacemakers have endocardial leads that are positioned in contact with the endocardium of the

Table 79-1. Five-Letter Pacemaker Code

Letter 1	Letter 2	Letter 3	Letter 4	Letter 5
Chamber Paced A = atrium V = ventricle D = dual O = none	Chamber Sensed A = atrium V = ventricle D = dual O = none	Sensing Response T = triggered* I = inhibited D = dual (A and V inhibited) O = none	Programmability P = simple M = multiprogrammable R = rate adaptive C = communicating O = none	Antitachycardia Functions P = pacing S = shock D = dual (shock + pace)

*In the triggered response mode, the pacemaker discharges or fires when it recognizes an intrinsic depolarization. As a result, pacemaker spikes occur during inscription of the QRS complex. Because this mode results in high-energy consumption and a shortened battery life and because the sensing response can be misinterpreted as pacemaker malfunction, this sensing mode is not used with modern pacemakers.

Table 79-2. Common Permanent Pacemakers

Code	Indication	Advantages	Disadvantages
VVI	Intermittent backup pacing; inactive patient	Simplicity; low cost	Fixed rate; risk of pacemaker syndrome
VVIR	Atrial fibrillation	Rate responsive	Requires advanced programming
DDD	Complete heart block	Atrial tracking restores normal physiology	No rate responsiveness; requires two leads and advanced programming
DDDR	Sinus node dysfunction; atrioventricular block and need for rate responsiveness	Universal pacer; all options available by programming	Complexity, cost, programming, and follow-up evaluation

right ventricle and, in the case of a dual-chamber device, the right atrium, using a subclavian or cephalic vein approach for insertion. On occasion, an epicardial lead may be implanted during open-heart surgery performed for another indication such as prosthetic valve insertion or correction of a congenital cardiac defect. Pacemaker leads, like power sources, continue to undergo major technical improvements.[1] Innovations include resilient plastic insulation surrounding the electrodes that reduces the chance of complete lead disruption or breakage (resulting in failure to pace or sense) or the chance of partial fracture (resulting in a "make or break" contact with intermittent failure to sense or pace). The expected incidence of lead disruption is approximately 2% per patient-year.[13] Endocardial leads are designed to fix actively to the atrial and ventricular endocardium using tined or screw-in tips. The expected incidence of lead displacement is about 2% for ventricular leads and 5% for atrial leads, whether actively or passively fixed to the endocardium.[13] A lead capable of active fixation is more commonly used in patients with cardiomyopathies and right ventricular dilation complicated by tricuspid regurgitation.

Pacemaker leads may be either bipolar or unipolar in configuration. A bipolar endocardial lead has both the negative (distal) and positive (proximal) electrodes, separated by about 1 cm, within the heart. A unipolar lead has the negative electrode in contact with the endocardial surface, and the positive pole is the metallic casing of the pulse generator. Each lead system has potential advantages and disadvantages.[12] The unipolar configuration is not compatible with ICD systems, is prone to oversensing of myopotentials and electromag-netic interference, but is of smaller diameter and less susceptible to fracture. The bipolar configuration is compatible with ICD systems but is larger and more prone to lead fractures; however, oversensing is rarely a problem. The selection of lead configuration usually depends on the experience and preference of the operator.

The Standard Electrocardiogram During Normal Cardiac Pacing

The modern pacemaker has two basic functions: to stimulate the heart electrically and to sense intrinsic cardiac electrical activity. Additional functions are available and noted in the pacemaker code system (Table 79-1, letters 4 and 5). The pacemaker delivers an electrical stimulus to either the atrium or ventricle if it does not recognize (sense) any intrinsic electrical activity from that chamber after a selected time interval. This interval is usually programmed at the time of implantation and can be changed noninvasively at a later time, if necessary, using a programming and "interrogating" device provided by the pacemaker manufacturer. If the pacemaker recognizes or senses an intrinsic atrial depolarization (P wave) or ventricular depolarization (QRS complex), the pacemaker inhibits or resets its output to prevent competition with the underlying intrinsic rhythm. The stimulus intensity and sensing threshold (amplitude of electrical activity that is detected as being intrinsic) are typically set at the time of implantation but can also be reprogrammed later.

The two basic functions of a pacemaker can be easily recognized and confirmed on a standard 12-lead elec-

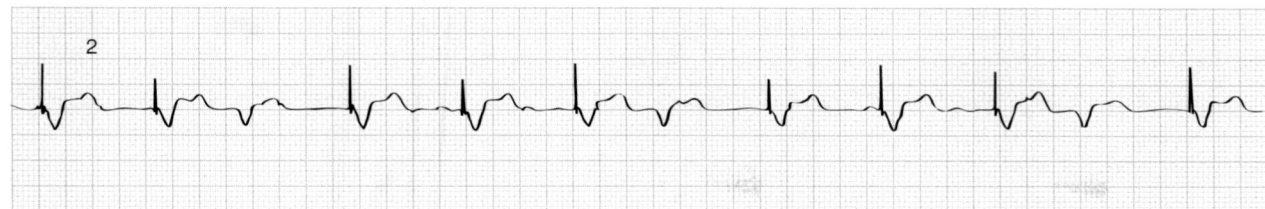

Figure 79-1. Normal VVI pacemaker (rhythm strip). This rhythm strip was recorded in a patient with a VVI pacemaker implanted for the treatment of symptomatic complete heart block. The pacing rate is approximately 75 beats/min (determined by measuring the time between consecutive pacemaker spikes). Each pacemaker spike is followed by a paced QRS complex. The third QRS from the left has a slightly different morphology than the paced QRS complexes. It is an intrinsic QRS complex that is sensed by the pacemaker, and a paced beat does not occur again until the programmed rate of the pacemaker is exceeded. The time interval between the spontaneous QRS and the next paced beat is about the same as the interval between consecutive pacemaker spikes. This sequence is subsequently repeated twice on this strip.

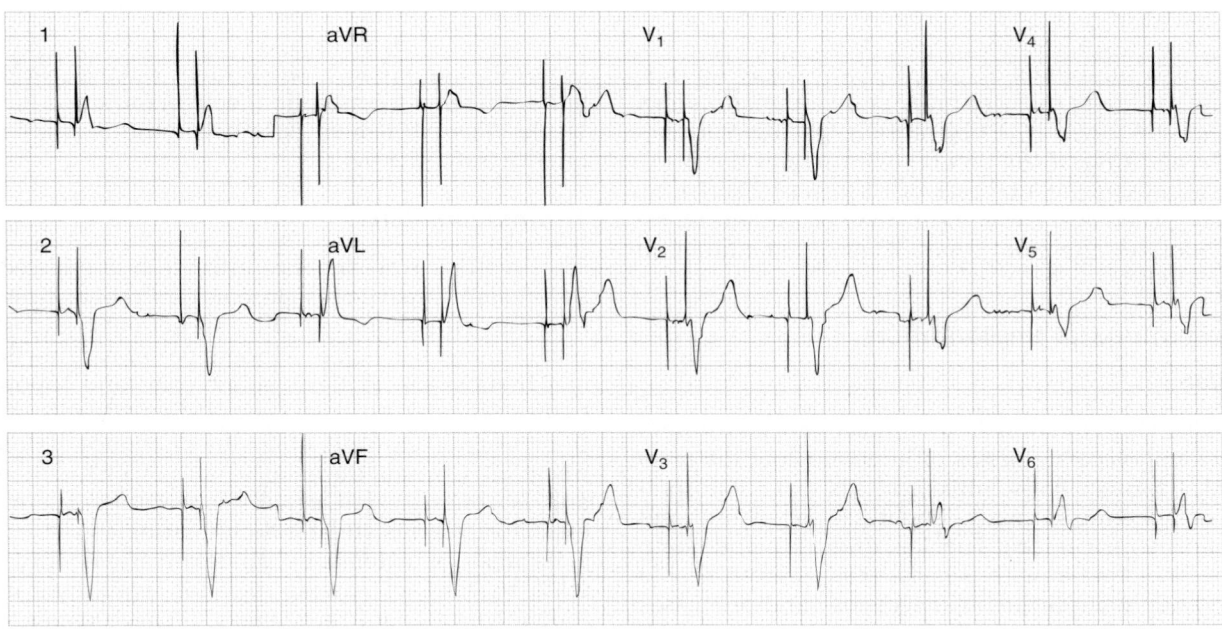

Figure 79-2. Normal DDD pacemaker (12-lead electrocardiogram). Each QRS complex is preceded by two pacemaker spikes. The first spike results in atrial depolarization, and the second produces a wide QRS complex. The QRS complex is conducted with a left bundle branch morphology, which is expected with endocardial pacing at the right ventricular apex.

trocardiogram (ECG) or rhythm strip. The normal function of a single-chamber VVI pacemaker is most easily recognized (Figure 79-1). After a programmed interval is surpassed during which intrinsic ventricular activity does not occur, a pacer "spike" or stimulus artifact appears. The pacer spike is a narrow deflection that is usually less than 5 mm in amplitude with a bipolar lead configuration and usually 20 mm or more in amplitude with a unipolar lead. A wide QRS complex appears immediately after the stimulus artifact. Depolarization begins in the right ventricular apex, and the spread of excitation does not follow normal conduction pathways. Characteristically, a left bundle branch block conduction pattern is seen. A right bundle branch pattern is abnormal and suggests lead displacement. In VVI pacing, the paced QRS complexes are independent of intrinsic atrial depolarization if present (AV dissociation).

The recognition of normal dual-chamber pacing is more complex owing to the interactive sensing and pacing of the right atrium and ventricle (Figure 79-2).[14] Pacing intervals are preprogrammed, may be changed noninvasively at a later time, and are generally specific to the patient's needs. Pacing rates and delay intervals typically vary from patient to patient. Dual-chamber devices are typically used in patients with nonfibrillating atria coupled with intact AV conduction. A normal-appearing QRS complex may follow an intrinsic "p" wave, owing to normal sinoatrial node discharge, if the intrinsic atrial depolarization is conducted to the ventricles. The intrinsic p wave and QRS complex inhibit the atrial and ventricular circuitry. A normal QRS complex follows a paced p wave if the paced atrial beat is conducted through the AV node and the programmed AV delay period is not exceeded. If it is not conducted to the ventricles (AV delay period exceeded), the pacemaker stimulates the ventricle, resulting in a paced p wave and a wide, paced QRS complex with left bundle branch block configuration. Recognition of the interactivity of the paced

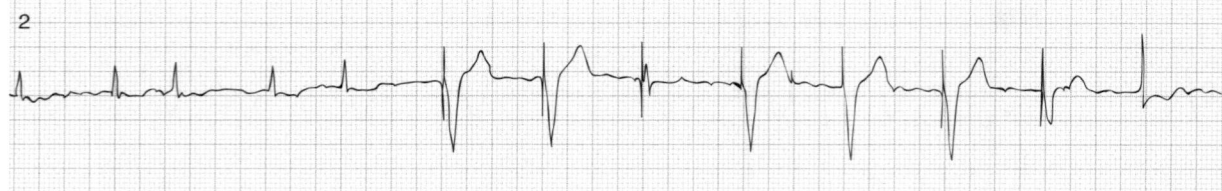

Figure 79-3. VVI pacemaker with fusion beats (pseudomalfunction). This VVI pacemaker was implanted in a patient with atrial fibrillation and intermittent symptomatic complete heart block. In the lead II rhythm strip, the first five QRS complexes are normal in morphology and irregular, as would be expected in atrial fibrillation. The next two QRS complexes are wide and preceded by a pacemaker spike. This represents normal sensing and pacing. The eighth QRS complex is narrow but preceded by a pacemaker spike. The spikes occur at a fixed and regular interval. In this instance, spontaneous ventricular depolarization had begun at about the time the pacemaker discharged. The 12th QRS complex in the sequence represents a fusion beat. Within the QRS complex of the 13th beat, a pacemaker spike is visible. Again, this represents nearly simultaneous conduction of a supraventricular beat and pacemaker electrical discharge. At first glance, this may appear to be failure to sense; however, the pacemaker is functioning normally and competing with the underlying rhythm.

chambers is important. A paced p wave may be mistaken for failure to sense or pace, and malfunction may be diagnosed when it is not present (pseudomalfunction). In addition, if the programmed rate of the pacemaker approximates the patient's intrinsic heart rate, fusion of paced and native beats may occur and represents another common type of pseudomalfunction (Figure 79-3).

Complications of Implantation

Infection

Pacemaker implantation is a surgical procedure and, like all surgery, carries a risk of infection, and the presence of a foreign body enhances this risk. The incidence of infection is small—about 2% for wound and subcutaneous pacemaker "pocket" infection and about 1% for bacteremia with sepsis. The presence of a foreign body complicates management, and few cases of bacteremia that develop after implantation can be managed with antibiotics alone. In most instances, reimplantation and replacement of the lead system are necessary.[15,16]

Pain and local inflammation at the site of the pacemaker are the first manifestations of a wound infection, cellulitis, or pocket infection. Approximately 20% to 25% of patients with a local infection have positive blood cultures. Bacteremia may occur in the absence of a focal infection and may arise with the typical manifestations of the systemic inflammatory response syndrome or sepsis. A hematoma of the pacemaker pocket may mimic a wound or pocket infection. Needle aspiration of the pocket, if performed, should be done with extreme caution, preferably under fluoroscopy, because the needle may cut the insulation surrounding the pulse generator or the portion of the pacemaker lead that lies within the pacemaker pocket.

When a local infection or bacteremia is suspected, blood cultures should be obtained and intravenous antibiotic therapy initiated. *Staphylococcus aureus* and *S. epidermidis* are the organisms isolated in approximately 60% to 70% of cases. Empirical antibiotic therapy should include vancomycin pending culture and sensitivity data. If blood cultures are positive, the pulse generator and pacemaker lead are usually

removed, temporary transvenous pacing performed, and intravenous antibiotic therapy continued for 4 to 6 weeks. The permanent pacemaker and lead are subsequently reimplanted.[17]

Thrombophlebitis

The incidence of venous obstruction associated with permanent transvenous pacemakers ranges from 30% to 50%, with about one third of patients having complete venous occlusion. Thrombosis of varying degrees can involve the axillary, subclavian, and innominate veins or the superior vena cava (SVC). The site of insertion does not appear to affect the incidence of this complication. Chronic thrombosis of the veins of the upper arm is common and usually asymptomatic owing to extensive venous collateral circulation.

Because of extensive collateralization, only about 0.5% to 3.5% of patients develop symptoms usually indicative of acute thrombosis.[18] These patients typically present with edema, pain, and venous engorgement of the arm ipsilateral to the site of lead insertion. Although rare, SVC syndrome resulting from pacemaker lead–induced thrombosis is reported. The signs and symptoms of lead-induced SVC syndrome are identical to those described in patients with SVC syndrome and malignancy. Whether pulmonary embolism is associated with pacemaker therapy and thrombosis is controversial.[18]

Although symptoms might suggest thrombosis, definitive diagnosis of acute thrombosis usually requires duplex sonography of the jugular venous system, conventional venography, or contrast-enhanced computed tomography. The symptoms typically respond to intravenous heparin therapy followed by long-term warfarin administration. Thrombolytic therapy is most effective if used early in management (within 7 to 10 days).

The "Pacemaker Syndrome"

After pacemaker implantation, a patient may present with new complaints or report a worsening of the symptoms that prompted evaluation and eventual pacemaker therapy. Such complaints often include syncope or near-syncope, orthostatic dizziness, fatigue, exercise intolerance, weakness, lethargy, chest fullness or pain, cough, uncomfortable pulsations in the neck or abdomen, right upper quadrant pain, and other non-specific symptoms.

These symptoms have been referred to as the pacemaker syndrome.[11,12] The etiology of this syndrome is the loss of AV synchrony and the presence of ventriculoatrial conduction, and it is most commonly encountered in the setting of VVI pacing but has been described with the DDI mode. With VVI pacing, the ventricle is electrically stimulated and depolarized, resulting in ventricular systole. If sinus node function is intact, the atria can be depolarized by a sinus impulse and contract when the tricuspid and mitral valves are closed. This contractile asynchrony results in an increase in jugular and pulmonary venous pressures and may produce symptoms of congestive heart failure. Atrial distention can result in reflex vasodepressor effects mediated by the central nervous system. Elevated levels of B-type natriuretic peptide (BNP) and diuresis are considered markers for the syndrome in its more severe forms. If the contribution of atrial contraction to late diastolic ventricular filling is important in maintaining an adequate cardiac output, basal and orthostatic hypotension may occur. DDI pacing in a patient with AV block may result in this syndrome if the sinus node discharge rate exceeds the programmed rate of the pacemaker.

Approximately 20% of patients report symptoms suggesting the pacemaker syndrome after pacemaker insertion. In most instances, symptoms are mild and patients adapt to them. In about one third of these patients, symptoms are severe. Treatment usually requires replacing a VVI pacemaker with a dual-chamber pacemaker or lowering the pacing rate of the VVI unit. If symptoms occur in a patient paced in the DDI mode, optimizing the timing of atrial and ventricular pacing is usually required. Patients appear to prefer dual-chamber pacing to the VVI modality.[19,20]

Although the pacemaker syndrome may be suspected in the emergency department in the patient with suggestive symptoms shortly after pacemaker implantation, consultation with a cardiologist is recommended. The same symptoms may be observed in patients with true pacemaker malfunction, which may necessitate pacemaker reprogramming or replacement of the pulse generator or pacemaker lead.

Pacemaker Malfunction

The term *pacemaker malfunction* refers specifically to problems with the circuitry or power source of the pulse generator, the pacemaker lead (most commonly displacement or fracture), or the interface between the pacing electrode and the myocardium (pacing or sensing threshold). In addition, environmental factors such as extracardiac or extracorporeal electrical signals may interfere with normal pacemaker function.[21,22] Using the standard ECG, pacemaker malfunction can be separated into three broad categories: (1) failure to capture (no pacemaker spikes or spikes not followed by an atrial or ventricular complex), (2) inappropriate sensing (oversensing or undersensing—spikes occur prematurely or

---

BOX 79-3. Causes of Pacemaker Malfunction

Failure to capture
- Lead disconnection, break, or displacement
- Exit block
- Battery depletion

Undersensing
- Lead displacement
- Inadequate endocardial lead contact
- Low-voltage intracardiac p waves and QRS complexes
- Lead fracture

Oversensing
- Sensing extracardiac signals: myopotentials
- T wave sensing

Inappropriate rate
- Battery depletion
- Ventriculoatrial conduction with pacemaker-mediated tachycardia
- 1:1 response to atrial dysrhythmias

---

do not occur even though the programmed interval is exceeded), or (3) inappropriate pacemaker rate. Symptomatic pacemaker malfunction after implantation occurs in less than 5% of patients and is rarely immediately life threatening. Malfunction is most commonly due to inappropriate sensing, followed by failure to capture.[13] Typical presentations and etiologies of pacemaker malfunction are listed in Box 79-3.

When the emergency physician suspects pacemaker malfunction, knowledge of the pacing modalities (see Table 79-1) and what is normal for a given pacing modality is critical when reviewing the ECG. Fortunately, patients are provided with important identifying information, usually in the form of a wallet card, after pacemaker implantation. The most important information for the emergency physician is provided in the five-letter code. If this information is not available, a standard posteroanterior and a lateral chest radiograph can provide critical information. A single lead in the apex of the right ventricle indicates a VVI pacemaker. With VVI pacing, only one stimulus artifact or spike is seen with each stimulated ventricular depolarization (see Figure 79-1). If sinus node activity is present, the paced QRS complex is dissociated from the intrinsic p waves. If separate leads are identified in the right atrium and right ventricle, the pacing modality is most often DDD or DVI, and paced p waves and QRS complexes (two spikes for each QRS complex) are seen (see Figure 79-2). However, although DDD and DVI units are capable of pacing both the right atrium and ventricle, only one spike may be seen (Figure 79-4). Failure to identify two spikes with a DDD or DVI unit can represent normal pacemaker function.

A magnet placed externally over the pulse generator is frequently used in the assessment of pacemaker function. The effect of such an intervention on pacemaker function, however, is often misunderstood by the noncardiologist. Magnet application does not inhibit or turn off a pacemaker. It does result in closure of a reed switch present within the pacemaker circuitry, con-

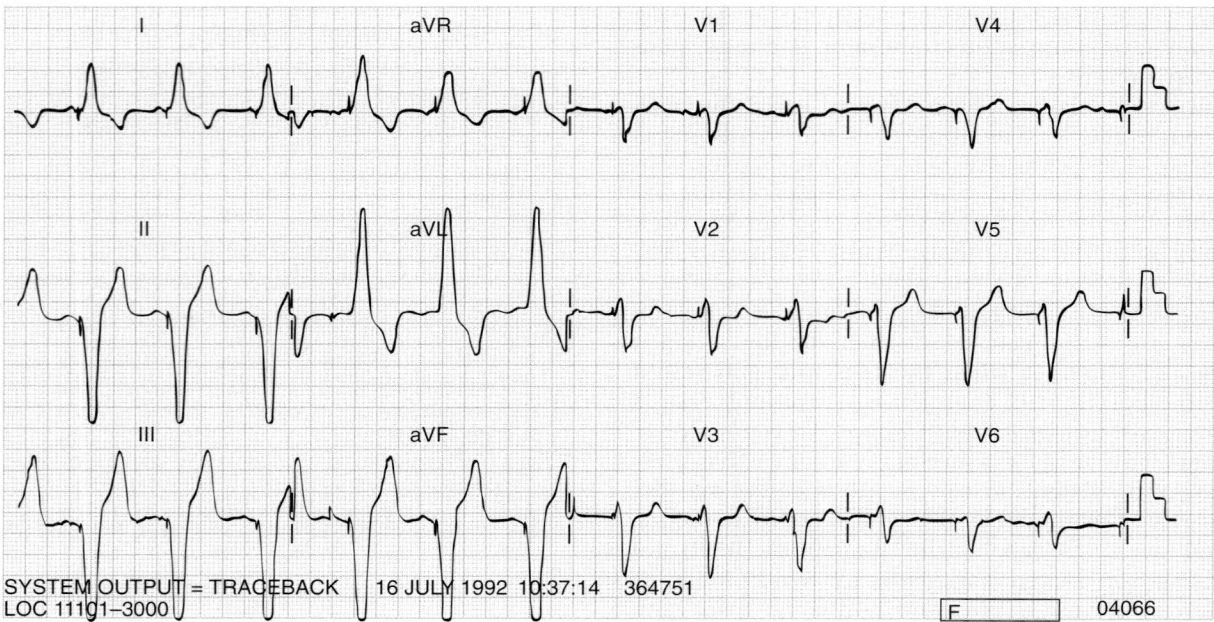

Figure 79-4. Normal DDD pacemaker (half-standard 12-lead electrocardiogram [ECG]). Three paced QRS complexes preceded by a stimulus artifact or spike are evident in leads I, II, and III. Paced QRS complexes occur after spontaneous or intrinsic p waves are sensed and atrio-ventricular (AV) conduction delay exceeds the pacemaker's programmed AV interval. The first QRS complex in the augmented leads, best seen in lead aVF, demonstrates both a paced p wave and a paced QRS complex. Although the pacemaker is a dual-chamber device, two spikes may not always be seen preceding every QRS complex and the presence of only one spike, or no spikes, should not be interpreted as evidence of pacemaker malfunction. Also evident on this ECG are the different amplitudes of the pacemaker spikes from lead to lead. When a single-lead rhythm strip is recorded, the selected lead should be the one in which the pacemaker spikes are most easily identified.

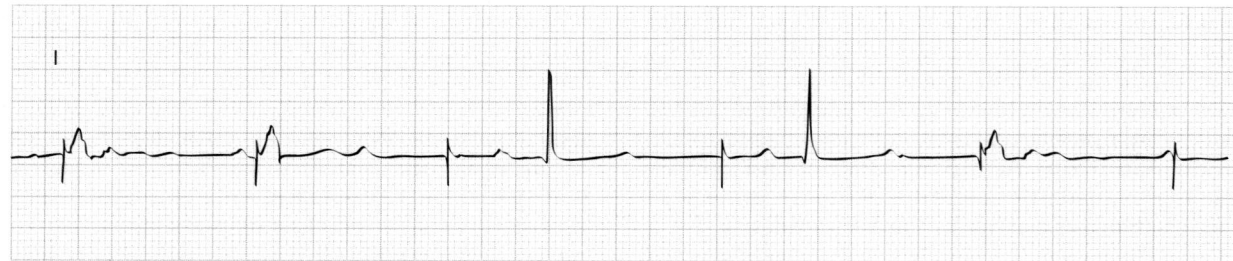

Figure 79-5. Intermittent failure to capture and slow pacing rate (lead I). This lead I rhythm strip demonstrates intermittent failure to capture of a VVI pacemaker. The first and second pacemaker spikes are followed by wide-paced QRS complexes; the third and fourth spikes are not. The pacemaker spikes occur at a rate of approximately 50/min. The device was programmed to pace at a rate of 75/min. This is a typical example of "end-of-life" pacing characteristics of a depleted battery.

verting the pacemaker to an asynchronous or fixed-rate pacing mode, and the pacemaker is no longer inhibited by the patient's intrinsic electrical activity. The technique is most commonly used when the patient's intrinsic heart rate exceeds the pacemaker's set rate and pacemaker function is inhibited. Magnet application then allows pacing to occur, and pacing rate and the presence of capture can be determined. Magnets are usually manufacturer specific, as are available external reprogramming devices.

Failure to Capture

Failure to capture may range from the complete absence of pacemaker spikes to spikes not followed by a stimulus-induced complex (Figure 79-5). A complete absence of pacemaker spikes may result from complete battery depletion, complete fracture of the pacemaker lead, or disconnection of the lead from the pulse generator unit.

Compared with the earlier mercury-zinc cells, the current lithium-iodine batteries are not prone to abrupt failure.[1,13] This power source displays typical end-of-life functional changes over a period of months and usually up to a year before complete depletion. Usually, the first sign of voltage depletion is a decrease in the programmed pacing rate. This change is gradual and should be noticed during the 1- to 3-month follow-up evaluations that pacemaker patients receive. When voltage output falls to a critical level, stimulus strength falls below the required threshold and failure to capture or intermittent failure to capture may be observed late in battery life. As a result, urgent or emergent battery replacement is rare.

Failure to capture, which may be complete or intermittent, is most commonly a lead problem. Lead displacement is the most common cause and is most likely to occur within the first month of pacemaker insertion. The chest radiograph may demonstrate the tip of the pacing catheter displaced from the right ventricular apex. The catheter tip is commonly found in the pulmonary outflow tract, where it may have intermittent contact with endocardium, resulting in intermittent failure to pace and sense. The atrial leads of dual-chamber devices are commonly displaced into the body of the right atrium, resulting in loss of contact between the pacing lead and the atrial endocardium.

Lead fracture, which is uncommon with the current polyurethane lead coating,[1] produces an insulation break, resulting in failure to capture as a result of current leakage. It can be detected as a change in pacing threshold. Lead fractures occur at predictable locations, usually at the site of attachment to the pulse generator or at abrupt angulations that serve as stress points. Inadequate contact of the lead with the pulse generator can mimic a lead fracture. On occasion, when a lead fracture is complete or nearly complete, a break in the catheter or its insulation can be detected on an over-penetrated posteroanterior chest radiograph. Loss of lead–pulse generator contact can be detected on the chest radiograph with close inspection of the pulse generator.

Exit block (the failure of an adequate stimulus to depolarize the paced chamber) can also result in failure to pace. Exit block should be considered when the pre-programmed pacing stimulus output fails to result in capture in the presence of a normally functioning pulse generator and an intact lead system. This problem is most commonly due to changes in the endocardium in contact with the pacing system. Etiologies include ischemia or infarction of the endocardium in contact with the electrodes, systemic hyperkalemia, and the use of class III antiarrhythmic drugs, such as amiodarone, which affect ventricular depolarization. Although other drugs are reported to alter pacemaker threshold, the effect is small and is rarely clinically important.[23] At the time of pacemaker insertion, stimulus strength, defined as the amplitude and duration of the electrical output, is always set substantially above the minimum required to result in an artificial electrical depolarization.

Inappropriate Sensing

For a pacemaker to function in a noncompetitive mode, it must be capable of sensing the intrinsic or "native" electrical activity of the heart. The electrical activity that is sensed is determined by the pacing modality (see Table 79-1). Sensing parameters are determined at the time of pacemaker insertion on the basis of the signal size of the intracardiac ECG and can be changed or fine tuned externally at a later time if needed.

Undersensing

Failure to sense may be complete or intermittent. It may result from a change in the sensing parameters selected at the time of insertion. This is most commonly encountered after acute right ventricular infarction or during the progressive fibrosis that accompanies many cardiomyopathies, causing intracardiac signals to decrease in amplitude. Lead displacement, fracture, and poor contact with the endocardium may also cause undersensing.

Undersensing is typically recognized electrocardiographically as the appearance of pacemaker spikes occurring earlier than the programmed rate. The spike may or may not be followed by a paced complex, depending on when it occurs during the cardiac refractory period (Figure 79-6). Failure of a stimulus spike to produce a complex when it occurs during the atrial or ventricular refractory period should not be interpreted as failure to pace.

Oversensing

In rare instances, the pacemaker may detect electrical activity that is not of cardiac origin. The result may be intermittent, irregular pacing or an apparent complete absence of pacemaker function. Myopotentials produced by the pectoralis muscle (Figure 79-7) and extracorporeal electrical signals are frequently oversensed when a unipolar lead system is used. T waves following an intrinsic ventricular depolarization are the most common oversensed cardiac signals. Common medical sources of electrical interference include electrocautery, which can cause temporary pacemaker inhibition, and magnetic resonance imaging, which can alter pacemaker circuitry and result in fixed-rate or asynchronous pacing. Electromagnetic interference

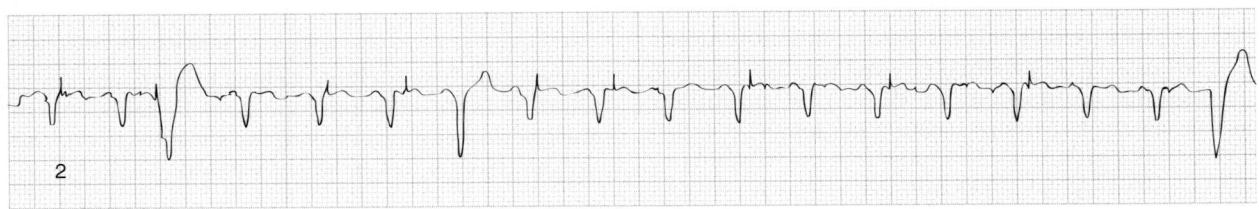

Figure 79-6. Failure to sense or undersensing (lead II). Pacemaker spikes are evident during inscription of the ST segment on this rhythm strip. These spikes do not produce QRS complexes because they occur during the ventricular refractory period of the preceding spontaneous QRS complex. The third QRS complex on the strip is a paced QRS complex. The device is capable of capture but is undersensing the spontaneous rhythm.

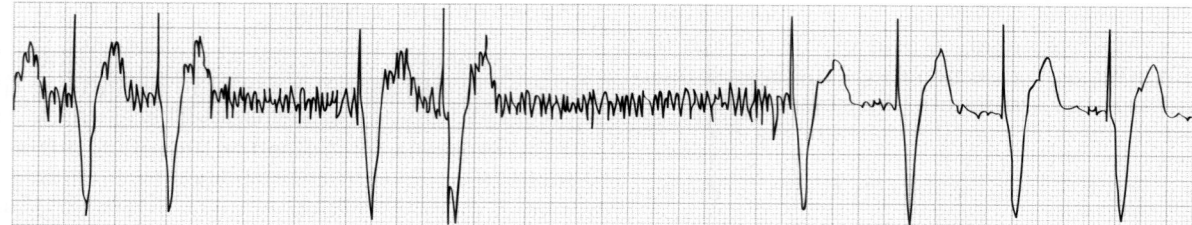

Figure 79-7. Oversensing (lead II). This VVI unipolar lead pacemaker is oversensing myopotentials produced by contraction of the pectoralis major. Myopotentials result in the undulating and irregular baseline seen in the middle of the strip. After muscular contraction ceases, normal pacing resumes (last four complexes on the strip).

resulting from close proximity to a microwave oven should not cause pacemaker problems with currently implanted pacemaker units.[23] Interference can be caused by the use of a digital cellular phone.[24] These devices may cause pacemaker inhibition, inappropriate ventricular tracking, or asynchronous pacing. Malfunction is most commonly seen when the phone is within 10 cm of the pulse generator and often occurs when the phone is applied to the ear ipsilateral to the site of the pacemaker pocket.

Inappropriate Pacemaker Rate

A pacing rate below the programmed rate is a typical finding in pulse generator depletion and does not occur abruptly with lithium-iodine batteries. An extreme increase in pacing rate, the so-called runaway pacemaker, is rarely, if ever, encountered with current pacemaker technology and circuitry in which upper rate limits are set (typically <140/min). An "endless loop" tachycardia may develop during dual-chamber pacing when ventriculoatrial conduction occurs and the resulting retrograde atrial depolarization results in a stimulated or paced ventricular depolarization.[21,22] If atrial flutter develops during dual-chamber pacing, flutter waves may be sensed and tracked, resulting in a rapid, paced ventricular rate. In both instances, the ventricular rate does not exceed its set upper limit. Patients with such rhythms may complain only of palpitations or symptoms of hemodynamic compromise. When such rhythms are detected, magnet application usually converts the pacemaker to a fixed rate in a competitive mode and terminates the tachyarrhythmia.

Management

History

The patient should be asked for the pacemaker identification card. The information on the card explains why a pacemaker was placed and the pacing modality used.

Most patients with pacemaker malfunction present with symptoms reminiscent of those that prompted pacemaker therapy: syncope, near-syncope, orthostatic dizziness, lightheadedness, dyspnea, or palpitations.

The majority of pacemaker complications and most instances of pacemaker malfunction occur within the first few weeks or months of pacemaker implantation. After wound healing, palpation of the pulse generator site should not elicit tenderness. A wound infection

or pocket infection typically arises with localized pain. Bacteremia secondary to infection of the pacing catheter, however, may arise only with fever and without other manifestations of the systemic inflammatory response syndrome. Pain in the arm ipsilateral to the site of insertion should suggest acute thrombophlebitis.

Patients who develop the pacemaker syndrome secondary to the loss of AV synchrony may present with nonspecific complaints of easy fatigability, generalized weakness, dyspnea, or an uncomfortable fluttering or "pounding" sensation in the neck or abdomen. Syncope or near-syncope may also occur, but these complaints should prompt an evaluation for true pacemaker malfunction. The pacemaker syndrome should be a diagnosis of exclusion.

Physical Examination

A pacemaker infection should be suspected in the presence of fever, even if another potential source of infection can be identified. Extremely low (<60) beats per minute or high pulse rates (>100 beats per minute in the resting patient) are suggestive of altered pacing parameters (battery depletion or pacemaker-mediated tachycardias). Hypotension may be present in either instance. Cannon "a" waves on inspection of the jugular venous pulse wave indicate AV asynchrony. Auscultation of lungs may reveal bibasilar rales if congestive heart failure is present.

During pacing, the first heart sound may vary in intensity as a result of AV dissociation (VVI mode), and the second heart sound may be paradoxically split when ventricular pacing occurs (the right ventricle is activated first). A pericardial friction rub may also be heard if the tip of the pacing catheter has perforated the wall of the right ventricle. Perforation, however, usually occurs at the time of pacemaker implantation and is usually recognized at that time. Although the pacing catheter traverses the tricuspid valve, tricuspid regurgitation is rarely heard unless there is myocardial disease such as right ventricular dilation that is common in the cardiomyopathies. Pedal edema may be present and is important if it is a new symptom or if chronic edema has recently worsened.

Chest Radiograph

A chest radiograph should be obtained to define pacing catheter tip position and to determine the number of pacing leads unless this information is available from another source. A ventricular pacing catheter tip in the right ventricular outflow tract or an atrial catheter tip in the SVC or right ventricle is always abnormal. The pulse generator site should also be examined on the radiograph. On occasion, disconnection of the lead from the pulse generator may be observed. In some cases, this is due to the patient's manipulation of the pulse generator ("twiddler's syndrome").[25]

12-Lead Electrocardiogram

A standard ECG and a long rhythm strip should be obtained in all patients. With bipolar pacing systems, the stimulus artifact may be extremely small and difficult to recognize in some leads (see Figure 79-4). Inspection of the rhythm strip may reveal failure to sense or pace, a low pacing rate, or an abnormally rapid rhythm, suggesting a pacemaker-mediated tachycardia.

Disposition of the Emergency Department Patient with a Pacemaker

As a result of the current design of modern pacemakers and the frequent follow-up evaluation of patients with pacemakers, life-threatening emergencies resulting from pacemaker malfunction requiring immediate emergency department intervention are rare. Most instances of malfunction are subtle and difficult to recognize without interrogation of the pacemaker using manufacturer-specific devices by someone skilled in the technique. In all instances of suspected pacemaker malfunction, the patient's cardiologist should be consulted.

Advanced Cardiac Life Support Interventions

Electrical defibrillation at recommended shock strengths (200, 300, and 360 J) can be safely performed in the patient with a pacemaker.[21] If the sternal paddle is placed adjacent to the sternum, it is at a safe distance (≥10 cm) from the pulse generator. Alternatively, defibrillation electrodes can be placed in an anteroposterior configuration. A cardiologist should check the pacing parameters of the unit if the resuscitation is successful. A chest radiograph should also be obtained after resuscitation to ensure that the pacing catheter was not displaced during chest compression, although this is an extremely uncommon occurrence.

Immediate return of pacing (capture) may not occur after defibrillation; this is more commonly the result of global myocardial ischemia and increased pacing threshold than an indication of pacemaker malfunction. Temporary transcutaneous pacing may be needed. Transcutaneous pacing can also be safely used because the anterior and posterior pacing electrodes, if properly positioned, are distant from the pulse generator. Attempting temporary transvenous pacing is usually not necessary and is unlikely to be successful, especially if undertaken without fluoroscopic guidance. Chronic venous thrombosis, which is common and most often asymptomatic after pacemaker insertion,

may preclude temporary catheter insertion through the neck veins. Insertion through the femoral vein is also difficult because the permanently implanted catheter may prevent entry into the right ventricle. Blind insertion may also dislodge the permanent catheter.

IMPLANTABLE CARDIOVERTER-DEFIBRILLATORS

The ICD was first used clinically in 1980. Technical refinements in this modality for treating ventricular dysrhythmias have progressed even more rapidly than refinements in the less complex standard pacemaker. More than 200,000 ICD implants have been performed worldwide.[2] A surge in the use of ICDs reflects improved survival with ICDs versus antiarrhythmic therapy in patients at risk for sudden death resulting from ventricular dysrhythmias.[7,8] Generally accepted indications for ICD implantation are noted in Box 79-2. Many patients still require drug therapy after ICD implantation to suppress ventricular dysrhythmias, minimize the frequency of ICD shocks, improve patients' tolerance, and decrease energy use, which prolongs ICD life.

Terminology and Components

The majority of ICDs are now placed percutaneously in a manner similar to that of the standard pacemaker. A transvenous electrode system has largely replaced epicardial lead placement, which required thoracotomy. An epicardial defibrillation lead may, on occasion, still be placed during coronary artery bypass surgery or in a few patients who cannot be defibrillated using existing transvenous electrode systems.

The typical modern ICD consists of components similar to those in the standard permanent pacemaker—namely, a power source, electronic circuitry, and lead system. In addition, the standard ICD has a high-voltage capacitor and complex microprocessor memory. The power source is lithium chemistry based with a battery life of 5 to 10 years. The longevity is largely determined by the frequency of shocks. All ICDs are also ventricular pacemakers, providing pacing for bradyarrhythmias. More complex pacing functions can also be incorporated if indicated. The lead system is implanted in a fashion similar to that described for pacemakers.[26-28]

The right ventricular lead is used for sensing and pacing, and shocks are typically delivered between a coil in the right ventricular lead and the pulse generator. If dual-chamber pacing is required, a second lead is placed in contact with the endocardium of the right atrium. A biphasic waveform is currently the preferred waveform for internal defibrillation. The shape and characteristics of the shock waveform vary among manufacturers. The biphasic waveform is more effective at lower energies than earlier monophasic waveforms and allows a smaller capacitor to be used, thereby reducing the size and increasing the comfort of the ICD unit.

The diagnostic and treatment functions of the ICD are determined at the time of implantation. In most instances, the cardioversion and defibrillation thresholds are determined at the time of ICD insertion by inducing ventricular tachycardia (VT) and fibrillation and adjusting the shock strength at a level above the minimum required to terminate the induced rhythm. Optimally, the required shock strength for defibrillation is less than half the maximum output (approximately 30 J) of the device. VT is typically managed using either low-energy shocks or programmed pacing that interrupts the VT reentrant circuit. Programmed pacing is less likely to have proarrhythmic effects and requires less energy, thereby extending battery life. In the setting of ventricular fibrillation (VF), ICDs are capable of delivering up to five additional discharges if the first shock fails.

The patient with an ICD should have close follow-up monitoring by a cardiologist familiar with ICD programming. It allows the cardiologist to determine the frequency of ICD activation (programmed antitachycardia pacing or shocks) and to confirm the programmed functions of the device. The majority of patients with ICDs have underlying heart disease, most commonly extensive atherosclerotic coronary artery disease, that is complicated by a low ejection fraction and congestive heart failure. The patient's medications and metabolic status, such as electrolyte disorders that accompany diuretic usage, may also affect ICD function.

Complications of Implantation

Complications of ICD implantation are nearly identical in type and frequency to those of permanent pacemaker implantation. They include infection of the wound, the subcutaneous pouch fashioned for the device, and the lead system as well as acute thrombophlebitis and chronic thrombosis of the veins traversed for lead insertion.[29,30] Management of these complications is similar to that for patients with permanent pacemakers.

Malfunction

Patients with ICD malfunction usually present to the emergency department with a limited number of specific symptoms (Box 79-4).

In contrast to patients with a permanent pacemaker, ICD patients are aware of when the ICD discharges to terminate VT or VF. The most common complaint of ICD patients is the occurrence of frequent shocks (i.e., occurring at a rate greater than they are accustomed to).[31] Increasing shock rate may be appropriate and not indicative of ICD malfunction if the patient is experiencing an increase in the frequency of VT or VF episodes. An increase in the frequency of episodes may occur in the setting of hypokalemia, hypomagnesemia, ischemia (with or without infarction) related to underlying coronary artery disease, or the proarrhythmic effect of drugs administered to decrease the frequency of ventricular tachyarrhythmias.

An increase in the shock frequency is a manifestation of ICD sensing malfunction if (1) a supraventricular tachyarrhythmia is inappropriately sensed as VT, (2) shocks are delivered for nonsustained VT, or (3) intra-

---

BOX 79-4. Causes of Implantable Cardioverter-Defibrillator Malfunction

Increase or abrupt change in shock frequency
- Increased frequency of VF or VT (consider ischemia, electrolyte disorder, or drug effect)
- Displacement or break in ventricular lead
- Recurrent nonsustained VT
- Sensing and shock of supraventricular tachyarrhythmias
- Oversensing of T waves
- Sensing noncardiac signals

Syncope, near-syncope, dizziness
- Recurrent VT with low shock strength (lead problem, change in defibrillation threshold)
- Hemodynamically significant supraventricular tachyarrhythmias
- Inadequate backup pacing for bradyarrhythmias (spontaneous or drug induced)

Cardiac arrest
- Assume malfunction, but probably due to VF that failed to respond to programmed shock parameters

VF, ventricular fibrillation; VT, ventricular tachycardia.

---

cardiac T waves detected by the ICD system are sensed as QRS complexes and the ICD interprets this as an increased heart rate. Temporary ICD deactivation with magnet application may be necessary if oversensing is the problem. Syncope, near-syncope, dizziness, or lightheadedness in the patient with an ICD may indicate undersensing of sustained VT or inappropriately low shock strength to terminate the rhythm. An approach to the evaluation of ICD malfunction is shown in Figure 79-8.

Advanced Cardiac Life Support Interventions

An ICD does not prevent sudden death in all patients at risk, and a patient with an ICD may present in cardiac arrest (2% annual incidence in implanted patients). Cardiac arrest is not necessarily an indication of ICD malfunction. Appropriate repeated shocks may have been delivered but were ineffectual. Alternatively, the ICD may not have sensed VF or the ventricular ectopic activity that typically precedes VF. Resuscitation efforts in the patient with an ICD should be undertaken in accordance with current recommendations. Transthoracic defibrillation can be performed in the standard fashion with a stacked sequence of shocks (200, 300, 360 J) if VF is the arrest rhythm. The sternal electrode or paddle should be placed in a parasternal location about 10 cm from the ICD subcutaneous pouch if the device has been implanted in the right deltopectoral area. If it has been implanted in the left deltopectoral region, this recommended safety distance is usually exceeded.

If the ICD discharges during manual chest compressions, the rescuer may feel a weak shock. There have been no reports of injury to rescuers from such discharges during resuscitation efforts. The device can be

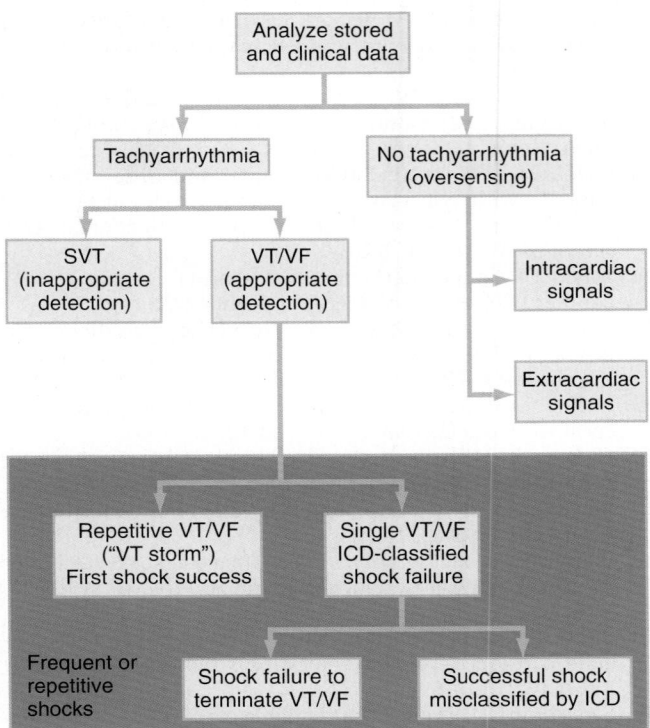

Figure 79-8. Approach to the patient with shocks. **Top,** Flow diagram for one or infrequent shocks. **Bottom,** Diagram for multiple or repetitive shocks. ICD, implantable cardioverter-defibrillator; SVT, supraventricular tachycardia; VT/VF, ventricular tachycardia/ventricular fibrillation. (Redrawn from Swerdlow CD, Zhang J: Implantable cardioverter defibrillator shocks: A troubleshooting guide. *Rev Cardiovasc Med* 2:61, 2001.)

function and preceding dysrhythmia episodes. Reprogramming may be necessary. If a lead problem is detected, reimplantation is required.

KEY CONCEPTS

- Pacemaker malfunction soon after implantation (within 6 to 8 weeks) is usually due to a lead problem, such as a lead displacement, or to pacemaker programming failure, such as a pacing rate too slow for the patient's needs.
- Pacemaker malfunction arises in a limited number of ways: failure to pace, oversensing, undersensing, and pacing at an inappropriate rate (too fast or too slow).
- With lithium-iodine batteries, abrupt failure is an unlikely cause of pacemaker malfunction.
- If a patient with a pacemaker presents with a fever of unclear etiology, pacemaker lead infection and endocarditis should be considered.
- Because paced ventricular complexes are conducted with a left bundle branch block pattern, a paced rhythm obscures the electrocardiographic diagnosis of acute myocardial infarction.
- Magnet application does not turn off a pacemaker. It does convert an inhibited or noncompetitive pacemaker to one that is not inhibited. Fixed-rate pacing and competition with the pacing underlying rhythm occur.
- Defibrillation is safe in patients with a pacemaker or ICD if paddles are placed at least 10 cm from the subcutaneous implant site of the device. Alternatively, anteroposterior defibrillation with adhesive defibrillation electrodes can be performed. There are no reports of injury to rescuers from ICD discharges during manual chest compressions.

deactivated with magnetic application during resuscitation efforts. Deactivation is probably more important in the immediate postresuscitation period because recurrent ventricular dysrhythmias are common at this time owing to prolonged global myocardial ischemia during the arrest period, reperfusion, and the hyperadrenergic state worsened by the use of intravenous epinephrine during resuscitation efforts. ICD malfunction should be assumed and these postresuscitation rhythms treated with standard pharmacologic agents (lidocaine, amiodarone). Although class 1 antidysrhythmic agents may raise the defibrillation threshold of the ICD, their impact on the defibrillation threshold during transthoracic countershock is clinically inconsequential owing to the high shock strengths that are used.

Disposition of the Emergency Department Patient with an Implantable Cardioverter-Defibrillator

As a result of the difficulty in documenting or excluding ICD malfunction in the patient with transient symptoms, the emergency physician should consult the patient's cardiologist regarding evaluation and therapy. In almost all instances, admission to a monitored setting with extended telemetric observation is necessary. ICD interrogation allows assessment of ICD

REFERENCES

1. Jeffrey K, Parsonnet V: Cardiac pacing, 1960-1985. A quarter century of medical and industrial innovation. *Circulation* 97:1978, 1998.
2. Josephson ME, Callans DJ, Buxton AE: The role of the implantable cardioverter-defibrillator for prevention of sudden cardiac death. *Ann Intern Med* 133:901, 2000.
3. Buckingham TA, Volgman AS, Wimer E: Trends in pacemaker use: Results of a multicenter registry. *PACE* 14:1437, 1991.
4. Bernstein AD, Parsonnet V: Survey of cardiac pacing in the United States in 1989. *Am J Cardiol* 69:331, 1992.
5. Bryce M, Spielman SR, Greenspan AM, Kotler MN: Evolving indications for permanent pacemakers. *Ann Intern Med* 134:1130, 2001.
6. Abraham WT, Hayes DL: Cardiac resynchronization therapy for heart failure. *Circulation* 108:2596, 2003.
7. Heidenreich PA, et al: Overview of randomized trials of antiarrhythmic drugs and devices for the prevention of sudden cardiac death. *Am Heart J* 144:422, 2002.
8. Ezekowitz JA, Armstrong PW, McAlister FA: Implantable cardioverter defibrillators in primary and secondary prevention: A systematic review of randomized, controlled trials. *Ann Intern Med* 138:445, 2003.
9. Gregoratos G, et al: ACC/AHA/NASPE 2002 guideline update for implantation of cardiac pacemakers and antiarrhythmia devices: A report of the American College of Cardiology/American Heart Association Task Force on Practice Guidelines (ACC/AHA/NASPE Committee on Pacemaker

Implantation), 2002. Available at www.acc.org/clinical/guidelines/pacemaker/pacemaker.pdf

10. Bernstein AD, et al: The revised NASPE/BPEG generic code for antibradycardia, adaptive-rate, and multisite pacing. *PACE* 25:260, 2000.

11. Glikson M, Hayes DL: Cardiac pacing. A review. *Med Clin North Am* 85:369, 2001.

12. Mitrani RD, et al: Cardiac pacemakers: Current and future status. *Curr Probl Cardiol* 24:341, 1999.

13. Hayes DL, Vlietstra RE: Pacemaker malfunction. *Ann Intern Med* 119:828, 1993.

14. Kusumoto FM, Goldschlager N: Device therapy for cardiac arrhythmias. *JAMA* 287:1848, 2002.

15. Chua JD, et al: Diagnosis and management of infections involving implantable electrophysiologic cardiac devices. *Ann Intern Med* 133:604, 2000.

16. Cardall TY, et al: Permanent cardiac pacemakers: Issues relevant to the emergency physician, part I. *J Emerg Med* 17:479, 1999.

17. Arber N, et al: Pacemaker endocarditis. Report of 44 cases and review of the literature. *Medicine (Baltimore)* 73:299, 1994.

18. Barakat K, Robinson NM, Spurrell RA: Transvenous pacing lead-induced thrombosis: A series of cases with a review of the literature. *Cardiology* 93:142, 2000.

19. Connolly SJ, et al: Dual-chamber versus ventricular pacing: Critical appraisal of current data. *Circulation* 94:578, 1996.

20. Ovsyshcher IE, Hayes DL, Furman S: Dual-chamber pacing is superior to ventricular pacing. Fact or controversy? *Circulation* 97:2368, 1998.

21. Cardall TY, et al: Permanent cardiac pacemakers: Issues relevant to the emergency physician, part II. *J Emerg Med* 17:697, 1999.

22. Sarko JA, Tiffany BR: Cardiac pacemakers: Evaluation and management of malfunctions. *Am J Emerg Med* 18:435, 2000.

23. Goldchlager N, et al: Environmental and drug effects on patients with pacemakers and implantable cardioverter/defibrillators. A practical guide to patient treatment. *Arch Intern Med* 161:649, 2001.

24. Hayes DL, et al: Interference with cardiac pacemakers by cellular telephones. *N Engl J Med* 336:1473, 1997.

25. Lal RB, Avery RD: Aggressive pacemaker twiddler's syndrome. Dislodgement of an active fixation ventricular pacing electrode. *Chest* 97:756, 1990.

26. Gollob MH, Seger JJ: Current status of the implantable cardioverter-defibrillator. *Chest* 119:1210, 2001.

27. Glikson M, Friedman PA: The implantable cardioverter defibrillator. *Lancet* 357:1107, 2001.

28. Pinski SL, Fahy GJ: Implantable cardioverter-defibrillators. *Am J Med* 106:446, 1999.

29. Pfeiffer D, et al: Complications of pacemaker-defibrillator devices: Diagnosis and management. *Am Heart J* 127:1073, 1994.

30. Smith PN, et al: Infections with nonthoracotomy implantable cardioverter-defibrillators: Can these be prevented? *PACE* 19:2156, 1998.

31. Swerdlow CD, Zhang J: Implantable cardioverter defibrillator shocks: A troubleshooting guide. *Rev Cardiovasc Med* 2:61, 2001.

CHAPTER

80 Heart Failure

John F. O'Brien and Jay L. Falk

Heart failure is a pathologic condition leading to a debilitating illness characterized by poor exercise tolerance and chronic fatigue along with high morbidity and mortality. *Heart failure* may be defined as the pathophysiologic state in which the heart is incapable of pumping a sufficient supply of blood to meet the metabolic requirements of the body or requires elevated ventricular filling pressures to accomplish this goal. The caveat that filling pressures must be normal acknowledges that a failing heart may continue to maintain systemic perfusion by using the compensatory Frank-Starling mechanism of preload reserve, resulting in the maintenance of normal stroke volume despite reduced ejection fraction. Conversely, low filling pressure with hypoperfusion indicates a pump-priming problem distinct from cardiac disease.

A complex neurohormonal regulatory system exists between the heart and multiple organ systems. Feedback loops mediated through a variety of vasoactive substances secreted by the kidneys, autonomic nervous system, adrenals, lungs, and vascular endothelium are most important. Perturbations of function in any of these organs affect the others. Accordingly, the cardiovascular system must be viewed as a dynamic one, continually adapting to optimize organ perfusion. Dysfunction of the heart or any component of the system results in hormonal and other compensatory responses, some of which are not precisely titrated and may themselves be maladaptive over time.

Heart failure is a progressive disease that begins long before signs and symptoms are evident. It is initially characterized by adaptive neurohormonal activation of the renin-angiotensin-aldosterone system, sympathetic nervous system, natriuretic peptides, endothelin, vasopressin, and other regulatory mechanisms. These initially compensate for cardiac dysfunction but neurohormonal mechanisms eventually lead to increased mechanical stress on the failing heart, causing maladaptive electrical and structural events, further impairment of systolic and diastolic function, and progressive cardiac fibrosis and apoptosis.[1] In many circumstances, heart failure occurs as a consequence of pathologic conditions involving the renal, peripheral vascular, or pulmonary system. The degree of myocardial dysfunction depends on both the amount of primary myocardial disease and the functional status of these other organ systems. Increasing knowledge of these neurohormonal interactions has led to progressive improvement in the management of congestive heart failure (CHF), with a shift from a hemodynamic to a neurohormonal model.

EPIDEMIOLOGY

Heart failure represents the only significant cardiovascular disease that is increasing in prevalence in our society and is a common cause of poor life quality and premature death. Nearly 5 million people in the United States have been diagnosed with heart failure, and almost 550,000 new cases are diagnosed annually.[2-4] The incidence approaches 10 per 1000 in persons older than 65 years, and CHF is the most common reason for hospital admission in this age group.[5] This prevalence results in an annual estimated health care cost of nearly $20 billion. The aging population, coupled with improvements in the medical therapy of heart failure, contributes to current expectations that the prevalence of this disease will continue to increase.

Heart failure carries a 50% mortality at 4 years after symptom onset.[6] Half of the patients with the most severe disease die within the first year after diagnosis. Progressive hemodynamic deterioration accounts for approximately 50% of deaths, but sudden death resulting from malignant ventricular dysrhythmias occurs in up to half of patients. Medical therapy has not decreased sudden dysrhythmic deaths but has improved overall outcome from pump failure. For example, in the Randomized Aldactone Evaluation Study (RALES), in which patients were being appropriately managed medically (95% were receiving angiotensin-converting enzyme [ACE] inhibitors), 2-year mortality was 46% for the placebo group and 35% for the spironolactone group.[7] ACE inhibitors as well as β-blockers decrease the death rate among patients with heart failure by both improving functional status and slowing the rate of progression of pump dysfunction. Hospital survival is improving steadily.[8]

The prognosis can be related to a number of factors, including age, ejection fraction, exercise tolerance, plasma norepinephrine and B-type natriuretic peptide (BNP) levels, cardiothoracic ratio on chest radiograph, renal function, and the presence of ventricular dysrhythmias. One third to one half of patients with heart failure have some degree of renal insufficiency, which is one of the strongest predictors of mortality in patients with heart failure. The American Heart Association (AHA) and American College of Cardiology (ACC) guidelines define heart failure related to systolic dysfunction as a left ventricular ejection fraction less than 40%.[4]

CELLULAR MECHANISMS

The heart is composed of a mass of individual striated muscle cells (myocytes) that form a branching syncytium. Each myocyte contains a central nucleus, mitochondria, an intracellular tubular system termed the *sarcoplasmic reticulum*, and numerous cross-banded strands termed *myofibrils* that traverse the length of the myocyte. The myofibrils, in turn, contain multiple subunits called sarcomeres. They form the basic functional unit of myocardial contraction and are arranged in series. Sarcomeres occupy approximately 50% of the mass of myocardial cells and are composed of the contractile proteins actin and myosin along with the regulatory proteins troponin and tropomyosin. These proteins are surrounded by invaginations of the myocardial cell membrane (sarcolemma) and the sarcoplasmic reticulum.

The sarcomere ranges in length from 1.6 to 2.2 μm, depending in part on the tension exerted on the muscle before contraction (preload). Sarcomere contraction occurs when the thin, double-helix actin is exposed to the thick myofilament myosin in the presence of Mg^{++} and adenosine triphosphate (ATP). This interaction, and thus myocyte contraction as well as relaxation, is controlled by the intracellular Ca^{++} level. When intracellular Ca^{++} is increased, it binds to the contraction regulatory protein troponin, which causes a conformational change in tropomyosin that exposes actin to myosin. In the presence of ATP, linkages are rapidly made and broken between actin and myosin, causing the actin to slide along the myosin filaments. This process generates muscle tension and ultimately myocyte contraction. A drop in intracellular Ca^{++} level reconforms the troponin-tropomyosin complex in such a way that myosin and actin linkages are broken, allowing sarcomere relaxation. Intracellular ionic calcium is the principal mediator of the inotropic state of the heart and is mainly stored and regulated by the sarcoplasmic reticulum. Most positive inotropic agents, including digitalis and catecholamines, act by increasing the availability of intracellular calcium in the vicinity of the myofibrils.

The normal cardiac index is 2.5 to 4.0 $L/min/m^2$ at rest. It is determined by the preload, afterload, heart rate, and contractility. In normal hearts, the collective force of contraction of the cardiac chamber is the sum of the forces generated by the individual myocytes. Myocyte force is in turn a function of the ability of the contractile proteins to generate power (inotropic state or contractility) as well as the degree of sarcomere stretch at the start of contraction (preload). Stretching the sarcomere progressively toward its optimal length of 2.2 μm increases the force of contraction by allowing the maximum number of actin-myosin myofilament interactions. This forms the basis of the Frank-Starling relation, which states that within physiologic limits, the force of ventricular contraction is directly related to the end-diastolic length of cardiac muscle.

Preload is the amount of force stretching the myofibril before contraction. In the intact ventricle, preload is produced by the venous return into the chamber resulting in stretch of the myofibrils constituting the chamber walls. The volume filling the chamber also results in the development of pressure that can be measured clinically in either ventricle. The pressure measured within a chamber is determined by both the

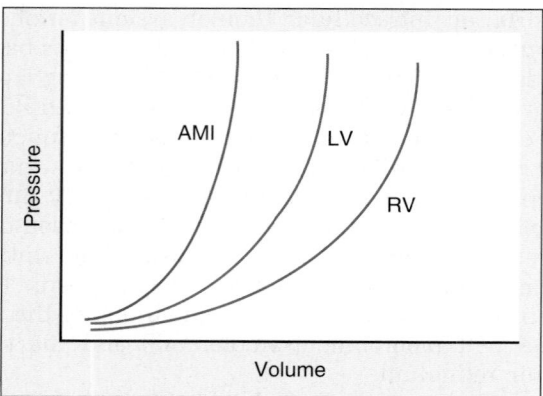

Figure 80-1. The end-diastolic pressure of the chamber is determined by the filling volume and the compliance characteristics of the chamber. The right ventricle (RV) is more compliant than the more muscular left ventricle (LV), which becomes stiffer still under conditions of ischemia or acute myocardial infarction (AMI).

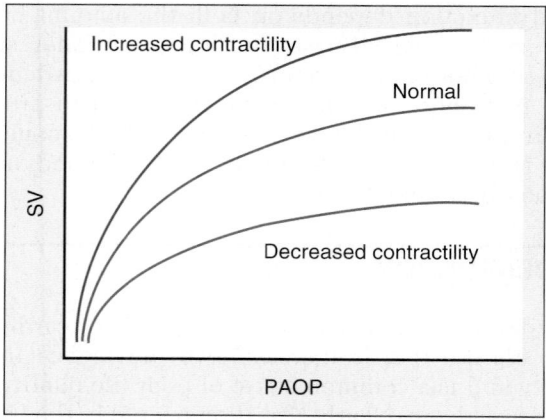

Figure 80-2. Increased preload, represented as pulmonary artery occlusion pressure (PAOP), results in increased stroke volume (SV) irrespective of the contractile state of the ventricle. At any level of contractility, an optimal PAOP is reached beyond which further increases in pressure may result in increased risk of pulmonary edema, with minimal incremental increase in SV.

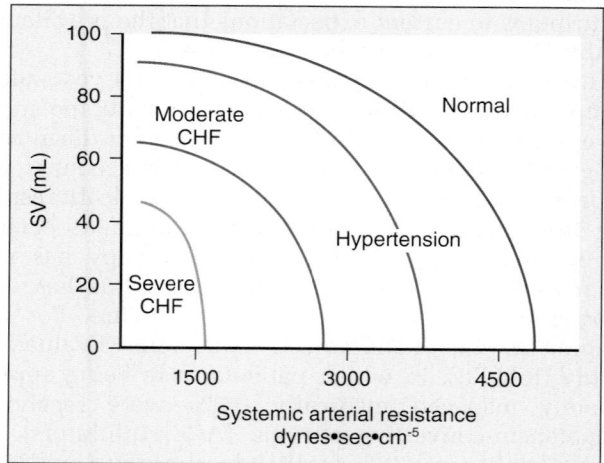

Figure 80-3. Normal hearts can perform pressure work against high peripheral resistance, maintaining cardiac output even in the presence of very high systemic arterial resistance. Failing hearts are more afterload sensitive and exhibit decreased stroke volume (SV) when confronted with high or high-normal resistances. CHF, congestive heart failure. (Modified from Weil et al: In Braunwald E (ed): *Heart Disease: A Textbook of Cardiovascular Medicine*, 4th ed. Philadelphia, WB Saunders, 1992.)

volume stretching the chamber wall and the compliance characteristics of the muscle. For this reason, pressure is only an indirect reflection of the preload. Changes in compliance may occur acutely (ischemia) or chronically (hypertrophy) and may substantially alter the relationship between chamber volume, pressure, and preload (Figure 80-1). These considerations notwithstanding, the bedside measurement of the pulmonary artery occlusion pressure (PAOP) by a balloon flotation pulmonary artery catheter remains a useful clinical tool in estimating preload of the left heart.

Optimal preload is the filling pressure that stretches ventricular myofibrils maximally and leads to the greatest stroke output per contraction. The actual optimal PAOP must be determined individually for each patient because it is affected by the loading conditions and compliance characteristics of the patient. For example, patients with acute myocardial infarction tend to have stiffer, less compliant left ventricles. In these patients, optimal PAOP ranges are higher. Irrespective of the inotropic state of the ventricle, optimizing preload results in the maximum stroke output for that ventricle (Figure 80-2). Ventricles with normal compliance accommodate larger volumes before the chamber pressure rises. Accordingly, if pressure is used to estimate preload, the normal ventricle has more dramatic increases in stroke output for similar increases in filling pressure (steeper Starling curve). The risk of pulmonary edema increases when PAOP rises significantly above normal ranges (6 to 12 mm Hg). In patients with low colloid osmotic pressures secondary to hypoalbuminemia, pulmonary edema may occur at even lower filling pressures.

Afterload represents the mural tension acting on myocardial cells during contraction. It is determined by the total peripheral vascular resistance and the cardiac chamber size. The peripheral resistance is affected by the total cross-sectional area of the circulation, the blood viscosity, and other factors. The arterioles are the major resistance vessels in the circulation. Flow is directly proportional to the fourth power of the vessel radius (Poiseuille's law). The larger the ventricular cavity, the more mural tension and thus myocardial work is required during contraction (law of Laplace). Failing ventricles cannot overcome increases in peripheral resistance in order to eject blood (Figure 80-3). In the presence of this afterload mismatch, these ventricles dilate further, increasing their end-diastolic volumes such that stroke volume is maintained, even with decreasing ejection fraction (preload reserve). Failing hearts are, therefore, extremely afterload sensitive.

For clinical purposes, afterload can be thought of as the pressure against which the heart must pump to eject blood. Blood pressure (BP) is determined by the product of the systemic vascular resistance and flow

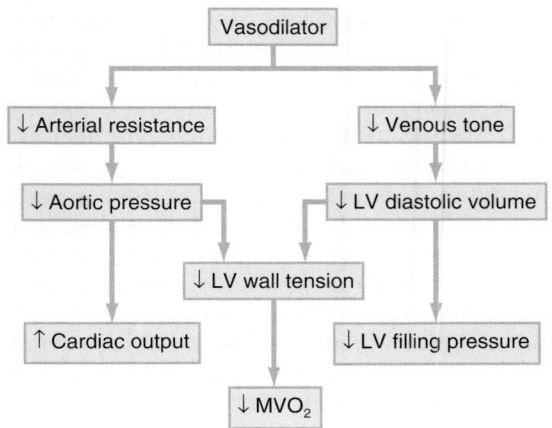

Figure 80-4. Arterial dilators decrease arterial resistance and result in increased cardiac output. Venodilators decrease venous return to the heart and relieve pulmonary congestion. Balanced agents (nitroprussides, angiotensin-converting enzyme inhibitors) do both. Decreased mural tension reduces myocardial oxygen demand (MVO$_2$) and may relieve ischemia. LV, left ventricular.

(BP = SVR × CO). Patients with heart failure and low cardiac output (CO) tend to maintain blood pressure by peripheral vasoconstriction mediated mainly by endogenous catecholamines and the renin-angiotensin-aldosterone system. Afterload reduction may be beneficial because it allows the conversion of pressure work into flow work (Figure 80-4). When blood pressure is decreased, cardiac output increases as long as preload is maintained. Because flow work is proportionally less oxygen demanding, afterload reduction therapy has the additional benefit of decreasing myocardial oxygen demands.

Heart rate and rhythmic contraction are important determinants of optimal cardiac output. As heart rate increases to the range of 150 to 160 beats/min in the adult, output increases progressively. Tachycardia above this level compromises diastolic filling time and leads to decreased cardiac output. Myocardial perfusion, which occurs during diastole, also becomes impaired by severe tachycardia. Stroke volume is maximized when atrial contraction "primes" the ventricular pumps before they contract. Accordingly, any derangement of intracardiac conduction or dysrhythmia can reduce stroke output. Loss of atrial priming can lead to marked deterioration in cardiac output, especially in diseased, stiffer hearts that require high filling pressures to optimize preload.

Contractility may be affected by a host of factors. Multiple physiologic depressants (hypoxia, hypercarbia, acidosis, ischemia) and pharmacologic depressants (e.g., many cardiac antidysrhythmic agents, calcium channel blockers, β-blockers, barbiturates, alcohol) decrease myocardial contractility. Correcting physiologic myocardial depressant factors and discontinuing certain medications with negative inotropic properties are important first steps in managing patients with heart failure. Inotropic agents enhance contractility and may improve hemodynamics both acutely (catecholamines) and chronically (cardiac glycosides).

PATHOPHYSIOLOGY OF ACUTE PULMONARY EDEMA

Pulmonary edema is classified clinically into cardiogenic and noncardiogenic forms. Most patients seen in the emergency setting with pulmonary edema have the acute cardiogenic variety, which results mainly from elevated pulmonary capillary hydrostatic pressure. Most commonly, cardiogenic pulmonary edema occurs with acute myocardial ischemia or infarction, cardiomyopathy, valvular heart disease, and hypertensive emergencies. In contradistinction, noncardiogenic pulmonary edema generally results from an alteration in the permeability characteristics of the pulmonary capillary membrane. The alteration may have such diverse causes as systemic sepsis or septic shock, inhalation injuries, drugs and toxins, aspiration syndromes, the fat emboli syndrome, neurogenic causes, and high altitude.

Cardiogenic pulmonary edema results primarily from increases in pulmonary capillary hydrostatic pressure that force a protein-sparse plasma ultrafiltrate across the pulmonary capillary membrane into the pulmonary interstitium. As in all forms of pulmonary congestion, this increase in fluid flux immediately results in an increase in the lymphatic drainage of fluid from the lung. These compensatory mechanisms may quickly become overwhelmed if large amounts of edema begin to accumulate in the pulmonary interstitium, ultimately leading to alveolar flooding. The increase in left ventricular end-diastolic pressure that causes the rise in pulmonary artery occlusion pressure may have a variety of causes, particularly myocardial ischemia. Increases in left ventricular end-diastolic pressures do not always reflect increases in plasma volume, although they generally do in patients with chronic heart failure. In patients with chronic CHF, neurohumoral mechanisms generally result in plasma volume expansion. In patients suffering from acute-onset cardiogenic pulmonary edema (as may result from acute myocardial ischemia, infarction, or abrupt increases in afterload), plasma volume is generally not expanded and may, in fact, be contracted. In this scenario, the acute challenge to a ventricle with minimal reserve results in an immediate decrease in ventricular compliance (diastolic dysfunction), with generation of high left ventricular pressures although there is no change in volume (see Figure 80-1). The pressures are reflected backward to the pulmonary capillaries, forcing a protein-sparse fluid from the plasma into the pulmonary interstitium. Volumes as large as 1 to 2 L may leave the plasma over a short time and create serious respiratory compromise.

Plasma volume studies in patients with acute cardiogenic pulmonary edema reveal that they have substantially lower plasma volumes than control patients. As therapy progresses, the plasma volume may expand as fluid is reabsorbed from the interstitial pulmonary space back into the plasma volume. These changes are reflected by initial hemoconcentration as evidenced by higher hematocrits and colloid osmotic pressures. It is important to understand this pathophysiologic scenario when treating patients with both acute pulmonary edema (APE) and systemic hypotension because despite the presence of pulmonary congestion, these patients may have low plasma volume (and low preload) and be in need of fluid challenge to rapidly restore preload, cardiac output, systemic perfusion, and blood pressure. Thus, careful volume infusion with aliquots of normal saline is usually the most appropriate initial resuscitation response for the hypoperfusing patient with acute-onset cardiogenic pulmonary edema.

COMPENSATORY MECHANISMS

Multiple compensatory mechanisms aid the heart in maintaining perfusion in response to an imposed hemodynamic burden or when significant numbers of myocytes are lost because of disease.

Increase in Stroke Volume

Increased stroke volume occurs in response to an increase in preload (the Frank-Starling mechanism). This compensatory mechanism is immediate and effective in improving cardiac output in response to acute cardiac demands. It is a limited response, however, because myofibril stretch to a sarcomere length beyond 2.2 μm does not increase further and may actually reduce stroke output. Also, this mechanism greatly increases myocardial oxygen demand, which may lead to dysfunction in the setting of significant coronary artery disease.

Increased Systemic Vascular Resistance

Increased systemic vascular resistance results in redistribution of a subnormal cardiac output away from skin, skeletal muscles, and kidneys to maintain normal blood flow to the brain and heart. This increased afterload also increases myocardial work greatly.

Development of Cardiac Hypertrophy

Development of cardiac hypertrophy is the primary chronic adaptation of the heart to compensate for pump failure. This hypertrophy occurs mainly by increasing the number of myofibrils per cell, as the heart has very limited ability to produce new cells (hyperplasia). New myofibrils arrange in series in response to an increase in chamber volume (leading to dilation over time) and in parallel when responding to higher pressure loads (leading to increased chamber wall thickness). In addition to myofibril hypertrophy, mitochondrial mass expands, leading to additional ATP provision for the expanded myofibril mass. Initially, hypertrophy leads to improved function of each myocardial cell but at a higher energy cost. Unfortunately, capillary mass may not increase significantly in response to myocyte hypertrophy. In addition, hypertrophy is associated with myosin synthesis shifts from V_1 to V_3 isoforms, with related slowing of the rate of contraction, prolon-

gation of the time to peak tension, and reduced rate of relaxation. With the continued influence of volume overload, myofibril mass expands more than mitochondrial mass and relative capillary blood flow is reduced, leading to progressive myocyte death (apoptosis) with fibrosis and increased stress on the remaining myocytes. This process appears to be a particular problem with aging, in which substantial diffuse loss of myocytes, increased fibrosis, and reactive hypertrophy of remaining myocytes have been demonstrated, even in hearts without known disease. Thus, the hypertrophic response, if allowed to continue, eventually becomes a destructive process that accelerates myocyte death and reduces pump function.

Neurohormonal Mechanisms

Neurohormonal mechanisms act to maintain blood pressure and vital organ perfusion and are activated by left ventricular dysfunction. Regrettably, these neurohormonal mechanisms also increase the hemodynamic burden and oxygen consumption of the failing ventricle and are counterproductive on a chronic basis.

Renal Neurohormonal Response

Decreased glomerular perfusion results in a reduction in the renal excretion of sodium. Renal arteriolar and adrenergic receptors stimulate renin release by the juxtaglomerular apparatus. Renin facilitates the conversion of the hepatically produced protein angiotensinogen to angiotensin I, which is further converted to angiotensin II by ACE. Angiotensin II is a potent vasoconstrictor and also an important stimulus for aldosterone release by the adrenal cortex. Aldosterone increases renal sodium retention and potassium excretion.

Renal adaptation to hypoperfusion occurs mainly through production of vasodilatory hormones such as prostacyclin, along with prostaglandins PGI_2 and PGE_2. Aspirin and other nonsteroidal anti-inflammatory drugs (NSAIDs) interfere with prostaglandin synthesis by inhibiting cyclooxygenase. Accordingly, except for the useful antiplatelet effect of low-dose aspirin, NSAIDs optimally should be avoided in patients with chronic heart failure because they may precipitate acute renal insufficiency with concomitant salt and water retention.

Central and Autonomic Nervous System Neurohormonal Response

The heart and great vessels contain sensory receptors that detect changes in perfusion. Metabolic receptors in muscles also exert inhibitory and excitatory influences on brainstem vasomotor neurons. Arginine vasopressin (antidiuretic hormone) is released from the pituitary gland in response to decreases in perfusion. Elevated vasopressin levels in heart failure increase volume overload while decreasing osmolality and adversely affect hemodynamics and cardiac remodeling while potentiating effects of angiotensin II and norepinephrine. Vasopressin antagonists hold promise in heart failure.[9]

Heart failure results in a generalized stimulation of sympathetic activity and inhibition of parasympathetic tone. Increased sympathetic outflow results in the release of increased epinephrine and norepinephrine from the adrenal glands and norepinephrine at peripheral sympathetic nerve endings. These elevated catecholamine levels stimulate surface receptors in the heart and blood vessels, increasing cardiac contractility, heart rate, and vascular tone. The resulting increased venous tone augments preload, which tends to maintain stroke output (preload reserve). Increased arterial smooth muscle tone increases afterload, which is deleterious to a failing ventricle incapable of maintaining stroke output against this resistance to flow. This adaptive mechanism therefore exacerbates myocardial dysfunction. Afterload reduction can permit improved stroke output as pressure work is converted to flow work (see Figure 80-4). Care must be taken to maintain adequate preload to achieve optimal benefit. Acutely, arterial blood pressure is improved and cardiac output increased by catecholamines but, chronically, a decrease in the number and affinity of surface catecholamine receptors occurs in myocardial tissue, reducing responsiveness to epinephrine and norepinephrine. Elevated catecholamines adversely affect myocardial perfusion, leading to progressive apoptosis and cardiac fibrosis.

Cardiac Neurohormonal Response

Increases in myocardial wall stretch activate the release of cardiac natriuretic peptides, which are structurally related peptides that are important in volume and sodium homeostasis. They include atrial natriuretic peptide, BNP, and C-type natriuretic peptide. All are elevated in patients with left ventricular dysfunction. The natriuretic peptides promote water and sodium excretion, promote peripheral vasodilation, and inhibit the renin-angiotensin-aldosterone system. A variety of natriuretic peptide receptors exist on endothelial cells, on vascular smooth muscle cells, on renal epithelial cells, and in the myocardium as well. Circulating natriuretic peptides are greatly increased in CHF as a result of increased synthesis. In early heart failure, they play a key role in compensation for left ventricular dysfunction. Attenuation of the renal response to natriuretic peptide occurs as heart failure progresses .

Vascular Endothelial Neurohormonal Response

Endothelial function plays an important role in local regulation of vasomotor tone. A family of endothelins, ET-1, ET-2, ET-3, and ET-4, are produced by endothelial and smooth muscle cells as well as neural, renal, pulmonary, and inflammatory cells in response to hemodynamic stress, hypoxia, catecholamines, angiotensin II, and many inflammatory cytokines.[10] ET-1 seems to be the most important endothelin and exerts its main vascular effects, vasoconstriction and cell proliferation, through specific ET_A and ET_B receptors on

vascular smooth muscle cells. ET_B receptor stimulation by ET-1 also increases prostacyclin and nitric oxide (NO) release, causing vasodilation. ET-1 plasma levels are elevated in patients with heart failure, correlate with symptoms as well as hemodynamic severity, and are associated with an adverse prognosis. Infusion of a mixed $ET_{A/B}$ antagonist, bosentan, improved systemic and pulmonary hemodynamics in both acute and chronic heart failure.[11] Selective ET_A and mixed $ET_{A/B}$ receptor antagonists show promise for hemodynamic and symptomatic improvements in patients with heart failure.

NO plays a critical role in the homeostasis of cardiac function.[12] Reduced synthesis or increased degradation of NO at the endothelial level appears to be detrimental in heart failure. Adding to this complex but increasingly recognized role of NO in heart failure, it appears that virtually all cell types constituting the myocardium produce NO. One of the three recognized nitric oxidase synthase isoforms, inducible NOS (iNOS), may actually produce excessive NO and suppress cardiac myocyte function in heart failure.[13]

MYOCARDIAL PATHOPHYSIOLOGY

Understanding heart failure requires recognition of the underlying pathologic conditions resulting in progressive myocardial dysfunction as well as the adaptive responses to this disease process. In addition, it is important to identify precipitating events that cause acute decompensation. If properly recognized, precipitating causes of acute decompensation of cardiac function can usually be more effectively treated than the underlying chronic condition. The short-term prognosis in patients who have an acute precipitating cause of heart failure is generally favorable, provided an effective therapeutic intervention is available. The prognosis is more guarded when the underlying disease process has progressed to a decompensated state.

PRIMARY DISEASE PROCESSES RESULTING IN HEART FAILURE

Heart failure can result from primary disease of the coronary arteries, myocardium, cardiac valves, pericardium, peripheral vessels, or lungs. Often, determining the etiology of heart failure is simpler early in its course than during its later stages. Early recognition also affords the opportunity for intervention that may prevent further progression of the syndrome.

Coronary Artery Disease

In developed countries, atherosclerotic coronary artery disease remains the leading cause of heart failure. Acute coronary thrombosis in vessels compromised by atheromatous plaques leads to focal myocardial necrosis, with resultant myocardial fibrosis and scarring. This process leads to areas of dyskinesis that result in decreased ejection fraction. When approximately 40% of the left ventricular muscle mass has been acutely infarcted, cardiogenic shock ensues. Aneurysmal dilation of infarcted areas with paradoxical motion during systole may disproportionately decrease ejection fraction. Transient loss of contractile function may result from episodes of myocardial ischemia that do not cause frank necrosis or from an ischemic zone surrounding an infarct. This so-called myocardial stunning may persist for several days.

Chronic coronary insufficiency leads to a more diffuse myocardial fibrosis, sometimes called ischemic cardiomyopathy. Revascularization of ischemic but not infarcted myocardial tissue provides a survival benefit in patients with CHF related to ischemic left ventricular systolic dysfunction. Diseases affecting the coronary microcirculation (e.g., vaso-occlusive sickle cell anemia and diabetes mellitus) result in similar pathology. Compensatory mechanisms may occur after large myocardial infarction and progressive cardiac disease, which are collectively termed ventricular remodeling. They include cardiac dilation, reactive hypertrophy, progressive fibrosis, and changes in wall conformation that may result from elevated chamber filling pressures as well as neurohumoral factors.

Cardiomyopathy

The cardiomyopathies are a group of disease processes that affect the myocardium primarily. Myocardial diseases resulting from coronary, valvular, and pericardial pathologies are excluded. Cardiomyopathy is categorized as primary, in which case the cause is unknown, or secondary to some identifiable cause or systemic illness. Clinically, patients with cardiomyopathy tend to present with three forms: dilated, hypertrophic, or restrictive.

Dilated Cardiomyopathy

Dilated cardiomyopathy is the most common form. It was formerly called congestive cardiomyopathy. In most cases, no definitive cause is identified. Rather, a variety of infectious, toxic, and metabolic agents probably contribute to the myocardial damage. Viral infection through secondary immunologic mechanisms, prolonged heavy alcohol consumption, cocaine use, and familial disease have all been associated with dilated cardiomyopathy.[14] Dilated cardiomyopathy is characterized by four-chamber cardiac enlargement, often with mural thrombi. Pump dysfunction is primarily systolic. Cardiac output may be normal at rest, but it does not increase adequately with exertion.

Hypertrophic Cardiomyopathy

Hypertrophic cardiomyopathy refers specifically to a form of hypertrophy not secondary to a hemodynamic load as may be imposed by conditions such as hypertension or valvular aortic stenosis. Approximately half of all cases of hypertrophic cardiomyopathy are familially linked. One third of the first-degree relatives of patients with hypertrophic cardiomyopathy have evidence of the disease. This disease is characterized by left ventricular hypertrophy, typically without chamber

enlargement but with characteristic excessive thickening of the upper left ventricular septum. There is abnormal systolic anterior motion of the anterior mitral valve leaflet that may result in a dynamic outflow obstruction to left ventricular ejection but causes a significant pressure gradient in only approximately a quarter of the patients. Diastolic dysfunction is the main pathologic abnormality. Increased stiffness of the hypertrophied cardiac muscle results primarily from elevated intracellular calcium levels. Histologic examination reveals a tissue pattern of bizarre disarrayed myocardial cells with variable degrees of fibrosis.

Hypertrophic cardiomyopathy is often clinically silent but is a common cause of sudden death in young adults, most often during or just after exertion. Dyspnea on exertion is the most common complaint among symptomatic patients. Exertional syncope is another common presentation. Symptoms are not always related to the severity of the outflow gradient. The classical finding in hypertrophic cardiomyopathy is a harsh systolic murmur heard best at the lower left sternal border and increased by maneuvers that decrease preload (e.g., Valsalva maneuver), decrease afterload (e.g., vasodilator therapy), or increase inotropicity (e.g., exercise). Young patients with syncope or dyspnea with suggestive clinical findings should undergo urgent echocardiography.

Patients with suspected or diagnosed hypertrophic cardiomyopathy should be cautioned to avoid strenuous exercise. β-Blockers, amiodarone, and calcium channel blockers are potentially beneficial. Digitalis, diuretics, nitrates, and β-agonists should in general be avoided in hypertrophic cardiomyopathy.

Restrictive Cardiomyopathy

Restrictive cardiomyopathy, the least common type of cardiomyopathy, occurs when cardiac muscle is infiltrated by other substances such as iron (hemochromatosis), protein (amyloidosis), granulomas (sarcoidosis), or fibrotic tissue. The chambers are stiff. Abnormalities in diastolic relaxation predominate, but systolic function is generally well preserved. Clinically, patients have sequelae of chronically elevated venous pressure such as peripheral edema, ascites, and congestive hepatomegaly. Restrictive cardiomyopathy is often difficult to differentiate from pericardial disease, even at catheterization. Computed tomography and magnetic resonance imaging can usually distinguish between restrictive cardiomyopathy and pericardial disease.

Myocarditis

Myocarditis is defined as an acute inflammatory reaction of the myocardium. Most cases of myocarditis go clinically unrecognized. In mild cases, nonspecific complaints of fatigue and dyspnea resolve after a short period of illness. Most commonly the result of a viral infectious process, myocarditis may also be caused by various other infectious agents, toxins, autoimmune disorders, and some physical agents. A small number of patients with acute myocarditis develop life-threatening dysrhythmias (e.g., Lyme disease) or progressive heart failure. Others may recover transiently only to develop a dilated cardiomyopathy after a latent period of weeks to years.

The clinical presentation of patients with myocarditis is generally nonspecific. Complaints of chest discomfort are often pleuritic and suggest associated pericarditis. Unexplained sinus tachycardia and nonspecific ST segment and T wave changes on the electrocardiogram (ECG) may be present. In some patients, acute myocarditis may simulate myocardial infarction with chest pain, ECG changes, and elevated cardiac enzyme levels. Chest radiography may show an enlarged heart. Echocardiography may reveal diffuse wall motion abnormalities and chamber dilation.

Valvular Heart Disease

Cardiac valvular disease is the third leading cause of heart failure, after ischemic heart disease and dilated cardiomyopathy. Acute valvular dysfunction may precipitate fulminant heart failure. Examples include acute mitral regurgitation secondary to papillary muscle dysfunction in acute myocardial infarction and acute aortic insufficiency secondary to bacterial endocarditis or aortic dissection. Most acute valvular dysfunction involves either the mitral or aortic valves and usually results in fulminant regurgitant lesions. Acutely stenotic lesions are predominantly restricted to mechanical catastrophes of prosthetic valves. Typical murmurs may be difficult to appreciate or even be absent in acute valvular insufficiency because of early equilibration of pressures across the defective valve. Accordingly, patients may present in extremis with fulminant pulmonary edema.

Acute mitral regurgitation commonly results from dysfunction of the valvular supporting apparatus, the papillary muscles and chordae tendineae. Infectious endocarditis and myxomatous degeneration are common causes of chordae tendineae rupture. Any cause of acute left ventricular dilation may cause functional mitral regurgitation. Papillary muscle dysfunction most commonly results from acute myocardial ischemia. Transient dysfunction may occur during episodes of angina pectoris, whereas permanent dysfunction and even papillary muscle rupture may occur early in the course of myocardial infarction. Papillary muscle failure days to weeks after infarction may lead to delayed cardiac decompensation.

Aortic dissection and infectious endocarditis are the most common causes of acute aortic regurgitation. Type A aortic dissection (involving the aortic arch) commonly disrupts the annulus of the aortic valve and may precipitate acute aortic insufficiency. Rapid surgical correction affords the only chance for survival. Type A dissections may also precipitate pericardial tamponade. Patients with infectious endocarditis may have fever, stigmata of intravenous drug use, and evidence of heart block. Acute endocarditis may cause valvular obstruction as a result of large vegetations. Outflow obstruction may also be seen with the rare conditions of atrial myxoma and air embolism. Syncope, obstruc-

tive shock, or acute heart failure in any patient with a prosthetic cardiac valve should be evaluated to demonstrate that the valve is operating normally.

Chronic Valvular Disease

Mitral insufficiency and aortic stenosis are most commonly associated with CHF. More than one valvular lesion can lead to complex clinical presentations. Knowing the precise valvular pathology may have important implications for emergency therapy for patients with heart failure. For example, patients with decompensated aortic stenosis should generally not receive vasodilator agents, as they cannot increase flow across a fixed obstruction and may become hypotensive. On the other hand, patients with mitral regurgitation benefit greatly from vasodilators, which improve antegrade flow by reducing afterload.

Pericardial Diseases

Pericardial diseases may significantly affect ventricular function, causing both decreased cardiac output and increased intracardiac pressures. Accumulation of fluid in the pericardial sac surrounding the heart may occur acutely in such conditions as blunt or penetrating trauma, acute pericarditis, uremia, or malignancy. The pericardium cannot stretch acutely. Accordingly, rapid fluid accumulation of as little as 100 mL may compromise cardiac filling and decrease cardiac output. Cardiac tamponade may be acutely fatal if not recognized and treated appropriately by pericardial decompression. The presence of elevated venous pressures, pulsus paradoxus, hypoperfusion, and tachycardia should prompt a rapid evaluation for cardiac tamponade. Echocardiography shows the presence of pericardial fluid and compromised ventricular filling. An alternative approach is bedside right heart catheterization, which demonstrates increased and equal diastolic pressures in all chambers.

Constrictive pericarditis is a rare clinical entity that restricts diastolic filling of all cardiac chambers because of a thickened and sometimes calcified pericardial sac. Symptoms are related to low cardiac output, often with prominent findings of right-sided heart failure. This clinical condition is difficult to distinguish from restrictive cardiomyopathy, although computed tomography and magnetic resonance imaging are generally helpful.

Pulmonary Disease

Pulmonary dysfunction reduces myocardial oxygen supply while increasing cardiac output demand by perfusing all tissues with suboptimally oxygenated blood. Hypoxia leads to pulmonary arteriolar vasoconstriction, which reduces lung vascular bed area, elevating pulmonary artery pressures. Chronic increases in pulmonary arterial pressure lead to right ventricular hypertrophy and dilation. When compensatory mechanisms fail, the patient shows clinical evidence of right-sided heart failure (cor pulmonale), usually with left ventricular output preserved, at least at rest. Causes of acute cor pulmonale (e.g., a large pulmonary embolus) may precipitate sudden systemic hypotension and even death caused by decreased left ventricular priming.

Distinguishing primary pulmonary disease causing predominantly right-sided heart failure from left ventricular failure with secondary right-sided dysfunction is clinically challenging. Both entities may arise with primarily wheezing or rhonchi. The chest radiograph may be difficult to interpret because both disease types cause interstitial changes. Hyperinflation depresses the diaphragm, which elongates the cardiac silhouette and may mask cardiomegaly.

CLASSIFICATION OF HEART FAILURE

Many different methods of classifying heart failure exist, including high versus low output, acute versus chronic, right sided versus left sided, systolic versus diastolic, and forward versus backward. Late in the disease process, these distinctions become blurred and somewhat artificial. Early in heart failure, they may be useful clinical descriptors suggesting particular causes and treatment strategies.

High-Output Versus Low-Output Failure

High-output failure refers to a hyperdynamic state with supranormal cardiac output and low arteriovenous oxygen difference (decreased oxygen extraction ratio) together with pulmonary congestion and peripheral edema as a consequence of elevated diastolic pressures. Diastolic dysfunction and circulatory overload contribute to the congestive symptoms. As the condition progresses, systolic myocardial dysfunction is superimposed on this background, symptoms progress, and at this point normal or even low cardiac output is present. Ultimately, untreated patients have classical CHF indistinguishable from other end-stage cardiomyopathies.

A persistent hyperdynamic state results in myocardial damage over time. The hyperdynamic state may result from increased preload (e.g., renal retention of salt and water, mineralocorticoids), decreased systemic vascular resistance (e.g., arteriovenous fistulas, pregnancy, cirrhosis, severe anemia, beriberi, thyrotoxicosis, Paget's disease, vasodilator medications), increased β-sympathetic activity, or persistent tachycardia. Early recognition of the hyperdynamic state may allow effective therapy of the underlying condition, thus avoiding the development of heart failure.

Low-output failure is the more typical variety of heart failure and occurs as a result of entities such as ischemic heart disease, dilated cardiomyopathy, valvular disease, and chronic hypertension. Low cardiac output (systolic dysfunction), high filling pressures (diastolic dysfunction), and an increased systemic oxygen extraction ratio (widened arteriovenous oxygen difference) characterize this more commonly encountered classical form of heart failure.

Acute Versus Chronic Heart Failure

The prototypical case of acute heart failure is that of the healthy person who develops a large myocardial infarction or acute valvular dysfunction. Chronic heart failure is best characterized by a disease state such as dilated cardiomyopathy, with gradual deterioration of cardiac function. In acute heart failure, the early presentation may be due to systolic dysfunction and hypoperfusion, often with APE resulting from the sudden reduction in chamber compliance (diastolic dysfunction) that accompanies acute ischemia or infarction. Chronic heart failure usually arises with symptoms related to fluid retention, with compensatory mechanisms adjusted so that normal perfusion exists, at least in the resting state.

Right-Sided Versus Left-Sided Heart Failure

The notion that one of the cardiac chambers can fail independently of the other is somewhat artificial. The right and left circulations are connected and, over time, output from the two chambers must be equal. Furthermore, the right and left ventricles share an interventricular septum, and dysfunction in one chamber may have immediate impact on the other. For example, acute right-sided heart failure from pulmonary hypertension secondary to acute respiratory failure causes bulging of the interventricular septum into the left ventricular chamber. This so-called septal shift results in decreased left ventricular preload and low cardiac output that is volume responsive. In addition, cardiac biochemical changes such as an abnormal catecholamine response affect all chambers. Chronic left-sided heart failure leads to pulmonary hypertension with resultant right-sided heart failure.

Nonetheless, the terms have some usefulness in identifying the predominant clinical presentation. Fluid accumulation "behind" the involved ventricle is responsible for many of the clinical manifestations of heart failure. For example, left ventricular failure leads primarily to pulmonary congestion with symptoms mostly of dyspnea and orthopnea. Patients with right-sided heart failure present with symptoms of systemic venous congestion such as pedal edema and hepatomegaly.

When previously normal patients have acute pathology, the concept of left- versus right-sided heart failure may be clinically useful. Patients with acute myocardial infarction of the anterior wall may present with APE. Yet, unlike patients with chronic heart failure, they generally do not have jugular venous distention or pedal edema because the central venous pressure remains normal. A chest radiograph reveals evidence of pulmonary venous congestion, interstitial edema, and, in fulminant cases, alveolar edema. Because there has not yet been time for cardiac dilation, the cardiac shadow is of normal size.

Patients with acute right ventricular infarction typically have jugular venous distention and hypotension, but often without rales. Bulging of the interventricular septum into the left ventricular chamber results in decreased left ventricular preload. The low cardiac output and hypotension are often responsive to fluid challenge. Jugular venous distention is a sign of right heart diastolic dysfunction. Failure to understand this may result in withholding of a therapeutic fluid challenge if distended neck veins are interpreted simply as a sign of heart failure.

Forward Versus Backward Heart Failure

Forward failure refers to inadequate systemic perfusion resulting from low cardiac output. Symptoms of forward failure include weakness, fatigue, oliguria, prerenal azotemia, and, in advanced cases, hypotension and cardiogenic shock. Backward failure refers to symptoms related to pressure that builds up "behind" a failing chamber. Pulmonary edema, hepatomegaly, and pedal edema are symptoms of backward failure.

Systolic Versus Diastolic Dysfunction

The classification of systolic and diastolic dysfunction allows specific treatment strategies.[15] Systolic dysfunction refers to impairment of contractility. Stroke output is reduced and forward flow is compromised. Systolic dysfunction is typically caused by myocyte destruction such as occurs in myocardial infarction or acute myocarditis. Asymptomatic left ventricular systolic dysfunction in patients 45 years of age or older has an estimated prevalence of 6% and is more common than systolic heart failure.[16,17] Diastolic dysfunction indicates a primary problem with the ability of the ventricles to relax and fill normally. In many cases, normal or even supernormal systolic function is preserved. Most cases of systolic dysfunction also involve some degree of diastolic dysfunction.

Echocardiographic and nuclear imaging techniques demonstrate that approximately 40% of patients with congestive symptoms have normal ejection fractions and suffer from diastolic dysfunction. Asymptomatic diastolic dysfunction is much more common than asymptomatic systolic dysfunction, occurring in 26% of patients 45 years of age or older in one study. Diastolic dysfunction is the predominant pathophysiologic problem in hypertrophic and restrictive cardiomyopathies, chronic hypertension, valvular aortic stenosis, and other conditions. Diastolic dysfunction occurs predominantly as a result of one of three mechanisms: impaired ventricular relaxation, increased ventricular wall thickness, or accumulation of myocardial interstitial collagen. Impaired relaxation (lusitropic) capacity of the myocardium leads to higher ventricular filling pressure, which results in congestive symptoms. Myocardial relaxation is an active, energy-requiring process. Failure of myocytes to relax may be secondary to low intracellular energy stores. Physiologic stresses causing increased cardiac demands can precipitate lusitropic abnormalities.

BOX 80-1. Classification System for Chronic Heart Failure: New York Heart Association Functional Classes

I. Asymptomatic on ordinary physical activity
II. Symptomatic on ordinary physical activity
III. Symptomatic on less than ordinary physical activity
IV. Symptomatic at rest

As with the other classification schemes, most patients with heart failure have components of both systolic and diastolic dysfunction. Patients with predominantly diastolic dysfunction, however, have the advantage of having intact myocardial contractile function. Hypertension is the most important factor leading to diastolic dysfunction. Caution in the treatment of diastolic dysfunction is also important. Because these stiffer hearts have steep pressure-volume curves, small reductions in diastolic filling volume, as may occur with aggressive diuretic therapy, may markedly decrease ventricular filling (see Figure 80-2). This preload deficiency may compromise stroke output.

CLINICAL EVALUATION OF PATIENTS WITH SUSPECTED HEART FAILURE

The New York Heart Association (NYHA) classification system is a time-honored categorization for patients with chronic heart failure (Box 80-1). Patients who present in extremis require aggressive management while history, physical examination, chest radiography, and laboratory evaluation proceed concurrently. Assessments for effective ventilation, adequate oxygenation, and reasonable systemic perfusion take priority. Patients should receive supplemental oxygen while intravenous access and cardiac monitoring as well as pulse oximetry are established. An ECG and chest radiograph should be obtained while the history is being taken. Careful consideration of the differential diagnosis is symptom based. The most common manifestation of acute heart failure is acute respiratory distress caused by pulmonary edema. Accordingly, the differential diagnosis includes exacerbation of chronic obstructive pulmonary disease or asthma, pulmonary embolus, pneumonia, anaphylaxis, and other causes of acute respiratory distress. Hypoperfusion may be caused by some of these as well as by sepsis syndrome, hypovolemia, hemorrhage, cardiac tamponade, tension pneumothorax, and other diseases.

Precipitating Causes of Heart Failure

Various stresses may result in acute cardiac decompensation (Box 80-2).

Systemic Hypertension

Sudden elevation of arterial pressure acutely increases afterload, which may precipitate the rapid onset of

BOX 80-2. Common Precipitating Causes of Acute Heart Failure

- Systemic hypertension
- Myocardial infarction or ischemia
- Dysrhythmia
- Systemic infection
- Anemia
- Dietary, physical, environmental, and emotional excesses
- Pregnancy
- Thyrotoxicosis or hypothyroidism
- Acute myocarditis
- Acute valvular dysfunction
- Pulmonary embolus
- Pharmacologic complications

heart failure. This event is particularly common when antihypertensive therapy is abruptly discontinued. Malignant hypertension, pheochromocytoma, and other states associated with high sympathetic outflow may be implicated. Cocaine and other sympathomimetic drugs of abuse may precipitate heart failure.

Myocardial Infarction and Ischemia

A new ischemic event may precipitate heart failure by impairing contractility and by decreasing left ventricular compliance. Pulmonary edema may occur rapidly in this setting, especially when large areas of myocardium are involved. In the compromised heart, ischemia may precipitate heart failure even when only small areas of cardiac muscle are involved.

Dysrhythmia

Both tachydysrhythmias and bradydysrhythmias can severely affect cardiac output. Acute dysrhythmias are a common cause of cardiac decompensation. Tachydysrhythmias compromise diastolic filling time and thus may reduce cardiac output. Concurrently, the shortened diastole impairs coronary perfusion and myocardial oxygen delivery while the tachycardia results in increased myocardial oxygen demand. These factors may precipitate ischemia, which may further impair contractility and exacerbate heart failure. The prevalence of atrial fibrillation in patients with heart failure increases from less than 10% in NYHA functional class I to approximately 50% in NYHA functional class IV.[18] Neurohormonal alterations, electrophysiologic changes, and mechanical factors create an environment in which heart failure predisposes to atrial fibrillation and atrial fibrillation exacerbates heart failure.[18] New-onset atrial fibrillation or other dysrhythmias that affect coordinated atrial priming of the ventricular pump may seriously reduce preload, especially in disease states with reduced ventricular compliance. Significant bradydysrhythmias may also reduce cardiac output simply by reducing the number of systolic ejections per minute (CO = stroke volume × heart rate).

Systemic Infection

Infection results in increased systemic metabolic demands that must be met by the heart. Pulmonary infection, which is common in patients with pulmonary vascular congestion, may add hypoxia to the metabolic stresses of fever, tachycardia, and increased tissue perfusion requirements. The sepsis syndrome is associated with a reversible form of myocardial depression, mediated by various cytokines, including interleukins-1, -2, and -6, as well as tumor necrosis factor.[19]

Anemia

In the presence of chronic anemia, oxygen delivery to tissues is maintained by increased cardiac output (isovolumic hemodilution). In patients with compensated myocardial dysfunction, this may be impossible, and increased pumping demands coupled with reduced coronary oxygen delivery may prompt the onset or exacerbation of heart failure.

Dietary, Physical, Environmental, and Emotional Excesses

Increased sodium ingestion, plasma volume expansion (e.g., transfusion), increased exertion, extremes of environmental temperature, and emotional upset are some of the important factors that may prompt cardiac decompensation.

Pregnancy

Cardiac output is normally increased significantly during pregnancy, which may lead to decompensation in women with underlying cardiac valvular disease or other cardiac pathology.

Thyroid Disorders

Heart failure may be a clinical manifestation in patients with previously compensated cardiac disease who develop hyperthyroidism, and hypothyroidism also adversely affects myocardial pump function.

Acute Myocarditis

A variety of infectious and inflammatory diseases, including viral agents and acute rheumatic fever, may precipitously impair myocardial contractility.

Acute Valvular Dysfunction

Almost all causes of acute heart failure resulting from cardiac valve dysfunction are secondary to aortic or mitral insufficiency. Mitral valve papillary muscle dysfunction or rupture may result from acute myocardial infarction, whereas acute aortic insufficiency is more commonly precipitated by acute bacterial endocarditis or aortic dissection. On occasion, acute valvular stenosis may occur, usually as a consequence of acute dysfunction of a prosthetic valve.

Pulmonary Embolus

The acute pulmonary hypertension and hypoxia that accompany pulmonary embolus may cause acute heart failure. Accordingly, this diagnosis should be entertained in patients who have unexplained heart failure and risk factors for pulmonary embolism.

Pharmacologic Complications

Patients with ischemic heart disease may be treated with β-blocking and calcium channel blocking agents. These drugs have negative inotropic effects and may precipitate overt heart failure if used in excessive doses. Many of the current antidysrhythmic agents may have this effect as well. Glucocorticoids, NSAIDs, vasodilator drugs, and others may result in sodium retention with substantial increases in plasma volume that may precipitate CHF.[20] NSAID agents in particular interfere with prostaglandin synthesis through cyclooxygenase inhibition, thereby impairing renal homeostasis in patients with heart failure. They also interfere with the effects of diuretics and ACE inhibitors. Noncompliance with medication regimens that have controlled hypertension or ischemia may also result in decompensation. A careful medication history and evaluation of the patient's compliance with that regimen is important in a search for precipitating factors.

History

A focused history should be taken for a patient in distress. The presence and character of chest pain, previous heart disease, cardiac catheterization, surgery, and other cardiac history are all explored. With patients unable to give a history, family members and old records are sources of information. A careful review of the patient's current medications may indicate ongoing disease processes. A more traditional history may be taken for patients who are less severely ill.

In patients with more gradual onset of heart failure, dyspnea on exertion is among the earliest complaints. Orthopnea is a type of dyspnea seen among patients with heart failure. The supine position enhances venous return to the heart, precipitating increases in diastolic cardiac pressure. Symptoms abate when the patient sits up and venous return decreases. Paroxysmal nocturnal dyspnea results from pulmonary congestion precipitated by plasma volume expansion that occurs as interstitial edema is reabsorbed into the circulation because venous hydrostatic pressures in the legs decrease during recumbency. Nocturia results from the same pathophysiologic process.

Physical Examination

Clammy, vasoconstricted patients with a thready pulse and delayed capillary refill may have systemic hypoperfusion despite adequate blood pressure (maintained by intense vasoconstriction). Persistently hypotensive patients require intra-arterial pressure monitoring. Noninvasive assessment of blood pressure in the vasoconstricted patient with low cardiac output is inaccu-

rate.[21] Cuff pressures in these patients typically reflect mean rather than systolic arterial pressure. Obtaining true intra-arterial pressure may make a substantial difference in the choice of therapeutic agent. For example, a patient with a cuff pressure of 80 mm Hg might receive a catecholamine vasoconstrictor to maintain coronary perfusion pressure despite the negative impact of these drugs on afterload and ischemia. If it were known that the *mean* intra-arterial pressure was 80 mm Hg, the same patient might more appropriately receive carefully titrated vasodilators (e.g., intravenous nitroglycerin) or nesiritide.

Because elevated afterload impairs ventricular ejection and places high oxygen demands on the myocardium, hypertension should be aggressively treated with systemic vasodilator therapy in patients with heart failure. This is important in patients who have active ongoing myocardial ischemia.

Physical examination of patients with APE resulting from acute myocardial infarction includes a search for surgically correctable lesions such as acute mitral regurgitation or ventricular septal defect. Patients with pulmonary congestion secondary to heart failure develop interstitial and alveolar pulmonary edema, causing reduced pulmonary compliance and decreased functional residual capacity. Crackles reflect alveolar flooding, often present in pulmonary edema. Peribronchial edema may cause wheezing, which can mimic bronchospastic disease and misdirect therapy. A positive response to bronchodilator therapy does not exclude heart failure.

Diagnostic Testing in Heart Failure

The upright chest radiograph may be one of the most useful tools available to distinguish cardiogenic pulmonary edema from other causes of dyspnea. An ECG is also indicated in most patients. The serum level of the natriuretic peptides correlates with the severity of heart failure and has prognostic significance.[22] BNP is a neurohormone synthesized in the ventricles that is released as pre-proBNP and then enzymatically cleaved to NH2-terminal-proBNP (NT-proBNP) and BNP in response to ventricular myocyte stretch. Blood measurements of NT-proBNP and BNP identify patients with heart failure.[23] Rapid, whole-blood BNP assays to evaluate possible heart failure are approved for clinical use.

The "breathing not properly" BNP Multinational Study was a prospective study of patients who presented to the emergency department with acute dyspnea and had BNP measured on arrival. BNP was accurate in diagnosing heart failure, and levels correlated with the severity of illness, with levels above 500 pg/mL making heart failure highly likely and levels of 100 to 500 pg/mL generally indeterminate. A low BNP level (less than 100 pg/mL) indicates that heart failure is highly unlikely.[24] Elevated BNP levels may also be seen in right-sided heart failure related to cor pulmonale or pulmonary embolism. BNP levels are not falsely elevated in patients with end-stage renal disease, and elevated BNP in this setting is present only with ventricular dysfunction.[25]

The BNP level correlates with ventricular function, NYHA classification, and prognosis. This screening modality may obviate the need for echocardiography, invasive monitoring, or both in selected clinical situations.[26] BNP provides a means of evaluating response to therapy. BNP levels have strong prognostic significance in ischemic heart disease. Results for 4300 patients in the Valsartan Heart Failure Trial confirmed that BNP levels are the strongest predictor of outcome in heart failure, compared with other neurohormones and clinical markers.[27]

TREATMENT OF HEART FAILURE

Of the patients with heart failure presenting to the emergency department, 21% are experiencing their first episode of heart failure and 79% have had prior hospital visits for the same condition.[28] An organized approach that (1) identifies the underlying cardiac pathology, (2) recognizes the acute precipitating event or events, and (3) controls the acute congestive state must be developed. The immediate therapeutic goals are to improve respiratory gas exchange, maintain adequate arterial saturation, and decrease pulmonary artery occlusion pressure while maintaining adequate cardiac and systemic perfusion. The acute congestive state may be controlled by (1) reducing the cardiac workload by decreasing both preload and afterload, (2) controlling excessive retention of salt and water, and (3) improving cardiac contractility. Patients may have a wide spectrum of symptoms and signs ranging from mild dyspnea on exertion to full-blown cardiogenic shock with hypotension and concomitant respiratory failure. The specific presentation dictates the appropriate clinical approach (Table 80-1).

In most patients, sitting upright while high-flow supplemental oxygen is administered and preload is decreased with morphine, nesiritide, nitrates, or furosemide results in prompt improvement.

Rapid-Onset Heart Failure

Common precipitants of rapid-onset heart failure include acute myocardial ischemia or infarction, medication noncompliance or toxicity, cardiac dysrhythmia, dietary indiscretion, acute hypoxia (e.g., pulmonary embolus, pneumonia), severe hypertension, acute valvular dysfunction, and increased hemodynamic demand secondary to trauma or infection (see Box 80-2). Iatrogenic causes of heart failure must also be considered, especially in patients who may have received overly aggressive volume resuscitation. Patients with known renal insufficiency often experience APE as a consequence of anemia, hyperkalemia, or salt and fluid overload and may require prompt hemodialysis.

Acute Pulmonary Edema

Many patients with rapid onset of pulmonary edema demonstrate adequate systemic perfusion with elevated blood pressure because of activation of various compensatory mechanisms. The ability of the left ventricle to generate systolic pressures above 160 mm Hg indicates the presence of considerable myocardial reserve.

Table 80-1. Agents Useful in the Treatment of Heart Failure

Agent	Route	Action Mechanism	PAOP	CI	BP	HR	Comment
Morphine	IV	Sympatholytic	↓↓↓	—	↓	↓	Excellent in APE, avoid in COPD
Nesiritide	IV	Natriuretic peptide	↓↓	↑↑	— or ↓		Potent reduction in neurohormonal activation
Nitroglycerin	Sublingual Transmucosal Transcutaneous	Direct smooth muscle dilator	↓↓	—	— or ↓	—	Venodilator or relieves ischemia
Nitroglycerin	IV		↓↓↓↓	↑	↓	—	Venodilator or vasodilator in larger doses, tachyphylaxis
Furosemide	Oral IV	Loop diuretic venodilator	↓↓	—	— or ↓	—	Electrolyte abnormalities
ACE inhibitors	Oral IV	Angiotensin-converting enzyme inhibition	↓↓	↑↑	↓↓	— or ↓	Improves outcome in chronic CHF, antihypertension
Nitroprusside	IV	Direct smooth muscle dilator	↓↓↓↓	↑↑↑	↓↓↓	— or ↓	Intra-arterial monitoring required Thiocyanate and cyanide toxicity
Digoxin	Oral IV	Increased Ca++ availability	↓	↑	—	↓	Most effective in atrial fibrillation with chronic CHF
Dobutamine	IV	β-Agonist	↓↓	↑↑	— or ↓	— or ↑	Safest catecholamine inotrope May cause hypotension
Dopamine	IV	β-, β-Dopaminergic agonist	—	↑↑	↑↑	↑	Effects differ with dose range
Levarterenol	IV	α-Agonist	↑	↑	↑↑↑↑	↑	Most effective vasopressor
Epinephrine	IV	α- and β-agonist	—	↑↑↑	↑↑↑	↑↑↑	High potential to induce ischemia
Amrinone	IV	Phosphodiesterase inhibitor	↓↓	↑↑	↓	↓	Nontitratable inotropic vasodilator
β-Blockers	Oral IV	β Blockade	↑↑	↓↓	↓↓	↓↓	May be useful chronically to treat diastolic dysfunction

ACE, angiotensin-converting enzyme; APE, acute pulmonary edema; CHF, congestive heart failure; COPD, chronic obstructive pulmonary disease; IV, intravenous; —, no effect; ↑ or ↓, increase or decrease on a relative scale of 1 to 4.

This group must be quickly distinguished from patients with pulmonary edema and evidence of hypoperfusion. Patients with hypertensive pulmonary edema are easier to manage because afterload reduction with the use of vasodilators is extremely effective.

Most patients with APE are diaphoretic because of intense sympathetic activation. Typical findings include crackles or wheezes, although both may be absent with decreased ventilation in more agonal patients. Jugular venous distention is present in approximately 50%, and one third of patients have peripheral edema. An S_3 gallop may be present in up to 25% but is often difficult to appreciate. An enlarged cardiac silhouette is seen on the chest radiograph in 70% of cases. These common clinical findings of chronic CHF are prevalent among patients with APE because most patients have acute exacerbations superimposed on chronic underlying disease.[28] The absence of jugular venous distention, pedal edema, and cardiomegaly is expected in previously healthy individuals with pulmonary edema resulting from an initial episode of acute myocardial ischemia. Accordingly, a normal-size heart on chest radiograph may be consistent with acute cardiogenic pulmonary edema. In addition, this finding should alert the emergency physician to the possibility of diastolic dysfunction, chronic obstructive pulmonary disease, or noncardiogenic pulmonary edema.

All patients with significant pulmonary edema have hypoxemia, which is sometimes profound. Accordingly, supplemental oxygen should be administered immediately through a high-flow face mask in spontaneously breathing patients. The typical acid-base disturbance of acute heart failure is a mixed picture. Most patients with fulminant APE have lactic acidosis, and many also have concomitant respiratory alkalosis resulting from the tachypnea stimulated by metabolic acidosis, hypoxemia, and decreased pulmonary compliance. A substantial minority of these patients present with respiratory acidosis. Underlying chronic lung disease need not be present for CO_2 retention to be manifest. The ratio of dead space to total ventilation (V_D/V_T) may be significantly increased from the pulmonary edema itself. Respiratory muscle fatigue may supervene and result in frank hypoventilation. Patients with inadequate respirations because of ventilatory failure or with severe hypoxia require immediate ventilatory support with supplemental oxygen and bag-valve-mask assisted breathing while medical therapy is initiated. Endotracheal intubation is reserved for apneic patients and those with respiratory distress, agitation, and hypoxemia not responsive to high-flow oxygen. Most spontaneously breathing patients respond rapidly to medical therapy. Even most hypercarbic patients can be managed without mechanical ventilation.

Noninvasive respiratory techniques show promise in treating severely compromised, but not agonal, APE patients. Continuous positive airway pressure (CPAP), biphasic positive airway pressure (BiPAP), and CPAP plus inspiratory pressure support (noninvasive positive pressure ventilation [NIPPV]) applied by an adjustable,

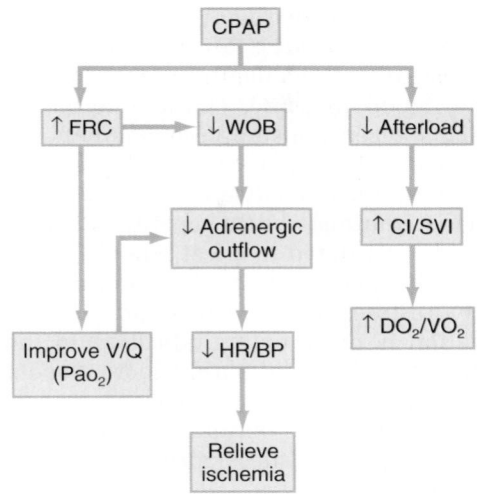

Figure 80-5. Continuous positive airway pressure (CPAP) recruits collapsed alveoli and increases functional residual capacity (FRC), which improves oxygenation and reduces work of breathing (WOB). These factors tend to reduce sympathetic tone, heart rate (HR), and blood pressure (BP), relieving myocardial ischemia. CPAP also acts as an afterload-reducing agent, which tends to improve directly cardiac index (CI) and systemic oxygen delivery (DO_2) and consumption (VO_2). PaO_2, partial pressure of oxygen in arterial blood; SVI, stroke volume index; V/Q, ventilation-perfusion ratio.

snugly fitting face mask increase functional residual capacity, improve oxygenation, reduce work of breathing, and result in decreased left ventricular preload and afterload by raising intrathoracic pressure (Figure 80-5). These techniques result in more rapid restoration of normal vital signs and oxygenation than supplemental oxygen alone. Even in studies using only CPAP, fewer patients required endotracheal intubation than in control groups. The addition of pressure support (NIPPV) further reduces the work of breathing and more rapidly improves hypercarbia than CPAP alone. Selected patients may benefit greatly from these techniques when appropriately applied in conjunction with pharmacotherapy.[29,30]

Acute Pulmonary Edema with Adequate Perfusion

Therapeutic interventions should be directed at decreasing both preload and afterload. Excessive preload reduction may result in an abrupt decrease in cardiac output, which could cause hypotension. This occurs more readily in patients with less compliant hearts (e.g., those with diastolic dysfunction, aortic stenosis, or acute myocardial infarction). Fluid challenge generally restores blood pressure quickly in these patients. In general, four categories of drugs should be considered initially: morphine sulfate, nesiritide, nitrates, and diuretics.

Morphine Sulfate

This opioid analgesic reduces pulmonary congestion through a central sympatholytic effect and release of vasoactive histamine that causes peripheral vasodilation. The result is decreased central venous return and reduced preload, lowering PAOP. In addition, through reduced systemic catecholamines, morphine decreases heart rate, blood pressure, cardiac contractility, and myocardial oxygen consumption. Patients with APE tend to be agitated as a result of air hunger. The calming effect of morphine is advantageous in this setting. Morphine is administered in repetitive 2- to 5-mg intravenous doses titrated to effect. Should oversedation result in hypoventilation, gentle stimulation usually effectively restores ventilatory effort. In APE, mild CO_2 retention is not a contraindication to the use of morphine because it results from acute alveolar flooding that is improved by the mechanisms just delineated. Patients who are obtunded at presentation are not given morphine unless airway support is first accomplished.

Nesiritide

Nesiritide, a recombinant human B-type natriuretic peptide, is frequently used in acute, decompensated heart failure. Nesiritide is a balanced vasodilator that reduces aldosterone and endothelin levels while increasing sodium and water excretion without a resultant reflex tachycardia. The Vasodilatation in the Management of Acute CHF (VMAC) trial[31] demonstrated that nesiritide is capable of symptom improvement similar to that produced by intravenous nitroglycerin in heart failure. Nesiritide improves hemodynamic function while creating a diuresis (natriuretic vasodilator), with preserved renal function.[32] Nesiritide is preferable to dobutamine or milrinone in acute decompensated heart failure. It may reduce hospital and intensive care unit lengths of stay. Because hypotension is unlikely to result from steady-dose infusions, most patients can be treated in step-down units rather than the intensive care unit. Intermittent infusions of nesiritide continue to be studied in the outpatient management of severe CHF.[32]

Nitrates

Organic nitrates activate the enzyme guanylate cyclase, leading to accumulation of cyclic guanosine monophosphate (cGMP). cGMP relaxes vascular smooth muscle by sequestering calcium in the sarcoplasmic reticulum. At lower doses, nitrates are primarily venodilators. They effectively decrease PAOP and are therefore very effective in the initial therapy of APE. At higher doses, intravenous nitroglycerin also causes arteriolar dilation that decreases blood pressure and afterload. Thus, myocardial pump function is improved while myocardial oxygen demands are decreased. Nitroglycerin may further reduce myocardial ischemia by its direct coronary vasodilator effect. Prolonged nitrate therapy over hours to days leads to tachyphylaxis secondary to depletion of intracellular sulfhydryl groups. Intermittent therapy with the smallest effective dose and occasional nitrate-free intervals minimizes tolerance.

Nitroglycerin may be initiated most expeditiously by the sublingual route. Hypotension from excessive preload reduction or vagally mediated idiosyncratic reactions may occur. Nitroglycerin should also be avoided in patients who have recently taken sildenafil or similar agents because it may precipitate refractory and possibly fatal hypotension. Patients with APE are often diaphoretic, with poor skin perfusion. Transcutaneous absorption may be erratic, and ointment applied earlier might be absorbed later in the course when skin perfusion is improved, resulting in "unexplained" hypotension. Transcutaneous nitroglycerin patches may ignite during defibrillation. These factors mitigate against the use of transcutaneous nitroglycerin in patients with APE. Intravenous nitroglycerin is a titratable agent with rapid onset and offset of action. Dosing begins at 10 to 20 µg/min by infusion pump and may be rapidly titrated upward in increments of 5 to 10 µg/min every 3 to 5 minutes. Dosages of 50 to 80 µg/min provide an antianginal effect and decreased preload in most cases. Dosages as high as 200 to 300 µg/min may be needed for maximal antihypertensive effect.

Loop Diuretics

Loop diuretics inhibit sodium resorption from the renal filtrate in Henle's loop in the medulla. The result is significant increases in renal salt and water excretion. In patients with volume overload, this diuretic action lowers plasma volume, decreasing preload and pulmonary congestion. Although intravenously administered loop diuretics have a rapid onset of action (5 to 10 minutes), symptom relief in patients with APE occurs much faster than it could from the diuretic effect alone. These improvements are probably the result of diuretic-induced neurohumoral changes. Furosemide is both a vasodilator (promotes both renal PGE_2 and natriuretic peptide secretion) and a vasoconstrictor (stimulates renin release). Loop diuretics (furosemide 1 mg/kg or bumetanide 1 mg/kg) should be administered to patients with hypertensive APE. The half-life of furosemide in patients with APE is double that in healthy volunteers, and frequent dosing should be avoided.

Patients with abrupt onset of APE who do not have underlying chronic CHF may have low plasma volumes at presentation. Diuresis in this group of patients may be unnecessary. Patients who fail to respond to loop diuretic administration may have severely compromised renal perfusion. Invasive hemodynamic monitoring may be beneficial in these patients. Diuretic therapy causes depletion of the important cations K^+ and Mg^{++}, which may be significant in patients already depleted by chronic diuretic therapy or other agents.

Nitroprusside

Nitroprusside is a potent direct smooth muscle relaxing agent that acts as a balanced vasodilator to reduce both preload and afterload. Continuous pressure monitoring is required in patients receiving this drug to avoid precipitous hypotension. Nitroprusside is an attractive drug for patients in hypertensive crisis with pulmonary edema if intra-arterial monitoring is available and can be combined with adequate nurse staffing, to avoid an inadvertent hypotensive emergency precipitated by the drug. In patients with acute myocardial ischemia or infarction, however, nitroglycerin is preferable because it avoids the coronary steal syndrome, in which less diseased vessels dilate and "steal" flow from more diseased vessels. These patients are also particularly vulnerable to unintended hypotension, an event more likely to occur with nitroprusside than nitroglycerin. Patients with renal failure may experience thiocyanate toxicity from high-dose infusions. Cyanide toxicity, recognized clinically by the presence of agitation and lactic acidosis, may occur in individuals with a genetic predisposition.

Other Therapies

Most patients with APE and adequate systemic perfusion respond promptly to treatment with oxygen, morphine, nesiritide, nitrates, and diuretics. Other previous therapies (e.g., rotating tourniquets, phlebotomy, and aminophylline) have no demonstrated efficacy in APE. Endotracheal intubation should be reconsidered if the patient develops severe respiratory deterioration unresponsive to NIPPV, significant cardiac dysrhythmias, or low cardiac output or has ongoing chest pain.

Treatment of Acute Pulmonary Edema in Hypotensive Patients

Patients with acute cardiogenic pulmonary edema and apparent systemic hypotension present a therapeutic dilemma. Coronary perfusion in patients with coronary artery disease depends on the pressure gradient between the aorta and left ventricular chamber in diastole. The combination of hypotension and elevated left-sided filling pressure dramatically decreases coronary perfusion and leads to further impairment of contractility from increased ischemia. Accordingly, vasopressor administration to maintain coronary perfusion pressure would be necessary if this set of conditions truly existed. Vasopressor therapy, however, has the potential to increase afterload, decrease cardiac output, increase myocardial oxygen demand, exacerbate ischemia, and precipitate dysrhythmias. Patients with this clinical condition uniformly have low cardiac output and intense peripheral vasoconstriction. Under these conditions, noninvasive assessment of arterial pressure is notoriously unreliable.[21] Gradients of 60 mm Hg between cuff systolic and true intra-arterial systolic pressures are common. Intra-arterial pressure monitoring should be instituted promptly in these patients, which may allow the judicious use of effective and myocardium-sparing venodilator agents and avoid the use of potentially dangerous vasopressors.

If the patient is truly hypotensive, aggressive measures are used to maintain or restore coronary perfusion pressure. In this setting, the patient is either in true cardiogenic shock (pulmonary edema, hypotension, and decreased peripheral perfusion) or volume depleted. Patients in true cardiogenic shock have lost as much as 40% of their ventricular muscle mass. They have both a low cardiac index (<2.2 L/min/m^2) and high left-sided filling pressures (PAOP > 15 mm Hg). Patients with depressed contractility and APE may also be plasma volume depleted, with a cardiac index less than 2.2 L/min/m^2 and PAOP less than 15 mm Hg. It is impossible to distinguish between these two subsets of patients by physical examination alone because both have signs of systemic hypoperfusion and pulmonary edema. Pulmonary artery catheterization may be needed to assess accurately the hemodynamic status of these individuals.

Of patients with acute myocardial infarction and clinical evidence of systemic hypoperfusion, nearly 25% have low PAOP, indicating the presence of hypovolemia. Fluid challenge alone in these patients results in restoration of hemodynamic stability in half the cases. Hypotensive patients with APE should receive judicious fluid challenge in the form of 250-mL saline boluses over 5 to 10 minutes. If the respiratory status is not deteriorating, repeated aliquots may be administered. If hypovolemia is contributing to the hypotension, this intervention should restore blood pressure and systemic perfusion without the need for vasopressors. If the patient has true cardiogenic shock, more aggressive interventions, including inotropic and vasopressor therapy, intra-aortic balloon counterpulsation, and endotracheal intubation with mechanical ventilation, may be needed. Although fluid challenge carries a potential risk in these patients, it is unlikely to have a substantial negative impact. Prompt hemodynamic monitoring allows precise titration of inotropic, vasopressor, and vasodilator therapies.

Catecholamine Inotropic Agents

In truly hypotensive patients who have been adequately volume repleted (cardiogenic shock), norepinephrine is probably the pressor of choice. It raises blood pressure and coronary perfusion pressure (α-vasoconstrictor effect) with the least increase in heart rate and contractility (lack of β effect) that could further increase myocardial oxygen demands. In cardiogenic shock, norepinephrine administration is a temporizing maneuver to maintain coronary perfusion while rescue strategies such as angioplasty, intra-aortic balloon pumping, or cardiac surgery are accomplished.

Dopamine is a naturally occurring catecholamine and a norepinephrine precursor. It has a dose-dependent effect on peripheral vascular tone and acts as a positive inotropic and chronotropic agent. Despite previous impressions, dopamine has no perfusion-sparing effect on the kidneys at any dose.[33] Epinephrine is a potent α and β agonist that maintains blood pressure and increases cardiac output. It is used primarily in cardiac surgery patients to combat the effects of myocardial stunning after operations using cardiopulmonary bypass. Dobutamine is a synthetic catecholamine that is mainly a β_2-receptor agonist with some β_1- and α-agonist activity. It is an inotropic vasodilator at therapeutic doses and should be used with caution in patients with borderline hypotension, as it occasionally reduces blood pressure further. Iso-proterenol is a potent β-agonist that causes profound tachycardia and vasodilation, making it dangerous to use in heart failure.

In patients with acute myocardial infarction or ischemia and severe left ventricular dysfunction, the use of a catecholamine may be counterproductive. Revascularization to reperfuse stunned or hibernating myocardium is preferable.

Digitalis

The cardiac glycosides inhibit the adenosine triphosphatase–dependent sodium-potassium pump in the cell membrane of the cardiac myocyte. This inhibition increases the availability of intracellular calcium to contractile proteins in myocardial cells, increasing the force of myocardial contraction, with modest inotropic effect. In the setting of acute myocardial infarction with pulmonary congestion, digitalis has minimal potency in improving hemodynamics compared with dobutamine. Digitalis preparations have little role in acute heart failure except to control the ventricular response rate in atrial flutter or fibrillation. Diltiazem offers a more promptly effective and safe alternative to digoxin in normotensive patients.[34]

Other Cardiotonic Agents

Amrinone is the prototype of phosphodiesterase type III inhibitors, which produce increased levels of cyclic adenosine monophosphate in the myocardium and peripheral smooth muscle. Only intravenous forms of amrinone and milrinone are approved by the Food and Drug Administration for use in heart failure. These vasodilating inotropic agents increase cardiac output and reduce left ventricular pressures without producing significant changes in heart rate and blood pressure. The positive inotropic effects of dobutamine and amrinone are additive, and concomitant use of both drugs appears to be better tolerated than aggressive dosing of dobutamine alone, with lower metabolic costs. Nevertheless, long-term use of milrinone has been shown to reduce survival in CHF in functional NYHA classes III and IV.[35] These agents appear to be prodysrhythmic. They may be useful on a short-term basis in patients awaiting heart transplantation. Amrinone use is somewhat risky, especially without invasive hemodynamic monitoring.

Treatment of Heart Failure without Pulmonary Congestion

On occasion, heart failure may lead to hypoperfusion without significant pulmonary congestion. For example, patients with dysfunction because of congestive cardiomyopathy may have had excessive diuresis or developed a dysrhythmia that has negatively affected pump function without creating pulmonary edema. Other entities to consider include septic shock and massive pulmonary embolus. Hypotension in this situation may not be pathologic because chronic adaptive changes and medical therapies may leave patients with a low blood pressure that is well tolerated. Clamminess, cyanotic extremities, altered mental status, metabolic acidosis, and decreased urine output are some of the important findings that help define significant hypoperfusion. If hypoperfusion is present, cautious volume challenge is instituted with isotonic crystalloid. Invasive hemodynamic monitoring is indicated because chamber filling pressures help define the cardiovascular pathology.

Acute right ventricular infarction is one important cause of hypoperfusion with jugular venous distention and absent pulmonary congestion. Approximately one third of patients with acute inferior infarction have significant right ventricular involvement, which leads to inadequate pulmonary perfusion and low left ventricular priming. These patients have hypotension that is often symptomatic. Jugular venous distention is prominent, but pedal edema is usually absent. These patients often have evidence of ST segment elevation or depression in the V_1 lead. Right-sided leads may provide further evidence of right ventricular infarction. Large volume fluid resuscitation along with inotropic support with norepinephrine or dopamine may be required to provide adequate preload to the left ventricle and restore blood pressure.

Treatment of Chronic Heart Failure

Patients with chronic heart failure often have complex multiorgan dysfunction and polydrug medical regimens. In this clinical setting, the potential impact of any therapeutic intervention on the entire spectrum of disease and compensatory mechanisms should be considered. For example, adding an NSAID to the medical regimen of a patient with chronic heart failure may negatively affect renovascular function and precipitate increased fluid retention and pulmonary edema.[20] Chronic heart failure often involves a much more gradual onset of symptoms, with a slow increase in dyspnea with minimal exertion, progressive orthopnea, fatigue, and other symptoms. U.S. guidelines approved by the AHA and ACC have introduced a new classification system for chronic heart failure that includes four categories: patients at risk, patients with asymptomatic left ventricular dysfunction, patients with symptomatic heart failure, and those with refractory heart failure (Table 80-2). The number of patients with asymptomatic heart failure is about fourfold greater than the number of patients with symptomatic heart failure.[36] A most important advance in the management of heart failure is to modify long-term maladaptive responses as well as achieve short-term functional improvement.[37] Ideally, treatment should be initiated in patients at risk to prevent disease progression. Atherosclerotic coronary artery disease, hypertension, diabetes mellitus, hyperlipidemia, cocaine and alcohol abuse, smoking, and obesity are significant risk factors for heart failure. Hypertension precedes heart failure in 75% of patients, particularly in blacks. About two thirds of patients with systolic heart failure have sig-

Table 80-2. Heart Failure Management Recommendations for Patients in New York Heart Association Class I or II with Stage A, B, or C Disease

Stage of Heart Failure	Management Recommendations
A (High risk of developing heart failure)	Risk factor management (e.g., control of hypertension, diabetes, lipid disorders; smoking cessation; avoidance of alcohol and illicit drugs) Use of ACE inhibitor in patients with atherosclerotic disease, hypertension, diabetes, or other risk factors Control of ventricular rate in patients with supraventricular tachyarrhythmias Treatment of thyroid disorders Periodic evaluation for signs and symptoms of heart failure Recommendations for stage A
B (Left ventricular dysfunction without symptoms)	Use of ACE inhibitor in patients with history of myocardial infarction or reduced ejection fraction regardless of history of myocardial infarction Use of β-blocker in patients with history of myocardial infarction or reduced ejection fraction regardless of history of myocardial infarction Valve replacement or repair in patients with hemodynamically important valvular disease Long-term use of systemic vasodilator in patients with severe aortic regurgitation Recommendations for stages A and B
C (Symptomatic left ventricular dysfunction)	Use of diuretic in patients with fluid retention Use of ACE inhibitor in all patients unless contraindicated Use of digitalis to treat symptoms unless contraindicated Discontinuation of drugs known to affect patient status adversely (e.g., nonsteroidal anti-inflammatory drugs, most antiarrhythmic drugs, calcium channel blockers) Use of spironolactone in patients with class IV symptoms, preserved renal function, normal potassium levels Exercise Use of angiotensin II receptor blocker in patients treated with digitalis, diuretics, or β-blockers who cannot tolerate ACE inhibitors because of cough or angioedema Use of hydralazine-nitrate combination in patients treated with digitalis, diuretics, or β-blockers who cannot take ACE inhibitors because of hypotension or renal insufficiency Addition of angiotensin II receptor blocker to ACE inhibitor Addition of nitrate, alone or with hydralazine, to ACE inhibitor, digitalis, diuretic, or β-blocker

ACE, angiotensin-converting enzyme.

nificant coronary artery disease. Control of hypertension reduces the risk of developing heart failure, as does control of dyslipidemias among patients with atherosclerosis. Appropriate lifestyle changes, including smoking cessation, weight reduction, restriction of salt and water intake, and modest exercise, reduce symptoms in heart failure and may delay progression. Substantial weight loss in patients with heart failure associated with obesity produces a reversal of many of the clinical manifestations and improves NYHA functional class in most patients.[38]

The use of BNP assays may assist in identifying patients with heart failure with more subtle clinical presentations.

Chronic Therapy

The mainstay of treatment for chronic heart failure and asymptomatic left ventricular dysfunction is vasodilator therapy, which benefits pump function by reducing both afterload and preload. The most important vasodilators for chronic heart failure are ACE inhibitors, angiotensin II receptor antagonists, nitrates, and calcium channel blockers. In general, exacerbations of chronic heart failure require admission if the cause of the exacerbation cannot be readily recognized and corrected, if the disease process has become unstable because of increased ischemia or new dysrhythmia, or if clinical deterioration of the patient appears likely.

Angiotensin-Converting Enzyme Inhibitors

ACE inhibitors provide the most effective therapy for left ventricular dysfunction. ACE inhibitors increase survival in all classes of chronic heart failure and also are useful to prevent the development of heart failure in patients with myocardial infarction and asymptomatic left ventricular dysfunction.[39,40] The actions of ACE inhibitors inhibit production of angiotensin II, producing direct vasodilation in addition to a natriuretic effect mediated by inhibition of aldosterone secretion. Additional ACE inhibitor effects include inhibition of the degradation of bradykinin and reduction of intrinsic endothelium-dependent vasoconstriction. ACE inhibitors are natriuretic vasodilators that reduce diuretic and potassium supplement requirements. Unlike other vasodilators, they do not induce reflex tachycardia.

The main side effects of ACE inhibitors are hypotension, deterioration of renal function, chronic cough secondary to bronchospasm, and upper airway angio-edema. ACE inhibitors should be initiated at low doses with careful attention to the potential for hypotension, with concomitant reduction in diuretic and potassium supplementation. Optimal ACE inhibitor dosing, however, appears to be neglected in many patients with CHF, particularly elderly patients.[41,42] In patients with chronic heart failure, high-dose aspirin (>325 mg/day) may impair some clinical benefits of ACE inhibitors.[43]

Angiotensin II Receptor Blockade

In heart failure patients intolerant of ACE inhibitors, angiotensin type 1 (AT_1) receptor blockers (ARBs) may have utility. ARBs appear to avoid the side effects of cough and bradykinin accumulation. Two studies comparing AT_1 receptor antagonists with ACE inhibitors in symptomatic heart failure failed to show superiority of either drug type.[44,45] Addition of AT_1 receptor antagonists to maximally tolerated doses of ACE inhibitors improves hemodynamic features in patients with chronic heart failure and enhances peak exercise capacity while alleviating symptoms. In a meta-analysis of 17 trials comparing angiotensin II receptor blockers with ACE inhibitors, ARBs were not superior to ACE inhibitors in reducing mortality or hospitalization for heart failure.[46] The combination of an ARB and an ACE inhibitor was superior to an ACE inhibitor alone for reducing hospitalizations but not mortality. ARBs are most useful in patients intolerant of ACE inhibitors.

Nitrates

Nitrate therapy, by virtue of a direct vasodilator effect, improves exercise tolerance in chronic heart failure. When used in combination with the arteriolar dilator hydralazine, it also prolongs survival in patients with CHF, but less so than ACE inhibitors. Nitrate therapy offers potential hemodynamic improvement in patients already taking ACE inhibitors.[47] The main problem with nitrate therapy appears to be rapid drug tolerance, which can be partially addressed by daily nitrate drug-free intervals.

Calcium Channel Blockers

First-generation calcium channel blockers (verapamil, diltiazem, and nifedipine) have not improved survival in chronic heart failure. Their use may precipitate clinical deterioration.[48] Second-generation dihydropyridines (nicardipine, amlodipine) have more moderate negative inotropic effects. Amlodipine reduces fatal and nonfatal cardiac events in nonischemic but not in ischemic heart disease.[49] There is no compelling evidence for the use of calcium channel blockers in heart failure, although they may be used in patients intolerant of β-blockers, ACE inhibitors, ARBs, and combined nitrates plus hydralazine.[50] Calcium channel blockers are indicated for the treatment of hypertension, angina, and dysrhythmias but should be used with caution, if at all, in patients with associated chronic heart failure.[51]

Diuretics

Patients with chronic heart failure exhibit a reduced ability to excrete a sodium and water load, with abnormal cardiac and hemodynamic adaptations to salt excess.[52] Loop diuretics, although commonly used, are associated with significant side effects, including hypovolemia, electrolyte disturbances (low K^+, Mg^{++}, and Na^+), hyperuricemia, and metabolic alkalosis. The hypokalemia and hypomagnesemia secondary to diuretic therapy are believed to be prodysrhythmic.

Spironolactone directly antagonizes aldosterone and significantly reduces mortality while improving left ventricular function in patients with severe heart failure (ejection fraction < 35%) already being treated with an ACE inhibitor and a loop diuretic, with or without digoxin. Spironolactone may lead to serious hyperkalemia in the presence of significant renal insufficiency or in patients taking supplemental potassium.

Cardiac Glycosides

Digoxin is of benefit in patients with all degrees of heart failure by reducing symptoms and improving quality of life and exercise tolerance.[53] Digoxin use reduces the rate of hospitalization in chronic heart failure, although it does not affect mortality. Digoxin should be used for most persistently symptomatic heart failure patients whose treatment already includes ACE inhibitors, diuretics, and β-blocker therapy when heart failure is caused by systolic dysfunction.

Phosphodiesterase Inhibitors

There is no indication for long-term amrinone or milrinone therapy, which increases morbidity and mortality in patients with severe chronic heart failure.[54] Other agents in this class have limited efficacy associated with increased mortality.

β-Blocker Therapy

Despite the apparent paradox of using agents that reduce myocardial contractility, β-adrenergic blocking agents have significant efficacy in chronic heart failure. Long-term activation of the sympathetic nervous system in heart failure, activation of the renin-angiotensin-aldosterone system, myocardial β-adrenergic receptor downregulation, and direct cardiotoxicity because of elevated norepinephrine levels are associated with adverse effects. An extensive meta-analysis revealed that β-blockers increase the ejection fraction by 29%, reduce mortality by 30%, and reduce hospitalization for heart failure by 40%.[55,56] The AHA/ACC guidelines recommend β-blockers in all patients with symptomatic left ventricular systolic dysfunction.[57]

β-Blockers should not normally be initiated in acute heart failure. They are most useful in chronic heart failure associated with other conditions in which there are indications for β-blocker therapy, including hypertension, angina pectoris, and significant dysrhythmias. Slow upward titration of β-blocker therapy facilitates maximal tolerability. Carvedilol, a third-generation α- and β-blocker with antioxidant properties, may be a particularly effective agent in chronic heart failure.[58]

Other Therapeutic Interventions in Chronic Heart Failure

Ultrafiltration and Renal Dialysis

Ultrafiltration reduces volume overload when diuretic therapy is inadequate.[59] Renal dialysis is important for heart failure treatment in end-stage renal disease. Potential complications of renal disease that may require special consideration include fluid overload, severe hyperkalemia, iatrogenic hypermagnesemia, uremic pericardial effusion, and drug toxicity (especially digitalis).

Sleep Apnea–Related Respiratory Support

Obstructive sleep apnea is more prevalent in chronic heart failure than previously recognized, and treatment with CPAP can be therapeutic.[60,61]

Antidysrhythmic Therapy

From 70% to 95% of patients with cardiomyopathy and CHF have frequent premature ventricular beats, and 40% to 80% develop nonsustained ventricular tachycardia.[62] An associated increased risk of sudden death exists in these patients. An extensive meta-analysis shows a 15% reduction in total mortality with amiodarone, with arrhythmic sudden death reduced by 29%.[63] In chronic heart failure, amiodarone prevented the development of atrial fibrillation and converted significantly more patients with atrial fibrillation to sinus rhythm.[64] Unfortunately, amiodarone and other antidysrhythmic agents have significant toxicities and may be prodysrhythmic.

Implantable Defibrillators

Implantable cardioverter-defibrillators (ICDs) have a mortality advantage over antiarrhythmics in chronic heart failure.[65] In the Multicenter Automatic Defibrillator Implantation Trial (MADIT),[66] in patients with previous myocardial infarction with ejection fraction below 35%, nonsustained ventricular tachycardia, and inducible ventricular tachycardia not suppressible by procainamide, ICD placement reduced sudden death by 54% at 2 years. The MADIT II study demonstrated a 29% reduction in all-cause mortality with ICDs in patients with a history of myocardial infarction and a left ventricular ejection fraction less than 30%. The economic as well as clinical impact of these studies awaits further clarification.[67]

In addition, patients with severe CHF with aberrant ventricular conduction benefit from atrioventricular sequential pacing.[68,69] Left or biventricular pacing or cardiac resynchronization therapy improves symptoms and exercise capacity and can reverse chronic cardiac dilation.[70,71] Also, ventricular pacing after atrioventricular node ablation appears more effective than pharmacologic therapy for CHF with chronic atrial fibrillation.[72]

Left Ventriculoplasty and Ventricular Assist Devices

Batista and colleagues stunned the medical community in 1996 by reporting a pilot trial of partial left ventriculoplasty in the treatment of chronic heart failure.[73] Simplistically, the surgery is a mechanical method of reducing left ventricular chamber size, which by Laplace's law should make the residual myocardium more efficient by reducing left ventricular workload. After a promising beginning, left ventriculoplasty has largely been abandoned because of failure to demonstrate long-term efficacy in heart failure.

Multiple implantable left ventricular assist devices have been in various trial stages for chronic heart failure as a bridge to transplantation and as a surgical alternative to chronic medical management.[74,75] Heart transplantation is still the most effective therapy for end-stage heart failure, with a 10-year survival rate after cardiac transplantation approaching 50%.[76] Although cardiac transplantation is associated with 84% survival at 1 year and 74.5% survival at 3 years in the United States,[77] the limited availability of donors (2500 heart transplants per year in the United States) makes alternative surgical techniques of interest in end-stage heart failure. Eventually, cell transplantation techniques using neonatal or fetal cardiac myocytes or even skeletal myoblasts may become viable techniques to repair the failing myocardium.[78]

SUMMARY

Diagnosis and management of patients with CHF in the emergency department remain important and challenging aspects of emergency medicine. Advances in the chronic medical management of CHF, including the routine use of digoxin, diuretics, ACE inhibitors, β-blockers, and spironolactone, have resulted in sustained symptomatic improvement and reduced 5-year mortality. Despite these advances, CHF exacerbation remains among the most frequent conditions resulting in emergency department visits and hospital admission. The increased number and types of pharmacologic agents used by these patients make it even more challenging to emergency physicians to care for heart failure appropriately. Abrupt-onset APE and cardiogenic shock complete the challenge for emergency physicians. Deliberate consideration of all differential diagnostic entities, careful physical examination, and utilization of the diagnostic tools available in the emergency department, combined with a sound understanding of the pathophysiology and pharmacotherapy reviewed in this chapter, allow rewarding results when caring for this frequently encountered, and ever challenging, diverse group of patients.

KEY CONCEPTS

- Patients with acute pulmonary edema and systemic hypotension may have acute plasma volume depletion and require a fluid challenge.

- In heart failure, patients with decompensated aortic stenosis should not receive vasodilator agents; in contrast, patients with mitral regurgitation benefit greatly.

- Patients with acute right ventricular infarction may present with distended neck veins, yet require a fluid challenge.

- Patients with acute cardiogenic pulmonary edema have low cardiac output and intense peripheral vasoconstriction. Noninvasive assessment of arterial pressure is notoriously unreliable.

- Approximately 50% of cases of heart failure involve mainly diastolic dysfunction.

- Aggressive treatment of risk factors for heart failure may prevent the development of heart failure.

- Neurohormonal mechanisms are deleterious in the long term in heart failure, and chronic therapy is important even in asymptomatic myocardial dysfunction to oppose these neurohormonal effects.

- The advent of BNP laboratory assays and therapeutic infusions are rapidly improving our capabilities to quantify objectively and treat acute heart failure.

REFERENCES

1. Sharma R, Anker SD: Immune and neurohormonal pathways in chronic heart failure. *Congest Heart Fail* 8:23, 2002.
2. Croft JB, et al: Heart failure survival among older adults in the United States: A poor prognosis for an emerging epidemic in the Medicare population. *Arch Intern Med* 159:505, 1999.
3. American Heart Association: *2002 Heart and Stroke Statistical Update*. Dallas, American Heart Association, 2001.
4. Hunt SA, et al: ACC/AHA guidelines for the evaluation and management of chronic heart failure in the adult: Executive summary. *J Am Coll Cardiol* 38:2101, 2001.
5. Musoudi FA, Havranek EP, Krumholz HM: The burden of chronic congestive heart failure in older persons: Magnitude and implications for policy and research. *Heart Fail Rev* 7:9, 2002.
6. Monchamp T, Frishman WH: Exercise as a treatment modality for congestive heart failure. *Heart Dis* 4:110, 2002.
7. Pitt B, et al: The effect of spironolactone on morbidity and mortality in patients with severe heart failure. Randomized Aldactone Evaluation Study Investigators. *N Engl J Med* 341;709, 1999.
8. Haldeman GA, et al: Hospitalization of patients with heart failure: National Hospital Discharge Survey, 1985 to 1995. *Am Heart J* 137:352, 1999.
9. Lee CR, et al: Vasopressin: A new target for the treatment of heart failure. *Am Heart J* 146:9, 2003.
10. Spieker LE, Lüscher TF: Will endothelin receptor antagonists have a role in heart failure? *Med Clin North Am* 87:459, 2003.
11. Kiowski W, et al: Evidence for endothelin-1-mediated vasoconstriction in severe chronic heart failure. *Lancet* 346:732, 1995.
12. Massion PB, et al: Nitric oxide and cardiac function: Ten years after, and continuing. *Circ Res* 93:388, 2003.
13. Linke A, Recchia F, Zhang X, Hintze TH: Acute and chronic endothelial dysfunction: Implications for the development of heart failure. *Heart Fail Rev* 8:87, 2003.
14. Baig MK, et al: Familial dilated cardiomyopathy: Cardiac abnormalities are common in asymptomatic relatives and may represent early disease. *J Am Coll Cardiol* 31:195, 1998.
15. Sheldon EL, Grossman W: Diastolic dysfunction as a cause of heart failure. *J Am Coll Cardiol* 22:49A, 1993.
16. Wang TJ, et al: The epidemiology of "asymptomatic" left ventricular systolic dysfunction: Implications for screening. *Ann Intern Med* 138:907, 2003.
17. Redfield MM, et al: Burden of systolic and diastolic ventricular dysfunction in the community: Appreciating the scope of the heart failure epidemic. *JAMA* 289:194, 2003.
18. Maisel WH, Stevenson LW: Atrial fibrillation in heart failure: Epidemiology, pathophysiology, and rationale for therapy. *Am J Cardiol* 91:2D, 2003.
19. Blum A, Miller H: Role of cytokines in heart failure. *Am Heart J* 135:181, 1998.
20. Feenstra J, et al: Drug-induced heart failure. *J Am Coll Cardiol* 33:1152, 1999.
21. Cohn JN: Blood pressure measurement in shock: Mechanisms of inaccuracy of auscultatory and palpatory methods. *JAMA* 199:118, 1967.
22. Stoupakis G, Klapholz M: Natriuretic peptides: Biochemistry, physiology, and therapeutic role in heart failure. *Heart Dis* 5:215, 2003.
23. McCullough PA, Omland T, Maisel AS: B-type natriuretic peptides: A diagnostic breakthrough for clinicians. *Rev Cardiovasc Med* 4:72, 2003.
24. Maisel A: B-type natriuretic peptide measurements in diagnosing congestive heart failure in the dyspneic emergency department patient. *Rev Cardiovasc Med* 3(Suppl 4):S10, 2002.
25. Cataliotti A, et al: Circulating natriuretic peptide concentrations in patients with end-stage renal disease: Role of brain natriuretic peptide as a biomarker for ventricular remodeling. *Mayo Clin Proc* 76:1111, 2001.
26. Nielsen OW, et al: Retrospective analysis of the cost-effectiveness of using plasma brain natriuretic peptide in screening for left ventricular systolic dysfunction in the general population. *J Am Coll Cardiol* 41:113, 2003.
27. Latini R, Masson S, de Angelis N, Anand I: Role of brain natriuretic peptide in the diagnosis and management of heart failure: Current concepts. *J Card Fail* 8:288, 2002.
28. Aghababian RV: Acutely decompensated heart failure: Opportunities to improve care and outcomes in the emergency department. *Rev Cardiovasc Med* 3(Suppl 4):S3, 2002.
29. Pang D, et al: The effect of positive pressure airway support on mortality and the need for intubation in cardiogenic pulmonary edema: A systematic review. *Chest* 114:1185, 1998.
30. Murray S: Bi-level positive airway pressure (BiPAP) and acute cardiogenic pulmonary oedema (ACPO) in the emergency department. *Aust Crit Care* 15:51, 2002.
31. Publication Committee for the VMAC Investigators: Intravenous nesiritide vs nitroglycerin for treatment of decompensated congestive heart failure: A randomized controlled trial. *JAMA* 287:1531, 2002.
32. Burger MR, Burger AJ: BNP in decompensated heart failure: Diagnostic, prognostic and therapeutic potential. *Curr Opin Investig Drugs* 2:929, 2001.
33. Smit AJ: Dopamine in heart failure and critical care. *Clin Exp Hypertens* 22:269, 2000.
34. Goldenberg IF, et al: Intravenous diltiazem for the treatment of patients with atrial fibrillation or flutter and moderate to severe congestive heart failure. *Am J Cardiol* 74:884, 1994.
35. Packer M, et al: Effect of oral milrinone on mortality in severe chronic heart failure. The PROMISE Study Research Group. *N Engl J Med* 325:1468, 1991.

36. Frigerio M, et al: Prevention and management of chronic heart failure in management of asymptomatic patients. *Am J Cardiol* 91:4F, 2003.

37. Katz AM: Pathophysiology of heart failure: Identifying targets for pharmacotherapy. *Med Clin North Am* 87:303, 2003.

38. Alpert MA: Management of obesity cardiomyopathy. *Am J Med Sci* 321:237, 2001.

39. Khalil ME, et al: A remarkable medical story: Benefits of angiotensin-converting enzyme inhibitors in cardiac patients. *J Am Coll Cardiol* 37:1757, 2001.

40. Jamali AH, et al: The role of angiotensin receptor blockers in the management of chronic heart failure. *Arch Intern Med* 161:667, 2001.

41. Gattis WA, et al: Is optimal angiotensin-converting enzyme inhibitor dosing neglected in elderly patients with heart failure? *Am Heart J* 136:43, 1998.

42. Van Veldhuisen DJ, et al: High- versus low-dose ACE inhibition in chronic heart failure: A double-blind placebo-controlled study of imidapril. *J Am Coll Cardiol* 32:1811, 1998.

43. Guazzi M, et al: Aspirin-angiotensin-converting enzyme inhibitor coadministration and mortality in patients with heart failure: A dose-related adverse effect of aspirin. *Arch Intern Med* 163:1574, 2003.

44. Brunner-LaRocca HP, Vaddadi G, Esler MD: Recent insight into therapy of congestive heart failure: Focus on ACE inhibition and angiotensin-II antagonism. *J Am Coll Cardiol* 33:1163, 1999.

45. Mazayex VP, et al: Valsartan in heart failure patients previously untreated with an ACE inhibitor. *Int J Cardiol* 65:239, 1999.

46. Jong P, et al: Angiotensin receptor blockers in heart failure: Meta-analysis of randomized controlled trials. *J Am Coll Cardiol* 39:463, 2002.

47. Mehra A, et al: Persistent hemodynamic improvement with short-term nitrate therapy in patients with chronic congestive heart failure already treated with captopril. *Am J Cardiol* 70:1310, 1992.

48. Elkayam U, et al: Calcium channel blockers in heart failure. *J Am Coll Cardiol* 22(Suppl A):139A, 1993.

49. Follath F, et al: Etiology and response to drug treatment in heart failure. *J Am Coll Cardiol* 32:1167, 1998.

50. Aronow WS: Left ventricular diastolic heart failure with normal left ventricular systolic function in older persons. *J Lab Clin Med* 137:316, 2001.

51. de Vries RJ, van Veldhuisen DJ, Dunselman PH: Efficacy and safety of calcium channel blockers in heart failure: Focus on recent trials with second-generation dihydropyridines. *Am Heart J* 139:185, 2000.

52. Volpe M, et al: Abnormalities of sodium handling and of cardiovascular adaptations during high salt diet in patients with mild heart failure. *Circulation* 88:1620, 1993.

53. Dec GW: Digoxin remains useful in the management of chronic heart failure. *Med Clin North Am* 87:317, 2003.

54. Packer M: The development of positive inotropic agents for chronic heart failure: How have we gone astray? *J Am Coll Cardiol* 22:119A, 1993.

55. Lechat P, et al: Clinical effects of β-adrenergic blockade in chronic heart failure: A meta-analysis of double-blind, placebo-controlled, randomized trials. *Circulation* 98:1184, 1998.

56. Foody JM, Farrell MH, Krumholz HM: Beta-blocker therapy in heart failure: Scientific review. *JAMA* 287:883, 2002.

57. Prichett AM, Redfield MM: Beta-blockers: New standard therapy for heart failure. *Mayo Clin Proc* 51:519, 2002.

58. Di Lenarda A, et al: Long-term effects of carvedilol in idiopathic dilated cardiomyopathy with persistent left ventricular dysfunction despite chronic metoprolol. *J Am Coll Cardiol* 33:1926, 1999.

59. Agostoni P, et al: Sustained improvement in functional capacity after removal of body fluid with isolated ultrafiltration in chronic cardiac insufficiency: Failure of furosemide to provide the same result. *Am J Med* 96:191, 1994.

60. Tkacova R, et al: Effects of continuous positive airway pressure on obstructive sleep apnea and left ventricular afterload in patients with heart failure. *Circulation* 98:2269, 1998.

61. Yan AT, Bradley TD, Liu PP: The role of continuous positive airway pressure in the treatment of congestive heart failure. *Chest* 120:1675, 2001.

62. Gorgels APM, et al: Ventricular arrhythmias in heart failure. *Am J Cardiol* 70:37C, 1992.

63. Amiodarone Trials Meta-Analysis Investigators: Effect of prophylactic amiodarone on mortality after acute myocardial infarction and in congestive heart failure: Meta-analysis of individual data from 6500 patients in randomized trials. *Lancet* 350:1417, 1997.

64. Deedwania PC, et al: Spontaneous conversion and maintenance of sinus rhythm by amiodarone in patients with heart failure and atrial fibrillation: Observations from the Veterans Affairs Congestive Heart Failure Survival Trial of Antiarrhythmic Therapy (CHF-STAT). *Circulation* 98:2574, 1998.

65. Estes NA 3rd, et al: Use of antiarrhythmics and implantable cardioverter-defibrillators in congestive heart failure. *Am J Cardiol* 91:45D, 2003.

66. Moss AJ, et al: Improved survival with an implanted defibrillator in patients with coronary disease at high risk for ventricular arrhythmia. Multicenter Automatic Defibrillator Implantation Trial Investigators. *N Engl J Med* 335:1933, 1996.

67. Boehmer JP: Device therapy for heart failure. *Am J Cardiol* 91:53D, 2003.

68. Auricchio A, et al: Effect of pacing chamber and atrioventricular delay on acute systolic function of paced patients with congestive heart failure. *Circulation* 99:2993, 1999.

69. Leclercq C, et al: Acute hemodynamic effects of biventricular DDD pacing in patients with end-stage heart failure. *J Am Coll Cardiol* 32:1825, 1998.

70. Leclercq C, Kass DA: Retiming the failing heart: Principles and current clinical status of cardiac resynchronization. *J Am Coll Cardiol* 39:194, 2002.

71. Gerber TC, et al: Left ventricular and biventricular pacing in congestive heart failure. *Mayo Clin Proc* 76:308, 2001.

72. Brignole M, et al: Assessment of atrioventricular junction ablation and VVIR pacemaker versus pharmacological treatment in patients with heart failure and chronic atrial fibrillation: A randomized, controlled study. *Circulation* 98:953, 1998.

73. Batista RJV, et al: Partial left ventriculectomy to improve left ventricular function in end-stage heart disease. *J Card Surg* 11:96, 1996.

74. Pennington DG, Oaks TE, Lohmann DP: Permanent ventricular assist device support versus cardiac transplantation. *Ann Thorac Surg* 68:729, 1999.

75. Young JB: Healing the heart with ventricular assist device therapy: Mechanisms of cardiac recovery. *Ann Thorac Surg* 71(3 Suppl):S210, 2001.

76. Vitali E, et al: Surgical therapy in advanced heart failure. *Am J Cardiol* 91:88F, 2003.

77. Keck BM, et al: Worldwide thoracic organ transplantation: A report from the UNOS/ISHLT International Registry for Thoracic Organ Transplantation. *Clin Transpl* 31,1996.

78. El Oakley RM, et al: Myocyte transplantation for myocardial repair: A few good cells can mend a broken heart. *Ann Thorac Surg* 71:1724, 2001.

81 Pericardial and Myocardial Disease

Nicholas J. Jouriles

PERICARDIAL DISEASE (PERICARDITIS)

PERSPECTIVE

Understanding of pericardial function and disease has increased greatly since Hippocrates described the pericardium in 460 B.C. as "a smooth tunic which envelops the heart and contains a small amount of fluid resembling urine." Galen provided the first description of a pericardial effusion and performed the first pericardial resection.[1] Lancisi first described the appearance of constrictive pericarditis at autopsy in 1728. Also in the 18th century, Laennec said, "There are few diseases attended by more variable symptoms and more difficult to diagnose than [pericarditis]."[1] This is still true today. During the 1930s, Beck researched and developed the practice of cardiac surgery. He is credited with first describing the clinical presentation of cardiac tamponade, which today is known as *Beck's triad* (hypotension, jugular venous distention, and muffled heart sounds).[2]

ETIOLOGY

The causes of acute and chronic pericardial disease are numerous (Box 81-1). Each of the disorders listed in Box 81-1 can produce acute pericarditis, with or without pericardial effusion. In addition, most of these disorders can progress to cardiac tamponade or constrictive pericarditis.

Most cases of pericarditis are idiopathic. Even exhaustive clinical testing identifies a specific etiology in only 22% of patients, with the remainder being considered idiopathic.[3] Molecular biology techniques show virus in many cases where prior methods could not establish a diagnosis. The most common viruses are coxsackievirus, adenovirus, rhinovirus, echovirus, and influenzavirus.[4]

EPIDEMIOLOGY

Acute pericarditis is a syndrome caused by inflammation of the pericardium. Although the exact incidence is unknown, autopsy series show an incidence of pericarditis ranging from 2% to 6%. Pericarditis accounts for approximately 1 in 1000 hospital admissions. It is more prevalent in men than in women and in adults than in children.

PRINCIPLES OF DISEASE

Pericardial Anatomy

The normal pericardium consists of parietal and visceral layers, with a narrow potential space between them. The thin visceral pericardium is closely applied to the epicardium of the heart and merges with the adventitia of the great arteries and veins at their attachment points. The parietal pericardium consists of a dense layer of collagen, approximately 1 mm thick, containing sparse elastic fibers. The position of the heart within the chest is stabilized by the attachment of the parietal pericardium to the manubrium and xiphoid anteriorly, to the diaphragm inferiorly, and to the vertebral column posteriorly. The phrenic nerves traverse the parietal pericardium laterally and are at risk when the pericardial sac is opened.

Pericardial Physiology

An ultrafiltrate of plasma, 15 to 60 mL of fluid, is normally contained in the pericardial space. Abnormal amounts of pericardial fluid can accumulate when the venous or lymphatic drainage of the heart is obstructed. Several functions of the pericardium are proposed: maintain the heart's position, lubricate the heart's surface, prevent the spread of infection or adhesion formation from adjacent thoracic structures, prevent cardiac overdilation, augment atrial filling, and maintain the normal pressure-volume relationships of the cardiac chambers. Patients with congenital absence (or surgical removal) of the pericardium show few, if any, problems.

PATHOPHYSIOLOGY

The inflammation of pericarditis is characterized by a granulocytic and lymphocytic infiltration of the pericardium. There is an increase in the number of antibodies in the pericardial fluid—specifically, antimyolemmal and antisarcolemmal antibodies.[4]

IDIOPATHIC PERICARDITIS

Clinical Features

The classic symptoms of pericarditis include chest pain, a variably present pericardial friction rub, and electrocardiogram (ECG) abnormalities. A prodrome of fever and myalgias may occur. Pericarditis chest pain

BOX 81-1. Etiology of Pericarditis

Infectious
- Viral
- Bacterial
- Fungal
- Parasite
- Rickettsia

Post Injury
- Trauma
- Surgery
- Myocardial infarction
- Radiation

Metabolic Diseases
- Uremia
- Medications

Systemic Diseases
- Rheumatoid arthritis
- Systemic lupus erythematosus
- Sarcoidosis
- Scleroderma
- Dermatomyositis
- Amyloidosis

Tumors

Aortic Dissection

is usually substernal and varies with respiration. It is classically, but not always, sharp or pleuritic in character. It is typically relieved by sitting forward and is worsened by lying down, deep inspiration, or swallowing. It uncommonly may mimic myocardial infarction (MI) pain. Pericarditis pain is usually retrosternal, can radiate to the trapezius muscles, and may present as isolated shoulder pain. Pain also can be felt over the diaphragm. Dyspnea is rare with pericarditis, but breathing may be shallow because of the pain.

The physical examination hallmark of acute pericarditis is the pericardial friction rub. The rub may be caused by friction between inflamed or scarred visceral and parietal pericardium or may result from friction between the parietal pericardium and adjacent pleura. It may be audible anywhere over the anterior chest wall but usually is best heard at the lower left sternal border. Friction rubs are best heard using the diaphragm of the stethoscope, with the patient in the sitting position holding his or her breath. The rub characteristically sounds "scratchy," "creaky," or "Velcro-like." The classic biphasic "to-and-fro" rub occurs in approximately 25% of cases and tends to be intermittent and migratory. Rubs vary with respiration, being loudest when the patient is sitting forward. The incidence of rubs in emergency department patients with pericarditis is unknown.

Diagnostic Strategies

The ECG typically evolves through four stages. These four stages occur over time, however, and the emergency physician rarely has the luxury of performing serial tracings. Stage 1, occurring in the first hours to days of illness, includes diffuse ST segment elevation seen in leads I, II, III, aVL, aVF, and V_2 through V_6 and reciprocal ST segment depression in aVR and V_1. Most patients with acute pericarditis have concurrent PR segment depression during stage 1 (Figure 81-1). In

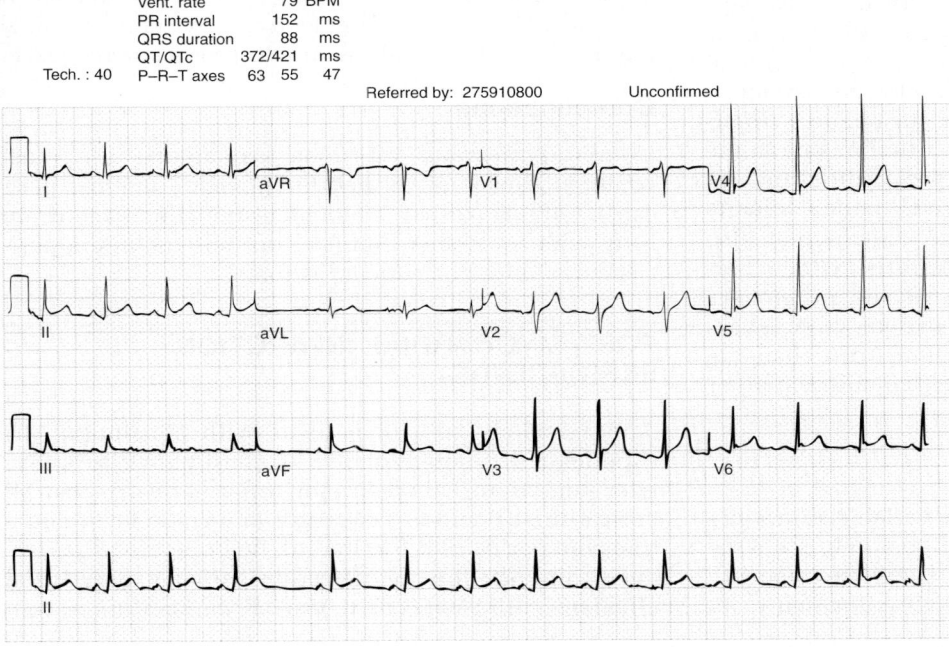

25mm/s	Med:		
10mm/mV	Age:	Ht:	Wt:
100Hz	Sex: M	Race: Cauc	
Pgm 010C/v78	Loc:	2 Room: 225	
Cart: 2	Option: 40		
	Vent. rate	79	BPM
	PR interval	152	ms
	QRS duration	88	ms
	QT/QTc	372/421	ms
Tech. : 40	P–R–T axes	63 55	47

Normal sinus rhythm with marked sinus arrhythmia
Acute pericarditis
Abnormal ECG

Referred by: 275910800   Unconfirmed

Figure 81-1. Electrocardiogram showing acute pericarditis. (Courtesy of the Ohio Chapter of the American College of Emergency Physicians.)

stage 2, the ST and PR segments normalize, but the T waves flatten. The characteristic finding of stage 3 is deep, symmetric T wave inversion. In stage 4, the ECG reverts to normal, although the T wave inversions may become permanent.[5]

The early ECG findings of acute pericarditis may be difficult to distinguish from those of acute MI, coronary artery spasm, or benign early repolarization. The differentiation of acute MI from acute pericarditis is essential because thrombolytic therapy is contraindicated in pericarditis because its use may precipitate hemorrhagic cardiac tamponade. In contrast to the ECG in acute MI, the ST segment elevations in stage 1 acute pericarditis are concave upward rather than convex upward, and simultaneous T wave inversions are not seen. Subsequent tracings do not evolve through a typical MI pattern, and Q waves do not appear.

Ventricular dysrhythmias are rare in pericardial disease. Patients with pericarditis who have ventricular dysrhythmias should be presumed to have concomitant myocarditis or underlying cardiac disease or to have been misdiagnosed.[6]

Echocardiography facilitates the definitive diagnosis of pericarditis with effusion. In addition, cardiac tamponade, increased pericardial thickness, pericardial tumors and cysts, constrictive pericarditis, and the congenital absence of the pericardium all can be diagnosed by echocardiography.

Some patients with acute pericarditis have elevated cardiac markers, caused by myopericarditis, myocarditis, or MI. The white blood cell count and erythrocyte sedimentation rate (ESR) may be elevated but are insensitive and nonspecific. Other laboratory studies should be directed at determining nonidiopathic causes of pericarditis.

Management and Disposition

Therapy of acute idiopathic pericarditis is symptomatic. Effective analgesia usually can be obtained with a nonsteroidal anti-inflammatory drug (NSAID) regimen. Aspirin, ibuprofen, ketorolac, and diclofenac are equally efficacious, and the choice of treatment should be based on side-effect profile for the patient. A 2-week trial of treatment should occur before a different class of NSAID is chosen.[7] Oral prednisone is the mainstay of therapy for chronic pericarditis and for acute pericarditis in patients who cannot tolerate NSAIDs. Methylprednisolone and colchicine also are effective for recurrent pericarditis. Other life-threatening conditions, including MI and pulmonary embolus, should be excluded. A patient with severe or intractable pain or with new or changing pericardial effusion should be placed in observation or hospitalized.

Complications

The clinical course of pericarditis is variable; one study showed that 60% of patients have complete recovery within 1 week, and 18% have complete recovery within 3 weeks.[8] Fifteen percent to 32% of patients can have recurrent pericarditis, which may require serial echocardiography to exclude effusion or tumor.

UREMIC PERICARDIAL DISEASE

Perspective and Etiology

Pericarditis was first recognized as a complication of uremia in 1936. It may occur secondary to end-stage renal disease or be associated with hemodialysis more frequently than peritoneal dialysis. Acute renal failure also is associated with pericarditis.[9] The etiology is unknown, but putative mechanisms include toxic metabolites, bleeding diathesis of uremia, and infectious or immunologic mechanisms. Because renal failure causes immune suppression, the evaluation of a chronic renal disease patient with pericarditis requires a diligent search for infectious causes.

Clinical Features and Diagnostic Strategies

Patients with uremic pericarditis present with chest pain, unexplained fever, and possibly a coarse friction rub. They also may have significant pretamponade effusions. The ECG in uremic pericarditis is often normal because little epicardial inflammation occurs.[9] In a dialysis patient, cardiac enlargement on chest radiograph in the absence of signs of volume overload or congestive heart failure (CHF) can be considered to represent pericardial effusion until proved otherwise by echocardiogram. Uremic pericarditis has an effusion that is fibrinous and often grossly bloody. Diagnostic pericardiocentesis may be indicated to exclude infection.

Management and Disposition

Uremic pericarditis causing pericardial effusion without hemodynamic compromise is initially treated with intensive dialysis, including daily treatments, if necessary. NSAIDs are ineffective.[7] Systemic steroids require 1 to 2 weeks of therapy to produce a response.

Complications

Uremic pericardial effusions are among the most common causes of cardiac tamponade.[9] Uremic pericardial effusions may be locular and difficult to drain fully with a catheter. Surgical options include a pericardial window or pericardiectomy.

POST–MYOCARDIAL INFARCTION PERICARDITIS

Approximately 20% of patients with transmural MIs experience a different quality of chest pain 2 to 4 days after infarction. This pain may represent early post-MI pericarditis. There is frequently low-grade fever and a transient pericardial friction rub that often requires frequent auscultation for detection. A large pericardial effusion is unusual. Early post-MI pericarditis is generally short-lived and disappears with 1 to 3 days of aspirin therapy.

The ECG changes of pericarditis usually are masked by the acute MI changes. Patients with early post-MI pericarditis have more dysrhythmias and heart failure. Pericarditis in acute MI may be an indicator of greater myocardial damage and poorer outcome.[10]

In 1956, Dressler[11] reported a syndrome of fever, pleuritis, leukocytosis, pericardial friction rub, and chest radiograph evidence of new pericardial or pleural effusions in 10 post-MI patients. Frequent relapses and a high incidence of friction rubs led Dressler to describe this syndrome as a delayed complication of MI in contrast to the well-known syndrome of early post-MI pericarditis.[11] The etiology of late post-MI pericarditis (Dressler's syndrome) may be immunologic. It also may be seen with pulmonary embolus and after pericardiotomy. Anticoagulants should be discontinued to reduce the risk of hemorrhagic effusion. Delayed, post-MI pericarditis is treated with NSAIDs or aspirin with steroids and colchicine the alternatives.

POSTTRAUMATIC PERICARDITIS

Perspective

Post–cardiac injury syndrome is defined as pericarditis after MI, cardiac surgery, or trauma.[12] The exact etiology is unknown. The incidence ranges from approximately 5% after MI to 30% after thoracic surgery or trauma. Pericarditis develops in 22% of patients with a penetrating cardiac injury, few of whom have cardiac tamponade.

Principles of Disease

Injury to the pericardium in blunt trauma may range from contusion to laceration or rupture. Some degree of traumatic pericarditis is found during surgery or at autopsy in many patients sustaining severe blunt trauma of the chest.

Penetrating wounds to the heart usually cause laceration of the pericardium and the myocardium, with secondary pericarditis and pericardial infections. Although the exact incidence is unknown, infection, tamponade, myocarditis, and inflammatory pericarditis may occur.

An immune pathogenesis is suggested by the development of cardiac autoantibodies, although these autoantibodies are common after injury, even in patients who do not develop pericarditis. Constrictive pericarditis occurs secondary to trauma. It may be due to pericardial blood, possibly secondary to the decreased resorptive power of damaged pericardium, with secondary fibrosis and constriction.[13]

Clinical Features

Signs and symptoms of post–cardiac injury syndrome include pericardial rub, fever, leukocytosis, high ESR, and chest pain. Although the diagnosis usually is established clinically, confirmation by echocardiography is helpful. The interval between injury and the onset of pericarditis ranges from 4 to 12 days.[12] During hospitalization, purulent pericarditis should be considered as a possible source of febrile illness in a trauma patient with multisystem organ failure.

Management and Disposition

Most patients respond to aspirin or NSAIDs. The use of steroids has not been shown to cause adverse effects in large studies. Uncomplicated pericarditis secondary to blunt trauma usually resolves. The patient should be observed until other life-threatening disease processes are excluded.

NEOPLASTIC PERICARDIAL DISEASE

Perspective

Malignant pericardial tumors typically present late, which makes diagnosis and treatment difficult. Malignant involvement of the pericardium is observed in 3.4% of general autopsies and 2% to 31% of cancer autopsies. The most common causes are lung cancer (30%), breast (23%), leukemia (9%), non-Hodgkin's lymphoma (9%), and Hodgkin's disease (8%). Primary malignancies of the pericardium are rare.[14,15]

Principles of Disease and Pathophysiology

The pattern of cardiac involvement by a malignant tumor is determined by the heart's lymphatic drainage system. Small lymphatics drain into a few vessels, which perforate the myocardium and drain into an epicardial plexus. The epicardial lymphatics drain into larger vessels, which accompany the coronary arteries to the aortic root. There they empty into the cardiac lymph nodes in the mediastinum between the innominate artery and the superior vena cava. The route of metastasis is usually retrograde from involved mediastinal lymph nodes to the relatively narrow passage at the root of the aorta. This is where obstruction to cardiac lymphatic drainage occurs.

Malignant pericardial effusions contribute directly to the patient's demise in 85% of cases. The large volume of the effusion and the tendency for rapid fluid accumulation frequently cause cardiac tamponade. Although the underlying disease process is often irreversible when tamponade develops, the patient's quality of life improves if tamponade is recognized and treated promptly.

Clinical Features

Primary cardiac neoplasms, such as angiosarcoma and teratoma, can present initially with symptoms consistent with benign, idiopathic pericarditis. The typical course is that of an acute pericarditis that resolves and subsequently recurs. Malignant pericardial disease is difficult to diagnose. Most patients are asymptomatic or have nonspecific symptoms, such as shortness of breath, cough, palpitations, ill-defined chest pain, weakness, dizziness, hiccups, or fatigue. Malignant pericardial effusion should be suspected in any cancer patient with a change in cardiorespiratory symptoms.

Diagnostic Strategies

The diagnostic workup for malignant pericardial effusion includes a strong clinical suspicion and an echocardiogram, computed tomography (CT), or magnetic resonance imaging (MRI). When a pericardial effusion is identified, pericardial fluid cytology is recommended if the underlying malignancy has yet to be diagnosed.

Management and Disposition

Treatment strategies for malignant pericardial effusion may include pericardiocentesis, local instillation of sclerosing or chemotherapeutic agents, systemic chemotherapy, cardiac radiation, and pericardial window. The method chosen depends on the primary tumor and the patient's expected length of survival.

The prognosis for patients with malignant pericardial disease depends on the type and extent of cancer. The outlook is better for breast cancer and lymphoma patients than for patients with lung cancer. Patients with a tumor diagnosed in the emergency department should be offered admission, as should all patients who are compromised or symptomatic.

RADIATION-INDUCED PERICARDITIS

Fewer than 5% of patients treated with radiation therapy develop pericarditis. The incidence has decreased with the advent of current radiation therapy techniques. The percentage of pericardial volume irradiated, dose, and fractionation help determine which patients will develop pericarditis.[16] Radiation-induced pericarditis is seen most commonly in patients with Hodgkin's lymphoma or breast cancer. Because patients with Hodgkin's disease are younger and have high survival rates, they represent most patients who develop radiation pericarditis. Pericardial effusion and constrictive pericarditis occur commonly in radiation pericarditis. Tumor recurrence also should be considered.

PERICARDIAL DISEASE RELATED TO SYSTEMIC CONNECTIVE TISSUE DISORDERS

Rheumatoid Arthritis

Pericarditis occurs in approximately one third of patients with rheumatoid arthritis (RA) during the course of their disease, usually within 3 years of the initial diagnosis. Rheumatoid pericardial disease is rarely clinically significant. Occasional patients develop chronic locular effusions, constrictive pericarditis, or cardiac tamponade; these patients usually have rheumatoid nodules, elevated circulating rheumatoid factor levels, and valvular heart disease. Pericar-

dial involvement should be suspected in any RA patient who experiences the onset of right-sided CHF. There are no suggestive ECG or chest radiograph findings. Elevated pericardial fluid, lactate dehydrogenase, and gamma globulin levels; rheumatoid factor; and low glucose level support the diagnosis. Corticosteroid treatment is useful in symptomatic cases.

Systemic Lupus Erythematosus

Pericarditis is found in more than 50% of patients with systemic lupus erythematosus (SLE) at autopsy. The effusion is usually thick and fibrinous. Either cardiac tamponade or constrictive pericarditis may develop. Lupus erythematosus cells may be identified in pericardial fluid specimens. Corticosteroid therapy is indicated for pericardial involvement in SLE.[17]

Other Connective Tissue Disorders

Approximately 33% of patients with Sjögren's syndrome show evidence of pericarditis. Giant cell arteritis produces granulomatous myocarditis that may respond to methylprednisolone. Cardiac abnormalities, particularly pericarditis, are seen in numerous patients with mixed connective tissue disease. Other connective tissue diseases that may cause pericarditis include ankylosing spondylitis, Reiter's syndrome, Behçet's disease, systemic sclerosis, and polyarteritis nodosa.

MISCELLANEOUS INFECTIOUS CAUSES OF PERICARDITIS

Other etiologies of pericarditis include *Rickettsia conorii,* which causes Mediterranean spotted fever (treated with doxycycline), *Mycoplasma pneumoniae* (treated with a macrolide), *Nocardia asteroides* (treated with pericardiectomy and long-term use of antibiotics such as sulfisoxazole), *Chlamydia trachomatis,* Epstein-Barr virus, cytomegalovirus infection, *Haemophilus actinomycetemcomitans* (treatment with chloramphenicol), and coccidioidomycosis (endemic in the southwestern United States). Viral and bacterial causes of pericarditis can coexist, such as varicella-zoster infection superinfected with *Staphylococcus aureus.* Bacterial superinfections associated with varicella are more common in children.

PERICARDIAL EFFUSION

Etiology and Clinical Features

The most common causes of pericardial effusion are viral or idiopathic pericarditis, malignancy, uremia, trauma, and radiation therapy. Drug reactions and autoimmune diseases are less common causes.

Pericardial effusion is often asymptomatic. Patients with known associated conditions (e.g., cancer or renal failure) who present with cough, fever, chest pain, or dyspnea may have an effusion.

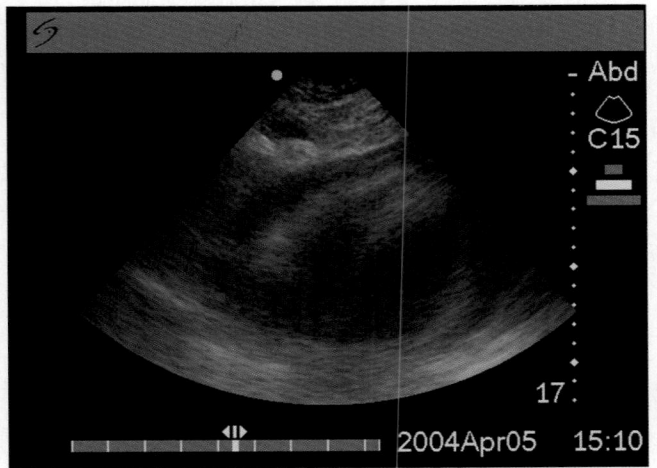

Figure 81-2. Bedside ultrasound showing a pericardial effusion. The effusion is best seen superior to the left ventricle at the top of the image. (Courtesy of Stephen Romisher, MD.)

Diagnostic Strategies

Pericardial effusion may present with an enlarged cardiac silhouette on chest radiograph, usually with normal pulmonary vascularity. A minimum of 200 to 250 mL of pericardial fluid is usually necessary to produce cardiomegaly on chest radiograph.

Echocardiography is the diagnostic modality of choice (Figure 81-2). It easily differentiates pericardial fluid from cardiac chamber enlargement and provides information about myocardial wall motion.

CT may be useful in diagnosing pericardial effusion when the echocardiogram is technically unsatisfactory. MRI also can be diagnostic. Nuclear scans may be useful in detecting purulent pericardial effusions.

Pericardiocentesis may be performed for either diagnostic or therapeutic purposes. Elective diagnostic pericardiocentesis is indicated in cancer patients (to differentiate malignant effusion from postradiation pericarditis), for failure to respond to usual treatment, or when bacterial infection is suspected. Common complications of pericardiocentesis include induction of cardiac dysrhythmias, pneumothorax, perforation of myocardium, laceration of coronary or internal mammary arteries, and liver laceration. Echocardiographic-guided pericardiocentesis is much safer than blind or ECG-guided pericardiocentesis and should be the procedure of choice.

Pericardial fluid should be analyzed for protein, glucose, specific gravity, cell count and differential, hematocrit, Gram stain, and culture. Other tests, depending on the clinical picture, include specific gravity, cytology, acid-fast stain, fungal smear, and connective tissue disease screening.

The gross appearance of the pericardial fluid provides a clue to the cause of the effusion. Serosanguineous effusions are associated most commonly with neoplasms, tuberculosis, uremia, radiation, and idiopathic pericarditis. Grossly bloody effusions are always ominous and are caused by blunt or pene-

trating trauma, postinfarction myocardial rupture, aortic dissection, coagulopathies, and iatrogenic cardiac perforation. Purulent pericardial fluid is seen with pneumonia, empyema, and bacterial endocarditis.

Pericardial effusions that are transudates (protein <3 g/100 mL and specific gravity <1.015) are usually due to systemic disorders, such as volume overload, CHF, or hypoproteinemia. Exudative effusions (protein content >3 g/100 mL and specific gravity >1.015) are generally caused by pericardial injury from malignancy or infection.

CARDIAC TAMPONADE

Etiology and Pathophysiology

Ten percent of all patients with cancer develop cardiac tamponade.[18] Cardiac tamponade should be suspected in patients with penetrating chest wounds. Cardiac tamponade is the result of compression of the myocardium by the contents of the pericardium. This compression usually is caused by fluid, but it may be gas, pus, blood, or a combination of factors.[18]

Cardiac tamponade is a physiologic continuum reflecting the amount of fluid, the rate of accumulation, and the nature of the heart. The three stages necessary for tamponade to develop include fluid filling the recesses of the parietal pericardium, fluid accumulating faster than the rate of the parietal pericardium's ability to stretch, and fluid accumulating faster than the body's ability to increase blood volume to support right ventricle filling pressure. The final result is increased pericardial pressure, which causes decreased cardiac compliance and decreased flow of blood into the heart, which leads to decreased cardiac output.[18] The most important factor in the development of tamponade is the rate of fluid accumulation. The main pathophysiologic derangement is reduced blood inflow.[19]

Symptoms and Signs

Cardiac tamponade symptoms are usually nonspecific. The patient may complain of chest pain, cough, or dyspnea. The classic triad of cardiac tamponade signs described by Beck is hypotension, distended neck veins, and muffled heart sounds. These signs may not be present if tamponade develops quickly. Initially the heart responds to tamponade by increasing heart rate to maintain output. This compensatory mechanism is maintained until late in the course. Decompensation occurs quickly.[19]

Diagnostic Strategies

The chest radiograph shows cardiomegaly only if there is a large accumulation of fluid (200 to 250 mL). The ECG classically shows decreasing voltage or electrical alternans (Figure 81-3), but the latter is rare. Echocardiography confirms the diagnosis when an effusion and paradoxical systolic wall motion are seen. Thermodilution catheters also can be diagnostic, showing equalization of right and left ventricular pressures.

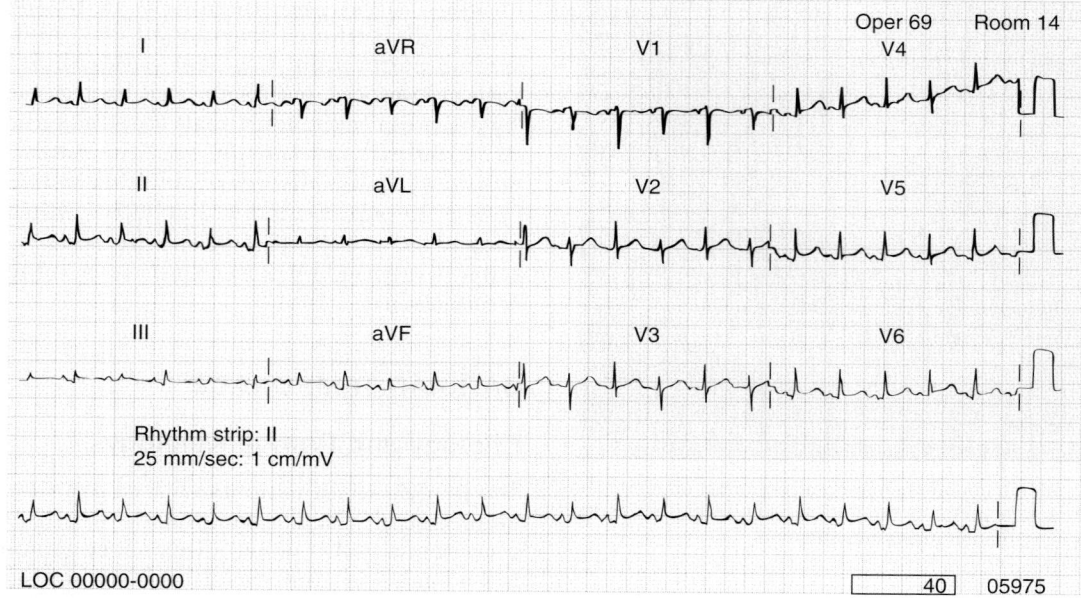

Figure 81-3. Electrocardiogram showing electrical alternans. (Courtesy of Drew Stephens, MD.)

Management and Prognosis

Initial treatment includes volume augmentation to the right ventricle with intravenous fluids to increase the filling pressure in an effort to overcome the pressure of pericardial constriction. Pericardiocentesis, preferably ultrasound guided, is the treatment of choice. Enough fluid should be withdrawn to stabilize the patient hemodynamically. If tamponade recurs, pericardiocentesis may be repeated, or a drainage catheter may be left in the pericardial space. A pericardiotomy ultimately may be necessary. Cardiac tamponade has a high mortality that depends on the severity and nature of the underlying disease, the time course of onset, and the rapidity of emergency department diagnosis and intervention.

PURULENT PERICARDITIS

Epidemiology and Etiology

Purulent pericarditis is a life-threatening process that is seen most commonly in hospitalized patients with systemic illnesses who develop sepsis. It can occur in any age group.[20] Etiologic organisms commonly include *Streptococcus, Staphylococcus, Haemophilus, Pseudomonas, Klebsiella, Escherichia coli,* meningococcus, *Legionella, Nocardia, Salmonella typhimurium, Salmonella enteritidis,* and *Clostridium septicum.* Fungal etiologies include *Candida, Aspergillus,* and *Histoplasma. Candida* pericarditis is found in three groups of patients: after cardiac surgery, with impaired host defenses, and with severe debilitating underlying diseases. *Histoplasma* infection of the pericardium occurs in endemic areas, including the Ohio and Mississippi River valleys.

Principles of Disease and Pathophysiology

Purulent pericarditis occurs by several mechanisms: (1) spread from an adjacent infection, such as pneumonia or empyema; (2) hematogenous spread from a distant site; (3) direct inoculation of bacteria (trauma or procedure); and (4) spread from an intracardiac source.[20] The most common mechanism is spread from a distant site.

Clinical Features and Diagnostic Strategies

Purulent pericarditis usually presents as a febrile illness lasting 2 to 3 days. Common presenting signs include tachycardia, dyspnea, hepatomegaly, elevated central venous pressure, chest pain, friction rub, and a leukocytosis. The most common presentation is a hospitalized patient with a serious underlying disease who initially improves after treatment of the primary process, but later develops fever, dyspnea, and chest pain.

The key to diagnosing purulent pericarditis successfully is to consider the diagnosis early in the patient's course. The diagnosis should be suspected in any febrile patient with multisystem illness who has a pericardial effusion. Pericardiocentesis is necessary to establish the diagnosis, to obtain fluid for microbiologic studies, and to relieve cardiac tamponade.

Management and Disposition

Although purulent pericarditis traditionally has been treated by pericardiectomy, placement of an indwelling catheter, coupled with lavage and drainage, may avoid the need for surgical drainage.[21] For either approach, use of intravenous antibiotics or antifungals is mandatory. Antibiotic treatment lasts 3 to 4 weeks; treatment is longer for antifungals.[22]

The overall survival rate for purulent pericarditis is approximately 30% with antibiotic therapy alone and 50% when combined with early surgical drainage, either open or percutaneous.[23] In addition to the initial complications related to sepsis and tamponade, long-term sequelae of purulent pericarditis include the development of constrictive pericarditis.

TUBERCULOUS PERICARDITIS

Tuberculous pericarditis is estimated to occur in 1% to 2% of patients with pulmonary tuberculosis.[24] Tuberculous pericarditis is more common in patients who are socioeconomically deprived or who have acquired immunodeficiency syndrome (AIDS) or another immunodeficiency state. Although rare, isolated tuberculous pericarditis still exists. Tuberculous pericarditis most commonly spreads to the pericardium by direct extension from the tracheobronchial tree, mediastinal or hilar lymph nodes, sternum, or spine.

In many patients, the chest radiograph shows an enlarged cardiac silhouette, but a pulmonary infiltrate is often absent. Pericardial fluid aspirates reveal acid-fast bacilli by smear or culture (which may require 4 to 6 weeks to become positive) in approximately 50% of all cases.[24] Diagnostic workup should include assessment for human immunodeficiency virus (HIV).

Patients with tuberculous pericarditis should be hospitalized and observed for evidence of cardiac tamponade. Triple-drug therapy should be started in the hospital and continued for at least 9 months.[24] Patients with chronic pericardial effusions may benefit from oral prednisone therapy. Patients with evidence of pericardial thickening, constrictive pericarditis, or hemodynamic compromise should be referred for surgical treatment. Pericardiocentesis may be a temporary measure until surgical treatment is available. When treatment is with medication and surgery, the current mortality rate is approximately 20%.[24]

OTHER CAUSES OF PERICARDITIS

Amyloid deposition can cause either restrictive cardiomyopathy (RCM) or constrictive pericarditis. Pericarditis can occur rarely as an extraintestinal complication of inflammatory bowel disease. Pericardial complications of inflammatory bowel disease are independent of the clinical course of the gut disorder.

Iatrogenic pericarditis also can be seen as a complication of an implantable defibrillator or an atrial lead of a permanent pacemaker. A polymicrobial bacterial pericarditis can occur after transbronchial needle aspiration or as a complication of endoscopic variceal sclerotherapy. Rarely, pericarditis also can be caused by erosion through the esophagus into the pericardium of a foreign body, such as a sewing needle or toothpick.

PERICARDITIS AND ACQUIRED IMMUNODEFICIENCY SYNDROME

Progressive dysfunction of multiple organ systems occurs in AIDS. Pericarditis is usually nonspecific in origin, but can be associated with Kaposi's sarcoma, lymphoma, or any infectious pathogen.

Less than 1% of patients with HIV develop acute pericarditis, but 40% have asymptomatic pericardial effusion. In 33% of these patients, the effusion is moderate or large in size. Pericardial effusion is more frequent in patients in the more advanced stages of HIV infection and is an independent predictor of decreased survival.[25] Although the etiology may differ, the clinical features and diagnostic evaluation of patients with AIDS-related pericarditis are the same as in patients without AIDS.

PERICARDIAL DISEASE AND PREGNANCY

Pericardial effusion and pericarditis occur rarely during pregnancy, usually during the third trimester. Both are usually asymptomatic. If the effusion enlarges, pericardial drainage and possibly pericardiotomy may be necessary. If constrictive pericarditis develops, cardiovascular complications may prevent the patient from carrying the pregnancy to term.

PNEUMOPERICARDIUM

Perspective and Etiology

Pneumopericardium and pyopneumopericardium are rare. Pneumopericardium also may be caused by diseases that can lead to formation of fistulae between the pericardial and pleural space, bronchial tree, or upper gastrointestinal tract (e.g., peptic ulcer disease, carcinoma of the esophagus or stomach, esophageal diverticulum). It may result from bronchial carcinoma or infection with gas-producing microorganisms, or it can be idiopathic. In most patients, pyopneumopericardium results from trauma, foreign body, ingestion of caustic substances, or invasive procedures (e.g., esophagoscopy, thoracentesis, endotracheal intubation).

Spontaneous pneumopericardium may complicate asthma, labor, barotrauma from positive pressure ventilation, or Valsalva maneuvers, such as might occur during weightlifting. Cocaine inhalation from positive-pressure devices also can cause pneumopericardium.[26] Pneumopericardium usually resolves spontaneously, but can lead to tension pneumopericardium, which requires decompression.

Pathophysiology

Pneumopericardium is caused most commonly by an increase in intra-alveolar pressure above atmospheric pressure, resulting in rupture of alveoli. Air dissects into the hilum and mediastinum, through the pericardial reflection on the pulmonary vessels, and into the pericardium.

Clinical Features and Diagnostic Strategies

Physical findings depend on the quantity of fluid and gas in the pericardial space. Heart sounds can be of variable intensity, can vary depending on body position, and sometimes have a metallic quality that may be accompanied by splashing sounds. *Hamman's sign* and *mediastinal crunch* are the terms used for a loud, crunching sound associated with pneumopericardium or pneumomediastinum. This is best heard with the patient in a left lateral recumbent position and is diagnostic for the presence of mediastinal air. The diagnosis of pneumopericardium is confirmed by chest radiograph, CT scan, or echocardiography. Tension pneumopericardium presents with clinical findings of acute cardiac tamponade.

Management

Stable patients with uncomplicated spontaneous pneumopericardium usually can be observed. In the rare patient with pneumopericardium who is stable after penetrating chest injury, after all other life-threatening injuries and complications are excluded, prolonged observation is indicated. There are no expected long-term sequelae. Tension pneumopericardium should be treated with emergency pericardiocentesis.

CONSTRICTIVE PERICARDITIS

Perspective and Etiology

Tuberculosis is still the leading cause of constrictive pericarditis in some countries, but accounts for only a few cases in Western cultures. Constrictive pericarditis may be a late consequence of viral pericarditis.[27] There is an increased incidence of constrictive pericarditis as a result of improved survival of patients with chronic renal disease. Other predisposing conditions include previous mediastinal irradiation, cardiac trauma, purulent pericarditis, cardiac actinomycosis, and postpericardiotomy adhesions.

Principles of Disease and Pathophysiology

Constrictive pericarditis is characterized by impaired diastolic filling from external cardiac compression caused by a thickened pericardium. It is usually the end result of fibrous reaction of the pericardium to some previous insult. In advanced cases, the visceral and parietal pericardial layers may be adherent. Impaired ventricular filling is the key pathophysiologic event.[22]

Because the pericardium limits volume, ventricular filling is rapid and completed within the first one third of diastole, after which left ventricular volume and pressure remain unchanged. Early ventricular filling followed by a period of unchanging pressure yields a corresponding dip and plateau pattern or square root sign on the left ventricular diastolic pressure curve.

Clinical Features

The symptoms and signs of constrictive pericarditis are virtually indistinguishable from those of CHF. Dyspnea, fatigue, and weight gain are the most common complaints. Hepatomegaly, marked pitting lower extremity edema, and ascites are seen on physical examination.[27] The presence of jugular venous distention differentiates this condition from liver disease. The characteristic auscultatory finding of constrictive pericarditis is a pericardial knock in early diastole, corresponding to the abrupt halt in ventricular filling. A friction rub also may be audible.

Diagnostic Strategies

The diagnosis is considered in a patient with right-sided heart failure symptoms that are greater than left-sided symptoms.[28] Heart size on the chest radiograph is typically small but may be increased by atrial enlargement. Pericardial calcification is helpful when present and may be seen on CT or MRI.[28] Liver function tests are consistent with passive congestion. ECG findings include low QRS voltage, nonspecific ST–T wave abnormalities, and atrial dysrhythmias.

Echocardiography may be helpful in differentiating constrictive pericarditis from RCM or cardiac tamponade, especially Doppler echocardiography. Cardiac catheterization and simultaneous measurement of right ventricular and left ventricular end-diastolic pressures or endomyocardial biopsy may be necessary for diagnosis.[22]

Differential Considerations and Management

Constrictive pericarditis often is confused with CHF because of the presence in both conditions of shortness of breath, elevated jugular venous pressure, hepatomegaly, and edema. A history of viral or bacterial pericarditis, radiation therapy, tuberculosis, chest trauma, or cardiac surgery should lead to consideration of constrictive pericarditis. The diagnosis also should be considered with signs of elevated venous pressure but no history of myocardial dysfunction. Patients with cirrhosis may have ascites and liver enlargement, but not jugular venous distention. Right ventricular infarction causes a hemodynamic picture similar to that of constriction, but the echocardiogram reveals abnormal right ventricular function and wall motion.

The hemodynamic picture in RCM is virtually identical to that of constrictive pericarditis; both are associated with signs of elevated venous pressure and small heart size. The echocardiogram may reveal the presence of infiltrative myocardial disease in patients with RCM. Pericardiectomy is the therapy of choice for constrictive pericarditis.

MYOCARDIAL DISEASE (MYOCARDITIS)

PERSPECTIVE

The term *myocarditis* was used initially by Sobernheim in 1837. Romberg reported the association with scarlet fever and typhus in 1891, and "isolated idiopathic interstitial myocarditis" was described by Fiedler in 1899. In 1941, Saphir proposed one of the first classification systems.[29] The 1995 World Health Organization/International Society and Federation of Cardiology classification of myocardial disease considers myocarditis an inflammatory cardiomyopathy, a subset of dilated cardiomyopathy (DCM).[30]

EPIDEMIOLOGY AND ETIOLOGY

Myocarditis is detected in almost 10% of routine autopsies, but often is not recognized clinically. The overall incidence is unknown.[31] The enteroviruses, especially the coxsackie B virus, and adenovirus predominate as causative agents. Coxsackie B virus usually causes infection during the summer months, but outbreaks do not occur every year. Other organisms that may cause myocarditis include influenza A and B, *Streptococcus*, mononucleosis, *Chlamydia, Mycoplasma,* parainfluenza, mumps, cytomegalovirus, rubeola, rubella, rabies, lymphocytic choriomeningitis virus, hepatitis A and B, and varicella zoster. Cytomegalovirus and *Toxoplasma gondii* have emerged as potential causes of myocarditis in cardiac transplant patients. Of patients dying of AIDS, 52% have myocarditis on autopsy. Worldwide, Chagas' disease is a leading cause of myocarditis, especially in South America.[32]

Mortality from myocarditis has not changed since before 1990. Approximately one third of patients have complete recovery; one third have ongoing cardiac dysfunction; and one third develop chronic heart failure, require transplantation, or die.[31]

PRINCIPLES OF DISEASE AND PATHOPHYSIOLOGY

Myocarditis presumably occurs by (1) necrosis from direct invasion of an offending infectious agent and its replication within or near myocytes; (2) destruction of cardiac tissue from infiltration of host cellular immune components or from cytotoxic effect of activated host humoral defenses or both, initiated by the infectious agent; or (3) the toxic effect of exogenous chemicals or endotoxins produced by a systemic pathogen.[33] Three stages are proposed: acute (within 3 days of infection), with viral cytotoxicity and focal necrosis; subacute (days 4 to 14), in which there is an increase in humoral factors, such as nitrous oxide synthetase, natural killer cells, and interleukin-2, which lead to autoimmune injury; and chronic (days 15 to 90), in which there is

diffuse myocardial fibrosis and cardiac dysfunction that may lead to DCM.[31]

Adenoviruses and enteroviruses may be associated with most cases of myocarditis in all age groups. Isolation of a coxsackievirus-adenovirus receptor shows how these two types of viruses, one RNA and one DNA, may enter the heart.[31,34] In neonates, the pathologic changes seem to be related more to direct viral damage, whereas adults seem more susceptible to immunologic damage.

Cardiac autoantibodies are present after myocarditis. There is also a higher concentration of IgG anti-α-myosin antibodies in patients with myocarditis and DCM than in controls.[35] Because myocarditis is linked to the development of DCM, idiopathic DCM after myocarditis may be predominately autoimmune in origin, resulting from either shared antigens or molecular mimicry.[36] The amino acid sequences of the coxsackie B virus and β myosin heavy chain protein are more than 50% similar. An immune response to the former yields damage to the latter (molecular mimicry).

CLINICAL FEATURES

Flulike complaints, including fever, fatigue, myalgias, vomiting, and diarrhea, are usually the first symptoms and signs of myocarditis. Altered vital signs include fever, tachycardia, tachypnea, and, uncommonly, hypotension. A tachycardia disproportionate to the temperature or apparent toxicity is a clinical clue. No symptom or sign is sensitive or specific. Cardiac examination is often unremarkable. CHF and dysrhythmias also occur, and unexplained CHF is a common manifestation of myocarditis. Approximately 12% of patients have chest pain. As a result, myocarditis is frequently a diagnosis of exclusion.[33]

In children, prominent physical findings include grunting respirations and intercostal retractions. Although most patients have clear lungs on auscultation, approximately 10% to 15% of patients have wheezing. Some postulate an overlap with respiratory syncytial virus infection.[31] Infants often have a fulminant syndrome characterized by fever, cyanosis, respiratory distress, tachycardia, and cardiac failure. When children have ventricular dysrhythmias, myocarditis and idiopathic DCM are commonly seen on endomyocardial biopsy, despite findings of structurally normal hearts by noninvasive studies.

DIAGNOSTIC STRATEGIES

Common ECG changes include sinus tachycardia and low electrical activity. There may be a prolonged corrected Q-T interval, atrioventricular block, or acute MI pattern abnormalities.

Cardiac markers are frequently elevated. The white blood cell count and ESR are nonspecific. The echocardiographic features of myocarditis are nonspecific, but can include multichamber dysfunction (e.g., reduced left ventricular ejection fraction, global hypokinesis,

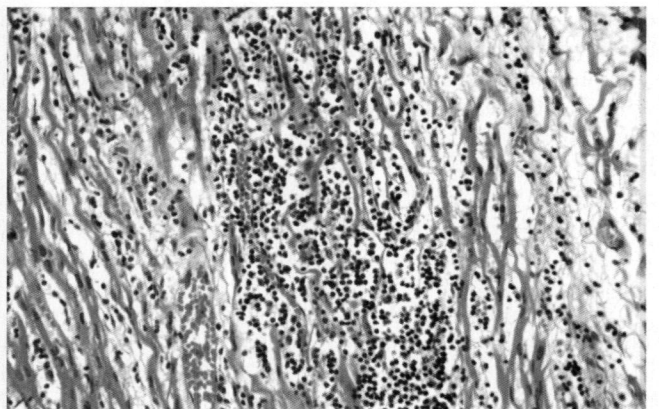

Figure 81-4. Myocardial biopsy showing myocarditis. Note the lymphocytic infiltrate.

and regional wall motion abnormalities). CT and MRI also may be diagnostic.

Indium-111 antimyosin antibodies bind specifically to exposed myosin in damaged myocardial cells, providing a noninvasive approach for the diagnosis of myocardial necrosis.[37] This approach also may be used to detect ongoing myocyte necrosis in myocarditis, acute MI, DCM, and cardiac transplant rejection.[38] Thallium-201 scanning also may establish a diagnosis.[39]

Viral titers are of low yield. A fourfold rise in viral titers or a high titer of viral specific IgM may help establish a viral etiology.

Endocardial biopsy, long considered the gold standard, has variable specificity and sensitivity (Figure 81-4).[31] Histologic criteria for myocarditis are present in only 5% to 30% of patients with clinically suspected myocarditis, 41% of patients with acute DCM, and 63% of patients with chronic DCM. Molecular genetic probes, such as polymerase chain reaction, are used to supplement standard histologic analysis. Results of one study show coxsackievirus and adenovirus to be the most common viral etiologies.[31] In addition, polymerase chain reaction analysis of tracheal aspirates of intubated patients with myocarditis show a correlation with endocardial biopsy.[40] Patients with virus present on biopsy tissue have a much worse clinical course.[41]

DIFFERENTIAL DIAGNOSIS

Myocarditis can masquerade as acute MI with severe chest pain, ECG changes, elevated cardiac enzymes, and heart failure. Patients with myocarditis are usually young (usually <35 years old) and have few risk factors for coronary artery disease. ECG abnormalities may be present beyond a single coronary artery distribution, or there may be global, rather than segmental, wall motion abnormalities on echocardiography.[42] The diagnosis of myocarditis also should be considered in an otherwise healthy patient who has symptoms and signs of CHF or dysrhythmias.

In myocarditis, chest pain continues, but there are no further ischemic ECG changes. Coronary arteriography

is usually normal, which should prompt consideration of endomyocardial biopsy. Myocarditis was found in more than 30% of patients with acute MI symptoms and normal coronary arteries in one study and in 78% in another.[39,42]

With nuclear scanning, myocarditis usually is characterized by a diffuse, faint, heterogeneous uptake of antimyosin antibody because myocyte necrosis is typically widespread. Acute MI almost always is characterized by an intense, localized uptake of antibody in the region of the occluded coronary artery. A normal antimyosin scan excludes acute MI and myocarditis.[37]

MANAGEMENT

Treatment for myocarditis is supportive therapy. Only bed rest is uniformly accepted as being of benefit. Patients with a fulminant clinical course require cardiac transplantation.

The demonstration of replicating enterovirus RNA in myocarditis suggests that the early phase of myocarditis may be treated early with antiviral agents, such as pleconaril or ribavirin.[31] Agents designed to act against the coxsackievirus-adenovirus receptor present an intriguing, theoretical approach.[34]

The subacute phases of myocarditis may respond to immunosuppressive therapy. There are reports of success in uncontrolled studies, but the National Institutes of Health–sponsored multicenter trial for myocarditis treatment did not establish the efficacy of immunosuppressive therapy.[43] Efforts to identify patient and treatment subsets in which immunosuppressive therapy may be beneficial are ongoing.

Because myocardial damage in myocarditis may be mediated by immunologic mechanisms, high-dose gamma globulin (intravenous immunoglobulin) therapy has been studied in a pediatric population. High-dose intravenous immunoglobulin may be associated with improved recovery of left ventricular function and better survival during the first year after presentation.[31,44]

In some cases of myocarditis, the deterioration of cardiac function is reversible if the patient survives the critical care phase with the aid of a cardiopulmonary support system. These devices have been used successfully over extended periods (70 days). They should be considered a treatment option in patients with fulminant myocarditis. This therapy or extracorporeal membrane oxygenation[31] may be tried before transplantation.[45]

DISPOSITION

All patients should be monitored, and patients with hemodynamic instability require intensive care. Paradoxically, patients with fulminant myocarditis have the best prognosis.[31] Complications of myocarditis include ventricular dysrhythmias, left ventricular aneurysm, and cardiac failure.

The mortality rate is 20% at 1 year and 56% at 4 years of follow-up, despite optimal medical management.

Ejection fraction and right ventricular function 1 year after initial presentation may be the best predictors of subsequent survival.[32] The long-term prognosis in patients who do not die is variable.

Patients who undergo transplantation because of myocarditis heart failure have decreased 1-year survival compared with patients transplanted for other reasons and have allograft rejection rates more than twice that of other recipients. This rejection often occurs within 2 weeks of transplantation.[46] The overall 5-year survival rate for children is 70%.[31]

CHAGAS' DISEASE

Chagas' disease is one of the leading causes of death and myocarditis in many countries in Latin America, particularly in Central America. Chaga's disease is caused by the protozoan *Trypanosoma cruzi*. Transmission to humans is by insect vector. The exact pathogenesis is unknown.[47]

Approximately 75% of seropositive patients with Chagas' disease never have cardiac symptoms. One fourth have angina-like chest pain, dysrhythmias, embolic episodes, heart failure, conduction abnormalities (bundle branch block, left anterior hemiblock, first-degree or higher atrioventricular block), multifocal ventricular premature contractions, and abnormal ST segment and T wave abnormalities in the precordial leads.[48] Ventricular tachycardia, sustained or nonsustained, is also common. Syncopal or near-syncopal episodes occur in nearly two thirds of patients.[48]

The diagnosis is established by showing serum parasites. It should be suspected in emergency department patients with new cardiac symptoms and a Latin American travel history.

In more than half of patients who die of chronic Chagas' disease, autopsy reveals a unique left ventricular apical aneurysm or scar, which is a reliable marker of the disease.[48] Echocardiography also may be suggestive. The extent of tissue damage correlates with the amount of parasites, which also can be found in histologic sections of infected tissues.

Chagas' disease is treated with the antitrypanosomal drug nifurtimox. Amiodarone may be useful to treat ventricular tachycardia.

TRICHINOSIS

Trichinosis is caused by ingestion of the cysts of *Trichinella spiralis* in undercooked meat. In the United States, the meat traditionally involved was pork, but trichinella has not been identified in domestic pork in decades, and today it is more likely to be wild game, such as bear or cougar. Larvae may be deposited in the myocardium, which incites an eosinophilic inflammatory reaction and necrosis of muscle fibers. The acute illness consists of fever, myalgias, muscle tenderness, neck stiffness, and a characteristic periorbital edema. Myocardial involvement is present in approximately 20% of clinically diagnosed cases and appears in the second or third week of illness, a time when other symptoms are declining. Cardiac manifestations include chest pain, dyspnea, cardiomegaly, dysrhythmias, and CHF. ECG findings, such as nonspecific ST–T wave abnormalities and conduction blocks, may appear transiently, even in the absence of cardiac symptoms. Peripheral eosinophilia and an elevated ESR are common.

The diagnosis usually is made by serologic studies or by biopsy of any symptomatic muscle group. Treatment usually involves corticosteroids and antihelmintic drugs. The prognosis for full recovery is good, with spontaneous remission of myocarditis in most patients. Myocardial involvement is the most common cause of death from trichinosis and is present in 94% of autopsies of fatal cases.[49]

DIPHTHERIA

Diphtheria is rare in the United States, with only 41 cases reported to the Centers for Disease Control and Prevention between 1980 and 1995. The incidence in the United States since 1980 has been 0.001 cases per 100,000 population. Most diphtheria patients in the United States are immigrants because diphtheria is more common outside the United States. People at risk include the nonimmunized (the Centers for Disease Control and Prevention reports 60% of adults in the United States >20 years old are not immunized) and people in contact with farm animals and unpasteurized dairy products. There is one report from the United States of a case of diphtheria in a previously immunized individual.[50]

Diphtheria is caused by the toxin of the gram-positive organism *Corynebacterium diphtheriae*. The principal manifestations of the illness are nasopharyngitis with membrane formation and respiratory obstruction, myocarditis, and polyneuritis. Myocardial involvement is clinically evident in 10% to 25% of cases and is the major cause of death. Early signs of myocarditis are tachycardia and faint heart sounds; this may progress to CHF. Cardiac markers are often elevated. Prolongation of the P-R interval and ST–T wave abnormalities occur within the first 2 weeks of onset. Other ECG abnormalities, such as bundle branch block or complete heart block, precede total circulatory collapse and are associated with a poor prognosis.

Specific therapy involves high-dose penicillin and diphtheria antitoxin. Treatment with oral carnitine, a cofactor in the transport of fatty acids to mitochondria, is associated with a lower incidence of heart failure, severe conduction blocks, and decreased mortality.

LYME DISEASE

Epidemiology and Clinical Features

Lyme disease is caused by infection with the spirochete *Borrelia burgdorferi* and is discussed in Chapter 132. Lyme disease–related carditis occurs a median of 21 days after the onset of erythema migrans.[51] Cardiac complications occur in 4% to 10% of patients, including conduction disturbances; bundle branch block; first-degree, second-degree, and third-degree heart block; cardiac arrest; dysrhythmias; and left ventricular dysfunction.

Lyme disease–related carditis should be suspected in otherwise healthy persons who have unexplained heart block and a history of potential exposure to ticks in an endemic area. Lyme disease is diagnosed by identification of the spirochete in blood, skin, or cerebrospinal fluid or by serologic testing. Silver staining of endomyocardial biopsy shows the spirochete. A screening ECG should be performed whenever the diagnosis of Lyme disease is suspected.

Atropine or isoproterenol may be used to treat first-degree or second-degree heart block or third-degree block that is hemodynamically stable. Placement of a temporary pacemaker is often required in unstable patients. Antibiotic therapy with intravenous penicillin G (20 million U/day) or oral tetracycline (250 mg four times/day) for 10 to 20 days is effective and can reverse atrioventricular block. Erythromycin should be prescribed in place of tetracycline in young children. Ceftriaxone also is effective. The role of antibiotics in preventing Lyme disease–related carditis is unknown. Prednisone (40 to 60 mg/day in divided doses, tapered by 5 to 10 mg/week) for the treatment of patients with Lyme disease–related carditis and conduction delays may prove useful.

ACQUIRED IMMUNODEFICIENCY SYNDROME–RELATED MYOCARDIAL DISEASE

Epidemiology

The cardiac manifestations of AIDS are diverse and cause death in at least 6% of patients with HIV.[52] The prevalence of left ventricular dysfunction in adult AIDS patients is approximately 20%. Myocarditis is described in approximately 46% of AIDS patients undergoing postmortem examination. Most AIDS patients exhibit cardiac involvement as their underlying disease worsens.

Etiology

The pathogenesis of HIV-related heart muscle disease is probably multifactorial. The direct etiologic role of HIV infection in cardiomyopathy is controversial. Cytomegalovirus infection is a major cause of morbidity in AIDS and can cause myocarditis, as can infection with Toxoplasma. Of AIDS patients with toxoplasmosis, 28% initially have cardiac symptoms, such as cardiomegaly, CHF, dysrhythmias, pericarditis, pericardial tamponade, or chest pain. Mycobacterium tuberculosis, Aspergillus fumigatus, coxsackie B virus, cryptococcal, and Histoplasma myocarditis also occur.

HIV disease treatment also may lead to cardiac toxicity. Pentamidine, which is structurally similar to procainamide, can cause torsades de pointes ventricular tachycardia.[52] Zidovudine and dideoxyinosine also can lead to cardiac dysfunction.

OTHER CAUSES OF MYOCARDITIS

Cardiac involvement of Legionella pneumophila is uncommon. Clinical symptoms resemble pericarditis and myocarditis. Dysrhythmias and conduction blocks occur. After treatment with erythromycin, normal cardiac function may return. In some cases, the heart is the only affected organ.

Cardiac Toxoplasma infection may lead to clinically significant disease. Infection occurs in patients with acute lymphocytic leukemia or lymphoma who are receiving chemotherapy. It is well described in recipients of bone marrow and cardiac transplantation. Immunocompromised patients with toxoplasmic myocarditis may have bundle branch block, CHF, pericarditis, and dysrhythmias as a result of lesions in the conducting system. Untreated toxoplasmic myocarditis is fatal.

Myocarditis associated with M. pneumoniae may be caused by direct invasion of the myocardium, an autoimmune mechanism, or intravascular coagulation. Miliary tuberculosis, including tuberculosis myocarditis, can lead to sudden death.[53] Granulomas within the myocardial conduction system can precipitate fatal dysrhythmias. Sudden death also can occur secondary to Chlamydia pneumoniae myocarditis.[54] Antibodies are present in the serum, and there are small foci of lymphocytic infiltrates and degenerative changes within the myocytes. Myocarditis, presumably mediated by exotoxin, is associated with Shigella infection.

Cardiac involvement of the conduction system and the pericardium also may occur in dermatomyositis and polymyositis. Patients are usually asymptomatic, but pericarditis, myocarditis, and dysrhythmias can occur.

DOXORUBICIN (ADRIAMYCIN) CARDIOTOXICITY

Acute and chronic cardiotoxicity occur secondary to the use of doxorubicin. Manifestations of acute cardiotoxicity include dysrhythmias, pericarditis, myocarditis, and left ventricular dysfunction.

COCAINE

Cocaine has various cardiac effects in addition to ischemia, including myocarditis and DCM. Myocarditis is a common autopsy finding in patients who die of cocaine abuse. The mechanism responsible for the cardiotoxic effects of cocaine is largely unknown. Theories include the following: (1) cocaine may have a direct effect on lymphocyte activity; (2) intravenous cocaine can increase natural killer cell activity in blood, which may be cytotoxic to myocardial cells; (3) there is a cocaine-related eosinophilic infiltrate that suggests a hypersensitivity reaction; and (4) catecholamine administration can induce a focal myocarditis.[55] Cocaine users are at increased risk for infection, and concomitant viral infection causing myocarditis is possible. Cocaine has a direct, negative inotropic effect on cardiac muscle.

Patients who die with detectable cocaine levels have myocarditis and myocardial contraction bands more often than controls. The severity of contraction-band necrosis correlates with the serum and urine concentrations of cocaine. Catecholamine excess caused by cocaine use may contribute to contraction-band necrosis, which may supply the anatomic substrate for ventricular dysrhythmias.

KAWASAKI DISEASE

Kawasaki disease, which is of unknown etiology, primarily affects children. The diagnosis is made based on clinical criteria. Twenty-five percent of all patients develop coronary artery abnormalities, usually several weeks after symptom onset. These are usually reversible, but may lead to aneurysm formation or secondary thrombosis and myocardial ischemia. Myocarditis occurs during the initial phase of the disease in 50% of patients. Rarely, myocarditis leads to cardiogenic shock or CHF. Pericarditis also occurs in 25% of patients.[56,57]

CARDIOMYOPATHIES AND SPECIFIC HEART MUSCLE DISEASE

Cardiomyopathies traditionally are classified into three categories according to the World Health Organization: (1) *dilated,* with ventricular dilation, contractile dysfunction, and CHF symptoms; (2) *hypertrophic,* with left ventricular hypertrophy, asymmetric septum involvement, and preserved contraction; and (3) *restrictive,* with impaired diastolic filling. In 1995, the World Health Organization changed its guidelines to reflect new insight into cardiac disease.[30] A variety of pathologic processes may initiate myocyte injury. When a threshold amount of injury occurs, common pathophysiologic pathways are activated. These pathways involve neurohumoral factors, immune factors, and cytokines. These factors contribute to myocyte dysfunction, which leads to remodeling. In response to disease, the heart remodels usually by hypertrophy or dilation. There is also an increase in interstitial fibrosis, which impairs ventricular filling; this leads to increased metabolic demands on the myocardium.[58,59] Whether the ultimate pathophysiologic derangement is the troponin complex, intracellular concentration of calcium, or myocardial subproteins, it is clear that sarcomere dysfunction is part of the clinical picture for the cardiomyopathies.[60]

In the past, cardiomyopathies were thought to be the result of environmental factors, such as toxins or poor nutrition. They are now thought to be caused by genetic factors.[59] Specifically, mutations of genes for myocardial protein components may lead to molecular changes in the sarcomere that lead to cardiomyopathy, although there is not yet a direct correlation between genotype, phenotype, and clinical presentation. The traditional splitting of cardiomyopathies into subtypes may evolve into a unified theory that shows all types of cardiomyopathy to be variations of a common genetic, anatomic, humoral, pathophysiologic process.

DILATED CARDIOMYOPATHY

Epidemiology and Etiology

DCM is a spectrum of disorders that have in common a dilated and failing heart for which no cause can be established. The diagnosis is one of exclusion. The incidence of DCM is estimated to be 7.5 cases per 100,000 persons per year. The true incidence is probably underestimated because many asymptomatic cases remain undiagnosed.[61] DCM is estimated to affect 4.5 million patients in the United States, causing 1 million hospitalizations, 300,000 deaths, and $17 billion in costs.[59] It is estimated that 30% of cases previously thought to be of unknown etiology may be secondary to infection.

DCM affects men more often than women, affects African Americans more than whites,[58] and may occur in any age group, with middle age (40 to 65 years old) being the most common. Risk factors include ethanol and tobacco abuse, pregnancy, hypertension, and infection. Among patients with DCM, approximately 25% have an inherited form.[58,59]

Pathophysiology

At the cellular level, myocyte necrosis and apoptosis occur, as does fibrosis, neurohumoral response (proliferative signaling), and cellular remodeling.[45] Myocardial overload initiates a vicious cycle of hypertrophic cell death that increases the burden of the remaining cells; this leads to signaling, more work, and cell death.[62]

Clinical Features

Symptoms of DCM have an insidious onset. Left-sided heart failure occurs as the initial manifestation in 75% to 85% of patients, with dyspnea (usually with exertion or while supine) the major symptom. Exacerbation of heart or renal disease, dietary indiscretion, and medication noncompliance are key contributors. Chest pain on exertion is the initial symptom in 8% to 20% of patients, and systemic or pulmonary emboli are the initial manifestation in 4%. Right-sided heart failure is a late and ominous sign.[61]

Diagnostic Strategies

ECG findings are nonspecific. There may be poor R wave progression, intraventricular conduction delay, or left bundle branch block pattern. Holter monitoring may show frequent premature ventricular contractions and occasional ventricular tachycardia, which is nonsustained. Sudden death is uncommon.[61]

The chest radiograph reveals cardiomegaly. Brain-type natriuretic peptide is mildly elevated in asymptomatic left ventricular failure and markedly elevated in overt heart failure.[58]

Echocardiography shows left ventricular dilation, reduced systolic function, and variable wall motion abnormalities. Abnormal ventricular contractility defines DCM, and an ejection fraction less than 45% is required for diagnosis. End-diastolic and systolic volumes are increased, as are pulmonary capillary wedge pressure and central venous pressure.[61]

Endomyocardial biopsy also may be necessary. Histologic abnormalities are nonspecific. New histochemical, immunologic, and molecular biologic techniques improve the diagnostic yield of biopsy tissue, especially the search for infectious causes.[58]

Management and Disposition

Therapy includes supportive measures, such as adequate rest, weight control, abstaining from tobacco, moderate salt and alcohol consumption, and reduced physical activity. Medical treatment includes measures that treat CHF. Because presentation to the emergency department usually includes pulmonary edema, emergency department treatment includes diuretics, oxygen, vasodilators, inotropic adjuncts and other measures.

Angiotensin-converting enzyme inhibitors are the treatment of choice.[62] They reduce morbidity and mortality.[58] Other afterload-reducing agents, such as isosorbide dinitrate and hydralazine, also prolong survival in patients with heart failure. Spironolactone and the angiotensin receptor–blocking agents, such as losartan, also prolong survival.[62] Implantable defibrillators improve survival in patients with known sudden death or ventricular tachycardia.[58] Antidysrhythmic use is not efficacious.[61] Digoxin may not alter mortality, but may lead to decreased symptoms and hospitalizations.[63] Its effectiveness is unclear for patients already receiving angiotensin-converting enzyme inhibitors.[58]

Several different β-blockers can reduce symptoms and improve left ventricular function, functional capacity, and survival.[62,64] In addition, the improvement in cardiac function that β-blockers have is associated with changes in expression of genes encoding for α and β myosin heavy-chain and sarcoplasmic reticulum calcium adenosine triphosphate, which shows that these medications work on a molecular basis.[65]

Anticoagulation is controversial. The incidence of systemic thromboembolism is about 2% per year. Trials in patients with low ejection fractions after MI show a decreased number of strokes in patients on warfarin (Coumadin).[66] Therapy aimed at B-type natriuretic peptide may prove to be effective.

Outcome

Because medical therapy usually fails, DCM is the leading indication for heart transplantation in adults and children. Mortality from DCM is 18% by 1 year, 35% by 5 years, and 50% by 10 years.[58] Patients with idiopathic DCM show progressive deterioration, with 75% of patients dying within 5 years of diagnosis. Survival at 5 years is reported at 50% and 75% with the use of neurohumoral antagonists.[58]

The clinical course for children is variable, with a 1-year mortality rate of 21% and a 5-year mortality of 36%.[68] There is a better prognosis in young children. Most deaths occur within the first 2 years. Some children show late, spontaneous, and unexplained improvement.

HYPERTROPHIC CARDIOMYOPATHY

Perspective

Although this condition has been known as idiopathic hypertrophic subaortic stenosis, obstructive cardiomyopathy, or hypertrophic obstructive cardiomyopathy, the currently accepted name is hypertrophic cardiomyopathy (HCM). The prevalence of HCM is estimated to be 0.1% to 0.2% of the general population. This is probably an underestimate because many patients are asymptomatic.[69] HCM may be more common in men than women and in African Americans than whites.

Principles of Disease

Anatomy

HCM is a disease involving abnormalities of heart muscle at anatomic, cellular, and genetic levels. The defining anatomic feature of HCM is a hypertrophied, nondilated left ventricle in the absence of another cause of left ventricular hypertrophy. The thickening is usually asymmetric and involves the septum more than the free ventricular wall. The extent of hypertrophy at any given site can vary greatly and bears significantly on the manifestation of the disease.[70] The dimensions of the left ventricular and right ventricular cavities are small or normal. Atrial dilation is another feature. Ventricular aneurysm formation also occurs.

Histologically, individual muscle cells are hypertrophied, showing a disorganized, characteristic whorled pattern. Sarcomere disarray is the histologic hallmark of HCM. In addition, abnormal fibrous tissue is often found in the left ventricle. The scarring mimics a healed MI.[59]

Pathophysiology

HCM is caused by mutations in genes that encode for sarcomere contractile proteins.[69] More than 100 different mutations are identified.[71] These mutations at the muscle fiber level cause differences in force stiffness ratio, maximum shortening velocity, and power.[69] Mutations of the β-myosin heavy chain gene seem to be the most significant. β-Myosin heavy chain is a contractile protein with enzyme activity responsible for hydrolyzing adenosine triphosphate. It makes up approximately 30% of the myocardial protein.[72]

Cardiac troponin-T constitutes approximately 5% of the total myofibrillar protein and is involved in regulation of calcium. A decreased quantity of stable cardiac troponin-T alters the stoichiometry of the sarcomere.[72] α-Tropomyosin protein constitutes 5% of the total myofibrillar protein. It bridges the binding of troponin protein complex to thin actin filament. Mutations for these proteins are present in patients with HCM.

In addition, genetic studies of families with HCM identify specific mutations that correlate with sudden cardiac death, intermediate risk for sudden cardiac death, and near-normal life expectancy.[72] In families with Arg403Gln mutation, less than half of affected family members survive past 45 years of age.[73] Genetics alone does not account for HCM. Even within the same family, the phenotypic expression among affected individuals sharing the same mutation varies markedly, indicating a role for environmental factors and possibly other factors.[59,72]

The hypertrophy in HCM may be a compensatory response to the cardiac protein abnormalities.[70] In vitro studies show that mutant β-myosin heavy chain protein exhibits impaired contractility and disrupts formation of the normal sarcomere. The heart's usual response to physiologic stress is hypertrophy, dilation, or a combination of both.[72] A gene mutation may lead to mutant protein that impairs cellular structure and function, probably by fibrous changes to the sarcomere.[59] This causes compensatory tissue hypertrophy that is manifest clinically as HCM.

Clinical Features

HCM occurs in all ages. The average age at diagnosis is 30 to 40 years. Approximately 2% of cases are diagnosed in children younger than 5 years old, and 7% are diagnosed before 10 years of age. The presentation of HCM varies widely. There usually are no presenting symptoms, although HCM may be discovered by screening relatives of patients who have HCM.

In many patients, the initial sign is sudden death, which usually occurs during exertion. Ninety percent of patients have shortness of breath. Other symptoms in decreasing order of frequency include chest pain, syncope, near-syncope, and palpitations. The severity of symptoms correlates roughly with the degree of hypertrophy and is independent of a systolic gradient.

Physical examination reveals a loud S_4 gallop and a harsh crescendo-decrescendo midsystolic murmur. This murmur is made louder by Valsalva's maneuvers or by standing. It becomes quieter when the patient lies down, squats, or does isometric exercises. Other physical findings may include a bifid arterial pulse, a double systolic or triple apex beat, reversed splitting of the second heart sound, and, rarely, a mitral leaflet septal contact sound.[70] Many dysrhythmias are seen in HCM, including premature atrial and ventricular contractions, multifocal ventricular ectopy, and ventricular and supraventricular tachydysrhythmias. In the emergency department, the diagnosis should be suspected in anyone with a family history, characteristic murmur, and cardiopulmonary symptoms (i.e., chest pain, dyspnea, dysrhythmia) not explained by other life-threatening conditions.

Diagnostic Strategies

Patients with suspected HCM should have an ECG, chest radiograph, and echocardiogram. The ECG is abnormal in approximately 90% of patients and shows a variety of patterns. The most common abnormalities are left ventricular hypertrophy, ST segment alterations, T wave inversion, left atrial enlargement, abnormal Q waves, and diminished or absent R waves in the lateral leads. The chest radiograph may be normal or show left ventricular or atrial enlargement.[74]

Echocardiography is the most important diagnostic strategy. Findings include left ventricular hypertrophy, left ventricular outflow tract narrowing, a small left ventricular cavity, and reduced septal motion.[70] The dynamic characteristic of HCM distinguishes it from the discrete forms of obstruction to ventricular flow. Doppler techniques are helpful in assessing the severity of this obstruction at rest and with provocative maneuvers.

Nuclear studies can be used to assess systolic and diastolic ventricular function and ventricular scarring. Electrophysiologic studies may show dysrhythmias but have not been shown to be more useful than clinical means in predicting sudden death.[75] Genetic screening may be helpful to predict other family members at risk.[70]

Differential Diagnosis

HCM mimics many disorders. In individuals who have a gradient and a loud systolic murmur, HCM may be confused with aortic stenosis, pulmonary stenosis, ventricular septal defect, or mitral regurgitation. In the absence of a murmur, symptoms may suggest mitral valve prolapse, left atrial myxoma, primary pulmonary hypertension, or coronary artery disease. ECG changes, such as severe left ventricular hypertrophy, deeply inverted T waves, or Q waves in the inferior and chest leads, without a history of preceding MI, should suggest HCM as well. Echocardiography is often helpful, but ultimately cardiac catheterization may be necessary to confirm the diagnosis.

Management

β-Blockers are the mainstay of therapy. The beneficial effects on symptoms (primarily dyspnea and chest pain) and exercise tolerance seem to be due largely to a decrease in the heart rate, which prolongs diastole and increases ventricular filling. β-Blockers also reduce inotropic response and lessen myocardial oxygen demand.[73] Calcium channel blockers also are useful. Verapamil reduces obstruction in patients with a gradient by decreasing contractility and improving diastolic relaxation and filling. It improves exercise capacity, and its negative effects on heart rate and blood pressure decrease oxygen consumption and the incidence of angina. Verapamil is contraindicated when conduction blocks are present, but should be considered when there is no response to β-blockers.

Nitrates, the traditional initial emergency department management for chest pain, are not indicated in HCM-associated chest pain because they decrease ventricular volume and outflow tract dimensions. Amiodarone is the drug of choice for treatment of ventricular dysrhythmias in HCM or when β-blockers or calcium blockers fail. Amiodarone also may control atrial fibrillation.[70] Automatic implantable cardioverter defibrillators are indicated for patients with sudden death or a history of two or more risk factors. Because 5% of patients with HCM develop subacute bacterial endocarditis, patients with HCM should receive antibiotic prophylaxis before undergoing diagnostic or therapeutic procedures.

Surgical treatment is reserved for patients with large (>50 mm Hg) systolic gradients, severe symptoms, and poor quality of life who do not respond to drug therapy. The most common procedure is septal myomectomy, in which a portion of the basal septum is resected. Success rates are 95%, with improvement in symptoms and quality of life despite the lack of effect on diastolic dysfunction or the other components of HCM. Dual-chamber pacing decreases outflow gradient and improves symptoms but does not improve outcome.[73]

Disposition

The natural history of HCM is variable and probably reflects the many different genetic etiologies. The annual mortality rate is 1%.[70] The annual incidence of sudden cardiac death is higher in young patients with HCM (6%) than in the elderly (1%).[72] The risk of cardiac death is 0.7% per year.[78]

The onset of atrial fibrillation in some patients with HCM may precipitate marked hemodynamic compromise and severe CHF. Cardioversion is indicated. Rate control and anticoagulation to prevent thromboembolism are the hallmarks of therapy for chronic atrial fibrillation. Embolic phenomena also can occur in HCM secondary to bacterial endocarditis, which most commonly affects the mitral valve.[73]

The best predictor of outcome may be the genetic defect. At present, clinical risk factors for sudden death are young age, syncope, malignant family history, cardiac functional status, outflow obstruction, sustained ventricular tachycardia, and ventricular tachycardia on ambulatory monitoring.[70] Syncope is the only independent predictor of sudden death.[79] Sudden death usually occurs with exercise. Patients with HCM who do not have the aforementioned risk factors may engage in low-intensity sports. Patients with HCM initially diagnosed in the emergency department should have strenuous physical activity specifically proscribed until cleared by their cardiologist. In the emergency department, patients with HCM who have angina, syncope, near-syncope, dysrhythmias, and abrupt changes in cardiopulmonary status should be hospitalized.

RESTRICTIVE CARDIOMYOPATHY

Perspective

The hallmark of RCM is a gradual and progressive limitation of ventricular filling secondary to myocardial lesions. RCM is the least common type of cardiomyopathy in countries where the most common etiology is amyloidosis. Other etiologies include sarcoidosis, hemochromatosis, scleroderma, neoplastic cardiac

infiltration, radiation heart disease, glycogen storage disorders, Fabry's disease, and Gaucher's disease. The most common cause of RCM worldwide is tropical endomyocardial fibrosis. Endomyocardial fibrosis is endemic to India, Africa, and Latin America. Symptoms include an initial viral-like illness followed by persistent fever, malaise, and the development of severe right-sided heart failure. Infectious and immunologic causes are proposed.

Only 2% of all childhood cardiomyopathies are RCM. Children also have a more rapid deterioration than adults, with only 29% survival at 4 years.[80] Some patients with RCM show an abnormal accumulation of desmin (the major intermediate filament of muscle) in a disorganized pattern. There is also an autosomal dominant inheritance of RCM in some families.[81] These two findings led to the hypothesis that RCM may have a pathophysiologic etiology in common with the other cardiomyopathies. This hypothesis is supported further by the finding of a mutation within the cardiac troponin I gene that leads to RCM. Similar to DCM and HCM, this finding supports the theory that the cardiomyopathies may be a spectrum of hereditary diseases of sarcomeric contractile proteins.[82]

Principles of Disease

Restriction of ventricular filling results in low end-diastolic ventricular volumes, high end-diastolic ventricular pressures, and decreased cardiac output. Systolic function is maintained. Grossly, there is atrial enlargement with nondilated ventricles. As the disease progresses, the ventricular cavities may become obliterated by fibrous tissue, scarring, or thrombus.

Clinical Features and Diagnostic Strategies

Symptoms are those of worsening diastolic dysfunction and include exercise intolerance (cardiac output cannot be increased because ventricular filling is compromised), elevated central venous pressure, peripheral edema, pulmonary edema, and S_3 and S_4 gallops on auscultation. Children can present with failure to thrive.[80]

Differentiation from constrictive pericarditis requires CT, MRI, or Doppler echocardiography. Occasionally, pericardial calcification can be seen on chest radiograph. This calcification favors a diagnosis of constrictive pericarditis over the diagnosis of RCM.

Echocardiography shows a thickened left ventricle and no change in the left ventricular isovolumic relaxation time with respirations, as occurs with constrictive pericarditis. Atrial dimensions are often increased, which is rarely true in constrictive pericarditis. Biopsy is the gold standard for making the diagnosis and can rule out treatable causes.

Management and Disposition

With few exceptions (e.g., hemochromatosis), there is no specific treatment for RCM. Treatment is symptomatic until transplantation. Close management is important because RCM has a relentless progression, with 90% of patients dying within 10 years of diagnosis.

PERIPARTUM CARDIOMYOPATHY

Perspective

Peripartum cardiomyopathy (PPCM) is uncommon. It represents less than 1% of the cardiovascular problems associated with pregnancy. PPCM is a form of DCM with symptoms and signs of heart failure that presents for the first time during the last 3 months of pregnancy or the first 6 months postpartum.

Etiology and Epidemiology

The etiology of PPCM is unknown. PPCM may be the result of a cardiovascular stressor during pregnancy, such as preeclampsia or cesarean section, superimposed on an underlying (and probably undiagnosed) cardiovascular disorder. Other proposed etiologies include myocarditis and nutrition factors. The incidence is estimated to be 1 case of PPCM per 3000 to 15,000 pregnancies[83] and is greater in women who are multiparous, have twin pregnancies, have gestational hypertension, have preeclampsia, are older than age 30, or are African American.[84]

Clinical Features and Diagnostic Strategies

Patients usually have symptoms of CHF, chest pain, palpitations, and occasionally thromboembolism. Physical examination often reveals tachycardia, tachypnea, pulmonary rales, an enlarged heart, and an S_3 heart sound.

The ECG may show left ventricular hypertrophy or nonspecific ST–T wave changes. On echocardiography, all four chambers are enlarged, with marked reduction in left ventricular systolic function. A small to moderate pericardial effusion may be found. PPCM is clinically identical to DCM.

Management and Disposition

Treatment of PPCM includes limitation of physical activity, β-blockers, alteration of preload with nitrates and diuretics, increase in ventricular contractility using agents such as digitalis, and afterload reduction. Hydralazine is an effective and safe afterload-reducing agent during pregnancy. Angiotensin-converting enzyme inhibitors may be started in the postpartum period.[84]

One third of patients with PPCM may die. Of survivors, half show complete or near-complete recovery of cardiac function within the first 6 months. Patients who do not recover completely show either continuous clinical deterioration or persistent left ventricular dysfunction. Subsequent pregnancies may be associated with relapses and a high risk of maternal mortality, although women with stable DCM before pregnancy often do well.[83] In the emergency department, patients with signs of hemodynamic instability or failure to maintain oxygenation should be admitted, and fetal monitoring should be initiated.

SPECIFIC HEART MUSCLE DISEASES

Amyloidosis

Disorders of amyloid deposition are divided into two categories: primary amyloidosis (associated with a high incidence of cardiac involvement) and amyloidosis secondary to multiple myeloma, RA, tuberculosis, or lymphoma, in which the heart is involved in approximately 50% of cases. Cardiac amyloidosis is a disease of the immune system in which cells of the reticuloendothelial system are stimulated to deposit amorphous material in the ventricle, coronary arteries, or valves. Massive amyloid deposition results in an increased cardiac weight and the diastolic dysfunction of RCM. CHF occurs in 85% of cases of cardiac amyloidosis. Standard CHF and antidysrhythmic therapy are indicated, although the dysrhythmias in amyloid heart disease are often refractory to treatment. The presence of high-grade atrioventricular block may require pacemaker insertion. The prognosis is poor, with death often resulting from progressive heart failure within 1 year of symptom onset.

Sarcoidosis

Cardiac granulomas are reported in approximately 25% of cases of systemic sarcoidosis. Granulomas are preferentially located in the septum (where they cause severe conduction defects, especially complete heart block), in the papillary muscles (causing mitral regurgitation), and in the ventricular walls (producing scarring and wall motion abnormalities). Cardiac involvement is clinically unrecognized in one third of these cases. The remaining two thirds present with dysrhythmias, conduction defects, or CHF. Complete heart block is the most common conduction block and is associated with a high risk of sudden death. Ventricular dysrhythmias also predispose to sudden death and are often refractory to therapy. Myocardial involvement in sarcoidosis is an indication for systemic corticosteroid therapy. Refractory cardiac failure and dysrhythmias are indications for heart transplantation.

Connective Tissue Disorders and Disease of the Myocardium

Myocarditis associated with various connective tissue diseases occurs more often than is recognized clinically. Cardiac abnormalities occur in RA, juvenile RA (Still's disease), mixed connective tissue disease, and primary Sjögren's syndrome. SLE is the connective tissue disease most commonly associated with cardiac abnormalities. Cardiac involvement in SLE includes pericarditis, endocarditis, and myocarditis.

Primary myocardial involvement is a major complication of diffuse scleroderma and develops as scleroderma worsens. Estimates of the frequency of myocardial involvement in scleroderma vary widely.

BOX 81-2. Specific Heart Muscle Diseases

Nutritional

Beriberi (vitamin B_1 deficiency), pellagra (vitamin B_6 deficiency), scurvy (vitamin C deficiency), hypervitaminosis D, kwashiorkor

Metabolic

Amyloidosis, glycogen storage disease type II (Pompe's disease), McArdle's syndrome, carnitine deficiency, hemochromatosis, acquired hemosiderosis, Fabry's disease, Tay-Sachs disease, Sandhoff's disease, GM_1 gangliosidosis, Niemann-Pick disease, Gaucher's disease, cardiac lipidosis, porphyria, Hurler's syndrome, other mucopolysaccharidoses, type II hyperlipoproteinemia (familial xanthomatosis), Hand-Schüller-Christian disease, gout, oxalosis, alkaptonuria, uremia

Hematologic

Leukemia, myeloma, sickle cell disease, sickle cell trait, thrombotic thrombocytopenic purpura, hereditary hemorrhagic telangiectasia, Henoch-Schönlein purpura

Neuromuscular

Duchenne's muscular dystrophy, Erb's (limb-girdle) muscular dystrophy, facioscapulohumeral muscular dystrophy, Friedreich's ataxia, myotonic dystrophy, myasthenia gravis, tuberous sclerosis

Toxic/Hypersensitivity

Ethanol, cobalt (beer-drinkers' cardiomyopathy), emetine, chloroquine, phenothiazines, lithium, tricyclic antidepressants, methysergide, cyclophosphamide, daunorubicin, doxorubicin (Adriamycin), heavy metals (arsenic, antimony, fluoride, mercury, lead), phosphorus, carbon monoxide, catecholamines, dextroamphetamine, phenylpropanolamine, venoms (scorpion, black widow, snake, wasp), tick paralysis

Physical

Radiation, hypothermia, electric shock, trauma, heatstroke

Miscellaneous

Sarcoidosis, rheumatoid arthritis, Reiter syndrome, Behçet's syndrome, transplant rejection, Noonan's syndrome, Wegener's granulomatosis, Reye's syndrome, inflammatory bowel disease, acquired immunodeficiency syndrome

Modified from Wenger NK, Ablemann WH, Robert WC: Cardiomyopathy and specific heart muscle disease. In Hurst JW, Schlant RC (eds): *The Heart*, 7th ed. New York, McGraw-Hill, 1990.

Presentation includes CHF, angina, and dysrhythmias. Pericardial disease also can occur. Azathioprine may be a beneficial adjunct to steroid therapy.

Sudden Death

Sudden death in patients younger than 21 years of age can be attributed to disease of the myocardium approximately 25% of the time. Cardiac etiologies include myocarditis, HCM, and anomalous coronary artery circulation. In patients with sudden death attributed to cardiac etiologies, prodromal symptoms are reported in more than half of the patients, most commonly chest pain (25%) in patients older than age 20 and dizziness (16%) in patients younger than 20.[85] The distribution of sudden death etiologies by age is as follows:

- Age less than 20 years—myocarditis 22% and HCM 22%

- Age 20 to 29 years—myocarditis 22% and HCM 13%
- Age 30 to 39 years—myocarditis 11% and HCM 2%

Coronary artery disease becomes the leading cardiac etiology (58%) in sudden death in people age 30 to 39 years. HCM is the cardiac disease most commonly found on postmortem diagnosis of athletes with sudden death. HCM and anomalous coronary arteries are seen more often in sports-related deaths than in deaths not related to sports.

Other Specific Heart Muscle Diseases

Box 81-2 lists the numerous other conditions associated with myocardial dysfunction.

KEY CONCEPTS

- Pericarditis must be differentiated from acute MI. Thrombolytic therapy is contraindicated in pericarditis because of the potential for hemorrhagic pericarditis or tamponade.
- Cardiac tamponade must be suspected (distended neck veins, hypotension, and muffled heart sounds), diagnosed (echocardiography), and treated (pericardiocentesis) quickly. If echocardiography is not readily available and the patient is unstable, pericardiocentesis may be diagnostic and therapeutic.
- Myocarditis should be considered in any patient with the combination of viral illness symptoms and signs of cardiac disease.
- The symptoms and signs of constrictive pericarditis are virtually indistinguishable from RCM.
- Lyme disease–related carditis should be suspected in otherwise healthy patients with unexplained heart block and potential exposure to ticks in an endemic area.
- β-Blockers are the mainstay of therapy for HCM; avoid nitrates.

REFERENCES

1. Spodick DH: Medical history of the pericardium. *Am J Cardiol* 26:447, 1970.
2. Beck CS: Two cardiac compression triads. *JAMA* 104:714, 1935.
3. Zayas R, et al: Incidence of specific etiology and role of methods for specific etiologic diagnosis of primary acute pericarditis. *Am J Cardiol* 75:378, 1995.
4. Maisch B, Risitc A: The classification of pericardial disease in the age of modern medicine. *Curr Sci* 4:13, 2002.
5. Chan T, Brady WJ, Pollack M: Electrocardiographic manifestations: Acute myopericarditis. *J Emerg Med* 17:864, 1999.
6. Spodick DH: Macrophysiology, microphysiology, and anatomy of the pericardium: A synopsis. *Am Heart J* 124:1046, 1992.
7. Shifferdecker B, Spodick D: Nonsteroidal anti-inflammatory drugs in the treatment of pericarditis. *Cardiol Rev* 11:211, 2003.
8. Mast HL, et al: Pericardial effusion and its relationship to cardiac disease in children with acquired immunodeficiency syndrome. *Pediatr Radiol* 22:548, 1992.
9. Gunukula S, Spodick D: Pericardial disease in renal patients. *Semin Nephrol* 21:52, 2001.
10. Correale E, et al: Pericardial involvement in acute myocardial infarction in the post-thrombolytic era: Clinical meaning and value. *Clin Cardiol* 20:327, 1997.

11. Dressler W: A post-myocardial infarction syndrome. *JAMA* 160:1379, 1956.

12. Kahn AH: The postcardiac injury syndromes. *Clin Cardiol* 15:67, 1992.

13. Wolfenden H, Newman DC: Constrictive pericarditis associated with trauma and pectus excavatum. *Aust N Z J Surg* 62:750, 1992.

14. Retter A: Pericardial disease in the oncology patient. *Heart Dis* 4:387, 2002.

15. Wilkes JD, et al: Malignancy-related pericardial effusion: 127 cases from the Roswell Park Cancer Institute. *Cancer* 76:1377, 1995.

16. Schultz-Hector S: Radiation-induced heart disease: Review of experimental data on dose response and pathogenesis. *Int J Radiat Biol* 61:149, 1992.

17. Moder KG, Miller TD, Tazelaar HD: Cardiac involvement in systemic lupus erythematosus. *Mayo Clin Proc* 74:275, 1999.

18. Spodick DH: Pathophysiology of cardiac tamponade. *Chest* 113:1372, 1998.

19. Vasquez A, Butman S: Pathophysiologic mechanisms in pericardial disease. *Curr Cardiol Rep* 4:26, 2002.

20. Park S, Bayer AS: Purulent pericarditis. *Curr Clin Top Infect Dis* 12:56, 1992.

21. Thavendrarajah V, et al: Catheter lavage and drainage of pneumococcal pericarditis. *Cathet Cardiovasc Diagn* 29:322, 1993.

22. Brook I: Pericarditis due to anaerobic bacteria. *Cardiology* 97:55, 2002.

23. Defouilloy C, et al: Intrapericardial fibrinolysis: A useful treatment in the management of purulent pericarditis. *Intensive Care Med* 23:117, 1997.

24. Fowler NO: Tuberculous pericarditis. *JAMA* 266:99, 1991.

25. Silva-Cardoso J, et al: Pericardial involvement in human immunodeficiency virus infection. *Chest* 115:418, 1999.

26. Ivey MJ, Gross BH: Back pain and fever in an elderly patient. *Chest* 103:1851, 1993.

27. Osterberg L, Vagelos R, Atwood JE: Case presentation and review: Constrictive pericarditis. *West J Med* 169:232, 1998.

28. Nishimura R: Constrictive pericarditis in the modern era. *Heart* 86:619, 2001.

29. Lieberman EB, Hutchins GM, Herskowitz A: Clinicopathologic description of myocarditis. *J Am Coll Cardiol* 18:1617, 1991.

30. Richardson P, et al: Report of the 1995 World Health Organization/International Society and Federation of Cardiology Task Force on the definition and classification of cardiomyopathies. *Circulation* 93:841, 1996.

31. Wheeler D, Kooy N: A formidable challenge: The diagnosis and treatment of myocarditis in children. *Crit Care Clin* 19:365, 2003.

32. Liu P, et al: Viral myocarditis: Balance between viral infection and immune response. *Can J Cardiol* 12:935, 1996.

33. Olinde KD, O'Connell JB: Inflammatory heart disease: Pathogenesis, clinical manifestations, and treatment of myocarditis. *Annu Rev Med* 45:481, 1994.

34. Bowles N, et al: Detection of viruses in myocardial tissues by polymerase chain reaction: Evidence of adenovirus as a common cause of myocarditis in children and adults. *J Am Coll Cardiol* 42:466, 2003.

35. Caforio A, et al: Circulating cardiac-specific autoantibodies as markers of autoimmunity in clinical and biopsy-proven myocarditis. *Eur Heart J* 18:270, 1997.

36. Sole MJ, Liu P: Viral myocarditis: A paradigm for understanding the pathogenesis and treatment of dilated cardiomyopathy. *J Am Coll Cardiol* 22:99A, 1993.

37. Narula J, et al: Brief report: Recognition of acute myocarditis masquerading as acute myocardial infarction. *N Engl J Med* 328:100, 1993.

38. Matsuura H, et al: Intraventricular conduction abnormalities in patients with clinically suspected myocarditis are associated with myocardial necrosis. *Am Heart J* 127:1290, 1994.

39. Sarda L, et al: Myocarditis in patients with clinical presentation of myocardial infarction and normal coronary angiograms. *J Am Coll Cardiol* 37:786, 2001.

40. Batra A, Lewis A: Acute myocarditis. *Curr Opin Pediatr* 13:234, 2001.

41. Why HJ, et al: Clinical and prognostic significance of detection of enteroviral RNA in the myocardium of patients with myocarditis of dilated cardiomyopathy. *Circulation* 89:2582, 1994.

42. Dec GW, et al: Viral myocarditis mimicking acute myocardial infarction. *J Am Coll Cardiol* 20:85, 1992.

43. Mason JW, et al: A clinical trial of immunosuppressive therapy for myocarditis. *N Engl J Med* 333:269, 1995.

44. Drucker NA, et al: Gammaglobulin treatment of acute myocarditis in the pediatric population. *Circulation* 89:252, 1994.

45. Kumpati G, McCarthy P, Hoercher K: Left ventricular assist device bridge to recovery: A review of the current status. *Ann Thorac Surg* 71:S103, 2001.

46. Brown CA, O'Connell JB: Myocarditis and idiopathic dilated cardiomyopathy. *Am J Med* 99:309, 1999.

47. Mengel JO, Rossi MA: Chronic chagasic myocarditis pathogenesis: Dependence on autoimmune and microvascular factors. *Am Heart J* 124:1052, 1992.

48. Case records of the Massachusetts General Hospital: Weekly clinicopathological exercises. Case 32-1993: A native of El Salvador with tachycardia and syncope. *N Engl J Med* 329:488, 1993.

49. Kociecka W: Trichinellosis: Human disease, diagnosis and treatment. *Vet Parasitol* 93:365, 2000.

50. Munford L, et al: Cardiac diphtheria in a previously immunized individual. *J Natl Med Assoc* 95:875, 2003.

51. Nagi K, Joshi R, Thakur R: Cardiac manifestations of Lyme disease: A review. *Can J Cardiol* 12:503, 1996.

52. Currie PF, Boon NA: Cardiac involvement in human immunodeficiency virus infection. *QJM* 86:751, 1993.

53. Chan AC, Dickens P: Tuberculous myocarditis presenting as sudden cardiac death. *Forensic Sci Int* 57:45, 1992.

54. Wesslen L, et al: Myocarditis caused by *Chlamydia pneumoniae* (TWAR) and sudden unexpected death in a Swedish elite orienteer [letter]. *Lancet* 340:427, 1992.

55. Cregler LL: Cocaine: The newest risk factor for cardiovascular disease. *Clin Cardiol* 14:449, 1991.

56. Barron KS, et al: Report of the National Institute of Health Workshop on Kawasaki Disease. *J Rheumatol* 26:170, 1999.

57. Burns JC, Kushner HL, Bastian JF, et al: Kawasaki disease: A brief history. *Pediatrics* 106:1, 2000.

58. Farrow G: Pathogenesis and treatment of cardiomyopathy. *Adv Intern Med* 47:1, 2001.

59. Seidman J, Seidman C: The genetic basis for cardiomyopathy: From mutation identification to mechanistic paradigms. *Cell* 104:557, 2001.

60. Morgensen J, Kubo T, Duque M: Idiopathic restrictive cardiomyopathy is part of the clinical expression of cardiac troponin I mutations. *J Clin Invest* 111:209, 2003.

61. Dec GW, Fuster V: Idiopathic dilated cardiomyopathy. *N Engl J Med* 331:1564, 1994.

62. Katz A: Pathophysiology of heart failure: Identifying targets for pharmacotherapy. *Med Clin North Am* 87:303, 2003.

63. Garg R, et al: The Digitalis Investigation Group: The effect of digoxin on mortality and morbidity in patients with heart failure. *N Engl J Med* 336:525, 1997.

64. Packer M, Bristow M, Cohn J: The effect of carvedilol on morbidity and mortality in patients with chronic heart failure. *N Engl J Med* 334:1349, 1996.

65. Lowes B, Gilbert E, Abraham W: Myocardial gene expression in dilated cardiomyopathy treated with beta blockers. *N Engl J Med* 346:1357, 2002.

66. Borrowman T, Love R, Mason JW: Dilated cardiomyopathy: Problems in diagnosis and management. *Chest* 115:569, 1999.

67. Peacock WF, Albert NM: Observation unit management of heart failure. *Emerg Clin North Am* 19:209, 2001.

68. Ciszewski A, et al: Dilated cardiomyopathy in children: Clinical course and prognosis. *Pediatr Cardiol* 15:121, 1994.

69. Fananapazir L: Advances in molecular genetics and management of hypertrophic cardiomyopathy. *JAMA* 281:1746, 1999.

70. Wigle E, et al: Hypertrophic cardiomyopathy: Clinical spectrum and treatment. *Circulation* 92:1680, 1995.

71. Sangwatanaroj S, et al: Mutations in the gene for cardiac myosin-binding protein C and late-onset familial hypertrophic cardiomyopathy. *N Engl J Med* 338:1245, 1998.

72. Roberts M, Roberts R: Recent advances in the molecular genetics of hypertrophic cardiomyopathy. *Circulation* 92: 136, 1995.

73. Spirito P, et al: The management of hypertrophic cardiomyopathy. *N Engl J Med* 336:775, 1997.

74. Lerakis S, Sheahan R, Stouffer G: Hypertrophic cardiomyopathy: Presentation and pathophysiology. *Am J Med Sci* 314:324, 1997.

75. Behr E, Elliott P, McKenna W: Role of invasive EP testing in the evaluation and management of hypertrophic cardiomyopathy. *Card Electrophysiol Rev* 6:482, 2002.

76. Maron B: Risk stratification and prevention of sudden death in hypertrophic cardiomyopathy. *Cardiol Rev* 10:173, 2002.

77. McKenna W, Firoozi S, Sharma S: Arrhythmias and sudden death in hypertrophic cardiomyopathy. *Card Electrophysiol Rev* 6:26, 2002.

78. Cannan C, et al: Natural history of hypertrophic cardiomyopathy: A population-based study, 1976 through 1990. *Circulation* 92:2488, 1995.

79. Kofflard M, Ten Cate F, van der Lee C: Hypertrophic cardiomyopathy in a large community population: Clinical outcome and identification of risk factors for sudden cardiac death and clinical deterioration. *J Am Coll Cardiol* 41:987, 2003.

80. Weller R, et al: Outcome of idiopathic restrictive cardiomyopathy in children. *Am J Cardiol* 90:501, 2002.

81. Zhang J, et al: Clinical and molecular studies of a large family with desmin-associated restrictive cardiomyopathy. *Clin Genet* 59:248, 2001.

82. Morgensen J, Kubo T, Duque M: Idiopathic restrictive cardiomyopathy is part of the clinical expression of cardiac troponin I mutations. *J Clin Invest* 111:209, 2003.

83. Bernstein P, Magriples U: Cardiomyopathy in pregnancy: A retrospective study. *Am J Perinatol* 18:163, 2001.

84. Mehta N, Mehta R, Khan I: Peripartum cardiomyopathy: Clinical and therapeutic aspects. *Angiology* 52:759, 2001.

85. Drory Y, et al: Sudden unexpected death in persons less than 40 years of age. *Am J Cardiol* 68:1388, 1991.

CHAPTER

82 Infective Endocarditis and Valvular Heart Disease

Susan M. Dunmire

INFECTIVE ENDOCARDITIS

Perspective

The term *infective endocarditis* (IE) has replaced the older classifications of *acute, subacute,* and *chronic* as they have become less meaningful in the antibiotic era. Although bacteria remain the most common etiology, virtually all organisms (including viruses, fungi, and rickettsiae) can cause endocarditis. Early diagnosis of endocarditis and identification of the causative organism play a significant role in the clinical outcome of this life-threatening disease.

Principles of Disease

In the United States, more recent studies indicate the incidence of IE is 1.7 to 6.2 cases per 100,000 person-years with a slight predominance in males.[1,2] In the preantibiotic era, the average age of a patient with IE was younger than 39 years. Currently, mean age has increased to 49 to 67 years, probably because of the increased prevalence of prosthetic heart valves and the increase in degenerative valve disease in an aging population.[3]

Most patients with bacterial endocarditis have one of the following predisposing factors: rheumatic or congenital heart disease, calcific degenerative valve disease, prosthetic heart valve, mitral valve prolapse (MVP), a history of intravenous (IV) drug use, or a history of endocarditis. Although the incidence of rheumatic heart disease has decreased, it remains an important predisposing factor for endocarditis with the mitral valve as the most common site of infection. Congenital cardiac lesions involving high-pressure gradients (e.g., ventricular septal defects, pulmonary stenosis, tetralogy of Fallot) place a patient at increased risk for IE. Calcific or degenerative disease of the aortic and the mitral valve is now recognized (owing to increased use of echocardiography) as being an extremely common entity in elderly patients.

Prosthetic valve endocarditis is a devastating complication of valve replacement. The incidence of endocarditis in prosthetic valve recipients ranges from 0.5% to 4% per year.[4] MVP is a particularly important and common predisposing factor for IE. The risk is greatest when regurgitant flow is identified by echocardiography or the presence of a murmur.

The incidence of IE associated with injection drug use is estimated at 150 to 2000 per 100,000 person-years.[5] Although any valve can be affected, it is the most common cause of right-sided endocarditis. The recurrence rate of endocarditis in injection drug users is approximately 41%, in contrast to a recurrence rate of less than 20% in other patients.[6,7] Endocarditis is a major risk factor for recurrence because infected valves heal with irregularities that become sites for future vegetations.

Pathophysiology

The classic lesion of endocarditis is the vegetation. It originates as a sterile thrombus on which microorganisms adhere and colonize. The initial thrombus may form at a site of trauma, inflammation, or abnormal turbulence induced by mechanical damage. In injection drug users, contaminants such as talc can injure the previously normal valve leaflets and produce a site for bacterial implantation. A subclinical bacteremia usually precedes the onset of symptoms of bacterial endocarditis by approximately 1 week. A variety of surgical procedures result in transient bacteremia, including dental procedures, cystoscopy, urethral dilation, endoscopic retrograde cholangiopancreatography, and esophageal dilation.[8,9]

The infective organism depends on the predisposing factor for endocarditis. *Streptococcus* remains the most common pathogen for left-sided endocarditis in patients with congenital valvular disease or MVP. There is an association between *Streptococcus bovis* endocarditis and coexisting gastrointestinal malignancy. *Staphylococcus* accounts for approximately 30% of native valve endocarditis and more than 80% of cases of bacterial endocarditis in patients with a history of injection drug use.[10] Coagulase-negative staphylococci are the most common infecting organisms in prosthetic valve endocarditis. *Staphylococcus lugdenesis* is a virulent coagulase-negative staphylococcus that infects native valves, resulting in rapid valve destruction and paravalvular abscess formation.[11]

The HACEK group (*Haemophilus aphrophilus, Actinobacillus, Cardiobacterium hominis, Eikenella corrodens,* and *Kingella kingae*) are fastidious gram-negative bacilli that can cause culture-negative (owing to fastidious nature and slow multiplication) endocarditis.[12] These organisms are known to result in large vessel septic thrombi. The fastidious *Bartonella* species of bacteria may cause endocarditis, particularly in disadvantaged, nutritionally compromised patients.[13]

Candida and *Aspergillus* species account for most cases of fungal endocarditis. Predisposing factors for fungal endocarditis include patients with long-term indwelling IV catheters, pacemakers, or implantable defibrillators; patients who are immunosuppressed because of malignancy, acquired immunodeficiency syndrome, or organ transplantation; and IV drug users. The large fungal vegetations often embolize, lodging in arteries. Because these patients usually have negative blood cultures, histologic and serologic study of these emboli may be the first clue to the presence of fungal endocarditis.

Clinical Features

Symptoms associated with IE are nonspecific and diverse. Many patients who present early during the bacteremic phase of the illness do not have a cardiac murmur and are indistinguishable from the large population of patients who present to the emergency department with a febrile viral illness, particularly during epidemic influenza season. In the absence of specific risks or a disproportionately ill appearance, the diagnosis of IE may be suspected only when the symptoms persist or the illness does not follow a typical course for viremia. The classic triad of fever, anemia, and heart murmur should suggest the presence of IE, but is rare. All presenting symptoms of IE are nonspecific. The most common symptoms are intermittent fever (85%) and malaise (80%). Fever is more common in an IV drug user with endocarditis (98%). Other symptoms (e.g., weakness, myalgias, dyspnea, chest pain, cough, headaches, and anorexia) vary widely in their incidence and are nonspecific. Thirty percent to 40% of patients have neurologic symptoms or signs, such as confusion, personality changes, decreased level of consciousness, or focal motor deficits. These symptoms are most commonly caused by embolization.

Almost all patients with IE have a cardiac murmur at some time during the course of their illness. The murmur may be absent in 15% of patients at the time of presentation. The most common murmurs are aortic, mitral, or tricuspid regurgitation. Fewer than 35% of IV drug users with endocarditis have a murmur on initial presentation.[14] This is most likely due to the fact that most endocarditis associated with IV drug use is right-sided, and consequently the murmur is much more difficult to elicit on physical examination.

Approximately 35% of patients have some form of vasculitic lesion, including petechiae, splinter hemorrhages, Osler's nodes, and Janeway lesions. Petechiae may be present on either a mucosal surface or the skin. Often the petechiae on mucous membranes or the conjunctivae have a pale center. These petechiae are nontender and do not blanch with pressure. Approximately 30% of patients have splenomegaly. Several ocular findings are associated with IE, including conjunctival or retinal hemorrhages. Retinal hemorrhages may be flame shaped or may have a pale center surrounded by a red halo (Roth's spots).

Diagnostic Strategies

Laboratory findings in bacterial endocarditis are nonspecific. Similar to virtually all infectious conditions, leukocytosis is insensitive (occurring in only approximately 50% of patients diagnosed with IE) and nonspecific. An elevated erythrocyte sedimentation rate or C-reactive protein may be present, but also is nonspecific. Most patients have a mild anemia, and more than 50% have microscopic hematuria as a result of embolic lesions of the kidney. Three blood cultures should be obtained on all patients with suspected endocarditis, with the first and last culture being drawn at least 1 hour apart. Approximately 90% to 95% of blood cul-

BOX 82-1. Duke Criteria for Diagnosis of Infective Endocarditis

Clinical diagnosis requires the following:
- Two major criteria
  or
- One major and three minor criteria
  or
- Five minor criteria

Major Criteria
- Positive blood cultures (of typical pathogens) from at least two separate cultures
- Evidence of endocardial involvement by echocardiography, such as the following:
  - Endocardial vegetation
  - Paravalvular abscess
  - New partial dehiscence of prosthetic valve
  - New valvular regurgitation

Minor Criteria
- *Predisposition:* Predisposing heart condition or IV drug use
- *Fever:* ≥38° C
- *Vascular phenomena:* Arterial emboli, septic pulmonary infarcts, mycotic aneurysm, conjunctival hemorrhages, or Janeway lesions
- *Immunologic phenomena:* Osler's nodes, Roth's spots, and rheumatoid factor
- *Microbiologic evidence:* Single positive blood culture (except for coagulase-negative staphylococcus or an organism that does not cause endocarditis)
- *Echocardiogram findings:* Consistent with endocarditis, but do not meet major criteria

BOX 82-2. Initial Therapy for Bacterial Endocarditis

Vancomycin
  Initial dose for adults: 15 mg/kg
  Initial dose for children: 10 mg/kg
  Subsequent dose for adults: 500 mg q 6 hr
  Subsequent dose for children: 10 mg/kg q 6 hr

Plus

Gentamicin
  Initial dose 1–3 mg/kg (subsequent dose 1 mg/kg q 8 hr)

Or

Ceftriaxone
  Adults: 1–2 g q 12 hr
  Children: 50–75 mg/kg q day

Plus

Gentamicin
  Initial dose 1–3 mg/kg (subsequent dose 1 mg/kg q 8 hr)

---

tures are positive unless antibiotics already have been administered.[15] An electrocardiogram (ECG) may show conduction abnormalities if an abscess has formed in the myocardium.

Transthoracic echocardiography (TTE) is a rapid, noninvasive tool for the diagnosis of vegetations. Although TTE is highly specific, it may be nondiagnostic in 20% of patients because of obesity, chronic obstructive pulmonary disease, and chest wall deformities. The sensitivity of TTE for the diagnosis of endocarditis is 60% to 70%.[16,17] Transesophageal echocardiography (TEE) is more invasive and time-consuming, but is far superior to TTE in diagnostic sensitivity for IE.[18,19] The negative predictive value of TEE for IE is greater than 92%.[20]

The Duke criteria stratify patients with suspected bacterial endocarditis into three distinct categories: definite, possible, and rejected (Box 82-1).[21] Proposed modifications to the Duke criteria expand the minor criteria to include an elevated C-reactive protein or erythrocyte sedimentation rate, new splenomegaly, splinter hemorrhages, or hematuria.[22] The specificity and sensitivity of the Duke criteria are estimated to be approximately 99% and 95%, respectively.[23-26]

Management

Appropriate antibiotics must be selected before the causative organism is known or before the diagnosis is proven. Box 82-2 provides guidelines for empiric therapy. It is helpful to obtain all necessary blood cultures before starting antibiotics. Patients who are IV drug users or have a prosthetic heart valve and are febrile should be admitted for evaluation of bacteremia and the possibility of endocarditis.[27] An exception would be a transient fever in an IV drug user that resolves spontaneously in the emergency department and is thought to be a result of an injected contaminant ("cotton fever").

Acute valve replacement is rarely necessary during the active episode of IE. Indications for surgery include severe congestive heart failure (CHF) resulting from valvular incompetence, paravalvular leak around a prosthetic valve, fungal endocarditis, and persistent bacteremia despite antibiotics.

With proper antibiotic therapy, patients defervesce within 1 week. The 5-year mortality rate for native valve endocarditis is 20%, but in the presence of a prosthetic valve, it is 20% to 60%.[28,29] The mortality for right-sided endocarditis in a patient with a history of injection drug use is approximately 10%.[30]

Prophylaxis

Antibiotic prophylaxis in patients undergoing procedures in the emergency department is important for patients with prosthetic heart valves, a history of endocarditis, or congenital cardiac malformations (Box 82-3). Antibiotics are thought to prevent IE by decreasing the degree of bacteremia and reducing the ability of bacteria to adhere to the valve surface. Common procedures for which prophylaxis is recommended are listed in Box 82-4.[31] Relatively clean procedures, such as suturing of clean lacerations, endotracheal intubation, or the placement of a central venous catheter, do not require prophylaxis. Table 82-1 summarizes recommendations for prophylaxis against bacterial endocarditis.

RHEUMATIC FEVER

Perspective

From 1920 to 1950, acute rheumatic fever was the leading cause of death in American children and the most common cause of heart disease in individuals younger than age 40. During the 1960s and 1970s, the incidence of rheumatic fever in developed countries declined dramatically because of widespread antibiotic use to treat streptococcal infections, declining preva-lence of the more virulent strains of group A strepto-cocci, and improved living conditions. In the mid-1980s, a resurgence of rheumatic fever occurred in several areas of the United States. This resurgence was thought to be caused by the emergence of a more viru-lent strain of group A streptococcus.[34] The incidence of rheumatic fever during epidemics of streptococcal pharyngitis is 3%, although sporadic cases of strepto-coccal sore throat rarely result in this disease. Children between the ages of 4 and 18 years are at greatest risk of developing rheumatic fever. In many developing nations, rheumatic fever continues to be a leading cause of death in infants and adolescents.

Principles of Disease

Although the exact pathogenesis of rheumatic fever is unclear, all affected individuals show an antibody response indicating a recent infection with group A beta-hemolytic streptococcus. The most popular theory is that rheumatic fever results from an abnormal immunologic response to group A streptococcus result-ing in antibodies that cross-react with certain tissues within the heart, joints, skin, and central nervous system.

Clinical Features

One third of patients with rheumatic fever do not remember having pharyngitis in the preceding month. The average latent period between pharyngitis and rheumatic fever is 18 days (range 1 to 5 weeks). In 1944, Jones[35] formulated major and minor criteria for the diagnosis of rheumatic fever. Revised in 1965 and further modified in 1984 and 1992, the Jones criteria remain the diagnostic basis for this disease (Box 82-5).[36] The diagnosis of rheumatic fever requires evidence of an antecedent streptococcal infection plus at least one major and two minor or two major manifestations from the Jones criteria. A presumptive diagnosis of recurrent rheumatic fever may be made if one major or more than three minor criteria are present in addition to recent evidence of a group A streptococcal infection. Use of the traditional Jones criteria may lead to underdiagno-sis of recurrent rheumatic fever.[37]

A migratory polyarthritis is the most common symptom of rheumatic fever. This polyarthritis often affects larger joints, such as the knees, ankles, elbows, and wrists, and the pain is usually much more severe

---

BOX 82-3. Moderate to High Risk Conditions for Bacterial Endocarditis

- Prosthetic heart valve
- History of endocarditis
- Congenital cardiac malformations, particularly cyanotic lesions (e.g., tetralogy of Fallot, transposition of great vessels)
- Rheumatic heart disease
- Mitral valve prolapse with regurgitation
- Hypertrophic cardiomyopathy

BOX 82-4. Indications for Endocarditis Prophylaxis

Prophylaxis Recommended
Prophylactic cleaning of teeth
Bronchoscopy (with rigid bronchoscope only)
Endoscopic retrograde cholangiopancreatography
Cystoscopy
Urethral dilation

Prophylaxis Not Recommended
Local anesthetic injections (nonintraligamentary)
Endotracheal intubation
Tympanostomy tube insertion
Transesophageal echocardiography
Endoscopy
Vaginal delivery
Urethral catheterization
Uterine dilation and curettage
Insertion or removal of an intrauterine device

From Dajani AS, et al: Prevention of bacterial endocarditis. *JAMA* 227:1794, 1997.

Table 82-1. Prophylactic Regimens for Bacterial Endocarditis

Dental Procedures	Agent	Regimen
Standard oral prophylaxis	Amoxicillin	*Adults*: 2 g 1 hr before procedure *Children*: 50 mg/kg 1 hr before procedure
Unable to take oral medication	Ampicillin	*Adults*: 2 g IM or IV 30 min before procedure *Children*: 50 mg/kg 30 min before procedure
Allergic to penicillin	Clindamycin	*Adults*: 600 mg orally 1 hr before procedure *or* 600 mg IV 30 min before *Children*: 20 mg/kg orally 1 hr before procedure *or* IV 30 min before
	Azithromycin or clarithromycin	*Adults*: 500 mg orally 1 hr before procedure *Children*: 15 mg/kg orally 1hr before procedure

From Dajani AS, et al: Prevention of bacterial endocarditis. *JAMA* 227:1794, 1997.

than physical findings suggest. Arthritis occurs early in the course of rheumatic fever and often coincides with a rising titer of streptococcal antibodies.

Forty percent of patients with rheumatic fever have a pancarditis manifested by a heart murmur, cardiomegaly, pericardial effusion, and occasionally CHF. The mitral valve is the most common valve affected by rheumatic fever, often resulting in mitral regurgitation and its classically high-pitched blowing systolic murmur.

Chorea (Sydenham's chorea, St. Vitus' dance) consists of random, rapid, purposeless movements usually of the upper extremities and face. It is a rare manifestation of rheumatic fever. Chorea may coexist with carditis, but it never occurs simultaneously with arthritis. If chorea is the only finding, diagnosis may become difficult because all other clinical and laboratory signs may be absent.

Erythema marginatum and subcutaneous nodules are found in fewer than 10% of cases of acute rheumatic fever; however, their presence should immediately suggest the diagnosis. Erythema marginatum is a non-pruritic, painless, evanescent "smoke ring" of erythema that commonly appears on the trunk and proximal extremities. Subcutaneous nodules are pea sized; nontender; and usually appear over the extensor surfaces of the wrists, elbows, knees, and occasionally the spine.

Fever is present during the acute phase of rheumatic fever. It rarely lasts more than 2 weeks and has no characteristic pattern.

Diagnostic Strategies

In diagnosing rheumatic fever, it is helpful to document a recent streptococcal infection. Although throat cultures are usually negative at the time of clinical onset of rheumatic fever, antistreptococcal antibody titers remain positive for 4 to 6 weeks after the streptococcal infection. The erythrocyte sedimentation rate and C-reactive protein level typically are elevated. Approximately 50% of patients have mild proteinuria or casts in their urine. There are no ECG findings pathognomonic of rheumatic fever, although a prolonged P-R interval is common and suggestive.

Management

Acute rheumatic fever can be prevented by appropriate treatment of streptococcal pharyngitis. Pharyngitis should be treated early with either a single injection of benzathine penicillin (600,000 U in children weighing <25 kg and 1.2 million U in adults) or a 10-day course of oral penicillin or erythromycin. If the oral route is chosen, it is important that a 10-day course be completed to eradicate the presence of streptococcus in the pharynx.

Management of acute rheumatic fever consists of treating the group A streptococcal infection, reducing inflammation, and evaluating for CHF. Patients with acute rheumatic fever must receive prophylaxis against streptococcal infections for at least 5 years with penicillin or erythromycin twice daily or an injection of benzathine penicillin once a month. Inflammation is responsive to salicylates and other anti-inflammatory agents. Corticosteroids are not indicated for treatment of arthritis; however, they are effective in treating carditis.

VALVULAR HEART DISEASE

Principles of Disease

Of the four heart valves, three (tricuspid, pulmonic, and aortic) are composed of three cusps, whereas the mitral valve has only two cusps. Each cusp is a double layer of endocardium that is attached at its base to the fibrous skeleton of the heart. The margins of the cusps are attached to muscular projections from the ventricles (papillary muscles) via tendinous cords (chordae tendineae). Contraction of the ventricle and consequently the papillary muscle results in the opening or closing of the valve depending on its location.

Mitral Valve Prolapse

Congenital MVP is an extremely common valvulopathy, affecting approximately 2.4% of the population.[38] Young women constitute most patients affected. Although MVP is usually an asymptomatic disorder discovered by routine physical examination or echocardiography, occasionally the patient may experience palpitations and chest pain. Rare complications of MVP include endocarditis, dysrhythmias, and sudden death. Patients with MVP may be encountered in a variety of clinical scenarios. Patients may have symptoms of palpitations or chest pain that may be related to the previously diagnosed MVP, or auscultation may reveal a new click or murmur.

Pathophysiology

Structurally, myxomatous proliferation of the spongiosa layer within the valve causes focal interruption of the fibrosa layer and allows abnormal stretching of the valve leaflet during systole. Although the anterior or the posterior leaflet may prolapse, involvement of the posterior leaflet has a greater association with mitral regurgitation and cardiovascular complications.[39,40] MVP may be associated with other connective tissue disorders, such as Marfan's syndrome; Ehlers-Danlos syndrome; and skeletal abnormalities, including pectus excavatum, a straight back, and severe scoliosis.

Clinical Features

The most common symptoms associated with MVP are palpitations and chest pain. Palpitations are caused most often by premature ventricular contractions; however, paroxysmal re-entrant supraventricular tachycardia and, rarely, ventricular tachycardia are reported.[41] The chest pain associated with MVP usually differs from angina pectoris in that it is sharp, localized, of variable duration, and nonexertional. Rarely the patient has pain mimicking angina, which may respond to nitroglycerin. Theories regarding the etiology of this pain include localized ischemia secondary to stretching of the papillary muscles and coronary artery spasm.

Fatigue, lightheadedness, and shortness of breath are other symptoms commonly associated with MVP. Exercise testing of MVP patients usually is normal. Generalized anxiety, panic attacks, and eating disorders commonly are described as part of the MVP syndrome. Most studies do not show any increase in incidence in panic disorder in patients with MVP.

The patient with MVP may show a wide variety of clicks and murmurs on cardiac auscultation. Approximately 20% of patients with MVP have the classic midsystolic click followed by a late systolic crescendo murmur heard best between the apex and the left sternal border, with the patient in the left lateral decubitus position. Any diagnostic maneuver that reduces end-diastolic ventricular volume, such as having the patient stand or perform Valsalva's maneuver, moves the click closer to S_1 and may accentuate a previously unheard click. This click is thought to result from snapping of the chordae tendineae during the prolapse of the valve.

Diagnostic Strategies

Diagnosis of MVP depends on detecting the typical auscultatory findings and is confirmed by echocardiography. In most patients, a thorough history and physical examination are sufficient to make the diagnosis. Echocardiography can be helpful in a patient suspected of having MVP with normal auscultatory findings. The ECG can have a variety of abnormalities in MVP, including ST segment depression in leads II, III, and aVF consistent with inferior ischemia, Q-T interval prolongation, and premature atrial and ventricular contractions.[42]

Complications

A variety of complications can occur with MVP. MVP is now the most common predisposing factor for IE in the United States and Western Europe. Risk factors for IE include the presence of mitral regurgitation or thickened valve leaflets or both.

MVP is associated with a variety of neurologic abnormalities, including migraine headaches and cerebrovascular events ranging from transient ischemic attacks to stroke.[43-45] Cerebral ischemic events may be secondary to sterile emboli from platelet and fibrin deposits on the defective mitral valve. Rarely, malignant ventricular dysrhythmias are associated with MVP resulting in sudden death. In a review of patients with sudden death related to MVP, risk factors included a history of syncope or near-syncope, a click and a late systolic or pansystolic murmur, ST-T segment abnormalities in the inferior or lateral leads, and multiple premature ventricular contractions.[46]

Management

Propranolol or other selective β-blockers may control symptoms such as palpitations, chest pain, and anxiety. Often, quiet reassurance and explanation of the disease entity suffice. Patients with severe mitral regurgitation or life-threatening dysrhythmias unresponsive to drug therapy may require valve replacement.

Mitral Stenosis

The most common cause of mitral stenosis is rheumatic heart disease. There usually is a latency period of approximately 20 years between rheumatic fever and the onset of symptoms from mitral stenosis. Without surgical intervention, steady deterioration occurs, resulting in 85% mortality 20 years after the onset of symptoms. Other, less common causes of mitral stenosis are congenital mitral stenosis, atrial myxoma, thrombus, and calcification of the mitral annulus and leaflets.

Pathophysiology

The stenosis of the mitral valve impedes flow from the left atrium to left ventricle, resulting in left atrial hypertension and eventually left ventricular failure and pulmonary edema. As the disease progresses, some patients develop severe pulmonary hypertension, which leads to right ventricular failure.

Clinical Features

Patients with hemodynamically significant mitral stenosis often complain of dyspnea on exertion, orthopnea, and hemoptysis. These symptoms are a result of left ventricular failure and pulmonary hypertension. The physician should examine the patient specifically for mitral stenosis in the setting of new-onset CHF. The following findings suggest mitral stenosis: a palpable diastolic thrill over the apex, a loud S_1, and an opening snap of the mitral valve in early diastole and a low-pitched, rumbling diastolic murmur heard best at the apex.

Although the chest x-ray may be normal, in more advanced cases, left atrial enlargement is present and results in straightening of the left heart border. Calcification of the mitral orifice occasionally can be seen. The most common ECG abnormalities include atrial fibrillation and evidence of left atrial enlargement (a notched P wave in lead II and a negative terminal deflection of the P wave in lead V_1).

Complications

Atrial fibrillation is the most common complication of mitral stenosis; the incidence may be 40% and depends on left atrial size. The sudden onset of atrial fibrillation can cause severe heart failure when accompanied by a rapid ventricular response. Embolic events are a serious complication of mitral stenosis. The incidence of embolism may be 20%, with approximately 75% of these affecting the brain.[47] Patients with right ventricular failure are prone to recurrent pulmonary emboli. Other complications are frequent respiratory infections and occasionally massive pulmonary hemorrhage from rupture of pulmonary bronchial venous connections. IE is rare with isolated mitral stenosis.

Mitral Regurgitation

Acute and chronic mitral regurgitation are two distinct disease entities. Acute mitral regurgitation is usually a catastrophic event resulting from the rupture of chordae tendineae or papillary muscle or perforation of the valve leaflet. Common causes include acute myocardial infarction, bacterial endocarditis, and trauma. Chronic mitral regurgitation is most commonly a result of rheumatic heart disease and often coexists with mitral stenosis. Other causes of chronic mitral regurgitation include MVP and connective tissue disorders, such as Marfan's syndrome and Ehlers-Danlos syndrome.

Pathophysiology

In acute mitral regurgitation, the regurgitant volume can be three to four times the forward flow, resulting in pulmonary edema and peripheral vascular collapse. In chronic mitral regurgitation, the left ventricle compensates by increasing stroke volume and maintaining cardiac output. Symptoms related to low output state, including fatigue and dyspnea on exertion, occur late in the disease, and patients commonly remain asymptomatic for their lifetime. Most patients eventually develop atrial fibrillation; however, CHF is uncommon.

Clinical Features

The clinical picture of acute mitral regurgitation is one of fulminant pulmonary edema; this often occurs in the setting of an acute myocardial infarction. The carotid pulse increases rapidly but is poorly sustained. Atrial and ventricular gallops are frequently present. The murmur of acute mitral regurgitation is a loud crescendo-decrescendo murmur ending before S_2 and heard best at the apex. The ECG in acute mitral regurgitation is notable for the absence of left atrial and ventricular hypertrophy. The chest x-ray usually reveals pulmonary edema and a normal cardiac silhouette.

Characteristic findings in chronic mitral regurgitation include a palpable left ventricular heave and thrill. The murmur is high-pitched, holosystolic, and heard best at the apex radiating to the axilla. The ECG usually reflects left atrial and ventricular hypertrophy. Atrial fibrillation is a common rhythm. Left atrial enlargement is commonly seen on the chest x-ray.

Management

When the diagnosis of acute mitral regurgitation is suspected, emergency echocardiography and cardiac catheterization are indicated to assess the degree of regurgitation and determine whether emergent surgery is indicated. Initial stabilization of the patient should include treatment of the pulmonary edema with nitrates, nitroprusside, morphine, and diuretics. In a hypotensive patient, an intra-aortic balloon pump may provide temporary stabilization before surgery.

Chronic mitral regurgitation is medically managed with diuretics, salt restriction, and digoxin. If the degree of regurgitation becomes debilitating, and the symptoms cannot be controlled by medications, surgery is indicated.

Aortic Stenosis

The cause of aortic stenosis (AS) varies according to the age of the patient. In patients younger than 65 years of age, the most common cause is a congenital bicuspid valve, whereas in patients older than 65 years, stenosis is usually a result of calcific degeneration of the valve cusp. Rheumatic heart disease is the second most common cause of AS in patients younger than age 65. In these patients, the mitral valve also usually is affected.

Pathophysiology

Significant obstruction of the left ventricular outflow tract is thought to occur when the valve orifice becomes less than 1 cm or when a pressure gradient across the valve exceeds 50 mm Hg. Compensatory left ventricular hypertrophy maintains stroke volume and cardiac output until the stenosis becomes critical, which is why symptoms appear late in the disease.

Clinical Features

The classic triad of symptoms from AS is (1) dyspnea on exertion from left ventricular failure, (2) angina, and (3) exertional syncope. Syncope is a result of either inadequate cerebral perfusion or occasional dysrhythmias. When symptoms occur, the life expectancy averages 5 years without operative intervention. When symptoms of heart failure occur, the life expectancy is less than 2 years.

The classic auscultatory finding in AS is a low-pitched, rasping crescendo-decrescendo systolic murmur heard best at the base and radiating into the carotids. Often the carotid pulse is diminished in intensity (parvus) and slow rising (tardus). The left ventricle is often hyperdynamic, with a palpable heave. Although the pulse pressure may be reduced in AS, this is not a constant finding. The ECG usually reveals left ventricular hypertrophy. Left ventricular enlargement may be seen on chest x-ray late in the disease.

Management

When symptoms occur in patients with AS, medical management has a limited role. These patients are at significant risk of sudden death and should be referred for valve replacement. A patient with critical AS maintains a delicate balance between preload and afterload. The addition of any medication that alters either of these parameters can lead to acute decompensation. Patients who have decompensated from AS most commonly are hypotensive. This usually can be treated with gentle fluid resuscitation; however, inotropic agents occasionally are necessary. An intra-aortic balloon pump can be used as a temporizing measure until the valve is replaced.

Aortic Regurgitation

Aortic regurgitation may be a chronic disease process evolving slowly over years, or it may occur acutely, presenting as fulminant heart failure. The most common cause of chronic aortic regurgitation is rheumatic heart disease or a bicuspid aortic valve. Acute aortic regurgitation most commonly is associated with fulminant endocarditis, aortic dissection, or trauma. A variety of connective tissue diseases, such as Marfan's syndrome, ankylosing spondylitis, rheumatoid arthritis, Takayasu's arteritis, and syphilitic aortitis, can predispose a patient to develop acute or chronic aortic regurgitation.

Pathophysiology

During acute aortic regurgitation, left ventricular diastolic pressure rises rapidly, resulting in left ventricular failure and fulminant pulmonary edema. In chronic aortic regurgitation, the left ventricle hypertrophies and dilates, allowing the heart to maintain cardiac output despite significant regurgitation.

Clinical Features

Patients with acute aortic regurgitation have severe CHF with symptoms of dyspnea, tachypnea, and occasionally chest pain. Decreased cardiac output results in cool, pale extremities and a resting tachycardia. The systolic and diastolic pressures are normal or low, and the pulse pressure is not widened. The first heart sound is diminished or absent because of early closure of the mitral valve. A short, soft diastolic murmur (regurgitation) and a midsystolic flow murmur may be present. The diagnosis of acute aortic regurgitation can be difficult because of the lack of physical findings. Acute mitral and aortic regurgitation should be considered in any patient presenting with new-onset CHF. Because acute therapy is quite similar, differentiating these two entities can await stabilization. The diagnosis can be made definitively by echocardiography.

In chronic aortic regurgitation, physical examination reveals a rapidly rising and falling carotid pulse (water-hammer or Corrigan's pulse). Other physical signs include nail pulsations (Quincke's sign), a to-and-fro murmur over the femoral artery (Duroziez's murmur), and head bobbing in severe cases. The pulse pressure is almost always widened. A high-pitched, blowing diastolic murmur at the left sternal border is characteristic. The Austin Flint murmur, a soft diastolic rumble caused by the regurgitant stream hitting the mitral valve, also may be present.

Management

Acute aortic regurgitation is a surgical emergency requiring immediate valve replacement. Medical stabilization should be attempted with the use of afterload reducers, diuretics, and, if necessary, an intra-aortic balloon pump while awaiting surgical therapy. In cases in which bacterial endocarditis is the cause of acute aortic regurgitation, the timing of surgery is controversial. The CHF of chronic aortic regurgitation can be managed with afterload reducers, nitrates, and digoxin. Aortic valve replacement should be considered when left ventricular failure occurs.

Tricuspid Stenosis and Regurgitation

Pathophysiology

Tricuspid stenosis is almost always rheumatic in origin and commonly coexists with mitral and aortic disease. Patients often complain of fatigue and symptoms related to increased venous congestion, such as edema, ascites, and hepatosplenomegaly. Left ventricular failure is rare and occurs only with associated aortic or mitral stenosis. Tricuspid regurgitation is most commonly the result of pulmonary hypertension; however, it also can be caused by rheumatic fever, right-sided endocarditis, and occasionally trauma.

Clinical Features

In tricuspid stenosis, physical examination reveals a prominent jugular venous "A" wave and a high-pitched diastolic murmur along the left sternal border that increases with inspiration. Hepatosplenomegaly usually is present.

Signs and symptoms of tricuspid regurgitation include dyspnea, painful hepatomegaly, ascites, and peripheral edema, reflecting associated pulmonary hypertension and right ventricular failure. On physical examination, a right ventricular heave is commonly present. The murmur is high-pitched, pansystolic, and best heard at the fourth intercostal space parasternally. A prominent P_2 and S_3 are often heard on auscultation. A right bundle branch block or atrial fibrillation may be present on ECG.

Management

Initial treatment of tricuspid stenosis and tricuspid regurgitation consists of fluid and salt restriction. Valve replacement eventually may be required.

Complications of Prosthetic Valves

Artificial heart valves are implanted in more than 40,000 patients per year in the United States. Prosthetic heart valves are separated into two groups: mechanical valves consisting of synthetic materials and bioprosthetic, or tissue, valves made with either porcine or bovine tissue cusps. The original mechanical valve, the Starr-Edwards caged-ball prosthesis, was first implanted in 1960. Since that time, many other designs for mechanical valves have been introduced, with the most common being the caged-ball, the tilting-disk, and the bileaflet hinged-disk prostheses. Dissatisfaction with the need for lifelong anticoagulation led to the development of bioprosthetic valves. Tissue valves are most commonly porcine but rarely may be made of hand-sewn human tissue. Although these valves offer the advantage of optional anticoagulation, they are much less durable than their mechanical counterparts. To evaluate a patient with a prosthetic valve properly, it is necessary to know the type, location, and age of the prosthesis. All patients are provided with a card containing this information at the time of their surgery.

All mechanical prostheses have a prominent metallic closure sound and a softer metallic opening click. Bioprostheses have opening and closing sounds similar to the native valve. Almost all prostheses result in some obstruction to flow, and when in the aortic position, a systolic ejection murmur is normal. A diastolic murmur is always pathologic and indicative of valve failure.

A posteroanterior and lateral chest x-ray study is helpful in determining the position of the prosthesis and evaluating the presence or absence of vascular congestion that may accompany valve dysfunction. A decreasing hematocrit may be a result of significant hemolysis indicating paravalvular leak or primary failure of the prosthesis. Coagulation studies are helpful only in the setting of suspected valve thrombosis, embolism, or hemorrhage and to check for adequate anticoagulation.

Early complications from prosthetic heart valves are often surgically related; later complications include embolization, valve obstruction from thrombus formation, endocarditis, hemolytic anemia, and primary failure of the valve. Thromboembolic events are the most serious complication of prosthetic valves. Thrombus formation can result in obstruction of the valve outlet or dislodgment of emboli into the systemic circulation. The risk of thrombus formation depends on the type and location of the prosthesis. Mechanical valves have a much higher incidence of thrombus formation than bioprosthetic valves. Patients with a thrombosed mechanical heart valve usually have an acute onset of hypotension, CHF, and an absent or muted metallic closure sound. Thrombosis also may develop subacutely with gradually worsening symptoms over periods lasting 6 months. Patients with mechanical valves usually require lifelong anticoagulation with warfarin with or without aspirin or dipyridamole. The international normalized ratio in these patients should be maintained in the range of 2.5 to 3.5. Patients with bioprosthetic valves usually require only aspirin. If the left atrium is dilated, however, warfarin may be recommended for mitral valve bioprostheses.

The incidence of IE in patients with prosthetic valves is approximately 0.5% per patient year. During the first two postoperative months, *Staphylococcus epidermidis* and other hospital-acquired organisms predominate. After the initial two months, the causative organisms are similar to those in native valve endocarditis.

Chronic hemolysis from the turbulence of blood flow past the prosthetic valve occurs in 70% of patients. The hemolysis is usually low grade in nature and responds well to iron therapy. The hemolysis occasionally can be severe, suggesting the possibility of a paravalvular leak or primary valve failure, both of which may require valve replacement. This chronic hemolysis may predispose the patient to cholelithiasis.

Primary valve failure in patients with prosthetic heart valves can lead to regurgitant blood flow, acute valvular occlusion, embolism of a piece of the prosthesis, or severe hemolysis. In bioprosthetic valves, primary tissue failure results from cuspal tears and perforations, calcification, and loss of pliability of the leaflets. Approximately 30% of aortic and mitral bioprosthetic valves have tissue failure at 10 years, necessitating replacement. Although mechanical valves are extremely durable, structural failures are reported. The Björk-Shiley 60-degree and 70-degree convexoconcave valves were withdrawn from the market in 1985 and 1983 because of a high incidence of strut fracture and resultant embolization of the tilting disk.[48] By 1985, more than 80,000 convexoconcave valves had been placed, and more than 4000 of them were the 70-degree model.[49] There are still some individuals with these prostheses in place who are at risk of strut fracture and disk escape. These patients experience the dramatic onset of CHF and hypotension. On physical examination, there is absence of the metallic closure sound and a regurgitant murmur. The murmur may be the only finding that differentiates this from valve thrombosis. A chest x-ray reveals the disk to be dislodged or absent.

🔑 KEY CONCEPTS

- Most patients with bacterial endocarditis have one of the following predisposing factors:
  Rheumatic or congenital heart disease
  Calcific degenerative valve disease
  Prosthetic heart valve
  History of IV drug use
  History of endocarditis
  MVP with regurgitant flow
- *Streptococcus viridans* is the most common cause of IE in patients with congenital valvular disease or MVP.
- *Staphylococcus* is the most common cause of endocarditis in patients with a history of IV drug use or prosthetic valves.
- Fewer than 35% of IV drug users and fewer than 20% of patients without IV drug use with IE have a murmur on initial presentation.
- Fever is the most common presenting sign in patients with IE.
- TEE is the diagnostic test of choice for IE.
- Rheumatic fever most commonly affects the mitral valve.
- The classic findings of chronic aortic regurgitation, including Corrigan's pulse, Quincke's sign, and Duroziez's murmur, are absent in acute aortic regurgitation.
- Absence of auscultated metallic closure sounds in a mechanical valve prosthesis should raise the suspicion of valve dysfunction (dislodgment or thrombosis).

REFERENCES

1. Berlin JA, et al: Incidence of infective endocarditis in the Delaware Valley, 1988-1990. *Am J Cardiol* 76:933, 1995.

2. Hogevik H, et al: Epidemiologic aspects of infective endocarditis in an urban population: A 5-year prospective study. *Medicine* 74:324, 1995.

3. Watanakunakorn C, Burkert T: Infective endocarditis at a large community teaching hospital, 1980-1990: A review of 210 episodes. *Medicine* 72:90, 1993.

4. Ghann JW, Cobbs CG: Infections of prosthetic valves and intravascular devices. In Mandel GI (ed): *Principles and Practices of Infectious Disease.* New York, John Wiley & Sons, 1985.

5. Frontera JA, Gradon JD: Right-side endocarditis in injection drug users: Review of proposed mechanisms of pathogenesis. *Clin Infect Dis* 30:374, 2000.

6. Pelletier LL, Petersdorf RG: Infective endocarditis: A review of 125 cases from the University of Washington Hospitals, 1963-1972. *Medicine* 56:287, 1977.

7. Welton DE, et al: Recurrent infective endocarditis: Analysis of predisposing factors and clinical features. *Am J Med* 66:932, 1979.

8. Dajani AS, et al: Prevention of bacterial endocarditis. *JAMA* 227:1797, 1997.

9. Hoesley CJ, Cobbs G: Endocarditis at the millenium. *J Infect Dis* 179(Suppl 2):S360, 1999.

10. Hecht SR, Berger M: Right-sided endocarditis in intravenous drug users: Prognostic features in 102 episodes. *Ann Intern Med* 117:560, 1992.

11. Lessing MA, et al: Native-valve endocarditis caused by *Staphylococcus lugdenesis. QJM* 89:855, 1996.

12. Wilson WR, et al: Antibiotic treatment of adults with infective endocarditis due to streptococci, enterococci, staphylococci, and HACEK microorganisms: American Heart Association. *JAMA* 274:1706, 1995.

13. Spach D, et al: *Bartonella (Rochalimaea)* species as a cause of apparent "culture negative" endocarditis. *Clin Infect Dis* 20:1044, 1995.

14. Delaney KA: The double challenge of endocarditis. *Emerg Med* 22:53, 1990.

15. Hoen B, et al: Infective endocarditis in patients with negative blood cultures: Analysis of 88 cases from a one year nationwide survey in France. *Clin Infect Dis* 20:501, 1995.

16. Shively BK, et al: Diagnostic value of transesophageal compared with transthoracic echocardiography in infective endocarditis. *J Am Coll Cardiol* 18:391, 1991.

17. Werner GS, et al: Infective endocarditis in the elderly in the era of transesophageal echocardiography: Clinical features and prognosis compared with younger patients. *Am J Med* 100:90, 1996.

18. Daniel WG, et al: Comparison of transthoracic and transesophageal echocardiography for detection of abnormalities of prosthetic and bioprosthetic valves in the mitral and aortic positions. *Am J Cardiol* 71:210, 1993.

19. Heidenreich PA, et al: Echocardiography in patients with suspected endocarditis: A cost effective analysis. *Am J Med* 107:198, 1999.

20. Lowry RW, et al: Clinical impact of transesophageal echocardiography in the diagnosis and management of infective endocarditis. *Am J Cardiol* 73:1089, 1994.

21. Durack DT, Lukes AS, Bright DK: New criteria for diagnosis of infective endocarditis: Utilization of specific echocardiographic findings: Duke Endocarditis Service. *Am J Med* 96:200, 1994.

22. Lamas CC, Eykyn SJ: Suggested modifications to the Duke criteria for the clinical diagnosis of native valve and prosthetic valve endocarditis: Analysis of 118 pathologically proven cases. *Clin Infect Dis* 25:713, 1997.

23. Heiro M, et al: Diagnosis of infective endocarditis: Sensitivity of the Duke vs. von Reyn criteria. *Arch Intern Med* 158:18, 1998.

24. Nettles RE, et al: An evaluation of the Duke criteria in 25 pathologically confirmed cases of prosthetic valve infective endocarditis. *Clin Infect Dis* 25:1401, 1997.

25. Hoen B, et al: The Duke criteria for diagnosing infective endocarditis are specific: Analysis of 100 patients with acute fever or fever of unknown origin. *Clin Infect Dis* 23:298, 1996.

26. Dodds GA, et al: Negative predictive value of the Duke criteria for infective endocarditis. *Am J Cardiol* 77:403, 1996.

27. Weisse AB, et al: The febrile parenteral drug abuser: A prospective study of 121 patients. *Am J Med* 94:274, 1993.

28. Verheul HA, et al: Effects of changes in management of active infective endocarditis on outcome in a 25-year period. *Am J Cardiol* 72:682, 1993.

29. Martin JM, Neches WH, Wald ER: Infectious endocarditis: 35 years of experience at a children's hospital. *Clin Infect Dis* 24:669, 1997.

30. Hecht SR, Berger M: Right-sided endocarditis in intravenous drug users: Prognostic features in 102 episodes. *Ann Intern Med* 117:560, 1992.

31. Dajani AS, et al: Prevention of bacterial endocarditis: Recommendations by the American Heart Association. *JAMA* 277:1794, 1997.

32. Veasy LG, et al: Resurgence of acute rheumatic fever in the intermountain area of the United States. *N Engl J Med* 316:421, 1987.

33. Hosier D, et al: Resurgence of rheumatic fever. *N Engl J Med* 316:422, 1987.

34. Kaplan EL, Johnson DR, Cleary PP: Group A streptococcal serotypes isolated from patients and sibling contacts during the resurgence of rheumatic fever in the United States in the mid-1980's. *J Infect Dis* 159:101, 1989.

35. Jones TD: The diagnosis of rheumatic fever. *JAMA* 126:481, 1944.

36. Dajani AS, et al: Guidelines for the diagnosis of rheumatic fever: Jones criteria, updated 1992. *Circulation* 87:302, 1993.

37. Ferrieri P, et al: Proceedings of the Jones Criteria Workshop. *Circulation* 106:2521, 2002.

38. Freed LA, et al: Prevalence and clinical outcome of mitral-valve prolapse. *N Engl J Med* 341, 1999.

39. Arvan S, Tunick S: Relationship between auscultatory events and structural abnormalities in mitral valve prolapse: A two-dimensional echocardiographic evaluation. *Am Heart J* 108:1298, 1984.

40. Kim S, et al: Relation between severity of mitral regurgitation and prognosis of mitral valve prolapse: Echocardiographic follow-up study. *Am Heart J* 132:348, 1996.

41. Savage DD, et al: Mitral valve prolapse in the general population: Part 3. Dysrhythmia: The Framingham study. *Am Heart J* 106:582, 1983.

42. Bhutto ZR, et al: Electrocardiographic abnormalities in mitral valve prolapse. *Am J Cardiol* 70:265, 1992.

43. Litman GI, Friedman HM: Migraine and the mitral valve prolapse syndrome. *Am Heart J* 96:610, 1978.

44. Jackson AC, et al: Mitral valve prolapse and cerebral ischemic events in young patients. *Neurology* 34:784, 1984.

45. Kouvaras G, et al: Association of mitral valve leaflet prolapse and cerebral ischaemic events in the young and early middle-aged patient. *QJM* 56:387, 1986.

46. Jeresaty RM: Sudden death in the mitral valve prolapse-click syndrome. *Am J Cardiol* 37:317, 1976.

47. Aberrantly WS, Willis PW III: Thromboembolic complications of rheumatic heart disease. *Cardiovasc Clin* 5:131, 1973.

48. Hendel PN: Björk-Shiley strut fracture and disc escape: Literature review and a method of disc retrieval. *Ann Thorac Surg* 47:436, 1989.

49. Ostermeyer J, et al: The Björk-Shiley 70-degree convexoconcave prosthesis strut fracture problem (present state of information). *Thorac Cardiovasc Surg* 35:71, 1987.

83 Hypertension

Richard O. Gray

PERSPECTIVE

For most of the 20th century, elevated blood pressure (BP) readings were thought to be associated with, but not causing, morbidity and mortality. Not until large population-based studies in the 1960s, such as the Framingham study, did physicians begin to focus on hypertension as a treatable risk factor for stroke, myocardial infarction (MI), peripheral vascular disease, congestive heart failure, and renal disease. Medical management of hypertension has reduced stroke mortality by 50% on an age-adjusted basis and is probably partially responsible for the decline in mortality from coronary artery disease. As a matter of public health, however, much remains to be done in the treatment of hypertension. Although approximately 75% of patients with chronically elevated BP are aware of their disease, as few as one half to one quarter of these patients are adequately treated.[1,2] Although hypertension may be epidemic, it rarely represents an emergency condition for the individual patient. In the absence of acute end-organ damage, it is rarely, if ever, necessary to lower a patient's BP acutely in the emergency department.

Hypertension is frequently encountered in the emergency department, where many factors can cause elevated BP. Anxiety and pain often cause transient hypertension, but evaluation of the patient for evidence of acute end-organ ischemia is important. Most patients, even those with an exacerbation of chronically elevated BP, show a substantial decrease in pressure without intervention during a short observation period in the emergency department.[3,4] Even if the patient's BP does remain elevated without end-organ damage, urgent treatment is rarely beneficial, and an appropriate referral for long-term management should be made.

PRINCIPLES OF DISEASE

Definition and Determination of Hypertension

The Joint National Committee on Prevention, Evaluation, and Treatment of High Blood Pressure in its seventh report has dramatically changed how it classifies hypertension. In adults, a systolic pressure less than 140 mm Hg and a diastolic pressure less than 90 mm Hg are considered normal. If the systolic pressure is between 140 and 159 mm Hg or if the diastolic pressure is between 90 and 95 mm Hg, the term *prehypertension* is now applied, reflecting that the lifetime incidence of hypertension in these individuals is twice that of individuals in the "normal" range.[2] The patient with a systolic pressure of 160 mm Hg or greater or a diastolic pressure over 95 mm Hg is considered to be hypertensive. If hypertension, as defined by these arbitrary values, is not controlled, the patient is at great risk for long-term morbidity and mortality.[2,5] In patients younger than 50 years, the diastolic pressure is the primary determinant of future cardiovascular risk. Diastolic hypertension is the most prevalent form of hypertension in patients younger than 50, whereas in the two thirds of adults older than 65 who have hypertension, systolic hypertension is more common and represents their greatest cardiovascular risk. Even isolated systolic hypertension in elderly patients is a significant risk factor for cardiovascular disease, especially when combined with other risk factors. In older patients, an elevated pulse pressure (determined by subtracting diastolic from systolic pressure) is an equally significant risk factor for stroke and MI.[6-8]

Proper technique is required to obtain accurate BP readings, with special attention to the cuff size. In patients with large extremities, a standard-size cuff may measure a falsely elevated BP. A larger cuff corrects this error and should be readily available in the emergency department. The cuff should be deflated slowly because with rapid deflation the inertia of the mercury column causes a gap between the actual pressure in the cuff and the measured pressure on the gauge. This gap may lead to falsely elevated levels. It is much easier to obtain an accurate reading with a slowly falling column of mercury. Aneroid instruments are somewhat less susceptible to this problem, but in general they are not as accurate. The systolic pressure should be recorded when the first tapping sound is heard as the cuff is deflated. Although several endpoints have been used to define diastolic pressure, the most widely accepted is the total disappearance of sound. In patients who do not have complete disappearance of these sounds, the point of distinct muffling should be recorded as the diastolic pressure.

A single elevated BP does not necessarily mean that the patient has hypertension. This is especially true in children.[9] BP measurement should be repeated after the patient is in a reclining position for at least 10 minutes and should be checked in both arms. If the second reading is also elevated or close to the hypertensive range, the patient should be advised of the potential for hypertension and referred for follow-up.

Pathophysiology

Hypertension is not a single disease but rather the result of a number of disease processes. By far the most common category is *essential hypertension*. No specific cause of essential hypertension has been identified, although many factors, including heredity, age, race, obesity, and the amount of dietary sodium, may contribute to the elevated BP.[10] Prehypertension has been intensely studied because patients who later become hypertensive may provide clues about the physiologic changes that eventually produce a fixed elevation of BP. Two major theories exist: (1) hypertension results from alterations in the contractile properties of smooth muscle in arterial walls and (2) alterations of arterial smooth muscle are a response to chronically elevated BP resulting from a primary failure of normal autoregulatory mechanisms. Research has focused on the role of calcium ions in vascular smooth muscle. Vascular tone depends on a transmembranous supply of calcium ions, and calcium antagonists suppress virtually all vasoconstrictive responses of vascular smooth muscles, including the peripheral resistance vessels.

Most patients with established hypertension have elevated peripheral arterial resistance and normal cardiac output. The findings are similar in the majority of prehypertensive individuals, many of whom have decreased plasma volume and elevated heart rate. This tachycardia seems to be caused not by an increased sympathetic tone but by a decreased parasympathetic tone. Autoregulatory mechanisms are blunted, and pharmacologic autonomic blockade has minimal effect on BP.

Many patients with hypertension have a very different circulatory status with an elevated cardiac output and hyperkinetic circulation. The increase in cardiac output results from an increase in both heart rate and stroke volume. There appears to be a large sympathetic component with an increase in both cardiac β-adrenergic and α-adrenergic tone. Autonomic blockade returns the BP readings to normal.

Renin, Angiotensin, and Aldosterone

The role of renin and angiotensin as a cause of essential hypertension is not clear. Renin is an enzyme produced by the kidney that splits off angiotensin I from a plasma globulin precursor.[11] Angiotensin I is converted by an enzyme in the lung to produce angiotensin II. Angiotensin II is a potent vasoconstrictor and also stimulates aldosterone production in the adrenal gland. Figure 83-1 depicts the renin-angiotensin-aldosterone axis. Patients with hypertension may be divided into clinical groups according to renin levels. Determining the renin-sodium profile, which is the plasma renin activity measured against the 24-hour urine sodium content, is especially useful in making this division.

In normal individuals, angiotensin effects depend on sodium levels. Inhibition of angiotensin-converting enzyme (ACE) has some effect on BP in normotensive individuals with normal total body sodium but greatly reduces BP in those with sodium depletion. When ACE inhibitors are administered to patients with hypertension, their acute effect on BP is closely related to the plasma renin activity. With chronic administration, however, the effect of ACE inhibitors on BP no longer correlates with pretreatment plasma renin activity.[12] Elevated renin and angiotensin levels are responsible for the hypertension seen in ischemic renal disease, and angiotensin is a major contributor to maintaining the progressive rise of BP in accelerated hypertension. In the latter condition, renin and angiotensin levels are increased because of areas of renal ischemia secondary to arteriolar necrosis. ACE inhibitors or angiotensin blockers are clearly the drugs of choice in hypertensive patients with diabetes or decreased left ventricular function, or both.

The role of hyperaldosteronism in essential hypertension is debatable.[13] Primary hyperaldosteronism may be more prevalent than previously recognized, with 8% to 32% of patients reported depending upon the population of patients screened. It should clearly be investigated among patients with refractory hypertension.[14] Hyperaldosteronism may occur with an isolated adrenal aldosteronoma, bilateral microscopic multinodular adrenal hyperplasia, macroscopic adrenal hyperplasia, a genetic form called glucocorticoid remediable hyperaldosteronism, or even adrenal carcinoma. Spontaneous hypokalemia in a patient with hypertension should suggest primary hyperaldosteronism, but this is not invariably present. Catecholamine levels may also be abnormal. Primary hyperaldosteronism is confirmed by a failure to inhibit aldosterone levels in the urine or plasma with sodium loading.

Renal Disease

Although essential hypertension is the most common form of hypertension, several specific causes do exist. Early identification of secondary hypertension is important because it may lead to cure or at least to a specific and much easier treatment regimen. Of these other causes, renal disease is the most prevalent. All types of renal disease have been associated with hypertension, although a direct relationship can be demonstrated only in cases of unilateral renal disease, in which the removal of the affected kidney cures the hypertension. This is clear in unilateral renal arteriostenosis. *Renovascular hypertension* results from the overproduction of renin secondary to reduced blood flow through the stenotic renal artery. The increased levels of renin lead to activation of the angiotensin pathway and resultant hypertension. The response to surgery is best predicted by determining renin levels in selective renal veins. If the renin level in the affected kidney is more than 50% higher than the level in the normal kidney, a complete or partial cure of the hypertension can be anticipated.

Another vascular lesion associated with arterial stenosis and hypertension is fibromuscular dysplasia of the renal arteries.[15,16] This disease is predominant in

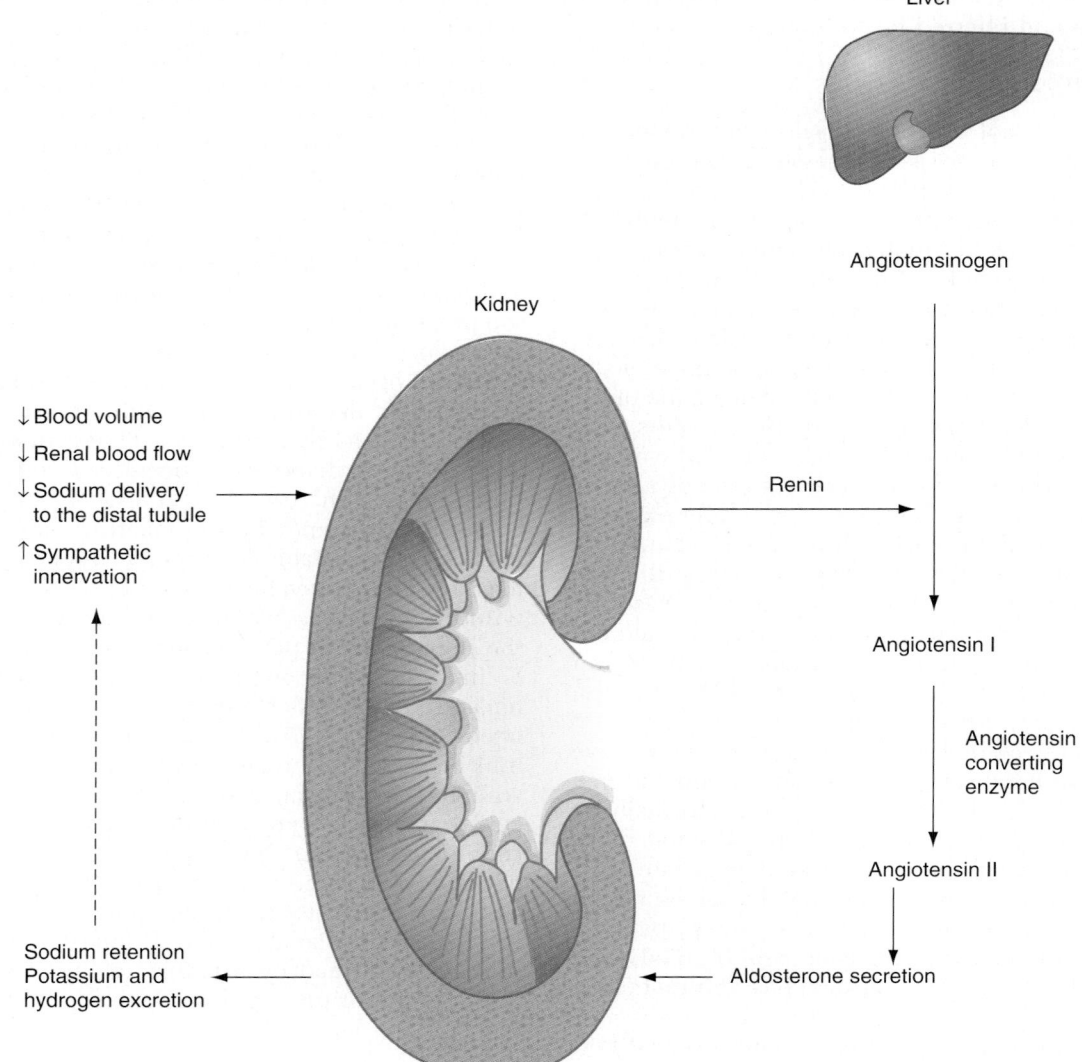

Liver

Angiotensinogen

Kidney

↓ Blood volume
↓ Renal blood flow
↓ Sodium delivery
    to the distal tubule
↑ Sympathetic
    innervation

Renin

Angiotensin I

Angiotensin
converting
enzyme

Angiotensin II

Sodium retention
Potassium and
hydrogen excretion

Aldosterone secretion

Figure 83-1. The renin-angiotensin-aldosterone axis. Solid lines represent stimulation, and dashed lines imply negative feedback mechanisms.

young white women, and flank bruits are often present. The various types affect different areas of the renal arteries. The result is progressive hypertension. Neither pharmacologic therapy nor surgical revision offers a cure, but both treatments reduce the progress of the disease process and help preserve functional renal mass.

Primary renal disease can produce hypertension, but the exact mechanism remains unknown. Up to 70% of patients with chronic pyelonephritis have elevated BP. Local ischemia within the kidney is suspected as the cause of hypertension. Some authors have suggested local microvascular renal disease as the final common pathway underlying essential hypertension as well.[14] Hypertension in patients with nonspecific glomerulonephritis may result from arteriolar lesions producing ischemia at the level of the individual nephron. With the exception of renin-secreting renal tumors, the exact cause of hypertension associated with the various nephropathies has not been determined.

Arterial Disease

Abnormalities of the large arteries can also produce hypertension. Although uncommon, coarctation of the aorta is an important cause of secondary hypertension, and early surgical intervention can greatly improve the patient's prognosis.[17] The triad of upper extremity hypertension, a systolic murmur best heard over the back, and delayed femoral pulses should alert the examiner to the diagnosis of coarctation. Hypertension associated with coarctation appears to result from the combined effects of mechanical obstruction and activation of the renin-angiotensin system.[18] Early diagnosis of coarctation is important because surgical repair has demonstrated a consistent and sustained lowering of BP. In adult patients, renal artery stenosis is an important cause of accelerated onset of significant hypertension, and renal artery ultrasonography or angiography is advisable (on an ambulatory basis) for patients with this type of onset of disease.

Loss of elasticity in the larger arteries associated with the aging process produces systolic hypertension as well as elevations in pulse pressure. Arteriosclerosis from the deposition of collagen and smooth muscle hypertrophy plays a major role in the age-dependent stiffness of the central vasculature. Previously, elevated systolic pressure was not considered significant and frequently was not treated. The current literature strongly suggests that isolated systolic hypertension is associated with an increased risk of stroke, heart disease, and renal failure and should be treated. The cause of reduced elasticity in the arteries associated with isolated systolic hypertension has not been fully determined. Endothelial dysfunction that develops over time with both aging and hypertension may play a critical role in this process. Other factors that decrease central vascular compliance include high dietary salt intake, tobacco use, elevated homocysteine levels, and diabetes.

Glucocorticoids

Excessive glucocorticoids are associated with hypertension, and the most common cause is iatrogenic steroid therapy. Endogenous overproduction is rare and results from excessive adrenocorticotropic hormone (ACTH) production by a pituitary tumor, ectopic ACTH production by a nonpituitary tumor, or glucocorticoid production by tumors of the adrenal cortex. These patients show other signs and symptoms of excessive glucocorticoids, including centripetal fat distribution, striae, easy bruising, muscular weakness, and poor healing. The hypertension associated with hyperadrenalism is usually not severe and can be controlled by treating the underlying disease process.

Thyroid and Parathyroid Disease

Both hyper- and hypothyroidism are associated with elevations in BP. In thyroid storm, patients are usually hypertensive and tachycardic and β-blockade is a mainstay of the acute management. Patients with hypothyroidism also present with hypertension as well as the other characteristic findings. Treatment of the hypothyroidism usually results in correction of the hypertensive state. Hypertension with hypercalcemia suggests hyperparathyroidism, which is another rare secondary cause of hypertension.

Sleep Apnea

Both obstructive and central forms of sleep apnea are associated with hypertension. Apnea itself is associated with a significant increase in BP. Approximately 50% of patients with sleep apnea have daytime hypertension, but many have other risk factors for hypertension such as obesity or alcohol consumption. Studies suggest that treatment of nocturnal hypoventilation may improve daytime BPs.[19,20]

Pheochromocytoma

Pheochromocytomas are responsible for less than 1% of cases of hypertension. More than 90% of these patients are curable with early diagnosis. Pheochromocytomas produce catecholamines and arise from cells of the sympathetic nervous system. The most common site is the adrenal medulla. Patients with neurofibromatosis (von Recklinghausen's disease) have an increased incidence of pheochromocytoma. Pheochromocytoma, medullary carcinoma of the thyroid, and parathyroid adenomas form the triad of multiple endocrine neoplasia (adenomatosis), type 2.

The characteristic feature of pheochromocytoma is paroxysms of hypertension associated with palpitations, tachycardia, malaise, apprehension, and sweating. Many patients have a persistently elevated BP interspersed with episodes of greater hypertension that occur sporadically and vary greatly in severity, frequency, and duration. These episodes may be related to physical and emotional stress, eating, position, or even micturition. A prodrome of apprehension and nonspecific abdominal pain progressing to headache, palpitations, and angina may be seen. Because of the episodic nature of this syndrome, the patient is often dismissed, and a diagnosis of hyperventilation syndrome or anxiety attack is made. An excessively elevated BP associated with these symptoms is enough to suggest a pheochromocytoma. Patients may also display increased BP when treated with β-blocking agents (β-blockers).

The diagnosis is confirmed with elevated urinary levels of catecholamines, metanephrines, and vanillylmandelic acid.[21] Usually in pheochromocytoma, all parameters are increased to more than twice the normal levels. Provocative pharmacologic testing to diagnose pheochromocytoma is no longer necessary. Treatment consists of α-blockade to control hypertension and subsequent β-blockade for the control of cardiac dysrhythmias. After the hypertension is adequately controlled, the tumor should be surgically removed.

Other Causes

The ingestion of foods containing large amounts of *tyramine* can cause episodic hypertension (Box 83-1). Tyramine causes release of norepinephrine stored in nerve endings. This response is normally transient; tyramine is rapidly destroyed by monoamine oxidase. Problems arise if a patient is being treated with a monoamine oxidase inhibitor (MAOI), which protects tyramine from destruction. Relatively small amounts of tyramine can cause severe and prolonged hypertension. A number of therapeutic agents can also induce a hypertensive crisis in patients taking MAOIs. These include meperidine, the amphetamines, ephedrine, reserpine, guanethidine, and tricyclic antidepressants. The hypertension can be controlled by using an α-blocking agent (α-blocker) such as phentolamine.

Excess catecholamine effect can result from the acute withdrawal of clonidine or β-blocker therapy.[22] *Clonidine* acts centrally as an α-adrenoreceptor agonist. The sudden withdrawal of this agent may result in catecholamine excess and severe hypertension 16 to 48 hours later. Many of the symptoms associated with clonidine withdrawal are similar to those of pheochro-

BOX 83-1. Foods and Drugs Causing Hypertensive Crisis in Patients Taking Monoamine Oxidase Inhibitors

Foods*
Natural or aged cheeses
Pickled herring
Chicken liver
Coffee in large amounts
Chocolate
Broad beans
Beer, wine
Snails
Yeast
Citrus fruits
Cream

Drugs
Sympathomimetic amines (e.g., amphetamines)
Methyldopa
Dopamine
Tryptophan
Reserpine
Guanethidine
Tricyclic antidepressants

---

*All contain significant amounts of tyramine except for broad beans, which contain dopamine.

BOX 83-2. Conditions Defining Hypertensive Crisis

Accelerated or Malignant Hypertension
Hypertensive encephalopathy
Microangiopathic hemolytic anemia
Acute renal failure

Aortic Dissection

Eclampsia/Preeclampsia

Severe Hypertension in the Setting of:
Myocardial ischemia
Left ventricular failure
Uncontrolled hemorrhage
Systemic reperfusion therapy for stroke or myocardial infarction

mocytoma, including anxiety, tremor, palpitations, and severe headache. Urinary catecholamine levels are markedly elevated. Treatment consists of restarting clonidine therapy or using α-blockers. This characteristic limits clonidine's usefulness as an antihypertensive agent in noncompliant patients.

Alcoholism or alcohol withdrawal may precipitate hypertension. Use of nonsteroidal anti-inflammatory agents, including the selective cyclooxygenase 2 inhibitors, may inhibit the antihypertensive effects of diuretics and drugs that work on the renin-angiotensin system.[23,24]

Emergency Department Presentation

Hypertension is seen in the emergency department in the following four general ways:
1. "Hypertensive emergency" or "hypertensive crisis" with acute end-organ ischemia
2. "Hypertensive urgency," a historical term related to arbitrarily elevated BP with nonspecific symptoms
3. Mild hypertension without end-organ ischemia
4. Transient hypertension related to anxiety or the primary complaint

CLINICAL PRESENTATION OF HYPERTENSIVE EMERGENCIES

A small number of hypertensive patients present with a true hypertensive emergency. BP is usually markedly elevated and there is evidence of *acute* dysfunction in the cardiovascular, neurologic, or renal organ system (Box 83-2). These conditions are true medical emergencies and mandate reduction of BP within 1 hour.[2,25]

In the past, the range of hypertensive emergencies included patients who presented with any emergent condition associated with a marked elevation of BP and patients without end-organ damage. The elevated BP in these patients is often a physiologic response to an acute condition, and aggressive treatment for hypertension may actually *increase* morbidity and mortality. This is especially true for patients with acute intracranial events.[26]

Hypertensive Encephalopathy

Throughout the normal range of BP, cerebral blood flow is maintained by fluctuations in the vascular tone of the cerebral resistance vessels known as *autoregulation*. Hypertensive encephalopathy is an uncommon syndrome resulting from an abrupt, sustained rise of BP that exceeds the limits of cerebral autoregulation of the small resistance arteries in the brain. Above a mean arterial pressure (MAP) of approximately 160 mm Hg, autoregulation may be unable to control cerebral blood flow, resulting in vasospasm, ischemia, increased vascular permeability, punctate hemorrhages, and brain edema. Immediate reduction of BP by 30% to 40% reverses the vasospasm. *Excessive reduction of BP must be avoided* to prevent increasing cerebral ischemia. In normal humans, autoregulation operates above an MAP of about 60 mm Hg. In patients with uncontrolled hypertension, however, the level of autoregulation is elevated, cerebral ischemia may occur at a much higher MAP, and BP reduction should generally not take the MAP below 100 mm Hg.

Hypertensive encephalopathy is (1) acute in onset and (2) reversible. Patients present with severe headaches, vomiting, drowsiness, and confusion. Seizures, blindness, focal neurologic deficits, or coma may occur. Papilledema is usually present, along with significant hypertensive retinopathy. Differential diagnosis includes strokes and intracranial hemorrhage (ICH), meningoencephalitis, brain tumors, and metabolic coma. Careful neurologic examination often differentiates between a space-occupying lesion and hypertensive encephalopathy because focal deficits from hypertensive encephalopathy usually do not follow a singular anatomic pattern. They may occur on opposite sides of the body or may have a patchy distribution. Computed tomography is usually normal, and the electroencephalogram shows only nonspecific abnormalities. The cerebrospinal fluid is clear, with an increased opening pressure and normal or increased protein.

Hypertensive encephalopathy is a true medical emergency; untreated patients develop increasing coma, and death may ensue within a few hours. The rapid *measured* reduction of BP is mandatory. The standard treatment regimen is intravenous (IV) nitroprusside with a careful reduction of the MAP by 25% or to a minimum diastolic pressure of 110 mm Hg over an hour. Use of an oral or nontitratable agent may result in excessive reduction of BP and irreversible cerebral ischemia. The standard agent in the United States has long been sodium nitroprusside, but fenoldopam mesylate and labetalol are now widely used, with nicardipine and enalaprilat gaining favor in some circles. Although fast-acting nifedipine has been widely used in the past for symptomatic hypertension, numerous serious adverse effects related to uncontrolled hypotension and sympathetic release have been reported, and its use in acute hypertension is contraindicated.[27-29]

All patients with hypertensive encephalopathy should be hospitalized, and establishment of an arterial line for BP monitoring is desirable.

Malignant Hypertension

Malignant (*accelerated*) hypertension is severe hypertension associated with evidence of acute and progressive damage to end organs. This syndrome can occur at any time in the clinical course of hypertension. The diastolic BP is usually greater than 130 mm Hg. Readings below this level are seldom associated with either malignant hypertension or hypertensive encephalopathy, although rarely either can occur with diastolic pressures as low as 110 mm Hg. *The vast majority of patients with diastolic pressures above 130 mm Hg do not develop either of these clinical syndromes.* Malignant hypertension affects only 1% of the hypertensive population.[25]

The pathologic process begins when a rapid, sustained rise in BP overwhelms the high-pressure autoregulatory mechanism, causing the small arterioles to dilate. As these vessels dilate, pressure in the proximal capillary beds increases, and fluid leaks into the tissues. The arterioles may rupture and leak plasma and blood, resulting in fibrin deposition into their walls. This combination of necrosis of myofibrils in smooth muscle cells, leaking of plasma, and fibrin deposition in the walls of arterioles is *fibrinoid necrosis* and is responsible for end-organ damage. These changes within the small arterioles are directly visible in the retina as linear hemorrhages dissecting along nerve fibers. The disruption of the arteriolar wall causes obstruction of the vessel and ischemia downstream. In the retina this produces a cotton-wool spot that consists of swollen, ischemic axons. The aggregation of materials within the ischemic axons produces a nuclear-like structure termed the *cytoid body*. Hard exudates, which consist of lipid deposits located deep in the retina, are also a common finding. These fine, punctate, shiny lesions can be distinguished from cotton-wool spots, which are larger and have blurred edges and a more diffuse appearance.

Patients with malignant hypertension appear ill and often present with complaints of severe headache, blurred vision, dyspnea, and chest pain or with symptoms of uremia. If untreated, it may result in acute renal failure, severe cardiac decompensation, MI, hypertensive cerebral hemorrhage, or hypertensive encephalopathy.

The diagnosis of malignant hypertension cannot be made on the basis of BP readings alone. In addition to elevated BP, these patients must demonstrate evidence of acute end-organ damage as a result of the hypertension. The physical examination may reveal an enlarged left ventricle and rales at the lung bases. Marked retinal findings are often present, including linear hemorrhages and cotton-wool patches. Acute elevation of blood urea nitrogen and serum creatinine or the presence of hematuria indicates involvement of the kidneys. Rarely, the blood smear reveals red cell fragments, and fibrin degradation products are elevated, giving a clinical picture compatible with microangiopathic hemolytic anemia. Left ventricular hypertrophy and strain are usually seen on the electrocardiogram (ECG). The chest radiograph may reveal cardiomegaly and evidence of congestive heart failure.

Malignant hypertension is treated by the judicious lowering of MAP by 25% of pretreatment levels over the initial minutes to hours, then toward a target of 160/100 over 2 to 6 hours, avoiding excessive falls in pressure that may precipitate renal, cerebral, or coronary ischemia.[2,25,30]

All patients with malignant hypertension should be hospitalized, and invasive BP monitoring may be preferable. An easily titratable agent is used, most often sodium nitroprusside, to avoid any episodes of hypotension.

Stroke Syndromes

Hypertension is often associated with stroke syndromes.[31] In most of these patients, elevated BP is the physiologic response to the stroke itself and is not the immediate cause. About 85% of strokes are nonhemorrhagic, and most patients who have embolic or thrombotic strokes without an associated hemorrhage do not sustain substantially elevated BP. These patients have mild to moderate hypertension that has little effect on the clinical course. In patients with long-standing hypertension, rapid reduction of the BP may further reduce cerebral blood flow and cause increased ischemia.

Except in cases of stroke caused by aortic dissection, antihypertensive therapy is not indicated and may be harmful. Some have recommended careful antihypertensive treatment for patients with persistent, extreme elevations of BP after a stroke (e.g., diastolic pressure >140 or MAP >130 mm Hg), but data are lacking. The best current advice is to limit reductions in BP for acute stroke patients to circumstances in which the BP elevation is causing injury to another end organ, for example, myocardial ischemia. In these cases, the BP should be lowered cautiously to mitigate the effects on the other end organ, but the ischemic neurologic deficit must not increase. When fibrinolytic therapy is administered, significant elevations of BP greatly increase the risk of secondary ICH, and patients with persistent pressures greater than 185/110 should not receive thrombolytic therapy.[29]

Patients with ICH often have a profound, reactive elevation of BP. In most patients with ICH, hypertension is secondary to the increased intracranial pressure (ICP) and to irritation of the autonomic nervous system. This type of hypertension often disappears rapidly and has little effect on clinical outcome. Deterioration in most patients with ICH results from hemorrhagic enlargement or edema. Data to support the pharmacologic lowering of BP in patients with ICH are lacking.[31] Persistent hypertension is associated with a poorer functional outcome after ICH, and traditionally many centers treat hypertension after ICH. Because cerebral perfusion pressure (CPP) depends on systemic pressure, this practice may not be beneficial. Although no conclusive evidence indicates that treating hypertension in the acute period after ICH is beneficial, modest reductions in BP (e.g., 20% reduction in MAP) have not been clearly associated with a worse outcome and may be advisable after discussion with the vascular neurosurgery consultant.

If BP reduction is pursued in these patients, labetalol is the agent of choice. Labetalol and other adrenergic blockers shift cerebral autoregulation to lower pressures in patients with intracranial mass lesions. This shift preserves cerebral blood flow at lower pressures. Adrenergic blockers also preserve reactivity to carbon dioxide partial pressure (P_{CO_2}).[31] ACE inhibitors also shift autoregulation but have not been extensively studied in patients with ICH or elevated ICP. Vasodilators, such as nitroprusside, increase ICP, impair cerebrovascular reactivity to changes in P_{CO_2}, and exacerbate any decrease in CPP for a given level of BP reduction.

Pulmonary Edema

Most patients with congestive heart failure have some degree of increased peripheral vascular resistance (PVR) and resultant hypertension; this is a normal response. The degree of BP elevation is moderate and does not represent a medical emergency. When poorly controlled, however, long-standing hypertension produces myocardial hypertrophy, which continues until the hypertrophy can no longer overcome the increased PVR; then the left ventricle begins to fail and dilates.

In most patients with this combination, the hypertension results from increased PVR caused by elevated catecholamines associated with the stress of pulmonary edema. With standard treatment of pulmonary edema, including morphine, nitrates, oxygen, ACE inhibitors, and furosemide, catecholamine levels fall and BP returns rapidly toward normal. In a small number of patients, pulmonary edema results from an abrupt, severe elevation of BP that precipitates acute left ventricular failure. The BP must be lowered to reverse this process. Nitroglycerin is usually the first drug used, but if it does not adequately reduce BP, nitroprusside should be the next choice. Nitroprusside does not cause sodium retention; it improves cardiac function, especially in the failing heart, and can be carefully titrated and rapidly reversed. ACE inhibition has also been used successfully as an adjunct in the acute treatment of pulmonary edema.[32,33] Although pressure often falls significantly with treatment of congestive heart failure, stroke syndromes can occur as a consequence of hypotension occurring during the treatment of acute pulmonary edema.[34]

Cardiac Ischemia

Hypertension and angina are often found together. If severe hypertension is present with concurrent angina, immediate lowering of BP is indicated to prevent myocardial damage. In most of these patients, nitroglycerin and an IV β-blocker, such as metoprolol, are the agents of choice. ACE inhibitors may be a useful adjunct and have also been shown to reduce mortality in patients with MI. Calcium channel blockers may be a useful alternative for patients unable to tolerate β-adrenergic blockade because of bronchospasm. Nitroprusside may induce a reflex tachycardia and must be used with caution in patients with cardiac ischemia. With systemic fibrinolytic therapy, the risk of ICH requires aggressive BP control.[35]

Renal Failure

The most important cardiovascular complication of chronic renal failure (CRF) is hypertension.[36,37] Uncontrolled hypertension accelerates the development of cardiovascular problems, which are the most common cause of death in both dialysis and transplant patients. Hypertension also causes further damage to diseased kidneys. Hypertension may appear at any time during the course of CRF and occurs in more than 80% of patients with advanced renal failure. Glomerular disease is associated with a higher incidence of hypertension than is tubulointerstitial disease. In the absence of hypertension, CRF worsens more slowly, and if hypertension is present but controlled, the progression of CRF can be delayed. Patients with renal failure secondary to malignant hypertension often demonstrate a transient worsening of renal function during their initial treatment period. After this initial period, renal function improves.

The primary cause of hypertension for patients with CRF is an actual or relative increase in extracellular volume secondary to sodium retention, as well as activation of the renin-angiotensin system in diseased kidneys. Glomerular disease is associated with greater sodium retention than tubulointerstitial disease. Diuretics to improve fluid balance and ACE inhibitors, angiotensin receptor blockers, or calcium channel blockers should be the first-line agents to control hypertension in patients with renal failure.[38] Patients with

CRF are frequently seen in the emergency department. If their BP is significantly elevated, the managing physician should be notified and the antihypertensive regimen adjusted.

Severe elevation of BP may lead to acute renal failure or may exacerbate CRF. Immediate reduction of BP is required. Nitroprusside is the drug of choice, although the IV calcium channel blocker nicardipine is a reasonable alternative.[27]

Pregnancy

Hypertension is one of the most common complications of pregnancy, involving 5% to 10% of all pregnancies (see Chapters 177 and 178). Antihypertensive agents may be needed but in most patients can be delayed until hospital admission. The exceptions are those women with severe preeclampsia or eclampsia, both of which represent hypertensive emergencies and can occur without an extreme elevation of BP. Any acute elevation of the diastolic BP above 100 mm Hg in the pregnant patient represents a true hypertensive emergency. The treatment of hypertensive emergencies of pregnancy should include reduction of BP, prevention and control of seizures, and early obstetric consultation. Although it may cause tachycardia and hypotension, the antihypertensive agent of choice in preeclampsia has classically been IV hydralazine.[39] Alternative antihypertensives include labetalol, nicardipine, and occasionally nitroprusside. Nitroprusside is relatively contraindicated because of the potential for accumulation of cyanide in utero. Because of this potential complication, nitroprusside should be reserved for those patients in whom other agents have failed. Oral nifedipine has also been used in this setting although, as in other conditions, overshoot hypotension has been observed.[40] Preeclampsia and eclampsia are true hypertensive emergencies and are discussed in Chapter 177.

Aortic Dissection

Aortic dissection is associated with a history of hypertension (see Chapter 84). Medical therapy consists of reducing BP to limit the extent of the dissection. The goals of medical therapy are to lower the BP to a systolic level of 100 to 120 mm Hg and to reduce the ejection force of the heart. The drugs of choice for reducing BP in patients with aortic dissection are a β-blocker to control tachycardia and a vasodilator such as nicardipine, nitroprusside, or fenoldopam. The combined α/β-blocker labetalol has been used successfully.[25,27]

MANAGEMENT OF HYPERTENSIVE EMERGENCIES

Vasodilators

Sodium Nitroprusside

Nitroprusside (Nipride, Nitropress) is a powerful vasodilator, with a direct effect on the smooth muscle of both resistance and capacitance vessels. Nitroprus-

Table 83-1. Summary of Drugs of Choice in the Treatment of Hypertensive Emergencies

Emergency	Drug(s) of Choice	Alternative or Second-Line Drugs
Accelerated hypertension, hypertensive encephalopathy	Nitroprusside, fenoldopam	Labetalol or nicardipine
Intracranial hemorrhage	Labetalol	Nitroprusside, nicardipine
Acute pulmonary edema	Nitroglycerin, nitroprusside	Fenoldopam, ACE inhibitor
Cardiac ischemia	Nitroglycerin, β-blockers	Nitroprusside, labetalol
Aortic dissection	Nitroprusside + β-blockers	Labetalol
Adrenergic crises	Phentolamine, nitroprusside + β-blockers	Labetalol
Eclampsia, preeclampsia	Labetalol	Nicardipine, hydralazine

ACE, angiotensin-converting enzyme.

side is considered the agent of choice for most hypertensive emergencies (Table 83-1). Its rate of onset is extremely rapid, and its duration of action is very short. Nitroprusside does not worsen angina. The cardiac response depends on the state of myocardial function. Because of the reduction of preload by venous dilation, the cardiac output often improves if congestive heart failure or borderline myocardial function is present. Because nitroprusside is a cerebral vasodilator, it may increase ICP secondary to increased cerebral blood flow. Nitroprusside is metabolized to thiocyanate and is excreted slowly by the kidneys. Cyanide is an intermediate metabolite, but cyanide toxicity is extremely rare. In the presence of renal failure or during prolonged nitroprusside therapy, the thiocyanate concentration may reach toxic levels of 10 mg/dL, and a clinical picture of weakness, hypoxia, nausea, tinnitus, muscle spasm, disorientation, and psychosis may develop. The prolonged use of nitroprusside may produce hypothyroidism by inhibition of iodine transport, and methemoglobinemia has occurred.

Nitroprusside must be used as an IV solution. As capacitance vessels dilate, the patient must be kept recumbent to prevent profound orthostatic hypotension. Because of nitroprusside's short half-life, stopping the infusion returns the BP to pretreatment levels within 1 to 10 minutes. The amount of BP reduction is dose related. Elderly patients and those receiving antihypertensive medications are more sensitive to nitroprusside's effects. In all patients the starting dose should be 0.25 to 1.0 µg/kg body weight per minute. The average dose required for the control of hypertension is 3.0 µg/kg/min. Dosages greater than 800 µg/min are seldom required and should not be used for long periods because of the accumulation of cyanide and thiocyanate. Patients treated with nitroprusside should be admitted to the intensive care unit for close monitoring of BP, preferably by an intra-arterial line. The drug should be diluted and given by an automatic infusion device. Nitroprusside is unstable in ultraviolet light, and the IV bag should be wrapped in opaque material. Only fresh solutions of nitroprusside less than 4 hours old should be used.

No type of hypertension has been found to be refractory to nitroprusside, although certain patients may not have an adequate response. Side effects are directly related to excessive vasodilation and resultant hypotension and can be avoided by careful monitoring of BP and regulation of infusion rate. Extreme caution must be taken to avoid the extravasation of nitroprusside because local necrosis can be severe. Nitroprusside has not been proved to be safe during pregnancy and should be avoided because of the potential effect of thiocyanate on fetal thyroid tissue, the risk of cyanide poisoning to the fetus, and the possibility of fetal methemoglobinemia.

Fenoldopam

Fenoldopam (Corlopam) is a peripheral dopamine-1 receptor agonist approved for the treatment of hypertensive emergencies. Dopamine-1 receptors are located postsynaptically in the systemic and renal vasculature and mediate systemic, renal, and mesenteric vasodilation as well as natriuresis. In contrast to treatment with nitroprusside, fenoldopam therapy improves renal function acutely in patients with malignant hypertension.[41] Fenoldopam does not cross the blood-brain barrier, has a rapid onset of action, and has an elimination half-life of 9 minutes.[42-44] Reflex tachycardia, flushing, and headache may be observed but hypotension occurs less often than with nitroprusside therapy.

The initial dose of fenoldopam is 0.1 µg/kg/min, and the dose is titrated in 0.1 µg/kg/min increments every 15 minutes until the desired effect is seen. The maximum recommended dose is 1.6 µg/kg/min. Fenoldopam represents a reasonable alternative to nitroprusside in the treatment of hypertensive emergencies without the concerns of light sensitivity and cyanide or thiocyanate toxicity and with a lower incidence of hypotensive episodes. Fenoldopam has been used in trials without invasive BP monitoring.[42]

Nitroglycerin

Nitroglycerin is a vasodilating agent that acts predominantly on the venous system, decreasing left ventricular end-diastolic pressure. At normal doses, nitroglycerin has little effect on arterial vascular tone and reduces BP by reducing preload and cardiac output. These effects may be undesirable in patients with impaired cerebral and renal perfusion. Nitroglycerin use should be limited to patients with cardiac ischemia or pulmonary edema. Nitroglycerin may be administered either sublingually or intravenously. Care must be exercised in patients with right ventricular dysfunction to avoid hypotension, which may exacerbate cardiac ischemia.

Hydralazine

Hydralazine (Apresoline) is a direct arteriolar vasodilator that was widely used in the past for the treatment of hypertensive emergencies of pregnancy. More recent studies, however, have shown that nicardipine and labetalol are superior agents in this setting.[45] The usual starting dose of hydralazine is 5 mg IV, with repeated doses of 5 to 10 mg every 20 minutes as needed to keep the diastolic pressure below 110 mm Hg. Typically, a latent period of 5 to 15 minutes is followed by a progressive and at times precipitous fall in BP lasting for up to 12 hours.[27] Hydralazine is also associated with significant reflex tachycardia, which may provoke angina in patients with coronary artery disease. Other common side effects are flushing, nausea, and headache. Chronic use is associated with a lupus-like syndrome that usually resolves with discontinuation of the medication.

β-Blockers

Labetalol

Labetalol (Trandate, Normodyne) is a selective α_1-blocker and nonselective β-blocker with a ratio of α/β-blockade between 1:3 and 1:7. It can be given orally or IV. Labetalol lowers BP by blockade of the α_1-receptors in vascular smooth muscle and the cardiac β-receptors. Because of the simultaneous β-receptor blockade, the usual reflex tachycardia associated with vasodilators does not occur. Labetalol does not cause the significant drop in cardiac output associated with other β-blockers. Although the oral administration of labetalol is less likely to produce orthostatic hypotension, IV use is marked by profound orthostatic changes. After IV labetalol the patient should be kept in the supine position for several hours. Labetalol does not affect cerebral blood flow or renal function.[27,31] With IV labetalol, BP generally falls within 5 to 10 minutes, with maximum effect in 30 minutes.

The initial dose of labetalol is 20 mg infused over 2 minutes. The BP should be rechecked every 5 minutes, and if only minimal change occurs, an additional dose is given every 10 minutes in increments of 20, 40, or 80 mg, to a total of 300 mg of labetalol, depending on BP response. Alternatively, after the initial loading dose an infusion may be started at 1 to 2 mg/min and titrated upward.[46,47] When given in this manner, labetalol appears to be a safe agent, with minimal adverse reactions. Because labetalol is a β-blocker, it is contraindicated in patients with congestive heart failure, heart block, and asthma. Labetalol also appears to be contraindicated for treatment of hypertension secondary to pheochromocytoma because it may result in paradoxical hypertension.

Labetalol therapy cannot be as closely controlled or as quickly reversed as nitroprusside therapy. However, use of labetalol may not require admission to an intensive care unit. Labetalol does not appear to exacerbate coronary artery disease or cause uncontrolled drops in BP.

The transition to oral therapy is smooth. After initial control of BP with IV labetalol, oral labetalol should be started when diastolic pressure rises 10 mm Hg. Labetalol is an excellent alternative to nitroprusside when constant BP monitoring is not feasible. Labetalol is superior as a single agent in patients who have aortic dissection or cardiac ischemia with intact left ventricular function.

Esmolol

Esmolol (Brevibloc) is an ultrashort-acting, selective β_1-blocker without intrinsic sympathomimetic activity. It typically has little effect on BP in normal individuals but may be very useful to control the reflex tachycardia seen with vasodilating agents such as nitroprusside. Esmolol is initiated with a loading dose of 500 µg/kg over 1 minute, followed by an infusion of 50 to 100 µg/kg/min. Maximal effect occurs in 5 minutes. If necessary, the patient receives another bolus of 500 µg/kg, and the drip is increased by 50 µg/kg/min. This cycle may be repeated every 5 minutes until the desired heart rate response is seen, up to a maximum dose of 300 µg/kg/min. Because the elimination half-life of esmolol is 9 minutes, any effect resolves within 30 minutes of discontinuing the infusion, with substantial recovery from β-blockade in 10 to 20 minutes. Contraindications are similar to those with labetalol, including cocaine overdose, pheochromocytoma, congestive heart failure, heart block, and reactive airway disease. Esmolol also causes tissue necrosis when extravasated into the soft tissue and may cause thrombophlebitis when infused into small veins.

α-Blockers

Phentolamine (Regitine) is an α-blocking agent used for the management of catecholamine-induced hypertensive crises (e.g., pheochromocytoma, MAOI crisis, cocaine overdose). Phentolamine is usually given IV in 1- to 5-mg boluses, although it may be given as an infusion at a rate of 5 to 10 µg/kg/min.[27,30] The effect is immediate and may last up to 15 minutes. Reflex tachycardia may be seen. When the BP is under control, oral *phenoxybenzamine*, a long-acting α-blocker, may be used.

Nicardipine

Nicardipine (Cardene) is a parenteral dihydropyridine calcium channel blocker that has become very popular in the treatment of postoperative hypertension. Nicardipine is titratable, is less negatively inotropic, and induces less tachycardia than nifedipine. Nicardipine acts predominantly as a vasodilator, but as with other calcium channel blockers, caution must be used when it is administered to patients with left ventricular failure. Nicardipine is administered as an infusion beginning at 5 mg/hr, increasing the infusion rate every 15 minutes until the desired reduction of BP has been achieved, to a maximum dose of 15 mg/hr. Onset of action is 5 to 15 minutes and duration of action 4 to 6 hours. As with labetalol, an oral form may facilitate the transition from acute to chronic therapy.

Nicardipine is heavily metabolized in the liver, and caution must be used in patients with cirrhosis. Nicardipine decreases the glomerular filtration rate in patients with compromised renal function, a trait shared by nitroprusside. As with the other vasodilators, headache, flushing, and tachycardia are the most common adverse reactions seen with nicardipine. Nicardipine has been best studied in pregnant patients and in the settings of postoperative and malignant hypertension, where it appears to be a less toxic alternative to nitroprusside.[2,27,30]

Enalaprilat and Enalapril

Enalaprilat (Vasotec) is a parenteral active metabolite of the ACE inhibitor enalapril. This drug has been studied in limited numbers of patients with true hypertensive emergencies. Hypotension has not been frequently reported with the use of enalaprilat, but caution should be used in patients who may be volume depleted. The acute dose is 0.625 to 5 mg administered as a single bolus. Peak effects generally occur in 15 minutes but may be delayed for hours. The response is not dose related, and one study showed an average drop in MAP of 35% at all doses and a 60% response rate.[48] Although no adverse effects were seen in the study, which excluded patients older than 80 and with known renovascular disease, such a significant drop in MAP might exceed the limits of vascular autoregulation in some patients. In fact, azotemia has been reported among older patients in studies of ACE inhibition after MI.[49]

Adverse effects that may be seen with ACE inhibitors such as enalaprilat include idiopathic angioedema, cough, and renal failure. Renal failure has been classically described in patients with bilateral renovascular disease. ACE inhibitors are considered toxic in the first trimester of pregnancy.

CLINICAL PRESENTATION OF AND MANAGEMENT OF HYPERTENSIVE URGENCY

Elevated BP without evidence of progressive end-organ involvement rarely mandates urgent antihypertensive therapy.[2] These patients appear to do well with a gradual lowering of BP on an ambulatory basis, without the inherent risks of cerebral and myocardial ischemia seen with acute reduction. It is unnecessary to lower BP acutely in the emergency department for patients with so-called hypertensive urgencies, and a growing body of literature suggests that this practice may actually cause increased risk to the patient.[50]

Patients with elevated BP who are asymptomatic or have nonspecific symptoms require an appropriate evaluation to rule out progressive end-organ disease, including a thorough history and physical examination paying special attention to the cardiovascular, funduscopic, and neurologic systems. Depending on the pre-

Table 83-2. Recommendations for Ambulatory Blood Pressure Therapy*

Blood Pressure Classification	Systolic Blood Pressure (mm Hg)	Diastolic Blood Pressure (mm Hg)	Lifestyle Modification	Initial Drug Therapy	
				Without Compelling Indication	*With Compelling Indication*
Normal	<120	and <80	Encourage		
Prehypertension	120-139	or 80-89	Yes	No antihypertensive drug indicated.	Drug(s) for compelling indications.†
Stage 1 hypertension	140-159	or 90-99	Yes	Thiazide-type diuretics for most. May consider ACEI, ARB, BB, CCB, or combination.	Drug(s) for the compelling indications.† Other antihypertensive drugs (diuretics, ACEI, ARB, BB, CCB) as needed.
Stage 2 hypertension	≥160	or ≥100	Yes	Two-drug combination for most‡ (usually thiazide-type diuretic and ACEI or ARB or BB or CCB).	

*Treatment determined by highest blood pressure category.
†Treat patients with chronic kidney disease or diabetes to blood pressure goal of <130/80 mm Hg.
‡Initial combined therapy should be used cautiously in those at risk for orthostatic hypotension.
ACEI, angiotensin-converting enzyme inhibitor; ARB, angiotensin receptor blocker; BB, β-blocker; CCB, calcium channel blocker.
Modified from the Seventh Report of the Joint National Committee on Prevention, Detection, and Treatment of High Blood Pressure. JNC7 complete report. *Hypertension* 42:1206, 2003.

sentation, laboratory testing may be helpful, including a urinalysis and electrolyte panel to evaluate renal function. In patients without any history of renal disease, a normal urinalysis obviates the need for blood tests of renal function.[51] A chest radiograph and ECG are obtained to evaluate patients with chest pain or symptoms of cardiac dysfunction. If initial evaluation fails to show any acute end-organ damage and myocardial ischemic symptoms are not present, the patient may be referred for outpatient evaluation within 7 days.

In some patients it is evident that ongoing chronic pharmacologic therapy is indicated. In the ambulatory setting the decision to initiate pharmacologic therapy for well-documented hypertension must be based on the degree of hypertension (Table 83-2). These recommendations are not without controversy.[2,52-54] In certain situations, it may be advisable to initiate or substantially modify the outpatient treatment of hypertension when the patient has been compliant with therapy and the therapy is clearly significantly inadequate. These dosing or agent adjustments are best done by discussing the strategy to be employed with the physician who will be responsible for ongoing management and then arranging appropriate follow-up. Numerous agents are used for the treatment of hypertension (Table 83-3). Other available agents contain drugs from two or more drug classes. The initial agent should be easy to take, well tolerated, and affordable for the patient and should have good efficacy. Because these factors may vary from patient to patient, accurate prediction of results is impossible. The choice of initial therapy is primarily empirical, but general guidelines exist. Large population-based studies comparing different classes of antihypertensive agents have established the thiazide diuretics such as hydrochlorothiazide at 25 to 50 mg once a day as the first-line agent of choice in the absence of compelling indications for other classes of antihypertensives.[2,55-57] These agents are inexpensive,

well tolerated, and easy to take. Other more expensive agents have so far failed to show better efficacy in preventing the cardiovascular complications of hypertension.

β-Blockers should probably be the second choice unless contraindicated.[2,8,55-58] Common starting doses of generic β-blockers include atenolol 25 to 50 mg and metoprolol 50 mg once or twice daily.

The best agent for uncomplicated hypertension remains an object of intense study. For patients with other health problems, specific classes of drugs have been shown to be particularly beneficial; the comorbid conditions should guide antihypertensive therapy. For patients with intact left ventricular function and a history of MI, a β-blocker is the agent of choice. On the basis of evidence of increased mortality, such patients should not be treated with immediate-release dihydropyridine calcium channel blockers.[59] For patients with diabetes, ACE inhibitors have benefits with respect to the preservation of renal function beyond that seen with BP control alone. In diabetic patients as well as in those with a history of left ventricular failure, an ACE inhibitor should be the drug of choice. Elderly patients with isolated systolic hypertension may benefit from the addition of a long-acting calcium channel blocker when diuretic monotherapy fails. Patients with prostatism or dyslipidemia may benefit from α-blocker therapy, although a report from a large prospective trial comparing the thiazide diuretic chlorthalidone with three other types of therapy showed an increased incidence of congestive heart failure and stroke in the group treated with the α-blocker doxazosin.[60]

Mild or Transient Hypertension

A vast majority of the hypertension encountered in the emergency department is either transient or mild. The

Table 83-3. Antihypertensive Drugs*

Drug	Trade Name	Usual Dose Range, Total mg/day and Interval	Common Side Effects and Comments
Diuretics (Common)			Short-term: increases cholesterol and glucose levels; biochemical abnormalities: decreases potassium, sodium, and magnesium levels, increases uric acid and calcium levels; rare: blood dyscrasias, photosensitivity, pancreatitis, hyponatremia
Thiazides			
Chlorothiazide	Diuril	125-500 qd	
Chlorthalidone	Hygroton	12.5-50 qd	
Hydrochlorothiazide	HydroDIURIL, Microzide, Esidrix	12.5-50 qd	
Polythiazide	Renese	2-4 qd	
Indapamide	Lozol	1.25-5 qd	
Metolazone	Mykrox, Zaroxolyn	0.5-1 (b-tid) 2.5-5 qd	
Loop Diuretics			
Bumetanide	Bumex	0.5-4 b-tid	
Furosemide	Lasix	40-240 b-tid	
Torsemide	Demadex	3-100 q-bid	
Potassium-Sparing Agents			Hyperkalemia may occur
Amiloride hydrochloride	Midamor	5-10 qd	
Triamterene	Dyrenium	25-100 qd	
Aldosterone Receptor Blockers			
Spironolactone	Aldactone	25-100 qd	
Eplerenone	Inspra	50-100 q-bid	
Adrenergic Inhibitors			Postural hypotension
Central α-Agonists			Sedation, dry mouth, bradycardia, withdrawal hypertension
Reserpine		0.05-0.25 qd	
Clonidine hydrochloride	Catapres, Catapres-TTS	0.2-1.2 b-tid 0.1-0.3 weekly	
Guanabenz acetate	Wytensin	4-8 bid	
Guanfacine hydrochloride	Tenex	0.5-2 qd	
Methyldopa	Aldomet	250-1000 bid	(Hepatitis and lupus-like syndrome)
α-Blockers			Postural hypotension
Doxazosin mesylate	Cardura	1-16 qd	
Prazosin hydrochloride	Minipress	2-20 b-tid	
Terazosin hydrochloride	Hytrin	1-20 qd	
β-Blockers			Bronchospasm, bradycardia, heart failure, may mask insulin-induced hypoglycemia; less serious: impair peripheral circulation, insomnia, fatigue, decreased exercise tolerance, hypertriglyceridemia (except agents with intrinsic sympathomimetic activity)
Acebutolol[1,2]	Sectral	200-800 qd	
Atenolol[1]	Tenormin	25-100 q-bid	
Betaxolol[1]	Kerlone	5-20 qd	
Bisoprolol fumarate[1]	Zebeta	2.5-10 qd	
Metoprolol tartrate[1]	Lopressor	50-300 bid	
Metoprolol succinate[1]	Toprol-XL	50-300 qd	[1]β, selective
Nadolol	Corgard	40-320 qd	[2]Intrinsic sympathomimetic activity
Penbutolol sulfate[2]	Levatol	10-20 qd	
Pindolol[2]	Visken	10-60 bid	
Propranolol hydrochloride	Inderal	40-480 bid	
	Inderal LA	40-480 qd	
Timolol maleate	Blocadren	20-60 bid	
Combined α- and β-Blockers			Postural hypotension, bronchospasm
Carvedilol	Coreg	12.5-50 bid	
Labetalol hydrochloride	Normodyne, Trandate	200-1200 bid	
Direct Vasodilators			Headaches, fluid retention, tachycardia
Hydralazine hydrochloride	Apresoline	50-300 bid	(Lupus syndrome)
Minoxidil	Loniten	5-100 qd	(Hirsutism)
Calcium Antagonists			Conduction defects, worsening of systolic dysfunction, gingival hypertrophy
Nondihydropyridines			
Diltiazem hydrochloride	Cardizem SR	50-300 bid	
	Cardizem CD, Dilacor XR, Tiazac	5-100 qd	
Verapamil hydrochloride	Isoptin SR, Calan SR	90-480 bid	(Constipation)
	Verelan, Covera-HS	120-480 qd	
Dihydropyridines			Pedal edema, flushing, headache, gingival hypertrophy
Amlodipine besylate	Norvasc	2.5-10 qd	
Felodipine	Plendil	2.5-20 qd	
Isradipine	DynaCirc	5-20 bid	
	DynaCirc CR	5-20 qd	
Nicardipine	Cardene SR	60-90 bid	
Nifedipine	Procardia XL, Adalat CC	30-120 qd	
Nisoldipine	Sular	20-60 qd	

Table 83-3. Antihypertensive Drugs*—cont'd

Drug	Trade Name	Usual Dose Range, Total mg/day and Interval	Common Side Effects and Comments
ACE Inhibitors			Common: cough; rare: angioedema, hyperkalemia, rash, loss of taste, leukopenia
Benazepril hydrochloride	Lotensin	5-40 q-bid	
Captopril (G)	Capoten	25-150 b-tid	
Enalapril maleate	Vasotec	5-40 q-bid	
Fosinopril sodium	Monopril	10-40 q-bid	
Lisinopril	Prinivil, Zestril	5-40 qd	
Moexipril	Univasc	7.5-15 q-bid	
Perindopril	Aceon	4-8 q-bid	
Quinapril hydrochloride	Accupril	5-80 q-bid	
Ramipril	Altace	1.25-20 q-bid	
Trandolapril	Mavik	1-4 qd	
Angiotensin II Receptor Blockers			Angioedema (very rare), hyperkalemia
Candesartan	Atacand	8-32 qd	
Eprosartan	Teveten	400-800 q-bid	
Losartan potassium	Cozaar	25-100 q-bid	
Valsartan	Diovan	80-320 qd	
Irbesartan	Avapro	150-300 qd	
Olmesartan	Benicar	20-40 qd	
Telmisartan	Micardis	20-80 qd	

*This list is only of single agents; multiple combination agents are also manufactured.

most common causes of transient hypertension are pain and anxiety. In these patients, end-organ ischemia is highly unlikely, and treatment of the primary process results in prompt resolution of their acute hypertension. For this reason, all patients without evident complications should be allowed to rest for 60 minutes and have their pressure reassessed or should simply be referred to their primary care physicians for repeated measurement days to a few weeks later. Most patients, even those with poorly treated chronic hypertension, show an improvement in their BP with watchful waiting.[4]

KEY CONCEPTS

- The presence or absence of acute target organ damage determines whether a hypertensive emergency exists.

- All patients with persistent and marked elevations in BP (e.g., diastolic BP over 110 mm Hg or systolic BP over 200 mm Hg) should be carefully evaluated for the presence of acute end-organ ischemia.

- The therapeutic goal for treatment of the majority of hypertensive emergencies is careful reduction of the BP with a titratable agent. Mean arterial pressure should be reduced by no more than 20% to 25% over minutes to hours. The diastolic pressure generally should not fall below 100 to 110 mm Hg. The exceptions to these rules may be patients with hypertensive complications of pregnancy, hypertensive emergencies of the pediatric population, and patients with aortic dissection.

- Patients without acute end-organ ischemia rarely require urgent management of their BP and may be safely referred for outpatient follow-up.

REFERENCES

1. Burt VL, et al: Prevalence of hypertension in the US adult population. Results from the Third National Health and Nutrition Examination Survey, 1988-1991. *Hypertension* 25:305, 1995.
2. Chobanian AV, et al: Seventh report of the Joint National Committee on Prevention, Detection, Evaluation, and Treatment of High Blood Pressure. *Hypertension* 42:1206, 2003.
3. Chiang WK, Jamshahi B: Asymptomatic hypertension in the ED. *Am J Emerg Med* 16:701, 1998.
4. Pitts SR, Adams RP: Emergency department hypertension and regression to the mean. *Ann Emerg Med* 31:214, 1998.
5. Kannel WB, Schwartz MJ, McNamara PM: Blood pressure and risk of coronary heart disease: The Framingham study. *Dis Chest* 56:43, 1969.
6. Cushman WC: The clinical significance of systolic hypertension. *Am J Hypertens* 11:182S, 1998.
7. He J, Whelton PK: Elevated systolic blood pressure and risk of cardiovascular and renal disease: Overview of evidence from observational epidemiologic studies and randomized controlled trials. *Am Heart J* 138:211, 1999.
8. Abate G, et al: Treatment of hypertension in the elderly. *Cardiologia* 44:427, 1999.
9. Bartosh SM, Aronson AJ: Childhood hypertension. An update on etiology, diagnosis, and treatment. *Pediatr Clin North Am* 46:235, 1999.
10. Kornitzer M, Dramaix M, De Backer G: Epidemiology of risk factors for hypertension: Implications for prevention and therapy. *Drugs* 57:695, 1999.
11. Allikmets K, Parik T, Viigimaa M: The renin-angiotensin system in essential hypertension: Associations with cardiovascular risk. *Blood Press* 8:70, 1999.
12. Brown NJ, Vaughan DE: Angiotensin-converting enzyme inhibitors. *Circulation* 97:1411, 1998.
13. Ganguly A: Primary aldosteronism. *N Engl J Med* 339:1828, 1998.

14. Oparil S, Zaman MA, Calhoun DA: Pathogenesis of hypertension. *Ann Intern Med* 139:761, 2003.

15. Youngberg SP, Sheps SG, Strong CG: Fibromuscular disease of the renal arteries. *Med Clin North Am* 61:623, 1977.

16. Klone, RA, Friedewald VE Jr: Case 6: Renovascular hypertension. *Am J Cardiol* 86:368, 2000.

17. Cheitlin MD: Coarctation of the aorta. *Med Clin North Am* 61:655, 1977.

18. Lipke DW, et al: Coarctation induces alterations in basement membranes in the cardiovascular system. *Hypertension* 22:743, 1993.

19. Becker HF, et al: Effect of nasal continuous positive airway pressure treatment on blood pressure in patients with obstructive sleep apnea. *Circulation* 107:68, 2003.

20. Faccenda JF, et al: Randomized placebo-controlled trial of continuous positive airway pressure on blood pressure in the sleep apnea-hypopnea syndrome. *Am J Respir Crit Care Med* 163:344, 2001.

21. Graves JW: Management of difficult-to-control hypertension. *Mayo Clin Proc* 75:278, 2000. Erratum in: *Mayo Clin Proc* 75:542, 2000.

22. Geyskes GG, Boer P, Dorhout Mees EJ: Clonidine withdrawal. Mechanism and frequency of rebound hypertension. *Br J Clin Pharmacol* 7:55, 1979.

23. White WB, et al: Effects of celecoxib on ambulatory blood pressure in hypertensive patients on ACE inhibitors. *Hypertension* 39:929, 2002.

24. Johnson AG, Nguyen TV, Day RO: Do nonsteroidal anti-inflammatory drugs affect blood pressure? A meta-analysis. *Ann Intern Med* 121:289,1994.

25. Kitiyakara C, Guzman NJ: Malignant hypertension and hypertensive emergencies. *J Am Soc Nephrol* 9:133,1998.

26. Barry DI: Cerebrovascular aspects of antihypertensive treatment. *Am J Cardiol* 63:14C, 1989.

27. Varon J, Marik PE: The diagnosis and management of hypertensive crises. *Chest* 118:214, 2000.

28. Grossman E, et al: Should a moratorium be placed on sublingual nifedipine capsules given for hypertensive emergencies and pseudoemergencies? *JAMA* 276:1328, 1996.

29. Guidelines 2000 for Cardiopulmonary Resuscitation and Emergency Cardiovascular Care. Part 7: The era of reperfusion: Section 2: Acute stroke. The American Heart Association in collaboration with the International Liaison Committee on Resuscitation. *Circulation* 102(Suppl):I204, 2000.

30. Vaughan CJ, Delanty N: Hypertensive emergencies. *Lancet* 356:411, 2000.

31. Adams RE, Powers WJ: Management of hypertension in acute intracerebral hemorrhage. *Crit Care Clin* 13:131, 1997.

32. Hamilton RJ, Carter WA, Gallagher EJ: Rapid improvement of acute pulmonary edema with sublingual captopril. *Acad Emerg Med* 3:205, 1996.

33. Sacchetti AR, McDermott P, Moakes ME, Moyer V: ICU use in acute pulmonary edema: Does ED management matter? [abstract]. *Ann Emerg Med* 30:430, 1997.

34. Hoshide S, et al: Hemodynamic cerebral infarction triggered by excessive blood pressure reduction in hypertensive emergencies [letter]. *J Am Geriatr Soc* 46:1179, 1998.

35. Guidelines 2000 for Cardiopulmonary Resuscitation and Emergency Cardiovascular Care. Part 7: The era of reperfusion: Section 1: Acute coronary syndromes (acute myocardial infarction). The American Heart Association in collaboration with the International Liaison Committee on Resuscitation. *Circulation* 102(8 Suppl):I172, 2000.

36. Zanchetti A: Impact of hypertension and antihypertensive treatment on organ damage. *Am J Cardiol* 84:18K, 1999.

37. Salvetti A, Mattei P, Sudano I: Renal protection and antihypertensive drugs: Current status. *Drugs* 57:665, 1999.

38. McCarthy JTM: A practical approach to the management of patients with chronic renal failure. *Mayo Clin Proc* 74:269, 1999.

39. Paller MS: Hypertension in pregnancy. *J Am Soc Nephrol* 9:314, 1998.

40. Vermillion ST, et al: A randomized, double-blind trial of oral nifedipine and intravenous labetalol in hypertensive emergencies of pregnancy. *Am J Obstet Gynecol* 181:858,. 1999.

41. Shusterman NH, Elliott WJ, White WB: Fenoldopam, but not nitroprusside, improves renal function in severely hypertensive patients with impaired renal function. *Am J Med* 95:161, 1993.

42. Tumlin JA, et al: Fenoldopam, a dopamine agonist, for hypertensive emergency: A multicenter randomized trial. Fenoldopam Study Group. *Acad Emerg Med* 7:653, 2000.

43. Post JB 4th, Frishman WH: Fenoldopam: A new dopamine agonist for the treatment of hypertensive urgencies and emergencies. *J Clin Pharmacol* 38:2, 1998.

44. Oparil S, et al: Fenoldopam: A new parenteral antihypertensive: Consensus roundtable on the management of perioperative hypertension and hypertensive crises. *Am J Hypertens* 12:653, 1999.

45. Walker JJ: Severe pre-eclampsia and eclampsia. *Baillieres Best Pract Res Clin Obstet Gynaecol* 14:57, 2000.

46. Cressman MD, et al: Intravenous labetalol in the management of severe hypertension and hypertensive emergencies. *Am Heart J* 107:980, 1984.

47. Lebel M, et al: Labetalol infusion in hypertensive emergencies. *Clin Pharmacol Ther* 37:615, 1985.

48. Hirschl MM, et al: Clinical evaluation of different doses of intravenous enalaprilat in patients with hypertensive crises. *Arch Intern Med* 155:2217, 1995.

49. Swedberg K, et al: Effects of the early administration of enalapril on mortality in patients with acute myocardial infarction. Results of the Cooperative New Scandinavian Enalapril Survival Study II (CONSENSUS II). *N Engl J Med* 327:678, 1992.

50. Zeller KR, Von Kuhnert L, Matthews C: Rapid reduction of severe asymptomatic hypertension. A prospective, controlled trial. *Arch Intern Med* 149:2186, 1989.

51. Karras DJ, et al: Urine dipstick as a screening test for serum creatinine elevation in emergency department patients with severe hypertension. *Acad Emerg Med* 9:27, 2002.

52. Jones DW, Hall JE: Seventh Report of the Joint National Committee on Prevention, Detection, Evaluation, and Treatment of High Blood Pressure and evidence from new hypertension trials. *Hypertension* 43:1, 2004.

53. Lenfant C, et al: Seventh report of the Joint National Committee on the Prevention, Detection, Evaluation, and Treatment of High Blood Pressure (JNC 7): Resetting the hypertension sails. *Hypertension* 41:1178, 2003.

54. Textor SC, Schwartz GL, Frye RL: The new hypertension guidelines from JNC 7: Is the devil in the details? *Mayo Clin Proc* 78:1078, 2003.

55. ALLHAT Officers and Coordinators for the ALLHAT Collaborative Research Group. The Antihypertensive and Lipid Lowering Treatment to Prevent Heart Attack Trial: Major outcomes in high-risk hypertensive patients randomized to angiotensin-converting enzyme inhibitor or calcium channel blocker vs diuretic: The Antihypertensive and Lipid-Lowering Treatment to Prevent Heart Attack Trial (ALLHAT). *JAMA* 288:2981, 2002. Erratum in: *JAMA* 289:178, 2003; *JAMA* 291:2196, 2003.

56. Zarnke KB: Recent developments in the assessment and management of hypertension: CHEP, ALLHAT and LIFE. *Geriatr Aging* 6:14, 2003.

57. Chalmers J: All hats off to ALLHAT: A massive study with clear messages. *J Hypertens* 21:225, 2003.

58. Ramsay LE, et al: The rationale for differing national recommendations for the treatment of hypertension. *Am J Hypertens* 11:79S; discussion 95S, 1998.

59. Kostis JB, et al: Association of calcium channel blocker use with increased rate of acute myocardial infarction in patients with left ventricular dysfunction. *Am Heart J* 133:550, 1997.

60. Major cardiovascular events in hypertensive patients randomized to doxazosin vs chlorthalidone: The antihypertensive and lipid-lowering treatment to prevent heart attack trial (ALLHAT). ALLHAT Collaborative Research Group. *JAMA* 283:1967, 2000.

CHAPTER

84 Aortic Dissection

Felix Ankel

PERSPECTIVE

Aortic dissection is a longitudinal cleavage of the aortic media created by a dissecting column of blood. The term "dissecting aortic aneurysm" has been inaccurately applied to this entity since 1819, when Laënnec first used the term *aneurysme dissequant*. The term *aortic dissection* is preferred to dissecting aortic aneurysm because the affected aorta is only rarely aneurysmal. In 1955, DeBakey outlined the principles that remain the basis for the surgical treatment of this entity. Medical treatment of aortic dissection was first advocated in the 1960s and is indicated for certain types of dissections.[1-4] In-hospital mortality for patients treated for aortic dissection is 27%.[4]

Epidemiology

Aortic dissection occurs more often in men and increases with age.[4,5] The incidence and prevalence are difficult to determine because of underreporting of this condition. Mortality is 1 to 5 per 100,000 population per year. Hypertension is the most common risk factor associated with aortic dissection and is seen in most patients.[4-6] A history of cardiac surgery is present in about 18%[4] and a bicuspid aortic valve in 14% of all patients with aortic dissections but more often in proximal dissections.[6] Atherosclerosis is rarely involved at the site of dissection.

Aortic dissection is uncommon before age 40 except in association with congenital heart disease, Ehlers-Danlos or Marfan syndrome, or giant cell arteritis. As many as 44% of patients with Marfan syndrome develop aortic dissection and account for about 5% of cases.[4,6,7] Women with Marfan syndrome are at particular risk during pregnancy.[8] In patients without connective tissue disease and with an aortic root size of less than 40 mm, pregnancy does not appear to be an independent risk factor.[9] Acute aortic dissection also occurs with stimulant use[10,11] and trauma.[12] It may also be seen in patients who undergo cardiac surgery[4] or intra-aortic balloon pump insertion.[13]

Blunt trauma from a high-speed deceleration injury usually causes traumatic aortic rupture, which is an entity distinctly different from aortic dissection (see Chapter 42).

PRINCIPLES OF DISEASE

Anatomy and Physiology

With each contraction, the heart swings from side to side, resulting in flexion of both the ascending aorta and descending aorta. The descending aorta flexes just distal to the left subclavian artery, where the mobile aorta is tethered. At an average of 70 heartbeats per minute, this sequence occurs about 37 million times a year, causing a repetitive stress on the aorta.

The aortic wall has three distinct layers: the intima, the media, and the adventitia. The media is composed of elastic tissue and smooth muscle. Dissection occurs through a degeneration of the media characterized by loss of smooth muscle cells and elastic tissue, accompanied by scarring, fibrosis, and hyalin-like changes. Pathologic studies show that this process is neither cystic nor necrotic; therefore, the old term *cystic medial necrosis* is no longer used.[14]

Pathophysiology

Medial degeneration, previously thought to be specific for aortic dissection, is now considered to be part of normal aging, although it is augmented by hypertension and with aortic dissection. The anatomic differences between the "normal" aorta and a dissection are *quantitative* rather than qualitative.[14]

The repetitive hydrodynamic forces produced by the ejection of blood into the aorta with each cardiac cycle contribute to weakening of the aortic intima and to medial degeneration. These hydrodynamic forces primarily affect the ascending aorta. Sustained hypertension intensifies these forces and results in an increase in medial degeneration. A bicuspid aortic valve may disrupt laminar flow and reorient the flow of blood toward the aortic wall, producing local injury. In

Marfan and Ehlers-Danlos syndromes, normal hydrodynamic forces act on an aortic media that is already weakened.

As a result of medial degeneration and repeated flexion of the aorta, hydrodynamic stress tears the aortic intima and a column of blood gains access into the aortic media. An alternative theory suggests that these forces damage the vasa vasorum of the aorta, which rupture and hemorrhage into the aortic media,[15] which may explain the absence of an intimal tear in some cases of dissection. Regardless of which of these theories is correct, the depth of penetration into the media and the distance and direction of dissection are at least partially determined by the degree of medial degeneration.

Once a dissecting hematoma is established in the media, migration of the hematoma occurs in an antegrade or retrograde fashion, or both, forming a "false lumen." The false lumen forms in the outer half of the media and propagates until it ruptures back into the "true lumen" of the aorta, resulting in a rare "spontaneous cure," or through the adventitia into the pericardial sac or pleural cavity. Because the outer wall of the aorta that contains the hematoma is thin, rupture is much more likely to occur to the outside. The most important factors favoring continued dissection of the aorta are (1) the degree of elevation of blood pressure and (2) the steepness (slope) of the pulse wave (dP/dt). Both of these hemodynamic factors must be controlled to halt migration of the hematoma.

Classification

Anatomic classification is important for diagnosis and therapy. The *Stanford classification* is based on the involvement of the ascending aorta. Type A dissections involve the ascending aorta; type B dissections do not (Figure 84-1). Dissections that involve the ascending aorta are much more lethal than those limited to the distal aorta and call for a different therapeutic approach. In the International Registry of Acute Aortic Dissection (IRAD), 62% of dissections are type A and 38% are type B.[2-4] Patients with distal dissections tend to be older, heavy smokers with chronic lung disease and more often with generalized atherosclerosis and hypertension compared with patients who have proximal aortic dissections.

Two other aortic conditions are closely related to aortic dissection: intramural hemorrhage[16,17] and penetrating aortic ulcer. Both groups of patients have clinical symptoms and management recommendations similar to those of patients with aortic dissection. An *intramural hemorrhage* is a contained hematoma within the aortic wall and occurs in about 10% of aortic dissections.[4] Rupture of the vasa vasorum is believed to be the initial event. *Penetrating atherosclerotic ulcers* of the aorta occur in older hypertensive patients with evidence of coronary artery disease. Computed tomography (CT) shows a focal ulceration without dissection, most commonly in the distal descending aorta. The progression of penetrating ulcers results in progressive aortic enlargement with saccular and fusiform aneurysm formation. Patients can have both an intramural hematoma and a penetrating atherosclerotic ulcer.[18]

A dissection is *acute* if it is of less than 2 weeks duration and *chronic* if present for more than 2 weeks.

CLINICAL FEATURES

History

Pain is by far the most common presenting complaint, affecting more than 90% of patients.[4,6,7] Most cases of painless aortic dissection are chronic in nature.[6] The pain is usually excruciating, occurs abruptly, is most severe at onset, and is typically described as "sharp"[4] more often than "tearing" or "ripping."

The location of the pain may help localize the dissection. Anterior chest pain is associated with the ascending aorta, neck and jaw pain with the aortic arch, pain in the interscapular area with the descending thoracic aorta, and pain in the lumbar area or abdomen with involvement below the diaphragm. Migration of the pain consistent with propagation of the dissection suggests aortic dissection but occurs in only 17% of cases.[4] The onset of aortic dissection is often accompanied by visceral pain symptoms, such as diaphoresis, nausea, vomiting, lightheadedness, and severe apprehension.

Syncope occurs early in aortic dissection in approximately 9% of cases and may be the sole presentation in some patients.[4,7] It most often heralds dissection into the pericardium, causing pericardial tamponade, but may occur from interruption of blood flow to the cerebral vasculature. Other causes of syncope secondary to aortic dissection are hypovolemia, excessive vagal tone, and cardiac conduction abnormalities. Neurologic symptoms such as focal weakness or change in mental status occur in up to 17% of cases.[4,6,7]

Physical Examination

Generally, the patient appears apprehensive. Most of the patients have a history of chronic hypertension that

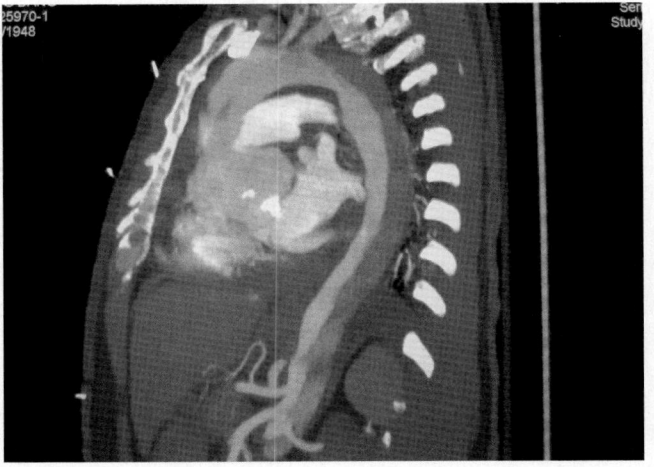

Figure 84-1. Computed tomographic reconstruction of Stanford type B or DeBakey type III dissection distal to the subclavian artery.

may be exacerbated by a catecholamine release related to the acute event. Severe hypertension refractory to medical therapy may occur if the dissection involves the renal arteries with subsequent renin release. If hypotension is present, either the dissection has progressed back into the pericardium with resulting pericardial tamponade or hypovolemia has occurred from rupture through the adventitia. *Pseudohypotension*, a condition in which the blood pressure in the arms is low or unobtainable and the central arterial pressure is normal or high, may be present. This results from the interruption of blood flow to the subclavian arteries.

Aortic regurgitation occurs in up to 32% of patients and is more common with type A dissections.[4,6] The murmur of aortic insufficiency may have a musical, vibrating quality with variable intensity, and congestive heart failure may develop. The patient with presumed aortic dissection should be examined carefully for findings that suggest hemorrhage into the pericardium or tamponade, such as jugular venous distention, muffled heart sounds, tachycardia, and hypotension.

When the integrity of one of the branches of the aorta is compromised, the expected ischemic findings occur. Pulse deficits and discrepancies in blood pressure between limbs can be helpful if present.[4,6,7] Usually these are present in the upper extremities and result from involvement of one or both of the subclavian arteries. Obstruction of one or both common iliac or superficial femoral arteries may produce pulse deficits in the lower extremities. Arterial obstruction may occur by either of two mechanisms. An intimal flap produced by the dissection may cover the true lumen of a branch vessel, or the dissecting hematoma may compress an adjacent true lumen. Frequent reexamination may detect transient pulse deficits.

Neurologic findings are related to the site of blood flow interruption. Proximal dissections are a more frequent cause of strokes or coma. Stroke treatment with a fibrinolytic agent in the patient with aortic dissection can be fatal. Distal dissections occluding the anterior spinal artery commonly cause ischemic paraparesis or ischemic peripheral neuropathy.[6]

In up to 3% of cases, a proximal dissection can dissect into the ostium of a coronary artery, most frequently the right coronary artery, and cause an acute myocardial infarction (MI), usually inferior-posterior.[4] Failure to identify the inciting aortic dissection with

incorrect administration of a fibrinolytic agent occurs in about 0.1% to 0.2% of MIs.[19] Distal extension of aortic dissections into the abdomen can cause mesenteric ischemia, renal failure, femoral pulse deficits, and lower extremity ischemia.[20]

DIAGNOSTIC STRATEGIES

Routine laboratory tests are of little value in the diagnosis of aortic dissection. Unless massive hemorrhage has occurred, the hemoglobin is normal or only modestly reduced. The leukocyte count is commonly mildly elevated.

Electrocardiography

The electrocardiogram (ECG) is often useful in excluding MI; however, 15% of patients with aortic dissection may have ECG abnormalities suggesting ischemia.[4,21] Proximal dissections that involve the right coronary artery may show an inferior wall MI. The ECG typically shows left ventricular hypertrophy in 26%, reflecting long-standing hypertension. Other findings include nonspecific ST-T wave changes and prior Q wave infarction. No abnormalities are noted on the ECG in 31% of cases (Table 84-1).[4]

Chest Radiography

Routine chest x-ray studies are abnormal in 80% to 90% of patients, but the abnormalities are nonspecific and rarely diagnostic.[4,6,7] Mediastinal widening occurs in the majority of cases[4,6]; may occur in the ascending aorta, aortic arch, or the descending portion of the thoracic aorta; and may be difficult to differentiate from the aortic tortuosity that is associated with chronic hypertension. A plain chest radiograph is inadequate to rule out aortic dissection. Up to 12% of patients with aortic dissection have a normal chest radiograph (see Table 84-1).[4,7]

The "calcium sign" is an uncommon radiographic manifestation of aortic dissection. Ordinarily, when intimal calcification is visible on a radiograph, it is butted up against the outer border of the aorta. With dissection of the aortic media, the calcium deposit becomes separated from the outermost portion of the aorta by more than 5 mm.

Table 84-1. Characteristics of Aortic Dissection from the International Registry of Acute Aortic Dissection[4]

	Chest Pain	Syncope	Aortic Insufficiency Murmur	Pulse Deficit	Normal CXR	Widened Mediastinum on CXR	Normal ECG	Ischemia	Left Ventricular Hypertrophy
All (n = 464)	73%	9%	32%	15%	12%	62%	31%	15%	26%
Type A (n = 289)	79%	13%	44%	19%	11%	63%	31%	17%	25%
Type B (n = 175)	63%	4%	12%	9%	16%	56%	32%	13%	32%

CXR, chest x-ray film; ECG, electrocardiogram.

Table 84-2. Sensitivities and Specificities of Imaging Modalities for Diagnosing Aortic Dissection

Test	TEE	CT	MRI
Sensitivity, %	98	94	98
Specificity, %	83	77	98

CT, computed tomography; MRI, magnetic resonance imaging; TEE, transesophageal echocardiography.
(From Nienaber CA, et al: The diagnosis of thoracic aortic dissection by noninvasive imaging procedures. *N Engl J Med* 328:1, 1993.

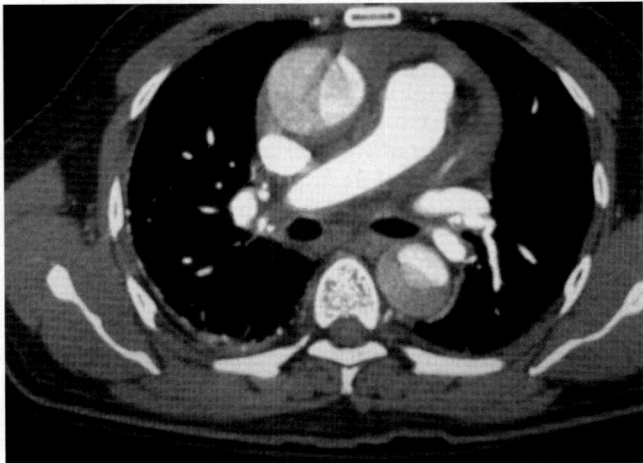

Figure 84-2. Computed tomography scan demonstrating the true lumen and false lumen.

Other helpful radiographic signs include a double-density appearance of the aorta suggesting true and false channels, a localized bulge along a normally smooth aortic contour, a disparity in the caliber between the descending and ascending aorta, obliteration of the aortic knob, and displacement of the trachea or nasogastric tube to the right by the dissection. Previous chest roentgenograms, when available, are useful for comparison.

Echocardiography

Transthoracic echocardiography (TTE) is an insensitive tool in the detection of aortic dissection because it does not visualize most of the descending aorta and imaging quality may not be optimal because of the patient's body habitus. While more sensitive imaging tests are being arranged, however, TTE can provide valuable information such as pericardial effusion or aortic regurgitation[22] and can help determine whether cardiac tamponade is the cause of hypotension in a patient with aortic dissection.

Transesophageal echocardiography (TEE) is highly sensitive[23] (Table 84-2) in the diagnosis of aortic dissection.[24] The proximity of the esophagus to the aorta and the ability to use higher transducer frequencies help to visualize the entire aorta and to detect pericardial effusion and aortic regurgitation.[23] TEE can be quickly performed at the patient's bedside with sedation or light anesthesia and requires no radiation or contrast agent injection. Visualization of the distal ascending aorta and proximal arch used to be difficult because of the interposition of the air-filled trachea and left main stem bronchus, but evaluation of this "blind spot" has been aided by biplane and multiplane probes.[23]

The diagnostic accuracy of TEE is dependent on the experience and availability of the echocardiographer. It is the primary diagnostic method in many institutions for detecting aortic dissection[4] and is the procedure of choice in unstable patients, in whom it can be done in the operating room coincident with induction of anesthesia.

Computed Tomography

A CT scan is a reliable test for diagnosing aortic dissection (see Table 84-2) and is the primary diagnostic test of choice in most institutions.[4] Findings suggestive of aortic dissection include dilatation of the aorta, identification of an intimal flap, and the clear demonstration of both the false and true lumina (Figure 84-2). Dynamic scanning, in which rapid scans are obtained at multiple levels immediately after a bolus injection of an intravenous (IV) contrast agent, improves the accuracy of the CT scan in the diagnosis of aortic dissection by allowing detection of differential filling rates in the true and false lumina (see Figure 84-1). Dynamic scanning performed with helical CT improves sensitivity and specificity.[25]

Aortography

Historically, aortography was the "gold standard" against which other modalities were measured. With the advent of TEE and CT scanning, however, aortography is rarely used as the initial diagnostic modality and is no longer the imaging modality of choice.[4] The findings of aortic dissection include (1) filling of a false channel or channels with or without an intervening intimal flap, (2) distortion of the true lumen by either a patent or thrombosed false lumen, (3) thickening of the aortic wall by more than 5 to 6 mm caused by a thrombosed false lumen, and (4) displaced intimal calcification. Aortography is accurate for determining the site of the intimal tear and the extent of the dissection. Aortic regurgitation is easily demonstrated with aortography, and it demonstrates the extent and location of dissection into aortic side branches.

With the use of other diagnostic modalities, the sensitivity of aortography has been shown to be as low as 77%.[26] Misdiagnoses occur in several situations. The intimal flap may not be visualized when it is located in a plane tangential to the x-ray beam. Thrombosis of the false channel may prevent visualization of either the intimal flap or a double lumen. The true and false lumina may opacify simultaneously and, therefore, may not be clearly delineated from one another.

Magnetic Resonance Imaging

Magnetic resonance imaging (MRI) is an appealing option in the detection of aortic dissection. Sensitivity and specificity are excellent (see Table 84-2).[27] The MRI scan shows the site of intimal tear, type and extent of dissection, presence of aortic insufficiency, and differential flow velocities in the true and false channels and in the aortic side branches. It requires no contrast material or ionizing radiation and is noninvasive. It is particularly useful in the evaluation of chronic aortic dissection, in the follow-up of postoperative patients, and for monitoring nonoperative patients for progression of the dissection. Its availability, however, is limited and it is difficult to perform in unstable patients.

Choice of Diagnostic Test

Although aortic dissection can be suspected on the basis of history and physical examination, diagnostic imaging is necessary to establish the diagnosis. With the high mortality in excess of 1% per hour after the onset of aortic dissection, a diagnostic study should be performed as soon as possible.[5] Frequently, more than one test is required to diagnose the condition and to assess associated complications.

The clinical services within the hospital involved in the diagnosis and treatment of patients with aortic dissection should prospectively agree on a strategy.[28] This strategy should consider (1) the technology available at the institution, (2) the institution-specific sensitivities and specificities for the diagnostic tests, (3) the benefits of diagnosing nondissecting causes of chest pain, and (4) the ease of obtaining each test, especially "after hours." Some tests (e.g., CT, MRI, aortography) may require moving a potentially unstable patient outside the emergency department. In IRAD, the initial choice of diagnostic test was CT in 61%, TTE or TEE in 33%, aortography in 4%, and MRI in 2% of patients.[4] "Real-world" sensitivities of diagnostic tests in IRAD were CT 93%, TEE 88%, aortography 87%, and MRI 100%, and patients averaged 1.85 imaging studies.[29]

DIFFERENTIAL CONSIDERATIONS

The differential diagnosis for the patient with symptoms suggestive of aortic dissection is extensive. Signs and symptoms associated with aortic dissection are variable and dependent on the extent of aortic and branch vessel involvement. Patients with the ultimate diagnosis of aortic dissection are often initially thought to have other conditions such as myocardial ischemia, congestive heart failure, or pulmonary embolus (PE).[6] Several clinical syndromes are particularly suggestive of aortic dissection: pain that progresses over hours or days from chest to neck to arms to abdomen, chest pain with concomitant neurologic deficits, and chest pain with pulse deficits.

Although chest pain is the most common symptom of aortic dissection, it is also the most common presenting complaint of at least three other serious and more common clinical entities: acute MI, PE, and pericarditis. An ECG can be helpful in excluding MI, although aortic dissection and MI may coexist as a result of the dissection proceeding retrogradely down a coronary artery and causing infarction. In cases in which aortic dissection is excluded, a CT scan may reveal other abnormalities that explain a patient's presentation (e.g., PE). TEE is helpful in identifying etiologies of chest pain other than aortic dissection (e.g., cardiac ischemia).

When the initial presentation of the aortic dissection is pain or dysfunction in an extremity from disruption of the blood supply, peripheral neurologic diagnoses should be included in the differential diagnosis. An aortic dissection may involve the carotid artery with the initial presentation mimicking that of a primary central nervous system lesion such as a stroke. The diagnosis of aortic dissection should be entertained in any patient with a new diagnosis of pericardial effusion, pericardial tamponade, or aortic insufficiency.

MANAGEMENT

Emergency Department

Early therapy for aortic dissection is critical and should be initiated while diagnostic tests are being performed. Opioids should be administered in adequate amounts for pain control and to decrease sympathetic tone.[30] Patients with aortic dissections are typically hypertensive. The two goals of medical management are to (1) reduce blood pressure and (2) decrease the rate of rise of the arterial pulse (dP/dt) to diminish shearing forces.[31] The use of β-adrenergic blockers is the cornerstone of aortic dissection management. Because vasodilators such as sodium nitroprusside increase the heart rate and may also increase the dP/dt, a β-blocker must be started before or in conjunction with vasodilator therapy to lower the dP/dt.

Esmolol is an ultrashort-acting β-blocker that is easily titrated. After mixing 5 g in 500 mL of 5% dextrose in water (D5W), an initial bolus of 500 μg/kg is given, followed by an infusion of 50 to 200 μg/kg/min. *Labetalol* has both α- and β-blocking activity and can be used as monotherapy. A suggested dose is an initial 20-mg IV bolus every 5 to10 minutes, incrementally increased to 80 mg IV until a target heart rate is reached or a total of 300 mg is given. A maintenance dose of labetalol is then given at 1 to 2 mg/hr. A target heart rate should be between 60 and 80 beats/min. If a patient is normotensive, a β-blocker should still be used to lower the dP/dt. In patients with a history of chronic obstructive pulmonary disease or at risk for bronchospasm, a selective β-blocker such as metoprolol or atenolol should be considered.

Sodium nitroprusside can be used, in conjunction with a β-blocker, to maintain the systolic blood pressure at 100 to 120 mm Hg or to the lowest level to maintain vital organ perfusion. Nitroprusside, 50 mg, is mixed in 500 mL of D5W and initially infused at a rate of 0.5 to 3 μg/kg/min.

The calcium channel blocker *nifedipine* is not recommended to treat aortic dissection. Nifedipine has minimal inotropic or chronotropic effects and may reflexively stimulate sympathetic activity and increase shear stress on the aortic wall.[31] IV *nitroglycerin* is often used initially in patients with hypertensive chest pain and suspected or uncertain aortic dissection. Nitroglycerin is a less effective arterial dilator than nitroprusside and less desirable than nitroprusside for the treatment of patients with aortic dissection. Nitroglycerin must, like nitroprusside, be accompanied by a β-blocker.

Patients presenting with hypotension secondary to aortic rupture or pericardial tamponade should be resuscitated with intravenous fluids and immediately transported to the operating room if they are to have a chance to survive. Blood pressure should be measured in all four limbs, if necessary, to ensure that this is not a pseudohypotension caused by an intimal flap obstructing the extremity in which the blood pressure is measured. In patients with electromechanical dissociation or marked hypotension, pericardiocentesis may raise the blood pressure while awaiting definitive surgery.

Surgery

Type A acute aortic dissections require prompt surgical treatment. The aortic segment containing the original intimal tear is resected when possible, with graft replacement of the ascending aorta to redirect blood into the true lumen. If aortic insufficiency is present, it can be corrected through aortic valve resuspension or replacement. Patients with type A dissections have an in-hospital mortality rate of 27% when treated surgically versus an in-hospital mortality of 56% when treated medically.

Definitive treatment of type B acute aortic dissections is less clear.[32] These patients in general tend to be worse surgical risks. Uncomplicated distal dissections have traditionally been treated with blood pressure control, and patients have an in-hospital mortality of 10% when treated in this manner.[3] Surgery has been reserved for patients who have persistent pain, uncontrolled hypertension, occlusion of a major arterial trunk, frank aortic leaking or rupture, or development of a localized aneurysm. These patients have an in-hospital, 30-day mortality of 32%. A "deadly triad" of absence of chest pain, hypotension, and branch vessel involvement is an independent predictor of in-hospital death.[3]

Interventional Therapy

In general, interventional endovascular techniques are not applicable to type A dissections. Interventional stent-graft and fenestration techniques are replacing surgery for complicated type B dissections in some centers, especially for patients with renal and mesenteric ischemia.[33,34] Patients managed with interventional therapy have an in-hospital mortality of 6.5%.[3] Interventional therapy for stable type B dissections is currently under study.

DISPOSITION

Patients who present with chronic aortic dissection have already survived their period of greatest mortality risk and are usually treated by blood pressure control and close monitoring unless complications mandate surgery. All patients who have sustained and survived an aortic dissection, regardless of the type of definitive therapy used, require careful long-term management. Major complications that may occur with time are redissection, the development of a localized aneurysm, and progressive aortic insufficiency.

KEY CONCEPTS

- Risk factors for aortic dissection include advanced age, hypertension, and connective tissue disorders such as Marfan or Ehlers-Danlos syndrome.
- Most patients with aortic dissection have chest pain, described as sudden onset, sharp, and migratory. Chest pain associated with neurologic symptoms or syncope should raise the suspicion of aortic disease.
- Physical examination findings may include pulse deficit, aortic insufficiency murmur, or neurologic findings.
- Diagnosis is difficult using only history, physical examination, and chest radiography. Computed tomography and transesophageal echocardiography are the confirmatory tests used most often.
- Treatment of type A proximal dissection is surgical. Treatment of uncomplicated type B distal dissection is usually medical, with a β-blocker and nitroprusside to control blood pressure and dP/dt shearing forces.

REFERENCES

1. Eagle KA, Isselbacher EM, DeSanctis RW, International Registry for Aortic Dissection (IRAD) Investigators: Cocaine-related aortic dissection in perspective. *Circulation* 105:1529, 2002.
2. Mehta RH, et al: Predicting death in patients with acute type A aortic dissection. *Circulation* 105:200, 2002.
3. Suzuki T, et al: Clinical profiles and outcomes of acute type B aortic dissection in the current era: Lessons from the International Registry of Aortic Dissection (IRAD). *Circulation* 108:312II, 2003.
4. Hagan PG, et al: The International Registry of Acute Aortic Dissection (IRAD): New insights into an old disease. *JAMA* 283:897, 2000.
5. Meszaros I, et al: Epidemiology and clinicopathology of aortic dissection. *Chest* 117:1271, 2000.
6. Spittell PC, et al: Clinical features and differential diagnosis of aortic dissection: Experience with 236 cases (1980 through 1990). *Mayo Clin Proc* 68:642, 1993.
7. Klompas M: Does this patient have an acute thoracic aortic dissection? *JAMA* 287:2262, 2002.
8. Elkayam U, Ostrzega E, Shotan A, Mehra A: Cardiovascular problems in pregnant women with the Marfan syndrome. *Ann Intern Med* 123:117, 1995.
9. Nienaber CA, Eagle KA: Aortic dissection: New frontiers in diagnosis and management: Part I: From etiology to diagnostic strategies. *Circulation* 108:628, 2003.
10. Swalwell CI, Davis GG: Methamphetamine as a risk factor for acute aortic dissection. *J Forensic Sci* 44:23, 1999.

11. Hsue PY, et al: Acute aortic dissection related to crack cocaine. *Circulation* 105:1592, 2002.

12. Rogers FB, Osler TM, Shackford SR: Aortic dissection after trauma: Case report and review of the literature. *J Trauma* 41:906, 1996.

13. Jacobs LE, Fraifeld M, Kotler MN, Ioli AW: Aortic dissection following intraaortic balloon insertion: Recognition by transesophageal echocardiography. *Am Heart J* 124:536, 1992.

14. Schlatmann TJ, Becker AE: Histologic changes in the normal aging aorta: Implications for dissecting aortic aneurysm. *Am J Cardiol* 39:13, 1977.

15. Lui RC, Menkis AH, McKenzie FN: Aortic dissection without intimal rupture: Diagnosis and management. *Ann Thorac Surg* 53:886, 1992.

16. Nienaber CA, Sievers HH: Intramural hematoma in acute aortic syndrome: More than one variant of dissection? *Circulation* 106:284, 2002.

17. von Kodolitsch Y, et al: Intramural hematoma of the aorta: Predictors of progression to dissection and rupture. *Circulation* 107:1158, 2003.

18. Ganaha F, et al: Prognosis of aortic intramural hematoma with and without penetrating atherosclerotic ulcer: A clinical and radiological analysis. *Circulation* 106:342, 2002.

19. Kamp TJ, Goldschmidt-Clermont PJ, Brinker JA, Resar JR: Myocardial infarction, aortic dissection, and thrombolytic therapy. *Am Heart J* 128:1234, 1994.

20. Pacifico L, Spodick D: ILEAD—Ischemia of the lower extremities due to aortic dissection: The isolated presentation. *Clin Cardiol* 22:353, 1999.

21. Hirata K, Kyushima M, Asato H: Electrocardiographic abnormalities in patients with acute aortic dissection. *Am J Cardiol* 76:1207, 1995.

22. Blaivas M, Sierzenski PR: Dissection of the proximal thoracic aorta: A new ultrasonographic sign in the subxiphoid view. *Am J Emerg Med* 20:344, 2002.

23. Keren A, et al: Accuracy of biplane and multiplane transesophageal echocardiography in diagnosis of typical acute aortic dissection and intramural hematoma. *J Am Coll Cardiol* 28:627, 1996.

24. Willens HJ, Kessler KM: Transesophageal echocardiography in the diagnosis of diseases of the thoracic aorta: Part 1. Aortic dissection, aortic intramural hematoma, and penetrating atherosclerotic ulcer of the aorta. *Chest* 116:1772, 1999.

25. Sommer T, et al: Aortic dissection: A comparative study of diagnosis with spiral CT, multiplanar transesophageal echocardiography, and MR imaging. *Radiology* 199:347, 1996.

26. Bansal RC, Chandrasekaran K, Ayala K, Smith DC: Frequency and explanation of false negative diagnosis of aortic dissection by aortography and transesophageal echocardiography. *J Am Coll Cardiol* 25:1393, 1995.

27. Laissy JP, et al: Thoracic aortic dissection: Diagnosis with transesophageal echocardiography versus MR imaging. *Radiology* 194:331, 1995.

28. Sarasin FP, Louis-Simonet M, Gaspoz JM, Junod AF: Detecting acute thoracic aortic dissection in the emergency department: Time constraints and choice of the optimal diagnostic test. *Ann Emerg Med* 28:278, 1996.

29. Moore AG, et al: Choice of computed tomography, transesophageal echocardiography, magnetic resonance imaging, and aortography in acute aortic dissection: International Registry of Acute Aortic Dissection (IRAD). *Am J Cardiol* 89:1235, 2002.

30. Nienaber CA, Eagle KA: Aortic dissection: New frontiers in diagnosis and management: Part II: Therapeutic management and follow-up. *Circulation* 108:772, 2003.

31. Grossman E, Ironi AN, Messerli FH: Comparative tolerability profile of hypertensive crisis treatments. *Drug Saf* 19:99, 1998.

32. Elefteriades JA, et al: Management of descending aortic dissection. *Ann Thorac Surg* 67:2002, 1999.

33. Dake MD, et al: Endovascular stent-graft placement for the treatment of acute aortic dissection. *N Engl J Med* 340:1546, 1999.

34. Shimono T, et al: Transluminal stent-graft placements for the treatments of acute onset and chronic aortic dissections. *Circulation* 106:241I, 2002.

35. Nienaber CA, et al: The diagnosis of thoracic aortic dissection by noninvasive imaging procedures. *N Engl J Med* 328:1, 1993.

CHAPTER

85 Abdominal Aortic Aneurysm

Howard A. Bessen

PERSPECTIVE

Most abdominal aortic aneurysms (AAAs) are true aneurysms. A true aortic aneurysm is a localized dilation of the aorta caused by weakening of its wall; it involves all three layers (intima, media, and adventitia) of the arterial wall (Figure 85-1). AAAs should not be confused with aortic dissections, which are sometimes incorrectly called "dissecting aortic aneurysms." In aortic dissection, blood enters the media of the aorta and splits (dissects) the aortic wall (see Chapter 84).

True aortic aneurysms and aortic dissections are very different diseases, with different complications, clinical presentations, diagnostic methods, and treatments.

A pseudoaneurysm (false aneurysm) is a collection of flowing blood that communicates with the arterial lumen but is not enclosed by the normal vessel wall; it is contained only by the adventitia or surrounding soft tissue. Pseudoaneurysms can arise from a defect in the arterial wall or a leaking anastomosis as a complication of AAA repair.

Aneurysms can develop in any segment of the aorta, but most involve the aorta below the renal arteries. The

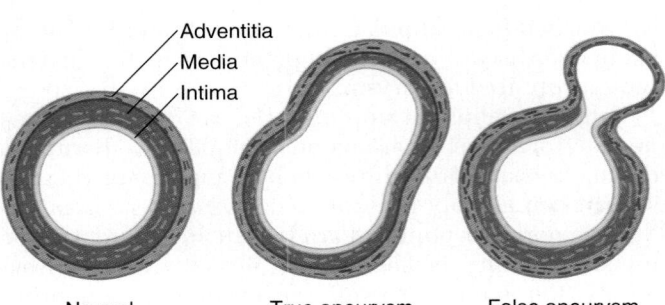

Adventitia
Media
Intima

Normal   True aneurysm   False aneurysm   Dissection

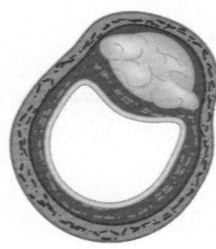

Figure 85-1. Types of aortic aneurysms. (Modified from LeRoy LL, et al: Imaging of abdominal aortic aneurysms. AJR *Am J Roentgenol* 152:785, 1989.)

Table 85-1. Prevalence of Abdominal Aortic Aneurysms (AAAs) in Selected Risk Groups

Group	Incidence (%)
Autopsy subjects aged 50 years or older[3,6]	2-4
Men aged 65 years or older[2,7]	5-10
Patients with occlusive peripheral vascular disease[8]	10-15
Brothers of patients with AAAs[9]	20-25
Patients with femoral or popliteal artery aneurysms[10,11]	35-40

diameter of the normal adult infrarenal aorta is approximately 2 cm, and a diameter of 3 cm or more can be used to define an AAA.[1]

Epidemiology

Abdominal aortic aneurysm is a disease of aging, and the prevalence of AAAs is expected to increase as the population of elderly patients grows. AAAs are rare before the age of 50 years but are found in 2% to 5% of the population older than 50.[1,2] The average age at the time of diagnosis is 65 to 70, and men are affected much more often than women.[3] The patient often has atherosclerotic occlusive disease that involves the coronary, carotid, or peripheral vessels, which may influence the clinical presentations, complications, and management.

Certain groups are at greatest risk for AAAs (Table 85-1). An AAA can be found in 5% to 10% of elderly men who are screened with ultrasonography and in an even higher percentage of patients with peripheral vascular disease. A family history of an AAA is a very strong risk factor; those with an affected first-degree relative have a 10- to 20-fold increased risk of developing an AAA. Awareness of these high-risk groups can speed the recognition of AAAs in these patients.

PRINCIPLES OF DISEASE

Pathophysiology

Abdominal aortic aneurysms have traditionally been attributed to atherosclerosis, but other factors probably contribute to their formation. Most patients with

advanced atherosclerosis have occlusive disease, not aneurysms. Biochemical abnormalities leading to the loss of elastin and collagen, the major structural components of the aortic wall, have been identified in patients with AAAs. The propensity to form aneurysms may have a genetic basis, but the exact mode of inheritance is uncertain. The Society for Vascular Surgery has recommended labeling the typical degenerative AAA as "nonspecific," rather than "atherosclerotic," to reflect this uncertain cause.

Abdominal aortic aneurysms sometimes result from specific causes, such as infection, trauma, connective tissue diseases, and arteritis. Such aneurysms are rare compared with nonspecific, degenerative aneurysms.

Natural History

Abdominal aortic aneurysms progressively enlarge, ultimately resulting in rupture of the aneurysm and fatal hemorrhage. Although other potential complications are possible, by far the most common and most important is rupture.

The most important factor determining the risk of rupture is the size of the aneurysm.[4,5] The rupture risk increases dramatically with increased aneurysm size, and most ruptured AAAs have diameters greater than 5 cm. However, no aneurysm is completely "safe."[2,6] Any aneurysm can rupture and may be the source of the symptoms causing the patient's emergency department presentation.

Rupture of an AAA usually occurs into the retroperitoneum, where hemorrhage may be temporarily limited by clotting and tamponade at the rupture site. Of patients with ruptures, 10% to 30% have free intraperitoneal rupture, which is often rapidly fatal.[7] Occasionally, rupture occurs into the gastrointestinal tract or the inferior vena cava.

Complications can also arise from intact AAAs. The walls of AAAs are often lined with clot and atheromatous material, which can embolize and occlude distal vessels. Aortic thrombosis may occur rarely. Patients can also have complications caused by impingement on adjacent structures.

In approximately 5% of AAAs, a dense inflammatory and fibrotic reaction develops in the aneurysm wall and adjacent retroperitoneal tissue. In these "inflammatory" AAAs, the periaortic fibrosis may incorporate and obstruct adjacent structures, such as the ureters.

The overwhelming concern in the patient with an AAA is the potential for rupture of the aneurysm. The natural history of expansion and rupture can be interrupted only by timely surgical repair.

CLINICAL FEATURES

Unruptured Aneurysms

The prevalence of symptoms in patients with unruptured AAAs is unknown. Patients may have symptoms that lead to the aneurysm's discovery and are believed to be caused by the aneurysm. These symptoms can include pain in the abdomen, back, or flank; an awareness of an abdominal mass or fullness; or a sensation of abdominal pulsations.[8]

The pain associated with stable, intact aneurysms has a gradual onset and a vague, dull quality. It is usually constant but may be described as throbbing or colicky. Acute or severe pain is an ominous symptom that suggests imminent or actual aortic rupture.

Most patients diagnosed with an AAA are entirely asymptomatic, and the aneurysm is discovered incidentally on physical examination, on a radiologic study done for other reasons, or in an ultrasonography aneurysm screening program. Symptoms usually do not develop until the aneurysm ruptures.

The diagnostic physical finding is a pulsatile, expansile abdominal mass. The aortic bifurcation is at the level of the umbilicus, and an AAA can be palpated at or above this level. The mass may extend below the umbilicus if the iliac arteries are aneurysmal. The right border of an AAA may be palpable to the right of midline, whereas a normal or tortuous aorta is usually not. Most intact AAAs are nontender; tenderness suggests aneurysm expansion or rupture.[8]

Symptomatic aneurysms are usually fairly large and are often palpable. Likewise, the patient with an aneurysm large enough to warrant elective repair often has a palpable abdominal mass.[8] However, an AAA may be difficult to palpate if the aneurysm is small or the patient is obese. Approximately 30% of nonruptured aneurysms measuring 3.0 to 3.9 cm by ultrasonography can be detected by abdominal palpation; 50% of aneurysms measuring 4.0 to 4.9 cm and 75% of aneurysms 5 cm or larger can be palpated.[9] There is virtually no risk of causing aneurysm rupture by abdominal palpation.

When the physical examination is suspicious for an AAA, the aorta often proves to be of normal size.[10] A tortuous aorta may appear enlarged, and prominent aortic pulsations, especially in a thin patient, may simulate an aneurysm. Aortic pulsations may be transmitted to an adjacent mass. Nonetheless, clinical suspicion of an AAA warrants further investigation.

An abdominal bruit is found in only 5% to 10% of patients with AAAs.[8] The presence of a bruit is a nonspecific finding because bruits can also originate in a stenotic renal, iliac, or mesenteric artery. A loud continuous bruit suggests the diagnosis of aortovenous fistula.

Perfusion distal to an AAA is usually well maintained, and most patients have normal femoral pulses.[8]

Diminished femoral pulses may result from iliofemoral occlusive disease or from hypotension in the patient with a ruptured aneurysm.

Thromboembolic complications can occur spontaneously or when atheromatous plaques are disrupted during invasive procedures such as angiography. Large emboli can acutely occlude major vessels such as the iliac, femoral, or popliteal artery, causing acute painful lower extremity ischemia with absent distal pulses. Rarely, the aneurysm itself can thrombose, rendering both lower extremities acutely ischemic.

More often, microemboli consisting of cholesterol crystals or clot obstruct small distal vessels, such as the digital arteries of the toes and arterioles and capillaries of the skin. These patients have livedo reticularis; one or more cool, painful, cyanotic toes; and palpable pedal pulses. This constellation of findings, often called the blue toe syndrome, is highly suggestive of a proximal source of emboli. When an AAA is the source, the aneurysm is often too small to palpate and may only be discovered after radiologic investigation.

Rarely, an intact AAA causes symptoms by compressing adjacent structures. Large, long-standing aneurysms can cause vertebral body erosion and severe back pain. Compression of the duodenum between the superior mesenteric artery and an AAA can cause duodenal obstruction, vomiting, and weight loss. Obstruction of the ureters in the patient with an inflammatory aneurysm can cause ureteral colic.

Ruptured Aneurysms

Pain-Hypotension-Mass Triad

Although the classic triad of a ruptured AAA is pain, hypotension, and a pulsatile abdominal mass, many patients have only one or two components of this triad, and an occasional patient has none of the classic features.

Rupture is often the first manifestation of an AAA. Some patients, however, have a previously diagnosed AAA, and a decision not to operate electively may have been made because the aneurysm was small or the patient was considered too high risk. If such a patient has acute symptoms, the presumptive diagnosis is aneurysm rupture.

Most patients with a ruptured AAA experience pain in the abdomen, back, or flank.[6,8] Pain is usually acute, severe, and constant and can radiate to the chest, thigh, inguinal area, or scrotum. The history of pain may be unobtainable if the patient's mental status is compromised by severe hypotension.

The mechanism of the pain associated with aneurysm rupture is poorly understood. It may be caused by expansion of the aortic wall or by stimulation of sensory nerves in the retroperitoneum. Identical pain can occur with intact but acutely expanding aneurysms, which may be impossible to differentiate clinically from ruptured aneurysms.[11,12] Acute pain in the patient with an AAA should be considered a symptom of rupture or impending rupture.

The duration of symptoms before presentation varies greatly. Some patients are seen shortly after severe pain and hypotension develop. In others, rupture is initially contained in the retroperitoneum, blood loss is small, and the presentation is delayed. The patient with a ruptured AAA occasionally has symptoms for several days or even weeks before seeking medical attention.[13] A long duration of symptoms does not exclude the diagnosis of ruptured AAA.

Rupture of an AAA may be accompanied by nausea and vomiting, and sudden hemorrhage can cause syncope or near-syncope.[8,14] Compensatory hemodynamic mechanisms may then return the blood pressure and cerebral perfusion to normal. Transient improvement in symptoms is fairly common but will be followed by hemodynamic deterioration if diagnosis and treatment are delayed.[14]

Ruptured AAAs are often large, and most patients have palpable abdominal masses.[8,13] As with intact aneurysms, a ruptured AAA may not be palpable if the aneurysm is small or the patient is obese. The examination may be difficult if abdominal guarding is present or if an ileus causes significant distention. Aortic pulsations may not be prominent if the blood pressure is low. When a mass is not palpable, the diagnosis is often delayed.

Hypotension is the least consistent part of the triad, occurring in only half to two thirds of patients,[7] and is often a late finding. When the initial blood loss is minor, vital signs are often normal. The patient with initially normal vital signs may deteriorate and become hypotensive suddenly and unpredictably.

Occasionally, rupture into the retroperitoneum is sealed and contained for many weeks or months.[15] Patients with this condition develop abdominal or back pain, presumably at the time of aneurysm leakage, that subsequently diminishes or resolves completely. If the diagnosis is made, evidence of chronic rupture (organized hematoma) is found at surgery. These patients can have chronic pain and may progress to free rupture and subsequent massive hemorrhage at any time.[15]

Aortoenteric Fistula

An AAA can rupture into the gastrointestinal tract (aortoenteric fistula) or inferior vena cava (aortocaval fistula). A primary aortoenteric fistula (AEF) is formed when an AAA erodes into the gastrointestinal tract, usually the third or fourth portion of the duodenum. A secondary AEF, a communication between the site of previous aortic surgery and the gastrointestinal tract, can occur as a late complication of AAA repair and should be considered as the leading diagnosis in any patient who presents with a severe gastrointestinal bleed and a history of aortic graft placement.

Early in the formation of a primary AEF, the bowel wall is eroded from the outside by the adjacent AAA. This can lead to the leakage of intestinal contents, with local infection and sometimes abscess formation. Eventually, breakdown of the aortic wall leads to an AEF and gastrointestinal bleeding.

The patient with an AEF may have abdominal or back pain, fever, or other signs of intraabdominal infection or gastrointestinal bleeding. Because most of these fistulas are into the duodenum, hemorrhage usually manifests as hematemesis or melena. The initial bleeding results from erosion of vessels in the bowel wall and is often minor. Later, often after several days to a week or longer, massive bleeding results from rupture into the intestinal lumen.

The possibility of a primary AEF should be considered in any patient older than 50 years with unexplained gastrointestinal bleeding. If an AAA is diagnosed by history, physical examination, or any other modality, the patient should be presumed to have an AEF until proven otherwise.

Aortovenous (Aortocaval) Fistula

An aortovenous (usually aortocaval) fistula arises when periaortic inflammation causes adherence of the aorta to an adjacent vein, with pressure on the vessel walls causing the development of an arteriovenous communication. If concomitant extravasation of blood into the retroperitoneum occurs, the clinical presentation is similar to that of other patients with ruptured AAAs, often with hypovolemic shock. More often the aneurysm ruptures into the vena cava without leaking externally, and the signs and symptoms of a large arteriovenous fistula dominate the clinical picture.[16]

As in other patients with AAAs, a patient with an aortovenous fistula may have abdominal or back pain. An aneurysm that becomes fistulous with the vena cava is usually large, and 80% to 90% are palpable. A continuous abdominal bruit can be auscultated in approximately 75% of patients with aortovenous fistulas, and 25% of patients have a palpable abdominal thrill.[16]

Shunting of blood from the arterial to the venous system increases venous pressure, venous volume, and venous return to the heart. Signs and symptoms of high-output congestive heart failure (dyspnea, jugular venous distention, pulmonary edema) are often present, and half the patients have signs of regional venous hypertension distal to the fistula.[16] The increased venous volume and pressure can cause lower extremity edema or cyanosis, and dilated superficial veins can be seen on the legs or abdominal wall. Distention and rupture of veins in the bladder mucosa can cause gross or microscopic hematuria; rectal bleeding can occur for similar reasons. Because of shunting of arterial blood into the venous system, the lower extremities may be cool with diminished pulses.

The patient with an aortovenous fistula often has renal insufficiency caused by decreased renal perfusion accompanying high-output congestive heart failure and by increased renal venous pressure. Hematuria in these patients may originate from the kidneys or the bladder. Hematuria is common when an aortovenous fistula is present but not in other patients with AAAs.[16] With an AAA and hematuria, computed tomography (CT) or aortography may be indicated to rule out aortovenous fistula formation.

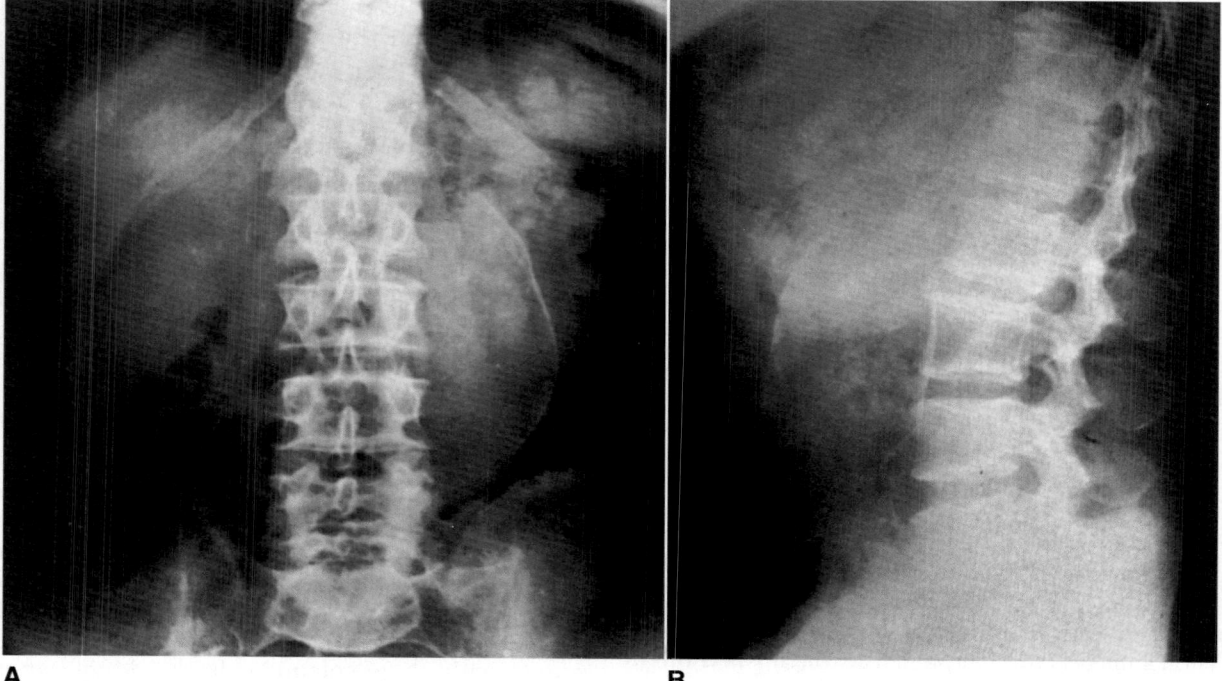

A   B

Figure 85-2. Anteroposterior **(A)** and lateral **(B)** views of large abdominal aortic aneurysms with calcification of aortic wall. (From Juergens JL, et al: *Peripheral Vascular Diseases*, 5th ed. Philadelphia, WB Saunders, 1980; by permission of the Mayo Foundation.)

DIAGNOSTIC STRATEGIES

Abdominal Radiography

If CT or ultrasonography is available, plain abdominal radiography may waste valuable time, because a normal plain film does not exclude the presence of an AAA and rarely identifies alternate pathology. However, AAAs large enough to cause symptoms are seen on plain abdominal radiographs in two thirds to three fourths of patients.[17] Radiographs obtained to investigate other causes of pain (e.g., bowel obstruction or back injury) may reveal signs of an AAA. If neither CT nor ultrasonography is immediately available, plain radiographs can usually be readily obtained and may be diagnostic.

The most common findings are curvilinear calcification of the aortic wall (Figure 85-2) or a paravertebral soft tissue mass. With rupture, the psoas or renal outlines may be obscured, although rupture cannot be reliably confirmed or excluded with plain films.

Abdominal aortic aneurysms can be seen on both anteroposterior and lateral radiographs. A lateral lumbar spine film (or cross-table lateral of the lumbar spine area) is often the easiest to evaluate because the right border of the aneurysm may overlie the spine on the anteroposterior view. In many cases, enough calcium is present in both lateral walls (on an anteroposterior view) or in the anterior and posterior walls (on a lateral view) to measure the aortic diameter and diagnose the presence of an aneurysm. If only the anterior wall is calcified (on the lateral view), the distance from the anterior wall calcification to the front of the vertebral bodies correlates well with the true aortic size.

Although plain radiographs are not the optimal diagnostic modality, in the proper clinical setting they can provide strong evidence that a patient's symptoms are caused by a ruptured aneurysm, allowing prompt mobilization of the surgical team.

Ultrasonography

Ultrasonography is virtually 100% sensitive in detecting AAAs (Figure 85-3), provided that a technically adequate study can be obtained.[1] Measurements of aortic diameter are very accurate. Because it is relatively inexpensive and requires no contrast agents or radiation exposure, ultrasonography is often chosen for nonemergency aneurysm diagnosis and used to follow patients with known aneurysms.

Ultrasonography has distinct advantages in the emergency evaluation of a patient with a suspected ruptured AAA.[18] It can be performed very rapidly at the patient's bedside, obviating the need to take a potentially unstable patient to the radiology suite. Ultrasonography is much more sensitive than abdominal radiography in detecting an AAA—if an aorta with a normal diameter throughout its entire abdominal course is visualized, the patient does not have an AAA. Ultrasonography sometimes provides alternative explanations for the patient's pain by revealing conditions such as acute cholecystitis.

Ultrasonography has certain limitations. It is more operator dependent than other diagnostic modalities and may be prone to technical or interpretive error. Even with elective studies, the aorta is sometimes not well visualized because of obesity or excess bowel gas. In many settings, ultrasonography is not immediately available and requires waiting for the arrival of a radi-

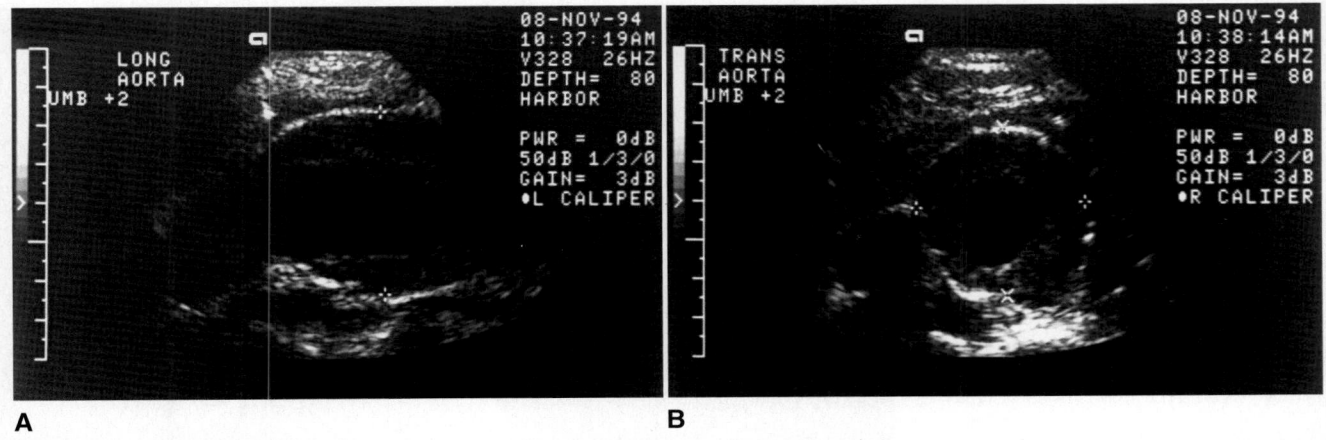

Figure 85-3. Longitudinal **(A)** and transverse **(B)** sonograms of an abdominal aortic aneurysm. Markers denote the outside of the aneurysm wall. The central patent lumen is surrounded by an echogenic mural thrombus. (Courtesy of Richard Rensio, MD.)

ologist or technologist. Importantly, although ultrasonography is extremely sensitive in demonstrating the presence of an AAA, it cannot be used to determine reliably whether an AAA has ruptured.

Rupture can be confirmed if free intraperitoneal or retroperitoneal blood is seen in the presence of an AAA. However, the sensitivity of emergency ultrasonography in detecting extraluminal blood is very low. The purpose of the study is to confirm or exclude the presence of an aneurysm; clinical information (or a CT scan) must be used to determine the likelihood of rupture. If ultrasonography reveals an AAA in an unstable patient, aneurysm rupture is presumed, and the patient requires immediate surgery.

Computed Tomography

As with ultrasonography, the abdominal CT scan is virtually 100% accurate in determining the presence or absence of an AAA and provides accurate measurements of the aortic diameter.[19] The CT scan is less subject to technical problems and interpretation errors than ultrasonography and is much more accurate in detecting extraluminal blood. CT is often used to help plan elective procedures because it can demonstrate the proximal and distal extent of the aneurysm, the status of the renal and visceral arteries, and unsuspected pathologic conditions that may influence operative management.[19]

Intravenous contrast material is usually administered in elective studies and is desirable, but not essential, in emergency situations.[19,20] If prolonged hypotension has occurred, it may be advisable to avoid intravenous contrast to prevent contrast-exacerbated nephropathy. Intravenous contrast will opacify the aortic lumen and distinguish the patent lumen from mural thrombus. It can demonstrate periaortic fibrosis because the soft tissue surrounding an inflammatory AAA often enhances. Intravenous contrast is not necessary to identify the aneurysm, however, and acute hemorrhage is well visualized on scans done without contrast.[19,20]

When evaluating a patient with a suspected ruptured AAA, a normal aortic diameter on CT scan excludes an

AAA as the cause of the patient's symptoms. CT scans provide more information than ultrasonography about other retroperitoneal or intraperitoneal disorders and may reveal diagnoses such as ureterolithiasis, pancreatitis, or diverticulitis. However, CT scans take longer to perform than ultrasonography and require moving the patient out of the emergency department. Therefore, obtaining a CT scan is appropriate only in hemodynamically stable patients.

The CT scan is much more sensitive than ultrasonography in detecting the retroperitoneal hemorrhage associated with aneurysm rupture. The reported sensitivity ranges from 77% to 100%.[21] Blood is seen as a retroperitoneal fluid collection adjacent to the aneurysm, often tracking into the perinephric space or along the psoas muscle (Figure 85-4).

Although CT scans are sensitive in detecting retroperitoneal blood, the scan results are sometimes misleading. Rarely, the CT scan is falsely positive for rupture and an intact aneurysm is found at surgery. This can occur when tumor, lymph nodes, inflammatory soft tissue, or bowel loops adjacent to the aorta are identified as blood.[19] False-negative scans are more serious; in these cases, an aneurysm is seen on the CT scan, but there is no evidence of hemorrhage. Typically, hemodynamic deterioration occurs a short time later, and a ruptured aneurysm is found at surgery.[22]

This situation can occur if hemorrhage is missed on the CT scan, or if rupture occurs shortly after the scan is completed. A CT scan cannot determine whether an AAA is the cause of the patient's pain or whether rupture of the aneurysm is imminent. Another cause of pain can be diagnosed only if the CT scan shows no aneurysm or shows an intact aneurysm and clearly demonstrates an alternative explanation for the patient's symptoms.

Other Diagnostic Modalities

Angiography has virtually no place in the emergency evaluation of the suspected ruptured AAA. Because contrast opacifies only the patent lumen and not mural thrombus, angiography often underestimates aneurysm size and can miss the aneurysm entirely.[19] In addition,

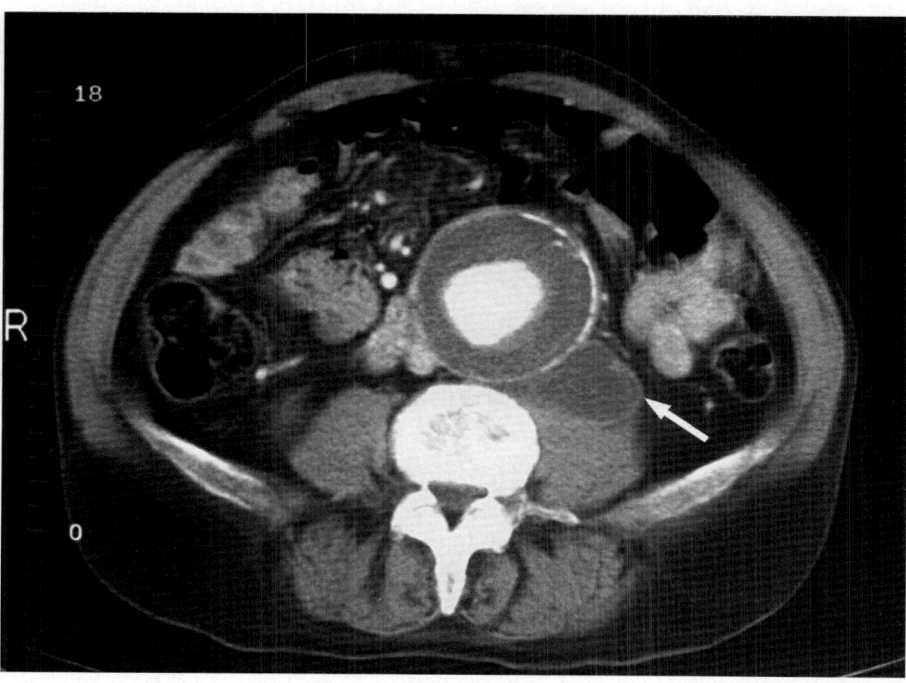

Figure 85-4. Computed tomography scan of ruptured abdominal aortic aneurysm, with calcification of the aortic wall and intraluminal thrombus. The patent lumen enhances with the administration of contrast material, but the periaortic hematoma (*arrow*) does not. (Courtesy of Richard Rensio, MD.)

angiography is time-consuming and performed away from the emergency department. Its use in the patient with an AAA is limited to helping plan elective surgery.

Magnetic resonance imaging and magnetic resonance angiography can also be used for elective preoperative assessment, but not for the evaluation of possible aortic rupture. Acutely hemorrhaged blood can be difficult to identify with magnetic resonance imaging, and the necessary monitoring equipment cannot be used.[19]

DIFFERENTIAL CONSIDERATIONS

Because the patient with a ruptured AAA usually has abdominal, back, or flank pain, with or without hypotension, common misdiagnoses are other disease processes causing these symptoms (Box 85-1). The sudden onset of pain often leads to the clinical suspicion of renal colic, with which AAA is often confused. Abdominal pain and tenderness can suggest pancreatitis, intestinal ischemia, or other intraabdominal disorders. The diagnosis of musculoskeletal back pain is especially dangerous because such patients are often discharged from the emergency department.

Presentation with epigastric pain and hypotension may lead to an admission diagnosis of acute myocardial infarction. Because the patient with a ruptured AAA often has coexistent coronary artery disease, blood loss from a ruptured aneurysm may diminish coronary perfusion and cause chest pain or electrocardiographic changes consistent with cardiac ischemia. These findings do not rule out the presence of a ruptured AAA.

To avoid missing the diagnosis, ruptured AAA should be considered in middle-age or elderly patients

---

BOX 85-1. Common Misdiagnoses in Patients with Ruptured AAAs

Renal colic
"Acute abdomen"
  Pancreatitis
  Intestinal ischemia
  Diverticulitis
  Cholecystitis
  Appendicitis
  Perforated viscus
  Bowel obstruction
Musculoskeletal back pain
Acute myocardial infarction

---

with any part of the classic triad. The diagnosis of ruptured AAA should also be considered when making the diagnoses listed in Box 85-1, especially when the diagnosis is not clear-cut or the patient is at high risk for an AAA.

MANAGEMENT

Ruptured Aneurysms

The patient with a ruptured AAA is unstable until the aorta is cross-clamped in the operating room or stabilized with endovascular techniques. No patient with a known or suspected aortic rupture should be considered stable, regardless of the initial vital signs or initial hemoglobin level. Patients taken to the operating room soon after emergency department arrival have a much higher survival rate than those in whom surgical care is delayed.[23]

When the patient arrives at the emergency department, large-bore intravenous access should be established with at least two lines and blood sent for crossmatching. At least 6 units of blood should be made available initially, with notification to the blood bank of the potential need for significantly more, because patients with ruptured AAAs have large transfusion requirements.[7] The surgical and anesthesia team should be notified immediately. Further management depends on hemodynamic stability and diagnostic certainty.

The hemodynamically unstable patient in whom a ruptured AAA has been diagnosed or is strongly suspected should be taken to the operating room as soon as possible. Diagnostic testing should be kept to a minimum. The diagnosis can often be made from the clinical presentation and abdominal examination, and bedside ultrasonography can quickly confirm or exclude the presence of an aneurysm. A CT scan is appropriate only if it can be obtained very quickly without compromising the patient's care. Time-consuming tests inappropriately delay definitive therapy and increase the risk of exsanguination. Hypotensive patients may have to be taken to the operating room based on a strong clinical presumption of the diagnosis, without definitive diagnostic imaging. Some of these patients will not have ruptured aneurysms, but they usually have other acute abdominal conditions requiring laparotomy.

Attempts to resuscitate these patients fully in the emergency department and normalize the vital signs should be avoided. Hypotensive patients need to be taken to the operating room so that the aorta can be clamped and hemorrhage stopped. Attempts to stabilize the patient in the emergency department are often fruitless and waste valuable time.

Fluid Resuscitation

The appropriate degree of preoperative volume resuscitation is controversial. Preoperative hypotension is the strongest predictor of mortality in the patient with a ruptured AAA.[7] However, correcting the hypotension before clamping the aorta may not improve mortality and may even be harmful.

It has been argued that hypotension slows bleeding in patients with AAA and allows local clot formation and tamponade of the rupture site. Raising the intravascular volume and blood pressure before clamping the aorta may dislodge clots and cause further bleeding.[24] Large volumes of crystalloid solution may contribute to bleeding by causing a dilutional coagulopathy. These concerns are similar to those in trauma patients with uncontrolled hemorrhage.

Alternatively, delaying resuscitation of hypotensive patients until they reach the operating room may have deleterious effects. The patient with a ruptured AAA often survives the surgery but dies in the early postoperative period. These deaths are caused by complications of prolonged hypotension, such as myocardial infarction, respiratory failure, and renal failure. The patient with a ruptured AAA is usually elderly, often has coexisting conditions, and tolerates hypovolemia and hypotension poorly.

No prospective studies have compared different preoperative fluid regimens in hypotensive patients with ruptured AAAs, and the optimal resuscitation strategy has not been determined. The priority in these patients is expeditious transportation to the operating room for definitive control of aortic hemorrhage. In the prehospital setting and in the emergency department before the availability of the surgeon and the operating room, the blood pressure should be raised with crystalloid or blood products to a level that maintains adequate cerebral and myocardial perfusion.[24] The goal is to prevent irreversible end-organ damage. An arbitrary blood pressure goal cannot be specified because the blood pressure necessary for vital organ perfusion varies among patients, but a reasonable target is 90 to 100 mm Hg systolic.

Aortic Clamping

Cross-clamping the aorta through a left lateral thoracotomy is sometimes performed in the operating room for severely hypotensive patients.[7] Thoracic aortic clamping adds the morbidity that comes with thoracotomy and may cause ischemic damage to the spinal cord and intraabdominal organs. Emergency department thoracotomy may be appropriate, however, when a patient with severe hemodynamic compromise or cardiac arrest fails to respond to standard resuscitative measures and cannot be taken quickly to the operating room.

Endovascular Approach

To date, ruptured AAAs have been repaired almost exclusively via open surgical techniques. Endovascular repair of ruptured aneurysms may now be feasible, even in unstable patients. The method of repair will clearly be the surgeon's decision and is institution dependent. Planning for the care of such patients should include development of a well understood protocol that advises the emergency department staff about which services to mobilize when ruptured AAA presents.

Diagnostic Confirmation

In the patient with acute abdominal or back pain but without hypotension, more time can be taken to confirm the presence of an AAA. If an AAA can be diagnosed with bedside testing (abdominal examination, plain radiographs, or ultrasonography), the surgeon will often proceed immediately to the operating room with a clinical diagnosis of aneurysm rupture, because a delay in surgery places the patient with a ruptured AAA at risk for sudden and unpredictable hemodynamic deterioration. If an AAA cannot be identified with bedside testing and the patient remains hemodynamically stable, an abdominal CT scan can be obtained to confirm or exclude the presence of an aneurysm. The patient who is sent for a CT scan must be monitored closely and taken to the operating room immediately if hemodynamic deterioration occurs.

The CT scan can also identify the retroperitoneal hemorrhage associated with rupture and confirm the need for an emergency procedure. The surgeon may want confirmation of rupture to avoid the problems of performing emergency surgery with an intact aneurysm. With emergency surgery, detailed anatomic evaluation and careful preoperative planning are often impossible, evaluation and optimization of the patient's cardiopulmonary and renal function may be precluded, and invasive hemodynamic monitoring may be unavailable. For these reasons, patients who are taken for emergency surgery and found to have intact, symptomatic aneurysms have a significantly higher mortality rate (20-25%) than patients undergoing elective aneurysm repair (approximately 5%).[4,8,12]

Once an AAA has been diagnosed, the decision to obtain a CT scan to distinguish a ruptured from an unruptured aneurysm should be made very cautiously and in close consultation with a surgeon. If a CT scan demonstrates an intact AAA and the decision is made to delay surgery, the patient must be closely observed for signs of rupture in an intensive care setting, and a clear alternate explanation for the patient's presentation (e.g., hypotension, syncope) must be established.

Patients may be hypertensive on admission because of pain or underlying chronic hypertension. Unlike the situation with aortic dissection, no evidence exists that lowering the blood pressure is beneficial in the patient with a ruptured AAA, and these patients are at risk of developing precipitous hypotension.

Surgery and Mortality

Ruptured AAA is uniformly fatal unless treated surgically. Thus, once this diagnosis is made, operative repair should be attempted in almost all patients.[7] Attempts have been made to identify patients with a very low likelihood of survival, and it has been suggested that surgery can be withheld in patients with prehospital or emergency department cardiac arrest. Survival has been reported in up to 25% of patients with preoperative cardiac arrest, however, and no variables that can be assessed in the emergency department are universally predictive of a fatal outcome.[3,7] Surgery is indicated unless the patient's life expectancy is very short because of underlying illnesses or the patient's quality of life is so poor that surgery is considered unreasonable.

Surgical mortality in patients with ruptured AAAs is approximately 50% and has shown little improvement in the past two decades.[25,26] Hypotension is the most important factor predicting a poor outcome; a low initial hematocrit also increases the likelihood of perioperative death.[7,24]

Operative mortality rates significantly underestimate the true lethality of the ruptured AAA. The patient with a ruptured AAA may die at home or may reach the hospital but die before surgery. When patients who do not reach the operating room are considered, the overall mortality rate is 80% to 90%.[27]

Intact, Asymptomatic Aneurysms

An incidental diagnosis of AAA can be made in the emergency department, or a patient with a known AAA presents to the emergency department. The decision to repair an asymptomatic aneurysm depends on the risk of aneurysm rupture, the patient's life expectancy and likelihood of dying from other causes, and the surgical risk. The latter factors are determined by the patient's age and coexisting illnesses. The risk of rupture is largely a function of aneurysm size.

In two recent clinical trials, patients with small (<5.5 cm) aneurysms were randomized to early surgery or close follow-up.[28,29] In the latter group, aneurysms were followed with serial ultrasonograms or CT scans, and surgery was performed only if symptoms developed, rapid expansion was documented, or a diameter of 5.5 cm was reached. Both studies showed equivalent survival rates in the two groups. As a result, fewer small aneurysms are now repaired electively, potentially leaving a larger group of patients who may present to the emergency department with complications of an AAA. It is important to note that the "watchful waiting" approach is appropriate only for asymptomatic aneurysms, and rupture of the AAA must be strongly considered when evaluating any symptoms in these patients.

Traditional Repair

The conventional technique for repair of AAAs is an open approach with a laparotomy. The aneurysm is opened longitudinally and repaired from within (Figure 85-5). A graft is inserted inside the aneurysm and anastomosed to uninvolved vessels above and below. When possible, a straight graft is used between the infrarenal and distal aorta. If the aneurysm involves the aortic bifurcation, or if iliac artery aneurysmal or occlusive disease is present, a bifurcation graft is used, with the distal anastomosis to the iliac or femoral arteries. The aneurysm wall is then closed around the graft to help separate it from adjacent structures.

Endovascular Repair

Many AAAs can now be repaired without laparotomy, using endovascular techniques.[4] A stent graft is placed into the femoral artery through a groin incision and is advanced under fluoroscopic guidance to a position that spans the aneurysm (Figure 85-6A). The contralateral iliac limb is then placed to form a bifurcated graft (Figure 85-6B). Straight (tube) grafts, placed in many patients early in the development of endovascular repair, are now rarely used because of a high failure rate.

Endovascular surgery avoids the morbidity of a laparotomy and may allow the repair of AAAs in some high-risk patients who might not tolerate conventional surgery. Detailed preoperative imaging and planning are often required, however, and few surgeons currently apply this technique to patients with ruptured aneurysms.[30] In addition, patients who have had endovascular aneurysm repair remain at risk for

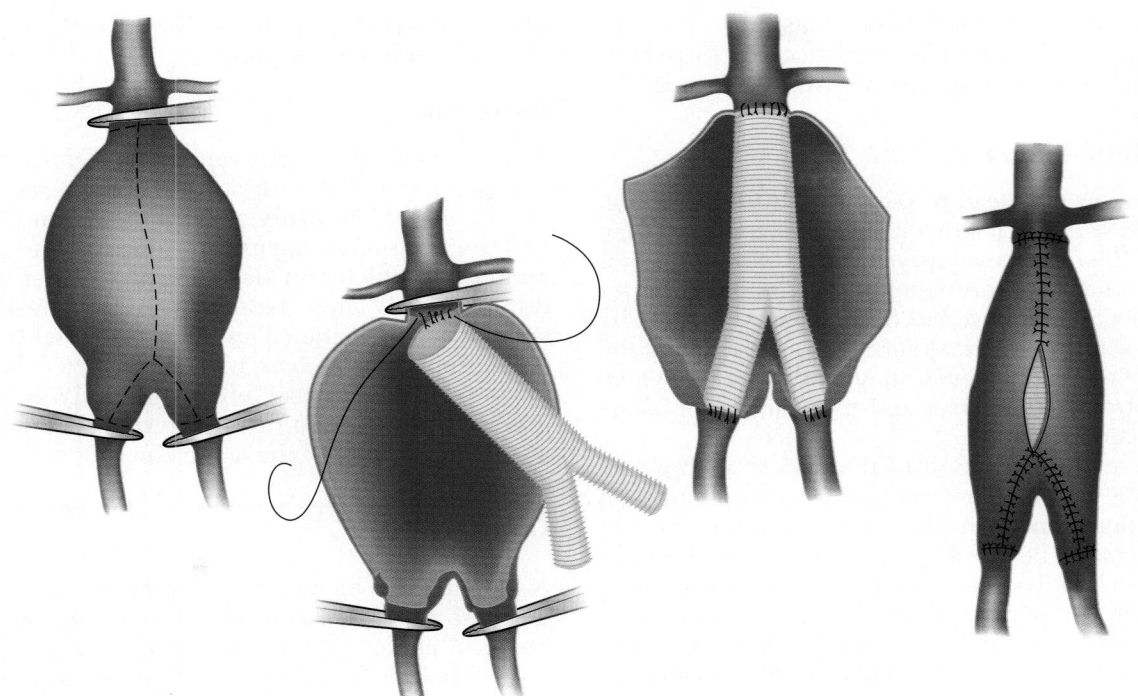

Figure 85-5. Steps in repair of an abdominal aortic aneurysm. See text for details. (From Kent KC, et al. Surgical principles for operative treatment of aortic aneurysms. In Lindsay J Jr [ed]: *Diseases of the Aorta*, Philadelphia, Lea & Febiger, 1994, p 287.)

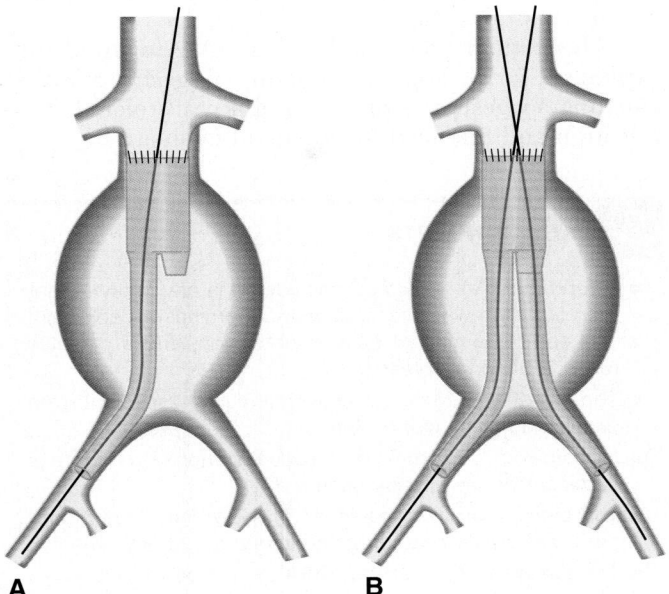

A   **B**

Figure 85-6. Endovascular repair of an abdominal aortic aneurysm. **A,** Aortic section with attached iliac limb. **B,** Addition of contralateral iliac limb. (From Blum U, et al: Endoluminal stent-grafts for infrarenal abdominal aortic aneurysm. *N Engl J Med* 336:13-20, 1997. Copyright © 1997, Massachusetts Medical Society.)

rupture of the aneurysm; the reported rupture rate is 1% per year.[31]

Survival

The mortality rate of elective AAA repair is now approximately 5%, in stark contrast to the results with ruptured aneurysms.[4] Patients who survive the operation have an excellent prognosis, with a long-term survival close to that of the general population. After repair of the aneurysm, long-term survival is primarily limited by associated cardiac disease.

LATE COMPLICATIONS OF REPAIR

Graft infection, AEF formation, and anastomotic aneurysm (pseudoaneurysm) formation can occur at any time from weeks to many years after the surgery.[32,34] These complications often occur together, their clinical presentations overlap, and they are diagnosed by similar means. Endoleak is a unique complication of endovascular aneurysm repair.

Graft Infection

Graft infection can result from contamination of the graft at surgery, spread of a contiguous infection, or hematogenous seeding. Infection can disrupt the anastomosis between native artery and graft, leading to leakage of blood and pseudoaneurysm formation. The infection can be localized to a portion of the graft, most often the inguinal portion of an aortofemoral graft, or can involve the entire graft.

Infection of the distal limb of an aortofemoral graft may be clinically evident, with local signs of infection or a palpable false aneurysm. Intraabdominal graft infection is often subtle, with low-grade fever and vague abdominal or back pain.[32] Abdominal tenderness or a palpable mass may be present at the leaking anastomosis. A CT scan should be obtained to evaluate suspected graft infection.[19] Collections of fluid or gas around the graft provide evidence of infection, although false-negative results occasionally occur.[32]

Aortoenteric Fistula

Graft infection may lead to secondary AEF formation. These fistulas, which are much more common than primary AEFs, can develop years after AAA repair or after aortoiliac or aortofemoral bypass surgery for peripheral vascular disease. Secondary AEFs usually form between the proximal aortic anastomosis and the distal duodenum. However, they can occur anywhere in the gastrointestinal tract and cause upper or lower gastrointestinal bleeding.[34]

The clinical presentation of the patient with a secondary AEF may be identical to that of a patient with graft infection alone, with fever and other signs of infection. More often, however, the patient with an AEF has gastrointestinal bleeding.[34] The bleeding can be acute or chronic, and its severity ranges from minor to massive.

An AEF must be considered in any patient with gastrointestinal bleeding and a history of abdominal aortic surgery. Most of these patients, however, ultimately prove to have other, more common causes of gastrointestinal bleeding.[35] The diagnostic approach depends on the patient's hemodynamic stability.

If the patient with a suspected AEF is unstable with massive bleeding, diagnostic testing may be dangerously time-consuming. In these patients, emergency laparotomy may be necessary to control hemorrhage and diagnose or exclude the presence of an AEF.[34,35] Stable patients can be evaluated with endoscopy or a CT scan.

Upper gastrointestinal endoscopy is often recommended as the initial diagnostic test.[34] Direct visualization of the fistula into the distal duodenum is sometimes possible. However, endoscopy cannot be relied on to identify an AEF, and its main value is in establishing another diagnosis. If an active bleeding site other than an AEF is clearly seen, emergency surgery can be avoided.

An abdominal CT scan can also be used to evaluate a suspected AEF.[19] Although imaging of the fistula is often impossible, graft infection is almost invariably present in patients with secondary AEFs, and the CT scan can demonstrate the associated infection. Radiographically distinguishing an AEF from intraabdominal graft infection alone may be difficult, but the distinction is not crucial because both need surgical management.

Pseudoaneurysm (Anastomotic Aneurysm)

Pseudoaneurysms can arise at the site of a leaking anastomosis.[36] They may be associated with graft infection or AEF formation but more often result from degeneration of the native vessel.

The patient with an anastomotic aneurysm may have pain or a pulsatile mass in the abdomen or groin. The aneurysm may give rise to distal emboli or may rupture and cause life-threatening hemorrhage. Suspected pseudoaneurysms can be evaluated with angiography, CT scans, or ultrasonography.[36]

Endoleak

After endovascular AAA repair, blood flow outside of the graft lumen but within the aneurysm sac is termed an *endoleak*.[37] As many as 20% of patients who have had endovascular aneurysm repair have persistent endoleaks, which may develop shortly after the procedure or much later. Because many endoleaks resolve spontaneously, patients are often observed for months before repair of the leak with secondary endovascular procedures or surgical intervention. With persistent leakage of blood into the aneurysm sac, the patient is at risk for rupture of the aneurysm.[31,37]

DISPOSITION

A patient with an acutely symptomatic AAA requires hospital admission and urgent or emergency surgical repair. A patient whose aneurysm is asymptomatic and discovered incidentally must be referred for consideration of elective repair. The patient with an AAA should be referred for an outpatient workup only if it is clear that the symptoms prompting the emergency department visit are unrelated to the aneurysm. If the patient is discharged, instructions should be given to seek medical attention immediately if abdominal, back, or flank pain develops.

In the patient who has had an AAA repaired, unexplained fever, abdominal pain, or gastrointestinal bleeding suggests the presence of a graft-related complication and the need for inpatient evaluation.

KEY CONCEPTS

- A ruptured AAA should be considered in any patient older than 50 years who presents with abdominal or back pain. The complete triad of pain, hypotension, and a pulsatile mass is often not present.
- The risk of rupture increases with aneurysm size, but even small aneurysms can rupture.
- In the patient with an AAA and acute symptoms, rupture is imminent or has already occurred.
- The patient with a ruptured AAA who is initially hemodynamically stable can suddenly deteriorate at any time.
- The patient with a ruptured AAA should be moved expeditiously to the operating room, bypassing complete resuscitation and time-consuming imaging.
- The patient who has had endovascular repair of an AAA remains at risk for aneurysm rupture.

REFERENCES

1. Lederle FA: Ultrasonographic screening for abdominal aortic aneurysms. *Ann Intern Med* 139:516, 2003.
2. Ashton HA, et al: The Multicentre Aneurysm Screening Study (MASS) into the effect of abdominal aortic aneurysm screening on mortality in men: A randomised controlled trial. *Lancet* 360:1531, 2002.

3. Chen JC, et al: Predictors of death in nonruptured and ruptured abdominal aortic aneurysms. *J Vasc Surg* 24:614, 1996.

4. Brewster DC, et al: Guidelines for the treatment of abdominal aortic aneurysms. Report of a subcommittee of the Joint Council of the American Association for Vascular Surgery and Society for Vascular Surgery. *J Vasc Surg* 37:1106, 2003.

5. Lederle FA, et al: Rupture rate of large abdominal aortic aneurysms in patients refusing or unfit for elective repair. *JAMA* 287:2968, 2002.

6. Noel AA, et al: Ruptured abdominal aortic aneurysms: The excessive mortality rate of conventional repair. *J Vasc Surg* 34:41, 2001.

7. Gloviczki P, et al: Ruptured abdominal aortic aneurysms: Repair should not be denied. *J Vasc Surg* 15:851, 1992.

8. Vohra R, et al: Long-term survival in patients undergoing resection of abdominal aortic aneurysm. *Ann Vasc Surg* 4:460, 1990.

9. Lederle FA, Simel DL: Does this patient have abdominal aortic aneurysm? *JAMA* 281:77, 1999.

10. Beede SD, et al: Positive predictive value of clinical suspicion of abdominal aortic aneurysm: Implications for efficient use of abdominal ultrasonography. *Arch Intern Med* 150:549, 1990.

11. Kvilekval KHV, et al: The value of computed tomography in the management of symptomatic abdominal aortic aneurysms. *J Vasc Surg* 12:28, 1990.

12. Sullivan CA, Rohrer MJ, Cutler BS: Clinical management of the symptomatic but unruptured abdominal aortic aneurysm. *J Vasc Surg* 11:799, 1990.

13. Akkersdijk GJM, van Bockel JH: Ruptured abdominal aortic aneurysm: Initial misdiagnosis and the effect on treatment. *Eur J Surg* 164:29, 1998.

14. Lederle FA, Parenti CM, Chute EP: Ruptured abdominal aortic aneurysm: The internist as diagnostician. *Am J Med* 96:163, 1994.

15. Sterpetti AV, et al: Sealed rupture of abdominal aortic aneurysms. *J Vasc Surg* 11:430, 1990.

16. Potyk DK, Guthrie CR: Spontaneous aortocaval fistula. *Ann Emerg Med* 25:424, 1995.

17. Loughran CF: A review of the plain abdominal radiograph in acute rupture of abdominal aortic aneurysms. *Clin Radiol* 37:383, 1986.

18. Kuhn M, et al: Emergency department ultrasound scanning for abdominal aortic aneurysm: Accessible, accurate, and advantageous. *Ann Emerg Med* 36:219, 2000.

19. Siegel CL, Cohan RH: CT of abdominal aortic aneurysms. *AJR Am J Roentgenol* 163:17, 1994.

20. Novelline RA, et al: Helical CT in emergency radiology. *Radiology* 213:321, 1999.

21. Adam DJ, et al: The value of computed tomography in the assessment of suspected ruptured abdominal aortic aneurysm. *J Vasc Surg* 27:431, 1998.

22. Greatorex RA, et al: Limitations of computed tomography in leaking abdominal aortic aneurysms. *BMJ* 297:284, 1988.

23. Hans SS, Huang RR: Results of 101 ruptured abdominal aortic aneurysm repairs from a single surgical practice. *Arch Surg* 138:898, 2003.

24. Brimacombe J, Berry A: A review of anaesthesia for ruptured abdominal aortic aneurysm with special emphasis on preclamping fluid resuscitation. *Anaesth Intensive Care* 2:311, 1993.

25. Bown MJ, et al: A meta-analysis of 50 years of ruptured abdominal aortic aneurysm repair. *Br J Surg* 89:714, 2002.

26. Heller JA, et al: Two decades of abdominal aortic aneurysm repair: Have we made any progress? *J Vasc Surg* 32:1091, 2000.

27. Choksy SA, Wilmink ABM, Quick CR: Ruptured abdominal aortic aneurysm in the Huntingdon district: A 10-year experience. *Ann R Coll Surg Engl* 81:27, 1999.

28. Lederle FA, et al: Immediate repair compared with surveillance of small abdominal aortic aneurysms. *N Engl J Med* 346:1437, 2002.

29. United Kingdom Small Aneurysm Trial Participants: Long-term outcomes of immediate repair compared with surveillance of small abdominal aortic aneurysms. *N Engl J Med* 346:1445, 2002.

30. Ohki T, Veith FJ: Endovascular grafts and other image-guided catheter-based adjuncts to improve the treatment of ruptured aortoiliac aneurysms. *Ann Surg* 232:466, 2000.

31. Harris PL, et al: Incidence and risk factors of late rupture, conversion, and death after endovascular repair of infrarenal aortic aneurysms: The EUROSTAR experience. *J Vasc Surg* 32:739, 2000.

32. McCann RL, Schwartz LB, Georgiade GS: Management of abdominal aortic graft complications. *Ann Surg* 217:729, 1993.

33. Hallett JW, et al: Graft-related complications after abdominal aortic aneurysm repair: Reassurance from a 36-year population-based experience. *J Vasc Surg* 25:277, 1997.

34. Peck JJ, Eidemiller LR: Aortoenteric fistulas. *Arch Surg* 127:1191, 1992.

35. Pabst TS, et al: Gastrointestinal bleeding after aortic surgery: The role of laparotomy to rule out aortoenteric fistula. *J Vasc Surg* 8:280, 1988.

36. Allen RC, et al: Paraanastomotic aneurysms of the abdominal aorta. *J Vasc Surg* 18:424, 1993.

37. van Marrewijk C, et al: Significance of endoleaks after endovascular repair of abdominal aortic aneurysms: The EUROSTAR experience. *J Vasc Surg* 35:461, 2002.

38. Zarins CK, et al: Endoleak as a predictor of outcome after endovascular aneurysm repair: AneuRx multicenter clinical trial. *J Vasc Surg* 32:90, 2000.

86 Peripheral Arteriovascular Disease

Tom P. Aufderheide

PERSPECTIVE

Treatments for peripheral arterial disease date from the late 18th century. In 1785, Hunter demonstrated complete thrombosis of an aneurysmal sac with a ligature proximal to a popliteal aneurysm.[1] In 1877, Eck reported the first successful anastomosis between two vessels, the portal vein and the inferior vena cava. In 1963, surgical embolectomy became widely established by the introduction of the Fogarty balloon catheter. Recent advances in noninvasive hemodynamic testing, imaging techniques, interventional devices, and chronic indwelling catheters present a wide range of new diagnostic and therapeutic challenges.

Arteries are classified into three categories on the basis of their size and histologic features: (1) large or elastic arteries (the aorta and its immediate proximal, larger branches, including the innominate, subclavian, common carotid, and pulmonary arteries), (2) medium-size or muscular arteries (located just distal to elastic arteries, including the common femoral, axillary, and carotid arteries), and (3) small arteries (usually <2 mm in diameter) that course in the substance of tissues and organs. This chapter considers disease manifestations in medium and small arteries.

PRINCIPLES OF DISEASE

Arterial Anatomy

All arteries possess three layers: the tunica intima, tunica media, and tunica adventitia. As peripheral arteries diminish in caliber, these three layers become progressively indistinct and are no longer identifiable at the level of the arteriole (precapillary vessel containing smooth muscle).

The tunica intima has an inner lining of endothelial cells surrounded by subendothelial connective tissue. The outer limit of the tunica intima is demarcated by a longitudinally dispersed layer of elastic fibers known as the *internal elastic lamina*. The single layer of continuous endothelium is a unique thromboresistant layer between blood and the potentially thrombogenic subendothelial tissues. The integrity of the endothelium is a fundamental requirement for maintenance of normal structure and function of the entire vessel wall. Endothelial injury can result in intraluminal thrombosis and may contribute to the initiation of atherosclerosis.

The tunica media is made up primarily of circular or spiral smooth muscle cells arranged in concentric layers. The outer limit of this layer is marked by a well-defined, external elastic membrane. The elastic content of the tunica media gives resilience to medium-sized arteries. In the aging process, the elastic fibers deteriorate and are replaced by fibrous tissue. This loss of elasticity results in stretching and elongation and accounts for the progressive tortuosity and development of arterial aneurysms with aging. Vascular smooth muscle cells are capable of many metabolic functions, may be important in lipid accumulation in the vessel wall during atherosclerosis, and participate in vasoconstriction and dilation.

The tunica adventitia is a poorly defined layer of connective tissue in which nerve fibers and small, thin-walled nutrient vessels (vasa vasorum) are dispersed. Medium-sized arteries contain more nerve fibers than larger vessels, reflecting the importance of their role in the autonomic regulation of blood flow.

The peripheral arterial vascular system can be considered as a single end-organ subject to a variety of pathologic conditions. This chapter describes eight basic pathophysiologic processes: atherosclerosis, aneurysm, embolism, thrombosis, inflammation, trauma, vasospasm, and arteriovenous fistula. Most peripheral arterial problems are caused by two of the eight pathologic processes: atherosclerosis and thrombosis.

Pathophysiology

Atherosclerosis

Atherosclerosis is a disease of large and medium-sized muscular arteries. The basic lesion, the *atheroma*, or fibrofatty plaque, is a raised focal plaque within the intima; it has a lipid core (mainly cholesterol, usually complexed to proteins and cholesterol esters) covered by a fibrous cap. As the plaques increase in size and number, they progressively encroach on the lumen of the artery and the adjacent media. Atheromas have two main effects: compromising arterial blood flow and weakening the walls of the affected arteries.

The distribution of atherosclerotic plaques is rather constant. The abdominal aorta has more atherosclerotic disease than the thoracic aorta, and aortic lesions tend to be much more common and prominent around the ostia of major branches. Other vessels greatly affected by atherosclerosis are the aortoiliac, femoral, and popliteal arteries; the descending thoracic aorta; the coronary arteries; the internal carotid arteries; and the circle of Willis. Vessels of the upper extremities are usually spared.

As atherosclerosis progresses, atheromas almost always undergo calcification, resulting in hard, brittle vessels. Ulceration of the luminal surface and rupture of the atheromatous plaques may result in discharge of the debris into the bloodstream, producing atheroemboli (cholesterol emboli). Fissured or ulcerated lesions can produce in situ thrombosis, causing acute intraluminal occlusion.

Hemorrhage into the plaque may further compromise the arterial lumen. Although atherosclerosis primarily affects the intima, in severe cases the tunica media undergoes pressure atrophy and loss of elastic tissue, with sufficient weakening to create aneurysmal dilation.

Aneurysms

A *true aneurysm* is an abnormal localized dilation of the intact vessel wall. In a pseudoaneurysm, the entire wall perforates or ruptures, and the extravasated blood is contained by the surrounding tissues, eventually forming a fibrous sac that communicates with the artery.

Mural and mechanical factors contribute to true aneurysm formation.[2] The major cause of aneurysms is a weakness or defect in the integrity of the arterial wall. The only aneurysms that develop in a normal arterial segment are poststenotic aneurysms, such as with coarctation. Acceleration of flow past a narrow point creates slower flow beyond the stenosis lateral to the jet stream, producing increased lateral pressure. Aneurysmal dilation accelerates, increasing the risk of rupture as diameter increases; Laplace's law states that the tension (lateral pressure) in the wall of a hollow viscus varies directly with its radius (tension = pressure × radius).

The most common cause of aneurysms is severe atherosclerosis resulting from thinning and destruction of the tunica media. Atheromatous ulcers covered by mural thrombi are common within an aneurysm. Such mural thrombi can form emboli that lodge in distal vessels. When an entire aneurysm is filled with thrombus material, arterial occlusion results.

Aneurysms cause clinical symptoms through (1) rupture with subsequent hemorrhage, (2) impingement on adjacent structures, (3) occlusion of a vessel by either direct pressure or mural thrombus formation, (4) embolism from mural thrombus, and (5) presentation as a pulsatile mass.

Arterial Embolism

An embolus is a blood clot or other foreign body that is carried by the blood to a site distant from its point of origin. Most emboli are the result of detached thrombus formation (thromboembolism). Less common sources include debris from ruptured atherosclerotic plaques, tumor debris, or foreign bodies. Unless otherwise specified, the term *embolus* in this chapter is defined as *thromboembolus*.

Thromboembolism

Most arterial emboli (85%) originate in thrombus formation in the heart. Left ventricular thrombus forma-tion resulting from myocardial infarction accounts for nearly 60% to 70% of arterial emboli. Atrial thrombi associated with mitral stenosis and rheumatic heart disease account for only 5% to 10% of arterial embolism.[3] Coexisting atrial fibrillation, often without mitral stenosis, is present in 60% to 75% of patients with peripheral arterial embolic events, since atrial fibrillation itself can predispose patients to intracardiac clotting.[4]

Acute arterial emboli often cause distal tissue infarction. Clinical outcome depends mostly on the amount of collateral circulation present but also on the size of the vessel and the degree of obstruction. Patients with long-standing atherosclerosis have well-developed collateral circulation, whereas sudden occlusion of a normal artery without collateral pathways results in severe ischemia. After acute obstruction, the embolus can propagate proximally or distally, fragment and embolize further to distal vessels, or precipitate associated venous thrombosis by initiating a localized inflammatory reaction.

Because vessel diameters change most abruptly at branch points, embolic occlusion most often occurs at major arterial bifurcations. The bifurcation of the common femoral artery is the most frequent site of arterial embolism, accounting for 35% to 50% of all cases.[3] The smaller femoral and popliteal arteries are involved twice as often as the larger aortic and iliac vessels, reflecting the small size of most emboli.

Cell death from arterial ischemia can produce high concentrations of potassium, lactic acid, and myoglobin in the extremity distal to an arterial occlusion. Their sudden release after revascularization can produce life-threatening hyperkalemia, metabolic acidosis, and myoglobinuria. This myonephropathic-metabolic syndrome accounts for approximately one third of the deaths from arterial embolism after revascularization.[5]

Atheroembolism

Atheroembolism refers to microemboli consisting of cholesterol, calcium, and platelet aggregates dislodged from proximal complicated atherosclerotic plaques that lodge in distal end arteries. In the central nervous system, atheroemboli cause transient ischemic attacks and strokes (cerebrovascular accidents). In the peripheral vascular system, atheroemboli characteristically present with cool, painful, and cyanotic toes, or the "blue toe syndrome."[6]

Atheroemboli are caused by a proximally located arterial lesion, usually atherosclerotic plaques or aneurysms. Bilateral distal extremity involvement usually implies an aortic source, whereas unilateral atheroemboli usually arise from sites distal to the aorta. Distal lesions are most common in the femoropopliteal arteries (60%) and the aortoiliac arteries (40%). Aortic lesions (e.g., aneurysms, polytetrafluoroethylene grafts) are a less common source of microemboli.[6]

Atheroemboli tend to lodge in arteries 100 to 200 μm in size, such as the digital arteries. Single atheroembolic events seldom result in tissue loss, but atheroemboli tend to cluster. If unrecognized, repeated events ultimately result in loss of collateral circulation, progressive symptoms, and extensive tissue infarction.[6]

Infectious emboli from bacterial endocarditis can produce septic infarcts that may convert to large abscesses. Rarely, cardiac and noncardiac tumors or foreign bodies may gain access to the arterial circulation and embolize. Primary or metastatic lung neoplasms, malignant melanoma, and bullet emboli have been reported. In patients with cyanotic congenital heart disease (e.g., patent foramen ovale), venous emboli may pass directly to the arterial circulation ("paradoxical" emboli). Although rare, this possibility should be considered in any patient with simultaneous arterial and venous emboli, particularly if a source of the arterial embolus is not evident.

Arterial Thrombosis

Thrombosis is the in situ formation of a blood clot within the noninterrupted arterial vascular system. Complicated atherosclerotic plaques are usually responsible for the two major factors that cause in situ thrombosis: (1) endothelial injury and (2) alterations in normal blood flow. Less common causes include acute vasculitis and trauma. Thrombosis is rare in normal arteries.[7]

Peripheral arterial thrombi are usually occlusive, although they may be limited to one wall (mural) in larger vessels. Peripheral arterial thrombi are usually firmly attached to the damaged arterial wall and infrequently embolize. The clot may propagate proximally and distally, which intensifies the ischemia.

Inflammation

Inflammatory arterial injury can be caused by drugs, irradiation, mechanical trauma, or bacterial invasion. The major cause of arteritis is noninfectious systemic necrotizing vasculitis (see Chapter 116). Most cases of infectious arteritis are caused by direct invasion of the arterial wall. Septicemia, intravenous drug abuse, or infective endocarditis is most often responsible. Certain fungal infections, particularly aspergillosis and mucormycosis, are frequently associated with vasculitis and thrombosis.

Trauma

Different types of vascular injury result in characteristic pathologic syndromes.[8] Partial arterial lacerations continue to bleed because the intact portion of the vessel wall prevents retraction and closure of the arterial wound. This may form an expanding hematoma, causing progressive deformity, pain, and nerve compression. Complete arterial transection usually has only moderate or insignificant bleeding because of arterial spasm of the transected ends of the artery and the formation of a temporary thrombus. Delayed hemorrhage in completely transected arteries may result from relaxation of arterial spasm, eventual liquefaction of the thrombus, or displacement of the thrombus by arterial pressure. Blunt injury may produce partial or complete intimal disruption. Dissection of the distal intima can lead to progressive obstruction and thrombosis. Complete occlusion may not occur for hours or days after injury. Vasospasm can accompany injuries that are adjacent to blood vessels; spontaneous resolution always occurs in the absence of arterial disruption or intimal injury.

Vasospasm

Vasospastic disorders (Raynaud's disease, Raynaud's phenomenon, livedo reticularis, acrocyanosis, erythromelalgia) produce an abnormal vasomotor response in distal small arteries. The exact cause of these disorders is unknown but is thought to be related to the autonomic innervation of the peripheral arterioles. The vasospastic disorders are characterized by the presence of ischemic symptoms and the absence of tissue loss. True organic changes within the arterial wall are absent. In contrast, patients with digital ulceration and gangrene always have fixed arterial occlusions in the distal extremity arteries.

Arteriovenous Fistulae

Abnormal communication between arteries and veins may result from congenital defects, rupture of an arterial aneurysm into an adjacent vein, penetrating injuries, and inflammatory necrosis associated with neoplasms or infection. Arteriovenous fistulae can occur in any region of the body. The artery proximal to the fistula becomes distended, tortuous, and aneurysmal. Similar changes occur in the venous side of the fistula. Proximal and distal veins respond to alterations in hemodynamics with intimal proliferation and fibrosis, followed by a decrease in the internal elastic lamina, resulting in distention, tortuosity, and aneurysm formation. The resultant chronic venous hypertension may cause dermatitis and ulceration of overlying skin. The size of the opening between artery and vein generally increases with time.

Approximately 60% of arteriovenous fistulae are associated with a false aneurysm.[9] False aneurysm formation can occur as part of the fistulous tract or as the result of arterial or venous dilation.[9]

The increase in cardiac output that occurs when blood switches from the arterial to the venous system can result in a widened pulse pressure or high-output cardiac failure.

CLINICAL FEATURES

History

Patients with peripheral arterial disease have pain, tissue loss (ulceration or gangrene), or a change in sensation or appearance (swelling, discoloration, or temperature change). Because the primary cause of peripheral arterial disease is atherosclerosis, related conditions providing evidence of atherosclerosis are cardiac disease, myocardial infarction, cardiac dysrhythmias (e.g., atrial fibrillation), stroke, transient ischemic attacks, and renal disease. Factors that increase the likelihood of atherosclerosis are cigarette smoking, diabetes, hypercholesterolemia, and hypertension.

Risk factors not related to atherosclerosis include prior injuries or surgeries, major illnesses, a history of phlebitis or pulmonary embolism, the presence of autoimmune disease or arthritis, and a history of prior coagulation abnormalities. Intravenous drug use can lead to arterial injury. Aortoiliac obstruction can cause sexual impotence in men (Leriche's syndrome).

Acute Arterial Occlusion

The patient with acute arterial occlusion usually exhibits some variant of the "five Ps": pain, pallor, pulselessness, paresthesias, and paralysis. Paresthesias and paralysis indicate limb-threatening ischemia that requires emergency surgical intervention regardless of the cause. In patients with non-limb-threatening ischemia, accurate differentiation between embolism and in situ thrombosis as the cause of acute arterial occlusion determines patient management. Arterial embolism is best managed by emergency Fogarty catheter embolectomy. Non-limb-threatening ischemia from in situ thrombosis is often aggravated by emergency surgical intervention and is therefore initially best managed nonoperatively, if possible (Figure 86-1). Acute arterial embolus usually occurs in patients without significant peripheral atherosclerosis and without well-developed collateral circulation. For this reason, acute embolus usually presents as sudden limb-threatening ischemia. Patients describe a sensation of

the leg's being "struck" by a severe shocking pain. Often the patient has to sit or fall to the ground during the event.

In situ thrombosis usually occurs in patients who have long-standing significant peripheral atherosclerosis and well-developed collateral circulation. For this reason, in situ thrombosis often is seen subacutely with non-limb-threatening ischemia. A history of claudication is common with in situ thrombosis and rare in patients with arterial embolus.

Chronic Arterial Insufficiency

Chronic arterial insufficiency causes two characteristic types of pain: intermittent claudication and ischemic pain at rest. The level of arterial occlusion and the location of intermittent claudication are closely correlated. Calf claudication is associated with femoral and popliteal disease. Patients complain of a cramping pain, reliably reproduced by the same degree of exercise and completely relieved by rest (usually 1 to 5 minutes). Aortoiliac occlusive disease typically causes claudication in the buttocks and hips, as well as the calves. The calf pain in aortoiliac disease is generally more severe than the buttock and thigh pain, which is more often described as an aching, discomfort, or weakness. Some patients even deny pain, complaining only that the thigh or hip "gives out" with exercise. Aortoiliac occlusive disease severe enough to produce bilateral claudication is almost always associated with impotence in men (Leriche's syndrome). Even in the absence of impotency, bilateral hip or thigh pain in a man should indicate the possibility of aortoiliac occlusive disease.

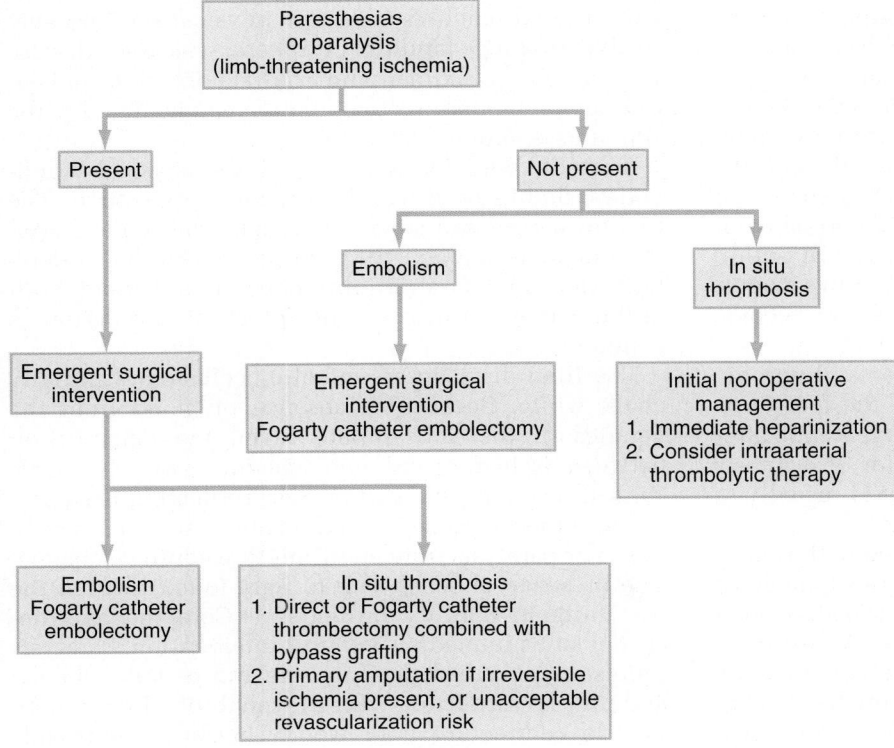

Figure 86-1. Clinical presentation and management of acute arterial occlusion.

Chronic arterial insufficiency may progress so that ischemic pain occurs at rest. Rest pain often begins in the feet and typically involves the foot distal to the metatarsals, awakening the patient from sleep. Ischemic rest pain is a severe, unrelenting pain aggravated by elevation and unrelieved by analgesics. Typically, patients sleep with the leg dangling over the side of the bed or sleep in a chair to improve perfusion pressure to the distal tissues. Patients have prompt relief of pain by any activity that involves a standing position.

Physical Examination

A systematic assessment of the peripheral vascular system includes palpation of the pulse volume in the pairs of brachial, radial, femoral, posterior tibial, and dorsalis pedis arteries documented on a 0 to 4+ scale. Carotid arteries should be gently palpated singly and findings similarly documented.

Approximately 10% of the population does not have one of the dorsalis pedis pulses.[10] The lower extremities should be examined for signs of chronic and advanced ischemia. Muscular atrophy, particularly in the lower extremities, and loss of hair growth over the dorsum of the toes and foot with thickening of the toenails resulting from slowness of nail growth are common signs of arterial insufficiency. As ischemia becomes more advanced, the skin becomes shiny, scaly, and "skeletonized" from atrophy of the skin, subcutaneous tissue, and muscle.

Any area in which ischemia is suspected can be tested by blanching with finger pressure; a delay in return of normal color on relieving the pressure (compared with that of the nonaffected extremity) implies reduced perfusion.

Buerger's sign provides reliable evidence of severe advanced ischemia. With the patient supine, the patient's feet are elevated more than 12 inches above the estimated level of the right atrium, and any change in the color of the feet is noted. If the color does not change, the patient dorsiflexes the feet five or six times; latent color changes induced by exercise are noted. With the patient sitting, the feet are then allowed to hang down over the side of the stretcher; the time of normal color return is recorded. Normal color should return within 10 seconds, and the veins should fill within 15 seconds. If the veins require more than 20 seconds to become distended, advanced ischemia is present.

With severely restricted arterial inflow and chronic dilation of the peripheral vascular bed, the foot turns chalk white on elevation and intensely hyperemic after 1 minute of dependency. Localized pallor or cyanosis associated with poor capillary filling is usually a prelude to ischemic gangrene or ulceration.

Doppler ultrasonography should be used in the emergency department in all patients with questionable or absent pulses. Doppler testing is more sensitive than palpation in detecting peripheral pulses. An estimate of blood flow to the lower extremities can be made by measuring the systolic blood pressure at the level of the ankle and comparing it to the brachial systolic pressure. With the patient supine, a blood pressure cuff is applied just proximal to the malleolus, inflated above brachial systolic pressure, and then deflated slowly. Ankle systolic pressure can be accurately measured with a Doppler probe placed over the dorsalis pedis or posterior tibial arteries. This pressure is normally 90% or more of the brachial systolic pressure; with mild arterial insufficiency, it is between 70% and 90%; with moderate insufficiency, between 50% and 70%; and with severe insufficiency, less than 50%.

Allen's test is helpful in assessing patency of the radial or ulnar artery distal to the wrist. The patient initially opens and closes the hand and then clenches the fist to expel as much blood from the hand as possible; the examiner then compresses the radial and ulnar arteries. When the patient opens the fist, the hand is pale. The examiner then releases pressure from the radial artery but maintains it on the ulnar artery. If the radial artery distal to the wrist is patent, the hand becomes pink rapidly; if it is occluded, the hand remains pale. The maneuver is then repeated by maintaining pressure on the radial artery while releasing the ulnar artery. A comparison can be made with the opposite hand.

Arterial Embolism

The physical examination can assist in differentiating between arterial embolism and in situ thrombosis in patients who have acute arterial occlusion. The sudden loss of a previously present pulse is the hallmark of arterial embolus. It is difficult to recognize this finding, however, if the prior pulse status of the limb is unknown or is abnormal as the result of associated atherosclerosis. A bounding pulse may be felt initially at the location of an embolus as a result of transmitted pulsations through the fresh clot. In general, patients with arterial embolus have few physical findings suggestive of long-standing peripheral vascular disease with normal, proximal, and contralateral limb pulses. Occasional tenderness to palpation can be noted at the site of an embolic occlusion.

If arterial embolus is suspected, the physical examination should be directed to identify its source. The two most common sites are (1) left ventricular mural thrombus secondary to a prior myocardial infarction and (2) left atrial thrombus in a patient with mitral valve disease. Coexistent atrial fibrillation is common.

The limb distal to an embolic occlusion is initially chalk white. Because of absence of blood from the venules of the subcapillary layer, the demarcation between ischemic and nonischemic tissue is sharp. With time, cyanosis may appear, indicating desaturation of blood with continued ongoing ischemia. Paresthesia or paralysis indicates limb-threatening ischemia. The presence of sensitivity to light touch is often the best guide to viability of the tissue. Complete anesthesia demands immediate surgical intervention. Paralysis represents severe skeletal muscle and neural ischemia and may be associated with irreversibility. Involuntary muscle contracture with woody hardness represents irreversible ischemia.

Table 86-1. Clinical Characteristics of Infected Aneurysms

	Mycotic Aneurysm	Infection of Atherosclerotic Arteries	Infection of Existing Aneurysm	Posttraumatic Infected False Aneurysm
Cause	Endocarditis	Bacteremia	Bacteremia	Drug addiction Trauma
Age (years)	30-50	>50	>50	<30
Incidence	Rare	Most common	Unusual	Very common
Location	Aorta Visceral Intracranial Peripheral	Atherosclerotic Aortoiliac Intimal defects	Infrarenal Aorta	Femoral Carotid
Bacteriology	Gram-positive cocci	*Salmonella* Others	*Staphylococcus* Others	*Staphylococcus aureus* Polymicrobial
Mortality	25%	75%	90%	5%

From Wilson SE, Van Wagenen P, Passaro E Jr: Arterial infection. *Curr Probl Surg* 15(9):1, 1978.

Arterial Thrombosis

Physical findings of in situ thrombosis are often accompanied by evidence of atherosclerotic occlusive disease. Proximal or contralateral limb pulses are usually diminished or absent. An identifiable source of an embolus, such as mitral valve disease or atrial fibrillation, is usually not present. Because of collateral circulation, demarcation of limb ischemia is less well defined in these patients (Table 86-1).

Carotid, renal, and femoral arteries may have bruits, and there may be evidence of abdominal aortic aneurysm. If an occlusion of the upper extremity vessels is suspected, the subclavian artery should be evaluated by palpating for thrills and listening for bruits in the supraclavicular fossa.

A funduscopic examination allows direct visualization of retinal arterioles that may yield evidence of arteriosclerosis or hypertension. Hollenhorst plaques (atheromatous emboli containing cholesterol crystals in the retinal arterioles) may be detected. Roth's spots (round or oval white spots seen near the optic disk) may be present in patients with infective endocarditis. Embolic phenomena can cause diverse end-organ damage: hemiplegia from cerebral emboli, flank pain with hematuria from renal emboli, left upper quadrant abdominal pain from splenic infarcts, and pleuritic pain with hemoptysis from pulmonary emboli. Septic pulmonary emboli from right-sided endocarditis may be confused with pneumonia.

Inflammation

Inflammatory vascular disease manifests primarily as skin involvement. Skin lesions typically appear as palpable purpura; other cutaneous manifestations of vasculitis include macules, papules, vesicles, bullae, subcutaneous nodules, ulcers, and recurrent or chronic urticaria. The skin lesions may be pruritic or even painful, with a burning or stinging sensation. Lesions more often occur in dependent areas: in the lower extremities in ambulatory patients or in the sacral area in bedridden patients. Edema accompanies some lesions, and hyperpigmentation often occurs in the areas of recurrent or chronic lesions.

Vasospasm

Vasospastic disorders cause a sharp border between ischemic and normal tissue. *Raynaud's disease* is characterized by intermittent attacks of triphasic color changes: pallor, cyanosis, and then rubor.[11] The most important element is pallor, during which the digits turn chalk white. Attacks generally last 15 to 60 minutes, and rewarming the hands restores normal color and sensation. Color changes do not occur above the metacarpophalangeal joints and rarely involve the thumb.

Two other vasospastic disorders have a characteristic appearance. *Livedo reticularis* is characterized by a persistent cyanotic mottling of the skin that has a typical fishnet appearance and may involve all parts of the extremities and trunk. *Acrocyanosis* is the least common vasospastic disorder and is characterized by persistent, painless, diffuse cyanosis of the fingers, hands, toes, and feet. Cyanosis usually intensifies with exposure to cold and decreases with warming. The involved parts are nearly always cold, exhibit excessive perspiration, and have normal arterial pulses.

Arteriovenous Fistulae

Arteriovenous malformations and fistulae, although rare, must be distinguished from vascular bruits or aneurysms. True aneurysms and arterial stenoses are associated with a systolic murmur. Pseudoaneurysms generally have a loud systolic and sometimes a separate faint diastolic murmur. Arteriovenous fistulae have a constant systolic and diastolic (to-and-fro) murmur heard best directly over the lesion and often associated with a palpable thrill, precisely analogous to the findings over a therapeutic arteriovenous fistula that has been established for hemodialysis. Unless congenital, arteriovenous fistulae occur at prior operative or trauma sites. The skin overlying the lesion may be warm, but distally the temperature is often decreased. Veins peripheral to the fistula are usually distended and varicose. Large and long-standing arteriovenous fistulae produce high cardiac output and widened pulse pressure. Tachycardia in these patients may suddenly decrease when the artery leading to the fistula or the fistula itself is occluded (Branham's sign).

DIAGNOSTIC STRATEGIES

An accurate diagnosis of peripheral arterial occlusive disease can be achieved in most patients by careful history and physical examination supplemented by bedside testing.

Noninvasive Assessment

Doppler ultrasonography measures blood flow velocity by detecting the frequency shift of sound waves reflected from red blood cells that move toward and away from the Doppler probe. The Doppler signal can be processed to generate a normal triphasic velocity waveform for recording and analysis. Progressive arterial narrowing alters the triphasic waveform to biphasic and finally monophasic shape. Such Doppler ultrasonographic waveform analysis can detect significant arterial occlusive disease, although it is less accurate in determining exact location.

Real-time B-mode ultrasonographic imaging uses differences in sound wave reflection from the interfaces between tissues with different acoustic impedances to provide anatomic detail of underlying structures. Ultrasonographic imaging is useful in detecting and evaluating atherosclerotic plaques and mural thrombi and in sizing aneurysms of the abdominal aorta, iliac, femoral, and popliteal arteries. B-mode ultrasonography is noninvasive, painless, less expensive than other modalities, and universally available. Bedside ultrasonographic studies can lead to rapid diagnosis of life-threatening conditions and reduce the number of delayed or invasive diagnostic procedures.[12] B-mode ultrasonographic imaging is the diagnostic procedure of choice for the initial evaluation and determination of the size of peripheral artery aneurysms.

Duplex scanning combines the image of B-mode ultrasonography and sophisticated on-line computer analysis of accurately sampled Doppler waveforms to allow simultaneous acquisition of both the image of a vascular structure and the characteristics of blood flow velocity within it. Duplex scanning permits noninvasive and accurate diagnosis of peripheral vascular, cerebrovascular, and venous disease.

Color imaging of blood flow has been combined with duplex scanning and is known as color-coded Doppler, Doppler angiography, or angiodynography. Color flow imaging is achieved by assignment of colors to the direction of blood flow detected by Doppler waveform signals. Red represents flow away from the ultrasonographic probe, and blue represents flow toward the probe. Color-coded Doppler, the procedure of choice for most conditions, allows noninvasive and accurate detection of atherosclerotic plaques and stenoses, their effect on intraluminal blood flow, and the presence of venous thrombosis.

Invasive Contrast Arteriography

Angiography is the definitive test of abnormal peripheral artery anatomy but is often inconclusive about the physiologic condition of the tissues. Adverse effects of contrast media and catheter-related complications must be weighed against the benefits of this procedure. Contrast media have a direct toxic effect on vascular endothelium; can produce renal failure, especially in diabetic patients; may cause peripheral vasodilation with hypotension; may result in seizures and stroke in neurologic patients; and can cause severe idiosyncratic and allergic reactions. Catheter-related complications, including embolization, catheter breakage, and vascular disruption, vary with operator skill and anatomic location but average 0.5%. Overall mortality rate from angiography is 0.03%.[13] Emergency angiography is usually required in the following circumstances: (1) acute arterial embolus or thrombosis if the clinical diagnosis is uncertain, (2) consideration of emergency vascular bypass grafting, and (3) characterization of vascular abnormality before emergency surgical correction. A decision to proceed with angiography should be made with the vascular surgeon.

Computed Tomography and Magnetic Resonance Imaging

Angiography using spiral computed tomography (CT), called computed tomography angiography, is the most useful diagnostic modality for the evaluation of the abdominal aorta.[14] In the peripheral arteriovascular system, computed tomography angiography is useful primarily for atherosclerotic, infected, and false aneurysms and for imaging the cerebral circulation. Magnetic resonance imaging has the capability for angiography (magnetic resonance angiography) that has been particularly useful in delineating cerebrovascular problems (see Chapter 99) and is seeing expanded use in the evaluation of peripheral vascular disease. The ability to make axial, coronal, and sagittal sections provides accurate visualization of anatomy. Magnetic resonance imaging detects changes in the relaxation variables of tissues before obvious structural changes, uniquely differentiating blood, thrombus, fat, and fibrosis.

MANAGEMENT OPTIONS

The management of acute arterial occlusion depends on the degree and cause of ischemia. Patients with limb-threatening ischemia from embolism receive emergency Fogarty catheter embolectomy. Patients with limb-threatening ischemia caused by in situ thrombosis require direct or Fogarty catheter thrombectomy combined with vascular bypass grafting. Thrombectomy alone often fails because of recurrent thrombosis. Patients who have a lesion that cannot be bypassed, who have evidence of irreversible ischemia, or who are too ill to tolerate revascularization are treated with primary amputation.

A patient with non-limb-threatening ischemia from embolism is treated with emergency Fogarty catheter embolectomy. Non-limb-threatening ischemia from in situ thrombosis is best managed nonoperatively with immediate systemic heparinization and possibly with intraarterial fibrinolytic therapy (see Figure 86-1).

Elective surgical repair of an asymptomatic atherosclerotic peripheral arterial aneurysm is usually accomplished by excision of the aneurysm with end-to-end anastomosis or graft interposition. Infected true and false peripheral aneurysms require aneurysm resection, debridement of infected tissue, and ligation of the proximal and distal uninfected arteries. Autogenous vein bypass through uninfected tissue planes is attempted. Prosthetic grafts carry a high risk of graft infection. The surgical approach to noninfected false aneurysms is similar to that of peripheral atherosclerotic aneurysms.

Patients with thoracic outlet syndrome who have cervical ribs, arterial involvement, or significant neurologic symptoms require surgical decompression with removal of anomalous fibromuscular bands and resection of the first rib, if present. Subclavian and subclavian-axillary aneurysms can be treated with resection and end-to-end anastomosis, graft reconstruction, or surgical revision. Patients with distal embolic occlusions are treated with Fogarty catheter embolectomy. Axillary and subclavian vein thromboses are best managed with surgical thrombectomy or systemic fibrinolytic therapy. Patients with only brachial plexus involvement and minimal signs and symptoms should be followed closely with conservative treatment.

Surgical treatment of peripheral arteriovenous fistulas requires interrupting the fistula tract and restoring both arterial and venous continuity with end-to-end anastomosis or graft interposition. If the anatomic location precludes surgical intervention, percutaneous transvascular embolization with liquid tissue adhesives (e.g., isobutyl 2-cyanoacrylate) is usually successful.

Noninvasive Therapy

Acute Anticoagulation with Heparin

Intravenous heparin remains an important initial emergency department therapy for patients with acute arterial embolism, acute arterial thrombosis, and subclavian vein thrombosis. Heparin should be immediately and empirically started at standard intravenous doses (80 U/kg by IV bolus, followed by a maintenance infusion of 18 U/kg/hr). Heparin quickly reduces thrombin generation and fibrin formation, minimizing clot propagation, which can intensify limb ischemia and jeopardize tissues. Relative contraindications include recent neurosurgery (especially within 2 weeks), major surgery within 48 hours, childbirth within 24 hours, a known bleeding diathesis, thrombocytopenia, a potentially hemorrhagic lesion, or active bleeding.

Fibrinolytic Therapy

Low-dose intraarterial fibrinolytic therapy is increasingly used for acute arterial occlusion. Patients with limb-threatening ischemia are not candidates for this therapy because clot lysis generally takes 6 to 72 hours. Patients cannot tolerate several more hours of ischemia without substantial tissue or limb loss, and immediate

Fogarty catheter embolectomy is still the treatment of choice in most patients with an acute arterial embolus. Consideration of fibrinolytic therapy is generally reserved for patients with in situ thrombosis and non-limb-threatening ischemia.

Intraarterial fibrinolytic agents induce clot lysis in the small, distal runoff vessels, decreasing outflow resistance and enabling the native artery to remain open longer. Fibrinolysis often uncovers a critical stenosis that, untreated, may lead to another episode of thrombosis. After successful fibrinolytic therapy, most patients require secondary bypass grafting or percutaneous transluminal angioplasty. Streptokinase, urokinase, and tissue plasminogen activator have all been used successfully. Intravenous administration of a fibrinolytic agent to treat arterial occlusion is less effective than direct administration into the clot. Clots more than 30 days old are more organized and less likely to achieve successful lysis.

Invasive Therapy

Fogarty Catheter Thrombectomy

The Fogarty catheter is most frequently used for iliac, femoral, and popliteal embolectomy, often with only local anesthesia.[15] Aortic saddle embolus is removed by sequentially passing the Fogarty catheter through bilateral common femoral arteriotomies.

Newly formed in situ thrombosis can often be successfully removed with the Fogarty catheter. An older thrombus adheres more firmly to the damaged vessel wall, requiring direct surgical thrombectomy. The Fogarty catheter is not used in the venous system because of the venous valves.

Peripheral Percutaneous Transluminal Angioplasty

The initial success and long-term patency achieved by angioplasty depend on the location of the lesion and the extent of atheromatous disease. Proximal larger caliber arteries (e.g., iliac, femoropopliteal) have the best initial and long-term results. Discrete stenotic lesions (<5 cm) have better long-term patency rates than those vessels that are diffusely involved or have multiple involved segments. Balloon angioplasty has become the accepted sole treatment for isolated stenotic lesions in the renal, iliac, and superficial femoral vessels.

Transluminal angioplasty with intravascular stent is used in more distal vessels, including the popliteal and tibial circulation, in cases of more diffuse lesions, and for patients who are prohibitive surgical risks.[16] Its value in these patients remains to be determined.

Recanalization devices include the percutaneous atherectomy catheter, percutaneous angioscope, hot-tip laser, excimer laser, and high-speed rotating wire and drill.

Grafting

Vascular grafting is associated with a variety of complications that can be diagnosed in the emergency department. Autogenous vein grafts (usually a reversed greater saphenous vein) provide excellent long-term patency for small arteries. Vein grafts respond to arterial pressure with gradual intimal proliferation and medial fibrosis. They may develop atherosclerosis, which can lead to graft stenosis and thrombosis. False aneurysms may form along the suture line.

Polytetrafluoroethylene prosthetic grafts are widely used in medium and large arteries that are impossible to bridge with smaller vein grafts. Prosthetic grafts have a higher rate of thrombosis than venous grafts. Distal emboli may result from poor fixation of luminal fibrin. If the prosthetic graft has not been adequately covered by viable tissue, it can erode into adjacent structures and hollow viscera. Prosthetic graft infection is a devastating complication requiring removal of the entire graft.

Vascular grafts can be used to bypass arterial occlusions and reconstruct a diseased arterial bifurcation, or they can be interposed between sections of resected artery. The two most common complications of both prosthetic and vein grafts are (1) thrombosis and (2) development of a false aneurysm at one or more suture lines. Bypass grafting is most often used as palliative treatment for symptoms of atherosclerotic occlusive disease. Patients with localized unilateral stenosis (<3 to 5 cm in length) may have a comparable rate of success with percutaneous transluminal angioplasty with or without stent placement.[17]

Patients with calf claudication from superficial femoral or popliteal occlusive disease usually do not experience rapid progression of disease if they stop smoking and maintain an active exercise regimen. Patients who have progression of disease, significant rest pain, or tissue loss require surgical revascularization.

Sympathectomy

Lumbar sympathectomy is no longer used for treatment of ischemia from arterial occlusion. The benefit of sympathectomy in patients with symptomatic Raynaud's phenomenon is unclear, but it remains a potential intervention to assist healing of superficial ischemic ulcers and relieve rest pain in patients with Buerger's disease.[18]

Hyperbaric Therapy

Scant objective evidence indicates that hyperbaric therapy alters the long-term course of chronic obliterative vascular disorders, presumably by accelerating formation of fine vessels. Success has been achieved with healing chronic diabetic ischemic ulcers and salvaging ischemic skin grafts and flaps.[19] Referral to a hyperbaric unit for consideration of chronic therapy should be made by the patient's primary care physician, diabetologist, or vascular surgeon and is not initiated from the emergency department.

SPECIFIC ARTERIOVASCULAR DISEASES

DISEASES OF CHRONIC ARTERIAL INSUFFICIENCY

Arteriosclerosis Obliterans

Arteriosclerosis obliterans (atherosclerotic occlusive disease, chronic occlusive arterial disease, obliterative arteriosclerosis) is the peripheral arterial presentation of atherosclerosis. Most often, arteriosclerosis obliterans affects the lower abdominal aorta, the iliac arteries, and the arteries supplying the lower extremities. Upper extremity manifestations are uncommon.

Arteriosclerosis obliterans is responsible for 95% of cases of chronic occlusive arterial disease. It is most common in persons older than 50 years, but as many as 19% of cases occur in patients between the ages of 30 and 49 years. Men are affected more often than women, 5:1 to 10:1. Approximately one third of patients with arteriosclerosis obliterans have coexistent coronary artery disease. The incidence of diabetes mellitus is 20% to 30%.[20]

As with other atherosclerotic diseases, risk factors for arteriosclerosis obliterans include cigarette smoking, hyperlipidemia, and hypertension. Of patients with arteriosclerosis obliterans, 70% to 90% are smokers when first examined, 75% have hyperlipidemia, and 30% have hypertension.[20]

Clinical Features and Differential Diagnosis

Acute arterial occlusion from embolism, thrombosis, or trauma is ruled out primarily by history. Atheromatous emboli from proximal ulcerated plaques or aneurysms can cause small scattered ischemic lesions in the toes, feet, or legs, which may cause blue toe syndrome (see Figure 86-3). The peripheral pulses are present in the blue toe syndrome. Exercise-induced claudication must be distinguished from the nocturnal muscle cramps that frequently occur during rest in elderly patients. Aortoiliac occlusive disease must be differentiated from osteoarthritis of the hip, in which symptoms tend to be more variable from day to day, are not relieved completely with rest, and are not reliably reproduced by the same amount of exercise. Pseudoclaudication from the cauda equina syndrome is caused by narrowing of the lumbar canal from spondylosis, disease of the intervertebral disks, or spinal cord tumor. Symptoms mimic intermittent claudication but are less closely related to exercise and rest than true claudication.

The cause of lower extremity ulcers should be carefully determined. Approximately 5% of lower extremity ulcerations are caused by arterial insufficiency.[21] These are usually located distal to the ankle, typically at the terminal portion of the digits, around the nail beds, or between the toes, caused by friction of one toe on another. Less common locations include the metatarsal heads, heel, and malleoli. Arterial insufficiency ulcers are painful but improve when the extremity is in a dependent position. They are associated with evidence of coexistent chronic arterial insufficiency (absence of hair growth on the dorsum of the feet, skin atrophy, absent pulses, and nail deformities). Ulcers are initially small, shallow, and dry. The base is gray, yellow, or black, with minimal or no granulation tissue. The rim of the ulcer is sharp and indolent, showing no signs of cellular proliferation or epithelialization.

Approximately 90% of lower extremity ulcers are caused by chronic venous insufficiency.[21] These typically occur proximal to or in the region of the ankle, especially near the medial malleolus. Venous stasis ulcers are only mildly painful and improve with elevation of the extremity. Evidence of long-standing chronic venous insufficiency, including edema, prominent superficial veins, and stasis dermatitis, is present. Ulcers are moderate in size, with a weeping base and extensive granulation tissue. A rapidly developing ulcer is more suggestive of venous insufficiency.

Most of the remaining lower extremity ulcers are caused by diabetic neuropathy, alone or with arterial insufficiency.[21] The location reflects sites of repeated trauma, including the toes, heels, and plantar surface of the feet, especially the metatarsal heads. Neurotrophic ulcers are characteristically painless. Patients may have evidence of coexistent peripheral arterial insufficiency. The ulcers are deep and penetrating, often with suppurative drainage caused by an associated underlying infection or chronic osteomyelitis. Neurotrophic ulcers are usually surrounded by a rim of thick callus.

Hypertensive ulcers are rare and reflect long-standing, uncontrolled hypertension. These ulcers are typically near the lateral malleolus and start as painful, reddish-blue areas of infarcted skin. A hemorrhagic bleb develops, then breaks down into a superficial ulcer, which can reach a size of 5 to 10 cm. The ischemic ulcer has sharply demarcated borders, little granulation tissue, and minimal drainage. The pain is the most severe of all lower extremity ulcers.

Multiple ischemic ulcerations above and below the ankle should suggest vasculitis or atheromatous embolization. Ulcers with regular edges in unusual locations may be factitial or may result from subcutaneous injection of illicit drugs. Thickened, rolled, and elevated edges with a central depression containing granulation tissue are characteristic of malignant ulcers.

Management

The first step in determining treatment is to identify patients whose symptoms are the result solely of arteriosclerosis obliterans without coexistent thromboembolic disease. Treatment is then dictated by the accurate classification of symptomatic patients into two groups: those with functional ischemia and those with

limb-threatening ischemia.[22] Initial assessments and treatments should be made in conjunction with appropriate vascular surgery consultation.

Patients with limb-threatening ischemia constitute a surgical emergency. Angiography should be arranged in consultation with a vascular surgeon to determine the presence of sufficiently localized disease to permit emergency bypass grafting.[22] Patients with functional ischemia may require outpatient arrangements for noninvasive vascular testing or elective invasive contrast arteriography to determine treatment options such as bypass grafting. Ischemic ulcers or skin lesions should be cultured in the emergency department. Systemic antibiotics to cover skin organisms should be instituted if infection is present. Wet to dry dressings may help debride ulcers containing fibrin, debris, or infection. Radiographs of the underlying bones should rule out osteomyelitis. Patients with ischemic rest pain require hospitalization even if they are not surgical candidates. Bed rest, a warm environment, and maintenance of the limb in a dependent position usually relieve pain.

Buerger's Disease (Thromboangiitis Obliterans)

First described by Buerger in 1908, thromboangiitis obliterans is an idiopathic inflammatory occlusive disease primarily involving the medium-sized and small arteries of the hands and feet.[23] Patients are usually men between 20 and 40 years of age who use tobacco, although recent reports indicate an increasing frequency of this disease in women. Buerger's disease affects all races but is more prevalent in the Middle and Far East. The incidence in the United States is 20 in 100,000.[24] The exact pathogenesis of Buerger's disease is unknown, but virtually all patients are smokers.

Thromboangiitis obliterans is characterized by segmental acute and chronic inflammation in the smaller arteries of both upper and lower extremities. The initial arterial inflammatory process progresses to affect the adjacent veins and nerves, often leading to associated venous thrombosis and progressive fibrous encasement of these structures. This is recognized clinically as painful, tender, reddened, or dark nodules over a peripheral artery with either a reduced or an absent pulse (phlebitis migrans).

Clinical Features

Clinical criteria for the diagnosis of Buerger's disease include (1) a history of smoking, (2) onset before the age of 50, (3) infrapopliteal arterial occlusive lesions, (4) either upper limb involvement or phlebitis migrans, and (5) absence of atherosclerotic risk factors other than smoking. A characteristic symptom of Buerger's disease is foot or instep claudication caused by infrapopliteal arterial occlusion. Intense rubor of the affected extremity, particularly with dependency, is also characteristic. Foot pulses may be absent in the presence of normal femoral and popliteal pulses. Involvement of the hands is often bilateral and symmetric, leading to the development of hand claudication or fingertip ulcers. Phlebitis migrans occurs early in the disease. Approximately 50% of patients experience Raynaud-type triphasic color response to cold. In the upper extremities, the digital arteries are usually more involved than the radial or ulnar arteries.[24]

Diagnostic Strategies

Adherence to diagnostic clinical criteria should be sufficient for emergency department diagnosis of Buerger's disease. Noninvasive vascular laboratory testing can confirm the diagnosis and determine the extent of involvement. Although rarely required, angiography demonstrates multiple segmental occlusions.

Differential Diagnosis

In patients older than 50 years who have signs of peripheral ischemia, arteriosclerosis obliterans is a more likely diagnosis. In young women, autoimmune diseases such as scleroderma or systemic lupus erythematosus should be considered.[24]

Management

Permanent complete abstinence from tobacco is the only known effective treatment for Buerger's disease. If a patient does not completely stop smoking, alternating periods of quiescence are followed by exacerbations, with severe arterial insufficiency. Patients who permanently abstain from smoking have a benign clinical course. Despite this, many individuals who have Buerger's disease continue to smoke even though severe pain at rest, tissue loss, and eventually amputation occur.

With early symptoms without threat of tissue loss, patient education and follow-up with a vascular surgeon are sufficient. Vascular surgery treatment options are varied for patients with severe symptoms or threatened tissue loss. Intractable pain can be controlled with epidural anesthesia. Intraarterial or intravenous prostaglandin E_1 and antithrombotic agents, including aspirin and heparin, have been used successfully.[24] Patients with large-vessel arterial occlusion may benefit from arterial reconstruction. Sympathectomy is still a potential treatment in advanced cases for cutaneous ulceration or relief of rest pain.[18] Because patients with Buerger's disease demonstrate good healing, intensive conservative treatment is usually successful in preventing surgical amputation.

DISEASES OF ACUTE ARTERIAL OCCLUSION

Arterial Embolism

Despite advances in diagnosis and treatment, acute arterial embolus continues to be associated with substantial morbidity and mortality. As in recent decades, the incidence of arterial embolic disease appears to be increasing. Approximately 50% of acute arterial occlu-

sions are caused by arterial embolism. The other 50% are caused by in situ thrombosis.[3]

Differential Diagnosis

Phlegmasia cerulea dolens is a massive iliofemoral deep venous thrombosis. The initial symptom may be acute onset of a swollen and painful leg. As swelling continues, secondary arterial insufficiency with associated pallor (*phlegmasia cerulea albens*) may occur. In cases of acute arterial embolus, leg swelling is not usually present, especially not at the onset of pain. In addition, acute embolus produces a sharply demarcated pallor; phlegmasia cerulea dolens causes a cyanotic-appearing leg.

Aortic dissection may involve the arteries of the upper or lower extremity and may mimic acute embolus. A history of progressive severe pain, the presence of aortic insufficiency, and involvement at multiple sites suggest dissection. Acute neurologic syndromes (e.g., transverse myelitis, spinal subarachnoid hemorrhage, ruptured intervertebral disk) may produce sudden onset of unilateral or bilateral lower extremity weakness or sensory loss that mimics an acute aortic saddle occlusion.

Cold, blue extremities may result from low-output states such as hypovolemia, decreased cardiac output, sepsis, dehydration, myocardial infarction, and pulmonary emboli in patients with long-standing atherosclerotic disease.

Management

Acute arterial embolus is a surgical emergency. The likelihood of limb salvage decreases after 4 to 6 hours. On the basis of clinical diagnosis alone, full doses of intravenous heparin should be administered immediately to minimize clot propagation. Patients whose history and physical examination clearly indicate an acute arterial embolus should undergo immediate Fogarty catheter embolectomy without prior angiography. In these patients, preoperative ultrasonography and angiography are rarely useful diagnostically and prolong the limb's ischemic status.

If the differentiation of acute embolus and in situ thrombosis is uncertain, pretreatment angiography is required and usually diagnostic. Patients with acute emboli generally show minimal signs of atherosclerosis, occlusion at the site of an arterial bifurcation, sharply demarcated cutoffs, and lack of flow distal to the occlusion. In patients with in situ thrombosis, arteriography shows diffuse atherosclerosis, occlusion at sites other than arterial bifurcations, a tapered irregular cutoff, and well-developed collateral vessels. In general, emboli tend to lodge at arterial bifurcations, whereas arterial thrombi do not (see Table 86-1).

Intraarterial thrombolytic therapy for acute embolus remains investigational. Immediate limb-threatening ischemia precludes consideration of treatment with thrombolytic therapy in most patients. Potential risks of thrombolytic therapy in arterial embolus patients with non-limb-threatening ischemia include partial clot lysis with further distal embolization or recurrent

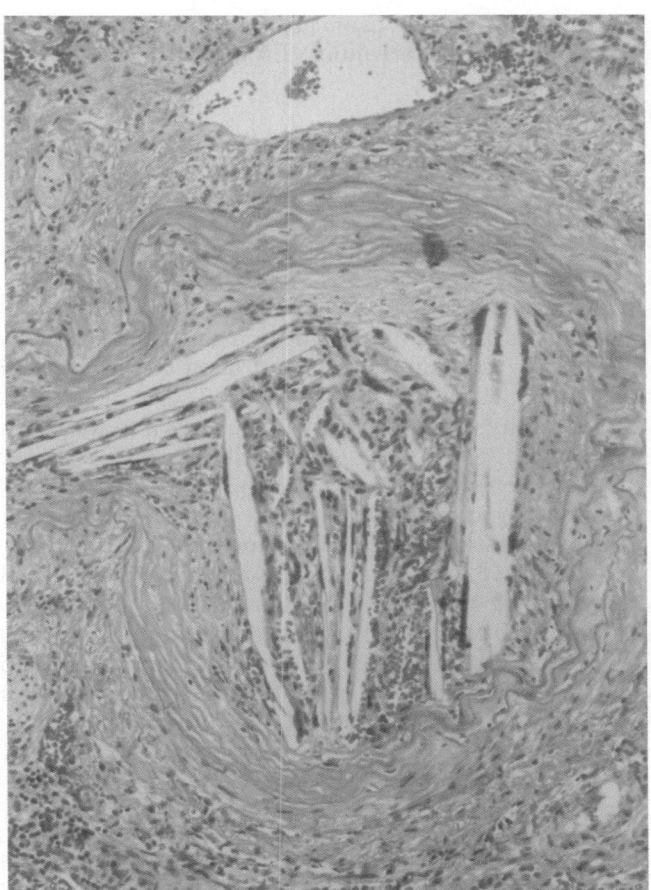

Figure 86-2. Photomicrograph of cholesterol embolus lodged in peripheral arteriole. (Courtesy of Arthur C. Aufderheide, MD.)

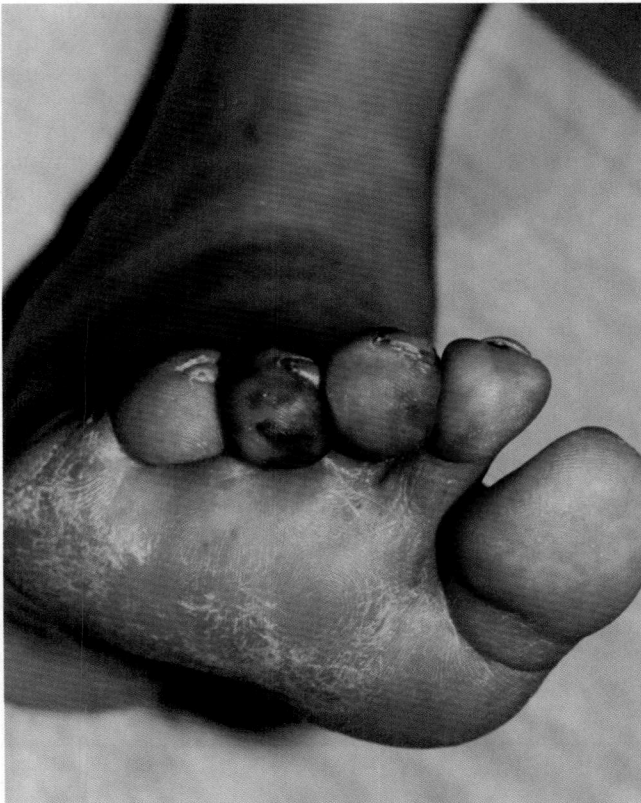

Figure 86-3. Clinical presentation of atheromatous emboli, or blue toe syndrome. (Courtesy of Gary R. Seabrook, MD.)

embolic events from the primary source of the initial embolus.[25]

Atheroembolism (Blue Toe Syndrome)

Atheroemboli are microemboli consisting of cholesterol, calcium, platelet aggregates, and hemorrhagic debris that break off from proximal atherosclerotic plaques or aneurysms and lodge in distal end arteries (Figure 86-2). In the central nervous system, atheroembolism causes transient ischemic attacks and strokes. In the peripheral vascular system, atheroemboli characteristically are found in the lower extremities with cool, painful cyanotic toes in the presence of palpable distal pulses (Figure 86-3).

Clinical Features

The typical presentation of atheroembolism is the sudden onset of a small painful area on the foot, typically the toe, which is cyanotic and tender.[26] If bilateral involvement is present, the distribution is not symmetric. Posterior tibial and dorsalis pedis pulses are present. The physical examination should be directed toward identification of a proximal source, such as an atherosclerotic aneurysm in the aorta, iliac, femoral, or popliteal arteries.

Differential Diagnosis

A variety of conditions can mimic the blue toe syndrome. Acrocyanosis is painless, has a symmetric distribution, and is located in the hands, nose, and lips. Poor peripheral perfusion as a result of low cardiac output must also be considered. Vasculitis typically has palpable purpuric lesions and is associated with constitutional symptoms of low-grade fever, myalgias, and weight loss. Previous frostbite may leave the extremities sensitive to cold. Local injury to the foot of the diabetic patient is easily differentiated.

Management

Treatment is directed toward identifying and removing the proximal source of atheroembolism. Angiography is the most accurate diagnostic method to determine the source of emboli. If the source is an aortic aneurysm and the patient is a surgical candidate, operative repair should be performed. Stenotic lesions in the iliac or femoral arteries can be treated with local endarterectomy, vascular bypass, or angioplasty.[16] Medical management with aspirin, dipyridamole, crystalline warfarin sodium (Coumadin), or steroids has variable results.

Arterial Thrombosis

Approximately 50% of acute arterial occlusions are caused by in situ thrombosis.[3] Acute arterial thrombosis is almost always superimposed on a complicated atherosclerotic lesion but can be caused by vasculitis or trauma. With limb-threatening ischemia, angiography can evaluate the feasibility of emergency bypass grafting. In patients with non-limb-threatening ischemia, angiography may be required if the clinical distinction of acute embolism and thrombosis is difficult (see Table 86-1).

Management

Systemic heparinization should be immediately established in the emergency department. Patients with severe limb-threatening ischemia require emergency direct or Fogarty catheter thrombectomy combined with bypass grafting. Simple thrombectomy alone often fails as a result of rethrombosis. Patients who have atherosclerotic disease not amenable to vascular bypass, who are too ill to tolerate revascularization, or who have irreversible ischemia require primary amputation. Patients with non-limb-threatening ischemia are initially best managed nonoperatively with heparin anticoagulation and consideration of treatment with low-dosage intraarterial thrombolytic therapy.

PERIPHERAL ARTERIAL ANEURYSMS

A true aneurysm is an abnormal localized dilation of the intact wall of any vessel caused by a combination of mural weakness and hemodynamic forces. Aneurysms enlarge at a rate governed by the cause of the lesion. Those caused by atherosclerosis progress slowly over years; those caused by trauma or infection enlarge over days, weeks, or months. The primary risk of central aneurysms (abdominal aorta, iliac arteries, and visceral arteries) is rupture (see Chapter 81). Peripheral arterial aneurysms rarely rupture; instead, they are complicated by thrombosis or embolism that jeopardizes distal tissues.[27]

The cause of an aneurysm depends on its anatomic location. Lower extremity aneurysms are most often atherosclerotic in origin. Upper extremity aneurysms are usually caused by localized trauma. Visceral aneurysms result from abnormal hemodynamics, atherosclerosis, or infectious causes.

Lower Extremity

Femoral and popliteal artery aneurysms almost always occur in older men with advanced atherosclerosis. Twenty-five percent of patients have distal atheroembolism or thromboembolism; an additional 15% have total occlusion from in situ thrombosis.[27]

Popliteal Aneurysms

Popliteal aneurysms are the most common peripheral aneurysms and occur bilaterally in approximately 60% of patients.[27] An abdominal aortic aneurysm occurs in almost 80% of patients with bilateral popliteal aneurysms. Most patients have claudication, thromboembolic events, atheroembolic events, or gangrene.

Aneurysmal dilation can cause venous compression with associated deep venous thrombosis.

Femoral Aneurysms

Femoral aneurysms are the second most common peripheral aneurysms and manifest similar to popliteal aneurysms. Femoral aneurysm dilation can also compress the femoral nerve, producing anterior thigh pain or weakness.

Diagnosis of both popliteal and femoral aneurysms is made by palpation of a pulsatile mass. Bilateral plain radiographs may show unilateral or bilateral calcified aneurysms. Ultrasonography and CT are diagnostic. Arteriography yields definitive diagnosis and indicates involvement of distal vessels. Patient with a lower extremity aneurysm should be evaluated for the presence of other aneurysms.

Asymptomatic patients often undergo elective surgical excision of the aneurysm and restoration of arterial continuity by end-to-end anastomosis or graft interposition. Simultaneous repair of coexisting abdominal aorta or contralateral extremity aneurysms combined with vascular bypass is typically done. Patients with limb-threatening thromboembolic events are first treated with Fogarty catheter embolectomy.[27]

Upper Extremity

Peripheral arterial aneurysms in the upper extremities are rare. Atherosclerosis generally spares the upper extremities, making localized trauma the most common cause.

Subclavian Artery Aneurysms

The causes of proximal subclavian artery aneurysms are thoracic outlet obstruction, trauma, and, rarely, atherosclerosis. Subclavian aneurysms from atherosclerosis represent severe disease, and 30% to 50% of patients so afflicted also have aortoiliac or other peripheral aneurysms.[28] Symptoms depend on the aneurysm's anatomic location. Patients may have chest, neck, and shoulder pain from acute expansion. Compression of the right recurrent laryngeal nerve can lead to voice change. Compression of the trachea can lead to stridor or other respiratory complaints. The chest radiograph may reveal a superior mediastinal mass, easily confused with a neoplasm.

Subclavian-Axillary Artery Aneurysms

The subclavian artery can be compressed by a complete cervical rib that articulates with the first rib, producing a poststenotic dilation in the proximal subclavian and distal axillary artery. This syndrome occurs more often in women and in the dominant upper extremity. Cervical ribs occur in only 0.6% of the population.[29]

Axillary Artery Aneurysms

Axillary artery aneurysms are most often caused by blunt trauma from inappropriate and prolonged use of crutches. Humerus fracture and anterior shoulder dislocation are less common causes.[28]

Subclavian, subclavian-axillary, and axillary artery aneurysms share the common complications of thromboembolism and limb-threatening ischemia, neuromuscular and sensory dysfunction from brachial plexus compression, and central nervous system ischemia produced by retrograde thromboembolism in the vertebral and right carotid circulation. A systolic bruit with a palpable thrill is common.

Arteriography to confirm the diagnosis and determine involvement of distal vessels is the diagnostic procedure of choice. Surgical treatment consists of aneurysm resection, vascular grafting, and reestablishment of arterial continuity.

Ulnar Artery Aneurysms (Hypothenar Hammer Syndrome)

The rare syndrome of ulnar artery aneurysm is associated with occupational trauma in which the heel of the palm is used to hammer, push, or twist objects.[30] Patients are often mechanics, carpenters, and machinists.

The ulnar artery fits snugly into the bony canal at the hypothenar eminence under the hook of the hamate bone. Long-term repetitive damage to this region results in aneurysm formation.[30] The aneurysm itself may secondarily develop a mural thrombus that repeatedly embolizes to the superficial palmar arch or to a digital artery. Symptoms consist of paresthesias, pain, coolness, and cyanosis, most often in the little and ring fingers and occasionally in the middle and index fingers. The thumb is characteristically spared because of its radial artery blood supply. Diagnosis is easily made by finding a pulsatile or nonpulsatile tender mass in the hypothenar eminence of the dominant hand. Allen's test may demonstrate occlusion of the ulnar artery. Angiography of the distal vessels is diagnostic. Proximal angiography rules out the subclavian and axillary arteries as embolic sources. Treatment requires surgical resection of the aneurysm and reestablishment of ulnar artery continuity. Adjunctive preoperative fibrinolytic therapy may be helpful.[30]

Viscera

Splenic Artery Aneurysms

Splenic artery aneurysms account for 60% of all visceral arterial aneurysms. They are the only aneurysms that are more common in women, with a female-to-male ratio of 4:1.[31] The development of aneurysms in the splenic artery has been attributed to systemic arterial fibrodysplasia, portal hypertension, and increased splenic arteriovenous shunting that occurs in pregnancy.

Splenic artery aneurysms are most often asymptomatic. Symptomatic patients exhibit vague left upper quadrant or epigastric discomfort and occasional radiation of pain to the left shoulder or subscapular area. Most splenic artery aneurysms are less than 2 cm in diameter; therefore, a pulsatile mass is not palpable. Occasionally, a systolic bruit can be heard.

Only 2% of splenic artery aneurysms result in life-threatening rupture.[31] More than 95% of ruptures occur in young women during pregnancy and can be confused with ectopic pregnancy or placental abruption.

Splenic artery aneurysms are usually an incidental discovery on the abdominal radiograph as signet ring calcifications in the left upper quadrant. Ultrasonography, CT, and magnetic resonance imaging can distinguish aneurysms from other cystic lesions in the left upper quadrant.[31] An angiogram is usually required to confirm the diagnosis. Symptomatic splenic artery aneurysms require immediate operative intervention, particularly in pregnant women or in women of childbearing age. The rate of maternal mortality from rupture during pregnancy is approximately 70%. Treatment is more controversial in asymptomatic patients. Transcatheter embolization has been successfully performed in some patients and is an alternative to surgery.[32]

Hepatic Artery Aneurysms

Hepatic artery aneurysms represent 20% of visceral artery aneurysms. The lesions are caused by atherosclerosis, infection (most often as a complication of intravenous drug abuse), major abdominal trauma, and polyarteritis nodosa. Hepatic artery aneurysms affect men twice as often as women and usually occur in patients older than 60 years of age.

Most aneurysms remain asymptomatic. Unruptured symptomatic aneurysms generally produce symptoms consistent with cholecystitis: vague, persistent, right upper quadrant or epigastric pain radiating to the back. Large aneurysms can cause severe upper abdominal discomfort, similar to that of pancreatitis. Hepatic artery aneurysms may rupture into the common bile duct, peritoneum, or adjacent hollow viscera. Mortality associated with hepatic artery rupture is 35%.

An abdominal bruit or palpable pulsatile mass is usually not present on physical examination. Aneurysmal calcification may be seen on a plain abdominal radiograph, but the diagnosis can be made reliably only by angiography. Ultrasonography and CT can be used to detect asymptomatic hepatic artery aneurysms.[32]

Because of the high mortality rate associated with aneurysmal rupture, an aggressive approach to patient management is warranted. Surgical resection of the aneurysm is performed in operative candidates. Transarterial catheter occlusion can be used in patients who are high surgical risks.[33]

Superior Mesenteric Artery Aneurysms

Superior mesenteric artery aneurysms are the third most common visceral aneurysms. Nearly 60% are infected aneurysms caused by nonhemolytic streptococci from left-sided bacterial endocarditis. Atherosclerosis and trauma are much less common causes. Patients are usually younger than 50 years of age; men and women are affected equally.

Patients generally have intermittent upper abdominal pain consistent with abdominal angina. Fifty percent have a pulsatile abdominal mass on physical examination. The stigmata of subacute bacterial endocarditis may be present. Plain abdominal radiographs may show a calcified aneurysm. Angiography is necessary to confirm the diagnosis.

Management of superior mesenteric artery aneurysm should address any underlying infectious process. The surgical approach is difficult and varies with the condition of the patient, the shape of the aneurysm (saccular or fusiform), and the intraoperative assessment of bowel viability.

Infected Aneurysms

Mycotic Aneurysms

The term *mycotic aneurysm* has been a source of confusion in the medical literature. No direct association exists with fungal disease. Although the term has been used to describe any infected aneurysm regardless of cause, it should be reserved for infected aneurysms resulting from bacterial endocarditis, as originally described in 1885 by Osler.[34,35]

Septic emboli from infective endocarditis implant in one of two ways. First, hematogenous seeding of bacteria can occur in nonaneurysmal arteries whose vessel walls have been damaged by preexisting atherosclerosis. Second, septic emboli can also become lodged in the vasa vasorum of larger vessels, causing vessel wall ischemia and infection. In smaller vessels, septic emboli tend to lodge at arterial bifurcations, arteriovenous fistulae, or sites of arterial stenosis. Mycotic aneurysms are most common in the aorta, superior mesenteric artery, and intracranial and femoral arteries.

The infecting organism in mycotic aneurysms reflects the bacteriology of infective endocarditis. *Streptococcus viridans* is the most common organism, although intravenous drug abusers are most often infected by *Staphylococcus aureus.* Patients who have mycotic aneurysms tend to be 30 to 50 years of age. The mortality rate is reported to be 25% (Table 86-2).[34,35]

Atherosclerotic Arteries

Currently, the most common cause of an infected aneurysm is sepsis with hematogenous spread of bacteria to atherosclerotic arteries. Large vessels (especially the aorta) rather than peripheral arteries are the most common site. Organisms associated with these infected aneurysms are *Salmonella, Staphylococcus,* and *Escherichia coli.* Patients tend to be older than 50 and to have well-established atherosclerosis. Perforation often occurs before diagnosis and carries a mortality rate of 75%.[35]

Preexisting Aneurysms

The incidence of infection in patients with preexisting atherosclerotic aneurysms is estimated at 3% to 4%. Some patients with ruptured aneurysms have a higher incidence of positive bacterial culture results than those who have elective surgical treatment of an asymptomatic aneurysm. Gram-positive organisms, especially *Staphylococcus,* predominate (60%). The rate of mortality is extremely high (90%) because of aneurysm rupture.[34,35]

Posttraumatic Pseudoaneurysms

Posttraumatic infected aneurysms result from invasive hemodynamic monitoring, angiography, and IV drug use. The most common artery affected is the femoral because of its involvement in groin injection. *S. aureus* is isolated in 30% to 70% of cases. Because of the more peripheral location and early identification, the mortality rate is low (5%).[36]

The clinical presentation of an infected aneurysm varies with anatomic location and underlying pathophysiologic process. Patients with infected abdominal aneurysms are often misdiagnosed. Onset is usually insidious; low-grade fever may be present for several months. Common findings are fever (75%), back and abdominal pain (33%), and palpable aneurysm (53%). More peripheral aneurysms, especially infected femoral pseudoaneurysms, are characterized by a tender groin mass, some manifestation of sepsis, or bleeding.[37] Almost all are easily palpable on physical examination. Although rare, fungal infections should be considered in patients who are chronically immunosuppressed, have been treated recently for disseminated fungal disease, or have diabetes mellitus.[37,38]

Laboratory findings are usually not diagnostic. Bacteremia often is continuous, and blood culture findings are positive for bacterial growth in approximately 70% of cases. Positive blood cultures in a patient with a preexisting aneurysm should prompt treatment as an infected aneurysm until disproven. Negative blood culture results alone do not rule out this diagnosis.

Table 86-2. Differentiation of Embolus from Thrombosis

Clinical Findings	Embolus	Thrombosis
Identifiable source for embolus	Usual, particularly atrial fibrillation	Less common
History of claudication	Rare	Common
Physical findings suggestive of occlusive disease	Few; proximal and contralateral limb pulses normal	Often present; proximal or contralateral limb pulses diminished or absent
Demarcation of ischemia	Sharp	Diffuse
Arteriography	Minimal atherosclerosis; sharp cutoff; few collaterals	Diffuse atherosclerosis, tapered, irregular cutoff; well-developed collaterals

From Brewster DC, Chin AK, Fogarty TJ: *Vascular Surgery.* Philadelphia, WB Saunders, 1990.

Angiography should be performed when an infected aneurysm is suspected.[38] Indium 111–labeled white blood cells are used to confirm or rule out infected aneurysms.[39]

Treatment must include both antibiotics and surgical repair. Antibiotic therapy is usually continued for at least 6 to 8 weeks, although some physicians advocate lifelong treatment after successful surgical repair.[40] The most important intervention is timely repair.[34,35] Without surgery, all patients will have aneurysm rupture with exsanguinating hemorrhage.[35]

Traumatic Aneurysms

Traumatic aneurysm refers to a pseudoaneurysm that follows perforation of the arterial wall, with formation of a perivascular hematoma. Chronic traumatic aneurysms may or may not be associated with an arteriovenous fistula. *Pseudoaneurysm* is a synonym for *false aneurysm.*

The usual presentation is a pulsatile mass found near the course of an extremity artery, with a history of trauma more than 1 month earlier.[41] The expanding aneurysm may compress associated peripheral nerves and produce neuropathy. Distal perfusion is usually well maintained, and thromboembolism is rare. A loud systolic and possibly a separate faint diastolic murmur are characteristic.

The diagnosis can be verified with many methods, including conventional angiography, digital subtraction arteriography, and CT. Surgical excision of the aneurysm is indicated as soon as possible to decrease the risk of complications, including rupture, thrombosis, or neurologic dysfunction caused by continued expansion.

VASOSPASTIC DISORDERS

Vasospastic disorders are characterized by an abnormal vasomotor response in the distal small arteries. Blood flow in the peripheral circulation is controlled by local, autonomic, and humoral mechanisms.[11] The cause of the heightened vasospastic response is unknown.

Raynaud's disease is the most common vasospastic disorder and occurs five or more times as often in women as in men. By definition, in cases of Raynaud's disease there is no evidence of an underlying cause. The diagnosis is correct in 95% of cases using these criteria: (1) episodes are precipitated by cold or emotion; (2) symptoms are bilateral; (3) gangrene is absent or is minimal and confined to the skin; (4) no disease or condition that could cause a secondary Raynaud's phenomenon is present; and (5) symptoms have been occurring for at least 2 years.[42]

The classic Raynaud's attack is triphasic: the fingers become white, then blue, and finally red. This is produced initially by complete closure of the palmar and digital arteries (and possibly arterioles), producing cessation of capillary perfusion. When a slight relaxation of arterial spasm occurs, a slight flow of blood returns into the dilated capillary bed, where it rapidly dissipates, producing cyanosis. Arterial spasm usually spontaneously resolves, arterial flow returns to baseline, but reactive hyperemia produces a red extremity. Attacks are often precipitated by cold and emotional stress. Raynaud's disease usually follows a benign course. True histologic changes within the vessel wall are absent. Reassurance, education, and continued primary care follow-up observation are the only treatment necessary for true Raynaud's disease.

Raynaud's phenomenon is Raynaud's disease that has an identifiable underlying disorder. Connective tissue disorders, including scleroderma, rheumatoid arthritis, and systemic lupus erythematosus, have the highest association with Raynaud's phenomenon. Treatment should be directed toward identifying the underlying disorder and minimizing threatened tissue loss if present.[42]

Benign livedo reticularis is caused by spasm of the dermal arterioles and may involve all parts of the upper and lower extremities, including the trunk. It is most common when skin is exposed to a cool environment. It is never associated with histologic vascular abnormality and quickly resolves when the exposed skin is covered or the environment is warmed. Secondary livedo reticularis can occasionally accompany peripheral vascular disease manifestations of other conditions similar to the causes of Raynaud's phenomenon.[42]

Acrocyanosis is the least common of the vasospastic disorders and is characterized by persistent, painless, symmetric cyanosis of the fingers, the hands, and less often the feet. The disease is benign and not associated with either vascular abnormality or an underlying disorder. Pain, trophic skin changes, and ulceration do not occur. This disorder occurs more often in women, is intensified by exposure to cold, and lessens with warming. The diagnosis is made by the bilateral and persistent nature of the findings, localized to the hands or feet in the presence of normal arterial pulsations. The involved extremities are nearly always cold; excessive perspiration is common. Except for reassurance and protection from cold, treatment is usually unnecessary.[42]

Primary erythromelalgia is a rare syndrome of paroxysmal vasodilation with burning pain, increased skin temperature, and redness of the feet and less often the hands. However, secondary erythromelalgia can occur in patients with underlying disease processes, most often systemic lupus erythematosus, myeloproliferative disorders, hypertension, venous insufficiency, or diabetes mellitus. Erythromelalgia is as common in children as adults, but in children it is less likely to be associated with an underlying systemic illness. Attacks are not triggered by cold and usually occur during modest ambient temperatures. Skin temperature of the involved digits is high compared with the patient's core temperature. Symptoms may remain mild for years or may become so severe that disability results. Tissue loss and trophic skin changes do not occur. Although rest, elevation of the extremities, and cold compresses or immersion in ice can provide temporary relief, no consistently effective treatment has been found for the multiple, often daily episodes of pain that occur with erythromelalgia.[42]

THORACIC OUTLET SYNDROME

Thoracic outlet syndrome involves compression of the brachial plexus, subclavian vein, or subclavian artery at the superior aperture of the thorax. Thoracic outlet syndromes were previously categorized by cause as scalenus anticus, costoclavicular, hyperabduction, cervical rib, or first thoracic rib syndromes. They are now most easily divided into three types—neurologic, venous, and arterial—depending on the predominant symptoms.

Compression of the brachial plexus causes the neurologic type of thoracic outlet syndrome and accounts for approximately 95% of all cases.[43] Symptoms begin between the ages of 20 and 50 years, with women predominating at a ratio of about 3:1. Compression or thrombosis of the subclavian vein constitutes the venous type of thoracic outlet syndrome and is responsible for 4% of all cases. It occurs most often in men 20 to 35 years of age. The arterial type of thoracic outlet syndrome is rare, occurring in approximately 1% of all cases, but is potentially the most serious of the three types. Men and women are affected equally in a bimodal age distribution of young adults (from cervical rib compression) and patients over age 50 (from localized atherosclerosis caused by arterial compression). Figure 86-4 demonstrates the relationship between anatomic abnormalities and neurovascular compression.

Principles of Disease

Roos[43] has described four basic concepts of thoracic outlet syndromes: (1) patients who have a thoracic outlet syndrome develop an anatomic abnormality predisposing them to symptoms under certain conditions; (2) brachial plexus compression or irritation constitutes approximately 95% of all thoracic outlet syndrome cases and is rarely caused by compression of the subclavian artery; (3) bedside testing for thoracic outlet syndrome based on positional compression of the subclavian artery is insensitive and unreliable; and (4) in advanced or refractory cases, the causative anatomic abnormalities must be surgically corrected.

The subclavian artery courses over the first rib between the scalenus anticus muscle anteriorly and the scalenus medius muscle posteriorly. From this point, it passes under the clavicle to the axilla, where the brachial plexus lies posteriorly and laterally. Four anatomic abnormalities have been associated with thoracic outlet syndrome.

Cervical rib syndrome results from an uncommon abnormality (0.5-0.7% of all chest radiographs), which is bilateral in 70% of patients.[43,44] It occurs twice as often in women as men. Most cervical ribs are incomplete, attached to a fibrous band on the scalene tubercle of the first rib. The site of compression is the scalene hiatus, made up of the scalene anterior muscle frontally, the scalene medius posteriorly, and the cervical rib inferiorly.

Figure 86-4. Interrelationships of muscle, ligament, and bone abnormalities in the thoracic outlet that may compress neurovascular structures. (From Urschel HC Jr: Management of thoracic outlet syndrome. *N Engl J Med* 286:1140, 1972.)

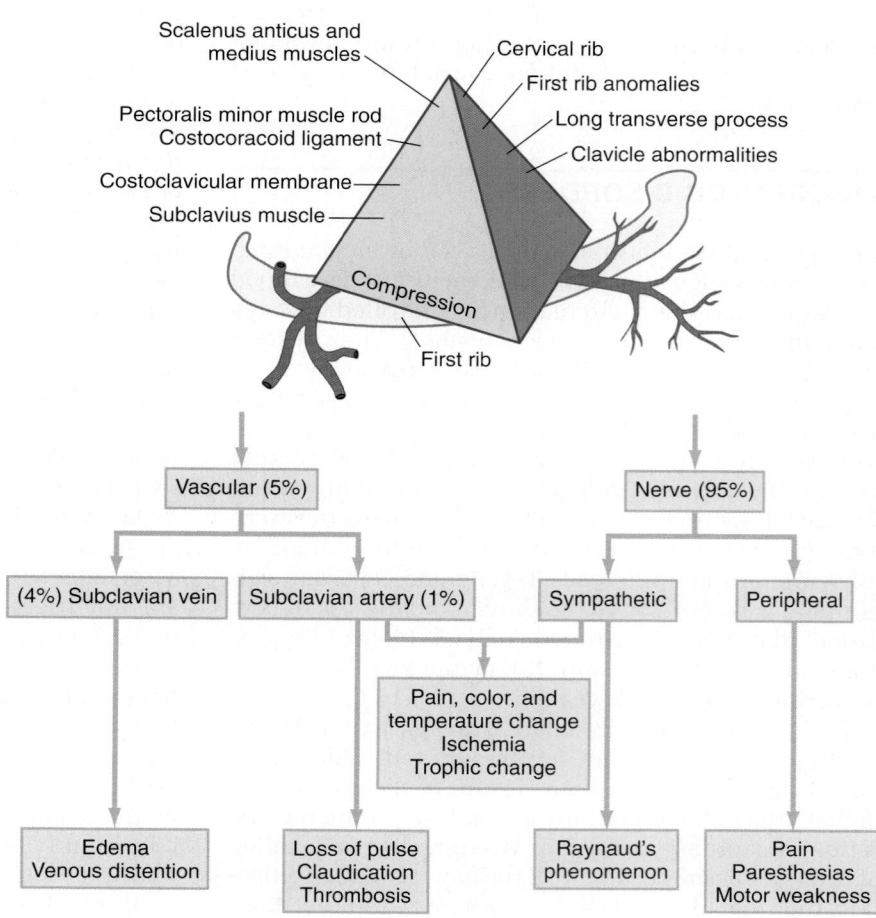

Scalenus anticus syndrome results when the neurovascular bundle is compressed as it passes through the interscalene triangle. The compression is caused by variations in the insertion of the anterior scalene muscle. In some patients, the subclavian artery passes through the body of the muscle.

Costoclavicular syndrome results when the shoulders are moved backward and downward. Causes include hypertrophy of the subclavius muscle, abnormalities of the first rib, and past clavicular fractures.

Hyperabduction syndrome results from the neurovascular compression that occurs when the arms are placed in the hyperabducted position. The site of compression is in the retroclavicular space anterior to the first rib or at the point where the neurovascular bundle passes beneath the pectoralis minor muscle.

The neurologic and venous compression type of thoracic outlet syndrome can be associated with any underlying anatomic abnormality. Bony abnormalities (cervical rib, first thoracic rib, or clavicle) are the most common causes of the arterial type of thoracic outlet syndrome (Figure 86-5A).

Clinical Features

Compression or irritation of the brachial plexus most often affects the lower two nerve roots, eighth cervical (C8) and first thoracic (T1), producing pain and paresthesias in the ulnar nerve distribution. The second most common anatomic pattern is involvement of the upper three nerve roots of the brachial plexus (C5, C6, and C7), with symptoms referable to the neck, ear, upper chest, upper back, and outer arm in the radial nerve distribution. Venous compression eventually progresses to intimal damage and subclavian vein thrombosis, with venous engorgement and swelling of the affected extremity. Persistent subclavian artery compression eventually results in poststenotic aneurysm formation and its pathologic sequelae.

Physical Examination

The Adson, costoclavicular, and hyperabduction maneuvers are unreliable as diagnostic tests.[45] Only 1% of all patients with thoracic outlet syndrome have involvement of the subclavian artery. Further-more, 92% of asymptomatic patients have variation in the strength of the radial pulse during positional changes.[43-45]

The most reliable test in screening for thoracic outlet syndrome is the elevated arm stress test (EAST).[45] With the patient sitting, the arms are abducted 90 degrees from the thorax and the elbows flexed 90 degrees, with the shoulders braced slightly behind the frontal plane. The patient is asked to open and close the fists slowly but steadily for a full 3 minutes and to describe any symptoms that develop. Normally, the patient performs this test without symptoms other than mild fatigue. The patient with thoracic outlet syndrome, however, usually has early heaviness and fatigue of the involved limb, gradual onset of numbness of the hand, and progressive aching through the arm and top of the shoulder. Within the 3 minutes, the patient usually drops the hand to the lap for relief of the progressive, crescendo distress that becomes intolerable. Patients with carpal tunnel syndrome may experience dysesthesias in the fingers but do not have shoulder or arm pain. Patients with cervical disk syndromes may have pain in the neck and shoulder but have no arm or hand symptoms.

The EAST evaluates all three types of thoracic outlet syndrome: neurologic, venous, and arterial. Radial pulses can be palpated by the examiner during the test. The presence of a radial pulse and a positive EAST test result are strong indications that the basis of symptoms is neurologic involvement of the brachial plexus.

The hands should be observed for changes in skin color, warmth, moisture, or muscular atrophy. Triceps muscle strength (innervated by C7) should be tested bilaterally. Muscle strength of the interosseous muscles (innervated by C8 and T1) should be tested by asking the patient to spread the fingers apart against resistance. The muscles innervated by the radial nerve are tested by the patient hyperextending the thumb and dorsiflexing the wrist against resistance. The median nerve innervates the thenar muscles, which can be tested by asking the patient to abduct the thumb away from the palm with the thumb pointing straight to the ceiling. Tinel's sign ("electric shock" to tips of fingers) is an indication of carpal tunnel compression of the median nerve and is elicited by percussing the volar aspect of the wrist. Gentle pressure with the thumb in the supraclavicular fossa over the brachial plexus may reproduce thoracic outlet symptoms after several seconds. The cervical spine and upper extremity reflexes should be assessed.

A blood pressure difference between the two arms is a reliable indication of arterial involvement. The blood pressure in the affected arm is lower. Doppler ultrasonography may be helpful in demonstrating comparatively reduced pressure over the pairs of radial, ulnar, and brachial arteries. The supraclavicular area should be auscultated bilaterally for subclavian bruits.

Ancillary Evaluation

Cervical spine radiographs with oblique views and chest radiographs are indicated in each patient for eval-

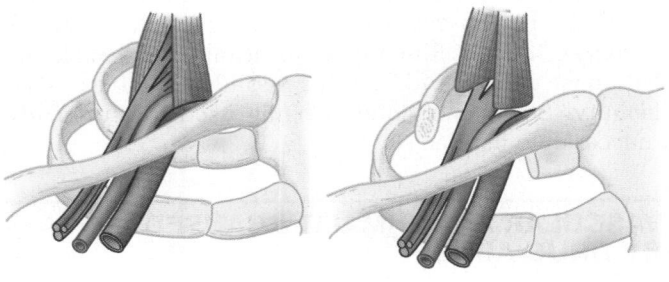

A   **B**

Figure 86-5. A, Thoracic outlet compression in costoclavicular space. **B,** Decompression of thoracic outlet by resection of first rib with disarticulation of the costochondral joint. (From Etheredge S, et al: *Am J Surg* 138:175, 1979.)

uation of skeletal abnormalities (first rib, cervical rib, clavicle deformity), trauma, arthritis, scoliosis, Pancoast tumor, or other pulmonary disease. Neurologic studies, including electromyography, nerve conduction times, and somatosensory-evoked potentials, are generally unreliable and do not provide objective evidence of thoracic outlet syndrome.[45] Patients suspected of having cervical disk or spinal cord disease may require cervical myelography, CT, or magnetic resonance imaging.

Arteriography is recommended with (1) obliteration of radial pulse on the EAST, (2) blood pressure 20 mm Hg less than that of the opposite asymptomatic limb, (3) suspected subclavian stenosis or aneurysm (bruit or abnormal supraclavicular pulsation), and (4) evidence of peripheral emboli in the upper extremity.[43] Venography is indicated if the patient has a history of intermittent or persistent edema of the hand or arm, peripheral unilateral cyanosis, or a prominent venous pattern over the arm, shoulder, or chest.[46]

Differential Diagnosis

The differential diagnosis of thoracic outlet syndrome includes herniated cervical disk, cervical spondylitis, spinal cord tumor, ulnar nerve compression at the elbow, carpal tunnel syndrome, orthopedic shoulder problems (sprain, rotator cuff injury, tendinitis), trauma, postural palsy, angina pectoris, and a variety of neuropathies, including multiple sclerosis, alcoholism, and diabetes.

Patients with a herniated cervical disk have more severe persistent pain radiating in a sharply demarcated dermatomal distribution (usually C4-5 or C5-6) and often have localized tenderness of the cervical spine at the affected level. Carpal tunnel syndrome is characterized by nocturnal symptoms of pain and paresthesias and an associated Tinel sign on physical examination. Brachial plexus compression and irritation can be confused with other vascular conditions, such as Raynaud's disease, vasospastic disorders, vasculitis, or arterial ischemia.[43] Unilateral symptoms should suggest thoracic outlet syndrome, whereas bilateral symptoms suggest a systemic process. Subclavian or axillary venous thrombosis from thoracic outlet syndrome must be differentiated from thrombophlebitis or mediastinal venous obstruction from a benign or malignant process (Pancoast's tumor).

Management

Treatment varies, depending on whether the involvement is neurologic, arterial, or venous. In patients with only brachial plexus involvement and with minimal signs and symptoms, conservative treatment with physiotherapy and shoulder girdle exercises is sufficient. Surgery is reserved for patients with significant neurologic signs and symptoms. This includes intolerable pain or progressive loss of function and strength of the arm or hand. First rib and anomalous muscle or fibrous tissue resection is the surgical treatment of choice and

provides consistent relief of symptoms and minimal morbidity (Figure 86-5B).[43]

Patients with arterial complications of thoracic outlet syndrome (thrombosis, thromboembolism, or acute ischemia) require immediate heparinization and angiography; Fogarty catheter embolectomy, if appropriate; and emergency or urgent surgical exploration. Patients with axillary and subclavian vein thromboses require immediate heparinization and venography and are treated with surgical thrombectomy or systemic fibrinolytic therapy.[47]

Disposition

The correct diagnosis of thoracic outlet syndrome can be achieved in more than 90% of patients with a careful history, physical examination, and bedside testing alone.[45] Neurologic, orthopedic, or vascular surgery consultation is indicated according to the pathologic condition.

PERIPHERAL ARTERIOVENOUS FISTULAE

Acquired peripheral arteriovenous fistulas are most often caused by trauma (gunshot wounds, stab wounds, or surgery). Malignancy, infection, and arterial aneurysms are less common sources. Patients generally seek medical care several months after an invasive surgical procedure or penetrating injury.

Differential Diagnosis

The correct diagnosis of an arteriovenous fistula can usually be made with clinical examination alone. A constant systolic and diastolic (to-and-fro) murmur associated with a palpable thrill is characteristic. Sixty percent of arteriovenous fistulae are also associated with a coexisting false aneurysm. Patients with peripheral venous disease may have similar cutaneous manifestations (varicose veins and stasis pigmentation) but lack vascular bruits. Infection in the form of bacterial endarteritis may complicate large fistulae.

Management

Acquired peripheral arteriovenous fistulae usually increase in size with time if surgery is delayed. Vessel dilation, peripheral ischemia, and cardiac output increase.[48] Transcatheter embolization with detachable balloons and liquid acrylic tissue adhesives (e.g., isobutyl 2-cyanoacrylate) is being used for surgically inaccessible fistulae.[49]

VASCULAR ABNORMALITY CAUSED BY DRUG ABUSE

Principles of Disease

The vascular complications of parenteral drug use have risen significantly in both frequency and severity since the late 1980s.[50] These intravenous or intraarterial injuries can result in acute arterial ischemia, infected pseudoaneurysms, lymphatic obstruction, or direct neurologic injury.

Acute arterial ischemia results from direct drug effects or endogenous catecholamine release after injection. Endothelial wall damage can stimulate platelet aggregation and thrombus formation. Precipitated crystals, talc, or foreign body emboli can cause arterial occlusion. Necrotizing arteritis can produce ischemia and is especially prevalent in patients who abuse intravenous methamphetamines.

Infected pseudoaneurysms associated with arteriovenous fistulae result from a through-and-through puncture of the artery with simultaneous contamination from either skin flora or organisms inoculated by contaminated needles or drug. These fistulae are the most common vascular lesions resulting from intravenous drug abuse. Secondary infection of the vascular structure may be covered by a surrounding soft tissue infection (cellulitis or abscess). Infected aneurysms at sites distant from the injection can occur.

Intravenous drug abusers can develop unilateral hand edema or "puffy hand syndrome" because of gradual obliteration of the superficial venous vessels and chronic lymphatic obstruction. Direct injury to adjacent nerves, polyneuritis, and ischemic neuritis can result from intravenous drug abuse. Coexisting serious or life-threatening infections include cellulitis, septicemia, and bacterial endocarditis.[50]

Clinical Features

Patients may withhold information about the use of intravenous drugs, so this possibility should be considered in all patients, especially patients with a fever. Objective evidence such as track marks may be present.

Distal ischemia after intraarterial injection most often occurs in the upper extremity after injection of the brachial or radial artery. The immediate onset of a severe, burning pain at the time of injection is a characteristic hallmark.[51] Patients have a painful, edematous upper extremity with patchy blue-purple skin discoloration. Distal pulses are generally present, but the skin temperature of the involved extremity is decreased. Because patients tend to seek attention early, the site of injection may be identifiable over the radial or brachial artery. Evidence of gangrene, pregangrenous changes, or neuromuscular deficits may accompany this syndrome.

Patients with infected pseudoaneurysms have a painful mass develop several days to weeks after injection, with resultant bleeding or "hitting pink." The mass is usually pulsatile, and 50% have an associated bruit.[50] Infected pseudoaneurysm is part of the differential diagnosis of cutaneous abscess or cellulitis in an intravenous drug user. Infected pseudoaneurysms are most often encountered in the lower extremities (80%). All patients should be carefully evaluated for sepsis, metastatic infection, and bacterial endocarditis. A peripheral vascular examination with careful documentation of pulses should be performed. A radiograph of the affected extremity can rule out a subcutaneous needle or foreign body. Angiography is the diagnostic procedure of choice for patients with suspected pseudoaneurysm or distal ischemia. Ultrasonography is often unable to distinguish an aneurysm from an abscess or cellulitis.

Management

Therapeutic considerations for acute ischemia from intraarterial injection are primarily conservative. Intraarterial vasodilators, heparin, low-molecular-weight dextran, fibrinolytic therapy, analgesics, systemic warming to stimulate vasodilation, antibiotics, elevation of the affected limb to promote venous drainage, and physical therapy have not significantly altered the outcome or amputation rate in this patient population. Surgical treatment is reserved for delayed amputation, with the goal of preserving as much tissue as possible. Gradual resolution of symptoms without surgical intervention is the most common outcome.

Patients with infected pseudoaneurysms require aneurysm resection, debridement of infected tissue, and ligation of the proximal and distal uninfected arteries. Autogenous vein bypass through uninfected tissue planes may require an extensive surgical approach.[52]

Methicillin-resistant *S. aureus* and gram-negative rods are increasing in frequency as the causative agents in infections and vascular injury resulting from drug abuse. Intravenous nafcillin is recommended for mild infections, nafcillin and a second- or third-generation cephalosporin for major infections, and vancomycin and a second- or third-generation cephalosporin or an aminoglycoside for patients who are bacteremic or overtly septic.[50]

PROBLEMS RELATED TO LONG-TERM CENTRAL VENOUS ACCESS

Hickman-Broviac Catheter

The Hickman-Broviac double-lumen catheter is in common use, with the smaller Broviac line used for the administration of intravenous therapy and the larger Hickman line reserved for additional venous access and blood withdrawal (Figure 86-6; see also Figure 86-8B). This catheter is generally inserted into the cephalic, subclavian, external, or internal jugular vein, with the distal tip just above the right atrium.[53] The proximal end exits through a subcutaneous tunnel from the lower anterior chest wall. A felt cuff (Dacron) is used to anchor it in place subcutaneously. The Hickman-Broviac catheter is made of polymeric silicone rubber that is of low thrombogenic potential but extremely flexible and soft. Because of the pliability of the material, the catheter must be treated gently. Clearing an obstructed catheter with a guidewire may perforate the catheter. Forcing fluid through the catheter by positive pressure carries the risk of catheter rupture or catheter embolus. For this reason, no syringe larger than 5 mL should be used for irrigation.

Figure 86-6. Selected catheters. **Top,** Double-lumen Hickman catheter. **Bottom,** Quinton-Mahurkar catheter.

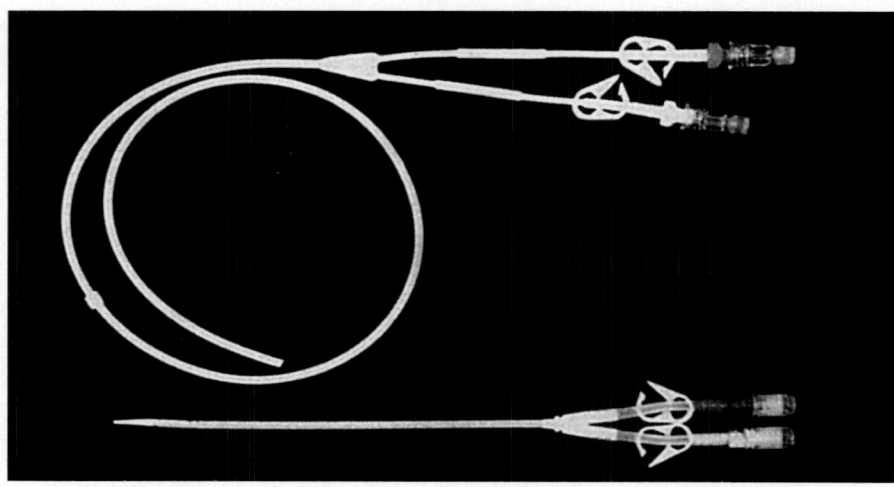

Routine Care and Use

The smaller Broviac line is most often used for the infusion of total parenteral nutrition or fat emulsions. This line should be irrigated with 6 mL of normal saline solution between different infusions to prevent mixing of incompatible solutions, development of precipitation, and resultant catheter occlusion. The larger Hickman line should be used to withdraw blood. This line should be irrigated with 6 mL of heparinized saline after blood withdrawal to prevent clot formation in the catheter lumen. When a clamp is used, it should be placed over a piece of tape wrapped around the line. The clamp should have a smooth surface, since teeth or prongs could sever or abrade the line.

Routine care and frequency of catheter dressing changes vary with the preference of the treating physician (unpublished data, Krzywda, 1990, and Quebbeman, 1990).[53,54] Most patients become skilled in routine catheter maintenance and are a reliable source of information. Absolute sterile technique is essential when manipulating the catheter.

Catheter Occlusion

Hickman catheters can exhibit complete or partial obstruction to flow in either line. Complete obstruction, in decreasing order of frequency, results from (1) clots within the catheter lumen, (2) precipitants within the catheter lumen, and (3) mechanical obstruction. In catheters that accept infusions at normal rates but cannot be aspirated, the causes, in decreasing order of frequency, are (1) catheter lodged against the wall of the vessel, (2) occluding fibrin sheath around the catheter tip, (3) ball valve or mural thrombus, and (4) central venous thrombosis. Patients who have intermittent complete occlusion and withdrawal occlusion have a type of mechanical obstruction called *pinch-off syndrome,* in which the catheter lumen is compromised from mechanical forces acting on it between the clavicle and the first rib. Clots within the catheter lumen, obstructing fibrin sheaths, and ball valve or mural thrombus often respond to low-dose intracatheter

---

BOX 86-1. Differential Diagnosis of Occluded Chronic Indwelling Catheters

Complete Occlusion
Clot in catheter lumen*
Precipitate in catheter lumen
Mechanical obstruction

Withdrawal Occlusion
Catheter against vessel wall
Fibrin sheath*
Ball valve/mural thrombus*
Subclavian vein thrombosis

Intermittent Complete Occlusion and Withdrawal Occlusion
Pinch-off syndrome

*Usually responds to low-dose intracatheter urokinase.

---

urokinase; central venous thrombosis, precipitants in the catheter lumen, and mechanical obstruction do not respond (Box 86-1).

Precipitants within the catheter lumen most often result from failure to clear the line with saline after total parenteral nutrition, flushing the line with a heparin solution instead. Heparin precipitates with total parenteral nutrition fluid, producing solids. Clots within the catheter lumen usually result from failure to flush the line with a heparinized saline solution after blood aspiration.

A chest radiograph should be obtained in all patients with persistently occluded catheters to confirm catheter position and integrity. The catheter tip should be positioned just above the right atrium.[53] Persistent right atrial placement can cause perforation of this thin-walled heart chamber or result in a right atrial thrombosis. Comparison with previous radiographs may be necessary to ensure lack of movement or displacement. In patients with withdrawal occlusion but appropriate catheter position, and without clinical evidence of subclavian vein thrombosis, the catheter may be lodged against the vessel wall. The patient's changing body position, raising the arms above the head, or performing the Valsalva maneuver may relieve withdrawal occlusion. If this is unsuccessful, further treatment can be considered when the presentation and history are consistent with a type of catheter occlusion that responds to low-dose intracatheter urokinase (see Box 86-1). Urokinase (5000 U) should be injected into the catheter and left for 30 minutes before aspiration is attempted. If this is also unsuccessful, a second dose of urokinase can be injected and the procedure repeated.[55] While contraindications to fibrinolytic agents should be considered, low-dose therapy for occluded catheters appears well tolerated.[55,56]

Mechanical obstruction has a variety of causes, including pinch-off syndrome. The catheter is intermittently obstructed during both administration and withdrawal of fluids. A chest radiograph demonstrates narrowing of the catheter lumen as it passes between the clavicle and the first rib. This condition is typically detected within 3 weeks after catheter placement; the catheter must be removed because of fragmentation or embolization if left in place.[57]

Because engorged collateral circulation or swelling in the affected extremity is not universally present with subclavian vein thrombosis, this diagnosis should be considered in all patients who are unresponsive to declotting attempts. Catheter removal with systemic heparinization or catheter maintenance with high-dose fibrinolytic therapy is a therapeutic option for subclavian vein thrombosis.[58,59] Mechanical occlusion is rare and requires catheter replacement with a surgical approach. Because of variations in approach by different consultants, early consultation is recommended in patients who have occluded central venous catheters (Figure 86-7).

Catheter Laceration

If an external catheter laceration or fracture occurs, the catheter should be clamped over tape distal to the laceration close to the chest wall. The catheter can be repaired as long as the damage is more than 4 cm from the chest wall. After clamping, as an interim measure, the next step is to insert a 14-gauge, 2-inch Angiocath into the catheter; remove the stylus; tape securely; and flush with heparin. The catheter can then be used while a repair kit is obtained.[60]

Catheter-Related Infections

Catheter infections can be categorized as local or systemic. Local infections primarily involve the skin and subcutaneous tissues surrounding the exit site with erythema, tenderness, and no clinical or laboratory evidence of sepsis. Skin organisms are primarily responsible for local infections, especially coagulase-negative staphylococci.[54] Studies show that local infections usually do not require catheter removal and resolve with antimicrobial therapy alone.[61]

The source of systemic infection in patients with Hickman-Broviac catheters may be difficult to localize, particularly in immunosuppressed patients. The most common sites of systemic infection in any patient with a central venous catheter, in decreasing order of frequency, are the urinary tract, the anorectal area, the upper respiratory tract, and the catheter.[54] The most common organisms causing catheter infection are coagulase-negative staphylococci, *S. aureus,* and *Candida albicans.* In immunocompromised patients with Hickman-Broviac catheters, gram-positive organisms now are responsible for more cases of sepsis than gram-negative bacteria. Accordingly, initial empiric therapy should include an antistaphylococcal drug, in addition to the usual gram-negative coverage. A good empirical regimen is Ancef (1 g) and gentamicin (1 mg/kg IV). All patients who have a suspected vascular access infection should have two blood culture samples drawn. Comparison of blood culture samples drawn simultaneously through the catheter and from a peripheral blood vessel may assist in determining whether the catheter is the source of infection. Infections that do not extend through the vessel wall (pericatheter infections) can be successfully treated without catheter removal. Catheter removal is mandatory in patients with continued positive blood culture results despite therapy and in those with vascular access infections caused by *Candida* species.[61]

Catheter-related septic central venous thrombosis can progress through and around the vessel wall to cause a perivascular infection or abscess. This rare but devastating complication is associated with serious morbidity and a reported mortality rate as high as 83%. Because of the lack of specific clinical findings, the most prominent diagnostic feature is continued bacteremia after catheter removal. Diagnosis is confirmed by venography or CT scan.[62] Removal of the catheter, intravenous administration of antimicrobials, and anticoagulation constitute appropriate initial therapy. Surgical treatment with thrombectomy and possible abscess drainage are indicated after failure of an adequate course of antibiotics and anticoagulation. Fibrinolytic agents have been used as an adjunct for catheter-related septic venous thrombosis, but the risk-benefit ratio has not been established.[63] In patients who require catheter removal, a quantitative culture of the number of organisms on the catheter's surface correlates well with a positive blood culture result for the same organism. This technique involves rolling the catheter on a culture medium. Broth culture of catheter tips may be less reliable in determining whether the catheter is the source of infection.[64]

Groshong Catheter

The Groshong catheter is a single, thin-walled silicone rubber catheter designed for prolonged venous cannulation. It differs from the Hickman-Broviac catheter in insertion, design, and maintenance. A decreased outer diameter to inner diameter ratio allows insertion into a smaller vein through a smaller introducer sheath. The

Figure 86-7. Approach to occluded indwelling catheter.

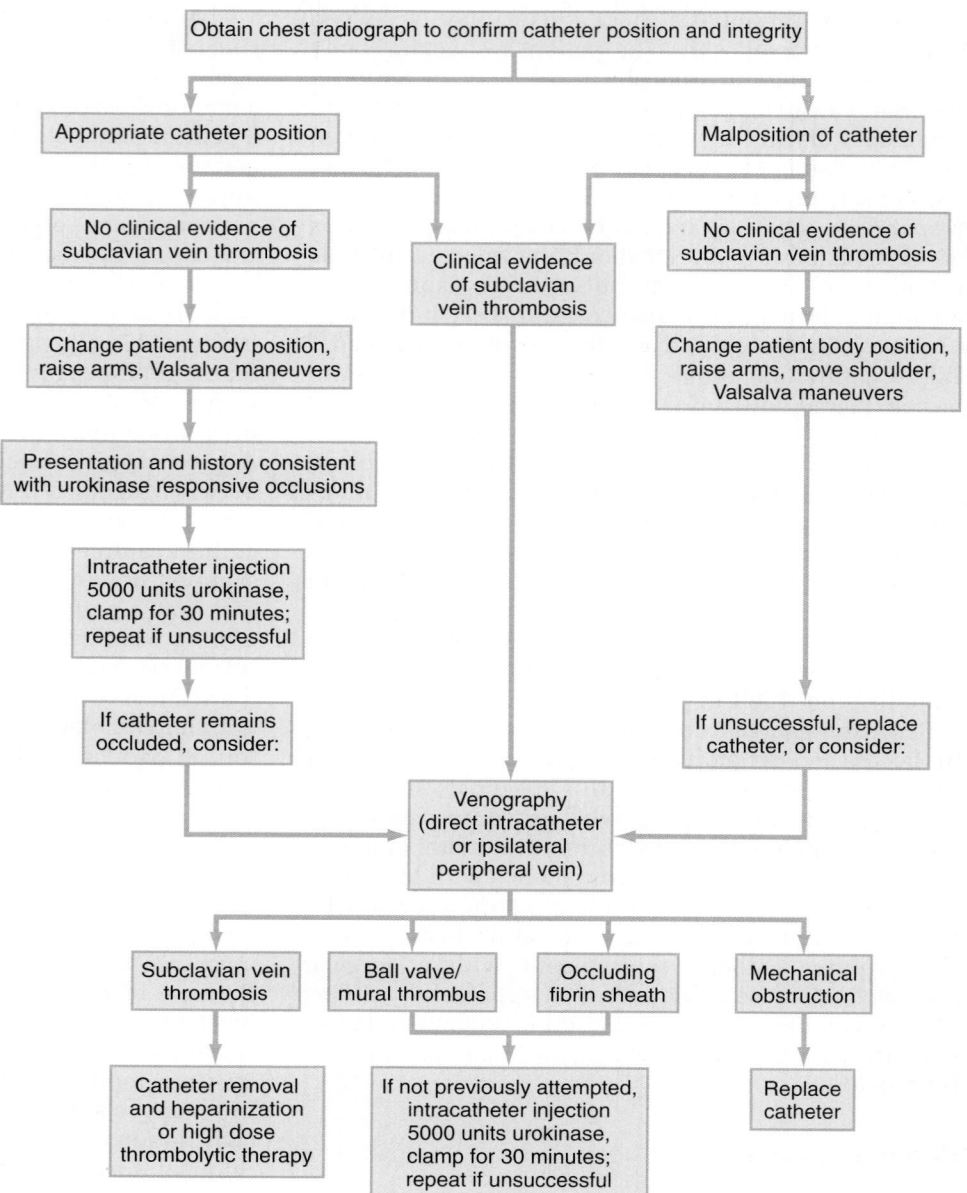

catheter can be inserted under local anesthesia without fluoroscopy, using the Seldinger technique and a peel-away catheter introducer sheath. After catheter placement in the subclavian, internal, or external jugular vein, a subcutaneous tunnel is created with a stainless steel tunneling device through which the catheter is threaded. A Dacron cuff stabilizes the catheter's placement in subcutaneous tissues and reduces the chance of inadvertent removal or retrograde infection.[65]

The Groshong catheter is constructed with a closed end and a vocal cord-type integral valve at the distal end (Figure 86-8A). This pressure-sensitive two-way valve at the intravascular end minimizes back-bleeding, eliminating the need for heparin flushes or external clamping, but permits blood sampling with gentle negative pressure. Patency of the catheter is maintained with 5 mL of saline flush once a week. A 20-mL saline irrigation is necessary after any blood transfusion or if blood is observed in the catheter

lumen. A 30-mL saline irrigation is performed before blood sampling after infusion of hyperalimentation solutions.

Groshong catheters offer the advantage of bedside placement, minimal back-bleeding, elimination of heparin flushes, and elimination of external clamping when changing injection caps or connecting tubing. A lower incidence of complete obstruction to flow from clots or precipitants within the catheter lumen, however, has not been shown.[66] Groshong catheters are otherwise subject to the same complications as described for Hickman-Broviac catheters.

Vascular Access for Hemodialysis

Quinton-Mahurkar Catheter

The Quinton-Mahurkar catheter is the preferred catheter for providing immediate and short-term vascular access for hemodialysis. Its advantages include

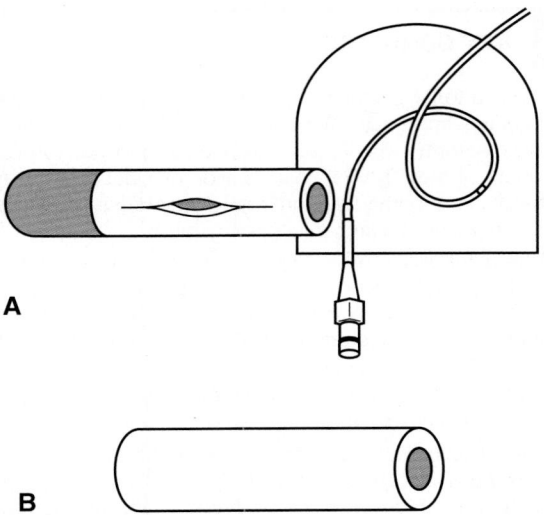

Figure 86-8. A, Groshong catheter with closed distal end and vocal cord-type valve. **B,** Hickman catheter with open distal end. (From Delmore JE, et al: Experience with Groshong long-term central venous catheter. *Gynecol Oncol* 34:216, 1989.)

bedside placement and a functional life up to 18 months.[67] This single, flexible, polyurethane cannula has two separate D-shaped channels, each connected by a molded Y piece to a color-coded external port (Figure 86-6B). To protect against a disconnected cap, each limb of the Y piece has an attached clamp. The Quinton-Mahurkar catheter is placed by the Seldinger technique, most often in the subclavian vein and less often in the femoral vein.

The mortality rate from central venous catheter hemodialysis is low (0 to 1.25 per 1000 catheterizations), but the morbidity rate is high, with a reported overall complication rate near 30%.[68] The most common complications are catheter-related infections and thrombosis.

A Quinton-Mahurkar catheter can be used to obtain blood samples. After blood withdrawal, the line should be flushed with more than 10 mL of normal saline solution, followed by 5000 U of heparin in 1 mL of saline to prevent intracatheter clot formation. The catheter can also be used for the administration of intravenous therapy. Routine care and use are otherwise similar to that previously described for chronic indwelling central venous catheters.

Cimino-Brescia Fistula and Prosthetic Bridge Fistula

The subcutaneous Cimino-Brescia fistula is the preferred means of vascular access for long-term hemodialysis. The fistula is created through a side-to-side and side-to-end anastomosis using the radial artery and the cephalic forearm vein. The high blood flow and pressure on the venous side of the fistula "arterialize" the veins, which takes 3 to 5 weeks. The Cimino-Brescia fistula is well tolerated by patients, has a low infection rate, and has the longest functional use of any vascular

access method. The fistula has a 90% patency rate at 12 months, which gradually decreases to approximately 75% at 4 years.

An alternative to the Cimino-Brescia fistula is the *arteriovenous bridge fistula.* Formed by a prosthetic conduit, this fistula connects a superficial artery (usually the radial or brachial) with a large antecubital vein. The prosthetic material is usually expanded polytetrafluoroethylene. Arteriovenous bridges can be constructed in the leg between the superficial femoral or femoral artery and the saphenous vein. Lower extremity arterial bridges have a higher blood flow rate and therefore are less likely to thrombose but are also associated with a higher rate of infection produced by their proximity to the bacteria-laden perineum.

Thrombosis

Thrombosis is the most common complication of a subcutaneous arteriovenous fistula or prosthetic graft. Emergency department personnel must avoid circumferential bandages, tourniquets, or blood pressure cuffs in the fistula-bearing arm because these objects restrict venous outflow and may predispose to thrombosis. A tourniquet should not be used. The opposite arm or the fistula itself can be used to acquire blood or vascular access (without using a tourniquet). Normal graft flow is clinically verified by feeling a thrill or hearing a bruit on auscultation. A strong palpable pulse with no matching thrill suggests venous outflow obstruction or early graft thrombosis. Thrombosis of arteriovenous fistulae requires temporary vascular access and definitive surgical intervention later, usually with the creation of a new fistula proximal to the thrombosed shunt.

Blood Withdrawal

Ideally, an alternate peripheral venipuncture site should be sought first before using a Cimino-Brescia fistula for blood withdrawal. When an alternate site is unavailable, however, the arteriovenous fistula is a reasonable choice. An individual skilled in venipuncture techniques should maintain absolute sterility with antiseptic (e.g., Betadine) skin preparation, sterile gloves, and sterile gauze. Tourniquets are contraindicated and unnecessary. Venipuncture should be performed on the well-developed venous side of the fistula. After blood acquisition, gentle pressure should be maintained for 5 minutes, with care taken not to occlude the vessel lumen. The site should then be observed for several minutes to ensure that bleeding does not occur. A prosthetic arteriovenous bridge fistula can also be used to obtain blood samples. Venipuncture is achieved by careful perforation of the superficial wall of the prosthetic graft; otherwise, the technique is identical.

Clinically differentiating a Cimino-Brescia fistula from a prosthetic arteriovenous bridge fistula may be difficult. The prosthetic portion of an arteriovenous bridge fistula connects the arterial to the venous vessels in an H shape and is tunneled for some distance beneath the skin, giving the appearance of a single, large blood vessel. The prosthetic fistula will have a thrill but will not be as pulsatile as a Cimino-Brescia fistula when gently palpated. If asked, most patients are knowledgeable about their fistula.

Peripheral intravenous access is also best established at an alternate site. When an alternate site is unavailable and the patient requires timely intravenous access, the Cimino-Brescia fistula or bridge fistula can be used, following the guidelines given for venipuncture. Careful attention to sterile technique, operator skill, and avoidance of tourniquets can provide timely venipuncture or intravenous therapy while preventing infectious or thrombotic complications. If an intravenous line is used in a fistula, early removal after alternative intravenous access is desirable.

Infection

Infections of an arteriovenous fistula or graft are potentially life threatening and are manifested by signs of septicemia and local inflammation. Once the diagnosis of infected fistula is considered, blood cultures should be obtained and intravenous antibiotics for gram-positive skin organisms administered. Prosthetic graft infection cannot be eradicated with intravenous antibiotics alone and requires prosthetic graft removal. Infections are the second leading cause of death of patients undergoing long-term dialysis.

Steal Phenomenon

Vascular steal from the ulnar artery via the palmar arch occasionally occurs in patients with atherosclerotic disease distal to the shunt, particularly diabetic patients. Patients with this condition may experience fingertip ischemia during periods of increased shunting (hemodialysis or increased activity). The steal phenomenon usually requires graft ligation with construction of a new fistula in the opposite extremity.

Venous Hypertension

Acute venous hypertension may occur in the first few weeks after fistula construction. This is a true surgical emergency. The early rise in venous pressure produces marked swelling of the extremity and severe venous stasis disease. Characteristic skin pigmentation, edema, and occasionally venous ulceration are seen. Management of venous hypertension requires hospitalization and urgent ligation of the vein immediately distal to the fistula before a potentially exsanguinating vessel rupture occurs.

Bleeding

Patients also present to the emergency department with bleeding from their fistula after dialysis. Persistent, gentle pressure, with care taken not to occlude blood flow, usually resolves this problem.

KEY CONCEPTS

- Acute arterial occlusion is a limb-threatening emergency requiring immediate heparinization and Fogarty catheter embolectomy. The clinical diagnosis is based on some variant of the "five Ps": pain, pallor, pulselessness, paresthesias, and paralysis. Confirmatory tests are unnecessary and increase the limb's ischemic status.

- Atheroembolism ("blue toe syndrome") is associated with cool, painful cyanotic toes in the presence of palpable distal pulses. A proximal source should be localized, most often an atherosclerotic aneurysm in the aorta or the iliac, femoral, or popliteal artery.

- Popliteal aneurysms are bilateral in 60% of patients and often coexist with an abdominal aortic aneurysm.

- The classic Raynaud attack is triphasic: the fingers become white, blue, then red. Raynaud's disease has no detectable underlying cause and usually has a benign course. Raynaud's phenomenon has an underlying disorder, usually connective tissue disease.

- The only reliable clinical test for detection of thoracic outlet syndrome is the elevated arm stress test (EAST).

- Complications of parenteral drug abuse include acute arterial ischemia, infected pseudoaneurysms, lymphatic obstruction, and direct neurologic injury.

- Acute venous hypertension can occur in the first few weeks after construction of an arteriovenous fistula. Hospitalization is required for ligation of the vein before a potentially exsanguinating vessel rupture occurs.

REFERENCES

1. Haimovici H: Landmarks and present trends in vascular surgery. In Haimovici H (ed): *Vascular Surgery,* 3rd ed. East Norwalk, Conn, Prentice Hall, 1989.
2. Rutherford RB: Arterial aneurysms: Etiologic considerations. In Rutherford RB (ed): *Vascular Surgery,* 5th ed. Philadelphia, WB Saunders, 2000.
3. Brewster DC, Chin AK, Fogarty TJ: Arterial thromboembolism. In Rutherford RB (ed): *Vascular Surgery,* 5th ed. Philadelphia, WB Saunders, 2000.
4. Kumagai K et al: Increased intracardiovascular clotting in patients with chronic atrial fibrillation. *J Am Coll Cardiol* 16:377, 1990.
5. Haimovici H: Muscular, renal and metabolic complications of acute arterial occlusions: Myonephropathic-metabolic syndrome. *Surgery* 85:461, 1979.
6. Bashore TM, Gehrig T: Cholesterol emboli after invasive cardiac procedures. *J Am Coll Cardiol* 42:217, 2003.
7. Cotran RS, Kumar V, Robbins SL: *Pathologic Basis of Disease,* 6th ed. Philadelphia, WB Saunders, 1999.
8. Bandyk DF: Vascular injury. In Condon RE, Nyhus LM (eds): *Manual of Surgical Therapeutics,* 9th ed. Boston, Little, Brown, 1996.
9. Elkin DC, Warren JV: Arteriovenous fistulas: Their effect on the circulation. *JAMA* 134:1524, 1947.
10. Perry MO: Acute limb ischemia. In Rutherford RB (ed): *Vascular Surgery,* 5th ed. Philadelphia, WB Saunders, 2000.
11. Flavahan NA, Flavahan S, Mitra S, Chotani MA: The vasculopathy of Raynaud's phenomenon and scleroderma. *Rheum Dis Clin North Am* 29:275, 2003.
12. Plummer D: Principles of emergency ultrasound and echocardiography. *Ann Emerg Med* 18:1291, 1989.

13. Hessel S, Adams D, Abrams H: Complications of angiography. *Radiology* 138:273, 1981.
14. Simoni G, et al: Helical CT for the study of abdominal aortic aneurysms in patients undergoing conventional surgical repair. *Eur J Vasc Endovasc Surg* 12:354, 1996.
15. Fogarty TJ, et al: A method of extraction of arterial emboli and thrombi. *Surg Gynecol Obstet* 116:241, 1963.
16. Ahn SS, Concepcion B: Indications and results of arterial stents for occlusive disease. *World J Surg* 20:644, 1996.
17. Morin JF, et al: Factors that determine the long-term results of percutaneous transluminal dilatation for peripheral arterial occlusive disease. *J Vasc Surg* 4:68, 1996.
18. Mills JL, Porter JM: Buerger's disease: A review and update. *Semin Vasc Surg* 6:14, 1993.
19. Rowe K: Hyperbaric oxygen therapy: What is the case for its use? *J Wound Care* 10:117, 2001.
20. Finsterer J, Dossenbach-Glaninger A, Krugluger W, et al: Risk-factor profile in severe, generalized, obliterating vascular disease. *South Med J* 97:87, 2004.
21. Litchfield R, et al: Differential diagnosis of leg ulcers. *JAMA* 78:364, 1979.
22. Kempczinski RF: The chronically ischemic leg: An overview. In Rutherford RB (ed): *Vascular Surgery,* 5th ed. Philadelphia, WB Saunders, 2000.
23. Buerger L: Thromboangiitis obliterans: A study of vascular lesions leading to presenile spontaneous gangrene. *Am J Med Sci* 136:567, 1908.
24. Mils JM, Porter JL: Buerger's disease (thromboangiitis obliterans). *Ann Vasc Surg* 5:570, 1991.
25. Working Party on Fibrinolysis in the Management of Limb Ischemia: Fibrinolysis in the management of lower limb peripheral arterial occlusion: A consensus document. *J Vasc Interv Radiol* 14:S337, 2003.
26. Sharma PV, Babu SC, Shah PM, et al: Changing patterns of atheroembolism. *Cardiovasc Surg* 4:573, 1996.
27. Graham LM: Femoral and popliteal aneurysms. In Rutherford RB (ed): *Vascular Surgery,* 5th ed. Philadelphia, WB Saunders, 2000.
28. Clark ET, Mass DP, Bassiouny HS, et al: True aneurysmal disease in the hand and upper extremity. *Ann Vasc Surg* 5:276, 1991.
29. Desai Y, Robbs JV: Vascular complications of thoracic outlet syndrome. *Eur J Vasc Endovasc Surg* 10:362, 1995.
30. Tatlor LM Jr: Hypothenar hammer syndrome. *J Vasc Surg* 37:697, 2003.
31. Zelenock GB, Stanley JC: Splanchnic artery aneurysms. In Rutherford RB (ed): *Vascular Surgery,* 5th ed. Philadelphia, WB Saunders, 2000.
32. Mandel SR, et al: Nonoperative management of peripancreatic arterial aneurysms: A 10-year experience. *Ann Surg* 205:126, 1987.
33. Pilleul F, Dougougeat F: Transcatheter embolization of splanchnic aneurysms/pseudoaneurysms: Early imaging allows detection of incomplete procedure. *J Comput Assist Tomogr* 26:107, 2002.
34. Akers DL, Fowl RJ, Kempczinski RF: Mycotic aneursym of the tibioperoneal trunk: Case report and review of the literature. *J Vasc Surg* 16:71, 1992.
35. Reddy DJ, Ernst CB: Infected aneurysms. In Rutherford RB (ed): *Vascular Surgery,* 5th ed. Philadelphia, WB Saunders, 2000.
36. Malanoski GJ, et al: *Staphylococcus aureus* catheter-associated bacteremia: Minimal effective therapy and unusual infectious complications associated with arterial sheath catheters. *Arch Intern Med* 155:1161, 1995.
37. Miller BM, et al: *Histoplasma* infection of abdominal aortic aneurysms. *Ann Surg* 197:57, 1983.
38. Shetty PC, et al: Mycotic aneurysms in intravenous drug abusers: The utility of intravenous digital subtraction angiography. *Radiology* 155:319, 1985.
39. Brunner MC, et al: Prosthetic graft infection: Limitations of indium white blood cell scanning. *J Vasc Surg* 3:42, 1986.
40. Oskoui R, Davis WA, Gomes MN: *Salmonella* aortitis: A report of a successfully treated case with a comprehensive review of the literature. *Arch Intern Med* 153:517, 1993.
41. Oiao ZR, Shi D: Surgical treatment of complicated traumatic aneurysm and arteriovenous fistula. *Chin J Traumatol* 6:213, 2003.
42. Spittel JA Jr: Vasospastic disorders. In Spittel JA Jr (ed): *Clinical Vascular Disease.* Philadelphia, FA Davis, 1983.
43. Sanders RJ, Cooper MA, Hammond, SL, Weinstein ES: Neurogenic thoracic outlet syndrome. In Rutherford RB (ed): *Vascular Surgery,* 5th ed. Philadelphia, WB Saunders, 2000.
44. Roos DB: Congenital anomalies associated with thoracic outlet syndrome. *Am J Surg* 132:771, 1976.
45. Roos DB: New concepts of thoracic outlet syndrome that explain etiology, symptoms, diagnosis and treatment. *Vasc Surg* 13:313, 1979.
46. Lang EK: Arteriography and venography in the assessment of thoracic outlet syndromes. *South Med J* 65:129, 1972.
47. Novak CB: Thoracic outlet syndrome. *Clin Plast Surg* 30:175, 2003.
48. Criado E, et al: Endovascular repair of peripheral aneurysms, pseudoaneurysms, and arteriovenous fistulas. *Ann Vasc Surg* 11:256, 1997.
49. Berenstein A, et al: Percutaneous embolization of arteriovenous fistulas of the external carotid artery. *AJNR Am J Neuroradiol* 7:937, 1986.
50. Ting AC, Chang SW: Femoral pseudoaneurysms in drug addicts. *World J Surg* 21:783, 1997.
51. Geelhoed GW, Joseph WL: Surgical sequelae of drug abuse. *Surg Gynecol Obstet* 139:749, 1974.
52. Trout HH, Smith CA: Lateral iliopopliteal arterial bypass as an alternative to obturator bypass. *Am Surg* 48:63, 1982.
53. Ahmed Z, Mohyuddin Z: Complications associated with different insertion techniques for Hickman catheters. *Postgrad Med J* 74:104, 1998.
54. Whitman ED: Complications associated with the use of central venous access devices. *Curr Prob Surg* 33:324, 1996.
55. Haire WD, Lieberman RP: Thrombosed central venous catheters: Restoring function with 6-hour urokinase after failure of bolus urokinase. *JPEN J Parenter Enteral Nutr* 16:129, 1992.
56. Earnshaw JJ: Fibrinolytic therapy in the treatment of acute limb ischemia. *Br J Surg* 78:261, 1991.
57. Hinke DH, et al: Pinch-off syndrome: A complication of implantable central venous access devices. *Radiology* 177:353, 1990.
58. Torremade JR, et al: The complications of central venous access systems: A study of 218 patients. *Eur J Surg* 159:323, 1993.
59. Fraschini G, et al: Local infusion of urokinase for the lysis of thrombosis associated with permanent central venous catheters in cancer patients. *J Clin Oncol* 5:672, 1987.
60. Anderson MA, Aker SN, Hickman RO: The double-lumen Hickman catheter. *Am J Nurs* 82:272, 1982.
61. Groeger JS, et al: Infectious morbidity associated with long-term use of venous access devices in patients with cancer. *Ann Intern Med* 119:1168, 1993.
62. Kaufman J, et al: Catheter-related septic central venous thrombosis: Current therapeutic options. *West J Med* 145:200, 1986.
63. Schuman ES, Winters V, Gross GF, Hayes JF: Management of Hickman catheter sepsis. *Am J Surg* 149:627, 1985.

64. Moyer MA, Edwards LD, Farley L: Comparative culture methods on 101 intravenous catheters: Routine, semiquantitative, and blood cultures. *Arch Intern Med* 143:66, 1983.
65. Pasquale MD, Canpbell JM, Magnant CM: Groshong versus Hickman catheters. *Surg Gynecol Obstet* 174:178, 1992.
66. Holloway RW, Orr JW: An evaluation of Groshong central venous catheters on a gynecologic oncology service. *Gynecol Oncol* 56:211, 1995.
67. Tan HK, et al: An ex-vivo evaluation of vascular catheters for continuous hemofiltration. *Ren Fail* 24:755, 2002.
68. Konner K: Complications of the vascular access for hemodialysis. *Contrib Nephrol* 142:193, 2004.

CHAPTER 87 Pulmonary Embolism and Deep Venous Thrombosis

Jeffrey A. Kline and Michael S. Runyon

PERSPECTIVE

This chapter discusses the diagnosis and treatment of venous thromboembolism (VTE), including deep venous thrombosis (DVT) and pulmonary embolism (PE), from the perspective of the emergency physician and provides a functional resource to help guide the clinician through the evaluation and treatment of VTE in the emergency department.

Pathophysiology of Thrombosis

Timely diagnosis and treatment of VTE can be facilitated by understanding the pathophysiology of thrombosis. VTE represents the end product of imbalanced clot formation versus clot breakdown. Fibrin represents the primary structural framework of embolized clots, and excessive fibrin deposition represents the primary nidus of VTE. Vertebrates (including humans) normally convert fibrinogen to fibrin in response to vascular injury and inflammation. Vascular injury exposes tissue factor that promotes fibrin formation, and inflammation increases the production of fibrinogen, stimulating fibrin deposition. Factors that enhance fibrin formation include systemic inflammation (which includes almost all so-called acquired states of hypercoagulability, such as antiphospholipid antibody syndromes) and genetic thrombophilias and neoplastic abnormalities that increase fibrin formation or decrease fibrinolysis. In particular, sluggish blood flow in large veins permits the process of fibrin deposition. Rudolf Virchow, a 19th-century pathologist, recognized the triad of venous injury, slow blood flow, and hypercoagulability as the cardinal factors that the clinician should use to classify a patient as at risk for excessive fibrin deposition relative to fibrin removal.[1] Most clinical decision rules for VTE incorporate these factors to help clinicians decide who has VTE and who does not. Notwithstanding its simplicity and elegance, from the perspective of diagnosis, Virchow's triad does not include the crucial issues of age or physiologic effects of VTE.

Epidemiologic studies show convincingly that age increases the likelihood of imbalanced clot formation.[2] Aging leads to venous valvular incompetence, which impairs venous return, and causes blood stasis; aging also increases the probability of an acquired hypercoagulability, such as malignancy. Older patients have more cumulative effects of inflammatory damage to venous endothelium and are more likely to be exposed to the independent risk factor of surgery. Older patients may be predisposed to dehydration, which probably accelerates clot deposition. Older patients are more likely to have heart and lung disease, and when PE is present, older patients are far more likely to manifest the adverse physiologic consequences of PE than younger patients with the same degree of obstructed vasculature.

DEEP VENOUS THROMBOSIS

DVT represents a disease spectrum ranging from a minimally symptomatic isolated calf vein thrombosis to a limb-threatening iliofemoral venous obstruction. Although the true incidence is unknown in the emergency department population, DVT accounts for approximately 600,000 hospital admissions per year.

Anatomy

The venous anatomy of the lower extremity can be divided into the deep and superficial systems. The superficial venous system consists primarily of the greater and short saphenous veins and the perforating veins. The deep venous system includes the anterior tibial, posterior tibial, and peroneal veins, collectively called the *calf veins.* The calf veins join together at the knee to form the popliteal vein, which extends proximally and becomes the femoral vein at the adductor canal. The femoral vein sometimes is called the *superficial femoral vein,* and this nomenclature may contribute to some confusion when interpreting radiology reports. Clinicians must be keenly aware that clot in the superficial femoral vein is indeed a DVT and should be

BOX 87-1. Differential Diagnosis of Deep Venous Thrombosis

Muscle strain/hematoma
Popliteal (Baker's) cyst
Lymphedema
Cellulitis
Vasculitis
Fracture
Superficial thrombophlebitis
Chronic venous insufficiency
Proximal venous compression (e.g., tumor, gravid uterus)
Congestive heart failure (swelling usually bilateral)
Hypoalbuminemia (swelling usually bilateral)

Table 87-1. Clinical Model for Estimating the Pretest Probability of Deep Vein Thrombosis

Clinical Feature	Score*
Active cancer (treated within the previous 6 mo or currently receiving palliative treatment)	1
Paralysis, paresis, or recent plaster immobilization of the lower extremities	1
Recently bedridden for ≥3 days or major surgery within 12 wk requiring general or regional anesthesia	1
Localized tenderness along the distribution of the deep venous system	1
Entire leg swollen	1
Calf swelling at least 3 cm larger than on the asymptomatic side (measured 10 cm below the tibial tuberosity)	1
Pitting edema confined to the symptomatic leg	1
Collateral superficial veins (nonvaricose)	1
Previously documented deep vein thrombosis	1
Alternative diagnosis at least as likely as deep vein thrombosis	–2

*A score of <2 indicates the probability of deep vein thrombosis is low.
Adapted from Wells PS, Anderson D, Bormanis J: Value of assessment of pretest probability of deep-vein thrombosis in clinical management. *Lancet* 350:1795, 1997.

treated as such. The femoral vein joins with the deep femoral vein to form the common femoral vein, which subsequently becomes the external iliac vein at the inguinal ligament. *Proximal DVT* refers to clot in the popliteal vein or higher, whereas *distal clot* refers to an isolated calf vein thrombosis.

Clinical Presentation

The initial symptoms of DVT can be as subtle and non-specific as a mild cramping sensation or sense of full-ness in the calf, without objective swelling, and may be difficult to differentiate clinically from myriad, other unrelated disorders (Box 87-1). It is precisely at this early stage, however, that DVT can be treated most effectively to minimize the potential morbidity and mortality associated with VTE. Likewise, the clinical signs of DVT vary and may include unilateral swelling, edema, erythema, and warmth of the affected extrem-ity; tenderness to palpation along the distribution of the deep venous system; dilation of superficial collateral veins; and a palpable venous "cord." The classic Homan's sign (pain felt in the calf or posterior aspect of the knee on passive dorsiflexion of the foot while the knee is extended) is insensitive and nonspecific for DVT and has no place in modern medicine.

Diagnosis

Estimation of the pretest probability of DVT is the initial step in the diagnostic strategy. This estimation may be accomplished either by the clinical gestalt of an experienced practitioner or in conjunction with a clin-ical decision tool, such as that derived and validated by Wells and colleagues (Table 87-1).[3]

Contrast venography has been considered the gold standard in the evaluation of DVT and has the advan-tage of being able to differentiate between acute and chronic thrombus. However, the invasive nature of the test, risk associated with contrast administration (including the potential for chemical phlebitis and ana-phylaxis), limited availability, and widespread avail-ability of alternative diagnostic tests have effectively restricted its use, Venous duplex ultrasonography has a sensitivity and specificity of approximately 95% for proximal DVT and is the diagnostic test of choice in

most centers.[4] A low-risk patient may have the diagno-sis of DVT effectively excluded by a single negative venous duplex ultrasound. However, a negative ultra-sound in a non–low-risk patient should prompt further evaluation, most commonly by a quantitative D-dimer measurement (with <500 ng/mL considered negative) or a repeat ultrasound in 5 to 7 days. A positive ultra-sound is sufficient to confirm the diagnosis of DVT. Ultrasound cannot image the pelvic veins or vena cava sufficiently.

The D-dimer is a protein derived from enzymatic breakdown of cross-linked fibrin, and an elevated plasma concentration indicates the presence of clot formed somewhere in the body within the past 72 hours. D-Dimer concentration is elevated with any con-dition that causes fibrin deposition, including malig-nancy, pregnancy, advanced age, prolonged bed rest, recent surgery, infection, inflammation, new indwelling catheters, stroke, and myocardial infarction. The magni-tude of the D-dimer concentration varies with the size of the clot and decreases with time, and the test sensitivity is lower with small or chronic clots. D-Dimer analysis may be useful in the evaluation of suspected DVT, but should not be relied on independently of pretest proba-bility. Specifically a negative D-dimer result excludes the diagnosis of DVT only in patients with a low pretest probability of disease.

The diagnostic accuracy of D-dimer measurement varies with the assay technique. The enzyme linked immunosorbent assay (ELISA) and turbidimetric tech-niques are the most quantitatively precise, and a D-dimer level of less than 500 ng/mL measured by either of these techniques may be used to exclude the diag-nosis of DVT in low-risk patients without further eval-uation. The immunofiltration D-dimer tests (Simplify [Agen, Inc, Brisbane, Australia] and IL-Test [Instru-mentation Laboratory, Lexington, Mass]) possess test characteristics similar to the ELISA and offer a significant advantage in that they may be performed rapidly (the Simplify assay may be completed at the bedside in <10 minutes). Latex fixation D-dimer measurements are less accurate and should not be used in the diagnostic evaluation of VTE. In the subset of moderate-risk to high-risk patients with a negative initial ultrasound, a normal D-dimer measurement effectively rules out DVT and obviates the need for serial ultrasonography.[5] Conversely a positive D-dimer in a moderate-risk to high-risk patient with a negative initial ultrasound should prompt a repeat ultrasound in 5 to 7 days.

Magnetic resonance imaging (MRI) can image the pelvic vasculature and vena cava, which is not possible with ultrasound. MRI does not require exposure to ionizing radiation, making it an attractive option for pregnant patients with suspected VTE. The clinical utility of MRI currently is limited by cost and availability.

Impedance plethysmography and strain-gauge plethysmography measure changes in venous outflow from the extremities to diagnose DVT. The reported sensitivities vary, and these tests are not widely used in the United States.

Treatment

When the diagnosis of DVT has been established, anticoagulation should be initiated, unless contraindicated, with weight-based unfractionated heparin (80 U/kg intravenous bolus followed by 18 U/kg/h infusion) or a low-molecular-weight heparin (e.g., enoxaparin, 1 mg/kg subcutaneously every 12 hours). Both forms of heparin work equally well, and both are safe in the absence of contraindications to anticoagulation. Treatment requires anticoagulation with warfarin for at least 3 months. The hospital stay can be shortened by giving the first dose of warfarin in the emergency department to avoid a possible 6- or 8-hour delay, which sometimes occurs in the process of consultation and admission. Evidence suggests that starting with a dose of 10 mg of warfarin sodium in most adults achieves a therapeutic effect faster and without increase in bleeding complications.[6] Selected patients may be considered for outpatient therapy with subcutaneous low-molecular-weight heparin and warfarin. This recommendation warrants caution inasmuch as it requires careful patient selection and education, availability of home health care, and close follow-up for laboratory monitoring and to assess for potential complications. Patients who cannot be anticoagulated and patients who have VTE recurrence despite anticoagulation should be considered for vena caval interruption.

Superficial Thrombophlebitis

Although thrombophlebitis of the superficial leg veins uncommonly evolves into a thromboembolic event, many patients with clinically suspected superficial thrombophlebitis have a synchronous DVT. Patients with clot in the greater saphenous vein that extends above the knee are at risk for progression to DVT via the saphenous-femoral junction and should be considered for anticoagulation. When DVT has been excluded, superficial thrombophlebitis should be treated symptomatically with nonsteroidal anti-inflammatory drugs, heat, and graded compression stockings (fitted to exert 30 to 40 mm Hg of pressure on the extremity). Increased ambulation and elevation of the extremity above the level of the heart while at rest help to decrease venous stasis. Routine anticoagulation is not indicated for superficial thrombophlebitis.

Isolated Calf or Saphenous Vein Thrombosis

The optimal management strategy for thromboses of the saphenous, tibial or peroneal veins remains controversial. Previously, isolated calf vein thrombosis was thought to be a benign self-limiting condition that carried a low risk of embolization and did not warrant anticoagulation. Longitudinal studies subsequently found that approximately 25% of isolated calf vein thromboses propagate proximally, prompting many experts to recommend treatment with anticoagulation as for DVT.[7] Others argue that a reasonable alternative in an otherwise healthy, ambulatory patient with an isolated calf thrombus and no other indication for anticoagulation is to prescribe antiplatelet therapy with aspirin (325 mg/day of enteric-coated acetylsalicylic acid) and arrange for close follow-up with serial duplex ultrasound scans (at 3-7 days) to evaluate for clot propagation.

Phlegmasia Cerulea Dolens (Painful Blue Leg)

Massive iliofemoral occlusion results in swelling of the entire leg with extensive vascular congestion and associated venous ischemia producing a painful, cyanotic extremity. There may be associated arterial spasm resulting in phlegmasia alba dolens (painful white leg or milk leg), which may mimic an acute arterial occlusion. Prompt consultation with a vascular surgeon should be obtained because these patients may require emergent thrombectomy. If timely consultation is not possible, early thrombolytic therapy may be a limb-salvaging procedure.

Upper Extremity Venous Thromboses

DVT of the upper extremity is less common than in the lower extremity and is associated most often with central venous catheters, pacemakers, and malignancies. Upper extremity DVT can cause PE, and all patients with upper extremity DVT require definitive treatment.[8-10] Treatment should be individualized to the particular clinical scenario, and, if present, central venous catheters should be removed from the affected extremity. Anticoagulation usually is indicated, and thrombolysis should be considered to treat apparent phlegmasia cerulea dolens of the arm.

Complications

Although the most feared complication of DVT is fatal PE, DVT also can cause or exacerbate chronic venous insufficiency, resulting in disabling pain and swelling, varicose veins, skin changes, and nonhealing ulcers.

PULMONARY EMBOLISM

Pathophysiology

PE results from a clot that formed hours, days, or weeks earlier in the deep veins that dislodges, travels through the venous system, traverses the right ventricle, and lodges in the pulmonary vasculature. During transit and after docking in the pulmonary vasculature, the embolism produces a highly variable set of sensations felt by the patient, and a wide range of physiologic perturbations observed by the physician. This variability contributes to the difficulty in diagnosing PE. No one knows exactly how many patients pass through the emergency department with PE because there is no reliable way of identifying missed cases. Assuming that emergency department populations have a risk for PE somewhere between hospitalized patients (who are at high risk for PE) and outpatients (who are at lower risk), approximately 1 in every 500 to 1000 emergency department patients has a PE.[2] Depending on the facility, emergency physicians probably correctly identify half of all patients with PE. About 10% of emergency department patients with PE die within 30 days even when PE is promptly diagnosed and treated.[11,12]

Table 87-2 presents a comprehensive listing of factors that significantly increase the probability of PE in a population of emergency department patients. Women drawn from emergency department populations seem to have a slight increase in risk of PE over men, but when the effect of oral hormones is removed, the risk of being female vanishes on statistical testing. Clini-

cians often question why variables that increase the probability of PE in epidemiologic studies are less useful as predictors in emergency department patients with signs and symptoms suggesting PE. Consider the social history variable of "smoking." It is probably true from an epidemiologic standpoint that people who smoke are at a significantly higher risk for venous clots compared with people who do not smoke. In the emergency department, however, the categorical presence of smoking in a given patient does not seem to increase that person's risk for PE compared with a nonsmoker with an otherwise identical clinical presentation. One hypothesis to explain this phenomenon is that smokers are simply more likely to have other lung problems that manifest a clinical presentation similar to PE.

Pathophysiology of Pulmonary Vascular Occlusion

The pulmonary vascular tree normally has a low resistance to fluid flow, and young persons without cardiopulmonary disease (e.g., congestive heart failure, chronic obstructive lung disease, advanced sarcoidosis, pulmonary fibrosis, scleroderma, and primary pulmonary hypertension) can tolerate at least 30% obstruction with trifling symptoms or signs. Pulmonary infarction is a more dramatic exception. Although a segmental pulmonary artery comprises only about one sixteenth of the entire pulmonary vascular circuit, a clot lodged deeply in a segmental artery can obstruct blood flow to a sufficient degree to cause tissue necrosis. The patient can feel focal, sharp, pleuritic pain and exhibit a splinting response to breathing. Over several days, the infarcted segment becomes consolidated on chest radiography and exudes a pleural effusion, manifesting an intense underlying inflammatory process.[13]

Table 87-2. Classic Risk Factors and Physiologic Findings for Pulmonary Embolism

Factor	Mechanisms	Strength of Association with PE in Emergency Department Populations
Inherited thrombophilia	Hypercoagulability	Unknown
Connective tissue disease	Inflammation	Unknown
Acquired thrombophilia	Hypercoagulability	Unknown
Carcinoma (all types, all stages)	Hypercoagulability	+
Limb or generalized immobility	Stasis	++
Prior PE or DVT	Multiple	+
Trauma within past 4 wk requiring hospitalization	Inflammation, venous injury and stasis	+++
Surgery within past 4 wk requiring general anesthesia	Inflammation, venous injury and stasis	++++
Smoking	Inflammation	Minimal
Estrogen	Hypercoagulability	++
Pregnancy/postpartum	Hypercoagulability	Minimal
Symptoms		
Chest pain	Ischemia, muscle strain	Minimal
Dyspnea	V/Q mismatch	+
Hemoptysis	Infarction	+++
Syncope	Vascular obstruction	Minimal
Signs		
Pulse rate >100 beats/min	Cardiac stress, baroreceptors	+++
Pulse oximetry reading <95%	V/Q mismatch	+++
Unilateral leg or arm swelling	Venous obstruction	++++

PE, pulmonary embolism; DVT, deep venous thrombosis; V/Q, ventilation perfusion.

The exact physiology of this process is unknown, but probably results in part from the consequences of chemokine production and hyperinflammation stimulated by normoxic ischemia.[14] Chest pain from noninfarcting PE can be highly variable and vague. About 30% of patients with definite PE deny any perception of chest pain.

In contrast, about 90% of patients with noninfarcting emboli experience dyspnea. The dyspnea may be constant and oppressive or may be intermittent and perceived only with exertion, possibly owing to an exercise-induced increase in pulmonary vascular resistance. The cause of rest dyspnea seems to be the clinical manifestation of distorted and irregular blood flow within the lung, referred to as *ventilation-perfusion inequality*. With each breath, a patient with PE wastes ventilation because of increased alveolar dead space (alveoli that are ventilated but not perfused). Lodged clot can redistribute blood flow to areas of the lung with already high perfusion relative to ventilation and as such cause more blue blood to pass through the lung without being fully oxygenated. This mechanism causes *venous admixture*, which probably represents the primary cause of hypoxemia with PE and the increased alveolar-arterial oxygen difference (the A-a gradient). About 15% of patients with PE have a normal A-a gradient of oxygen (with normal defined as age in years/4 + 4), however, and the A-a gradient is abnormally high in most patients who are evaluated for PE, but ultimately are found to not have PE.[15] In a multicenter registry of 348 patients with PE, 37 (10.6%) had a pulse oximetry reading of 100% at the time of arrival to the emergency department, while breathing room air. Despite its shortcomings as a single diagnostic step, the presence of hypoxemia (pulse oximetry <95%, breathing room air) that cannot be explained by a known disease process definitely increases the probability of PE. Conversely, lack of hypoxemia can be used together with other criteria to justify not pursuing a workup for PE (Box 87-2). Additionally, when PE is diagnosed, the severity of hypoxemia represents a powerful independent predictor of patient outcome.[11]

PE also causes highly variable hemodynamic effects. In the emergency department, about half of all patients with PE have a heart rate greater than 100 beats/ min.[16-18] Tachycardia from PE probably results from impaired left ventricular filling, leading to a pathophysiologic process that parallels that of hemorrhagic shock

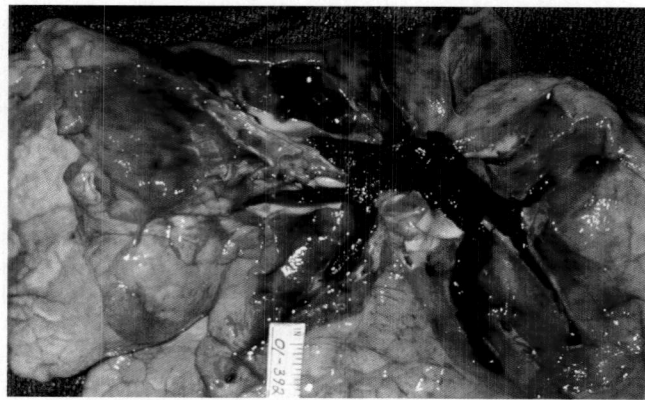

Figure 87-1. Massive pulmonary embolism observed on autopsy. This man died as a result of a large clot burden that plugged the distal lobar arterial branches, eventually producing nearly complete obstruction to blood flow and subsequent cardiac arrest. This man had vague respiratory symptoms for 2 weeks causing him to see a physician who diagnosed bronchitis. The patient was given a prescription for azithromycin.

(see Chapter 4). When PE obstructs more than 50% of the vasculature, it usually causes an acute increase in right ventricular pressure. In contrast to the left ventricle, the right ventricle does not show an elastic response to acutely increased afterload; it quickly dilates and "gives up the fight," showing echocardiographic hypokinesis early in the course. In about 40% of cases, the right ventricular damage persists for at least 6 months and probably longer. Arterial hypotension represents an ominous hemodynamic consequence of PE; it occurs in only about 10% of patients, but signifies a fourfold increase in risk of death compared with normotensive patients.[12] In its most extreme form, PE can obstruct the right ventricular outflow entirely, either by casting the entire pulmonary vascular tree (Figure 87-1) or by acutely occluding the main pulmonary artery. Pulseless electrical activity (PEA) is the most common electrocardiogram (ECG) result from obstructive PE.[19,20] The survival rate from cardiac arrest from PE is abysmally low, even if the arrest is witnessed and heroic treatment measures are initiated.

Diagnosis

Virtually any emergency department visit related to weakness, shortness of breath, dizziness or syncope, pain, extremity discomfort, or nonspecific malaise or functional deterioration could represent PE. A patient with PE typically presents with 2 to 3 days of shortness of breath, now worsened enough to seek care. The chest pain usually is vaguely described. A few patients have focal pleuritic chest pain, but many say nonspecifically that their chest hurts with breathing, usually on the lateral aspects. Purely substernal chest pain is a rare presentation for PE and in general points more toward a cardiac or other origin. Many physicians use the logic that if the symptoms did not start suddenly, this somehow reduces the probability of PE to a level that justifies no further workup. This perception is incorrect because less than half of outpatients with PE

BOX 87-2. Criteria to Support a Decision Not to Initiate a Workup on a Low-Risk Patient

Age <50
Pulse rate <100 beats/min
Oxygen saturation >94%
No hemoptysis
No unilateral leg swelling
No recent major surgery or trauma
No prior pulmonary embolism or deep venous thrombosis
No hormone use

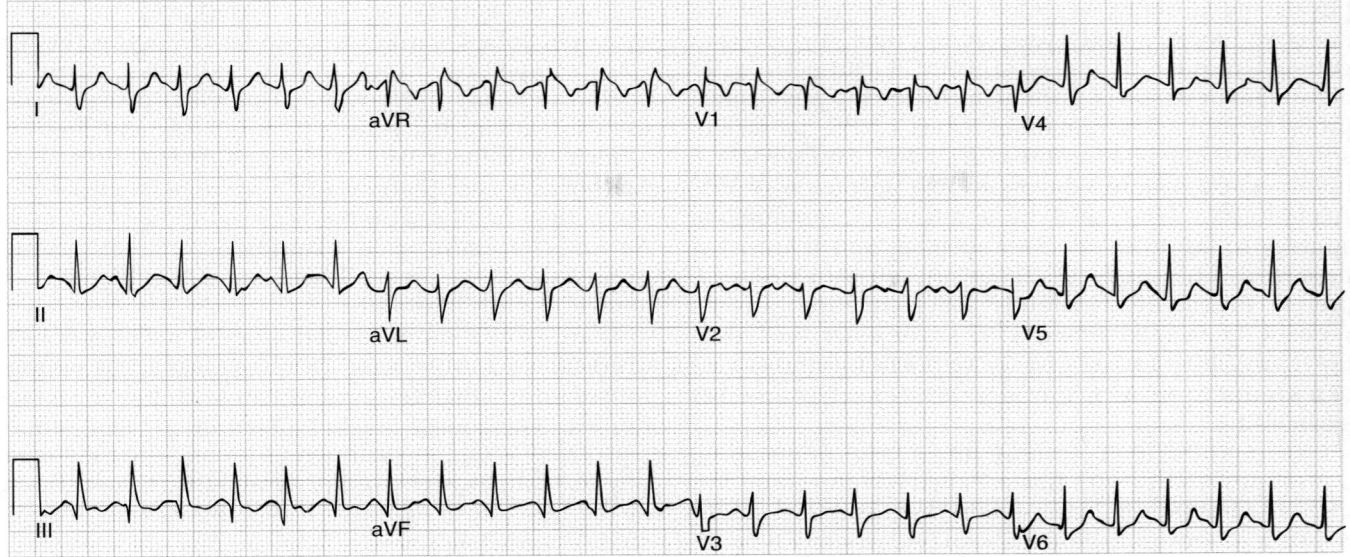

Figure 87-2. Initial electrocardiogram tracing from an 18-year-old woman on oral contraceptives who presented to the emergency department with syncope. Several findings consistent with pulmonary embolism are shown, including tachycardia, the S1Q3T3 pattern, and an incomplete right bundle branch block. Computed tomography angiography revealed extensive bilateral pulmonary emboli, and surface echocardiography documented severe right heart dysfunction.

describe either their dyspnea or chest pain sensation as "sudden onset." When the antemortem histories of patients who die suddenly and unexpectedly from PE are reconstructed by interviewing family and examining medical records, it is discovered that most have complained of nagging symptoms for weeks before collapse; 40% already had seen a physician for care.[20]

PE with lung infarction can present with a clinical picture that is similar to lobar pneumonia, including focal chest pain, fever, and unilateral rales on auscultation. A fever greater than 103° F suggests infection rather than infarction. An occasional clue to pulmonary infarction is the onset of pain and blood-red hemoptysis on the same day, whereas lobar pneumonia usually presents with productive cough for a few days followed by rust-tinged sputum.

The physical examination sometimes can provide specific information about the presence of PE, including the presence of unilateral leg asymmetry, suggesting presence of DVT. Jugular venous distention in a patient with severe dyspnea and clear lung fields on auscultation suggests pure right heart failure. The presence of wheezing suggests bronchospasm, which is not seen commonly in PE and makes the diagnosis less likely (but does not exclude it). Bilateral rales suggest the diagnosis of left ventricular failure, although localized rales often are heard over infarcted lung tissue. Acoustically gifted clinicians may hear an accentuated pulmonic component of the second heart sound, or a right ventricular S_3 sound.

Chest radiography seldom provides specific information, but it is useful to suggest alternative diagnoses, such as pneumonia, congestive heart failure, or pneumothorax. Unilateral basilar atelectasis increases the probability of PE.[18] If symptoms have been present for 3 days or more, pulmonary infarction sometimes shows

an apex-central, pleural-based, wedge-shaped area of infiltrate, incarnating the elusive "Hampton's hump." Unilateral lung oligemia (Westermark's sign) is a rare radiographic manifestation of a large PE.

Likewise, a 12-lead ECG provides more information about the presence of alternative diagnoses, such as pericarditis or cardiac ischemia, than the presence of PE. When PE causes ECG changes, this is usually a result of acute or subacute pulmonary hypertension. The most common effects of pulmonary hypertension on ECG are rapid heart rate, symmetrical T-wave inversion in the anterior leads (V1-V4), the McGinn-White S1Q3T3 pattern, and incomplete or complete right bundle branch block (Figure 87-2).[21]

After processing the data obtained from the history and physical examination (with or without ECG and chest x-ray data), emergency physicians often are driven to evaluate for PE based on unexplained symptoms or signs. Symptoms include dyspnea or atypical chest pain, syncope, or seizure; signs include tachycardia, tachypnea, or hypoxemia. In the emergency department, unexplained symptoms and signs are as important as predictors of the presence of PE as the triad described by Virchow. In a multicenter registry of prospectively studied emergency department patients with PE, 40% had no identifiable classic risk factor for thrombosis. The decision to pursue the diagnosis of PE seems to be a complex process that is based on the patient's particular presentation and that appropriately does not rely on the presence or absence of population risk factors.

In some cases, PE can be excluded with reasonable certainty based on data that are available at the bedside, gathered only by the medical history and physical examination. Multicenter studies of urban academic emergency departments have suggested that emergency physicians currently evaluate about 1% to 2% of all patients for PE. Each year, more than 16 million patients present to the emergency department with chest pain or dyspnea. Although emergency physicians probably still miss numerous cases of PE, there are simply not sufficient resources available to image definitively every patient who raises any suspicion of PE. Accordingly, there must be a rational, reproducible strategy to guide the decision-making and diagnostic processes. This strategy should rely on estimation of pretest probability. Methods for estimating pretest probability can be referred to as *implicit* (meaning the clinician's best guess) or *explicit* (meaning use of a scoring system or flow algorithm to categorize the probability).[22]

One approach to the workup for PE is to compare the pretest probability with the so-called test threshold for PE.[23] The test threshold represents the theoretical cutoff point in pretest probability, above which some type of workup should be initiated and below which the clinician can justify not starting the workup. For PE, the test threshold is approximately 2%.[24] Patients with a pretest probability less than 2% are more likely to be harmed than benefited by a workup and vice versa for patients with a pretest probability greater than 2%. The question becomes how to quantify the pretest probability in an accurate way. One method is to use the unstructured approach, in which the clinician draws from his or her own experience and surmises the probability of PE to be less than 2%. This method is easy to use and allows the inherent flexibility of human thought. This approach is subject, however, to the conditions in the emergency department at the time (e.g., is one less likely to pursue a relatively low-likelihood diagnosis when the department is very busy), conditions of the clinician (e.g., fatigue, dysphoria, subjective feelings about the patient), and the availability of diagnostic studies (e.g., daytime versus nighttime, weekday versus weekend). In addition, there is the variability between clinicians. Two practitioners may not agree that a 19-year-old with cough and pleuritic chest pain, a normal chest radiograph, and no other risk factors has less than a 2% probability of PE. Decision rules help to deal with these problems because they are structured and more transparent. In a validation study, patients with a Canadian score less than 2 had a 1.3% probability of PE,[25] but this finding had not been repeated as of 2004. To help reduce the probability of PE to a level below the test threshold, the PE rule-out criteria (or PERC rule) were derived and tested in two validation populations (see Box 87-2).[24]

The PERC rule suggests a rationale to avoid unnecessary testing in a low-risk patient with a sign or symptom partially suggestive of PE. This rule should not be used, however, to supplant clinical judgment or in cases in which the patient is deemed by the treating clinician to be at moderate or high risk for PE. If validated in larger studies, these criteria potentially could be used in patients with chest pain or shortness of breath to avoid further evaluation for PE. Patients without any symptoms or signs of PE (e.g., no chest pain, no shortness of breath, no dyspnea on exertion,

normal or normalized vital signs, and no recent syncope) do not warrant workup for PE, unless there is some compelling clinical indication to the contrary.

PE also is less likely when some other disease process can explain the patient's complaints and findings —such as asthma causing bronchospasm proven by findings on auscultation and a spirometric test—and the patient is otherwise not believed to be at high risk for PE. The finding that a confirmed alternative diagnosis reduces the probability of coincident PE has been shown in multiple settings.

There is now an expanded array of diagnostic tests available to evaluate for PE. The diagnostic options include a qualitative or quantitative D-dimer, venous duplex sonography of the extremities, ventilation-perfusion (V/Q) lung scintigraphy, computed tomography (CT) angiography of the chest and CT venography of the legs (these two may be combined into a single study), formal pulmonary angiography, and magnetic resonance angiography and venography. Because of variation in availability of clinical testing and differences in patient populations, it is not possible to construct a single algorithm for the evaluation of PE that covers all possibilities. The flow algorithms provided here are predicated on the following goals: (1) to identify as many emergency department patients as possible who have PE; (2) to avoid mislabeling (and anticoagulating) patients who do not have PE; and (3) to use available resources efficiently and effectively (Figure 87-3).

First, the workup for PE always starts with the physician estimate of pretest probability. For a patient with a relatively concerning clinical picture (e.g., implicit suspicion or explicit score suggesting a pretest probability >40%), it makes little sense to start with a screening strategy such as the D-dimer. In these cases, the D-dimer is likely to be positive, and even if it is negative, there is insufficient evidence to support using it to exclude the diagnosis in patients with other than a low pretest probability of PE. Because the half-life of circulating D-dimer is less than 8 hours, some experts worry that the sensitivity of the D-dimer decreases if the patient's symptoms have been present for longer than 3 days. The type of D-dimer test influences the test sensitivity. Qualitative tests, such as the whole-blood agglutination assays (SimpliRED) or the immunofiltration assays (IL test, Simplify) and latex fixation tests, have sensitivities of 80% to 90% and specificities of 60% to 65% in ED populations. Meta-analyses have shown that quantitative tests, either ELISA or immunoturbidimetric tests using a cutoff of 500 FEU/mL (an *FEU* is a fibrinogen equivalent unit, usually reported by hospital laboratories as a mass value of 500 ng/mL or 0.50 µg/mL), have sensitivities of about 94% and specificities of about 55%. Although high D-dimer concentrations (e.g., >2500 ng/mL) more strongly suggest the presence of PE, as opposed to a nonspecific cause, no cutoff of D-dimer concentration can be used to confirm the diagnosis.

The posttest probability where the clinician can exclude the diagnosis of PE safely using a D-dimer as the only test must be approximately 1%, which is reasonably equivalent to imaging.[22] This combination can

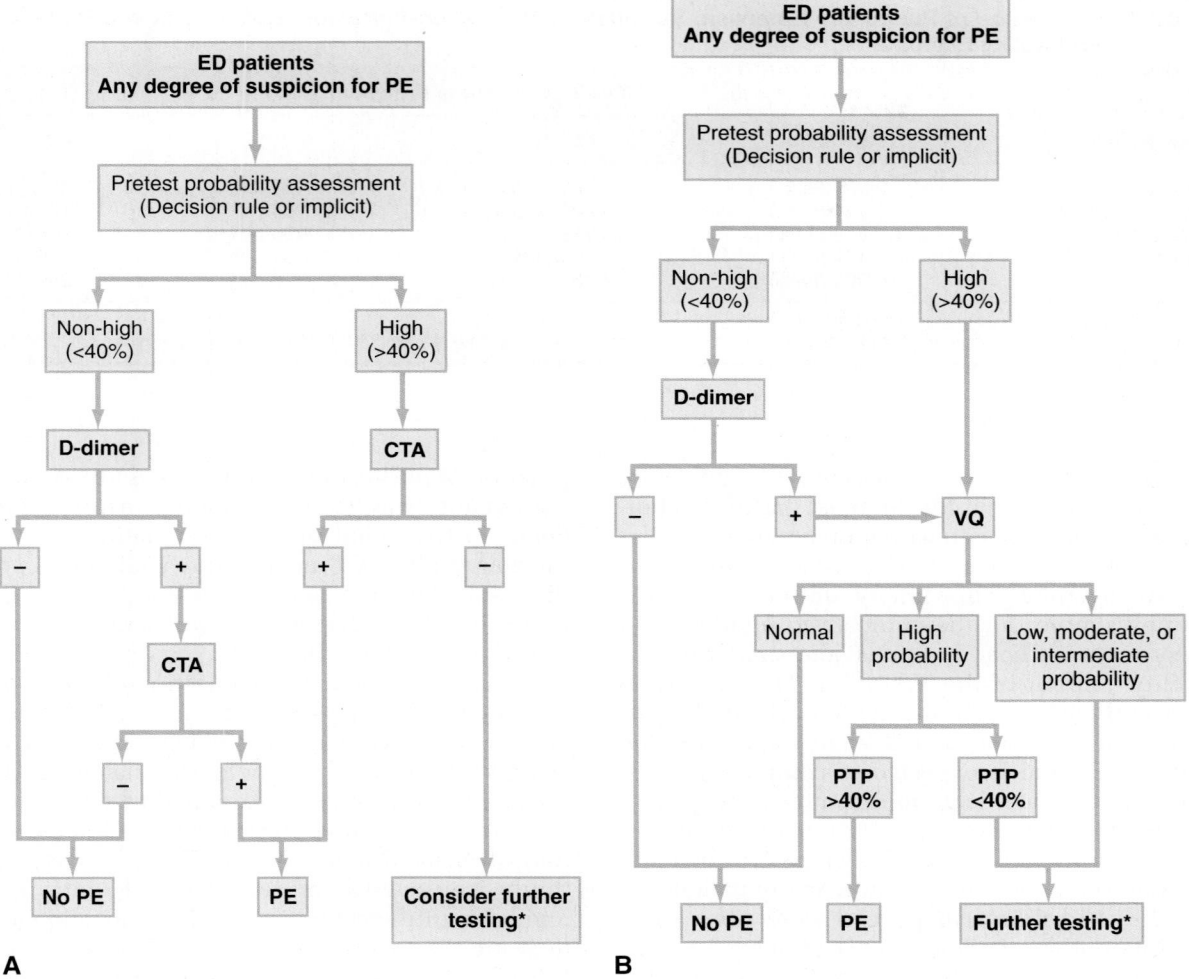

Figure 87-3. A and **B,** Suggested algorithms to evaluate for pulmonary embolism (PE) in the emergency department (ED). These algorithms include the use pretest probability (PTP), the quantitative D-dimer assay, and pulmonary vascular imaging (computed tomography angiography [CTA]). **A,** Algorithm incorporating contrast-enhanced CTA. A negative D-dimer is an immunoturbidimetric assay or enzyme-linked immunosorbent assay that returns a concentration less than 500 FEU (ng)/mL. **B,** Algorithm incorporating ventilation-perfusion (V/Q) scanning. *May require patient admission. Additional testing: *option 1:* "crossover" to perform either V/Q scanning or CT for algorithms **A** and **B**; *option 2:* perform lower extremity venous ultrasound, and if initial venous ultrasound is negative, repeat the lower extremity venous ultrasound in 1 week; *option 3:* perform formal pulmonary angiography.

be achieved by several routes that include the combination of pretest probability assessment and either qualitative or quantitative D-dimer testing. By this rationale, it is safe to assume that an ELISA D-dimer concentration less than 500 ng/mL excludes the presence of PE, if the pretest probability is less than 40%. When the pretest probability is relatively high, or the screening D-dimer is positive, pulmonary vascular imaging, by either V/Q scanning or CT angiography, is advised. Although neither V/Q scanning nor CT angiography is perfect, both can be combined with pretest probability to diagnose and exclude the presence of PE.

The relative accuracy and precision of the V/Q scan were shown in the Prospective Investigation of Pulmonary Embolism Diagnosis (PIOPED) study, which compared the results of V/Q scanning with the most accurate criterion standard test possible—formal pulmonary angiography (Table 87-3).[26] This multicenter study showed that a high-probability V/Q scan can be used to diagnose PE, and a normal V/Q scan excludes

the diagnosis of PE with a degree of certainty that is acceptable to the medical community. A moderate probability or indeterminate scan requires additional testing, either formal pulmonary angiography or a CT angiography. Except in patients with a low pretest probability, a low-probability V/Q scan requires additional testing. Suggestions include either CT angiography or venous duplex ultrasonography of the legs. The latter should be repeated at least once, 5 to 7 days later, if negative at the initial presentation. In patients with a chest radiograph that shows airspace disease, the specificity of V/Q scanning can be expected to decrease, and the relative diagnostic utility of CT angiography can be expected to increase.

Most academic centers now employ CT angiography as the primary method of evaluating for PE.[27] Images can be obtained in a few seconds, so that the time required for the test primarily depends on scanner availability, transport time, transferring the patient to and from the CT table, and radiologist interpretation

Table 87-3. Prevalence of Pulmonary Embolism Stratified by Ventilation-Perfusion Scan Result and Pretest Probability Estimate

V/Q Scan Result	Clinician Estimate of Pretest Probability for PE			
	80-100%	*20-79%*	*0-19%*	*All*
High probability	28/29 (96%)	70/80 (88%)	5/9 (56%)	103/118 (87%)
Intermediate probability	27/41 (66%)	66/236 (28%)	11/68 (16%)	104/345 (30%)
Low probability	6/15 (40%)	30/191 (16%)	4/90 (4%)	40/296 (14%)
Near-normal/normal	0/5 (0%)	4/62 (6%)	1/61 (2%)	5/128 (4%)
Total	61/90 (68%)	170/569 (30%)	21/228 (9%)	252/887 (28%)

V/Q, ventilation-perfusion; PE, pulmonary embolism.
Adapted from The PIOPED Investigators: Value of the ventilation/perfusion scan in acute pulmonary embolism. *JAMA* 263:2753, 1990.

time. One of the greatest advantages of CT angiography over V/Q scanning is that for the most part the radiologist indicates the test is positive or negative, similar to the results of conventional catheter-based pulmonary angiography. This binary output makes CT angiography simpler for the clinician to interpret and to integrate into medical decisions compared with the "probability" output of the V/Q scan. The PIOPED II study currently is being conducted to evaluate the performance characteristics of CT angiography for the evaluation of PE and is expected to complete recruitment in 2004. To date, large multicenter management studies have found a lower than 1% rate of subsequent anticoagulation in patients with negative CT angiography, but questions remain as to how many patients in these studies had untreated PE and were never diagnosed.[28] The authors believe that a growing concern exists about the false-positive rate of CT angiography. At present, the best evidence available suggests that CT angiography has *about* a 90% sensitivity and a 90% specificity.[29,30]

When the results of CT angiography seem questionable in view of clinical suspicion, it is often worth the time to investigate issues of image acquisition quality that can affect the certainty of the radiologist's call on the presence or absence of PE. Good contrast enhancement of the pulmonary vasculature probably is the most important factor determining the diagnostic quality of CT angiography. Poor heart function complicates the timing of vascular opacification, but using bolus-timing software that is readily available on almost all CT scanners today essentially should eliminate this factor. Obesity also can compromise image quality and must be considered when determining the appropriate scanning parameters for each patient (i.e., mAs, kVp). Motion artifact can severely degrade the quality of the images, as can severe intrinsic lung disease, such as stage 4 sarcoidosis or bulky carcinoma that can distort the vasculature and give false-positive appearances.[31] Technical aspects that seem associated with better accuracy of the interpretation include specialty training of the reader, review of images in cine mode on a picture archival and communication system (PACS), a greater number of detectors on the scanner, and thinner collimation of the x-ray beam. There is no quantitative method to fold these findings into the com-

putation of posttest probability except to say that if the scan quality was good, this should inspire more confidence in the radiologist's interpretation. As with any imaging study, if CT angiography quality was poor, and the results do not match the clinical picture, PE cannot be excluded or diagnosed with certainty, and more testing should be performed.

Clinicians often raise the question of the importance of isolated subsegmental pulmonary embolus either missed or detected by CT angiography. This concern can arise because of a radiologist's statement that subsegmental clot cannot be excluded by CT angiography, or more recently, as a consequence of increased detection of isolated subsegmental filling defects on more thinly collimated images acquired with a higher number multidetector scanner. No firm evidence exists to guide the treating clinician in these circumstances. When two radiologists independently evaluate CT angiography, their agreement on the presence of isolated subsegmental filling defects is poor.[32,33] The same lack of agreement in subsegmental clots holds for formal pulmonary angiography.[34] It is important that this lack of agreement refers to scans without other larger defects seen by either radiologist. Our opinion is that if the patient has no evidence of DVT, no signs of cardiopulmonary stress, and no ongoing major risk for thrombosis, isolated subsegmental findings or no findings together comprise a nonissue, and for either case, withholding anticoagulation would afford more benefit than harm. If a patient with negative CT angiography has signs of pulmonary hypertension or hypoxemia or has a known thrombophilia, further testing is advised. These patients are at a high risk for PE, and as such, we recommend a V/Q scan be performed. Unless the V/Q scan yields a normal or high-probability result, a formal pulmonary angiogram is advised. In reality, radiologists often are reluctant to perform these tests after good-quality, negative CT angiography study. Another option is to perform duplex ultrasound of the extremities, which can clinch the diagnosis if positive. A negative sonogram does not exclude the diagnosis, however, and should be repeated in 5 to 7 days.

CT angiography can provide additional information to enhance its utility in the emergency department. First, without requiring any additional contrast injection, the legs can be scanned a few seconds later to

BOX 87-3. Frequency of Potentially Important Non–Pulmonary Embolism Diagnoses Disclosed on Computed Tomography

Pneumonia (6%)*
Unsuspected pericardial effusion (1%)
Mass suggesting new carcinoma (1%)
Aortic dissection (0.5%)
Pneumothorax (0.5%)

*Percentage of all 1025 emergency department patients who underwent computed tomography to evaluate for pulmonary embolism.

provide a CT venogram, which can evaluate for DVT.[35] Indirect CT venography has been shown to be equally accurate as venous ultrasound, and when two radiologists interpret CT venography independently, the rate of agreement is good.[36] CT pulmonary angiography often provides information about alternative processes that might explain the patient's symptoms (Box 87-3). Pneumonia is the most common alternative diagnosis found in emergency department patients.[37] It can be hypothesized that in about 10% of emergency department patients evaluated for PE, the CT scan as a single test could (1) show absence of PE; (2) provide evidence of alternative disease, which can be used with other evidence to reduce the probability of PE to a reasonably low level to stop the workup; and (3) facilitate treatment for the alternative disease.

Management

Anticoagulation

A high-probability V/Q scan, positive CT angiography, or ultrasound evidence of DVT in a patient with a symptom or sign suggesting PE confirms the diagnosis and mandates initiation of therapy. Either unfractionated heparin (80 U/kg intravenous bolus, followed by 18 U/kg/hr intravenous infusion) or fractionated heparin (e.g., enoxaparin, 1 mg/kg subcutaneously or intravenously every 12 hours) represents current standard treatment for most patients with PE. At present, no published evidence has proved the superiority of either form of heparin over the other. Both forms of heparin work equally well, and both are safe in the absence of contraindications to anticoagulation. Heparin provides several known benefits, including the reduction in formation of new clot (which can occur rapidly as clot volume increases exponentially with existing clot mass), and reduces the theoretical transient hypercoagulable effect of warfarin treatment, thought to be mediated by relative decrease in circulating protein C activity. Heparin also possesses antichemokine and antimitogenic properties that may help prevent inflammatory-mediated damage in the lung vasculature. As with DVT, administration of the first 10-mg dose of warfarin in the emergency department can help shorten the hospital stay.

Physicians often question when to administer heparin based on pretest probability, before the results of imaging are known. Published evidence has not addressed this question directly. This choice would seem to confer more benefit than harm when the implicit or explicit pretest probability of PE exceeds 40%, the patient has no major contraindication to anticoagulation, and imaging would delay heparin initiation for greater than 2 hours. The intransitive logic used to support the 2-hour statement derives from the fact that about one third of all normotensive patients who die from PE during hospitalization die within 24 hours of diagnosis.

For a patient diagnosed with PE in presence of a major contraindication to anticoagulation, such as a recent cerebral hemorrhage or a 7-day old large cerebral infarction, the appropriate consultant should be contacted for urgent placement of an inferior vena caval filter. If vena caval interruption cannot be performed within 12 hours, one option is to perform a baseline head CT scan, then start an unfractionated heparin infusion at 18 U/kg/hr (without a bolus), admit the patient to the intensive care unit for neurologic checks every 15 minutes, and monitor the partial thromboplastin time every 4 hours. The rationale for unfractionated heparin is that it can be reversed more reliably (by discontinuing the heparin drip and administering protamine, 1 mg/kg intravenously) than fractionated heparin.

Most patients with PE look and feel better the day after starting heparin anticoagulation, and more than half go on to a nearly full recovery of pre-PE health status. The in-hospital mortality of patients diagnosed with PE who remain hemodynamically stable while in the emergency department is about 10%. Another 10% to 20% complain of persistent dyspnea and exercise intolerance that permanently degrades their quality of life. Systolic hypotension (<90 mm Hg) represents a highly specific and moderately sensitive indicator of severe PE. In particular, persistent hypotension from PE increases the mortality rate dramatically.[12] In the absence of hypotension, several parameters available at the bedside can help with prognosis. A heart rate that is persistently above the systolic blood pressure indicates more severe clot, as does a pulse oximetry reading less than 95%.[11] Presence of prior congestive heart failure or advanced chronic obstructive pulmonary disease serves to magnify the severity of PE. Laboratory studies that portend a worse outcome include an elevated serum troponin measurement or an elevated brain natriuretic peptide or pro-brain natriuretic peptide concentration.[38-42] Echocardiography that shows right ventricular hypokinesis or dilation also increases the probability of death from PE. Table 87-4 summarizes the diagnostic accuracy of these predictors for the outcome of in-hospital death, shock, or respiratory failure.

Thrombolytic Therapy

Thrombolytic therapy in suspected or proven PE is controversial. Administration of alteplase to patients with PE results in more rapid symptomatic improvement than standard antithrombotic therapy alone[43] and

Table 87-4. Predictors of Short-Term Complications from Pulmonary Embolism

Predictor	Criteria	Sensitivity (%)*	Specificity (%)
Troponin I	>0.4 ng/mL or T >0.04 ng/mL	60	85
Pulse oximetry	<95%, breathing room air	90	64
Brain natriuretic peptide	>90 pg/mL	85	75
Echocardiography	RV dilation or hypokinesis	86	39

*Sensitivity and specificity for the predication of circulatory shock requiring vasopressor treatment, need for intubation, or death during hospitalization. RV, right ventricular.

Table 87-5. Food and Drug Administration–Approved Fibrinolytic Regimens for Acute Treatment of Pulmonary Embolism

Streptokinase	1 million U infused over 24 hr
Urokinase	1 million U bolus followed by 24-hr infusion at 300,000 U/hr
Alteplase	15-mg bolus followed by 2-hr infusion of 85 mg. Discontinue heparin during infusion

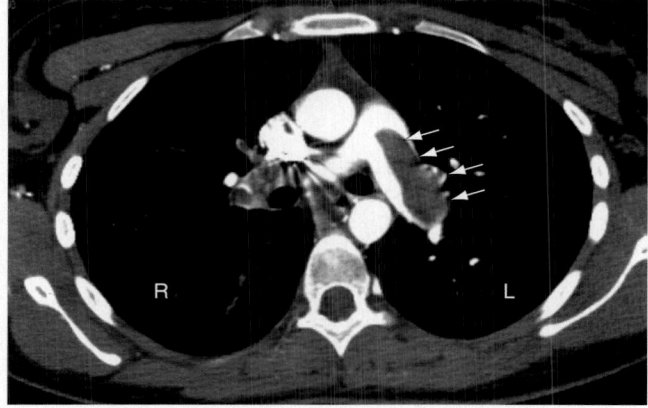

Figure 87-4. Massive pulmonary embolism observed on a contrast-enhanced computed tomography (CT) scan of the chest. This CT scan was obtained at the level of the bifurcation of the main pulmonary artery. The left main branch of the pulmonary artery shows a massive filling defect *(arrows)*. The patient was a young woman who recently began taking oral contraceptive pills who presented to the emergency department after passing out at work after a 1-week duration of dyspnea. The clinicians had a high suspicion for pulmonary embolism and ordered a CT scan immediately. The patient showed orthodeoxia and reverse orthostasis of blood pressure (hypoxemia and worsened hemodynamic findings when supine). She was treated with anticoagulation and emergent surgical embolectomy and survived with excellent outcome. Her DNA was examined by polymerase chain reaction testing, and both alleles were found to have the factor V Leiden mutation.

causes more rapid normalization of right ventricular function.[44] Alteplase administration also increases the risk of hemorrhage, however. It is not known how many patient lives would be saved—or definitively improved—by the addition of thrombolytic treatment to heparin therapy versus the number of patients who would experience a fatal or life-threatening bleeding event as a result of thrombolytic treatment.[45] On balance, the benefit/risk analysis argues that fibrinolysis is of greatest value in the subset of patients with PE who are likely to die, develop circulatory shock, or progress to respiratory failure in the first week. The criteria in Table 87-4 facilitate the identification of these high-risk patients. In the absence of a contraindication to thrombolytic therapy (see Chapter 94), a patient with even one documented episode of systolic hypotension, persistent hypoxemia, an elevated troponin, or an elevated plasma concentration of brain natriuretic peptide likely would benefit from thrombolytic therapy. If possible, consultation with cardiology or cardiac surgery should be obtained before administering fibrinolytic therapy for patients with PE who are not in extremis. The Food and Drug Administration–approved regimens for thrombolysis are shown in Table 87-5.

The clinical course of patients with obstructive PE can be unpredictable. Many patients with massive PE remain stable in the emergency department. Other patients "look fine" on arrival, but progressively deteriorate over hours as right ventricular function declines. Three percent of emergency department patients have no hypotension while in the emergency

department, but experience cardiac arrest and die within 24 hours.[11] A patient can be stable and then hypotensive within minutes because of the effect of variable right ventricular outflow obstruction from a large clot perched in the main pulmonary artery. The massive filling defect illustrated in Figure 87-4 represents a huge PE in a 19-year-old woman from our emergency department who would develop severe hypotension with cyanosis when supine, but was normotensive without severe distress when sitting upright. Additional mechanisms of rapid instability include new embolization of clot material, release of mediators of pulmonary vasospasm, sudden brady-asystolic arrhythmias, or respiratory failure. Clues to oncoming cardiopulmonary decompensation include worsening respiratory distress and worsening hypoxemia, a rising shock index (the heart rate divided by the systolic blood pressure), systolic arterial blood pressure less than 90 mm Hg, and syncope or a seizure-like convulsive episode while in the emergency department. A particularly ominous finding is the evolution on ECG from a narrow-complex tachycardia to an incomplete right bundle branch block to a complete right bundle branch block (Figure 87-5). This progression (or regression) is evidence of life-threatening pulmonary hypertension and incipient cardiac arrest.[21]

Increasing arterial partial pressure of carbon dioxide with a decreasing pulse oximetry defines respiratory failure and predicts a clinical course heading toward respiratory arrest. Respiratory failure mandates endotracheal tube intubation using standard rapid sequence intubation with either ketamine or etomidate used for induction of anesthesia before neuromuscular blockade

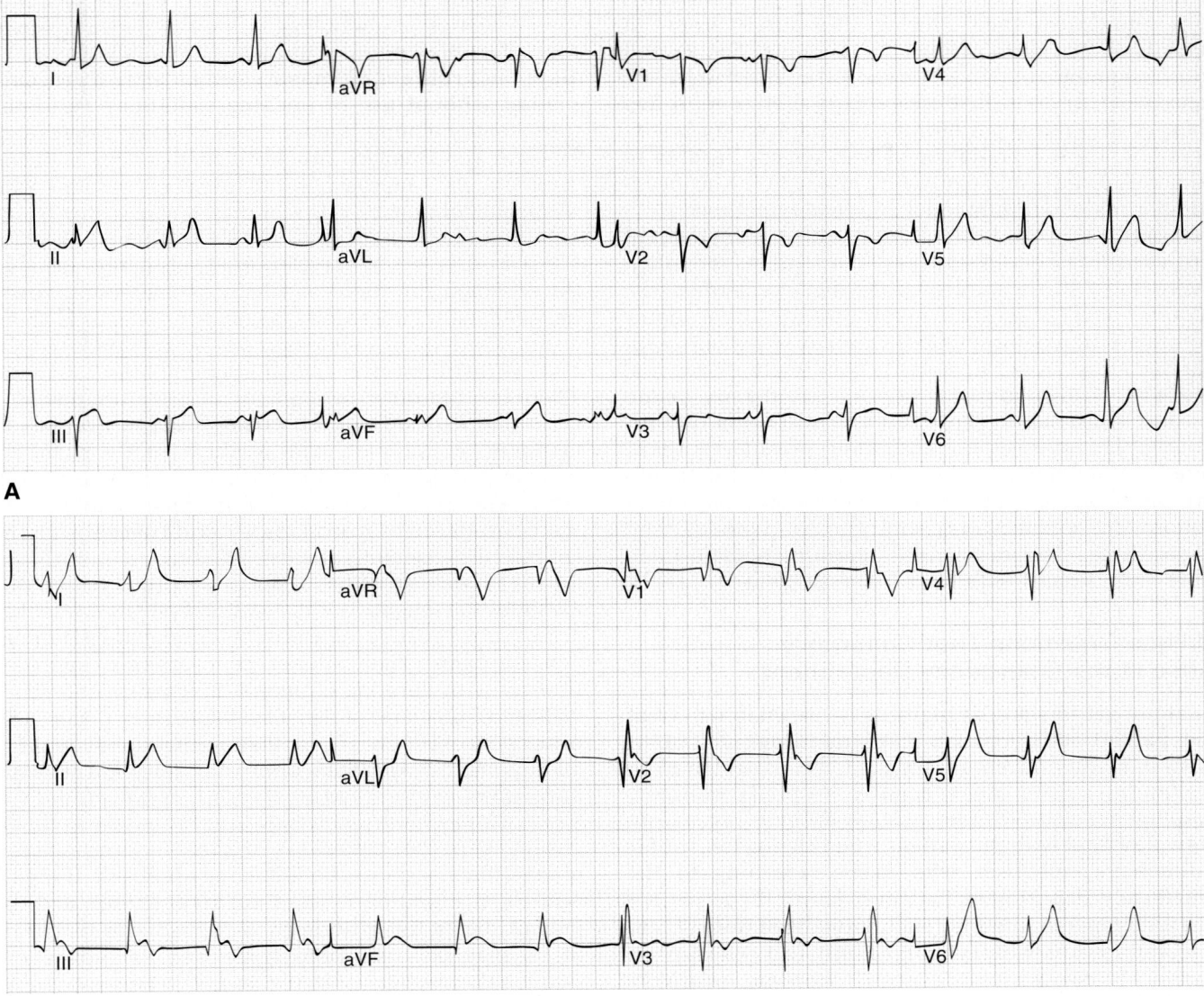

Figure 87-5. A and **B,** Serial electrocardiograms obtained 2 minutes apart show the progression from a narrow complex rhythm **(A)** to a right bundle branch block pattern **(B)** in a patient with massive bilateral pulmonary emboli. Shortly after the second tracing was obtained, the patient developed cardiovascular collapse refractory to vigorous resuscitation efforts.

(see Chapter 1). Other induction agents that depress cardiac function or reduce preload may precipitate severe hypotension and should be avoided. In the case of impending respiratory or cardiac arrest, fibrinolytic therapy should be strongly considered. For patients with known floating thrombi in the right heart or for patients with severe refractory hypotension, surgery is the most likely intervention to save the patient's life. Surgical embolectomy requires extracorporeal cardiopulmonary bypass and an experienced cardiothoracic surgeon. Surgery may be the best option for patients who have severe PE with a contraindication to fibrinolysis; however, extracorporeal perfusion requires intensive heparin anticoagulation, and the patient's mental status cannot be monitored during surgery—a key concern in patients with high risk of intracranial hemorrhage. Catheter thrombectomy also may be life-

saving and can be performed in an awake patient, but requires that the patient be sent to the relatively uncontrolled environment of the interventional radiology suite.

In the worst case, PE can cause cardiac arrest. In the prehospital setting, the arrest often initially appears to occur suddenly and unexpectedly. Most patients with incipiently fatal PE have overt respiratory distress, syncope or seizure, or a high heart rate relative to the systolic blood pressure before arrest. Compared with pure cardiac causes of arrest, a higher percentage of patients with arrest from PE have the initial arrest event witnessed, in particular by health care providers. First responders most commonly observe PEA as the initial cardiac arrest rhythm (>20 depolarizations per minute without palpable pulses). The mechanism for PEA seems to be pure right ventricular outflow obstruction complicated by impaired right ventricular contractility. Ultrasound performed during PEA arrest from PE usually shows weak cardiac contractions. The second most common rhythm observed after arrest from PE is asystole, or an agonal escape type rhythm with less than 20 complexes per minute. Mechanisms for brady-asystolic arrest include septal wall tension leading to ischemia or ischemic-equivalent effect on the atrioventricular node and infranodal conducting pathways.

Regardless of the initial rhythm, the development of pulselessness from PE imparts a horrendous mortality, exceeding 70% in published studies. Numerous case reports have suggested heroic results from bolus administration of thrombolytic therapy to patients with cardiac arrest from PE. Notwithstanding these reports, the goal is to administer fibrinolytic therapy before cardiac arrest supervenes. The administration of fibrinolytic therapy does not absolutely preclude surgical intervention. Patients who have been treated with a fibrinolytic agent can undergo sternotomy or thoracotomy for embolectomy and survive without fatal hemorrhage. The decision to perform embolectomy ultimately resides with the cardiac surgeon.

Unique Questions That Commonly Arise in the Emergency Department

I cannot get imaging at night. Is it reasonable to treat the patient with heparin until morning? The short answer to this question is yes, if the patient has no contraindications. Many smaller hospitals routinely employ this method, using a single dose of enoxaparin.

How do I deal with the patient who is being treated for pulmonary embolism who keeps returning to the emergency department for chest pain? If the patient has a therapeutic international normalized ratio (1.5 to 2.5) and returns with symptoms only (e.g., chest pain, dyspnea) and without syncope, appears relatively comfortable, has normal vital signs, and has no new changes suggesting pulmonary hypertension on ECG (in particular, no S1Q3T3 pattern and no T wave inversion in leads V1 through V4), follow-up imaging is probably not needed. Other causes of chest pain (especially acute coronary syndrome) must be considered (see Chapters 19 and 77). In the absence of an identified alternative diagnosis, symptomatic care with an anti-inflammatory agent is safe and reasonable therapy for the return complaint of chest pain. Persistent dyspnea at rest raises more concerns of unresolved or recurrent thrombosis with secondary effects, including bronchospasm or, worse, pulmonary vascular hyperplasia with pulmonary hypertension. Repeat pulmonary vascular imaging may provide evidence of unresolved or new clot. More importantly, a transthoracic echocardiogram can disclose evidence of persistent right ventricular dysfunction and pulmonary hypertension. Symptomatic patients with unresolved filling defects and pulmonary hypertension can progress to chronic thromboembolic pulmonary hypertension. To prevent this decline, patients who return to the emergency department with persistent rest dyspnea and have unresolved filling defects and pulmonary

hypertension should be admitted or referred to a pulmonologist or pulmonology clinic that has a program that offers the option of pulmonary thrombectomy.

How can I rule out pulmonary embolism in a pregnant patient without use of ionizing radiation? PE is the most common nontraumatic cause of death in pregnant women, so clinicians are justified to adopt a liberal "rule-out PE" approach to all pregnant women with dyspnea. Pulmonary V/Q scanning is safe in pregnancy and provides almost no risk to the fetus. A chest CT scan delivers about 250 mrad of energy, whereas the common threshold at which fetomaternal experts believe fetal teratogenicity becomes a concern is about 5 rad. The mother's abdomen can be shielded, but the fetus will still receive a small fraction of the 250 mrad. There is a rapidly growing body of literature that suggests that exposure of the young brain to even small amounts of radiation can produce subtle cognitive deficits later in life, and at present the long-term consequences of CT scanning of pregnant patients are unknown. It seems logical to try to rule out PE with the D-dimer in pregnant patients; if D-dimer is negative in a patient believed to be at low pretest probability, this excludes the diagnosis. Coagulation systems are hyperactive in pregnancy, elevating the circulating D-dimer concentration. The D-dimer concentration increases linearly with duration of normal pregnancy, and about 75% of all pregnant patients evaluated for PE have a D-dimer concentration greater than the abnormal cutoff of 500 ng/mL.[46] About 60% of healthy pregnant patients have a D-dimer less than 1000 ng/mL, however, and virtually all pregnant patients with a PE have a D-dimer greater than 1000 ng/mL. A reasonable interpretation of these data suggests the following approach. If the D-dimer concentration is less than 1000 ng/mL, and the patient meets the criteria in Box 87-2, the diagnosis of PE may be considered reasonably excluded, and pulmonary vascular imaging is not necessary. As an additional margin of safety, a negative venous ultrasound of the lower extremities excludes DVT and helps reduce the probability of PE by about half. V/Q scanning, if normal, excludes the diagnosis. A high-probability V/Q scan establishes the diagnosis, and heparin (which does not cross the placental barrier) can be initiated. If neither normal nor high probability, the V/Q scan is nondiagnostic, and further imaging (perhaps beginning with venous duplex ultrasound of the legs) is indicated.

How do I evaluate the patient with possible pulmonary embolism who is too obese to fit in a CT or V/Q scanner? When a patient weighs more than 400 lb, the imaging options become limited because many CT and gamma scanner tables cannot accommodate body mass greater than 400 lb. We recommend an attempt to perform compression venous ultrasound of the lower extremities to rule out DVT. Although often technically suboptimal in a massively obese patient, venous ultrasound occasionally provides positive evidence of DVT, ostensibly clinching the diagnosis. Another option is to decide to anticoagulate empirically based on a moderate-to-high pretest probability and a D-dimer concentration that exceeds 1000 ng/mL. The adequate regimen for anticoagulation is uncertain, but many experts recommend subcutaneous enoxaparin, 1 mg/kg of actual body weight up to a maximum of 200 μ/kg.

 KEY CONCEPTS

- Deep vein thrombosis often presents as a crampy sensation in the calf.
- "Sudden onset" is useless as a discriminator for presence or absence of PE.
- A D-dimer concentration <500 ng/mL can rule out PE or DVT in non–high-risk patients.
- A patient with a pretest probability <2% probably should not be tested for PE.
- A patient with PE and a pulse oximetry reading <95% has an increased risk for a bad outcome.

REFERENCES

1. Dalen JE: Pulmonary embolism: What have we learned since Virchow? Natural history, pathophysiology, and diagnosis. *Chest* 122:1440, 2002.
2. White RH: The epidemiology of venous thromboembolism. *Circulation* 107(23 Suppl 1):I4, 2003.
3. Wells PS, Anderson D, Bormanis J: Value of assessment of pretest probability of deep-vein thrombosis in clinical management. *Lancet* 350:1795, 1997.
4. Kearon C, et al: Noninvasive diagnosis of deep venous thrombosis. *Ann Intern Med* 128:663, 1998.
5. Schutgens RE, et al: Combination of a normal D-dimer concentration and a non-high pretest clinical probability score is a safe strategy to exclude deep venous thrombosis. *Circulation* 107:593, 2003.
6. Kovacs MJ, et al: Comparison of 10-mg and 5-mg warfarin initiation nomograms together with low-molecular-weight heparin for outpatient treatment of acute venous thromboembolism: A randomized, double-blind, controlled trial. *Ann Intern Med* 138:714, 2003.
7. Meissner MH, et al: Early outcome after isolated calf vein thrombosis. *J Vasc Surg* 26:749, 1997.
8. Hingorani A, et al: Upper extremity deep venous thrombosis and its impact on morbidity and mortality rates in a hospital-based population. *J Vasc Surg* 26:853, 1997.
9. Kommareddy A, Zaroukian MH, Hassouna HI: Upper extremity deep venous thrombosis. *Semin Thromb Hemost* 82:89, 2002.
10. Luciani A, et al: Catheter-related upper extremity deep venous thrombosis in cancer patients: A prospective study based on doppler US. *Radiology* 220:655, 2001.
11. Kline JA, et al: Use of pulse oximetry to predict in-hospital complications in normotensive patients with pulmonary embolism. *Am J Med* 115:203, 2003.
12. Goldhaber SZ, Visani L, De Rosa M: Acute pulmonary embolism: Clinical outcomes in the International Cooperative Pulmonary Embolism Registry (ICOPER). *Lancet* 353:1386, 1999.
13. Bynum LJ, Wilson JE: Characteristics of pleural effusions associated with pulmonary embolism. *Arch Intern Med* 136:159, 1976.
14. Zagorski J, et al: Chemokines accumulate in the lungs of rats with severe pulmonary embolism induced by polystyrene microspheres. *J Immunol* 171:5529, 2003.
15. Kline JA, Johns KL, Coluciello SA, Israel EG: New diagnostic tests for pulmonary embolism. *Ann Emerg Med* 35:168, 2000.
16. Kline JA, Nelson RD, Jackson RE, Courtney DM: Criteria for the safe use of D-dimer testing in emergency department patients with suspected pulmonary embolism: A multicenter United States study. *Ann Emerg Med* 39:144, 2002.
17. Wells PS, et al: Derivation of a simple clinical model to categorize patients' probability of pulmonary embolism: Increasing the models utility with the SimpliRED D-dimer. *Thromb Haemost* 83:416, 2000.
18. Wicki J, et al: Assessing clinical probability of pulmonary embolism in the emergency ward: A simple score. *Arch Intern Med* 161:92, 2001.
19. Courtney DM, Sasser H, Pincus B, Kline JA: Pulseless electrical activity with witnessed arrest as a predictor of sudden death from massive pulmonary embolism in outpatients. *Resuscitation* 49:265, 2001.
20. Courtney DM, Kline JA: Identification of prearrest clinical factors associated with outpatient fatal pulmonary embolism. *Acad Emerg Med* 8:1136, 2001.
21. Daniel KR, Courtney DM, Kline JA: Assessment of cardiac stress from massive pulmonary embolism with 12-lead electrocardiography. *Chest* 120:2474, 2001.
22. Kline JA, Wells PS: Methodology for a rapid protocol to rule out pulmonary embolism in the emergency department. *Ann Emerg Med* 42:266, 2003.
23. Pauker SG, Kassirer JP: The threshold approach to clinical decision making. *N Engl J Med* 302:1109, 1980.
24. Kline JA, et al: Clinical criteria to prevent unnecessary diagnostic testing in emergency department patients with suspected pulmonary embolism. *J Thromb Haemost* 2:1247, 2004.
25. Wells PS, et al: Excluding pulmonary embolism at the bedside without diagnostic imaging: Management of patients with suspected pulmonary embolism presenting to the emergency department by using a simple clinical model and D-dimer. *Ann Intern Med* 135:98, 2001.
26. PIOPED Investigators: Value of the ventilation/perfusion scan in acute pulmonary embolism. *JAMA* 263:2753, 1990.
27. Kline JA, Jones AE: Availability of technology to evaluate for pulmonary embolism in academic emergency departments in the United States. *J Thromb Haemost* 11:2240, 2003.
28. Musset D, et al: Diagnostic strategy for patients with suspected pulmonary embolism: A prospective multicentre outcome study. *Lancet* 360:1914, 2002.
29. van Beek EJ, et al: Lung scintigraphy and helical computed tomography for the diagnosis of pulmonary embolism: A meta-analysis. *Clin Appl Thromb Hemost* 7:87, 2001.
30. Safriel Y, Zinn H: CT pulmonary angiography in the detection of pulmonary emboli: A meta-analysis of sensitivities and specificities. *Clin Imaging* 26:101, 2002.
31. Remy-Jardin M, et al: CT angiography of pulmonary embolism in patients with underlying respiratory disease: Impact of multislice CT on image quality and negative predictive value. *Eur Radiol* 12:1971, 2002.
32. Ruiz Y, et al: Prospective comparison of helical CT with angiography in pulmonary embolism: Global and selective vascular territory analysis: Interobserver agreement. *Eur Radiol* 13:823, 2003.
33. van Rossum AB, et al: Pulmonary embolism: Validation of spiral CT angiography in 149 patients. *Radiology* 201:467, 1996.
34. Diffin DC, et al: Effect of anatomic distribution of pulmonary emboli on interobserver agreement in the interpretation of pulmonary angiography. *AJR Am J Roentgenol* 171:1085, 1998.
35. Richman PB, et al: Contribution of indirect computed tomography venography to computed tomography angiography of the chest for the diagnosis of thromboembolic disease in two United States emergency departments. *J Thromb Haemost* 1:652, 2003.

36. Garg K, Kemp JL, Russ PD, Baron AE: Thromboembolic disease: Variability of interobserver agreement in the interpretation of CT venography with CT pulmonary angiography. *AJR Am J Roentgenol* 176:1043, 2001.

37. Richman PB, Courtney DM, Kline JA: Prevalence and significance of non-thromboembolic findings on chest computerized tomography angiography performed to rule-out pulmonary embolism: A multi-center study of 1025 emergency department patients. *Acad Emerg Med* 11:642, 2004.

38. Tulevski II, Mulder BJ, van Veldhuisen DJ: Utility of a BNP as a marker for RV dysfunction in acute pulmonary embolism. *J Am Coll Cardiol* 39:2080, 2002.

39. Kruger S, Merx MW, Graf J: Utility of brain natriuretic peptide to predict right ventricular dysfunction and clinical outcome in patients with acute pulmonary embolism. *Circulation* 108:e94, 2003.

40. Kucher N, et al: Low pro-brain natriuretic peptide levels predict benign clinical outcome in acute pulmonary embolism. *Circulation* 107:1576, 2003.

41. Kucher N, Printzen G, Goldhaber SZ: Prognostic role of brain natriuretic peptide in acute pulmonary embolism. *Circulation* 107:2545, 2003.

42. ten Wolde M, et al: Brain natriuretic peptide as a predictor of adverse outcome in patients with pulmonary embolism. *Circulation* 107:2082, 2003.

43. Konstantinides S, et al: Heparin plus alteplase compared with heparin alone in patients with submassive pulmonary embolism. *N Engl J Med* 347:1143, 2002.

44. Goldhaber SZ, Haire WD, Feldstein ML, Miller M: Alteplase versus heparin in acute pulmonary embolism: Randomised trial assessing right-ventricular function and pulmonary perfusion. *Lancet* 341:507, 1993.

45. Agnelli G, Becattini C, Kirschstein T: Thrombolysis vs heparin in the treatment of pulmonary embolism: A clinical outcome-based meta-analysis. *Arch Intern Med* 162:2537, 2002.

46. Giavarina D, Mezzena G, Dorizzi RM, Soffiati G: Reference interval of D-dimer in pregnant women. *Clin Biochem* 34:331, 2001.

Section V **GASTROINTESTINAL SYSTEM**

CHAPTER

88 Esophagus, Stomach, and Duodenum

Mark J. Lowell

ESOPHAGEAL OBSTRUCTION

Perspective

Ingestion of foreign objects and esophageal food bolus impactions occur commonly. Although most pass spontaneously, approximately 10% to 20% require a nonoperative intervention and less than 1% require surgical removal. Death as a result of foreign body ingestion or impaction is exceedingly rare.[1] Most foreign body ingestions occur in children between the ages of 6 months and 6 years, with coins being the most commonly impacted objects. In adults, foreign body ingestion tends to occur in prisoners, alcoholics, psychiatric patients, and mentally impaired patients; many have a tendency for repetitive ingestion. Most adult impactions are due to pieces of food, particularly meat and bones. Patients with preexisting esophageal abnormalities are at greater risk for foreign body impaction. Denture wearers are also at increased risk because of impaired oral sensation.

Principles of Disease

The adult esophagus is approximately 25 to 30 cm in length. Superiorly, it begins in the hypopharynx as a transverse slit posterior to the larynx and approximately at the level of the cricoid cartilage. On either side of this cephalad slit are the piriform recesses, which are blind pouches that may occasionally harbor a foreign body. Throughout its course, the esophagus has four natural areas of narrowing that may cause impaction of a foreign body: at the cricopharyngeus muscle (the upper esophageal sphincter), the aortic arch, the left main stem bronchus, and the diaphragmatic hiatus. Most impactions occur in the proximal third of the esophagus and, if large enough, can impinge on the trachea, leading to airway compromise.

The esophagus comprises two main bands of muscle: an inner circular layer and an outer longitudinal layer. The resting tone of these muscles causes the inner epithelium to fold in on itself, effectively obliterating the lumen. Elastic fibers enable the esophageal lumen to expand and allow passage of a food bolus. The upper one third of the esophagus, including the cricopharyngeus muscle, contains striated muscle to allow the voluntary initiation of swallowing. The middle portion of the esophagus is a mixture of skeletal and smooth muscle, and the distal third comprises only smooth muscle.

Although it is relatively fixed at its origin, the esophagus becomes mobile as it traverses the mediastinum. Thus, it can be easily displaced by adjacent structures such as an enlarged left atrium or ventricle, a goiter, or a mediastinal tumor. Displacement of the esophagus may alter its shape enough to impede the passage of a food bolus or foreign body.

Clinical Features

Esophageal obstruction may be partial or complete. The patient with complete obstruction is unable to swallow, is often drooling, and may be violently retching in an attempt to regurgitate the obstructing bolus. The patient may complain of pain from the neck to the substernal and epigastric area, although the perceived level of obstruction may not correlate with the actual site of the obstruction.

A proximal obstruction may arise as a "café coronary," characterized by sudden cyanosis and collapse caused by food (usually an unchewed piece of meat) lodging in the upper esophagus or oropharynx leading to airway obstruction. Similarly, "steakhouse syndrome" results when a large piece of food, usually improperly chewed, is swallowed and causes esophageal obstruction in the distal esophagus. The obstruction may be transient with spontaneous passage of the bolus or may be complete or partial. Intense discomfort develops shortly after swallowing a large piece of meat, and the patient is usually unable to swallow anything else. Ingestion of alcohol and absence of teeth are predisposing factors. Although obstruction may occur in a patient with a normal esophagus, abnormalities such as carcinoma, peptic stricture, or a Schatzki ring are identified in almost 90% of patients with an esophageal obstruction.[2] Schatzki's ring is a fibrous, diaphragm-like stricture near the gastroesophageal junction present in up to 15% of the population.

Aside from naturally occurring areas of anatomic narrowing, there are other pathologic causes of esophageal stenosis that may lead to symptoms of obstruction. Intrinsic causes of luminal narrowing include carcinoma and webs. An esophageal web is a thin structure composed of mucosa and submucosa. Although webs can occur in isolation, they are also seen in the Plummer-Vinson syndrome, which is characterized by anterior webs, dysphagia, iron deficiency anemia, cheilosis, spooning of the nails, glossitis, and thin friable mucosa in the mouth, pharynx, and upper esophagus. Women 30 to 50 years of age are usually affected. Patients usually present with dysphagia that is initially intermittent and worse with solids. If untreated, it may progress and become constant.[3]

Extrinsic compression of the esophagus can occur in a variety of conditions. In the neck, thyroid enlargement from goiter or carcinoma may cause dysphagia. Symptoms may also be seen with a pharyngoesophageal or Zenker diverticulum, a progressive outpouching of the pharyngeal mucosa as a result of increased pressure generated by failure of proper relaxation of the cricopharyngeus muscle. Noisy deglutition, dysphagia, foul breath, and a palpable compressible mass in the neck may be present. Laryngotracheal aspiration when the patient is supine results from the emptying of contents from the diverticulum.

Congenital anomalies of the aortic arch may cause dysphagia in both children and adults. In children, respiratory symptoms are also usually present and commonly predominate. In adults, an anomalous right subclavian artery is the most common vascular cause for dysphagia, which often does not become symptomatic until the fourth decade of life. The most common symptoms in adults are dyspnea on exertion and dysphagia. Vascular compression of the esophagus with dysphagia may also occur with aneurysms of the aortic arch and great vessels. Bronchogenic carcinoma can cause dysphagia by direct involvement of the esophagus or by compression with nodes.

Esophageal foreign bodies can occur atypically in small children or mentally impaired individuals. They may present with choking, refusing to eat, vomiting, blood-stained secretions, or respiratory distress.

Diagnostic Strategies

Plain radiographs of the neck should be obtained if a foreign body in the throat is suspected. Coins are easily visualized. Disk batteries have a characteristic radiographic "double-density" appearance.[4] Small bones or radiopaque objects may occasionally be visualized. Air in the tissues may be present if perforation has occurred. However, failure to demonstrate a foreign body on radiographs does not rule out its presence. Traditionally, contrast studies have been performed next; however computed tomography (CT) scans have been used successfully to identify foreign bodies, particularly chicken and fish bones, and may be more sensitive than plain films or barium examinations.[5,6] Other nonorganic objects (e.g., Lego pieces) have also been successfully visualized with CT.[7] CT scans have the additional value of visualizing changes in the surrounding tissues associated with perforation.

Handheld metal detectors have been reported to be useful screening devices for metallic foreign bodies in children. They may also be of use in finding radiolucent metallic foreign bodies such as aluminum pull tabs. They do not, however, localize the object.[8]

If available, endoscopy is helpful to diagnose and treat esophageal foreign bodies. When endoscopy is unavailable, a radiographic contrast study may help in diagnosis. However, in addition to the risk of aspiration, the presence of contrast agents may make endoscopy more difficult. It is therefore advisable to consult with the endoscopist before performing any study in a patient with a suspected esophageal foreign body. If an esophageal perforation is suspected, a water-soluble contrast agent (e.g., diatrizoate meglumine [Gastrografin]) should be used first because barium induces an inflammatory response in tissues. Failure to visualize a clinically suspected perforation warrants a repeated examination utilizing barium as the contrast agent. Because barium may obscure subsequent endoscopic visualization, a minimal amount of thin barium should be used. The use of a swallowed barium-soaked cotton ball to identify the site of obstruction is not recommended because it adds an additional foreign body that then needs to be removed. Plain radiographs followed by contrast studies have false-negative rates of less than 1% and false-positive rates of less than 20%.[9,10] Because of the risk of complications, a patient who is suspected of having ingested a sharp object should undergo evaluation up to and including endoscopy.[1]

Differential Considerations

Esophageal foreign bodies must be distinguished from foreign bodies in the airway. This distinction can be especially difficult in small children. Radiographically, esophageal foreign bodies usually lie in the frontal plain and are best visualized in anteroposterior views. Tracheal foreign bodies tend to lie sagittally.

Patients with esophageal obstruction may present with retrosternal pain that can appear similar to that in an acute ischemic cardiac syndrome. The presence of odynophagia suggests an underlying mucosal lesion.

Management

Flexible endoscopy by an experienced endoscopist is the procedure of choice for removal of esophageal foreign bodies, as it is effective and relatively safe with a complication rate of 8%.[11]

Upper Esophagus

Oropharyngeal foreign bodies can usually be removed with a Kelly clamp or McGill forceps under direct visualization. Smooth upper esophageal foreign bodies can often be removed with a Foley catheter. This procedure requires an experienced technician, a cooperative patient, and fluoroscopic guidance. The patient is placed in a prone position, and the catheter is passed into the esophagus past the point of the foreign body impaction. The balloon is then inflated and the catheter withdrawn, pulling the foreign body with it. Controversy exists regarding the safety of this technique because there is no direct control of the foreign body.[12-14] Prophylactic endotracheal intubation may be warranted to prevent the foreign body from entering the airway. When these maneuvers fail to dislodge the esophageal foreign body, consultation with a qualified endoscopist is indicated.

Lower Esophagus

Lower esophageal obstruction is usually the result of an impacted food bolus and can often be treated effectively in the emergency department. Administration of 1 mg of glucagon intravenously (up to a total of 2 mg) may cause enough relaxation of the esophageal smooth muscle to allow passage of the bolus in approximately 50% of patients.[15,16] Because glucagon affects smooth muscle only, it is effective only for impactions in the lower esophagus. Many emergency physicians give the patient a trial of glucagon while arranging for endoscopy. Side effects of glucagon include vomiting, nausea, dizziness, and flushing. Glucagon should not be used in patients with sharp-edged, potentially damaging foreign bodies or in patients with insulinoma, pheochromocytoma, or Zollinger-Ellison syndrome.[17]

Effervescent agents are sometimes effective in accelerating the passage of an obstructing food bolus. Although the mechanism of action is unclear, it is hypothesized that the carbon dioxide released from bubbles escaping the fluid acts to disrupt the impacted food bolus and to distend the distal esophagus. The administration of carbonated beverages (including soft drinks) results in the passage of the obstructing food bolus in 60% to 80% of patients treated.[18,19] Studies combining the use of glucagon and an effervescent agent show rapid relief of symptoms in 65% to 75% of patients.[20,21] It has been recommended that effervescent agents be avoided in cases of complete obstruction and cases in which an obstruction has been present for over 24 hours because of the theoretical potential of inducing perforation of a possibly ischemic distal esophagus.[22] The use of meat tenderizer (papain) to soften a food bolus is not recommended. Although intact mucosa is resistant to papain's effects, an inflamed mucosa becomes much more inflamed when exposed to this proteolytic enzyme and is more likely to perforate.[23]

Patients with sharp-edged, distal foreign bodies, those who have contraindications to use of the aforementioned agents, and those who do not respond to treatment should be evaluated with endoscopy. It is unclear whether CT or contrast radiographic studies, performed to document the presence of obstruction, are of any benefit in symptomatic patients.

Endoscopy should be performed immediately for patients experiencing significant distress and for children with impaction of an alkaline button battery. These batteries contain concentrated sodium or potassium hydroxide in addition to metals such as zinc, lithium, and mercury. Leakage of any of these can lead to systemic toxicity. Larger batteries have a greater risk of impaction and leakage. Batteries that pass into the stomach should be followed radiographically and clinically to ensure passage. Assistance with the management of a patient with button battery ingestion can be obtained though the National Button Battery Ingestion Hotline at (202) 625-3333.

Urgent intervention is also indicated for sharp objects, disk batteries, coins in the proximal esophagus, and impactions that impair the handling of secretions.[24] It is unclear whether patients with mild to moderate symptoms of esophageal obstruction from a suspected food bolus require immediate endoscopy. In such cases, some authors believe that emergent intervention is unnecessary if the patient is still able to handle secretions because the bolus often passes on its own.[25] Others believe that the softened bolus makes endoscopic removal more difficult and predisposes to complications.[26] Any object remaining in the esophagus for more than 24 hours carries a higher risk of complications.

Most authors advocate follow-up endoscopic evaluation in all cases after an esophageal obstruction to rule out underlying pathologic conditions.

Stomach

Certain foreign bodies that pass into the stomach still require endoscopic retrieval. Objects longer than 5 cm or wider than 2.5 cm in diameter (e.g., toothbrushes, spoons) rarely pass the stomach. All sharp and pointed foreign bodies (e.g., toothpicks, bones) should be removed before they pass the stomach because 15% to

35% may cause intestinal perforation.[27] Smaller objects that pass into the stomach can be followed with stool inspections and with serial radiographs if necessary to ensure passage. Objects that remain in the stomach for more than 3 to 4 weeks or that remain in the same intestinal location for more than 1 week should be considered for surgical removal.[28]

ESOPHAGEAL PERFORATION

Perspective

Esophageal perforation is a potentially life-threatening condition that must be identified and treated early to minimize morbidity and mortality. Although first reported by Boerhaave in the early 1700s as a result of forceful vomiting, it can also result from any Valsalva-like maneuver, including childbirth, cough, or heavy lifting. In modern times, spontaneous perforation accounts for only 15% of cases, with iatrogenic injuries accounting for the remainder. These usually occur as a complication of upper endoscopy, dilation, sclerotherapy, or other gastrointestinal (GI) procedures. It has also been reported as a complication of both nasogastric tube placement and endotracheal intubation, including the use of the esophagotracheal Combitube.[29,30] Other causes of perforation include foreign body ingestion, caustic substance ingestion, severe esophagitis, carcinoma, and direct injury related to blunt or penetrating trauma.

Principles of Disease

More than 90% of spontaneous esophageal ruptures occur in the distal esophagus. In contrast, rupture resulting from blunt trauma to the neck or thorax usually occurs in the proximal and middle third of the esophagus. Most iatrogenic injuries occur at the pharyngoesophageal junction because the wall in this area is thin and there is no serosal layer to reinforce it. Another site of frequent iatrogenic injury is the esophagogastric junction. In this area, the esophagus curves anteriorly and to the left as it enters the abdomen, and an endoscope has a greater likelihood of perforating the posterior wall. Other factors predisposing to iatrogenic perforation include anterior cervical osteophytes, Zenker's diverticulum, esophageal strictures, and malignancies.[9]

When a perforation occurs, saliva and gastric contents can enter the mediastinum. Rapid spread of an infectious or inflammatory response to the surrounding tissues and organs occurs because of the thinness of the esophageal wall. Changes in intrathoracic pressure during respiration draw contaminants deeper into the mediastinum. The presence of gastric enzymes and other foreign material in the mediastinum induces an intense inflammatory response that may result in enough fluid buildup to displace adjacent structures.

Clinical Features

The presenting features vary with the site of injury. Patients with an upper esophageal perforation usually present with neck or chest pain, dysphagia, respiratory distress, and fever. Odynophagia, nausea, vomiting, hoarseness, or aphonia may also result.

Patients with perforation of the lower esophagus may present with abdominal pain, pneumothorax, hydropneumothorax, and pneumomediastinum.[31] The pain often radiates into the back, to the left side of the chest, and to the left or both shoulders.[32] Most patients have mediastinal or cervical emphysema, which may be noted by palpation or by a "crunching" sound heard during auscultation (Hamman's sign). Abdominal examination may reveal epigastric or generalized abdominal tenderness, often with guarding and involuntary rigidity. Patients with severe mediastinitis may present in fulminant shock.

Pain or fever following esophageal instrumentation should be considered an indication of perforation until proved otherwise. It should be noted that symptoms related to iatrogenic perforation may not appear until several hours after the procedure.

Diagnostic Strategies

Radiographic studies are used to establish the diagnosis of an esophageal perforation. A chest radiograph and an upright abdominal radiograph are usually obtained first. Radiographic abnormalities may be detected in up to 90% of patients and include findings such as subcutaneous emphysema, pneumomediastinum, mediastinal widening, pleural effusion, or pulmonary infiltrate.[33] Radiographic changes may not be present in the first few hours after the perforation.

Patients with suspected perforation should have contrast radiographic studies performed. Barium sulfate is superior in identifying small perforations; however, it may incite an inflammatory response in tissues. For this reason, water-soluble agents (e.g., Gastrografin) should be used first. If a clinically suspected perforation is not identified, the examination should be repeated using barium.

CT of the chest may be used if a contrast study does not demonstrate a clinically suspected perforation. Findings such as mediastinal air, extraluminal contrast material, or fluid collections or abscesses adjacent to the esophagus confirm a perforation. These can be found after the initial perforation has healed. CT scan also allows evaluation of other adjacent areas that may suggest an alternative diagnosis. Endoscopy may be useful, especially in cases of trauma; however, small perforations may be difficult or impossible to visualize. Laboratory studies are usually not helpful early after a perforation, although an elevated white blood count may be noted.

Differential Considerations

Misdiagnosis occurs in more than half of patients with esophageal rupture because the differential diagnosis includes the numerous causes of chest and abdominal pain, including pulmonary embolism, acute myocardial infarction, aortic dissection, perforated ulcer, pneumothorax, lung abscess, pericarditis, or pancreatitis. It is important that esophageal perforations be diagnosed as soon as possible because the morbidity and mortality of the disorder increase with time.

Management

Certain patients with esophageal perforation require aggressive management. These include patients with Boerhaave's syndrome, clinically unstable patients, patients with perforations that contaminate the mediastinum or pleura, patients with intra-abdominal perforations, or patients with perforations with an associated pneumothorax.[34] Broad-spectrum intravenous antibiotics should be initiated early. The combination of a second-generation cephalosporin and an aminoglycoside usually provides adequate coverage.[35] Patients should be kept with nothing by mouth, and a nasogastric tube should be considered to eliminate oral and gastric secretions. Early surgical consultation is warranted.

There is growing evidence that some iatrogenic perforations can be managed conservatively with close observation in certain low-risk patients. These patients include those who are clinically stable (minimal symptoms and fever with no clinical signs of shock), those whose perforation resulted from endoscopic injury after dilation, and those who present a long time after their procedure and have demonstrated no ill effects. The last patients usually have small perforations of the cervical esophagus.[36-38] Most authors advocate treatment with suction and antibiotics as noted previously.

ESOPHAGITIS

Perspective

Esophagitis is defined as inflammation of the esophagus. The most common cause of esophagitis is gastroesophageal reflux disease (GERD). Other important causes of esophagitis include infectious esophagitis, pill esophagitis, and injuries from the effects of caustic ingestion, radiation, or sclerotherapy.

Principles of Disease

Infectious Esophagitis

Esophageal infections in the immunocompetent host are relatively rare. Iatrogenic alterations in host defenses through the use of immunosuppressive agents, potent chemotherapeutic agents, and broad-spectrum antibiotics have increased the incidence of esophageal infections. The spread of the human immunodeficiency virus (HIV) has also led to an increase in esophageal infection, although the epidemiology has been changing as more effective antiretroviral agents have become available. In addition to iatrogenic immunosuppression, diseases that weaken immunologic defenses in otherwise normal hosts can predispose the esophagus to infections. These conditions include diabetes mellitus, alcoholism, underlying malignancy, use of corticosteroids, and advanced age. Changes that occur in the mucosal barrier of the esophagus as a result of these conditions result in

an increased susceptibility to infection. The *Candida* species (primarily *Candida albicans*) are the most common esophageal pathogens.

The use of inhaled steroids for asthma has led to candidal infection in otherwise healthy patients. As empirical antifungal prophylaxis in immunosuppressive states has become more common, viral esophagitis has become more prominent. Herpes simplex 1 and cytomegalovirus are the most common viral pathogens. Bacteria, mycobacteria, other fungi, and parasitic organisms such as *Trypanosoma cruzi*, *Cryptosporidium*, and *Pneumocystis* are uncommon causes of infectious esophagitis and are usually diagnosed by culture or biopsy.

Pill Esophagitis

Pill esophagitis is estimated to occur in approximately 10,000 people per year in the United States.[39] However, because most cases are unreported, the true incidence is unknown. It results when a pill or capsule fails to pass into the stomach and remains in contact with the esophageal mucosa for a prolonged period. The contents can become exposed, resulting in inflammation and injury. It has been reported in all age groups. Predisposing factors include advanced age, decreased esophageal motility, and extrinsic compression. Large pills are more likely to be retained, as are those coated with gelatin. It should be noted that pills can stick to a normal esophagus, especially when taken without water or while in the supine position. Any area of the esophagus can be affected, although sites of natural compression may be more susceptible. Sustained-release compounds may be more damaging than standard preparations. Injury can range from minor irritation to frank ulceration, hemorrhage, and ultimately stricture formation. Some of the more common offending medications include antibiotics (especially the tetracycline family) and antivirals, aspirin and other nonsteroidal anti-inflammatory drugs (NSAIDs), potassium chloride, quinidine, ferrous sulfate, alprenolol, alendronate, and pamidronate.

Other Causes

Esophagitis from caustic substance ingestion occurs most commonly in children, although adults may ingest a caustic substance in a suicide attempt. Strongly acidic or alkaline substances are the offending agents. The degree of injury depends on the concentration of the substance, the volume ingested, and the time in contact with tissue. Strong acids produce coagulation necrosis, which results in eschar formation that usually limits the damage. In contrast, alkali produces liquefaction necrosis, which continues to cause injury as long as the substance is in contact with tissue.[40]

Patients undergoing radiation treatment for underlying malignancy may develop esophagitis. The degree of injury is related to the total dosage of radiation received. The mucosa becomes inflamed and friable. Agents used during sclerotherapy can also cause esophagitis.

Clinical Features

Esophagitis, regardless of etiology, most commonly arises with dysphagia (difficulty swallowing) or odynophagia (painful swallowing). Chest pain is frequently present, and esophageal bleeding, ranging from localized oozing as a result of inflammation to frank hemorrhage, can occur. Ulceration and perforation can result in mediastinitis.

Infectious Esophagitis

Most commonly, infectious esophagitis causes severe odynophagia. Dysphagia of both solids and liquids may also be present. Pain may be so severe that the patient refuses to eat or drink. Chest pain may also be present and may be described as acute in onset, constant, and not affected by standard antacid measures. Heartburn and nausea may also be presenting symptoms. Some immunocompromised patients may have fever or bleeding without dysphagia or odynophagia.

Pill Esophagitis

Patients with pill esophagitis present with odynophagia. Most patients have no prior history of esophageal disease and present with sudden onset of pain worsened by swallowing. Dysphagia may be present. Although some patients may present complaining of a pill that has become "stuck," the history of pill ingestion may be difficult to obtain because symptoms may begin hours after the offending pill is taken. Atypical presentations include a burning type of pain suggesting GERD as the etiology.

Other

Patients with caustic injuries may present with pain in the mouth, chest, or epigastrium. Dysphagia and vomiting may be present. Patients may be drooling. Airway compromise may be present because of direct tissue injury or resulting edema. Later, perforation may occur, and strictures are a common long-term complication. Radiation-induced esophagitis usually causes odynophagia and dysphagia. Strictures may ultimately develop.

Diagnostic Strategies

Endoscopy is the best method of diagnosing both pill-induced and infectious esophagitis. With infectious esophagitis, direct visualization may reveal characteristic signs of infection, such as white plaques of *Candida* or herpetic vesicles. Definitive diagnosis can be made through brushings and biopsies. Radiographic studies are usually not helpful because the findings are nonspecific. A strong clinical suspicion is necessary to diagnose pill esophagitis. The other causes of esophagitis are usually clinically apparent.

Differential Considerations

Other causes of esophageal pain include GERD, esophageal motility disorder, foreign body, and perforation. Chest pain may also be a component, and there-fore an acute coronary syndrome must be considered. Esophageal pain is more likely to be positional and related to swallowing.

Management

Infectious Esophagitis

For infectious esophagitis, therapy should be directed at the causative organism. Patients with normal immune systems and mild cases of candidal esophagitis can be treated with clotrimazole troches (10 mg dissolved in the mouth five times a day for 1 week) or nystatin (1 to 3 million units by mouth four to five times per day for 2 weeks). Some of the newer anti-fungal agents such as fluconazole (200 mg by mouth daily for 3 to 4 weeks), ketoconazole (300 to 400 mg by mouth daily for 3 to 4 weeks), or itraconazole (100 to 200 mg by mouth daily for 3 to 4 weeks) may be used for more advanced infections in patients with compromised immune systems. They may also be used for a shorter duration in patients with less severe infections.

Initial treatment for herpes simplex esophagitis includes antivirals such as acyclovir (400 mg by mouth five times per day for 7 to 14 days or 5 to 10 mg/kg intravenously [IV] every 8 hours for 7 to 14 days), famciclovir (500 mg by mouth three times a day for 7 to 14 days), or valacyclovir (500 mg by mouth twice a day for 7 to 14 days).[9] For cytomegalovirus, initial treatment can begin with ganciclovir (5 mg/kg IV every 12 hours for 2 to 3 weeks) or foscarnet (60 mg/kg IV every 8 hours or 90 mg/kg IV every 12 hours for 2 to 3 weeks).[41]

If the causative organism cannot be adequately identified or if the patient is severely debilitated, admission to the hospital may be required. Patients discharged from the emergency department should receive appropriate follow-up (e.g., gastroenterology, infectious disease). In addition to antibiotic therapy directed at the infecting organism, treatment with antacids, topical anesthetics, or sucralfate may provide symptomatic relief.

Pill Esophagitis

If a patient with suspected pill esophagitis has persistent symptoms, endoscopy may be necessary. It also helps to determine alternative etiologies. No data exist supporting any specific treatment, although intuitively antacid medication may prevent further erosion of damaged mucosa.[42] Symptoms may take up to 6 weeks to resolve.

The best treatment for pill esophagitis is prevention. Patients should be instructed to drink at least 4 ounces of liquid with any pill. All medications should be taken by the patient when in an upright position, and the patient should remain upright for several minutes after medication ingestion. Patients with underlying esophageal abnormalities or those who are bedridden should avoid the use of pills whenever practical.

Other

Management of caustic injuries includes rinsing of the mouth and dilution of the substance with water.

Airway compromise or involvement may require aggressive management. Emesis or gastric lavage is contraindicated because it reexposes tissues to the agent. Charcoal is not indicated. Patients usually undergo delayed endoscopy to evaluate the extent of injury. A patient who presents with a history of caustic substance ingestion without obvious clinical findings should be admitted and observed.

Treatment of radiation esophagitis is supportive. Patients who cannot eat or drink because of radiation injury to the esophagus should be admitted for intravenous fluid therapy.

GASTROESOPHAGEAL REFLUX DISEASE

Perspective

Asymptomatic reflux of gastric contents from the stomach into the esophagus occurs in most people several times a day as a normal physiologic phenomenon. When reflux becomes symptomatic or histopathologic alteration in the upper GI or respiratory tract results from these episodes, GERD is said to exist. In the United States, symptomatic reflux in the form of heartburn occurs daily in 7% of adults, weekly in 14%, and monthly in 40%.[43]

Principles of Disease

Although the anatomic relationship between the cardia of the stomach and the left side of the esophagus prevents reflux of gastric contents into the esophagus, the major barrier to gastroesophageal reflux is the lower esophageal sphincter (LES). A defective LES is believed to be the primary mechanism in pathologic reflux by allowing a larger volume of refluxate to enter the esophagus.[44] When reflux does occur, gravity, peristalsis, normal swallowing of saliva, and secretions from esophageal glands help clear refluxed gastric contents back into the stomach. Factors also operate at the mucosal level to minimize the damage caused by refluxate.

Besides (or in addition to) a defective LES, other mechanisms that may lead to GERD include esophageal motility abnormalities, increased intragastric pressure (e.g., obesity, pregnancy), acid hypersecretion, gastric outlet obstruction, and conditions that cause delayed gastric emptying (e.g., gastroparesis, neuromuscular disease). The presence of a hiatal hernia (a prolapse of a portion of the stomach through the diaphragmatic esophageal hiatus), formerly thought to be synonymous with GERD, may be a factor in the initiation of GERD pathogenesis by interfering with the function of the LES. However, hiatal hernia is thought to play a greater role in sustaining GERD, as one is found in approximately 90% of patients with severe GERD and its complications.[45,46]

Clinical Features

Symptoms

The most common manifestation of GERD is reflux esophagitis, of which the most common symptom is

---

BOX 88-1. Agents and Conditions Related to Gastroesophageal Reflux

Decreased Lower Esophageal Sphincter Pressure
Anticholinergic drugs
Benzodiazepines
Caffeine
Calcium channel blockers
Chocolate
Ethanol
Estrogen
Fatty foods
Nicotine
Nitrates
Peppermint
Progesterone
Pregnancy

Decreased Esophageal Motility
Achalasia
Diabetes mellitus
Scleroderma

Increased Gastric Emptying Time
Anticholinergic drugs
Diabetic gastroparesis
Gastric outlet obstruction

---

heartburn, defined as a burning sensation that begins in the subxiphoid area and radiates toward the neck. Reflux may also cause a dull discomfort, localized pressure, or severe squeezing pain across the middle of the chest. This type of pain has been postulated to be a result of acid-induced esophageal spasm, but this is believed to be uncommon. The patient may appear comfortable or may have associated diaphoresis, pallor, nausea, and vomiting, leading to the consideration of an ischemic cardiac syndrome. A detailed history is often helpful in differentiating cardiac chest pain from reflux, although the distinction may not be possible in the emergency department.

Other symptoms of GERD include regurgitation (the spontaneous appearance of acid or bitter material in the mouth or pharynx) and water brash (a vagally mediated hypersalivation response that may produce as much as 10 mL of saliva in 1 minute). Dysphagia and odynophagia may also be presenting complaints and may be associated with more serious complications.

Any condition or agent that decreases LES pressure, decreases esophageal motility, or prolongs gastric emptying predisposes patients to reflux (Box 88-1). Positions that place the esophagus in a dependent position to the stomach or increase intra-abdominal pressure tend to precipitate reflux. Stooping, bending, leaning forward, Valsalva-type maneuvers, and assuming a supine position are common precipitants.

GERD can manifest itself in extraesophageal locations. Reflux-induced asthma may result from either aspiration of gastric contents into the lung or activation of a vagal reflex arc from the gut to the lung. Although both asthma and GERD have been shown to coexist in many individuals, it is difficult to identify GERD as the etiology of the asthma, and there is no diagnostic test to define which patients have GERD-associated asthma.[47-49] Chronic persistent cough (without wheezing) can also result from reflux.[50]

If the refluxate reaches the proximal esophagus, otolaryngologic manifestations may result, even in the absence of esophageal symptoms. Laryngeal and tracheal stenosis can result from repeated exposure to refluxate; it is postulated that subglottic stenosis in patients intubated for prolonged periods may be due to GERD.[51] GERD may also cause hoarseness, dysphonia, cough, globus sensation, repetitive throat clearing, and frequent sore throat or laryngitis.[52] Refluxate that enters the oropharynx may lead to gingivitis, halitosis, or dental problems such as erosion of the lingual sides of the teeth as a result of acid exposure. Otalgia and hiccups can also result from reflux.[53]

Complications

Repetitive exposure to acid can lead to changes in the esophageal mucosa. Continued reflux can lead to thinning of the normal stratified squamous epithelial layer. With the development of esophagitis, an inflammatory response occurs within the mucosa and submucosa with infiltration of polymorphonuclear leukocytes. The inflammatory response is the result of chemical irritation of the esophageal mucosa from reflux of gastric acid, pepsin, and bile acids. Both acid and alkaline refluxes produce the same pathologic changes. Continued exposure can lead to further endoscopically visible changes of erosion, ulceration, and scarring. Ultimately, stricture formation may result. The most severe histologic consequence of GERD is replacement of the normal stratified squamous epithelium with metaplastic columnar epithelium in a condition known as Barrett's metaplasia. Histologically, it is characterized by a villous architecture with goblet cells. There is a strong correlation between the development of Barrett's metaplasia and adenocarcinoma of the esophagus.

Diagnostic Strategies

GERD is a common problem, and additional diagnostic testing in the emergency department is rarely necessary, assuming other more serious etiologies of the patient's symptoms have been excluded. Patients with dysphagia, odynophagia, or bleeding should be referred for further study.

Differential Considerations

One should consider acute ischemic cardiac syndromes as a possible cause of chest pain in adults. Radiation of pain is an inconstant finding in both esophageal and cardiac chest pain. The pain seen with reflux may radiate into the neck, jaws, shoulders, back, arms, and abdomen. Radiation into the back is more often ascribed to the esophagus. Radiation of pain into one arm or into the neck or jaw is not helpful in distinguishing ischemic cardiac pain from esophageal pain. Radiation of pain into the abdomen is present approximately three times more often in reflux than in ischemic heart disease. Radiation into both arms is rarely seen in reflux, whereas it may be present in approximately one quarter of patients with ischemic heart disease. Precipitation of pain by exercise and relief by rest may occur in pain from reflux as well as in ischemic heart disease. Emotional precipitation of pain occurs in reflux, although it is also seen with coronary artery disease.[54] The occurrence of reflux after meals is another important feature in the history. A feeling of fullness after meals occurs commonly in reflux and is helpful in differentiating it from coronary artery disease.

Relief of chest pain from reflux by antacids is a key point in the history; however, one should not place too much weight upon this point as evidence against a cardiac etiology. The relief is often short lived, and pain may recur in a short time. Esophageal pain may be brought on by swallowing. The physical examination in patients with esophageal reflux is not usually helpful in diagnosis. Thus, the history is by far the most valuable aid. It is important to maintain an acute awareness of the diverse presentations of ischemic heart disease and to be cautious in attributing chest pain to esophageal causes solely on the basis of historical elements. Other GI disorders such as gastritis, esophagitis, peptic ulcer disease, and biliary tract disease should be considered in the differential.

Management

Earlier treatment guidelines for GERD recommended lifestyle modification solely as an initial approach; however, this approach has been shown to have little therapeutic benefit without concomitant medical management.[55,56] Lifestyle modifications, still an important aspect of treatment, include avoiding the fully recumbent position during sleep in an effort to decrease the number of reflux episodes and to facilitate clearance of refluxate. The following should also be avoided: eating before retiring at night, the wearing of tight garments, the performance of heavy physical exercise after meals, the use of anticholinergic drugs, or the consumption of foods or use of agents that decrease LES tone, such as cigarettes and alcohol. Direct irritants to the esophagus such as coffee, citrus fruits, and tomato-based products should also be avoided.[57] Overweight patients may experience relief with weight loss. Avoidance of fatty foods and consumption of smaller meals may also help alleviate symptoms.

The pharmacologic therapy of GERD includes agents that neutralize acids, decrease acid production, act on the LES or affect motility, and protect the mucosa. Many patients initially self-medicate with antacids or over-the-counter-strength H_2 receptor antagonists, both of which have been demonstrated to relieve and prevent symptoms.[58] The most effective treatment for GERD is reduction of acid production with either an H_2 blocker or a proton pump inhibitor (PPI). These agents do not stop the reflux but rather reduce the potency of the refluxate. Many trials have demonstrated the efficacy of H_2 blockers and PPIs for esophagitis; however, the PPIs are more effective at healing esophagitis.[59] PPIs have been shown to provide rapid

Table 88-1. Summary of Histamine Receptor Antagonists

	GERD	PUD*
Cimetidine	800 mg bid or 400 mg qid	800 mg qhs or 400 mg bid
Famotidine	20 or 40 mg bid	40 mg qhs or 20 mg bid
Nizatidine	150 mg bid	300 mg qhs or 150 mg bid
Ranitidine	150 mg bid	300 mg qhs or 150 mg bid

*Maintenance dose for PUD is half the qhs dose.
GERD, gastroesophageal reflux disease; PUD, peptic ulcer disease.

Table 88-2. Summary of Proton Pump Inhibitors*

	GERD	PUD or NSAID-Induced Ulcers†
Esomeprazole	20 mg qd or 40 mg qd	40 mg PO qd
Lansoprazole	30 mg qd or 30 bid	30 mg PO qd
Omeprazole	20 mg qd or 20 bid	20 mg PO qd
Pantoprazole	40 mg qd or 40 bid	40 mg PO qd
Rabeprazole	20 mg qd or 20 bid	20 mg PO qd

*All doses should be taken before breakfast; second doses (when necessary) should be administered prior to the evening meal.
†Patients with duodenal ulcer should be treated for 4 weeks; patients with gastric ulcer should be treated for 8 weeks.
GERD, gastroesophageal reflux disease; NSAID, nonsteroidal anti-inflammatory drug; PUD, peptic ulcer disease.
Adapted from Wolfe MM, Sachs G: Acid suppression: Optimizing therapy for gastroduodenal ulcer healing, gastroesophageal reflux disease, and stress-related erosive syndrome. *Gastroenterology* 118:S9, 2000.

symptomatic relief and healing of esophagitis in the highest percentage of patients. H$_2$ blockers are regarded as less potent than the PPIs but are effective and may be used in patients with mild to moderate GERD. Choices of H$_2$ blockers and PPIs are listed in Tables 88-1 and 88-2. All of these agents are now generally regarded as safe and effective.

Prokinetic agents treat GERD by increasing LES pressure. They may also be used for patients whose symptoms suggest a superimposed motility disturbance (e.g., regurgitation, choking, abdominal distention). In addition to improving propulsive activity of the stomach and small and large intestine, the increased esophageal peristalsis and LES tone would make it effective therapy for reflux by improving the clearance of refluxate.[60] Cisapride (Propulsid) was formerly used for this purpose but was withdrawn from the marketplace by the manufacturer because of adverse cardiac effects. Metoclopramide, a dopamine antagonist, may be used for these patients, but its efficacy has not been conclusively demonstrated and it has significant side effects, some of which are irreversible (e.g., tardive dyskinesia).[61] Baclofen has been used with some success in selected patients.[62] Candidates for this type of therapy are probably best chosen by a gastroenterologist.

Another agent that may be of benefit in refractory cases of symptomatic esophageal reflux is sucralfate, the salt of aluminum hydroxide and sucrose octasulfate. It may have an advantage in that it also absorbs

and inactivates bile salts.[63,64] However, this is not a Food and Drug Administration–approved indication for its use.

Although the emergency physician can initiate antireflux therapy, the patient with clinically suspected reflux should be referred to a gastroenterologist to confirm the diagnosis and provide follow-up care. Further diagnostic evaluation including esophageal pH monitoring, an upper GI series, esophageal manometry, or esophagoscopy may be necessary, especially for patients who fail to respond to all of the preceding measures. Medically refractory patients may be candidates for antireflux surgery.

GASTRITIS

Perspective

Strictly speaking, gastritis is a histologic diagnosis denoting inflammation of the gastric mucosa. Hence, the diagnosis of gastritis can be made only by endoscopy and biopsy. However, it is common practice for clinicians to use the term *gastritis* to refer to symptoms of dyspepsia. To confuse the picture further, gastroenterologists frequently use the term to refer to the endoscopic finding of an edematous, friable mucosa. However, without accompanying inflammation, this is more appropriately termed gastropathy rather than gastritis.[65] Controversy exists regarding how best to classify the entities that cause gastritis or gastropathy. This section considers gastritis and gastropathy together as one entity because the distinction makes little difference in the emergency department setting. Regardless of the cause, up to 50% of the population have endoscopic evidence of gastritis or gastropathy by age 50.

Principles of Disease

The most common cause of gastritis is infection with *Helicobacter pylori*. Although most patients are asymptomatic at the time of initial exposure, acute infection with *H. pylori* can cause severe gastritis and upper GI symptoms. Suppurative gastritis (also known as *acute phlegmonous gastritis*) can result from a bacterial infection of the stomach wall, usually from gram-positive cocci or gram-negative rods. Patients usually have an underlying mucosal abnormality such as cancer, ulcer, or preexisting gastritis.[66] Less common infectious causes of gastritis include mycobacterial, viral, parasitic, and fungal organisms.

Gastritis can also result from exposure to drugs. Aspirin or other NSAIDs are the most common offending agents. Inflammation occurs as a result of prostaglandin inhibition both locally and systemically and is probably a precursor to gastric ulcer formation. Other drugs implicated in causing gastritis are potassium preparations and iron supplements. Gastritis can result from both short- and long-term exposure to ethanol, although some authors feel that the long-term effects are more likely due to *H. pylori* rather than to the ethanol itself.

The presence of corrosive agents in the stomach can induce gastritis. Intrinsic substances such as bile or ingested substances such as acids, alkali, and corrosive agents can induce an inflammatory response and subsequent gastritis.

Any condition that causes hypovolemia or hypotension, or both, can lead to gastritis. Ulcer formation may ultimately result. This may be a major causative factor in intensive care unit patients who develop gastritis and upper GI bleeding.

Other causes of gastritis include radiation, autoimmune reactions, Crohn's disease, and sarcoidosis. These disorders can be diagnosed only by biopsy.

Clinical Features

There are no symptoms that are characteristic of gastritis. Acute gastritis may cause abdominal pain, nausea, and vomiting, although most patients are asymptomatic unless ulcers or other complications develop. By definition, it is not possible to diagnose gastritis or gastropathy on the basis of clinical features alone. However, a good clinical history such as recent NSAID use or alcohol ingestion in the setting of the foregoing symptoms supports a presumptive clinical diagnosis of gastritis.

Acute infection with *H. pylori* may cause epigastric abdominal pain, nausea, and vomiting. Systemic signs such as fever are usually absent. Symptoms may last days to weeks. If the infection goes untreated, chronic gastritis may result. Patients with phlegmonous gastritis usually appear toxic. Patients with gastritis as a result of decreased mucosal blood flow may present with symptoms of abdominal pain and upper GI bleeding in addition to those of their underlying disease.

Complications of gastritis include perforation and gastric outlet obstruction.

Diagnostic Strategies

Because the presumptive diagnosis of gastritis is made empirically, no specific diagnostic tests are necessary. Ancillary tests should be ordered as clinically indicated to rule out other possible diagnoses or to assess for complications of gastritis such as bleeding, obstruction, or perforation.

Differential Considerations

Before making the diagnosis of gastritis, other diseases that cause nausea, vomiting, and upper abdominal pain must be excluded. These include pancreatitis, biliary tract disease, and small bowel obstruction. The possibility of an acute coronary syndrome should also be considered, particularly in elders.

Management

Therapy of presumptive gastritis should be directed toward any suspected underlying etiology. Acid suppression may improve symptoms of dyspepsia in patients taking NSAIDs. Patients with persistent symptoms should be referred to a gastroenterologist for further diagnostic evaluation.

PEPTIC ULCER DISEASE

Perspective

Gastric and duodenal ulcers are usually grouped together as peptic ulcer disease (PUD) because of the similarity in their pathogenesis and treatment. Approximately 4 million people in the United States are affected by PUD each year.[67] The annual cost to the health care system is estimated to be over $15 billion.[68] Increased understanding of the etiology and pathogenesis of PUD over the past decade has led to the advent of new and effective therapies. PUD is now considered to have two main etiologies: *H. pylori* infection and NSAID use. Approximately 1% of PUD is caused by increased levels of circulating gastrin from gastrin-secreting tumors (Zollinger-Ellison syndrome). These patients have increased parietal cell mass and hypersecretion of acid leading to ulcer formation.

Principles of Disease

Histologically, the stomach is composed of different types of cells with varying secretory functions. Mucous cells secrete acidic mucus, parietal cells secrete hydrochloric acid (through the hydrogen-potassium adenosine triphosphatase [Na^+,K^+-ATPase], the proton pump) and intrinsic factor, chief cells secrete pepsinogens, and enterochromaffin-like cells release substances such as histamine and gastrin. Acid secreted by the over 1 billion parietal cells can generate a hydrogen ion concentration gradient of greater than 1 million to 1 within the lumen of the stomach.

Many mechanisms exist to protect the gastric mucosa from the digestive effects of the hydrochloric acid, proteolytic enzymes, bile, and other injurious substances to which it is exposed. Normally, a gastric mucosal barrier to intraluminal gastric acid is present and prevents the back-diffusion of hydrogen ions from the gastric lumen. Sodium ions are barred from moving in the opposite direction. This ionic impermeability protects the gastric mucosa from damage in a hostile environment. Damage to the gastric mucosal barrier from any cause (Box 88-2) allows hydrogen ions and digestive enzymes to make contact with the gastric mucosa, leading to inflammation, bleeding, and potential ulceration.

BOX 88-2. Substances and Conditions That Damage the Gastric Mucosal Barrier

Bile
Cigarette smoking
Ethanol
Glucocorticoids
Helicobacter pylori
Nonsteroidal anti-inflammatory drugs
Pancreatic secretions
Shock conditions
Stress

The identification of *H. pylori* has proved to be a landmark discovery that has changed our understanding of PUD. *H. pylori* is an S-shaped, gram-negative rod whose natural habitat is the human stomach between the epithelial cell surface and the overlying mucus. Infection with *H. pylori* is a primary risk factor for development of PUD. It is estimated that 70% to 80% of patients with duodenal ulcer and 60% to 70% of patients with gastric ulcer are infected with *H. pylori*. *H. pylori* is more prevalent in lower socioeconomic groups and is probably spread by the fecal-oral route, although oral-to-oral and iatrogenic transmissions have also been suggested. It is found in all age groups, although it is believed that infection is acquired during childhood. Its presence is believed to cause mucosal inflammation that disrupts the normal defense mechanisms and leads to ulceration. It also increases the risk of gastric carcinoma and, less often, lymphoma. Not all people infected with *H. pylori* develop PUD, and it is unclear what role environmental and host factors (such as diet) play. It is now accepted that almost all non–NSAID-related ulcers are due to *H. pylori*. Eradication of infection with *H. pylori* results in more rapid healing of ulcers, prevents relapse, and diminishes the rate of ulcer complications. The most effective means of diagnosis and optimal management, including the most effective antibiotic regimens, are still being defined. Currently available tests include a urea breath test, urea blood tests, antibody testing, stool antigen testing, and direct mucosal biopsy during endoscopy. As yet, none of these are of practical use for the emergency department patient.

The second most common cause of peptic ulcer formation is the use of NSAIDs. NSAIDs have both a direct and an indirect effect on the gastric mucosa. NSAIDs are weak acids that remain in the nonionized form in the acidic milieu of the stomach lumen. This allows free diffusion into the mucosal cells, where ionization occurs. Because ionized forms cannot cross the cell membrane, the NSAID becomes "ion trapped" within the cell. The increased intracellular concentration of NSAID damages the cell, most likely as a result of inhibition of mucosal prostaglandin secretion, reduced mucus production, and diminished cell turnover.[69] Because administration of enteric-coated NSAIDs that are not absorbed in the stomach does not diminish the incidence of ulcer formation, a second systemic mechanism of injury must also exist. It is believed that the inhibition of cyclooxygenase by NSAIDs leads to a diminished level of protective prostaglandins in the stomach. In addition, the antiplatelet aggregation effect of NSAIDs may increase the amount of bleeding associated with the development of NSAID-induced ulcers. NSAIDs differ in their ulcerogenic potential, with etodolac, nabumetone, and salsalate having lower risks of GI toxicity. The newer cyclooxygenase-2 specific inhibitors (celecoxib, rofecoxib, and valdecoxib) have been shown to have a better GI safety profile than traditional NSAIDs and may be a better choice for high-risk patients. However, they should not be used in patients with known active or healing ulcers. Also, the

safety benefit is lost if patients are concurrently taking aspirin.[70]

Certain patients are at high risk for NSAID-induced gastroduodenal toxicity. These include those with a prior history of an ulcer or hemorrhage, patients older than 60 years, those receiving higher doses of NSAIDS, and those with concurrent use of glucocorticoids or anticoagulants.[71] These patients should be considered for ulcer prophylaxis with misoprostol or lansoprazole.

PUD also occurs in infants and children. Infants with PUD usually present with poor feeding, vomiting, or failure to thrive, but hematemesis may be the first sign. Toddlers and preschool children may have abdominal pain or vomiting and bleeding. Eighty percent of ulcers in this age group are stress ulcers. Older children and adolescents usually have primary PUD, with presentations similar to those of adults.

Clinical Features

Presenting Symptoms

Although 1% to 2% of patients with ulcers are asymptomatic, the most common symptom of PUD is abdominal pain.[72] Classically, ulcer pain is described as nonradiating epigastric pain of a burning, gnawing, or "hunger-like" quality. However, patients may also describe pain in other areas of the abdomen, the chest, or the back; the pain may also be vague or crampy. It usually occurs 2 to 5 hours after a meal or at night. Pain that awakens a patient from sleep between midnight and 3 AM is classical for ulcer disease, because in most people gastric acid output is highest at about 2 AM. Ulcer pain is usually not present on awakening in the morning because gastric acid output is at its lowest at this time. Colicky pain is rarely gastric or duodenal in origin. Well-defined periods of exacerbation and remission are usually present with duodenal ulcer and aid in the diagnosis. A constant pain lasting from weeks to months is uncommonly caused by ulcer disease. Relief of pain after eating is another feature of gastric or duodenal ulcer. The pain from duodenal ulcer is usually worse immediately preceding a meal, and the complex of pain-eating-relief is typical for duodenal ulcer.

Although some patients with ulcers may vomit, alternative diagnoses such as gastric volvulus, gastric outlet obstruction, small bowel obstruction, pancreatitis, or biliary tract disease should be considered in patients who present with epigastric pain and vomiting. Relief of abdominal pain with antacids is an important aspect of the history. Antacids usually afford relief of pain in both PUD and gastritis. Ninety percent of patients with PUD have pain relief with antacids, and 75% with gastritis have relief. Patients with duodenal ulcer usually experience pain relief within 5 minutes after taking an antacid.

Physical findings in patients with PUD are usually minimal. Mild epigastric tenderness may be elicited. A positive stool guaiac may be evidence of a bleeding ulcer, but other causes of occult bleeding must be considered.

Complications

The most serious complications of PUD include hemorrhage, perforation, penetration, and gastric outlet obstruction. Hemorrhage is the most common complication, occurring in 15% of patients. Older patients are at greater risk. Approximately 7% of patients experience perforation, which occurs when an ulcer erodes through the wall and leaks air and digestive contents into the peritoneal cavity. Penetration is pathologically similar to perforation, except that the ulcer erodes into another organ such as the liver (usually from a gastric ulcer) or the pancreas (usually from a duodenal ulcer) instead of into the peritoneal cavity. Gastric outlet obstruction occurs in 2% of ulcer patients as a result of edema and scarring near the gastroduodenal junction. Symptoms may manifest as gastroesophageal reflux, early satiety, weight loss, abdominal pain, and vomiting.

Pain patterns may be helpful in diagnosing some of the complications of PUD. Pain from a perforated duodenal ulcer is usually appreciated first in the epigastrium but becomes generalized within a short time. Vomiting is present in 50% of patients, and peritoneal findings usually result. Pneumoperitoneum commonly occurs after duodenal ulcer perforation, and the accumulated air under the diaphragm may cause referred pain to the shoulder. One or both shoulders may be involved, depending on the location of the free air.

A history of ulcer-like anterior abdominal pain that begins to radiate into the back suggests penetration of a duodenal ulcer. The pain is usually described as steady and is perceived at the level of the lower thoracic and upper lumbar vertebrae. Relief of the pain with antacids and food often vanishes, and the pain becomes refractory to treatment. Also, pain radiation may occur to the chest, right upper quadrant, and left upper quadrant in up to 20% of patients. The sudden onset of pain, especially if unrelated to eating, suggests either ulcer perforation or gastric volvulus.

Diagnostic Strategies

The initial diagnosis of PUD is usually made clinically. Ancillary tests may be of benefit in evaluating possible complications of PUD in patients who present in distress. They may also be of benefit in providing indirect evidence of another disease. A complete blood count may diagnose anemia, and liver enzymes may help elucidate a hepatic or biliary tree etiology. Electrolytes may provide indirect evidence of disease, and amylase and lipase should be considered to rule out pancreatitis and may provide indirect evidence of a posterior penetrating ulcer.

Abdominal and chest radiographs should be ordered if obstruction, perforation, or penetration is suspected or if a pulmonary etiology is being considered, although negative films do not definitively rule out these diagnoses. Electrocardiography should be performed in any patient suspected of having a cardiac etiology for the pain. Any female patient of childbearing age should have a pregnancy test performed. As noted earlier, several methods exist for diagnosing infection with *H. pylori*, although at this time none is of practical application in the emergency department.

Differential Considerations

Fifty percent of patients with symptoms of dyspepsia have no identifiable etiology. These patients are classified as having nonulcer dyspepsia (NUD). The official criteria for diagnosing NUD are chronic recurrent upper abdominal pain or discomfort for a period of at least 1 month, with symptoms present more than 25% of the time, and absence of evidence of organic disease.[73]

NUD may be caused by peptic ulcers that are not yet large enough to appear endoscopically. Gastritis related to hypersecretion of gastric acid, *H. pylori* infection, bile reflux, or viral infection may cause NUD, although these should be identifiable endoscopically or pathologically. Maldigestion or malabsorption of carbohydrates can arise as NUD in patients with lactase deficiency or in patients who consume large quantities of nonabsorbable sugars such as sorbitol, mannitol, and fructose. Intestinal parasites such as *Giardia lamblia* or *Strongyloides stercoralis* may cause NUD, as can chronic pancreatitis. NUD may also be caused by gastric motility disorders, which have been reported in 25% to 60% of patients with NUD. Abnormalities in the biliary tract, such as increased resting pressure of the sphincter of Oddi, or incomplete relaxation of the sphincter upon gallbladder contraction may lead to bile duct distention and pain.[74]

Many other disorders can produce epigastric pain that mimics the pain of an ulcer. It can be difficult to distinguish between gastritis and PUD. The discomfort associated with gastritis is often mild to moderate in severity and described as a hot, burning pain or bloating. In particular, burning pain is twice as common in gastritis as in PUD. Esophageal disorders such as GERD, esophagitis, or esophageal spasm can arise with abdominal symptoms. Mesenteric ischemia ("abdominal angina") should be considered, especially in elder patients and those with underlying vascular disease or atrial fibrillation. Aortic dissection, other intra-abdominal processes such as the biliary tract and pancreatic disease, and atypical presentation of an acute cardiac syndrome or other intrathoracic process should be considered in the differential diagnosis. Finally, abdominal pain may be the presenting symptom in psychiatric patients with somatoform disorder. These patients have an altered perception of visceral pain and have an increased sensation of pain when the stomach or small intestine is dilated.

Management

The initial treatment of presumptive PUD includes lifestyle changes (cessation of smoking and the use of alcohol and aspirin) and initiation of a bland diet with frequent small feedings (although no study has proved the effectiveness of dietary changes). Because PUD is a result of either infection with *H. pylori* or NSAID use, initial treatment should be based on the presumed

BOX 88-3. Suggested Treatment Regimens for *Helicobacter pylori*

Triple Therapy

Clarithromycin 500 mg bid for 14 days

Plus

Amoxicillin 1 g bid for 14 days

Or

Metronidazole 500 mg bid × 14 days

Plus

A proton pump inhibitor (PPI)

Quadruple Therapy

Bismuth subsalicylate (Pepto-Bismol) 525 mg PO qid × 14 days

Plus

Metronidazole 500 mg bid × 14 days

Plus

Tetracycline 500 mg PO qid

Plus

A PPI or H₂ blocker

---

etiology. For NSAID-related ulcers, treatment should begin by discontinuing the offending agent and beginning a PPI. There is probably no benefit in changing to a selective cyclooxygenase-2 inhibitor.

If NSAIDs are not being used by a patient with suspected PUD, it is currently recommended to treat for *H. pylori* infection. Dyspeptic symptoms without proven ulcer may also be an indication for treatment, but that decision may best be left to a gastroenterologist. Antacid therapy may be started with a PPI or H₂ blocker. Nonendoscopic testing for *H. pylori* is available (e.g., antibody detection, urea breath test); however, its role in the evaluation of emergency department patients is not yet defined.

There are a few recommended regimens combining antibiotics with acid-suppressing agents for treatment of *H. pylori* infection (Box 88-3). There are also commercially available combination products that may be prescribed that may assist in compliance (PrevPac, which contains lansoprazole, amoxicillin, and clarithromycin; and Helidac, which contains bismuth subsalicylate, metronidazole, and tetracycline).[75] Most gastroenterologists recommend continued therapy with antisecretory agents following the antibiotic-containing regimens.

H₂ blockers have not been demonstrated to prevent the formation of ulcers when given concurrently with NSAID therapy; PPIs have been demonstrated to be of some benefit and should be used in patients with gastroduodenal ulcers who must continue using NSAIDs.[76]

GASTRIC VOLVULUS

Perspective

Gastric volvulus is a rare cause of severe abdominal pain that occurs when the stomach rotates upon itself more than 180 degrees, creating a closed-loop obstruction. Only 400 cases have been reported in the literature, although its true incidence is unknown because some types of volvulus are intermittent and resolve spontaneously. It most commonly occurs in persons 40 to 50 years of age and is usually associated with the presence of a paraesophageal hernia. Approximately 20% of cases occur in infants younger than 1 year and are due to congenital diaphragmatic defects.[77] If an acute volvulus is not identified and corrected early, it may lead to gastric ischemia, perforation, and death. The mortality from acute gastric volvulus is 15% to 20%.

Principles of Disease

The stomach is fixed at only two points, the esophagocardiac junction and the pylorus. The remainder of the organ is relatively distensible and mobile and can occupy various positions within the abdomen. When a person is supine, the stomach lies entirely above the umbilicus, whereas it descends below the umbilicus in the erect position. Regardless of its position, the stomach maintains its familiar morphology because of ligamentous attachments to the surrounding organs. A primary (or subdiaphragmatic) volvulus occurs when the stabilizing ligaments are too lax or are congenitally abnormal in such a way that the stomach is able to twist upon itself. Approximately one third of cases are of this type.

Secondary (or supradiaphragmatic) volvulus occurs in patients with diaphragmatic defects such as a paraesophageal hiatal hernia, an elevated diaphragm, gastric ulcer or carcinoma, diaphragmatic paralysis, extrinsic pressure on the stomach from other organs, or abdominal adhesions.[78] The combination of one of these factors and ligamentous laxity makes a volvulus more likely to occur.

Gastric volvulus can be classified on the basis of its axis of rotation. The most common form is organoaxial volvulus, which occurs when the stomach twists on its long axis. Less commonly, the stomach folds on its short axis from the lesser to greater curvature and is classified as a mesenteroaxial volvulus. Approximately one third of cases of gastric volvulus are of this type.

Clinical Features

Presenting Symptoms

The presenting features of a gastric volvulus can be variable, depending on the type. Primary volvulus may arise with the sudden onset of severe abdominal pain. The upper abdomen may demonstrate marked distention. Patients with secondary volvulus may have their predominant symptoms in their chest, with pain radiating to the back and shoulders along with accompanying dyspnea. The abdominal examination may be unremarkable. Vomiting is usually present and may be persistent and severe. The combination of severe epigastric pain and distention, vomiting, and inability to pass a nasogastric tube (Borchardt's triad) should increase the level of suspicion for a gastric volvulus.

A volvulus may be chronic if the rotation is minimal and there is no vascular compromise. Symptoms usually consist of mild intermittent upper abdominal pain. Early satiety, dyspnea, bloating, eructation, and upper abdominal fullness may be present. It is unknown how often a chronic volvulus can lead to an acute volvulus.

Complications

If not recognized, volvulus can lead to bowel ischemia and necrosis of the stomach. Untreated, this may lead to shock and death. Fortunately, the frequency of gastric infarction is low (reported between 5% and 28% for organoaxial volvulus) because of the redundant blood supply of the stomach. Other complications include ulceration, perforation, hemorrhage, pancreatic necrosis, and omental avulsion.

Diagnostic Strategies

A plain abdominal radiograph often demonstrates a large, gas-filled loop of bowel in the abdomen or chest. A barium swallow may help visualize the abnormality. There are no laboratory findings specific for volvulus, although elevations in amylase and alkaline phosphatase have been reported.

Differential Considerations

The differential diagnosis of gastric volvulus includes any disease that can arise with sudden upper abdominal pain and vomiting. Perforated peptic ulcer, gastric outlet obstruction, biliary tract disease, and acute pancreatitis should be considered. Symptoms of a volvulus may suggest an acute cardiac syndrome.

Management

The goal of treatment of an acute gastric volvulus is reduction. Mortality increases with delayed diagnosis because of complications of ischemia. Acutely, one should attempt passage of a nasogastric tube, which may occasionally reduce the volvulus. Patients without signs of gastric infarction may undergo an attempt at endoscopic reduction. Following reduction, recurrence is prevented by surgically repairing any predisposing defects.

DYSPHAGIA

Perspective

Precise motor control of the act of swallowing is necessary to ensure that food is successfully transferred from the mouth through the esophagus into the stomach. This includes the muscles of the oropharynx, the upper esophageal sphincter (UES), the body of the esophagus, and the LES. Failure at any one of these levels results in a motility disorder, the primary symptom of which is dysphagia, which literally means "difficulty swallowing."

Principles of Disease

Normal Physiology

Swallowing is a complex phenomenon requiring both voluntary and involuntary skeletal muscle activity. Control of swallowing is coordinated by the swallowing center in the medulla. Afferent sensory input involves the trigeminal, glossopharyngeal, vagus, and spinal accessory cranial nerves; efferent motor activity travels through the trigeminal, facial, glossopharyngeal, vagus, and hypoglossal cranial nerves. The act of swallowing begins a process of both simultaneous and sequential activity in all three esophageal zones. A rapidly progressive pharyngeal contraction transfers the food bolus through a relaxed UES into the esophagus, where a moving ring-like contraction begins in the upper esophagus and propagates distally, making the transition from striated to smooth muscle, culminating with the propulsion of the bolus through a relaxed LES. Three mechanisms have been described that regulate the peristaltic wave, ensuring a smooth transition from the striated muscle in the upper esophagus to the smooth muscle of the middle and lower esophagus and coordination of UES and LES activity. These mechanisms are sequential firing of vagal afferents that begin in the brainstem, an intramural neural mechanism that responds to local stimuli, and myogenic propagation of the contraction through the myocytes themselves.[79]

Physiologically, swallowing can be divided into oral, pharyngeal, and esophageal phases. The oral phase involves preparation of the food bolus by mastication and lubrication. The tongue then propels the bolus into the pharynx by progressive anteroposterior contractions. In the pharyngeal phase of swallowing, events are initiated by delivery of the food bolus to the oropharynx. Voluntary contraction of the pharyngeal muscles seals the nasopharynx by elevation of the soft palate. The oropharynx is sealed by the upward movement of the tongue against the palate. The larynx and hyoid bone are elevated to seal off the respiratory passage. The cricopharyngeus muscle, or UES, relaxes, and the bolus is swept into the esophagus by sequential peristaltic waves initiated in the upper pharynx. During the esophageal phase, the bolus is propelled toward the stomach by sequential peristaltic waves. Peristalsis can be initiated by swallowing or in response to luminal distention of the gut or changes in the pH or osmotic environment of the mucosa. The lower sphincter normally maintains a degree of tone sufficient to prevent reflux of gastric contents. When the food bolus reaches the lower sphincter, the sphincter relaxes to allow passage of the bolus and then regains its degree of resting tone.

Pathophysiology

Disturbances of the interactions between the components of the upper GI tract lead to a motility disorder. The motor disorders of the body of the esophagus are only now beginning to be understood. The major primary esophageal motility disorders are achalasia, diffuse esophageal spasm, hypercontractile esophagus

BOX 88-4. Causes of Dysphagia

Neuromuscular

Vascular
Cerebrovascular accident

Immunologic
Dermatomyositis
Multiple sclerosis
Myasthenia gravis
Polymyositis
Scleroderma

Infectious
Botulism
Diphtheria
Poliomyelitis
Rabies
Sydenham's chorea
Tetanus

Metabolic
Lead poisoning
Magnesium deficiency

Other
Alzheimer's disease
Amyotrophic lateral sclerosis
Brain tumor
Depression
Diabetic neuropathy
Familial dysautonomia
Muscular dystrophies
Metabolic myopathies (e.g., thyrotoxicosis)
Parkinson's disease

Obstructive
Aortic aneurysm
Esophageal motility disorder (e.g., achalasia, diffuse esophageal spasm, hypertensive LES, nutcracker esophagus, etc.)
Esophageal rings
Esophageal stricture
Esophageal webs
Esophagitis
Foreign bodies
Hypertrophic cervical spurs
Inflammatory lesions
Left atrial enlargement
Mediastinal mass
Neoplasm
Thyroid enlargement
Vascular anomalies (e.g., enlarged aorta, aberrant subclavian artery)
Zenker's diverticulum

Other
Alcoholism
Decreased saliva production (Sjögren's syndrome, post-irradiation)
Diabetes
Functional
Gastroesophageal reflux disease
Post-operative

("nutcracker esophagus"), and nonspecific motor disorder. Of these, the only two that are well defined are achalasia and diffuse esophageal spasm. Controversy exists about whether the other entities are true disease states because symptoms are not always associated with manometric abnormalities and correction of the abnormalities does not always result in symptom improvement. Motor disorders may be the primary cause of other esophageal abnormalities such as GERD or esophageal diverticula.

Clinical Features

Dysphagia at any age is abnormal and requires evaluation. Although dysphagia has many causes, a thorough history reveals the diagnosis in most patients (Box 88-4).[80-82] One should determine the location where the bolus sticks; the duration of the dysphagia and whether symptoms are intermittent or progressive; whether solids, liquids, or both are involved; whether it is associated with pain; and whether the patient has any previous gastroesophageal history (e.g., esophageal reflux). Any family history of neurologic disease should be obtained.

The examination should include a thorough evaluation of the head and neck and a detailed neurologic examination. The patient should be observed while swallowing. Difficulty in initiating the swallow, misdi-

rection of the bolus with regurgitation or aspiration, and unusual posturing of the patient when swallowing should be noted. Many patients with neuromuscular disorders depend on gravity to swallow, and having the patient swallow in the prone position may be helpful in diagnosis.

Oropharyngeal Dysphagia

Oropharyngeal causes of dysphagia inhibit the initiation of swallowing. Patients complain that "food gets stuck" upon swallowing, often pointing to the cervical region when describing their symptoms. Coughing, choking, or drooling may be associated. Neuromuscular diseases cause approximately 80% of oropharyngeal dysphagias, with most remaining etiologies being localized structural lesions. Most neuromuscular causes of dysphagia result in misdirection of the bolus, sticking, and the need for repeated swallowing attempts. Patients may drool and turn the head and neck to the side to facilitate swallowing. Liquids, especially of extreme temperatures, usually cause dysphagia more commonly than solids, and symptoms are more often intermittent. Progressive unremitting dysphagia is usually not caused by neuromuscular disorders of the oropharynx. Cerebrovascular accidents are probably the most common cause of neuromuscular dysphagia, especially those involving the vertebrobasilar system and posteroinferior cerebellar arteries and when some degree of dysarthria is present. The mechanism in such cases is pharyngeal weakness, with failure of the cricopharyngeus muscle to relax. Weakness of the tongue may occur, resulting in poor transfer of the bolus, or weakness of the buccal muscles may produce drooling and difficulty initiating the swallow.[83]

The second most common cause of neuromuscular dysphagia is polymyositis or dermatomyositis. These disorders are characterized by inflammatory and degenerative changes in striated muscle that can produce dysphagia from weakness of the palate, pharynx, and upper esophagus. Dysphagia is seen in approximately 25% of patients with these disorders at the time of treatment.[84]

A cause of oropharyngeal dysphagia that deserves particular mention is myasthenia gravis. Two thirds of patients with myasthenia gravis may have dysphagia, and occasionally it is the presenting symptom. The dysphagia becomes progressively worse with repeated swallowing attempts and is temporarily reversible with edrophonium.

Disorders in the pharyngeal phase of swallowing may lead to misdirection of the food bolus, pain, sticking, or multiple swallowing attempts. Tongue weakness can result in oral regurgitation. Inability to seal the nasopharynx because of obstruction or muscular weakness can cause nasal regurgitation. Inefficient laryngeal elevation from muscular weakness or a fixed larynx can result in laryngotracheal aspiration. Delayed aspiration can occur with pharyngeal weakness and with pooling of food in the piriform recesses or in a diverticulum. Inability to contract the pharyngeal muscles is often compounded by failure of the cricopharyngeus to relax. Failure of relaxation of the cricopharyngeus with or without pharyngeal weakness causes misdirection of the food bolus or necessitates repeated swallowing attempts. Inflammatory lesions of the tongue or oropharynx can result in odynophagia and even complete inability to swallow because of pain.

Esophageal Dysphagia

Dysphagia from upper esophageal lesions is usually perceived 2 to 4 seconds after the initiation of swallowing. Dysphagia that the patient localizes to the substernal or retrosternal area may be anatomically accurate, but localization to the neck may be referred from anywhere in the esophagus.

Esophageal dysphagia can be caused by intrinsic or extrinsic lesions. Strictures, webs, rings, and carcinoma are some of the more common causes. Approximately one half of patients with esophageal dysphagia who have no readily identifiable cause may have a motor disorder. Achalasia is a disorder of unknown cause in which there is a marked increase in the resting pressure of the LES and absent peristalsis in the body of the esophagus. Although it can occur at any age, most patients are between 20 and 40 years of age. Dysphagia is the most common presenting symptom and usually begins insidiously with equal frequency for solids

and liquids. Patients may report that maneuvers that increase esophageal pressure (raising arms above the head, standing erect with back straight) help pass the food. Odynophagia from esophageal spasm may also be seen early in the course of achalasia. The symptoms are often worse with rapid eating and during periods of stress. The patient may also report chest pain as a symptom. As dilation occurs above the sphincter, retention of undigested food in the esophagus occurs and the patient may be aware of gurgling while eating. Regurgitation of the undigested material can occur after a meal (prompting consideration of the diagnosis of an eating disorder) or with changes in position or vigorous exercise. The regurgitated food usually has no acid taste, although bacterial contamination may lead to fermentation of the undigested food. Laryngotracheal aspiration may occur, especially at night, and may cause nocturnal coughing. Physical examination is usually unremarkable except for weight loss.[85] Radiographically, a dilated esophagus is seen proximal to a narrowed gastroesophageal junction that has a beak-like appearance.

The second type of intrinsic motor disorder of the esophagus is diffuse esophageal spasm. Manometrically, simultaneous prolonged strong esophageal contractions are noted to be interspersed over normal peristaltic waves. If a barium swallow is obtained during a spasm, findings such as a "corkscrewing" or curling of the esophagus may be noted. Diffuse spasm may be precipitated by swallowing very hot or cold liquids. Symptoms include chest pain, dysphagia, or both.

Nutcracker esophagus is the term used to describe prolonged, high-intensity peristaltic waves. Many authors feel that this represents a variant of diffuse esophageal spasm. Nonspecific motor disorder includes repetitive esophageal contractions, nontransmitted esophageal contractions, or low-amplitude esophageal contractions.[86]

Diagnostic Strategies

Given the myriad causes of dysphagia, a careful history and physical examination are essential. Patients with oropharyngeal dysphagia should have laboratory studies and central nervous system imaging as indicated. Nasopharyngoscopy may be also be performed to rule out obvious structural abnormalities. If these are nondiagnostic, patients may be referred for a swallowing study (videoesophagram). Patients with esophageal dysphagia in whom carcinoma, radiation or caustic injury, or achalasia is suspected should undergo a barium swallow. If a motor disorder is suspected, a swallowing study may prove helpful as well, but this may not detect intermittent dysfunction. In such cases, referral to a gastroenterologist for manometric examination may be required. At that time, additional provocative studies can be performed.

Differential Considerations

The differential diagnosis of lower esophageal dysphagia includes acute coronary syndromes. Substernal chest pain is the main symptom in 80% to 90% of patients with esophageal motility disorders. The chest pain can be similar to angina, described as crushing or squeezing with patterns of radiation similar to those of cardiac chest pain. Nitroglycerin may relieve the pain of spasm as well, further confusing the picture.

Symptoms that suggest an esophageal etiology of chest pain are pain that is prolonged and nonexertional, pain that interrupts sleep, pain related to meals, relief with antacids, and presence of other symptoms of esophageal disease such as heartburn, dysphagia, or regurgitation.[87] Because of considerable overlap in symptoms, the emergency physician must exclude a cardiac diagnosis before attributing chest pain to an esophageal cause.

Management

Appropriate management of the patient with dysphagia is based upon the identified or suspected etiology. Most patients with no readily identifiable etiology can be evaluated in follow-up; however, it is prudent to admit patients who are at high risk for aspiration. Patients in whom an esophageal motility disorder is suspected should be referred to a gastroenterologist because the diagnosis is usually made manometrically. Achalasia is the only motility disorder for which reasonably good studies support specific treatment. Pharmacologic therapy is directed at decreasing the tone of the LES. Nitrates and calcium channel blockers have been used with some success; however, reflux symptoms may be exacerbated.[88] Other therapies used with some degree of success have included botulinum toxin injection, pneumatic dilation, and surgical intervention.

Although no definitive therapy has been described for any of the other motility disorders, the emergency physician should be familiar with those that may be used in the treatment of these disorders. It should be noted that medical therapy of esophageal motility disorders is rather limited, and clinical results are usually minimal. Anticholinergic drugs such as hyoscyamine sulfate (Levsin) or dicyclomine (Bentyl) have also been used because they decrease the amplitude of esophageal peristalsis and LES pressure.[89] These drugs may also exacerbate reflux symptoms because they cause delayed gastric emptying and decreased esophageal peristalsis.

Calcium channel blockers decrease both LES pressure and the amplitude of esophageal contractions. Nifedipine has been used successfully in some patients.[90] Diltiazem has been shown to be effective in patients with nutcracker esophagus.[91] Verapamil has been shown to decrease LES pressure when administered IV to healthy volunteers, but no effects have been noted with an oral dose.[92,93] Psychotropic medications such as alprazolam and trazodone have been used to treat some esophageal motility disorders. Although no study has demonstrated specific beneficial manometric effects, it is believed that the improvement may be secondary to treatment of an underlying functional disorder such as panic attacks or depression.[94]

PHARMACOLOGIC AGENTS FOR UPPER GASTROINTESTINAL DISORDERS

Antacids

By the time most patients present with upper GI complaints, most have already tried some form of antacid therapy because these agents are readily available as over-the-counter preparations. Antacids afford pain relief in most patients with PUD. Doses with low neutralizing capacity (as low as 30 mEq) promote ulcer healing. Antacids may also work by binding bile acids or inhibiting pepsin.

The choice of antacid should be individualized. The magnesium-containing antacids can produce diarrhea in up to 25% of patients. Magnesium-containing antacids can also lead to an increase in serum magnesium levels and should be avoided or used with caution in patients with impaired renal function. Aluminum-containing antacids may lead to constipation, and prolonged use may lead to phosphate depletion. Calcium-containing antacids have been marketed both as neutralizing acid and as a means of calcium supplementation, especially for postmenopausal women. Calcium-containing antacids have been traditionally believed to cause the most acid rebound, a paradoxical increase in gastrin secretion and acid production. Calcium antacids can also lead to constipation, and their excess consumption can lead to hypercalcemia, alkalosis, and renal insufficiency (the milk-alkali syndrome).

Antacids can also decrease the absorption of warfarin, digoxin, some anticonvulsants, and some antibiotics. The recommended dose of antacids in the treatment of PUD is 400 mmol/day divided over four doses, usually delivered 1 and 3 hours after meals and at bedtime. Antacids are the least expensive drugs available to treat PUD, but their use is somewhat limited by side effects and inconvenient dosing schedules.

Histamine Blockers

Histamine is the primary stimulus to gastric acid secretion. It binds to the type 2 histamine receptor (H_2) located on the basolateral portion of the parietal cell to stimulate the release of hydrochloric acid. The discovery of the ability of H_2 blockers to inhibit gastric acid production was a major advance in antiulcer therapy because ulcers cannot develop in the absence of acid. These drugs are highly selective competitive inhibitors of histamine for the H_2 receptor on parietal cells and reduce both the volume of gastric juice and its hydrogen ion concentration. All of the currently available H_2 blockers are rapidly absorbed after an oral dose, reaching peak levels within 1 to 2 hours. All have half-lives of approximately 2 to 3 hours, so the effects last for about 6 hours. Most are now available over the counter in lower dosage strength. H_2 blockers are effective in treating duodenal ulcer and, to a lesser extent, gastric ulcer, although they are not as effective as the PPIs. They are widely prescribed for symptoms of dyspepsia and work well in patients with episodic heartburn. All H₂ blockers are mainly hepatically and renally metabolized with the exception of nizatidine, which is almost exclusively renally metabolized. Dosages of all these agents should be reduced in patients with renal failure.

H₂ blockers are safe and generally well tolerated. Side effects are rare, including central nervous system effects such as somnolence, dizziness, and confusion. Transient increases in liver enzymes may be noted. Some patients may exhibit abnormalities in cardiac conduction, as there are H₂ receptors in the heart. Cimetidine has been shown to cause gynecomastia. Dosing of the various agents is summarized in Table 88-1.

Proton Pump Inhibitors

The H⁺,K⁺-ATPase (proton pump) is located on the apical portion of the parietal cell and is responsible for the production of hydrogen ions in gastric acid. PPIs are the most potent inhibitors of gastric acid secretion. They work by irreversibly binding to stimulated proton pumps to block secretion of hydrogen ions. Although they have no effect on the volume of gastric juice produced, production of acid can be reduced by up to 95%. Both basal and stimulated gastric acid secretions are reduced. The antisecretory effects last up to 72 hours. PPIs should be administered before the first meal of the day, as the number of proton pumps is maximized after a fasting state. At the cellular level, additional proton pumps are continually recruited to produce more acid in response to stimulation; therefore, several doses of a PPI are necessary to achieve maximal antacid effect. The use of these medications on an as-needed basis would not be expected to provide a good clinical response. H₂ blockers are more suitable for this purpose.[95]

PPIs are hepatically metabolized, and dosage should be modified in patients with hepatic failure. Side effects are usually minimal. Although there are questions regarding the safety of long-term acid suppression leading to hypergastrinemia and hypochlorhydria, the 15-year experience with omeprazole has not demonstrated any clinically significant consequences.[96] PPIs may be used at significantly higher dosages in patients with Zollinger-Ellison syndrome.[97] Dosing of the various agents is summarized in Table 88-2. It should be noted that pantoprazole is currently the only PPI available in an intravenous formulation.

Prostaglandins

Prostaglandins exert protective effects on the gastric mucosa by inhibiting acid secretion and decreasing the amount of cyclic adenosine monophosphate generated in response to histamine. Inhibition of gastric acid secretion, increased secretion of mucus and bicarbonate, and stimulation of mucosal blood flow have all been demonstrated.[98] Misoprostol (Cytotec) is an analogue of prostaglandin E₁ with a longer duration of action and greater potency than endogenous prostaglandins. It should be used only for prevention of NSAID-induced gastric ulcers in high-risk patients. The dose is 200 μg four times a day with food, but crampy abdominal pain and diarrhea may require the use of a somewhat less effective dose of 100 μg four times a day.[99] Misoprostol is an abortifacient and therefore is contraindicated in any female patient of childbearing age who is not using contraception.

Other Agents

Sucralfate (Carafate) binds to epithelial cells and especially to ulcerated surfaces, providing a protective layer that inhibits further acid damage. Its mechanism of action is not completely understood, although it has been shown to enhance epithelial growth, suppress acid secretion, and inhibit growth of H. pylori. The usual dose is 1 g four times a day given 30 to 60 minutes before meals.

Bismuth compounds such as bismuth subsalicylate (Pepto-Bismol) decrease pepsin activity, increase mucus secretion, and form a barrier to further acid damage in ulcer craters. They also increase prostaglandin synthesis and retard hydrogen ion diffusion through the mucosal barrier.[100] Bismuth may also help heal ulcers through its bactericidal action on H. pylori. Bismuth compounds are not approved for the treatment of peptic ulcers.

KEY CONCEPTS

- The combined use of glucagon and an effervescent agent can cause rapid relief of acute lower esophageal obstruction in up to 75% of patients.
- Radiographic contrast studies of patients with suspected perforation of the esophagus or stomach should first be performed with water-soluble agents such as Gastrografin.
- GERD treatment includes lifestyle modification and therapy with H₂ receptor antagonists (mild cases) or a proton pump inhibitor (moderate to severe cases).
- Peptic ulcer disease results primarily from NSAID use or infection with H. pylori.
- Proton pump inhibitors are the most effective means of suppressing gastric acid secretion.

REFERENCES

1. Eisen GM, et al: Guideline for the management of ingested foreign bodies. *Gastrointest Endosc* 55:802, 2002.
2. Choudhry U, Boyce HW: Treatment of esophageal disorders caused by medications, caustic ingestion, foreign bodies, and trauma. In Wolfe MM (ed): *Therapy of Digestive Disorders*. Philadelphia, WB Saunders, 2000.
3. Pope CE II: Rings, webs, diverticula. In Sleisenger MH, Fordtran JS (eds): *Gastrointestinal Diseases*, 5th ed. Philadelphia, WB Saunders, 1993.
4. Maves MD, Lloyd TV, Carithers JS: Radiographic identification of ingested disc batteries. *Pediatr Radiol* 16:154, 1985.
5. Eliashar R, et al: Computed tomography diagnosis of esophageal bone impaction: A prospective study. *Ann Otol Rhinol Laryngol* 108:708, 1999.
6. Watanabe K, et al: The usefulness of computed tomography in the diagnosis of impacted fish bones in the oesophagus. *J Laryngol Otol* 112:360, 1998.
7. Applegate KE, et al: Spiral CT scanning technique in the detection of aspiration of LEGO foreign bodies. *Pediatr Radiol* 31:836, 2001.

8. Doraiswamy NV, et al: Metal detector and swallowed metal foreign bodies in children. *J Accid Emerg Med* 16:123, 1999.

9. Brady PG: Esophageal foreign bodies. *Gastroenterol Clin North Am* 20:691, 1991.

10. Taylor RB: Esophageal foreign bodies. *Emerg Med Clin North Am* 5:301, 1987.

11. Eisen GM, et al: Complications of upper GI endoscopy. *Gastrointest Endosc* 55:784, 2002.

12. Taylor RB: Esophageal foreign bodies. *Emerg Med Clin North Am* 5:301, 1987.

13. Campbell JB, Quattromani FL, Foly LC: Foley catheter removal of blunt esophageal foreign bodies: Experience with 100 consecutive children. *Pediatr Radiol* 13:116, 1983.

14. Ginaldi S: Removal of esophageal foreign bodies using a Foley catheter in adults. *Am J Emerg Med* 3:64, 1985.

15. Glauser J, et al: Intravenous glucagon in the management of esophageal food obstruction. *J Am Coll Emerg Physicians* 8:228, 1979.

16. Ferrucci JT, Long JA: Radiologic treatment of food impaction using intravenous glucagon. *Radiology* 125:25, 1977.

17. Votey S, Dudley JP: Emergency ear, nose, and throat procedures. *Emerg Med Clin North Am* 7:117, 1989.

18. Mohammed SH, et al: Dislodgement of impacted esophageal foreign bodies with carbonated beverages. *Clin Radiol* 37:589, 1986.

19. Rice BT, et al: Acute esophageal food impaction treated by gas-forming agents. *Radiology* 146:299, 1983.

20. Kaszar-Siebert DJ, et al: Treatment of acute esophageal food impaction with a combination of glucagon, effervescent agent, and water. *AJR Am J Roentgenol* 154:533, 1990.

21. Robbins MI, et al: Treatment of acute esophageal food impaction with glucagon, an effervescent agent, and water. *AJR Am J Roentgenol* 162:325, 1994.

22. Choudhry U, Boyce HW: Treatment of esophageal disorders caused by medications, caustic ingestion, foreign bodies, and trauma. In Wolfe MM (ed): Therapy of Digestive Disorders. Philadelphia, WB Saunders, 2000.

23. Webb WA: Management of foreign bodies of the upper gastrointestinal tract. *Gastroenterology* 94:204, 1988.

24. Faigel DO, Fennerty MB: Miscellaneous diseases of the esophagus. In Yamada T, et al (eds): *Textbook of Gastroenterology*. Philadelphia, Lippincott Williams & Wilkins, 1999.

25. Webb WA: Management of foreign bodies of the upper gastrointestinal tract. *Gastroenterology* 94:204, 1988.

26. Brady PG: Esophageal foreign bodies. *Gastroenterol Clin North Am* 20:691, 1991.

27. Webb WA: Management of foreign bodies of the upper gastrointestinal tract. *Gastroenterology* 94:204, 1988.

28. Eisen GM, et al: Guideline for the management of ingested foreign bodies. *Gastrointest Endosc* 55:804, 2002.

29. Ahmed A, Aggarwal M, Watson E: Esophageal perforation: A complication of nasogastric tube placement. *Am J Emerg Med* 16:64, 1998.

30. Richards CF: Piriform sinus perforation during esophageal-tracheal Combitube placement. *J Emerg Med* 16:37, 1998.

31. Faigel Douglas O, et al: Miscellaneous diseases of the esophagus. In Yamada T (ed): *Textbook of Gastroenterology*. Philadelphia, Lippincott Williams & Wilkins, 1999.

32. Datta CK, Brannon JV: Spontaneous rupture of esophagus (Boerhaave syndrome): A review of literature and a case presentation. *W Va Med J* 75:180, 1979.

33. Younes Z, Johnson D: The spectrum of spontaneous and iatrogenic esophageal injury. *J Clin Gastroenterol* 29:306, 1999.

34. Baehr PH, McDonald GB: Esophageal disorders caused by infection, systemic illness, medications, radiation, and trauma. In Feldman M, Sleisenger MH, Scharscmidt BF (eds): *Sleisenger and Fordtran's Gastrointestinal and Liver Disease*, 6th ed. Philadelphia, WB Saunders, 1998.

35. Orringer MB: Tumors, injuries, and miscellaneous conditions of the esophagus. In Greenfield LJ (ed): *Surgery: Scientific Principles and Practice*. Philadelphia, JB Lippincott, 1993.

36. Baehr PH, McDonald GB: Esophageal disorders caused by infection, systemic illness, medications, radiation, and trauma. In Feldman M, Sleisenger MH, Scharscmidt BF (eds): *Sleisenger and Fordtran's Gastrointestinal and Liver Disease*, 6th ed. Philadelphia, WB Saunders, 1998.

37. Niezgoda JA, McMenamin P, Graeber GM: Pharyngoesophageal perforation after blunt neck trauma. *Ann Thorac Surg* 50:615, 1990.

38. Sawyer R, Phillips C, Vakil N: Short- and long-term outcome of esophageal perforation. *Gastrointest Endosc* 41:130, 1995.

39. Kikendall JW: Pill esophagitis. *J Clin Gastroenterol* 28:298, 1999.

40. Swann LA, Munter DW: Esophageal emergencies. *Emerg Med Clin North Am* 14:557, 1996.

41. Banerjee S, et al: Treatment of gastrointestinal infections. *Gastroenterology* 118:S48, 2000.

42. Faigel DO, Fennerty MB: Miscellaneous disease of the esophagus. In Yamada T, et al (eds): *Textbook of Gastroenterology*. Philadelphia, Lippincott Williams & Wilkins, 1999.

43. Nebel OT, Frones MF, Castell DO: Symptomatic gastroesophageal reflux: Incidence and precipitating factors. *Am J Dig Dis* 21:953, 1976.

44. Kahrilas PJ: GERD pathogenesis, pathophysiology, and clinical manifestations. *Cleve Clin J Med* 70(Suppl 5):S4, 2003.

45. Mittal RK: Hiatal hernia: myth or reality? Proceedings of a symposium: First Multi-Disciplinary International Symposium on Supraesophageal Complications of Reflux Disease. *Am J Med* 103:33S, 1997.

46. Cameron AJ: Barrett's esophagus: Prevalence and size of hiatal hernia. *Am J Gastroenterol* 94:2054, 1999.

47. Harding SM, et al: Asthma and gastroesophageal reflux: Acid suppressive therapy improves asthma outcome. *Am J Med* 100:395, 1996.

48. Larrain A, et al: Medical and surgical treatment of nonallergic asthma associated with gastroesophageal reflux. *Chest* 99:1330, 1991.

49. Sontag SJ: Gastroesophageal reflux and asthma. Proceedings of a Symposium: First Multi-Disciplinary International Symposium on Supraesophageal Complications of Reflux Disease. *Am J Med* 103:84S, 1997.

50. Ing AJ: Cough and gastroesophageal reflux. Proceedings of a Symposium: First Multi-Disciplinary International Symposium on Supraesophageal Complications of Reflux Disease. *Am J Med* 103:91S, 1997.

51. Gaynor EB: Gastroesophageal reflux as an etiologic factor in laryngeal complications of intubation. *Laryngoscope* 98:972, 1998.

52. Kahrilas PJ: Gastroesophageal reflux disease. *JAMA* 276:983, 1996.

53. Katz PO: Treatment of gastroesophageal reflux disease: Use of algorithms to aid in management. *Am J Gastroenterol* 94(Suppl):S3, 1999.

54. Davies HA: Anginal pain of esophageal origin: Clinical presentation, prevalence, and prognosis. *Am J Med* 92:5S, 1992.

55. DeVault KR, Castell DO: Updated guidelines for the diagnosis and treatment of gastroesophageal reflux disease. *Am J Gastroenterol* 94:1434, 1999.

56. Dent J, et al: An evidence-based appraisal of reflux disease management: The Genval Workshop Report. *Gut* 44(Suppl 2):1, 1999.

57. Fisher RS: Treatment of gastroesophageal reflux disease. In Wolfe MM (ed): *Therapy of Digestive Disorders.* Philadelphia, WB Saunders, 2000.

58. Wolfe MM: H2-receptor antagonists vs OTC medications: How beneficial have they been? *Pract Gastroenterol* 20:10, 1996.

59. Chiba N, et al: Speed of healing and symptom relief in grade II to IV gastroesophageal reflux disease: A meta-analysis. *Gastroenterology* 112:1798, 1997.

60. Fisher RS: Treatment of gastroesophageal reflux disease. In Wolfe MM, et al (eds): *Therapy of Digestive Disorders.* Philadelphia, WB Saunders, 2000.

61. Maton PN: Profile and assessment of GERD pharmacotherapy. *Cleve Clin J Med* 70(Suppl 5):52, 2003.

62. Pandolfino JE, et al: Motility-modifying agents and management of disorders of gastrointestinal motility. *Gastroenterology* 118(Suppl):S32, 2000.

63. Williams RM, et al: Multicenter trial of sucralfate suspension for the treatment of reflux esophagitis. *Am J Med* 83:61, 1987.

64. Richter JE: A critical review of current medical therapy for gastroesophageal reflux disease. *J Clin Gastroenterol* 8:72, 1986.

65. Yardley JH, Hendrix TR: Gastritis, gastropathy, duodenitis, and associated ulcerative lesions. In Yamada T (ed): *Textbook of Gastroenterology*, 3rd ed. Philadelphia, Lippincott Williams & Wilkins, 1999.

66. Tytgat GNJ: Gastritis. In Bouchier IAD, et al: *Gastroenterology: Clinical Science and Practice*, 2nd ed. Philadelphia, WB Saunders, 1993.

67. Munnangi S, Sonnenberg A: Time trends of physician visits and treatment patterns of peptic ulcer disease in the United States. *Arch Intern Med* 157:1489, 1997.

68. Del Valle J, et al: Acid peptic disorders. In Yamada T (ed): *Textbook of Gastroenterology*, 3rd ed. Philadelphia, Lippincott Williams & Wilkins, 1999.

69. Del Valle J, et al: Acid peptic disorders. In Yamada T (ed): *Textbook of Gastroenterology*, 3rd ed. Philadelphia, Lippincott Williams & Wilkins, 1999.

70. Cryer B: Nonsteroidal anti-inflammatory drug injury. In Sleisenger MH, Fordtran JS (eds): *Gastrointestinal Diseases*, 5th ed. Philadelphia, WB Saunders, 1993, p 419.

71. Lanza FL: A guideline for the treatment and prevention of NSAID-induced ulcers. Members of the Ad Hoc Committee on Practice Parameters of the American College of Gastroenterology. *Am J Gastroenterol* 93:2037, 1998.

72. Kuipers EJ, et al: The prevalence of *Helicobacter pylori* in peptic ulcer disease. *Aliment Pharmacol Ther* 9(Suppl 2):59, 1995.

73. Talley NJ, et al: Functional dyspepsia: A classification with guidelines of diagnosis and management. *Gastroenterol Int* 4:145, 1991.

74. Fisher RS, Parkman HP: Management of nonulcer dyspepsia. *N Engl J Med* 339:1376, 1998.

75. Howden CW, Hunt RH: Guidelines for the management of *Helicobacter pylori* infection. *Am J Gastroenterol* 93:2330, 1998.

76. Wolfe MM, et al: Acid suppression: Optimizing therapy for gastroduodenal ulcer healing, gastroesophageal reflux disease, and stress-related erosive syndrome. *Gastroenterology* 118(Suppl):S19, 2000.

77. Miller DL, et al: Gastric volvulus in the pediatric population. *Arch Surg* 126:1146, 1991.

78. Godshall D, Mossallam U, Rosenbaum R: Gastric volvulus: Case report and review of the literature. *J Emerg Med* 17:837, 1999.

79. Diamant NE: Neuromuscular mechanisms of primary peristalsis. Proceedings of a Symposium: First Multi-Disciplinary International Symposium on Supraesophageal Complications of Reflux Disease. *Am J Med* 103:40S, 1997.

80. Mathog RH, Fleming SM: A clinical approach to dysphagia. *Am J Otolaryngol* 13:133, 1992.

81. Richter JE: Heartburn, dysphagia, odynophagia, and other esophageal symptoms. In Sleisenger MH, Fordtran JS (eds): *Gastrointestinal Diseases*, 5th ed. Philadelphia, WB Saunders, 1993.

82. Hess GP: An approach to throat complaints: Foreign body sensation, difficulty swallowing, and hoarseness. *Emerg Med Clin North Am* 5:313, 1987.

83. Seaman WB: Pharyngeal and upper esophageal dysphagia. *JAMA* 235:2643, 1976.

84. Tandan R, Bradley WG: Dermatomyositis and polymyositis. In Isselbacher KJ, et al (eds): *Harrison's Principles of Internal Medicine*. New York, McGraw-Hill, 1994.

85. Pitcher JL: Dysphagia in the elderly: Causes and diagnosis. *Geriatrics* 28:64, 1973.

86. Clouse RE: Motor disorders. In Sleisenger MH, Fordtran JS (eds): *Gastrointestinal Diseases*, 5th ed. Philadelphia, WB Saunders, 1993.

87. Alban-Davies H, et al: Angina-like esophageal pain: Differentiation from cardiac pain by history. *J Clin Gastroenterol* 7:477, 1985.

88. Kikendall JW, Mellow MH: Effect of sublingual nitroglycerin and long-acting nitrate preparations on esophageal motility. *Gastroenterology* 79:703, 1980.

89. Katzka DA, Castell DO: Esophageal motor disorders and chest pain. In Bayless TM (ed): *Current Therapy in Gastroenterology and Liver Disease*, 4th ed. St Louis, Mosby, 1994.

90. Richter JE, et al: Oral nifedipine in the treatment of noncardiac chest pain in patients with the nutcracker esophagus. *Gastroenterology* 93:21, 1987.

91. Cattau EL Jr, et al: Diltiazem therapy for symptoms associated with the nutcracker esophagus. *Am J Gastroenterol* 86:272, 1991.

92. Becker BS, Burakoff R: The effect of verapamil on lower esophageal sphincter pressure in normal subjects and in achalasia. *Am J Gastroenterol* 78:773, 1983.

93. Allen M, et al: Comparison of calcium channel blocking agents and an anticholinergic agent on esophageal function. *Aliment Pharmacol Ther* 1:153, 1987.

94. Katzka DA, Castell DO: Esophageal motor disorders and chest pain. In Bayless TM (ed): *Current Therapy in Gastroenterology and Liver Disease*, 4th ed. St Louis, Mosby, 1994.

95. Wolfe MM, et al: Acid suppression: Optimizing therapy for gastroduodenal ulcer healing, gastroesophageal reflux disease, and stress-related erosive syndrome. *Gastroenterology* 118(Suppl):S9, 2000.

96. Laine L, et al: Potential gastrointestinal effects of long-term acid suppression with proton pump inhibitors. *Aliment Pharmacol Ther* 14:651, 2000.

97. Shamburek RD, Schubert ML: Control of gastric acid secretion. *Gastrointest Pharmacol* 21:527, 1992.

98. Walt RP: Misoprostol for the treatment of peptic ulcer and antiinflammatory drug-induced gastroduodenal ulceration. *N Engl J Med* 327:1575, 1992.

99. Graham DY, Agrawal NM, Roth SH: Prevention of NSAID-induced gastric ulcer with misoprostol: Multicentre, double-blind, placebo-controlled trial. *Lancet* 2:1277, 1988.

100. Hixson LJ, et al: Current trends in the pharmacotherapy for gastroesophageal reflux disease. *Arch Intern Med* 152:717, 1992.

HEPATIC DISORDERS

The liver is one of the largest organs in the body, serving a multitude of critical functions. The average weight of the normal adult liver is 1500 g. It receives approximately 30% of the resting cardiac output through the portal vein and the hepatic artery. The liver can be affected by a variety of disorders, and because of its varied synthetic and metabolic functions, liver disease may manifest with a broad range of clinical signs and symptoms. Acute and chronic diseases of the liver are common in the general population and represent a common cause for presentation to the emergency department.

Hepatitis

Perspective

Hepatitis is a generic term referring to inflammation of the liver. Hepatitis is most commonly a consequence of viral infection but can be secondary to bacterial, fungal, or parasitic infection; a result of toxic exposure; a side effect of prescribed medication; or a consequence of an immunologic disorder. Hepatitis in its generic context represents the most common variety of liver disease encountered by the emergency physician.

Viral Hepatitis

Although many viruses are associated with some degree of measurable liver inflammation, the most significant and potentially severe cases of viral hepatitis are caused by type A (infectious), type B (serum), type C (posttransfusion), and delta viruses. Although a common cause of hepatitis, Epstein-Barr virus, the causative agent of mononucleosis, is more important clinically for its nonhepatic effects.

Epidemiology

The number of cases of hepatitis A has declined steadily from a rate of 11.7 cases per 100,000 in 1997 to 4.0 cases per 100,000 in 2001.[1,2] The number of reported cases of hepatitis B declined by more than 60% in the interval between 1990 and 2001, and the number of new cases of hepatitis C declined by about 80% during this time period.[1] The reduced rates of hepatitis A and B are most likely a consequence of broad use of effective vaccines, and hepatitis C rates are probably down because of modern blood bank screening techniques and possibly reduced risk behaviors.[3]

Hepatitis A virus (HAV), the causative agent of hepatitis A, is an RNA enteroviral picornavirus. It is spread by the fecal-oral route either directly or through contaminated water or foodstuffs. Transmission by blood is a theoretical possibility but is exceedingly rare. HAV can occur sporadically but is notorious for its association with epidemics generally linked to common source outbreaks. HAV infection is common worldwide; serologic evidence of previous infection exists in almost 100% of the adult population in some regions. In the United States, close to half of all urban-dwelling adults are seropositive for antibody for HAV. Approximately one third of reported cases occur in children younger than 15 years, and the fewest cases are in patients older than 40.[4] The incidence of hepatitis A infection varies among ethnic groups. In the United States, the incidence among American Indians and Alaskan natives is 121 per 100,000 population: Asians have an incidence of 5 per 100,000 population.[4] High rates of seropositivity in association with the relatively small number of reported episodes support the idea that many cases may be asymptomatic. Occult disease appears to be more common in children, and 70% may be asymptomatic.[4] The typical incubation period for hepatitis A is 30 days, with a range of 15 to 45 days. Viremia is of relatively short duration and is most prominent before the onset of symptoms. Fecal shedding and the period of greatest infectivity occur before the onset of symptomatic disease and have generally waned by the time jaundice appears (Figure 89-1). HAV is not associated with a chronic carrier state.

Hepatitis B virus (HBV) is contained in a 42-nm structure called the *Dane particle*. Within this enveloped virion are the viral DNA, DNA polymerase, hepatitis B surface antigen (HBsAg), and hepatitis B core antigen (HBcAg). Hepatitis B e antigen (HBeAg), detectable in the serum of infected patients, is thought to be a degradation product of HBcAg.[5] Compared with HAV, for which there is only a single antigenic variety, there are eight subtypes of HBV as defined by surface antigen. HBV is principally transmitted by parenteral exposure but can also be transmitted by intimate contact. The highest rates of infection are among intravenous (IV) drug users and homosexual men. Blood transfusion, previously a common source of infection, has been eliminated because of modern blood bank screening techniques.

HBsAg has been detected in a variety of bodily secretions, including saliva, semen, stool, tears, urine, and vaginal secretions. Although the presence of HBsAg is

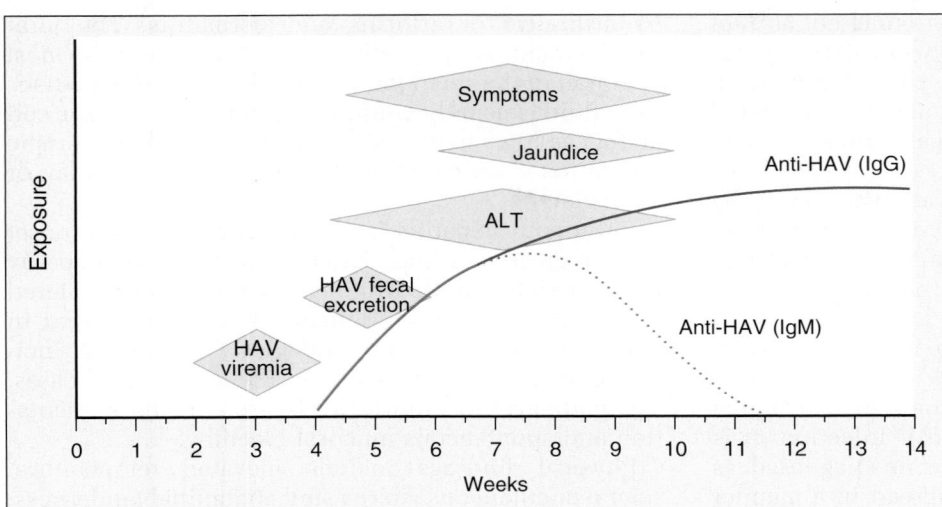

Figure 89-1. Acute hepatitis A virus (HAV) infection. ALT, alanine aminotransferase; IgG, immunoglobulin G.

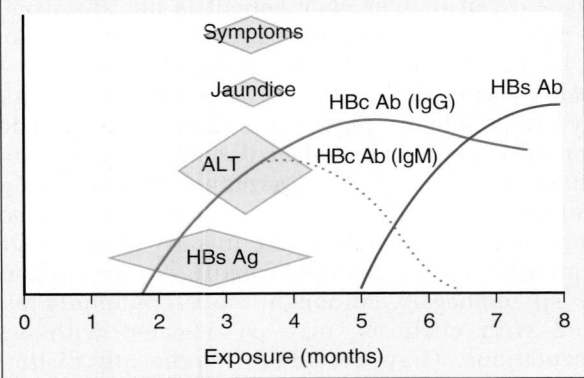

Figure 89-2. Acute hepatitis B virus infection. Ab, antibody; Ag, antigen; ALT, alanine aminotransferase; HBc, hepatitis B core; HBs, hepatitis B surface; IgG, immunoglobulin G.

Table 89-1. Prevalence of Hepatitis B Serologic Markers

Population	HBsAg (%)	All Markers
Immigrants from areas with endemic HBV	13	70-85
Intravenous drug users	7	60-80
Homosexual males	6	35-80
Household contacts of HBV carriers	3-6	30-60
Health care workers, frequent blood exposure	1-2	15-30
Health care workers, infrequent blood exposure	0.3	3-10
Prisoners (men)	1-8	10-80
Healthy adults, first time blood donors	0.3	3-5

HBsAg, hepatitis B surface antigen; HBV, hepatitis B virus.
Modified from Protection against viral hepatitis. Recommendations of the Immunization Practices Advisory Committee (ACIP). *MMWR Recomm Rep* 39(RR-2):1, 1990.

not synonymous with infectivity, HBV DNA has been identified in several of these fluids and is likely to be infectious. The typical interval between exposure and onset of clinical illness is between 60 and 90 days; however, serologic markers of infection generally appear within 1 to 3 weeks (Figure 89-2).[6] Approximately 10% of adults and 90% of neonates infected with HBV become chronic carriers of HBsAg.[7] These groups serve as important reservoirs of infection and major sources of exposure risk for the health care worker. The overall prevalence of HBsAg in the United States is low but can be significant in certain subpopulations (Table 89-1). Health care workers who routinely come in contact with blood have a prevalence of HBsAg of 1% to 2%, and 15% to 30% show serologic evidence of previous infection.[8]

What was historically referred to as non-A non-B hepatitis is caused by at least two distinct RNA viruses, hepatitis C and hepatitis E. Hepatitis C, linked to transfusions, is common in the United States. Hepatitis E, which is associated with fecal-oral transmission, is encountered most often in Asia, Africa, and the Soviet Union. The historic risk of hepatitis in patients receiving blood transfusions was about 0.45% per unit transfused. The screening of donor blood for surrogate markers (aminotransferases) and antibody to hepatitis C has decreased this risk to 0.03% per unit.[9] Although hepatitis C is most often associated with transfusions, only 10% of patients with this disease report a previous history of having received blood or blood products. Approximately 4% to 8% of cases are linked to occupational exposure in health care workers, and 23% to 60% are associated with IV drug use.[10] Patients infected with human immunodeficiency virus (HIV) have an incidence of coinfection with hepatitis C of 15% to 30%. This rate approaches 50% to 90% in those who acquired HIV by parenteral drug use.[8] In 40% to 57% of cases of hepatitis C, no source of infection is identified.[10] The incubation period of hepatitis C is 30 to 90 days, with a mean of 50 days. Hepatitis E has an incubation period of 15 to 60 days. Approximately 50% of patients with hepatitis C go on to develop chronic hepatitis, and cirrhosis develops in 20% of this group within a decade.[11] In the United States it is estimated that 2.7 million people are chronically infected with HCV.[12]

Hepatitis delta virus (HDV) was discovered by Rizzetto and colleagues in 1977 in liver specimens from patients with chronic HBV infection.[13] It is a defective RNA virus that can infect only patients who are actively producing HBsAg, which is required for its viral coating. In the United States the incidence of HDV antibody is between 4% and 30% of patients with chronic HBV infection.[14,15] As a consequence of the routine association with chronic HBV infection, it is likely that many cases of HDV are misdiagnosed as acute or reactivated HBV. HDV is spread in a manner similar to HBV, being most common among IV drug users, promiscuous homosexual men, and hemophiliacs. Infection with HDV can occur either concomitantly with HBV (coinfection) or after earlier HBV infection (superinfection). In cases of coinfection, the course of the illness is generally dominated by HBV; however, HDV seems to be associated with an increased risk of fulminant disease.[16] In cases of superinfection, the presentation may be acute self-limited disease to fulminant hepatitis or chronic infection.

Hepatitis G virus (HGV), also referred to as hepatitis GB virus type C, is the most recently identified virus associated with hepatitis. It is an RNA virus in the Flaviviridae family. Transmission of HGV seems to occur through blood transfusion, through parenteral exposure to blood or blood products, and possibly during intimate sexual contact. The virus has been identified in patients with acute and chronic hepatitis. However, it is generally thought to be an innocent bystander with disease manifestations attributed to coinfection with another hepatitis virus.[17,18]

Principles of Disease

The pathophysiology of viral hepatitis is not completely understood. In the most common varieties of hepatitis, liver injury appears to be related to the development of the immunologic response to infection rather than to the cytopathologic effect of the virus. HDV appears to be an exception, having significant direct cytotoxic potential.

Clinical Features

The clinical presentation of viral hepatitis is highly variable. A significant number, possibly a majority, of cases are asymptomatic. The protean nature of symptoms and the common occurrence of anicteric disease can result in misdiagnosis. The most common symptoms are malaise, fever, and anorexia, followed by nausea, vomiting, abdominal discomfort, and diarrhea. The first symptom leading to physician consultation is commonly jaundice. A small number of patients with hepatitis B develop a prodromal illness characterized by arthralgia or arthritis and dermatitis. The joint involvement is generally polyarticular and is most common in the small joints of the hands and the wrists. Joint fluid is usually noninflammatory but can have cell counts as high as 90,000 cells/mm^3. The characteristic dermatitis is urticarial but may be macular, papular, or petechial.

Fulminant hepatitis is characterized by acute onset and progresses to hepatic failure and encephalopathy over a period of days. Although most often encountered with HBV and HDV, fulminant hepatitis can occur in association with all viral etiologies.[19] The overall incidence of fulminant hepatitis is 1% to 2% of all cases. The hallmarks of fulminant disease are altered mentation and spontaneous mucosal bleeding.

Physical findings include elevated temperature, scleral or cutaneous icterus, and abdominal tenderness. If significant vomiting has occurred, tachycardia and supine or orthostatic hypotension may be noted. Hepatomegaly may be detected and is generally characterized by a smooth, homogeneous, and tender liver surface. Even if liver enlargement is not appreciated, the patient often has tenderness to percussion over the lower right ribs. Scleral icterus is generally noticeable earlier than cutaneous discoloration, particularly in people of pigmented races. Muddy sclera, commonly found among black patients, may obscure or confuse this finding. An alternative in this setting is examination of sublingual or subungual surfaces. Scleral icterus is usually not clinically apparent until serum bilirubin is above 2.5 mg/dL. Spider angiomas and splenomegaly, although more commonly associated with cirrhosis, may be detected with acute presentations. Gray or acholic stools are distinctly uncommon.

Diagnostic Strategies

Laboratory tests are critically important in diagnosing hepatitis and determining the specific cause. The most useful tests are measurements of the hepatic aminotransferases and bilirubin. Typically, hepatitis is associated with elevations (10-fold to 100-fold) of serum aspartate aminotransferase (AST) and alanine aminotransferase (ALT), with ALT generally elevated in excess of AST. Bilirubin may be moderately increased (5 to 10 mg/dL) and occasionally is markedly elevated (15 to 25 mg/dL). Hyperbilirubinemia typically emerges several days to a week or more after the onset of clinical symptoms. Both direct bilirubin and indirect bilirubin are elevated in nearly equal proportions. Alkaline phosphatase and lactate dehydrogenase may be elevated but are rarely more than two to three times normal. The prothrombin time (PT) or international normalized ratio (INR) is useful in assessing the degree of hepatic synthetic dysfunction. Elevation of the PT or INR may be the first clue to a complicated course. The white blood cell count is generally not useful in the diagnosis because values range from low overall counts with a lymphocytic predominance to marked polymorphonuclear leukocytosis.

Table 89-2. Serologic Markers in Hepatitis

Serologic Marker	Abbreviation	Interpretation
Antibody to HAV	Anti-HAV	A combination of IgG and IgM antibody defining infection with HAV, acute or past
IgM antibody to HAV	Anti-HAV IgM	Antibody to HAV, indicating acute infection
Hepatitis B surface antigen	HBsAg	Surface antigen associated with acute or chronic HBV infection
Hepatitis B e antigen	HBeAg	Antigen associated with active infection, acute or chronic, and indicative of high infectivity
Antibody to B surface antigen	HBsAb	Antibody indicative of acute or past infection or immunization
Antibody to B core antigen	HBcAb	A combination of IgG and IgM antibody defining infection with HBV, acute or past
IgM antibody to B core antigen	HBcAb-IgM	Antibody to B core antigen, indicating acute infection with HBV
Antibody to B e antigen	HBeAb	Antibody to e antigen, possibly representing resolving HBV infection and decreased infectivity
Antibody to HDV	Anti-HDV	Antibody defining infection with HDV; HBsAg should be present
Antibody to HCV	Anti-HCV	A new antibody that defines infection with HCV, acute or past

HAV, hepatitis A virus; HBV, hepatitis B virus; HCV, hepatitis C virus; HDV, hepatitis Delta virus; IgG, immunoglobulin G.

Although determination of the precise cause of hepatitis can rarely be achieved in the emergency department, it is important to initiate this evaluation as soon as possible. Identification of the causative agent has a significant impact on prognosis and public health issues. In this regard, it is important to be able to interpret the significance of certain serologic tests (Table 89-2).

Acute hepatitis A is diagnosed by the presence of immunoglobulin M (IgM) HAV antibody, whereas prior infection is determined by the measurement of an immunoglobulin G (IgG) antibody. Acute hepatitis B is characterized by the presence of HBsAg and IgM antibody to HBcAg. HBsAg alone does not establish the diagnosis of acute hepatitis B because it can be either absent late in the course of acute disease or present chronically unrelated to the cause of the current episode. Anti-HBcAg antibody is generally the best indicator of previous HBV infection, whereas anti-HBsAg antibody is the best marker for immunity to HBV.

Currently, the diagnosis of hepatitis C is based on the exposure history and the elimination of other causes. The serologic assay for an antibody to this virus facilitates a definitive diagnosis, but there can be a delay between the onset of symptoms and the development of assayable antibody.[20,21] Furthermore, the HCV test does not distinguish acute from chronic infection.

Diagnosing hepatitis D requires an aggressive search because the disease can easily be mistaken for acute or chronic HBV infection. A serologic test for the antibody to HDV (anti-HDV) is available. The presence of this antibody in conjunction with IgM antibody to HBcAg suggests coinfection with HDV and HBV. Anti-HDV in association with IgG antibody to HBcAg supports the diagnosis of superinfection.

The temporal relationships between infection, clinical symptoms, and serologic responses for the two most common causes of viral hepatitis, HAV and HBV, are delineated in Figures 89-1 and 89-2.

Differential Considerations

The protean nature of the symptoms and signs associated with viral hepatitis makes the differential diagnosis of this disorder quite broad. Beyond a variety of nonhepatic viral illnesses, one must consider all of the infectious, chemical, and immunologic etiologies of hepatic inflammation in addition to biliary tract disease. A viral cause is often suggested by the exposure and medical history but requires serologic tests for confirmation. Alcoholic hepatitis is usually associated with a history of chronic or excessive alcohol consumption, less marked elevation of hepatic transaminases, and AST levels elevated above those of ALT. Extrahepatic obstruction, cholecystitis, and cholelithiasis are excluded by their lack of association with significant elevation of aminotransferases; however, abdominal ultrasonography may be required to eliminate these other causes.

Management

Treatment of viral hepatitis is primarily symptomatic. It is often necessary to correct fluid and electrolyte imbalances secondary to poor oral intake or excessive diarrhea or vomiting. Antiemetics may allow resumption of adequate oral intake, thereby avoiding hospital admission. In the anorectic or nauseous patient, fluid intake should be encouraged, with avoidance of solids until they are palatable. Medications requiring primarily hepatic metabolism generally do not need to be discontinued or the dosage modified unless there is significant hepatic dysfunction. Nonessential drugs with hepatotoxic potential should be avoided. Alcohol consumption should be completely discontinued until signs of liver injury have disappeared. Although a variety of active interventions (e.g., corticosteroid administration) have been suggested, no reliable data suggest that such therapies offer clear benefit; they may even be harmful.

Complications of acute hepatitis are most commonly related to fluid or electrolyte imbalance as a result of inadequate oral intake or refractory emesis. Severe vomiting can result in upper gastrointestinal bleeding as the result of an esophageal tear. The most severe complication of acute disease is the development of liver failure heralded by the emergence of hepatic encephalopathy. Most patients with viral hepatitis have self-limited disease that goes on to symptomatic and histologic resolution in 2 to 4 weeks. Approximately 10% of patients with hepatitis B and as many as 50% of those with hepatitis C develop chronic disease. Some of these patients go on to develop cirrhosis and eventually die.

Disposition

Hospital admission is rarely required for patients with viral hepatitis and is generally reserved for the individual with significant fluid and electrolyte imbalance or refractory vomiting. Patients with less severe illness may require hospitalization for concomitant medical problems or if suitable living arrangements are not available. Altered sensorium or prolongation of the PT beyond 5 seconds or INR beyond 1.5 may suggest fulminant disease or an increased likelihood of a complicated course, necessitating admission for observation. The emergence of fulminant disease should lead to consideration of transfer to a facility that can offer liver transplantation.

Anxiety about disease communicability may affect the ease of a disposition. Patients with possible HAV infection should be advised to practice meticulous personal hygiene, not to share toiletries, and to ensure cleaning of utensils and kitchenware between uses. In patients with suspected HBV or HDV infection, the relatively low risk of transmission in lieu of intimate personal contact or parenteral exposure should be emphasized.

Viral hepatitis is a reportable disease, and the emergency physician is required to notify the health department. The emergency physician should provide immunoprophylaxis for the patient's family members and close personal contacts. Although the nature of prophylaxis depends on the specific viral cause, it is wise to offer γ-globulin to household contacts immediately unless they are known to have been previously immunized, pending serologic determination. Table 89-3 outlines the guidelines for immunoprophylaxis. Patients with HAV infection who process or handle food must not return to work while potentially infectious. Although infectivity is greatly diminished by the time jaundice emerges, it is best to delay return to work until after jaundice has cleared.

Special Considerations

There has been effective preexposure and postexposure prophylaxis for HBV for almost two decades. The rates of seropositivity for HBV infection among health care workers have historically been high compared with the general population (see Table 89-1). Health care workers in an emergency department are at increased risk because of frequent contact with blood and interaction with high-risk patients. Seropositivity among emergency department nurses is 30% and among emergency department physicians is between 12% and 15% (see Table 89-1).[16,22-24] The 1-year risk of infection among nonimmunized emergency department physicians is about 0.25%, with a 30-year risk approaching 7.5%. During a 30-year career, the risk of death from hepatitis B is estimated at 1:540.[25] Markers for hepatitis C were identified in 18% of patients in an inner city emergency department; the health risk this might pose to staff is unknown.

All emergency department personnel involved in patients' care or custodial work should be vaccinated for HBV before or soon after employment. The vaccine is highly effective and associated with minimal acute or delayed toxicity. A complete three-injection series of vaccine produces protective antibody in approximately 95% of individuals.[26] Optimal immunologic response results from deltoid injection.[27] HBV immune globulin (HBIG) is recommended for immediate passive immunization in individuals not previously immunized but exposed to potentially infective material. HBIG alone diminishes the risk of HBV infection by 75%.[28] Unvaccinated, exposed people should receive HBIG 0.06 mL/kg intramuscularly (IM) in addition to the HB vaccine. Concerns related to the potential risk of HIV infection from γ-globulin preparations are unfounded. Figure 89-3 outlines an approach for managing health care workers exposed to blood or other potentially infectious secretions.

A safe and effective vaccine for HAV is available; however, health care workers are not currently on the list of those recommended for routine immunization.[4]

The risk of seroconversion after percutaneous exposure from an HCV-positive source is about 1.8%.[8] Despite health care workers' theoretical risk of blood-borne HCV exposure, the prevalence of HCV infection in this group is approximately 1% to 2%, the same as in the general population.[8] There is no effective vaccine for HCV, and despite some evidence to suggest effectiveness of interferon in acute hepatitis C, there is no accepted pre- or postexposure prophylaxis regimen.[29]

Universal precautions, the use of gloves, masks, protective eye wear, and gowns, represent the first and best means of defense when dealing with potentially infective bodily fluids.

KEY CONCEPTS

- Viral hepatitis is a common emergency department disorder that can be caused by several agents.
- Clinical presentation is highly variable, with many cases, particularly in children, being asymptomatic.
- The process of identifying the etiologic agent should be initiated in the emergency department because it affects both prognosis and public health interventions.
- Many of the etiologic agents of viral hepatitis represent a potential threat to health care workers, necessitating proper precautions when handling potentially infectious body fluids and pre- and postexposure prophylaxis.

Table 89-3. Postexposure Hepatitis Prophylaxis

Hepatitis A	
Nature of Exposure	*Recommended Treatment*
Close personal contact	ISG 0.02 mL/kg IM
Daycare center	
Employee	ISG 0.02 mL/kg IM
Attendee	ISG 0.02 mL/kg IM
School contacts	None
Hospital contacts	None
Workplace contacts	None
Food-borne source	
Within 2 weeks of exposure	ISG 0.02 mL/kg IM
After 2 weeks of exposure	None
After common source outbreaks have begun to occur	None

Hepatitis B

		Exposed Individual	
Nature of Exposure	*Source*	*Unvaccinated*	*Vaccinated*

Percutaneous/mucosal	HBsAG⁺	1. HBIG*
		2. HB vaccine†
			1. Test HBsAb; if −, then
			  a. HBIG
			  b. HB vaccine

	Known source
	  High-risk HBsAg⁺
		1. HB vaccine
		2. Test source; if +, then HBIG
			1. Test HBsAb; if − and source HBsAg⁺
			  a. HBIG
			  b. HB vaccine

	Low-risk HBsAg⁺	1. HB vaccine	1. None
	Unknown source	1. HB vaccine	1. None
Intimate sexual	HBsAg⁺	1. HBIG 2. HB vaccine‡	1. None
Household/workplace	HBsAg⁺	1. None	1. None
Perinatal	HBsAg⁺	1. HBIG§ 2. HB vaccine	NA

Hepatitis C

Unknown benefit from prophylaxis; ISG 0.06 mL/kg IM can be considered for parenteral exposures from patients with evidence of viral hepatitis and negative serologies

Hepatitis Delta

Same as for hepatitis B

*HBIG: hepatitis B immune globulin, dose 0.06 mL/kg IM.
†HB vaccine, hepatitis B vaccine, dose 10-20 μg IM deltoid depending on variety of vaccine used (adequate vaccination requires three injections, so all patients should be referred for follow-up).
‡Vaccine required only if repeated sexual contacts are likely to occur over an extended period of time and the source becomes a chronic carrier.
§Dose of HBIG 0.5 mL.
HBsAg, hepatitis B surface antigen; ISG, immune serum globulin.
Modified from Protection against viral hepatitis. Recommendations of the Immunization Practices Advisory Committee (ACIP). *MMWR Recomm Rep* 39(RR-2):1, 1990.

Alcohol-Related Liver Disease

Perspective

An estimated 10 million people are chronic alcoholics.[30] Alcohol and its metabolites are toxic to most organ systems and contribute to disease or death from many different causes. The liver is the most common site of injury from chronic ethanol ingestion. Alcoholic liver disease is ranked as the fourth leading cause of death among men aged 25 to 64 years living in urban areas. Cirrhosis, most commonly linked to chronic alcohol consumption, is the ninth most common overall cause of death and years of productive life lost.[31]

Principles of Disease

Alcohol is largely eliminated by metabolic degradation in the liver. Approximately 2% to 15% of alcohol is excreted unchanged in the urine or expired air.[32] The precise pathogenesis of alcoholic liver disease is unknown and probably multifactorial. Coexistent malnutrition, accumulation of toxic metabolites (e.g., acetaldehyde), excessive production of reduced nicotinamide adenine dinucleotide (NADH), and induction of microsomal enzymes related to the metabolism of alcohol and alteration of immune function all may play a role.[32]

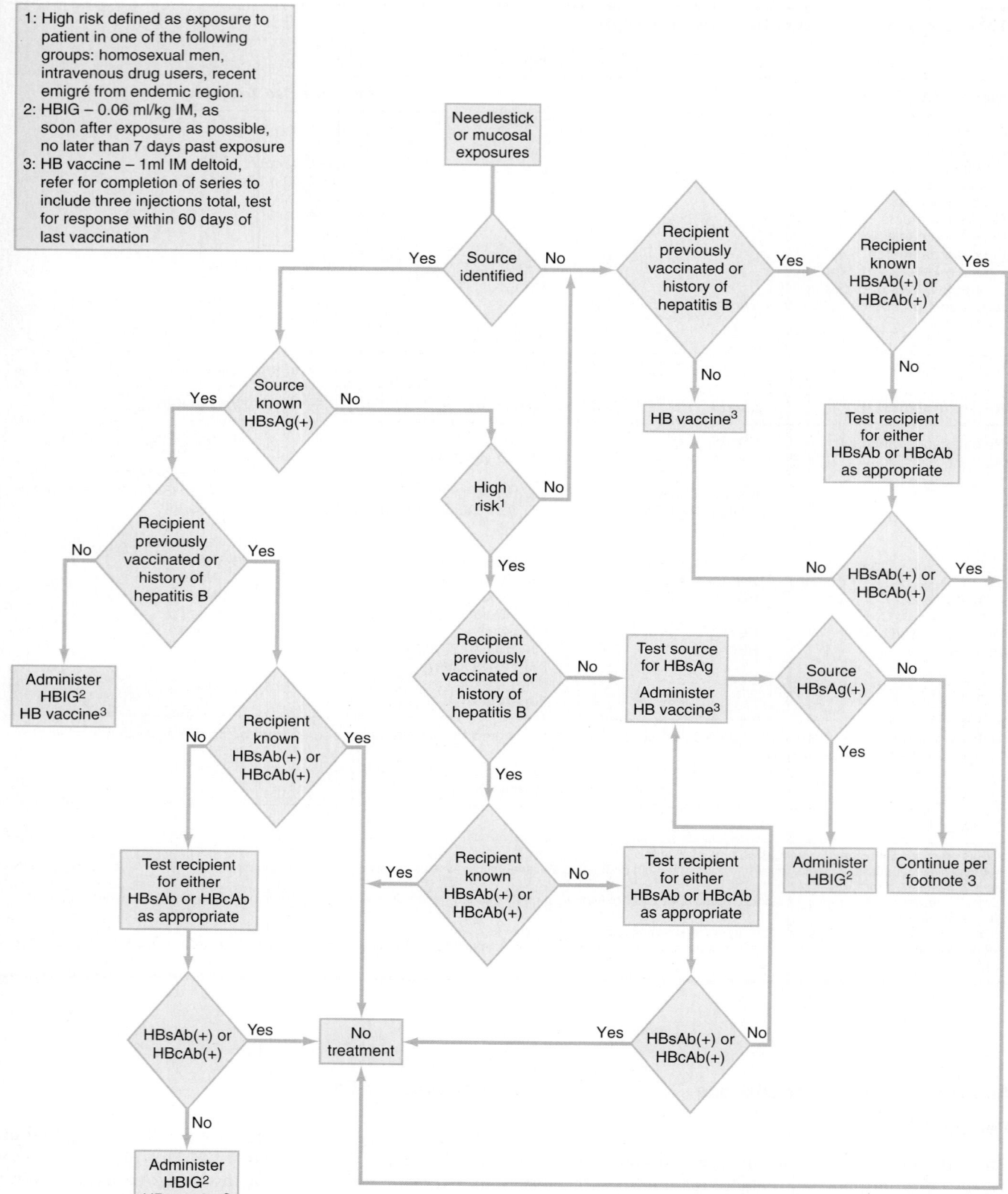

1: High risk defined as exposure to patient in one of the following groups: homosexual men, intravenous drug users, recent emigré from endemic region.
2: HBIG – 0.06 ml/kg IM, as soon after exposure as possible, no later than 7 days past exposure
3: HB vaccine – 1ml IM deltoid, refer for completion of series to include three injections total, test for response within 60 days of last vaccination

Figure 89-3. Management of health care workers exposed to blood or other infectious secretions. Ab, antibody; Ag, antigen; HB, hepatitis B; HBc, HB core; HBIG, HB immune globulin; HBs, HB surface.

Regardless of the precise mechanism of injury, there appears to be genetic heterogeneity in susceptibility to liver damage. Women and possibly American Indians appear to have an increased propensity for injury compared with white men.[33,34] A study of Portuguese adults identified certain histocompatibility antigens associated with increased risk of ethanol-related hepatic injury.[35] Although susceptibility to alcohol varies, there is a rough correlation between the amount of ethanol ingested and the risk of developing liver disease. The risk of liver injury increases as daily consumption exceeds 80 g of ethanol daily in men and 20 g in women. For men this is equivalent to a six-pack of beer, four to six glasses of wine, or three to four mixed drinks daily.[30]

The most common variety of alcohol-induced liver disease is steatosis. Fatty infiltration of the liver is most likely a consequence of altered fatty acid metabolism resulting from a diminished $NAD^+/NADH$ ratio, which favors triglyceride production. Fatty infiltration appears to depend on the duration and amount of alcohol consumed and, in general, is reversible when the patient stops drinking. Beyond enlargement of the liver, which is usually painless, this tends to be a benign disorder.

Clinical Features

Alcoholic hepatitis is a potentially severe form of alcohol-induced liver disease. Most cases are probably subclinical, but the spectrum of presentation can range from nausea, vomiting, and abdominal pain to acute liver failure.

Physical findings include tachycardia, fever, and supine or orthostatic hypotension. Abdominal tenderness is usually present, especially in the right upper quadrant. Coexistent fatty infiltration may produce palpable hepatomegaly; cirrhosis from chronic disease may result in a small, nonpalpable liver. The characteristic physical signs of cirrhosis (gynecomastia, spider angioma, muscle wasting, ascites, and palmar erythema) may be present. Jaundice can be noted in patients with a bilirubin level of at least 2.5 mg/dL.

Diagnostic Strategies

Laboratory tests reveal moderate elevations of AST and ALT. Values in excess of 10 times normal are unusual, even in severe cases associated with eventual liver failure. Compared with levels in viral hepatitis, a relative predominance of AST over ALT is expected. Bilirubin is commonly elevated. The white blood cell count is often high, with a polymorphonuclear leukocytosis in the range of 10,000 to 20,000. The PT and INR provide a rough assessment of hepatic dysfunction. An acutely elevated PT or prolonged INR in a patient not suspected of chronic cirrhotic disease suggests a complicated course. Electrolyte or acid-base disturbances may occur as a consequence of excessive vomiting or alcoholic ketoacidosis.

Differential Considerations

The differential diagnosis of alcoholic hepatitis is quite broad and includes a variety of other alcohol-related gastrointestinal maladies (e.g., gastritis, pancreatitis). Patients often have several ethanol-induced diseases simultaneously. The broad differential of hepatitis must be entertained; however, the clinical history and aminotransferase profile should facilitate accurate diagnosis. Mild aminotransferase elevation and marked bilirubin elevation are consistent with alcoholic hepatitis; ultrasonography helps differentiate this from common duct obstruction. Serum for anti-HAV IgM and HBcAg-IgM should be sent for testing, but results are usually not available to establish these diagnoses in the emergency department.

Management

Management of alcoholic hepatitis is principally supportive. Fluid and electrolyte imbalance must be corrected, usually requiring parenteral fluid replacement; antiemetics may mitigate the need for IV treatment. Alcohol may suppress gluconeogenesis and therefore cause hypoglycemia. Blood glucose should be measured and supplemented as indicated. Many alcoholics are malnourished, and if thiamine deficiency is suspected, it should be given in a dose of 50 to 100 mg IM or IV before glucose administration to avoid inducing acute Wernicke's encephalopathy. Ethanol-induced magnesium wasting may not be apparent on serum magnesium measurement, and replacement should be given empirically unless there is a contraindication such as renal failure or known hypermagnesemia. Magnesium can be given as a sulfate salt in a dose of 1 g IV or IM or as oral replacement in a dosage of 200 to 1000 mg daily as an oxide, chloride salt, or amino acid conjugate.

The overall nutritional status of the patient should be addressed with the administration of a high-calorie, vitamin-supplemented diet. Protein content may require restriction if evidence of cirrhosis and incipient encephalopathy exists. Coexisting gastritis should be treated with histamine 2 antagonists, proton pump inhibitors, or antacids. The patient should be evaluated for gastrointestinal bleeding and treated appropriately. Corticosteroids, propylthiouracil, and insulin-glucagon infusions have been investigated for treatment of alcoholic hepatitis and look promising in severe cases, but they have not gained acceptance as part of routine management.[30,36-38]

Disposition

Disposition is determined by the patient's clinical state: the degree of fluid and electrolyte abnormality, the ability to retain oral intake, the coexistent diagnoses or complications, and the patient's social situation. Admission to the hospital is generally not required. All patients should be advised to abstain from further alcohol ingestion and should be provided referral for detoxification or alcohol dependence treatment.

Cirrhosis

Principles of Disease

Cirrhosis is a generic term for an end stage of chronic liver disease characterized by destruction of hepatocytes and replacement of normal hepatic architecture with fibrotic tissue and regenerative nodules. *Laënnec's cirrhosis* is a diffuse process that involves the entire lobule and is most often related to chronic alcohol ingestion. From 10% to 20% of chronic alcoholics develop this type of cirrhosis. Amount and duration of alcohol ingestion, heredity, and underlying nutritional status all seem to play some role in the development of this disorder. *Postnecrotic cirrhosis* is usually nonhomogeneous, characterized by regions of fibrosis and hepatocyte loss alternating with normal areas. It is most often a consequence of chronic hepatitis of divergent etiologies: infectious (viral, bacterial, fungal), drug induced, or metabolic. *Biliary cirrhosis* is much less common and is a consequence of chronic extrahepatic biliary obstruction or a primary disorder of autoimmune-mediated intrahepatic duct inflammation and scarring. Nonalcoholic fatty liver disease has become an increasingly recognized cause of *cryptogenic cirrhosis*. This still poorly understood disease, with features similar to Laënnec's cirrhosis, is more common in obese patients and those with type 2 diabetes mellitus.[39]

Clinical Features

The clinical manifestations of cirrhosis are related to loss of hepatocytes, leading to metabolic and synthetic dysfunction, or to fibrosis and altered hepatic architecture, resulting in impaired portal blood flow and portal hypertension. Typically, the patient with cirrhosis complains of chronic fatigue and poor appetite. With the exception of those with biliary cirrhosis, many patients with cirrhosis can be asymptomatic until they develop some dramatic complication such as gastrointestinal bleeding, ascites, or hepatic encephalopathy. Patients with biliary cirrhosis generally complain of pruritus or develop obvious jaundice before end-stage cirrhosis or complications develop. Primary biliary cirrhosis may be associated with other immune-mediated disorders; these patients may have signs and symptoms characteristic of scleroderma or the CREST syndrome (calcinosis cutis, Raynaud's phenomenon, esophageal motility disorder, sclerodactyly, and telangiectasia).[40]

Physical examination may reveal muscle wasting, thinning of the skin with patchy ecchymosis, spider angioma, palmar erythema, Dupuytren's contracture, and, in men, gynecomastia or testicular atrophy. Jaundice is generally absent in mild or early cases. The liver may not be palpable if it is extensively scarred, but a large regenerative nodule, tumor, or fatty infiltration can result in hepatomegaly. Ascites is common, particularly in advanced disease, and may be present in association with a characteristic pattern of abdominal wall vein distention known as caput medusae.

Diagnostic Strategies

Laboratory tests are not specific. Aminotransferase levels are rarely more than minimally elevated. Bilirubin may be increased but usually not until cirrhosis is far advanced. Elevation of alkaline phosphatase out of proportion to other liver enzymes is suggestive of biliary cirrhosis. Coagulation studies are commonly abnormal, and the serum albumin level is low as a result of impaired hepatic synthetic function. Mild to moderate anemia and thrombocytopenia are often present in Laënnec's cirrhosis. Elevated blood urea nitrogen (BUN) or creatinine should suggest dehydration or hepatorenal syndrome.

Ancillary tests are rarely of use in the emergency setting. Ultrasonography is highly sensitive for the detection of ascites, but a carefully performed physical examination can generally yield equivalent results. Patients with ascites and fever or abdominal pain should have paracentesis performed to eliminate the possibility of spontaneous bacterial peritonitis (SBP). Nuclear or computed tomography (CT) scan imaging may reveal a hepatic or splenic appearance characteristic of cirrhosis and portal hypertension but, in general, these tests should be deferred to an elective setting.

Management

Treatment of cirrhosis in the emergency department is limited. Fluid and electrolyte imbalances should be corrected, and vitamin and nutritional supplements should be provided. Most patients can be discharged with referral to a general internist for further evaluation and treatment. Ascites associated with respiratory compromise or significant discomfort can be treated with paracentesis and removal of 2 or more liters of fluid. Removal of very large quantities of ascites can result in fluid and electrolyte abnormalities and hemodynamic instability. If SBP is a consideration, diagnostic paracentesis should be done.

A low-sodium diet in conjunction with an aldosterone antagonist may be of use in the chronic management of ascites. A low dose of a thiazide or loop diuretic may accelerate resolution of ascites and is probably safe if the patient has coexistent peripheral edema and normal renal function. Coagulopathy noted before a planned invasive procedure or in conjunction with active bleeding should be corrected with fresh frozen plasma. Uncomplicated prolongation of PT or

INR can be treated with vitamin K supplement, but this is often ineffective. Gastrointestinal bleeding should be treated aggressively. Early consultation with a gastroenterologist for endoscopy often permits identification of a bleeding site and initiation of appropriate adjunctive treatment. An elevated creatinine level may herald the onset of hepatorenal syndrome and requires admission for optimal fluid and electrolyte management.

Complications of cirrhosis include gastrointestinal bleeding, ascites with or without infection, encephalopathy, and hepatorenal syndrome. Although gastrointestinal bleeding is often related to esophageal or gastric varices, more than half of cases result from some other source (e.g., gastritis or a duodenal ulcer). Ascites occurs as a consequence of portal hypertension, impaired hepatic lymph flow, hypoalbuminemia, and renal salt retention. Ascites generally causes few symptoms beyond abdominal distention and discomfort. However, massive ascites can lead to respiratory embarrassment. SBP is an important and often subtle complication. Encephalopathy occurs as a result of impaired hepatic metabolic function and portal hypertension. Hepatorenal syndrome is defined as renal failure occurring in the setting of cirrhosis without obvious renal pathology. The mechanism of this almost universally fatal complication is not understood. An otherwise unexplained elevation of creatinine or BUN suggests an emerging hepatorenal state.

KEY CONCEPTS

- Cirrhosis is an advanced stage of liver disease from a variety of causes.
- The emergency department presentation of patients with cirrhosis is most often due to a complication such as ascites, variceal bleeding, or hepatic encephalopathy.
- Impaired hepatic synthetic and metabolic function in patients with cirrhosis may require correction of coagulopathy before invasive procedures and modification of medication dosing.

Hepatic Encephalopathy

Principles of Disease

Hepatic encephalopathy is a clinical state of disordered cerebral function occurring because of acute or chronic liver disease. The pathophysiology of hepatic coma is complex and related to the diseased liver's failure to perform adequately its normal metabolic functions. Ammonia, formed primarily in the gastrointestinal tract by the action of bacteria on proteinaceous compounds, is a common marker of this process. Normally, absorbed ammonia is converted to urea in the liver. In severe hepatic disease, ammonia accumulates, crosses the blood-brain barrier, and combines sequentially with α-ketoglutarate and glutamate to form glutamine. Serum ammonia levels correlate inconsistently with the severity of encephalopathy, but there is a close asso-

Table 89-4. Grades of Hepatic Encephalopathy

Grade	Clinical Description
I	Disordered sleep, irritability, depression, mild cognitive dysfunction
II	Lethargy, disorientation, confusion, personality changes, asterixis
III	Somnolence or marked disorientation, confused speech, inability to follow commands, possible asterixis
IV	Coma

ciation with cerebrospinal fluid (CSF) glutamine levels.[41] Whether glutamine is itself toxic or simply represents a marker for disordered central nervous system (CNS) metabolism is unknown. Other agents presumed to play a role in the pathophysiology of this disorder include mercaptans, octopamine, γ-aminobutyric acid, and the aromatic amino acids, particularly tryptophan.

Clinical Features

The clinical manifestations of hepatic encephalopathy vary depending on the severity of the process, from mild cognitive dysfunction, irritability, and confusion to profound coma. Table 89-4 summarizes the four stages of hepatic encephalopathy. Asterixis, a low-amplitude, alternating flexion and extension of the wrist when it is held in extension, is characteristic of mild to moderate degrees of encephalopathy. A similar finding may be elicited in the dorsiflexed foot or in the head with extension of the neck. Fetor hepaticus, a musty breath odor presumably caused by mercaptans, may be detected in severe cases.

Physical examination commonly reveals signs of cirrhosis, including spider angiomas, testicular atrophy, muscle wasting, superficial bruising, gynecomastia, and ascites.

Diagnostic Strategies

Laboratory tests may be normal or indicate fulminate liver failure or chronic cirrhosis. Serum ammonia levels are generally elevated but do not necessarily correlate with the severity of encephalopathy. Laboratory tests reflective of hepatic synthetic function, albumin and protime, are generally abnormal. The electroencephalogram is abnormal in most cases, but the pattern of generalized slowing with high-voltage bursts of triphasic or delta waves characteristic of hepatic encephalopathy is not specific.[41]

Differential Considerations

The differential considerations in patients with hepatic encephalopathy include all causes of altered sensorium. The diagnosis can be narrowed if there is a history of previous episodes of hepatic encephalopathy or it is recognized the patient has severe underlying liver disease and physical signs are supportive. It may be useful to obtain a full electrolyte panel, glucose, toxicology screen, and, if conditions warrant, a head CT scan and CSF examination to eliminate potentially life-threatening conditions.

Management

Aggressive management of the patient with hepatic encephalopathy may reverse the condition. As with any comatose patient, the airway is assessed first, not only to determine the need for respiratory support but also for prevention of aspiration. The patients are generally hemodynamically stable but have an increased incidence of gastrointestinal bleeding. Hypokalemia, alkalosis, and gastrointestinal bleeding contribute to increased ammonia production or absorption and must be corrected when detected. Relatively mild degrees of hyponatremia, hypoglycemia, azotemia, or dehydration often have a disproportionate effect on cerebral function and require immediate correction. All CNS depressant drugs must be discontinued, and care should be taken not to prescribe even mild sedatives.

Lactulose and neomycin represent the principal therapeutic agents in the management of this disorder. Lactulose is a poorly absorbed sugar metabolized to lactic acid by colonic bacteria. The lactic acid causes acidification of the fecal stream, resulting in the trapping of ammonia as ammonium in the stool. Lactulose is also a cathartic. The usual dosage of lactulose is 15 to 30 mL orally three or four times daily or in a quantity sufficient to result in several loose bowel movements daily. The principal adverse effect is excessive diarrhea, with resultant fluid and electrolyte imbalance. Neomycin is a poorly absorbed aminoglycoside. It is believed to act by reducing colonic bacteria responsible for the production of ammonia. Neomycin is administered orally at a dosage of 0.5 g every 4 to 6 hours. Ototoxicity or renal injury may occur in patients with impaired renal function. In obtunded patients, lactulose and neomycin can be administered by nasogastric tube. An alternative route for neomycin is rectal enema. Long-term management requires diet modification with significant protein restriction.

Alternative therapies, still undergoing clinical evaluation, include metronidazole, levodopa, branched-chain amino acid infusions, bromocriptine, and more recently the benzodiazepine antagonist flumazenil.[42-46] The molecular absorbent recirculating system (MARS) utilizes albumin in a dialysis solution to bind and remove circulating toxins. Limited experience with this novel experimental approach to treat liver failure and hepatic encephalopathy indicates that it is safe and cost effective.[47,48]

Disposition

Although most patients with hepatic encephalopathy require hospitalization, individuals with grade I or II encephalopathy without complicating factors and a supportive home environment can be managed at home. In addition to a prescription for lactulose, a diet with limited amounts of protein is essential to effective ongoing management.

KEY CONCEPTS

- The differential diagnosis of hepatic encephalopathy includes all causes of altered sensorium. The correct diagnosis may be determined by the clinical setting, but the broad differential may require additional testing, including chemistry and CSF studies, toxicology, and a head CT scan.
- Management of hepatic encephalopathy includes correction of underlying electrolyte abnormalities and strict protein restriction.

Spontaneous Bacterial Peritonitis

Perspective

Spontaneous bacterial peritonitis is an acute bacterial infection of ascites in patients with liver disease, without an apparent external or intraabdominal focus of infection. The syndrome is not new, but it was not until the late 1960s and early 1970s that this potentially fatal disorder was commonly recognized. Although the disease occurs most often in patients with cirrhosis related to alcohol, it can occur in any patient with ascites secondary to cirrhosis.[49,50] Retrospective studies have identified SBP in 5% to 27% of patients admitted to the hospital with cirrhosis and ascites.[51]

Principles of Disease

The pathophysiology of SBP remains speculative but is most likely related to a combination of impaired phagocytic function in the liver with portal systemic hypertension, which can cause bowel mucosal edema and transmural migration of enteric organisms. Additional contributing factors may include impaired opsonic and complement activity in ascitic fluid. The bacteriology of SBP reveals a predominance of gram-negative enteric organisms. *Escherichia coli* is most common, isolated in 47% to 55% of cases, followed by *Streptococcus* sp (18% to 26%), *Klebsiella* sp (11%), and *Streptococcus pneumoniae* (8% to 20%).[49,51] Polymicrobial and anaerobic infections have been reported but are not common.

Clinical Features

The clinical presentation can be variable, ranging from the acute onset of severe abdominal pain, fever, chills, and hemodynamic instability to the slow, insidious onset of abdominal discomfort, low-grade fever, or hepatic encephalopathy. Although by definition ascites must be present for SBP to occur, free peritoneal fluid may not always be clinically apparent. An elevated temperature may not be detected in 20% to 50% of cases.[52]

Physical examination may vary from only mild tenderness to abdominal rigidity and guarding with rebound tenderness. One study identified a positive peritoneal fluid culture rate of 1.5% of patients with what was judged to be asymptomatic ascites.[53] This finding underscores the exceptionally broad spectrum of manifestations and often very minimal physical findings of this disorder and the need to consider the diagnosis of SBP in any patient with ascites who presents with abdominal pain or unexplained clinical deterioration.

Diagnostic Strategies

Diagnosis is made by culture of the ascitic fluid. However, treatment decisions should be made in advance of these results. An ascitic fluid granulocyte count of more than 500 cells/mm³ correlates with positive cultures in more than 90% of cases; however, emergency department treatment for SBP should be initiated if the neutrophil count is greater than 250 cells/mm³.[50-52,54,55] A positive result from a urine reagent strip for leukocyte esterase has a high degree of correlation with a clinically significant elevation of neutrophil cell count.[56] If available for testing, an ascitic fluid pH of less than 7.34 or a pH gradient between arterial blood and ascitic fluid of more than 0.10 is also a reliable early indicator of SBP.[54-57] Other laboratory parameters (e.g., aminotransferase, bilirubin, and peripheral blood count) are commonly abnormal but are nonspecific and more often are a consequence of underlying liver disease than infection. A PT and INR should be obtained in advance of paracentesis, and fresh frozen plasma should be administered if significant coagulopathy is identified.

Differential Considerations

The differential diagnosis of SBP includes all of the entities that may lead to peritonitis and abdominal pain in patients with or without liver disease.

Management

Treatment of SBP requires IV antibiotics. The choice of agents is driven by the anticipated bacteriology of the process. A third-generation cephalosporin such as cefotaxime is considered to be a drug of choice with a demonstrated cure rate of 85%.[52] An alternative is an ampicillin-sulbactam combination. Ampicillin and an aminoglycoside are also effective but involve an increased risk of renal toxicity.

Disposition

SBP is a risk in any patient with ascites. The risk of SBP is markedly increased in patients with ascitic fluid protein levels less than 1 g/dL.[51,52,58] Other important risk factors include serum bilirubin level greater than 3.2 mg/dL, platelet count less than 98,000/mm³, and a previous history of SBP.[59] Antibiotic prophylaxis of high-risk patients can reduce SBP incidence by 60% to 80% and be cost effective.[51,52,58,60] Recommended regimens include norfloxacin 400 mg daily and ciprofloxacin 750 mg once weekly.[51,52,61] If a high-risk patient with ascites is identified in the emergency department and contraindications are absent, prophylactic therapy should be initiated. Referral to a primary care physician or gastroenterology specialist is recommended.

KEY CONCEPTS

- SBP should be considered in any patient with ascites presenting with abdominal pain, fever, or unexplained clinical deterioration.
- The diagnosis is dependent upon sampling of ascitic fluid and measurement of cell count. An ascitic fluid granulocyte count greater than 250 cells/mm³ is an indication for antibiotic treatment. Urine reagent strips that test for leukocyte esterase may provide a convenient bedside screening test of ascitic fluid.
- Identification of high-risk patients with ascites is an indication for initiation of SBP prophylaxis with an ortho-quinolone antibiotic.

Drug-Induced Liver Disease

Perspective

In addition to alcohol, a variety of other chemical agents can induce injury to the liver. Most of these agents are commonly prescribed medicinals or drugs available over the counter. Although hepatic injury represents a relatively small proportion of all adverse drug reactions, it may account for up to 5% of hospital admissions for jaundice.[62] Drug-induced liver disease is one of the most common reasons for market withdrawal of drugs by the Food and Drug Administration and is responsible for about 50% of the cases of fulminate liver failure in the United States.[63] For reasons not entirely clear, the incidence of liver injury related to drugs appears to increase with patients' age. Notable exceptions include valproic acid and aspirin, which more often cause hepatic damage in children.

Principles of Disease

The pathogenesis of liver injury from drug exposure is variable. It may occur as a result of a direct cytotoxic effect of the primary agent or, as is more often the case, a major or minor metabolite. Alternatively, toxicity can be related to a hypersensitivity or allergic reaction. Antimetabolites (e.g., azathioprine, comfrey tea) have been associated with hepatic injury caused by veno-occlusive disease, whereas oral contraceptives have been implicated in cases of hepatic vein thrombosis.[64,65]

Not all agents commonly associated with hepatic toxicity cause injury in all patients. This variability is a consequence of variations in metabolic pathways, simultaneous ingestion of other substances that may facilitate toxicity, amount and duration of drug exposure, or patients' idiosyncrasy. For example, isoniazid appears to have differential toxicity depending on both the patient's age and the rate of conversion to a particular toxic metabolite, acetyl hydrazine. Acetaminophen is relatively nontoxic when taken in the usually recommended amounts but universally toxic and potentially fatal when taken in significant excess (see Chapter 146).

Generally, drugs that induce liver injury cause hepatocellular necrosis or cholestasis. Although specific agents tend to cause damage characterized by a partic-

Table 89-5. Common Agents Involved in Hepatic Injury

Agent	Injury Pattern
Acetaminophen	Cytotoxic
Amiodarone	Cytotoxic
Amphotericin	Cytotoxic
Anabolic steroids	Cholestatic, veno-occlusive
Azathioprine	Cytotoxic, cholestatic, veno-occlusive
Carbamazepine	Cytotoxic, cholestatic
Chlorpromazine	Cholestatic
Cis-platinum	Cytotoxic
Contraceptive steroids	Cholestatic, hepatic vein thrombotic
Cyclophosphamide	Cytotoxic
Erythromycin estolate	Cholestatic
Gold salts	Cytotoxic, cholestatic
Haloperidol	Cholestatic
Isoniazid	Cytotoxic
Ketoconazole	Cytotoxic
Lovastatin	Cytotoxic
Methotrexate	Cytotoxic
Methoxyflurane	Cytotoxic
Methyldopa	Cytotoxic
Phenobarbital	Cholestatic
Phenytoin	Cytotoxic
Quinidine	Cytotoxic
Salicylate	Cytotoxic
Tetracycline	Cytotoxic, fatty infiltrative
Valproic acid	Cytotoxic
Verapamil	Cholestatic

ular pattern of injury, there is considerable overlap. Cellular necrosis is commonly associated with anesthetic agents (e.g., halothane, the antimicrobials amphotericin and ketoconazole, or the antidysrhythmic amiodarone). A cholestatic picture is characteristic of chlorpromazine, haloperidol, anabolic or oral contraceptive steroids, and erythromycin estolate.

Clinical Features

Many patients with drug-induced liver disease are asymptomatic, with injury apparent only by moderate elevations of aminotransferase levels. Others may experience painless jaundice resulting from agents associated with cholestatic pathology or from acute hepatitis indistinguishable from virally induced disease.

Physical examination varies depending on the nature of the underlying pathology. The liver can be enlarged and tender. A rash is frequently seen in halothane-induced hepatitis, consistent with its presumed allergic causation. Aminotransferase levels are commonly elevated but only mildly so in cholestatic cases. Bilirubin is often elevated, most dramatically in cases associated with cholestasis. Eosinophilia is frequently seen in cases of chlorpromazine- and halothane-induced injury.

It can be difficult to differentiate drug-induced liver injury from infectious causes or extrahepatic biliary obstruction. A careful history in conjunction with knowledge of the drugs commonly associated with hepatic toxicity should facilitate diagnosis (Table 89-5). On occasion, particularly in cases with a cholestatic presentation, abdominal ultrasonography and liver biopsy may be necessary.

Management

The offending agent or agents should be discontinued and appropriate supportive measures instituted, as in the treatment of acute hepatitis. For patients with cholestasis and significant pruritus, a bile acid sequestering agent such as cholestyramine may provide relief. If an allergic mechanism is suspected, corticosteroids may be of benefit.[63] Although drug-induced liver disease is generally a benign disorder, it can be associated with fulminant hepatic failure or the development of cirrhosis.

Disposition

Patients with mild cases of drug-induced hepatitis can be managed effectively as outpatients. Telephone consultation with a gastroenterology specialist is recommended to aid in the diagnosis and ensure reliable follow-up. Severe cases should be admitted to the hospital, and if signs of fulminate hepatitis are apparent, consideration should be given to transfer to a center with the capacity to perform liver transplantation.

Hepatic Abscesses

Hepatic abscesses fall into two broad categories, pyogenic and amebic. Although there may be similarities in clinical presentation, the pathophysiology and treatment differ significantly.

Pyogenic Abscess

Principles of Disease

Pyogenic hepatic abscess is uncommon, present in only 8 to 16 cases per 100,000 hospital admissions. The disorder increases in frequency with patients' age and is distributed equally between men and women.[66] Liver abscesses are most commonly associated with biliary tract obstruction or cholangitis but may also be related to diverticulitis, pancreatic abscess, omphalitis, appendicitis, inflammatory bowel disease, or bacteremia of any cause.[67,68] In a significant number of cases no underlying cause for liver abscess is identified.[69]

Solitary and multiple abscesses occur with approximately equal frequency, most often in the right lobe of the liver. Patients with multiple lesions tend to be more severely ill, with worse prognoses. Both anaerobic and aerobic organisms are causative; *E. coli*, *Klebsiella*, *Pseudomonas*, *Enterococcus* sp, anaerobic streptococci, and various *Bacteroides* species are the microbes most commonly isolated.[70]

Clinical Findings

Clinical presentation is characterized by the onset of high fever, chills, right upper quadrant pain, nausea, and vomiting. Patients generally present acutely and appear quite ill, particularly if there is underlying cholangitis. A more insidious chronic presentation, although atypical, has been described. Physical findings include elevated temperature, right upper quadrant tenderness, hepatomegaly, and occasionally dullness to percussion and decreased breath sounds over the right lower chest. Jaundice may be apparent,

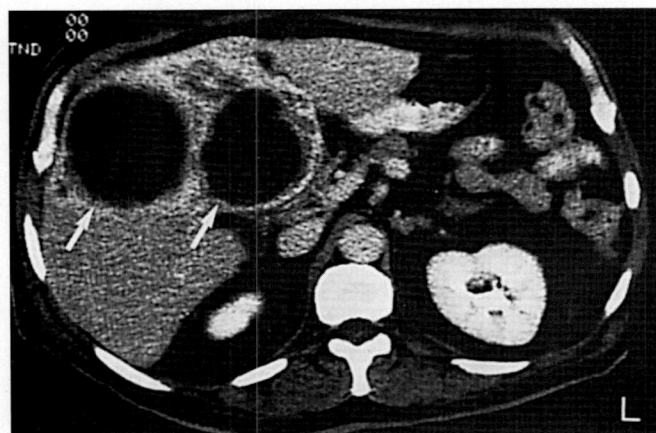

Figure 89-4. Contrast computed tomography scan of liver showing large cystic masses with irregular, contrast-enhancing borders in a patient with pyogenic liver abscess caused by *Streptococcus milleri*.

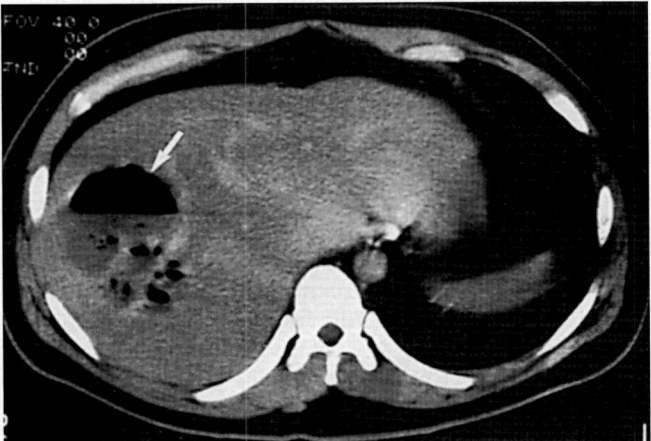

Figure 89-5. Contrast computed tomography scan of liver showing pyogenic liver abscess. Complex cystic mass with air-fluid level caused by gas-producing *Klebsiella* sp pneumonia.

especially if coexistent biliary tract obstruction is present.

Diagnostic Strategies
Laboratory findings include leukocytosis in 70% to 80% of cases, elevated alkaline phosphatase in up to 90%, and bilirubin in excess of 2 mg/dL in 50% of patients. Serum aminotransferase levels are commonly elevated to two to four times normal.[66] Chest radiographs may reveal a right pleural effusion, a basilar atelectasis, or an elevated right hemidiaphragm.[71]

Many imaging techniques are useful in delineating hepatic abscesses, including ultrasonography, nuclear scan with technetium or gallium, CT scan (Figures 89-4 and 89-5), and magnetic resonance imaging (MRI) scan. In the emergency department, ultrasonography and the CT scan are the most sensitive and expeditious modalities.

Differential Considerations
The differential diagnosis of pyogenic hepatic abscess includes amebic liver abscess, hepatitis and cholangi-

tis, and pancreatic and subphrenic abscess. Although clinical evaluation may not allow definitive diagnosis, appropriate use of imaging techniques generally does.

Management
The initial treatment of a pyogenic hepatic abscess consists of hemodynamic stabilization, IV antibiotics, and pain control. Pending definitive microbial identification, broad-spectrum antibiotic coverage should be provided. Triple antibiotic coverage is warranted and should include an aminoglycoside or third-generation cephalosporin for gram-negative coverage, metronidazole or clindamycin for anaerobes, and ampicillin for streptococcal species. Definitive treatment requires abscess drainage. Drainage is usually done percutaneously, with open surgical drainage reserved for complex cases associated with intraperitoneal soiling, intestinal perforation, or biliary obstruction.[72-74]

Complications include rupture of the abscess into the peritoneal cavity or an adjacent anatomic structure (e.g., the thoracic cavity, lung, pericardium).

Disposition
Patients with pyogenic hepatic abscess uniformly require admission to the hospital. Consultation with a general surgeon, gastroenterologist, or interventional radiologist is necessary.

Amebic Abscess

Principles of Disease
Amebiasis is one of the most common protozoan infections worldwide. Up to 10% of the world's population and approximately 1% to 2% of the U.S. population may be infected. Transmission is generally by the fecal-oral route and usually a consequence of ingesting contaminated water or foodstuffs. The illness is more common in homosexual men, presumably as a result of oral-anal contact during sexual activity. One limited but fatal outbreak of intestinal disease in the Midwest was traced to a contaminated colonic irrigation apparatus.[75] Although intestinal disease is by far the most common manifestation of infection, extraintestinal disease is not rare, with the liver most commonly affected. *Entamoeba histolytica* is the only ameba responsible for invasive disease, and evidence suggests that only certain varieties of *E. histolytica* are pathogenic.[76] Pathogenic amebae reach the liver after invasion of the intestinal mucosa and move through the portal vein. As with a pyogenic abscess, involvement of the right liver lobe is more common.

Clinical Features
The clinical presentation is generally acute, with fever, chills, abdominal pain, nausea, and vomiting. Coexistent diarrhea is common in children but is present in less than one third of adults. Careful questioning of patients without diarrhea often yields a history of intestinal illness several weeks before. Many patients complain of cough, which can serve to misdirect attention from the liver. Chronic illness of several months' duration, although less common than the acute presentation, has been described.[77]

Physical examination reveals an elevated temperature, right upper quadrant tenderness, hepatomegaly, and dullness with decreased breath sounds over the right lower chest.

Diagnostic Strategies

Laboratory parameters are not specific. Neutrophilic leukocytosis is common. Alkaline phosphatase is elevated in 75% of cases and aminotransferases in 50%. Hyperbilirubinemia is uncommon and when present is indicative of biliary obstruction. The chest radiograph may reveal a right pleural effusion, basilar atelectasis, or an elevated right hemidiaphragm. Ultrasound imaging of the liver can be diagnostic, revealing a peripherally based mass with well-circumscribed borders and an inhomogeneous hypoechoic center. Technetium, CT, and MRI scanning are alternative imaging modalities if ultrasonography is inconclusive.

Diagnosis is supported by identifying a pathogenic protozoan in the stool. However, even in cases of invasive intestinal disease, the yield may be low. Serologic testing is generally required to establish a definitive diagnosis. Agar gel diffusion, counterimmunoelectrophoresis, and rapid enzyme immunoassay are positive in most cases.[78,79] Indirect hemagglutination remains positive for an extended period and is therefore not helpful in establishing the presence of acute infection.

Differential Considerations

In a review of 75 cases of amebic liver abscess seen in a single emergency department over 5 years, the correct diagnosis was made in the emergency department in only 31.5% of patients.[80] The differential diagnosis of an amebic liver abscess includes pyogenic abscess, followed by biliary tract disease, hepatitis, pneumonia, appendicitis, and pancreatitis. Respiratory symptoms and abnormal chest radiograph may cause confusion with pulmonary illnesses. Hepatic imaging is helpful in establishing the correct diagnosis; however, differentiation from pyogenic illness may still be difficult.

Management

Management consists of supportive therapy and initiation of amebicidal therapy. Metronidazole, 750 mg by mouth or IV three times daily for 7 days, is the treatment of choice. Most patients respond to this regimen. Percutaneous catheter drainage is required only in refractory or complicated cases.

The most serious complication of amebic liver disease is rupture into adjacent anatomic structures. Involvement of the lung occurs in 20% to 35% of cases of extrahepatic disease, often arising with signs and symptoms of massive pleural effusion or consolidative pneumonia. Rupture into a bronchus can arise with cough productive of an anchovy paste–like substance, necrotic debris, or frank hemoptysis. Abdominal pain with peritonitis can result from rupture into the abdominal cavity. Involvement of the pericardium is occasionally seen with lesions in the left lobe of the liver and can be catastrophic, either acutely as a consequence of pericardial tamponade or chronically from constrictive pericarditis.

Disposition

Selected patients with amebic liver abscess can be managed as outpatients. This approach is best suited for individuals with mild clinical disease, stable living circumstances, and access to medications as well as follow-up care. Patients with more severe disease, evidence of complications, or questionable social circumstances should be admitted to a medical service.

Miscellaneous Disorders of the Liver

Chronic Hepatitis

Chronic hepatitis is defined as persistent inflammation of the liver for at least 6 months. *Chronic persistent hepatitis* (CPH) is characterized clinically by a lack of symptoms, persistent mild complaints, or intermittent episodes of moderate hepatitis. Despite persistent elevation of aminotransferases, CPH rarely progresses to hepatic failure or cirrhosis. *Chronic active hepatitis* (CAH), on the other hand, commonly progresses to cirrhosis. CAH may initially follow a clinical course indistinguishable from that of CPH; however, biopsy of the liver, even early in the disease, reveals diffuse inflammation, bridging necrosis, and evidence of scarring and macronodular cirrhosis.[81]

The causes of chronic hepatitis include all of the recognized etiologies of acute hepatitis, but it is rare with HAV. It may occur in 5% to 10% of patients with HBV infection, in 50% to 60% of those with HCV, and probably in an even greater percentage of patients with HDV infection.[15,82-84] The incidence of chronic disease of other etiologies is closely related to the reversibility of the metabolic or immunologic disorder or to the duration of exposure to the incriminated toxic substance.

Chronic hepatitis, in its precirrhotic stage, rarely causes emergency department presentations. It is not unusual, however, for an elevated aminotransferase to be detected during the course of evaluation of some seemingly unrelated entity. Evaluation is generally limited to obtaining a careful history and ordering appropriate viral serologies (HBsAg, HBeAg, and anti-HCV). The active treatment of CAH goes beyond the bounds of the emergency department. Referral to an internist or gastroenterology specialist is advisable.

Liver Disease in Pregnancy

The two primary hepatic disorders associated with pregnancy are benign cholestasis and acute fatty liver. Cholestasis is common and appears to have a familial linkage. Onset is in the third trimester and is heralded by the development of progressive pruritus. Bilirubin may be elevated but not dramatically, and jaundice is uncommon. Laboratory tests reveal elevated alkaline phosphatase, 5′-nucleotidase, and bilirubin. Although the chief concern for the mother is discomfort from pruritus, the illness can bode poorly for the fetus, with increased incidences of prematurity, stillbirth, and fetal distress.[85] Malabsorption of vitamin K can result in serious coagulopathy in the fetus, predisposing to spontaneous intracranial hemorrhage.[86] Treatment is supportive and should include subcutaneous vitamin

K for the mother prepartum and the newborn after delivery. Cholestasis resolves without incident after delivery.

Acute fatty liver of pregnancy is a malignant disorder that, if unrecognized, can progress rapidly to maternal and fetal demise. The incidence is about 1 in 7000 live births.[87] The illness occurs in the latter part of the third trimester and is more common in primigravidas and twin pregnancies.[86] The initial clinical features include fatigue, anorexia, nausea, and vomiting. Abdominal pain may be present, most prominently in the midepigastrium and right upper quadrant. Physical examination may reveal mild jaundice and abdominal tenderness. The liver may not be palpable because of the enlarged uterus.

Abnormal laboratory findings include moderate elevation of aminotransferases (5 to 10 times normal) and bilirubin, hypoglycemia, and evidence of disseminated intravascular coagulation (prolonged PT and partial thromboplastin time, hypofibrinogenemia, elevated fibrin split products, and thrombocytopenia). Treatment involves aggressive fluid and electrolyte support, glucose administration, and immediate delivery. Liver disease generally resolves without permanent sequelae after delivery.[87]

Hepatic Cancer

Hepatocellular carcinoma is the most common primary hepatic malignancy. It is especially common in underdeveloped areas of the world, particularly in regions where chronic HBV infection is prevalent. In parts of China and Africa, the incidence of hepatocellular carcinoma approaches 100 in 100,000; in the United States, it is 4 or 5 per 100,000.[88] It has been estimated that HBV is causally related to the development of hepatoma in 75% to 90% of cases worldwide.[89] Associations beyond HBV include infection with *Clonorchis* and schistosomiasis, chronic alcoholic liver disease, primary biliary cirrhosis, hemochromatosis, and several chemical agents (e.g., estrogens, androgens, thorium dioxide [Thorotrast], vinyl chloride).[90] Metastases to the liver from gastrointestinal, lung, breast, or other origins are more common in the United States than primary malignancy.

The clinical presentation of hepatic carcinoma or metastases is nonspecific. Symptoms may include nausea, vomiting, jaundice, or right upper quadrant abdominal pain. Physical examination may reveal signs of recent weight loss or cachexia. Hepatocellular carcinoma is linked with cirrhosis; many of these patients present with manifestations of that process. An enlarged liver, particularly in patients with a history of cirrhosis, is strongly suggestive of malignant transformation. Although laboratory tests (e.g., blood count, aminotransferase measurements, bilirubin measurement) are often abnormal, they are nonspecific and generally of little aid in diagnosis. α-Fetoprotein is often elevated in patients with a hepatoma but is nonspecific and of limited use in diagnosis. Ultrasound imaging, CT scan, and MRI scan of the liver are all effective means of identifying tumor. Liver biopsy is recommended for the definitive diagnosis of hepatoma; biopsy of an alternative site may be preferable in cases of metastatic disease.

Management in the emergency department is limited to supportive measures, provision of analgesic agents, and possibly nutritive supplementation. Hepatitis B serologies should be obtained in cases of hepatoma to determine linkage with chronic HBV infection and to assess infection risk to family members.

Liver Transplantation

Human orthotopic liver transplantation was pioneered in the 1960s, and approximately 4000 liver transplantations are now performed annually in the United States. The 5-year survival is generally reported in the range of 80%, but complications are common.[91,92] Early complications include bleeding, acute rejection, vascular and biliary tract problems, and infection. Delayed complications include malignancy, recurrence of underlying disease, infection, chronic rejection, medication toxicity, and renal failure. Many early complications are manifest during the immediate postoperative period while the patient is in the hospital or being closely observed by the transplantation team. Delayed complications may occur a year or more after transplantation.

The clinical signs that cause emergency department presentation are related to the nature of the underlying problem. The signs of malignancy or recurrence of underlying disease mirror those in the patient without a transplant. Infectious complications are relatively straightforward when common pyogenic organisms are involved; however, liver transplant recipients are at increased risk for opportunistic infections as a consequence of their immunosuppressive therapy. These include cytomegalovirus (CMV), herpes simplex and herpes zoster, *Pneumocystis carinii*, and various fungal organisms and may arise with subtle signs and symptoms. Chronic rejection is manifest with signs of low-grade temperature elevation, fatigue, and jaundice. Expected laboratory abnormalities include elevated bilirubin, transaminases, prolonged PT or INR, and low serum albumin. Renal failure may not be clinically apparent until the glomerular filtration rate has declined significantly. Routine serum creatinine measurement is the best means of identifying this disorder early, when successful intervention is still possible.

The most common immunosuppressive agents used after liver transplantation include corticosteroids, cyclosporin, tacrolimus, and azathioprine. Corticosteroid toxicity may produce glucose intolerance, osteoporosis, gastric ulceration, and muscle wasting. Cyclosporin and tacrolimus can cause renal impairment, which is the most common dose-limiting effect of these agents. Azathioprine can be hepatotoxic but is more often associated with bone marrow suppression, placing the patient at increased risk for infectious complications and bleeding diathesis.

Management of patients with complications related to liver transplantation is directed by the nature of the problem. Infections are evaluated and managed in the usual fashion with emphasis on evaluation of the patients' underlying immune function and a search for uncommon pathogens. There should be a low threshold for measurement of complete blood count, glucose, BUN, creatinine, serum electrolytes, transaminases, bilirubin, and albumin and coagulation studies. Hepatobiliary imaging is indicated if tumor, vascular occlusion, or biliary tract obstruction is suspected. Ultrasonography with Doppler interrogation can be particularly useful in the emergency department setting. Consultation with a transplant specialist is recommended for any patient with a problem potentially related to the transplanted organ or immune modulating medications.

BILIARY TRACT DISORDERS

Cholelithiasis

Perspective

The biliary tract comprises the hepatic bile canaliculi, intrahepatic and extrahepatic bile ducts, the common bile duct, and the gallbladder. Bile, required for absorption of fats and fat-soluble nutrients, is produced in the canaliculi. During the fasting state, approximately 50% of the bile produced flows directly into the duodenum; the other half is stored in the gallbladder. The gallbladder serves to acidify and concentrate the bile and can store up to 50 mL of bile for immediate availability at the time of feeding. The presence of food in the stomach, in particular fat, results in both vagal impulses and the secretion of cholecystokinin-pancreozymin, which serve as potent stimuli for gallbladder contraction. Removal of the gallbladder generally is not associated with measurable changes in intestinal fat absorption or clinical symptoms.[93]

The principal cause of biliary tract disease is related to the development of gallstones. It is estimated that 20% of women and 8% of men have gallstones, resulting in approximately 500,000 operations annually.[94]

Principles of Disease

There are two categories of gallstones. *Cholesterol stones* most commonly occur as a consequence of an elevated concentration of cholesterol in bile relative to the other principal constituents, bile acids and phospholipids. Bile acids and lecithin, the primary bile phospholipid, act in concert to solubilize cholesterol. As cholesterol levels rise or bile acids and lecithin levels decline, cholesterol has an increasing tendency to form crystals. These crystals, particularly in an incompletely emptying gallbladder, serve as a nidus for stone formation. Factors associated with an enhanced risk of cholesterol stone formation include increased age, female gender, massive obesity, rapid weight loss, cystic fibrosis, parity, drugs (e.g., clofibrate and oral contraceptive agents), and familial tendency. The hereditary risk of cholelithiasis is most dramatically demonstrated by the high concordance for stone formation in monozygotic twins and the exceedingly high incidence of cholelithiasis in Pima Indians.[95]

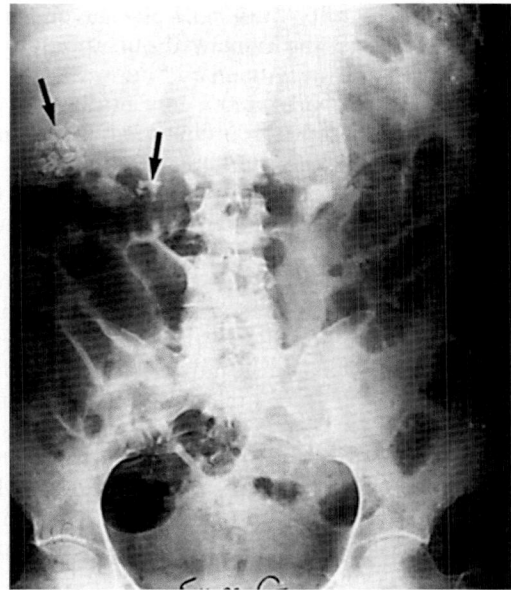

Figure 89-6. Plain flat plate (kidney, ureter, bladder) radiograph of abdomen with calcified gallstones and pancreatic calcifications. This patient also has bilateral staghorn calculi and calcified iliac vessels.

There are two varieties of *pigmented stones*: black and brown. Black stones occur exclusively in the gallbladder and contain a high concentration of calcium bilirubinate. They are more commonly encountered in elders and have a strong association with disease causing intravascular hemolysis (e.g., sickle cell anemia and hereditary spherocytosis). Brown stones are associated with infection and can form in both the gallbladder and the intrahepatic and extrahepatic bile duct system. Although bacterial infections are most commonly incriminated, parasites (e.g., *Ascaris lumbricoides* and *Clonorchis sinensis*) have also been linked to brown stone formation.[96] Both types of pigmented stones contain calcium bilirubinate and therefore may be visible on plain abdominal radiographs. For a stone to be radiopaque, it must contain at least 4% calcium by weight (Figure 89-6).

Clinical Features

The most common clinical manifestation of cholelithiasis is biliary colic. The pathophysiology of this process is not entirely clear, but it appears to be related to the passage of small stones from the gallbladder through the cystic duct into the common bile duct. The term *colic* is often misleading; these individuals commonly complain of steady pain rather than intermittent or cramping discomfort. The pain is most often perceived in the right upper quadrant but may be located in a wide region of the upper abdomen. Radiation of pain, if it occurs, is generally to the base of the scapula or shoulder. Associated symptoms include nausea and vomiting, which may be severe enough to lead to fluid and electrolyte imbalance. Patients with biliary colic commonly admit to similar self-limited occurrences in the past and may offer an association between symptom onset and eating. A relationship between fatty food ingestion and symptoms is as likely to occur in patients with gallstones as it is in those without. Physical examination usually reveals mild tenderness without guarding or rebound in the right upper quadrant or epigastric region.

Diagnostic Strategies

There are no pathognomonic clinical laboratory findings; most commonly obtained test results are within normal limits. Important tests to obtain include ALT and AST to evaluate for the presence of hepatitis, bilirubin and alkaline phosphatase for evidence of common duct obstruction, and amylase or lipase for the presence of pancreatitis.

The diagnosis of biliary colic is made clinically in conjunction with demonstration of stones in the gallbladder. Plain radiographs have little role in the evaluation of cholelithiasis because only 10% of stones have sufficient calcium to allow visualization.[97] Ultrasonography is the procedure of choice for investigating the gallbladder. Ultrasound imaging can be performed rapidly, is highly sensitive, and provides the added utility of permitting evaluation of surrounding structures (Figure 89-7). Ultrasonography can also be employed by the emergency physician at the bedside, adding further convenience to the patient and reducing turnaround times.[98] Oral cholecystography with iopanoic acid is an alternative when ultrasonography either is not available or cannot be performed successfully. This technique can identify gallstones in 95% of patients with cholelithiasis in whom visualization of the gallbladder can be achieved. However, in large series, as many as 25% of patients' gallbladders are not visualized after a single dose of iopanoic acid and 8% after a second dose.

Differential Considerations

The differential diagnosis of biliary colic includes cholecystitis, peptic acid disease of the stomach or duodenum, pancreatitis, and hepatitis. Patients with cholelithiasis may occasionally present with chest pain, and cardiopulmonary syndromes must be considered. The clinical history in conjunction with normal laboratory test values (ALT, AST, and amylase and alkaline phosphatase), gallstones on ultrasound imaging, and minimal or no tenderness in the right upper quadrant favors the diagnosis of cholelithiasis. If abnormal, a chest radiograph or electrocardiogram may help differentiate cardiopulmonary and biliary pathology.

Management

The initial management of biliary colic is directed at fluid and electrolyte correction and symptom relief. Vomiting is managed with antiemetics and, if necessary, nasogastric suction. Pain can often be controlled with antispasmodics (e.g., glycopyrrolate), nonsteroidal anti-inflammatory agents, and, if necessary, opiate analgesic agents. Clinically evident volume depletion should be treated with IV fluids.

The definitive management of cholelithiasis usually involves surgical removal of the gallbladder; however, other options exist. Oral administration of bile acid (e.g., chenodeoxycholate or ursodeoxycholate) over a period of months to years can result in dissolution of small to medium-size stones, whereas methyl *tert*-butyl ether irrigation of the gallbladder has been shown to dissolve stones over a period of hours or days.[99,100] Extracorporeal shock wave lithotripsy has been successful in a selected cohort of patients with solitary stones less than 20 mm in diameter.[101]

The most common complication of biliary colic is fluid and electrolyte imbalance as a result of vomiting. Other adverse consequences include Mallory-Weiss tear from uncontrolled emesis and cholangitis from unrecognized and persistent common bile duct obstruction.

Special Considerations

Biliary colic is an uncommon disease in children and, when it occurs, is most often associated with an underlying hemolytic disorder (e.g., sickle cell anemia or spherocytosis). Acute management of biliary colic is the same for children as adults.

Cholelithiasis may be encountered in pregnant women. Diagnosis in this population is made more difficult by the common occurrence of nausea and vomiting, particularly in the first trimester, and the presence of an enlarged uterus in later pregnancy, which interferes with anatomic relationships and abdominal examination. Ultrasound imaging is of considerable diagnostic use in this setting. Treatment in the emergency department is comparable to that for the nonpregnant patient; however, definitive therapy is generally delayed until after parturition.

Cholecystitis

Perspective

Acute cholecystitis is defined as sudden inflammation of the gallbladder. The incidence ranges from 5% to 19% of patients undergoing surgery for biliary tract

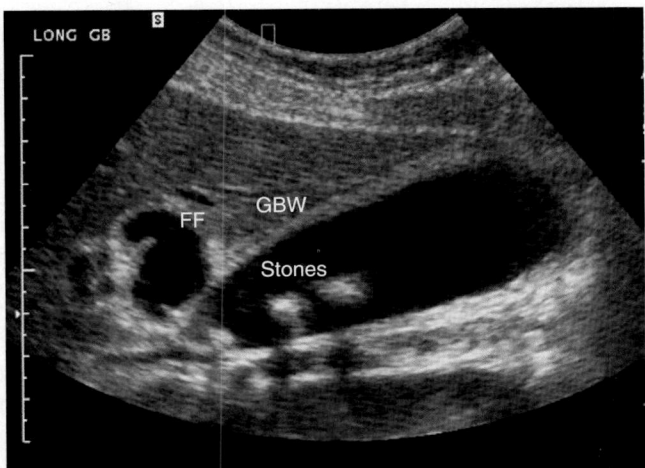

Figure 89-7. Gallbladder with gallstone (stones), thickened gallbladder wall (GBW), and pericholecystic fluid (FF), together representing the sonographic signs of cholecystitis.

disorders. The risk factors for cholecystitis are similar to those for cholelithiasis: female gender, increasing age and parity, and obesity.[102] Although gallstones play a prominent role in the pathogenesis of cholecystitis, approximately 2% to 12% of cases are categorized as acalculous.[103]

Principles of Disease

Obstruction of the cystic duct appears to be the critical factor in the development of gallbladder inflammation. Gallstones are identified in 95% of patients with cholecystitis and may be located in the common bile duct in many patients with acalculous cholecystitis. Causes of cystic duct obstruction unrelated to stone disease include tumor, lymphadenopathy, fibrosis, parasites, and kinking of the duct. Regardless of cause, obstruction of the cystic duct leads to filling and distention of the gallbladder. The ensuing inflammatory reaction may be related to mucosal ischemia from increased hydrostatic pressure or to the action of cytotoxic products of bile metabolism (e.g., lysophosphatidylcholine).[104] Although bacteria are isolated from the bile of inflamed gallbladders in 50% to 75% of cases, the role of infection in the pathogenesis of cholecystitis is not completely understood.[105] Coliforms (e.g., *E. coli*) represent the most common isolates, but anaerobes have been identified in as many as 40% of cases.

Clinical Features

The most common presenting symptom of cholecystitis is pain, usually in the right upper quadrant. Although the pain may initially be described as colicky, it becomes constant in virtually all cases. A prior history of similar but less severe and self-limited symptoms is a valuable diagnostic clue, as is a prior history of documented gallstones. Radiation of pain is generally to the tip of the scapula on the right. Nausea and vomiting are generally present, and the patient may complain of fever.

Physical examination reveals tenderness in the right upper quadrant or epigastric region, often with guarding or rebound. Murphy's sign (tenderness and an inspiratory pause elicited by palpation of the right upper quadrant during a deep breath) is compatible with, but not specific for, gallbladder inflammation. Fever and tachycardia are commonly absent, and cholecystitis should remain a diagnostic consideration in the absence of these findings in patients with abdominal pain and right upper quadrant pain and tenderness.[106]

Diagnostic Considerations

A polymorphonuclear leukocytosis with left shift is common but has been reported to be in a normal range in 27% to 40% of patients.[106,107] Serum aminotransferase, bilirubin, and alkaline phosphatase may be mildly elevated but are more often within normal limits. An elevated amylase or lipase should suggest the diagnosis of pancreatitis, either instead of or in addition to cholecystitis. Plain abdominal radiographs may reveal calcified stones, gas in the gallbladder, or an upper quadrant sentinel loop. However, these findings are so uncommon and nonspecific that plain film radiographs are not recommended unless other diagnostic considerations are present.

Ultrasound imaging is the most useful test in the emergency department setting. Visualization of the gallbladder without identification of stones has an extremely high negative predictive value for cholecystitis, whereas the presence of stones, a thickened gallbladder wall, and pericholecystic fluid has a positive predictive value in excess of 90% (see Figure 89-7).[108]

Nuclear scintigraphy with technetium-99m–labeled iminodiacetic acid (IDA) is generally considered the most sensitive and specific imaging test for cholecystitis. IDA administered IV is taken up by hepatocytes and secreted into the bile canaliculi. Failure to outline the gallbladder within 1 hour of administration of IDA in the presence of hepatic and common duct visualization proves cystic duct obstruction. In the appropriate clinical setting, this finding is diagnostic of cholecystitis. Conversely, visualization of the gallbladder and common duct within 1 hour of administration has a negative predictive value of 98%.[109] Scintigraphy with IDA loses its sensitivity as serum bilirubin rises above 5 to 8 mg; however, scintigraphy with diisopropyl IDA (diisopropyl iminodiacetic acid or mebrofenin) allows visualization of the biliary tree in patients with total serum bilirubin in the range of 20 to 30 mg.[110]

Differential Considerations

Diagnostic considerations in the patient suspected of having cholecystitis include hepatitis, hepatic abscess, pyelonephritis, right lower lobe pneumonia or pleurisy, pancreatitis, peptic acid disease of the duodenum with perforation or penetration, and appendicitis. Up to 20% of patients with acute cholecystitis may be misdiagnosed when only clinical criteria are considered.[111] Accurate diagnosis often requires the use of sonographic or, less commonly, scintigraphic studies.

Management

Basic supportive measures provide the foundation for initial management of acute cholecystitis. Volume status should be optimized with IV crystalloid administration. Emesis can be managed with antiemetics and nasogastric suction. Nasogastric suctioning may have the added benefit of diminishing the stimulus for biliary secretion and excretion, thereby adding to pain relief. Narcotic analgesic agents are useful for pain control. Despite the questionable role of microbial infection in the pathogenesis of cholecystitis, antibiotics are recommended. Unless clinical evidence of sepsis exists, coverage with a single broad-spectrum antibiotic (e.g., a second-generation or third-generation cephalosporin) is adequate.

The most serious complication of cholecystitis is gangrene of the gallbladder, with necrosis and perforation. Localized perforation may lead to pericholecystic abscess or fistula formation, the latter predisposing to gallstone ileus at a later date. Patients with diabetes mellitus are at increased risk for bacterial invasion of the gallbladder wall and the development of emphysematous cholecystitis.

Disposition

Admission for antibiotics and pain management is required. Surgery is recommended for patients with cholecystitis; however, the best timing for operation is not certain. Surgery is usually performed after symptoms have subsided but during the acute hospitalization. Immediate cholecystectomy or cholecystotomy is reserved for the complicated case in which the patient has gangrene or perforation.

Special Considerations

Cholecystitis is uncommon in the pediatric age group but, when it occurs, should be managed as it is in the adult. When cholecystitis occurs in the pregnant woman, it poses challenging diagnostic and therapeutic issues. Initial therapy is identical to that for the nonpregnant patient, but the issue of surgical intervention requires an individualized consultation between surgeon and obstetrician.

Acalculous cholecystitis occurs in approximately 5% to 14% of cases.[74] It is more common in elders and is most often encountered in patients who are recovering from nonbiliary tract surgery. Over the past decade, acalculous disease has been increasingly encountered as a complication of advanced acquired immunodeficiency syndrome (AIDS), usually secondary to infection with CMV or *Cryptosporidium*. Compared with calculous disease, acalculous cholecystitis tends to have a more acute and malignant course with a mortality rate as high as 41%.[112] The same techniques are used to diagnose acalculous disease as for other forms of cholecystitis but are less sensitive and specific. Sonographic findings include thickening of the gallbladder wall, pericholecystic fluid, and lack of response to cholecystokinin. Scintigraphic findings are the same as in calculous disease.

Emphysematous cholecystitis is an uncommon variant of cholecystitis, occurring in approximately 1% of cases. It is characterized by the presence of gas in the gallbladder wall, presumably consequent to the invasion of the mucosa by gas-producing organisms (e.g., *E. coli, Klebsiella* sp, and *Clostridium perfringens*). It is more common in diabetic patients, has a male predominance, and is acalculous in up to 50% of cases.[113,114] Clinical presentation and physical findings are similar to those in cholecystitis. Plain radiographs or CT scans of the abdomen will reveal gas in the gallbladder wall. Because of a high incidence of gangrene and perforation, emergency cholecystectomy is recommended.[106] Antibiotic coverage should include penicillin, an aminoglycoside, and clindamycin or an ampicillin-sulbactam combination agent. Mortality in emphysematous cholecystitis is approximately 15%.[114]

KEY CONCEPTS

- The vast majority of patients with cholecystitis have gallstones; however, approximately 5% have acalculous disease. This group of patients tends to have more severe disease and is at increased risk for complications.
- Despite an unclear relationship between bacterial infection and pathophysiology, antibiotic therapy is recommended.
- Patients with acalculous and emphysematous cholecystitis are at increased risk for gangrene and perforation and should have emergent cholecystectomy.

Cholangitis

Perspective

Acute obstructive cholangitis was first described by Charcot in 1877. In one large series, it was reported to occur in approximately 8% of patients admitted for biliary tract disease.[115] Cholangitis is most often a consequence of common duct blockage by a gallstone but may be associated with malignancy or a benign stricture.

Principles of Disease

The key factors in the pathogenesis of cholangitis are obstruction, elevated intraluminal pressure, and bacterial infection. Incomplete obstruction occurs more commonly than complete blockage.[115] Bacteria may gain access to the obstructed common duct either in a retrograde manner from the duodenum, through lymphatics, or from portal vein blood. The most commonly encountered organisms are similar to those encountered in other varieties of biliary tract disease: *E. coli, Klebsiella, Enterococcus,* and *Bacteroides*.

Clinical Features

Patients most often experience fever, chills, nausea, vomiting, and abdominal pain. The classical triad of physical findings first described by Charcot are right upper quadrant pain, fever, and jaundice. Although these findings are compatible with cholangitis, they can also be seen with both cholecystitis and hepatitis. Sepsis is a common complication and may be heralded by tachycardia, tachypnea, and frank hypotension. The presence of Charcot's triad along with the clinical signs of sepsis and altered sensorium is referred to as Reynolds' pentad.

Diagnostic Considerations

Common laboratory abnormalities include polymorphonuclear leukocytosis, hyperbilirubinemia, elevated alkaline phosphatase, and moderately increased aminotransferases. Arterial blood gas measurements are useful to assess base deficit as an early sign of sepsis.

Sonography can be helpful if it demonstrates common and intrahepatic ductal dilation, whereas identification of stones in the gallbladder or common duct suggests the underlying cause of obstruction

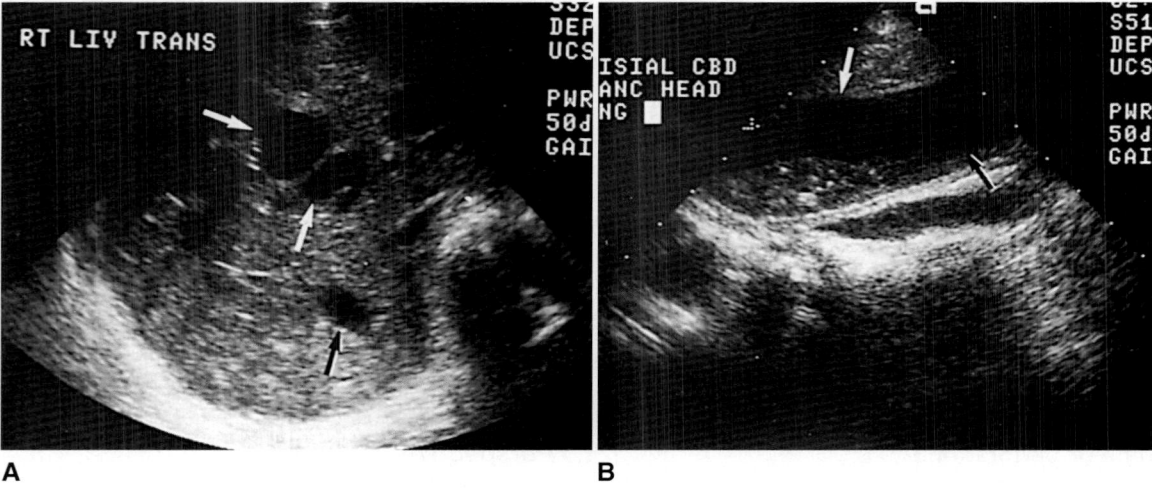

Figure 89-8. Abdominal ultrasound images. **A,** Multiple dilated intrahepatic ducts in patient with common bile duct obstruction. **B,** Significant dilated common bile duct in the same patient. Duct measures 2 cm.

(Figure 89-8). Although nuclear scintigraphy cannot determine the cause, it appears to be a more sensitive means to diagnose early obstruction. Several studies have demonstrated a high incidence of nonvisualization of the biliary tree with cholescintigraphy in patients with common duct obstruction when sonography failed to identify dilation.[116,117]

Alternative imaging techniques include CT scanning, percutaneous transhepatic cholangiography (THC), and endoscopic retrograde cholangiopancreatography (ERCP). Although these techniques may be more expensive and time consuming, the latter two have the added benefit of offering potential therapeutic benefit. Endoscopic cholangioscopy can permit culture of bile, direct removal of obstructing stones, or decompression of the biliary tree by sphincterotomy or stent placement.[118]

Differential Considerations

Although patients with cholangitis generally have a higher fever and appear more ill than those with cholecystitis, there can be considerable variability and overlap. The presence of jaundice is the clinical sign most helpful in differentiating these two disorders. An elevated bilirubin is characteristic of cholangitis and uncommon in cholecystitis. Ultrasonographic evidence of dilated common and intrahepatic ducts is usually required to distinguish cholangitis from cholecystitis.

Management

Treatment of cholangitis includes hemodynamic stabilization with crystalloid fluid and, if necessary, vasopressors. Broad-spectrum antibiotic coverage should be initiated immediately after blood cultures are obtained. Ampicillin, an aminoglycoside, and clindamycin or metronidazole are suggested. Mezlocillin, an acylureidopenicillin with activity against gram-positive, gram-negative, and anaerobic organisms, is secreted into the bile and may be a reasonable single-agent alternative to triple-drug therapy.[119] The key to successful treatment is early biliary tract decompression. This can be achieved with THC, ERCP, or surgery.

Disposition

Patients with cholangitis require admission, preferably to a monitored setting. Prompt consultation with a service that can provide biliary tract decompression (surgery, interventional radiology, or gastroenterology) is necessary.

KEY CONCEPTS

- Cholangitis is an emergent condition resulting from extrahepatic bile duct obstruction and bacterial infection.
- Effective management requires prompt administration of broad-spectrum antibiotics and early biliary tract decompression.
- Biliary tract decompression can be achieved surgically, transhepatically, or by ERCP.

Sclerosing Cholangitis

Sclerosing cholangitis is an idiopathic inflammatory disorder affecting the biliary tree. It is characterized by diffuse fibrosis and narrowing of the intrahepatic and extrahepatic bile ducts. It is commonly associated with inflammatory bowel disease, particularly ulcerative colitis; however, in 25% of cases it appears as an isolated disorder.[120]

Patients may arrive at the emergency department with complaints of weight loss, lethargy, jaundice, and pruritus. Rarely, these patients develop infective cholangitis. Prompt diagnosis may be more difficult in these cases because of the sclerotic nature of the bile ducts and the failure to demonstrate dilation on ultrasound imaging. Surgical exploration or ERCP is often required for diagnosis. The management of noninfected cases is primarily symptomatic. Cholestyramine, a bile acid sequestrant, may diminish pruritus.

AIDS Cholangiopathy

Patients with advanced HIV disease, generally with CD4 counts less than 200/mm³, may develop any one of a series of disorders collectively referred to as AIDS cholangiopathy. These disorders include bile duct stricture, papillary stenosis, or sclerosing cholangitis.[121] The precise pathophysiology is not completely understood but is related to infection with either CMV, *Cryptosporidium*, microsporidia, or *Mycobacterium avium* complex. The clinical presentation may be similar to that with other causes of cholangitis with fever and right upper quadrant pain. Laboratory values include increased levels of alkaline phosphatase and minor elevation of transaminases. As compared with other etiologies of cholangitis, bilirubin is less commonly elevated. Ultrasonography is generally helpful in identifying bile duct stricture, thickening, or dilation. IDA scans are useful as they are in other causes of cholangitis. Management involves endoscopic sphincterotomy or stent placement in conjunction with treatment of the underlying infective agent.

Porcelain Gallbladder

The porcelain gallbladder is a dramatic radiographic finding caused by either linear or punctate calcifications within the gallbladder wall. Most patients are women, with a mean age in the 50s. Gallstones are commonly present. The gallbladder may be palpable in the right upper quadrant and is usually nontender. Patients with this disorder should be referred for cholecystectomy because of the high incidence of associated carcinoma.

Malignancy

Carcinoma of the biliary tract is uncommon. Gallbladder carcinoma is the most common malignancy, accounting for 5% of all cancers found at autopsy. It occurs predominantly in women older than 50.[122] Cholelithiasis and porcelain gallbladder appear to be major risk factors. Metastatic disease to regional nodes and the liver is common at the time of initial diagnosis because of the relatively silent nature of early disease. Symptoms include chronic right upper quadrant pain and jaundice. Physical examination may reveal a palpable mass in the right upper quadrant. These tumors occasionally perforate, and the patient may have symptoms of pericholecystic abscess. Noninvasive imaging techniques may be of some aid in identifying the tumor. Ultrasound imaging is more sensitive than the CT scan, but even the sequential use of both tests fails to identify malignancy in 49% of cases.[123] Radionuclide imaging is nonspecific, revealing no image in most circumstances.

Carcinoma of the extrahepatic bile ducts is less frequent than gallbladder malignancy and is more common in men. Jaundice is the most frequent finding. A palpable gallbladder (Courvoisier's sign) may be present on physical examination in one third of cases.[124] Diagnosis is suggested by the presence of dilated intrahepatic and extrahepatic bile ducts on sonography. THC and ERCP may delineate better the location and extent of tumor. Scirrhous carcinomas may have a radiographic appearance similar to that of sclerosing cholangitis and may be effectively differentiated only with surgical biopsy. Both gallbladder and ductal carcinomas have a similarly dismal prognosis, with 5-year survival in the range of 5% to 13%.[125]

Carcinoma of Vater's ampulla is more common in elders and in males. The critical location of the ampulla results in relatively early symptoms and thus more prompt diagnosis. Ultrasound imaging is the most useful initial imaging technique, but gastrointestinal endoscopy and ERCP are generally necessary to provide the definitive diagnosis. Early diagnosis contributes to the more favorable prognosis, with 5-year survival ranging from 32% to 62%.[126]

REFERENCES

1. Summary of notifiable diseases—United States, 1997. *MMWR Morb Mortal Wkly Rep* 46:3, 1998.
2. Summary of notifiable diseases—United States, 2001. *MMWR Morb Mortal Wkly Rep* 50:1, 2003.
3. Prevention and control of infections with hepatitis viruses in correctional settings. Centers for Disease Control and Prevention. *MMWR Recomm Rep* 52(RR-1):1, 2003.
4. Prevention of hepatitis A through active or passive immunization: Recommendations of the Advisory Committee on Immunization Practices (ACIP). *MMWR Recomm Rep* 48(RR-12):1, 1999.
5. Lee HS, Vyas GN: Diagnosis of viral hepatitis. *Clin Lab Med* 7:741, 1987.
6. Edwards MS: Hepatitis B serology: Help in interpretation. *Pediatr Clin North Am* 35:503, 1988.
7. Thomas HC: Hepatitis B viral infection. *Am J Med* 85(Suppl 2A):135, 1988.
8. Sulkowski MS, Thomas DL: Hepatitis C in the HIV-infected patient. *Clin Liver Dis* 7:261, 2003.
9. Donahue JG, et al: The declining risk of post-transfusion hepatitis C virus infection. *N Engl J Med* 327:369, 1992.
10. Non-A, non-B hepatitis—Illinois. *MMWR Morb Mortal Wkly Rep* 38:529, 1989.
11. Alter MJ, et al: The natural history of community acquired hepatitis C in the United States. *N Engl J Med* 327:1899, 1992.
12. Alter M, et al: The prevalence of hepatitis C virus infection in the United States, 1988 through 1994. *N Engl J Med* 341:556, 1999.
13. Rizzetto M, et al: Immunofluorescence detection of a new antigen-antibody system associated to hepatitis B virus in liver and in serum of HBsAg carriers. *Gut* 18:997, 1977.
14. Chatzinoff M, Friedman LS: Delta agent hepatitis. *Infect Dis Clin North Am* 1:529, 1987.
15. Bonino F, Smedile A, Verme G: Hepatitis delta virus infection. *Adv Intern Med* 32:345, 1987.
16. Govindarajan S, et al: Fulminate B viral hepatitis: Role of delta agent. *Gastroenterology* 86:1417, 1984.
17. Alter M, et al: Acute non-A-E hepatitis in the United States and the role of hepatitis G virus infection. *N Engl J Med* 336:741, 1997.
18. Alter H, et al: The incidence of transfusion-associated hepatitis G virus infection and its relation to liver disease. *N Engl J Med* 336:747, 1997.
19. Lee W: Acute liver failure. *N Engl J Med* 329:1862, 1993.
20. Cossart Y: Laboratory investigation of hepatitis C: A review. *Pathology* 31:102, 1999.

21. Hoofnagle JH: Hepatitis. In Mandell GL, Douglas RG, Bennett JE (eds): *Principles and Practice of Infectious Disease*. New York, Churchill Livingstone, 1990.

22. Smedile A, et al: Influence of delta infection on severity of hepatitis B. *Lancet* 2:945, 1982.

23. Trott A: Hepatitis B exposure and the emergency physician: Risk assessment and hepatitis vaccine update. *Am J Emerg Med* 5:54, 1987.

24. Iserson KV, Criss EA: Hepatitis B: Prevalence in emergency physicians. *Ann Emerg Med* 14:119, 1985.

25. Iserson KV, Criss EA, Wright AL: Hepatitis B and vaccination in emergency physicians. *Am J Emerg Med* 5:227, 1987.

26. Update on hepatitis B prevention. *MMWR Morb Mortal Wkly Rep* 36:353, 1987.

27. Suboptimal response to hepatitis B vaccine given by injection into the buttock. *MMWR Morb Mortal Wkly Rep* 34:105, 1985.

28. Recommendations for protection against viral hepatitis. *MMWR Morb Mortal Wkly Rep* 34:312, 1985.

29. Lauer GM, Walker BD: Hepatitis C virus infection. *N Engl J Med* 345:41, 2001.

30. Diehl AM: Alcoholic liver disease. *Med Clin North Am* 73:815, 1989.

31. Premature mortality in the United States: Public health issues in the use of years of potential life lost. *MMWR Morb Mortal Wkly Rep* 35(2 Suppl):1S, 1986.

32. Lieber CS: Alcoholic liver disease: New insights in pathogenesis lead to new treatments. *J Hepatol* 32(Suppl 1):113, 2000.

33. Morgan MY, Sherlock S: Sex related differences among 100 patients with alcoholic liver disease. *Br Med J* 1:939, 1977.

34. Lamarine RJ: Alcohol abuse among Native Americans. *J Community Health* 13:143, 1988.

35. Monteiro E, et al: Histocompatibility antigens: Marker for susceptibility to and protection from alcoholic liver disease in a Portuguese population. *Hepatology* 8:455, 1988.

36. Bird GL, Williams R: Treatment of advanced alcoholic liver disease. *Alcohol Alcohol* 25:197, 1990.

37. Bird G, et al: Insulin and glucagon infusion in acute alcoholic hepatitis: A prospective randomized controlled trial. *Hepatology* 14:1097, 1991.

38. Carithers RL Jr, et al: Methylprednisolone therapy in patients with severe alcoholic hepatitis: A randomized multicenter trial. *Ann Intern Med* 110:685, 1989.

39. Angulo P: Nonalcoholic fatty liver disease. *N Engl J Med* 346:1221, 2002.

40. Heathcote J: The clinical expression of primary biliary cirrhosis. *Semin Liver Dis* 17:23, 1996.

41. Fraser C, Arieff AI: Hepatic encephalopathy. *N Engl J Med* 313:865, 1985.

42. Mousseau DD, Butterworth RF: Trace amines in hepatic encephalopathy. *Prog Brain Res* 106:277, 1995.

43. Scollo-Lavizzori G, Steinmann E: Reversal of hepatic coma by benzodiazepine antagonist (R015-1788). *Lancet* 1:1324, 1985.

44. Butterworth RF: Pathophysiology of hepatic encephalopathy: A new look at ammonia. *Metab Brain Dis* 17:221, 2002.

45. Kircheis G, et al: Clinical efficacy of L-ornithine-L-aspartate in the management of hepatic encephalopathy. *Metab Brain Dis* 17:453, 2002.

46. Kircheis G, Haussinger D: Management of hepatic encephalopathy. *J Gastroenterol Hepatol* 17:S260, 2002.

47. Hassanein T, et al: Albumin dialysis in cirrhosis with superimposed acute liver injury: Possible impact of albumin dialysis on hospitalization costs. *Liver Int* 23:61, 2003.

48. Jalan R, et al: Extracorporeal liver support with molecular adsorbents recirculating system in patients with severe acute alcoholic hepatitis. *J Hepatol* 38:24, 2003.

49. Conn HO, Fessel JM: Spontaneous bacterial peritonitis in cirrhosis: Variations on a theme. *Medicine (Baltimore)* 50:161, 1971.

50. Wilcox CM, Dismukes WE: Spontaneous bacterial peritonitis: A review of pathogenesis, diagnosis and treatment. *Medicine (Baltimore)* 66:447, 1987.

51. Guarner C, Soriano G: Spontaneous bacterial peritonitis. *Semin Liver Dis* 17:203, 1997.

52. Gilbert J, Kamath P: Spontaneous bacterial peritonitis: An update. *Mayo Clin Proc* 70:365, 1995.

53. Evans LT, et al: Spontaneous bacterial peritonitis in asymptomatic outpatients with cirrhotic ascites. *Hepatology* 37:897, 2003.

54. Stassen WN, et al: Immediate diagnostic criteria for bacterial infection of ascitic fluid: Evaluation of ascitic fluid polymorphonuclear leukocyte count, pH, and lactate concentration, alone and in combination. *Gastroenterology* 90:1247, 1986.

55. Hallak A: Spontaneous bacterial peritonitis. *Am J Gastroenterol* 84:345, 1989.

56. Castellote J, et al: Rapid diagnosis of spontaneous bacterial peritonitis by use of reagent strips. *Hepatology* 37:893, 2003.

57. Attali P, et al: pH of ascitic fluid: Diagnostic and prognostic value in cirrhotic and noncirrhotic patients. *Gastroenterology* 90:1255, 1986.

58. Andreu M, et al: Risk factors for spontaneous bacterial peritonitis in cirrhotic patients with ascites. *Gastroenterology* 104:1133, 1993.

59. Guarner C, et al: Risk of a first community-acquired spontaneous bacterial peritonitis in cirrhotics with low ascitic fluid protein levels. *Gastroenterology* 117:414, 1999.

60. Das A: A cost analysis of long term antibiotic prophylaxis for spontaneous bacterial peritonitis in cirrhosis. *Am J Gastroenterol* 93:1895, 1998.

61. Rolachon A: Ciprofloxacin and long-term prevention of spontaneous bacterial peritonitis: Results of a prospective controlled trial. *Hepatology* 22:1171, 1995.

62. Lewis JH, Zimmerman HJ: Drug-induced liver disease. *Med Clin North Am* 73:775, 1989.

63. Lee WM: Drug-induced hepatotoxicity. *N Engl J Med* 349:474, 2003.

64. Rollins BJ: Hepatic veno-occlusive disease. *Am J Med* 81:297, 1986.

65. Maddrey WC: Hepatic vein thrombosis (Budd-Chiari syndrome): Possible association with the use of oral contraceptives. *Semin Liver Dis* 7:32, 1987.

66. Rustgi AK, Richter JM: Pyogenic and amoebic liver abscess. *Med Clin North Am* 73:847, 1989.

67. Chu KM, et al: Pyogenic liver abscess. An audit of experience over the past decade. *Arch Surg* 131:148, 1996.

68. Greenstein AJ, Sachar DB: Pyogenic and amebic abscesses of the liver. *Semin Liver Dis* 8:210, 1988.

69. Seeto R, Rockey D: Pyogenic liver abscess. Changes in etiology, management, and outcome. *Medicine (Baltimore)* 75:99, 1996.

70. Srivastava ED, Mayberry JF: Pyogenic liver abscess: A review of aetiology, diagnosis and intervention. *Dig Dis* 8:287, 1990.

71. Barnes PF, et al: A comparison of amoebic and pyogenic abscesses of the liver. *Medicine (Baltimore)* 66:472, 1987.

72. Rajak CL, et al: Percutaneous treatment of liver abscesses: Needle aspiration versus catheter drainage. *AJR Am J Roentgenol* 170:1035, 1998.

73. Ch YS, et al: Pyogenic liver abscess: Treatment with needle aspiration. *Clin Radiol* 52:912, 1997.

74. Chou F, et al: Single and multiple pyogenic liver abscesses: Clinical course, etiology, and results of treatment. *World J Surg* 21:384, 1997.

75. Amebiasis associated with colonic irrigation—Colorado. *MMWR Morb Mortal Wkly Rep* 30:101, 1981.

76. Sargeunt PG, Williams JE, Grene JD: The differentiation of invasive and non-invasive *Entamoeba histolytica* isoenzyme electrophoresis. *Trans R Soc Trop Med Hyg* 75:519, 1978.

77. Katzenstein D, Rickerson V, Braude A: New concepts of amoebic liver abscess derived from hepatic imaging: Serodiagnosis and hepatic enzymes in 67 consecutive cases in San Diego. *Medicine (Baltimore)* 61:237, 1982.

78. Kraoul L, et al: Evaluation of a rapid enzyme immunoassay for diagnosis of hepatic amoebiasis. *J Clin Microbiol* 35:1530, 1997.

79. Parija S, Karki B: Detection of circulating antigen in amoebic liver abscess by counter-current immunoelectrophoresis. *J Med Microbiol* 48:99, 1999.

80. Hoffner R, et al: Common presentation of amebic liver abscess. *Ann Emerg Med* 34:351, 1999.

81. Boyer JL: Chronic hepatitis—A perspective on classification and determinants of prognosis. *Gastroenterology* 70:1161, 1976.

82. Balisteri WF: Viral hepatitis. *Pediatr Clin North Am* 35:637,1988.

83. Garcia G, Gentry KR: Chronic viral hepatitis. *Med Clin North Am* 73:971, 1989.

84. Payne JA: Chronic hepatitis: Pathogenesis and treatment. *Dis Mon* 34:109, 1988.

85. Reyes H: Review: intrahepatic cholestasis. A puzzling disorder of pregnancy. *J Gastroenterol Hepatol* 12:211, 1997.

86. Rustgi VK: Liver disease in pregnancy. *Med Clin North Am* 73:1041, 1989.

87. Castro M, et al: Reversible peripartum liver failure: A new perspective on the diagnosis, treatment, and cause of acute fatty liver of pregnancy, based on 28 consecutive cases. *Am J Obstet Gynecol* 181:389, 1999.

88. Di Bisceglie AD: Hepatocellular carcinoma: Molecular biology of its growth and relationship to hepatitis B virus infection. *Med Clin North Am* 73:985, 1989.

89. Beasley RP: Hepatitis B virus: The major etiology of hepatocellular carcinoma. *Cancer* 61:1942, 1988.

90. Lisker-Melman M, Martin P, Hoofnagle JH: Conditions associated with hepatocellular carcinoma. *Med Clin North Am* 73:999, 1989.

91. Savitsky EA, et al: Evaluation of orthotopic liver transplant recipients presenting to the emergency department. *Ann Emerg Med* 31:507, 1998.

92. Hussain HK: Imaging of hepatic transplantation. *Clin Liver Dis* 6:247, 2002.

93. Krondyl A, Vavrinkova H, Michalec C: Effect of cholecystectomy on the role of the gallbladder in fat absorption. *Gut* 5:607, 1964.

94. Young M: Acute diseases of the pancreas and biliary tract. *Emerg Med Clin North Am* 7:555, 1989.

95. Comess LJ, Bennett PH, Burch TA: Clinical gallbladder disease in Pima Indians. *N Engl J Med* 277:894, 1967.

96. Maki T: Pathogenesis of calcium bilirubinate gallstones: Role of *E. coli*, β-glucuronidase and coagulation by inorganic ions, polyelectrolytes and agitations. *Ann Surg* 164:90, 1966.

97. Carroll BA: Preferred imaging techniques for the diagnosis of cholecystitis and cholelithiasis. *Ann Surg* 210:1, 1989.

98. Cardenas E: Limited bedside ultrasound imaging by emergency medicine physicians. *West J Med* 168:188, 1998.

99. Tomida S, et al: Long-term ursodeoxycholic acid therapy is associated with reduced risk of biliary pain and acute cholecystitis in patients with gallbladder stones: A cohort analysis. *Hepatology* 30:6, 1999.

100. Petroni ML, et al: Repeated bile acid therapy for the long-term management of cholesterol gallstones. *J Hepatol* 25:719, 1996.

101. Thistle JL, Peterson BT: Biliary lithotripsy: A perspective. *Ann Intern Med* 111:868, 1989.

102. Friedman GD, Kannel WB, Dawber TR: The epidemiology of gallbladder disease: Observations in the Framingham study. *J Chronic Dis* 19:273, 1966.

103. Kadakia SC: Biliary tract emergencies. *Med Clin North Am* 77:1015, 1993.

104. Jivegard L, Thornell E, Svanik J: Pathophysiology of acute obstructive cholecystitis: Implications for nonoperative management. *Br J Surg* 74:1084, 1987.

105. Nahrwold DL: Acute cholecystitis. In Sabiston DC Jr (ed): *Textbook of Surgery,* 14th ed. Philadelphia, WB Saunders, 1991.

106. Singer AJ, et al: Correlation among clinical, laboratory, and hepatobiliary scanning findings in patients with suspected acute cholecystitis. *Ann Emerg Med* 28:267, 1996.

107. Gruber PJ, et al: Presence of fever and leukocytosis in acute cholecystitis. *Ann Emerg Med* 28:273, 1996.

108. Cooperberg PL, Jibney RG: Imaging the gallbladder. *Radiology* 163:605, 1987.

109. Weissman HS, et al: An update in radionuclide imaging in the diagnosis of cholecystitis. *JAMA* 246:1354, 1981.

110. Grossman SJ, Joyce JM: Hepatobiliary imaging. *Emerg Med Clin North Am* 9:853, 1991.

111. Halasz NA: Counterfeit cholecystitis: A common diagnostic dilemma. *Am J Surg* 130:189, 1975.

112. Kalliafas S, et al: Acute acalculous cholecystitis: Incidence, risk factors, diagnosis, and outcome. *Am Surg* 64:471, 1998.

113. Garcia-Sancho Tellez L, et al: Acute emphysematous cholecystitis. Report of twenty cases. *Hepatogastroenterology* 46:2144, 1999.

114. Joshi N: Infections in patients with diabetes mellitus. *N Engl J Med* 341:1906, 1999.

115. Salk RP, et al: Spectrum of cholangitis. *Am J Surg* 130:143, 1975.

116. Kaplun L, et al: The early diagnosis of common duct obstruction using cholescintigraphy. *JAMA* 254:2431, 1985.

117. Miller DR, Egbert RM, Braunstein P: Comparison of ultrasound and hepatobiliary imaging in the early detection of acute total common duct obstruction. *Arch Surg* 119:1933, 1984.

118. Brugge W, Van Dam J: Pancreatic and biliary endoscopy. *N Engl J Med* 341:1808, 1999.

119. Gerecht WB, et al: Prospective randomized comparison of mezlocillin therapy along with combined ampicillin and gentamicin therapy for patients with cholangitis. *Arch Intern Med* 149:1279, 1989.

120. Schaffner F: Sclerosing cholangitis. In Berk JE (ed): *Gastroenterology,* vol 6, 4th ed. Philadelphia, WB Saunders, 1985.

121. Tanowitz H, et al: Gastrointestinal manifestations. *Med Clin North Am* 80:1395, 1996.

122. Fromm D: Carcinoma of the gallbladder. In Sabiston DC Jr (ed): *Textbook of Surgery,* 13th ed. Philadelphia, WB Saunders, 1986.

123. Fultz PJ, Skucas J, Weiss SL: Comparative imaging of gallbladder cancer. *J Clin Gastroenterol* 10:683, 1988.

124. Orloff MJ, Marassi NP: Tumor of the extrahepatic bile ducts. In Berk JE (ed): *Gastroenterology,* vol 6, 4th ed. Philadelphia, WB Saunders, 1985.

125. Arnaud JP, et al: Primary carcinoma of the gallbladder—Review of 143 cases. *Hepatogastroenterology* 42:811, 1995.

126. Hayes DH, et al: Carcinoma of the ampulla of Vater. *Ann Surg* 206:572, 1987.

CHAPTER

90 Pancreas

Sally A. Santen and Robin R. Hemphill

The pancreas is a retroperitoneal organ extending across the posterior abdomen in the epigastrium (Figure 90-1). The head of the pancreas sits in the loop of the first part of the duodenum, whereas the tail lies against the hilum of the spleen. The main pancreatic duct goes from the tail through the body to the head of the pancreas and with the common bile duct enters the second part of the duodenum through the sphincter of Oddi. Accessory ducts and anomalies are not uncommon. Anterior to the pancreas from right to left are the transverse colon, the lesser sac of the omentum, and the stomach. Posterior are the bile duct, portal vein, splenic vein, vena cava, aorta, and superior mesenteric artery. To the left are the psoas muscle, kidney, and adrenal gland. Because of the close proximity, inflammation of the pancreas not only may injure these structures but also can mimic a variety of diseases.

The pancreas has essential exocrine and endocrine functions. Exocrine products include amylase, lipase, trypsin, chymotrypsin, elastase, carboxypeptidase, phospholipase, and other enzymes. In addition, bicarbonate is produced in greatest quantity from this organ. The bicarbonate serves to neutralize gastric acids as well as the enzymes that break down proteins, carbohydrates, and fats. Cholecystokinin, pancreozymin, and secretin, as well as other factors, control secretion of these enzymes. The endocrine functions of the pancreas are managed by insulin, glucagon, pancreatic polypeptide, and somatostatin.

In the general population, diabetes is the most common disorder of the pancreas, followed by pancreatitis. Acute pancreatitis is an inflammatory process of the pancreas usually associated with abdominal pain, elevated pancreatic enzymes, and variable involvement of other regional tissues or remote organ systems. Pancreatic abscesses, necrosis, and pseudocysts are complications of pancreatitis. Repeated bouts of pancreatitis of any etiology may ultimately result in chronic pancreatitis because of permanent alterations in function and morphology. Chronic pancreatitis is an ongoing inflammation of the pancreas, which may be interrupted by spells of acute pancreatitis.

Pancreatic tumors may develop from the endocrine or nonendocrine structures. These tumors may cause acute pancreatitis but usually arise in a more indolent fashion. The most common is adenocarcinoma originating from the pancreatic ducts. Chronic pancreatitis is a risk factor for pancreatic cancer.

ACUTE PANCREATITIS

Perspective

The first reports of pancreatitis date to the 1700s, and the first accurate study and description were completed by Fitz in 1889.[1] He noted that performing surgery in the early stages of this disease was "extremely hazardous." Since then, our understanding of pancreatitis has evolved; however, treatment remains largely supportive rather than curative. Advances in care have decreased hospital mortality for all patients with pancreatitis from 10% to 15% 20 years ago to 4% to 7% more recently.[2] Most patients with pancreatitis have a mild course; however, 10% to 15% of cases are severe and have a mortality rate of 20% to 50%.[2,3] Children are at increased risk for mortality, with rates of approximately 10%.[4] Severity is also increased in obese patients,[5,6] and in all patients disease progression and outcome are difficult to predict at onset.[7]

As indicated, pancreatitis can be divided into mild or severe, with severity of the disease being defined by the presence of organ failure or local complications such as necrosis, pseudocysts, or abscess.[8] The gravity of the impending illness may not be apparent at the initial presentation. Death in the first week is usually from pulmonary failure, multiorgan failure, or cardiovascular collapse.[8] Later deaths are more likely to be from infective complications.[9] Approximately 40% of cases of fatal pancreatitis remain undiagnosed prior to autopsy. Therefore, pancreatitis should be suspected in moribund patients with multiorgan failure, particularly in elders.

The incidence of acute pancreatitis in the United States is 100 per 100,000, although this incidence varies with the age, gender, and social characteristics of the population studied.[10,11] Gallstones are the most common obstructive cause of pancreatitis and occur more commonly in women than men, with peak symptomatic incidence between 50 and 60 years of age. Some anatomic variations of the duct result in increased risk of obstruction.[12] Many gallstones are asymptomatic; however, 3% to 7% of patients with gallstones develop pancreatitis.[11] Alcoholic pancreatitis is more common in men than women. In most (but not all) populations, alcohol is the second leading cause of pancreatitis after obstructive causes. In chil-

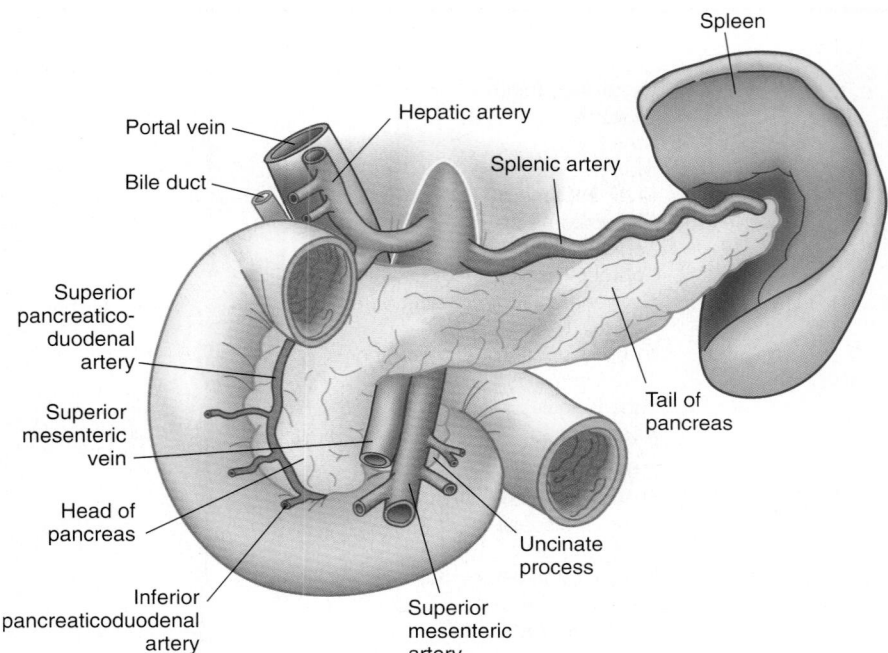

Figure 90-1. Diagrammatic representation of the anterior view of the pancreas. (Redrawn from Feldman M, Friedman LS, Sleisenger MH (eds): Sleisenger and Fordtran's Gastrointestinal and Liver Disease: Pathophysiology, Diagnosis, Management, 7th ed. Philadelphia, Elsevier, 2002.)

dren, trauma is the most common identifiable cause of acute pancreatitis.[4,13]

Principles of Disease

Pathophysiology

The pathogenesis of pancreatitis is multifactorial although poorly understood. The initial cause of pancreatitis is thought to include direct cellular toxicity or increased ductal pressure. Many mechanisms are recognized, including obstruction of the pancreatic or bile ducts, direct toxicity of the pancreatic cells from toxins or infections, trauma, and idiopathic causes. Regardless of the etiology, the final common pathway is premature activation of pancreatic enzymes such as trypsinogen and zymogen either in the ducts or in the acinar cells.[5,12,14] This activation causes the release of enzymes that are intended to digest dietary proteins and fats but instead lead to cellular breakdown and pancreatic tissue autodigestion. Initially, the injury is localized, creating focal pancreatic injury and edema. With increasing severity, the inflammation causes necrosis of the pancreas and spreads to the surrounding fat and tissues. There may be necrosis of the pancreatic ducts as well as the vascular structures, leading to hemorrhage.[15,16] Necrosis of more than 30% of the pancreas increases both morbidity and mortality.[17]

The enzyme activation, inflammation, and necrosis commonly create a fluid collection in 30% to 50% of patients with severe pancreatitis.[18] Over time, a fibrinous or granulation wall may develop around this fluid collection, creating a pseudocyst. Thus, pseudocysts are not present in the initial phases of pancreatitis but instead develop over 4 to 6 weeks. Fluid collections, necrotic areas, or pseudocysts may become infected in 1% of cases, usually after several weeks.[18]

Inflammation of the pancreas can affect surrounding tissues. Irritation of the surrounding bowel is common, creating bowel wall edema, ileus, and third spacing of fluid. Formation of ascites is common and together with bowel edema can cause significant intravascular fluid loss and hypotension.

Because of the release of inflammatory mediators, the initial localized inflammatory response caused by pancreatitis may cause a systemic immune response syndrome resulting in multiple organ failure. This is a sepsis-like response and any organ system can be involved, potentially resulting in myocardial depression, adult respiratory distress syndrome (ARDS), disseminated intravascular coagulation, or renal failure.[19]

Etiology

Eighty percent of pancreatitis is caused by either gallstones (45%) or alcoholism (35%) (Box 90-1).[5] The exact mechanism of biliary pancreatitis is not clear. Either a stone within the bile duct applies transmural pressure on the pancreatic duct or a stone in the common channel of the pancreatic duct and common bile duct causes obstruction. Obstruction or pressure on the pancreatic duct causes bile reflux or increased pressure of pancreatic secretions. Either mechanism leads to the activation of pancreatic enzymes, setting off the cascade of pancreatitis. Many cases that were presumed to be idiopathic are actually due to small stones, sludge, or crystals that are too small to be seen by ultrasound examination but may be noted on endoscopic retrograde cholangiopancreatography (ERCP).[20]

Alcohol is the cause of about 35% of pancreatitis cases. The mechanism by which alcohol is toxic to the pancreas is not well understood. Possible mechanisms include toxic effects of the ethanol metabolite acetaldehyde, ethanol-related lipid metabolism, or spasm of the

BOX 90-1. Etiology of Pancreatitis

Toxic
Alcohol, methanol
Drugs
Scorpion bites in Trinidad

Metabolic
Hypercalcemia (often from hyperparathyroid)
Hyperlipidemia and hypertriglyceridemia (>1000 mg/dL)

Obstructive
Biliary tract disease
Ampullary tumors
Pancreas divisum with obstruction of the accessory duct
Periampullary duodenal diverticula
ERCP and postpancreatography
Pancreatic neuroendocrine tumors
Pancreatic carcinoma
Sphincter of Oddi fibrosis, stricture, tumor, or hypertension

Infectious
Viral
Adenovirus
Coxsackievirus
CMV
EBV
Echovirus
Hepatitis A, B, C virus
HIV
Varicella
Rubella

Other Infections
Aspergillus
Campylobacter
Clonorchiasis
Cryptococcus

Cryptosporidium
Dysentery
MAI
Mumps
Mycobacterium TB
Mycoplasma sp.
Legionella sp.
Leptospirosis
Salmonella typhimurium
Scarlet fever
Streptococcal food poisoning
Toxoplasma
Tuberculosis
Ascariasis

Other Etiologies
Diabetic mellitus, DKA
Crohn's disease
Cystic fibrosis
Emboli (atherosclerotic)
Hemochromatosis
Hereditary pancreatitis
Hypothermia
Vasculitis
Lupus
Polyarteritis nodosa, malignant hypertension
Ischemia from hypoperfusion
Perforated ulcer
Postoperative
Pregnancy
Reye's syndrome
Trauma
Uremia
Idiopathic

CMV, cytomegalovirus; DKA, diabetic ketoacidosis; EBV, Epstein-Barr virus; ERCP, endoscopic retrograde cholangiopancreatography; HIV, human immunodeficiency virus; MAI, *Mycobacterium avium* intracellulare; TB, tuberculosis.

sphincter of Oddi. Patients with alcoholic pancreatitis have usually had 5 to 10 years of chronic alcohol use before the onset of pancreatitis.[5,21] Underlying chronic pancreatitis may precede and follow exacerbations of acute pancreatitis.

In addition to alcohol, a number of other medications and toxins cause pancreatitis, including didanosine, pentamidine, organophosphates, and selected scorpion bites. The list of definite and potential drugs causing pancreatitis is quite extensive (Box 90-2). Another cause of pancreatitis is hypertriglyceridemia, with levels less than 500 mg/dL being implicated, although often the level is above 1000 mg/dL. In pregnancy, both gallstones and increased triglycerides levels can cause pancreatitis.[5] When this occurs, both maternal and fetal mortality is high (20%).

Both blunt and penetrating abdominal trauma can disrupt the ductal system and the pancreatic cells, setting off the enzyme cascade that results in acute pancreatitis. Pancreatitis may also develop in 1% to 10% of ERCP procedures, resulting from iatrogenic ductal injury.[22] Likewise, postoperative pancreatitis is well recognized and is associated with a higher mortality than other etiologies.

Although both viral and bacterial etiologies for pancreatitis are known, the two most common viral causes of pancreatitis are mumps and Coxsackie B. Pancreatitis is more common in patients with human immunodeficiency virus (HIV) than in the general population.[22] In addition to the common etiologies, this population is at risk for pancreatitis from opportunistic infections, HIV-specific medications, and acquired immunodeficiency syndrome (AIDS)–related cancers.[23,24] Ultimately, the cause of acute pancreatitis is idiopathic in about 10% of cases.[15]

The etiology of pancreatitis in adults and children is similar, although incidences are different. Trauma (including child abuse), infection, and idiopathic causes make up 70% of the etiologies in children.[3] Hereditary pancreatitis is an autosomal dominant trait with the onset frequently noted during childhood. Other causes include infections and congenital anomalies.[25] In elders, gallstones are the most common cause of acute pancreatitis, causing up to 55% of the cases.[26]

BOX 90-2. Drug-Induced Pancreatitis

Definite	Possible
Acetaminophen	Bumetanide
Azathioprine	Carbamazepine
Cimetidine	Chlorthalidone
Cisplatin	Clonidine
Corticosteroids	Colchicine
Didanosine	Cyclosporin
Erythromycin	Cytarabine
Estrogens	Diazoxide
Ethyl alcohol	Enalapril
Furosemide	Ergotamine
I-Asparaginase	Ethacrynic acid
Mercaptopurine	Indomethacin
Metronidazole	Isoniazid
Methyldopa	Isotretinoin
Nitrofurantoin	Mefenamic acid
Octreotide	Opiates
Organophosphates	Phenformin
Pentamidine	Piroxicam
Ranitidine	Procainamide
Tetracycline	Rifampin
Salicylates	Thiazides
Sulfonamides, trimethoprim-sulfamethoxazole, sulfasalazine	
Sulindac	
Valproic acid	

Clinical Features

Pancreatitis should be suspected in all patients with epigastric abdominal pain, regardless of age. When the diagnosis has been made, the etiology and complications related to the disease should be sought.

By history, almost all patients have abdominal pain, most commonly in the midepigastric area; however, the pain can also be in the right or left upper quadrant. If significant inflammation is present, the pain may be diffuse and the patient may have difficulty localizing the discomfort. Typically, the onset of symptoms is relatively rapid, and the symptoms increase in severity over 30 to 60 minutes. The pain is generally described as constant and severe and may radiate to the midback. The degree of pain does not correlate with the severity of disease. Even though gallstones are frequently the cause of pancreatitis, the onset of pain is not usually related to eating. Nausea and vomiting often accompany the pain. Although the discomfort may be improved by lying on the side or sitting up, more typically there is little relief with position change, moving, eating, vomiting, or bowel movement. Colicky pain or pain that waxes and wanes suggests another diagnosis. Approximately 50% of patients have a history of similar abdominal pain that may represent biliary colic or mild pancreatitis.[27]

On physical examination, vital signs may be stable but are frequently abnormal. Hypotension, tachycardia, and shock indicate severe disease with complications or an alternative diagnosis. Vital signs may also be influenced by pain (tachycardia, tachypnea, hyperten-sion) or alcohol withdrawal (tachycardia, hyperten-sion, fever). A low-grade fever is present in about half of patients with pancreatitis after 1 to 3 days even in the absence of infection.[15,17] High fever is uncommon during the acute presentation of pancreatitis because infection is generally a late complication. Pulse oxime-try should be measured as acute hypoxia is an indica-tor of systemic complication and severe disease.

Patients with pancreatitis generally appear restless and in moderate distress. They may be jaundiced if an obstructing stone is present. The cardiopulmonary examination may be significant for rales or diminished breath sounds if the patient is hypoventilating because of pain or if a pleural effusion is present. Observation of the abdomen may be normal or notable for disten-tion. Only rarely is there evidence of blood within the peritoneum or retroperitoneum resulting from severe hemorrhagic pancreatitis. Blood within these areas is classically described by Cullen's sign (discoloration around the umbilicus) and Grey Turner's sign (dis-coloration of the flank). Auscultation of the abdomen may reveal normal, decreased, or absent bowel sounds depending on whether the patient has a concomitant ileus. Because the pancreas is a retroperitoneal organ, palpation of the abdomen generally reveals epigastric guarding, with rebound tenderness being a less common finding. Murphy's sign may be present if the pancreatitis developed secondary to a biliary source. Very rarely, the physician may see evidence of sub-cutaneous fat necrosis, which appears as red nodules most prominent on the extremities. Other physical findings such as the stigmata of alcoholism or xan-thomas of hyperlipidemia may help point to the etiology of the pancreatitis.

Complications

Complications are common and may be related to local damage as well as systemic injury. The multiorgan involvement arises from the direct release of pancreatic enzymes into the bloodstream and, perhaps more important, from the initiation of the systemic inflam-matory response through mediators. Most of the major organ systems can be affected.[7,12,17]

Shock may result from multiple sources of volume loss. Fluid sequestration occurs in both the pancreas and the bowel lumen and wall. There may also be hemorrhage into necrotic pancreatic tissue. In addition, release of vasodilator and cardiodepressive substances may occur.

About 18% to 30% of patients may have pulmonary complications, including (1) degradation of surfactant by pancreatic phospholipases; (2) pleural effusions (more commonly on the left and frequently with ele-vated amylase); (3) hypoxia from atelectasis, hypoven-tilation, and intrapulmonary shunting; and (4) ARDS. Although ARDS from the loss of surfactant as well as from the inflammatory mediators causing capillary leak is rare, it carries a 60% mortality.[6]

Metabolic complications of pancreatitis include both hyperglycemia and hypocalcemia. Hyperglycemia is

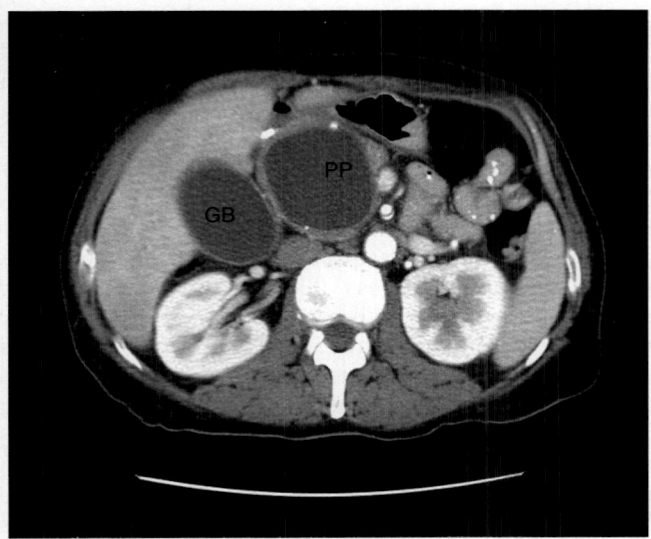

Figure 90-2. Pancreatic pseudocyst formation. In this patient, the pseudocyst was so large as to compress the common bile duct, causing obstructive jaundice. GB, gallbladder; PP, pancreatic pseudocyst.

caused by decreased insulin and increased glucagon. Hypocalcemia is caused by (1) sequestration or saponification of calcium in areas of fat necrosis; (2) hypoalbuminemia, hypomagnesemia, and hyperglucagonemia; and (3) inactivation of parathyroid hormone.

Coagulopathy develops from circulating proteases affecting the coagulation cascade. Acute tubular necrosis can cause acute renal failure and results from circulating inflammatory mediators or from hypotension and hypoperfusion.

Late complications occur after the second week of illness and include local structure involvement, abscess formation (1% to 4%), gastrointestinal bleeding from stress ulcers, splenic vein thrombosis, rupture of pancreatic pseudoaneurysms, fistula formation, splenic rupture, venous thrombosis, and right hydronephrosis.[5] Pancreatic pseudocysts develop in 1% to 8% of patients after 4 to 6 weeks and are more common in alcoholic pancreatitis (Figure 90-2).[28] Long-term complications of pancreatitis include recurrent or chronic pancreatitis, diabetes mellitus, and digestive and malabsorption problems.

Diagnostic Strategies

Laboratory Tests

The diagnosis of acute pancreatitis and its differentiation from other abdominal disorders depend on careful clinical assessment in conjunction with abnormality of certain laboratory values and supportive radiographic findings. The elevation of amylase has been the cornerstone of the diagnosis of pancreatitis, although it is an imperfect assay.

Amylase is an enzyme that cleaves carbohydrates. It is produced primarily in the salivary glands and pancreas, although it can also be found in small amounts in the fallopian tubes, ovary, testis, muscle, intestines,

and other organs. Elevations of amylase may be seen in normal individuals as well as in ectopic pregnancy, macroamylasemia, parotitis, renal failure (decreased clearance), mesenteric ischemia, bowel obstruction or infarction, perforated duodenal ulcer, acute peritonitis from other causes, and other diseases.[29] Pancreatic amylase can be differentiated from these other sources by electrophoresis, a test that is not readily available in the emergency department. Because of the other nonspecific sources of amylase, elevations of amylase lack specificity for the diagnosis of pancreatitis.[27,30] In acute pancreatitis amylase rises within 6 to 24 hours and peaks in 48 hours, becoming normal in 5 to 7 days. Thus, sensitivity of amylase decreases after the first 24 to 48 hours.

In addition to the unclear origin of amylase, there are several other limitations to using amylase to diagnose acute pancreatitis. The use of different assays and the lack of an international standard lead to varying measured levels of "normal" or "elevated" across institutions. Complicating matters, there is no universal "gold standard" to diagnose pancreatitis; amylase, autopsy, computed tomography (CT), and laparoscopy have all been used. Thus, amylase is commonly used as an imperfect standard with which to make the diagnosis of pancreatitis because of its low cost and rapid availability. However, it is difficult to determine the precise value of this test to the clinician trying to make the initial diagnosis, particularly in the presence of an unclear clinical presentation. According to one author, the sensitivity of amylase for the diagnosis of pancreatitis ranges from 79% to 95% depending on the comparative choice of gold standard test.[29] As expected, the sensitivity and specificity of amylase vary depending upon the cutoff value selected to make the diagnosis of pancreatitis. With a cutoff value of total amylase that is at the upper limit of normal, the sensitivity is 91% to 100%, but the specificity is 71% to 98%. Increasing the cutoff value to approximately three times the normal value increases the specificity to about 100% but decreases the sensitivity to as low as 61%.[31] The higher cutoff of amylase results in a related drop in sensitivity that is unacceptable for a serious disease such as acute pancreatitis. In up to 25% of patients with pancreatitis, especially in alcoholics and patients with hypertriglyceridemia or chronic pancreatitis, the amylase can be normal.[29] The emergency physician should be aware that mild amylase elevations in patients presenting with acute abdominal pain of unclear etiology, particularly in elders, should raise the suspicion of an acute surgical abdomen. Essentially, amylase levels alone, whether normal, mildly elevated, or extremely elevated, do not diagnose pancreatitis unless accompanied by the appropriate clinical picture.

Lipase is a pancreatic enzyme that hydrolyzes triglycerides and has been used as both an adjunctive and an alternative test for the diagnosis of pancreatitis. Unfortunately, its use has many of the same pitfalls as amylase. In the presence of pancreatic inflammation, lipase increases within 4 to 8 hours and peaks at 24 hours. The levels stay elevated longer than those of amylase, falling over 8 to 14 days.[29] Lipase, like amylase, exists in other tissues and tends to be elevated in similar clinical situations. Improved assays have rendered lipase more specific than amylase. Yet, there are still cases of nonpancreatic elevations of lipase, such as elevations with duodenal ulcers or bowel obstruction and idiopathic elevations.[31,32] Comparisons between amylase and lipase are limited by the lack of a true gold standard for the diagnosis of pancreatitis as well as the choice of cutoff values used for the diagnosis. Despite these limitations, lipase is at least equally sensitive and probably more specific than amylase (specificity 80% to 99%). At five times the upper limits of normal, lipase is 60% sensitive and 100% specific. The use of two times the upper limit of normal for lipase has been recommended to decrease the possibility of missing the diagnosis of pancreatitis.[29] Using elevation of either amylase or lipase as evidence of disease increases the sensitivity but decreases the specificity. Requiring both levels to be elevated does the reverse. Several expert authors recommend using lipase over amylase when seeking the diagnosis, but this remains a point of debate, particularly when considering the entire differential diagnosis of pancreatitis.[6,15,29,33]

The degree of elevation of amylase or lipase is not a marker of disease severity.[12,32] In a study of patients with pancreatitis, those with amylase elevation less than three times normal had the same severity of disease as those with higher elevations of amylase. In fact, alcoholics frequently have lower amylase levels but may develop more severe disease than nonalcoholic patients.[34] In a patient with prolonged abdominal pain or the history of pancreatitis, an elevated amylase for longer than a week may suggest pseudocyst or pancreatic abscess. Use of the amylase-to-lipase ratio has not proved helpful in the determination of a specific etiology of pancreatitis.[30]

There are several new tests still under development to aid in diagnosis. However, at this time, none of these has yet proved useful in diagnosing acute pancreatitis.[15,31]

In evaluating a patient with abdominal pain, amylase or lipase levels, or both, along with other blood tests are necessary to narrow the differential, detect complications, and determine prognosis. With this in mind, additional testing should consist of a complete blood count (CBC), lactate dehydrogenase (LDH), and a comprehensive metabolic panel (including liver enzymes, calcium, renal function, and glucose). Patients with liver disease should have coagulation studies performed to determine the degree of liver dysfunction. Arterial blood gas tests should be used selectively in patients who are acidotic or hypoxic. Magnesium levels should be determined in alcoholics and in patients with electrolyte abnormalities. Both hypocalcemia and hyperglycemia are common in pancreatitis, with the hyperglycemia resulting from glucagon and insulin abnormalities. Calcium is best determined using the ionized calcium level. Serum calcium is falsely lowered because of low albumin levels that may be present in patients with pancreatitis. The creatinine and blood urea nitrogen may indicate both the presence of hypovolemia and renal involvement.

Table 90-1. Sensitivity and Specificity for the Etiology of Pancreatitis of Liver Enzymes[35]

	Sensitivity (%)	Specificity (%)	PPV (%)
ALT >150 mmol/L	48	96	95
AST	44	95	87
Alkaline phosphatase >300 units/L	24	95	87
Bilirubin 2.8 mg/dL	38	93	89

ALT, alanine aminotransferase; AST, aspartate transaminase; PPV, positive predictive value.

Elevation in liver enzymes may result from a biliary etiology of pancreatitis or from other diseases of the liver or biliary tract. In addition, liver enzymes may increase from the pressure on the common bile duct that results from the surrounding pancreatic inflammation. Mild elevations of bilirubin are common in all types of pancreatitis as well as many other liver disorders. For the patient diagnosed with pancreatitis, higher elevations of aspartate transaminase (AST) and LDH are related to a worse prognosis according to Ranson's criteria.

When liver enzymes are elevated, the pattern of elevation may help determine the etiology of the pancreatitis (Table 90-1). Alanine aminotransferase (ALT) is the best single marker for biliary etiology; levels greater than three times baseline support the diagnosis of biliary pancreatitis.[5,6,35] The higher the elevation of ALT, the greater the specificity and predictive value for gallstones. ALT levels more than 150 IU/L have 96% specificity, positive predictive value of 95%, and 48% sensitivity for gallstone pancreatitis. Significant rises in AST, alkaline phosphatase, and bilirubin are also more likely to be related to biliary pancreatitis but are not as sensitive as ALT.[35]

The CBC may be notable for an elevated white blood cell count and the hematocrit may be either high or low. Early in the course, the hematocrit may be elevated because of third space volume loss. A decrease in hematocrit is a poor prognostic factor because it indicates intra-abdominal hemorrhage and severe pancreatitis. An electrocardiogram should also be obtained early to determine whether the patient's abdominal pain may be cardiac in origin.

There are several scoring systems for judging the prognosis for the patient with acute pancreatitis. The most commonly used are Ranson's criteria, which were developed in 1974 (Box 90-3) and are a two-step list of primarily laboratory parameters, determined at admission and after 48 hours, to predict mortality from pancreatitis.[36,37] Five criteria on admission note the degree of local inflammation, whereas the six criteria at 48 hours note the development of systemic complications. Ranson noted that the model did not work well for patients with gallstone pancreatitis and revised the criteria to reflect the improved mortality. Although Ranson's criteria have a 90% negative predictive value,

BOX 90-3. Ransom's Criteria

At Admission	**Within 48 Hours of Admission**
Age >55 years	Hematocrit fall >10%
WBC >16,000/mm^3	BUN rise >5 mg/dL
Glucose >200 mg/dL	Calcium <8 mg%
LDH >350 IU/L	PO_2 <60 mm Hg
AST >250 SF units	Base deficit >4 mEq/L
	Fluid sequestration >6 L

Substitute if Gallstone Induced Admission	**Within 48 Hours of Admission**
Age >70 years	Hematocrit fall >10%
WBC >18,000/mm^3	BUN rise >2 mg/dL
Glucose >220 mg/dL	Calcium <8 mg%
LDH >400 IU/L	Base deficit >5 mEq/L
AST >250 SF units	Fluid sequestration >4 L

Add the Total Number of Signs at 48 Hours		**Mortality**	
0-3	5-6	1%	40%
3-4	>7	15%	100%

AST, aspartate transaminase; BUN, blood urea nitrogen; LDH, lactate dehydrogenase; WBC, white blood cells.

BOX 90-4. Severe Pancreatitis

Local Complications of the Pancreas
Pseudocyst
Related ascites
Fistula
Pancreatic necrosis

Systemic Complications
Infection (by culture)
Refractory hypotension
Renal failure (creatinine >2.0 mg/dL if no renal insufficiency or rise >1 mg/dL)
New onset pulmonary insufficiency (O_2 saturation <90% without chronic pulmonary disease)
Symptomatic pulmonary effusion
ARDS
New onset cardiac dysfunction
Acidemia (pH <7.25)
Gastrointestinal bleeding (>500 mL/24 hours)
New onset DIC (platelet ≤100,000 mm^3, fibrinogen <1 g/L, FSP elevated)

ARDS, adult respiratory distress syndrome; DIC, disseminated intravascular coagulation; FSP, fibrin split products.

the obvious drawback to the use of this system in the emergency department is that the scoring cannot be completed until 48 hours after diagnosis.[6,38] Although it is a simple and well-known scoring system, relying on it may result in delayed recognition of illness severity.[21] The Acute Physiology and Chronic Health Evaluation (APACHE-II) system may also be used to judge severity.[38-40] This score includes 12 physiologic variables, age, and chronic health status to generate a total point score. The score can be determined on admission and throughout the hospital stay. Different studies use different cutoff numbers to determine sensitivity and specificity. In one study, APACHE-II scores greater than 7 at admission indicated severe disease with a sensitivity of 68% and specificity of 67%.[39] A score greater than 13 is associated with a high likelihood of death.[5] An APACHE-III scoring system has also been developed and includes additional physiologic variables. However, a study did not find that it was better able to predict outcome in patients with acute pancreatitis.[41] The difficulty with the APACHE scores is that they are time consuming to calculate because they include multiple variables. Both the Ranson and APACHE scores are better in predicting for patients with disease of low to moderate severity. In severe disease the scoring system becomes less accurate.[12] In patients with AIDS, Ranson's criteria may not be as accurate because of HIV-induced changes in laboratory values such as calcium and LDH.[24,25]

Because numerous factors contribute to disease severity and prognosis in patients with acute pancreatitis, an expert consensus of gastroenterologists has developed a uniform definition for severe pancreatitis.[15] This definition includes extensive local injury or systemic complications (Box 90-4), a level greater than

2 on Ranson's criteria at 48 hours, or an APACHE score greater than 7.[18,24] Again, because some markers of severity do not develop until later in the disease course, the search continues for early methods to detect patients who have a high risk for clinical deterioration. Several laboratory tests such as serum C-reactive protein, urinary trypsinogen activation peptides, and interleukins are still being evaluated and show some promise.[32,42]

Radiographic Studies

Abdominal radiographs are frequently ordered for patients with abdominal pain. Although these films do not help diagnose acute pancreatitis, they may help exclude other causes of abdominal pain such as bowel obstruction or perforation. In pancreatitis, abdominal radiographs may show an ileus with a sentinel jejunal loop or spasm of the transverse colon and dilation of the ascending colon. Pancreatic calcifications of chronic pancreatitis or gallstones may also be seen. The chest radiograph included in an abdominal series may show left-sided or bilateral pleural effusions, atelectasis, or ARDS. Up to 80% of radiographs in patients with pancreatitis have some abnormal finding.[21] Unfortunately, many of these findings are nonspecific.

Because laboratory tests cannot completely exclude gallstones as the etiology of pancreatitis, another diagnostic test is recommended.[5] CT and ultrasonography (US) are complementary studies in the evaluation of pancreatitis. US images the biliary tract with better accuracy than CT; however, the pancreas itself as well as pseudocysts are less well visualized by US because of overlying bowel gas, which is present in more than half of cases. It is recommended that US be performed within the first 24 hours of admission to determine whether gallstones or dilation of the common bile duct is present.[8,34] In one study comparing CT and US among patients with pancreatitis, US resulted in a change in treatment in 55% of patients compared with no changes after CT; CT was 39% sensitive for biliary disease whereas US was 83% sensitive.[43] In another study US was 94% sensitive for gallstones but only 19% sensitive for common bile duct stones and 38% sensitive for common bile duct dilation.[44] Because of these limitations, when gallstone pancreatitis is highly suspected, ERCP may be necessary to determine the presence of and to remove common bile duct stones early in the hospital stay.[45] Magnetic resonance cholangiopancreatography is a noninvasive test that can image the pancreas and may be used to help determine the cause of acute pancreatitis.[46]

There are several reasons to perform CT in pancreatitis. CT helps to rule out other causes of abdominal pain; allows evaluation for potential peripancreatic complications such as hemorrhage, pseudocyst, abscess, or vascular abnormalities; and helps determine the extent of any pancreatic necrosis.[31,47] The Atlanta International Symposium recommended CT in patients with (1) an uncertain diagnosis; (2) severe clinical pancreatitis, abdominal distention, tenderness, temperature higher than 102° F, and leukocytosis; (3) a Ranson score of more than 3 or APACHE score of more than 8; (4) no improvement within 72 hours; and (5) acute deterioration. The main indication for obtaining a CT scan in the emergency department is to exclude other diagnoses; however, if the patient is significantly ill and can tolerate the procedure, early CT may help determine whether complications are already present. Patients with a clear diagnosis of pancreatitis and without evidence of obstructive etiology may have an imaging study, CT or US or both, performed as necessary as an inpatient. If a CT scan is obtained, dynamic helical CT with oral and intravenous contrast material is recommended to help differentiate unopacified bowel from a pancreatic abscess or pseudocyst. Studies have shown that contrast material does not worsen pancreatitis in humans; however, if the patient cannot tolerate the contrast agent, a noncontrast study is still helpful.[31,48] CT may also be used to stage the severity and prognosis of acute pancreatitis.[5] Grades A (no abnormality) and B (focal or diffuse pancreatic enlargement) indicate lower levels of inflammation. Grade C represents mild peripancreatic inflammation and is associated with an increased risk of complications. Grade D (enlarged pancreas with fluid in the anterior pararenal space) and grade E (enlarged pancreas with two or more fluid collections) are associated with a significant risk of infection and mortality up to 15%.

Differential Considerations

Pancreatitis must be differentiated from other abdominal processes, cardiopulmonary disorders, and systemic diseases (Box 90-5). A number of acute surgical conditions may mimic pancreatitis and may also cause elevated amylase. Examples include bowel perforation,

BOX 90-5. Differential Diagnosis for Pancreatitis

Abdominal Disorders
Perforated viscus
Peptic ulcer disease
Cholecystitis, gallbladder colic
Cholangitis
Gastroenteritis
Nephrolithiasis or pyelonephritis
Bowel obstruction
Mesenteric ischemia
Abdominal aortic aneurysm
Ectopic pregnancy

Cardiopulmonary Disorders
Myocardial infarction
Pericarditis
Pneumonia
ARDS
Pleural effusion

Systemic Diseases
Sickle cell crisis

ARDS, adult respiratory distress syndrome.

peritonitis, ischemic bowel, small and large bowel obstruction, and ruptured ectopic pregnancy.

Management

The management of pancreatitis is primarily supportive and has multiple objectives. The first is volume replacement. Because of vomiting and fluid sequestration, most patients with pancreatitis are dehydrated. Fluids should be replaced with normal saline, and several liters may be required. Vital signs and urine output should be used to judge the adequacy of volume replacement. Electrolytes should be monitored and replenished.

A second objective is pain control. Abdominal pain associated with pancreatitis is severe and generally requires narcotic analgesia. Meperidine historically has been used in pancreatitis and biliary disease. Although morphine may increase the tone of the sphincter of Oddi, there is no evidence to show that it worsens the disease process in pancreatitis.[49] In fact, most narcotics may affect the function of the sphincter of Oddi, but none have been more problematic than the others. One can consider starting with 4 to 10 mg of morphine or 25 to 50 mg of meperidine (Demerol) and titrating the dose as needed for pain. Patient-controlled analgesia may be the most effective method of pain control.[34] Antiemetics are indicated to control nausea or vomiting.

A third objective is to ensure adequate nutrition. In the past, patients were allowed nothing by mouth and nasogastric suctioning was initiated because of concern that oral intake would stimulate the release of pancreatic enzymes. However, randomized clinical trials involving patients with mild to moderate pancreatitis have shown no benefit from either fasting or use of nasogastric suctioning.[50,51] Currently, nasogastric suction is indicated only in cases of intractable vomiting or ileus, and some enteral feeding should begin as soon as tolerable. Some evidence suggests that early enteral nutrition may improve outcomes even in severe pancreatitis[52]; however, if oral feedings are not tolerated or are inadequate, parenteral feedings should be initiated.[3]

Objective four is reevaluation for complications of pancreatitis. Hypotension should be corrected with large volumes of normal saline (up to 6 L). Invasive hemodynamic monitoring may become necessary. Airway control is appropriate for respiratory failure or continued shock. Hyperglycemia should be treated cautiously as it may self-correct as the pancreatitis resolves. Hypocalcemia may be the result of decreased albumin or hypomagnesemia, and ionized calcium and magnesium levels should be checked before initiating replacement therapy. If there is true hypocalcemia and the patient is experiencing symptoms, treatment is appropriate. Calcium gluconate should be used if the calcium must be replenished. However, the serum potassium should be normalized before calcium replacement because calcium causes intravascular potassium shifts.

In the case of gallstone pancreatitis, gastroenterology consultation is appropriate to discuss the use of ERCP. Early operative removal of gallstones and the gallbladder has been shown to increase mortality[53]; however, early removal of common bile duct stones by ERCP may reduce morbidity. At this time, there are conflicting opinions regarding the optimal timing of ERCP in the presence of gallstone pancreatitis.[54] Early endoscopic sphincterotomy (in 24 to 48 hours) and stone removal are recommended in the setting of cholangitis, sepsis, and evidence of severe obstructive pancreatitis.[5,7,44,55] In mild pancreatitis, early ERCP has not consistently been shown to improve morbidity. In addition, there is approximately a 5% rate of pancreatitis with ERCP and papillotomy as well as other complications associated with the procedure (bleeding and perforation). Given the ongoing controversy, it is appropriate to involve the consultant early in the case so that a well-coordinated plan can be created.

Theoretically, the following medications should moderate the course of pancreatitis. Histamine 2 (H_2) blockers decrease the release of secretin by inhibition of gastric acid, glucagon directly suppresses pancreatic exocrine secretion, and octreotide inhibits pancreatic secretion. However, these therapies have not been shown to be clinically effective.[5-7] Other approaches using inhibitors of inflammatory mediators have also failed to show clinical improvement.[5-7,19] For patients with severe pancreatitis, an H_2 blocker, although not helpful for the acute disease, may decrease stress-induced ulcers.

In patients with severe pancreatitis and evidence of sepsis, broad-spectrum antibiotics should be started. Use of antibiotics in patients with severe pancreatitis with or without evidence of necrotized pancreatic tissue is controversial. Evidence exists that prophylactic antibiotics may be effective in reducing subsequent infection.[5,7,9,56] However, there is also some evidence suggesting that use of prophylactic antibiotics in any patient with severe pancreatitis may increase the risk of fungal infection. Use of percutaneous drainage helps to determine whether infection is present, but this is an invasive procedure. The current recommendation, despite some ongoing controversy, is to begin broad-spectrum antibiotics in patients with severe acute pancreatitis.[3,15,52]

Surgical intervention or percutaneous drainage may be necessary for cases of infected pancreatic necrosis, infected pseudocyst, or unresolved pseudocyst. Surgery is preferred when percutaneous drainage is not effective or not possible (extensive pancreatic necrosis or deteriorating clinical status).[17,35]

Disposition

The course of acute pancreatitis is unpredictable and complications may occur hours or days after the onset of illness; therefore, all patients with acute pancreatitis should be admitted to the hospital.[52,57] Patients with evidence of severe pancreatitis should be admitted to the intensive care unit, especially if there is evidence of pulmonary insufficiency or cardiovascular problems such as hypotension or poor urine output. This recommendation includes patients with a score of more than 2 on Ranson's criteria on admission or other evidence of organ failure, local complications, or significant comorbidities.[5]

In smaller hospitals without appropriate intensive care facilities, patients with evidence of severe pancreatitis should be transferred. If one suspects or confirms the cause of pancreatitis to be gallstones, discussion with another specialist (gastroenterologist or surgeon) is necessary. Pediatric patients have increased morbidity and mortality with pancreatitis and should be considered for early transfer to a pediatric specialty center.

CHRONIC PANCREATITIS

Principles of Disease

Chronic pancreatitis is an ongoing inflammatory process leading to irreversible structural damage and impairment of exocrine and endocrine pancreatic function. Normal pancreatic structure is replaced with fibrotic tissue, resulting in pancreatic ducts that are strictured in some areas and dilated in others. The incidence is about 4 per 100,000.[12] In 70% to 80% of cases, the etiology is chronic alcohol use. The risk increases with the duration and amount of alcohol consumption.[57] Ingestion of alcohol at more than 150 g/day for an average of 5 to 15 years is associated with the development of chronic pancreatitis; 5% to 15% of chronic alcoholics develop this disease.[12,58-60] It is possible that individuals sensitive to small amounts of alcohol may also develop chronic pancreatitis. Three theories exist regarding the mechanism by which alcohol causes chronic pancreatitis: (1) direct cellular toxicity, (2) alcohol-induced precipitation of proteinaceous fluid in the ductules that causes obstruction and calcification, and (3) injury caused by recurrent acute pancreatitis leading to irreversible damage and chronic inflammation.[59,60] Chronic pancreatitis can continue even after the cessation of alcohol use, although it is more commonly associated with alcoholic relapse.

Other less common causes of chronic pancreatitis include ductal obstruction, hereditary pancreatitis, cystic fibrosis, trauma, autoimmune diseases, hyperparathyroidism, α_1-antitrypsin deficiency, hyperlipidemia, and tropical pancreatitis (cassava fruit is implicated).[58,61,62] Idiopathic chronic pancreatitis occurs in about 10% of patients. In the 25% of cases with unknown causes, occult alcohol use may be the culprit. In children, the most common causes are cystic fibrosis and hereditary pancreatitis.

Chronic pancreatitis has several different classifications. One useful system uses both underlying pathology and probable etiology. Chronic calcific pancreatitis, usually seen in alcoholics, is characterized by patchy fibrosis, ductal injury, intraductal protein plugs, and stones. Chronic obstructive pancreatitis results from obstruction of the main pancreatic duct by tumors or strictures. Chronic inflammatory pancreatitis is seen in association with autoimmune diseases and is characterized by diffuse fibrosis and inflammatory changes. The final type is a silent perilobular fibrosis with an unclear etiology.[63,64]

As in acute pancreatitis, chronic inflammation can cause local injury such as pseudoaneurysms, splenic vein thrombosis, pancreatic ascites, or pancreatic fistulas. Pancreatic pseudocysts occur in up to 25% of chronic pancreatitis cases.[61] Rarely, pseudocysts can erode into vascular structures or can become infected. Narrowing of the bile duct from extrinsic pressure or strictures may lead to elevated liver enzymes and jaundice. Approximately 5% of patients develop duodenal obstruction secondary to inflammation around the head of the pancreas. Thus, the acutely ill patient with chronic pancreatitis may be manifesting the primary disease or a complication. The most common endocrine complication is the presence of glucose intolerance in many patients with chronic pancreatitis. Over years, insulin-dependent diabetes develops in between 30% and 50% of patients. Patients with chronic pancreatitis have an increased risk of pancreatic carcinoma of about 4%, as do patients with hereditary pancreatitis.

Chronic pancreatitis is associated with high morbidity in terms of pain and complications. In addition, patients with chronic pancreatitis have an excess mortality of about 20%; however, the cause of death is more likely to be related to other consequences of alcoholism rather than pancreatitis.[59]

Clinical Features

Patients with chronic pancreatitis may present with chronic pain, complications, or an acute flare of the chronic underlying disease. These flares may be severe, and if the patient is relatively well during the interim it may be difficult to distinguish this episode from a recurrent bout of acute pancreatitis.[58] When present, the pain is epigastric, usually radiating to the back and associated with nausea and vomiting. Often, the patient can relate the similarity to previous attacks of acute pancreatitis or flares of chronic pancreatitis. Use of alcohol or eating exacerbates the pain. There is no correlation between remaining pancreatic function and the degree of pain.[12] However, a few studies have shown that the pain diminishes over years of chronic disease for some patients.[58] Patients may have weight loss from malabsorption or decreased intake because of nausea and vomiting or because eating may precipitate the pain.

Over time, about 15% of patients with chronic pancreatic disease may develop symptoms of pancreatic exocrine function insufficiency including malabsorption, diarrhea, steatorrhea, or weight loss. Malabsorption occurs after approximately 90% of the pancreas is nonfunctional. Functional endocrine insufficiency develops in approximately one third to two thirds of patients with chronic disease.[53] The symptoms primarily manifest as hyperglycemia; however, the development of diabetic ketoacidosis is rare. Hypoglycemia is multifactorial, resulting from an insufficiency of glucagon, decreased liver glucose stores, malnourishment, and hypoglycemic medications.

On physical examination, patients may appear in significant discomfort. Their general appearance is frequently one of chronic illness from alcoholism, poor nutrition, and malabsorption. On abdominal examination there is frequently tenderness without peritoneal signs. The abdomen should be carefully palpated for a mass that might represent a pseudocyst or tumor. Stigmata of chronic alcohol abuse may also be present. Jaundice may be noted from pressure on the common bile duct or from alcohol-related liver injury.

Diagnostic Strategies

The diagnosis of chronic pancreatitis is frequently made clinically rather than from laboratory values. The serum levels of amylase and lipase are initially mildly elevated in chronic pancreatitis, but as the disease progresses, these levels become normal. As in acute pancreatitis, the degree of elevation of amylase and lipase is not prognostic. In the patient with the appropriate clinical picture, normal amylase and lipase values are consistent with a diagnosis of chronic pancreatitis.

Blood work should include a CBC, and the complete metabolic profile should be checked. The white blood cell count is usually normal. There may be elevations of hepatic enzymes (alkaline phosphatase, bilirubin, or transaminases) either from alcoholic hepatitis or from compression on the biliary duct by pancreatic inflammation or a mass in the head of the pancreas. Elevations in serum glucose may also be seen; hypoglycemia is less common. Sudan stain of the stool may show fat globules. Decreases in albumin and calcium are common because of the chronic nature of the disease.

Although abdominal radiographs are not necessary, pancreatic calcifications are pathognomonic and are seen in 30% to 50% of patients, usually related to chronic alcohol-induced pancreatitis (Figure 90-3).[12,58]

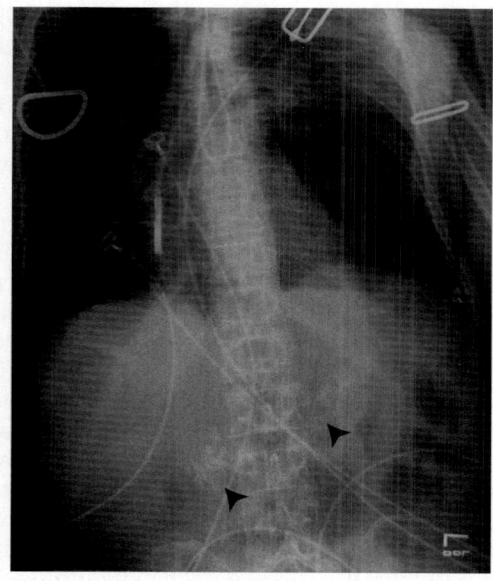

Figure 90-3. Pancreatic calcifications *(arrowheads)* throughout the pancreas as seen in chronic pancreatitis. (Incidental finding of feeding tube in main stem bronchus.) (Image contributed by Ronald Arildsen.)

Patients with calcifications have probably had pancreatitis for several years; therefore, these patients should be evaluated for long-term complications such as diabetes and malabsorption.

Abdominal imaging in the emergency department with CT scan or US is not necessary for patients with chronic pancreatitis. Imaging should be reserved for cases in which the diagnosis is in question or the pain is prolonged, significantly increased, or unresponsive to treatment. Although US is useful in diagnosing the cause of acute pancreatitis, it is less useful in chronic pancreatitis, with a sensitivity of 75% and specificity of 80% to 90%.[12,15,58] The primary findings on US are pancreatic calcifications and ductal abnormalities. CT is 90% sensitive for the diagnosis of chronic pancreatitis and is the preferred modality when imaging is indicated. It also makes the diagnosis of complications such as pseudocysts.[58] CT findings consistent with chronic pancreatitis are dilated intrapancreatic ducts and microcalcifications.

Although endoscopic retrograde pancreatography (ERP) is not an emergency department procedure, it can be helpful in diagnosing pancreatic duct abnormalities and measuring pancreatic function. Some gastroenterologists consider the ductal abnormalities seen on ERP and endoscopic US to be the gold standard for the diagnosis of chronic pancreatitis.[15] In the future, magnetic resonance imaging cholangiopancreatography may assume a greater role in the evaluation of chronic pancreatitis.

Differential Considerations

The diagnosis of chronic pancreatitis is usually straightforward in the alcoholic patient with elevated amylase or lipase who has chronic abdominal pain and a history of similar previous flares of pancreatitis. The diagnosis may be more difficult when the amylase and lipase are normal. However, the emergency physician should not be lulled into complacency and forget that other abdominal processes (unrelated to the pancreas or complications of pancreatitis) must be considered in the differential (see Box 90-5). In addition, other chronic abdominal diseases such as peptic ulcers, irritable bowel, gallstones, and endometriosis may arise with recurrent abdominal pain. Finally, narcotic-dependent patients in withdrawal may have vomiting and abdominal pain that may be difficult to differentiate from chronic pancreatitis.[59]

Management

The initial management of chronic pancreatitis is supportive. Depending upon the patient's clinical status and electrolyte levels, fluids and electrolytes may need to be replaced. An "alcohol cocktail" with thiamine, multivitamins, and folate is often indicated because patients are frequently malnourished. Antiemetics should be used to treat recurrent emesis.

Management of pain is one of the most difficult aspects of treatment. Patients may have normal laboratory values despite significant pain, and patients with chronic pain syndromes may not exhibit signs of autonomic hyperactivity when experiencing exacerbations of their underlying disease. In patients unknown to the emergency department, this situation may lead to concern that the patient is drug seeking. Although this possibility is ever present in the emergency department setting, the emergency physician should err on the side of treatment in all cases except those of documented abuse. Nonsteroidal analgesics are the preferred treatment but often are not adequate.[61] Either morphine or meperidine may be used and should be titrated. Tramadol (Ultram) was used effectively in one study.[65] The use of narcotics may be needed over extended periods. Non-narcotic modulators of pain such as selective serotonin reuptake inhibitors or gabapentin may be helpful for chronic pain.[15] In the ideal medical system, the primary care physician or a pain management specialist monitors the narcotic prescription because narcotic dependence may become an issue.[64]

The removal of inciting factors, especially alcohol, is important. Patients with significant pain should have nothing by mouth, although as in acute pancreatitis, a nasogastric tube is not indicated. The use of oral pancreatic replacement enzymes increases the amount of trypsin in the duodenum and may provide a negative feedback to the release of pancreatic secretions, thus treating malabsorption.[12] Therefore, pancreatic replacement enzymes may also decrease the pain in some patients.[58] Studies of the effectiveness of pancreatic enzyme replacement on pain yielded contradictory results. In theory, proton pump inhibitors or H_2 receptor blockers may reduce pancreatic stimulation; however, these have not been shown to decrease pain or improve recovery.[12]

Beyond the emergency department treatment, endoscopic dilation, ductal stone removal, or stenting of the pancreatic ducts may be a helpful treatment adjunct.

Common bile duct stenting may also be necessary because obstruction occurs in about 5% to 10% of cases.[12] Surgery such as pancreatic head resection, lateral pancreaticojejunostomy, or Whipple pancreatoduodenectomy is sometimes an option when conservative treatment has failed. Pancreatic pseudocysts in chronic pancreatitis are less likely to resolve spontaneously and should be drained either endoscopically, by US, or by an open procedure. Celiac plexus blocks have also been used with minimal success for pain control.[61]

Disposition

In general, patients with chronic pancreatitis are managed as outpatients and present to the emergency department with exacerbations or complications. Because acute pancreatitis can occur in patients with chronic pancreatitis, the same prognostic indicators for severity of acute pancreatitis should be noted. Patients with severe disease should be admitted to the intensive care unit. Patients with dehydration, abdominal pain unresponsive to medications, or a questionable diagnosis should be admitted for evaluation and treatment. After a careful emergency department evaluation, the patient who is not dehydrated, who has stable vital signs, and whose pain has been controlled may be treated as an outpatient with close follow-up.

PANCREATIC CANCER

Perspective

Pancreatic cancer is not commonly an emergency department diagnosis; however, it may be found incidentally on an abdominal CT scan, or a patient with known cancer may present with complications of the disease. Pancreatic cancer is a particularly lethal cancer, with death occurring in approximately 99% of patients. It is the fourth most common cause of cancer-related mortality in the United States. The disease is diagnosed in approximately 10 people per 100,000 per year and the incidence has increased threefold over the past 40 years.[26] Because there are few early symptoms, few patients (<20%) are diagnosed at an early stage. The 5-year survival is only 3% despite aggressive surgery and advances in chemotherapy.[66,67]

Principles of Disease

Little is known about the etiology of pancreatic cancer. Heavy smoking increases the risk by two to three times. Chronic alcohol use also increases the risk. In some studies, chronic pancreatitis increased the risk of pancreatic cancer approximately 4% in patients observed over 20 years. Pancreatic cancer may be more common in diabetic patients, although this may be the result of development of diabetes in patients with pancreatic cancer.[67] There is a small familial aggregation of pancreatic cancer.[67,68]

Ductal adenocarcinomas make up 95% of malignant pancreatic tumors. The pancreatic head is the location of origin in about 70% of cases. The tumor extends locally into adjacent structures and can metastasize by hematogenous or lymphatic spread to liver, peritoneum, lungs, bones, and brain. Neuroendocrine tumors, such as gastrinomas, vasoactive intestinal peptide tumors (VIPomas), and glucagonomas, make up the remaining cases.[69] These types of tumors have a better prognosis.

Clinical Features

The presentation of pancreatic adenocarcinoma is variable because progression of the disease is indolent. The tumor has usually been present for several months before the cancer is diagnosed; therefore, patients may present with pain of long duration or with one of the many complications of this cancer.[70] One of the most common presentations is weight loss, which is usually the result of anorexia rather than malabsorption. The abdominal pain is usually a dull, constant pain in the epigastrium that may radiate to the back. The patient may present with jaundice from common bile duct obstruction. Progressive jaundice develops in about 75% of patients. An enlarged and palpable, but painless, gallbladder in the presence of jaundice is most commonly associated with pancreatic cancer (termed Courvoisier's sign). Glucose intolerance may also develop. As the tumor enlarges, patients may develop evidence of bowel obstruction. Pancreatic cancer (as well as other cancers) may render patients hypercoagulable and result in thromboembolic presentations. Varices and gastrointestinal bleeding may be caused by compression of the portal system by the tumor.

Neuroendocrine tumors of the pancreas are rare and arise with symptoms that are the result of the hormones that they produce. For example, insulinomas may arise with hypoglycemia. Gastrinomas are related to Zollinger-Ellison syndrome and recurrent peptic ulcers. VIPomas arise with extreme watery diarrhea, hypokalemia, and achlorhydria. Glucagonomas occur with glucose intolerance and necrolytic migratory erythema. Some tumors produce multiple hormones.[69] Other nonfunctional tumors may also be noted incidentally on CT as small pancreatic masses. Diagnosis is made by abnormal levels of hormones and the appropriate clinical syndrome. Fifty percent of pancreatic neuroendocrine tumors are malignant.[71]

Diagnostic Strategies

The diagnosis of pancreatic cancer may be made by US, although a CT scan provides better imaging of the cancer. Percutaneous US, CT-guided biopsy, or ERCP-guided biopsy can be used to obtain a tissue diagnosis. Histologic samples are needed to differentiate ductal adenocarcinoma from islet cell tumors, other metastatic cancers, and lymphoma. Serologic markers have not proved satisfactory for diagnosis or follow-up, although several oncogenes and tumor markers are under study (CA19-9 and carcinoembryonic antigen).

Management

Complete resection of the carcinoma is the only effective treatment. Unfortunately, few tumors (5% to 10%)

are diagnosed at a stage at which this may be possible. In patients with unresectable tumors, the median survival after diagnosis is approximately 6 months. Palliative surgery may be performed to relieve obstruction. Biliary drainage by percutaneously or ERCP-placed stents may also improve jaundice. Chemotherapy and radiation therapy may decrease tumor size to ease pain and prolong survival in some patients.[72] Treatment of neuroendocrine tumors is aimed at both tumor growth by excision and hormone excess.[72]

In the emergency department, patients may present with complications of the cancer such as bowel obstruction, jaundice, or pain control issues. Given the grim prognosis of the disease and significant pain associated, narcotics should not be withheld and end of life issues should be addressed with patients by their oncologist.

KEY CONCEPTS

- Most cases of acute pancreatitis are caused by gallstones (45%) and alcoholism (35%). Other etiologies include medications, toxins, and trauma.

- The clinical spectrum of acute pancreatitis ranges from mild (epigastric discomfort often associated with vomiting) to life threatening (severe abdominal pain in the presence of an acute abdomen and hemodynamic instability related to systemic complications). The mortality in severe pancreatitis approaches 30%.

- There is no perfect test for diagnosing acute pancreatitis. The most useful tests include serum amylase and lipase. Unfortunately, both tests can be normal in up to 25% of cases, and mild elevations are not specific for acute pancreatitis and can be seen in many other acute surgical disorders causing abdominal pain. Both tests are highly specific for pancreatitis when serum levels are elevated five times above the upper limits of normal.

- Emergent abdominal CT should be performed in patients with clinically suspected pancreatitis who appear acutely ill (to exclude peripancreatic complications such as hemorrhage, pseudocyst, or abscess) and in patients with an uncertain diagnosis (to exclude other surgical causes of acute abdominal pain).

- Because the course of acute pancreatitis is unpredictable, all patients should be hospitalized for pain control, hydration, observation, and the management of complications. Patients with severe pancreatitis (having more than two of Ranson's criteria, an APACHE score over 7, or evidence of systemic complications) should be cared for in an intensive care unit.

REFERENCES

1. Leach SD, Gorelick FS, Modlin IM: Acute pancreatitis at its centenary. *Ann Surg* 212:109, 1990.
2. Bank S, Singh P, Pooran N, Stark B: Evaluation of factors that have reduced mortality from acute pancreatitis of the past 20 years. *J Clin Gastroenterol* 351:50, 2002.
3. Yousaf M, McCallion K, Diamond T: Management of severe acute pancreatitis. *Br J Surg* 90:407, 2003.
4. Benifla M, Weizman Z: Acute pancreatitis in childhood. *J Clin Gastroenterol* 37:169, 2003.
5. Steinberg WM: Diagnosis and management of acute pancreatitis. *Cleve Clin J Med* 64:182, 1997.
6. Steinberg W, Tenner S: Acute pancreatitis. *N Engl J Med* 330:1198, 1994.
7. Tenner S, Banks PA: Acute pancreatitis: Nonsurgical management. *World J Surg* 21:143, 1997.
8. British Society of Gastroenterology: United Kingdom guidelines for the management of acute pancreatitis. *Gut* 42:S1, 1998.
9. Kramer KM, Levy H: Prophylactic antibiotics for severe acute pancreatitis: The beginning of an era. *Pharmacotherapy* 19:592, 1999.
10. Go VLW: Etiology and epidemiology of pancreatitis in the United States. In Bradley EL (ed): *Acute Pancreatitis: Diagnosis and Therapy*. New York, Raven Press, 1994, pp 235-241.
11. Moreau JA, et al: Gallstone pancreatitis and the effect of cholecystectomy: A population based cohort study. *Mayo Clin Proc* 63:466, 1988.
12. Banks PA: Acute and chronic pancreatitis. In Feldman M, Scharschmidt BF, Sleisenger MH (eds): *Gastrointestinal and Liver Disease*. Philadelphia, WB Saunders, pp 838-863.
13. Jackson WD: Pancreatitis: Etiology, diagnosis, and management. *Curr Opin Pediatr* 13:447, 2001.
14. Steer ML: Pathogenesis of acute pancreatitis. *Digestion* 58:46, 1997.
15. Mitchell RMS, Byrne MF, Baille J: Pancreatitis. *Lancet* 361:1447, 2003.
16. Balthazar EJ, Freeney PC, vanSonnenberg E: Imaging and intervention in acute pancreatitis. *Radiology* 194:297, 1994.
17. Baron TH, Morgan DE: Acute necrotizing pancreatitis. *N Engl J Med* 340:1412, 1999.
18. Bradley E: A clinically based classification system for acute pancreatitis. *Arch Surg* 128:586, 1993.
19. Horman J: The role of cytokines in the pathogenesis of acute pancreatitis. *Am J Surg* 175:76, 1998.
20. Lee SP, Nicholls JF, Park HZ: Biliary sludge as a cause of acute pancreatitis. *N Engl J Med* 326:589, 1992.
21. Ranson JHC: Etiologic and prognostic factors in human acute pancreatitis. *Am J Gastroenterol* 77:633, 1982.
22. Freeman ML, et al: Risk factors for post-ERCP pancreatitis: A prospective, multicenter study. *Gastrointest Endosc* 54:425, 2001.
23. Manocha AP, et al: Prevalence and predictors of severe acute pancreatitis in patients with acquired immune deficiency syndrome (AIDS). *Am J Gastroenterol* 94:784, 1999.
24. Dutta SK, Ting CD, Lai LL: Study of the prevalence, severity and etiologic factors associated with acute pancreatitis in patients infected with human immunodeficiency virus. *Am J Gastroenterol* 92:2044, 1997.
25. Benkov KJ, Compton CC: Weekly CPC exercises. *N Engl J Med* 340:215, 1999.
26. Gloor B, Ahmed Z, Uhl W, Buchler MW: Pancreatic disease in the elderly. *Best Pract Res Clin Gastroenterol* 16:159, 2002.
27. Ranson JHC: Diagnostic standards for acute pancreatitis. *World J Surg* 21:136, 1997.
28. Maringhini A, et al: Pseudocysts in acute nonalcoholic pancreatitis. *Dig Dis Sci* 44:1669, 1999.
29. Vissers RJ, Abu-Laban RB, McHugh DF: Amylase and lipase in the emergency department evaluation of acute pancreatitis. *J Emerg Med* 17:1027, 1999.
30. Kusnierz-Cabala B, Kedra B, Sierzega M: Current concepts on diagnosis and treatment of acute pancreatitis. *Adv Clin Chem* 37:47, 2003.
31. Yadav D, Agarwal N, Pitchumoni CS: A critical evaluation of laboratory tests in acute pancreatitis. *Am J Gastroenterol* 97:1309, 2002.
32. Frank B, Gottlieb K: Amylase normal, lipase elevated: Is it pancreatitis? *Am J Gastroenterol* 94:463, 1999.

33. Banks PA: Practice guidelines in acute pancreatitis. *Am J Gastroenterol* 92:377, 1997.

34. Lankisch PG, Burchard-Reckert S, Lehnick D: Underestimation of acute pancreatitis: Patients with only a small increase in amylase/lipase levels can also have or develop severe acute pancreatitis. *Gut* 44:542, 1999.

35. Tenner S, Dubner H, Steinberg W: Predicting gallstone pancreatitis with laboratory parameters: A meta-analysis. *Am J Gastroenterol* 89:1863, 1994.

36. Ranson JHC, Rifkind KM, Turner JW: Prognostic signs and nonoperative peritoneal lavage in acute pancreatitis. *Surg Gynecol Obstet* 143:209, 1976.

37. Ranson JHC, et al: Prognostic signs and operative management in acute pancreatitis. *Surg Gynecol Obstet* 139:69, 1974.

38. Agarwal N, Pitchumoni L: Assessment of severity in acute pancreatitis. *Am J Gastroenterol* 86:1385, 1991.

39. Wilson C, Heath DDI, Imrie CW: Prediction of outcome in acute pancreatitis: A comparative study of APACHE II, clinical assessment and multiple factor scoring systems. *Br J Surg* 77:1260, 1990.

40. Sanctis JT, et al: Prognostic indicators in acute pancreatitis: CT vs APACHE. *Clin Radiol* 52:842, 1997.

41. Chatzicostas C, et al: Comparison of Ranson, APACHE II and APACHE III scoring systems in acute pancreatitis. *Pancreas* 4:331, 2002.

42. Treister SL, Kowdley KV: Prognostic factors in acute pancreatitis. *J Clin Gastroenterol* 34:167, 2002.

43. Harvey RT, Niller WT: Acute biliary disease: Initial CT and follow-up US vs. initial US and follow-up CT. *Radiology* 213:831, 1999.

44. Liu CL, Lo CM, Fan ST: Acute biliary pancreatitis: Diagnosis and management. *World J Surg* 21:149, 1997.

45. Pezzilli R, et al: Ultrasonographic evaluation of the common bile duct in biliary acute pancreatitis patients. *J Ultrasound Med* 18:391, 1999.

46. Barich MA, Yucel EK, Ferrucci JT: Magnetic resonance cholangiopancreatography. *N Engl J Med* 341:258,1999.

47. Dazell DP, Scharling ES, Ott DJ, Wolfman NT: Acute pancreatitis: The role of diagnostic imaging. *Crit Rev Diagn Imaging* 39:339, 1998.

48. Balthazar EJ: Acute pancreatitis: Assessment of severity with clinical and CT evaluation. *Radiology* 223:603, 2002.

49. Thompson DR: Narcotic analgesic effects on the sphincter of Oddi: A review of the data and therapeutic implications in treating pancreatitis. *Am J Gastroenterol* 96:1266, 2001.

50. Naeije R, et al: Is nasogastric suction necessary in acute pancreatitis? *Br Med J* 2:659, 1978.

51. Levant JA, et al: Nasogastric suction in the treatment of alcoholic pancreatitis: A controlled study. *JAMA* 229:51, 1974.

52. Kahl S, Zimmermann S, Malfertheiner P: Acute pancreatitis: Treatment strategies. *Dig Dis* 21:30, 2003.

53. Kelly TR, Wagner DS: Gallstone pancreatitis: A prospective randomized trial of the timing of surgery. *Surgery* 104:600, 1988.

54. Fogel EL, Sherman S: Acute biliary pancreatitis: When should the endoscopist intervene? *Gastroenterology* 125:229, 2003.

55. Fan ST, et al: Early treatment of acute biliary pancreatitis by endoscopic papillotomy. *N Engl J Med* 328:228, 1993.

56. Pederzoli P, et al: A randomized multi-center clinical trial of antibiotic prophylaxis of septic complications in acute necrotizing pancreatitis with imipenem. *Surg Gynecol Obstet* 176:480, 1993.

57. Beckingham IJ, Bornman PC: Acute pancreatitis. *BMJ* 322:595, 2001.

58. Mergener K, Baillie J: Chronic pancreatitis. *Lancet* 350:1379, 1997.

59. Apte MV, Keogh GW, Wilson JS: Chronic pancreatitis: Complications and management. *J Clin Gastroenterol* 29:225, 1999.

60. Ammann RW, Mauellhaupt B: Progression of alcoholic acute to chronic pancreatitis. *Gut* 35:552, 1994.

61. Bornman PC, Beckham IJ: Chronic pancreatitis. *BMJ* 322:660, 2001.

62. Steer ML, Waxman I, Freedman S: Medical progress: Chronic pancreatitis. *N Engl J Med* 332:1482, 1995.

63. Sarles H: Definition and classification of pancreatitis. *Pancreas* 6:470, 1991.

64. Strate T, Knoefel WT, Yekebas E, Izbicki JR: Chronic pancreatitis: Etiology, pathogenesis, diagnosis and treatment. *Int J Colorectal Dis* 18:97, 2003.

65. Wilder-Smith CH, et al: Effect of tramadol and morphine on pain and gastrointestinal motor function in patients with chronic pancreatitis. *Dig Dis Sci* 44:1107, 1999.

66. Rosewicz S, Wiedenmann B: Pancreatic carcinoma. *Lancet* 349:485, 1997.

67. O'Meara AT: Pancreatic cancer: Evidence-based diagnosis and treatment. *Clin Obstet Gynecol* 45:855, 2002.

68. Rocha Lima CM, Centeno B: Update on pancreatic cancer. *Curr Opin Oncol* 14:424, 2002.

69. Chun J, Foherty GM: Pancreatic endocrine tumors. *Curr Opin Oncol* 13:52, 2001.

70. Bornman PC. Beckingham IJ. Pancreatic tumours. *BMJ* 322:721, 2001.

71. Eriksson G, Oberg K: Neuroendocrine tumors of the pancreas. *Br J Surg* 87:128, 2000.

72. Hugier M, Mason NP: Treatment of cancer of the exocrine pancreas. *Am J Surg* 177:257, 1999.

91 Disorders of the Small Intestine

Susan P. Torrey and Philip L. Henneman

SMALL BOWEL OBSTRUCTION

Perspective

The signs and symptoms of intestinal obstruction have been recognized for centuries. This clinical entity has historically been treated with a variety of interventions, including enemas and inflation of the rectum, metallic mercury ingestion, therapeutic bleeding, and percutaneous intestinal puncture.[1,2] By the late 19th century, proximal intestinal decompression was reliably utilized to provide temporary symptomatic relief of intestinal obstruction. Advances in this century, including the development of antibiotics and improved surgical techniques, have significantly improved the prognosis for patients with small bowel obstruction (SBO).

Patients with SBO account for 20% of hospital admissions for acute abdominal complaints.[2-4] Approximately 300,000 operations are performed in the United States each year for relief of intestinal obstruction.[5] Aggressive treatment has resulted in a current mortality of less than 5%, a substantial improvement over the expected 60% mortality associated with this disease in 1900.[6] When strangulation complicates SBO, however, the mortality rate increases to as much as 30%.[7] Death from SBO occurs most often in the elderly or in patients with significant underlying illness.

The term *mechanical obstruction* implies a physical barrier to the flow of intestinal contents. Within this definition, *simple obstruction* refers to the situation in which the intestinal lumen is partially or completely occluded at one or more points, thus producing proximal intestinal distention, but without compromise of the intestinal vascular supply. A *closed-loop obstruction* implies that a segment of bowel is obstructed at two sequential sites, usually by twisting about a constricting adhesive band or hernia opening. This mechanism of obstruction has a high risk of compromising intestinal blood flow with resulting intestinal ischemia, a condition referred to as *strangulation obstruction*. It is important to note that not all closed-loop obstructions are associated with intestinal ischemia and that other types of obstruction may eventually involve vascular compromise.

In contrast to mechanical obstruction, *neurogenic* or *functional obstruction* occurs when intestinal contents fail to pass through the bowel lumen because of disturbances in gut motility rather than actual blockage. This entity is also commonly referred to as an *adynamic ileus.* When intestinal peristalsis fails, dilation of the involved intestinal tract develops. Adynamic ileus is most commonly seen after abdominal surgery but can be caused by other common medical conditions (Box 91-1). Focal decrease in peristaltic activity may occur because of a localized inflammatory process (e.g., pancreatitis, cholecystitis, or appendicitis) and result in gas and fluid accumulation in an isolated segment of bowel. This segmental ileus is called a *sentinel loop*.

Pseudo-obstruction refers to a poorly understood disorder of intestinal motility associated with a number of medical conditions, including amyloidosis, collagen vascular disease, diabetes, hypothyroidism, and several metabolic disorders (hypokalemia, hypocalcemia, and uremia). The signs and symptoms of intestinal obstruction are present, but there is no evidence of an underlying lesion or cause on diagnostic evaluation. Correction of any underlying disease process and supportive care are recommended, but the results of treatment are often disappointing.

Principles of Disease

There is a relationship between the progressive physiologic changes that occur in patients with SBO and the corresponding clinical manifestations. Mechanical SBO initially causes mild proximal intestinal distention that results from the accumulation of normal gastrointestinal secretions and swallowed air above the obstructing lesion. This distention stimulates peristalsis above and below the obstruction, which accounts for the frequent loose bowel movements that may accompany partial and even complete SBO in the early stages.[1,2] Early bowel distention stimulates epithelial cell secretory activity, resulting in the addition of more fluid, increasing bowel dilation, and the creation of a self-perpetuating process. This situation is worsened by the inability of the distended bowel to absorb fluid and electrolytes at a normal rate. Further increases in intraluminal pressure result in capillary and lymphatic obstruction with subsequent edema of the bowel wall. Perforation occurs if this process continues uninterrupted. In addition, vomiting and intraperitoneal fluid sequestration further compound volume losses, leading to extracellular fluid depletion, hypovolemia, and, eventually, shock.

The rise in intraluminal pressure is much more abrupt with a closed-loop obstruction because the intestinal contents are also prevented from retrograde flow. Strangulation occurs with the development of venous congestion, small vessel rupture, intramural and mesenteric hemorrhage, and arterial insufficiency. It is also not uncommon for the loop of distended bowel

BOX 91-1. Causes of Adynamic Ileus

Abdominal trauma
Infection (retroperitoneal, pelvic, intrathoracic)
Laparotomy
Metabolic disease (hypokalemia)
Renal colic
Skeletal injury (rib fracture, vertebral fracture)
Medications (e.g., narcotics)

BOX 91-2. Lesions Causing Small Bowel Obstruction

Intrinsic
   Congenital (atresia, stenosis)
   Inflammatory (Crohn's disease, radiation enteritis)
   Neoplasms (metastatic or primary)
   Intussusception
   Traumatic (hematoma)
Extrinsic
   Hernias (internal and external)
   Adhesions
   Volvulus
   Compressing masses (tumors, abscesses, hematomas)
Intraluminal
   Foreign body
   Gallstones
   Bezoars
   Barium
   Ascaris infestation

to twist on itself further, resulting in large artery occlusion. Either sequence of events then progresses rapidly from intestinal ischemia to infarction.

Necrosis of the bowel and leakage of contaminated contents cause bacterial peritonitis and sepsis. Although the proximal small bowel normally contains few bacteria, this changes quickly during times of intestinal stasis. Simple intestinal obstruction has been shown to be associated with increased bacterial translocation to mesenteric lymph nodes. In one series, 59% of the patients undergoing laparotomy for simple SBO had bacteria (most commonly *Escherichia coli*) cultured from mesenteric lymph nodes, compared with only 4% of patients operated on for other reasons.[1,3]

The most common causes of SBO are listed in Box 91-2. In developed countries, postoperative adhesions are now responsible for more than 50% of all cases. It is estimated that as many as 15% of abdominal surgeries eventually result in SBO from adhesion.[8] A particularly high incidence of SBO is found after gynecologic or intestinal surgery as well as in patients who have previously undergone surgery in the presence of peritonitis or significant abdominal trauma.[6] Other important causes of SBO include hernias and neoplasms, each with an incidence of approximately 15%.[1-3] The incidence of obstruction related to hernias has been steadily decreasing in developed countries because of elective treatment of external hernias.[9] Although hernias account for a relatively small proportion of bowel obstruction, it is important to recognize

this etiology because it is associated with a high rate of strangulation (28% with hernias versus 8% with adhesive obstruction[3]). Anatomically, strangulation occurs because many obstructions caused by hernias are of the closed-loop type. When neoplasm is associated with SBO, the cause is most often colon cancer, followed by pancreatic, gastric, and gynecologic malignancies.

There are several less common causes of SBO that are pertinent to the practice of emergency medicine. *Gallstone ileus* is rare in the general population but accounts for 25% of nonstrangulated SBO in patients older than 65.[10,11] In this entity, a gallstone erodes through an inflamed gallbladder wall into a loop of adjacent small bowel. The stone then passes through the bowel lumen until it meets some narrowing, typically at the distal ileum, where it produces mechanical obstruction. Given the population of elderly patients in whom this problem occurs, it is not surprising to find 15% to 18% mortality. Another unique cause of SBO is an *obturator hernia*. This hernia typically occurs in elderly emaciated women with significant concomitant medical illness but no previous abdominal surgery.[12] It is believed that women with a wider pelvis and more oblique obturator canal are predisposed to the development of obturator hernia in the presence of decreased preperitoneal fat related to emaciation and chronic increased intra-abdominal pressure related to associated medical disease. This hernia is difficult to detect and often diagnosed only when it arises as SBO. Both of these uncommon causes of SBO occur in elderly patients, a group that is becoming an increasing percentage of the emergency department population.

Another uncommon but noteworthy cause of SBO is *small bowel volvulus*. This condition results from abnormal twisting of a loop of bowel around the axis of its own mesentery. Although volvulus of the colon (sigmoid and cecum) is common, volvulus of the small bowel is rare. Primary small bowel volvulus occurs in an otherwise normal abdominal cavity and is seen most often in adult patients in Africa, the Middle East, and the Indian subcontinent. It is rarely seen in Europe and North America. Secondary causes of small bowel volvulus include malformation and malrotation of the intestine or tethering of the loop of bowel at its apex as a result of postoperative adhesions.[13] Early surgical intervention is important because this classical closed-loop obstruction is associated with a high incidence of strangulation, 60% in one series.

Intussusception occurs in all age groups but is primarily a disease of infancy and early childhood, constituting the most common cause of SBO in early childhood. Only 5% of all intussusceptions occur in adults, and intussusception accounts for only 5% of SBO in adults.[14] An intussusception occurs when a segment of bowel telescopes into an adjacent segment, resulting in obstruction and ischemic injury to the intussuscepting segment. In contrast to the idiopathic nature of most childhood intussusceptions, a mechanical cause is present in more than 90% of adult cases. Tumors, either benign or malignant, act as the lead point of intussusception in more than 65% of adult cases. There have been several reports of adult intussusception associated with acquired immunodeficiency syndrome (AIDS). In this setting, the lesions are generally in the ileum, and intussusception has been associated with lymphoma or unusual inflammatory processes, including atypical mycobacterial infection.

Signs and symptoms caused by intussusception in the adult are nonspecific and may occasionally be chronic or recurrent in nature. Abdominal pain is a prominent complaint, often associated with symptoms suggestive of obstruction (nausea, vomiting, and abdominal distention). Radiographic features of intussusception are also nonspecific. Plain films may reveal evidence of partial or complete bowel obstruction. It has been recommended that ultrasonography may be useful in the diagnosis of adult and pediatric cases. The mainstay of diagnosis, however, remains contrast studies, typically abdominal computed tomography (CT) with an oral contrast agent. Although reduction of the intussusception may occur during contrast studies, surgery is recommended for adults because of the high incidence of pathologic lesions as a cause of intussusception.[15]

Clinical Features

History

Patients with SBO typically complain of regularly recurrent bouts of poorly localized abdominal pain lasting from seconds to minutes. The painful spasms occur every few minutes with proximal intestinal obstruction and less frequently with more distal obstruction. The pain is described as crampy in nature, and each episode has a characteristic crescendo-decrescendo pattern. A change in the description of the pain from intermittent and colicky to constant and severe may signal the development of complications, such as intestinal ischemia or perforation.

In general, the more proximal the obstruction, the greater the patient's discomfort and the shorter the delay between onset of symptoms and presentation. Several hours of severe colicky pain in association with bilious vomiting and mild abdominal distention are typical of proximal intestinal obstruction, whereas a day or two of progressively worsening pain and more prominent abdominal distention is typical of distal intestinal obstruction. When vomiting does occur with distal intestinal obstruction, it is often feculent from bacterial proliferation. Patients with complete intestinal obstruction eventually develop obstipation, whereas patients with early or partial obstruction may continue to pass stool or flatus.

Physical Examination

The physical examination should begin with a brief but thorough assessment of the patient's degree of distress, vital signs, and general condition. These important parameters determine the urgency of the evaluation and management of the patient.

Examination of the abdomen should include inspection for distention and a careful search for surgical scars and external hernias. Auscultation may reveal hyperactive bowel sounds, in particular rushes or high-pitched "tinkles" produced by forceful peristaltic efforts. Late in the course of bowel obstruction, the bowel sounds may become hypoactive or absent. Percussion may elicit tympany with distal obstruction and ileus. Palpation may reveal a tender mass, especially with a closed-loop cause of obstruction. A rectal examination should be performed to evaluate the rectal vault and to check for gross or occult blood. A prospective study of patients with abdominal pain defined six clinical variables that had high sensitivity and positive predictive value for the diagnosis of bowel obstruction.[16] These are a history of previous surgery, history of constipation, age older than 50, vomiting, abdominal distention, and increased bowel sounds.

The presence of peritoneal signs usually indicates late obstruction with complications, including strangulation. However, aggressive abdominal palpation in the setting of bowel dilation can give the false impression of peritonitis, because quick compression-decompression of dilated bowel may elicit a significant pain response. Determining the presence of pain with cough or gentle shaking of the patient's pelvis along with percussion tenderness is often helpful in differentiating peritonitis from pain related to rapid decompression of dilated loops of bowel. Other clues to serious complications include alterations of the vital signs with tachycardia, hypotension, and fever indicating early sepsis. Unfortunately, a number of studies document that even experienced physicians cannot reliably distinguish between strangulation and simple intestinal obstruction on the basis of examination alone.[2,3]

Complications

Complications associated with SBO include hypovolemia, intestinal ischemia and infarction, peritonitis and sepsis, and respiratory compromise from elevation of the diaphragm or aspiration of gastrointestinal material. The incidence of complications is, in part, related to the degree of intestinal dilation, which in most cases is directly related to delays in presentation, diagnosis, and initiation of appropriate treatment. Early diagnosis and management in the emergency department can prevent or minimize much of the preoperative morbidity associated with this disease.

Complications related to surgical management of SBO include recurrence of the obstruction, hemorrhage, wound infection, abscess formation, sepsis, and short bowel syndrome.[2] Much of the eventual postoperative morbidity and mortality is related to the patient's underlying medical condition. Whether the condition is treated surgically or conservatively, the long-term recurrence rate of adhesive SBO is significant—53% after an initial episode and 83% after second and further episodes.[6]

Diagnostic Strategies

Routine laboratory testing yields nonspecific findings. Leukocytosis is common with both simple and strangulated obstructions and is not a reliable marker for intestinal compromise. Serum markers of intestinal compromise and ischemia, including creatine phosphokinase (CPK), amylase, and lactate, are elevated late in the course of bowel obstruction. Electrolyte and renal function tests are appropriate if significant volume loss is evident.

Conventional and special radiographic examinations of the abdomen are the most useful diagnostic adjuncts for the evaluation of patients with suspected SBO. These studies may confirm or exclude the presence of bowel obstruction; identify the site, severity, and cause of the obstruction; and help distinguish simple obstruction from strangulation.[4,17,18] Answers to these pivotal questions determine the need for urgent surgical intervention versus a period of conservative, nonoperative management.

An adequate plain film examination of the abdomen requires at least two films, one with the patient supine and the other with the patient in the upright or decubitus position. An upright chest film may be added to exclude the presence of free subdiaphragmatic gas, an uncommon finding in bowel obstruction. Plain films demonstrate the presence of SBO in 50% to 60% of cases and are suggestive of obstruction in another 20% to 30%.[17] The cause of obstruction is rarely demonstrated on conventional abdominal radiographs. The ability to predict the site of obstruction correctly is often limited by fluid-filled loops or abnormal positioning of small bowel. Despite these potential limitations, plain radiographs are still the appropriate starting point for the diagnostic evaluation of a patient with suspected SBO.

Typical plain film findings with SBO are distended loops of small bowel proximal to the site of obstruction followed by normal or collapsed bowel distal to the obstruction. The supine view may show dilated loops of bowel that are sharply angulated or arranged in a series of parallel segments reminiscent of a stepladder. Upright or decubitus films may demonstrate multiple intraluminal air-fluid levels (Figure 91-1). In general, the greater the number of dilated loops of bowel, the more distal the site of obstruction. Colonic gas is usually negligible unless the films are obtained early in the course of the obstruction or in the presence of a partial SBO.[4]

When the obstructed intestine contains more fluid than gas, the classical findings just described may be absent. In this setting, small pockets of gas may become trapped between the valvulae conniventes of the small bowel and may appear as an oblique series of round radiolucencies on the upright film—the so-called string of pearls or string of beads sign, which is very suggestive of SBO.

Two subtle plain film findings suggest the presence of a closed-loop obstruction: the coffee bean sign and the pseudotumor sign.[4] The coffee bean sign refers to distended, air-filled, and U-shaped bowel loops that are separated by edematous bowel wall. The pseudotumor sign refers to the presence of a fluid-filled loop of bowel that resembles a mass. These are revealing signs concerning the type of obstruction but are seldom seen or properly interpreted.

Patients with adynamic ileus or gastroenteritis may have plain film findings that are similar to those of

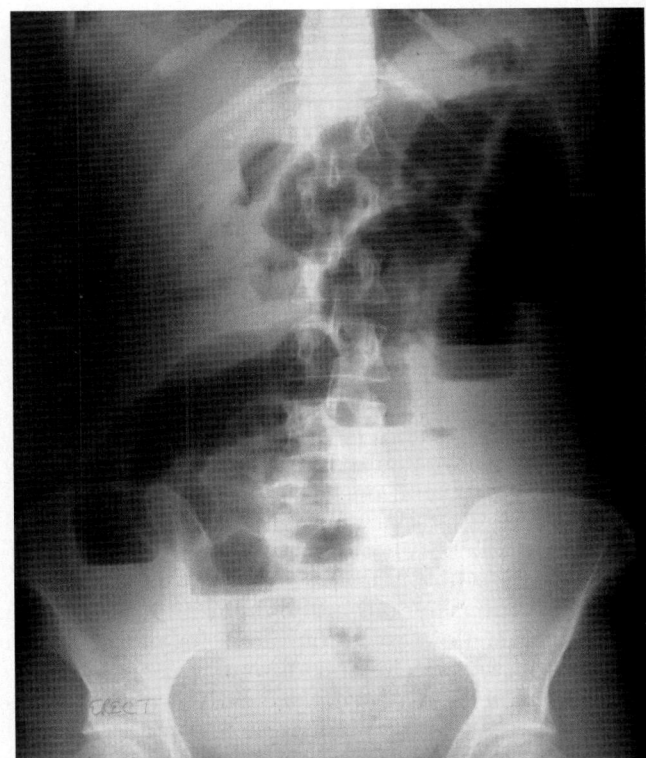

Figure 91-1. Upright abdominal film revealing multiple air-fluid levels and small bowel dilation, consistent with a diagnosis of small bowel obstruction.

intestinal obstruction. In this setting, however, the radiologic findings tend to involve the entire gastrointestinal tract, including the colon, and air-fluid levels are not as prominent as with mechanical obstruction. The air-filled loops of bowel are also not dilated in gastroenteritis or other causes of adynamic ileus.

Since the first reports describing the role of CT in bowel obstruction in the early 1990s, this modality has been increasingly utilized. It is considered complementary to standard radiography in the evaluation of SBO. CT has been shown to be an excellent way to demonstrate intussusception, volvulus, and extraluminal lesions such as abscesses and tumors.[18] This modality is especially helpful and should be used as an early imaging technique in the setting of known abdominal malignancy or inflammatory bowel disease or when an abdominal mass is discovered on examination. CT scans have high sensitivity, specificity, and accuracy in the diagnosis of SBO.[19,20] In high-grade obstructions, in particular, these numbers are greater than 90%.[4] CT can demonstrate both closed-loop obstruction and findings suggestive of strangulation.[4,21-26] In the vast majority of cases, CT is not required in the emergency department to make the diagnosis of bowel obstruction. Its main use is in better defining the site of obstruction and possible cause.[18-22]

Differential Considerations

The diagnosis of SBO should be considered in a patient with abdominal pain and vomiting, especially if there is a prior history of abdominal surgery. It is often difficult to distinguish among mechanical obstruction, adynamic ileus, and pseudo-obstruction on clinical grounds alone.

Other clinical diagnoses that should be considered range from benign to life threatening and include pregnancy, gastroenteritis, cholelithiasis and cholecystitis, pancreatitis, peptic ulcer disease, appendicitis, ischemic bowel syndromes, and myocardial infarction. Each of these diagnoses has typical signs, symptoms, and diagnostic findings that help to differentiate it from SBO, but in the early presentation it may be a surprising challenge to exclude each diagnosis from the differential list.

Management

The initial management of SBO has remained largely unchanged for several decades and consists of aggressive fluid resuscitation, bowel decompression, and timely surgical consultation.

All patients with SBO should be admitted to the hospital. Intravenous hydration should be initiated with an isotonic crystalloid solution administered through large-bore catheters. Enteral decompression by nasogastric suction should take place early in the patient's course to remove accumulated gas and fluid proximal to the obstruction. There is no convincing argument for the use of a long intestinal tube (e.g., Cantor, Miller-Abbott) over a nasogastric tube.[27,28] Placement of a nasogastric tube is a noxious procedure for patients. Topical anesthetics applied to the nasopharynx and posterior pharynx may improve the patient's tolerance of the procedure.

There is no convincing research to recommend routine use of antibiotics in the conservatively managed patient. However, the demonstration of bacterial proliferation during intestinal stasis and obstruction suggests that broad-spectrum antibiotics are appropriate when surgery is planned and when there is a suggestion of vascular compromise or intestinal perforation.[2] Antibiotic use should provide coverage of gram-negative and anaerobic organisms that colonize the intestinal contents (e.g., second-generation cephalosporins).

"Never let the sun set or rise on a bowel obstruction" is an oft-quoted surgical adage that has stood the test of time because of the preoperative difficulty in distinguishing strangulation from simple bowel obstruction.[1,2] Proponents of early surgical intervention cite the similar clinical and radiographic presentations of simple and strangulated obstructions and argue that any delay in surgical therapy may increase morbidity. Although there is no debate about the need for surgery if there are signs of peritoneal irritation or fever, most surgeons advocate a trial of conservative therapy in the absence of findings suggestive of strangulation. Up to 75% of patients with partial SBO and 35% to 50% of those with complete obstruction have resolution of symptoms when treated with intravenous fluid and bowel decompression alone.[29-31] Patients with early postoperative bowel obstruction, adhesive obstruction, and obstruction secondary to Crohn's disease are more likely to respond to nonoperative management. Surgical intervention should be planned if substantial relief is not attained within a short time after nasogastric tube placement or if symptoms persist after 48 hours of conservative treatment. A practical point is that obstruction occurring in a patient without a previous history of laparotomy is not likely to be caused by peritoneal adhesions. Such de novo obstruction and the underlying cause usually are not resolved without surgery.

Neither advanced age nor known abdominal malignancy is a contraindication to operative intervention. Patients with known abdominal cancer who do not have widespread intra-abdominal metastases should be treated like any other patients with SBO. They should receive a trial of bowel decompression followed by surgery if resolution of the symptoms is not evident. From 20% to 40% of patients with abdominal neoplasms and SBO have a benign cause of the obstruction.[32,33] In addition, the incidence of strangulation with obstruction related to malignancy is uniformly reported to be low. Therefore, a trial of tube decompression is a safe and often successful option.

A therapeutic approach that is gaining support for the management of SBO is laparoscopy.[34-37] Bowel obstruction has traditionally been a relative contraindication for laparoscopy because of the potential for bowel distention and the risk of enteric injury. However, as experience with this surgical approach has increased, surgeons have begun to demonstrate that this is a safe and effective method of diagnosing and treating acute bowel obstruction in selected patients, particularly in those with obstruction caused by adhesions.

Disposition

The diagnosis or serious consideration of SBO requires surgical consultation and admission to hospital for definitive management.

KEY CONCEPTS

- More than 50% of SBO cases are caused by postoperative adhesions. Two other leading causes are various hernias (15%) and neoplasms (15%).
- The diagnosis of SBO is usually made on the basis of plain radiographs, with the upright abdominal radiograph revealing air-fluid levels and dilated loops of small bowel in the majority of cases.
- Emergency department management should include volume assessment and resuscitation, plain radiographs, bowel decompression, and surgical consultation. A significant percentage of SBO cases caused by adhesions may be managed without surgery.

ACUTE MESENTERIC ISCHEMIA

Perspective

Acute mesenteric ischemia primarily affects patients older than 50 years, especially those with significant cardiovascular or systemic disease. The acute form of this disease results in the rapid development of intestinal injury and is much more common than the chronic form of mesenteric ischemia. Chronic mesenteric ischemia results when splanchnic blood flow is inadequate to support fully the functional demands of the intestines yet not so compromised as to threaten bowel viability. The incidence of acute mesenteric ischemia is difficult to determine but has been reported as 0.1% of hospital admissions, and several authors report increasing occurrence in our aging population.[38,39] Acute vascular compromise of the intestine remains an important and life-threatening cause of acute abdominal pain in patients presenting to the emergency department.

Acute mesenteric ischemia was described in the 18th and 19th centuries in sporadic reports; however, an understanding of the underlying pathophysiology awaited the classical experimental work of Litten in 1875, when he described the results of ligation of mesenteric vessels in animals.[40] In 1895, Elliot described the first patient to recover after resection of an infarcted intestine that was probably due to mesenteric venous thrombosis. He created two stomas and reanastomosed them 2 weeks later. Thus, the diagnosis of gangrenous bowel by laparotomy and its treatment by resection with anastomosis, a sequence of events that is still common today, were first performed more than 100 years ago.

The concept of mesenteric revascularization as the treatment of acute mesenteric ischemia was introduced in the 1950s. Even with the advent of this significant surgical advance, however, morbidity and mortality rates remained high. Today, most physicians use an aggressive approach to the patient with suspected acute mesenteric ischemia, as first proposed in the 1970s. The single most important step in this approach is early diagnosis.

Acute mesenteric ischemia actually has four distinct etiologies, each associated with a group of risk factors, signs and symptoms on presentation, and varying nuances in the evaluation and management of the patient. The most common cause of acute mesenteric ischemia is arterial embolus, which accounts for at least 50% of cases. Arterial thrombosis and venous occlusion by thrombosis each represent 15% of acute presentations. The remaining 20% of mesenteric ischemia cases are caused by nonocclusive vascular disease.[41,42] The importance of early diagnosis and aggressive intervention in patients with suspected acute mesenteric ischemia is underscored by mortality rates that climb to 70% to 90% when intestinal infarction has occurred.[43] The mortality of this lethal disease has changed little in the last several decades and probably will not change until a reliable screening test for the disease is found.

Principles of Disease

The severity of intestinal injury is inversely proportional to mesenteric blood flow and is a function of the state of the systemic circulation, the number and caliber of involved vessels, the status of the collateral circulation in the region, and the duration of the ischemia.[41,42,44] The extent of the damage ranges from reversible impairments in mucosal function to transmural infarction and necrosis of part or all of the bowel served by the compromised vasculature.

Blood supply to the abdominal organs derives from three major vessels: the celiac trunk, the superior mesenteric artery (SMA), and the inferior mesenteric artery (IMA). Abdominal organs receive their blood supply on the basis of embryologic development. The esophagus, stomach, proximal duodenum, liver, gallbladder, pancreas, and spleen are supplied by the celiac trunk. The SMA supplies the distal duodenum, jejunum, ileum, and colon to the splenic flexure. The descending and sigmoid colon and rectum are supplied by the IMA. There is an abundant system of collateral vessels and significant territorial overlap of blood flow that can be clinically significant.[45,46]

Approximately 25% of the cardiac output is delivered to the small and large intestines, with two thirds going to the SMA distribution and one third to the IMA.[41] Eighty percent of this flow is destined for perfusion of the mucosa because of its high metabolic requirement. Accordingly, the visceral mucosa is very sensitive to decreased perfusion. With the onset of hypoperfusion, a redistribution of intramural blood flow favoring the superficial layers of the mucosa takes place. Below a critical level of blood flow, however, the intestinal villi become ischemic and significant alterations in mucosal function occur.

The countercurrent exchange mechanism in the small intestinal villi initiates and perpetuates ischemic damage to the tissue.[41,46] As epithelial cells become necrotic, there is release of endothelial factors that lead to the attraction and activation of neutrophils and macrophages into the ischemic tissue. These cells release protease enzymes, tissue necrosis factor, platelet activating factor, arachidonic acid byproducts, and toxic oxygen radicals that cause further endothelial damage, increased vascular permeability, vasoconstriction, inflammation, and further necrosis. This initial ischemic insult is compounded if and when perfusion is reestablished because restoration of blood flow permits further recruitment of inflammatory cells to the area. Ischemic disruption of the normally impenetrable mucosal barrier allows the release of bacteria, toxins, and vasoactive mediators into the systemic circulation. Cardiac depression, multisystem organ failure, septic shock, and death may occur even before the development of intestinal ischemia. Necrotic changes can be seen as soon as 10 to 12 hours after the onset of symptoms but may develop in a more delayed fashion.

Mesenteric Arterial Embolism

The median age of patients presenting with mesenteric arterial emboli is 70 years. Approximately two thirds of these patients are women. The vast majority of arterial emboli resulting in acute mesenteric ischemia involve the SMA. The source of SMA emboli is usually the heart, either left atrial or ventricular thrombi that fragment during or after a dysrhythmia, or valvular lesions. Emboli consisting of tumor and cholesterol have also been reported.[47] Emboli typically lodge 4 to 7 cm from the vessel's origin at a point of anatomic narrowing such as the takeoff of a major arterial branch. More than 50% of SMA emboli are found immediately

BOX 91-3. Factors Associated with Mesenteric Arterial Embolism

Coronary artery disease
   Post–myocardial infarction mural thrombi
   Congestive heart failure
Valvular heart disease
   Rheumatic mitral valve disease
   Nonbacterial endocarditis
Arrhythmias
   Chronic atrial fibrillation
Aortic aneurysms or dissections
Coronary angiography

distal to the origin of the middle colic artery. Risk factors for mesenteric arterial emboli include coronary artery disease, valvular heart disease, and arrhythmias, in particular atrial fibrillation.[48] Risk factors are listed in Box 91-3. It is important to recognize these in an effort to improve early consideration and diagnosis of this disease.

Mesenteric Arterial Thrombosis

The SMA, which originates from the ventral surface of the abdominal aorta at a 45-degree angle, is commonly narrowed by atherosclerosis. This is the most common site for thrombus formation in the mesenteric circulation. In contrast to arterial embolism, the more proximal nature of thrombus formation results in greater visceral damage and a less favorable prognosis. SMA thrombosis usually occurs in patients with chronic, severe, visceral atherosclerosis. Up to 50% of these patients give a history of "abdominal angina" or abdominal pain after meals. Thus, risk factors associated with mesenteric arterial thrombosis include older age, diffuse atherosclerosis (coronary, cerebral, or peripheral vascular disease), and hypertension.

Nonocclusive Mesenteric Ischemia

This entity has been defined only in the last 50 years, as intraoperative and postmortem examinations have revealed ischemic bowel without obvious vascular obstruction.[38,49] The pathogenesis of nonocclusive mesenteric ischemia is multifactorial, but a common pathway involves mesenteric vasoconstriction, usually in response to low-flow states associated with decreased cardiac output or the administration of vasoactive medications. Factors contributing to the development of nonocclusive mesenteric ischemia include many systemic diseases associated with hypotension as well as medications that produce splanchnic vasoconstriction (Box 91-4). Nonocclusive mesenteric ischemia is seen in patients of all ages and often develops during hospitalization for other medical or surgical problems.

Mesenteric Venous Thrombosis

Mesenteric venous thrombosis is the least common cause of acute mesenteric ischemia. It occurs in a

BOX 91-4. Factors Associated with Mesenteric Venous Thrombosis

Hypercoagulable states
   Polycythemia vera
   Sickle cell disease
   Antithrombin III deficiency
   Protein C or S deficiency
   Malignancy
   Myeloproliferative disorders
   Estrogen therapy/oral contraceptive pill
   Pregnancy
Inflammatory conditions
   Pancreatitis
   Diverticulitis
   Appendicitis
   Cholangitis
Trauma
   Operative venous injury
   Postsplenectomy
   Blunt or abdominal trauma
Miscellaneous
   Congestive heart failure
   Renal failure
   Decompression sickness
   Portal hypertension

BOX 91-5. Factors Associated with Nonocclusive Mesenteric Ischemia

Cardiovascular disease leading to low-flow states
   Congestive heart failure
   Arrhythmias
   Cardiogenic shock
   Post-cardiopulmonary bypass
Preceding hypotensive episode
   Septic shock
Drug-induced splanchnic vasoconstriction
   Digoxin
   Vasopressors
   Ergot alkaloid poisoning
   Cocaine abuse

younger population of patients, and the mortality rate is lower than that associated with other causes, ranging from 20% to 50%.[50,51] Mesenteric venous thrombosis can rarely occur as a primary diagnosis, but it often occurs in association with an underlying medical condition, including hypercoagulable states, inflammatory processes within the abdomen, local trauma, and conditions associated with relative venous stasis (Box 91-5). Historically, up to 60% of patients with mesenteric venous thrombosis have a history of peripheral deep venous thrombosis.[41]

Clinical Features

History

The clinical findings associated with acute mesenteric ischemia, regardless of the cause of the vascular compromise, are fairly nonspecific. Nonetheless, the presentation is sufficiently characteristic that acute mesenteric ischemia should be considered in the population of patients at risk. Patients older than 50 years with any of the previously discussed risk factors for mesenteric ischemia, who experience sudden onset of abdominal pain that is severe enough to call it to the attention of a physician and that lasts for more than 2 hours, should be suspected of having acute mesenteric ischemia.[38,52]

On initial presentation the patient with acute mesenteric ischemia typically complains of severe, poorly localized, colicky abdominal pain. Associated symptoms may include nausea, vomiting, and frequent bowel movements as the bowel attempts to empty itself. The most consistent finding is pain that is out of proportion to the physical findings. This characteristic finding is noted because only visceral structures are initially ischemic, and the parietal peritoneum is spared. Mesenteric ischemia can also be more subacute in its presentation, with the insidious onset of less severe and vague abdominal pain, abdominal distention, and occult gastrointestinal bleeding.

Physical Examination

In the early phases of mesenteric ischemia, physical examination findings may be nondiagnostic. As the disease process continues, abdominal distention and diffuse abdominal tenderness without guarding develop. Transmural intestinal injury leads to peritoneal signs (involuntary guarding and rebound tenderness). Late in the ischemic episode, the abdomen is grossly distended, with absent bowel sounds and exquisite tenderness to palpation. Heme-positive stool develops in 25% of patients and often occurs as a relatively late finding.[41] Historical details and physical findings referable to other parts of the body may suggest the etiology of the acute impairment in mesenteric blood flow.

Complications

Delays in diagnosis permit progression of the disease process and the development of transmural intestinal ischemia, with its correspondingly high morbidity and mortality. Yet, even with early diagnosis and aggressive management, a complicated course is to be expected. Secondary reperfusion injury is common, and bowel initially believed to be viable at the time of operation may become ischemic and infarct in the postoperative period. Other postoperative complications include wound infections, intra-abdominal abscesses, sepsis, and pneumonia. This population of patients is also at risk for many life-threatening complications (including myocardial infarction, pulmonary embolism, and renal failure) because of their significant concurrent illnesses.

Diagnostic Strategies

Routine laboratory and standard radiographic evaluations are usually not helpful in the diagnosis of mesenteric ischemia. An increase in the peripheral white blood cell count is a common but nonspecific finding, and although a normal count makes the diagnosis of acute intestinal ischemia less likely, it does not exclude

the diagnosis. Hemoconcentration, metabolic acidosis with base deficit, and hyperamylasemia are present in more than half of the cases of acute mesenteric ischemia but are likewise nonspecific findings. A significant emphasis has been placed on the role of serum lactate levels in ischemia, but a consensus regarding their utility is yet to be reached.[39] The sensitivity of this serum marker is high, approaching 100% when bowel infarction is present, but it has a disappointing specificity, ranging from 42% to 87% in varying series.[53,54] A retrospective review of mesenteric ischemia noted an elevated serum lactate level at the time of diagnosis to be most useful as a significant predictor of mortality and suggested that the presence of unexplained acidosis in patients at risk should prompt a search for reversible causes of mesenteric ischemia.[55] The seromuscular enzyme CPK rises 3 to 4 hours after vascular occlusion but has limited specificity and sensitivity. Other seromuscular enzymes (lactate dehydrogenase, aspartate transaminase) and mucosal enzymes (alkaline phosphatase) are even less sensitive and specific than CPK.[41]

The first radiologic examination that should be done in a patient with suspected mesenteric ischemia is a plain abdominal radiograph series (supine and upright) to rule out bowel obstruction or free air. Plain radiographs are most often normal in the presence of acute mesenteric vascular compromise. By the time any changes characteristic of acute intestinal ischemia are apparent, transmural damage has already taken place. Subtle signs of acute mesenteric ischemia on plain abdominal radiographs include adynamic ileus, distended air-filled loops of bowel, and bowel wall thickening from submucosal edema or hemorrhage. In advanced stages of ischemia, pneumatosis of the bowel wall may be detected as intraluminal gas dissects into the submucosa.[42,56] Another late, and often preterminal, sign of necrotic bowel is the presence of gas within the portal venous system.

Further radiographic examinations should be selected judiciously. Intraluminal barium contrast evaluations are contraindicated because residual contrast material can limit visualization of the mesenteric vasculature during diagnostic angiography.[42] Duplex ultrasonography may be of some benefit in visualizing flow in the SMA and celiac axis. Unfortunately, many patients suspected of having mesenteric ischemia often have dilated, air-filled loops of bowel, which makes ultrasonography extremely difficult.

Because of the availability, improved quality, and speed of CT, this radiologic test is often used for assessing undiagnosed abdominal pain in high-risk patients in the emergency department. In the setting of intestinal ischemia, a CT scan is capable of demonstrating edema of the bowel wall and mesentery, abnormal gas patterns, intramural gas, ascites, and, occasionally, direct evidence of mesenteric venous thrombosis. Although some studies find CT scanning to be as sensitive as angiography,[57,58] it should not be considered the first study of choice. Nonetheless, the diagnosis of acute mesenteric ischemia is occasionally made by CT imaging given the prevalence of this test in the evaluation of abdominal pain. Finally, one must keep in

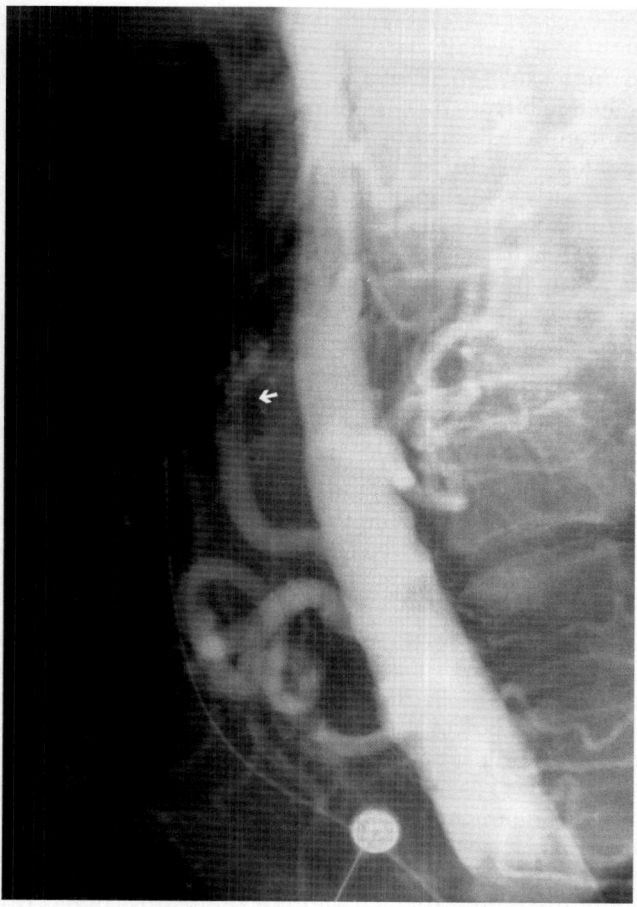

Figure 91-2. Angiogram demonstrating a superior mesenteric artery embolus (*arrow*). (Courtesy of Mark LeQuire, MD, Department of Radiology, Carolinas Medical Center, Charlotte, NC.)

mind that, as with plain films, a large percentage of patients may have normal or nonspecific CT findings, and thus the diagnosis of mesenteric ischemia cannot be ruled out on the basis of a normal CT scan.[39]

Angiography remains the "gold standard" in the diagnosis of mesenteric ischemia and is unique among other diagnostic modalities in that it may assist with both diagnosis and therapy. Preoperative angiography is useful in the diagnosis of either mesenteric artery embolus or thrombus. It allows identification of the site and type of occlusion as well as evaluation of the splanchnic circulation, thus facilitating plans for prompt revascularization. Classically, the angiographic finding with SMA embolus is the "mercury meniscus" sign appearing 3 to 8 cm distal to the origin of the SMA (Figure 91-2). Thrombosis of the SMA typically reveals an occlusion just distal to the origin of the vessel. In addition, angiography provides a definitive diagnosis of nonocclusive mesenteric ischemia. Arteriographic signs of nonocclusive disease include diffuse or focal tapering of mesenteric arterial branches, alternating segments of narrowing and dilation of intestinal branches ("sausage sign"), poor intramural vessel filling, and mesenteric arcade vasospasm.[41] There are two clinical situations, however, in which angiography is contraindicated in the setting of nonocclusive

disease: shock and vasopressor therapy.[39] In these instances, diagnosis during laparotomy is preferred because the underlying mesenteric arterial vaso-constriction may result in either a false-positive or false-negative diagnosis of acute mesenteric ischemia. Broad criteria for selection of patients must be used if early diagnosis and effective intervention are to be possible. Therefore, a significant number of negative angiograms should be accepted.[38]

Differential Considerations

Mesenteric ischemia occurs most often in patients older than 50 years, but the diagnosis should be considered in all patients, regardless of age, who have sudden onset of severe abdominal pain. The severe and colicky nature of the pain may also suggest chole-cystitis, peptic ulcer disease, perforation of bowel, nephrolithiasis, diverticulitis, and bowel obstruction. The significant pain, often out of proportion to the physical findings, may also suggest the possibility of pancreatitis and abdominal aortic aneurysm rupture. The urgency of efficiently identifying acute mesenteric ischemia would recommend that this diagnosis be considered in a large population of patients, particularly in patients at risk because of underlying illness or chronic medical therapy that produces vasoconstric-tion. In practice, the diagnosis of acute mesenteric ischemia is often made after other disorders have been excluded.

Management

Early diagnosis achieved by aggressive utilization of angiography remains the key to a successful outcome. Therapeutic intervention should take place as soon as the diagnosis of acute mesenteric ischemia is made if tissue salvage is to be maximized and mortality minimized.

Initial resuscitative efforts should include correction of hypovolemia and hypotension as well as any accompanying metabolic abnormalities. In the population of patients at risk for mesenteric ischemia, successful resuscitation may require invasive hemodynamic monitoring. Control of arrhythmias, congestive heart failure, and other factors contributing to relative hypoperfusion of the bowel is a priority. Medications with vasoconstrictive properties should be discontin-ued immediately. If vasopressors must be used to support blood pressure, the lowest possible dose should be infused, and α-agonists should be avoided, with inotropes being the preferred agents. Enteral decompression by nasogastric tube placement is rec-ommended. Broad-spectrum antibiotic therapy that covers bowel flora should be initiated early, particu-larly when surgery is anticipated.

When the patient is stabilized, routine laboratory and plain film examination can be performed to exclude other more common causes of abdominal pain. If an expeditious evaluation does not reveal an alternative diagnosis, angiography should be performed. Even when the decision to operate has been made on clini-cal grounds, a preoperative angiogram may improve management of the patient at laparotomy.[41] In addition, when the diagnosis of acute mesenteric arterial compromise is confirmed, infusion of papaverine through the angiography catheter directly into the SMA reduces or eliminates mesenteric vasoconstriction. Papaverine is a potent inhibitor of phosphodiesterase, the enzyme necessary for degradation of cyclic adenosine monophosphate (cAMP). Increased cAMP levels cause vascular smooth muscle relaxation and relief of vasoconstriction. Because papaverine is 90% metabolized by the liver on its first pass, few if any systemic effects are noted during its use. The dosing is a 60-mg bolus into the SMA, followed by continuous infusion of 30 to 60 mg/hour at a concentration of 1 mg/mL.[41] Use of this vasodilator in both nonocclusive and occlusive forms of mesenteric ischemia has improved survival 20% to 50%.[59]

The surgical management of acute mesenteric ischemia is both challenging and controversial. Treatment principles range from pharmacologic manipulation without operation to revascularization procedures to bowel resection. The underlying cause of intestinal hypoperfusion is often not amenable to surgical correction, as with mesenteric venous occlusion and nonocclusive disease, and the role of operation may be limited to the resection of already infarcted bowel.

If a revascularization procedure is to be undertaken in the presence of arterial occlusive disease, it is completed before any evaluation of bowel viability is performed. The reason behind this therapeutic sequence is that bowel that initially appears irreversibly damaged may exhibit significant recovery on restoration of blood flow. Obviously necrotic bowel is resected, but in the presence of extensive ischemic damage, the surgeon may choose to leave bowel of questionable viability in place and to reevaluate its viability during a subsequent operation.[59-61] This "second-look" operation, typically performed 12 to 24 hours after the initial procedure, may permit a more limited resection.

Percutaneous transluminal angioplasty has been described for both acute and chronic mesenteric ischemia from thrombosis of the SMA. In the acute setting, it appears to be associated with an increased risk of recurrence and potential for extensive bowel loss.[41] With chronic intestinal ischemia, particularly in elderly patients who are poor surgical candidates, mesenteric angioplasty is a good option, with the majority of patients having complete symptomatic improvement and continued relief of symptoms during follow-up.[62]

Intra-arterial infusion into the SMA of thrombolytic agents has been used successfully for mesenteric ischemic following acute emboli,[63,64] but only on a case report basis. These patients were selected with emboli confirmed by angiography, had no peritoneal signs, and had normal abdominal films revealing no ileus. Close monitoring and frequent clinical reassessment, as well as serial angiograms, are necessary after the infusion of thrombolysis. The main drawbacks to the use of thrombolytic agents are the difficulty in assessing bowel viability without laparotomy, the possible time delay of 12 to 18 hours before clot resolution, and the poten-

tial for clot fragmentation and involvement of more distal branches that are less amenable to surgical revascularization.[61]

In the patients surviving the initial episode of acute mesenteric ischemia, recurrent thrombosis is a potential problem requiring long-term anticoagulation. Warfarin (Coumadin) is started after mesenteric arterial embolism and mesenteric venous thrombosis. Antiplatelet therapy is begun after mesenteric arterial thrombosis and nonocclusive mesenteric ischemia. The 2-year mortality after mesenteric ischemia is as high as 70%. This grave prognosis, however, is mainly related to cardiovascular comorbidity rather than recurrent mesenteric ischemic events.[65]

Disposition

The consideration of acute mesenteric ischemia in a differential diagnosis of abdominal pain should lead to a surgical consultation. All patients with a clinical presentation suggestive of this life-threatening diagnosis require an aggressive, multidisciplinary approach to the diagnosis and management. The important role of the emergency physician on this team is to coordinate an efficient evaluation and appropriate referral. Although the prognosis for patients with acute mesenteric ischemia remains dire, one potential place for improvement in survival occurs during initial resuscitation and evaluation in the emergency department.

KEY CONCEPTS

- There are four separate acute mesenteric ischemia syndromes. The majority of cases are caused by embolic occlusion of the SMA. The remainder are due to SMA thrombosis, venous thrombosis, and nonocclusive arterial ischemia. Each of the syndromes has a specific set of risk factors or associated medical conditions that are helpful in differentiating them from one another.
- The diagnosis of acute mesenteric ischemia may be suggested by pain out of proportion to examination findings, heme-positive stool, elevated serum lactate levels, and classical findings on plain film or CT scans, but none of these provide enough sensitivity to ensure a diagnosis before bowel infarction occurs.
- An aggressive approach to diagnosis and management, including early utilization of angiography, has provided some improvement in the prognosis of acute mesenteric ischemia, although mortality from this disease is still greater than 50%.

REFERENCES

1. Holder WD: Intestinal obstruction. *Gastroenterol Clin North Am* 17:317, 1988.
2. Bass KN, Jones B, Bulkley GB: Current management of small-bowel obstruction. *Adv Surg* 31:1, 1998.
3. Bauer AJ, et al: Ileus in critical illness: Mechanisms and management. *Curr Opin Crit Care* 8:152, 2002.
4. Maglinte DDT, et al: The role of radiography in the diagnosis of small-bowel obstruction. *AJR Am J Roentgenol* 168:1171, 1997.

5. Ray NF, et al: Abdominal adhesiolysis: Inpatient care and expenditures in the United States in 1994. *J Am Coll Surg* 186:1, 1998.

6. Barkan H, Webster S, Ozeran S: Factors predicting the recurrence of adhesive small-bowel obstruction. *Am J Surg* 170:361, 1995.

7. Ellis H: The clinical significance of adhesions: Focus on intestinal obstruction. *Eur J Surg* 163(Suppl 577):5, 1997.

8. Beck DE, et al: Incidence of small-bowel obstruction and adhesiolysis after open colorectal and general surgery. *Dis Colon Rectum* 42:241, 1999.

9. Miller G, et al: Etiology of small bowel obstruction. *Am J Surg* 180:33, 2000.

10. Reisner RM, Cohen JR: Gallstone ileus: A review of 1001 reported cases. *Am Surg* 60:441, 1994.

11. Lobo DJ, et al: Gallstone ileus: Diagnostic pitfalls and therapeutic successes. *J Clin Gastroenterol* 30:72, 2000.

12. Lo CY, Lorentz TG, Lau PWK: Obturator hernia presenting as small bowel obstruction. *Am J Surg* 167:396, 1994.

13. Roggo A, Ottinger LW: Acute small bowel volvulus in adults. *Ann Surg* 216:135, 1992.

14. Begos DG, et al: The diagnosis and management of adult intussusception. *Am J Surg* 173:88, 1997.

15. Takeuchi K, et al: The diagnosis and treatment of adult intussusception. *J Clin Gastroenterol* 36:18, 2003.

16. Bohner H, et al: Simple data from history and physical examination help to exclude bowel obstruction and to avoid radiographic studies in patients with acute abdominal pain. *Eur J Surg* 164:777, 1998.

17. Maglinte DDT, et al: Reliability and role of plain film radiography and CT in the diagnosis of small-bowel obstruction. *AJR Am J Roentgenol* 167:1451, 1996.

18. Suri S, et al: Comparative evaluation of plain films, ultrasound and CT in the diagnosis of intestinal obstruction. *Acta Radiol* 40:422, 1999.

19. Donckier V, et al: Contribution of computed tomography to decision making in the management of adhesive small bowel obstruction. *Br J Surg* 85:1071, 1998.

20. Frager D, et al: CT of small-bowel obstruction: Value in establishing the diagnosis and determining the degree and cause. *AJR Am J Roentgenol* 162:37, 1994.

21. Maglinte DDT, et al: Obstruction of the small intestine: accuracy and role of CT in diagnosis. *Radiology* 188:61, 1993.

22. Stewart ET: CT diagnosis of small-bowel obstruction. *AJR Am J Roentgenol* 158:771, 1992.

23. Ha HK, et al: Differentiation of simple and strangulated small-bowel obstructions: Usefulness of known CT criteria. *Radiology* 204:507, 1997.

24. Balthazar EJ, Liebeskind ME, Macari M: Intestinal ischemia in patients in whom small bowel obstruction is suspected: Evaluation of accuracy, limitations, and clinical implications of CT in diagnosis. *Radiology* 205:519, 1997.

25. Frager D, et al: Detection of intestinal ischemia in patients with acute small-bowel obstruction due to adhesions or hernia: Efficacy of CT. *AJR Am J Roentgenol* 166:67, 1996.

26. Peck JJ, Milleson T, Phelan J: The role of computed tomography with contrast and small-bowel follow-through in management of small bowel obstruction. *Am J Surg* 177:375, 1999.

27. Fleshner PR, et al: A prospective, randomized trial of short versus long tubes in adhesive small-bowel obstruction. *Am J Surg* 170:366, 1995.

28. Ellozy SH, et al: Early postoperative small-bowel obstruction. *Dis Colon Rectum* 45:1214, 2002.

29. Sosa J, Gardner B: Management of patients diagnosed as acute intestinal obstruction secondary to adhesions. *Am Surg* 59:125, 1993.

30. Seror D, et al: How conservatively can postoperative small bowel obstruction be treated? *Am J Surg* 165:121, 1993.

31. Choi H, Chu K, Law W. Therapeutic value of Gastrografin in adhesive small bowel obstruction after unsuccessful conservative treatment. *Ann Surg* 236:1, 2002.

32. Butler JA, et al: Small bowel obstruction in patients with a prior history of cancer. *Am J Surg* 162:624, 1991.

33. Tang E, Davis J, Silberman H: Bowel obstruction in cancer patients. *Arch Surg* 130:832, 1995.

34. Wullstein C, Gross E. Laparoscopic compared with conventional treatment of acute adhesive small bowel obstruction. *Br J Surg* 90:1147, 2003.

35. Francois V, et al: Postoperative adhesive peritoneal disease: Laparoscopic treatment. *Surg Endosc* 8:781, 1994.

36. Ibrahim IM, et al: Laparoscopic management of acute small-bowel obstruction. *Surg Endosc* 10:1012, 1996.

37. Strickland P, et al: Is laparoscopy safe and effective for treatment of acute small-bowel obstruction? *Surg Endosc* 13:695, 1999.

38. Vicente DC, Kazmers A. Acute mesenteric ischemia. *Curr Opin Cardiol* 14:453, 1999.

39. Ruotolo RA, Evans SRT: Mesenteric ischemia in the elderly. *Clin Geriatr Med* 15:527, 1999.

40. Boley SJ, Brandt LJ, Sammartano RJ: History of mesenteric ischemia: The evolution of a diagnosis and management. *Surg Clin North Am* 77:275, 1997.

41. Castellone JA, Powers RD: Ischemic bowel syndromes: A comprehensive, state-of-the-art approach to emergency diagnosis and management. *Emerg Med Rep* 18:189, 1997.

42. McKinsey JF, Gewertz BL: Acute mesenteric ischemia. *Surg Clin North Am* 77:307, 1997.

43. Mamode N, Pickford I, Lieberman P: Failure to improve outcome in acute mesenteric ischemia: Seven year review. *Eur J Surg* 165:203, 1999.

44. Walker JS, Dire DJ: Vascular abdominal emergencies. *Emerg Med Clin North Am* 14:571, 1996.

45. Rosenblum JD, Boyle CM, Schwartz LB: The mesenteric circulation: Anatomy and physiology. *Surg Clin North Am* 77:289, 1997.

46. Mitsudo S, Brandt LJ: Pathology of intestinal ischemia. *Surg Clin North Am* 72:43, 1992.

47. Krupski WC, Selzman CH, Whitehill TA: Unusual causes of mesenteric ischemia. *Surg Clin North Am* 77:471, 1997.

48. Howard TJ, et al: Nonocclusive mesenteric ischemia remains a diagnostic dilemma. *Am J Surg* 171:405, 1996.

49. Bassiouny HS: Nonocclusive mesenteric ischemia. *Surg Clin North Am* 77:319, 1997.

50. Rhee RY, Gloviczki P: Mesenteric venous thrombosis. *Surg Clin North Am* 77:327, 1997.

51. Kumar S, Sarr MG, Kamath PS. Mesenteric venous thrombosis. *N Engl J Med* 345:1683, 2001.

52. Bradbury AW, Brittenden J, Ruckley CV: Mesenteric ischaemia: A multidisciplinary approach. *Br J Surg* 82:1446, 1995.

53. Lange H, Jackel R: Usefulness of plasma lactate concentration in the diagnosis of acute abdominal disease. *Eur J Surg* 160:381, 1994.

54. Murray MJ, et al: Serum lactate levels as an aid to diagnosing acute intestinal ischemia. *Am J Surg* 167:575, 1994.

55. Newman TS, et al: The challenging face of mesenteric infarction. *Am Surg* 64:611, 1998.

56. Wolf EL, Sprayregen S, Bakal CW: Radiology in intestinal ischemia: Plain films, contrast, and other imaging studies. *Surg Clin North Am* 72:107, 1992.

57. Klein HM, et al: Diagnostic imaging of mesenteric infarction. *Radiology* 197:79, 1995.

58. Taourel PG, et al: Acute mesenteric ischemia: Diagnosis with contrast-enhanced CT. *Radiology* 199:632, 1996.

59. Endean ED, et al: Surgical management of thrombotic acute intestinal ischemia. *Ann Surg* 233:801, 2001.

60. Mansour MA. Management of acute mesenteric ischemia. *Arch Surg* 134:328, 1999.

61. Schneider TA, et al: Mesenteric ischemia: Acute arterial syndromes. *Dis Colon Rectum* 37:1163, 1994.
62. Allen RC, et al: Mesenteric angioplasty in the treatment of chronic intestinal ischemia. *J Vasc Surg* 24:415, 1996.
63. Regan F, Karlstad RR, Magnuson TH: Minimally invasive management of acute superior mesenteric artery occlusion: Combined urokinase and laparoscopic therapy. *Am J Gastroenterol* 91:1019, 1996.
64. Turégano-Fuentes P, et al: Acute arterial syndromes in mesenteric ischemia. *Dis Colon Rectum* 38:778, 1995.
65. Klempnaueer J, et al: Long-term results after surgery for acute mesenteric ischemia. *Surgery* 121:239, 1997.

CHAPTER

92 Acute Appendicitis

Jeannette M. Wolfe and Philip L. Henneman

PERSPECTIVE

Epidemiology

Appendicitis is a common condition requiring emergency surgery. About 7% of people will develop appendicitis sometime during their lifetime. Most cases occur in adolescents and young adults, with the incidence in men being slightly higher than in women.[1,2] The incidence of appendicitis in the United States has actually decreased since the early part of the century. This may be due to increased fiber in American diets causing more formed stools or to improved hygiene causing fewer enteric infections.[3]

Historical Perspective

The earliest evidence of appendicitis is suggested by the presence of right lower quadrant adhesions in an Egyptian mummy from the Byzantine era. In 1492, Leonardo da Vinci drew pictures of the colon and the appendix and called the structure an "orecchio," which literally means "ear." Claudius Amyand removed the first appendix incidentally in 1735 during the repair of a scrotal hernia in an 11-year-old boy. The appendix had perforated and a cutaneous fecal draining fistula had developed.[4] The half-hour operation was done without anesthesia and the boy fully recovered. In the early 1800s during the Lewis and Clark expedition, the only trip mortality was the death of Charles Floyd, who is rumored to have died from a ruptured appendix.[5]

In 1880 in Europe, Lawson Tait performed the first successful planned appendectomy by removing a gangrenous appendix from a 17-year-old woman. Six years later, Reginald Fitz, a pathologist, coined the term *appendicitis* when he read his classic paper at the first meeting of the Association of American Physicians. Fitz correctly described many of the pathophysiologic changes associated with appendicitis and advocated early surgery. Three years later, Charles McBurney described a point "determined by the pressure of one finger" between "one and a half and two inches from the anterior spinous process" which, when palpated, was associated with the greatest discomfort in patients with acute appendicitis (McBurney's point). The general acceptance that appendicitis was a surgical disease did not occur until several decades had passed. Early surgical intervention became popular in the early 1900s around the time that King Edward VII perforated his appendix and was operated on days before his coronation.[4,6]

PRINCIPLES OF DISEASE

Pathophysiology

The appendix is a hollow, muscular, closed-ended tube arising from the posterior medial surface of the cecum, about 3 cm below the ileocecal valve. Its average length is approximately 10 cm and its normal capacity is 0.1 to 0.3 mL. The role of the appendix in human physiology is unknown, but it may serve some type of immunologic function, as suggested by the presence of abundance of lymphoid tissue.[2] Innervation of the appendix is derived from sympathetic and vagus nerves from the superior mesenteric plexus. Afferent fibers that conduct visceral pain from the appendix accompany the sympathetic nerves and enter the spinal cord at the level of the tenth thoracic segment. This causes referred pain to the umbilical area.

The anatomic location of the appendix affects the clinical presentation as well as the subsequent risk of developing appendicitis. In a study of 10,000 autopsies, the appendix was located behind the cecum in the retrocecal fossa in 65% of cases and in the pelvis in 31% of cases.[7] This ratio is somewhat reversed in patients who are operated on for appendicitis. It is possible that a retrocecal appendix is less likely to become obstructed due to the position of its lumen.[8]

The majority of patients develop appendicitis because of an acute obstruction of the appendiceal lumen. This is usually from an appendicolith, but obstruction can also be caused by calculi, tumor, parasite, or foreign object. Of historical note, one of the more common causes of acute appendicitis from foreign objects in the early 19th century was from ingested lead shells buried in quail meat.[9]

After acute obstruction, intraluminal pressures rise, as mucosal secretions are unable to drain. The resulting distension stimulates visceral afferent pathways and is perceived as a dull, poorly localized pain. Abdominal cramping may occur due to hyperperistalsis. Next, ulceration and ischemia develop as the intraluminal pressure exceeds the venous pressure, and bacteria and polymorphonuclear cells begin to invade the appendiceal wall. The appendix may appear grossly normal at this time with evidence of pathology apparent only by microscopic examination.[10] With time, the appendix becomes swollen and begins to irritate surrounding structures, including the peritoneal wall. The pain now becomes more localized to the right lower quadrant. Continued swelling and hypoxia lead to gangrene (presence of necrosis) and ultimately, perforation through the appendiceal serosal layer. This can lead to abscess formation or diffuse peritonitis. The time required for the appendix to perforate is highly variable but usually occurs within 24 to 36 hours from onset of symptoms.[3] Elderly patients are prone to earlier perforation due to anatomical changes in the appendix associated with aging, such as a narrowed appendiceal lumen, thinner mucosal lining, decreased lymphoid tissue, and atherosclerosis.[11]

In about one third of cases, no direct cause of obstruction is noted; in these cases, it is surmised that inflammation is caused by viral, bacterial, or parasitic infection with subsequent mucosal ulceration or lymphoid hyperplasia.[2,3]

CLINICAL FEATURES

History

Appendicitis is classically described as starting with the vague onset of dull periumbilical pain, and the development of anorexia, nausea, and vomiting. The pain then migrates to the right lower quadrant and a low-grade temperature may develop. In most instances, the patient has not experienced pain similar to this episode in the past.[2] Unfortunately, the presentation can be highly variable. If the appendix is retrocecal or retroiliac, the pain may start in the right lower quadrant without migration and may be blunted by the presence of overlying bowel.[12] If the appendix is elongated, the pain may be referred to the flank, pelvis, or right upper quadrant. Other less typical symptoms seen with appendicitis are increased urinary frequency and the desire to defecate.[2,3]

Physical Examination

The most common finding on physical examination is localized abdominal tenderness, usually in the right lower quadrant. The pain may be noted over McBurney's point, an area 2 cm from the anterior superior iliac spine. However, since only 35% of patients have the base of their appendix within 5 cm

of this point, the pain of appendicitis can be localized in other areas of the abdomen.[13]

Other physical examination findings include guarding and rigidity. Guarding is usually voluntary and the patient can often be persuaded to relax. Rigidity is involuntary and implies more significant underlying pathology.[2] Both of these findings reflect the tensing of the abdominal wall musculature to protect the underlying bowel.

Rovsing's sign is present when tenderness is referred to the right lower quadrant when the left lower quadrant is palpated. Psoas sign is the increase of pain when the psoas muscle is stretched as the patient is asked to extend the hip. Obturator sign is the elicitation of pain as the hip is flexed and externally rotated.

Rebound tenderness is a late finding in patients with appendicitis and usually occurs only after the appendix is significantly inflamed or ruptured. The presence of rebound tenderness can be suspected if the patient reports abdominal pain with coughing or gentle rocking of their pelvis. Classically, rebound tenderness is detected by gradually pressing over the area of tenderness for 5 to 10 seconds and then quickly withdrawing the hand to just above the skin level. A positive response is when the patient reports increased pain as the hand is removed. Patients with rebound tenderness are very uncomfortable with this maneuver and it should not be repeated unnecessarily.[12]

Isolated rectal tenderness may rarely be the only site of localized pain in patients with a low-lying appendix. In general, however, rectal tenderness has a very limited diagnostic value, especially if there is concurrent right lower quadrant pain and tenderness.[14,15] Although a single rectal examination may provide other important information, such as the discovery of a rectal mass or occult blood, multiple examinations are not justified.

Although any of the above signs may be present in patients with acute appendicitis, a review of 10 studies that evaluated 13 signs and symptoms of appendicitis identified certain findings as having a high positive likelihood ratio of identifying patients with appendicitis. These were right lower quadrant pain, rigidity, and migration of initial periumbilical pain to the right lower quadrant.[2] Conversely, the presence of pain for more than 48 hours, a history of previous episodes of similar pain, the lack of migration and right lower quadrant pain, and the lack of worsening pain with movement or cough make appendicitis less likely.[2,14] Vital signs are often normal, particularly early in the course. A low-grade fever is present in about 15% of patients; this increases to about 40% if perforation has occurred.[16]

Special Considerations

Children

Young children with acute appendicitis are frequently misdiagnosed and the correct diagnosis is often made only after perforation has occurred. This may be because many common childhood illnesses are associated with nausea, anorexia, and vomiting, and young

Table 92-1. Abdominal Pain in Women

More Suggestive of Appendicitis
Anorexia, pain and tenderness localized to the right lower quadrant, normal or minimally abnormal pelvic examination findings (i.e., isolated right adnexal tenderness)

More Suggestive of Pelvic Inflammatory Disease
Several days of symptoms, history of pelvic inflammatory disease, hunger, diffuse lower abdominal pain, bilateral adnexal tenderness, cervical motion tenderness, vaginal discharge

children may have difficulty communicating their discomfort.[17] Children may be more prone to perforation due to the thinness of the appendiceal wall. They also may be more likely to develop diffuse peritonitis because their omentum is less developed and unable to wall off infection.[18]

Women

The diagnosis of acute appendicitis in women of childbearing age is especially problematic. As many as 45% of women with symptomatology suggestive of appendicitis will have a normal appendix at surgery, and as many as one third of women with true appendicitis are initially misdiagnosed. Gynecologic disease can easily masquerade as appendicitis due to the close proximity of the right ovary, fallopian tube, and uterus to the appendix.[19–21] In two studies, about one fourth of women with signs suggestive of acute appendicitis ultimately were found to have gynecologic disease. The clinical and laboratory distinction between these two entities can be very difficult (Table 92-1).[2,22] Of note, although cervical motion tenderness is more common in patients with pelvic inflammatory disease, it does not differentiate women with and without appendicitis. In one study, almost one in four women with acute appendicitis were noted to have cervical motion tenderness.[19] Because disease recognition is probably most difficult in women of childbearing age, ancillary testing with ultrasonography, computed tomography (CT), or ultimately laparoscopy can be very helpful.

Pregnant Women

Pregnant women carry an overall risk of developing appendicitis similar to that of the general population.[23,24] Of the three trimesters, appendicitis appears to occur slightly more often in the second trimester. The reason for this is unknown. The diagnosis of appendicitis during pregnancy can be difficult, as early symptoms of appendicitis such as nausea and vomiting occur frequently in a normal pregnancy. Laboratory values are even less helpful, as a leukocytosis is common during pregnancy. The enlargement of the uterus may change the location of the appendix. A recent study, however, looked at pregnant patients with appendicitis and found that even when appendicitis occurred in the third trimester, the vast majority of patients still had right lower quadrant pain.[25]

Because the correct diagnosis is often delayed, the rate of perforation is about two to three times higher

in pregnant patients. Although maternal death from appendicitis is extremely rare, fetal abortion is about 20% in cases in which the appendix is perforated.[23,24] Because morbidity is high, extra caution should be taken in pregnant women with abdominal pain. The liberal use of ultrasonography and early surgical and gynecologic consultation will optimize patient care.

Elderly Patients

Elderly patients are three times more likely to have a perforated appendix at surgery compared with the general population. There appear to be multiple causes for this, including anatomical age-related changes of the appendix, which weaken the appendiceal wall. Older people may also delay seeking medical care for many reasons, including early nonspecific symptoms, reluctance or inability to leave the home, and difficulties in accurately communicating worsening symptoms. Diagnosis can be further delayed after physician examination due to atypical presentations and minimally elevated laboratory test results.[11,26]

Complications

The complication rate after the removal of a normal appendix or an acutely inflamed appendix is about 3% and increases approximately three to four times if perforation occurs.[16] The most common complication is infection. Localized wound infection occurs in about 2% to 7% and deep intra-abdominal abscess occurs in 0.8% to 2% of cases, with the higher percentages representing cases in which perforation had occurred.[27] Other complications include a prolonged ileus, small bowel obstruction, pneumonia, and urinary retention and infection. In adult women, perforation may cause obstruction of the fallopian tubes and later fertility problems.[28] Although some investigators have suggested that fallopian tube damage from a ruptured appendix may account for significant tubal infertility, this has not been confirmed by more recent studies.[29,30]

The mortality rate of uncomplicated appendicitis is less than 0.1% but increases to about 3% to 4% with perforation in patients with comorbidities or advanced age.[31] Although reported perforation rates vary significantly from study to study, the overall average is about 20% to 30%. This increases greatly at the extremes of age. Elderly patients have perforation rates of about 30% to 60% and children younger than 3 years of age can have perforation rates as high as 80% to 90%.[11,18]

Delay in definitive management of patients with acute appendicitis can lead to increased perforation rates and complications. This delay can be due to one or more of the following factors: patient delay in seeking medical care, physician delay in consulting a surgeon, excessive testing, administrative delay due to patient transfer based on insurance status, surgical delay in the decision to operate, or hospital delay in the availability of the operating room. Several recent studies have suggested that in cases of complicated appendicitis, the greatest delay was attributed to patient delay in seeking medical evaluation.[12,32] In one study, the average time for patients to seek medical care was 17 hours for simple appendicitis versus 32 for perforated disease.[1] Uninsured and medicaid patients have the highest adjusted risk for ruptured appendix and this is believed to be due to late presentation due to the fear of the financial burden of acute medical management.[33,34]

DIAGNOSTIC STRATEGIES

Laboratory Testing

Leukocyte Count. About 80% to 90% of patients with acute appendicitis have an elevated white blood cell count above 10,000/mm^3. This percentage is slightly lower in elderly patients and very young patients.[16,35-38] Unfortunately, the leukocyte count is nonspecific and often elevated with other types of abdominal pain. Repeated testing of the leukocyte count after an observation period is also of limited value, since about 25% of patients with acute appendicitis do not experience a rise from their initial count.[36]

C-Reactive Protein. The sensitivity of C-reactive protein level varies from 40% to 99%, depending on the study. A recent meta-analysis suggests that the overall sensitivity of C-reactive protein level is approximately 62% and the specificity is 66%, which limits its usefulness as a diagnostic tool.[39]

Urinalysis. A urinalysis is helpful in differentiating urinary tract disease from acute appendicitis. Mild sterile pyuria may be seen in patients with appendicitis, especially if the appendix is irritating the ureter. Significant pyuria (more than 20 white blood cells per high-power field) is very suggestive of urinary tract pathologic condition.[17]

Pregnancy Test. This should be done on all women of childbearing age, as a positive test finding broadly expands the differential diagnosis of right lower quadrant pain.

Diagnostic Scores

Although some retrospective studies have shown a benefit in using diagnostic scoring systems for appendicitis that assign a numerical value to different aspects of the history and physical examination findings, these scores have inconsistent results when prospectively studied and appear to be particularly inaccurate when applied to female patients.[2,40]

Imaging Studies

Plain Radiographs. Plain abdominal radiographs are not useful in diagnosing appendicitis because of their very low sensitivity and specificity and are not recommended in the evaluation of appendicitis unless there is a significant concern of bowel obstruction or free air.[41]

Barium Enemas. Barium enemas have a sensitivity of about 80% to 90% for detecting appendicitis, and the diagnosis is essentially ruled out if the entire appendix is filled with contrast.[42,43] The limiting factor of this technique, however, is that a normal appendiceal lumen is often not well visualized. Barium enemas are most helpful when another colon pathologic condition is high in the differential diagnosis.[42]

Nuclear Medicine Scans. The use of nuclear imaging with tagged white blood cells has been well studied as a diagnostic tool for acute appendicitis.[44-46] The reported sensitivities of nuclear scans depend on the tag used and range between 88% and 98%. The overall utility of these scans is limited, since any process causing inflammatory changes in the lower abdomen can lead to a false-positive scan.

Ultrasonography. Graded compression ultrasonography has been prospectively shown to improve the clinical accuracy of the diagnosis of acute appendicitis.[47-49] It may be particularly helpful in women of childbearing age, in whom pelvic pathologic conditions can mimic appendicitis. It is also often advocated as the initial imaging modality in children and pregnant patients to spare them radiation exposure. The reported sensitivity and specificity of ultrasonography for acute appendicitis in most studies is 75% to 90% and 85% to 95%, respectively.[47,49-53]

Ultrasonography is considered positive for appendicitis if the appendix is noncompressible and has a diameter of greater than 6 mm. Ultrasonography is inexpensive, requires no exposure to radiation or dye, adds no extra time for contrast filling, and has had long-standing success in diagnosing pelvic pathologic conditions in women. It also allows the ultrasonographer to correlate the patient's pain with the direct visualization of underlying abdominal contents. The major disadvantage of ultrasonography is that the visualization of an abnormal appendix is operator dependent and can be especially difficult in patients who are obese, have strictures, or have a retrocecal appendix. It also may be limited in patients who have significant tenderness and cannot tolerate the graded compression. Once the appendix has perforated, it also becomes more difficult to identify it by ultrasonography. The visualization of a normal appendix is even more problematic, with reported rates of only 2% to 45%.[49,54] Therefore, although a positive ultrasonographic study finding for appendicitis has a very high positive predictive value (about 90%), a negative study finding, unless the appendix is clearly visualized, is not helpful unless an alternative pathologic condition is identified.[55] For this reason, it is appropriate, after a negative ultrasonography study finding, to perform either in-hospital observation or a CT scan if the patient's symptoms have not improved.[22,47]

Computed Tomography Scan. Abdominal pelvic CT scanning has been prospectively studied and shown to improve the clinical accuracy of the diagnosis of appendicitis.[49,56,57] CT findings suggestive of appendicitis include an enlarged appendix (diameter greater than 6 mm), pericecal inflammation, the presence of an appendicolith (Figure 92-1), or a periappendiceal phlegmon or abscess. The sensitivity (87%-100%) and specificity (89%-98%) of CT scan varies by study and technique and by how authors categorize inconclusive scans in their statistical analyses.[42,49,50,57-61] Of the different CT techniques, thin-cut, helical CT with rectal

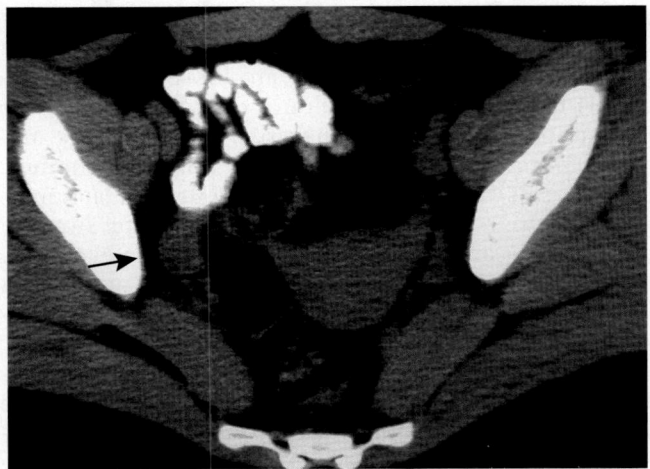

Figure 92-1. Oral contrast-enhanced CT scan of acute appendicitis. *Arrow* points to swollen appendix.

contrast appears to be the most sensitive, with sensitivities as high as 98%. This technique allows the patient to be scanned immediately after administration of the contrast medium and avoids oral and intravenous administration. It also usually shows opacification and distention of the cecal region, which allows better identification of the appendix.[60,61] Unfortunately, rectal contrast may not be conceptually or practically acceptable to some patients or radiology technicians. Oral contrast abdominal pelvic CT is an alternative choice but requires a 60- to 90-minute delay after contrast administration for distal small bowel opacification, may be poorly tolerated in the nauseous patient, and may delay emergency department patient disposition. Although certain institutions have published high sensitivity and specificity rates with non-contrast-enhanced CT scans, these findings have not been reproducible in other settings.[56,61,62] Periappendiceal fat streaking, which is an important CT sign of appendicitis, can easily be missed in a non-contrast-enhanced CT scan in thin patients or children with scant intraperitoneal fat. In these patients, an enteric contrast-enhanced CT scan should be strongly considered to clearly identify the appendiceal region. Intravenous administration of contrast medium can help diagnose very early appendicitis by enhancing appendiceal wall inflammation, but in most instances it adds little additional information. Its use is not routinely recommended because it increases cost and the potential for dye-related complications.

Computed tomography scanning has some advantages over ultrasonography in the diagnostic workup of appendicitis. With CT, the appendix can usually be visualized (with a contrast-enhanced scan), the technique is not operator dependent, the technique is standardized, and an alternative pathologic lesion is often identified. An added benefit of CT is that the identification of CT signs of appendicitis is relatively straightforward and can be easily learned. This is important because the initial interpretation of the CT scan often determines patient disposition, and these scans may be initially read by junior radiology residents after hours.[47]

The biggest disadvantages of CT scan are the radiation exposure and the expense. Routine full abdominal and pelvic CT scanning results in at least 900 rads of radiation exposure and total charges for the combined examination can exceed $2000. Radiation exposure can be decreased by up to two thirds by doing a limited 15 cm scan through the cecum and pelvis. This exposes the patient to approximately 300 rads or the equivalent of radiation exposure from one abdominal plain radiograph. It also decreases the overall cost of the scan.[61] Finally, CT scan is not 100% accurate, so it is important to remind all patients with a "negative" scan that they should be re-evaluated if their symptoms progress or do not resolve.[63] This is especially true in patients evaluated within the first few hours of symptoms, since early appendicitis results in only histologic changes that will not be seen on a CT scan.

Magnetic Resonance Imaging. Data on using magnetic resonance imaging (MRI) for the evaluation of appendicitis are limited. Some studies suggest that MRI may be very sensitive in diagnosing appendicitis. The potential benefits of MRI are that it spares the patient ionizing radiation, and that the entire appendix is usually visualized.[64,65] Few emergency departments have access to MRI for this use currently.

Laparoscopy

Laparoscopy can be performed for diagnosis or definitive treatment. Historically, its greatest advantage was in the clarification of the diagnosis of appendicitis versus gynecologic disease in young female patients. As an enteric contrast-enhanced CT scan can now usually visualize the appendix, the use of diagnostic laparoscopy with its anesthetic risks has decreased significantly.

In-Hospital Observation

Despite the increased tendency to pursue diagnostic imaging in patients with right lower quadrant abdominal pain, recent literature suggests that most cases of appendicitis can still be accurately diagnosed by performing serial physical examinations.[66] In a recent review of 12 studies using active inpatient observation in patients with an equivocal diagnosis of appendicitis, the negative appendectomy rates were about 6% without an increase in perforation rates. The cost-effectiveness of this approach was not addressed in the review.

DIFFERENTIAL DIAGNOSIS

An elongated appendix can irritate almost any abdominal structure, so the differential diagnosis of appendicitis includes essentially any pathologic condition that can cause abdominal pain (Table 92-2). Of note, the diagnosis of gastroenteritis should be made with caution and only in patients with vomiting and diarrhea.

Table 92-2. Differential Diagnosis for Appendicitis

All	Women	Children
Nonspecific abdominal pain	Ovarian cyst	Henoch-Schönlein purpura
Gastroenteritis	Ovarian torsion	Testicular torsion
Ascending diverticulitis	Pelvic inflammatory disease	Epiploic appendagitis
Gallbladder disease	Ectopic pregnancy	Mesenteric adenitis/ileocolitis
Inflammatory bowel disease		Meckel's diverticulum
Renal colic		

MANAGEMENT

Patients should be kept NPO and undergo a complete physical examination including a rectal and pelvic examination. Dehydrated patients should receive bolus intravenous crystalloid fluid. Parenteral antiemetics should be given to patients who are nauseated or vomiting. Patients who are in moderate to severe pain should be given judicious amounts of opioid medication such as morphine or fentanyl. Several small studies have suggested that it is unlikely that pain medication will mask important abdominal findings and that its administration is therefore safe and humane.[67,68] Depending on local surgical preference or institutional policy, surgical consultation prior to medication administration may be indicated, but only if it can be done in a timely fashion (Figure 92-2).

A urine dipstick analysis is suggested for all patients, and although the data show that a white blood cell count is not specific for appendicitis, most surgeons still request one. All women of childbearing age should also have a pregnancy test.

Controversy exists regarding when and how to best utilize advanced imaging techniques. Some authors have shown that CT scanning significantly decreases the rate of negative laparotomies, even in patients with a high clinical suspicion of appendicitis.[47,49,54,60,69–71] Others believe that diagnostic imaging studies are overutilized and that this practice has not improved patient care.[72,73] This view is supported by a recent population-based study suggesting that negative laparotomy and perforation rates have remained at about 15% and 25% even with the increased use of CT and ultrasonography.[74] The results of this study, however, should be interpreted cautiously because the database the authors used prohibited detection of any direct relationship of CT or ultrasonography to clinical outcomes.

Considering both these views, it appears that diagnostic imaging is most helpful if done in a select group of patients. We suggest, after initial physical examination and laboratory tests, stratifying patients by risk. Excessive imaging in patients who are at low risk for appendicitis will result in increased false-positive findings, as there is low prevalence of disease in this population. Patients can be considered low risk if they have minimal physical findings, are hungry, and have a strong alternative diagnosis; have multiple previous episodes of similar pain; or have symptoms for more than 3 days. The other distinct group of patients that may not benefit from imaging are those patients who are within their first few hours of symptoms. These patients are at risk for false-negative study findings, and their "normal" scan may provide false reassurance. In both sets of patients, the best course of action is probably to educate them about worsening signs of appendicitis and arrange for them to be re-evaluated immediately if their symptoms progress or in 12 to 24 hours if they have not improved. Ideally, this conversation should be documented in the chart.

Patients with "equivocal" signs of appendicitis should be considered for diagnostic testing or active observation. Surgical input by phone or formal consultation may be appropriate prior to imaging, depending on local surgical preference.

"Equivocal" patients include women of childbearing age, who are especially difficult to clinically diagnose as they can have negative laparotomy rates as high as 40% to 45% even with clinical presentations highly suggestive of appendicitis. Therefore, advanced imaging should be strongly considered in this subgroup.[22] Ultrasonography may be the most appropriate initial study in pregnant women or in cases in which there is a high suspicion for gynecologic disease by history or an abnormal pelvic examination finding; otherwise, an enteric contrast-enhanced CT scan should be obtained.

Other subgroups of equivocal patients are more difficult to define because of variable inclusion criteria among published studies. It appears reasonable that men, children, and older women with a suspicious presentation for appendicitis but who lack at least one of its classic findings (new-onset periumbilical pain migrating down to the right lower quadrant associated with tenderness and anorexia) and have no clear alternative diagnosis be considered "equivocal." Ultrasonography is often considered the initial imaging study in children because it does not expose the child to radiation, and it can be performed without sedation. A limited-cut helical CT scan with enteric contrast (either rectal or oral) is also an option that should be strongly considered as the first imaging choice in overweight children or at institutions where appendiceal ultrasonograms have poor sensitivities. It is important to realize that if ultrasonography is chosen and interpreted as negative, a follow-up CT scan or admission for serial observation should be done unless the patient's examination findings have improved.[47,75] For men and older women who present with equivocal signs of appendicitis, an enteric contrast-enhanced CT scan is probably the best diagnostic imaging study. It is important to reiterate that although a "negative" CT scan is reassuring, no study is 100% sensitive, and adequate follow-up should be arranged for all patients sent home from the emergency department with abdominal pain.

Male patients, children, and older women with a classic presentation of appendicitis are considered to be at high risk for appendicitis. Male patients with a classic presentation are found to have appendicitis more than 90% of the time, and imaging adds little to the workup.[75] In these cases, the surgeons should be

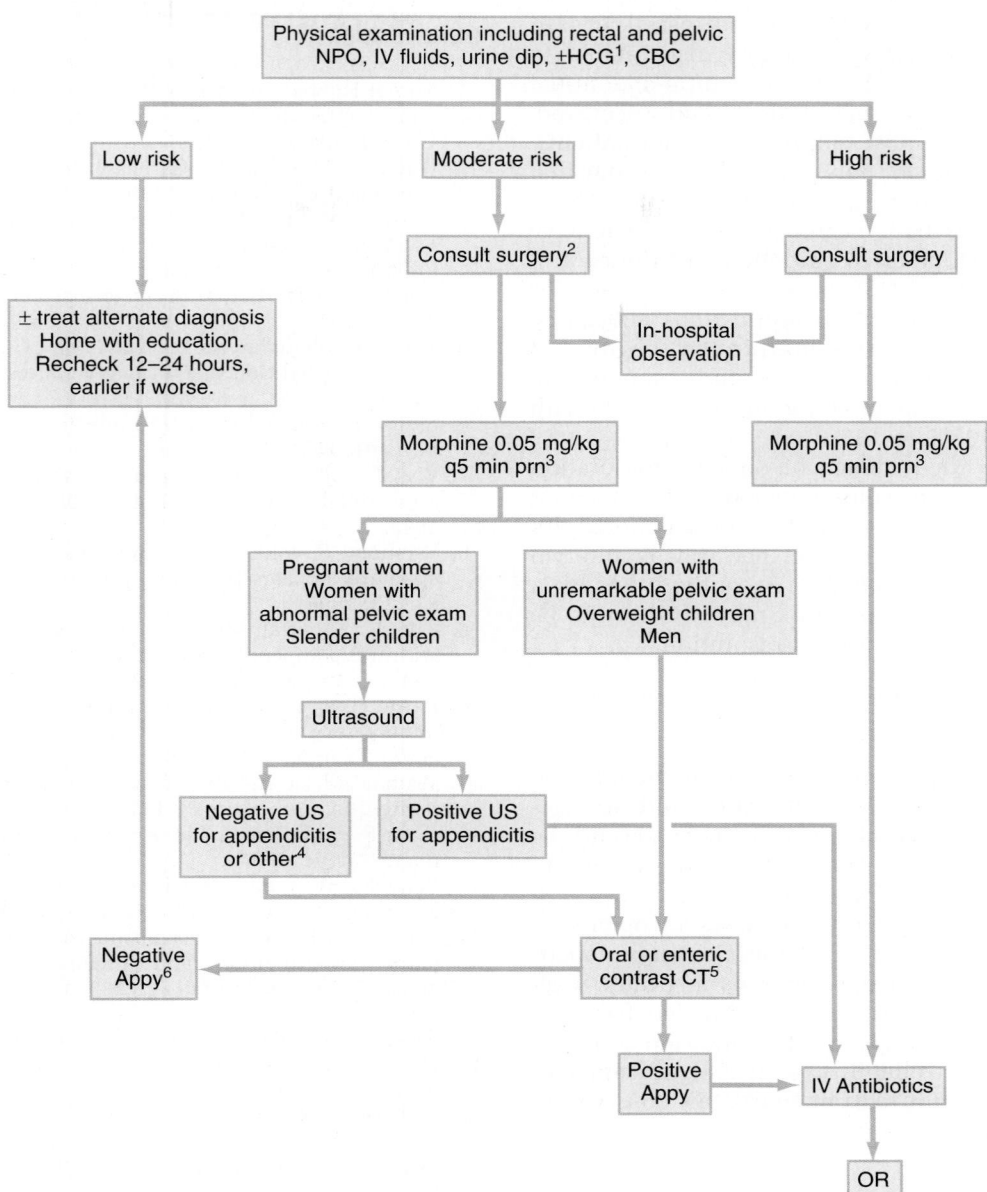

1. Consult Ob/Gyn immediately if unstable pregnant patient. 2. Timing and type of surgical consultation with be dependent upon local preferences. 3. Pain medication should be given as soon as possible in uncomfortable patients. If the surgeon desires to examine the patient unmedicated, the physical examination should be done in a timely fashion so the patient can then be medicated. 4. A negative ultrasound that does not visualize a normal appendix does not rule out appendicitis. Unless other convincing pathology is found or the patient's exam has improved, enteric CT or in-hospital observation should be considered. 5. Rectal contrast abdominal pelvic CT is the preferred study. 6. In-hospital admission should be considered in patients who have significant pain or have required substantial amounts of opioids

Figure 92-2. Suggested emergency department management of patients with possible appendicitis.

consulted immediately for an operative intervention. Once the decision to operate has been made, prophylactic antibiotics should be given to cover gram-negative and anaerobic organisms as this practice has been proven to decrease postoperative wound infections.[76] Intravenous second-generation cephalosporins such as cefotetan or cefoxitin provide good coverage. If there is a high suspicion of perforation, then broader antibiotic coverage should be given (i.e., gentamicin and metronidazole, levofloxacin, or combination β-lactam/β-lactamase inhibitor therapy).[77]

The appendix can be surgically removed either through the traditional open technique or through laparoscopy. A Cochrane review of 45 randomized studies favored laparoscopic removal.[78] They concluded that laparoscopic appendix removal resulted in less frequent wound infections, less postoperative pain on day 1, shorter lengths of hospital stay, shorter time to return to normal activity, and decreased overall costs. However, laparoscopic surgery also tended to slightly increase the risk of deep intra-abdominal abscess, especially if perforation had occurred. Laparoscopy may be most helpful in female patients, as it allows inspection for pelvic pathologic lesions that may masquerade as acute appendicitis.

Some institutions have begun to develop extensive operative and postoperative guidelines for the care of appendicitis patients.[79–81] The use of these guidelines has decreased postoperative complications and costs, and they appear to be most helpful in the subgroup of patients with perforation. In one study, the use of guidelines decreased the infection rate in patients with perforation from 33% to 13%.[79]

For patients with evidence of obvious perforation and abscess formation, some surgeons prefer to non-operatively drain the abscess and treat the patient with intravenous antibiotics and then perform an interval appendectomy 6 weeks later.[82,83] Recently, it has even been suggested that the appendix may not have to be removed after successful abscess resolution.[83]

DISPOSITION

If the suspicion for appendicitis is low, the patient can be sent home after extensive education and arrangement for follow-up. Discharged patients should be encouraged to start on a liquid diet and advance to solids if their symptoms improve.

Patients who require significant doses of opiates to control their pain while they are in the emergency department should not be discharged without a specific diagnosis that can be safely treated on an outpatient basis.[84]

If follow-up cannot be arranged, if there are concerns of patient or family reliability, or if a significant language or transportation barrier exists, an observation admission should be considered.

 KEY CONCEPTS

- Classic appendicitis is a clinical diagnosis.
- Patients with a low risk of appendicitis can be sent home with close follow-up and education about progressive symptoms.
- Patients with equivocal findings of appendicitis should undergo advanced diagnostic imaging or in-hospital serial examinations.
- Patients with a high risk of appendicitis should undergo prompt surgical evaluation without further imaging.
- Ultrasonography is an appropriate initial test in pregnant patients, women of childbearing age with suspicion of pelvic pathologic condition, and in thin children.
- Helical CT scan with enteric contrast (ideally rectal) is considered the initial test in all males and in females of non-childbearing age with equivocal signs of appendicitis.
- Pain medicine in judicious amounts is appropriate for patients with suspected appendicitis, especially if imaging studies are planned.
- Antibiotics should be given preoperatively.

REFERENCES

1. Korner H, et al: Incidence of acute non perforated and perforated appendicitis: Age-specific and sex-specific analysis. *World J Surg* 21:313, 1997.
2. Wagner J, Mckinnery P, Carpenter J: Does this patient have appendicitis? *JAMA* 276:1589, 1996.
3. Feldman M, Sleisenger MH, Scharschmidt BF: *Sleisenger & Fordtran's Gastrointestinal and Liver Disease*, 6th ed. Philadelphia, W.B. Saunders, 1998, pp 1778-1785.
4. Seal A: Appendicitis: A historical review. *Can J Surg* 24:427, 1981.
5. Vastag B: Medicine on the Lewis and Clark Trail: Exhibit explores expedition's medical adventures. *JAMA* 289:1227, 2003.
6. Smith S: Appendicitis, appendectomy and the surgeon. *Bull Hist Med* 70:414, 1996.
7. Wakely CPG: The position of the vermiform appendix as ascertained by an analysis of 10,000 cases. *J Anat* 67:227, 1933.
8. Varshney S, Johnson CD, Rangnekar GV: The retrocecal appendix appears to be less prone to infection. *Br J Surg* 83:223, 1996.
9. Klingler PJ, et al: Management of ingested foreign bodies within the appendix: A case report with review of the literature. *Am J Gastroenterol* 92:2295, 1997.
10. Barrat C, et al: Does laparoscopy reduce the incidence of unnecessary appendicectomies? *Surg Laparosc Endosc Percutan Techniques* 9:27, 1999.
11. Watters JM, et al: The influence of age on the severity of peritonitis. *Can J Surg* 39:142, 1996.
12. Eldar S, et al: Delay of surgery in acute appendicitis. *Am J Surg* 173:194, 1997.
13. Ramsden W, et al: Is the appendix where you think it is—and if not does it matter? *Clin Radiol* 47:100, 1993.
14. Andersson RE, et al: Diagnostic value of disease history, clinical presentation, and inflammatory parameters of appendicitis. *World J Surg* 23:133, 1999.
15. Dixon JM, et al: Rectal examination in patients with pain in the right lower quadrant of the abdomen. *BMJ* 302:386, 1991.
16. Hale DA, et al: Appendectomy: A contemporary appraisal. *Ann Surg* 225:252, 1997.
17. McLario D, Rothrock S: Understanding the varied presentation and management of children with acute abdominal disorders. *Pediatr Emerg Med Rep* November 1997, p 113.
18. Chung JL, et al: Diagnostic value of C-reactive protein in children with perforated appendicitis. *Eur J Pediatr* 155:529, 1996.
19. Bongard F, Landers DV, Lewis F: Differential diagnosis of appendicitis and pelvic inflammatory disease. *Am J Surg* 150:90, 1985.
20. Webster DP, et al: Differentiating acute appendicitis from pelvic inflammatory disease in women of childbearing age. *Am J Emerg Med* 11:569, 1993.
21. Barry J Jr, Malt RA: Appendicitis near its centenary. *Ann Surg* 200:567, 1984.
22. Borgstein PJ, et al: Acute appendicitis—a clear-cut case in men, a guessing game in young women: A prospective study on the role of laparoscopy. *Surg Endosc* 11:923, 1997.
23. Al-Mulhim AA: Acute appendicitis in pregnancy: A review of 52 cases. *Int Surg* 81:295, 1996.
24. Hee P, Viktrup L: The diagnosis of appendicitis during pregnancy and maternal and fetal outcome after appendectomy. *Int J Gynecol Obstet* 65:129, 1999.
25. Mourad J, Elliott J, Erickson L, et al: Appendicitis in pregnancy: New information that contradicts long-held clinical beliefs. *Am J Obstet Gynecol* 182:1027, 2000.
26. Roosevelt GE, Reynolds SL: Does the use of ultrasonography improve the outcome of children with appendicitis? *Acad Emerg Med* 5:1071, 1998.

27. Chung R, Rowland D, Li P, Diaz J: A meta-analysis of randomized controlled trials of laparoscopic versus conventional appendectomy. *Am J Surg* 177:250, 1999.

28. Malt RA: The perforated appendix. *N Engl J Med* 315:1546, 1986.

29. Urbach D, Cohen M: Is the perforation of the appendix a risk factor for tubal infertility and ectopic pregnancy? An appraisal of the evidence. *Can J Surg* 42:101, 1999.

30. Andersson R, Lambe M, Bergstrom R: Fertility patterns after appendicectomy: Historical cohort study. *BMJ* 318:963, 1999.

31. Fauci A, et al (eds): *Harrison's Principles of Internal Medicine*, 14th ed. New York, McGraw Hill, 1998, pp 1658-1660.

32. Hale DA, et al: Appendectomy: Improving care through quality improvement. *Arch Surg* 132:153, 1997.

33. Braveman P, et al: Insurance-related differences in the risk of ruptured appendix. *N Engl J Med* 331:444, 1994.

34. O'Toole SJ, et al: Insurance-related differences in the presentation of pediatric appendicitis. *J Pediatr Surg* 31:1032, 1996.

35. Paajanen H, et al: Are serum inflammatory markers age dependent in acute appendicitis? *J Am Coll Surg* 184:303, 1997.

36. Lyons D, et al: An evaluation of the clinical value of the leucocyte count and sequential counts in suspected acute appendicitis. *Br J Clin Pract* 41:794, 1987.

37. Lau W, et al: Leucocyte count and neutrophil percentage in appendicectomy for suspected appendicitis. *Austr N Z J Surg* 59:359, 1989.

38. Elangovan S: Clinical and laboratory findings in acute appendicitis in the elderly. *J Am Board Fam Pract* 9:75, 1996.

39. Hallan S, Asberg A: The accuracy of C-reactive protein in diagnosing acute appendicitis: A meta-analysis. *Scand J Clin Lab Invest* 57:373, 1997.

40. Malik AA, Wani NA: Continuing diagnostic challenge of acute appendicitis: Evaluation through modified Alvarado score. *Austr N Z J Surg* 68:504, 1998.

41. Roa P, et al: Plain abdominal radiography in clinically suspected appendicitis: Diagnostic yield, resource use and comparison with CT. *Am J Emerg Med* 17:325, 1999.

42. Rao PM, Boland GW: Imaging of acute right lower abdominal quadrant pain [comment: Clin Radiol 54:271, 1999]. *Clin Radiol* 53:639, 1998.

43. Okamoto T, et al: The appearance of a normal appendix on barium enema examination does not rule out a diagnosis of chronic appendicitis: Report of a case and review of the literature. *Surg Today* 27:550, 1997.

44. Rypins E, et al: 99m Tc anti-CD 15 monoclonal antibody (Leu Tach) imaging improves diagnostic accuracy and clinical management in patients with equivocal presentation of appendicitis. *Ann Surg* 235:232, 2002.

45. Kao CH, et al: Tc-99m HMPAO-labeled WBC scans to detect appendicitis in women. *Clin Nucl Med* 21:768, 1996.

46. Lin WY, et al: 99Tcm-HMPAO-labelled white blood cell scans to detect acute appendicitis in older patients with an atypical clinical presentation. *Nucl Med Commun* 18:75, 1997.

47. Kaiser S, Frenckner B, Jorulf H: Suspected appendicitis in children: US and CT-A prospective randomized study. *Radiology* 223:633, 2002.

48. Chen SC, et al: Abdominal sonography screening of clinically diagnosed or suspected appendicitis before surgery. *World J Surg* 22:449, 1998.

49. Garcia Pena B, et al: Ultrasonography and limited computed tomography in the diagnosis and management of appendicitis in children. *JAMA* 282:1041, 1999.

50. Balthazar E, et al: Acute appendicitis: CT and US correlation in 100 patients. *Radiology* 190:31, 1994.

51. Vermeulen B, et al: Acute appendicitis: Influence of early pain relief on the accuracy of clinical and US findings in the decision to operate. A randomized trial. *Radiology* 210:639, 1999.

52. Franke C, et al: Ultrasonography for diagnosis of acute appendicitis: Results of a prospective multicenter trial. Acute Abdominal Pain Study Group. *World J Surg* 23:141, 1999.

53. Rice H, et al: Does early ultrasonography affect management of pediatric appendicitis? A prospective analysis. *J Pediatr Surg* 34:754, 1999.

54. Simonovsky V: Sonographic detection of normal and abnormal appendix. *Clin Radiol* 54:533, 1999.

55. Pohl D, et al: Appendiceal ultrasonography performed by nonradiologists: Does it help in the diagnostic process? *J Ultrasound Med* 17:217, 1998.

56. Peck J, et al: The clinical role of noncontrast helical computed tomography in the diagnosis of acute appendicitis. *Am J Surg* 180:133, 2000.

57. Balthazar EJ, Rofsky NM, Zucker R: Appendicitis: The impact of computed tomography imaging on negative appendectomy and perforation rates. *Am J Gastroenterol* 93:768, 1998.

58. Malone AJ, et al: Diagnosis of acute appendicitis: Value of unenhanced CT. *AJR* 160:763, 1993.

59. Lane MJ, et al: Unenhanced helical CT for suspected acute appendicitis. *Am J Roentgenol* 168:405, 1997.

60. Rao PM, et al: Helical CT technique for the diagnosis of appendicitis: Prospective evaluation of a focused appendix CT examination. *Radiology* 202:139, 1997.

61. Rao PM, et al: Helical CT combined with contrast material administered only through the colon for imaging of suspected appendicitis. *Am J Roentgenol* 169:1275, 1997.

62. Horton M, et al: A prospective trial of computed tomography and ultrasonography for diagnosing appendicitis in the atypical patient. *Am J Surg* 179:379, 2000.

63. Yoshiko M, et al: Enhanced CT in the diagnosis of acute appendicitis to evaluate the severity of disease: Comparison of CT findings and histological diagnosis. *Radiation Med* 19:97, 2001.

64. Inescur L, et al: Acute appendicitis: MR imaging and sonographic correlation. *AJR* 168:669, 1997.

65. Hormann M, et al: MR imaging in children with nonperforated acute appendicitis: Value of unenhanced MR imaging in sonographically selected cases. *Am J Roentgenol* 171:467, 1998.

66. Jones PF: Suspected acute appendicitis: Trends in management over 30 years. *Br J Surg* 88:1570, 2001.

67. Thomas S, et al: Effects of morphine analgesia on diagnostic accuracy in emergency department patients with abdominal pain: A prospective randomized trial. *J Am Coll Surg* 196:18, 2003.

68. Wolfe JM, et al: Does morphine change the physical examination in patients with acute appendicitis? *Am J Emerg Med* 22:280, 2004.

69. Rhea JT, et al: A focused appendiceal CT technique to reduce the cost of caring for patients with clinically suspected appendicitis. *Am J Roentgenol* 169:113, 1997.

70. Rao PM, et al: Effect of computed tomography of the appendix on treatment of patients and use of hospital resources. *N Engl J Med* 338:141, 1998.

71. Rao PM, et al: Introduction of appendiceal CT: Impact on negative appendectomy and appendiceal perforation rates. *Ann Surg* 229:344, 1999.

72. Morris K, et al: The rational use of computed tomography scans in the diagnosis of appendicitis. *Am J Surg* 183:547, 2002.

73. Reich J, et al: Use of CT scan in the diagnosis of pediatric acute appendicitis. *Pediatr Emerg Care* 16:241, 2000.

74. Flum D, Morris A, Koepsell T, Dellinger E: Has misdiagnosis of appendicitis decreased over time? A population-based analysis. *JAMA* 286:1748, 2001.

75. Wilson E, et al: Computed tomography in the diagnosis of appendicitis: When are they indicated? *Arch Surg* 136:670, 2001.
76. Bauer T, et al: Antibiotics prophylaxis in acute nonperforated appendicitis. *Ann Surg* 209:307, 1989.
77. Helmer K, et al: Standardized patient care guidelines reduce infectious morbidity in appendectomy patients. *Am J Surg* 186:608, 2002.
78. Sauerland S, Lefering R, Neugebaur E: Laparoscopic versus open surgery for suspected appendicitis (Cochrane review). *Cochrane Databases Syst Rev* 1:CD001546, 2002.
79. Helmer K, et al: Standardized patient care guidelines reduce infectious morbidity in appendectomy patients. *Am J Surg* 183:608, 2002.
80. Krishner S, et al: Intra-abdominal abscess after laparoscopic appendectomy for perforated appendicitis. *Arch Surg* 136:438, 2001.
81. Katkhouda N, et al: Intraabdominal abscess rate after laparoscopic appendectomy. *Am J Surg* 180:456, 2000.
82. Yamini D, et al: Perforated appendicitis: Is it truly a surgical urgency? *Am Surgeon* 64:970, 1998.
83. Ein SH, Shandling B: Is interval appendectomy necessary after rupture of an appendiceal mass? *J Pediatr Surg* 31:849, 1996.
84. Rusnak R, Borer J, Fastow J: Misdiagnosis of acute appendicitis: Common features discovered in cases after litigation. *Am J Emerg Med* 12:397, 1994.

CHAPTER

93 Acute Gastroenteritis

Robert A. Bitterman and David K. Zich

INVASIVE BACTERIAL ENTERITIS (Table 93-1)

Campylobacter Enteritis

Epidemiology

Campylobacter is the most common bacterial cause of diarrhea in patients who seek medical attention and is found in the stools of 5% to 14% of these patients.[1,2] Most cases occur in young children, but people of all ages are affected. The disease is more common during the summer months. Opportunistic infections with *Campylobacter* species are often found in homosexual men or patients with acquired immunodeficiency syndrome (AIDS), even in the absence of symptoms of diarrhea or proctitis. *Campylobacter* species are a common cause of "backpacker's diarrhea," along with *Giardia,* both of which are frequently acquired by drinking from wilderness water sources.

Pathophysiology

Campylobacter organisms are small gram-negative bacteria. *C. jejuni, C. coli,* and *C. fetus* are the most common subspecies isolated. *C. cinaedi* and *C. fennelliae* are isolated almost exclusively from homosexual men. *Campylobacter* species produce disease primarily by direct invasion of the colonic epithelium and may induce inflammatory changes that are endoscopically indistinguishable from inflammatory bowel disease.

Infection is transmitted by the fecal-oral route through contaminated food and water or by direct contact with fecal material from infected animals or persons. The primary reservoirs for *Campylobacter* species are chickens and common birds such as pigeons, blackbirds, starlings, sparrows, and canaries.[3]

Clinical Presentation

The incubation period for *Campylobacter* enteritis is approximately 2 to 5 days. Disease onset is usually rapid, consisting of fever, cramping abdominal pain, and diarrhea. Constitutional symptoms of anorexia, malaise, myalgias, and headache are the rule, and some patients experience backache, arthralgias, and vomiting. The clinical picture can mimic that of acute appendicitis. The diarrhea often lags 24 to 48 hours after the onset of fever and abdominal pain. Typically, the stools are loose and bile-colored but progress to become watery, grossly bloody, or melanotic more than 40% of the time. Either gross or occult blood is found in the stool of 60% to 90% of patients with *Campylobacter* gastroenteritis. At the height of the illness, patients usually pass eight to ten stools or more per day.[1]

Most patients are well within a week or less; however, diarrhea can persist for weeks. Rare cases have been fatal. Relapses are common although generally milder than the original episode.

Diagnostic Strategies

Diagnosis is made by stool culture. Laboratory findings include a leukocytosis and stool positive for occult or gross blood and fecal leukocytes. Blood cultures are sometimes positive. Sigmoidoscopy reveals a nonspecific inflammatory colitis, and *Campylobacter* infection must be considered before a new diagnosis of inflammatory bowel disease is made.

Differential Considerations

The differential diagnosis of campylobacteriosis includes all organisms that produce typical infectious diarrhea or fecal leukocytes, but particularly salmo-

Table 93-1. Epidemiologic Aspects of Invasive Bacterial Enteritis

Pathogen	Sources	Incubation Period (I) and Duration (D) Untreated	Features
Campylobacter	Contaminated food/water, wilderness waters (backpacker's diarrhea), birds, animals	I: 2-5 days D: 5-14 days	May cause bloody diarrhea May mimic acute appendicitis or inflammatory bowel disease; recurrence common
Salmonella	Grade A shell eggs, poultry, unpasteurized milk, domestic pets	I: 8-24 hr D: 2-5 days	Family and cafeteria-type food poisoning outbreaks common; increased incidence in patients with cancer or immunodeficiency
Shigella	Person-to-person, confined populations, poor hygiene, water-borne	I: 24-48 hr D: 4-7 days	Toxigenic watery diarrhea, followed by invasive picture; may produce severe dysentery
Yersinia	Food/water/milk, person-to-person, dogs, cats, pigs	I: 12-48 hr D: 5-14 days	Appendicitis/terminal ileitis-like syndrome; postinfection polyarthritis; long duration of fecal excretion of the organism
Vibrio parahaemolyticus	Raw or inadequately cooked seafood, especially shrimp	I: 8-24 hr D: 1-2 days	High attack rates, summer months; self-limited
Escherichia coli O127:H7	Raw ground beef, raw milk, meats, person-to-person, water-borne, travel	I: 3-8 days D: 5-10 days	Bloody diarrhea/hemorrhagic colitis; hemolytic uremic syndrome or thrombotic thrombocytopenic purpura
Plesiomonas	Uncooked shellfish, travel	I: 1-2 days D: 5-20 days	Severe abdominal cramps and vomiting, with dehydration
Bacillus anthracis	Infected herbivores, undercooked meat, bioterrorism	I: 1-6 days D: Weeks	Oral ulcers, neck swelling, lymphadenopathy, fever, gastrointestinal hemorrhage, possible ascites

nellosis, shigellosis, and *Escherichia coli* 0157:H7 infection.

Management

Treatment with antibiotics is not needed for patients whose condition is clinically improved when stool culture results become available. According to the Infectious Disease Society of America 2001 consensus statement, erythromycin, 500 mg twice a day for 5 days is the recommended first-line therapy.[4] Azithromycin 500 mg for 3 days is acceptable as well. Ciprofloxacin 500 mg bid can be used and was previously the treatment of choice, but there is alarming resistance to the fluoroquinolones, thought mainly due to antibiotic use in the poultry industry. Roughly 10% of *Campylobacter* is now resistant in the United States, and there is more than 80% resistance in Thailand. *Campylobacter* organisms are generally resistant to trimethoprim-sulfamethoxazole (TMP-SMX) as well. Suggested antibiotic regimens are listed in Table 93-2. Relapses can occur, but the likelihood is decreased with appropriate antibiotic treatment.[5] Because *Campylobacter* infection is an invasive enteritis, antimotility agents are not recommended unless treatment with antibiotics is also given.

Complications of *Campylobacter* are rare. Cholecystitis, pancreatitis, and massive gastrointestinal bleeding have all been documented, as have meningitis, endocarditis, and osteomyelitis. In addition, a definite association has been made with Guillain-Barré syndrome. Guillain-Barré syndrome associated with *Campylobacter* infection tends to be more severe than Guillain-Barré syndrome from other triggers and can occur even with asymptomatic infections. Luckily, the incidence is estimated at less than 1 per 1000 cases.[6]

Salmonellosis

Epidemiology

Salmonella causes more than 2 million infections in the United States each year, most occurring during the summer months.[7,8] It accounts for 10% to 15% of all cases of acute food poisoning reported to the Centers for Disease Control and Prevention (CDC).[3,9] The organism affects people of all age groups but particularly children.

Almost all *Salmonella* infections are acquired by the ingestion of contaminated food or drink.[9,10] Direct person-to-person transmission can occur, but most human infections are related to the vast reservoir of salmonellosis in lower animals. Poultry products constitute the most common source of *Salmonella*. Unpasteurized milk and domestic pets are other sources. Approximately 10% of household dogs and cats excrete *Salmonella,* and pet reptiles, such as turtles, snakes, and iguanas, have been responsible for outbreaks of salmonellosis.[7,11,12] Rattlesnake meat and medicinal preparations have been associated with *Salmonella arizonae* infections, especially among Hispanic populations in the southwestern United States.

Cooking contaminated foods decreases the possibility of infection but does not eliminate it. *Salmonella* can survive cooking deep inside certain foods, where temperatures may not reach the lethal range. Very large outbreaks of *Salmonella* infection have been traced to contaminated, unbroken, grade A shell eggs.[7] Although the organism is present in the uncracked egg, thorough cooking usually eradicates or reduces it to clinically insignificant levels.

Common raw egg-based sources of *Salmonella* infections include hollandaise sauce, homemade eggnog,

Table 93-2. Antibiotic Therapy for Diarrhea in Immunocompetent Adults

Pathogen	Antibiotic*†	Dose
Campylobacter	1. Erythromycin	500 mg PO bid × 5 days
	2. Azithromycin	500 mg PO qd × 3 days
Salmonella	1. Ciprofloxacin	500 mg PO bid × 7 days
	2. Azithromycin	1 g PO ×1, then 500 mg qd × next 6 days
Shigella	1. Ciprofloxacin	500 mg PO bid × 3 days
	2. TMP-SMX	160 mg/800 mg PO bid × 3 days
Yersinia	1. TMP-SMX	160 mg/800 mg PO bid × 3 days
	1. Ciprofloxacin	500 mg PO bid × 3 days
Vibrio parahaemolyticus	1. Not recommended	
Vibrio cholerae	1. Ciprofloxacin	1 g PO × 1 + IV fluids
	2. Doxycycline	300 mg PO × 1 + IV fluids
	3. TMP-SMX	160 mg/800 mg PO bid × 3 days + IV fluids
Escherichia coli O157:H7	1. None recommended	
Enterotoxigenic *Escherichia coli*	Mild symptoms: ciprofloxacin	750 mg PO × 1 dose
	1. Ciprofloxacin	500 mg PO bid × 3 days
	2. TMP-SMX	160 mg/80 mg PO bid × 3 days
Plesiomonas hominis	1. TMP-SMX	160 mg/80 mg PO bid × 3 days
	2. Ciprofloxacin	500 mg PO bid × 3 days
Clostridium difficile		
Diarrhea	1. Metronidazole	250 mg PO qid × 10-14 days
	2. Vancomycin	125 mg PO qid × 10-14 days
Colitis	1. Metronidazole or vancomycin	500 mg PO qid × 10-14 days; 1 g IV q day
Aeromonas	1. TMP-SMX	160 mg/800 mg PO bid × 3 days
	2. Ciprofloxacin	500 mg PO qid × 3 days
Bacillus anthracis	1. Ciprofloxacin	400 mg IV q 12 hours
	2. Doxycycline	100 mg IV q 12 hours
Giardia lamblia	1. Metronidazole	250 mg PO tid × 5 days
	2. Furazolidone	100 mg PO qid × 7-10 days
Entamoeba histolytica (confirmed by	1. Paromomycin	500 mg PO tid × 7 days
PCR or other test to be distinct from	2. Iodoquinol	650 mg PO tid × 20 days
E. dispar)	3. Diloxanide furoate	500 mg PO tid × 10 days
Severe symptoms: start treatment with metronidazole	Metronidazole (severe)	750 mg PO tid × 10 days followed by above
Cryptosporidium	1. Paromomycin	500–750 mg PO qid × 14-21 days
	2. Indomethacin	500 mg PO tid
Isospora belli	1. TMP-SMX	160 mg/800 mg PO qid × 10 days then bid for 3 wk
Cyclospora cayetanensis	1. TMP-SMX	160 mg/800 mg PO bid × 7 days
Strongyloides stercoralis	1. Ivermectin	200 μg/kg/PO day × 1-2 days
	2. Thiabendazole	50 mg/kg/day in two doses × 2 days (max 3 g/day)
Enterobius vermicularis	1. Mebendazole or pyrantel pamoate	100 mg PO × 1 dose, repeated after 2 wk
		11 mg/kg PO × 1 dose (max 1 g), repeated after 2 wk
	2. Albendazole	400 mg PO × 1 dose, repeated after 2 wk

*Another quinolone agent, norfloxacin, can be substituted for ciprofloxacin in the treatment of diarrheas. The equivalent dosage is 400 mg bid.
†1 indicates drug of first choice; 2 indicates alternative drug(s).
PCR, polymerase chain reaction; TMP-SMX, trimethoprim-sulfamethoxazole.

Caesar salad dressing, and French toast mix. *Salmonella enteritidis* is the species universally associated with egg-related infections. Patients convalescing from *Salmonella*-related enterocolitis and persons with asymptomatic infection may continue to excrete *Salmonella* organisms for weeks or months, thus serving as sources of infection.

Pathophysiology

Ingested *Salmonella* organisms penetrate the intestinal mucosal cells and lodge in the lamina propria. The subsequent inflammatory reaction produces the gastroenteritis. Different *Salmonella* serotypes show marked variations in invasive potential and are associated with particular presentations: *Salmonella typhi* with enteric fever (typhoid fever), *S. choleraesuis* with septicemia, *S. typhimurium* with acute gastroenteritis, and *S. enteritidis* infections from grade A shell eggs.[7]

Relatively large numbers of *Salmonella* must be ingested to produce illness. However, a carrier state can be induced with ingestion of 10 to 100 times fewer bacteria. In infants and adults with certain underlying diseases, a much smaller inoculum may produce illness. Decreased gastric acidity or an alteration of intestinal flora resulting from the administration of antibiotics can impressively reduce the size of the required inoculum. Approximately one third to one half of patients hospitalized with salmonellosis have some type of major underlying disease, such as leukemia, lymphoma, cancer, or AIDS. The incidence of *Salmonella* enteric fever is markedly increased in immunodeficient patients with cancer or AIDS.[13,14] Patients with sickle cell anemia, other hemolytic anemias, or AIDS are unusually susceptible to *Salmonella* bacteremia.[13] Protracted salmonellosis and higher morbidity and mortality rates occur in patients older than 65 years of age.

Clinical Presentation

Family outbreaks and sporadic cases are more common than large epidemics. After an incubation period of 8 to 48 hours, the typical patient with *Salmonella* gastroenteritis presents with fever, colicky abdominal pain, and loose, watery diarrhea, occasionally with mucus and blood. Nausea and vomiting are common but are rarely severe or protracted. Mild to moderate diffuse abdominal tenderness is present in most patients, but occasionally severe tenderness and even rebound can be present. Symptoms usually abate within 2 to 5 days, and recovery is uneventful.

Diagnostic Strategies

Diagnosis is made by stool culture. The peripheral white blood cell count is usually normal unless bacteremia is present. Fecal leukocyte test results are positive, and sometimes occult blood is also present in the stool. Blood cultures are occasionally positive, and culture samples should be obtained from all severely ill patients. The possibility of an underlying disease or immunodeficiency state should be considered in every patient with a severe *Salmonella* infection.

Differential Considerations

Family or communal outbreaks can suggest staphylococcal-related food poisoning, but this entity has a shorter incubation period, is not associated with fever, and produces the typical toxigenic, noninvasive, diarrheal picture. Vomiting is also much more prominent in cases of staphylococcal food poisoning than in most cases of *Salmonella* infection.

Management

Most patients with *Salmonella* gastroenteritis will have clinically improved by the time their culture results are available. These patients do not require antibiotic treatment. Patients whose condition is not improving should be treated to effect cure, and those who represent a public health risk should be treated to eradicate the carrier state and prevent spread of the organism. The antibiotics effective for outpatient management of *Salmonella* gastroenteritis include one of the following: either ciprofloxacin (500 mg bid) or norfloxacin (400 mg bid) for 5 to 7 days, or azithromycin (1 g by mouth) then 500 mg a day for the next 6 days.[2,5] TMP-SMX can also be used if the organism is susceptible. Ciprofloxacin is effective in the treatment of chronic *S. typhi* carriers. However, treatment with fluoroquinolones can actually prolong shedding of non-*typhi* species. Patients requiring inpatient therapy are best treated with intravenous ceftriaxone until results of sensitivity studies become available.[15,16]

Follow-up with the patient's primary care physician should be arranged. Food handlers and health care personnel should not be allowed to work until the carrier state has abated. Repeated stool cultures and further decisions regarding job or school situations will be required. Personal hygiene should be stressed because untreated patients may continue to shed infective

BOX 93-1. Notifiable Foodborne Diseases and Conditions*

Bacterial
Botulism
Brucellosis
Cholera
Escherichia coli O157:H7
Hemolytic uremic syndrome, postdiarrheal
Salmonellosis
Shigellosis
Typhoid fever

Viral
Hepatitis A

Parasitic
Cryptosporidiosis
Cyclosporiasis
Trichinosis

---

*In the United States, additional reporting requirements may be mandated by state and territorial laws and regulations. Details on specific state reporting requirements are available from the Council of State and Territorial Epidemiologists (http://www.cste.org) and Centers for Disease Control and Prevention (http://www.cdc.gov).

From the American Medical Association, Centers for Disease Control and Prevention, Center for Food Safety and Applied Nutrition, et al: Diagnosis and management of foodborne illnesses: A primer for physicians. *MMWR Recomm Rep* 50(RR-2):1-69, 2001.

organisms in the stool for weeks or even months. As with other invasive pathogens, the use of antimotility drugs alone is contraindicated. These drugs prolong fever and diarrhea and increase the incidence of bacteremia and the carrier state in patients with *Salmonella* enteritis. However, administration of loperamide is safe when given concomitantly with an appropriate antibiotic.

Prevention of salmonellosis depends on adequate cooking and minimizing the time that foods are allowed to stand at room temperature to reduce the chance of bacterial growth to an infectious inoculum. Careful personal hygiene, including hand washing, is also important. Salmonella is a nationally notifiable disease (Box 93-1).

Shigellosis

Epidemiology

Shigellosis, or bacillary dysentery, is worldwide in distribution and particularly common in countries lacking effective sanitation. Approximately 25,000 to 40,000 cases are reported annually in the United States, but many more undoubtedly occur. *Shigella sonnei* is responsible for approximately 75% of the infections occurring in this country; *S. flexneri* causes most of the remaining cases, with *S. dysenteriae* responsible for a small percentage of cases.[2]

Shigella infections are common in confined populations, such as those in mental or penal institutions, in nursing homes, or on American Indian reservations. Spread is by the fecal-oral route, and humans are the only natural hosts. *Shigella* can be found in large numbers around the bases of toilets used by infected persons, and the organism readily passes through toilet tissue onto the fingers. *Shigella* can be recovered in cultures taken as long as 3 hours after contamination. In the last few years, a number of large outbreaks have been associated with recreational water venues such as swimming pools, water parks, fountains, hot tubs, and spas.[17]

Pathophysiology

Unlike *Salmonella,* which requires a very large inoculum to produce disease, as few as 50 to 100 *Shigella* bacilli can cause infection. No other enteric pathogen is so efficient in producing overt disease in humans. Infection is generally superficial, localized to the epithelial lining of the mucosa; therefore, bowel perforation or invasion into the bloodstream is extremely rare. Bleeding occurs from superficial ulcerations of the mucosa.

Many patients infected with *Shigella* do not develop dysentery but have only a watery diarrhea of short duration. The watery diarrhea is caused by exotoxin-induced secretion of water and electrolytes by the small bowel, whereas the bloody mucoid dysentery is the result of colonic mucosal invasion by the organisms. Systemic manifestations may also be toxin induced, because bacteremia is rarely found.

Clinical Presentation

The incubation period is usually 24 to 48 hours, and the clinical manifestations vary considerably, often appearing in a bimodal fashion. Mild, watery diarrhea with few if any constitutional symptoms or asymptomatic infection occurs in a significant proportion of infected individuals. Colicky abdominal pain, followed shortly by high fever and diarrhea, is the more common clinical presentation. The stools are liquid and green, contain shreds of mucus and undigested food, and average 7 to 12 daily. Only 20% to 30% of patients with culture-proven cases develop bloody mucoid stools.

When true dysentery develops, it is ordinarily preceded by a recognizable period of watery diarrhea lasting a few hours to a few days. Patients with dysentery have grossly bloody diarrhea, tenesmus, and significant constitutional symptoms, such as fever, nausea, vomiting, headache, and myalgias. Convulsions and other neurologic manifestations are common in infected children. If symptoms are severe enough, profound dehydration and even circulatory collapse can occur.

Generally, shigellosis is a self-limited disease. Patients become afebrile in 3 to 4 days, and the abdominal cramping and diarrhea resolve within 1 week. A significant number of untreated patients will continue to shed organisms in the stool for 2 or more weeks, and approximately 10% of patients will have a relapse unless treated with antibiotics.

Diagnostic Strategies

Most cases of shigellosis remain undiagnosed. Patients seen in the emergency department with mild, watery diarrhea and few if any constitutional symptoms are sent home with conservative management, and no investigative procedures are performed. However, shigellosis should be considered in every patient with an acute febrile illness associated with diarrhea, especially those patients who appear ill or who have dysenteric stools.

Fecal white blood cells, usually in large numbers, are present in cases of shigellosis, regardless of the gross appearance of the stool.[2] Thus, finding leukocytes in watery stools can help identify shigellosis even in the absence of classic dysenteric stools. Occult blood is usually present in the stools of infected patients. Blood leukocytosis is common, and a significant leftward shift in the differential count is almost always present. Blood cultures for *Shigella* are rarely positive. Sigmoidoscopic examination reveals diffuse mucosal inflammation, often with multiple ulcerations.

A definitive diagnosis of shigellosis is made with stool culture. Stool cultures are positive in more than 90% of cases when obtained during the first 3 days of illness; however, only approximately 75% are positive if samples are obtained more than 1 week after the onset of diarrhea.

Differential Considerations

The differential diagnosis includes salmonellosis, *Campylobacter* enteritis, *E. coli* 0157:H7 infection, amebic dysentery, and ulcerative colitis.

Management

Treatment primarily involves the correction of fluid and electrolyte abnormalities. Discharged patients whose stool cultures return positive for *Shigella* organisms may require antibiotics. If *S. sonnei* or *S. flexneri* is cultured, the decision to administer antibiotics is based on the patient's clinical condition and the feasibility of sanitary control. Asymptomatic or improving patients do not need to be treated with antibiotics unless treatment is necessary for public health measures. Patients whose condition is not improving should be treated. Antibiotics shorten the clinical course and eradicate the pathogen from the stool, often within 48 hours.[18] Whenever *S. dysenteriae* is isolated, the patient should be treated to prevent outbreaks of dysentery, even if the patient is asymptomatic when the culture result returns.

In the United States, more than 50% of *Shigella* organisms are resistant to ampicillin, and 25% to 45% are resistant to TMP-SMX.[2,5] Significant resistance has not yet been found to the quinolone agents ciprofloxacin or norfloxacin, and one of them should be considered the drug of choice unless sensitivity studies demonstrate that the organism is sensitive to either ampicillin or TMP-SMX. Treatment is required for only 3 days in immunocompetent patients.

Antimotility agents may prolong the fever, diarrhea, and excretion of *Shigella* in the stools and are contraindicated in patients with invasive shigellosis. However, they may be safe when used simultaneously with antibiotics. Follow-up stool cultures should be done in patients treated for *S. dysenteriae* to ensure eradication of the organism. Follow-up cultures, however, are not necessary in patients treated for *S. sonnei* or *S. flexneri,* provided that the patient's condition improves clinically. Shigellosis is a nationally notifiable disease.

Yersinia enterocolitica Gastroenteritis

Epidemiology

Yersinia enterocolitica, a gram-negative aerobic bacterium, is a member of the family Enterobacteriaceae. *Y. enterocolitica* is increasingly being recognized as a human pathogen all over the world, particularly in Scandinavia, Europe, Canada, and Japan. In some areas, such as Ontario and Quebec, Canada, it is now more common than *Shigella* and is approaching the incidence of *Salmonella* as a cause for gastroenteritis in children. In the United States, it is increasingly diagnosed as a cause of gastroenteritis and other enteric syndromes that can mimic appendicitis. *Yersinia* infections are most common in childhood.[2,3]

Pathophysiology

Yersiniosis is an invasive infection of the intestine, particularly the terminal ileum, and the mesenteric lymph nodes. Infection originates from contaminated food or drink. The consumption of contaminated milk or contaminated raw pork has accounted for sporadic cases and several large outbreaks. Fecal-oral transmission to humans from a variety of animals, particularly dogs, cats, and pigs, and direct person-to-person spread probably occur, but communicability appears to be low.[19]

Clinical Presentation

The initial clinical picture of *Yersinia* enterocolitis resembles that of infection by other invasive intestinal organisms: fever; colicky abdominal pain; watery, greenish, and sometimes bloody diarrhea; and constitutional symptoms of anorexia, vomiting, and malaise. However, in cases of *Y. enterocolitica* gastroenteritis, the abdominal pain and diarrhea usually persist for 10 to 14 days, or longer.

A substantial number of patients with yersiniosis, in particular adolescents and young adults, develop an ileocecitis. In these cases, lower abdominal pain with little or no diarrhea predominates and may perfectly mimic acute appendicitis. Large outbreaks have been traced to contaminated milk, largely because physicians noticed an extraordinary rise in the number of negative appendectomies.[19] Postinfection manifestations, such as erythema nodosum or a persistent polyarthritis, occur in as many as 2% to 5% of patients, mainly adults.[2]

Diagnostic Strategies

Leukocytosis sometimes occurs with *Yersinia* enterocolitis, and blood cultures are almost always negative. Fecal stains show leukocytes, as in other invasive diarrheas, and occasionally red blood cells. If performed, contrast radiography of the small bowel shows mucosal abnormalities consistent with terminal ileitis. Radio-

graphic studies of the large bowel and sigmoidoscopy usually reveal normal colonic mucosa. Ultrasonography can show a typical sonographic picture of bacterial ileocecitis and may differentiate bacterial enteritis from acute appendicitis.

Culturing the organism from the stool is the only definitive way to diagnose yersiniosis. Stool cultures require special techniques and a long time for growth. Patients with *Yersinia* enterocolitis often continue to shed organisms in the stools well into convalescence, long after the diarrhea subsides. The mean duration of fecal shedding is approximately 6 weeks.

Differential Considerations

The diagnosis should be suspected when a patient has prolonged abdominal pain and diarrhea after what appears to be a common, usually self-limited gastroenteritis syndrome, or the patient has symptoms similar to those of an appendicitis or mesenteric adenitis. *Y. enterocolitica* infection should also be considered in the differential diagnosis of regional enteritis, which it can closely mimic.

Management

Generally, *Y. enterocolitica* infection is self-limited at the diarrheal stage and resolves without treatment. As with other invasive gastrointestinal pathogens, antiperistaltic drugs are not recommended unless the patient is simultaneously treated with antibiotics.

Treatment with antibiotics has not been proven essential or efficacious in the management of uncomplicated *Yersinia* enterocolitis or in the pseudoappendicitis syndrome. However, because *Yersinia* organisms take a long time to grow on culture, in most studies the duration of illness before antibiotics were started was 1 to 2 weeks. *Yersinia* organisms are usually susceptible to TMP-SMX, which is the treatment of choice when antibiotic therapy is indicated.[15] The drug does not decrease the fecal shedding of the organism. Doxycycline in combination with an aminoglycoside is another alternative, as are quinolones as a single agent.[5] In immunocompetent adults, a 3-day course is sufficient; the course is 7 to 10 days if the patient is immunocompromised. Treatment should be considered in patients who are still significantly ill at the time culture results return, particularly if the patients are immunocompromised or have a significant underlying medical illness, or in cases in which the fecal shedding could represent a public health hazard. In those patients who interact with potentially susceptible individuals, appropriate steps should be taken to ensure they do not propagate their infection. However, *Yersinia* is not a mandatory reportable disease.

Vibrio parahaemolyticus Gastroenteritis

Epidemiology

Vibrio parahaemolyticus bacilli are gram-negative marine vibrios present in the coastal seawaters of the United States, Japan, and other temperate zone nations.

V. parahaemolyticus is the most common cause of bacterial enteritis in Japan, causing up to 70% of cases. It has also been implicated in many outbreaks of acute diarrheal illness in the coastal areas of the United States, often from eating raw oysters.[20-22] Raw fish is the most common source in Japan, whereas inadequately cooked seafood, usually shrimp, is the most common in the United States. Several epidemics of *V. parahaemolyticus* infections have occurred on cruise ships.[23] Food poisoning from vibrios can be partly explained by the fact that vibrios are not detected by standard techniques used to check fishing waters, nor are they eliminated by the usual commercial decontamination procedures for shellfish.[24,25]

The illness appears to be limited to the warmer months of the year, when large numbers of vibrios are present in coastal seawaters and the temperature favors bacterial multiplication in unrefrigerated seafood. *V. parahaemolyticus* grows rapidly at room temperature, and within 3 to 4 hours a few organisms can multiply into an infectious inoculum. Attack rates are quite high, but there is no evidence of secondary spread among family members of infected patients.[21]

Pathophysiology

Unlike other vibrios, *V. parahaemolyticus* produces disease by an infectious process rather than one mediated through an enterotoxin. It causes an intense, inflammatory response in the intestinal mucosa. Stools contain numerous leukocytes and are occasionally grossly bloody. *V. parahaemolyticus* appears to be pathogenic only for humans; no other known host exists. Vibrios are not found in the feces of asymptomatic persons.

Clinical Presentation

Symptoms usually appear 8 to 12 hours after the ingestion of contaminated food, but the incubation period can range from 4 to 48 hours. The most predominant symptom is acute diarrhea, but the volume of fluid lost is generally not large. Moderately severe abdominal cramps usually occur, and many patients also exhibit systemic symptoms of fever, nausea, and headache. Vomiting can occur but generally is not prominent. The illness is almost invariably self-limited and seldom lasts longer than 24 to 48 hours.[21]

V. parahaemolyticus infection should be suspected when a common source outbreak of acute diarrheal disease occurs in persons exposed to fresh or frozen seafood. It should also be considered when fecal white blood cells are present in cases of acute diarrhea linked to food poisoning.

Diagnostic Strategies

The diagnosis of *V. parahaemolyticus* infection can be confirmed within 24 hours by culturing the stools on thiosulfate citrate-bile salts sucrose agar.

Management

Because the disease is self-limited, most patients require no therapy. Antibiotic treatment does not shorten the course or the duration of pathogen excretion, although tetracycline and fluoroquinolones have been effective against the organism in vitro. An occasional patient may require fluid replacement. Antimotility agents are not indicated.

Because *V. parahaemolyticus* is widely present in coastal waters, the only effective preventive measures are adequate cooking, refrigeration, and hygienic practice in the preparation of seafood for human consumption.

Hemorrhagic *Escherichia coli* Serotype 0157:H7 Gastroenteritis

Epidemiology

Escherichia coli serotype 0157:H7 is an important and common cause of bloody diarrhea in the United States, Canada, the United Kingdom, and South America. Its incidence is about the same as that of *Shigella* in many parts of the United States, particularly in the Pacific Northwest.[26] Infection is most common in children and elderly adults. Patients with a previous gastrectomy are also at risk, probably because of loss of the gastric acidity defense. Large outbreaks of *E. coli* 0157:H7 hemorrhagic colitis have occurred, primarily in nursing homes, with mortality rates as high as 35%.[3,7,27,28]

Inadequately cooked hamburger has caused many large outbreaks.[29] *E. coli* 0157:H7, present in the intestines of healthy cattle, contaminates the meat during slaughter, and the grinding process then transfers the organisms from the surface of the meat to the interior. The U.S. Department of Agriculture food safety regulations now require that hamburger be cooked thoroughly, to the point that the juices are no longer pink, to effectively kill *E. coli* organisms. Outbreaks have also occurred from apple cider, raw milk, contaminated municipal water supplies, and person-to-person spread in daycare centers.[30] Food handlers with *E. coli* 0157:H7–related diarrhea have contaminated meals responsible for institutional outbreaks. Person-to-person spread occurs, and this explains the secondary infections that occur later in workers caring for persons with *E. coli* 0157:H7 colitis.[7,27]

Pathophysiology

Escherichia coli 0157:H7 is one of more than 30 serotypes of *E. coli* known to produce *Shigella*-like toxins called *vertoxins,* which are cytotoxic to the intestinal vascular endothelial cells and cause hemorrhagic colitis. *E. coli* 0157:H7 does not cause an invasive infection.[26,31]

Clinical Presentation

After an incubation period of 4 to 9 days, patients initially produce watery diarrhea that becomes bloody hours to days later. More than 95% of patients report bloody stools.[26] The amount of blood varies, but stools passed may consist wholly of blood, and the infection may masquerade as gastrointestinal bleeding from noninfectious causes. The bloody diarrhea is typically accompanied by severe abdominal cramps, pain, and often vomiting. Fever is not a prominent symptom and, if present, is usually low grade. This helps differentiate *E. coli* 0157:H7 from other invasive organisms that can be treated empirically with antibiotics. Fecal leukocytes are found but in small numbers, in contrast to the sheets of white blood cells seen in *Shigella* dysentery. Endoscopic, histologic, and radiographic studies demonstrate only nonspecific changes consistent with an inflammatory hemorrhagic colitis.[26]

Uncomplicated infection resolves spontaneously over 7 to 10 days. A carrier state may last another 1 to 2 weeks, but it also resolves spontaneously. Chronic diarrhea is rare.[32]

Complications

Escherichia coli 0157:H7 hemorrhagic colitis has been associated with two serious complications, hemolytic uremic syndrome (HUS) and thrombotic thrombocytopenic purpura. HUS is more common in children, especially those younger than 4 years, occurring in 20% to 25% of cases. Approximately 5% to 10% of elderly patients in nursing home outbreaks acquire HUS, and 50% to 80% of these patients die. Thrombocytopenic purpura is seen in 2% to 3% of cases, most often in immunosuppressed patients. HUS or thrombocytopenic purpura typically occurs 5 to 20 days after the onset of infection, and the diarrhea can be totally resolved and forgotten by the time a diagnosis is established. Death from *E. coli* 0157:H7 hemorrhagic colitis alone or from one of the complications occurs primarily among elderly patients.[28,33]

Diagnostic Strategies

Diagnosis requires specific stool culture techniques. In addition to the routine battery of media used for stool cultures, specimens should be plated onto sorbitol-MacConkey medium. The 0157:H7 strains of *E. coli* are sorbitol negative at 18 to 24 hours on this medium and can be rapidly identified using various serologic tests, such as latex agglutination or fluorescent antibody testing. DNA probes aid in the diagnosis and are used by the CDC to determine the etiology of widespread outbreaks.[34]

Differential Considerations

Hemorrhagic *E. coli* infections are misdiagnosed as ischemic colitis, inflammatory bowel disease, intussusception, or another infectious colitis. The examining physician should test for *E. coli* 0157:H7 when considering a diagnosis of one of these entities.

Management

Antibiotic therapy does not shorten the clinical course or eradicate the organism. Moreover, treatment with antibiotics to which the organism is resistant may increase the risk of developing HUS by eliminating competing bowel flora. However, the degree to which antibiotic treatment truly increases the risk of HUS remains controversial.[26,27,33] Retrospective studies in adults show an increased association between antibiotic use and the development of HUS but may have been biased because antibiotics could preferentially have been prescribed for the more serious cases, which would have a propensity to develop HUS regardless. Since treatment does not eradicate the organism or shorten the course of illness, however, combined with some level of risk for developing HUS, treatment of known *E. coli* O157:H7 is not indicated.

Before culture results are available to rule out this pathogen, empiric treatment of bloody diarrhea should be approached with caution. Empiric antibiotic treatment for diarrheal illness is not recommended in children because HUS is more common in this demographic population. For adults, empiric antibiotic treatment of bloody diarrhea is recommended only for patients with a temperature higher than 38.5° C to avoid HUS. *E. coli* O157:H7 does not cause a high fever; if fever is present, it is due to another pathogen. In this case, empiric antibiotics may be warranted.

Aeromonas hydrophila Gastroenteritis

Epidemiology

Aeromonas species are gram-negative, facultative, anaerobic, rod-shaped bacteria of the family Vibrionaceae. *Aeromonas* organisms are ubiquitous in fresh and brackish water in the United States and also contaminate the food supply.[2,8] Drinking untreated water, usually from private wells or springs, causes most cases of diarrhea from *Aeromonas* bacteria.[20] *Aeromonas* infection has not been associated with consumption of shellfish. Predisposing factors include age, underlying systemic or localized gastrointestinal disease such as colon cancer or inflammatory bowel disease, and recent hospitalization or antibiotic treatment. *Aeromonas* infection causes 10% to 15% of all cases of diarrhea in children. It does occur in normal adults but is most often seen in immunocompromised patients. It is a particularly common cause of diarrhea in patients with AIDS.[13,14]

Pathophysiology

The exact mechanism by which *Aeromonas* species produce diarrhea has not yet been explained. Both enterotoxins and cytopathic toxins may be produced, and the organisms may have some invasive characteristics.

Clinical Presentation

Typical symptoms are watery diarrhea, abdominal cramps, vomiting, and occasionally fever. Children tend to have a more acute, severe illness than adults. In untreated patients, diarrhea persists for 2 to 10 weeks, with more prolonged illness in adults than in children. Generally, fecal leukocytes and occult blood are absent from the stool; however, patients can have a severe colitis, including fever, fecal leukocytes, and bloody diarrhea, which can mimic Crohn's disease or ulcerative colitis. An association of inflammatory bowel disease exists with acute *Aeromonas*-associated diarrhea. What role, if any, *Aeromonas* species play in the activation of inflammatory bowel disease remains unknown.

Diagnostic Strategies

Diagnosis is made by stool culture, but *Aeromonas* infection should be strongly suspected in children or immunocompromised patients with diarrhea, particularly those with a history of drinking from untreated water sources.

Management

Antibiotic treatment results in prompt resolution of all symptoms. Treatment also eradicates the organism from the stools. Double-strength TMP-SMX is the drug of choice, but the quinolones also effectively treat *Aeromonas*-related diarrhea.[5,15] Treatment is recommended for 3 days.

Plesiomonas shigelloides Gastroenteritis

Epidemiology

Plesiomonas shigelloides is a gram-negative, facultative, anaerobic bacterium of the family Vibrionaceae. *Plesiomonas* has been recovered in up to 17% of immunocompetent patients who have acute diarrhea.[13,14] Infection is strongly associated with eating uncooked shellfish, usually raw oysters, in the 48 hours before the onset of illness. A strong association also exists between *Plesiomonas* infection and foreign travel, especially to Mexico. Sporadic diarrheal illness occurs in both normal and immunocompromised hosts. Large outbreaks have occurred, usually resulting from oyster consumption.[8]

Pathophysiology

The mechanism of disease production is enteroinvasion by the organisms. *Plesiomonas* does not appear to produce enterotoxins.

Clinical Presentation

The incubation period is only 1 to 2 days. Most patients have significant diarrhea and vomiting, severe abdominal cramps, and some degree of dehydration. Stools are generally bloody and contain mucus, with fecal leukocytes present. Symptoms last anywhere from 5 to 40 days and are usually shorter in children and longer in adults.

Diagnosis of *P. shigelloides* infection should be considered in patients with a typical invasive-appearing diarrhea, especially if the stools are bloody or when the onset of illness occurs shortly after the ingestion of raw shellfish or foreign travel, particularly to Mexico.

Diagnostic Strategies

Definitive diagnosis is by stool culture. However, the laboratory must be notified when this pathology is considered because unless oxidase testing is done, *Plesiomonas* species may be indistinguishable from normal Enterobacteriaceae on nonselective culture media. Patients with *Plesiomonas* infections should be evaluated for possible immunodeficiency.

Management

Antibiotic treatment results in rapid clinical and bacteriologic cure. *P. shigelloides* is usually resistant to ampicillin but susceptible to TMP-SMX, the quinolones, cephalothin, gentamicin, and chloramphenicol. Current recommended treatment is TMP-SMX, 160 mg/800 mg twice daily for 3 days, ciprofloxacin, 500 mg twice daily, or norfloxacin, 400 mg twice daily for 3 days.[5] Follow-up evaluation is not necessary, unless the patient is immunodeficient or does not respond clinically.

Bacillus anthracis

Epidemiology

Although gastrointestinal anthrax is rare, large outbreaks still occur in endemic regions throughout the world. Anthrax has also been used as a weapon of bioterrorism in regions not normally susceptible to the disease. As early as the 1930s, groups have experimented with anthrax-impregnated chocolate as a weapon against their enemies.[35,36] Awareness of the spectrum of clinical presentations of gastrointestinal anthrax is important not only for the welfare of the patient, but for prompt notification of potential terrorist activity.

Traditionally, gastrointestinal infection has been estimated at less than 1% of all human anthrax cases. Ninety-five percent of cases mainly involved cutaneous symptoms and 5% were limited mostly to the respiratory tract. However, since gastrointestinal anthrax can cause only mild and self-limited symptoms, many persons with the disease may not seek medical treatment or get diagnosed in a medical setting. Therefore, the actual number of gastrointestinal anthrax cases may be much greater than suspected.[37]

Areas endemic for anthrax exist in all continents containing tropical and subtemperate regions. Thailand, India, Iran, Gambia, and Uganda have all reported deaths from gastrointestinal anthrax.[37] Within the United States, naturally occurring anthrax exposure has been documented in several areas, including Minnesota.[38] Although there is no predilection to time of year in endemic areas, it is more common in animals after substantial rainfall following a period of drought.[39]

Populations at risk for naturally occurring anthrax are those in rural, agricultural areas who have ingested undercooked meat contaminated with anthrax spores. As with many other organisms, the pediatric population seems to be most at risk for serious or fatal illness.

Pathophysiology

Bacillus anthracis is a nonmotile, rodlike, gram-positive anaerobic bacillus that produces central oval-shaped spores. It is introduced into the food chain most often after ingestion by herbivores such as cattle. The animal usually becomes visibly ill, and the meat is often identifiable as abnormal after slaughter, preventing human exposure. Even when the meat reaches a consumer, adequate cooking usually reduces the inoculum to harmless levels. However, if the meat is undercooked, or the organism is intentionally introduced to food products, a high rate of infectivity results. Water-borne transmission has not been documented.

When swallowed, anthrax spores stick to the gastrointestinal epithelium, germinate, and create multiple superficial ulcerations. Lesions have been identified from the oral cavity to the cecum. The vegetative cells may, at times, migrate into the bloodstream, where they rapidly multiply and can cause septicemia. *Bacillus anthracis* protects itself with an antiphagocytic capsule and produces two exotoxins, lethal and edema toxins.

Clinical Presentation

A minority of patients who ingest anthrax remain asymptomatic, and, in endemic areas, adults are often thought to have some natural immunity through prior exposure. Of those who do develop symptoms, presentation can vary widely from mild watery diarrhea to fulminant upper and lower gastrointestinal bleeding, septicemia, and death. The incubation period for gastrointestinal symptoms varies from 1 to 6 days, with larger inocula and more severe disease developing earlier. For disease confined to the oropharynx, patients usually present with complaints of sore throat, fever, dysphagia, hoarseness, and painful neck swelling. The swelling results from marked lymphadenopathy and tissue edema and can become severe enough to compromise breathing.[37]

Much information concerning intestinal anthrax has been derived from two large outbreaks in Uganda and Thailand.[37] The majority of these patients presented with isolated diarrhea. A minority also developed nausea, vomiting, and severe abdominal pain with distension. Most patients are febrile above 39° C, and blood in both the vomitus and diarrhea is common.

Lesions throughout the gastrointestinal tract are often surrounded by significant edema and can lead to obstruction, necrosis, and perforation. Intra-abdominal lymphadenopathy and splenomegaly occur. The lymphatic tissue often becomes hemorrhagic, and ascites may form with fluid shifts large enough to cause shock and even death.

In cases of primary gastrointestinal anthrax, the superficial mucosa is always involved, with ulcerations visible on endoscopic examination. This is in contrast to disseminated infection from pulmonary anthrax, in which the lesions begin submucosally due to seeding from the bloodstream. These can then secondarily ulcerate to the surface of the gastrointestinal tract epithelium. Untreated, gastrointestinal anthrax may last weeks and can be, but is not always, fatal.

Diagnostic Strategies

Diagnosis of *B. anthracis* in cases of oropharyngeal disease is best made by swabbing the oral lesions for culture. Blood cultures are recommended for all suspected cases of anthrax but are usually negative in patients with isolated oropharyngeal involvement. A gram-stained smear from the lesions will demonstrate numerous polymorphonuclear leukocytes and gram-positive bacilli. In addition to culture, studies of serum antibody to anthrax antigens may confirm the diagnosis.

Diagnosis of the gastrointestinal variant of anthrax relies more on cultures obtained from blood and, if possible, ascitic fluid. Culture of the diarrheal stool yields positive results in a minority of cases. Serum antibody tests for anthrax antigens can again be helpful.

Differential Considerations

Oropharyngeal anthrax lesions are sometimes confused with paratonsillar abscess. The marked swelling of the lesions is secondary to edema and should not yield pus if incision and drainage are performed. Gastrointestinal anthrax can cause enough upper gastrointestinal bleeding to be confused with variceal rupture. Patients with marked ascites and abdominal pain may present similarly to those with end-stage liver disease with peritonitis.

Management

Traditionally, intravenous or intramuscular penicillin has been used to treat gastrointestinal anthrax. There are documented cases of penicillin resistance, however, and one must assume that a resistant strain would be chosen for use as a weapon of bioterrorism. Therefore, current recommendations from the CDC are to treat gastrointestinal cases in the same manner as cases of respiratory anthrax, with ciprofloxacin 400 mg IV every 12 hours or doxycycline 100 mg IV every 12 hours. Even with aggressive antibiotics, the disease carries a 4% to 40% rate of mortality, depending on host factors and the size of the inoculum.

TOXIN-INDUCED BACTERIAL GASTROENTERITIS (Table 93-3)

Staphylococcal Food Poisoning

Epidemiology

Staphylococcus-related food poisoning is caused by the multiplication of an enterotoxin-forming strain of *Staphylococcus* organisms in the food before ingestion. Food contamination with *Staphylococcus* is extremely common because the organism is ubiquitous in the environment. It can be isolated from the hands of approximately 50% of the population. Most protein-rich foods support the growth of *Staphylococcus*, especially ham, eggs (even hard-boiled), custard-filled pastries, mayonnaise, and potato salad.[3,40] Contaminated foods left at room temperature for only a few hours will allow proliferation of the organism and production of sufficient enterotoxin to cause disease. Foods containing sufficient enterotoxin to produce violent illness are usually normal in appearance, odor, and taste. Large outbreaks are common, particularly in institutions.[3,7,8]

Pathophysiology

Staphylococcus enterotoxin is heat-stable and, once it is present in food, reheating or even boiling will not

Table 93-3. Epidemiologic Aspects of Toxin-Induced Bacterial Enteritis

Pathogen	Sources	Incubation Period (I) and Duration (D) Untreated	Features
Preformed toxins			
Staphylococcus	Food handler related; potato salad, mayonnaise, confections	I: 1-6 hr D: 6-10 hr	Very high attack rates, large outbreaks
Bacillus cereus emetic toxin	Fried rice	I: 2-4 hr D: 10 hr	High attack rate, almost always fried rice
Bacillus cereus diarrheal toxin	Vegetables, meats, especially gravies	I: 6-14 hr D: 24-36 hr	Food reheated or sitting out for long periods
Scombroid	Mahimahi, tuna, bluefish	I: 5-60 min D: 6 hr	Peppery or bitter taste, histamine intoxication, high attack rates
Ciguatera	Large, predacious, coral reef fish	I: 2-6 hr D: 7-14 days	High attack rates, gastrointestinal and neurologic symptoms with paresthesias, hot/cold reversal, worse with alcohol
Toxins produced after colonization			
Clostridium perfringens	Meat, poultry, gravies, "steam table" meats	I: 6-24 hr D: 24 hr	Food reheated or sitting out for long periods
Vibrio	Seafood, especially raw shellfish	I: 24-48 hr D: 6-8 days	Summer months, dehydration common
Escherichia coli	Usually unsanitary drinking water	I: 24-72 hr D: 1-7 days	Travelers, dehydration common in children
Clostridium difficile	Overgrowth of normal flora	I: 5-14 days D: Variable	Antibiotic-associated colitis, cytopathic toxin
Aeromonas	Untreated drinking water	I: 1-5 days D: 2-10 wk	Common and severe in children, chronic watery diarrhea in adults, occasionally mimics inflammatory bowel disease

prevent illness. The toxin has no local effect on the digestive tract. It is absorbed, and symptoms are mediated by a direct effect of the absorbed toxin on the central nervous system. The disease can be reproduced by the parenteral injection of the enterotoxin.[40]

Clinical Presentation

The illness has an explosive onset, beginning 1 to 6 hours after ingestion of the contaminated food. Cramping and abdominal pain, with violent and often-repeated retching and vomiting, are the predominant symptoms. Diarrhea is variable; it is usually mild, occasionally absent entirely, and infrequently profuse. Fever is occasionally present. Staphylococcal food poisoning is short-lived, usually subsiding in 6 to 8 hours and rarely lasting as long as 24 hours. Patients are often recovering by the time they seek medical attention. Attack rates are very high, often greater than 75% of the population at risk.[40] The short incubation period and multiple cases in persons eating the same meal are highly suggestive of this disease. Examination of the stool is noncontributory, and no practical laboratory test is available to confirm the diagnosis. The epidemiologic circumstances, however, usually provide adequate suggestive evidence.

Management

Rapid, uncomplicated, spontaneous recovery is the rule. Parenteral antiemetic agents help control vomiting. Intravenous fluids to correct saline depletion are needed in 10% to 15% of patients, particularly in the young or debilitated. Antibiotics are of no value because staphylococcal food poisoning is caused by preformed enterotoxin and not by viable microorganisms. Strict personal hygiene of food handlers and immediate refrigeration of foods not due for immediate consumption are the most important preventive measures. Ordinary refrigerator temperatures prevent production of the enterotoxin. Food should not be allowed to stand at room temperature for long periods before being served.

Clostridium perfringens Food Poisoning

Epidemiology

Clostridium perfringens is probably the most common cause of acute food poisoning in the United States, constituting almost one fourth of all bacteria-associated food-borne illnesses. Most cases occur in large outbreaks and are caused by the ingestion of meat or poultry heavily contaminated with C. perfringens type A heat-resistant spores.[3,8,41] The organism is also ubiquitous in the environment and in human and animal feces. Typically, poisoning results from ingesting food that is cooked more than 24 hours before consumption, allowed to cool slowly at room temperature, and then served either cool or rewarmed. During this period of incubation, spores that survived cooking germinate, and clostridia grow to sufficient numbers to constitute an infectious inoculum.

Pathophysiology

Ingestion of live organisms is required to produce disease, but illness is not caused by infection; rather, it is from an enterotoxin produced by sporulation of the organism in the gastrointestinal tract. The enterotoxin is responsible for all the symptoms of *C. perfringens* food poisoning.

Clinical Presentation

Symptoms usually appear within 6 to 12 hours but can occur up to 24 hours after ingestion of the contaminated food. Frequent, watery diarrhea and moderately severe abdominal cramping are the major symptoms. Fever, nausea, and vomiting are rare. The illness is self-limited and rarely lasts for more than 24 hours.

Clostridium perfringens food poisoning should be considered in a patient who has an acute onset of abdominal cramps and diarrhea shortly after eating a suspect meat or poultry dish and when others who ate the same meal are similarly ill. Leukocytes and erythrocytes are not present on stool examination.

Complications

A rare type of *Clostridium* food poisoning, termed *enteritis necroticans,* occurs after the ingestion of foods heavily contaminated with the type C strain of *C. perfringens*. The illness is characterized by an acute onset of severe abdominal pain, vomiting, diarrhea, prostration, and shock and may be rapidly fatal. Postmortem examination reveals a diffuse, hemorrhagic, necrotizing enteritis of the jejunum, ileum, and colon.

Management

Occasionally, a patient will need intravenous fluid replacement. Antibiotics are of no value because of the natural history of the disease. Food poisoning from *C. perfringens* can be prevented by avoiding long periods of warming or cooling of foods that have already been cooked.

Bacillus cereus Food Poisoning

Epidemiology

Bacillus cereus is an aerobic, spore-forming, gram-positive rod that is a common cause of food-borne illness. The organism is ubiquitous in soil and in raw, dried, and processed food. As with other bacterial pathogens commonly isolated from raw foodstuffs and the environment, the disease is associated with improper food handling.[8]

B. cereus causes two distinct clinical syndromes: an emetic form produced by a heat-stable, *Staphylococcus*-like enterotoxin and a diarrheal form resulting from a heat-labile enterotoxin similar to that of *E. coli*. The emetic form is almost always caused by the ingestion of contaminated fried rice; the diarrheal syndrome is usually associated with meats or vegetables.[3,42]

Pathophysiology

Bacillus cereus is found in uncooked rice. Its heat-resistant spores survive boiling and then germinate when boiled rice is left unrefrigerated (a common practice in Chinese restaurants to avoid clumping of grain). The vegetative forms then multiply and produce toxin. Flash frying or brief rewarming before serving

is often not sufficient to destroy the preformed, heat-stable toxin. Spores also survive cooking, and if the food is left sitting at room temperature, they will germinate. The vegetative forms then grow and produce toxin.

Clinical Presentation

The emetic syndrome is clinically indistinguishable from that caused by staphylococcal enterotoxin. After an incubation period of 2 to 3 hours, profound vomiting and abdominal cramping occur in all patients. Diarrhea is present in approximately 25% to 30% of persons affected. The duration is short, usually less than 10 hours, and patients recover uneventfully.

The diarrheal syndrome begins after an incubation time of 6 to 14 hours and is characterized by diarrhea in all patients and by abdominal cramps in approximately 75%. Vomiting occurs in only 20% of cases. The duration of illness ranges from 20 to 36 hours. Symptoms are essentially the same as for food poisoning produced by *C. perfringens*, although vomiting is even less common with *C. perfringens*.

Bacillus cereus food poisoning should be suspected whenever an illness predominantly found in the upper gastrointestinal tract develops less than 6 hours after eating fried rice, or whenever a predominantly lower intestinal tract illness occurs 6 to 24 hours after a suspect meal, usually of meats or vegetables.

Diagnostic Strategies

Isolation of 10^5 or more organisms from incriminated foods confirms the diagnosis. Stool cultures are sometimes positive, but the organisms can also be present in the stools of healthy persons.[42]

Management

Both syndromes are generally mild and self-limited. Antibiotics are not indicated because symptoms are mediated by enterotoxins. Parenteral antiemetic agents effectively comfort patients presenting with violent vomiting. *B. cereus* food poisoning is preventable if boiled rice and other cooked foods are promptly eaten or refrigerated and not left to sit at room temperature.

Cholera and Noncholera Vibrios

Epidemiology

Other halophilic marine *Vibrio* species in addition to *V. parahaemolyticus* have shown a dramatic increase as a cause for acute gastroenteritis associated with seafood. Their epidemiology is identical to that of *V. parahaemolyticus:* ubiquitous in coastal seawater, outbreaks associated with the eating of raw or inadequately cooked shellfish, and an incidence markedly limited to the warmer months of the year.[21] Outbreaks of true cholera continue to occur sporadically along the Gulf coast of the United States from inadequately cooked crabs or oysters.[21] Cholera outbreaks in South America and India have led to an increasing number of cases of cholera imported into the United States.[43]

Pathophysiology

The difference between these species and *V. parahaemolyticus* lies in the mechanism of pathogenesis. *V. parahaemolyticus* produces disease directly by an invasive intestinal infection, whereas these strains produce an enterotoxin in vivo that is responsible for the diarrhea. Therefore, symptoms resemble those of other forms of enterotoxin-induced gastroenteritis and not those caused by invasive pathogens. The enterotoxin of the noncholera vibrio is antigenically similar to *V. cholerae* enterotoxin and produces a similar diarrheal illness, although it is much less severe.[21]

Clinical Presentation

Patients experience copious watery diarrhea, abdominal cramps, and often nausea and vomiting within 24 to 48 hours after ingesting contaminated seafood. Almost half lose enough fluids to require hospitalization. A low-grade fever may occur. The median duration of illness is approximately 7 days, quite unlike the 1- to 2-day course of *V. parahaemolyticus* infection.[21]

Another *Vibrio* species, *Vibrio vulnificus,* can produce an invasive gastroenteritis. *V. vulnificus* is also associated with eating raw seafood, especially raw oysters. Septicemia is common, and the mortality rate approaches 50% in patients with significant underlying diseases, particularly chronic liver disease.[24,25] Physicians should advise all patients with chronic liver disease, alcoholism, AIDS, other immunodeficiency states, and any significant chronic disease to avoid all raw shellfish.[24,25]

Diagnostic Strategies

Because these are noninvasive vibrios, unlike *V. parahaemolyticus,* stained fecal smears will not show leukocytes or erythrocytes. Stool cultures will quickly identify the organisms if plated on appropriate thiosulfate citrate bile salts sucrose medium.

Management

Most patients will lose enough fluids to require rehydration therapy. The World Health Organization oral rehydration formula has been used successfully to treat cholera worldwide.[43] In the emergency department, use of either oral or intravenous fluid hydration is dictated by the clinical picture. The role of antibiotics in the treatment of intestinal infections caused by noncholera vibrios is not clearly established. However, appropriate antibiotics have been shown to decrease both the severity and the duration of cholera and may have the same effect on the diarrheal disease caused by these marine vibrios.[21] Choices include a single oral dose of either ciprofloxacin, 1 g, or doxycycline, 300 mg, or 3 days of double-strength TMP-SMX twice a day. Prevention, as with *V. parahaemolyticus,* depends on proper handling and avoidance of inadequately cooked seafood. Cholera is a nationally reportable infection.

Scombroid Fish Poisoning

Epidemiology

Scombroid fish poisoning is a growing problem in the United States. The disease takes its name from the suborder Scombroidea (e.g., tuna, mackerel, and related species) and results from the ingestion of a wide variety of dark meat fish. The fish species most commonly implicated are mahimahi, tuna, and bluefish.[44] Restaurants serve these fish under various names such as mackerel, swordfish, bonito, dolphin, amberjack, or the generic "tuna salad sandwich."

Most cases occur in Hawaii and Florida, followed by California, New York, Washington, and Connecticut. However, scombroid poisoning can occur in any location where "fresh fish" are flown in on a regular basis.

Pathophysiology

Scombroid fish poisoning results from the ingestion of heat-stable toxins produced by bacterial action on the dark meat of the fish. The responsible bacteria are normal constituents of the surface marine flora of the fish rather than contaminants. The histidine decarboxylase activity of these organisms produces histamine and histamine-like substances, which cause the symptoms of scombroid fish poisoning. High levels of histamine in the fish correlate directly with the occurrence of the illness. Formation of the scombrotoxins is directly related to improper preservation and refrigeration of the fish from the time they are caught until the time they are cooked. Generally, the problem is caused by improper refrigeration by the supplier, rather than being the fault of the restaurant serving the fish.

Clinical Presentation

The symptoms of scombroid fish poisoning resemble those of histamine intoxication. While eating the fish, the patient may note a metallic, bitter, or peppery taste. Symptoms usually develop abruptly within 20 to 30 minutes and consist of facial flushing, diarrhea, severe, throbbing headache, palpitations, and abdominal cramps. Sometimes dizziness, dry mouth, nausea, vomiting, and urticaria also occur. The facial flushing resembles a sunburn and can extend over the entire skin surface. The conjunctivae are usually injected. The duration of the major symptom complex is generally less than 6 hours, and although weakness and fatigue persist longer, the clinical course is usually benign. The attack rate is very high; most persons sharing the same toxic fish will become ill.

Management

Parenteral antihistamine therapy, such as diphenhydramine, 50 mg, or cimetidine, 300 mg, intramuscularly or intravenously, usually promptly relieves all symptoms. Rarely, intravenous fluids are necessary. The disease is preventable if fish are properly handled, especially if they are refrigerated early and adequately. This is not an allergic reaction, so patients should not be told they are allergic to these fish, nor should they be prohibited from eating them again in the future.

Ciguatera Fish Poisoning

Epidemiology

Ciguatera fish poisoning is a common public health problem, with appreciable economic significance. It is endemic in tropical regions but is found worldwide. It is responsible for more than half of all fish-related food poisonings in the United States.[2,4] Fish caught around Hawaii and Florida cause the most cases, but because the responsible ocean fish are now commonly transported inland, cases can be seen virtually anywhere in the country.[45]

Ciguatoxin is produced by the marine dinoflagellate *Gambierdiscus toxicus,* which attaches itself to marine algae and is passed up the food chain. The lipid-soluble toxin accumulates in the tissues of the larger predacious coral reef fish, with the highest concentrations in the viscera and roe. It does not affect the fish in any way. Only humans suffer its ill effect when the toxin is ingested.

More than 400 fish species that frequent coral reefs have been implicated as ciguatoxin carriers, but fewer than 50 are commercially important species. Red snapper, grouper, amberjack, barracuda, sea bass, sturgeon, jack tuna, king mackerel, and moray eels are the most common carriers.[46,47]

Pathophysiology

Ciguatera fish poisoning results from the ingestion of the neurotoxin *ciguatoxin.* Ciguatoxin is heat and acid stable, odorless, and tasteless. It is not deactivated by cooking or freezing, nor is it eliminated by drying, salting, smoking, marinating, or pickling. It is not possible to predict whether a fish contains sufficient amounts of the toxin to produce illness.[46-48] Ciguatoxin has both anticholinesterase and cholinergic properties, but its toxicity is probably due to its inhibition of calcium regulation through passive cell membrane sodium channels.[46]

Clinical Presentation

Ciguatera fish poisoning is most commonly seen in the spring and summer months. The incubation period is approximately 2 to 6 hours, but a delay of 12 to 24 hours is not unusual. Attack rates are very high; 80% to 90% of those exposed become ill. Symptoms tend to be related to the amount of toxin ingested and vary considerably in their severity. If not fully recovered from an initial ingestion of ciguatoxin, a person is likely to have much more serious symptoms from a second ingestion.[46-48]

Classically, patients develop both gastrointestinal and neurologic symptoms. The gastrointestinal symptoms (e.g., nausea, vomiting, profuse watery diarrhea, crampy abdominal pain, and diaphoresis) tend to appear first. The constellation of neurologic symptoms consists largely of dysesthesias and paresthesias around the throat and the perioral area; "burning feet," which may resemble alcoholic peripheral neuropathy; "loose, painful teeth"; and sometimes central nervous system changes, such as ataxia, weakness, vertigo, visual hallucinations, and even confusion and coma.[47,49]

Distortion of temperature perception is vividly described by patients with ciguatera poisoning. Presenting as sensory reversal dysesthesia in which cold objects are perceived to be warm and vice versa, this symptom is highly suggestive of ciguatera fish as the source of illness. Another classic feature is either a return or a worsening of all the symptoms after ingestion of alcohol.[46-48]

Ciguatera poisoning lasts an average of 1 to 2 weeks, but at least half of its victims are still symptomatic at 8 weeks. The neurologic symptoms, particularly the paresthesias and dysesthesias, tend to persist longer than the gastrointestinal symptoms and have been reported up to years later. It can be a chronic, nagging problem.

Differential Considerations

Ciguatera fish poisoning should be strongly considered in patients with a combination of gastrointestinal and neurologic symptoms, particularly dysesthesias. Sensory reversal dysesthesia and marked worsening of the symptoms with alcohol ingestion are highly suggestive of ciguatera toxicity.

The disease is sometimes misdiagnosed as acute gastroenteritis with "hyperventilation syndrome" because of the combination of gastrointestinal symptoms and paresthesias, particularly when they occur about the mouth and acral areas. Similarly, ciguatera toxicity has sometimes been ascribed to malingering because the paresthesias are often transient and vague and lack traditional dermatome patterns.

Other disorders that should be considered include paralytic or neurotoxic shellfish poisoning, eosinophilic meningitis, botulism, organophosphate insecticide poisoning, and tetrodotoxin poisoning.[45,46]

Management

Treatment is primarily supportive. Intravenous fluids are given to replace volume losses from vomiting and diarrhea, and analgesics are given as needed. In severe cases, the toxin may display some anticholinesterase activity, manifested as bradycardia and hypotension, which can be treated with atropine and dopamine. Patients must be told to abstain from alcohol of any kind until symptoms have completely resolved.

Pruritus may be managed with an H_1 antagonist such as cetirizine at a dosage of 10 mg once daily. Amitriptyline, 25 mg bid, can bring about a dramatic reduction in both the pruritus and the dysesthesias, two of the most disturbing and protracted symptoms.

Dramatic recovery from ciguatera fish poisoning has been reported after the use of intravenous mannitol, 1 g/kg of a 20% solution infused over 30 minutes.[47,49] In all the patients, central nervous system manifestations were markedly reduced within minutes after mannitol infusion. These reports are as yet empiric and uncontrolled, and the mechanism of action is unclear; nevertheless, the use of mannitol should be considered in patients who are seriously ill from ciguatera fish poisoning.[47,49]

Enterotoxigenic *Escherichia coli*

Epidemiology

Enterotoxin-producing *E. coli* is recognized as a major cause of acute diarrheal disease throughout most of the world. In some U.S. cities, enterotoxin-producing *E. coli* has been responsible for 60% to 80% of moderate to severe cases of pediatric diarrheal disease. It is also a major cause of diarrhea in adults, particularly in persons traveling to underdeveloped areas, such as Mexico, the Middle East, Asia, and parts of the Mediterranean. The disease has been most intensely studied in North American visitors to Mexico, where it occurs in 40% to 60% of travelers studied, often incapacitating them or forcing a change in their plans.[50]

Infection is acquired from contaminated food or drink. Unpeeled fruits, leafy vegetables, unsanitary drinking water, and ice prepared from impure water are the most common sources. Most tourists are careful about their food and drink, but there seems to be a poor correlation between individual eating habits and the incidence of traveler's diarrhea.

Pathophysiology

For an *E. coli* strain to cause diarrhea, it must possess both a surface factor that allows colonization (although not invasion) of the small intestine and the ability to secrete an enterotoxin that causes the outpouring of fluids and electrolytes into the small bowel lumen. The enterotoxin-induced secretion occurs in the absence of any demonstrable histologic damage to intestinal epithelial cells or to the capillary endothelial cells.[2]

Escherichia coli produces both heat-labile and heat-stable toxins. The heat-labile enterotoxin causes secretion of water and electrolytes into the intestinal lumen by the stimulation of adenyl cyclase, which results in an increase in cyclic adenosine monophosphate. The heat-stable toxin probably exerts its effect through the stimulation of guanylate cyclase in mucosal cells and tends to have a more rapid onset of action. Either or both toxins can be produced by any enterotoxic strain of *E. coli.* The intestinal fluid losses are qualitatively identical to those in cholera and other toxigenic diarrheas.[2]

Clinical Presentation

After an incubation period of 24 to 72 hours, an abrupt onset of watery diarrhea follows. Severity varies from a fulminant, cholera-like disease to the much more common and milder *turista*, in which the symptoms of mild, watery diarrhea and abdominal cramps are more troublesome than life threatening. Fever is unusual. Vomiting occurs in fewer than half of affected adults and is seldom responsible for significant fluid losses. Even in severe cases, the diarrhea seldom lasts longer than 48 to 72 hours, and the response to either oral or intravenous fluids is uniformly good. Milder disease generally subsides more gradually, occasionally persisting for 1 week or longer.

Escherichia coli enterotoxin-induced disease should be suspected when a child or adult has frequent, watery diarrhea and few other symptoms. It is often passed off as "mild, nonspecific gastroenteritis" and resolves spontaneously. Anyone who acquires toxigenic diarrhea while visiting a developing nation probably has this disease. *E. coli* is by far the most common cause of traveler's diarrhea.

Diagnostic Strategies

No easy, rapid means of laboratory diagnosis of enteropathogenic *E. coli* exists because *E. coli* is part of the normal colonic flora, and its ability to produce enterotoxin is not restricted to any specific serotype. Stool preparations show no erythrocytes or leukocytes.

Management

Because this is almost always a self-limited disease, no treatment other than maintaining hydration is required. However, if the organism is identified while symptoms are still active, or if the patient is traveling in an endemic area, antibiotics can improve symptoms rapidly. For milder symptoms, a single dose of ciprofloxacin 750 mg by mouth in addition to loperamide should be effective. For more severe symptoms, TMP-SMX 160 and 800 mg or standard doses of a fluoroquinolone for 3 days should eradicate the organism.

Clostridium difficile Antibiotic-Associated Enterocolitis

Epidemiology

Severe colitis can occur as a result of oral or parenteral administration of several antimicrobial drugs, particularly clindamycin. Other antibiotics that have been associated with colitis include lincomycin, ampicillin, cephalosporins, tetracycline, penicillin, chloramphenicol, sulfa products, and erythromycin. *Clostridium difficile,* a toxin-producing bacterium, is the cause of antibiotic-induced colitis. Infection with this organism occurs primarily in adults. Patients with constipation and those treated with constipating agents, especially diphenoxylate hydrochloride (Lomotil), or narcotics are particularly prone to developing antibiotic-associated colitis. These conditions favor multiplication of the clostridia and a build-up of toxin in the colon.[51]

Many cases of *C. difficile* colitis are of nosocomial origin, transmitted among hospitalized patients by the hands of hospital personnel or from patient to patient. Up to 20% of inpatients acquire the organism, although only about a third become symptomatic.[51,52] Some nosocomial infections occur even in the absence of antibiotic therapy.[53]

Pathophysiology

The disease is unique in that an organism normally found in the colon causes illness only after the administration of antimicrobial agents. *C. difficile* bacteria proliferate when the normal bowel flora is substantially reduced by antibiotic therapy. The organisms must then produce sufficient quantities of a cytopathic toxin for the disease to occur. This cytopathic toxin destroys the colonic mucosa rather than inducing the secretion of fluids and electrolytes, as occurs with other types of toxin-induced diarrhea.[52]

The mucosa becomes hyperemic and edematous. Raised, yellowish-white plaques, loosely adherent to the mucosa, occur in patches, primarily in the rectosigmoid area, but can occur in any part of the colon. The disease was named *pseudomembranous enterocolitis* because of these pseudomembrane-like plaques.

Clinical Presentation

Symptoms may appear during the course of antimicrobial therapy or commonly up to 3 or 4 weeks after discontinuation of antibiotics. There are even reports of *C. difficile* producing illness as late as 6 months after completion of antibiotic therapy. Because the toxin alters the intestinal mucosa, the illness presents more like an invasive diarrhea than a toxigenic one. Typically, patients have fever, crampy abdominal pain, and watery, sometimes bloody diarrhea. Fecal leukocytes are generally but not invariably present. Children tend to have more severe infections than adults. The disease continues to have a significant rate of mortality.[7,53]

Diagnostic Strategies

Stool toxin assays are the primary method to diagnose *C. difficile* infection.[51,52,54] Although quite sensitive and specific, they require 48 to 72 hours for completion. Stool cultures can confirm the presence of *C. difficile* in the feces of patients with AAC. However, a positive stool culture is not diagnostic because *C. difficile* is often present in the feces of normal subjects or in persons receiving antibiotics who do not have an enteritis. Cultures are seldom used clinically but are often part of epidemiologic studies.[5,51,52] In patients with typical history and physical examination findings, a tentative diagnosis can be made by sigmoidoscopy or colonoscopy.

Differential Considerations

It is important to differentiate diarrhea with colitis from simple antibiotic-associated diarrhea. Three percent to 10% of all patients treated with antibiotics, particularly children, develop diarrhea not associated with *C. difficile* toxin. These patients experience mild, watery diarrhea and no associated constitutional symptoms or evidence of a cytopathic toxin–induced colitis.

Management

Many cases of antibiotic-associated colitis are self-limited, provided that the offending agent is discontinued. If discontinuing the antibiotic does not resolve the diarrhea, or if the diarrhea is severe, empiric antibiotic treatment should be started promptly to eradicate *C. difficile.* Either oral metronidazole or oral vancomycin can be used. The dosage of metronidazole is 250 mg PO four times daily for 10 to 14 days. Metronidazole is also effective when administered intravenously. The dose of vancomycin is 125 to 250 mg PO four times daily for 10 to 14 days, except in critically ill patients, for whom the recommended dosage is 500 mg PO four times daily for 10 to 14 days.[5,51,52] Patients significantly ill with colitis should be admitted to the hospital and started on both intravenous metronidazole and oral vancomycin.[53]

Vancomycin is generally not effective if given intravenously because it does not reach effective intraluminal concentrations. Because vancomycin is much more expensive than metronidazole and both seem to be equally effective, oral vancomycin is reserved for patients who do not respond to metronidazole therapy or for those who are extremely ill at the time of presentation.

Patients generally become afebrile and show clinical improvement within 36 to 72 hours; the diarrhea resolves over 5 to 7 days, even though toxin assays and stool cultures may remain positive for weeks. Five percent to 55% (average 25%) of patients suffer a relapse regardless of the antibiotic chosen, its dosage, or the duration of treatment. Nearly all of these patients will respond to another course of antibiotic therapy.[5,52]

Adding the yeast *Saccharomyces boulardii,* 500 mg PO twice daily for 4 weeks, to antibiotic treatment has been shown to dramatically decrease the number of recurrences of *C. difficile*–associated disease in patients with previous episodes. However, no benefit results are seen when *S. boulardii* is given to patients with an initial episode.[5,55] No serious adverse reactions have occurred with the use of *S. boulardii.*[55]

Although toxicity from parenteral vancomycin is common, no adverse effects have been reported with its oral use in the treatment of *C. difficile* colitis. Antimotility or constipating agents are contraindicated in these patients because of the risk of toxic megacolon and the possibility of increasing the level of cytopathic toxin in the colon.

ACUTE VIRAL GASTROENTERITIS

Etiology and Epidemiology

Viral gastroenteritis is the second leading cause of illness in the United States. Although several virus families have been implicated, including caliciviruses, coronaviruses, and parvoviruses, two have predominated in the last decade. Noroviruses, which include the Norwalk virus, are primarily responsible for disease in adults and older children, whereas human reovirus–like agents, also called *rotaviruses,* cause most diarrheal disease in infants and young children. Rotaviruses also cause epidemics in adults, especially those in contact with sick children, such as parents and hospital personnel.[56,57]

These viruses have a low infectious dose, and attack rates may reach 50%. The incubation period is short, so explosive outbreaks are common. Norovirus is transmitted by several routes and is relatively stable in the environment, making it particularly prone to spread.[58] Both viruses can be transmitted from person to person by the fecal-oral route, but water- or food-borne outbreaks are also common. Large outbreaks of norovirus infection have occurred from municipal or semipublic water sources, recreational swimming, stored water on cruise ships, cafeteria sandwiches, food handlers, or shellfish.[59] The ingestion of raw oysters has caused many large outbreaks.[59] Nosocomial spread of infection is also common.[60] Astrovirus and picornaviruses are common causes of diarrhea in HIV-infected patients.[57,61]

Pathophysiology

Viruses distort the absorptive cells of the microvilli of the small bowel, decreasing their absorptive surface and causing diarrhea from decreased absorption of fluid and electrolytes. The histologic picture resembles tropical sprue, and transient malabsorption of fats and sugars, which may persist for a week or more after infection, occurs in patients with viral gastroenteritis.[57]

Virus-induced diarrheal stools contain more sodium, chloride, and bicarbonate than normal stools, but this is not comparable to the almost isotonic fluid loss of bacterial toxin–induced diarrhea. Potassium loss is usually not significant unless symptoms are prolonged.

Clinical Presentation

Viral gastroenteritis occurs primarily in two epidemiologically distinct clinical forms. Outbreaks caused by rotaviruses are usually sporadic, are occasionally epidemic, and typically occur in the winter months in infants and children 6 to 24 months of age. The incubation period is 24 to 72 hours, followed by an abrupt onset of vomiting, watery diarrhea, and low-grade fever, but little or no associated abdominal pain. Vomiting is a prominent and constant early manifestation of rotavirus enteritis but rarely persists beyond the first 36 hours. The diarrhea generally lasts for 4 to 7 days and may be followed by steatorrhea in approximately 20% to 40% of patients. Many children become significantly dehydrated, requiring hospitalization and intravenous fluid replacement, but the disease is rarely life threatening.

Overt clinical disease can occur among family and adult contacts of ill children, but it is uncommon. Most adults with rotavirus infections are asymptomatic. When symptoms do occur, they are usually mild, perhaps because these episodes are reinfections; 60% to 90% of older children and adults have antibodies to rotaviruses.[56,57]

The second clinical entity is characteristically epidemic and is responsible for family and community-wide outbreaks of gastroenteritis among school-age children, family contacts, and adults. This form is generally caused by the Norwalk virus. After an incubation period of 20 to 36 hours, diarrhea, nausea, and mild abdominal cramps occur. Vomiting is not prominent. Fever is generally absent. Anorexia, headache, malaise, and myalgias may be present. The illness is self-limited, usually lasting only 24 to 48 hours. Generally, most adults have mild symptoms, and most do not seek medical attention.[56,57]

Diagnostic Strategies

The diagnosis of rotavirus gastroenteritis should be considered in children with significant vomiting, diarrhea, low-grade fever, moderate dehydration, and a normal white blood cell count, especially in those 6 to 24 months old who become symptomatic during the winter months. An elevated blood urea nitrogen level and a compensated metabolic acidosis are common findings. Serum electrolytes indicate that the dehydration is usually isotonic.

In adults, the diagnosis of viral gastroenteritis is usually one of exclusion. The physician diagnoses viral enteritis when a patient has mild intestinal symptoms, the patient does not appear ill, and further history and physical examination uncover no reason to suspect a bacterial pathogen, inflammatory disease, or any other cause. No investigation beyond the physical examination is usually required. Some patients may have mild bacterial infections, but these are also generally self-limited, and treatment is not different.

A laboratory diagnosis can be made by demonstration of the viruses in stools by electron microscopy or various methods used for the detection of viral antigens, such as counterimmunoelectrophoresis or enzyme-linked immunoabsorbent assay. With rotavirus illness, large numbers of viruses are present in the stools, and these antigen detection methods are quite sensitive. Specific Rotazyme testing is probably indicated only in more serious cases of diarrhea. Fecal leukocytes and erythrocytes are not found in cases of viral gastroenteritis.[57]

Management

The most important aspect of therapy for acute viral gastroenteritis is fluid replacement. Many children require hospitalization, with intravenous fluid and electrolyte repletion. No specific antiviral therapy is indicated. Antidiarrheal agents are not recommended in children. In adults, they are generally not needed but may provide some symptomatic relief. Because viral spread is primarily by the fecal-oral route, scrupulous hand washing and other hygienic practices are the best preventive measures.

PROTOZOAN GASTROINTESTINAL INFECTION (Table 93-4)

Coccidia: *Cryptosporidium* and *Isospora belli*

Epidemiology

Cryptosporidium and *Isospora* are intestinal protozoan parasites that commonly cause diarrhea in the young of many animal species such as cattle, lambs, pigs, goats, cats, dogs, chickens, and birds. In humans, cryptosporidiosis is a worldwide problem, most often seen in persons who handle animals, children in daycare centers, healthy homosexual men, and immunocompromised patients.[62,63] *Cryptosporidium* is the most common cause of chronic diarrhea in persons with

Table 93-4. Epidemiologic Aspects of Protozoan Gastroenteritis

Pathogen	Sources	Incubation Period (I)	Features
Entamoeba histolytica	Fecally contaminated food and water sources	3 wk to 4 mo	Infection may be commensal or intermittently symptomatic or produce severe dysentery
Giardia lamblia	Water-borne, fecal-oral, daycare centers, travelers, backpackers, AIDS, homosexual men	1-3 wk	5-10% of U.S. population, malabsorption syndromes or commensal
Coccidia			
Cryptosporidium and *Isospora*	Fecal-oral, water-borne, animals, daycare centers, AIDS	5-10 days	Profuse watery diarrhea, self-limited in the immunocompetent, persistent in the immunocompromised
Cyclospora cayetanensis	Fresh fruit, berries, lettuce, water supply	1 wk	Explosive, protracted, watery diarrhea; fatigue, weight loss
Strongyloides stercoralis	Occupational exposure to soil, travel to endemic areas in United States (Kentucky, Tennessee, Ohio) or overseas	Weeks to months	Eosinophilia, sepsis, and hyperinfection syndrome in AIDS patients
Enteromonas hominis	Fecal-oral, homosexual men	?	Chronic watery diarrhea, especially in children

AIDS, acquired immunodeficiency syndrome.

AIDS.[13,14] Congenital immunodeficiency and treatment with cancer chemotherapeutics or other immunosuppressive drugs are also predisposing factors. The organism is highly infectious and is easily transmitted. Nosocomial spread, household contact infections, and large outbreaks in daycare centers or in other facilities where personal hygiene is poor occur commonly.[63] In addition to zoonotic spread and person-to-person spread, indirect transmission occurs by exposure to fecally contaminated environmental surfaces, toys, food, and recreational water venues such as community swimming pools, water parks, decorative fountains, hot tubs, and spas.[17] *Cryptosporidium* oocysts are highly resistant to chlorine and common disinfectants. Large outbreaks have originated from community swimming pools.[64]

The oocysts are also small (2 to 6 μm) and may not be removed from contaminated water by standard filtration systems used in the treatment of public water supplies. Cases have been reported of thousands of people contracting cryptosporidiosis from contamination of filtered public water systems that meet federal and state standards for drinking water.[65] Contamination of rivers and streams by *Cryptosporidium* has been reported in a number of states.[11] In children, cryptosporidiosis is more common in the late summer and early fall and is often associated with intestinal infection from other organisms, particularly *Giardia*.

Isosporiasis is generally an opportunistic infection. It occurs primarily in patients with AIDS, especially Haitians with AIDS, and in homosexual men. In the homosexual community, isosporiasis is a sexually transmitted disease similar to giardiasis and amebiasis.[66,67]

Pathophysiology

The pathophysiology is the same for both coccidial organisms. Disease is acquired by ingestion of oocysts. Excystation occurs, and trophozoites and all other developmental stages are found only at the surface of the intestinal epithelial membranes; no tissue invasion occurs. Profuse fluid loss results from a combination of enterotoxin-induced secretions and malabsorption. In cryptosporidiosis, a biliary reservoir may contribute to the chronicity of the infection and the inability to eradicate the organism.[63]

Clinical Presentation

The clinical presentations of cryptosporidiosis and isosporiasis are indistinguishable. After an incubation period of approximately 1 week, symptoms may develop insidiously or suddenly. Infection is characterized by profuse watery diarrhea, crampy abdominal pain, anorexia, nausea, malaise, weight loss, and flatulence. The diarrhea and abdominal pain are often exacerbated by eating. Immunocompromised patients can have enormous stool fluid losses: 3 to 4 L/day is common, and losses may reach 10 to 20 L/day. Physical examination usually reveals only signs of dehydration. Minimal diffuse abdominal tenderness may be present, and fever and leukocytosis are uncommon. Eosinophilia does not occur. Stool examinations for blood or fecal leukocytes are almost uniformly negative in adults but occasionally are positive in children.[17,20,63]

The patient's immune status is the primary determinant of whether the infection is self-limited or persistent. Diarrhea in immunocompetent persons usually resolves after 1 to 3 weeks, but it can continue longer or become chronic. In immunodeficient patients, especially those with AIDS, chronic, persistent diarrhea is common, causing significant discomfort and morbidity unless the infection is responsive to treatment.[13,14,67]

Asymptomatic infections can occur from either *Cryptosporidium* or *Isospora,* and a carrier state has been demonstrated for *Cryptosporidium.*[67] In one U.S. study of immunocompetent patients who underwent upper endoscopy for a variety of reasons, 13% were found to harbor cryptosporidia in the second portion of the duodenum. None of the patients had diarrhea.

Diagnostic Strategies

The diagnosis of either coccidial infection is made by documenting the oocysts in the stool. Acid-fast stains are the current preferred method; they are fast, simple, inexpensive, and reliable. Yeasts are morphologically similar to coccidia but are not acid fast. Patients with diarrhea from *Cryptosporidium* generally excrete large numbers of oocysts continually, so the organism can be readily identified in the stools by experienced examiners. *Isospora* oocysts, however, can be shed only intermittently and in much smaller numbers, so multiple stool samples often must be obtained and concentrated to successfully identify this parasite.[66,68]

Management

In immunocompetent persons, *Cryptosporidium* infection is generally self-limited; symptomatic therapy and fluid replacement are sufficient. No proven effective antibiotic treatment has been found for cryptosporidiosis.[5,63,69] Immunocompetent patients shed oocysts in the stools when symptomatic and continue shedding oocysts for up to 6 weeks after resolution of their clinical illness, creating a public health risk.[62]

Treatment of cryptosporidiosis in immunocompromised patients is usually ineffective. The most successful interventions occur when the underlying immunodeficiency can be reversed. Patients taking immunosuppressive agents generally recover if the drugs can be discontinued. Patients with AIDS usually continue to have significant watery diarrhea until death. Prostaglandin inhibitors, such as indomethacin, may decrease the secretory diarrhea.[70] Aggressive treatment of human immunodeficiency virus (HIV) infection with antiretroviral regimens is probably the best treatment for *Cryptosporidium* diarrhea in patients with AIDS because it directly enhances host defenses and immunity by suppression of HIV replication.[63] Patients severely infected with *Cryptosporidium* are often incontinent and have large numbers of infectious oocysts in their feces, so strict enteric precautions are necessary to prevent nosocomial spread. If enhancing the immune system fails and symptoms continue to be severe, nitazoxanide 0.5 to 1 g twice daily combined with antidiarrheals has had limited effect. Paromomycin (Humatin, 500 to 750 mg three or four times daily) is also sometimes used to ameliorate cryptosporidiosis, particularly in combination with azithromycin, but no good evidence exists that any drug is routinely effective.[5,69,71,72]

In contrast to cryptosporidiosis, isosporiasis responds promptly to antibiotic therapy. The treatment of choice for isosporiasis in immunocompetent adults is TMP-SMX 160 mg/800 mg twice daily for 10 days. In immunocompromised adults, the dosage is increased to four times daily for 10 days and then extended twice daily for 3 weeks. In patients with sulfonamide sensitivity, pyrimethamine 50 to 75 mg daily may be effective.[66] Chronic suppressive therapy with either twice-daily doses of TMP-SMX or daily doses of pyrimethamine is often required because *Isospora* infection recurs in more than 50% of patients.[66,67]

Patients seen in the emergency department whose examination for parasites later reveals *Cryptosporidium* or *Isospora* should be contacted. Recovering patients need only have the diagnosis and its ramifications explained to them. Patients who are not recovering, and those who are known or thought to be immunosuppressed, should have appropriate treatment and follow-up arranged. Cryptosporidiosis is a notifiable disease.

Coccidia: *Cyclospora cayetanensis*

Epidemiology

Cyclospora is a coccidian parasite widely distributed throughout the world that produces disease very similar to that caused by *Cryptosporidium* and *Isospora*. It is acquired from contaminated foods, primarily fresh fruit, raspberries and other berries, lettuce, and contaminated water supplies.[73-75] It is occasionally the cause of traveler's diarrhea. It infects all classes of vertebrates, reptiles, and rodents, and the vast majority of cases occur during the spring and summer seasons, often in large outbreaks.[72,75] The average incubation period is 1 week.[76]

Pathophysiology

The exact mode of *Cyclospora* transmission and mechanism of disease is unclear. The organism is ingested in the oocyst stage, sporulates in the gut, and produces an explosive watery diarrhea. The histologic picture looks similar to that of tropical sprue, but it is unknown whether symptoms are toxin induced or secondary to direct infection of the small bowel.[76]

Clinical Presentation

Typically, the patient presents with an acute onset of explosive watery diarrhea and abdominal cramps. Constitutional symptoms are relatively mild, and fever is uncommon. The disease is generally self-limited in immunocompetent hosts but may last as long as 2 to 3 weeks, and relapsing diarrhea is common. Sustained fatigue and weight loss are common.[73,75,76]

Diagnostic Strategies

The clinical picture may be suggestive, but finding the oocysts in the stools confirms the diagnosis. Fecal leukocytes are absent. The oocysts measure 8 to 10 μm in diameter and are difficult to distinguish from *Cryptosporidium*. In fact, the CDC will not accept the diagnosis unless confirmation is made by an experienced reference laboratory. In some studies, the disease was misdiagnosed in up to 70% of cases, creating "pseudo-outbreaks." Health departments that identify *Cyclospora* infection should contact the CDC's Parasitic Division for confirmation.[73,74]

Differential Considerations

The primary confusing organism is *Cryptosporidium* because the symptoms of infection with the two entities are often indistinguishable. *Cryptosporidium* tends to be associated with animal contact, daycare centers, and immunocompromised patients. *Isospora* and *Aeromonas hydrophila* infections should also be considered in the differential diagnosis.

Management

The disease tends to be self-limited in immunocompetent persons, but treatment with sulfa medications is very effective for cyclosporiasis, unlike treatment for cryptosporidiosis.

The drug of choice is double-strength TMP/SMX one tablet twice daily for 7 days in immunocompetent patients, and one tablet four times daily for 10 days and then one tablet three times per week in AIDS patients. The pediatric dose is TMP 5 mg/kg plus SMX 25 mg/kg twice daily for 7 days. Thorough washing of fresh produce before consumption decreases, but does not eliminate, the risk of transmission. Irradiation may be a future solution.[5,73,74,76] Cyclosporiasis is a reportable disease.

Giardiasis

Epidemiology

Giardia is the most common cause of water-borne diarrheal outbreaks in the United States.[23,68,77] The mode of transmission in large outbreaks is contamination of municipal water supplies with cyst-infested feces from humans or animals, particularly beavers or muskrats, but also dogs, raccoons, and other animals. Campers and backpackers commonly acquire giardiasis, called "backpackers' diarrhea," from drinking fecally contaminated water from the "pristine mountain streams."[68] Only rarely is *Giardia* infection communicated by contaminated food.

Giardia can be spread by sexual or other close person-to-person contact in which fecal contamination may occur, particularly among homosexual men, and in daycare centers and institutions for the mentally challenged. The prevalence is 5% to 10% in the general U.S. population, 5% to 25% in homosexual men, and 25% to 30% in children in daycare centers.[68]

Many cases of acute symptomatic giardiasis in the United States are found in persons returning home from travel elsewhere. Travelers to any underdeveloped country can acquire giardiasis, but it is especially common in those who visit the republics of the former Soviet Union, the Caribbean states, and Latin America, where the water supplies appear to be heavily contaminated with *Giardia* cysts.[50] Visitors to the former Soviet Union, particularly the city of Leningrad, experience attack rates approaching 60%, and the disease is ruefully known among its victims as "the Trotskys."[78,79]

Patients with decreased gastric acidity, for any reason, are more susceptible to *Giardia* infection. Giardiasis is also more frequent in patients with various immunoglobulin deficiencies; a relative deficiency of intestinal IgA may be the reason.

Pathophysiology

Giardia trophozoites infect the duodenum, jejunum, and upper ilium. Encystation occurs in the gut lumen, and cysts passed in the feces remain viable for long periods. After the cysts are ingested by the next host, excystation to the active trophozoites occurs in the proximal small bowel, completing the life cycle. The trophozoites multiply rapidly. A single diarrheal stool may contain billions of parasites or hundreds of millions of cysts. The trophozoites are capable of superficial invasion of the mucosa, but malabsorption probably causes most symptoms.

Clinical Presentation

Most patients harboring *Giardia* are asymptomatic. The most common symptoms of acute infection are abdominal distention, colicky pain with audible borborygmi, flatulence, and frequent stools that are pale, loose, explosive, and often offensive smelling. The onset is usually sudden and follows an incubation period of 1 to 3 weeks. It can persist or be chronically intermittent and produce a malabsorption-like illness, particularly in patients with an immunoglobulin deficiency.

Diagnostic Strategies

Routine tests (e.g., blood counts, electrolytes, or radiographic studies) are generally not helpful. Eosinophilia does not occur. Stool examination is the primary means of diagnosis. In the acute phase of *Giardia* infection, rapid bowel transit allows trophozoites as well as the more hardy cystic form of the parasite to appear in the stool. Trained observers using standard stool examination techniques will readily identify *Giardia* in more than 95% of acute cases if three or more stool specimens are studied. Detecting *Giardia* in cases of subacute, chronic, or asymptomatic infection, however, can be difficult. The trophozoites may be passed only intermittently and in small numbers. Concentration techniques should be used to improve the chances of finding the cysts in the stools. Diagnosis may require small bowel sampling techniques such as duodenal-jejunal aspiration by endoscopy or duodenal-jejunal biopsies. Stool antigen tests can also be diagnostic.[79]

Differential Considerations

Enteromonas hominis, a flagellate parasite like *Giardia,* can produce an intestinal infection that mimics giardiasis. *Enteromonas* is found most commonly in children and homosexual men. Even when all techniques fail to confirm a clinically suspected case of giardiasis, an empiric diagnosis can be supported by a successful trial of appropriate antibiotics.

Management

All patients harboring *Giardia* should be treated, even if they are asymptomatic. Asymptomatic cyst passers, especially children and food handlers, pose a threat of infection to others and are at risk of developing intermittent chronic symptoms.[79] The treatment of choice in both asymptomatic and symptomatic patients is metronidazole 250 mg three times daily for 5 days for adults and 5 mg/kg three times daily (maximum

250 mg three times daily) for 5 days for children.[5,79] Furazolidone is the only alternative drug available as a suspension, which may be helpful in treating children. However, its cure rates average only 80%. The recommended dosage is 100 mg four times daily for adults or 1.5 mg/kg four times daily for children, up to the adult dose, for a total of 7 to 10 days. Nausea and vomiting are common side effects, and rarely a hemolytic anemia occurs in patients with glucose-6-phosphate dehydrogenase deficiency.[5,79]

Giardiasis must be considered a family infection. To prevent reinfections, other household members and sexual contacts should be examined and, if found to harbor the parasite, treated appropriately.[79]

Acute Intestinal Amebiasis

Epidemiology

Entamoeba histolytica is a ubiquitous organism infecting at least 10% of the world's population but originally thought to cause clinical disease in only 10% of those who carry it. This number is probably an underestimate, however; recent studies have confirmed the presence of a morphologically indistinguishable ameba, *E. dispar*, as a separate nonpathogenic species that also colonizes the human gut and is probably responsible for the majority of asymptomatic infections originally attributed to *E. histolytica*. Distinguishing the two organisms can be accomplished through enzyme-linked immunosorbent assay or polymerase chain reaction evaluation, with polymerase chain reaction testing slightly more reliable.[80] High-risk groups include travelers, homosexual men, patients with AIDS, and institutionalized persons. Most cases acquired in the United States are asymptomatic; acute amebic dysentery is rare and most often occurs in travelers returning from underdeveloped countries where the disease is endemic.[81]

Entamoeba histolytica exists in trophozoite and cystic forms. The trophozoites infect the colon and may produce symptomatic disease. Infectious cysts are passed in the feces and are highly resistant to environmental factors. Transmission is usually from ingestion of cysts present in fecally contaminated food or water. Homosexual men commonly acquire amebic infection from cysts ingested through anal-oral sexual practices. When these patients present with diarrhea, a diligent search for other organisms should be completed before ascribing symptoms to amebas. Co-infection with other enteric pathogens occurs frequently in homosexual men.[13,14]

Pathophysiology

The factors that determine whether infection with *E. histolytica* will be commensal or invasive are poorly understood. Variable strain virulence and host susceptibility are determinants. In young children, pregnant women, persons with malnutrition or underlying systemic disease, or persons taking corticosteroids, amebiasis is often more fulminant.[82]

Invasive trophozoites characteristically produce colonic ulcerations that have rounded or punched-out margins and are elevated by a submucosal inflammatory reaction from the advancing trophozoites. The bases of the ulcers are covered with whitish or yellowish exudate. Usually, no diffuse mucosal inflammation exists between ulcers. However, should diffuse inflammation occur, the picture becomes indistinguishable from that of idiopathic ulcerative colitis or Crohn's disease. Less than 1% of infections will spread outside the intestines. Complications can include liver and brain infection, as well as pleural or pericardial effusions.[83]

Clinical Presentation

In many patients, *E. histolytica* lives commensally without producing symptoms. Acute amebic dysentery follows an incubation period as short as 1 week or as long as 1 year. The onset is abrupt, with fever; severe abdominal cramps; profuse, bloody diarrhea; and tenesmus. Chronic amebic dysentery is the common symptomatic form. The onset is gradual. Usually, intermittent diarrhea is present with two to four foul-smelling stools daily, often containing blood-streaked mucus. Vague abdominal cramps, flatulence, weight loss, and low-grade fever are present. Symptomatic periods may alternate with asymptomatic periods lasting for months to years. The only physical finding may be slight right lower quadrant tenderness and occasional tender hepatomegaly. The diagnosis is elusive because cysts or trophozoites are difficult to detect.

The stools of patients with symptoms contain mucus and leukocytes, although not in large numbers. Eosinophilia does not occur except in rare cases of ameboma. Liver function test results are generally normal unless the disease is complicated by liver abscess, which is the most common serious complication of amebic colitis.[81]

Diagnostic Strategies

Definitive diagnosis of intestinal amebiasis depends on laboratory identification of the organisms in the stools. Polymerase chain reaction testing can then distinguish *E. histolytica* from *E. dispar*. The stools must be examined before the administration of antibiotics, antidiarrheal agents, antacids, or enemas, or performing radiographic procedures using barium sulfate. All of these agents destroy trophozoites or distort cysts and thus interfere with the recovery of amebas. A rectal biopsy or mucosal exudate obtained at sigmoidoscopy may reveal the amebas, even when multiple previous stool examinations have been negative. To obtain mucosal exudate, a glass or metal pipette must be used because amebas adhere to cotton swabs.

Serologic tests are quite sensitive and specific for active amebic infection. Because administration of steroids to patients with amebic colitis is potentially fatal, and identification of the parasite in stools is difficult, a serologic test for amebiasis should be done in all newly diagnosed cases of inflammatory bowel disease before initiation of steroid therapy.[84]

Differential Considerations

Amebiasis should always be considered in cases of acute dysentery-like colitis and in the differential diagnosis of any chronic diarrhea, especially when the feces contain blood-streaked mucus. Amebiasis should also be suspected in homosexual men with acute colitis. Patients with AIDS, however, rarely develop amebic dysentery.[13,85] Patients with nondysenteric amebiasis are often misdiagnosed as having irritable bowel syndrome, diverticulitis, or regional enteritis.

Management

Substantial controversy existed over whether asymptomatic cyst passers should be treated. However, given that it is now possible to distinguish between nonpathogenic *E. dispar* and *E. histolytica*, it is possible to make an accurate diagnosis and prudent to treat *E. histolytica*, even in all asymptomatic carriers. If only *E. dispar* is identified, treatment is unnecessary. When differentiation is not possible and the patient is asymptomatic, treatment is not recommended unless there is an increased likelihood for *E. histolytica*. Such would be the case for patients with high specific antibody titers, a history of close contact with a patient with invasive amebiasis, or a patient with symptoms in the face of an outbreak of amebiasis. In symptomatic patients who are diagnosed with *E. histolytica/E. dispar* infection, other pathogens should be ruled out before assuming *E. histolytica* as the cause.[86]

For treatment of benign cyst passers, aminosidine (Paromomycin) 500 mg by mouth three times a day for 7 days should be effective. Other therapy includes oral iodoquinol 650 mg PO three times a day for 20 days, or diloxanide furoate 500 mg PO three times a day for 10 days. For mild to moderate intestinal infection, metronidazole is added (see Table 93-2).[5] Treatment with metronidazole should precede treatment with aminosidine. Aminosidine can cause diarrhea as a side effect, making it difficult to assess the patient's response to the metronidazole if both are given together.[87] Patients with severe infections and systemic illness such as dehydration or hypotension should be hospitalized. Therapy is usually effective, but relapses can occur. Standard precautions to prevent fecal-oral spread are the best preventive measures.

Enterobiasis

Epidemiology

Enterobius vermicularis, also known as *pinworm* or *seatworm,* is perhaps the most prevalent parasite in the United States. It is estimated that 20% to 30% of all children are infected with pinworms; 200 million people are infected annually wordwide, 40 million in the United States alone. Adult worms are small, spindle-shaped, white to yellowish round worms that live in the cecum and adjacent portions of the large and small bowel. The female averages 10 mm in length, and the male is 3 mm. The gravid female migrates through the anal canal at night and oviposits her eggs (usually more than 10,000) onto the perineal area. The eggs become infective larvae 4 to 6 hours after deposition and, once ingested, the larvae are released in the small intestine and migrate down to the cecum. Approximately 1 month from the time of ingestion, newly developed, gravid females are again discharging eggs.[68]

The human body is the only natural host of *E. vermicularis.* The most common means of infection, particularly in children, is by the direct transfer of eggs from the anus to the mouth by way of contaminated fingers. Retrograde infection, which happens primarily in adults, may sometimes occur. In this situation, larvae hatch in the perineal region, re-enter the anus, and migrate to the cecum. Spread within family and children's groups occurs readily, either by direct transfer of eggs or by airborne transmission. The eggs, which are relatively resistant to desiccation, also contaminate night clothes and bed linens, where they remain viable and infective for 2 to 3 weeks.

Pathophysiology

Because *E. vermicularis* does not penetrate the mucosa, there are no anatomic lesions. The movement of the worms or the presence of the eggs on the perineum usually causes local tingling or itching. Scratching causes irritation of the skin, which can lead to excoriations, eczematous dermatitis, and secondary bacterial infections. In women, gravid female worms can migrate through the vagina and uterus into the fallopian tubes, where they may evoke vaginitis, endometritis, or salpingitis. Young girls with pinworms may have a much higher incidence of urinary tract infections than persons not infected.[68]

Clinical Presentation

The most common symptom is pruritus ani. This usually occurs at night in relation to the nocturnal migration and oviposition. Scratching may lead to secondary skin changes and bacterial infection. Restlessness, insomnia, and enuresis are probably a result of the pruritus.

Diagnostic Strategies

Adult worms may be recognized in the perineal area, and in suspected cases nocturnal examination of this area using a flashlight may confirm infection. Worms can sometimes also be seen on the surface of stool. The most reliable way to diagnose infection is to examine material taken from the perineal area for ova. The cellophane tape test is simple and reliable. The tape is folded, sticky side out, over the end of a tongue blade, pressed firmly against the perineal area, and then spread on a glass slide with toluene and examined under the low power of a microscope. The typical eggs are identified easily.

A single cellophane tape test will detect approximately 50% of infections. If done daily for 3 days, the test will detect 90% of infections; after 5 days, it will detect 99%. Examining stool specimens for ova is rarely helpful, but scrapings from under the fingernails may reveal the ova.[68] Eosinophilia is not found because the worm does not have a tissue phase.

Management

All infected individuals in a family or communal group should be treated simultaneously. It is the usual accepted practice to treat empirically all other members of the same group at the same time, even if they are not infected. The drugs of choice are albendazole, 400 mg by mouth once, mebendazole (Vermox), a single oral dose of 100 mg chewed well, or pyrantel pamoate (Antiminth), a single oral dose of 11 mg/kg (maximum 1 g). With all of the treatments, a second dose should be administered 2 weeks later. The repeat dose is needed because mature worms seem to be more vulnerable than young worms. Although the maturation process takes 1 to 2 months, a second dose is effective in eradicating all stages of the life cycle in 90% to 95% of infections.[5]

The ease of airborne dissemination of the eggs, their resistance to desiccation, and the poor hygienic practices of children increases the likelihood of reinfection. Ova are also resistant to ordinary fumigants and disinfectants, making control in schools, institutions, and the home very difficult.

Miscellaneous Protozoan Infections

Infections with other parasites appear to be increasing in the United States, primarily as a result of widespread international travel and the AIDS epidemic. Substantial increases have been noted with *Strongyloides stercoralis*, *E. hominis*, and *Blastocystis hominis* (Table 93-5).[13,14]

DIARRHEA IN PATIENTS WITH AIDS

Epidemiology

Diarrhea is the most common manifestation of gastrointestinal disease in patients with AIDS and may be the presenting symptom or a life-threatening compli-

Table 93-5. Causes of Diarrhea in Patients with AIDS

Frequency	Organism
Most common	*Cryptosporidium*
	Cytomegalovirus
Common	*Entamoeba histolytica* (probably commensal, not causative)
	Giardia lamblia
	Mycobacterium avium-intracellulare
	Salmonella species, especially *typhimurium*
	Aeromonas hydrophila
	Microsporidia
	Astrovirus/picornavirus
	Clostridium difficile
	Campylobacter jejuni
Less common	Viruses—herpes simplex, rotavirus, adenovirus, Norwalk agent
	Cyclospora
	Isospora belli
	Enteromonas hominis
	Strongyloides stercoralis
	Blastocystis hominis
	Shigella species
	Yersinia enterocolitica

AIDS, acquired immunodeficiency syndrome.

cation of the disease. The occurrence rate is greater than 90% in developing countries and 50% to 60% in the United States.[13,14,70,85,88]

Patients who are HIV positive and those with active AIDS are more susceptible to infection both from the usual enteric organisms and from opportunistic organisms. Diarrheal diseases are much more problematic in AIDS patients because of the patients' diminished immunity and underlying poor nutritional status.[13,14] A vastly different profile of pathogens causes diarrhea in AIDS patients compared with immunocompetent individuals. Also, the ramifications of the disease are significantly more serious, requiring a much more aggressive diagnostic evaluation and treatment regimen.

Pathophysiology

Mucosal biopsy specimens in patients with AIDS show crypt epithelial cell degeneration, villous atrophy, chronic inflammation, and often mild fibrosis. These nonspecific changes may be associated with many inflammatory or infectious processes but, because a significant percentage of AIDS patients with diarrhea have no pathogen identified, HIV itself may produce an enteropathy.[67,70,85,88]

In the homosexual population, unprotected receptive anal intercourse and anal-oral contact among multiple partners provide exposure to a diverse spectrum of enteric pathogens. In the heterosexual intravenous drug–abusing population, infection spreads primarily from water- and food-borne transmissions of the organisms. Patients with AIDS are unable to combat these intestinal pathogens, probably because of a combination of their T-lymphocyte functional deficiency and underlying HIV-induced enteropathy.

Etiology

A known enteric pathogen can be identified in approximately 80% to 85% of AIDS patients with diarrhea. Multiple organisms may be present in as many as 20% to 25% of patients. Homosexual men with AIDS develop diarrhea more often than other AIDS patients.[13,88]

Cryptosporidium and cytomegalovirus infections are the two most common causes. The incidence of each is 15% to 40%.[14,85,88] Chronic persistent diarrhea is most often from one of the coccidia, *Cryptosporidium* or *Isospora belli*. Cytomegalovirus and *Mycobacterium avium-intracellulare* also produce a chronic illness, although most patients die within 6 months of diagnosis. In underdeveloped countries, the coccidia are by far the most common cause of diarrhea in patients with AIDS; *Cryptosporidium* is the etiologic agent in more than 50% of patients and *Isospora* in approximately 15%.[67]

Salmonella infections, especially *S. typhimurium*, are common in immunocompromised hosts.[85] One unusual source of *Salmonella* is rattlesnake meat preparations. Hispanic persons in particular use rattlesnake powder or capsules as a treatment for a variety of ailments. *S. arizonae* is the usual species associated with rattlesnake meat.[89]

Entamoeba histolytica, although commonly found, is generally considered commensal. It is rare for amebae to cause invasive disease in patients with AIDS.[67] For unknown reasons, *Campylobacter, Shigella, Yersinia, V. parahaemolyticus,* viruses (non-cytomegalovirus), *Neisseria gonorrhoeae,* and *Chlamydia trachomatis* are unusual causes of diarrhea in patients with AIDS.

Astrovirus and picornavirus infections commonly cause diarrhea in AIDS patients.[61] The protozoan parasite *Microsporidia* may account for as much as 50% of the unexplained chronic, watery, nonbloody diarrhea that occurs with HIV infection.

Clinical Presentation

In AIDS patients, diarrhea presents in one of three ways. First, at the time of HIV seroconversion, patients usually experience diarrhea, nausea, anorexia, and malaise in association with an acute infectious mononucleosis–like syndrome. Second, diarrhea may be the presenting symptom of full-blown AIDS, with associated fever, malaise, anorexia, and significant weight loss. The most common presentation, however, is for diarrhea to start well after AIDS has been clinically apparent. These patients typically have a chronic debilitating infection that rarely remits spontaneously. It is often accompanied by profound weight loss, major nutritional impact, and a diminished sense of well-being. Many cases are refractory to treatment and persist until death, or may even be the cause of death.[70,85,88]

In AIDS patients, the presenting signs and symptoms generally do not allow one to consistently classify diarrheas, as is done for the immunocompetent host. This is in part because many patients with AIDS have multiple, concomitant enteric pathogens. However, some clinical pictures are typical. Patients with a fulminating clinical course usually have a disseminated infection, such as infection with cytomegalovirus or *M. avium-intracellulare.* Massive weight loss is also associated with those two organisms and the coccidia, *Cryptosporidium* or *Isospora.* Voluminous, watery diarrhea is usually due to one of the coccidial organisms. Patients with a proctocolitis-like picture most often have herpes simplex virus or cytomegalovirus infection. Strongyloidiasis should be considered in any immunocompromised patient who deteriorates suddenly and has polymicrobial sepsis, meningitis, or adynamic ileus.[85]

Complications

The most common complications are dehydration and malnutrition resulting from both fluid loss and malabsorption. Cytomegalovirus can produce gastrointestinal hemorrhage, perforation, or toxic megacolon. *M. avium-intracellulare* often produces severe anemia, weight loss, and a rapid downhill course of persistent weakness, malaise, and malabsorption. Bacteremia can be found in as many as 40% to 45% of AIDS patients with diarrhea, usually caused by *M. avium-intracellulare* or *Salmonella* species.[13,14,70]

Diagnostic Strategies

The diagnostic approach for AIDS patients with diarrhea is entirely different from that in an immunocom-

---

BOX 93-2. Diagnostic Protocol for Evaluating Diarrhea in Patients with AIDS

A. Initial evaluation—indicated in all patients
   1. Stool cultures for enteric bacteria—*Salmonella, Shigella, Campylobacter, Yersinia*
   2. Stool examinations by various stains, especially acid-fast stains, for ova, parasites, and mycobacteria; *C. difficile* toxin assay
   3. Blood cultures
   4. Proctosigmoidoscopy in patients with clinically severe colitis or a proctocolitis picture, especially male homosexuals
B. Further evaluation—indicated if initial study results are negative or to look for multiple organisms present if a patient fails to respond to appropriate therapy for an identified pathogen
   1. Repeat stool cultures and examinations, possibly add culture for viruses
   2. Proctosigmoidoscopy or gastroduodenoscopy performed to obtain duodenal fluid and small bowel and colonic biopsies, which are examined for:
      a. Duodenal fluid examination for ova and parasites
      b. Duodenal and colonic biopsies cultured for mycobacteria, cytomegalovirus, and herpes simples; colonic biopsy tissue is also cultured for bacterial enteric pathogens (add gonorrhea and chlamydia testing in patients with acute proctitis)
      c. Biopsy specimens examined by multiple stains (e.g., acid-fast, hematoxylin-eosin, Giemsa, silver, periodic acid-Schiff) for protozoa, mycobacteria, and cells containing viral inclusion bodies

---

petent host. In 80% to 90% of cases, one or more enteric pathogens are found; of the pathogens identified, 55% to 75% are treatable.[13,14,70,88] Known pathogens are detected less frequently in patients being treated with antiviral agents.[13] Diarrhea in AIDS patients is generally not self-limiting but requires medical intervention to effect resolution. Therefore, each patient deserves a diagnostic evaluation (Box 93-2), although the approach and intensity of the diagnostic workup remain controversial. AIDS patients with diarrhea should have one or more stool specimens cultured for enteric bacteria and examined by multiple stain preparations for ova, parasites, and mycobacteria. The usual bacterial enteric pathogens are readily identified, but the protozoan infections can be difficult to detect. Multiple stool specimens may have to be examined to diagnose *Giardia lamblia* and *Isospora belli,* in part because these oocysts are generally shed only intermittently and in small numbers. In patients with severe diarrhea from *Cryptosporidium,* the first stool examination is usually positive, but in less severe cases additional samples may have to be studied to make the diagnosis. Specialized techniques are necessary to detect most of the viral agents.

Blood cultures are a valuable diagnostic adjunct. Bacteremia may be found in up to 40% of patients, and in 20% of cases, a positive blood culture may be present when the stool cultures and examinations fail to reveal a pathogen.[85] The most common organisms that produce bacteremia are *M. avium-intracellulare*, *Salmonella*, and occasionally *Shigella* or *Campylobacter*. Most cases of *M. avium-intracellulare* bacteremia occur in heterosexual intravenous drug abusers. A routine complete blood cell count demonstrating eosinophilia suggests parasitic infection with *Strongyloides stercoralis*.[85]

If results of these diagnostic tests are negative, endoscopy should be performed to obtain mucosal biopsy samples from the rectum or colon. Rectal biopsy, which can be performed easily even in seriously ill patients, is an indispensable tool in the diagnosis of CMV infection.[13] Viral inclusion bodies with clear halos typical of CMV can be demonstrated. Stained examinations of the biopsy tissue may also diagnose *M. avium-intracellulare*, *Cryptosporidium*, or *Giardia* infections that were missed on stool examinations. Herpes simplex virus can be identified microscopically by detecting multinucleated giant cells or through cultures obtained at the time of endoscopy.

Small bowel biopsies and duodenal aspirates are indicated when stool examination, cultures, and sigmoidoscopy fail to lead to a diagnosis. Small bowel studies are most helpful for detecting *Cryptosporidium*, cytomegalovirus, *M. avium-intracellulare*, *Giardia*, or *I. belli*.[13,14]

Differential Considerations

Kaposi's sarcoma, even if it involves the bowel, rarely produces diarrhea. Symptomatic oral and esophageal candidiasis is common in patients with AIDS, but diarrhea from *Candida* has not been reported. Diarrhea can be a side effect of drugs used to treat AIDS, such as dideoxyinosine (ddI), and must be differentiated from infectious causes.[14,67,88]

Antibiotic-associated colitis from *C. difficile* should be considered when the diarrhea follows antibacterial therapy. Ulcerative colitis can mimic or be mimicked by cytomegalovirus colitis.[13] Aphthous ulceration, particularly of the colon, should be considered when cultures and endoscopy biopsy specimens fail to reveal evidence of infection with common infectious pathogens, herpes simplex virus, or cytomegalovirus. Empiric corticosteroid therapy may cause dramatic improvement in these patients.[90] Acute proctitis should be differentiated from diarrhea or acute colitis, because the investigative evaluation and treatment regimens are distinctly different.

Management

Treatment of diarrhea in patients with AIDS includes diet, antimotility agents, and antimicrobial agents. Diets that are lactose-free and low in fat often diminish the diarrhea caused by malabsorption. Patients should avoid intestinal stimulants such as caffeine, raw or inadequately cooked seafood, rattlesnake preparations, and untreated water. Varying success has been reported with the standard antimotility agents, such as diphenoxylate or loperamide. In patients with cryptosporidiosis, these agents commonly cause a marked increase in crampy abdominal pain. Long-acting morphine sulfate derivatives have provided better clinical relief.[13,85]

Specific antimicrobial therapy can lead to marked symptomatic improvement in 55% to 75% of patients in whom a pathogen has been identified (Table 93-6). Many patients show substantial improvement after therapy, even when the organism or the diarrhea has not been eliminated. Antimicrobial therapy should be dictated by the results of the diagnostic evaluation. Empiric use of antimicrobial agents is not indicated; no one antimicrobial agent can possibly provide reasonable coverage of the wide variety of causative organisms found in these patients. This is in distinct contrast to the situation encountered in immunocompetent patients. The possibility of infection by multiple organisms must always be considered, especially when patients do not respond to known effective antimicrobial agents for an identified pathogen.

Ganciclovir, a nucleoside analogue similar to acyclovir, is effective in inducing clinical remission in up to 80% of patients with gastrointestinal cytomegalovirus.[5,14,85,91,92] Foscarnet is also effective. The dosage of both drugs should be reduced in patients with low creatinine clearance.[5,92] However, treatment of the other most common cause of diarrhea in patients with AIDS, cryptosporidiosis, has been much less successful.[5,13,67,69] Paromomycin, particularly in combination with azithromycin, may be beneficial.[5,72,76] Infection with *I. belli* and *C. cayetanensis* can be cured with TMP-SMX.[5,66] *M. avium-intracellulare* is poorly responsive to therapy, and generally death ensues within 6 to 8 months of diagnosis. Virtually all of the other organisms listed in Table 93-5 are susceptible to the usual therapeutic agents, although higher dosages and longer courses of treatment are often required. Recurrences of either the opportunistic organisms or the usual enteric organisms are common. Chronic suppressive antimicrobial therapy may be indicated to prevent relapse or reinfection.[85] Patients with AIDS enteropathy or infectious enteritis who are not responsive to antimicrobial therapy may respond to zidovudine (AZT) because it enhances host immunity by suppressing HIV replication.

TRAVELER'S DIARRHEA

Epidemiology

It is said that "travel expands the mind and loosens the bowels." Diarrhea is by far the most common health problem of the 12 million people who travel from an industrialized nation to a developing country each year. Travel to high-risk areas such as Mexico, Latin America, Africa, the Middle East, or Asia is associated with diarrheal attack rates of 30% to 50%. However, few travelers to industrialized countries develop diarrhea. Among visitors to the United States, the attack rate is less than 4%. Traveler's diarrhea is more common in young adults than in elderly adults.[78,93]

Table 93-6. Treatment of Pathogens Causing Diarrhea in Patients with AIDS

Organism/Treatment Regimen	Comments
Cytomegalovirus	
Foscarnet 90 mg/kg IV q12hr × 14-21 days (diluted in 100 mL D₅W, infused over at least 1 hr)	
Ganciclovir 5 mg/kg q12hr IV × 14 days (diluted in 100 mL D₅W, infused over 1 hr)	Effective, but 75% recurrence rate within 8 to 9 weeks; maintenance therapy may be warranted
Cryptosporidium	
Paromomycin 1 g PO bid × 12 weeks *plus* azithromycin 600 mg qd × 4 wk	Disease generally chronic, despite treatment
Somatostatin analogue	
Antiviral therapies	
Indomethacin 50 mg PO q8hr	
Cyclospora cayetanensis	
TMP-SMX 160 mg/800 mg qid PO × 10 days, then 1 tab PO 3×/wk	
Entamoeba histolytica	
Paromomycin 500 mg PO tid × 7 days	Treat only if distinguished from *E. dispar*, or for severe symptoms. Look for other causes as well.
Proceed with metronidazole 750 mg PO tid × 10 days for severe symptoms	
Giardia lamblia	
Metronidazole 250-750 mg PO tid × 5 to 10 days	Patient's symptoms may resolve despite continued enteric presence of *Giardia*
Mycobacterium avium-intracellulare	
Clarithromycin 500 mg PO bid *plus* ethambutol PO 15 mg/kg/day	
Antituberculous regimens or ciprofloxacin 500-750 mg PO bid × 10-14 days	Mixed results with antituberculous drugs, more drug resistant than tuberculous strains of mycobacteria; little evidence that treatment prolongs life
Salmonella species	
Ciprofloxacin 500-750 mg PO bid × 10-14 days or azithromycin 1 g day 1, then 500 mg × 10 days	Bacteremia common; maintenance therapy often required
Ceftriaxone 1-2 g IV q12hr × 7-10 days	
Herpes simplex virus	
Acyclovir 5 mg/kg PO or IV tid × 7-10 days	Proctitis picture, especially in homosexual men
Campylobacter jejuni	
Erythromycin 500 mg bid × 7-10 days or azithromycin 500 mg qd × 5-7 days	40% recurrence rate; high rate of fluoroquinolone resistance
Isospora belli	
Trimethoprim-sulfamethoxazole (TMP-SMX) 160 mg/800 mg PO qid × 10 days, then bid for 3 weeks	50% recurrence rate; chronic suppressive therapy usually recommended
Aeromonas hydrophila	
Ciprofloxacin 500 mg PO bid × 3 days or TMP-SMX 160 mg/800 mg PO bid × 3 days	Associated with drinking untreated water
Enteromonas hominis	
Metronidazole 250-750 mg PO tid × 10 days	Increasingly common in homosexual men, possibly commensal; treatment indicated when no other pathogens found in the presence of appropriate symptoms
Blastocystis hominis	
Metronidazole 750 mg PO tid × 10 days or furazolidone 100 mg PO qid × 7-10 days	Possibly more common in children
Shigella species	
Ciprofloxacin 500 mg PO bid × 7 days	Most species resistant to ampicillin, and increasing resistance is found to TMP-SMX
Yersinia	
Ciprofloxacin 500 mg PO bid × 7 days	Appendicitis-like picture; bacteremia possible
Strongyloides stercoralis	
Ivermectin 200 µg/kg/d × 1-2 days or thiabendazole 25 mg/kg po bid × 2 days	Migration of the larvae through the bowel wall may be accompanied by gram-negative bacteremia and a hyperinfection syndrome in AIDS patients; in disseminated strongyloidiasis, therapy should be continued for at least 5 days

Pathophysiology

The syndrome is caused by an infection acquired by ingesting fecally contaminated food or water. High-risk items include raw leafy vegetables, raw or undercooked meats or seafood, unpeeled fruits, unpasteurized dairy products, tap water, and ice. Once an organism is ingested, rapid and dramatic change occurs in the traveler's intestinal flora. When the ingested inoculum overcomes an individual's defense mechanisms, diarrhea develops. Most often, this is from the elaboration of enterotoxins that produce a secretory diarrhea. When organisms are invasive, rather than toxigenic, a typical infectious enteritis develops.

Etiology (Table 93-7)

Enterotoxigenic *E. coli* is responsible for 40% to 50% of all cases of traveler's diarrhea and can be acquired anywhere in the world. The organisms adhere to the wall of

Table 93-7. Causes of Traveler's Diarrhea

Agent	Estimated Incidence (%)*
Bacteria (approximately 80–85%)	
Enterotoxigenic *Escherichia coli*	45-50
Shigella	8-12
Campylobacter	7-9
Enteroinvasive *E. coli* (hemorrhagic strain 0157:H7)	5-6
Salmonella	3-5
Others, such as *Vibrio,* *Aeromonas, Plesiomonas,* shigelloides, *Yersinia,* other types of *E. coli*	1-5
Viruses (approximately 5–10%)	
Rotavirus	5-10
Norwalk agent and others	0-5
Parasites (approximately 5–6%)	
Giardia lamblia	4-5
Cryptosporidium	3-4
Entamoeba histolytica	0-1
Strongyloides stercoralis	0-1
Unknown	5-10

*Rough estimates, which vary depending on destination.

the small bowel, where they multiply and produce an enterotoxin that causes fluid secretion and diarrhea. The other infectious bacterial agents, particularly *Shigella, Salmonella,* and *Campylobacter,* account for 20% to 30% of cases. *V. parahaemolyticus* is an increasingly common cause because of its association with raw or inadequately cooked seafood. The organism commonly causes diarrhea in persons traveling to Japan or Asia or those vacationing on cruise ships.[23,50,78,93]

Plesiomonas shigelloides is typically associated with uncooked shellfish, especially oysters. It is also associated with travel to Mexico. *Plesiomonas* produces a typical invasive enteritis. *E. coli* 0157:H7 and enteroinvasive *E. coli* each cause up to 5% of cases of traveler's diarrhea.[3,7] Another type of *E. coli,* enteroadherent *E. coli,* may be the cause of a significant number of the previously undiagnosed cases of traveler's diarrhea.[94] Norwalk virus and rotavirus may cause up to 10% of cases of traveler's diarrhea in visitors to Mexico.[50] *Giardia* is the most common parasite acquired by travelers and accounts for 3% to 5% of all cases. Travelers to the former Soviet Union, particularly Leningrad and Moscow, have a very high risk for acquiring giardiasis. Amebiasis is rare.[78]

Clinical Presentation

Traveler's diarrhea typically begins abruptly and results in four or five loose or watery stools per day for 1 to 3 days. Approximately one third of patients are temporarily confined to bed, and the symptoms last more than a week in 10% of patients. Onset is usually within the first 3 to 4 days of travel but can occur at any time, including after the patient arrives home. Patients may not associate their diarrhea with recent travel because the incubation time of the infection, particularly if it is parasitic, may have been long enough to allow them to return home before the symptoms began.

Associated symptoms include abdominal cramps, nausea, bloating, urgency, and occasionally vomiting, fever, chills, headache, malaise, tenesmus, and bloody stools. Symptoms depend on whether the cause is "toxigenic" or "infectious." Traveler's diarrhea may ruin one's trip, but it is rarely life threatening.

Prevention

Diet

Traditionally, instruction regarding food and beverage preparation has been touted to prevent traveler's diarrhea. Most travelers, however, do not follow such advice. Ideally, a tourist should eat foods that are freshly prepared and served piping hot. High-risk foods should be assiduously avoided, and travelers should follow the Peace Corps adage of "boil it, cook it, peel it, or forget it." Thirsty travelers should be advised to avoid ice and to drink beverages such as tea and coffee that are made with boiled water, canned or bottled carbonated beverages, and wine.[50] Boiling water is by far the most reliable method to make it safe for drinking and brushing teeth. Travelers and outdoor enthusiasts should be advised to bring the water to a vigorous boil and allow it to cool without adding ice. Boiling destroys virtually all bacteria, viruses, and parasitic cysts. A pinch of salt in each quart improves the taste. When boiling is not feasible, water can be chemically disinfected with 2% tincture of iodine drops or tetracycline hydroperiodide tablets, such as Globaline or Potable Aqua, available from pharmacies and sporting goods stores.

Nonantimicrobial Medications

The nonantimicrobial agent most studied in the prevention of traveler's diarrhea is bismuth subsalicylate (Pepto-Bismol). Two tablets, or 2 ounces, taken four times per day decreases the incidence of traveler's diarrhea by 65%. This dosage, however, contains the daily equivalent of eight 5-grain aspirin tablets. Bismuth subsalicylate should not be used in patients who are allergic to salicylates, those taking large doses of salicylates for arthritis, and patients taking oral anticoagulants, uricosuric drugs, or methotrexate. Salicylates have antiplatelet effects, inhibit the activity of uricosuric drugs, and increase the toxicity of methotrexate by decreasing its renal clearance. Pepto-Bismol also turns the tongue and stool black and may cause mild tinnitus and interfere with the bioavailability of doxycycline.

Antiperistaltic agents such as diphenoxylate and loperamide are not effective prophylactic agents. Controlled studies have indicated that the use of diphenoxylate actually increases the incidence of traveler's diarrhea; slowing of the gut allows more time for organisms to colonize and elaborate toxin or produce infection.[94]

Antimicrobials

The risks of prophylactic treatment with antibiotics include allergic reactions, skin rashes, photosensitivity reactions, serious hematologic reactions, Stevens-Johnson syndrome, and antibiotic-induced infections such as antibiotic-associated colitis or *Candida* vaginitis.[50] The main argument, however, against the widespread use of prophylactic antibiotics in millions of travelers each year has been the risk of emergence of resistant organisms. Resistance to doxycycline is now found in many parts of the world. TMP-SMX resistance is common in tropical areas. The quinolones are the most effective agents but have up to 80% resistance to some organisms in parts of Southeast Asia.[5,50,94-96]

In addition, if a prescription for a suitable antibiotic based on regional resistance patterns accompanies the traveler, taking one dose in combination with loperamide immediately after the onset of diarrhea will often halt symptoms within hours. For these reasons, prophylactic use of antibiotics before the onset of symptoms is no longer recommended, except in cases of significant concurrent illness or immunocompromised states.[96,97]

For persons requiring prophylaxis, a single daily dose of prophylactic antibiotics such as ciprofloxacin (500 mg), or norfloxacin (400 mg) in combination with bismuth subsalicylate 2 tablets (262 mg/tablet) or 30 mL four times daily (with meals and every hour) can effectively prevent traveler's diarrhea in up to 90% of persons. The regimen is started the day before travel and continued until 2 days after returning home. TMP-SMX can also be used but is not recommended as a first-line agent because of significant resistance.

Management

Diet
In most patients, fluid and electrolyte balances can be maintained by drinking potable fruit juices, bottled beverages, or caffeine-free soft drinks.

Nonantimicrobial Medications
Adsorbents such as kaolin or pectin are ineffective in treating traveler's diarrhea. They may give the stools more consistency but have not been shown to decrease cramps or the frequency of stooling or to shorten the course of an infectious diarrhea. Nonantimicrobial agents such as bismuth subsalicylate, paregoric, codeine, diphenoxylate, or loperamide may provide prompt but temporary symptomatic relief.

Loperamide (initial dose 4 mg followed by 2 mg after each unformed stool for 2 days; total dosage no more than eight 2-mg capsules/day) has been shown to provide significantly more relief than bismuth subsalicylate (30 mL PO every 30 minutes for 3 to 5 hours on each of 2 days; 240 mL/day).[94] Antimotility agents alone, however, should never be given to patients when an invasive bacterial infection is suspected, and they should be discontinued if symptoms persist longer than 48 hours.

Antimicrobials
Antibiotics have a role in the treatment of all clinical presentations of traveler's diarrhea. Antibiotic therapy can provide prompt relief of symptoms, decrease the rate of stooling, and shorten a typically 1- to 3-day illness to a few hours.[78,98,99] In cases of mild toxigenic, nondysenteric traveler's diarrhea, a single dose of

ciprofloxacin 750 mg in combination with loperamide often resolves the symptoms within an hour. When the course is extended to 3 days, response rates of up to 98% are attained. In patients with high fever, bloody stools, or the typical bacterial/invasive picture, the treatment of choice is norfloxacin, 400 mg twice daily, or ciprofloxacin, 500 mg twice daily, in combination with loperamide. The duration of treatment is generally 3 days, although one double dose may be all that is necessary.[95,98]

Persons with dysentery failing to respond to one antibiotic should promptly be switched to another. Azithromycin may be effective in cases in which fluoroquinolones either cannot be used or are ineffective. The quinolone agents are not recommended for use in children and pregnant women.[94]

A summary of current recommendations for the prevention and treatment of traveler's diarrhea is outlined in Box 93-3. Further detailed information on traveler's diarrhea and the other medical problems of travelers can be found at the Center for Preventive Services section of the CDC's website, www.cdc.gov/travel.htm. The website contains a plethora of travel-related information. The CDC's "Yellow Book," *Health Information for International Travel,* can be downloaded for free at www.cdc.gov/travel/reference.htm, and the CDC provides up-to-the-minute travel information through its traveler's hotline phone number, 877-FYI-TRIP.

BOX 93-3. Current Recommendations for the Prevention and Treatment of Traveler's Diarrhea

1. Provide instruction regarding sensible dietary practices and drinking water management.
2. Reserve prophylaxis for patients who have special circumstances including severe concurrent illness or immunosuppression. The basis of this recommendation is threefold: first, the modest benefit from bismuth subsalicylate as opposed to its aspirin-related complications; second, the ramification of widespread use of prophylactic antibiotics in terms of adverse medication reactions or the emergence of resistant organisms; third, the availability of highly successful treatment strategies.
3. Other patients who request prophylaxis should be steered toward the use of bismuth subsalicylate rather than antibiotics.
4. For those requiring prophylaxis, one of the quinolones, norfloxacin or ciprofloxacin, is recommended.
5. For all patients, it is reasonable to institute prompt antimicrobial therapy once traveler's diarrhea occurs.
   a. Toxigenic/nondysentery: loperamide combined with one dose of ciprofloxacin 750 mg orally.
   b. Infectious/dysentery: norfloxacin or ciprofloxacin—alone or in combination with loperamide bid × 3 days.
   c. The rare traveler with persistent symptoms, particularly fever, chills, or blood or mucus in stools, unresponsive to antimicrobial therapy within 24 to 48 hours, should seek immediate medical attention.

KEY CONCEPTS

- Contact isolation precautions should be followed for all patients with significant diarrhea that continues while the patient is in the emergency department.

- Most otherwise healthy patients presenting with diarrhea do not require laboratory testing or antibiotic therapy.

- Fecal testing should be reserved for those patients who are systemically ill, are febrile, have significant comorbid disease, have bloody stool, or report recent antibiotic use or for whom there is a strong suspicion of exposure to a treatable or reportable pathogen.

- Empiric treatment of diarrhea in adults with a fluoro-quinolone or TMP-SMX is acceptable for traveler's diarrhea and when inflammatory diarrhea is present with a low risk of *E. coli* O157:H7 as its cause. This includes patients with a temperature greater than 38.5° C in combination with bloody diarrhea. False-positive blood in stools may come from aggravation of hemorrhoids or perianal irritation secondary to copious stooling. Fecal leukocytes or lactoferrin testing may help distinguish inflammatory diarrhea but has a low specificity. Stool testing should be performed before all empiric treatment.

- Avoid milk and other lactose-containing foods because gastroenteritis often leads to transient lactose intolerance. Caffeine products may also worsen diarrhea. However, bowel rest is not necessary or advantageous and patients should be encouraged to eat and drink what they find palatable during the illness.

- Risks of empiric antibiotic treatment include adverse and allergic reactions, possible increase in the risk of hemolytic uremic syndrome in the case of *E. coli* O157:H7, prolonged shedding of non-*typhi* species of *Salmonella*, and increased organism resistance.

- Treatment should be considered in patients who are still significantly ill at the time that culture results are reported, particularly if they are immunocompromised or have a significant underlying medical illness, or in cases in which the fecal shedding could represent a public health hazard.

- Patients with sickle cell anemia, other hemolytic anemias, or AIDS are unusually susceptible to *Salmonella* bacteremia.

- Although risk associated with antimotility agents may be overstated, these agents are still not recommended for treatment of invasive enteritis unless antibiotics are also used.

- In patients with *Y. enterocolitica* gastroenteritis, the abdominal pain and diarrhea usually persist for 10 to 14 days or longer. A substantial number of patients with yersiniosis, in particular adolescents and young adults, develop an ileocecitis. In these cases, lower abdominal pain with little or no diarrhea predominates and may perfectly mimic acute appendicitis.

- The symptoms of scombroid fish poisoning, which resemble histamine intoxication and usually develop abruptly within 20 to 30 minutes of eating the fish, consist of facial flushing, diarrhea, severe, throbbing headache, palpitations, and abdominal cramps, and generally last less than 6 hours. The mainstay of therapy is antihistamine administration.

- Many cases of *C. difficile* antibiotic-associated enterocolitis are self-limited, provided that the offending agent is discontinued. When stopping the antibiotic does not resolve the diarrhea, or when the diarrhea is severe, empiric antibiotic treatment should be started promptly. Either oral metronidazole or oral vancomycin can be used to eradicate *C. difficile* colitis.

- *Giardia* is the most common cause of water-borne diarrheal outbreaks in the United States. Most patients harboring *Giardia* are asymptomatic. The most common symptoms of acute infection are abdominal distention, colicky pain with audible borborygmi, flatulence, and frequent stools. All patients harboring *Giardia* should be treated, even if they are asymptomatic.

- Diarrhea is the most common manifestation of gastrointestinal disease in patients with AIDS and may be either the presenting symptom or a life-threatening complication of the disease. Diarrhea in the AIDS patient is generally not self-limiting but requires medical intervention to effect resolution. Therefore, each patient deserves a diagnostic evaluation.

- Enterotoxigenic *E. coli* is responsible for 40% to 50% of all cases of traveler's diarrhea and can be acquired anywhere in the world. Prophylactic antibiotics are no longer recommended for otherwise healthy patients, but quick resolution of diarrhea is possible with prompt treatment.

REFERENCES

1. Altekruse SF, et al: Campylobacter jejuni: An emerging food-borne pathogen. *Emerg Infect Dis* 5:1, 1999.

2. Goodman L, et al: Infectious diarrhea. *Dis Mon* 45:268, 1999.

3. Tauxe RV: Emerging food-borne diseases: An evolving public health challenge. *Emerg Infect Dis* 3:1, 1997.

4. Guerrant RL, et al: Practice guidelines for the management of infectious diarrhea. *Clin Infect Dis* 32:331, 2001.

5. Editorial Board: Drugs for parasitic infections. *Med Lett* 3:1, 2000.

6. Allos M: *Campylobacter jejuni* infections: Update on emerging issues and trends. *Clin Infect Dis* 32:1201, 2001.

7. Angulo FJ, Swerdlo DL: *Salmonella enteritidis* infections in the United States. *J Am Vet Med Assoc* 213:1729, 1998.

8. Mead PS: Food-related illness and death in the United States. *Emerg Infect Dis* 5:607, 1999.

9. Olsen SJ, et al: Surveillance for food borne-disease outbreaks: United States, 1993-1997. *MMWR Morb Mortal Wkly Rep* 49(SS-1), 2000.

10. VanBeneden CA, et al: Multinational outbreak of salmonella infections due to contaminated alfalfa sprouts. *JAMA* 281:158, 1999.

11. Meriman J, Hoar B, Angulo FJ: Iguanas and *Salmonella marina* infection in children: A reflection of the increased incidence of reptile-associated salmonellosis in the US. *Pediatrics* 99:399, 1997.

12. Centers for Disease Control and Prevention: Reptile-associated salmonellosis: Selected states, 1996, 1998. *MMWR Morb Mortal Wkly Rep* 48:1009, 1999.

13. Weber R, et al: Enteric infections and diarrhea in HIV-infected persons. *Arch Intern Med* 159:1473, 1999.

14. Angulo FJ, Swerdlow DL: Bacterial enteric infections in persons infected with HIV. *Clin Infect Dis* 21(Suppl 1):S84, 1995.

15. Editorial Board: Choice of antimicrobial drugs. *Med Lett* 36:53, 1994.

PART THREE MEDICINE AND SURGERY • Section V Gastrointestinal System

16. Smith ME: Comparison of ofloxacin and ceftriaxone for short-course treatment of enteric fever. *Antimicrob Agents Chemother* 38:1716, 1994.

17. Centers for Disease Control and Prevention: Outbreak of cryptosporidiosis associated with a water sprinkler fountain: Minnesota. *MMWR Morb Mortal Wkly Rep* 47:856, 1998.

18. Murphy S, et al: Ciprofloxacin and loperamide in the treatment of bacillary dysentery. *Ann Intern Med* 118:582, 1993.

19. Oloughlin EV, Gall DJ, Pai CH: *Yersinia enterocolitica*: Mechanisms of microbial pathogenesis and pathophysiology of diarrhea. *J Gastroenterol Hepatol* 5:2, 1990.

20. Centers for Disease Control and Prevention: Surveillance for waterborne disease outbreaks, United States 1997-1998. *MMWR Morb Mortal Wkly Rep* 49(SS-4):1, 2000.

21. Hlady WG, Klontz KC: The epidemiology of vibrio infections in Florida. *J Infect Dis* 173:1176, 1996.

22. Centers for Disease Control and Prevention: Outbreak of *Vibrio parahaemolyticus* infections associated with eating raw oysters: Pacific Northwest, 1997. *MMWR Morb Mortal Wkly Rep* 47:457, 1998.

23. Koo D, Maloney K, Tauxe R: Epidemiology of diarrheal disease outbreaks on cruise ships, 1986 through 1993. *JAMA* 275:545, 1996.

24. Hlady WG, Mullen RC, Hopkins RS: Vibrio vulnificus from raw oysters: Leading cause of reported deaths from foodborne illness in Florida. *J Fla Med Assoc* 80:536, 1993.

25. Mouzin E, et al: Prevention of *Vibrio vulnificus* infections: Assessment of regulatory educational strategies. *JAMA* 278:576, 1997.

26. Dundass, Todd WT: *E. coli* 0157:H7 review article, current opinion. *Infect Dis* 11:171, 1998.

27. MacDonald KL, Osterholm MT: The emergence of *Escherichia coli* 0157:H7 infection in the United States: The changing epidemiology of food-borne disease. *JAMA* 269:2264, 1993.

28. Slutsker L, et al: *Escherichia coli* 0157:H7 diarrhea in the United States: Clinical and epidemiologic features. *Ann Intern Med* 126:505, 1997.

29. Centers for Disease Control and Prevention: *Escherichia coli* O157:H7 infections associated with eating a nationally distributed commercial brand of frozen ground beef patties and burgers: Colorado, 1997. *MMWR Morb Mortal Wkly Rep* 46:777, 1997.

30. Cody SH, et al: An outbreak of *Escherichia coli* 0157:H7 infection from unpasteurized commercial apple juice. *Ann Intern Med* 120:202, 1999.

31. Tarr PI, et al: *Escherichia coli* 0157:H7 and the hemolytic uremic syndrome: Importance of early cultures in establishing the etiology. *J Infect Dis* 162:553, 1990.

32. Belongia EA, et al: Transmission of *Escherichia coli* 0157:H7 infection in Minnesota child day-care facilities. *JAMA* 269:883, 1993.

33. Boyce TG, Sverdlow DL, Griffin PM: *Escherichia coli* 0157:H7 and the hemolytic-uremic syndrome. *N Engl J Med* 333:364, 1995.

34. Bender JB, et al: Surveillance for *E. coli* O157:H7 infections in Minnesota by molecular subtyping. *N Engl J Med* 337:338, 1997.

35. Harris S: Japanese biological warfare research on humans: A case study of microbiology and ethics. *Ann N Y Acad Sci* 666:21, 1992.

36. Daley S: In support of apartheid: Poison whisky and sterilization. *New York Times*, June 11, 1998, A3.

37. Sirisanthana T, et al: Anthrax of the gastrointestinal tract. *Emerg Infect Dis* 8:649, 2002.

38. Centers for Disease Control and Prevention: Human ingestion of *Bacillus anthracis*-contaminated meat, Minnesota, August 2000. *MMWR Morb Mortal Wkly Rep* 49:813, 2000.

39. Beatty M, et al: Gastrointestinal anthrax: Review of the literature. *Arch Intern Med* 163:2527, 2003.

40. Centers for Disease Control and Prevention: Outbreak of staphylococcal food poisoning associated with pre-cooked ham: Florida, 1997. *MMWR Morb Mortal Wkly Rep* 46:1189, 1997.

41. Lund BM: Food-borne disease due to *Bacillus* and *Clostridium* species. *Lancet* 336:982, 1990.

42. Centers for Disease Control and Prevention: *Bacillus cereus* food poisoning associated with fried rice at two child daycare centers: Virginia, 1993. *MMWR Morb Mortal Wkly Rep* 43:177, 1994.

43. Centers for Disease Control and Prevention: Imported cholera associated with a newly-described toxigenic *Vibrio cholera* 0139, 1993. *MMWR Morb Mortal Wkly Rep* 42:501, 1993.

44. Bishai WR, Sears CL: Food poisoning syndromes. *Gastroenterol Clin North Am* 22:579, 1993.

45. Morris PD, Campbell DS, Freeman JI: Ciguatera fish poisoning: An outbreak associated with fish caught from North Carolina coastal waters. *South Med J* 83:380, 1990.

46. Gollop JH, Pon EW: Ciguatera: A review. *Hawaii Med J* 51:91, 1992.

47. Beadle A: Ciguatera fish poisoning. *Military Med* 162:319, 1997.

48. Centers for Disease Control and Prevention: Ciguatera fish poisoning: Texas, 1997. *MMWR Morb Mortal Wkly Rep* 47: 692, 1998.

49. Blythe DG et al: Clinical experience with IV mannitol in the treatment of ciguatera. *Bull Soc Pathol Exot* 85:425, 1992.

50. Editor: Advice for travelers. *Med Lett* 40:470, 1998.

51. Gerding BN et al: Clostridium difficile-associated diarrhea and colitis. *Infect Control Hosp Epidemiol* 16:459, 1995.

52. Kelly CP, LaMont JT: *Clostridium difficile* infection. *Ann Rev Med* 49:375, 1998.

53. Frost F et al: Increasing hospitalization and death possibly due to *Clostridium difficile* diarrheal disease. *Emerg Infect Dis* 4:1, 1998.

54. Bartlett JG: How to identify the cause of antibiotic-associated diarrhea. *J Crit Illness* 9:1063, 1994.

55. McFarland LV, et al: A randomized placebo-controlled trial of *Saccharomyces boulardii* in combination with standard antibiotics for *Clostridium difficile* disease. *JAMA* 271: 1913, 1994.

56. Kapikian AZ: Viral gastroenteritis. *JAMA* 269:627, 1993.

57. Kapikian AZ: Overview of viral gastroenteritis. *Arch Virol Suppl* 12:7, 1996.

58. Brown T: Update on emerging infections: News from the Centers for Disease Control and Prevention. *Ann Emerg Med* 42:417, 2003.

59. Daniels NA, et al: A food-borne outbreak of gastroenteritis associated with Norwalk-like viruses: First molecular traceback to deli sandwiches contaminated during preparation. *J Infect Dis* 181:1467, 2000.

60. Kohn MA, et al: An outbreak of Norwalk virus gastroenteritis associated with eating raw oysters. *JAMA* 273:466, 1995.

61. Grohmann GS, et al: Enteric viruses and diarrhea in HIV-infected patients. *N Engl J Med* 329:14, 1993.

62. Cordell RL, Addiss DG: Cryptosporidiosis in child care settings: A review of the literature and recommendations for prevention and control. *Pediatr Infect Dis J* 13:310, 1994.

63. Guerrant RL: Cryptosporidiosis: An emerging, highly infectious threat. *Emerg Infect Dis* 3:1, 1997.

64. Bell A, et al: A swimming pool-associated outbreak of cryptosporidiosis in British Columbia. *Can J Public Health* 84:334, 1993.

65. MacKenzie WR, et al: A massive outbreak in Milwaukee of *Cryptosporidium* infection transmitted through the public water supply. *N Engl J Med* 331:161, 1994.

66. Ackers JP: Treatment of isosporiasis. *Semin Gastrointest Dis* 8:33, 1997.
67. Mannheimer SB, Soave R: Protozoal infections in patients with AIDS. *Dis Clin North Am* 8:483, 1994.
68. Cevallos AM, Farthing MJG: Parasitic infections of the gastrointestinal tract. *Curr Opin Gastroenterol* 6:112, 1990.
69. White AC, et al: Paromomycin for cryptosporidiosis in AIDS: A prospective, double-blind trial. *J Infect Dis* 170:419, 1994.
70. Simon D, Brandt LJ: Diarrhea in patients with the acquired immunodeficiency syndrome. *Gastroenterol* 105:1238, 1993.
71. Armitage K, et al: Paromomycin and azithromycin treatment of cryptosporidiosis. *Arch Intern Med* 152:2497, 1992.
72. Smith NH, et al: Combination drug therapy for cryptosporidiosis in AIDS. *J Infect Dis* 178:900, 1998.
73. Centers for Disease Control and Prevention: Outbreaks of cyclosporiasis in the United States and Canada 1997. *MMWR Morb Mortal Wkly Rep* 46:521, 1997.
74. Colley DG: Widespread food-borne cyclosporiasis outbreaks present major challenges. *Emerg Infect Dis* 2:354, 1996.
75. Herwaldt BL, et al: An outbreak in 1996 of cyclosporiasis associated with imported raspberries. *N Engl J Med* 336:1548, 1997.
76. Sterling CR, Ortega YR: Cyclospora: An enigma worth unraveling. *Emerg Infect Dis* 5:20, 1999.
77. Centers for Disease Control and Prevention: Giardiasis surveillance: United States, 1992-1997. *MMWR Morb Mortal Wkly Rep* 49(SS-7):1, 2000.
78. Chak A, Banwell JG: Traveler's diarrhea. *Gastroenterol Clin North Am* 22:549, 1993.
79. Ortega YR, Adam RD: Giardia: Overview and update. *Clin Infect Dis* 25:545, 1997.
80. Gonin P, et al: Detection and differentiation of *Entamoeba histolytica* and *Entamoeba dispar* isolates in clinical samples by PCR and enzyme-linked immunosorbent assay. *J Clin Microbiol* 41:237, 2003.
81. Weinket R, et al: Prevalence and clinical importance of *Entamoeba histolytica* in two high-risk groups: Travelers returning from the tropics and male homosexuals. *J Infect Dis* 161:1029, 1990.
82. Berkelman RL: Emerging infectious diseases in the United States 1993. *J Infect Dis* 170:272, 1994.
83. Haque R, et al: Current concepts: amebiasis. *N Engl J Med* 348:1565, 2003.
84. Farmer RG: Infectious causes of diarrhea in the differential diagnosis of inflammatory bowel disease. *Med Clin North Am* 74:29, 1990.
85. Smith PD, et al: NIH Conference: Gastrointestinal infections in AIDS. *Ann Intern Med* 116:63, 1993.
86. World Health Organization: World Health Organization/Pan American Health Organization/UNESCO report of a consultation of experts on amoebiasis. *Wkly Epidemiol Rec* 72:97, 1997.
87. Stauffer W, et al: *Entamoeba histolytica*: An update. *Curr Opin Infect Dis* 16:479, 2003.
88. Sanchez-Mejoradag G, Ponce de Leons S: Clinical patterns of diarrhea in AIDS: Etiology and prognosis. *Rev Invest Clin* 46:187, 1994.
89. Babu K, et al: Isolation of salmonellae from dried rattlesnake preparations. *J Clin Microbiol* 28:361, 1990.
90. Bach MC, et al: Aphthous ulceration of the gastrointestinal tract in patients with AIDS. *Ann Intern Med* 112:465, 1990.
91. Buckner FS, Pomeroy C: Ganciclovir treatment of cytomegalovirus gastroenteritis. *Clin Infect Dis* 17:644, 1993.
92. Dietrerich DT, et al: Treatment of cytomegalovirus infections in AIDS. *Am J Gastroenterol* 88:542, 1993.
93. Black RE: Epidemiology of traveler's diarrhea and relative importance of various pathogens. *Rev Infect Dis* 12(Suppl 1):S73, 1990.
94. Ericsson CD: Traveler's diarrhea. *Curr Opin Gastroenterol* 6:100, 1990.
95. DuPont HL, Ericsson CD: Drug therapy: Prevention and treatment of traveler's diarrhea. *N Engl J Med* 328:1821, 1993.
96. Diemert DJ: Prevention and self-treatment of travelers' diarrhea. *Prim Care* 29: 843, 2002.
97. Day LJ, et al: Ciprofloxacin use and misuse in the treatment of travelers' diarrhea. *Am J Med* 114:771, 2003.
98. Taylor DN, et al: Treatment of travelers' diarrhea: Ciprofloxacin plus loperamide compared with ciprofloxacin alone. *Ann Intern Med* 114:731, 1991.
99. Petruccelli BP, et al: Treatment of traveler's diarrhea with ciprofloxacin and loperamide. *J Infect Dis* 165:557, 1992.

CHAPTER

94 Large Intestine

Michael A. Peterson

IRRITABLE BOWEL SYNDROME

Perspective

Irritable bowel syndrome (IBS) is a chronic non–life-threatening disorder characterized by abdominal pain and an alteration in bowel habits. An extremely common disorder, estimates put the prevalence of IBS in the North American population at 10% to 15%,[1] with women affected twice as often as men. Although only a third of patients who have the clinical syndrome ever seek medical attention, IBS accounts for more than 10% of all visits to primary care physicians and more than 25% of all visits to gastroenterologists.[2] IBS is said to be more of an impairment to quality of life than diabetes or renal failure.

There are no specific physical or laboratory abnormalities that define IBS. IBS is defined by clinical criteria and usually is diagnosed after other more serious diagnoses are excluded. A new diagnosis of IBS is difficult in the emergency department because many of the studies required to exclude other conditions are not readily available. Undiagnosed patients are usually discharged with a diagnosis of "abdominal pain of unclear etiology" or the equivalent. Undiagnosed patients and even patients with known IBS presenting with acute symptoms pose a diagnostic challenge. Symptoms of IBS overlap with other conditions, including some that are life-threatening and which must be excluded before discharge.

Principles of Disease

Although the cause of IBS is unknown, it is associated with several pathologic physiologic findings that suggest it is a disorder of altered gut motility, gut sensation, and perception of intestinal activity. IBS initially was thought to be primarily a psychiatric disorder because there are no visible anatomic abnormalities and because stress is an exacerbating factor. Physiologic testing has now shown that patients with IBS have disturbances in the rhythmic pattern of electrical activity in the intestine and in how the intestine responds to stimulation. Patients with IBS seem to be more attuned to the activity in their abdomens as well, sensing different phases of intestinal motor activity and intestinal content movement more than people without IBS.

Psychiatric conditions often coexist in patients with IBS, ranging from generalized anxiety disorder to major depression. There is also an association with prior sexual abuse.[2] In women, symptoms are often related to the menstrual cycle, suggesting a hormonal influence. A familial predisposition for symptoms of IBS has been reported, suggesting a genetic component.

Clinical Features

The diagnosis of IBS is defined by clinical criteria in a patient who has no other organic explanation for the symptoms. There are several published sets of clinical criteria, one of which is the Rome II criteria (Box 94-1). Patients with IBS exhibit symptoms intermittently, with the typical patient averaging symptoms on 1 out of every 3 days. Complaints include abdominal pain, bloating, and constipation or diarrhea. Pain is typically relieved with defecation; pain that persists suggests another diagnosis. Commonly a mucoid discharge from the rectum accompanies diarrhea. Upper gastrointestinal symptoms such as nausea and dyspepsia can also

---

BOX 94-1. Rome II Criteria for Irritable Bowel Syndrome

Abdominal pain or discomfort for ≥12 weeks over past 1 year *and* 2 of the following:
1. Relief of discomfort with defecation
2. Association of discomfort with altered stool frequency
3. Association of discomfort with altered stool form

From Brandt LJ, et al: Systematic review on the management of irritable bowel syndrome in North America. *Am J Gastroenterol* 97:S7, 2002.

BOX 94-2. Differential Diagnosis in Irritable Bowel Syndrome

Constipation Predominant
- Bowel obstruction
- Cancer
- Adult-onset Hirschsprung's disease
- Rectocele
- Paradoxical closure of the anus during defecation

Diarrhea Predominant
- Bacterial/parasitic intestinal infection
- Inflammatory bowel disease
- Lactose intolerance
- Malabsorption
- Radiation proctocolitis

Painful
- Inflammatory bowel disease
- Ureteral colic
- Bowel obstruction
- Diverticular disease
- Gastroesophageal reflux/ulcer
- Liver or pancreatic disease
- Lead toxicity
- Porphyria

---

occur. Patients may present to the emergency department with an exacerbation of their previous symptoms or with a new abdominal complaint and often report they are undergoing a period of stress. Physical examination may reveal mild abdominal tenderness that is focal, varying in location, or diffuse.

Pain that is progressive, keeps the patient awake at night, or is associated with anorexia or significant abdominal tenderness suggests an alternate diagnosis. Fever, abdominal mass, and rectal bleeding also are atypical for IBS. In the absence of symptoms suggesting another diagnosis, the clinical criteria have a specificity ranging from 87% to100%, although sensitivity may be only 60%.[2] Patients diagnosed with IBS through correct use of the clinical criteria and who are followed for many years rarely have the diagnosis changed.[2]

Diagnostic Strategies

The diagnosis of IBS usually is made in the primary care setting and not in the emergency department. A typical primary care evaluation for IBS may include a complete blood count, thyroid studies, stool for ova and parasites, evaluation for lactose intolerance, and possibly lower gastrointestinal endoscopy. The role of the emergency physician is to exclude other more urgent causes of the patient's symptoms. In the emergency department, testing for pancreatitis, hepatitis, biliary colic, or urologic disorders, including urolithiasis, is appropriate based on the pattern of the presenting complaints.

Differential Considerations

The differential of symptomatic IBS depends on the predominant symptoms and includes a host of disorders (Box 94-2). Patients may present with pain, constipation, diarrhea, or any combination of the three.

Management

Not all patients with IBS require treatment. It is recommended that therapy be initiated only if symptoms diminish the quality of life.[1] Because no curative therapy is available, treatment is directed toward the relief of symptoms. Diet, behavioral, and pharmacologic therapies all are used in IBS. Therapy is subdivided by the type of IBS: constipation predominant, diarrhea predominant, or constipation-diarrhea combination. Dietary suggestions include a low-fat diet, reduced nondigestible sugars, and avoidance of gas-forming foods, although none of these has any proven benefit. Fiber supplementation may aid constipation-predominant IBS.

Medications with antispasmodic activity, such as anticholinergics and calcium channel blockers, are used for abdominal cramping, and peripherally acting narcotics, such as loperamide, are used to reduce diarrhea. Osmotic laxatives, such as lactulose, are sometimes helpful in constipation. Tricyclic antidepressants have been effective in certain classes of patients with IBS. Serotonin receptor antagonists, such as alosetron, and prokinetic agents also are used (Box 94-3).

Behavioral therapy may benefit patients who are unresponsive to medication, but high-quality evidence on its effectiveness is lacking. Nontraditional therapies such as arrowroot, artichoke leaf, and some Chinese traditional herbal medicines are supported by limited scientific evidence.[2]

Disposition

IBS is not a life-threatening disease and can be managed on an outpatient basis as long as other disorders have been excluded. The search for optimal therapy usually involves empiric trials until the correct fit is found. This process is best accomplished through a well-established primary care relationship. The disorder is chronic, but with appropriate therapy many patients experience significant improvement in their quality of life.

DIVERTICULAR DISEASE

Perspective

Diverticular disease is an affliction of middle age that seems to be a direct consequence of the diet of modern Western civilization. Diverticular disease was virtually unknown in the Western world before the 20th century and is still rare in other cultures. In 1925, only 9% of people older than age 50 in the United States had diverticula; by 1968, the percentage had increased to 30%.[3] Today it is estimated that 5% to 10% of people older than 45 years old and 80% of people older than 85 years old have diverticula.[4] The overall annual incidence is estimated at 200/100,000 adult population (40 to 75 years old).[3] Diverticula are less common in people younger than age 40 (representing only about 2% to 5% of all patients with the disease).[5] The proliferation of this disease was coincident with the invention and widespread use of the flour rolling mill, which removes the fiber-containing outer part of wheat. This coincidence has prompted the labeling of diverticulosis as a "modern deficiency disease,"[3] which is supported by the fact that adding fiber back into the diet seems to be protective against the development of diverticulosis.[6] In rural Africa and Asia where the diet contains a higher fiber content diverticular disease is virtually unknown.[7]

Diverticulosis denotes the presence of diverticula in the colon. Most patients with this condition are asymptomatic. *Diverticulitis* denotes inflammation of diverticula, which is usually a painful disorder. *Complicated diverticulitis* occurs when there is more extensive disease, including abscess formation, peritonitis, intestinal obstruction, or fistula formation.

Principles of Disease

The wall of the colon is penetrated at regular intervals by blood vessels that supply the internal intestinal layers. These vessels are the *vasa recta*. The site of vessel penetration is apparently the weakest part of the colon wall because it is at these sites that diverticula form. Although the exact pathogenic mechanism is unknown, the current theory is that diverticula form in response to increased intracolonic pressures generated when the colon is processing smaller non–fiber-containing stools. Higher pressures lead to a herniation of colonic mucosa through the intestinal wall at the vasa recta creating small, saclike appendages. These appendages (diverticula) usually measure 5 to 10 mm in diameter, but on rare occasions can grow into huge sacs measuring many centimeters *(giant colonic diverticulum)*. Diverticula are asymptomatic in most individuals but sometimes become obstructed, presumably with inspissated stool. When obstructed, inflammation sets in and microperforations of the sac occur, resulting in inflammation of pericolonic structures and abdominal pain.

In the Western world 85% of diverticular disease occurs in the left colon,[4] usually the sigmoid. This is not the case in Japan, where right-sided diverticular disease is more common. Japanese-Hawaiians consuming a low-fiber Western diet have a significantly increased incidence of diverticular disease but it remains in the right colon.[3] This finding suggests that diet plays a significant role in the formation of diverticula, but that the location of diverticula is genetically determined.

A spectrum of disease can occur when diverticular inflammation begins. In *uncomplicated diverticulitis* only the pericolonic fat is inflamed. With time, a phlegmon, abscess, or gross perforation may occur. Any extension of disease beyond the pericolonic fat is considered *complicated diverticulitis*. The involved colonic segment may fistulize to any adjacent organ, most commonly the bladder (65% of all fistulae).[7] Adjacent bowel may become obstructed by mass effect from an abscess or may exhibit an inflammatory ileus. Recurrent episodes of diverticulitis can lead to strictures in the colon with subsequent colonic obstruction.

Diverticula also can bleed, presumably from erosion into the mucosal wall by dried stool trapped in the diverticular sac. Severe hemorrhage occurs in 3% to 5% of all patients with diverticulosis and accounts for about 40% of all lower gastrointestinal hemorrhage.[3] Bleeding notably occurs in the absence of inflammation and is typically painless. Nonsteroidal anti-inflammatory drug use is known to be associated with this complication.[7]

Clinical Features

Diverticulosis

Commonly asymptomatic, patients with diverticulosis sometimes have nonspecific abdominal complaints including bloating, crampy pain, excessive gas, or a change in bowel habits.[8] Approximately 10% to 30% of patients with diverticulosis develop diverticulitis.[3,5]

Diverticulitis

Because most diverticula found in Western society form in the left colon, the typical presentation of diverticulitis is persistent left lower quadrant pain and tenderness. Occasionally pain is first felt in the hypogastrium before localizing to the left lower quadrant.[4] Referred pain may occur in the penis, scrotum, or suprapubic region. Right-sided diverticulitis may present as right lower quadrant pain and is impossible to distinguish clinically from appendicitis. Additional findings suggest various complications: Diffuse tenderness is associated with gross perforation or abscess rupture; dysuria, with a colovesical fistula; mass, with an abscess; and vomiting and abdominal distention, with intestinal obstruction. Fecal matter or gas emanating from the vagina suggests a colouterine fistula. Almost any adjacent organ can be involved in the inflammatory process. Patients who have been recently diagnosed with diverticulitis who are being treated as outpatients with oral antibiotics and who present to the emergency department with continuing or worsening symptoms should be evaluated for the possibility of an abscess.

Special care must be taken with elderly or immunocompromised patients since clinical signs and symptoms are much less dramatic, even with more severe disease. Perforation is more common in these patients, presents with less significant findings, and carries a high mortality rate.[4]

Diagnostic Strategies

Uncomplicated Diverticulitis

The clinical diagnosis of uncomplicated diverticulitis is made in a patient in the correct age range exhibiting focal left lower quadrant pain and tenderness in the absence of symptoms or signs that suggest an alternative diagnosis. No mass or peritoneal irritation should be encountered on examination, and the patient should otherwise appear well. If the patient fits this clinical picture treatment can be initiated on an empiric basis, and no laboratory tests or diagnostic imaging is required. Ancillary tests primarily are performed to exclude alternative diagnoses or the presence of complicated diverticulitis. When the diagnosis is unclear, studies to exclude gynecologic, renal, hepatic, biliary, or pancreatic disease may be indicated depending on the patient's presentation and degree of distress. Computed tomography (CT) of the abdomen should be considered for elderly and immunocompromised patients to exclude the possibility of a subtle presentation of complicated diverticulitis.

Complicated Diverticulitis

Abdominal Computed Tomography

Abdominal CT is the preferred method of evaluation in complicated diverticulitis. CT has the advantage of evaluating the colon and the structures around it, so it can make the diagnosis of diverticulitis and simultaneously evaluate the extent of disease. CT can also be used to guide percutaneous drainage of diverticular abscesses. Findings on CT consistent with diverticulitis include the presence of diverticula, inflammation of pericolonic fat, thickening of the bowel wall greater than 4 mm, free abdominal air, and an abscess.[4,5,9] CT can also help make an alternate diagnosis when diverticulitis is absent. CT is relatively noninvasive and is well tolerated by ill patients. Sensitivity and specificity for diverticulitis range from 69% to 95% and 75% to 100%.[7]

A negative CT scan cannot absolutely exclude diverticulitis. Small abscesses within the colon or mesocolon can be missed, as can the diverticula themselves. It may also be difficult to differentiate between carcinoma and diverticulitis on CT.[5] Marked bowel wall thickening associated with diverticulitis looks like cancer,[4] and contrast enema or endoscopy may be required to differentiate between the two. Occasionally metastatic disease is seen in the liver as proof of cancer, making the diagnosis more straightforward.

Barium Enema

Although double-contrast barium examination is the standard for the diagnosis of asymptomatic diverticula, it should be avoided in the setting of diverticulitis. The potential for preexisting occult perforation and subsequent risk of barium peritonitis limits its utility. Barium enema may be employed after the acute episode to exclude the diagnosis of carcinoma.

Water-Soluble Contrast Enema

A water-soluble contrast enema is the preferred method of imaging if a contrast enema needs to be performed in the acute setting. Water-soluble contrast material shows less detail than barium, but is still useful. Findings consistent with diverticulitis include the presence of diverticula along with extravasation of contrast material into an abscess cavity or into the peritoneum. Findings also can show a fistula or evidence of compression of the colon by an extrinsic mass. Because contrast material usually collects only in the intestinal lumen, contrast enemas give less information than CT about the extent of disease outside of the colon.

Ultrasound

Ultrasound can detect several findings suggesting diverticulitis including fluid collections around the colon, thickened hypoechoic bowel wall, or hyperechoic areas adjacent to the bowel wall suggesting pericolonic inflammation. Tenderness over an abnormal-appearing colon suggests that the colon is the source of the patient's pain. Occasionally diverticula can be visualized by ultrasound. As is often the case, the sensitivity of ultrasound for these findings varies significantly with the experience of the ultrasound operator. Because bowel gas inhibits the ability to image with ultrasound, adequate visualization of the bowel can be a problem. Currently the role for ultrasound in the evaluation of diverticulitis is not well defined.

Endoscopy

Endoscopy is limited in the acute setting by its more invasive nature, the risk of perforation,[5,10] and the logistics of arranging this procedure emergently. Although the endoscope is able to visualize diverticula and other pathology within the lumen of the colon, it is unable to evaluate the extent of extracolonic disease.

Plain Radiography

Plain films of the abdomen are not likely to be helpful in the diagnosis of diverticulitis unless either intestinal obstruction or perforation is suspected.

Differential Considerations

A patient who presents with more serious disease usually undergoes laboratory testing and diagnostic imaging and poses less of a diagnostic dilemma. A patient with milder disease who may be diagnosed on clinical grounds alone presents more of a challenge. One of the most serious diagnostic questions is whether or not the patient may have colonic carcinoma; however, it is usually safe to wait until after the acute episode has resolved to investigate this possibility. Additional diagnoses to consider include colitis (either inflammatory or ischemic); ureteral stones; inguinal hernia; and pelvic pathology, including ectopic pregnancy, pelvic inflammatory disease, and ovarian pathology with or without ovarian torsion. Appendicitis should be suspected when symptoms are predominantly right-sided. Diffuse abdominal pain should

---

BOX 94-4. Oral Antibiotic Therapy for Uncomplicated Diverticulitis

- Trimethoprim/sulfamethoxazole double-strength tablets BID *and* metronidazole, 500 mg q 6 hr
- Ciprofloxacin, 500 mg BID, *and* metronidazole, 500 mg q 6 hr
- Amoxicillin/clavulanate, 500/125 mg TID

All oral regimens should be taken for 7 to 10 days.

From Gilbert DN, Moellering RC Jr, Eliopoulos GM, Sande MA (eds): *The Sanford Guide to Antimicrobial Therapy,* 34th ed. Hyde Park, Vt, Antimicrobial Therapy, Inc, 2004.

---

prompt an evaluation for other life-threatening problems including leaking abdominal aortic aneurysm, peritonitis, hemoperitoneum from ectopic pregnancy, and bowel obstruction.

Management

Diverticulosis

All patients diagnosed with diverticulosis should be placed on a high-fiber diet, which has been shown to reduce abdominal symptoms and recurrent bouts of diverticulitis.[7] It is not known whether the common advice to avoid eating foods such as small seeds and nuts that may obstruct diverticula has merit.[7]

Uncomplicated Diverticulitis

Uncomplicated diverticulitis in an immunocompetent, nonelderly patient can be managed on an outpatient basis with oral antibiotics (Box 94-4). Coverage for gram-negative aerobic and anaerobic bacteria is required. Patients may be placed on a liquid diet for comfort, although this is not mandatory. Nonsteroidal anti-inflammatory drugs or narcotics are appropriate for pain control but many authors recommend avoiding morphine sulfate because it increases intraintestinal pressure and theoretically can precipitate perforation.[4] A high-fiber diet prevents recurrent diverticulitis for 5 years in 70% of patients.[5]

Patients with significant comorbid conditions or other problems including inability to tolerate oral liquids, poor social support, or inability to comply with follow-up in a reasonable time frame (2 to 3 days), should be considered for admission to the hospital. Admitted patients generally are treated with intravenous antibiotics (Box 94-5) and placed on bowel rest, although patients admitted for social reasons can be treated with oral medications.

Complicated Diverticulitis

Patients with complicated diverticulitis should be admitted to the hospital and treated with intravenous antibiotics. Emergent surgical intervention is indicated for all patients with peritonitis or perforation. Continuing clinical decline, sepsis resistant to medical management, or a high level of suspicion for carcinoma warrants urgent surgical consultation. Small (<5 cm) abscesses are treated with intravenous antibiotics alone (see Box 94-5), whereas larger abscesses are drained either percutaneously with imaging guidance or surgically. Bowel obstruction during an attack of diverticulitis is usually self-limited and resolves with conservative management. Chronic recurrent diverticulitis can result in stricture, which requires surgical intervention. Fistulae are usually repaired surgically. A significantly dilated cecum (>10 cm) or gas in the bowel wall should prompt early consultation with a surgeon about the possibility of bowel necrosis and impending perforation.[4]

Definitive Management

It is not known whether diverticula improve with medical or dietary treatment. The only proven way to eradicate diverticula is to remove the affected segment of colon surgically. Most patients who recover from their first attack of diverticulitis are likely to remain asymptomatic for many years. With subsequent attacks the likelihood of recurrence increases. Elective resection of diverticula typically is reserved for patients who have had more than one attack of diverticulitis. Some authors suggest that younger patients (<40 years old) undergo elective resection after their first bout of diverticulitis because of concerns about a higher risk for a second attack, but this is controversial.[11] Most resections can be done laparoscopically with a single-stage procedure (no colostomy).[11] Estimates on recurrence of diverticular disease after resection vary from 3% to 27%.[4,5,7,8,11]

Disposition

Uncomplicated Diverticulitis

Young, immunocompetent patients may be sent home on oral antibiotics with follow-up in 2 to 3 days to determine the success of treatment. Patients are cautioned to return to the emergency department if their condition worsens. Patients not significantly improved at follow-up should undergo diagnostic imaging to rule out an abscess and be admitted for intravenous antibiotics. Of patients treated medically for their first attack of diverticulitis, 95% remain symptom-free for the next 2 years,[4] and 80% to 90% remain symptom-free permanently.[11] Patients with recurrent episodes of diverticulitis should be referred to a surgeon for outpatient consultation for elective resection. All patients should undergo an evaluation for colon cancer when the acute episode has resolved because the incidence of coexistent cancer has been reported to be 9%.[3]

Complicated Diverticulitis

All patients require hospitalization for intravenous antibiotics and bowel rest. Most patients (65% to 85%) recover with medical management alone; the rest require surgical intervention. Outcomes are generally good, with mortality rates ranging from 1% to 6% for all patients, increasing to 12% to 18% for patients requiring surgery.[3]

LARGE BOWEL OBSTRUCTION

Perspective

Large bowel obstruction (LBO) is much less common than small bowel obstruction, but LBO is a more ominous condition because it is frequently associated with malignant disease. Half of all operative cases involving LBO in the United States are due to colorectal cancer. Adhesions, a common cause of small bowel obstruction, cause only 1% to 8% of LBO.[12] Other causes of LBO include volvulus, diverticular disease, fecal impaction, strictures (often related to inflammatory bowel disease or chronic colon ischemia), adhesions, hernia, and pseudo-obstruction. Most causes are managed surgically, but pseudo-obstruction responds well to medical management alone.

Principles of Disease

When mechanical obstruction occurs secondary to an obstructing lesion, either inside the bowel (carcinoma) or outside the bowel (diverticular abscess, volvulus), the bowel becomes increasingly dilated with air and fluid that cannot be passed distally. As the distention increases the intraluminal pressure increases. When intraluminal pressure approaches systolic blood pressure, blood flow to the bowel wall is compromised and edema sets in, with subsequent transudation of fluid into the lumen. Transudation along with decreased resorption of intraluminal fluid leads to dehydration. Eventually, as arterial flow to the bowel wall is compromised, ischemia and gangrene occur. Translocation of bacteria from compromised bowel can lead to sepsis. Perforation of the bowel wall follows if the process is not interrupted.[12]

Pseudo-obstruction, also called *Ogilvie's syndrome,* occurs through a completely different mechanism. Pseudo-obstruction is defined as LBO in which no obstructing lesion can be identified. This condition is usually found in patients with significant acute comorbid conditions.[13] Typically patients have a history of significant spine or retroperitoneal trauma, severe electrolyte disturbances, or narcotic exposure. Although the exact mechanism is unknown, it is believed to be a malfunction of autonomic control of the bowel. Normal balance between parasympathetic and sympathetic input is disrupted resulting in changes in motility that lead to obstruction. When the obstruction is in place, the pathophysiologic changes are the same as the changes described for mechanical obstruction.

Clinical Features

The typical presenting complaints of LBO are abdominal pain, abdominal distention, obstipation, and vomiting. The time frame in which these symptoms develop varies based on the rapidity of onset of the obstruction. LBO associated with a volvulus can develop rapidly, whereas obstruction from cancer tends to be gradual. Patients presenting later in the course of obstruction may be significantly dehydrated. Significant fever or tachycardia should prompt an investigation for gangrene and perforation. A palpable abdominal mass may represent a tumor, an abscess, or simply distended bowel. A rectal examination is helpful to look for an obstructing rectal mass or large volume of hard stool in the rectal vault consistent with fecal impaction.

Diagnostic Strategies

Electrolyte measurements may be helpful in guiding fluid and electrolyte replacement therapy. A significantly elevated white blood cell count should raise suspicion for gangrenous bowel whereas anemia suggests the possibility of colorectal cancer.

Plain Radiographs

A distended colon is the hallmark of LBO (Figure 94-1), although small bowel may be distended as well if the ileocecal valve is incompetent. In some cases gas-filled small bowel may obscure visualization of the colon and lead to the misdiagnosis of small bowel obstruction. An abrupt cutoff at the distal end of the obstructed colonic segment suggests a possible pseudo-obstruction. Cecal diameters exceeding 12 cm are of concern because this finding is associated with a higher risk of perforation.[13] The actual location and cause of the LBO is not usually evident on plain films.

Computed Tomography

CT is a valuable tool for determining the cause of the obstruction especially if the cause is a diverticular abscess or intussusception.[12] It is typically less helpful in pseudo-obstruction, where either colonoscopy or a water-soluble contrast enema is needed to make the diagnosis.

Colonoscopy and Water-Soluble Contrast Enema

Patients in whom the cause of obstruction is not known and who are not candidates for urgent surgical intervention should undergo either a water-soluble contrast enema or colonoscopy to determine the etiology of the

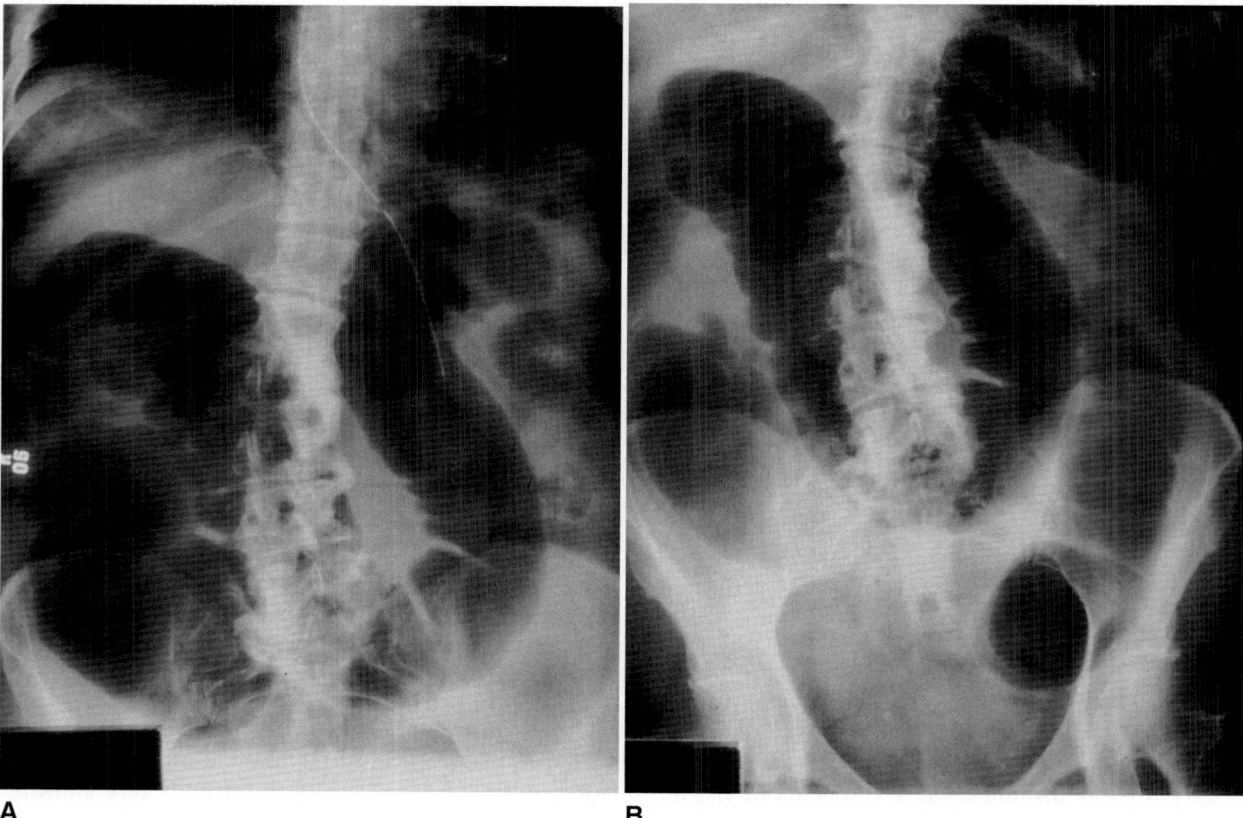

A   **B**

Figure 94-1. Large bowel obstruction at sigmoid colon caused by carcinoma. **A,** Erect. **B,** Supine.

obstruction. This diagnostic strategy is much more accurate in ruling out pseudo-obstruction than imaging.

Differential Considerations

The most common causes of LBO are colorectal cancer (53%), volvulus (17%), diverticulitis (12%), and compression from metastatic disease (6%). Other less common causes are strictures, incarcerated hernia, fecal impaction, adhesions, and pseudo-obstruction.[12]

Management

Management in the emergency department is symptomatic. Rehydration, electrolyte replacement, and pain management are the first concerns. Gastric decompression with a nasogastric tube may be helpful in cases of vomiting or when there is evidence of significant fluid or gas build-up in the small intestine. No additional fluid or solids should be administered by mouth. Antibiotics are indicated if gangrene or perforation is suspected (see Box 94-5). Definitive management depends on the cause of the obstruction, which may or may not be determined in the emergency department. Select diverticular abscesses may be drained percutaneously, whereas a sigmoid volvulus or pseudo-obstruction can be decompressed endoscopically. Diverticular disease and sigmoid volvulus eventually require an elective surgical procedure to prevent recurrence, although this often can be delayed. Carcinoma, cecal volvulus, strictures, intussusception, adhesions, and hernias are primarily dealt with surgically.

As long as there is no immediate concern for perforation, pseudo-obstruction is managed for the first 24 hours with bowel rest, hydration, and management of any acute comorbid conditions. If the colon fails to decompress, colonoscopic or pharmacologic intervention (neostigmine)[13] may be attempted with surgery reserved for refractory cases.

Fecal impaction is generally managed definitively in the emergency department through digital disimpaction or enema instillation. Particularly helpful are retention enemas where the patient retains the enema fluid in the rectum for 15 minutes or longer. Occasionally disimpaction is technically difficult enough to warrant general anesthesia.

Disposition

Most cases of LBO require procedural intervention (surgical, endoscopic, or percutaneous abscess drainage) to achieve resolution. All patients require hospitalization and consultation with a specialist capable of performing the appropriate procedure. Emergency surgical consultation is warranted in patients with evidence of gangrenous bowel or perforation.

VOLVULUS

Perspective

Volvulus of the colon occurs when a loop of bowel twists and obstructs the intestinal lumen. If severe enough, the twist may involve and compromise the vas-

cular supply to the loop of colon. The incidence of colonic volvulus is 2.65 cases per 100,000 population per year,[14] accounting for 1% to 7% of all LBOs.[15] Volvulus occurs in all age groups but older adults are affected most often, with a mean age of 60 to 70 years.[14] One third of cases in the developed world involve institutionalized patients.[15] Most cases are divided equally between the sigmoid colon and the cecum although volvulus can occur in all other areas of the colon. Sigmoid volvulus is typically a disease of older patients. Mortality rates with sigmoid volvulus exceed 50% in patients who present with gangrenous bowel.[14] In the absence of gangrenous bowel the risk of death is about 10%. Cecal volvulus is the most common cause of bowel obstruction in pregnancy. Pregnant women account for 12% of all cases of cecal volvulus.

Principles of Disease

Sigmoid Volvulus

The anatomic requirement for a sigmoid volvulus is a long redundant section of sigmoid that is attached to the abdominal wall by a narrow strip of mesentery. The narrow attachment allows the mesentery to twist on itself and obstruct the intestinal lumen. It is not clear whether this is a congenital condition or occurs as part of the aging process. After the colon twists on itself, the proximal colon continues to force gas and liquid into the obstructed segment causing a sometimes massive dilation of the distal colon. Significant electrolyte disturbances can occur secondary to third spacing and respiratory compromise occasionally occurs from massive abdominal distention. Left untreated the vascular supply can become compromised resulting in gangrene and perforation.

The exact precipitator of an acute episode of volvulus is not clear. A high-fiber diet has been implicated because a significant increase in the disease is noted in patients who are switched to a high-fiber diet.[14] Chronic constipation has been associated with volvulus, but it is unclear how the two conditions are related. Residents of long-term care facilities and patients with neurologic or psychiatric diseases also are predisposed to sigmoid volvulus, possibly as a result of alterations in colonic motility. There does not seem to be an association with prior surgery.

Cecal Volvulus

As in sigmoid volvulus, a mobile segment of cecum is a prerequisite to the disease. This mobility seems to be due to an incomplete fusion of the cecal mesentery to the posterior abdominal wall. Cadaver studies show that 10% of the adult population has ceca that are mobile enough to cause torsion.[15] Ten percent of cecal volvulus is due to a variant called *cecal bascule* in which the cecum does not twist but merely folds over on itself[12]; symptoms and management are the same. The tendency for cecal volvulus may be related to "maneuvering room" available for the colon within the abdomen. Persons with less space in the abdomen for the colon to move about seem to be more predisposed to volvulus in general. Women are less susceptible than men, possibly because of their wider pelvic brim. This situation changes in pregnancy when the abdomen becomes crowded with a distended uterus, and a higher incidence of volvulus is seen. Gangrene of the bowel is common and occurs in 20% of patients with cecal volvulus.[16]

Clinical Features

Sigmoid Volvulus

The hallmark of sigmoid volvulus is the triad of abdominal pain, distention, and constipation. There is variability in the extent to which the sigmoid colon can twist on itself, so the presentation of sigmoid volvulus varies from subtle to dramatic. Everything from minor abdominal discomfort that has been present for many days to severe acute abdominal pain associated with gross abdominal distention and unstable vital signs has been described. Sometimes the diagnosis is not made until the patient has been hospitalized for some time. Many patients have a history suggestive of previous episodes of volvulus that self-reduced.

The physical examination may reveal a distended tympanitic abdomen, often with most of the distention in the upper abdomen but primarily on one side. Patients may look remarkably well for the amount of distention that is encountered. Significant abdominal pain, fever, lack of bowel sounds, peritonitis or cardiovascular instability suggest gangrenous bowel and should prompt immediate surgical consultation. The absence of these findings does not exclude gangrene however. The length of symptoms alone is not predictive of gangrene of the bowel.[14]

Cecal Volvulus

The clinical triad of abdominal pain, distention, and constipation seen in sigmoid volvulus also is seen in cecal volvulus, but many patients lack one or more of these findings. Vomiting is seen in only about 50% of patients.

Diagnostic Strategies

Sigmoid Volvulus

The diagnosis of sigmoid volvulus can be made on plain films in 80% of cases.[14] A grossly distended loop of colon lacking haustral markings is typical and is seen just as often in the right side of the abdomen as in the left (Figure 94-2). The bowel may appear as if it were a "bent inner tube." Free air may be seen on an upright chest x-ray or lateral decubitus film of the abdomen in patients who have a perforation. Gas backing up into the rest of the colon may obscure the typical appearance of sigmoid volvulus on plain films, leading to a significant number of nondiagnostic studies.[14] Cecal volvulus and bowel obstruction from other causes may have a similar radiographic appearance. When the diagnosis is in doubt contrast enema may be helpful. Contrast material fills up the colon to the tapering point of torsion, giving a "bird's beak" appearance to the column of contrast material (Figure 94-3).

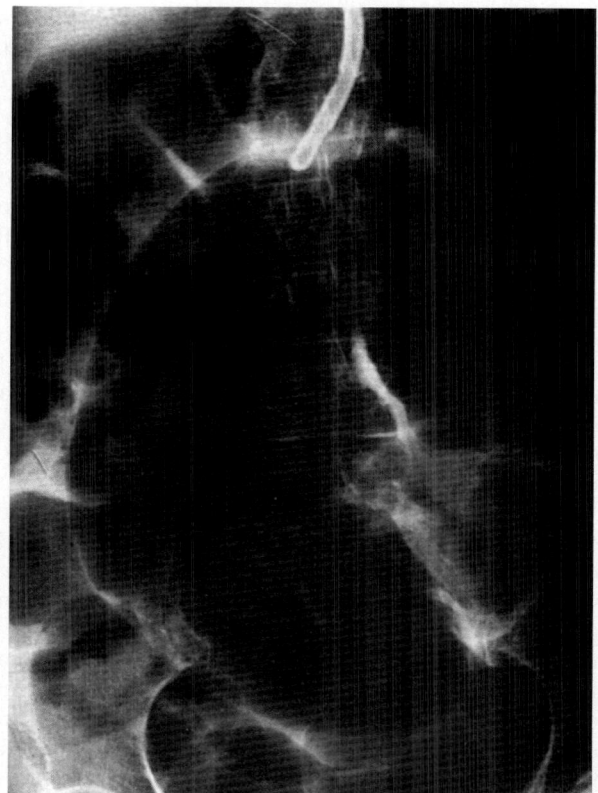

Figure 94-2. Plain film of abdomen shows large, dilated loop characteristic of sigmoid volvulus.

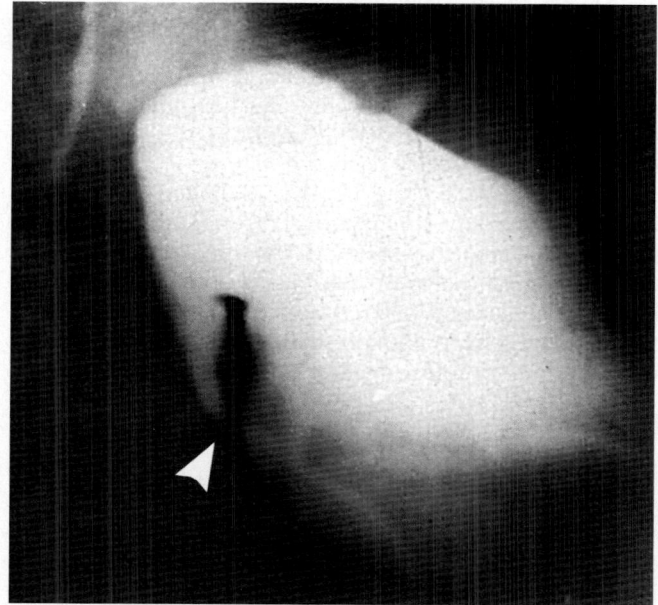

Figure 94-3. Characteristic "bird's beak" sign of volvulus shown on barium enema.

Cecal Volvulus

Plain films are often helpful in establishing a diagnosis of cecal volvulus, but in 50% of cases the diagnosis cannot be made definitively on the plain film.[14,16] The cecum should be markedly dilated and may contain an

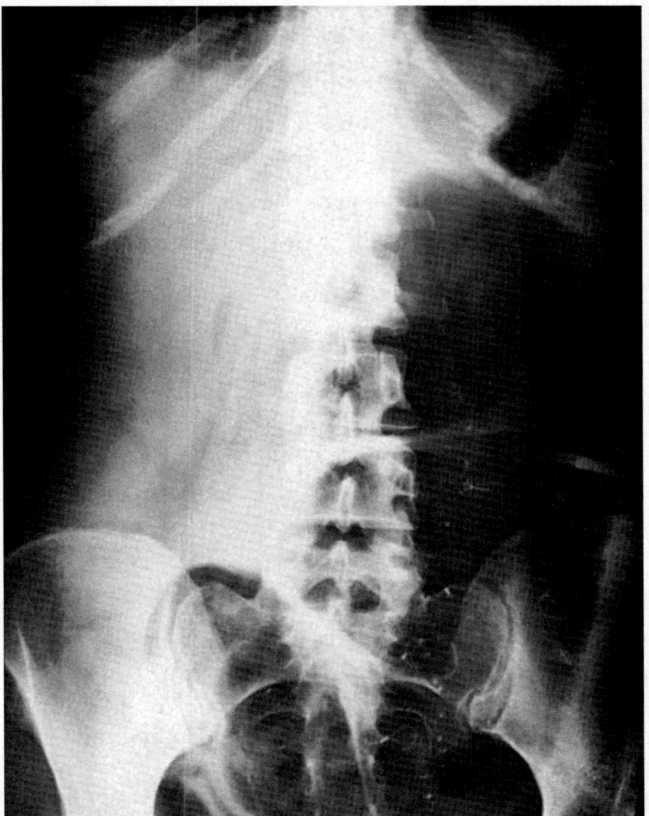

Figure 94-4. Plain film shows distended colon characteristic of cecal volvulus. Note presentation in left lower quadrant and absence of right-sided gas shadows.

obstructed proximal end of the bowel lumen is identified, and a lubricated rubber tube is inserted through the obstruction. With decompression of gas and liquid stool the bowel is able to undergo self-detorsion. Endoscopic decompression is successful in 50% to 90% of cases.[12,14] If the patient has gangrenous bowel or does not respond to endoscopic decompression, surgery is indicated. Recurrence rates are estimated at 60%[14]; elective resection of the redundant sigmoid is recommended after resolution of the acute episode. The mortality rate associated with sigmoid volvulus is 20% overall and exceeds 50% in the subpopulation with gangrene.

Cecal Volvulus

The proximal nature of the cecum makes it unavailable for detorsion via endoscope, so detorsion is done surgically. After detorsion, the cecum typically is fixed to the abdominal wall or the redundant section is resected.[17] Recurrence is rare after surgical repair.

Disposition

All patients with volvulus require admission to the hospital for detorsion and surgical intervention to prevent recurrence.

INTUSSUSCEPTION

Perspective

In contrast to in children, intussusception in adults is rare. It accounts for only 1% to 3% of cases of adult bowel obstruction. Most adult intussusceptions (80%) are of the small bowel, and although only 10% of children have a pathologic lesion as the cause of the intussusception, 90% of adults do. In the colon most of the lesions are malignancies.[18] Intussusception in adults is often unsuspected before being revealed on a CT scan or during laparotomy. The condition occurs over a wide variety of ages; the mean age of presentation is 65 years.[19]

Principles of Disease

The exact mechanism of intussusception is unknown, but it is believed that a lesion ("lead point") changes the motility properties of the intestine and allows a

air-fluid level. The small bowel is often distended as well. In contrast to sigmoid volvulus, the distal colon should have paucity of gas (Figure 94-4). The classic "coffee bean" sign, a large oval gas shadow with a line down the middle representing bowel bent over on itself, may be seen in the midabdomen. Free air suggests perforation and requires emergent surgical consultation. A common mistake is misinterpreting the plain film as showing a sigmoid volvulus. If the diagnosis is unclear, a contrast enema is helpful in showing the site of torsion. On CT a mesocolon "whirl sign" may be seen indicating a twisted segment of mesentery.[17]

Differential Considerations

Any process that causes LBO may mimic volvulus (Box 94-6).

Management

Sigmoid Volvulus

Although spontaneous reduction of a sigmoid volvulus can occur, it is infrequent enough to mandate a proactive approach to treatment. If there is no clinical evidence of gangrenous bowel, endoscopic detorsion should be attempted by an experienced operator. Using the endoscope, the bowel is first examined for any signs of gangrene. If the bowel is healthy, the twisted, proximal segment to invaginate into a more distal segment. As peristaltic activity pushes the invaginated segment, its mesentery, and mesenteric blood vessels farther down the bowel, eventually the blood supply can be compromised and ischemia may occur. Edema associated with the intussusception can lead to a mechanical obstruction of the bowel.

Clinical Features

Intussusception in adults presents in one of two patterns. The first is that of acute partial intestinal obstruction. Fewer than 20% of intussusceptions cause complete obstruction.[20] With this pattern, the typical presenting complaint is abdominal pain. Vomiting, bleeding, and constipation may be present but often are not. The abdomen may be distended, and bowel sounds are often decreased. A mass is seldom palpated, and although each of the individual findings can be present, the classic triad of abdominal pain, mass, and heme-positive stools seen in children is rarely found in adults. The second presentation is much more subtle, with intermittent abdominal pain for months or years. The diagnosis is usually made only when the pain becomes unrelenting or has been persistent enough to prompt imaging.

Diagnostic Strategies

Plain Radiography

Plain radiographs are a reasonable screening test in a patient suspected of having bowel obstruction, but they usually show only nonspecific large bowel dilation.

Computed Tomography

Typically used in the evaluation of abdominal pain and bowel obstruction, CT usually detects the intussusception.[19]

Ultrasound

Ultrasound is also accurate in detecting intussusception but is not as useful as CT in excluding other diagnoses. A transverse view of the intussusception appears as a "donut" or a "target." A longitudinal view has an ultrasound appearance similar to a kidney ("pseudo-kidney sign").

Barium Enema

Although a barium enema can show intussusception and even reduce it, it is a less desirable study than either CT or ultrasound for initial diagnosis. In contrast to children, reduction of intussusception in adults is not desired before surgery because of concerns about spreading malignant cells from malignant lead points. Barium enema should never be used in patients suspected of having a bowel perforation.

Differential Considerations

The differential diagnosis includes other causes of bowel obstruction (Box 94-6 and Box 94-7).

BOX 94-7. Causes of Small Bowel Obstruction

- Adhesions
- Hernias
- Neoplasm
- Adynamic ileus
- Inflammatory bowel disease
- Intussusception
- Volvulus
- External compression from masses (infectious or neoplastic)
- Gallstones
- Bezoars
- Pseudo-obstruction

Management

Surgery is required in most cases. Emergency department management is supportive and aimed at optimizing fluid status, recognizing gangrene or perforation, administering antibiotics if compromised bowel is suspected, and securing surgical consultation in the appropriate time frame. Because of the high incidence of malignancy, reduction is often not attempted in adults before surgical exploration.[19] Occasionally intussusception may resolve spontaneously, but an evaluation to exclude a pathologic lead point still must be undertaken.

Disposition

Because of the surgical nature of this disease, all patients require admission to the hospital.

INFLAMMATORY BOWEL DISEASE

Perspective

Inflammatory bowel disease (IBD) includes two clinically similar but distinct diseases: Crohn's disease (CD) and ulcerative colitis (UC). Both diseases are characterized by chronic and unpredictable relapsing inflammation of the gastrointestinal tract from causes that have not been definitively identified. Significant morbidity occurs from acute exacerbations of inflammation. It is estimated that more than 1 million people in the United States are affected by IBD,[21] divided approximately equally between CD and UC.[22] The annual incidence of CD is 5 cases per 100,000. The long-term management of IBD is a complex stepwise process that involves multiple medications and surgery. The goals of the emergency physician are (1) to recognize potential new cases of IBD, (2) to consider and exclude serious complications in IBD patients, and (3) to identify IBD patients who need in-hospital care. Treatment plans are best developed in consultation with a physician experienced in the long-term management of IBD.

Principles of Disease

Ulcerative Colitis

UC causes inflammation and ulceration throughout the colon and rectum, but spares the small intestine. Inflammation is more superficial than that found in CD. Typically inflammation exists as one continuous lesion originating in the rectum and extending varying distances into the colon, although more recently cases of discontinuous disease ("skip lesions") similar to CD have been reported in UC.[23] The concordance rate among identical twins is low (6% to 14%) suggesting that more than genetic factors are involved in the development of UC.[24] Stress can trigger exacerbations and cigarette smoking has a protective effect, suggesting environmental factors at work. Appendectomy at an early age is protective suggesting the immune system may play a role. In animal models of IBD, the disease does not occur in animals kept in a bacteria-free environment, suggesting bowel flora are a necessary ingredient for disease. One unifying theory is that UC represents a genetic predisposition to develop an inflammatory reaction to normal intestinal flora.

Crohn's Disease

The cause of CD is unknown, but genetic, environmental, immunologic, and infectious causes all have been implicated as possible causative or contributory factors.[22] Concordance between identical twins is 45% to 50%, suggesting a strong genetic predisposition that is modified by other factors.[24] Africans have a low incidence of CD but African Americans have an incidence similar to white Americans.[22] The first genetic mutation associated with CD was described in 2001 and is associated with 10% to 20% of cases of CD.[23] An association between a strain of *Mycobacterium* and CD has been hypothesized with the evidence being convincing enough to spur legislation in the United Kingdom to eradicate this potential pathogen from the food chain.[25] Although the onset of the disease can occur at any time, CD affects young patients, with onset of disease typically in the teens and 20s. Inflammation in CD is deep, involving the entire colonic wall. The disease is not limited to the colon and rectum as it is in UC, but may affect any part of the gastrointestinal tract. CD is found most often in the distal small intestine and colon and less commonly in the esophagus, duodenum, or stomach.[26] Because of the transmural nature of the inflammation, patients may develop intestinal strictures or fistulae to adjacent organs.

Clinical Features

Typical presenting complaints in patients with IBD include abdominal pain, often crampy, and tenesmus with loose or diarrheal stools. Blood may be present in the stool. CD patients may have a history of nocturnal diarrhea; a complaint that helps differentiate CD patients from patients who have IBS. Weight loss is common. The physical examination may reveal significant tenderness or an abdominal mass representing an abscess. External evidence of CD may be evident in the anal area with fissures, ulcerated hemorrhoids, strictures, or cutaneous abscesses. Extraintestinal manifestations include inflammatory conditions of the skin, eyes, and joints. In children growth and sexual development may be affected. Onset of symptoms usually occurs before age 30,[21] although the diagnosis can be difficult to make in its early stages.

Patients often present with a previous diagnosis of IBD and worsening abdominal symptoms. A common reason for relapse is the interruption of the medications that have kept the patient in remission. Many patients become complacent during quiescent periods and stop taking their medications. IBD requires continuous, lifelong maintenance therapy. Adherence to therapy has been shown to reduce the risk of cancer and acute attacks.[21] The complications of IBD include common ones such as fistulae, strictures, and abscesses, and less common but life-threatening complications, such as fulminant colitis, toxic megacolon, and intestinal perforation.

Toxic Megacolon

Toxic megacolon is a pathologic dilation of the colon resulting from inflammation of the smooth muscle layers of the intestine. Muscle inflammation leads to paralysis, dilation, and potentially perforation if left untreated. The hallmark of toxic megacolon is colon dilation in the presence of an inflammatory condition of the colon in a patient who appears systemically toxic. Presence of inflammation and toxicity differentiates toxic megacolon from other disorders that cause colon dilation including mechanical obstruction, pseudo-obstruction, or congenital or acquired megacolon.[27]

Toxic megacolon is typically caused by IBD or infectious colitis. Triggering events may include recent ingestion of anticholinergics, antimotility agents, narcotics, or antidepressants. Patients usually have experienced symptoms of colitis, often severe, for several days before the onset of toxic megacolon. Abdominal pain, fever, tachycardia, and abdominal distention are present. Plain radiographs are diagnostic and show a colon with a diameter of 6 cm or greater, although this finding may not be present in early stages. Treatment involves aggressive fluid hydration, intravenous corticosteroids, antibiotics covering bowel flora (see Box 94-5), and an evaluation for potential infections, especially in immunocompromised patients. The mortality rate has decreased since the 1970s to less than 2% as a result of the early recognition and aggressive treatment.

Diagnostic Strategies

There are no specific laboratory tests available to diagnose IBD. Laboratory abnormalities can occur for a variety of reasons. Electrolyte abnormalities may occur secondary to significant diarrhea, or anemia may occur from bloody stools. The erythrocyte sedimentation rate can be elevated and useful for categorizing the severity of the disease. Stools contain fecal leukocytes, but stool cultures and ova and parasite examinations should be normal.

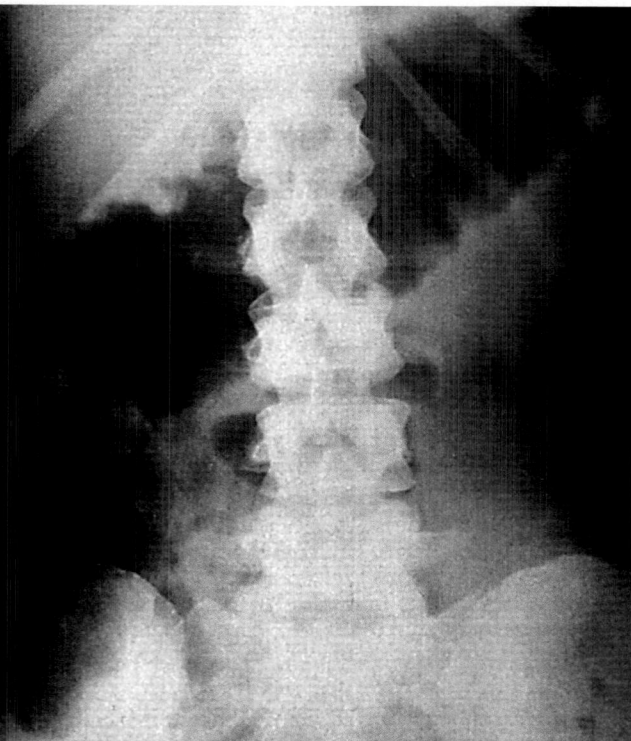

Figure 94-5. Toxic megacolon secondary to ulcerative colitis. Smooth indentations along margin of colon represent pseudopolyps.

Plain radiography is not helpful in the diagnosis of uncomplicated disease, but may show bowel obstruction, toxic megacolon, or free air from a perforation (Figure 94-5). Plain films should be limited to patients suspected of having these complications. Contrast studies can reveal lesions suspicious for IBD including ulcerations of the mucosal surface, fistulae, or strictures. In Europe, where ultrasound technicians are more experienced in the application, ultrasound is used to identify active disease and look for complications.[23] Ultrasound is much less commonly used in the United States. Magnetic resonance imaging can locate affected bowel segments and identify fistulae, stenoses, and abscesses. CT is the best study routinely available to evaluate extraluminal complications. CT colonography ("virtual colonoscopy"), although good at identifying cancerous lesions of the colon, does not show the typical lesions of IBD.[23] Endoscopic evaluation with biopsy is usually required to confirm the diagnosis.

Differential Considerations

Symptoms are protean and overlap with many common abdominal conditions, including appendicitis, infectious colitis, ischemic colitis, radiation colitis, diverticular disease, cancer, and bowel obstruction.

Management

Medical management is the mainstay of therapy for most IBD patients. Salicylates, steroids, antimetabolites, and immunosuppressive agents play a role in CD and UC (Box 94-8). The choice of agents depends on

BOX 94-8. Medications Used in the Treatment of Inflammatory Bowel Disease

- 5-Aminosalicylic acid agents
  - Sulfasalazine
  - Mesalamine
- Antibiotics
  - Metronidazole*
  - Ciprofloxacin
  - Rifaximin
  - Tobramycin
- Corticosteroids
  - Prednisone
  - Hydrocortisone
  - Methylprednisolone
  - Budesonide
- Antimetabolites
  - Azathioprine
  - 6-Mercaptopurine
  - Methotrexate
- Immunosuppressants
  - Cyclosporine
- Anti–tumor necrosis factor antibodies
  - Infliximab

*Beneficial in Crohn's disease only.

classification of the disease into either *mild to moderate* disease or *severe* disease (Box 94-9).

5-Aminosalicylic acids (5-ASA) are the first line of therapy for disease that is not severe. These agents can be administered orally, or rectally if the disease is in or near the rectum. Sulfasalazine is one of the original drugs in this category. Its dose range is limited by sulfa toxicity at higher doses which is manifested by headache, stomach upset, and nausea. Serious side effects including bone marrow suppression can occur. A newer 5-ASA derivative, mesalamine, has less toxicity allowing higher dosages. When an acute flare of IBD is in remission, the patient may be continued on 5-ASA derivatives for maintenance therapy.

Antibiotics are used primarily in CD, although they may be used in UC as well. Metronidazole and ciprofloxacin may be used as maintenance therapy in CD but do not seem to affect UC. Studies suggest that tobramycin or rifaximin may offer some benefit in UC, but further evaluation is needed.[28]

Oral corticosteroids are used in patients with moderate to severe disease or patients who are unresponsive to a 5-ASA agent. Steroids should be tapered when remission is achieved to avoid typical steroid side effects. Intravenous corticosteroids are reserved for hospitalized patients with severe disease. Budesonide, a newer oral corticosteroid, is degraded on its first pass through the bloodstream and has fewer systemic side effects.

The immunomodulating drugs azathioprine and 6-mercaptopurine are used in patients resistant to other therapies or to wean steroid-dependent patients off steroids. Emergency physicians must assess for marrow suppression from these medications and pancreatitis, which can occur in 15% of patients.[29]

BOX 94-9. Disease Severity in Inflammatory Bowel Disease

Ulcerative Colitis
Mild Disease
- ≤4 stools per day
- May have some blood
- No systemic signs of toxicity (fever, tachycardia, anemia, elevated erythrocyte sedimentation rate)

Moderate Disease
- >4 stools per day
- Minimal signs of toxicity

Severe Disease
- >6 bloody stools per day *and*
- Signs of systemic toxicity

Crohn's Disease
Mild
- Ambulatory and able to eat
- No toxicity
- No significant abdominal pain or mass

Moderate
- Mild disease that has failed treatment
- May have some systemic toxicity

Severe
- Persistent symptoms on corticosteroids
- High fever, persistent vomiting
- Intestinal obstruction
- Rebound tenderness
- Cachexia
- Abscess

Adapted from Hanauer SB, Present DH: The state of the art in the management of inflammatory bowel disease. *Rev Gastroenterol Disord* 3:81, 2003.

The immunosuppressant agent cyclosporine is used in severe cases, often when patients are not surgical candidates. Although most patients tolerate it well, cyclosporine has significant potential toxicity including myelosuppression, electrolyte disturbances, and hepatic and nephrotoxicity.[21] Opportunistic infections including *Pneumocystis* pneumonia have been known to occur.[24]

Infliximab, an antibody to human tumor necrosis factor-α, is useful in advanced cases of IBD. It generally has a benign side-effect profile[22] but carries a risk of opportunistic infections, including tuberculosis and fungal infections. Surgery is reserved for patients with severe disease refractory to medical management or for patients with complications. Indications for surgical intervention include intestinal obstruction, significant bleeding, abscess formation, or fistulae. A colectomy is curative for UC, but there is no curative surgery for CD.

Disposition

Consultation with a gastroenterologist is recommended before patient disposition. Most patients with an uncomplicated mild to moderate exacerbation of IBD need only to restart their maintenance therapy if it was interrupted or add oral corticosteroids to their regimen.

Patients with severe disease need hospitalization for administration of parenteral corticosteroids. Bowel rest does not seem to be beneficial unless the patient needs surgical intervention.[28] Emergent surgical consultation should be sought for life-threatening hemorrhage, evidence of perforation, or toxic megacolon. Urgent surgical intervention is indicated if the bowel is obstructed. Abscesses may be treated percutaneously with imaging guidance or by surgery.[26] Chronic fistulae are initially treated medically.[29] Patients discharged home need to be followed closely by the physician monitoring their disease to ensure that remission is achieved in a timely fashion and that the patient complies with the suppressive therapy after the acute event. For patients in remission endoscopic monitoring for cancer is required on an ongoing basis, although the exact frequency of examination has not yet been defined.[29] The estimated prevalence of cancer in CD patients is significant at 2%,[26] and patients with UC have a 15 times greater chance of developing colorectal cancer than the general population.[24]

COLONIC ISCHEMIA

Perspective

Colonic ischemia (CI) is the most common of the intestinal ishemic disorders. Estimates place the incidence of CI at 1 of every 2000 hospitalizations. Its presentation overlaps with many other significant abdominal diseases, and it is difficult to diagnose without endoscopic visualization of the colonic mucosa. Although elderly people are most at risk, the condition can occur in all age groups. Both sexes are equally affected. In one study, more than 50% of persons admitted with CI were initially diagnosed with IBD. Because there is no specific treatment, and outcomes are usually good, the difficulty in making the diagnosis does not cause significant morbidity.

Principles of Disease

The exact cause of CI is unknown. Isolated CI without small bowel involvement is usually due to microvascular disease of the colon and not to large vessel (mesenteric artery) occlusion. The primary insult is a low blood flow state precipitated by a variety of causes. The colonic vascular system lacks the redundancy that is found in the small bowel, predisposing it to ischemic insults. Colonic arterioles seem to be particularly sensitive to vasoconstrictive influences, and the rapid-growing intestinal mucosa is especially vulnerable to interruptions in blood flow. In addition, high intraluminal pressures that normally develop within the colon can alter intestinal perfusion significantly. CI can occur in any part of the colon, including the rectum, but for unknown reasons it occurs in the left colon 75% of the time.[30]

CI represents a spectrum of disease whose manifestations vary with the extent of the ischemic insult. Most CI is self-limited and resolves completely with conservative therapy. With a prolonged or severe insult scarring or stricturing of the colon may occur. If the ischemia is transmural, gangrene and intestinal perforation are possibilities. Chronic mild inflammation results in intermittent symptoms similar to IBD.

Clinical Features

The presentation of CI may vary but typically involves the acute onset of mild crampy abdominal pain in the left lower quadrant with abdominal distention and bloody diarrhea.[30,31] One third of patients may present without pain.[30] Nausea and vomiting can occur with obstruction secondary to a stricture or an ileus. Tenderness over the affected colon may be present but is often not dramatic. Peritoneal findings, fever, and a significantly elevated white blood cell count suggest gangrenous bowel and perforation. Toxic megacolon is a recognized complication.

Diagnostic Strategies

There are no sensitive or specific biochemical markers for CI, although biochemical abnormalities such as elevated serum lactate, phosphate, and alkaline phosphate levels may be present. These abnormalities may be absent in milder disease[30] and often are not present in more significant disease until after irreversible damage has occurred. A complete blood count to exclude significant anemia and to look for a leukocytosis suggestive of perforation is appropriate. Serum electrolytes should be checked if diarrhea or vomiting has been significant or prolonged. Stool blood and white blood cells are common findings in several of the entities that present similarly to CI including IBD and infectious colitis. A positive occult stool guaiac should insure that the patient is eventually evaluated for colonic carcinoma.

Plain Radiographs

Plain radiographs often show only nonspecific dilated bowel. Findings specific for CI occur in only 20% of patients. The classic findings are intraluminal prominences representing submucosal hemorrhage and swelling, known as *thumbprinting*. Thumbprinting also can be seen occasionally with other disorders, including IBD, colonic infections, or hemorrhage secondary to anticoagulants. Other findings consistent with CI include wall thickening and ahaustral segments. Air in the portal venous system or bowel wall suggests imminent intestinal infarction.

Barium Enema

Thumbprinting is detected more often by barium enema than by plain films, but this study has largely been replaced by colonoscopy.

Colonoscopy

Colonoscopy is the preferred method to diagnose CI because it visualizes the abnormal colonic mucosa better than barium enema and can be used to take biopsy specimens to differentiate between cancer and other non-CI causes of colitis. Colonoscopy can also detect necrotic bowel by its distinct cyanotic or black appearance. If colonoscopy is delayed, findings consistent with CI may have already improved or resolved.

Computed Tomography

Although CT does not allow the definitive diagnosis of CI, it can exclude other disorders. CT shows several findings in the colon suggestive of CI including thumbprinting, wall thickening, and luminal narrowing.

Angiography

Angiography is not usually helpful in either the diagnosis or the management of CI. In most cases of CI the blood flow defect is at the microvascular level and has resolved by the time the patient presents for evaluation.[30-32] The exception is when only the ascending colon is affected; this suggests a superior mesenteric artery thrombosis. Angiography is indicated in these cases.

Differential Considerations

The symptoms of CI are nonspecific and overlap with numerous other disorders including IBD, radiation proctocolitis, and infectious colitis. If strictures are present, the possibility of diverticulitis or colon cancer should be considered.

Management

In the absence of surgical complications the treatment of CI is supportive and includes hospitalization for bowel rest, hydration, and pain management. Nonsteroidal anti-inflammatory drugs are best avoided if there is any evidence of bleeding. Broad-spectrum antibiotics covering bowel flora are indicated for patients with more significant symptoms (see Box 94-5). If CI is precipitated by an episode of hypotension, the cause of hypotension must be sought and treated aggressively and cardiac output must be maximized.[33] Vasopressors should be avoided, as should steroids which may facilitate bowel perforation.[31] Colonic distention if present can be reduced through the use of a rectal tube. Decompression of the colon may result in a lowering of transmural pressure and improved colonic perfusion. Sepsis, peritoneal findings, free abdominal air, significant fever, massive bleeding, and a significant leukocytosis suggest bowel necrosis or perforation and should prompt emergent surgical consultation.

Disposition

Patients with mild symptoms and no significant abdominal tenderness or bleeding can be managed as outpatients and referred for colonoscopy. Stool studies including cultures for bacteria, microscopy for ova and parasites, and a *Clostridium difficile* titer are helpful if the diagnosis is uncertain. Patients with more significant findings, especially if the diagnosis of gangrenous bowel cannot be excluded, require admission to the hospital. A high mortality rate (60%) is expected for patients undergoing emergent surgery. Most patients improve without surgical intervention and only 5% have a recurrence of CI.[30]

RADIATION PROCTOCOLITIS

Perspective

Radiation proctocolitis is a common side effect of radiation therapy, occurring in 50% to 75% of patients receiving radiation to the pelvis. The disease has two distinct presentations: acute and chronic. *Acute radiation proctocolitis* begins during or shortly after a course of radiation therapy, usually is easily diagnosed, and is self-limited. *Chronic radiation proctocolitis* typically begins anytime up to 2 years after the end of radiation therapy, although 10% of cases have onset delayed beyond 2 years. Some cases have occurred decades later. Approximately 5% to 10% of patients with pelvic radiation develop chronic radiation proctocolitis.[34] Patients with more severe acute radiation proctocolitis seem to be prone to chronic proctocolitis.[35] Because of its nonspecific presentation and delayed appearance the diagnosis of chronic radiation proctocolitis can be challenging.

Principles of Disease

Radiation damages tissue through the creation of oxygen free radicals which damage cellular DNA. The faster the growth rate of cells the more this DNA damage affects their function. For this reason radiation is an effective treatment for neoplastic disease, but also is damaging to rapidly growing normal tissue such as intestinal epithelium.

Acute Radiation Proctocolitis

Intestinal epithelium is normally sloughed and replaced at a rapid rate. After the start of radiation therapy growth of replacement epithelium is slowed, but sloughing continues at the pre-exposure rate. This mismatch leads to gaps in the epithelium. Over time these gaps coalesce into ulcerations. In addition, edema and inflammatory changes of the submucosa cause excessive mucous secretion and bleeding. When radiation therapy has ended, the cycle of damage stops and healing occurs over the next few weeks.

Chronic Radiation Proctocolitis

The pathologic mechanism in chronic radiation proctocolitis is entirely different from acute radiation proctocolitis. Chronic radiation proctocolitis results from a progressive endarteritis with abnormal tissue collagen deposition. Over time affected bowel gradually becomes ischemic, leading to ulceration, scarring, and narrowing of the bowel lumen. Frank necrosis and perforation, although uncommon, can occur in more severe cases. The long-term outcomes in chronic radiation proctocolitis have not been well studied, but it seems that patients who develop fistulae and bleeding strictures have the poorest prognosis.[35]

Clinical Features

Acute radiation proctocolitis presents as abdominal pain and bleeding and tenesmus. Onset during the course of radiation therapy, typically after several treatments, suggests the diagnosis.

Chronic radiation proctocolitis has a more insidious onset with a variety of presentations including ulcerative disease, stricture with or without obstruction, fistulae, or bowel perforation. Symptoms may be similar to acute disease with tenesmus, diarrhea, and urgency. Bleeding can occur but is usually not hemodynamically significant. Decreased caliber of stool with increased straining or constipation suggests a stricture. Fistulae can occur between affected bowel and any adjacent organ, but the most common fistulae are rectovaginal. Some patients may have anal sphincter dysfunction and loss of bowel control. Symptoms tend to have a significant negative impact on the quality of life.[35]

Diagnostic Strategies

The diagnosis of acute radiation proctocolitis is made clinically based on the development of typical symptoms in the setting of radiation therapy. Further evaluation is usually not warranted.

Chronic radiation proctocolitis is typically a diagnosis of exclusion. Endoscopy can be suggestive, revealing pale, thickened, and friable mucosa with prominent telangiectasias. Biopsy specimens often show only nonspecific chronic inflammation. In some cases endoscopy may be technically difficult because of scarring and reduced mobility of the intestine. Barium enema is an acceptable alternative when endoscopy is problematic, as long as bowel perforation is not a concern.

Differential Considerations

In chronic radiation proctocolitis, the possibility that symptoms are due to recurrence of the initial malignancy or a new malignancy induced by radiation exposure must be entertained. Symptoms of chronic radiation proctocolitis generally are clinically indistinguishable from other causes of bowel inflammation including IBD, infectious colitis, and ischemic colitis.[36]

Management

Treatment of acute radiation proctocolitis is symptomatic and a therapeutic plan should be developed in conjunction with the patient's radiation therapist. Steroid enemas to reduce inflammation and water-absorbing stool softeners to reduce mucus-containing diarrhea are helpful. Reduction of the daily radiation dose also can reduce symptoms significantly.

Chronic radiation proctocolitis treatment is also symptomatic. If rectal involvement is significant, stool softeners, analgesics, anti-inflammatory agents (e.g., sulfasalazine) and sucralfate enemas are helpful. Metronidazole is beneficial when added to anti-inflammatory therapy. Symptoms often resolve over several months of medical treatment. If bleeding is significant, endoscopic laser photocoagulation may be effective although recurrence of bleeding is common.[34] Minimally symptomatic strictures can be managed initially with stool softeners and enemas as needed. Some strictures have a reversible edema component, so the extent of narrowing may improve after treatment. Fistulae and significant strictures generally require surgical repair.

Approximately 20% of all patients with chronic radiation injury to the intestinal tract require some type of surgical intervention. Biopsy specimens of ulcerations associated with chronic injury should be obtained to exclude malignancy.

Disposition

Suspected perforation mandates emergent surgical consultation, and signs of bowel obstruction should prompt urgent surgical consultation. Unless symptoms are severe, patients with acute and chronic radiation proctocolitis usually can be managed at home under the care of their radiation therapist or gastroenterologist. For acute disease, symptoms typically resolve several weeks after radiation treatments have been completed. Mild chronic disease typically resolves with medical therapy, but more severe symptoms often require laser photocoagulation or surgical intervention.[34]

 KEY CONCEPTS

- New or atypical symptoms in a patient with known IBS should prompt an evaluation for other abdominal pathology.
- A new diagnosis of IBS should be left to the primary care setting; the purpose of the emergency department evaluation is to exclude other abdominal disorders.
- A positive fecal occult blood test should never be assumed to be caused by diverticula. An appropriate investigation to exclude malignancy is essential.
- Uncomplicated diverticulitis can be diagnosed and treated without imaging in many patients.
- An LBO should prompt an evaluation for malignancy.
- Gangrene or perforation should be suspected whenever there is persistent unexplained tachycardia, fever, or remarkable abdominal tenderness.
- Volvulus often appears as a nonspecific large bowel obstruction on plain films.
- Although typically a disease of older persons, volvulus can occur at any age.
- Most adult intussusception is associated with a significant cause, often a malignancy.
- Adult intussusception usually presents as partial small bowel obstruction and rarely has the classic triad of abdominal pain, mass, and heme-positive stool that is seen in children.
- IBD is a lifelong relapsing disorder that can be treated by a variety of therapies. Management decisions are best made in consultation with the physician who will be providing ongoing care for the patient.
- Treatment of uncomplicated IBD depends on the clinical classification of disease severity (see Box 94-9).
- A new diagnosis of IBD in elderly patients should be made only after the exclusion of CI.
- Any evidence of blood in the stool should prompt an evaluation for colon cancer.
- Chronic radiation proctocolitis should be considered in anyone with a history of radiation to the pelvis or abdomen who presents with symptoms of gastrointestinal inflammation. This is true regardless of how long ago the radiation therapy was received.

REFERENCES

1. American College of Gastroenterology Functional Gastrointestinal Disorders Task Force: Evidence-based position statement on the management of irritable bowel syndrome in North America. *Am J Gastroenterol* 97:S1, 2002.
2. Hasler WL: The irritable bowel syndrome. *Med Clin North Am* 86:1525, 2002.
3. Mimura T, Emanuel A, Kamm MA: Pathophysiology of diverticular disease. *Best Pract Res Clin Gastroenterol* 16:563, 2002.
4. Ferzoco LB, Raptopoulos V, Silen W: Acute diverticulitis. *N Engl J Med* 338:1521, 1998.
5. Wong WD, et al: Practice parameters for the treatment of sigmoid diverticulitis—supporting documentation. The Standards Task Force, The American Society of Colon and Rectal Surgeons. *Dis Colon Rectum* 43:290, 2000.
6. Aldoori WH, et al: A prospective study of dietary fiber types and symptomatic diverticular disease in men. *J Nutr* 128:714, 1998.
7. Stollman NH, Raskin JB: Diagnosis and management of diverticular disease of the colon in adults. Ad Hoc Practice Parameters Committee of the American College of Gastroenterology. *Am J Gastroenterol* 94:3110, 1999.
8. Fearnhead NS, Mortensen NJ: Clinical features and differential diagnosis of diverticular disease. *Best Pract Res Clin Gastroenterol* 16:577, 2002.
9. Halligan S, Saunders B: Imaging diverticular disease. *Best Pract Res Clin Gastroenterol* 16:595, 2002.
10. Buchanan GN, Kenefick NJ, Cohen CR: Diverticulitis. *Best Pract Res Clin Gastroenterol* 16:635, 2002.
11. Surgical treatment of diverticulitis. Patient Care Committee of the Society for Surgery of the Alimentary Tract (SSAT). *J Gastrointest Surg* 3:212, 1999.
12. Lopez-Kostner F, Hool GR, Lavery IC: Management and causes of acute large-bowel obstruction. *Surg Clin North Am* 77:1265, 1997.
13. Saunders MD, Kimmey MB: Colonic pseudo-obstruction: The dilated colon in the ICU. *Semin Gastrointest Dis* 14:20, 2003.
14. Gibney EJ: Volvulus of the sigmoid colon. *Surg Gynecol Obstet* 173:243, 1991.
15. Frizelle FA, Wolff BG: Colonic volvulus. *Adv Surg* 29:131, 1996.
16. Rabinovici R, et al: Cecal volvulus. *Dis Colon Rectum* 33:765, 1990.
17. Madiba TE, Thomson SR: The management of cecal volvulus. *Dis Colon Rectum* 45:264, 2002.
18. Eisen LK, Cunningham JD, Aufses AH Jr: Intussusception in adults: Institutional review. *J Am Coll Surg* 188:390, 1999.
19. Takeuchi K, et al: The diagnosis and treatment of adult intussusception. *J Clin Gastroenterol* 36:18, 2003.
20. Haas EM, et al: Adult intussusception. *Am J Surg* 186:75, 2003.
21. Hanauer SB, Present DH: The state of the art in the management of inflammatory bowel disease. *Rev Gastroenterol Disord* 3:81, 2003.
22. Knutson D, Greenberg G, Cronau H: Management of Crohn's disease—a practical approach. *Am Fam Physician* 68:707, 2003.
23. Scholmerich J: Inflammatory bowel disease. *Endoscopy* 35:164, 2003.
24. Farrell RJ, Peppercorn MA: Ulcerative colitis. *Lancet* 359:331, 2002.
25. Greenstein RJ: Is Crohn's disease caused by a mycobacterium? Comparisons with leprosy, tuberculosis, and Johne's disease. *Lancet Infect Dis* 3:507, 2003.
26. Schraut WH: The surgical management of Crohn's disease. *Gastroenterol Clin North Am* 31:255, 2002.

27. Sheth SG, LaMont JT: Toxic megacolon. *Lancet* 351:509, 1998.
28. Rizzello F, et al: Review article: Medical treatment of severe ulcerative colitis. *Aliment Pharmacol Ther* 17(Suppl 2):7, 2003.
29. Hanauer SB, Sandborn W: Management of Crohn's disease in adults. *Am J Gastroenterol* 96:635, 2001.
30. Cappell MS: Intestinal (mesenteric) vasculopathy: II. Ischemic colitis and chronic mesenteric ischemia. *Gastroenterol Clin North Am* 27:827, 1998.
31. Alapati SV, Mihas AA: When to suspect ischemic colitis: Why is this condition so often missed or misdiagnosed? *Postgrad Med* 105:177, 1999.
32. Brandt LJ, Boley SJ: AGA technical review on intestinal ischemia. American Gastrointestinal Association. *Gastroenterology* 118:954, 2000.
33. American Gastroenterological Association Medical Position Statement: Guidelines on intestinal ischemia. *Gastroenterology* 118:951, 2000.
34. Otchy DP, Nelson H: Radiation injuries of the colon and rectum. *Surg Clin North Am* 73:1017, 1993.
35. Denton A, et al: Non-surgical interventions for late radiation proctitis in patients who have received radical radiotherapy to the pelvis. *Cochrane Database Syst Rev* CD003455, 2002.
36. Leupin N, et al: Acute radiation colitis in patients treated with short-term preoperative radiotherapy for rectal cancer. *Am J Surg Pathol* 26:498, 2002.

CHAPTER

95 Anorectum

Wendy C. Coates

PERSPECTIVE

Patients present to the emergency department with a variety of anorectal complaints. These may be self-limited in nature or may be a harbinger of an underlying medical condition. It is incumbent upon the emergency physician to demonstrate sensitivity and maintain a professional demeanor when dealing with patients who may find it difficult to discuss historical details and their physical complaints openly.

PRINCIPLES OF DISEASE

The anorectum marks the end of the alimentary canal. From its beginning at the rectosigmoid junction at the level of the third sacral vertebra (S3), the rectum follows the sacral curvature for 12 to 15 cm, then sharply turns posteriorly and inferiorly at the puborectalis muscle (Figure 95-1). Here the anal canal begins its 4-cm course to the anal verge, the orifice where stool exits the body. It is supported by three muscle groups, the levator ani and the internal and external anal sphincters. Anal valves are located 2 cm proximal to the anal verge at the dentate line. Above the valves are the anal crypts that contain mucous glands to lubricate the area during defecation. They are a nidus for abscess and fistula formation if occluded. Proximal to the crypts are the columns of Morgagni, where the epithelium of the anal canal changes from pink columnar (like the rectum) to squamous.[1-3]

The superior, middle, and inferior hemorrhoidal arteries provide the blood supply to the anorectum. They arise from the inferior mesenteric, internal iliac, and internal pudendal arteries, respectively. The superior hemorrhoidal veins drain into the portal system, and the inferior hemorrhoidal veins drain into the caval system. Lymphatic drainage is to the inferior mesenteric nodes above the dentate line and to the inguinal nodes from all areas of the anorectum.[2]

Sympathetic and parasympathetic nervous systems function together to retain the contents of the rectum until evacuation is desired. Continence is maintained when sympathetic fibers from L1 to L3 (upper rectum) and presacral nerves (lower rectum) inhibit contraction of rectal smooth muscle and L5 fibers cause the internal sphincter to contract. Elimination occurs when parasympathetic fibers from the anterior roots of S2 to S4 cause the rectal wall to contract and the internal sphincter to relax. Voluntary external sphincter control is mediated by motor branches of the pudendal nerve (S2, S3) and the perineal branch of S4. The levator ani is supplied by the pudendal nerve and pelvic branches of S3 to S4 fibers. Sensory perception of rectal distention involves extramural receptors to parasympathetic fibers from S2 to S4. The abundant sensory nerve endings of the distal anal epithelium perceive sensations that are transmitted by the pudendal nerve.[2]

Defecation begins as the rectum becomes distended, the internal sphincter relaxes, and stool enters the anal canal. At an appropriate time and place, the external sphincter is relaxed to complete the process of elimination. Sometimes voluntary straining is needed to assist in the passage of stool. On performing the Valsalva maneuver, the abdominal muscles contract, the rectal angle straightens, and the pelvic floor descends. To postpone defecation, the external sphincter contracts voluntarily. This contraction relaxes the rectal

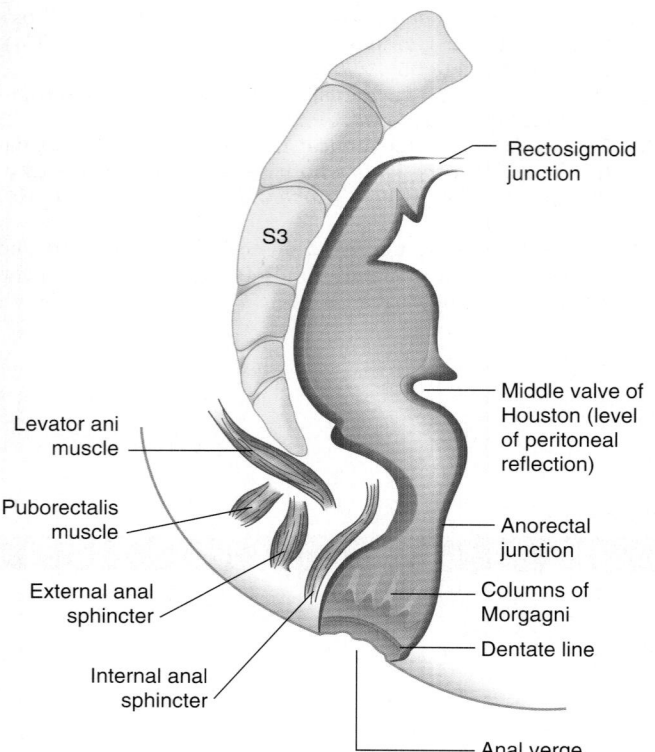

Figure 95-1. Anorectal anatomy.

Rectosigmoid junction

S3

Levator ani muscle

Puborectalis muscle

External anal sphincter

Internal anal sphincter

Middle valve of Houston (level of peritoneal reflection)

Anorectal junction

Columns of Morgagni

Dentate line

Anal verge

BOX 95-1. Medical History

Anorectal History
Pain
Bleeding
Swelling
Itching
Discharge
Urgency

GI History
Change in bowel habits (straining, flatus, color, consistency, frequency)
Nausea or vomiting
Incontinence of stool
Underlying GI disease (Crohn's disease, cancer, polyps)

Systemic Disease History
Diabetes mellitus
Coagulopathy
Cancer
HIV

Sexual History of the Anus
Penetration
Known STDs
Assault

GI, gastrointestinal; HIV, human immunodeficiency virus; STD, sexually transmitted disease.

---

wall and quells the urge to defecate unless there is an underlying sphincter disorder or an overwhelming volume of stool.[4]

CLINICAL FEATURES

History

A complete history of anorectal and gastrointestinal (GI) symptoms and the presence of systemic disease elucidates the diagnosis of most anorectal disorders (Box 95-1 and Figure 95-2). Common complaints include bleeding, swelling, pain, itching, and discharge. The standard questions of time and circumstances of onset, duration, quality, and exposure to radiation should be asked. Alterations in bowel habits of the individual patient should be noted. These include changes in color, frequency, or consistency of the stool and the presence of straining, flatus, and incontinence of solid or liquid stool. People with underlying GI disorders (e.g., Crohn's disease, cancer, or polyps) are predisposed to different presentations of anorectal problems. Similarly, those with underlying systemic diseases such as acquired immunodeficiency syndrome (AIDS), cancer, diabetes mellitus, and coagulopathies are susceptible to serious complications of anorectal conditions. Finally, patients should be asked directly about the use of the anus for sexual purposes.[5,6]

Rectal Bleeding

The color, amount, and relationship to defecation are important factors in establishing the cause of rectal bleeding. Approximately 10% to 20% of the population experiences rectal bleeding at some time.[7] Pain and bright red blood signify anal fissures or hemorrhoids. Fissure pain is sharp, sudden in onset, and not associated with swelling, whereas pain from a prolapsed or thrombosed hemorrhoid is gnawing, continuous, and of more gradual onset. Painless rectal bleeding occurs in internal hemorrhoids, cancer, or precancerous lesions.

The relationship of bleeding to defecation is important. Visible blood on the toilet paper is usually caused by anal fissures or external hemorrhoids; however, minute quantities can result from any irritating condition. Bright red blood that drips into the toilet bowl or streaks around the stool is caused by internal hemorrhoids. Blood mixed with stool originates proximal to the rectum, whereas melena indicates a very proximal source. Bloody mucus is associated with cancer, inflammatory bowel disease, and proctitis.[1,7]

Swelling and Masses

Patients who complain of a swelling near the anus or have the sensation of rectal fullness often list hemorrhoids as their chief complaint. Painful swellings that bleed are usually thrombosed hemorrhoids, but other painful lesions such as abscesses, pilonidal disease, and hidradenitis suppurativa must be considered. Painless, itchy swellings may be caused by condylomata acuminata or secondary syphilis. A mass protruding through the anal orifice may signal rectal prolapse.[1] Perianal and rectal carcinoma should be considered in

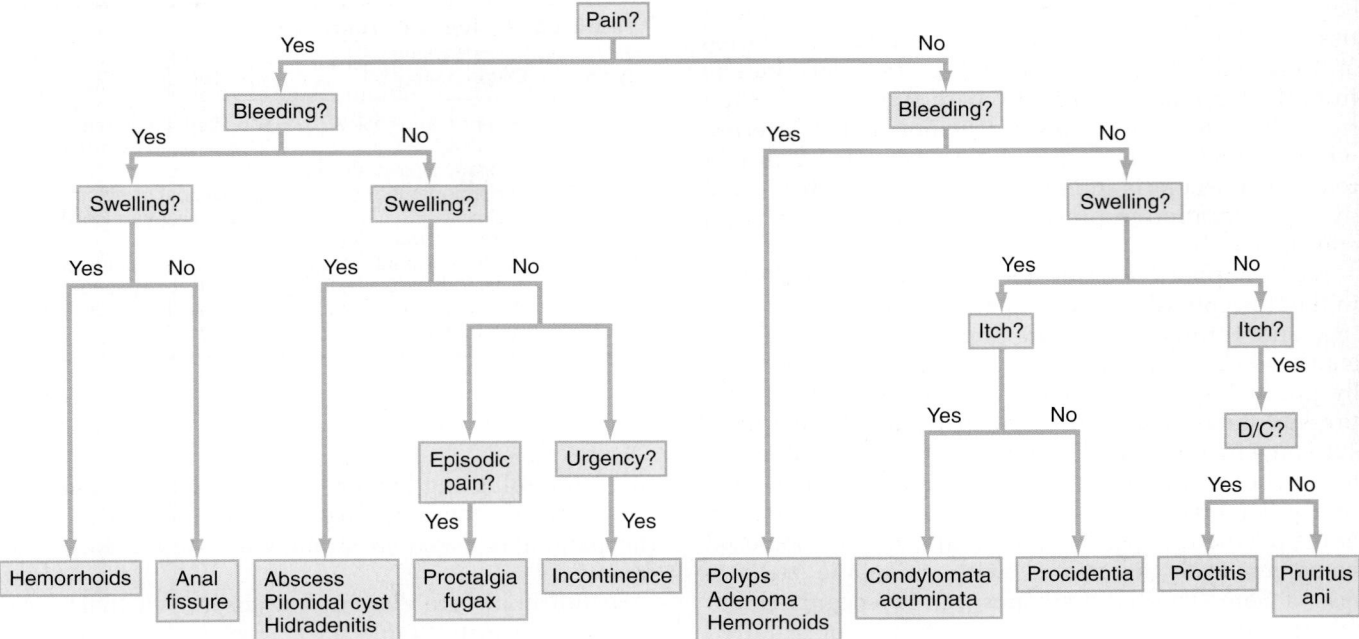

Figure 95-2. Algorithm for anorectal complaints.

older persons and those with long-standing anorectal complaints.[5]

Pain and Itching

Severe, episodic anorectal pain that is not associated with bleeding or swelling is proctalgia fugax. Perianal itching (pruritus ani) is caused by any lesion that makes hygiene difficult to maintain.

Physical Examination

The physical examination should take place in private, respecting the patient's modesty. The patient can then relax the external sphincter to facilitate a complete examination. The patient is placed in the left lateral decubitus position and covered with a sheet. The buttocks are inspected for dermatologic manifestations of disease and then gently spread apart to expose the anal orifice. Elements of personal hygiene are noted, in addition to anatomic disruptions such as fissures, skin tags, lesions, hemorrhoids, or abscesses. The patient is asked to strain to assess the integrity of the pelvic floor and note prolapse of hemorrhoids or rectal mucosa. Next, a well-lubricated gloved finger is placed flat against the anal opening, exerting gentle pressure until the external sphincter relaxes and allows the finger to enter the anus. Anal sphincter tone can be assessed by asking the patient to squeeze the anal muscles against the examining finger. By sweeping the finger in a circumferential manner, accessible areas of the anorectum can be examined for masses and areas of tenderness. The cervix or prostate is palpated through the rectal wall. A bidigital examination reveals masses and tender areas at the distal portion of the anal canal and perineum. Upon withdrawal, the contents on the glove can be assessed for frank or occult blood, mucus, or pus.[1]

Direct visualization can be accomplished by anoscopy. With the patient similarly positioned, the lubricated anoscope is inserted into the anus with the obturator in place. The obturator is removed and a circumferential view of the rectal mucosa is possible. Attention is directed to sites of bleeding, hemorrhoids, masses, or abnormal tissue and finally the dentate line and anal epithelium.

MANAGEMENT OF SPECIFIC ANORECTAL PROBLEMS

Hemorrhoids

Perspective

When the Philistines defeated the Israelites, the book of I Samuel reports the fate of the avengers: "A deadly panic had seized the whole city, since the hand of God had been very heavy upon it. Those who escaped death were afflicted with hemorrhoids, and the outcry from the city went up to the heavens."[8] In 1815 the battle of Waterloo marked the defeat of Napoleon's army. Speculation purports that the great leader suffered from hemorrhoids at the time of his defeat.[9] Hemorrhoidal disease continues to afflict modern humans with a 4.4% incidence in the U.S. population. Both sexes are affected, and there is an increased frequency among whites, rural dwellers, and those from high socioeconomic classes.[10-12]

Principles of Disease

The cause of hemorrhoids is controversial. The anal vascular cushion theory is the most widely accepted. Rather than forming a continuous ring around the anal canal, the submucosa forms three distinct cushions of tissue that are richly supplied with small blood vessels and muscle fibers. Blood supply to these cushions is from the superior rectal artery with some contribution from the middle and inferior hemorrhoidal arteries, which explains why hemorrhoidal bleeding is bright red. The muscularis submucosa cushions the anal canal during defecation to prevent injury and to aid in fecal continence.[13]

As the supportive tissue deteriorates, usually starting in the third decade, venous distention, prolapse, bleeding, and thrombosis occur. Some controversy exists about whether straining and constipation cause this by producing venous backflow when intra-abdominal pressure increases.[1,13] In pregnant women, direct pressure on a hemorrhoidal vein can produce symptomatic hemorrhoids. Up to one third of pregnant women experience hemorrhoids in the last trimester of pregnancy or the postpartum period. The incidence of thrombosed hemorrhoids is associated with traumatic deliveries.[14,15] Some familial predisposition is recognized, but whether this is a result of genetic factors or acquired factors such as diet is unknown. Hemorrhoids are not varicose veins; they are normal structures that manifest symptoms when the muscularis submucosa weakens and the anal cushions are displaced distally.[13] Conditions that increase sphincter tone correlate with a higher prevalence of hemorrhoids.[11] Portal hypertension does not cause hemorrhoids. The incidence of symptomatic hemorrhoids is similar in patients with and without portal hypertension. Rectal bleeding in this population may be caused by rectal varices that are vascular communications between the superior and middle hemorrhoidal veins.[11,12] A major exception to this observation occurs in the pediatric population; children with portal hypertension are susceptible to hemorrhoidal exacerbations.[16,17]

Clinical Features

A careful history is needed to confirm the presence of hemorrhoids because many patients use this term to refer to any perianal condition. Bleeding with defecation is the most common complaint, and unless the hemorrhoids are thrombosed, it is usually painless. Patients report seeing variable amounts of bright red blood on the toilet paper or in the toilet bowl. Many complain of swelling, itching, mucoid discharge, or simply the presence of a moist perianal area. Further history should address recent stool patterns, such as diarrhea or constipation; chronic medical problems, such as portal hypertension or bleeding disorders; and a dietary and family history.

Hemorrhoidal symptoms are exacerbated by frequent bowel movements, prolonged sitting, heavy lifting, and straining while defecating. Although straining is cited as a cause of hemorrhoids, it may also be a result of them when the patient is constipated from the fear of defecating. Physical examination should address the type and degree of hemorrhoids. This can be accomplished by a visual inspection at rest and during straining. Nonprolapsing hemorrhoids can be visualized on anoscopy as a focus of bleeding or as they bulge when the patient is asked to strain while the anoscope is removed.[1]

Hemorrhoids are classified according to their location and severity (Table 95-1). External hemorrhoids originate below the dentate line and receive their blood supply from the inferior hemorrhoidal plexus. They are covered with modified squamous epithelium (anoderm) and resemble the surrounding skin. Two syndromes are common. First, the veins beneath the skin of the hemorrhoid become dilated and the surrounding subcutaneous tissue becomes engorged, causing swelling or pressure after defecation. Painless, bright red bleeding may occur. Second, the veins can become thrombosed as clots form within them (Figure 95-3A). This produces acute pain and tenderness to palpation. A bluish discoloration is often noted.

Internal hemorrhoids originate above the dentate line and receive their blood supply from the superior hemorrhoidal plexus (Figure 95-3B). They are covered with a mucosal surface consisting of transitional or columnar epithelium that looks very different from the surrounding anoderm. They are classified according to severity (Table 95-2). Symptoms range from mild, painless bleeding with defecation to irreducible prolapse with unremitting and debilitating pain. First-degree internal hemorrhoids protrude into the lumen of the anal canal, causing a feeling of fullness. Because there are no sensory nerve endings in the mucosal wall, they do not cause pain. Second-degree internal hemorrhoids temporarily prolapse outside the anal canal during defecation but spontaneously return to their normal position at the end of the bowel movement. Both of these are amenable to medical management. Third-degree internal hemorrhoids prolapse spontaneously or during defecation and remain outside the body until they are manually replaced into the anal canal. A throbbing pressure-like pain may accompany bleeding and improves when the hemorrhoids are reduced. Fourth-degree internal hemorrhoids cannot be reduced and are permanently prolapsed. Continued prolapse leads to the formation of a thrombus with possible progression to gangrene. Definitive treatment for the intense pain and thrombosis is surgical.[1,18]

Table 95-1. Types of Hemorrhoids

Type	Origin	Epithelium
External	Inferior hemorrhoidal plexus Proximal to dentate line	Modified squamous epithelium (anoderm)
Internal	Superior hemorrhoidal plexus Distal to dentate line	Transitional or columnar epithelium (mucosa)
Mixed	Superior and inferior hemorrhoidal plexus Proximal and/or distal to dentate line	Transitional, columnar, or modified squamous epithelium (mucosa and anoderm)

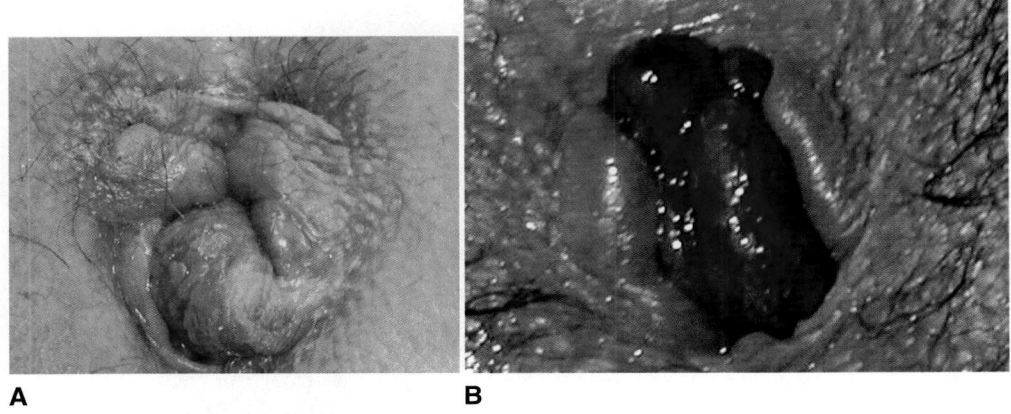

A   **B**

Figure 95-3. Thrombosed hemorrhoids. **A,** External. **B,** Internal. Note the engorged external hemorrhoids that surround the thrombosed internal hemorrhoids. (**A,** Courtesy of Michelle Lin, MD, Harbor-UCLA Medical Center; **B,** courtesy of Gershon Effron, MD, Sinai Hospital of Baltimore. In Seidel HM, et al: *Mosby's Guide to Physical Examination*, 4th ed. St. Louis, Mosby, 1999.)

Table 95-2. Classification of Internal Hemorrhoids by Severity

Type	Prolapse	Mode of Reduction	Treatment
First-degree	None	N/A	Medical management
Second-degree	During defecation	Spontaneous	Medical management
Third-degree	May be spontaneous or during defecation	Manual	Medical management Optional surgical repair
Fourth-degree	Permanently	Irreducible	Surgical repair

BOX 95-2. The WASH Regimen

Warm water
Analgesic agents
Stool softeners
High-fiber diet

Management

The symptoms of nonthrombosed external and non-prolapsing internal hemorrhoids can be ameliorated by the standard regimen—warm water, analgesics, stool softeners, and high-fiber diet (WASH)—aimed at overcoming the problems that led to their formation (Box 95-2). Anal canal pressures decrease significantly in warm water (40°C).[19] Patients can direct a shower stream at the area for several minutes or take sitz baths. Mild oral analgesic agents reduce the pain. The use of topical anesthetics, steroid creams, and suppositories is controversial. Prolonged use of topical corticosteroids produces atrophic skin changes and is discouraged.[1] Stool softeners can make the passage of stool easier, to avoid straining. A high-fiber diet (20 to 30 g of dietary fiber per day) produces stool that is passed more easily.

Patients with second- or third-degree internal hemorrhoids also benefit from this regimen; however, permanent resolution of their symptoms may require surgical intervention (Table 95-3). These patients can be discharged from the emergency department with the WASH regimen and referred to a surgeon for

Table 95-3. Surgical Management of Hemorrhoids

Classification	Management
Thrombosed external hemorrhoids	Excision in emergency department
Second- and third-degree internal hemorrhoids	Elective surgical repair Banding Sclerotherapy Hemorrhoidectomy
Fourth-degree hemorrhoids (nonthrombosed)	Nonemergent hemorrhoidectomy
Thrombosed or gangrenous fourth-degree internal hemorrhoids	Emergent hemorrhoidectomy

banding, sclerotherapy, or elective hemorrhoidectomy. Patients with acute, gangrenous, fourth-degree internal hemorrhoids should be referred for emergent hemorrhoidectomy.[18]

Acutely thrombosed external hemorrhoids can be excised (not incised and drained) in the emergency department to provide prompt relief within the first 48 hours after the onset of symptoms (Figure 95-4). Incision results in incomplete evacuation of the clot, subsequent rebleeding, and swelling. Excision provides long-term relief and prevents the formation of skin tags.[20] If not excised, the thrombosed external hemorrhoid and its associated symptoms resolve spontaneously after several days when the hemorrhoid ulcerates and leaks the dark accumulated blood. Residual skin tags may persist.[1] It is not common for emer-

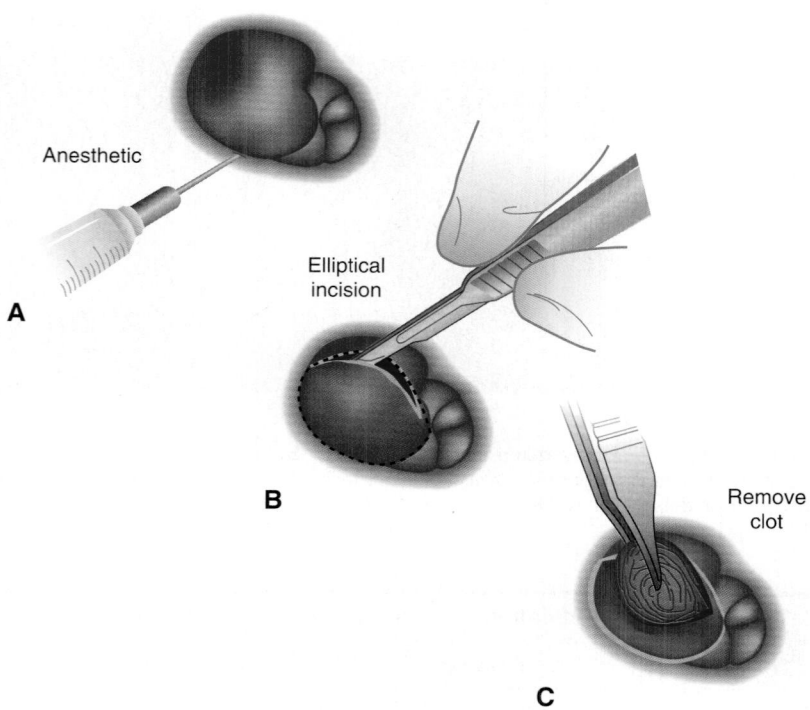

Figure 95-4. Excision of thrombosed external hemorrhoid. **A,** Field block with local anesthetic. **B,** An elliptical incision is made around the hemorrhoid. **C,** The thrombosed hemorrhoid is removed. (From Larson S, et al [eds]: *Atlas of Emergency Procedures*. St. Louis, Mosby, 2001)

Anesthetic

Elliptical incision

A

B

Remove clot

C

gency physicians to perform this procedure in pediatric patients, pregnant women, or immunocompromised patients. Conservative therapy with topical nifedipine (0.3%) with lidocaine (1.5%) gel is under investigation. Its purported effectiveness is related to its ability to modulate resting sphincter tone and, therefore, reduce the pain and inflammation of the thrombosed hemorrhoids.[21]

Anal Fissures

Principles of Disease

The development of an anal fissure is the most common cause of the sudden onset of intensely painful rectal bleeding. A superficial tear in the anoderm results when a hard piece of feces is forced through the anus, usually in patients who are constipated. Although anyone can experience an anal fissure, it is most common in the 30- to 50-year age bracket.[22] It is the most commonly encountered anorectal problem in pediatric patients, especially infants.[23,24] Men and women are affected equally. Most fissures occur along the posterior midline where the skeletal muscle fibers that encircle the anus are weakest. Anterior midline fissures are more common in women than men.[1,22] Fissures that occur elsewhere should alert the emergency physician to diseases such as leukemia, Crohn's disease, human immunodeficiency virus (HIV) infection, tuberculosis (TB), or syphilis.[25]

Fissures not treated promptly may become chronic and display a classical "fissure triad" of deep ulcer, sentinel pile, and enlarged anal papillae (Figure 95-5). A sentinel pile forms when the skin at the base of the fissure becomes edematous and hypertrophic. A resolving sentinel pile can form a permanent skin tag and may be associated with a fistulous tract.

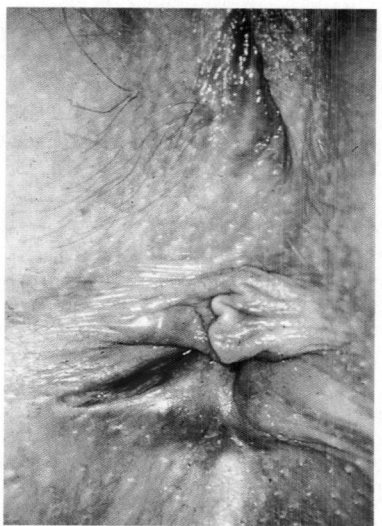

Figure 95-5. Lateral anal fissure. (Courtesy of Gershon Effron, MD, Sinai Hospital of Baltimore. In Seidel HM, et al: *Mosby's Guide to Physical Examination*, 4th ed. St. Louis, Mosby, 1999.)

Clinical Features

The patient complains of a sudden, searing pain during defecation that may be accompanied by a small amount of bright red blood on the stool or toilet paper. This is followed by a nagging, burning sensation that lasts for a few hours from internal sphincter spasm. Subsequent bowel movements are excruciating, and the external sphincter can exhibit a reflex spasm. Physical examination must be performed cautiously to avoid further spasm and pain. The depth of the fissure, its orientation to the midline, and the presence of a coexisting sentinel pile or edema are noted. Rectal examination during an acute exacerbation is often impossible because of pain and sphincter spasm.[22]

Management (Box 95-3)

Treatment using the WASH regimen (see Box 95-2) focuses on eliminating constipation with a bulking agent, stool softener, and high-fiber diet. Warm sitz baths and limited use of topical anesthetic creams may be helpful. Parental encouragement to pediatric patients helps prevent encopresis that can result from a fear of painful bowel movements. Most acute, uncomplicated fissures resolve in 2 to 4 weeks. Topical agents aimed at reducing sphincter pressures have been studied in the adult population and may be effective therapy for this group, especially those who suffer from chronic disease. Hyperbaric oxygen has been used successfully as an adjunctive therapy.[26]

Nitroglycerin (0.4%) ointment applied topically to the anoderm two or three times daily has been shown to relieve the pain associated with anal fissures. Although it was not associated with more rapid healing, patients receiving this therapy reported a higher level of comfort during the healing process. The typical side effect of a vasodilatory headache may be experienced by some patients.[27]

Nifedipine gel (0.2%) in combination with lidocaine (1.5%) applied to the anal area twice daily is effective in promoting healing and reducing discomfort in the management of anal fissures. The mechanism of healing is thought to be the reduction of anal canal pressures by local calcium channel blockade.[28,29] When the efficacy of calcium channel blockers was compared directly with application of nitrates, the rates of healing and recurrence were similar; however, the incidence of side effects was lower in one study.[30]

Injection of botulinum toxin (2.5 to 5.0 million units, 0.1 to 0.2 mL of Botox preparation) is effective in relaxing the sphincter tone by inhibiting acetylcholinesterase release but may cause temporary, reversible fecal incontinence.[29] Injection into the external (rather than internal) sphincter muscles may reduce this undesirable side effect. It has been used successfully by colorectal surgeons[31-35] but has not yet been studied as a primary treatment in the emergency department. In comparison with the topical treatments, botulinum toxin is superior in its rate of permanent healing; however, the first line of therapy is still topical agents because of their cost, ease of application, and side effect profiles.[35] Long-term treatment of recurrent fissures focuses on reducing resting anal pressures and may require anal dilation under anesthesia or surgical correction of the internal sphincter to reduce its tone.[27,31]

Abscesses and Fistulas

Principles of Disease

Anorectal abscesses and fistulas are most common in adults who are 30 to 50 years old, and men are afflicted more often than women (2 : 1 to 7 : 1).[1,36] There is also an increased incidence in infants (85% male) associated with congenital abnormalities.[37-40]

One probable cause of anorectal abscesses is occlusion of the ducts of the mucus-producing anal glands at the base of the anal crypts (the cryptoglandular theory). Abscesses are also caused by inflammatory bowel disease, trauma, cancer, radiation injury, and infection (TB, lymphogranuloma venereum, actinomycosis).[1,36,39,41] Common bacterial causative agents are *Staphylococcus aureus*, *Escherichia coli*, *Streptococcus*, *Proteus*, and *Bacteroides*.

Management

General Approach

Abscesses are the acute manifestations of a continuum of anorectal infections, whereas fistulas are the chronic sequelae. Symptoms vary depending on the site of infection, but incision and drainage are required in all cases (Table 95-4). Delay of medical management may allow extension of the infection and eventual compromise of the sphincter mechanism.[42] Adjunctive antimicrobial therapy is indicated in patients who are immunocompromised, diabetic, or have valvular heart

BOX 95-3. Treatment of Anal Fissures

WASH regimen
Nitroglycerin ointment (0.4%) bid-tid
Nifedipine gel (0.2%) bid with lidocaine (1.5%)
Botulinum toxin (Botox) 0.1–0.2 mL
Anal dilatation under anesthesia
Surgical excision

Table 95-4. Types of Abscesses

	Perianal	Ischiorectal	Intersphincteric	Supralevator	Postanal
Incidence	40%-45%	20%-25%	20%-25%	<5%	5%-10%
Location	Outside and verge	Buttocks	Lower rectum	Above levator ani	Deep to external sphincter
Symptoms	Painful perianal mass	Buttock pain	Rectal fullness	Perianal and buttock pain	Rectal fullness / Pain near coccyx
Fever, ↑WBC	−	±	±	+	+
Associated fistula	++	+	+++	+++	−
ED incision and drainage	+	±	−	−	−

ED, emergency department; WBC, white blood cells; −, does not occur; ±, occurs sometimes; ++, occurs often; +++, usually occurs.

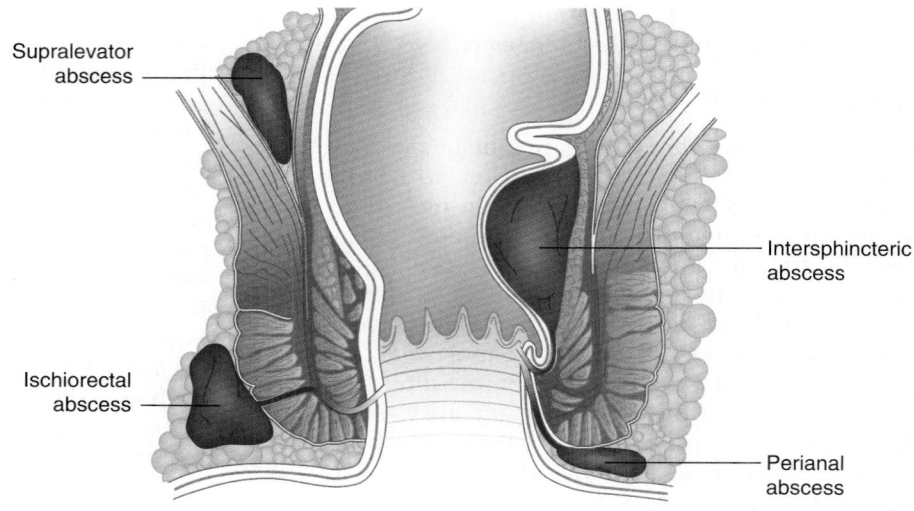

Figure 95-6. Location of common anorectal abscesses. (Modified from Gordon PH, Nivatvonghs S: *Principles and Practice of Surgery for the Colon, Rectum, and Anus.* St. Louis, Quality Medical Publishing, 1992.)

Supralevator abscess

Intersphincteric abscess

Ischiorectal abscess

Perianal abscess

disease. Tetanus status should be verified. The sites of anorectal abscess formation are depicted in Figure 95-6. The difficulty in diagnosis is that pain often precedes physical findings of a mass or fluctuance. Approximately 34% of patients with AIDS develop anorectal abscesses and fistulas. In addition to the usual organisms, many are infected with opportunistic ones. HIV-infected patients appear more likely to have incomplete fistulous tracts than their seronegative cohorts. This condition prevents adequate spontaneous drainage and highlights the urgency of treating these patients promptly. A small incision is desirable when possible because wound healing may be impaired. Supplemental antimicrobial therapy is required.[43]

Treatment of Specific Abscesses

Perirectal and Perianal Abscesses. Perirectal and perianal abscesses are the most common (40% to 45%) and produce painful swelling at the anal verge that is worsened by defecating or sitting. Most patients are afebrile. Physical examination reveals localized tenderness, erythema, swelling, and fluctuance. If tolerated, anoscopy may reveal pus in the anal crypts. Incision and drainage in the emergency department with eventual emergency department discharge are possible in the absence of comorbid factors (e.g., diabetes mellitus, extremes of age, and immunocompromised hosts). Some patients may be unable to tolerate the procedure without general or regional anesthesia. Incision and drainage should not take place in a sterile surgical procedure area. The WASH regimen (see Box 95-2) may alleviate postprocedure discomfort. Antibiotics are unnecessary in healthy adults except in cases involving associated cellulitis.[6]

Ischiorectal Abscess. Approximately 20% to 25% of abscesses form outside the sphincter muscles in the buttocks, and patients complain of severe pain. The diagnosis is obvious if there is an indurated mass on the buttocks but is more difficult if the abscess is deep. Patients often have fever and leukocytosis.[1] If there is no induration, a needle aspirate can confirm the pres-

ence of pus. Although many patients require drainage under general anesthesia, superficial abscesses can be treated in the emergency department in a fashion similar to that used for the perianal abscess. If the patient is febrile, a short course of antibiotics, such as cephalexin, may be considered, beginning with a parenteral dose prior to drainage followed by 3 to 7 days of an oral agent.[1]

Intersphincteric Abscess. One fourth of abscesses form in the space deep to the external sphincter and inferior to the levator ani. The infection tracks cephalad and may appear to be a mass in the rectum and confused with a thrombosed internal hemorrhoid. Patients complain of continuous rectal pressure and a throbbing pain exacerbated by defecation or sitting. They may be febrile and have leukocytosis. There may be no external evidence of inflammation, but rectal examination reveals an erythematous, indurated, sometimes draining mass. Associated fistulas and inguinal lymphadenopathy are common. Drainage in the operating room is required so that the entire abscess and fistula network can be treated.[36]

Supralevator Abscess. Accounting for fewer than 5% of abscesses, supralevator abscesses cause perianal and buttock pain associated with fever and leukocytosis. External evidence of this disease is usually absent, which often delays the diagnosis. Approximately 23% of patients are obese or have diabetes mellitus, and others have concurrent disorders such as Crohn's disease, pelvic inflammatory disease, or diverticulitis.[1] A tender mass may be palpated on rectal or pelvic examination. Emergency surgical treatment is indicated.[36]

Postanal Abscess. Postanal abscesses are uncommon and occur posterior to the rectum, deep to the external sphincter, and inferior to the levator ani. Patients complain of severe rectal discomfort and coccygeal pain. They are usually febrile and have continuous pain that does not change with position. Rectal examination is painful, but anal drainage is rare. Many of these abscesses are missed on initial presentation, and patients are diagnosed with lumbosacral strain, proctalgia fugax, sciatica, or coccygodynia. Patients often return in a few days with an abscess draining at the skin. Treatment is surgical.[1]

Horseshoe Abscess. Occasionally, a large, communicating, horseshoe-shaped abscess forms in the ischiorectal, intersphincteric, or supralevator space. Surgical management is necessary.

Necrotizing Infection. A delay in the management of an anorectal abscess may lead to the destruction of tissue, especially in the diabetic or immunocompromised host. Widespread cellulitis, necrotic tissue, and gas on radiography suggest the possibility of necrotizing fasciitis, Fournier's gangrene, or tetanus. Wide surgical debridement, broad-spectrum antibiotics with anaerobic coverage, and tetanus prophylaxis are required.[1]

Treatment of Fistulas

A fistula is a connection between two epithelium-lined surfaces. Anorectal fistulas develop in 50% to 67% of patients with ischiorectal abscesses.[42] Other causes include Crohn's disease, trauma, foreign body reactions, TB, and cancer. Evidence to support these diagnoses should be sought because the anorectal complaint may be the presenting symptom of the fistula. Patients notice a recurrent or persistent perianal discharge that becomes painful when one of the openings becomes occluded. Bidigital rectal examination may reveal a tract in the perineum or canal. Probing of fistulous tracts is not recommended because the danger of creating a new tract outweighs the benefit of identifying the path of the existing fistula. Diagnostic evaluation may include intrarectal ultrasonography, fistulography with radiopaque dye, or radiolabeled white cell scanning during surgery.[36,39,44,45] Spontaneous resolution of fistula-in-ano is rare. Because most fistulas produce recurrent abscesses if untreated, all patients should be referred for surgical management. Immediate or delayed fistulotomy, fistulectomy, or treatment with fibrin glue may be done.[36,45,46]

Pilonidal Disease

Principles of Disease

Little nests of hair in the sacrococcygeal area were first described in 1847 by Anderson (Latin *pilus*, hair; *nidus*, nest), who originally believed the lesions to be scrofula.[47] One hundred fifty years later, physicians have yet to agree on the cause and best mode of treatment. Pilonidal abscesses and subsequent sinus tracts afflict young adults with a 4 : 1 male predominance and are more common in obese and hirsute individuals. The disease is rare in persons older than 40 years, even among those who were afflicted in their youth. The lesions arise in the midline of the sacrococcygeal area in the natal cleft and should not be confused with anal fistulas, perirectal abscesses, hidradenitis suppurativa, or granulomatous diseases (syphilis, TB).[1] Much of our understanding of pilonidal disease comes from experi-

ence in World War II, when the condition was rampant among jeep drivers.[4,48,49]

The debate between congenital predisposition and acquired disease seems to favor the latter.[48,50,51] This theory asserts that bacteria enter the usually sterile hair follicle and produce inflammation and edema that occlude the opening to the skin surface. The contents expand until the hair follicle ruptures, and the material spreads into the subcutaneous fatty tissue, where a foreign body reaction leads to abscess formation. The purulent material subsequently tracks cephalad and drains to the skin through a laterally displaced epithelialized tract. Diagnosis is made by establishing the presence of a painful, fluctuant area in the presacral skin. In chronic or recurrent disease, visible or palpable tracts of 2- to 5-cm length may be identified with openings approximately 5 cm above the anus. These sinuses usually contain hairs and cellular debris.[48,49]

Management

Treatment options vary from conservative therapy to extensive surgical management.[48,52] Antibiotics can supplement surgical drainage in cases accompanied by cellulitis but should never be the primary mode of treatment.[1] Emergency department management of pilonidal disease involves drainage of the acute abscess for relief of symptoms. To prevent reaccumulation of debris, a longitudinal incision off the sacral midline should be made. To decrease the usual 40% recurrence rate, the patient can be referred for follicle removal and unroofing of sinus tracts after the acute inflammation subsides (usually 1 week). A higher cure rate with shaving the hairs in the natal cleft every 3 weeks has been reported. For patients whose disease is recalcitrant, wide excision and plastic surgery techniques are used.

Hidradenitis Suppurativa

Perianal hidradenitis suppurativa is an infection of the apocrine glands.[53] It is most common in young adults and is related to poor skin hygiene, hyperhidrosis, obesity, acne, diabetes mellitus, and smoking. Patients are commonly misdiagnosed with pilonidal disease or fistula in ano. The differential diagnosis also includes sebaceous cysts, furuncles, granulomas (TB or syphilis), and Crohn's disease. Occluded apocrine ducts are infected with strains of *Staphylococcus*, *Streptococcus*, *E. coli*, or *Proteus*. Extension through the dermis spreads the infection to neighboring ducts, and a network of sinus tracts forms. This cycle leads to extensive scarring.[51,54]

Patients complain of a pustule in the perianal area, which may be associated with fever, leukocytosis, and malaise. One or more tender pustules may drain pus and have surrounding cellulitis. Local lymphadenopathy is common. Treatment begins with careful attention to perianal hygiene, warm compresses, and broad-spectrum antibiotics. Drainage of isolated lesions may provide symptomatic relief, but the recurrence rate approaches 40%. Referral to a surgeon for wide excision of advanced chronic disease may be necessary.[55,56]

Proctalgia

Perspective

Anorectal pain (proctalgia) that does not arise from one of the organic disorders described earlier can be severe and difficult to treat. The two most common causes are levator ani syndrome and proctalgia fugax. These can be distinguished by their patterns of affliction. Other causes of pelvic pain, such as tumors, cauda equina syndrome, and endometriosis, must first be considered.[57]

Levator Ani Syndrome

A constant, dull pressure in the sacrococcygeal region that is precipitated by defecation or prolonged periods of sitting suggests levator ani syndrome. The patient usually has tenderness of the levator muscles, which are often found to be firmly contracted on examination. It affects both men and women. No standard treatment regimen has been studied, but there are anecdotal reports that sitz baths, levator ani muscle massage, and muscle relaxants can provide some relief.[57,58]

Proctalgia Fugax

Proctalgia fugax is an intensely painful spasm in the rectal area that begins abruptly and lasts for several minutes. It is attributed to a sudden spasm of the levator muscle complex or the sigmoid colon. People who frequent the toilet are at greatest risk, and women are more commonly affected than men. A psychogenic predisposition is described by Pilling, who found that professionals, managers, and perfectionists are more likely to be afflicted.[59]

Proctalgia fugax can begin abruptly during sleep, defecation, urination, or intercourse. The character of the pain has been compared with a charley horse. It lasts less than 30 minutes and may radiate to the coccyx or perineum. Symptoms during recurrent episodes are consistent for an individual, but each patient has a unique constellation of symptoms.[1] Treatment is often unrewarding, but recommendations include bowel regimens, upward manual pressure on the anus, diazepam, and topical nitrates.[57]

Fecal Incontinence

Perspective

Fecal incontinence is an embarrassing condition that affects parous women, elders, and people with a variety of neurologic or traumatic complaints. The delicate balance among the pelvic floor muscles, sphincters, and anorectal sensation is disrupted.[4] Complete incontinence is the inability to control passage of solid feces. Partial incontinence occurs when there is a loss of control of the passage of flatus or liquid feces.[60]

Principles of Disease

There are many causes of fecal incontinence (Box 95-4).[4,61] Injury to muscles and nerves may result

---

BOX 95-4. Causes of Fecal Incontinence

Traumatic
Nerve injured in surgery
Spinal cord injury
Obstetric trauma
Sphincter injury

Neurologic
Spinal cord lesions
Dementia
Autonomic neuropathy (e.g., diabetes mellitus)
Obstetrics: pudendal nerve stretched during surgery
Hirschsprung's disease

Mass Effect
Carcinoma of anal canal
Carcinoma of rectum
Foreign body
Fecal impaction
Hemorrhoids

Medical
Procidentia
Inflammatory disease
Diarrhea
Laxative abuse

Pediatric
Congenital
    Meningocele
    Myelomeningocele
    Spina bifida
After corrective surgery for imperforate anus
Sexual abuse
Encopresis

---

from accidental trauma or surgery for anorectal disorders. Similarly, injury or stretching during childbirth can cause immediate or delayed problems. Spinal cord and cauda equina lesions and the autonomic neuropathy of diabetes mellitus can cause progressive incontinence. Liquid feces may seep around tumors or foreign bodies of the rectum or anal canal. A common "foreign body" is a large impacted stool that occurs in elders or those with underlying megacolon. Explosive diarrhea from laxative abuse, inflammation, or infection can temporarily overwhelm a normal sphincter mechanism. Partial incontinence after surgery to correct imperforate anus is common.[62] It occurs in children with congenital neurologic conditions such as meningocele, myelomeningocele, and spina bifida. Young children (4 to 7 years) with emotional stress may develop encopresis.[22,63] In otherwise healthy children, sexual abuse involving the anus must be considered.[64]

Clinical Features

The physical examination should address the local and systemic factors described previously. The anorectum should be assessed for masses, hemorrhoids, evidence of previous surgery, and neuromuscular function. The anocutaneous reflex, or "anal wink," is elicited by touching the skin near the anus with a pin and observing the resulting constriction.[4] Sphincter function is assessed by asking the patient to squeeze the examiner's finger.

Management

The approach to management of fecal incontinence depends on the cause. Structural and inflammatory conditions may be diagnosed with anoscopy. In cases of transient incontinence caused by diarrhea, a high-fiber diet along with brief therapy with loperamide or opioids has been shown to solidify stool and enhance rectal compliance.[61]

Neuromuscular causes of fecal incontinence can be diagnosed by anorectal physiologic testing. In addition to conservative treatment measures described for transient incontinence, Kegel exercises, biofeedback training, or surgical repair may be necessary.[61,65]

Pruritus Ani

Principles of Disease

Patients with pruritus ani complain of an uncontrollable urge to scratch the perianal area. Approximately 1% to 5% of the population seek medical attention for this condition during their lifetime. Others rely on self-treatment to soothe less severe symptoms. The period of peak incidence is during the fifth and sixth decades of life, and it occurs more often in men.[66] The condition is more common in the summer months and is more noticeable at night. The sensation of itching arises when the richly innervated perianal skin becomes irritated. Patients scratch vigorously in an effort to relieve the itching, which leads to a vicious circle that results in greater irritation and excoriation. The causes of pruritus ani are summarized in Box 95-5.[66-69]

The most common cause is the presence of feces on the perianal skin. Conditions ranging from poor personal hygiene to anatomic disorders of the anorectum allow feces to accumulate in the area. Patients may not clean the area thoroughly after defecation. Disruptions in the anorectal anatomy can lead to uncontrollable fecal collection on the perianal skin. Obesity, deep perianal clefts, copious hair, hemorrhoids, posthemorrhoidal skin tags, rectal mucosal prolapse, anal fissures, and fistulas make the area difficult to clean effectively. Decreased air circulation from wearing tight pants or synthetic undergarments may exacerbate symptoms.

Foods (e.g., caffeine, spicy or citrus foods, tea, and beer) and drugs (e.g., quinidine, colchicine, tetracycline, intravenous hydrocortisone) augment the irritant quality of the feces by altering its pH. Perfumed soaps and drugs, especially local anesthetic creams and ointments, can produce a contact dermatitis. Prolonged usage of hemorrhoidal preparations containing local anesthetic and topical corticosteroid can exacerbate the symptoms. Other dermatologic conditions include psoriasis, seborrhea, lichen simplex, and lichen sclerosus.

Systemic diseases and local infections can produce perianal itching. Chronic renal failure, diabetes mellitus, thyrotoxicosis, myxedema, polycythemia vera,

---

BOX 95-5. Causes of Pruritus Ani

Dermatitis

Fecal irritation
Poor hygiene
Anorectal conditions: Fissure, fistula, hemorrhoids, skin tags, perianal clefts
Systemic: Caffeine, tea, beer, spicy foods, citrus fruits, quinidine, IV hydrocortisone, colchicine, tetracycline

Contact Dermatitis
Anesthetic agents, topical corticosteroids, perfumed soap

Systemic Diseases

Dermatologic
Psoriasis, seborrhea
Lichen simplex or sclerosus

Nondermatologic
Chronic renal failure, myxedema, diabetes mellitus, thyrotoxicosis, polycythemia vera
Vitamins A or D deficiency, iron deficiency
Cancers: Bowen's, Paget's, Hodgkin's diseases

Infectious Agents

STDs
Syphilis
HSV
HPV

Other Agents
Scabies
Pinworm
Bacterial infection
Fungal infection

HPV, human papillomavirus; HSV, herpes simplex virus; STD, sexually transmitted disease.

---

deficiencies of iron or vitamins A or D, and certain cancers (Bowen's, Paget's, Hodgkin's diseases) are systemic causes. Local conditions include pinworms (*Enterobius vermicularis*), scabies (*Sarcoptes scabiei*), bacterial or fungal infections, and dermatologic manifestations of sexually transmitted diseases (e.g., syphilis, herpes simplex virus [HSV], cytomegalovirus, human papillomavirus).

Management

A careful history and physical examination can identify the etiology of pruritus ani. Questions related to hygienic care of the anus, coexisting anorectal or systemic conditions, diet, and sexual practices must be asked. Pinworms can be identified by applying transparent tape to the perianal area and attaching it to a glass slide. Visualization of eggs under low power of a microscope confirms the diagnosis. The treatment is mebendazole (Vermox) 100 mg orally. An alternative treatment is pyrantel pamoate (Antiminth) 1 g orally (11 mg/kg to a maximum of 1 g for pediatric patients). The dose of either may need to be repeated in 2 weeks. Scabies and pediculosis pubis should be treated with 1% lindane lotion or 5% permethrin cream.[66,69] Dermatitis caused by a fungal infection is characterized by sharply demarcated borders and is treated with clotri-mazole or nystatin cream. Definitive treatment of con-comitant anorectal conditions (e.g., fissures, fistulas, hemorrhoids, skin tags, rectal prolapse) can prevent recurrence of pruritus ani.

Underlying systemic diseases that have perianal manifestations should be treated. Education on per-sonal hygiene is of the utmost importance. Patients should be instructed to clean the area thoroughly with lukewarm water after each bowel movement and pat (rather than rub) it dry with a tissue or towel that is free of chemical irritants. Loose-fitting underwear and exposure to fresh air may aid in alleviating symp-toms. The treatment of acute dermatitis includes a short course of topical corticosteroids, calamine lotion, and systemic antihistamines.[66,69] Some success with topical application of capsaicin cream has been reported.[65,70] Prevention of recurrent bouts of pruritus ani requires compliance with impeccable anal hygiene

and minimizing the factors that caused the initial exacerbation.

Sexually Transmitted Diseases and Proctitis

Management

General Approach

The incidence of sexually transmitted diseases (STDs) has increased in the past few decades, and anorectal transmission is of particular concern in the patient with HIV.[69] Semen has a concentrated viral load, and the damaged epithelium of ulcerated anoderm makes an easy portal for entry of the virus.[71] The constellation of infectious diseases that afflicts the anus, rectum, and colon is often termed the "gay bowel syndrome," although it also affects women who engage in anal intercourse. A summary of common infections and treatment guidelines may be found in Table 95-5. Sur-

Table 95-5. Sexually Transmitted Diseases of the Anorectum

Type	Findings	Treatment
Ulcerative		
LGV	Unilateral inguinal adenopathy Fever, malaise Mucoid or bloody discharge	Doxycycline 100 mg PO bid × 21 days If pregnant or allergic to tetracyclines; erythromycin 500 mg PO qid × 21 days

HSV	Rectal pain, tenesmus, constipation
	Bloody mucoid discharge
	Vesicles and ulcerations
	Fever, malaise, myalgias, paresthesias
		First episode:
		  Perianal: acyclovir 400 mg PO tid or
		    Famciclovir 250 mg PO bid × 7-10 days or
		    Valacyclovir 1 g PO daily for 7-10 days
		  Proctitis: acyclovir 800 mg PO tid × 7-10 days
		  Recurrent: acyclovir 400 mg PO tid for 5 days or
		    Acyclovir 200 mg PO 5× per day for 5 days or
		    Acyclovir 800 mg PO bid for 5 days or
		    Famciclovir 125 mg PO bid for 5 days or
		    Valacyclovir 500 mg PO bid for 3-5 days or
		    Valacyclovir 1 g PO daily for 5 days

Early (primary) syphilis	Chancre Tenesmus, pain, mucoid drainage Inguinal lymphadenopathy	Benzathine penicillin G 2.4 MU IM once Alternatives: doxycycline or erythromycin

Chancroid (*H. ducreyi*)	Inflammatory lesion progresses to ulcer
	Inguinal adenitis-bubo
		Azithromycin 1 g PO once or
		  Ceftriaxone 250 mg IM once or
		  Ciprofloxacin 500 mg PO bid ×3 days or
		  Levofloxacin 500 mg PO for 7 days or
		  Erythromycin 500 mg PO tid ×7 days

CMV	Tenesmus, diarrhea, weight loss	Ganciclovir with appropriate disposition
Idiopathic (usually HIV+)	Eccentric, deep, poor healing, multiple	Symptomatic relief or surgical referral
Nonulcerative		
Condylomata acuminata (HPV)	Keratinized vegetative growths in anus or skin Asymptomatic, or pruritus ani, or bleeding	Podophyllin topically or cryotherapy Consider home therapy with podofilox 0.5% solution or gel for limited involvement

Gonorrhea (*N. gonorrhoeae*)	Pruritus ani
	Tenesmus
	Purulent yellow discharge
		Cefixime 400 mg PO once or
		  Ceftriaxone 125 mg IM once or
		  Ofloxacin 400 mg PO once or
		  Ciprofloxacin 500 mg PO once or
		  Levofloxacin 250 mg PO once
		For pregnant patients: spectinomycin 2 g IM one plus
		Erythromycin 500 mg PO qid ×7 days

Chlamydia (*C. trachomatis*)	Mucoid or bloody discharge
	Tenesmus
		Azithromycin 1 g PO once or
		  Doxycycline 100 mg PO ×7 days or
		  Ofloxacin 300 mg PO bid ×7 days
		For pregnant patients: erythromycin 500 mg PO qid ×7 days

Syphilis (secondary)	Maculopapular rash Condyloma latum	Benzathine penicillin G 2.4 MU IM once Alternatives: doxycycline or erythromycin

CMV, cytomegalovirus; HIV, human immunodeficiency virus; HPV, human papillomavirus; HSV, herpes simplex virus; LGV, lymphogranuloma venereum.

gical repair for benign anorectal conditions in HIV-positive patients should be undertaken early in the course of the disease when potential wound healing and patients' wellness are at their best.[71] Empirical therapy is indicated for patients who have recently practiced anally receptive intercourse and present with a rectal discharge. The recommended regimen is ceftriaxone 125 mg intramuscularly for one dose plus doxycycline 100 mg twice a day orally for 7 days.[72] All patients with anorectal infections should be referred for HIV testing. The possibility of sexual assault should be considered and managed appropriately.[72-74]

Treatment of Specific Sexually Transmitted Diseases

Gonorrhea. Gonorrhea is caused by the gram-negative diplococcus *Neisseria gonorrhoeae* and is most prevalent in young adults. Routine screening in homosexual men reveals that 55% are infected, although not all manifest symptoms.[71] It is postulated that gonorrhea is a cofactor for transmission of HIV.[75] Proctitis (inflammation of the rectum) results from anal intercourse or autoinoculation from vaginal secretions and becomes symptomatic after a 5- to 7-day incubation period. Symptomatic patients complain of pruritus ani, tenesmus, and bloody or thick purulent yellow drainage. Anoscopy reveals proctitis and mucus in the anal crypts. Recovery of the organism directly from the crypts doubles the likelihood of identifying the organism on Gram's stain. Water should be used to lubricate the anoscope because many lubricants contain an antibacterial agent. Symptoms of disseminated gonococcal infection, such as arthritis, skin lesions, perihepatitis, endocarditis, and meningitis, may occur.[76]

Chlamydia and Lymphogranuloma Venereum. *Chlamydia trachomatis*, an intracellular organism that is endemic to the tropics, is the most common STD in the United States.[72,77] It causes proctitis in people who practice anal or oral-anal intercourse. Common symptoms include mucoid or bloody rectal discharge, tenesmus, and burning. Some people are asymptomatic carriers of the organism. Lymphogranuloma venereum is a more serious manifestation caused by specific strains of *C. trachomatis* that starts as a painful anal or perianal ulceration. Prominent unilateral lymph nodes coalesce to form a bubo, which must be distinguished from secondary syphilis. Patients often have systemic complaints of fever and malaise. Anoscopic examination reveals an erythematous, friable mucosa. Rectal cultures are generally unreliable because the organism is intracellular. Diagnosis is best achieved by immunofluorescent antibody testing. In its final stage, rectal strictures and rectovaginal fistulas may form.[60]

Herpes Simplex Virus. Herpes proctitis is caused by both HSV-1 and HSV-2, but HSV-2 is responsible for approximately 90% of cases.[76,78] There is a 95% seroprevalence of HSV-2 in the HIV-positive population.[71] Herpes genital infections occur in people who practice oral-anal or anal intercourse. Symptoms appear 1 to 3 weeks after exposure. Those with proctitis complain of severe rectal pain, bloody mucoid discharge, tenesmus, constipation, and sometimes sacral paresthesias and

urinary difficulties. Systemic complaints of fever, malaise, and myalgias may be present.[76,78] Physical examination and anoscopy may be impossible without anesthesia. Single or coalesced vesicles and ulcerations occur in the perianal area and rectum, and anoscopy reveals an erythematous, friable, ulcerated rectal mucosa. Chronic mucocutaneous HSV infection is considered diagnostic for AIDS. Definitive diagnosis with viral or immunofluorescent staining relies on proper collection of fluid and scrapings from the base of the vesicle.[1,76]

Syphilis. The number of reported cases of syphilis is increasing. Up to 75% of homosexual men are infected with *Treponema pallidum*, the motile spirochete responsible for the disease.[76] During anal intercourse, the organism enters the rectal mucosa or anoderm and causes an ulcer (chancre) to form within 2 to 6 weeks. The chancre heralds the primary phase of syphilis and may resemble an anal fissure that is not located in the midline.[79] Most patients experience discomfort during defecation, mucoid discharge, tenesmus, and inguinal adenopathy. Primary syphilis can be confused with lymphoma, but the diagnosis can be made by visualizing spirochetes on dark field microscopy from scrapings at the base of the ulcer.[78] Serologic testing is useful several weeks after the appearance of the chancre. Treponemal tests such as the fluorescent treponemal antibody test become positive earlier than the Venereal Disease Research Laboratory (VDRL) or rapid plasma reagin (nontreponemal) test.[78] Patients infected with HIV may take longer to test positive, and in some cases test results remain negative despite infection.[76] Patients with AIDS have a high incidence of neurosyphilis regardless of the stage of syphilis at the time they seek treatment.[80]

In some patients the chancre goes unnoticed, and they are seen initially with secondary syphilis, marked by the appearance of a maculopapular rash that characteristically involves the palms and soles or of condyloma latum. The latter is a spirochete-laden, weeping, verrucous lesion in the perianal area that emits a foul odor.[76] It is easily distinguishable from condyloma acuminatum, which has a drier, more keratinized appearance. Serologic testing results are usually positive. Tertiary syphilis is rare but may be revealed as a rectal gumma with severe perianal pain and paralysis of the sphincters, which may initially cause it to be mistaken for cancer.[76]

Chancroid. Chancroid is caused by the gram-negative bacillus *Haemophilus ducreyi* and begins as an inflammatory pustule or macule that ruptures to form an irregularly shaped ulcer. In several days, painful inguinal adenitis develops. It is often a diagnosis of exclusion. All antimicrobial therapy, especially single-dose ceftriaxone, is less effective in HIV-positive patients.

Condylomata Acuminata (Genital Warts). Condylomata acuminata, the most commonly encountered anorectal STD, are caused by human papillomavirus. They are most often found in homosexual men but can be seen in heterosexual men, women, and children. The mode of transmission is primarily through sexual

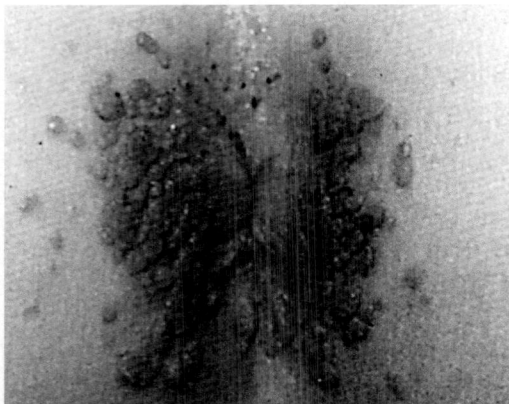

A

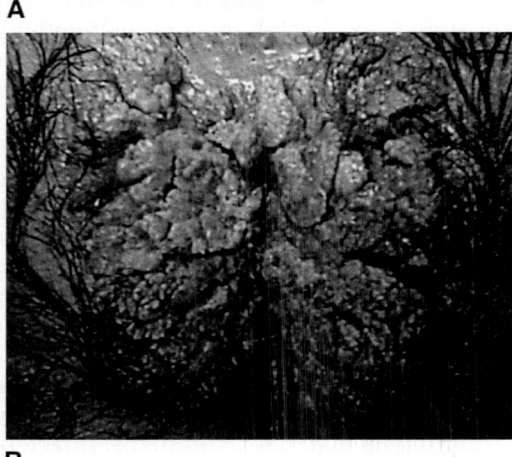

B

Figure 95-7. Condylomata acuminata in a child (**A**) and in an adult (**B**).

intercourse, but it can occur through close contact with infected persons, as often happens in pediatric cases in which an infected person is changing a diaper and transmits the virus to the infant because of poor hand-washing techniques. It is incumbent upon the evaluating physician to consider sexual abuse in these cases.[24] Because one half of HIV-positive patients have anal warts, HIV testing is recommended in patients with this diagnosis.[71,81] The pink-to-gray warts are a result of hyperplastic epithelial growth and appear as vegetative papilliform growths (Figure 95-7). They may coalesce to form a massive patch that obscures the anal verge.[35] Many patients are asymptomatic or complain of pruritus ani, a "hemorrhoid," or bleeding. Evaluation should include anoscopy because the warts often grow within the anal canal. Failure to treat the internal lesions results in recurrence.[1,35,64] The differential diagnosis includes the condyloma latum of secondary syphilis, which has a more flat, moist appearance. Squamous cell carcinoma should be considered if the lesions are indurated. Progression to intraepithelial neoplasia has been reported to be related to the level of immunosuppression.[69]

Outpatient treatment with 0.5% podofilox solution or gel is limited to mild cases of external lesions.[65] Multiple applications of podophyllin resin by the physician may be required. This derivative of the plant

BOX 95-6. Anorectal Lesions in the Patient with HIV

Common Conditions
Anal fissure
Abscess and fistula
Hemorrhoids
Pruritus ani
Pilonidal disease

Common STDs
Gonorrhea
Chlamydia
Herpes
Chancroid
Syphilis
Condyloma acuminata

Atypical Conditions
Infectious: TB, CMV, actinomycosis, cryptococcus
Neoplastic: lymphoma, Kaposi's sarcoma, squamous cell carcinoma
Other: idiopathic anal ulcer

CMV, cytomegalovirus; STD, sexually transmitted disease; TB, tuberculosis.

Podophyllum emodi is a powerful skin irritant, and meticulous application is necessary. Alternative treatments include bichloroacetic acid, immunotherapy, laser, chemotoxic agents, cryotherapy, electrocoagulation, and excision.[35]

Ulcerative Lesions in the Patient with HIV. Anal intercourse has led to a proliferation of anorectal STDs. Most patients who are HIV positive have current or past STD infection, which may be the initial reason for seeking medical attention. One third are anorectal complaints that fall into three categories: (1) routine proctologic conditions seen in the general population, (2) STDs, and (3) opportunistic infections (Box 95-6). The treatment of routine conditions and common STDs is similar except that wound healing may be slower in the patient with HIV.

In immunocompromised patients, the differential diagnosis of ulcerative anorectal lesions should include opportunistic infections, lymphoma, and Kaposi's sarcoma. Approximately 10% of patients with AIDS develop cytomegalovirus proctitis with tenesmus, diarrhea, and weight loss. The only clue may be the presence of an anal ulcer that may be indistinguishable from a fissure. Further diagnostic testing and treatment are required. Patients with AIDS often exhibit idiopathic anal ulcerations with pain and bleeding. Before making this diagnosis, other possible causes of the lesions must be considered (see Box 95-6). Symptomatic relief can often be achieved by the WASH regimen (see Box 95-2), but recalcitrant lesions may require surgical excision.[73,83,84]

Radiation Proctitis

Radiation-induced injury caused by treatment of gynecologic, urologic, and GI malignancies occurs most commonly in the rectum. Because of the ability to deliver localized radiation to organs in the pelvis, the dose of radiation for treatment of malignancies is often higher than when treating other forms of cancer.[85,86] Immediate radiation proctitis is usually self-limited and responds to symptomatic treatment. Delayed radiation proctitis can present up to 2 years after the exposure to radiation and may predispose the patient to subsequent rectal malignancies as a result of damage to DNA.[86]

Signs and symptoms of radiation proctitis include bleeding, ranging from spotting to hemorrhage, tenesmus, diarrhea, pain, fistula-in-ano, and rectal strictures.[87] Diagnosis is achieved by rectal mucosal biopsy, a procedure best performed under sedation or anesthesia.

Treatment regimens include the use of anti-inflammatory agents, botulinum toxin injection, enemas with short-chain fatty acids, oral sucralfate therapy, hyperbaric oxygen therapy, or sclerosing therapy.[88] Supportive therapy can be given for the individual symptoms that the patient experiences.

Procidentia

Rectal prolapse, or procidentia, is a disease of the extremes of age. It is complete if all bowel layers protrude and incomplete if only the mucosal layer is involved. In adults, complete procidentia is most common in older women with a history of excessive straining while stooling. The cause is a laxity of attachment structures, and it is often accompanied by uterine prolapse or a cystocele. Patients complain of an anal mass during defecation, coughing, or sneezing. It may cause incontinence, bloody or mucoid discharge, and a foul odor. Physical examination reveals a red, ulcerated mass protruding from the anus (Figure 95-8). Sphincter tone may be weakened. Reduction should be attempted and, when successful, patients discharged with agents to relieve constipation. Surgical repair is often necessary.[89-91]

In children, procidentia may herald the presence of malnutrition or cystic fibrosis and occurs during the first 2 years of life. Boys are more commonly affected than girls. Children usually have a mucosal prolapse.[22,92] The parent reports protrusion during defecation with small amounts of mucus or blood. It must be distinguished from a protruding juvenile polyp and intussusception. Reduction of procidentia should be attempted with sedation, if necessary.[1] Medical management is successful because the disease is usually self-limited.[90,92]

Anorectal Foreign Bodies

Perspective

The incidence of anorectal foreign bodies is on the rise with the increasing popularity of the anus for sexual gratification. Rectal foreign bodies are also found in children, psychiatric patients, and victims of assault or as a result of iatrogenic injury. Most objects are introduced directly into the anus, but some become lodged there after oral ingestion. It is important to identify and remove foreign bodies to prevent mucosal lacerations, intestinal obstruction, sepsis, and peritonitis. In many cases, removal can be done safely in the emergency department.

Clinical Features

Objects Inserted into the Anus

In a few cases, the foreign body is introduced iatrogenically. The two most common are the enema tip and the broken rectal thermometer.[93] However, in most cases the foreign body is placed deliberately by the patient or sexual partner for medicinal or sexual purposes. Objects that are commonly retrieved include fruits and vegetables; household items, especially those whose dimensions resemble the penis; and those purchased specifically with an anal erotic intent.[94-98] By the time patients arrive at the emergency department, they have most likely tried to remove the foreign body at home. The history of injury is often reluctantly given or is vague and inconsistent. The emergency physician should attempt to ascertain the history in a nonjudgmental manner: to learn the type of foreign body involved, how long it has been there, what attempts have been made to remove it, and whether the patient has fever, abdominal pain, or rectal bleeding. The possibility of assault should always be considered.[98]

Physical examination of the anorectum begins with an external examination for signs of trauma followed by digital rectal examination and anoscopy, which may reveal the foreign body, a lax sphincter, or a mucosal injury. Abdominal examination may demonstrate signs of perforation or obstruction. The foreign body may be visible on abdominal radiographs, or its presence may be inferred by a nonspecific gas pattern, free air, or signs of intestinal obstruction. If perforation is suspected, water-soluble contrast medium can be introduced to delineate radiolucent foreign bodies.[93]

Orally Ingested Foreign Bodies

Some foreign bodies that are ingested orally, especially toothpicks and fish or chicken bones, pass through the GI tract and subsequently become lodged in the rectum

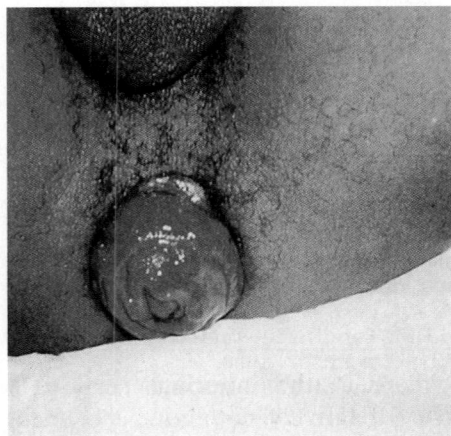

Figure 95-8. Prolapse of the rectum. (Courtesy of Gershon Effron, MD, Sinai Hospital of Baltimore. In Seidel HM, et al: *Mosby's Guide to Physical Examination*, 4th ed. St. Louis, Mosby, 1999.)

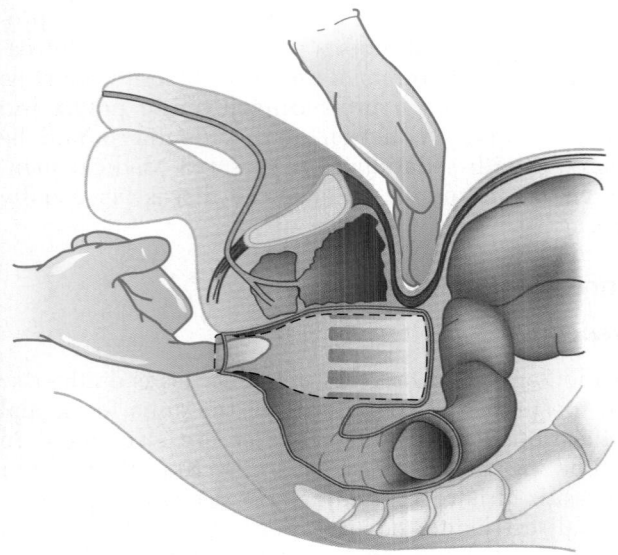

Figure 95-9. Removal of foreign body from the rectum.

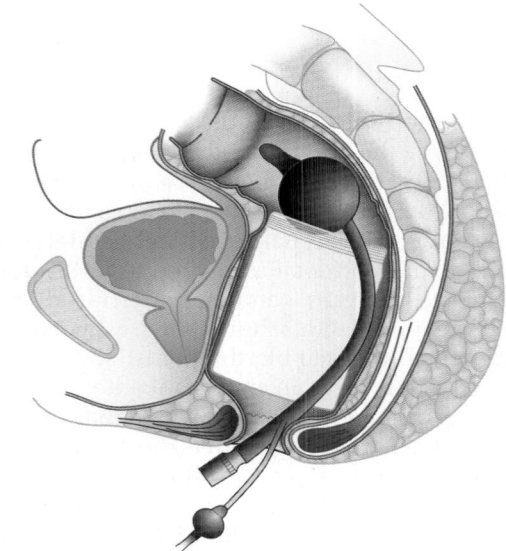

Figure 95-10. Foley catheter–assisted removal of a rectal foreign body.

or anal crypts.[98] Patients at highest risk for ingested foreign bodies are children, especially those in the first 2 years of life; psychiatric patients; and body packers who ingest condoms containing drugs.

Management

Optimal treatment depends on the location and type of object found. Generally, objects that are soft and low lying (<10 cm from the anal verge) can be removed safely in the emergency department. Large, hard, fragile objects and those that have migrated proximally are difficult to remove without anal dilation under general anesthesia and instrumentation to assist in the passage through the sacral curve and sphincters. Premedication with a benzodiazepine is helpful to relax both the sphincter and the patient, but the patient should remain awake to assist in expulsion by performing the Valsalva maneuver at the appropriate time.[98] With the patient in the lithotomy position, suprapubic pressure can assist in removal (Figure 95-9). Other positions may be more appropriate for a particular foreign body. Several methods are effective for removal. The easiest is to grasp an edge of the foreign body with forceps and apply traction while the patient bears down. Most foreign bodies in the rectum do not have a convenient place to grasp, and other methods are needed. A Foley catheter can be placed beside the foreign body and the balloon inflated proximal to it (Figure 95-10). This breaks the suction of the rectal wall mucosa and provides a way to guide the object out of the rectal vault. Hollow objects may be filled with plaster of Paris, with an inset, inflated Foley catheter to be used as a handle.[98]

Other creative ways to remove foreign bodies in the emergency department have been successful, and an individualized strategy for each patient is essential. After the removal of the foreign body, all patients should undergo sigmoidoscopy to look for mucosal tears and perforations.[95-98] Discharge instructions should warn the patient of signs and symptoms of perforation, peritonitis, and sepsis.

🗝 **KEY CONCEPTS**

- Patients who seek treatment for nonspecific anorectal complaints should be evaluated for the presence of underlying systemic disease (e.g., cancer, diabetes mellitus) because the anus may herald associated conditions.

- Patients with any STD should be evaluated for HIV infection and questioned about the use of the anus for sexual purposes.

- Anorectal conditions can be differentiated according to an algorithm (Figure 95-2) that addresses the presence or absence of pain, bleeding, swelling, and pruritus, in combination with an assessment of the patient's overall health.

- Most anorectal conditions can be symptomatically improved by adhering to the WASH regimen: warm water, analgesics, stool softeners, high-fiber diet.

REFERENCES

1. Corman ML: *Colon and Rectal Surgery*, 4th ed. Philadelphia, JB Lippincott, 1998.
2. Marcio J, et al: Anatomy and physiology of the rectum and anus. *Eur J Surg* 163:723, 1997.
3. Moore KL: *Clinically Oriented Anatomy*, 4th ed. Baltimore, Williams & Wilkins, 1999.
4. Thorson AG: Anorectal physiology. *Surg Clin North Am* 82:1115, 2002.
5. Gopal DV: Diseases of the rectum and anus: A clinical approach to common disorders. *Clin Cornerstone* 4:34, 2002.
6. Janicke DM, Pundt MR: Anorectal disorders. *Emerg Med Clin North Am* 14:757, 1996.
7. Jones R, Farthing M: The management of rectal bleeding. *Br J Clin Pract* 47:155, 1993.
8. *New American Bible*. New York, World Publishing Company, 1970.
9. Welling DR, et al: Piles of defeat: Napoleon at Waterloo. *Dis Colon Rectum* 31:303, 1988.

10. Hulme-Moir M, Bartolo DC: Hemorrhoids. *Gastroenterol Clin North Am* 30:183, 2001.
11. Nisar PJ, Scholefield JH: Managing haemorrhoids. *BMJ* 327:847, 2003.
12. Sardinha TC, Corman ML: Hemorrhoids. *Surg Clin North Am* 82:1153, 2002.
13. Thomson WHF: The nature of haemorrhoids. *Br J Surg* 62:542, 1975.
14. Abramowitz L, et al: Anal fissure and thrombosed external hemorrhoids before and after delivery. *Dis Colon Rectum* 45:650, 2002.
15. Wald A: Functional anorectal and pelvic pain. *Gastroenterol Clin North Am* 30:243, 2001.
16. Heaton ND, et al: Symptomatic hemorrhoids and anorectal varices in children with portal hypertension. *J Pediatr Surg* 27:833, 1992.
17. Heaton ND, et al: Incidence of haemorrhoids and anorectal varices in children with portal hypertension. *Br J Surg* 80:616, 1993.
18. Orkin BA, et al: Hemorrhoids: What the dermatologist should know. *J Am Acad Dermatol* 41:449, 1999.
19. Dodi G, et al: Hot or cold in anal pain? A study in the changes in internal sphincter pressure profiles. *Dis Colon Rectum* 29:248, 1986.
20. Jongen J, et al: Excision of thrombosed external hemorrhoid under local anesthesia: A retrospective evaluation of 340 patients. *Dis Colon Rectum* 46:1226, 2003.
21. Perrotti P, et al: Topical nifedipine with lidocaine ointment vs. active control for treatment of chronic anal fissure: Results of a prospective, randomized, double-blind study. *Dis Colon Rectum* 45:1468, 2002.
22. Metcalf AM: Anal fissure. *Surg Clin North Am* 82:1291, 2002.
23. Matt JG: Proctologic problems in infants and children: An analysis of 308 cases. *Dis Colon Rectum* 3:511, 1960.
24. Behrman R, Kliegman RM, Jenson HB (eds): *Nelson's Textbook of Pediatrics*, 17th ed. Philadelphia, WB Saunders, 2003.
25. Rosen L, et al: Practice parameters for the management of anal fissure. *Dis Colon Rectum* 35:206, 1992.
26. Cundall JD, et al: Use of hyperbaric oxygen to treat chronic anal fissure. *Br J Surg* 90:452, 2003.
27. Bailey HR, et al: A study to determine the nitroglycerin ointment dose and dosing interval that best promote the healing of chronic anal fissures. *Dis Colon Rectum* 45:1192, 2002.
28. Antropoli C, et al: Nifedipine for local use in conservative treatment of anal fissures. *Dis Colon Rectum* 42:1011, 1999.
29. Nelson R: A systematic review of medical therapy for anal fissure. *Dis Colon Rectum* 4:422, 2004.
30. Ezri T, Susmallian S: Topical nifedipine vs. topical glyceryl trinitrate for treatment of chronic anal fissure. *Dis Colon Rectum* 46:805, 2003.
31. Jost WH: One hundred cases of anal fissure treated with botulinum toxin: Early and long-term results. *Dis Colon Rectum* 40:1029, 1997.
32. Brisinda D, et al: Safety of botulinum neurotoxin treatment in patients with chronic anal fissure. *Dis Colon Rectum* 46:419, 2003.
33. Brisinda G, Maria G: Botulinum toxin in the treatment of chronic anal fissure. *Dis Colon Rectum* 46:1144, 2003.
34. Mitka M: Colon and rectal surgeons are trying Botox treatment, too. *JAMA* 288:439, 2002.
35. Helton WS: 2001 consensus statement on benign anorectal disease. *J Gastrointest Surg* 6:302, 2002.
36. Nelson R: Anorectal abscess fistula: What do we know? *Surg Clin North Am* 82:1139, 2002.
37. Endo M, et al: Analysis of 1992 patients with anorectal malformations over the last two decades in Japan. Steering Committee of Japanese Study Group of Anorectal Anomalies. *J Pediatr Surg* 34:435, 1999.
38. Festen C, van Harten H: Perianal abscess and fistula-in-ano in infants. *J Pediatr Surg* 33:711, 1998.
39. Macdonald A, Wilson-Storey D, Munro F: Treatment of perianal abscess and fistula-in-ano in children. *Br J Surg* 90:220, 2003.
40. Murthi GV, et al: Perianal abscess in childhood. *Pediatr Surg Int* 18:689, 2002.
41. Venkatesh KS, Ramanujam P: Fibrin glue application in the treatment of recurrent anorectal fistulas. *Dis Colon Rectum* 42:1136, 1999.
42. Hughes LE: Clinical classification of perianal Crohn's disease. *Dis Colon Rectum* 35:928, 1992.
43. Cataldo PA, et al: Intrarectal ultrasound in the evaluation of perirectal abscess. *Dis Colon Rectum* 36:554, 1993.
44. Corfitsen MT, et al: Anorectal abscesses in immunocompromised patients. *Eur J Surg* 158:51, 1992.
45. Oliver I, et al: Randomized clinical trial comparing simple drainage of anorectal abscess with and without fistula track treatment. *Int J Colorectal Dis* 18:107, 2003.
46. Sentovich SM: Fibrin glue for anal fistulas: Long-term results. *Dis Colon Rectum* 46:498, 2003.
47. Anderson AW: Hair extracted from an ulcer. *Boston Med Surg J* 37:74, 1847.
48. Chintapatla S, et al: Sacrococcygeal pilonidal sinus: Historical review, pathological insight and surgical options. *Tech Coloproctol* 7:3, 2003.
49. Hull TL, Wu J: Pilonidal disease. *Surg Clin North Am* 82:1169, 2002.
50. Haworth JC, Zachary RB: Congenital dermal sinuses in children—Their relation to pilonidal sinus. *Lancet* 2:10, 1955.
51. Billingham RP: Anorectal miscellany: Pilonidal disease, anal cancer, Bowen's and Paget's diseases, foreign bodies, and hidradenitis suppurativa. *Prim Care* 26:171, 1999.
52. Khatri VP, et al: Management of recurrent pilonidal sinus by simple V-Y fasciocutaneous flap. *Dis Colon Rectum* 37:1232, 1994.
53. Paletta C, Jurkiewicz MJ: Hidradenitis suppurativa. *Clin Plast Surg* 14:383, 1987.
54. Mitchell KM, Beck DE: Hidradenitis suppurativa. *Surg Clin North Am* 82:1187, 2002.
55. Bocchini SF, et al: Gluteal and perianal hidradenitis suppurativa: Surgical treatment by wide excision. *Dis Colon Rectum* 46:944, 2003.
56. Slade DEM, Powell BW, Mortimer PS: Hidradenitis suppurativa: Pathogenesis and management. *Br J Plast Surg* 56:451, 2003.
57. Wald A: Functional anorectal and pelvic pain. *Gastroenterol Clin North Am* 30:243, 2001.
58. Hetrick DC, et al: Musculoskeletal dysfunction in men with chronic pelvic pain syndrome type III: A case-control study. *J Urol* 170:828, 2003.
59. Pilling LF, et al: The psychologic aspects of proctalgia fugax. *Dis Colon Rectum* 8:372, 1965.
60. Hyman NH: Anorectal disease: How to relieve pain and improve other symptoms. *Geriatrics* 52:75, 1997.
61. Tariq SH, Morley JE, Prather CM: Fecal incontinence in the elderly patient. *Am J Med* 115:217, 2003.
62. Pena A, et al: Reoperative surgery for anorectal anomalies. *Semin Pediatr Surg* 12:118, 2003.
63. Loening-Baucke V: Encopresis. *Curr Opin Pediatr* 14:570, 2002.
64. Ozturk H, et al: Management of anorectal injuries in children: An eighteen-year experience. *Eur J Pediatr Surg* 13:249, 2003.
65. Norton C, Wilson-Barnett J, Redfern S, Kamm MA: Randomized controlled trial of biofeedback for fecal incontinence. *Gastroenterology* 125:1320, 2003.
66. Jones DJ: Pruritus ani. *BMJ* 305:575, 1992.
67. Harrington CL, et al: Dermatological causes of pruritus ani. *BMJ* 305:955, 1992.

68. Marks MM: The influence of intestinal pH on anal pruritus. *South Med J* 61:1005, 1968.
69. Paré AA, Gottesman L: Anorectal diseases. *Gastroenterol Clin North Am* 26:367, 1997.
70. Lysy J, et al: Topical capsaicin—A novel and effective treatment for idiopathic intractable pruritus ani: A randomised, placebo controlled, crossover study. *Gut* 52:1323, 2003.
71. Law CLH, et al: Nonspecific proctitis: Association with human immunodeficiency virus infection in homosexual men. *J Infect Dis* 165:150, 1992.
72. Sexually transmitted diseases treatment guidelines 2002. Centers for Disease Control and Prevention. *MMWR Recomm Rep* 51(RR-6):1, 2002.
73. Kazal HL, et al: The gay bowel syndrome: Clinicopathologic correlation in 260 cases. *Am Clin Lab Sci* 6:184, 1976.
74. Pesola GR, Westfal RE, Kuffner CA: Emergency department characteristics of male sexual assault. *Acad Emerg Med* 6:792, 1999.
75. Kim AA, Kent CK, Klausner JD: Risk factors for rectal gonococcal infection amidst resurgence in HIV transmission. *Sex Transm Dis* 30:813, 2003.
76. Viamonte M, et al: Ulcerative disease of the anorectum in the HIV+ patient. *Dis Col Rectum* 36:801, 1993.
77. Cook RL, et al: Prevalence of chlamydia and gonorrhoea among a population of men who have sex with men. *Sex Transm Infect* 78:190, 2002.
78. Holmes KK, et al (eds): *Sexually Transmitted Diseases*, 3rd ed. New York, McGraw-Hill, 1999.
79. Craib KJ, et al: Rectal gonorrhea as an independent risk factor for HIV infection in a cohort of homosexual men. *Genitourin Med* 71:150, 1995.
80. Bordon J, et al: Neurosyphilis in HIV infected patients. *Eur J Clin Microbiol Infect Dis* 14:864, 1995.
81. Karon JM, et al: HIV in the United States at the turn of the century: An epidemic in transition. *Am J Public Health* 91:1060, 2001.
82. Bassi O, et al: Primary syphilis of the rectum—Endoscopic and clinical features. *Dis Colon Rectum* 34:1024, 1991.
83. Wilcox CM, Schwartz DA: Idiopathic anorectal ulceration in patients with human immunodeficiency virus infection. *Am J Gastroenterol* 89:599, 1993.
84. Miles AJG, et al: Persistent ulceration of the anal margin in homosexuals with HIV infection. *J R Soc Med* 84:87, 1991.
85. Ajlouni M: Radiation-induced proctitis. *Curr Treat Options Gastroenterol* 2:20, 1999.
86. Johnston MJ, Robertson GM, Frizelle FA: Management of late complications of pelvic radiation in the rectum and anus: A review. *Dis Colon Rectum* 46:247, 2003.
87. Babb RR: Radiation proctitis: A review. *Am J Gastroenterol* 91:1309, 1996.
88. Denton AS, et al: Systematic review for non-surgical interventions for the management of late radiation proctitis. *Br J Cancer* 87:134, 2002.
89. Madbouly KM, et al: Clinically based management of rectal prolapse. *Surg Endosc* 17:99, 2003.
90. Karulf RE, Madoff RD, Goldberg SM: Rectal prolapse. *Curr Probl Surg* 38:771, 2001.
91. Hyman NH: Anorectal disease: How to relieve pain and improve other symptoms. *Geriatrics* 52:75, 1997.
92. Corman ML: Rectal prolapse in children. *Dis Colon Rectum* 28:535, 1985.
93. Hellinger MD: Anal trauma and foreign bodies. *Surg Clin North Am* 82:1253, 2002.
94. Losanoff JE, Kjossev KT: Rectal "oven mitt": The importance of considering a serious underlying injury. *J Emerg Med* 17:31, 1999.
95. Ooi BS, et al: Management of anorectal foreign bodies: A cause for obscure anal pain. *Aust NZ J Surg* 68:852, 1998.
96. Thomson SR, et al: Iatrogenic and accidental colon injuries—What to do? *Dis Colon Rectum* 37:496, 1994.
97. Fry RD: Anorectal trauma and foreign bodies. *Surg Clin North Am* 74:1491, 1994.
98. Johnson SO, Hartranft TH: Nonsurgical removal of a rectal foreign body using a vacuum extractor. Report of a case. *Dis Colon Rectum* 39:935, 1996.

Section VI GENITOURINARY SYSTEM

CHAPTER

96 Renal Failure

Allan B. Wolfson

EVALUATION OF RENAL FUNCTION

Perspective

The kidneys are responsible for the excretion of certain end products of metabolism (e.g., urea, creatinine, and uric acid) and for control of the concentration of many body fluid constituents (e.g., sodium, potassium, chloride, and hydrogen ions). Plasma is filtered at the glomerulus, creating an ultrafiltrate that is then processed by the proximal and distal tubules and collecting duct. More than 99% of the filtrate is reabsorbed by the tubules; the remainder passes through the ureters, bladder, and urethra and is excreted as urine. The glomerular filtrate contains virtually no red blood cells (RBCs), and its composition is similar to that of interstitial fluid except that it has a protein concentration only 0.02 that of plasma. Water, electrolytes, and small molecules (e.g., glucose and uric acid) are reabsorbed from the glomerular filtrate across the tubular epithelium and are taken up into the plasma of the peritubular capillaries. Other substances are secreted by the tubular epithelium into the urine. The amount of glomerular filtrate formed per minute by both kidneys, termed the glomerular filtration rate (GFR), averages 125 mL/min in adult men and about 100 mL/min in women.

Although renal dysfunction may ultimately result in disturbances in volume regulation, acid-base balance, and electrolyte metabolism, patients often have the cardinal manifestations of hematuria, proteinuria, or azotemia. The last is defined as an increased serum concentration of the end products of protein metabolism, as reflected principally by urea and creatinine. The evaluation of renal disease in the emergency department requires the intelligent use of urinalysis, serum and urine chemical determinations, and renal imaging studies to assess the degree of renal dysfunction and to take the first steps in determining its cause.

After discussing these diagnostic studies, this chapter outlines the approach to patients with hematuria, proteinuria, acute renal failure (ARF), or chronic renal failure. Related topics, including urinary tract infection (UTI), urinary tract tumors, nephrolithiasis, renal trauma, acid-base disorders, and treatment of electrolyte abnormalities, are discussed in greater detail in other chapters.

Diagnostic Strategies

Urine Volume

Because urine flow does not diminish until the GFR is sharply decreased, urine volume is a poor indicator of renal dysfunction. In fact, urine volume often increases as concentrating ability is lost with advancing renal dysfunction; patients with renal failure typically produce isosthenuric urine. Oliguria, defined as a urine volume of 100 to 400 mL per 24 hours, may be seen with prerenal (blood flow–dependent), intrinsic (intrarenal), or postrenal (obstructive) causes of ARF. Alternating oliguria and anuria, although uncommon, is a classical indicator of intermittent obstruction that occurs as urine collects behind an obstructing stone or tumor and then is allowed to flow past as the obstructing material shifts position.

Urinalysis

The standard urinalysis consists of dipstick screening for heme pigment, protein, glucose, ketones, pH, leukocyte esterase, and nitrite and microscopic examination of a spun specimen of freshly voided urine.

Heme

Heme pigment catalyzes the oxidation of orthotoluidine by peroxidase, a reaction that is used to produce a color change on the dipstick reagent strip. The dipstick detects both free hemoglobin (or myoglobin) and hemoglobin contained in RBCs but is more sensitive to the former. Although as few as 3 RBCs per high-power field (HPF) can be detected, the dipstick may fail to identify from 10% to 15% of patients with microscopic hematuria, as defined by more than 5 RBC/HPF. The sensitivity of the dipstick can be decreased by substances in the urine that alter the hemoglobin molecule. Vitamin C, for example, can cause a false-negative test result when present in the urine in large quantities. False-negative findings also occur in dilute urine and in urine containing large amounts of protein. False-positive results can be produced by chlorine or other oxidizing agents. A positive dipstick result should prompt microscopic examination of the urine. If red cells are seen, the diagnosis of hematuria is confirmed. If the dipstick result is positive but findings on microscopic examination are negative, pigmenturia (myoglobin or free hemoglobin) should be suspected.

Protein

Urine containing large amounts of protein tends to foam when shaken, but visual inspection alone cannot reliably detect proteinuria. The dipstick test for protein, using the color change of tetrabromophenol blue, can detect protein at concentrations of 10 to 15 mg/dL but does not reliably yield positive results until the concentration is greater than 30 mg/dL. Moreover, the relation between color intensity and protein concentration is only approximate. The dipstick is three to five times more sensitive to albumin than to globulins and immunoglobulin light chains (e.g., Bence Jones protein), an important limitation. False-positive results are caused by alkaline urine, hematuria, or prolonged immersion of the dipstick in the urine. False-negative results are seen with dilute urine. The sulfosalicylic acid (SSA) test is more sensitive to proteinuria, detecting as little as 5 mg/dL of nonalbumin or albumin protein. Eight drops of 20% SSA are added to 2 mL of urine; turbidity appears if protein is present. False-positive findings may be caused by radiographic contrast agents, penicillin, or sulfonylurea drugs. False-negative results occur in alkaline urine. All specimens that produce a positive dipstick result should be retested using SSA; if the SSA result is significantly more positive than that of the dipstick, a urine electrophoresis should be performed to detect nonalbumin proteins such as the light chains associated with multiple myeloma.[1]

Microscopic Examination

After the urine is dipped with the test strip, 10 mL is placed in a conical test tube and spun at 2000 rpm for 5 minutes (higher speeds may break up casts). The supernatant is discarded. The sediment is resuspended in the residual urine, and a drop is placed on a slide and covered with a cover slip. The periphery of the cover slip, where casts tend to concentrate, is scanned under low power. The slide is then scanned under high power for red cells, white cells, renal tubular epithelial cells, oval fat bodies, bacteria, and crystals. Although some inaccuracy is involved in gauging the degree of hematuria by examining the spun-urine sediment, more reliable quantitative techniques are cumbersome and are rarely available to the clinician. Observations are recorded as the number of cells seen per high-power field. A level of 2 to 3 RBC/HPF in adult men or 2 to 4 RBC/HPF in adult women is commonly accepted as normal; in many studies a finding of 5 RBC/HPF is considered the threshold of abnormality.[2,3]

Casts are formed from urinary Tamm-Horsfall protein, a product of the tubular epithelial cells that gels at low pH and high concentration and when mixed with albumin, red cells, tubular cells, or cellular debris.

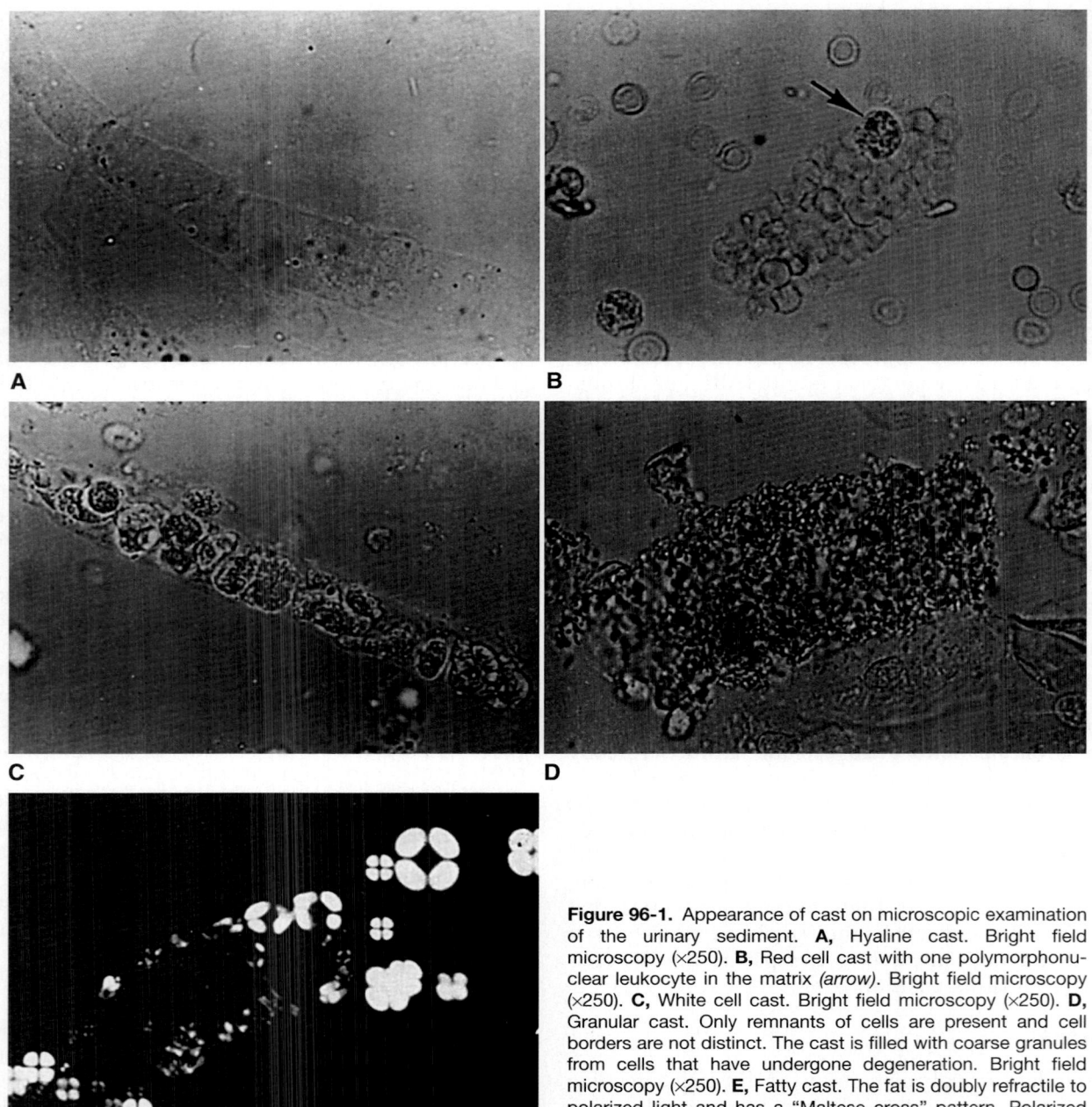

Figure 96-1. Appearance of cast on microscopic examination of the urinary sediment. **A,** Hyaline cast. Bright field microscopy (×250). **B,** Red cell cast with one polymorphonuclear leukocyte in the matrix *(arrow)*. Bright field microscopy (×250). **C,** White cell cast. Bright field microscopy (×250). **D,** Granular cast. Only remnants of cells are present and cell borders are not distinct. The cast is filled with coarse granules from cells that have undergone degeneration. Bright field microscopy (×250). **E,** Fatty cast. The fat is doubly refractile to polarized light and has a "Maltese cross" pattern. Polarized microscopy (×250). (Courtesy of the American Society of Clinical Pathologists.)

The composition of a cast thus reflects the contents of the tubule. Casts are described and classified according to their appearance or constituents (e.g., hyaline, red cell, white cell, granular, or fatty casts) (Figure 96-1). Hyaline casts, those that are devoid of contents, are seen with dehydration, after exercise, or in association with glomerular proteinuria. Red cell casts indicate glomerular hematuria, as seen in glomerulonephritis; the presence of even a few red cell casts is significant. White cell casts imply the presence of renal parenchymal inflammation. Granular casts are composed of cellular remnants and debris. Fatty casts, like oval fat bodies, are generally associated with heavy proteinuria and the nephrotic syndrome but have been noted to

occur in a substantial proportion of patients with nonglomerular renal disease as well.

Casts may also be classified by size and appearance as hyaline, broad, or waxy. In chronic renal disease, casts may be broad (>3 white blood cell [WBC] diameters wide) because of enlargement of the nephrons that are still functioning; they have finely dispersed granules and appear waxy. The term *telescoped sediment* refers to a combination of cellular casts and broad and waxy casts, suggesting ongoing damage of the remaining nephrons.

Microscopic examination of the urinary sediment can be helpful in establishing the cause of ARF. A sediment without formed elements or with only hyaline casts is characteristic of prerenal azotemia or obstruction. Red cell casts suggest glomerulonephritis or vasculitis. Fatty casts are seen in the nephrotic syndrome and also suggest glomerular disease. In acute tubular necrosis (ATN), the urinary sediment commonly shows granular casts and renal tubular epithelial cells. Large numbers of polymorphonuclear leukocytes are observed in interstitial nephritis, papillary necrosis, and pyelonephritis. Eosinophil-containing casts (appreciated only after staining the sediment) are typical of allergic interstitial nephritis. Uric acid crystals suggest uric acid nephropathy but are extremely nonspecific; oxalic acid or hippuric acid crystals may be seen in ethylene glycol ingestion.

Serum and Urine Chemical Analysis

Creatinine and Blood Urea Nitrogen

Creatinine is formed from the breakdown of muscle creatine. The amount produced is proportional to muscle mass and is normally stable from day to day. Creatinine is filtered at the glomerulus, and a small amount is secreted by the tubule. Creatinine clearance, which usually parallels GFR closely, can be determined from a 24-hour urine collection, but in the absence of the information provided by this time-consuming procedure, GFR is commonly estimated from the serum creatinine.

The normal range of the serum creatinine level extends from 0.5 mg/dL in thin persons to 1.5 mg/dL in muscular individuals. Spurious elevations can be caused by acetoacetate (which cross-reacts with creatinine in the commonly used assays) and by certain medications that either cross-react in the assay or reversibly inhibit tubular creatinine secretion despite a normal GFR. Serum creatinine concentration is a function of the amount of creatinine entering the blood from muscle, its volume of distribution, and its rate of excretion. Because the first two are usually constant, changes in serum creatinine concentration generally reflect changes in GFR. Under steady-state conditions, if the GFR is halved, the serum creatinine doubles. Abrupt cessation of glomerular filtration causes the serum creatinine to rise by 1 to 2 mg/dL/day. Thus, a daily increment of less than 1 mg/dL suggests that at least some renal function has been preserved. Rhabdomyolysis releases creatine into the plasma and may cause the serum creatinine to increase by more than 2 mg/dL/day.

The blood urea nitrogen (BUN) also rises with renal dysfunction but is influenced by many extrarenal factors as well. Increased protein intake, gastrointestinal (GI) bleeding, and the catabolic effects of fever, trauma, infection, or drugs such as tetracycline and corticosteroids all increase protein turnover and result in increased hepatic urea production and increased BUN. Conversely, BUN tends to be decreased in patients with liver failure or protein malnutrition.

When glomerular filtrate has been formed, renal urea clearance is largely a function of flow rate. Urea clearance is thus decreased in patients with prerenal azotemia or acute obstruction, despite preservation of tubular function. In these individuals the BUN/ creatinine ratio, normally approximately 10:1, is usually greater than 10:1, whereas this ratio is usually not markedly increased in cases of uncomplicated intrinsic ARF.

Urine Sodium and Fractional Excretion of Sodium

Measurement of the urine sodium (UNa) concentration provides information on the integrity of tubular reabsorptive function. Normally, UNa concentration parallels sodium (Na) intake. Low UNa concentration thus indicates not only intact reabsorptive function but also the presence of a stimulus to conserve Na. The UNa concentration, as well as the fractional excretion of sodium (FENa), an additional measure of tubular sodium handling, helps distinguish between the two most common causes of ARF: prerenal azotemia and ATN (Table 96-1).

Urinary indices are most helpful in oliguric patients. In euvolemic individuals who are in sodium balance and who have a moderate sodium intake and normal renal function, UNa is less than 20 mEq/L and FENa is less than 1%.[4,5] As the stimulus for sodium reabsorption increases, both UNa and FENa decrease.

In general, an oliguric patient with a UNa concentration less than 20 mEq/L and FENa less than 1% should be considered to have prerenal azotemia, whereas UNa greater than 40 mEq/L and FENa greater than 1% suggest ATN. Values in patients with prerenal azotemia overlap somewhat with those of patients with nonoliguric ATN, particularly if the renal injury is mild and some capability to retain sodium has been preserved. Thus, intermediate values of UNa and FENa are of little discriminatory use. The administration of mannitol or a loop diuretic within the several hours preceding urine collection may also make interpretation of urine values difficult because the urinary sodium tends to be higher and the urine less concentrated, causing the results in a patient with prerenal azotemia to resemble those of a patient with intrinsic renal failure (Box 96-1).

In glomerulonephritis, the urinary indices generally reflect intact tubular sodium handling, but the diagnosis is better made by urine microscopy. In obstructive uropathy, the values of the urinary indices depend on

Table 96-1. Typical Urinary Findings in Prerenal Azotemia and Acute Tubular Necrosis

Laboratory Test	Prerenal Azotemia	Acute Tubular Necrosis
Urinalysis	Normal, or hyaline casts	Brown granular casts, cellular debris
Urine sodium concentration (mEq/L)	<20	>40
Fractional excretion of sodium (%)	<1	>1
Urine/plasma creatinine ratio	>40	<20

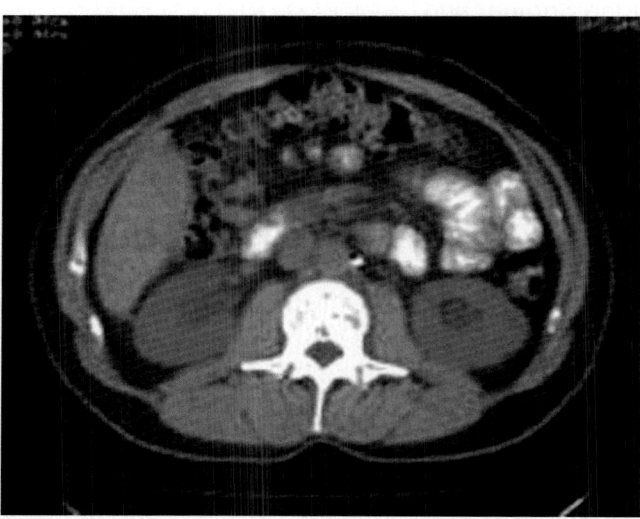

Figure 96-2. Computed tomography scan of bilateral hydronephrotic kidneys without intravenous contrast medium.

the duration of obstruction and cannot be relied on to indicate either the presence or absence of obstruction.

Radiography

Renal imaging is often helpful in evaluating the patient with kidney dysfunction, particularly when obstruction is suspected. Contrast-enhanced computed tomography (CT) scanning provides an anatomic image of the urinary tract but does not give a precise evaluation of renal function. The classical findings of obstruction are kidneys that are normal to large in size, nephrograms that become increasingly dense, and delayed opacification of dilated collecting systems. Contrast-enhanced CT subjects the kidneys of an already azotemic patient to the risk of an additional potential insult from the contrast agent (Figure 96-2). Patients with a baseline

serum creatinine level greater than 2.5 mg/dL are estimated to have approximately a 33% chance that a further significant decrease in renal function will develop, compared with an approximately 2% chance in individuals with a normal baseline creatinine level. The newer, more expensive, nonionic contrast agents may have less potential for nephrotoxicity, but study results have not been consistent.[6] In patients with preexisting renal insufficiency, therefore, techniques such as ultrasonography and CT scanning that do not involve contrast administration are much preferred.

Computed Tomography

Noncontrast CT scanning may be useful in evaluating some azotemic patients. Hydronephrosis can be recognized without the use of contrast material. Dilated ureters can also often be seen without contrast enhancement and the level of obstruction determined. Moreover, the cause of obstruction (e.g., lymphoma, retroperitoneal hemorrhage, metastatic cancer, or retroperitoneal fibrosis) can often be delineated as well. CT scanning is the technique of choice for visualizing ureteral obstruction at the level of the bony pelvis. Occasionally, obstruction severe enough to result in renal failure may not cause detectable proximal dilation of the urinary tract. Bilateral ureteral obstruction produced by malignancy or retroperitoneal fibrosis is the most important cause of this nondilated obstructive uropathy. When noninvasive studies produce negative results, the diagnosis must be made by retrograde pyelography or by antegrade pyelography through a percutaneous nephrostomy.

Ultrasonography

Ultrasonography allows accurate measurement of renal dimensions and is a reliable and safe method of excluding obstruction as a cause of ARF. The normal kidney shows an echo-free renal parenchyma surrounding the echogenic central urothelium of the renal pelvis and calices. The sonographic appearance of obstruction is that of an enlarged central sonolucent area that spreads the normal central echo densities. A similar pattern may be produced by renal cysts, but without associated ureteral dilation. Dilation of the collecting system is generally apparent within 24 to 36 hours of the onset of obstruction, but obstruction may be overlooked in patients who are evaluated early in the development of obstructive ARF.

MANAGEMENT

Approach to Hematuria

Principles of Disease

Microscopic hematuria is often discovered incidentally on routine urinalysis, but as little as 1 mL of blood in 1 L of urine can cause grossly appreciable hematuria, an occurrence that usually induces the patient to seek medical attention.

Normal individuals pass up to 1 million RBCs into the urine during any 24-hour period. Counts greater than this correspond roughly to the presence of more than 5 RBC/HPF in the spun urine sediment. Although the presence of blood in the urine is not invariably a sign of disease, the finding of hematuria calls for an effort to rule out any treatable underlying disorder. Both gross and microscopic hematuria are caused by similar disorders, but the amount of blood in the urine does not correlate with the severity or the seriousness of the condition causing it.[2,3]

The causes of hematuria can be divided into hematologic, renal, and postrenal causes; renal causes may be further classified as glomerular or nonglomerular (Box 96-2).[3] Overall, the most common causes of nontraumatic hematuria, in roughly descending order of occurrence, are kidney stones, carcinoma of the kidney or bladder, urethritis, UTI, benign prostatic hyper-

trophy, and glomerulonephritis. The differential diagnosis can be narrowed by taking into account the patient's age and sex (Table 96-2) and by distinguishing between upper and lower urinary tract sources. When gross hematuria is present, cystoscopy can determine whether blood is emerging from one or both ureteral orifices, thereby defining a source in the upper tract. Red cell casts indicate a renal source, as does associated proteinuria (>500 mg in 24 hours). When differentiating between proteinuria produced by renal parenchymal disease and that simply produced by admixture of urine with extravasated blood, a useful rule of thumb is that 1 mL of whole blood contains approximately 5 billion RBCs and approximately 50 mg of albumin.

The evaluation of the emergency department patient who has gross or microscopic hematuria should begin with a complete history so that the pattern and character of the hematuria can be defined. Blood noted only on initiation of voiding suggests a urethral source, whereas blood noted only in the last few drops of urine suggests a prostatic or bladder neck source. Total hematuria (i.e., hematuria present throughout urination) suggests a source in the bladder, ureter, or kidney. Brown or smoky-colored urine usually has a renal source. Blood clots indicate a nonglomerular renal or lower urinary tract source of bleeding. Hematuria may rarely be cyclic or associated with menses, suggesting endometriosis of the ureter or bladder. Flank pain suggests calculus, neoplasm, renal infarction, obstruction, or infection as cause. Symptoms of frequency, dysuria, or suprapubic pain suggest cystitis or urethritis; in adult men, perineal pain, dysuria, and terminal hematuria suggest prostatitis.

Other clues to the cause should be sought by careful questioning. Because glomerulonephritis or interstitial nephritis may be caused by a variety of bacterial, viral, and parasitic infections, a history of recent infection is important. In particular, a recent sore throat suggests the possibility of poststreptococcal glomerulonephritis; a history of foreign travel or residence abroad may suggest schistosomiasis or tuberculosis. Symptoms suggestive of a multisystem disorder (e.g., systemic lupus erythematosus) should also be sought, as should a history of human immunodeficiency virus infection.[7] Because drugs may cause acute interstitial nephritis (AIN),[8] papillary necrosis, or hemorrhagic cystitis, a complete medication history should be elicited. When

---

BOX 96-2. Causes of Hematuria

Hematologic
  Coagulopathy
  Sickle hemoglobinopathies
Renal (glomerular)
  Primary glomerular disease
  Multisystem disease (e.g., systemic lupus erythematosus, Henoch-Schönlein purpura, hemolytic uremic syndrome, polyarteritis nodosa, Wegener's granulomatosis, Goodpasture's syndrome)
Renal (nonglomerular)
  Renal infarction
  Tuberculosis
  Pyelonephritis
  Polycystic kidney disease
  Medullary sponge kidney
  Acute interstitial nephritis
  Tumor
  Vascular malformation
  Trauma
  Papillary necrosis
Postrenal
  Stones
  Tumor of ureter, bladder, urethra
  Cystitis
  Tuberculosis
  Prostatitis, urethritis
  Foley catheter placement
  Exercise
  Benign prostatic hypertrophy

Table 96-2. Most Common Causes of Hematuria by Age

	<20 yr	20-40 yr	40-60 yr	40-60 yr
Sex	♂ and ♀	♂ and ♀	♂	♀
Causes of hematuria	Glomerulonephritis UTI	UTI Stone Trauma Carcinoma (bladder, kidney)	Carcinoma (bladder) Stone UTI Carcinoma (kidney) BPH if >60	UTI Stone Carcinoma (bladder, kidney)

BPH, benign prostatic hyperplasia; UTI, urinary tract infection.
Adapted from Restrepo NC, Carey PO: Evaluating hematuria in adults. *Am Fam Physician* 40:149, 1989.

hematuria is associated with anticoagulant use, significant underlying disease can be identified in at least 70% of patients.[9] The family history should be elicited because it may provide a clue to the presence of polycystic or other familial kidney disease, sickle cell disease, or renal calculi. A history of strenuous exercise is important; 15% to 20% of normal individuals exhibit hematuria after strenuous exercise. The mechanism is unclear, but the hematuria resolves spontaneously within a few days.

Clinical Features

On physical examination, findings of arthritis, skin lesions, hypertension, or edema suggest underlying glomerulonephritis. Because endocarditis or atrial fibrillation may cause renal embolism, the physician should check for a new heart murmur or an irregular rhythm. Costovertebral angle tenderness suggests pyelonephritis or stone disease, and a palpably enlarged kidney suggests polycystic kidney disease or renal malignancy. The prostatic examination may offer clues to the presence of prostatitis, benign prostatic hypertrophy, or cancer. Examination of the external genitalia may reveal a urethral meatal lesion that may be the source of bleeding; in adult women, a pelvic examination should be performed to exclude vulvovaginal sources of blood.

Laboratory

Evaluation of hematuria in the emergency department should include assessment of the blood pressure and measurement of the BUN and serum creatinine levels to gauge the patient's underlying renal function, but urinalysis can be expected to provide more specific information. Red urine that is dipstick negative and free of red cells on microscopy may be caused by ingestion of beets, red berries, or food coloring; by urate crystals; or by drugs such as phenazopyridine (Pyridium) and rifampin. A finding of red cell casts, other casts, or lipiduria or significant proteinuria in combination with hematuria suggests intrinsic renal disease, and appropriate referral should be made. (The urine should be examined as soon as possible after voiding because structures such as red cell casts may disintegrate over time.) Microscopic hematuria usually does not produce a positive dipstick test result for protein, but gross hematuria may contribute enough protein to cause a positive result; thus, a finding of proteinuria should be confirmed and the amount quantitated in a 24-hour urine collection. Hematuria in combination with pyuria or bacteriuria suggests UTI; infection should be treated and hematuria reassessed after therapy has been completed. Even if white cells or organisms are not seen on urinalysis, the urine should be cultured to rule out hemorrhagic cystitis, especially when lower tract symptoms are present. Eosinophiluria (appreciable on Wright's stain or Hansel's stain of the urine sediment) suggests AIN.

Blood studies should be ordered only as necessary to gauge renal function and to confirm causes suggested by the clinical presentation. In the emergency department, routine ordering of the full gamut of chemical and serologic studies necessary to rule out all possible causes of hematuria is rarely appropriate. In particular, a platelet count and coagulation studies are extremely unlikely to be helpful in the absence of a suggestive history or other specific clinical clues.

Radiography and Ultrasonography

The role of urinary tract imaging studies in the immediate evaluation of hematuria is also limited. Visualization of the urinary tract is generally helpful only when the history suggests renal colic or other disorders of the upper urinary tract (e.g., polycystic kidney disease, tumor, or obstruction). Helical CT scanning without contrast has emerged as the imaging modality of choice.[10-12] Ultrasonography can be used to determine kidney size and shape and to detect renal masses or obstruction. Further imaging studies, if indicated, should be planned after urologic consultation.

If no upper tract lesions are identified on initial imaging studies, cystoscopy is usually the next step in evaluation because it is the most effective means of visualizing the bladder and the male urethra. It is the initial study of choice for patients with active gross hematuria; in fact, some urologists prefer to perform endoscopic procedures promptly during an acute bleeding episode to maximize the chance of localizing the source. In older patients whose urinalysis shows only hematuria and whose history and physical examination are otherwise unhelpful, urinary cytologic examination may also be undertaken.

Patients with hematuria who have no other abnormality revealed by urinalysis; who are otherwise asymptomatic; who are not azotemic, hypertensive, or severely anemic; and who have no evidence of intrinsic renal disease may be monitored as outpatients. (A possible exception may be the patient with a known bleeding disorder.) Others should generally be admitted to the hospital for prompt evaluation. Extensive outpatient evaluation of an isolated episode of hematuria is usually not undertaken in patients younger than 40 years unless hematuria is persistent, but most patients older than 40 should undergo a thorough evaluation after even a single episode of hematuria.

The cause of hematuria can be determined on initial medical and urologic evaluation in 70% to 80% of cases. In others, a diagnosis of small calculi, occult bladder tumor, arteriovenous malformation, or early glomerulonephritis is made only after repeated examination or the development of further signs or symptoms. In 5% to 10% of cases no cause can be determined.

Approach to Proteinuria

Principles of Disease

During a 24-hour period, the kidneys normally filter 180 L of plasma containing approximately 12 kg of protein. The 1 to 2 L of urine produced from this filtrate contains only 40 to 80 mg of protein in normal individuals. Abnormal proteinuria is defined as excretion of more than 150 mg per 24 hours in adults or more than 140 mg/m^2 per 24 hours in children. Patients with mild to moderate degrees of proteinuria are commonly identified incidentally on routine urinalysis; patients with more severe degrees of proteinuria often seek medical attention because of edema or other effects of hypoproteinemia.

Proteinuria may be classified broadly as glomerular or tubular. *Glomerular proteinuria*, the more common type, results from increased permeability of the glomerular capillaries to plasma proteins. With alteration in the glomerular capillary barrier (e.g., with the nephrotic syndrome and the many varieties of primary and secondary glomerulonephritis), albumin and globulins, which under normal circumstances are restricted from the glomerular ultrafiltrate because of their ionic charge and size, are lost into the urine. Protein losses of 10 g or more per day are not uncommon. *Tubular proteinuria* occurs in patients with normal glomeruli when the smaller proteins that are normally filtered at the glomerulus and then reabsorbed in the tubule appear in the urine because of tubular or interstitial abnormality. This occurs in disorders such as urinary tract obstruction, sickle cell disease, and other causes of acute or chronic interstitial nephritis. In these disorders, daily urinary protein losses rarely exceed 2 g. The term *overflow proteinuria* refers to the urinary loss of small proteins that are present in the blood in excessive concentrations and appear in the glomerular filtrate in amounts exceeding the normal tubular reabsorptive capacity (e.g., the light chains produced in multiple myeloma).

Miscellaneous causes of transient proteinuria include exertion, stress, and fever. Low-grade proteinuria can occur during an otherwise normal pregnancy. *Orthostatic proteinuria* is characterized by the occurrence of proteinuria during periods when the patient is upright but not during recumbency; the condition is usually transient and benign. However, persistent proteinuria is a marker for renal disease even in the absence of azotemia or an abnormal urine sediment.

Excretion of more than 2 g of protein in 24 hours is likely to be caused by a glomerular process, whereas excretion of less than 2 g is typical of tubular overflow or orthostatic proteinuria. In the nephrotic syndrome, protein losses exceed the liver's capacity to synthesize albumin and result in hypoalbuminemia. This leads to decreased plasma oncotic pressure and accumulation of edema fluid in the extravascular interstitial space. Increased aldosterone secretion and further retention of salt and water ensue. Thus, edema is the clinical hallmark of the nephrotic syndrome and is often the initial complaint of patients who have significant proteinuria. Edema ranges in severity from mild dependent peripheral edema or periorbital swelling to frank anasarca with pleural effusions and ascites. Nephrotic-range proteinuria is defined arbitrarily as being greater than 3.5 g per 24 hours.

Patients with the nephrotic syndrome are at increased risk for thromboembolic events, including deep venous thrombosis of the lower extremity, renal vein thrombosis, and pulmonary embolism. The reason

BOX 96-3. Causes of the Nephrotic Syndrome

Primary Renal Disease

Multisystem Disease
Diabetes mellitus
Collagen vascular disease
Systemic lupus erythematosus
Rheumatoid arthritis
Henoch-Schönlein purpura
Polyarteritis nodosa
Wegener's granulomatosis
Amyloidosis
Cryoglobulinemia

Drugs and Toxins
Heroin
Captopril
Heavy metals
Nonsteroidal anti-inflammatory drugs
Penicillamine
Others

Allergens

Infection
Bacterial
Infective endocarditis
Poststreptococcal
Syphilis
Viral
Hepatitis B
Human immunodeficiency virus
Cytomegalovirus
Protozoal
Malaria
Toxoplasmosis

Malignancy
Solid tumors
Multiple myeloma
Lymphoma
Leukemia

Miscellaneous
Hereditary nephritis
Preeclampsia
Malignant hypertension
Reflux nephropathy
Transplant rejection

for this propensity appears to be a hypercoagulable state that may be related in part to urinary loss and decreased plasma levels of antithrombin III, proteins, and fibrinolytic factors.[1] Hyperlipidemia is another typical feature of the nephrotic syndrome; the mechanism is thought to be related indirectly to hypoalbuminemia and decreased oncotic pressure or viscosity. However, the major clinical significance of the nephrotic syndrome is that it indicates the presence of an underlying renal process or systemic disease affecting the glomerulus (Box 96-3).

Clinical Features

Evaluation of the patient with proteinuria focuses not only on gauging the severity of proteinuria and the likelihood of complications but also on identifying any associated signs of underlying renal disease or systemic illness. One should seek to elicit a history of recent illnesses (including pharyngitis), use of medications or drugs, or a past history of proteinuria, hypertension, edema, or renal disease. In young female patients, the possibility of pregnancy should be kept in mind because pregnancy can exacerbate previously inapparent renal disease; in late pregnancy, proteinuria may be the first sign of preeclampsia. Clues to the presence of systemic diseases that commonly affect the kidneys (e.g., diabetes or collagen vascular disease) should be sought as well. On physical examination the emergency physician should evaluate the blood pressure, note the presence or absence of edema, and assess for signs of systemic disease or renal insufficiency.

Laboratory

The laboratory evaluation of the patient with protein-uria should include urinalysis and measurement of the BUN and serum creatinine. Special attention should be given to detecting lipiduria in the form of oval fat bodies (desquamated fat-laden renal epithelial cells), fatty casts, or free fat droplets. The identification of lipiduria is made easier by the characteristic appearance of lipid droplets when viewed under the polarizing microscope ("Maltese crosses") (see Figure 96-1E).

Although the finding of isolated proteinuria may or may not be clinically important, proteinuria is almost always significant when it occurs in combination with hematuria. RBCs and red cell casts suggest glomeru-lonephritis; proteinuria with pyuria may be seen with AIN. The combination of proteinuria and glycosuria suggests diabetic nephropathy. A 24-hour urine collection should be ordered to provide an accurate measure of GFR and to quantitate protein excretion.

Abnormal findings on the history, physical examination, or laboratory evaluation greatly increase the probability of the presence of significant renal disease, and early referral to an internist or nephrologist is indicated. However, in the absence of edema, azotemia, hypertension, active urine sediment, or known systemic illness affecting the kidney, patients with proteinuria may be referred to their primary care provider for follow-up observation. Because transient, mild proteinuria is not uncommon in healthy individuals, patients with mild proteinuria indicated by dipstick (particularly if the urine is concentrated) should have dipstick testing repeated at follow-up observation before further evaluation is undertaken. Persistent proteinuria may require referral to a nephrologist; in some cases renal biopsy is necessary to establish a diagnosis and guide management.

ACUTE RENAL FAILURE

Perspective

ARF is a generic term used to describe a precipitous decline in kidney function. Its hallmark is progressive azotemia caused by the accumulation of nitrogenous end products of metabolism, but this is commonly accompanied by a wide range of other disturbances depending on the severity and duration of renal dysfunction. These include metabolic derangements (e.g., metabolic acidosis and hyperkalemia), disturbances of body fluid balance (particularly volume overload), and a variety of effects on almost every organ system (Box 96-4).

The causes of ARF may be divided into those that decrease renal blood flow (prerenal), produce a renal parenchymal insult (intrarenal), or obstruct urine flow (obstructive or postrenal ARF). Identification of either a prerenal or a postrenal cause of ARF generally makes the prompt initiation of specific corrective therapy possible; if these two broad categories of ARF can be excluded, an intrarenal cause is implicated. The renal

---

BOX 96-4. Clinical Features of Acute Renal Failure

Cardiovascular
Pulmonary edema
Arrhythmia
Hypertension
Pericarditis
Pericardial effusion
Myocardial infarction
Pulmonary embolism

Metabolic
Hyponatremia
Hyperkalemia
Acidosis
Hypocalcemia
Hyperphosphatemia
Hypermagnesemia
Hyperuricemia

Neurologic
Asterixis
Neuromuscular irritability
Mental status changes

Somnolence
Coma
Seizures

Gastrointestinal
Nausea
Vomiting
Gastritis
Gastroduodenal ulcers
Gastrointestinal bleeding
Pancreatitis
Malnutrition

Hematologic
Anemia
Hemorrhagic diathesis

Infectious
Pneumonia
Septicemia
Urinary tract infection
Wound infection

From Brady HR, Brenner BM, Clarkson MR, Lieberthal W: Acute renal failure. In Brenner BM: *The Kidney*, 6th ed. Philadelphia, WB Saunders, 2000, pp 1201-1246.

---

parenchymal causes of ARF can be usefully subdivided into those primarily affecting the glomeruli, the intrarenal vasculature, or the renal interstitium.[5] The term *acute tubular necrosis* denotes another broad category of intrinsic renal failure that cannot be attributed to specific glomerular, vascular, or interstitial causes (Figure 96-3).[5]

Principles of Disease

Prerenal Azotemia

Decreased renal perfusion that is sufficient to cause a decrease in the GFR results in azotemia. The possible causes can be grouped into entities causing intravascular volume depletion, volume redistribution, or decreased cardiac output (Box 96-5). Individuals who have preexisting renal disease are particularly sensitive to the effects of diminished renal perfusion.

Prerenal azotemia is characterized by increased urine specific gravity, BUN/creatinine ratio greater than 10:1, UNa concentration less than 20 mEq/dL, and FENa less than 1%. The condition can generally be corrected readily by expanding extracellular fluid volume, augmenting cardiac output, or discontinuing vasodilating antihypertensive drugs. However, severe prolonged prerenal azotemia can eventuate in ATN.

Patients who have congestive heart failure (CHF) or cirrhosis form an important subset of those with prerenal azotemia. These individuals are often salt overloaded and water overloaded, yet their effective intra-arterial volume is decreased. Administration of diuretics has the potential to decrease intravascular volume further, resulting in decreased glomerular filtration and prerenal azotemia. For some patients with

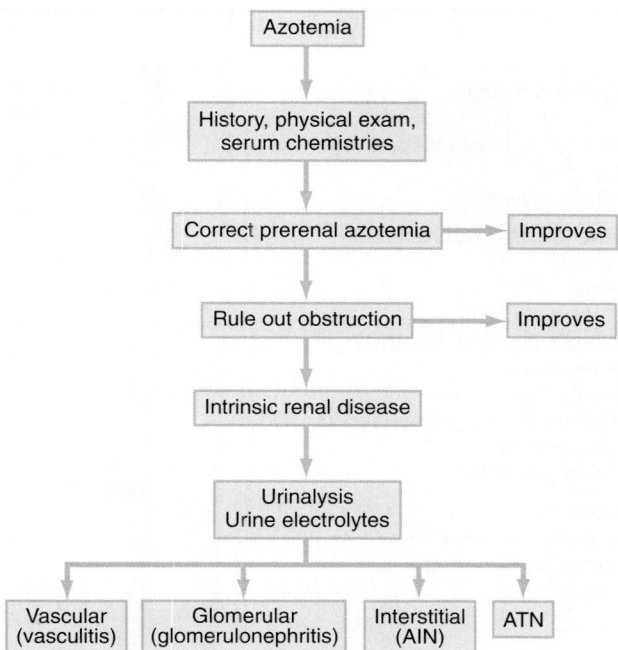

Figure 96-3. Evaluation of azotemia.

BOX 96-6. Causes of Postrenal Acute Renal Failure

Intrarenal and Ureteral
Kidney stone
Sloughed papilla
Malignancy
Retroperitoneal fibrosis
Uric acid or oxalic acid crystal precipitation
Sulfonamide, methotrexate, acyclovir, or indinavir precipitation

Bladder
Kidney stone
Blood clot
Prostatic hypertrophy
Bladder carcinoma
Neurogenic bladder

Urethra
Phimosis
Stricture

BOX 96-5. Causes of Prerenal Azotemia

Volume Loss	Cardiac
Gastrointestinal: vomiting, diarrhea, nasogastric drainage	Myocardial infarction
	Valvular disease
Renal: diuresis	Cardiomyopathy
Blood loss	Decreased effective arterial volume
Insensible losses	Antihypertensive medication
Third space sequestration	Nitrates
Pancreatitis	
Peritonitis	**Neurogenic**
Trauma	Sepsis
Burns	Anaphylaxis
	Hypoalbuminemia
	Nephrotic syndrome
	Liver disease

advanced CHF or hepatic disease, a state of chronic stable prerenal azotemia may be the best achievable compromise between symptomatic volume overload and severe renal hypoperfusion.[13]

Glomerular perfusion may also be decreased in patients with normal intravascular volume and normal renal blood flow who take angiotensin-converting enzyme (ACE) inhibitors or, more commonly, prostaglandin inhibitors. All nonsteroidal anti-inflammatory drugs (NSAIDs), including aspirin, inhibit prostaglandin synthesis. Renal vasodilator prostaglandins are critical in maintaining glomerular perfusion in patients with conditions such as CHF, chronic renal insufficiency, and cirrhosis, in which elevated circulating levels of renin and angiotensin II act to diminish renal blood flow and GFR. In this setting, decreased production of vasodilator prostaglandins may result in acute

intrarenal hemodynamic changes and a reversible decrease in renal function. This phenomenon is also seen with the newer, selective cyclooxygenase 2 inhibitor class of NSAIDs.[14,15] Other risk factors include advanced age, diuretic use, renovascular disease, and diabetes. This entity is distinct from other renal complications of NSAIDs, including interstitial nephritis and papillary necrosis.

Renal insufficiency secondary to NSAIDs is generally reversible after cessation of the causative agent. For patients who are at increased risk but require treatment with NSAIDs, a short-acting preparation (e.g., ibuprofen) should be prescribed and follow-up monitoring of renal function and serum potassium level should be undertaken in days rather than weeks. If renal function is unchanged after a short course of treatment, adverse effects from continuing therapy are unlikely, although other potential mechanisms for the production of renal dysfunction (e.g., interstitial nephritis) should be kept in mind.

Postrenal (Obstructive) Acute Renal Failure

Obstruction is an eminently reversible cause of ARF and should be considered in every patient with newly discovered azotemia or worsening renal function. Obstruction may occur at any level of the urinary tract but is most commonly produced by prostatic hypertrophy or by functional bladder neck obstruction (e.g., secondary to medication side effects or neurogenic bladder) (Box 96-6). Intrarenal obstruction may result from intratubular precipitation of uric acid crystals (e.g., with tumor lysis), oxalic acid (as in ethylene glycol ingestion), myeloma proteins, methotrexate, sulfadiazine, acyclovir, or indinavir.[16] Bilateral ureteral obstruction (or obstruction of the ureter of a solitary kidney) may be caused by retroperitoneal fibrosis, tumor, surgical misadventure, stones, or blood clots. A sudden deterioration of renal function in the setting of

BOX 96-7. Intrinsic Renal Diseases That Cause ARF

Vascular
Large vessel
  Renal artery thrombosis or stenosis
  Renal vein thrombosis
  Atheroembolic disease
Small and medium vessel
  Scleroderma
  Malignant hypertension
  Hemolytic uremic syndrome
  Thrombotic thrombocytopenic purpura
  HIV-associated microangiopathy

Glomerular
Systemic diseases
  Systemic lupus erythematosus
  Infective endocarditis
  Systemic vasculitis (e.g., periarteritis nodosum, Wegener's granulomatosis)
  Henoch-Schönlein purpura
  HIV-associated nephropathy
  Essential mixed cryoglobulinemia
  Goodpasture's syndrome
Primary renal disease
  Poststreptococcal glomerulonephritis
  Other postinfectious glomerulonephritis
  Rapidly progressive glomerulonephritis

Tubulointerstitial
Drugs (many)
Toxins (e.g., heavy metals, ethylene glycol)
Infections
Multiple myeloma

Acute Tubular Necrosis
Ischemia
  Shock
  Sepsis
  Severe prerenal azotemia
Nephrotoxins
  Antibiotics
  Radiographic contrast agents
  Myoglobinuria
  Hemoglobinuria

Other
Severe liver disease[22]
Allergic reactions
NSAIDs[23]

ARF, acute renal failure; HIV, human immunodeficiency virus; NSAID, nonsteroidal anti-inflammatory drug.

---

diabetes mellitus, analgesic nephropathy, or sickle cell disease should suggest papillary necrosis.

Treatment of postrenal ARF consists of relief of the obstruction. In the absence of infection, full renal recovery is said to be possible even after 1 to 2 weeks of total obstruction, although the serum creatinine level may not return to baseline for several weeks. Because the onset of irreversible loss of renal function with obstruction appears to be gradual, a few days' delay in diagnosis is generally considered acceptable. Still, common sense dictates that obstructions should be detected and relieved as expeditiously as possible.

Intrinsic Acute Renal Failure

Of the specific intrarenal disorders that cause ARF, glomerulonephritis, interstitial nephritis, and abnormalities of the intrarenal vasculature are amenable to specific therapy and thus should be carefully considered as possible causes. However, these entities are responsible for only 5% to 10% of cases of ARF in adult inpatients; most are due to ATN. The incidence of glomerular, interstitial, and small vessel disease is much greater in adults who develop ARF outside the hospital. In children, these entities account for approximately half the cases of ARF (Box 96-7).[5]

Glomerular Disease

Acute glomerulonephritis may represent a primary renal process or may be the manifestation of any of a wide range of other disease entities (see Box 96-7). Patients may have dark urine, hypertension, edema, or

CHF (secondary to volume overload) or may be completely asymptomatic, in which case the diagnosis results from an incidental finding on urinalysis. The hematuria associated with glomerular disease may be microscopic or gross and may be persistent or intermittent. Proteinuria, although often in the range of 500 mg/day to 3 g/day, is not uncommonly in the nephrotic range. Hematuria, proteinuria, or red cell casts are very suggestive of glomerulonephritis. In fact, red cell casts are essentially diagnostic of active glomerular disease, although occasionally they are seen with other types of renal disease. Conversely, the absence of red cell casts, proteinuria, and hematuria essentially excludes glomerulonephritis as the cause of ARF.

The specific diagnosis of acute glomerulonephritis caused by primary renal disease is often ultimately made by renal biopsy. However, when glomerulonephritis is secondary to a systemic disease such as systemic lupus erythematosus, the patient's clinical signs and symptoms, in combination with the results of laboratory assessment, aid considerably in narrowing the differential diagnosis. As a rule, extensive laboratory testing to identify the cause of acute glomerulonephritis is not indicated in the emergency department and is more appropriately performed as part of an inpatient evaluation.

Interstitial Disease

AIN is most commonly precipitated by drug exposure or by infection. Drug-induced AIN is poorly understood, but the absence of a clear relationship to the dose and the recurrence of the syndrome on rechallenge with the offending agent suggest that an immunologic mechanism is responsible. The most commonly incriminated drugs are the penicillins, diuretics, anticoagulants, and NSAIDs. AIN has been reported in association with bacterial, fungal, protozoan, and rickettsial infections.

Patients with AIN classically have rash, fever, eosinophilia, and eosinophiluria, but it is common for one or more of these cardinal signs to be absent. Pyuria, gross or microscopic hematuria, and mild proteinuria are observed in some cases. A definite diagnosis sometimes can be made only on renal biopsy. Treatment of AIN is directed at removing the presumed cause; infections should be treated and offending drugs discontinued. Renal function generally returns to baseline over several weeks, although chronic renal failure has been reported to occur.

Intrarenal Vascular Disease

Vascular disease of the kidney can be classified according to the size of the vessel that is affected. Disorders such as renal arterial thrombosis or embolism, which affect large blood vessels, must be bilateral (or must affect a single functioning kidney) to produce ARF. Whether to attribute such cases of ARF to prerenal or intrarenal vascular causes is a matter of semantics. The most common cause of thrombosis is probably trauma; thrombosis may also occur after angiography or may be secondary to aortic or renal arterial dissection. Renal atheroembolism is thought to occur commonly—at least on a microscopic level—after arteriography but is an uncommon cause of ARF. Similarly, patients with chronic atrial fibrillation or infective endocarditis may throw emboli to the kidney but rarely suffer ARF as a result. Renal arterial embolism can cause acute renal infarction, generally manifested by sudden flank, back, chest, or upper abdominal pain. Urinary findings, including hematuria, are variable. Fever, nausea, and vomiting are not uncommon; in some cases, evidence of embolization to other vessels provides a useful clue. The diagnosis is usually made by renal flow scanning or arteriography. Surgical embolectomy has been reported to restore function when undertaken within several hours of occlusion, but significant return of function has been documented in patients operated on as long as 6 weeks after total occlusion. This is presumably because they develop collateral circulation in association with a preexisting partial occlusion.

An interesting but relatively uncommon type of ARF occurs when an ACE inhibitor is given to a patient with underlying bilateral renal artery stenosis (or unilateral stenosis in a solitary functioning kidney). With inhibition of angiotensin synthesis, efferent arteriolar tone is not maintained and GFR decreases. The condition is reversible with cessation of therapy.

Several diseases that affect the smaller intrarenal vessels can cause ARF (see Box 96-7). Patients whose disease is severe enough to cause ARF are also generally found to have hypertension, microangiopathic hemolytic anemia, and other systemic and organ-specific manifestations.

Infection with *Escherichia coli* O157:H7 has emerged as a major cause of hemolytic-uremic syndrome, an important cause of ARF in children.[17]

Malignant hypertension, although much less common since the advent of more effective antihypertensive therapy, has by no means disappeared. Patients with scleroderma (systemic sclerosis) may have "scleroderma renal crisis,"[18] characterized by malignant hypertension and rapidly progressive renal failure. Whereas vasculitis associated with glomerular capillary inflammation typically causes gross or microscopic hematuria and formation of red cell casts, vascular involvement of the medium-size vessels, such as that produced by scleroderma, often spares the preglomerular vessels and tends not to produce an active urine sediment. Extrarenal manifestations (rash, fever, arthritis, pulmonary symptoms) are usually evident.

For both malignant hypertension and scleroderma renal crisis, appropriate treatment can produce a gratifying remission of ARF. Patients with malignant hypertension have been reported to recover renal function after aggressive antihypertensive therapy, with temporary maintenance with dialysis if necessary.[19] For individuals who have scleroderma renal crisis, specific therapy with ACE inhibitors has been shown to result in improvement in renal function in a significant proportion of patients.[20]

Acute Tubular Necrosis

The term *ATN* refers to a generally reversible deterioration of kidney function associated with a variety of renal insults. Oliguria may or may not be a feature. The diagnosis is made after prerenal and postrenal causes of ARF and disorders of glomeruli, interstitium, and intrarenal vasculature have been excluded. These discrete categories do overlap in a few disorders. For example, ARF associated with multiple myeloma or ethylene glycol toxicity is associated with both intrarenal obstruction and interstitial disease as well as a probable direct toxic effect on the renal tubule itself.

The most common precipitants of ATN are renal ischemia during surgery or after trauma and sepsis. The remainder of cases occur in the setting of medical illness, most commonly as a result of the administration of nephrotoxic aminoglycoside antibiotics or radiocontrast agents or in association with rhabdomyolysis. Multiple causes can be identified in some cases; in others a definitive cause is never established.

Several competing theories have been put forward to explain the pathophysiology of ATN.[21] One proposes that casts and cellular debris physically obstruct the tubular lumen, which leads to an increase in intratubular pressure and a consequent decrease in net glomerular filtration pressure. Another theory holds that damage to the renal tubular epithelium allows backleak of glomerular filtrate into the peritubular capillaries. Other investigators suggest a primarily vascular mechanism for renal failure in which afferent arteriolar vasoconstriction or efferent arteriolar vasodilation is sufficient to decrease glomerular filtration. Yet another view emphasizes the importance of changes in glomerular capillary permeability.

Decreased renal perfusion results in a continuum of renal dysfunction that ranges from transient prerenal azotemia at one extreme to ATN at the other. Early during the period of renal ischemia, renal function can be restored completely by restoring renal blood flow, but at some point, continued hypoperfusion results in renal dysfunction unresponsive to volume repletion, and ATN supervenes. ATN may occur in the absence of frank hypotension; even modest renal ischemia may result in ATN in susceptible individuals. Individual susceptibility to ATN may be related to the balance of prostaglandin-mediated vasopressor and vasodilatory influences on the renal vasculature.

Postischemic ATN can occur in the setting of volume loss from the GI tract (upper or lower), skin, or kidneys or can result from severe hemorrhage or major burns. Heatstroke is commonly associated with the development of ATN, which is thought to result from a combination of volume loss, hyperpyrexia, and rhabdomyolysis. Another cause of ATN is hyperglycemic hyperosmolar nonketotic coma, which can be associated with loss of as much as 25% of total body water. ATN is also seen in the setting of cardiogenic shock, sepsis, and the "third spacing" of fluids in pancreatitis and peritonitis.

ATN is common in postoperative patients, although not all cases can be attributed to intraoperative hypotension or hemorrhage. Concomitant sepsis, increased age, preexisting renal disease, and other comorbidities are associated with a worse outcome.[22,23]

Nephrotoxins are the other major cause of ATN. Among the most prominent of these are the endogenous pigments myoglobin and hemoglobin. Rhabdomyolysis and ARF resulting from crush injuries first received widespread attention after their description in survivors of the London blitz during World War II, but many other causes of pigment nephropathy have been reported (Box 96-8). Hypotension secondary to fluid loss into damaged muscle is thought to worsen the effects of myoglobinuria on the renal tubule, as is acidosis. Hemolysis, resulting in the release of hemoglobin into the circulation and hemoglobinuria, can cause ATN but usually only in the presence of coexisting dehydration, acidosis, or other causes of decreased renal perfusion. ATN may be produced by the hemolysis of as little as 100 mL of blood.

ATN associated with rhabdomyolysis is often oliguric; it is characterized by rapid increases in the serum creatinine, potassium, phosphorus, and uric acid levels.[24,25] Creatine released from muscle is metabolized to creatinine, which may result in serum creatinine increases of more than 2 mg/dL/day, in contrast to the increase of 0.5 to 1.0 mg/dL/day typically seen in other forms of ARF. The BUN/creatinine ratio is often less than 10:1. Intracellular potassium released from damaged muscle may raise the serum potassium by 1 to 2 mEq/L in several hours. Likewise, phosphate released from muscle may cause dramatic increases in the serum phosphate level. Uric acid, produced by metabolism of purines released from damaged muscle, may accumulate to levels high enough to suggest acute uric acid nephropathy.

The urine dipstick yields a positive result for heme in only 50% of patients with rhabdomyolysis because myoglobin is rapidly cleared from the serum and therefore may be undetectable in the urine at the time of presentation. Thus, a negative urine dipstick result does not rule out the diagnosis. Serum creatine phosphokinase (CPK) is cleared much more slowly and is therefore a much more sensitive test.

No biochemical parameter can be used to predict which patients who have rhabdomyolysis will develop ARF. In one classical study of patients in whom alcoholism, muscle compression, and seizures were the most common causes of rhabdomyolysis, ARF developed in only one third. Neither the height of the serum CPK elevation, the presence or absence of myoglobinuria, nor the degree of hyperkalemia correlated well with the development of ARF.[24]

Antibiotics and radiographic contrast agents are other nephrotoxins that are commonly implicated in the development of ATN. Aminoglycosides are the most commonly implicated antibiotics. Higher doses and longer duration of therapy are associated with higher serum drug levels, leading to greater accumulation of drug in the renal parenchyma and a greater likelihood of nephrotoxicity. Increased age, impaired renal function, dehydration, and exposure to other nephrotoxins are additional risk factors. Once-daily administration of a somewhat higher dose is associated with less nephrotoxicity but equal effectiveness.[26,27]

Aminoglycoside-induced ATN typically has a gradual onset. Clinically significant renal dysfunction usually occurs only after several days and often after more than a week of therapy. However, renal failure can develop as long as 10 days after a drug has been discontinued, an observation that appears to be explained by the prolonged tissue half-life characteristic of these agents. Renal function returns to normal after an average of 6 weeks, but the condition occasionally progresses to permanent renal injury.

Radiographic contrast agents are a common cause of hospital-acquired renal insufficiency. Renal failure produced by these agents may be defined as an increase in serum creatinine level of 25% over baseline with a temporal relation to contrast medium administration and

---

BOX 96-8. Causes of Pigment-Induced Acute Renal Failure

Rhabdomyolysis and myoglobinuria	Myopathy
Vigorous exercise	Alcoholism
Arterial embolization	Hypokalemia
Status epilepticus	Hypophosphatemia
Status asthmaticus	Hemoglobinuria
Coma-induced and pressure-induced myonecrosis	Transfusion reactions
	Snake envenomation
	Malaria
Heat stress	Mechanical destruction of RBCs by prosthetic valves
Diabetic ketoacidosis	G6PD deficiency

RBC, red blood cells.

in the absence of other identifiable causes. Contrast-induced ATN encompasses a spectrum ranging from asymptomatic nonoliguric renal insufficiency to severe renal failure requiring dialysis, but most cases are mild. It can occur after any procedure involving intravascular contrast. Typically, an increase in the serum creatinine level is noted within 3 days of exposure, with a return to normal within 10 to 14 days.

The most important risk factors for contrast-induced ATN are preexisting renal insufficiency, diabetes mellitus, multiple myeloma, age older than 60 years, volume depletion, and higher doses of contrast material. Of these, preexisting renal insufficiency is the most important.[28] Diabetic patients with a serum creatinine level less than 1.5 mg/dL are at low risk for the development of contrast-induced ATN, whereas those whose serum creatinine is greater than 1.5 mg/dL are at significant risk.[29] Multiple myeloma, particularly when dehydration is present, is another reasonably well-documented risk factor. Advanced age also appears to make ATN more likely, possibly because of decreased renal mass and cortical blood flow. Volume depletion appears to be an independent risk factor, and aggressive volume expansion before contrast exposure has been shown to have a protective effect.[30,31] Finally, large doses and repeated doses of contrast material are associated with increased risk of ATN, particularly if two studies are performed within 72 hours of one another. Use of low-osmolality contrast media appears to be associated with a lower risk of nephrotoxicity than use of standard high-osmolality agents.[6,32,33,34]

Oral N-acetylcysteine has been shown to have some protective effect when given prophylactically for 2 days before coronary angiography.[35,36] A rapid intravenous (IV) regimen, administered with IV saline, also appeared to prevent nephrotoxicity, but the overall clinical effect was modest.[37] The mechanism of this protective effect remains unclear,[38] and the regimen has not yet been tested in patients with moderate to severe degrees of renal dysfunction.

Clinical Features

When the presence of azotemia or renal failure has been discovered, the emergency physician should first consider potentially life-threatening complications (e.g., hyperkalemia and pulmonary edema). Assuming these have been satisfactorily ruled out, the next step is to determine whether the condition represents ARF or is the result of preexisting renal disease. The clinical distinction between ARF and chronic renal failure is often difficult; old records and laboratory results are invaluable. The finding of small kidneys on abdominal radiography or bone changes of secondary hyperparathyroidism on hand films suggests that renal failure is chronic. Anemia, hypocalcemia, and hyperphosphatemia, on the other hand, should not be relied on to identify patients who have chronic renal failure because these abnormalities can develop rapidly in ARF.

In evaluating the patient with azotemia, the history, physical examination, and laboratory studies should seek clues to the cause and identify signs and symptoms of uremia, volume overload, or other complications of renal failure. In attempting to identify the cause of azotemia, the general strategy is to rule out both prerenal and postrenal causes before considering the many intrinsic renal causes. First, potential sources of volume loss and causes of decreased cardiac output should be sought in the history, and the patient should be questioned about lightheadedness, bleeding, GI fluid loss, abnormal polyuria, or symptoms of CHF. In men, a history of nocturia, frequency, hesitancy, or decrement of urinary stream suggests prostatic obstruction. A history of lower tract symptoms or of abdominal or pelvic tumor in either sex should likewise be elicited, as should a history of kidney stones or chronic UTI. A documented history of acute anuria (defined as the production of urine at less than 100 mL/day) is most often the result of high-grade urinary tract obstruction, although it may also accompany severe volume depletion, severe acute glomerulonephritis, cortical necrosis, or bilateral renal vascular occlusion. Intermittent anuria, on the other hand, is characteristic of obstructive disease.

The patient should be questioned about medication use and possible exposure to radiographic contrast agents or other exogenous toxins. A history of pharyngitis, hypertension, dark-colored urine, rash, fever, or arthritis suggests intrinsic renal disease or a multisystem disorder. In older patients, symptoms that suggest multiple myeloma should be elicited.

The physical examination should focus on signs of volume depletion such as orthostatic hypotension, tachycardia, and decreased skin turgor; documented short-term changes in body weight offer a valuable clue in assessing volume status, particularly in chronically ill patients. In addition, suspected bleeding should be specifically excluded. Similarly, volume overload should be sought by assessment of jugular venous distention and attention to the presence of rales, an S_3 gallop, or edema.

An attempt to percuss the bladder should be made. A distended bladder is percussible when it contains 150 mL of urine, and the dome is palpable abdominally when it contains 500 mL. Ultrasonography can be used to detect bladder distention if there is a question of urinary retention.[39]

Prostate examination in adult men or pelvic examination in adult women should not be neglected. Rash, purpura, pallor, or petechiae should be noted, as should arthritis, musculoskeletal tenderness, or findings suggestive of infection or malignancy.

Diagnostic Strategy

Laboratory

The laboratory evaluation should begin with a careful dipstick and microscopic urinalysis and measurement of urine output. BUN, serum creatinine, UNa, and FENa levels should be determined to help evaluate renal function and to provide clues to the cause of ARF. A complete blood count, serum electrolyte calcium, phosphorus, and magnesium levels, electrocardiogram

(ECG), and chest radiograph should be ordered to establish the patient's baseline status and to provide information about possible complications. Other studies may be of value in the emergency department when the history or physical findings suggest a specific role in immediate diagnosis or management.

Prerenal azotemia should be suspected in the setting of volume loss, volume redistribution, or decreased effective renal perfusion. It is typically associated with a normal urinalysis, high BUN/creatinine ratio, increased urine osmolality, UNa concentration less than 20 mEq/L, and FENa less than 1%. A rapid response to volume repletion is also characteristic.

Urethral or bladder neck obstruction is documented by the finding of significant amounts of residual urine in the bladder on catheterization after the patient has voided or attempted to void spontaneously. It should be emphasized that the ability to void does not rule out obstruction. In fact, the urine volume in the presence of obstruction may vary from zero to several liters per day. Flank pain is likewise an insensitive marker for obstruction. Urine indices and the BUN/creatinine ratio tend not to be helpful, although an increase in the latter is common in obstruction. The presence of a renal parenchymal disorder can often be diagnosed by its manifestations on microscopic urinalysis or by associated extrarenal manifestations (e.g., with multisystem disease) or the clinical setting (e.g., recent exposure to a new medication). In the absence of these clues, the failure to find evidence for prerenal or postrenal causes in a patient with ARF may also be taken as presumptive evidence of an intrarenal parenchymal process. Among these, the emergency physician should keep in mind the possibility of an acute or ongoing vascular insult because timely intervention may be important in preserving ultimate renal function.

Radiography and Ultrasonography

Significant hydronephrosis is usually readily demonstrable by ultrasonography and may indicate either upper or lower tract obstruction. In questionable cases, or if bilateral ureteral obstruction is strongly suspected clinically, the next step is retrograde urography performed by a urologist.[40] CT imaging is less useful in this setting; in fact, IV contrast material may compound the injury to the kidney.

Management

Emergency department management of ARF is directed to reversing decreases in GFR and urine output (if possible) while minimizing further hemodynamic and toxic insults, maintaining normal fluid and electrolyte balance, and managing other complications of ARF as required. Because renal failure alters the metabolism and action of many drugs, often in ways that are not predictable, the physician must exercise care when prescribing all medications. A compendium of guidelines for drug dosing in renal failure, such as the one by Aronoff and colleagues,[41] is of great help for this purpose.

After ensuring that the vital signs are adequate and that the patient is in no immediate danger from volume or metabolic derangements, the next step is to correct prerenal and postrenal factors, if any are identified. Intravascular volume should be repleted in hypovolemic patients and maintained in euvolemic patients by matching input to measured and insensible output. Inadequate cardiac output should be augmented when possible. Postrenal or obstructive ARF is treated by restoration of normal urine outflow. Bladder outlet obstruction may be relieved by passage of a Foley catheter, whereas upper tract obstruction may require percutaneous nephrostomy.

When prerenal and postrenal factors have been ruled out, the challenge to the emergency physician is to identify the cause of intrinsic renal ARF, keeping in mind the multitude of known possible causes (see Box 96-7). The clinical setting and physical and laboratory findings often allow the differential diagnosis to be considerably narrowed. The clinical picture is often most consistent with the broad category of ATN.

It has been noted repeatedly that patients who have oliguric ARF have a significantly higher mortality rate and a much greater risk of complications than those who are not oliguric. The difference in prognosis may simply reflect a more severe renal insult in patients who are oliguric, however, and it is not clear that interventions aimed at converting oliguric to nonoliguric ARF have an effect on renal function or mortality.[42] Nevertheless, because nonoliguric patients are easier to manage, an attempt to increase urine flow is warranted.

Loop diuretics or mannitol is often effective in increasing urine flow when intravascular volume deficits are corrected. Although furosemide has been shown to decrease dialysis requirements and complications caused by volume overload, it has not been shown to shorten the clinical course or affect mortality.[43-45] Mannitol appears to be most useful when given at the time of or shortly after the renal insult; the recommended dose is 12.5 to 25 g intravenously. If urine output does not increase, further doses may cause hyperosmolality and clinically significant intravascular volume overload in patients with impaired renal function.[46]

Dopamine (1 to 3 μg/kg/min) and atrial natriuretic peptide have also been used, with and without furosemide, in an effort to increase urine output, but their efficacy has not been validated in prospective studies.[47-49]

Certain specific considerations apply to toxin-induced ATN. Pigment-induced ATN may be prevented by avoidance of hemolysis and muscle injury and by correction of the factors (e.g., dehydration, acidosis) that are known to predispose patients with pigmenturia to the development of renal failure. When hemolysis or rhabdomyolysis has occurred, treatment is directed at eliminating the cause and preventing the development of renal failure.

Mannitol has been shown to prevent ARF in experimental models of myoglobinuria, presumably by inducing osmotic diuresis and decreasing intratubular deposition of pigment. Furosemide, on the other hand, has not consistently shown a beneficial effect. Other studies have suggested that myoglobin precipitates in an acid urine but not in an alkaline urine. Thus, aggressive volume repletion, alkalinization, and mannitol infusion have been recommended after crush injuries to reduce the likelihood or severity of ARF.[50] This regimen also helps control hyperkalemia. When ARF has occurred, management is similar to that of other forms of ARF, but early dialysis may be required to control rapidly developing hyperkalemia, hyperphosphatemia, and hyperuricemia.

Patients who have contrast-induced ATN require only supportive therapy but should be hospitalized and seen by a nephrologist. A more significant role for the emergency physician is in preventing the occurrence of contrast-induced ATN, particularly by recognizing risk factors in patients for whom contrast studies are being considered. BUN and serum creatinine levels should be checked before contrast exposure in patients with risk factors. Moreover, before contrast medium is administered to a high-risk patient, it should be established that there is a compelling reason to perform the contrast study and that there is no adequate alternative to using a contrast agent. The patient should be volume repleted before the study, the administered dose of contrast agent should be kept as low as possible, and multiple studies should be avoided, as should concomitant use of other nephrotoxins. IV saline, given before and after contrast agent administration, may be protective.[30,31]

Volume and Metabolic Complications

In addition to these general measures aimed at minimizing decreases in GFR and increasing urine output, an important component of the management of ARF is the prevention or control of systemic complications. Particularly important are metabolic derangements (e.g., hyperkalemia, hypocalcemia, hyperphosphatemia, and metabolic acidosis) and complications of volume overload (e.g., hypertension and CHF).

Hyperkalemia, the most common metabolic cause of death in patients with ARF, results from an inability to excrete endogenous and exogenous potassium loads. In oliguric patients the serum potassium level typically increases by 0.3 to 0.5 mEq/L/day, but greater increases occur in catabolic, septic, or traumatized patients and in the presence of acidosis or exogenous potassium loads from diet or medication.

Hyperkalemia results in serious disturbances in cardiac electrophysiology that may culminate in cardiac arrest. Although some hyperkalemic patients note muscular weakness, most are generally asymptomatic until major manifestations of cardiotoxicity supervene. Thus, hyperkalemia is particularly dangerous and should be considered and sought out. ECG changes correlate only roughly with the serum potassium level. Mild hyperkalemia (K$^+$ <6.0 mEq/L) may be cautiously observed without specific treatment while all exogenous sources of potassium are eliminated. If the serum potassium level is greater than 6.5 mEq/L and particularly if ECG changes are present, urgent intervention is necessary. When cardiotoxicity must be reversed immediately (e.g., when there is hemodynamic compromise), IV calcium (10 mL of 10% calcium gluconate or calcium chloride over 2 minutes) is the treatment of choice. IV insulin (given with glucose to prevent hypoglycemia) and IV bicarbonate temporarily shift potassium to the intracellular space. Bicarbonate should be used with caution in patients with renal failure because of its potential to cause volume overload and to provoke hypocalcemic tetany or seizures. The safety and efficacy of inhaled albuterol in hyperkalemic patients with *chronic* renal failure have been well documented; like insulin and bicarbonate, this agent causes potassium to move into cells, thereby controlling hyperkalemia for 2 hours or more.[51,52] Elimination of potassium from the body is promoted by using a potassium-binding ion exchange resin (sodium polystyrene sulfonate [Kayexalate]), by enhancing urinary potassium excretion, or by dialysis.

Hypocalcemia is a common feature of ARF and can develop rapidly after its onset. Vitamin D–dependent intestinal absorption of calcium is decreased in ARF because of decreased renal synthesis of 1,25-dihydroxyvitamin D. Another factor promoting hypocalcemia is the complexing of calcium with retained phosphate. Rhabdomyolysis-associated ARF in particular is often associated with the deposition of complexed calcium in muscle and other tissues. Asymptomatic hypocalcemia requires no immediate treatment, but incipient or frank tetany should be treated with IV calcium (10 to 20 mL of 10% calcium gluconate over several minutes).

Hyperphosphatemia resulting from decreased renal elimination of phosphate is another common feature of ARF. The serum phosphorus level usually ranges from 6 to 8 mg/dL but may be much higher with rhabdomyolysis or in catabolic states. A calcium-phosphate product greater than 70 may result in metastatic soft tissue calcification. Hyperphosphatemia is often treated with oral calcium-based antacids that bind ingested phosphate in the gut.

Acids produced in normal metabolic processes accumulate in ARF and are buffered in part by serum bicarbonate, resulting in a decrease in the serum bicarbonate level and high-anion-gap metabolic acidosis. Compensatory hyperventilation may be mistakenly attributed to primary cardiac failure or volume overload. The metabolic acidosis associated with ARF is usually mild, and treatment is not generally necessary if the serum bicarbonate level is greater than 10 mEq/L. Overzealous correction may result in hypokalemia, hypocalcemia, or volume overload.

Hypermagnesemia complicates ARF when patients are given magnesium-containing antacids or laxatives. Thus, these products, as well as magnesium itself (e.g., when given for treatment of arrhythmia or wheezing), should be avoided in the setting of ARF.

Hyperuricemia, resulting from decreased renal clearance, is typically in the range of 9 to 12 mg/dL but may be much higher in catabolic patients. For reasons that are unclear, gout rarely complicates ARF. A urinary uric acid/creatinine ratio in excess of 1 suggests that hyperuricemia is the *cause,* rather than the result, of ARF. In this case, diuretics, alkalinization of the urine, and dialysis may be necessary.

Disturbances of volume regulation can be expected to occur in most patients with ARF. Some nonoliguric patients excrete salt and water sufficiently well that intravascular volume depletion occurs if adequate fluid replacement is not provided. Volume depletion prolongs recovery from ARF. Much more commonly, ARF is complicated by volume overload because sodium and water excretion may be inadequate to match even modest intakes. Volume overload is largely responsible for the hypertension often seen in ARF and commonly leads to CHF and pulmonary edema. Iatrogenic volume overload is particularly common and can be prevented only by careful attention to fluid intake and output using prudent estimates of insensible loss. Volume overload can be treated with diuretics or IV nitroglycerin while preparations are being made to initiate dialysis.

Organ System Effects

The clinician should be alert to the numerous other important systemic and organ-specific effects of renal failure. Only the more prominent of these can be mentioned here.

Uremia impairs host defenses, particularly leukocyte function. Infection occurs in 30% to 70% of patients with ARF and is a significant cause of morbidity and mortality. Thus, patients with fever require prompt investigation and aggressive treatment.

Pericarditis, which has a prevalence of 12% to 20% in dialyzed patients with end-stage renal disease (ESRD), may also occur in patients with ARF. Chest pain that is worse in a recumbent position is the most common symptom, and most patients have a pericardial friction rub. Fever is common. The ECG may show ST-T wave elevation, low voltage, electrical alternans, or atrial fibrillation. The presence of pericardial effusion is identified most accurately by echocardiography; tamponade, with typical clinical signs, occurs in some patients. In contrast to the situation in chronic renal failure, pericarditis or pericardial effusion in the setting of ARF is generally an indication for the urgent initiation of dialysis. Patients who have hemodynamically significant tamponade require surgical drainage of the effusion or, occasionally, emergency pericardiocentesis.

Neurologic abnormalities in ARF may be precipitated by electrolyte abnormalities, medications, or uremia. Common symptoms in uremic patients include lethargy, confusion, agitation, asterixis, myoclonus, and seizures.

Anorexia, nausea, vomiting, gastritis, and pancreatitis are also associated with ARF. GI hemorrhage is seen in 10% to 30% of patients; it results from a combination of stress and impaired hemostasis. GI hemorrhage is one of the leading causes of death in ARF.

Impaired erythropoiesis, shortened RBC survival, hemolysis, hemodilution, and GI blood loss all play a role in the normocytic normochromic anemia that usually accompanies ARF. Although mild thrombocytopenia may be present, it is the qualitative defect in platelet function associated with ARF that is more significant and that contributes to these patients' bleeding tendencies. In patients with active bleeding or in whom an invasive procedure is being contemplated, the prolonged bleeding time can be corrected pharmacologically. Infusion of 10 U of cryoprecipitate normalizes the bleeding time in 1 to 2 hours, with a return to baseline in 24 hours. Administration of 1-deamino-8-D-arginine vasopressin (DDAVP) shortens the bleeding time within 30 minutes.

Disposition

Patients who have new-onset ARF should be admitted to the hospital. If nephrology consultation and dialysis facilities are not available, transfer to another institution is advisable, provided that volume and metabolic abnormalities are adequately controlled and the patient is hemodynamically stable.

Decisions regarding dialysis are generally made by the nephrology consultant and take into account many factors, including laboratory test result abnormalities and the presence or absence of symptoms of uremia (e.g., nausea, vomiting, and change in mental status). Many consultants choose to initiate dialysis when the BUN level exceeds 100 mg/dL or the serum creatinine level exceeds 10 mg/dL. Intractable volume overload and life-threatening hyperkalemia are the two most common indications for emergency dialysis.

CHRONIC RENAL FAILURE

Perspective

The management of patients with chronic renal failure requires the emergency physician to consider different issues from those that are of most concern in patients with ARF. The most obvious difference is in the pace of evolution of the patient's illness. An individual with ARF has, by definition, a relatively rapidly evolving clinical course and thus is much more susceptible to the development of clinical manifestations requiring prompt attention. In contrast, a patient with chronic renal disease has most commonly experienced a slowly progressive course of decreasing renal function over months or years and is likely to have either slowly progressive symptoms or acute problems brought on by superimposed illness, trauma, or other physiologic stress. The most common problems requiring emergent intervention are severe hyperkalemia and symptomatic volume overload.

In addition, barring renal transplantation, chronic renal failure is an essentially irreversible condition generally characterized by a relentless decrease in renal function. Thus, whereas preservation of renal function may be a high priority in the patient with known ARF, one does not as a rule need to be concerned with efforts to reverse the process presumed to have caused chronic renal failure nor even perhaps with efforts to determine the exact cause. On occasion, however, there may be a reversible component of renal failure that should be addressed. In some cases, the underlying pathologic process affecting the kidneys may be arrested or treated; much more commonly, correctable extrarenal factors (e.g., volume depletion or urinary tract obstruction) may be identified.

Finally, in the patient with chronic renal failure who has an acute problem, the focus must be the identification and treatment of intercurrent illness that has caused clinical decompensation, with the goal of returning the patient to a stable, chronically compensated status.

Principles of Disease

The standard terminology for chronic renal failure has changed.[53] *Chronic kidney disease* denotes kidney damage or decreased renal function for 3 months or more and is characterized by irreversible nephron loss and scarring. *Chronic renal insufficiency*, which denotes a condition in which GFR has been moderately reduced but not to a degree sufficient to cause clear clinical symptoms, has been replaced by an indication of the degree to which GFR is reduced. The term *end-stage renal disease*, now termed *kidney failure*, describes a condition in which renal function has diminished to a low level and in which serious, life-threatening manifestations can be expected to occur without dialysis or transplantation. At this stage, the kidneys are often shrunken and diffusely scarred to such a degree that it may be impossible to make an etiologic diagnosis, even on pathologic examination.

The causes of chronic renal failure are numerous; their relative frequency depends primarily on the population studied. As with ARF, they can be conveniently classified (Box 96-9) as prerenal (vascular), intrinsic renal (glomerular and tubulointerstitial), and postrenal (obstructive). Glomerular disease accounts for approximately one third to one half the cases of ESRD, of which diabetic nephropathy forms the largest group. Hypertensive nephrosclerosis is another important cause, particularly among blacks, in whom it may be the cause of 25% or more of cases of ESRD. Among children and adolescents, reflux nephropathy is the most common cause of ESRD. Renal failure related to IV drug use or to human immunodeficiency virus disease is a major consideration in some populations. Clues to other specific causes may be gained from elements of the history, physical examination, or laboratory and imaging studies. Although determining the underlying cause of chronic renal failure can permit the underlying disease to be treated and make possible some improvement in renal function in some cases, this is the exception rather than the rule.

Uremia

Regardless of the underlying cause, progressive loss of renal function eventually results in a recognizable syn-

BOX 96-9. Major Causes of Chronic Renal Failure

Vascular
Renal arterial disease
Hypertensive nephrosclerosis

Glomerular
Primary glomerulopathies
Focal sclerosing glomerulonephritis (GN)
Membranoproliferative GN
Membranous GN
Crescentic GN
IgA nephropathy
Secondary glomerulopathies
Diabetic nephropathy
Collagen vascular disease
Amyloidosis
Postinfectious
HIV nephropathy

Tubulointerstitial
Nephrotoxins
Analgesic nephropathy

Hypercalcemia/ nephrocalcinosis
Multiple myeloma
Reflux nephropathy
Sickle nephropathy
Chronic pyelonephritis
Tuberculosis

Obstructive
Nephrolithiasis
Ureteral tuberculosis
Retroperitoneal fibrosis
Retroperitoneal tumor
Prostatic obstruction
Congenital

Hereditary
Polycystic kidney disease
Alport's syndrome
Medullary cystic disease

drome termed uremia. Despite the presence of often impressive laboratory abnormalities, clinical manifestations do not generally appear until GFR has been reduced to perhaps 15% to 20% of normal. Up to that point, the remaining functioning nephrons compensate reasonably well for those that have been injured or destroyed. Beyond that point, the kidney can no longer maintain normal serum levels of certain solutes, and metabolic by-products, collectively termed *uremic toxins*, are retained. These poorly defined substances are thought to be responsible for many of the clinical manifestations of uremia.

Uremia is characterized by derangements in homeostasis and metabolism and by specific effects in multiple organ systems. Homeostatic disturbances generally develop gradually. As the patient becomes unable to excrete an ingested salt or water load promptly, external balance of sodium and water is affected; volume overload or hypernatremia or hyponatremia may result. Inability to concentrate the urine is an early manifestation of renal insufficiency and may be manifested as nocturia. Potassium homeostasis is likewise disrupted, and a relatively small potassium load may lead to dangerous hyperkalemia. Acid-base balance is affected as the kidney fails to clear the daily metabolic acid load because of a decreased ability to excrete ammonium and phosphate; the result is a non-anion-gap acidosis in the earlier stages of chronic renal failure and a superimposed anion-gap acidosis as GFR decreases further. Calcium and phosphate metabolism is affected early on; retention of phosphate and progressive loss of the kidney's capacity to synthesize 1,25-dihydroxycholecalciferol, the active form of vitamin D, lead to hypocalcemia, secondary hyperparathyroidism, and eventually to the development of renal osteodystrophy.

Uremia causes less dramatic but no less serious derangements in protein, carbohydrate, and lipid metabolism. Nitrogenous by-products of protein catabolism are retained in the blood and are the presumed cause of many of the diverse abnormalities of organ function in renal failure. Most patients with ESRD show decreased glucose tolerance, although it is rarely severe enough to require treatment unless there is a history of overt diabetes. In the latter case, insulin or other hypoglycemic therapy may need to be continued but generally in a lower dosage than required before renal failure supervened because the normal kidney has a major role in insulin degradation. Alterations in lipid metabolism result in elevated low-density lipoproteins and hypertriglyceridemia in many ESRD patients.

Clinical Features

Uremia has specific effects on a variety of organ systems. Many of these manifestations are relieved by dialysis, but others are not. A number have been attributed in some degree to retention of nitrogenous wastes and to the previously noted derangements in vitamin D and parathyroid hormone metabolism.

Cardiovascular

The cardiovascular system is perhaps most dramatically affected.[54,55] Many of the manifestations can be attributed to the effects of chronic volume overload, anemia, hyperlipidemia, alterations in calcium and phosphorus metabolism, and volume- and hormonally mediated hypertension.[55-58] Pericarditis, with or without pericardial fluid accumulation, is also common in ESRD, particularly among patients who have not had dialysis.

Pulmonary

Similarly, some patients develop uremic pleuritis, with or without associated pleural fluid collections. So-called uremic lung, manifested radiographically by "bat-wing" perihilar infiltrates, represents pulmonary edema and is almost always caused by volume overload or myocardial dysfunction. Noninflammatory pleural effusion caused by volume overload is also fairly common. Of special importance to the emergency physician is the fact that the radiographic appearance of pulmonary edema may at times be misleading, simulating an infectious lobar infiltrate or even assuming a nodular appearance in some cases.[59]

Neurologic

Neurologic dysfunction is common in advanced uremia and is usually manifested by lethargy, somnolence, difficulty concentrating, or frank alteration in mental status. Seizures may also occur, although causes other than uremia alone must be ruled out. Uremic encephalopathy is also commonly manifested by hiccups, asterixis, or myoclonic twitching. The last should not be confused with tetany caused by hypocalcemia, which is also common in untreated patients

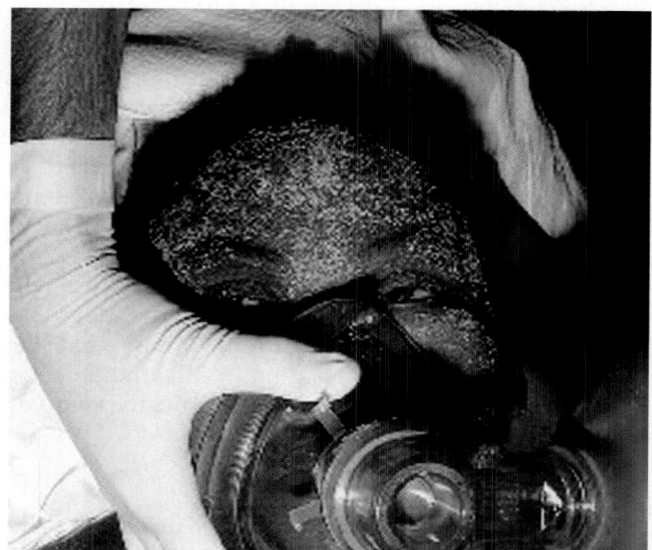

Figure 96-4. Uremic frost. Note the fine white powder on the skin of this patient with end-stage renal disease.

with ESRD. In the peripheral nervous system, uremia often causes cramps and a distal sensorimotor neuropathy. A troublesome and characteristic complaint is the "restless legs syndrome," in which there is persistent neuropathic discomfort in the legs that patients find can be relieved only by movement.

Gastrointestinal

Anorexia, nausea, and vomiting are nearly constant features of uremia. These symptoms are thought to be caused by accumulation of nitrogenous wastes because they are often relieved, even in the undialyzed patient, by introduction of a low-protein diet and seem to correlate roughly with the BUN level.

Dermatologic

The skin of the patient with chronic renal failure has a characteristic yellowish tinge. "Uremic frost," the result of deposition of urea from evaporated sweat on the skin, is a classical finding that, like "uremic fetor," is seen only rarely now with the widespread use of dialysis (Figure 96-4). Diffuse pruritus is often a major source of discomfort for the ESRD patient; in some cases it may be caused by calcium deposition in the skin secondary to derangements in calcium metabolism.

Musculoskeletal

The bones and joints are sites of problems for many patients, particularly those with long-standing renal disease. The complex disturbances of calcium and phosphate metabolism in ESRD result in renal osteodystrophy, a term encompassing several overlapping varieties of bone disease that can cause symptoms of bone pain or frank fractures.[60,61] Patients with chronic renal disease are generally treated with long-term oral calcium and vitamin D in an effort to prevent both secondary hyperparathyroidism and uremic osteodystrophy. Occasional patients have a poor response to therapy and require parathyroidectomy.

A particular type of arthritis caused by deposition of calcium hydroxyapatite or calcium oxalate crystals in joints is seen in some patients,[62] as are periarticular calcium deposition, spontaneous tendon rupture, myopathy, and carpal tunnel syndrome.

Immunologic

Infection remains a leading cause of mortality associated with renal failure.[63,64] Uremic patients have long been noted to have an increased susceptibility to infection, even when not challenged by the invasive procedures necessitated by dialysis. Both humoral and cellular immunities have been shown to be affected. Although the relative importance of each in the pathogenesis of infection in renal failure has not yet been clarified, defects in cellular immunity appear to be more significant clinically. Nevertheless, although patients with renal failure should be considered to be immunocompromised, most infections in ESRD patients are caused by common pathogens rather than opportunistic organisms.

Hematologic

A rather severe normochromic normocytic anemia, with a hematocrit commonly in the range of 18% to 25%, is nearly universal in untreated ESRD, except among patients with polycystic disease. It is primarily caused by the kidneys' decreased production of erythropoietin, a hormone that stimulates red cell production by the bone marrow. Other contributing factors are increased red cell hemolysis, nutritional deficiencies, and increased bleeding secondary to platelet dysfunction.

Although platelet number is generally normal in uremia, the bleeding time is prolonged because of defective platelet adhesiveness and activation. A common manifestation is the numerous ecchymoses seen in many patients with chronic renal failure.

Diagnostic Strategies

The patient with chronic renal failure, particularly one who is not yet receiving dialysis, is likely to present to the emergency department with one of the manifestations previously noted. In cases in which the diagnosis of renal failure has not previously been made, patients most commonly have nonspecific complaints, often of insidious onset, such as generalized weakness, poor appetite, or deterioration of mental functioning. The initial laboratory finding of a reasonably well-tolerated but rather severe anemia may be the first clue to the diagnosis, which is subsequently confirmed by elevated BUN and serum creatinine levels. A prudent next step is to check the ECG for evidence of immediately life-threatening hyperkalemia before proceeding with further laboratory and radiographic investigations.

Once it is established that the patient is in no immediate danger, the emergency physician should attempt to establish that renal failure is indeed chronic rather

BOX 96-10. Causes of Chronic Renal Failure with Normal or Large Kidney Size	
Polycystic kidney disease	Multiple myeloma
Amyloidosis	Glomerulonephritis (some)
Diabetic nephropathy	Obstructive uropathy (some)
Malignant hypertension	

than acute. An explicit history to that effect obtained from previous medical records or from the patient or family provides the most straightforward and reliable confirmation, as does the presence of a dialysis access device on physical examination. If such a history is unavailable, the finding of bilaterally small kidneys (readily detected on plain abdominal films or by ultrasonography) is equally good evidence. However, the converse is not necessarily true. A finding of normal-sized or large kidneys does not rule out chronic renal failure (Box 96-10); in this case additional diagnostic steps are required to establish the diagnosis. Another good indication of chronicity is the presence of renal osteodystrophy (particularly of the osteitis fibrosa cystica type) on x-ray films of the hands and clavicles because these radiographic changes probably require at least a year to develop. Of course, a convincing history of the long-standing presence of the presenting symptoms or of symptoms such as nocturia may be helpful in suggesting chronicity, as may a history of familial kidney disease such as polycystic kidney disease or Alport's syndrome. Laboratory abnormalities such as anemia, acidosis, hyperuricemia, hypocalcemia, and hyperphosphatemia can occur in patients with *acute* renal failure as early as 10 days after onset. Although urinary findings likewise tend not to be helpful, the presence of reliably demonstrated broad waxy casts on microscopic examination is suggestive of chronicity, whereas the finding of an "active" sediment (e.g., red cell casts) is good evidence for an acute process.

Although, as a rule, chronic renal failure is irreversible and slowly progressive, the emergency physician should be able to exclude the possibility of potentially reversible factors (in effect, to rule out "acute on chronic" renal failure) and to be sure that treatable causes of chronic renal failure, disorders that if treated might allow for some return of renal function, have not been overlooked. These potentially reversible factors and treatable causes of chronic renal failure are important to keep in mind because they represent the emergency physician's only potential opportunity to reverse the patient's disease rather than simply to manage and ameliorate the results of it (Box 96-11).

Primary among superimposed reversible factors are those that lead to decreased renal perfusion. Of these, the most common is volume depletion. Regardless of the initiating cause, the process is exacerbated by the diseased kidney's impaired ability to conserve sodium and to concentrate the urine appropriately. Decreased renal perfusion caused by cardiac dysfunction of any cause is another extremely common and potentially reversible factor. An uncommonly encountered but

BOX 96-11. Reversible Factors and Treatable Causes of Chronic Renal Failure

Reversible Factors	Treatable Causes
Hypovolemia	Renal artery stenosis
Congestive heart failure	Malignant hypertension
Pericardial tamponade	Acute interstitial nephritis
Severe hypertension	Hypercalcemic nephropathy
Catabolic state/protein loads	Multiple myeloma
Nephrotoxic agents	Vasculitis (e.g., systemic
Obstructive disease	lupus erythematosus,
Reflux disease	Wegener's granulomatosis,
	polyarteritis nodosa)
	Obstructive nephropathy
	Reflux nephropathy

BOX 96-12. Mechanisms of Drug Toxicity in Renal Failure

Excessive drug level
Impaired renal excretion of drug
Impaired renal excretion of active metabolite
Impaired hepatic metabolism
Increased sensitivity to drug
Changes in protein binding
Changes in volume of distribution
Changes in target organ sensitivity
Metabolic loads administered with drug
Misinterpretation of measured serum drug level (i.e., change in therapeutic range)

From Wolfson AB, Singer I: Hemodialysis-related emergencies: Part I. *J Emerg Med* 5:533, 1987.

important vascular cause of reversible deterioration of renal function is scleroderma renal crisis, a syndrome of accelerated hypertension and severe vasoconstriction in patients with underlying scleroderma that can be reversed by timely treatment with ACE inhibitors.[20]

Increased catabolism caused by infection, trauma, surgery, corticosteroids, or GI bleeding is another reversible factor that is often responsible for worsening azotemia and developing uremic symptoms.

Drugs and toxins constitute another important group of reversible factors. Not only may these agents exacerbate renal insufficiency by causing intravascular volume depletion (diuretics), decreased renal perfusion (antihypertensive agents), or increased catabolism (tetracycline), they can also cause ATN (radiographic contrast material), AIN (many drugs), or inhibition of renal prostaglandin synthesis (NSAIDs). Particularly noteworthy is the dramatic decrease in renal function produced when an ACE inhibitor is administered to a patient with renal insufficiency caused by bilateral renal artery stenosis (or renal artery stenosis in a solitary kidney).[65]

Postrenal reversible factors are also important because of their frequency, particularly obstructive disease in the older male patient and reflux nephropathy in the child. Papillary necrosis should remain a consideration in the diabetic patient, the patient with sickle cell disease, and the patient with a history of long-term analgesic use. Stone disease, retroperitoneal fibrosis, and even rarer entities such as ureteral tuberculosis should also not be overlooked.

Finally, treatment of the underlying disorder that has caused chronic renal failure can occasionally result in the return of some renal function, most notably in cases of myeloma kidney, some forms of secondary glomerulonephritis, and severe hypertensive disease. Although this consideration must relate to long-term care and follow-up, it is appropriate that the emergency physician consider this issue to ensure that appropriate evaluation and disposition are arranged.

Management

Individuals with chronic renal failure constitute a group of patients who merit special attention from the emergency physician. These patients are susceptible to infection, bleeding, and the numerous other complications associated with renal failure per se as well as those that may be associated with the underlying disorder that was the cause of renal failure. Moreover, these patients are more than normally vulnerable to the effects of any intercurrent illness or trauma and the physiologic stresses thereby imposed on a more or less delicately compensated physiologic state. Those who are maintained with chronic hemodialysis or peritoneal dialysis (PD) are subject to potential complications entailed by the dialytic therapy itself.

Patients with chronic renal failure are also "special" in that they are uniquely susceptible to iatrogenic illness. First, they are less able to handle fluid and solute loads than are normal individuals. Just as important, the presence of renal failure significantly alters the metabolism and action of many drugs, often in ways that are not predictable a priori[66] (Box 96-12). Thus, the dose and schedule of every administered agent, even apparently innocuous ones such as antacids, laxatives, antiemetics, or multivitamin preparations, should be carefully considered. For this purpose the emergency physician should have access to a compendium such as the one by Aronoff and colleagues[41] or be able to consult frequently with the hospital pharmacy. In light of these considerations, when evaluating the patient with chronic renal failure in the emergency department, the emergency physician should be prepared not only to make a diagnosis and initiate appropriate treatment but also to do so while keeping in mind the predictable consequences of chronic renal failure and the necessary modifications of standard treatment they imply. In general, the emergency physician should consult with the patient's nephrologist when the initial evaluation has been completed because management and follow-up monitoring after the patient leaves the emergency department are often complex.

In the United States, most patients with advancing chronic renal disease are eventually treated with dialysis, but several true emergencies may develop in the patient with ESRD before chronic dialysis has been

Table 96-3. Treatment of Hyperkalemia

	Dose	Onset/duration of Action	Mechanism of Action	Comments
Calcium gluconate (10%) or calcium chloride (10%)	10 ml IV (May repeat × 2 prn q5-10 min)	1-5 min/~1 hr	Antagonizes membrane effects of K^+	ECG monitoring required Do not mix with HCO_3^- Beware: Hypercalcemia
Sodium bicarbonate	50 mg IV (May repeat × 1 prn)	~10-15 min/1-2 hr	Intracellular movement of K^+	Beware: Volume overload Hypertonicity Alkalosis (Seizures)
Albuterol	10-20 mg (nebulized) by inhalation	30 min/2^+ hr	Intracellular movement of K^+	Relatively free of significant side effects; tachycardia
Glucose/insulin	10-20 units regular insulin per 100 g glucose	30 min/while infusion continued	Intracellular movement of K^+	Beware: Hyperglycemia Hypoglycemia Infused volume may be decreased by using D10, D20, or D50
Kayexalate	25 g in 25 mL 70% sorbitol PO q6h ± 50 g in 50 mL 70% sorbitol by retention enema q6hr	Hours/while continued	Exchange of K^+ for Na^+	Beware: Na^+ overload Enema must be retained × 30-45 min
Dialysis	Hemodialysis Peritoneal dialysis	Minutes/while continued	Removal of K^+ from blood	HD may remove 50 mEq/hr (beware K^+ rebound) PD may remove 15 mEq/hr
IV diuretics (IV fluid if hypovolemic)	Minutes/while diuresis continued (depending on renal function)		Urinary K^+ excretion	Only in patients with residual renal function

ECG, electrocardiogram; HD, hemodialysis; PD, peritoneal dialysis.
From Wolfson AB, Singer I: Hemodialysis-related emergencies—Part II. *J Emerg Med* 6:61, 1988.

instituted. Specific diagnostic and therapeutic considerations apply to the management of these conditions regardless of whether they occur in dialyzed or undialyzed patients.

Hyperkalemia

Potentially the most rapidly lethal complication of chronic renal failure that the emergency physician must deal with is severe hyperkalemia. As a rule, this condition is clinically silent until it arises with potentially life-threatening manifestations.[67] Thus, hyperkalemia must be looked for in every patient with chronic renal disease. These individuals can become severely hyperkalemic when required to handle even modest exogenous and endogenous potassium loads; moreover, even drugs such as β-blockers and ACE inhibitors that have only minimal effects on the serum potassium in normal individuals can cause hyperkalemia in these patients. The inadvertent use of succinylcholine in patients with ESRD can rapidly result in life-threatening hyperkalemia.

An ECG should be obtained whenever hyperkalemia is a possibility, and if signs of hyperkalemia are noted, appropriate therapy should be started immediately, even before laboratory confirmation of a high serum potassium level. ECG changes may be completely absent even when hyperkalemia is severe, however.[68] Thus, a normal ECG does not make laboratory confirmation of a normal serum potassium level unnecessary. A potassium level of 6 mEq/L should be considered potentially dangerous even though many patients with ESRD chronically tolerate levels somewhat above this

without ECG changes. A patient with chronic renal failure who is in cardiac arrest should be assumed to be hyperkalemic and treated accordingly while the usual resuscitative measures are taken.

The most rapidly effective treatment for hyperkalemia is IV calcium, which transiently reverses the cardiac manifestations of hyperkalemia without altering the serum potassium level or total-body potassium (Table 96-3). Calcium should be given to buy time in which more definitive measures can take effect. It makes little sense to administer calcium in response to an elevated serum potassium level in the absence of manifestations of hyperkalemia on the ECG.

In treating hyperkalemia, the emergency physician must also keep in mind the ESRD patient's limited ability to tolerate volume and solute loads (see Table 96-3). Thus, repeated doses of IV sodium bicarbonate risk causing volume overload and precipitating pulmonary edema. IV glucose and insulin act less rapidly and also require volume administration. However, if the patient's condition permits, the latter method is preferred because sodium administration can be avoided and hyperkalemia can be controlled for as long as the infusion is continued. Another effective temporizing measure is administration of inhaled albuterol to promote movement of potassium into cells while more definitive maneuvers are being instituted.[51,52]

To remove potassium from the body, sodium polystyrene sulfonate (Kayexalate), a resin that exchanges sodium for potassium ions, can be administered orally or rectally. This drug can continue to control the potassium for hours and, despite the modest sodium load it entails, can be effective as a temporizing measure until

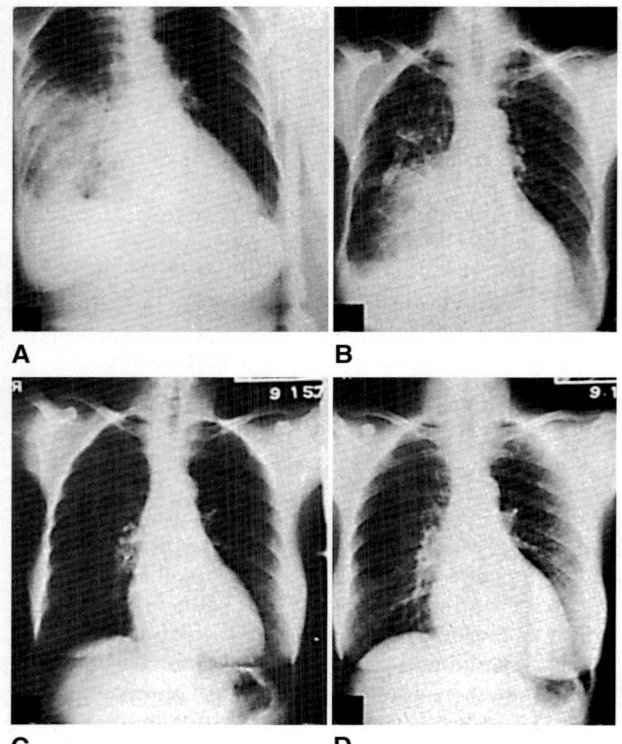

Figure 96-5. Pulmonary edema simulating right lower lobe pneumonia in a dialysis patient. Infiltrate improved drastically, and heart size returned to normal after dialysis and ultrafiltration. **A,** Chest x-ray film immediately before dialysis showing cardiomegaly and right lower lobe infiltrate interpreted as pneumonia. **B,** Chest x-ray film 5 hours after initiating dialysis with 2-kg weight reduction. There was marked improvement of infiltrate. **C** and **D,** Return of normal lung and cardiac size. (From Kjellstrand C, et al: In Drukker W, Parson FM, Maher JF [eds]: Replacement of Renal Function by Dialysis. Boston, Martinus Nijhoff, 1983, pp 536-568.)

dialysis (if necessary) can be instituted. In patients who still retain some renal function, the most effective way to treat hyperkalemia may be to administer an IV diuretic such as furosemide (if the patient is not hypovolemic) and to give volume if necessary. Large doses of diuretic may be necessary to induce a satisfactory diuresis. In light of the potential for ototoxicity with the use of loop-active diuretics, these drugs should be administered by slow infusion rather than by bolus. They should probably be avoided in patients who are also receiving other potentially ototoxic agents. During the course of any of these therapeutic interventions, both the ECG and the serum potassium must be monitored frequently.

Pulmonary Edema

Perhaps the most common emergency complaint in the patient with chronic renal failure is pulmonary edema secondary to volume overload. Surprisingly, the diagnosis is not always straightforward. The patient may have a suggestive history of increasing dyspnea on exertion or paroxysmal nocturnal dyspnea, but physical examination may not reveal the expected signs of CHF and even chest radiography may be deceptive (Figure 96-5).[58] A history of recent weight gain or of the

BOX 96-13. Treatment of Pulmonary Edema in Renal Failure

Dialysis
    Hemodialysis
    Hemofiltration
    Peritoneal dialysis
Oxygen
Nitroglycerin
Morphine
Diuretics
Nitroprusside

patient being considerably over "dry weight" (typically >5 pounds) is the most reliable clue, and in the absence of convincing evidence of another cause for dyspnea, the emergency physician should assume that volume overload is the cause and treat accordingly.

Treatment of pulmonary edema in the patient with chronic renal failure is of necessity somewhat different from that used with other patients (Box 96-13).[69,70] Arrangements for initiation of dialysis should be made as soon as possible because it is the most rapidly effective means to decrease intravascular volume in the absence of renal function. Other immediate measures should be instituted in the meantime. Although such measures may occasionally prove effective enough to avoid dialysis temporarily in patients who possess some residual renal function, the emergency physician should nevertheless anticipate that the extent and rapidity of response to even extremely aggressive medical therapy short of dialysis will be inadequate.

The patient should be placed in the sitting position and high-flow oxygen should be administered by mask. The use of continuous or bilevel positive airway pressure delivered by face mask has been reported to be a useful adjunct in patients with ESRD, as it is in patients without renal failure.[71,72] Sublingual or topical nitroglycerin, or both, can be administered immediately and functions rapidly to reduce both preload and afterload; an IV infusion can be begun promptly and titrated to effect. IV nitroprusside may have an advantage in producing more arteriolar dilation if the patient is hypertensive. IV morphine increases venous capacitance, but as with non–renal failure patients, its routine use as a first-line drug in pulmonary edema has become less common. Bumetanide is an appropriate alternative for patients who are allergic to furosemide. The use of ethacrynic acid has been associated with permanent deafness in patients with renal failure.

Infection

Because infection is a major cause of morbidity and mortality among patients with ESRD,[63,64] the possibility of serious infection should be entertained even when the expected classical findings are not all present.[62] For example, bacteremia may be manifested by fever alone, just as it is in other patients with impaired immunity. Pneumonia may arise with only vague dyspnea or malaise, symptoms that may be attributed to volume overload or uremia. Thus, all diagnostic possibilities should be pursued, and empirical broad-spectrum antibiotic coverage is often advisable until infection has been ruled out in the hospital. Bacteremia resulting from vascular access infection is quite common in patients receiving hemodialysis, as is peritonitis in patients undergoing continuous ambulatory PD.

UTI can occur even in patients with minimal urine output or those with long-standing renal failure. Urinary stasis is undoubtedly a predisposing factor.[73] In patients with lower tract symptoms, infection can usually be diagnosed by urinalysis or culture performed on a few drops of urine; oral antibiotic therapy is usually effective. Upper UTI arising with a clinical picture typical of pyelonephritis or renal colic is seen most commonly in patients with polycystic kidney disease and requires parenteral therapy. A clinical diagnosis can be made presumptively in the emergency department, but invasive measures are sometimes necessary to document infection and guide therapy. For infected cysts, lipid-soluble antibiotics (e.g., clindamycin or trimethoprim-sulfamethoxazole) offer the best antibiotic penetration; surgical intervention for refractory infection sometimes becomes necessary, however.[74]

Dialysis

Over the past several decades, dialysis techniques have been developed as a substitute for several of the functions of the normal kidney. Dialysis can normalize fluid balance, correct electrolyte and other solute abnormalities, and remove uremic toxins or drugs from the circulation when the patient's kidneys are unable to do so. Dialysis can also, but generally to a lesser degree, reverse some uremic symptoms and permit better long-term control of hypertension, anemia, and renal osteodystrophy.

There are two major dialysis modalities: hemodialysis and PD. Each is based on technology wherein the patient's blood comes into contact with a semipermeable membrane on the other side of which is a specially constituted balanced physiologic solution. Water and solutes diffuse across the membrane by moving along concentration and osmotic gradients, effectively normalizing the blood's composition.

In hemodialysis, the patient's heparinized blood is pumped through an extracorporeal circuit where it comes into contact with an artificial membrane across which fluid and solute movement occurs. The amount of fluid transferred can be controlled by adjusting the pressure difference across the membrane. Because high blood flow rates (typically at least 200 mL/min) are necessary to achieve reasonable clearances, hemodialysis requires special access to the patient's circulation, generally through a surgically created arteriovenous fistula or an implanted artificial graft. Some patients are dialyzed through a surgically placed tunneled subclavian catheter, most commonly when hemodialysis must be performed before a peripheral access has had a chance to mature or after all of a patient's peripheral sites for access have been exhausted. Chronic hemodialysis is typically performed three times a week for 3 to 5 hours per treatment, either at home or at a specially staffed dialysis unit.

The vascular access must be treated with care because hemodialysis cannot be performed without it.[66] Careless manipulation or puncture can result in bleeding, infection, or thrombosis that may result in loss of the access. The involved arm should not be used for blood pressure determinations, and a tourniquet should not be applied.

In general, blood should be drawn and IV lines established in other locations. In exceptional circumstances, if no other site is available and it is essential to obtain blood samples quickly, the fistula or graft may be used, but with precautions. A tourniquet should not be applied, the area should be cleansed scrupulously before the puncture, and extreme care should be taken not to puncture the back wall of the access. After the puncture, firm but nonocclusive pressure should be applied for at least 10 minutes. The presence of a thrill both before and after the procedure should be documented. Similar precautions are taken in the exceptional cases in which the fistula or graft must be used for IV access. If this is done, an automated infusion pump is essential to control the infusion rate into these relatively high-pressure blood vessels.

In PD, the patient's peritoneum functions as the dialysis membrane. Water and solutes diffuse from the peritoneal capillaries across this membrane to equilibrate with sterile dialysate that has been infused into the peritoneal cavity. For acute PD, dialysate is infused and drained hourly (or even more frequently) for approximately 48 hours through a percutaneously placed stiff temporary catheter. In chronic ambulatory peritoneal dialysis (CAPD), the technique in which patients with ESRD perform dialysis themselves at home, dialysate is infused through a surgically implanted Silastic catheter (Tenckhoff catheter) that penetrates the peritoneum and abdominal musculature, passes through a subcutaneous tunnel, and exits through the skin of the lower abdominal wall. Externally the catheter is attached to sterile plastic tubing to which is connected a sterile bag of dialysate. Dialysate is allowed to dwell in the peritoneal cavity for 4 to 8 hours. The patient typically exchanges the fluid four times a day, 7 days a week, discarding the bag of drained fluid and sterilely attaching a bag of fresh fluid, which is then infused. CAPD is a form of continuous dialysis, and although it is substantially less efficient on an hourly basis than hemodialysis, it achieves a total weekly clearance comparable to that obtained with thrice weekly hemodialysis. A similar technique, continuous cyclic peritoneal dialysis (CCPD), uses an automatic cycler to perform shorter exchanges while the patient sleeps at night and may offer advantages over CAPD for some patients.[75]

In contrast to hemodialysis, in which a relatively isosmolar dialysate is used and excess intravascular fluid is removed by adjusting the pressure under which the blood is pumped, PD uses a hyperosmolar dialysate to remove intravascular fluid by osmotic forces. The typical 1.5% glucose solution generally continues to remove fluid for at least 4 hours before it has substantially equilibrated with the blood. Patients usually use a more concentrated solution (e.g., 4.25% glucose) for fluid removal during the long overnight exchange.

PD offers patients with ESRD greater independence than hemodialysis, avoids the dangers of anticoagulation, and achieves smoother control of volume and hypertension without the intermittent rapid shifts of solute typical of hemodialysis. In addition, medications such as insulin and antibiotics can be administered intraperitoneally, allowing smoother absorption and more stable blood levels. The main disadvantage of PD is a significant incidence of bacterial peritonitis, which is, however, usually readily treatable.

Indications for Dialysis

The decision to initiate chronic dialysis in the patient with ESRD is generally made by the patient's nephrologist in the setting of gradually decreasing GFR and slowly progressive manifestations of renal failure. The absolute value of the BUN or serum creatinine is generally used only as a rough guide to when chronic dialysis should be instituted. Provision of vascular or peritoneal access usually has been arranged weeks to months before the anticipated initiation of dialysis to allow the access to mature and to minimize any avoidable mechanical complications of the procedure.

For the patient who comes to the emergency department with ARF, however, as well as for the patient with chronic renal failure who develops acute problems, it is the emergency physician who must be prepared to make the decision to arrange for dialysis to be provided emergently (Box 96-14). How urgently dialysis must be initiated depends on not only the severity and acuteness of the presenting problem but also the availability of technical facilities and trained dialysis personnel and the effectiveness of available temporizing measures for the problem at hand.

The most common problem requiring emergent dialysis, particularly in the patient with ESRD, is pulmonary edema secondary to volume overload. Generally, the inciting cause is overingestion of fluid and salt in excess of the patient's greatly diminished renal excretory capacity. Despite the effectiveness of temporizing measures, many of these patients require immediate dialysis—either emergency hemodialysis or, in the case of the PD patient, intensification of the usual PD regimen. Hemodialysis takes time to initiate but, once instituted, can be expected to lead to dramatic

improvement in the patient's status within a few minutes. In contrast, the success of PD in this situation depends on whether the patient can be adequately sustained for the several hours usually required for even hourly PD exchanges to effect clinically significant changes in intravascular volume status.

A related problem that may require emergent, or at least urgent, dialysis is malignant hypertension, particularly when associated with hypertensive encephalopathy or cardiovascular decompensation. Because hypertension in most patients with renal failure is at least in part volume dependent, correction of volume overload, even if clinically inapparent, is a central component of therapy. Temporizing measures such as the administration of IV sodium nitroprusside or nitroglycerin often permit hypertension to be controlled sufficiently that dialysis can be delayed for several hours, but prolonged administration of sodium nitroprusside carries an increased risk of thiocyanate toxicity in patients with renal failure. In many cases, hypertension and associated symptoms are difficult to control until dialysis permits volume overload to be corrected. Because the blood pressure is often dramatically responsive to reduction of circulating volume, it is recommended that other antihypertensive agents with more prolonged effects be withheld until after dialysis has been able to reduce circulating volume.

Severe hyperkalemia is another common indication for emergent or urgent dialysis, particularly in the patient with ARF who is hypercatabolic. In the patient with chronic renal failure, hyperkalemia is usually caused by excessive potassium intake, but endogenous causes such as hemolysis or rhabdomyolysis must be kept in mind as well.[67] A variety of available temporizing measures can be used with varying effectiveness and for various durations to control the serum potassium level, but dialysis remains the most effective means of removing potassium from the body. For rapid control of the serum potassium, hemodialysis, with its high clearance rates, is preferred to PD. However, because PD can be continued on a 24-hour basis, it can probably remove at least as great an amount of potassium as daily hemodialysis, and it eliminates the rebound increase in serum potassium often seen after hemodialysis in patients who have been chronically hyperkalemic. Moreover, PD can often be initiated more easily in a patient who has not previously been dialyzed and is less likely to cause complications related to rapid solute shifts. The rapidity of the fall in the serum potassium with either modality is difficult to predict because 98% of total body potassium resides in the intracellular space and equilibrates rapidly with the blood.

Other severe electrolyte and acid-base disturbances may sometimes require emergent dialysis. Occasional patients with renal failure and severe hypercalcemia uncontrollable by other modalities (e.g., individuals with multiple myeloma causing both renal failure and hypercalcemia) may require dialysis. The occasional patient with renal failure who develops severe hypermagnesemia after inappropriate therapy or magnesium ingestion may require immediate dialysis to reverse

---

BOX 96-14. Indications for Emergency Dialysis

Pulmonary edema
Severe uncontrollable hypertension
Hyperkalemia
Other severe electrolyte or acid-base disturbances
Some overdoses
Pericarditis (possibly)

life-threatening paralysis or cardiac dysrhythmia. Severe metabolic acidosis in the setting of renal failure is another indication for emergent dialysis, particularly if volume overload precludes the administration of reasonable amounts of bicarbonate. Of note, bicarbonate can also precipitate tetany and convulsions if administered intravenously (e.g., to treat acidosis or hyperkalemia) to a patient with hypocalcemia.

A somewhat unusual but related situation is one in which a patient with renal failure has taken an overdose or inadvertently been administered medication that is ordinarily cleared by the kidneys. If the agent is adequately dialyzable and its continued presence in the circulation poses a significant risk to the patient, immediate dialysis can be lifesaving. An example of such a situation is the ingestion of methanol or ethylene glycol by a dialysis patient. Similarly, ill-advised use of magnesium-containing cathartics or phosphate-containing enemas by patients with ESRD can lead to dangerous hypermagnesemia and hyperphosphatemia, respectively, and may require urgent dialysis.

The serum creatinine and BUN levels themselves should not be considered indications for dialysis. A creatinine of 10 mg/dL or a BUN of 100 mg/dL is often used as a guideline for beginning chronic dialysis in the patient with progressive renal failure. In dialyzed patients, however, the serum creatinine is often considerably greater than 10 mg/dL but is a reflection more of total body muscle mass than the adequacy of dialysis. The BUN is a somewhat better indicator; the level in well-dialyzed individuals is generally in the 50 to 80 mg/dL range and is over 100 mg/dL in less well dialyzed patients. However, neither blood level correlates more than roughly with uremic symptoms even in undialyzed patients or has any direct bearing on how urgently dialysis should be initiated.

The occurrence of uremic symptoms such as nausea, vomiting, lethargy, or twitching indicates a need for dialysis but does not require dialysis to be initiated immediately unless symptoms are severe. Pericarditis, even in the absence of cardiac tamponade, is often considered an indication for urgent dialysis,[76] but it is not uncommon for pericarditis to occur in well-dialyzed ESRD patients as well.[77,78] In a previously undialyzed patient with progressive renal insufficiency, the appearance of pericarditis indicates that it is time to initiate dialysis, although not necessarily on an emergency basis.

Complications of Dialysis Therapy

The emergency physician must be familiar with the particular problems associated with ESRD and dialysis to manage acute problems referred from the dialysis unit or those occurring at home or in the interdialysis period.[61,64,66,79-81] Consultation with the nephrologist or dialysis nurse is important in arranging a consistent care plan for the dialysis patient with an emergent condition and in ensuring appropriate further acute care or follow-up monitoring.

Hemodialysis. *Vascular access–related complications.* The performance of hemodialysis depends on reliable vascular access, and it is the vascular access device that is responsible for complications of dialysis that most often require evaluation in the emergency department.[82] These problems must be attended to promptly to minimize the risk of losing the patient's dialysis "lifeline."

Bleeding from the dialysis puncture site can occur hours after a hemodialysis treatment, either spontaneously or after inadvertent minor trauma to the site. Patients are usually able to control the bleeding by applying pressure to the area, but they need to be evaluated to exclude significant blood loss. Such bleeding can almost always be stopped by applying firm pressure to the access site; the emergency physician must be careful not to occlude and possibly cause thrombosis of the vessel by compressing it too vigorously, and the presence of a thrill immediately after the procedure should be documented on the chart. It may be necessary to keep the patient in the emergency department for a time to be sure that bleeding does not recur. Recurrent bleeding, especially from an aneurysm or pseudoaneurysm, should be evaluated by a vascular surgeon.

Similarly, if the patient complains that the thrill in the access has been lost, a vascular surgeon should be consulted immediately. Although thrombolytic agents such as urokinase or streptokinase are sometimes used, definitive treatment is generally surgical revision.[61,82] The access device should not be forcefully manipulated or irrigated because rupture of the vessel or venous embolization may result.

Infection of the vascular access is not uncommon and can result in persistent or recurrent bacteremia as well as loss of the access.[82,83] Infection appears to be a consequence of contamination at the time of puncture for dialysis; most infections are caused by staphylococci typical of skin flora. Infections are more likely to occur in grafts than in native fistulas.[64,82] The signs and symptoms of an access infection—redness, warmth, and tenderness over the site—are often obvious, but in many cases patients manifest no localizing findings and have only fever or a history of recurrent episodes of fever and documented bacteremia.[61] For this reason, it is common practice to obtain blood cultures for all hemodialysis patients who have a fever without an obvious source of infection and to treat them presumptively for an access infection. However, a careful search for other sources of infection should be made before concluding that inapparent access infection is the cause. Infections such as odontogenic abscess, extremity cellulitis (particularly in diabetics), and perirectal abscess can easily be missed.

Although some nephrologists prefer to admit all dialysis patients with fever to the hospital, it is often possible to manage these individuals on an outpatient basis, provided they otherwise feel well and do not appear to be septic and provided they can care for themselves at home and return promptly if their condition worsens. This course is made more practical by the fact that they can be loaded with IV antibiotics that dependably maintain adequate blood levels until the time of the next scheduled dialysis treatment, at which time the culture and sensitivity test results can be checked and therapy adjusted accordingly. IV vancomycin is often the drug of choice in this situation because most access infections are staphylococcal and because this drug is only minimally hemodialyzable and needs to be given only every 5 to 7 days in the chronic dialysis patient. If a gram-negative infection is also thought to be reasonably likely, as in a patient who has had recent episodes of gram-negative bacteremia, a loading dose of a second drug (e.g., a third-generation cephalosporin or an aminoglycoside) can also be administered. Patients can be reloaded with these drugs at the end of the next hemodialysis if cultures prove to be positive.

Non–vascular access–related complications. It is not surprising that the hemodialysis procedure itself, which entails invasion of the vasculature, anticoagulation, and often massive shifts of fluid and solutes, is often associated with acute complications such as hypotension, shortness of breath, chest pain, and neurologic abnormalities.

Hypotension that occurs after dialysis is most commonly the result of an acute reduction in circulating intravascular volume and the failure of the patient's homeostatic mechanisms to compensate for it. Because hemodialysis is episodic, each treatment must remove the excess fluid that has accumulated over the period since the last dialysis (generally 2 to 3 days), and patients are often relatively volume overloaded at the beginning of each treatment. With rapid removal of extracellular fluid, there is inadequate time for transcellular fluid shifts to replace intravascular volume. Antihypertensive medications, particularly β-blockers that are required when the patient is in a volume-expanded state, can contribute to the hypotension when intravascular volume is normalized.

Most episodes of hypotension that occur during hemodialysis either resolve spontaneously or are readily managed by either a decrease in blood flow rate or the infusion of small volumes of saline (to effect transient volume expansion) or hypertonic solutions (to reverse transiently acute hypo-osmolality). Patients with significant hypotension who do not respond to these maneuvers are often brought to the emergency department for further evaluation. Dialysis patients should be considered to be at risk for acute myocardial infarction, acute dysrhythmia, and sepsis. These are common causes of hypotension among all emergency patients, and consideration should first be given to these entities[66] (Box 96-15).

Acute hemorrhage is also not uncommon in dialysis patients. Almost all patients are now routinely treated with epoetin or darbepoetin to prevent severe anemia,[84,85] but untreated individuals typically have low baseline hemoglobin levels, and acute blood loss may result in symptomatic angina or CHF. Serum levels of clotting factors are normal in ESRD, but patients are routinely anticoagulated for each hemodialysis treatment. Transient thrombocytopenia may occur during the dialysis procedure, but the qualitative platelet defect characteristic of renal failure represents the most important factor in bleeding that continues beyond the peridialytic period.[86] This abnormality is only partially reversed by dialysis but can be corrected by adminis-

1550

BOX 96-15. Differential Diagnosis of Hypotension in Hemodialysis Patients

Hypovolemia	Hypercalcemia or
Excessive fluid removal	hypocalcemia
Hemorrhage	Hypermagnesemia
Septicemia	Vascular instability
Cardiogenic shock	Drug related
Dysrhythmia	Dialysate related
Pericardial tamponade	Autonomic neuropathy
Myocardial infarction	Excessive access
Myocardial or valvular	arteriovenous flow
dysfunction	Anaphylactoid reaction
Electrolyte disorders	Air embolism
Hyperkalemia or hypokalemia	

From Wolfson AB. Singer I: Hemodialysis-related emergencies: Part I. *J Emerg Med* 5:533, 1987.

tration of DDAVP, which causes increased release of factor VIII–von Willebrand factor (VWF) polymers from vascular endothelium. DDAVP has been used successfully to normalize the bleeding time in preparation for surgery in the patient with chronic renal failure. Cryoprecipitate and conjugated estrogen have both been shown to produce similar effects for a longer period.[86]

GI bleeding, often caused by angiodysplasia or peptic ulcer disease, is common and can be dramatic.[87,88] Occult hemorrhage, however, can challenge the emergency physician's diagnostic skills because symptoms and signs of volume loss tend to be overshadowed by local manifestations of bleeding into a closed space. Thus, spontaneous retroperitoneal or pleural hemorrhage tends to arise with flank pain or with chest pain and shortness of breath, respectively.

Occasionally, acute hypotension may be caused by anaphylaxis or an anaphylactoid reaction to some component of the dialyzer or the dialysate; these should be considered if the history is suggestive. Acute pulmonary embolism and acute air embolism are two less likely possibilities. The former, although it does occur occasionally in dialysis patients, is unusual. The latter, although reported occasionally in the past, has been all but eliminated by improved dialysis unit monitoring equipment and safety mechanisms.

The emergency physician, however, should not neglect to consider two additional entities in the differential diagnosis of hypotension that are of particular importance in the ESRD patient—acute pericardial tamponade and severe, life-threatening hyperkalemia.

Acute pericardial tamponade may be the result of either sudden pericardial hemorrhage or a compensated pericardial effusion becoming suddenly symptomatic in the presence of acute correction of elevated preload. The clinical features of tamponade in the dialysis patient are similar to those in other populations, but the common preexistence of cardiomegaly may make the chest x-ray film difficult to interpret unless it shows the typical "water bottle" shape and a definite increase in heart size from previous examinations.

Similarly, the finding of an elevated central venous pressure is of little use in differentiating tamponade from underlying right-sided heart failure. Even a bedside ultrasonographic examination that shows pericardial fluid, although suggestive, is not proof that tamponade is present because many dialysis patients chronically have appreciable pericardial effusions that do not cause hemodynamic compromise.[77,78] Ultrasonographic demonstration of right ventricular diastolic collapse is more specific, but a definitive diagnosis of tamponade depends on the direct demonstration of equal pressures in the right and left atria on cardiac catheterization.

Emergency pericardiocentesis must occasionally be performed in the emergency department to relieve acute tamponade, but there is often enough time for the patient to be transported to the catheterization suite or operating room for safer and more definitive therapy in a controlled setting.[66] If immediate pericardiocentesis is believed to be necessary, however, the emergency physician should not hesitate to perform this potentially lifesaving procedure, despite the many potential complications and the increased risk of bleeding in patients with ESRD. Similarly, in the case of a dialysis patient who is in cardiac arrest, pericardiocentesis should generally be attempted if initial resuscitative efforts have not been successful.

Severe life-threatening hyperkalemia, although unusual in a dialyzed patient, can occur in the presence of underlying catabolic illness or with a prolonged period of hypotension and low flow. Patients who are hyperkalemic can have profoundly slow heart rates, particularly if they have been treated with β-blockers or calcium channel blockers. If a dialysis patient is in cardiac arrest, it should be assumed that hyperkalemia is present, and separate IV infusions of calcium and bicarbonate should be given immediately.

Shortness of breath in dialysis patients is generally caused by volume overload. In the patient who becomes short of breath while being dialyzed, however, other causes must be sought, primarily sudden cardiac failure, pericardial tamponade, or pleural effusion or hemorrhage. Air embolism and anaphylactoid reactions are unusual causes. Often, pneumonia or underlying airway disease is responsible.

Chest pain during dialysis must be taken seriously because almost one half of ESRD patients die of cardiovascular causes, and it is likely that most episodes of chest pain occurring during dialysis are ischemic in origin.[63,89,90] Most dialysis patients have risk factors for coronary artery disease, related to either ESRD itself or the underlying condition that led to renal failure, and many have well-documented coronary disease.[54] ESRD is commonly associated with hypertension, hyperlipidemia, and carbohydrate intolerance; in addition, dialysis patients may be anemic, and many are chronically volume overloaded. During hemodialysis these underlying factors may be added to acute physiologic stresses such as transient hypotension and hypoxemia that are often associated with the dialysis procedure, which increases myocardial oxygen demand while decreasing oxygen delivery.

In evaluating the ESRD patient with presumed ischemic chest pain, the physician must keep in mind the potentially reversible factors that may have precipitated the episode. Particularly when a patient whose angina has been stable begins to experience more frequent or more severe anginal episodes, the emergency physician should determine whether increasing anemia, poorly controlled hypertension, or uncorrected volume overload is a factor. Coronary artery disease appears to become symptomatic with a lesser degree of obstruction than in other populations.

Patients who repeatedly experience chest pain during dialysis should undergo a complete evaluation so that the extent of their coronary disease can be defined and optimal management planned. After repeated, frequent hospital admissions to rule out myocardial infarctions because of chest pain during dialysis, it may be reasonable for the patient's nephrologist and cardiologist to set guidelines for further admissions.

The presence of renal failure and its associated electrolyte and acid-base disturbances does not in general obscure the usual ECG changes of angina or acute myocardial infarction. The pattern of the change of serum cardiac enzymes with acute infarction is also not altered by ESRD, although the baseline level of these enzymes may be higher than in the general population. Troponin I appears to perform best as a marker of infarction in ESRD patients.[91-93] Treatment of ischemic chest pain is the same as for other populations.

Among nonischemic causes of chest pain, pericarditis should always be a consideration, even in the well-dialyzed patient. The presentation is essentially the same as in nonrenal patients; fever, a friction rub, or atrial dysrhythmias may be associated findings, and signs of pericardial effusion or early tamponade should be sought. Indomethacin is often effective in relieving pain, but some patients eventually require further measures, such as pericardiocentesis with corticosteroid instillation or pericardial stripping. Patients with pericarditis often receive more frequent or intensified dialysis because pericarditis is thought to be a marker for inadequate dialysis.[76]

Neurologic dysfunction during or immediately after hemodialysis is most often caused by disequilibrium syndrome, a constellation of symptoms and signs that is thought to be due to rapid changes in body fluid composition and osmolality during hemodialysis. It usually occurs only in patients who have a high BUN and are first initiating hemodialysis. The syndrome does not occur with PD. Typically, patients have headache, malaise, nausea, vomiting, and muscle cramps, but in more severe cases there may be altered mental status, seizures, or coma. Symptoms resolve over several hours as fluid and solutes are redistributed across cell membranes.

It is dangerous, however, to attribute an altered mental status to disequilibrium syndrome unless other potential causes have been ruled out (Box 96-16), particularly when symptoms persist, fluctuate, or worsen during a reasonable period of observation.[79] Likewise, when seizures occur during dialysis, it is tempting but unwise to attribute them to disequilibrium syndrome without considering other potentially serious causes,

BOX 96-16. Differential Diagnosis of Altered Mental Status in Dialysis Patients

Structural
Cerebrovascular accident
    (particularly hemorrhage)
Subdural hematoma
Intracerebral abscess
Brain tumor

Metabolic
Disequilibrium syndrome
Uremia
Drug effects
Meningitis

Hypertensive
    encephalopathy
Hypotension
Postictal state
Hypernatremia or
    hyponatremia
Hypercalcemia
Hypermagnesemia
Hypoglycemia
Severe hyperglycemia
Hypoxemia
Dialysis dementia

even in patients who have had seizures in the past. In particular, the finding of any new focal neurologic abnormality calls for, at a minimum, an immediate head CT scan to detect intracranial hemorrhage. Similarly, if there is fever or other evidence of infection, meningitis must be a serious consideration. The emergency physician should also consider hyperglycemia and hypoglycemia (especially in the diabetic patient), electrolyte abnormalities, hypoxic states, hypotension of any cause, and other toxic or metabolic causes. The treatment of seizures in patients with ESRD is essentially the same as in other populations.

Complications of Peritoneal Dialysis. As with hemodialysis, most of the complications of PD are related to the dialysis access device, in this case the peritoneal catheter.[64] In contrast to hemodialysis, however, the dialytic process in PD occasions few immediate difficulties. Whatever volume or metabolic problems develop are often a consequence of the fact that the typical PD patient is seen by a doctor or nurse only once a month.

Peritonitis is the most common complication of PD. Fortunately, it is in general much less severe than other types of peritonitis and can be treated readily on an outpatient basis despite the continued presence of a foreign body—the Tenckhoff catheter—in the peritoneal cavity.[64,94] Occasionally, when an episode of peritonitis responds poorly to antimicrobial therapy or when a patient has repeated episodes of peritonitis caused by the same organism, the catheter must be removed and the patient sustained with hemodialysis until the infection is completely cleared and a new catheter can be placed. Repeated infections do, however, carry the risk of permanently altering peritoneal permeability or effective surface area and necessitating a permanent switch to hemodialysis.

Peritonitis in CAPD patients is presumably caused by inadvertent bacterial contamination of the dialysate or tubing during an exchange or by extension of an infection of the exit site or the subcutaneous tunnel into the peritoneal cavity. The majority of cases of peritonitis are caused by *Staphylococcus aureus* or *Staphylococcus epidermidis* and most of the remainder (approximately 20%) by gram-negative enteric organisms.[94]

Fungal infections are uncommon but are generally refractory to medical therapy and are often considered an indication for catheter removal.[95] Polymicrobial infection suggests direct contamination from the GI tract and mandates a search for the site of perforation or fistula, although such a source is identified only in a distinct minority of cases.[96]

The diagnosis of peritonitis is usually made by the patient when a cloudy dialysis effluent is noted, corresponding to the appearance of WBCs in the dialysate. Peritonitis is often, but by no means invariably, accompanied by nonspecific abdominal pain, malaise, or fever. Even in the absence of cloudy fluid, when a patient has fever or abdominal symptoms, it is advisable to consider peritonitis and to check the fluid because early peritonitis may arise atypically. In more severe cases, peritonitis is accompanied by nausea, vomiting, severe pain, and hypotension, requiring admission to the hospital and consideration of the possibility of acute surgical disease.

In the emergency department, the diagnosis of peritonitis is confirmed by the finding of more than 100 WBC/mm^3 in the peritoneal fluid, with more than 50% neutrophils, or by a positive Gram stain. A sample of fluid should be obtained for analysis, preferably by a specialized dialysis nurse, if available. Fluid should be sent for cell count and differential, Gram stain, and culture.

Occasionally, an otherwise asymptomatic patient who has recently begun PD notes the appearance of cloudy peritoneal fluid that proves on examination to contain many WBCs with a predominance of eosinophils. This condition, called eosinophilic peritonitis, is thought to represent a transient allergic reaction to some component of the fluid delivery system.[97] Peritoneal fluid cultures are negative and the condition resolves without antibiotic therapy.

PD-associated peritonitis can usually be treated with an initial intraperitoneal loading dose of antibiotic, followed by a 10- to 14-day course of intraperitoneal antibiotics, of which some may be administered by the patient on an outpatient basis. Patients with PD are taught how to inject antibiotics into the dialysis bag at the time of an exchange and the proper sterile technique to be used. After making the diagnosis, the emergency physician should make contact with the patient's nephrologist or dialysis nurse specialist to discuss the choice of antibiotic and to agree on plans for outpatient management and follow-up evaluation or occasionally, if peritonitis is severe or if outpatient management is precluded by psychosocial considerations, for hospitalization.

A common treatment regimen is a loading dose of vancomycin, 30 mg/kg intraperitoneally, followed by further intraperitoneal doses once weekly. An alternative is a regimen of intraperitoneal cefazolin or a third-generation cephalosporin, with or without gentamicin. These are given as a loading dose followed by maintenance doses administered intraperitoneally once daily at the time of an exchange (Table 96-4). Heparin (1000 U) may also be added to each 2-L bag for the first few days of treatment to help reduce the formation of

Table 96-4. Antibiotic Dosages for Treatment of PD-Associated Peritonitis[93]

Drug	Dose
Cefazolin	1 g or 15 mg/kg body weight IP in one exchange daily
Vancomycin	30 mg/kg body weight IP q5–7 days
Gentamicin	0.6 mg/kg body weight IP in one exchange daily
Ceftazidime	1 g IP in one exchange daily

IP, intraperitoneally; PD, peritoneal dialysis.

fibrin strands that may obstruct the catheter. Patients who usually receive insulin by the intraperitoneal route may have to increase their insulin dosage for a few days until the infection is under control. Patients should be seen by the dialysis nurse in 48 hours to check on the response to therapy and to adjust antibiotic therapy as necessary after reviewing the results of culture and sensitivity testing.

Catheter contamination or leaks from the catheter, tubing, or dialysate bag should be managed in the same fashion as frank peritonitis. The site and cause of leakage should be identified, and damaged elements should be replaced promptly. Occasionally, when there is leakage of peritoneal fluid from around the catheter, surgical correction is necessary.

Individuals who have severe abdominal pain, vomiting, ileus, chills or high fever, or hypotension should be admitted to the hospital. Likewise, patients with severe underlying illness and those who cannot reliably perform exchanges or administer antibiotics at home as necessary require inpatient management. Dialysis exchanges should be continued on the same schedule. The inpatient antibiotic regimen is essentially the same as that used for outpatients.

Perhaps the most serious potential pitfall in caring for the PD patient with abdominal pain or other signs of peritonitis is to overlook other serious intra-abdominal conditions whose presentation may mimic that of peritonitis.[98,99] PD patients are at increased risk for abdominal wall or inguinal hernia because of chronically increased intra-abdominal pressures; previous abdominal surgery also places them at risk for hernia as well as for obstruction secondary to adhesions. The manifestations of serious disorders unrelated to dialysis (e.g., acute appendicitis, diverticulitis, cholecystitis, acute pancreatitis, ischemic bowel, or perforated viscus) may also be attributed to ordinary PD-associated peritonitis, with the potential for disastrous consequences. The accessibility of the peritoneal fluid for examination may prove helpful in documenting the presence of an inflammatory process, but it also has the potential to mislead the emergency physician concerning its cause. A finding of brownish or fecal material in the peritoneal drainage should suggest a ruptured viscus until proved otherwise, and immediate surgical consultation should be sought. Detection of localized tenderness, a palpable mass, or an incarcerated hernia on physical examination can be extremely helpful in making the diagnosis. Abdominal radiography may be useful for demonstrating the presence of ileus, but pneumoperitoneum may be caused by the introduction of air during a recent fluid exchange rather than by a perforated viscus.[100] Thus, keeping in mind the possibility that disorders other than peritonitis may underlie the patient's symptoms, the emergency physician should maintain a lowered threshold for requesting surgical consultation or admitting the patient to the hospital for observation.

An often alarming but generally harmless occurrence is the appearance of a grossly bloody dialysate in a young female PD patient who is otherwise asymptomatic. Unless other findings are present, this is attributable to a small degree of retrograde menstruation that is thought to be common in many women. Scant, irregular menses are the rule in ESRD; conception can occur but is uncommon, and viable delivery is rare.

Infection of the catheter exit site is another relatively common problem for which the CAPD patient may seek care in the emergency department.[101] This infection tends to be caused by typical skin flora and is manifested by the usual local signs of infection. Although not serious in themselves, exit site infections should be taken seriously because they may lead to infection of the subcutaneous tunnel, which can cause repeated episodes of peritonitis and may ultimately necessitate removal of the catheter. Any visible exudate should be cultured and a Gram stain performed, and an oral antibiotic such as cephalexin should be started, pending the results of culture and sensitivity testing. The patient should be instructed to cleanse the site meticulously several times a day using povidone-iodine or peroxide solution.

Tunnel infections can be difficult to detect on physical examination and may be suspected only after the patient has several bouts of peritonitis caused by the same organism. As with other closed-space infections, they tend to be difficult to eradicate unless the tunnel is partially unroofed and drained.

PD patients may also present to the emergency department with any of several basically mechanical problems, of which the most common is inability to drain the dialysate completely at the time of an exchange. Occasionally, this is simply caused by kinking or inadvertent clamping of the external catheter or tubing, but more often it is the result of catheter obstruction by fibrinous debris or kinking or migration of the catheter within the peritoneal cavity, often associated with constipation. Catheter position is best assessed initially by plain abdominal radiographs. Specific intervention may be guided by a contrast catheterogram. Fibrinolytic agents have been used successfully to open occluded catheters, but surgical intervention for catheter replacement is often required.

PD patients generally care for themselves completely between routine visits to the nephrologist and dialysis nurse specialist. One consequence of this highly desirable independence, however, is that they may gradually develop volume or metabolic disturbances between visits. Although patients are instructed to weigh themselves daily and to measure their pulse and blood pressure frequently, some become progressively volume overloaded. The result may be only minor worsening of blood pressure control, but occasionally a patient develops acute pulmonary edema and requires immediate attention in the emergency department. Treatment strategies are the same as for hemodialysis patients, but even with hourly exchanges of 4.25% glucose dialysate solution, improvement may not be rapid, particularly when the presence of 2 L of fluid in the peritoneal cavity restricts lung expansion.

PD patients can also become volume depleted, particularly when oral intake is poor or when there has been significant GI fluid loss yet volume continues to be removed by dialysis. Oral or IV rehydration and further instruction on maintaining normal volume status are generally all that is necessary.

Severe metabolic disturbances are much less common among patients with PD than hemodialysis patients because dialysis is being performed essentially continuously and the blood remains in near equilibrium with the dialysate. Significant disturbances do occasionally occur, usually in association with hypercatabolic states, major dietary indiscretions, or significant GI fluid loss. One interesting derangement that occurs occasionally in diabetic patients receiving PD is a syndrome of severe hyperglycemia (sometimes even despite continuation of the usual insulin dose) resulting from absorption of glucose from hyperosmolar dialysate, with associated nonspecific symptoms of malaise, weakness, and headache. Although glucose levels may be as high as 1500 mg/dL in these individuals, they cannot undergo an osmotic diuresis and remain clinically euvolemic. Correction of hyperglycemia must be undertaken carefully to avoid causing rapid osmolar and volume shifts.

 KEY CONCEPTS

Acute Renal Failure
- The causes of ARF can be classified prerenal, postrenal, and intrinsic renal causes.
- Management of ARF should be directed first at potentially lethal complications such as hyperkalemia or volume overload and then at reversal of the underlying cause of renal dysfunction. It is important to avoid any further hemodynamic or toxic insults to the kidneys if possible.
- The patient's impaired renal function must be considered when fluid administration regimens and drug dosages are prescribed.

Chronic Renal Failure
- Patients with chronic renal failure have a limited ability to handle fluid and solute loads and altered metabolism of many drugs; therefore, fluid administration regimens and drug dosages should be checked carefully.
- The most rapidly lethal complication of chronic renal failure is hyperkalemia. This entity should always be considered a possibility, and appropriate diagnostic and therapeutic interventions should be instituted when indicated.
- Patients with renal failure often present with varying degrees of volume overload. Volume overload should generally be the first diagnostic consideration when dyspnea is the presenting complaint.

REFERENCES

1. Orth SR, Ritz E: The nephrotic syndrome. *N Engl J Med* 338:1202, 1998.
2. Sutton JM: Evaluation of hematuria in adults. *JAMA* 263:2475, 1990.
3. Cohen RA, Brown RS: Microscopic hematuria. 348:2330, 2003.
4. Klahr S, Miller SB: Acute oliguria. *N Engl J Med* 338:671, 1998.
5. Singri N, Ahya SN, Levin ML: Acute renal failure. *JAMA* 289:747, 2003.
6. Sandler CM: Contrast-agent-induced acute renal dysfunction—Is iodixanol the answer? *N Engl J Med* 348:551, 2003.
7. Kimmel P, Barisoni L, Kopp JB: Pathogenesis and treatment of HIV-associated renal diseases: Lessons from clinical and animal studies, molecular pathologic correlations, and genetic investigations. *Ann Intern Med* 139:214, 2003.
8. Cruz DN, Perazella MA: Drug-induced acute tubulointerstitial nephritis: The clinical spectrum. *Hosp Pract (Off Ed)* 33:151, 1998.
9. Van Savage JG, Fried FA: Anticoagulant associated hematuria: A prospective study. *J Urol* 153:1594, 1995.
10. Chen MYM, Zagoria RJ: Can noncontrast helical computed tomography replace intravenous urography for evaluation of patients with acute urinary tract colic? *J Emerg Med* 17:299, 1999.
11. Sourtzis S, et al: Radiologic investigation of renal colic: Unenhanced helical CT compared with excretory urography. *Am J Radiol* 172:1491, 1999.
12. Viewig J, et al: Unenhanced helical computerized tomography for the evaluation of patients with acute flank pain. *J Urol* 160:1465, 2000.
13. Dagher L, Moore K: The hepatorenal syndrome. *Gut* 49:729, 2001.
14. Perazella MA, Tray K: Selective cyclooxygenase-2 inhibitors: A pattern of nephrotoxicity similar to traditional nonsteroidal anti-inflammatory drugs. *Am J Med* 111:64, 2001.
15. Whelton A, et al: Effects of celecoxib and naproxen on renal function in the elderly. *Arch Intern Med* 160:1465, 2000.
16. Perazella MA: Drug-induced renal failure: Update on new medications and unique mechanisms of nephrotoxicity. *Am J Med Sci* 325:349, 2003.
17. Garg AX, et al: Long-term renal prognosis of diarrhea-associated hemolytic uremic syndrome: A systematic review, meta-analysis, and meta-regression. *JAMA* 290:1360, 2003.
18. Adams BD: Scleroderma renal crisis [letter]. *Ann Emerg Med* 42:713, 2003.
19. Bakir AA, Bazilinski N, Dunea G: Transient and sustained recovery from renal shutdown in accelerated hypertension. *Am J Med* 80:172, 1986.
20. Steen VD, et al: Outcome of renal crisis in systemic sclerosis: Relation to availability of angiotensin converting enzyme (ACE) inhibitors. *Ann Intern Med* 113:352, 1990.
21. Brady HR, et al: Acute renal failure. In Brenner BM (ed): *The Kidney*, 6th ed. Philadelphia, WB Saunders, 2000, pp 1201-1246.
22. Nash K, Hafeez A, Hou S: Hospital-acquired renal insufficiency. *Am J Kidney Dis* 39:930, 2002.
23. Brivet FG, Kleinknecht DJ, Loirat P, Landais PJ: Acute renal failure in intensive care units—Causes, outcome, and prognostic factors of hospital mortality: A prospective multicenter study. *Crit Care Med* 24:192, 1996.
24. Gabow PA, Kaehny WD, Kelleher SP: The spectrum of rhabdomyolysis. *Medicine (Baltimore)* 61:141, 1982.

25. Zager RA: Rhabdomyolysis and myohemoglobinuric acute renal failure. *Kidney Int* 49:314, 1996.

26. Barza M, et al: Single or multiple daily doses of aminoglycosides: A meta-analysis. *BMJ* 312:338, 1996.

27. Hatala R, Dinh T, Cook DJ: Once-daily aminoglycoside dosing in immunocompetent adults: A meta-analysis. *Ann Intern Med* 124:717, 1996.

28. Lautin EM, et al: Radiocontrast-associated renal dysfunction: Incidence and risk factors. *Am J Radiol* 157:49, 1991.

29. Parfrey PS, et al: Contrast material-induced renal failure in patients with diabetes mellitus, renal insufficiency, or both. *N Engl J Med* 320:143, 1989.

30. Trivedi HS, et al: A randomized prospective trial to assess the role of saline hydration on the development of contrast nephropathy. *Nephron Clin Pract* 93:C29, 2003.

31. Mueller C, et al: Prevention of contrast media–associated nephropathy. *Arch Intern Med* 162:329, 2002.

32. Barrett BJ, Carlisle EJ: Metaanalysis of the relative nephrotoxicity of high- and low-osmolality iodinated contrast media. *Radiology* 188:171, 1993.

33. Rudnick MR, et al: Nephrotoxicity of ionic and nonionic contrast media in 1196 patients: A randomized trial. *Kidney Int* 47:254, 1995.

34. Aspelin P, et al: Nephrotoxic effects in high-risk patients undergoing angiography. *N Engl J Med* 348:491, 2003:

35. Kay J, et al: Acetylcysteine for prevention of acute deterioration of renal function following elective coronary angiography and intervention: A randomized controlled trial. *JAMA* 289:553, 2003.

36. Diaz-Sandoval LJ, et al: Acetylcysteine to prevent angiography-related renal tissue injury (the APART trial). *Am J Cardiol* 89:356, 2002.

37. Baker CS, et al: A rapid protocol for the prevention of contrast-induced renal dysfunction: The RAPPID study. *J Am Coll Cardiol* 41:2114, 2003.

38. Curhan GC: Prevention of contrast nephropathy. *JAMA* 289:606, 2003.

39. Aquilera PA, Choi T, Durham BA: Ultrasound-guided suprapubic cystostomy catheter placement in the emergency department. *J Emerg Med* 26:319, 2004.

40. Lyons K, Matthews P, Evans C: Obstructive uropathy without dilatation: A potential diagnostic pitfall. *Br Med J (Clin Res Ed)* 296:1517, 1988.

41. Aronoff GR, et al: *Drug Prescribing in Renal Failure: Dosing Guidelines for Adults.* Philadelphia, American College of Physicians, 2002.

42. Esson ML, Schrier RW: Diagnosis and treatment of acute tubular necrosis. *Ann Intern Med* 137:744, 2002.

43. Lameire N, Vanholder R, Van Biesen W: Loop diuretics for patients with acute renal failure: Helpful or harmful? *JAMA* 288:2599, 2002.

44. Shilliday IR, et al: Loop diuretics in the management of acute renal failure: A prospective, double-blind, placebo-controlled, randomized study. *Nephrol Dial Transplant* 12:2592, 1997.

45. Mehta RL, et al: Diuretics, mortality, and nonrecovery of renal function in acute renal failure. *JAMA* 288:2547, 2002.

46. Better OS, Rubinstein I, Winaver JM, Knochel JP: Mannitol therapy revisited (1940-1997). *Kidney Int* 52:886, 1997.

47. Marik PE, Iglesias J: Low-dose dopamine does not prevent acute renal failure in patients with septic shock and oliguria. *Am J Med* 107:387, 1999.

48. Bellomo R, et al: Low-dose dopamine in patients with early renal dysfunction: A placebo-controlled randomized trial. *Lancet* 356:2139, 2000.

49. Lewis J, et al: Atrial natriuretic factor in oliguric acute renal failure. *Am J Kidney Dis* 36:767, 2000.

50. Better OS, Stein JH: Early management of shock and prophylaxis of acute renal failure in traumatic rhabdomyolysis. *N Engl J Med* 322:825, 1990.

51. Allon M, Dunlay R, Copkney C: Nebulized albuterol for acute hyperkalemia in patients on hemodialysis. *Ann Intern Med* 110:426, 1989.

52. Montoliu J, et al: Treatment of hyperkalemia in renal failure with salbutamol inhalation. *J Intern Med* 228:35, 1990.

53. Levey AS, et al: National Kidney Foundation practice guidelines for chronic kidney disease: Evaluation, classification, and stratification. *Ann Intern Med* 139:137, 2003.

54. Luke RG: Chronic renal failure—A vasculopathic state. *N Engl J Med* 339:841, 1998.

55. Sarnak MJ, et al: Kidney disease as a risk factor for development of cardiovascular disease: A statement from the American Heart Association Councils on Kidney in Cardiovascular Disease, High Blood Pressure Research, Clinical Cardiology, and Epidemiology and Prevention. *Circulation* 108:2154, 2003.

56. Goodman WG, et al: Coronary-artery calcification in young adults with end-stage renal disease who are undergoing dialysis. *N Engl J Med* 342:1478, 2000.

57. Coresh J, et al: Epidemiology of cardiovascular risk factors in chronic renal disease. *J Am Soc Nephrol* 9:S24, 1998.

58. Muntner P, et al: The prevalence of nontraditional risk factors for coronary heart disease in patients with chronic kidney disease. *Ann Intern Med* 140:9, 2004.

59. Kohen JA, Opsahl JA, Kjellstrand CM: Deceptive patterns of uremic pulmonary edema. *Am J Kidney Dis* 7:456, 1986.

60. Llach F, Bover J: Renal osteodystrophies. In Brenner BM (ed): *The Kidney*, 6th ed. Philadelphia, WB Saunders, 2000, pp 2103-2186.

61. Ifudu O: Care of patients undergoing hemodialysis. *N Engl J Med* 339:1054, 1998.

62. Hoffman GS, et al: Calcium oxalate microcrystalline-associated arthritis in end-stage renal disease. *Ann Intern Med* 97:36, 1982.

63. Port FK: Mortality and causes of death in patients with end-stage renal failure. *Am J Kidney Dis* 15:215, 1990.

64. Pastan S, Bailey J: Dialysis therapy. *N Engl J Med* 338:1428, 1998.

65. Hricik DE, et al: Captopril-induced functional renal insufficiency in patients with bilateral renal-artery stenoses or renal-artery stenosis in a solitary kidney. *N Engl J Med* 308:373, 1983.

66. Wolfson AB, Singer I: Hemodialysis-related emergencies: Part I. *J Emerg Med* 5:533, 1987.

67. Palevsky PM, Singer I: Disorders of potassium metabolism. In Wolfson AB (ed): *Endocrine and Metabolic Emergencies.* New York, Churchill Livingstone, 1990, pp 17-44.

68. Szerlip HM, Weiss J, Singer I: Profound hyperkalemia without electrocardiographic manifestations. *Am J Kidney Dis* 7:461, 1986.

69. Anderson CC, Shahvari MBG, Zimmerman JE: The treatment of pulmonary edema in the absence of renal function. *JAMA* 241:1008, 1979.

70. Gehm L, Propp DA: Pulmonary edema in the renal failure patient. *Am J Emerg Med* 7:336, 1989.

71. Huff JS, Whelan TV: CPAP as adjunctive treatment of severe pulmonary edema in patients with ESRD. *Am J Emerg Med* 12:388, 1994.

72. Sacchetti A, et al: ED management of acute congestive heart failure in renal dialysis patients. *Am J Emerg Med* 11:644, 1993.

73. Chaudhry A, Stone WJ, Breyer JA: Occurrence of pyuria and bacteriuria in asymptomatic hemodialysis patients. *Am J Kidney Dis* 21:180, 1993.

74. Sklar AH, et al: Renal infections in autosomal dominant polycystic kidney disease. *Am J Kidney Dis* 10:81, 1987.

75. De Fijter CWH, et al: Clinical efficacy and morbidity associated with continuous cyclic compared with continuous ambulatory peritoneal dialysis. *Ann Intern Med* 120:264, 1994.

76. Lundin AP: Recurrent uremic pericarditis: A marker of inadequate dialysis. *Semin Dial* 3:5, 1990.

77. Elkayam U, et al: Pericardial involvement in asymptomatic patients undergoing long-term hemodialysis: An echocardiographic study. *Eur J Cardiol* 11:445, 1980.

78. Frommer JP, Young JB, Ayus JC: Asymptomatic pericardial effusion in uremic patients: effect of long-term dialysis. *Nephron* 39:296, 1985.

79. Wolfson AB, Singer I: Hemodialysis-related emergencies: Part II. *J Emerg Med* 6:61, 1988.

80. Wolfson AB: End-stage renal disease: Emergencies related to dialysis and transplantation. In Wolfson AB, Harwood-Nuss AH (eds): *Renal and Urologic Emergencies*. New York, Churchill Livingstone, 1986, pp 23-50.

81. Denker BM, Chertow GM, Owers WS Jr: Hemodialysis. In Brenner BM (ed): *The Kidney*, 6th ed. Philadelphia, WB Saunders, 2000, pp 2373-2453.

82. Feldman HI, Kobrin S, Wasserstein A: Hemodialysis vascular access morbidity. *J Am Soc Nephrol* 7:523, 1996.

83. Marr KA, et al: Catheter-related bacteremia and outcome of attempted catheter salvage in patients undergoing hemodialysis. *Ann Intern Med* 127:275, 1997.

84. Eschbach JW, et al: Recombinant human erythropoietin in anemic patients with end-stage renal disease. *Ann Intern Med* 111:992, 1989.

85. Kaufman JS, et al: Subcutaneous compared with intravenous epoetin in patients receiving hemodialysis. *N Engl J Med* 339:578, 1998.

86. Eberst ME, Berkowitz LR: Hemostasis in renal disease: Pathophysiology and management. *Am J Med* 96:168, 1994.

87. Zuckerman GR, et al: Upper gastrointestinal bleeding in patients with chronic renal failure. *Ann Intern Med* 102:588, 1985.

88. Blackstone MO: Angiodysplasia and gastrointestinal bleeding in chronic renal failure. *Ann Intern Med* 103:805, 1985.

89. Bleyer AJ, Russell GB, Satko SG: Sudden and cardiac death rates in hemodialysis patients. *Kidney Int* 55:1553, 1999.

90. Herzog CA: Acute myocardial infarction in patients with end-stage renal disease. *Kidney Int* 56:S130, 1999.

91. Martin GS, Becker BN, Schulman G: Cardiac troponin-I accurately predicts myocardial injury in renal failure. *Nephrol Dial Transplant* 13:1709, 1998.

92. Watnick S, Perazella MA: Cardiac troponins: Utility in renal insufficiency and end-stage renal disease. *Semin Dial* 15:66, 2002.

93. McCullough PA, et al: Performance of multiple cardiac biomarkers measured in the emergency department in patients with chronic kidney disease and chest pain. *Acad Emerg Med* 9:1389, 2002.

94. Keane WF, et al: Adult peritoneal dialysis–related peritonitis treatment recommendations, 2000 update. Available at:
http://www.ispd.org/2000_treatment_recommendations.html

95. Goldie SJ, et al: Fungal peritonitis in a large chronic peritoneal dialysis population: A report on 55 episodes. *Am J Kidney Dis* 28:86, 1996.

96. Holley JL, Bernardini J, Piraino B: Polymicrobial peritonitis in patients on continuous peritoneal dialysis. *Am J Kidney Dis* 19:162, 1992.

97. Gokal R, et al: "Eosinophilic" peritonitis in continuous ambulatory peritoneal dialysis (CAPD). *Clin Nephrol* 15:328, 1981.

98. Steiner RW, Halasz NA: Abdominal catastrophes and other unusual events in continuous ambulatory peritoneal dialysis patients. *Am J Kidney Dis* 15:1, 1990.

99. McDonald RJ, et al: Concomitant surgical illness in CAPD patients [abstract]. *Perit Dial Int* 8:89, 1988.

100. Kiefer T, et al: Incidence and significance of pneumoperitoneum in continuous ambulatory peritoneal dialysis. *Am J Kidney Dis* 22:30, 1993.

101. Piraino B, Bernardini J, Sorkin M: The influence of peritoneal catheter exit-site infections on peritonitis, tunnel infections, and catheter loss in patients on continuous ambulatory peritoneal dialysis. *Am J Kidney Dis* 8:436, 1986.

CHAPTER

97 Sexually Transmitted Diseases

Diane M. Birnbaumer and Christine Anderegg

PERSPECTIVE

More than 300 million new cases of curable sexually transmitted diseases (STDs) are diagnosed worldwide each year, and these cases are seen frequently in emergency department settings. Twelve million new STD cases are diagnosed annually in the United States,[1] giving the United States the highest rate of STDs in the industrialized world.

Patients with STDs present with a variety of symptoms that most commonly involve the genitalia but can also include abdominal pain, dermatologic conditions, and systemic illness. To prevent both complications and spread of these diseases, accurate and timely diagnosis and treatment are crucial.

As with many other illnesses, history and physical examination provide much of the clinical information needed to diagnose STDs. Patients should be questioned about their current and previous symptoms and their duration, as well as any prior history of STDs, recent sexual contacts, use of contraceptives (particularly barrier devices such as condoms), and types of sexual practices; women should additionally be questioned about their menstrual history. Physical examination should focus on the symptomatic area, often the genitalia. Evidence of skin lesions and their type as well as presence of discharge should be noted. Examination of the skin and lymph nodes may be an important component of the examination, particularly in the cases of syphilis or gonorrhea. Examination of symptomatic joints for septic arthritis may indicate gonococcal arthritis and disseminated gonococcal infection.

The STDs can be split into two large categories: those that manifest with genital ulcers with or without adenopathy, and those that are nonulcerative, which most frequently manifest with genital discharge (Table 97-1).

DISORDERS CHARACTERIZED BY GENITAL LESIONS WITH OR WITHOUT ADENOPATHY

When a patient presents with a "sore" on or near the genitalia, physicians must be aware that the patient may be using this term to refer to genital warts, scabies, premalignant lesions, or other conditions, in addition to STDs. Certain components of the history and physical examination can provide crucial information to help narrow the diagnosis to a specific infection (Table 97-2). History and examination should focus on the characteristics of the lesion or lesions, the presence of adenopathy, and the presence or absence of systemic symptoms. In regard to the lesions, it is important to determine whether they are single or multiple, painful or painless, and indurated or soft, whether they have irregular or regular borders, and how they began (e.g., vesicle, papule). If the patient has lymphadenopathy, one should note whether it is unilateral or bilateral and the presence of fluctuance and pain.

When evaluating a patient with an ulcerative lesion, herpes simplex virus (HSV) testing and syphilis serology should be undertaken; if feasible, a darkfield examination of the lesion is also useful. In addition, patients should also be referred for human immunodeficiency virus (HIV) testing, because ulcerative genital lesions increase the risk of acquiring HIV infection. Despite testing, one quarter of patients with an ulcerative lesion will have no laboratory-confirmed diagnosis.[1]

Comprehensive test results are often not available during the patient's emergency department evaluation; therefore, treatment should be considered for the more likely diagnoses based on history and physical examination findings. The most common ulcerative diseases in the United States are herpes and syphilis; herpes occurs much more frequently than syphilis.[1] In rare outbreaks, chancroid can occur.[1]

Herpes

In the United States, genital herpes is the most common cause of ulcerative STDs, with 50 million people infected with the virus and 200,000 to 300,000 new symptomatic cases annually.[1] One in five sexually active adults is infected with the virus. Most commonly caused by herpes simplex virus type 2 (HSV-2), genital herpes can also be caused by HSV-1. In pregnant

Table 97-1. Differential Diagnosis of Sexually Transmitted Diseases

Ulcerative	Nonulcerative
Herpes genitalis	Gonorrhea
Syphilis (primary)	Chlamydia
Chancroid	Nongonococcal urethritis
Lymphogranuloma venereum	Secondary/tertiary syphilis
Granuloma inguinale (donovanosis)	Candidal vaginitis
Molluscum contagiosum	Trichomonas
Genital warts	Bacterial vaginosis
Pediculosis	Endometriosis
Scabies	
Pyoderma	
Trauma	
Excoriations	
Behçet's disease	
Fixed drug eruption	
Yeast infection	

Table 97-2. Characteristics of Ulcerative Sexually Transmitted Diseases

Disease	Nature of Genital Ulcer	Incubation Period	Painful	Inguinal Adenopathy	Diagnostic Tests
Syphilis	Indurated, sharply demarcated, with red, smooth base; heals spontaneously	9-90 days; average 2-3 weeks	No	Firm rubbery nodes; nontender	Darkfield examination; serology
Herpes simplex	Multiple, small grouped vesicles on a red base, which form shallow ulcers; may coalesce; resolve spontaneously but recurrence is common	2-7 days	Yes	Bilateral, firm, tender	Culture, serology
Chancroid	Irregular, sharply demarcated borders with undermined edges, shallow, often multiple	3-6 days	Yes	Unilateral most common; overlying erythema, fixed and tender, suppuration may occur	Culture
Lymphogranuloma venereum	Usually single lesion, papule or ulcer, transient, frequently not noticed	5-21 days	No	Unilateral most common; firm, tender, matted fixed; may suppurate or form fistulae	Lymphogranuloma venereum complement fixation (serology)

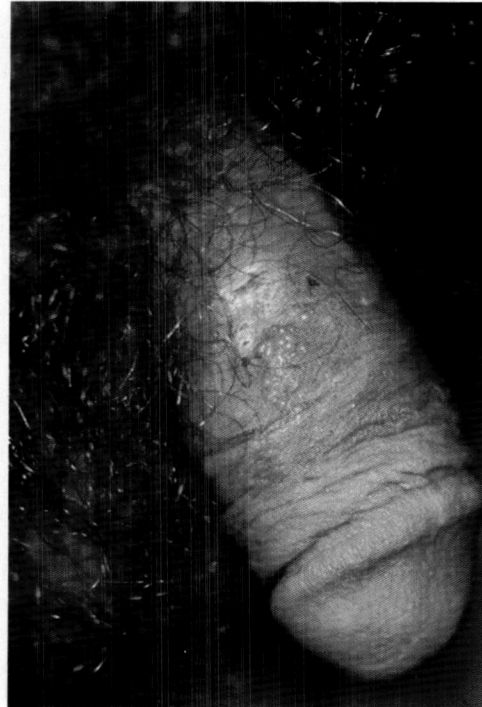

Figure 97-1. Genital herpes lesions on the penile shaft.

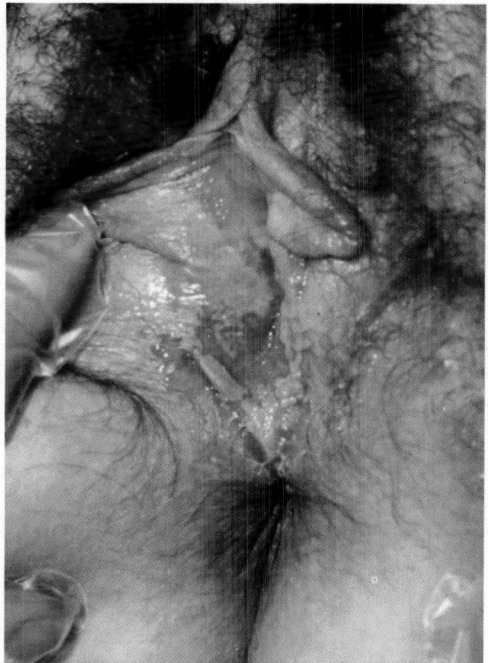

Figure 97-2. Coalescent primary herpes lesions on the vulva.

patients, herpes can cause a devastating congenital infection, although the incidence of this has decreased. In addition, HSV infection plays a major role in the transmission of HIV, as the lesions can increase the risk of both acquisition and transmission of HIV.

Clinically, genital herpes manifests as either primary herpes infection or recurrence. In primary infections, the degree of illness depends on whether the patient has preexisting circulating antibodies to either HSV-1 or HSV-2: those with antibodies tend to have a milder initial syndrome than those without. With primary infection in patients without antibiotics, the patient develops symptoms after a 2- to 7-day incubation period. The syndrome begins with genital lesions that tend to be painful, shallow, multiple, and grouped (Figure 97-1); in women, they may coalesce into large ulcerative lesions on the perineum (Figure 97-2). Systemic symptoms may include low-grade fever, myalgias, headache, and fatigue. Adenopathy, usually bilateral, mildly tender, and nonfluctuant, develops during the second or third week of the illness. The local symptoms peak at about 8 to 10 days, and it takes 2 to 4 weeks for the lesions to completely heal. Viral shedding can last as long as 3 weeks. In some cases, sacral radiculopathy may develop, with urinary retention, constipation, and sensory changes in the perineal region. Aseptic meningitis and transverse myelitis are uncommon complications. In patients with circulating antibodies to the herpesvirus, genital lesions alone usually characterize the initial infection.

As the symptoms of primary infection recede, the virus takes residence in the spinal cord ganglia and becomes latent, residing there for the lifetime of the patient. Symptomatic recurrences are the rule, occurring

in 60% to 90% of patients. In contrast to the prolonged syndrome and systemic symptoms of primary infection, recurrences are much shorter in duration and tend to cause only mild local symptoms. Many patients will be warned of an impending recurrence by a prodrome, often characterized by paresthesias, burning, or itching at the site of the subsequent lesions. Although it is known that the patient can shed the virus during a recurrence, data suggest that patients infected with HSV-2 shed the virus during asymptomatic periods as well.

Population screening with serologic tests for HSV-2 suggest that many people become infected with the virus without symptoms (or "knowledge").[2,3] Current data suggest that patients with only serologic evidence for past infection may be a potential reservoir for transmission of the virus.

Diagnosis

Although the diagnosis of genital herpes is usually made clinically, confirmatory testing should be strongly considered, particularly in women of childbearing age. Several methods are available, including viral culture and antigen testing methods of the lesions as well as new type-specific serologic testing of the blood; positive results of any of these tests is considered definitive.[4] The Tzanck test, used in the past for diagnosis of herpes infection, is no longer recommended because of its lack of sensitivity.

Although viral culture of a lesion traditionally has been and still is considered to be the gold standard, this test takes 3 to 10 days to get results and false-negative results are common, usually because of improper specimen collection, storage, or transportation. Antigen testing has been disappointing, with results often less sensitive than results of culture. In addition, some

Table 97-3. Sexually Transmitted Diseases Treatment Guidelines

Disease	Recommended Treatment Regimen	Alternative(s)
Chlamydia	Azithromycin 1 g PO in a single dose *or* Doxycycline 100 mg PO bid × 7 days	Erythromycin base 500 mg PO qid × 7 days *or* Ofloxacin 300 mg PO bid × 7 days *or* Levofloxacin 500 mg PO qd × 7 days
Gonorrhea	Cefixime 400 mg PO in a single dose *or* Ceftriaxone 125 mg IM × 1 *or* Ciprofloxacin 500 mg PO × 1* *or* Ofloxacin 400 mg PO × 1*	Spectinomycin 2 g IM × 1
Syphilis, primary or secondary	Benzathine penicillin G 2.4 million units IM × 1	
Syphilis, late latent	Benzathine penicillin G 2.4 million units IM in 3 doses, 1 week apart	
Herpes simplex, first episode	Acyclovir 400 mg PO tid × 7-10 days *or* Acyclovir 200 mg PO 5×/day × 7-10 days *or* Famciclovir 250 mg PO tid × 7-10 days *or* Valacyclovir 1 g PO bid × 7-10 days	
Herpes simplex, recurrent	Acyclovir 400 mg PO tid × 5 days *or* Acyclovir 200 mg PO 5×/day × 5 days *or* Acyclovir 800 mg PO bid × 5 days *or* Famciclovir 125 mg PO bid × 5 days *or* Valacyclovir 1 g PO qd × 5 days *or* Valacyclovir 500 mg PO bid × 5 days	
Herpes simplex, suppressive	Acyclovir 400 mg PO bid *or* Famciclovir 250 mg PO bid *or* Valacyclovir 500 mg PO qd *or* Valacyclovir 1 g PO qd	
Chancroid	Azithromycin 1 g PO ×1 *or* Ceftriaxone 250 mg IM ×1 *or* Ciprofloxacin 500 mg PO bid × 3 days *or* Erythromycin base 500 mg PO tid × 7 days	
Lymphogranuloma venereum	Doxycycline 100 mg PO bid × 21 days	Erythromycin base 500 mg PO qid × 21 days

*Due to resistance, quinolones cannot be used to treat gonorrhea acquired in Asia or Hawaii, or in cases diagnosed in California or Arizona.

antigen testing cannot distinguish between HSV-1 and HSV-2. Although the newly available serologic testing is type-specific, patients with new acquisition of the virus may take up to 6 weeks to show positive antibodies. This test is most useful in patients presenting with symptoms consistent with herpes but with negative culture or antigen testing findings.[2-4] In the newly presenting patient, culture for virus isolation is the recommended diagnostic test.

Treatment

Although genital herpes is incurable and outbreaks are self-limited, treatment decreases the duration of symptoms in patients with primary infection, can shorten or abort recurrences, and decreases the amount and duration of viral shedding and therefore potential infectivity. In patients with frequent recurrences (six or more per year), suppressive therapy can decrease the number of these episodes by up to 80%. The mainstays of treatment are the antiviral drugs acyclovir, valacyclovir, and famciclovir[1] (Table 97-3). None of these agents can eliminate the virus, but their use can control symptoms, at least while the drug is being taken. Acyclovir has been shown to be safe for up to 6 years' continuous use as a suppressive agent; the other antivirals are proven safe for 1 year.[1]

Patient education is critical in cases of genital herpes. The importance of testing the patient's sexual partner or partners should be emphasized, and the patient should be told that he or she might transmit the virus and infect a sexual partner even during asymptomatic periods. If the patient is a woman of childbearing age, she must be instructed to inform her physician of her history of genital herpes if she becomes pregnant.

Neonatal herpes is a devastating and potentially fatal infection seen most often in women who acquire the infection during their pregnancy,[3] whether or not the patient is symptomatic. Cesarean section is the preferred method of delivery if the patient has active lesions at the time of onset of labor. As the antiviral agents used to treat genital herpes have not been proven safe during pregnancy, the decision to use these agents should be made in conjunction with both the patient and the patient's physician.

Bartholin Cyst and Abscess

The Bartholin glands are located inferiorly on either side of the vaginal opening. The glands normally secrete fluid through their openings on the sides of the vestibule. The ducts and glands are only palpable or visible when obstructed, infected, or inflamed. When the duct of the gland becomes obstructed, a simple cyst develops, which is usually painless. Patients with a Bartholin gland cyst typically report a lump at the lateral introitus, and on examination, an ovoid mass can be palpated on the mucosal surface of the lateral posterior introitus, just above the posterior fourchette. Treatment is usually incision and drainage using local anesthesia with a Word catheter placement and sitz baths.

A Bartholin abscess develops when a Bartholin cyst becomes secondarily infected. The majority of abscesses involve the anaerobic and aerobic bacteria normally found in the vagina. However, they can also be due to sexually transmitted infections, including infection with *Neisseria gonorrhoeae* and *Chlamydia trachomatis*. Other commonly implicated bacteria include *Bacteroides* species, *Escherichia coli*, and other gram-negative organisms. Patients with a Bartholin abscess present with swelling and pain at the lower lateral vaginal opening and may report a lump or mass near the labia. On examination, patients may have a swollen and painful labia, and a tender, fluctuant mass can be palpated on the posterolateral margin of the vaginal vestibule. Cellulitis may be present with surrounding edema and erythema. Treatment options include incision and drainage, with the incision on the mucosal surface of the vestibule. Iodoform gauze can be used as a packing material to promote ongoing drainage, but it is preferable to use a Word catheter for this purpose. This small catheter is placed into the incision, and the balloon on the catheter is then inflated with 2 to 4 mL of water or saline. The catheter is left in place for 6 to 8 weeks until epithelialization along the catheter tract has occurred. Although this treatment is adequate in most patients, some patients who have recurrent infections may require marsupialization, creating a permanent fistula that prevents recurrent abscess formation. Antibiotics are not usually necessary unless there is significant surrounding cellulitis. Patients should be instructed to start sitz baths within 24 hours of emergency department discharge to promote drainage. Patients should follow up for reexamination of the wound within 48 hours. Because many Bartholin abscesses are caused by sexually transmitted organisms, the abscess should be cultured and routine testing for STDs performed, and patients should be treated with appropriate antibiotic therapy to cover chlamydia and gonorrhea.

Syphilis

Syphilis, also known as the "Great Imitator," is caused by the spirochete *Treponema pallidum* and earns its nickname from its ability to infect any organ of the body.

The organism is fragile and does not survive on dry surfaces. Transmission occurs during exposure of moist skin to an infected area, usually the genitalia, although inoculation can occur virtually anywhere on the body. In 2001, 6103 cases of primary and secondary syphilis were reported in the United States.[1]

If untreated, syphilis typically progresses through several stages, as follows.

1. *Primary*. The primary lesion, called a *chancre*, occurs after an incubation period that varies from 9 to 90 days, averaging 2 to 4 weeks. This lesion occurs at the site of inoculation and begins as a papule that then becomes ulcerative. Typically, the chancre is painless

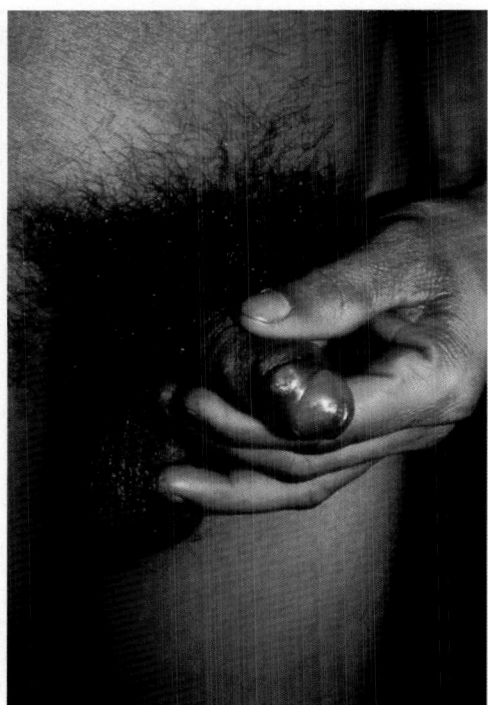

Figure 97-3. Primary syphilitic chancre on the penis.

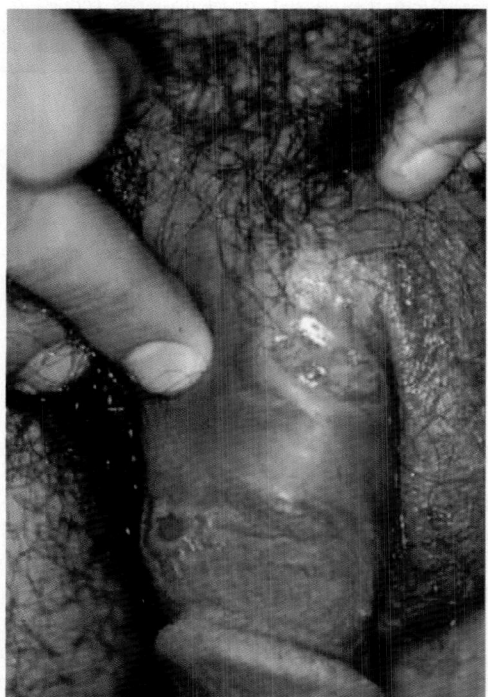

Figure 97-4. Two primary syphilitic lesions on the penile shaft.

and single and has a smooth, slightly raised edge, with sharply defined borders and a clean base (Figure 97-3); occasionally, patients present with more than one lesion (Figure 97-4). Untreated, the chancre lasts for 2 to 6 weeks and resolves spontaneously, and the patient progresses to the secondary stage of the disease.

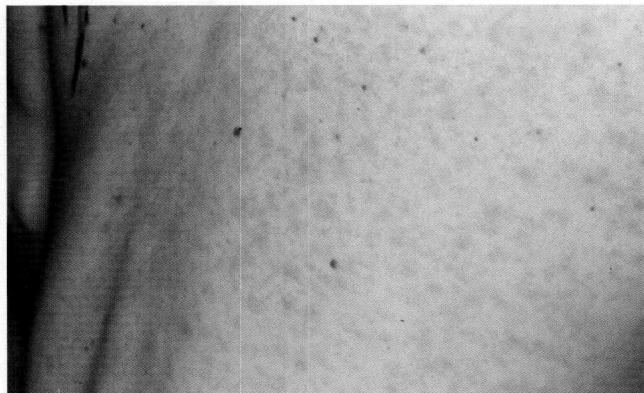

Figure 97-5. The rash of secondary syphilis.

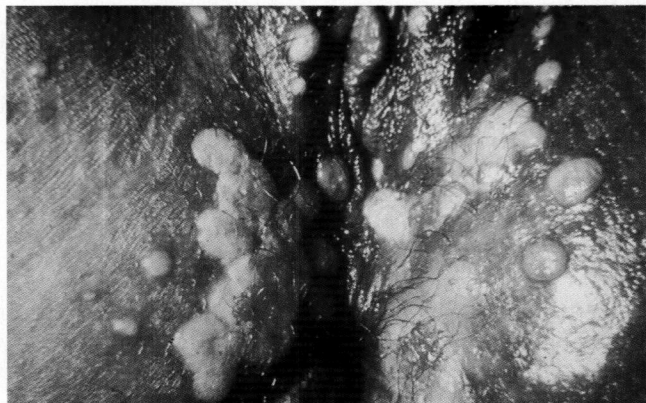

Figure 97-7. Condyloma lata of secondary syphilis.

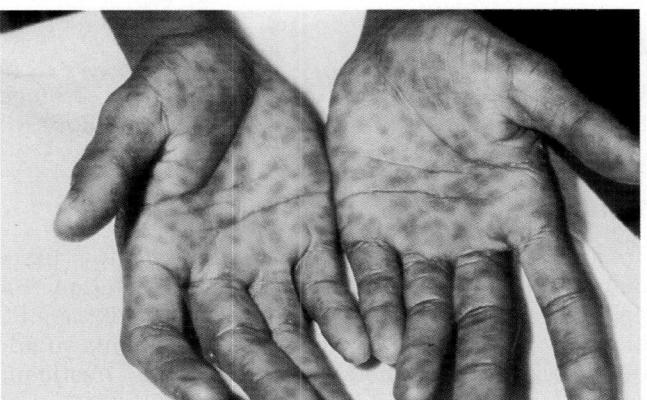

Figure 97-6. Palmar rash due to secondary syphilis.

Adenopathy is not a predominant feature of primary syphilis. If the chancre is on the genitalia, bilateral, painless, nonfluctuant, and slightly enlarged inguinal adenopathy may occur several days after appearance of the primary chancre.[5]

2. *Secondary.* Five to eight weeks after resolution of primary syphilis, the patient develops signs and symptoms of the secondary stage of the disease. The most common symptom is a total body rash (Figure 97-5). This rash begins on the trunk with a fine macular rash, which then spreads outward to the arms and legs, and may involve the palms and soles (Figure 97-6). As it progresses, it becomes papulosquamous and may appear slightly annular, often resembling the rash of pityriasis rosea. Mucous patches can be seen on the tongue, which are the oral manifestations of the skin rash. Condyloma lata (Figure 97-7) can develop, characterized by broad-based papules with flat moist tops, occurring in the perineal region and involving the anus, between the buttocks, and the labia. Constitutional symptoms are common during this stage, including fatigue, low-grade fever, malaise, headache, arthralgias, and generalized lymphadenopathy. Adenopathy may occur virtually anywhere in the body, including epitrochlear nodes. The nodes are discrete, nontender, and rubbery. Like the primary stage, secondary syphilis

will resolve spontaneously if untreated, and the patient enters the latent or tertiary stage of infection.

3. *Latent.* Once the clinical symptoms of secondary syphilis resolve, the patient's infection may become latent. There are no clinical symptoms during this stage, and laboratory testing is the only means to identify these individuals. Latent syphilis is divided into two categories: *early latent* syphilis is that which is acquired within the preceding year, and all other cases of latent syphilis are either *late latent* syphilis or latent syphilis of unknown duration.

4. *Tertiary.* After a latent period of at least 3 to 4 years, the patient may present with symptoms of tertiary syphilis. This stage predominantly involves the cardiovascular and nervous systems. Patients may present with thoracic aortic aneurysms, meningitis, peripheral neuropathy (tabes dorsalis), and gummatous lesions of the mucous membranes. Although common in the preantibiotic era, tertiary syphilis is now uncommon in the United States.[1,5,6]

Diagnosis

The only rapid means of diagnosing syphilis is the darkfield examination. This method involves viewing scrapings or fluid from lesions of primary or secondary syphilis under a darkfield microscope to identify the spirochete. Unfortunately, the sensitivity of darkfield microscopy is approximately 80%, and many hospitals and clinics do not have this technique routinely available.[7]

Serologic testing is the current standard for diagnosing secondary, latent, and tertiary syphilis. There are two types of serologic tests: nontreponemal (VDRL, RPR) and treponemal (MHA-TP and FTA-ABS). Both tests are necessary for definitive diagnosis. Nontreponemal tests measure nonspecific antibodies in the serum of patients with syphilis, and the titers vary with the stage and activity of disease. These tests become positive about 2 weeks after the primary chancre appears and are measured quantitatively. Titers are used to follow response to treatment. Because these tests are nonspecific to the treponeme and false-positive results can occur, positive test results should be confirmed with the more specific treponemal tests. Treponemal tests measure antibodies specific to the spirochete *T. pallidum.* These tests are more expensive and difficult to perform than the nonspecific tests, and as their titers do not predictably vary with treatment, the main value of these tests is in confirming positive nontreponemal test findings.[4,7]

Treatment

A one-time dose of benzathine penicillin G, 2.4 million U IM, is the treatment of choice for treating primary and secondary syphilis[1] (see Table 97-3 for alternative treatment regimens and for treatment of latent and tertiary syphilis). Sexual partners need to be evaluated; partners within the last 90 days should be tested but treated presumptively; and former partners of move than 90 days ago should be evaluated and treated if indicated. Because syphilis increases the risk of acquisition of HIV, all patients should be referred for testing. To ensure response to treatment, patients should be reexamined clinically and serologically 6 and 12 months after treatment. Successful treatment is confirmed by either a nonreactive nontreponemal test or a fourfold or greater decrease in titers after 6 months. Because syphilis is a reportable disease, patients with positive test results should be reported to the public health department.

In the pregnant patient with syphilis, congenital syphilis with its devastating outcome is a significant concern. Parenteral penicillin G is the only therapy with documented efficacy in these instances. In pregnant women with syphilis at any stage with a reported penicillin allergy, treatment with penicillin is still recommended after desensitization.[1]

Lymphogranuloma Venereum

Lymphogranuloma venereum is a chronic sexually transmitted disease caused by specific serotypes of *Chlamydia trachomatis.* Although this disease is prevalent in many tropical countries, it is rare in the United States and is seen primarily in patients who have traveled to endemic areas. The incubation period is 3 days to 3 weeks. A transient genital lesion that is small, is painless, and often goes unnoticed by the patient characterizes initial infection. Seven to 30 days after the primary lesion disappears, the secondary stage develops, characterized by involvement of the lymphatic channels and nodes of the genitalia, pelvis, and rectum. The patient usually presents at this secondary stage, when regional lymphadenitis appears. Inguinal lymphadenopathy is most often unilateral, and enlargement of the glands above and below Poupart's ligament give the characteristic lymphogranuloma venereum "groove sign." The enlarged nodes are often painful, with overlying erythema, but are not usually fluctuant. The nodes either eventually break down, with the formation of multiple draining sinuses, or form a hard inguinal mass without suppuration. Late complications result from the blockage of lymphatic channels by the infection, resulting in distal lymphedema.

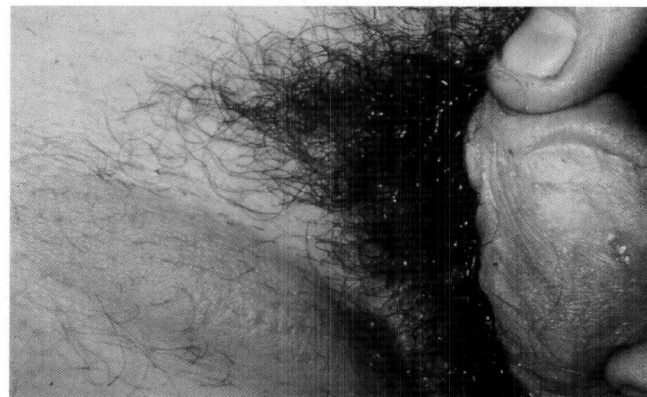

Figure 97-8. Ulcerative lesions of the penis from chancroid with accompanying fluctuant, tender, erythematous lymphadenitis (bubo).

Diagnosis

Diagnosis is based on the clinical picture and serologic testing. Other causes of inguinal lymphadenopathy and genital ulcers must be ruled out.

Treatment

Treatment is curative and prevents ongoing tissue damage. The preferred treatment is doxycycline, 100 mg PO bid for 3 weeks. Erythromycin base 500 mg PO qid × 21 days is an alternate regimen.[1] Patients should refer their sexual partners for evaluation and treatment, and all patients should be referred for HIV testing.

Chancroid

Chancroid is caused by *Haemophilus ducreyi,* a small gram-negative bacterium. This disease is common in developing countries[6] but rare in the United States, with only 38 cases reported to the Centers for Disease Control and Prevention (CDC) in 2001.[1] Outbreaks of chancroid have been reported in the United States, however, and physicians should be aware of the characteristics of this disease to recognize these occasional outbreaks when they occur.

Clinically, chancroid is characterized by multiple, painful genital ulcerations and inguinal bubo formation (Figure 97-8). After an incubation period of less than 1 week, the patient develops a short-lived, small, tender, red papule at the site of inoculation. This lesion rapidly ulcerates, and the patient develops multiple shallow, painful ulcers with sharply demarcated edges and purulent bases that last 1 to 2 weeks; in some patients, these lesions coalesce. Inguinal lymph node involvement is seen in 50% of patients, occurring 1 week after the ulcers begin. Typically, the patient develops a unilateral large, painful, fluctuant lymph node (bubo) in the groin. Overlying skin is thinned and erythematous, and suppuration is common. These buboes can spontaneously rupture.

On a clinical basis, it may be difficult to distinguish chancroid from genital herpes. The presence of a large, fluctuant bubo strongly suggests chancroid. However, if only ulcers are present, the patient can have either disease. Because herpes is much more common in the United States than chancroid (which tends to occur in isolated outbreaks), herpes should be the first diagnosis considered.

Diagnosis

Haemophilus ducreyi is difficult to culture, so diagnosis is based on clinical presentation and is often a diagnosis of exclusion, after other diseases such as herpes and syphilis are ruled out by testing. Definitive diagnosis requires isolation and identification of *H. ducreyi*, a fastidious organism requiring a special growth medium not routinely available. Since definitive diagnosis can be elusive, probable diagnosis can be made if all of the following criteria are met: (1) the patient has one or more painful genital ulcers; (2) the patient has no evidence of *T. pallidum* infection by darkfield examination or serologic testing; (3) the clinical presentation, appearance of genital ulcers, and regional lymphadenopathy are typical for chancroid; and (4) a test for HSV performed on the ulcer exudates is negative. When local outbreaks are known, the microbiology laboratory can prepare the special medium required to grow this organism to confirm cases as well as to follow containment of the infection.

The two recommended curative treatment regimens are one dose of azithromycin 1 g PO or one dose of ceftriaxone 250 mg IM (see Table 97-3 for more treatment options).[1] Co-infection with syphilis or HSV occurs in about 10% of patients who have chancroid acquired in the United States. Chancroid is a cofactor for HIV transmission, so all patients should be referred for HIV and other STD testing. Sexual partners of patients with chancroid should be examined and treated if they had sexual contact with the patient during the 10 days preceding the patient's onset of symptoms. To confirm response to treatment, patients should be referred for re-examination 3 to 7 days after initiation of therapy.

Drainage of buboes is not recommended, because these nodes usually respond to appropriate antibiotic treatment. If deemed necessary, nodes can be aspirated from the superior aspect of the fluctuant area with a needle; reaspiration is usually not necessary because the nodes respond quickly to antimicrobial treatment.

Granuloma Inguinale

Granuloma inguinale (donovanosis) is caused by *Calymmatobacterium granulomatis*, an intracellular gram-negative rod. The disease is rare in developed countries but is endemic in tropical and semitropical regions, including India, Papua New Guinea, central Australia, and southern Africa. The disease is presumed sexually transmitted, with an incubation period of 8 to 80 days.

Clinically, the disease manifests as chronic, painless, progressive ulcerative lesions. The lesions are irregular, clean-based granulomatous ulcers that are highly vascular ("beefy red appearance") and bleed easily on contact. The ulcer feels hard when palpated. Regional lymphadenopathy does not occur. As the lesion enlarges, it can be quite mutilating to the genitalia,

causing urethral stenosis over a period of months to years. Left untreated, it may result in lymphatic obstruction, producing genital edema and eventually lower extremity elephantiasis. In men, the sites of predilection are the prepuce, the coronal sulcus, and the frenulum. In women, lesions are typically found on the labia, but vaginal and cervical lesions can also occur.

Diagnosis is difficult and requires identification of the infectious agent, which appears as short, pleomorphic rods with bipolar staining. Donovan bodies may be seen within histiocytes on tissue crush preparation or biopsy. The causative organism is very difficult to culture.

Treatment halts progression of the lesions, but relapse can occur up to 18 months after apparently successful treatment. Recommended regimens include doxycycline 100 mg PO bid for at least 3 weeks or until the lesions have healed, or trimethoprim-sulfamethoxazole (Bactrim DS), one tablet PO bid for 3 weeks. Alternate regimens include ciprofloxacin 750 mg PO bid, erythromycin base 500 mg PO qid, or azithromycin 1 g PO weekly; all regirrens should be for at least 3 weeks (see Table 97-3).

Patients should be followed clinically until signs and symptoms have resolved. Persons who have had sexual contact with the patient within 60 days of symptom onset should be examined and offered therapy. Patients should be screened for other STDs.

Condylomata Acuminata

Anogenital warts are caused by the human papilloma virus (HPV), and more than 30 types of HPV can infect the genital tract. HPV infections are most often sexually transmitted, and lesions are most common at the site of greatest trauma during sexual intercourse. Most HPV cases are asymptomatic or subclinical, with only approximately 1% resulting in clinically apparent warts. Most visible genital warts are caused by HPV types 6 and 11 and are benign. Other HPV types have been associated with external genital squamous intraepithelial neoplasia, however, as well as vaginal, anal, and cervical intraepithelial dysplasia and squamous cell carcinoma.

Warts may be single or multiple (Figure 97-9). Warts on the warm, moist, nonhairy skin tend to be soft and nonkeratinized, whereas those on the dry hairy skin are more firm and keratinized. The lesions can be broad-based, pedunculated, or pigmented. Depending on the size and location, warts can be painful, friable, or pruritic. Warts that are indurated, fixed, ulcerated, and darkly pigmented may require biopsy to rule out carcinoma.

Diagnosis is usually made clinically. In women, a speculum examination is indicated to evaluate the patient for intravaginal and cervical lesions. Occasionally, HPV infections may be confused with the condyloma lata of syphilis. If there is any doubt about the diagnosis, or if warts have high-risk characteristics, biopsy and darkfield microscopy of tissue are indicated, as well as serologic testing for syphilis.

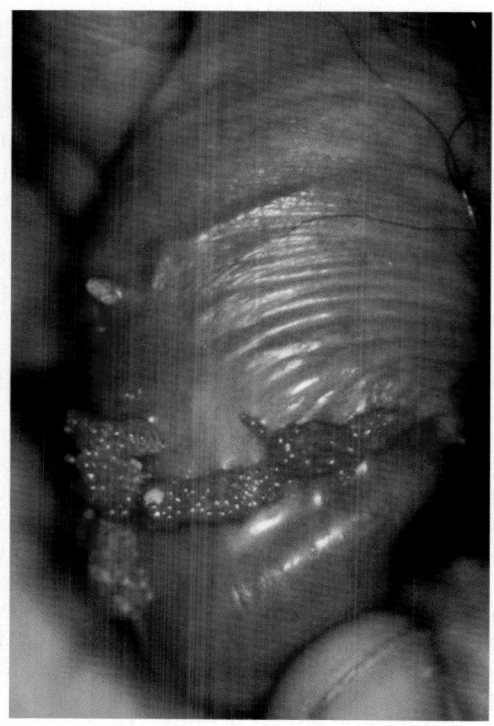

Figure 97-9. Genital warts due to human papilloma virus.

Treatment is aimed at removal of symptomatic warts, including those that cause obstructive symptoms of the urethral meatus or rectum.. Although treatment may lead to wart-free periods, there are no data that show that treatment affects the course of disease in the patient or these patients or reduces infectivity. If left untreated, visible genital warts may resolve spontaneously, remain unchanged, or increase in number.

There are many available treatment options, and no evidence suggests that any of the available treatments is superior to the others; all have significant failure and recurrence rates. For patient-applied regimens, the patient must be able to identify and reach the warts to be treated with these methods. Provider-administered regimens often require ongoing treatments on a weekly basis and are usually best administered by a primary care physician, who can follow the patient for response to therapy. In general, warts located on moist surfaces respond better to topical treatments than do the keratinized warts found on drier surfaces.

Patient preference, available resources, and physician experience should guide treatment. Most of these treatments are administered by the patient's primary care physician and not through the emergency department.

Treatment regimens can be divided into patient-applied and provider-administered. Patient-applied regimens include the following:

- Podofilox 0.5% solution or gel, applied twice a day for 3 days, followed by 4 days of no therapy. This may be repeated, as necessary, for up to four cycles.
- Imiquimod 5% cream, applied once daily at bedtime, three times a week for up to 16 weeks. The treatment

area should be washed with soap and water 6 to 10 hours after application.

Provider-administered regimens include the following:

- Cryotherapy with liquid nitrogen or cryoprobe. This may need to be repeated every 1 to 2 weeks.
- Podophyllin resin, 10% to 25%
- Trichloroacetic acid or dichloroacetic acid 80% to 90%
- Surgical removal

Podophyllin and podophyllum resin should be avoided in pregnant patients because of possible teratogenic effects. Imiquimod is also not approved for use during pregnancy. Immunosuppressed patients are more likely to have poor response to treatment, increased relapse rates, and dysplasia and need close follow-up. All patients need screening for other sexually transmitted infections. Treatment of partners is not necessary.[1]

DISORDERS CHARACTERIZED BY GENITAL DISCHARGE

Patients with diseases that fall into this group tend to present with urethral or cervical discharge and do not have ulcerations or significant lymphadenopathy. These infections include chlamydia, gonorrhea, nongonococcal urethritis, trichomoniasis, bacterial vaginosis, candidiasis, and pelvic inflammatory disease. Bacterial vaginosis and candidiasis are not sexually transmitted diseases but are often diagnosed in patients undergoing evaluation for sexually transmitted diseases. Chlamydia and gonorrhea, the two most common nonulcerative STDs, can also cause vaginal discharge, especially in the setting of mucopurulent cervicitis, and both tend to cause urethral discharge in men. These two infections commonly occur concurrently, and clinical manifestations of these two infections are similar. It is usually not possible to distinguish between the two diseases based on signs and symptoms alone, and patients are often appropriately treated presumptively for both infections (see Table 97-1).

Chlamydia

In the United States, chlamydia causes an estimated 3 to 5 million cases annually, making it the most commonly reported sexually transmitted disease.[1] The causative organism is *Chlamydia trachomatis*, an obligate intracellular organism that infects columnar and pseudostratified columnar epithelial surfaces.[4,7] Infection with *C. trachomatis* can cause a variety of symptoms, including urethritis, cervicitis, epididymitis, proctitis, prostatitis, pelvic inflammatory disease (PID), and perihepatitis, also known as Fitz-Hugh–Curtis syndrome.

Symptoms appear after an incubation period of 1 to 3 weeks. Although urethritis is the most common symptom in men, men can also present with epididymitis or both in combination. When symptomatic, women may report symptoms ranging from dysuria to peritonitis. Often, women have only vague, nonspecific symptoms of vaginal discharge or bleeding, abdominal or pelvic pain, or some combination thereof. Unfortunately, infection is commonly asymptomatic; estimates show that up to 75% of infected women and 50% of infected men have no symptoms. The highest rate of infection is in sexually active adolescent females, with infection rates as high as 10% in this group. Up to 40% of women with untreated chlamydia infection develop PID, with the subsequent increased risk of ectopic pregnancy and infertility. Because of the high rate of asymptomatic infection and the increased risk for developing PID and its sequelae, screening of high-risk patients (those with multiple sexual partners) for disease may be appropriate in the emergency department as long as adequate follow-up is ensured. The CDC recommends chlamydia testing for all women with cervical infections and all pregnant patients.[1]

Until recently, the gold standard for diagnosing chlamydia was cell culture. Unfortunately, this test is labor-intensive, is fraught with difficulties, and takes days for definitive results. Although other nonculture techniques (DNA probe and latex agglutination testing) have been used in the 1990s to make the diagnosis of chlamydia, new, recently available tests utilizing nucleic amplification techniques have better sensitivity and specificity than culture and are rapidly becoming the new gold standard. These nucleic acid amplification tests (NAATs) include ligase chain reaction, polymerase chain reaction (PCR), strand displacement amplification, and transcript-mediated amplification. All techniques amplify nucleic acid sequences specific to the organism being tested and do not require viable organisms. NAATs have sensitivities better than culture (>90% versus 60-80%, respectively), with specificities greater than 99%. These new NAATs are more sensitive than other nonculture tests (DNA probe testing, latex agglutination testing) by 17% to 35%.[4,8-10] NAATs can be performed on swabs (endocervical or urethral) and urine. Sensitivities of NAATs are lower when performed on urine than on endocervical swabs,[9,11] making endocervical swabs the test of choice in females. Urine screening using NAATs is adequate for symptomatic males, and urethral swabs are generally not necessary.[8,10,11] In sexual abuse cases, culture should still be performed in addition to the NAAT for medicolegal purposes.[1]

Treatment of chlamydia consists of azithromycin 1 g PO as a single dose or doxycycline 100 mg PO bid for 7 days.[1] Coinfection with gonorrhea is common, so treating patients for both diseases is recommended unless gonorrhea is definitively ruled out (see Table 97-3 for alternative regimens). Patients should be instructed to abstain from sexual intercourse for 7 days after completion of treatment (either single-dose therapy or the 7-day regimen of doxycycline). Sexual partners need to be tested and treated, and the index patient should be instructed to abstain from sexual intercourse until all sexual partners are treated. Follow-up for test of cure is not required unless symptoms persist or reinfection is suspected.

Nongonococcal Urethritis

Nongonococcal urethritis is characterized by urethral discharge, dysuria, or urethral pruritus. Although *C. trachomatis* is implicated in many cases,[12] the cause in some cases is unknown. All patients with suggestive presenting symptoms should be evaluated for both gonorrhea and chlamydia. The diagnosis is made by Gram stain (>5 white blood cells [WBCs] per high-power field and no gram-negative diplococci),[1] positive leukocyte esterase test on urinalysis, or more than 10 WBCs per high-power field on urinalysis. Treatment consists of azithromycin 1 g (single oral dose) or doxycycline 100 mg PO bid for 7 days.[1] In women, other causes of vaginal discharge must be ruled out, including chlamydia, trichomoniasis, and candidiasis.

Gonorrhea

Gonorrhea is the second most frequently reported STD after chlamydia, with an estimated 600,000 new *N. gonorrhoeae* infections in the United States each year.[1] As infection affects columnar or transitional epithelium, this organism affects the urethra, rectum, cervical canal, pharynx, upper female genital tract, and conjunctival sac.

The most common clinical presentation in men is acute urethritis, characterized by dysuria and a penile discharge (Figure 97-10), starting within 1 to 14 days of exposure. On examination, the patient may have urethral meatal erythema and a purulent urethral discharge. Patients may present with epididymitis, although this is uncommon.

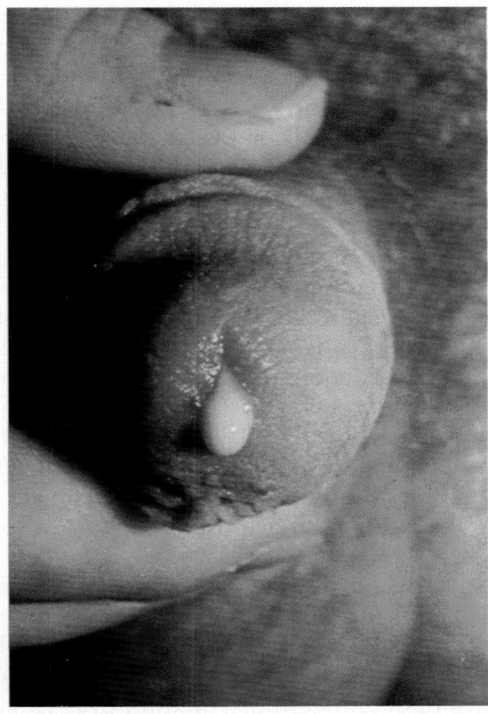

Figure 97-10. Purulent urethral discharge in a patient with gonorrhea.

In women, primary infections are often asymptomatic or produce only vague symptoms such as vaginal discharge, abnormal vaginal bleeding, abdominal or pelvic pain, dyspareunia or dysuria, and frequency. Patients may not present until complications such as pelvic inflammatury disease (PID) have occurred, and up to 20% of women with untreated gonorrhea develop PID. Like chlamydia, symptomatic and asymptomatic gonorrhea infection can cause PID with subsequent tubal scarring that may lead to infertility or ectopic pregnancy.

Gonorrhea can also infect the oropharynx and anorectal area. Gonococcal infection of the pharynx is often asymptomatic, but in symptomatic cases patients present with sore throat and exudative tonsillitis. Most cases are self-limited. Anorectal involvement is more common in individuals who engage in receptive anal intercourse. Like pharyngeal infection, it is often asymptomatic. When symptomatic, patients complain of rectal discomfort or pain, tenesmus, constipation, dyspareunia, pruritus ani, and purulent or mucoid anal discharge or bleeding. Anoscopy reveals friable mucosa and mucopurulent exudate.

Gonococcal conjunctivitis can be a sight-threatening infection, so recognition of this infection is crucial. This infection can occur in newborns (acquired during passage through an infected birth canal) and in adults, who often acquire the infection by direct inoculation from organisms on the fingers and then rubbed onto the eye. Symptomatic conjunctivitis is characterized by beefy red conjunctiva, chemosis, and purulent eye discharge that is often copious. If untreated, it can progress to corneal ulceration or, in severe cases, gonococcal endophthalmitis.

Disseminated gonococcal infection (DGI) results from gonococcal bacteremia and occurs more frequently in women than men. Typically, it presents with the arthritis-dermatitis syndrome, characterized by a combination of any or all of the following: fevers, chills, oligoarticular arthritis or arthralgias, rash, and tenosynovitis. The rash of DGI is pustular acral skin lesions, usually found peripherally on the extremities. The lesions are described as necrotic pustules on an erythematous base and are tender to palpation. These lesions represent septic emboli to small blood vessels during bacteremia. Joint involvement, the second most common manifestation of DGI, manifests with an acute monoarticular or oligoarticular septic arthritis. The knees are most commonly involved, followed by elbows, ankles, wrists, and small joints of the hands and feet. The involved joint is erythematous, is warm, often has an effusion, and is painful to range of motion. Other manifestations of DGI, although very rare, include hepatitis, myocarditis, endocarditis, and meningitis.

Definitive diagnosis of DGI is confirmed by isolating gonococci from the blood, synovial fluid, or infected skin; unfortunately, such isolation has relatively poor sensitivity. Presumptive diagnosis of DGI is based on the appropriate clinical presentation, plus isolation of gonococci from a source site.

Diagnosis

Diagnostic tests for gonorrhea include Gram stain, culture, and NAATs. Gram stain is most useful in symptomatic men with urethritis or in patients with gonococcal conjunctivitis. In these cases, it is an excellent diagnostic test, with a sensitivity and specificity approaching 100%,[13,14] and results are available rapidly. However, this test is less useful in asymptomatic men and all women, owing to its decreased sensitivity in these groups.

Culture for gonorrhea is considered the gold standard for diagnosis.[13] Because this test can be used to isolate the organism for antimicrobial testing and determination of antibiotic sensitivities, it is useful in areas of rapidly emerging resistance. However, the utility of this test may be limited by improper specimen collection and handling. To maximize the yield of gonococcal culture, inoculating the specimen directly onto the appropriate medium optimizes viability of the organisms. If the specimen is from a sterile site, such as cerebrospinal fluid or synovial fluid, a nonselective medium such as chocolate agar is best. Specimens from nonsterile sites such as the cervix, urethra, rectum, or oropharynx, where normal bacterial flora are present, should be inoculated on selective media such as Martin-Lewis agar. If not transported immediately to the laboratory, specimens should be incubated at 35° to 36.5° C in a carbon dioxide–enriched atmosphere after collection and transported to the laboratory in a carbon dioxide–enriched atmosphere.[4,13,14]

The NAATs have good sensitivity and excellent specificity for detection of gonorrhea from endocervical, urethral, and urine samples. These tests are approved by the Food and Drug Administration for the detection of *C. trachomatis* and *N. gonorrhoeae* in endocervical swabs from women, urethral swabs from men, and urine from both men and women.[13] Although sensitivities of NAATs are comparable with culture (95-99%), selected NAATs may be less sensitive when performed on urine than when performed on endocervical specimens or male urethral swabs. Therefore, in symptomatic patients, NAATs of endocervical swabs from women or urethral swabs from males are good alternatives to gonococcal culture, particularly when appropriate techniques for maximizing organism viability and culture cannot be achieved.[13-15]

Although NAATs are useful for diagnosing cervical and urethral gonorrhea, culture is required for diagnosing organisms from sites such as the oropharynx, synovial fluid, anorectal area, and cerebrospinal fluid. In addition, culture is the test of choice when the results will be used as evidence in legal investigations.

Treatment

There are several recommendations for single-dose therapy for gonorrhea (see Table 97-3); the most universally recommended are single doses of ceftriaxone 125 mg IM or cefixime 400 mg PO.[1] Although quinolones are listed as possible choices, the increasing frequency of quinolone-resistant strains in Asia, Hawaii, and California has led to the recommendation that these agents not be used to treat gonorrhea acquired in these areas.[1] Because co-infection with chlamydia is so common, treatment for presumptive chlamydia should also be provided unless co-infection can be ruled out. Sexual partners need referral for evaluation, testing, and treatment. Patients should be instructed to avoid sexual intercourse until therapy is completed and until they and their sexual partners are no longer symptomatic. Referral for HIV testing should be offered.

Because emergency departments are often used as a source of primary health care, the role of emergency departments in screening and treating STDs has been debated. A major area of difficulty in using emergency departments for this purpose is that many test results are not available during the emergency department visit, and treatment decisions are therefore made presumptively. Errors are made in both overtreating and undertreating STDs in this setting. Although it has been shown that health care providers are significantly overtreating women who test negative for gonorrhea and chlamydia,[16] one third of patients who test positive for STDs in the emergency department are not treated during the initial visit, and the majority of untreated patients do not return for subsequent treatment.[16-18] As a result, providers must weigh the cost of overtreatment against the risk of untreated disease. Because these diseases pose a significant public health risk, it is recommended that patients be treated presumptively in the emergency department unless good follow-up for test results can be ensured.

Trichomonas

Trichomoniasis is caused by *Trichomonas vaginalis*, a flagellated protozoan. It is the most common nonviral sexually transmitted disease in the world, with an estimated 173 million new infections worldwide in 1999. As with other vaginal infections, up to 50% of infected women are asymptomatic. The most common presenting symptoms include dysuria, vulvar irritation or itching, and vaginal discharge, often described as thin, malodorous, and yellow-green. Affected patients may also report lower abdominal pain, discomfort, or dyspareunia. Males are frequently asymptomatic, and most often present as partners of infected women. Trichomonas has been implicated as a cause of nongono-coccal urethritis in men, possibly responsible for up to 20% of cases.[19] Rarely, men report purulent urethral discharge or symptoms consistent with prostatitis or epididymitis.

On physical examination, vaginal discharge is noted in up to 70% of patients, ranging in description from thin and scanty to the classic description of thick, frothy yellow discharge. Vaginal pH is above 4.5. Punctate mucosal hemorrhages of the cervix ("strawberry" cervix) has been described in 2% to 10% of patients. The history and examination findings are not sensitive or specific enough to make the diagnosis on clinical grounds alone, however.

The diagnosis is most often made by microscopic examination of a wet-mount slide, but this method has a sensitivity of only 60% to 70%, and sensitivity varies with the skill and thoroughness of the examiner. Culture is more sensitive than wet mount but is not widely performed. Results are not available in a timely manner for emergency department diagnosis and treatment, and few clinical laboratories have the culture material. In men, urine sediment can be examined for trichomonads and can also be sent for culture. PCR is being studied as an alternate method for diagnosis of trichomoniasis. Several PCR primers have been studied and each has demonstrated higher sensitivity than wet mount or culture.[20,21] PCR has also been found to be highly specific, exceeding 95%. In addition, PCR analysis of specimens obtained from the distal vagina had a higher sensitivity and specificity for diagnosis of trichomoniasis than wet mount or culture of specimens obtained during a speculum examination, suggesting a role for less invasive diagnostic techniques such as vaginal introitus swabs.[20,22] Despite these promising studies, results of PCR testing are not available for point-of-care testing. At this point, the most promising role for PCR testing for trichomonas is as part of a combination screening test with chlamydia and gonorrhea.[21]

The only drug approved by the Food and Drug Administration for treatment of trichomoniasis in the United States is metronidazole, with a recommended single dose of 2 g PO. Alternate therapy is metronidazole 500 mg PO bid for 7 days (see Table 97-4). These recommendations are the same in HIV-positive women with trichomoniasis. Topical metronidazole is available but is less efficacious for treatment of trichomoni-

Table 97-4. Characteristics of Vulvovaginitis by Cause

	pH	Discharge Appearance	Wet Mount	Treatment
Bacterial vaginosis	>4.5	Gray, white, milky/creamy; amine odor present	Clue cells present	Metronidazole 500 mg PO bid × 7 days or clindamycin cream 2% intravaginally qhs × 7 days or metronidazole gel 0.75% intravaginally bid × 5 days
Trichomonas	>4.5	Gray, yellow, greenish or white; often frothy; homogeneous	Trichomonads present	Metronidazole 2 g PO × 1 or metronidazole 500 mg PO bid × 7 days
Candida	<4.5	White, often curdy	Mycelia present	Fluconazole 150 mg PO × 1 or intravaginal agents

asis than oral preparations and is not recommended for use.

Trichomoniasis has been associated with premature rupture of membranes, premature labor, low birth weight, and post-hysterectomy infection. Symptomatic pregnant women should be treated with a single dose of metronidazole, 2 g PO. Metronidazole does not appear to be associated with an increased teratogenic risk during pregnancy.[23] The role for treatment of asymptomatic pregnant women infected with trichomonas is less clear, and routine screening and treatment of asymptomatic women are not recommended.[24]

Because of the disulfiram-like reaction that can be seen in patients taking metronidazole, patients should be counseled to avoid alcohol during therapy and for 72 hours after the last dose of oral metronidazole. Sexual partners of patients with *T. vaginalis* should be treated, and patients should be instructed to avoid sex until they and their partners are clinically cured.

Candida

Vulvovaginal candidiasis is most often caused by *Candida albicans* but can be caused by other candida species and other yeasts. It is estimated that 75% of women will have at least one episode of yeast vulvovaginitis in their lifetime, and 40% to 45% will have two or more episodes.

Common presenting symptoms include vulvar itching or soreness, vaginal discharge, dyspareunia, and dysuria. Characteristic examination findings are vulvar erythema, vulvar edema or excoriation, and raised, white adherent vaginal plaques. Satellite lesions can also be seen. Vaginal pH is normal (<4.5). Because none of these symptoms or signs is specific for candidiasis and the history and examination findings are relatively unreliable,[25] diagnostic testing is indicated.

Diagnosis is typically based on wet-mount microscopy using potassium hydroxide preparation or Gram stain demonstrating yeast or pseudohyphae. The sensitivities of these tests range from 40% to 70%. Culture is considered the gold standard, but 10% to 20% of asymptomatic women harbor *Candida* species and other yeasts in the vagina. Latex agglutination tests are also available but do not seem to offer benefit over microscopy.[25]

Multiple short-course topical preparations are available for treatment and result in an 80% to 95% cure rate in patients who complete therapy (see Table 97-4 for recommended regimens). Fluconazole is the only oral agent that is approved by the Food and Drug Administration for the treatment of candidiasis. Many of the topical preparations are available over the counter. Self-medication with over-the-counter preparations should only be advised for women who have been diagnosed previously with vulvovaginal candidiasis and have recurrence of the same symptoms. Unnecessary or inappropriate use of over-the-counter preparations is common, can lead to contact or irritant vulvar dermatitis, and may delay treatment of other causes of vulvovaginitis. In addition, patients should be counseled that vaginal preparations are oil-based and may weaken latex condoms and diaphragms.

Candidal infections can be divided into complicated and uncomplicated types. Uncomplicated vaginitis is seen in 90% of patients and is characterized by mild to moderate symptoms due to *Candida albicans* in a normal host. It responds readily to short-course treatments. Complicated infections, with severe or recurrent symptoms (four or more episodes of vulvovaginal candidiasis each year), tend to occur in hosts with complicating medical problems (e.g., immunosuppression, poorly controlled diabetes mellitus) and require longer courses of treatment (e.g., 7-14 days of topical therapy or a 150-mg oral dose of fluconazole repeated 3 days later).[26] Vulvovaginal candidiasis in HIV-positive patients is not considered complicated and should be treated as uncomplicated vulvovaginal candidiasis.

Vulvovaginal candidiasis occurs frequently during pregnancy and may be more difficult to cure. Only topical azole therapies, applied for 7 days, are recommended for use during pregnancy; fluconazole is contraindicated.

There is no evidence to support treatment of asymptomatic sexual partners. In addition, there is no direct association between yeast infection and other STDs, and no difference in yeast isolation rates in STD versus non-STD patients.

Bacterial Vaginosis

Bacterial vaginosis occurs due to a shift in bacterial flora in the vagina, with the normal H_2O_2-producing *Lactobacillus* species being replaced with high concentrations of a polymicrobial group, including anaerobic bacteria (*Prevotella*, *Mobiluncus*, and *Bacterioides* species), *Gardnerella vaginalis*, and *Mycoplasma hominis*, and an attendant increase in the vaginal pH from 4.5 to as high as 7.0. Bacterial vaginosis is the most common cause of vaginal discharge and malodor. However, up to 50% of women with bacterial vaginosis are asymptomatic.

The most common symptom is vaginal discharge, often with an offensive vaginal odor, which may be accentuated after coitus (the pH of semen induces a physiologic "whiff test," releasing a fishy odor). Vaginal pruritus and irritation are not common complaints. On examination, a thin, white, homogeneous discharge is present.

Diagnosis can be made using the Amsel criteria (Table 97-4).[27] Three of the four criteria must be present for diagnosis:
1. A thin, white, homogeneous discharge
2. Presence of clue cells in microscopic examination. True clue cells are epithelial cells that are so heavily stippled with bacteria that the cell borders are obscured. Epithelial cells with few bacteria do not classify as clue cells.
3. pH of vaginal fluid > 4.5
4. A fishy odor of vaginal discharge before or after the addition of 10% KOH (whiff test)

Diagnosis can also be made with Gram stain, determining the relative concentration of bacterial morphotypes (Nugent criteria). Culture isolation of *G. vaginalis* is not useful, as it can be cultured from the vagina of more than 50% of healthy women and is therefore not specific. Other diagnostic modalities include a DNA probe-based test (Affirm VP III) and card tests, which detect elevated pH as well as the presence of elevated amine concentration (FemExam test) or proline amino-peptidase (Pip Activity TestCard). The card tests indicate the presence of two of the four criteria recommended for diagnosis by the CDC, so they must be used in correlation with microscopy or appropriate examination findings and are not used in isolation to make the diagnosis.

All women who have symptomatic disease require treatment. Bacterial vaginosis is associated with an increased risk of acute upper genital tract infection by the various organisms associated with upper tract infection.[28] It is not known whether treatment of bacterial vaginosis reduces the risk of ascending infection, so screening for and treatment of bacterial vaginosis in asymptomatic women is not recommended at this time. Bacterial vaginosis has also been associated with endometritis and PID. It is also associated with vaginal cuff cellulitis after invasive procedures, including endometrial biopsy, hysterectomy, and placement of an intrauterine device, and there may be some role for preprocedural prophylaxis in certain patients. Recommended treatment regimens include metronidazole 500 mg PO bid for 7 days, metronidazole gel 0.75% 5 g intravaginally every day for 5 days, or clindamycin cream 2%, 5 g intravaginally at bedtime for 7 days. The vaginal cream may be less efficacious than oral metronidazole. Alternative regimens include metronidazole 2 g PO in a single dose, or clindamycin 300 mg PO bid for 7 days. However, the alternative regimens have lower efficacy for bacterial vaginosis. Patients should be advised to avoid alcohol during treatment with metronidazole. Treatment of partners does not affect response to therapy or recurrence rates in clinical trials and is therefore not recommended.[29]

Bacterial vaginosis during pregnancy is associated with premature rupture of membranes and preterm labor, preterm birth, and postpartum endometritis. Studies have not demonstrated a benefit of treatment for asymptomatic pregnant patients; however, among women with a previous preterm birth or those who are at high risk for preterm birth, treatment with metronidazole has been shown to reduce the risk of spontaneous preterm birth.[30-32] The treatment of asymptomatic bacterial vaginosis in pregnant women does not reduce the occurrence of preterm delivery. Recommended treatment regimens in pregnancy include metronidazole 250 mg PO tid for 7 days or clindamycin 300 mg PO bid for 7 days. Topical agents are not recommended for use during pregnancy.[1] Metronidazole use during pregnancy has no demonstrated association with teratogenic or mutagenic effects in newborns.

Other Causes of Genital Discomfort

Many other conditions manifest with vulvovaginal itching or discharge. The differential diagnosis includes the sexually transmitted and vaginal infections discussed previously, as well as allergic or chem-ical vaginitis, atrophic vaginitis, scabies, pediculosis pubis (genital lice), and vaginal foreign bodies.

Chemical vaginitis is most commonly associated with the use of douches, scented soaps, or feminine hygiene products. In addition, some women with a latex allergy may present with vaginal itching and discomfort after intercourse with a partner who uses condoms. Diagnosis is by history, and discontinuing use of the offending agent is usually sufficient treatment.

Atrophic vaginitis occurs when levels of circulating estrogens decrease after menopause. Patients may report increased vaginal itching, vulvar discomfort, and dyspareunia. Other sources of infection, such as candida, must be ruled out because relative lack of estrogen predisposes to vaginal and vulvar infections. Treatment consists of topical estrogen creams.

The mite *Sarcoptes scabiei* causes scabies infestation, and any part of the body may be affected. Transmission is by skin contact. The main symptom is pruritus, which is caused by a hypersensitivity reaction to mite excrement. The diagnosis is made clinically by identification of characteristic silvery lines seen in the skin where the mites have burrowed. There may also be papules or nodules, especially in the genital area. Scrapings viewed under light microscopy reveal mites, confirming the diagnosis. Treatment regimens include permethrin 5% cream, applied to the whole body from the neck down and washed off after 12 hours. Treatment should be repeated in 1 week. Antihistamines and topical creams may give symptomatic relief. Potentially contaminated clothes and bedding should be washed at high temperature, or not used for 72 hours (mites die when separated from the human host for 72 hours). Sexual and household contacts should be treated. Other treatment choices include lindane, crotamiton (Eurax) cream, or 5% sulfur ointment. Lindane should not be used on infants or during pregnancy.

Phthirus pubis is a crab louse transmitted by close body contact. Adult lice infest pubic hair, body hair, and occasionally the eyebrows and eyelashes. Eggs (nits) adhere to the hairs. The main symptom is pruritus due to hypersensitivity reaction to the feeding lice. Diagnosis is based on finding adult lice or eggs. A number of treatments are available. Lotions are likely more effective than shampoos and should be applied to all body hair. Treatment regimens include permethrin 1% cream rinse, malathion 0.5%, or lindane 1% cream. Sexual partners should be treated. Patients should be screened for other STDs.

Pelvic Inflammatory Disease

Perspective

Pelvic inflammatory disease is a spectrum of disorders of the female upper genital tract, including any combination of endometritis, salpingitis, peritonitis, or tubo-ovarian abscess. The serious complications of PID (infertility, ectopic pregnancy, and chronic pelvic pain) account for a significant proportion of non-HIV STD morbidity in the United States and afflict approximately 25% of diagnosed patients.[33] PID is reported to be the most common serious infection in women of reproductive age and causes approximately 30% of infertility cases, 50% of ectopic pregnancies, and many cases of chronic pelvic pain.[34] Approximately 750,000 cases of PID are diagnosed annually in the United States, with an estimated direct medical cost in 1998 of $1.8 billion and an average per-person cost of $2150. Estimated average lifetime costs for women who developed major complications were $6350 for chronic pelvic pain, $6840 for ectopic pregnancy, and $1270 for infertility.[33]

Principles of Disease

Pelvic inflammatory disease is an ascending infection, with the infecting microorganisms spreading from the cervix and vagina to the upper portions of the genital tract. The most commonly implicated organisms are *Chlamydia trachomatis* and *Neisseria gonorrhoeae*. However, the cause of PID is often polymicrobial, and various microorganisms have been recovered from the upper genital tract of patients with acute PID, including gonorrhea, chlamydia, genital mycoplasmas, and anaerobic and aerobic bacteria from endogenous vaginal flora such as *Prevotella* sp, peptostreptococci, *Gardnerella vaginalis*, *E. coli*, *H. influenzae*, and aerobic streptococci.[35,36] Although organisms that are associated with sexual transmission are those most commonly found with PID, this infection can be caused by nonsexually acquired organisms.

Risk factors for PID include young age, multiple sexual partners, cigarette smoking, and menses. Intrauterine contraceptive devices have previously been implicated as a major risk factor for PID; however, IUDs increase the risk of PID only in the first month after insertion.

Clinical Features

Owing to the wide variety of presenting signs and symptoms, acute PID is challenging to diagnose. The most common presenting symptom is lower abdominal pain. Other common symptoms include dyspareunia, abnormal bleeding, and abnormal cervical or vaginal discharge. Common signs include lower abdominal tenderness, cervical motion or adnexal tenderness (most often bilateral) on bimanual examination, and fever greater than 38° C.[1,36,37]

Many women with PID demonstrate mild, vague, or subtle symptoms, often not recognized as PID. Unrecognized PID is probably as common, if not more common, than clinically apparent disease, and it is estimated that up to two thirds of cases go unrecognized. *Silent* or *atypical PID* is a term that has been used to describe women with documented tubal infertility who have no history of being diagnosed with PID despite confirmed chronic inflammatory residua. Unrecognized or atypical PID is usually characterized by abdominal pain, abnormal uterine bleeding, and mucopurulent endocervical discharge.

Patients can also present with right upper quadrant pain and tenderness, which may be preceded or accompanied by the signs and symptoms of PID. This syndrome, known as *perihepatitis* or Fitz-Hugh–Curtis

syndrome, has been associated with both gonococcal and chlamydial salpingitis. Up to 10% of patients with PID develop this syndrome, depending on the organisms implicated as the cause of the PID.

Unfortunately, the clinical diagnosis of PID is insensitive. One study comparing clinical diagnosis with laparoscopic findings showed that the clinical diagnosis of PID is no more accurate than chance when compared with biopsy-confirmed diagnosis.[38] Other laparoscopic studies support these findings, with sensitivities of the clinical examination ranging from 50% to 75%.[34,39] No single historical physical or laboratory finding is adequately sensitive or specific to make the diagnosis of PID. Because of the difficulty in making this diagnosis and the serious long-term sequelae of PID, the CDC recommends that clinicians maintain a low threshold for diagnosing and treating patients for PID.

The CDC recommends empiric treatment of PID in sexually active young women if the following minimum criteria are present without other identifiable causes:
- Uterine tenderness, adnexal tenderness, or both
- Cervical motion tenderness

Controversy also surrounds what constitutes cervical motion tenderness. Although the traditional "chandelier sign" of severe tenderness has been taught as the criterion standard, studies indicate that the patient herself should be questioned about her degree of pain. If it is more than the usual discomfort experienced by the patient during a pelvic examination, this should be considered positive for cervical motion tenderness.

Other criteria that support the diagnosis of PID but are not necessary to make the diagnosis include the following:
- Oral temperature greater than 38° C
- Abnormal cervical or vaginal mucopurulent discharge
- Presence of WBCs on wet mount of vaginal secretions
- Elevated erythrocyte sedimentation rate
- Elevated C-reactive protein level
- Laboratory documentation of cervical infection with gonorrhea or chlamydia

When more criteria for diagnosis are met, the specificity increases but the sensitivity decreases. The absence of WBCs on wet mount makes the diagnosis of PID unlikely, and in these cases other causes of abdominal pain should be sought. Ultrasonography may also be useful in the diagnosis of PID, especially in identifying tubo-ovarian abscess or pyosalpinx. If the diagnosis is unclear, particularly in patients who present with fever and peritoneal signs, further testing is indicated. In these cases, computed tomography may rule out other causes of peritoneal clinical findings, such as appendicitis or diverticulitis, and in some cases laparoscopy may be necessary to determine the cause of the patient's illness.

Differential Diagnosis

The differential diagnosis of lower abdominal pain in young women is broad. Other common diagnoses

Table 97-5. Treatment for Pelvic Inflammatory Disease

	Parenteral Treatment	Oral Treatment
Regimen A	Cefotetan 2 g IV bid *or* cefoxitin 2 g IV q6h *plus* doxycycline 100 mg PO or IV q12h	Ofloxacin 400 mg PO bid × 14 days *or* levofloxacin 500 mg PO qd × 14 days *with or without* metronidazole 500 mg PO bid × 14 days
Regimen B	Clindamycin 900 mg IV q8h *plus* gentamicin loading dose IV 12 mg/kg IV or IM followed by maintenance 1.5 mg/kg IV or IM q8h. May substitute with single daily dosing regimen	Ceftriaxone 250 mg IM × 1 *or* cefoxitin 2 g IM × 1 and probenecid 1 g PO × 1 *plus* doxycycline 100 mg PO bid × 14 days *with or without* metronidazole 500 mg PO bid × 14 days
Alternate regimens	Ofloxacin 400 mg IV bid *or* levofloxacin 500 mg IV qd *with or without* ampicillin/sulbactam 3 g IV q6h *plus* doxycycline 100 mg PO or IV bid	

include ectopic pregnancy, acute appendicitis, endometriosis, ovarian cysts, and functional abdominal pain.

Management

The goal of treatment in PID is to prevent the chronic sequelae of infection. Treatment regimens must provide broad-spectrum coverage of likely pathogens, including gonorrhea, chlamydia, anaerobes, gram-negative bacteria, and streptococci. Although it is recommended that endocervical testing be done in these patients, negative results do not preclude upper tract infection. Delaying treatment may increase the risk of developing long-term sequelae.[37]

No studies have clearly demonstrated differences in efficacy of parenteral versus oral therapy, or inpatient versus outpatient treatment. The decision to hospitalize a patient must be based on the clinical presentation and other comorbid or complicating factors. The CDC suggests the following criteria for hospitalization:

- Surgical emergencies such as appendicitis cannot be excluded.
- The patient is pregnant.
- The patient does not respond clinically to oral antimicrobial therapy.
- The patient is unable to follow or tolerate outpatient oral regimens.
- The patient has a severe illness, nausea and vomiting, or high fever.
- The patient has a tubo-ovarian abscess.

It has also been recommended that patients with an intrauterine device be treated on an inpatient basis due to a high rate of adnexal inflammatory masses in these patients.

Parenteral and oral regimens are listed in Table 97-5. If outpatient treatment is chosen, patients must be reevaluated within 24 to 48 hours to assess response to oral therapy. If there is no response, the patients should be admitted for parenteral antibiotics and confirmation of the diagnosis.

Patients should demonstrate significant clinical improvement, such as defervescence, reduction in abdominal tenderness, and reduction in uterine, adnexal, and cervical motion tenderness, within 3 days of initiation of therapy. Sexual partners of patients diagnosed with PID should be evaluated and empirically treated for gonorrhea and chlamydia. Patients should be counseled to avoid sexual intercourse until both they and their partners have completed treatment. It is recommended by some specialists that patients with documented gonorrhea and chlamydia be reevaluated for test of cure in 4 to 6 weeks after completion of therapy, although this is not universally practiced.

REFERENCES

1. Sexually transmitted diseases treatment guidelines 2002. Centers for Disease Control and Prevention. *MMWR Recomm Rep* 51(RR-9):1, 2002.
2. Koutsky LA, et al: Underdiagnosis of genital herpes by current clinical and viral-isolation procedures. *N Engl J Med* 326:1533, 1992.
3. Kulhanjian JA, et al: Identification of women at unsuspected risk of primary infection with herpes simplex virus type 2 during pregnancy. *N Engl J Med* 326:916, 1992.
4. Judson FN, Ehret J: Laboratory diagnosis of sexually transmitted infections. *Pediatr Ann* 23:361, 1994.
5. Hook EW, Marra CM: Acquired syphilis in adults. *N Engl J Med* 326:1060, 1992.
6. Singh AE, Roamnowski B: Syphilis: Review with emphasis on clinical, epidemiologic, and some biologic features. *Clin Microbiol Rev* 12:187, 1999.
7. Clyne B, Jerrard D: Syphilis testing *J Emerg Med* 18:361, 2000.
8. Toye B, et al: Diagnosis of *Chlamydia trachomatis* infections in asymptomatic men and women by PCR assay. *J Clin Microbiol* 34:1396, 1996.
9. Black C, et al: Head to head multicenter comparison of DNA probe and nucleic acid amplification tests for Chlamydia trachomatis infection in women performed with an improved reference standard. *J Clin Microbiol* 40:3757, 2002.
10. Cheng H, et al: Relative accuracy of nucleic acid amplification tests and culture in detecting chlamydia in asymptomatic men. *J Clin Microbiol* 39:3927, 2001.
11. Schachter J, et al: Noninvasive tests for diagnosis of chlamydia trachomatis infection: Application of ligase chain reaction to first-catch urine specimens of women. *J Infect Dis* 172:1411, 1995.
12. Heller M: Chlamydial infections. *Ann Emerg Med* 13:170, 1984.
13. Johnson RE, Newhall WJ, Papp JR, et al. Screening tests to detect *Chlamydia trachomatis* and *Neisseria gonorrhoeae* infections—2002. *MMWR Recomm Rep* 51(RR-15):1; quiz, CE1, 2002.
14. Koumans E, et al: Laboratory testing for *Neisseria gonorrhoeae* by recently introduced nonculture tests: A performance review with clinical and public health considerations. *Clin Infect Dis* 27:1171, 1998.

15. Smith K, et al: Evaluation of ligase chain reaction for use with urine for identification of *Neisseria gonorrhoeae* in females attending a sexually transmitted disease clinic. *J Clin Microbiol* 33:455, 1995.
16. Levitt MA, et al: Clinical management of chlamydia and gonorrhea infection in a community teaching emergency department: Concerns in overtreatment, undertreatment, and follow-up treatment success *J Emerg Med* 25:7, 2003.
17. Bachmann LH, et al: Patterns of Chlamydia trachomatis testing and follow-up at a University Hospital Medical Center. *Sex Transm Dis* 26:496, 1999.
18. Todd CS, Haase C, Stoner BP: Emergency department screening for asymptomatic sexually transmitted infections. *Am J Public Health* 91:461, 2001.
19. Schwebke JR, Hook EW: High rates of trichomonas vaginalis among men attending a sexually transmitted diseases clinic: Implications for screening and urethritis management. *J Infect Dis* 188:465, 2003.
20. Crucitti T, et al: Comparison of culture and different PCR assays for detection of *Trichomonas vaginalis* in self collected vaginal swab specimens. *Sex Transm Infect* 79:393, 2003.
21. Madico G, et al: Diagnosis of trichomonas vaginalis infection by PCR using vaginal swab samples. *J Clin Microb* 36:3205, 1998.
22. Heine P, et al: Polymerase chain reaction analysis of distal vaginal specimens: A less invasive strategy for detection of trichomonas vaginalis. *Clinic Infect Dis* 24:985, 1997.
23. Burtin P, et al: Safety of metronidazole in pregnancy: A meta-analysis. *Am J Obstet Gynecol* 172:525, 1995.
24. Klebanoff MA, et al: Failure of metronidazole to prevent preterm delivery among pregnant women with asymptomatic trichomonas vaginalis infection. *N Engl J Med* 345:487, 2001.
25. Abbott J: Clinical and microscopic diagnosis of vaginal yeast infection: A prospective analysis. *Ann Emerg Med* 25:587, 1995.
26. Rex JH, et al: Practice guidelines for the treatment of candidiasis. *Clin Infect Dis* 30:662, 2000.
27. Hay P: National guideline for the management of bacterial vaginosis. Clinical Effectiveness Group (Association of Genitourinary Medicine and the Medical Society for the Study of Venereal Diseases). *Sex Transm Infect* 75(Suppl 1):S16, 1999.
28. Peipert JF, Montango AB, Cooper AS, Sung CJ: Bacterial vaginosis as a risk factor for upper genital tract infection. *Am J Obstet Gynecol* 177:1184, 1997.
29. Colli E, et al: Treatment of male partners and recurrence of bacterial vaginosis: A randomized trial. *Genitourin Med* 73:267, 1997.
30. McDonald JM, et al: Impact of metronidazole therapy on preterm birth in women with bacterial vaginosis flora (*Gardnerella vaginalis*): A randomized, placebo controlled trial. *Br J Obstet Gynecol* 104:1391, 1997.
31. Hauth JC, et al: Reduced incidence of preterm delivery with metronidazole and erythromycin in women with bacterial vaginosis. *N Engl J Med* 333:1732, 1995.
32. Carey JC, et al: Metronidazole to prevent preterm delivery in pregnant women with asymptomatic bacterial vaginosis. *N Engl J Med* 342:534, 2000.
33. Yeh JM, Hook EW, Goldie SJ: A refined estimate of the average lifetime cost of pelvic inflammatory disease. *Sex Transmit Dis* 30:369, 2003.
34. Eschenbach DA, et al: Acute pelvic inflammatory disease: Associations of clinical and laboratory findings with laparoscopic findings. *Obstet Gynecol* 89:184, 1997.
35. Westrom L, Wolner-Hanssen P: Pathogenesis of pelvic inflammatory disease. *Genitourin Med* 69:9, 1993.
36. McCormack WM: Pelvic inflammatory disease. *N Engl J Med* 330:115, 1994.
37. Ross JDC: National guideline for the management of pelvic infection and perihepatitis. *Sex Transm Inf* 75(Suppl 1):S54, 1999.
38. Sellors J, et al: The accuracy of clinical findings and laparoscopy in pelvic inflammatory disease. *Am J Obstet Gynecol* 164:113, 1991.
39. Morcos R, et al: Laparoscopic versus clinical diagnosis of acute pelvic inflammatory disease. *J Reprod Med* 38:53, 1993.

CHAPTER

98 Selected Urologic Problems

John Kahler and Ann L. Harwood-Nuss

PERSPECTIVE

Individuals who come to the emergency department with genitourinary complaints often warrant a rapid, but thorough general physical examination. Regions of particular concern include the kidneys, bladder, prostate, and external genitalia.

The Urologic Examination

Kidneys

The kidneys are not usually palpable in adults. The best method of palpation is illustrated in Figure 98-1.

The right kidney is normally lower than the left. Auscultation over the upper abdominal quadrants and the costovertebral angle should be performed in search of bruits. The presence of a bruit in these areas may signify renal artery stenosis, aneurysm, or an arteriovenous malformation.

Bladder

Similarly, the bladder is not palpable in its normal, empty state. When the bladder contains in excess of 150 mL of fluid, it may be palpable or percussible. A bladder that contains 500 mL or more of fluid can often be seen and palpated as a suprapubic mass. Percussion

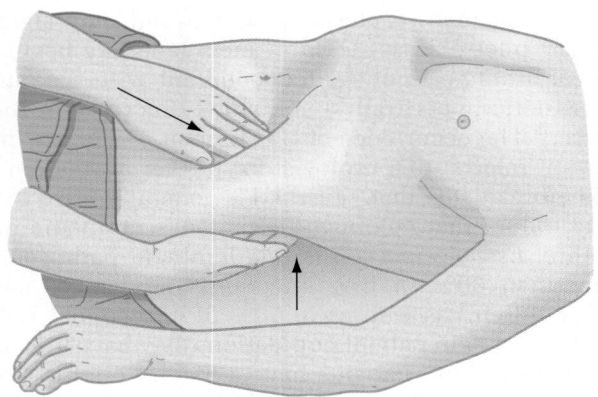

Figure 98-1. Method of palpation of the kidney. The posterior hand lifts the kidney upward. The anterior hand feels for the kidney. The patient then takes a deep breath, which causes the kidney to descend. As the patient inhales, the fingers of the anterior hand are plunged inward at the costal margin. If the kidney is mobile or enlarged, it can be felt between the two hands. (Modified from Smith DR: *General Urology*, 9th ed. Los Altos, Calif, Lange Medical, 1978.)

is probably the most reliable method of detecting a distended bladder.

Penis

If the patient is uncircumcised, the foreskin should be retracted to inspect for the possibility of infection or tumor. The urethral meatus should be examined for both adequacy of size and proper location. The meatus should be separated with the examiner's thumb and forefinger to search for neoplasm, discharge, or inflammatory lesions.

Scrotum

The contents of the scrotum should be palpated. The testes are best examined by gently palpating with the thumb and first finger for consistency, masses, or unusual tenderness. A normal testis is firm and mobile. A hard area within the testis must be considered a neoplasm until proved otherwise, and immediate referral is warranted. The epididymis should be examined. An acutely inflamed epididymis is usually too tender to permit a thorough examination. Nodular induration of the epididymis suggests tuberculosis or other chronic inflammation. A mass that is revealed by transillumination may represent a spermatocele. A cystic mass around the testis is likely to be a hydrocele, but it should be noted that 10% of testicular neoplasms cause a reactive hydrocele.

Rectum

A rectal examination is an essential portion of a urologic examination in men and should not be deferred. A 360-degree sweep of the interior of the rectum should be done (looking for masses) before careful palpation of the prostate. The surface of a normal adult prostate is approximately the size of a half-dollar, with discrete lateral margins and a firm consistency. The size of the prostate on examination bears little relationship to the degree of urinary obstruction that might be present.

SPECIFIC DISORDERS

Urinary Tract Infections

Perspective

Background

Urinary tract infection (UTI) is now considered the most frequently occurring bacterial infection.[1] It accounts for 7 to 8 million outpatient visits, 1 million hospitalizations annually,[2] and over a third of all hospital-acquired infections.[3] To obtain a better understanding of UTI, it is helpful to review some important terms.

Bacteriuria is the presence of bacteria in the urine.

Urinary tract infection describes an inflammatory response of urothelium to microorganisms in the urinary tract. This term does not distinguish between upper and lower tract infections.

Cystitis refers to inflammation of the bladder resulting in increased urinary frequency, urgency, dysuria, and suprapubic pain. Cystitis can be separated into bacterial and nonbacterial (e.g., radiation) causes.

Acute pyelonephritis is a UTI of the renal parenchyma and collecting system manifested by the clinical syndrome of fever, chills, and flank pain.

Uncomplicated urinary tract infection is an infection that involves a structurally and functionally normal urinary tract. The causative pathogen can generally be eradicated with a short course of standard antibiotics. This type of infection usually occurs in women.

Complicated urinary tract infection is an infection associated with underlying neurologic, structural, or medical problems, all of which may reduce the efficacy of standard antimicrobial therapy. Male patients with UTIs generally fall into this category.

Urethritis refers to inflammation of the urethra.

Epidemiology

UTI is a problem that affects all age groups.[4-8] The prevalence of UTI in febrile infants is approximately 5%, regardless of whether UTI is suspected.[9] UTI is more common in boys during the neonatal period but becomes more common in girls during infancy and thereafter.[10,11] When bacteriuria is seen in preschool boys, it is almost always associated with congenital anomalies of the urinary tract. It has been estimated that 0.8% to 1.5% of children have bacteriuria.

Once adulthood is reached, the prevalence of bacteriuria increases in women. It is estimated that 10% to 20% of women will experience a UTI. The prevalence of bacteriuria in young, sexually active women is 2% to 4% and gradually increases to 5% to 10% at 70 years of age and to approximately 20% by 80 years of age.[6]

Bacteriuria in adult men is uncommon unless cystoscopy or catheterization has been performed. The prevalence is less than 1% from childhood through middle age, but increases to 1% to 3% by 60 to 65 years of age and to 10% by 80 years of age. In institutionalized men and women the prevalence of bacteriuria is increased to approximately 25% and 40%, respectively.[6] UTI associated with catheter use is the most common nosocomial infection in the United States and accounts for over 1 million cases annually.[1]

Principles of Disease

Physiology

The urine is sterile along the entire urinary tract from the glomerulus to the external sphincter in men and to the bladder neck in women. The urinary tract maintains its sterility by means of various defenses.[1] A major mechanism is complete emptying. Free, unobstructed flow of urine within the kidney and down the ureter along with complete evacuation of the bladder is essential. Abnormal anatomy or physiology or the presence of a foreign body may compromise the host defense mechanisms and predispose to infection.[1]

In men, the distal end of the urethra is inhabited by staphylococci, streptococci, and diphtheroid organisms. Nevertheless, men do not generally become infected without predisposing causes.

In women, the urethra is short and close to the vulvar and perirectal areas. The organisms that cause UTI in women usually arise from the fecal reservoir and initially colonize the vaginal introitus and periurethral area. These factors contribute, in part, to the much higher incidence of UTI in women.

Pathophysiology

Bacteria most often enter the urinary tract via ascent through the urethra and into the collecting system. Infrequently, bacterial infection of the urinary tract arises from hematogenous or lymphatic sources.

Numerous abnormalities of the urinary tract interfere with its natural resistance to infection.[12,13] Obstruction from any cause, with resultant stasis of urine, is a major factor. Urinary calculi may cause obstruction and increased susceptibility to the development of UTI. Any obstruction or impediment to the free flow of urine or complete bladder emptying results in a greatly increased incidence of UTI. It is crucial that infection in the face of obstruction be diagnosed and relieved promptly.

Vesicoureteral reflux in children plays an important role in UTIs, particularly upper tract infections. Reflux caused by congenital abnormalities or by bladder overdistention (as seen in advanced prostatic hypertrophy) also predisposes to infection. Incomplete bladder emptying may predispose to UTI because of a large residual pool of urine, although this mechanism has been challenged.[14,15] Various underlying disease states are also associated with an increased frequency of UTI. Diabetic patients have a higher incidence of bacteriuria. Women with sickle cell trait also have a higher incidence of bacteriuria.

As noted earlier, UTIs are more common in women. Marriage, sexual activity, and pregnancy all represent important precipitating factors in the development of UTI in women. There is a 4% to 10% incidence of UTI in pregnant women. Bacteriuria should be sought, confirmed, and promptly treated in this population, as will be discussed.

In young men, bacteriuria is rare and may signify urinary tract disease. UTIs in men generally begin to appear at 50 years of age (concomitant with the onset of prostatic hypertrophy) and slowly increase in incidence.[16] The occurrence of UTI in men of any age may warrant referral to a urologist for further evaluation.

The organisms that cause UTIs generally arise from enteric flora that colonize the patient's perineum and urethra. *Escherichia coli* is the dominant pathogen in more than 80% of first infections in women, men, and children,[1] as well as in 50% of nosocomial UTIs; however, certain patient populations may have unusual organisms. These patients have a history of either frequent hospitalization or multiple courses of antibiotics given for other diseases. Both these settings predispose to alterations in the normal gastrointestinal flora. In some disease states the initial episode of infection in the urinary tract may be caused by an unusual pathogen. Typically, this patient group includes those with asthma, chronic obstructive pulmonary disease, or sickle cell disease. A urine culture and sensitivity test should be performed before initiating therapy in this patient population. Patients who fall into this category should be considered to have complicated UTIs and be treated accordingly.

Any instrument or catheter passed through the urethra carries bacteria into the bladder. For ambulatory patients the risk is small. A single catheterization in an outpatient setting carries a risk of infection of 1% to 3%.[14] In pregnant or debilitated patients, this risk increases substantially to 10% to 15%.[14]

Bacteriology

The majority of UTIs are caused by gram-negative aerobic bacilli that arise from the gastrointestinal tract. Of these, *E. coli* is the dominant pathogen in more than 80% of cases.[1] *Staphylococcus saprophyticus*, a coagulase-negative gram-positive organism, is the second most common cause of UTI and accounts for approximately 11% of cases.[17-19] This species is present in normal skin flora, including the perineal area, but only in low numbers, and it does not appear to be of fecal origin. Sometimes it is falsely identified as *Staphylococcus albus* or *Staphylococcus epidermidis*. Other less common bacteria may be responsible for infection and include *Proteus*, *Klebsiella*, and *Enterobacter*.[18] Unusual microorganisms may be found in institutionalized or hospitalized patients and in patients with complicated UTIs. The uropathogens in these patients include more resistant strains of *E. coli*, *Klebsiella*, *Proteus*, and *Enterobacter*, as well as *Pseudomonas*, *Enterococcus*, *Staphylococcus*, *Providencia*, *Serratia*, *Morganella*, *Citrobacter*, *Salmonella*, *Shigella*, *Haemophilus influenzae*, *Mycobacterium tuberculosis*, and fungi.[18,20]

Uropathogenic organisms may elaborate various factors that affect their virulence, including aerobactin, hemolysins, and fimbriae (pili). Fimbriae, also called *adhesions*, are proteinaceous structures that can attach to specialized receptor sites on host cells. Attachment of bacteria to vaginal and uroepithelial cells ultimately leads to a higher incidence of UTI.[14,18,21]

The virulence factor of greatest importance is the resistance transfer plasmid. A plasmid is an extrachromosomal piece of DNA that can be transferred among strains and species of bacteria. Transmission of this genetic material may confer resistance to multiple classes of antibiotics enzymatically. Plasmids may be responsible for 80% to 90% of antimicrobial resistance.[14]

Clinical Features

Signs and Symptoms

Clinically, a UTI is suspected on the basis of symptoms of urethritis, cystitis, or pyelonephritis. The symptoms vary with age. In infancy, initial symptoms may include irritability, fever, vomiting, diarrhea, and failure to thrive. Preschool children with UTI have vomiting, diarrhea, generalized abdominal pain, and febrile seizures. Fever alone is not an adequate indicator of the severity of infection in children because it may be absent in patients with significant renal scarring. In older children and adults, the inflammatory response that occurs with UTIs may result in urinary urgency, frequency, dysuria, suprapubic pain, flank pain, back pain, hematuria, and fever.

In general, clinical symptoms associated with lower UTIs are localized to the genitourinary system and include urgency, dysuria, frequency, and suprapubic pain. In addition to these symptoms, a patient with an upper UTI may manifest back and flank pain and constitutional symptoms such as fever, vomiting, and malaise.

Many studies have documented that the correlation between clinical symptoms and the presence and extent of infection is not exact.[15,21-23] Stamm and coauthors reported that 30% to 50% of women with symptoms restricted to the lower urinary tract in fact have silent (or subclinical) infection of the kidney.[24]

Differentiation between upper and lower tract infection is important and entails an understanding of the differences in pathology and the pharmacokinetics of antibiotic delivery. Infection of the bladder generally involves only the superficial mucosa, and high urinary concentrations of antibiotics can easily be achieved. The kidney, in contrast, tends to become infected in the medullary tissue, where it is far more difficult to achieve therapeutic concentrations of antimicrobial agents.

Diagnostic Strategies

Laboratory Tests

Urine Collection Methods. The diagnostic value of microscopic examination depends on the quality of the specimen obtained. In neonates, suprapubic aspiration is a safe procedure for obtaining a urine specimen, but it is invasive. Alternatively, in children younger than 6 months, urethral catheterization is more often successful and, like suprapubic aspiration, carries a very low complication rate. Urine collected in a perineal "bag" is the least invasive but useful only if the culture is negative because of high contamination rates. If a UTI is suspected, urine should not be collected by perineal bag but preferably by catheterization or rarely by suprapubic aspiration.

In older children, a sterile midstream urine sample can be collected from boys. In girls, if the voided specimen is free of cellular elements (epithelial cells), it is probably acceptable for analysis. If not, it is appropriate to catheterize the patient.

Recommendations regarding urine collection methods in women vary widely. One authority states that it is impossible for an adult woman to cleanse herself properly and collect a midstream voided specimen without perineal contamination. It has shown that up to 50% of women with sterile bladder urine grow 1000 to 100,000 bacterial colony-forming units (CFUs) per milliliter from a midstream clean-catch specimen.[25] This finding assumes major significance in the emergency department evaluation, in which accurate, initial supportive evidence for the diagnosis of UTI is important.

Sterile catheterization is the quickest and most accurate method of obtaining a urine specimen from an adult woman. It is safe and atraumatic and carries an exceedingly small risk of infection (1% to 3% in most series). This risk increases, however, to 20% if the patient is pregnant, elderly, or debilitated. If the clinician chooses to not catheterize the patient, a clean-catch, midstream urine specimen should be sought. To assess the possibility of perineal contamination of a urine specimen, it may be helpful to observe the ratio of leukocytes to vaginal epithelial cells. The lower the ratio, the more likely it is that the leukocytes are vaginal contaminants.

In men, the time as well as effort spent instructing adult men in the proper technique of cleansing and collecting a midstream specimen is not efficacious. The specimen is not affected significantly by lack of cleansing or by the timing of specimen collection.[26] It is *not* appropriate to catheterize an adolescent or adult man simply for the purpose of collecting a urine specimen.

Urinalysis. Urine cultures constitute the majority of cultures performed by microbiology laboratories, and various screening tests have been developed for the purpose of reducing this burden and its attendant costs. The goal of urine screening tests is to reliably select specimens that will provide negative cultures so that the laboratory can more appropriately focus its attention on higher yield studies.

The most commonly used screening tests measure urinary leukocyte esterase and nitrite. Leukocyte esterase is an enzyme found in neutrophils, and nitrite is produced from urinary nitrate by nitrate reductase, which is present in gram-negative bacteria. Both can be detected by a color change on dipstick testing. The two tests are often combined to improve overall accuracy. Indirect urine dipstick tests for pyuria or bacteriuria are inexpensive and easy to perform and may aid in making the diagnosis of UTI. However, they should be used with caution because they can be less sensitive than microscopic examination of urine (urinalysis). Urine dipstick testing for leukocyte esterase has shown a sensitivity of 75% to 96% in detecting pyuria associated with UTI. However, a meta-analysis of screening tests for UTI in children demonstrated that a dipstick test for leukocyte esterase and nitrite may be equal to microscopic urinalysis in its ability to detect UTI.[27]

The ability of traditional screening tests to detect UTI in young children appears to be much lower than in older children and adults.[28,29] For this reason, additional screening measures have been proposed, such as Gram stain and hemocytometry.[30,31] A urine culture should be performed in all infants and children being examined for UTI.[28,29]

It has been proposed that symptomatic patients who are normal hosts and have a positive leukocyte esterase test (in the absence of other indications for urine culture) can be treated empirically without culture. In symptomatic patients, a negative leukocyte esterase or nitrite test should be followed by urine microscopy. In adults, urine culture should be performed only if the microscopic analysis is also negative or if the patient is at risk for bacteremia.

Urine Microscopy. Urine microscopy is another commonly used method of providing clinicians with rapid results and reducing the number of urine cultures performed.[32-34] Some 96% of infected urine specimens contain 10 or more white blood cells (WBCs) per cubic millimeter when counted by a hemocytometer.[35] Various counting chamber methods detect pyuria with an accuracy approaching the hemocytometer.[19,36] Unfortunately, these tests are not widely available, and thus direct microscopy is commonly used.

The accuracy of direct microscopy is compromised by a lack of standardization of the technique. Common sources of variability include specimen collection and transport, centrifugation speed and duration, decanting and resuspension techniques, staining, and the threshold used for significant numbers of WBCs or bacteria. One method, the slide centrifuge test, avoids many of these sources of error, and high sensitivity and specificity have been reported.[37] Microscopic inspection of uncentrifuged, Gram-stained urine has also given good results.[30,34]

Although no accepted level of pyuria is diagnostic of UTI, Stamm maintains that when pyuria is carefully quantitated with a hemocytometer chamber, pyuria will be found in nearly all cases of acute UTI caused by coliforms.[35] In patients with a low-count coliform infection, those with fewer than eight WBCs/mm³ of urine will have no demonstrable infection. In patients with more than eight WBCs/mm³, 85% will have documented infection (coliforms, staphylococci, or *Chlamydia*). Despite these controversies and limitations, microscopic examination of urine to identify bacteria remains the most readily available and reliable test for a presumptive diagnosis of UTI in most patient populations.

The presence of bacteria on microscopic examination in a symptomatic patient may confirm infection. However, its absence does not exclude it. The limitation imposed by the microscope on the volume of urine may result in a false-negative error. The volume of urine seen under a high-power field (×570) is approximately 1/30,000 mL. Previous studies have demonstrated that a minimum bacterial count of 30,000/mL must be present for isolation in the urinary sediment.[38] It can be concluded that a negative urinalysis for bacteria does not exclude the presence of bacteria in concentrations less than 30,000/mL. By combining the laboratory findings of pyuria and bacteriuria, in addition to clinical symptoms, the diagnostic yield can be further improved.

Any study of urine must be performed immediately after collection. Urine specimens that are allowed to sit become alkaline, with subsequent dissolution of the cellular elements and multiplication of bacteria, thus providing the clinician with markedly unreliable results.

A properly centrifuged specimen should be spun at 2000 rpm for 5 minutes, the supernatant decanted, and the sediment placed on a glass slide with a cover slip. A second slide should be similarly prepared for staining. Gram stain will aid in differentiating leukocytes, epithelial cells, and bacteria.

In an unstained, uncentrifuged specimen, the presence of one organism per oil immersion field indicates a urine culture of greater than 10^4 bacteria/mL. If the urine is Gram stained, one might detect the presence of more than 10^5 bacteria/mL. If the urine is centrifuged and Gram stained, one should be able to detect the presence of more than 10^4 bacteria/mL.

If the Gram stain is positive for gram-negative rods, pyuria is also usually present. Coliform infection is the most likely cause. Of these patients, 95% grow in excess of 10^4 coliforms/mL of midstream urine. Gram-stained urine is negative in most patients with low-count bacterial infections and in many infections caused by *S. saprophyticus* and *Chlamydia*. Gram stain can rule in infection, but it cannot rule it out. Women with no pyuria and a negative Gram stain constitute approximately 25% of patients in whom low-count infection is diagnosed.

Urine Culture. Definitive diagnosis of UTI is based on isolation of significant numbers of bacteria on urine culture. Traditionally, growth of 10^5 CFUs/mL has been used as the statistically significant number for the presence of UTI. However, using an absolute number is fraught with limitations. The presence of 10^5 CFUs/mL of bacteria in cultures from a child's urine is associated with a 95% likelihood of infection, whereas 10^4 CFUs/mL is associated with a 50% likelihood of infection.[39]

The symptom complex of dysuria, frequency, urgency, and suprapubic pain may be caused by a wide variety of infectious organisms in numbers far less than the traditional 100,000 CFUs/mL. In addition, these same symptoms may represent a significant upper tract infection or may be caused by urethritis.

Since the benchmark studies by Kass, a quantitative culture of midstream urine revealing 10^5 CFUs/mL has been the criterion to diagnose acute bacterial cystitis.[38] His studies, however, were performed in patients with pyelonephritis and asymptomatic bacteriuria. Patients suspected of having a lower UTI were not examined. Subsequently, a distinction was made between acute symptomatic abacteriuria (acute urethral syndrome, pyuria-dysuria syndrome) and acute symptomatic bacteriuria (acute bacterial cystitis). This distinction is made solely on the number of bacteria isolated when cultured. It is postulated that women with a traditionally negative urine culture ($<10^5$ CFUs/mL) have infection localized to the urethra, which accounts for the low concentration or absence of bacteria.

A follow-up study by Stamm and coworkers revealed that 46% of women with dysuria who have a negative urine culture ($<10^5$ CFUs/mL) are found to have bacteriuria with suprapubic aspiration.[24] This suggests that there is probably no difference in urinary tract disease or treatment implications between the cystitis group and a significant number of patients thought to have acute urethral syndrome. Of patients with clinical cystitis, 30% to 50% have negative urine cultures according to traditional criteria.[40] Conceptually, patients in both groups should be combined into one: lower UTI. Data suggest that the presence of more than 100 CFUs/mL of a known uropathogen (i.e., significant bacteriuria) in a clean voided urine specimen from a symptomatic woman with dysuria is a sensitive and specific indicator of UTI.

The presence of bacteria on culture in the absence of clinical symptoms does not always indicate infection. Women often carry large numbers of pathogenic bacteria on the perineum, and uncircumcised men may harbor large quantities of uropathogenic bacteria on their foreskin. The presence of bacteria in these regions may contaminate otherwise sterile bladder urine during collection.[40]

In this era of cost containment in medicine, it is only natural that this test should be assessed for its relevance to patient care. A number of studies indicate that patients with frequency, dysuria, urgency, and suprapubic pain should be treated on the basis of symptoms only; however, urinalysis and culture are performed on all women in whom the diagnosis is uncertain, as well as those who have host (e.g., structural abnormalities) or comorbid (e.g., immunocompromised, pregnant) factors requiring definitive identification of the organism by culture. In general, the list of indications for urine culture (Box 98-1) represents those same high-risk groups reflected in Box 98-2.

The emergency physician customarily orders urine culture and sensitivity without due consideration for the clinical usefulness of both components. In vitro sensitivities seem to contribute little to the general management of most patients with UTI. There is often poor correlation between the therapeutic response and in vitro testing. It also represents an additional cost to the patient with minimal contribution to the therapeutic plan for most outpatients. The exception is a patient who has a complicated UTI.

Imaging

The majority of patients with acute cystitis or pyelonephritis do not need emergency imaging of the urinary tract. In certain clinical settings, however, emergency imaging is indicated. Patients with either unusually severe signs and symptoms or an atypical clinical picture may be candidates. For example, a

BOX 98-1. Groups in Which Urine Culture is Indicated

1. Children
2. Adult men
3. Immunocompromised patients
4. "Treatment failure" (recently completed course of antibiotics with persistent urinary symptoms)
5. Patients with symptoms in excess of 4 to 6 days
6. Elderly patients at risk for bacteremia
7. Toxic-appearing patients with signs and symptoms suggestive of pyelonephritis or bacteremia
8. Pregnant women
9. Patients with known chronic or recurrent renal infection
10. Patients with known anatomic urologic abnormalities
11. Patients in whom urinary tract obstruction is suspected (e.g., stones, benign prostatic hypertrophy)
12. Patients with serious medical diseases, including diabetes mellitus, sickle cell anemia, cancer, or other debilitating diseases
13. Patients with alcoholism, drug dependence
14. Recently hospitalized patients
15. Patients taking antibiotics
16. Patients recently instrumented (e.g., cystoscopy, catheterization)

BOX 98-2. High-Risk Groups

Compromised hosts with infected urine warrant a conservative approach. In general, the duration of therapy and liberal admission criteria should all be considered carefully. This group is at increased risk for subclinical pyelonephritis, complicated urinary tract infection (UTI), or antibiotic-resistant pathogens

Risk Factors*
1. Urban emergency department
2. Lower socioeconomic status
3. Hospital-acquired infection
4. Indwelling catheter
5. Recent urinary tract instrumentation
6. Known urinary tract abnormality or stone disease
7. Relapse after treatment of UTI
8. UTI before 12 years of age
9. Pyelonephritis or more than three UTIs in the past year
10. Symptoms >7 days before treatment
11. Recent antibiotic use
12. Diabetes
13. Immunosuppression (renal failure, chronic illness, drug or alcohol abuse, cancer, elderly)
14. Pregnancy
15. Sickle cell anemia and trait

*Modified from Johnson JR, Stamm WE: Urinary tract infections in women: Diagnosis and Treatment. *Ann Intern Med* 111: 906, 1989

patient with the classic signs and symptoms of pyelonephritis but unremarkable urinalysis findings may have an obstructive process that has prevented the pyuria and bacteriuria from reaching the bladder. Another example is a patient with a known history of UTI under treatment who has persistent fever, chills, and general toxicity. Perhaps one of the most sensitive predictors of a complicated infection (e.g., abscess) is the persistence of fever beyond 72 hours after the institution of antimicrobial therapy.[40] Pyelonephritis with obstruction from any cause can rapidly lead to an abscess with resultant loss of nephrons and sepsis. Emergency imaging is thus indicated in this circumstance.

First episodes of UTI in selected patients, such as males and girls younger than 4 years, generally require evaluation after resolution of the UTI. These patients are at increased risk for structural anomalies, and if untreated, recurrent UTI or complications such as hydronephrosis, renal scarring, and ultimately, renal failure may develop. Several imaging studies may be useful in these patients. Intravenous or excretory urography (pyelography) provides both structural and functional information about the upper urinary tract.[41] However, recent work has focused on gaining this information through safer, less invasive, and less costly methods. Ultrasound has compared favorably with intravenous pyelography (IVP) in several studies. Radionuclide cystograms compare favorably with voiding cystourethrograms in the diagnosis of vesicoureteral reflux and give less ionizing radiation to the gonads by a factor of 50 to 100. Voiding cystourethrography is the traditional method for initial evaluation of the genitourinary tract. Computed tomography (CT) is exceptional for diagnosing upper tract complications such as varying degrees of pyelonephritis, abscesses, pyonephrosis, granulomatous infections, and infected cysts. As with IVP, its disadvantages include cost, radiation exposure time, and contrast-induced reactions.

Ultrasound. Ultrasound is useful in the evaluation of patients with potential urinary obstruction. It is a sensitive tool for detecting intrarenal and perinephric abscesses and the presence of hydroureter. It is less accurate in determining the presence of a partially obstructing ureteral stone. Ultrasound can also detect the presence of pyelonephritis and congenital anomalies in pediatric patients.[42-44] Regardless of the age group, this procedure is relatively inexpensive and avoids the hazards of contrast and radiation exposure.

Intravenous Pyelography. IVP has higher sensitivity and specificity for determining the presence of obstruction than ultrasound does. Hydration of the patient is indicated before this study. It is also prudent to obtain renal function studies (blood urea nitrogen [BUN], creatinine) to rule out existing renal dysfunction because patients with preexisting renal disease, diabetes, and multiple myeloma have an increased risk of adverse reactions to contrast media. IVP is not sensitive for detecting the presence of pyelonephritis. With the wide availability of CT, IVP has become less commonly used in the emergency department setting.

Radionuclide Scans. Radionuclide scans are also gaining popularity in the early evaluation of UTI. A dimercaptosuccinic acid scan is the most sensitive method of identifying pyelonephritis and is the imaging study of choice in infant girls with UTI and fever.

Computed Tomography of the Abdomen. A contrast-enhanced CT scan of the abdomen is perhaps the best test for assessing the kidneys. It has the highest sensitivity for detecting abscess, obstruction, and acute inflammation.[45] As with IVP, its disadvantages include cost, radiation exposure, and contrast-induced reactions. CT without contrast can be performed in patients with renal insufficiency and is the preferred study in patients with clinical concern for urolithiasis. CT is still limited by its availability in some places.

Urinary Tract Infection in High-Risk Populations

Pregnancy

UTI during pregnancy represents a special situation. The incidence of infection in pregnancy is approximately 10%. Maternal complications include a 20% to 40% incidence of acute pyelonephritis and an increased incidence of postpartum chronic pyelonephritis. The physiologic changes that occur within the urinary tract of pregnant women include ureteral and renal pelvis dilation and reduced peristalsis throughout the collecting system. During the last trimester, minimal ureteral contractions occur in many patients.

The prevalence of bacteriuria in women does not change with pregnancy.[46] However, in contrast to bacteriuria in nonpregnant females, bacteriuria in pregnant women, even if they are asymptomatic, must be treated. Complications that may result from untreated bacteriuria in pregnancy include premature labor, perinatal mortality, maternal anemia, and maternal pyelonephritis.[42,47]

Reasonable antibiotic choices include amoxicillin, cephalexin, and nitrofurantoin. Some authors recommend trimethoprim-sulfamethoxazole (TMP-SMX) if used before the third trimester. Single-dose therapy is not recommended. Hospital admission should be considered in patients who are in their last trimester and who appear ill or have evidence of pyelonephritis and would benefit from treatment with parenteral antibiotics. Although pregnant patients with UTI are being treated as outpatients more often than in the past, conservative treatment and close follow-up are warranted.

Diabetes and Sickle Cell Disease

Diabetic patients with bacteriuria also have an increased risk for the development of pyelonephritis, but treatment of asymptomatic bacteriuria has not been proved to be beneficial and should not be standard therapy at this time.[48] Papillary necrosis and perinephric abscess represent two grave complications for this group.

Patients with sickle cell anemia have also shown a predilection for the development of papillary necrosis and generalized renal microvascular compromise.

Indwelling Catheters

Treatment of asymptomatic bacteriuria in patients with indwelling catheters is not indicated. Antibiotic treat-

Table 98-1. Differential Diagnosis of Dysuria Syndromes: Laboratory Findings

	Pyuria	Microscopic Hematuria or Bacteriuria	Urine Culture (>10² CFUs/mL)	Abnormal Vaginal Fluid or Cervical Smear	Culture of Genital Lesions, Cervix, or Urethra Positive for Herpes Simplex Virus, Gonorrhea, *Chlamydia trachomatis*
Acute pyelonephritis	+	+	+	−	−
Acute cystitis	+	±	+	−	−
Urethritis caused by sexually transmitted disease:					
Herpes simplex virus	+	−	−	±	+
Neisseria gonorrhoeae	+	−	−	+	+
Chlamydia trachomatis	+	−	−	+	+
Vulvovaginitis (bacterial vaginosis, trichomoniasis, yeast, genital herpes simplex)	−	−	−	+	±
Noninflammatory dysuria (trauma, irritant, allergy)	−	−	−	−	−

From Stamm WE: Protocol for diagnosis of urinary tract: Reconsidering the criterion for significant bacteriuria. *Urology* 32(2 Suppl):6, 1988.

Table 98-2. Differential Diagnosis of Dysuria Syndromes: Physical Examination

	Vaginal or Cervical Discharge, Vulvar Lesions	Suprapubic Tenderness	Flank Tenderness, Fever
Acute pyelonephritis	−	±	−
Acute cystitis	−	±	−
Urethritis caused by sexually transmitted disease:			
Herpes simplex virus	+	−	−
Neisseria gonorrhoeae	+	−	−
Chlamydia trachomatis	+	−	−
Vulvovaginitis (bacterial vaginosis, trichomoniasis, yeast, genital herpes simplex)	+	−	−
Noninflammatory dysuria (trauma, irritant, allergy)	−	−	−

From Stamm W: Protocol for diagnosis of urinary tract: Reconsidering the criterion for significant bacteriuria. *Urology* 32(2 Suppl):6, 1988.

ment results in the development of resistant microorganisms, whereas removal of the catheter leads to the spontaneous elimination of bacteria in many patients. Treatment of patients with symptomatic bacteriuria who cannot have the catheter removed includes antibiotic therapy, replacement of the catheter, and strong consideration for hospital admission because this group of patients is at risk for infection with unusual pathogens and bacteremia.

Differential Considerations

Bacterial UTI is the most common cause of dysuria, with low-count infections (10^2 to 10^4 organisms/mL) representing one subgroup.[39] It is important, however, to consider acute urethritis and acute vaginitis in these patients, as well as mechanical trauma or irritation (Tables 98-1 to 98-3 and Figure 98-2). Urethritis caused by *Chlamydia* may be seen in patients with acute dysuria; in fact, *Chlamydia* may be present in up to 20% of women with dysuria.[24] In general, if historical information reveals the presence of multiple sexual partners, a recent change in sexual partners, or a sexual partner with dysuria or discharge, *Chlamydia* should

Table 98-3. Clinical Differentiation of Major Causes of Dysuria

Cause	Clinical Features
Urinary tract infection	Internal dysuria Frequency, urgency, voiding small volumes Abrupt onset Suprapubic pain Often associated with diaphragm use Presence of pyuria Presence of hematuria (50% of patients)
Sexually transmitted disease	Internal dysuria Occasional history of frequency, urgency, voiding small volumes Gradual onset History of new or multiple sexual partners Vaginal discharge
Vaginitis	External dysuria Gradual onset Vaginal discharge Vaginal odor Pruritus

From Stamm W: Protocol for diagnosis of urinary tract: Reconsidering the criterion for significant bacteriuria. *Urology* 32(2 Suppl):6, 1988.

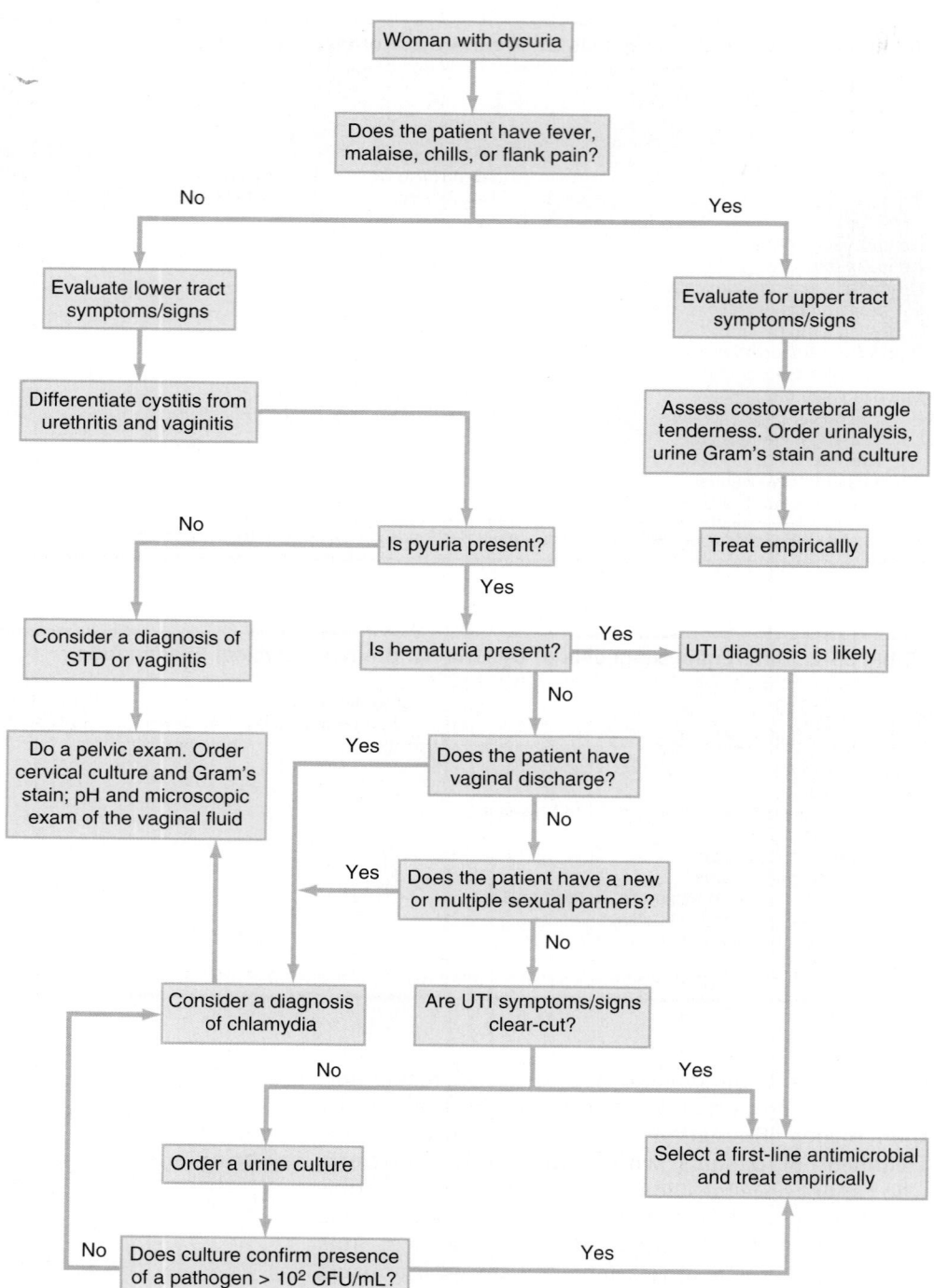

Figure 98-2. Diagnostic protocol for women with dysuria. CFU, colony-forming units; STD, sexually transmitted disease; UTI, urinary tract infection. (From Stamm WE: Protocol for diagnosis of urinary tract: Reconsidering the criterion for significant bacteriuria. *Urology* 32(2 Suppl):6, 1988.)

be strongly considered. A pelvic examination should be performed, with appropriate cultures obtained to detect *Chlamydia* and/or *Neisseria gonorrhoeae*. Other causes of acute dysuria include *Trichomonas* and herpes simplex virus.

The dysuria of vaginitis is most often described as "external," the sensation being caused by the passage of urine over inflamed introital tissue. Elderly women may complain of dysuria secondary to atrophic vaginitis. In either case a pelvic examination may be required. Urinary frequency and urgency are seldom if ever associated with a vaginal cause of dysuria.

Acute bacterial cystitis afflicts 6% to 10% of the adult female population each year. The symptoms of dysuria, frequency, urgency, and suprapubic discomfort are associated with significant bacteriuria.

Bacterial infection of the bladder is the most likely cause of dysuria in female patients (60% to 70%). Most demonstrate positive urine cultures with growth exceeding 10^5 CFUs/mL of bacteria. However, as described earlier, this number is not absolute inasmuch as 30% to 50% of patients have low-count bacterial infections as a cause of their symptoms. It has been suggested that low bacterial counts may represent an early

Table 98-4. Treatment Regimens for Bacterial Urinary Tract Infections

Condition	Characteristic Pathogens	Mitigating Circumstances	Recommended Empirical Treatment*
Acute uncomplicated cystitis in women	*Escherichia coli, Staphylococcus saprophyticus, Proteus mirabilis, Klebsiella pneumoniae*	None	3-day regimens: oral trimethoprim-sulfamethoxazole, trimethoprim, norfloxacin, ciprofloxacin, ofloxacin, lomefloxacin, or enoxacin[†]
		Diabetes, symptoms for >7 days, recent UTI, use of diaphragm, age >65 yr	Consider 7-day regimen: oral trimethoprim-sulfamethoxazole, trimethoprim, norfloxacin, ciprofloxacin, ofloxacin, lomefloxacin, or enoxacin[†]
		Pregnancy	Consider 7-day regimen: amoxicillin, macrycrystalline nitrofurantoin, cefpodoxime proxetil, or trimethoprim-sulfamethoxazole[†]
Acute uncomplicated pyelonephritis in women	*E. coli, P. mirabilis, K. pneumoniae, S. saprophyticus*	Mild to moderate illness, no nausea or vomiting—outpatient therapy	Oral[‡] trimethoprim-sulfamethoxazole, norfloxacin, ciprofloxacin, ofloxacin, lomefloxacin, or enoxacin for 10-14 days
		Severe illness or possible urosepsis—hospitalization required	Parenteral[§] trimethoprim-sulfamethoxazole, ceftriaxone, ciprofloxacin, ofloxacin, or gentamicin (with or without ampicillin) until fever gone; then oral[‡] trimethoprim-sulfamethoxazole, norfloxacin, ciprofloxacin, ofloxacin, lomefloxacin, or enoxacin for 14 days
		Pregnancy—hospitalization recommended	Parenteral[§] ceftriaxone, gentamicin (with or without ampicillin), aztreonam, or trimethoprim-sulfamethoxazole until fever gone; then oral[‡] amoxicillin, a cephalosporin, or trimethoprim-sulfamethoxazole for 14 days
Complicated UTI	*E. coli, Proteus* species, *Klebsiella* species, *Pseudomonas* species, *Serratia* species, enterococci, staphylococci	Mild to moderate illness, no nausea or vomiting—outpatient therapy	Oral[‡] norfloxacin, ciprofloxacin, ofloxacin, lomefloxacin, or enoxacin for 10-14 days
		Severe illness or possible urosepsis—hospitalization required	Parenteral[§] ampicillin and gentamicin, ciprofloxacin, ofloxacin, ceftriaxone, aztreonam, ticarcillin-clavulanate, or imipenem-cilastatin until fever gone; then oral[‡] trimethoprim-sulfamethoxazole, norfloxacin, ciprofloxacin, ofloxacin, lomefloxacin, or enoxacin for 14-21 days

*Treatments listed are those to be prescribed before the etiologic agent is known (Gram staining can be helpful); they can be modified once the agent has been identified. The recommendations are the authors' and are limited to drugs currently approved by the Food and Drug Administration, although not all the regimens listed are approved for these indications. Fluoroquinolones should not be used in pregnancy. Trimethoprim-sulfamethoxazole, although not approved for use in pregnancy, has been widely used. Gentamicin should be used with caution in pregnancy because of its possible toxicity to eighth nerve development in the fetus.

[†]Multiday oral regimens for cystitis are as follows: trimethoprim-sulfamethoxazole, 160 to 800 mg every 12 hours; trimethoprim, 100 mg every 12 hours; norfloxacin, 400 mg every 12 hours; ciprofloxacin, 250 mg every 12 hours; ofloxacin 200 mg every 12 hours; lomefloxacin, 400 mg every day; enoxacin, 400 mg every 12 hours; macrocrystalline nitrofurantoin, 100 mg four times a day; amoxicillin, 250 mg every 8 hours; and cefpodoxime proxetil, 100 mg every 12 hours.

[‡]Oral regimens for pyelonephritis and complicated UTI are as follows: trimethoprim-sulfamethoxazole, 160 to 800 mg every 12 hours; norfloxacin, 400 mg every 12 hours; ciprofloxacin, 500 mg every 12 hours; ofloxacin, 200 to 300 mg every 12 hours; lomefloxacin, 400 mg every day; enoxacin, 400 mg every 12 hours; amoxicillin, 500 mg every 8 hours; and cefpodoxime proxetil, 200 mg every 12 hours.

[§]Parenteral regimens are as follows: trimethoprim-sulfamethoxazole, 160 to 800 mg every 12 hours; ciprofloxacin, 200 to 400 mg every 12 hours; ofloxacin 200 to 400 mg every 12 hours; pentamicin, 1 mg/kg of body weight every 8 hours; ceftriaxone, 1 to 2 g every day; ampicillin, 1 g every 6 hours; imipenem-cilastatin, 250 to 500 mg every 6 to 8 hours; ticarcillin-clavulanate, 3.2 g every 8 hours; and aztreonam, 1 g every 8 to 12 hours.

Modified from Stamm W, Hooton TM: Management of urinary tract infections in adults. *N Engl J Med* 329:1328, 1993.

phase of UTI. Finding over 100 CFUs/mL in a voided urine specimen from a symptomatic woman is a clear indicator of a true coliform infection.[49]

Management

Lower UTI

Options for treating uncomplicated lower UTI include single-dose therapy, short-course therapy (3 to 5 days), and the more traditional 7- to 10-day course of therapy (Table 98-4).

E. coli remains the most common urinary pathogen and is susceptible to many antibiotic regimens. Emerging resistance to TMP-SMX has been noted in 15% to 32% of organisms.[50] In some areas of Europe resistance to TMP-SMX is approaching 50%.[51] Risk factors for UTI from TMP-SMX–resistant *E. coli* include recent use of antibiotics (especially TMP-SMX), recent travel to areas with a high prevalence of resistance, and age younger than 3 years with daycare attendance.[52] Resistance to TMP-SMX shows geographic as well as hospital-to-hospital variance.

Controlled trials in large population groups have demonstrated that single-dose therapy is not as effective as other regimens. Proponents of single-dose therapy cite improved compliance, reduced cost, and a lower incidence of adverse effects as advantages. Cure rates of almost 90% have been reported for trimethoprim combined with a sulfonamide. Cure rates are much less satisfactory for the β-lactam antibiotics.[18,53,54]

Three days of therapy is more effective than single-dose therapy. It shares the advantages of improved compliance, low cost, and reduced side effects and is currently the recommended duration of therapy for uncomplicated lower UTI. Hooton and associates found TMP-SMX to be the most cost-effective 3-day regimen when compared with other commonly used antibacterials.[55] Studies indicate that 3-day therapy is effective in pregnancy; it is generally a recommended option, although it is unclear whether this regimen can be used for all lower UTIs or only for asymptomatic bacteriuria.

The fluoroquinolones have now become first-line agents in most areas because of emerging TMP-SMX resistance.[50] They are considered first-line agents in regions where the incidence of TMP-SMX resistance has approached 10% to 20%. Ciprofloxacin is the most commonly used drug and offers twice-daily dosing. Ciprofloxacin extended-release preparations have been developed and have been shown to be effective and offer once-a-day dosing, which may improve compliance.[2] Gatifloxacin and levofloxacin offer once-daily dosing, have the broadest activity, and have same-dose bioequivalency between oral and parenteral administration.

Because of significant differences in cost, TMP-SMX is still considered a first-line agent in areas without TMP-SMX resistance. Cost must be weighed against advantages, including improved efficacy in the treatment of complicated UTI because of host factors, resistant organisms, and difficult-to-treat pathogens such as *Pseudomonas*. Fluoroquinolones damage developing cartilage in animal studies and should not be used in children.

Seven-day therapy generally offers no benefit over shorter courses. However, it remains an option in pregnancy and with other high-risk conditions (e.g., diabetes) that result in unacceptably lower cure rates with shorter regimens.

Patients with risk factors for subclinical upper tract infection (see Box 98-2) require traditional treatment with 7 to 10 days of antimicrobial therapy. In addition, these patients need close follow-up to determine response to therapy.

For lower UTI, numerous antimicrobial agents are highly effective. Nitrofurantoin and trimethoprim are excellent drugs for acute bacterial cystitis.[56] Nitrofurantoin is inexpensive and maintains low serum and high urine levels, with a bacterial resistance pattern that remains unchanged. Adverse reactions are primarily secondary to gastrointestinal disturbance, but they may be alleviated by using the macrocrystalline form (Macrodantin).

Folate antagonists such as trimethoprim have a broader spectrum of activity than nitrofurantoin does. In patients with acute uncomplicated UTI, antimicrobial susceptibility patterns may be as high as 99%.[54] The addition of sulfamethoxazole further broadens the spectrum to include *Proteus* and *Klebsiella*. Folate antagonists have a higher incidence of adverse effects than nitrofurantoin does, predominantly gastrointestinal upset, yeast vaginitis, and rash. Addition of the sulfa component further increases the likelihood of side effects.[54]

Except in pregnancy, ampicillin and amoxicillin should not be used empirically as first-line drugs for the treatment of acute UTI. There is a high recurrence rate with ampicillin-resistant strains, and they are unable to effectively eradicate the vaginal reservoir of pathogenic bacteria.

A useful adjunctive therapy for UTIs is phenazopyridine (Pyridium). It produces topical analgesia in the urinary tract and helps relieve the symptoms of dysuria. Patients should be cautioned, however, that body secretions/excretions (e.g., tears, urine) will turn orange. This side effect can stain contact lenses and alarm unknowing patients.

It is controversial whether the time-honored dictum to "force fluids" is beneficial for patients with lower tract infection. It may result in enhanced bacterial washout from the bladder, or it may decrease the concentration of antibiotics. A sounder recommendation is to emphasize regular and frequent bladder emptying. Avoidance of prolonged deferral of voluntary voiding applies to all patients. Individuals who appear symptomatic after intercourse should be encouraged to void before the sexual act. Avorn and colleagues demonstrated that ingestion of 300 mL of cranberry juice per day decreases bacteriuria with pyuria in elderly women.[57]

Upper UTI

Subclinical pyelonephritis must be considered in the differential diagnosis of any woman with acute dysuria. It occurs most commonly in indigent populations. In several studies, up to 80% of women seen in this setting had upper tract infection or at least tissue invasion. Approximately 30% of patients with symptoms of lower UTI actually have subclinical upper UTI. There also appears to be a relationship between the level of infection and the duration of symptoms. Patients who demonstrate upper tract involvement have symptoms exceeding 5.9 days.[58] Kunin asserts that the most useful guide to upper tract infection is clinical toxicity.[19] However, subclinical pyelonephritis should be considered when certain "red flags" are present (see Box 98-2). If a patient has one or more of the listed risk factors, urinalysis and culture should be performed. If pyuria or WBC casts are present, it is strongly recommended that treatment consist of a conventional full course of antibiotics. Follow-up of these patients is important and should be emphasized.

Mild to moderate pyelonephritis not meeting admission criteria can be safely treated on an outpatient basis

Table 98-5. Signs and Symptoms of Urinary Tract Infection

Newborn	Infant	Preschooler	School-Age Child
Poor feeding	Poor feeding	Abdominal pain	Fever
Vomiting	Vomiting	Vomiting	Enuresis
Jaundice	Diarrhea	Strong-smelling urine	Increased frequency of urination
Hypothermia	Fever	Fever	Dysuria
Fever	Strong-smelling urine	Enuresis	Urgency
Failure to thrive		Increased frequency of urination	Costovertebral angle tenderness (flank pain)
Sepsis		Dysuria	
		Urgency	

with a fluoroquinolone for 10 to 14 days (first-line agent) or TMP-SMX (second-line agent). In many centers, observation units have evolved and offer a short-stay (<24 hours) option for milder cases in which the emergency physician is uncomfortable with outpatient therapy. Severe upper UTI requiring admission should initially be treated with parenteral antibiotics and then with oral therapy once the patient has been afebrile for 24 to 48 hours. Oral therapy should be continued for 2 weeks. Twenty percent of cultures are resistant to ampicillin, cephalothin, and sulfonamides.[58] Therefore, most authors recommend initiating therapy with a fluoroquinolone. Follow-up of these patients is important and should be emphasized. Hospitalization is required in the presence of clinical toxicity (fever, tachycardia, hypotension, vomiting), inability to take oral medications, an immunocompromised state, pregnancy, or urologic abnormalities.

Urinary Tract Infection in Children

Perspective
UTI is a major bacterial disease of childhood. The risk of UTI developing before 11 years of age is 3% in girls and 1% in boys.[59] An estimated 0.8% to 1.5% of children have bacteriuria. The incidence of UTI in the neonatal period is higher in boys but becomes higher in girls during infancy and thereafter. In children aged 1 to 3 months, UTI is associated with a high incidence of sepsis (30%).[6] After 3 months of age, there is a decrease in the incidence of sepsis associated with UTI (5%).[6] Vesicoureteral reflux is a common risk factor for UTI and renal scarring in children.[27,60] Data suggest that the incidence of scar formation after acute pyelonephritis may be as high as 37%.[60]

Principles of Disease
As in adults, *E. coli* is the predominant pathogen. There are age-related differences worth noting, however. In older boys, *Proteus* is often isolated during UTI, whereas in newborn children, *Klebsiella* is the causative agent.

The route of infection is age related. In the newborn period, it is thought that the bacteria are blood-borne (and often associated with generalized sepsis). In the older age group, as in adults, the ascending urethral route is primarily responsible for generating infection of the urinary tract. Interestingly, in 13% of children an

upper respiratory tract infection precedes the development of UTI.[59]

Clinical Features
Pyelonephritis may be present *without* overt symptoms. UTI is often overlooked in children because of inappropriate emphasis placed on classic signs and symptoms with little regard to age variables. Nonspecific findings should be considered the rule and not the exception (Table 98-5). Generally, a febrile patient with a UTI indicates pyelonephritis. An elevated BUN level or hypertension in a child older than 2 months strongly suggests bilateral hydronephrosis or advanced renal parenchymal disease.

Neonates. Generalized septicemia is often the major manifestation of neonatal UTI.[4] Classically, feeding difficulties, irritability, and sluggishness are seen in this age group. Bacteremia is present in nearly 50% of cases.[59]

Age 1 Month to 3 Years. This age group has the most deceptive manifestation of UTI. Nonspecific findings are typical. Fever, irritability, abdominal pain, vomiting, and failure to thrive are often seen. Occasionally, gross hematuria may be present.

Age 3 to 11 Years. In girls, abdominal pain, newly developed enuresis, and irritative voiding symptoms should alert the emergency physician to the possible existence of UTI. In boys, fever is present in association with UTI in more than 50% of cases. Varying degrees of hematuria and irritative symptoms (urgency, dysuria) are present. *Proteus* is a common pathogen in this particular group. Most cases are simple, uncomplicated infections responsive to commonly used antimicrobial agents. However, certain features, if present, should alert the emergency physician to the possibility of serious underlying disease of the urinary tract. The most significant factors include a raised or palpable bladder, hypertension, abnormalities in electrolytes, acidosis, elevated BUN level, evidence of dribbling, poor urinary stream, and straining to void. If any of these factors are noted, prompt urologic referral should be considered. In addition, if one is concerned about an obstructive process with an acute febrile UTI, performance of emergency imaging is essential.

Diagnostic Strategies
Laboratory studies useful for diagnosing an infection of the urinary tract as discussed in the previous section

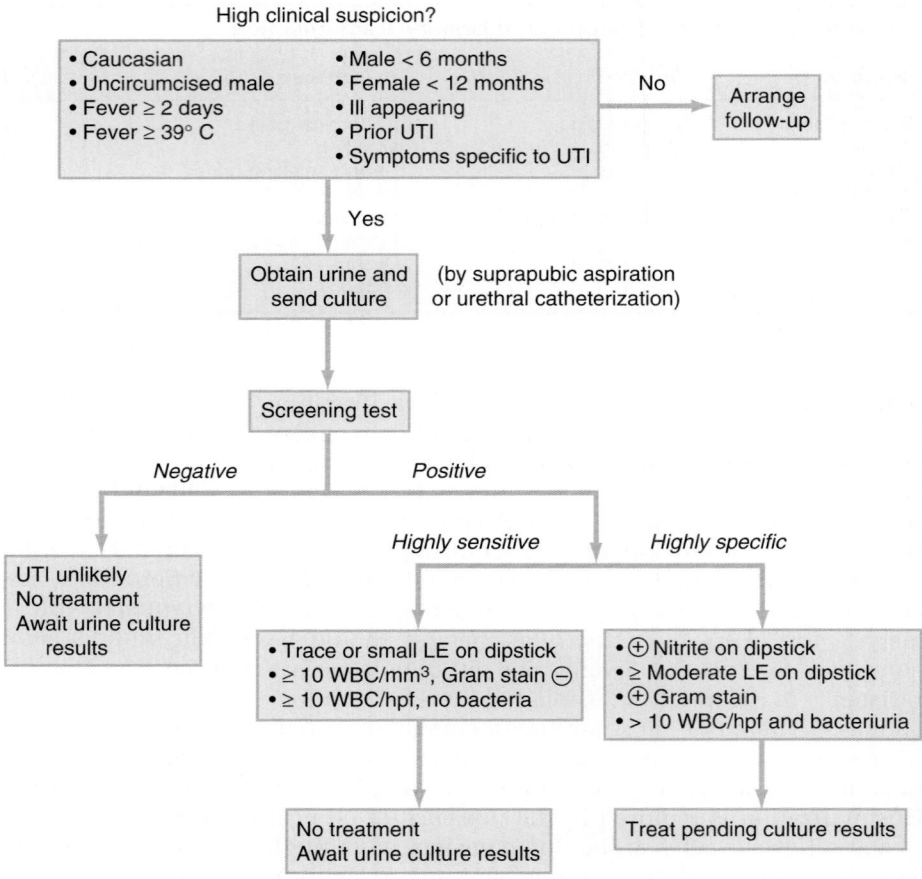

Figure 98-3. Screening for urinary tract infection (UTI) in febrile children (aged 2 to 23 months) in the emergency department. LE, leukocyte esterase; hpf, high-power field; WBC, white blood cell. (From Shaw KN, Gorelick MH: UTI in the pediatric patient. *Pediatr Clin North Am* 46:1111, 1999.)

apply to children as well. However, presumptive treatment may be indicated in high-risk patients based on clinical predictors and screening tests,[59] as shown in Figure 98-3. Additional studies are dictated by the clinical setting and include renal function studies, a complete blood count (CBC), serum electrolytes, CT, voiding cystourethrography, and ultrasonography. Renal cortical scintigraphy has proved to be the most sensitive method of detecting pyelonephritis.[61-63]

Urine collection often poses a challenge in a child with a suspected UTI. The following techniques represent acceptable methods of urine collection:

- Urethral catheterization is acceptable in all infants. Aseptic technique ensures a low risk of introducing bacteria. It is the preferred method of urine collection.
- Suprapubic aspiration is a superb, reliable method if urine is able to be withdrawn, but it is seldom used these days. For patients 12 months or younger, it is a useful method and carries an incidence of adverse effects similar to that of urethral catheterization.
- Plastic bag collection is a reasonably reliable method, but the perineum (in girls) and the glans (in boys) should be properly cleansed before application of the bag. It is a less reliable form of collection and is associated with a high incidence of skin contamination.
- A clean-catch urine specimen is preferred in cooperative and continent male patients.

Management and Disposition

As in adults, there are many therapeutic options for children with UTI. Sulfonamides, nitrofurantoin, TMP-SMX, cephalosporins, and aminopenicillins are all effective.[29] Newborns and young infants should be treated with ampicillin and gentamicin as inpatients, and sulfonamides should be avoided. Traditionally, inpatient treatment with parenteral antibiotics has been the rule for young children with suspected pyelonephritis. Recent evidence, however, suggests that oral therapy is acceptable in children with uncomplicated infections.[64] However, the clinician should manage these patients conservatively, and hospital admission is advised for children who are dehydrated, severely ill, or not tolerating oral fluids or those who have underlying structural abnormalities of the genitourinary system. In addition, family dynamics, which could affect compliance with medication, should be taken into account when deciding on the disposition of a child with UTI.

The appropriate duration of therapy is currently a subject of debate. Some authors believe that in children with uncomplicated lower UTI, short-course therapy can be used instead of the traditional 10-day therapy.[56,65] Short-course (3-day) therapy is more widely accepted in adolescent girls. Once the decision to discharge a child has been made, the parents should be advised of signs of toxicity and the importance of compliance with medications. Parents should be encouraged to return the child for subsequent evaluation if signs of toxicity occur. The child should be seen in follow-up 2 to 3 days after the emergency department visit and again 2 to 3 weeks later (or 7 to 10 days after completing the antibiotic course).

Urinary Tract Infection in Men

Perspective
The incidence of UTI in men is estimated to be 10 times lower than that in women.[66] The route of infection in men is generally ascending, from the urethra to the prostate, bladder, and kidney. Pathogenic organisms responsible for UTI in men are similar in type, regardless of the site of infection in the genitourinary tract. *E. coli* causes 80% of infections in men. Infections of the urethra (urethritis) may be due to *Chlamydia* and/or gonorrhea, and patients may be asymptomatic. Dipstick testing of the urine may demonstrate leukocyte esterase, and appropriate cultures should be sent if suspected (see further discussion of urethritis elsewhere in text).[67,68] It is unusual for either cystitis or pyelonephritis to occur in a normal host. The emergency physician should actively seek predisposing factors, as discussed later.

Specific Disorders
Cystitis. Cystitis is rare in the absence of trauma or instrumentation. Chronic prostatitis, prostatic hyperplasia with obstruction, and previous instrumentation are the most common predisposing causes. Lack of circumcision and homosexuality are other recognized risk factors.[17] Commonly, men with cystitis have symptoms of urinary urgency, frequency, dysuria, nocturia, suprapubic pain, and often low back pain. Gross hematuria occasionally occurs, but fever, chills, and flank pain are generally absent. On physical examination, there may be suprapubic tenderness. Pneumaturia may be present and is indicative of an infection with gas-forming bacteria. It may also more commonly represent the presence of a vesicoenteric fistula, which is most often caused by diverticulitis, although rectosigmoid carcinoma and regional enteritis are associated diseases as well. If fever and chills are present in association with irritative symptoms *and* difficulty voiding, acute bacterial prostatitis should be strongly considered. The most common pathogens found in men with cystitis are *E. coli*, *Proteus*, and *Providencia*.

A voided urine specimen should reveal pyuria, bacteriuria, and varying degrees of hematuria. Urine culture is essential.

If there are no signs of toxicity, the patient can generally be treated as an outpatient with any of the urinary antibacterial agents (TMP-SMX, nitrofurantoins, sulfonamides, or fluoroquinolones). However, three qualifying factors must always be addressed when dealing with UTIs in men:
1. Obstruction. It is imperative that urinary obstruction be eliminated as a pathogenic mechanism. Infection and obstruction together can be catastrophic and may lead to sepsis. Obstruction at the level of the prostate in older men is common and should be considered. Catheterization or ultrasound may be indicated to rule out retention. Obstruction (need to differentiate partial from complete) of the upper tracts by urinary calculi should be suggested by the history, in which case abdominal CT or ultrasound is indicated.
2. Genitourinary tract anomalies. UTIs in men are often secondary to underlying, serious disease of the genitourinary tract. Therefore, all these patients should be referred to a urologist for diagnostic studies if indicated. Urologic evaluation may not be warranted in those who respond promptly to therapy.[17,66]
3. Catheterization. Urethral catheterization should not be used to collect a urine specimen in a man unless there is urinary retention. An inability to produce a specimen in the presence of infectious symptoms should be a major clue regarding the cause of the infection. If retention is suspected, however, catheterization for collection of residual urine is indicated. Referral and probably admission are also prudent.

Pyelonephritis. Classically, the clinical features in men with acute pyelonephritis are those of flank and costovertebral angle pain, chills and fever, urinary frequency, urgency, and dysuria. The only characteristically helpful sign is costovertebral angle tenderness over the affected kidney. Generalized malaise, nausea, and vomiting are often seen as signs of systemic toxicity, and physicians must be diligent in identifying impending gram-negative sepsis.

A voided urine specimen usually reveals leukocytes, occasional leukocyte casts, varying numbers of red blood cells (RBCs), and bacteria. Urine culture is essential. Blood cultures should be performed if the clinical picture suggests sepsis. A CBC, renal function studies, and electrolyte studies are recommended. Uncomplicated pyelonephritis should *not* produce detectable alterations in the BUN level.

For an *adult* male with pyelonephritis, hospitalization may be required. Ultrasonography, abdominal CT, or IVP is indicated if there is a question of obstruction, which is often caused by calculi, strictures, or prostatic hypertrophy. Catheterization for collection of residual urine may be indicated if urinary retention is suspected.

Antibiotic therapy should be instituted in the emergency department *only* after samples for urine culture and blood culture are taken. Appropriate oral therapy includes TMP-SMX, trimethoprim, or an oral fluoroquinolone. Intravenous therapies include TMP-SMX, gentamicin, a fluoroquinolone, or a third-generation cephalosporin.

Prostatitis. Prostatitis is a diagnosis seldom clearly established by objective evidence. The prevalence of prostatitis is thought to be around 9%.[66] Indirect parameters often lead physicians to the diagnosis. The history and physical examination provide clues; irritative voiding symptoms and the finding of a tender or "boggy" prostate are suggestive.

Bacterial prostatitis is an infection of the prostate caused primarily by gram-negative organisms. More than 80% of cases are caused by strains of *E. coli*; 20%

are caused by *Klebsiella*, *Enterobacter*, *Proteus*, and *Pseudomonas* species. Mixed bacterial infections are uncommon. Tuberculous prostatitis may be found in patients with renal tuberculosis. The question of how bacteria infect the prostate gland remains unanswered. Although various routes have been postulated, none have been firmly substantiated.

Acute Bacterial Prostatitis. Acute bacterial prostatitis is an acute febrile illness characterized by chills, low back pain, and perineal pain. Irritative symptoms of voiding are present, including frequency, urgency, dysuria, and varying degrees of bladder outlet obstruction and retention. Patients often also have constitutional symptoms of arthralgia, myalgia, and generalized malaise.

Prostate examination reveals a tender, swollen gland that is firm and warm to touch. If the patient has a spontaneous urethral exudate, it may reveal leukocytes and bacteria. Palpation of an acutely inflamed prostate should be limited and performed with caution to avoid the possibility of precipitating bacteremia or sepsis. Fortunately for the clinician, cystitis usually accompanies acute bacterial prostatitis. Thus, culture of voided bladder urine generally reveals the responsible pathogen.

Antimicrobial therapy has been shown to be beneficial and is recommended.[69] In nontoxic patients a prolonged course of antibiotics such as for 4 to 6 weeks is required and may be repeated if only partial success is achieved. The following list represents an appropriate selection of drugs:

1. Ciprofloxacin, 500 mg orally twice daily; norfloxacin, 400 mg orally twice daily; or ofloxacin, 400 mg by mouth twice daily for 30 days.
2. Trimethoprim with sulfamethoxazole (Bactrim), one double-strength tablet by mouth twice daily for 30 days.

If the patient is toxic with fever, chills, or urinary retention, hospitalization and parenteral antibiotics are warranted.[70,71]

The following antibiotic choices are appropriate:

1. Ciprofloxacin, 400 mg IV every 12 hours, or levofloxacin, 500 mg IV every 24 hours.
2. Ceftriaxone, 2 g IV every 24 hours with or without gentamicin 3 to 5 mg/kg/day.

If the patient is having painful urinary retention, urethral catheterization should be avoided. Suprapubic needle aspiration or catheterization is much safer and more comfortable than urethral catheterization for initial management. A urologist should be consulted in this situation.

General support measures for outpatients should include bed rest, analgesics, antipyretics, hydration, and stool softeners. Nonsteroidal agents may be useful.

Chronic Prostatitis. Emergency physicians most often deal with chronic prostatitis when an acute exacerbation of the disease occurs. Clinical manifestations vary widely, but most patients complain of some degree of irritative voiding symptoms (frequency, urgency, dysuria), low back and perineal pain, and occasionally myalgia.[69,72] Fever and chills are uncommon except during an acute exacerbation of the chronic infection. A history of previous episodes of acute prostatitis may be absent.

The physical examination is often unremarkable, including examination of the prostate. The hallmark of chronic bacterial prostatitis is relapsing UTI caused by the same organism. Chronic bacterial prostatitis is the most common cause of recurrent UTI in men.

Antimicrobial therapy is recommended for the treatment of chronic prostatitis. Unfortunately, most antimicrobials diffuse poorly from plasma into prostatic fluid. The fluoroquinolones achieve the highest concentrations in the prostate and are the drugs of choice, with cure rates around 64%. The recommended dosages are as follows: ciprofloxacin, 500 mg twice daily for 30 days; norfloxacin, 400 mg twice daily for 30 days; enoxacin, 400 mg twice daily for 30 days; or ofloxacin, 300 mg twice daily for 6 weeks.

TMP-SMX (Bactrim or Septra) is also useful with cure rates of 44% to 50%. The dosage is one double-strength tablet twice daily, but the optimal duration of therapy is unclear and may range from 4 to 16 weeks

Renal Calculi

Perspective

Background

Renal calculi are a common clinical problem seen in the emergency department. In the United States the prevalence of renal calculi is 7% in men and 3% in women.[73] Renal calculi are seen commonly in middle age, with nearly 70% of all ureteral calculi occurring between the ages of 20 and 50 years. Recurrence of renal calculi is common, with rates approaching 50%.[74] It is believed that most ureteral calculi originate in the kidney and then pass into the collecting system.

Epidemiology

Various clinical syndromes involve metabolic alterations and are thus associated with an increased likelihood of stone formation (Box 98-3).[75]

BOX 98-3. Risk Factors for Urolithiasis

Metabolic
   Crohn's disease
   Milk-alkali syndrome
   Primary hyperparathyroidism
   Hypernitraturia
   Hyperuricosuria
   Sarcoidosis
   Recurrent UTI
   Renal tubular acidosis (type I)
   Gout
   Laxative abuse
Positive family history
Hot arid climates (southeast US)
Male gender (white > black)
Prior kidney stone
Dehydration

Risk factors include age, male gender, and family history. Many conditions are associated with an increased risk for calculus formation, including primary hyperparathyroidism, milk-alkali syndrome, sarcoidosis, Crohn's disease, laxative abuse, recurrent UTI, and renal tubular acidosis (type I).

Renal calculi form primarily as a result of metabolic abnormalities. Renal colic is more prevalent in hot, arid climates as opposed to wet climates.[76] In the United States the area of highest incidence of stone disease is the Southeast.

Patient occupation is also a risk factor. Kidney stones are most prevalent in white professional men with sedentary lifestyles.

Recurrence of renal calculi is common. In a study of patients with a first stone, recurrence rates of 37% and 50% were demonstrated at 1 and 5 years, respectively.[77] The incidence of recurrence is biphasic, with peaks at 1, 2, and 8 years.

Principles of Disease

Multiple pathogenic factors interact to cause the formation of renal calculi. Renal calculi can be stratified into the following types: calcium, struvite, uric acid, and cystine.

Most stones (75%) are composed of calcium oxalate alone or in combination with calcium phosphate. Hyperexcretion of calcium is a major contributor to stone formation and occurs in various clinical settings. The major dietary sources of calcium are cheese and milk, and hypercalciuria may occur in adults who ingest more than 1 quart of milk daily. Many conditions predispose to hypercalciuria and the development of calculi. Perhaps the most common is hyperparathyroidism, in which calculi develop in 67% of patients.[77] Peptic ulcer disease may also predispose to calculi formation. These patients tend to ingest large amounts of calcium with food, in addition to absorbed alkali (sodium bicarbonate) and antacids.

The other major component of calcium stones, oxalate, is also influenced by diet. Hyperoxaluria occurs in the presence of small bowel disease—Crohn's disease, ulcerative colitis, and radiation enteritis. Magnesium-ammonium-phosphate (struvite) stones represent approximately 15% of all renal calculi. Struvite stones occur almost exclusively in patients with UTI and are often referred to as "infection stones." They form as a result of urea-splitting organisms such as *Proteus*, *Providencia*, *Klebsiella*, *Pseudomonas*, and *Staphylococcus*. A distinctive feature of these calculi is the common occurrence of staghorns and coffin-lid crystals, often in the presence of alkaline urine.

Uric acid stones account for 10% of all stones in the United States. The basic causative factor is excessive excretion of uric acid in urine. Approximately 25% of patients with symptomatic gout have uric acid calculi, and the incidence of uric acid stones increases with the use of uricosuric agents. A distinctive feature of uric acid stones is their radiolucency. These calculi infrequently cause staghorns.

Cystine stones are rare and represent only 1% of stones. They are caused by an inborn error of metabolism that results in increased secretion of cystine. Cystine forms staghorns.

Pathophysiology

Impaction along the genitourinary tract is a serious complication of renal calculi and can cause several physiologic changes. Once obstruction occurs, there is a rapid redistribution of renal blood flow that results in a decrease in the glomerular filtration rate. As glomerular and tubular function decreases, renal excretion shifts to the unaffected kidney. Obstruction causes a rapid decrease in ureteral peristaltic activity. In the presence of infection, both renal and ureteral function may be impaired. Complete obstruction of the ureters may lead to loss of renal function, with an increased incidence of irreversible damage after 1 to 2 weeks. Rupture of the renal calyx may also occur. Partial obstruction is associated with a lower likelihood of renal injury, but it may still result in irreversible damage.

Calculus size and location are important determinants for the resultant degree of disease; however, the major cause of progressive renal damage is the presence of infection. Because the stone behaves as a foreign body and leads to stasis and obstruction, decreases in host resistance increase the incidence of infection. Subsequent infectious complications include pyelonephritis, perinephric abscess, and bacterial sepsis.

The most important factor that relates to passage of a calculus though the genitourinary tract is its size. The critical size for spontaneous passage is 5 mm. Approximately 90% of stones that are smaller than 5 mm and located in the lower part of the ureter pass spontaneously within 4 weeks. This number decreases to 15% for stones between 5 and 8 mm. In contrast, 95% of stones larger than 8 mm become impacted along the genitourinary tract, and lithotripsy or surgical removal is generally required. Intervention can be performed in most cases in an outpatient setting.

Ureteral stones originate in the kidney, with gravity and peristalsis contributing to their passage along the ureter. Renal calculi seldom cause complete obstruction. There are five sites along the ureter where calculi are likely to become impacted (Figure 98-4). First, a stone may lodge in the calyx of the kidney or pass into the renal pelvis and become lodged at the ureteropelvic junction. The relatively large renal pelvis (1 cm) narrows abruptly at its distal portion, where it equals the diameter of its adjoining ureter (2 to 3 mm). The third region is near the pelvic brim where the ureter arches over the iliac vessels posteriorly into the true pelvis. The most constricted area along the ureter, and a common location for impaction, is at the ureterovesicular junction. This location is the site where the ureter enters the muscular coat of the bladder (intramural ureter). At the time of diagnosis, up to 75% of stones are located in the distal third of the ureter. Finally, calculi may become lodged in the vesical orifice.

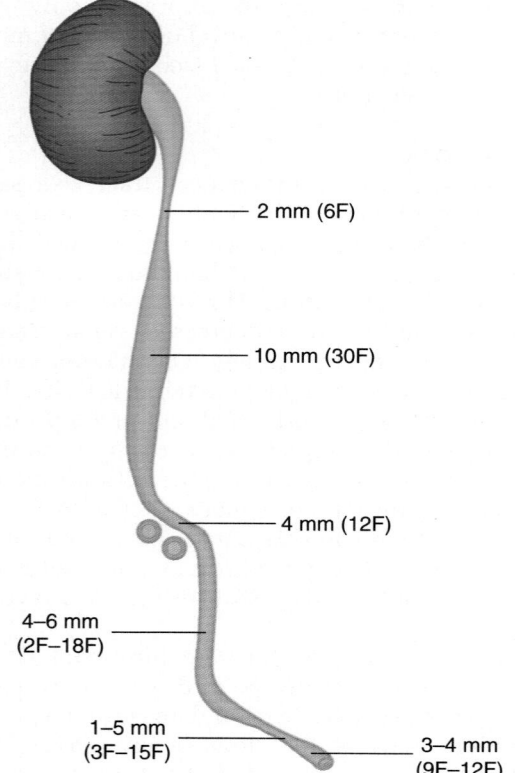

2 mm (6F)

10 mm (30F)

4 mm (12F)

4–6 mm
(2F–18F)

1–5 mm
(3F–15F)

3–4 mm
(9F–12F)

Figure 98-4. Variations in caliber of the ureter. (After Eisendrath, Rolnick; from Lich R Jr, et al: Childhood disorders and diseases. In Harrison JH, et al [eds]: *Campbell's Urology,* vol 1, 4th ed. Philadelphia, WB Saunders, 1978.)

Clinical Features

Signs and Symptoms

The classic symptoms of renal colic typically occur during the night or early morning. It is usually abrupt in onset with a crescendo of extreme pain that begins in the flank, extends laterally around the abdomen, and radiates into the groin. Pain may radiate to the testicles in men and the labia majora in women. A constant, underlying dull ache in the flank is common between episodes of colic. The cause of colicky, severe flank pain is hyperperistalsis of the smooth muscle of the calyces, pelvis, and ureter, whereas the cause of a dull ache can be attributed to acute obstruction and renal capsular tension.

Autonomic nerve fibers that serve the kidney, testicle, and ovary are involved in the transmission of pain with renal calculi, and the location of the stone may be suggested by the pattern of pain. A stone located high in the ureter may cause pain that radiates to the testicle (or ovary). As the stone approaches the bladder, the pain may shift to the scrotum or vulva. Symptoms of urinary urgency and frequency often develop as the stone nears the bladder.

Gastrointestinal symptoms of nausea and vomiting are common in patients with renal colic. A third of patients experience gross hematuria, with or without blood clots in the urine. A history of fever and chills

strongly suggests superimposed infection and should be regarded as a true emergency.

Physical Examination

The diagnosis of renal colic is often made from the doorway. Simply observing the patient can often lead to the correct diagnosis. A patient with renal colic often has severe pain and is pacing or writhing in pain on the stretcher unable to find a comfortable position. Vomiting is common. The skin is usually pale, cool, and clammy. Fever is not generally noted but, if present, strongly suggests infection. The abdominal examination may reveal signs of an early ileus with hypoactive bowel sounds. A decrease in peristalsis often accompanies renal colic, but abdominal tenderness is usually absent. It is essential that the abdomen be auscultated in search of bruits over the abdominal aorta and iliac vessels because the clinical manifestations of aortic abdominal aneurysms may mimic those of renal colic.

Diagnostic Strategies

Laboratory Tests

Urinalysis. The initial diagnostic step in the management of suspected renal colic is urinalysis. This simple noninvasive test provides a variety of helpful information. Generally, a dipstick test is performed first to evaluate for the presence of blood and infection. If abnormal, it is usually followed by microscopic analysis.

Sediment. RBCs are generally found in the urine of patients with urolithiasis. However, the absence of RBCs in urine does not exclude the diagnosis. Ten percent to 20% of patients with urolithiasis documented by IVP have no microscopic hematuria. Furthermore, there is no correlation between the degree of obstruction and the absence of hematuria.[78] Sterile pyuria can occur in the absence of infection as a result of ureteral inflammation. However, bacteriuria should be sought, especially if other clinical signs of infection are present, such as fever and chills. Culture should always be performed when infection is suspected.

Urinary pH. The mean urinary pH is 5.85. Urinary pH greater than 7.6 should raise suspicion for the presence of urea-splitting organisms because the kidney will not, under normal conditions, produce urine in this alkaline range. Renal tubular acidosis and ingestion of absorbable alkali must also be considered. A pH less than 5 is often associated with the formation of uric acid calculi.

Crystalluria. Examination of the crystals present may provide a clue to the type of stone.

Other Laboratory Tests. Serum uric acid levels are elevated in 50% of all uric acid stone formers and may be of use. Measurement of BUN and serum creatinine levels should be done if indicated (solitary kidney, transplanted kidney, history of renal insufficiency).

A CBC may reveal a slightly elevated WBC count in patients with renal calculi that is thought to be due to demargination. However, a count higher than 15,000 WBCs/mm³ or a significant left shift on the dif-

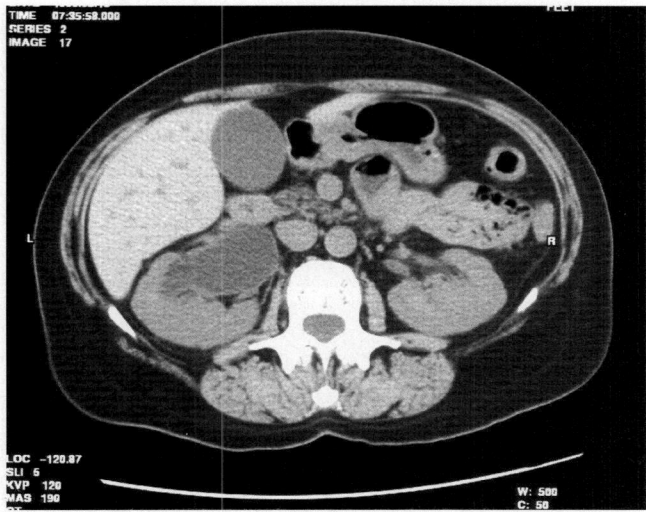

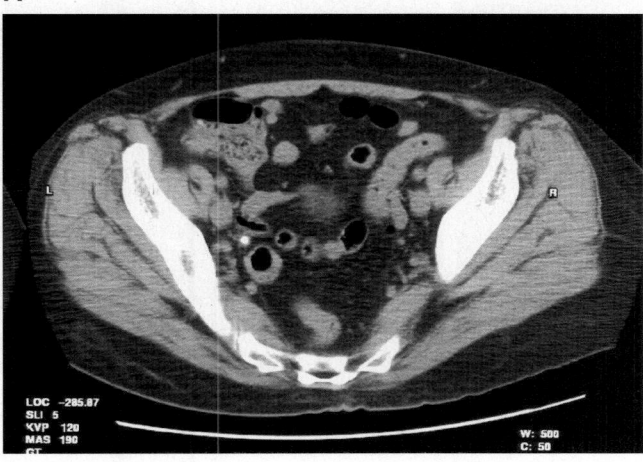

Figure 98-5. Computed tomography images of a patient with renal colic. **A,** Right-sided hydronephrosis. **B,** Right ureteral calculi.

ferential suggests active infection. Serum calcium and phosphorus levels can help screen for hyperparathyroidism, sarcoidosis, and other disorders of calcium metabolism, but this metabolic workup is generally performed in the outpatient setting.

Imaging

Imaging is not needed in all patients with renal colic. If the patient's signs and symptoms are atypical, the diagnosis is in question, the patient appears toxic, high-grade obstruction is suspected, or it is the patient's first episode, imaging should be pursued.

Computed Tomography. Non–contrast-enhanced spiral CT has become the standard imaging modality in many centers. It has been shown to be sensitive and specific (97% and 96%, respectively) in detecting both ureteral calculi and ureteral obstruction.[79-81] Other advantages include its ability to detect calculi as small as 1 mm in diameter and direct visualization of complications such as hydroureter, hydronephrosis (Figure 98-5), and ureteral edema.[82] CT is superior to other imaging modalities in its ability to recognize other pathology (malignancy, renal abscess, abdominal aortic

aneurysm). It also has the advantage of lack of contrast exposure, short duration of testing, and ease of interpretation. There are few contraindications to CT imaging, but the patient's weight is often an exclusion if more than 250 to 300 lb. It is also not the preferred modality in pregnant patients because of radiation exposure.

Intravenous Pyelography. IVP remains the most accurate imaging modality for renal colic in centers without CT access. It is very accurate, with the diagnosis of calculous disease able to be established in 96% of cases, and it can quantify the presence and severity of obstruction. Contraindications to the use of urographic contrast media include renal insufficiency and previous reaction to contrast material. The incidence of serious contrast medium reactions is extremely low. Its value is also limited by the complexity and length of time needed to perform the procedure.

After injection of a standard urographic contrast medium, a radiograph is taken at 5 minutes. The most reliable and earliest indicator of a calculus is the delay in appearance of contrast medium in the 5-minute film. If only a nephrogram is seen at 5 minutes on the affected side, the patient should return to the emergency department after 60 to 120 minutes has passed. If contrast medium is excreted on the affected side, the degree of hydronephrosis and the intensity of obstruction of the kidney can be assessed by the rate of elimination of the dye. The degree of dilation of the ureter above the calculus should be noted. Often, the findings may be subtle—there may be only mild dilation of the ureter and calyces.

A helpful finding is columnization. In general, in the absence of a pathologic condition, the ureter should not be seen in its entirety on a single film. The ureter is a dynamic structure, not a passive conduit. Normally, it is in various phases of peristalsis. With the onset of obstruction, peristalsis does not cease, but the increase in volume within the ureter results in columnization of urine and is manifested as such during an excretory urogram.

The pyelogram should not be terminated before dye is allowed to reach the level of the obstructing stone. A column of dye ending at the calculus must be demonstrated for true confirmation to be made.

Occasionally, the patient may become pain free during the radiographic procedure. This may be caused by two phenomena: the hyperosmolar load of contrast medium often "assists" in passage of the stone, or the cessation of pain may signify the onset of complete obstruction.

Ultrasonography. An alternative to IVP and CT is ultrasound. Ultrasound is less reliable at detecting small (<5 mm) ureteral and midureteral stones. Though only 64% sensitive in detecting calculi, ultrasound shows hydronephrosis with a sensitivity of 85% to 94% and a specificity of 100% (Figure 98-6).[83] In a patient with a history of calculi whose symptoms suggest new renal colic, ultrasound may be the study of choice. It is also the study of choice when trying to rule out hydronephrosis in a pregnant patient with pyelonephritis if obstructive urolithiasis is also a concern.

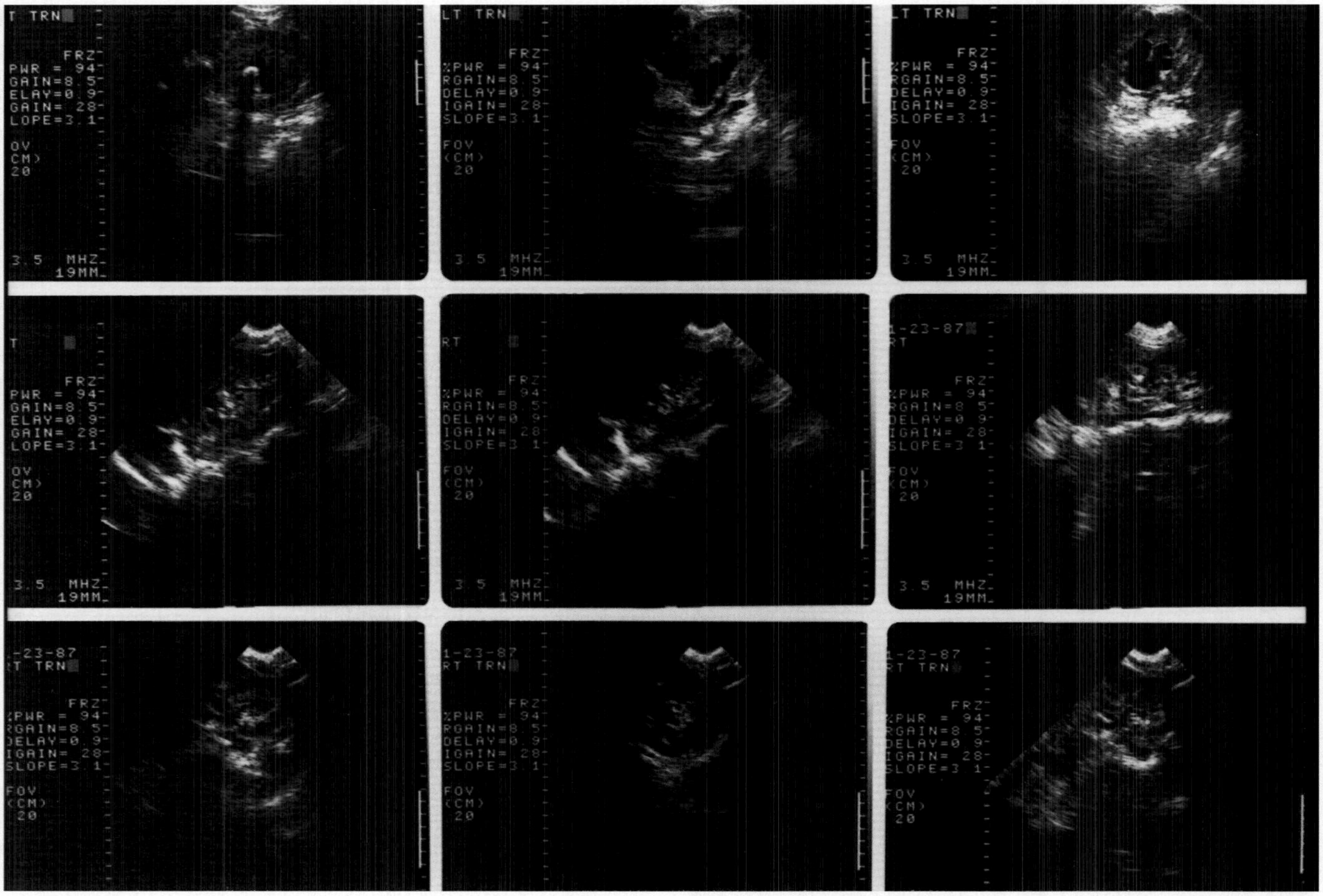

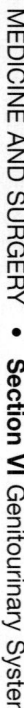

A

Figure 98-6. Ultrasound of a patient with renal colic. **A,** A long 1-1 axis view demonstrates hydronephrosis.

Radiography of the Kidney, Ureter, and Bladder. A kidney, ureter, bladder (KUB) film is the standard initial radiograph done before injecting contrast medium during IVP. It is of limited utility on its own except in cases in which it is used as a progress film after CT has already identified a radiopaque stone. A KUB film is not a reliable study to diagnose urolithiasis because it provides only presumptive evidence of calculi (<70% specificity), so it should be followed by a more definitive study.[84,85] The most common radiographic densities seen on KUB films are phleboliths in the pelvic veins, which are spherical with a hollow (lucent) center, whereas calculi are usually irregularly shaped. Calcified mesenteric lymph nodes may also add confusion; however, these densities change in position on subsequent films.

Most calculi (90%) are radiopaque, including calculi composed of calcium oxalate, cystine, calcium phosphate, or magnesium-ammonium-phosphate (Figures 98-7 and 98-8). Uric acid stones, blood clots, and sloughed papillae are seen as "negative" shadow on radiographs. The most commonly overlooked calculi lie in the region over the sacrum, where small stones are often obscured by this bony density.

Differential Considerations

A number of significant clinical entities can produce flank pain (Box 98-4) and should be considered in patients with symptoms suggestive of renal colic. Such conditions include acute abdominal aneurysm, pyelonephritis, carcinoma, renal tuberculosis, papillary necrosis, and vascular compromise.

Acute pyelonephritis can cause severe renal pain. Urinalysis should aid in the differential diagnosis by the findings of pyuria and bacteriuria; however, infection occasionally occurs in the presence of an obstructive stone and is a true urologic emergency. In this setting, it is vital to perform imaging (renal CT, ultrasound, IVP) to rule out hydronephrosis, which may warrant immediate urologic intervention (ureteral stents).

Renal carcinoma may also produce flank pain, especially if there has been hemorrhage within the tumor. An abdominal flat-plate radiograph (KUB) may demonstrate calcifications overlying the renal shadow that are often seen in renal neoplasms. IVP may suggest the diagnosis, but CT is the preferred diagnostic study.

Calculous disease complicates renal tuberculosis in 10% of all cases. The finding of sterile pyuria may

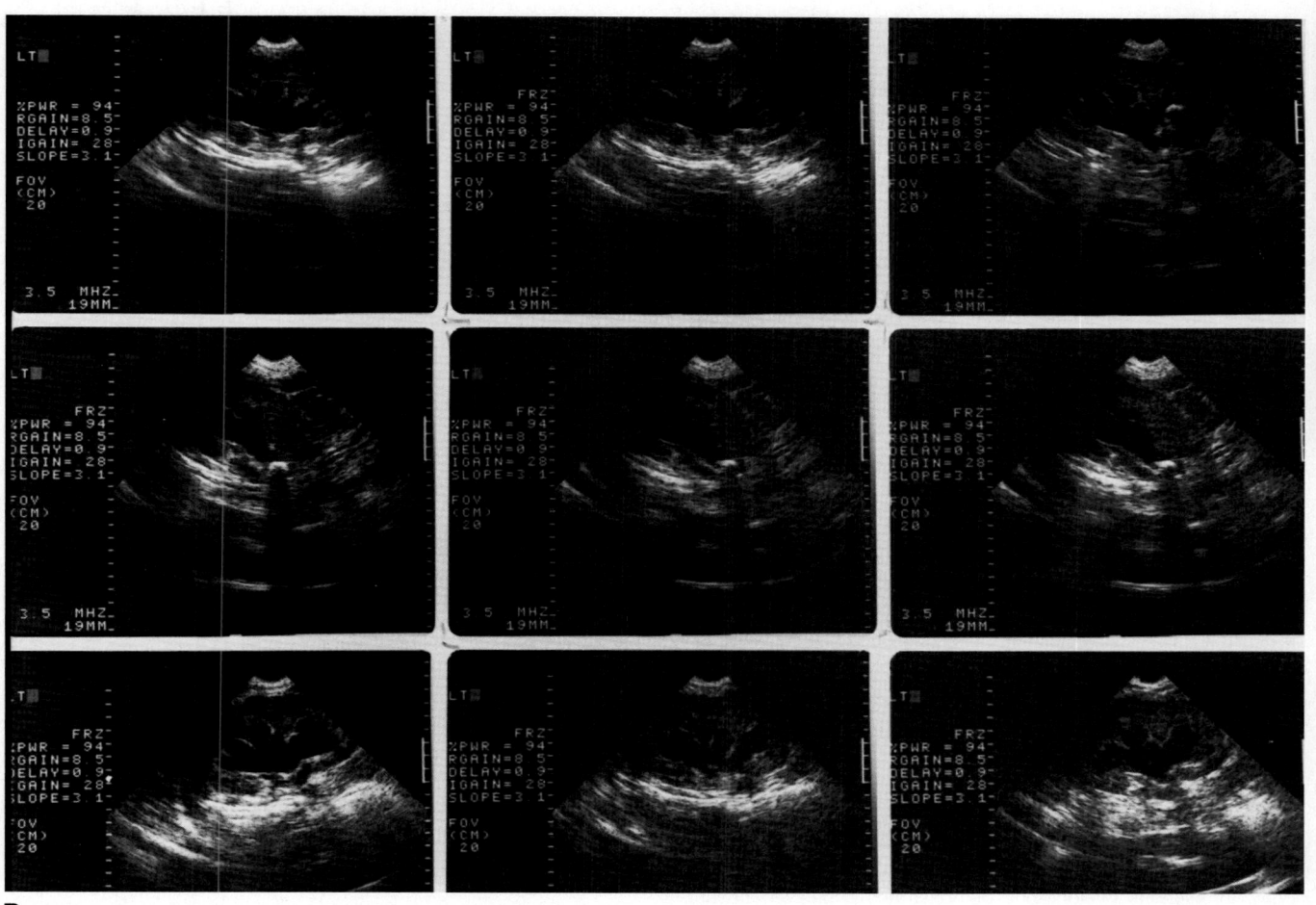

B

Figure 98-6, cont'd. B, A transverse cut shows a calcification with an acoustic shadow in the renal calyx.

suggest renal tuberculosis, and identification of acid-fast bacilli in urine confirms the diagnosis.

Papillary necrosis may cause renal colic as a result of passage of sloughed papillae down the ureter. It is most often seen in diabetics and in patients with a history of acute or chronic UTI. Sloughed papillae may be visualized on imaging but be mistaken for an obstructive stone.

Renal pain, either colicky or noncolicky, is also produced by acute vascular compromise of a kidney. The pain of renal infarction is severe and occasionally associated with microscopic or gross hematuria. The acute vascular changes may be secondary to renal artery embolism, renal vein thrombosis, dissection of the renal artery, rupture of a renal artery aneurysm, aortic dissection, or abdominal aortic aneurysm. If a vascular etiology is suspected, a contrast-enhanced CT scan or an angiogram should be performed. The most common of these relatively rare processes is renal artery embolism, which is most often of cardiac origin (atrial fibrillation, subacute bacterial endocarditis, mural thrombus). An immediate angiogram is indicated because early diagnosis allows possible salvage of the ischemic kidney. Most renal artery aneurysms are small and seldom manifest themselves. Approximately 60% of renal artery aneurysms are calcified.[83] Dissection or rupture of a renal artery aneurysm is rare and causes shock and flank pain. Renal vein thrombosis often demonstrates microscopic hematuria and proteinuria. The KUB film may show an increased renal shadow, and in the early stages, IVP reveals decreased function of the affected kidney. Predisposing factors for renal vein thrombosis include nephrotic syndrome, malignancies, and pregnancy.

A renal or perinephric abscess may cause flank pain, fever, and a palpable mass. Ultrasonography or CT should be performed. A chest film may demonstrate a pleural effusion or elevation of the diaphragm. Both these entities are emergencies and require hospitalization for adequate management and determination of the underlying causes.

Management

Patients with ureteral stones are generally in agonizing pain. Often, the history, physical examination, and finding of hematuria allow a presumptive diagnosis to be made. The first priority is usually pain control. Non-steroidal anti-inflammatory drugs (NSAIDs) are first-line agents, but parenteral administration (intravenous ketorolac) is often necessary because of vomiting. Ketorolac (Toradol) provides rapid effective analgesia

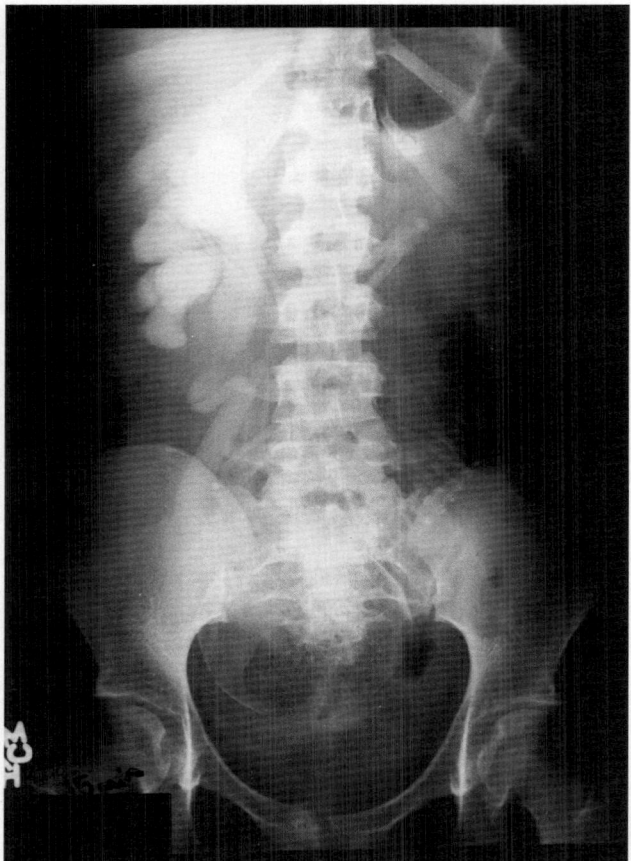

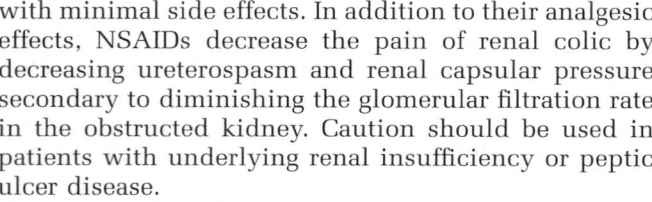

Figure 98-7. In a near-term pregnant woman with an obstructed left kidney, intravenous pyelography demonstrates a delayed nephrogram. The right kidney has physiologic hydronephrosis from ureteral compression by the fetal head.

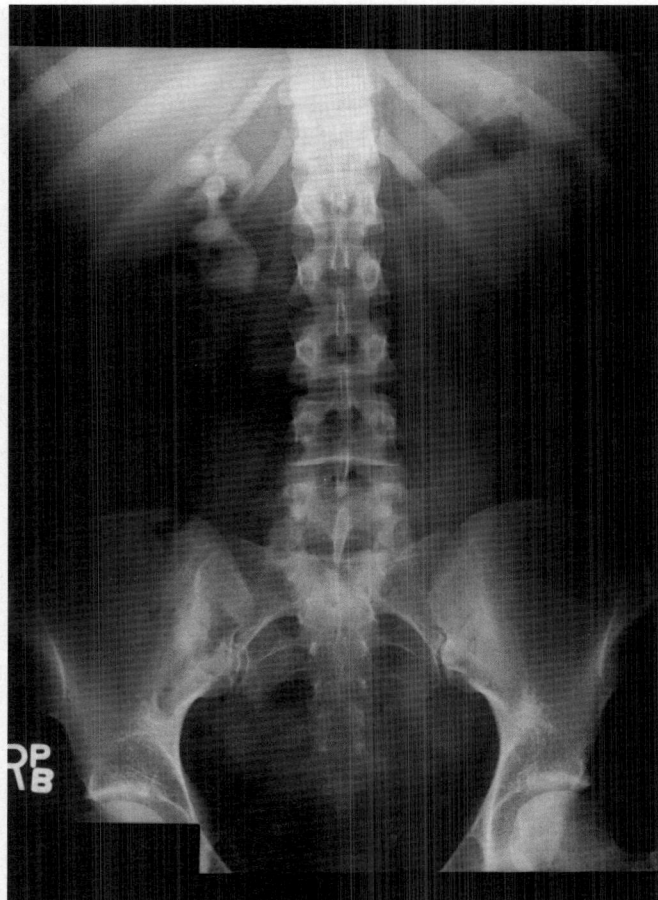

Figure 98-8. Kidney-ureter-bladder film demonstrating a staghorn calculus in the right kidney.

with minimal side effects. In addition to their analgesic effects, NSAIDs decrease the pain of renal colic by decreasing ureterospasm and renal capsular pressure secondary to diminishing the glomerular filtration rate in the obstructed kidney. Caution should be used in patients with underlying renal insufficiency or peptic ulcer disease.

Narcotics (morphine sulfate, meperidine, or hydromorphone) are also very effective in providing rapid analgesia, but they have a higher incidence of side affects than NSAIDs do. Renal colic is a complaint commonly used by individuals seeking narcotics.[73] Factors suggesting malingering include multiple drug allergies (e.g., ketorolac, nalbuphine [Nubain], ibuprofen [Motrin]), multiple emergency department visits with nondiagnostic imaging, specific drug and dose requests by the patient, noncooperative behavior, and a history of multiple emergency department visits for other painful conditions. There is little evidence in the literature to support the use of anticholinergics for the treatment of acute colic.

Outpatient Management

Most patients with ureteral calculi may be discharged with appropriate referral and careful instructions from the emergency physician after adequate pain control. The patient should be instructed to drink a moderate

amount of fluids, to take analgesics as needed for pain, and to engage in activity as tolerated. Proper discharge instructions should include work and driving restrictions while taking any narcotics. In addition, patients should strain all urine, and commercially available strainers are available for this purpose. If not available, patients may simply void into a glass jar and the calculus will be visible at the bottom. The stone should be saved and submitted to the urologist for analysis. Patients should be instructed to return immediately for intractable or severe pain, persistent nausea and vomiting, fever or chills, or difficulty voiding. Finally, an outpatient urologic evaluation should be scheduled (within 2 weeks).

Indications for Admission

Hospital admission should be sought for patients who are severely dehydrated, have unrelenting pain or vomiting, or have an underlying urinary infection (Box 98-5). Sepsis and renal damage are risks in the presence of obstruction and infection. Infected urine in the setting of an obstructive stone is a true urologic emergency, and simply admitting the patient to a floor is not adequate. These patients require immediate urologic consultation in the emergency department to evaluate the need for drainage and relief of the obstruction (usually in the form of stenting). If signs of sepsis

BOX 98-4. Differential Diagnosis of Urolithiasis

Urologic Disease
Upper Urinary Tract
Renal infarct
Renal parenchymal tumors
Urothelial tumors
Papillary necrosis
Pyelonephritis
Hemorrhage (blood clot)

Ureter
Urothelial tumors
Hemorrhage (blood clot)
Previous surgery (e.g., stricture)
Metastatic tumors

Lower Urinary Tract
Urothelial tumors
Urinary retention

Nonurologic Disease
Intra-abdominal
Peritonitis (especially appendicitis)
Biliary colic
Intestinal obstruction

Vascular
Abdominal aortic aneurysm
Superior mesenteric artery occlusion

Retroperitoneal
Retroperitoneal lymphadenopathy
Retroperitoneal fibrosis
Tumor

Gynecologic
Cervical cancer
Endometriosis
Ovarian vein syndrome

Musculoskeletal

From Lingeman J: Calculous disease of the kidney and bladder. In Harwood-Nuss A (ed): *The Clinical Practice of Emergency Medicine*, 2nd ed. Philadelphia, JB Lippincott, 1996.

BOX 98-5. Indications for Hospital Admission

Absolute
Obstructing stone with signs of urinary infection
Intractable nausea/vomiting
Severe pain requiring parenteral analgesics
Urinary extravasation
Hypercalcemic crisis

Relative
Significant comorbidities complicating outpatient
 management
High-grade obstruction
Leukocytosis
Size of stone
Solitary kidney/intrinsic renal disease
Social

(tachycardia, fever, hypotension, shock) are present, antibiotics and fluid resuscitation should be administered while awaiting urologic evaluation. Immediate operative intervention may be indicated to provide drainage and relieve the obstruction. The size of the stone is of less concern in the acute setting.

A patient who returns to the emergency department with colic may not need a repeat imaging study if the stone was identified previously. In this case a KUB film may localize the stone. Urologic consultation is recommended.

Treatment Options

Several treatment options are available to the urologist for the management of stones that do not pass spontaneously. Optimal therapy depends on the size, location, and composition of the stone. Extracorporeal shock wave lithotripsy (ECSWL) has proved very effective for stones located in the kidney, with a greater than 85% clearance rate. Upper ureteral stones may also be cleared with a high success rate when ECSWL is per-

formed after ureteroscopic manipulation of the stone to a more proximal position. Percutaneous nephrolithotomy, which establishes a tract from the skin to the collecting system, is used for stones too large or hard for ECSWL. Stones unresponsive or unlikely to respond to other techniques may require surgical removal.

Vesical Calculus

Although calculi generally form in the kidneys, they may also originate in the bladder. There is evidence for assuming that bladder stones are a different entity from renal stones. In the United States, bladder stones occur almost exclusively in elderly men, most often as a complication of other urologic disease. The most common cause is infection of residual bladder urine with urea-splitting organisms *(Proteus)*. The other common cause of vesical stones is an indwelling catheter. Predisposing causes to the formation of bladder stones include bladder neck obstruction (usually secondary to prostatic hyperplasia), neurogenic bladder, vesical diverticula, irradiation, and schistosomiasis.

The symptoms are most often pain on voiding and hematuria. The patient may complain of a sudden interruption of the urinary stream, which strongly suggests a vesical stone that intermittently obstructs the bladder outlet. Frequency, urgency, and dysuria are seen in up to 50% of patients, and UTI is common.

Physical examination is rarely rewarding because signs may be minimal. Rectal examination may reveal an enlarged prostate or a prostatic malignancy. Poor sphincter tone may suggest a neurogenic bladder. Urinalysis generally reveals pyuria and bacteriuria; hematuria is commonly seen as well. Plain radiographs of the pelvis reveal a bladder stone in 50% of cases. IVP may demonstrate obstructive changes in the upper tracts or bladder diverticula.

Acute Scrotal Mass

Perspective

The onset of acute scrotal pain and swelling can present a major challenge to the emergency physician. It should be considered a major medical emergency and

Figure 98-9. Testes, epididymis, ductus deferens, and glands of the male reproductive system. (From Seeley RR, et al [eds]: *Anatomy and Physiology,* 1st ed. New York, McGraw-Hill, 1989.)

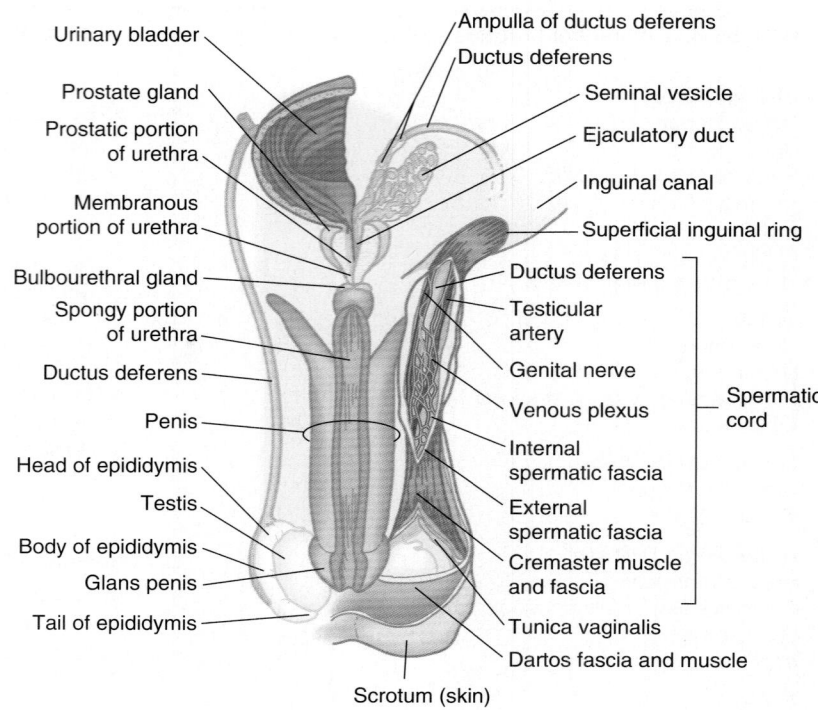

approached rapidly. Patients with an acute scrotal mass may have widely variable signs and symptoms, including a painless mass, severe sharp pain, dull pain, or pain that radiates to the abdomen or thighs. The emergency physician must act quickly to identify emergency conditions in these patients.

Principles of Disease

Anatomy

Knowledge of testicular landmarks is essential for examination of a patient with an acute scrotal mass. Figure 98-9 demonstrates the normal anatomy of the scrotum and testis. A normal scrotum is relatively symmetrical, and both testicles are of equal mass and volume. A normal testis is found in the vertical axis with a slight forward tilt, and the epididymis is above the superior pole in the posterolateral position.

Physical Examination

The testis should be examined by grasping it between the first and second fingers and the thumb. Particular attention should be paid to any tenderness to palpation, discrepancies in size, loss of testicular landmarks, or discoloration. In addition, the epididymis should be nontender and soft and have a noticeable smooth ridge posterolateral to the testis. Testing of the cremasteric reflex is a very helpful part of the scrotal examination. The cremasteric reflex is elicited by stroking or pinching the inner aspect of the thigh and observing a more than 0.5-cm elevation of the ipsilateral testicle.

Differential Considerations

The emergency physician must act quickly to rule out the most devastating causes first, such as testicular torsion. The most common causes of an acute scrotal mass are testicular torsion, epididymitis, torsion of appendages, testicular tumor, orchitis, and hernia/hydrocele.

Specific Disorders

Testicular Torsion

Perspective. Testicular torsion is estimated to occur in three to four patients per year in a large general hospital (or 1 in 4000).[86] The average salvageability rate remains low in most series, with approximately 50% testicular loss from either atrophy or orchiectomy.[86] There are two peak periods in which torsion is likely to occur: in the first year of life and at puberty. One series reports an age range of 5 months to 41 years, with an average age of 16.2 years. Clearly, torsion is not limited to the pubertal period. Testicular torsion is 10 times more likely in an undescended testis. It should be high in the differential diagnosis when a patient has a painful inguinal mass and an empty scrotum.

Principles of Disease. Most torsions are caused by an underlying bilateral anatomic abnormality. The tunica vaginalis is capacious with a high insertion about the spermatic cord. The result is a redundant cord. The testis then "dangles" in the scrotum and is mobile. This phenomenon has been likened to the clapper of a bell, hence the term *bell-clapper deformity* of the testicle.

The initial effect of testicular torsion is obstruction of venous return. As twisting of the cord persists, thrombosis of the vein is followed by arterial thrombosis. The degree of obstruction is a function of the degree of rotation. If the rotation is incomplete, edema and congestion occur. Necrosis develops in a testicle with complete obstruction, and infarction promptly develops when arterial thrombosis occurs. Clinically, there is rapid swelling and edema of the testis and scrotum, with erythema of the scrotal skin following soon after.

The amount of damage is related to the duration and extent of vascular obstruction. A salvage rate of 80% to 100% is possible if the pain has lasted less than 6 hours.[86] Continuous pain for 24 hours is usually associated with testicular infarction.

Clinical Features. A well-recognized phenomenon may provide an early clue—nearly 41% of patients report a history of *similar* pain that resolved spontaneously. The pain of torsion usually begins suddenly in the scrotum, but its location may be inguinal or lower abdominal. It is often associated with nausea and vomiting, which are thought to be secondary to sudden occlusion of the testicular vascular supply. Torsion commonly occurs either after exertion or during sleep. Most patients have a notable absence of urinary symptoms.

The diagnosis of testicular torsion is often made more difficult by extreme pain, which permits only superficial examination of the affected hemiscrotum. Generally, the hemiscrotum is swollen, tender, and firm. A reactive hydrocele may be present. The classic signs of a high-riding testis with a transverse lie are not always detectable. Loss of the cremasteric reflex is strongly associated with torsion. The presence of the cremasteric reflex virtually excludes the diagnosis, although rare cases have been reported.[87] In infants and children, many of the signs are often absent.

Examination of the opposite testis is essential and should be performed with the patient standing. The basic anatomic abnormality that predisposes to testicular torsion is the bell-clapper deformity. Hence, the contralateral testicle may be noted to lie in the horizontal axis.

Diagnostic Strategies. Urinalysis should be performed, but it may be unremarkable in patients with testicular torsion. Similarly, a CBC often reveals an absence of leukocytosis. Although the CBC and urinalysis can be of help, these studies should not delay definitive testing. Color Doppler ultrasound has become the test of choice at most hospitals to diagnose testicular torsion if the clinical diagnosis is uncertain. Color Doppler ultrasound has a sensitivity (86% to 100%) and specificity (100%) similar to that of radioisotope scans (80% to 100%, 89% to 100%). In addition to being more specific, color Doppler ultrasound is more rapid and often more practical than radioisotope scans.

Management. The first step in management of suspected testicular torsion is consultation with a urologist. Intravenous access should be obtained, analgesia provided, and nothing-by-mouth status maintained. Manual detorsion should be attempted in most cases while steps are being taken for definitive surgical exploration. Manual detorsion is not considered curative, but rather a temporizing technique only. Torsion of a testicle may occur in either direction, but usually the anterior portion twists medially. After appropriate parenteral analgesics, the anterior portion of the testicle should be twisted laterally unless it appears to shorten the cord or worsen the torsion, in which case detorsion in the reverse direction should be attempted.

Cord blocks should be attempted only by the consulting urologist.

No procedure should delay surgical intervention. If torsion is suspected based on the history and physical examination (no urethral discharge, no cremaster reflex), the place to prove or disprove it is the operating room.

Disposition. Rapid diagnosis of testicular torsion is essential. Once the diagnosis has been established, emergency surgical scrotal exploration and bilateral orchidopexy are performed.

Epididymitis

Perspective. Epididymitis is the most common intrascrotal inflammatory disease. It is also the most common misdiagnosis in patients with testicular torsion. Epididymitis is generally a disease of adult men, with the average age being 25 years. It rarely affects prepubertal children in the absence of underlying urinary tract disease. Epididymitis accounts for more than 600,000 visits to physicians each year in the United States and is responsible for more days lost from military service than any other disease.[86]

Principles of Disease

Bacterial epididymitis is usually the result of retrograde ascent of urethral and bladder pathogens. In rare instances, epididymitis may result from hematogenous spread. In the initial stages of epididymitis, there is cellular inflammation that begins in the vas deferens and descends to the lower pole of the epididymis. This descent explains the initial common symptoms of flank and groin pain (secondary to vasitis). The inflammatory process in the lower pole progresses and eventually involves the remaining epididymis and the testis.

In the acute phase the epididymis is swollen and indurated with involvement of both the upper and lower poles. The spermatic cord is thickened. The testis may become edematous secondary to passive congestion or the inflammatory process (orchitis). Resolution of the process may be complete and without sequelae, but peritubular fibrosis often develops and occludes the ductules. If the process is bilateral, it may result in sterility.

Pathophysiology. Studies clearly implicate *C. trachomatis* as a major etiologic agent. Through the use of epididymal aspirates during acute epididymitis, it has been demonstrated that in men 35 years and older, *E. coli* is the predominant pathogen, whereas in men younger than 35 years, *Chlamydia* and *N. gonorrhoeae* are the major pathogens.[88] Moreover, nearly two thirds of all cases of acute epididymitis in the younger group are caused by *C. trachomatis*. In addition to the usual pathogens (*Chlamydia*, *Neisseria*, coliform bacteria), many other organisms are known to cause acute epididymitis, most often in association with systemic infections (e.g., blastomycosis, meningococcus).[88]

The most common cause of non–sexually transmitted bacterial epididymitis in men older than 35 years is infection with coliform organisms or *Pseudomonas* species. Gram-positive cocci are also important pathogens. This age group distinction is important not only from the standpoint of therapy but also because bacterial epididymitis in men older than 35 years is commonly associated with underlying urologic pathology.

An older patient (>35 years) with epididymitis may give a history of recent genitourinary tract manipulation. Acute or chronic bacterial prostatitis is also an important predisposing condition for the development of epididymitis. In an obtunded, febrile patient with a catheter, it is wise to examine the genitalia to rule out epididymitis as a cause.

The two most common causes of sexually transmitted bacterial epididymitis in young men are *C. trachomatis* and *N. gonorrhoeae*, with *C. trachomatis* clearly the dominant organism (nearly two thirds of all cases in the younger age group). Most patients infected with *Chlamydia* do not complain of urethral discharge but have a demonstrable discharge characteristic of nongonococcal urethritis. A sexual history should be obtained, although there is evidence that patients may carry *C. trachomatis* for long periods before clinical epididymitis develops. Of patients with gonococcal epididymitis, 21% to 30% have no history of urethral discharge and no demonstrable discharge 50% of the time. A sexual history is important, but the patient may be reluctant to give a history of recent exposure. Underlying urologic pathology is rare in this age group.

Syphilitic epididymitis probably occurs more often than generally believed. It may occur early in the secondary stage or 8 to 9 years after onset of the disease. Diffuse thickening of the superior aspect of the epididymis and rubbery nodules may be palpable.[86] The diagnosis is usually presumptive, having been made on the basis of evidence of syphilis elsewhere. Tuberculous epididymitis is often (41%) the earliest indication of renal tuberculosis, but it usually follows a subacute or chronic course rather than an acute one. Typically, one might expect to find beading or thickening of the vas deferens. The most common lesion is a "cold abscess" located in the tail of the epididymis, although the disease may cause the more classic, painful inflammation seen with the more usual pathogens. The diagnosis is further suspected by the urine sediment, which typically reveals abacterial pyuria. The diagnosis is confirmed by isolating *M. tuberculosis* in urine. Amiodarone has also been implicated as a cause of noninfectious epididymitis.

Clinical Features. The pain of epididymitis is usually more gradual in onset and reaches a peak over a period of days, not hours. In 95% of cases of epididymitis there is a febrile state with an average temperature of 38° C (100.4° F). However, nearly 20% of patients with torsion are also mildly febrile. Urinary tract symptoms may precede the pain.

Examination of the affected scrotum is often difficult. The extreme sensitivity and diffuse changes often mask distinguishing landmarks. In general, edema and erythema of the scrotum are *not* noted in the *early* stage of acute epididymitis. The cremasteric reflex is usually present.

Pain most often begins gradually in the scrotum or groin, radiates along the spermatic cord, and frequently intensifies over the next few hours. The degree of epididymal swelling varies, but the epididymis often reaches twice normal size over a 3- to 4-hour period. Fever and generalized toxicity may be seen. A urethral discharge or associated irritative voiding symptoms may accompany the swelling and pain.

There may be tenderness over the groin, lower part of the abdomen, and scrotum. The scrotal skin is usually erythematous and warm. After the initial 3 to 4 hours, the epididymis may be indistinguishable from the testis because of passive congestion. The spermatic cord may be edematous as well.

Diagnostic Strategies. Urinalysis may or may not reveal evidence of bacterial infection. *Chlamydia* is not identified in routine examination of the sediment, whereas *E. coli* is. If a urethral discharge is present, it must be examined for gram-negative intracellular diplococci and other bacteria. The presence of intracellular gram-negative diplococci on Gram stain of the urethral smear correlates nearly 100% of the time with cultures for *N. gonorrhoeae*.

Leukocytosis in the range of 10,000 to 30,000 WBCs/mm^3 is often present. Leukocytosis suggests epididymitis, as does the presence of pyuria in the urine sediment. However, only overwhelming evidence of infection should prevent a strong consideration of torsion as the diagnosis because just 50% of patients with epididymitis have pyuria or bacteria. A urethral Gram stain and culture are indicated, especially for patients younger than 35 years.

The presence of pyuria, bacteriuria, dysuria, or fever does not exclude a diagnosis of torsion. Any patient with an equivocal examination requires perfusion imaging by color Doppler ultrasonography or nuclear scintigraphy. The diagnosis of epididymitis is confirmed by normal to increased testicular blood flow.

Differential Considerations. For both age groups, it is recommended that the genitalia be examined carefully to rule out other diseases. Three intrascrotal processes commonly confused with epididymitis are torsion, torsion of the testicular appendage, and tumor of the testicle. These conditions are addressed in their respective sections.

Management. Treatment of sexually transmitted epididymitis in adults is listed in Table 98-6. Treatment of epididymitis secondary to coliform infection should be guided by the results of urine analysis and culture. Treatment may be accomplished with various effective antimicrobials, including sulfonamides, TMP-SMX, ampicillin, cephalosporins, and fluoroquinolones. One should not forget the importance of treating the sexual partners of patients with sexually transmitted bacterial epididymitis.

In addition to appropriate antibiotics, general supportive measures are recommended, including bed rest, scrotal support, analgesics, sitz baths, or ice packs. The patient should be referred to a urologist for follow-up. In general, the acute inflammatory process subsides within 2 weeks, although it may be a month or more before the epididymis returns to its normal size.

Complications of the disease include infertility (most often seen in sexually transmitted epididymitis), abscess formation (seen in gonococcal epididymitis),

Table 98-6. Treatment of Epididymitis

Drug of Choice	Dose/Route	Alternative
Presumed Sexually Acquired		
Ceftriaxone	250 mg IM	Ciprofloxacin, 500 mg PO Ofloxacin, 400 mg PO
	followed by	
Doxycycline	100 mg PO bid × 10 days	
	or	
Tetracycline	500 mg qid × 10 days	
Presumed Nonsexually Acquired*		
Trimethoprim-sulfamethoxazole	One double-strength tablet PO bid × 14 days	Ciprofloxacin, 500 mg PO bid × 14 days Ofloxacin, 400 mg PO bid × 14 days

*Adjust antibacterial therapy with results of urine culture.

and chronic epididymitis. Ultrasound is indicated for patients not responsive to medical therapy.

Disposition. Patients in the older age group should be approached conservatively from the standpoint of admission since many have urologic pathology as an underlying factor. Patients of any age with systemic signs of toxicity (fever, chills, nausea, vomiting) or complications of acute epididymitis should be hospitalized and treated with parenteral antibiotics. Scrotal abscesses should be sought because emergency surgical debridement and drainage are necessary.

Torsion of Appendages

Perspective. A normal scrotum has several vestigial appendages that may undergo torsion and cause an acute, painful scrotal mass. The testicular and epididymal appendages are two vestigial remnants that are commonly involved. Torsion of the appendages is most frequently seen in preadolescent boys between 3 and 13 years of age. Torsion of the appendix testis is most common, followed by torsion of the epididymal appendix.

Principles of Disease. The appendix testis is a müllerian duct remnant that is attached to the superior pole of the testis between the testis and the epididymis. The appendix epididymis is a wolffian duct remnant attached solely to the epididymis.

The cause of torsion of the appendage is unclear. However, the effects of estrogen before puberty have been thought to cause enlargement and subsequent strangulation of the involved appendage.[89] Similar to testicular torsion, twisting causes obstruction, secondary edema, and sharp pain as the tissue becomes necrotic.

Clinical Features. A twisted appendage is typically manifested as an acute scrotal pain and a discrete, painful testicular mass. However, the symptoms are usually less severe than in testicular torsion. Unlike testicular torsion, a history of previous episodes is uncommon, as are complaints of nausea, vomiting,

fever, dysuria, and penile discharge. If the lesion is seen early, it might be rewarding to transilluminate the scrotum. The appendage may appear as a blue-black dot. With progressive edema it is not uncommon for a reactive hydrocele to develop and mask the small, tender mass of a twisted appendage.

Diagnostic Strategies. Urinalysis of midstream urine should be performed, but it does not generally demonstrate pyuria or bacteriuria. Color Doppler ultrasound and nuclear scintigraphy are the diagnostic procedures of choice. An imaging study that demonstrates normal to increased blood flow helps establish the diagnosis.

Differential Considerations. Other diagnoses such as testicular torsion, epididymitis, and testicular tumor must be considered.

Management and Disposition. If testicular torsion can be ruled out with certainty, conservative measures generally remain the standard of care, including scrotal support, pelvic rest, and analgesia. Resolution of symptoms can be expected within 7 to 10 days. Surgical excision is reserved for severe or refractory cases.

Testicular Tumors

Perspective. Tumor of the testis is the most common malignancy in young men, and it occurs at an average age of 32 years. Testicular cancer accounts for 1% of all cancer in men. The differential diagnosis between tumor, torsion, and epididymitis can be extremely difficult. In fact, epididymitis is the most common *incorrect* diagnosis made in cases of testicular tumor (6% to 16% incidence).[86] There is an increased prevalence in patients with cryptorchidism in both the nondescended and descended testis.

The vast majority of testicular cancers are seminomas, followed by embryonal cell cancer and teratoma. The cancer spreads by the lymphatic system.

Clinical Features. Clinically, the emergency physician might be confronted with diffuse swelling of the scrotum and its contents, with neither the classically severe pain of torsion or epididymitis nor the palpably hard, painless growth of testicular carcinoma. Although tumors are generally painless ("heaviness" is commonly reported), the patient may have sudden testicular pain because of acute hemorrhage within the tumor. This acute hemorrhage causes an expanding mass effect on the nonpliable tunica albuginea.

Diagnostic Strategies. Findings on urinalysis should be normal in the presence of tumor. The key to diagnosis is identification of a distinct *intratesticular* mass. Color Doppler ultrasonography is the initial diagnostic imaging study. A chest radiograph or chest CT may be considered if metastatic spread is suspected. Abdominal CT may be indicated for staging purposes.

Management. Suspicion of a testicular tumor is an indication for immediate referral and hospitalization. Radical orchiectomy with high ligation of the spermatic cord is the preferred surgical procedure. The radiosensitive nature of seminomas makes the combined treatment of orchiectomy and radiation therapy beneficial for early-stage seminomas. The highly effective chemotherapy agent cisplatin has also improved survival rates.

Orchitis

Perspective. Orchitis is an acute infection involving the testis. Because the testis possesses a relatively high threshold of resistance to infection, orchitis is rare without an initial epididymitis. Additionally, orchitis occurs significantly less often than prostatitis or epididymitis. As in epididymitis, the testis may become infected with a wide variety of organisms.

The two major distinguishing causes of orchitis are blood-borne bacterial infection and viral infection. Pyogenic bacterial orchitis is usually secondary to bacterial involvement of the epididymis, with testicular spread occurring secondarily. The most frequent bacterial pathogens are *E. coli*, *Klebsiella*, and *Pseudomonas*. Viral orchitis is most commonly caused by mumps. It is rarely seen in prepubertal boys but occurs in 20% to 30% of postpubertal boys with mumps.[86] Granulomatous orchitis occurs in association with syphilis and mycobacterial and fungal diseases, most often in an immunocompromised host.

Clinical Features. A patient with pyogenic orchitis is usually acutely ill with fever, marked discomfort, and swelling of the testicle. It is common to see a reactive hydrocele, and the testis is swollen and exquisitely tender. The most frequent picture is that of coexistent epididymo-orchitis. In general, presumptive signs of infection are present, such as pyuria, leukocytosis, and fever.

A patient with viral orchitis has testicular pain and swelling that commonly begin 4 to 6 days after the onset of parotitis but may occur without parotid involvement. The disease is unilateral in 70% of patients. The clinical course varies, but resolution generally occurs in 4 to 5 days. More than 50% of testes involved with mumps orchitis suffer from atrophy; however, this atrophy seldom results in infertility.

Diagnostic Strategies. Urinalysis, urine culture, and blood cultures should be performed. If granulomatous orchitis is suspected, its diagnosis depends on specific cultures and often on histologic stains. The diagnosis of testicular torsion should be excluded. If epididymo-orchitis is present, it is a difficult entity to distinguish from torsion. Therefore, if the diagnosis is uncertain, color Doppler ultrasonography should be performed.

Management. Treatment of pyogenic bacterial orchitis includes antibiotics targeting *E. coli*, *Klebsiella pneumoniae*, *Pseudomonas aeruginosa*, staphylococci, or streptococci. Local scrotal measures as outlined in the section on epididymitis are helpful. Admission to the hospital is generally required for patients with systemic signs and symptoms.

Treatment of viral orchitis is supportive only. Admission is guided by the clinical picture, which may range from mild swelling and discomfort to marked pain, high fever, and constitutional symptoms.

Inguinal Hernia and Acute Hydrocele

Both inguinal hernia and acute hydrocele are reasonable considerations in the differential diagnosis of an acute scrotal mass. However, both should be readily distinguished by careful physical examination.

Acute Urinary Retention

Perspective

Acute urinary retention (AUR) can be defined as the sudden inability to pass urine. Although there are numerous causes (Box 98-6), a patient with AUR is most often an elderly man with prostatic hypertrophy.

AUR is a common problem in men with advancing age. It is estimated that at least one episode of AUR will develop in 10% and 33% of men in their 70s and 80s, respectively.[90] In women a common cause of urinary retention is an atonic, decompensated bladder that has

---

BOX 98-6. Causes of Acute Urinary Retention in Adults

Penis
Phimosis
Paraphimosis
Meatal stenosis
Foreign body constriction

Urethra
Tumor
Foreign body
Calculus
Urethritis (severe)
Stricture
Meatal stenosis (female)
Hematoma

Prostate Gland
Benign prostatic hypertrophy
Carcinoma
Prostatitis (severe)
Bladder neck contracture
Prostatic infarction

Neurologic Causes
Motor paralytic
  Spinal shock
  Spinal cord syndromes
Sensory paralytic
  Tabes dorsalis
  Diabetes
  Multiple sclerosis
Syringomyelia
Spinal cord syndromes
Herpes zoster

Drugs
Antihistamines
Anticholinergic agents
Antispasmodic agents
Tricyclic antidepressants
α-Adrenergic stimulators
  "Cold" tablets
  Ephedrine derivatives
  Amphetamines

Psychogenic Problems

From Sacknoff EJ, Dretler SP: Urologic emergencies. In Wilkins E (ed): *MCH Textbook of Emergency Medicine*. Baltimore, Williams & Wilkins, 1978.

resulted from years of infrequent voiding. In young patients, urinary retention may be an early manifestation of neurologic disease (e.g., multiple sclerosis, tabes dorsalis, diabetes, syringomyelia). Less common causes of urinary retention include phimosis, paraphimosis, and meatal stenosis.

Psychogenic urinary retention is rare and should be a diagnosis of exclusion only after appropriate studies on bladder function have been performed by a urology specialist.

AUR may be drug induced, especially in patients who are susceptible (e.g., an elderly man with mild bladder neck obstruction). Drug categories that may directly cause retention include antihistamines, anticholinergics, antispasmodics, and tricyclic antidepressants. Medications that induce bladder neck hypertonicity and thereby result in AUR include ephedrine compounds, amphetamines, and certain "cold" tablets (Box 98-7).

The most common cause of urinary retention in men older than 50 years is prostatic hyperplasia with bladder neck obstruction. Other, less common causes of obstruction in men include carcinoma of the prostate, bladder carcinoma, urethral stricture (secondary to infection or injury), and an atonic or neurogenic bladder.

Clinical Features

In elderly men, symptoms and signs may include a progressive decrease in the force and caliber of the urinary stream, nocturia, dribbling, previous history of retention, or urologic procedures such as catheterization, dilation for strictures, and prostatectomy (Box 98-8). Constitutional symptoms such as bone pain and weight loss (suggesting carcinoma of the prostate) should be sought in these patients.

If infection is also present, symptoms such as dysuria, frequency, and urgency may be reported.

Physical examination in men may reveal an enlarged prostate gland, but a normal-sized gland does not eliminate it as a source of obstruction. A nodular, firm mass may also be palpated and suggests carcinoma of the prostate.

A bladder containing 150 mL or more of urine should be palpable and percussible.

Diagnostic Strategies

Laboratory studies should be obtained to assess renal function. With both postrenal and prerenal obstruction, the BUN-to-creatinine ratio is elevated. In lower urinary tract obstruction, BUN may be increased because of significant reabsorption. Urinalysis should always be performed to ascertain the presence of coexisting infection. Hematuria suggests the presence of infection, tumor, or calculi.

Imaging studies (IVP, ultrasonography, CT) are rarely indicated in the emergency department and are generally reserved for patients with evidence of infection or signs of systemic toxicity.

Management

Initial efforts to relieve painful urinary retention are best approached with a standard urethral catheter. A 16 or 18 French urethral catheter with a 5-mL balloon may be used. Lidocaine jelly should be inserted into the urethra first, not only to anesthetize the urethra but also to lubricate and distend it.

BOX 98-7. Pharmacologic Agents That May Contribute to Acute Urinary Retention

β-Agonists
Isoproterenol
Terbutaline

Narcotics
Morphine
Meperidine
Hydromorphone (Dilaudid)

Anticholinergics
Atropine
Belladonna
Benztropine (Cogentin)
Cyclic antidepressants
Antihistamines
Phenothiazines
Propantheline (Pro-Banthīne)
Methantheline
Ipratropium bromide
Monoamine oxidase

Musculotropic Relaxants (of the Detrusor)
Flavoxate (Urispas)
Nifedipine
Dicyclomine (Bentyl)
Oxybutynin (Ditropan)
Hyoscyamine (Cytospaz)
Estrogen
Diazepam
Indomethacin (NSAIDs)

NSAIDs, nonsteroidal anti-inflammatory drugs.

BOX 98-8. Symptoms of Urinary Retention

Obstructive Symptoms
Urinary hesitancy
Straining to void
Decrease in size and force of urinary stream
Interruption of urinary stream
Sensation of incomplete emptying
Previous episode of urinary retention

Irritative Symptoms
Urinary frequency
Urinary urgency
Dysuria (usually secondary to infection)
Nocturia or nocturnal incontinence

Modified from Lapides J: *Fundamentals of Urology*. Philadelphia. WB Saunders, 1976.

If a standard urethral catheter cannot be passed, the next step is to attempt to pass a coudé catheter. This type of catheter has an upward deflection in its distal 3 cm, which allows it to pass over an enlarged median lobe of the prostate. It also allows the tip of the catheter to be directed toward the roof of the urethra. The floor of the urethra is more lax, whereas the roof is relatively fixed. A coudé catheter can avoid impingement on the urethral fold.

If an 18 French or coudé catheter will not pass into the bladder, further effort at instrumentation should be stopped. The use of filiforms and followers as well as metal sounds may result in serious tissue damage and should be undertaken by a urologic specialist.

If no consultant is available or if immediate bladder decompression is needed, percutaneous bladder aspiration may be performed. It is important to ensure that the bladder is palpable and distended to minimize complications. If doubt exists, a 22-gauge needle on a syringe should be passed through the skin to see whether urine can be aspirated. This should be done one to two fingerbreadths above the symphysis pubis and directed toward the anus. Alternatively, ultrasound-directed cystostomy may be performed. Depending on availability, a number of devices may be used, including the Cystocath, the Bonana, and the Argyle-Ingram catheter. If these devices are not available, a central venous set may be used, with the 12- to 18-inch tubing inserted into the bladder before the needle is withdrawn (Figure 98-10).[91]

Traditionally, gradual decompression has been recommended to prevent complications such as hematuria, hypotension, and postobstructive diuresis.

The risk of hematuria with release of AUR is 2% to 16%. However, there have been no reported cases of severe hematuria requiring invasive treatment.[92]

Hypotension has been reported after decompression in patients with AUR. AUR results in an increase in systemic blood pressure as a result of stimulation of the vesicovascular reflex. The reduction in blood pressure after decompression may simply be normalization of systolic blood pressure. Patients at risk for hypotension after decompression include those with advancing age or hypovolemia, in whom the ability to compensate appropriately to sudden changes in systolic blood pressure is altered.

Postobstructive diuresis is thought to result from a combination of factors, including osmotic diuresis, involvement of natriuretic and diuretic factors, disordered nephron function, altered tubular permeability, and disturbance of sodium-regulating hormones.[92] Patients with comorbid conditions (renal disease, fluid overload) appear to be at greatest risk for postobstructive diuresis.

Figure 98-10. Cystostomy tube placement. **A**, Anesthetizing trocar track. After a skin wheal (a) is raised, the suprapubic track for the trocar is anesthetized, including the rectus fascia (b). Anesthetizing until the bladder is penetrated will ensure total comfort for patient during insertion of the trocar. **B**, Needle localization of the bladder. A spinal needle may be used even during insertion of the trocar to locate the bladder. **C**, Trocar position. Advance the trocar until its sheath, as well as the point, is fully in the bladder. **D**, Tubing position. Insert enough tubing so that it will not pull out of the bladder when the bladder empties. (From Robert JR, Hedges JR: *Clinical Procedures in Emergency Medicine.* Philadelphia, WB Saunders, 1985.)

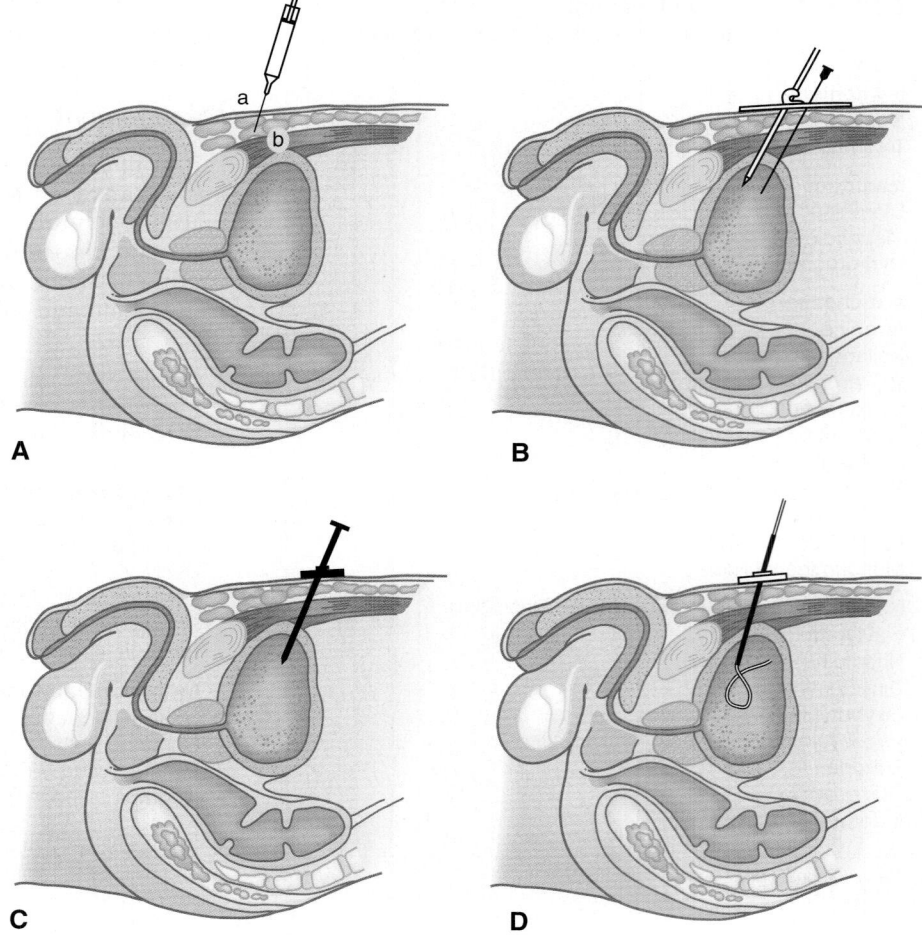

A

B

C

D

Nyman and associates report that gradual emptying of the bladder, though traditionally recommended, has unproven efficacy.[92] No controlled studies have demonstrated that gradual emptying of the bladder reduces the risk for complications. In addition, to avoid large alterations in vesicular pressure, urine would need to be removed in fractions of 50 mL or less, a practice that is impractical in the emergency department. Surveys of well-intentioned nurses who practice gradual emptying showed that the majority release more than 750 mL initially before clamping the catheter. Though common practice, this technique's physiologic effects are similar to those of complete bladder emptying. Based on an extensive literature review, Nyman and colleagues recommend quick, complete emptying of the obstructed urinary bladder in all instances.[92]

Disposition

Consultation or immediate referral (or both) is the rule in patients with AUR. After bladder drainage and consultation, patients may be discharged with an indwelling catheter. Patients with signs of serious infection, decreased renal function, volume overload, or an inability to care for themselves without reliable home care should be hospitalized.

Removal of the catheter is not prudent because reaccumulation of urine and recurrence of AUR are inevitable.

Hematuria

Perspective

Hematuria is a clinical condition commonly seen by emergency physicians. The prevalence of asymptomatic microscopic hematuria in adult men and postmenopausal women has been reported to range from 10% to as high as 20%.[93] The emergency physician's understanding of the evaluation, workup, and appropriate disposition is essential. Gross or microscopic hematuria should be considered a harbinger of serious urologic disease. In fact, *patients with gross hematuria have an approximately five times higher incidence of life-threatening conditions than do those with microhematuria.*[94]

Principles of Disease

Bleeding from the lower and middle urinary tract causes approximately 60% of all cases of hematuria. A considerable number are caused by bladder neoplasms. Urologic malignancies have been reported to occur in 2.2% to 12.5% of patients with microscopic hematuria and up to 20% of patients older than 50 years with gross hematuria. A large prospective study of patients with gross hematuria on two of three urinalyses found a potentially life-threatening lesion in 9.1% of these patients.[95,96]

Other sources of bleeding from the bladder commonly include infection of the bladder (hemorrhagic cystitis), varices of the bladder, diverticula, bladder stones, and postradiation changes. Anticoagulation at currently recommended levels does not predispose

---

BOX 98-9. Most Frequent Causes of Hematuria by Age and Gender

Age 0-20 Years
Acute glomerulonephritis
Acute UTI
Congenital urinary tract anomalies with obstruction

Age 20-40 Years
Acute UTI
Bladder cancer
Urolithiasis

Age 40-60 Years (Women)
Acute UTI
Bladder cancer
Urolithiasis

Age 40-60 Years (Men)
Acute UTI
Bladder cancer
Urolithiasis

Age 60 Years and Older (Women)
Acute UTI
Bladder cancer

Age 60 Years and Older (Men)
Acute UTI
Benign prostatic hyperplasia
Bladder cancer

UTI, urinary tract infection.
From Restrepo NC, Carey PO: Evaluating hematuria in adults. *Am Fam Physician* 40:149, 1989. Modified from Gillenwater JY (ed): *Adult and Pediatric Urology.* St Louis, CV Mosby, 1987.

---

patients to hematuria. Identifiable genitourinary tract disease is present in most anticoagulated patients with microscopic or gross hematuria.[97] Hemorrhage from the prostate is most often caused by a benign lesion. In fact, bleeding from benign prostatic hyperplasia is the most common cause of gross hematuria in men 60 years and older (Boxes 98-9 and 98-10, and Table 98-7).

An attack of renal colic associated with gross hematuria is probably caused by a bleeding site in the kidney or ureter. If a "wormlike" clot is passed, a neoplasm of the kidney or renal pelvis should be suspected.

Hematuria can be divided into glomerular and nonglomerular categories. Hematuria of glomerular origin is frequently associated with dysmorphic erythrocytes, RBC casts, and significant proteinuria in the 2+ to 3+ range on dipstick. IgA nephropathy (Berger's disease) is the most common cause of glomerular hematuria. In contrast, nonglomerular hematuria results in uniformly round erythrocytes and absence of erythrocyte casts and proteinuria.

Clinical Features

An appropriate medical history may assist in the evaluation (Box 98-11). Certain distinguishing historical features aid the clinician in narrowing the differential diagnosis.

BOX 98-10. Common Causes of Hematuria

Prerenal
Coagulopathy (e.g., hemophilia, idiopathic thrombocytopenic purpura)
Anticoagulation (e.g., use of warfarin sodium [Coumadin, Panwarfin, Sofarin], heparin sodium)
Collagen vascular disease (e.g., systemic lupus erythematosus, scleroderma)
Sickle cell disease, sickle cell trait

Renal
Glomerular
Glomerulonephritis
Lupus nephritis
Benign familial hematuria
Alport's syndrome
Vascular abnormalities (vasculitis, arteriovenous malformation, infarct)

Nonglomerular
Pyelonephritis
Polycystic kidney disease
Granulomatous disease (tuberculosis, cryptococcosis)
Xanthogranulomatous pyelonephritis
Interstitial nephritis
Papillary necrosis secondary to phenacetin use
Malignant neoplasm (renal cell carcinoma)

Postrenal
Calculus
Ureteritis
Cystitis
Prostatitis
Benign prostatic hyperplasia
Epididymitis
Urethritis
Malignant neoplasm (transitional cell carcinoma)

False
Vaginal bleeding
Recent circumcision
Factitious (automanipulation)
Pigmenturia
  Myoglobinuria
  Hemoglobinuria
  Porphyria
  Intake of certain foods (beets, blackberries, rhubarb)
  Intake of certain drugs (quinine sulfate [Quine, Quinamm], phenazopyridine HCl [Baridium, Pyridium], rifampin [Rifadin, Rimactane], cascara sagrada)

BOX 98-11. Medical History of Patients with Hematuria

Exclude pseudohematuria—drugs, vegetable dyes, pigments
Factitious—Munchausen syndrome, narcotic-seeking behavior
Bleeding diathesis
Clots—indicate nonglomerular bleeding; large, thick clots (bladder); small, stringy clots (upper tract)
Gross hematuria—relationship to exercise, infection
Relationship of gross hematuria to urinary stream—initial (urethra distal to the urogenital diaphragm), total (bladder proper or upper urinary tract), terminal (bladder neck or prostatic urethra)
Painful hematuria—urinary tract infection or calculus, papillary necrosis, passage of clots, obstruction, loin pain–hematuria syndrome, glomerulonephritis
Genitourinary history—flank trauma or pain frequency; nocturia; dysuria; previous stones, tissue passage, or infections; vaginal or penile discharge; sexual activity; presence of urinary catheter
Relationship to menstruation—endometriosis
Sickle cell disease or trait
Medications
Systemic symptoms—fever, rash, joint pain, weight loss
Infectious etiology—night sweats, sore throat, impetigo, tooth extraction or other invasive procedures, diarrhea, travel to areas endemic for *Schistosoma haematobium*
Risk factors for urologic cancer—age >40 years, tobacco use, analgesic abuse, pelvic irradiation, cyclophosphamide, *S. haematobium*, occupational exposure to dyestuffs and rubber compounds
Family history—hematuria, renal disease, sickle cell disease, deafness, bleeding diathesis
Previous testing—blood pressure, urinalysis, serum chemistries, intravenous pyelogram
Pregnancies—proteinuria, hypertension (and month of onset)

suggests hemophilia and polycystic kidney disease, respectively. Papillary necrosis should be suspected in diabetics, sickle cell patients, and analgesic abusers. The classic features of urolithiasis, sudden flank pain, and hematuria are common historical complaints. Another common initial historical complaint is hematuria, dysuria, and frequency consistent with UTIs.

Diagnostic Strategies

Laboratory Studies

Microscopic hematuria can be identified by two methods: dipstick and microscopic examination of urinary sediment. The dipstick is positive only with lysis of RBCs or with myoglobinuria. The dipstick detects hemoglobin in a concentration greater than 0.003 mg/L. This concentration corresponds to 10,000 RBCs/mm^3 or 1 to 2 RBCs per high-power field of spun urine. Most urine specimens containing RBCs test positive on the dipstick, but the presence of only a few RBCs may be missed during microscopic examination. Urine should be centrifuged for 3 to 5 minutes and examined carefully to distinguish hematuria from

In the presence of glomerular disease, children, typically young boys, have hematuria, an erythematous rash, and fevers suggesting immunoglobulin nephropathy, or Berger's disease. A family history of deafness, renal disease, and hematuria is linked to Alport's nephritis. A rash, arthritis, and hematuria are seen with systemic lupus erythematosus. Hematuria, hemoptysis, and microscopic anemia are common manifestations of Goodpasture's syndrome. A preceding upper respiratory infection, pharyngitis, skin infection, or rash with associated hematuria suggests poststreptococcal glomerulonephritis.

In the presence of nonglomerular disease, a family history of bleeding disorders or renal cystic disease

Table 98-7. Results of Hematuria Evaluation in 1000 Adults

Condition	Total No.	Insignificant	Significant		Life Threatening
			Requiring Observation	*Requiring Treatment*	
Glomerulonephritis	12	0	10	0	2
Renal adenocarcinoma	10	0	0	0	10
Pyelonephritis	7	0	6	1	0
Simple renal cyst	6	0	6	0	0
Renal tubular ectasia	3	0	3	0	0
Papillary necrosis	3	0	3	0	0
Atrophic kidney	1	0	1	0	0
Diffuse intervascular coagulation from stomach cancer	1	0	0	0	1
Pelvic kidney	1	0	1	0	0
Renal arteriovenous fistula	1	0	1	0	0
Renal contusion	1	0	1	0	0
Familial hematuria	1	0	1	0	0
Total renal (%)	47 (4.7)	0	33	1	13
Renal calculus	34	2	22	10	0
Renal pelvic transitional cell cancer	5	0	0	0	5
Ureteropelvic junction obstruction	1	0	1	0	0
Total renal pelvic (%)	40 (4.0)	2	23	10	5
Ureteral calculus	6	0	4	0	2
Ureteral transitional cell cancer	3	0	0	0	3
Total ureteral (%)	9 (0.9)	0	4	0	5
Bladder transitional cell cancer	65	0	0	0	65
Cystitis	43	10	4	29	0
Bladder neck varicosities	33	30	3	0	0
Cystitis cystica	30	29	1	0	0
Bladder neck contracture	8	0	8	0	0
Bladder calculus	6	0	6	0	0
Radiation cystitis	3	0	3	0	0
Interstitial cystitis	2	0	0	2	0
Bladder adenocarcinoma	1	0	0	0	1
Bladder diverticulum	1	0	1	0	0
Positive cytology	1	0	1	0	0
Sigmoid metastases	1	0	0	0	1
Total bladder (%)	194 (19.7)	69	27	31	67
Urethritis/trigonitis	377	355	20	2	0
Benign prostatic hyperplasia	143	107	27	9	0
Recurrent benign prostatic hyperplasia	22	6	8	8	0
Meatal stenosis	20	6	0	14	0
Urethral carbuncle	19	18	0	1	0
Urethral stricture	10	1	3	6	0
Prostate adenocarcinoma	1	0	0	0	1
Urethral prolapse					
Total urethral (%)	593 (59.2)	493	59	40	1
Total diagnostic (%)	883 (88.3)	564 (56.4)	146 (14.6)	(82) 8.2	91 (9.1)

From Mariani A et al: The significance of adult hematuria: 1000 hematuria evaluations including a risk benefit and cost effectiveness analysis. *J Urol* 141:350, 1989.

hemoglobinuria and myoglobinuria. The presence of erythrocytes establishes the diagnosis of hematuria. RBC casts indicate that the source of bleeding is from the kidney at the glomerular level. RBC and WBC casts degenerate quickly (as do most cellular elements), so the urine must be examined within 1 hour. Warmth and alkalinity cause rapid lysis and can lead to false-negative results. To optimally visualize erythrocytes, phase-contrast microscopy is recommended, although conventional light microscopy is acceptable.

Imaging

Emergency imaging studies performed in the emergency department to evaluate nonglomerular hematuria include limited renal ultrasonography, tailored excretory urography with CT, magnetic resonance imaging, and spiral CT without contrast. Because preexisting renal insufficiency is the most important risk factor for renal failure after contrast administration, serum creatinine determination is recommended before any contrast study.[97] If the patient's creatinine is higher than 1.1 mg/dL, there is evidence that sodium bicarbonate infusion may help decrease the subsequent incidence of contrast nephropathy.[98]

Differential Considerations

Exercise-Induced Hematuria

Strenuous exercise can cause transient hematuria both through direct glomerular excretion of erythrocytes in urine and through repetitive minor trauma to the bladder (runner's hematuria). In either case, symptoms should resolve spontaneously within 48 hours.[97] Exercise-induced hematuria that does not resolve after 48 hours commonly results from punctate hemorrhagic lesions, suggestive of bladder cancer, and can be diagnosed by cystoscopy.

Pseudohematuria

Red urine may result from urinary pigments that give a pink-red color to the urine. Microscopic examination of the sediment reveals no RBCs. The major causes include anthocyanins in beets and berries, phenolphthalein in alkaline urine, phenazopyridine (Pyridium), heavy concentrations of urates, porphyria, and vegetable dyes for food coloring.

Disposition

The emergency physician must be cognizant of the acute evaluation and treatment of hematuria and the appropriate and timely disposition of patients with hematuria. Specifically, a complete urologic evaluation is necessary for the evaluation of tumors. The likelihood of tumors developing within 2 to 5 years after a complete and negative hematuria evaluation is 0% to 3%.[99] Current recommendations include urinalysis and cytologic evaluation for 3 consecutive years in patients with resolution of hematuria or persistent asymptomatic microhematuria. Patients with gross hematuria should be re-evaluated in all instances.[97]

KEY CONCEPTS

- Infected urine in the setting of obstructive urolithiasis is a urologic emergency.
- Aortic abdominal aneurysm is most commonly misdiagnosed as nephrolithiasis.
- Testicular torsion is most commonly misdiagnosed as epididymitis.
- Genitourinary neoplasm should always be considered in patients with nontraumatic hematuria.
- Urinary tract infection in young children should be treated conservatively and always requires follow-up studies for anatomic evaluation.

REFERENCES

1. Foxman B: Epidemiology of urinary tract infections: Incidence, morbidity, and economic costs. *Am J Med* 113:5S, 2002.
2. Patton JP, Nash DB, Abrutyn E: Urinary tract infections: Economic considerations. *Med Clin North Am* 75:495, 1991.
3. Talan DA, Naber KG, Palou J, Elkharrat D: Extended-release ciprofloxacin (Cipro XR) for treatment of urinary tract infections. *Int J Antimicrob Agents* 23(Suppl 1)S54, 2004.
4. Pattaragarn A, Alon US: Urinary tract infection in childhood. Review of the guidelines and recommendations. *Minerva Pediatr* 54:401, 2002.
5. Santen S, Altieri M: Pediatric urinary tract infection. *Emerg Med Clin North Am* 19:3, 2001.
6. Dairiki-Shortliffe L, McCue J: Urinary tract infection at the age extremes: Pediatrics and geriatrics. *Am J Med* 113:S55, 2002.
7. MacNeily A: Pediatric urinary tract infections: Current controversies. *Can J Urol* 8(Suppl 1):18, 2001.
8. Nicolle LE: Urinary tract infection in the elderly. *J Antimicrob Chemother* 33:99, 1994.
9. Hoberman A, et al: Prevalence of urinary tract infection in febrile infants. *J Pediatr* 123:17, 1993.
10. Shaw K, Gorelick M: Urinary tract infection in the pediatric patient. *Pediatr Clin North Am* 46:6, 1999.
11. Lindert K, Dairiki Shortliffe L: Evaluation and management of pediatric urinary tract infections. *Urol Clin North Am* 26:4, 1999.
12. Gupta K: Increasing prevalence of antimicrobial resistance among uropathogens causing acute uncomplicated cystitis in women. *JAMA* 281:736, 1999.
13. Childs S: Management of UTIs. *Am J Med* 85:15, 1988.
14. Brettman LR: Pathogenesis of urinary tract infections: Host susceptibility and bacterial virulence factors. *Urology* 32:9, 1988.
15. Hampson SJ, et al: Does residual urine predispose to urinary tract infection? *Br J Urol* 70:506, 1992.
16. Boscia JA, et al: Epidemiology of bacteriuria in an elderly ambulatory population. *Am J Med* 80:208, 1986.
17. Richmann M, et al: Risk factors for bacteriuria in men. *Urology* 43:617, 1994.
18. Mariani P, Terndrup TE: Urinary tract infection in women. In Harwood-Nuss A (ed): *The Clinical Practice of Emergency Medicine,* 2nd ed. Philadelphia, JB Lippincott, 1996.
19. Kunin CM: Urinary tract infections in females. *Clin Infect Dis* 18:1, 1994.
20. Stamm WE, Hooton TM: Management of urinary tract infections in adults. *N Engl J Med* 329:1328, 1993.
21. Cox C: Comparison of intravenous fleroxacin with ceftazidime for treatment of complicated urinary tract infections. *Am J Med* 94:1185, 1993.
22. Andriole VT: Urinary tract infections in the '90s: Pathogenesis and management. *Infection* 20(Suppl 4):S251, 1992.
23. Sheldon CA, Gonzalez R: Differentiation of upper and lower urinary tract infections. *Med Clin North Am* 68:321, 1984.
24. Stamm WE, et al: Causes of the acute urethral syndrome in women. *N Engl J Med* 303:409, 1980.
25. Busch R, Huland H: Correlation of symptoms and results of direct bacterial localization in patients with urinary tract infections. *J Urol* 132:282, 1984.
26. Lipsky BA, et al: Diagnosis of bacteriuria in men: Specimen collection and culture interpretation. *J Infect Dis* 15:847, 1987.
27. Gorelick MH, Shaw KN: Screening tests for UTI in children: A meta-analysis. *Pediatrics* 104:54, 1999.
28. Shaw KN, et al: Clinical evaluation of a rapid screening test for urinary tract infections in children. *J Pediatr* 118:733, 1991.
29. Schlager TA, Lohr JA: Urinary tract infection in outpatient febrile infants and children younger than 5 years of age. *Pediatr Ann* 22:505, 1993.
30. Lockhart GR, et al: Use of urinary Gram's stain for detection of urinary tract infection in infants. *Ann Emerg Med* 25:31, 1995.
31. Hoberman A, et al: Enhanced urinalysis as a screening test for urinary tract infection. *Pediatrics* 91:1196, 1993.
32. Morgan MG, McKenzie H: Controversies in the laboratory diagnosis of community-acquired urinary tract infection. *Eur J Clin Microbiol Infect Dis* 12:491, 1993.
33. Carroll KC, et al: Laboratory evaluation of urinary tract infections in an ambulatory clinic. *Clin Microbiol Infect Dis* 101:100, 1992.
34. Weinberg AG, et al: Urine screen for bacteriuria in symptomatic pediatric outpatients. *Pediatr Infect Dis J* 10:651, 1991.

35. Stamm WE: Measurement of pyuria and its relation to bacteriuria. *Am J Med* 75:53, 1983.

36. Saito A, Kawada Y: Reliability of pyuria detection method. *Infection* 22:S36, 1994.

37. Goswitz JJ, et al: Utility of slide centrifuge Gram's stain versus quantitative culture for diagnosis of urinary tract infection. *Clin Pathol* 99:132, 1993.

38. Kass EH: Bacteriuria and the diagnosis of infections of the urinary tract with observation on the use of methionine as a urinary antiseptic. *Arch Intern Med* 100:179, 1957.

39. Kunin CM, White LV, Hua TH: A reassessment of the importance of "low-count" bacteriuria in young women with acute urinary symptoms. *Ann Intern Med* 119:454, 1993.

40. Schaeffer AJ: Infections of the urinary tract. In Walsh, et al (eds): *Campbell's Urology*. Philadelphia, WB Saunders, 1998.

41. Kanel KT, et al: The intravenous pyelogram in acute pyelonephritis. *Arch Intern Med* 148:2144, 1988.

42. McNicholas MMJ, Griffin JF, Cantwell DF: Ultrasound of the pelvis and renal tract combined with a plain film of abdomen in young women with urinary tract infection: Can it replace intravenous urography? *Br J Radiol* 64:221, 1991.

43. MacKenzie JR, et al: The value of ultrasound in the child with an acute urinary tract infection. *Br J Urol* 74:240, 1994.

44. Dinkel E, et al: Renal sonography in the differentiation of upper from lower urinary tract infection. *AJR Am J Roentgenol* 146:775, 1986.

45. Goldman SM, Fishman EK: Upper urinary tract infection: The current role of CT, ultrasound, and MRI. *Semin Ultrasound CT MR* 12:335, 1991.

46. Bint AJ, Hill D: Bacteriuria of pregnancy: An update on significance, diagnosis, and management. *J Antimicrob Chemother* 33:93, 1994.

47. Stamey TA: *Pathogenesis and Treatment of UTI*. Baltimore, Wilkins & Wilkins, 1980.

48. Harding GK, et al: Antimicrobial treatment in diabetic women with asymptomatic bacteriuria. *N Engl J Med* 347:1576, 2002.

49. Stamm WE, et al: Diagnosis of coliform infection in acutely dysuric women. *N Engl J Med* 307:463, 1982.

50. McLaughlin SP, Carson CC: Urinary tract infections in women. *Med Clin North Am* 88:417, 2004.

51. Gupta K, Hooton TM, Stamm WE: Increasing antimicrobial resistance and the management of uncomplicated community acquired urinary tract infections. *Ann Intern Med* 135:41, 2001.

52. Stamm W: An epidemic of urinary tract infections [editorial]? *N Engl J Med* 345:14, 2001.

53. Dyer IE, Sankery TM, Dawson JA: Antibiotic resistance in bacterial UTI, 1991-97. *West J Med* 169:265a, 1988.

54. Norrby SR: Short-term treatment of uncomplicated lower urinary tract infections in women. *Rev Infect Dis* 12:458, 1990.

55. Hooton TM, et al: Randomized comparative trial and cost analysis of 3-day antimicrobial regimens for treatment of acute cystitis in women. *JAMA* 273:41, 1995.

56. Greenberg RN, et al: Randomized study of single dose, three-day, and seven-day treatment of cystitis. *J Infect Dis* 153:277, 1986.

57. Avorn J, et al: Reduction of bacteriuria and pyuria after ingestion of cranberry juice. *JAMA* 271:751, 1994.

58. Fang LS, Tolkoff-Rubin NE, Rubin RH: Clinical management of urinary tract infection. *Pharmacotherapy* 2:91, 1982.

59. Shaw KN, Gorelick MH: UTI in the pediatric patient. *Pediatr Clin North Am* 46:1111, 1999.

60. Jakobsson B, Berg U, Svensson L: Renal scarring after acute pyelonephritis. *Arch Dis Child* 70:111, 1994.

61. Benador D, et al: Cortical scintigraphy in the evaluation of renal parenchymal changes in children with pyelonephritis. *J Pediatr* 124:17, 1994.

62. Kim SB, et al: Clinical value of DMSA planar and single photon emission computed tomography as an initial diagnostic tool in adult women with recurrent acute pyelonephritis. *Nephron* 67:274, 1994.

63. Gleeson FV, et al: Imaging in urinary tract infection. *Arch Dis Child* 66:1282, 1991.

64. Hoberman A, et al: Oral vs. IV therapy for UTI in young febrile children. *Pediatrics* 104:79, 1999.

65. Petersen KE: Short-term treatment of acute urinary tract infection in girls. *Scand J Infect Dis* 23:213, 1991.

66. Krieger JN, Ross SO, Simonsen JM: Urinary tract infections in healthy university men. *J Urol* 149:1046, 1993.

67. Stamm WE, et al: *Chlamydia trachomatis* urethral infections in men. *Ann Intern Med* 100:47, 1984.

68. McNagny SE, et al: Urinary leukocyte esterase test: A screening method for the detection of asymptomatic chlamydial and gonococcal infections in men. *J Infect Dis* 165:573, 1992.

69. Hua VN, Schaeffer AJ: Acute and chronic prostatitis. *Med Clin North Am* 88:2, 2004.

70. Krieger JN: Prostatitis revisited: New definitions, new approaches. *Infect Dis Clin North Am* 17:395, 2003.

71. Wagenlehner FME, Naber KG: Prostatitis: The role of antibiotic treatment. *World J Urol* 21:105, 2003.

72. Khastigir J, Dickinson AJ: Where do we stand with chronic prostatitis? An update. *Hosp Med* 64:732, 2004.

73. Saklayem MG: Medical management of nephrolithiasis. *Med Clin North Am* 81:785, 1997.

74. Ahlstrand C, Tiselius HG: Recurrences during a 10-year follow up after final renal stone episode. *Urol Res* 18:397, 1990.

75. Teichman J: Acute renal colic from ureteral calculus. *N Engl J Med* 350:7, 2004.

76. Borghi L, et al: Hot occupation and nephrolithiasis. *J Urol* 150:1757, 1993.

77. Seftel A, Resnick MI: Metabolic evaluation of urolithiasis. *Urol Clin North Am* 17:159, 1990.

78. Stewart DP, et al: Microscopic hematuria and calculus-related ureteral obstruction. *J Emerg Med* 8:693, 1990.

79. Miller O, et al: Prospective comparison of unenhanced spiral computed tomography and intravenous urogram in the evaluation of acute flank pain. *Urology* 52:6, 1998.

80. Bird V, et al: A comparison of unenhanced helical computerized tomography findings and renal obstruction determined by furosemide ^{99m}technetium mercaptoacetyl-triglycine diuretic scintirenography for patients with acute renal colic. *J Urol* 167:4, 2002.

81. Vieweg J, et al: unenhanced helical computerized tomography for the evaluation of patients with acute flank pain. *J Urol* 160:3, 1998.

82. Sheley RC, et al: Helical CT in the evaluation of renal colic. *Am J Emerg Med* 17:279, 1999.

83. Sinclair D, et al: The evaluation of suspected renal colic: Ultrasound scan versus excretory urography. *Ann Emerg Med* 18:556, 1989.

84. Mutgi A, et al: Renal colic: Utility of the plain abdominal radiograph. *Arch Intern Med* 151:1589, 1991.

85. Zangerle KF, Iserson KV, Bjelland JC: Usefulness of abdominal flat plate radiographs in patients with suspected ureteral calculi. *Ann Emerg Med* 14:316, 1985.

86. Swartz D: The acute scrotal mass. In Harwood-Nuss A (ed): *The Clinical Practice of Emergency Medicine,* 2nd ed. Philadelphia, JB Lippincott, 1996.

87. Rabinowitz R: The importance of the cremasteric reflex in acute scrotal swelling in children. *J Urol* 132:89, 1984.

88. Berger RE, et al: The clinical use of epididymal aspiration cultures in the management of selected patients with acute epididymitis. *J Urol* 124:60, 1980.

89. Skoglund RW, et al: Torsion of testicular appendage: Presentation of 43 cases. *J Urol* 104:604, 1970.
90. Emberton M, Anion K: Acute urinary retention in men: An age old problem. *BMJ* 318:921, 1999.
91. Stewart C: Urinary tract infections in men. In Harwood-Nuss A (ed): *The Clinical Practice of Emergency Medicine.* Philadelphia, JB Lippincott, 1991.
92. Nyman MA, et al: Management of acute urinary retention: Rapid vs gradual decompensation and risk of complications. *Mayo Clin Proc* 72:951, 1997.
93. Thaller TR, Wang LP: Evaluation of asymptomatic microscopic hematuria in adults. *Am Fam Physician* 60:1143, 1999.
94. Mariani AJ, et al: The significance of adult hematuria: 1000 hematuria evaluations including a risk benefit and cost effectiveness analysis. *J Urol* 141:350, 1989.
95. Stewart DP, et al: Microscopic hematuria and calculus-related ureteral obstruction. *J Emerg Med* 8:693, 1990.
96. Sinclair D, et al: The evaluation of suspected renal colic: Ultrasound scan versus excretory urography. *Ann Emerg Med* 18:556, 1989.
97. Mariani AJ: A prospective analysis of 1930 patients with hematuria to evaluate current diagnostic practice. *J Urol* 165:545, 2001.
98. Merten GJ, et al: Prevention of contrast-induced nephropathy with sodium bicarbonate: A randomized controlled trial. *JAMA* 291:2328, 2004.
99. Rasmussen OO, et al: Recurrent unexplained hematuria and the risk of urologic cancer: A follow up study. *Scand J Urol Nephrol* 22:335, 1989.

Section VII **NEUROLOGY**

CHAPTER

99 Stroke

Rashmi U. Kothari, Todd J. Crocco, and William G. Barsan

PERSPECTIVE

Background

Stroke is the third leading cause of death in the United States and the leading cause of adult disability.[1] It affects more than 700,000 patients a year, with an in-hospital mortality of almost 15% and a 30-day mortality of 20% to 25%.[2-4] Although 50% to 70% of stroke survivors regain functional independence, 15% to 30% are permanently disabled, and 20% require institutional care at 3 months. The current cost of stroke is estimated to be greater than $53 billion a year.[1] In terms of emergency care, almost 2% of all 911 calls and 4% of hospital admissions from the emergency department are for patients with potential strokes.[5,6]

Stroke can be defined as any vascular injury that reduces cerebral blood flow (CBF) to a specific region of the brain causing neurologic impairment. The onset of symptoms may be sudden or stuttering and may result in transient or permanent loss of neurologic function. Approximately 80% of all strokes are ischemic in origin, caused by the occlusion of a cerebral vessel.[3,4] The rest are hemorrhagic strokes caused by the rupture of a blood vessel into the parenchyma of the brain (intracerebral hemorrhage [ICH]) or into the subarachnoid space (subarachnoid hemorrhage). Only ischemic stroke and ICH are discussed in this chapter.

In the past, treatment for stroke consisted of stabilization, observation, and rehabilitation. In recent years, with a better understanding of the pathophysiology of neuronal injury and the introduction of new therapies, there has been a shift to early evaluation and treatment. Current interventional treatment regimens include blood pressure management, anticoagulation, thrombolytic therapy, catheter-based interventions, and surgery. The key to success is early identification and treatment of stroke patients before neurologic deficits become irreversible. Emergency physicians play an integral role in the decision-making process involved in the care of these critically ill patients.[7]

PRINCIPLES OF DISEASE

Pathophysiology

The cerebral vasculature supplies the brain with a rich flow of blood that contains the critical supply of oxygen and glucose necessary for normal brain function. When a stroke occurs, immediate alterations in CBF and extensive changes in cellular homeostasis occur. A complete interruption of CBF, which is rare, results in loss of consciousness within approximately 10 seconds and death of vulnerable pyramidal cells of the hippocampus within minutes. In stroke, collateral circulation helps maintain some blood flow to the ischemic region. The normal CBF is 40 to 60 mL/100 g of brain/min. When CBF decreases to less than 15 to 18 mL/100 g of brain/min, several physiologic changes occur. The brain loses electrical activity and becomes electrically "silent," although neuronal membrane integrity and function remain intact. Clinically the areas of the brain maintaining electrical silence manifest a neurologic deficit, even though the brain cells are viable. When CBF is less than 10 mL/100 g of brain/min, membrane failure occurs with a subsequent increase in the extracellular potassium and intracellular calcium and eventual cell death.

The *ischemic penumbra* is the area of the brain surrounding the primary injury, which is preserved by a tenuous supply of blood from collateral vessels. This border zone of neuronal tissue is the area of greatest interest to investigators for possible salvage in ischemic and hemorrhagic stroke.[8] As defined by CBF, the ischemic penumbra constitutes brain tissue with blood flow of 10 to 18 mL/100 g of brain/min in which electrical silence is present, but irreversible damage has not yet occurred. In ischemic stroke, the duration of occlusion plays a crucial role in neuronal survival.[9] Increasing the duration of occlusion increases the irreversibility of deficits and the amount of cerebral infarction. In experimental animals, occlusion of cerebral vessels usually results in a reversible neurologic deficit if the occlusion lasts less than 2 hours. After 6 hours of occlusion, neurologic deficits in most animal studies are irreversible. In ischemic stroke trials, fibrinolytic or antiplatelet agents have been used to recanalize occluded arteries and reperfuse ischemic areas of the brain within the 2- to 6-hour therapeutic window.[10-14] Clinical investigators evaluating neuroprotective agents have focused primarily on a longer window of 24 hours in patients with ischemic and hemorrhagic stroke.[15-19] Studies using magnetic resonance imaging (MRI) and positron emission tomography in humans support this longer time window in some patients.[8,20] To date, however, no neuroprotective agents have shown significant clinical efficacy in human trials.

In patients with ICH, physical compression, edema, and inflammation secondary to the hematoma are thought to play an important role in secondary injury.[21,22] Similar to ischemic stroke trials, investigators have begun looking at the feasibility of ultra-early hematoma evacuation within this 2- to 6-hour window in patients with ICH.[23]

Anatomy and Physiology

Blood is supplied to the brain by the anterior and posterior circulation. The anterior circulation originates from the carotid system and perfuses 80% of the brain, including the optic nerve, retina, and frontoparietal and anterior-temporal lobes. The first branch off the internal carotid artery is the ophthalmic artery, which supplies the optic nerve and retina. As a result, the sudden onset of painless monocular blindness (amaurosis fugax) identifies the stroke as involving the anterior circulation (specifically the ipsilateral carotid artery) at or below the level of the ophthalmic artery. The internal carotid arteries terminate by branching into the anterior and middle cerebral arteries at the circle of Willis.

The anterior cerebral artery supplies the basal and medial aspects of the cerebral hemispheres and extends to the anterior two thirds of the parietal lobe. The middle cerebral artery supplies the lenticulostriate branches that supply the putamen, part of the anterior limb of the internal capsule, the lentiform nucleus, and the external capsule. Main cortical branches of the middle cerebral artery supply the lateral surfaces of the cerebral cortex from the anterior portion of the frontal lobe to the posterolateral occipital lobe. Although the posterior circulation is smaller and supplies only 20% of the brain, it supplies the brainstem (which is crucial for normal consciousness, movement, and sensation), cerebellum, thalamus, auditory and vestibular centers of the ear, medial temporal lobe, and visual occipital cortex. The posterior circulation is derived from the two vertebral arteries that ascend through the transverse processes of the cervical vertebrae. The vertebral arteries enter the cranium through the foramen magnum and supply the cerebellum via the posterior inferior cerebellar arteries. They join to form the basilar artery, which branches to form the posterior cerebral arteries.

The extent of injury in either an anterior or a posterior stroke depends on the vessel involved and the presence of collateral blood flow distal to the vessel occlusion. A patient with excellent collateral blood flow from the contralateral hemisphere may have minimal clinical deficits despite a complete carotid occlusion. In contrast, a patient with poor collateral flow may have hemiplegia with the same lesion.

EPIDEMIOLOGY

Ischemic Stroke

It is estimated that there are 430,000 first-ever, ischemic strokes per year in the United States, of which 10% to 15% are transient ischemic attacks (TIAs). These may occur either from in situ thrombosis or embolic obstruction from a more proximal source, usually the heart. In more than a third of these first-ever strokes, no cause is found (Table 99-1).[24,25]

Approximately one third of all ischemic strokes are thrombotic in nature. These can be due to either large or small vessel occlusions.[24,25] There is a higher incidence of large vessel occlusions among men than women and among whites than African Americans.[24,25] Common areas for large vessel occlusions are cerebral vessel branch points, especially in the distribution of the internal carotid artery. Thrombosis usually results from clot formation in the area of an ulcerated atherosclerotic plaque (which occurs in the area of turbulent blood flow, such as vessel bifurcations). There is a

Table 99-1. Estimated Number of First-Ever Strokes/Transient Ischemic Attacks in the United States

Stroke Subtype	Estimated Number
Large vessel	69,000 (16%)
Small vessel/lacunae	76,000 (17.5%)
Cardioembolic	113,000 (26%)
Stroke of uncommon mechanisms	15,000 (3.5%)
Infarcts of unknown etiology	157,000 (36.5%)
Total stroke/TIAs	430,000 (100%)

Data from references 24 and 25.

marked reduction of flow when the stenosis occludes more than 90% of the blood vessel diameter. As further ulceration and thrombosis occur, platelets adhere to the region. A clot then either embolizes or occludes the artery.

Lacunae or small vessel strokes involve small terminal sections of the vasculature and more commonly occur in African Americans and patients with diabetes and hypertension.[24] A history of hypertension is present in 80% to 90% of patients who have lacunar strokes. The subcortical areas of the cerebrum and brainstem are often involved. The infarctions range in size from a few millimeters to 2 cm and occur most commonly in the basal ganglia, thalamus, pons, and internal capsule. They may be caused by small emboli or by a process termed *lipohyalinosis,* which occurs in patients with hypertensive cerebral vasculopathy. Although nearly 20 lacunar syndromes have been described, the most common of these lacunar syndromes are pure motor strokes, pure sensory strokes, and ataxic hemiparesis. Because they are subcortical and well localized, lacunar strokes do not cause cognitive impairment, aphasia, or simultaneous sensorimotor findings.

A quarter of all ischemic strokes are cardioembolic in nature.[24,25] Embolization of a mural thrombus in patients with atrial fibrillation is the most common source of these emboli, and patients who have atrial fibrillation are 5 to 17 times more likely to develop a stroke than patients who do not have atrial fibrillation.[26] Almost 20% of stroke patients have atrial fibrillation on their admission electrocardiogram (ECG).[26,27] Strokes resulting from atrial fibrillation are more likely to involve large cerebral vessels, be more severe, and have a higher mortality rate than strokes not associated with atrial fibrillation.[26,27] Noncardiac sources of emboli may arise from diseased portions of extracranial arteries and result in an artery-to-artery embolus. One common example is amaurosis fugax, in which emboli from a proximal carotid plaque embolizes to the ophthalmic artery causing transient monocular blindness.

Approximately 1% to 2% of patients with acute myocardial infarctions have a subsequent stroke within the first month after their cardiac event.[28,29] Half of these strokes occur within the first 5 days of the myocardial infarction.[29] Independent predictors of who will develop a stroke after an acute myocardial infarction are a history of atrial fibrillation (new-onset or chronic), prior stroke, and ST segment elevation.[29] The use of aspirin has been shown to reduce the incidence of post–myocardial infarction stroke by 42%.[30]

Approximately 3% to 4% of all strokes occur in patients between the ages of 15 and 45 years. Although atherosclerosis is the most common cause in older patients, younger patients have causes that are often uncommon and reversible. Pregnancy, the use of oral contraceptives, antiphospholipid antibodies (e.g., lupus anticoagulant and anticardiolipin antibodies), protein S and C deficiencies, and polycythemia all predispose patients to sludging or thrombosis and increase their risk of stroke. Fibromuscular dysplasia of the cerebral vasculature also may lead to stroke, and in rare instances, prolonged vasoconstriction from a migraine syndrome causes stroke. Recreational drugs such as cocaine, phenylpropanolamine, and amphetamines are potent vasoconstrictors that have been associated with ischemic and hemorrhagic stroke. Vascular dissections are often associated with severe trauma, but can occur from such mild events as turning the head sharply.

A TIA is a neurologic deficit that has complete clinical resolution within 24 hours. TIAs are an important warning sign for the future development of cerebral infarction. Approximately 10% of patients who experience a TIA develop a stroke within 3 months of the sentinel event, and half of these occur within the first 2 days.[31] Most TIAs last less than 5 minutes, but the course can be variable.[32] Three or more TIAs occurring within 72 hours are termed *crescendo TIAs.* Although there is a strong relationship between "carotid territory" TIAs and extracranial carotid artery disease, at least 50% of patients with carotid territory TIAs do not have angiographically demonstrable arterial disease. The cause of TIAs in these patients without arterial lesions is unknown. Although clinical deficits resolve within 24 hours, evidence of infarction can be found with computed tomography (CT) in 64% of patients and with MRI in 81% of patients.[33,34] Almost half of all patients 65 years old and older with "first-ever TIAs" have MRI evidence of a previous, clinically silent, cerebral infarction.[34] These silent infarcts are usually deep, less than 1 cm, and often involve the nondominant right hemisphere.

Hemorrhagic Stroke

Spontaneous ICH causes 8% to 11% of all acute strokes and is twice as common as subarachnoid hemorrhage. It has a 30-day mortality of 50%, with half of patients dying in the first 2 days. Among survivors, only one in five is living independently at 1 year.[35] There is a higher incidence of ICH among men than women and among Asians than whites, and it occurs more commonly in young and middle-aged African Americans than whites of similar age.[2]

ICH may occur in association with long-standing hypertension (hypertensive hemorrhage), in the elderly with amyloid angiopathy, or in patients with arteriovenous malformations (AVMs). Hypertensive hemorrhage results from degenerative changes in the small penetrating arteries and arterioles leading to the formation of microaneurysms, most commonly in penetrating vessels of the middle cerebral artery. Two thirds of cases occur within the region of the basal ganglia (Box 99-1). The hematoma that forms usually enlarges,

---

BOX 99-1. Location of Hypertensive Hemorrhages

Putamen	44%
Thalamus	13%
Cerebellum	9%
Pons	9%
Other cortical areas	25%

causing local tissue injury and a subsequent increase in intracranial pressure (ICP).

ICH due to amyloid angiopathy tends to be lobar in nature. It occurs more commonly in the elderly, and there is a higher incidence among whites than African Americans. Sudden increases in blood pressures that occur with such drugs as phenylpropanolamine and cocaine can cause ICH. Other causes include the use of anticoagulants, tumors, and AVMs (especially in the young).

Bleeding from an AVM may be subarachnoid, intraparenchymal, or both. In AVMs, the hemorrhage into the subarachnoid space generally is confined to the area of the AVM, and the major clinical presentation is due to the intraparenchymal involvement with focal neurologic deficits. AVMs are more likely to bleed into the ventricles and subarachnoid space than are hypertensive intracerebral hemorrhages and usually have a less disruptive impact on cerebral function. An AVM producing hemorrhage is more common in younger patients than hypertensive ICH. These patients may have no history of hypertension.

CLINICAL FEATURES

Ischemic Stroke

The signs and symptoms of an ischemic stroke may occur suddenly and without warning or may have a stuttering, insidious onset. Disruption of the flow to one of the major vascular limbs of the cerebral circulation results in physiologic disruption to the anatomic area of the brain supplied by that blood vessel. Ischemic strokes can be classified as anterior or posterior circulation strokes depending on the vasculature involved. The presence of neurologic deficits depends on collateral flow. In addition to the vascular supply involved, ischemic strokes can be described further by the temporal presentation of their neurologic deficits. A "stroke in evolution" is one in which focal neurologic deficits worsen over the course of minutes or hours. Approximately 20% of anterior circulation strokes and 40% of posterior circulation strokes show evidence of progression. Anterior circulation strokes may progress within the first 24 hours, whereas posterior strokes may progress for 3 days. Propagation of a thrombus is postulated as a likely mechanism for progression. Anterior circulation strokes (involving primarily the carotid, anterior cerebral, or middle cerebral arteries) rarely present with complete loss of consciousness, unless it occurs in the previously unaffected hemisphere of a patient who has experienced a prior contralateral stroke. Occlusions in the anterior cerebral artery mainly affect frontal lobe function. The patient has altered mentation coupled with impaired judgment and insight and the presence of primitive grasp and suck reflexes. Bowel and bladder incontinence can occur. Paralysis and hypesthesia of the lower limb opposite the side of the lesion is characteristic. Leg weakness is greater than arm weakness in anterior cerebral distribution stroke. Apraxia or clumsiness occurs in the patient's gait.

Marked motor and sensory disturbances are the hallmarks of occlusion of the middle cerebral artery. These disturbances occur on the side of the body contralateral to the side of the lesion and are usually worse in the arm and face than the leg. Involvement may occur in only part of an extremity or in the face but almost always is accompanied by numbness in the same region as the motor loss. Hemianopsia, or blindness in one half of the visual field, occurs ipsilateral to the lesion. Agnosia, or the inability to recognize previously known subjects, is common, and aphasia may be present if the lesion occurs in the dominant hemisphere. Patients often have a gaze preference toward the affected hemisphere because of disruption of the cortical lateral gaze centers. The clinical aphorism is that a patient looks *at* a destructive lesion (stroke) but *away from* an irritative lesion (seizure focus).

Aphasia, a disorder of language in which the patient articulates clearly but uses language inappropriately or understands it poorly, is also common in dominant-hemisphere stroke. Aphasia may be expressive, receptive, or a combination of both. *Wernicke's aphasia* occurs when the patient is unable to process sensory input such as speech and fails to understand verbal communication (receptive aphasia). *Broca's aphasia* is the inability to communicate verbally in an effective way, even though understanding may be intact (expressive aphasia). Aphasia should be distinguished from dysarthria, which is a motor deficit of the mouth and speech muscles; a dysarthric patient articulates poorly but understands words and word choices. Aphasia is important to recognize because it usually localizes a lesion to the dominant (usually left) cerebral cortex in the middle cerebral artery distribution. *Aphasia* and *dysphasia* are terms that are used interchangeably but must be distinguished from *dysphagia,* which is difficulty in swallowing.

Pathology in the vertebrobasilar system (i.e., posterior circulation strokes) can cause the widest variety of symptoms and as a result may be the most difficult to diagnose. The symptoms reflect cranial nerve deficits, cerebellar involvement, and involvement of neurosensory tracts. The brainstem also contains the reticular activating system, which is responsible for mediating consciousness, and the emesis centers. In contrast to anterior circulation strokes, patients with posterior circulation stroke can present with loss of consciousness and frequently have nausea and vomiting. The posterior cerebral artery supplies portions of the parietal and occipital lobes, and vision and thought processing are impaired. *Visual agnosia,* the inability to recognize seen objects, and *alexia,* the inability to understand the written word, may occur. A third nerve palsy may occur, and the patient may experience homonymous hemianopsia. One of the more curious facets of this syndrome is that the patient may be unaware of any visual problem (visual neglect). Vertigo, diplopia, visual field defects, weakness, paralysis, dysarthria, dysphagia, syncope, spasticity, ataxia, and nystagmus may occur with vertebrobasilar artery insufficiency. Posterior circulation strokes also show crossed deficits, such as motor deficits on one side of the body and sensory loss on the other. In contrast, anterior circulation strokes always have findings limited to one side of the body.

A focused neurologic examination should assess level of consciousness, speech, cranial nerve function, motor and sensory function, and cerebellar function. The patient's level of consciousness and fluency of speech can be assessed rapidly in a dialogue with the patient to determine the presence of dysarthria or aphasia. The patient's head should be evaluated for signs of trauma. Pupillary size, reactivity, and extraocular movements provide important information about brainstem function, particularly cranial nerves III through VI; an abnormal third nerve function may be the first sign of tentorial herniation. Gaze preference suggests brainstem or cortical involvement. Central facial nerve weakness from a stroke should be distinguished from the peripheral causes of cranial nerve VII weakness. With a peripheral lesion, the patient is unable to wrinkle the forehead. Determination of facial sensation, eyebrow elevation and squinting, smiling symmetry, gross auditory acuity, gag reflex, shoulder elevation, sternocleidomastoid strength, and tongue protrusion completes the cranial nerve evaluation.

Motor and sensory testing is performed next. Muscle tone can be assessed by moving a relaxed limb. Proximal and distal muscle group strength should be assessed against resistance. Pronator drift of the arm is a sensitive sign of motor weakness and can be tested simultaneously by having the patient sit with eyes closed, arms outstretched, and palms toward the ceiling for 10 seconds. Asymmetric sensation to pain and light touch may be subtle and difficult to detect. Double simultaneous extinction tests for sensory neglect can be tested easily by simultaneously touching the right and left limbs. The patient may feel the right and left sides being touched individually but may not discern one side being touched when both are touched simultaneously. Similarly the ability to discern a number gently scratched on a forearm, *graphesthesia,* is another easily tested cortical parietal lobe function. These tests can help differentiate a pure motor deficit of a lacunar stroke from a sensorimotor middle cerebral artery deficit.

Cerebellar testing and the assessment of reflexes and gait complete the examination. Finger-to-nose and heel-to-shin evaluations are important tests of cerebellar functions. Asymmetry of the deep tendon reflexes or a unilateral Babinski sign may be an early finding of corticospinal tract dysfunction. Gait testing is commonly omitted, yet is one of the most informative parts of the neurologic examination. Observing routine ambulation and heel-to-toe walking can assess subtle ataxia, weakness, or focal cerebellar lesions.

The National Institutes of Health Stroke Scale (NIHSS) is a useful and rapid tool for quantifying neurologic deficit in patients with stroke and can be used in determining treatment options.[36] It has been shown to be reproducible and valid and correlates well with the amount of infarcted tissue on CT scan.[37,38] The baseline NIHSS can determine patients appropriate for fibrinolytic therapy and patients at increased risk of

Table 99-2. Clinical Findings Associated with Ischemic Strokes, Intracranial Hemorrhage, and Subarachnoid Hemorrhage from the Stroke Data Bank, Harvard and Lausanne Stroke Registries

Symptom	Ischemic Stroke (%)	ICH (%)	SAH (%)
Headache	11-17	33-41	78-87
Vomiting	8-11	29-46	45-48
Decreased LOC	13-15	39-57	48-68
Seizure	0.3-3	6-7	7

ICH, intracranial hemorrhage; LOC, level of consciousness; SAH, subarachnoid hemorrhage.
Data from Bogousslausky J, Van Melle G, Regli F: The Lausanne Stroke Registry: Analysis of 1000 consecutive patients with first stroke. *Stroke* 19:1083,1988; Foulkes MA, et al: The Stroke Data Bank: Design, methods, and baseline characteristics. *Stroke* 19:547, 1988; and Mohr JP, et al: The Harvard Cooperative Stroke Registry: A prospective registry. *Neurology* 28:754, 1978.

hemorrhage. In addition, the NIHSS has been used as a prognostic tool to predict outcome and is currently being used by some stroke centers to stratify patients into treatment trials.[36,39]

Hemorrhagic Stroke

The classic presentation of ICH is the sudden onset of headache, vomiting, severely elevated blood pressure, and focal neurologic deficits that progress over minutes. Similar to ischemic stroke, the patient often has a motor and sensory deficit contralateral to the brain lesion. The patient may present with agitation and lethargy, but may progress quickly to stupor or coma. One third have significant growth in hemorrhage volume within the first few hours.[40] Although headache, vomiting, and coma are common, significant proportions of patients do not have these findings and may present similarly to patients with ischemic stroke (Table 99-2).

Airway and mental status are of paramount importance in patients with ICH because they can deteriorate precipitously. The respiratory pattern also may be affected in hemorrhagic stroke. Cheyne-Stokes respirations (increasing and decreasing depth of respirations with periods of apnea) may occur with a large ICH. Putaminal hemorrhages may cause deep, irregular respirations, whereas patients with cerebellar hemorrhage may have a normal respiratory pattern.

The pupillary examination can be extremely helpful in determining the location and extent of the insult. Pontine hemorrhage classically presents with pinpoint pupils because of the interruption of the descending sympathetic tracts and unopposed parasympathetic stimulation. Dilated pupils may result from bleeding into the putamen, whereas blood in the thalamus may present with anisocoria, miosis, or a sluggish pupillary response. Cranial nerve abnormalities may result from cerebellar hemorrhages. The parasympathetic fibers course along the outside of cranial nerve III. As a result, compression of the nerve results in loss of pupillary reactivity before anisocoria. As noted previ-

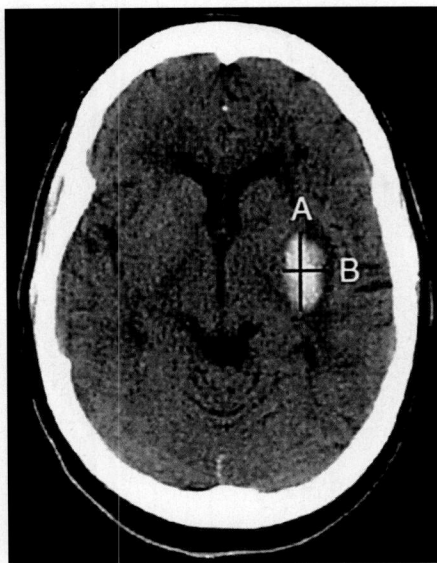

Figure 99-1. The CT slice with the largest area of hemorrhage is identified. The largest diameter of the hemorrhage on this slice is measured in centimeters (A). The largest diameter 90 degrees to A on the same slice is measured (B). C is the approximate number of 10-mm slices on which the intracerebral hemorrhage was seen. The volume of the hemorrhage equals A multiplied by B, multiplied by C, divided by 2 (ABC/2).

ously, the physical examination may be insufficient to distinguish an ischemic stroke from an ICH, and radiographic confirmation is required.

Similar to ischemic stroke, a careful neurologic examination is important in localizing the region and extent of injury. A baseline NIHSS and Glasgow Coma Scale can be used to assess stroke severity, although the Glasgow Coma Scale may be more feasible to follow neurologic deterioration.

Poor prognostic indicators for patients with ICH include a decreased level of consciousness on arrival, intraventricular hemorrhage, and an ICH volume of greater than 40 mL, all of which can be assessed in the emergency department. The ABC/2 technique is a quick and accurate method of measuring ICH volume at the bedside (Figure 99-1).[41]

DIFFERENTIAL DIAGNOSIS

Ischemic Stroke

Extra-axial collections of blood secondary to trauma can mimic stroke. An epidural or subdural hematoma can cause altered mental status, focal neurologic signs, and rapid progression to coma. Elderly patients, who are the age group at highest risk for stroke, can be victims of recurrent falls that lead to chronic subdural hematomas. Carotid dissection may occur after neck trauma or sudden hyperextension and may occur with focal neurologic findings, as with an aortic dissection that extends into the carotid arteries. The diagnosis is supported by a compatible history, contrast angiography, or magnetic resonance angiography (MRA).

Other structural lesions that may cause focal neurologic signs include brain tumor and abscesses. Air embolism should be suspected in the setting of marked atmospheric pressure changes, such as scuba diving or during medical procedures or injuries that may allow air into the vascular system. Seizures, altered mental status, and focal neurologic findings also may occur with air embolism.

Similar to stroke, giant cell arteritis is a disease of the elderly. It may cause severe headache, visual disturbances, and, rarely, aphasia and hemiparesis. Other symptoms include intermittent fever, malaise, jaw claudication, morning stiffness, and myalgias. The diagnosis is confirmed by temporal artery biopsy. Collagen vascular diseases, such as polyarteritis nodosa, lupus, and other types of vasculitis, may cause stroke syndromes.

Metabolic abnormalities also can mimic stroke syndromes. Hypoglycemia is often responsible for an altered mental status and is a well-known cause of sustained focal neurologic findings that persist for several days.[41] Wernicke's encephalopathy causes ophthalmoplegia, ataxia, and confusion that can be mistaken for signs of cerebellar infarction.

Migraine is another entity that may present with focal neurologic findings, with or without headache. A seizure followed by Todd's postictal paralysis may mimic stroke. Bell's palsy, labyrinthitis, peripheral nerve palsy, and demyelinating diseases all may mimic stroke. Ménière's disease may be difficult to distinguish from a posterior circulation stroke or TIA. Dizziness, vertigo, hearing loss, and tinnitus in Ménière's disease are common, whereas difficulties with vision, speech, or other focal symptoms are uncommon.

Hemorrhagic Stroke

The differential diagnosis for ICH is similar to that of ischemic stroke and includes migraine, seizure, tumor, abscess, hypertensive encephalopathy, and trauma. Hypertensive encephalopathy and migraine also can present with headache, nausea, and vomiting. Although focal neurologic signs are uncommon, they may occur with these entities. With hypertensive encephalopathy, patients usually have marked elevation in blood pressure and other evidence of end-organ injury, including proteinuria, cardiomegaly, papilledema, and malignant hypertensive retinopathy. These patients usually improve significantly with treatment of hypertension. Migraines often are associated with an aura, and the patient often has a history of similar headaches. The differentiation between intracerebral hemorrhage and labyrinthitis can be especially difficult in the elderly. The abrupt onset of vertigo, vomiting, and nystagmus can represent a peripheral process, such as labyrinthitis, or a central process, such as cerebellar or brainstem infarct or hemorrhage. Age older than 40 years and a history of hypertension or other risk factors for ICH increase the possibility of a cerebellar hemorrhage. Findings specifically referable to the brainstem must be sought; these include hiccups, diplopia, facial numbness, dysphagia, and ataxia. Vertiginous patients often have a strong desire to remain immobile with their eyes closed, but this must not preclude a thorough cranial nerve and cerebellar examination, including gait. Gross ataxia should be present with cerebellar stroke and absent with labyrinthine disease. A head CT scan should be strongly considered in patients older than age 40, to assist in differentiating labyrinthitis and cerebellar hemorrhage.

DIAGNOSTIC STRATEGIES

Ischemic Stroke

Although clinical data can help establish the diagnosis, cause, and location of the stroke, confirmatory diagnostic tests often are required to establish the final etiology or to eliminate other causes of the deficits. The immediate emergency department evaluation should include a blood glucose determination, cranial CT scan, and an ECG.

An emergent noncontrast cranial CT scan is the standard imaging technique for evaluating a patient with a potential stroke in the emergency department.[42] It can quickly differentiate an ischemic stroke from ICH and other mass lesions. This information is crucial for subsequent therapeutic decisions. A CT scan can identify almost all parenchymal bleeds greater than 1 cm and 95% of all subarachnoid hemorrhages. Most ischemic strokes do not have gross signs of infarction on routine CT scan for at least 6 to 12 hours, depending on the size of the infarct. Subtle, ultra-early changes have been noted, however, in a third of stroke patients evaluated by CT within 3 hours of symptom onset. These ultra-early changes include the hyperdense artery sign (acute thrombus in a vessel), sulcal effacement, loss of the insular ribbon, loss of gray-white interface, mass effect, and acute hypodensity (Figure 99-2). Additionally, a CT scan with angiography can be used to identify the presence of intravascular thrombosis, vasculature dissection, or stenosis.

The clinical importance of these findings in regard to administering fibrinolytic therapy within less than 3 hours of symptom onset is questionable because the ability of treating physicians to identify these findings reproducibly is poor, and their significance is questionable.[43,44] Only acute hypodensity and mass effect have been shown to be associated with an increased risk of intracerebral hemorrhage after fibrinolysis (compared with treated patients without these findings). These findings do not exclude appropriate patients from fibrinolytic therapy, however, because patients' chances for excellent neurologic outcome at 3 months with these findings was better than for placebo-treated patients, and their risk of symptomatic ICH, severe disability, or death at 3 months was no different.[43] Patients with a hyperdense artery sign and acute hypodensity of one third the middle cerebral artery distribution tend to have a poorer prognosis; however, their outcomes are still better when treated with recombinant tissue plasminogen activator (rt-PA) than not treated.[43] A cranial CT scan with contrast is rarely indicated on an

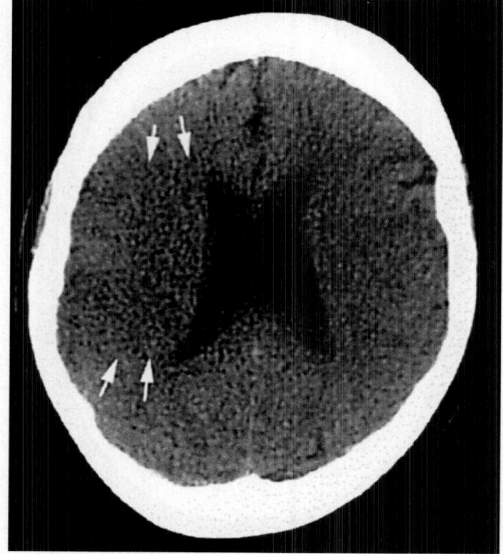

A

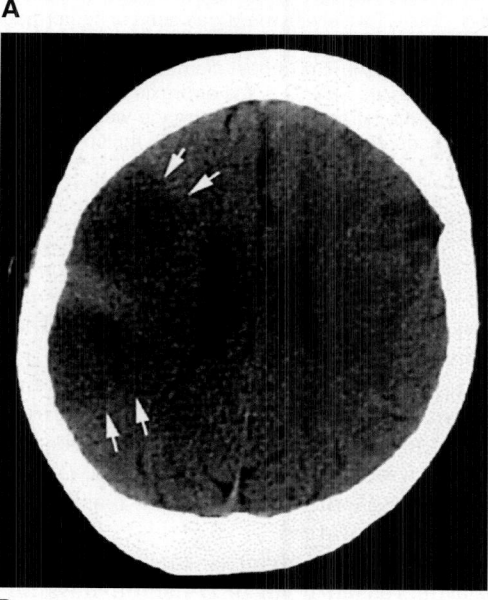

B

Figure 99-2. A, CT scan taken 2 hours, 50 minutes after large right middle cerebral artery occlusion. There are subtle, ultra-early ischemic changes, including loss of the gray-white interface *(arrows)* and subtle evidence of sulcal effacement. **B,** CT scan of same patient approximately 8 hours after symptom onset shows acute hypodensity *(arrows)* and more prominent sulcal effacement.

emergency basis if the noncontrast cranial CT scan is normal.

An ECG should be obtained because atrial fibrillation and acute myocardial infarction are associated with 60% of all cardioembolic strokes. The hematologic evaluation should include a complete blood count with platelet count and coagulation studies. Toxicologic screen and cardiac isoenzymes should be considered if appropriate. Elevated blood viscosity even when hematocrit levels are not frankly polycythemic can affect blood flow and prognosis. A platelet count can identify thrombocytosis or thrombocytopenia that may precipitate a thrombosis or hemorrhage. Coagulation studies are especially helpful for patients in whom anticoagulation is being considered or patients with a hemorrhagic stroke. Cocaine or amphetamine ingestion should be considered with an ischemic or a hemorrhagic stroke in patients younger than 40 years old.

Other ancillary diagnostic tests to consider include an echocardiogram, carotid duplex scan, angiogram, and MRI or MRA. Some centers perform these studies as part of an observation unit protocol in the emergency department. An echocardiogram can identify a mural thrombus, tumor, patent foramen ovale, or valvular vegetation in patients in whom a cardioembolic stroke is suspected. Echocardiogram also should be considered in patients younger than 65 years old with no obvious etiology for their stroke. Carotid duplex scanning may be helpful in patients with known or suspected high-grade carotid stenosis who have worsening neurologic deficit or crescendo TIAs.[45,46] These patients may be candidates for heparinization or emergent carotid endarterectomy. Carotid duplex studies can accurately identify carotid stenosis of greater than 60%, but an angiogram is required to distinguish 95% stenosis from a complete occlusion. Angiography is the definitive test to show stenosis or occlusion of large and small blood vessels of the head and neck. It can detect subtle abnormalities, such as dissection, which may not be shown with other imaging techniques.

The role of MRI in the emergency department evaluation of stroke continues to evolve. MRI can visualize ischemic infarcts earlier and identify acute posterior circulation strokes more accurately than CT. Availability, difficulty in accessing critically ill patients, and scan time limit its general use, however. In addition, although MRI can identify acute intracerebral hemorrhage, it is considered less accurate at differentiating ischemia from hemorrhage.[47,48] Advances in MRA technology have allowed a noninvasive method of showing large vessel occlusions of the anterior and posterior circulation, although small intracranial vascular occlusions may not be readily apparent. With the improvement in MRA speed and resolution, MRA is quickly replacing conventional angiography as the diagnostic gold standard for identifying occlusion or stenosis in select patients. Diffusion-weighted imaging and perfusion-weighted imaging are newer MRI techniques that take minutes to perform and may allow differentiation between reversible and irreversible neuronal injury.[8,49]

Hemorrhagic Stroke

The hematologic evaluation should be performed in the same manner as in the ischemic stroke patient. Particular attention should be directed to the presence of a coagulopathy. A drug screen should be obtained to evaluate for use of sympathomimetics if substance abuse is suspected. Increased sympathetic outflow due to the hemorrhage may lead to an increase in dysrhythmias. Dysrhythmias also may signal impending brainstem compression from an expanding hemorrhage.

As in ischemic stroke, the cranial CT scan is the diagnostic test of choice to evaluate for an ICH.[35] CT reliably diagnoses 95% of ICHs, although very small lesions may not be visible. Hemorrhages of several days' age may appear as isodense regions.

Table 99-3. NINDS Recommended Stroke Evaluation Targets for Potential Thrombolytic Candidates

	Target Time-Frames
Door to physician	10 min
Door to CT completion	25 min
Door to CT reading	45 min
Door to treatment	60 min
Access to neurologic expertise*	15 min
Access to neurosurgical expertise*	2 hr

*By phone or in person.
NINDS, National Institute of Neurological Disorders and Stroke.

MANAGEMENT

Ischemic Stroke

With the focus on rapid recognition, evaluation, and treatment of stroke, emergency departments have attempted to streamline the care of these patients to meet recommended time goals (Table 99-3). This streamlining has led to the development of various stroke protocols, critical pathways, and acute interventional stroke teams that are often initiated in the prehospital phase before the patient arrives at the emergency department.

In the prehospital setting, the focus should be on airway, breathing, and circulation; rapid identification; early hospital notification; and rapid transport.[50] Although it is unusual for patients with ischemic stroke to be unresponsive on presentation, an altered ability to communicate, secondary to dysphasia, may be present. The ischemic stroke patient usually can maintain the airway, unless the brainstem is affected, or there is significant cerebral edema compressing the opposite hemisphere. Patients with intact protective airway reflexes should be placed on oxygen if hypoxic (oxygen saturation <95%),[51] with the head of the bed slightly elevated[52] and a monitor and intravenous line established.

Overhydration should be avoided to prevent cerebral edema. Shock or significant dehydration in a patient with an ischemic stroke should be treated promptly, however, because it may contribute to decreased CBF in the ischemic region. Dextrose-containing solutions should be avoided in normoglycemic patients suspected of having a stroke because elevated blood glucose levels may worsen an ischemic deficit.[53-56] Prehospital personnel should attempt to ascertain the patient's blood glucose rapidly. If this is not possible, glucose should be given only to diabetic patients in whom hypoglycemia is strongly suspected. ECG monitoring is necessary because of the frequency of cardiac causes of ischemic stroke.[26,28,29]

The circumstances surrounding the stroke and concomitant medical conditions should be ascertained.

The initial prehospital responders should document the exact time of stroke onset and the level of neurologic functioning; reversible defects may resolve completely by the time the patient has arrived at the hospital. The level of consciousness, gross focal motor deficits, difficulty with speech, clumsiness, facial asymmetry, and any other focal deficits should be noted. Prehospital stroke scales have been developed to assist in differentiating stroke from nonstroke patients and to identify potential fibrinolytic candidates.[57-60] Early recognition, notification and transport by prehospital personnel have been shown to be valuable in enabling early treatment.[50]

In the emergency department, airway, breathing, and circulation should be reassessed on an ongoing basis because patients may deteriorate rapidly. Even patients with subacute stroke may deteriorate precipitously. These patients may be found 1 to 2 days after the event has occurred and may have concomitant illnesses, including aspiration pneumonia, dehydration, hypothermia, rhabdomyolysis, or myocardial ischemia. Fever should be thoroughly evaluated, identifying the source of infection and treating promptly. There is strong evidence that even minor degrees of hyperthermia produce worsening of the neurologic injury.[61]

Blood Pressure Management of Ischemic Stroke

The management of blood pressure in patients with acute ischemic stroke and TIA is controversial because of limited data. Current guidelines for the management of hypertension in patients with acute ischemic stroke recommend that antihypertensive treatment be re-served for patients with markedly elevated blood pressures, unless fibrinolytic therapy is planned or specific medical indications are present.[50,62] These medical indications include (1) acute myocardial infarction, (2) aortic dissection, (3) true hypertensive encephalopathy, or (4) severe left ventricular failure. A similar approach to the acute management of blood pressure in patients with TIA is recommended.

Oral or parenteral agents should be withheld unless the patient's systolic pressure is greater than 220 mm Hg, diastolic pressure is greater than 120 mm Hg, or mean arterial pressure is greater than 130 mm Hg (Table 99-4). If parenteral agents are used, labetalol and enalapril are favored because of ease of titration and limited effect on cerebral blood vessels. Sublingual nifedipine and sublingual nitroglycerin are not recommended because they can produce a precipitous decrease in blood pressure.

If fibrinolytic therapy is planned, stringent control of blood pressure is indicated to reduce the potential for bleeding after the thrombolytic is administered (see Table 99-4).[63,64] Thrombolytic therapy is not recommended for patients who consistently have a systolic pressure greater than 185 mm Hg or diastolic pressure of 110 mm Hg at the time of treatment. Simple measures can be used to try lowering blood pressure below this level. Recommended approaches include the use of nitroglycerin paste or one or two doses of 10 to 20 mg of labetalol intravenously. If more aggressive measures are required to reduce blood pressure to less than 185/110 mm Hg, the use of tPA is not recommended. When thrombolytic therapy has been initiated, blood pressure must be monitored closely and hypertension treated aggressively.

Table 99-4. Emergency Antihypertensive Therapy for Acute Ischemic Stroke

Blood Pressure*	Treatment
Nonthrombolytic Candidates	
DBP > 140 mm Hg	Sodium nitroprusside (0.5 µg/kg/min). Aim for 10-20% reduction in DBP
SBP > 220, DBP > 120, or MAP[†] > 130 mm Hg	10-20 mg labetalol[‡]　IV push over 1-2 min. May repeat or double labetalol every 20 min to a maximum dose of 150 mg.
SBP < 220, DBP > 120, or MAP[†] > 130 mm Hg	Emergency antihypertensive therapy is deferred in the absence of aortic dissection, acute myocardial infarction, severe congestive heart failure, or hypertensive encephalopathy
Thrombolytic Candidates	
Pretreatment	
SBP > 185 or DBP > 110 mm Hg	1-2 inches of nitropaste or 1-2 doses of 10-20 mg labetalol[‡] IV push. If BP is not reduced and maintained to <185/110 mm Hg, the patient should not be treated with TPA
During and after treatment	
Monitor BP	BP is monitored every 15 min for 2 hr, then every 30 min for 6 hr, then every 1 hr for 16 hr
DBP > 140 mm Hg	Sodium nitroprusside (0.5 µg/kg/min)
DBP > 230 or DBP 121-140 mm Hg	(1) 10 mg labetalol[‡] IVP over 1–2 min. May repeat or double labetalol every 10 min to a maximum dose of 150 mg or give the initial labetalol bolus, then start a labetalol drip at 2 mg/min. (2) If BP not controlled by labetalol, consider sodium nitroprusside
SBP 180–230 or DBP 105-120 mm Hg	10 mg labetalol[‡] IV push. May repeat or double labetalol every 10-20 min to a maximum dose of 150 mg or give initial labetalol bolus, then start a labetalol drip at 2 mg/min

BP, blood pressure; DBP, diastolic blood pressure; MAP, mean arterial pressure; SBP, systolic blood pressure; TPA, tissue plasminogen activator.
*All initial blood pressures should be verified before treatment by repeating reading in 5 minutes.
[†]As estimated by one third the sum of systolic and double diastolic pressure.
[‡]Labetalol should be avoided in patients with asthma, cardiac failure, or severe abnormalities in cardiac conduction. For refractory hypertension, alternative therapy may be considered with sodium nitroprusside or enalapril.

Acute Drug Therapy

Two major strategies for acute stroke treatment have been evaluated: recanalization and neuroprotection. To date, only the use of intravenous tPA has been approved by the U.S. Food and Drug Administration for treatment of patients with acute ischemic stroke. These recommendations initially were based on the results of the National Institutes of Neurological Disorders and Stroke (NINDS) trial, although subsequent analysis of other studies has supported its use.[65-68] There has been concern regarding the safety of the use of tPA in community practice.[69] A meta-analysis of non–trial-related use of tPA ($n = 2639$) in community practice showed, however, that tPA had similar efficacy and safety as that reported in the NINDS trial.[70]

The current recommendation for rtPA is that it be administered intravenously at a dose of 0.9 mg/kg to a maximum of 90 mg (10% of the dose given as a bolus followed by an infusion lasting 60 minutes). Treatment must be initiated within 3 hours of the onset of ischemic symptoms in patients who meet strict inclusion and exclusion criteria (Box 99-2). Intravenous tPA is not recommended when the time of stroke onset cannot be ascertained reliably, including strokes recognized on awakening. In addition, caution should be used in treating patients with large strokes (NIHSS ≥20) or early CT changes of a recent major infarction (e.g., acute hypodensity or mass effect) because they are at increased risk of symptomatic hemorrhage.[71] Prior studies have shown the importance of adhering to the inclusion and exclusion criteria established by the NINDS trial.[72,73] The use of intravenous tPA beyond the 3-hour window has not been shown to be clinically beneficial, although a meta-analysis of these studies suggests that there may be benefit in a specific subset of patients.[11-13,65] Streptokinase is not recommended for use in patients with acute ischemic strokes. Other intravenous fibrinolytic agents are currently being investigated.

Advances in catheter-based fibrinolysis have been promising and suggest the possibility of extending the therapeutic window beyond the current 3-hour limit.[36,74,75] In the PROACT II study, patients were 58% more likely to have little or no neurologic disability at 90 days when treated with prourokinase 6 hours after stroke onset compared with placebo. The symptomatic hemorrhage rate (10%) was similar to that seen with intravenous tPA. A combination of low-dose intravenous tPA followed by intra-arterial therapy is currently being evaluated for patients with large strokes.[36]

More recent studies have focused on the use of antiplatelet agents in acute ischemic stroke. Data from two large trials involving almost 40,000 patients indicate that early use of aspirin in patients with acute ischemic stroke who were not treated with a fibrinolytic agent was associated with a small, but significant reduction in stroke recurrence and mortality.[76,77] These studies in combination would suggest that for every 1000 stroke patients treated with aspirin, about 9 deaths or nonfatal recurrences would be prevented in the first few weeks and approximately 13 fewer patients would be dead or dependent at 6 months. The need for acute administration of aspirin in the emergency department is unclear because patients were given aspirin 48 hours after stroke onset. Aspirin should not be given for the first 24 hours in patients receiving a fibrinolytic agent because this has been associated with an increased risk of ICH and death.[78]

The use of low-molecular-weight or unfractionated heparin is common in patients with acute ischemic stroke or TIAs, but its value is unproven. Some studies suggest that heparin may reduce the risk of subsequent ischemic stroke but increase the risk of hemorrhagic stroke. To date, no studies have definitively established the efficacy of anticoagulants in the management of acute ischemic stroke.[79] Heparin sometimes is considered, however, in patients at high risk of stroke progression; this includes patients with crescendo TIAs, TIA secondary to a cardioembolic source, a high-grade carotid stenosis, posterior circulation TIA, and evolving strokes. Heparin should not be initiated in patients with suspected endocarditis or in any patient until a CT scan has ruled out intracranial bleeding. Because of the lack of consistent evidence of efficacy, the most prudent course for an emergency physician is to deter-

---

BOX 99-2. Fibrinolytic Therapy for Acute Ischemic Stroke: Inclusion and Exclusion Criteria

Inclusion Criteria
1. Age ≥18 years
2. Clinical diagnosis of ischemic stroke causing a measurable neurologic deficit
3. Time of symptom onset well established to be <180 minutes before treatment would begin

Exclusion Criteria
1. Evidence of intracranial hemorrhage on noncontrast head CT
2. Only minor or rapidly improving stroke symptoms
3. High clinical suspicion of subarachnoid hemorrhage even with normal CT
4. Active internal bleeding (e.g., gastrointestinal bleed or urinary bleeding within last 21 days)
5. Known bleeding diathesis, including but not limited to:
   Platelet count <100,000/mm³
   Patient has received heparin within 48 hours and had an elevated activated partial thromboplastin time (greater than upper limit of normal for laboratory)
   Recent use of anticoagulant (e.g., warfarin sodium) and elevated prothrombin time >15 seconds
6. Within 3 months of intracranial surgery, serious head trauma, or previous stroke
7. Within 14 days of major surgery or serious trauma
8. Recent arterial puncture at noncompressible site
9. Lumbar puncture within 7 days
10. History of intracranial hemorrhage, arteriovenous malformation, or aneurysm
11. Witnessed seizure at stroke onset
12. Recent acute myocardial infarction
13. On repeated measurements, systolic pressure <185 mm Hg or diastolic pressure <110 mm Hg at time of treatment, requiring aggressive treatment to reduce blood pressure to within these limits

mine the need for heparin therapy in conjunction with the patient's neurologist or the admitting physician.

Numerous neuroprotective agents aimed at preventing the cascade of physiologic steps that occur after ischemia and lead to cell death have been studied. These have included antioxidants, calcium channel blockers, N-methyl-D-aspartate inhibitors, glycine, and glutamate receptor antagonists. Although promising in animal and small human trials, none have been shown to be effective in larger, phase III trials.[80-82]

Other innovative approaches for stroke care also are being investigated. Mild to moderate hypothermia is being investigated as a possible neuroprotective strategy. Desmoteplase, a thrombolytic agent that is reportedly more specific for fibrin-bound plasminogen, is being studied in acute ischemic stroke patients within 9 hours of symptom onset. Additionally, glycoprotein IIb/IIIa inhibitors, such as abciximab and eptifibatide, are being studied alone or in combination with rt-PA.[83] Such combinations may increase the efficacy of rt-PA and reduce the symptomatic intracranial hemorrhage rate. Finally, a variety of mechanical retrieval devices are being investigated. Some preliminary results using this interventional strategy have shown neurologic improvement without any instances of symptomatic intracerebral hemorrhage.[84]

Intracerebral Hemorrhage Management

A patient with a potential ICH requires rapid assessment and transport to a facility that has CT scanning capability and intensive care management. The prehospital management is similar to that for ischemic stroke. The circumstances surrounding the event and other concomitant medical conditions also should be ascertained. An evaluation of the initial level of consciousness, Glasgow Coma Scale, any gross focal deficits, difficulty with speech, clumsiness, gait disturbance, or facial asymmetry should be noted.

Supportive care involving attention to airway management and perfusion is of the highest priority. Patients with hemorrhagic stroke are more likely to have an altered level of consciousness that may progress rapidly to unresponsiveness requiring emergent endotracheal intubation. Because of increased ICP and intracranial bleeding, manipulation of the airway should be performed as atraumatically as possible. Intravenous access and cardiac monitoring should be initiated. Evaluation of blood glucose and appropriate dextrose and naloxone administration should be considered in any patient with altered mental status.

There is considerable disagreement regarding optimal blood pressure management in a patient with ICH. Hypertension may cause deterioration by increasing ICP and potentiating further bleeding from small arteries or arterioles. Hypotension may decrease CBF, worsening brain injury. In general, recommendations for treatment of hypertension in patients with ICH are more aggressive than those for patients with ischemic stroke. The current consensus for ICH is to recommend

antihypertensive treatment with parenteral agents for systolic pressures greater than 160 to 180 mm Hg or diastolic pressures greater than 105 mm Hg. Treatment for lower blood pressures is controversial.[35,50] Nitroprusside is the agent most commonly recommended because one can obtain a rapid and consistent lowering of the blood pressure to the desired level, and adjustments can be rapidly made. Nitroprusside provides a rapid onset, is titratable, and has no effect on mental status. Disadvantages include the need for careful monitoring (ideally with an indwelling arterial catheter) and the theoretical risk of worsening the hemorrhage secondary to the vasodilatory effects of nitroprusside on cerebral vessels. Labetalol is another therapeutic option.

Hyperventilation and diuretics, such as furosemide and mannitol, are useful when ICH is complicated by signs of progressively increasing ICP, clinical deterioration associated with mass effect, or impending uncal herniation.[35] These interventions should not be used prophylactically. Diuretics and mannitol move fluid from the intracranial compartment, reducing cerebral edema. Although this effect may be temporarily helpful in the acute setting, the brain tissue re-equilibrates, and rebound swelling can occur and worsen the patient's clinical status. These agents also can cause dehydration and lead to hypotension. The use of steroids in cerebral hemorrhage, previously a common practice, may be harmful and is not recommended. Other experimental modalities include barbiturate coma and hypothermia.

Seizure activity can cause neuronal injury, elevations in ICH, and destabilization of an already critically ill patient. In addition, nonconvulsive seizure may contribute to coma in 10% of patients in a neurologic intensive care unit.[35] Seizure prophylaxis (phenytoin, 18 mg/kg) should be considered for patients with ICH, especially patients with lobar hemorrhage.

Surgery is not beneficial in most cases of ICH. Selected patients with sizable lobar hemorrhage and progressive neurologic deterioration may benefit from surgical drainage. Surgery is more efficacious in patients with cerebellar hemorrhage. The clinical course in cerebellar hemorrhage is notoriously unpredictable. Patients with minimal findings may deteriorate suddenly to coma and death with little warning. For this reason, most neurosurgeons consider emergent surgery for patients with cerebellar hemorrhage within 48 hours of onset.

DISPOSITION

Ischemic Stroke and Transient Ischemic Attack

"Stroke center" definitions have been proposed, and a national certification process is now evolving despite considerable political controversy. It has been recommended that emergency medical services personnel should transport patients with symptoms consistent with an acute stroke to emergency facilities capable of initiating fibrinolytic therapy within 1 hour of hospital arrival. At a minimum, this recommendation requires emergent CT capabilities, an institutional "acute stroke protocol," and a physician versed in the use of thrombolytic therapy. Intensive care monitoring and neurosurgery capabilities should be available within 2 hours of drug initiation, either at the treating hospital or by helicopter or ground transport to an appropriate health care facility (see Table 99-3).[85]

In most cases, when the diagnosis of an acute stroke or stroke syndrome is established and the patient is stabilized, the patient should be hospitalized for further evaluation and treatment. Patients may deteriorate over the first 24 hours and require close in-hospital monitoring. In addition, patients often require prolonged rehabilitation, including physical therapy and assistance to regain ability to perform activities of daily living. Most patients can be managed on a general medical or telemetry unit. Patients with large acute hemispheric strokes (at risk for herniation), patients with significant posterior circulation findings, and patients treated with a fibrinolytic agent should be monitored in a step-down or intensive care unit for at least 24 hours. In some cases, patients with multiple previous strokes who have been thoroughly evaluated and who experience mild new episodes or have a completed stroke days to weeks after the event may be treated at home when it is deemed appropriate by the patient's physician and family.

Patients with new-onset TIAs warrant hospital admission for evaluation and workup because of the substantial short-term risk of stroke and other adverse events.[31] The exception is a patient with only minimal anterior circulation symptoms, who can have an extensive emergency department evaluation. In these patients, the emergency department evaluation must include a CT scan, a carotid Doppler, MRA, or CT angiography of the anterior circulation and an echocardiogram (if indicated). A medically or surgically treatable cause for TIAs (e.g., high-grade carotid stenosis or a mural thrombus) should be sought, which would require in-hospital treatment, such as anticoagulation, antiplatelet agents, or carotid endarterectomy. If the patient's symptoms have resolved completely, the workup is negative, and close neurologic follow-up is arranged, the patient can be considered for outpatient therapy. The decision to start the patient on an antiplatelet agent should be made in conjunction with the neurologist.

Hemorrhagic Stroke

All patients with an acute hemorrhagic stroke in whom surgical intervention is a consideration should be admitted to an intensive care unit under the care of a neurologist or a neurosurgeon. If this is unavailable at the evaluating institution, the patient should be transported to an appropriate institution.

KEY CONCEPTS

- Patients presenting with the signs and symptoms of an acute ischemic stroke within 3 hours of symptom onset should be evaluated for thrombolytic therapy within the following recommended target time frames:

  Door to physician: 10 minutes

  Door to CT completion: 25 minutes

  Door to CT reading: 45 minutes

  Door to drug treatment: 60 minutes

- Carotid Doppler, MRA, or CT angiography studies are recommended before discharging a patient with TIA.

- Avoid overaggressive blood pressure management in patients with acute ischemic stroke.

- Accurate time of symptom onset should be documented for all patients with stroke.

- Assessment of gait is essential to rule out posterior circulation stroke in patients presenting with vertigo.

REFERENCES

1. American Heart Association: *Heart Disease and Stroke Statistics—2004 Update.* Dallas, Tex, American Heart Association, 2003.
2. Broderick J, et al: The Greater Cincinnati/Northern Kentucky Stroke Study: Preliminary first-ever and total incidence rates of stroke among blacks. *Stroke* 29:415, 1998.
3. Williams GR, et al: Incidence and occurrence of total (first-ever and recurrent) stroke. *Stroke* 30:2523, 1999.
4. Kolominksky-Rabas PL, et al: A prospective community-based study of stroke in Germany—the Erlangen Stroke Project (ESPro). *Stroke* 29:2501, 1998.
5. Kothari RU, et al: Emergency physicians: Accuracy in the diagnosis of stroke. *Stroke* 26:2238, 1995.
6. Kothari RU, et al: Frequency and accuracy of prehospital diagnosis of acute stroke. *Stroke* 26:937, 1995.
7. Smith RW, et al: Emergency physician treatment of acute stroke with recombinant tissue plasminogen activator: A retrospective analysis. *Acad Emerg Med* 6:618, 1999.
8. Baird AE, et al: Enlargement of human cerebral ischemic lesion volumes measured by diffusion-weighted magnetic resonance imaging. *Ann Neurol* 41:581, 1997.
9. Marler JR, et al: Early stroke treatment associated with better outcome: The NINDS rt-PA stroke study. *Neurology* 55:1649, 2000.
10. The NINDS rt-PA Stroke Study Group: Tissue plasminogen activator for acute ischemic stroke. *N Engl J Med* 333:1581, 1995.
11. Clark W, et al, for the ATLANTIS Stroke Study Investigators: Recombinant tissue-type plasminogen activator (Alteplase) for ischemic stroke 3 to 5 hours after symptom onset—the ALANTIS study: A randomized controlled trial. *JAMA* 282:2019, 1999.
12. Hacke W, et al: Intravenous thrombolysis with recombinant tissue plasminogen activator for acute hemispheric stroke. The European Cooperative Acute Stroke Study. *JAMA* 274:1, 1995.
13. Hacke W, et al, for the Second European-Australasian Acute Stroke Study Investigators: Randomized double-blind placebo-controlled trial of thrombolytic therapy with intravenous alteplase in acute ischaemic stroke (ECASS II). *Lancet* 352:1245, 1998.
14. The Abciximab in Ischemic Stroke Investigators: A randomized, double-blinded, placebo-controlled, dose-escalation study. *Stroke* 31:601, 2000.

15. Clark WM, et al, for the Citicholine Stroke Study Group: A randomized efficacy trial of citicholine in patients with acute ischemic stroke. *Stroke* 31:2592, 1999.

16. Grotta J: The US and Canadian Lubeluzole Stroke Study Group: Lubeluzole treatment of acute ischemic stroke. *Stroke* 28:2338, 1997.

17. Gammans RE, et al: ECCO 2000 Study of Citicholine for treatment of acute ischemic stroke. Presented at the 25th International Stroke Conference, New Orleans, February 10-12, 2000.

18. Diener HC, European and Australian Lubeluzose Ischaemic Stroke Study Group: Multinational randomized controlled trial of lubeluzole in acute ischaemic stroke. *Cerebrovasc Dis* 8:172, 1998.

19. RANTTAS Investigators: A randomized trial of tirilazad mesylate in patients with acute stroke (RANTTAS). *Stroke* 27:1453, 1996.

20. Marchal G, et al: Prolonged persistence of substantial volumes of potentially viable brain tissue after stroke: A correlative PET-CT study with voxel-based data analysis. *Stroke* 27:599, 1996.

21. Wagner KR, et al: Lobar intracerebral hemorrhage model in pigs: Rapid edema development in perihematomal white matter. *Stroke* 27:490, 1996.

22. Xi G, et al: Role of blood clot formation on early edema development after experimental intracerebral hemorrhage. *Stroke* 29:2580, 1998.

23. Zuccarello M, et al: Early surgical treatment for supratentorial intracerebral hemorrhage: A randomized feasibility study. *Stroke* 30:1833, 1999.

24. Woo D, et al: Incidence rates of first-ever ischemic stroke subtypes among blacks: A population-based study. *Stroke* 30:2517, 1999.

25. Petty GW, et al: Ischemic stroke subtypes: A population-based study of incidence and risk factors. *Stroke* 30:2513, 1999.

26. Jorgensen HS, et al: Acute stroke with atrial fibrillation—the Copenhagen Stroke Study. *Stroke* 10:1765, 1996.

27. Lin HJ, et al: Stroke severity in atrial fibrillation—the Framingham Study. *Stroke* 27:1760, 1996.

28. Maggioni AP, et al: Cerebrovascular events after myocardial infarction: Analysis of the GISSI trial. *BMJ* 302:1428, 1991.

29. Mooe T, Eriksson P, Stegmayr B: Ischemic stroke after acute myocardial infarction—a population based study. *Stroke* 28:762, 1997.

30. ISIS-2 (Second International Study of Infarct Survival) Collaborative Group: Randomized trial of intravenous streptokinase, oral aspirin, both, or neither among 17,187 cases of suspected acute myocardial infarction: ISIS-2. *Lancet* 2:349-360, 1988.

31. Johnston SC, Gress DR, Browner WS, Sidney S: Short-term prognosis after emergency department diagnosis of TIA. *JAMA* 284:2901, 2000.

32. American Heart Association: *Heart and Stroke Facts.* Dallas, Tex, American Heart Association, 2003.

33. Fazekas F, et al: Magnetic resonance imaging correlates of transient cerebral ischemic attacks. *Stroke* 27:607, 1996.

34. Bhadelia RA, et al, for the CHS Collaborative Research Group: Prevalence and associations of MRI-demonstrated brain infarcts in elderly subjects with a history of transient ischemic attack—the Cardiovascular Health Study. *Stroke* 30:383, 1999.

35. Broderick JP, et al: Guidelines for the management of spontaneous intracerebral hemorrhage: A statement for healthcare professionals from a special writing group of the Stroke Council, American Heart Association. *Stroke* 30:905, 1999.

36. Lewandowski CA, and the EMS Bridging Trial Investigators: Combined intravenous and intra-arterial r-TPA versus intra-arterial therapy of acute ischemic stroke—Emergency Management of Stroke (EMS) Bridging Trial. *Stroke* 30:2598, 1999.

37. Brott T: Utility of the NIH Stroke Scale. *Cerebrovasc Dis* 2:241, 1992.

38. Lyden P, et al, and The National Institute for Neurological Disorders and Stroke rt-PA Study Group: A proposed revision of the NINDS Stroke Scale: Results of a factor analysis. *Stroke* 30:2347, 1999.

39. DeGraba TJ, et al: Progression in acute stroke—value of the initial NIH Stroke Scale score on patient stratification in future trials. *Stroke* 30:1208, 1999.

40. Brott T, et al: Early hemorrhage growth in patients with intracerebral hemorrhage. *Stroke* 28:1-5, 1997.

41. Kothari RU, et al: The ABCs of measuring intracerebral hemorrhage volumes. *Stroke* 27:1304, 1996.

42. Gilman S: Imaging the brain. *N Engl J Med* 338:812, 1998.

43. The NINDS t-PA Stroke Study Group: Intracerebral Hemorrhage after intravenous t-PA therapy for ischemic stroke. *Stroke* 28:2109, 1997.

44. Grotta J, et al, for the NINDS rtPA Stroke Study Group: Agreement and variability interpreting early CT changes in stroke patients qualifying for intravenous r-tPA therapy. *Stroke* 30:1528, 1999.

45. Executive Committee for the Asymptomatic Carotid Atherosclerosis Study: Endarterectomy for asymptomatic carotid artery stenosis. *JAMA* 273:1421, 1995.

46. Barnett HJ, et al: Benefit of carotid endarterectomy in patients with symptomatic moderate or severe stenosis. North American Symptomatic Carotid Endarterectomy Trial Collaborators. *N Engl J Med* 339:1415, 1998.

47. Schellinger PD, et al: A standardized MRI stroke protocol—comparison with CT in hyperacute intracerebral hemorrhage. *Stroke* 30:765, 1999.

48. Linfante I, et al: MRI features of intracerebral hemorrhage within 2 hours from symptom onset. *Stroke* 30:2263, 1999.

49. Tong DC, et al: Correlation of perfusion and diffusion weighted MRI with NIHSS score in acute (<6.5 hour) ischemic stroke. *Neurology* 50:864, 1998.

50. Emergency Stroke Care Task Force: Acute stroke. In Cummins RO (ed): *Advanced Cardiac Life Support,* 1997 edition. Dallas, Tex, American Heart Association, 1997 pp 10-1 to 10-28.

51. Ronning OM, Guldvog B: Should stroke victims routinely receive supplemental oxygen? A quasi-randomized controlled trial. *Stroke* 30:2033, 1999.

52. Elizabeth J, et al: Arterial oxygen saturation and posture in acute stroke. *Age Aging* 22:269, 1993.

53. Weir CJ, et al: Is hyperglycemia an independent predictor of poor outcome after acute stroke? Results of a long-term follow-up study. *BMJ* 314:1303, 1997.

54. Broderick JP, et al: Hyperglycemia and hemorrhagic transformation of cerebral infarcts. *Stroke* 26:4848, 1995.

55. Yip PK, et al: Effect of plasma glucose on infarct size in focal cerebral ischemia-reperfusion. *Neurology* 41:899, 1991.

56. Chew W, et al: Hyperglycemia augments ischemic brain injury: In vivo MR imaging spectroscopic study with nicardipine in cats with occluded middle cerebral arteries. *AJNR Am J Neuroradiol* 12:603, 1991.

57. Kothari R, et al: Early stroke recognition: Developing an out-of-hospital NIH Stroke Scale. *Acad Emerg Med* 4:986, 1997.

58. Kothari RU, et al: Cincinnati Prehospital Stroke Scale: Reproducibility and validity. *Ann Emerg Med* 33:373, 1999.

59. Kidwell CS, et al: Design and retrospective analysis of the Los Angeles Prehospital Stroke Screen (LAPSS). *Prehosp Emerg Care* 2:27, 1998.

60. Kidwell CS, et al: Identifying stroke in the field: Prospective validation of the Los Angeles Prehospital Stroke Screen (LAPSS). *Stroke* 31:71, 2000.

61. Ginsberg MD, Busto R: Combating hyperthermia in acute stroke: A significant clinical concern. *Stroke* 29:529, 1998.

62. Adams JHP, et al: Guidelines for the management of patients with acute ischemic stroke. *Stroke* 25:1901, 1994.

63. Brott T, et al, and The National Institute for Neurological Disorders and Stroke rt-PA Study Group: Hypertension and its treatment in the NINDS rt-PA Stroke Trial. *Stroke* 29:1504, 1998.

64. A special Writing Group of the Stroke Council, American Heart Association Guidelines for Thrombolytic Therapy for Acute Stroke. A supplement to the guidelines for the management of patients with acute ischemic stroke. *Circulation* 94:1167, 1996.

65. Wardlaw JM, del Zoppo G, Yamaguchi T: Thrombolysis for acute ischaemic stroke. *Cochrane Review,* The Cochrane Library, Issue 4. Oxford, Update Software, 1999.

66. Kwiatkowski TG, et al, for the NINDS r-tPA Stroke Study Group: Effects of tissue plasminogen activator for acute ischemic stroke at one year. *N Engl J Med* 340:1781, 1999.

67. Hill MD, et al: Methodology for the Canadian Activase for Stroke Effectiveness Study (CASES). *Can J Neurol* 28:232, 2001.

68. The ATLANTIS, ECASS, and NINDS rt-PA Study Group Investigators: Better outcome with early stroke treatment: A pooled analysis of ATLANTIS, ECASS, and NINDS rt-PA stroke trials. *Lancet* 363:768, 2004.

69. Katzan IL, et al: Use of tissue-type plasminogen activator for acute ischemic stroke: The Cleveland area experience. *JAMA* 283:1151, 2000.

70. Graham GD: Tissue plasminogen activator for acute ischemic stroke in clinical practice: A meta-analysis of safety data. *Stroke* 34:2847, 2003.

71. The National Institute of Neurological Disorders t-PA Stroke Study Group: Generalized efficacy of t-PA for acute stroke: Subgroup analysis of the NINDS t-PA Stroke Trial. *Stroke* 28: 2119, 1997.

72. Tanne D, et al: Initial clinical experience with IV tissue plasminogen activator for acute ischemic stroke: A multicenter survey. *Neurology* 53:424, 1999.

73. Lopez-Yunez AM, et al: Protocol violations in community-based rt-PA stroke treatment are associated with symptomatic intracerebral hemorrhage. *Stroke* 32:12, 2001.

74. del Zoppo GT, Higashida HT, Furlan AJ, for the PROACT Investigators: PROACT: A phase II randomized trial of recombinant pro-urokinase by direct arterial delivery in acute middle cerebral artery stroke. *Stroke* 29:4, 1998.

75. Furlan A, et al, for the PROACT investigators: Intra-arterial Pro-urokinase for acute ischemic stroke: The PROACT II study: A randomized controlled trial. *JAMA* 282:2003, 1999.

76. International Stroke Trial Collaborative Group: The International Stroke Trial (IST): A randomized trial of aspirin, subcutaneous heparin, both, or neither among 19,435 patients with acute ischaemic stroke. *Lancet* 349:1569, 1997.

77. Chinese Acute Stroke Trial Collaborative Group: CAST: Randomized placebo-controlled trial of early aspirin use in 20,000 patients with acute ischaemic stroke. *Lancet* 349:1641, 1997.

78. Multicentre Acute Stroke Trial–Italy (MAST-I) Group: Randomized controlled trial of streptokinase, aspirin, and combination of both in treatment of acute ischaemic stroke. *Lancet* 346:1509, 1995.

79. Coull BM, et al: Anticoagulants and antiplatelet agents in acute ischemic stroke. *Stroke* 33:1934, 2002.

80. Clark WM, et al, for the Citocholine Stroke Study Group: A randomized efficacy trial of citocholine in patients with acute ischemic stroke. *Stroke* 31:2592, 1999.

81. Grotta J, the US and Canadian Lubeluzole Ischemic Stroke Study Group: Lubeluzole treatment of acute ischemic stroke. *Stroke* 28:2338, 1997.

82. Gammans RE, et al: ECCO 2000 Study of Citicholine for treatment of acute ischemic stroke. Presented at the 25th International Stroke Conference, New Orleans, February 10-12, 2000.

83. The Abciximab in Ischemic Stroke investigators: Abciximab in Acute Ischemic Stroke: A randomized, double-blind, placebo-controlled, dose-escalation study. *Stroke* 31:601, 2000.

84. Mechanical embolus retrieval in cerebral ischemia (MERCI). Abstract presented at 29th International Stroke Conference, San Diego, February 2004.

85. Barsan WG: Recommendations: Emergency department panel. In Marler JR, Jones PW, Emr M (eds): Proceedings of a National Symposium on Rapid Identification and Treatment of Acute Stroke (NIH Publication No. 97-4239). Bethesda, Md, National Institute of Neurological Disorders and Stroke, 1997, pp 151-156.

CHAPTER

100 Seizures

Charles V. Pollack, Jr.

PERSPECTIVE

A *seizure* is the clinical manifestation of excessive, abnormal cortical neuron activity. The physical manifestation depends on the area of brain cortex involved and, to a lesser extent, on the specific underlying abnormality. Patients who have recurring seizures without consistent provocation have *epilepsy,* although this term encompasses many disparate clinical syndromes.

Seizures may occur also as a predictable response to certain toxic, pathophysiologic, or environmental stresses; these are *reactive* or *secondary seizures,* and patients who have them do not have epilepsy. In the United States, 10% of people have at least one seizure in their lifetime; the incidence of epilepsy is less than 1%.[1]

The evaluation of seizure patients in the emergency department may be complex and difficult. A careful history must be elicited to determine the presence of ictal events that represent epilepsy or exposure to ictogenic stimuli (e.g., alcohol or cocaine), significant underlying illness (e.g., meningitis, hypoxemia, hypoglycemia, or intracranial mass), or contributing causes (e.g., sleep deprivation in an epileptic). The physical examination should focus on the identification of focal neurologic abnormalities, systemic illness, and signs of toxic exposure. If the patient continues to seize, airway protection and abortive therapy must be provided. Laboratory and radiographic evaluation that is guided by historical and physical findings may be limited or unnecessary in some cases. Finally, an appropriate disposition of a seizure patient from the emergency department requires an understanding of the underlying illness, likelihood of recurrence, indications for maintenance pharmacologic therapy, and state reporting regulations.

In addition to the distinction between primary (epileptic) and secondary (reactive) seizures, there are many other classifications of ictal events.[2-6] Seizures are termed *generalized* or *focal (partial)* depending on their clinical manifestations. The former type of seizure results from the abnormal electrical event that simultaneously involves both cerebral hemispheres and is accompanied by loss of consciousness; in the latter, abnormal activity is limited to part of one cerebral hemisphere only. Generalized seizures usually are characterized by rhythmic, tonic-clonic muscle contractions, or *convulsions,* although *nonconvulsive generalized seizures* also occur. Partial seizures can be differentiated further into seizures during which consciousness is maintained *(simple partial)* and seizures during which consciousness is impaired *(complex partial).* Finally, partial seizures may become generalized *(partial with secondary generalization).*

Inexperienced witnesses may provide insufficient histories to categorize seizures. A rule of thumb remains, however, when an accurate history is available: Secondary seizures typically are generalized, not partial, in nature. The definitive differentiation among these classifications may require electroencephalogram (EEG) recording *during* the seizure, sometimes in association with simultaneous video recording.

Seizures in children, as in adults, are classified as primary (idiopathic) and secondary (symptomatic or reactive). The term *cryptogenic* is used sometimes when seizures are thought to be secondary, but no cause has been identified. The history is the most important diagnostic tool in evaluating seizures in children. The actual seizure activity usually is not observed, and the emergency physician must rely on a detailed and accurate history for diagnosis.

Other important terms to describe ictal events include *status epilepticus,* in which seizures occur serially without an intervening return to a normal neurologic condition; *spasm,* which is a specific, debilitating seizure syndrome that occurs in infants; and *myoclonus,* which refers to rhythmic, shocklike muscle contractions also typical for specific seizure syndromes. The *postictal period* is a variable time interval after a seizure, usually characterized by impaired consciousness, but sometimes also marked by self-limited focal paralysis or neurogenic pulmonary edema.

PRINCIPLES OF DISEASE

The pathophysiology of seizures at the neuronal level is incompletely understood, with most of what is known coming from animal studies in which either electrical or pharmacologic stimulation is applied directly to brain cortex. To produce generalized ictus, stimuli must be applied to both hemispheres simultaneously. Some studies show the concept of recruitment, which occurs when the initiating neurons' abnormal, increased electrical activity activates adjacent neurons and propagates until the thalamus and other subcortical structures are recruited. The clinical seizure activity typically, but not always, reflects the focus of initiation.[1,7,8]

What prompts such initiation is unclear. Proposed mechanisms include disruption of normal structure—whether congenital, maturational, or acquired (as with scar tissue)—and disruption of local metabolic or biochemical function. The latter mechanism is better elucidated because the roles of two neurotransmitters—acetylcholine, which is excitatory to cortical neurons, and γ-aminobutyric acid (GABA), which is inhibitory—are better recognized. In sensitive neurons, such as those at an ictogenic focus, subtle changes in the local concentrations of these neurotransmitters can produce sustained membrane depolarization, ultimately followed by local hyperpolarization and recruitment. Recruitment may follow contiguous paths or extend along diverse integrated circuits that are deep and across the midline.[1,7,8]

When the ictal discharge extends below the cortex to deeper structures, the reticular activating system in the brainstem may be affected, altering consciousness. In generalized seizures, the focus is often subcortical and midline, which explains the prompt loss of consciousness and bilateral involvement.[8,9] Seizures are typically self-limited; at some point, the hyperpolarization subsides, and the electrical discharges from the focus terminate. This termination may be related to reflex inhibition, loss of synchrony, neuronal exhaustion, or alteration of the local balance of acetylcholine and GABA in favor of inhibition.[8,9]

The systemic manifestations of convulsive ictal activity include hypertension, tachycardia, tachypnea, and hyperglycemia from sympathetic stimulation. With more prolonged convulsions, skeletal muscle damage, lactic acidosis, and, rarely, frank rhabdomyolysis may ensue.[1,8,10,11] Autonomic discharge and bulbar muscle involvement may result in urinary or fecal incontinence, vomiting (with significant aspiration risk), tongue biting, and airway impairment.

CLINICAL FEATURES

Primary Seizures in Adults

Primary ictal events in adults include events of genetic and of idiopathic origin. Onset is typically during childhood or adolescence, but occasionally idiopathic seizures may begin de novo in adulthood. Because idiopathic seizures are rare, the emergency physician should evaluate thoroughly a first-time seizure in an adult.

Focal seizures in adults may be classified as simple partial, complex partial, or evolving into generalized seizures. Simple partial seizures are limited in electrical focus to one cerebral hemisphere and do not cause loss of consciousness. Consciousness usually is assessed by the ability to respond to external stimuli. Although the specific function of the initiating neurons determines the clinical manifestation of the ictal event (i.e., motor, somatosensory, special sensory, autonomic, or psychic), such clinical manifestations are not sufficiently specific for anatomic localization without performing an EEG. Typical features of simple partial seizures include focal clonic movements; paresthesias; visual, auditory, olfactory, or gustatory experiences; sweating and flushing; dysphasia; a sense of déjà vu; or a sense of unwarranted fear.[7] Motor signs, which by definition remain ipsilateral in simple partial seizures, may spread contiguously in a stepwise fashion *(Jacksonian march)* because neuron recruitment occurs in the motor cortex. There is generally no postictal state after a simple partial seizure.

Complex partial seizures are ictal events that involve impairment but not loss of consciousness, either at onset or evolving from focal activity. Amnesia for the ictal event is a consistent finding in a complex partial seizure, although during the episodes the patient may remain responsive to the surroundings. Complex partial seizures typically involve automatisms that are specific to the individual, such as lip smacking, repeated swallowing or verbal phrases, or picking at one's clothing. Complex partial seizures generally are associated with an aura, such as a specific smell, taste, visual hallucination, or intense emotional feeling. In contrast to generalized seizures, patients maintain higher cortical function during complex partial seizures; patients may drive automobiles, ride bicycles, or play musical instruments. *Psychomotor epilepsy* and *temporal lobe seizure* are other terms applied to such complex partial seizures. This terminology is considered outdated, however, because seizures that originate in the temporal lobe may be generalized, simple, or complex partial seizures. Partial seizures may progress rapidly to generalized seizures. A postictal state is common after complex partial seizures and may persist for hours.[1,7,8]

Generalized seizures in adults may be convulsive or nonconvulsive. By definition, patients lose consciousness in a generalized seizure, and no aura is present. Some patients may experience a brief, vague prodrome or dysphoric state just before the ictal event. Convulsive generalized seizures are typified by the grand mal seizure, in which the patient loses consciousness; stiffens with generalized muscular hypertonus; then rhythmically, violently contracts multiple, bilateral, and usually symmetric muscle groups. The muscular force may be sufficiently vigorous to result in posterior shoulder dislocation or fractures of thoracic spine vertebral bodies; significant tongue and buccal injuries also may occur from repeated biting. Dysautonomia,

including transient apnea, is a potential manifestation of convulsive generalized seizures; urinary incontinence occurs more often than fecal incontinence. A generalized convulsive seizure is followed by a postictal state, headache, and drowsiness that may persist for hours. This state must be differentiated in the emergency department from altered consciousness attributable to other causes. Ictal and interictal EEG findings are abnormal.[1,7,8]

Nonconvulsive generalized seizures include absence, or petit mal, seizures; myoclonic seizures; tonic seizures; and atonic seizures. Absence seizures in adults are subclassified further as *typical* or *atypical.* Typical absence ictus is characterized by the sudden cessation of normal, conscious activity followed by a nonconvulsive, dissociative state that persists for a few seconds to several minutes before suddenly terminating. Eye movements, blinking, or automatisms may be present. There is no postictal state. Absence seizures typically begin in childhood but occasionally develop in older adults, in whom brief 3-Hz, spike-and-wave discharges occur on the EEG. Atypical absence seizures are marked by more complicated motor signs, coexistence with other forms of generalized seizures, inconsistent postictal confusion, and irregular EEG abnormalities.[1,7,8]

Myoclonic and *tonic seizures* are manifested by sudden, brief muscle group contractions without a loss of consciousness. When the entire body is involved, the patient falls ("drop attack"). Atonic seizures also result in drop attacks, which are so unexpected that significant injury may result. Because there is typically no postictal state associated with these episodes, an altered level of consciousness should prompt the emergency physician to investigate for head trauma or a toxic or metabolic abnormality.

Status epilepticus is defined as serial seizure activity without interictal recovery or prolonged, continuous seizure activity that lasts longer than 30 minutes and may occur with any type of seizure.[12] The clinical significance can range from life-threatening in convulsive generalized status to negligible in typical absence. The most common cause of status epilepticus is discontinuation of anticonvulsant medication. This situation may be compounded by barbiturate withdrawal when phenobarbital therapy is abruptly withdrawn. Patients may present for the first time with a primary seizure disorder in status. There are many other causes of status epilepticus (Box 100-1).[13,14]

Complex partial status, although not life-threatening, also should be treated vigorously to avoid prolonged antegrade amnesia.[7] Clonic simple partial status, also termed *epilepsia partialis continua,* may occur in adults as a result of hyperosmolar conditions, such as nonketotic hyperglycemia or uremia, and should prompt a thorough metabolic evaluation in the emergency department.[14]

All classes of primary seizures may recur sporadically, randomly, or predictably. Cyclical recurrence has been reported with awakening, sleep deprivation, and menses, among other factors. Seizures also may be triggered by photic stimulation (particularly strobe lights),

BOX 100-1. Status Epilepticus: Common Etiologies

Metabolic Encephalopathies
Hyponatremia
Hypocalcemia
Hypoglycemia
Hepatic or renal failure

Infectious Encephalopathies
CNS abscess
Meningitis
Encephalitis

CNS Lesions
Neoplasm
Arteriovenous malformations
Acute hydrocephalus
Intracerebral hematomas
Cerebrovascular accident

Intoxications
Cyclic antidepressants
Lead
Strychnine
Camphor

specific musical compositions, and tactile stimulation.[1,8,9] The most common cause of recurrent primary seizures is medication noncompliance.[7]

Reactive Seizures in Adults

Reactive or secondary seizures do not result from genetic or idiopathic causes. The conditions that cause reactive seizures may be static (e.g., anatomic scarring), progressive (e.g., degenerative cortical disorders), or transient (e.g., acute electrolyte derangements).

Seizures Caused by Metabolic Derangements

Hypoglycemia is a common metabolic cause of reactive seizures. Ictal activity can occur when the plasma glucose level is less than 45 mg/dL, although some patients may manifest neurologic disturbances at higher levels.[15] A rapid bedside glucose test should be an integral part of seizure evaluation in an emergency department patient without known epilepsy. Convulsive and nonconvulsive seizures and generalized and partial seizures all may occur during hypoglycemia.[15] Patients at the extremes of age are particularly susceptible to glucose stress during acute illness. Hypoglycemia also may result from insulin reaction, a deliberate insulin or hypoglycemic agent overdose, or poor nutrition. Hypoglycemic seizures respond to glucose therapy; anticonvulsants are unnecessary.

Cation derangements are another common metabolic cause of ictal activity.[16,17] Hypo-osmolar and hyperosmolar states can precipitate seizures. Disorders of sodium—the primary cation in the extracellular fluid compartment and the primary determinant of serum osmolarity—are most common. Hyponatremia is the most commonly identified electrolyte disorder in hospitalized patients, and sodium levels less than 120 mEq/L are often complicated by seizures.[18] The rate at which the sodium level decreases, and not the absolute magnitude of the decrease, determines the risk of neurologic manifestations.[17] As a result, correcting hyponatremia should be undertaken slowly in the emergency department, unless seizures are persistent, in which case administration of hypertonic (3%) saline may be indicated. Hypernatremia, which typically occurs as a result of a dehydrating illness or lack of access to free water in the very young and the very old, also is associated with seizures, particularly when serum sodium levels are greater than 160 mEq/L. Hypernatremia also should be corrected slowly.[17]

Hypercalcemia reduces neuronal excitability and rarely causes seizures; significant hypocalcemia (7.5 mEq/L) is associated, however, with ictal activity. Hypocalcemia may result from hypoparathyroidism, renal failure, or acute pancreatitis and typically is associated with hypomagnesemia, which also can precipitate seizures, particularly at serum levels less than 1 mEq/L. Hypomagnesemia is seen most often as a result of poor nutrition, especially in alcoholics. Patients with significant hypomagnesemia or hypocalcemia should be treated for both disorders empirically.[17]

Nonketotic hyperosmolar hyperglycemia also is associated with seizure activity. Partial seizures, including partial status, predominate and do not respond to anticonvulsants, but rather to gradual correction of fluid deficits and glucose excess.[15,19]

Seizures may complicate the course and treatment of renal failure.[20] Ictal activity occasionally complicates uremic encephalopathy, is more common in conjunction with acute fluid and electrolyte shifts during dialysis (dialysis disequilibrium syndrome), and can occur as a complication of immunosuppressive therapy after a renal transplant.

Thyroid disease may be associated with generalized seizures. Seizures are the presenting sign of hypothyroidism in 20% of patients but are a less common feature of thyrotoxicosis.[21,22] Seizures also occur with hypoparathyroidism as a direct result of secondary hypocalcemia.[22] Seizures occur in one third of patients with hepatic encephalopathy; phenytoin is considered a first-line treatment because benzodiazepines induce coma in these patients.[15,23]

High anion gap acidosis is the most likely acid-base disorder to be associated with seizures.[24] Benzodiazepines should be given for these seizures in the emergency department as specific treatment is initiated for the underlying metabolic derangement. Seizures also may be a feature of cerebral hypoxia that results from suffocation, respiratory failure, circulatory collapse, or carbon monoxide poisoning.

Hypertensive encephalopathy also can cause seizures. The underlying problem must be addressed while seizure control is attempted with benzodiazepines.[25] Acute intermittent porphyria is an uncommon illness often associated with seizures. Treatment includes glucose and hematin.[23]

Seizures Caused by Infectious Diseases

Infectious diseases can cause seizures independent of a purely febrile mechanism. These seizures generally result from primary central nervous system (CNS) infections, but occasionally arise from other septic sources. The most important ictogenic infections are meningitis, encephalitis, cerebral abscess, cerebral parasitosis, and the protean CNS manifestations of human immunodeficiency virus (HIV) disease and its associated opportunistic infections.

Seizures can occur as a result of the acute inflammatory response or as sequelae to bacterial or viral meningitis. During the acute course of their illness, 15% to 40% of patients with meningitis have at least one seizure; this is more common at the extremes of age.[26] Partial seizures predominate in most cases, although generalized seizures also occur.[27] After meningitic seizures are terminated with benzodiazepines, phenytoin or phenobarbital therapy should be initiated temporarily.[28]

All viral meningoencephalitides are associated with seizures. These seizures are typically partial motor events, and postictal paralysis is common, particularly with herpetic infections.[15,29] Seizures are the presenting sign in one third of cerebral abscess cases. Although ictal activity is usually generalized, any focal manifestations help establish the location of the lesion.[30]

The parasitic CNS infection neurocysticercosis is relatively common in areas of the United States with immigrants from Latin America. Seizures complicate 50% to 90% of neurocysticercosis cases.[31] Latent syphilis also may be a cause of adult-onset seizures. Primary HIV disease of the CNS and its attendant infectious and mass lesion complications, such as from toxoplasmosis and lymphoma, are a significant cause of generalized and partial seizures.[15]

Seizures Caused by Drugs and Toxins

The list of substances reported to cause seizures either as an idiosyncratic side effect of therapeutic use or as a manifestation of toxic overdose is enormous.[32] The recognition of this etiologic category is crucial in the emergency department. Seizure activity should be viewed as a dire sign of toxicity and may herald the onset of life-threatening instability.

Seizures may occur after therapeutic doses of antimicrobials, cardiovascular agents, neuroleptics, and sympathomimetics.[33] Seizures also may result from exposure to plant toxins, insecticides and rodenticides, and hydrocarbons. The most common drug-associated and toxin-associated seizures occur, however, in conjunction with illicit drugs, such as cocaine, amphetamines, and phencyclidine; with overdoses of anticholinergic agents, such as cyclic antidepressants and antihistamines; as a manifestation of withdrawal from ethyl alcohol and sedative-hypnotics; and with toxic levels and deliberate overdoses of diverse medications, such as aspirin, theophylline, isoniazid, lithium, and the anticonvulsants phenytoin and carbamazepine.[34-36] Standard emergency department therapeutic measures are usually effective in toxic seizures.

In some cases, specific antidotal therapy is available, such as alkalinization for cyclic antidepressant and salicylate overdoses, pyridoxine for isoniazid overdose, and hemodialysis for salicylate and lithium toxicity.

Because of its prevalence in urban emergency department patient populations, cocaine toxicity warrants special mention.[37] Seizures may occur after isolated recreational use or chronic abuse, after overdose, and in "body packers" and "body stuffers."[38] Cocaine-related seizures may be a manifestation of direct CNS toxicity or an indirect result of hypoxemia from cardiac toxicity. Cocaine seizures are usually generalized but occasionally are partial.[39] Seizures in cocaine-intoxicated patients must be managed as part of the overall toxic reaction, which often includes high fever, rhabdomyolysis, and cardiac arrhythmias. Benzodiazepines are the appropriate initial drug therapy.

Ethyl alcohol is another common toxic cause of seizures. Of 472 adult hospital admissions for new-onset seizures, 41% were related to alcohol abuse.[40] Ictal events may occur with acute inebriation but are more common during withdrawal from alcohol.[41-43] Withdrawal seizures are typically generalized, are recurrent, and may begin within 6 hours of cessation or decrease of alcohol consumption. Via a phenomenon termed *kindling,* the risk and severity of seizures increase with each episode of withdrawal. Kindling implies that with each episode of alcohol withdrawal, the seizure threshold is lower. Alcoholic patients with seizures must be evaluated for other related, concomitant ictogenic problems (e.g., hypoglycemia, electrolyte derangements, head trauma, coingestion of other toxins, and pregnancy). The preferred treatment for alcohol-associated seizures is benzodiazepines; these drugs substitute for the GABA-enhancing effect of ethanol in the CNS.

Seizures Caused by Trauma

Posttraumatic seizures can occur as an acute result of blunt or penetrating head trauma and as posttraumatic sequelae. Immediate posttraumatic seizures occur within 24 hours of injury. Epidural, subdural, and intracerebral hematomas and traumatic subarachnoid hemorrhages all can be acutely ictogenic, particularly as intracranial pressure rises. Immediate posttraumatic seizures are more common in children than in adults.[44] The onset of seizure activity more often is delayed for at least several hours, however. Early posttraumatic seizures occur within 1 week of injury, whereas late posttraumatic seizures occur after 1 week. Within the first year after significant head trauma, the incidence of seizures is at least 12 times that of the general population.[45]

The severity of head injury correlates with the likelihood of posttraumatic seizures. The incidence of seizures after injury with neurologic deficit without dural violation is 7% to 39%; when the dura is disrupted, the incidence is 20% to 57%.[45] Imaging studies should be performed urgently because the likelihood of identifying significant cerebral edema, cerebral contusions, hematomas, and depressed skull fractures is relatively high.[46]

Seizures Associated with Malignancy or Vasculitis

Seizures are a common manifestation of primary and metastatic CNS neoplasms. They also may complicate cancer treatment because of postsurgical scarring or chemotherapy-related electrolyte derangements, hematologic abnormalities, or immunosuppression. Although any CNS tumor can be ictogenic, low-grade and slow-growing primary neoplasms (e.g., well-differentiated gliomas and oligodendrogliomas) are implicated most commonly.[47] In these cases, seizures that are most often partial with secondary generalization may be the initial manifestation of the mass. A new-onset seizure in a patient with a non-CNS primary malignancy, such as melanoma and tumors of the lung, breast, colon, germ cells, or renal cells, should prompt consideration of CNS metastasis and warrants neuroimaging.

Seizures also may be the presenting manifestation of CNS vasculitis seen in patients with systemic lupus erythematosus and polyarteritis nodosa. These are commonly complex partial seizures that give a general indication of the acute inflammatory focus. Sometimes secondary generalization follows.[48]

Seizures Caused by Strokes, Arteriovenous Malformations, and Migraines

Infarctive or hemorrhagic stroke is the cause of new-onset seizures in 54% of elderly patients.[49] The overall incidence of seizures with stroke ranges from 4% to 15%; more than half occur within the first week after stroke. The incidence of epilepsy after stroke is 4% to 9%.[50] Seizures that occur acutely with stroke are thought to result from local metabolic alterations in the CNS; these events are transient, and the seizures are often focal and self-limited. Seizures that develop later are more likely to be generalized.

Focal seizures also occur in conjunction with unruptured cerebrovascular aneurysms and arteriovenous malformations.[15] Arteriography may be required to confirm the diagnosis; unruptured arteriovenous malformations are easier to detect on an enhanced cranial computed tomography (CT) scan than are smaller unruptured aneurysms. Seizures also may coexist with vascular headaches coincidentally, via migrainous activation of an epileptic focus, or after vascular headache has induced cerebral infarction that becomes an epileptic focus.[51]

Seizures Caused by Degenerative Disease of the Central Nervous System

Approximately 5% of patients with multiple sclerosis develop focal or generalized seizures during their illness. These seizures must be differentiated from tonic spasms that occur in multiple sclerosis. Patients with demyelinating disease also should be evaluated for the other types of reactive seizures.[15]

CNS degeneration associated with aging increases the risk of reactive seizures and epilepsy.[52] Alzheimer's dementia seems to be a significant risk factor for developing new-onset seizures.[53] The elderly also are more likely to have other ictogenic problems (e.g., stroke, brain neoplasm, toxic and metabolic disturbances, and blunt head trauma from falls). Maintenance treatment of elderly patients with epilepsy is often complicated by drug-drug interactions, and breakthrough seizures may result even when patients are compliant. Emergency department management of these patients must include a thorough evaluation for causes of reactive seizures, even though the incidence of primary seizures increases after age 60 years.

Gestational Seizures

Seizures associated with pregnancy are divided into two categories: *gestational epilepsy,* in which hormonal and metabolic changes exacerbate underlying epilepsy or adversely influence serum levels of anticonvulsants, and *eclampsia* or *toxemia,* which is a gestational hypertensive encephalopathy manifested by seizures, hypertension, coma, proteinuria, and edema. For the former, antiepileptic therapy should be tailored by the patient's neurologist and obstetrician to maximize seizure control and minimize the risk of teratogenic effects.[54] Convulsive generalized status epilepticus in pregnancy jeopardizes the mother and the fetus. Emergency physicians should develop a standing protocol for managing pregnancy-related seizures in conjunction with their consulting obstetricians because of the controversy in this area.

Psychogenic Seizures

Psychogenic seizures, or pseudoseizures, are functional events that may be associated with alterations in consciousness, abnormal movements and behaviors, and autonomic changes. They are not the result of abnormal CNS electrical activity. Pseudoseizures may be primarily motor and mimic convulsive generalized seizures that are usually readily recognizable, or they may be primarily behavioral and analogous to complex partial seizures, in which case even experienced observers have difficulty differentiating them from true ictus.

Although simultaneous video and EEG recordings may be required to confirm the diagnosis, several typical characteristics of pseudoseizures may aid in differentiating them.[55,56] In general, patients with pseudoseizures tend to be of lower intelligence or have an underlying anxiety or hysterical personality disorder. The emergency department evaluation of these patients is difficult because seizures and pseudoseizures can coexist. All but obviously functional abnormalities should be treated as true ictus pending formal neurologic evaluation. Many patients with pseudoseizures are not deliberately attempting to mislead the examining physician. The long-term treatment of patients with confirmed pseudoseizures may include direct confrontation, intensive psychotherapy, and a placebo.

POSTICTAL STATES

The postictal state that follows most generalized seizures typically is characterized by a decreased level of arousal and responsiveness, disorientation, amnesia, and headache. These conditions may persist for only a few minutes or for many hours and may not be consistent from seizure to seizure. The most important consideration for the emergency physician managing the postictal state is to monitor and investigate the altered mental status after a seizure; otherwise, dangerous underlying metabolic or toxic abnormalities may be overlooked. At the minimum, airway positioning maneuvers, pulse oximetry, rapid glucose determination, and cardiac rhythm monitoring are necessary.

There are two unusual postictal manifestations: postictal paralysis and neurogenic pulmonary edema. Postictal paralysis (or Todd's paralysis) may follow generalized or complex partial seizures and is a focal motor deficit that may persist for 24 hours. Weakness of one extremity or a complete hemiparesis may occur; in the latter case, the patient must be safely restrained to avoid falls caused by a combination of weakness and diminished responsiveness resulting from the postictal state. Todd's paralysis indicates a high likelihood of an underlying structural cause for the seizure.

Neurogenic pulmonary edema is a relatively common, although often subclinical, complication of any structural CNS insult, including a seizure, trauma, or hemorrhage. Neurogenic pulmonary edema probably is caused by centrally mediated sympathetic discharge and generalized vasoconstriction, coupled with increased pulmonary capillary membrane permeability. After a seizure, neurogenic pulmonary edema can be confused clinically and radiographically with aspiration pneumonia. Neurogenic pulmonary edema is managed with ventilatory support, including positive end-expiratory pressure and other aggressive measures to reduce intracranial pressure. Hypoxia or other clinical evidence of pulmonary congestion after a seizure should prompt consideration of neurogenic pulmonary edema.[57]

DIAGNOSTIC STRATEGIES

First-Time Seizures

The essential components of the seizure evaluation in the emergency department are discussed in Chapter 16. An accurate and thorough history of the ictal event, any known or potential precipitants or exposures, and the patient's medical problems must be obtained. A thorough physical examination, including a complete neurologic examination, is essential. Any identified focal neurologic deficits must be followed for progression or resolution. Appropriate ancillary studies may be comprehensive, but if precipitants (e.g., hypo-

glycemia or intoxication) are known, studies may be comparatively limited. There is more debate regarding the role of neuroimaging for seizures in the emergency department.

A cranial CT scan is indicated in any age group when there is suspicion of head trauma, elevated intracranial pressure, intracranial mass, persistently abnormal mental status or focal neurologic abnormality, or HIV disease. An American College of Emergency Physicians expert panel[58] made the following recommendations: For patients with first-time seizure, a CT scan should be performed immediately when the provider suspects a serious structural lesion. This suspicion may be based on the presence of a new focal deficit, persistent altered mental status, fever, recent trauma, persistent headache, history of cancer, anticoagulant use, suspicion or known history of AIDS, age older than 40, and partial-complex seizure. Scans reasonably may be obtained on an outpatient, follow-up basis for patients who have recovered completely from the ictal event and for whom no apparent cause has been elucidated; if follow-up is unlikely or even questionable, the CT scan should be obtained in the emergency department to ensure its completion. In patients with known epilepsy and recurrent seizures, the same considerations apply, but, in addition, epilepsy patients with a change in seizure pattern, prolonged postictal state, or persistent abnormal mental status should be scanned in the emergency department.

Initiating anticonvulsant therapy after a single seizure is an issue of considerable controversy. The prompt treatment of any underlying ictal cause discovered in the emergency department is always appropriate. Disposition plans must be individualized. In one study, 46% of adults with new-onset seizures required admission, most for abnormal CT scans or persistent focal abnormalities; 95% of patients who required admission were identified correctly by using an emergency department evaluation consistent with the recommendations given here.[59]

Recurrent Seizures

The initial stabilization of a patient with a known seizure disorder does not differ from that for a new-onset patient; this includes a rapid blood glucose determination. Because the most common cause of seizures in a known seizure patient is noncompliance with medications, the levels of prescribed anticonvulsants should be measured.[7] Supratherapeutic and toxic levels of some anticonvulsants, such as phenytoin and carbamazepine, whether attained chronically or after acute overdose, can *cause* seizures. As a result, the emergency physician must be cautious about giving a full loading dose of anticonvulsants to patients on long-term therapy before checking a serum level. Meanwhile, a thorough history and physical examination should focus on intercurrent illness or trauma, drug or alcohol use, potential adverse drug-drug interactions with anticonvulsants, a recent change in anticonvulsant dosing regimens, or a change in ictal pattern or characteristics. Clinical indications should tailor the selection of other laboratory or radiographic tests.

DIFFERENTIAL CONSIDERATIONS

Even when witnessed in the emergency department, other abnormal movements and states of consciousness can be confused with ictal activity. Disorders in the differential diagnosis include syncope, hyperventilation and breath holding, certain toxic and metabolic states, transient ischemic attacks, narcolepsy, some movement disorders, and other psychogenic maladies.[7,8,60] Syncope—whether vasodepressive (e.g., "vagal" or micturition syncope), orthostatic, or arrhythmogenic (e.g., paroxysmal ventricular tachycardia or fibrillation, long Q-T syndrome)—may be confused with ictal events; differentiating among these may be particularly difficult when episodes are recurrent.

A sudden loss of consciousness followed by abnormal movements can be ictal or syncopal in origin—hence the consideration "fit versus faint." In one series of patients with episodic attacks of unconsciousness, epilepsy was diagnosed in 40%, and syncope was confirmed in 44%.[61] Generally, ictal tonic-clonic movements are much more forceful and are more prolonged than the "twitches" sometimes associated with fainting. In addition, most seizures are characterized by a postictal state—with the important exception of atonic drop attack ictus—that syncope patients do not manifest. The cause of an unwitnessed, unprovoked loss of consciousness with a fall, after which the patient presents to the emergency department, may be difficult to classify. Suggestions of an ictal diagnosis include retrograde amnesia, loss of continence, and evidence of tongue biting.

Hyperventilation syndrome can be associated with mood disturbances, paresthesias, and posturing movements of the distal extremities.[62] Toxic and metabolic disorders that may mimic ictus include delirium tremens and alcoholic blackouts; the alteration in consciousness associated with hypoglycemia and acute intermittent porphyria; the buccolingual spasms of phencyclidine intoxication; and tonic spasms caused by tetanus, strychnine, and camphor.[7] Nonictal CNS events, such as transient ischemic attacks, transient global amnesia, and atypical migraines, may present similarly to absence seizures and postictal states such as Todd's paralysis. Carotid sinus hypersensitivity, which can even result from a too-tight necktie, may cause drop attacks.[63] Narcolepsy (recurrent irresistible daytime sleepiness), especially when it occurs with cataplexy (sudden falls), may be associated with hallucinations and abnormal movements. It can be differentiated from seizure activity by the history and response to stimulation. Movement disorders, such as hemiballismus and tics, usually are associated with other neurologic problems. Finally, dissociative states such as fugue and panic attacks can be confused with seizures. An EEG is an appropriate diagnostic option in unclear cases.

MANAGEMENT

Immediate Management

Emergency department management of a seizing patient begins with active, anticipatory airway management. In generalized ictus, the gag reflex is suppressed, and vomiting is often complicated by aspiration of gastric contents. The patient should be placed in a left lateral decubitus position; any dentures should be removed. A bite-block should be placed to protect the tongue and allow access for suctioning.

If the patient is persistently apneic or if there is an unavoidable airway threat, the patient should be endotracheally intubated for definitive protection. A benzodiazepine should be used as an induction agent in the hope that its action might terminate the seizure or obviate the need for tracheal intubation. Trismus may necessitate neuromuscular blockade in selected patients.

In general, the first-line pharmacologic treatment of any active seizure activity is a parenteral benzodiazepine. The intravenous route is preferred, but diazepam also may be given rectally, endotracheally, or intraosseously.[64-66] Because benzodiazepines directly enhance GABA-mediated neuronal inhibition, they affect clinical and electrical manifestations of seizures. Benzodiazepines are effective in terminating ictal activity in 75% to 90% of patients.[67]

Benzodiazepines available to the emergency physician include diazepam (Valium), lorazepam (Ativan), and midazolam (Versed) (Table 100-1). In comparison studies, no one drug is clearly superior. All three may be used in patients regardless of age, and all share the following characteristics: relatively short duration of anticonvulsant action, sedation, and the potential for hypotension and respiratory depression. Pertinent differences among benzodiazepines are the efficacy of diazepam when administered rectally, endotracheally, or intraosseously; a relatively longer duration of seizure suppression with lorazepam; and efficacy of the rectal and intramuscular routes of administration for midazolam. Lorazepam generally is recommended for alcohol withdrawal seizures.[68]

Second-line abortive anticonvulsant therapy consists of phenytoin (Dilantin) and phenobarbital. Phenytoin suppresses neuronal recruitment but does not suppress electrical activity at the ictogenic focus.[14] Phenytoin neither sedates patients nor causes respiratory depression, but rapid intravenous administration of phenytoin in its propylene glycol diluent may cause hypotension and cardiac bradydysrhythmias. Phenytoin's onset of action is 10 to 30 minutes, and intravenous administration typically requires at least 20 minutes.[69] The duration of action is approximately 24 hours. Continued benzodiazepine dosing is appropriate while phenytoin achieves adequate brain levels.

If levels of phenytoin or phenobarbital are subtherapeutic in a patient already being treated for seizures, loading doses can be given intravenously, or, alternatively, an adjusted oral dosing schedule can be prescribed to boost the serum level over 24 to 48 hours.

Table 100-1. Drugs Used in the Abortive Treatment of Seizures and Status Epilepticus in the Emergency Department

Drug	Adult Dose	Comments
Diazepam	0.2 mg/kg IV at 2 mg/min up to 20 mg	
Lorazepam	0.1 mg/kg IV at 1-2 mg/min up to 10 mg	
Midazolam	2.5-15 mg IV	
	0.2 mg/kg IM	
Phenytoin	20 mg/kg IV at ≤50 mg/min	Use continuous cardiac and blood pressure monitoring during infusion
Fosphenytoin	15-20 PE/kg at 100-150 mg PE/min; may be given IM	Safety in pediatric patients has not been established
Phenobarbital	20 mg/kg IV at 60-100 mg/min	May be given as IM loading dose
Valproate	20 mg/kg PR	Dilute 1:1 with water; slow onset
Propofol	1-3 mg/kg IV, then 1-15 mg/kg/hr	Critical care monitoring required
Pentobarbital	5 mg/kg IV at 25 mg/min, then titrate to EEG	Intubation, ventilation, and pressor support are required
Isoflurane	Via general endotracheal anesthesia	Monitor with EEG

EEG, electro-encephalogram; PE, phenytoin sodium equivalents; PR, per rectum.

Oral loading of phenytoin is associated with fewer adverse events than loading with either intravenous phenytoin or fosphenytoin, but its use may be limited when therapeutic activity is required urgently.[70]

The phenytoin prodrug fosphenytoin is water soluble and can be administered quickly without significant toxicity.[71] Fosphenytoin achieves a free phenytoin level of $2\mu g/mL$ in 15 minutes, as opposed to 25 minutes with phenytoin itself.[72] Cost analyses of phenytoin versus fosphenytoin use have shown conflicting results. Clinically, fosphenytoin has several advantages: It is better tolerated, safer, and more stable than phenytoin; it can be given more rapidly intravenously; and it can be given intramuscularly. Using fosphenytoin carries the potential for therapeutic drug monitoring errors and a delayed hypotensive response. Use of fosphenytoin should be considered when convulsive status is refractory to benzodiazepines.

Anticonvulsant experience with phenobarbital is derived primarily from studies of pediatric populations. Phenobarbital is a CNS depressant that decreases ictal and physiologic cortical electrical activity. Sedation and depression of respiratory drive and blood pressure must be anticipated, and some physicians prefer nonsedating phenytoin for this reason.[73] The onset of action of phenobarbital is 15 to 30 minutes, and the duration of action is 48 hours. Appropriate emergency department dosing regimens for phenytoin and phenobarbital are listed in Table 100-1. Although such agents are being given to abort ongoing seizure activity, the emergency physician must search for other underlying reversible causes. This search might prompt administration of dextrose for hypoglycemia, pyridoxine for isoniazid overdose, or magnesium for eclampsia.

Abortive treatment for eclamptic seizures is a subject of much debate. Magnesium is *not* an anticonvulsant, and its efficacy in some eclamptic seizures is largely unexplained; its clinical effect may be a manifestation of local neuromuscular blockade that masks continuing ictal activity.[8,54] Benzodiazepines are often effective in the short-term; phenytoin also may be efficacious in eclampsia. Emergency physicians, in consultation with obstetricians, should develop a protocol by which eclamptic seizures are managed. The typical dose of magnesium sulfate is 4 to 6 g via intravenous bolus followed by a 1 to 2 g/hr infusion along with hydralazine. Because hypermagnesemia may cause respiratory arrest, it is essential to monitor patients for hyporeflexia, which precedes respiratory compromise.

Nonpregnant patients who continue to seize in the emergency department despite management with benzodiazepines, phenytoin, or phenobarbital are likely to meet the clinical criteria for status epilepticus. Additional therapeutic measures include using valproate, barbiturate coma, and general inhalational anesthesia. Valproate, which increases GABA concentration, may be given rectally in status epilepticus (see Table 100-1).[74] It is absorbed slowly, but may be of use in polydrug-resistant seizures or before prolonged transport when trying to avoid barbiturate coma or general anesthesia. Valproate also may be administered intravenously, but published experience with this route is limited.[75] Another alternative is afforded by the use of propofol, a nonbarbiturate anesthetic agent with hypnotic and anticonvulsant activity. Studies suggest that propofol acts at a location other than the benzodiazepine binding site and modifies the chloride channel in a way that is different from, and possibly synergistic with, benzodiazepines and barbiturates. Several case reports and two small studies showed efficacy in the management of refractory status epilepticus. Propofol usually is administered as an intravenous loading dose of 1 to 3 mg/kg; this is followed by an infusion of 1 to 15 mg/kg/hr.[76]

Barbiturate coma is effective in terminating seizures by facilitating GABA, although it also suppresses all brainstem function. Previous neurologic consultation is advisable because barbiturate coma may induce respiratory arrest, myocardial depression, and hypotension, while decreasing intracranial pressure and increasing cerebral perfusion. The preferred agent for barbiturate coma is pentobarbital (see Table 100-1). Patients require intubation and ventilatory support, continuous cardiac monitoring, and invasive hemodynamic monitoring. Pressors may be required to support the blood pressure.

Isoflurane anesthesia is one final alternative in the management of refractory ictus. Halothane is associated

Table 100-2. Important Adverse Effects and Drug-Drug Interactions of Anticonvulsants

Drug	Important Adverse Effects	Significant Drug-Drug Interactions
Carbamazepine	Dizziness, drowsiness, aplastic anemia, agranulocytosis, rash, hepatotoxicity, teratogenicity	Warfarin, digitalis, calcium channel blockers, tetracycline, erythromycin, oral contraceptives, theophylline
Phenytoin	Gingival hyperplasia, elevated transaminases, nystagmus, rash, myopathy, drug-induced lupus, teratogenicity, "dilantin hypersensitivity syndrome"	Corticosteroids, quinidine, theophylline, cimetidine, digoxin, ciprofloxacin, oral contraceptives, isoniazid, warfarin, disulfiram, cotrimoxazole
Fosphenytoin	Nystagmus, dizziness, pruritus, paresthesia	
Phenobarbital	Drowsiness, hepatitis, teratogenicity, decreased IQ with long-term use in children	Corticosteroids, warfarin, tetracycline, propranolol, quinidine, theophylline, oral contraceptives
Ethosuximide	Drowsiness, ataxia, dizziness, nausea	Isoniazid
Clonazepam	Drowsiness, ataxia	Other CNS depressants
Valproate	Thrombocytopenia, tremor, nausea, hypatotoxicity	Aspirin, erythromycin, isoniazid
Gabapentin	Somnolence, fatigue, ataxia, dizziness, gastrointestinal upset, dyspnea	None significant
Lamotrigine	Rash, dizziness, ataxia, blurred vision, nausea	Carbamazepine, phenobarbital, phenytoin and fosphenytoin, primidone, valproic acid
Felbamate	Anorexia, vomiting, insomnia, somnolence, aplastic anemia, hepatotoxicity	Carbamazepine, phenobarbital, phenytoin and fosphenytoin, primidone, valproic acid
Topiramate	Dizziness, somnolence, ataxia, confusion, fatigue, paresthesias, speech difficulties, diplopia, impaired concentration, nausea	Other anticonvulsants, carbonic anhydrase inhibitors

CNS, central nervous system.

with more hemodynamic and hepatotoxic complications. Isoflurane suppresses electrical seizure foci and is easily titratable. Patients treated with barbiturate coma or inhalational anesthesia require intubation and mechanical ventilation. Intubation of a seizing patient is best facilitated by using a benzodiazepine as an induction agent and lidocaine (1 mg/kg) as a pretreatment medication. Lidocaine reduces the increase in intracranial pressure that reflexively results from laryngoscopy and intubation.

The visual manifestations of convulsive ictus are extinguished by neuromuscular blockade. When a seizing patient is paralyzed and intubated, the emergency department cannot assume that pharmacologic therapy has terminated the seizure. Anticonvulsants should be administered, and EEG monitoring of the patient should be arranged. Without EEG, detection of seizure activity in a heavily sedated or paralyzed patient is difficult.

Long-Term Management

Identifying a new-onset seizure disorder in the emergency department should prompt consideration for further management in the following three areas: pharmacologic, psychosocial, and legal. The primary dilemma concerns whether to initiate prophylactic anticonvulsant therapy after one seizure. The decision to treat should be based on (1) the risk of seizure recurrence; (2) the presence of any underlying, predisposing disease; and (3) the risk of anticonvulsant therapy. The risk of seizure recurrence is difficult to estimate in the emergency department. The presence of EEG abnormalities suggests greater risk, but this information is usually unavailable in the emergency department. Other factors associated with an increased risk of recurrence are partial (versus generalized) ictus, status epilepticus, a history of intracranial surgery or

trauma, and the presence of a persistent neurologic abnormality, such as Todd's paralysis. In adults, the overall risk of seizure recurrence after a single, unprovoked seizure in a prospective study of patients without correctable predisposing factors was 14% at 1 year, 29% at 3 years, and 34% at 5 years.[77] By way of comparison, some studies report that more than one in five seizure patients can have adverse effects from anticonvulsants significant enough to cause a change in therapy.

The presence of specific underlying conditions may affect the decision to institute long-term therapy. Many authorities recommend treatment after an initial seizure in HIV-positive patients. Alcohol-related seizures are notoriously unresponsive to anticonvulsants. Prophylaxis against posttraumatic seizures beyond the first week after injury is probably unnecessary,[78] but the occurrence of early posttraumatic seizures should prompt at least short-term initiation of therapy.[79]

The side effects of anticonvulsants can be debilitating for the patient (Table 100-2). The side effects must be considered before initiating therapy, particularly in women of reproductive age, because anticonvulsants are teratogenic and may precipitate failure of oral contraceptives.

In the absence of specific underlying conditions that increase risk of recurrence, most authorities do not recommend initiation of anticonvulsant therapy from the emergency department after a single unprovoked seizure in adults.[7] If the seizure was provoked, the decision should be based on whether the provoking factor can be corrected; if it cannot, anticonvulsant therapy should be instituted. Anticonvulsant dosing regimens in known epileptic patients should be modified only in consultation with the patient's physician.

Drug monotherapy is always preferable in anticonvulsant regimens. The preferred drugs for convulsive generalized seizures are phenytoin, carbamazepine,

Table 100-3. Drugs Used for Long-term Anticonvulsant Therapy in Adults

Drug	Indications	Dose (mg/kg/day)	Therapeutic Range (μg/mL)	Daily Doses
Carbamazepine	Partial, GCS	15-25	8-12	3-4
Phenytoin	Partial, GCS	3-8	10-25	1-3
Phenobarbital	Partial, GCS	2-4	15-40	1
Primidone*	Partial, GCS	10-20	5-15	4
Ethosuximide	Absence	10-30	40-100	2
Clonazepam	Absence	0.03-0.3	0.01-0.05	2
Valproate	All	15-60	50-100	4
Felbamate	Partial, GCS, atonic	1200-3600 mg/day	N/A	3

*Primidone is a congener of phenobarbital.
GCS, generalized convulsive seizure; N/A, not applicable.

valproate, phenobarbital, and felbamate (Table 100-3). The preferred drugs for nonconvulsive generalized seizures are ethosuximide and valproate. Drugs recommended for treatment of partial seizures are carbamazepine, phenytoin, phenobarbital, valproate, and felbamate. Dosing should be initiated in the emergency department, although there is no clear consensus regarding whether a full loading dose of phenytoin or phenobarbital should be given.

The psychological and social implications of the new diagnosis of a seizure disorder should not be underestimated. Fear of seizures and stigmatization are common; employability and insurability may be adversely affected. Although the emergency physician is not usually in a suitable position to arrange for counseling, referral to local epilepsy support groups may be helpful.

Finally, there are legal implications of diagnosing a new-onset seizure disorder. Each state has regulations regarding driving privileges in patients with seizures, and some states require reporting by the physician. The emergency physician should obey these regulations and inform patients accordingly. Patients also should be advised to refrain from hazardous or isolated activities until cleared to do so by their physician. The need for a MedicAlert bracelet or other medical condition identifier should be stressed.

KEY CONCEPTS

- The possibility of reactive seizures should be considered in all seizure patients who present to the emergency department, including patients with a history of epilepsy. The most common cause of reactive seizures is hypoglycemia. The most common cause of recurrent primary seizures is medication noncompliance.

- Nonconvulsive seizures may be confused with nonictal states, including psychiatric disorders. The presence of repetitive eye movements, blinking, or automatisms suggests the diagnosis.

- Neuroimaging is recommended for seizure patients when there is suspicion of head trauma, elevated intracranial pressure, intracranial mass, persistently abnormal mental status or focal neurologic abnormality, or HIV disease.

- Primary abortive therapy for seizures in the emergency department is a benzodiazepine; second-line therapy includes phenytoin or phenobarbital.

REFERENCES

1. Hauser WA, Hesdorffer DC: *Epilepsy: Frequency, Causes and Consequences.* New York, Demos, 1990.
2. Benbadis SR: Epileptic seizures and syndromes. *Neurol Clin* 19:251, 2001.
3. Gram L: Epileptic seizures and syndromes. *Lancet* 336:161, 1990.
4. Commission on Classification and Terminology of the International League Against Epilepsy: Proposal for revised clinical and electroencephalographic classification of epileptic seizures. *Epilepsia* 30:389, 1989.
5. Commission on Classification and Terminology of the International League Against Epilepsy: Proposal for revised clinical and electroencephalographic classification of epileptic seizures. *Epilepsia* 22:489, 1981.
6. Luders HO, Acharya J, Baumgartner C, et al: Semiological seizure classification. *Epilepsia* 39:1007, 1998.
7. Shneker BF, Fountain NB: Epilepsy. *Dis Mon* 49:7, 2003.
8. Engel J: *Seizures and Epilepsy.* Philadelphia, FA Davis, 1989.
9. Laidlaw J, Richens A (eds): *A Textbook of Epilepsy,* 3rd ed. London, Churchill Livingstone, 1988.
10. Orringer CE, et al: Natural history of lactic acidosis after grand mal seizures. *N Engl J Med* 297:796, 1977.
11. Meldrum BS, Horton RW: Physiology of status epilepticus in primates. *Arch Neurol* 28:1, 1973.
12. Aicardi J, Chevrie JJ: Convulsive status epilepticus in infants and children: A study of 239 cases. *Epilepsia* 11:187, 1970.
13. Aminoff MJ, Simon RP: Status epilepticus: Causes, clinical features, and consequences in 98 patients. *Am J Med* 69:657, 1980.
14. Bancaud J: Kojewnikow's syndrome (epilepsia partialis continua) in children. In Roger J, et al (eds): *Epileptic Syndromes in Infancy, Childhood, and Adolescence.* London, John Libbey, 1985.
15. Weiner WJ (ed): *Emergent and Urgent Neurology.* Philadelphia, JB Lippincott, 1992.
16. Pollack CV: Medical etiologies of altered mental status. *Top Emerg Med* 13:54, 1991.
17. Riggs JE: Neurologic manifestations of electrolyte disturbances. *Neurol Clin* 20:227, 2002.
18. Halperin ML: Clinical approach to disorders of salt and water balance: Emphasis on integrative physiology. *Crit Care Clin* 18:249, 2002.
19. Trence DL: Hyperglycemic crises in diabetes mellitus type 2. *Endocrinol Metab Clin N Am* 30:817, 2001.
20. Palmer CA: Neurologic complications of renal disease. *Neurol Clin* 20:23, 2002.
21. Tonner DR, Schlechte JA: Neurologic complications of thyroid and parathyroid disease. *Med Clin North Am* 77:251, 1993.

22. Goldberg PA: Critical issues in endocrinology. *Clin Chest Med* 24:583, 2003.
23. Rothstein JD, Herlong HF: Neurologic manifestations of hepatic disease. *Neurol Clin* 7:563, 1989.
24. Riley LJ, Ilson BE, Narins RG: Acute metabolic acid-base disorders. *Crit Care Clin* 5:699, 1987.
25. Varon J: The diagnosis and management of hypertensive crisis. *Chest* 118:214, 2000.
26. Handrick W, Adasser S: Seizures during bacterial meningitis. *Antibiot Chemother* 45:239, 1992.
27. Rosman NP, et al: Seizures in bacterial meningitis. *Pediatr Neurol* 1:278, 1985.
28. Shelton MM, Marks WA: Bacterial meningitis: An update. *Neurol Clin* 8:605, 1990.
29. Roos KL: Encephalitis. *Neurol Clin* 17:813, 1999.
30. Tattevin P: Bacterial brain abscesses: A retrospective study of 94 patients admitted to an intensive care unit. *Am J Med* 115:143, 2003.
31. Carpio A: Neurocysticercosis: An update. *Lancet Infect Dis* 2:751, 2002.
32. Kunisaki TA, Augenstein WL: Drug- and toxin-induced seizures. *Emerg Med Clin North Am* 12:1027, 1994.
33. Mokhlesi B: Toxicology in the critically ill patient. *Clin Chest Med* 24:689, 2003.
34. Hedges D: Antipsychotic medication and seizures: A review. *Drugs Today (Barc)* 39:551, 2003.
35. Zimmerman JL: Poisonings and overdoses in the intensive care unit: General and specific management issues. *Crit Care Med* 31:2794, 2003.
36. Newton EH, Shih RD, Hoffman RS: Cyclic antidepressant overdose: A review of current management strategies. *Am J Emerg Med* 12:392, 1994.
37. Shanti CM: Cocaine and the critical care challenge. *Crit Care Med* 31:1851, 2003.
38. Pollack CV, et al: Case conference: Two crack cocaine body stuffers. *Ann Emerg Med* 21:1370, 1992.
39. Ogunyemi AO, et al: Complex partial status epilepticus provoked by "crack" cocaine. *Ann Neurol* 26:785, 1989.
40. Earnest M, Yarnell P: Seizure admissions to a city hospital: The role of alcohol. *Epilepsia* 17:387, 1976.
41. Freedland ES, McMicken DB: Alcohol-related seizures: Part I. Pathophysiology, differential diagnosis, and evaluation. *J Emerg Med* 11:463, 1993.
42. Freedland ES, McMicken DB: Alcohol-related seizures: Part II. Clinical presentation and management. *J Emerg Med* 11:605, 1993.
43. McMicken DB, Freedland ES: Alcohol-related seizures. *Emerg Med Clin North Am* 12:1057, 1994.
44. Yablon SA: Posttraumatic seizures. *Arch Phys Med Rehabil* 74:983, 1993.
45. Hauser WA: Prevention of post-traumatic epilepsy. *N Engl J Med* 323:540, 1990.
46. Frey LC: Epidemiology of posttraumatic epilepsy: A critical review. *Epilepsia* 44(Suppl 10):11, 2003.
47. Wen PY: Neurologic complications of solid tumors. *Neurol Clin* 21:107, 2003.
48. Nadeau SE: Neurologic manifestations of connective tissue disease. *Neurol Clin* 20:151, 2002.
49. Asconapé JJ, Penry JK: Poststroke seizures in the elderly. *Clin Geriatr Med* 7:483, 1991.
50. Labovitz DL, Hauser WA, Sacco RL: Prevalence and predictors of early seizure and status epilepticus after first stroke. *Neurology* 57:200, 2001.
51. Förderreuther S: Headache associated with epileptic seizures: Epidemiology and clinical characteristics. *Headache* 42:649, 2002.
52. Drury I, Beydoun A: Seizure disorders of aging: Differential diagnosis and patient management. *Geriatrics* 48:52, 1993.
53. Mendez M: Seizures in elderly patients with dementia: Epidemiology and management. *Drugs Aging* 20:791, 2003.
54. Lipstein H: A current concept of eclampsia. *Am J Emerg Med* 21:223, 2003.
55. Boon PA, Williamson PD: The diagnosis of pseudoseizure. *Clin Neurol Neurosurg* 95:1, 1993.
56. Riggio S: Psychogenic seizures. *Emerg Med Clin North Am* 12:1001, 1994.
57. Pender ES, Pollack CV: Neurogenic pulmonary edema: Case reports and review. *J Emerg Med* 10:45, 1992.
58. American College of Emergency Physicians: Clinical policy for the initial approach to patients with a chief complaint of seizure, who are not in status epilepticus. *Ann Emerg Med* 22:875, 1993.
59. Henneman PL, DeRoos F, Lewis RJ: Determining the need for admission in patients with new-onset seizures. *Ann Emerg Med* 24:1108, 1994.
60. Morrell MJ: Differential diagnosis of seizures. *Neurol Clin* 11:737, 1993.
61. Moss AJ, et al: The long Q-T syndrome: Prospective longitudinal study of 328 females. *Circulation* 84:1136, 1991.
62. Perkins GD, Joseph R: Neurologic manifestations of the hyperventilation syndrome. *J Soc Med* 79:48, 1986.
63. Huang SKS, et al: Carotid sinus hypersensitivity in patients with unexplained syncope: Clinical, electrophysiologic, and long-term follow-up observations. *Am Heart J* 116:989, 1988.
64. Seigler RS: The administration of rectal diazepam for the acute management of seizures. *J Emerg Med* 8:155, 1990.
65. Rusli M, et al: Endotracheal diazepam: absorption and pulmonary pathologic effects. *Ann Emerg Med* 16:314, 1987.
66. Lathers CM, Jim KF, Spivey WH: A comparison of intraosseous and intravenous routes of administration for antiseizure agents. *Epilepsia* 30:472, 1989.
67. Henriksen O: An overview of benzodiazepines in seizure management. *Epilepsia* 39(Suppl 1):S2, 1998.
68. Bleck TP: Management approaches to prolonged seizures and status epilepticus. *Epilepsia* 40:S59, 1999.
69. Smith BJ: Treatment of status epilepticus. *Neurol Clin* 19:347, 2001.
70. Swadron SP, et al: A comparison of phenytoin-loading techniques in the emergency department. *Acad Emerg Med* 11:244, 2004.
71. Luer MS: Fosphenytoin. *Neurol Res* 20:178, 1998.
72. Working Group on Status Epilepticus: Treatment of convulsive status epilepticus. *JAMA* 270:854, 1993.
73. Brown T: The pharmacokinetics of agents used to treat status epilepticus. *Neurology* 40:28, 1990.
74. Lowenstein DH, Alldredge BK: Status epilepticus. *N Engl J Med* 338:970, 1998.
75. Hodges BM, Mazure JE: Intravenous valproate in status epilepticus. *Ann Pharmacother* 35:1465, 2001.
76. Stecker MM, Kramer TH, Raps EC: Treatment of refractory status epilepticus with propofol: Clinical and pharmacokinetic findings. *Epilepsia* 39:18, 1998.
77. Hauser WA, et al: Seizure recurrence after a first unprovoked seizure: An extended follow-up. *Neurology* 40:1163, 1990.
78. Bernardo LS: Prevention of epilepsy after head trauma: Do we need new drugs or a new approach? *Epilepsia* 44(Suppl 10):27, 2003.
79. Beghi E: Overview of studies to prevent posttraumatic epilepsy. *Epilepsia* 44(Suppl 10):21, 2003.

101 Headache

Thomas Kwiatkowski and Kumar Alagappan

Headache is a common complaint, more frequent than the common cold, and accounts for approximately 2 million visits to the emergency department per year in the United States.[1] In addition, many more patients present with headache as part of a constitutional illness, making the symptom of headache one of the most frequent complaints seen in the emergency department.

Headache is divided into *primary* and *secondary* disorders. The primary headache disorders include migraine, cluster, and tension-type headaches, which represent greater than 90% of headaches seen in clinical practice.[2] Secondary headache disorders include a variety of organic illnesses in which head pain is a symptom of an identifiable, distinct pathologic process. To facilitate a standardized approach to headache, the International Headache Society (IHS) published the "Classification and diagnostic criteria for headache disorders, cranial neuralgias and facial pain" in 1988.[3] This comprehensive and widely accepted system includes 13 categories of headache disorders and uses specific operational diagnostic criteria to define each headache type (Box 101-1). A revised classification system will soon be available that offers better separation of primary and secondary headaches and more standardization and better criteria for secondary headaches.[4]

The vast majority of patients presenting with headache have a benign primary headache disorder requiring symptomatic treatment and referral. The challenge for the emergency physician is to identify the very small subset of patients who have headache as a symptom of a serious or potentially life-threatening disease.

PRIMARY HEADACHE DISORDERS

Migraine Headache

Principles of Disease

Migraine is a common, chronic, sometimes incapacitating neurovascular disorder, characterized by attacks of severe headache, autonomic nervous system dysfunction, and in some patients an aura involving neurologic symptoms.[5]

Migraine headaches account for approximately 1 million visits to the emergency department per year.[6] They typically begin in the second decade of life, peaking in early to midadolescence, and are more prevalent among women (18%) than men (6%).[7,8] During childhood, however, there is no gender differ-

ence in the prevalence of migraine.[2] After menarche there is a relationship between migraine headache and menses in about 15% of female migraineurs, possibly related to fluctuating estrogen and progesterone levels. After menopause, women also tend to experience fewer migraine headaches. The lifetime prevalence of migraine is at least 18%.[5]

Historically, migraine headaches have been considered to be vascular in origin. According to this hypothesis, an initial phase of cerebral vasoconstriction resulting in neurologic symptoms (migraine with aura) was followed by a vasodilatory phase, manifested by the typical pounding headache of migraine. Appropriate changes in blood flow have been demonstrated for the classical migraine attack, and pain relief provided by vasoconstriction further supported this hypothesis.[9] However, this mechanism does not fully explain the entire spectrum of migraine attacks, and migraine is no longer thought to be caused by a primary vascular event.[5] It is now believed that the pathophysiologic cause of migraine may actually originate in the brainstem within its descending and ascending circuitry, including the ascending pain-modulating projections from the midbrain raphe nuclei.[10] Evidence suggests a perturbation of neural activity within this serotonergic system as an important precursor to migraine.[11] Changes in serotonergic activity can alter the cranial circulation, triggering a "vascular phase." In addition to constriction and dilatation of intracranial and extracranial arteries, this neurovascular reaction activates the nociceptive trigeminal vascular system.[12,13] Neural connections between cerebral blood vessels and the trigeminal nerve release neuropeptides that can induce a painful neurogenic or sterile inflammation.[14]

Agonists of the 5-hydroxytryptamine (5-HT) (1B/1D) receptor, such as sumatriptan or dihydroergotamine (DHE), block the inflammatory process. Effective prophylactic agents are believed to act as antagonists of the $5HT_2$ receptor site.[15]

Migraine is further divided into two major categories. Migraine without aura, or "common migraine," is the most frequent form of migraine and accounts for about 80% of all cases (Box 101-2). "Classical migraine," or migraine with aura, has specific reversible neurologic symptoms that precede the actual headache (Box 101-3) and is seen less frequently.

Clinical Features

Migraine headaches tend to be chronic and recurrent. The headache is often unilateral, pulsating in quality,

BOX 101-1. International Headache Society Classification of Headache

1. Migraine
2. Tension-type headache
3. Cluster headache and chronic paroxysmal hemicrania
4. Miscellaneous headaches unassociated with structural lesion
5. Headache associated with head trauma
6. Headache associated with vascular disorders
7. Headache associated with nonvascular intracranial disorder
8. Headache associated with substances or their withdrawal
9. Headache associated with noncephalic infection
10. Headache associated with metabolic disorder
11. Headache or facial pain associated with disorder of cranium, neck, eyes, ears, nose, sinuses, teeth, mouth, or other facial or cranial structures
12. Cranial neuralgias, nerve trunk pain, and deafferentation pain
13. Headache not classifiable

BOX 101-2. Migraine Without Aura (Common Migraine)

International Headache Society Criteria
A. At least five attacks fulfilling criteria in B, C, D, and E.
B. Attack lasts 4 to 72 hours with or without treatment.
C. Headache has at least two of the following characteristics:
   1. Unilateral location
   2. Pulsating quality
   3. Moderate to severe intensity
   4. Aggravated by walking up stairs or similar routine physical activity
D. During headache, at least one of the following:
   1. Nausea or vomiting (or both)
   2. Photophobia and phonophobia
E. History, physical, and neurologic examination and, if appropriate, diagnostic tests to exclude related organic disease.

BOX 101-3. Migraine With Aura (Classic Migraine)

International Headache Society Criteria
A. At least two attacks that fulfill criterion B.
B. At least three of the four characteristics must be present before the diagnosis of classic migraine can be made.
   1. One or more fully reversible aura symptoms indicating focal cerebral cortical or brainstem dysfunction (or both).
   2. At least one aura symptom develops gradually over more than 4 minutes or two or more symptoms occur in succession.
   3. No single aura symptom lasts longer than 60 minutes.
   4. Headache begins during aura or follows with a symptom-free interval of less than 60 minutes (headache may begin before aura).
C. An appropriate history, physical, and neurologic examination with appropriate diagnostic tests must be performed to exclude related organic diseases.

moderate to severe in intensity, and exacerbated by routine activities. The side of the headache can vary with individual attacks, and the headache may be bilateral in 40% of patients. The onset is usually gradual and the attacks typically last from 4 to 72 hours. Headache frequency is quite variable, and some patients experience several episodes per month. Associated symptoms include nausea, vomiting, anorexia, photophobia, phonophobia, osmophobia (aversion to odors), blurred vision, lightheadedness, and nasal congestion. Some patients have cognitive impairments producing forgetfulness, irritability, and depression, whereas others may be manic, with outbursts of anger that can be disruptive in the emergency department setting. Many patients have dramatic light and sound sensitivity and seek a cool, dark, and quiet room.

The aura of classical migraine consists of focal neurologic symptoms that precede and herald the migraine attack. By definition, the aura is fully reversible and typically lasts 10 to 20 minutes, although it may continue for as long as 1 hour. The most common aura is visual and may include scintillating scotomas (bright rim around an area of visual loss), teichopsias (subjective visual image perceived with eyes open or closed), fortification spectrums (zigzagged wall of fortress slowly drifting across visual field), photopsias (poorly formed brief flashes or sparks of light), or blurred vision. Less common auras include somatosensory phenomena such as tingling or numbness, motor disturbances, and cognitive or language disorders.[16]

Ophthalmoplegic migraine is a rare syndrome associated with paresis of one or more ocular nerves, most commonly the third cranial nerve. Patients typically present with ipsilateral headache associated with extraocular muscle paresis and occasionally pupillary changes. The ophthalmoplegia or pupillary changes may last for days to weeks and, rarely, may become permanent.[17] Because of the neurologic findings, secondary causes including intracranial aneurysm and mass lesion must be ruled out.

Hemiplegic migraine is characterized by episodic hemiparesis or hemiplegia as an aura to the migraine attack. The progression of the motor deficit is slow or marching in quality and in most cases is accompanied by a sensory disturbance as well. The neurologic symptoms last 30 to 60 minutes, followed by a severe pulsating headache. Rarely, the motor deficit is persistent, resulting from a true migraine-induced stroke.

Basilar artery migraine arises with an aura referable to the brainstem and is associated with multiple neurologic findings, including visual symptoms (often total blindness), dysarthria, tinnitus, vertigo, bilateral paresthesias, paresis, and altered level of conciousness.[18] The symptoms are stereotyped and resolve spontaneously.

Status migrainosus is a severe migraine headache that persists longer than 72 hours. Associated symptoms are debilitating, and patients often require hospitalization for pain management and supportive care.

Many factors can trigger migraine headaches in predisposed individuals. Common precipitants include sleep deprivation, stress, hunger, hormonal changes including menstruation, and the use of certain drugs including oral contraceptives and nitroglycerin.[6] In addition, some patients report specific food sensitivities including chocolate, caffeine, and foods rich in tyramine, monosodium glutamate, and nitrates.[19,20] Alcohol, specifically red or port wine, has also been implicated. In others, certain sensory stimuli such as a strong glare or strong odors, loud noises, or weather changes can trigger an attack.[21]

Differential Diagnosis

Because of their complex symptoms, migraine headaches may be difficult to distinguish from other secondary causes of headache. Other diagnoses that mimic migraine include ruptured berry aneurysm, arteriovenous malformation, intracranial mass lesions, giant cell arteritis, and cerebrovascular disease.

Diagnostic Evaluation

Routine neuroimaging is not necessary for patients with typical recurrent migraine headaches. However, neuroimaging must be considered for patients with new-onset headaches, headaches with a progressive course or change in pattern, headaches that never alternate sides, and headaches associated with any neurologic findings or seizures. Such patients have a substantially higher likelihood of a secondary cause such as tumor, arteriovenous malformation, or structural lesion.[22] In addition, patients who present with a severe headache or "worst headache of their life" require a lumbar puncture (LP) to rule out subarachnoid hemorrhage if a computed tomography (CT) scan is negative.

Treatment

The pharmacologic treatment of migraine is divided into abortive therapies, which attempt to limit the intensity and duration of a given episode, and prophylactic therapies, which are intended to decrease the frequency and intensity of attacks.[23] The goals of acute migraine therapy include treating attacks rapidly and consistently to avoid headache recurrence, restoring the patient's ability to function, and minimizing the use of backup and rescue medications.[21]

Patients who are unable to control their headaches at home often present to the emergency department for better pain control or supportive therapy. There are several approaches to treating the acute headache episode, depending on the severity of the attack (Table 101-1). In addition, patients with a history of migraine may relate specific interventions that have been successful. The choice of agents depends on several factors, including the patient's prior response to specific therapies, the existence of comorbid conditions, and the presence or absence of nausea or vomiting. Gastric stasis is common during acute migraine attacks and may limit the effectiveness of oral agents.

For mild to moderate attacks, the IHS recommends simple analgesics such as acetaminophen or nonsteroidal anti-inflammatory drugs (NSAIDs). In the presence of nausea or vomiting, adding an agent such as metoclopramide enhances the absorption and effectiveness of these medications. Appropriate doses and possible side effects are listed in Table 101-1.

For moderate to severe attacks, several classes of medications are available to treat the pain in addition

Table 101-1. Selected Medications for Acute Migraine Attacks

Medication	Dose and Route Administered	Comments
Mild to Moderate		
Acetaminophen	500 mg to 1000 mg PO	Gastrointestinal upset
Aspirin	650 mg to 1000 mg PO	Gastrointestinal upset
Ibuprofen	600 mg to 800 mg PO	Gastrointestinal upset
Naproxen sodium	275 mg to 550 mg PO	Gastrointestinal upset
Tolfenamic acid	200 mg to 600 mg PO	Gastrointestinal upset
Moderate to Severe		
Dihydroergotamine	1 mg IV or IM; may be repeated in 1 hr	Gastrointestinal upset (pretreat with antiemetic)
Triptans		Chest pain, throat tightness, flushing. Contraindicated
Sumatriptan	6 mg SC; may be repeated once in 1 hr if partial response	with hypertension, coronary artery disease,
Sumatriptan	25-100 mg PO	peripheral vascular disease, and pregnancy.
Rizatriptan	5-10 mg PO	Cannot be used within 24 hours of ergot usage.
Zolmitriptan	2.5-5 mg PO	
Naratriptan	1-2.5 mg PO	
Prochlorperazine	10 mg IV or IM; may be repeated in 30 to 60 min.	Sedation and dystonic reaction
Metoclopramide	10 mg IV	Dystonic reaction
Ketorolac	30 mg IV or 30 to 60 mg IM	Gastrointestinal upset; avoid medication in elderly and in patients with renal insufficiency.
Meperidine	50-100 mg IM or IV	Opioids less efficacious than other treatment modalities
Refractory Attack, Status Migrainosus		
Dihydroergotamine	1 mg IV q8h	Use in conjunction with antiemetic (e.g., metoclopramide, prochlorperazine).
Steroids	Various regimens	Gastrointestinal bleeding, infection, cataracts, aseptic necrosis, memory disturbances

to the nausea and vomiting that frequently accompany the headache. Specific agents available for treating severe migraine include DHE and the triptans. DHE should be given intravenously (IV) at 1.0 mg slowly over 2 minutes and can be repeated in 1 hour if pain control has not been achieved. Because DHE can cause nausea and vomiting, patients should be pretreated with an antiemetic such as metoclopramide 10 mg IV or prochlorperazine 5 mg IV. Repeated administration of the intravenous form of DHE has been shown to be very effective in patients with intractable migraine and status migrainosus. Contraindications to using DHE include pregnancy, breast-feeding, poorly controlled hypertension, coronary artery disease, and peripheral vascular disease. DHE should not be used if the patient has already taken any drug in the triptan class.

Sumatriptan, the first approved medication of the triptan class, is a selective 5-HT(1B/1D) receptor agonist. Other triptans that are available include zolmitriptan, naratriptan, and rizatriptan, but only sumatriptan is available for subcutaneous administration and it is the most common preparation used in the emergency department. The initial dose is 6 mg subcutaneously, which may be repeated once in 1 hour if the patient has a partial response to the first dose. Common side effects include tingling, flushing, warm or hot sensations, and heaviness in the chest. Sumatriptan has contraindications similar to those for DHE and should not be used within 24 hours of administration of an ergotamine-containing medication or DHE.[24] In addition to subcutaneous sumatriptan, several triptans are available in oral formulation for the treatment of acute migraine attacks.

Neuroleptics have also been shown to be effective in treating acute migraine attacks. Prochlorperazine can be administered as a slow 10-mg IV bolus, which can be repeated once in 30 to 60 minutes.[13,25] The most common side effects after parenteral administration include sedation, postural hypotension, and extrapyramidal symptoms including acute dystonic reactions.

Narcotic analgesics such as meperidine should be reserved for patients who do not respond or have contraindications to standard migraine therapies. Although frequently used, narcotics have been shown to be less efficacious than other treatments and are associated with a risk of addiction; however, some patients obtain relief with this class of medications.

The use of steroids for the treatment of migraine remains controversial. Anecdotal evidence suggests that they may be effective for prolonged migraine attacks that are refractory to standard therapies and for treating status migrainosus (a migraine attack lasting more than 72 hours).[10,26]

Occasionally, patients do not respond to initial therapy in the emergency department and require hospitalization for continued pain control and supportive therapy.

Prophylactic Therapy

Prophylactic therapy is indicated for patients who have frequent attacks (more than two to three episodes per month), prolonged attacks lasting more than 48 hours, or attacks that are severe and debilitating. Of note, prophylactic medications are seldom more than 55% to 65% effective.[27]

Several classes of medications are used for the prophylaxis of migraine. Many of these medications have significant side effects, especially among women of childbearing age; therefore, after headaches have decreased, attempts should be made to taper and discontinue treatment when possible.

β-Adrenergic blocking agents reduce both the frequency and severity of migraine headache and are the most widely used drugs for recurrent migraine.[6] Propranolol has been the most extensively studied medication. However, patients who do not respond to propranolol may respond to another drug in this class, including atenolol, metoprolol, timolol, or nadolol.[28] Contraindications to β-blockers include pregnancy, asthma, heart failure, Raynaud's phenomenon, and diabetes mellitus.[10]

Other medications used for migraine prophylaxis include calcium channel blockers, tricyclic antidepressants, anticonvulsants including divalproex sodium and sodium valproate, and monoamine oxidase inhibitors.[10,28]

Methysergide, a semisynthetic ergot preparation, has also been widely used for prophylaxis. It is a potent peripheral serotonin antagonist with a presumed mechanism similar to that of other ergot drugs. It is contraindicated in patients with coronary artery or peripheral vascular disease. Its prolonged use has been associated with retroperitoneal, pulmonary, and endocardial fibrosis.[29]

Cluster Headache

Perspective

Cluster headache is the only headache syndrome that is more common in men than in women. It typically occurs in young to middle-aged adults who smoke, with a peak incidence in the late 20s.[30] The headaches tend to occur repeatedly over a defined time interval, hence the term "cluster." Several attacks can occur in 1 day, and a typical cluster period may last 6 to 8 weeks. Several precipitating factors have been implicated, most notably the ingestion of alcohol. Stress and climatic changes may also play a role in susceptible individuals.

Clinical Features

Cluster headaches occur suddenly with little warning, and several episodes can occur within a 24-hour period. Each headache lasts from a few minutes up to 2 hours. The patient typically complains of a unilateral, sharp, stabbing pain in the eye, which may awaken him or her from sleep. The attacks tend to occur exclusively in the territory of the trigeminal nerve.[31] Unlike patients with migraine, the cluster headache patient presents in a predictable fashion (i.e., holding his or her eye, rocking, rubbing the head, and pacing). The attack subsides rapidly, often leaving the patient exhausted.

Up to 30% of patients have a partial Horner's syndrome with ptosis and miosis.[32] The eye is often injected and tearing, and many patients have unilateral nasal congestion.[9]

Differential Diagnosis

Other headache disorders that mimic cluster include migraine, trigeminal neuralgia, and chronic paroxysmal hemicrania (CPH). With migraine, the clinical presentation, gender, and age distribution are usually different. With trigeminal neuralgia, the pain peaks within seconds, lasts only a couple of minutes, and can be provoked by specific trigger points on the face or oral mucosa. CPH is a brief unilateral headache that recurs at least 15 times a day, often induced by rotation or turning of the head or by pressure on the cervical spine.[33]

Treatment

Because cluster headaches are abrupt in onset, treatment must be initiated rapidly to be effective. At present, sumatriptan 6 mg subcutaneously is the preferred abortive therapy for the majority of patients if given very early after the onset of the attack[34]; however, by the time a patient presents to the emergency department, the headache has usually progressed and symptomatic treatment is indicated. High-flow oxygen at a rate of 7 to 10 L/min has been shown to abort the headache within several minutes.[35] DHE 1.0 mg IV or intramuscularly has also been shown to be effective, but it is less practical than oxygen administration and has more side effects. For patients who do not respond to these measures, intranasal application of cocaine[27] or lidocaine to produce anesthesia of the sphenopalatine region has been advocated by some but has not gained widespread acceptance.[36]

In addition to acute therapies, several medications have been shown to be effective for the prophylactic treatment of cluster headaches. A short course of oral prednisone may effectively abort a cluster attack in some patients. A recommended regimen is 60 mg of prednisone daily for 10 days, followed by a 1-week taper.[36] To prevent breakthrough headaches after the steroid taper, patients may require the concurrent administration of another prophylactic agent (e.g., verapamil, lithium carbonate, or methysergide).

Tension Headache

Perspective

Tension headache is the most common recurrent pain syndrome, affecting more than 75% of the population.[37] Women are affected more frequently than men, and most patients are middle aged. The headaches do not cause significant disability, and patients are able to continue with their normal daily activities.[38] The median frequency of headaches is six per month, and stress and lack of sleep are implicated as triggering factors.[39,40] The average duration of the headache is 4 to 13 hours, with a maximum of 72 hours.[40]

Little is known about the pathophysiology of tension headache.[37] There is no clear evidence that increased muscle activity is present, and tender areas of the scalp and neck can be found with both tension and migraine headaches. Evidence suggests that tension and migraine headaches may be part of a continuum with similar pathophysiology.

Clinical Features

Patients typically complain of a tight, band-like discomfort around the head that is nonpulsating and dull. They may also experience tightening of the neck muscles. The majority do not seek medical assistance because the headache is usually mild in intensity and of relatively short duration. Occasionally, the discomfort can build up slowly and fluctuate in severity over several days. Unlike those of migraine, symptoms do not worsen with physical activity, and accompanying symptoms such as nausea, vomiting, phonophobia, or photophobia are unusual. Anxiety and depression may coexist with chronic tension headache, which by definition occurs more than 15 days a month and can be daily and unremitting.[30]

Differential Diagnosis

Tension headache is the least distinct of all the primary headache disorders, and its diagnosis is based mainly on the absence of features that would suggest another diagnosis. The lack of specificity often results in the clinician hesitating to make the diagnosis without other diagnostic investigations to exclude organic disease.[41] The most common disorders mimicking tension headache include idiopathic intracranial hypertension, oromandibular dysfunction, cervical spondylosis, sinus or eye disease, and intracranial masses.

Treatment

For the majority of individuals, simple analgesics such as aspirin, acetaminophen, or NSAIDs are adequate for pain control. Because tension-type headache is more common in sedentary individuals, a regular exercise program may help.[30] Patients with chronic symptoms may exhibit signs of depression or anxiety, and these patients often respond to medications and nonpharmacologic regimens that treat these conditions. Some nonpharmacologic regimens are meditation, massage, and biofeedback. For long-term management, psychotherapy may be of value in teaching patients to deal with tension effectively.

SECONDARY HEADACHE DISORDERS

Subarachnoid Hemorrhage

Principles of Disease

Subarachnoid hemorrhage (SAH) refers to extravasated blood in the subarachnoid space. The blood activates meningeal nociceptors, leading to diffuse occipital pain along with signs of meningismus. SAH accounts for up to 10% of all strokes and is the most common cause of sudden death from a stroke.[42]

Approximately 80% of patients with nontraumatic SAH have ruptured saccular aneurysms.[43] Other causes include arteriovenous malformations, cavernous angiomas, mycotic aneurysms, neoplasms, and blood dyscrasias. SAH may be caused secondarily by an intraparenchymal hematoma that dissects its way into the subarachnoid space.

The risk for aneurysmal SAH increases with age, with most cases occurring between 40 and 60 years of age.[44] In children and adolescents, aneurysms are uncommon, and when SAH occurs it is usually secondary to an arteriovenous malformation.[45] It is estimated that 5% of the general population harbors a berry aneurysm, and the risk of rupture may increase with aneurysmal size. Other risk factors associated with SAH include hypertension, smoking, excessive alcohol consumption, and sympathomimetic drugs.[46,47] Increased systolic blood pressure values and long-term hypertension before aneurysm rupture seem to predict fatal SAH independently of aneurysm size or the patient's age or sex at the time of rupture.[48] There is a familial association of cerebral aneurysms with several diseases, including autosomal dominant polycystic kidney disease, coarctation of the aorta, Marfan's syndrome, and Ehlers-Danlos syndrome type IV.

Of all patients presenting to the emergency department with headache, 1% to 4% have SAH. Many patients with SAH die before reaching the hospital, with prehospital mortality ranging from 3% to 26%.[43] Because of the significant morbidity and mortality (50%) associated with this condition and the high likelihood of clinical deterioration in patients who are initially misdiagnosed, emergency physicians should consider SAH and be familiar with its presentation.[43]

Clinical Features

The majority of patients with SAH present with a sudden, cataclysmic "thunderclap" headache, which is often described as the worst headache of their life. The onset of headache may be associated with exertional activities such as exercise, the Valsalva maneuver, or sexual intercourse in up to 20% of patients.[42] One study demonstrated that moderate to extreme physical exertion in the previous 2-hour period was associated with a tripling of the risk of SAH.[49] Associated symptoms include nausea and vomiting in about 75% of patients, neck stiffness in 25%, and seizures in 17%.[44] Some patients experience a headache within the previous 6 to 8 weeks, indicating a warning leak or sentinel hemorrhage. Physical findings depend on the extent of the SAH. Meningismus is present in more than 50% of patients,[45] and up to 20% have focal findings.[46] Funduscopic examination may reveal retinal or subhyaloid hemorrhages, and patients may also have an isolated third or sixth nerve palsy. Oculomotor (third) nerve compression secondary to an expanding aneurysm leads to pupillary dilation. About 50% of patients with a ruptured aneurysm are restless or have an altered level of consciousness. Although the majority do not

Table 101-2. Hunt and Hess Clinical Grading Scale for Cerebral Aneurysms and Subarachnoid Hemorrhage

Grade	Condition
0	Unruptured aneurysm
1	Asymptomatic or minimal headache and slight nuchal rigidity
2	Moderate or severe headache, nuchal rigidity; no neurologic deficit other than cranial nerve palsy
3	Drowsiness, confusion, or mild focal deficit
4	Stupor, moderate to severe hemiparesis
5	Deep coma, decerebrate posturing, moribund appearance

have focal neurologic signs, when present, they may indicate the site of the aneurysm.[50]

The patient's prognosis is related to neurologic status at admission. The Hunt and Hess scale stratifies patients according to their clinical signs and symptoms at the time of presentation and is predictive of outcome (Table 101-2).[42,51] Patients who present with a grade I or II hemorrhage tend to have a good prognosis, and patients in grades IV or V tend to do poorly. These patients have an altered mental status, ranging from stupor to deep coma, together with focal neurologic findings. Patients with grade III hemorrhage present with drowsiness or confusion and are at risk for rapid clinical deterioration.

Diagnostic Studies

When the diagnosis of SAH is considered, a CT scan should be ordered emergently. Figure 101-1 shows an example of SAH on a CT scan. For acute hemorrhage less than 24 hours old, the sensitivity of CT in identifying hemorrhage is greater than 90%; however, it decreases to approximately 50% by the end of the first week.[43] When the CT scan is negative, a lumbar puncture (LP) should be performed. Using LP as a first strategy, postulated to be cost effective in carefully selected patients who have completely normal physical examinations, may be safe but has not been studied clinically.[52] To differentiate a traumatic LP from SAH, the patient's cerebrospinal fluid (CSF) should be spun and the supernatant observed for xanthochromia. The yellowish pigmentation is secondary to the metabolism of hemoglobin to pigmented molecules of oxyhemoglobin and bilirubin, a process that takes approximately 12 hours to occur.[53,54] The method of comparing the red blood cell count in the first and last tubes of CSF has been shown to be unreliable.[43] CSF xanthochromia in association with a negative CT scan is diagnostic of SAH. After the diagnosis is established, angiography should be performed to study the vascular anatomy and identify the source of hemorrhage in patients who are candidates for surgical intervention.

Most authorities agree that the presence of xanthochromia as measured by spectrophotometry, which is much more sensitive than visual inspection,[43] is the primary criterion for a diagnosis of SAH. However, because xanthochromia may require up to 12 hours to

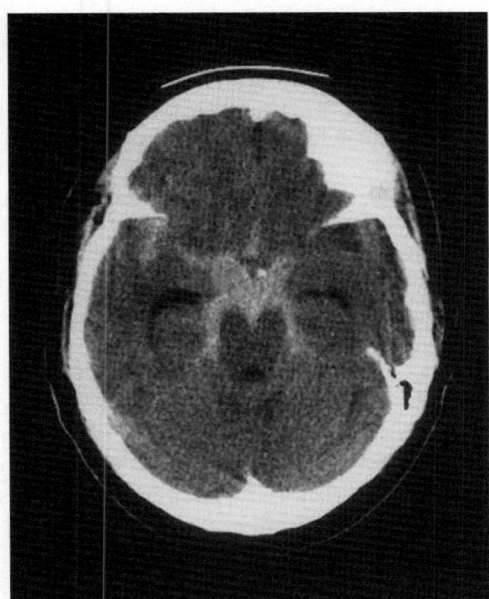

Figure 101-1. Cerebral aneurysm. Shown is a computed tomography (CT) scan of an aneurysmal subarachnoid hemorrhage. The CT scan of a 55-year-old woman shows subarachnoid blood within the interpeduncular and ambient cisterns and the right sylvian fissure caused by a ruptured aneurysm at the junction of the right carotid artery and the posterior communicating artery. (From Soliman E, Kader A, Perez N: Cerebral aneurysm. Online article at eMedicine.com. http://www.emedicine.com/med/topic3468.htm, picture 8.)

be present after the initial bleeding, patients with persistently bloody CSF without xanthochromia should undergo vascular imaging when the level of clinical suspicion of SAH is high.[43]

Up to 90% of patients with SAH have cardiac arrhythmias or electrocardiogram findings suggestive of acute cardiac ischemia, which may lead to an erroneous primary cardiac diagnosis.[43] Typical electrocardiographic findings include ST-T wave changes, U waves, and QT prolongation.[55]

Treatment

The management of SAH is complex and includes initial resuscitation, stabilization, and emergent neurosurgical consultation. The goals of management are to treat the acute medical and neurologic complications, prevent recurrent hemorrhage, and forestall the ischemic complications of vasospasm.[56] Because of an altered level of consciousness, patients with SAH of grade III or higher are at risk for respiratory depression and hypercapnia, which can lead to further increases in intracranial pressure (ICP); therefore, these patients may require early endotracheal intubation. Blood pressure must also be closely monitored because of the risk of continued bleeding or recurrent hemorrhage. Nimodipine, a calcium channel blocker, should be started soon after a diagnosis of aneurysmal SAH is made to lessen the likelihood of ischemic stroke. Because nimodipine may cause transient hypotension in some patients, hemodynamic monitoring is required

during its administration. The recommended dose is 60 mg by mouth or nasogastric tube every 4 hours. A Cochrane review concluded that treatment with antifibrinolytics (e.g., aminocaproic acid) does not improve overall outcome because the reduction in the rate of rebleeding is offset by an increase in poor outcome caused by cerebral ischemia.[57]

Analgesics, including opioids, should be used for persistent headache. In patients who are nauseated or at risk for vomiting, antiemetics must also be administered. Agitated patients require sedation, and all patients should be placed at bed rest in a quiet and dark environment. Clinically evident seizures should be treated with anticonvulsants, but the prophylactic use of these drugs is controversial.[55] The majority of these patients require hemodynamic and ICP monitoring in an intensive care setting. The role of surgery (e.g., aneurysmal clipping) versus endovascular coil embolization is not yet fully defined.[58]

Brain Tumor

Principles of Disease

Headache is the most common presenting complaint with brain tumor and occurs in about 50% of patients.[59] The majority of patients are elderly and have a cerebral metastasis as a cause of their headache.[60] The most common causes are lung and breast carcinoma followed by malignant melanoma and carcinomas of the kidney and gastrointestinal tract.[50] Primary brain tumors are much less common and typically occur in adults younger than 50 years.

The headache can be caused by several mechanisms, including direct involvement or traction on pain-sensitive structures such as meninges or larger cerebral vessels, or occur as a symptom of increased ICP. The pain patterns produced are highly variable, depending on the location of the mass and the structures involved.[50] Headaches are often but not always on the same side as the tumor. With increased ICP, the pain is often bifrontal or bioccipital and may be accompanied by vomiting. Brain tumors may also disrupt sleep, awakening the patient during the night. This may be related to increases in cerebral pressure that occur with recumbency and sleep-related carbon dioxide retention.[9]

Clinical Presentation

The typical patient presents with complaints of a worsening headache that has been present for weeks to months. The headache may have been present initially only on awakening, gradually becoming continuous. The classical triad of brain tumor headache—sleep disturbances, severe pain, and nausea and vomiting—is seen in only one third of patients.[61] Vomiting, when present, may be projectile and not preceded by nausea. If increased ICP is present, the headache is often bilateral and worsened by coughing, sneezing, bending, defecation, and sexual intercourse.[62] Although patients may not complain of focal neurologic deficits, abnormal findings are often found with neurologic testing.[63]

Other presentations include seizures, personality changes, and cognitive difficulties.

Diagnostic Evaluation

The diagnosis of brain tumor is often suspected from the history and neurologic examination. Neuroimaging with CT or magnetic resonance imaging (MRI) is the most efficient way to confirm the diagnosis. Contrast enhancement on CT often improves the identification of the underlying mass lesion and helps differentiate it from other causes, including abscess, hematoma, or vascular malformation.[64]

Treatment

Management consists of urgent referral to neurosurgery and treatment of any acute complications, including increased ICP and seizures. For patients who present with symptoms suggestive of increased ICP (e.g., headache, nausea, vomiting, confusion, weakness), treatment with steroids has been shown to be beneficial. Dexamethasone is the high-potency steroid used most often to treat edema associated with brain tumors. It has several advantages over other glucocorticoids, including a longer half-life, reduced mineralocorticoid effect, and a lower incidence of cognitive and behavioral complications.[63] The exact dose of steroids necessary for each patient varies, depending on the histology, size, and location of the tumor and the amount of edema present. In general, most patients require between 8 and 16 mg of dexamethasone per day. An appropriate starting dose in the emergency department is 10 mg IV followed by 4 mg every 6 hours.

Patients with a seizure (generalized or partial) should receive anticonvulsant therapy. Appropriate first-line agents include phenytoin, carbamazepine, and valproic acid. Empirical or prophylactic treatment does not appear to delay or prevent the onset of seizure activity and may expose the patient to unnecessary complications and toxicity.[63]

Giant Cell Arteritis

Principles of Disease

Giant cell arteritis, or temporal arteritis, is a systemic inflammatory process of the small and medium-sized arteries. Extracranial branches of the aortic arch and the ophthalmic vessels are most commonly involved, but the process may affect any artery in the body.[64] The mean age of onset is 71 years and it is rare before age 50. Females are more commonly affected than males.

Clinical Presentation

Headache is the most common initial manifestation of giant cell arteritis and occurs in more than 70% of patients.[65] The headache can be continuous or intermittent and is often worse at night or on exposure to cold. The pain may be described as sharp, throbbing, boring, or aching and is usually localized to the temporal region but may occur anywhere in the head. There may be tenderness over the scalp in the area of the temporal artery, with pain exacerbated when wearing a hat or resting the head on a pillow. Patients may also experience jaw claudication secondary to vascular insufficiency of the masseter and temporalis muscles. Systemic symptoms including fever, anorexia, and weight loss are often present. About 40% of patients complain of pain in their large proximal joints, with symptoms referable to the neck, torso, and lower back. Typically, pain and stiffness are worse in the morning and improve as the day goes on.[65] This condition, known as *polymyalgia rheumatica*, can occur in the absence of giant cell arteritis.

The most serious complication of giant cell arteritis is permanent visual loss, which eventually occurs in 36% of untreated cases.[66] Amaurosis fugax can also occur before permanent visual loss. Other complications include peripheral neuropathies, transient ischemic attacks, and stroke.

Diagnostic Evaluation

The physical examination may reveal tender and indurated superficial scalp arteries that may be pulseless. Visual acuity and visual field testing and a thorough funduscopic examination should also be performed.

The majority of patients have a significant elevation of the erythrocyte sedimentation rate (ESR), usually over 50 mm/hr and often over 100 mm/hr, although an elevated ESR is not specific for the disorder and a normal value does not rule out the diagnosis. Other laboratory abnormalities include mild to moderate anemia, elevated C-reactive protein, and liver function abnormalities.[50] An elevated platelet count (>400,000) may be a risk factor for permanent visual loss.[67] The diagnosis is confirmed by temporal artery biopsy. Because this is a patchy disease, multiple biopsies of a long segment of the artery may need to be examined.

Treatment

Because of the risk of visual loss, giant cell arteritis is a medical emergency and treatment should be initiated promptly when the diagnosis is suspected. Steroids are the mainstay of therapy; the recommended initial dose of prednisone ranges from 60 to 120 mg/day. Symptomatic response usually occurs rapidly over days, although therapy must be continued for months, with close ESR monitoring.

Carotid and Vertebral Dissection

Principles of Disease

Carotid and vertebral dissections are more common than previously realized. They are the most frequent cause of stroke in persons younger than 45 years, accounting for approximately 20% of all cases in this age group.[68] Although dissections may occur spontaneously, careful history taking frequently identifies an association with sudden neck movement or trauma preceding the event [68,69] Reported mechanisms include neck torsion, chiropractic manipulation, coughing, minor falls, and motor vehicle accidents. Early symptoms and signs are often subtle, and in the absence of neurologic findings delays in diagnosis are common.

The pathologic lesion is intramural hemorrhage within the media of the arterial wall. The hematoma can be localized or extend circumferentially along the length of the vessel, resulting in partial or complete occlusion. Platelet aggregation and thrombus formation also occur, further compromising vessel patency or causing distal embolization. The timing of these events is variable, and a patient may experience symptoms of cerebral ischemia days to years after dissection.[70,71]

Clinical Presentation

The typical presentation of the patient with carotid or vertebral dissection is the abrupt onset of pain in the neck or face. Neurologic findings usually occur within the first few hours, but autopsy studies have shown that strokes may occur months later.[68]

Carotid Dissection

The classical triad of symptoms for carotid dissection includes unilateral headache, ipsilateral partial Horner's syndrome, and contralateral hemispheric findings that may include aphasia, neglect, visual disturbances, or hemiparesis. The headache is often severe and throbbing but may be subacute and similar to previous headaches. Acute severe retro-orbital pain in a previously healthy person with no history of cluster headaches is particularly suggestive of carotid dissection.[9] Most patients eventually develop signs of cerebral ischemia. Warning symptoms include transient ischemic attacks, amaurosis fugax, episodic lightheadedness, and syncope. Spontaneous dissection of the carotid artery has a favorable prognosis and recurrence is uncommon.[71] Factors associated with a worse prognosis include older age, occlusive disease on angiography, or stroke as the initial presenting symptom.[72]

Vertebral Dissection

Vertebral artery dissections are less common than carotid dissections. The classical presentation is that of a relatively young person with severe unilateral posterior headache and neurologic findings.[73] The majority of patients develop a rapidly progressive neurologic deficit with symptoms of brainstem and cerebellar ischemia. Common findings include vertigo, severe vomiting, ataxia, diplopia, hemiparesis, unilateral facial weakness, and tinnitus.[74] Spontaneous vertebral artery dissection appears to be relatively rare. Approximately 10% of patients who develop a vertebral dissection die during the acute phase, secondary to massive stroke. For patients who survive, the prognosis is usually good.[69]

Diagnosis and Treatment

The diagnosis of dissection may prove to be difficult. A CT scan should be obtained first but is often normal in uncomplicated dissection. Further imaging studies including MRI, magnetic resonance angiography, or

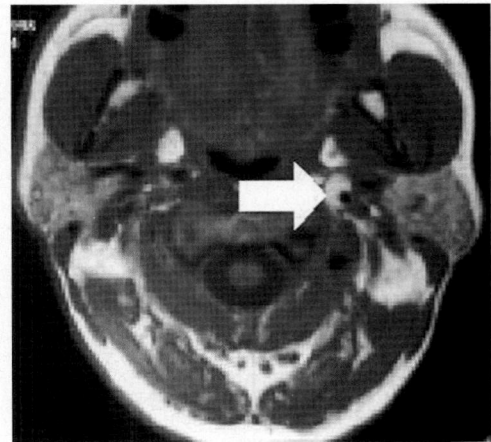

Figure 101-2. Axial T1-weighted magnetic resonance image demonstrating a crescent sign *(arrow)* in a patient with a left internal carotid artery dissection. (From Kidwell C: Dissection syndromes. Online article at eMedicine.com. http://www.emedicine.com/neuro/topic99.htm, picture 2.)

catheter angiography are required to confirm the diagnosis.[68] Figure 101-2 shows an example of carotid artery dissection on MRI. Duplex imaging is of limited value.[68] Treatment is aimed at stroke prevention and usually includes early anticoagulation followed by antiplatelet therapy.

Identifying patients with dissection is challenging. More than 50% of patients see their physician for symptoms before admission. The emergency physician must consider this diagnosis in any young patient who presents with head or neck pain with focal neurologic findings.

Idiopathic Intracranial Hypertension

Principles of Disease

Idiopathic intracranial hypertension (IIH) is also known as *pseudotumor cerebri* or benign intracranial hypertension. The term *idiopathic intracranial hypertension*, however, is preferred because this disorder is not always benign and may have significant neurologic sequelae in affected individuals.

IIH is a relatively common neurologic disease seen primarily in young obese women of childbearing age. Several predisposing factors have been identified, including the use of oral contraceptives, anabolic steroids, tetracyclines, and vitamin A.[75]

Pathophysiology and Clinical Features

The pathophysiology of this disease remains controversial, with increased brain water content and decreased CSF outflow considered the two major causative factors.[76] The most prominent symptom is generalized headache, which is often gradual in onset and of moderate intensity. There is no specific localizing pattern, although in some patients it is worsened by eye movement. It may awaken patients from sleep and is exacerbated by bending forward and the

BOX 101-4. Diagnostic Criteria for Idiopathic Intracranial Hypertension (IIH)

- Increased intracranial pressure (ICP) (>200 mm H_2O) measured by opening pressure from a lumbar puncture
- Signs and symptoms of increased ICP, with absence of localizing signs
- No mass lesions or ventricular enlargement on neuroimaging
- Normal or low cerebrospinal fluid protein and normal cell count
- No clinical or neuroimaging suspicion of venous sinus thrombosis[76]

Valsalva maneuver, which impede cerebral venous return.

Visual complaints are common, and patients may experience transient visual obscuration several times a day secondary to ischemia of the visual pathways. These episodes can be followed by prolonged periods of visual loss, which can become permanent in up to 10% of patients.[77] Patients may also complain of nausea, vomiting, and dizziness. On physical examination, patients have papilledema and visual field defects, including an enlarged blind spot initially followed by loss of peripheral vision. Occasionally, a sixth nerve palsy is noted.

Diagnosis

The diagnosis of IIH should not be made without neuroimaging and measurement of ICP. The diagnostic criteria are listed in Box 101-4.

Treatment

Predisposing factors (e.g., discontinuation of implicated medications) should be corrected. Symptomatic treatment often includes lowering ICP and managing the headache. Acetazolamide (a carbonic anhydrase inhibitor) can be used to decrease CSF production alone or with a loop diuretic such as furosemide. Steroids have also been used, although their mechanism of action is unclear. Prolonged therapy is problematic, and rebound IIH often occurs when doses are tapered. Repeated LPs can be attempted, but most patients find this approach objectionable. In patients with impending visual loss or incapacitating symptoms, a ventricular shunt or optic nerve sheath fenestration may be indicated.

Posttraumatic Headache

Headache is the most common symptom following minor head injury. It is often part of a complex syndrome that can include dizziness, fatigue, insomnia, irritability, memory loss, and difficulty with concentration. The prevalence of headache with posttraumatic syndrome is not known because most patients are not admitted for this condition. There are approximately 2 million closed head injuries per year, and it is estimated that 30% to 50% of these patients develop posttraumatic headache (PTHA).[78] Acute PTHA develops hours to days after the injury and resolves within 8 weeks. Chronic PTHA may last from several months to years and may mimic other forms of headache, including tension and migraine headaches. The presence of headache, dizziness, or nausea on initial presentation is strongly associated with the development of chronic PTHA.[79]

Patients who develop PTHA after minor head injuries have normal neurologic examinations and normal neuroimaging studies. The pathophysiology of their symptoms is unclear and may include both anatomic and functional components. Most patients are more concerned about the cause of the headache rather than the headache itself.

Treatment is symptomatic. For acute PTHA, analgesics such as acetaminophen or NSAIDs are adequate for pain control. For chronic PTHA, treatment must be individualized depending on the type of headache and associated symptoms the patient is experiencing. Novel therapies, such as antidepressants and β-blockers, may be effective in selected patients.

Acute Glaucoma

Patients with acute angle closure glaucoma present with sudden onset of severe pain localized to the affected eye that may radiate to the ear, sinuses, teeth, or forehead.[62] Visual symptoms, including blurriness, halos around lights, and scotomas, are typically present, and many patients also experience nausea and vomiting. The underlying pathophysiology is congenital narrowing of the anterior chamber angle that, under certain conditions, closes, resulting in a significant rise in intraocular pressure (IOP). Episodes can be precipitated by entering a low-light environment such as a movie theater, with resultant pupillary dilatation, or by the use of medications such as mydriatics (e.g., dilated ocular examination), sympathomimetics (e.g., pseudoephedrine), or agents with anticholinergic properties (e.g., antiemetics, antihistamines, antipsychotics, and antidepressants).[75,80]

Physical examination reveals a red eye with a fixed, middilated pupil, corneal clouding, and shallow anterior chamber. The diagnosis is confirmed by demonstrating markedly elevated IOP in the range of 60 to 90 mm Hg (normal <21 mm Hg).

Treatment includes topical miotics, topical β-blockers, oral carbonic anhydrase inhibitors (e.g., acetazolamide 250 mg four times daily), IV osmotic agents (e.g., mannitol), and prompt referral to an ophthalmologist. The potential for diagnostic confusion between acute glaucoma, iritis, and cluster headache must be recognized. Although cluster headache may arise with pain, nausea, and a red eye, vision is not affected and the pupil is generally small and ptotic (from an oculosympathetic paresis).[81] Acute iritis also arises with a painful red eye, but only acute angle closure glaucoma is associated with markedly elevated IOP.

Postdural Puncture Headache

Principles of Disease and Pathophysiology

Headache is the most common complication of LP, occurring in up to 40% of patients.[82] The incidence is highest in the 18- to 30-year age group and uncommon in young children and adults older than 60. Although the onset is often immediate, patients may not report symptoms for several days. In the majority of affected individuals, the duration of headache is less than 5 days.[82,83]

The cause of postdural puncture headache (PDPH) is not entirely clear. The most likely explanation is a persistent CSF leak that exceeds CSF production, resulting in CSF hypotension. If sufficient CSF is lost, the brain descends in the cranial vault when the patient assumes the upright position, leading to increased traction on the pain fibers.[84] Thus, the headache is characteristically positional and increases with the upright position and decreases with recumbency. The amount of time a patient remains recumbent after LP does not appear to affect the incidence of headache.[9]

Certain factors have been implicated as causes of PDPH, including the size or diameter of the spinal needle, the orientation of the bevel during the procedure, and the amount of fluid withdrawn. Smaller diameter needles cause less leakage, and it is postulated that inserting the needle with the bevel up (i.e., bevel pointing up when the patient is in the lateral position) minimizes damage to the dural fibers. Using atraumatic needles or pencil-point needles (e.g., Whitaker[85] or Sprotte[86]) has also been shown to reduce significantly the incidence of PDPH.[87]

Clinical Features

PDPH is typically bilateral, throbbing, and exacerbated by the upright position. Associated symptoms include neck stiffness; nausea; vomiting; auditory disturbances, including tinnitus and hearing loss (hypoacusis); and ocular symptoms, including blurred vision and diplopia.[84]

Treatment

Most PDPHs resolve spontaneously within a few days with bed rest, adequate hydration, and mild analgesics. For persistent headaches, methylxanthine agents have been found to help some patients. Oral caffeine (300 mg every 4 to 6 hours), caffeine sodium benzoate (500 mg in 1 L of fluid), or theophylline (300 mg PO every 8 hours) may be effective.[82] For severe headaches lasting more than 24 hours, an epidural blood patch (autologous blood clot) relieves the headache in the majority of patients.[83]

Intracranial Infection

Headache is commonly seen in patients with intracranial infections, including meningitis, brain abscess, encephalitis, and acquired immunodeficiency syndrome. The severity and type of headache vary depending on the specific infection.

With acute bacterial meningitis, the patient often has a severe bursting headache that rapidly increases in severity over a short period.[88] These patients typically have significant meningismus, with positive Kernig's and Brudzinski's signs. With viral meningitis, patients may also complain of severe headache and nuchal rigidity, but the course is more indolent than that with bacterial meningitis.

The severity of headache associated with encephalitis depends on the type of virus involved. For example, the headache is usually mild with mumps encephalitis. However, with herpes simplex infection, the headache is abrupt and severe and frequently associated with confusion, fever, altered level of consciousness, seizures, and focal neurologic signs.

Patients with brain abscess often have headache as their presenting complaint.[89] As the infection progresses, vomiting, focal neurologic signs, and depressed level of consciousness typically develop.

Headache is a frequent complaint in patients with human immunodeficiency virus infection and can be caused by a number of conditions, including aseptic meningitis, toxoplasmosis, cryptococcal or tuberculous meningitis, or cytomegalovirus encephalitis.

In the majority of cerebral infections, the mechanism of head pain includes meningeal irritation and increased ICP. In addition, headache may be a general reaction to fever or the toxic products of the infecting agent.[90]

Hypertensive Headache

Contrary to common belief, hypertension is not an important cause of headache, and the occurrence of headache and hypertension in the same patient is often coincidental.[91] Whether some patients with mild to moderate hypertension suffer from headache caused by elevated blood pressure is uncertain. The rate of blood pressure increase is more important as a cause of headache than the absolute blood pressure value. Diastolic pressures lower than 130 mm Hg are rarely the cause of headache.[65]

Nonetheless, the association of headache with severe hypertension is well documented. Acute, severe headache is a prominent symptom of hypertensive encephalopathy, and most patients have a blood pressure in the range of 250/150 mm Hg. Other conditions include headache secondary to toxic agents (e.g., drug-induced hypertension), pheochromocytoma, and eclampsia.

The headache of severe hypertension is typically diffuse, worse when the patient awakes in the morning, and gradually subsides over the course of the day.[91] Treatment is directed at lowering the blood pressure; in most cases, the headache is relieved within 24 hours. In patients with hypertensive encephalopathy, the headache may persist for days until brain edema has resolved.

Cervicogenic Headache

Cervicogenic headache refers to headaches that originate from disorders of the neck. Diagnosis is based on the presence of the following three distinct sets of symptoms:[92]

1. Unilateral headache triggered by movements of the head or neck or certain head positions
2. Unilateral headache triggered by pressure on the neck
3. Unilateral headache spreading to the neck or possibly the ipsilateral shoulder or arm

Many of these headaches are reported after a whiplash injury. Even though neck structures play a primary role in the pathophysiology of some headaches, clinical patterns indicating a neck-headache relationship have not been adequately defined.

Medication-Induced Headache

Medication use, abuse, or withdrawal can be a cause of headache, and the term *medication-induced headache* is used to describe these conditions. Medication-induced headache is underdiagnosed and often difficult to manage. Although not well understood, it tends to occur in patients with a primary headache disorder (e.g., migraine, tension type) who use immediate relief medications, often in excessive quantities.[93] Medications that have been implicated include NSAIDs, aspirin or acetylsalicylic acid (ASA), acetaminophen, barbiturate-analgesic combinations plus caffeine with or without codeine, opioids, caffeine, and ergotamine. A key factor in medication overuse headache is preemptive use of drugs, in anticipation of—rather than for—headache.[30] Women are affected more commonly than men, and the most frequently affected age group is between 30 and 40 years.[94] The headache itself is variable and may be accompanied by asthenia, nausea, anxiety, depression, and difficulty with concentration. Typically, it is worse on awakening in the morning and after physical exertion.

The symptomatic medication that leads to the development of this disorder initially provides some pain relief to the patient, but over time tolerance develops, and larger doses are required to obtain symptomatic improvement.[94]

Treatment typically requires complete withdrawal of the medication being overused to achieve long-term results. In addition, these patients require a comprehensive education and follow-up program involving pharmacologic, dietary, and behavioral components.[94]

Trigeminal Neuralgia

Trigeminal neuralgia is a painful unilateral affliction of the face, characterized by brief electric shock–like (lancinating) pains limited to the distribution of one or more divisions of the trigeminal nerve. Pain is commonly evoked by trivial stimuli (e.g., washing, shaving, smoking, talking, and brushing teeth) but may also occur spontaneously.[95] Individual attacks are brief, lasting a few seconds to less than 2 minutes, and are stereotyped in the individual patient. The lightning-like pains and unilateral grimaces so characteristic of

trigeminal neuralgia led to the designation of the term *tic douloureux*.[95] The diagnosis is straightforward in most patients on the basis of clinical criteria. However, because these symptoms can also be caused by an underlying mass lesion, CT or MRI is indicated in previously undiagnosed patients and when sensory loss or motor dysfunction is present.

Several drugs have been effective in treating trigeminal neuralgia, including carbamazepine, phenytoin, and baclofen; however, about 30% of patients fail to respond to medical therapy.[96] In these patients, surgical management, including alcohol or glycerol injection or microvascular decompression, may be indicated.[95]

Cough and Exertional Headache

In some patients, severe headache can be provoked by coughing, sneezing, laughing, heavy lifting or exertion, and the Valsalva maneuver. The pain starts within a few seconds of the precipitant and is typically brief when associated with cough but can last as long as 24 hours when associated with exertion. The headache is bilateral and throbbing in nature and in the majority of patients resolves spontaneously without persistent neurologic symptoms (e.g., neck stiffness or photophobia). In some patients, the headache may be secondary to structural lesions, especially in the posterior fossa[97]; therefore all previously undiagnosed patients require CT, or preferably MRI, followed by LP to rule out intracranial disease including SAH. For patients with recurrent benign exertional headache, treatment includes avoiding the underlying triggering mechanism and using analgesics as necessary. For patients with exertional headache, NSAIDs including indomethacin have been effective.

Coital Headache

Coital cephalgia is a recurrent, benign headache associated with sexual activity and is more common in men than in women. It can occur just before, during, or immediately after orgasm. The headaches are usually dull and throbbing and last from minutes to hours. Occasionally, some patients experience a sudden, explosive headache that occurs during orgasm. In these patients, SAH should be ruled out.[97,98]

High-Altitude Headache

Headache is one of the cardinal manifestations of acute mountain sickness and can occur at altitudes higher than 5000 feet above sea level in unacclimatized individuals. The headache is throbbing in nature, located in the temporal or occipital areas, and is probably caused by a mild increase in ICP secondary to brain swelling.[99] It is worse at night or in the early morning and exacerbated by the Valsalva maneuver or bending forward.[100] Other findings associated with high-altitude illness include fatigue, nausea, vomiting, dizziness, insomnia, and an altered mental status. Pulmonary edema and cerebral edema occur with severe cases. The treatment for these conditions includes supplemental oxygen and descent to a lower altitude.

KEY CONCEPTS

- Headache is a common presenting complaint in the emergency department. The emergency physician must distinguish between benign primary headache disorders and the more serious and potentially life-threatening secondary causes of headache.

- The majority of patients do not have abnormal neurologic findings; therefore, the key to a successful diagnosis is a thorough and systematic history.

- Patients with the following headache presentations are at risk for serious underlying disease: sudden explosive headache; first or worst headache; new-onset headache after age 50; headache associated with papilledema, alteration in or loss of consciousness, or focal neurologic symptoms; headache after head trauma; subacute headache with increasing frequency or severity; headache associated with fever, cancer, or immunosuppression; and headache triggered by exertion, sexual activity, or Valsalva maneuver.[101]

- The need for diagnostic studies is dictated by the suspected secondary cause of headache.

REFERENCES

1. Centers for Disease Control and Prevention: *Vital and Health Statistics of the Centers for Disease Control and Prevention/National Center of Health Statistics, National Hospital Ambulatory Medical Survey: Emergency Department Survey*, 1995.
2. Saper JR: Headache disorders. *Med Clin North Am* 83:663, 1999.
3. Daroff RB: Classification and diagnostic criteria for headache disorders, cranial neuralgias and facial pain, Headache Classification Committee of the International Headache Society. *Cephalalgia* 8:1, 1988.
4. Mikta M: Experts sort out headache classification, new guidelines for physicians to debut. *JAMA* 290:736, 2003.
5. Goadsby PJ, Lipton RB, Ferrari MD: Migraine—Current understanding and treatment. *N Engl J Med* 346:257, 2002.
6. Diamond S, Diamond ML: Emergency treatment of migraine: Insights into current options. *Postgrad Med* 101:169, 1997.
7. Silberstein S, Merriam G: Sex hormones and headache 1999 (menstrual migraine). *Neurology* 53:S3, 1999.
8. Boyle CA: Management of menstrual migraine. *Neurology* 53:S14, 1999.
9. Kanner RM: Headache and facial pain. In Portenoy RK, Kanner RM (eds): *Pain Management: Theory and Practice*. Philadelphia, FA Davis, 1996, pp 51-78.
10. Capobianco DJ, Cheshire WP, Campbell JK: An overview of the diagnosis and pharmacologic treatment of migraine. *Mayo Clin Proc* 71:1055, 1996.
11. Raskin NH: On the origin of head pain. *Headache* 28:254, 1988.
12. Barre F: Cocaine as an abortive agent in cluster headache. *Headache* 22:69, 1982.
13. Bell R, et al: A comparative trial of three agents in the treatment of acute migraine headache. *Ann Emerg Med* 19:1079, 1990.
14. Moskowitz MA: The neurobiology of vascular head pain. *Ann Neurol* 16:157, 1984.
15. Silberstein SD: Serotonin (5-HT) and migraine. *Headache* 34:408, 1994.
16. Campbell JK: Manifestations of migraine. *Neurol Clin* 8:841, 1990.
17. Troost BT: Ophthalmoplegic migraine. *Biomed Pharmacother* 50:49, 1996.
18. Bickerstaff ER: Basilar artery migraine. *Lancet* 1:15, 1961.
19. Moffert AM, Sash M, Scott DF: Effect of chocolate in migraine: A double-blind study. *J Neurol Neurosurg Psychiatry* 37:445, 1974.
20. Monro J, Carini C, Brostoff J: Migraine is a food-allergic disease. *Lancet* 2:719, 1984.
21. Snow V, Weiss K, Wall EM, Mottur-Pilson C: Pharmacologic management of acute attacks of migraine and prevention of migraine headache. *Ann Intern Med* 137:840, 2002.
22. Frishberg BM: Neuroimaging in presumed primary headache disorders. *Semin Neurol* 17:373, 1997.
23. Baumel B: Migraine: A pharmacologic review with newer options and delivery modalities. *Neurology* 44:S13, 1994.
24. Edmeads J: Advances in migraine therapy: Focus on oral sumatriptan. *Neurology* 45:S3, 1995.
25. Lane PL, McLellan BA, Baggoley CJ: Comparative efficacy of chlorpromazine and meperidine with dimenhydrinate in migraine headache. *Ann Emerg Med* 18:360, 1989.
26. Edmeads J: Emergency management of headache. *Headache* 28:675, 1988.
27. Diener HC, Limmroth V: The treatment of migraine. *Rev Contemp Pharmacother* 5:271, 1994.
28. Tfelt-Hansen P: Prophylactic pharmacotherapy of migraine: Some practical guidelines. *Neurol Clin* 15:153, 1997.
29. Graham JR, et al: Fibrotic disorders associated with methysergide therapy for headache. *N Engl J Med* 274:359, 1966.
30. Steiner TJ, Fontebasso M: Headache. *BMJ* 325:881, 2002.
31. Mathew NT: Cluster headache. *Semin Neurol* 17:313, 1997.
32. Sturm JW, Donnan GA: Diagnosis and investigation of headache. *Aust Fam Physician* 27:587, 1998.
33. Nappi G, Russell D: Symptomatology of cluster headache. In Olesen J, Tfelt-Hansen P, Welch KMA (eds): *The Headaches*, 2nd ed. Philadelphia, Lippincott Williams & Wilkins, 2000, pp 717-724.
34. Ekbom K: Sumatriptan in the management of cluster headache. *Rev Contemp Pharmacother* 5:311, 1994.
35. Fogan L: Treatment of cluster headache: A double-blind comparison of oxygen v. air inhalation. *Arch Neurol* 42:362, 1985.
36. Ekbom K, Solomon S: Management of cluster headache. In Olesen J, Tfelt-Hansen P, Welch KMA (eds): *The Headaches*, 2nd ed. Philadelphia, Lippincott Williams & Wilkins, 2000.
37. Jensen R: Pathophysiological mechanisms of tension-type headache: A review of epidemiological and experimental studies. *Cephalalgia* 19:602, 1999.
38. Spira PJ: Tension headache. *Aust Fam Physician* 27:597, 1998.
39. Jensen R, Paiva T: Symptomatology of episodic tension-type headache. In Olesen J, Tfelt-Hansen P, Welch KMA (eds): *The Headaches*, 2nd ed. Philadelphia, Lippincott Williams & Wilkins, 2000, pp 619-626.
40. Iversen HK, et al: Clinical characteristics of migraine and episodic tension-type headache in relation to old and new diagnostic criteria. *Headache* 30:514, 1990.
41. Schoenen J, Jensen R: Differential diagnosis and prognosis of tension-type headache. In Olesen J, Tfelt-Hansen P, Welch KMA (eds): *The Headaches*, 2nd ed. Philadelphia, Lippincott Williams & Wilkins, 2000, pp 635-638.
42. Becker KJ: Epidemiology and clinical presentation of aneurysmal subarachnoid hemorrhage. *Neurosurg Clin North Am* 9:435, 1998.
43. Edlow JA, Caplan LR: Avoiding pitfalls in the diagnosis of subarachnoid hemorrhage. *N Engl J Med* 342:29, 2000.

44. Locksley HB: Report on the cooperative study of intracranial aneurysms and subarachnoid hemorrhage, Sect. V, Part I: Natural history of subarachnoid hemorrhage, intracranial aneurysms and arteriovenous malformations: Based on 6368 cases in the Cooperative Study. *J Neurosurg* 25:219, 1966.

45. Linn F, et al: Prospective study of sentinel headache in aneurysmal subarachnoid hemorrhage. *Lancet* 344:590, 1994.

46. Levine S, et al: Cerebrovascular complications of the use of the "crack" form of alkaloidal cocaine. *N Engl J Med* 323:699, 1990.

47. Broderick JP, et al: Major risk factors for aneurysmal subarachnoid hemorrhage in the young are modifiable. *Stroke* 34:1375, 2003.

48. Juvela S: Prehemorrhage risk factors for fatal intracranial aneurysm rupture. *Stroke* 34:1852, 2003.

49. Anderson C, et al:. Triggers of subarachnoid hemorrhage. Role of physical exertion, smoking, and alcohol in the Australasian Cooperative Research on Subarachnoid Hemorrhage Study (ACROSS). *Stroke* 34:1771, 2003.

50. Newman LC, Lipton RB: Emergency department evaluation of headache. *Neurol Clin* 16:285, 1998.

51. Hunt WE, Hess RM: Surgical risk as related to time intervention in the repair of intracranial aneurysm. *J Neurosurg* 28:14, 1968.

52. Schull MJ: Lumbar puncture first: An alternative model for the investigation of lone acute sudden headache. *Acad Emerg Med* 6:131, 1999.

53. Fishman RA: *Cerebrospinal Fluid in Diseases of the Nervous System*. Philadelphia, WB Saunders, 1992.

54. Roost KT, et al: The formation of cerebrospinal fluid xanthochromia after subarachnoid hemorrhage: Enzymatic conversion of hemoglobin to bilirubin by the arachnoid and choroid plexus. *Neurology* 22:973, 1972.

55. Sawin PD, Loftus CM: Diagnosis of spontaneous subarachnoid hemorrhage. *Am Fam Physician* 55:145, 1997.

56. Adams HP, del Zoppo GJ, von Kummar R: *Management of Stroke: A Practical Guide for the Prevention, Evaluation and Treatment of Acute Stroke*. Caddo, Okla, Professional Communications, 1998.

57. Roos Y, et al: Antifibrinolytic therapy for aneurysmal subarachnoid hemorrhage. A major update of a Cochrane review. *Stroke* 34:2308, 2003.

58. Claiborne Johnston S, et al: Recommendations for the endovascular treatment of intracranial aneurysms. *Stroke* 33:2536, 2002.

59. Forsyth PA, Posner JB: Headaches in patients with brain tumors: A study of 111 patients. *Neurology* 43:1678, 1993.

60. Zimm S, et al: Intracerebral metastases in solid-tumor patients: Natural history and results of treatment. *Cancer* 48:384, 1981.

61. Patchell RA, Posner JB: Neurologic complications of systemic cancer. *Neurol Clin* 3:729, 1985.

62. Welch KMA, et al: Headache in the emergency room. In Olesen J, Tfelt-Hansen P, Welch KMA (eds): *The Headaches*, 2nd ed. Philadelphia, Lippincott Williams & Wilkins, 2000, pp 993-1000.

63. Newton HB, et al: Clinical presentation, diagnosis, and pharmacotherapy of patients with primary brain tumors. *Ann Pharmacother* 33:816, 1999.

64. Moltyaner Y, Tenenbaum J: Temporal arteritis: A review and case history. *J Fam Pract* 43:294, 1996.

65. Hellmann D: Temporal arteritis. A cough, toothache, and tongue infarction. *JAMA* 287:2996, 2002.

66. Keltner JL: Giant-cell arteritis: Signs and symptoms. *Ophthalmology* 89:1101, 1982.

67. Liozon E, et al: Risk factors for visual loss in giant cell (temporal) arteritis: A prospective study of 174 patients. *Am J Med* 111:211, 2001.

68. Norris JW, Beletsky V: Cervical arterial dissection. *Adv Neurol* 92:119, 2003.

69. Stahmer SA, Raps EC, Mines DI: Carotid and vertebral artery dissections. *Emerg Med Clin North Am* 15:677, 1997.

70. Bogousslavsky J: Dissections of the cerebral arteries: Clinical effects. *Curr Opin Neurol* 1:63, 1988.

71. Hart RG, Easton JD: Dissections of cervical and cerebral arteries. *Neurol Clin* 1:155, 1983.

72. Pozzati E, et al: Long-term follow-up of occlusive cervical carotid dissection. *Stroke* 21:528, 1990.

73. Caplan LR, Tettenborn B: Vertebrobasilar occlusive disease: Review of selected aspects. *Cerebrovasc Dis* 2:256, 1992.

74. Mokri B: Traumatic and spontaneous extracranial internal carotid artery dissections. *J Neurol* 237:356, 1990.

75. Sztajnkrycer M, Jauch EC: Unusual headaches. *Emerg Med Clin North Am* 16:741, 1998.

76. Sorensen PS, Corbett JJ: High cerebrospinal fluid pressure. In Olesen J, Tfelt-Hansen P, Welch KMA (eds): *The Headaches*, 2nd ed. Philadelphia, Lippincott Williams & Wilkins, 2000, pp 823-830.

77. Corbett JJ, et al: Visual loss in pseudotumor cerebri: Follow-up of 57 patients from five to 41 years and a profile of 14 patients with permanent severe visual loss. *Arch Neurol* 39:461, 1982.

78. Packard RC: Epidemiology and pathogenesis of posttraumatic headache. *J Head Trauma Rehabil* 14:9, 1999.

79. de Kruijk JR, et al: Prediction of post-traumatic complaints after mild traumatic brain injury: Early symptoms and biochemical markers. *J Neuro Neurosurg Psychiatry* 73:727, 2002.

80. Gobel H, Martin T: Ocular disorders. In Olesen J, Tfelt-Hansen P, Welch KMA (eds): *The Headaches*, 2nd ed. Philadelphia, Lippincott Williams & Wilkins, 2000, pp 899-904.

81. Hedges TR: An ophthalmologist's view of headache. *Headache* 19:151, 1979.

82. Evans RW: Complications of lumbar puncture. *Neurol Clin* 16:83, 1998.

83. Tarkkila PJ, Miralles JA, Palomaki EA: The subjective complications and efficiency of the epidural blood patch in the treatment of postdural puncture headache. *Reg Anesth* 14:247, 1989.

84. Duffy PJ, Crosby ET: The epidural blood patch: Resolving the controversies. *Can J Anaesth* 46:878, 1999.

85. Dittmann M, et al: Spinal anaesthesia with 29-gauge Quincke point needles and post dural puncture headache in 2378 patients. *Acta Anaesthesiol Scand* 38:691, 1994.

86. Sathi S, Stieg PE: "Acquired" Chiari I malformation after multiple lumbar punctures: Case report. *Neurosurgery* 32:306, 1993.

87. Thomas S, Jamieson DRS, Muir KW: Randomised controlled trial of atraumatic versus standard needles for diagnostic lumbar puncture. *BMJ* 321:986, 2000.

88. Drexler ED: Severe headaches: When to worry, what to do. *Postgrad Med* 87:164, 1990.

89. Weinke T, et al: *Cryptococcus* in AIDS patients: Observations concerning CNS involvement. *J Neurol* 236:38, 1989.

90. Marinis M, Welch M: Headache associated with intracranial infection. In Olesen J, Tfelt-Hansen P, Welch KMA (eds): *The Headaches*, 2nd ed. Philadelphia, Lippincott Williams & Wilkins, 2000, pp 841-848.

91. Strandgaard S, Henry P: Arterial hypertension. In Olesen J, Tfelt-Hansen P, Welch KMA (eds): *The Headaches*, 2nd ed. Philadelphia, Lippincott Williams & Wilkins, 2000, pp 819-822.

92. Sjaastad O, Fredriksen TA, Pfaffenrath V: Cervicogenic headache: Diagnostic criteria. *Headache* 30:725, 1990.

93. Mathew NT: Transformed migraine, analgesic rebound, and other chronic daily headaches. *Neurol Clin* 15:167, 1997.
94. Zed PJ, Loewen PS, Robinson G: Medication-induced headache: Overview and systematic review of therapeutic approaches. *Ann Pharmacother* 33:61, 1999.
95. Terrence C, Jensen T: Trigeminal neuralgia and other facial neuralgias. In Olesen J, Tfelt-Hansen P, Welch KMA (eds): *The Headaches*, 2nd ed. Philadelphia, Lippincott Williams & Wilkins, 2000, pp 929-938.
96. Newton HB, et al: Clinical presentation, diagnosis, and pharmacotherapy of patients with primary brain tumors. *Ann Pharmacother* 33:816, 1999.
97. Pascual J, et al: Cough, exertional and sexual headaches: An analysis of 72 benign and symptomatic cases. *Neurology* 46:1520, 1996.
98. Banerjee A: Coital emergencies. *Postgrad Med J* 72:653, 1996.
99. Hackett PH, Roach RC: Current concepts: High-altitude illness. *N Engl J Med* 345:107, 2001.
100. Harris MD, et al: High-altitude medicine. *Am Fam Physician* 57:1907, 1998.
101. Kaniecki R: Headache assessment and management. *JAMA* 289:1430, 2003.

CHAPTER

102 Delirium and Dementia

Jeffrey Smith and Jennifer Seirafi

PERSPECTIVE

Emergency physicians are often confronted with patients who present with signs and symptoms of a confusional state.. The confusional state can be a harbinger of serious medical conditions or psychiatric disorders, and the emergency physician has a unique opportunity to diagnose these patients accurately and manage them appropriately. The emergency physician must decide what intervention is required, what emergency department diagnostic evaluation is necessary, who needs hospitalization, and who can be safely discharged. This chapter is divided into the topics of delirium and dementia. The focus is on the key pathophysiology and clinical features of delirium and dementia and the management of these patients.

Organic brain syndrome is a term that encompasses a host of abnormal cognitive states in which the unifying and defining feature is confusion (i.e., the inability to think with normal speed and clarity). Organic brain syndrome loosely defines a group of cognitive disorders that are secondary to central nervous system (CNS) disease, systemic disorders, or substance-related disorders. Organic brain syndrome is a rather nebulous term that the *Diagnostic and Statistical Manual of Mental Disorders: DSM-IV-TR*, text revision, eschews because the "organic" connotation implies that "functional" mental disorders are without a biologic basis.[1] In general, acute organic brain syndrome is synonymous with delirium, and chronic organic brain syndrome is synonymous with dementia. The essential finding present in both of these conditions is a confusional state manifest as global cognitive impairment. Global impairment involves all aspects of higher cortical function; patients may manifest disordered behavior, emotions, judgment, language, abstract thinking, and psychomotor activity. These disorders encompass a wide spectrum of behavioral abnormalities. Although certain aspects of the global impairment are more pronounced in certain individuals, minor deficiencies in other areas of cognitive functioning are usually present.

Several key features best distinguish delirium from dementia. These include the time course of disease evolution; the presence of autonomic system involvement; the level of disturbance of consciousness, orientation, and perception; and the acuity of the underlying disease process. Delirium is characterized by a disturbance in level of consciousness caused by widespread cerebral dysfunction. It is acute in onset and typically hours to days in duration, although resolution can take weeks. The patient usually has some autonomic system abnormalities, as seen in the prototypical condition of delirium tremens, with fever, tachycardia, hypertension, and diaphoresis. Delirium is a direct consequence of an acute systemic or CNS disturbance or insult. Dementia, on the other hand, tends to follow a more gradual course, with the evolution occurring over months to years. Although patients with dementia exhibit confusion, there is usually no disturbance in level of consciousness or perception. There are minimal or no manifestations of autonomic nervous system abnormalities. Most cases of dementia originate in the CNS, and many are irreversible.

When evaluating patients with a confusional state, the physician must keep in mind some basic guidelines:
1. He or she must decide whether this state represents delirium or dementia. The diagnosis may seem obvious. However, early symptoms and signs may go unrecognized by the physician unless an adequate history is obtained from the patient and family members and a careful examination, including a brief mental status examination, is performed.

2. Supportive care must be provided. This care may vary from aggressive airway and cardiovascular support to pharmacologic or physical restraint to simply placing the patient in a quiet room.
3. A diligent search must be initiated for the underlying disease process causing the global cognitive impairment.
4. The underlying illness that has been identified must be treated when possible. This is especially crucial with the delirious patient because immediate initiation of therapy can prevent permanent disability.

Physicians are commonly asked to distinguish a psychiatric or functional condition from an acute or chronic organic brain syndrome. Although the distinction may seem intuitively obvious to some physicians, it is not always readily apparent in the emergency setting. In a busy emergency department the physician must resist the temptation to distinguish psychiatric from organic illnesses prematurely on the basis of a single item in a patient's history or a previous psychiatric illness. To "clear" a patient medically for admission to a psychiatric or detoxification unit, a careful history and examination should be conducted to exclude a medical condition masquerading as a psychiatric disorder. In some patients it is not always possible to exclude a medical problem compounding an apparent psychiatric illness during a brief emergency department stay, and the medical evaluation should continue after these patients are hospitalized.

DELIRIUM

Delirium can be defined as an acute or subacute state of cognitive dysfunction caused by an underlying medical condition. Terms that have been used interchangeably with delirium include *acute organic brain syndrome, acute confusional state, reversible cerebral dysfunction, metabolic encephalopathy, toxic encephalopathy,* and *febrile delirium.* The word delirium is derived from the Latin *delirare,* which literally means "to go out of the furrow" (*lira,* Latin, "furrow"), but is used figuratively to mean crazy or deranged.[2]

Several key features are necessary to make a diagnosis of delirium (Box 102-1). Patients with delirium have disturbances in consciousness, cognition, and perception. These disturbances tend to occur over a short period of time (hours to days). The disturbance in consciousness may arise as an inability to focus attention. Deficiencies in cognition may be manifest as disorientation and memory deficits. Perceptual disturbances include hallucinations or delusions. The delirious patient may be somnolent or agitated, and the thought process may range from mildly disturbed to grossly disorganized. The clinical presentation may be subdued or explosive, and the course can fluctuate over minutes to hours. The patient's sleep-wake cycle may be altered or reversed; agitation is often present during the night. The patient's behavior is unpredictable. Historically, delirium referred to the hyperactive, agitated, emotionally labile patient (i.e., the individual with acute phencyclidine [PCP] intoxication or delirium tremens).

However, it is important to recognize that the spectrum of delirium is broad and can encompass hyperactive, depressed, and mixed states of consciousness.

The exact incidence of delirium in the overall emergency department population is unknown. However, the prevalence of delirium among elderly emergency department patients is approximately 10%.[3] Among hospitalized patients, the prevalence of delirium has been noted to be approximately 10% on a general medical service (16% to 24% in patients older than 70 years), 40% on the neurology service, 8% to 12% on the psychiatric service, and 35% to 80% on the geriatric service.[4] Geriatric patients are at particularly high risk for developing delirium; the incidence is also higher in women, whites, and young children.

Several predisposing factors for the development of delirium have been identified. Advanced age, dementia, and underlying medical illness are the factors most strongly associated with delirium, but multiple medications, drugs, and alcohol are also associated with delirium.[5] Severe psychological stress and sleep deprivation may facilitate the development of delirium. When delirium has developed, the patient's basic personality, coping style, intelligence, and level of education can modify manifestations of the acute disability.

Pathophysiology

At a cellular level, delirium is the result of widespread alteration in cerebral metabolic activity, with secondary deregulation of neurotransmitter synthesis and metabolism. Elders are particularly susceptible to any change in cerebral biochemical activity. Both the cerebral cortex and the subcortical structures are affected, producing changes in arousal, alertness, attention, information processing, and normal sleep-wake cycle.

Although the exact pathophysiology is not well understood, multiple neurotransmitters have been implicated in causing delirium. Acetylcholine transmission may be one of the important factors in the development of delirium. In addition to anticholinergic medicines causing delirium, serum anticholinergic activity is increased in older patients with delirium.[6] Increased serotonin levels have been found in hepatic encephalopathy, serotonin syndrome, sepsis, and psychedelic drug ingestion.[7] Some of the disturbances that occur in delirium are deficiencies of substrates for oxidative metabolism (e.g., glucose, oxygen); disturbances of ionic passage through excitable membranes; an increase in cytokines; an imbalance of normal noradrenergic, serotonergic, and cholinergic homeostasis; and, in some cases, synthesis of false neurotransmitters.[8] Drugs and exogenous toxins can produce delirium by direct effects on the CNS. Although the limbic system appears particularly vulnerable to the effects of these drugs, the cerebral hemispheres and the brainstem can also be profoundly affected.

Tricyclic antidepressants can cause delirium by causing cholinergic inhibition; sedative hypnotics such as the benzodiazepines depress activity in the CNS, especially in the limbic system, thalamus, and hypothalamus. Phenothiazines and other major tranquilizers accumulate in the brain at four times the plasma concentration and have similar depressant effects on the CNS. Barbiturates suppress axon impulse transmission. Narcotics affect CNS activity primarily by interacting with various opioid receptor sites. Depending on the opioid receptor type, the physiologic response may be analgesia, euphoria, sedation, dysphoria, delusions, or hallucinations. Psychedelic drugs probably act as agonists at serotonin receptor sites and increase activity in the cerebral cortex and limbic forebrain. PCP inhibits reuptake of dopamine, norepinephrine, serotonin, and γ-aminobutyric acid and may also act as a false neurotransmitter.

Hyperthermia and hypothermia can cause delirium, probably as a result of changes in the cerebral metabolic rate. In hypothermia, cerebral metabolism decreases 6% to 7% for each 1° C decrease in temperature from 35° C to 25° C. Temperature-dependent enzyme systems in the brain are unable to function at low temperatures. In hyperthermia, cellular damage with uncoupling of oxidative phosphorylation begins to occur at temperatures greater than 42° C. Patients suffering from heat stroke may have cerebral edema, degenerative neuronal changes (especially involving Purkinje cells of the cerebellum), and petechiae in the walls of the third and fourth ventricles. Delirium occurring at temperatures below 40° C is multifactorial in origin and not solely caused by increased core temperature.

Delirium caused by metabolic abnormalities such as hyponatremia, hypernatremia, hyperosmolarity, and hypercapnia is associated with a variety of metabolic disturbances at the neuronal and astrocyte levels, including impaired energy supplies, changes in resting membrane potentials, and changes in cellular morphology. The high brain ammonia concentration that occurs in hepatic encephalopathy may interfere with cerebral energy metabolism and the sodium-potassium adenosine triphosphatase pump. False neurotransmitters are present in patients with hepatic encephalopathy, and structurally there are increases in the number and size of astrocytes. Acute encephalopathy in renal

Table 102-1. Causes of Delirium ("I Watch Death")

Cause	Form
Infectious	Sepsis, encephalitis, meningitis, syphilis central nervous system (CNS) abscess
Withdrawal	Alcohol, barbiturates, sedative-hypnotics
Acute metabolic	Acidosis, electrolyte disturbance, hepatic and renal failure, other metabolic disturbances (glucose, Mg^{++} Ca^{++})
Trauma	Head trauma, burns
CNS disease	Hemorrhage, cerebrovascular accident, vasculitis, seizures, tumor
Hypoxia	Acute hypoxia, chronic lung disease, hypotension
Deficiencies	B_{12}, hypovitaminosis, niacin, thiamine
Environmental	Hypothermia, hyperthermia, endocrinopathies; diabetes, adrenal, thyroid
Acute vascular	Hypertensive emergency, subarachnoid hemorrhage, sagittal vein thrombosis
Toxins/drugs	Medications, street drugs, alcohols, pesticides, industrial poisons; carbon monoxide, cyanide, solvents, etc.
Heavy metals	Lead, mercury

Modified from Wise MG: Delirium: differential diagnosis for delirium: Critical items (I WATCH DEATH). In Yudofsky SC, Hales RE (eds): *The American Psychiatric Press Textbook of Neuropsychiatry,* 2nd ed. Washington, DC, American Psychiatric Publishing, 1992.

failure is caused at least partially by increased permeability of the blood-brain barrier to toxic substances such as organic acids. Changes in brain water volume probably play a role in the cognitive impairment that occurs in diabetic ketoacidosis, the nonketotic hyperosmolar state, and hyponatremia.

Most patients who have delirium have reduced cerebral metabolic activity. This reduction in cerebral metabolism is reflected by a decrease in the frequency of electroencephalogram (EEG) background activity. Exceptions are hyperthermia, sedative-hypnotic withdrawal, delirium tremens, and certain drug-induced states in which the cerebral metabolism is either normal or increased.

Etiology

The causes of delirium are legion (Table 102-1). Prescribed, over-the-counter, and illicit drugs are common causes of delirium. Among elders, medications are the most common cause of delirium, accounting for 22% to 39% of cases.[9] Acute cognitive dysfunction may be secondary to drug overdose, withdrawal, or adverse or idiosyncratic reactions. Delirium that begins when patients are taking a drug can disappear after the drug is stopped. However, abrupt discontinuation of other substances such as ethanol can precipitate delirium.

The list of commonly prescribed drugs causing delirium is quite extensive and includes antibiotics (antifungal, antimalarial, and antiviral agents; numerous antibacterial agents including the quinolones and macrolides), anticholinergic drugs (antihistamines, antispasmodics, tricyclic antidepressants), anticonvulsants, anti-inflammatory agents (corticosteroids, salicylates, nonsteroidal anti-inflammatory drugs), various cardiovascular medications (β-blockers, antidysrhythmics, antihypertensives, cardiac glycosides), sympathomimetics (phenylpropanolamine), sedative hypnotics, narcotics (transdermal fentanyl [Duragesic], morphine sulfate [Roxanol], hydromorphone HCl [Dilaudid], oxycodone HCl [OxyContin]), miscellaneous drugs (aminophylline, cimetidine, lithium, chlorpropamide), over-the-counter medications that have anticholinergic properties, and caffeine-containing products.[10-12]

Many "street" drugs with significant abuse potential such as hallucinogens, amphetamines, PCP, cocaine, and methylenedioxymethamphetamine (MDMA, ecstasy) can cause delirium.[13] Intoxication with any of the alcohols (e.g., ethanol, methanol, and ethylene glycol) can cause acute delirium. Ethanol withdrawal causes a full spectrum of symptoms ranging from mild anxiety to florid delirium tremens with agitation and autonomic hyperactivity. Delirium can also occur as part of the withdrawal syndrome associated with barbiturates, sedative hypnotics, opiates, and sympathomimetics.

Exposure to industrial chemicals (e.g., carbon disulfide, heavy metals, insecticides, cyanide, and carbon monoxide) can cause a wide range of symptoms that include acute delirium. In addition, ingestion of certain plants (e.g., nutmeg, foxglove, jimsonweed, and psilocybin-containing mushrooms) can cause delirium.

An acute confusional state can be one of the protean manifestations of a metabolic or nutritional abnormality. The most common metabolic disorder causing acute organic brain syndrome is diabetes mellitus. Hypoglycemia is the most common and readily reversible cause of acute confusion in the diabetic patient. Other causes of acute cognitive impairment in the diabetic patient are hyperglycemia, hyperosmolarity, and acid-base abnormalities. Fluid and electrolyte disorders can cause an altered sensorium, particularly in children and elders. Severe dehydration, hypernatremia, hyponatremia, hypercalcemia, hypomagnesemia, hypermagnesemia, hypophosphatemia, or hyperphosphatemia can cause delirium. Other metabolic causes include hypoxemia, hepatic insufficiency, renal insufficiency, and dysfunction of various endocrine glands, including hyperthyroidism, hypothyroidism, Cushing's syndrome, and hyperparathyroidism. Deficiency of niacin, pyridoxine, folic acid, and vitamin B_{12} may be associated with acute confusional states.

Delirium can be a prominent feature of any systemic infection, particularly in the very young, elders, or immunocompromised patients. Infectious and host factors together determine the degree of cognitive impairment. Extracranial infections that are associated with delirium include sepsis (particularly gram-negative sepsis), subacute bacterial endocarditis, legionnaires' disease, Rocky Mountain spotted fever, malaria, typhoid fever, toxic shock syndrome, and several viral infections, including influenza. Patients with CNS infections, including meningitis, encephalitis, and intracerebral abscess, may have acute cognitive dysfunction.

Acute delirium can occasionally be the first manifestation of an intracranial space-occupying lesion such as a subdural hematoma, tumor (especially frontal lobe), or hydrocephalus. The size and location of the lesion determine whether focal neurologic findings are present.

Other less common causes of delirium include CNS infarction in the distribution of the nondominant middle cerebral artery and the posterior cerebral artery. Patients who have collagen vascular disease with CNS vasculitis may have prominent neuropsychiatric manifestations, including acute delirium. Remote effects of visceral neoplasms unrelated to the presence of metastases can cause paraneoplastic encephalopathy, with symptoms of confusion, catatonia, and dementia.

Patients who are immunocompromised may have multiple and unusual causes of acute delirium. Patients with immunosuppression secondary to malignancy, drugs, or human immunodeficiency virus type 1 (HIV-1) infection may have acute brain dysfunction secondary to infection, complications of drug therapy, or the underlying disease itself. Patients with HIV-1 infection may experience delirium caused by various CNS infections (toxoplasmosis, *Cryptococcus* infection, cytomegalovirus infection, herpes simplex infection, retroviral, or bacterial) or CNS malignancy (lymphoma) with minimal focal neurologic findings. In addition, patients with HIV-1 infection may have delirium secondary to various approved or investigational drugs.

Acute confusional states have been reported to be a more common herald of the onset of physical illness in elders than fever, pain, and tachycardia.[14] In addition, elders are very susceptible to the toxicities of many commonly prescribed drugs, especially medications with anticholinergic properties.[15,16] Some of the most commonly prescribed drugs for elders, including cimetidine, ranitidine (Zantac), codeine, warfarin, isosorbide, theophylline, nifedipine (Procardia), ciprofloxacin, diltiazem, and digoxin, have been shown to cause significant impairments in tests of recent memory and attention in normal elders. Factors that predispose older adults to delirium include the aging brain, reduced capacity for homeostatic regulation, impaired vision and hearing, and age-related changes in the pharmacokinetics and pharmacodynamics of drugs. The etiology of delirium in elders is usually multifactorial.[9] Common causes include infections (especially pneumonia and urinary tract), congestive heart failure, myocardial infarction, ischemic bowel, hypovolemia, sodium depletion, dehydration, malnutrition, and pain. Alcoholism and alcohol withdrawal symptoms are also common in elders.

Clinical Findings

The clinical manifestations of delirium are as variable as the causes. The clinical presentation can be so subtle as to go unrecognized or be dramatic enough to disrupt the entire emergency department. The natural history of a patient's delirium can progress from apathy to marked agitation over the course of hours.

The nonspecific prodromal symptoms such as anxiety, restlessness, and insomnia typically progress over hours to days. The most consistent features of delirium are global cognitive impairment, relatively rapid onset of symptoms, and a clinical course that fluctuates over a period of hours to days. The fluctuation in symptoms over hours can be striking. Patients may be agitated and confused at home yet appear subdued and behave more appropriately during the emergency department evaluation.

Key aspects of cognitive impairment should become evident during a careful history and examination. Disturbance in attention is central to the diagnosis of delirium. The patient is easily distractible and has difficulty remaining focused on a particular topic or interacting with a single individual. Disorientation often accompanies the deficit in attention, but this finding is not invariably present. The patient is usually disoriented to time and occasionally to place; in extreme cases, there may be disorientation to person. Delirium, however, may be present in a patient who is completely oriented to person, place, and time. A mental status examination that consists solely of questions that assess orientation does not detect delirium in these instances.

The patient with delirium always has some degree of memory impairment. One of the hallmarks of delirium is impairment in short-term memory, with inability to learn and assimilate new information. Remote memory, or memory of past events, is usually preserved. Thought processes and speech may be disorganized. Disturbance in the sleep-wake cycle often occurs early in the course of delirium. A history of insomnia, restlessness, daytime sleepiness, and disturbances in sleep continuity can often be elicited from the patient, family, or friends. Characteristically, the sleep-wake cycle is reversed because patients sleep during the day and are awake throughout the night.

Perceptual disturbances, including misperception of the environment, poorly formed delusions, and hallucinations, are common in patients with acute organic brain syndrome. The delirious patient may experience visual, auditory, tactile, gustatory, or olfactory hallucinations, in contrast to patients with acute functional psychosis, who typically experience only auditory hallucinations. In addition, the delirious patient has a reduced capacity to modulate fine emotional expression and may demonstrate emotional lability. The patient typically manifests undue readiness to laugh, cry, or become angry and may shift rapidly from one form of emotional expression to another.

The cognitively impaired patient may provide an unreliable history, lacking key clinical information. Valuable information can often be obtained from family, friends, and prehospital personnel. One should inquire about the patient's medical history and current medical problems, including diabetes, hypertension, kidney or liver disease, and any neurologic or psychiatric problems. It is important to determine whether the patient is immunosuppressed or has risk factors that may predispose to an immunosuppressed state (prior transfusions, multiple sexual partners, homosexual activity, intravenous [IV] drug use, immunosuppressive therapy, or underlying malignancy). A detailed medication history, including the use of prescribed and over-the-counter medications, dietary supplements, and alcohol or substance abuse, is essential. It is important to identify when the symptoms began and whether any prior episodes of similar problems have occurred. Prehospital personnel should be able to provide information about the home environment, medication bottles belonging to the patient or found near the patient, and the possibility of trauma.

The physical examination should begin with a careful assessment of vital signs, including pulse oximetry, noting the presence of any abnormality. The delirious patient often manifests abnormal vital signs. The examination should include assessment of the head for signs of trauma and the pupils for symmetry of light reflex; funduscopic examination for hemorrhage or papilledema; examination of the ears for hemotympanum; evaluation of the neck for nuchal rigidity, bruits, and thyroid enlargement; evaluation of the heart and lungs; evaluation of the abdomen for organomegaly and ascites; and examination of the extremities for cyanosis. The skin should be carefully examined for rashes, petechiae, ecchymosis, splinter hemorrhages, and needle tracks. The neurologic examination should include assessment of the cranial nerves, motor strength, sensation, and presence of abnormal movements (e.g., tremor, asterixis, and myoclonus). The reflexes should be assessed for symmetry and presence of hyperreflexia or hyporeflexia. Overlap exists between findings that typically suggest a metabolic or structural neurologic problem. Asterixis is a hallmark of metabolic encephalopathy but can be seen in focal brain disease. Likewise, focal neurologic signs that are typically associated with structural CNS lesions can also be present in various metabolic abnormalities such as hypoglycemia, hyperglycemia, hepatic encephalopathy, uremia, and hypercalcemia.

A brief mental status examination should be performed in all patients suspected of having acute brain dysfunction. Although the concept is rather obvious, few physicians proceed beyond questions about the patient's orientation to person, place, and time when assessing mental status.[17,18] A physician's inability to diagnose subtle forms of delirium is directly related to failure to perform mental status testing, which all too often is perceived by physicians as time consuming, awkward to administer, and difficult to interpret.

Mental status testing should include assessment of orientation, memory, attention, concentration, constructional tasks, spatial discrimination, arithmetic ability, and writing. These aspects of cognitive functioning can be assessed in approximately 5 minutes. Typically, disorientation to the environment begins with inability to recall the date, followed by disorientation to day of the week, time, month, year, and then eventually to place; only in the most severe cases is the person unable to identify self. Memory assessment requires testing the patient's ability to repeat short series of words or numbers (immediate recall), to learn new information (short-term memory), and to retrieve previously stored information (long-term memory). Constructional apraxia is the inability to perform constructional tasks, such as drawing geometric figures or clock faces or connecting dots. Dysnomia (inability to name objects correctly) and dysgraphia (impaired writing ability) are two of the most sensitive indicators of delirium. Almost all acutely confused patients have writing impairments, including spatial disorganization, misspelling, and tremor.[19]

No single bedside cognitive test that can be administered quickly is ideal. Most of the studies evaluating the ability of the various tests to detect organic cognitive impairment have been performed on hospitalized patients. The Mini-Mental Status Examination (MMSE) developed by Folstein and colleagues has been validated more than any other test.[18] For hospitalized patients, this test has a sensitivity of 87% and a specificity of 82% for detecting organic brain syndrome.[20] Some investigators report slightly better results when the test is modified and age is added as a variable in the analysis.[21] The MMSE is a very resilient instrument for providing objective measures of mental status changes but it lacks measures of executive function and is insensitive to early signs in patients with mild dementia. As a result, the MMSE needs to be supplemented by other brief tests such as the category fluency test (e.g., name as many animals as possible in 1 minute) and the phonemic fluency test (e.g., name as many words beginning with the letter F as possible in 1 minute).[22]

The MMSE is one of the easiest and most reliable bedside tests that can be administered in the emergency department. It consists of a short series of questions that test orientation, registration (memory), attention, calculation, recall, and language (Figure 102-1). The registration section tests both immediate and short-term memory; the recall section also assesses short-term memory. The ability to recall two out of three objects has 81% sensitivity and 74% specificity for excluding organic brain syndrome. Asking the patient to subtract serial 7s backward from 100 tests attention, concentration, and arithmetic ability. This test is specific but not sensitive for absence of an organic brain syndrome; 40% to 50% of nondelirious, nondemented people fail to perform this test correctly. The MMSE can be performed in less than 5 minutes. A total score of 23 or below is considered abnormal and suggests an organic brain syndrome.

Another useful diagnostic tool is the Confusional Assessment Method (CAM); it has a sensitivity of 93% to 100% and specificity of 90% to 95%.[23] This simple tool has four key features used for screening for delirium: acute onset and fluctuating course, inattention, disorganized thinking, and altered level of consciousness. To make the diagnosis of delirium, the first two features and one of the last two must be present. It has been proved to be a valuable tool because of its ease and interobserver reliability. In addition, it has been shown to be more sensitive than clinical impression alone.[24]

Any bedside cognitive test has limitations. Very mild degrees of cognitive impairment can be missed with bedside screening tests. The patient's level of education and general intelligence can substantially affect the outcome. Furthermore, a single bedside test is ahistor-

Maximum Score	
	Orientation
5	What is the (year)(season)(date)(day)(month)?
5	Where are we (city)(state)(country)(hospital)(floor)?
	Registration
3	Name three objects: one second to say each. Ask the patient for all three after you have said them. Give one point for each correct answer. Repeat them until all three are learned. Count trials and record number.
	Attention and calculation
5	Serial sevens backwards from 100 (stop after five answers). Alternatively, spell WORLD backward.
	Recall
3	Ask for the three objects repeated above. Give one point for each correct answer.
	Language and praxis
2	Show a pencil and watch, and ask subject to name them.
1	Ask the patient to repeat the following; "no ifs, ands or buts."
3	(Three-stage command): "Take this paper in your right hand, fold it in half, and put it on the floor."
1	Read and obey the following: "Close your eyes." (Written on a piece of paper)
1	Write a sentence. (Must contain a noun, verb, and be sensible. Ignore grammar and punctuation.)
1	Copy this design (interlocking pentagons). Must contain all angles and two must intersect.

Figure 102-1. Mini-Mental Status Examination. (Redrawn from Folstein MF, Folstein SE, McHugh PR: "Mini-mental state": A practical method for grading the cognitive state of patients for the clinician. *J Psychiatr Res* 12:189, 1975.)

ical; it reflects a patient's cognitive functioning at only one point in time. To establish a diagnosis of delirium (or dementia), the physician must show that there has been a decline from the patient's baseline cognitive functioning.

Once it is established that a patient is in a delirious state, it is often difficult to determine the cause of delirium immediately. Delirium is a nonspecific CNS manifestation of a multitude of structural or metabolic insults. The history and physical examination may not immediately establish the specific cause of the acute brain dysfunction. Further evaluation is usually necessary to arrive at the cause of the delirium.

All medications or drugs that the patient is taking should be reviewed. It is usually the history and not the physical examination that leads the physician to suspect a specific overdose or adverse reaction to medication as the cause of the patient's delirium. The physical examination is not often helpful in determining the specific drug or class of drugs causing acute cognitive impairment. The one exception to this rule is toxidromes, which are constellations of signs and symptoms characteristic of intoxication with certain drugs or classes of drugs (see Chapter 145). Toxidromes can result from a chemical ingestion or exposure. Reversal of the symptoms with an antidote can confirm the diagnosis; however, when the history is not helpful, specific toxicology screens based on the physician's clinical suspicion may be useful.

Diagnostic Evaluation and Ancillary Studies

Delirium represents a true medical emergency because certain causes of delirium, when untreated, result in increased morbidity or death. Although some of the causes of delirium require diagnostic testing beyond the scope of what is obtainable or appropriate in the emergency department, many readily reversible causes can be diagnosed by a number of basic, readily available tests.

The following laboratory tests can be helpful in evaluating the delirious patient: a complete blood count (CBC) (hemoglobin, leukocyte count with differential, platelet count, and mean corpuscle volume), serum electrolytes, glucose, calcium, and urinalysis. The CBC may suggest unusual but potentially treatable abnormalities, such as thrombotic thrombocytopenic purpura, megaloblastic anemia, hyperviscosity from myelogenous leukemia, and unsuspected infection. The anion gap should be determined in all patients with altered mental status; an elevated anion gap (>15 mEq/L) may indicate the presence of unmeasured anions, such as sulfate in renal failure, ketoacids in diabetic or alcoholic ketoacidosis, lactate in postictal or hypotensive patients, and exogenous toxins such as ethylene glycol, methanol, or salicylates. A pulse oximeter measurement should be obtained for all patients (as part of initial vital signs) to screen for hypoxemia; if it is abnormal, an arterial blood gas measurement should be obtained. Febrile patients with suspected occult infection should have urinalysis and a chest radiograph. In elders, an electrocardiogram (ECG) should be obtained to exclude a silent acute coronary syndrome as a cause of the delirium. Ammonia level should be considered in patients with cirrhosis, ascites, or asterixis. Results of this initial screen may be normal, necessitating further evaluation. Despite these diagnostic evaluations, no cause is found for delirium in up to 16% of patients.[9]

Toxicology screens, although commonly overused as diagnostic tests, have limited utility in the evaluation of most patients with delirium. A toxicologic evaluation is appropriate in the presence of a specific toxidrome and when no obvious cause of the alteration in sensorium can be identified and the delirium is not resolving quickly. Laboratory techniques for toxicology screens consist of gas-liquid chromatography, high-performance liquid chromatography, immunoassays, and chemical and spectrometric techniques. Each of these general techniques can be adapted to detect a wide number of drugs and chemicals or focused to detect and quantitate certain drugs. Immunoassays are most widely used for discrete analysis. Immunoassays are very sensitive, with some quantitative ability, and have a rapid turnaround time of less than 1 hour. Gas chromatographic techniques are used for broad screens. Because various drugs have similar chromatographic patterns, the more information the clinician can provide to the laboratory, the better the yield of the toxicology screen. Gas chromatography–mass spectroscopy is more sensitive, can assay multiple drugs quantitatively compared with gas chromatography and immunoassays, and permits accurate determination of virtually any toxin. Unfortunately, this sophisticated system is expensive, with limited availability, has a prolonged turnaround time of more than 8 hours, and requires greater technical expertise.[25]

Additional laboratory studies that may be appropriate when the cause of delirium remains unknown include thyroid function studies, tests for vitamin B_{12}, folic acid, rapid plasma reagin (RPR), serum antinuclear antibodies, and urinary porphobilinogen, and screens for heavy metals. Although the results of such tests do not aid in the emergency physician's diagnosis, it may be reasonable to order these studies in conjunction with the admitting consultant.

Patients with a history of trauma, prior neurosurgical procedures, immunodeficiency, or focal neurologic findings should have a head computed tomography (CT) scan performed to detect structural lesions causing delirium. A noncontrast head CT scan is excellent for detecting acute and subacute subdural hematomas; subarachnoid hemorrhage; subacute, chronic infarctions; and most cerebral contusions. Contrast-enhanced CT scans are superior in detecting isodense subdural hematomas, some CNS mass lesions, and enhancing lesions such as those of toxoplasmosis in the immunocompromised host. Most patients with delirium have a normal or nondiagnostic head CT scan, and this does not completely exclude a primary CNS cause of the delirium. Early infarctions, small brainstem lesions, meningitis or encephalitis, closed head injuries, sagittal vein thrombosis, and small isodense subdural hematomas may be missed on a CT scan. In addition, approximately 2% to 10% of subarachnoid hemorrhages are not detected by head CT scan and require lumbar puncture (LP) for diagnosis. The role of magnetic resonance imaging (MRI) in the evaluation of the delirious patient has not been fully or clearly established. The MRI scan is superior to the CT scan in detecting small intercerebral and brainstem lesions, small brain contusions, certain encephalitides, and abnormalities of white matter (i.e., leukoencephalopathy). MRI perfusion scans are sensitive in detecting an acute vascular event. Another imaging technique that is potentially useful beyond the emergency department evaluation is positron emission tomography (PET) scanning, which provides information regarding cerebral metabolic activity.

An LP and cerebrospinal fluid (CSF) analysis are essential parts of the emergency department evaluation in selected patients with delirium. Patients with fever and cognitive dysfunction, even without meningismus, should have an LP performed in the emergency department to rule out meningitis. This is true particularly for a patient who is immunocompromised and unlikely to show all the classical signs of meningitis. Patients with underlying malignancies, hepatic or renal failure, acquired immunodeficiency syndrome (AIDS), elderly patients, alcoholics, and patients receiving chronic immunosuppressive therapy such as antimetabolites and steroids may not have the typical symptoms and signs of headache, fever, and stiff neck. Patients with focal neurologic findings, immunocompromised states, or findings of increased intracranial pressure should have a head CT before the LP. They should receive antibiotics in the emergency department before the CT scan. Patients with subacute presentations suggestive of a CNS infection (i.e., symptoms that develop over days to weeks) who do not appear toxic can have antibiotic therapy delayed until after the head CT scan and LP. Chronic tuberculous or cryptococcal meningitis does not require initiation of treatment while the patient is in the emergency department.

The spinal fluid should be sent for routine studies, including cell count, protein, glucose, Gram stain, acid-fast smear, India ink stain, Venereal Disease Research Laboratory (VDRL) test, and culture. Cryptococcal antigen should be obtained in selected patients. Patients with AIDS who have cryptococcal meningitis may have normal or nondiagnostic CSF cell counts, protein, and glucose levels; the diagnostic sensitivity is increased to 95% with an India ink stain and CSF cryptococcal antigen.

Although rarely practical in the emergency setting, the EEG can be a valuable diagnostic tool in determining the presence of delirium. In the case of severe delirium, bilateral diffuse symmetrical abnormalities are a relatively consistent feature. In most cases, the findings consist of a generalized slowing from the baseline activity, a nonspecific finding present in both delirium and dementia. The EEG shows nonfocal slow activity in the range 5 to 7 cycles/sec, a state that rapidly returns to normal as the delirium clears. Such slowing correlates well with the clinical evidence of reduced alertness and wakefulness and with diminished cerebral blood flow, oxygen consumption, and metabolic rate. This generalized slowing may or may not be associated with superimposed fast activity, which is usually secondary to alcohol withdrawal or psychoactive substances. In mild cases of delirium, the EEG lacks sensitivity. Normal EEG activity is between 8 and 12 cycles/sec. An individual's EEG can be slowed from its normal baseline with mild metabolic encephalopathy, but if that baseline is within upper normal limits and the slowing is not substantial, the EEG result is interpreted as normal. Serial EEG studies would reveal the abnormality because recovery of the patient from delirium would be accompanied by acceleration of the EEG rhythm. Furthermore, clinical changes often precede EEG changes, and normalization of the EEG often trails the return to baseline cognitive status.

Differential Diagnosis

Although many etiologies for delirium must be considered, the differential diagnosis is more limited. The differential diagnosis for the patient who has apparent delirium also includes functional psychiatric disorders and dementia. Depression, mania, paranoia, and schizophrenia may resemble delirium. Several clinical features are helpful in distinguishing between organic and functional syndromes (Table 102-2). Delirium represents a global cognitive process with clouding of the sensorium, multiple cognitive deficits, and abnormal vital signs. Functional psychiatric syndromes typically have an onset early in life, the patient is oriented, sensorium is usually clear, and cognition is normal. Patients with psychiatric disorders are occasionally unable or unwilling to cooperate with a complete mental status evaluation. In these instances, inconsistent responses to cognitive questions of similar difficulty, prior psychiatric history, normal vital signs, nonfocal neurologic examination, normal laboratory test results, and a normal EEG result support the diagnosis of a psychiatric disorder.

Table 102-2. Comparison of Delirium and Acute Psychosis

Characteristic	Delirium	Acute Psychosis
Onset	Acute	Acute
Vital signs	Typically abnormal (fever, tachycardia)	Normal
Prior psychiatric history	Uncommon	Common
Course	Rapid fluctuating	Stable
Psychomotor activity	Variable	Variable
Involuntary activity	Possible asterixis, tremor	Absent
Cognition function		
Orientation	Usually impaired	Occasionally impaired
Attention	Globally impaired	May be disorganized
Concentration	Globally impaired	Impaired
Hallucinations	Visual, visual and auditory	Primarily auditory
Delusions	Transient, poorly organized	Systematized
Speech	Pressured, slow, possibly incoherent	Usually coherent
Course	Typically resolves	Responds to therapy, recurrence common

Dementia, like delirium, is characterized by global cognitive impairment. Unlike delirium, dementia tends to be an insidious process that develops over months to years with little fluctuation over hours or days. Typically, the patient's vital signs are normal. Dementia occurs primarily in elders. However, it is important to remember that patients with dementia are at risk for developing delirium.

Management

Delirium is a medical emergency. The outcome depends on the cause of the delirium, the patient's overall health status, and the timeliness of treatment. The presence of hyperactive or hypoactive delirium has some prognostic significance. The hypoactive form of delirium tends to be more common in elders and has a worse overall prognosis, perhaps because it often goes unrecognized.[4] Some patients with delirium have a self-limiting course, whereas others ultimately progress to chronic cognitive impairment, coma, or death. The initial approach to the delirious patient should focus on diagnosing and treating the conditions that can cause increased morbidity if ignored while providing supportive measures for patients who have a self-limited course.

Prehospital care for the delirious patient should first address the patient's airway, breathing, and circulation. If it is impossible to determine whether the patient has normal oxygen saturation by pulse oximetry during transport, the patient should receive supplemental oxygen to treat potential hypoxemia. If the possibility of trauma exists, the cervical spine should be properly immobilized. An IV line should be established to provide normal saline or Ringer's lactate solution, and the serum glucose level should be determined by a bedside method. If the patient is hypoglycemic or if the serum glucose level cannot be assessed, the patient should receive 50 mL of 50% IV dextrose solution or 1 mg of intramuscular (IM) glucagon. For the patient who is neurologically depressed, naloxone hydrochloride should be administered by IV or IM injection. All patients should have a cardiac monitor. Combative patients should be restrained to protect both the patient and the prehospital personnel. Prehospital care providers should attempt to obtain a history of the patient's recent health, current medical problems, significant past medical history, and a comprehensive medication list from family members or friends at the scene. Whenever possible, a family member or friend should be encouraged to go to the hospital to provide additional information and all medications should be brought to the hospital.

Patients who have acute delirium should be screened quickly for readily reversible causes such as hypoglycemia, hypoxia, and narcotic overdose. Acute intoxication from a number of drugs or chemical agents, including tricyclic antidepressants, ethylene glycol, cholinesterase inhibitors, anticholinergic agents, carbon monoxide, and cyanide, requires prompt attention. Although supportive measures are the mainstay of treatment in most poisonings and intoxications, most of these toxins have specific antidotes.

Other conditions requiring immediate medical intervention include infections such as acute meningitis, encephalitis, or overwhelming sepsis. Patients who have signs of acute meningitis or overwhelming sepsis should optimally receive antibiotics within 30 minutes of arrival to the emergency department. Other emergency conditions that may arise as delirium and require immediate intervention include severe hypothermia, hyperthermia, and CNS vascular conditions, including hypertensive encephalopathy, acute epidural or subdural hematoma, subarachnoid hemorrhage, and acute cerebrovascular accidents. Patients with Wernicke's encephalopathy require immediate treatment with 100 mg of IV thiamine, with titration of additional doses until the ophthalmoplegia resolves. Resistance to thiamine may result from hypomagnesemia because magnesium is a cofactor for thiamine transketolase. Glucose administration in patients with severe thiamine deficiency may precipitate Wernicke's encephalopathy. The specific treatment of delirium tremens (and other alcohol withdrawal syndromes) involves the substitution of a long-acting drug that is cross-tolerant for the alcohol. Benzodiazepines are the agents of choice for inducing sedation.

Other causes of delirium are treated by supportive care in the emergency department while the identified abnormality is gradually corrected. Delirium secondary to dehydration, hyponatremia, hypernatremia, hypercalcemia, and hepatic or renal disease gradually resolves over hours to days with appropriate treatment. Acute organic brain syndrome secondary to substance abuse usually resolves over several hours as the patient detoxifies.

Supportive care for all patients with delirium includes providing an appropriate environment with adequate lighting, minimizing sensory overload, placing the patient in an area that can be easily observed by staff, and addressing the patient by name. Utilization of sitters may be necessary, because patients may require constant supervision. Whenever possible, sensory impairments should be minimized by replacing glasses and hearing aids.[26] Delirious patients should not remain unobserved, and stretcher side rails should be up at all times. It is important to protect the patient from self-harm or from injuring other patients or staff. In cases of hyperactive delirium, the patient may need to be restrained physically initially to protect both the patient and staff until pharmacologic control takes effect. Restraints should be viewed only as a temporizing action because they can increase agitation and the risk of injury to the patient.[27] Physical restraints in agitated patients have been associated with significant injuries and even death by asphyxiation and should not be used as a substitute for pharmacologic control.[28]

Pharmacologic restraint has become the cornerstone in behavioral management. Classes of drugs that have been used for delirium include the antipsychotics and benzodiazepines. The ideal sedating drug should have the following characteristics: low toxicity, ease of administration, short half-life, minimal effects on the cardiovascular and respiratory systems, and no effect on the seizure threshold. Antipsychotic medications that have been used to treat delirium include phenothiazines, butyrophenones, and the newer atypical antipsychotic agents.[29-33] Although no one drug is ideal, the butyrophenones, specifically haloperidol (Haldol), are considered the drugs of choice for control of agitation in acute delirium based on extensive clinical experience.[19] There is increasing evidence that the newer atypical antipsychotic agents (risperidone, olanzapine, ziprasidone, aripiprazole) may have better efficacy and fewer side effects than haloperidol in managing acute agitation.[29] These atypical antipsychotics are associated with fewer extrapyramidal side effects (especially akathisia and dystonia) and less sedation and have been shown to be more effective in controlling agitation acutely.[29-33] Phenothiazines and droperidol can cause orthostatic hypotension, lower the seizure threshold, and have anticholinergic effects, making them unacceptable for the treatment of delirium.

Droperidol, a butyrophenone pharmacologically similar to haloperidol, has similar sedating properties plus a potent antiemetic effect. Droperidol has been reported to have a faster onset of action than haloperidol.[34] However, in December 2001, the Food and Drug Administration gave a black box warning regarding the association of droperidol usage with QT prolongation and torsades de pointes, and its usage has been significantly curtailed.[35] The opioids morphine and meperidine (Demerol) are capable of inducing dysphoria and can exacerbate respiratory depression and hepatic encephalopathy. They should not be used for behavior control in the agitated delirious patient. Diazepam (Valium) should be avoided as a treatment for agitated behavior in most delirious patients because of its long half-life, respiratory depression, and risk of drug accumulation with repeated dosing. The benzodiazepines, however, are the drugs of choice for delirium caused by withdrawal from alcohol or sedative hypnotics in which a long duration of action is desirable.

Haloperidol is a potent dopamine-blocking medication with virtually no anticholinergic and minimal hypotensive effects. The main effect of the drug acutely is tranquilization. The drug can be easily titrated with IV administration. Although extrapyramidal side effects are common when it is administered on a regular basis for psychosis, the incidence of these side effects in patients receiving IV haloperidol for delirium with agitation is relatively low.[36] Studies of the acute administration of haloperidol report an 8% to 30% incidence of extrapyramidal side effects, with akathisias being most common and acute dystonia occurring in less than 10% of patients.[31,37] Haloperidol can prolong the QTc interval, but this effect is clinically insignificant in the vast majority of patients and does not require a pretreatment ECG. Caution should be used with patients taking medications that prolong the QTc (e.g., class Ia and III antiarrhythmics, certain antibiotics, inhibitors of the cytochrome P-450 system) and patients with acute coronary ischemia or uncompensated congestive heart failure.[38] Dosing should vary with the patient's level of agitation, age, and response to treatment. In most patients, 2 to 5 mg is well tolerated as an initial dose and can be titrated as needed. Higher doses may be required for younger patients and are generally well tolerated. Daily doses in excess of 100 mg have been given safely for agitated patients in the critical care setting. For elders, a lower initial dose of 0.50 to 1.0 mg has been recommended.[39]

Several well-controlled studies have shown that the combination of haloperidol and lorazepam (either intramuscularly or intravenously) can achieve more rapid control of agitated behavior than haloperidol alone.[37] In addition, the combination of a benzodiazepine with haloperidol may further reduce the already low incidence of extrapyramidal neuromuscular symptoms, such as acute dystonia, parkinsonism symptoms (e.g., rigidity and akinesia), and akathisia, which may occur with haloperidol alone.[37] Lorazepam (Ativan) seems to be particularly effective as an adjunct to haloperidol and poses minimal risk to the patient. Both drugs have short half-lives and do not have clinically important major active metabolites.

The atypical antipsychotics can be used acutely for management of agitation. These drugs have multiple mechanisms of action including antagonism of α_2-adrenergic, serotonin, dopamine, and histamine receptors. These drugs block the reuptake of dopamine and serotonin, and the newer drugs also have dopamine agonist effects (aripiprazole).[29] Compared with haloperidol, several of these atypical agents (ziprasidone, olanzapine) have been shown to control agitation more effectively with less sedation and fewer extrapyramidal side effects.[30-33,42] Resperidone has also been reported to be successful in controlling agitation in delirious patients, including elderly patients, starting with a dose of 0.25 to 0.50 mg.[39-41] Atypical antipsychotic agents for acute agitation have been slow to be adopted in clinical practice because of the limited studies of management of agitation and the significant clinical experience with haloperidol and lorazepam.

It is not possible to obtain informed consent regarding proposed diagnostic and therapeutic interventions from a patient suffering from delirium. In such cases, implied consent exists when a true emergency is present or clinically suspected because common law recognizes that a reasonable person would want to receive treatment in a true emergency even if impaired awareness at the time of treatment precludes giving informed consent. The physician may render treatment without informed consent to an incompetent patient in a life-threatening emergency situation. A delirious patient who needs urgent but not emergent medical treatment is in a legally ambiguous situation, and the treating physician has several options.[43] When time allows, the physician should involve the designated durable medical power of attorney and other significant others or family members in the evaluation and treatment process. This may be particularly appropriate when there are several equally effective treatment alternatives, particularly when risks are associated with the evaluation and treatment. A less desirable option for the physician is to obtain a second clinical opinion before proceeding. Ultimately, the course the emergency physician takes when caring for the delirious patient depends on the time available for obtaining consent or appointing an alternative decision-making authority; the risk-to-benefit ratio of diagnostic or therapeutic measures; the availability, sympathy, and decisiveness of family members; and knowledge of the patient's preferences. In addition, the emergency physician must remember to document these proceedings carefully.

Disposition

Patients with delirium secondary to acute drug intoxication may be discharged provided the process readily reverses itself during a short period of observation and the drug has no potentially serious delayed toxicity. Acute intoxication with ethanol, cocaine, heroin, MDMA, or PCP typically clears while the patient is in the emergency department. For most patients delirious from metabolic, infectious, or CNS processes, admission to the hospital is necessary for further diagnostic evaluation and treatment. The only readily reversible metabolic problem associated with delirium that can be completely managed in the emergency department is hypoglycemia.

For most patients without significant underlying medical illness who have delirium, the outcome is full recovery. After an episode of acute delirium, younger patients may experience mild cognitive dysfunction that lasts weeks to months. Elders, on the other hand, often experience persistent decline in their baseline level of functioning, with a loss of at least one activity of daily living after acute delirium.[44,45] Geriatric patients with delirium have longer hospital stays and longer rates of institutional care.[46] Delirium in elders hospitalized without baseline dementia is associated with higher 1-year mortality rates.[47] For elders, an episode of delirium, especially for those with baseline cognitive impairment, can have significant long-term consequences.

DEMENTIA

Dementia is a gradually progressive deterioration of cognitive function. Dementia is not a single disease entity but refers to a highly variable clinical syndrome. As with delirium, there are many different causes, and the prognosis depends on the underlying cause. A particular dementia can be classified as either potentially reversible or irreversible. Although most patients with dementia have an irreversible disease process, approximately 10% of dementias are reversible.[48] The emergency physician should recognize the signs and symptoms of potentially reversible forms of dementia, promptly identify the manifestations of acute illness in the demented patient, and be aware of the normal progression of irreversible dementias.

In 1907, Alzheimer described the clinical history and postmortem findings of a 50-year-old female patient with progressive dementia.[49] For decades, Alzheimer's disease was considered to be an uncommon dementia of younger patients known as "presenile" dementia. The more common dementia of elderly patients was believed to be secondary to atherosclerotic cerebrovascular disease and was referred to as "senile" dementia. Over the past 30 years, research has shown that the neuropathologic changes in the two are identical. Today, these two categories of primary degenerative dementias are collectively referred to as *Alzheimer's disease*. Alzheimer's dementia accounts for more than half of all dementias; the remaining cases are attributable to more than 50 known causes.

In 2003, the prevalence of Alzheimer's disease in the United States was 4.1 million; this number is expected to triple in the next 50 years.[50] It is the 12th leading cause of death in the United States. The prevalence is about 1% at age 60 but doubles every 5 years until it reaches 30% to 50% by 85 years of age.[51] The National Institutes of Health calculates that by 2030 there will be approximately 10 million people with Alzheimer's dementia.[52] The true incidence of dementia is unknown, and the disease is commonly underdiagnosed in lower socioeconomic groups and rural areas. Diagnosing dementia is problematic, and the true epidemiology of this disorder is beyond our current understanding.[53]

The American Psychiatric Association has defined criteria necessary for the diagnosis of dementia (Box 102-2). Several clinical features deserve emphasis. Intellectual impairment must involve both short-term and long-term memory. The cognitive impairment commonly involves abstract thinking, judgment, and other higher cortical functions. Although mild decline in intellectual functioning can be part of the normal aging process, gross intellectual impairment and confusion should not be considered part of normal aging. Another important feature in the diagnosis of dementia is that the cognitive disturbance must significantly interfere with interpersonal relationships, work, and social activities of the individual.

BOX 102-2. Diagnostic Criteria for Dementia

A. The development of multiple cognitive deficits manifested by both of the following:
  1. Memory impairment (impaired ability to learn new information or to recall previously learned information)
  2. One (or more) of the following cognitive disturbances:
    a. Aphasia (language disturbance)
    b. Apraxia (impaired ability to carry out motor activities despite intact motor function)
    c. Agnosia (failure to recognize or identify objects)
    d. Disturbance in executive functioning (i.e., planning, organization, sequencing, abstracting)
B. The cognitive deficits cause significant impairment in social or occupational functioning and represent a significant decline from a previous level of functioning.
C. The deficits do not occur exclusively during the course of a delirium.

Modified from American Psychiatric Association: *Diagnostic and Statistical Manual of Mental Disorders,* 4th ed, text revision, Washington, DC, American Psychiatric Association, 2000.

BOX 102-3. Classification of Dementias

Primary Cortical Dementias
Alzheimer's disease
Pick's disease

Primary Subcortical Dementias
Huntington's chorea
Parkinson's disease
Progressive supranuclear palsy
Secondary dementia
Drug/toxin-induced
Metabolic or electrolyte disturbance
Intracerebral disorders
Trauma
Mass effect (tumor, hematoma, abscess)
Hydrocephalus
Cerebrovascular disease (multi-infarct dementia)
Endocrinopathies
Infectious (intracranial) chronic meningitis, encephalitis, abscess. HIV-1, slow virus, neurosyphilis
Nutritional
Psychiatric (pseudodementia)
Other (e.g., collagen vascular disease, paraneoplastic)

HIV-1, human immunodeficiency virus type 1.

Dementia can be classified according to the degree of cognitive impairment. Mild dementia implies some impairment of work and social activities; however, the capacity for independent adequate personal hygiene and independent living remains intact. With moderate dementia, independent living is hazardous and some degree of supervision is necessary. In severe dementia, continual supervision and often custodial care are needed.

Demented patients often have longer hospitalizations for the same acute medical illness than those without dementia, and the life expectancy of demented patients is 6 to 8 years less than that for nondemented age-matched control subjects.[54]

Etiology

Dementia may be caused by more than 50 different disease states (Box 102-3). Broadly, dementia may be classified as either primary degenerative dementia or secondary dementia; the latter category includes all the potentially reversible dementias. Primary degenerative dementias include Alzheimer's disease, vascular dementia, dementia with Lewy bodies, the subcortical dementias involving the basal ganglia and thalamus (e.g., progressive supranuclear palsy, Huntington's chorea, Parkinson's disease), and *dementia of the frontal lobe type,* which includes Pick's disease. Most dementia is Alzheimer's type. Vascular dementia is also common, accounting for approximately 10% to 20% of all dementias. Dementia with Lewy bodies, clinically manifested by prominent extrapyramidal movements, has been found to be the second most common type of dementia.[55] A smaller percentage of dementias are attributable to causes such as anoxic encephalopathy,

hepatolenticular degeneration, tumors, and slow virus infections.

Adverse drug reactions and metabolic abnormalities in patients can cause either an acute delirium or a gradual progressive dementia. Drug-induced dementia occurs primarily in elders and can be caused by various psychotropic drugs (e.g., sedative-hypnotics, minor or major tranquilizers, lithium, antidepressants), antihypertensive medications, anticonvulsants, anticholinergics, and miscellaneous medications such as L-dopa. Dementia may also be caused by heavy metals and other exogenous agents, such as carbon monoxide, carbon disulfide, and trichloroethylene.

Endocrinopathies that can cause secondary dementia include hypothyroidism, hyperthyroidism, parathyroid disease, Addison's disease, Cushing's disease, and panhypopituitarism. Nutritional deficiencies that cause dementia include thiamine deficiency (Wernicke's syndrome), niacin deficiency (pellagra), vitamin B_{12} deficiency, and folate deficiency. Dementia can be caused by intracranial space-occupying lesions and hydrocephalus. Repetitive intracranial trauma, such as boxers sustain, can produce a chronic organic brain syndrome without evidence of hematoma or significant contusion (dementia pugilistica).[56] Intracranial processes that may eventually lead to a chronic organic brain syndrome include infections with slow viruses, HIV-1, chronic meningitis (tubercular or fungal), brain abscess, and neurosyphilis. A patient with dementia who has an HIV-1 infection should be evaluated for the cause of the dementia and should not be assumed to have cognitive impairment solely resulting from direct HIV-1 infection. Toxoplasmosis, cryptococcal meningitis, herpes virus, cytomegalovirus, varicella-zoster, papovavirus (progressive multifocal leukoencephalopathy), and malignancy can cause progressive cognitive impairment in this compromised group of patients and must be excluded.[57]

Depression in elders may closely mimic dementia. Diagnosing pseudodementia, or depression masquerading as dementia, can be difficult and may require therapeutic interventions to confirm the clinical diagnosis of depression. Confounding the issue, depression often coexists with dementia; one study found that 12% of patients with dementia were depressed.[58]

Pathophysiology

Dementia is characterized by many different pathophysiologic findings. Alzheimer's disease is the best-understood dementia and involves several characteristic anatomic, pathologic, and neurochemical changes. On a broad scale, there is cortical atrophy most prominent in the temporal and hippocampal regions, caused by progressive synaptic and neuronal loss in the cerebral gray matter.[59] This atrophy is generally followed by loss of white matter (subcortical atrophy). Atrophy secondary to neuronal death is an important manifestation of Alzheimer's disease. Cell loss does occur with the normal aging process but not to the extent seen in senile dementia. The brain of the patient with Alzheimer's disease typically has diffuse atrophy, with widening of the sulci and some dilation of the cerebral ventricles, but these characteristics can be found in some normal elders. Also, not all patients with dementia have gross cerebral atrophy. There is no ischemic component to this disease.

Histologic findings characteristic of Alzheimer's disease are neurofibrillary tangles and senile plaques. The neurofibrillary tangles are intraneuronal paired helical filaments composed of the abnormally phosphorylated protein tau, the structural protein involved in the regeneration of neurites.[52] In demented patients, these tangles occur in great numbers throughout the cerebral cortex; only limited numbers can be seen in nondemented elders (primarily in the hippocampus region) and in a variety of other diseases. The density of neocortical tangles correlates with the severity of dementia.[60] Senile plaques are extracellular lesions composed of degenerating neuronal processes and abnormal beta-amyloid protein. These plaques are extensively spread throughout the cerebral cortex. The plaques can be numerous when the dementia is clinically mild.[61] Other consistent neurohistopathologic changes in Alzheimer's disease include granulovascular degeneration, Hirano bodies, beta-amyloid deposition in the small cortical blood vessels, and neuronal loss in the limbic area.[62]

Many biochemical abnormalities have been described in patients with Alzheimer's disease. The neurons using acetylcholine as a neurotransmitter in the hippocampus, parietal, and temporal areas are susceptible to these pathologic changes.[63] There is a decrease in the neurotransmitter acetylcholine in patients with dementia. The enzyme choline acetyltransferase synthesizes acetylcholine in the brain. Levels of this enzyme decrease with aging; however, in patients with Alzheimer's disease, the levels may decline to 20% of those of age-matched control subjects.

There are several risk factors for Alzheimer's disease: age, family history, female gender, low education level, and history of head trauma. New research has led to the discovery of new risk factors and possible mechanisms causing Alzheimer's disease.[64] One allele for the apolipoprotein E gene (ApoE) on chromosome 19 has been associated with both familial and sporadic late-onset Alzheimer's disease.[65] Apolipoprotein E is responsible for transporting the cholesterol and phospholipids necessary for dendritic and synaptic repair. There are several allelic variants, but those homozygous or heterozygous for the E-4 variant have an increased risk for the development and expression of the disease.[66] Abnormalities on chromosomes 1, 14, and 19 have been associated with Alzheimer's disease. Free radicals have been postulated to cause crosslinking of beta-amyloid, and antioxidants have been shown to reduce the formation of beta-amyloid.[67] Also, there may be an inflammatory response associated with Alzheimer's disease; this is supported by data indicating that anti-inflammatory therapy has an inverse association with Alzheimer's disease.[68,69]

The frontotemporal dementias (FTDs) are less prevalent than Alzheimer's disease and are categorized by a frontal and temporal atrophy caused by cell death. Five types of neuropathology can be present, depending on the subtype of FTD. Pick's disease, the classical FTD, involves Pick bodies, which are intracytoplasmic argyrophilic inclusions in the frontal and anterior cortex and hippocampus.[68] The most common histologic finding in the FTD is prominent cell loss and gliosis in the frontal and temporal cortex termed *dementia lacking distinctive histology.*[69]

Dementia with Lewy bodies is characterized by extrapyramidal features and cognitive impairment. The Lewy body, an eosinophilic structure found in the neuron, is the hallmark of Parkinson's disease but is found in other dementias. Other dementias with extrapyramidal features include Huntington's disease, Wilson's disease, and progressive supranuclear palsy.

Approximately 10% to 20% of dementias are secondary to multiple vascular insults to the CNS (multiinfarct dementia [MID]). The multiple infarcts typically involve the cerebral hemispheres and basal ganglia. MID often has an earlier age of onset than Alzheimer's disease and occurs more often in adult men and patients who have risk factors for atherosclerosis. Uncontrolled hypertension, diabetes, atrial fibrillation, tobacco use, hypercholesterolemia, and hypercoagulable states may greatly increase the risk of MID. Usually, the patient has a history of cerebrovascular infarcts; however, a small number of patients with MID do not have a history of prior strokes. Approximately 29% of dementias are a mixed variety and contain components of both ischemic cerebrovascular disease and Alzheimer's dementia.[70]

Slow virus infections of the CNS can cause a progressive dementia that is irreversible. In slow virus infections, months to years pass between infection with the virus and the appearance of clinical illness. When the diagnosis has been established, progression may occur over several months or years. Slow virus infections of the CNS are caused by both conventional viruses and unconventional virus-like agents known as prions. The conventional viruses tend to provoke a mild inflammatory response before the onset of clinical symptoms, whereas the unconventional viruses are insidious, residing within the cells for long periods without causing detectable cytopathic changes. There is a variable presence of elevated levels of circulating antibodies or no detectable immune response. *Prion* refers to a proteinaceous infectious particle that seems to have the ability to start a chain reaction that changes the shape of benign protein molecules into abnormal, slowly destructive forms. Prions are present in Creutzfeldt-Jakob disease (CJD) and variant CDJ.[71]

The CNS inflammatory conditions caused by conventional viruses include subacute sclerosing panencephalitis from the measles virus, progressive multifocal leukoencephalopathy (PML) from the JC virus (a papovavirus), progressive rubella encephalitis, and infection from HIV. The unconventional viral infections include kuru, CJD, and variant CJD (which appears linked to bovine spongiform encephalopathy, the causative agent in "mad cow disease"). The latter diseases cause a fine vacuolation of the nervous tissue;

hence, they are referred to as *subacute spongiform viral encephalopathies.*

Progressive multifocal leukoencephalopathy (PML) occurs in patients who have immunodeficiency (e.g., AIDS), are taking immunosuppressive medication, or have an underlying malignancy. This disease is consistently associated with disorders of cell-mediated immunity. It is usually caused by a reactivation of the latent JC virus, which resides in either the brain or lymphatic system. The oligodendrocytes are infected by the virus, causing widespread demyelination.

One of the most prevalent slow virus infections causing progressive dementia is HIV-1 infection. HIV may produce a primary neurotrophic disorder in addition to causing the immunologic compromise that permits other viruses to replicate and damage nervous tissue. The most prevalent dementia caused by HIV is HIV dementia or AIDS dementia complex, which occurs in about one quarter of patients with AIDS. The exact pathology is still unclear, but it is believed to be caused by the HIV-1 virus targeting the microglia and the macrophages, which may produce cytotoxic substances such as tumor necrosis factor and interleukins. Pathologic changes, mostly in the hippocampus and basal ganglia, include atrophy, ventricular dilation, and fibrosis; microscopically, there are multinucleated giant cells, perivascular mononuclear inflammation, and neuronal loss.[72,73]

Several of the potentially reversible causes of dementia are also associated with neuropathologic or neurochemical abnormalities. There is evidence suggesting that neurochemical abnormalities may contribute to the depression in pseudodementia. Normal pressure hydrocephalus (NPH) generally affects a younger age group; 50% of patients are younger than 60. Most of the conditions that cause hydrocephalus involve a defect involving the arachnoid villi in the uptake of CSF, which results in gradual ventricular dilation. Primary hydrocephalus is not associated with any predisposing neurologic disease. Secondary hydrocephalus results from some antecedent disorder, such as subarachnoid hemorrhage, head injury, or meningitis.

Several drugs may cause subacute or chronic cognitive dysfunction, particularly in elders. Because elders have diminished CNS cholinergic reserves, medications with anticholinergic properties such as tricyclic antidepressants can often tip the scales to cognitive impairment. Drug-induced dementia may be dose related or idiosyncratic. Discontinuation of the suspected drug is frequently the only way to exclude a medication as the cause of cognitive dysfunction.

Ethanol, a commonly abused substance, can cause more than one type of chronic organic brain syndrome. The neurotoxicity of ethanol appears to be independent of thiamine deficiency. Alcoholism can cause cerebral cortical atrophy, but no single alcohol-related dementia syndrome exists. It is estimated that approximately 20% of chronically demented patients have a history of alcoholism. One rare progressive dementia attributable to alcoholism is Marchiafava-Bignami disease, which is similar clinically to frontal lobe dementias and pathologically involves destruction of the central regions of the corpus callosum.[74] Korsakoff's psychosis, which results from thiamine deficiency, is primarily a memory disorder; intellectual functioning is not impaired to the same degree as in the primary degenerative dementias.

Clinical Features

The symptoms, signs, and progression of chronic cognitive impairment are rarely so diagnostic as to permit identification of the specific cause of the dementia. Typically, gradual progression of symptoms is independent of the specific causes. Because Alzheimer's disease is the most common cause of dementia, a more detailed discussion of the progression of this entity is presented.

Senile dementia begins insidiously. Signs and symptoms of cognitive dysfunction may be present for months to years before the diagnosis is made. The earliest symptoms and signs of Alzheimer's disease are often vague and nonspecific because the patient manifests anxiety, depression, insomnia, frustration, and somatic complaints that are often more prominent than the memory loss. Patients often deny any cognitive deficits and change the subject of conversations frequently rather than admit their increasing forgetfulness. The subtle signs of dementia are often overlooked by physicians in this phase of the disease.[75] Depression is often the initial sign of Alzheimer's disease and is present in up to 40% of cases.[76] Early in the illness, short-term memory is affected, with forgetfulness of recent events such as appointments and names of new acquaintances. Patients often repeat questions. The memory impairment may cause them to withdraw from social situations and recreational pursuits. Complex tasks may cause anxiety and confusion. The patient often has difficulty with interpersonal relationships. The patient's affect may be shallow and labile, and minor events may trigger inappropriate laughter or tears. Compensation for early deficits includes excessive orderliness and avoidance of situations in which the defects may be observed. Patients in this early phase who are treated with antidepressants with strong anticholinergic properties may have their symptoms worsen. Sedative-hypnotics prescribed for anxiety may also increase cognitive dysfunction.

As the dementia progresses, cognitive deficits are more obvious and should be readily apparent on a mental status examination. Recent memory is clearly impaired, and there may be some impairment of remote memory. Most patients demonstrate language deficits and difficulty with spontaneous speech.[77] They have difficulty naming objects (anomia). They may demonstrate circumstantiality and tangentiality in their thought processes. They make errors in judgment and easily become lost or confused. Receptive dysphasia, dyslexia, dysgraphia, and dyspraxia may be apparent in more than 50% of patients, and as many as 50% have delusions, usually of the paranoid type.[78] Atypical presentations of Alzheimer's disease include aphasia, visual agnosia, right parietal lobe syndrome, focal neurologic findings, extrapyramidal signs, gait disturbances, and pure memory loss. In the final stage of dementia, patients have marked cognitive impairment, with profound memory disturbances and significant personality changes. These patients suffer from apraxia, the loss of fine motor skills. They are often bedridden and unable to perform any of the routine activities of daily living.

Family or friends usually bring the patient to the emergency department because of a sudden worsening in mental status, a change in the patient's activities (e.g., refusal to eat), or a change in the ability of the caregiver to manage the patient. Many elders with dementia have a superimposed delirium on presentation to the emergency department. Acute confusion superimposed on a baseline dementia may be a more common herald of the onset of physical illness in demented elders than fever, pain, or tachycardia. Precipitating events causing deterioration in mental status include stroke, silent myocardial infarction, pain (i.e., ischemic bowel, dissecting aneurysm), dehydration, and infection. Systemic illnesses more commonly cause acute cognitive decline than primary cerebral events. The most common sites of infection are the urinary tract and lungs.

Because Pick's disease dementia affects the frontal and temporal lobes, patients often have frontal lobe release signs, including dramatic behavioral changes of disinhibition and social inappropriateness. In contrast, patients with Alzheimer's disease initially have memory problems with preservation of social skills until later in the disease process.

Several basal ganglia degenerative disorders have dementia as a prominent finding. These include Huntington's, Parkinson's, and Wilson's diseases and supranuclear palsy. Several features distinguish cortical and subcortical dementias (Table 102-3). The most striking feature of these dementias is the movement disorder that tends to occur early in the illness. Other features of these dementias include slowness of speech, hypotonia, and dysarthria, which occur early and progress to mutism.

Patients with vascular dementia have a stepwise deterioration in mental status with each cerebrovascular insult. The clinical presentation may follow one of two scenarios. In the more common scenario, the patient has suffered several strokes that involve large volumes of cortical and subcortical structures in both hemispheres. The patient exhibits dementia along with other neurologic disabilities (e.g., focal weakness, hyperreflexia, extensor plantar response). The other group of patients have a more subtle presentation. These individuals are characteristically hypertensive and suffer multiple tiny infarcts (lacunae) that involve deep subcortical structures. There may be no focal neurologic residua except progressive dementia with psychomotor retardation.

The clinical manifestations of slow virus CNS infections are protean. After an insidious onset of mental deterioration in subacute sclerosing panencephalitis, there is a rapid progression that is associated with myoclonic jerks, incoordination, and ataxia. In PML, neurologic signs and symptoms reflect diffuse asymmetric involvement of both cerebral hemispheres. Sporadic CJD, of unknown etiology, tends to affect older persons, with a rate of disease among 50- to 70 year-old persons of 1 per million. These patients have rapidly evolving dementia with myoclonus. The hallmarks of the disorder are mental deterioration, multisystem neurologic signs, myoclonus, and typical EEG changes that evolve over months. Most patients die within the first 6 months after the onset of clinical symptoms. Variant CJD appears linked to consumption of certain beef products of animals with bovine spongiform encephalopathy (mad cow disease). Variant CJD affects younger patients (median age 24) with key features including early affective symptoms progressing to cognitive impairment and gait disturbances, and ultimately leading to progressive neurologic deterioration. The incubation period appears to be in the range of 10 to 15 years and most patients die within 14 months.[71]

AIDS dementia is a subacute dementia with an insidious onset and gradual progression that is often accompanied by motor system abnormalities. The early cognitive impairment includes poor recall, impaired concentration, and difficulty in performing complex sequential tasks. Initially, the symptoms may appear to be manifestations of a depressive illness. Slowing of verbal and motor responses and reduced spontaneity are typically present. A normal level of consciousness may be maintained into the late stages of the illness. The AIDS dementia complex may be more acute after surgery, use of psychoactive drugs, infections, and other stresses. The AIDS dementia complex is primarily of a subcortical nature with a predilection for involvement of frontal white matter. Aphasia and apraxia are uncommon; however, verbal and motor slowing occur.

The most common treatable dementia is pseudodementia, or depression. The clinical distinction between depression and dementia is difficult, and the coexistence of depression and dementia is common in mildly demented individuals. A number of distinguishing features may suggest that the problem is depression rather than dementia (Table 102-4). The onset of cognitive changes in pseudodementia can often be pinpointed, and symptoms are usually of short duration before medical help is sought. The progression of symptoms is rapid and the family is usually aware of the severity of the dysfunction. The patient commonly has a history of psychiatric illness. Patients with pseudodementia usually complain of cognitive dysfunction and empha-

Table 102-3. Characteristics of Cortical Versus Subcortical Dementia

Characteristic	Cortical	Subcortical
Appearance	Unremarkable	Disheveled
Activity	Normal	Slow
Gait	Normal	Posturing, ataxic
Movements	Normal	Tremor, chorea, slow
Speech	Normal	Slow, dysarthric
Language	Anomia, paraphasia	Normal
Cognition	Impaired	Impaired
Memory	Disordered learning	Forgetful
Visual-spatial	Constructional deficit	Sloppy

Table 102-4. Comparison of Dementia and Pseudodementia

Characteristic	Dementia	Pseudodementia (Depression)
Onset	Insidious	More precise, rapid
Prior psychiatric history	Absent	Present
Demeanor	Unconcerned	Distressed
	Conceals deficits	Emphasizes deficits
	Struggles at tasks	Limits effort
	Loss of social skills	Social skills intact
Affect	Shallow, labile	Depressive, pervasive
Cognitive function	Attention impaired	Attention preserved
	Cooperative	Poor effort, despair
	Recent memory more impaired than remote memory	Impaired recent and remote memory
	Consistent testing performance	Variable performance of similar tasks
Course	Chronic, progressive	Response to therapy

size their failures and disabilities. The affective change is often pervasive and the patient makes little effort to perform simple tasks. Loss of social skills usually occurs early in the illness, and patients communicate a strong sense of distress and inability to function. Intellectual functioning in pseudodementia is often difficult to assess because of lack of cooperation of the patient or inconsistent findings on neuropsychometric testing. Attention and concentration are often intact, but patients commonly give answers such as "I don't know" on tests of orientation, concentration, and memory. Memory loss for recent and remote events is usually equally severe, and there may be marked variability in the performance of tasks that have similar degrees of difficulty. Tasks of high capacity (e.g., testing delayed memory with distraction) may be helpful in identifying the depressed patient.[79]

The classical triad of progressive dementia, ataxia, and urinary incontinence occurs in patients with NPH, which affects younger patients than primary degenerative dementia. More than half of the reported cases involve individuals younger than 60 years. Hydrocephalus secondary to prior head trauma or infection has a more favorable prognosis than primary hydrocephalus.

Approximately 20% of reversible dementia is secondary to an intracranial mass. Patients may exhibit focal or nonfocal neurologic findings. A nonfocal neurologic examination can be caused by a tumor in the frontal, subfrontal (i.e., large prolactinoma), or temporal lobe region and occasionally by an extracerebral mass such as a subdural hematoma or meningioma.[80]

Of reversible dementias, 10% to 15% are secondary to medications or chemical intoxications. Elders may have increased susceptibility to the toxicities of commonly prescribed drugs. Age-related changes in metabolism can prolong the half-lives of many medications. Polypharmacy is a common problem in elders, which increases the likelihood of adverse drug interactions. A temporal relationship does not always exist between initiation of a medication and onset of cognitive impairment. Furthermore, alcoholism is common in elders and may contribute to chronic cognitive impairment. The clinical presentation of a patient with a drug-related or toxin-related dementia may be indistinguishable from that of a patient with a primary degenerative process.

Differential Diagnosis

Subacute or chronic cognitive decline may be secondary to a dementing illness or a manifestation of senescent forgetfulness, delirium, or depression.

Senescent forgetfulness is an inevitable reality of aging. Mild impairment of both short-term and long-term memory is usually present. Unlike dementia, the cognitive disturbance in senescent forgetfulness does not interfere with work or customary social activity.

In most cases, the clinical distinction between delirium and dementia is obvious. In both delirium and dementia, global cognitive processes are impaired. Dementia has an insidious onset, whereas delirium typically is abrupt in presentation. Dementia is a slowly progressive condition; delirium has a fluctuating course, varying over the span of hours. The level of consciousness is usually normal in dementia and reduced or agitated in delirium. Hallucinations and fluctuations in psychomotor activity are typically present in delirium and absent from dementia. The dexamethasone suppression test, EEG, CT scan, neuropsychological testing, and amobarbital interview are not completely reliable in diagnosing pseudodementia.

Diagnostic Strategies

The emergency department evaluation of the patient with possible dementia should include a medical and psychiatric history plus a collateral history from family and friends. Physical examination should include a detailed neurologic examination with mental status evaluation. Dementia is often unrecognized in the patient who is alert, pleasant, and cooperative. A systematic mental status examination can play a key role in the early identification of dementia in patients who have maintained social and conversational ability.

All patients who have a dementing illness require a basic laboratory and radiologic evaluation to detect treatable dementia (Box 102-4). A thorough physical examination is usually not helpful in detecting treatable dementias because of the considerable clinical overlap with irreversible dementias. The basic laboratory evalu-

BOX 102-4. Diagnostic Evaluation for Dementia

History (patient, family, friends)
Review of medications
Physical examination, including neurologic evaluation
Mental status examination

Laboratory Evaluation
CBC
Electrolyte, glucose levels
Liver, renal function studies
Urinalysis
Thyroid function studies
VDRL, FTA

Radiographic Evaluation
Chest radiograph
Head CT scan

Additional Evaluation
Blood and urine screens for drugs, heavy metals
Erythrocyte sedimentation rate
HIV screen
Antinuclear antibody
Oxygen saturation, ABG
Serum B_{12} and folate
Lumbar puncture
MRI head scan
EEG
Neuropsychometric testing
Evoked potentials (visual, brainstem auditory, somatosensory)

ABG, arterial blood gases; CBC, complete blood count; CT, computed tomography; EEG, electroencephalogram; FTA, fluorescent treponemal antibody; HIV, human immunodeficiency virus; VDRL, Venereal Disease Research Laboratory.

ation should include CBC, determination of electrolytes and glucose levels, tests of liver and renal function, thyroid function tests, serologic tests for syphilis, and antibody tests for HIV infection. It is important that a serum fluorescent treponemal antibody absorption (FTA-ABS) test be performed in addition to a VDRL test because the serum VDRL may yield negative results in patients who have tertiary syphilis. The radiologic evaluation should include a noncontrast head CT scan; if it is normal, a contrast-enhanced CT or MRI may be obtained electively during follow-up care.

Certain patients require additional laboratory evaluation, which may include serum B_{12} and folate levels, erythrocyte sedimentation rate, fluorescent antinuclear antibody (FANA), urine corticosteroid levels, and urine screens for drugs and heavy metals. Selected patients should undergo an LP with CSF analysis, MRI scanning, PET scan, EEG (in CJD, characteristic slowing and periodic complexes may be present), neuropsychological testing, visual evoked potentials, brainstem auditory evoked potentials, and somatosensory evoked potentials.

In Alzheimer's disease, a cranial CT scan may be normal or show cerebral atrophy, especially in the gyri of the association areas of the cerebral cortex. Cerebral atrophy is a function of age and can occur in both normal and demented patients. The basic usefulness of the CT scan in the evaluation of dementia is to exclude the presence of hydrocephalus and space-occupying lesions. The EEG is rarely helpful in establishing the diagnosis of senile dementia.

No test allows the clinician to distinguish readily between dementia and pseudodementia. The dexamethasone suppression test may be used clinically to detect endogenous depression. In the normal individual, administration of IV dexamethasone suppresses release of adrenocorticotropic hormone (ACTH) by the pituitary and produces decreased cortisol production. The dexamethasone suppression test result is abnormal in 50% of patients with depressive illness (cortisol production is not suppressed by dexamethasone) and only 4% of healthy subjects. Some have found this test helpful in detecting pseudodementia, but it lacks specificity. The evaluation needed to diagnose pseudodementia or concomitant dementia and depression is beyond the scope of emergency department care. A carefully monitored trial of antidepressants is occasionally necessary to confirm the presence of depression.

Treatment and Disposition

Several questions arise when treating a patient with apparent subacute or chronic cognitive impairment. Why was the patient taken to the emergency department? What precipitating events have caused a worsening in the baseline mental status? Is there a reversible component of the apparent dementia? Is there a superimposed delirium? Reversible dementias and conditions causing worsening of baseline dementia require early diagnosis and treatment of the underlying disorder if prior cognitive function is to be restored.

Determining reversible causes of dementia during the emergency department evaluation is occasionally possible on the basis of the history, physical examination, and head CT scan. Most treatable dementias are secondary to depression, NPH, intracranial mass lesions, and medications. These conditions should be apparent with a careful bedside evaluation and a CT scan. Few reversible causes of dementia can be readily treated in the emergency department; most patients require hospitalization. Occasionally, individuals who have a gradual decline in cognitive function without an underlying acute medical condition can receive further evaluation on an outpatient basis. Close medical follow-up and strong family support are essential elements when deciding on the feasibility of an outpatient evaluation.

Pharmacotherapy for dementia includes two drugs that have been approved by the Food and Drug Administration for the treatment of mild to moderate Alzheimer's disease. These agents are tacrine (Cognex) and donepezil (Aricept). They work by reducing the metabolism of acetylcholine. Other cholinesterase inhibitors include rivastigmine tartrate and galantamine. These drugs do not halt the underlying disease process. They are also associated with peripheral side effects and elevation of liver enzymes. Yet, these therapies represent short-term hope for patients with Alzheimer's disease. Vitamin E is currently recommended as possibly reducing the progression of Alzheimer's disease.[81] The key to altering the course of the disease is halting synaptic loss. The main goal in the management of patients with dementia is supportive care. Patients should be in an environment that ensures their personal safety. Employment of home health aides or custodians and occasionally institutionalization may be necessary. Patients should receive adequate supervision to ensure proper nutrition, hydration, and skin care.

Occasionally, medications are needed for symptomatic treatment of agitation, sleep disturbance, and depression. These patients typically do not improve with anxiolytics. Agitation can be controlled with a small dose of the butyrophenone haloperidol (Haldol). The cardiovascular toxicity of this drug is minimal, and it is well tolerated in elders. Clozapine has been shown to be effective in treating psychosis associated with both Alzheimer- and Parkinson-type dementias.[81] A newer atypical antipsychotic, ziprasidone (Geodon), may also be useful for this purpose.[31] Temazepam (Restoril) is the drug of choice for sleep disturbance. The half-life of temazepam is 8 to 10 hours for patients of all ages, and the drug bypasses the oxidative hepatic enzyme system.[82] The shorter acting sedative triazolam (Halcion) should be avoided because it does not maintain sleep throughout the night and may exacerbate mental confusion.[82]

The goal in the management of vascular dementia is to prevent further vascular insult by controlling precipitating factors such as hypertension. The prognosis ultimately depends on the underlying cerebrovascular status. The only slow virus infection that may respond to treatment, with some reversal of the cognitive dysfunction, is HIV infection.

Occasionally, patients are taken to the emergency department because of family stress from continuous care of the patient. An honest discussion with family members regarding the home situation often reveals the reason for the present difficulty in managing the patient. A brief nursing home stay or other institutional stay (respite program) may give the family time to mobilize resources to resume care of the patient. Coordinating evaluation, treatment, and ongoing supportive care can be time consuming. A social worker can play a vital role in attempting to deliver comprehensive care to the demented patient.

KEY CONCEPTS

- Delirium is a medical emergency. The delirious patient requires prompt evaluation and treatment. A thorough investigation of possible causes of the delirium should be undertaken in the emergency department. This investigation may require laboratory and radiographic examinations.

- Dementia has many causes, some of which may be reversible with accurate diagnosis. One should resist the temptation to classify dementia as a "futile" disease and search for underlying medical conditions that may be worsening a dementing illness.

- One should be wary of attributing behavioral disturbances to psychiatric illness in the presence of abnormal vital signs.

REFERENCES

1. American Psychiatric Association: *Diagnostic and Statistical Manual of Mental Disorders: DSM-IV-TR*, text revision. Chicago, American Psychiatric Association, 2000.
2. Hunter R, Macalpine I: *Three Hundred Years of Psychiatry*. London, Oxford University Press, 1963.
3. Hustey FM, Meldon SW: The prevalence and documentation of impaired mental status in elderly emergency department patients. *Ann Emerg Med* 39:248, 2002.
4. Inouye SK: Delirium in hospitalized older patients. *Clin Geriatr Med* 14:745, 1998.
5. Elie MJ: Delirium risk factors in elderly hospitalized patients. *J Gen Intern Med* 13:204,1998.
6. Mach JR, et al: Serum anticholinergic activity in hospitalized elderly with delirium: A preliminary study. *J Am Geriatr Soc* 43:491, 1995.
7. Chan D, Brennan NJ: Delirium: Making the diagnosis, improving the prognosis. *Geriatrics* 54:28, 1999.
8. Adams RD, Victor M, Ropper AH: *Principles of Neurology*, 6th ed. New York, McGraw-Hill, 1997.
9. Inouye SK: The dilemma of delirium: Clinical and research controversies regarding diagnosis and evaluation of delirium in hospitalized elderly medical patients. *Am J Med* 97:278, 1994.
10. Chen WH, et al: Low dose propranolol-induced delirium: 3 cases reported and a review of the literature. *Kaohsiung J Med Sci* 10:40, 1994.
11. Leinonen E, et al: Delirium during fluoxetine treatment: A case report. *Ann Clin Psychiatry* 5:255, 1993.
12. Rivera W, et al: Central nervous system toxicity manifestations of drug toxicity. *Emerg Med Rep* 24:12, 2003
13. Alciati A, et al: Three cases of delirium after "ecstasy" ingestion. *J Psychoactive Drugs* 31:167, 1999.
14. Hodkinson HM: *Common Symptoms of Disease in the Elderly*. Oxford, Blackwell, 1976.
15. Hohl CM, et al: Polypharmacy, adverse drug-related events, and potential adverse drug interactions in elderly patients presenting to an emergency department. *Ann Emerg Med* 38:661, 2001.
16. Tune L, et al: Anticholinergic effects of drugs commonly prescribed for the elderly: Potential means for assessing risk of delirium. *Am J Psychiatry* 149:1393, 1992.
17. Lewis LM, et al: Unrecognized delirium in geriatric patients. *Am J Emerg Med* 13:142,1995.
18. Folstein MF, Folstein SE, McHugh PR: "Mini-mental state": A practical method for grading the cognitive state of patients for the clinician. *J Psychiatr Res* 12:189, 1975.
19. American Psychiatric Association Practice Guidelines: Practice guidelines for the treatment of patients with delirium. *Am J Psychiatry* 156:5(Suppl), 1999.
20. Petersen RC: Practice parameter: Early detection of dementia: Mild cognitive impairment (an evidenced-based review). *Neurology* 56:1133, 2001.
21. Feher EP, et al: Establishing the limits of the mini-mental state. *Arch Neurol* 49:87, 1992.
22. Duff Canning SJ, et al: Diagnostic utility of abbreviated fluency measures in Alzheimer disease and vascular dementia. *Neurology* 62:556, 2004.
23. Inouye SK, et al: Clarifying confusion: The confusion assessment method: A new method for detection of delirium. *Ann Intern Med* 113:941, 1990.
24. Zou Y, et al: Detection and diagnosis of delirium in the elderly: Psychiatrist diagnosis, confusion assessment method or consensus diagnosis? *Int Psychogeriatr* 10:303, 1998.
25. Osterloh J: Laboratory testing in emergency toxicology. In Ford MD: *Clinical Toxicology*, 1st ed. Philadelphia, WB Saunders, 2001, pp 51-60.

26. Inouye SK, Charpentier PA: A predictive model for delirium in hospitalized elderly medical patients based on admission characteristics. *Ann Intern Med* 119:474, 1993.

27. Inouye SK, Charpentier PA: Precipitating factors for delirium in hospitalized elderly persons: Predictive model and interrelationship with baseline vulnerability. *JAMA* 275:852, 1996.

28. Pollanen MS, et al: Unexpected death related to restraint from excited delirium: A retrospective study of deaths in police custody and in the community. *CMAJ* 158:1603, 1998.

29. Seeman P: Atypical antipsychotics: Mechanism of action. *Can J Psychiatry* 47:27, 2002.

30. Daniel DG, et al: Intramuscular (IM) ziprasidone 20 mg is effective in reducing acute agitation associated with psychosis: A double-blind, randomized trial. *Psychopharmacology* 155:128, 2001.

31. Brook S, et al: Intramuscular (IM) ziprasidone compared with intramuscular haloperidol in the treatment of acute psychosis. *J Clin Psychiatry* 61:933, 2000.

32. Battaglia J, et al: Calming versus sedative effects of intramuscular olanzapine in agitated patients. *Am J Emerg Med* 21:192, 2003.

33. Wright P, et al: Double blind, placebo-controlled comparison of intramuscular olanzapine and intramuscular haloperidol in the treatment of acute agitation. *Am J Psychiatry* 158:1149, 2001.

34. Bailey P, Norton R, Karan S: The FDA droperidol warning: Is it justified? *Anesthesiology* 97:288, 2002.

35. Thomas H, Schwartz E, Petrilli R: Droperidol versus haloperidol for chemical restraint of agitated and combative patients. *Ann Emerg Med* 21:407, 1992.

36. Schillevoort I: Risk of extrapyramidal syndromes with haloperidol, risperidone, and olanzapine. *Ann Pharmacother* 35:1517, 2001.

37. Battaglia J, et al: Haloperidol, lorazepam, or both for psychotic agitation: A multicenter, prospective, double-blind emergency department study. *Am J Emerg Med* 15:335, 1997.

38. Sharma ND, et al: Torsades de pointes associated with intravenous haloperidol in critically ill patients. *Am J Cardiol* 81:238, 1998.

39. Liptzin B: Delirium. In Sadavoy J, et al (eds): *Comprehensive Review of Geriatric Psychiatry*, 2nd ed. Washington, DC, American Psychiatric Press, 1996, pp 487-492, 903-991.

40. Sipahimalani A, Massand PS: Use of risperidone in delirium: Case reports. *Ann Clin Psychiatry* 9:105, 1997.

41. Ravona-Springer R, et al: Delirium in elderly patients treated with risperidone: A report of three cases. *J Clin Psychopharmacol* 18:171, 1998.

42. Sipahimalani A, Masand PS: Olanzapine in the treatment of delirium. *Psychosomatics* 39:422, 1998.

43. Naess AC: Patient autonomy in emergency medicine. *Med Health Care Philos* 4:71, 2001.

44. Inouye SK, et al: Does delirium contribute to poor hospital outcomes? A three site epidemiologic study. *J Gen Intern Med* 13:234, 1998.

45. O'Keefe S, Lavan J: The prognostic significance of delirium in older hospitalized patients. *J Am Geriatr Soc* 45:174, 1997.

46. Cole MG, Primeau FJ: Prognosis of delirium in elderly hospital patients. *CMAJ* 149:41, 1993.

47. McCusker J, et al: Delirium predicts 12-month mortality. *Arch Intern Med* 457, 2002.

48. Weytingh MD, Bossuyt PMM, van Crevel H: Reversible dementia: More than 10% or less than 1%? A quantitative review. *J Neurol* 242:446, 1995.

49. Alzheimer A: Uber eine eigenartige Erkrankung der Hirnrinde. *Allerg Z Psychiatr* 64:146, 1907.

50. Sadik K: The increasing burden of Alzheimer disease. *Alzheimer Dis Assoc Disord* 17(Suppl 3):S75, 2003.

51. Carr DB, Goate A, Phil D, Morris JC: Current concepts in the pathogenesis of Alzheimer's disease. *Am J Med* 103(Suppl):3S, 1997.

52. National Institutes of Health, National Institute on Aging: Progress Report on Alzheimer's Disease, 1999 (NIH Publication No. 99-4664). Bethesda, Md, U.S. Department of Health and Human Services, 1999.

53. Kukull WA: Dementia epidemiology. *Med Clin North Am* 86:573, 2002.

54. Antonelli IR, et al: Unrecognized dementia: Sociodemographic correlates. *Aging* 4:327, 1992.

55. McKeith IG, et al: Consensus guidelines for the clinical and pathologic diagnosis of dementia with Lewy bodies (DLB): Report of the consortium on DLB international workshop. *Neurology* 47:1113, 1996.

56. Roberts GW, Allsop D, Bruton C: The occult aftermath of boxing. *J Neurol Neurosurg Psychiatry* 53:373, 1990.

57. Belman AL: HIV-1 infection and AIDS. *Neurol Clin* 20:983, 2002.

58. Forsell Y, Winblad B: Major depression in a population of demented and nondemented older people: Prevalence and correlates. *J Am Geriatr Soc* 46:27,1998.

59. Gauthier S, et al: Alzheimer's disease: Current knowledge, management and research. *CMAJ* 157:1047, 1997.

60. Morris JC, et al: Very mild Alzheimer's disease: Informant-based clinical, psychometric, and pathologic distinction from normal aging. *Neurology* 41:469, 1991.

61. Morris JC, et al: Cerebral amyloid deposition and diffuse plaques in "normal" aging: Evidence for presymptomatic and very mild Alzheimer's disease. *Neurology* 46:707, 1996.

62. Morris JC: Relationship of plaques and tangles to Alzheimer's disease phenotype. In Goate AM, Ashall F (eds): *The Pathobiology of Alzheimer's Disease*. San Diego, Academic Press, 1995, pp 193-223.

63. de Silva HA, et al: Abnormal function of potassium channels in platelets of patients with Alzheimer's disease. *Lancet* 352:1590, 1998.

64. Strittmatter WJ, et al: Apolipoprotein E: High avidity binding to beta-amyloid and increased frequency of type 4 allele in late onset Alzheimer's disease. *Proc Natl Acad Sci USA* 90:1977, 1993.

65. Roses AD: Apolipoprotein E affects the rate of Alzheimer disease expression: Beta-amyloid burden is secondary consequence dependent on APOE genotype and duration of disease. *J Neuropathol Exp Neurol* 53:429, 1994.

66. Selkoe DJ: Alzheimer's disease: Genotypes, phenotypes, and treatments. *Science* 275:630, 1997.

67. Breitner JCS, et al: Inverse association of anti-inflammatory treatments and Alzheimer's disease: Initial results of a co-twin control study. *Neurology* 44:227, 1994.

68. Knopman DS: An overview of common non-Alzheimer dementias. *Clin Geriatr Med* 17:281, 2001.

69. Giannakopoulos P, Hof PR, Bouras C: Dementia lacking distinctive histopathology: Clinicopathological evaluation of 32 cases. *Acta Neuropathol (Berl)* 89:346, 1995.

70. Holmes C, et al: Validity of current clinical criteria for Alzheimer's disease, vascular dementia and dementia with Lewy bodies. *Br J Psychiatry* 174:45, 1999.

71. Tyler KL: Creutzfeldt-Jakob disease. *N Engl J Med* 384:681, 2003.

72. Bensalem MK, Berger JR: HIV and the central nervous system. *Compr Ther* 28:23, 2002.

73. Sotrel A, Dal Canto MC: HIV-1 and its causal relationship to immunosuppression and nervous system disease in AIDS: A review. *Hum Pathol* 31:1274, 2000.

74. Weiner WJ, Goetz CG: *Neurology for the Non-Neurologist*. Philadelphia, Lippincott Williams & Wilkins, 1999.

75. Solari A, et al: Agreement in the clinical diagnosis of dementia: Evaluation of a case series with mild cognitive impairment. *Neuroepidemiology* 13:89, 1994.

76. Finkel SI: Behavioral and psychologic symptoms of dementia. *Clin Geriatr Med* 19:799, 2003.
77. Ross GW, Cummings JL, Benson DF: Speech and language alterations in dementia syndromes: Characteristics and treatment. *Aphasiology* 4:339,1990.
78. Lachner G, Engel RR: Differentiation of dementia and depression by memory tests: A meta-analysis. *J Nerv Ment Dis* 182:34, 1994.
79. Brisman MH, et al: Reversible dementia due to macroprolactinoma: Case report. *J Neurosurg* 79:135, 1993.
80. Doody RS, et al: Practice parameter: Management of dementia (an evidence-based review). *Neurology* 56:9, 2001.
81. Low-dose clozapine for the treatment of drug-induced psychosis in Parkinson's disease. The Parkinson Study Group. *N Engl J Med* 340:757, 1999.
82. Tariot PN, et al: Pharmacologic therapy for behavioral symptoms of Alzheimer's disease. *Clin Geriatr Med* 17:359, 2001.

CHAPTER

103 Brain and Cranial Nerve Disorders

Brian Stettler and Arthur M. Pancioli

Neurologic pathology can be difficult to diagnose in the emergency department. Clinical entities that can be particularly vexing include cranial nerve pathology, cerebral venous thrombosis, and multiple sclerosis. This chapter discusses several neurologic disorders that present significant diagnostic and therapeutic challenges to the emergency physician (Table 103-1).

TRIGEMINAL NEURALGIA

Perspective

Trigeminal neuralgia, or *tic douloureux*, is a syndrome featuring painful paroxysms in one or more distributions of the trigeminal nerve. It is relatively uncommon, with an annual occurrence of 4 individuals per 100,000, and it is more common in women than in men, with a female-to-male ratio of 1.7:1. Individuals affected are most commonly between 50 and 69 years of age, and symptoms occur more commonly on the right side of the face.[1]

Pathophysiology

Trigeminal neuralgia is an idiopathic disorder. One long-standing theory relates the cause to compression of the trigeminal nerve root caused by a tortuous blood vessel in the posterior fossa, an arteriovenous malformation, or a tumor. In surgical case series, vascular compression of the trigeminal nerve root is found in 80% to 90% of cases.[2,3] Notably, however, structural lesions such as these are not found in all patients with trigeminal neuralgia.[4]

Clinical Features

Trigeminal neuralgia arises with unilateral facial pain, typically characterized as lancinating paroxysms of pain in the lips, teeth, gums, or chin. The pain is commonly associated with physical triggers such as chewing, brushing teeth, shaving, washing or touching the affected area of the face, swallowing, or exposure to hot or cold temperature in the affected area. Trigeminal neuralgia is most commonly found in the maxillary and mandibular divisions of the trigeminal nerve. Rarely, trigeminal neuralgia occurs in the ophthalmic division alone. Patients tend to have clusters of the pain that last a few seconds to several minutes. The attacks can occur during the day or night but rarely occur during sleep.[4,5]

Diagnostic Strategies

A careful history and physical examination should be performed to rule out other painful facial disorders including odontogenic infections, sinus disease, otitis media, acute glaucoma, temporomandibular joint disease, and herpes zoster. Patients with no local findings to explain the painful syndrome require a careful neurologic examination. The presence of a neurologic deficit should prompt suspicion of a structural lesion, including aneurysm, tumor, or other intracranial lesion such as multiple sclerosis (MS). Notably, 2% to 4% of patients with trigeminal neuralgia also have MS.[6] Patients with normal head and neck examinations and no neurologic deficits who have episodic, unilateral facial pain associated with nonpainful triggers are likely to have trigeminal neuralgia.

Management

Since the 1960s, the medical treatment of choice for trigeminal neuralgia has been the anticonvulsant carbamazepine. This treatment is, however, based on uncontrolled studies, and the mechanism of action of anticonvulsant therapy for trigeminal neuralgia is unclear. The true efficacy of medical therapy is difficult to assess because of a high rate of spontaneous remission. Nonetheless, carbamazepine appears to be an effective and well-tolerated treatment. The initial dosage of carbamazepine is 100 mg twice daily, then increased to three times daily. The dose may be

Table 103-1. The Cranial Nerves: Normal Function and Pathologic Considerations

Cranial Nerve	Clinical Function Relevant to Emergency Medicine	Pathologic Features	Possible Causes
Cranial nerve I: olfactory nerve	Sense of smell	Unilateral anosmia	*Trauma:* Skull fracture or shear injury interrupting olfactory fibers traversing the cribriform plate *Tumor:* Frontal lobe masses compressing the nerve
Cranial nerve II: optic nerve	Vision	Unilateral vision loss	*Trauma:* Traumatic optic neuropathy *Tumor:* Orbital compressive lesion *Inflammatory:* Optic neuritis (MS) *Ischemic:* Ischemic optic neuropathy
Cranial nerve III: oculomotor nerve	Extraoculomotor function via motor fibers to levator palprae, superior rectus, medial rectus, inferior rectus, inferior oblique muscles Pupillary constriction via parasympathetic fibers to constrictor pupillae and ciliary muscles	Ptosis caused by loss of levator palpebrae function Eye deviated laterally and down Diplopia Dilated, nonreactive pupil Loss of accommodation	*Trauma:* Herniation of the temporal lobe through the tentorial opening causing compression and stretch injury to the nerve *Ischemic:* Especially in diabetes. microvascular ischemic injury to nerve causes extraocular muscle paralysis, but usually is papillary sparing (often painful) *Vascular:* Intracranial aneurysms may press on the nerve leading to dysfunction Myasthenia gravis can lead to atraumatic ocular muscle palsy
Cranial nerve IV: trochlear nerve	Motor supply to the superior oblique muscle	Inability to move eye downward, and laterally Diplopia Patients tilt head toward unaffected eye to overcome inward rotation of affected eye	Trauma is the most common cause of nerve dysfunction
Cranial nerve V: trigeminal nerve	Motor supply to muscles of mastication and to tensor tympani Sensory to face, scalp, oral cavity (including tongue and teeth)	Partial facial anesthesia Episodic, lancinating facial pain associated with benign triggers such as chewing, brushing teeth, light touch	*Trauma:* Facial bone fracture may injure one section leading to area of facial anesthesia Tic douloureux
Cranial nerve VI: abducens nerve	Motor supply to the lateral rectus muscle	Inability to move affected eye laterally Diplopia upon attempting lateral gaze	*Tumor:* Lesions in the cerebellopontine angle Any lesion, vascular or otherwise, in the cavernous sinus may compress nerve *Elevated intracranial pressure (ICP):* Because of its position and long intracranial length, increased ICP from any cause may lead to injury and dysfunction of the nerve
Cranial nerve VII: facial nerve	Motor supply to muscles of facial expression Parasympathetic stimulation of the lacrimal, submandibular, and sublingual glands Sensation to the ear canal and tympanic membrane	*Hemifacial paresis:* Lower motor neuron lesion with entire side of face paralyzed Upper motor neuron lesion leaves forehead musculature functioning Abnormal taste Sensory deficit around ear Intolerance to sudden loud noises	*Lower motor neuron:* *Infection (viral):* The likely cause of Bell's palsy *Lyme disease:* The most common cause of bilateral cranial nerve VII palsy in areas where Lyme disease is endemic Bacterial infection extending from otitis media *Upper motor neuron:* Stroke, tumor
Cranial nerve VIII: vestibulocochlear nerve	Hearing and balance	Unilateral hearing loss Tinnitus Vertigo, unsteadiness	*Tumors:* Acoustic neuroma Mimics Ménières's disease, perilymphatic fistula
Cranial nerve IX: glossopharyngeal nerve	General sensation to posterior third of tongue Taste for posterior third of tongue Motor supply to the stylopharyngeus	Clinical pathology referable to the nerve in isolation is very rare Occasionally painful paroxysms beginning in the throat and radiating down the side of the neck in front of the ear but behind the mandible	Brainstem lesions Glossopharyngeal neuralgia
Cranial nerve X: vagus nerve	Motor to striated and muscles of the pharynx, larynx, and tensor (veli) palatini Motor to smooth muscles and glands of the pharynx, larynx, thoracic and abdominal viscera Sensory from larynx, trachea, esophagus, thoracic and abdominal viscera	*Unilateral loss of palatal elevation:* Patients complain that on drinking liquids the fluid refluxes through the nose *Unilateral vocal cord paralysis:* Hoarse voice	Brainstem lesion Injury to the recurrent laryngeal nerve during surgery
Cranial nerve XI: spinal accessory nerve	Motor supply to the sternocleidomastoid and trapezius muscles	Downward and lateral rotation of the scapula and shoulder drop	Trauma to the nerve
Cranial nerve XII: hypoglossal nerve	Motor supply to the intrinsic and extrinsic muscles of the tongue	*Tongue deviations:* Upper motor neuron lesion causes the tongue to deviate toward the opposite site Lower motor neuron lesion causes the tongue to deviate toward the side of the lesion, and the affected side atrophies over time	Stroke or tumor can cause upper motor neuron lesion Amyotrophic lateral sclerosis (ALS) can cause bilateral lower motor neuron lesion with atrophy Metastatic disease to the skull base may involve the nerve

increased by 100 mg/day up to a maximum of 1200 mg/day. Because of potential side effects of carbamazepine, complete blood count and liver function studies should be performed periodically. Additional medical therapies include phenytoin, baclofen, valproate sodium, lamotrigine, and gabapentin. None of these therapies, however, has been shown to be more effective than carbamazepine.[5]

Surgical management has been an option for patients since the 1950s and includes both peripheral approaches and central procedures. Peripheral strategies include medication injection or cryotherapy designed to block temporarily, or permanently ablate, branches of the peripheral trigeminal nerve. Although these are relatively effective initially, recurrence is common. Repeated nerve blocks are not recommended because of a high risk of permanent facial anesthesia.

Central procedures can be divided into percutaneous approaches and open approaches. Percutaneous destruction of the trigeminal ganglion can be done through radiofrequency ablation, thermal ablation, glycerol injection, or balloon microcompression. These procedures have the risk of corneal anesthesia, oculomotor paresis, or masticatory weakness.[7]

Open surgical management is the surgical option of choice in most centers. Open surgical treatments include microvascular decompression of the nerve with or without partial ablation. Although the open microvascular decompression procedure has proved very effective, with 80% to 95% of patients achieving pain relief, the surgery can have significant side effects.[8] These include hearing loss, facial anesthesia, cerebrospinal fluid (CSF) leak, brainstem or cerebellar injury, headaches, meningitis, and death.[9] Gamma knife radiosurgery, a minimally invasive, highly directed stereotactic radiosurgery, has also been associated with good outcomes in trigeminal neuralgia. This highly specialized technique requires extremely sophisticated stereotactic radiofrequency equipment and is available only in specialized centers.[10,11]

Disposition

Patients with suspected trigeminal neuralgia should be referred for specialty evaluation. Patients with any physical findings during the head and neck examination should not be considered to have trigeminal neuralgia, and patients with any neurologic deficit require urgent imaging studies to rule out a mass or vascular abnormality.

KEY CONCEPTS

- Patients commonly visit multiple physicians in multiple settings before a definitive diagnosis of trigeminal neuralgia is established.
- Alertness to the possibility of trigeminal neuralgia may provide the patient with more rapid and appropriate specialty consultation and therapy.

FACIAL NERVE PARALYSIS

Perspective

Facial nerve paralysis is an emotionally devastating disorder for the patient and a diagnostic challenge for the emergency physician. The acute onset of symptoms often prompts a visit to the emergency department, where early diagnosis and early appropriate therapy can improve a patient's chance for recovery of function of the facial nerve. The acute onset of facial nerve paralysis affects approximately 20 to 25 individuals per 100,000 per year without geographic, gender, or race predilections.[12,13]

Principles of Disease

The facial nerve innervates the muscles of facial expression and the muscles of the scalp and external ear in addition to the buccinator, platysma, stapedius, stylohyoid, and posterior belly of the digastric muscles. The sensory portion of the nerve supplies the anterior two thirds of the tongue with taste and portions of the external auditory meatus, soft palate, and adjacent pharynx with general sensation. The parasympathetic portion supplies secretomotor fibers for the submandibular, sublingual, lacrimal, nasal, and palatine glands.[14]

The facial nerve originates from the pontomedullary junction of the brainstem and enters the internal auditory meatus with cranial nerve VIII. Within the temporal bone, the facial nerve gives off four major branches: the greater and lesser superficial petrosal nerves, the nerve to the stapedius muscle, and the chorda tympani. The facial nerve exits the temporal bone at the stylomastoid foramen and enters the parotid gland, where it divides to supply the muscles of facial expression.[14,15]

Pathophysiology

Although the complete differential diagnosis for facial nerve paralysis is lengthy, the causes pertinent to emergency medicine can be grouped into several categories: infectious, traumatic, and neoplastic.

Infection

Bell's Palsy

Bell's palsy, also commonly called *idiopathic facial paralysis*, has long been postulated to have a viral cause. This disease entity is characterized by an abrupt onset of a lower motor neuron paresis that can progress over 1 to 7 days to complete paralysis. Figure 103-1 shows an example of the facial paralysis. A prodromal illness is described by 60% of patients. Symptoms frequently associated with the facial paresis include ear pain, a perception of sensory change on the involved side of the face, decreased tearing, an overflow of tears upon the cheek (epiphora), abnormally acute hearing (hyperacusis), and an impairment or perversion of taste (dysgeusia).[16]

Treatment approaches can be medical or surgical. The primary medical therapies for Bell's palsy center on reducing inflammatory changes to the nerve with corticosteroids and treating the presumed viral cause. If these therapies are unsuccessful, surgical decompression may be considered.

The use of corticosteroids for Bell's palsy has been controversial. Their use is based on the belief that edema of the nerve, confined within the facial canal, is causing or contributing to the nerve injury. On the basis of this theory, most experts currently recommend a course of prednisone with an initial dose of 1 mg/kg/day for 7 to 10 days with or without a short taper.[12,15,17,18] Therapy should be started as soon as possible, ideally within the first 24 hours, but should be considered for patients without contraindications who seek treatment within 1 week of symptom onset.[17]

A number of publications have advanced the belief that Bell's palsy may be caused by herpes virus infection. One study demonstrated herpes simplex virus type 1 DNA in the endoneural tissue of 11 of 14 patients with Bell's palsy but not in control subjects.[19] In one trial involving 99 patients, patients treated with prednisone and acyclovir had a more favorable recovery than patients treated with prednisone alone.[20] Despite a lack of strong scientific evidence, antiviral agents are now routinely used in the treatment of Bell's palsy. Recommended antiviral regimens include acyclovir 400 to 800 mg orally five times daily for 10 days. The newer oral antiviral agents such as valacyclovir and famciclovir have better oral absorption, are better tolerated, and have been recommended as alternatives to acyclovir.[15,17,18,21] As with steroid therapy, although earlier treatment is preferred, treatment should be considered for patients who present within 1 week of symptom onset.

Ramsay Hunt Syndrome (Herpes Zoster Oticus)

Ramsay Hunt syndrome is characterized by unilateral facial paralysis, a herpetiform vesicular eruption, and vestibulocochlear dysfunction. The vesicular eruption may occur on the pinna, external auditory canal, tympanic membrane, soft palate, oral cavity, face, and neck as far down as the shoulder. There is considerably more pain than is associated with Bell's palsy, and the pain is frequently out of proportion to physical findings. In addition, outcomes are worse than with Bell's palsy, with a lower incidence of complete facial recovery and the possibility of sensorineural hearing loss. Therapy is similar to that for Bell's palsy. Both prednisone and antiviral therapy for 7 to 10 days are advocated.[15,22,23]

Lyme Disease

Lyme disease is the most frequent vector-borne infection in the United States. It is caused by the spirochete *Borrelia burgdorferi* and is spread by the bite of ticks of the genus *Ixodes*. Neurologic manifestations can occur in any phase of the disease, and the incidence of facial palsy in patients with neurologic involvement is 35% to 51%. In regions where Lyme disease is endemic, it has been shown to be the leading cause of facial paralysis in children, causing one half of all cases of facial nerve paralysis.[24,25]

Bilateral facial nerve paralysis is rare but can occur with systemic infections. The two diseases most commonly associated with bilateral simultaneous onset of facial paralysis are Lyme disease and infectious mononucleosis. The emergency physician should consider bilateral facial paralysis to be a manifestation of Lyme disease until further testing can confirm or refute this diagnosis.[18,24-26]

Bacterial

Facial paralysis can result from acute bacterial infections of the middle ear, mastoid, or external auditory canal. In the preantibiotic era, facial paralysis was associated with acute otitis media in approximately 2% of cases. Now, however, facial paralysis occurs in only 0.16% of cases of otitis media.[15] Treatment involves intravenous antibiotics and myringotomy for decompression. Malignant otitis externa is another bacterial infection that can be associated with facial paralysis. It is most commonly seen among immunocompromised and diabetic patients and is usually caused by a pseudomonal infection. Treatment involves prolonged intravenous antipseudomonal antibiotic therapy and may require surgical debridement.[18,27]

Trauma

Among patients with head trauma, the facial nerve is the most commonly injured cranial nerve. The cause is generally a temporal bone fracture with nerve transection. Surgical exploration is warranted if there is firm evidence that the nerve has been transected, indicated by a sudden onset of complete unilateral facial paralysis, loss of electrical activity, and evidence of a displaced fracture involving the facial canal.

Neoplasm

Tumors of the facial nerve itself, or tumors anywhere along the course of the facial nerve that invade or compress the nerve, may lead to facial paralysis. Typically, the course is progressive over at least 3 weeks. A sudden onset of paralysis, however, does not rule out an underlying tumor because facial paralysis secondary to a neoplasm has a sudden onset in approximately 25% of cases.[15] In patients who suffer from recurrent ipsilateral facial paralysis, significant pain, prolonged symptoms, or any other cranial nerve abnormality, the suspicion of a tumor should be high.

Clinical Features

A thorough history and physical examination can often identify the cause of acute facial paralysis. The history should focus on symptom onset, concentrating on timing and rapidity of onset and looking for any associated symptoms. A rapid onset of facial paralysis with dysgeusia and hyperacusis preceded by a viral prodrome leads the clinician toward a diagnosis of Bell's palsy. A history of recurrent ipsilateral paralysis or slow progression of symptoms should alert the physician to the possibility of a tumor. Associated cranial nerve abnormalities, although occasionally seen with Bell's palsy, should also alert the physician to the possibility of a tumor. The Ramsay Hunt syndrome causes significant pain and a vesicular rash, although the rash may follow the facial paresis by a few days. Significant anatomic abnormalities on visual or otoscopic inspection of the ipsilateral ear are found with bacterial otitis media and otitis externa. Finally, systemic symptoms or bilateral facial paresis, especially in endemic areas, should raise the possibility of Lyme disease.

Diagnostic Strategies

The diagnostic workup of a facial nerve paresis is based on the clinician's suspicion that the patient has a disease process other than Bell's palsy. If the clinical history is classical for Bell's palsy, no imaging or laboratory studies are required. Notably, any history of possible exposure merits serologic evaluation for Lyme disease if the patient lives in or has visited an endemic area. Although outpatient testing including electroneurography may ultimately be performed, this is not a part of the emergency department evaluation.

The physical finding of a "central" seventh nerve paralysis (upper face sparing) should prompt an imaging workup with computed tomography (CT) or magnetic resonance imaging (MRI), and consideration should be given to the possibility of an acute stroke or other hemispheric lesion. History or physical examination findings suggestive of a possible tumor require imaging to rule out a neoplasm. The study of choice depends on the institution and the consultant.

Disposition

The vast majority of patients who present with a seventh nerve paralysis have Bell's palsy and may be discharged with treatment and short-term follow-up. Patients with a possible hemispheric process, such as stroke or tumor, should be admitted for further evaluation. Patients who might have Lyme disease should receive antibiotics and referral if they appear nontoxic and admission if they are systemically ill.

Patients with a peripheral facial nerve paralysis should have the ipsilateral eye patched and consideration should be given to ophthalmologic follow-up because of the high rate of corneal abrasions and corneal dryness associated with the inability to blink properly or completely close the eye.

KEY CONCEPTS

- The literature highlights significant potential benefit for patients with Bell's palsy when they are treated early in the course with a combination of corticosteroids and antiviral medication.
- Lyme disease should be considered in the differential of Bell's palsy, especially in endemic regions. Simultaneous bilateral facial paralysis excludes Bell's palsy and is suggestive of Lyme disease.
- Slowly progressive facial paralysis is suggestive of a neoplasm.
- Recurrent unilateral paralysis may occur with Bell's palsy but is frequently (30%) seen in tumor patients.
- Patients who have facial muscle paresis with intact forehead movement should be considered to have an upper motor neuron lesion until proved otherwise.

ACOUSTIC NEUROMA

Perspective

Acoustic neuroma is a rare but important cause of sensorineural hearing loss. Patients with asymmetric hearing loss or unilateral tinnitus should be evaluated to rule out acoustic neuroma and thereby prevent further neurologic damage. The annual incidence of acoustic neuroma is 1 case per 100,000. The female-to-male ratio is 1.5:1. Acoustic neuroma is rarely bilateral, occurring in approximately 5% of cases and generally occurring with type II neurofibromatosis. Acoustic neuromas, although histologically benign, can cause neurologic damage through direct compression on the eighth cranial nerve and the other structures in the cerebellopontine angle.[29]

Principles of Disease

An acoustic neuroma, also referred to as a schwannoma, arises from the Schwann cells covering the vestibular branch of the eighth cranial nerve as it passes through the internal auditory canal. The tumor compresses the cochlear (acoustic) branch of the eighth cranial nerve, causing hearing loss, tinnitus, and dysequilibrium. Continued growth of the tumor may result in compression of structures in the cerebellopontine angle, where the facial and trigeminal nerves may be compressed and damaged. Larger tumors may further encroach upon the brainstem and if large enough may compress the fourth ventricle, ultimately resulting in signs of increased intracranial pressure (ICP).[30]

Clinical Features

Asymmetric sensorineural hearing loss is the hallmark of acoustic neuroma. However, up to 15% of patients have normal results on an audiogram. These patients typically have symptoms such as unilateral tinnitus, imbalance, headache, fullness in the ear, otalgia, or facial nerve weakness. Thus, patients with asymmetric symptoms should be evaluated further for acoustic neuroma even with the occurrence of a normal audiogram.[31]

Acoustic neuromas are extremely slow-growing tumors. Therefore, symptom onset is generally quite gradual. In one series of 126 cases, the average time from symptom onset to discovery of an acoustic neuroma was approximately 4 years.[32]

Diagnostic Strategies

Any abnormality found during the history or physical examination that might indicate acoustic neuroma should be evaluated with an audiogram. If this test is normal and symptoms remain unexplained, gadolinium-enhanced MRI may be warranted. This imaging technique is extremely sensitive and has led to earlier diagnosis and a decrease in the mean size at detection of acoustic neuromas. The smaller the tumor at the time of diagnosis, the more options there are for therapy and the potential prognosis is better.[29]

Differential Considerations

The majority of disease entities in the differential considerations for acoustic neuroma cause symmetric sensorineural hearing loss. Asymmetric sensorineural hearing loss has few causes other than acoustic neuroma. Ménière's disease may present a diagnostic dilemma because it can be asymmetric. However, the tinnitus of Ménière's disease is usually intermittent, whereas the tinnitus of acoustic neuroma is typically continuous. In addition, patients with Ménière's disease typically describe true vertigo, whereas patients with an acoustic neuroma are more likely to describe imbalance or dysequilibrium.

Acoustic neuromas account for 80% of all cerebellopontine angle tumors. Among all other lesions, meningioma is the most common. Meningiomas more frequently cause symptoms of facial palsy or trigeminal nerve abnormality. There may be, however, considerable similarity between the clinical picture of a meningioma and that of an acoustic neuroma in the cerebellopontine angle.[33]

Management

Acoustic neuroma may be removed surgically or with stereotactic radiation. Injuries to the trigeminal, facial, and acoustic nerves and to the cerebellum are all possible complications of these procedures.

Disposition

Patients with suspected acoustic neuroma should be referred for an audiogram and evaluation by specialists in either otolaryngology or neurosurgery.

 KEY CONCEPTS

- The onset of unilateral auditory symptoms requires evaluation and referral.
- Neurologic symptoms of lower cranial nerve dysfunction, ataxia, or raised ICP may be caused by a benign tumor of the cerebellopontine angle.
- The smaller the tumor at diagnosis, the lower the risk of definitive treatment.

DIABETIC CRANIAL MONONEUROPATHY

Perspective

Cranial mononeuropathies are uncommon but when they occur often lead to an emergency department visit. Cranial mononeuropathies attributed to diabetes most often affect the extraocular muscles. The oculomotor nerve is the most commonly affected cranial nerve, followed in order by the trochlear and abducens nerves. In one large series, the incidence of cranial nerve palsies was 1.0% among diabetics and 0.1% among nondiabetics.[34,35]

The incidence of third, sixth, and seventh cranial nerve palsies in diabetic versus nondiabetic patients has been studied.[34] Overall, the incidence of cranial nerve palsies in diabetic patients was found to be higher than in nondiabetic patients. The incidence of diabetic complications in patients with specific nerve palsies was also evaluated. Only 1 out of 9 patients with facial palsy (11%) had diabetic complications, whereas 7 out of 10 patients with ophthalmoplegia (70%) demonstrated diabetic complications. Hence, ophthalmoplegia appears to be closely related to diabetes and facial palsy is less strongly correlated with it.[34]

Principles of Disease

Diabetic mononeuropathy appears to be caused by ischemia of the affected cranial nerve caused by occlusion of an intraneural nutrient artery serving the nerve. This occlusion causes injury primarily to the center of the nerve because the core fibers are more dependent on the supply from such nutrient arteries. The peripheral fibers are less affected because part of their blood supply comes from collateral vessels. In the oculomotor nerve, the preservation of the circumferentially located parasympathetic fibers explains the pupillary sparing that is usually found in this syndrome. In two studies, the microvascular changes of the intraneural arteries that led to occlusion were noted in diabetics but absent in nondiabetics.[36,37]

Clinical Features

Patients typically complain of an acute onset of unilateral, retroocular, and supraorbital pain, diplopia, and ptosis.[35] Physical findings of a third cranial nerve palsy include the inability to move the eye superiorly and medially. It is also accompanied by ptosis. The pupillary light reflex is usually present. Although less common, the fourth and sixth cranial nerves may be affected. With a fourth cranial nerve palsy the patient is unable to move the eye inferolaterally, and with a sixth cranial nerve palsy the patient is unable to move the eye laterally. Because of the long intracranial course of the sixth nerve, a patient with an isolated sixth nerve palsy should be evaluated for an intracranial lesion or increased ICP.[38]

Differential Considerations

Cranial nerve dysfunction requires a thorough history and physical examination, including a detailed neurologic examination, and cranial imaging such as MRI. Diabetic mononeuropathy must be considered a diagnosis of exclusion, and the differential diagnosis includes trauma, tumor, vertebrobasilar ischemia, and hemorrhage into the brainstem.[39]

Management

Analgesics, patching the affected eye, and antiplatelet therapy constitute the required therapy. The prognosis is good, with complete resolution expected within the first year. If the neuropathy does not improve within 3 to 6 months or if more than one nerve is affected, another cause should be sought.

 KEY CONCEPTS

- Diabetic neuropathy is a diagnosis of exclusion because no definitive diagnostic testing is available.
- Both ischemic and hemorrhagic brainstem lesions must be ruled out in the case of an acute ophthalmoplegia.
- An extraocular mononeuropathy is sufficiently common in patients with diabetes mellitus that the occurrence in isolation should lead the physician to evaluate the patient for previously undiagnosed diabetes.

CEREBRAL VENOUS THROMBOSIS

Perspective

There are no precise studies of the epidemiology of cerebral venous thrombosis (CVT). In a case series, the mean age of patients was approximately 38 years, with a female-to-male ratio of 1.5:1.[40]

Principles of Disease

Cerebral blood is drained by several major veins, which lead into the dural sinuses. The major dural sinuses are the superior sagittal sinus, the inferior sagittal sinus, the straight sinus, the lateral sinuses, and the sigmoid sinuses. As with venous thrombosis in other locations, there are multiple causes and predisposing factors that may ultimately lead to CVT. Underlying causes are often divided into infectious and noninfectious categories. Infectious causes include local infections, such as sinusitis, otitis media, facial cellulitis, and systemic infections. Noninfectious causes include direct injury to the cerebral venous system by trauma, surgery, tumor, dehydration, or any other condition that may predispose a patient to a hypercoagulable state.[40]

Clinical Features

The symptoms associated with CVT are quite varied. This variability stems from differences in thrombus location and acuity of thrombus formation. Headache is the primary feature of CVT in 74% to 90% of affected patients.[40,41] Papilledema is noted in 45% of cases.[41] Lethargy, decreased level of consciousness, or mental status changes may be seen. Seizures are seen in 50% of patients in the acute phase.[40] In addition to the location and acuity of thrombosis formation, a patient's symptom onset varies depending on the extent of collateral vessel growth in the venous territory. Early thrombotic changes may be well compensated for by the collateral venous drainage. Symptoms appear only when the compensation for venous thrombosis is no longer sufficient. Variability in collateralization between patients adds to the variability and time course of symptoms. One study of 102 patients with CVT documented a mean delay of 14 days between the onset of first symptoms and hospital arrival.[42] The incidence of focal neurologic findings on clinical examination at the time of presentation varies between series, ranging from 25% to 71%, and includes seizures.[40,41] Because of the broad spectrum of clinical features, the clinician must have a high degree of clinical suspicion of CVT in the presence of unexplained headache, especially when combined with focal neurologic deficit, papilledema, or seizures.

Diagnostic Strategies

The "gold standard" for the diagnosis of CVT has long been cerebral angiography. The advent of MRI and magnetic resonance venography (MRV) has significantly improved diagnostic accuracy. CT scanning is also useful in the initial workup of the patient with possible CVT, but CT is not sensitive or specific enough to confirm or exclude it reliably. Findings on CT that are consistent with CVT include hyperdensity of a thrombosed sinus, brain edema, or hemorrhage from swelling secondary to venous congestion. In addition, patients with ventricles that appear smaller than expected for the patient's age may have a CVT.

Similarly to CT scanning, MRI can demonstrate local changes secondary to venous congestion, such as brain edema or hemorrhage. In addition, MRI can demonstrate the possibility of CVT on the basis of lack of a "flow void." On a normal MRI scan, a flow void would indicate the presence of blood flow within the sinus. The absence of a flow void indicates a possible thrombus. Diagnostic accuracy, however, is greatly improved through use of MRV. This technique takes advantage of the MRI signal characteristics of flowing blood to create images of venous structures. Combining these imaging techniques further enhances diagnostic accuracy. The presence of a given sinus on conventional MRI and a lack of flow on the MRV are diagnostic of a sinus thrombosis. This combined approach has diagnostic sensitivity similar to that of angiography.[40,43]

Because patients often present with headache, a lumbar puncture (LP) is commonly performed as part of the evaluation. Elevated opening pressure on the LP should heighten clinical suspicion for CVT in the absence of other disorders causing elevated ICP. There have been several small studies on the usefulness of D-dimer to exclude CVT when MRI imaging is not available or practical as a screening tool. Although the reported sensitivities are fair at 83% to 100%, larger prospective studies need to be done for further evaluation of the usefulness of D-dimer in this disease process.[44,45]

Differential Consideration

CVT is difficult to diagnose, and the clinician must be alert to the possibility of CVT to detect it. There are numerous causes of nonspecific headache in the differential for CVT. Unexplained headache with either CT findings suggestive of possible CVT or clinical history suggestive of hypercoagulability may lead the clinician to pursue advanced imaging to evaluate a patient for possible CVT.

Management

CVT is a relatively rare disease, and there is a lack of controlled studies evaluating therapy for this condition. Current therapeutic consensus rests on the use of standard heparin to prevent further clot formation and to promote recanalization.[40,41,46,47] Previously, intravenous heparin was the only option for therapy for patients with CVT. In one placebo-controlled randomized trial involving 20 patients, anticoagulation with heparin to a target partial thromboplastin time of 80 to 100 seconds demonstrated benefit, even in patients in whom intracranial hemorrhage was seen on CT before anticoagulation.[48] In another study of 60 patients randomly assigned to placebo versus low-molecular-weight heparin, no statistical benefit was shown for treatment.[49]

Catheter-based intervention with thrombolysis has been attempted in multiple case series using either urokinase or tissue plasminogen activator. Thrombolysis was shown to be relatively safe and relatively successful in very small case series.[47] In one nonrandomized study of 40 patients, 20 received systemic heparin and 20 received catheter-based infusion of urokinase followed by systemic heparin. Despite initially worse neurologic function in the thrombolysis group, there was a significant difference in neurologic function at discharge favoring thrombolysis.[50] Although this therapy is promising, it should be considered only for cases with symptoms of decreased level of consciousness, elevated ICP, or rapidly deteriorating neurologic status.

Disposition

All patients with suspected CVT should be admitted to a unit capable of giving a high level of care with neurologic consultation. Patients should receive heparin if no contraindication exists, and catheter-based thrombolysis should be considered.

KEY CONCEPTS

- CVT is a relatively rare entity that should be suspected in patients with headache who have predisposing factors (head and neck infections or hypercoagulable states) and any of the following: seizures, an altered sensorium, papilledema, focal neurologic deficits, or increased ICP on LP in the absence of an intracranial mass lesion.
- The onset may be insidious with a considerable delay between onset and arrival in the treatment setting.
- CT scanning is not adequate to rule out CVT. MRI with MRV is recommended.

MULTIPLE SCLEROSIS

Perspective

MS is an inflammatory disease that affects the central nervous system (CNS). Although the exact etiology remains uncertain, the pathologic manifestation of this inflammatory disease is a demyelination of discrete regions (plaques) within the CNS with a relative sparing of axons. The clinical picture is highly variable but is classically characterized by episodes of neurologic dysfunction that evolve over days and resolve over weeks.

MS has an overall prevalence in the United States of 0.1%. The peak age at onset is 25 to 30 years, with women being slightly younger at onset than men. The incidence in women exceeds that of men by a ratio of 1.8:1. The worldwide prevalence is greatest in the United Kingdom, Scandinavia, and North America. Epidemiologic studies indicate that both genetic and environmental factors are associated with the disease incidence. Data indicating that genetics influence the disease process include a 30% concordance rate among monozygotic twins. In addition, 20% of patients with MS have at least one affected relative. Indicators of environmental influences include the observation that MS is more common in temperate climates. It is rare between 23 degrees north and south latitudes but has a rising incidence above and below 50 degrees north and south latitudes. Although no exact environmental factor has been identified, if a person emigrates from an area of high prevalence to an area of low prevalence before the age of 20, the risk is diminished. MS is rare in Africans and Asians, but African Americans have a higher incidence than their relatives who remain in Africa.[51] In addition, reports of clusters or mini-epidemics support environmental factors. Thus, an environmental cause superimposed on genetic susceptibility appears likely.[52,53]

Principles of Disease

MS is considered to be an organ-specific autoimmune disease. One theory proposes that genetic factors interact with an environmental trigger or infection to establish pathologically autoreactive T cells in the CNS. After a long and variable latency period (typically 10 to 20 years), a systemic trigger, such as a viral infection or superantigen, activates these T cells. The activated T cells, upon reexposure to the autoantigen, initiate the inflammatory response. A complex immunologic cascade ensues that leads to the demyelination characteristic of MS. This releases CNS antigens that are hypothesized to initiate further episodes of autoimmune-induced inflammation. The mechanisms underlying the autoimmunity in MS are unknown.[54]

Clinical Features

The clinical picture of MS displays marked heterogenicity. The classical clinical syndrome consists of recurring episodes of neurologic symptoms that are rapidly manifest over days and slowly resolve. Variability occurs in age of onset, location of CNS lesions, frequency and severity of relapses, and the degree and time course of progression.

The clinical features of MS can be divided in a manner similar to the divisions of a neurologic examination. They can be divided into aspects of cognitive impairment, cranial nerve dysfunction, impairment of motor pathways, impairment of sensory pathways, impairment of cerebellar pathways, and impairment of bowel, bladder, and sexual functions.[51]

Patients with MS have frequent complaints of poor memory, distractibility, and a decreased capacity for sustained mental effort. Formal neuropsychological testing suggests that cognitive involvement is common and underreported. Specifically, neuropsychological testing has shown that 43% to 65% of patients with MS have cognitive impairment.[55] Notably, there is a correlation between the MRI-based total lesion load and cognitive impairment.[56]

Cranial nerve dysfunction is common in MS. The most common associated cranial nerve abnormality is optic neuritis, a unilateral syndrome characterized by pain in the eye and a variable degree of visual loss affecting primarily central vision. Within 2 years of an attack of optic neuritis, the risk of MS is approximately 20%, and within 15 years it is approximately 45% to 80%.[57,58] Optic neuritis is often the first symptom of MS.[59,60]

Because of lesions in the vestibuloocular connections, the oculomotor pathways may also be affected. This effect may be manifest as diplopia or nystagmus. The nystagmus may be severe enough that the patient complains of oscillopsia (a subjective oscillation of objects in the visual field). Cranial nerve impairment may also include impairment of facial sensation, which is relatively common. Unilateral facial paresis may also occur. In addition, the occurrence of trigeminal neuralgia in a young person may be an early sign of MS.

Motor pathways are also commonly involved. Specifically, corticospinal tract dysfunction is common in patients with MS. Paraparesis or paraplegia is all too common and occurs with greater frequency than upper extremity lesions because of the common occurrence of lesions in the motor tracts of the spinal cord. In patients with significant motor weakness, spasms of the legs and trunk may occur when the patient attempts to stand

from a seated position. This is manifested on physical examination as spasticity that is typically worse in the legs than the arms. The deep tendon reflexes are markedly exaggerated, and sustained clonus may be demonstrated. Although these symptoms are frequently bilateral, they are generally asymmetric.[51]

Sensory manifestations are a frequent initial feature of MS and are present in nearly all patients at some point during the course of the disease. Sensory symptoms are commonly described as numbness, tingling, "pins and needles" paresthesias, coldness, or swelling of the limbs or trunk.[51]

Impairment of the cerebellar pathway results in significant gait imbalance, difficulty with coordinated actions, and dysarthria. Physical examination reveals the typical features of cerebellar dysfunction including dysmetria, dysdiadochokinesia (an impairment of rapid alternating movements), a breakdown in the ability to perform complex movements, an intention tremor in the limbs and head, truncal ataxia, and dysarthria.[51]

Impairment of bowel, bladder, and sexual functions is also common. The extent of sphincter and sexual dysfunction usually parallels the motor impairment in the lower extremities. Urinary frequency may progress to urinary incontinence with progression of the disease. An atonic bladder may develop, which empties by simple overflow and is often associated with the loss of perception of bladder fullness and anal and genital hypoesthesia. Constipation becomes common over time, and almost all patients with paraplegia require special measures to maintain bowel habits. Sexual dysfunction, although frequently overlooked, is common in MS. Approximately 50% of patients become completely sexually inactive secondary to this disease.[51]

Diagnostic Strategies

Although there are no laboratory tests diagnostic for MS, one clinical feature remains relatively unique to this disease. Uhthoff's phenomenon is the syndrome in which small increases in the patient's body temperature can temporarily worsen current or preexisting signs or symptoms of MS. Activities such as exercise, a hot bath, exposure to a warm environment, or fever can bring about Uhthoff's phenomenon. This phenomenon reflects subclinical demyelination or preexisting injury to nerves without obvious significant clinical involvement prior to heat exposure or temperature elevation.[51]

The clinical diagnosis rests on the patient having at least two clinical episodes with different neurologic symptoms that occur at different times. Thus, MS has commonly been described as having lesions that differ in time and space. It has also been described as a relapsing-remitting disorder with symptoms that fluctuate over time.

CSF analysis is abnormal in 90% of cases. Fifty percent of patients have pleocytosis with more than five lymphocytes per high-power field in the CSF. Approximately 70% of patients have an elevated γ-globulin, with immunoglobulin G (IgG) ranging from

10% to 30% of the CSF total protein. Electrophoresis of the CSF demonstrates oligoclonal bands of IgG in 85% to 95% of patients who have a diagnosis of MS. Note, however, that oligoclonal bands of IgG also occur in neurosyphilis, fungal meningitis, and other CNS infections. LP should be considered for all patients with suspected MS, but mass lesions and elevated ICP should be considered and ruled out before LP.[61]

MRI is a sensitive test for lesions consistent with MS and is also useful as a marker of disease severity.[62] In patients with an initial neurologic event consistent with CNS demyelination and an MRI with multiple white matter lesions, the 5-year risk of developing MS is 60%. Patients with similar clinical syndromes and a normal MRI have a 5-year risk of less than 5%.[63]

Differential Considerations

Other diseases that affect the CNS white matter may appear clinically and radiographically similar to MS. Considerable care must be taken to exclude these disease processes before making a diagnosis. These include CNS tumors (especially lymphomas and gliomas), spinal cord compression, vasculitides, Behçet's disease, neurosarcoidosis, postinfectious and postvaccinal encephalomyelitis, human immunodeficiency virus (HIV) encephalopathy, Lyme disease, and vitamin B_{12} deficiency.

Management

Therapy for MS has essentially three arms. The first arm consists of therapies aimed at halting the progression of the disease. The second arm is designed to treat acute exacerbations, and the third arm consists of therapies designed to modify complications.

Therapies aimed at halting disease progress are primarily based on the use of interferon-β or glatiramer acetate. There are two forms of interferon-β: β-1b and β-1a. The interferons are a group of natural compounds that have antiviral and immunomodulatory actions. The side effects include influenza-like symptoms, depression, anxiety, and confusion. In one study, 560 patients with MS were randomly assigned to receive subcutaneous recombinant interferon-β-1a in doses of either 22 or 44 μg or placebo three times a week for 2 years. The relapse rate was significantly lower at 1 and 2 years with both doses of interferon-β-1a than with placebo. Time to first relapse was prolonged by 3 and 5 months in the 22 and 44 μg groups, respectively. The accumulation of burden of disease and number of active lesions on MRI were lower in both treatment groups than in the placebo group. The authors concluded that subcutaneous interferon-β-1a is an effective treatment for relapsing-remitting MS in terms of relapse rate, defined disability, and all MRI outcome measures in a dose-related manner, and it is well tolerated.[64]

Glatiramer acetate (previously called *copolymer 1*) is a mixture of synthetic polypeptides designed to mimic myelin basic protein. The mechanism of action by which glatiramer acetate exerts its effect is unknown.

However, it is thought to act by modifying the immune processes responsible for the pathogenesis of MS. In one study, 251 patients with relapsing-remitting MS were randomly assigned to receive daily subcutaneous injections of glatiramer acetate or placebo for 24 months. Patients receiving glatiramer acetate had significantly fewer relapses and were more likely to be neurologically improved, whereas those receiving placebo were more likely to worsen. This drug is generally quite well tolerated.[65]

Current recommendations for relapsing-remitting MS are to initiate treatment with interferon-β or glatiramer acetate. These therapies have been demonstrated to decrease the volume of plaques seen on MRI and to diminish relapses.[54]

Acute exacerbations should also be targets for therapy. Although most exacerbations resolve without therapy, steroids have been demonstrated to diminish the duration of acute exacerbations. More than 85% of patients with relapsing and remitting MS show improvement with intravenous methylprednisolone. Steroids have been shown in controlled trials to speed the recovery of the visual loss of optic neuritis when compared with placebo. In addition, when patients with acute optic neuritis are treated with high-dose steroids, the 2-year rate of development of MS is reduced, although this effect diminishes over time.[58,66]

The current standard therapy for an acute exacerbation in MS is intravenous methylprednisolone. A typical dose administered intravenously is 250 to 500 mg every 12 hours for 3 to 7 days. It remains controversial whether this should be followed by an oral prednisolone taper. Complications of methylprednisolone therapy include fluid retention, gastrointestinal hemorrhage, anxiety, psychosis, infection, and osteoporosis.

There are several therapies directed toward the complications of MS. The associated spasticity is generally treated with baclofen. Baclofen is a highly effective therapy aimed at reducing the painful flexor and extensor spasms. A major side effect is drowsiness, which generally diminishes with continued use. Higher dose therapy can cause confusion, especially in the setting of baseline cognitive impairment. For patients with intractable spasticity, baclofen is available for intrathecal administration by either bolus therapy or continuous implanted pump therapy. Additional therapies for spasticity include tizanidine, diazepam, and dantrolene.

The tremor and ataxia associated with MS are occasionally treated with propranolol, diazepam, or clonazepam. The results of these therapies, however, are generally unsatisfactory. Pain is often associated with MS and affects the shoulders, pelvic girdle, and face. The facial pain may be indistinguishable from that of trigeminal neuralgia. Treatment options include carbamazepine, baclofen, or tricyclic antidepressants. Fatigue, which is common, may be treated with amantadine. These drugs produce partial relief for a minority of patients. In controlled studies, the effect of these medications is only slightly better than that of placebo.[54]

Disposition

Patients with a history of MS who seek treatment in the emergency department for significant symptoms must first be evaluated to rule out other, non–MS-related pathology. Also, systemic illness, especially infections, can cause an exacerbation and must be ruled out. If the problem is thought to be an exacerbation of MS, most patients require admission for intravenous steroid therapy. An alternative to admission may be to initiate intravenous steroids in the emergency department, and arrange for next-day follow-up with the primary care physician or neurologist if outpatient intravenous steroid administration is an option. Most important is the awareness of the emergency physician in order to identify early symptoms of MS or a recurrence so that appropriate therapy may be instituted.

 KEY CONCEPTS

- The diagnosis of MS should be considered in young to middle-aged patients who present with recurring episodes of neurologic impairment. Optic neuritis is often the first symptom.

- Patients with apparent recurring or relapsing MS should be evaluated to rule out other CNS pathology and possible exacerbating factors such as infections before the symptoms are attributed to an exacerbation of MS.

- Optimal therapy for patients with MS involves consultation with the patient's primary care provider or neurologist to provide consistent disease management.

- Intravenous methylprednisolone effectively promotes earlier resolution of recurrences and has been shown to speed recovery of vision loss from optic neuritis.

REFERENCES

1. Katusic S, et al: Incidence and clinical features of trigeminal neuralgia, Rochester, Minnesota 1945-1984. *Ann Neurol* 27:89, 1990.
2. Patel NK, et al: How accurate is magnetic resonance angiography in predicting neurovascular compression in patients with trigeminal neuralgia? A prospective, single-blinded comparative study. *Br J Neurosurg* 17:60, 2003.
3. Fukuda H, Ishikawa M, Okumura R: Demonstration of neurovascular compression in trigeminal neuralgia and hemifacial spasm with magnetic resonance imaging. Comparison with surgical findings in 60 consecutive cases. *Surg Neurol* 59:93, 2003.
4. Tenser RB: Trigeminal neuralgia: Mechanisms of treatment. *Neurology* 51:17, 1998.
5. Delzell JE, Grelle AR: Trigeminal neuralgia: New treatment options for a well known cause of facial pain. *Arch Fam Med* 8:264, 1999.
6. Jensen TS, et al: Association of trigeminal neuralgia with multiple sclerosis: Clinical and pathological features. *Acta Neurol Scand* 65:182, 1982.
7. Taha JM, Tew JM Jr: Comparison of surgical treatments for trigeminal neuralgia: Reevaluation of radiofrequency of rhizotomy. *Neurosurgery* 38:865, 1996.
8. Chen JF, Lee ST: Comparison of percutaneous trigeminal ganglion compression and microvascular decompression for the management of trigeminal neuralgia. *Clin Neurol Neurosurg* 105:203, 2003.
9. McLaughlin M, et al: Microvascular decompression of cranial nerves: Lessons learned after 4400 operations. *J Neurosurg* 90:1, 1999.
10. Kondziolka D, et al: Gamma knife radiosurgery for trigeminal neuralgia. *Arch Neurol* 55:1524, 1998.
11. Shetter AG, et al: Gamma knife radiosurgery for recurrent trigeminal neuralgia. *J Neurosurg* 97(Suppl 5):536, 2002.
12. Adour KK, et al: The true nature of Bell's palsy: Analysis of 1000 consecutive patients. *Laryngoscope* 88:787, 1978.
13. Hauser W, et al: Incidence and prognosis of Bell's palsy in the population of Rochester, Minnesota. *Mayo Clin Proc* 46:258, 1971.
14. Facial Nerve. In Standring S: *Gray's Anatomy*. London, Churchill Livingstone, 2005, pp 513-515.
15. Jackson CG, von Doersten PG: The facial nerve: Current trends in diagnosis, treatment, and rehabilitation. *Med Clin North Am* 83:179, 1999.
16. Marenda SA, Olsson JE: The evaluation of facial paralysis. *Otolaryngol Clin North Am* 30:669, 1997.
17. Knox GW: Treatment controversies in Bell's palsy. *Arch Otolaryngol Head Neck Surg* 124:821, 1998.
18. Ruckenstein M: Evaluating facial paralysis: Expensive diagnostic tests are often unnecessary. *Postgrad Med* 103:187, 1998.
19. Murakami S, et al: Bell's palsy and herpes simplex virus: Identification of viral DNA in endoneurial fluid and muscle. *Ann Intern Med* 124:27, 1996.
20. Adour KK, et al: Bell's palsy treatment with acyclovir and prednisone compared with prednisone alone: A double-blind, randomized, controlled trial. *Ann Otol Rhinol Laryngol* 105:371, 1996.
21. Axelsson S, Lindberg S, Stjernquist-Desatnik A: Outcome of treatment with valacyclovir and prednisone in patients with Bell's palsy. *Ann Otol Rhinol Laryngol* 112:197, 2003.
22. Dickins JR, et al: Herpes zoster oticus: Treatment with intravenous acyclovir. *Laryngoscope* 98:776, 1998.
23. Uri N, et al: Acyclovir in the treatment of Ramsay Hunt syndrome. *Otolaryngol Head Neck Surg* 129:379, 2003
24. Dotevall L, Hagberg LL: Successful oral doxycycline treatment of Lyme disease–associated facial palsy and meningitis. *Clin Infect Dis* 28:569, 1999.
25. Cook SP, et al: Lyme disease and seventh nerve paralysis in children. *Am J Otolaryngol* 18:320, 1997.
26. Smith V, Traquina DN: Pediatric bilateral facial paralysis. *Laryngoscope* 108:519, 1998.
27. Joseph EM, Sperling NM: Facial nerve paralysis in acute otitis media: Cause and management revisited. *Otolaryngol Head Neck Surg* 118:694, 1998.
28. Jackson CG, et al: Facial paralysis of neoplastic origin: Diagnosis and management. *Laryngoscope* 90:1581, 1980.
29. The Consensus Development Panel: National Institutes of Health Consensus Development Conference statement on acoustic neuroma. *Arch Neurol* 51:201, 1994.
30. Selesnick SH, Jackler RK: Clinical manifestations and audiologic diagnosis of acoustic neuromas. *Otolaryngol Clin North Am* 25:521, 1992.
31. Wright A, Bradford R: Management of acoustic neuroma. *BMJ* 311:1141, 1995.
32. Selesnick SH, et al: The changing clinical presentation of acoustic tumors in the MRI era. *Laryngoscope* 103:431, 1993.
33. Harvey SA, Haberkamp TJ: Pitfalls in the diagnosis of CPA tumors. *Ear Nose Throat J* 70:290, 2000.
34. Watanabe K, et al: Characteristics of cranial nerve palsies in diabetic patients. *Diabetes Res Clin Pract* 10:19, 1990.
35. Thomas PK: Clinical features and investigation of diabetic somatic peripheral neuropathy. *Neuroscience* 4:341, 1997.
36. Asbury AK, et al: Oculomotor palsy in diabetes mellitus: A clinico-pathological study. *Brain* 93:555, 1970.

37. Brown MJ, Asbury AK: Diabetic neuropathy. *Ann Neurol* 15:2, 1984.

38. Clements RS, Bell DSH: Diabetic neuropathy peripheral and autonomic syndromes. *Postgrad Med* 71:50, 1982.

39. Fujioka T, et al: Ischemic and hemorrhagic brain stem lesions mimicking diabetic ophthalmoplegia. *Clin Neurol Neurosurg* 97:167, 1995.

40. Villringer A, Einhäupl KM: Dural sinus and cerebral venous thrombosis. *New Horiz* 5:332, 1997.

41. Wasson J, Redenbaugh J: Transverse sinus thrombosis: An unusual cause of headache. *Headache* 37:457, 1997.

42. Villringer A, et al: Pathophysiological aspects of cerebral sinus venous thrombosis (SVT). *J Neuroradiol* 21:72, 1994.

43. Provenzale JM, et al: Dural sinus thrombosis: Findings on CT and MRI and diagnostic pitfalls. *AJR Am J Roentgenol* 170:777, 1998.

44. Lalive PH, et al: Is measurement of D-dimer useful in the diagnosis of cerebral venous thrombosis? *Neurology* 61:1057, 2003.

45. Tardy B, et al: D-dimer levels in patients with suspected acute cerebral venous thrombosis. *Am J Med* 113:238, 2002.

46. Preter M, et al: Long-term prognosis in cerebral venous thrombosis: Follow-up of 77 patients. *Stroke* 27:243, 1996.

47. Frey JL, et al: Cerebral venous thrombosis: Combined intrathrombus rTPA and intravenous heparin. *Stroke* 30:489, 1999.

48. Einhäupl KM, et al: Heparin treatment in sinus venous thrombosis. *Lancet* 338:597, 1991.

49. de Bruijn SF, Stam J: Randomized, placebo-controlled trial of anticoagulant treatment with low-molecular-weight heparin for cerebral sinus thrombosis. *Stroke* 30:484, 1999.

50. Wasay M, et al: Nonrandomized comparison of local urokinase thrombolysis versus systemic heparin anticoagulation for superior sagittal sinus thrombosis. *Stroke* 32:2310, 2001.

51. Francis GS, et al: Inflammatory demyelinating diseases of the central nervous system. In Bradley WG, et al (eds): *Neurology in Clinical Practice.* Boston, Butterworth-Heinemann, 1996, pp 1308-1343.

52. Kurtzke JF, et al: Multiple sclerosis in the Faroe Islands: Transmission across four epidemics. *Acta Neurol Scand* 91:321, 1995.

53. Hogenkamp WE, et al: The epidemiology of multiple sclerosis. *Mayo Clin Proc* 72:871, 1997.

54. Giovannoni G, Miller D: Multiple sclerosis and its treatment. *J R Coll Physicians Lond* 33:315, 1999.

55. Rao SM, et al: Cognitive dysfunction in multiple sclerosis. I. Frequency, patterns, and prediction. *Neurology* 41:685, 1991.

56. Swirsky-Sacchetti T, et al: Neuropsychological and structural brain lesions in multiple sclerosis: A regional analysis. *Neurology* 42:1291, 1992.

57. Wray S: Optic neuritis: Guidelines. *Curr Opin Neurol* 8:72, 1995.

58. Beck RW, et al: The effect of corticosteroids for acute optic neuritis on the subsequent development of multiple sclerosis. *N Engl J Med* 329:1764, 1993.

59. Ebers GC: Optic neuritis and multiple sclerosis. *Arch Neurol* 42:702, 1985.

60. Kidd D: Presentations of multiple sclerosis. *Practitioner* 243:24, 1999.

61. Mehta PD: Diagnostic usefulness of cerebrospinal fluid in multiple sclerosis. *Crit Rev Clin Lab Sci* 28:233, 1991.

62. Lee KH, et al: Magnetic resonance imaging of the head in the diagnosis of multiple sclerosis: A prospective 2-year follow-up with comparison of clinical evaluation, evoked potentials, oligoclonal banding, and CT. *Neurology* 41:657, 1991.

63. Morrissey SP, et al: The significance of brain magnetic resonance imaging abnormalities at presentation with clinically isolated syndromes suggestive of multiple sclerosis: A 5-year follow-up study. *Brain* 116:135, 1993.

64. Anonymous: Randomised double-blind placebo-controlled study of interferon β-1a in relapsing/remitting multiple sclerosis. PRISMS (Prevention of Relapses and Disability by Interferon β-1a Subcutaneously in Multiple Sclerosis) Study Group. *Lancet* 352:1498, 1998.

65. Johnson KP, et al: Extended use of glatiramer acetate (Copaxone) is well tolerated and maintains its clinical effect on multiple sclerosis relapse rate and degree of disability. *Neurology* 50:701, 1998.

66. Beck RW, et al: A randomized, controlled trial of corticosteroids in the treatment of acute optic neuritis. *N Engl J Med* 326:581, 1992.

CHAPTER 104

Spinal Cord Disorders

Andrew D. Perron and J. Stephen Huff

PERSPECTIVE

Spinal cord disorders encompass a wide range of pathologic entities and may affect all age groups. Some spinal cord disorders may have catastrophic outcomes if not recognized early in the clinical course. The ultimate neurologic outcome of many of these disorders may depend on an expeditious recognition by the emergency physician with appropriate initial diagnostic actions, neuroimaging, management, and consultation

for definitive therapy. As with so many disease processes affecting the nervous system, knowledge of the anatomic organization of the spinal cord and skill in taking a history and performing a neurologic examination are required for the emergency physician to make a correct diagnosis and manage these patients appropriately. This chapter generally concerns processes affecting the spinal cord and its vascular supply and processes compressing the spinal cord. Direct trauma and mechanical instability of the spinal column are discussed in Chapter 40.

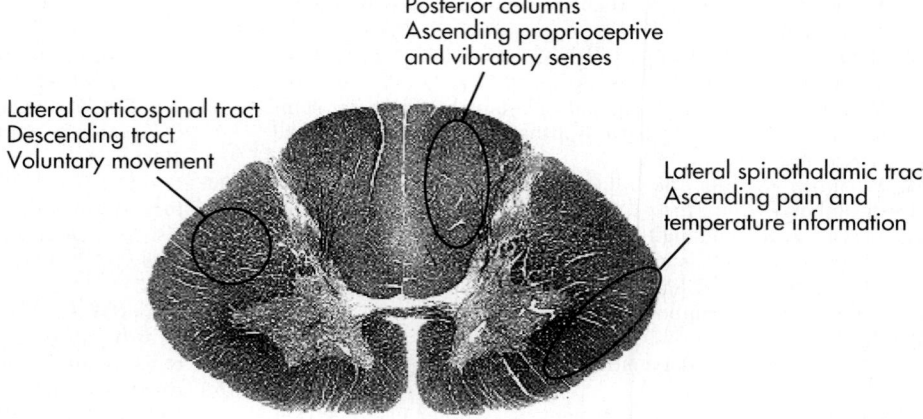

Figure 104-1. Simplified spinal cord anatomy showing clinically essential motor and sensory tracts. (Photomicrograph courtesy of John Sundsten, Digital Anatomist Project, University of Washington.)

Posterior columns
Ascending proprioceptive and vibratory senses

Lateral corticospinal tract
Descending tract
Voluntary movement

Lateral spinothalamic tract
Ascending pain and temperature information

PRINCIPLES OF DISEASE

Anatomy

In adults, the spinal cord is approximately 40 cm long and extends from the foramen magnum, where it is continuous with the medulla oblongata, to the body of the first or second lumbar vertebra. Similar to the brain, the spinal cord is covered by three meningeal layers: the inner pial layer, the arachnoid, and the outer dural layer. At its lower end, the spinal cord tapers into the conus medullaris, where several segmental levels are represented in a small area. The lumbar and sacral nerve roots form the cauda equina as they descend caudally in the thecal sac before exit of the spinal canal at the respective foramina. The non-neural filum terminale runs from the tip of the conus and inserts into the dura at the level of the second sacral vertebra.

There are two symmetric enlargements of the spinal cord that contain the segments that innervate the limbs. The cervical enlargement (cord level C5-T1) gives rise to the brachial plexus and subsequently to the peripheral nerves of the upper extremity. The lumbar enlargement (L2-S3) gives rise to the lumbosacral plexus and peripheral nerves of the lower extremity. The space surrounding the spinal cord within the spinal canal is reduced in the area of the enlargements, potentially leaving the cord more vulnerable to compression in these regions. At each segmental level, anterior (ventral) and posterior (dorsal) roots arise from rootlets along the anterolateral and posterolateral surfaces of the cord. At each level, the anterior root conveys the outflow of the motor neurons in the anterior horn of the spinal cord, and the posterior root contains sensory neurons and fibers that convey sensory inflow.

The arterial supply of the spinal cord is derived primarily from two sources. The single anterior spinal artery arises from the paired vertebral arteries. This anterior spinal artery runs the entire length of the cord in the midline anterior median sulcus and supplies roughly the anterior two thirds of the spinal cord. Blood supply to the posterior third of the spinal cord derives from the smaller paired posterior spinal arteries. The anterior and the posterior spinal arteries receive segmental contributions from radicular arteries, the largest being the radicular artery of Adamkiewicz, which typically originates from the aorta between T8 and L4. The venous drainage of the cord largely parallels the arterial supply.

The internal anatomy of the spinal cord is divided into central gray matter, which contains cell bodies and their processes, and surrounding white matter, where the ascending and descending myelinated fiber tracts are located. These fiber tracts are organized into discrete bundles, with the ascending tracts conveying sensory information and the descending tracts conveying the efferent motor impulses and visceral innervation.

For clinical purposes, neuroanatomy of the spinal cord may be greatly simplified (Figure 104-1). Major ascending sensory tracts are represented on the right side of Figure 104-1, with motor tracts on the left side. The posterior columns carry afferent ascending proprioceptive and vibratory information on the ipsilateral side of the cord to the area stimulated; decussation of these fibers occurs in the medulla so that contralateral cortical representation ultimately occurs. In a portion of the lateral column of white matter, the lateral spinothalamic tract conveys afferent information about pain and temperature. (Tracts are named with their point of origin first so that the spinothalamic tract arises in the spinal cord and travels to the thalamus.) The tract is laminated so that sacral fibers are represented most laterally. Crossing of fibers from this tract occurs near the level of entry of the spinal nerve; a cord lesion affecting one lateral spinothalamic tract results in decreased or absent pain and temperature perception below the level of injury on the contralateral side of the body.

For clinical purposes, the major descending motor tract is represented in the lateral corticospinal tract (which, as the name implies, originates in the cortex and flows toward the spinal cord). This tract also is anatomically organized, with efferent motor axons to the cervical area located medially and the sacral efferent axons located laterally. Decussation of this descending tract occurs in the medulla. The cell bodies of the lower motor neurons (anterior horn cells) are in the ventral portion of the gray matter of the spinal cord.

Classification of Spinal Cord Syndromes

The anatomic organization of the spinal cord lends itself to a corresponding anatomic pathophysiologic classification of cord dysfunction. The different anatomic syndromes may be the final clinical picture of a variety of clinical processes either extrinsic or intrinsic to the spinal cord. Frequently the syndromes exist in partial or incomplete forms.

Complete (Transverse) Spinal Cord Syndrome

Complete spinal cord lesions may occur as either acute or subacute pathologic processes. A complete spinal cord lesion is defined as a total loss of sensory, autonomic, and voluntary motor innervation distal to the spinal cord level of injury. Reflex responses mediated at the spinal level, such as muscle stretch ("deep tendon") reflexes, may persist, although they also may be absent or abnormal. Autonomic dysfunction may be manifest with hypotension (neurogenic shock) or priapism. The most common cause of the complete transverse cord syndrome is trauma, although this anatomic syndrome is nonspecific as to etiology.[1,2] Other causes of acute complete cord syndrome include infarction, hemorrhages, and entities causing extrinsic compression. Of patients who develop complete transverse syndromes that persist for more than 24 hours, 99% do not have a functional recovery.[3,4] An important point to consider before diagnosing a complete cord lesion is that any evidence of cord function below the level of injury denotes a partial rather than a complete lesion. Signs such as persistent perianal sensation ("sacral sparing"), rectal sphincter tone or voluntary rectal sphincter contraction, or voluntary toe movement suggest a partial cord lesion, which has a better prognosis than a complete lesion.[1]

Spinal shock refers to the loss of muscle tone and reflexes with complete cord syndrome during the acute phase of injury. The intensity of the spinal shock increases with the height of the level in the spinal cord.[5] Spinal shock typically lasts less than 24 hours but has been reported occasionally to last days to weeks.[5,6] A marker of spinal shock is loss of the bulbocavernosus reflex, which is a normal cord-mediated reflex that may be preserved in complete cord lesions. The bulbocavernosus reflex involves involuntary reflex contraction of the anal sphincter in response to a squeeze of the glans penis or a tug on the Foley catheter. The termination of the spinal shock phase of injury is heralded by the return of the bulbocavernosus reflex; increased muscle tone and hyperreflexia follow later.[5,6]

Incomplete Spinal Cord Lesions

Incomplete spinal lesions are characterized by preservation of function of various portions of the spinal cord. Of all incomplete spinal lesions, most can be classified into one of three clinical syndromes: central cord syndrome, Brown-Séquard syndrome, or anterior cord syndrome (Table 104-1).

Central Cord Syndrome

Central cord syndrome, first described by Schneider and colleagues in 1954, is the most prevalent of the partial cord syndromes.[7,8] It is characterized by bilateral motor paresis, with upper extremities affected to a greater degree than lower extremities and distal muscle groups affected to a greater degree than proximal muscle groups. Sensory impairment and bladder dysfunction are variable. At times, burning dysesthesias in the upper extremities may be the dominant feature.[9] Central cord injury affects the central gray matter and the central portions of the corticospinal and spinothalamic tracts. It is caused most often by a hyperextension injury, with the postulated mechanism being squeezing or pinching of the spinal cord anteriorly and posteriorly by inward bulging of the ligamentum flavum. The most common mechanism is a fall, followed by a motor vehicle crash.[10] The result is contusion to the spinal cord, with the central portion being most affected. This injury classically occurs in elderly individuals with degenerative arthritis and spinal stenosis in the cervical area, but may affect any patient with cervical canal narrowing of any etiology (e.g., congenital narrow canal as seen in achondroplasia or canal narrowing from disk protrusion or tumor). The prognosis for patients with central cord syndrome varies, depending on the degree of injury at presentation and patient age.[10,11] In patients younger than 50 years old, more than 80% regain bladder continence, and approximately 90% return to ambulatory status. In patients older than 50, only 30% regain bladder function, with approximately 50% regaining ambulation.[11]

Brown-Séquard Syndrome

Brown-Séquard syndrome, first described in 1846 by the physician for whom it is named,[12] may be an anatomic or functional hemisection of the spinal cord. Usually the result of penetrating injuries,[13] Brown-Séquard syndrome also may be the result of compressive or intrinsic lesions. The syndrome has been reported in association with spinal cord tumors, spinal epidural hematoma, vascular malformations, cervical spondylosis, and radiation injury; as a complication of spinal instrumentation; and resulting from degenerative disk disease.[13] The syndrome in its pure form is characterized by ipsilateral loss of motor function and proprioception/vibration with contralateral loss of pain and temperature sensation below the spinal cord level of injury. Because fibers associated with the lateral spinothalamic tract ascend or descend one to two cord segments before crossing to the contralateral side, ipsilateral anesthesia (pain and temperature modalities) may be noted one or two segments above the lesion, although this observation is variable. Most patients with Brown-Séquard syndrome have only partial syndromes of sensory and motor impairment, and the classic pattern is not seen.[11,13,14] Brown-Séquard syndrome has the best prognosis of any of the incomplete spinal cord syndromes. Eighty percent to 90% of patients with Brown-Séquard syndrome regain bowel and bladder function, 75% regain ambulatory status,

Table 104-1. Spinal Cord Syndromes

	Sensory	Motor	Sphincter Involvement
Central cord	Variable	Upper extremity weakness, distal > proximal	Variable
Brown-Séquard syndrome	Ipsilateral position and vibration loss Contralateral pain and temperature loss	Motor loss ipsilateral to cord lesion	Variable
Anterior cord syndrome	Loss of pin and touch Vibration, position preserved	Motor loss or weakness below level	Variable
Transverse cord syndrome—complete	Loss of sensation below level of cord injury	Loss of voluntary motor function below cord level	Sphincter control lost
Conus medullaris syndrome	Saddle anesthesia may be present, or sensory loss may range from patchy to complete transverse pattern	Weakness may be of upper motor neuron type	Sphincter control impaired
Cauda equina syndrome	Saddle anesthesia may be present, or sensory loss may range from patchy to complete transverse pattern	Weakness may be of lower motor neuron type	Sphincter control impaired

and 70% become independent in their activities of daily living.[11]

Anterior Cord Syndrome

Anterior cord syndrome is characterized by loss of motor function, pinprick, and light touch below the level of the lesion, with preservation of posterior column function, including some touch, position, and vibratory sensation. Although most reports of anterior spinal syndrome are in cases that follow aortic surgery,[15] the syndrome has been reported after severe hypotension, infection, myocardial infarction, vasospasm from drug reaction, and aortic angiography.[16] This lesion may result from a cervical hyperflexion

injury resulting in a cord contusion or by protrusion of bony fragments or herniated cervical disk material into the spinal canal. Rarely, it is produced by laceration or thrombosis of the anterior spinal artery or a major radicular feeding vessel.[11] Patients present with the characteristic neurologic findings noted earlier. Functional recovery varies, with most improvement made in the first 24 hours but little improvement thereafter.[4] Although anterior cord lesions from ischemia are usually incomplete, patients without motor function at 30 days have little or no likelihood of regaining any motor function by 1 year.[17] Overall, only 10% to 20% of patients with this entity regain some muscle function, and even in this group there is little power or coordination.[11]

Conus Medullaris Syndrome/Cauda Equina Syndromes

The separation of conus medullaris and cauda equina lesions in clinical practice is difficult because the clinical features of the disorders overlap. Additionally, a combined lesion may occur that masks clear clinical symptoms or signs of either an upper or a lower motor neuron type of injury. The conus medullaris is the terminal end of the spinal cord located at approximately L1 in adults. The conus medullaris syndrome may involve disturbances of urination (usually manifested as a denervated, autonomic bladder that presents clinically with overflow incontinence) and sphincter involvement or sexual dysfunction. Sensory involvement may affect the sacral and coccygeal segments, resulting in saddle anesthesia. Pure lesions of the conus medullaris are rare.[18] Upper motor neuron signs, such as increased motor tone and abnormal reflexes, may be present, but their absence does not exclude the syndrome. The conus medullaris syndrome can be caused by central disk herniation, neoplasm, trauma, or vascular insufficiency. Because the conus is such a small structure, with lumbar and sacral segments represented in a small area, a lesion usually causes bilateral symptoms. This may help distinguish lesions of the conus from lesions of the cauda equina, which are often unilateral.[18]

The *cauda equina* ("horse's tail") is the name given to the lumbar and sacral nerve roots that continue on within the dural sac caudal to the conus medullaris. The etiology of the cauda equina syndrome is usually a ruptured, midline intervertebral disk, most commonly occurring at the L4-5 level. Tumors and other compressive masses also may cause the syndrome. Similar to the conus medullaris syndrome, patients generally present with progressive symptoms of fecal or urinary incontinence, impotence, distal motor weakness, and sensory loss in a saddle distribution. Muscle stretch reflexes also may be reduced. The presence of urinary retention is the most consistent finding, with a sensitivity of 90%.[19] Low back pain may or may not be present.

CLINICAL FEATURES

History

Weakness, sensory abnormalities, and autonomic dysfunction are the cardinal symptoms of spinal cord dysfunction. The tempo and degree of impairment often reflect the disease process. A history of cancer should suggest the possibility of metastatic disease. Recent trauma raises the possibility of vertebral fracture or disk protrusion. Past medical history is vital because a history of coagulopathy or other systemic processes may be elicited.

Physical Examination

The physical examination pertinent to spinal cord dysfunction involves testing in three areas: (1) motor function, (2) sensory function, and (3) reflexes. Each component is best tested with the anatomic organization of the spinal cord in mind to help determine the location of the spinal cord dysfunction.

Motor Function

Testing of motor function encompasses examination of muscle bulk, tone, and strength. Muscle bulk is easily examined in large motor groups, such as the thigh or calf muscles, the biceps, or the triceps. Inspection of the intrinsic hand muscles also may be helpful for determining muscle bulk; wasting may be evident as hollowed or recessed regions of the hand. Decreased mass, asymmetry, or fasciculations should be noted. Tone is tested with repeated passive knee, elbow, or wrist flexion, with the examiner feeling for abnormally increased or decreased resistance. Rapid pronation and supination of the forearm is another useful method to assess tone. Increased tone may indicate spasticity or an upper motor neuron lesion, whereas decreased tone corresponds with lower motor neuron, motor end plate, or muscular problems. Finally, motor strength is graded in the upper and the lower extremities. A rectal examination is performed to assess voluntary sphincter contraction, resting tone, and, as described previously, the bulbocavernosus reflex. Motor grading for the neurologic examination is relatively straightforward. Scored on a 0-to-5 scale, neuromuscular functioning is graded as follows:

0. No firing of the muscle is present.
1. The muscle fires, but is unable to move the intended part.
2. The muscle is able to move the intended part with gravity eliminated.
3. The muscle is able to move the intended part against gravity.
4. The muscle is able to move the intended part, but not at full strength.
5. Full muscular strength is present.

Sensory Function

Sensory testing requires a cooperative patient and an attentive examiner. The spinal cord–related modalities that may be clinically useful for emergency physicians include pinprick, light touch (contralateral lateral spinothalamic tract), and proprioception (ipsilateral posterior column). Testing of the patient's response to pinprick, light touch, and proprioception in all four extremities is necessary if a neurologic injury is suspected. Testing of sacral dermatomes may be an important part of the examination in some patients. As previously noted, sacral sparing is an important finding that indicates spinal cord dysfunction may be incomplete. The sensory fibers from sacral dermatomes are more peripherally located in the ascending fiber bundles; central or partial cord lesions may ablate sensation in the extremities, yet allow some perception of sensation in the sacral area.

Reflexes

Muscle stretch ("deep tendon") reflexes may be tested rapidly at the bedside. Responses are graded on a 0-to-

Table 104-2. Clinical Characteristics of Neuromuscular Diseases

	History	Strength	DTR	Sensation	Wasting
Myelopathy	Trauma, infection, cancer	Normal to decreased	Increased	Normal to decreased	No
Motor neuron disease (ALS)	Progressive difficulty swallowing, speaking, walking	Decreased	Increased	Normal	Yes
Neuropathy	Recent infection Ascending weakness	Normal or decreased Distal > proximal	Decreased	Decreased	Yes
Neuromuscular junction disease	Food (canned goods) Tick exposure Easy fatigability	Normal to fatigue	Normal	Normal	No
Myopathy	Thyroid disease Previous similar episodes	Decreased Proximal > distal	Normal	Normal	Yes

ALS, amyotrophic lateral sclerosis; DTR, deep tendon reflex.

4+ scale, with 2 being normal. Hyperactive reflexes suggest upper motor neuron disease (affecting the neurons or their outflow from the brain or spinal cord), as does sustained clonus. Reflexes may be diminished or absent when sensation is lost or when lower motor neuron disease is present. Diseases of muscles or neuromuscular junctions also may decrease reflexes. In acute cord injury, reflexes may be diminished in the acute phase. The bulbocavernosus reflex may be helpful in this assessment.

DIAGNOSTIC STRATEGIES

Historical or physical examination findings that suggest spinal cord dysfunction prompt further investigations. The basic strategy is to detect or exclude extrinsic compressive lesions or other potentially treatable entities. Magnetic resonance imaging (MRI) has changed the diagnostic approach to patients with suspected spinal cord dysfunction. Plain radiographs and computed tomography (CT) scans may show bony and some soft tissue abnormalities. Conventional radiographs and CT scans are required in patients with trauma or suspected bony involvement by tumor or degenerative processes, but MRI shows many of these abnormalities and defines the spinal cord. Tissue damage patterns within the cord, such as hemorrhage and edema, also may be detected with MRI. CT myelography may be requested by some consultants. Institutions vary in procedures that are available. After imaging studies exclude compressive lesions or other masses affecting the spinal cord, the possibility of inflammatory or demyelinating etiologies remains, and lumbar puncture may be useful in diagnosis.

DIFFERENTIAL CONSIDERATIONS

The prime principle in management of spinal cord dysfunction is to consider and exclude potentially treatable problems. The clinical assessment of spinal cord dysfunction is limited to detecting weakness, sensory alterations, sphincter dysfunction, and perhaps reflex abnormalities. Pain in the back may be present depending on the pathologic process. Because potential functional loss and impact on quality of life are great, the detection of a process where some intervention is possible assumes great importance. A likely diagnosis of spinal cord infarction may be entertained, but the pursuit of a treatable process, such as spinal cord compression from an epidural hematoma, should be seriously considered.[20] This discovery process may involve specialty consultation or obtaining studies not readily available in many emergency settings, such as MRI. As a general rule, liberal consultation and imaging are suggested when the possibility of spinal cord dysfunction is considered. The history may suggest an etiology and guides the tempo of investigation.

The picture of a complete transverse spinal cord syndrome with paraplegia, sensory loss at a clear anatomic level, and sphincter dysfunction cannot be fully simulated by other anatomic lesions. Incomplete or evolving spinal cord syndromes may be imitated by other processes, however. It is always prudent to consider an anatomic differential diagnosis—the classic "where is the lesion"—during the diagnostic process (Table 104-2). Progressive lower extremity weakness and sensory alteration may represent cord dysfunction, but could reflect an intracranial vertex mass with bilateral cortical dysfunction. Another example is that of a patient with a rapidly progressive paralysis with areflexia and quadriplegia; ascending paralysis (Landry-Guillain-Barré syndrome) at times may mimic an acute cord lesion. Ataxia rarely has been reported as an isolated finding with spinal cord compression.[21]

Generally, pathologic processes involving the spinal cord may be divided into processes affecting the cord or its blood supply primarily, such as demyelination, infection, or infarction, and processes that compress the cord, most often originating outside the dura (Box 104-1). *Myelitis* is a comprehensive term for spinal cord inflammation with dysfunction, and the etiologies are legion. Although a variety of entities may cause cord compression, the clinical presentation is often similar. The tempo of the process may yield a different clinical picture. In chronic compression, muscle wasting and abnormal reflexes may be present, whereas both of these may be lacking in acute compression. When the

Box 104-1. Nontraumatic Etiologies of Spinal Cord Dysfunction

Processes Affecting the Spinal Cord or Blood Supply Directly
Demyelination
   Multiple sclerosis
   Transverse myelitis
Spinal Arteriovenous Malformation/Subarachnoid Hemorrhage
   Syringomyelia
   Traumatic
   Tumor
Idiopathic Spastic Paraparesis
   HIV myelopathy
   Other myelopathies
   Spinal cord infarction
Compressive Lesions Affecting the Spinal Cord
Spinal Epidural Hematoma
   Spinal epidural abscess
   Diskitis
   Neoplasm
   Metastatic
   Primary CNS

HIV, human immunodeficiency virus; CNS, central nervous system.

examiner finds a neurologic deficit in concert with back pain, a spinal cord lesion should be strongly considered and ultimately ruled in or out. Atypical presentations for these lesions are the norm, and a low threshold for investigation is important.

MANAGEMENT

Just as the clinical manifestations of spinal cord dysfunction are nonspecific as to etiology, the treatment for many of the disease entities is often nonspecific. Steroids traditionally have been accepted therapy in spinal cord trauma, although this use has been coming into question in the medical literature[22-24]; they also are employed with many causes of cord compression, although rigorous clinical studies supporting this use are lacking. Radiation treatment is recommended for cord compression by tumor. Surgical consultation for decompression may be considered, although the indications for surgery and timing of surgery are controversial. Involvement of consultants and discussion of what may be understudied therapies are suggested. The specific diagnosis is needed for treatment and guides therapy. A discussion of specific disease processes follows.

SPECIFIC DISEASE PROCESSES

As noted earlier, spinal cord disorders may be grouped into lesions resulting from processes intrinsic to the cord and vasculature and lesions causing extrinsic compression. The order of this discussion roughly follows the organization of Box 104-1.

Intrinsic Cord Lesions

Multiple Sclerosis

Principles of Disease
Demyelination denotes a disease process with the prominent feature of partial or complete loss of the myelin sheath surrounding the axons of the central nervous system. Multiple sclerosis (MS) is the most common example of such a process; spinal cord involvement may dominate the clinical picture.

Clinical Features
Central nervous system lesions that are "scattered in time and space" are the hallmark of MS. The demyelinated segments do not transmit action potentials normally, resulting in a wide variety of spinal cord findings, depending on the location and extent of the demyelination. In addition to patchy motor and sensory findings, patients with MS may complain of bladder dysfunction, tremor, or evidence of a transverse partial or complete cord syndrome mimicking a compressive spinal lesion.[25,26] There may be a history of optic neuritis or transient visual problems. Spinal cord lesions in MS primarily involve the lateral corticospinal tracts, the posterior columns, and the lateral spinothalamic tracts. Motor system dysfunction is the most frequent manifestation of MS involvement of the spinal cord, usually as a result of lesions in the lateral corticospinal tracts.

The examination of these patients is often characterized by paresis, increased muscle tone, hyperreflexia, clonus, and a Babinski response. Spinal cord involvement also may result in dysautonomias. Signs of other central nervous system involvement, such as pallor of the optic disks, may be present.

Diagnostic Strategies
Spinal MRI is the imaging test of choice for the diagnosis because it can exclude motor symptoms and show lesions suggesting MS.[26-28] Cranial MRI may be helpful in showing other central nervous system lesions. Cerebrospinal fluid (CSF) testing for myelin basic protein and oligoclonal bands also is a diagnostic option, but no CSF abnormalities are entirely specific for MS.[29,30] Oligoclonal bands in the CSF may aid in the diagnosis, but they are significant only if not present in the serum as well.[29]

Differential Considerations
The differential diagnosis includes systemic lupus erythematosus, Lyme disease, neurosyphilis, human immunodeficiency virus (HIV) myelopathy, and others.

Management
MS exacerbations may be treated with high-dose methylprednisolone followed by a tapering dose of prednisone. Corticosteroids have been shown to be useful in shortening the time required for recovery from an exacerbation of MS.[26] Consultation and referral are indicated. Immunosuppressive therapy in patients with the chronic progressive form of the disease has met with

variable success.[25,26] Because numerous disorders can mimic MS, the definitive diagnosis of the disease usually is not made in the emergency department.[31]

Transverse Myelitis

Principles of Disease

Acute transverse myelitis refers to acute or subacute spinal cord dysfunction characterized by paraplegia, a transverse level of sensory impairment, and sphincter disturbance. It is relatively rare, with a reported annual incidence of 1 per 1.3 million population. The presentation may be mimicked by compressive lesions, trauma, infection, or malignant infiltration. The exact pathogenesis is unknown, although it is noted to follow viral infection in approximately 30% of patients and commonly is termed *postinfectious myelitis*.[32] Other postulated etiologies include infectious, autoimmune, and idiopathic.[33,34] No apparent cause for acute transverse myelitis is found in 30% of patients.[32] Progression of symptoms is usually rapid, with 66% reaching maximal deficit by 24 hours.[35] Symptoms may progress, however, over days to weeks. The thoracic cord region is affected most often by this process (60% to 70%),[35] and the cervical spinal cord is rarely affected.[36]

Clinical Features

In addition to motor, sensory, and urinary disturbances, patients with acute transverse myelitis may complain of back pain and may have low-grade fever, raising concern for spinal epidural abscess. As with MS, the examination of patients can be characterized by weakness progressing to paresis, hypertonia, hyperreflexia, clonus, and a Babinski response. Spinal cord involvement also can result in dysautonomias.

Diagnostic Strategies

Evaluation for acute transverse myelitis is done primarily with emergent MRI to exclude compressive lesions. CSF studies are normal in 40% and show only mildly elevated protein or pleocytosis in the remaining 60%.[37] The most essential aspect of the treatment of acute transverse myelitis is to eliminate a potentially treatable cause, such as spinal epidural abscess, neoplasm, or hematoma.

Differential Considerations

The differential diagnosis for transverse myelitis includes MS, spinal epidural abscess, spinal neoplasm, and hematoma.

Management

Treatment with steroids is of unknown benefit. Anecdotal reports of improvement after steroid administration exist,[35,38] but other investigators have found no benefit to their use.[37] Consultation is suggested, and admission usually is required.

The clinical course of acute transverse myelitis varies, ranging from complete recovery to death from progressive neurologic compromise.[34] Maximal improvement usually occurs within 3 to 6 months.[39] At the 5-year follow-up of patients with this disease, 30% had a good recovery, 25% had a fair recovery, 30% had a poor recovery, and 15% died as a result of complications of the disease.[40]

Spinal Subarachnoid Hemorrhage

Principles of Disease

Intraspinal hemorrhage is rare and occurs in the same anatomic locations as do intracranial hemorrhages: epidural, subdural, subarachnoid, and intramedullary.[41] Spinal subarachnoid hemorrhage usually is caused by an arteriovenous malformation.[41,42] Other etiologies include hemorrhage from tumors and cavernous angiomas or spontaneous hemorrhage secondary to anticoagulation therapy.[43,44] Bleeding may occur exclusively in the subarachnoid space or within the substance of the spinal cord itself.

Clinical Features

Patients present with the paroxysmal onset of excruciating back pain at the level of the hemorrhage. This pain also may be in a radicular distribution or into the flank. Patients may complain of headache and exhibit cervical rigidity if the blood migrates into the intracranial subarachnoid space simulating an intracranial subarachnoid hemorrhage.

The patient presents with variable neurologic deficits depending on the magnitude and anatomic location of the hemorrhage. Typically, these deficits include extremity numbness, weakness, or sphincter dysfunction.[45] Nuchal rigidity or signs of meningeal irritation may be present.

Diagnostic Strategies

The diagnostic study of choice is MRI. Lumbar puncture also confirms the diagnosis of blood in the CSF.

Differential Considerations

The differential diagnosis includes epidural abscess, tumor, transverse myelitis, ischemia from an aortic catastrophe such as dissection, or anterior spinal artery thrombosis.

Management

Treatment depends on the etiology of the hemorrhage. Neurosurgical referral is obtained for further evaluation and for clot evacuation if compression is present. Angiography may be recommended if arteriovenous malformation is suspected.

Syringomyelia

Principles of Disease

Syringomyelia is the condition of having a cavitary lesion within the substance of the spinal cord. A syrinx is usually a chronic progressive lesion, and its location within the cord determines the neurologic findings on examination.

Clinical Features

Headache and neck pain are the most common complaints, followed by sensory disturbance, gait disorder, and lower cranial nerve dysfunction.[46] The classic pattern of sensory deficit is a loss of pain and temperature sensation in the upper extremities, with preservation of proprioception and light touch. This phenomenon is described as a "disassociative anesthesia" because of the discrepant loss of sensory modalities. The sensory deficit often is described as being in a "capelike" distribution over the shoulders and arms. The anatomic basis for the neurologic findings of syrinx is due to its central location near the central canal. Here it may compress the crossing fibers of the lateral spinothalamic tract that carry pain and temperature fibers. Crude touch, position, and vibratory sensation typically are unaffected. Sensory fibers from the lower limbs are similarly spared.

The symptoms of syringomyelia develop and progress based on the intracavitary pressure and location of the syrinx. The most common features on physical examination are lower limb hyperreflexia, weakness and wasting in the hands and arms, dissociated sensory loss, and gait disorder. Symptoms may be exacerbated by sneeze, cough, or Valsalva maneuver.[47] Ninety percent of patients who develop this process have Arnold-Chiari I malformation (cerebellar tonsils and medulla project into the spinal canal).[48] Syrinx also may result from spinal cord trauma (often months to years later) or compressive tumors or as a sequela of meningitis.[49]

Diagnostic Strategies
Syrinx is best seen on MRI. No other study currently in widespread use can equal the diagnostic ability of MRI.

Differential Considerations
The differential diagnosis for syrinx includes intrinsic spinal tumor and demyelination.

Management
If the diagnosis is considered, it is not necessary to perform emergent imaging if follow-up can be arranged because this is usually a slowly progressive process. In patients for whom MRI is obtained and the diagnosis is made, referral to a neurologic surgeon should be made because symptoms progress in about two thirds of patients.[50]

Idiopathic Spastic Paraparesis

Idiopathic spastic paraparesis is a progressive disorder characterized by progressive weakness and signs of spasticity of the lower extremities. This disorder sometimes also is referred to as *primary lateral sclerosis,* which describes the demyelination pattern in the lateral column of the spinal cord. Typically this disorder occurs in older men. Sometimes a heritable form may be discovered. It is a diagnosis of exclusion.[51-53]

Human Immunodeficiency Virus Myelopathy

HIV myelopathy typically occurs in patients with advanced disease. Weakness, gait disturbance, sphincter dysfunction, sensory abnormalities, and signs of spasticity are present in this progressive process. This is a diagnosis of exclusion because etiologies such as toxoplasmosis, lymphoma, varicella zoster, and cytomegalovirus may simulate this clinical picture in immunocompromised patients. Pathologically, vacuolization of myelin sheaths in the cord may be found. Treatment is directed at the retroviral infection, although there is no proven treatment.[54,55]

Spinal Cord Infarction

Spinal cord infarction is another diagnosis of exclusion. Aortic dissection, surgery, and global ischemia are the more common causes, although this disorder may occur as a complication of systemic lupus erythematosus or be cryptogenic. An anterior spinal cord syndrome is the most common clinical picture. Some recovery may occur, although generally less than in cerebral stroke. The site of clinical dysfunction may be distant from the site of vascular occlusion.[56]

Extrinsic Cord Lesions

Spinal Epidural Hematoma

Principles of Disease
Spinal epidural hematoma is a relatively rare condition resulting from a variety of etiologies. Its incidence is 0.1 per 100,000 patients per year.[57,58] Traumatic etiologies include post lumbar puncture or epidural anesthesia and a complication of spinal surgery. Spinal epidural hematoma is more likely to occur in anticoagulated or thrombocytopenic patients or in patients with liver disease or alcoholism.[59,60] Spontaneous bleeding is rare, but may be seen from spinal arteriovenous malformation or vertebral hemangioma. Approximately one quarter to one third of all cases are associated with anticoagulation therapy, including low-molecular-weight heparin.[2,61,62]

Clinical Features
The patient usually presents with sudden, severe, constant back pain with a radicular component. It may be noted to follow a straining episode. The pain may be enhanced by percussion over the spine and maneuvers that increase intraspinal pressure, such as coughing, sneezing, or straining.[63] The pain often causes the patient to seek care before the development of neurologic signs, possibly leading to delays in diagnosis.[41] Neurologic deficits follow and may progress over hours to days.[58] Anticoagulant use or coagulation abnormality may be present.

The patient is in significant distress from the pain. Motor and sensory findings depend entirely on the level and size of the hematoma, but can include weakness, paresis, loss of bowel or bladder function, and virtually any sensory deficit.

Diagnostic Strategies
MRI, as with virtually all suspected intrinsic spinal disorders, is the diagnostic study of choice.[63]

Differential Considerations
The differential diagnosis includes abscess, epidural neoplasm, acute disk herniation, and spinal subarachnoid hemorrhage.

Management

Recovery without surgery is rare, and surgical consultation for consideration of emergent decompressive laminectomy must be obtained. Overall mortality is 8%.[58] Functional recovery is related primarily to the length of time the symptoms are present. Recovery after 72 hours of symptoms is rare,[64] but has been reported.[65]

Spinal Epidural Abscess

Principles of Disease

Spinal epidural abscess is an infectious process usually confined to the adipose tissue of the dorsal epidural space where there is a rich venous plexus. It is an uncommon disease with an overall frequency of 0.2 to 1.2 per 10,000 hospital admissions.[66,67] Major risk factors include diabetes, intravenous drug abuse, chronic renal failure, alcoholism, and immunosuppression.[68,69] Although the disease may present in subacute or chronic forms, the acute presentation is seen most frequently by the emergency physician. Thoracic and lumbar sites of infection predominate, with cervical epidural abscess being much less common.[70,71] Infection typically extends over four to five spinal vertebral segments.[72] The dura mater limits the spread of an epidural infection, making subdural or intraspinal spread uncommon. Hematogenous spread of infection to the epidural space is the most common source (26% to 50% of cases),[41,72] either to the epidural space or to the vertebra with extension to the epidural space. Skin and soft tissue infection is the most frequently reported identified source (15%),[68,72] with *Staphylococcus aureus* being the most prevalent organism cultured in more than 50% of cases.[68,72,73] Other frequently identified pathogens include aerobic and anaerobic streptococcus, *Escherichia coli,* and *Pseudomonas aeruginosa.* Multiple organisms are identified in approximately 10% of cases, whereas in 40% no organism is identified.[73]

Clinical Features

The classic clinical presentation of spinal epidural abscess begins with a backache that progresses to localized back pain often associated with tenderness to percussion. Fever, sweats, and rigors are common, reported in 30% to 75% of patients.[41,72,73] The classic triad of back pain, fever, and progressive neurologic deficits is present in only a few patients, however, and delayed clinical diagnosis is common.[66] Radicular symptoms may not be present initially, but usually develop as the disease progresses.

If untreated, patients develop myelopathic signs, usually beginning with bowel and bladder disturbance. Weakness ensues, followed by paraplegia or quadriplegia. Approximately 10% of patients with spinal epidural abscess present with encephalopathy.[66,72]

Diagnostic Strategies

MRI is the imaging modality of choice and needs to be obtained emergently if the diagnosis is entertained. Other diagnostic testing may include a complete blood count because leukocytosis is commonly present with an average white blood cell count of 13,000/mm^3 to 16,000/mm^3.[72] The erythrocyte sedimentation rate, although not specific for epidural abscess, is virtually always elevated with this condition.[66,67,72] Plain films are usually normal, unless there is osteomyelitis of an adjacent vertebral body. Lumbar puncture is relatively contraindicated, but often is performed as part of evaluation for meningitis. CSF findings are consistent with a parameningeal infection showing elevation of protein and some cellular response.

Differential Considerations

Any compressive spinal lesion, including tumor or blood, can mimic spinal epidural abscess.

Management

Urgent surgical consultation for decompression is required. Antibiotics effective against the most common organisms (particularly *S. aureus*) should be started empirically. One such regimen that covers gram-positive and gram-negative organisms is a third-generation cephalosporin plus vancomycin, both given intravenously, plus rifampin given orally.

Outcome is related to the speed of diagnosis before the development of myelopathic signs. The disease is fatal in 18% to 23%, and patients with neurologic deficit rarely improve if surgical intervention is delayed more than 12 to 36 hours after onset of paralysis.[66,72] Patients operated on before development of neurologic symptoms almost universally have a good outcome.[67]

Diskitis

Principles of Disease

Diskitis is an uncommon primary infection of the nucleus pulposus, with secondary involvement of the cartilaginous end plate and vertebral body. It may occur after surgical procedures or spontaneously, the latter being more common in pediatric patients.[74,75] There is an increased incidence of diskitis in immunocompromised patients and in patients with systemic infections. An acute and a chronic disease course have been described, with the acute course being more common.[74]

Clinical Features

Patients present with moderate to severe pain, localized to the level of involvement and exacerbated by almost any movement of the spine. Radicular symptoms are present in 50% to 90% of cases.[76] The lumbar spine is the most common site of disease. Elevated temperature is noted in more than 90% of patients.[74] Patients experience pain with range of motion. Neurologic deficits are the exception with diskitis.

Diagnostic Strategies

Plain radiographs usually are not helpful for early diagnosis, but destruction of the disk space is highly suggestive if present. Plain films become positive after 2 to 4 weeks of disease. In addition to disk space narrowing, plain films may show irregular destruction of the vertebral body end plates. Often there is a latent period (2 to 8 weeks) between the onset of back pain and the development of other clinical symptoms or physical examination findings. MRI is the radiographic study of choice because it not only can diagnose diskitis, but also it can rule out paravertebral or epidural abscess. Laboratory studies often show an elevated erythrocyte sedimentation rate, but the white blood cell count is usually normal.[74,75] *S. aureus* is the most common organism, but gram-negative, fungal, and tuberculous infections all have been recognized.

Differential Considerations
The differential diagnosis includes spinal epidural abscess, neoplasm, and hematoma.

Management
With timely diagnosis and treatment, outcome is generally good, and medical treatment with intravenous antibiotics is usually curative. Surgery is often not necessary.[74,75]

Neoplasm

Principles of Disease
Spinal cord tumors are classified according to their relationship to the dura and spinal cord (extradural, intradural/extramedullary, and intradural/intramedullary). Spinal cord tumors produce neurologic symptoms by compression, invasion, or destruction of myelinated tracts. The resulting neurologic symptoms are directly related to the growth rate and the location of the tumor. Spinal cord tumors account for 4% to 10% of central nervous system tumors, but only 1% of all cancers. Primary tumors occur with an incidence of 1 per 1 million population.[77] Most tumors of the spinal cord are metastatic in origin, however. Approximately 10% of patients with known cancer are diagnosed with a spinal metastasis at some point in the course of their disease, and 5% to 10% of patients ultimately diagnosed with cancer first present with a spinal metastasis.[2] Lung cancer, breast cancer, and lymphoma represent more than 50% of the primary malignancies that subsequently develop spinal metastasis, spreading by the hematogenous route and direct extension. Most metastases occur in the thoracic spine, and nearly 20% have disease at multiple levels.[2,78,79]

Clinical Features
In 95% of patients with spinal neoplasm, the initial complaint is pain, either in the back at the level of the tumor or in a radicular distribution. Pain often is characterized as dull, constant, and aching and is said to worsen often with recumbency (in contrast to the pain of herniated disk).[41] Nighttime pain that is severe is characteristic of spinal neoplasm.[80] Any action that increases intraspinal pressure (Valsalva maneuver, sneeze, cough) may be associated with increased pain. Neurologic deficits vary, depending on the location of the lesion. Besides a thorough neurologic examination, a search for possible primary sites should be done on the physical examination.

Diagnostic Strategies
Plain radiographs are usually the initial diagnostic test, and 70% to 85% of patients with spinal column involvement show some abnormality on these films.[77,80] Patients with neurologic findings and suspicious findings on plain films are candidates for emergent MRI or CT myelography. In patients with a known history of neoplasm and new back pain, some authors recommend skipping plain films and proceeding directly to MRI because plain films can be misleading or nondiagnostic.[81] MRI has not been shown, however, to be a cost-effective screening tool for neoplasm in patients presenting with back pain and no known history of malignancy.[82]

Differential Considerations
The differential diagnosis includes any of the compressive lesions (blood, infection). Tumor also can mimic intrinsic lesions, such as transverse myelopathy and cord infarction.

Management
Acute compressive myelopathy from neoplasm is an oncologic emergency. Immediate treatment is required to preserve function and prevent deterioration. When paraplegia and incontinence occur, less than 5% of patients regain ambulatory status.[1,83] Of patients who are ambulatory at the time of diagnosis, 60% remain ambulatory.[41] High-dose steroids, radiotherapy, and surgery all may be necessary acute interventions, and consultation with neurosurgeons, neurologists, oncologists, and therapeutic radiologists may be necessary.

 KEY CONCEPTS

- Patients with rapid onset and progression of spinal cord symptoms should receive specialized imaging and consultation in the emergency department.
- MRI frequently is required to make a definitive diagnosis for spinal syndromes.
- With compressive lesions of the spinal cord, duration of neurologic dysfunction is directly related to ultimate neurologic outcome. The diagnosis must be made expeditiously and definitive therapy begun as soon as possible.

REFERENCES

1. Wagner R, Jagoda A: Spinal cord syndromes. *Emerg Med Clin North Am* 15:699, 1997.
2. Johnston RA: The management of acute spinal cord compression. *J Neurol Neurosurg Psychiatry* 56:1046, 1993.
3. Guthkelch AN, Fleischer AS: Patterns of cervical spine injury and their associated lesions. *West J Med* 147:428, 1987.
4. Bohlman HH, Freehafer AF, Dejak J: The results of treatment of acute injuries of the upper thoracic spine with paralysis. *J Bone Joint Surg* 67:360, 1985.
5. Shewman DA: Spinal shock and "brain death": Somatic pathophysiological equivalence and implications for the integrative unity rationale. *Spinal Cord* 37:313, 1999.
6. Atkinson PP, Atkinson J: Spinal shock. *Mayo Clin Proc* 71:384, 1996.

7. Merriam WF, et al: A reappraisal of acute traumatic central cord syndrome. *J Bone Joint Surg* 688:708, 1986.

8. Schneider RC, Cherry G, Pantek H: The syndrome of acute central spinal cord injury, with special reference to the mechanics involved in hyperextension injury of the cervical spine. *J Neurosurg* 11:546, 1954.

9. Maroon JC: "Burning hands" in football spinal cord injuries. *JAMA* 238:2049, 1977.

10. Tow AM, Kong KH: Central cord syndrome: Functional outcome after rehabilitation. *Spinal Cord* 36:156, 1998.

11. Kirschblum SC, O'Connor KC: Predicting neurologic recovery in traumatic cervical spinal cord injury. *Arch Phys Med Rehabil* 79:1456, 1998.

12. Brown-Séquard CE: Lectures on the physiology and pathology of the central nervous system and the treatment of organic nervous affections. *Lancet* 2:593, 659, 755, 821, 1868.

13. Rumana CS, Baskin DS: Brown-Séquard syndrome produced by cervical disc herniation: Case report and literature review. *Surg Neurol* 45:359, 1996.

14. Koehler PJ, Endtz LJ: The Brown-Séquard syndrome: True or false? *Arch Neurol* 43:921, 1986.

15. Gharagozloo F, et al: Spinal cord protection during surgical procedures on descending thoracic and thoracoabdominal aorta: Review of current techniques. *Chest* 109:799, 1996.

16. Rogers FB, et al: Isolated stab wound to the artery of Adamkiewicz: Case report and review of the literature. *J Trauma Injury Infection Crit Care* 43:549, 1997.

17. Waters RL, et al: Recovery following ischemic myelopathy. *J Trauma* 35:837, 1993.

18. Kim SW: The syndrome of acute anterior lumbar spinal cord injury. *Clin Neurol Neurosurg* 92:249, 1990.

19. Kostiuk JP, et al: Cauda equina syndrome and lumbar disc herniation. *J Bone Joint Surg* 68A:386, 1986.

20. Huff JS: Spinal epidural hematoma associated with cocaine abuse. *Am J Emerg Med* 12:350, 1994.

21. Hainline B, Tuszynski MH, Posner JB: Ataxia in epidural spinal cord compression. *Neurology* 42:2193, 1992.

22. Coleman WP, et al: A critical appraisal of the reporting of the National Acute Spinal Cord Injury Studies (II and III) of methylprednisolone in acute spinal cord injury. *J Spinal Disord* 13:185, 2000.

23. Hurlbert RJ: Methylprednisolone for acute spinal cord injury: An inappropriate standard of care. *J Neurosurg* 93(1 Suppl):1, 2000.

24. Canadian Association of Emergency Physicians: Steroids in acute spinal cord injury. *Can J Emerg Med* 5:9, 2003.

25. Rodriguez M: Multiple sclerosis: Basic concepts and hypothesis. *Mayo Clin Proc* 64:570, 1989.

26. Ransohoff RM: Multiple sclerosis: New concepts of pathogenesis, diagnosis, and treatment. *Comp Ther* 15:39, 1989.

27. Miller DH, et al: Magnetic resonance imaging in isolated noncompressive spinal cord syndromes. *Ann Neurol* 22:714, 1987.

28. Gebarski S: The initial diagnosis of multiple sclerosis: Clinical impact of magnetic resonance imaging. *Ann Neurol* 17:469, 1985.

29. Swanson JW: Multiple sclerosis: Update in diagnosis and review of prognostic factors. *Mayo Clin Proc* 64:577, 1989.

30. Warren KG, Catz I: The relationship between levels of cerebrospinal fluid myelin basic protein and IgG measurements in patients with multiple sclerosis. *Ann Neurol* 17:475, 1985.

31. Herndon RM, Brooks B: Misdiagnosis of multiple sclerosis. *Semin Neurol* 5:94, 1985.

32. Dawson DM, Potts F: Acute nontraumatic myelopathies. *Neurol Clin* 9:585, 1991.

33. Jeffrey DR, Mandler RN, Davis LE: Transverse myelitis: Retrospective analysis of 33 cases, with differentiation of cases associated with multiple sclerosis and parainfectious events. *Arch Neurol* 50:532, 1993.

34. Kalita J, Misra UK, Mandal SK: Prognostic predictors of acute transverse myelitis. *Acta Neurol Scand* 98:60, 1998.

35. Kelley CE, Matthews J, Noskin GA: Acute transverse myelitis in the emergency department: A case report and review of the literature. *J Emerg Med* 9:417, 1991.

36. Misra UK, Kalita J: Transverse myelitis: Neurophysiological and MRI correlation. *Paraplegia* 32:593, 1994.

37. Dunne K, Hopkins IJ, Shield JK: Acute transverse myelopathy in childhood. *Dev Med Child Neurol* 28:198, 1986.

38. Dowling PC, Bosch VV, Cook SD: Possible beneficial effect of high-dose intravenous steroid therapy in acute demyelinating disease and transverse myelitis. *Neurology* 30:33, 1980.

39. Sureda B, et al: Severe acute transverse myelitis: Prognostic factors. *Arch Neurobiol (Madr)* 51:13, 1988.

40. Lipton HL, Teasdale RD: Acute transverse myelopathy in adults: A follow-up study. *Arch Neurol* 28:252, 1973.

41. Schmidt RD, Markovchik V: Nontraumatic spinal cord compression. *J Emerg Med* 2:189, 1992.

42. Aminoff MJ, Barnard RO, Logue V: The pathophysiology of spinal vascular malformations. *J Neurol Sci* 23:255, 1988.

43. Marconi F, et al: Spinal cavernous angioma producing subarachnoid hemorrhage: Case report. *J Neurosurg Sci* 39:75, 1995.

44. Cordan T, et al: Spinal subarachnoid hemorrhage attributable to schwannoma of the cauda equina. *Surg Neurol* 51:373, 1999.

45. Morgan MK, Marsh WR: Management of spinal dural arteriovenous malformations. *J Neurosurg* 70:832, 1989.

46. Rossier AB, et al: Posttraumatic cervical syringomyelia. *Brain* 108:439, 1985.

47. Elghazawi AK: Clinical syndromes and differential diagnosis of spinal disorders. *Radiol Clin North Am* 29:651, 1991.

48. Davis CH, Symon L: Mechanisms and treatment in posttraumatic syringomyelia. *Br J Neurosurg* 3:669, 1989.

49. Caplan LR, Norohna AB, Amico LL: Syringomyelia and arachnoiditis. *J Neurol Neurosurg Psychiatry* 53:106, 1990.

50. Dworkin GE, Staas WE: Posttraumatic syringomyelia. *Arch Phys Med Rehabil* 66:329, 1985.

51. Bird TD: Idiopathic progressive spastic paraparesis. *JAMA* 274:1191, 1995.

52. Younger DS, et al: Primary lateral sclerosis: A clinical diagnosis reemerges. *Arch Neurol* 45:1304, 1988.

53. Pringle CE, et al: Primary lateral sclerosis. *Brain* 115:495, 1992.

54. Simson DM, Berger JR: Management of the HIV-infected patient. *Med Clin North Am* 80:1363, 1996.

55. de Silva SM, et al: Zoster myelitis: Improvement with antiviral therapy in two cases. *Neurology* 47:923, 1996.

56. Cheshire WP, et al: Spinal cord infarction: Etiology and outcome. *Neurology* 47:321, 1996.

57. Tekkok IH, et al: Extradural hematoma after continuous extradural anaesthesia. *Br J Anaesth* 67:112, 1991.

58. Hejazi N, Thaper PY, Hassler W: Nine cases of nontraumatic spinal epidural hematoma. *Neurol Med Chir* 38:718, 1998.

59. Dickman CA, et al: Spinal epidural hematoma associated with epidural anaesthesia: Complications of systemic heparinization in patients receiving peripheral vascular thrombolytic therapy. *Anesthesiology* 72:947, 1990.

60. Mattle H, et al: Nontraumatic spinal epidural and subdural hematomas. *Neurology* 37:1351, 1987.

61. Lederle FA, et al: Spinal epidural hematoma associated with warfarin therapy. *Am J Med* 100:237, 1996.

62. Wysowski DK, et al: Spinal and epidural hematoma and low-molecular-weight heparin. *N Engl J Med* 338:1774, 1998.

63. Boukobza M, et al: Spinal epidural hematoma: Report of 11 cases and review of the literature. *Neuroradiology* 36:456, 1994.

64. Groen RT, Van Alphen HA: Operative treatment of spontaneous spinal epidural hematomas: A study of the factors

determining postoperative outcome. *Neurosurgery* 39:494, 1996.

65. Enomato T, et al: Spontaneous spinal epidural hematoma: Report of a case. *Neurol Surg* 8:875, 1980.

66. Sampath P, Rigamonti D: Spinal epidural abscess: A review of epidemiology, diagnosis, and treatment. *J Spinal Disord* 12:89, 1999.

67. Rigamonti D, Liem L, Sampath P: Spinal epidural abscess: Contemporary trends in etiology, evaluation, and treatment. *Surg Neurol* 52:189, 1999.

68. Curling OD, Gower DJ, McWhorter JM: Changing concepts in spinal epidural abscess: A report of 29 cases. *Neurosurgery* 27:185, 1990.

69. Koppell BS, Tuchman AJ, Mangiardi JR: Epidural spinal infection in intravenous drug abusers. *Arch Neurol* 12:1331, 1988.

70. Nussbaum ES, et al: Spinal epidural abscess: A review of 40 cases and review. *Surg Neurol* 38:225, 1992.

71. Corboy JR, Price RW: Myelitis and toxic, inflammatory and infectious disorders. *Curr Opin Neurol Neurosurg* 6:564, 1993.

72. Hlavin ML, et al: Spinal epidural abscess: A ten-year perspective. *Neurosurgery* 27:177, 1990.

73. Danner RL, Hartman BJ: Update of epidural abscess: 35 cases and a review of the literature. *Rev Infect Dis* 9:265, 1987.

74. Maiuri F, et al: Spondylodiscitis: Clinical and magnetic resonance diagnosis. *Spine* 22:1741, 1997.

75. Honan M, White GW, Eisenberg GM: Spontaneous infectious discitis in adults. *Am J Med* 100:85, 1996.

76. Malik GM, McCormick P: Management of spine and intervertebral disc space infection. *Contemp Neurosurg* 10:1, 1988.

77. Constantini S, Epstein FJ: Primary spinal cord tumors. In Levin VA (ed): *Cancer in the Nervous System.* New York, Churchill Livingstone, 1996, pp 127-137.

78. Schiff D, O'Neill BP, Suman VJ: Spinal epidural metastasis as the initial manifestation of malignancy: Clinical features and diagnostic approach. *Neurology* 49:452, 1997.

79. Schiff D, O'Neill BP: Intramedullary spinal cord metastases: Clinical features and treatment outcome. *Neurology* 47:906, 1996.

80. Abdu WA, Provencher M: Primary bone and metastatic tumors of the cervical spine. *Spine* 23:2767, 1998.

81. Husband DJ, Grant KA, Romaniuk CS: MRI in the diagnosis and treatment of suspected malignant spinal cord compression. *Br J Radiol* 74:15, 2001.

82. Jarvik JG, et al: Rapid magnetic resonance imaging vs radiographs for patients with low back pain: A randomized controlled trial. *JAMA* 289:2810, 2003.

83. Wong D, Fornasier V, MacNab I: Spinal metastasis: The obvious, the occult, and the imposters. *Spine* 15:1, 1990.

CHAPTER

105 Peripheral Nerve Disorders

E. John Gallagher

PERSPECTIVE

Background

The nervous system is traditionally divided into central (CNS) and peripheral (PNS) components. The PNS can be further subdivided into 12 cranial and 31 spinal nerves. Disorders of the cranial nerves, whether central or peripheral in origin, are discussed in Chapter 103. Because diseases of the neuromuscular junction and the myopathies are located distal to the neuron itself, they are also considered separately in Chapter 104. Radiculopathies, which are disorders of the roots of the PNS, are so commonly associated with musculoskeletal neck and back pain that they are mentioned only briefly here and are discussed in detail in Chapter 51.

The simplest approach to diseases of the PNS parallels the CNS model of separating focal from nonfocal disease. In the PNS, the first broad category is the focal group, which can be divided into those with evidence of single versus multiple lesions of peripheral nerves, known respectively as *simple mononeuropathies* and *multiple mononeuropathies* (or *mononeuropathy multiplex*). The second broad category, which constitutes the nonfocal group of peripheral neuropathies, contains the polyneuropathies. These tend to produce bilaterally symmetrical symptoms and signs, reflecting the widespread nature of the underlying pathologic process.

An extension of this approach to the PNS, which is applicable to emergency practice, is proposed in Figure 105-1.

The template in Figure 105-1 is derived from a goal-directed history and physical examination targeted at answering the following three questions, each of which corresponds to a stratum of the algorithm in Figure 105-1:

- Are the sensorimotor signs and symptoms symmetrical or asymmetric?
- Are the sensorimotor signs and symptoms distal or both proximal and distal?
- Is the modality involved exclusively motor, sensory, or mixed sensorimotor?

By systematically combining responses to these questions, one can identify seven discrete categories of peripheral neuropathy, each of which contains a finite set of possible diagnoses. Because pure motor or sensory findings tend to occur mainly in an asymmetric, distal distribution, this is the only category in Figure 105-1 subdivided into pure motor and pure sensory abnormalities.

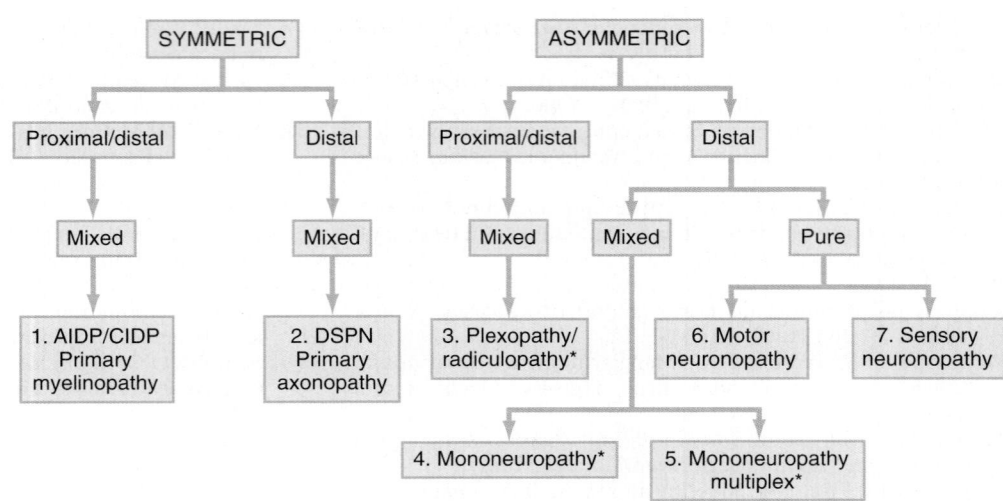

Figure 105-1. An approach to peripheral neuropathy in the ED. AIDP, Acute inflammatory demyelinating polyneuropathy (Guillain-Barré); CIDP, chronic inflammatory demyelinating polyneuropathy; DSPN, distal symmetrical polyneuropathy. *A proximal distribution of sensorimotor findings may dominate the clinical picture in patterns 3, 4, and 5, depending on the location of the lesion(s).

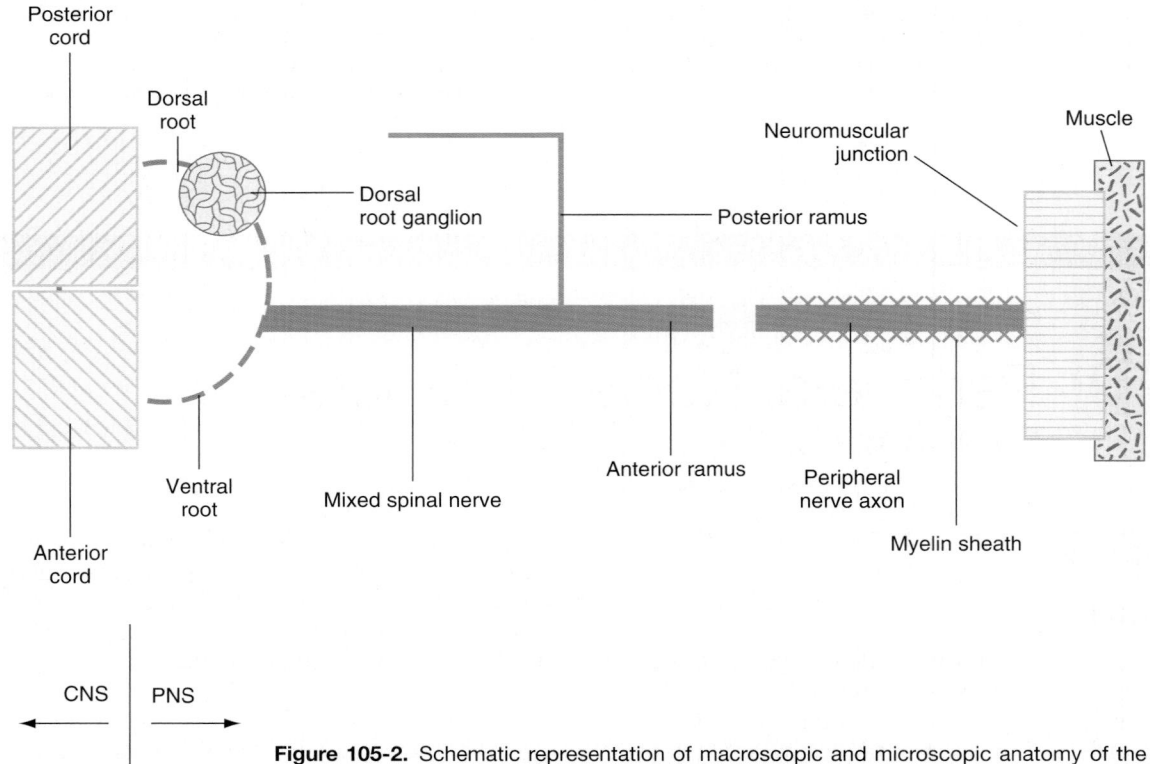

Figure 105-2. Schematic representation of macroscopic and microscopic anatomy of the PNS and its interface with the CNS. See text for explanation.

Epidemiology

Although Guillain-Barré syndrome (GBS) is the most commonly encountered emergent peripheral neuropathy in developed countries, its annual incidence is just over 1 case per 100,000 population.[1] In contrast to the low incidence of acute peripheral neuropathies, several of which are associated with short-term mortality, the vast majority of peripheral neuropathies seen in the emergency department are subacute or chronic and are associated not with mortality but with long-term morbidity.

Current estimates suggest that about 1.5% of the U.S. population suffers from peripheral neuropathy.[2]

According to the American Diabetes Association, about 17 million Americans (more than 6% of the population) have diabetes mellitus, and roughly 60% of these individuals have peripheral neuropathy.[3]

PRINCIPLES OF DISEASE

Anatomy

The spinal component of the PNS is shown schematically in Figure 105-2. This does not include the cranial nerves, which are discussed in Chapter 103. The anterior and posterior nerve roots exit the spinal cord at each segmental level. Just distal to the dorsal root ganglion they converge to form a mixed (motor and sensory) spinal nerve, of which there are 31 pairs: 8 cervical, 12 thoracic, 5 lumbar, 5 sacral, and 1 coccygeal. The spinal nerves immediately bifurcate into anterior (ventral) and posterior (dorsal) rami. The posterior ramus travels to the back. The anterior ramus innervates the anterolateral portion of the body and supplies all peripheral nerves for the upper and lower extremities through the brachial and lumbosacral plexus, respectively. Interweaving of fibers occurs within a plexus, producing a mixed sensorimotor innervation of peripheral nerves exiting the plexus.

In addition to the motor and sensory modalities of the PNS, the autonomic nervous system has a peripheral component. Anatomically and functionally, the autonomic nervous system is divided into two parts: a sympathetic (thoracolumbar) component and a parasympathetic (craniosacral) component. Autonomic dysfunction may cause systemic abnormalities, such as orthostasis, or local problems, such as atrophic, dry skin.

Pathophysiology

The PNS has only three basic responses to a wide array of pathologic stimuli. As shown in Figure 105-2, these are (1) the myelinopathies (primary site of involvement is limited to the myelin sheath surrounding the axon), (2) the axonopathies (primary site of involvement is the axon, with or without secondary demyelination), and (3) the neuronopathies (cell body of the neuron itself is the primary site of involvement, ultimately affecting the entire peripheral nerve). Although overlap occurs, each of these prototypes has a distinctive clinical presentation, electrophysiologic profile, and microscopic appearance.

Electrophysiologic testing, that is, nerve conduction studies (NCSs) and needle electromyography (EMG), detects underlying pathologic abnormalities. Because neither test is appropriate to the emergency department setting, they are discussed only briefly here. Information gathered from NCSs and EMG can be used to obtain objective information on the anatomic distribution of involvement (symmetrical versus asymmetrical and distal versus proximal and distal) and the modalities involved (sensory, motor, or mixed). NCSs and EMG can also identify the level of the neuraxis affected by the disease process (i.e., root, plexus, or nerve); if the nerve is affected, electrophysiologic testing can help determine whether the lesion is mononeuropathic (either caused by an isolated mononeuropathy or mononeuropathy multiplex) or polyneuropathic. Finally, EMG and NCSs can distinguish axonal from myelinopathic disease, further narrowing the differential diagnosis. Prognosis is determined by the nature of pathologic involvement of the PNS. Primary demyelination spares the axon and thus carries the best prognosis. The prognosis is worse in axonopathies because reestablishing nerve function is dependent on the much slower process of axonal regeneration. Neuronopathies, which begin with primary

BOX 105-1. Causes of Acute, Emergent Weakness

Autoimmune
Demyelinating
  Guillain-Barré syndrome
  Chronic inflammatory demyelinating polyneuropathy (CIDP)
Myasthenia gravis

Toxic
Botulism
Buckthorn
Seafood
  Paralytic shellfish toxin
  Tetrodotoxin (puffer fish, newts)
Tick paralysis
Metals
  Arsenic
  Thallium

Metabolic
Dyskalemic syndromes
  Acquired (especially with thyrotoxicosis)
  Familial
Hypophosphatemia
Hypermagnesemia
Porphyria

Infectious
Poliomyelitis
Diphtheria

destruction of the nerve cell body, produce pure motor or pure sensory syndromes. Eventually the entire nerve is affected, resulting in the worst prognosis of the three.

CLINICAL FEATURES

The differential diagnosis for any patient coming to the emergency department with sensory, motor, or sensorimotor complaints, particularly if localized to the extremities, should include a peripheral neuropathy. Within this group, patients with focal weakness should be seen first because they are at greatest risk for respiratory compromise. Box 105-1 lists the causes of acute, emergent weakness, defined as entities that may affect respiration. Although several of these are myopathies (see Chapter 106) rather than peripheral neuropathies, they are lumped together because it is important to identify patients at risk for respiratory failure early in the emergency department workup.

As soon as the emergent causes of weakness listed in Box 105-1 have been excluded—which is possible in the overwhelming majority of patients—the individuals with focal weakness should be assessed next to exclude CNS disease (e.g., stroke) (see Chapter 99). One can then proceed through the systematic approach to peripheral neuropathy discussed previously and outlined in Figure 105-1. Another way to look at the algorithm displayed in Figure 105-1 is shown in Table 105-1, with the distinguishing features of each of the seven peripheral neuropathic patterns described by

Table 105-1. Patterns and Prototypes of Peripheral Neuropathies

Type	Pattern	Prototypical Disease	Distribution		Modalities
I	Proximal and distal, symmetric, sensorimotor polyneuropathy	GBS	P/D	S	M > S
II	Distal, symmetric, sensorimotor polyneuropathy	Diabetic DSPN	D	S	S > M
III	Proximal and distal, asymmetric, sensorimotor neuropathy	Brachial plexopathy	P/D	A	S, M
IV	Distal, asymmetric, sensorimotor mononeuropathy (single nerve involved)	CTS (median mononeuropathy)	D	A	S, M
V	Distal, asymmetric, sensorimotor mononeuropathy multiplex (multiple nerves involved)	Vasculitic mononeuropathy multiplex	D	A	S, M
VI	Distal, asymmetric, pure motor neuronopathy	ALS	D	A	M
VII	Distal, asymmetric, pure sensory neuronopathy	Pyridoxine toxicity	D	A	S

A, Asymmetric distribution; ALS, amyotrophic lateral sclerosis; CTS, carpal tunnel syndrome; D, distally located; DSPN, distal symmetric polyneuropathy; GBS, Guillain-Barré syndrome; P/D, both proximally and distally located; S, symmetric (right and left) distribution; M, motor findings present; S, sensory modalities affected.

BOX 105-2. Demyelinating Polyneuropathies

Guillain-Barré syndrome
    Fisher variant of GBS (ophthalmoplegia and ataxia)
    Axonal GBS
    Sensory GBS
    Autonomic GBS
Chronic inflammatory demyelinating polyradiculoplexo-
    neuropathy (CIDP)
Malignancy
HIV
Hepatitis B
Buckthorn
Diphtheria

---

distribution and modality and represented by a disease prototype.

Type 1: Demyelinating Polyneuropathies

The pattern of symmetrical weakness, usually worse distally, accompanied by variable sensory findings is characteristic of acute GBS. This pattern is discussed first because it is the most common cause of weakness associated with acute respiratory failure seen in emergency practice.

Guillain-Barré Syndrome

GBS is a heterogeneous and unpredictable disorder, with marked variation in latency between antecedent infection (if any is recalled) and symptom onset. The clinical signs, cadence of disease progression, degree of respiratory compromise, laboratory findings, and time required for convalescence are also highly variable. Alternative eponyms for GBS include *Landry-Guillain-Barré* and *Guillain-Barré-Strohl* syndrome. The most common form of GBS is an acute inflammatory demyelinating polyneuropathy. Less common variants include acute axonal GBS, acute sensory GBS, and the Miller-Fisher syndrome, which involves cranial nerves early in the disease process (Box 105-2).[4]

The majority of patients seek treatment days to weeks after resolution of an upper respiratory or gastrointestinal illness, presenting with progressive, symmetrical distal (and usually to a lesser extent proximal) weakness. Signs and symptoms are worse in the lower extremities and are associated with diminution or loss of deep tendon reflexes (DTRs), variable sensory findings, and sparing of the anal sphincter. Urinary retention secondary to autonomic dysfunction may occur, contributing to a clinical picture easily mistaken for a spinal cord lesion or conus medullaris syndrome.

Of the several causes of emergent weakness listed in Box 105-1, GBS is by far the most common. It is also the most frequent type of demyelinating polyneuropathy listed in Box 105-2. In practice, patients with symmetrical weakness of relatively acute onset, decreased or absent DTRs, and variable degrees of sensory loss should be managed as if they have GBS or one of its variants, which places them at risk for respiratory compromise. Conversely, patients with predominantly sensory signs and symptoms are less likely to develop acute respiratory distress and have a more favorable prognosis.[5]

About half of patients with GBS have autonomic dysfunction, experience a peak of disease severity within a week of onset, have some form of cranial nerve involvement (usually VII), and suffer long-term sequelae of their illness. Nearly one third require ventilatory support. Both the mortality and the recurrence rate are about 3%.[6]

In addition to electrophysiologic testing, there are three ancillary tests that may be helpful in the diagnosis of GBS. Cerebrospinal fluid (CSF) analysis is useful when it demonstrates the characteristic picture of markedly elevated protein with only a mild pleocytosis. In the clinical setting of suspected GBS, this finding is highly specific. Early in the disease, however, patients may have normal CSF values. Consequently, a normal CSF cannot be used to exclude GBS because of the limited sensitivity of this test. Selective enhancement of the anterior spinal nerve roots on magnetic resonance imaging (MRI) is suggestive, but not diagnostic, of GBS.[7] In more serious cases, axonal degeneration occurs, particularly in association with antecedent

BOX 105-3. Distal Sensorimotor Polyneuropathies

Diabetes mellitus
Alcoholism
Neoplastic or paraneoplastic
Hereditary motor and sensory neuropathies
   (Charcot-Marie-Tooth)
Cryptogenic sensorimotor polyneuropathies (CSPN)
HIV
Toxins
   Organic or industrial agents
      Acrylamide
      Allyl chloride
      Carbon disulfide
      Ethylene oxide
      Hexacarbons
      Methyl bromide
      Organophosphate-induced delayed polyneuropathy
         (OPIDP)
      Polychlorinated biphenyls (PCBs)
      Trichloroethylene
      Vacor
   Metals
      Arsenic
      Gold
      Mercury (inorganic)
      Thallium
   Therapeutic agents
      Amiodarone

Antiretrovirals
Dapsone
Disulfiram
Isoniazid
Metronidazole
Nitrofurantoin
Paclitaxel (Taxol)
Phenytoin
Statins (HMG-CoA reductase inhibitors)
Thalidomide
Vinca alkaloids (vincristine, vinblastin)
Nutritional
   Beriberi (thiamine or vitamin B_1)
   Pellagra (niacin, B vitamins)
   Pernicious anemia (vitamin B_{12})
   Pyridoxine deficiency (vitamin B_6)
End-organ dysfunction
   Acromegaly
   Chronic pulmonary disease
   Hypothyroidism
   Renal failure (uremic neuropathy)
Paraproteinemias
   Amyloidosis
   Monoclonal gammopathy of unknown significance (MGUS)
   Multiple myeloma
   Waldenström's macroglobulinemia
Porphyria

HMG-CoA, hydroxymethylglutaryl coenzyme A.

Campylobacter jejuni infection.[8] There is increasing evidence that the broad clinical spectrum of GBS may parallel a balance between circulating humoral and lymphocytic cell–mediated inflammation directed against neural tissue.[9]

Management

Individuals with suspected GBS must have their respiratory function followed with forced expiratory volume in 1 second (FEV_1) or peak flow rate. Patients unable to perform these tests and those with values less than 100% predicted should have an arterial blood gas obtained. Evidence of alveolar hypoventilation (elevated carbon dioxide [PCO_2]) in a patient with an unsecured airway requires a level of intensive monitoring that is impractical in many emergency departments. Therefore, patients with weakness, CO_2 retention, or other evidence of early ventilatory failure should be considered for prophylactic intubation.[10]

Among patients with possible GBS who have normal pulmonary function, extensor neck strength can be monitored to predict impending ventilatory failure. Patients with probable GBS should receive neurologic consultation and be admitted to the hospital. Either plasma exchange or intravenous immunoglobulin should be administered. There is sound evidence that both are superior to placebo and that combination or sequential therapy confers no therapeutic advantage over either intervention alone. Corticosteroids are no longer recommended for treatment of GBS.[11] The

marked elevation in blood pressure seen in some patients with GBS should not be treated because it is typically transient and may be followed by precipitous and unpredictable hypotension.

Type 2: Distal Symmetrical Polyneuropathies

Most polyneuropathies are characterized by a pattern of distal, symmetrical sensorimotor findings, worse in the lower than upper extremities, with a stocking-glove distribution of sensory abnormalities that gradually diminishes as one moves proximally. The motor findings and loss of DTRs, which lag behind the sensory features, follow a similar pattern of progression from distal to proximal. The diffuse, distal, symmetrical nature of this pattern is most consistent with a toxic-metabolic disease process, as yet unidentified, that causes a length-dependent axonopathy. Only the most common causes of distal symmetrical polyneuropathies (DSPN) are discussed, with a more complete listing of other causes shown in Box 105-3.

Diabetic Distal Symmetrical Polyneuropathy

DSPN is the most common type of peripheral neuropathy seen in emergency practice, with the preponderance of cases occurring in diabetics. Initial symptoms usually consist of "positive" sensory complaints (e.g., dysesthesias such as tingling or burning) beginning on the plantar surfaces of both feet. At the early stages of a typical DSPN, there may be some asymmetry.[12] At this juncture, it may be impossible to distinguish a focal neuropathic process such as a mononeuropathy from a polyneuropathy, although in this location, prior probability strongly favors a polyneuropathy. As the process advances, the plantar surfaces of both feet become dysesthetic before the dorsum of either foot is involved. Weakness of dorsiflexion of the big toe is usually the first motor sign, followed by weakness of foot dorsiflexion, footdrop, loss of ankle jerks, and later a "steppage gait."

Sensory loss continues to move proximally, and before it reaches the knees, the finger tips are usually involved. DTRs are progressively lost, as is proprioception. If the latter becomes severe, patients may develop sensory ataxia. As the neuropathy continues to progress, sensory abnormalities ultimately involve all modalities and extend to a diamond-shaped periumbilical area. Far advanced disease may affect sensation over the skull vertex and facial midline structures. Atrophy and areflexia occur as weakness worsens. Severely impaired patients may be unable to ambulate or grasp objects.

Management

As is the case with virtually all peripheral neuropathies, referral is indicated for management of diabetic DSPNs. However, if discomfort is severe, the etiology of the neuropathy seems likely to be diabetic, and referral is delayed, it may be necessary to provide the patient with some symptomatic relief. Because treatment of neuropathic pain has traditionally been linked to etiology rather than underlying mechanism, the choice of pharmacologic agents is empirical with substantial practice variation in the United States and worldwide.[13] If one bases drug choice solely on placebo-controlled randomized clinical trials, the tricyclic antidepressants and anticonvulsants appear to have the best NNTs (number of patients needed to treat in order to provide at least 50% relief of symptoms in one patient). These are generally in the range 3 to 5, with confidence intervals whose upper limits reach 10 in some instances.[14] Imipramine or amitriptyline may be started at a dose of 25 mg at bedtime (10 mg in elderly patients) and titrated slowly up to a dose of 300 mg. Carbamazepine, 200 to 400 mg every 8 hours or four times daily, should also be considered, as should gabapentin.[15] The latter was effective at a dose of 3600 mg/day but showed no advantage over placebo at a dose of 900 mg/day.[16] Tramadol in two studies also showed an NNT below five.[14] Although tramadol is a mixed opioid, development of dependence in long-term use appears to be uncommon. Among the selective serotonin reuptake inhibitors (SSRIs), paroxetine and bupropion appear to be effective, but fluoxetine does not.[17] The summary NNT for the SSRIs has a confidence interval that reaches 50, suggesting that, pending further data, these agents should be considered second-line drugs.[14] Topical capsaicin provides relief in some patients, but the burning associated with its application has limited its usage. Improving glycemic control can prevent, diminish, or reverse early diabetic DSPNs.

Alcoholic Distal Symmetrical Polyneuropathy

Although the association between alcoholism and peripheral neuropathy has been well established for centuries, demonstration of a direct neurotoxic effect of alcohol remains elusive. The preponderance of evidence, from both observational studies in humans and experimental data from animal models, suggests that the association between alcohol and peripheral neuropathy may be confounded by nutritional status (i.e., deficiency states might be the true underlying cause of alcoholic peripheral neuropathy).

The clinical and pathologic picture of alcoholic neuropathy is similar to that of the DSPN of diabetes. However, in alcoholism severe myopathy and cerebellar degeneration often complicate the clinical picture.[18] Autonomic skin changes with atrophy and hair loss accompany the sensorimotor abnormalities. Often other systemic effects of alcoholism are so severe that the patient may not notice the neuropathic symptoms. All patients with suspected alcoholic DSPN should receive dietary supplements and referral for outpatient management.

Human Immunodeficiency Virus Neuropathies

With the widespread use of highly active and effective antiretroviral treatment, peripheral neuropathies have become the most common neurologic complication of human immunodeficiency virus (HIV) infection. The typical HIV neuropathy is a DSPN, which appears to be triggered by a combination of dideoxynucleoside therapy and poorly characterized immune-mediated mechanisms associated with HIV.[19] These patients require referral for specialized care. In addition to standard therapies for DSPN, lamotrigine has been shown to be moderately effective in the treatment of HIV-associated painful neuropathies.[20]

Toxic and Metabolic Neuropathies

Many toxic agents and metabolic derangements produce a typical DSPN. Box 105-3 lists some of the most common toxic and metabolic causes of peripheral neuropathy. On the basis of preliminary results from a case-control study, the statins have been added to this list.[21]

Type 3: Asymmetric Proximal and Distal Peripheral Neuropathies (Radiculopathies and Plexopathies)

Radiculopathies that conform to this pattern are discussed in detail in Chapter 103. Plexopathies, which are summarized in Box 105-4, are discussed briefly in this chapter because they are uncommon and often traumatic. Generally, a plexopathy, whether brachial or lumbosacral, is identified by a process of elimination (i.e., a pattern of sensorimotor and reflex abnormalities

BOX 105-4. Asymmetric Proximal/Distal Peripheral Neuropathies

Brachial Plexopathy
Open
    Direct plexus injury (knife or gunshot wound)
    Neurovascular (plexus ischemia)
    Iatrogenic (central line insertion)
Closed
    Traction injuries
      "Stingers"
      Traction neurapraxia
      Partial or complete nerve root avulsion
    Radiation
    Neoplastic
    Idiopathic brachial plexitis
    Thoracic outlet

Lumbosacral Plexopathies
Open
Closed
    Traction injuries
      Pelvic double vertical shearing fracture
      Posterior hip dislocation
      Retroperitoneal hemorrhage
    Vasospastic (deep buttock injection)
    Neoplastic
    Radiation
    Idiopathic lumbosacral plexitis
    Infectious
      Herpesvirus (sacrococcygeal)
        Herpes simplex II
        Herpes zoster
      Cytomegalovirus (CMV) polyradiculopathy (HIV)

that fit neither a radicular nor individual peripheral nerve distribution). Although this approach does not exclude a mononeuropathy multiplex on physical examination alone, a careful history should determine whether the patient is at risk for developing a mononeuropathy or plexopathy on the basis of underlying disease.

Radiation (actinic) plexopathy occurs after a variable period of latency following treatment, which may extend to 20 years or more. Almost all series include women who received radiation treatment for breast cancer. Among neoplastic causes, most originate from lung or breast. Patients with probable neoplastic brachial plexopathy need imaging studies and may require immediate radiation therapy. Pain control is the focus of management.

Thoracic outlet syndrome remains a controversial disorder.[22] Although the pendulum has swung over the past 50 years from a postulated vascular cause of thoracic outlet syndrome to a neurogenic etiology, current evidence supporting the high prevalence of compression of the brachial plexus as a cause of thoracic outlet syndrome is in fact only slightly better[23] than earlier evidence favoring a vascular etiology.[24] Cardiothoracic surgeons argue that the syndrome is common, although objective data other than reported postoperative improvement are lacking. Neurologists, on the other hand, maintain that it is rare and due to compression of the medial or lower portion of the brachial plexus by a cervical rib or fibrous band.[25] The syndrome is characterized by gradually progressive weakness and wasting of median and ulnar hand muscles with ulnar forearm and hand sensory signs and symptoms. Patients with this clinical picture should be referred for NCSs and EMG, which are said to be diagnostic.[25] The treatment of true neurogenic thoracic outlet syndrome requires surgical removal of the rib or aberrant fibrous band to decompress the brachial plexus.[26] An excellent discussion of this entity from a different perspective can be found in Chapter 86.

Because of the complexity of plexopathies, there is no reason to expect that one can or should do more in the emergency department than localize the probable pathologic process to the brachial or lumbosacral plexus. Depending on severity and suspected etiology, one should either admit or refer the patient to a neurologist with experience in PNS disease.

Type 4: Isolated Mononeuropathies

The pattern of asymmetric, sensorimotor, usually distal, peripheral neuropathy is characteristic of a mononeuropathy. Mononeuropathies are of two main types: isolated and multiple. Multiple mononeuropathies, which are less prevalent in emergency practice than isolated mononeuropathies, are commonly known by the term *mononeuropathy multiplex*. They are discussed in the next section, as a type 5 peripheral neuropathy. The isolated mononeuropathies are discussed here.

Isolated mononeuropathies are usually caused by trauma, either blunt or penetrating. If the trauma is blunt, the injury may be secondary to compression from an internal or external source. Entrapment neuropathies are a subset of compression neuropathies occurring at anatomic locations where nerves traverse potentially constricting compartments or tunnels.[27] Isolated mononeuropathies may be acute, intermittent, or chronic and continuous. Antecedent peripheral neuropathy may be a risk factor for development of compression neuropathy (so-called double-crush syndrome), particularly in diabetics.[28] The isolated mononeuropathies are listed in Box 105-5 and discussed here.

Radial Mononeuropathy

The radial nerve arises from C5-T1 roots. As shown in Figure 105-3, after exiting the brachial plexus, it passes behind the proximal humerus in the spiral groove, taking a lateral (radial) course down the upper arm.

At about the level of the antecubital fossa, it bifurcates into the posterior interosseous (pure motor) and superficial radial (pure sensory) nerves. The radial nerve controls extension of the fingers, thumb, wrist, and elbow (triceps). In contrast to the median and ulnar nerves, the radial nerve provides only *extrinsic* motor innervation to the hand (i.e., it does not supply motor fibers to any muscles that both originate and insert within the hand). In further contrast to the median and ulnar nerves, which supply most of the sensation to the

BOX 105-5. Isolated Mononeuropathies

Upper Extremity
Radial nerve
  Axilla
  Humerus
  Elbow (posterior interosseous neuropathy)
  Wrist (superficial cutaneous radial neuropathy)
Ulnar nerve
  Axilla
  Humerus
  Elbow
    Condylar groove
    Cubital tunnel
  Wrist (Guyon's canal)
  Hand
    Superficial terminal ulnar neuropathy
    Deep terminal ulnar neuropathy
      Proximal hypothenar
      Distal hypothenar
Median nerve
  Axilla
  Humerus (musculocutaneous mononeuropathy)
  Forearm
    Anterior interosseus
    Pronator syndrome (?)

  Wrist (carpal tunnel)
  Hand (recurrent motor branch)
Suprascapular mononeuropathy
  Axillary mononeuropathy

Lower Extremity
Sciatic nerve
Femoral nerve
  Illiacus compartment (proximal)
  Saphenous mononeuropathy (distal)
Lateral femoral cutaneous (meralgia paresthetica)
Peroneal nerve
  Common peroneal mononeuropathy (fibular head, popliteal fossa)
  Deep peroneal mononeuropathy (anterior compartment)
Tibial nerve
  Popliteal fossa (proximal)
  Tarsal tunnel (distal)
Sural nerve
  Popliteal fossa, calf (proximal)
  Fifth metatarsal base (distal)
Plantar nerve
  Distal to tarsal tunnel
  Interdigital neuropathies (Morton's neuroma)
Obturator mononeuropathy

Figure 105-3. Radial nerve, major branches, right arm, lateral view. (From Stewart JD: *Focal Peripheral Neuropathies*, 3rd ed. Philadelphia, Lippincott Williams & Wilkins, 2000.)

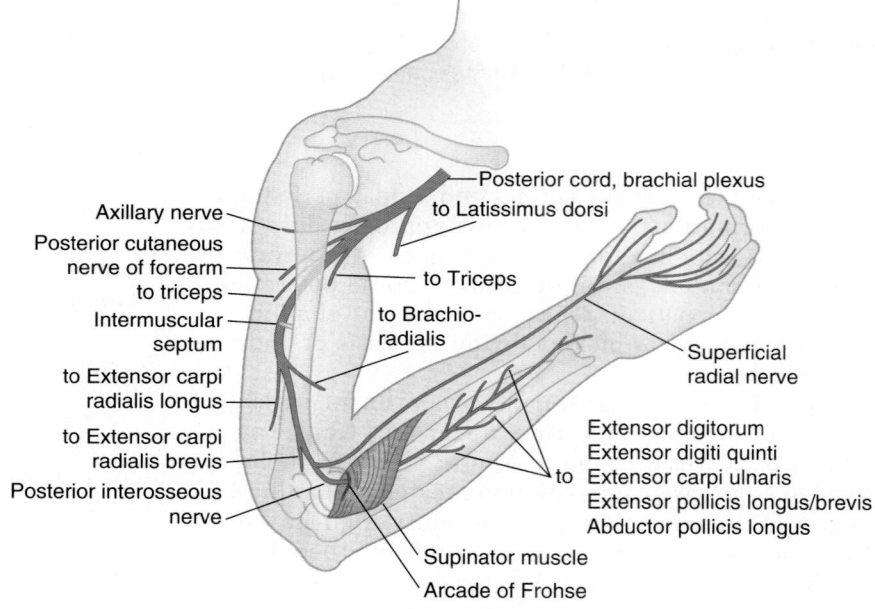

hand, the radial nerve makes a contribution only to a cutaneous dorsal area overlying the first dorsal interosseus muscle, sometimes extending part of the way up the dorsum of the thumb, index, and long finger.

Radial mononeuropathy caused by involvement at the level of the axilla is uncommon. When it occurs, it is usually associated with other upper extremity mononeuropathies or a brachial plexopathy. Although improper use of crutches may cause this syndrome, it usually occurs after an extended period of uncon-

sciousness during which the arm is positioned in such a way that prolonged, deep compression is applied to the axilla. Axillary radial mononeuropathy is distinguished from the more common humeral form by the finding of triceps involvement in addition to typical wrist and finger drop. Triceps involvement occurs because the innervation to the triceps is proximal to the point where the nerve is most vulnerable as it winds around the humeral shaft (see Figure 105-3).

Most radial mononeuropathies are due to so-called Saturday night palsies. The euphemism is apparently derived from the association of radial mononeuropathy with improper positioning of the arm during deep, commonly inebriated sleep. Consequently, the radial nerve is trapped for a prolonged period between the humeral shaft and some firm surface, causing an external compression mononeuropathy. "Bridegroom's palsy" is another eponym for radial mononeuropathy, so named because the radial nerve may be compressed by the bride's head resting on the bridegroom's arm during sleep.

Because innervation of the wrist and finger extensors occurs distal to this area of the humeral shaft, findings are characterized by wrist and finger drop and mild numbness over the skin of the first dorsal interosseus muscle. Depending on the level, degree, and duration of compression, some fascicles of the nerve may remain functional, resulting in a partial radial mononeuropathy. Thus, the superficial radial nerve may remain intact, resulting in no loss of sensation, or loss of wrist and finger extension may be incomplete.

Because the finger drop of radial mononeuropathy places the hand at a mechanical disadvantage, examination of ulnar function by testing interossei may produce false-positive findings of weakness. To adjust for this, the examiner should ask the patient to place the palm on a horizontal supporting surface such as a stretcher. With the fingers extended and no longer "dropped" at the metacarpophalangeal joints, interosseous strength can now be fairly tested. Failure to perform this maneuver may cause misdiagnosis of a simple radial mononeuropathy as a brachial plexopathy in an effort to explain what appears to be radial and partial ulnar nerve involvement.

About 90% of radial nerve palsies occurring during sleep, coma, or anesthesia recover fully, usually within 6 to 8 weeks. Evidence of denervation on EMG studies predicts a slower rate of recovery. Tourniquet injuries to the radial nerve usually recover spontaneously within 2 to 4 months. If axonal degeneration is seen on electrophysiologic testing, recovery may take longer, although virtually all radial mononeuropathies caused by tourniquets eventually resolve. About 75% of radial nerve injuries associated with a closed humeral shaft fracture recover spontaneously. In contrast, surgical intervention is needed to free the nerve from entrapment associated with complex fractures.

While patients are waiting for spontaneous recovery to occur, the hand should be maintained in about 60 degrees of dorsiflexion. Although a simple dorsal plaster or fiberglass splint treats the wristdrop, atrophy, contractures, and function of the hand can be improved if wide rubber bands anchored to the splint at a point proximal to the wrist are attached to individual fingers to provide passive dorsiflexion.

Ulnar Mononeuropathy

The ulnar nerve includes C7-T1 roots and passes through the brachial plexus to descend medially, without branching, to the ulnar (medial) condylar groove at the elbow. It then enters the cubital canal, where it gives off branches to the ulnar wrist flexor and the deep flexors of the fourth and fifth digits.

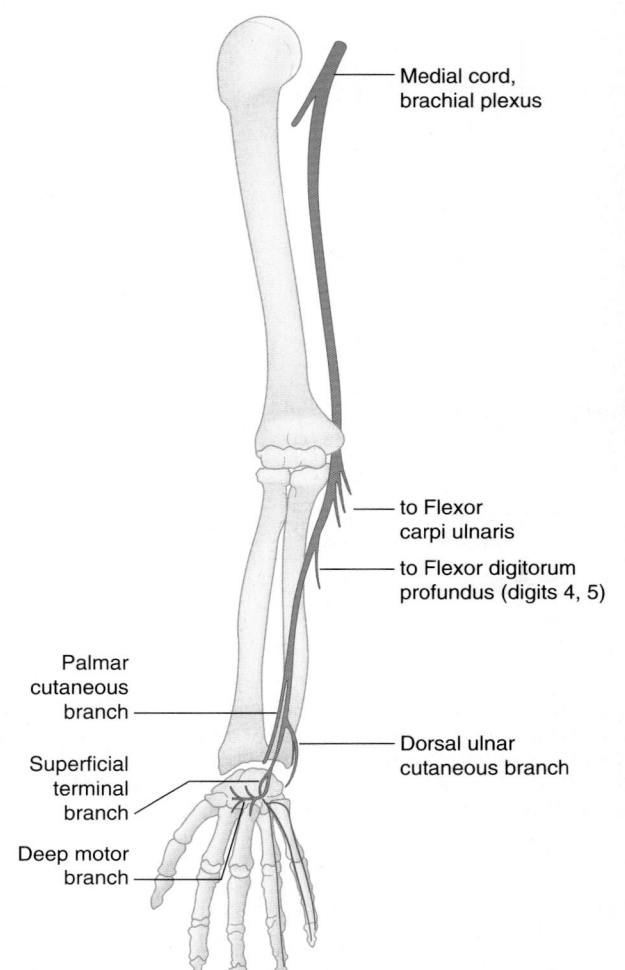

Figure 105-4. Ulnar nerve, major branches, right arm, anterior view. (From Stewart JD: *Focal Peripheral Neuropathies*, 3rd ed. Philadelphia, Lippincott Williams & Wilkins, 2000.)

Just proximal to the wrist, two important sensory branches leave the main trunk to supply cutaneous sensation to part of the hand (Figure 105-4). These are the palmar and dorsal cutaneous branches, which do *not* pass through Guyon's canal. The palmar branch supplies sensation to the hypothenar eminence, and the dorsal branch innervates the ulnar side of the dorsum of the hand, extending out nearly to the tips of the fifth and ulnar half of the fourth digits.

At the wrist, the nerve enters Guyon's canal (Figure 105-5) between the pisiform and hook of the hamate, then bifurcates into the superficial terminal sensory branch and the deep motor branch.

The superficial sensory nerve supplies ulnar sensation to the palmar side of the fifth and half of the fourth digit (see Figure 105-5). The deep motor nerve supplies the hypothenar muscles, then crosses to the radial side of the palm to innervate the ulnar intrinsics (all interossei and the ulnar lumbricals of the fourth and fifth digits), terminating in the first dorsal interosseus. The interossei abduct and adduct the fingers and are all innervated by the ulnar nerve. The lumbrical muscles flex the metacarpal phalangeal joints and are evenly

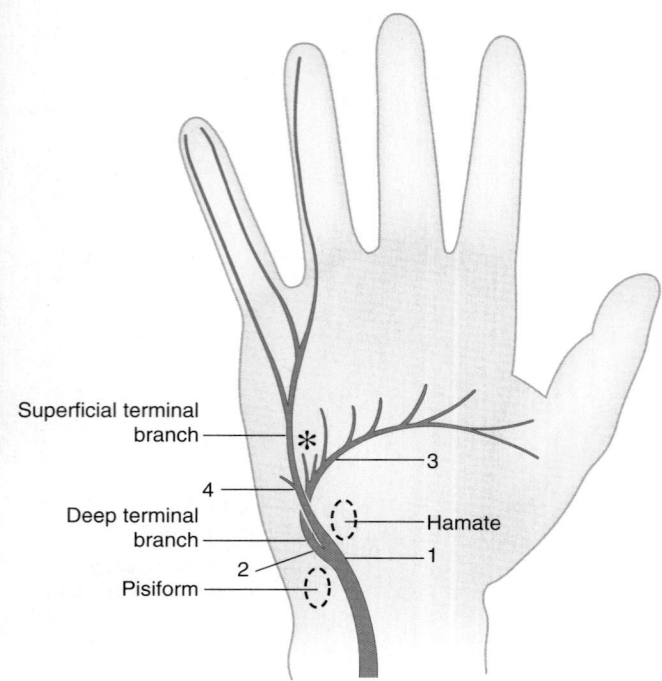

Figure 105-5. Distal ulnar nerve and branches, right hand, palmar view. Numbers indicate four main sites of distal ulnar mononeuropathy in the wrist and hand. * denotes hypothenar branches. (From Stewart JD: *Focal Peripheral Neuropathies*, 3rd ed. Philadelphia, Lippincott Williams & Wilkins, 2000.)

divided between the ulnar (fourth and fifth) and median (second and third) digits. The ulnar nerve can be thought of as the complement to the median nerve in the hand because it supplies all of the muscles and all palmar sensation not innervated by the median nerve.

The ulnar nerve may be injured at two locations near the elbow: in the ulnar condylar groove and distally in the cubital canal. Because the condylar groove is shallow, the ulnar nerve runs superficially in this location and is vulnerable to injury, usually from external pressure or from a fracture or dislocation. The ulnar nerve has a propensity to develop a "tardy ulnar palsy," occurring years after a traumatic event. Many of these delayed ulnar mononeuropathies can be localized to the elbow on electrophysiologic testing.

Some ulnar mononeuropathies occur secondary to compression just proximal to entry into the cubital canal or are entrapped within the canal itself. Transient symptoms may occur during prolonged flexion or with repeated flexion and extension at the elbow.

Although distinguishing a condylar from a cubital ulnar mononeuropathy is difficult, it is usually possible to localize the problem to the region of the elbow or the wrist. In addition to prior probability heavily favoring the elbow, the presence of sensory abnormalities in an ulnar distribution in the hand and fingers (i.e., usually including the fifth digit and "splitting" the fourth digit) strongly suggests that the lesion is at the level of the elbow rather than the wrist. The ulnar cutaneous innervation to the hand branches off from the main trunk

proximal to the nerve entering Guyon's canal (see Figures 105-4 and 105-5). Thus, a lesion at the wrist should not produce sensory abnormalities, whereas one at the elbow would be expected to do so.

Compression of the ulnar nerve within Guyon's canal is rare. When it does occur, it affects all of the ulnar intrinsics (i.e., the two ulnar [fourth and fifth] lumbricals) and all the interossei. However, the ulnar extrinsics (i.e., the deep flexors of the fourth and fifth digits) are not affected, nor is the ulnar flexor of the wrist. The only sensory abnormalities are those in the distribution of the superficial terminal sensory branch, sparing other areas of ulnar innervation (see Figure 105-5).

There are three ulnar mononeuropathies that occur distal to Guyon's canal in the hand. The two most common ones involve the deep terminal branch, either proximal or distal to the separation of the hypothenar branches (see Figure 105-5). If the lesion is proximal, it produces weakness of all the ulnar innervated muscles of the hand without sensory loss. If it is distal, the hypothenar ulnar intrinsics are spared but the picture is otherwise similar. Usually, this occurs secondary to a laceration or repeated compression in the hand from use of certain tools, a cane, or the handle of a crutch.

Involvement of the superficial terminal branch (see Figure 105-5) arises as pure sensory loss of the palmar surface of the fifth digit and ulnar half of the fourth digit caused by direct compression of this branch just distal to Guyon's canal. The dorsal surface of these two digits should have normal sensation except for the distal tips. This configuration of findings is due to the intact innervation provided by the dorsal and palmar cutaneous branches that enter the hand without passing through Guyon's canal (see Figure 105-4).

Median Mononeuropathy

The median nerve arises from C5-T1 spinal nerve roots and exits the brachial plexus through the lower trunk (Figure 105-6). Median mononeuropathy is usually diagnosed as carpal tunnel syndrome (CTS), which is the most common of all entrapment neuropathies. Although the patient may complain of bilateral symptoms, a careful history usually reveals that symptoms in one hand preceded those in the other. Awakening at night and shaking the hand is a common symptom of CTS. Symptoms are often worsened by activity. For unclear reasons, the pain may spread as high as the arm or shoulder, although the paresthesias are generally confined to the fingers. Many patients on initial questioning state that their entire hand is involved, although this is not supported by careful sensory examination. Complaints that the hands are clumsy or weak, especially when holding a glass or opening a screw-top container, are frequent. The skin of the fingers innervated by the median nerve may be drier and rougher to the touch than the corresponding ulnar skin, depending on the duration of entrapment.[29]

Because the nerve has already given off motor branches to the median extrinsic muscles to the hand,

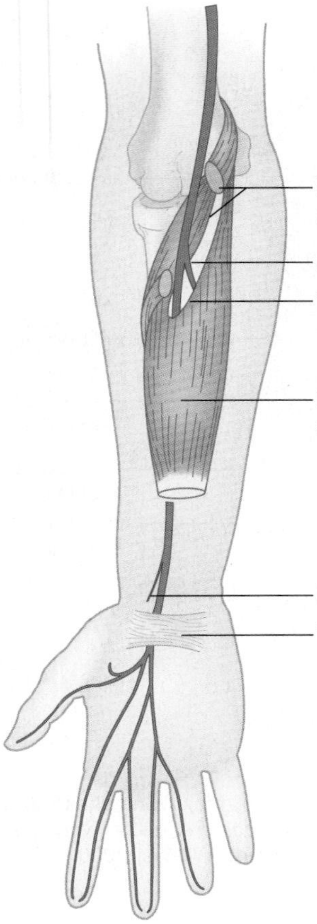
Pronator teres muscle
(superficial and deep heads)
Anterior interosseous nerve
"Sublimis bridge"
Flexor digitorum
superficialis muscle
Palmar cutaneous branch
Transverse carpal ligament

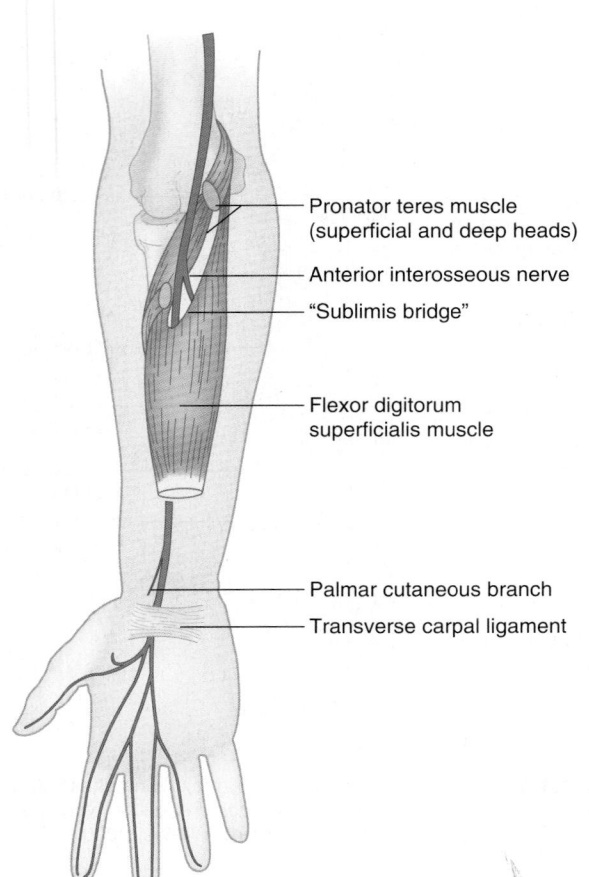

Figure 105-6. Median nerve, major branches, right arm, anterior view. (From Stewart JD: *Focal Peripheral Neuropathies*, 3rd ed. Philadelphia, Lippincott Williams & Wilkins, 2000.)

when there is motor involvement in CTS it is confined to the median intrinsics, which innervate the *l*umbricals (flexion of the metacarpal phalangeal joints), and subserve thumb *o*pposition, *a*bduction, and *f*lexion, known as the LOAF muscles. However, the hallmark of CTS is sensory involvement, with motor abnormalities occurring later. The typical pattern of sensory innervation of the hand by the median, ulnar, and radial nerves shows marked individual variation. The most specific finding for CTS is splitting of the fourth digit (i.e., normal sensation of the ring finger on the ulnar palmar side with abnormal sensation on the median [radial] palmar side of the same finger). The most sensitive finding is abnormal sensation of the distal palmar tip of the index finger. If sensory findings are absent in the presence of motor findings consistent with median nerve involvement, it is highly unlikely that the patient has CTS, and an alternative diagnosis should be sought. If neither sensory nor motor symptoms are evident, none of the provocative tests originally reported to reproduce the sensory symptoms of CTS—of which the most common are Tinel's sign (percussion of the median nerve at the wrist) and Phalen's sign (maximal palmar flexion at the wrist)—has shown adequate sensitivity or specificity to determine which patients should be referred for electrodiagnostic studies.[30-32] As suggested earlier, the best way to examine patients for sensory findings is to touch the distal palmar tips very lightly, asking the patient whether the sensation feels "abnormal."

BOX 105-6. Conditions Associated with Carpal Tunnel Syndrome

Acromegaly
Amyloid
Diabetes mellitus
Hypothyroidism
Pregnancy
Renal failure

CTS appears to be associated with the conditions listed in Box 105-6. Of these, the two most common are diabetes mellitus and pregnancy. CTS associated with systemic illness is commonly bilateral. Although CTS in pregnancy may be self-limiting, about half the women in one series were still symptomatic at 1-year follow-up.[33] All patients with suspected CTS should be referred for NCSs. However, because of the dissociation between clinical and electrodiagnostic indicators of CTS early in the disease, patients with normal electrodiagnostic findings in the presence of symptoms suggestive of CTS (with or without signs) should have an MRI.[34] or sonogram.[35] At present, the sensitivity of MRI is good but its specificity is poor.[36] Sonography appears promising but has not yet been well studied. Thus, if all diagnostic studies in a symptomatic patient are negative, or if only the MRI is positive, they should be repeated within a few months if symptoms do not resolve.[29] This recommendation is based on the theory that the CTS will progress over time to the point that an objective indicator such as the NCS will become positive.

Because of the possibility of development of a disabling "median hand" after inadvertent direct injection of the median nerve, one should not inject the carpal tunnel with steroids in the emergency department. The physician to whom the patient is referred can decide after NCS whether to recommend splinting, injection, or surgical division of the transverse carpal ligament. Endoscopic repair appears to provide excellent results.[37]

Sciatic Mononeuropathy

The sciatic nerve includes L4-S3 spinal nerve roots that pass through the lumbosacral plexus and divide into two terminal branches: the common peroneal and tibial nerves. As shown in Figure 105-7, the nerve exits the pelvis through the sciatic notch, passes behind the hip, and remains deep in the thigh until its terminal bifurcation in the proximal popliteal fossa.

Lesions of the sciatic nerve occur with posterior hip dislocation or with virtually any form of penetrating or blunt trauma that causes formation of a buttock

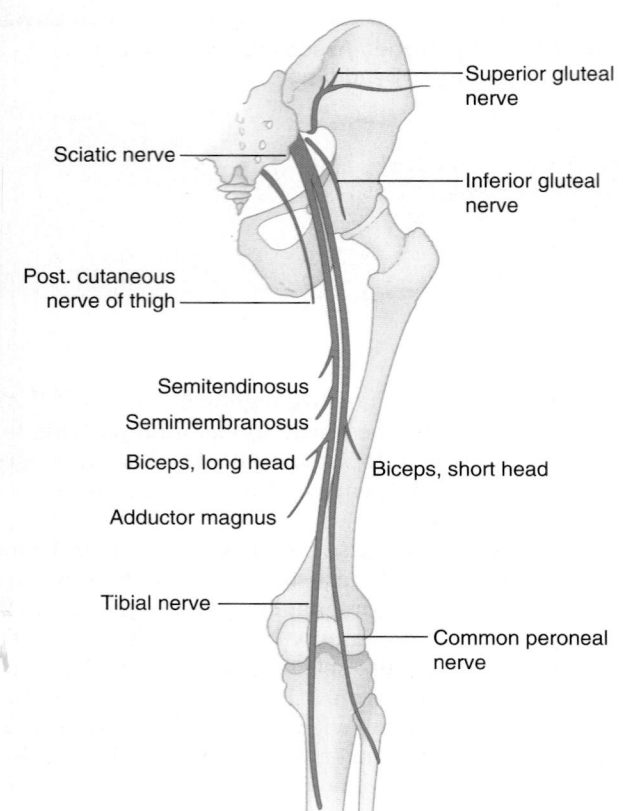

Figure 105-7. Sciatic nerve, major branches, right leg, posterior view. (From Stewart JD: *Focal Peripheral Neuropathies*, 3rd ed. Philadelphia, Lippincott Williams & Wilkins, 2000.)

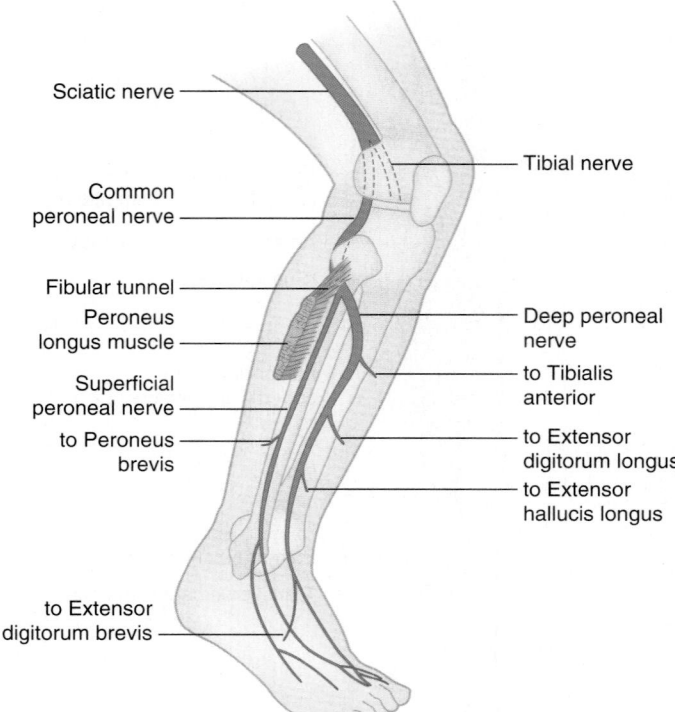

Figure 105-8. Common peroneal nerve, major branches, right leg, anterolateral view. (From Stewart JD: *Focal Peripheral Neuropathies*, 3rd ed. Philadelphia, Lippincott Williams & Wilkins, 2000.)

hematoma. Other causes include deep gluteal injection and prolonged supine immobilization on a firm surface. Because the sciatic nerve innervates the hamstrings and provides all sensorimotor function distal to the knee, a complete sciatic mononeuropathy is a devastating injury. Ambulation is extremely difficult because of inability to flex the knee and a flail foot (i.e., neither flexion nor extension is possible at the ankle). Fortunately, many sciatic mononeuropathies are incomplete. For unknown reasons, a partial lesion typically involves only the trunk of the sciatic nerve, which subsequently becomes the common peroneal nerve, sometimes making the two difficult to distinguish from one another clinically. On electrophysiologic studies, evidence of involvement of gluteal muscles or of any muscles innervated by the tibial nerve readily distinguishes a partial sciatic mononeuropathy from a lesion of the common peroneal nerve. Treatment of footdrop requires a posterior splint to maintain the ankle at 90 degrees until a brace can be obtained (see "Common Peroneal Mononeuropathy").

Lateral Femoral Cutaneous Mononeuropathy

Lateral femoral cutaneous mononeuropathy (meralgia paresthetica) is a common syndrome believed to be caused by injury to this pure sensory nerve as it passes through or over the inguinal ligament, where it may become entrapped or kinked. Along with facial nerve neuropathy, meralgia paresthetica is one of the most commonly reported mononeuropathies associated with HIV. External pressure and obesity may also contribute to nerve injury, causing numbness and dysesthesia over the skin of the upper lateral thigh. Regression usually occurs spontaneously, but recurrence is common and may require a release procedure for the inguinal ligament.

Common Peroneal Mononeuropathy

The common peroneal nerve is a continuation of one trunk of the sciatic nerve. It is most vulnerable to injury where it winds around the fibular neck (Figure 105-8). It then passes through the fibular canal and bifurcates into its terminal branches, the superficial and deep peroneal nerves. The superficial peroneal nerve innervates the peroneal muscles (foot everters) and supplies sensation to the lateral, distal lower leg and dorsum of the foot. The deep peroneal nerve traverses the anterior compartment and supplies innervation to the dorsiflexors of the foot and toes, plus cutaneous sensation between the first and second toes.

Most common peroneal mononeuropathies are idiopathic and thought to be related to compression where the nerve is superficially located lateral to the fibular neck. Because this common neuropathy is often noted on awakening, it may be secondary to position during sleep. Leg crossing may also be a risk factor for development of this mononeuropathy. The most striking feature of a complete common peroneal mononeuropathy is footdrop caused by weakness of foot dorsiflexion. At testing, the everters of the foot are also weak, but the inverters, which are innervated by the tibial nerve, remain strong. This is the single most reliable clinical feature distinguishing sciatic from common peroneal mononeuropathy. Analogous to radial mononeuropathy in the upper extremity, sensory abnormalities in the leg and foot are inconstant and easily overlooked in peroneal mononeuropathy. Most patients with peroneal palsy recover. Those who do not should be studied electrophysiologically to ensure that the point of compression is not proximal to the fibular neck (i.e., in the popliteal fossa). If the point of peroneal injury appears to be in the region of, or distal to, the fibular neck on EMG, patients whose footdrop does not resolve should be considered candidates for exploration to determine whether the nerve is compressed within the fibular canal.

Treatment of common peroneal palsy may require a posterior splint to maintain the ankle at 90 degrees until the nerve regenerates. This splinting prevents the foot from falling into sustained equinus (plantar flexion), which in turn allows the intermalleolar distance to narrow, effectively locking the talus out of the ankle mortice.

The treatment of isolated mononeuropathies depends on their etiology, location, and natural history of spontaneous recovery. All penetrating neuropathies should have surgical exploration and repair performed. Blunt trauma may cause a mononeuropathy indirectly by entrapment of a nerve within a fracture, hematoma, or compartment, requiring surgical intervention. Alternatively, nerves may be injured at a point where they are superficial, either by a single direct blow or by sustained pressure caused by immobility (pressure palsies). Most of these resolve spontaneously over time, depending on the severity of injury and length of the nerve. If entrapment can be confirmed by imaging or electrophysiologic studies, a release procedure is indicated. In many instances, when there is disagreement between clinical and EMG findings, MRI may be helpful in selecting patients for exploration by visualizing entrapment or traction.[38] Characteristic sonographic findings have also been reported in several mononeuropathies.[39]

The mononeuropathies that do not require timely surgical exploration should be referred for further workup to confirm the location of the neuropathic lesion.

Type 5: Mononeuropathy Multiplex

Mononeuropathy multiplex (Box 105-7) is characterized by an asymmetric, sensorimotor, usually distal pattern of peripheral neuropathy. As with isolated mononeuropathies, sensory abnormalities tend to be located in the same general anatomic region as the accompanying motor findings. Whether DTRs are affected depends on which nerves are involved. For example, if the process includes the femoral nerve, the knee jerk is likely to be diminished or absent.

Vasculitis

Mononeuropathy multiplex is strongly associated with vasculitis, which is the most common indication for sural nerve biopsy in most series. However, because diabetes mellitus is far more prevalent than vasculitis, the most common cause of mononeuropathy multiplex among emergency department patients is likely to be diabetes.

Diabetes Mellitus

Although the role of ischemia in diabetic neuropathies is controversial, evidence for a vascular cause is stronger in the asymmetric diabetic multiple mononeuropathies than in the more common DSPNs seen in diabetes.

Lyme Disease

The PNS manifestations of Lyme disease can be divided into early and late. The early PNS syndromes commonly include facial nerve involvement (rarely other cranial nerve palsies) and radiculoneuritis. Late PNS involvement occurs as a DSPN, mononeuropathy multiplex, or radiculoneuropathy. The most common neurologic abnormality in Lyme disease is unilateral or bilateral facial nerve palsy, usually occurring within a month of exposure. Patients may also complain of headache and constitutional symptoms. Early in the course of Lyme, severe neuritic pain may develop in a radicular distribution, often in or near the dermatome where the tick bite occurred. There may also be associated sensory changes, motor weakness, and decreased reflexes consistent with nerve root involvement. Patients with chronic Lyme disease present with sensory symptoms, particularly distal paresthesias in the lower extremities. Less commonly, they develop a picture consistent with mononeuropathy multiplex or a radiculopathy. The latter is much less severe than the early radiculoneuritis of Lyme.

BOX 105-8. Objective Clinical Findings Consistent with Amyotrophic Lateral Sclerosis

Upper Motor Neuron Signs
Hyperreflexia
   Sustained clonus, especially at ankle
   Finger flexors and jaw jerk
Spasticity, especially of gait
Positive Babinski sign

Lower Motor Neuron Signs
Positive motor phenomena
   Fasciculations
   Cramps
Negative motor phenomena
   Asymmetric distal weakness
   Atrophy

Combined Upper and Lower Motor Neuron Signs
Dysarthria
Dysphagia
Respiratory compromise

BOX 105-9. Sensory Neuronopathies (Ganglionopathies)

Herpes
   Herpes simplex I and II
   Varicella zoster (shingles)
Inflammatory sensory polyganglionopathy (ISP)
Paraneoplastic
Primary biliary cirrhosis
Sjögren's syndrome (keratoconjunctivitis sicca)
Toxin induced
   Pyridoxine (vitamin B_6) overdose
   Metals
      Platinum (cisplatin)
      Methyl mercury
Vitamin E deficiency

The most useful diagnostic tests for patients with suspected Lyme disease are a serum enzyme-linked immunosorbent assay, Western blot, and a CSF examination. CSF abnormalities suggestive of Lyme disease are a lymphocytic pleocytosis, elevated protein, and normal glucose. The CSF is almost always abnormal in early radiculitis, sometimes abnormal with isolated facial palsy, and typically normal in chronic Lyme disease. Facial nerve palsy without CSF abnormalities may be treated with oral doxycycline 100 mg twice a day for 2 weeks. Intravenous ceftriaxone is the drug of choice for all other neurologic syndromes associated with Lyme disease. The adult dose is 2 g/day, and the pediatric dose is 75 to 100 mg/kg/day. Treatment with ceftriaxone should be continued for at least 2 weeks.

Type 6: Amyotrophic Lateral Sclerosis

Although amyotrophic lateral sclerosis (ALS) and motor neuron disease (MND) are often used synonymously, the latter represents a spectrum of diseases ranging from primary lateral sclerosis, in which degeneration is confined to upper motor neurons, to progressive muscle atrophy, in which only lower motor neurons are involved. ALS, which requires the presence of both upper and lower motor neuron findings, resides in the middle of this spectrum, representing the most common form of MND.

In ALS, the primary pathologic process in the PNS component of the disease is a neuronopathy of the anterior horn cell. Because this structure is located proximal to the point where motor and sensory fibers merge to form mixed spinal nerve roots, the signs and symptoms of MND are purely motor (see Figure 105-2). In the CNS, there is loss of Betz cells from the motor cortex with secondary degeneration of the corticospinal tracts. Box 105-8 lists some representative upper, lower, and mixed motor signs. Patients typically demonstrate

asymmetric distal weakness without sensory findings. Positive motor phenomena in the form of fasciculations are found in almost all patients at diagnosis but are rarely an initial complaint. Although there is electrophysiologic evidence of autonomic involvement in ALS, this is generally subclinical.

Most patients with an asymmetric, distal, pure motor neuropathy have ALS, for which only supportive treatment is available. All patients coming to the emergency department in whom this diagnosis is suspected should be referred for electrophysiologic confirmation against standardized criteria. Confirmation is particularly important because multifocal motor neuropathy, a rare disease that masquerades as ALS, responds dramatically to cyclophosphamide and immunoglobulin administration.[40]

Type 7: Sensory Neuronopathy (Ganglionopathy)

This category of peripheral neuropathy is characterized by a selective or predominant involvement of the dorsal root ganglion, producing a relatively pure sensory syndrome analogous to the pure motor syndrome of ALS. Although all sensory modalities are affected, proprioception is profoundly altered, leading to sensory ataxia and loss of DTRs without weakness. The distribution is typically asymmetric and distal at the outset, but depending on severity and extent of progression, it may become functionally symmetrical. Sensory ganglionopathies can now be confirmed by MRI of the spinal cord and surrounding areas, showing degeneration of central sensory projections that localize the disease process to the dorsal root ganglion.[41] Some of the more common causes of this type of peripheral neuropathy are listed in Box 105-9.

ANCILLARY DIAGNOSTIC TESTING

Relatively few blood tests contribute to the diagnosis of peripheral neuropathy, and only a small number of these are available in the emergency department. CSF

BOX 105-10. Ancillary Diagnostic Testing in Suspected Peripheral Neuropathy

Obtained in Most Patients
Complete blood count (CBC)
Erythrocyte sedimentation rate (ESR)
Glucose
Creatine kinase (CK)
Creatinine

Obtained Only if Indicated
Human chorionic gonadotropin (HCG)
Magnesium
Phosphate
Vitamin B_{12}
Hemoglobin A_{1c}
Serum protein electrophoresis (SPEP) with immune fixation electrophoresis (IFE)
VDRL or RPR screen with fluorescent treponemal antibody-absorption (FTA-ABS) test, as appropriate
Thyroid function
HIV

Lyme enzyme-linked immunosorbent assay (ELISA) and Western Blot
Rheumatoid factor and antinuclear antibody
Blood, urine, hair, or nails for metal, depending on suspected chronicity of exposure
Specific serum antibodies to components of PNS
CSF for cells, protein, Lyme titer
Electrodiagnostic testing
   Nerve conduction studies
   Electromyography
Neurodiagnostic imaging
   MRI
   CT
   Sonography
Quantitative sensory testing
Nerve biopsy
   Sural
   Intraepidermal nerve fiber density

may be helpful in Guillain-Barré and Lyme disease. Additional tests that may be indicated in patients referred for evaluation are listed in Box 105-10, along with others that may be ordered selectively, depending on the clinical picture. Expensive batteries of tests purporting to measure a wide variety of antibodies to components of peripheral neuropathies are commercially available but have not been shown to be useful as screening tests.

 KEY CONCEPTS

- Although peripheral neuropathies only rarely cause respiratory compromise, GBS is by far the most common peripheral neuropathic cause of respiratory arrest.

- Any patient with symmetrical weakness, distributed both proximally and distally, with loss or diminution of DTRs and variable sensory abnormalities, should be managed as having GBS.

- When GBS and the other causes of weakness listed in Box 105-1 have been excluded, diseases that place respiratory function at risk have been removed from the differential diagnosis. This effectively eliminates the short-term mortality from peripheral neuropathy.

- In the emergency department, it is not usually possible to arrive at the diagnosis of a specific peripheral neuropathy because of the need for confirmatory ancillary testing that is beyond the scope of emergency practice. Rather, the focus should be on identifying one of seven categorical patterns of peripheral neuropathy shown in Figure 105-1 and listed in Table 105-1.

- One of these seven patterns can usually be identified by combining three clinical features that are readily obtainable from a goal-directed history and physical: (1) right-left symmetry or asymmetry, (2) proximal-distal location, and (3) sensorimotor modalities affected. This approach is summarized as an algorithm in Figure 105-1.

- Identification of one of the seven types of peripheral neuropathy determines the need for ancillary diagnostic testing, therapeutic intervention, disposition, and the timing of neurologic referral.

REFERENCES

1. Pascuzzi RM, Fleck JD: Acute peripheral neuropathy in adults: Guillain-Barré syndrome and related disorders. *Neurol Clin* 15:529, 1997.
2. Carter GT, Galer BS: Advances in the management of neuropathic pain. *Phys Med Rehabil Clin N Am* 12:447, 2001.
3. American Diabetes Association: Facts and figures [Online]. http://www.diabetes.org/info/facts/facts.jsp, 2003.
4. Winer JB: Treatment of Guillain-Barré syndrome. *QJM* 95:717, 2002.
5. Oh SJ, LaGanke C, Claussen GC: Sensory Guillain-Barré syndrome. *Neurology* 56:82, 2001.
6. Barohn RJ, Saperstein DS: Guillain-Barré syndrome and chronic inflammatory demyelinating polyneuropathy. *Semin Neurol* 18:49, 1998.
7. Byun WM, et al: Guillain-Barré syndrome: MR imaging findings of the spine in eight patients. *Radiology* 208:137, 1998.
8. Tam CC, Rodrigues LC, O'Brien SJ: Guillain-Barré syndrome associated with *Campylobacter jejuni* infection in England, 2000-2001. *Clin Infect Dis* 37:307, 2003.
9. Kieseier BC, Hartung HP: Therapeutic strategies in the Guillain-Barré syndrome. *Semin Neurol* 23:159, 2003.
10. Wijdicks EF, Henderson RD, McClelland RL: Emergency intubation for respiratory failure in Guillain-Barré syndrome. *Arch Neurol* 60:947, 2003.
11. Hughes RA, et al: Practice parameter: Immunotherapy for Guillain-Barré syndrome: Report of the Quality Standards Subcommittee of the American Academy of Neurology. *Neurology* 61:736, 2003.
12. Latov N, et al: Diabetic neuropathy. *Interdisciplinary Med* 4:1, 1999.
13. Woolf CJ, Mannion RJ: Neuropathic pain: Aetiology, symptoms, mechanisms, and management. *Lancet* 353:1959, 1999.
14. Sindrup SH, Jensen TS: Pharmacologic treatment of pain in polyneuropathy. *Neurology* 55:915, 2000.
15. Henstreet B, Lapointe M: Evidence for the use of gabapentin in the treatment of diabetic peripheral neuropathy. *Clin Ther* 23:520, 2002.
16. Gorson K, et al: Gabapentin in the treatment of painful diabetic neuropathy: A placebo controlled double blind crossover trial. *J Neurol Neurosurg Psychiatry* 66:251, 1999.

17. Semenchuk MR, Sherman S, Davis B: Double-blind randomized trial of bupropion-SR for the treatment of neuropathic pain. *Neurology* 57:1583, 2001.
18. Preedy VR, et al: Alcoholic skeletal muscle myopathy: Definitions, features, contribution of neuropathy, impact and diagnosis. *Eur J Neurol* 8:677, 2001.
19. Luciano CA, Pardo CA, McArthur JC: Recent developments in the HIV neuropathies. *Curr Opin Neurol* 16:403, 2003.
20. Simpson DM, et al: Lamotrigine for HIV-associated painful sensory neuropathies. *Neurology* 60:1508, 2000.
21. Faist K, et al: Statins and risk of polyneuropathy. *Neurology* 58:1333, 2002.
22. Parziale JR, et al: Thoracic outlet syndrome. *Am J Orthop* 29:353, 2000.
23. Lee GW, et al: Documentation of brachial plexus compression in the thoracic inlet with quantitative sensory testing. *J Reconstr Microsurg* 16:15, 2000.
24. Roos DB: Historical perspectives and anatomic considerations: Thoracic outlet syndrome. *Semin Thorac Cardiovasc Surg* 8:183, 1996.
25. Goetz CG (ed): *Textbook of Clinical Neurology*, 2nd ed. Philadelphia, Elsevier, 2003, pp 597-598.
26. Nannapaneni R, Marks SM: Neurogenic thoracic outlet syndrome. *Br J Neurosurg* 17:144, 2003.
27. England JD: Entrapment neuropathies. *Curr Opin Neurol* 12:597, 1999.
28. Vinik AI: Diabetic neuropathy: Pathogenesis and therapy. *Am J Med* 107:17S, 1999.
29. Padua L, et al: Multiperspective assessment of carpal tunnel syndrome: A multicenter study. Italian CTS Study Group. *Neurology* 53:1654, 1999.
30. Szabo RM, et al: The value of diagnostic testing in carpal tunnel syndrome. *J Hand Surg [Am]* 24:704, 1999.
31. Kuhlman KA, Hennessey WJ: Sensitivity and specificity of carpal tunnel syndrome signs. *Am J Phys Med Rehabil* 76:451, 1997.
32. De Smet L, et al: Value of clinical provocative tests in carpal tunnel syndrome. *Acta Orthop Belg* 61:177, 1995.
33. Padua L, et al: Carpal tunnel syndrome in pregnancy. Multiperspective follow-up of untreated cases. *Neurology* 59:1643, 2002.
34. Andre V, et al: Clinical, electrophysiological and MRI correlations in carpal tunnel syndrome. *J Radiol* 80:721, 1999.
35. Kele H, et al: The potential value of ultrasonography in the evaluation of carpal tunnel syndrome. *Neurology* 61:389, 2002.
36. Jarvik JG, et al: MR nerve imaging in a prospective cohort of patients with suspected carpal tunnel syndrome. *Neurology* 58:1597, 2002.
37. McNally SA, Hales PF: Results of 1245 endoscopic carpal tunnel decompressions. *Hand Surg* 8:111, 2003.
38. Sawaya RA: Idiopathic sciatic mononeuropathy. *Clin Neurol Neurosurg* 101:256, 1999.
39. Hide IG, et al: Sonographic findings in the anterior interosseus nerve syndrome. *J Clin Ultrasound* 27:459, 1999.
40. Chaudhry V: Multifocal motor neuropathy. *Semin Neurol* 18:73, 1998.
41. Lauria G, et al: Clinical and magnetic resonance imaging findings in chronic sensory ganglionopathies. *Ann Neurol* 47:104, 2000.

CHAPTER

106 Neuromuscular Disorders

Peter Shearer and Andrew Jagoda

PERSPECTIVE

Disorders of the neuromuscular unit can cause dramatic clinical pictures, including acute respiratory failure, although they more often have subtle symptoms. Morbidity and mortality are often related to failure of the muscles that maintain airway integrity and drive respiration. In most cases, the pathophysiology of these disorders is well understood and permits an organization and understanding that is based on the level of the nervous system affected. This facilitates an approach that is based on signs and symptoms, the findings of which direct the urgency of diagnostic testing and treatment.

Processes involving the brainstem and brain can usually be differentiated from those in the spinal cord and in the peripheral nervous system on the basis of historical and physical findings. In general, lesions at the level of the brainstem or above produce unilateral weakness; bilateral weakness caused by lesions above the spinal cord is generally associated with a change in mental status or cranial nerve involvement. Lesions of the central nervous system result in upper motor neuron signs that include spasticity, hyperreflexia, and extensor plantar reflexes. As a corollary, when bilateral upper motor neuron signs are found in conjunction with normal mental status, diagnostic testing including neuroimaging should focus on looking for a lesion in the spinal cord.

PRINCIPLES OF DISEASE

The neuromuscular unit is divided into four components: the anterior horn cells of the spinal cord, the peripheral nerve, the neuromuscular junction, and the muscle being innervated. The level of the pathology determines associated signs and symptoms (Table 106-1). *Myelopathies* are processes involving the spinal cord. *Radiculopathies* are processes involving the nerve roots as they leave the spinal cord. *Neuropathies* involve the peripheral nerves, and *myopathies* are processes involving the muscles.

Table 106-1. Clinical Characteristics of Neuromuscular Diseases

Disease	History	Strength	DTR	Sensation	Wasting
Myelopathy	Trauma, infection, cancer	Normal to decreased	Increased	Normal to decreased	No
Motor neuron disease (ALS)	Progressive difficulty swallowing, speaking, walking	Decreased	Increased	Normal	Yes
Neuropathy	Recent infection Ascending weakness	Normal or decreased Distal > proximal	Decreased	Decreased	Yes
Neuromuscular junction disease	Food (canned goods) Tick exposure Easy fatigability	Normal to fatigue	Normal	Normal	No
Myopathy	Thyroid disease Previous similar episodes	Decreased Proximal > distal	Normal	Normal	Yes

ALS, amyotrophic lateral sclerosis; DTR, deep tendon reflex.

Neuropathies involve the axon itself or the myelin sheath (or the Schwann cells that make the myelin sheath) of the nerve. Nerve conduction studies can differentiate the locations of involvement. As the conduction along the axon is disrupted, the subsequent delay in transmission first causes symptoms in the muscles controlled by longer nerve axons, resulting in a history of weakness beginning in the distal extremities. As the myelin destruction or axonal degeneration progresses, patients usually note a slowly progressive course of symptoms.

The motor nerve branches into multiple terminals as it approaches the muscle. The neuromuscular junction is composed of the presynaptic membrane, the postsynaptic membrane, and the synaptic cleft. The neurotransmitter is acetylcholine (ACh). The motor synapse is a nicotinic receptor, whereas muscarinic synapses link the central nervous system with the autonomic nervous system. Disorders of the postsynaptic nicotinic receptors produce weakness. Postsynaptic ACh receptors are continually turned over at a rate that is related to the amount of stimulation. A disorder of transmission often leads to increased production of ACh receptors. Myasthenia gravis (MG) is the prototype of neuromuscular junction diseases.

CLINICAL FINDINGS

History

The history of patients with complaints of weakness initially focuses on establishing the acuity and progression of onset and the potential for airway compromise. Any complaint of difficulty breathing or swallowing raises suspicion of bulbar involvement and concern for life-threatening deterioration. The history must elicit whether the weakness is muscular or nonspecific generalized fatigue. Weakness implies the inability to exert normal force, whereas fatigue implies a decrease in force with repetitive use. When muscular weakness exists, the clinician should determine whether it is focal or generalized, proximal or distal. The history of present illness must include the duration of symptoms, exacerbating and mitigating factors, and presence of associated symptoms such as fever, weight loss, and bowel or bladder changes.

The patient should be asked about the presence of a preexisting neuromuscular disorder; an acute exacerbation or end-stage degeneration of some genetic muscular dystrophies and MG may be the cause of the current difficulty. Prior episodes or a family history of weakness suggests the familial forms of the periodic paralyses. A history of a recent illness (often respiratory or diarrheal) supports a diagnosis of postinfectious autoimmune causes of weakness such as transverse myelitis or Guillain-Barré syndrome (GBS). Past history or risk factors for cancer may indicate a metastatic tumor as the cause of a compressive myelopathy. Questions about recent travel can help exclude tick bites or snakebites, and a dietary history may elicit shellfish toxin ingestion or the ingestion of canned goods suggesting botulism.

Physical Examination

The physical examination should first assess the patient's airway and ventilation and then proceed to localize the level of the lesion. The presence of swallowing and a strong cough suggest that the patient has sufficient protective and ventilatory reserve. The muscles used to lift the head off the bed may weaken before those of respiration and should be assessed. A patient who is not yet intubated but is complaining of shortness of breath or difficulty breathing should have frequent vital capacity measurements. Normally, these values range from 60 to 70 mL/kg. When the forced vital capacity reaches 15 mL/kg, intubation is necessary. If vital capacity cannot be measured, a maximal negative inspiratory force is easily determined. A negative inspiratory force less than 15 mm Hg suggests the need for endotracheal intubation. An easy bedside assessment used to follow ventilatory status is to have the patient count numbers with one breath.[1] With sequential performance of this test, a decline in respiratory function is detected as the patient fails to count as high as before. Arterial blood gas is not necessarily helpful because functional reserve can be severely diminished by the time a patient develops either hypercarbia or hypoxia.

The assessment of vital signs is important because some causes of weakness may result in dysregulation of the autonomic system. A systematic neurologic examination should assess the patient's mental status, cranial nerves, motor function, sensory function, deep tendon reflexes (DTRs), and coordination, including cerebellar function. The motor examination begins by determining whether the weakness is unilateral or bilateral and which muscle groups are involved. Key components of the examination include motor strength, muscle bulk, and presence of fasciculations. Box 106-1 provides the grading system used in motor strength assessment. Table 106-2 provides the findings used to distinguish upper motor neuron from lower motor neuron processes.

Differential Considerations

Myelopathies

A myelopathy shows signs of upper motor neuron dysfunction. Without upper motor neuron function, muscle weakness is present with increased spinal reflexes, including an extensor plantar reflex (Babinski response). The same reflex arcs eventually creates spasticity in the affected muscles. The weakness is ascending in nature, and there is often bladder and bowel involvement. When sensory findings are present, they often define the distinct level of the lesion.

Motor Neuron Disease

Amyotrophic lateral sclerosis is the prototypical disease process resulting from a degeneration of the motor neuron without sensory involvement. These patients may complain of dysarthria or dysphagia; however, the characteristic findings are those of combined upper and lower motor neuron dysfunction. Consequently, findings include hyperreflexia, muscle wasting, and fasciculation. Pain is not a component of the clinical picture.

Poliomyelitis affects the anterior horn cells and results in lower motor neuron disease without sensory involvement. The weakness can be symmetrical or more often asymmetric. Patients initially have a clinical picture similar to that of viral meningitis, with fever and neck stiffness. Currently, most cases follow exposure of an immunocompromised host to the oral polio vaccine, and this should be sought in the history. The cerebrospinal fluid analysis resembles that of viral meningitis.

Neuropathies

Weakness from a neuropathy is often noted in distal muscles first and ascends. Grip strength or footdrop may be noted first. As all outflow from the spinal cord is affected, DTRs are diminished or absent. Patients exhibit varying degrees of altered sensation, muscle wasting, and fasciculation depending on the duration of the symptoms.

Diseases of the Neuromuscular Junction

Disorders of the neuromuscular junction cause progressive motor fatigability. The initial depolarization of the muscle causes stimulation of a maximum number of receptors, producing a normal, or nearly normal, strength response. Repeated stimulation leads to diminishing motor strength, which is caused by blockage of the receptors (as in MG) or by a decrease in the amount of ACh released (as in botulism). A decrease in the release of ACh may produce a combination of nicotinic and muscarinic effects leading to anticholinergic findings such as decreased visual acuity, confusion, urinary retention, tachycardia, low-grade fever, and dry, flushed skin. In the case of Lambert-Eaton myasthenic syndrome, weakness is more pronounced at the beginning of muscle use and improves with repeated use as more ACh builds up in the synaptic cleft with each stimulation.

Myopathies

These disorders usually produce generalized, symmetrical weakness. Reflexes are present but markedly decreased, whereas sensation is preserved. Myopathies caused by inflammatory processes (i.e., viral myositis) may cause muscle tenderness and, over time, some wasting may occur as a result of disuse.

DIAGNOSTIC STRATEGIES

Laboratory Studies

Serum potassium, calcium, and phosphorus should be assessed in patients with acute weakness. Thyroid

---

BOX 106-1. Grading Score for Motor Strength

5 = Normal strength
4 = Weak but able to resist examiner
3 = Moves against gravity but unable to resist examiner
2 = Moves but unable to resist gravity
1 = Flicker but no movement
0 = No movement

Table 106-2. Distinguishing Upper Motor Neuron (UMN) from Lower Motor Neuron (LMN) Involvement

Motor Neuron	DTR	Muscle Tone	Atrophy	Fasciculations	Babinski
UMN	Increased	Increased	No*	No	Present
LMN	Decreased	Decreased	Yes	Yes	Absent

*Not significant, but can occur.
DTR, deep tendon reflex.

function tests are recommended in cases of suspected myopathies. A creatine kinase (CK) level assesses for muscular inflammation; a urinalysis should be performed for the presence of myoglobinuria and possible rhabdomyolysis.

Special Studies

Magnetic resonance imaging (MRI) is the preferred test for suspected cases of acute myelopathy. Computed tomography of the spinal cord with myelography can help to differentiate compressive (herniation, abscess, tumor) from noncompressive causes when MRI is not available. Cerebrospinal fluid analysis has limited use in the evaluation of weakness. It is indicated when GBS or transverse myelitis is suspected.

SPECIFIC DISORDERS

Disorders of the Neuromuscular Junction

Myasthenia Gravis

Perspective
It is rare for the emergency physician to diagnose a new case of MG; more commonly, patients with established disease come to the emergency department with an exacerbation. In addition, the emergency physician must be cognizant of medication interactions in patients with MG.

Principles of Disease
MG has a prevalence of 50 to 125 per million.[2] Age of onset is bimodal, with the first peak among women in the 20s and 30s and a second peak among men in the sixth and seventh decades.

MG results from autoantibodies directed against the nicotinic acetylcholine receptor (AChR) at the neuromuscular junction. This leads to complement-mediated destruction of AChRs with a decrease in the total number of available receptors. The autoantibodies further compete with ACh for binding at remaining receptors. Thus, with repeated stimulation of the same muscle, fewer and fewer sites are available and fatigue develops.

Fatigability and muscular weakness are the hallmarks of MG. Considering the slow clinical progression of MG and the low likelihood of complications from its progression, the importance of suspecting the diagnosis is to facilitate proper referral for further evaluation.

Clinical Features
Ocular symptoms are often the first manifestation of MG. The typical symptoms are ptosis, diplopia, or blurred vision. Ocular muscle weakness may be the first sign in up to 40% of patients, although 85% of patients with MG eventually have ocular involvement. When present, ptosis is often worse toward the end of the day. Respiratory failure is rarely the initial symptom of MG. Even so, up to 17% of patients may have weakness of the muscles of respiration.[3] Bulbar muscles may be involved, producing dysarthria or dysphagia.

The Lambert-Eaton myasthenic syndrome is a rare disorder often associated with small cell carcinoma of the lung. Autoantibodies cause inadequate release of ACh from nerve terminals, affecting both nicotinic and muscarinic receptors. With repeated stimulation the amount of ACh in the synaptic cleft increases, leading to an increase in strength, the opposite of that seen with MG. The classical syndrome includes weakness that increases with use of muscles, particularly proximal hip and shoulder muscles; hyporeflexia; and autonomic dysfunction, most commonly seen as dry mouth.[4] Management primarily focuses on treating the underlying neoplastic disorder, although plasmapheresis and immunoglobulin G have been reported to be useful.[5]

Diagnostic Strategies
New-Onset Myasthenia Gravis. The diagnosis of MG is based on clinical findings and a combination of serologic testing, electromyographic testing, and the edrophonium test. The first two tests are not usually done in the emergency department, although serum can be sent for AChR antibody testing. Results are positive in 80% to 90% of patients with MG. Many patients who are seronegative still respond to traditional therapy aimed at lowering levels of circulating antibodies, suggesting that antibodies are present but not detected.[2]

The edrophonium (Tensilon) test is a simple pharmacologic test that can be performed safely at the patient's bedside. The sensitivity and specificity of the test have not been well documented, and there are reports of false positives in cases of botulism and in cases of MG occurring concurrently with other disorders. It is performed by measuring the distance from the upper to the lower eyelid in the most severely affected eye before and after the intravenous administration of the short-acting acetylcholinesterase (AChE) blocking agent edrophonium. Because some patients have a severe reaction to edrophonium, an intravenous test dose of 1 to 2 mg is given first. If no adverse reaction is found and the patient does not dramatically improve in 30 to 90 seconds, a second dose of 3 mg is given. If there is still no response, a final dose of 5 mg is given for a total maximum dosage of 10 mg.[6]

Because of potential bradycardia from edrophonium, atropine should be available at the bedside. Also, because of the potential cholinergic effect of increased airway secretions, this test should be used with caution in asthmatics and patients with chronic obstructive pulmonary disease.

Another bedside test is the ice test. Cooling decreases symptoms in MG,[7] and heat exacerbates symptoms.[8] In a patient with ptosis who is suspected of having MG, the distance between the upper and lower lids is measured (as in the edrophonium test). An ice pack is then applied to the affected eye for approximately 2 minutes, and the distance between the lids is measured again. A prospective evaluation of this approach that compared patients with MG and patients without MG found the test to be positive (an improvement in dis-

BOX 106-2. Drugs that May Exacerbate Myasthenia Gravis

Cardiovascular
β-Blockers
Calcium channel blockers
Quinidine
Lidocaine
Procainamide

Antibiotics
Aminoglycosides
Tetracyclines
Clindamycin
Lincomycin
Polymyxin B
Colistin

Other
Phenytoin
Neuromuscular blockers
Corticosteroids
Thyroid replacement

tance of at least 2 mm) in 80% of patients with MG and in no patients without MG.[9]

Acute Myasthenic Crisis. Myasthenic crisis is defined as respiratory failure leading to mechanical ventilation.[1] It occurs in 15% to 20% of patients with MG,[10,11] usually within the first 2 years of disease onset. Although it is potentially life-threatening, the mortality from this complication of MG has declined from 40% to 5% since the 1960s with the use of better and more aggressive intensive care unit techniques.

Underlying infection, aspiration, and changes in medications—stopping anticholinergic medications or taking a new medication that precipitates weakness—most often set off crisis, but the precipitant may not be found in up to 30% of cases.[12] Some patients experience a severe increase in weakness on starting steroids for chronic therapy. Other precipitants can be surgery and pregnancy (Box 106-2).[1]

The initial step in managing the patient in crisis is stabilization of the airway. In less severe cases in which intubation is not imminent, it is imperative to monitor ventilatory status in the emergency department pending intensive care unit admission. Airway compromise can be detected by various mechanisms already discussed.

It is important to look for signs of myasthenic crisis in any patient with MG who presents to the emergency department, even with no complaint of weakness. Many commonly used drugs can adversely affect the treatment of a patient with MG (see Box 106-2). A patient with stable MG who has an acute medical or surgical condition requires a full neurologic examination. The decision to admit or discharge a patient from the emergency department should take into account the potential for neurologic deterioration in patients with MG.

Management

Cholinesterase Inhibitors. Pyridostigmine (60 to 120 mg every 4 to 6 hours) and neostigmine (15 to 30 mg every 4 to 6 hours) are the backbone of chronic outpatient therapy and provide symptomatic improvement, although they are not directed at the underlying immunologic basis of the disease. This class of drugs inhibits the hydrolysis of ACh, leading to increased circulating ACh to stimulate the decreased number of receptors and to compete with the antibodies for binding sites. The most common side effects are those of excessive cholinergic stimulation, such as increased airway secretions and increased bowel motility. At extremes there may be bradycardia or even worsening of weakness, simulating a myasthenic crisis. These drugs are often used as adjunctive therapy to control symptoms while other therapy is being instituted, after which they are often discontinued.[13]

The use of intravenous pyridostigmine in the setting of acute exacerbation is controversial. In a review of various therapies for myasthenic crisis, pyridostigmine alone or in combination with prednisolone or plasma exchange appeared comparable to plasma exchange alone. The study reported that 11 of the 63 patients treated for MG crisis suffered cardiac arrest and that 7 of the 10 patients who developed asystole had received pyridostigmine, although there is no evidence that the pyridostigmine was the cause.[12] In addition, some authors reported that most patients with crisis have not responded to AChE inhibition and may benefit from a rest period from AChE inhibitors.[14]

Thus, cholinergic drug therapy should be discontinued during crisis when the patient is intubated. In addition, pyridostigmine may complicate mechanical ventilation by increasing the production of pulmonary secretions.

It has been proposed that acute decompensation and excessive muscarinic stimulation can be caused by overmedication with AChE inhibitors. The prevalence and importance of this cholinergic crisis are debated in the literature. Nevertheless, the physical examination should distinguish a cholinergic crisis from an exacerbation of the disease. The weakness comes from the excessive stimulation of AChRs by the additional ACh, preventing repolarization, and thus no further muscle contractions can be stimulated. Muscarinic effects of AChE inhibition may include excessive sweating, salivation, lacrimation, miosis, tachycardia, and gastrointestinal hyperactivity.

Immunosuppressant Drugs. Immunosuppressant drugs are often used for the chronic control of MG. Although they have no role in the acute management of a myasthenic crisis, they may be started before extubation of a patient recovering from crisis. Corticosteroids, azathioprine, and cyclosporine have all been used. Of note, the initiation of corticosteroids in patients with moderate to severe weakness may actually precipitate a worsening of weakness or even myasthenic crisis.

Thymectomy. Although the association between thymoma and MG is still not fully elaborated, it is well known that thymectomy for patients with thymoma can lead to remission of MG or enable a reduction in other medications. Thymectomy for patients with MG but without thymoma has been shown to have similar benefits and is recommended for patients younger than 60. Thymectomy in patients between adolescence and 60 years of age leads to remission or improvement in up to 50% of cases.[14] The onset of improvement after thymectomy is often delayed for 2 to 5 years.

Immunomodulatory Therapy. Plasma exchange (plasmapheresis) and intravenous immune globulin (IVIG) can be used for patients with severe exacerbations or preoperatively in patients with stable MG.

Plasma exchange removes the AChR antibodies and other immune complexes from the blood. The fall in AChR levels is associated with improvement in symptoms of MG. There is a risk of complications from hypotension or anticoagulation. Because of safety concerns, clinical trials have not been done in children. Although there are no randomized controlled studies of the efficacy of plasma exchange, it is an accepted therapy and is recommended by the American Academy of Neurology for acute exacerbations and for preoperative prophylaxis.[15] Research is exploring plasmapheresis with a staphylococcal protein A immunoaimmunoadsorption system that is more selective for the antibodies.

Small, uncontrolled studies and case reports of IVIG for patients not responsive to other therapies began to appear in the 1970s. It is difficult to compare these studies because different protocols and preparations have been used. From 50% to 90% of patients treated with IVIG have some improvement after infusion. Current consensus suggests a dose of 0.4 g/kg/day for 5 days in cases of uncontrolled acute exacerbations.

There are no blind, controlled comparisons of plasma exchange versus IVIG. One study concluded that IVIG is as effective as plasma exchange.[16] Another retrospective study comparing the two techniques found that plasma exchange leads to improved ventilatory status at 2 weeks compared with IVIG, but it has a higher complication rate.[17] The decision to institute either therapy is based on the input of the consulting neurologist and the resources available at the admitting hospital.

Botulism

Principles of Disease

Botulism is a toxin-mediated illness that can cause acute weakness leading to respiratory insufficiency. In 1998 the Centers for Disease Control and Prevention (CDC) reported 116 cases of botulism in the United States, 65 of which were categorized as infantile botulism.[18] *Clostridium botulinum* is an anaerobic, spore-forming bacterium. Three of eight known toxins produced by *C. botulinum* cause human disease. These are toxin types A, B, and E. Although most cases are isolated events associated with improperly preserved canned foods,[19] there has been an increase in the incidence of botulism from wound infections. In 1995 and 1996, 42 cases of wound botulism were reported in

heroin users who injected subcutaneously,[20] and in 2003, 4 more cases in Washington were reported from black tar heroin. Botulism is also thought to be a potential agent in bioterrorism.

Toxin type E is associated with preserved or fermented fish and marine mammals. These are the most important sources of botulism in Alaska, Japan, Russia, and Scandinavia.[21] The botulinum toxin works by binding irreversibly to the presynaptic membrane of peripheral and cranial nerves, inhibiting the release of ACh at the peripheral nerve synapse. As new receptors are generated, the patient improves.

Clinical Features

The toxin blocks both voluntary motor and autonomic functions. Because the disorder is at the neuromuscular junction, there is no sensory deficit and no sense of pain. The onset of symptoms is 6 to 48 hours after the ingestion of tainted food. There may or may not be accompanying signs and symptoms of gastroenteritis, with nausea, vomiting, abdominal cramps, diarrhea, or constipation. The classical feature of botulism is a descending, symmetrical flaccid paralysis. The muscles often affected first are the cranial nerves and bulbar muscles, and the patient presents with diplopia, dysarthria, and dysphagia, followed later by generalized weakness. There may be associated blurring of vision. Because the toxin decreases cholinergic output, anticholinergic signs may be seen in the form of constipation, urinary retention, dry skin and eyes, and increased temperature. Pupils are often dilated and not reactive to light. This can be a point of differentiation from MG. DTRs are normal or diminished.

Infantile botulism results from the ingestion of *C. botulinum* spores that are able to germinate and produce toxin in the high pH of the gastrointestinal tract of infants. The same spores are not active in the gut of adults because of the lower pH. It occurs in infants between the age of 1 week and 11 months and has been implicated as a cause of sudden infant death syndrome. Because spores can survive in honey, it is recommended that it not be fed to infants. The clinical presentation includes constipation, poor feeding, lethargy, and weak cry; consequently, this diagnosis must be in the differential of the floppy infant.[22]

Diagnostic Strategies

The diagnosis is made by both clinical findings and exclusion of other processes. The toxin can be identified in serum and stool, but the assay is not commonly available in most hospitals and requires a prolonged turnaround time. If the suspected food source is available, it should also be tested for the toxin.

Management

The treatment is initially focused on stabilizing the airway and supportive measures. There is trivalent antitoxin that can shorten the disease course, although it is not clear that the antitoxin decreases ventilator dependence. Nevertheless, the antitoxin should be administered as soon as possible. It is made from horse

Tick Paralysis

Principles of Disease

The pathogenesis of tick paralysis, also known as *tick toxicosis*, is not fully understood. It is known that a toxin is injected while the tick feeds, and it is referred to as an *ixovotoxin*. The toxin appears to diminish the release of ACh at the neuromuscular junction and also reduces nerve conduction velocity. It may also have effects at autonomic ganglia, leading to pupillary signs.

Clinical Features

Tick paralysis is an acute, ascending, flaccid motor paralysis that can be confused with GBS, botulism, and MG. It typically begins with the development of an unsteady gait, followed by ascending, symmetrical, flaccid paralysis. Although symptoms usually begin 1 to 2 days after the female tick has attached and begun to feed, delays of up to 6 days have been reported.[23] There may be associated ocular signs, such as fixed and dilated pupils, that can help distinguish it from GBS.

Management

A tick can be removed using forceps to grasp it as closely as possible to the point of attachment. Care must be taken not to leave mouth parts in the patient's tissue. Although symptoms may resolve rapidly after removal of the tick, supportive measures such as intubation should not be withheld pending resolution of symptoms. It has been noted that the *Ixodes holocyclus* tick in Australia elaborates a toxin that is very similar to botulinum toxin and that after removal of this tick symptoms may worsen during the succeeding 24 to 48 hours.[24] Recovery in these patients may also be prolonged.

Disorders of the Muscles

Perspective

Newly acquired weakness originating at the muscular level can be divided into two types: inflammatory and toxic-metabolic. Inflammatory disorders usually produce pain and tenderness, but metabolic disorders do not.

Inflammatory Disorders

Principles of Disease

The most common inflammatory myopathies are polymyositis (PM) and dermatomyositis (DM). PM may be idiopathic in nature, occur secondary to infections (viral or bacterial), or be seen in conjunction with other disorders such as sarcoidosis or hypereosinophilic syndromes. Inflammatory myopathies cause weakness, pain, and tenderness of the muscles involved. They must be distinguished from simple myalgias related to a fever or cramping that may suggest a myotonia (inability to relax the muscle).

Clinical Features

DM and PM can occur at any adult age, although DM may also affect children. There is a slightly increased incidence in women. An associated increased risk of malignancy, especially breast, ovary, lung, gastrointestinal, and lymphoproliferative disorders, has been noted after the diagnosis of DM or PM, although the reported rate of malignancy varies widely. Proximal muscle weakness predominates and leads to complaints of difficulty rising from a seated position or climbing stairs and weakness in lifting the arms over the head. There is often pain and tenderness in these proximal muscles as well. There is a decrease in reflexes as the weakened muscles fail to contract. Thus, the decrease in reflexes is in proportion to the decrease in strength. Fasciculations are not seen, and atrophy is a very late finding.

DM is similar to PM, but it is also associated with classical skin findings. These are more prominent in childhood but are also found in adults. They include a periorbital heliotrope and erythema and swelling of the extensor surfaces of joints. The facial rash is usually photosensitive and may also involve the exposed areas of the chest and neck.

Diagnostic Strategies

Electrolyte abnormalities must be ruled out and the serum CK checked. If possible, the skeletal muscle isoform (MM) should be distinguished from the cardiac muscle isoform (MB). The CK must be interpreted in light of the entire clinical picture. The presence of an elevated CK does not establish the cause of weakness as a myopathy because some neuropathies can also produce an elevated CK. Similarly, a normal CK does not rule out a myopathy as the cause of weakness. Electromyography and muscle biopsy are used to confirm the diagnosis.[25]

Management

PM and DM are usually managed with oral prednisone in a dose of 1 to 2 mg/kg day. When steroids prove ineffective and during acute exacerbations, cytotoxic drugs such as azathioprine or methotrexate are added. Fortunately, the degree of rhabdomyolysis seen with the inflammatory myopathies is not sufficient to cause renal impairment.

Metabolic Disorders

Perspective

Acute, generalized muscle weakness can be seen with severe electrolyte abnormalities of any cause: hypokalemia, hyperkalemia, hypocalcemia, hypercalcemia, hypomagnesemia, and hypophosphatemia. Acute painless myopathies can also be seen with endocrine disorders involving the thyroid, parathyroid, or adrenal glands.

Of particular interest are several disorders referred to collectively as the *periodic paralyses*. This group of entities includes familial periodic paralysis (FPP) of the hyperkalemic and hypokalemic forms and thyrotoxic periodic paralysis (TPP), which is similar to hypokalemic FPP except that it is associated with hyperthyroidism.

Familial Periodic Paralysis

Principles of Disease. Patients with FPP experience intermittent attacks of extremity weakness associated with either hyperkalemia or hypokalemia, although the latter is more common. It is most often associated with an inherited genetic mutation.[26] Patients usually report a personal and family history of similar episodes.

Clinical Features and Diagnostic Strategies. Patients may suffer either isolated or recurrent episodes of flaccid paralysis. The lower limbs are involved more often than the upper, although both can be affected. Bulbar, ocular, and respiratory muscles are usually not involved.[27] Onset is rapid; a prodrome of myalgias and muscle cramps may occur but is uncommon; mental status and sensory function are typically preserved, but reports of sensory nerve involvement have been documented.[28] Males are more often affected than females, and there is a higher incidence in Asians, particularly Japanese, although it does occur in other ethnic groups.

Attacks may be induced by the injection of insulin, epinephrine, or glucose. The onset of symptoms often follows a high carbohydrate intake (with subsequent insulin rise) and a period of rest.[29] A typical complaint is the acute onset of weakness noted on waking in the morning after a large meal the preceding evening. An electrocardiogram, which should be done immediately in all patients suffering from acute paralysis, demonstrates signs of hyperkalemia or hypokalemia. An immediate potassium level should be ordered; in the hypokalemic form, the potassium level during an attack falls to values below 3.0 mEq/L.

Management. Many cases resolve spontaneously with supportive care alone. The mainstay of management is the treatment of the underlying electrolyte imbalance. In the hypokalemic state the total body potassium is not depleted but has shifted intracellularly.[30,31] Thus, in the repletion of potassium, caution is necessary to prevent overtreatment. For this reason, intravenous potassium should be used sparingly; one or two 10 mEq doses of potassium chloride (KCl), each administered over 1 hour, should be the maximum given intravenously. This can be done in parallel with 40 mEq oral potassium repletion and retesting of serum potassium levels. Intravenous hydration helps to redistribute the body's potassium stores.

Thyrotoxic Periodic Paralysis

The clinical picture of TPP is almost identical to that of hypokalemic FPP, and indeed a small number of patients with hypokalemic FPP have hyperthyroidism. In TPP, symptoms related to hyperthyroidism are often present at the same time the patient develops weakness. The relation of the hyperthyroidism to hypokalemia is probably due to increased sodium-potassium adenosine triphosphatase activity[32] but research is limited. Treatment of the hyperthyroid symptoms, such as tachycardia, may help the treatment of the paralysis as well. There is one case report of TPP in which the patient's weakness did not respond to

potassium replacement until propranolol was given to treat tachycardia.[33] There is probably a genetic feature underlying this disorder because there is a higher incidence of repeated attacks of hypokalemic periodic paralysis among Japanese and Chinese patients with hyperthyroidism. It is important that all patients have thyroid function testing done after a first episode of hypokalemic paralysis.

KEY CONCEPTS

- In patients with bilateral upper motor neuron signs and a normal mental status, neuroimaging of the spinal cord should be strongly considered.

- In patients presenting with acute neuromuscular weakness, complaints of difficulty in breathing or swallowing should heighten suspicion of bulbar involvement with possible airway compromise. In such patients, a forced vital capacity less than 15 mL/kg or a maximal negative inspiratory force less than 15 mm Hg are potential indications for mechanical ventilation.

- Botulism usually arises as a painless descending paralysis, often first affecting the cranial nerves and bulbar muscles, without sensory deficits or significant alteration of consciousness. The treatment is airway management and administration of antitoxin.

REFERENCES

1. Thomas CE, et al: Myasthenic crisis: Clinical features, mortality, complications and risk factors for prolonged intubation. *Neurology* 48:1253, 1997.
2. Drachman DB: Myasthenia gravis. *N Engl J Med* 330:1797, 1994.
3. Massey JM: Acquired myasthenia gravis. *Neurol Clin* 15:577, 1997.
4. O'Neill JH, Murray NM, Newsom-Davis J: The Lambert-Eaton myasthenic syndrome. A review of 50 cases. *Brain* 111:577, 1988.
5. Penn AS: Lambert-Eaton myasthenic syndrome. In Rowland LP (ed): *Merritt's Textbook of Neurology*, 9th ed. Philadelphia, Williams & Wilkins, 1995.
6. Seybold ME: Office Tensilon test for ocular myasthenia gravis. *Arch Neurol* 43:842, 1986.
7. Borenstein S, Desmedt JE: Local cooling in myasthenia: Improvement of neuromuscular failure. *Arch Neurol* 32:152, 1975.
8. Gutmann L: Heat-induced myasthenic crisis. *Arch Neurol* 37:271, 1980.
9. Golnik KC, et al: An ice test for the diagnosis of myasthenia gravis. *Ophthalmology* 106:1282, 1999.
10. Fink ME: Treatment of the critically ill patient with myasthenia gravis. In Ropper AH (ed): *Neurological and Neurosurgical Intensive Care*, 3rd ed. New York, Raven Press, 1993.
11. Cohen MS, Younger D: Aspects of the natural history of myasthenia gravis: Crisis and death. *Ann NY Acad Sci* 377:670, 1981.
12. Mayer SA: Intensive care of the myasthenic patient. *Neurology* 48(Suppl 5):S70, 1997.
13. Berrouschot J, et al: Therapy of myasthenic crisis. *Crit Care Med* 25:1228, 1997.
14. Mayer SA: Therapy of myasthenic crisis [letter]. *Crit Care Med* 26:1136, 1998.

15. Gajdos PH, et al: Clinical trial of plasma exchange and high-dose intravenous immunoglobulin in myasthenia gravis. *Ann Neurol* 41:789, 1997.
16. Quershi AI, et al: Plasma exchange versus intravenous immunoglobulin treatment in myasthenic crisis. *Neurology* 52:629, 1999.
17. Summary of Notifiable Diseases, United States, 1998. *MMWR Morb Mortal Wkly Rep* 47:1, 1999.
18. Shapiro RL, et al: Botulism in the United States: A clinical and epidemiologic review. *Ann Intern Med* 129:221, 1998.
19. Passaro D, et al: Wound botulism associated with black tar heroin among injecting drug users. *JAMA* 279:859, 1998.
20. Mines D, et al: Poisonings: food, fish, shellfish. *Emerg Med Clin North Am* 15:58, 1997.
21. Jagoda A, Renner G: Infant botulism: Case report and clinical update. *Am J Emerg Med* 8:318, 1990.
22. Tick paralysis—Washington, 1995. *MMWR Morb Mortal Wkly Rep* 45:325, 1996.
23. Felz MW, et al: A six-year-old girl with tick paralysis. *N Engl J Med* 342:90, 2000.
24. Bartt R: Autoimmune and inflammatory disorders. In Goetz CG (ed): *Goetz Textbook of Clinical Neurology*. Philadelphia, WB Saunders, 1999.
25. Rowland LP: Familial periodic paralyses. In Rowland LP (ed): *Merritt's Textbook of Neurology*, 9th ed. Philadelphia, Williams & Wilkins, 1995.
26. Ober KP: Thyrotoxic periodic paralysis in the United States: Report of 7 cases and review of the literature. *Medicine (Baltimore)* 71:109, 1992.
27. Inshasi J: Dysfunction of sensory nerves during attacks of hypokalemic periodic paralysis. *Neuromuscul Disord* 9:227, 1999.
28. Miller D, et al: Severe hypokalemia in thyrotoxic periodic paralysis. *Am J Emerg Med* 7:584, 1989.
29. Cannon L, et al: Hypokalemic periodic paralysis. *J Emerg Med* 4:287, 1986.
30. Miller JD, et al: Nonfamilial hypokalemic periodic paralysis and thyrotoxicosis in a 16-year-old male. *Pediatrics* 100:413, 1997.
31. Shayne P, Hart A: Thyrotoxic periodic paralysis terminated with intravenous propranolol. *Ann Emerg Med* 24:734, 1994.
32. Chan A, et al: In vivo and in vitro sodium pump activity in subjects with thyrotoxic periodic paralysis. *BMJ* 303:1096, 1991.
33. Rowland LP: Familial periodic paralysis. In Rowland LP (ed): *Merritt's Textbook of Neurology*, 9th ed. Philadelphia, Williams & Wilkins, 1995.

CHAPTER

107 Central Nervous System Infections

Frank W. Lavoie and John R. Saucier

PERSPECTIVE

Background

Central nervous system (CNS) infections have always been among the most perplexing and devastating illnesses. "Epidemic cerebrospinal fever," classically described by Viesseux in 1805, was associated with almost universal mortality.[1] The first American epidemic of meningococcal meningitis was recorded in 1806.[2] Since that time, epidemiologic changes have occurred in concert with advances in understanding of disease processes and evolution of effective treatment strategies.

The etiologic spectrum of CNS infection has changed considerably as a result of the development and aggressive use of antibiotics and the epidemic emergence of immunocompromising disorders such as infection with the human immunodeficiency virus (HIV). Some of the research on CNS infections has markedly increased in sophistication, which provides insights into pathogenesis, including the role of host mechanisms such as cytokines and other immune components. The pathophysiologic alterations are increasingly understood at the cellular and molecular levels.

Likewise, diagnostic tools have been developed that allow precise pathogen identification, most recently using molecular technologies such as polymerase chain reaction (PCR) tests for viral nucleic acids in cerebrospinal fluid (CSF). The initial treatment methodologies began by demonstrating the efficacy of antiserum treatment by Flexner in 1913 and of antibiotics by Colebrook and Kenny in 1936.[3,4] The mortality rates were decreased further with the use of high-dose penicillin by Dowling and colleagues in the 1940s.[5] Unfortunately, despite historical advances, the morbidity and mortality of these disorders remain considerable.

Definitions

CNS infections comprise a broad spectrum of disease entities. *Meningitis* is defined as inflammation of the membranes of the brain or spinal cord and is also called *arachnoiditis* or *leptomeningitis*. *Encephalitis* denotes inflammation of the brain itself, whereas *myelitis* refers to inflammation of the spinal cord. The terms *meningoencephalitis* and *encephalomyelitis* describe more diffusely localized inflammatory processes. Collections of infective and purulent materials may form within the CNS as abscesses. Abscesses may be intraparenchymal, in epidural or subdural intracranial locations, or may be found in intramedullary or epidural spinal locations.

This chapter focuses on the more common acute and subacute CNS infections. Infections of the nervous system with HIV or human T lymphotrophic virus, rabies virus, polio or hepatitis viruses, *Borrelia burgdorferi* (Lyme disease), *Treponema* organisms (syphilis), parasites, rickettsia, and the chronic and slow infections of the CNS (subacute sclerosing panencephalitis, progressive multifocal leukoencephalopathy, and the prion-mediated spongiform encephalopathies, such as Creutzfeldt-Jakob disease, bovine spongiform encephalopathy, and kuru) are not addressed.

Epidemiology

Bacterial meningitis is a common disease worldwide. Meningococcal meningitis is endemic in parts of Africa, and epidemics commonly occur in other countries, including the United States. A variety of other pathogens are also causative.[6-10] The overall incidence of bacterial meningitis in the United States is 5 to 10 cases per 100,000 people per year.[11] Men are affected more often than women.[11] The incidence of bacterial meningitis increases in late winter and early spring, but the disease may occur at any time of the year.

Because most cases are unreported, the actual incidence of viral meningitis is unknown. It is estimated to affect between 11 and 27 individuals per 100,000 people.[12] A prominent increase of cases is seen in summer months, which is concurrent with seasonal predominance of the enterovirus group of the picornaviruses.

The same organisms responsible for viral meningitis may also be associated with encephalitis. Encephalitis is, however, far less common, and the ratio of cases of meningitis to encephalitis varies according to the specific pathogen. Arbovirus infection is transmitted by an insect vector, although clinical disease develops in only a small percentage of the people bitten. Before 1999, approximately 19,000 cases of encephalitis were hospitalized in the United States annually. Since then, there has been a rapid increase because of the West Nile virus (WNV). In 2003, more than 8000 additional cases were hospitalized because of WNV alone.[13,14]

Approximately 2000 cases of brain abscess occur in the United States annually.[15] Although CNS abscesses may occur at any age and any time of year, they are more commonly seen in men than women.[16,17] CNS abscesses are associated with local contiguous and remote systemic infections, intravenous (IV) drug use, neurologic surgery, and cranial trauma. Brain abscess secondary to otitis media most often occurs in pediatric or older adult populations. When associated with sinusitis, it most often arises among young adults. Increasingly, CNS abscesses are seen in the immunocompromised population, particularly those with HIV infection, and among bone marrow and solid organ transplant recipients. However, antimicrobial prophylaxis of immunosuppressed patients and more aggressive treatment of otitis and sinusitis have decreased the overall incidence to 0.9 per 100,000 person-years.[15]

PRINCIPLES OF DISEASE

Etiology

Meningitis

Meningeal inflammation may be caused by a variety of disease processes, but the infectious etiologies predominate. Some of the more common and important infectious etiologic agents in CNS infection, with emphasis on the United States, are listed in Boxes 107-1 and 107-2.[6-10,18] Among the bacterial etiologies, *Streptococcus pneumoniae* remains the predominant pathogen in adult patients, followed by *Neisseria meningitidis* and *Listeria monocytogenes*.[19,20] *N. meningitidis* is the predominant organism in adults younger than 45 years. Five major serogroups cause most meningococcal disease worldwide (A, B, C, Y, and W-135). Serogroup A accounts for the majority of cases of meningococcal meningitis in developing nations.[21] Serogroup distribution for invasive disease has

---

BOX 107-1. Bacterial, Fungal, and Parasitic Pathogens in Central Nervous System Infection

Bacterial
Bacillus sp.
Bacteroides
Borrelia burgdorferi (Lyme disease)
Other Enterobacteriaceae
Escherichia coli
Haemophilus influenzae
Listeria monocytogenes
Mycobacterium tuberculosis
Mycoplasma
Neisseria meningitidis
Proteus
Pseudomonas aeruginosa
Staphylococcus aureus
Streptococci
Streptococcus pneumoniae
Treponema (syphilis)
Others

Fungi
Blastomyces
Candida
Cladosporium
Coccidioides
Cryptococcus
Histoplasma
Paracoccidioides
Others

Parasites
Amoebae
Taenia solium (cysticercosis)
Toxoplasma gondii
Others

Rickettsia
Rickettsia rickettsii (Rocky Mountain spotted fever)
Others

BOX 107-2. Viral Etiologies in CNS Infection

Arboviruses
  Bunyaviruses
    California encephalitis virus
  Alphaviruses
    Eastern equine encephalitis virus
    Western equine encephalitis virus
    Venezuelan equine encephalitis virus
  Flaviviruses
    Japanese B encephalitis virus
    Colorado tick fever virus
    St. Louis encephalitis virus
    West Nile virus
  Others
Herpes viruses
  Herpes simplex viruses (HSV)
  Epstein-Barr virus
  Cytomegalovirus
  Varicella-zoster virus
Enteroviruses
  Coxsackieviruses
  Echoviruses
  Poliovirus
Lymphocytic choriomeningitis virus (LCMV)
Retroviruses
  Human immunodeficiency virus (HIV)
  Human T lymphotrophic virus (HTLV)
Paramyxoviruses
  Measles virus
  Mumps virus
Rabies virus
Others

BOX 107-3. Noninfectious Meningitides

Drug-induced meningitis
  Nonsteroidal anti-inflammatory drugs (NSAIDs)
  Trimethoprim
  Isoniazid
  Others
Carcinomatous meningitis
Serum sickness
Vasculitis
Systemic lupus erythematosus
Behçet's disease
Sarcoidosis
Others

changed markedly in the United States, with B, C, and Y now most commonly responsible.[22-25] These pathogens account for the bulk of cases in nontraumatic meningitis, although virtually any organism can be encountered, particularly among patients who are elderly, alcoholic, or immunosuppressed and those who have cancer. Regional variations should also be considered. For example, Lyme meningitis has become more prevalent in the northeastern United States.

Meningeal infection may also occur in association with a dural leak secondary to neurosurgery or neurotrauma. *S. pneumoniae*, *Staphylococcus aureus*, *Pseudomonas aeruginosa*, and coliform bacteria are seen most commonly in this population.

Viral meningitis may likewise be caused by a variety of etiologic agents.[18] Enteroviruses are statistically encountered most commonly.[26] Unfortunately, precise definition of the etiologic agent is often impossible. Fungal and parasitic meningitides are additional concerns, particularly among immunocompromised patients.[8,9]

Noninfectious meningitides include drug-induced meningitis, carcinomatous meningitis, CNS involvement in serum sickness, vasculitis, systemic lupus erythematosus, Behçet's disease, sarcoidosis, and others (Box 107-3). The differentiation of noninfectious from infectious etiologies can occasionally be perplexing.

Encephalitis

Arboviruses and herpes simplex virus (HSV), a human herpes virus (HHV), are the most common causes of endemic and sporadic cases of encephalitis, respectively. Children are the most vulnerable to infection with these viruses, although adults are also commonly affected. Epidemics of viral encephalitis have been attributed to a wide variety of viral agents. WNV, a flavivirus, first infected humans in the New York City area and rapidly spread to 47 states by 2003.[27] Varicella, herpes zoster, HHV 6 and 7, and Epstein-Barr virus have been increasingly reported to be the cause of encephalitis in immunocompetent hosts.[28,29] Vaccinia encephalitis has been recognized in those receiving vaccination for smallpox.[30] Postinfectious encephalomyelitis is also induced by a variety of viral pathogens, most commonly by the measles virus.[31] However, *Mycoplasma pneumoniae* and idiopathic causes are becoming more common in developed countries.

Central Nervous System Abscess

The etiologies of CNS abscess are multiple and reflect the primary infective process and the immune state of the human host. A variety of mixed pathogens may be responsible for intracranial abscesses. Streptococci, particularly the *Streptococcus milleri* group, have been identified in nearly 50% of brain abscesses.[32] Anaerobic bacteria, predominantly *Bacteroides* species, are commonly seen when the primary infectious process is chronic otitis media or pulmonary disease. *S. aureus* is also often identified, particularly after cranial penetration from surgery or trauma.[33] The Enterobacteriaceae are an additional common isolate. Opportunistic fungal and parasitic etiologies are often seen in the immunosuppressed.[32]

Culture of epidural and subdural abscesses more often yields a single organism, with streptococci most commonly seen when associated with contiguous spread and *S. aureus* and gram-negative rods most commonly encountered after neurologic trauma.[9] Etiologic agents in spinal abscess are similarly varied. *S. aureus* is most commonly encountered.

Pathophysiology

Bacterial Meningitis

The pathogenetic sequence in bacterial meningitis has been well characterized.[8,9,34,35] The first step is nasopharyngeal colonization and mucosal invasion. Although colonization rates vary, virulent microbes use secretion of immunoglobulin A proteases and induce ciliostasis of mucosal cells. After penetration occurs by a variety of mechanisms, bacterial intravascular survival occurs because of evasion of the complement pathway. The varying capsular properties of each organism protect the bacteria. The third step occurs when the bacteria cross the blood-brain barrier to enter the CSF. The dural venous sinuses, cribriform plate area, and choroid plexus have all been implicated as potential sites of invasion. Although the mechanism of invasion is not completely understood, host defense mechanisms within the CSF are often ineffective; there are low levels of complement, immunoglobulin, and opsonic activity. Bacterial proliferation then occurs, which stimulates a convergence of leukocytes into the CSF.

Meningeal and subarachnoid space inflammations are also associated with the release of cytokines into the CSF, most notably tumor necrosis factor and interleukins 1 and 6.[34,36] This results in increased permeability of the blood-brain barrier, cerebral vasculitis, edema, and increased intracranial pressure. A subsequent decrease in cerebral blood flow leads to cerebral hypoxia. Glucose transport into the CSF is decreased coincidentally with an increased use by brain, bacteria, and leukocytes, which depresses CSF glucose concentrations. The increased permeability leads to increased CSF proteins.

Viral Meningitis and Encephalitis

Viruses enter the human host through the skin, as in arbovirus injection from a mosquito vector; through the respiratory, gastrointestinal, or urogenital tract; or by receipt of infected blood products or donor organs.[37,38] Viral replication subsequently occurs outside the CNS, most often followed by hematogenous spread to the CNS. Additional routes into the CNS include retrograde transmission along neuronal axons and direct invasion of the subarachnoid space after infection of the olfactory submucosa.[39,40]

Fortunately, most systemic viral infections do not result in meningitis or encephalitis. The development and subsequent magnitude of viral infection depend on the virulence of the specific virus, the viral inoculum level, and the state of immunity of the human host. The tropism of the virus for specific CNS cell types also influences the focality of disease and its manifestations.[39] Particular viruses may preferentially attack cortical, limbic, or spinal neurons, oligodendria, or ependymal cells. An example is the tropism of HSV for the temporal lobes and the development of temporal lobe seizures and behavioral changes in afflicted patients.

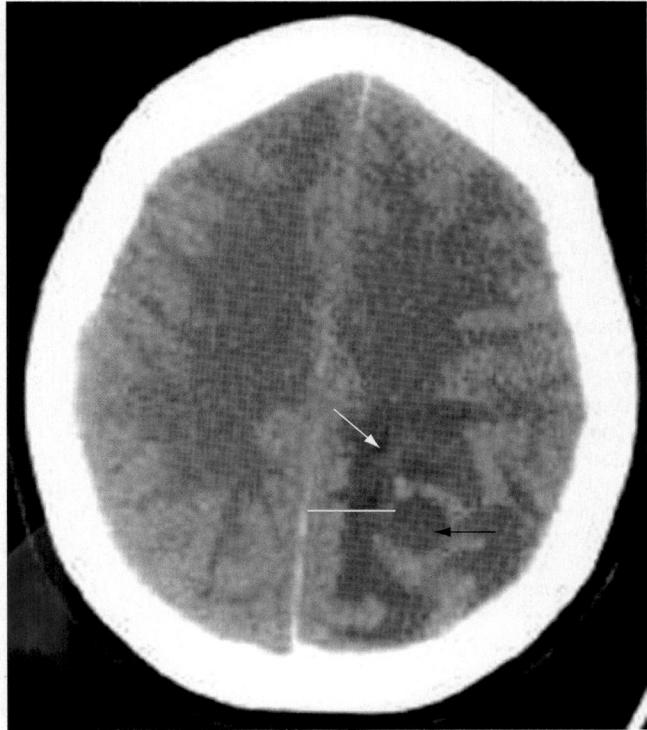

Figure 107-1. Central nervous system abscess: computed tomography of an intraparenchymal abscess (arrows).

Fungal Meningitis

Fungal meningitis probably develops in much the same way as bacterial meningitis, although this has been incompletely studied. Pulmonary exposure followed by hematogenous spread is the primary pathogenetic mechanism in most cases. Immune system defects or immunosuppression compromises host defense mechanisms, with ensuing development of CNS infection.

Central Nervous System Abscess

Intraparenchymal brain abscesses, subdural empyema, or intracranial or spinal epidural abscesses form by inoculation of the CNS from contiguous spread of organisms from a sinus, middle ear, or dental infection or metastatic seeding from a distant site, usually from pulmonary infection, endocarditis, or osteomyelitis[16,33] (Figure 107-1). The primary infection can be identified in 75% to 85% of cases. These conditions may also follow surgery or penetrating cranial trauma, particularly when bone fragments are retained in brain tissue. Otogenic abscesses occur most commonly in the temporal lobe in adults and cerebellum in children, whereas sinogenic abscesses typically occur in frontal areas.[32] Multiple brain abscesses suggest hematogenous spread of organisms, although solitary lesions may also occur. The pulmonary system is the most common source of hematogenous spread.[9]

BOX 107-4. Host Factors Predisposing to Meningitis

Age <5 yr
Age >60 yr
Male gender
Low socioeconomic status
Crowding (e.g., military recruits)
Splenectomy
Sickle cell disease
African-American race
Alcoholism and cirrhosis
Diabetes
Immunologic defects
Recent colonization
Dural defect (e.g., traumatic, surgical, congenital)
Continuous infection (e.g., sinusitis)
Household contact with meningitis patient
Thalassemia major
Intravenous drug abuse
Bacterial endocarditis
Ventriculoperitoneal shunt
Malignancy

CLINICAL FEATURES

Symptoms and Signs

Numerous host factors have been implicated in the acquisition of meningitis (Box 107-4).[41] Although these factors alone and in combination increase the risk of meningitis, the disease often occurs in patients with none of these factors.

Many patients with meningitis present with advanced disease; in these patients, the diagnosis of acute meningitis is strongly suspected. The constellation of symptoms that may classically occur in an acute CNS infection consists of fever, headache, photophobia, nuchal rigidity, lethargy, malaise, altered sensorium, seizures, vomiting, and chills.[7,41]

Unfortunately, more subtle presentations are also common. Immunosuppressed and geriatric patients present a diagnostic challenge because the classical signs and symptoms of meningitis may not be present. Although some degree of fever is present in most patients, as are a headache and neck stiffness, meningitis should be carefully considered in any immunosuppressed patient with symptoms or signs of infectious disease. Often, the only presenting sign of meningitis in the elderly patient is an alteration of mental status. However, a meta-analysis suggested that the absence of fever, stiff neck, and mental status change excludes meningitis in immunocompetent adults.[42]

The presentation of fungal meningitis can be obscure even in the healthy adult population. Headache, low-grade fever, lassitude, and weight loss may be present but often to such a mild degree that the correct diagnosis is not initially considered.[7] This is also true of tuberculous meningitis, which often has a protracted course and a vague nonspecific presentation consisting of fever, weight loss, night sweats, and malaise, with or without headache and meningismus.[6]

The physical findings in meningitis vary, depending on the host, causative organism, and severity of the illness. Nuchal rigidity or discomfort on flexion of the neck is common. Kernig's and Brudzinski's signs are present in approximately 50% of adults.[9] Described in 1882 by Vladimir Kernig, Kernig's sign is present in the patient if the examiner is unable, because of resistance and hamstring pain, to straighten the patient's leg passively to a position of full knee extension when the patient is lying supine with the hip flexed to a right angle. Jozef Brudzinski initially described five signs, two of which are currently utilized.[2] The contralateral sign is present if an attempt to flex the hip passively on one side is accompanied by a similar movement of the other leg. The neck sign is present if attempts to flex the neck passively are accompanied by flexion of the hips. The absence of jolt accentuation of headache with this maneuver may be useful in obviating the need for lumbar puncture (LP) in a patient with low suspicion for meningitis.[43] Deep tendon reflexes may be increased, and ophthalmoplegia may be present—especially of the lateral rectus muscles.

The systemic findings may include an obvious source of infection such as sinusitis, otitis media, mastoiditis, pneumonia, or urinary tract infection. Various manifestations of endocarditis may be present. Arthritis may be seen with *N. meningitidis* and occasionally with other bacteria.[41] Petechiae and cutaneous hemorrhages are widely reported with meningococcemia but also occur with *Haemophilus influenzae*, pneumococcal organisms, *L. monocytogenes*, and echovirus infections, in addition to staphylococcal endocarditis.[41] Endotoxic shock with vascular collapse often develops in severe meningococcal disease, but shock may be present in the advanced stages of any bacterial meningitis. Any determination of a serious systemic infection should encourage rather than dissuade the clinician from considering the possibility of a concomitant CNS infection.

Patients with encephalitis may also have symptoms of meningeal irritation. An alteration of consciousness occurs in virtually all patients. Fever, headache, and a change of personality are also usually present.[44] Hallucinations and bizarre behavior may precede motor, reflex, and other neurologic manifestations by several days, occasionally prompting an initial diagnosis of a psychiatric disorder. Because focal neurologic deficits and seizures occur much more commonly with encephalitis than meningitis, there may also be diagnostic confusion with a brain abscess. Distinguishing the etiologic agent in encephalitis is clinically difficult, although HSV encephalitis results in a higher incidence of dysphasia and seizures.[45] In some patients, WNV produces a myelitis that affects the anterior horn cells of the spinal column, resulting in a flaccid paralysis with a clear sensorium, similar to findings in polio or Guillain-Barré syndrome.[27]

Patients with intracranial abscess may be indistinguishable from those with meningitis or encephalitis. Most patients with intraparenchymal abscess have a subacute course of illness, with symptoms progressing during the course of 2 or more weeks. However, nuchal

BOX 107-5. Complications of Bacterial Meningitis

Immediate
Coma
Loss of airway reflexes
Seizures
Cerebral edema
Vasomotor collapse
Disseminated intravascular coagulation (DIC)
Respiratory arrest
Dehydration
Pericardial effusion
Death
Others

Delayed
Seizure disorder
Focal paralysis
Subdural effusion
Hydrocephalus
Intellectual deficits
Sensorineural hearing loss
Ataxia
Blindness
Bilateral adrenal hemorrhage
Death
Others

rigidity and fever are present in fewer than 50% of cases. Focal neurologic deficits are present in most of these patients. A large number of patients exhibit papilledema, which is a rare finding in meningitis. An abrupt neurologic deterioration that results from uncal herniation or rupture into the ventricular system may occur.

Patients with a subdural or epidural abscess most often have headache, fever, and focal signs, although more subtle presentations are common. Most of the patients with spinal abscess typically present with spinal pain and other symptoms and signs of cord compression but not necessarily with fever.[46]

Complications

Bacterial Meningitis

The immediate complications of bacterial meningitis include coma (with loss of protective airway reflexes), seizures, cerebral edema, vasomotor collapse, disseminated intravascular coagulation, respiratory arrest, dehydration, syndrome of inappropriate secretion of antidiuretic hormone, pericardial effusion, and death (Box 107-5).[10] Various delayed complications include multiple seizures, focal paralysis, subdural effusions, hydrocephalus, intellectual deficits, sensorineural hearing loss, ataxia, blindness, bilateral adrenal hemorrhage (Waterhouse-Friderichsen syndrome), peripheral gangrene, and death.[41]

The case fatality rate for pneumococcal meningitis averages 20% to 25%, with higher fatality rates occurring in patients with serious underlying or concomitant disease or advanced age.[47,48] The prognosis is related to the degree of neurologic impairment on presentation. Overall, 20% to 30% of the survivors of pneumococcal

meningitis have some residual neurologic deficit.[41] The case fatality rate for *Listeria* meningitis may be as high as 40%.[20]

With the advent of antibiotic therapy, the mortality from meningococcal meningitis has markedly decreased to less than 20%, but it remains substantially higher in elderly patients or in those who also have meningococcemia.[48] Although most of the complications and sequelae are less common than with pneumococcal disease, the incidence of Waterhouse-Friderichsen syndrome is dramatically higher when meningococcemia is present.[41] The overall mortality rate in community-acquired gram-negative meningitis has been less than 20% since the introduction of the third-generation cephalosporins.[8]

Viral Meningitis

With rare exceptions, the overall prognosis for complete recovery from viral meningitis is excellent. Various complications related to the systemic effects of the particular virus include orchitis, parotitis, pancreatitis, and various dermatoses. Usually all of these complications resolve without sequelae.[18]

Viral Encephalitis

The outcomes in viral encephalitis are dependent on the infecting agent. Encephalitis caused by Japanese encephalitis virus, Eastern equine virus, and St. Louis encephalitis virus is severe, with high mortality rates and virtually universal neurologic sequelae among survivors.[49] WNV produces encephalitis in only 0.5% of those infected, yet it resulted in 120 deaths in 2003.[14] Western equine virus and California encephalitis virus cause milder infections, and death is rare. The incidence of neurologic sequelae is highly variable and appears to depend on both the host and the infecting agent.[49]

The mortality from HSV encephalitis before the use of acyclovir was 60% to 70%. Acyclovir treatment has reduced the mortality to approximately 30%.[31] Common sequelae observed among survivors include seizure disorders, motor deficits, and changes in mentation.

Tuberculous Meningitis

Death from tuberculous meningitis in the adult age group ranges from 10% to 50% of cases, with the incidence directly proportional to the patient's age and the duration of symptoms before presentation. Focal ischemic stroke may result from the associated cerebral vasculitis. In advanced disease, up to 25% of patients may require some neurosurgical procedure for obstruction (ventriculoperitoneal shunt or drainage).[50] In most patients some neurologic deficit develops, but severe long-term sequelae among survivors are unusual.[6,50]

Fungal Meningitis

Common CNS complications with fungal meningitis include abscesses, papilledema, neurologic deficits, seizures, bone invasion, and fluid collections. Direct invasion of the optic nerve results in ocular abnormalities in up to 40% of patients with cryptococcal meningitis.[7] The mortality rate is high but variable and is related to the timeliness of diagnosis, underlying illness, and therapeutic regimens.

Central Nervous System Abscess

With the early diagnosis afforded by the use of the cranial computed tomography (CT) scan; appropriate antimicrobial therapy; and combined management approaches with surgery, aspiration, and medical therapy, the mortality from brain abscess has declined dramatically from approximately 50% to less than 20%.[16,51] A seizure disorder is the most common sequela of intracranial abscess, occurring in 80% of patients.[8] Other neurologic sequelae of intracranial abscesses, including focal motor or sensory deficits or changes in mentation, are common. Complications of spinal abscess primarily result from cord compression, including paralysis, motor and sensory deficits, and bowel and bladder dysfunction. Generalized spread of CNS infection and death may also occur.[46]

DIAGNOSTIC STRATEGIES

Lumbar Puncture

General Considerations

Because the consequences of missing a CNS infection are devastating, CNS infection must be presumed to be present until excluded. The possibility of the diagnosis of meningitis mandates LP unless the procedure is contraindicated by the presence of infection in the skin or soft tissues at the puncture site or the likelihood of brain herniation.[31] Adherence to this principle prevents a delay in diagnosis, which substantially increases the morbidity and mortality of the disease. Some patients have clinically obvious bacterial meningitis, and CSF examination serves primarily to help identify the organism, thereby facilitating the appropriate treatment. Most patients, however, present more of a diagnostic problem, and analysis of the CSF fluid constitutes the critical step in the elucidation of the presence of CNS infection.

Increased Intracranial Pressure

In most patients with bacterial meningitis, LP may be safely performed without antecedent neuroimaging studies. As this may not be the case in other brain pathologies, in many circumstances it is advisable to obtain a CT scan of the head before performing an LP (Box 107-6).[52] These indications must be carefully weighed against the patient's condition, the probability of meningitis, and the availability of the CT or magnetic resonance imaging (MRI) scan.[8]

It has been conventionally asserted that an LP in the presence of increased intracranial pressure may be harmful or fatal to the patient. Although data to address this concern are limited, the presence of focal neurologic signs does appear to be associated with a dramatic

---

BOX 107-6. Indications for Computed Tomography Scan before Lumbar Puncture in Suspected Bacterial Meningitis

Immunocompromised state
History of
   Stroke
   Mass lesion
   Focal infection
   Head trauma
Seizure within last 7 days
Abnormal level of consciousness
Inability to answer questions or follow commands
   appropriately
Abnormal visual fields or paresis of gaze
Focal weakness
Abnormal speech

---

increase in complications from LP. These patients may deteriorate precipitously during or after the procedure.[53]

Patients with a markedly depressed sensorium that precludes careful neurologic examination or those with a focal neurologic deficit, papilledema, seizures, or evidence of head trauma must be considered to be at risk for a herniation syndrome that may be exacerbated by an LP. If the presentation is an acute, fulminating, febrile illness and bacterial meningitis is the concerning diagnosis, early initiation of antimicrobial therapy is mandatory because of the association of prognosis and time to treatment.[54] The algorithmic alternatives are therefore (1) immediate LP followed by initiation of antibiotic treatment before obtaining the results or (2) initiation of antibiotic treatment followed by a cranial CT scan and then an LP. The latter choice of empirical treatment with antibiotics is now the routine in many institutions. This reflects the efficacy of current methodologies of identification of causative organisms by means other than bacteriologic cultures.

Cerebrospinal Fluid Analysis

Opening Pressure

The normal CSF pressure in an adult varies from 50 to 200 mm H_2O. This value applies only to patients in the lateral recumbent position and may increase several-fold when the patient is in the sitting position. The pressure is often elevated in bacterial, tuberculous, and fungal meningitides and a variety of noninfectious processes.[44] Pressure may be falsely elevated when the patient is tense or obese or has marked muscle contraction.

Collection of Fluid

At least three sterile tubes each containing at least 1 to 1.5 mL of CSF should be obtained and numbered in sequence. A fourth tube may be desirable should later studies such as viral cultures or a Venereal Disease Research Laboratories (VDRL) test for syphilis become necessary. The fluid should be sent to the laboratory

Table 107-1. Analysis of Cerebrospinal Fluid

Test	Normal Value	Significance of Abnormality
Cell count	<5 WBC/mm³ <1 PMN/mm³ <1 eosinophil/mm³	Increased WBC counts are seen in all types of meningitis and encephalitis; increased PMN count suggests bacterial pathogen
Gram's stain	No organism	Offending organism identified 80% of time in bacterial meningitis, 60% if patient pretreated
Turbidity	Clear	Increased turbidity with leukocytosis, blood, or high concentration of microorganisms
Xanthochromia	None	Presence of RBCs in spinal fluid for 4 hr before lumbar puncture; occasionally caused by traumatic tap (if protein > 150 mg/dL) or hypercarotenemia
CSF-to-serum glucose ratio	0.6 : 1	Depressed in pyogenic meningitis or hyperglycemia; lag time if glucose given IV
Protein	15-45 mg/dL	Elevated with acute bacterial or fungal meningitis; also elevated with vasculitis, syphilis, encephalitis, neoplasms, and demyelination syndromes
India ink stain	Negative	Positive in one third of cases of cryptococcal meningitis
Cryptococcal antigen	Negative	90% accuracy for cryptococcal disease
Lactic acid	<35 mg/dL	Elevated in bacterial and tubercular meningitis
Bacterial antigen tests	Negative	>95% specific for organism tested; up to 50% false-negative rate
Acid-fast stain	Negative	Positive in 80% of cases of tuberculous meningitis if >10 mL of fluid

CSF, cerebrospinal fluid; PMN, polymorphonuclear; RBC, red blood cell; WBC, white blood cell.

for immediate analysis of turbidity, xanthochromia, glucose, protein, cell count and differential, Gram's stain, bacterial culture, and antigen testing (Table 107-1). In certain cases an India ink stain, a bacteriologic stain for acid-fast bacilli, or a VDRL test should be obtained. When only a small amount of fluid can be obtained, the most important studies are the cell count with differential, Gram's stain, and bacterial cultures. Ideally, the cell count should be performed on both the first and third or fourth tubes to help differentiate true CSF pleocytosis from contamination of the specimen by a traumatic LP.

Turbidity

The CSF should be assessed immediately for turbidity or cloudiness by the person performing the LP. Because normal CSF is completely clear and colorless and should be indistinguishable from water, any degree of turbidity is pathologic. Leukocytosis is the most common cause of CSF turbidity; counts greater than 200 cells/mm³ usually cause clinically detectable changes in CSF clarity.[55]

Cell Count and Differential

Normal adult CSF contains no more than 5 leukocytes/mm³ with at most one granulocyte (polymorphonuclear [PMN] leukocyte)[41,55,56]; therefore, the presence of more than one PMN or a total cell count of more than 5 cells/mm³ should be considered evidence of CNS infection. In addition, the presence of any eosinophil in the CSF is abnormal, although occasionally basophils may be seen in the absence of disease.[55] Pretreatment with a few doses of antibiotics, although possibly diminishing the yield of Gram's staining and cultures, should not affect the CSF cell counts in meningitis.[8,19,57,58]

The cell counts in bacterial meningitis are usually markedly elevated, sometimes exceeding 10,000 cells/mm³, and demonstrate a dramatic granulocytic

shift.[41] In general, counts exceed 500 cells/mm³, with a preponderance of PMN leukocytes. However, the initial CSF analysis exhibits lymphocytosis (lymphocyte count greater than 50%) in 6% to 13% of all cases of bacterial meningitis. When only the patients with bacterial meningitis with fewer than 1000 cells/mm³ are considered, 24% to 32% have a predominance of lymphocytes.[59,60] In addition, the same population of patients often has only a mild disturbance of CSF glucose and protein levels. In well-established viral meningitis and encephalitis, counts are usually less than 500 cells/mm³, with nearly 100% of the cells being mononuclear.[26] Early (less than 48 hours) presentations may reveal significant PMN pleocytosis and hence be indistinguishable from presentations in early bacterial meningitis.[61]

Similarly, normal cell counts and differentials, although reassuring, do not absolutely exclude bacterial meningitis.[56] Any patient thought to have a clinical syndrome compatible with meningitis requires hospital admission with frequent reevaluation, repeated LP, and antimicrobial therapy. In some patients who have symptoms or signs of meningitis and have a normal initial CSF analysis, CSF pleocytosis may develop within 24 hours; the causative organism may be cultured from the original "normal" CSF.

Brain abscess and parameningeal infections, such as subdural empyema or epidural abscess, usually display CSF cell counts and differentials similar to those of viral meningitis and encephalitis, although the CSF may also be normal.

A traumatic LP is suggested by the presence of a clot in one of the tubes or the clearing of the CSF and a decreasing red blood cell (RBC) count from tubes one to three. In the presence of a traumatic LP, one may estimate the true degree of CSF white blood cell (WBC) pleocytosis with the following formula[55]:

$$\text{True CSF WBC} = \text{measured CSF WBC}$$
$$[(\text{CSF RBC} \times \text{blood WBC})/\text{blood RBC}]$$

Table 107-2. Gram's Stain Characteristics of Selected Meningeal Pathogens

Pathogen	Typical Characteristics
Staphylococci	Gram-positive cocci: singles, doubles, tetrads, clusters
Streptococcus pneumoniae	Gram-positive cocci: paired diplococci
Other streptococci	Gram-positive cocci: pairs and chains
Listeria monocytogenes	Gram-positive rods: single or chains
Neisseria meningitidis	Gram-negative cocci: negative paired diplococci; kidney or coffee bean appearance
Haemophilus influenzae	Gram-negative coccobacilli: "pleomorphic" bacilli
Enterobacteriaceae (including Escherichia coli)	Gram-negative rods
Pseudomonas aeruginosa	Gram-negative rods

Alternatively, when peripheral cell counts are normal, the CSF from a traumatic LP should contain about 1 WBC per 700 RBCs.

Gram's Stain

A properly performed Gram's stain of a centrifuged specimen of CSF identifies the causative organism approximately 80% of the time in cases of bacterial meningitis.[57] Gram's stain characteristics of the most commonly encountered organisms are described in Table 107-2. The yield from this procedure is diminished by 20% to 30% when there has been prior treatment with antibiotics.[8] Misidentification of gram-positive organisms as gram negative is also known to occur more commonly among pretreated patients because organisms with damaged walls stain unpredictably.

Xanthochromia

Xanthochromia refers to the yellowish discoloration of the supernatant of a centrifuged CSF specimen. Xanthochromia is abnormal and results from the lysis of RBCs and release of the breakdown pigments oxyhemoglobin, bilirubin, and methemoglobin into the CSF. This process normally begins within 2 hours, and pigments may persist up to 30 days[62]; therefore early analysis of the LP specimen is essential. If a traumatic tap has introduced enough plasma to raise the CSF protein level to 150 mg/dL or more, blood pigments may cause xanthochromia. If the CSF protein level is less than 150 mg/dL, however, and systemic hypercarotenemia does not exist, xanthochromia of a centrifuged CSF specimen should suggest that subarachnoid hemorrhage has occurred.[55,62]

Glucose

When the serum glucose is normal, the CSF glucose is usually between 50 and 80 mg/dL. The CSF glucose is normally in a ratio of 0.6 : 1 to the serum glucose, except with marked systemic hyperglycemia, when the ratio is closer to 0.4 : 1. Therefore a CSF-to-serum glucose ratio of less than 0.5 in normoglycemic subjects or 0.3 in hyperglycemic subjects is abnormal and may represent the impaired glucose transport mechanisms and increased CNS glucose use associated with pyogenic meningitis.[41,55] Mild decreases in the CSF glucose level may occur with certain viral and parameningeal processes. However, bacterial or fungal meningitis should be presumed to be the cause of low CSF glucose, termed hypoglycorrhachia, until each is clearly excluded.[63] If the serum glucose level has increased rapidly—for example, after IV administration of 50% dextrose in water—equilibration in the CSF may take up to 4 hours, and therefore the interpretation of CSF-to-serum glucose ratios may be unreliable.

Protein

The normal CSF protein level in adults ranges from 15 to 45 mg/dL. An elevated CSF protein, usually higher than 150 mg/dL, commonly occurs with acute bacterial meningitis.[41] When a traumatic LP has occurred, the CSF protein can be corrected for the presence of blood by subtracting 1 mg/dL of protein for each 1000 RBCs.[55] Elevated CSF protein concentrations can result from any cause of meningitis, subarachnoid hemorrhage, CNS vasculitis, syphilis, viral encephalitis, neoplasms, and demyelination syndromes.[55] A greatly elevated CSF protein level (>1000 mg/dL) in the presence of a relatively benign clinical presentation should suggest fungal disease.[7]

India Ink Preparation

India ink staining of the CSF should be performed when a diagnosis of cryptococcal meningitis is being considered. The demonstration of budding organisms (Figure 107-2) is virtually diagnostic for cryptococcal disease but occurs in only one third of the cases.[7] A more definitive diagnostic test is the cryptococcal antigen.

Lactic Acid

Although nonspecific, elevations in CSF lactic acid concentrations (>35 mg/dL) are potentially indicative of bacterial meningitis. Normal lactate levels (<35 mg/dL) are seen in patients with viral meningitides.

Antigen Detection

Counterimmunoelectrophoresis (CIE), latex agglutination, and coagglutination are methods of detecting specific antigens. These tests are particularly useful in patients receiving antibiotic treatment before CSF sampling because the tests depend on the presence of only an antigen and not viable organisms.

The CIE techniques that are performed for the most common bacterial pathogens demonstrate high sensitivity and specificity for bacterial antigens, particularly when performed on CSF, blood, and urine simultaneously. Latex agglutination techniques are, however, more rapid and sensitive and are replacing the use of CIE in many facilities. Although reported results vary,

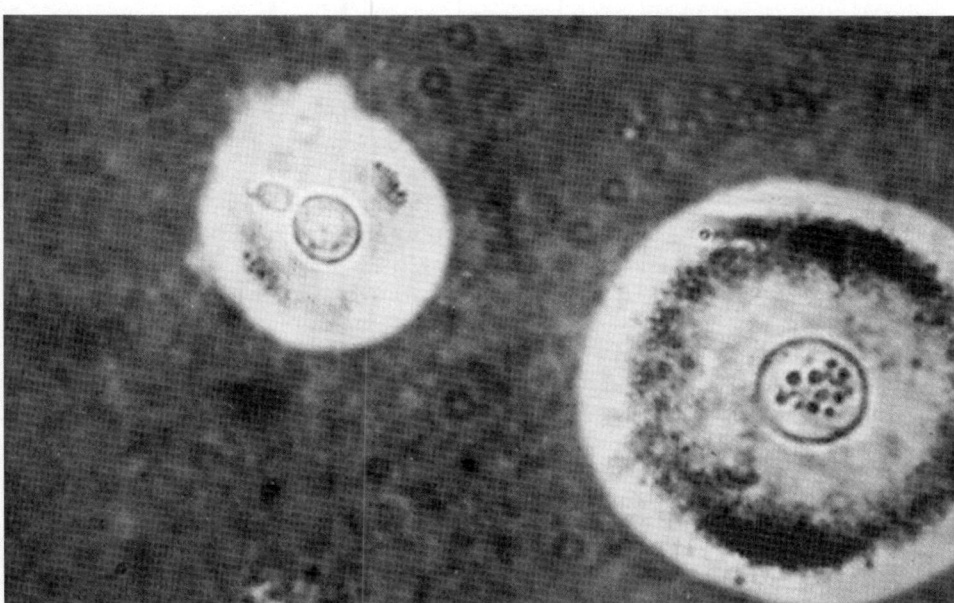

Figure 107-2. India ink staining of the cerebrospinal fluid.

the sensitivities of antigen tests are 50% to 90% for *Neisseria* organisms, 50% to 100% for *S. pneumoniae*, and approximately 80% for *H. influenzae*. A specific agglutination test for cryptococcal antigen is also highly sensitive (90%) and specific. Cultures are always indicated because a negative antigen test does not exclude the possibility of any particular bacterial or fungal etiology.

Antigen and antibody testing is also being used to identify viral and atypical pathogens. These have particular utility in HSV encephalitis. Enzyme-linked immunosorbent assays can detect HSV antibody production.[64] Unfortunately, the appearance of antibody in CSF occurs too late to aid in any therapeutic decision analysis. PCR amplification and the identification of HSV DNA have demonstrated a sensitivity of 95% to 100% and a specificity of 100% early in the disease and have markedly decreased the need for diagnostic brain biopsy in this disorder.[65-67] PCR has improved the diagnosis of tuberculous meningitis, with a sensitivity of 80% to 85% and a specificity of 97% to 100%, and is superior to standard techniques.[68-70] PCR has additionally been shown to be superior in identifying bacteria, enteroviruses, and other viral etiologies in both immunocompromised and immunocompetent patients.[71,72] Reported sensitivities of detection in CSF by PCR for *N. meningitidis*, *H. influenzae*, and *S. pneumoniae* are 88%, 100%, and 92%, with nearly 100% specificity.[73,74] The sensitivities of bacteriologic culture are much lower, especially for *N. meningitidis* at 37% to 55% and *H. influenzae* at 50%.[74-76]

In addition, PCR assays have nearly tripled the yield of viral culture in identifying the etiologic agent.[77] In studies of enteroviral meningitis, sensitivities and specificities for PCR ranged from 86% to 100% and 92% to 100%, respectively.[78] PCR has been shown to be at least as sensitive as culture technique in detecting cryptococcal meningitis. Quantitative PCR may be

of benefit in monitoring response to therapy in some forms of severe disease.[28]

The growing availability of these molecular techniques does not, however, suggest that they should be routinely employed. Most cases of acute bacterial meningitis are readily diagnosed and treated on the basis of the standard Gram stain and culture. PCR should be reserved for less clear presentations, patients pretreated with antibiotics, and cases in which concern exists for tuberculous, cryptococcal, and treatable viral CNS infections.[79]

Bacteriologic Cultures

Although results are not available for emergency management, bacteriologic cultures of CSF should be performed. Bacterial culture yields are significantly decreased in patients pretreated with antibiotics. Viral cultures may also be indicated.

Other Tests

A variety of additional, nonspecific tests of CSF have been advocated. These include measuring CSF lactate dehydrogenase, C-reactive protein, and the limulus lysate test; however, none of these have demonstrated a high degree of clinical usefulness. Likewise, the evaluation of CSF chloride as a diagnostic aid for tuberculous meningitis is no longer clinically relevant.

Neuroimaging Techniques

A cranial CT scan or MRI scan is indicated in the evaluation of any patient with presumed CNS infection in whom there is the possibility of an intracranial abscess, intracranial hemorrhage, or mass lesion. In the diagnostic evaluation of acute meningitis, however, a CT scan should not unnecessarily delay LP or antimicrobial therapy. The CT scan may also show hypodense lesions in the temporal lobes in patients with HSV encephalitis, although an MRI scan reveals this abnormality much earlier in the disease process. A contrast-enhanced cranial CT scan or MRI scan is invaluable in the diagnosis of a CNS abscess.[16] MRI scanning is also helpful in the evaluation of other infectious and non-infectious encephalitides.

Additional Investigations

As with other infectious diseases, the complete blood count with differential is a nonspecific adjunct in the diagnostic evaluation of a patient suspected to have a CNS infection. The peripheral cell counts are often normal in the presence of significant disease and may even be depressed, particularly in elderly or immuno-suppressed persons. A "normal" leukocyte count and differential should not dissuade the emergency physician from performing a diagnostic LP, obtaining a CT scan, or otherwise pursuing the diagnosis of a CNS infection.

Even when antimicrobial therapy has already been administered, two or three blood cultures should be obtained for all patients who are being evaluated for a CNS infection. The blood cultures can identify the causative organisms more often when the meningitis is caused by pneumococcus than meningococcus. Although blood cultures are not immediately useful in the acute diagnosis of meningitis in the emergency department, they may be of considerable clinical importance later in the management of the disease. The cultures are helpful in identifying a causative organism in only a small minority of cases of brain abscess.

As many as 50% of patients with pneumococcal meningitis also have evidence of pneumonia on an initial chest x-ray study. This association occurs in fewer than 10% of the cases of meningitis caused by H. influenzae type B and N. meningitidis and in approximately 20% of cases of meningitis caused by other organisms. The identification of a pulmonary infection on chest radiography may assist in identification of causative organisms and appropriate antimicrobial therapy in approximately 10% of cases of brain abscess.[16]

Other ancillary investigations such as echocardiography, cultures of other body fluids, and bone scans may be undertaken as necessary to evaluate coexistent or complicated disease. Serum electrolytes, glucose, urea nitrogen, and creatinine levels should be measured to facilitate the interpretation of the CSF glucose level and to establish the level of renal function and the state of electrolyte balance. Although organism-specific abnormalities are uncommon, hyponatremia has been associated with tuberculous meningitis.

A number of characteristic but not pathognomonic electroencephalographic (EEG) abnormalities have been associated with HSV type 1 encephalitis. The presence of focal or lateralized EEG abnormalities in the presence of an encephalitis syndrome should be considered strong evidence supporting a diagnosis of HSV encephalitis.[80]

DIFFERENTIAL CONSIDERATIONS

Patients with meningitis may have symptoms and signs ranging from mild headache with fever to frank coma and shock. To facilitate the discussion of diagnosis and treatment, meningitis may be divided into three clinical syndromes: acute meningitis, subacute meningitis, and chronic meningitis.

Acute meningitis encompasses patients with obvious signs and symptoms of meningitis who are evaluated in less than 24 hours after the onset of their symptoms and who rapidly deteriorate. In many of these patients the diagnosis of meningitis is not in doubt, and the crucial step is to initiate antimicrobial therapy immediately. The most likely pathogens in this syndrome are S. pneumoniae and N. meningitidis. Although H. influenzae has been reported in this context, it is not commonly implicated in the adult population.[10,19]

In the syndrome of subacute meningitis, the symptoms and signs causing the patient to seek care have developed during a period of 1 to 7 days. This syndrome includes virtually all cases of viral meningitis, along with most of the bacterial and some of the fungal etiologies.[8,9] The differential diagnosis depends on the symptoms and signs at presentation. Among elderly and immunosuppressed individuals, a change in the patient's mental status may be the only presenting sign in meningitis. Even when a fever is present, the patient's change in mental status may be misattributed to another disease outside the CNS, such as pneumonia or urinary tract infection; neck stiffness may be misattributed to degenerative joint disease. The elderly patient is at high risk for meningitis and, rather than constituting a diagnostic endpoint, the identification of an infection outside the CNS in such a patient is a clear indication for LP because of the risk of bacteremic seeding by the involved organisms.

The differential diagnosis of encephalitis and brain abscess occurs in the context of the subacute meningitis syndrome. Brain abscess should be considered, especially if fever is minimal or absent or if there are focal neurologic findings. The presence of fever, altered sensorium, headache, seizures, and personality change is consistent with encephalitis. In addition, diagnoses such as subdural empyema, brain tumor, subarachnoid hemorrhage, subdural hematoma, and traumatic intracranial hemorrhage should be considered. In these circumstances a cranial CT scan should be obtained before performing an LP.

The spectrum of chronic meningitis includes some of the viral meningitides as well as meningitis caused by tubercle bacilli, syphilis, and fungi. Many of the patients in this group have had symptoms for at least 1 week before presentation and generally have a prolonged indolent course marked by difficult and changing diagnoses and multiple therapies.[6,7] In addition to tuberculous, fungal, and syphilitic meningitides, the differential diagnosis of the chronic meningitis syndrome is extensive (Box 107-7).[9]

MANAGEMENT

Prehospital Care

The field stabilization and transport of the patient with a suspected CNS infection are dictated by the patient's condition. In cases in which the patient is stable and alert with normal vital signs, application of oxygen and rapid transport suffice, with or without establishing an IV line. If an altered mental status is present, protection or establishment of an adequate airway may be necessary. Shock, if present, may require IV crystalloid infusion. Seizures may usually be managed supportively through protection of the patient's airway and prevention of injury, although prolonged or recurrent seizures may require IV anticonvulsants.

Assessment and Stabilization

Septic shock, hypoxemia, seizures, cerebral edema, and hypotension resulting from dehydration require aggressive management. When possible, a thorough history should be obtained from the patient, family members, or ambulance personnel with particular emphasis on preexisting conditions that may complicate the patient's disease. Examples include recent neurosurgery, trauma, a history of leukopenia, immunocompromise, or diabetes mellitus.

BOX 107-7. Differential Considerations in Chronic Meningitis

Tuberculous meningitis
Fungal central nervous system (CNS) infections
Tertiary syphilis
CNS neoplasm
Lupus cerebritis
Sarcoidosis
Rheumatoid arthritis
Granulomatous angiitis
Various encephalitides
Toxic encephalopathies
Metabolic encephalopathies
Multiple sclerosis
Chronic subdural hematoma
Others

Hypotension or shock should be treated as indicated with isotonic crystalloid infusion, high-flow oxygen, and pressors. IV dextrose may be required for hypoglycemia secondary to depletion of glycogen stores. Alcoholic or nutritionally compromised patients should also receive 50 to 100 mg of thiamine IV. In cases of moderate to severe hypotension, central venous pressure monitoring should be initiated and used as a guide for additional IV fluids or vasopressors.

Active airway management with endotracheal intubation may be required, particularly in cases of coma, recurrent seizures, or severe accompanying pulmonary infection. Cardiac monitoring may also be necessary, particularly in elderly patients, those with known coronary disease, and those with an altered mental status. Seizures are a particularly prominent component of the clinical presentation in patients with a brain abscess but may also occur with any CNS infection, especially when an underlying seizure disorder is present.

If acute cerebral edema or an elevated intracranial pressure is present, it should be managed by immediate intubation and adequate ventilation. Osmotic agents such as mannitol or diuretics such as furosemide may be used, but caution should be exercised if shock or uncontrolled hypotension is present. If diuretics or osmotic agents are administered, the emergency physician must ensure that the patient does not become volume depleted and hypotensive.

Definitive Therapy

Bacterial Meningitis

Therapy for bacterial meningitis requires antibiotics that penetrate the blood-brain barrier and achieve adequate CSF concentrations, are bactericidal against the offending organism in vivo, and maintain adequate tissue levels to treat the infection effectively.

Until the pathogenetic organism is identified, broad-spectrum coverage of the most common pathogens is necessary (Table 107-3). Many authorities recommend cefotaxime or ceftriaxone, plus vancomycin to cover potentially resistant organisms.[81] High-dose ampicillin is also added if concern exists about *Listeria*.[81] In patients allergic to penicillin and cephalosporins, meropenem or chloramphenicol plus vancomycin may be effective while awaiting the outcome of desensitization techniques.[81]

Table 107-3. Antimicrobial Therapy for Bacterial Meningitis

Organism	Treatment of Choice	Alternative Treatment
Neisseria meningitidis	Penicillin G, 4 million units IV q4h	Chloramphenicol 50 mg/kg IV q6h (maximum dose 1 g)
Streptococcus pneumoniae	Penicillin G, 4 million units IV q4h	Chloramphenicol 50 mg/kg IV q6h (maximum dose 1 g), OR vancomycin 15 mg/kg IV q6-12h, plus rifampin 600 mg IV or PO qd
Haemophilus influenzae	Ceftriaxone 2 g IV q12h	Chloramphenicol 50 mg/kg IV q6h (maximum dose 1 g)
Listeria monocytogenes	Ampicillin 2 g IV q4h, plus gentamicin 2 mg/kg IV loading, then 1.7 mg/kg q8h	Trimethoprim-sulfamethoxazole 240 mg/1200 mg IV q6h

After the pathogen is identified, more targeted therapy can be instituted. It is prudent to refer to a current antimicrobial reference to guide therapy in all instances, given rapid changes in etiologic spectrum, drug resistance, and available agents.

Corticosteroid treatment is additionally recommended in acute bacterial meningitis. Animal studies demonstrate the salutary effects of the administration of corticosteroids in experimental pneumococcal meningitis, including reduced brain edema, CSF pressure, and CSF lactate levels.[82] Earlier resolution of the clinical and CSF stigmata of meningitis and a decrease in long-term hearing loss are observed in infants and children given dexamethasone with cefuroxime or ceftriaxone compared with those receiving the antibiotic alone, particularly when *H. influenzae* is the offending agent.[83,84] In adult bacterial meningitis, an absolute risk reduction of 10% for unfavorable outcome is seen when dexamethasone is given either 15 minutes before or concomitantly with antibiotics and continued for 4 days at 6-hour intervals.[85] This benefit is greatest in those with *S. pneumoniae*. No benefit has been seen in *N. meningitidis* infection.

Viral Meningitis

No specific agents are available for treating most types of viral meningitis. Investigational agents in development may reduce symptoms in enterovirus meningitis[86]; however, with the exception of HSV meningitis, the viral meningitides contracted in the United States are generally characterized by a short, benign, self-limited course followed by a complete recovery. The primary therapeutic consideration in cases of viral meningitis is therefore the validity of the diagnosis. Early cases of viral meningitis may be indistinguishable from bacterial meningitis, and this confusion may not be resolved by CSF analysis; therefore, when any doubt exists about the veracity of the diagnosis, appropriate cultures should be obtained and the patient admitted to the hospital. Antimicrobial therapy for presumed bacterial meningitis may be initiated on the basis of the clinical presentation or may be withheld pending the outcome of close clinical observation and repeated LP in 8 to 12 hours.

Viral Encephalitis

Specific therapy for meningoencephalitis from HHV is available. Acyclovir remains the current choice and is capable of substantially improving the patient's outcome. When the diagnosis of herpes meningoencephalitis is suspected or established, IV acyclovir should be administered in a dose of 10 mg/kg every 8 hours.[81] Ganciclovir, foscarnet, and cidofovir are also effective in HHV infections, and pleconaril has been effective in enteroviral disease. Additional antiviral treatments are in development.[27,28,86]

Tuberculous Meningitis

Early chemotherapeutic intervention in acute tuberculous meningitis improves the patient's prognosis. A strong clinical suggestion of this disease is an adequate indication to begin antituberculous therapy. A standard treatment regimen consists of isoniazid, rifampin, pyrazinamide, and ethambutol or streptomycin.[81] Corticosteroids have also been shown to decrease secondary complications.[81,87]

Fungal Meningitis

The treatment of fungal meningitis is complex.[7] Four agents are commonly used: amphotericin B, flucytosine, miconazole, and fluconazole. Of these, amphotericin B, either alone or in combination with flucytosine, is the most commonly recommended initial therapeutic regimen.[81] These diseases are rarely acutely life threatening but rather are slowly progressive. Prolonged therapy, often with multiple agents, is necessary. The initiation of antifungal therapy is rarely indicated in the emergency department.

Central Nervous System Abscess

The treatment of cerebral abscess is complex, and neurosurgical consultation is indicated. The location, size, and number of abscesses influence the choice of medical management, surgical excision, aspiration, or a combination of these modalities.[32] In general, small multiple abscesses are more appropriately treated medically, whereas large, surgically accessible lesions should be excised. Empirical antimicrobial therapy before identification of specific organisms by aspiration or surgical excision should be guided by the principles of CSF penetration and the coverage of likely pathogens.

Otogenic and sinogenic abscesses are often treated with cefotaxime or ceftriaxone plus metronidazole.[81] Abscesses with traumatic or neurosurgical causes should have antimicrobial coverage for *S. aureus* or methicillin-resistant *S. aureus*. Patients at high risk for tuberculous, fungal, or parasitic abscess should also receive coverage for the suspected etiologic agent. Corticosteroids should be reserved specifically for managing any attendant cerebral edema; in other circumstances, steroid use is associated with increased mortality.

Chemoprophylaxis

Among household contacts the incidence of transmission of meningococcus is approximately 5%; therefore, it is recommended that household contacts of bacteriologically confirmed cases receive rifampin (adults, 600 mg; children older than 1 month, 10 mg/kg; children younger than 1 month, 5 mg/kg) orally every 12 hours for a total of four doses.[81] In addition, these contacts should be advised to watch for fever, sore throat, rash, or any symptoms of meningitis. They should be hospitalized with appropriate IV antimicrobial therapy if there are signs that active meningococcal disease is developing because rifampin is ineffective against invasive meningococcal disease. Intimate, nonhousehold contacts who have had mucosal exposure to the patient's oral secretions should also receive rifampin prophylaxis. Health care workers are not at increased risk for the disease and do not require prophylaxis unless they have had direct mucosal contact with the patient's secretions, as might occur during mouth-to-mouth resuscitation, endotracheal intubation, or nasotracheal suctioning. Ciprofloxacin 500 mg by mouth (adults only) and ceftriaxone 250 mg intramuscularly (125 mg intramuscularly for children younger than 15 years) provide single-dose alternatives.[81]

There is no indication for chemoprophylaxis in pneumococcal meningitis. Rifampin prophylaxis for the contacts of patients with *H. influenzae* type B meningitis is recommended for nonpregnant household contacts when there are children younger than 4 years of age in the household[81] (adults, 600 mg by mouth; children, 20 mg/kg by mouth daily for 4 days).

Immunoprophylaxis

A quadrivalent vaccine based on the polysaccharide capsule and conferring protection against group A, C, Y, and W-135 meningococci has been in routine use by the U.S. military since the 1980s.[88] However, the capsular polysaccharide vaccines used to immunize adults are neither immunogenic nor protective in children younger than 2 years because of poor antibody response. In addition, no licensed vaccine is currently available against the serogroup B meningococcus.[25] The serogroup B capsular polysaccharide has proved to be poorly immunogenic in both adults and children.[89] The sequence variation of the surface proteins and cross-reactivity of the group B polysaccharide with human tissues have further impeded efforts to develop a successful vaccine. Efforts to enhance the immunogenicity and protective efficacy of meningococcal vaccines have focused on using conjugate methods that link polysaccharides and carrier proteins. Serogroup C and serogroup C + Y conjugate vaccines have been developed and utilized effectively.[90] Current recommendations for the quadrivalent vaccine are evolving. The vaccine is recommended in established meningococcal epidemics and for travelers to countries where meningococcal disease is currently epidemic. Elective vaccination of college freshmen has been recommended by the Advisory Committee on Immunization Practices (ACIP) in the United States and public health authorities in the United Kingdom.[25,91] The United Kingdom has also implemented universal childhood immunization with a group C conjugate vaccine.[90]

The development of effective pneumococcal vaccines has been hampered by the large number of serotypes of the organism. A small number of serotypes, however, is responsible for most clinical pneumococcal disease, and a 23-valent vaccine effective against many of these principal serotypes has been developed.[92] The recommendations for this polyvalent pneumococcal vaccine are targeted primarily at prevention of pneumonia, despite a potential beneficial effect for meningitis. A single dose of the vaccine should be considered for elderly or debilitated patients, especially those with pulmonary disease, and for patients with impaired splenic function, splenectomy, or sickle cell anemia.[93] A heptavalent conjugated pneumococcal vaccine has also been developed and is recommended for universal childhood immunization by the ACIP.[94] A conjugate vaccine effective against *H. influenzae* type B has been developed for use in the pediatric, but not adult, population. It appears to be approximately 90% protective and has a very low incidence of adverse reactions.[95-97] Modern childhood immunization against *H. influenzae* type b has raised the average age of patients afflicted with *Haemophilus* meningitis to 25 years and decreased the incidence of meningitis of any etiology by 55%.[98]

Vaccination is also available to confer immune protection against Japanese encephalitis virus, and it is recommended for people performing extensive outdoor activities or spending more than 30 days in endemic areas during transmission seasons.[99,100] The reported protective efficacy of the vaccine is approximately 90%. Although there is no current human vaccine for the WNV, vaccines for nonhuman mammals have been developed.[27]

DISPOSITION

With the exception of viral meningitis, all but the most chronic CNS infections require initial inpatient evaluation and treatment. Bed rest, analgesics, and the institution of appropriate IV antimicrobials are indicated.

Some patients with suspected viral meningitides merit hospitalization. These include patients with more severe disease, immunocompromise, suspicion of HSV meningitis, or potential nonviral causes. Some authorities manage patients with classical presentations of viral meningitis as outpatients and ensure close follow-up within 24 hours. Others admit all patients until the more serious causes, such as early bacterial meningitis or encephalitis, can be excluded with certainty.

KEY CONCEPTS

- CNS infection should be considered in all patients with headache, neck stiffness, fever, altered sensorium, or diffuse or focal neurologic findings.
- Lumbar puncture with sampling of cerebrospinal fluid is the only reliable method of assessing the presence or absence of meningitis. In the absence of contraindications, any suspicion of meningitis mandates performance of LP.
- Early initiation of antimicrobial therapy is mandatory in any case of suspected acute CNS infection. Antibiotic administration must not be delayed for CSF analysis or performance of neuroimaging studies.
- Antibiotic chemoprophylaxis should be assured for close contacts of patients with meningitis resulting from *Neisseria meningitidis* or *Haemophilus influenzae*. Single-dose and multiple-dose regimens are available.
- Vaccination against *N. meningitidis* is recommended for certain at-risk populations but does not afford protection against serogroup B infection.
- Concomitant CNS infection should be strongly considered in any patient with another severe systemic infection, such as urinary tract infection or pneumonia.

REFERENCES

1. Viesseux M: Mémoire sur le maladie qui a regré à Geneve au printemps de 1805. *J Med Chir Pharm* 11:163, 1805.
2. Roos KL: Acute bacterial meningitis. *Semin Neurol* 20:293, 2000.
3. Flexner S: The results of serum treatment in 1300 cases of epidemic meningitis. *J Exp Med* 17:553, 1913.
4. Colebrook L, Kenny M: Treatment of human puerperal infections and experimental infections in mice with prontosil. *Lancet* 1:1279, 1936.
5. Dowling HF, et al: The treatment of pneumococcal meningitis with massive doses of systemic penicillin. *Am J Med Sci* 217:149, 1949.
6. Alvarez S, McCabe WR: Extrapulmonary tuberculosis revisited: A review of experience at Boston City and other hospitals. *Medicine (Baltimore)* 63:25, 1984.
7. Salaki JS, et al: Fungal and yeast infections of the central nervous system. *Medicine (Baltimore)* 63:108, 1984.
8. Lambert HP (ed): *Infections of the Central Nervous System.* Philadelphia, BC Decker, 1991.
9. Tyler KL, Martin JB (eds): *Infectious Diseases of the Central Nervous System.* Philadelphia, FA Davis, 1993.
10. Durand ML, et al: Acute bacterial meningitis in adults: A review of 493 episodes. *N Engl J Med* 328:21, 1993.
11. Fraser DW, et al: Bacterial meningitis in Bernalillo County, New Mexico: A comparison with three other American populations. *Am J Epidemiol* 100:29, 1974.
12. Beghi E, et al: Encephalitis and aseptic meningitis, Olmsted County, Minnesota, 1950-81: I. Epidemiology. *Ann Neurol* 16:283, 1984.
13. Khetsuriani N, et al: Burden of encephalitis-associated hospitalizations in the United States, 1988-1997. *Clin Infect Dis* 35:175, 2002.
14. Centers for Disease Control and Prevention: West Nile virus activity, United States, October 30-November 5, 2003. *MMWR Morb Mortal Wkly Rep* 52:1080, 2003.
15. Calfee DP, Wispelwey B: Brain abscess. *Semin Neurol* 20:353, 2000.
16. Yand SY: Brain abscess: A review of 400 cases. *J Neurosurg* 55:794, 1981.
17. Mathiesen GE, et al: Brain abscess. *Clin Infect Dis* 25:763, 1997.
18. Specter S, et al (eds): *Neuropathogenic Viruses and Immunity.* New York, Plenum, 1992.
19. Luby JP: Infections of the central nervous system. *Am J Med Sci* 304:379, 1992.
20. Hussein AS, Shafran SD: Acute bacterial meningitis in adults. *Medicine (Baltimore)* 79:360, 2000.
21. Ahlawat S, et al: Meningococcal meningitis outbreak control strategies. *J Commun Dis* 32:264, 2000.
22. Centers for Disease Control and Prevention: Serogroup Y meningococcal disease: Illinois, Connecticut, and selected areas, United States, 1989-1996. *MMWR Morb Mortal Wkly Rep* 45:1011, 1996.
23. Centers for Disease Control and Prevention: Summary of notifiable diseases, United States, 1997. *MMWR Morb Mortal Wkly Rep* 46:10, 1997.
24. Jackson LA, et al: Serogroup C meningococcal outbreaks in the United States: An emerging threat. *JAMA* 273:383, 1995.
25. Postgraduate Institute for Medicine: *The Changing Epidemiology of Meningococcal Disease in the United States with an Emphasis on College Health Issues.* Englewood, Colo, Postgraduate Institute for Medicine, 1999.
26. Nowak DA, Boehmer R, Fuchs HH: A retrospective clinical, laboratory, and outcome analysis in 43 cases of acute aseptic meningitis. *Eur J Neurol* 10:271, 2003.
27. Solomon T, et al: West Nile encephalitis. *BMJ* 326:7394, 2003.
28. Redington JJ, Tyler KL: Viral infections of the nervous system. *Arch Neurol* 59:712, 2002.
29. Aberle SW, Puchhammer-Stockl E: Diagnosis of herpesvirus infections of the nervous system. *J Clin Virol* 25(Suppl 1):S79, 2002.
30. Thorne CD, et al: Emergency medicine tools to manage smallpox (vaccinia) vaccination complications: Clinical practice guidelines and policies and procedures. *Ann Emerg Med* 42:5, 2003.
31. Rowland LP (ed): *Merritt's Textbook of Neurology*, 9th ed. Baltimore, Williams & Wilkins, 1995.
32. Wispelwey B, Scheld W: Brain abscess. *Semin Neurol* 12:273, 1992.
33. Small M, et al: Intracranial suppuration 1968-1982: A 15-year review. *Clin Otolaryngol* 9:315, 1984.
34. Qualiarello V, Scheld W: Bacterial meningitis: Pathogenesis, pathophysiology, and progress. *N Engl J Med* 327:864, 1992.
35. Tunkel MD, et al: Bacterial meningitis: Recent advances in pathophysiology and treatment. *Ann Intern Med* 112:610, 1990.
36. Saukkonen K, et al: The role of cytokines in the generation of inflammation and tissue damage in experimental gram-positive meningitis. *J Exp Med* 171:439, 1990.
37. Root RK, Sande MA (eds): *Viral Infections: Diagnosis, Treatment, and Prevention.* New York, Churchill Livingstone, 1993.
38. Charatan F: Organ transplants and blood transfusions may transmit West Nile virus. *BMJ* 325:566, 2002.
39. Johnson RT: The pathogenesis of acute viral encephalitis and postinfectious encephalomyelitis. *J Infect Dis* 155:359, 1987.
40. Whitley RJ: Viral encephalitis. *N Engl J Med* 323:242, 1990.
41. Geiseler PJ, et al: Community-acquired purulent meningitis: A review of 1316 cases during the antibiotic era, 1954-1976. *Rev Infect Dis* 2:725, 1980.
42. Attia J, et al: Does this adult patient have acute meningitis? *JAMA* 282:2, 1999.
43. Uchihara T, Tsukagoshi H: Jolt accentuation of headache, the most sensitive sign of CSF pleocytosis. *Headache* 31:167, 1991.
44. Whitley RJ, et al: Herpes simplex encephalitis: Clinical assessment. *JAMA* 247:317, 1982.
45. Studahl M, et al: Acute viral encephalitis in adults—A prospective study. *Scand J Infect Dis* 30:215, 1998.
46. Maslen DR, et al: Spinal epidural abscess. *Arch Intern Med* 153:1713, 1993.
47. Sangster G, et al: Bacterial meningitis 1940-79. *J Infect* 5:245, 1982.
48. Wenger JD, et al: Bacterial meningitis in the United States, 1986B: Report of a multistate surveillance study. *J Infect Dis* 162:1316, 1990.
49. Anderson JR: Viral encephalitis and its pathology. *Curr Top Pathol* 76:23, 1988.
50. Kennedy DH, Fallon RJ: Tuberculous meningitis. *JAMA* 241:264, 1979.
51. Sennaroglu L, Sozeri B: Otogenic brain abscess, a review of 41 cases. *Otolaryngol Head Neck Surg* 123:751, 2000.
52. Hasbrun R, et al: Computed tomography of the head before lumbar puncture in adults with suspected meningitis. *N Engl J Med* 345:24, 2001.
53. van Creel H, et al: Lumbar puncture and the risk of herniation: When should we first perform CT? *J Neurol* 249:129, 2002.
54. Radetsky M: Duration of symptoms and outcome in bacterial meningitis: An analysis of causation and the implications of a delay in diagnosis. *Pediatr Infect Dis J* 11:694, 1992.
55. Conly JM, Ronald AR: Cerebrospinal fluid as a diagnostic body fluid. *Am J Med* 75:102, 1983.

56. Onorato IM, et al: A "normal" CSF in bacterial meningitis. *JAMA* 244:1469, 1980.
57. Pickens S, et al: The effects of pre-admission antibiotics on the bacteriological diagnosis of pyogenic meningitis. *Scand J Infect Dis* 10:183, 1978.
58. Jarvis CW, Saxena KM: Does prior antibiotic treatment hamper the diagnosis of acute bacterial meningitis? *Clin Pediatr* 11:201, 1972.
59. Powers WJ: Cerebrospinal fluid lymphocytosis in acute bacterial meningitis. *Am J Med* 79:216, 1985.
60. Arevalo CE, et al: Cerebrospinal fluid cell counts and chemistries in bacterial meningitis. *South Med J* 82:1123, 1989.
61. Huang QS, et al: An echovirus type 33 winter outbreak in New Zealand. *Clin Infect Dis* 37:650, 2003.
62. Kooiker JC: Spinal puncture and cerebrospinal fluid examination. In Roberts JR, Hedges JR (eds): *Clinical Procedures in Emergency Medicine*, 2nd ed. Philadelphia, WB Saunders, 1991, pp 969-984.
63. Leonard JM: Cerebrospinal fluid formula in patients with central nervous system infection. *Neurol Clin* 4:3, 1986.
64. Aurelius E: Herpes simplex encephalitis B: Early diagnosis and immune activation in the acute stage and during long-term follow-up. *Scand J Infect Dis* 89:3, 1993.
65. Gufford T, et al: Significance and clinical relevance of the detection of herpes simplex virus DNA by the polymerase chain reaction in cerebrospinal fluid from patients with presumed encephalitis. *Clin Infect Dis* 18:744, 1994.
66. Aslanzadeh J, Skiest DJ: Polymerase chain reaction for detection of herpes simplex virus encephalitis. *J Clin Pathol* 47:554, 1994.
67. Cinque P, et al: The role of laboratory investigation in the diagnosis and management of patients with suspected herpes simplex encephalitis: A consensus report. The EU Concerted Action on Virus Meningitis and Encephalitis. *J Neurol Neurosurg Psychiatry* 61:339, 1996.
68. Kearns AM, et al: A rapid polymerase chain reaction technique for detecting *M. tuberculosis* in a variety of clinical specimens. *J Clin Pathol* 51:922, 1998.
69. Desai MM, Pal RB: Polymerase chain reaction for the rapid diagnosis of tuberculous meningitis. *Indian J Med Sci* 56:546, 2002.
70. Rafi A, Naghily B: Efficiency of polymerase chain reaction for the diagnosis of tuberculous meningitis. *Southeast Asian J Trop Med Public Health* 34:357, 2003.
71. Read SJ, Kurtz JB: Laboratory diagnosis of common viral infections of the central nervous system by using a single multiplex PCR screening assay. *J Clin Microbiol* 37:1352, 1999.
72. Casas I, et al: Viral diagnosis of neurological infection by RT multiplex PCR: A search for entero- and herpesviruses in a prospective study. *J Med Virol* 57:145, 1999.
73. Corless CE, et al: Simultaneous detection of *Neisseria meningitidis, Haemophilus influenzae,* and *Streptococcus pneumoniae* in suspected cases of meningitis and septicemia using real-time PCR. *J Clin Microbiol* 39:1553, 2001.
74. Porritt RJ, Mercer JL, Munro R: Detection and serogroup determination of *Neisseria meningitidis* in CSF by polymerase chain reaction (PCR). *Pathology* 32:42, 2000.
75. Richardson DC, et al: Evaluation of a rapid PCR assay for diagnosis of meningococcal meningitis. *J Clin Microbiol* 41:3851, 2003.
76. Singhi SC, et al: Evaluation of polymerase chain reaction (PCR) for diagnosing *Haemophilus influenzae* b meningitis. *Ann Trop Paediatr* 22:347, 2002.
77. Hukkanen V, Vuorinen T: Herpesviruses and enteroviruses in infections of the central nervous system: A study using time-resolved fluorometry PCR. *J Clin Virol* 25(Suppl 1):S87, 2002.
78. Romero JR: Reverse-transcriptase polymerase chain reaction detection of the enteroviruses. *Arch Pathol Lab Med* 123:1161, 1999.
79. Thompson RB, Bertram H: Laboratory diagnosis of central nervous system infections. *Infect Dis Clin North Am* 15:1047, 2001.
80. Lai CW, Gragasin ME: Electroencephalography in *herpes simplex* encephalitis. *J Clin Neurophysiol* 5:87, 1988.
81. Gilbert DN, et al: *Guide to Antimicrobial Therapy 2003.* Hyde Park, Vt, Antimicrobial Therapy, 2003.
82. Tauber MG, et al: Effects of ampicillin and corticosteroids on brain water content, cerebrospinal fluid pressure, and cerebrospinal fluid lactate levels in experimental pneumococcal meningitis. *J Infect Dis* 151:528, 1985.
83. Lebel MH, Freij BJ: Dexamethasone therapy for bacterial meningitis: Results of two double-blind, placebo-controlled trials. *N Engl J Med* 319:964, 1988.
84. McIntyre PB, et al: Dexamethasone as adjunctive therapy in bacterial meningitis. *JAMA* 278:925, 1997.
85. DeGans J, VanDeBeek D: Dexamethasone in adults with bacterial meningitis. *N Engl J Med* 347:20, 2002.
86. Rotbart HA, et al: Treatment of human enterovirus infections. *Antiviral Res* 38:1, 1998.
87. Kumarvelu S, et al: Randomized controlled trial of dexamethasone in tuberculous meningitis. *Tuber Lung Dis* 75:203, 1994.
88. Zangwill KM, et al: Duration of antibody response after meningococcal polysaccharide vaccination in U.S. Air Force personnel. *J Infect Dis* 169:847, 1994.
89. Morley SL, et al: Immunogenicity of a serogroup B meningococcal vaccine against multiple *Neisseria meningitidis* strains in infants. *Pediatr Infect Dis J* 20:1054, 2001.
90. Soriano-Gabarro M, Stuart JM, Rosenstein NE: Vaccines for the prevention of meningococcal disease in children. *Semin Pediatr Infect Dis* 13:182, 2002.
91. Centers for Disease Control and Prevention: Meningococcal disease and college students. Recommendations of the Advisory Committee on Immunization Practices (ACIP). *MMWR Recomm Rep* 49(RR-7):13, 2000.
92. Butler JC, et al: Pneumococcal polysaccharide vaccine efficacy B—An evaluation of current recommendations. *JAMA* 270:1826, 1993.
93. Centers for Disease Control and Prevention: Prevention of pneumococcal disease: Recommendations of the Advisory Committee on Immunization Practices (ACIP). *MMWR Recomm Rep* 46(RR-8):1, 1997.
94. Jacobson RM, Poland GA: The pneumococcal conjugate vaccine. *Minerva Pediatr* 54:295, 2002.
95. Peltola H, et al: Prevention of *Haemophilus influenzae* type B bacteremic infections with capsular polysaccharide vaccine. *N Engl J Med* 310:1561, 1984.
96. Vadheim CM, et al: Eradication of *Haemophilus influenzae* type B disease in southern California: Kaiser-UCLA vaccine study group. *Arch Pediatr Adolesc Med* 148:51, 1994.
97. Madore DV: Impact of immunization on *Haemophilus influenzae* type B disease. *Infect Agents Dis* 5:8, 1996.
98. Thompson RB, Bertram H: Laboratory diagnosis of central nervous system infections. *Infect Dis Clin North Am* 15:1047, 2001.
99. Centers for Disease Control and Prevention: Inactivated Japanese encephalitis virus vaccine: Recommendations of the Advisory Committee on Immunization Practices (ACIP). *MMWR Recomm Rep* 42(RR-1):1, 1993.
100. Zhou B, Jia L, Xu X: A large-scale study on the safety and epidemiological efficacy of Japanese encephalitis live vaccine (SA14-14-2) in endemic areas (Chinese). *Zhonghua Liu Xing Bing Xue Za Zhi* 20:38, 1999.

CHAPTER

108 Thought Disorders

Robert S. Hockberger and John R. Richards

PERSPECTIVE

Although unusual or bizarre behavior dates back more than 3000 years, no detailed descriptions of behavior resembling modern schizophrenia can be found before 1800. In the 1800s, Morel introduced the term *dementia praecox* to describe a progressive deterioration of mental functioning and behavior with onset in adolescence to early adult life.[1] In 1911 Bleuler detailed the specifics of this disorder, which he termed *schizophrenia,* or "split-mindedness."[2] Early authorities differed in their views regarding the pathophysiology of the disorder. Early treatments for schizophrenia included ice water immersion, the use of barbiturates or insulin to induce prolonged narcosis or coma, seizure induction with pentylenetetrazol (Metrazole), electroconvulsive therapy, and frontal leukotomy.[3] The effectiveness of these treatments was marginal at best, and until more recent times most schizophrenic patients were relegated to lifelong institutionalization.

Modern-era pharmacotherapy of schizophrenia, principally with chlorpromazine and haloperidol, began in the early 1950s. This treatment proved so successful that, by the 1960s, most psychiatrists believed that schizophrenia could be successfully managed in the outpatient setting. In 1965, the Community Mental Health Centers Act initiated the release of medicated schizophrenic patients into the community.[4] Unfortunately, inadequate family support, the unavailability of jobs and low-cost housing, and the lack of funding for social services and outpatient psychiatric care left these individuals isolated without the tools needed for resocialization. This situation has improved little during the past 40 years, and currently 20% to 40% of homeless people in the United States have major mental illness.[5] The emergency department serves as the primary entry point into the mental health care system for many of these individuals and is the only source of treatment for many chronically ill mental patients.

PRINCIPLES OF DISEASE

Schizophrenia is currently viewed as a heterogenous disorder that results from the interaction of biologic and environmental factors. Studies involving adopted twins whose biologic parents have schizophrenia demonstrate a strong genetic basis for the disorder. Although the overall incidence of schizophrenia in the general population is approximately 1%, it increases to almost 10% in first-degree biologic relatives of individuals with the disorder.[6] Research on drugs that mimic schizophrenic-like psychoses, as well as drugs that alleviate the disorder, implicates involvement of the dopaminergic, serotonergic, cholinergic, and glutamatergic systems in the pathophysiology of schizophrenia.[7-10]

Evidence increasingly suggests that schizophrenia is a neurodevelopmental disorder resulting from the influence of environmental factors on genetically predisposed individuals. Disruptions in fetal brain development, caused by perinatal hypoxia, poor nutrition, influenza infection, and other insults, may set the stage for development of schizophrenia decades later.[1] Models of schizophrenia have suggested that two or more insults to brain development are required over the life span rather than only one early-life event.[11] New imaging techniques have documented structural brain abnormalities, most of which appear to be developmental rather than degenerative, in many patients with schizophrenia.[7] Evidence supports the existence of a progressive continuum of psychotic illness.[1,12,13] The continuum begins with unipolar depression, progressing to bipolar illness, then to schizoaffective psychoses, and finally to schizophrenia, depending on the extent of the developmental defect.

CLINICAL FEATURES

Overt signs of schizophrenia usually become manifest during adolescence or early adult life. If questioned carefully, however, many patients describe a childhood marked by few interpersonal relationships and a sense, on the part of themselves and others, that they were withdrawn and somewhat eccentric.

Phases of Schizophrenia

The development of schizophrenia almost invariably passes through three phases.[14] The *premorbid phase* is characterized by the development of "negative" symptoms that cause deterioration from a previous level of personal, social, and intellectual functioning. Typically, patients progressively withdraw from social interactions and neglect personal appearance and hygiene. It becomes increasingly difficult for them to function at work and school and, ultimately, in their home environment.

The *active phase* is usually precipitated by a stressful event that results in the development of "positive" symptoms such as active delusions, hallucinations, and bizarre behavior. Patients may become agitated or

BOX 108-1. Summary of *DSM-IV* Criteria for Schizophrenia

A. Presence of two (or more) characteristic symptoms for 1 month (or more) unless treated
  1. Delusions
  2. Hallucinations
  3. Disorganized speech (derailment or incoherence)
  4. Grossly disorganized or catatonic behavior
  5. Negative symptoms: affect flattening, alogia (poverty of speech), avolition (unable to perform goal-directed activities)
  Note: only one symptom above is required if delusions are bizarre or hallucinations consist of a running commentary.
B. Sharp deterioration from prior level of functioning (i.e., work, self-care, interpersonal relations)
C. Continuous signs of disturbance for 6 months (or more)
D. Schizoaffective disorder and mood disorder when psychotic features have been ruled out
E. Not caused by substance abuse, medication, or a general medical condition

Modified from *Diagnostic and Statistical Manual of Mental Disorders*, ed 4-TR, Washington, DC, 2000, American Psychiatric Association.

BOX 108-2. Pharmacologic Agents that May Cause Acute Psychosis

Antianxiety Agents
Alprazolam
Chlordiazepoxide
Clonazepam
Clorazepate
Diazepam
Ethchlorvynol

Antibiotics
Isoniazid
Rifampin

Anticonvulsants
Ethosuximide
Phenobarbital
Phenytoin
Primidone

Antidepressants
Amitriptyline
Doxepin
Imipramine
Protriptyline
Trimipramine

Cardiovascular Drugs
Captopril
Digitalis
Disopyramide
Methyldopa
Procainamide
Propranolol
Reserpine

Miscellaneous Drugs
Antihistamines
Antineoplastics
Bromides
Cimetidine
Corticosteroids
Disulfiram
Heavy metals

Drugs of Abuse
Alcohol
Amphetamines
Cannabis
Cocaine
Hallucinogens
Opioids
Phencyclidine
Sedative-hypnotics

exhibit a hypervigilant withdrawal state characterized by rocking or staring. It is during this phase that they are most likely to be brought to the emergency department by family, friends, coworkers, or the police.

The *residual phase* resembles the premorbid phase in that patients are left with impaired social and cognitive ability, marked by bizarre ideation or vague delusions and accompanied by peculiar behavior, poor personal hygiene and grooming, and social isolation. Most schizophrenic patients require a sheltered environment to function adequately. Despite a wide spectrum of severity, the general course for most patients is one of gradual deterioration with periodic episodes of psychotic decompensation, often precipitating another visit to the emergency department.

Criteria for Schizophrenia

The clinical criteria for the diagnosis of schizophrenia are outlined in the fourth edition of the *Diagnostic and Statistical Manual of Mental Disorders* (DSM-IV-TR) (Box 108-1).[14] (1) The patient must exhibit two or more of the following symptoms: delusions, hallucinations, disorganized speech, grossly disorganized or catatonic behavior, and negative symptoms such as flattening of affect, poverty of speech, or inability to perform goal-directed activities. (2) There must be a sharp deterioration from the patient's prior level of functioning (work, school, self-care, or interpersonal relations), and there must be continuous signs of disturbance (including prodromal symptoms) for at least 6 months. (3) The diagnoses of schizoaffective disorder and mood disorder with psychotic features must be excluded. (4) Most important for emergency physicians, the presence of medical conditions that can mimic or cause psychotic symptoms must be excluded. Such conditions

include substance abuse, the side effects of some medications, and certain medical disorders (Boxes 108-2 and 108-3).

Delusions

The DSM-IV defines *delusions* as "erroneous beliefs that usually involve a misinterpretation of perceptions or experiences."[14] The delusions seen with schizophrenia are most often persecutory, religious, or somatic. They most often involve loss of control over the mind or body, such as having one's thoughts stolen, feeling that one is being manipulated by some outside force, or the belief that one's internal organs are rotting away.

Hallucinations

A *hallucination* is a sensory experience that does not exist, except in the mind of the person experiencing it. Although the hallucinations seen with schizophrenia can involve any sensory modality (auditory, visual, olfactory, gustatory, or tactile), auditory hallucinations (hearing voices) that are pejorative or threatening are especially common.

Disorganized Speech

Patients with schizophrenia experience loosening of associations; that is, their thoughts shift randomly from one topic to another without a logical connection. Their speech often shows lack of content or not saying much when talking. *Neologisms* (nonsense words invented

BOX 108-3. Medical Disorders that May Cause Acute Psychosis

Metabolic Disorders
Hypercalcemia
Hypercarbia
Hypoglycemia
Hyponatremia
Hypoxia

Inflammatory Disorders
Sarcoidosis
Systemic lupus erythematosus
Temporal (giant cell) arteritis

Organ Failure
Hepatic encephalopathy
Uremia

Neurologic Disorders
Alzheimer's disease
Cerebrovascular disease
Encephalitis (including HIV)
Encephalopathies
Epilepsy
Huntington's disease
Multiple sclerosis
Neoplasms
Normal-pressure hydrocephalus
Parkinson's disease
Pick's disease
Wilson's disease

Endocrine Disorders
Addison's disease
Cushing's disease
Panhypopituitarism
Parathyroid disease
Postpartum psychosis
Recurrent menstrual psychosis
Sydenham's chorea
Thyroid disease

Deficiency States
Niacin
Thiamine
Vitamin B_{12} and folate

by the patient) and *perseverations* (frequently repeated words or phrases) are common. Occasionally, the person's speech may be so severely disorganized that it is totally incoherent, termed *word salad*.

Grossly Disorganized or Catatonic Behavior

As a result of their delusions, hallucinations, and disorganized thinking, schizophrenic patients have great difficulty formulating and producing goal-directed behavior. They are often found wandering about, disheveled, malnourished, apparently talking to themselves, and exhibiting unpredictable and untriggered agitation, such as shouting or swearing. It is this behavior that usually prompts family members, friends, or the police to bring them to the emergency department.

Patients exhibiting catatonia appear to be completely unaware of their environment, maintain a rigid posture, and resist efforts to be moved.

Negative Symptoms

Three negative symptoms—flattening of affect, alogia, and avolition—account for a significant degree of the morbidity associated with schizophrenia. Patients with a *flattened affect* exhibit little facial expressiveness, eye contact, or body language. *Alogia*, or poverty of speech, is manifested by brief, laconic, empty replies to questioning. *Avolition* is characterized by an inability to initiate and persist in goal-directed activities. The emergency physician must be cautious in using the presence of negative symptoms to support a diagnosis of schizophrenia because similar symptoms can be produced by severe depression, chronic environmental understimulation, and treatment with neuroleptic medications.

DIAGNOSTIC STRATEGIES

Patients with Known Psychiatric Disorders

Patients with known psychiatric disorders who present with a mild to moderate exacerbation of their symptoms secondary to noncompliance with neuroleptic medication do not require extensive laboratory evaluation.[15] Because some of these patients may have coexisting substance abuse or undiagnosed medical disorders, a complete history and physical examination, along with urine toxicology studies, are indicated for most patients.[16-18] Patients exhibiting severe exacerbation of symptoms accompanied by marked agitation, violent behavior, or significantly abnormal vital signs should receive more extensive evaluation.

Patients without Known Psychiatric Disorders

Schizophrenia is a clinical diagnosis (see Box 108-1). Unfortunately, many toxicologic and medical disorders can mimic schizophrenia. Patients with the apparent new onset of psychosis and those with known psychiatric disorders who experience a severe exacerbation of symptoms or exhibit signs or symptoms of organic disease should receive a comprehensive medical evaluation to exclude toxicologic and medical disorders.[19-22]

DIFFERENTIAL CONSIDERATIONS

Medical Disorders

Certain medications and medical disorders may affect thought processes, causing persons to exhibit abnormal behavior (see Boxes 108-2 and 108-3). This behavior may range from mild personality changes to apparent acute psychosis, even in the absence of an underlying psychiatric disorder.[1] Factors that should alert the

Table 108-1. Factors in Differentiating Organic and Functional Psychosis: "MADFOCS"

	Organic	Functional
Memory deficits	Recent impairment	Remote impairment
Activity	Psychomotor retardation	Repetitive activity
	Tremor	Posturing
	Ataxia	Rocking
Distortions	Visual hallucinations	Auditory hallucinations
Feelings	Emotional lability	Flat affect
Orientation	Disoriented	Oriented
Cognition	Islands of lucidity	Continuous scattered thoughts
	Perceives occasionally	Unfiltered perceptions
	Attends occasionally	Unable to attend
	Focuses	
Some other findings	Age >40	Age <40
	Sudden onset	Gradual onset
	Physical examination often abnormal	Physical examination normal
	Vital signs may be abnormal	Vital signs usually normal
	Social immodesty	Social modesty
	Aphasia	Intelligible speech
	Consciousness impaired	Awake and alert

Modified from Frame DS, Kercher EE: Acute psychosis: Functional vs. organic. *Emerg Med Clin North Am* 9:123, 1991.

emergency physician to a medical disorder include (1) history of substance abuse or a medical disorder requiring medication, (2) patient's age greater than 35 years without previous evidence of psychiatric disease, (3) recent fluctuation in behavioral symptoms, (4) hallucinations that are primarily visual in nature, (5) presence of lethargy, (6) abnormal vital signs, and (7) poor performance on cognitive function testing, particularly orientation to time, place, and person. These and other factors may be helpful in differentiating functional (psychiatric) from organic (medical) causes of abnormal behavior and can be organized for easy recall into the mnemonic MADFOCS (Table 108-1).[23]

Although the classical textbook differentiation between functional and organic causes of abnormal behavior is straightforward, the evaluation of individual patients may be difficult.[20] A patient with underlying psychiatric disease may develop a medical disorder, which may worsen the patient's behavioral symptoms and further cloud the distinction between functional and organic disease. This evaluation is particularly difficult in the emergency department when previous medical or psychiatric history is not available, the patient is uncooperative, and the time frame to make a disposition is brief. When the clinical differentiation between functional and organic disease is unclear on the basis of available information, a patient should be evaluated to exclude a toxicologic or medical disorder.

Psychiatric Disorders

A previously undiagnosed patient who presents with an acute functional psychosis may ultimately be given one of several psychiatric diagnoses.[14] A *brief psychotic disorder* involves the sudden onset of psychotic symptoms during the immediate postpartum period or in response to any major stress, such as the loss of a loved one or the psychological trauma of combat, and lasts from several days to 1 month. Patients with *schizophreniform disorder* have similar symptoms that last longer than 1 month but less than 6 months. Approximately one third of individuals initially given the diagnosis of schizophreniform disorder recover within 6 months; the other two thirds retain their symptoms and ultimately are diagnosed as having schizophrenia. Patients with mood disorders may develop psychotic symptoms. If these symptoms are present only during periods of mood disturbance, the diagnosis of *mood disorder with psychotic features* is applied; if they persist longer than 2 weeks in the absence of prominent mood symptoms, the diagnosis of *schizoaffective disorder* is made. Patients with *personality disorders* may occasionally develop brief psychotic episodes when under stress.

Ganser's syndrome is a symptom complex, considered to be emotional in origin, in which the patient may appear to have amnesia, hallucinations, or alterations in consciousness, usually in association with physical complaints. An individual with Ganser's syndrome may have psychotic symptoms for no apparent gain except to assume the role of the psychiatric patient.

Persons with a *delusional disorder* experience nonbizarre delusions that may dominate their lives. They may believe that famous people are in love with them (erotomanic type), that they have extraordinary powers with a special relationship to a deity or a famous person (grandiose type), that their sexual partner is unfaithful (jealous type), that they are being malevolently treated in some way (persecutory type), or that they have some physical defect or general medical condition (somatic type). Although patients with somatic delusions may experience tactile or olfactory hallucinations related to the delusional theme (e.g., the sensation of being infested with insects), the other features associated with schizophrenia are not present.

MANAGEMENT

General Approach

Patients with thought disorders may be agitated and hyperactive, may be withdrawn but hypervigilant, or may complain of somatic delusions. In addition, they may have paranoid ideation, may be angry that they have been brought to the emergency department against their will, or may be frightened because they have been confronted by the police, restrained, and isolated. The presence of such patients in the emergency department may be disconcerting to staff because these patients are known to be potentially irrational, erratic, and unpredictable in their behavior. Although emergency personnel must remain calm, empathetic, and reassuring in their interactions with patients exhibiting a thought disorder, they must also take steps to ensure staff safety whenever dealing with patients at risk for sudden violence. Such patients include those who have manifested violent behavior before coming to the emergency department, those who physically or verbally threaten staff, and those who demonstrate an escalating level of agitation despite verbal attempts to calm them.

Each patient should have a complete history and physical examination performed, including a detailed mental status evaluation, to rule out the existence of an organic brain syndrome. Valuable information can be obtained from family members, friends, coworkers, neighbors, paramedical personnel, police, or previous medical records (see Table 108-1).[23]

The most important step in evaluating a patient with a suspected thought disorder is the assessment of the patient's thought processes through a psychiatric interview. This interview attempts to establish a positive physician-patient relationship, to make a correct diagnosis, and to gather the information necessary to render an optimal disposition. The interview should be conducted in a quiet, comfortable room with adequate privacy. The examiner should be sitting, and if possible the interview should proceed to completion without interruption. If the patient is believed to be potentially dangerous but is not in need of immediate restraint, the interview should take place in an open area with security personnel nearby.

The emergency physician should begin with an introduction and should express the desire to be "of help" to the patient. The interview should begin with open-ended questions designed to assess the patient's complaint and understanding of the current circumstances. Good opening questions include "Do you understand why you have been brought here today?"; "You seem to be upset. Can you tell me why?"; and "Do you have any idea why you might be having these symptoms?" The patient's appearance, body language, affect, and speech should be observed during the responses to these questions.

The second portion of the psychiatric interview consists of a formal mental status examination, which may be initiated in a nonthreatening manner by stating, "I am now going to ask you a few questions to see how well you are concentrating." The patient should first be asked questions regarding orientation to time, place, and person because this is the most sensitive test for differentiating organic from functional disease. Patients who are disoriented should have a detailed medical evaluation to exclude the presence of an organic brain syndrome. Patients who are oriented should be assessed for attention, memory, intellectual functioning, and judgment in an attempt to determine their specific diagnosis, their potential for danger to themselves or others, and their degree of dysfunction and ability to care for themselves in the outpatient setting.

Rapid Tranquilization

When psychotic patients exhibit behavior that is violent or so disorganized and uncooperative that clinical evaluation is impossible, the temporary use of physical restraints is indicated while rapid tranquilization is initiated (see Chapter 189). The technique of rapid tranquilization uses serial doses of a high-potency antipsychotic agent until target symptoms, such as agitation and excessive psychomotor activity, are improved. The goal is to facilitate cooperation of the patient without causing unnecessary sedation, which would inhibit further medical and psychiatric assessment. Oral, intramuscular (IM), or intravenous (IV) doses can be given every 30 to 60 minutes until the patient becomes calmer and more cooperative. If the patient is willing, an oral concentrate is preferred because it implies consent and can take effect almost as quickly as IM administration.

Haloperidol (Haldol), a butyrophenone, is the agent most widely used for rapid tranquilization in the United States.[24-26] The initial dose is 5 to 10 mg IM or IV for young to middle-age patients and 0.5 to 2.0 mg IM or IV for elderly patients. Although rapid tranquilization with haloperidol quickly reduces tension, anxiety, and hyperactivity, delusions and hallucinations may not resolve for several weeks. *Droperidol* (Inapsine), another butyrophenone, has also been extensively used for this indication in doses from 2.5 to 5.0 mg IM or IV.[27,28] Compared with haloperidol, droperidol has a faster onset and shorter duration of action and causes slightly more sedation. However, a U.S. Food and Drug Administration (FDA) "black box" warning was published in 2001 because of reports of a potential association between droperidol and prolonged QT interval, torsades de pointes, and sudden death.[29] Despite subsequent studies supporting both the efficacy and safety of droperidol, the FDA warning has resulted in a significant decrease of its use in the emergency department.[30,31] Neuroleptics should not be used for pregnant or lactating females, phencyclidine overdose, or anticholinergic drug–induced psychosis. In addition, they should not be used as the sole agent to manage agitation in patients with drug or alcohol withdrawal.

The newer atypical antipsychotic agents appear to have a broader spectrum of response with less side effects than the typical agents. Both olanzapine (Zyprexa) and risperidone (Risperdal) are available in a dissolvable oral tablet and should be considered for patients who accept oral medication. However, oral administration of a pharmacologic agent during an acute episode of agitation and psychosis may be difficult to impossible. *Ziprasidone* (Geodon) is the only member of the newer atypical antipsychotics that is currently approved in the United States for IM injection.[32] The dose is 20 mg IM and can be repeated every 4 hours. It has been shown to be as effective as or more effective than haloperidol for sedation and with fewer extrapyramidal side effects, but it has not yet been widely used in the emergency department setting.[33,34]

Benzodiazepines are effective in managing agitation in patients who have alcohol or sedative-hypnotic withdrawal, cocaine intoxication, or a contraindication to neuroleptic use. Benzodiazepines are helpful adjuncts to neuroleptic medication in providing rapid tranquilization, particularly in patients exhibiting combativeness or severe agitation, when a greater degree of sedation is desired. *Lorazepam* (Ativan), 1 to 2 mg, is frequently mixed with haloperidol, 5 mg, in the same syringe and administered IM or IV for this purpose. One disadvantage of benzodiazepines is the potential for respiratory depression with large doses, which requires close monitoring after administration.

Outpatient Management

The outpatient treatment of schizophrenia involves maintenance therapy using neuroleptic agents, family counseling, and social rehabilitation. Emergency physicians rarely prescribe outpatient neuroleptic medications but should be familiar with the complications associated with their long-term use.

Box 108-4 lists the most common neuroleptic medications currently used in the United States.[35-41] The mechanism of action is related to the blockade of dopamine receptors in the central nervous system, particularly dopamine D_2 receptors in the basal ganglia and limbic portions of the forebrain. The earlier, less potent drugs, of which chlorpromazine is the prototype, cause more pronounced sedation, orthostatic hypotension, and cardiovascular toxicity. This is the result of a combination of anticholinergic, antihistaminic, and anti–α-adrenergic effects. The newer, more potent agents (e.g., haloperidol) are safer, especially in older patients, because of their relative lack of these adverse affects. However, these more potent drugs are associated with a higher incidence of extrapyramidal symptoms, such as dystonias, akathisia, akinesia, and rigidity.

The high frequency of severe adverse reactions, poor compliance by patients, and the large number of patients with symptoms that are refractory to traditional antipsychotic agents have resulted in new alternative agents. These "atypical" neuroleptic agents block serotonin to a greater extent than dopamine, resulting in a low incidence of extrapyramidal side effects. *Clozapine* is particularly effective in patients who have not responded to other antipsychotic drugs.[39] However, clozapine is expensive, has a side effect

profile similar to that of the low-potency antipsychotic agents, and causes agranulocytosis in approximately 1% of patients.[36] It is recommended only for the treatment of patients with refractory psychosis. *Olanzapine*, *quetiapine*, and the newest agent, *aripiprazole*, are similar to clozapine but have fewer side effects and less risk of agranulocytosis.[35] *Risperidone*, another newer neuroleptic agent with improved effects on negative symptoms, has been found to be superior to haloperidol in several short-term trials.[39-42] *Ziprasidone* is the only newer atypical antipsychotic agent currently approved for IM injection in the United States; the other atypical drugs are approved for oral administration only. Unfortunately, this, coupled with the expense and limited availability of these newer antipsychotic agents, limits their utility for treating acute psychosis in the emergency department. Ziprasidone, risperidone, and quetiapine have been associated with QT interval prolongation similar to that seen with droperidol but have not been found to be associated with sudden cardiac death.[43]

Because of the high incidence of extrapyramidal symptoms in patients treated with high-potency neuroleptics, it is common practice to administer antiparkinsonian drugs (e.g., benztropine, procyclidine, trihexyphenidyl) at the same time, either to treat the adverse effects or to prevent them. Prophylactic treatment is most useful in patients with a history of extrapyramidal symptoms, those receiving high doses of high-potency antipsychotic agents, and those in whom the occurrence of these symptoms is likely to increase the risk of noncompliance.

Noncompliance with antipsychotic medication remains a leading cause of psychiatric hospitalization. Patients with recurrent psychotic relapses caused by noncompliance are candidates for treatment with long-acting injectable antipsychotic drugs, usually given every 2 weeks. Two such agents available in the United States are fluphenazine decanoate and haloperidol decanoate.[44]

Complications of Neuroleptic Drug Therapy

Dystonia

Acute dystonia, the most common adverse effect seen with neuroleptic agents, occurs in 1% to 5% of patients. This reaction is caused by a disruption of the dopaminergic-cholinergic balance in the nigrostriatal pathways of the basal ganglia, resulting in cholinergic dominance.[45] Dystonic reactions, which can occur at any point during long-term therapy and up to 48 hours after administration of neuroleptics in the emergency department, involve the sudden onset of involuntary contraction of the muscles of the face, neck, or back. The patient may have protrusion of the tongue (buccolingual crisis), deviation of the head to one side (acute torticollis), sustained upward deviation of the eyes (oculogyric crisis), extreme arching of the back (opisthotonos), or rarely laryngospasm. These symptoms tend to fluctuate, decreasing with voluntary activity and increasing under emotional stress, which occasionally misleads emergency physicians to believe they are factitious.

Dystonic reactions should be treated with IM or IV benztropine (Cogentin), 1 to 2 mg, or diphenhydramine (Benadryl), 25 to 50 mg. IV administration usually results in an almost immediate reversal of symptoms. Patients should receive oral therapy with the same medication for 48 to 72 hours to prevent recurrent symptoms.[45]

Akathisia

Akathisia is a state of motor restlessness characterized by a physical need to be moving constantly. It occurs most often in middle-aged patients during the first few months of therapy. Patients are usually pacing the room and expressing a sense of inner tension that is not relieved by activity. If asked, they do not want to be constantly moving but feel physically compelled to do so. This reaction can easily be mistaken for a decompensating psychosis, leading to a vicious circle in which more medication is given to treat a side effect caused by the same drug. This misdiagnosis can be avoided by carefully evaluating the patient for the exacerbation of positive psychotic symptoms, which are not increased by akathisia. Akathisia is treated with β-blockers (e.g., propranolol, 30 to 60 mg/day) or anticholinergic drugs (e.g., benztropine, 1 mg twice to four times daily). A new potential agent for the treatment of akathisia is glycine, a nonessential amino acid that stimulates glutamatergic neurotransmission.[46] In addition, if possible, the dosage of the antipsychotic agent should be lowered.

Pseudoparkinsonism and Akinesia

A clinical picture can occur that may be indistinguishable from Parkinson's disease, particularly in elderly patients during the first month of therapy. Treatment with anticholinergic agents (e.g., benztropine) or antiparkinsonian drugs is usually effective. Akinesia, which is characterized by immobility, withdrawal, and lack of motivation, may be mistaken for a postpsychotic depression. It is responsive to antiparkinsonian drugs, but symptoms usually resolve gradually over time.

Tardive Dyskinesia

The most feared neurologic complication of chronic neuroleptic drug treatment is tardive dyskinesia. This syndrome usually appears after several years of treatment and is characterized by involuntary movements, especially of the face and tongue, that are described as writhing, grimacing, and choreoathetoid in nature. The earliest manifestation is often a curling or twisting movement of the tongue. The onset of these symptoms can be falsely attributed to psychological factors because they intensify under emotional stress, fatigue, and voluntary activity and disappear with sleep.

The reported prevalence of tardive dyskinesia ranges from 0.5% to 70%, with a mean value of 24%.[45] The incidence of the disorder appears to be directly related to the duration of treatment, total cumulative dosage, evidence of preexisting brain damage, and age of the patient. It is more common in elderly women and patients with associated mood disorders. For patients with mild symptoms, discontinuing or lowering the dosage of antipsychotic agents or switching to a newer atypical neuroleptic agent, along with cotreatment with benzodiazepines, may reverse the symptoms. Patients with moderate to severe symptoms are difficult to treat, but some have variable degrees of improvement when treated with reserpine or tetrabenazine along with discontinuation of neuroleptic treatment.[45]

Orthostatic Hypotension

All the antipsychotic agents can cause orthostatic hypotension, an effect related to α-adrenergic blockade. This complication is less common with the more potent agents (e.g., haloperidol). Typically, episodes are mild in severity and brief in duration. Symptomatic patients should be treated with oxygen, Trendelenburg's position, and IV crystalloid fluid administration. Pressor agents (e.g., dopamine) should be used only for severe, symptomatic episodes that fail to respond to the previous measures. Agents with β-agonist activity (e.g., epinephrine, isoproterenol) are contraindicated in these patients.

Neuroleptic Malignant Syndrome

Neuroleptic malignant syndrome (NMS) is a life-threatening complication of neuroleptic drug treatment that affects 0.5% to 1% of patients.[47] It is seen with both typical and atypical neuroleptic agents, usually occurs in the first few weeks after initiation of treatment, but can also be seen after a recent increase in drug dosage or after parenteral treatment with high doses of neuroleptic agents. NMS is characterized by high fever, severe muscle rigidity, altered consciousness, autonomic instability, and elevated serum creatine kinase levels. Additional complications can include respiratory failure, gastrointestinal hemorrhage, hepatic and renal failure, coagulopathy, and cardiovascular collapse.

The pathophysiology of NMS is not well understood, but it is thought to be related to dopamine depletion in the central nervous system, which leads to defective thermoregulation in the hypothalamus. Predisposing factors include exhaustion, dehydration, and the use of long-acting depot neuroleptics. Treatment consists of recognition and discontinuation of the neuroleptic agent, fever reduction, rehydration with IV fluids, and general supportive measures. *Dantrolene*, a direct-acting muscle relaxant, should be used in severe cases. It can be administered by continuous rapid IV push at a minimum initial dose of 1 mg/kg, repeated until symptoms subside or up to a maximum cumulative dose of 10 mg/kg. For severe symptoms, dopamine agonists such as bromocriptine, levodopa, and amantadine have shown encouraging results. Because of earlier recognition and treatment, mortality rates with NMS have decreased from 30% to less than 10%.[48]

DISPOSITION

The ultimate disposition of the acutely psychotic patient depends on the underlying cause of the psychosis, whether the patient is a danger to self or others, and the presence of social support in the community. Hospitalization is indicated for patients experiencing their first psychotic episode, for patients deemed to be a danger to themselves (suicidal) or others (homicidal), for patients who are grossly debilitated, for patients who are moderately debilitated but have no social support system within the community, and for patients with either functional or organic psychosis that does not clear with a brief period of treatment and observation in the emergency department. The decision to hospitalize psychotic patients is complex and imprecise and often must be made in a short period with limited information.

A psychiatric short-procedure unit offers a cost-effective alternative to hospitalization.[49] After stabilization, patients are moved from the emergency department to a separate treatment area, where they are treated for a period of 12 to 24 hours by a small staff of consultants. This unit is used for rapid tranquilization, individual and family crisis intervention, amobarbital interviews, electroconvulsive therapy, and evaluation of patients for underlying medical problems.

KEY CONCEPTS

- In patients exhibiting abnormal behavior, an organic etiology is suggested by (1) new onset of symptoms in a patient older than 35 years, (2) rapid onset of symptoms in a previously normal person, (3) visual hallucinations, (4) abnormal vital signs, and (5) lethargy or disorientation.

- Physical restraints should be considered for patients who have violent behavior, verbally threaten staff, or demonstrate escalating agitation despite verbal attempts to calm them. Restraints should be removed after sedation has been achieved.

- Rapid tranquilization is best accomplished with the use of high-potency neuroleptics (e.g., haloperidol, ziprasidone). Benzodiazepines (e.g., lorazepam) are a helpful adjunct for patients with severe agitation.

REFERENCES

1. Jones P, Cannon M: The new epidemiology of schizophrenia. *Psychiatr Clin North Am* 21:1, 1998.
2. Tomlinson WK: Schizophrenia: History of an illness. *Psychiatr Med* 8:1, 1990.
3. Tueth MJ: Schizophrenia: Emil Kraepelin, Adolph Meyer, and beyond. *J Emerg Med* 13:805, 1995.
4. Lewis G, et al: Schizophrenia and city life. *Lancet* 340:137, 1992.
5. Opler LA, et al: Symptom profiles and homelessness in schizophrenia. *J Nerv Ment Dis* 182:174, 1994.
6. Schwab SG, et al: Support for a chromosome 18p locus conferring susceptibility to functional psychoses in families with schizophrenia, by association and linkage analysis. *Am J Hum Genet* 63:1139, 1998.
7. Michels R, Morzuk PM: Progress in psychiatry. *N Engl J Med* 329:552, 1993.
8. Lieberman JA, et al: Serotonergic basis of antipsychotic drug effects in schizophrenia. *Biol Psychiatry* 44:1099, 1998.
9. Tandon R: Cholinergic aspects of schizophrenia. *Br J Psychiatry* S37:7, 1999.
10. Tamminga CA: Schizophrenia and glutamatergic transmission. *Crit Rev Neurobiol* 12:21, 1998.
11. McGrath JJ, et al: The neurodevelopmental hypothesis of schizophrenia: A review of recent developments. *Ann Med* 35:86, 2003.
12. Harrison PJ: The neuropathology of schizophrenia: A critical review of the data and their interpretation. *Brain* 122:593, 1999.
13. Crow TJ, Harrington CA: Etiopathogenesis and treatment of psychosis. *Annu Rev Med* 45:219, 1994.
14. *Diagnostic and Statistical Manual of Mental Disorders*, 4-TR ed. Washington, DC, American Psychiatric Association, 2000.
15. Olshaker JS, et al: Medical clearance and screening of psychiatric patients in the emergency department. *Acad Emerg Med* 4:124, 1997.
16. Breslow RE, Klinger BI, Erickson BJ: Acute intoxication and substance abuse among patients presenting to a psychiatric emergency service. *Gen Hosp Psychiatry* 18:183, 1996.
17. Elangovan N, et al: Substance abuse among patients presenting at an inner-city psychiatric emergency room. *Hosp Community Psychiatry* 44:782, 1993.
18. Dhossche D, Rubinstein J: Drug detection in a suburban psychiatric emergency room. *Ann Clin Psychiatry* 8:59, 1996.

19. Tintinalli JE, Peacock FW IV, Wright MA: Emergency medical evaluation of psychiatric patients. *Ann Emerg Med* 23:859, 1994.
20. Henneman PL, Mendoza R, Lewis RJ: Prospective evaluation of emergency department medical clearance. *Ann Emerg Med* 24:672, 1994.
21. Smith ML: Atypical psychosis. *Psychiatr Clin North Am* 4:895, 1998.
22. Hutto B: Subtle psychiatric presentations of endocrine diseases. *Psychiatr Clin North Am* 21:905, 1998.
23. Frame DS, Kercher EE: Acute psychosis: Functional vs. organic. *Emerg Med Clin North Am* 9:123, 1991.
24. Currier GW, Trenton A: Pharmacological treatment of psychotic agitation. *CNS Drugs* 16:777, 2002.
25. Hillard JR: Emergency treatment of acute psychosis. *J Clin Psychiatry* 59:57, 1998.
26. Battaglia J, et al: Haloperidol, lorazepam, or both for psychotic agitation? A multicenter, prospective, double-blind, emergency department study. *Am J Emerg Med* 15:335, 1997.
27. Thomas IT: Droperidol vs haloperidol for chemical restraint of agitated and combative patients. *Ann Emerg Med* 21:407, 1992.
28. Richards JR, Derlet RW, Duncan DR: Chemical restraint for the agitated patient in the emergency department: Lorazepam versus droperidol. *J Emerg Med* 16:567, 1998.
29. Richards JR, Schneir AB: Droperidol in the emergency department: Is it safe? *J Emerg Med* 24:441, 2003.
30. Chase PB, Biros MH: A retrospective review of the use and safety of droperidol in a large, high-risk, inner-city emergency department patient population. *Acad Emerg Med* 9:1402, 2002.
31. Shale JF, et al: A review of the safety and efficacy of droperidol for the rapid sedation of severely agitated and violent patients. *J Clin Psychiatry* 64:500, 2003.
32. Bellvier TJ: Continuum of care: Stabilizing the acutely agitated patient. *Am J Health Syst Pharm* 59:512, 2002.
33. Daniel DG, et al: Intramuscular ziprasidone 20mg is effective in reducing acute agitation associated with psychosis: A double-blind randomized trial. *Psychopharmacology* 115:128, 2001.
34. Brook S, et al: Intramuscular ziprasidone compared with intramuscular haloperidol in the treatment of acute psychosis. *J Clin Psychiatry* 61:933, 2000.
35. Cain JM: Schizophrenia. *N Engl J Med* 334:34, 1996.
36. Alvir JM, et al: Clozapine-induced agranulocytosis: Incidence and risk factors in the United States. *N Engl J Med* 329:162, 1993.
37. Fleischhacker WW: New developments in the pharmacotherapy of schizophrenia. *J Neural Transm Suppl* 64:105, 2003.
38. Breier A, et al: Effects of clozapine on positive and negative symptoms in outpatients with schizophrenia. *Am J Psychiatry* 151:20, 1994.
39. Marder SR, Meibach RC: Risperidone in the treatment of schizophrenia. *Am J Psychiatry* 151:825, 1994.
40. Tran PV, et al: Double-blind comparison of olanzapine versus risperidone in the treatment of schizophrenia and other psychotic disorders. *J Clin Psychopharmacol* 17:407, 1997.
41. Breier AF, et al: Clozapine and risperidone in chronic schizophrenia: Effects on symptoms, parkinsonian side effects, and neuroendocrine response. *Am J Psychiatry* 156:294, 1999.
42. Leucht S, et al: Efficacy and extrapyramidal side-effects of the new antipsychotics olanzapine, quetiapine, risperidone, and sertindole compared to conventional antipsychotics and placebo: A meta-analysis of randomized controlled trials. *Schizophr Res* 35:51, 1999.
43. Trenton AJ, Currier GW, Zwemer FL: Fatalities associated with therapeutic use and overdose of atypical antipsychotics. *CNS Drugs* 17:307, 2003.
44. Davis JM, et al: Depot antipsychotic drugs: Their place in therapy. *Drugs* 47:741, 1994.
45. Fernandez HH, Friedman JH: Classification and treatment of tardive syndromes. *Neurologist* 9:16, 2003.
46. Heresco-Levy U, et al: Efficacy of high-dose glycine in the treatment of enduring negative symptoms of schizophrenia. *Arch Gen Psychiatry* 56:29, 1999.
47. Viejo LF, et al: Risk factors in neuroleptic malignant syndrome. A case-control study. *Acta Psychiatr Scand* 107:45, 2003.
48. Caroff SN, et al: Neuroleptic malignant syndrome in the critical care unit. *Crit Care Med* 30:2609, 2002.
49. Mok H, Watler C: Brief psychiatric hospitalization: Experience with an urban short-stay unit. *Can J Psychiatry* 40:415, 1995.

CHAPTER

109 Mood Disorders

Douglas A. Rund and Marshall G. Vary

PERSPECTIVE

Happiness and sorrow are common emotions but usually cause no impairment in functioning or threat to life. Mood disorder, by contrast, can significantly impair physical, social, and family functioning and can cause psychological pain, physical pain, and a negative perception of physical health. The term *mood disorders* replaced the term "affective disorders" in the fourth edition of the *Diagnostic and Statistical Manual of Mental Disorders* (DSM-IV-TR).[1] *Mood* refers to an "enduring emotional orientation that colors the person's psychology," whereas *affect* normally refers to "the outward and changeable manifestation of a person's emotional tone."[2] *Dysphoria* means depressed mood or feeling. The DSM-IV-TR assigns psychiatric diagnoses to patients by assessing specific observable and measurable symptoms and signs, facilitating appropriate psychiatric evaluation, and communicating with psychiatric consultants. Research regarding the neurobiology of mood disorders and genetics may ultimately permit classification of mood disorders by specific, genetically predisposed pathophysiology derangements.

Epidemiology

Psychiatric problems account for at least 5.4% of all emergency department visits and the rate of psychiatric related visits has increased 15% since 1992.[3] The World Health Organization ranks major depression as one of the most prevalent diseases in the world.[4] In the 2002 National Comorbidity Survey of Psychiatric Disorders, the lifetime prevalence of major depressive disorders in the United States was 16.2% and for the previous 12 months was 6.6%. Prominent associated disorders included anxiety disorders (almost 60%), substance use disorders (24%), and impulse control disorder (30%).[5] Patients with substance abuse comorbidity have higher emergency department utilization than patients without such comorbidity.[6] Patients with chronic illness have a much higher prevalence of undiagnosed depression than the general population. The lifetime suicide risk for persons with major untreated depressive illness is 15%.[7] Mood disorders are becoming more common and have increased in every generation born after 1910.[8]

The prevalence of bipolar disorders (manic-depressive disorders) is substantially lower than that of major depression. The overall lifetime prevalence of a manic episode is 1.6% (1.7% for women and 1.6% for men).

PRINCIPLES OF DISEASE

Current neurobiologic concepts provide the basis for various pharmacologic treatments. The psychosocial theories of depression consider the complex interaction of genetics, environment, and experience, providing the basis for understanding the various psychotherapeutic approaches to treatment.

Neurotransmitters

In the fourth century BC, Hippocrates believed that the body contained four essential humors: blood, phlegm, yellow bile, and black bile. Harmony in the brain required a harmony of humors. "Disharmony" produced mental illness. In the second century, Galen believed that "melancholia" resulted from an excess of black bile acting on the brain. Such excesses were thought to be caused by noxious stomach vapors, grief, anxiety, excessive wine, and advancing age. Proposed treatments included bloodletting, surgery, special diets, and exercise.[9]

Modern theories regarding the pathophysiology of mood disorders and monoamine neurotransmitters (e.g., norepinephrine) were developed 40 years ago.[10] *Reserpine,* an antihypertensive medication, depleted cerebral concentrations of norepinephrine and caused clinical depression in a large proportion of patients. *Imipramine,* by increasing cerebral concentrations of norepinephrine at various synaptic sites, alleviated symptoms of depression.

Neurons interact at synapses, where neurotransmitters released at presynaptic sites interact with postsynaptic receptors. Neurotransmitters identified thus far include the biogenic amines (serotonin, norepinephrine, dopamine, glutamate, histamine, acetylcholine, γ-aminobutyric acid, glycerin), certain neuropeptides, and neurotropic factors.

Complex processes in the nervous system cause depression or mania. If the concentrations of neurotransmitters at synaptic sites were the only factors responsible for alleviation of depression, the therapeutic effect of an antidepressant agent would be almost immediate. However, clinical improvement with these agents takes several weeks and is highly individually variable. Emphasis has now shifted to the study of neurobehavioral systems, intricate regulatory mechanisms, development of preferred neural circuits, the effect of environment on phenotype expression, and gene transcriptors.[11]

Cerebral Anatomy

Certain areas of the brain are involved in processes that become abnormal during episodes of depression and mania.[12,13] Stress activates neurons in the locus ceruleus, resulting in increased alertness, decreased appetite, increased heart rate, increased cortisol production, and other features of a stress response. The response can be dampened by neurons in the cerebral cortex. Prolonged stress, from which escape appears hopeless, seems to decrease the activity of neurons in the locus ceruleus. Another noradrenergic system, the median forebrain bundle, elicits reward-seeking behavior when stimulated. Prolonged stress decreases levels of norepinephrine in this region and may explain the lack of energy and interest that accompany depression.[14,15]

Serotonergic neurons are located in the brainstem dorsal raphe and project diffusely throughout the brain. The serotonergic system seems to enhance sleep, appetite, libido, and circadian rhythms. Activation decreases aggressive behavior in animal models.[16,17]

Dopaminergic pathways include the tuberoinfundibular system, originating in the hypothalamus (prolactin secretion); the nigrostriatal system, originating in the substantia nigra (involuntary motor activity); the mesolimbic pathway, in the ventral tegmentum; and the mesocortical pathway, originating in the ventral tegmentum.[18] These pathways regulate emotion, pleasure, learning, and reinforcement. The mesocortical pathway extends to frontal cortical regions that regulate complex cognition concentration and motivation.[19]

Endocrine System

The cortical-hypothalamic-pituitary-adrenocortical system is affected in many patients with depression, causing increased levels of plasma cortisol, apparently from an impaired biofeedback loop regulating cortisol. The thyroid axis malfunctions in 5% to 10% of depressed patients. Thyroid-stimulating hormone levels are elevated, and thyroid replacement therapy facilitates treatment in certain patients.[20]

Genetics

Family studies have repeatedly demonstrated a relationship between genetic inheritance and mood disorders.[21] Monozygotic and dizygotic twins have a high concordance rate, 70% and 35%, respectively, for mood disorder.[22] The mechanisms of genetic transmission are still undetermined but may relate to the synthesis, transport, and action of serotonin and other transmitters.[23,24] The inherited susceptibility to depression may manifest only during severe stress or serious illness.[25]

Psychosocial Theories

The complex neural mechanism that regulates mood responds to and is modified by each person's experience, including events in early childhood, reward and punishment during growth and development, interpersonal relationships, and various kinds of loss. Psychosocial theories of mood disorder form the basis for psychotherapy. Freud noted that personal loss included grief and sadness, but that depression also involved guilt and lowered self-esteem.[26] Freud theorized that suicide in depressed patients is a manifestation of aggression that has been turned against the self in a person otherwise unable to express anger toward loved ones.

The interpersonal theory of depression emphasizes guilt, disputes between partners and family members, role transitions in families and relationships, and problems with social skills necessary to sustain a fulfilling relationship. Cognitive theories have also been applied to depressed individuals, especially when the content of a depressed person's thought involves self-blame, hopelessness, and helplessness. The concept of "learned helplessness" first developed when animals were blocked from escape and subjected to repeated noxious stimuli such as electric shock. They eventually stopped trying to escape and became apathetic, even when escape became available.[27] The concept was later applied to humans and adapted to construct a behavioral mode of therapy for depression.

CLINICAL FEATURES

Major Depressive Disorder

Major depressive disorder is characterized by one or more major depressive episodes, as defined by DSM-IV-TR criteria (Boxes 109-1 and 109-2). A major depressive episode is characterized by disturbances in four major areas: mood, psychomotor activity, cognition, and vegetative function.[28] The patient must exhibit or

---

BOX 109-1. Summary of DSM-IV Criteria for Major Depressive Episode

A. Five or more of the following symptoms present almost every day during the same 2-week period and representing a change from previous functioning; at least one of the symptoms is either (1) depressed mood or (2) loss of interest or pleasure. **NOTE:** Do not include symptoms caused by a general medical condition, and do not include mood-incongruent delusions or hallucinations.
  1. Depressed mood (can be irritable mood in children and adolescents)
  2. Loss of interest or pleasure in activities
  3. Significant weight loss when not dieting or weight gain or decrease or increase in appetite
  4. Insomnia or hypersomnia
  5. Psychomotor agitation or retardation
  6. Fatigue or loss of energy
  7. Feelings of worthlessness or excessive or inappropriate guilt
  8. Diminished ability to think or concentrate, or indecisiveness
  9. Recurrent thoughts of death (not just fear of dying), recurrent suicidal ideation, or a suicide plan or attempt
B. Symptoms do not meet criteria for a "mixed episode."
C. Symptoms cause clinically significant distress or impairment in social, occupational, or other functioning.
D. Symptoms are not caused by direct physiologic effects of a substance (e.g., drug of abuse, medication) or a general medical condition (e.g., hypothyroidism).
E. Symptoms are not better accounted for by bereavement; after the loss of a loved one, the symptoms persist for longer than 2 months or are characterized by marked functional impairment, morbid preoccupation with worthlessness, suicidal ideation, psychotic symptoms, or psychomotor retardation.

Modified from the *Diagnostic and Statistical Manual of Mental Disorders*, 4th ed, Text Revision. Washington, DC, 2000, American Psychiatric Association.

---

experience at least five symptoms for a minimum of 2 weeks.

Mood Disturbances

Depressed mood is painful and referred to as being anguished, sad, gloomy, dejected, unhappy, discouraged, or in low spirits. The mood may also involve feelings of anxiety and irritability. The patient's feelings can be so intensely painful that suicide may be seen as the only way to terminate the agony.

Anhedonia refers to the inability to experience pleasure or interest in formerly pleasurable or satisfying activities. The patient must have actually stopped doing the formerly pleasurable activities, for example, an avid tennis or golf player who gives up playing entirely. Questions can help to elicit loss of interest or pleasure: "When were you last feeling well?"; "When you were feeling well, what kinds of things did you do for enjoyment?"; "Are you doing those things now?"; and "Are you enjoying them?"[29]

BOX 109-2. Factors in Evaluating Depression: "IN SAD CAGES"

INterest
Sleep
Appetite
Depressed mood
Concentration
Activity
Guilt
Energy
Suicide

Change in Psychomotor Activity

Psychomotor disturbances can take the form of retardation or agitation. *Psychomotor retardation* includes significant slowing of thought processes and physical activity. The patient is slow to answer questions and moves slowly or not at all. Questioning such patients in the emergency department may be frustrating when the answers come slowly, in short words or phrases, and are low in volume and lack inflection. The "body language" of depression includes sitting slumped over, arms folded, mouth turned down, and eyes closed or downcast. Such slowing clearly affects the patient's work, school, or family functioning. Symptoms may be erroneously attributed to worsening dementia in elderly persons. An alternative presentation is *psychomotor agitation,* in which the patient fidgets, paces, rubs the skin, and is unable to sit still. Other common, almost stereotypical manifestations include hand wringing and tugging at the hair.

Vegetative symptoms include disturbances in three major areas: sleep, appetite, and sexual function. Depressed patients typically report some form of sleep disorder, such as difficulty falling asleep, middle insomnia, or the classic symptoms of early-morning wakening and inability to fall back to sleep. Some depressed patients may report sleeping 12 to 14 hours a day and inability to arise in the morning. This may be a more common symptom in depressed teenagers. The depressed patient may lose appetite and weight or may gain weight in a short time. Loss of interest in sexual activity and impotence can be considered vegetative symptoms; they may accompany depression or may be part of the anhedonia associated with depressed mood.

Cognitive Dysfunction

Depressed patients are unable to concentrate or think properly, which can cause significant dysfunction in a job or profession. Thought content is negative, such as recurrent thoughts of guilt, failure, worthlessness, and self-criticism. Suicide may preoccupy the patient's thinking and may reinforce feelings of helplessness, perpetuating self-reproach. The patient may formulate a definite plan for ending life. Depressed patients must be questioned about suicidal thoughts and plans, which allow them to describe their pain and may provide them with some relief (see Chapter 113).

Psychosis

Psychosis may accompany severe depression. Hallucinations and delusions are classified as mood congruent or mood incongruent. *Mood-congruent* delusions reflect the depressed mood. The patient may report, for example, being "already dead" or feeling like "my insides have rotted away." Hallucinations typically consist of voices saying extremely unpleasant things or punishing the patient for previous wrongs. *Mood-incongruent* delusions do not reflect the depressed mood as clearly and include the paranoid delusions of being followed and having one's thoughts controlled by external forces.

Masked Depression

Mood disorders may not be clear at presentation. The depressed patient may have only vague physical symptoms, such as weakness, fatigue, headache, or complaints of pain. Patients may not be aware of their depression and are often heavy utilizers of medical care. Such symptoms may be the presenting features of a masked, or *hidden,* depression. Clues suggesting mood disturbance include the recent onset of a set of unusual behaviors, trouble at work or job loss, marital difficulties, or self-destructive behavior (e.g., substance abuse, sexual promiscuity).

Children and Adolescents

A common and overt presentation of depression in an older child or teenager is a suicide attempt. Such patients should be considered depressed and unstable until subsequent assessment differentiates depression from other conditions in these age groups, including transient psychoses, anxiety disorders, high levels of life stress, and substance abuse.

Symptoms of depression in children and adolescents generally follow the same criteria as for adults. Some children are misdiagnosed as having attention deficit disorder, especially if symptoms involve poor concentration, listlessness, agitation, and withdrawal from daily activities. Depression in these age groups is often misunderstood, masked in its presentation, or simply overlooked by friends, parents, teachers, and physicians. Adequate treatment maximizes the child's potential and minimizes the serious negative impact depression can have on multiple spheres of development. An overdose that "clears" is only the tip of a major issue for each child or adolescent patient and the family.

Elderly Persons

Depression is common in elderly persons; losses and grief, serious health issues, and loss of autonomy create a setting conducive to depression. The classic symptoms of moderate to severe depression, with or without psychosis, are typically seen. Depressed patients can present with symptoms involving memory loss, inattention, withdrawal from daily activities, confusion, and lapses in personal and social hygiene that suggest dementia rather than depression. When such symptoms result from depression, the condition is called *pseudodementia*. Serious depression in elderly patients is a highly treatable, reversible condition. Distinguishing it from dementia is essential for further diagnostic and therapeutic follow-up.

Other Depressive Disorders

Seasonal Affective Disorder

Seasonal affective disorder is a subclassification of major depressive disorder that is diagnosed when major depression occurs during seasons with less daylight (fall and winter), then either resolves or changes to manic episodes in seasons with more daylight, for at least 2 consecutive years. Phototherapy is an effective and safe treatment for this "winter depression,"[30] which appears to be mediated by ultraviolet radiation through the retina.

Postpartum Depression

Symptoms of depression are common in the postnatal period. Up to 65% of mothers report some depressed mood after childbirth, often called "baby blues." Almost one quarter of mothers feel "moderately depressed" or "very depressed" in the postpartum period. Forty-four percent of these women report symptoms lasting a few days, 16% have symptoms a few months, 3.9% are still depressed 1 year after the birth, and 1.5% report thoughts of suicide.[31]

Postpartum depression seems to be more prevalent in those who have mood disorder, are unemployed, or have no assistance with infant care. Severe postpartum depression may negatively influence development in the child.[32]

Dysthymic Disorder

Dysthymic disorder is a long-standing, fluctuating, low-grade depression. Some features of a major depressive episode may be present, but marked changes in appetite or psychomotor disturbance are not typically observed. Depressed mood typically begins early in life, and the individual may report having always been depressed. Affected individuals typically are able to carry out their work assignments diligently, but they gain little pleasure from the leisure activities others find enjoyable, such as recreation, time with family, or sexual activity.

Bipolar Disorders

Bipolar disorder is lifelong, with episodic exacerbation of symptoms and deterioration of function characterized by extreme mood swings. Patients with bipolar disorder thus require different forms and intensities of treatment at different times. *Bipolar I disorder* includes at least one *manic* episode, and patients have typically had one or more major depressive episodes. *Bipolar II*

BOX 109-3. Summary of DSM-IV Criteria for Manic Episode

A. Distinct period of abnormally and persistently elevated, expansive, or irritable mood, lasting at least 2 weeks (or any duration if hospitalization is necessary).
B. During the period of mood disturbance, three or more of the following symptoms have persisted (four if the mood is only irritable) and have been present to a significant degree:
   1. Inflated self-esteem or grandiosity
   2. Decreased need for sleep (e.g., feels rested after only 3 hours of sleep)
   3. More talkative than usual or pressure to keep talking
   4. Flight of ideas or subjective experience that thoughts are racing
   5. Distractibility (i.e., attention too easily drawn to unimportant or irrelevant external stimuli)
   6. Increase in goal-directed activity (either socially, at work or school, or sexually) or psychomotor agitation
   7. Excessive involvement in pleasurable activities that have a high potential for painful consequences (e.g., buying sprees, sexual indiscretions, foolish investments)
C. Symptoms do not meet criteria for a "mixed episode."
D. Mood disturbance is sufficiently severe to cause marked impairment in occupational functioning or social activities or to necessitate hospitalization to prevent harm to self or others, or psychotic features are present.
E. Symptoms are not caused by direct physiologic effects of a substance (e.g., drug of abuse, medication) or a general medical condition (e.g., hyperthyroidism).

Modified from the *Diagnostic and Statistical Manual of Mental Disorders*, 4th ed, Text Revision. Washington, DC, 2000, American Psychiatric Association.

---

disorder involves a *hypomanic* episode and at least one major depressive episode. A hypomanic episode includes the features of a manic episode without psychosis, marked impairment of function, or the need for hospitalization.

Manic Episode

As defined by DSM-IV-TR criteria (Box 109-3), to be considered manic the disturbance must be severe enough to cause psychosis, the need for hospitalization, or marked impairment in functioning. Bipolar disorders are much less common than major depressive disorder. The overall prevalence of a manic episode is 1.6% in both women and men.[33]

Patients who are experiencing a manic episode may be gregarious, humorous, and engaging. An alternative presentation is one of belligerence and irritability. Initial clues to mania include a history of the patient's behavior immediately before the evaluation and any prior history of bipolar disorder or a history of taking medications almost exclusively prescribed for bipolar disorder, such as lithium. In most cases, the manic patient will be brought to the emergency department by someone else (e.g., family, police, emergency medical services). They often try to leave as soon as possible, display impaired judgment and impulsivity, and may need to be restrained.

Pressured speech is one of the first clinical signs of mania. The patient keeps talking, with no interruption between thoughts or sentences. The speech may be loud and rapid, with creative, amusing, or trivial and irrelevant content. The patient may tell jokes, use puns, or play other word association games. A hallmark of mania is *grandiosity,* which involves feelings of inflated self-esteem and great personal importance. The patient may describe a massive undertaking such as "uniting the world's churches" or "solving world poverty."

Manic patients have decreased or no need for sleep and typically report being awake for days during a manic episode. They may be involved in a massive project (e.g., writing a novel), may completely disregard consequences of actions, may have difficulty with spending (e.g., credit cards revoked), and may engage in risky behavior (e.g., sexual liaisons with strangers, risky driving) An accurate history must be obtained from family or others who know the patient's behavior.

Manic patients may present to the emergency department as trauma patients, injured by an action reflecting the patient's grandiosity (e.g., attempting to fly), impulsivity, or belligerence (e.g., fighting, resisting arrest). A manic episode may be punctuated by abrupt periods of tearfulness and profound depression, including suicidal ideation. When depressive and manic features occur concurrently in such a manner, the disorder is termed *mixed* or *bipolar, mixed phase.*

Cyclothymic Disorder

Cyclothymic disorder is characterized by a life of mood swings of insufficient severity to meet criteria for a bipolar disorder. Persons with this disorder may have a chaotic life, characterized by frequent mood swings, unstable relationships, and uneven school or work performance.

Mood Disorders Caused by General Medical Condition

Certain medical illnesses have a well-known association with mood disorder (Box 109-4). In Parkinson's disease, electrical stimulation to a certain area of the substantia nigra alleviates symptoms of depression. Stimulation of an area only 2 mm away can cause acute reversible symptoms of depression, such as crying, not wanting to live, and hopelessness.[34] Parkinson's disease has a well-known association with depression, with up to 40% of parkinsonian patients demonstrating major depression.[35]

Certain malignancies have a well-known association with depression, including pancreatic carcinoma, brain neoplasm, and disseminated malignancy (e.g., lymphoma).[36] Coronary artery disease,[37] myocardial infarction, stroke, end-stage renal disease, acquired immunodeficiency syndrome, several endocrine diseases, and connective tissue disease are also associated with major depressive disorder.[38] After a myocardial infarction, patients with depression experience a 3.5-fold increase in cardiovascular mortality compared with patients without depression after a myocardial infarction.[39] Patients with depression appear to be more likely to develop stroke, diabetes, and osteoporosis than those who are not depressed.[40,41]

Slowly emerging is the concept that in patients with depression related to medical conditions, the depression is different in some respects than primary depression. Depression in the medically ill, for instance, responds less favorably to antidepressant medication than primary depression.[42] Two other issues arise in the assessment of patients with depression and serious medical illness (e.g., malignancy, acquired immunodeficiency syndrome). First, depression must be distinguished from the symptoms and signs associated with serious medical illness (e.g., weight loss, loss of energy, slowing of activity, sleep disturbance, loss of ability to concentrate). Alternative criteria for depression can be substituted for DSM-IV-TR criteria in patients with serious medical illness: *depressed appearance* for loss of appetite, *social withdrawal* for sleep disturbance, *pessimism* or *self-pity* for energy loss, and *nonreactive mood* for difficulty concentrating. Second, it is important to determine whether the depression associated with terminal, rapidly progressive, or painful illness is understandable or appropriate. Although patients with such diseases may understandably be sad, most do not have major depression. The treatment of major depression in such patients can greatly improve their quality of life.

Mood Disorders Caused by Medications or Other Substances

Certain medications are associated with symptoms of mood disorders (Box 109-5). A medication-induced mood disorder should be considered if the patient has no history of depression before taking the medication.

Intoxication or chronic heavy use of alcohol, sedatives, hypnotics, anxiolytics, narcotics, and other

---

BOX 109-4. Medical Illnesses Associated with Onset of Depression

Neurologic
Parkinson's disease
Stroke
Multiple sclerosis
Head trauma
Sleep apnea

Neoplastic
Pancreatic carcinoma
Brain tumor
Disseminated carcinomatosis

Endocrine
Hypothyroidism
Hyperthyroidism
Cushing's disease
Addison's disease
Diabetes mellitus

Infectious
Human immunodeficiency virus

Cardiac
Coronary artery disease
Myocardial infarction

Renal
End-stage renal disease
Renal dialysis

Connective Tissue
Lupus erythematosus
Rheumatoid arthritis

Substance Abuse
Alcohol
Drugs of abuse

BOX 109-5. Medications that Can Cause Depressive or Manic Symptoms

Depressive Symptoms

Antihypertensives
β-Blockers
Captopril
Clonidine
Diltiazem
Enalapril
Nifedipine
Prazosin
Thiazide diuretics

Anticonvulsants
Phenytoin
Valproic acid

Hormones
Anabolic steroids
Contraceptives
Corticosteroids
Thyroid hormone

Sedative-Hypnotics
Barbiturates
Benzodiazepines

Manic Symptoms
Psychiatric Agents
Antidepressants
Bupropion
Loxapine
Monoamine oxidase inhibitors

Antibiotics
Acyclovir
Chloroquine
Interferon
Isoniazid
Norfloxacin
Ofloxacin
Sulfonamides

Other Agents
Amantadine
Bromocriptine
Cyclobanzaprine
Cycloserine
Digitalis
Disopyramide
Levodopa
Metoclopramide
Nonsteroidal anti-inflammatory drugs
Phenylpropanolamine
Theophylline
Thyroid hormone

depressants can cause symptoms of a major depressive episode. Stimulants such as cocaine, phencyclidine, hallucinogens, and amphetamines can cause symptoms of a manic episode. Mood disorder symptoms can also develop during withdrawal. To qualify for this diagnosis, the symptoms must not occur exclusively during delirium and must cause significant distress or impairment of functioning..

When the mood disorder predates the period of substance abuse or lasts longer than 1 month after the period of abuse, the diagnosis may be an underlying mood disorder, such as a major depressive disorder or bipolar disorder, with a comorbid substance abuse or dependence diagnosis.

Substance abuse is typically seen in patients who self-treat underlying depressive or bipolar symptoms, especially adolescents.

DIAGNOSTIC STRATEGIES

The initial history and physical examination should focus on the presenting complaints and evaluate the possibility that drug abuse, medications, or a general medical condition may be responsible for the patient's condition. The diagnosis of a mood disorder is based on history and observation of the patient's ability and style in relating to family and medical staff. The patient's body language may be helpful. Precipitating events (e.g., loss of job or relationship), accompanying symptoms (e.g., hallucinations, delusions, anxiety dis-

order, mania), and suicidal intent should be assessed. The patient's history should be confirmed through interviews with family, friends, or eyewitnesses to the events that precipitated the emergency department visit. A tentative diagnosis can be established using DSM-IV-TR criteria. Laboratory tests to investigate medical conditions may be necessary (see Box 109-4), but no tests can confirm or exclude mood disorders.

DIFFERENTIAL CONSIDERATIONS

Medical disorders, medications, and substance abuse or withdrawal not only can cause but also can mimic mood disorders. The patient who presents with agitation, for example, might have hypoxia, cocaine intoxication, or alcohol-sedative withdrawal. The patient with symptoms and signs of depression may have an unrecognized malignancy or sedative intoxication.

Antidepressant medications are used to treat a variety of disorders, such as anxiety, obsessive-compulsive disorder, posttraumatic stress disorder, pain syndromes, smoking cessation, and vasodepressor syncope. Patients taking antidepressant medication are often not being treated for depression.

Grief and *bereavement* are normal human reactions to the acute loss of another person, health, social position, or job. The period of mourning is characterized by sadness, diminished sense of well-being (somatic complaints), sleeplessness, and sadness triggered by thoughts of the loss. Normal grief, however, does not include guilt, loss of self-esteem, feelings of worthlessness, suicidal intent, psychomotor retardation, or occupational dysfunction.

Adjustment disorders are behavioral or emotional disorders that occur in response to an identifiable stress or stressors. The emotional component can involve sadness, low self-esteem, suicidal behavior, hopelessness, helplessness, or other self-threatening behavior. Acute adjustment disorder occurs within 3 months of the stressor and does not last longer than 6 months. The stressors are typically not as severe as those precipitating bereavement reaction, and the responses are often more maladaptive. The teenager who ends a romantic relationship, for instance, may attempt drug overdose in response to the stress. In such cases, adjustment disorder is a more likely diagnosis than major depressive episode. The pattern of recurrent maladaptive behavioral responses to stress may be lifelong, but the acute episode should resolve within 6 months.

Borderline personality disorder is characterized by unstable personal relationships, unstable self-image, and inappropriate behaviors. The disorder may include chronic feelings of emptiness, which may be misdiagnosed as depression, or lability of mood, which may be mistaken for mania or hypomania. Borderline patients typically live lives of crisis and constant conflict.

Dementia can be confused with depression. Dementia is characterized by abnormal mental status, including abnormalities in tests of memory, calculation, and judgment. Delirium with waxing and waning sensorium, hallucinations, and delusions may involve disorganization, agitation, and restlessness, which might first be considered features of mania or agitated depression.

Differential considerations for manic symptoms include the manic phase of bipolar disorder, stimulant abuse (e.g., cocaine, amphetamines), hallucinogen abuse, alcohol or sedative withdrawal, delirium, hyperthyroidism, other medical conditions causing agitation, brief reactive psychosis, schizoaffective disorder, and schizophrenia.

MANAGEMENT

Emergency Department Stabilization

The creation of a safe and stable environment must be a first priority in management. The patient with an acute manic episode may be disruptive, refuse medical evaluation, and make repeated attempts to leave the emergency department. Hospital security personnel should be summoned early and, depending on the patient's behavior, can remain to show that disruptive behavior will not be tolerated. When necessary, security personnel can apply physical restraints and search the patient for weapons.

Initiating treatment for a mood disorder is not typically done in the emergency department. An exception is the acute manic episode (or possibly a severe depressive episode with psychosis) with behavior so extreme that the patient or others are threatened. Such cases may well involve significant hallucinations, delusions, and other features of psychoses. In such cases an antipsychotic agent is often indicated. For years, clinicians have used intramuscular or oral haloperidol with or without lorazepam to calm such patients. A typical regimen for "rapid tranquilization" is an initial dose of 5 mg haloperidol with 2 mg lorazepam intramuscularly and patient reassessment in 30 to 45 minutes for resolution of "target" symptoms such as agitation. The patient is then monitored for improvement in hallucinations, delusions, agitation, or violent behavior, and another 5-mg dose is administered after 30 to 60 minutes as needed.[43] Most patients usually respond after one or two doses. Benztropine (Cogentin), 1 to 2 mg, is often given initially to prevent extrapyramidal symptoms. Droperidol was popular for this purpose but has fallen out of favor because of a "black box" Food and Drug Administration warning about prolongation of QT intervals and torsades de pointes ventricular arrhythmias associated with its use.[44]

A newer class of agents are the "atypical" antipsychotic medicines, which currently include ziprasidone, risperidone, and olanzapine. The atypical agents are favored because they produce few of the side effects associated with conventional antipsychotic agents, such as acute dystonia, other extrapyramidal symptoms, and sedation. Ziprasidone is currently the only atypical antipsychotic available for intramuscular use. A dose of 20 mg is used initially and can be repeated in 4 hours.[45,46] Small doses of lorazepam can be used in the interim if needed. Both risperidone and olanzapine are available in rapidly dissolving tablet form and can be used if the patient accepts oral medications (see

Chapter 108).[47-50] Immediate psychiatric consultation should begin during the initiation of rapid tranquilization, since patients undergoing rapid tranquilization will generally require hospitalization (Box 109-6).

Long-Term Treatment

Depression

Effective treatment modalities for depression are grouped into three broad categories: antidepressant medication, psychotherapy, and electroconvulsive therapy (ECT).

Antidepressant Therapy

Many equally effective antidepressants are available for first-episode uncomplicated major depression. After 4 to 6 weeks of therapy, the response rate is usually 60% or greater for all agents. However, 10% to 15% of patients quit medication trials,[51] and many patients in general medical practice are inadequately treated.[52]

Coexistent medical illness, psychotic or bipolar symptoms, substance use, and recurrent or refractory depressive symptoms must be considered in the choice of a medication for treatment of depression. Sensitivity to the side effects of the tricyclic antidepressants and the significant risks of serious side effects with monoamine oxidase inhibitors, along with strict dietary limitations, have led to a significant rise in the use of selective serotonin-reuptake inhibitors as first-line treatment for depression. Side effects of selective serotonin-reuptake inhibitors include dizziness, sedation, peripheral anticholinergic symptoms, weight gain, sexual dysfunction, neurologic symptoms, cardiovascular symptoms, insomnia, and anxiety. Another antidepressant, ECT, thyroid hormone, or other psychoactive medication can be added for patients with treatment-resistant depression.

Psychotherapy

Brief psychotherapy based on the cognitive-behavioral approach is often initially employed in patients with major depression. Interpersonal psychotherapy, psychodynamic psychotherapy, and group or marital/family therapy are also used with some patients. Psychosocial therapeutic support typically includes community-based support groups that focus on specific individual, occupational, or family/marital issues that arise in depression and are amenable to group and supportive intervention.

Depressed patients benefit most from a combination of somatic therapy (medication and/or ECT) and psychotherapy. All patients with incomplete therapeutic response, recurrent depression, or comorbid conditions (e.g., anxiety/panic, substance abuse) should receive multimodal treatment.[53]

Electroconvulsive Therapy

Electroconvulsive therapy has a high therapeutic success rate and an excellent safety profile but is not a first-line treatment for uncomplicated major depression. In part, this is a result of an undeserved reputation among laypersons that ECT causes "permanent brain damage." Indications for ECT include severe depression with malnutrition, severe psychosis with agitation, continuing significant suicide risk with ongoing suicidal behaviors, and prolonged catatonia. ECT is a first-line treatment for patients with recurrent depression who previously had a positive response to ECT. ECT is more often used as a second-line treatment for patients with moderate to severe depression who have not responded to trials of medication or who cannot tolerate the medication because of side effects or concurrent medical conditions.

Bipolar Disorders

Bipolar disorder is treated primarily with mood stabilizing drugs, including lithium, valproate, and carbamazepine. Almost all bipolar patients require a mood stabilizer during exacerbation of depression or mania, and most patients benefit from a mood stabilizer for ongoing supportive maintenance treatment as well. Lithium was the first highly effective mood-stabilizing agent for the treatment of bipolar patients.[54] Valproate is a very effective mood stabilizer with dose-related side effects, most of which clear after an initial period of treatment or with reduced dosage.[55] Valproate can be instituted rapidly in acutely manic bipolar patients.[56] Both lithium and valproate serum levels are routinely monitored during therapy. The therapeutic window is much wider for valproate than for lithium. Carbamazepine also has dose-related side effects but has potentially lethal reactions as well, including blood dyscrasias, exfoliative dermatitis, pancreatitis, and hepatic failure. These conditions are rare and are not reliably predicted by laboratory monitoring.

Mood-stabilizing medications usually take 3 or more weeks to become effective.[57] Some bipolar patients require antipsychotic medications and benzodiazepines in the interim to control symptoms. Some patients with bipolar disorder have persistent psychotic symptoms requiring continuing use of a major neuroleptic, such as haloperidol, ziprasidone (Geodon), risperidone (Risperdal), olanzapine (Zyprexa), or quetiapine (Seroquel).[58] After 3 weeks, a second mood-stabilizing medication or ECT is often added for patients who have a partial response to an initial mood-stabilizing course of treatment.[59] For bipolar patients with a depressive episode, the addition of an antidepressant medication is often helpful.

Bipolar patients are sensitive to psychosocial stressors, changes in medication dosage, and medical illness. This sensitivity can lead to a marked worsening in a patient's level of adaptation and functioning. It is helpful to understand these precipitating stressors when developing a therapeutic support plan for patients. Psychosocial therapeutic support, including individual psychotherapy, supportive community groups, family/marital treatment, and occupational support, are important in both the acute phase and the maintenance phase of treatment for bipolar patients.

KEY CONCEPTS

- Patients with apparent mood disorders should be evaluated for a medical disorder, medication effect, or drug use that can mimic both depression and mania. A mental status examination is helpful in this assessment.
- Mood disorders should be suspected in patients with multiple, vague, nonspecific complaints, or in patients who are frequent, heavy utilizers of medical care.
- The differentiation of depression and dementia in elderly patients can be difficult but is important, since depression often responds dramatically to treatment, whereas dementia does not respond.
- Patients with mood disorders should be assessed for their potential for violence or self-harm before discharge.
- Patients who have harmed themselves or who have positive responses when questioned about features of depression should be assessed for suicide risk.

REFERENCES

1. American Psychiatric Association: *Diagnostic and Statistical Manual of Medical Disorders,* 4th ed, Text Revision. Washington, DC, American Psychiatric Association, 2000.
2. Dubovsky SL, Buron R: Mood disorders. In *Textbook of Psychiatry,* 3rd ed. Washington, DC, American Psychiatric Press, 1999.
3. Hazlett SB, McCarthy ML, Londner MS, Onyike CH: Epidemiology of adult psychiatric visits to U.S. emergency departments. *Acad Emerg Med* 11:193, 2004.
4. World Health Organization: *The World Health Report 2002: Reviewing Risks, Promoting Healthy Life.* Geneva, World Health Organization, 2002.
5. Kessler RC, et al: The epidemiology of major depressive disorder: Results from the National Comorbidity Survey Replication (NCS-R). *JAMA* 289:3095, 2003.
6. Curran GM, et al: Emergency department use of persons with comorbid psychiatric and substance abuse disorders. *Ann Emerg Med* 41:659, 2003.
7. Mueller TI, Deon AC: Recovery, chronicity and levels of psychopathology in major depression. *Psychiatr Clin North Am* 19:85, 1996.
8. Cross-National Collaborative Group: The changing rate of major depression: Cross-national comparisons. *JAMA* 268:3098, 1992.
9. Colp R Jr: Psychiatry: Past and future. In Sadock BJ, Sadock VA (eds): *Comprehensive Textbook of Psychiatry.* Philadelphia, Lippincott Williams & Wilkins, 1999.
10. Schildkraut JJ: The catecholamine hypothesis of affective disorders: A review of supporting evidence. *Am J Psychiatry* 122:509, 1965.

11. Thase ME: Mood disorders: Neurobiology. In Sadock BJ, Sadock VA (eds): *Comprehensive Textbook of Psychiatry.* Philadelphia, Lippincott Williams & Wilkins, 1999.

12. Bremner JD, et al: Regional brain metabolic correlates of alpha-methylparatyrosine-induced depressive symptoms: Implications for the neural circuitry of depression. *JAMA* 289:3125, 2003.

13. Thase ME, Howland RH: Biological processes in depression: An updated review and integration. In Beckhamee EE, Leber WR (eds): *Handbook of Depression,* 2nd ed. New York, Guilford, 1995.

14. Petty F, et al: Learned helplessness sensitizes hippocampal norepinephrine to mild restlessness. *Biol Psychiatry* 35:901, 1994.

15. Weiss JM: Stress induced depression: Critical neurochemical and electrophysiological change. In Madden J IV (ed): *Neurobiology of Learning Emotion and Affect.* New York, Raven, 1991.

16. Higley TD, et al: Cerebrospinal fluid monoamine and adrenal correlates of aggression in free ranging rhesus monkeys. *Arch Gen Psychiatry* 49:436, 1992.

17. Brown GL, Linnoila MI: CSF serotonin metabolite (5-H1AA) studies in depression impulsivity and violence. *J Clin Psychiatry* 51(suppl 4):31, 1990.

18. Kandel ER, et al: *Principles of Neural Science,* 3rd ed. New York, Elsevier, 1991.

19. Spoont MR: Modulatory role of serotonin in neural information processing: Implications for human psychopathology. *Psychol Bull* 112:330, 1992.

20. Joffe RT, et al: A placebo-controlled comparison of lithium and triiodothyronine augmentation of tricyclic antidepressants in unipolar refractory depression. *Arch Gen Psychiatry* 50:387, 1993.

21. Tsuang MT, Farone SV: The inheritance of mood disorders. In Hall LL (ed): *Genetics and Mental Illness: Evolving Issues for Research and Society.* New York, Plenum, 1996.

22. Kendler KS, Prescott CA: A twin study of major depression. *Arch Gen Psychiatry* 56:39, 1999.

23. Mann J, et al: Possible association of a polymorphism of the tryptophan hydroxylase gene with suicidal behavior in depressed patients. *Am J Psychiatry* 154:1451, 1997.

24. Zhang H, et al: Serotonin receptor gene polymorphism in mood disorders. *Biol Psychiatry* 41:768, 1997.

25. Roy A: Genetics of suicide in depression. *J Clin Psychiatry* 60(suppl 2):12, 1999.

26. Freud S: Mourning and melancholia. In *Complete Psychological Works of Sigmund Freud,* vol 4. London, Hogwarth, 1975.

27. Suomi SJ: Early stress and emotional reactivity in rhesus monkeys. In Ciba Foundation Symposium: *Childhood Environment and Adult Disease.* Chichester, England, Wiley, 1991.

28. Akiskal MS: Mood disorders: Clinical features. In Sadock BJ, Sadock VA (eds): *Comprehensive Textbook of Psychiatry.* Philadelphia, Lippincott Williams & Wilkins, 1999.

29. Goldberg RJ: *Practical Guide to the Care of the Psychiatric Patient,* 2nd ed. St Louis, Mosby, 1998.

30. Lam RW, et al: Effects of light therapy on suicidal ideation in patients with winter depression. *J Clin Psychiatry* 61:30, 2000.

31. Najman JM, et al: Postnatal depression—myth and reality: Maternal depression before and after the birth of a child. *Soc Psychiatry Psychiatr Epidemiol* 35:19, 2000.

32. Whiffen VE, Gotlib IM: Infants of postpartum depressed mothers: Temperament and cognitive status. J Abnorm Psychol 98:274, 1989.

33. Hendrick V, et al: Gender and bipolar illness. J Clin Psychiatry 61:393, 2000.

34. Bejjani B-P, et al: Transient acute depression induced by high frequency deep brain stimulation. *N Engl J Med* 340:1476, 1999.

35. Cummings JL: Depression and Parkinson's disease: A review. *Am J Psychiatry* 149:443, 1992.

36. McDaniel JS, et al: Depression in patients with cancer: Diagnosis, biology, and treatment, *Arch Gen Psychiatry* 52:89, 1995.

37. Gonzalez MB, et al: Depression in patients with coronary artery disease. *Depression* 4:57, 1996.

38. Evans DL, et al: Depression in the medical setting: Biopsychological interactions and treatment considerations. *J Clin Psychiatry* 60:40, 1999.

39. Gilbody S, Whitty P, Grimshaw J, Thomas R: Educational and organizational interventions to improve the management of depression in primary care: A systematic review. *JAMA* 289:3145, 2003.

40. Pignone MP, et al: Screening for depression in adults: A summary of the evidence for the US Preventive Services Task Force. *Ann Intern Med* 136:765, 2002.

41. Insel TR, Charney DS: Research on major depression: Strategies and priorities. *JAMA* 289:3167, 2003.

42. Popin MK: Consultation-liaison psychiatry. In Jacobson JL, Jacobson AM (eds): *Psychiatry Secrets,* 2nd ed. Philadelphia, Hanley and Belfus, 2004.

43. Nockwitz R, Rund DA: Psychotropic medications. In Tintinalli JE, et al (eds): *Emergency Medicine: A Comprehensive Study Guide*, 6th ed., Columbus, Ohio, McGraw-Hill, 2003.

44. Horowitz BZ, Bizovi K, Moreno R: Droperidol—behind the black box warning. *Acad Emerg Med* 9:615, 2002.

45. Daniel DG, Potkin SG, Reeves KR, et al: Intramuscular (IM) ziprasidone 20 mg is effective in reducing acute agitation associated with psychosis: A double-blind randomized trial. *Pharmacology* 155:128, 2001.

46. Brook S, et al: Intramuscular ziprasidone compared with intramuscular haloperidol in the treatment of acute psychosis. *J Clin Psychiatry.* 61:933, 2000.

47. Allen MH, et al: The Expert Consensus Guideline Series: Treatment of behavioral emergencies. *Postgrad Med* May(Spec No):1, 2001.

48. Currier GW, Simpson GM: Risperidone liquid concentrate and oral lorazepam versus intramuscular haloperidol and intramuscular lorazepam for treatment of psychotic agitation. *J Clin Psychiatry* 62:153, 2001.

49. Citrome L: Atypical antipsychotics for acute agitation: New intramuscular options offer advantages. *Postgrad Med* 112:85, 2002.

50. Battaglia J, et al: Calming versus sedative effects of intramuscular olenzapine in agitated patients. *Am J Emerg Med* 21:192, 2003.

51. McIntyre JS, et al: *Practice Guideline for Major Depressive Disorder in Adults.* Washington, DC, American Psychiatric Association, 1996.

52. Gilbody S, et al: Educational and organizational interventions to improve the management of depression in primary care: A systematic review. *JAMA* 289:3145, 2003.

53. Scott J: Treatment of chronic depression. *N Engl J Med* 342:1518, 2000.

54. Schou M: *Lithium Treatment of Manic-Depressive Illness: A Practical Guide,* 5th ed. New York, Karger, 1993.

55. McElroy SL, et al: Valproate in the treatment of bipolar disorder: Literature review and clinical guidelines. *J Clin Psychopharmacol* 12:42S, 1992.

56. Hirschfeld RMA, et al: Safety and tolerability of oral loading divalproex sodium in acutely manic bipolar patients. *J Clin Psychiatry* 60:815, 1999.

57. Compton MT, Nemeroff CB: The treatment of bipolar depression. *J Clin Psychiatry* 61:57, 2000.

58. Sernyak MJ, Woods SW: Chronic neuroleptic use in manic-depressive illness. *Psychopharmacol Bull* 29:375, 1993.

59. Mukherjee S, Sackeim HA, Schnurr DB: Electroconvulsive therapy of acute manic episodes: A review. *Am J Psychiatry* 151:169, 1994.

110 Anxiety Disorders

Eugene E. Kercher and Joshua L. Tobias

Anxiety is essential to the human condition. Confrontation with anxiety can relieve us from boredom, sharpen our sensitivity, and create the tension which is necessary to preserve human existence.

Rollo May

Acute anxiety and apprehension are common in emergency department patients. Many medical entities mimic anxiety disorders, and up to 42% of patients thought to have anxiety disorders are later found to have organic disease. Emergency physicians must thoroughly assess the anxious patient and recognize and appropriately treat any underlying medical conditions.[1]

PERSPECTIVE

Anxiety is defined as a specific unpleasurable state of tension that forewarns the presence of danger. This uneasiness stems from the anticipation of some imminent danger, the source of which is largely unknown and unrecognized. Vigilance is a positive consequence of anxiety, helping people to recognize threats quickly, which produces more learning and more intelligence. The capacity to experience anxiety and the capacity to plan are therefore related, with anxiety accompanying intellectual activity as its "shadow."[1]

Anxiety facilitates performance up to a point of "moderate" stress. Beyond this point, further increases in anxiety may lead to deterioration of performance. In addition to the well-described adrenergic responses to stress that contribute to survival, nonadaptive responses may also be a source of stress to the patient. The threshold for pain decreases, and the person becomes more aware of bodily discomfort. Respiratory, cardiovascular, gastrointestinal, genitourinary, and neuromuscular complaints become prominent.[1]

Pathologic anxiety (anxiety disorders) occurs when anxiety surpasses a normal response to the "threat" at hand and interferes with normal functioning. Some patients may be unaware that underlying anxiety causes their symptoms, whereas others may be consciously anxious.[2]

The emergency physician should not assume that anxiety is purely functional, because physical discomfort often triggers an anxiety attack. The anxiety state makes significant metabolic demands that may actually cause a marginally compensated organ system to fail. Emergency physicians must be able to distinguish between the anxiety and the illness and, if necessary, treat both entities.

EPIDEMIOLOGY

Millions of individuals each year seek help for what is broadly construed as anxiety or nervousness. Anxiety disorders are among the most prevalent psychiatric disorders, with approximately 25% of the U.S. population experiencing pathologic anxiety during their lifetime.[3] Anxiety is the most common psychiatric problem seen by primary care physicians, with 20% of these patients receiving benzodiazepines for 6 months.[4] Most people who use primary care services have significant mood and anxiety symptoms, such as panic disorders, generalized anxiety disorders, and depression. Patients with chronic illness and those who make frequent medical visits have higher rates of anxiety and depression. Anxiety is a prominent complaint in 15% of medical outpatients and 10% of medical inpatients.[4] The prevalence of anxiety disorders surpasses that of any other mental health disorder, including substance abuse. In view of the close relationship between alcohol abuse and anxiety disorders, the substance abuser is frequently found self-medicating an underlying anxiety disorder.[5]

Anxiety disorders are associated with marked impairment of physical and psychosocial function as well as quality of life. Most patients improve if treated, but only 25% of patients with an anxiety disorder receive treatment. This low treatment rate is a result of failure to diagnose, a high degree of patient denial, and physician discomfort with diagnosis and therapy.[6]

PRINCIPLES OF DISEASE

Noradrenergic, serotonergic, and other neurotransmitter systems may be biologic substrates of anxiety disorders. Anxious subjects are in a state of "overpreparedness," as indicated by physiologic measures. Heightened arousal has been demonstrated in normal subjects made anxious in the laboratory by a variety of adrenergic-stimulating procedures. Catecholamines increase in normal people as a response to stress, and any change in stimulation seems to increase catecholamine excretion. Anxiety reactions may originate as a central nervous system (CNS) arousal state that secondarily provokes peripheral events. The CNS arousal center may be the locus ceruleus, which contains at least 50% of all neurons in the CNS and is the origin of most norepinephrine pathways in the brain. Neurons, using norepinephrine as the neurotransmitter, send afferent projections to wide areas of the brain by a number of pathways. Other authorities implicate heightened serotonin activity as the basis for anxiety.[7]

The "benzodiazepine model" is based on the effects of anxiolytic drugs, specifically benzodiazepines, on various paradigms for provoking "anxiety" in animals. The neurotransmitter γ-aminobutyric acid is the principal inhibitory neurotransmitter in the CNS.[8] It decreases anxiety by hyperpolarizing other neurons, resulting in less neuronal discharge. Levels of most neurotransmitters in the brain, including γ-aminobutyric acid, decrease with age, which may predispose the older person to anxiety.[7]

Other investigators have found anxiety reactions associated with aberrant metabolic changes induced by lactate infusion and hypersensitivity of the brainstem to carbon dioxide receptors. Newer research is focusing on the regulatory centers found in the cerebral hemispheres. The hippocampus and the amygdala, which regulate emotion and memory, appear to be key areas involved in an individual's response to fear.[9] Family studies suggest that genetic factors are implicated in anxiety, but the precise nature of the inherited vulnerability is unknown. Psychological factors, as outlined in psychodynamic, behavioral, and cognitive theories, also play a causative role in the generation of anxiety in biologically predisposed individuals.[9]

CLINICAL FEATURES

Although some anxiety is routinely expected of a visit to the emergency department, anxiety is frequently a significant clinical issue. Patients encounter a world of internal and external dangers: uncomfortable procedures; forced intimacy with strangers; the atmosphere of illness, pain, and death; and separation from loved ones and familiar surroundings. They typically experience uncertainty about their illness and its implications for their capacity to work and maintain social and family relationships.

The anxious patient is a diagnostic challenge. Anxiety may represent (1) the patient's reaction to the meaning and implications of medical illness and the medical setting; (2) a manifestation of the physical disorder itself; or (3) the expression of an underlying psychiatric disorder. Anxiety as a symptom may be difficult to distinguish from anxiety as a syndrome in the emergency department, where there may be an overlap between normal situational anxiety or fear, anxiety-like symptoms resulting from a variety of organic disease states and their treatments, and the characteristic presentation of anxiety itself.

In recent years, increasing attention has been paid to the role of serious medical illness and invasive procedures in producing marked anxiety reactions that approach or meet criteria for posttraumatic stress disorder.[10]

The physical symptoms of autonomic arousal (e.g., tachypnea, tachycardia, diaphoresis, lightheadedness) may be the only manifestation of anxiety (Box 110-1). When present, affective symptoms range from mild

BOX 110-1. Somatic Symptoms of Anxiety

Respiratory
Hyperventilation
Sense of dyspnea

Cardiovascular
Palpitations
Chest discomfort
Awareness of missed beats

Gastrointestinal
Dry mouth
Difficulty in swallowing
Epigastric discomfort
Excessive flatulence
Frequent or loose stools

Genitourinary
Frequent or urgent micturition
Failure of erection
Amenorrhea
Menstrual discomfort

Neuromuscular
Tremor
Aching muscles
Prickling sensations
Headache
Dizziness, tinnitus

edginess to terror and panic.[2] Anxiety associated with organic causes is more likely to manifest with physical symptoms and less likely to be associated with avoidance behavior.[11]

DIFFERENTIAL CONSIDERATIONS

Medical Illness Manifesting as Anxiety

Anxiety disorders may manifest as apparent physical disease, and many physical diseases are accompanied by symptoms of anxiety. Differentiating between these two scenarios can be a daunting task. Moreover, many anxious patients also experience significant depression, which should also be evaluated and treated.[12] Several factors help distinguish an organic anxiety syndrome from a primary anxiety disorder (Box 110-2).[13]

Anxiety can be classified as endogenous or exogenous. Endogenous anxiety, which arises spontaneously, is not a response to an identifiable external stress or symbolic conflict, although patients may later develop conflicts and additional fears to explain their anxiety. Exogenous anxiety is an understandable but exaggerated response to an external stress or a psychological conflict (Box 110-3).[1] With anxiety, the somatic symptoms can be so prominent that they occupy most of the patient's attention, making it difficult to differentiate between endogenous and exogenous causes. The *Diagnostic and Statistical Manual of Mental Disorders* (DSM-IV) provides a classification of anxiety disorders that includes anxiety caused by general medical conditions (Box 110-4).[14]

BOX 110-2. Predictors of Organic Anxiety Syndrome

1. Onset of anxiety symptoms after age 35.
2. Lack of personal or family history of an anxiety disorder.
3. Lack of childhood history of significant anxiety phobias, or separation anxiety.
4. Lack of avoidance behavior.
5. Absence of significant life events generating or exacerbating the anxiety symptoms.
6. Poor response to antipanic agents.

BOX 110-3. Types of Exogenous Anxiety

- **Traumatic anxiety** is an overwhelming state of panic occurring in the face of great stress, such as rape or a severe physical or medical illness.
- **Separation anxiety** occurs in the face of separation or the threat of separation from a significant person or position.
- **Castration anxiety** is a morbid fear of bodily injury.
- **Instinctual anxiety** is a fear of "something inside welling up" and causing loss of control.
- **Conscience anxiety** is a fear of being "found out" for not acting up to one's standards.
- **Reactionary anxiety** is a response to normal life events, such as birth, marriage, death, loss of position, poverty, and deterioration of physical and mental well-being.

From Kercher EE: Anxiety. *Emerg Med Clin North Am* 9:161, 1991.

BOX 110-4. Definitions of Anxiety Disorders

- **Panic attack** is a discrete period in which there is a sudden onset of intense apprehension, fearfulness, or terror, often associated with feelings of impending doom.
- **Agoraphobia** is an anxiety about, or avoidance of, places or situations from which escape might be difficult.
- **Panic disorder with agoraphobia** is characterized by both recurrent unexpected panic attacks and agoraphobia.
- **Agoraphobia without a history of panic disorder** is characterized by the presence of agoraphobia and panic-like symptoms without a history of unexpected panic attacks.
- **Specific phobia** is characterized by clinically significant anxiety provoked by exposure to a specific feared object or situation, often leading to avoidance behavior.
- **Social phobia** is characterized by clinically significant anxiety provoked by exposure to certain types of social or performance situations, often leading to avoidance behavior. Blushing is the cardinal characteristic symptom.
- **Obsessive-compulsive disorder** is characterized by obsessions that cause marked anxiety or distress and by compulsions that serve to neutralize anxiety.
- **Posttraumatic stress disorder** is characterized by experiencing of an extremely traumatic event, accompanied by symptoms of increased arousal and by avoidance of stimuli associated with trauma.
- **Acute stress disorder** is characterized by symptoms similar to those of posttraumatic stress disorder that occur immediately in the aftermath of an extremely traumatic event.
- **Generalized anxiety disorder** is characterized by at least 6 months of persistent and excessive anxiety and worry.
- **Anxiety disorder caused by a general medical condition** is characterized by prominent symptoms of anxiety that are judged to be a direct physiologic consequence of a general medical condition.
- **Substance-induced anxiety disorder** is characterized by prominent symptoms of anxiety that are judged to be a direct physiologic consequence of a drug of abuse or medication or toxin exposure.
- **Anxiety disorder not otherwise specified** is included for coding (1) disorders with prominent anxiety or phobic avoidance that do not meet criteria for specific anxiety disorders and (2) anxiety symptoms with inadequate or contradictory information.

From American Psychiatric Association: *Diagnostic and Statistical Manual of Mental Disorders*, 4th ed, Text Revision. Washington, DC, 2000, American Psychiatric Association.

Anxious patients are frequently convinced that their problem is purely physical. The emergency physician must realize that the anxious patient is not in control of the symptoms, is not faking, and often cannot immediately identify the correct precipitant. Because the patient may be uncomfortable, uncooperative, impatient, and unreasonable, triage medical personnel must recognize that the patient believes an illness truly exists and is not being consciously manipulative. Anxiety caused by physical illness is usually suggested by the patient's physical findings. The patient should be evaluated for exacerbation of known preexisting disease as well as for symptoms that suggest the onset of new illness. The emergency physician must keep in mind that anxiety is associated with increased medical risk in the acute exacerbation of chronic illness.[15]

Of the medical illnesses causing anxiety symptoms, 25% are neurologic in nature, 25% are endocrine disorders, and 12% are cardiovascular problems, collagen vascular disorders, and chronic infections. The most common organic cause of anxiety is alcohol and drug use, in which symptoms arise from either intoxication or, more typically, withdrawal states.[11]

Cardiac Diseases

Patients with various psychiatric conditions may present to the emergency department with reports of chest pain. Several studies indicate that a panic disorder affects approximately 30% of noncardiac chest pain patients.[16]

The symptoms of myocardial infarction and angina pectoris are crushing chest pain, shortness of breath, choking or smothering sensations, palpitations, heavy perspiration, and a feeling of impending death. These are also the primary symptoms of acute anxiety, but in cases of anxiety the pain is rarely the worst symptom and the patients are generally younger.[8] When the differentiation between myocardial infarction and acute anxiety is unclear, patients should be approached as though they have a cardiac event. Cardiac dysrhythmias can cause palpitations, discomfort, dizziness, respiratory distress, and fainting. An anxious patient with a panic disorder will frequently have similar symptoms. Fortunately, most dysrhythmias can be documented and characterized by an electrocardiogram.

Mitral valve prolapse syndrome can be associated with panic attacks indistinguishable from a panic disorder.[17] Benzodiazepines can be used to provide symptomatic relief to patients who experience chest pain. In a recent study, benzodiazepines were found to reduce anxiety, pain, and cardiovascular activation. It has been hypothesized that by reducing circulating catecholamines, benzodiazepines may cause coronary vasodilatation, prevent dysrhythmias, and block platelet aggregation.[18]

Endocrine Diseases

The DSM-IV lists the most common endocrine disorders associated with anxiety states as hypoparathyroidism, hyper- and hypothyroidism, hypoglycemia, pheochromocytoma, and hyperadrenocorticism.[13] Anxiety is the predominant symptom in 20% of patients with hypoparathyroidism. Other symptoms include paresthesias, muscle cramps, muscle spasm, and tetany. Although most cases result from past surgical removal of the parathyroid glands during thyroidectomy, there are many other causes. The diagnosis of hypoparathyroidism is suggested by a low serum calcium level and a high phosphate level and confirmed by a parathyroid hormone assay.[19]

Fourteen percent of diabetic patients suffer from a generalized anxiety disorder, and another 27% to 40% exhibit elevated anxiety symptoms. There is evidence that diabetic patients who are treated with anti-anxiety medication experience not only a reduction in anxiety but also a decrease in glycosylated hemoglobin and high-density lipoprotein levels.[20] Many patients with anxiety, somatoform, or characterologic disorders are convinced that they have reactive hypoglycemia. A normal sevum glucose level during an attack can exclude this diagnosis.

One half of the patients with pheochromocytoma have acute attacks of anxiety, headache, sweating, flushing, hypertension, and diarrhea. Pheochromocytoma attacks, like panic attacks, can be precipitated by emotional stress. Pheochromocytoma attacks not only cause crushing abdominal and back pain and vomiting but also sweating of the whole body. The sweating in panic attacks is more likely to be confined to the hands, feet, and forehead. Measuring urinary or plasma catecholamines and metabolites can diagnose a pheochromocytoma.[21]

Hyperthyroidism is one of the most frequently encountered endocrine diseases associated with anxiety. As with panic disorders, hyperthyroidism is associated with acute episodic anxiety. Thyrotoxicosis causes anxiety, palpitations, perspiration, hot skin, rapid pulse, active reflexes, diarrhea, weight loss, heat intolerance, proptosis, and lid lag.[22] Psychiatric symptoms can also be the first sign of hypothyroidism, occurring in approximately 2% to 12% of reported cases along with organic mental deficits. Characteristic

symptoms include anxiety and progressive mental slowing associated with diminished recent memory, speech deficits. and diminished learning ability. The development of severe anxiety disorders in hypothyroid states is related to both the rapidity of change of thyroid hormone levels and the absolute levels encountered. In general, the serum concentration of thyroid-stimulating hormone, also known as thyrotropin and free thyroxine, will suffice in the emergency department to make the diagnosis of thyroid emergencies.[23]

Respiratory Diseases

Most conditions causing airway compromise or impairing gas exchange would never be mistaken for a psychiatric disorder. However, certain conditions that cause hypoxemia or hypercarbia can manifest with significant anxiety. More than one third of the patients with chronic obstructive pulmonary disease have anxiety disorders, including 8% to 25% with a panic disorder.[24]

As in panic disorders, asthma is characterized by episodic attacks of dyspnea and anxiety. Anxiety can also precipitate and prolong asthma attacks. Patients with severe asthma are twice as likely to have an anxiety disorder, four times as likely to have a panic attack, five times as likely to have a panic disorder, and almost five times as likely to have a phobia compared with nonasthmatic people. Pure panic is easily differentiated from pure asthma by good air movement with normal lung sounds. It should be noted, however, that a number of studies have shown that the coexistence of anxiety disorders increases rates of asthma-related morbidity and mortality.[25]

Acute shortness of breath in any patient should never be dismissed lightly. It is important to remember that patients with pulmonary embolism can present with only shortness of breath as the major symptom. These patients can be distinguished by close attention to history and examination, assessing risk factors for thromboembolic disease and use of basic investigations (e.g., pulse oximetry, electrocardiogram, chest radiography, arterial blood gas analysis, and D-dimer).[26]

Neurologic Disorders

Neurologic conditions that affect a range of different neuroanatomic structures can be associated with anxiety symptoms. Temporal lobe seizures, tumors, arteriovenous malformation, and infarction all have been reported to manifest with panic attacks.

Electroencephalography and anticonvulsant trials may be appropriate when the patient's condition is refractory to conventional treatment. Anxiety often accompanies a transient ischemic attack and may be the major presenting symptom if the transient ischemic attack has resolved by the time the patient reaches the emergency department. In patients with Huntington's disease, anxiety is reported as the most common prodromal symptom. Anxiety occurs in up to 40% of patients with Parkinson's disease and 37% of patients with multiple sclerosis. Similarly, anxiety is common in patients with moderate Alzheimer's disease. The existence of anxiety disorders plays an important role in the prognosis and associated impairment among patients who have had cerebral vascular accidents with neurologic sequelae. Anxiety and depression are associated with left-hemispheric strokes and anxiety alone with right-hemispheric strokes. And finally, anxiety disorders are also reported after traumatic brain injury.[27]

Drug Intoxication and Withdrawal States

Amphetamines, cocaine, and sympathomimetic drugs are abused for their euphoric and mind-altering properties. However, patients who use these drugs will become agitated, anxious, or panicky when the drugs are taken in large doses and with prolonged use. Many illicit drug users believe marijuana reduces their anxiety, but the depersonalization experience can provoke severe anxiety, fearfulness, and agoraphobic symptoms.[28] Amyl nitrite is used medically as a short-acting vasodilator. It is abused primarily as a sexual stimulant, for prolonging and intensifying arousal, erection, and orgasm, but it can also cause brief panic anxiety.[28] LSD can produce "bad trips," which are often associated with severe generalized anxiety. The effects of LSD are typically abolished within an hour by atypical antipsychotic medications.[28]

Caffeine is a common stimulant and can provoke anxiety symptoms.[28] Lower doses of caffeine can be pleasantly stimulating, but higher doses cause hyperalertness, hypervigilance, motor tension, tremors, gastrointestinal distress, and anxiety. The acute symptoms of caffeine intoxication and generalized anxiety disorder are almost identical.

Stimulants such as ephedra and ephedrine-based compounds are found in many nutritional supplements and are listed by such herbal names as ma huang and khat. Yohimbine is used as a stimulant or aphrodisiac but can also produce extreme anxiety. It produces panic and anxiety so reliably that it has been useful in experimental anxiety research.[28] Khat is a botanical stimulant that results in symptoms that are stronger than those elicited by caffeine but weaker than those elicited by amphetamines.

Sedative-hypnotic drugs (e.g., benzodiazepines, barbiturates, meprobamate, methaqualone, chloral hydrate, paraldehyde, ethchlorvynol, glutethimide) are taken to relieve anxiety or sleeplessness, but their discontinuation can cause sedative withdrawal and rebound anxiety. The severity of the withdrawal syndrome depends on the drug, dosage, duration of use, and speed of elimination. In general, the intermediate-acting sedative-hypnotics (4-6 hours) cause the worst withdrawal symptoms. These symptoms include hyperalertness, motor tension, muscle aches, agitation, anxiety, insomnia, hyperactive reflexes, postural hypotension, tremulousness, nausea, vomiting, convulsions, delirium, and death.[28]

Benzodiazepine withdrawal is rarely fatal but can be very unpleasant. Severe rebound anxiety can occur with discontinued use after only a few weeks, even with recommended therapeutic doses. Lorazepam and alprazolam are short-acting agents and their abrupt discontinuation frequently causes panic attacks. Normal people may experience this rebound as stimulating. Although antidepressants are rarely abused, their abrupt withdrawal can also cause an abstinence syndrome of insomnia, vivid nightmares, and extreme anxiety.[28]

In cases of alcohol withdrawal, patients present with severe anxiety symptoms in the context of acute or protracted abstinence syndromes, but it is unclear whether this anxiety is an independent psychiatric disorder or a temporary syndrome related solely to withdrawal.[29]

Anxiety in Primary Psychiatric Disorders

Even in the domain of mental illness, a panic disorder is a diagnosis of exclusion. Several mental illnesses cause panic attacks as their secondary manifestation. The presence of panic often influences the treatment and outcome of the primary mental illness. Panic attacks can occur as part of a bipolar (manic-depressive) disorder, in either the manic or the depressed phase. In manic and hypomanic disorders, the patient's predominant affect is usually cheerful and euphoric but may also be dysphoric, with irritability and extreme anxiety of panic proportions.[30]

Panic attacks are often seen with schizophrenia, especially early in its course. Fearfulness, tension, agitation, immobility, disorganized thinking, dilated pupils, extreme insecurity, suspiciousness, and delusions of reference and persecution may characterize schizophrenic panic attacks. The hallucinations often have derogatory accusative content. Social anxiety is a common and disabling condition in outpatients with schizophrenia that is unrelated to clinical psychotic symptoms.[31]

Patients with somatoform disorders report a variety of somatic symptoms, including panic attacks, and claim to have most of the physical symptoms they are asked about. However, patients with "pure" anxiety disorders tend to be hypochondriacal. Patients with somatization are more likely to improve transiently on active medication or placebo but rarely respond so well that they stop seeking unnecessary medical attention. Patients with panic disorders, however, seek at least as much psychiatric attention as those with somatoform disorders.[32]

Approximately 50% of patients with a primary panic disorder develop major depression and many others are bothered by some degree of depression in mood. Twenty percent of patients with depression have panic attacks; the remainder have considerable anxiety. Depression with panic attacks responds less well to treatment. Agitated depression with anxiety and psychosis, sometimes called "involutional melancholia," responds well to electroconvulsive therapy. Depression with anxiety and hostility responds well to antidepressants, but benzodiazepines can exacerbate symptoms.[33]

Posttraumatic stress disorder is an anxiety disorder characterized by the re-experiencing of an extremely traumatic event. The symptoms are closely related to and worsened by reminders of the trauma. The "flashbacks," in which patients re-experience the original trauma, can have the same symptoms as panic attacks. These patients often avoid crowds or social situations.[34]

A panic disorder is one of the easier psychiatric diseases to feign because most of the symptoms can be duplicated by intentional hyperventilation. Functional hyperventilation can be distinguished from organic hyperventilation by its irregularity and interruptions by sighs. When in doubt, formal psychiatric evaluation is indicated, particularly before prescribing a potentially dangerous or addictive drug therapy.

A phobia (an irrational fear) is considered normal in children. The objects of fear tend to be things that seem to be dangerous to children (e.g. spiders, snakes, bats, cats, enclosed places, the dark, open spaces). Phobia becomes a disorder when it interferes with an individual's day-to-day life.[35] Agoraphobia is a fear of leaving home, particularly alone. Approximately one half of agoraphobic patients do not have panic attacks. Those with panic attacks are more likely to seek treatment, whereas those with uncomplicated agoraphobia tend to stay at home. Agoraphobia without panic attacks may not differ fundamentally from simple phobias. Most panic disorder patients have multiple phobias, including agoraphobia. The agoraphobia is believed to result from the panic patient's increasing attempts to avoid places or situations in which the panic attacks would be particularly inconvenient or difficult to control. Agoraphobic patients particularly avoid places from which escape would be difficult (e.g., bridges, crowded theaters). When they attend theaters, they favor seats on the aisle and near the door. Panic attacks in agoraphobic patients are more likely to include fear of losing control, whereas those not associated with agoraphobia are more likely to include dyspnea and dizziness.[36]

A social phobia is characterized by clinically significant anxiety provoked by exposure to specifically feared objects or situations, often leading to avoidance behavior. Social phobias prevent patients from participating in such activities as public speaking, performing, visiting, using public showers or rest rooms, or eating in public places.

An obsessive-compulsive disorder (OCD) is characterized by recurrent, obtrusive, unwanted thoughts (obsessions), such as fears of contamination, and compulsive behaviors or rituals (compulsions), such as hand-washing or rechecking on things thought either undone or lost. OCD is classified as an anxiety disorder because (1) anxiety or tension is often associated with obsessions and resistance to compulsions, (2) anxiety or tension is often immediately relieved by yielding to compulsions, and (3) OCD often occurs in association with anxiety disorders. The obsessions and intrusive thoughts increase anxiety, and the compulsions and repetitive behaviors decrease anxiety but with significant disruption of one's life.[10]

Reactive anxiety or situational anxiety occurs in reaction to stressful situations (e.g., onset of serious medical illness). The criteria for an adjustment disorder with anxiety include the development of significant anxiety in response to an identifiable stressor.[10]

MANAGEMENT

Initial Evaluation

Anxious patients should be placed in a quiet area for evaluation. Some patients calm down when removed from the emergency department environment. If the emergency physician cannot calm the patient, supportive family members may help. Often a known and trusted face helps anxious patients make order out of their inner turmoil. Prior discussion and clarification with the family are essential to elicit their support.[1]

Once the patient is calm, a more formal evaluation can begin with the asking of open-ended questions and careful observation of the patient's responses. Questions regarding drug or alcohol use should be delayed until rapport has been established. Reassurance should not be premature, because this important interventional technique is more effective when it is delayed until after the patient's specific concerns are clarified.[1]

The extent of the medical workup for the patient with significant anxiety will vary depending on the patient's age and health status, the nature of the anxiety, and the range and severity of associated symptoms. The following factors should be considered: (1) potential contributory medical illness (e.g., thyroid dysfunction, hypoglycemic episodes in diabetes, hyperparathyroidism, dysrhythmias, chronic obstructive pulmonary disease, seizure disorders); (2) the possibility of substance use (e.g., caffeine, amphetamines, cocaine) and withdrawal states (e.g., alcohol, sedative-hypnotics); and (3) the anxiogenic effects of medications (e.g., β-andrenergic agonists, theophylline, corticosteroids, thyroid hormones, and sympathomimetic agents).

If a somatic concern is the major component of the acute anxiety attack, a physical examination with particular attention to the area of complaint is appropriate, even when there is overwhelming evidence of a functional cause to the patient's complaints. Anxiety attacks are stressful experiences in themselves and can cause deterioration in marginally compensated organ systems. Careful evaluation reassures the patient and avoids the problem of a premature "medical clearance." Abnormal vital signs and low pulse oximetry readings suggest an organic cause of anxiety symptoms.[10]

Because of the physical nature of these symptoms, patients often seek treatment in the emergency department rather than in a psychiatric setting. A calm manner and willingness to listen usually relieves some of the patient's initial anxiety. An anxiety or panic reaction may be precipitated by the loss of a significant relationship, a job, a living situation, or self-esteem, as well as by physical illness or injury. Once the patient describes a trigger event, the physician should restate it, as if experiencing a similar situation. This gives the patient authoritative approval for expressing embarrassing feelings. A patient who has frequent anxiety reactions is usually suggestible and will respond to reassurance. Conversely, an anxious or unsympathetic physician may only compound the problem.[1]

Even an apparently calm patient may communicate anxiety through worried looks, nervousness, pressured speech, or covert assaults on the physician's competence. Also, a physician may empathetically respond to the patient's overt or hidden anxiety by becoming somewhat anxious. This is a strong clue that the patient's anxiety is real and significant. Without this self-awareness, physicians may focus on a patient's physical symptoms, rather than on the irrational anxiety. In a crowded emergency department, the emergency physician's emotional isolation and limited patient interaction becomes even more pronounced. The pressure to see patients quickly results in limited interactions that may lead to misdiagnosis of anxiety disorders and excessive and unnecessary medical workups.

A careful medical evaluation is important. However, excessive focus on unlikely illness suggests to the patient a reason to worry, avoids recognition of crucial psychological factors, and may increase anxiety and the severity of symptoms.

After organic illness, medications, and obvious psychiatric causes of the acute anxiety state have been ruled out, the physician should determine whether the anxiety is endogenous or exogenous in nature (see Box 110-3). If the anxiety is paroxysmal, unpredictable, and accompanied by agoraphobia, an endogenous component is likely to be present. Such patients should be referred to a psychiatrist for evaluation and treatment. If the anxiety appears to be related to an identifiable external event or circumstance, the patient should be encouraged to discuss his or her feelings with a mental health worker. Talking about fears allows the anxious patient some sense of mastery and control over events. These patients often require ongoing advice, support, and assistance in mobilizing necessary resources from family members, friends, and social agencies to achieve realistic expectations.

Anxiety is common in elderly patients, with prevalence rates conservatively estimated from 10% to 15%. Anxiety disorders may be the most common psychiatric ailments experienced by older adults and the least studied in that age group. Older patients with anxiety often have somatic complaints. These patients require a careful investigation for underlying medical illness, other psychiatric conditions, and the use of over-the-counter and prescription drugs.[37]

Pharmacologic Treatment

Use of intravenous medication is rare but may be necessary when an anxiety state renders a patient so helpless and out of control that there is a significant threat of safety to self or others. Intravenous medication is also appropriate for the anxious patient experiencing a significant medical illness or undergoing a medical procedure. Morphine is effective in controlling the anxiety associated with congestive heart failure, acute myocardial infarction, and acute pulmonary embolism. Lorazepam in 1- to 2-mg increments every 20 minutes can be helpful in alleviating the anxiety associated with substance withdrawal states. Midazolam can reduce anxiety and increase amnesia for emergency department procedures.

In the past few years, emergency physicians and the public have become increasingly concerned about the growing use of benzodiazepines in the United States. More than 1 million Americans are physically dependent on tranquilizers. When tranquilizers are given in place of understanding, support, and intrapersonal therapies, patients are taught to rely on the external support of a pill rather than on inner resources.[8]

Patients with endogenous anxiety (panic attacks with or without agoraphobia) should be referred to a psychiatrist to establish a good therapeutic relationship before using anxiolytic medication. Benzodiazepines, tricyclics, selective serotonin-reuptake inhibitors, and monoamine oxidase inhibitors are safe and effective in endogenously anxious patients who are under psychiatric care (Table 110-1). Recurrence rates of panic attacks are high when drug therapy is discontinued.[8]

Benzodiazepines can be prescribed for motivated patients with acute exogenous anxiety for time-limited stress. Patients who are cooperative, employed, educated, married, and aware of their problems on a

Table 110-1. Pharmacotherapy for Anxiety Disorders

	SSRIs	TCAs	MAOIs	Benzodiazepines	Buspirone	CBT
Panic disorder	+	+	+	+	−	+
Generalized anxiety disorder	+	+	+	+	+	+
Social phobia	+	−	+	+	−	+
Specific phobia	−	−	−	+/−	−	+
PTSD	+	+/−	+	+/−	−	+
OCD	+	−*	+	+/−†	+/−†	+

*Clomipramine is effective.
†Used adjunctively with serotonergic antidepressant.
CBT, cognitive-behavioral therapy; MAOIs, monoamine oxidase inhibitors; OCD, obsessive-compulsive disorder; PTSD, posttraumatic stress disorder; SSRIs, selective serotonin-reuptake inhibitors; TCAs, tricyclic antidepressants.

psychological basis are more likely to respond. Benzodiazepines can be given in one or two daily doses to make use of their short half-lives; alternatively, a bedtime dose may minimize daytime sedation and still manifest a daytime anxiolytic effect. Benzodiazepines should not be prescribed for more than 1 week, since patients who do not improve within a week are unlikely to benefit from the drug. Patients with a history of alcoholism or drug abuse, who are excessively and emotionally dependent, or who become anxious in response to normal stress are at greater risk of drug dependency. Dependence and abstinence syndromes have been reported to occur with low doses of tranquilizing drugs, especially if they are taken for more than 8 months. Short-acting benzodiazepines (e.g., lorazepam, oxazepam) should be prescribed at low dosages for patients with liver disease or organic brain syndrome and for those taking medications that either depress CNS function or inhibit benzodiazepine metabolism and clearance. Withdrawal rebound symptoms are more common with discontinuation of benzodiazepines than with other anti-anxiety treatments. Short-acting benzodiazepines produce a more severe abstinence syndrome when they are stopped abruptly. Clonidine, in gradually decreasing doses, may ameliorate benzodiazepine withdrawal. For some patients, switching from a short-acting agent (e.g., alprazolam) to a long-acting agent (e.g., clonazepam) can be helpful before initiating a taper.[38]

Buspirone is a nonbenzodiazepine tranquilizer that does not appear to cause dependency. Buspirone is effective in treating generalized anxiety disorders. Because of a therapeutic lag in efficacy of several weeks and the need for dose titration, buspirone has had variable and sometimes disappointing results in clinical practice, particularly when used in patients with prior exposure to benzodiazepines.[38]

Many psychiatrists use β-blockers to treat anxiety associated with tremor, tachycardia, and stage fright. Because of the risk of extrapyramidal side effects, neuroleptic drugs should be reserved for episodes of psychotic anxiety.[38]

Monoamine oxidase inhibitors demonstrate high effectiveness in the treatment of social phobia, panic, generalized anxiety disorders, OCD, and comorbid conditions (e.g., atypical depression). Monoamine oxidase inhibitors (phenelzine and tranylcypromine) can be difficult to tolerate and require dietary restrictions.

Tricyclic antidepressants (TCAs) are effective for panic disorders and generalized anxiety disorders but ineffective for social phobias. TCAs, with the exception of clomipramine, are largely ineffective for OCD. TCAs are also effective for depressive and anxiety symptoms associated with posttraumatic stress disorder. TCAs include imipramine, nortriptyline, desipramine, amitriptyline, and doxepin. The TCAs have largely been supplanted by the selective serotonin-reuptake inhibitors as first-line interventions for the treatment of anxiety and depressive disorders.[38]

Selective serotonin-reuptake inhibitors have become first-line treatment for most anxiety disorders because of their broad spectrum of efficacy. Selective serotonin-reuptake inhibitors are tolerated better and are safer than the previous classes of antidepressants. They also have a lower potential for physical dependence than the benzodiazepines. Selective serotonin-reuptake inhibitors include fluoxetine, sertraline, paroxetine, fluvoxamine, venlafaxine, nefazodone, mirtazapine, and gabapentin.[38] Long-term use of antidepressants and benzodiazepines for anxiety disorders is often required to maintain ongoing benefit and prevent relapse.

Nonpharmacologic Therapy

Psychotherapies can be helpful for individuals whose psychological makeup, coping style, interpersonal dynamics, and situational stressors contribute to their pathologic anxiety. Supportive, insight-oriented, family, and other types of therapy can be helpful when these factors appear prominently in the patient's presentation.[8]

Cognitive-behavioral therapy is predicated on the theory that the distress and impairment associated with anxiety and panic are mediated by maladaptive cognitive responses that promote anxiety and avoidance. The core components of cognitive-behavioral therapy for panic disorder include correction of cognitive misperceptions and overreactions to anxiety symptoms, breathing retraining, muscle relaxation, and exposure and desensitization to phobic situations.[8,10]

Meditation (e.g., Zen, yoga, transcendental) has been proposed by many authorities, but few clinical data support its efficacy in treating anxiety disorders.[15] Biofeedback appears promising for the treatment of generalized anxiety disorder.[39] Hypnotic suggestion may be effective because anxious patients tend to be cognitively scattered, unable to focus their attention, and highly suggestible. A hypnotic state can often be induced by certain stimuli.[40]

These nonpharmacologic techniques take anxious patients out of the future, about which they are frightened, and place them into the present. These techniques should be reinforced by the development of a physically and psychologically healthy lifestyle. A significant social support system not only protects against vulnerability to illness but also is highly anxiolytic. Regular exercise (e.g., dancing, swimming, bicycling, walking, jogging) also promotes tranquility. Encouraging activity that focuses on hand-eye-ear coordination (e.g., painting, playing keyboard, needlework) helps anxious patients regain and maintain control by bringing them into the present.[1]

DISPOSITION

Many patients with anxiety-related symptoms can be effectively treated in the emergency department with the following general measures:

1. Rule out organic illnesses and medications associated with anxiety.
2. Determine whether anxiety is endogenous or exogenous.
3. Rule out depression.

4. Evaluate the patient's capacity for self-awareness.
5. Assess techniques that have worked in the past.
6. Support coping skills.
7. Give the patient as much control over the care plan as feasible.
8. Offer ongoing support when the patient's strengths are limited.
9. Clarify what is currently frightening the patient.
10. Apply adjunctive techniques as appropriate for the patient's personality and the physician's preference (e.g., hypnotic suggestion, breathing exercises).

Patients with a panic disorder associated with suicidal or homicidal ideation or with severe depression require urgent psychiatric attention and admission to the hospital. Other patients with suspected endogenous or severe exogenous anxiety disorders should be referred for psychiatric evaluation. The Anxiety Disorders Association of America can be contacted (240-485-1001) for a national registry of clinicians and treatment programs specializing in anxiety disorders or can be found online at www.adaa.org.

 KEY CONCEPTS

- Up to 40% of patients thought to have anxiety disorders are later found to have organic disease. Anxiety can accompany the onset of serious disease and may itself cause increased metabolic demands, which can cause a marginally compensated organ system to fail.
- Anxiety caused by physical illness is usually suggested by the patient's physical findings but may require adjunctive testing.
- Anxiety affects at least 10% to 15% of elderly patients.
- Intravenous medication may be necessary for patients who are a significant threat to themselves or others and for anxious patients with significant medical illness.
- Limited benzodiazepine therapy may be helpful for select patients with exogenous anxiety.

REFERENCES

1. Kercher EE: Anxiety. *Emerg Med Clin North Am* 9:161, 1991.
2. Benjamin GC: Anxiety disorders. In Rosen P, et al (eds): *Emergency Medicine: Concepts and Clinical Practice*, 3rd ed. St Louis, Mosby, 1992.
3. Kessler RC, et al: Lifetime and twelve-month prevalence of DSM III-R psychiatric disorders in the United States: Results from the National Comorbidity Survey. *Arch Gen Psychiatry* 51:8, 1994.
4. Leon AC, et al: Prevalence of mental disorders in primary care: Implications for screening. *Arch Fam Med* 4:857, 1995.
5. Kushner MG, Sher KJ, Erickson MA: Prospective analysis of the relation between DSM-III anxiety disorders and alcohol use disorders. *Am J Psychiatry* 156:723, 1999.
6. Pollack HM, Smoller JW: The longitudinal course and outcome of panic disorder. *Psychiatr Clin North Am* 18:789, 1995.
7. Johnson MR, Lydiard RB: The neurobiology of anxiety disorders. *Psychiatr Clin North Am* 18:681, 1995.
8. Hollander E, Simeon D, Gorman JM: Anxiety disorders. In Hales RE, et al (eds): *Textbook of Psychiatry*. Washington, DC, American Psychiatric Press, 1999.
9. Doefler LA, Obert J, DeCosimo D: Symptoms of post-traumatic stress disorder following myocardial infarction and coronary artery bypass surgery. *Gen Hosp Psychiatry* 16:193, 1994.
10. Pollack MH, Smoller JW, Lee DK: Approach to the anxious patient. In Stern TA, Herman JB, Slavin PL (eds): *Guide to Psychiatry in Primary Care*. New York, McGraw-Hill, 1998.
11. Gorman JM, Coplan JD: Comorbidity of depression and panic disorder. *J Clin Psychiatry* 57(suppl 10):34, 1996.
12. Rosenbaum JF, et al: Anxiety. In Cassem NH, Stern TA, Rosenbaum JF, Jellinek MS (eds): *Massachusetts General Hospital Handbook of General Hospital Psychiatry*, 4th ed. St Louis, Mosby, 1998.
13. American Psychiatric Association: *Diagnostic and Statistical Manual of Mental Disorders*, 4th ed, Text Revision. Washington, DC, American Psychiatric Association, 2000.
14. Davies, SJ, et al: Association of panic disorder and panic attacks with hypertension. *Am J Med* 107:310, 1999.
15. Fleet RP, et al: Detecting panic disorder in emergency department chest pain patients: A validated model to improve recognition. *Ann Behav Med* 19:124, 1997.
16. Kanton WJ: Chest pain, cardiac disease and panic disorder. *J Clin Psychiatry* 51:27, 1990.
17. Worthington JJ, et al: Panic disorder in emergency ward patients with chest pain. *J Nerv Ment Dis* 185:274, 1997.
18. Huffman JC, Stern TA: The use of benzodiazepines in the treatment of chest pain: A review of the literature. *J Emerg Med* 25:427, 2003.
19. Fitzpatrick LA, Arnold A: Hypoparathyroidism. In DeGroot LJ, et al (eds): *Endocrinology*. Philadelphia, WB Saunders, 1995.
20. Grigsby AB, et al: Prevalence of anxiety in adults with diabetes: A systematic review. *J Psychosom Res* 53:1053, 2002.
21. Starkman MN, Cameron OG, Nesse RM, Zelnik T: Peripheral catecholamine levels and the symptoms of anxiety: Studies in patients with and without pheochromocytoma. *Psychosom Med* 52:129, 1990.
22. Dement MM, et al: Depression and anxiety in hyperthyroidism. *Arch Med Res* 33:552, 2002.
23. Ringel MD: Management of hypothyroidism and hyperthyroidism in the intensive care unit. *Crit Care Clin* 17:59, 2001.
24. Karajgi B, et al: The prevalence of anxiety disorders in patients with chronic obstructive pulmonary disease. *Am J Psychiatry* 147:200, 1990.
25. Goodwin RD, Jacobi F, Thefeld W: Mental disorders and asthma in the community. *Arch Gen Psychiatry* 60:1125, 2003.
26. Mehta TA, Sutherland JG, Hodgkinson DW: Hyperventilation: Cause or effect? *J Accid Emerg Med* 17:376, 2000.
27. Stein DJ, Hugo FJ: Neuropsychiatric aspects of anxiety disorders. In Yudofsky SC, Hales RE: *Neuropsychiatry and Clinical Neurosciences*, 4th ed. Washington DC, American Psychiatric Publishing, 2002.
28. Weiss RD, Greenfield SF, Mirin SM: Intoxication and withdrawal syndromes. In Hyman SE, Tesar GE (eds): *Manual of Psychiatric Emergencies*, 3rd ed. Boston, Little, Brown, and Co, 1994.
29. Schuckit MA, Hessebrock V: Alcohol dependence and anxiety disorders: What is the relationship? *Am J Psychiatry* 151:1723, 1994.
30. Sasson Y, et al: Bipolar comorbidity: From diagnostic dilemmas to therapeutic challenge. *Int J Neuropsychopharmacol* 6:139, 2003.
31. Tibbo P, Swainson J, Chue P, LeMelledo JM: Prevalence and relationship to delusion and hallucinations of anxiety disorders in schizophrenia. *Depress Anxiety* 17:65, 2003.

32. Barsky AJ: Hypochondriasis: Medical management and psychiatric treatment. *Psychosomatics* 37:48, 1996.

33. Zimmerman M, Chelminski I: Generalized anxiety disorder in patients with major depression: Is DSM-IV's hierarchy correct? *Am J Psychiatry* 160:504, 2003.

34. Howard S, Hopwood M: Post-traumatic stress disorder: A brief overview. *Aust Fam Physician* 32:683, 2003.

35. Boyd JH, et al: Phobia: Prevalence and risk factors. *Soc Psychiatry Psychiatr Epidemiol* 25:314, 1990.

36. Craske MG, DeCola JP, Sachs AD, Pontillo DC: Panic control treatment for agoraphobia. *J Anxiety Disord* 17:321, 2003.

37. Sheikh JI: Anxiety and panic disorders. In Busse EW, et al (eds): *Textbook of Geriatric Psychiatry*. Washington, DC, American Psychiatric Press, 1996.

38. Shatzberg AF, Nemeroff CB: *Textbook of Psychopharmacology*, 2nd ed. Washington, DC, American Psychiatric Press, 1998.

39. Rice KM, Blanchard GB, Purcell M: Biofeedback treatments of generalized anxiety disorder: Preliminary results. *Biofeedback Self Regul* 18:93, 1993.

40. Spiegel MD, Maldonado JR: Hypnosis. In Hales RE, et al (eds): *Textbook of Psychiatry*. Washington, DC, American Psychiatric Press, 1999.

CHAPTER

Somatoform Disorders

Thomas B. Purcell

PERSPECTIVE

Many patients have functional (nonorganic) complaints, but nonpsychiatrists often fail to recognize these subtle presentations of psychiatric disease. In the emergency department, this lack of recognition is probably the result of limited time and the emergency physician's focus on action rather than toward passive listening. Even when psychiatric pathology has been identified or is strongly suspected, emergency physicians are reluctant to attribute somatic complaints to functional etiologies.[1] Nevertheless, proper diagnosis and treatment of patients with functional complaints are essential. Misidentification and mismanagement unnecessarily prolong patients' distress and add to the overall burden on the health care delivery system.

Between 25% and 72% of patients' visits to primary care physicians have been attributed to psychosocial distress manifest as somatic complaints.[2] The prevalence of somatization has risen over the last 30 to 40 years, possibly because of a general decline of patients' tolerance for mild and self-limited ailments.[3,4]

CLINICAL FEATURES

Most physicians have experienced somatization; up to 80% of all medical students become convinced they have a disease.[5] *Somatization* refers to a tendency to experience and communicate psychological distress in the "body language" of physical symptoms in the absence of organic pathology.[6] Patients seek medical attention because they are convinced that their symptoms reflect real physical disease.[7-11]

The term *somatoform disorders* embraces all disorders that have somatization as a common factor. In some cases, a demonstrable physical disorder does exist (often iatrogenic) but the patient's complaints are out of proportion to the physical findings.[8] The symptoms are not feigned nor are under the voluntary control of the patient.[12,13] Almost any complaint involving any body system may occur, with patients often complaining of fashionable diseases recently popularized by the media.[11] The *environmental somatization syndrome* refers to individuals convinced that their symptoms are caused by exposure to chemical or physical components of the external environment, such as poisonous substances, electromagnetic fields, or ergonomic stress attributed to repetitive movements.[14] In general, it is the *multiplicity* of symptoms, rather than the specific symptom, that is more indicative of somatization.[15,16] In women with more than five and in men with more than three unexplained somatic complaints, the likelihood of a diagnosable psychiatric disorder doubles.[15,17,18]

In general, patients with somatoform disorders tend to be women between ages 20 and 60 who have fewer than 12 years of education, are widowed or divorced, and exhibit low self-esteem. They tend to be self-conscious, vulnerable to stress, anxious, hostile, and depressed.[6,8] Certain categories of patients, such as women with chronic pelvic pain, have a high rate of sexual or physical abuse in childhood.[19] Somatizers have difficulty describing their feelings in words, a phenomenon termed *alexithymia* ("without words for mood"), resulting in alternative (somatic) forms of expression.[20] They steadfastly insist that their symptoms are caused by serious physical disorders even in the presence of conclusive evidence to the contrary.[8] Somatization may be unconsciously motivated by a desire to assume the "sick role" and seek the privileges afforded to a sick person by society, such as release from normal obligations and absolution from blame for their condition.[20,21]

Individual somatic complaints such as headache, low energy levels, and recurrent abdominal pain are

BOX 111-1. Criteria for the Diagnosis of Somatization Disorder

1. There must be a history of medically unexplained physical symptoms beginning before the age of 30 years.
2. A history of all of the following:
   a. Pain related to at least four different sites (e.g., head, abdomen, back, joints, chest) or functions (e.g., during menstruation, during urination)
   b. At least two gastrointestinal symptoms other than pain
   c. At least one sexual or reproductive symptom other than pain (e.g., sexual indifference, irregular menses)
   d. At least one symptom or deficit suggesting a neurologic condition not limited to pain (e.g., paralysis, lump in the throat, blindness)
3. Either the above symptoms must not be explainable by any known medical condition or, when there is a related general medical condition, the complaints or impairment must be out of proportion to what might be reasonably expected.
4. The symptoms must not be intentionally produced or feigned.

common in children and adolescents in the general population and generally are not associated with significant social or emotional impairment. Pronounced polysymptomatic somatization, although uncommon in this age group, may occur in late childhood or early adolescence, and these patients are at increased risk for coexistent or later development of major depression, anxiety disorders, panic attacks, and drug and alcohol abuse.[22,23]

Somatoform disorders may be subdivided into four specific disorders, each with a somewhat different clinical picture and management approach: somatization disorder, conversion disorder, pain disorder, and hypochondriasis.

Somatization Disorder

Historically referred to as *hysteria* and *neurasthenia*, somatization disorder was given the eponym "Briquet's syndrome" by Guze in 1975 to avoid the pejorative implications that had come to be associated with the traditional terms.[24,25] The malady is chronic or repetitive, dating from young adulthood, with numerous physical symptoms and complaints involving a variety of organ systems but few or no physical findings to explain those symptoms.[26-29]

The diagnosis of somatization disorder requires several criteria (Box 111-1).[12] This diagnosis is rarely made in the emergency department, even though it may be suspected, because the proper investigation of this disorder involves time-consuming interviews and may require four to six visits before the establishment of a definitive diagnosis.[1] A short list of symptoms provides a rapid screen for this disorder.[30] The seven symptoms that may best discriminate between patients with and without somatization disorder are (1) dysmenorrhea, (2) the sensation of a "lump" in the throat, (3) vomiting, (4) shortness of breath, (5) burning in the sex organs, (6) painful extremities, and (7) amnesia lasting

hours to days. Tested prospectively among patients displaying at least two of these seven symptoms, the diagnosis of somatization disorder is correctly predicted with a sensitivity of 93% and a specificity of 59%. When four or more of these seven symptoms are present, the specificity rises to 100%. Although this screening test may identify patients at high risk for somatization disorder, such patients should still be evaluated more thoroughly to confirm the diagnosis.

True somatization disorder is relatively uncommon, having a prevalence of 0.06% to 2% among the general population and up to 9% among hospitalized patients.[7,12,18,30] It tends to run in families and is rarely diagnosed in men,[9,10,12,31,32] although in some cultures the prevalence in men and women may be the same.[18] The typical patient is a woman in her 40s who has a 25- to 30-year history of multiple vague complaints, usually headache, dizziness, nausea and vomiting, syncope, abdominal pain and bowel trouble, fatigue, palpitations, dyspareunia, and dysmenorrhea.[19,29,32-34] Symptoms usually date back to the patient's teens and 20s, with menstrual complaints being common in these age groups.[7,12,29]

Only 33% of patients recover during 10- to 20-year follow-up,[35] and new symptoms requiring medical attention tend to surface at least every year.[7] Despite a "lifetime of suffering," the life span of these patients is normal.[36]

Somatization disorder is associated with lower socioeconomic groups, alcoholism and other addictions,[13,32,37] and poor education; fewer than 25% graduate from high school.[18,32] Many have occupational, interpersonal, and marital problems.[7,32]

The health care utilization and functional impairment of these patients are astounding. Expenditures for physician services are 14 times greater and overall health care expenditures 9 times greater than for unaffected patients. The typical patient spends 7 days in the hospital each year and 7 days sick in bed each month (compared with less than a half-day for a control population). More than 82% stop work because of their health.[32] When the diagnosis is recognized, however, medical resource use among these patients tends to become normal.[38]

Patients with somatization disorder describe their symptoms in dramatic exaggerated fashion using colorful language, with great detail about how their lives have been disrupted. They usually admit to being sickly throughout life. Although extensive, their narrative suggests no clear diagnostic constellation. Patients offer detailed accounts of multiple prior medical encounters, termed "doctor shopping," and often display multiple abdominal scars because they undergo two to three times the number of surgeries of other patients.[1,32] Their medical records have numerous and exotic test results, and they faithfully consume an impressive array of medications acquired from multiple primary care physicians and specialists. They report allergies to a comprehensive list of antibiotics and analgesics.

These patients are often emotional and vain, exhibit limited interpersonal skills, and have few close personal relationships.[29] They are typically dependent (especially on the physician) and often seductive (yet sexually unresponsive) and highly manipulative.

Of these patients, 68% fulfill the criteria for *histrionic personality disorder*.[39] Somatization disorder may be closely related to some anxiety and affective disorders; more than 80% of patients with somatization disorder report a lifetime history of major depression and 68% a history of anxiety.[32,33,40,41] These individuals may threaten or attempt suicide. Completed suicide is usually associated with psychoactive substance abuse.[7] Women with this disorder tend to marry men with antisocial personalities. The husband is often overly solicitous, demanding that his wife receive many clinical studies and quick, decisive action. Predictably, he usually shows some degree of dissatisfaction with physicians in general.[29]

Patients who do not meet the full criteria of somatization disorder but have suggestive symptoms for 6 months or longer may be classified as having *undifferentiated somatoform disorder*, which is treated similarly to somatization disorder.[12]

Conversion Disorder

Also known as *hysterical neurosis, conversion type*, the rare conversion disorder is characterized by the sudden onset and dramatic presentation of a single symptom, typically simulating some nonpainful neurologic disorder for which there is no pathophysiologic or anatomic explanation.[7] The symptoms, generally conforming to the patient's own idiosyncratic ideas about illness, are not under the patient's voluntary control. Some symptoms provide gratification for unconscious dependency needs; other symptoms provide escape from painful external emotional stimuli (e.g., hysterical paralysis in battle).[37,38] Although the symptoms may have a symbolic relationship to the precipitating factors, this is often not the case.[28] The most common conversion symptoms are voluntary motor or sensory functions and are therefore called *pseudoneurologic* (Box 111-2).[12] The most common presentations to the emergency department include pseudoseizures, syncope or coma, and paralysis or other movement disorders.[42]

Most patients are women, except for those in military service and industrial accidents.[12,38] Conversion disorder appears in adolescence and early adulthood (but may have later onset) and is more common among lower socioeconomic groups. Symptoms tend to be of sudden onset, waxing and waning in response to environmental stresses.[7,9,10,28,37] The history may show similar symptoms in the past, as well as anxiety, depression, phobias, and sexual disturbances.[28] Up to 29% of patients have a history of past psychiatric illness.[42] Patients may describe their conversion symptoms with a lack of appropriate concern about their profound bodily dysfunction (*la belle indifférence*). Although this time-honored feature has been classically associated with conversion disorder, it may be absent in more than 50% of patients and is also seen in organic disease.[43]

BOX 111-2. Presentations of Conversion Disorder

1. Motor disturbances:
   a. Tremors (that worsen when attention is called to the movements)
   b. Seizures (wild, thrashing, writhing, often mimicking copulation)
   c. Paralysis or paresis (often a monoplegia, stocking-glove weakness, with normal reflexes and limb circumferences)
   d. Aphonia (wherein the patient can whisper and cough normally and vocal cords move normally with respiration)
   e. Coordination disturbances
2. Sensory disturbances:
   a. Anesthesia (the patient may not find this symptom disturbing)
   b. Blindness and tunnel vision[15,16]
3. An occasional patient may present with other nonneurologic symptoms such as vomiting or pseudocyesis[13]

Pain Disorder

Also termed *somatoform pain disorder*,[7] this condition is similar to conversion disorder in that stressful events are translated into somatic symptoms. The primary and often exclusive symptom is distressful pain that (1) is not intentionally feigned, (2) is persistent in nature, (3) limits daily function, (4) involves one or more organ systems, and (5) cannot be pathophysiologically explained.[12,13,28] The pain most frequently occurs in the face, low back, neck, or pelvic area and causes significant functional impairment, ultimately becoming a major focus in the patient's life.[4,9,10,12,19] One half of all patients have some precipitating traumatic event at the outset (e.g., motor vehicle accident, industrial injury).[7] Chronic pain behavior patterns are typically fixed within 3 months after the onset of symptoms, and patients who do not resume normal activities within 2 weeks deserve reevaluation and a careful psychosocial review.[4] Associated features include frequent visits to physicians despite medical reassurance (doctor shopping), excessive use of analgesics, requests for surgery, and eventually the role of permanent invalid after the pain has forced the patient to discontinue gainful employment.[4,7]

Onset occurs most often in the 30- to 50-year-old age group but can occur at any age. Symptoms such as headaches or musculoskeletal pain are more likely in women.[7,9,12] The pain often approximates real pain from physical disease that the patient has experienced in the past (e.g., the patient with a history of pancreatitis may develop recurrent epigastric pain when stressed). Frequent surgical intervention may produce multiple and genuine iatrogenic pain symptoms.[19]

Hypochondriasis

The term hypochondriasis comes from *regio hypochondriaca*, a Latin term referring to the upper lateral regions of the abdomen inferior to the costal cartilages, especially the area of the spleen, which early physicians presumed to be the seat of this disorder. Hypochondriasis has four characteristics: (1) physical symptoms disproportionate to demonstrable organic disease; (2) a fear of disease and a conviction that one is sick, leading to "illness-claiming behavior" (a compulsive insistence on being considered a physical cripple); (3) a preoccupation with one's own body; and (4) persistent and unsatisfying pursuit of medical care (doctor shopping) with a history of numerous procedures and surgeries and eventual return of symptoms.[28]

These unfortunate patients manifest both a heightened awareness and an unrealistic interpretation of normal physical signs or sensations, such as bowel habits, heartbeat, sweating, or peristalsis. These sensations are perceived as abnormal, noxious, and alarming, a phenomenon known as *amplification*.[31] These aberrant perceptions result in a chronic morbid preoccupation with bodily functions and a lingering fear of having a disease despite medical reassurance.[7,12,13,28] A distinguishing feature of hypochondriasis is that the patient's symptoms do exist and often are confirmed by physical examination, but the patient exaggerates and misinterprets them.

Hypochondriasis is relatively common. Its prevalence in general medical practice ranges from 4% to 9%.[12] It has a peak incidence among men in their 30s and women in their 40s, affecting men and women in about the same proportions.[9,10,20] Hypochondriacs have an increased sense of responsibility for, and place high value on, their personal health and physical appearance. They have an acute sense of body vulnerability and a heightened aversion to death and aging.[31] There is a strong correlation of hypochondriasis with major depression.[41] A milder form of this disorder may be an exaggerated interest in bodily function and health ("health nuts").[44]

The hypochondriac complains at length and in detail, using medical jargon. The complaints focus on the head, neck, and trunk, often in the form of pain. Hypochondriacs often believe they have lost control of their lives and have been characterized as "experts at defeating doctors in order to feel more powerful."[28] Consequently, physicians perceive hypochondriacal patients as more angry and hostile than other patients.[45] The diagnosis may be suggested when the physician feels "frustration, helplessness, or anger associated with a wish to be rid of the patient."[21,28]

Reactive hypochondriasis, or transient hypochondriasis, is an acute response to a psychosocial stress or life crisis, such as an acute myocardial infarction, terminal illness, or recent loss of a family member. In contrast to true hypochondriasis, this form is reversible and does respond to reassurance.[28,44]

DIAGNOSTIC STRATEGIES

Physicians are generally unwilling to consider somatoform disorders in their initial differential diagnosis. The often dramatic presentation of symptoms creates a sense of urgency to take action, a fear of undiscovered medical illness, and a subsequent exhaustive evaluation of every complaint. Repetitive or extensive diagnostic testing rarely excludes organic disease with absolute certainty, however, and may yield false-positive results, prompting further testing. Somatizing patients are more likely to have morbidity from repeated or invasive evaluations than from undiagnosed organic disease.[1,2]

Yielding to the temptation to institute further diagnostic procedures or interventions typically leads to a temporary improvement, closely followed by renewal of symptoms and mutual physician-patient disappointment. This gives rise to inevitable conclusions on the part of the patient ("another quack") and on the part of the physician ("another crock"), leading to an unsatisfactory parting of ways and a perpetuation of the doctor-shopping cycle.[46]

Managed care and capitated reimbursement have created an additional quandary by restricting the supply of care in a time of rising demand for care from patients whose symptoms are relatively minor.[3,15] The most effective diagnostic tool with somatizers is the interview.[2] Evaluation starts with a thorough but focused history and, if available, a review of the patient's medical record. This is followed by a careful problem-oriented physical examination, with meticulous inspection of the area of complaint, and simple or routine diagnostic testing, when appropriate, until attaining a reasonable level of diagnostic certainty.[2,15] Further investigations or hospital admissions should be initiated solely on the basis of new objective signs of disease and only after confirming that the tests have not been performed. One rule of thumb in ordering laboratory tests is to do exactly what would be done if the patient were not a somatizer.[15,21] However, the clinician must resist the impassioned entreaties of the patient when it is clear that further complex or hazardous studies are unlikely to be productive.[9,10,15,47]

Multiple medical and surgical consultations generally prove counterproductive. Hypochondriacs perceive this as a test of their claim to illness and respond simply by propagating and demonstrating symptoms with redoubled zeal.[28]

DIFFERENTIAL CONSIDERATIONS

Distinguishing between the various somatoform disorders is less important than the diagnosis of treatable organic disease or the detection of anxiety and depression, which are both more common and more likely to respond to treatment.[2] Coexistent depression or anxiety disorder should always be considered.[40,48] Patients who have a relatively recent onset of somatization are more likely than patients with long-standing complaints to be exhibiting subtle signs of acute psychosis, organic brain syndrome, grief reaction, depression, or anxiety.

Depression

Approximately 50% to 70% of depressed patients consult their physician for various somatic complaints.[49] Depressed patients may not be aware of a depressed mood or may feel their depression is secondary to the somatic symptoms.[48] As a result, depression is the psychiatric disorder most often mistaken for somatoform disorder.[13]

Although somatoform disorders often coexist with depression, the two conditions must be distinguished. Depression is worse in the morning, better at night, and often associated with a positive family history. The patient is reluctant to describe the symptoms and has vegetative signs of depression (e.g., sleep disturbances, decreased appetite with weight loss).[47,50] Pain is a common symptom, particularly headache and pain involving the back, chest, or pelvic area.[48,49] Somatoform disorders, on the other hand, are worse at the end of the day, and patients have a marked propensity to discuss their symptoms, usually do not have a family history, and show no vegetative signs.[28]

In general, elderly patients do not have more physical symptoms than younger patients. Multiple somatic complaints should not be dismissed as a normal consequence of aging but rather considered a symptom of another underlying problem, usually depression or medical disease. Older patients may communicate somatic complaints as a way of expressing anger and provoking guilt among family members.[20]

Anxiety

Patients with acute anxiety often hyperventilate and frequently exhibit physical signs of increased sympathetic activity. They may be hypervigilant and irritable and may show signs of muscular tension.[28] They may offer a history of excessive worrying about their health, feeling "on edge" or irritable, having difficulty relaxing, or sleeping poorly or having trouble falling asleep and report symptoms of headache, tingling, dizzy spells, and diarrhea.[50] Notably, in patients with somatoform disorders there is a high prevalence of anxiety disorders, especially generalized anxiety disorder.[51]

Physical Illness

When patients with somatization disorder develop true organic disease, they present similarly to other patients, with specific complaints, clear chronology, and objective findings that should be appropriately investigated.[29] Unfortunately, subjective reports of distress are often not dependable in these patients, and the emergency physician must rely on more objective evidence, including the physical examination and routine laboratory tests.[21] Multiple physical symptoms starting late in life are frequently the result of physical disease.[7,12] In addition, patients who have a short duration of symptoms are more likely to have organic disease.

Although any organic disease may be mistaken for a somatoform disorder, the occasionally bizarre and atypical manifestations and presentations of the disorders listed in Box 111-3 merit special consideration.[13]

Factitious Disease and Malingering

Patients with somatoform disorders are not deliberately feigning illness; they are exhibiting the result of an

---

BOX 111-3. Organic Disease That May Be Mistaken for Somatoform Disorders

Endocrine disorders: hyperparathyroidism, thyroid disorders, Addison's disease, insulinoma, panhypopituitarism
Poisonings: botulism, carbon monoxide, heavy metals
Porphyria
Multiple sclerosis
Systemic lupus erythematosus
Wilson's disease
Myasthenia gravis
Guillain-Barré syndrome
Uremia

---

unconscious behavior modification. In the past they have unintentionally secured secondary gain from the sick role in the form of sympathy, encouragement, attention, support, and relief from responsibilities and challenges without significant loss of self-esteem.[44] In contrast, factitious disorder and malingering are both characterized by the intentional and conscious simulation or production of disease (see Chapter 112). Because such deception is difficult to uncover in the emergency department, these patients are often mistaken for having a somatoform disorder.

MANAGEMENT

The symptoms of conversion disorder may provide a protective coping value for the patient, and the physician should be cautious about removing them without first providing adequate psychological support and treatment. Otherwise, new symptoms may arise to replace previous ones. The external precipitating stress or cause of anxiety should be removed if possible. These patients require psychiatric evaluation and management,[9,10] and psychiatric consultation in the emergency department can be beneficial.[42]

Recurrence is common, but the prognosis associated with an individual episode of conversion disorder is good and the likelihood of recovery from symptoms exceeds that of other somatoform disorders.[12,20,38] Factors associated with a good prognosis include (1) good premorbid health, (2) absence of organic illness or concomitant major psychiatric syndromes, (3) acute and recent onset, (4) definite precipitation by a stressful event, and (5) presenting symptoms of paralysis, aphonia, or blindness.[12]

Reassurance

Young patients with no underlying medical or psychiatric illnesses who present with somatization in response to a clear psychosocial stress can often be reassured successfully with an appropriate explanation of their symptoms.[2] Patients with chronic somatization, however, perceive this as an official denial of their sick role and are almost invariably unwilling to accept reassurance. Because they desire the acknowledgment and recognition that come with the designation of illness, which they feel is rightfully theirs, they are disappointed when no pathologic condition is discovered. Conversely, they are elated when given a diagnosis, but they resist recovery because subconsciously the "specter of cure" poses a threat to their sick role.[44] Accordingly, attempts to cure the condition are countered with side effects, allergic reactions, and new symptoms. Such patients require another management strategy.[2]

Legitimization of Symptoms

Most patients with chronic somatization interpret a psychological explanation for their symptoms as an accusation of lying or feeblemindedness. It is important to convince them that the emergency physician believes in their symptoms and will not try to "talk them out of it." The priority is to listen and truly understand what the patient is feeling and trying to convey. Suffering is always a subjective phenomenon and, in that sense, is genuine in these patients.[21] The physician should convey empathy for the patient's physical discomfort. If the physician acknowledges the legitimacy of the claim to illness and assures the somatizer of ongoing care, limits may be set on the patient's illness behavior.[2,9,10,15,20,28]

Patients should be allowed to tell their story without interruption. They should be told that they have an illness that causes them to experience many symptoms but that these symptoms will not lead to medical deterioration.[1,52] The physician should offer only guarded projections regarding chances for complete "cure" of the condition. Ironically, this may be better received by these patients than overly optimistic assurances because the former serves to safeguard their sick role and shifts the physician away from an adversarial position.[15,47]

Diagnosis

Diagnostic labels are of critical importance for somatizers, but the precise meaning of the term should be clarified for the patient to avoid misinterpretation. Explanations for symptoms that incorporate somatic responses and descriptions such as hyperventilation, tension headache, muscle tension, muscle strain, chest wall muscle spasm, or stress may be better accepted than purely psychiatric diagnoses. This reassures the patient that the emergency physician shares the belief that the symptoms result from socially acceptable ailments while allowing more in-depth explanations that incorporate the relationship of bodily function to psychological stress. This, in turn, serves as a preparation for future psychiatric consultation or psychotropic medication.[2,8-10,47]

At times, the best approach may be to share the diagnostic uncertainty with the patient, using such terms as "atypical pain" or "multiple complaints following injury."[2] On a broader scale, managed care organizations must be encouraged to educate their enrollees about the process of somatization, the negative side effects of medications and other interventions, and the range of bodily symptoms in healthy people.[3]

Medications

Patients with somatoform disorder have a high affinity for medications and are reluctant to discontinue drugs, even those with no benefit.[28] The emergency physician should avoid drugs that produce an abstinence syndrome or dependence and those that cannot be safely continued indefinitely.[29] Pain medications, if given, should be prescribed for regular intervals, not "as needed."[28] Patients with somatoform pain disorder may benefit significantly from treatment with antidepressants, including tricyclic antidepressants.[53] Patients with somatization disorder with major depression may also improve with pharmacologic management of the depression.[41]

Therapy should be kept simple and limited to exercise, diet, physical therapy, and vitamins when possible.[47] Hospitalization and narcotics should be avoided. Benign remedies, such as lotions, nutritional supplements, elastic bandages, and heating pads, may be helpful.[15,21] Drug regimens should be simplified and only the most distressing symptoms addressed. Before starting any type of symptomatic drug treatment, specific target symptoms should be identified. The goal is to restore function and to make the target symptoms tolerable, not to remove them completely. If emergency department patients request an increase in dosage or a stronger medication, they should be told to review their medications with their regular physician before any changes are made. Insistent patients may be informed that long-term opioid use is associated with significant adverse effects, especially constipation, sedation, impaired cognition, and progressive development of tolerance and addiction.[21]

Mental Health Consultation

Patients with somatoform disorders have difficulty confronting their own emotions, view psychiatric evaluation as threatening to their sick role, and take offense at any suggestion that their fears or beliefs may be unwarranted.[7,11] They usually resist psychiatric consultation and interpret it as an attempt to be "dumped on the psychiatrist."[28] Nevertheless, psychiatric consultation may be appropriate (1) to confirm the diagnosis or discuss medications, (2) when the patient has coexistent manifestations of chronic depression or psychosis, (3) when symptoms suddenly change or become bizarre, (4) when the patient expresses suicidal ideation or severely disruptive behavior, (4) when current management is not working, or (5) when the patient requests psychotherapy.[2,9,10,28] Favorable prognostic indicators include youth, acute onset, concurrent anxiety or depression, and limited medical comorbidity.[54]

Many patients accept psychological treatment under the rubric of "stress management" as long as it targets physical symptoms and somatic distress.[15] Group therapy techniques presented as education rather than psychotherapy have had some limited success.[55] Patients should be reassured that continuity of care with the primary physician will be provided to avoid the false interpretation that the referral is an abandonment.[2]

Physician Attitudes

Somatizing patients often take over the interview. They may subtly or overtly question the physician's competence or may demand inappropriate tests, stronger medications, or specialty referrals. Emergency physicians caring for these patients predictably react with feelings of uncertainty, helplessness, anger, or guilt. Such feelings may interfere, consciously or unconsciously, with patients' care and result in extensive workups and referrals as well as overmedication or undermedication. Strategies for dealing with these feelings begin with recognition and acknowledgment. Discussing these feelings with colleagues and consultants, sharing with the patient the responsibility for care, and modifying therapeutic expectations are helpful.[2,47]

Treatment Goals

Somatizing patients have a need to be ill. Attaining invalid status enables them to be cared for and nurtured. It offers them a sense of self-importance and respect not otherwise available to them, as well as an honorable release from noxious personal and vocational responsibilities and duties.[37] To attempt a cure poses a threat to this role, and unduly positive projections by physicians are therefore understandably met with disappointment, disbelief, and even thinly veiled reproaches regarding their professional competence.[4,15,47] Thus, the goal of therapy must be *control of disability* rather than cure.[20,54] The course of management most likely to prove successful begins with performing a sympathetic and thorough problem-oriented history and physical examination, then offering the patient the paradoxical reassurance that he or she will probably always be ill. When pain is the dominant feature, the patient should not be promised complete relief; rather, a major task of the patient should be to "learn to live with some pain."[20]

Treatment goals should focus on modification of illness behavior and improvement of functional status.[37] Achievable endpoints include (1) decreased frequency and urgency of medical use, in particular a reduction in emergency department and unscheduled office visits; (2) avoidance of expensive and hazardous procedures; (3) improved work or school performance; (4) more social activities; and (5) better personal relationships.[2,9,13,21]

These principles apply equally to pediatric patients with somatoform disorders. Unnecessary tests and procedures, in addition to placing the patient at risk, may encourage somatization. Physician acknowledgment of the patient suffering's and family concerns, a "rehabilitative" approach emphasizing return to normal activities prior to definitive symptom relief, rewarding healthy behavior and discouraging the sick role, assumption by the patient of responsibility for coping with the symptoms, and treatment of coexistent anxiety or depression are the cornerstones of therapy.[23,56]

Patients with somatoform disorder have been described as the "least insightful, the least introspective and the least cognitively oriented patients one is likely to encounter."[29] Understanding the link between emotional and somatic distress need not be a treatment goal for these patients, and insight-oriented psychotherapy is neither productive nor cost effective.[2,15,20,21,29] On the other hand, both the emergency physician and the patient must accept fundamental alterations in the traditional paternalistic physician-patient relationship. Increasing responsibility for health and disease management must be incrementally turned over to the somatizing patient.[20]

DISPOSITION

Appropriate referral for "continued vigilance" should be provided for the patient. Outpatient tests or hospitalization should be avoided unless clear objective signs indicate a need for diagnostic investigation or therapeutic intervention.[20,29]

As a rule, management is best carried out by a single primary care physician who becomes the gatekeeper for all medical consultation and care.[1,8-10,13,15,20,28,47,54] The patient should be told that no alarming findings have come to light, that further testing and additional medications are not indicated at this time, and that ongoing care and periodic reassessment are indicated and will be arranged. Patients with chronic somatization should initially be seen every 2 to 4 weeks, even if their symptoms are stable. The visits should be on a time-contingent, not a need-contingent, basis. For the patient, this severs the association between medical contact and the necessity for worsening or additional symptoms and complaints. It also decreases the patient's fear of abandonment by the physician and permits repeated evaluation for early detection of objective signs of organic disease.[2,13,20] The patient seems to value the visit to the physician more highly than any treatment.[29]

KEY CONCEPTS

- The behavior of patients with somatoform disorders is unconsciously driven. They are not "faking" the symptoms or their distress.
- Short-term management should include the legitimization of symptoms, communication of compassion, and assurance that ongoing vigilance of the patient's medical condition will be arranged and maintained.
- Long-term cure of somatization disorder is unlikely. However, a steady state of symptom coping with improved function is an achievable goal. This can be done only in the primary care setting, not in the emergency department.
- New objective clinical findings should be medically evaluated. Otherwise, laboratory tests, specialty consultations, initiation of medications, and hospitalization should be avoided. Care decisions should be deferred to the patient's primary care physician when possible.

1. Zoccolillo MS, Cloninger CR: Excess medical care of women with somatization disorder. *South Med J* 79:532, 1986.

2. Gordon GH: Treating somatizing patients. *West J Med* 147:88, 1987.

3. Barsky AJ, Borus JF: Somatization and medicalization in the era of managed care. *JAMA* 274:1931, 1995.

4. Gillette RD: Behavioral factors in the management of back pain. *Am Fam Physician* 53:1313, 1996.

5. Woods SM, Natterson J, Silverman J: Medical students' disease: Hypochondriasis in medical education. *J Med Educ* 41:785, 1966.

6. Swartz M, et al: Somatization symptoms in the community: A rural/urban comparison. *Psychosomatics* 30:44, 1989.

7. *Diagnostic and Statistical Manual of Mental Disorders*, 3rd ed. Washington, DC, American Psychiatric Association, 1987.

8. Lipowski ZJ: Somatization: A borderland between medicine and psychiatry. *CMAJ* 135:609, 1986.

9. Smith RC: A clinical approach to the somatizing patient. *J Fam Pract* 21:294, 1985.

10. Smith RC: Somatization in primary care. *Clin Obstet Gynecol* 31:902, 1988.

11. Stewart DE: The changing faces of somatization. *Psychosomatics* 31:153, 1990.

12. *Diagnostic and Statistical Manual of Mental Disorders*, 4th ed. Text Revision. Washington, DC, American Psychiatric Association, 2000.

13. Ries RK, et al: The medical care abuser: Differential diagnosis and management. *J Fam Pract* 13:257, 1981.

14. Göthe CJ, Odont CM, Nilsson CG: The environmental somatization syndrome. *Psychosomatics* 36:1, 1995.

15. Barsky AJ: A 37-year-old man with multiple somatic complaints. *JAMA* 278:673, 1997.

16. Ciccone DS, Just N, Bandilla EB: Non-organic symptom reporting in patients with chronic non-malignant pain. *Pain* 68:329, 1996.

17. Katon W, et al: Somatization: A spectrum of severity. *Am J Psychiatry* 148:34, 1991.

18. Escobar JI, et al: Somatic symptom index (SSI): A new and abridged somatization construct. *J Nerv Ment Dis* 177:140, 1989.

19. Badura AS, et al: Dissociation, somatization, substance abuse, and coping in women with chronic pelvic pain. *Obstet Gynecol* 90:405, 1997.

20. Ford CV: *The Somatizing Disorders: Illness as a Way of Life.* New York, Elsevier Biomedical, 1983.

21. Servan-Schreiber D, Kolb R, Tabas G: The somatizing patient. *Prim Care* 26:225, 1999.

22. Zwaigenbaum L, et al: Highly somatizing young adolescents and the risk of depression. *Pediatrics* 103:1203, 1999.

23. Campo JV, Fritsch SL: Somatization in children and adolescents. *J Am Acad Child Adolesc Psychiatry* 33:1223, 1994.

24. Guze SB: The validity and significance of the clinical diagnosis of hysteria (Briquet's syndrome). *Am J Psychiatry* 132:138, 1975.

25. De Gucht V, Fischler B: Somatization: A critical review of conceptual and methodological issues. *Psychosomatics* 43:1, 2002.

26. Epstein RM, Quill TE, McWhinney IR: Somatization reconsidered: Incorporating the patient's experience of illness. *Arch Intern Med* 159:215, 1999.

27. McWhinney IR, Epstein RM, Freeman TR: Lingua medica: Rethinking somatization. *Ann Intern Med* 126:747, 1997.

28. Dubovsky SL, Weissberg MP: Hypochondriasis. In Dubovsky SL, Weissberg MP: *Clinical Psychiatry in Primary Care*, 3rd ed. Baltimore, Williams & Wilkins, 1986.

29. Murphy GE: The clinical management of hysteria. *JAMA* 247:2559, 1982.

30. Othmer E, DeSouza C: A screening test for somatization disorder (hysteria). *Am J Psychiatry* 142:1146, 1985.

31. Barsky AJ, Wyshak G: Hypochondriasis and related health attitudes. *Psychosomatics* 30:412, 1989.

32. Smith GR, Monson RA, Ray DG: Patients with multiple unexplained symptoms: Their characteristics, functional health, and health care utilization. *Arch Intern Med* 146:69, 1986.

33. Barsky AJ, et al: The clinical course of palpitations in medical outpatients. *Arch Intern Med* 155:1782, 1995.

34. Kapoor WN, et al: Psychiatric illnesses in patients with syncope. *Am J Med* 99:505, 1995.

35. Coryell W, Norten SG: Briquet's syndrome (somatization disorder) and primary depression: Comparison of background and outcome. *Compr Psychiatry* 22:249, 1981.

36. Coryell W: Diagnosis-specific mortality: Primary unipolar depression and Briquet's syndrome (somatization disorder). *Arch Gen Psychiatry* 38:939, 1981.

37. Quill TE: Somatization disorder: One of medicine's blind spots. *JAMA* 254:3075, 1985.

38. Kent DA, Tomasson K, Coryell W: Course and outcome of conversion and somatization disorders: A four-year follow-up. *Psychosomatics* 36:138, 1995.

39. Morrison J: Histrionic personality disorder in women with somatization disorder. *Psychosomatics* 30:433, 1989.

40. Rogers MP, et al: Prevalence of somatoform disorders in a large sample of patients with anxiety disorders. *Psychosomatics* 37:17, 1996.

41. Smith GR: The epidemiology and treatment of depression when it coexists with somatoform disorders, somatization, or pain. *Gen Hosp Psychiatry* 14:265, 1992.

42. Dula DJ, DeNaples L: Emergency department presentation of patients with conversion disorder. *Acad Emerg Med* 2:120, 1995.

43. Barnert C: Conversion reactions and psychophysiologic disorders: A comparative study. *Psychiatry Med* 2:205, 1971.

44. Barsky AJ, Klerman GL: Overview: Hypochondriasis, bodily complaints, and somatic styles. *Am J Psychiatry* 140:273, 1983.

45. Kellner R, et al: Anxiety, depression, and somatization in DSM-III hypochondriasis. *Psychosomatics* 30:57, 1989.

46. Sternbach RA: Varieties of pain games. *Adv Neurol* 4:423, 1974.

47. Lichstein PR: Caring for the patient with multiple somatic complaints. *South Med J* 79:310, 1986.

48. Lipowski ZJ: Somatization and depression. *Psychosomatics* 31:13, 1990.

49. Katon W: Depression: Somatization and social factors [editorial]. *J Fam Pract* 27:579, 1988.

50. Goldberg D, et al: Detecting anxiety and depression in general medical settings. *BMJ* 297:897, 1988.

51. Stein DJ: Comorbidity in generalized anxiety disorder: Impact and implications. *J Clin Psychiatry* 62(Suppl 11):29, 2001.

52. Johns M: Communicating effectively with a patient who has somatization disorder. *Am Fam Physician* 59:2639, 1999.

53. Fishbain DA, et al: Do antidepressants have an analgesic effect in psychogenic pain and somatoform pain disorder? A meta-analysis. *Psychosom Med* 60:503, 1998.

54. Barsky AJ: Hypochondriasis: Medical management and psychiatric treatment. *Psychosomatics* 37:48, 1996.

55. Kashner TM, et al: Enhancing the health of somatization disorder patients: Effectiveness of short-term group therapy. *Psychosomatics* 36:462, 1995.

56. Campo JV, Fritz G: A management model for pediatric somatization. *Psychosomatics* 42:467, 2001.

Factitious Disorders and Malingering

Thomas B. Purcell

PERSPECTIVE

Patients may present to the emergency department with symptoms that are intentionally produced or simulated. The inducements that generate this behavior define two distinct varieties: factitious disorders and malingering.

Factitious disorders are characterized by symptoms or signs that are intentionally produced or feigned by the patient in the absence of apparent external incentives.[1,2] These patients constitute approximately 1% of general psychiatric referrals. This percentage is somewhat lower than that seen in emergency medicine and other clinical settings because acceptance of psychiatric treatment is unusual in these patients.[1,3] Among patients referred to infectious disease specialists for fever of unknown origin, 9.3% of the disorders are factitious.[4] Between 5% and 20% of patients followed in epilepsy clinics have psychogenic seizures, and in some primary care settings the number reaches 44%.[5] Among patients submitting kidney stones for analysis, up to 3.5% have been found to be fraudulent.[6]

Munchausen's syndrome, the most dramatic and exasperating of the factitious disorders, was originally described in 1951.[7] This fortunately rare syndrome takes its name from Baron Karl F. von Munchausen (1720-1797), a noted raconteur who amused his friends with fantastic and entertaining but untrue personal anecdotes. The diagnosis is appropriately applied to only 10% to 20% of patients with factitious disorders.[1,8] Other names applied include the "hospital hobo syndrome" (patients wander from hospital to hospital seeking admission), peregrinating (wandering) problem patients, hospital addict, polysurgical addiction, laparotomaphilia migrans, Kopenickades syndrome, Ahasuerus syndrome, and hospital vagrant.[3,9,10]

An especially pernicious variant of Munchausen's syndrome involves the simulation or production of factitious disease in children by a parent or caregiver. Also known as Polle syndrome[9] and factitious disorder by proxy,[11] *Munchausen syndrome by proxy* (MSBP) was first described in 1977.[12] The syndrome excludes straightforward physical abuse or neglect and simple failure to thrive; mere lying to cover up physical abuse is not MSBP.[13,14] The key discriminator is motive: the mother is making the child ill so that she can vicariously assume the sick role with all its benefits. Mortality from MSBP is 9% to 31%.[14,15] Children who die are generally younger than 3 years, and the most frequent causes of death are suffocation and poisoning.[14] Permanent disfigurement or permanent impairment of function resulting directly from induced disease or indirectly from invasive procedures, multiple medications, or major surgery occurs in at least 8% of these children.[14,16]

Malingering is the simulation of disease by the intentional production of false or grossly exaggerated physical or psychological symptoms, motivated by external incentives such as avoiding military conscription or duty, avoiding work, obtaining financial compensation, evading criminal prosecution, obtaining drugs, gaining hospital admission (for the purpose of obtaining free room and board), or securing better living conditions.[2,17-19] The most common goal among such "patients" presenting to the emergency department is obtaining drugs, whereas in the office or clinic the gain is more commonly insurance payments or industrial injury settlements.[20] Because of underreporting, the true incidence of malingering is difficult to gauge, but estimates include a 1% incidence among mental health patients in civilian clinical practice, 5% in the military, and as high as 10% to 20% among patients presenting in a litigious context.[18]

CLINICAL FEATURES

Factitious Disorders

With a factitious disorder, the production of symptoms and signs is compulsive in that the patient is unable to refrain from the behavior even when its risks are known. The behavior is voluntary only in the sense that it is deliberate and purposeful (intentional) but not in the sense that the acts can be fully controlled.[2] The underlying motivation for producing these deceptions, securing the sick role, is primarily unconscious.[8,21,22] Individuals who readily admit that they have produced their own injuries (e.g., self-mutilation) are not included in the category of factitious disorders.[11] Presentations may be acute, in response to an identifiable recent psychosocial stress (termination of romantic relationship, threats to self esteem), or a chronic life pattern, reflective of the way the person deals with life in general.[23] The symptoms involved may be either psychological or physical.

Psychological Symptoms

This disorder is the intentional production or feigning of psychological (often psychotic) symptoms suggestive of a mental disorder. Stimulants may be used to induce restlessness or insomnia, hallucinogens to create altered levels of consciousness, and hypnotics to produce lethargy. This psychological factitious condition is less common than factitious disorders with physical symptoms and is almost always superimposed on a severe personality disorder.[2,11]

Physical Symptoms

The intentional production of physical symptoms may take the form of fabricating symptoms without signs (e.g., feigning abdominal pain), simulation of signs suggesting illness (e.g., fraudulent pyuria, induced anemia), self-inflicted pathology (e.g., producing abscesses by injecting contaminated material under the skin), or genuine complications from the intentional misuse of medications (e.g., diuretics, hypoglycemic agents).[19] These patients are predominantly unmarried women younger than 40 years. They typically accept their illness with few complaints and are generally well-educated, responsible workers or students with moral attitudes and otherwise conscientious behavior.[19,24,25] Many are in health care occupations, including nurses, aides, and physicians.

These patients are willing to undergo incredible hardship, limb amputation, organ loss, and even death to perpetuate the masquerade.[19] Although multiple hospitalizations often lead to iatrogenic physical conditions, such as postoperative pain syndromes and drug addictions, patients continue to crave hospitalization for its own sake. They typically have a fragile and fragmented self-image and are susceptible to psychotic, and even suicidal, episodes.[24] Interactions with the health care system and relationships with caregivers provide the needed structure that stabilizes the patients' sense of self. The hospital may be perceived as a refuge, sanctuary, or womb-like environment.[3,19,21,26] Some patients are apparently driven by the conviction that they have a real, but as yet undiscovered, illness. Consequently, artificial symptoms are contrived to convince the physician to continue a search for the elusive disease process.[19] Factitious illness behavior has even emerged on the Internet. "Virtual support groups" offering person-to-person communications through chat rooms and bulletin boards have been perpetrated by individuals, under the pretense of illness or personal crisis, for the purpose of extracting attention or sympathy, acting out anger, or exercising control over others.[27]

There has been increasing recognition of factitious illness produced by children (distinct from the MSBP described later). These children, ranging in age from 8 to 18 years, are typically "bland, flat and indifferent during their extensive medical interventions . . . depressed, socially isolated and often obese."[28] Among the most common presentations are fever without clear etiology, diabetic ketoacidosis, purpura, and recurrent infections. The prognosis is good if identification and psychotherapeutic intervention can be carried out at a young age.[28]

Munchausen's Syndrome

The uncommon patient with true Munchausen's syndrome has a prolonged pattern of "medical imposture," usually years in duration. The behavior usually begins before age 20 and is diagnosed between ages 35 and 39. Twice as many men are affected as women.[3,29] Patients' entire adult lives may consist of trying to gain admission to hospitals and then steadfastly resisting discharge. Their career of imposture usually lasts about 9 years but has continued unabated for as long as 50 years.[3] The quest for repeated hospitalizations often takes these patients to numerous and widespread cities, states, and countries.[2]

These individuals see themselves as important people, or at least related to such persons, and their life events are depicted as exceptional.[29] They possess extensive knowledge of medical terminology. Frequently there is a history of genuine disease, and the individual may exhibit objective physical findings.[24]

The symptoms presented are "limited only by the person's medical knowledge, sophistication, and imagination."[2] The alleged illnesses involved have been termed *dilemma diagnoses* in that investigators rarely can totally rule out the disorder, clarify the cause, or prove that it did not exist at one time.[3] Common presentations are those that most reliably result in admission to the hospital, such as abdominal pain, self-injection of a foreign substance,[9,10] feculent urine, bleeding disorders, hemoptysis, paroxysmal headaches, seizures, shortness of breath, asthma with respiratory failure,[3,30] chronic pain,[22] acute cardiovascular symptoms (e.g., chest pain, induced hypertension and syncope),[29] renal colic and spurious urolithiasis,[6] fever of unknown origin (hyperpyrexia figmentatica),[4,10] profound hypoglycemia, and coma with anisocoria.[31] Such self-induced conditions themselves may prove highly injurious or even lethal.[9]

The patient usually presents to the emergency department during evenings or on weekends so as to minimize accessibility to psychiatric consultants, personal physicians, and past medical records.[10,24] In teaching institutions these patients typically present in July, shortly after the change in resident house officers.[3] They relate their history in a precise, dramatic, even intriguing fashion, embellished with flourishes of pathologic lying and self-aggrandizement. Pseudologica fantastica, or pathologic lying, is a distinctive peculiarity of these patients. In a chronic, often lifelong behavior pattern, the patient typically takes a central and heroic role in these tales, which may function as a way to act out fantasy.[32] The history quickly becomes vague and inconsistent, however, when the patient is questioned in detail about medical contacts.[2,26] Attempts to manage the complaint on an outpatient basis are adamantly resisted.[22] Once admitted, the patient initially appeals to the physician's qualities of nurturance and omnipotence, lavishing praise on the caregivers. Behavior rapidly evolves, however, as the patient creates havoc on the ward by insisting on excessive attention while ignoring both hospital rules and the prescribed therapeutic regimen.[2] When the hoax is uncovered and the patient confronted, fear of rejection abruptly changes into rage against the treating physician, closely followed by departure from the hospital against medical advice.[9,10,22]

Munchausen Syndrome by Proxy

The diagnosis of MSBP depends on specific criteria (Box 112-1).[14] The presenting complaints typically evade definitive diagnosis and are refractory to conventional therapy for no apparent reason.[14] The symptoms are usually more than five in number, presented in a confused picture, are unusual or serious, and, by design, are unverifiable. They invariably occur when the mother is alone with the child or otherwise unobserved.[33] In 72% to 95% of cases, simulation or production of illness occurs while the victim is hospitalized.[14]

Simulated illness, faked by the mother without producing direct harm to the child (e.g., adding blood to a urine specimen), is present in 25% of cases. *Produced illness*, which the mother actually inflicts on the child (e.g., injection of feces into an intravenous line), is found in 50% of cases. Both simulated and produced illnesses are found in 25% of cases.[14]

MSBP most commonly arises with factitious bleeding, seizures, central nervous system (CNS) depression, apnea, diarrhea, vomiting, fever, and rash.[14] Reported techniques of simulation or production of disease include administration of drugs or toxins (e.g., chronic arsenic poisoning, ipecac, warfarin, phenolphthalein, hydrocarbons, salt, imipramine, laxatives, CNS depressants), caustics applied to the skin, and nasal aspiration of cooking oil.[12,14-16,24,34] Techniques of asphyxiation include (1) covering the mouth or nose with one or both hands, a cloth, or plastic film and (2) inserting the fingers into the back of the mouth. In such instances, even struggling infants may sustain no cutaneous markings.[35] Cases involving seizures are common and may involve third-party witnesses. On personal questioning, however, these witnesses frequently deny the occurrence of seizure activity.[14]

In a variant of MSBP termed *serial Munchausen syndrome by proxy*, there may be a history of similar strange presentations in multiple siblings, although typically only one child is involved at a time.[15,16,35] In 9% of such cases there is a history of siblings who died under mysterious circumstances.[14]

Perpetrator Characteristics

Ninety-eight percent of perpetrators are biologic mothers from all socioeconomic groups.[14] Many have a background in health professions or social work, features of Munchausen's syndrome themselves, or a past history of psychiatric treatment, marital problems, or suicide attempts.[14,15] Depression, anxiety, and somatization are common, but frankly psychotic behavior by the mother is atypical.[14,16] Perpetrators of MSBP have an inherent skill in manipulating health workers and child protection services.[36] They are pleasant, socially adept, cooperative, and appreciative of good medical care. They often choose to stay in the hospital with their child, cultivate unusually close relationships with hospital staff, and thrive on the staff's attention.[12-14,16,34] This affable relationship with the medical team rapidly changes to excessive anger and denial when confronted with suspicions.[16]

Most of these mothers have had an abusive experience early in life, and they use the health care system as a means to satisfy personal nurturing demands.[33,37] They often cannot distinguish their needs from the child's and satisfy their own needs first. They derive a sense of purpose from the medical and nursing attention gained when their children are in the hospital.[13,14,16,37] Alternatively, the behavior may enable the mothers to escape from their own physical or psychological illnesses, marital difficulties, or social problems.[33]

Victim Characteristics

Victims of MSBP are equally male and female children. The mean age at diagnosis is 40 months, and the mean duration from the onset of signs and symptoms to diagnosis is 15 months.[14] A known physical illness that explains part of the symptoms is common among these children.[37] Most have a history of significant failure to thrive and have been hospitalized in more than one institution. Delays in many areas of performance and learning, difficulty with family relationships, attention deficit disorder, or clinical depression may coexist.[16] Victims of MSBP are also found among the elderly population, although this is uncommon.[38]

Malingering

Malingering is frequently found in association with *antisocial personality disorder*. On questioning, malingerers are vague about prior hospitalizations or treatments. The physicians who previously treated them are usually unavailable. At times, malingerers may be careless about their symptoms and abandon them when they believe no one is watching.[24] In some "patients," such as those seeking drugs, homeless persons seeking hospital admission on a cold night, or prisoners wanting a holiday from incarceration, the secondary gain may be clear. In other persons the external incentive may be obscure.

In contrast to the person with factitious disorders, the malingerer prefers *counterfeit mental illness* because it is objectively difficult to verify or disprove. Amnesia is the most common psychological presentation, followed by paranoia, morbid depression, suicidal ideation, and psychosis.[18]

DIAGNOSTIC STRATEGIES

Factitious Disorders

Initial diagnosis is often delayed because the possibility of factitious disease is not considered, physicians may be unfamiliar with this problem, or the patient does not exhibit the type of personality expected with this behavior.[6] Diagnosis may be confounded by genuine medical illnesses predating and coexisting with a factitious disorder. For example, patients with factitious hypoglycemia may have a history of insulin-dependent diabetes mellitus, or factitious skin disorders may be preceded by true dermatologic diseases.[1] Identification of a factitious disorder is usually made in one of four ways: (1) the patient is accidentally discovered in the act, (2) incriminating items are found, (3) laboratory values suggest nonorganic etiology, or (4) the diagnosis is made by exclusion.[11] Wallach provides a useful review of the laboratory diagnosis of factitious disorders including feigned endocrine, hematologic, genitourinary, gastrointestinal, and infectious disorders.[39]

Suspected MSBP requires a detailed description of the event or illness and a search for caregiver witnesses, who should be interviewed personally. Although it is essential to see the child when the symptoms are present, the parents show great ingenuity at frustrating this effort.[37] Additional history of unusual illness in siblings and parents should be sought. Child victims who are verbal should be interviewed in private regarding foods, medicines, and their recollection of the symptoms or events. Prior medical records of the victim and, if possible, the siblings should be examined, although parents may impede such data gathering.

The major obstacle to early discovery of MSBP is its omission from the differential diagnosis. When it is considered, the diagnosis is generally made easily and quickly.[14] A suspected diagnosis may be confirmed through separation of the parent from the child (with consequent cessation of symptoms), covert video surveillance during hospitalization, or toxin screens.[16,33,35] In the majority of cases, the caregiver attempts to induce episodes surreptitiously while in the hospital, often during the first day of admission.[14,33]

Malingering

Malingering should be strongly suspected with any combination of certain factors (Box 112-2).[2,40] A definitive diagnosis of malingering can be established only by securing the patient's confession, a rare circumstance.[41] Because malingering constitutes criminal behavior, documentation of this diagnosis must be made with care.[18] In the absence of proof of wrongdoing, it is best to assume that the patient is not a malingerer but rather a common somatizer.[41]

DIFFERENTIAL CONSIDERATIONS

Patients with factitious disorders are distinguished from malingerers because their desired hospitalization

BOX 112-2. Characteristics of Malingering

1. Medicolegal context of the presentation (e.g., the patient was referred by his or her attorney)
2. Marked discrepancy between the person's claimed stress or disability and objective findings
3. Poor cooperation during the diagnostic evaluation or poor compliance with previously prescribed treatment regimens
4. The person exhibits, or has a history of, antisocial behavior.

or surgery seems to offer no secondary gain other than granting the sick role.[2,9,20] The clinical presentation of the majority of patients with factitious disorders, unlike those with Munchausen's syndrome, is relatively subtle and convincing. The complaints are generally chronic in nature rather than emergent and precipitous, and there are no obvious associated behavioral aberrations.[19] Malingering is usually associated with less chronicity than factitious disorder, and malingerers are more reluctant to accept expensive, possibly painful, or dangerous tests or surgery.[20]

MANAGEMENT

Treatment options for factitious disorders depend on the patient's characteristics. Although it is challenging, managing common forms of factitious disorder can be more rewarding, especially with adolescents, than managing Munchausen's syndrome.[1,8,21,26] Cases stemming from an underlying depression have a more favorable prognosis than those associated with borderline personalities.[24]

The best approach to patients with factitious disorder, other than Munchausen's syndrome and MSBP, remains an area of controversy. Direct nonaccusatory confrontation has been advocated as "the foundation of effective management" when coupled with the assurance that an ongoing relationship with a physician will be provided.[3,19,20,24] This may be the first step in the acceptance of outpatient therapy.[3]

Others point out that confrontation is ineffective in most patients and may even be counterproductive in that it threatens to undermine a needed psychological defense. Enforced recognition of external objective reality, while simultaneously disallowing the patient's subjective experience, may generate even more dysfunction to legitimize and maintain symptoms or may place the patient at risk for suicide.[8,11,26,42,43] Some patients may relinquish this defense if they feel safe in doing so and may abandon a claim to disease if some face-saving option is offered. This approach, termed the *therapeutic double bind* or *contingency management*, involves informing the patient that a factitious disorder may exist. The patient is further told that failure to respond fully to medical care would constitute conclusive evidence that the patient's problem is not organic but rather psychiatric. The problem is therefore reframed or redefined in such a way that (1) symptoms and their resolution are both legitimized and (2) the patient has little choice but to accept and respond to a proposed course of action or seek care elsewhere.[8,43]

Individuals with Munchausen's syndrome typically demonstrate overt sociopathic traits or a borderline personality disorder and are demanding and manipulative, especially regarding analgesics.[4,8] They have been described as "essentially untreatable," and successful management of this condition is, in fact, considered reportable. Early confrontation or limit setting, especially regarding drug use, is advocated.[8,10,19,22,24] Although Munchausen patients typically do not want to be examined extensively, a thorough physical examination should be performed to rule out physical pathology.

MSBP constitutes a form of child (or elder) abuse, and appropriate action to protect the victim, including notification of welfare services, should take immediate priority.[35,38] When the diagnosis has been established and the parents confronted, psychiatric care should be made immediately available to the parents because maternal suicide is a significant risk.[14]

Malingerers do not want to be treated. Because they are "gaming the system" for personal advantage, the last thing they want is an accurate identification of their behavior and appropriate intervention. The emergency physician should maintain clinical neutrality, offering the reassurance that the symptoms and examination are not consistent with any serious disease.

Some authors have characterized patients' use of medical resources under false pretenses as criminal behavior, and several states have enacted legislation against the fraudulent acquisition of medical services. Successful prosecution of such behavior has been reported.[44] Conversely, patients with factitious disorders can and do sue. In dealing with such patients, it is advisable to involve hospital administration and risk management. Clandestine searches are inadvisable, and respect for the patient's confidentiality should be maintained.[11]

DISPOSITION

Patients with factitious disorder should receive primary care follow-up and ongoing care. If acceptable, psychiatric referral should be arranged. Referral to other medical specialists or hospitalization should be avoided when possible.

The manner of presentation and the unavailability of past medical history often allow patients with Munchausen's syndrome to achieve hospital admission. If the patient is discharged from the emergency department, outpatient primary care follow-up and psychiatric referral should be offered, although both are likely to be refused.[22]

Because perpetrators of MSBP typically induce symptomatic episodes soon after hospitalization, admission of the victims (children or elderly persons) without taking appropriate precautions may actually place them at increased risk.[14] Visits by the suspected perpetrator should be closely supervised, and no food, drink, or medicines should be brought in by the family. Protective services should be notified. Out-of-home placement of children in established cases of MSBP is advisable, and best outcomes are seen among children taken into long-term care at an early age without access to their mother. Children allowed to return home have a high rate of repeated abuse.[36] In 20% of reported deaths the parents had been confronted and the child sent home to them, subsequently to die.[14]

After courteous but assertive reassurance, suspected malingerers should be offered primary care follow-up if the symptoms do not resolve. These individuals may become threatening when they are either denied treatment or overtly confronted.[17]

 KEY CONCEPTS

- Emergency department patients who have consciously synthesized symptoms and signs may be divided into two broad diagnostic categories: (1) those with obvious secondary gain (malingering), who control their actions, and (2) those with a motivation of achieving the sick role (factitious disorders), who cannot control their actions.
- Emergency department management of patients suspected of fabricating disease includes a caring attitude and a search for objective clinical evidence of treatable medical or psychiatric illness.
- Unnecessary tests, medications, and hospitalizations should be avoided in the absence of objective evidence of a medical or psychiatric disease, and patients should be referred for ongoing primary care.
- In cases of suspected Munchausen's syndrome by proxy involving children or elderly persons, protection of the victim takes first priority.

REFERENCES

1. Sutherland AJ, Rodin GM: Factitious disorders in a general hospital setting: Clinical features and a review of the literature. *Psychosomatics* 31:392, 1990.
2. *Diagnostic and Statistical Manual of Mental Disorders*, 4th ed. Text Revision. Washington, DC, American Psychiatric Association, 2000.
3. Burkle FM, Calabro JJ, Parks FB: Munchausen's syndrome presenting as a respiratory failure requiring intubation. *Ann Emerg Med* 16:203, 1987.
4. Aduan RP, et al: Factitious fever and self-induced infection: A report of 32 cases and review of the literature. *Ann Intern Med* 90:230, 1979.
5. Riggio S: Psychogenic seizures. *Emerg Med Clin North Am* 12:1001, 1994.
6. Gault MH, Campbell NR, Aksu AE: Spurious stones. *Nephron* 48:274, 1988.
7. Asher R: Munchausen syndrome. *Lancet* 1:339, 1951.
8. Eisendrath SJ: Factitious physical disorders: Treatment without confrontation. *Psychosomatics* 30:383, 1989.
9. Nichols GR, Davis GJ, Corey TS: In the shadow of the baron: Sudden death due to Munchausen syndrome. *Am J Emerg Med* 8:216, 1990.
10. Scully RE, Mark EJ, McNeely BU: Weekly clinicopathological exercises, case records of the Massachusetts General Hospital: Case 28-1984. *N Engl J Med* 311:108, 1984.

11. Wise MG, Ford CV: Factitious disorders. *Prim Care* 26:315, 1999.
12. Meadow R: Munchausen syndrome by proxy: The hinterland of child abuse. *Lancet* 1:343, 1977.
13. Meadow R: What is, and what is not, "Munchausen syndrome by proxy"? *Arch Dis Child* 72:534, 1995.
14. Rosenberg DA: Web of deceit: A literature review of Munchausen syndrome by proxy. *Child Abuse Negl* 11:547, 1987.
15. Alexander R, Smith W, Stevenson R: Serial Munchausen syndrome by proxy. *Pediatrics* 86:581, 1990.
16. Lacey SR, et al: Munchausen syndrome by proxy: Patterns of presentation to pediatric surgeons. *J Pediatr Surg* 28:827, 1993.
17. Dubovsky SL, Weissberg MP: Hypochondriasis. In Dubovsky SL: *Clinical Psychiatry in Primary Care*, 3rd ed. Baltimore, Williams & Wilkins, 1986.
18. Lipian MS, Mills MJ: Malingering. In Sadock BJ, Sadock VA (eds): *Comprehensive Textbook of Psychiatry*, 7th ed. Philadelphia, Lippincott Williams & Wilkins, 2000.
19. Reich P, Gottfried LA: Factitious disorders in a teaching hospital. *Ann Intern Med* 99:240, 1983.
20. Ries RK, et al: The medical care abuser: Differential diagnosis and management. *J Fam Pract* 13:257, 1981.
21. Eisendrath SJ: Factitious physical disorders. *West J Med* 160:177, 1994.
22. Fishbain DA, et al: Munchausen syndrome presenting with chronic pain: Case report. *Pain* 35:91, 1988.
23. Goldstein AB: Identification and classification of factitious disorders: An analysis of cases reported during a ten year period. *Int J Psychiatry Med* 28:221, 1998.
24. Ford CV: *The Somatizing Disorders: Illness as a Way of Life.* New York, Elsevier Biomedical, 1983.
25. Krahn LE, Li H, O'Connor MK: Patients who strive to be ill: Factitious disorder with physical symptoms. *Am J Psychiatry* 160:1163, 2003.
26. Spivak H, Rodin G, Sutherland A: The psychology of factitious disorders: A reconsideration. *Psychosomatics* 35:25, 1994.
27. Feldman MD: Munchausen by Internet: Detecting factitious illness and crisis on the Internet. *South Med J* 93:669, 2000.
28. Libow JA: Child and adolescent illness falsification. *Pediatrics* 105:336, 2000.
29. Ludwigs U, et al: Factitious disorder presenting with acute cardiovascular symptoms. *J Intern Med* 236:685, 1994.
30. Bernstein JA, et al: Potentially fatal asthma and syncope: A new variant of Munchausen's syndrome in sports medicine. *Chest* 99:763, 1991.
31. Bretz SW, Richards JR: Munchausen syndrome presenting acutely in the emergency department. *J Emerg Med* 18:417, 1999.
32. Newmark N, Adityanjee, Kay J: Pseudologia fantastica and factitious disorder: Review of the literature and a case report. *Compr Psychiatry* 40:89, 1999.
33. Samuels MP, et al: Fourteen cases of imposed upper airway obstruction. *Arch Dis Child* 67:162, 1992.
34. Fisher GC, Mitchell I: Is Munchausen syndrome by proxy really a syndrome? *Arch Dis Child* 72:530, 1995.
35. Mitchell I, et al: Apnea and factitious illness (Munchausen syndrome) by proxy. *Pediatrics* 92:810, 1993.
36. Davis P, et al: Procedures, placement, and risks of further abuse after Munchausen syndrome by proxy, non-accidental poisoning, and non-accidental suffocation. *Arch Dis Child* 78:217, 1998.
37. Eminson DM, Postlethwaite RJ: Factitious illness: Recognition and management. *Arch Dis Child* 67:1510, 1992.
38. Ben-Chetrit E, Melmed RN: Recurrent hypoglycaemia in multiple myeloma: A case of Munchausen syndrome by proxy in an elderly patient. *J Intern Med* 244:175, 1998.
39. Wallach J: Laboratory diagnosis of factitious disorders. *Arch Intern Med* 154:1690; 1994.
40. Levine SS, Helm ML: An AIDS diagnosis used as focus of malingering. *West J Med* 148:337, 1988.
41. Smith RC: Somatization in primary care. *Clin Obstet Gynecol* 31:902, 1988.
42. Ugurlu S, et al: Factitious disease of periocular and facial skin. *Am J Ophthalmol* 127:196, 1999.
43. Teasell RW, Shapiro AP: Strategic-behavioral intervention in the treatment of chronic nonorganic motor disorders. *Am J Phys Med Rehabil* 73:44, 1994.
44. Feldman MD: Factitious disorders and fraud [letter]. *Psychosomatics* 36:509, 1995.

CHAPTER

113 Suicide

Stephen A. Colucciello

PERSPECTIVE

Although suicide has occurred in all societies since the beginning of recorded history, attitudes toward suicide have differed dramatically among various eras and cultures. Seneca viewed suicide as the ultimate expression of personal freedom, but later Judeo-Christian religions have routinely condemned it. Shakespeare portrayed suicide sympathetically and expressed either pity or admiration for the victim.[1]

In the United States, suicide is illegal in 49 states, and only since 1994 has assisted suicide of terminally ill patients been sanctioned in Oregon. On the Internet, suicide help groups provide active advice on methods, and numerous bulletin boards condemn them. More than 100,000 sites about suicide now appear on the Internet.[2]

Two facts are especially important to the emergency department. First, many suicide attempts occur during an acute crisis, such as a personal loss or the exacerbation of an underlying psychiatric disorder. This acute crisis is usually time limited and may be resolvable or treatable. Second, except for the acutely psychotic patient, suicidal patients are usually ambivalent about dying. The attitude and approach of the emergency physician can help a patient choose crisis resolution rather than death.

Definitions

The term *suicide,* from the Latin *suicidum* (to kill the self), refers to a continuum of thought and action that runs from ideation to completion of the act.[3] *Parasuicide* is used by the British to describe an attempted suicide that is more of a gesture than a serious act. Statistically, there are 10 to 40 suicide attempts for every completed act.[4] *Chronic suicidal behavior* consists of recurrent self-destructive acts, such as heavy drinking in the presence of alcoholic liver disease. *Occult suicide* is applied to self-destructive acts disguised as accidents, such as the intoxicated, depressed driver in an apparently accidental car crash. *Silent suicide* refers to the act of slowly killing oneself by nonviolent means, such as starvation or noncompliance with essential medical treatment. Silent suicide is most common in elderly patients and is frequently unrecognized.

A *suicide pact* involves an agreement between two people who are intimately involved and accounts for 0.6% of all suicides.[5] *Mass suicide* or *group suicide* involves a number of willing and sometimes not-so-willing persons, such as members of an apocalyptic cult.

Epidemiology

Suicidal ideation is common, with as many as one in three people considering suicide during their lifetime.[6] Suicide is the eighth leading cause of death in the United States, claiming more than 31,000 lives annually, with an overall rate of 10.7 per 100,000 population in 2001.[7]

Suicide rates vary with age, gender, race, and marital status. Suicides are highest among older individuals, particularly elderly white men. White men commit 73% of all suicides in the United States.[7] Whites and Native Americans are much more likely to commit suicide than African Americans, Hispanics, or Asians. Marriage decreases the likelihood of suicide, but separated or divorced people have a higher rate of suicide than those who never had a close relationship.

Women attempt suicide three to four times more often than men, whereas men are three to four times more likely to succeed. Worldwide, Chinese and Indian women have higher rates of suicide than women of other nationalities.[8] Pregnant women have a significantly lower risk than women of childbearing age who are not pregnant. Motherhood seems to protect against suicide, except that postpartum depression is associated with a higher than normal suicide rate. In general, men have a higher incidence of alcoholism and tend to use more lethal methods, such as firearms.

Most people who attempt suicide have one or more known risk factors (Box 113-1). Individuals with the highest risk include those with psychiatric disorders, alcohol or substance abusers, adolescents, elderly persons, and patients with certain chronic illnesses. In patients hospitalized for psychiatric disorders, the first month after discharge carries a high risk of suicide.[9]

BOX 113-1. Risk Factors for Suicide

Demographics
White men older than 65 years
Women older than 60 years
Males 15 to 24 years old

Psychiatric Disorders
Major depression
Bipolar disorder
Schizophrenia
Borderline personality disorder
Panic disorder

Substance Abuse
Alcoholism
Drug abuse (especially cocaine)

Medical History
Prior suicide attempts
Chronic pain or illness
Physical or sexual abuse
Recent psychiatric hospital discharge
Terminal illness

Family History
Family violence
Suicide in family

Social Factors
Firearm in home
Living alone
Separated, widowed, or divorced
Unemployed
Recent personal loss
Incarceration

Emotional Factors
Hopelessness
Chronic loneliness
Fixation on death

A strong association may exist between suicide risk and bisexuality or homosexuality in men.[10] Unemployment appears to be a risk factor for suicide among 18- to 24-year-old men.[11] Homeless people with mental illness are at particularly high risk for suicidal behavior, only in part because of the high prevalence of traditional risk factors.

Suicide completers and suicide attempters represent separate but overlapping populations.[12] Although 10% to 15% of suicide attempters ultimately complete suicide, 60% to 70% of suicide completers have no prior history of attempts and commit suicide on the first known attempt.[13] In individuals who committed suicide while not in contact with mental health services, nearly one third of cases (32%) have no concurrent mental disorder.[14]

PATHOPHYSIOLOGY AND ETIOLOGY

Societal, Psychiatric, and Biologic Factors

There are many motivations for attempting suicide. It may be seen as the only escape from a terminal disease or intense chronic pain. It may be an act of revenge or political protest. Most suicide attempts occur in individuals with intense feelings of hopelessness, guilt, or self-hatred, often compounded by the exacerbation of an underlying psychiatric disorder or by the occurrence or perception of a great personal loss. The underlying causes for suicide are similar for adults and adolescents; however, adolescents tend to romanticize suicide, and "copycat" suicides are frequent after the suicide of celebrities or friends. Regardless of the motivation, most suicide attempters are ambivalent, and their attraction to death is usually counterbalanced by a desire to live. This internal conflict is reflected in the high ratio of attempted to completed suicides, and the fact that most people consult a physician shortly before their death.

Psychoanalysts explain suicide in terms of psychic forces. Freud believed that suicide stems from aggression, initially directed toward another person, which ultimately turns against the self. Depression and suicide in the Freudian model represent internalized anger. Many authorities have recognized this association between aggression and suicide. In the United States, more than 1000 deaths each year result from murder-suicides. The perpetrators are usually young men with intense sexual jealousy, depressed mothers, or despairing elderly men. Their victims are usually female sexual partners, young children, or blood relatives. The dual risk for suicide and violence is greatest in alcoholics.[15]

The impulses that lead to suicide differ between violent and nonviolent people. "Suicidality" is correlated with anger, fear, and suspiciousness in violent individuals and with feelings of sadness and despair in nonviolent persons. The psychic roots of suicide may arise from childhood trauma. Chronic loneliness during childhood is associated with subsequent suicide attempts during adolescence, and a history of sexual molestation is linked to suicide attempts in women and adolescents. Current research suggests a biologic basis for depression and suicide involving the serotonergic and dopaminergic systems. People who attempt suicide have altered serotonin receptor function and low serotonin levels.[16,17] These abnormalities may be regulated through serotonergic-related genes in persons with major depression.[18] Other genetic studies report polymorphisms in the tryptophan hydroxylase gene that is involved in the synthesis of serotonin. The genetic susceptibility to suicide, however, may affect individuals only when associated with psychiatric illness or stress.[19] The rate of suicide is twice as high in families of suicide victims, and a family history of suicide predicts suicide independent of severe mental disorder.[20]

Depressed patients who attempt suicide excrete less homovanillic acid in their urine and produce less dopamine than depressed patients who have not attempted suicide. Low concentrations of dopamine and serotonin metabolites in the cerebrospinal fluid also correlate with suicidal behavior. Suicide attempts in women vary with estrogen levels, with 42% of attempts occurring during the first week of the menstrual cycle.[21]

Neuroanatomy may also influence suicidality; suicide victims have smaller right-sided parahippocampi than control subjects.[22] No laboratory tests can identify individuals at increased risk for suicide; however, research holds promise for biologic markers that might be used in the future.

Some drugs, including reserpine, benzodiazepines, and barbiturates, are associated with depression and suicidal behavior, although no clear relationship exists between any single antidepressant and the occurrence of suicide. Cases of patients who commit suicide shortly after the initiation of antidepressant medications are explained by the "mobilization of energy" theory.[23,24] According to this theory, patients who are profoundly depressed may develop the energy to attempt suicide only as their condition improves with treatment. Such patients must be monitored very closely during their initial phase of treatment.

Methods of Attempting Suicide

Most completed suicides involve firearms (70%), whereas most attempted suicides involve the ingestion of drugs or poisons (72%).[24] Episodes involving firearms are 2.6 times more lethal than the second most lethal suicide method, suffocation.[25] Preventing access to firearms can reduce the proportion of fatal firearm-related suicides by 32% among minors and 6.5% among adults. In 1994, 19,750 suicides involved firearms in the United States.[26] Guns represent the most common method of suicide in all victim subgroups, especially among older persons and adolescents, and the use of guns has increased dramatically in the past decade, recently replacing ingestion as the major cause of suicide among women.[27] The simple presence of a gun in the home represents an independent risk factor for firearm-related suicide, but not by non-firearm means.[28] This is particularly true for adolescents, whose risk for suicide increases five to 10 times when there is a gun in the household.[29-30] Suicide by handgun is often associated with drug or alcohol use.[32] The rate of gun-related suicide is 57 times higher in the first week after purchasing a handgun.[33]

After gun-related deaths, men tend to hang themselves, whereas women are more likely to commit suicide by poisoning. Antidepressant overdose is the most common cause of suicide by ingestion.[34] Cyclic antidepressants are associated with more deaths because of their widespread use and high potential for lethality. Most patients hospitalized for self-poisoning have ingested drugs prescribed by their physicians for depression.[35] Selective serotonin-reuptake inhibitors, including fluoxetine (Prozac), sertraline (Zoloft), and paroxetine (Paxil) are less lethal when taken in overdose and are replacing cyclic antidepressants.

The method of suicide depends on many factors, including psychic issues of self-hate, the desire for a peaceful versus violent death, and the availability of fatal means. Those who jump to their death are more likely single, unemployed, or psychotic. Those who use firearms are more likely to be male, to be alcoholic, to have been arrested, or to have an antisocial or borderline personality disorder.[36] Communities with tall buildings and bridges have higher rates of suicide from falls, whereas suicide by gunfire occurs more often in areas where firearms are prevalent.

"Suicide by cop" occurs when a suicidal individual intentionally provokes a police officer by orchestrating a lethal situation where the officer is forced to shoot in self-defense or to protect other civilians. This may account for as many as 11% of officer-involved shootings in Los Angeles.[37] Certain individuals carry a suicide note; some offer an eerie postmortem apology to the police officer who ultimately kills them.

CLINICAL FEATURES

Psychiatric Illness

Although most psychiatric patients never attempt suicide, most people who commit suicide have either a diagnosable psychiatric illness or alcoholism. Exceptions include those with mental retardation, dementia, and agoraphobia.[38] Patients with an affective disorder, especially major depression, are at highest risk.[39-41] Approximately 15% to 20% of people with major depression commit suicide, usually while under psychiatric care.[42] Individuals who experience hopelessness, anhedonia (loss of ability to experience pleasure), and mood cycling are at highest risk. Approximately 10% of schizophrenic patients will kill themselves. Psychotic patients who commit suicide are most often unmarried whites with high intelligence quotient (IQ) scores.[43] Patients with borderline personality disorders are also predisposed to commit suicide. Women with borderline personality disorder who attempt suicide often have a history of childhood sexual abuse and impulsive behavior. The risk is especially high when patients require hospitalization for psychiatric illness and is greatest the first month after discharge.[44,45]

Approximately 40% of patients with panic disorder attempt suicide at some point in their lives. These patients usually have an additional comorbid psychiatric diagnosis (e.g., borderline personality disorder, substance abuse, emotional instability). Posttraumatic stress disorder, sustained by military combat personnel and disaster survivors, is also associated with suicide.

Alcoholism and Substance Abuse

Almost 25% of all suicides involve alcoholics, and estimates of the lifetime risk of suicide from chronic alcoholism range from 3% to 25%.[46] Alcoholics who commit suicide usually have multiple risk factors, including major depressive episodes, unemployment, medical illness, and interpersonal loss. In psychiatric patients, the use of alcohol increases depression and suicidal behavior.

Substance abuse among mentally ill patients is increasingly common. Patients with the dual diagnoses of substance abuse and a psychiatric disorder are particularly prone to violence in the emergency department. Psychoactive substance abuse is associated with a greater frequency, repetitiveness, and lethality in suicide attempts than are most other medications.

Nearly one half of all adolescents who attempt suicide use drugs shortly before the attempt, and alcohol intoxication is strongly associated with suicide by firearms.[47] Cocaine use is particularly dangerous; in New York City, 20% of all suicide victims younger than 61 years of age used cocaine within days of their death. Among young Hispanic men, nearly one half of the suicide victims have toxicologic screens positive for cocaine.[48] In general, cocaine abusers choose violent means of self-destruction, especially firearms.

Adolescents

Suicide among adolescents has quadrupled during the last 40 years and is now the second leading cause of death (after accidents) in people between 5 and 19 years of age.[5,15] Although some authorities believe that the rise in adolescent suicide simply corresponds to changing demographics in the United States, others believe that the increase is related to a growing sense of hopelessness, increased economic pressures, and access to firearms.[16] In a survey of high-school students in North Carolina, 24% had seriously considered suicide, 19% had planned suicide, and 9% had actually attempted suicide during a 1-year period.[49]

Adolescent girls are more likely to attempt suicide, whereas adolescent boys are more likely to complete suicide; the ratio of attempted to completed suicides is 25:1 for adolescent girls and 3:1 for boys.[50] Most adolescents who complete suicide have made previous suicide threats.

The majority of youths who kill themselves meet criteria for diagnosable psychiatric disorders, and both alcohol and substance abuse play a significant role in teenage suicide attempts. Adolescents with panic attacks are twice as likely to make suicide attempts as adolescents without panic attacks.[51] Gay, lesbian, bisexual, or "not sure" youths may also be more prone to self-harm.[52]

Nearly 40% of youths in runaway programs report prior suicide attempts.[53] Young people may also be influenced by movies or television shows that feature suicide. Teenage suicides increase after television broadcasts on the subject.

From 1989 to 1995, suicide by firearm in young people increased dramatically.[54] The firearm-related suicide rate in U.S. adolescents is 11 times higher than the combined rates of 25 other industrialized countries.[55] Having a gun in the home places the troubled adolescent in great danger, and storing the gun in a locked cabinet or separating it from the ammunition does not deter suicide attempts.[56] Surprisingly, up to 23% of adolescents who have attempted suicide report that their families continue to keep firearms and ammunition in the home despite their suicide attempt.

Older Adults

The highest rates of suicide occur in elderly people. In 1992, suicide was the third leading cause of injury-related deaths among older U.S. residents, after deaths from falls and motor vehicle crashes.[57] Older Americans use highly lethal methods when attempting suicide and, unlike adolescents, rarely stage an attempt that permits rescue. Self-inflicted gunshot wounds account for 88% of elder suicides.

White men older than 65 years of age account for approximately 80% of suicide deaths, whereas self-injury among elderly people belonging to minority groups is rare.[58] Suicide among older adults is especially common in those with prior suicide attempts or major depression. Severity of depression is the strongest predictor of suicide in the elderly population.[59] Physicians often overlook signs of depression in older patients, even though most who commit suicide see their primary care physician during the month before their death. Elderly people also have more chronic illnesses that predispose to suicide. One study showed that perceived poor health, poor sleep quality, and limited presence of a relative or friend to confide in are also associated with suicides among elderly people.[60]

Chronic Illness

Patients with terminal illnesses may commit suicide to end their suffering and to reduce the emotional and financial burden on their families. Diseases more highly associated with suicide include cancer, stroke, renal failure, congestive heart failure, and chronic lung disease. A history of cancer is an especially strong risk factor in elderly people.

The acquired immunodeficiency syndrome (AIDS) epidemic has also increased suicide rates, and the relative risk of suicide in men with AIDS is nearly 37 times higher than in uninfected men. Patients who are positive for human immunodeficiency virus but do not have AIDS-defining conditions are more likely to be suicidal than those with active disease.[61]

History

Recognition of Depression and Suicide Potential

Recognition of suicide potential is relatively straightforward in patients who present shortly after a suicide attempt, as well as in individuals who complain of depression or express suicidal ideation during their evaluation. The potential for suicide should also be addressed in patients with any acute problem related to chronic alcoholism, substance abuse, or any psychiatric disorder. Silent suicide is possible with patients who present to the emergency department repeatedly because of noncompliance with treatment of their medical disorders. Occult suicide should be suspected in patients who "unintentionally" overdose or have had "accidental" gunshot wounds, lacerated wrists, automobile crashes, or falls from heights.

Patients Who Present After a Suicide Attempt or Have Suicidal Ideation

Patients in the emergency department after a suicide attempt with a normal mental status should be queried

regarding the specifics of the act after medical evaluation and treatment are initiated. Suicidal patients may give inaccurate histories or may even refuse to speak to the physician. Because most people who attempt suicide communicate their intent to others at some point, an attempt should be made to interview family, friends, police, and paramedics regarding the patient's recent actions and possible motivations. They may also provide information regarding the specifics of the current suicide attempt. Although some physicians worry that current federal laws regarding patient privacy conflict with the need to obtain information with the family, an emergency exception to the Health Insurance Portability and Privacy Act (HIPPA) rule exists. Section 164.512(j), "Uses and Disclosures to Avert a Serious Threat to Health or Safety," allows physicians to disclose protected health information without individual authorization "based on a reasonable belief that use or disclosure of the protected health information was necessary to prevent or lessen a serious and imminent threat to health or safety of an individual or of the public."[62]

Once the patient is medically stable, the presence of risk factors for successful suicide should be determined. Such factors may include a history of previous suicide attempts or psychiatric care; a history of excessive alcohol or drug use, both acutely and long term; family history of suicide; and signs of depression, including a sense of hopelessness. Patients who have a history of deliberate-self harm (self-poisoning, cutting, burning, or hitting oneself) have a higher risk of suicide, especially male patients.[63] The patient's marital status and social support are important factors, and the motivation for and the seriousness of the suicide attempt are assessed. Some physicians interview patients to see whether they can provide their own lists of "reasons why they want to live"—a sort of reverse score for suicidality. If discharge is being considered, patients should be asked whether they would harm themselves if they were released from the emergency department. Additional demographic information may be helpful (see Box 113-1). The SAD PERSONS mnemonic can be used to document salient points and facilitate subsequent communications with primary care providers or psychiatrists (Table 113-1).

Table 113-1. Modified SAD PERSONS Scale

Factor	Points Assigned
Sex (male)	1
Age (<19 or >45 years)	1
Depression or hopelessness	2
Previous attempts or psychiatric care	1
Excessive alcohol or drug use	1
Rational thinking loss	2
Separated, divorced, or widowed	1
Organized or serious attempt	2
No social supports	1
Stated future intent	2

From Hockberger RS, Rothstein RJ: *J Emerg Med* 6:99, 1988.
Five points or fewer: questionable outpatient treatment; *6 or more points*: emergency psychiatric treatment/evaluation: *more than 9 points*: psychiatric hospitalization.

Patients Suspected of Occult or Silent Suicide Attempts

Patients who are not overtly depressed or suicidal but who exhibit one or more of the high-risk presentations previously described should be assessed in a sympathetic but direct manner using a "graduated" approach. First, rapport should be established during an assessment of the presenting complaint. This should include a general medical and psychiatric history, as well as an evaluation of the patient's home, work, and social situation, followed by specific questions regarding the signs and symptoms of depression. The emergency physician should ask direct questions regarding suicide, such as, "Have you ever had the thought that life is not worth living?"; "Do you have thoughts of killing yourself now?"; and "What plans, if any, have you made to do this?" Patients who are not depressed or suicidal are generally not offended by this approach, and it does not place the concept of suicide into the mind of someone who has not been considering it. Patients who are depressed or suicidal are often thankful and relieved for the intervention.

Physical Examination

Suicidal patients should be examined closely for evidence of drug ingestion, trauma, or an associated medical illness. Examination of the patient's mental status, vital signs, pupils, skin, and nervous system is helpful in detecting organic conditions, particularly the toxidromes associated with common ingestions (see Chapter 145). Patients with altered mentation should be assessed to determine whether their condition is caused by an organic (medical) or functional (psychiatric) cause (Table 113-2). Physical findings associated with chronic disease, alcoholism, and substance abuse should be sought. The physical examination is often overlooked or performed in a cursory manner in patients with psychiatric complaints. Up to 50% of patients with an acute psychiatric presentation harbor unrecognized medical illnesses.[64]

DIAGNOSTIC STRATEGIES

Routine toxicologic screening tests are unnecessary in the evaluation of suicidal patients. Nearly all patients with dangerous overdoses and poisonings demonstrate clinical signs within several hours of ingestion. While the likelihood of potentially lethal acetaminophen ingestion is small in patients who deny taking acetaminophen, the emergency physician should consider measuring the acetaminophen level in patients with intentional overdose.[65] An electrocardiogram should be obtained if cyclic antidepressant overdose is suspected. Patients with acute depression, particularly if newly diagnosed, may need screening tests for underlying medical disorders. However, a primary care physician or psychiatrist can safely perform this evaluation during follow-up.

MANAGEMENT

Prehospital Care

The prehospital management must focus on the patient's injuries and potential harm from poisoning or overdose. If the patient refuses to be transported to the hospital or becomes aggressive, emergency medical personnel should involve law enforcement officers. All states give police the right to place individuals into protective custody if they are suspected of being a danger to self or others. The presence of law enforcement officers, or even the threat of calling the police for assistance, usually ensures patient cooperation during transport. In hospitalized psychiatric patients, patients transported to the medical facility by police have an independent risk factor for an imminent suicide attempt.[66]

Emergency Department

The clinical assessment of suicide potential requires an empathetic approach. Patients feel more comfortable discussing personal issues when health care personnel are friendly, nonjudgmental, and supportive. Unfortunately, emergency department staff may be unsympathetic toward patients who attempt suicide because of religious or philosophic beliefs, lack of formal psychiatric training, or inadequate time and personnel to provide appropriate psychiatric evaluation. They may perceive the patient's behavior as abusive or manipulative and may become frustrated regarding ineffective disposition and follow-up options. Failure to anticipate and overcome these factors can result in inadequate patient assessment and reinforce these patients' already low self-esteem.

Medical Clearance

The first priority in managing patients is medical stabilization and treatment of injuries, poisoning, or overdose. The second priority is the identification and treatment of associated medical conditions that may cause a patient's altered mental status or violent behavior. Patients with significant injury, poisoning, or other medical problems should be hospitalized, sometimes in an intensive care setting, where their medical prob-

Table 113-2. Factors in Differentiating Organic from Functional Psychosis

	Onset	Age of Onset	Hallucinations	Orientation
Organic	May be acute	Any age	Often visual	Often disoriented
Functional	Subacute to chronic	14 to 40 years	Usually auditory	Normal

lems can be treated while they remain under constant observation. Five to 40 inpatients commit suicide for every 100,000 hospitalizations.[67,68]

Suicide Precautions

Most suicide attempts involve minor injury or overdose that can be definitively treated in the emergency department. These patients must be protected from additional self-harm while in the emergency department. Suicidal patients who are calm and cooperative should be placed in an area where they can be safely observed by staff. Having a dedicated "sitter" to watch the patient is helpful and may decrease the need for restraints. The sitter should accompany the patient when leaving the area to use the rest room or smoke. No potentially suicidal patient should be allowed to leave the emergency department before an evaluation is completed. The use of family members as "sitters" is discouraged because they may collude with the suicidal patient to leave the emergency department or may not intervene if the patient attempts to leave.

Security personnel should search all potentially suicidal patients. Having the patient change into a hospital gown facilitates removal of weapons and other possessions that might be used to inflict injury, such as belts, neckties, and long shoelaces. The patient's room should be cleared of all potentially harmful objects, including medications, instruments, and glass objects.

Use of Restraints

Mechanical and chemical restraint use is based primarily on the physician's impression regarding the immediate risk of elopement or subsequent suicide attempt. Placing a depressed patient in mechanical restraints can impair rapport with the patient and contribute to the patient's diminished self-esteem. Chemical restraints may calm a violent patient but may make subsequent psychiatric evaluation more difficult.

Nevertheless, restraints may be essential for uncooperative, violent, or psychotic patients and for those at high risk for elopement or self-harm. Restraints may be required for a brief period when emergency department staffing precludes a high level of observation.

Determination of Risk

Once a patient has demonstrated suicidal behavior or ideation, the emergency physician must determine whether the risk is imminent (i.e., within 48 hours), short term (i.e., within days to weeks), or long term.[6] The likelihood of an impending repeat attempt will drive disposition, whether psychiatric hospitalization, emergency psychiatric consultation, or discharge and referral for follow-up. The physician should also consider the potential lethality of the method chosen; for example, ingesting a handful of birth control pills is less worrisome than shooting oneself or setting oneself on fire.

Although the emergency physician should determine an individual patient's likelihood for committing suicide if discharged, this assessment is far from an exact science. No single psychological test can accurately predict suicidal attempts.[69] In a group of 4800 psychiatric patients who were followed prospectively over 5 years, 44% of all suicides where not foreseen by the psychiatrist.[70] In another group of individuals who completed suicides after evaluation by an emergency psychiatric service,[71] no specific factors could be identified that predicted imminent suicide.

There are at least 31 different English-language scales devised to predict the risk of suicide, but the vast majority are not designed for or suitable for use in the emergency department.[72] One study evaluated six clinical scales to identify high-risk patients: the Modified SAD PERSONS scale, revised Beck Depression Inventory, Beck Anxiety Inventory, Beck Hopelessness Scale, Beck Scale for Suicidal Ideation, and the High-Risk Construct Scale.[73] As with most studies regarding clinical scales, the outcome measured was psychiatric hospitalization admission for suicide risk and not completed suicide or future suicide attempts. All of the scales had 100% sensitivity and negative predictive value, but lower specificity and positive predictive value (ranges, 38-90% and 28-71%, respectively). Although scoring systems might help in determining the need for hospitalization, prospective studies show that most systems cannot predict future attempts at self-harm.[74,75] Nevertheless, the emergency physician should still attempt to determine a patient's immediate risk for self-harm and, when indicated, communicate the assessment to other health care providers.

The SAD PERSONS mnemonic provides a "suicide score" (see Table 113-1) and is well suited for use in the emergency department. Two points are given for each of four high-risk factors: (1) complaints of depression or hopelessness, (2) existence of an organic brain syndrome or acute psychosis, (3) presence of a well-conceived plan or life-threatening presentation, and (4) expression of determination or ambivalence regarding future suicidal behavior. One point is assigned for other important but less significant factors: male gender; age younger than 19 or older than 45 years; a history of previous suicide attempts or psychiatric care; stigmata of chronic alcoholism or substance abuse or the history of recent increased use of these substances; a patient who is separated, divorced, or widowed; and the absence of social support systems, such as close family, friends, job, or active religious affiliation.

A SAD PERSONS score of 6 or more has a sensitivity of 94% and a specificity of 71% compared with formal psychiatric evaluation in identifying the need for hospitalization in patients who present immediately after a suicide attempt.[76] A score of less than 6 has a negative predictive value of 95%. No deaths were noted in patients with low scores evaluated at 6 to 12 months.

A rapid Risk of Suicide Questionnaire was administered to adolescents at a large children's hospital.[77] The four most useful questions on the Risk of Suicide Questionnaire were the following:
1. Are you here because you tried to hurt yourself?

2. In the past week, have you been having thoughts about killing yourself?
3. Have you ever tried to hurt yourself in the past?
4. Has something very stressful happened to you in the past few weeks?

Any positive answer on this rapid screen correlated with potential risk for self-harm when compared to a longer Suicidal Ideation Questionnaire; however, the study did not compare the Risk of Suicide Questionnaire with the need for hospitalization or suicidal outcomes.

Suicide assessment should be based on information obtained from the patient after the metabolism of any drugs or alcohol. Patients who complain of depression or state ambivalence regarding their future intentions to commit suicide while intoxicated may disavow these feelings once they are sober (but may still be at risk despite the disavowal). In addition, the information obtained from a potentially suicidal patient might be confirmed through a family member or friend. Patients who are determined to commit suicide may give false or misleading information.

The crises that precipitate suicide attempts often are time limited, usually lasting from a few hours to a few days. If a crisis has passed or can be adequately addressed, the risk of subsequent suicide is substantially diminished. Hospitalization or emergency psychiatric evaluation should be strongly considered when a patient cannot or will not participate in an evaluation of the current crisis or when the problem is unlikely to be resolved.

Ultimately, the assessment of suicide risk remains a highly individualized process. The crisis that precipitated the suicide event, the patient's current emotional state, and the presence or absence of a supportive home environment must also be considered. When emergency physicians are uncertain regarding the need for hospitalization, they should err on the side of caution and either admit the patient for psychiatric care or request emergency psychiatric evaluation.

A psychiatric social worker or other paraprofessional may assist the emergency physician in gathering information and in making decisions about the need for hospitalization; however, the emergency physician still must make an independent judgment about the patient's suicide risk.[78]

Involuntary Commitment

Many patients who are severely depressed or suicidal will agree to be hospitalized for further evaluation and care; however, some may express reticence at being hospitalized. Patients refuse recommended medical treatment usually because of anger or fear. Patients may be angry for being brought to the emergency department against their wishes or for having to wait for evaluation. Alternatively, they may fear the loss of control associated with hospitalization or the perceived negative stigma associated with a psychiatric disorder. When a patient is reluctant to be hospitalized, the emergency physician should attempt to identify and address the specific concerns. The patient's family and friends may help convince the patient to accept voluntary hospitalization. If these attempts are unsuccessful, involuntary admission is necessary if the physician believes the patient may inflict self-harm. Depression itself is not the criterion for involuntary commitment; the standard generally involves the imminent risk of harm to self or others.

Civil commitment statutes differ among the 50 states and the District of Columbia. One analysis revealed that nearly 85% of the jurisdictions require dangerousness to self to be the result of a mental illness, and only two jurisdictions mandate attempts at involuntary commitment if a person is deemed to be an imminent harm to self.[79]

Controversy surrounds the efficacy of commitment as a long-term preventive measure.[67] Involuntary commitment has not been proven to prevent future suicide and may even precipitate adverse psychiatric consequences (e.g., increased feelings of hopelessness and dependency) or cause rebellion in some patients. Many authorities believe that people who are determined to kill themselves will probably prevail despite the best efforts of family members and health care professionals.[6] Still, despite the lack of hard data, involuntary commitment remains a primary intervention when patients are deemed acutely suicidal.

DISPOSITION

Most patients who attempt suicide or have symptoms of depression can be safely managed as outpatients, if the risk for subsequent suicide is judged acceptably low (Box 113-2). Before discharging a patient, the emergency physician should address the crisis that precipitated the suicide attempt. The patient should also be considered low risk for subsequent suicide (e.g., low SAD PERSONS score). Some emergency physicians ask the patient to form a verbal or written "contract" with them. This "no harm" agreement usually involves patients vowing not to hurt themselves and agreeing to return to the emergency department to seek help if the situation worsens before follow-up. Although the "no

---

BOX 113-2. Factors for Patients at Low Risk for Suicide

1. Few significant risk factors (e.g., low SAD PERSONS score)
2. Stable and supportive home environment
3. Patient agrees to "no harm" contract and will return to emergency department if situation worsens
4. Family member or friend staying with or available to patient
5. Phone contact with health care provider responsible for follow-up
6. Specific appointment made for follow-up within 24 to 48 hours
7. No gun in home

harm" agreement has not been validated, some believe this is a reasonable approach, whereas others believe that it provides only a false sense of security for the physician. On its own, it will certainly not absolve the clinician from malpractice liability if the patient commits suicide.[80]

If the patient is to be discharged, a family member or friend should agree to stay with the patient or to be immediately available to the patient until follow-up is provided. The patient should be discharged to a stable and supportive home environment that is free of guns and lethal medications.

Adequate disposition may include a conversation with the ongoing provider. If possible, the follow-up appointment should be scheduled within 24 to 48 hours of discharge from the emergency department and should be specific regarding the location and time. This approach maximizes patient compliance with follow-up. Providing a card that indicates how to contact an available physician may be helpful.[81]

DOCUMENTATION

Documentation is important when patients are committed or discharged. If a patient requires involuntary commitment, the emergency physician should document why the patient is a danger to self. If the patient is to be discharged, the record should reflect that the patient is low risk and does not intend self-harm after leaving the emergency department. Documenting that there is no gun in the home is useful. The use of pre-formatted charts may improve documentation.[82]

PREVENTION

The incidence of suicide parallels the incidence of alcoholism, drug abuse, and psychiatric disease in society. Although most suicide prevention programs have been found to be of questionable value, legislation to control access to lethal drugs and handguns is effective. In Japan, for example, laws requiring prescriptions for all sedative and hypnotic drugs led to a decrease in their use for suicide, with no increase in the use of other methods.[83] In Canada, suicide decreased after gun control laws were tightened.[84]

Despite great interest in the prevention of suicide, uncertainty remains regarding which (if any) interventions are effective to prevent future attempts at self-harm.[85] No strong evidence suggests that antidepressants prevent self-harm in patients with prior suicide attempt. However, one small study did show an advantage to depot flupenthixol versus placebo in multiple repeaters.[86] In another small study, dialectic behavior therapy was more effective than standard aftercare in preventing further episodes of self-harm.[87]

Suicide attempts correlate with future suicide. In one study on survivors of self-poisoning, the 5-year mortality rate from suicide was 65.5 times greater than expected in the female group (compared to a control group who did not attempt self-harm) and 41.5 times greater among males.[88]

KEY CONCEPTS

- Suicide is often provoked by a treatable or reversible short-term crisis.
- Suicidal patients frequently see a physician shortly before their death.
- The most complete information can be elicited with an empathetic approach to the patient and communication with family members, friends, health care providers, and others.
- Suicide precautions in the emergency department include appropriate use of "sitters" and, when necessary, physical and chemical restraints and involuntary commitment.
- The emergency physician should identify risk factors for suicide, even though determination of suicide risk is difficult. The SAD PERSONS score can be of help in documenting this assessment.
- If patients are sent home because their risk of suicide is low, ensure a safe and supportive gun-free environment and early psychiatric follow-up.

REFERENCES

1. Kirkland LR: To end itself by death: Suicide in Shakespeare's tragedies. *South Med J* 92:660, 1999.
2. Thompson S: Internet sites may encourage suicide. *Psychiatr Bull* 23:449, 1999.
3. Brent DA, et al: Risk factors for adolescent suicide: A comparison of adolescent suicide victims with suicidal inpatients. *Arch Gen Psychiatry* 45:581, 1988.
4. McAlpine DE: Suicide: Recognition and management. *Mayo Clin Proc* 62:778, 1987.
5. Brown M: Epidemiology of suicide pacts in England and Wales. *BMJ* 315:286, 1997.
6. Hirschfeld RM, Russell JM: Assessment and treatment of suicidal patients. *N Engl J Med* 337:910, 1997.
7. Centers for Disease Control and Prevention: CDC website. Available at: http://www.cdc.gov/nchs/products/pubs/pubd/hus/listables.pdf#Mortality
8. Brockington L: Suicide in women. *Int Clin Psychopharmacol* 16(Suppl 2):S7, 2001.
9. Ho TP: The suicide risk of discharged psychiatric patients. *J Clin Psychiatry* 64:702, 2003.
10. Remafedi G, et al: The relationship between suicide risk and sexual orientation: Results of a population-based study. *Am J Public Health* 88:57, 1998.
11. Blakely TA, Collings SC, Atkinson J: Unemployment and suicide: Evidence for a causal association? *J Epidemiol Comm Health* 57:594, 2003.
12. Maris R: The relationship of nonfatal suicide attempts to completed suicides. In Maris R, et al (eds): *Assessment and Prediction of Suicide*. New York: Guilford, 1992, pp 362-380.
13. Kleespies PM, Dettmer EL: An evidence-based approach to evaluating and managing suicidal emergencies. *J Clin Psychol* 56:1109, 2000.
14. Owens C, et al: Suicide outside the care of mental health services: A case-controlled psychological autopsy study. *Crisis J Crisis Intervent Suicide* 24:113, 2003.
15. Greenwald DJ, Reznikoff M, Plutchik R: Suicide risk and violence risk in alcoholics: Predictors of aggressive risk. *J Nerv Ment Dis* 182:3, 1994.
16. McBride PA, et al: The relationship of platelet 5-HT2 receptor indices to major depressive disorder, personality traits, and suicidal behavior. *Biol Psychiatry* 35:295, 1994.
17. Arango V, et al: Quantitive autoradiography of alpha 1- and alpha 2-adrenergic receptors in the cerebral cortex of controls and suicide victims. *Brain Res* 630:271, 1993.

18. Mann JJ, et al: Possible association of a polymorphism of the tryptophan hydroxylase gene with suicidal behavior in depressed patients. *Am J Psychiatry* 154:1451, 1997.

19. Roy A, et al: Genetics of suicide in depression. *J Clin Psychiatry* 60(suppl 2):12, 1999.

20. Runeson B, Asberg M: Family history of suicide among suicide victims. *Am J Psychiatry* 160:1525, 2003.

21. Fourestie V, et al: Suicide attempts in hypoestrogenic phases of the menstrual cycle. *Lancet* 2:1357, 1986. [Erratum: *Lancet* 1:176, 1987.]

22. Altshuler LL, et al: The hippocampus and parahippocampus in schizophrenia, suicide, and control brains. *Arch Gen Psychiatry* 47:1029, 1990. [Erratum *Arch Gen Psychiatry* 48:422, 1991.]

23. Gunnell D, Frankel S: Prevention of suicide: Aspirations and evidence. *BMJ* 308:1227, 1994.

24. Birkhead GS, et al: The emergency department in surveillance of attempted suicide: Findings and methodologic considerations. *Public Health Rep* 108:323, 1993.

25. Shenassa ED, Catlin SN, Buka SL: Lethality of firearms relative to other suicide methods: A population based study. *J Epidemiol Commun Health* 57:120, 2003.

26. Zwerling C, et al: The choice of weapons in firearm suicides in Iowa. *Am J Public Health* 83:1630, 1993.

27. Meehan PJ, Saltzman LE, Sattin RW: Suicides among older United States residents: Epidemiologic characteristics and trends. Am J Public Health 81:1198, 1991.

28. Wiebe DJ: Homicide and suicide risks associated with firearms in the home: A national case-control study. *Ann Emerg Med* 41:71, 2003.

29. Killias M: International correlations between gun ownership and rates of homicide and suicide. *Can Med Assoc J* 148:1721, 1993.

30. Kellerman AL, Reay DT: Protection or peril? An analysis of firearm-related deaths in the home. *N Engl J Med* 314:1557, 1986.

31. Brent DA, et al: Firearms and adolescent suicide: A community case-control study. *Am J Dis Child* 147:1066, 1993.

32. Peterson LG, et al: Self-inflicted gunshot wounds: Lethality of method versus intent. *Am J Psychiatry* 142:228, 1985.

33. Wintemute GJ, et al: Mortality among recent purchasers of handguns. *N Engl J Med* 341:1583, 1999.

34. Kapur S, Mieczkowski T, Mann JJ: Antidepressant medications and the relative risk of suicide attempt and suicide. *JAMA* 268:3441, 1992.

35. Prescott LF, Highley MS: Drugs prescribed for self poisoners. *Br Med J Clin Res Ed* 290:1633, 1985.

36. De Moore GM, Robertson AR: Suicide attempts by firearms and by leaping from heights: A comparative study of survivors. *Am J Psychiatry* 156:1425, 1999.

37. Hutson HR, et al: Suicide by cop. *Ann Emerg Med* 32:665, 1998.

38. Risk for suicide is increased for most mental disorders where patients require treatment in a hospital setting. *Evidence-Based Med* 2:156, 1997.

39. Henriksson MM, et al: Mental disorders and comorbidity in suicide. *Am J Psychiatry* 150:935, 1993.

40. Winokur G, Black DW: Psychiatric and medical diagnoses as risk factors for mortality in psychiatric patients: A case control study. *Am J Psychiatry* 144:208, 1987.

41. Asnis GM, et al: Suicidal behaviors in adult psychiatric outpatients. Part I. Description and prevalence. *Am J Psychiatry* 150:108, 1993.

42. Isometsa ET, et al: Suicide in major depression. *Am J Psychiatry* 151:530, 1994.

43. Westermeyer JF, Harrow M, Marengo JT: Risk for suicide in schizophrenia and other psychotic and nonpsychotic disorders. *J Nerv Ment Dis* 179:259, 1991.

44. Goldacre M, Seagroatt V, Hawton K: Suicide after discharge from psychiatric inpatient care. *Lancet* 342:283, 1993.

45. Allgulander C: Suicide and mortality patterns in anxiety, neurosis, and depressive neurosis. *Arch Gen Psychiatry* 51:708, 1994.

46. Murphy GE, et al: Multiple risk factors predict suicide in alcoholism. *Arch Gen Psychiatry* 49:459, 1992.

47. Rich CL, et al: Some difference between men and women who commit suicide. *Am J Psychiatry* 145:718, 1988.

48. Marzuk PM, et al: Prevalence of cocaine use among residents of New York City who committed suicide during a one-year period. *Am J Psychiatry* 149:371, 1992.

49. Garrison CZ, et al: Aggression, substance use, and suicidal behaviors in high school students. *Am J Public Health* 83:179, 1993.

50. Rosenberg ML, et al: The emergence of youth suicide: An epidemiologic analysis and public health perspective. *Annu Rev Public Health* 8:417, 1987.

51. Pilowsky DJ, Wu LT, Anthony JC: Panic attacks and suicide attempts in mid-adolescence, *Am J Psychiatry* 156:1545, 1999.

52. Garofalo R, et al: Sexual orientation and risk of suicide attempts among a representative sample of youth. *Arch Pediatr Adolesc Med* 153:487, 1999.

53. Rotheram-Borus MJ: Suicidal behavior and risk factors among runaway youths. *Am J Psychiatry* 150:103, 1993.

54. Cummings P, LeMier M, Keck DB: Trends in firearm-related injuries in Washington State. *Ann Emerg Med* 32:37, 1998.

55. Centers for Disease Control and Prevention: Rates of homicide, suicide, and firearm-related death among children in 26 industrialized countries. *MMWR* 46:101, 1997.

56. Brent DA, et al: The presence and accessibility of firearms in the homes of adolescent suicides: A case-control study. *JAMA* 266:2989, 1990.

57. Centers for Disease Control and Prevention: Suicide among older persons—United States, 1980-1992. *MMWR* 45:3, 1996.

58. Casey DA: Suicide in the elderly: A two-year study of data from death certificates. *South Med J* 84:1185, 1991.

59. Alexopoulos GS, et al: Clinical determinants of suicidal ideation and behavior in geriatric depression. *Arch Gen Psychiatry* 56:1048, 1999.

60. Turvey CL, et al: Risks factors for late-life suicide: A prospective, community-based study. *Am J Geriatr Psych* 10:398, 2002.

61. McKegney FP, O'Dowd MA: Suicidality and HIV status. *Am J Psychiatry* 149:396, 1992.

62. Federal Register / Vol. 65, No. 250 / Thursday, December 28, 2000 / Rules and Regulations. Available at http://www.hhs.gov/ocr/part4.pdf

63. Hawton K, Zahl D, Weatherall R: Suicide following deliberate self-harm: Long-term follow-up of patients who presented to a general hospital. *Br J Psychiatry* 182:537, 2003.

64. Henneman PL, Mendoza R, Lewis RJ: Prospective evaluation of emergency department medical clearance. *Ann Emerg Med* 24:672, 1994.

65. Lucanie R, Chiang WK, Reilly R: Utility of acetaminophen screening in unsuspected suicidal ingestions. *Vet Hum Toxicol* 44:171, 2002.

66. King EA, Baldwin DS, Sinclair JM, Campbell MJ: The Wessex Recent In-Patient Suicide Study, 2: Case-control study of 59 in-patient suicides. *Br J Psychiatry* 178:537, 2001.

67. Robertson WD: Poisonings in the United States. *Am J Emerg Med* 6:544, 1988.

68. Hogarty SS, Rodaitis CM: A suicide precautions policy for the general hospital. *J Nurs Admin* 17:36, 1987.

69. Maris RW: Suicide. *Lancet* 360:319, 2002.

70. Pokorny AD: Prediction of suicide in psychiatric patients. *Arch Gen Psychiatry* 40:249, 1983.

71. Harris MR, et al: Completed suicides and emergency psychiatric evaluations: The Louisville experience. *J Kentucky Med Assoc* 98:210, 2000.

72. Brown GK: A Review of Suicide Assessment Measures for Intervention Research with Adults and Older Adults. Available at www.nimh.nih.gov/research/adultsuicide.pdf

73. Cochrane-Brink KA, Lofchy JS, Sakinofsky I: Clinical rating scales in suicide risk assessment. Gen Hosp Psychiatry 22:445, 2000.

74. Goldstein RB, et al: The prediction of suicide: Sensitivity, specificity, and predictive value of a multivariate model applied to suicide among 1906 patients with affective disorders. Arch Gen Psychiatry 48:418, 1991.

75. Maris RW: Suicide and life-threatening behavior: Introduction. Suicide Life Threat Behav 21:1, 1991.

76. Hockberger RS, Rothstein RJ: Assessment of suicide potential by non-psychiatrists using the SAD PERSONS score. J Emerg Med 6:99, 1988.

77. Horowitz LM, et al: Detecting suicide risk in a pediatric emergency department: Development of a brief screening tool. Pediatrics 107:1133, 2001.

78. Armitage DT, Townsend GM: Emergency medicine, psychiatry and the law. Emerg Med Clin North Am 11:869, 1993.

79. Werth JL Jr: U.S. involuntary mental health commitment statutes: Requirements for persons perceived to be a potential harm to self. Suicide Life Threat Behav 31:348, 2001.

80. Simon RI: The suicide prevention contract: Clinical, legal, and risk management issues. J Am Acad Psychiatry Law 27:445, 1999.

81. Morgan HG, Jones EM, Owen JH: Secondary prevention of non-fatal deliberate self-harm: The green card study. Br J Psychiatry 163:111, 1993.

82. Crawford MJ, Turnbull G, Wessely S: Deliberate self harm assessment by accident and emergency staff: An intervention study. J Accid Emerg Med 15:18, 1998.

83. Lester D, Abe K: The effect of controls on sedatives and hypnotics on their use for suicide. J Toxicol Clin Toxicol 27:299, 1989.

84. Lester D, Leenaars A: Suicide rates in Canada before and after tightening firearm control law. Psychol Rep 72:787, 1993.

85. Hawton K, et al: Deliberate self-harm: Systematic review of efficacy of psychosocial and pharmacological treatment in preventing repetition. BMJ 317:441, 1998.

86. Montgomery SA, Roy D, Montgomery DB: The prevention of recurrent suicidal acts. Br J Clin Pharmacol 15(suppl 2):183, 1983.

87. Linehan MM, et al: Cognitive-behavioral treatment of chronically parasuicidal borderline patients. Arch Gen Psychiatry 48:1060, 1991.

88. Rygnestad T: Mortality after deliberate self-poisoning: A prospective follow-up study of 587 persons observed for 5279 person years-risk factors and causes of death. Soc Psychiatry Psychiatr Epidemiol 32:443, 1997.

Section IX IMMUNOLOGIC AND INFLAMMATORY

CHAPTER

114 Arthritis

Douglas W. Lowery III

PERSPECTIVE

Evaluating and managing the inflamed joint remains a critical core competency for emergency physicians. Unfortunately, as the population ages and medical complexities increase, the typical appearance of a "red hot joint" is becoming more rare. Nevertheless, because of the tremendous pain and disability associated with joint inflammation, patients with the gamut of arthritic maladies present frequently for emergency evaluation.[1]

History

Rheumatic diseases have been described for thousands of years. Hippocrates wrote of musculoskeletal complaints and joint inflammation. Differences in presentation of joint disease were noted, but distinctions were not made until the 1680s, when Sydenham described gout, rheumatism, and chorea. Despite the historical awareness of joint ailments, minimal success in classifying them into recognizable entities occurred, until the beginning of the 19th century. The phrase *rheumatic fever* was coined in 1808, but not until 1880 was a relationship to streptococcal infection proposed. Simi-larly, Swediaur noted a relationship between urethritis and arthritis in 1784, but discovery of gonococcal arthritis waited until 1883. Ankylosing spondylitis was first mentioned in 1831 but was not accurately described until the 1930s. In 1876, Garrod postulated that acute gout resulted from monosodium urate deposits in the joints, but the ultimate proof of that hypothesis had to wait until the mid-1900s, when additional technologic advances facilitated the more specific characterization and investigation of many rheumatic conditions.[2]

Heberden described his "nodes" as early as 1802, and Bouchard described his in 1884; but the entity of osteoarthritis was not clearly defined until 1907. In 1819, Brodie described synovitis with its potential to destroy cartilage. This was a basic step toward understanding rheumatoid arthritis. Rheumatoid factor was first measured in the 1940s. The other connective tissue diseases, systemic lupus erythematosus, systemic sclerosis, and polymyositis were all described in the middle to late 1880s. Reiter's disease was named after the author of a report of the typical joint manifestations occurring after dysentery.[2] Although understanding of rheumatologic disorders continues to increase,

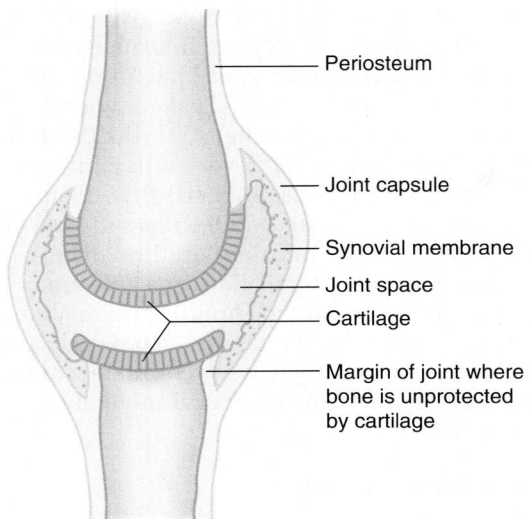

Figure 114-1. Clinical anatomy of the joint. (From Branch WT: *Office Practice of Medicine,* 2nd ed. Philadelphia, WB Saunders, 1987.)

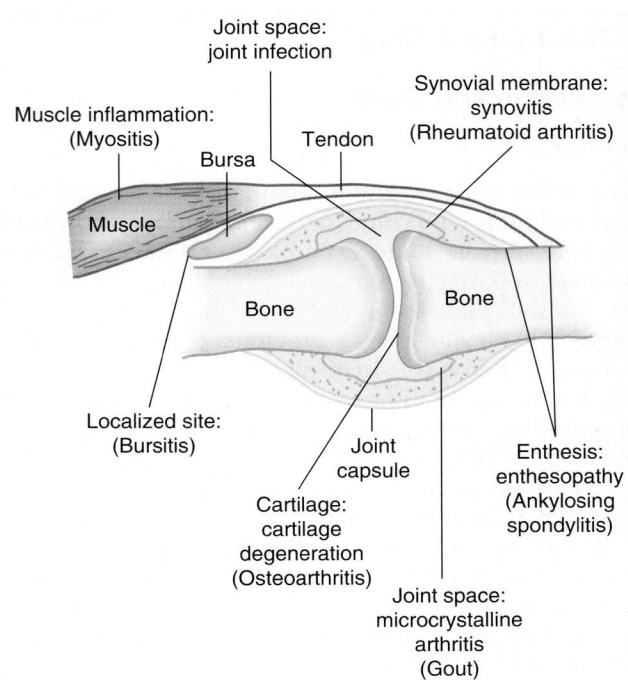

Figure 114-2. Sites and types of rheumatic disease. (From Wyngaarden JB, Smith LH [eds]: *Cecil Textbook of Medicine,* 18th ed. Philadelphia, WB Saunders, 1988.)

improved treatments are still required. Substantial disability and chronic pain create significant cost to the patient and society.[3]

PRINCIPLES OF DISEASE

Anatomy and Physiology

Joints are designed to bear weight and allow motion with as little wear as possible.[4] Three classes of joints are identified: synarthroses (suture lines of the skull), amphiarthroses (fibrocartilaginous unions of the pubic symphysis and the lower third of the sacroiliac joint), and diarthroses (moving joints). The most common type is the diarthrosis or synovial joint, which consists of two ends of subchondral bone (one convex, one concave) almost completely covered by articular cartilage. The cartilage consists of a matrix of collagen fibers and proteoglycans, which are synthesized by the chondrocytes within it. The cartilaginous surfaces are well lubricated and slide against each other. The joint is surrounded by a capsule that is supported by ligaments, tendons, and muscle and is lined with a synovial membrane (Figure 114-1).

Cartilage is deformable, compressible, and lubricated by synovial fluid secreted by cells of the synovial membrane lining the joint space. The synovium is up to three cells thick and consists of two cell types: type A cells, which contain lysosomes, and type B cells, which synthesize the fluid. Both types multiply in synovitis and interact with the vasculature to produce arthritis.[5] Joint fluid has a high viscosity because of its major component, a polysaccharide, hyaluronic acid. The fluid also contains water, glucose, electrolytes, and proteins of low molecular weight.

Pathophysiology

Mechanical trauma to a joint causes a decrease in the number of proteoglycans, probably by causing disequilibrium of anabolism and catabolism.[6] If the trauma is minor and transient, some regeneration of the articular cartilage by the chondrocytes may occur; but if the trauma is persistent, the damage is irreparable.

Marked inflammation of the joint is characterized by a predominance of polymorphonuclear cells (PMNs) exuding into the synovial cavity. Viscosity decreases because of decreased hyaluronic acid, the major contributor to synovial fluid viscosity. The trigger for this inflammatory reaction is different with different diseases. In nongonococcal bacterial arthritis, the cells of the synovial lining phagocytize bacteria. In gout and pseudogout, crystals are released from cells lining the synovium by conditions that precipitate an acute attack: minor trauma, ingestion of drugs or foods that raise the uric acid level, and alcohol. The joint inflammation in rheumatoid arthritis, rheumatic fever, and disseminated gonococcal arthritis has an immunologic basis. Reiter's syndrome is probably an immunologic "reactive" arthritis.

The PMNs release lysosomal enzymes that elicit a severe inflammatory reaction and ultimately degrade the components of the joint.[7] In rheumatoid arthritis, the "pannus" of proliferating cells erodes into the articular cartilage and bone. Erosions of bone occur in those portions of the joint cavity in which the bone is not covered by cartilage (a portion just distal to the attachment of the capsule). Subchondral bone is resorbed, an effect that is manifested radiologically as juxta-articular osteoporosis. Figure 114-2 shows the sites at which rheumatic disease occurs.

CLINICAL FINDINGS

Symptoms and Signs

History

Pain is the most common complaint of patients with joint problems who come to the emergency department. The pain may be acute or chronic, or an acute episode in a person with chronic disease. The patient may have had similar pain before, so it is important to know whether a diagnosis was previously made and what treatment, if any, was instituted.

A key determination to make is whether the source of the inflammation or pain is articular or periarticular (outside the joint capsule). True arthritis produces generalized joint pain, warmth, swelling, and tenderness. Discomfort increases with both passive and active motion of the joint because the inflamed synovium is exquisitely sensitive to stretching and because all parts of the joint are involved in the inflammatory process. By contrast, periarticular inflammation (bursitis, tendinitis, or localized cellulitis) tends to be more focal. Tenderness and swelling do not occur uniformly across the joint, and pain is produced only with certain movements, with the most common being resisted active contraction or passive stretching of the affected muscles or tendons.

If the site of the patient's pain is articular and not periarticular, the next step is to determine whether the arthritis is monarticular or polyarticular. Although certain disease entities (i.e., rheumatoid arthritis, gonococcal arthritis) can be placed in both categories, this basic approach of classification by number of joints involved can assist in narrowing the differential diagnosis (Table 114-1).

If polyarticular, the arthritis may be symmetric (e.g., rheumatoid or drug induced) or asymmetric (e.g., rubella, acute rheumatic fever, or gonococcal). In addition, it may also be migratory (e.g., gonococcal or rubella), subsiding in one area before presenting in another, or additive, remaining in the first joint and progressing to additional joints.

The distribution of joint involvement may give some clues to the disease: the first metatarsophalangeal joint is classically affected in gout; the metacarpophalangeal

(MP) joints and proximal interphalangeal (PIP) joints in rheumatoid arthritis; the distal interphalangeal (DIP) joints and first carpometacarpal joint in osteoarthritis; and the knee in septic arthritis, pseudogout, and gout.

Patients with any inflammatory arthritis may have low-grade fever, but high fever with chills is more likely to be caused by septic arthritis. Concomitant renal stones suggest gout, genital ulcerations occur in Reiter's syndrome, and purulent urethral discharge suggests gonococcal arthritis or Reiter's syndrome.

The emergency physician should inquire about what medications a patient is taking. Isoniazid, procainamide, and hydralazine can precipitate lupus, and thiazides can increase the serum uric acid level, leading to gouty arthritis.

Physical Examination

A thorough physical examination should be performed that specifically searches for evidence of particular rheumatic diseases. The skin, eyes, cardiac, pulmonary, and neurologic systems should be examined carefully. Some of the findings may indicate long-standing disease (e.g., tophi in gout, Heberden's nodes in osteoarthritis, swan-neck deformity in rheumatoid arthritis, skin lesions in psoriasis), whereas others may indicate an acute process (e.g., pustular lesions of gonococcemia, mucocutaneous lesions of Reiter's syndrome) (Table 114-2).

Joint Examination

Each joint in question should be specifically examined for the following attributes[8]:
1. Warmth and effusion
2. Synovial thickening
3. Deformity
4. Range of motion
5. Pain on motion
6. Tenderness (generalized or localized, articular or periarticular)

When evaluating the spine, the patient should stand, and the vertebral column should be assessed for abnormal curvature or asymmetry. The patient should then bend forward to assess for the limitation of the lumbar spine motion that occurs in ankylosing spondylitis. Sacrum and anterior iliac crests are palpated to elicit pain in the sacroiliac joints.

A shoulder affected by chronic arthritis or bursitis will have atrophy of the deltoid muscle. Generalized tenderness and pain, both at rest and with active and passive motion, suggest joint involvement. Localized tenderness and pain associated with active movement are more likely to be periarticular in origin. Having the patient place the hands behind the head and then the back tests for external and internal rotation, respectively.

Early signs of joint inflammation in the elbow are limitation of extension and an increase in the normal angle at which the patient holds the elbow at the side. The hand and wrist provide many clues to the presence of long-standing rheumatic diseases: MP and PIP joints are affected in rheumatoid arthritis; and the first car-

Table 114-1. Cause of Joint Pain

Articular		Periarticular
Monarticular	**Polyarticular**	
Osteoarthritis	Rheumatoid arthritis	Bursitis
Septic arthritis	Systemic lupus erythematosus	Tendinitis
Gout	Viral arthritis	Cellulitis
Pseudogout	Rheumatic fever	
Trauma	Reiter's syndrome	
Hemarthrosis	Lyme disease	
	Serum sickness	
	Drug-induced	

Table 114-2. Clinical Signs of Rheumatic Diseases

	Findings	Diseases
Scalp, hair	Alopecia, skin lesions	SLE, psoriasis
Skin	Pustular lesions	Gonococcemia
	Malar rash	SLE, dermatomyositis
	Rash on elbows, knees	Psoriasis
	Rash on dorsum of hands	Dermatomyositis
	Tightening of skin	Scleroderma
	Erythema chronicum migrans	Lyme disease
	Hyperkeratotic lesions	Reiter's syndrome
	Rash	Rubella
	Tophi	Gout
	Track marks	Injection drug use
	Erythema marginatum	Rheumatic fever
	Subcutaneous nodules	Rheumatoid arthritis
Eyes	Dryness	Sjögren's syndrome
	Iritis, uveitis	HLA B27 disease
	Conjunctivitis	Reiter's syndrome
	Icterus	Hepatitis
Oral mucosa	Dryness	Sjögren's syndrome
	Ulcerations	SLE, Reiter's syndrome
Pulmonary	Interstitial fibrosis	Scleroderma
	Pleuritis	SLE, rheumatoid arthritis
Cardiac	Friction rubs	Rheumatoid arthritis, SLE
	Murmurs	Endocarditis, Rheumatoid arthritis
Gastrointestinal examination	Enlarged, tender liver	Hepatitis
Neurologic	Peripheral nerve findings	Vasculitis
Genitalia	Lesions, urethral discharge	Reiter's syndrome, gonococcemia

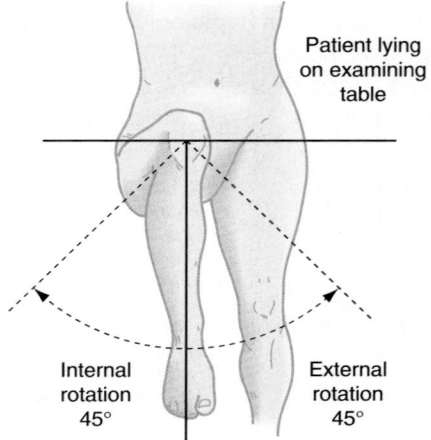

Figure 114-3. Testing for intrinsic disease of the hip joint. (From Branch WT: *Office Practice of Medicine,* 2nd ed. Philadelphia, WB Saunders, 1987.)

An effusion of the knee joint is relatively easy to detect when it appears as a ballotable fullness medially and laterally. Small effusions can be detected by examining for a transmitted fluid wave. Fullness of the popliteal fossa may indicate a Baker cyst. Passive range of motion may elicit crepitus or clicking. Tibiotalar joint effusions produce swelling under the medial malleolus and make it difficult to palpate the extensor hallucis longus tendon. Tenderness, warmth, and swelling of the great toe metatarsophalangeal (MTP) joint occur in cases of gout but can also occur with osteoarthritis and rheumatoid arthritis. Sausage-like swellings of the toes are seen in Reiter's syndrome.

DIAGNOSTIC STRATEGIES

Laboratory Tests

Laboratory tests other than synovial fluid analysis are of limited diagnostic value for evaluating acute arthritis in the emergency department.[10] The two most general screening tests are a complete blood cell count and an erythrocyte sedimentation rate (ESR). Infective bacterial arthritis usually causes an elevated white blood cell (WBC) count. Many of the chronic rheumatic diseases have a mild associated anemia. The ESR can be used to screen for inflammatory arthritis because the ESR is elevated in almost all such cases. Rheumatoid factor, antinuclear antibody, antistreptolysin O titers, and Lyme serologies are useful for follow-up but have no role in the acute emergency department evaluation. The serum uric acid level is not helpful in diagnosing acute gouty arthritis; in the acute phase of the disease, the serum uric level may be normal.

Radiology

Plain radiographs are of more diagnostic help in patients with chronic disease than in those with acute arthritis. The radiograph of a joint should be surveyed using the following systematic approach, summarized by the mnemonic SECONDS:

pometacarpal, PIP, and DIP joints are affected in osteoarthritis. The fingers may be swollen or sausage-like in appearance, an indication of psoriasis or Reiter's syndrome. Subluxation at the MP joints, ulnar deviation, and swan-neck deformities occur in rheumatoid arthritis. The nails may have pitting characteristic of psoriatic arthritis. Although the wrist may not be obviously swollen, discomfort and decreased range of motion, particularly on extension, may indicate synovial involvement.

Inflammation affecting the hip joint can be reported by the patient as pain in the anterior thigh, knee, or in the groin. A hip joint effusion will cause the patient to hold the hip partially flexed. An externally rotated and abducted leg in a neonate suggests infection even if the child is afebrile.[9] Range of motion of the hip is most easily tested by flexing the hip, bending the knee at a right angle, and rotating the heel medially and laterally to test for external and internal rotation, respectively (Figure 114-3).[8] Marked irritability and decreased range of movement confirm hip joint involvement.

Table 114-3. Common Radiologic Findings in Arthritis

Arthritis	Findings
Acute arthritis (gout, pseudogout, septic arthritis)	Soft tissue swelling
Late septic arthritis (need at least 8-10 days to see changes)	Subchondral bone destruction Periosteal new bone Loss of joint space Osteoporosis Late joint-space narrowing
Late pseudogout (knee, hip, radiocarpal, midcarpal, all MP)	Linear calcification in cartilage Asymmetrical joint-space narrowing Reactive sclerosis Osteophyte formation Subchondral cyst formation Lack of osteoporosis
Degenerative arthritis (acromioclavicular, first carpometacarpal, first MTP, DIP, knee, hip, cervical spine, lumbosacral spine)	Asymmetrical joint-space narrowing Sclerosis of juxta-articular bone Bone spurs and cysts—adjacent to severe cartilage degeneration No osteoporosis
Tuberculous arthritis (knee, hip, shoulder)	Soft-tissue swelling Marked demineralization Bony rarefaction Little reactive sclerosis Late: bony destruction Joint space preserved
Late rheumatoid arthritis (wrist, MP, PIP, MTP, first IP, foot, atlantoaxial, glenohumeral)	Symmetrical joint-space narrowing Osteoporosis of periarticular bone Marginal erosions (no overhanging margins as in gout) Little reactive bone formation

DIP, distal interphalangeal; IP, interphalangeal; MP, metacarpophalangeal; MTP, metatarsophalangeal; PIP, proximal interphalangeal.

Soft tissue swelling
Erosions
Calcification
Osteoporosis
Narrowing (joint space)
Deformity
Separation (fractures)[11]

Common findings that help distinguish the different forms of arthritis are set out in Table 114-3. Other radiologic modalities are available but are not usually performed as part of a routine workup in an emergency setting. Ultrasonography is useful in evaluating joint effusions and lesions of tendons, ligaments, and skeletal muscle, particularly of the shoulder region.[12]

Computed tomography scan in the axial plane can detect sacroiliac joint disease in difficult cases and is the preferred method for evaluating the sternoclavicular joint.[13] Both sonography and the computed tomography scan have been used to evaluate joint effusions in children with transient synovitis. A magnetic resonance imaging scan is excellent for (1) imaging cruciate ligaments of the knee, (2) detecting early edema in periarticular structures and fluid collection in tendon sheaths, and (3) determining the extent of cartilage destruction.[14] A contrast-enhanced magnetic resonance imaging scan can differentiate synovitis from synovial fluid and is useful in patients with rheumatoid arthritis.[15]

Scintigraphy makes use of technetium-99m methylene diphosphonate (^{99m}Tc MDP); thus, a ^{99m}Tc MDP scan can detect osteomyelitis and stress fractures. After intravenous injection, the radioisotope is absorbed onto hydroxyapatite crystals at the juxta-articular subchondral cancellous bone, which becomes vascular with inflammation. Gallium scanning is less dependent on blood flow; gallium accumulates where there is a proliferation of serum proteins and leukocytes. Gallium scanning is helpful if searching for infection, especially in the presence of healing fractures or postoperatively, but it is expensive.[12,14,16]

Arthrocentesis

Arthrocentesis provides critical diagnostic information for evaluation of the acutely inflamed joint. The procedure, which involves puncturing and aspirating a joint space, is safe and well tolerated by the patient when properly performed.[17,18] Arthrocentesis may also be performed for therapeutic reasons, providing substantial relief to patients suffering from hemarthroses, as well as acute and chronic arthritides.[19]

The emergency indications for arthrocentesis in evaluating joint pain include obtaining joint fluid for analysis, draining tense hemarthroses in patients with hemophilia (after the appropriate clotting factor replacement), and for the instillation of analgesics and anti-inflammatory agents for the treatment of acute and chronic arthritis. Emergency arthrocentesis is contraindicated if infection of any kind covers the area to be punctured because of the risk of introducing infection into the joint space. At times, determining whether periarticular tissues are infected or simply inflamed can be quite difficult, and caution is advised in such instances. Arthrocentesis is relatively contraindicated when bleeding diatheses are present or when patients are undergoing anticoagulant therapy, owing to the risk of bleeding in the joint space.[17] Bacteremia is a relative contraindication for arthrocentesis as well. Arthrocentesis of prosthetic joints should only be performed to rule out infection. The primary complications of arthrocentesis are infection in the joint space, bleeding into the joint space, allergic reaction to anesthetic agents, and long-term corticosteroid-related complications. Dry tap, a situation in which no fluid is aspirated after joint puncture, has been reported but is relatively rare in arthrocentesis of the larger joints. Dry tap is a more common complication in patients with a history of chronic arthritis owing to anatomic abnormalities in the synovium and periarticular tissues.[20]

As with any procedure, careful preparation is the key to success. The patient should be positioned comfortably, with adequate exposure and cushioned support for the joint. Muscle tension during the procedure can reduce the joint volume, making the procedure more difficult; thus, every opportunity to provide for the patient's comfort should be employed. Bony landmarks should be carefully palpated. Using aseptic technique, the skin should be prepared with an appropriate surgical scrub. Adequate local anesthesia can be achieved either by use of a vapor coolant, or by local infiltration with anesthetic solution such as 1% or 2% lidocaine.[17] Using an 18- to 22-gauge needle attached to a syringe, the physician punctures the joint space and aspirates joint fluid while carefully avoiding abrasion of the articular cartilage. As much fluid as possible should be removed before withdrawal of the needle.

Synovial Fluid Examination

Analysis of synovial fluid is especially useful for identifying crystalline and suppurative causes of acute arthritis; therefore, synovial fluid should always be analyzed for appearance (color, clarity), cell count, differential, Gram stain for organisms, and crystal analysis. A positive Gram stain is diagnostic for septic arthritis, but a Gram stain that is negative for bacteria does not rule out septic arthritis.

The cell count helps distinguish the noninflammatory fluid of osteoarthritis and traumatic arthritis from the inflammatory fluid that occurs in most other forms of arthritis. A rough estimate can be made on a wet mount preparation: one to two WBCs per high-power field (hpf) is consistent with a noninflammatory effusion; more than 20 WBCs/hpf suggests severe inflammation or infection.[21,22] Joint fluid in septic arthritis usually has more than 50,000 WBCs/mm³. However, low WBC counts can occur early in infectious arthritis and in partially treated infections; high WBC counts

(greater than 50,000/mm³) can occur in rheumatoid arthritis, gout, and pseudogout. Most of the WBCs in both septic and severe inflammatory arthritis are PMNs. Prediction rules regarding cell count and the likelihood of septic arthritis are common but are in no way absolute, and cell counts should not be used to rule out a septic cause.[23] Rather, bacterial cultures should be obtained if there is any suspicion of infection. Fungal and mycobacterial cultures should only be obtained in cases of persistent monarthritis or oligoarthritis, or in immunocompromised patients.[18] Other tests (i.e, synovial fluid glucose, lactic acid, viscosity, mucin clot, and total protein) have limited utility in ruling out infection and are no longer routinely recommended.[17,18,23] Collecting the synovial fluid in the appropriate container is vital for obtaining accurate results. Specimens for cellular analysis should be submitted in tubes with ethylenediaminetetraacetic acid anticoagulant (lavender top), whereas specimens for crystal analysis should be transported in tubes with liquid heparin (green top). Chemical analysis, serology, and viscosity should be analyzed on fluid submitted in a red top tube. Specimens submitted for Gram stain and culture should be plated as soon as possible, especially if *Neisseria gonorrhea* is suspected as the causative organism (Table 114-4).

Special tests of synovial fluid include analysis for crystals as well as glucose and viscosity. Crystal analysis is best performed using polarizing microscopy of a drop of synovial fluid or postcentrifugation sediment placed on a slide with cover slip. Monosodium urate crystals are usually needle shaped, negatively birefringent (yellow when parallel to the compensator and

Table 114-4. Synovial Fluid Interpretation

Diagnosis	Appearance	WBCs/mm³	Polymorphonuclear Leukocytes (%)	Glucose (% Blood Level)	Crystals Under Polarized Light	Culture
Normal	Clear	<200	<25	95-100	None	Negative
Degenerative joint disease	Clear	<4000	<25	95-100	None	Negative
Traumatic arthritis	Straw-colored, bloody, xanthochromic, occasionally with fat droplets	<4000	<25	95-100	None	Negative
Acute gout	Turbid	2000-50,000	>75	80-100	Negative birefringence*; needle-like crystals	Negative[†]
Pseudogout	Turbid	2000-50,000	>75	80-100	Positive birefringence*; rhomboid crystals	Negative
Septic arthritis	Purulent/turbid	5000-50,000	>75	<50	None	Usually positive
Rheumatoid arthritis/ seronegative arthritis (Reiter's disease, psoriatic arthritis, ankylosing spondylitis, inflammatory bowel disease)	Turbid	2000-50,000	50-75	~75	None	Negative

*Negative birefringence means that crystals appear yellow when lying parallel to the axis of the slow vibration of light of the first-order red compensator. With the same orientation to the compensator, positive birefringence crystals appear blue. When the crystals lie perpendicular to the axis, the opposite is true—that is, negative birefringence crystals are blue, and positive ones are yellow. A polarizing microscope is necessary for this distinction to be made.
[†]May be coexisting infection.
WBC, white blood cell.
From Benjamin GC: Arthrocentesis. In Roberts JR, Hedges JR (eds): *Clinical Procedures in Emergency Medicine*, 3rd ed. Philadelphia, WB Saunders, 1998.

blue when perpendicular), and range in size from 2 to 10 μm. Calcium pyrophosphate crystals, in contrast, are polymorphic, assuming the shape of rhomboids, rods, or even needles. They are positively birefringent (yellow when perpendicular to the compensator, blue when parallel), and can be as large as 10 μm.[17,18,24] Monosodium urate crystals can persist in synovial fluid even after resolution of a gouty attack.[25] Synovial fluid glucose analysis, when performed, should be evaluated only in the context of concomitant serum glucose. The normal ratio of synovial fluid glucose to serum glucose is 95%. Because severe inflammation decreases synovial fluid glucose, any ratio of synovial fluid to serum glucose less than 50% is suggestive of the severe inflammation of septic arthritis. However, because other arthritides, such as rheumatoid arthritis, can cause severe inflammation, glucose determination is not useful for ruling in or ruling out the diagnosis of septic arthritis. Finally, inflammation causes the loss of hyaluronate, which imparts viscosity to synovial fluid. Thus, inflammatory processes cause a less viscous synovial fluid. By measuring the maximum length of a drop of synovial fluid as it is falls from a syringe, viscosity can be measured. A drop of normal synovial fluid will elongate to 5 to 10 cm as it falls away from the syringe, whereas an inflammatory process will result in a much shorter length or even discrete drops.

Electrocardiography

Electrocardiography may prove useful in the evaluation of a patient with arthritis for whom a diagnosis of acute rheumatic fever is being considered. Electrocardiography is indicated for patients with arthritis who have a history of chest pain or complaints that might be related to the heart, or physical examination findings of a new or changing heart murmur, evidence of congestive heart failure, or cardiomegaly. In patients with carditis, prolongation of the P-R interval is the most common finding, and if pericarditis is present, acute diffuse ST segment elevations may be noted. PR prolongation is one of the minor Jones criteria for acute rheumatic fever.[26]

DIFFERENTIAL CONSIDERATIONS

The differential diagnosis of arthritis in the emergency department is best considered in terms of patterns of the number and distribution of joints involved, as well as the chronicity of the symptoms (Box 114-1).

MANAGEMENT

The emergency department approach and management, from diagnosis to treatment, of patients complaining of joint pain varies depending on the number and distribution of joints involved. Figure 114-4 and Figure 114-5 describe guidelines for the diagnostic strategies for patients with monarticular, pauciarticular, and polyarticular presentations. After a diagnosis is made, treatment varies by underlying pathology.

BOX 114-1. Differential Diagnosis of Arthritis in the Emergency Department

Monarticular
Septic arthritis
Gout
Pseudogout
Osteoarthritis
Trauma/hemarthrosis
Charcot's joint

Polyarticular

Symmetric
Gonococcal arthritis
Viral arthritis
Lyme disease
Drug-induced arthritis
Reiter's syndrome
Rheumatic fever
Seronegative spondyloarthropathies

Asymmetric
Gonococcal
Acute rheumatic fever
Lyme
Systemic lupus erythematosus
Immune complex diseases (viral)
Reiter's syndrome
Reactive

Monarticular Arthritis

Septic Arthritis

A patient with monarticular arthritis should be considered to have septic arthritis until proven otherwise.

Pathophysiology and Epidemiology
Bacterial pathogens reach joint spaces by hematogenous spread, by direct inoculation, and by direct spread from bony or soft tissue infections. The synovium becomes infected before the release of fluid and enzymes that degrade the articular cartilage. In children, hematogenous spread from a remote source is the most common cause. Joint infection by *Staphylococcus* organisms occurs as a result of trauma or skin infection.[27] Early or delayed postoperative infections occur in up to 10% of patients who undergo joint surgery and are more common with obese patients, those taking steroids, patients with underlying systemic disease, patients who have had previous procedures, and after long procedures.[14] Spread of infection from osteomyelitis into a joint predominantly occurs in children during the year before growth plate closure. Once in the joint, bacterial growth and invasion can occur essentially unchecked, resulting in a clinical syndrome manifest by the rapid onset of joint pain, swelling, redness, warmth, and decreased range of motion.[28] The resulting septic arthritis, unless rapidly recognized and treated, can result in serious and prolonged morbidity, disability, and even mortality.[29]

Many populations are at increased risk of septic arthritis, including elderly people, patients with pros-

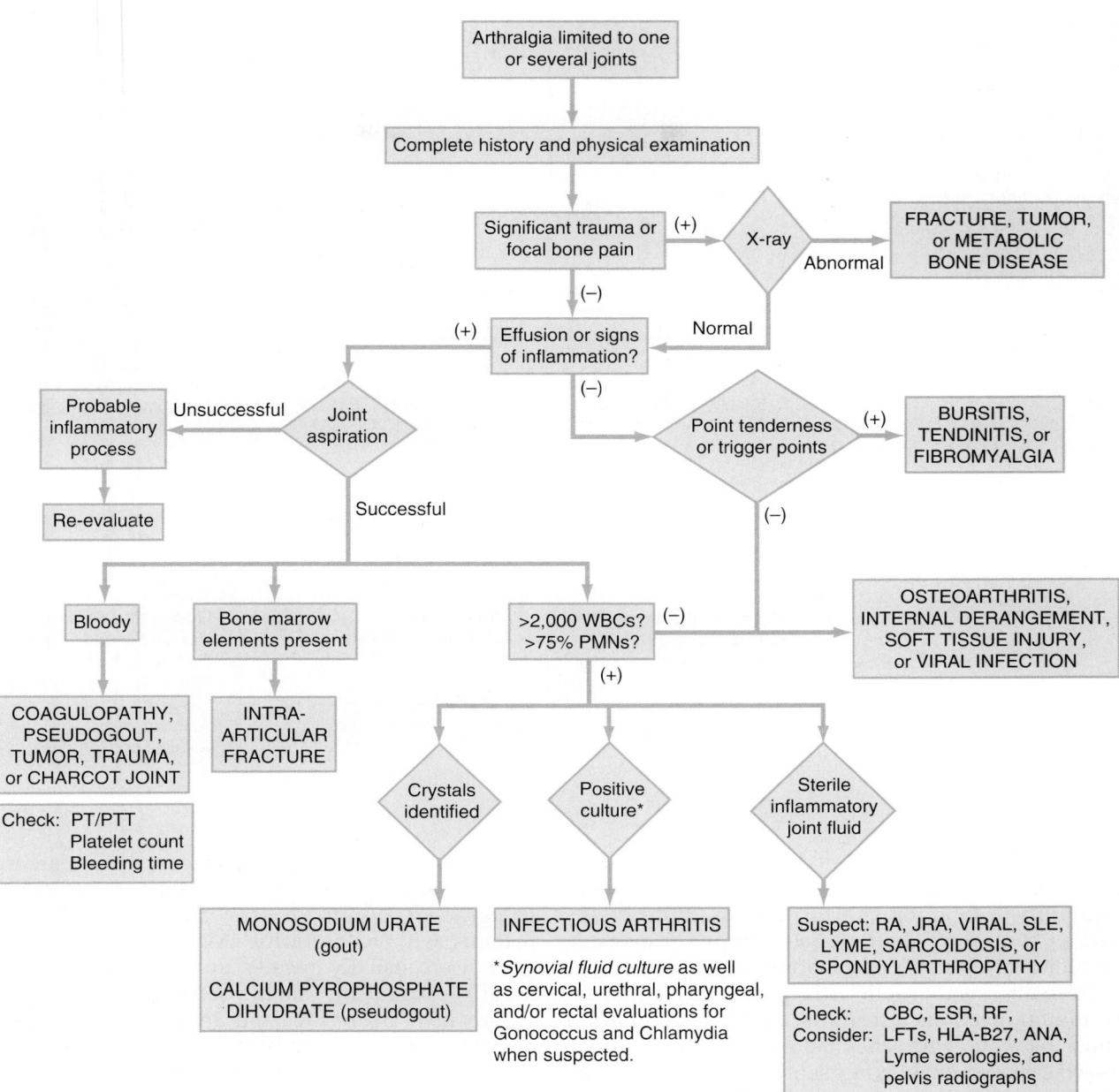

Figure 114-4. An initial approach to the patient with symptoms in one or a few joints. The majority of diagnoses will be determined by the history and physical examination findings. ANA, antinuclear antibodies; CBC, complete blood cell count; ESR, erythrocyte sedimentation rate; JRA, juvenile rheumatoid arthritis; LFTs, liver function tests; PMNs, polymorphonuclear neutrophils; PT, prothrombin time; PTT, partial thromboplastin time; RA, rheumatoid arthritis; RF, rheumatoid factor; SLE, systemic lupus erythematosus; WBCs, white blood cells. (From American College of Rheumatology Ad Hoc Committee on Clinical Guidelines. *Arthritis Rheum* 39:1, 1997.)

thetic joints, injection drug users, and immuno-compromised patients such as those with human immunodeficiency virus or chronic diseases.[28-34] Often the presentations of these special populations are unusual. Septic arthritis in injection drug users usually involves the axial skeleton but can involve the extremities.

Individuals at risk for nongonococcal septic arthritis are those with poor immune defenses: the very young, elderly patients and those with chronic debilitating disease, patients taking immunosuppressive drugs, and intravenous drug abusers, as well as those with prosthetic joints and after arthrocentesis.[28] Septic arthritis often occurs in patients with underlying chronic arthritis, most commonly in patients with rheumatoid arthritis and particularly those taking steroids. It is also seen in those with osteoarthritis and crystal arthritis. The diagnosis of infectious arthritis in a patient with known crystal arthritis can be difficult. An acute flare of pseudogout or gout can cause fever, and crystals may be present in an infected joint.[35,36] Indeed, an acute septic arthritis may cause a high count of crystals, which are released as the articular cartilage is destroyed.[37] Gram stain and culture must always be done on joint fluid, even when a diagnosis of crystal arthritis is made by light microscopy.

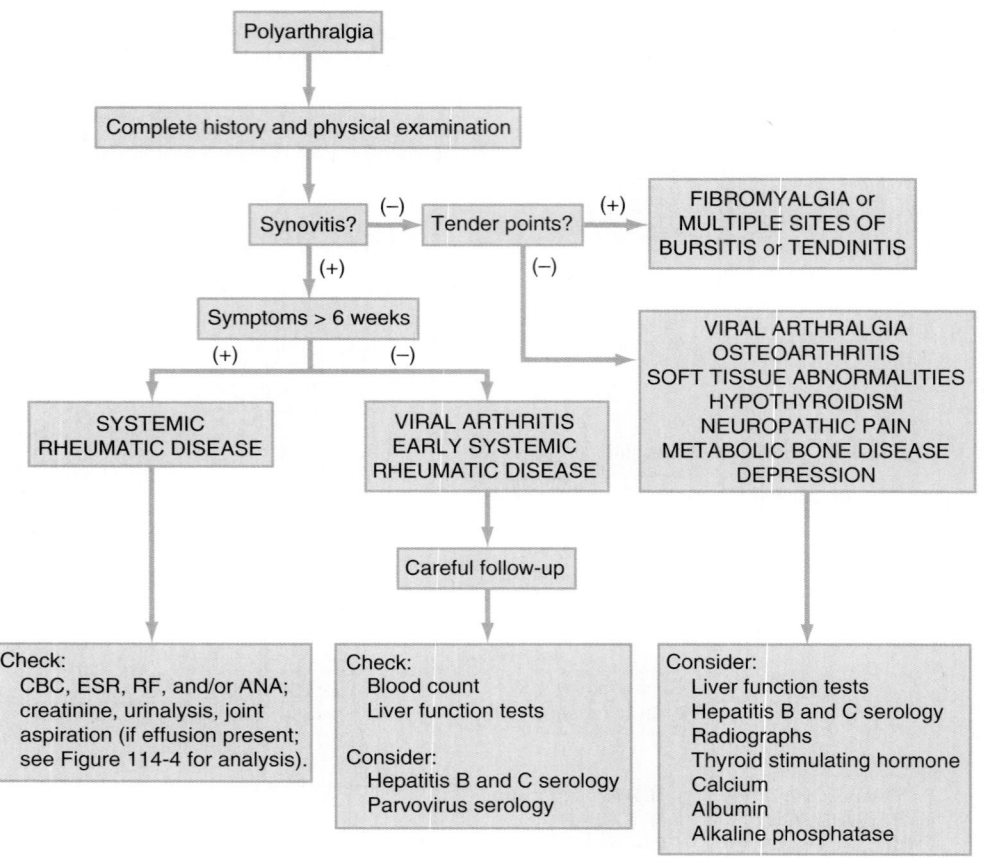

Figure 114-5. An initial approach to the patient with polyarticular joint symptoms. ANA, antinuclear antibodies; CBC, complete blood cell count; ESR, erythrocyte sedimentation rate; RF, rheumatic factor. (From American College of Rheumatology Ad Hoc Committee on Clinical Guidelines. *Arthritis Rheum* 39:1, 1997.)

Immunocompromised patients pose a challenge in diagnosis and management because of their increased susceptibility to suppurative arthritis in multiple joints as well as because of their altered immune response, which alters the clinical constellation of symptoms and signs normally seen in septic arthritis. Further, patients prone to noninfectious arthritides, such as hemophiliacs and patients with rheumatoid arthritis, are at increased risk for developing septic arthritides. As a result, one needs a high degree of vigilance in ruling out septic arthritis as the cause of joint pain in such patients.[28,31]

The microbiology of septic arthritis has remained fairly constant over time. Overall, *S. aureus* is still the most common cause of septic arthritis. The remaining cases of monarthritis are caused by other staphylococci, streptococci, gram-negative organisms, and anaerobes in relatively constant proportions.[38] *Neisseria gonorrhoeae* accounts for only 20% of cases of monarticular septic arthritis, whereas it is a more common pathogen in patients presenting with polyarthritis, which is the usual presentation. The microbiology of septic arthritis in several unique populations contrasts with this, although *Staphylococcus aureus* is the most common pathogen in most populations. Infants younger than 6 months of age are at risk for *Escherichia coli* as well as group B streptococci, and children from 6 to 24 months are at risk for staphylococci, *Kingella kingae*, and, in the prevaccination era, *Haemophilus influenzae*.[39] Immunization programs have reduced the incidence of

H. influenzae by 95%. Pneumococci remain an articular pathogen in the pediatric age group as well.[40] *N. gonorrhoeae* occurs in less than 10% of pediatric patients with monarthritis. Monarthritis in injection drug users usually results from *S. aureus* or gram-negative organisms such *Pseudomonas aeruginosa*, *Enterobacter* organisms, and *Serratia marcescens*.[34]

Infections can complicate arthrocentesis, arthroscopy, and joint replacement procedures.[17,41] The complication rate varies from 0.04% to 4%. Most infectious complications are early, usually within days or weeks. Organisms causing iatrogenic infections after arthrocentesis and arthroscopy are most commonly *S. aureus*, *S. epidermidis,* and gram-negative rods. Intra-articular infection after injection of corticosteroids may be masked by the lingering effects of the anti-inflammatory agents themselves, as well as by the underlying arthritides and their associated immunosuppressive medications. Again, a high degree of suspicion for bacterial infection must be maintained. In the case of prosthetic joints, infections may surface as long as 1 year after the procedure. The presence of any concurrent bacterial infection is a contraindication to joint replacement. *S. aureus* is the most common infecting organism after joint replacement, followed by mixed infections, gram-negative bacteria, and, finally, anaerobes.

Clinical Features

The clinical features of bacterial arthritis vary based on the host's concurrent medical conditions. Patients usually complain of pain in the joint, which is often swollen and hot. Infectious arthritis typically affects a single joint, most commonly the knee (40-50%), hip (13-20%), shoulder (10-15%), wrist (5-8%), ankle (6-8%), elbow (3-7%), and the small joints of the hand or foot (5%).[32] In approximately 20% of cases, several joints may be involved at the same time. Even in cases of septic polyarthritis, however, the knees are the most common sites of infection. In addition to joint pain, 80% of patients have a history of fever, although only 20% report shaking chills.[28] Predisposing factors include a history of trauma, surgical procedures, or injection drug use. Clinically, affected joints in immunocompetent hosts are red, swollen, warm, and exquisitely tender to touch or motion. Most, but not all, patients are febrile at presentation. Laboratory evaluation should include complete blood cell count, ESR, and blood cultures. Elevated sedimentation rate is more common than leukocytosis in septic arthritis. Blood cultures will grow the causative organism approximately 50% of the time.[42] Radiographs demonstrate only soft tissue swelling if present; the bony changes of septic arthritis are long-term findings and are not usually present on the initial examination.

The definitive diagnostic test for septic arthritis is arthrocentesis with examination of the synovial fluid. Purulent fluid with elevated WBC counts is typical. However, WBC counts may be low in bacterial arthritis, especially in immunocompromised hosts, and a low WBC count alone should not be used to rule out septic arthritis. In fact, the WBC count is greater than 50,000 WBCs/mm^3 in only 50% to 70% of patients. The percentage of PMNs is usually higher than 85%. Gram stain will show bacteria in 50% to 70% of infected joints.[28] Synovial fluid cultures for both aerobic and anaerobic organisms should be obtained.

Management

The key to successful treatment of septic arthritis is accurate diagnosis. Substantial delays in diagnosis directly worsen prognosis. Empiric antibiotic therapy should be based on Gram stain or the presumptive consideration of likely organisms. Once the diagnosis is made, hospital admission is indicated for incision and drainage of the affected joint and administration of intravenous antibiotics. The antibiotic regimen should be adjusted based on final culture results and sensitivities. In the hospital, daily aspirations of the joint fluid, along with irrigation of the joint using a large-bore needle or arthroscopy, can be performed. Failure to respond to therapy in 5 to 7 days, the presence of osteomyelitis, involvement of the hips or shoulders, or involvement of any prostheses usually mandates open arthrotomy for drainage. Parenteral narcotic analgesics and immobilization will control pain and discomfort. Antibiotic therapy should continue parenterally for 2 to 4 weeks, depending on the response to therapy, and should be followed with 2 to 6 weeks of oral antibiotic therapy at a high dose.[28,38,42,43] The ultimate clinical outcome is determined by the duration of symptoms before treatment, the number of infected joints, the age of the patient, the immune status of the patient, pre-ceding joint pathologic conditions, and the sensitivity and persistence of the causative organism.[28]

Gouty Arthritis

History

Greek writers such as Hippocrates described what is now known as gout. Podagra was the foot goddess, a bad-tempered virgin, who attacked victims after they overindulged.[44] For many centuries, this disease was thought to be limited to men who had indulged in dietary or sexual excess.[2] Benjamin Franklin's advice was, "Be temperate in wine, in eating, girls and sloth or the gout will seize you and plague you both."[45]

Pathophysiology and Epidemiology

Gout is the deposit of uric acid crystals from a super-saturated extracellular fluid. Uric acid can be overproduced in myeloproliferative or lymphoproliferative diseases or underexcreted in the kidney. Risk factors include obesity or weight gain during young adulthood, hypertension, diabetes, alcohol consumption, proximal loop diuretics, and lead exposure.[46,47] During an attack of gouty arthritis, the crystals are ingested by PMNs, resulting in an inflammatory reaction.[46]

Gouty arthritis occurs most commonly in middle-age men and postmenopausal women. Men often have a history of increased alcohol consumption, dietary excess, or other precipitating event such as stress of illness or surgery.[48] Not all patients with elevated uric acid levels or even crystals present in joint fluid have acute attacks. Women are relatively protected from gouty arthritis until menopause, because estrogens increase the renal excretion of uric acid. Postmenopausal women who sustain attacks of gouty arthritis are more often taking diuretic therapy and have a greater degree of renal insufficiency; the attacks often occur in fingers previously involved with osteoarthritis.[48] Increased levels of uric acid (greater than 5.1 in men, 4.0 in women) are usually present for 20 years before the first attack. Gouty attacks have been observed to occur in cardiac intensive care patients on nitroglycerin infusion during or within 12 hours of discontinuation, perhaps from the ethanol that is part of the mixture.[49] Organ transplant recipients have a high incidence of gout related to cyclosporine-induced hyperuricemia. Often, patients with an acute gouty arthritis have a normal uric acid level, possibly because of the uricosuric effect of pain-induced stress hormones.[47]

Clinical Presentation

Gouty attacks most commonly occur in the great toe MTP joint (up to 75%), the tarsal joints, the ankle, and the knee. Usually only one joint is involved initially, although up to 40% of patients can experience polyarticular involvement. The pain is excruciating at the onset and the joint is so sensitive that some patients cannot even tolerate the weight of a sheet on the joint. Systemic symptoms may be minimal or absent or the patient may be febrile, mimicking a picture of septic arthritis. Without treatment, the attack is self-limiting, lasting for several days to weeks, and is followed by an intercritical period of weeks to years. Subsequent attacks get closer together, involve more joints, and last longer. Long-term sequelae include renal stones and tophi (foreign body granulomas with the crystals as a nidus), which form in the musculotendinous unit (olecranon bursa, Achilles tendon, ulnar surface of the forearm, hands, knees, feet, toes, fingers, and even the helix of the ear).

The emergency department patient may either be experiencing a first attack or have a known history of gout with a recurrent episode. Cellulitis and septic arthritis need to be excluded, particularly if the knee is the joint involved; all of these patients may have fever, leukocytosis, and an elevated ESR. A uric acid level is not helpful in the diagnosis of gout in the acute setting because it can be normal. Renal function should be checked. During an acute attack, radiographs of the affected joint will only show soft-tissue swelling. Long-standing disease produces asymmetric bone erosions as a result of crystal deposits, with overhanging margins.

The definitive diagnosis of gouty arthritis is made by seeing negative birefringent joint fluid crystals with a polarizing microscope (a yellow crystal against a red background) and having a negative joint fluid culture.

Management

The therapy for gout can be separated into treatment of the acute and the chronic condition. Colchicine or non-steroidal anti-inflammatory drugs (NSAIDs) are used to stop the acute gouty attack. Patients who have severe pain also benefit from a regional block and may require minimal additional analgesia.

Colchicine, which inhibits microtubule formation, is most effective if administered within the first 24 hours of an episode. It inhibits the inflammatory response to crystals in the joint. Intravenous colchicine, more frequently used in the past, is free of the gastrointestinal side effects associated with oral colchicine.[50] The oral dosage regimen is 0.6 mg orally every hour until the pain is controlled, up to a maximum of 6 mg or until side effects supervene. Patients may have severe nausea and vomiting or diarrhea from oral colchicine. After a full course of colchicine is given, no more should be used for a week. Because it is effective for pseudogout and other crystal arthritides, it cannot be used to make the specific diagnosis of gout, although a gratifying therapeutic response does help distinguish crystal arthritis from septic arthritis. Colchicine is contraindicated in patients with hematologic, renal, and hepatic dysfunction.

The NSAIDs are very effective for analgesia with an acute attack of gouty arthritis but can have gastrointestinal and renal side effects. The NSAID most commonly used is indomethacin, in dosages of 75 mg to 200 mg/day for several days with tapering of the dose as the inflammation decreases. One regimen is 50 mg three times a day for 2 days, followed by 25 mg three times a day for 3 days. NSAIDs are contraindicated in patients with peptic ulcer disease and gastrointestinal bleeding and relatively contraindicated in patients with inflammatory bowel disease, congestive heart failure, asthma, and renal insufficiency. They interact with warfarin (Coumadin), oral hypoglycemics, and anticonvulsants.[51] Ketoprofen may be as effective as indomethacin and has fewer contraindications.[52] Patients who recognize the "twinges" of an impending attack are instructed to start indomethacin, 25 mg three times a day; and colchicine, 0.6 mg three times a day, to abort a full-blown attack. In resistant cases, oral prednisone (40 mg/day for 3 to 5 days, then tapering by 5 mg/day) or intramuscular adrenocorticotropic hormone can be used. Adrenocorticotropic hormone is also recommended for those patients with contraindications to NSAIDs. The dose of adrenocorticotropic hormone is 40 IU to 80 IU given intramuscularly.[50,51,53,54] Uric acid lowering agents should *not* be started during an acute attack.

Long-term therapy of gout is designed to decrease serum uric acid levels either by decreasing production (allopurinol) or increasing excretion (probenecid). Most physicians treat hyperuricemia only in cases of frequent gouty attacks, tophi, joint destruction, or renal stones. Allopurinol is given in doses from 100 mg/day for mild disease to more than 600 mg/day for severe tophaceous disease. It works by decreasing uric acid production through the inhibition of xanthine oxidase. Allopurinol can cause a sometimes-fatal syndrome of exfoliative rash, fever, hepatitis, and renal failure seen 1 to 6 weeks after initiation of therapy. Those at risk usually have preexisting renal insufficiency or are taking diuretics. Probenecid, a uricosuric agent, can affect the serum levels of many commonly prescribed drugs (i.e., penicillin, ampicillin, and aspirin). Patients already taking uric acid therapy may have an acute gouty attack, which should be managed as outlined previously; the regimen of the uric acid agent should not be changed in the emergency department for fear of precipitating another acute episode. In patients prone to recurrent acute attacks of gout, colchicine 0.5 mg twice daily reduced the frequency of attacks by 75% to 85% and attenuated the severity of attacks that did occur.[55] Colchicine may be given prophylactically for 6 to 12 months as a way of suppressing flareups.

Pseudogout

Calcium pyrophosphate dihydrate crystal-deposition disease (also called *pseudogout*) is in the differential diagnosis of monarticular arthritis. It may also appear as asymptomatic calcific deposits in articular hyaline or fibrocartilaginous tissues on radiographs, as pseudorheumatoid arthritis with involvement of multiple symmetric joints, or as systematic symptoms with a gout-like picture: severe monarticular attacks precipitated by illness such as stroke, myocardial infarction, and surgery, separated by asymptomatic intervals.[56] The knee is most commonly involved, followed by the wrist, ankle, and elbow.[57] More than one joint can be involved.

Twenty-five percent of patients with pseudogout present acutely when crystals are shed from cartilaginous tissues into the synovial cavity and then elicit an inflammatory response. The average attack is not as severe as that of acute gout.[58] In general, these patients are between the sixth and eighth decades in age and have a history of previous arthritic attacks. Although the most common form is idiopathic, pseudogout specifically occurs in patients with hyperparathyroidism, hemochromatosis, hypothyroidism, hypomagnesemia, hypophosphatemia, and Wilson's disease.[56]

Laboratory testing usually reveals leukocytosis and elevated ESR. Radiographs of the affected joint may show calcification in joints (knee, wrist, and symphysis pubis), tendon insertions, ligaments, and bursae.[59] Joint fluid examination shows the weakly positive birefringent crystals of calcium pyrophosphate dihydrate. The crystals appear rhomboidal on regular light microscopy. The presence of joint fluid crystals and radiographic calcifications are required for a definite diagnosis of pseudogout.[56] The patient's symptoms may mimic septic arthritis, so joint fluid should be gram-stained and cultured. A serum calcium level may detect unsuspected hyperparathyroidism.

Treatment for an acute attack is similar to the therapy for acute gout: NSAIDs or oral colchicine, although the latter is not as effective as with gout.[60] As in gouty arthritis, colchicine, 0.6 mg twice daily, can be administered prophylactically to prevent subsequent episodes.[61] Aspiration with or without steroid injection can also be used.[56]

A variant form of pseudogout exists in which calcium apatite crystals are present. The arthropathy has a short history and is rapidly progressive and destructive. Shoulders and knees are involved, effusions are cold, and pain is the most common presentation. Radiographs are notable for marked destructive changes and fewer than expected osteophytes.[62] Apatite crystals may be detected by a wet preparation of synovial fluid stained with alizarin red S.[58]

Osteoarthritis (Degenerative Joint Disease)

Osteoarthritis (degenerative joint disease) is the most common form of arthritis in the adult population. Patients with osteoarthritis are elderly: men predominate until 60 years of age, then women predominate. The disease is characterized by loss of articular cartilage and reactive changes at the margins of the joint and in subchondral bone.[63] Patients with degenerative joint disease can present with an acute flare-up in a joint that has been chronically affected. The initial damage begins in the cartilage, which degenerates; subsequently, subchondral bone fractures occur and osteophytes are formed in an attempt to repair the damage. Synovitis is more common in advanced disease because of the release of inflammatory mediators by the damaged joint parts, precipitated by trauma or basic calcium phosphate crystals. Articular cartilage that has been lost does not regenerate and may leave the patient with a painful bone-to-bone interface.

The chief complaint in osteoarthritis is pain. A lack of systemic symptoms helps distinguish those patients from those with rheumatoid arthritis. The hands are predominantly affected in some patients with osteoarthritis. Bouchard's and Heberden's nodes (osteophyte spurs) are visible and palpable at the PIP and DIP joints, respectively, and are more common in women. The knee has crepitus on active and passive motion. The quadriceps muscle may be atrophied because of disuse. Many patients have involvement of the hip and walk with a limp.[64] The great toe MTP joint is commonly affected (bunion formation).

Results of routine laboratory tests are usually normal. ESR may be elevated. Radiographs of an osteoarthritic joint show asymmetric joint-space narrowing, osteophyte formation at the joint margins, and subchondral cyst formation without osteoporosis. The synovial fluid is generally noninflammatory with fewer than 2000 cells/mm^3 and few PMNs.[65] Occasionally, crystals may be seen. A diagnosis of osteoarthritis can be made in patients with knee pain and radiographic evidence of osteophytes and whose age is greater than 50 years or who have crepitus or stiffness of more than 30 minutes after nonuse.

Treatment includes judicious exercise for muscle strengthening, relief of muscle spasm, and support for the joint. Analgesics, such as acetaminophen, are the drug of first choice. Acetaminophen is comparable to ibuprofen for the short-term treatment of knee osteoarthritis.[66] If acetaminophen fails to provide relief from symptoms, patients can be started on NSAIDs, although it is not obvious that they are needed for early osteoarthritis. They may be no more efficacious than acetaminophen and the risk of side effects is significant.[67,68] Ultimately, those patients with completely denuded cartilage in the hip and knee will need joint replacement.

Polyarthritis

The differential diagnosis of polyarticular arthritis is much broader than monarticular arthritis. It is helpful to divide polyarticular presentations into two groups. Acute presentations (<6 weeks) include gonococcal arthritis, viral arthritis (e.g., rubella, hepatitis), Lyme disease, Reiter's syndrome, and rheumatic fever. Chronic polyarticular presentations are caused by rheumatoid arthritis, systemic lupus erythematosus, scleroderma, psoriatic arthritis, dermatomyositis, and other autoimmune diseases. The diseases may also be distinguished on the basis of symmetric or asymmetric presentations. Rheumatoid arthritis and lupus tend to be symmetric, the others asymmetric. The spondyloarthropathies (ankylosing spondylitis, reactive arthritis, psoriatic arthritis, and the arthropathy of inflammatory bowel disease) involve predominantly larger joints, whereas psoriatic arthritis affects the small joints of the hands.

Gonococcal Arthritis

Typically, the patient is a young woman (4:1 ratio to men) who has symptoms develop during her menstrual period, in her last two trimesters of pregnancy, or even postpartum.[69] Of the 1 to 3 million patients with gonorrhea in the United States, each year 1% develop disseminated infection.[28] Clinically, the illness begins with fever, chills, and a migratory tenosynovitis and arthralgias that progress to arthritis, predominantly in the knee, ankle, or wrist. The tendon sheaths of the wrists and hands are often involved. The tenosynovitis and arthritis is thought to be an immune-mediated phenomenon. A characteristic rash in two thirds of patients accompanies the tenosynovitis and arthritis—a countable number of hemorrhagic necrotic pustules that have a red surrounding and a pustular center and typically first appear on the distal extremities, including the sides of the fingers. This full clinical spectrum is called the *arthritis/dermatitis syndrome.* Rarely does the patient report cervicitis or urethritis. A similar syndrome has recently been recognized as a result of *Neisseria meningitidis* infection.[70] The differential diagnosis includes Reiter's syndrome, polyarticular septic arthritis, hepatitis B arthritis, and rheumatic fever.[69]

Blood cultures generally give a poor yield for *Neisseria gonorrhoeae* and do not correlate with positive synovial fluid cultures, which in general are positive for gonococcus in no more than 50% of cases. The Gram stain is positive more often than the culture.[69] The synovial fluid is inflammatory (30,000-100,000 cells/mm^3).[71] Cervical, urethral, rectal, and pharyngeal cultures are positive in up to 75% of cases. For the best yield, all orifices (synovium, blood, cervix, urethra, rectum, pharynx, and skin lesions) should be cultured and plated at the bedside on chocolate agar or Thayer-Martin medium.[28] Cultures take 48 hours to turn positive, so the initial diagnosis of gonococcal arthritis is a clinical one; it is the diagnosis to be excluded in any young patient with a fever, migratory polyarthritis, and polytendinitis.

Patients with gonococcal arthritis need to be admitted to the hospital—if they are unable to comply with treatment—to confirm the diagnosis, rule out endocarditis, and treat purulent synovitis. The current treatment recommendations call for ceftriaxone 1 g IM or IV daily, and for 24 to 48 hours after improvement. Cefixime, 400 mg twice daily, or ciprofloxacin, 500 mg twice daily, is then given orally for a total of 7 days of antibiotics. During treatment, penicillin, amoxicillin, or tetracyclines can be substituted if the *N. gonorrhea* strain is found to be susceptible. β-Lactam-allergic patients can be treated with spectinomycin 2 g IM every 12 hours.[71]

Viral Arthritis

The two viruses that most commonly cause arthritis are rubella and hepatitis B, but arthritis can also occur with mumps, adenoviruses, Epstein-Barr virus, and enteroviruses. The pathophysiology of arthritis in the viral diseases appears to be deposition of soluble immune complexes in the synovium with resultant inflammation. Patients with rubella arthritis often are young women. The characteristic rash has usually appeared several days before, and patients may have just arthritic symptoms. The arthritis is acute, symmetric, and usually polyarticular, but it can occur in only one joint. Generally it resolves within weeks but

in some patients lasts months to years.[72] A history of a recent rubella infection or vaccination helps make the diagnosis. The rubella virus can be isolated from synovial fluid, so joint fluid can be sent for viral culture. The joint fluid initially may be noninflammatory, but if the arthritis persists, the fluid may become inflammatory.

The arthritis of hepatitis B usually occurs with or follows the prodromal syndrome of fever and lymphadenopathy or may be the only presenting symptom. It often precedes the onset of jaundice, seems to occur in conditions of antigen abundance, and clears with the production of antibodies. Immune complexes in the synovial fluid seem to be responsible for the inflammatory, serum-sickness type of reaction. The arthritis may be sudden and severe. The PIP, knee, ankle, and MP joints are most commonly involved. Salicylates may be helpful for the joint complaints. Serologic tests for rheumatoid arthritis are negative.

Lyme Disease

Lyme disease is caused by a spirochete, *Borrelia burgdorferi.* It is named for the location of its original discovery in Lyme, Connecticut. Its current geographic prevalence is primarily in three areas: (1) from Massachusetts to Maryland on the East Coast; (2) Wisconsin and Minnesota in the Midwest; and (3) California, Oregon, Utah, and Nevada in the West. The vector for this spirochete is the tick, *Ixodes dammini,* on the East Coast and in the Midwest and *Ixodes pacificus* in the West. Arthritis is a late manifestation of the disease. The initial illness is seen in the late spring and early summer.[73] A week after a bite from an infected tick, patients may develop a characteristic skin lesion, erythema chronicum migrans, at the site of the bite. The lesion has a bright red border with central clearing and quickly multiplies, spreading to the thigh, groin, and axilla, and rarely lasts more than 30 days.[73,74] Other early symptoms of the disease are fever, fatigue, severe lethargy, and other viral complaints, such as arthralgias, myalgias, and headache. Neurologic abnormalities (commonly Bell's palsy and less commonly meningitis and radiculoneuritis) or cardiac abnormalities (predominantly fluctuating atrioventricular block sometimes presenting as syncope and often requiring temporary pacing) may develop in the second stage, 4 weeks after the bite.[73,75,76] This stage represents hematogenous dissemination of the spirochetes. At that time, results of serologic testing are more likely to be positive.

Within 6 months of the inoculum, 50% to 60% of patients with untreated disease develop frank arthritis, asymmetric, most commonly in large joints, particularly the knees.[77,78] Patients have minimal joint pain and usually are afebrile. Large joint effusions are common in the knee.[73,77] Fifty percent may have had preceding intermittent musculoskeletal pain with pain on motion of the affected region without effusions or swelling.[79] The severity of the initial presentation is predictive of the subsequent arthritis.[80] From 10% to 15% of patients can develop recurrent intermittent attacks of monarticular or pauciarticular arthritis, with episodes of tendinitis or bursitis between the attacks.[76] Chronic arthritis is more common in patients who are positive for HLA-DR4.[81] The differential diagnosis consists of gonococcal arthritis and septic arthritis, acute rheumatic fever, rheumatoid arthritis, and Reiter's syndrome. A history of a previous tick bite or a history of the rash is helpful in making the diagnosis. The joint fluid is an inflammatory one with a predominance of PMNs. Serum immunofluorescent antibody assays are usually negative until approximately 6 weeks, when immunoglobulin M peaks and indicates active disease.[82] Immunoglobulin G antibodies are detected when the arthritis presents and peak at 12 months. False-positive titers can be caused by syphilis, but the different clinical presentations should distinguish the diseases. The diagnosis of Lyme disease is a clinical one, and serologic testing should be used discriminantly to confirm the diagnosis.[76]

In the early stages, treatment is effective in shortening the duration of symptoms and preventing later disease, so if the clinical findings and epidemiology make the disease suspect, medication should be given before the serologic results are available.[81] No evidence seems to recommend prophylactic therapy after a bite even in an endemic area, except perhaps in pregnant patients or with prolonged attachment in small children.[77] Doxycycline, 100 mg twice daily; amoxicillin, 500 mg four times daily; or cefuroxime, 500 mg twice daily, is recommended for the treatment of early Lyme disease. Erythromycin 250 mg four times daily and azithromycin, 500 mg on day 1 and 250 mg on following days, are less effective clinically. Treatment is for 20 to 30 days, although the shorter course may not completely eliminate the organism.[73] Amoxicillin is used instead of doxycycline for pregnant and lactating women and for children younger than 8 years of age. The same drugs can be used for cases with mild neurologic and cardiac disease, but their course of therapy needs to be longer. More severe disease needs 20 million units of IV penicillin or 2 g of IV ceftriaxone daily.[81,83] Persistent arthritis requires either 2.4 million units of IM benzathine per week for 3 weeks, or 4 million units of IV penicillin G or 2 g of IV ceftriaxone daily for 2 weeks. Treatment failure is most commonly seen in patients who do not have the disease and were mistakenly diagnosed and treated. A patient with chronic symptoms and a negative immunoglobulin G titer does not have Lyme disease and should not be started on antibiotics.

Seronegative Spondyloarthropathies

The seronegative spondyloarthropathies share the characteristics of sacroiliac involvement, peripheral inflammatory arthropathy, absence of rheumatoid factor, pathologic changes around the enthesis (ligamentous and tendinous insertion into bone), and a genetic component related to the HLA-B27 marker. The most important of these chronic polyarthritic inflammatory diseases are ankylosing spondylitis, reactive arthritis (including Reiter's syndrome), psoriatic arthritis, and the arthropathy of inflammatory bowel disease. Some clinical overlap exists, but each does have its own distinctive features that will help distinguish one from the other. One feature common to all the spondyloarthropathies is the concept of a genetic predisposition that encounters an environmental stimulus.

Patients with ankylosing spondylitis generally have back discomfort with radiologic evidence of sacroiliitis. There is a male predominance. Radiologically, there is a symmetric squaring of the margins of the vertebral bodies, and later the development of a "bamboo spine." The presentation is subacute or chronic-insidious back discomfort of more than 3 months' duration, with morning stiffness that improves with exercise in someone younger than 40 years of age. Uveitis is the most common extra-articular manifestation. The peripheral joints are involved in up to 30% of patients with enthesopathic involvement—plantar fasciitis and Achilles tendinitis. The goal of therapy is to control pain, decrease inflammation with NSAIDs, and begin strengthening exercises.[84,85]

Reiter's syndrome represents the clinical manifestation of a reactive arthritis that occurs in genetically susceptible hosts after infection with *Chlamydia trachomatis* in the genitourinary tract, or *Salmonella*, *Shigella*, *Yersinia*, or *Campylobacter* organisms in the gastrointestinal tract. *Salmonella* enteritis leads to reactive arthritis in up to 4% of cases; *Shigella flexneri* is the most common stool isolate causing Reiter's syndrome. Even human immunodeficiency virus has been implicated. Reactive arthritis is generally a disease of young men 15 to 35 years of age in whom arthritis develops 2 to 6 weeks after an episode of urethritis or dysentery. Because cervicitis is often asymptomatic, the diagnosis is more problematic in women. The syndrome is predominantly polyarticular and asymmetric. The weight-bearing joints of the lower extremities are commonly involved: knees, ankles, and feet, particularly the heels ("lover's heel").[86]

Other physical signs appear early and may be gone when the musculoskeletal complaints persist. Patients may have conjunctivitis early in the disease. This ocular component of the illness may progress to iritis, uveitis, or corneal ulceration. In up to 10% of patients, the oral mucosa and tongue may have initially painless lesions that develop into shallow painful ulcers. Similar lesions are seen on the glans penis (balanitis circinata), particularly in uncircumcised men (20% of patients). Penile lesions of circumcised men are more psoriatic in appearance. Fingers and toes may swell and appear sausage-like, a phenomenon that also occurs in psoriatic arthritis. In 10% of patients, hyperkeratotic lesions of keratoderma blennorrhagia (waxy plaques) develop on the palms and soles and look like pustular psoriasis. Patients may have inflammation at the insertion of the Achilles tendon, and up to one third of patients have low back pain and have limitation of vertebral movement on range of motion.[86]

Synovial fluid is inflammatory, with a predominance of PMNs. *Chlamydia*, *Salmonella*, and *Yersinia* antigens have been found in the synovial membrane and even in the joint fluid, but cultures are sterile. The ESR and WBC count are often increased, but these are not specific for the disease. The HLA-B27 antigen occurs in approximately 80% of patients who have the disease. Rheumatoid factor and antinuclear antibody test findings are typically negative. Early x-ray films show an enthesopathic picture, particularly at the interphalangeal joint of the great toe. This finding is related to the changes seen where ligaments attach to bone and occurs at the sacroiliac joints, ischial tuberosities, greater trochanter, and Achilles insertion. A fluffy periostitis characteristic for the seronegative arthropathies is seen. An asymmetric sacroiliitis of the vertebral bodies can occur. Ankylosing spondylitis, which may be confused with the spinal lesions of Reiter's syndrome, typically has symmetric and continuous bambooing of the spine.[86]

Patients with reactive arthritis respond well to NSAIDs, particularly indomethacin, up to 200 mg/day. Tetracyclines have improved recovery time for patients with chlamydia-triggered reactive arthritis, but not for arthritis with a gastrointestinal cause. Patients may have a single episode (the mean length of an episode is 4 to 7 months); may have recurrent bouts of arthritis; or may have a continuous spectrum of disease generally involving the ankles and calcaneus. Ankylosing spondylitis and occasionally aortic insufficiency are late complications.[86]

Of patients with inflammatory bowel disease, 20% develop acute migratory, inflammatory polyarthritis of the larger joints of the lower extremities. This generally occurs at the same time as flare-ups of the bowel disease. Psoriatic arthropathy occurs in up to 20% of patients with psoriasis. Several forms exist: asymmetric oligoarthropathy (with sausage digits), symmetric polyarthropathy, spondylitis (asymmetric as in Reiter's syndrome), DIP involvement, and arthritis mutilans.[86]

Acute Rheumatic Fever

Acute rheumatic fever is believed to result from group A streptococcal pharyngitis, although the exact mechanisms of disease initiation are unclear.[26] The incidence of acute rheumatic fever has been in a long state of decline in developing countries, especially after the discovery of antibiotics. However, reports of outbreaks in developed countries still occur.[87] It is proposed that an abnormal humoral response to streptococcal antigens leads to arthritis, carditis, valvulitis, and chorea in genetically susceptible individuals, who tend to range from 5 to 20 years of age. The clinical syndrome, then, classically consists of recurring, self-limited episodes of fever associated with polyarthritis, carditis/valvulitis, rash, subcutaneous nodules, or chorea occurring 2 to 3 weeks after an episode of streptococcal pharyngitis.[88] Unchecked advancement of the cardiac manifestations leads to both short- and long-term morbidity and mortality.

Clinically, the diagnosis of acute rheumatic fever is based on the revised Jones criteria. Over the past 50 years, the Jones criteria have undergone several revisions to improve their diagnostic accuracy.[89] The presence of two major, or one major and two minor, criteria

---

BOX 114-2. 1992 Jones Criteria for Diagnosis of Acute Rheumatic Fever

Major Manifestations	Minor Manifestations
Polyarthritis	Clinical findings
Carditis	Arthralgia
Chorea	Fever
Erythema marginatum	Laboratory findings
Subcutaneous nodules	Elevated acute phase reactants
	Erythrocyte sedimentation rate
	C-reactive protein
	Prolonged PR interval on ECG

Plus:
Supporting evidence of prior group A streptococcal infection (elevated or increasing streptococcal antibody titer, positive rapid strep test or bacterial throat culture, recent scarlet fever).

Special Writing Group of the Committee on Rheumatic Fever, Endocarditis and Kawasaki Disease of the Council on Cardiovascular Disease in the Young of the American Heart Association: Guidelines for the diagnosis of rheumatic fever: Jones criteria, 1992 update, *JAMA* 268:2069–2073, 1992. Copyrighted (1992), American Medical Association.

---

in the presence of supporting evidence of prior group A streptococcal infection is required (Box 114-2).[90] The major manifestations of rheumatic fever include polyarthritis, carditis, chorea, erythema marginatum, and subcutaneous nodules. Migratory arthritis is present in the majority of patients and usually affects the large joints. Owing to the availability and efficacy of anti-inflammatory agents, the migratory arthritis is often short-lived and far from classic.[88] Rheumatic fever involves the heart in about half of patients, causing both cardiac dysfunction and valvular abnormalities. Pericarditis, congestive heart failure, valvular dysfunction, and cardiomegaly all indicate cardiac involvement of acute rheumatic fever. Echocardiography has been recommended even for patients with no clinical evidence of carditis.[87,91] Neurologic dysfunction in acute rheumatic fever can lead to chorea (also known as Sydenham's chorea), weakness, and even behavioral disturbances. Careful neurologic evaluation will demonstrate sparing of sensory functions even in the presence of these other startling findings. The rash of erythema marginatum as well as subcutaneous nodules may also be present in patients with acute rheumatic fever. Erythema marginatum is manifested by the appearance of well-demarcated, pinkish areas of non-pruritic rash, usually on the trunk, but sometimes spreading to the proximal limbs. The plaques demonstrate central clearing and may last only hours. Subcutaneous nodules, on the other hand, are firm, nontender nodules usually located under the skin overlying bony prominences.

The laboratory workup for possible acute rheumatic fever consists of pharyngeal cultures, ESR, C-reactive protein, and antibody to streptolysin O. The last is helpful in patients with joint involvement as the only clinical manifestation. Anti-DNase B, if available, increases the sensitivity to 95%. The streptozyme test also documents recent streptococcal infection. The synovial fluid is an inflammatory one with an average of 16,000 WBCs, no crystals, and a negative culture.

Poststreptococcal reactive arthritis is a closely related but distinct clinical entity in which patients have some but not all of the diagnostic criteria for acute rheumatic fever. Reactive arthritis is a clinical syndrome characterized by a sterile oligoarthritis associated with bacterial infection in a distant site. In poststreptococcal reactive arthritis, carditis is rare, and the arthritis is often severe. Controversy exists about the relationship and diagnosis of this entity to acute rheumatic fever.[92,93]

Treatment is benzathine, 1.2 million U IM or 2 g of oral penicillin V per day for 10 days (erythromycin if the patient is penicillin-allergic). Penicillin can be given as monthly benzathine, 1.2 million U IM or 250 mg orally per day (or 500 mg to 1 g sulfadiazine) through adolescence or up to 5 years from the last episode to prevent recurrences (up to 75% of cases). The arthritis responds well to salicylates, 6 to 8 g/day for adults and 80 to 100 mg/kg/day for children or NSAIDs.[94] They may need to be continued for 2 months or until the ESR is normal. Carditis can be treated with 40 to 60 mg prednisone for 2 weeks to decrease the inflammatory response in the myocardium.[88]

Rheumatoid Arthritis

Although rheumatoid arthritis is a chronic disease, at least 20% of patients have an acute presentation.

The disease develops in women two to three times more often than in men, with a peak incidence between the fourth and sixth decades of life. There appears to be a genetic predisposition related to the HLA-DR4 haplotype. Immune complexes are formed that stimulate PMNs to release the enzymes that ultimately cause joint destruction. The synovial cells increase dramatically in number and produce even more inflammatory substances. A pannus of granulation tissue is formed that ultimately destroys the joint.[95]

Patients commonly see a physician after a prodromal period of fatigue, weakness, and musculoskeletal pain that may last weeks to months. The patient's joints begin to swell in a symmetric and additive pattern, particularly the hands (MP and PIP joints), wrists, and elbows. The foot, however, may be the initial site of involvement and is affected in more than 90% of patients with rheumatoid arthritis, particularly the great and little toe MTP joints. The DIP joints of the fingers are not involved, which helps distinguish rheumatoid arthritis from osteoarthritis, reactive arthritis, and psoriatic arthritis.[96]

Acute presentations may have only warm, tender, swollen joints that may be difficult to distinguish from a viral arthropathy. Tenosynovitis can occur. Acute pericarditis is not related to the duration of disease and also may be an early presentation. In the patient with long-standing rheumatoid arthritis, long-term changes may be observed. These include MP and PIP swelling,

ulnar deviation, swan-neck and boutonnière deformities of the hands, and limitation of dorsiflexion of the wrist. The knee is often affected, on the short term with effusion and on the long term with muscle atrophy and Baker's cysts.[96] Bursae in the retrocalcaneal region are common complications. Extra-articular complications include subcutaneous nodules (associated with more severe disease), vasculitis of the skin, pulmonary fibrosis, mononeuritis multiplex, and Sjögren's and Felty's syndromes. Patients with long-standing rheumatoid arthritis may have degeneration of the transverse ligament develop that keeps the dens of C2 close to the posterior aspect of the anterior part of the C1 ring.

The workup of the patient in whom rheumatoid arthritis is suspected should be directed at excluding other causes of arthritis, such as septic arthritis. Rheumatoid factor, which is an antibody against gamma globulin, is positive in approximately 85% of patients with rheumatoid arthritis but even if negative does not exclude the diagnosis.[96] ESR and C-reactive protein levels may be elevated but are also elevated in other rheumatologic diseases.

Early radiographic features of rheumatoid arthritis are soft-tissue swelling and juxta-articular osteoporosis leading to uniform joint-space narrowing. The magnetic resonance imaging scan is useful early in the disease by demonstrating erosions before they can be seen on conventional x-ray study. Arthrocentesis must be done. The fluid should be evaluated for purulence and crystals and undergo Gram stain and culture. The cell count is usually inflammatory, between 4000 and 50,000, with more PMNs (75%) than seen with crystal disease. The joint fluid glucose level is usually low.

Excessive movement increases inflammation, so the initial treatment is rest in combination with suppression of the inflammation by medications. The joints should be splinted, the upper extremities for 3 weeks and the lower extremities for 8 weeks. The plan is to decrease the pain, inflammation, and side effects as much as possible.[97]

The mainstay of therapy in the past was the pyramid approach, with salicylates used alone as the first-line medication. Other medications were added only as the disease progressed. Because the first 12 to 18 months are critical in preventing major joint damage, particularly in aggressive disease, salicylates are no longer being used as solo agents.[98] Instead, a "bridge concept" of coadministering different classes of medications has emerged.[98] These include steroids, gold, penicillamine, azathioprine, methotrexate, cyclosporine, and sulfasalazine. Oral prednisone, 5 mg to 7.5 mg daily, has been used effectively to control inflammation, and methotrexate and sulfasalazine have been used in combination without any increase in the significant side effects of methotrexate alone. For mild disease, most clinicians still use the salicylates or other NSAIDs, which have their gastrointestinal and renal toxicities related to their inhibition of cyclooxygenase. A scoring system has been used to best predict patients at greatest risk for gastrointestinal complications, including age, dose, and concurrent steroid use.[97] Acetylsalicylic acid in its original form has gastrointestinal and platelet toxicity. The enteric-coated form has decreased gastrointestinal effects but is not as well absorbed, and the nonacetylated form has fewer hypersensitivity reactions, less gastrointestinal toxicity, and no effect on platelet function. All take up to 2 weeks to reach peak effective serum levels. If NSAIDs are chosen, patients may need to try at least three different types before a reduction in symptoms occurs. In addition, NSAIDs have gastrointestinal toxicity (a problem in the elderly), change platelet function, and should not be used in patients with renal or cardiac failure.

DISPOSITION

The challenge in the emergency department management of arthritis is in ruling out septic causes. If a patient is diagnosed with nongonococcal septic arthritis based on a positive Gram stain or culture, or based on strong clinical suspicion even in the face of a negative Gram stain, the patient should be admitted with emergency orthopedic consultation for parenteral antibiotics and evaluation for possible arthroscopy or arthrotomy. Patients in whom a disseminated gonococcal infection is suspected should be admitted for parenteral antibiotics and orthopedic consultation, except in cases in which the patient is well-appearing, the symptomatology is mild, and the patient is able to comply with the daily follow-up plans. Patients with noninfectious causes of arthritis can be discharged, assuming their pain is controlled.

KEY CONCEPTS

- The number of joints involved and the distribution of joint involvement help to pinpoint the most likely cause of arthritis.
- Monarthritis is septic arthritis until proven otherwise.
- The most definitive test for evaluating an inflamed joint for the possibility of bacterial infection is examination of synovial fluid.
- Negative Gram stain of synovial fluid does not rule out bacterial arthritis.
- Delays in the diagnosis and treatment of septic arthritis worsen outcomes.

REFERENCES

1. Schned ES, Reinertsen JL: The social and economic consequences of rheumatic disease. In Klippel JH (ed): *Primer on the Rheumatic Diseases,* 11th ed. Atlanta, Arthritis Foundation, 1997.
2. Benedek TG: History of the rheumatic diseases. In Klippel JH (ed): *Primer on the Rheumatic Diseases,* 11th ed. Atlanta, Arthritis Foundation, 1997.
3. Felson DT: Epidemiology of the rheumatic diseases. In Koopman WJ (ed): *Arthritis and Allied Conditions: A Textbook of Rheumatology,* 13th ed. Baltimore, Williams & Wilkins, 1997.
4. Simkin PA: The musculoskeletal system: Joints. In Klippel JH (ed): *Primer on the Rheumatic Diseases,* 11th ed. Atlanta, Arthritis Foundation, 1997.
5. Goldring MB: Articular cartilage. In Klippel JH (ed): *Primer on the Rheumatic Diseases,* 11th ed. Atlanta, Arthritis Foundation, 1997.
6. Knudson W, Kuettner KE: Structure: Proteoglycans. In Klippel JH (ed): *Primer on the Rheumatic Diseases,* 11th ed. Atlanta, Arthritis Foundation, 1997.
7. Abramson SB: Mediators of inflammation, tissue destruction and repair: Cellular constituents. In Klippel JH (ed): *Primer on the Rheumatic Diseases,* 11th ed. Atlanta, Arthritis Foundation, 1997.
8. Cash JM: Evaluation of the patient: History and physical examination. In Klippel JH (ed): *Primer on the Rheumatic Diseases,* 11th ed. Atlanta, Arthritis Foundation, 1997.
9. Middleton DB: Infectious arthritis. *Primary Care* 20:4, 1993.
10. Shmerling RH, Liang MH: Evaluation of the patient: Laboratory assessment. In Klippel JH (ed): *Primer on the Rheumatic Diseases,* 11th ed. Atlanta, Arthritis Foundation, 1997.
11. Beachley MC: Radiology of arthritis. *Primary Care* 20:4, 1993.
12. Scott WW: Evaluation of the patient: Imaging techniques. In Klippel JH (ed): *Primer on the Rheumatic Diseases,* 11th ed. Atlanta, Arthritis Foundation, 1997.
13. Winalski CS, Shapiro AW: Computed tomography in the evaluation of arthritis. *Rheum Dis Clin North Am* 17:543, 1991.
14. Mitchell M, et al: Septic arthritis. *Radiol Clin North Am* 26:1295, 1988.
15. Missenbaum MA, Adams MK: MRI in rheumatology, *Rheum Dis Clin North Am* 20:2, 1994.
16. Lopez-Longo F, et al: Primary septic arthritis in heroin users: Early diagnosis by radioisotope imaging and geographic variations in the causative agents. *J Rheumatol* 14:991, 1987.
17. Benjamin GC: Arthrocentesis. In Roberts JR, Hedges JR (eds): *Clinical Procedures in Emergency Medicine,* 3rd ed. Philadelphia, WB Saunders, 1998.
18. Hasselbacher P: Arthrocentesis, synovial fluid analysis, and synovial biopsy. In Klippel JH (ed): *Primer on the Rheumatic Diseases,* 11th ed. Atlanta, Arthritis Foundation, 1997.
19. Schaffer TC: Joint and soft-tissue arthrocentesis. *Primary Care* 20:4, 1993.
20. Roberts WN, et al: Dry taps and what to do about them: A pictorial essay on failed arthrocentesis of the knee. *Am J Med* 100:461, 1996.
21. Shmerling RH: Synovial fluid analysis: A critical appraisal. *Rheum Dis Clin North Am* 20:2, 1994.
22. Clayburne G, Baker DG, Schumacher HR: Estimated synovial fluid leukocyte numbers on wet drop prep as a potential substitute for actual leukocyte counts. *J Rheumatol* 19:60, 1992.
23. Javors JM, Weisman MH: Principles of diagnosis and treatment of joint infections. In Koopman WJ (ed): *Arthritis and Allied Conditions: A Textbook of Rheumatology,* 13th ed. Baltimore, Williams & Wilkins, 1997.
24. Krey PR, Lazaro DM: *Analysis of Synovial Fluid.* Summit, NJ, Ciba-Geigy, 1992.
25. Pascual E, et al: Synovial fluid analysis for diagnosis of intercritical gout. *Ann Intern Med* 131:756, 1999.
26. Gibofsky A, Zabriskie JB: Rheumatic fever: Etiology, diagnosis, and treatment. In Koopman WJ (ed): *Arthritis and Allied Conditions: A Textbook of Rheumatology,* 14th ed. Baltimore, Williams & Wilkins, 1997.
27. Barton LL, Dumkle LM, Habib FH: Septic arthritis in childhood. *Am J Dis Child* 141:898, 1987.
28. Mahowald ML: Infectious disorders: Septic arthritis. In Klippel JH (ed): *Primer on the Rheumatic Diseases,* 11th ed. Atlanta, Arthritis Foundation, 1997.
29. Baker DG, Schumacher RH: Current concepts: Acute monoarthritis. *N Engl J Med* 329:1013, 1993.

30. Vassilopoulos D, et al: Musculoskeletal infections in patients with human immunodeficiency virus infection. *Medicine* 76:284, 1997.
31. Gilbert MS, et al: Long-term evaluation of septic arthritis in hemophiliac patients. *Clin Orthop* 328:54, 1996.
32. Dubost J, et al: Polyarticular septic arthritis. *Medicine* 72:296, 1993.
33. Sack K: Monarthritis: Differential diagnosis. *Am J Med* 102:30S, 1997.
34. Brancos MA, et al: Septic arthritis in heroin addicts. *Semin Arthritis Rheum* 21:81, 1991.
35. Baer PA, et al: Coexistent septic and crystal arthritis: Report of 4 cases and literature review. *J Rheumatol* 13:604, 1986.
36. Esterhai JL, Gelb I: Adult septic arthritis. *Orthop Clin North Am* 22:3, 1991.
37. Jobanputra P, Gibson T: Case report: Diagnosis of pseudogout and septic arthritis. *Br J Rheumatol* 26:379, 1987.
38. Ike RW: Bacterial arthritis. In Koopman WJ (ed): *Arthritis and Allied Conditions: A Textbook of Rheumatology,* 13th ed. Baltimore, Williams & Wilkins, 1997.
39. Yagupsky P, et al: Epidemiology, etiology and clinical features of septic arthritis in children younger than 24 months. *Arch Pediat Adolesc Med* 149:537, 1995.
40. Bradley JS, et al: Pediatric pneumococcal bone and joint infections. *Pediatrics* 102:1376, 1998.
41. Armstrong RW, Bolding F, Joseph R: Septic arthritis following arthroscopy: Clinical syndromes and analysis of risk factors. *J Arthrop Rel Surg* 8:213, 1992.
42. Mikhail IS, Alarcon GS: Nongonococcal bacterial arthritis. *Rheum Dis Clin North Am* 19:2, 1993.
43. Kim HK, Alman B, Cole WG: A shortened course of parenteral antibiotic therapy in the management of acute septic arthritis of the hip. *J Pediatr Orthop* 20:44, 2000.
44. Cornelius R, Schneider MA: Gouty arthritis in the adult. *Radiol Clin North Am* 26:1267, 1988.
45. Vawter RL, Antonelli MA: Rational treatment of gout. *Postgrad Med J* 91:2, 1992.
46. Terkeltaub RA: Gout: Epidemiology, pathology, and pathogenesis. In Klippel JH (ed): *Primer on the Rheumatic Diseases,* 11th ed. Atlanta, Arthritis Foundation, 1997.
47. Edwards NL: Gout: Clinical and laboratory findings. In Klippel JH (ed): *Primer on the Rheumatic Diseases,* 11th ed. Atlanta, Arthritis Foundation, 1997.
48. Lally EV, Ho G, Kaplan SR: The clinical spectrum of gouty arthritis in women. *Arch Intern Med* 146:2222, 1986.
49. Shergy WJ, Gilkeson GS, German DC: Acute gouty arthritis and intravenous nitroglycerin. *Arch Intern Med* 148:2505, 1988.
50. Star VL, Hochberg MC: Prevention and management of gout. *Drugs* 45:2, 1993.
51. Pratt PW, Ball GB: Gout: Treatment. In Klippel JH (ed): *Primer on the Rheumatic Diseases,* 11th ed. Atlanta, Arthritis Foundation, 1997.
52. Altman RD, et al: Ketoprofen versus indomethacin in patients with acute gouty arthritis: A multicenter, double blind comparative study. *J Rheumatol* 15:1422, 1988.
53. Diamond HS: Control of crystal induced arthropathies. *Rheum Dis Clin North Am* 15:557, 1988.
54. Emmerson BT: Drug therapy: The management of gout. *N Engl J Med* 334:445, 1996.
55. Paulus HE, et al: Prophylactic colchicine therapy of intercritical gout: A placebo-controlled study of probenecid-treated patients. *Arthritis Rheum* 34:1489, 1991.
56. Ryan LM: Calcium pyrophosphate dihydrate crystal deposition. In Klippel JH (ed): *Primer on the Rheumatic Diseases,* 11th ed. Atlanta, Arthritis Foundation, 1997.
57. Masuda I, Ishikawa K: Clinical features of pseudogout attacks: A survey of 50 cases. *Clin Orthop* 229:173, 1988.
58. Beutler A, Schumacher HR: Gout and pseudogout: When are arthritic symptoms caused by crystal deposition? *Postgrad Med* 95:2, 1994.
59. Bonafede RP: Evaluating CPPD crystal deposition: An important disease of aging. *Geriatrics* 48:59, 1988.
60. Agarwal AK: Gout and pseudogout. *Primary Care* 20:4, 1993.
61. Alvarellos A, Spilberg I: Colchicine prophylaxis in pseudogout. *J Rheumatol* 13:804, 1986.
62. Dieppe P: Apatites and miscellaneous crystals. In Klippel JH (ed): *Primer on the Rheumatic Diseases,* 11th ed. Atlanta, Arthritis Foundation, 1997.
63. Fife RS: Osteoarthritis: Epidemiology, pathology, and pathogenesis. In Klippel JH (ed): *Primer on the Rheumatic Diseases,* 11th ed. Atlanta, Arthritis Foundation, 1997.
64. Hurwitz DE, et al: Gait compensations in patients with osteoarthritis and their relationship to pain and passive hip motion. *J Orthop Res* 15:629, 1997.
65. Hochberg MC: Osteoarthritis: Clinical features and treatment. In Klippel JH (ed): *Primer on the Rheumatic Diseases,* 11th ed. Atlanta, Arthritis Foundation, 1997.
66. Bradley JD, et al: Comparison of an inflammatory dose of ibuprofen, an analgesic dose of ibuprofen and acetaminophen in the treatment of patients with osteoarthritis. *N Engl J Med* 325:87, 1991.
67. Brandt KD: Should osteoarthritis be treated with nonsteroidal anti-inflammatory drugs? *Rheum Dis Clin North Am* 19:3, 1993.
68. Brandt KD: Should nonsteroidal anti-inflammatory drugs be used to treat osteoarthritis? *Rheum Dis Clin North Am* 19:1, 1993.
69. Scopelitis E, Martinez-Osuna P: Gonococcal arthritis. *Rheum Dis Clin North Am* 19:2, 1993.
70. Rompalo AM, et al: The acute arthritis-dermatitis syndrome. *Arch Intern Med* 147:281, 1987.
71. Goldenberg DL: Gonococcal arthritis and other neisserial infections. In Koopman WJ (ed): *Arthritis and Allied Conditions: A Textbook of Rheumatology,* 13th ed. Baltimore, Williams & Wilkins, 1997.
72. Naides SJ: Infectious disorders: Viral arthritis. In Klippel JH (ed): *Primer on the Rheumatic Diseases,* 11th ed. Atlanta, Arthritis Foundation, 1997.
73. Schoen RT: Identification of Lyme disease. *Rheum Dis Clin North Am* 20:3, 1994.
74. Wright SW, Trott AT: North America tick borne disease. *Ann Emerg Med* 17:964, 1988.
75. Williams DN, Schned ES: Lyme disease: Recognizing its many manifestations. *Postgrad Med J* 87:139, 1990.
76. Sigal LH: Lyme disease: Testing and treatment—who should be tested and treated for Lyme disease and how? *Rheum Dis Clin north Am* 19:1, 1993.
77. Kalish R: Lyme disease. *Rheum Dis Clin North Am* 19:2, 1993.
78. Steere AC: Musculoskeletal manifestations of Lyme disease. *Am J Med* 98:44S, 1995.
79. Kolstoe J, Messner RP: Lyme disease: Musculoskeletal manifestations. *Rheum Dis Clin North Am* 15:649, 1989.
80. Steere AC, Schoen RT, Taylor E: The clinical evolution of Lyme arthritis. *Ann Intern Med* 107:725, 1987.
81. Sigal LH: Infectious disorders: Lyme disease. In Klippel JH (ed): *Primer on the Rheumatic Diseases,* 11th ed. Atlanta, Arthritis Foundation, 1997.
82. Magnarelli LA: Lab diagnosis of Lyme disease. *Rheum Dis Clin North Am* 15:735, 1989.
83. Steere AC: *Borrelia burgdorferi.* In Mandell GL, Bennett JE, Dolin R (eds): *Mandell, Douglas, and Bennett's Principles and Practice of Infectious Diseases,* 5th ed. Philadelphia, Churchill Livingstone, 2000.
84. Taurog JD: Seronegative spondyloarthropathies: Epidemiology, pathology, and pathogenesis. In Klippel JH (ed): *Primer on the Rheumatic Diseases,* 11th ed. Atlanta, Arthritis Foundation, 1997.
85. Khan MA: Seronegative spondyloarthropathies: Ankylosing spondylitis. In Klippel JH (ed): *Primer on the*

Rheumatic Diseases, 11th ed. Atlanta, Arthritis Foundation, 1997.

86. Arnett FC: Seronegative spondyloarthropathies: Reactive arthritis (Reiter's syndrome) and enteropathic arthritis. In Klippel JH (ed): *Primer on the Rheumatic Diseases*, 11th ed. Atlanta, Arthritis Foundation, 1997.

87. Veasy LG, et al: Resurgence of acute rheumatic fever in the intermountain area of the United States. *N Engl J Med* 316:421, 1987.

88. Gibofsky A, Zabriskie JB: Rheumatic fever. In Klippel JH (ed): *Primer on the Rheumatic Diseases,* 11th ed. Atlanta, Arthritis Foundation, 1997.

89. Shiffman RN: Guideline maintenance and revision: 50 years of the Jones criteria for diagnosis of rheumatic fever. *Arch Ped Adol Med* 149:727, 1995.

90. Special Writing Group of the Committee on Rheumatic Fever, Endocarditis, and Kawasaki Disease of the Council on Cardiovascular Disease in the Young of the American Heart Association: Guidelines for the diagnosis of rheumatic fever: Jones criteria, 1992 update. *JAMA* 268:2069, 1992.

91. Veasy LG: Echocardiography for diagnosis and management of rheumatic fever. *JAMA* 269:2084, 1993.

92. Aviles RJ, et al: Poststreptococcal reactive arthritis in adults: A case series. *Mayo Clin Proc* 75:144, 2000.

93. Jansen TL, Janssen M, VanRiel PL: Acute rheumatic fever or post-streptococcal reactive arthritis: A clinical problem revisited. *Br J Rheumatol* 37:335, 1998.

94. Amigo MC, Martinez-Lavin M, Reyes P: Acute rheumatic fever. *Rheum Dis Clin North Am* 19:2, 1993.

95. Goronzy JJ, Weyand CM: Rheumatoid arthritis: Epidemiology, pathology, and pathogenesis. In Klippel JH (ed): *Primer on the Rheumatic Diseases,* 11th ed. Atlanta, Arthritis Foundation, 1997.

96. Anderson RJ: Rheumatoid arthritis: Clinical and laboratory features. In Klippel JH (ed): *Primer on the Rheumatic Diseases,* 11th ed. Atlanta, Arthritis Foundation, 1997.

97. Paget SA: Rheumatoid arthritis: Treatment. In Klippel JH (ed): *Primer on the Rheumatic Diseases,* 11th ed. Atlanta, Arthritis Foundation, 1997.

98. Healy LA, Wilske KR: Reforming the pyramid: A plan for treating rheumatoid arthritis in the 1990s. *Rheum Dis Clin North Am* 15:615, 1989.

CHAPTER

115 Tendinopathy and Bursitis

Ted Koutouzis and Stephen L. Adams

TENDINOPATHY

Perspective

Diseases of rheumatism have long been of concern to physicians, with evidence that many of the aphorisms of Hippocrates had some reference to this area of the healing arts. In the mid-1600s, Sydenham, a physician who himself had gout, described gout, acute rheumatism, and Syndenham's chorea and hence began to identify distinctions among various processes of musculoskeletal complaints and joint inflammations.[1] Today, given the increased participation of people in athletics and fitness, the emergency physician may see a wide variety of patients with tendinopathies presenting to the emergency department.[2] In fact, for many, athletic pursuits and fitness have become a vocation and avocation alike. Although physical activities may well have dramatic health benefits, they may also predispose one to significant morbidity. Many overuse syndromes have increased in incidence. Approximately half of all sports participants will be injured at some time, and of these injuries, up to one half will involve a tendinopathy. Among athletes, studies have indicated that tendinopathies have been involved in approximately 30% of running-related injuries and in nearly 40% of tennis injuries.[3,4] In the workplace, the incidence of work-related musculoskeletal disorders reported is higher in those occupations that involve repetitive motion, localized contact stress, awkward positions, vibrations, and forceful exertion. Studies have demonstrated that improvements in ergonomic design can reduce the incidence of tendinopathies.[5]

Important not only because of their prevalence, tendinopathies often take on the frustrating character of chronicity. Patients may have symptoms for extended periods of time in spite of appropriate therapy.[6] The management of tendinopathy focuses on identification of the cause of discomfort, elimination of sources of primary tendinopathy, treatment modalities such as protection, relative rest, application of ice, compression and elevation as necessary, modification of behavior to minimize or eliminate sources of continuing irritation, provision of appropriate analgesic medication and, importantly, referral for appropriate follow-up.[7,8]

Principles of Disease

Tendons are collagenous structures that connect muscle to bone. They transmit the forces originating in the muscle to the bone, which enables joint motion.[7] The diagnosis of *tendinitis*, a commonly used term implying an "inflammation of the tendon," has long been attached to many overuse injuries.[2] Many practitioners now advocate use of the term *tendinosis* as a more accurate reflection of the pathologic process, given that histologic findings consistent with inflammation are not clearly evident in pathoanatomic studies.[2,9] Although it has been noted that reliable, well-conducted epidemiologic studies have not been performed for most tendinopathies, the histopathologic substratum, in many cases, is degenerative.[2] The term *tendinopathy* is used throughout this chapter to refer to the injured tendon, as it encompasses the pathology seen in such injuries.[2]

Mechanical overload and repetitive microtrauma to the musculotendinous unit are thought to be the major precipitating causes of most tendinopathies. This is as a result of extrinsic and/or intrinsic factors modifying the pathophysiologic state.[10] Intrinsic factors, such as malalignment, poor muscle flexibility, muscle weakness, or imbalance can result in excessively high or frequent mechanical loads during normal activity. Extrinsic factors, such as poor ergonomic design or excessive duration, frequency, or intensity of activity can also contribute to the development of a tendinopathy. Many injuries have a multifactorial origin. Individual factors can contribute as well. For example, a younger athlete may develop a tendinopathy as a result of mechanical overload on the basis of repetitive exercise and poor technique, whereas an older athlete with previously occult underlying tendon degeneration and decreased vascularity may see the symptoms of a tendinopathy develop with minimal exercise.[10]

Under optimal conditions, such as appropriate athletic training, the musculotendinous units are able to adapt to tension overload. This occurs through an increase in the ability of bone to increase its load-bearing capacity, and an increase in size and strength by hypertrophy of existing muscle fibers. An enhancement of tendon and ligament strength occurs by an increase in collagen content, collagen cross linking, and mucopolysaccharide content.[8] Unfortunately, in many athletes, sufficient time may not be allotted for this adaptive process to occur. For instance, a runner may increase mileage, intensity, or both with excessive alacrity, not allowing time for the cellular changes that are required to adapt to the increased stresses. Poor technique and improper equipment may also contribute to the development of an overuse syndrome.[8]

As the damaged tendon goes through several stages in the healing process, it may take 6 to 12 weeks for structural organization and collagen cross linking to return the tendon to its preinjured strength.[8]

As the healing process ensues, unrestricted activity is generally avoided. However, atrophy associated with immobilization should be avoided because the strength in healing tendons and ligaments increases faster when controlled forces are applied. Consequently, flexibility forces, isometric contractions, and a measured return to resistive exercises have been suggested as long as pain is not produced.[8] In essence, a prescription for good follow-up is important in caring for the patient with tendinopathy.

Some areas with common presentations of tendinopathies are diagrammed in Figure 115-1.

Clinical Features

History

The history of the patient presenting with a tendinopathy can be quite variable, although certain clinical aspects are often seen. A recent history of repetitive stress may be obtained by inquiring about changes in sports or other recreational activities, work activities, or changes in the workplace. Many patients initially report no such changes, but when prompted to consider activities over several weeks or months (including sports equipment utilized, workplace ergonomic features, protective boots, or other features), they may recall a potential inciting change or activity. Occasionally, no cause is identified for an inciting mechanical overload. A history of infectious disease, fluoroquinolone therapy, or other systemic illness should also be obtained.[11-13]

Pain is the most common symptom of the patient who presents with tendinopathy. Increasing discomfort, nonradiating, at the site of the affected tendon is a general symptom.[7] The pain can be acute or chronic, or can be an acute exacerbation of an existing tendinopathy. The discomfort is frequently described as more severe subsequent to periods of rest. Unlike the discomfort of morning stiffness associated with arthritis, the pain of tendinopathy may resolve after initial movement, only to manifest itself as a throbbing pain after completion of exercise. The patient may have had prior similar epsiodes.[7] Continued episodes may be accompanied by an increased severity in pain. Consequently, it may be helpful to know whether a diagnosis was made (and how) and which treatment rendered (if any) was successful.

Physical Examination

In the evaluation of the patient with a tendinopathy, a thorough, directed musculoskeletal examination should be performed. Inspection, looking for signs of edema, effusion, erythema, atrophy, deformity, symmetry, or trauma can be helpful. Palpation of the tendon, noting warmth or evidence of crepitation on movement, is important. Evidence of tenderness over the tendon, especially localized, reproducing the patient's pain should be elicited.[7] Underlying bony tenderness (and consideration of other differential diagnoses, including avulsion fracture and osteomyelitis) should be assessed as well. Motor evaluation, in particular passive and active range of motion (and symptoms elicited during the examination), strength (and evidence of weakness or pain), and joint involvement and stability should be noted.

In narrowing the diagnosis, it is important to determine whether the source of pain is articular (within the joint capsule) or periarticular (around the joint capsule). In general, arthritis produces generalized joint pain, warmth, swelling, and tenderness. The discomfort of arthritis increases with both passive and active motion of the joint. By contrast, the pain of a tendinopathy tends to be more localized.[7] Tenderness and swelling do not occur uniformly across the joint,

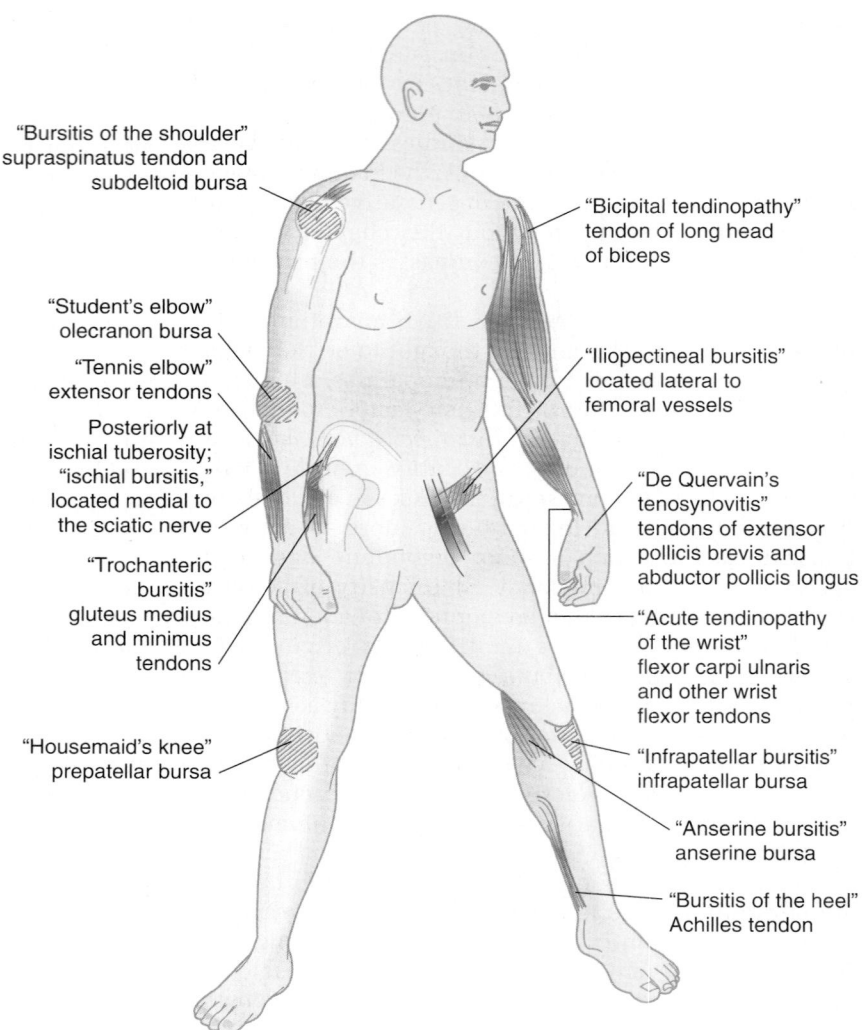

Figure 115-1. Location of common sites for tendinopathy or bursitis. (Modified from Branch WT: *Office Practice of Medicine,* 2nd ed. Philadelphia, WB Saunders, 1987.)

"Bursitis of the shoulder" supraspinatus tendon and subdeltoid bursa

"Student's elbow" olecranon bursa

"Tennis elbow" extensor tendons

Posteriorly at ischial tuberosity; "ischial bursitis," located medial to the sciatic nerve

"Trochanteric bursitis" gluteus medius and minimus tendons

"Housemaid's knee" prepatellar bursa

"Bicipital tendinopathy" tendon of long head of biceps

"Iliopectineal bursitis" located lateral to femoral vessels

"De Quervain's tenosynovitis" tendons of extensor pollicis brevis and abductor pollicis longus

"Acute tendinopathy of the wrist" flexor carpi ulnaris and other wrist flexor tendons

"Infrapatellar bursitis" infrapatellar bursa

"Anserine bursitis" anserine bursa

"Bursitis of the heel" Achilles tendon

and pain may be produced only with certain movements, most commonly with resisted active contraction or passive stretching of the affected muscles or tendons.

Specific Tendinopathies

Shoulder

Tendinopathy of the shoulder is not uncommon. Given the anatomy of the shoulder and the multiple tendons necessary to assist in the stability and motor functions of the relatively mobile shoulder, patients with symptoms of tendinopathy are ubiquitous. The causes of nontraumatic shoulder discomfort are myriad: impingement syndrome, including subacromial bursitis or rotator cuff tendinopathy, bicipital tendinopathy, calcific tendinopathy, and adhesive capsulitis, as well as others.[14]

Impingement Syndrome and Rotator Cuff Tendinopathies

The shoulder joint is predisposed to soft tissue injury because of its extensive range of motion and unique anatomic structure. While inherently unstable, the muscles of the rotator cuff (supraspinatus, infraspina-

tus, teres minor, and subscapularis) and the glenohumeral ligaments serve to stabilize the joint. The muscles of the rotator cuff originate from the scapula (hence their nomenclature) and their tendinous insertion is found on the fibrous capsule of the glenohumeral joint after traversing through the subacromial space. The presence of the subacromial bursa, as for all bursae, serves to ensure fluidity of movement but may itself become inflamed as a part of an impingement syndrome.[14] Impingement of the tendons occurs because of their unique position interposed between the humeral head and the acromion, which may predispose to a chronic tendinopathy. The functional arc of the elevated shoulder is forward and in the anterior plane.[15] As a result of this position, the greater tuberosity of the humerus may compress (impinge) the ligaments of the rotator cuff (usually the supraspinatus) against the undersurface of the anterior third of the acromion. Because of the insertion of the tendon of the long head of the biceps, it too may be involved as part of the impingement syndrome.[16] Development of this tendinopathy may be a result of overuse of the extremity that leads to microtrauma of the tendinous fibers, or due to individual anatomic differences (congenital or from the process of aging, such as osteophytic changes) that predispose to tendinopathy, or both. Other entities that may be indicted in the syndrome include subacromial bursitis, bicipital tendinopathy, and calcific tendinopathy.[14]

More than 30 years ago, Neer noted that 95% of rotator cuff tears are associated with impingement (if one does not include those tears due to a one-time traumatic event).[15,17] He described three progressive stages of the impingement syndrome as a result of overuse.[15,17] The first stage, frequently seen in athletes younger than 25 years of age who participate in sports that require repetitive overhead motions of the shoulder (e.g., swimming or baseball),[17,18] is characterized by edema and hemorrhage within and around the tendon. The pain may be characterized as a dull ache over the anterolateral shoulder, extending from the shoulder to the middle upper arm, often occurring after an activity involving flexion and abduction of the arm. Point tenderness may be elicited over the greater tuberosity. No weakness or loss of motion is generally present. This condition has been described as reversible. Conservative therapy, consisting of relative rest, application of ice, nonsteroidal anti-inflammatory drugs (NSAIDs), activity modification, and appropriate referral, is indicated.[15] In the second stage, as mechanical trauma continues, fibrosis and thickening of the tendon and subacromial bursa can occur. This generally affects patients between 25 and 40 years of age. The pain becomes constant and may worsen at night. Active motion may be limited by pain, and any activity involving overhead movement exacerbates the symptoms. Passive range of motion should be preserved and, on physical examination, pain is more diffuse and intense. The third stage has symptoms similar to the second stage but may involve a prolonged history of shoulder problems. The range of motion of the shoulder is usually decreased, either due to disuse or to a partial rotator cuff tear.[17] Pathologically, tendon degeneration and attrition may be present. Partial-thickness tears may occur or extend with minor trauma or stress. Complete tears of the rotator cuff, biceps tendon rupture, and osteophytic bony changes are sometimes seen.[14,15,17]

Physical examination in the evaluation of a rotator cuff tendinopathy includes maneuvers that can exacerbate the symptoms of impingement. Because the supraspinatus is most often the tendon involved, a physical examination sign (sometimes referred to as *Jobe's sign,* after Dr. Frank Jobe, team physician of the Los Angeles Dodgers, or the *empty can test,* describing the position of emptying aluminum cans) is helpful in isolating the supraspinatus tendon with resistance testing. With the arms abducted at 90 degrees in the scapular plane (30 degrees anterior to the coronal plane), the arms are then internally rotated with the thumbs pointed downward. The examiner places a downward force on the arms, and the patient is instructed to resist the examiner and keep the arms parallel to the floor. Weakness or pain would be considered a positive finding. If the patient is unable to resist the force of the examiner, isolated supraspinatus weakness should be suspected.[15,19]

Another sign of rotator cuff tendinopathy is Neer's test, which suggests mechanical impingement with decrease of the subacromial space. The examiner forward-flexes the arm, which causes impingement of the greater tuberosity of the humerus with the anterior and inferior edge of the acromium. The patient's shoulder should then be fully flexed to 180 degrees. A positive result occurs if there is pain produced at the end range of the arc.[15,19]

Hawkin's sign, also indicative of mechanical impingement, is performed by forcibly internally rotating the proximal humerus while forward-flexed and abducted to 90 degrees. Pain with this maneuver indicates a positive finding.[14,15,19]

A sign of complete rotator cuff tear is the drop arm test, in which the arm is passively abducted at 90 degrees and the patient is asked to maintain the abduction. If the arm drops to the side, a large rotator cuff tear must be considered.[17,20]

The shrug sign is exhibited when a patient with acute macrotrauma to the rotator cuff is asked to abduct the arm at 90 degrees and appears to be giving a shrug with that side. This movement results from the scapula attempting to abduct the arm without the assistance of the rotator cuff.[21] Patients with adhesive capsulitis (frozen shoulder) have limitation of active and passive range of motion.[22]

Bicipital Tendinopathy

The tendon of the long head of the biceps, given its insertion into the humerus in proximity to the rotator cuff, can be associated with the impingement syndrome. The patient with bicipital tendinopathy may report pain in the anterior shoulder that radiates down to the radius. Discomfort occurs when rolling on the shoulder at night or when attempting to reach a hip pocket or a back zipper. Focal tenderness elicited by palpation in the groove between the greater and lesser tuberosities of the humerus is elicited by Yergason's test. This test is performed by having the patient flex the elbow to 90 degrees with the arm against the body and resisting supination of the forearm. Pain in the area of the proximal tendon is considered to be a positive finding and indicative of bicipital tendinopathy.[16,19]

Another physical examination tool in the diagnosis of bicipital tendinopathy is that of Speed's test. With the elbow extended and the forearm supinated, the patient is instructed to resist forward flexion of the adducted shoulder at 60 degrees. Pain in the area of the proximal biceps tendon (bicipital groove) is indicative of a positive finding. (This may also be suggestive, however, of labral pathology.[16])

Calcific Tendinopathy

Calcific tendinopathy is an aptly named condition in which the deposition of calcium hydroxyapatite crystals occurs in or around the tendons of the rotator cuff. The cause is unknown but has been postulated to be related to continuous microtrauma.[14] It can manifest as either an acute or a chronically painful condition. Although it can affect any of the rotator cuff tendons, it seems to have a predilection for the supraspinatus.

The symptoms are similar to those of an impingement syndrome, and the condition generally affects people older than 40 years of age. Calcium deposition occurs over time and then undergoes spontaneous resorption. This resorptive phase is thought to be the painful aspect, but the severity of the symptoms is not related to the size of the deposit.[14] Some practitioners have suggested that acute attacks of calcific tendinopathy also occur secondary to crystal release from the tendon, often after trauma.[23]

On physical examination, there may be specific tenderness over the greater tuberosity as well as symptoms consistent with impingement. Radiographic evaluation will confirm evidence of calcification in or around the rotator cuff tendons. The presence of calcium in the tendon does not necessarily affirm the origin of the pain, as asymptomatic patients may have evidence of calcification on a routine radiograph.[24]

Treatment is conservative and consists of brief sling immobilization (beware adhesive capsulitis) and analgesia such as NSAIDs.[14] Localized disruption in the resorptive phase by needle lavage under fluoroscopy or in the operating suites has been noted to be an efficacious therapy.[24] The use of corticosteroids is controversial. Ultrasonography and extracorporeal shock wave therapy have also been utilized.[24] Follow-up care is important because calcific tendinopathy has been described as the best-known cause of reactive cuff failure.[14]

Elbow

Increasingly, athletes of all ages and skill levels are participating in sports involving overhead arm motions; consequently, elbow injuries are increasingly seen.[25] As might be expected, tendinopathy can occur in these areas through overuse and repetitive microtrauma. From an anatomic and functional perspective, the extensors and supinators of the wrist attach to the lateral elbow, and the flexors and pronators attach medially.

Lateral epicondylitis, which can occur in more than half of athletes using overhead arm motions, manifests as pain on the lateral elbow where the common extensor muscles meet the lateral humeral epicondyle.[25] This pathologic condition begins with overuse of the wrist extensor musculature. Repetitive microtraumatic injury can lead to degeneration of the extensor origin and subsequent failure of the tendon.[25]

Medial epicondylitis is characterized by pain and tenderness at the flexor-pronator tendinous origin at the medial elbow, with pathologic lesions commonly located at the interface between the origin of the pronator teres and flexor carpi radialis. People who play golf, pitch baseballs, and bowl may develop this condition as a result of the repetitive valgus stress placed on the soft tissues of the medial elbow.[25]

Lateral Epicondylitis

Lateral epicondylitis ("tennis elbow") is a painful elbow condition that occurs at the insertion of the common extensor tendon (extensor carpi radialis brevis) onto the lateral epicondyle of the humerus. Although it occurs in many tennis players, epidemiologic studies suggest that fewer than 5% of patients with such a syndrome actually play tennis. Activities such as driving in screws, use of a wrench, and repetitive work on an assembly line have also been implicated. Symptoms often begin as a dull ache on the outer (lateral) aspect of the elbow.[18,23,26] The discomfort can be exacerbated by activities that involve extension or supination of the wrist, such as grasping and twisting. Cozen's test is performed by having the patient keep the fist clenched while extending the wrist. The examiner grasps the forearm with the left hand while the right pulls his hand toward flexion against the patient's resistance. A positive finding is pain at the lateral epicondyle, reproducing the patient's symptoms.[27]

Active extension of the long finger against resistance with the elbow in extension can also reproduce the pain over the lateral epicondyle at the insertion of the extensor carpi radialis brevis. A similar sign, referred to as "the finger-snapping test," is characteristic for an enthesopathy of the extensor carpi radialis brevis. If the test is negative, it is assumed that the pain is caused by spondylogenic, arthrogenic, or neurogenic phenomena.[28]

Radiographs can be helpful in cases with atypical or prolonged symptoms and to rule out other pathologic conditions. Approximately 20% of patients demonstrate tendon calcification or a reactive exostosis at the tip of the epicondyle.[26]

The differential diagnosis of lateral epicondylitis would include posterior interosseus nerve entrapment (motor aspect of radial nerve in forearm). Other associated lesions include plica, synovitis, chondromalacia, and adolescent osteochondral defect.[26]

In up to 95% of patients, their condition improves with conservative therapy.[25] Initial efforts include making the patient more comfortable with the standard principles of protection, relative rest, cryotherapy, compression, elevation, medication (NSAIDs), and modalities of physical therapy. The term *relative rest* implies the avoidance of abuse and not the absence of activity. Activities that aggravate the pain should be eliminated, and an attempt to protect the tendon through such strategies as a reduction in playing time or intensity should be considered. Control of force loads by bracing, improved performance technique, and use of appropriate equipment should also be considered. Follow-up evaluation should be ensured.[26]

The pain of the less common medial epicondylitis ("pitcher's elbow," "golfer's elbow") can result from microtrauma at the site of the insertion of the flexor carpi radialis on the medial epicondyle. It is important to differentiate medial epicondylitis from other causes of medial elbow pain, including medial ulnar collateral ligament injury. As a result of repetitive valgus stress placed on the joint, microtraumatic injury and valgus instability at the ligament can occur. With disruption of the medial ulnar collateral ligament, abnormal stress is placed on the articular surfaces, which may lead to degenerative changes and the formation of osteophytes.[25,29] The pain of medial epicondylitis can be reproduced by having the patient's arm fully extended in supination. The physician then places the resisting hand on the palmar side of the fist and challenges the patient to prevent extension of the wrist (i.e., flexion against resistance).[30]

Wrist

De Quervain's Tenosynovitis

The wrist and hand comprise several tendons that pass through thick, fibrous retinacular tunnels. These help prevent subluxation of the tendons and act as a pulley system. Overuse syndromes are thought to result from changes of the synovial lining between these tendons and retinaculum. De Quervain's tenosynovitis involves the synovial lining of the abductor pollicis longus and extensor pollicis brevis. Although the term *tenosynovitis* indicates an inflammation of the tendon sheath, it has been noted that there are many potential forms of tenosynovitis. Classic acute inflammatory changes that are characteristic of tenosynovitis may be related to systemic manifestations of disease (e.g., rheumatoid arthritis, gout); tenosynovitis related to de Quervain's syndrome is referred to by some practitioners as *stenosing tenosynovitis*.[13] The pathology of de Quervain's tenosynovitis does not generally involve inflammation, as the primary pathologic change seen is thickening of the extensor retinaculum covering the first dorsal compartment of the wrist.[13] It has been suggested that de Quervain's disease is a result of intrinsic degenerative mechanisms rather than extrinsic inflammatory ones.[31]

The history may consist of chronic, repetitive trauma or unaccustomed repetitive efforts such as firm grasping and movement of the hand in a radial direction. Occasionally, direct trauma has been implicated.[13] The discomfort of de Quervain's tenosynovitis can be localized over the radial styloid process. Radiation of pain proximally to the forearm or distally down the thumb has been noted. The pain is generally constant but may be exacerbated by maneuvers that include grasping, abduction of the thumb, and ulnar deviation of the wrist. In many cases of De Quervain's tenosynovitis, the onset is gradual and not associated with a history of acute trauma.[13]

On physical examination, slight swelling may be seen over the radial styloid. Crepitation may be palpable over the tendons with flexion/extension of the thumb. An increase in the tensile load (passive stretching or active contraction) in the abductor pollicis longus or extensor pollicis brevis increases pain.[13] Finkelstein's test, which exacerbates the discomfort of de Quervain's tenosynovitis, is the most pathognomonic physical sign. The patient is instructed to hold the affected thumb in the palm by the fingers and then to ulnar-deviate the wrist. Pain will occur near the radial styloid, which is also the point of tenderness. Pain with this maneuver is considered to be a positive finding.[13] Routine laboratory study findings and radiographs are characteristically normal.[13]

The differential diagnosis includes scaphoid fracture and osteoarthritis of the carpometacarpal joint, which has pain caused by longitudinal traction and compression. Tuberculous tenosynovitis can manifest with a tenosynovitis of the extensor tendon of the thumb, and gonococcal tenosynovitis has been reported as an extensor tenosynovitis as well.[12,32]

Conservative treatment consists of rest, a thumb spica splint, anti-inflammatory medications, and prompt, appropriate referral. Some authors note that this treatment may not be sufficient and recommend that cortisone injection is necessary to abate the course of the disease. Surgical release of the A-1 pulley in the first dorsal compartment may also be indicated if conservative treatment fails.[8,33]

Knee

Patellar Tendinopathy

Patellar tendinopathy or "jumper's knee" often, as may be surmised by the name, occurs in sports that have jumping as a part of the activity. The patient may report tenderness at the inferior pole of the patella. This discomfort may abate with activity early in the tendinopathy and, as is not uncommon in the history of a tendinopathy, progresses to the point of discomfort during exercise and at rest. With the knee flexed at 30 degrees (quadriceps relaxed), tenderness may be localized to the deep surface of the proximal attachment of the patellar tendon at the inferior pole of the patella. However, healthy active athletes sometimes have tenderness on examination as well.[33-36]

The differential diagnosis includes patellofemoral syndrome, which is generally arises with a nonsporting activity or a recreational, low-impact sporting activity with vague, anterior knee pain that occurs at rest. There is minimal tenderness or tenderness of the patellar facets only.[35]

Imaging with ultrasonography and magnetic resonance imaging (MRI) may reflect collagen degeneration but is generally adjunctive to the distinctive history and physical examination findings. It is noted that some asymptomatic jumping athletes have similar appearances to those affected, and that prognosis and outcome are not predicted by such imaging.[35]

Conservative management includes load reduction and relative rest. Complete immobilization is contraindicated because the tensile load stimulates collagen production and directs its alignment. Treatment includes appropriate medication, cryotherapy, and referral for physical therapy modalities and biomechanical correction.[35]

Ankle

Achilles Tendinopathy

Achilles tendinopathy is a common overuse syndrome that typically affects male athletes. The Achilles tendon, named for the mythological Achilles, whose heel was not immersed in the River Styx as his mother dipped him in the river for its protective powers, arises from the medial and lateral heads of the gastrocnemius muscle and the deep layers of the soleus muscle and inserts on the calcaneal tuberosity. A major function is plantar flexion of the foot. It is the strongest and largest tendon in the body and can withstand tensile loads of up to eight times the body's weight during running.[37]

The Achilles tendon is vulnerable to injury from either trauma or overuse. A tendinopathy can also develop as a result of systemic disease (e.g., ankylosing spondylitis, Reiter's syndrome, gout, pseudogout). The use of fluoroquinolones has also been related to an Achilles tendinopathy.[11]

The occurrence of Achilles tendinopathy is highest among individuals who participate in middle- and long-distance running, orienteering, track and field, tennis, badminton, volleyball, and soccer.[38] Some studies have noted an almost 10% annual incidence of Achilles disorders in elite runners.[38] In some large studies, the most common clinical diagnosis of Achilles disorders is tendinopathy (55-66%) followed by insertional problems (retrocalcaneal bursitis and insertional tendinopathy) (20-25%).[38] Many cases of Achilles tendinopathy are thought to be multifactorial in origin. Body mechanics and environmental factors (e.g., uneven terrain), may apply valgus or varus stress to the tendon. Technique, equipment, and body mechanics can also contribute to the development of this tendinopathy. Anatomically, the vascular supply to the tendon creates a watershed area approximately 2 to 6 cm above the calcaneal insertion. This is thought to be responsible for clinical symptoms and the pathologic disruption commonly seen at this site.

The patient's history should provide the majority of the information to make the diagnosis of Achilles tendinopathy.[38] Pain, a cardinal symptom of Achilles tendinopathy, may lead the patient to seek medical help. Some practitioners have noted that the patient's symptoms reflect the degree of the tendon abnormality. As is common in many tendinopathies, in the early phase, pain after strenuous activities is reported, whereas in the later phase pain may be associated with activity and even occur at rest. At this point, the patient is often unable to perform sporting activities.[38]

On physical examination, inspection of the contour of the muscle-tendon unit and areas of swelling and erythema should be evaluated. Acutely in Achilles tendinopathy, the tendon may be diffusely swollen and exhibit tenderness on palpation, usually greatest in the middle third. Typically, in the patient who has acute symptoms of tendinopathy, the area of swelling and tenderness does not move with dorsiflexion of the ankle joint.[38] On palpation, local heat, crepitation, and palpable tendon nodules or defects should be noted. Examination for ankle instability and biomechanical faults may be considered as well.[38]

As noted, a tendinopathy may progress through a series of stages. Initially, the tendon sheath becomes inflamed. With repeated stress, scar tissue formation and degeneration of the tendon may occur, thereby reducing its strength. Clinically, the patient may note pain, decreased range of motion, and, if chronic, morning stiffness.[37] As with other cases of tendinopathy, treatment with relative rest, application of ice, and NSAIDS should be initiated. Depending on the cause of the tendinopathy, correction of limb malalignment with the use of orthotics or heel wedges may be indicated. Changes in the training environment and duration and intensity may also be modified to eliminate undue stress. Obviously, amelioration of conditions that predispose to the tendinopathy is warranted.

Achilles Tendon Rupture

An important consideration in the differential diagnosis of the patient who presents with Achilles tendon pain is that of rupture. Although some practitioners have indicated that rupture of the Achilles tendon occurs when preceded by tendon damage,[39] it is possible for untrained athletes to apply excessive force and rupture the tendon, even in the absence of prior changes of tendinopathy. Partial and complete rupture may occur, most commonly in 30- to 40-year-old men. Complete rupture is more common in the middle-aged recreational athlete. Historically, the patient may note a "popping" sensation followed by acute weakness and inability to continue the exercise or sport. The patient may report that it felt as though someone kicked him or her in the back of the ankle, or if playing a racket sport, may report that it felt as if he or she were struck on the calf with the ball.

On physical examination, a rent in the tendon can sometimes be palpated. If enough time has elapsed to allow hematoma formation, bogginess may be noted over the injured area of the tendon. It is important to note that the ability to plantar-flex the foot is not incompatible with a complete rupture of the Achilles tendon. There are multiple plantar flexors of the foot and toes. Muscles such as the tibialis posterior, flexor digitorum longus, flexor hallucis longus, peroneus brevis, and peroneus longus can remain functional and therefore disguise a complete rupture with the ability to plantar-flex the foot.[37,40] Simmonds' (Thompson's) test can be performed to evaluate for complete rupture. With the patient prone and feet hanging over the edge of the bed, the examiner squeezes the calf muscles at their widest point and looks for passive plantar flexion. The absence of plantar flexion is considered a positive finding, indicative of a complete tear of the Achilles tendon. The presence of plantar flexion does not, however, negate the possibility of a partial tear of the Achilles tendon.[40]

The therapeutic approach to Achilles tendon rupture is somewhat controversial and dependent on several variables. Appropriate consultation with an orthopedist is essential. A conservative approach, including immobilization in a leg (short versus long) cast in the equinus position may be indicated.[41] Some authors note that complete ruptures in active athletes should be treated surgically in most cases.[42] Although other risks and benefits must be taken into consideration, some studies indicate that early surgery may be indicated, as the risk for Achilles tendon re-rupture is less.[41,42]

Diagnostic Strategies

Plain Radiographs

In the emergency department, the diagnosis of tendinopathy is generally made on clinical grounds.

However, radiologic studies may be indicated to either affirm the diagnosis or eliminate other causes in the differential diagnosis. Plain radiographs may be helpful in excluding bony abnormalities (e.g., fracture, foreign body, tumor, osteomyelitis).

Ultrasonography has been noted by some practitioners to be the modality of choice for evaluating tendon pathologic conditions.[43] Ultrasonography can be especially useful when other conditions (e.g., gouty arthritis) obscure the findings of concomitant tendinopathy. Currently, the availability of this modality for tendinopathy is limited in the emergency department.[44] In cases of acute or chronic tendinopathy, one or more of the following features can be seen: loss of the fibrillar echotexture, focal tendon thickening, diffuse thickening, focal hypoechoic areas, extended hypoechogenicity, irregular and ill-defined borders, microruptures, and peritendinous inflammatory edema.[44] Hypoechoic areas surrounding tendons provide evidence for surrounding soft tissue inflammation. In addition to tendinopathy, tendon tears, both partial and complete, can be delineated by ultrasonography.[44]

Magnetic resonance imaging has been used to visualize pathologic conditions of the tendon. It is able to provide high intrinsic tissue contrast, which permits the distinction between normal tendons and abnormal tendons, as well as providing the high spatial resolution that permits detailed anatomic structures to be identified. The resolution of the tendon by MRI can aid in the diagnosis of Achilles tendon disorders, which include rupture (complete or partial), postoperative assessment of tendinous healing, tendinopathy, tenosynovitis, and various tumors of the Achilles tendon.[45]

Management

A key to the appropriate management of the patient with a tendinopathy is to provide for appropriate consultation and referral. Known inciting causes should be sought in the history and ameliorated. Many patients with tendinopathy can initially be managed conservatively, depending on the tendon affected, with protection, relative rest, cryotherapy, and NSAIDs, but timely and appropriate follow-up and arrangement for modalities available in the setting of physical therapy are indicated.

The involved part should be put at relative rest. If indicated the shoulder should not be immobilized for more than a few days because of the concern of the development of adhesive capsulitis. Patients with lateral epicondylitis often benefit from a forearm brace. De Quervain's tenosynovitis should be immobilized by splinting in a thumb spica. Corticosteroid therapy may be indicated. Achilles tendinopathy, depending on cause, can benefit from a heel lift or splint in slight plantar flexion. Appropriate consultation and referral should be ensured and are key in the therapy of these often lingering diseases.

Cryotherapy (cold treatments, 20 minutes at a time every several hours, for the first 24 to 48 hours) may be beneficial. NSAIDs are also sometimes indicated to provide some pain relief. Graduated range-of-motion exercises may be useful after the period of immobilization.

The use of corticosteroid injection in the emergency department is controversial. Steroids should not be injected into such major tendons as the Achilles tendon and patellar tendon, which may be at risk for spontaneous rupture if already weakened.

Disposition

Most patients with tendinopathy are safely discharged home with proper discharge instructions, relative rest of the tendon, analgesia, and appropriate follow-up. The exception is elderly or disabled patients for whom the tendinopathy renders them unable to perform the activities of daily living. Although appropriate rest and analgesia provide symptomatic relief, underlying causes should be sought and modified.

BURSITIS

Perspective

Bursae are closed, round, flat sacs lined by synovium.[46-48] They occur at areas of friction between skin and underlying ligaments and bone. The bursa permits the lubricated movement of soft tissues over areas of potential impingement (e.g., subacromial bursa) and friction (e.g., olecranon bursa, prepatellar bursa). Many bursae are nameless, and new bursae can form as a result of frequent irritation.[46,47] The two most common identifiably inflamed bursae likely to be seen in the emergency department are the olecranon and the prepatellar, and when these bursae are inflamed, they are generally recognizable over the extensor surface of the elbow or the knee, respectively.

Principles of Disease

Bursae become inflamed for many reasons. Many cases of bursitis are idiopathic in nature, but common identifiable causes of inflammation include infection (most often due to *Staphylococcus aureus*), trauma (which may predispose to infection), rheumatologic disorders (e.g., gout, pseudogout, ankylosing spondylitis, psoriatic arthritis), and other systemic diseases.

Clinical Features

Olecranon and Prepatellar Bursitis

Less than half of patients who present to the emergency department with olecranon or prepatellar bursitis have an infectious origin.[47,49,50] Distinguishing septic from nonseptic bursitis is not always straightforward, either on clinical grounds or as a result of diagnostic testing.[49] On a historical basis, septic bursitis generally is associated with a shorter period before presentation than nonseptic bursitis; however, other characteristics may not provide definitive clues in distinguishing between the infected and noninfected bursa.[51] Patients at risk for septic bursitis include those with impaired host defenses, including alcoholism, leukopenia, diabetes mellitus, chronic renal failure, and chronic steroid therapy.[47] It may also be seen more commonly in people in occupations in which repetitive knee (e.g., carpet layer) or elbow (e.g., miner) trauma is common.[47]

The olecranon bursa, on the extensor surface of the elbow, is the only bursa of the elbow joint and is easily traumatized, resulting in inflammation, pain, and swelling. Septic bursitis involves the olecranon much more commonly than the prepatellar bursa.[49] Infection can occur from local trauma (e.g., puncture wound, laceration), but may also be present in the absence of visible trauma. Hematogenous bacterial seeding has been described as rare, probably due to the limited vascular supply of the bursal tissue.[47] However, some series have noted up to an 8% incidence of an associated bacteremia.[46] Although it may occur very uncommonly, an association between trochanteric bursitis and bacterial endocarditis has been made, and subacromial bursitis has been reported to have been septic.[52]

On physical examination, localized swelling and fluctuance are usually present.[47] In the septic bursa, tenderness is present in more than 90% of patients, and evidence of a traumatic wound (e.g., abrasion, laceration) is evident in half.[47] A nontender bursal effusion is usually present in the nonseptic (e.g., traumatic, idiopathic) types of bursitis, although up to 45% of patients have mild tenderness, and one fourth have mild peribursal edema, warmth, and erythema.[47] Fever is more commonly seen in patients with septic than in those with nonseptic bursitis.[46] Most patients with septic bursitis present with swelling and peribursal cellulitis, and there may be peribursal soft tissue inflammation.[47] Crystal-induced bursitis may reflect an acute inflammatory process, and the concomitant existence of septic bursitis in a patient with gouty bursitis has been described.[47]

Passive range of motion should be painless, with the exception of full flexion, at which point there may be discomfort as the inflamed bursa is compressed. Evidence of diminished range of motion, generalized joint swelling, or other signs and symptoms of joint involvement (e.g., joint pain, warmth, and joint effusion) should raise concern in the differential diagnosis of septic arthritis. Although the olecranon and prepatellar bursae generally do not communicate with the joint space, one must consider this possibility in the differential diagnosis, especially if trauma is involved and the integrity of the underlying joint is disrupted.[47,51] Arthrocentesis (to rule out septic arthritis) may then be indicated.[47]

Differential Diagnosis

Conditions that mimic bursitis include underlying fracture and osteomyelitis. Radiographs and bone scans may be necessary to exclude these conditions. Other diagnoses in the differential diagnosis of the nontraumatic causes of nonseptic bursitis include rheumatoid arthritis, gout, pseudogout, scleroderma, ankylosing spondylitis, systemic lupus erythematosus,

hypertrophic pulmonary osteoarthropathy, Whipple's disease, oxalosis, and idiopathic hypereosinophilic syndrome.[46]

Diagnostic Strategies

One of the key decisions to be made in the evaluation and treatment of olecranon and prepatellar bursitis is to distinguish between septic and nonseptic bursitis. Aspiration of the bursa may be indicated in making the definitive diagnosis.[48,49,53] Some authors have described the treatment of the olecranon bursitis as "controversial" and note that "some experts support aspiration and evaluation of the effusion in all cases, even if the area is not red and is only minimally tender. Others feel that aspiration only increases the risk of infection and prefer to treat empirically with antibiotics and NSAIDs or antibiotics alone."[23] And yet other authors, as a result of a prospective study (without a nonaspirated control group) in the emergency department, have favored the "aspiration of all bursae for diagnosis and as a part of treatment."[49] This concept has been questioned by others who have commented that the general practice of "expectant treatment with antibiotics" without aspiration or surgical treatment should be compared with those wounds that are aspirated.[54] Still others suggest that "initial treatment of a septic bursitis includes aspiration of all fluid, appropriate culturing, and antibiotic therapy."[48]

Although a discussion of the technique of bursal aspiration is beyond the scope of this chapter, it should be performed observing sterile technique. A lateral approach utilizing an 18- to 20-gauge needle has been recommended.[47] Other authors have described a distal approach when aspirating the olecranon bursa.[49] Anecdotal reports of sinus drainage as a result of aspiration from the center of the bursa have been noted in emergency medicine lore. In a prospective study of almost 50 patients with bursitis who underwent aspiration, only 3 developed a draining sinus, all around the center of the bursa and not at the site of aspiration (performed at the distal aspect in olecranon bursitis, and from the lateral aspect in prepatellar bursitis).[49] In cases of septic bursitis, the aspirate may appear to be purulent, serosanguineous, or straw-colored.[47] In the case of nonseptic bursitis, the aspirate may vary from bloody aspirate to straw-colored.[47] Aspirate of an inflamed bursa should be sent for evaluation of white blood cell (WBC) count (with differential), microscopy for crystals (if crystalline disease is suspected), Gram stain, and appropriate cultures and sensitivities.[49,50] Some practitioners have suggested the use of a glucose level in the aspirate as an indicator of bacterial infection, but this has been shown to be neither very sensitive nor specific.[46]

Organisms found either on Gram stain or culture are diagnostic for septic bursitis.[46] If organisms are not seen on Gram stain, the WBC count may give an indication as to whether the cause is infectious. Most cases of an infected bursa manifest a highly inflammatory fluid. The noninfected bursa usually has a WBC count of less than 1500/µL (predominantly mononuclear cells) and uncommonly above 10,000/µL. The septic bursa has been reported to have WBC counts that range from fewer than 1000/µL to 300,000/µL (predominantly polymorphonuclear cells).[46] A bursal fluid WBC count greater than 5000/µL[3] suggests bursal fluid infection, even in the presence of a negative Gram stain.[23] *Staphylococcus aureus* is most the common organism in bursal infection.[47]

Management

Those patients who have olecranon or prepatellar bursal inflammation with suspicion (clinical or laboratory) of infection should be treated with appropriate antibiotics. Oral antibiotic therapy (some recommend 14 days) and treatment on an outpatient basis in the patient with uncomplicated bursitis and no underlying disease has been recommended as initial therapy.[47] Empiric therapy (including coverage for *S. aureus* and *Streptococcus* species) may be indicated until definitive culture results are available.[47] Most cases can be managed with outpatient antibiotics as long as close follow-up can be ensured. Those with a purulent aspirate may require repeat aspiration at 1- to 3-day intervals if the effusion persists.[47] It should be noted that in the treatment of bursitis caused by *S. aureus* there have been apparent therapeutic failures with erythromycin.[47] Close follow-up and repeat aspiration may be indicated. In any case, appropriate follow-up to assess response to therapy should be arranged. Warm soaks and wound care are also indicated. Surgical excision and drainage may also be necessitated.[50]

In the absence of infection, acute olecranon bursitis is treated with the administration of NSAIDs and application of a Jones type of compression dressing with an elastic bandage to prevent recurrent swelling. Systemic causes of bursitis (e.g., crystalline disease) should be treated appropriately. Avoiding local trauma is important to treat and successfully prevent bursitis.[47] Recurrent olecranon bursitis may be caused by an underlying bone spur that needs resection.[47] Steroids should not be instilled in a bursa if any suspicion of infection exists.[47,48] Steroid injection into a nonseptic bursa has been utilized as a treatment modality, but significant complications, such as skin atrophy over the bursa (20%), chronic pain with pressure applied to the elbow (30%), and the development of septic bursitis (10%) have been noted.[47] Other complications of intrabursal injection include bleeding, postinjection flare as a result of release of microcrystals, and tendon rupture.[23] In the emergency department, awaiting culture results and arranging for appropriate follow-up seems prudent. It should be noted that the bursal sac, with recent injection of a long-acting steroid, may reveal evidence of birefringent crystals under microscopy.[46]

Disposition

Patients without underlying medical problems who present with uncomplicated septic bursitis may be discharged on appropriate oral antibiotics.[47] Those with underlying diseases (e.g., immunocompromise, leukopenia, diabetes) and those with systemic toxicity or severe bursal infection (e.g., purulent drainage) should be considered for intravenous antibiotics and inpatient therapy. Patients with a purulent aspirate may need repeat aspiration. Close follow-up is necessary to ensure response to therapy. Those patients with presumed nonseptic bursitis should have close follow-up as well.[47]

Other Types of Bursitis

Subacromial Bursitis

The subacromial bursa lies between the tendon and the acromion. Subacromial bursitis is thought to be nearly synonymous with supraspinatus tendinopathy and may be involved in the stages of rotator cuff impingement. Pain and tenderness, localized to the lateral aspect of the shoulder, and signs of impingement may be noted on physical examination.[14]

Trochanteric Bursitis

The trochanteric bursa has both deep and superficial components. The deep bursa is between the greater trochanter and the tensor fascia lata; the superficial bursa is between the greater trochanter and the skin. Generally, middle-aged or older women report acute or chronic pain over the bursal area as well as the lateral thigh. Lying on the hip and walking may exacerbate the pain. Trochanteric bursitis can occur as a complication of rheumatoid arthritis. On examination, the pain of superficial bursitis may be reproduced by hip adduction and the pain of deep trochanteric bursitis reproduced with hip abduction. The hip joint itself should have normal examination findings.[55] There has been a report of a trochanteric bursitis associated with bacterial endocarditis.[52]

Ischiogluteal Bursitis

The ischiogluteal bursa is located adjacent to the ischial tuberosity and overlies the sciatic and posterior femoral cutaneous nerve. Inflammation, known as *weaver's bottom,* is described as pain over the center of the buttocks with radiation down the back of the leg. Sitting on a hard surface exacerbates the pain, and palpation over the ischial tuberosity causes discomfort.[56]

Iliopsoas Bursitis

The iliopsoas bursa is the largest bursa around the hip. It lies between the iliopsoas tendon and the lesser trochanter. The pain of iliopsoas bursitis radiates down the medial thigh to the knee and is increased on hip extension.[23]

Anserine Bursitis

The anserine bursa lies deep to the three tendons (sartorius, gracilis, and semitendinosus) that form the pes anserina ("foot of the goose"). It lies superficial to the medial collateral ligament.[50,57] Irritation over this area produces a fluctuant swelling on the medial aspect of the knee just below the medial femoral epicondyle.[57] At one time known as "cavalryman's disease," it now mainly occurs disproportionately in overweight women in association with osteoarthritis of the knee.[48] It can be characterized by a relatively abrupt onset of medial knee pain with localized discomfort.[48]

KEY CONCEPTS

Tendinopathy

- Mechanical overload and repetitive microtrauma are key underlying mechanisms in the development of tendinopathy. Patients most often present with a history of progressively worsening localized pain after work or sport-related activities that are repetitive in nature.

- Tendinopathy may also be associated with nonmechanical causes, including systemic manifestations of diseases and the use of fluoroquinolones.

- The diagnostic use of ultrasonography and MRI in the evaluation of tendinopathy has become widespread but is currently of limited use in the emergency department setting.

- Most patients with tendinopathy can initially be treated with conservative measures such as protection, relative rest, application of ice, medication, and elevation. Overuse syndromes can take at least 6 to 12 weeks to heal. Patients should be informed of this and have appropriate referral for follow-up.

- Operative treatment may be indicated for selected cases of tendon injury that require primary repair (e.g., rupture of the Achilles tendon) or that have failed conservative treatment (e.g., impingement syndrome) and are amenable to surgical amelioration.

Bursitis

- The possibility of an infectious cause should be considered in all cases of bursitis.

- The definitive diagnosis of bursitis in the emergency department is made by aspiration of the bursa and evaluation of the fluid.

- Septic bursitis is most commonly caused by *Staphylococcus aureus*.

- Nonseptic bursitis may include such origins as traumatic, idiopathic, and rheumatologic (e.g., gout, pseudogout).

- Other conditions, such as septic arthritis, osteomyelitis, or underlying fracture, should be considered in the differential diagnosis of bursitis.

- The emergency management of bursitis includes treatment with appropriate medication, rest, application of ice, compression, and elevation as well as prompt referral for appropriate follow-up. Hospitalization should be considered for severe local infections, for patients who are immunosuppressed, and in the presence of high fever or systemic toxicity.

REFERENCES

1. Benedek TG: History of the rheumatic diseases. In Klippel JH (ed): *Primer on the Rheumatic Diseases,* 11th ed. Atlanta, Arthritis Foundation, 1997, pp 1-5.
2. Maffuli N, Wong J, Almekinders LC: Types and etiologies of tendinopathy. *Clin Sports Med* 22:675, 2003.
3. James SL, Bates BT, Osternig LR: Injuries to runners. *Am J Sports Med* 6:40, 1978.
4. Gruchow HW, Pelletier D: An epidemiologic study of tennis elbow: Incidence, recurrence, and effectiveness of prevention strategies. *Am J Sports Med* 7:234, 1979.
5. Bernacki EJ, et al: An ergonomics program designed to reduce the incidence of upper extremity work related musculoskeletal disorders. *J Occup Environ Med* 41:1032, 1999.
6. Almekinders LC, Almekinders SV: Outcome in the treatment of chronic overuse sports injuries: A retrospective study. *J Orthop Sports Phys Ther* 19:157, 1994.
7. Khan K, Cook J: The painful nonruptured tendon: Clinical aspects. *Clin Sports Med* 22:711, 2003.
8. Fulcher SM, Kiefhaber TR, Stern PJ: Upper-extremity tendinitis and overuse syndromes in the athlete. *Clin Sports Med* 17:433, 1998.
9. Cook JL, et al: Reproducibility and clinical utility of tendon palpation to detect patellar tendinopathy in young basketball players. *Br J Sports Med* 35:65, 2001.
10. Archambault JM, Wiley JP, Bray RC: Exercise loading of tendons and the development of overuse injuries: A review of current literature. *Sports Med* 20:77, 1995.
11. Khaliq Y, Zhanel GG: Fluoroquinolone-associated tendinopathy: A critical review of the literature. *Clin Infect Dis* 36:1404, 2003.
12. Chen WS, Eng HL: Tuberculous tenosynovitis of the wrist mimicking de Quervain's disease. *J Rheum* 21:763, 1994.
13. Moore JS: De Quervain's tenosynovitis: Stenosing tenosynovitis of the first dorsal compartment. *J Occup Environ Med* 39:990, 1997.
14. Blake R, Hoffman J: Emergency department evaluation and treatment of the shoulder and humerus. *Emerg Med Clin North Am* 17:859, 1999.
15. Neer CS II: Anterior acromioplasty for the chronic impingement syndrome in the shoulder: A preliminary report. *J Bone Joint Surg Am* 54:41, 1972.
16. Neviaser TJ: The role of the biceps tendon in impingement syndrome. *Orthop Clin North Am* 18:383, 1987.
17. Barry NN, McGuire JL: Overuse syndromes in athletes. *Rheum Dis Clin North Am* 22:515, 1996.
18. Rizio L, Uribe JW: Overuse injuries of the upper extremity in baseball. *Clin Sports Med* 20:453, 2001.
19. Wolin PM, Tarbet JA: Rotator cuff injury: Addressing overhead overuse. *Phys Sportsmed* 25:54, 1997.
20. Wolf WB III: Shoulder tendinoses. *Clin Sports Med* 11:871, 1992.
21. Blevins FT, Hayes WM, Warren RF: Rotator cuff injury in contact athletes. *Am J Sports Med* 24:263, 1996.
22. Belzer JP, Durkin RC: Common disorders of the shoulder. *Primary Care* 23:365, 1996.
23. Richards CF, Koutouzis TK: Tendonitis and bursitis. In Marx JA (ed): *Rosen's Emergency Medicine: Concepts and Clinical Practice,* vol 2, 5th ed. St. Louis, Mosby, 2002, pp 1599-1607.
24. Hurt G, Baker CL Jr: Calcific tendinitis of the shoulder. *Orthop Clin North Am* 34:567, 2003.
25. Field LD, Savoie FH: Common elbow injuries in sport. *Sports Med* 26:193, 1998.
26. Nirschl RP, Ashman ES: Elbow tendinopathy: Tennis elbow. *Clin Sports Med* 22:813, 2003.
27. DeGowin EL, DeGowin RL: The spine and extremities. In *Bedside Diagnostic Examination.* New York, Macmillan, 1976, p 647.
28. Coenen W: A diagnostic sign in so-called epicondylitis humeri radialis. Zeitschr Orthop Grenzgebiete 124:323, 1986.
29. McCarroll JR: Overuse injuries of the upper extremity in golf. *Clin Sports Med* 20:469, 2001.
30. Sapira JD: The musculoskeletal system. In Orient JM (ed): *The Art and Science of Bedside Diagnosis.* Baltimore, Williams & Wilkins, 1990, pp 415-433.
31. Clarke MT, Lyall HA, Grant JW, Matthewson MH: The histopathology of de Quervain's disease. *J Hand Surg Br* 23:732, 1998.

32. Craig JG, van Holsbeeck M, Alva M: Gonococcal arthritis of the shoulder and septic extensor tenosynovitis of the wrist: Sonographic appearances. *J Ultrasound Med* 22:221, 2003.
33. Rettig AC: Wrist and hand overuse syndromes. *Clin Sports Med* 20:591, 2001.
34. Cook JL, et al: Reproducibility and clinical utility of tendon palpation to detect patellar tendinopathy in young basketball players. *Br J Sports Med* 35:65, 2001.
35. Cook JL, Khan KM, Maffulli N, Purdam C: Overuse tendinosis, not tendonitis. *Phys Sportsmed* 28:31, 2000.
36. Gecha SR, Torg E: Knee injuries in tennis. *Clin Sports Med* 7:435, 1988.
37. Barry N, McGuire J: Musculoskeletal medicine. *Rheum Dis Clin North Am* 22:515, 1996.
38. Paavola M, et al: Achilles tendinopathy. *J Bone Joint Surg Am* 84:2062, 2002.
39. Cetti R, Junge J, Vyberg M: Spontaneous rupture of the Achilles tendon is preceded by widespread and bilateral tendon damage and ipsilateral inflammation: A clinical and histopathologic study of 60 patients. *Acta Orthop Scand* 74:78, 2003.
40. Simmonds FA: The diagnosis of the ruptured achilles tendon. *The Practitioner* 179:56-58, 1957.
41. Bhandari M, et al: Treatment of acute Achilles tendon ruptures: A systematic overview and metaanalysis. *Clin Orthop* Jul(400):190, 2002.
42. Schepsis AA, Jones H, Haas AL: Achilles tendon disorders in athletes. *Am J Sports Med* 30:287, 2002.
43. Rasmussen OS: Sonography of tendons. *Scand J Med Sci Sports* 10:360, 2000.
44. Grassi W, et al: Sonographic imaging of tendons. *Arthritis Rheum* 43:969, 2000.
45. Panageas E, et al: Magnetic resonance imaging of pathologic conditions of the Achilles tendon. *Orthop Rev* 19:975, 1990.
46. Zimmerman B III, Mikolich DJ, Ho G Jr: Septic bursitis. *Semin Arthritis Rheum* 24:391, 1995.
47. McAfee JH, Smith DL: Olecranon and prepatellar bursitis: Diagnosis and treatment. *West J Med* 149:607, 1988.
48. Neustadt DH: Injection therapy of bursitis and tendinitis. In Roberts JR, Hedges JH (eds): *Clinical Procedures in Emergency Medicine,* 2nd ed. Philadelphia, WB Saunders, 1991, pp 835-847.
49. Stell IM: Management of acute bursitis: Outcome study of a structured approach. *J R Soc Med* 92:516, 1999.
50. Stell IM: Septic and non-septic olecranon bursitis in the accident and emergency department: An approach to management. *J Accident Emerg Med* 13:351, 1996.
51. Ho G Jr, Tice AD: Comparison of nonseptic and septic bursitis: Further observations on the treatment of septic bursitis. *Arch Intern Med* 139:1269, 1979.
52. García-Porrúa C, González-Gay MA, Ibañez D, García-País MJ: The clinical spectrum of severe septic bursitis in Northwestern Spain: A 10 year study. *J Rheumatol* 26:663, 1999.
53. Adams SL: Bursitis and tendinopathy. In Wolfson AB (ed): *Harwood-Nuss' Clinical Practice of Emergency Medicine,* 4th ed. Philadelphia, Lippincott Williams & Wilkins, 2005.
54. McMullan JJ: Management of acute bursitis [letter]. *J R Soc Med* 93:54, 2000.
55. Leonard MH: Trochanteric syndrome: Calcareous and non-calcareous tendonitis and bursitis about the trochanter major. *JAMA* 168:175, 1958.
56. Swartout R, Compere EL: Ischiogluteal bursitis: The pain in the arse. *JAMA* 227:551, 1974.
57. DeGowin EL, DeGowin RL: In *Bedside Diagnostic Examination.* New York, Macmillan Publishing, 1976, p 738.

CHAPTER

116 Systemic Lupus Erythematosus and the Vasculitides

Clare T. Sercombe

SYSTEMIC LUPUS ERYTHEMATOSUS

Perspective

Systemic lupus erythematosus (SLE) is a multisystem autoimmune disease with systemic complications, including renal failure and neurologic compromise. Symptoms and clinical courses vary widely, but patients with a known diagnosis of SLE are at risk for certain complications. Use of corticosteroids and immunosuppressive agents for therapy makes these patients challenging when they come to the emergency department.

Background

The disease was originally described by Biett in 1822. The term lupus erythematosus was used by Cazanave to describe the cutaneous manifestations in 1851. Osler first described many of the visceral manifestations in 1904.[1] The term *lupus,* which means "wolf" in Latin, was used to describe the skin lesion, differentiating it from lupus vulgaris. It was not until 1949 that the lupus erythematosus cell was identified, allowing Haserick to describe the autoimmune nature of the disease.[2,3]

Epidemiology

The prevalence is 17 to 48 per 100,000 people in North America and northern Europe.[4] The highest incidence, for women in their childbearing years, is 1 per 1000 in white women and 1 per 250 in black women.[5] Seven women present with the disease for every man, with an 11:1 ratio during the childbearing years.[6] Factors thought to increase the prevalence include familial cases and a lupus-like syndrome caused by certain medications, including hydralazine, isoniazid, and procainamide.

Principles of Disease

In part, the underlying mechanism is an autoimmune response with production of autoantibodies and a failure of the body to suppress them.[7] There is a polyclonal activation of B cells with exaggerated production of autoantibodies. The abnormal cellular and humoral response to the formation of these autoantibodies is modified by genetic, environmental, and hormonal factors. Genetic factors include familial association and relationship to certain human leukocyte antigen (HLA) genotypes. Environmental factors include exposure to sunlight. Autoantibodies are also found in laboratory workers who handle SLE sera. Exposure to certain drugs can also produce an SLE-like syndrome. Hormonal factors include an association with estrogens, which may explain the higher prevalence in women. There may also be a link to Klinefelter's syndrome.[7] The different manifestations in different patients may reflect the varied autoantibodies produced, the varied organs targeted, and the individual patients' responses to the autoantibodies. These autoantibodies may induce immune complex formation or interact directly at the site, binding to tissue, resulting in different disease manifestations. Pathologic findings are manifestations of the inflammation, inflammatory vasculitis, noninflammatory blood vessel damage, and immune complex deposition.

Clinical Features

The triad of fever, joint pain, and rash in a woman of childbearing age should suggest the diagnosis of SLE; however, the disease ranges from mild illness with cutaneous abnormalities to severe life-threatening complications such as renal failure and lupus cerebritis.

The American Rheumatism Association Revised Criteria for the Classification of Lupus were published in 1982.[8] These criteria consist of 11 conditions that are associated with SLE. Patients must have four criteria present, serially or simultaneously, to be given the diagnosis of SLE (Box 116-1).

Rheumatologic

Almost all patients with SLE have arthralgias and myalgias at some time during the course of their disease. As in rheumatoid arthritis, the inflammation of the hands, specifically the proximal interphalangeal and the metacarpophalangeal joints, is symmetrical. Although the initial presentation can mimic that of rheumatoid arthritis, joint deformities are less common. Thirty percent of patients develop hitchhiker's thumb, a hyperextension of the interphalangeal joint of the thumb. Tenosynovitis and tendon rupture may also occur, especially in patients taking corticosteroids. Avascular necrosis of the large joints, especially the femoral heads, can also be seen with ischemia caused by the vasculitis or as a complication of the large doses of corticosteroids used to treat SLE.

Dermatologic

The cutaneous manifestations include the characteristic malar or butterfly rash of acute cutaneous SLE. This facial eruption, seen in up to 40% of patients with SLE,[4] may be the first sign of SLE or may accompany flares of the disease. It can be exacerbated by exposure to ultraviolet light. Discoid lupus consists of an erythematous raised plaque with scales usually on the face, head, or neck. This can be associated with alopecia. Only 10% of patients with discoid lupus have SLE, whereas up to 25% of patients with SLE develop skin lesions consistent with discoid lupus.[9] Mucous membrane lesions can be seen with small, shallow ulcerations and are present in up to 19% of patients.[4] Vasculitic lesions such as ulcerations, purpura, and digital infarcts may occur.

Renal

Clinical nephritis, defined as persistent proteinuria, is seen in approximately 50% of patients, although mesangial and glomerular immunoglobulin deposition is seen in almost all patients with SLE. Most patients have no symptoms from their lupus nephritis until it progresses to nephrotic syndrome or frank renal failure.

Serum creatinine is an insensitive indicator of early renal disease because many nephrons must be involved before any elevation is seen. In patients with renal disease, the urinalysis shows hematuria, proteinuria, and red blood cell casts. Patients with active urine sediment may benefit from aggressive therapy with steroids or other immunosuppressive therapy. With aggressive treatment, survival has increased to 95% at 5 years and 75% to 80% at 10 years in Western Europe and the United States.[10] Indications for treatment include worsening renal failure, decreasing serum complement levels, increasing anti–double-stranded DNA (dsDNA) levels, and nephritic urinary sediment, especially when accompanied by increasing or nephrotic-range proteinuria. Renal biopsy can be useful in making treatment decisions. High-dose corticosteroids with immunosuppressive agents as therapy for renal disease are controversial. Patients who have end-stage SLE renal disease have survival rates similar to those of other patients receiving dialysis, approaching 85% at 5 years.[11] Although patients receiving dialysis experience an improvement of their nonrenal SLE manifestations, they run a high risk of dying from severe SLE or infection in their first year of dialysis. Renal transplantation has been successful in these patients, and recurrent nephritis in the allograft is rare.[12,13]

Neurologic

Nervous system manifestations are varied and include seizures, stroke, psychosis, migraines, and peripheral neuropathies.[14,15] These symptoms may appear early in the course of the disease but are rarely the initial sign of SLE. Central nervous system (CNS) involvement occurs in approximately 50% of patients with SLE.[16] Seizures are the most common manifestation in up to 70% of patients with CNS involvement.[15] Strokes are also common, especially in association with antiphospholipid syndrome (APS). Frank psychosis can be seen, either as a manifestation of SLE or as a result of corticosteroid use. Lupus cerebritis should be considered in any patient with SLE who exhibits a change in behavior or mental status. Presence of infection should also be considered, especially in patients receiving immunosuppressive agents. These patients are at risk for bacterial, fungal, and tuberculous infections in addition to abscesses. Other causes include uremia and hypertensive encephalopathy. Mononeuritis multiplex and peripheral neuropathy have also been described.

A computed tomography (CT) scan is useful in patients with gross focal neurologic deficit to assess for bleeding or edema associated with an embolic stroke. A magnetic resonance imaging (MRI) scan is much more sensitive for small infarcts, edema, or evidence of vasculitis. Full recovery from neuropsychiatric manifestations is approximately 70% to 85%; however, the mortality from such events is 10% to 15%.[16]

Cardiac

Pericarditis is the most common cardiac manifestation of SLE, reported in 30% of patients.[17,18] The diagnosis may be determined on the basis of electrocardiographic (ECG) findings alone, or patients may have signs and symptoms of fever, tachycardia, chest pain, and transient cardiac rubs. Pericarditis is associated with effusion in 20% of patients; however, this rarely progresses to tamponade.[17] Purulent pericarditis related to *Staphylococcus aureus* and tuberculosis has been reported in patients taking steroids. Purulent pericarditis, which is exudative with a high protein and white blood cell count,[18] may mimic the effusion seen with SLE, which causes a transudative, serous fluid. Pericarditis in SLE is generally benign and responds well to corticosteroids.

Myocarditis resembling cardiomyopathy is clinically diagnosed in fewer than 10% of patients with SLE but is found in 40% of patients at autopsy.[19] Some degree of left ventricular dysfunction may be found in a large number of patients with SLE.[20] It may be accompanied by congestive heart failure, ventricular dysrhythmia, tachycardia, or nonspecific ECG changes. Severe myocarditis should be treated with large doses of systemic corticosteroids, control of hypertension, and correction of volume overload.

A noninfectious endocarditis, as described by Libman and Sachs, produces vegetative growths on the valves that are usually clinically silent; however, these may be complicated by infection, valvular dysfunction, and, rarely, thromboembolism.[21] Libman-Sachs vegetations are seen in up to 10% of patients with SLE.[22] The mitral valve is most commonly involved, although all four valves may have vegetations. Valvular dysfunction may occur independent of vegetations secondary to valvulitis, mucoid degeneration, or aortic dissection. The aortic valve has the highest incidence of hemodynamically significant regurgitation, followed by the mitral valve.

Vasculitis of the coronary arteries or accelerated atherosclerosis related to corticosteroid use may cause coronary ischemia. Mortality from coronary artery disease (CAD) is seen in up to 30% of patients with SLE despite improved survival in renal and cerebral SLE.[23] Coronary vasculitis, although rare, is best treated with steroids, whereas the atherosclerosis is best treated with conventional methods including aspirin, nitrates, β-blockers, angioplasty, or bypass surgery. Treatment differences make the distinction between the two entities important. The diagnosis can be made by coronary angiography, with evidence of aneurysmal dilatation of the coronary arteries seen in patients with vasculitis.[17] Patients with SLE, hypertension, smoking, and hypercholesterolemia are at significantly increased risk for CAD[17,23] and should be treated aggressively for these problems as well as screened regularly for CAD.

Patients with SLE tend to have systemic hypertension secondary to lupus nephritis and steroid use, with all of the resultant complications of hypertension. The incidence has been reported as 25% to 50% of patients with SLE. Hypertension is noted in the patients who take high, long-term doses of corticosteroids.

Pulmonary

Pleural effusions and pleurisy are common. Pleural effusions, seen in 12% of SLE patients, are usually exudative in nature. Pleural fluid glucose levels are usually similar to serum glucose levels, in contrast to those of rheumatoid arthritis, in which the pleural fluid glucose level is very low. Other manifestations include pulmonary infarcts and hemorrhage. Lupus pneumonitis causes diffuse interstitial infiltrates, although patients have usually had the disease for several years before they suffer from pneumonitis. Bacterial, fungal, and opportunistic infections must be considered, especially in patients taking immunosuppressive agents, before a diagnosis of lupus pneumonitis is given. Patients with SLE are particularly at risk for pneumococcal disease, in part because of autosplenectomy or splenic dysfunction. Patients with SLE may also develop chronic interstitial infiltrates leading to pulmonary fibrosis. These patients need inpatient treatment, and their conditions may progress to chronic hypoxia, pulmonary hypertension, and right-sided heart failure.[24]

Gastrointestinal

Gastrointestinal complaints in SLE are common, ranging from oral ulcerations to the much more serious intestinal vasculitis. Oral ulcerations usually accompany disease flares. Esophageal dysmotility is occasionally seen, but it is much less common than in patients with scleroderma. Patients with intestinal pseudoobstruction may have crampy abdominal pain and a clinical and radiographic picture consistent with obstruction. They should be observed for resolution. Pancreatitis can result from either an SLE flare or corticosteroid therapy. Spontaneous bacterial peritonitis is also described. Elevated liver function tests are common, usually the result of the medications given to treat SLE, such as azathioprine. However, infection with cytomegalovirus while taking immunosuppressive agents may also occur. Portal hypertension caused by scarring and fibrosis is seen in 4% of patients.[24] The most serious complication is intestinal vasculitis, a syndrome of abdominal pain, bloody diarrhea, and evidence of vasculitis elsewhere. This vasculitis may progress to perforation or gangrene, resulting in peritonitis.

Hematologic

Hematologic and vasculitic problems are complex. Anemia, affecting up to 40% of patients, may result from hemolysis or chronic disease. Thrombocytopenia occurs in 25% of patients. Treatment for severe thrombocytopenia is controversial, with some authors advocating use of vinca alkaloids and intravenous γ-globulin.[25] Splenectomy is controversial, with some believing splenectomy exacerbates the disease. Thrombotic thrombocytopenic purpura and immune idiopathic thrombocytopenic purpura have also been reported in patients with SLE.[14]

Diagnostic Strategies

The diagnosis of SLE is often confirmed with antinuclear antibodies (ANAs). Positive ANAs occur in more than 95% of patients with SLE.[4] The degree of positivity of the test is important, with higher titers having a positive predictive value. ANAs may also be positive in elderly patients taking certain medications such as hydralazine and procainamide as well as with subacute bacterial endocarditis, infectious hepatitis, and other immune diseases such as primary biliary cirrhosis. Five percent to 7% of healthy people may also have a positive ANA.[26] Antibodies to dsDNA and anti-Smith (anti-Sm) antibodies are most specific for SLE.[27] Patients with disease flares may show an increase in their ANA or dsDNA titers. Decreases in complement levels for C3 and C4 also correlate with disease flares in certain patients. The erythrocyte sedimentation rate (ESR) is a very poor index of disease activity. Patients who have an ESR of 50 to 100 mm/hr often show minimal disease activity. C-reactive protein levels often remain low except in the presence of concurrent infection. Patients with SLE may have a false-positive Venereal Disease Research Laboratory (VDRL) or Rapid Plasma Reagin (RPR) result.

A normochromic, normocytic anemia is common in SLE. Leukopenia is common with disease flares as well. Thrombocytopenia occurs in up to 25% of patients. Urinalysis and serum creatinine may be useful tests in patients showing evidence of disease flare, to demonstrate worsening nephritis. Active urine sediment with excretion of red blood cell casts and increasing proteinuria is worrisome.

Management

The treatment of SLE is controversial because the manifestations and severity vary widely among patients. General recommendations include avoidance of stress and fatigue, which can exacerbate symptoms. Approximately one third of patients are photosensitive and should avoid sunlight and use sunscreen. Oral contraceptives may also exacerbate symptoms, and only low-estrogen oral contraceptives should be used.

Acetaminophen may be useful for mild to moderate pain control. Drug therapy starts with anti-inflammatory agents. Aspirin and nonsteroidal anti-inflammatory drugs (NSAIDs) have been used to treat the minor inflammatory complaints such as arthralgias, pleurisy, and pericarditis. The maximum recommended doses of these agents are usually needed. These agents should be avoided in patients with severe gastrointestinal complications or thrombocytopenia. Patients with lupus nephritis should also avoid NSAIDs because the inhibitory effect on prostaglandins may reduce renal function, confusing the clinical picture of worsening renal failure. Some NSAIDs, including ibuprofen, have also been associated with aseptic meningitis, with headache, fever, and meningismus.[28] Cerebrospinal fluid studies in these patients show lymphocytosis, elevated protein levels, and sterile culture.

Corticosteroids are usually the next agent of choice. Topical application controls most cutaneous manifestations. Oral corticosteroids are prescribed in dosages that control disease activity. Minor disease activity (e.g., arthralgias, fatigue, and pleurisy) is usually controlled with 0.5 mg/kg or less in a single daily dose. With minor symptoms, however, anti-inflammatory and antimalarial drugs have been advocated to avoid the long-term complications of corticosteroids. Major disease activity (e.g., hemolytic anemia and severe thrombocytopenia) is usually controlled with prednisone 1.0 mg/kg/day. With lupus cerebritis and acute worsening of lupus nephritis, methylprednisolone 1.0 g intravenously (IV) once daily may be given for several days. Treatment of glomerulonephritis with long-term steroids has not been proved to alter the outcome or course in patients with SLE, and their long-term use remains controversial.[14,29] When tapering, corticosteroids may be changed to an alternate-day dosing regimen; however, some patients may experience disease flares at these dosages and come to the emergency department.

Antimalarial drugs are also effective for the cutaneous and musculoskeletal manifestations of SLE. Hydroxychloroquine and chloroquine are given on an outpatient basis in a loading dose for 4 weeks, followed by maintenance dosing when these symptoms are under control. Withdrawal of the drug may result in disease flare. The antimalarial agents can result in two major ophthalmologic side effects. Corneal deposits, easily seen on slit-lamp examination in patients who complain of floaters in the visual field, are reversible with drug withdrawal or decreased dosage. The second complication, an irreversible retinopathy, is unrelated to the corneal deposits. All patients with SLE who take antimalarial medications should be observed biannually by an ophthalmologist to detect evidence of retinopathy that may lead to blindness. If evidence of retinopathy appears, patients should stop taking the antimalarial medication under a rheumatologist's supervision.

Immunosuppressive agents (e.g., azathioprine, methotrexate, and cyclophosphamide) are reserved for patients with severe renal or cerebral disease in whom other therapies have failed or for patients who have not tolerated corticosteroids.[29] Studies examining the use of immunosuppressants have shown decreased chronic renal scarring and reduced likelihood of end-stage renal disease without an increase in mortality.[30] The toxicities of such drugs are numerous and include infections, myelosuppression, and future risk of neoplasms.[29]

Newer treatments include autologous marrow stem cell transplantation, intravenous immunoglobulins, and mycophenolate mofetil, an inhibitor of purine synthesis.[10,31] All of the trials involving patients are small, of short duration, or anecdotal. A controlled clinical trial with significant power is needed to prove the efficacy of these therapies in patients with SLE.[31]

Special Considerations

Drug-Induced Lupus
Drug-induced lupus was first described in 1954 by Dustan and colleagues and Perry and Schroeder.[32,33]

Table 116-1. Drugs Implicated in Lupus-like Syndromes

System	Drug	Risk
Cardiovascular	Procainamide	High
	Quinidine	
	Practolol*	High
Antihypertensive	Hydralazine	High
	Methyldopa	
	Reserpine	
Antimicrobial	Isoniazid	Moderate
	Penicillin	
	Sulfonamides	
	Streptomycin	
	Tetracycline	
	Nitrofurantoin	
Anticonvulsant	Phenytoin	Moderate
	Mephenytoin	Moderate
	Ethosuximide	Moderate
	Primidone	
Antithyroid	Propylthiouracil	Low
	Methylthiouracil	Low
Psychotropic	Chlorpromazine	Low
	Lithium carbonate	
Miscellaneous	D-Penicillamine	High
	Methysergide	Low
	Phenylbutazone	
	Allopurinol	
	Gold salts	
	Aminoglutethimide	

*Removed from market because of lupus-like syndrome.

Procainamide was first implicated in 1962 by Ladd.[34] Since then, a large number of agents have been implicated, with hydralazine and procainamide being the most common (Table 116-1). The clinical manifestations vary, with most patients experiencing arthralgias and occasional pleuropericardial manifestations. The full manifestations are present in less than 1% of patients taking high-risk drugs, although a positive ANA titer can be found in more than 50% of patients taking high-risk drugs.[35] The patients are usually women, middle-aged or older, and rarely blacks, but these findings may be representative of the group of patients taking these drugs. The condition is usually reversible when the agents are stopped, with resolution within days or weeks; however, manifestations lasting for years have been reported. In patients with significant pleuropericardial disease, a short course of tapered steroids has been used successfully when the implicated medication has been discontinued.

Antiphospholipid Antibody Syndrome
The lupus anticoagulant and anticardiolipin antibody are antiphospholipid antibodies that bind to the prothrombin activator complex. This binding results in a prolongation of the partial thromboplastin time (PTT) but is clinically associated with clotting. This disorder can be seen in patients with SLE, but it also occurs in the healthy population, in patients with human immunodeficiency virus (HIV), in some malignancies, and with drug-induced lupus. Patients without evidence of SLE have a much lower incidence of complications. A prolonged PTT that is not corrected when

Arterial occlusion
   Extremity gangrene
   Stroke
   Myocardial infarct
   Other visceral infarct
   Aortic occlusion
Venous occlusion
   Peripheral venous occlusion
   Visceral venous occlusion
      Budd-Chiari syndrome
      Portal vein occlusion
Recurrent fetal loss
Thrombocytopenia
Coombs' positive hemolytic anemia
Livedo reticularis
Neurologic abnormalities
   Chorea
   Multiple sclerosis–like syndrome
   Transient ischemic attacks
Valvular heart disease
Sudden multisystem arterial occlusion

Modified from Sammaritano LR, et al: Commonly agreed clinical manifestations of antiphospholipid antibody syndrome, *Semin Arthritis Rheum* 20:81, 1990.

the patient's sample is mixed 50:50 with normal serum suggests the presence of an inhibitor; the lupus anticoagulant and anticardiolipin antibody can then be found with further testing.

The spectrum of the clinical manifestations of antiphospholipid antibody syndrome (APS) is wide. Some patients may have repeated episodes of arterial or venous clotting, including recurrent strokes and pulmonary emboli. Elevated serum creatinine values may be a result of renal vein thrombosis, seen on CT with contrast, mimicking worsening nephritis. Multiple spontaneous abortions have been reported (Box 116-2).

This syndrome may also be associated with thrombocytopenia, with clinically significant bleeding, and with neuropsychiatric disorders believed to be secondary to cerebral ischemia and infarcts.[36] Patients who have evidence of APS may still undergo surgery, with routine precautions for deep venous thrombosis. Despite the prolonged PTT, there is minimal risk for prolonged bleeding unless thrombocytopenia is also present. Any patient with APS and a documented thrombosis is anticoagulated with an International Normalized Ratio (INR) target of 2.5 to 3.0.

Pregnancy

Recurrent spontaneous abortions have been seen in patients with APS. Subcutaneous heparin with low-dose aspirin throughout pregnancy is currently the treatment of choice to prevent further fetal wastage. As the pregnancy progresses, there is a risk of worsening manifestations of SLE and nephritis. These patients are also at risk for pregnancy-induced hypertension. In patients who do not respond to subcutaneous heparin with continued fetal wastage, monthly doses of intravenous γ-globulin may be effective, although this increases the risk of preeclampsia and preterm delivery.[10] Patients with evidence of thrombosis and APS should receive anticoagulation and be admitted for further workup Corticosteroids in combination with aspirin have shown some benefit in maintaining the pregnancy. Although they cross the placenta and show little evidence of fetal harm, corticosteroids are a second-line agent because of complications of long-term, high-dose therapy. Other medications, including NSAIDs, antimalarials, and immunosuppressive agents, should be stopped. These patients should be referred to a high-risk obstetrician early in the pregnancy.

Neonatal lupus syndrome is usually diagnosed by dermatologic manifestations of lupus and is associated with transient anemia and thrombocytopenia. Neonates can also experience congenital complete heart block that may require permanent pacing.[14] The congenital heart block has been associated with transmission of a maternal antibody to anti-SSA (Ro).

Complications of Therapy

The complications of SLE itself are many and varied because of the systemic nature of the illness. Treatment of the disease causes further complications. Treatment with NSAIDs can worsen lupus nephritis, either by causing interstitial nephritis or by inhibiting prostaglandins.

Corticosteroids are associated with well-known, long-term complications including steroid-induced diabetes, osteoporosis and resultant fractures, weight gain, pancreatitis, osteonecrosis, accelerated atherosclerosis, and, most important, immunosuppression. Patients receiving steroid therapy should be monitored for evidence of infection and should be evaluated for any episode of fever. Patients taking corticosteroids should also be given stress-dose steroids with hydrocortisone 100 mg IV every 8 hours for any systemic infection, surgery, delivery, or obvious stressor.

Patients using antimalarial agents are at risk for dose-related corneal deposits, which can be managed by outpatient drug discontinuation and rheumatology follow-up. The retinopathy associated with antimalarial agents is irreversible and may progress to blindness. Prompt attention by an ophthalmologist is important.

Patients taking immunosuppressive agents are also at risk for infection, especially with gram-negative organisms, encapsulated gram-positive organisms, herpes zoster, and opportunistic organisms. Febrile patients who are receiving azathioprine, methotrexate, or cyclophosphamide should be admitted whether a source is evident or not because gram-negative or streptococcal sepsis occurs in this population. Patients with localized herpes zoster should be admitted for intravenous acyclovir administration to prevent viral dissemination.

Disposition

Because of the systemic and varied nature of the disease, there are no hard and fast rules about admission for complications of SLE. Patients without a previous diagnosis of lupus may be admitted for workup and treatment of possible connective tissue disease if they have symptoms that warrant immediate diagnosis (e.g., pericarditis, myocarditis, pleural effusion or infiltrates, evidence of vasculitis, or renal insufficiency). In the patient who has monoarticular or polyarticular arthritis, the joint can be aspirated in the emergency department if fluid is present. Further workup can be done on an outpatient basis by the primary care physician or a rheumatologist. NSAIDs may alleviate the symptoms.

Patients with known SLE may come to the emergency department for a flare of their disease, for new systemic complaints, or for fevers. Patients with known disease can usually tell the emergency physician whether the problem is consistent with a previous flare versus a new complaint. Patients with worsening disease who take large doses of steroids or immunosuppressive agents should be admitted for consideration of other diagnoses or more aggressive therapy. Patients with known disease and increasing arthritic pain, or mild flare without fever, may be effectively treated with an increase in their NSAID or corticosteroid dosages and prompt follow-up with their rheumatologists.

Patients with evidence of lupus nephritis and worsening renal failure should be admitted for aggressive therapy with steroids or immunosuppressive agents. The serum creatinine level may be elevated, but it is a poor indicator of disease. Proteinuria may be present, or red blood cell casts may be seen on urinalysis. Treatment for lupus nephritis should be done in conjunction with a rheumatologist or nephrologist. Consideration of renal vein thrombosis is necessary in patients with evidence of APS or nephrotic syndrome.

Mental status changes in the patient with SLE should be approached as in any workup for mental status changes because lupus cerebritis is a diagnosis of exclusion. Laboratory examination for electrolyte imbalances, evidence of hypoxia or hypoglycemia, and a toxicology screen should be performed. A CT scan to assess for hemorrhage, especially in the hypertensive, thrombocytopenic, or anticoagulated patient, should be performed. Lumbar puncture to evaluate for infection should be performed if the patient is febrile or immunocompromised. MRI may reveal abnormalities with increased signal intensity in the area of involvement. Cerebral ischemia may cause acute mental status changes as a result of a lupus vasculitis or thrombosis associated with APS. Consultation with a rheumatologist is prudent before giving high-dose steroids for lupus cerebritis. Patients with seizures should be treated in the routine manner and workup of new-onset seizures done with the help of a neurologist.

Patients with cardiac or pulmonary complaints should be admitted for observation or therapy. Those who take corticosteroids are at high risk for CAD.

Patients with chest pain should be aggressively evaluated for myocardial infarction. If pericarditis is suspected, evaluation of pericardial effusion may be necessary, although tamponade is rare. Patients with myocarditis should be observed for evidence of congestive heart failure and dysrhythmias. Patients taking immunosuppressive agents should be given antibiotic prophylaxis for invasive dental and genitourinary procedures.

Pulmonary complaints are quite difficult to evaluate in the outpatient setting. Patients with fever and infiltrates may have community-acquired pneumonia, especially pneumococcal disease, but opportunistic infection, atypical tuberculosis, and lupus pneumonitis need to be considered. Sputum culture and pulmonary consultation may be appropriate, especially in the hypoxic patient. Hypoxic patients should also be evaluated for pulmonary embolism and for a history of antiphospholipid antibody with thrombosis. Patients with pleural effusions should be admitted to have diagnostic thoracentesis and treatment. Pleural effusions may be complicated by infection, tuberculosis, or malignancy.

Patients with abdominal pain present a diagnostic challenge because most of them are young women of childbearing age. Workup should include a pelvic examination and pregnancy test. Laboratory examination may not be helpful without baseline values because many patients are chronically anemic and the white blood cell count may be elevated in those taking corticosteroids. Evidence of an increased anion gap or metabolic acidosis may be indicative of lactic acidosis. Abdominal films may be helpful to show bowel wall thickening or free air. Consultation with a surgeon, overnight observation for serial examinations, or a CT scan may be necessary to diagnose vasculitic problems, abscess in immunocompromised patients, or routine causes of abdominal pain. Even if the patient has a common cause of abdominal pain (e.g., pelvic inflammatory disease, pancreatitis, peptic ulcer disease, or biliary colic), admission may be necessary for administration of stress-dose steroids and workup of fever.

SLE predisposes patients to anemia and thrombocytopenia. Patients should be admitted if there is evidence of active hemolysis with decreased hematocrit or if hemolysis is evident on the blood smear. Patients with thrombocytopenia should be admitted if there is evidence of bleeding or if platelet counts are severely decreased ($<50,000/mm^3$). If the patient is actively bleeding, platelet transfusion is appropriate; however, rapid destruction of the platelets may occur. Simultaneous administration of intravenous corticosteroids and intravenous γ-globulin aids in increasing the platelet count and decreasing the amount of platelet destruction.

Patients with evidence of arterial or venous thrombosis should be admitted for anticoagulation and possible embolectomy. Anticoagulation can be achieved acutely with heparin, although large doses are occasionally needed to overcome the antibody effect. The PTT, if not elevated, can be followed to assess for evidence of adequate anticoagulation, with careful observation for bleeding in patients who are also thrombocytopenic. Otherwise, patients with prolonged PTT and evidence of the lupus anticoagulant can be monitored with thrombin times if necessary. Patients with an INR of less than 2.5 should still be considered to have a possible thrombus if they have a history of APS.

Pregnant patients with SLE should have early follow-up with a high-risk obstetrician. Emergency delivery for the pregnant patient with SLE should include stress-dose steroid administration and close observation of the neonate for congenital complete heart block. Emergent cardiac pacing may be necessary.

Patients experiencing overwhelming sepsis or shock should be given stress-dose steroids in the emergency department with hydrocortisone 100 mg IV. Broad-spectrum antibiotics may also be given empirically after appropriate cultures are obtained. Adrenal insufficiency from abrupt discontinuation of steroids is another possible cause of shock. If the patient is unstable, admission to the intensive care unit is warranted.

KEY CONCEPTS

- Patients with SLE can have multiple and varied symptom complexes. The diagnosis should be considered in patients with fever, rash, or unexplained systemic complaints.

- Patients with deep venous thrombosis without risk factors should be considered for APS. Patients with evidence of thrombosis should receive anticoagulation and be admitted for further workup.

- Febrile patients with SLE receiving immunosuppressive therapy should be hospitalized and treated aggressively because they have a high risk for gram-negative or streptococcal sepsis.

- Patients with worsening renal function or with involvement of the heart, lungs, or CNS should be hospitalized for aggressive treatment to prevent progression of the disease and symptoms.

- Patients with symptoms of coronary ischemia should be aggressively treated. Even young patients with risk factors for CAD should be evaluated for coronary ischemia.

THE VASCULITIDES

Perspective

The vasculitic syndromes are a spectrum of multisystem diseases characterized by inflammation and destruction of the blood vessels. The pathophysiology is not well described, and systemic manifestations vary depending on the location, the size of the vessel involved, and whether the vasculitis is a primary or secondary disease state.

Background

The first classical description of a vasculitic syndrome was in 1866 by Kussmaul and Maier. This syndrome is

BOX 116-3. Classification of Vasculitis

Large Vessel Disease
Arteritis
Temporal (giant cell) arteritis
Takayasu's arteritis
Arteritis associated with Reiter's syndrome, ankylosing spondylitis

Medium and Small Vessel Disease
Polyarteritis Nodosa
Primary (idiopathic)
Associated with viruses
　Hepatitis B or C
　Cytomegalovirus
　Herpes zoster
　HIV
Associated with malignancy
　Hairy cell leukemia
Other
　Familial Mediterranean fever

Granulomatous Vasculitis
Wegener's granulomatosis
Lymphomatoid granulomatosis

Behçet's Disease

Kawasaki Disease (Mucocutaneous Lymph Node Syndrome)

Predominantly Small Vessel Disease
Hypersensitivity Vasculitis (Leukocytoclastic Vasculitis)
Henoch-Schönlein purpura
Mixed cryoglobulinemia
Serum sickness
Vasculitis associated with connective tissue diseases
　SLE
　Sjögren's syndrome
Vasculitis associated with specific syndromes
　Primary biliary cirrhosis
　Lyme disease
　Chronic active hepatitis
　Drug-induced vasculitis

Churg-Strauss Syndrome

Goodpasture's Syndrome

Erythema Nodosum

Panniculitis

Buerger's Disease (Thrombophlebitis Obliterans)

HIV, human immunodeficiency virus; SLE, systemic lupus erythematosus.

now known as polyarteritis nodosa.[37] Since then, a number of well-described disease states have been attributed to vasculitic syndromes. In 1952, Zeek presented the first classification system.[38] This system has been revised several times with great difficulty because of the broad spectrum of disease and large overlap between syndromes (Box 116-3).

Principles of Disease

Vasculitic syndromes are thought to arise because immune complexes are deposited in vessel walls and the complement system is activated. The complement system then stimulates accumulation of polymorphonuclear cells at the site and release of lysosomal enzymes, resulting in vessel wall damage and necrosis. The clinical manifestations of this process depend on the size of the immune complexes, the mechanics of blood flow through the vessel, the vessel permeability, and the site of deposition.

The relationship between immune complexes and the subsequent development of vasculitis is best studied in the infectious causes of vasculitis. Hepatitis B surface antigen has been demonstrated to be an inciting antigen.[39] Other infectious agents known to be associated with vasculitis include cytomegalovirus, herpes zoster, parvovirus, hepatitis A, hepatitis C, and HIV.[39-42] Malignancies such as hairy cell leukemia, some lymphomas, and the myeloproliferative disorders are also associated. Immune complexes are rarely found in some other vasculitic syndromes, such as polyarteritis nodosa and Wegener's granulomatosis, because of rapid clearing of the complexes.

It is important to differentiate thrombosis and vasculitis because treatments are dramatically different. APS can mimic vasculitis, especially when present in patients without SLE. Yet in SLE, both vasculitis and thrombosis from APS may be present.

Large Vessel Vasculitides

Temporal Arteritis

Temporal or giant cell arteritis is characterized by granulomatous inflammation with multinucleated giant cells. The distribution is most common in branches of the carotid artery but may involve any large or medium artery. The disease is most commonly seen in women in the sixth and seventh decades of life.

The classical symptoms of temporal arteritis are consistent with ischemia to the organs fed by branches of the internal and external carotid artery: visual loss in one eye, temporal artery tenderness, and jaw claudication. Some patients experience central retinal occlusion or transient diplopia. Patients may complain of nonspecific, vague symptoms such as malaise, weight loss, and fever. Headache may be the initial complaint. There is also an association with polymyalgia rheumatica, with patients complaining of early morning shoulder girdle stiffness.

Although the diagnosis is made clinically, helpful laboratory findings include elevated ESR (usually greater than 100 mm/hr on a Westergren blot), elevated C-reactive proteins, and anemia. The definitive diagnosis is made by temporal artery biopsy.

Most patients are extremely sensitive to glucocorticoids, and treatment should be started for any patient with a high clinical suspicion of temporal arteritis. The steroids do not significantly change the results of the biopsy and may prevent progression to visual loss. Prednisone should be started at a dosage of 1 mg/kg/day until biopsy can be performed. Patients with severe disease or impending visual loss should be hospitalized and given high-dose steroids until the diagnosis is obtained. Most patients tolerate slow tapering of the steroid dosage, although relapse rates are lower in those who use them longer (1 to 2 years).[43]

Takayasu's Arteritis

Takayasu's arteritis (pulseless disease) is a chronic, recurrent, inflammatory vascular disease that affects the aorta, proximal portions of its major branches, and the pulmonary arteries.[44] It is characterized by lymphocytic infiltration and fibrosis of the vessels, resulting in marked thickening of the intima and adventitia and leading to eventual obstruction of the arteries and ischemic complications. Women are predominantly affected, usually in the second and third decades of life. A high incidence is seen in Japanese women.

In the prepulseless or early phase, the diagnosis is difficult. Fatigue, weight loss, and low-grade fever predominate. Hypertension is frequently seen secondary to aortic or renal artery involvement. With progression of the disease, ischemic symptoms appear with diminished pulses, claudication, retinopathy, and visual loss. Strokes, syncope, subclavian steal syndrome, abdominal pain, and coronary ischemia are also reported.

Early diagnosis is difficult because symptoms are nonspecific. Later, acute phase reactants are elevated and bruits may be auscultated. Definitive diagnosis is made with arteriography and demonstrates stenotic lesions, poststenotic dilation, aneurysms, and increased collateral circulation.

Treatment with prednisone 1 mg/kg/day induces remission in up to 50% of patients.[45] Other cytotoxic agents such as methotrexate, cyclophosphamide, or azathioprine may be added to achieve remission if relapses occur. Infections may complicate therapy. Hypertension may be treated with calcium channel blockers and angiotensin-converting enzyme inhibitors. Antiplatelet agents may be of benefit. Bypass grafting and endarterectomy are useful in patients with significant disease.

Medium Vessel Vasculitides

Polyarteritis Nodosa and Microscopic Polyangiitis

Polyarteritis nodosa (PAN) is characterized by acute inflammation and fibrinoid necrosis of small and medium vessels.[46] The etiology is unknown. Viral hepatitis B or C is associated with a vasculitis identical to PAN but is treated differently.[46] PAN is also linked with drug reactions, serum sickness, and HIV. PAN is more common in men than women. A distinction has been made between PAN and microscopic polyangiitis (MPA). PAN includes vasculitis associated with nervous system and gastrointestinal tract involvement, whereas MPA is associated with nerve, glomerular, and lung tissue. Classical PAN is also perinuclear antineutrophil cytoplasmic antibody (p-ANCA) negative; MPA is p-ANCA positive, although it is not specific for the disease. Both are excluded if chronic hepatitis B or C is found.

The early clinical picture consists of constitutional symptoms of fever, malaise, arthralgias, and myalgias. PAN then progresses to peripheral neuropathy and bowel ischemia, complicated by hypertension related to renal artery inflammation. MPA is characterized by glomerulonephritis, alveolar hemorrhage, and often rapidly progressing glomerulonephritis.

The diagnosis is made by the clinical pattern and histopathology seen on biopsy. After endocarditis and concomitant infections are ruled out as a cause of the vasculitis, biopsy of the involved segment may reveal the diagnosis. Abdominal angiography may be useful to demonstrate small berry aneurysms, but these may not be present early in the course of the illness.

Treatment for both PAN and MPA is corticosteroids, especially in cases without organ involvement. Patients with severe disease may need additional therapy with immunosuppressive agents such as cyclophosphamide.[46] Patients with MPA have a higher rate of relapse. Active viral hepatitis, if present, should be treated with antiviral therapy.

Granulomatous Vasculitis

Wegener's granulomatosis is a necrotizing granulomatous vasculitis involving the respiratory tract, kidneys, and to variable degrees the medium to small vessels in other organs. The disease is extremely rare, with a slightly increased incidence in men compared with women. The mean age of onset is 45 years.

Patients first complain of upper respiratory tract symptoms with sinusitis, otitis, and nasal ulceration. Destruction of the sinus walls may also occur. Lower respiratory tract symptoms include cough, dyspnea, hemoptysis, and asymptomatic pulmonary infiltrates, occasionally with cavitation. Tracheal stenosis occurs in 13% of patients.[47] Renal involvement is a later finding with glomerulonephritis, which may be aggressive, in 85% of patients.[39,48] Eye involvement includes conjunctivitis and scleritis caused by granulomatous deposition in the sclera. Skin lesions include ulcers, nodules, and granuloma formation. Nervous system involvement, usually a late feature of the disease, is seen in one third of patients and includes cerebral vasculitis, granulomatous deposition in cranial nerves, and peripheral nerve vasculitis resulting in neuropathies.[49] Coronary vasculitis, pericarditis, and conduction defects are rare.[22]

Laboratory examination includes findings of a markedly elevated ESR, normochromic normocytic anemia, and occasionally thrombocytopenia. Urinalysis may show hematuria, active sediment excretion, proteinuria, and red blood cell casts. Antibodies against cytoplasmic components of polymorphonuclear cells (c-ANCA) have been found to be sensitive and specific for a diagnosis of Wegener's granulomatosis.[48] ANAs are usually absent. The chest x-ray study shows multiple sharply demarcated nodular densities, predominantly in the lower lung fields, with pleural effusions in 25% of patients.[47] Lymphadenopathy is rarely seen on radiography.

Diagnosis of Wegener's granulomatosis is confirmed by an open lung biopsy.

Treatment with corticosteroids alone does little to alter the prognosis, and most patients die from renal disease within a year of diagnosis. The use of cyclophosphamide and corticosteroids in combination induced remissions in up to 90% of patients.[47] Complications of this therapy include increased risk of infection, especially disseminated herpes zoster and *Pneumocystis carinii* pneumonia.

Patients with known Wegener's granulomatosis with flares of renal disease should be admitted for intravenous corticosteroid administration. Patients suspected to have Wegener's granulomatosis should be admitted for diagnosis and possible therapy. Renal transplantation has been successful in patients who progress to end-stage renal disease.

Lymphomatoid granulomatosis, often confused with Wegener's granulomatosis, is characterized by destructive infiltration of lymphocytoid and plasmacytoid cells. The lower respiratory tract disease is the most prevalent, and upper respiratory tract involvement is rarely seen. Involvement of the kidney with deposition of granulomata is rare; but, in contrast to findings in Wegener's granulomatosis, no vasculitis or glomerulonephritis is present. The spleen, lymph nodes, and bone marrow are usually spared. Malignant lymphoma develops in 50% of patients.[39] There are no specific laboratory findings, although, in contrast to that in Wegener's granulomatosis, the ESR is usually normal or only mildly elevated and the c-ANCA is negative. The chest x-ray study shows multiple nodules similar to those seen in metastatic cancer.

Diagnosis is made by biopsy, usually of lung tissue. Treatment is the same as for Wegener's granulomatosis. Remissions with corticosteroids and cyclophosphamide are seen in 50% of patients, except in those who are also diagnosed with malignant lymphoma, in whom mortality is 90%.[39]

Behçet's Disease

Behçet's disease is a chronic relapsing vasculitis characterized by oral ulceration, genital ulceration, and uveitis. The prevalence of Behçet's disease is 1 in 1000 in Japan to 1 in 150,000 in the United States and Europe.[50] It affects men more often than women, mainly young adults. In Japan, it has been linked to histocompatibility antigen HLA-B5.

Recognizing recurrent, painful aphthous ulcers that involve the oral mucosa and genitals makes the clinical diagnosis. Eye involvement includes iritis, uveitis, and optic neuritis, all of which can lead to blindness. The hallmark of Behçet's disease, a hypopyon uveitis, is seen rarely. CNS vasculitis, resulting in meningoencephalitis, intracranial hypertension, or a multiple sclerosis–like syndrome, can also occur. Gastrointestinal ulceration has been reported in Japanese patients, including ileocecal perforation. Skin lesions, including erythema nodosum and cutaneous vasculitis, may occur. Cardiac involvement is rare.[22] Nondeforming arthritis involving the knees and ankles has been described. Laboratory examination is nonspecific.

The diagnosis of Behçet's disease is made when a consistent clinical syndrome is associated with a nonnecrotizing perivascular infiltrate of lymphocytes and monocytes on biopsy of affected tissue. The disease is well controlled with glucocorticoids at 1 mg/kg/day. Gastrointestinal disease can be controlled with sulfasalazine 2 to 6 g/day. Patients with eye involvement should be referred to an ophthalmologist. Serious manifestations of uveitis and CNS involvement warrant use of azathioprine or cyclophosphamide, and patients should be admitted to the hospital. Deep venous thrombosis associated with Behçet's disease rarely results in pulmonary emboli but should be treated with systemic anticoagulation.

Small Vessel Vasculitides

Hypersensitivity Vasculitis

Hypersensitivity vasculitis describes a group of clinical syndromes characterized by small vessel vasculitis with a known or presumed inflammatory precipitating antigen, including drugs and infectious organisms, with immune complex deposition. Leukocytoclastic vasculitis describes the pathologic findings in the vessels, primarily the postcapillary venules, with infiltration by polymorphonuclear leukocytes with or without destruction of vessel walls.[39] In later stages, red blood cell extravasation and dermal necrosis are seen. The diseases can be seen at any age and have no gender predominance. Common drugs that cause this vasculitis include the penicillins, sulfa drugs, nonsteroidal anti-inflammatory agents, and streptokinase.

The syndromes in this category have similar clinical findings. The skin is the most commonly involved organ, with appearance of skin lesions abruptly after exposure to an infectious precipitating antigen or within 1 to 2 days of taking a drug. The lesions are described as flat, erythematous purpuric papules or palpable purpura, usually on dependent portions such as lower extremities. The lesions may coalesce, forming patches, and may progress to bullae if the destruction is severe. Lower extremity edema is often associated. Burning or pain is often associated with the skin lesions. Other organs may be involved to varying degrees. Systemic symptoms of fever, malaise, and weight loss are common. Laboratory examination is nonspecific, with a mildly elevated ESR and mild leukocytosis.

Several characteristic hypersensitivity vasculitic syndromes have been described.

Henoch-Schönlein Purpura

Henoch-Schönlein purpura (HSP) affects mainly the arterioles and capillaries, with peak incidence between 4 and 11 years of age, although adults may also be affected. The syndrome occurs most often in the spring after a viral upper respiratory infection.[39] Other inciting agents associated with HSP include insect stings and drugs.

The rash is accompanied by arthralgias of the lower extremities, most commonly the ankles, with swollen tender joints. Frank arthritis is usually absent. Gastrointestinal complaints, seen in 70% of patients, include abdominal pain, nausea, vomiting, and diarrhea, associated with blood and mucus per rectum.[48] Renal involvement occurs in 50% of patients with hematuria and red blood cell casts; however, it rarely progresses to renal failure.[51] Nervous system involvement is rare, especially in children.[49] The syndrome is relapsing and remitting over several weeks.

The immune complex deposition is immunoglobulin A, with antigens to drugs, infectious agents, foods, insect bites, and immunizations implicated in the pathogenesis. Most patients do well with supportive care and explanation of the relapsing and remitting nature of the disease. Treatment of the precipitating infection or discontinuation of the drug is necessary, if it is known. Children with more severe arthralgias and abdominal pain benefit from prednisone at 1 mg/kg/day orally. Adults who have symptoms may be given prednisone 60 mg/day. Prolonged renal impairment occurs in 25% of patients[39]; however, the benefits of steroids in the renal prognosis are controversial.

Mixed Cryoglobulinemia

Cryoglobulins are immunoglobulins and immune complexes that precipitate in the cold (4° C) and dissolve on rewarming. The syndrome of mixed cryoglobulinemia involves purpura, arthralgias, lymphadenopathy, and demonstration of the presence of cryoglobulins. Middle-aged women are most commonly affected. Some precipitating antigens, such as hepatitis A, B, and C, cytomegalovirus, or Epstein-Barr virus, have been demonstrated, although most precipitants are unknown.[53]

Clinically, patients have polyarthralgias, purpura, and Raynaud's phenomenon. Hepatomegaly, splenomegaly, and lymphadenopathy are common. Recurrent palpable purpura occurs in virtually all patients.[47] The most serious involvement is renal deposition of the cryoglobulins, resulting in glomerulonephritis. Patients may have fulminant or slowly progressive chronic renal disease. Laboratory examination demonstrates an elevated ESR, decreased serum complement levels, and the presence of cryoglobulins.

Diagnosis is made clinically in the presence of cryoglobulins; however, it may be difficult to distinguish from SLE or HSP. Treatment depends on the extent of involvement. Patients with disease limited to the skin may try low-dose steroids, and patients with systemic manifestations are usually started on prednisone 60 mg/day orally. Cyclophosphamide has been helpful in controlling systemic disease and allows decreases in steroid dosages. Interferon may be useful in treating hepatitis C–related cryoglobulinemia. Patients with underlying diseases such as multiple myeloma and lymphoproliferative disorders should have their underlying disorders treated.

Serum Sickness

Serum sickness and serum sickness–like reaction usually occur after ingestion of a known antigen, such as penicillin or sulfa medications. A cutaneous vasculitis is common in the disorder. Usually, symptoms start 12 to 36 hours after ingestion if there is a previously immunizing exposure, but they may occur up to 10 days after antigen exposure. The manifestations seen in serum sickness are due to immune complex deposition but not to systemic vasculitis as described in this chapter.

Churg-Strauss Syndrome

Churg-Strauss syndrome (allergic granulomatosis and angiitis), first described in 1951 by Churg and Strauss, is characterized by granulomatous vasculitis of multiple organs, with hypereosinophilia in patients with asthma and allergic rhinitis. The vasculitis usually involves the veins and venules of the lower respiratory tract. The exact incidence is unknown, and there is an overlap of pulmonary vasculitides. The mean age is 44 years, with men affected more often than women.

Patients have systemic symptoms of fever, weight loss, and malaise. Pulmonary symptoms are predominant, with a history of asthma for at least 2 years before diagnosis.[52] Skin lesions occur in 60% to 70% of patients, with subcutaneous nodules or palpable purpura present. Pericarditis can lead to constrictive pericarditis. Myocarditis can be seen, manifesting as congestive heart failure.[22] Gastrointestinal symptoms caused by infiltration of the small bowel or stomach walls are associated with infarction, perforation, or bloody diarrhea. Renal disease is much less prominent. The neurologic manifestation is mainly mononeuritis multiplex, found in up to 80% of patients.[49]

Laboratory examination reveals a persistent eosinophilia greater than 1000/mm^3, often up to an absolute count of 5000 to 20,000/mm^3.[39] Patients may have antineutrophil cytoplasmic antibodies directed against myeloperoxidase (p-ANCA), also seen in PAN. The chest x-ray study can show patchy, fleeting infiltrates known as Löffler's syndrome, consolidation, or cavitation.

The diagnosis of Churg-Strauss syndrome is made by biopsy, usually of skin or lung tissue. The patient may also have an elevated immunoglobulin E. Churg-Strauss syndrome is extremely responsive to corticosteroids, with usual dosing of prednisone at 60 mg/day orally. The prognosis is much improved with treatment, with 5-year survival greater than 50% in contrast to 25% in untreated patients.[39] Cytotoxic agents have no proven benefit.[39]

Goodpasture's Syndrome

Goodpasture's syndrome is characterized by glomerulonephritis and pulmonary hemorrhage associated with antibody to glomerular basement membrane. The etiology is unknown, and the disease may occur at any age but primarily affects young men.

Clinically, the patients have cough, dyspnea, and hemoptysis. Initially, the pulmonary hemorrhage may be mild, or it may be severe and life threatening. Hypoxia is common. Fever, arthralgias, and malaise are also present. The renal manifestations are varied; some patients have normal renal function, others a rapidly progressing glomerulonephritis. Patients may also have

skin involvement with palpable purpura. Laboratory examination is notable for elevated ESR and urinalysis with red blood cell casts. On blood testing, antiglomerular basement membrane (anti-GBM) antibodies can be measured, but the level of circulating antibodies does not correlate with the severity of the disease. Complement levels are normal and, in contrast to findings in Wegener's granulomatosis, c-ANCA tests are negative. A chest radiograph shows hilar pulmonary infiltrates.

The differential diagnosis includes SLE and Wegener's granulomatosis. Diagnosis is made by renal biopsy. Lung tissue shows pulmonary alveolar hemorrhage, with similar linear deposition of antibodies along the alveolar basement membrane.

Management of the airway is the first priority in patients with severe pulmonary hemorrhage. Treatment with methylprednisolone 10 to 15 mg/kg IV is necessary if rapidly progressive glomerulonephritis or severe pulmonary hemorrhage complicates the patient's course. The use of cytotoxic agents such as cyclophosphamide, as well as plasmapheresis (2 to 4 L/day of plasma), has been associated with improvement in pulmonary hemorrhage and glomerular lesions if extensive renal damage has not yet occurred.

The prognosis is varied. Some patients have minimal renal involvement and may have occasional flares of pulmonary hemorrhage. These patients should be admitted to the hospital to be observed for airway complications and for development of renal disease. Most patients have renal involvement, with development of rapidly progressive glomerulonephritis within weeks and an extremely poor prognosis if untreated. These patients should be admitted for high-dose steroids and renal biopsy, if indicated, to guide management with cytotoxic agents and plasmapheresis. Patients who progress to end-stage renal disease are candidates for transplantation if anti-GBM antibodies return to undetectable levels; otherwise, the disease may recur in the transplanted kidney.

Erythema Nodosum

Erythema nodosum is a vasculitis of the venules in the subcutaneous layers of the skin. The cause is unclear, but it is usually the result of a hypersensitivity vasculitis from infections, drugs, or a systemic disease. The disease is seen most commonly in spring and fall. Women are more commonly affected than men, with a peak incidence in the third decade of life.[54] The lesions most often appear on the shin. The subcutaneous nodules are initially red but then have a blue hue as they resolve. Patients may have just the nodules or may have systemic symptoms, including fever and malaise. Arthralgias are seen in 90% of patients at some time during the disease course.[54] Hilar lymphadenopathy may be present.

Patients who have erythema nodosum should be considered for underlying diseases such as viral upper respiratory tract infection, streptococcal infection, sarcoidosis, tuberculosis, and drug exposure. Much rarer causes include inflammatory bowel diseases, histoplasmosis, *Yersinia*, *Salmonella*, *Chlamydia*, coccidioidomycosis, psittacosis, and autoimmune diseases such as SLE. Drugs implicated include penicillins, sulfa drugs, aspartame, phenytoin (Dilantin), and oral contraceptives. The eruption can last up to 6 weeks. NSAIDs may be useful in controlling the arthralgias. Disposition depends on suspicion of underlying disease but is usually outpatient follow-up.

Panniculitis

Subcutaneous nodules manifest vasculitis of the subcutaneous fat layer surrounding the venules. Biopsy of the involved subcutaneous tissue shows fat cell necrosis, infiltration of inflammatory cells with macrophages, and vasculitis. Several forms of panniculitis exist. Diseases associated with panniculitis are erythema nodosum, erythema induratum, lupus profundus, pancreatitis, α_1-antitrypsin deficiency, light-chain paraproteinemia, and C_1 inhibitor deficiency.

Erythema nodosum can exist as a manifestation of systemic disease or as a hypersensitivity to drugs (as discussed previously). Erythema induratum (Bazin's disease) is a vasculitis of the skin of the calf associated with tuberculosis and is typically seen in girls and young women. The bilateral lesions begin as nodules but then ulcerate and scar. The disease is chronic and recurrent. Mycobacteria are rarely found in the lesions. Therapy is supportive with dressing changes and elevation, unless evidence of active tuberculosis is found elsewhere.[54]

Lupus profundus is inflammation of the subcutaneous fat seen in SLE. It occurs in approximately 2% of patients with SLE.[55] Patients have subcutaneous nodules in the scalp, face, breasts, thighs, and buttocks. The lesions ulcerate and then heal. Of patients with lupus profundus, 50% eventually develop systemic manifestations of SLE.[55] The differential includes erythema nodosum, but in lupus profundus the lesions are usually more chronic and nontender.

Patients with pancreatitis or pancreatic cancer may have disseminated fat necrosis with lesions identical to those of nodular panniculitis. The fat necrosis is commonly found in periarticular sites. Patients also have fever and arthritis. Sinus tracts may be present with drainage. This form of panniculitis is thought to be due to the release of pancreatic enzymes into the vessels with necrosis at distal sites. Eosinophilia is commonly seen. Prognosis is poor, and the only treatment is to treat the underlying disorder.

KEY CONCEPTS

- The diagnosis of systemic vasculitis is difficult and should be considered in patients with rash and pulmonary or renal complaints.
- Consultation with a rheumatologist is helpful for determining management when patients have flares of a known vasculitis.
- Febrile patients receiving immunosuppressive therapy or corticosteroids have a high risk for sepsis or disseminated viral infections and should be treated aggressively.

REFERENCES

1. Osler W: On the visceral manifestations of the erythema group of skin diseases. *Am J Med Sci* 127:1, 1904.
2. Hargraves MM, et al: Presentation of two bone marrow elements: The "tart" cell and the "LE" cell. *Proc Staff Meet Mayo Clin* 24:234, 1949.
3. Haserick JR: Blood factor in acute disseminated lupus erythematosus. *Arch Dermatol* 61:889, 1950.
4. Patel P, Werth V: Cutaneous lupus erythematosus: A review. *Dermatol Clin* 20:373, 2002.
5. Fessel WJ: Systemic lupus erythematosus in the community: Incidence, prevalence, outcome and first symptoms; the high prevalence in black women. *Arch Intern Med* 134:1027, 1974.
6. Manzi S: Epidemiology of systemic lupus erythematosus. *AM J Manag Care* 16:S474, 2001.
7. Pisetsky DS: Systemic lupus erythematosus: Epidemiology, pathology and pathogenesis. In Klippel JH (ed): *Primer on the Rheumatic Diseases*, 11th ed. Atlanta, Arthritis Foundation, 1997, pp 246-250.
8. Tan EM, et al: The 1982 revised criteria for the classification of systemic lupus erythematosus (SLE). *Arthritis Rheum* 25:1271, 1982.
9. Gilliam JM: Systemic lupus erythematosus in the skin. In Lahita RG (ed): *Systemic Lupus Erythematosus*. New York, Wiley, 1992.
10. Ruiz-Irastorza G, et al: Systemic lupus erythematosus. *Lancet* 357:1027, 2001.
11. Correia P, et al: Why do lupus patients with nephritis die? *Br Med J (Clin Res Ed)* 290:126, 1985.
12. Nossent HC, et al: Systemic lupus erythematosus after renal transplantation: Patient and graft survival and disease activity. *Ann Intern Med* 114:183, 1991.
13. Cheigh JS, et al: A multicenter study of outcome in systemic lupus erythematosus in patients with end-stage renal disease: Long-term follow-up on the prognosis of patients and the evolution of lupus activity. *Am J Kidney Dis* 16:189, 1990.
14. Robinson DR: Systemic lupus erythematosus. In Dale DC, Federman DD (eds): New York, Scientific American, 1996.
15. Futrell N: Connective tissue disease and sarcoidosis of the central nervous system. *Curr Opin Neurol* 7:201, 1994.
16. van Dam AP: Diagnosis and pathogenesis of CNS lupus. *Rheumatol Int* 11:1, 1991.
17. Doherty NE, Siegal RJ: Cardiovascular manifestations of systemic lupus erythematosus. *Am Heart J* 110:1257, 1985.
18. Remetz MS, Matthay RA: Cardiovascular manifestations of connective tissue disease. *J Thorac Imaging* 7:49, 1992.
19. Hallegua DS, Wallace DJ: How accelerated atherosclerosis in SLE has changed our management of the disorder. *Lupus* 9:228, 2000.
20. Ansari A, et al: Cardiovascular manifestations of systemic lupus erythematosus: Current perspective. *Prog Cardiol Dis* 27:421, 1985.
21. Leung WH, et al: Cardiac abnormalities in systemic lupus erythematosus: A prospective M-mode, cross-sectional and Doppler echocardiographic study. *Int J Cardiol* 27:367, 1990.
22. Libman E, Sacks B: A hitherto undescribed form of valvular and mural endocarditis. *Arch Intern Med* 33:701, 1924.
23. Remetz MS, Matthay RA: Cardiovascular manifestations of connective tissue disorders. *J Thorac Imaging* 7:49, 1992.
24. Ansari A, et al: Vascular manifestations of systemic lupus erythematosus. *Angiology* 37:423, 1986.
25. Gladman DD, Urowitz MB: Systemic lupus erythematosus: Clinical and laboratory features. In Klippel JH (ed): *Primer on the Rheumatic Diseases*, 11th ed. Atlanta, Arthritis Foundation, 1997, pp 251-257.

26. Dall'Era M, Davis JC: Systemic lupus erythematosus. *Post-grad Med* 114:31, 2003.
27. Mills JA: Systemic lupus erythematosus. *N Engl J Med* 330:1871, 1994.
28. Wibener HL, Littman BH: Ibuprofen-induced meningitis in systemic lupus erythematosus. *JAMA* 239:1062, 1978.
29. Balow JE: Lupus nephritis: Natural history, prognosis, and treatment. *Clin Immunol Allergy* 6:353, 1986.
30. Klippel JH: Systemic lupus erythematosus: Treatment. In Klippel JH (ed): *Primer on the Rheumatic Diseases*, 11th ed. Atlanta, Arthritis Foundation, 1997, pp 258-261.
31. Fayez FH, et al: Treatment of lupus nephritis. *Drugs* 63:257, 2003.
32. Dustan HP, et al: Rheumatic and febrile syndrome during prolonged hydralazine therapy. *JAMA* 154:23, 1954.
33. Perry HM, Schroeder HA: Syndrome simulating collagen disease caused by hydralazine (Apresoline). *JAMA* 154:670, 1954.
34. Ladd AT: Procainamide-induced lupus erythematosus. *N Engl J Med* 267:1357, 1962.
35. Harmon CE, Portanova JP: Drug-induced lupus: Clinical and serological studies. *Clin Rheum Dis* 8:121, 1982.
36. Love PE, Santoro SA: Antiphospholipid antibodies: Anti-cardiolipin and the lupus anticoagulant in systemic lupus erythematosus (SLE) and in non-SLE disorders. *Ann Intern Med* 112:682, 1990.
37. Kussmaul A, Maier K: Uber eine bischer nicht beschreibene eigenthumliche Arterienerkrankung (periarteritis nodosa), die mit Morbus Brightii und rapid fortschreitender allge-meiner Muskellahmung einhergeht. *Dtsch Arch Klin Med* 1:484, 1866.
38. Zeek PM: Periarteritis nodosa: Critical review. *Am J Clin Pathol* 22:777, 1952.
39. Valente RM, et al: Vasculitis and related disorders. In Kelly WN, et al (eds): *Textbook of Rheumatology*, 5th ed. Philadelphia, WB Saunders, 1997.
40. Calabrese LH, et al: Systemic vasculitis in association with human immunodeficiency virus infection. *Arthritis Rheum* 32:569, 1989.
41. Lehman TJA: Connective tissue disease and nonarticular rheumatism. In Klippel JH (ed): *Primer on the Rheumatic Diseases*, 11th ed. Atlanta, Arthritis Foundation, 1997, pp 398-403.
42. Calabrese LH: Vasculitis and infection with the human immunodeficiency virus. *Rheum Dis Clin North Am* 17:131, 1991.
43. Fauci AS, et al: The spectrum of vasculitis: Clinical, patho-logic, immunologic, and therapeutic considerations. *Ann Intern Med* 89:660, 1978.
44. Kerr GS, et al: Takayasu's arteritis. *Ann Intern Med* 120:919, 1994.
45. Harris ED: Systemic vasculitis. In Dale DC, Federman DD (eds): New York, Scientific American, 1995.
46. Mandell BF: Systemic vasculitic syndromes. In Dale DC, Federman DD (eds): New York, Scientific American, 2000.
47. Hoffman GS, et al: Wegener granulomatosis: An analysis of 158 patients. *Ann Intern Med* 116:488, 1992.
48. Tervaert JWC, Kallenberg C: Neurologic manifestations of systemic vasculitides. *Rheum Dis Clin North Am* 19:913, 1993.
49. Mandell BF: Systemic vasculitis. In Dale DC, Federman DD (eds): New York, Scientific American, 1997.
50. O'Duffy JD: Behçet's disease. In Klippel JH (ed): *Primer on the Rheumatic Diseases*, 11th ed. Atlanta, Arthritis Foun-dation, 1997, pp 307-309.
51. Koskimies O, et al: Renal involvement in Schönlein-Henoch purpura. *Acta Paediatr* 63:357, 1974.
52. Boulware DW, et al: Pulmonary manifestations of rheumatic disease. *Clin Rev Allergy* 3:249, 1985.
53. Myers AR: Cryoglobulinemia. In Schumacher HR Jr (ed): *Primer on the Rheumatic Diseases*, 9th ed. Atlanta, Arthri-tis Foundation, 1988.
54. Hurwitz S: *Clinical Pediatric Dermatology*, 2nd ed. Philadelphia, WB Saunders, 1993.
55. Foster DW: The lipodystrophies and other rare disorders of adipose tissue. In Isselbacher KJ, Braunwald E (eds): *Harrison's Principle of Internal Medicine*, 13th ed. New York, McGraw-Hill, 1994.

CHAPTER

117 Allergy, Hypersensitivity, and Anaphylaxis

T. Paul Tran and Robert L. Muelleman

PERSPECTIVE

Over millions of years, the human immune system has evolved an immense repertoire of cells and proteins that work in concert for the purpose of preserving the self (autologous) and protecting the body from harmful nonself (foreign). The immune system is divided into two subsystems according to the type of response. The *innate* immune system is encoded in the germline and provides nonspecific pathogen recognition and elimi-nation. The *adaptive* immune system, on the other hand, provides specific pathogen recognition and sub-sequent pathogen elimination by genetic rearrangement during the life of the individual, continually changing in response to continual antigenic stimulation. Despite the enormous complexity, the immune system gener-ally effects defense functions with impeccable fidelity, producing desired immunity. It can, however, some-times overreact, causing allergy and allergic diseases.

Cases of allergy and anaphylaxis have been docu-mented since the days of antiquity. Pharaoh Menes reportedly died in 2641 BC of anaphylaxis. In 1902, Portier and Richet[1] discovered that although a dog tol-erated an injection of an extract of the tentacles of a jel-lyfish the first time, it died within minutes when injected again several weeks later. They coined the term *anaphylaxis* from Greek (*ana*, against; *phylax*, guard or protect), meaning "against protection." For this and subsequent work in anaphylaxis, Richet was awarded the Nobel Prize in Medicine and Physiology in 1913. Today, we use the term anaphylaxis to refer to an infrequent but life-threatening allergic syndrome, characterized by multiorgan involvement, respiratory insufficiency, hypotension, and precipitated within minutes of exposure to a particular allergen in a sensitized patient. Common allergens that can induce an anaphylactic reaction include pharmacologic agents, foods, insect stings, and latex. Deaths from anaphylaxis usually result from acute respiratory failure (caused by orolaryngeal edema or bronchospasm) or cardiovascular collapse.

Allergy and allergic diseases span a continuum of immune disorders ranging from the emergent anaphylaxis to the less acute allergic syndromes. The latter include commonly evaluated disorders such as atopic dermatitis, contact dermatitis, allergic rhinoconjunctivitis, acute and chronic urticaria, angioedema, and mastocytosis. This chapter focuses on anaphylaxis and the immunologically related disorders of urticaria, angioedema, and mastocytosis.

Immunopathology

Allergies in general, and anaphylaxis in particular, are diseases of immune-mediated injury that result in immediate-type hypersensitivity reactions. A two-stage process is usually involved. A predisposed individual first becomes *sensitized* to an allergen when he or she develops immunoglobulin E (IgE) antibodies when exposed to the allergen for the first time, through either the inhalation, ingestion, or parenteral route (also known as *sensitization*). The IgE fixation upregulates the receptor (FcεRI) and prepares the mast cells for future activation. Within minutes of reexposure, the allergen-IgE interaction causes a release of preformed and newly synthesized mediators from mast cells and basophils. Clinical diseases are expressed depending on the response of the target organs to these mediators. Differences in target organ responses account for the differences in clinical manifestations. The most commonly affected organs are rich in mast cells and include the skin, eye, nose, respiratory tract (airway and lung), gastrointestinal tract, and cardiovascular system.

The term *anaphylactoid* reaction refers to a syndrome clinically similar to anaphylaxis but is not mediated by IgE. Although the exact mechanisms are unknown, anaphylactoid reactions seem to result from direct degranulation of mast cells and basophils and may follow a single, first-time exposure to certain agents. In this chapter, anaphylaxis refers to a general adverse immunologic or allergic syndrome not limited by an IgE-mediated mechanism, obviating the need for the term anaphylactoid reaction.

Causes and Incidence

The exact incidence of anaphylaxis is not known but is generally thought to be less than 1% in the general U.S. population. The annual incidence rates average 21 per 100,000 person-years in one study.[2] Other authorities, however, think the risks and burden of anaphylaxis are much higher with incidence of at least 1.21%, and up to 42 million Americans are at risk for having an anaphylactic attack at some time in their lifetime, resulting in up to 1500 deaths annually.[3,4] One emergency department experience over a 4-month period showed that of 19,122 visits to the emergency department, 17 (~0.09%) were for anaphylaxis.[5]

The cause of anaphylaxis remains unidentified in more than one third of the cases.[6] In the cases in which a cause can be determined, food, stings by insects of the order Hymenoptera, pharmacotherapeutic agents, exercise, and latex are the most common etiologic agents. Among these, food is the most common group, accounting for approximately one third of cases.[6] Peanuts and crustaceans are the most frequent offenders. Insect stings, particularly bee and wasp stings, are an important cause of anaphylaxis and account for 25 to 50 deaths per year in the United States.[7] Penicillin allergy occurs at a frequency of one to five reactions per 10,000 treatments of patients and 1 per 50,000 to 100,000 treatments resulting in a fatality.[8] Up to 0.9% of normal individuals taking aspirin experience anaphylaxis.[9] Another important therapeutic agent that can cause severe reactions is radiocontrast medium (RCM).[10] Such reactions occur in 0.22% of patients given the older hyperosmolar contrast agents but in only 0.04% of patients given the newer nonionic agents. Exercise can be an important cause of anaphylaxis, reported as being responsible for 7% of cases in one study.[6]

In the past two decades, the newest, most significant agent causing allergic reactions and anaphylaxis has been latex, widely used in the manufacture of medical products such as latex gloves and latex medical devices.[11] Latex is the natural rubber derived from the commercial rubber tree *Hevea brasiliensis*, which is native to the southern Amazon and harvested commercially from plantations in Southeast Asia and Africa. The functional unit is a rubber particle coated with a layer of proteins, lipids, and phospholipids to provide structural integrity. Latex allergy refers to sensitivity to either the proteins or the chemical products contained in the latex products. The sensitivity reaction can be delayed (type IV) contact dermatitis or an immediate hypersensitivity (type I) reaction such as asthma, urticaria, and anaphylaxis. The prevalence of latex sensitivity in the general population seems to range from 0.1% to 1%.[12,13] Health care workers are at increased risk, with 5% to12% showing sensitivity to latex.[14]

Risk Factors for Anaphylaxis

It is unclear whether race, sex, occupation, and geographic location predispose individuals to the risks of anaphylaxis.[15,16] The risk of anaphylaxis appears to be lower in the very young and elders, presumably because of immaturity of the immune system and an attenuated immune response in these two groups, respectively. The dose, frequency, duration, and route of administration of a drug also affect the tendency to develop an anaphylactic reaction, with the parenteral and topical routes of administration more strongly associated with more severe reactions than the oral route. One interesting aspect of drug-related anaphylaxis is the constancy of administration. An anaphylactic reaction may not occur in a susceptible patient as long as a drug is administered at regular intervals. The same patient may, however, experience an anaphylactic reaction if the drug is resumed after an interruption of therapy. Atopy also predisposes patients to a higher risk of anaphylaxis. Lastly, the more distant the last exposure, the lower the risks of anaphylaxis upon reexposure, presumably because of some forgetfulness of the immune memory.

PRINCIPLES OF DISEASE

Development of the Immune System and Mechanism of Immune-Mediated Injury

The adaptive and innate immune systems originate from the common pluripotential hematopoietic stem cells, which are derived from the yolk sac and later reside in the bone marrow. These stem cells differentiate and develop into the lymphoid precursor cells and the colony-forming unit for granulocyte, erythroid, myeloid, and megakaryocyte (CFU-GEMM) stem cells. The lymphoid precursor cells in turn differentiate into *b*ursa-equivalent lymphocytes (B cells), *t*hymus-derived lymphocytes (T cells), and natural killer (NK) cells; the CFU-GEMM cells, in the meantime, develop into mast cells, basophils, and others (Figure 117-1). When the body encounters a foreign pathogen, the cellular components of the adaptive immune system (B and T cells) interact with the cellular components and soluble products of the innate immune system (macrophages, dendritic cells, neutrophils, NK cells, eosinophils, basophils, mast cells, cytokines, and acute-phase protein and complement systems) to mount a concerted defense aimed at neutralizing and removing the harmful pathogen.[17]

T Cell Development

Lymphoid precursor cells migrate from the bone marrow into the thymus, where they progress through ontogeny. Under regulation by cytokines and cell-cell interaction, these precursors undergo gene rearrangement and positive and negative selection. In the process, T cells acquire the T cell antigen receptors and various surface markers and eventuate into two main T cell lineages. Using the cluster of differentiation (CD) classification, there are principally two types of mature T cells that eventuate out of the thymus: CD_4^+, also called helper T cells, and CD_8^+, also called suppressor T cells. Depending on the type of cytokine produced, T helper cells are subdivided into type 1 helper cells (Th1) and type 2 helper cells (Th2), with opposing activities.[18] Th1 cells secrete interferon-γ and interleukin 2 (IL-2), which inhibit IgE production and IgE isotype switching; Th2 cells secrete IL-3, IL-4, IL-5, IL-6, IL-10, and IL-13, which stimulate IgE production and IgE isotype switching. The balance of these stimu-

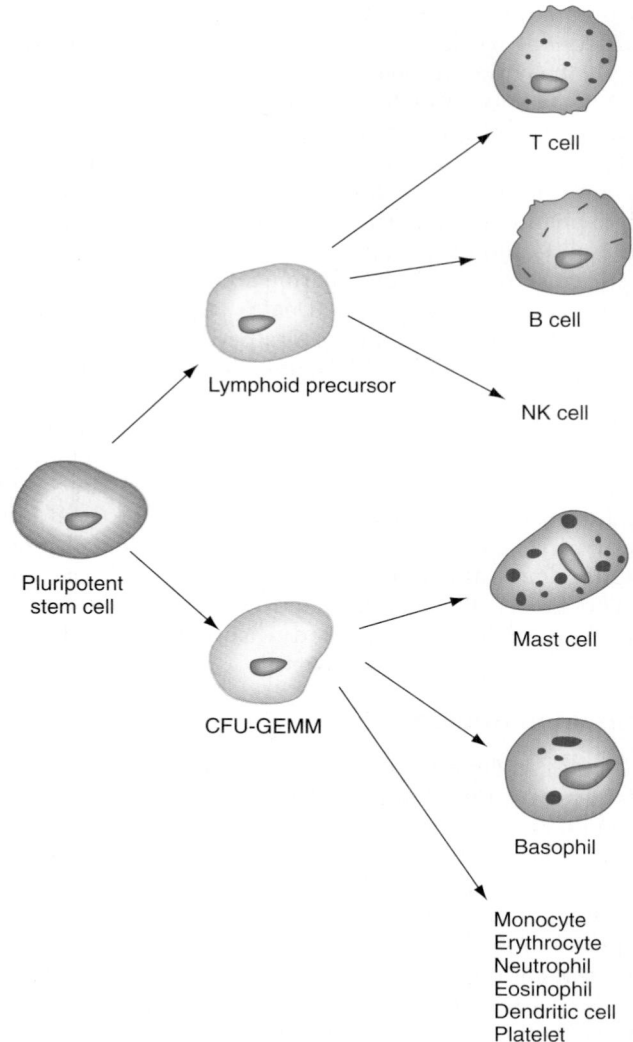

Figure 117-1. Developmental pathways of the immune and hematopoietic systems. CFU-GEMM, colony-forming unit for granulocyte, erythroid, myeloid, and megakaryocyte; NK, natural killer. (Redrawn from Shearer WT, Fleisher TA: The immune system. In Middelton E, et al [eds]: *Allergy: Clinical and Practice.* St. Louis, Mosby, 1998, pp 1-13.)

latory and inhibitory activities of the Th1 and Th2 cells is believed to determine an individual's propensity to developing allergic disease or *atopy*.[19]

B Cell Development and Immunoglobulins

B cell ontogeny can be divided into antigen-independent and antigen-dependent stages. During the antigen-independent stage, B cells mature in primary lymphoid organs (bone marrow and fetal liver), where they undergo gene rearrangement in a stochastic fashion and acquire various surface markers. Later during the antigen-dependent stage in the secondary lymphoid organs (lymph nodes and spleen), B cells differentiate into memory B cells and plasma cells and are ready to secrete immunoglobulins. Throughout B cell ontogeny, B cell maturation, isotype switching, and immunoglobulin production are driven by activated T cells,

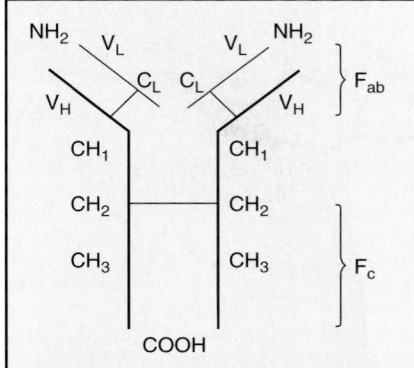

Immunoglobulin molecule Ig is composed of a pair of heavy chains and a pair of light chains with variable (V) and constant (C) domains.

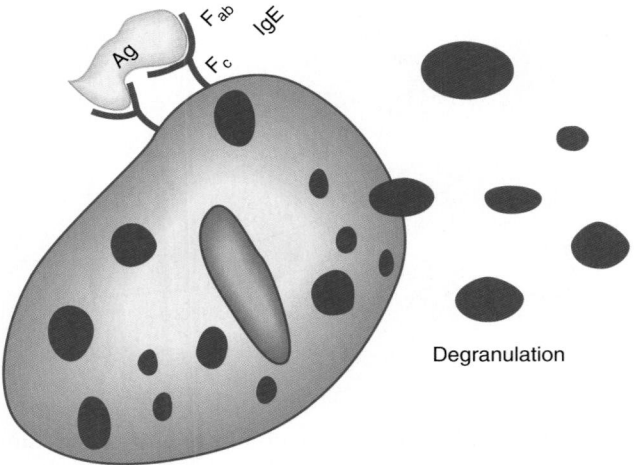

Figure 117-2. Activation of mast cells with degranulation of mast cell mediators by antigen (Ag) cross-linking adjacent immunoglobulin E (IgE) on cell surface.

cytokines produced therein, and by interaction with antigen and bone marrow stromal cells.

Immunoglobulins are protein molecules composed of two identical polypeptide heavy chains and two identical polypeptide light chains, which are covalently linked by disulfide bonds (Figure 117-2). The heavy (H) chains have one variable domain, V_H, and three or four constant domains, C_H. The light (L) chains have one variable domain, V_L, and one constant domain, C_L. The variable domains of the heavy and light chains together form a pair of identical antigen binding sites and, together with the adjacent constant heavy domain pair, make up the Fab (antibody-binding fragment) region of the immunoglobulin molecule. The remaining constant domains of the heavy chains together form the Fc (crystallizable fragment) region of the immunoglobulin molecule. The Fc binds to the surface receptors of effector cells such as mast cells, B cells, or macrophages. There are five isotypes or classes of immunoglobulins, IgG, IgA, IgM, IgD, and IgE, with isotype IgG having four subclasses (IgG1, IgG2, IgG3, IgG4) and IgA two subclasses (IgA1 and IgA2). The body usually produces

IgM antibodies when it first encounters an antigen. Repeated antigenic exposure, however, may cause the constant region of the IgM to switch to another class (IgA, IgG, or IgE), in a process called isotype switching. Isotype IgE (and IgG4) is the most important antibody in the pathogenesis of allergic disease and anaphylaxis.

Characteristics of the Immune System

Four distinguishing characteristics of the immune system differentiate it from other systems in the body.

1. Antibodies, found in blood and tissue fluids and on the surface of the B cells themselves, and receptors on T cells are highly specific for antigen; they can bind and distinguish antigens with nearly identical chemical structures.

2. The species of antibodies and T cell receptors are enormously diverse. There are up to 10^{15} types of antibodies and a similar number of T cell receptors that are available to bind antigens (all from less than 400 genes).[20]

3. Besides the brain, the immune system is the only system that has memory. After the first (primary) exposure to an allergen, a subsequent (secondary) challenge—days to years later—can elicit an accelerated and augmented immune response. Both the cellular and humoral arms are activated, resulting in a higher antibody titer, enhanced affinity of the antibodies for the antigen, and increased T cell reactivity. Immunologic memory is the basis for prophylactic immunization.

4. The immune system is able to discriminate self from nonself.

Classification of Reactions

The original classification of immunopathologic reactions, proposed by Coombs and Gell, lists four types of hypersensitivity reactions. Alternative classifications, such as the Sell classification,[21] have been proposed to reflect our increased understanding of immunopathology. In this chapter, the traditional Coombs and Gell classification is adopted. Type I (immediate hypersensitivity) is IgE (and IgG4) mediated and accounts for most allergic and anaphylactic reactions observed in humans. Type II (cytotoxic) is IgG (and IgM) mediated. Complement-fixing IgG or IgM engages cell-bound antigen, activating the classical complement pathway and anaphylatoxin production. Anaphylatoxins C3a and C5a stimulate mediator release and may produce the same action as the classical mediators of anaphylaxis at the target tissue level. Type III (immune complex) is IgG or IgM complex mediated. Circulating soluble antigen-antibody immune complexes migrate from the circulation to deposit in the perivascular interstitial space, which may activate the complement system. Anaphylactic reactions to blood transfusions or blood component therapy, including serotherapy (immunoglobulin administration), are clinical examples of the overlap of type II and type III reactivity; thus, they have been classified as complement-mediated or immune complex–mediated anaphylaxis. Type IV (delayed hypersensitivity) is T cell mediated

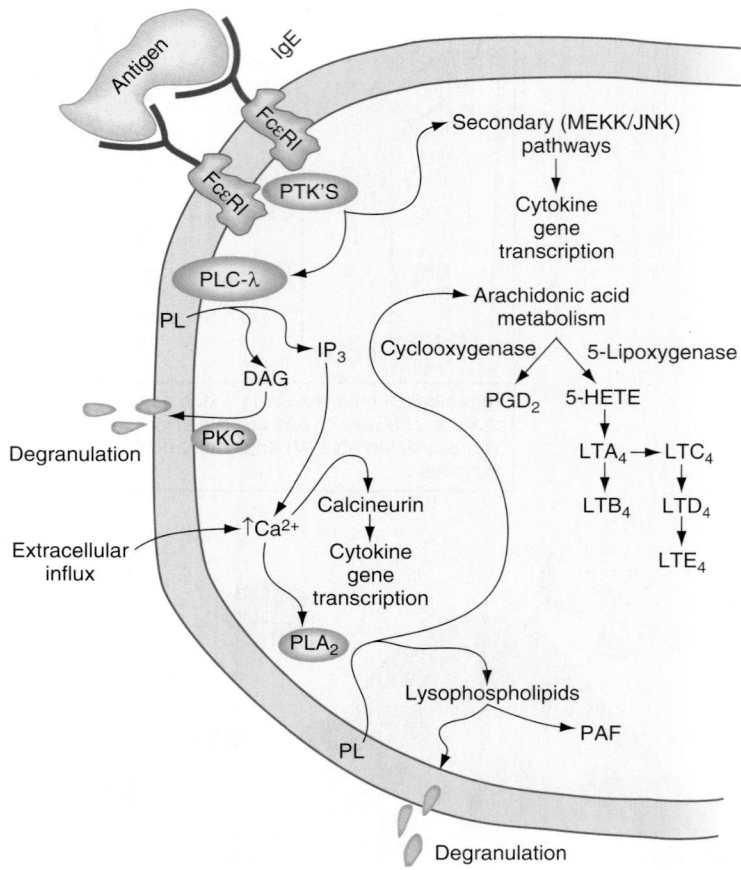

Figure 117-3. Signal transduction sequence following the cross-linking of adjacent immunoglobulin E (IgE) on surface of mast cell (see text for description). DAG, diacylglycerol; HETE, hydroxyeicosatetraenoic (acid); IP_3, inositol triphosphate; LTA_4, leukotriene A_4; PAF, platelet-activating factor; PGD_2, prostaglandin D_2; PKC, protein kinase C; PLA_2, phospholipase A_2; PTK, protein tyrosine kinase. (Redrawn from Kinet JP: The high-affinity IgE receptor [Fc epsilon RI]: From physiology to pathology. *Annu Rev Immunol* 17:931, 1999.)

and has no documented relationship to the pathogenesis of anaphylaxis.

PATHOPHYSIOLOGY

Mast cells (and basophils) possess surface receptors that have high affinity for the Fc portion of IgE (FcεRI).[15,16] After the initial sensitization exposure, subsequent challenges with an appropriate multivalent antigen or immune complex cause aggregation or clustering of surface IgE molecules. This clustering sets off a cascade of conformational and biochemical events, leading to the degranulation of preformed mediators and the generation of various chemicals from mast cells (and basophils). These mediators and chemicals cause enhanced capillary permeability, vasodilation, smooth muscle contraction, sensory nerve stimulation, myocardial depression, and activation of secondary inflammatory pathways with chemotaxis and inflammatory cell infiltration in the target tissues. The end results are the classical signs and symptoms of flushing syndrome, urticaria and angioedema, pruritus, nausea, vomiting, diarrhea, abdominal pain, chest pain, dyspnea, wheezing, respiratory insufficiency and failure, dizziness, syncope, hypotension, and shock.

Classical anaphylactic reactions are mediated by IgE-dependent degranulation, whereas anaphylactoid reactions involve direct (IgE-independent) degranulation of mast cells and basophils. Many cases of anaphylaxis caused by foods, drugs, insect bites, and stings and some cases of food-dependent and exercise-induced anaphylaxis are mediated through an IgE-dependent mechanism. Many other cases of anaphylaxis caused by radiocontrast agents, aspirin and nonsteroidal anti-inflammatory drugs (NSAIDs), blood transfusions, opioids, biologicals, and thermomechanical physical factors such as sunlight or cold and the majority of cases of idiopathic anaphylaxis are mediated by an IgE-independent mechanism. Reactions to radiocontrast agents are believed to involve multimediator complement activation and activation of the contact system. Aspirin and NSAIDs are believed to cause anaphylaxis through abnormal metabolism or arachidonic acid (AA). Incompatible blood transfusions involve cytotoxic and immune complex–mediated anaphylactoid reactions.

Immunoglobulin E–Mediated Signal Transduction System

In the IgE-dependent mechanism, the cascade of events starts with the cross-linking of the receptors FcεFI on the mast cell by multivalent antigens, which causes the phosphorylation of a number of protein tyrosine kinases (PTKs) and immunoreceptor tyrosine activation motifs (Figure 117-3).[22-24] Phosphorylation of PTKs leads to several events, one of which is the phosphorylation of phospholipase C γ (PLC-γ). Phosphorylated PLC-γ generates diacylglycerol (DAG) and inositol

BOX 117-1. Mediators of Activated Mast Cells and Basophils

Preformed Mediators
Histamine
Tryptase
Chymase
Carboxypeptidase A
Cathepsin G
Proteoglycans

Lipid-Derived Metabolites
LTB_4
LTC_4
PGD_2
Platelet-activating factor (PAF)

Cytokines
TNF-α
IFN-γ
GM-CSF
IL-4, 5, 6, 13

GM-CSF, granulocyte-macrophage colony-stimulating factor; IL-4, interleukin-4; IFN-γ, interferon-γ; LTB_4, leukotriene B_4; PGD_2, prostaglandin D_2; TNF-α, tumor necrosis factor α.

triphosphate (IP_3) from membrane phospholipids. DAG in turn activates protein kinase C (PKC), which promotes exocytosis. IP_3 mobilizes intracellular calcium stores, causing intracellular calcium to increase, which leads to more influx of calcium from extracellular space. Spikes in intracellular calcium activate a number of calcium-gated kinases, including phospholipase A_2 (PLA_2). Cytosolic PLA_2 cleaves AA from membrane phospholipids to form lysophospholipids. Lysophospholipids, such as DAG, facilitate the fusion of secretory granules with the cell membrane, leading to the exocytosis of the secretory granules. Lysophospholipids can also be acetylated to produce platelet-activating factor (PAF). Increases in intracellular calcium also promote cytokine gene transcription by the calcineurin pathway. Phosphorylation of PTKs also promotes AA metabolism and more cytokine gene transcription by other secondary pathways (mitogen-activated protein kinase kinase kinase/c-Jun N-terminal kinase [MEKK/JNK] pathways), although the detailed mechanisms are not well elucidated. AA serves as the substrate in the lipoxygenase and cyclooxygenase pathways to generate prostanoid prostaglandin D_2 (PGD_2) and leukotrienes LTB_4, LTC_4, LTD_4, and LTE_4.

Mediators of Anaphylaxis

The many mediators released by the mast cells and basophils can be categorized into three main groups: preformed mediators, lipid-derived metabolites (arachidonic metabolism), and cytokines (Box 117-1). Of the preformed mediators, histamine is the most clinically apparent and responsible for the immediate symptoms. Histamine is an essential mediator in immediate hypersensitivity and inflammation, and infusion of his-

tamine has been shown to produce the majority of the clinical features of anaphylaxis syndrome.[25] Histamine is produced and stored in preformed granules (pg) in mast cells and basophils, at about 1 to 2 pg/cell.[26] There are three classes of histamine receptors—H_1, H_2, and H_3—that mediate the activity of histamine in the body.[27] H_1 receptor stimulation produces bronchial, intestinal, and uterine smooth muscle contraction; increased vascular permeability; nasal mucus production; coronary artery spasm; and increased eosinophil and neutrophil chemokinesis and chemotaxis. H_2 receptor stimulation increases the rate and force of ventricular and atrial contraction, gastric acid secretion, airway mucus production, and vascular permeability while also causing bronchodilation and inhibition of basophil histamine release. H_3 receptors, found in neurons (in the central nervous system) and peripheral tissues, control the synthesis and release of histamine. The role of the other preformed mediators in mast cell and basophil degranulation syndrome is not well delineated.

In contrast to the preformed mediators, cytokines and lipid metabolites are elaborated de novo following the activation of mast cells and basophils (see Figure 117-3). The biochemical details of the cytokines are not well understood but are believed to involve immunoregulation of several kinases. Prostanoids and the leukotrienes are the other mediators generated from AA. The leukotrienes—LTB_4, LTC_4, LTD_4, and LTE_4—also referred to as cysteinyl leukotrienes or slow-reacting substances of anaphylaxis, are synthesized from AA by the lipoxygenase pathway. They are involved in cholinergic-independent bronchial and bronchiolar wall smooth muscle contraction, increased vascular permeability, and increased mucous gland production. These cysteinyl leukotrienes have a slow onset but are 10 to 1000 times as potent as histamine in causing bronchoconstriction when administered by aerosol.[26] They also have a longer duration of action and potentiate the effects of other bronchoconstrictors such as histamine. The prostaglandins, prostacyclins, and thromboxanes are synthesized from AA by the cyclooxygenase pathway. These AA metabolites produce many of the same clinical symptoms as the leukotrienes. In humans, the main prostaglandin produced is PGD_2, which is approximately 30 times as potent as histamine in causing bronchoconstriction.

PAF is an unstored phospholipid and the most potent compound known to cause aggregation of human platelets with subsequent release of platelet-derived vasoactive mediators. Its other actions include neutrophil activation and chemotaxis and ileal and parenchymal lung strip smooth muscle contraction. PAF has been demonstrated to produce many of the important clinical manifestations of anaphylaxis, including decreased myocardial contractile force, coronary vasoconstriction, pulmonary edema, and a prolonged increase in total pulmonary resistance with a decrease in dynamic compliance. Indeed, blockage of PAF with experimental antagonists leads to improved cardiac function, suggesting that PAF may be involved in the late cardiac dysfunction and lethality associated with anaphylaxis.[28]

Physiologic Effects

The chemical mediators just described collectively effect the syndrome of anaphylaxis.[29] Increased vascular permeability can lead to urticaria, angioedema, laryngeal edema, nasal congestion, or gastrointestinal swelling with abdominal cramping and vomiting. Vasodilation can lead to flushing, headaches, reduced peripheral vascular resistance, hypotension, and syncope. Contraction of smooth muscle can lead to bronchospasm, abdominal cramping, or diarrhea. Pulmonary vessel vasoconstriction can lead to pulmonary hypertension, pulmonary edema, and decreased cardiac filling pressures. Coronary vasoconstriction can lead to myocardial ischemia and decreased myocardial contractile force. Changes in atrial chronotropy and ventricular and atrial isotropy can lead to cardiac dysrhythmias. In addition to the direct actions on the target tissues, these preformed mediators, lipid-derived mediators, and cytokines activate a number of inflammatory pathways, including the complement system, clotting and clot lysis systems, and kallikrein-kinin (contact) system, to contribute to the clinical manifestations of allergy and anaphylaxis.

Cardiovascular collapse in anaphylaxis has classically been described as a result of peripheral vasodilation, enhanced vascular permeability, leakage of plasma, and intravascular volume depletion (the "empty ventricle" syndrome). However, hemodynamic reports for humans experiencing anaphylactic shock indicate that the explanation may be more complicated. In a variety of clinical settings, hypotension in anaphylaxis has been associated with increased cardiac index, increased cardiac index with decreased peripheral vascular resistance, decreased cardiac index, decreased cardiac index with decreased peripheral vascular resistance, and decreased cardiac index with increased peripheral vascular resistance. In the setting of decreased cardiac index and decreased peripheral vascular resistance, a small reduction in oxygen delivery and large reductions in oxygen consumption and oxygen extraction ratios are present, causing reduced organ perfusion and metabolic acidosis.

Pathologic features identified at autopsy in fatal cases of anaphylaxis are most commonly observed in the respiratory and cardiac systems. These include orolaryngeal edema, pulmonary hyperinflation, peribronchial vascular congestion, intra-alveolar hemorrhage, pulmonary edema, increased tracheobronchial secretions, eosinophilic infiltration of the bronchial walls, and varying degrees of myocardial damage. Other autopsy findings include urticarial eruptions, angioedema, visceral congestion, submucosal edema, and hemorrhagic gastritis. Notably, autopsy findings may also be normal after an anaphylactic death.[30] A summary of the physiologic effects and clinical signs and symptoms is given in Table 117-1.

ETIOLOGY

Numerous agents are known to cause anaphylactic reactions in humans. They can be categorized in a number of ways: by chemical family (proteins, polysaccharides, and haptens), by function (foods, pharmacotherapeutics [e.g., antibiotics, immunotherapeutics], and insect stings), or by immunopathogenetic mechanism. The last classification is adopted in this chapter. Etiologic agents are classified as IgE mediated, immune complex mediated, nonimmunologic activators, or AA modulators (Box 117-2). Reactions without identifiable causative agents are classified as physically induced or IA. The number of substances capable of eliciting an anaphylactic reaction is continuously expanding because of the introduction of new diagnostic and ther-

---

BOX 117-2. Etiologic Agents and Pathogenetic Mechanisms of Anaphylaxis

IgE-Mediated Agents
Foods (eggs, peanut, tree nuts, cow's milk, fruits, shellfish, shrimp, other crustaceans, many others)
Antibiotics (penicillins, cephalosporins, sulfonamides, nitrofurantoin, tetracycline, streptomycin)
Other therapeutics (methylparaben, human diploid cell rabies vaccine, egg-based vaccines: measles, mumps, rubella, vasopressin, antilymphocyte globulin)
Insect stings (Hymenoptera venoms, fire ant stings)
Latex
Allergens used in immunotherapy
Heterologous and human sera
Hormones (insulin, methylprednisolone, parathormone, estradiol, progesterone, corticotropin)
Enzymes (trypsin, streptokinase, chymotrypsin, chymopapain, L-asparaginase)
Polysaccharides (dextran, iron dextran)
Local anesthetics (mostly ester family, procaine, tetracaine, benzocaine)

Direct Mast Cell Degranulation
Radiocontrast media (RCM)
Opiates
Curare, d-tubocurarine
Protamine
Polysaccharides (some are IgE mediated)
ACE inhibitor used during hemodialysis with certain HD membranes
Ethylene oxide gas on dialysis tubing

Immune Complex Mediated
Whole blood (transfusion reaction to formed elements)
Immunoglobulin administration

Arachidonic Acid Metabolism
Aspirin and NSAIDS (presumed)
Benzoates (presumed)
Food colorants (tartrazine [possibly])

Physical Factors
Exercise
Temperature (heat or cold)

Idiopathic
Factitious
Undifferentiated somatoform idiopathic anaphylaxis
Idiopathic

ACE, angiotensin-converting enzyme; HD, hemodialysis; IgE, immunoglobulin E; NSAID, nonsteroidal anti-inflammatory drug.
Modified from Kemp SF, Lockey RF: Anaphylaxis: A review of causes and mechanisms. *J Allergy Clin Immunol* 110:341, 2002.

Table 117-1. Clinical Manifestations of Anaphylaxis and Related Pathophysiology

Organ System	Reaction	Symptoms	Signs	Pathophysiology
Respiratory Tract Upper	Rhinitis	Nasal congestion Nasal itching Sneezing	Nasal mucosal edema Rhinorrhea	Increased vascular permeability Vasodilation Stimulation of nerve endings
	Laryngeal edema	Dyspnea Hoarseness Throat tightness Hypersalivation	Laryngeal stridor Supraglottic and glottic edema	As above, plus increased exocrine gland secretions
Lower	Bronchospasm	Cough Wheezing Retrosternal tightness Dyspnea	Cough Wheeze, rhonchi Tachypnea Respiratory distress Cyanosis	As above, plus bronchiole smooth muscle contraction
Cardiovascular System	Circulatory collapse	Light-headedness Generalized weakness Syncope Ischemic chest pain	Tachycardia Hypotension Shock	Increased vascular permeability Vasodilation Loss of vasomotor tone Increased venous capacitance
	Dysrhythmias	As above, plus palpitations	ECG changes: Tachycardia Nonspecific and ischemic ST- T wave changes Right ventricular strain Premature atrial and ventricular contractions Nodal rhythm Atrial fibrillation	Decreased cardiac output Decreased mediator-induced myocardial suppression Decreased effective plasma volume Decreased preload Decreased afterload Hypoxia and ischemia Dysrhythmias Iatrogenic effects of drugs used in treatment Preexisting heart disease
	Cardiac arrest		Pulseless ECG changes: Ventricular fibrillation Asystole	
Skin	Urticaria	Pruritus Tingling and warmth Flushing Hives	Urticaria Diffuse erythema	Increased vascular permeability Vasodilation
	Angioedema	Nonpruritic extremity, periorbital and perioral swelling	Nonpitting edema, frequently asymmetric	Increased vascular permeability
Eye	Conjunctivitis	Ocular itching Increased larcrimation Red eye	Conjunctival inflammation	Stimulation of nerve endings
Gastrointestinal Tract		Dysphagia Cramping abdominal pain Nausea and vomiting Diarrhea (rarely bloody) Tenesmus	Nonspecific	Increased mucus secretions Gastrointestinal smooth muscle contraction
Miscellaneous Central Nervous System		Apprehension Sense of impending doom Headache Confusion	Anxiety Seizures (rarely) Coma (late)	Secondary to cerebral hypoxia and hypoperfusion Vasodilation
Hematologic	Fibrinolysis and disseminated intravascular coagulation	Abnormal bleeding and bruising	Mucous membrane bleeding, disseminated intravascular coagulation Increased uterine tone Vaginal bleeding Urinary incontinence	Mediator recruitment and activation Uterine smooth muscle contraction Bladder smooth muscle contraction
Genitourinary		Pelvic pain Vaginal bleeding Urinary incontinence		

ECG, electrocardiographic.

apeutic agents; the most significant new agent in the last two decades is natural rubber latex.

Immunoglobulin E–Mediated Agents

This diverse group of agents is functionally categorized into foods, antibiotics, latex, other therapeutic agents, and Hymenoptera stings.

Foods

Foods are the major identifiable causative agents, accounting for approximately one third of the cases of anaphylaxis.[6] A variety of foods ranging from the well known such as nuts, shellfish, and eggs to the obscure such as chamomile tea (which may have cross-reactivity with ragweed) have been identified. Cow's milk, egg, peanut, soy, wheat, fish, shellfish, and tree nuts are, however, the foods that most commonly cause anaphylaxis.[6] Even for a person with a known history of food allergy, it may be difficult to avoid foods that may cause allergic reactions because their identity may be obscured in processing. Because allergenic foods are first absorbed transmucosally, symptoms of food ana-phylaxis may first appear localized to the upper airway of the respiratory tract. When anaphylactic allergens are administered parenterally, symptoms of anaphy-laxis tend to be more cardiovascular and systemic. Allergic reactions to foodstuffs are more common in children, ranging from 0.3% to 7.5%.[31]

Therapeutic and prophylactic use of large quantities of antibiotics is common in the production of beef cattle, swine, fish, poultry, and sometimes vegetables and fruits. Along with antibiotics, sodium and potassium bisulfites and metabisulfites are used as preservatives in foods. Sulfites have been used as antioxidants in the food and restaurant industry to prevent discoloration of vegetables (e.g., salad bars, avocado dips), fruits, and potatoes and to preserve fruit and vegetable juices. They are also used to prevent bacterial contamination and oxidation of wines, beers, and distilled beverages. Sensitivity to ingested sulfites has been well documented, especially among the asthmatic population.[32] Establishing a particular foodstuff or preservative as the causative agent of anaphylaxis can be difficult.

Antibiotics

Benzylpenicillin, semisynthetic penicillin, and cephalosporins are the most significant antimicrobial agents causing anaphylaxis. The first penicillin-induced anaphylactic fatality was reported in 1949.[33] Because of their low molecular weights, these antimicrobials do not themselves possess antigenic properties. Immunologically, they are haptens, simple chemicals that are not antigenic in themselves but become antigenic after the chemicals or their metabolites form a stable bond with the host proteins. Certain binding properties of particular drugs make them more likely to induce sensitization. Although patients often report a history of penicillin allergy, this usually does not stand up to close scrutiny.[34] Depending on the studies, the fre-

quency of allergic reactions to penicillin varies from 0.01% to 0.05% of administrations of penicillin (1 to 5 reactions per 10,000) with an anaphylactic reaction rate less than 0.01% and a fatality rate less than 0.002% (less than one fatality per 50,000 million penicillin administrations).[8] Parenterally administered penicillin is responsible for most severe anaphylactic reactions with rare fatalities from oral penicillin administration.[35,36] The extensive use of this drug in unsuspected sources, such as foods, in which it is used as a bacteriostatic agent, may make it difficult to ascertain historically that penicillin is not the causative agent.

Cephalosporins share the β-lactam ring structure and side chains of the penicillins and have been incriminated for allergic cross-sensitivity in up to 8.1% of patients.[37] It is unclear which epitope is responsible for the cross-reactivity. Patients who have urticaria or anaphylactic reactions after taking penicillin are about four times more likely to have an adverse reaction to cephalosporins. Even in this setting, risks of an anaphylactic reaction to cephalosporins are still less than 0.1%. Although it may be prudent to administer a class of antibiotics other than the cephalosporins when a well-documented significant history of penicillin allergy is obtained, if no other antibiotic choices are available, the first dose of cephalosporin can be administered orally under medical supervision and observation.[38]

Latex

Allergy to natural rubber latex in gloves and other medical products has become a serious health issue for health care providers, patients, and rubber industry workers.[39] Latex antigens can be proteins or other chemical contaminants present in latex. For glove wearers, latex antigens are adsorbed onto the cornstarch powder, serving as a contact allergen, or they can become airborne allergens when the gloves are discarded or can be leached from latex during normal use. The prevalence and severity of reactions have rapidly increased and may be related to the expanded use of latex gloves after the issuance of universal precautions in 1987, even though some authorities have questioned this relationship.[40] Groups at higher risk include spina bifida patients, health care workers, latex industry workers, and patients with a history of atopy or multiple surgical procedures. The prevalence of latex allergy in the occupationally unexposed general population remains low at less than 1%.[13]

The most common symptoms of latex allergy include allergic urticaria, rhinitis, conjunctivitis, and occupational asthma. There is evidence that patients with specific food allergies are predisposed to latex allergy.[41] Allergy to latex can be an immediate hypersensitivity IgE-mediated reaction (type I) that can lead to anaphylaxis or delayed (type IV) contact dermatitis.[14] The true risks of latex-induced anaphylaxis are not known, but in a review of anaphylaxis incidents in 50 children, 27% were due to latex allergy.[42] Diagnostic tools include serologic assays and skin prick testing. There is no effective prophylaxis for latex allergy. In fact, routine use of the H_2 blocker ranitidine for gastroesophageal reflux was reported to increase the risk of a heart conduction block in a case of anaphylaxis caused by latex.[43] Avoidance of latex-containing products is currently the recommended approach.[44]

Insect Stings

Hymenoptera venoms and fire ant stings are responsible for significant anaphylactic morbidity and mortality. The first recorded fatality caused by anaphylaxis was probably the hieroglyphic-documented death of King Menes of Egypt in 2641 BC, when he succumbed to the sting of a wasp or hornet. Stinging hymenopteran insects account for approximately 25 to 50 deaths annually in the United States, with several more deaths probably unrecognized and unreported.[45] Allergic sensitization to Hymenoptera has been reported in 0.4% to 4% of the general population.[46] The principal offenders (in decreasing order of frequency) are the yellow jackets, honeybees, wasps, and yellow and bald-faced hornets. The imported fire ant has become a significant pest responsible for anaphylaxis, spreading from the Atlantic and Gulf coasts inland.[47] The introduction of killer (Africanized) bees in Brazil and their subsequent migration make them a significant cause of sting-induced anaphylaxis in parts of Texas, Arizona, and the southwestern United States[48]

The Hymenoptera venoms are complex mixtures of pharmacologically and biochemically active substances. Honeybee venom has been subjected to the greatest amount of research and contains two major enzymes—hyaluronidase and PLA—and other peptides, including a mast cell–degranulating peptide. Yellow jacket venom contains not only phospholipases A and B and hyaluronidase but also kinins. Hornet venom has, in addition, acetylcholine. Wasp venom has not been extensively studied. Fire ant venom is mostly a nonproteinaceous alkaloid suspension containing PLA and hyaluronidase.

Other Therapeutic Agents

Heterologous sera that were used in diphtheria and tetanus equine antitoxins in the past can act as whole antigenic markers. In fact, until the advent of penicillin, these two therapeutic agents were the most common iatrogenic causes of anaphylaxis in humans. The use of human antisera was associated with a marked reduction in the incidence of serum-induced anaphylactic reactions. In fact, no adverse reactions were noted on repeated immunization using human tetanus antisera in approximately 250 patients who had previous anaphylactic reactions to equine tetanus antisera.[49] Equine antisera are still used in the administration of antilymphocyte serum and in the management of venomous snake bites. Although anaphylactic reactions are rare (1 : 500,000), the equine antiserum should still be diluted and pretested.

Since the development of heterologous insulin hormone therapy for the management of diabetes mellitus, local and systemic allergic complications have been recognized. A large percentage of local reactions were eliminated with the introduction of purified, single-peak pork insulin. With the introduction of Humulin, an insulin preparation prepared from recombinant DNA, the incidence of anaphylaxis and insulin resistance has declined dramatically.

Allergen extracts are used diagnostically in skin testing and therapeutically in immunotherapy (also known as hyposensitization or desensitization). Exposure to therapeutic pollens, by injection or inhalation, can result in local allergic or systemic anaphylactic reactions.[50] High-dose therapy, too frequent administration, or inadvertent intravascular injection increases the risk of anaphylaxis with immunotherapy.

Although corticosteroids are used in the management of acute allergic syndromes and anaphylaxis, adverse reactions to these medications have been observed after parenteral administration.[51] Skin testing may demonstrate the specific class of steroids responsible for hypersensitivity, and substitution of a different class should be considered.

Local anesthetics occasionally produce adverse reactions. Most of these reactions are not allergic in nature but are related to a direct effect of the medication.[52,53] True allergic reactions are rare and are most commonly seen with local anesthetics from the ester family (e.g., procaine, tetracaine, benzocaine). Allergic reactions to local anesthetics belonging to the amide family (e.g., lidocaine, bupivacaine, mepivacaine, dibucaine) are extremely rare if they occur at all. Multidose vials of lidocaine contain the preservative methylparaben, which belongs structurally to the ester family. This preservative has been implicated in allergic reactions in patients with a history of previous lidocaine hypersensitivity.[54] Pure lidocaine (without the methylparaben preservative) should be used intravenously (as in Bier's block).

Anaphylactic reactions have occurred after the administration of egg embryo–grown vaccines, including the combined measles, mumps, and rubella (MMR), yellow fever, and influenza vaccines. A patient who is able to tolerate eggs orally, even if the patient has previously experienced anaphylaxis and shows a positive skin test to eggs, is likely to tolerate the vaccines. Anaphylactic reactions have also occurred against ethylene oxide (ETO), which is used to sterilize hemodialyzers. ETO can bind with human proteins such as human serum albumin (HSA), thus rendering the ETO-HSA complex allergenic.[55]

Immune Complex–Mediated Agents

Anaphylactic-type reactions are uncommon complications after the administration of whole blood and immunoglobulins. The fixation of antibodies to formed elements such as red blood cells, platelets, and leukocytes and soluble components activates the complement system. This is particularly relevant in IgA-deficient patients exposed to multiple transfusions, who may have produced antibodies to IgA present in previous transfusions. With subsequent transfusions, an antigen (IgA)–anti-IgA antibody (IgG) immune complex forms, and subsequent activation of the complement cascade may occur.

Nonimmunologic Activators

Many of the opioid analgesics can be potent agents of histamine release. It is unclear how much cross-sensitivity is present among these agents. Although most of these reactions appear to be a result of direct histamine release, some evidence exists that, rarely, some reactions are true IgE-mediated reactions.

RCM rarely can cause anaphylactoid reactions.[10] They are hypertonic, water-soluble compounds that are administered by intravascular or intrathecal injection. The older hyperosmolar agents can cause a reaction in up to 5.6% of patients, with fatalities in up to 0.01%.[56] Subsequent studies put the risks of a serious reaction to high-osmolar contrast media at 0.22%, with 11.7 fatalities per million injections.[57] The newer lower osmolar agents cause allergic reactions much less frequently. The risk of a serious reaction is approximately 0.04%, with an estimated 3.9 fatalities per million injections.[58]

The pathophysiology of RCM reactions is uncertain but is believed to be nonimmunologic. Suggested mechanisms include direct histamine release, alternative complement pathway activation, and activation of the contact system.[10]

Modulators of Arachidonic Acid Metabolism

Interruption of arachidonic metabolism by aspirin and other NSAIDs has been postulated as the mechanism responsible for anaphylactoid reactions resulting from these agents, although AA modulation, anaphylatoxin generation, and direct histamine release may all be partially responsible.[59,60] The incidence of anaphylactoid reactions to aspirin and NSAIDs varies widely, depending on the population. The incidence of anaphylactoid reactions to aspirin ranges from 0.9% in a healthy population to 97% in adults with asthma and rhinosinusitis or nasal polyps. Most aspirin-sensitive patients can tolerate sodium salicylate or acetaminophen as an aspirin substitute. Of note, one of many food additives, tartrazine (foods, drugs, and cosmetics [FD&C] yellow dye number 5), is a stable azo coloring agent present in thousands of foods and drugs in the United States.[61] The exact mechanism of tartrazine sensitivity is unknown, although modulation of AA metabolism and several other theories have been proposed.[62]

Physically Induced Anaphylaxis

Thermomechanical and physical factors (heat, cold), especially exercise, have increasingly been recognized as etiologic agents in certain anaphylactic-like incidents.[63] The mechanism remains unclear, but releases of mast cell and basophil mediators have been implicated. Patients with exercise-induced anaphylaxis are generally dedicated athletes who may have a personal or family atopic history. Exercise-induced anaphylaxis has been demonstrated in some cases to depend on previous ingestion of food to which the patient may be subclinically sensitive.[64] Provocative foods, if identified, should be avoided. Patients should discontinue the exercise when they experience pruritus. When exercise is continued beyond this point, clinical deterioration is likely in susceptible individuals. Prophylactic treatment with an antihistamine as a single agent or in combination with other agents may be helpful. Avoidance of precipitating factors, modification of exercise, and use of a self-injectable epinephrine kit have been recommended for patients with exercise-induced anaphylaxis.

Idiopathic Anaphylaxis

IA refers to mediator-induced anaphylaxis without a discernible cause. In the United States, it is estimated that 20,000 to 47,000 patients annually see allergists for signs and symptoms of IA.[65] A specific causative agent cannot be found historically, and laboratory studies including a complete blood count with differential leukocyte count, erythrocyte sedimentation rate, blood chemistries, complement levels, C1 esterase inhibitor levels, serum and urinary histamine levels, urinalysis, skin testing, and occasionally more specialized tests when clinically indicated are all nondiagnostic. Food diaries and efforts to find systemic disease are often fruitless. Although IA may be life threatening, it is usually responsive to conventional therapies including antihistamines, sympathomimetics, and steroids.[66] Some cases of IA may be caused by kissing[67] or conversion disorders.[68] The overall prognosis for IA is good, but certain patients may experience recurrent IA despite intensive prophylactic administration of antihistamines, sympathomimetics, or steroids.[69] Sometimes IA can represent "progesterone" anaphylaxis.[15] Women suffering from this disorder may present with recurrent episodes of anaphylaxis that are temporally related to the menstrual cycle. Other patients may have anaphylactic reactions to injection of medroxyprogesterone or luteinizing hormone–releasing hormone.

CLINICAL FEATURES

Anaphylaxis in humans primarily affects organs that are rich in mast cell—the cutaneous, upper and lower respiratory, cardiovascular, neurologic, and gastrointestinal systems. Anaphylactic reactions range from mild to fatal with variable durations of attack. The clinical expression depends on the degree of hypersensitivity; the quantity, route, and rate of antigen exposure; the pattern of mediator release; and the target organ sensitivity and responsiveness. Most anaphylactic reactions become clinically evident within minutes (average 5 to 30 minutes) after a parenteral exposure and hours (average 2 hours) after ingestion of the triggering antigen.[15] Most fatalities occur within the first 30 minutes after antigenic exposure. Delay of several hours or even days can, however, occur in rare situations. Symptoms can sometimes resolve and recur hours later in what has been termed *biphasic anaphylaxis*.[70] In general, the sooner the clinical syndrome is manifest after antigenic exposure, the more severe the reaction. Anaphylactic reactions after parenteral antigenic exposure are usually more immediate in onset, more rapidly progressive, and more severe in quality than those occurring after topical or oral exposures. Rapid progression from mild urticaria and bronchospasm to shock or asphyxia may occur in minutes. Fatal cases of anaphylaxis are usually caused by cardiovascular and respiratory disturbances. Although urticaria and angioedema are the most common presenting symptoms (88%) in anaphylaxis,[15] fatal anaphylaxis syndromes with laryngeal edema and circulatory collapse can occur even in the absence of any premonitory warning symptoms or signs or cutaneous manifestations.[71]

The first clinical manifestation of anaphylaxis usually involves the skin; the patient experiences generalized warmth and tingling of the face, mouth, upper chest, palms, soles, or the site of antigenic exposure. Pruritus is a nearly universal feature and may be accompanied by generalized flushing and urticaria, and nonpruritic angioedema may also be evident initially. This may be followed by mild to severe respiratory distress. The patient may describe a cough; a sense of chest tightness, dyspnea, and wheeze from bronchospasm; or throat tightness, dyspnea, odynophagia, or hoarseness associated with laryngeal edema or oropharyngeal angioedema. Hypotension or dysrhythmias may be manifest as light-headedness or syncope. Any of these clinical patterns may occur independently of, in combination with, or in association with nasal congestion and sneezing; ocular itching and tearing; cramping abdominal pain with nausea, vomiting, diarrhea, and tenesmus; incontinence; pelvic pain; headache; or a sense of impending doom.

The physical examination may reveal tachypnea, tachycardia, and hypotension. Laryngeal stridor, hypersalivation, hoarseness, and angioedema indicate upper airway obstruction, whereas coughing, wheezing, rhonchi, and diminished air flow suggest lower respiratory tract bronchoconstriction. Tachycardia and hypotension suggest circulatory collapse. Commonly observed dysrhythmias include sinus tachycardia, premature atrial and ventricular contractions, nodal rhythm, and atrial fibrillation. Other electrocardiographic changes include nonspecific and ischemic ST-T wave changes, right ventricular strain, and intraventricular conduction defects. The patient may have a depressed level of consciousness, but this is rarely due to seizure activity. Urticaria, angioedema, rhinitis, and conjunctivitis may be evident. A summary of the observed clinical manifestations of anaphylaxis along with their related pathophysiology is presented in Table 117-1.

DIAGNOSTIC STRATEGIES

The truism that a good history and physical examination and a high index of suspicion offer the best diagnostic tool is even more self-evident in the diagnosis of anaphylaxis. Several other diagnostic modalities should be considered concurrently to rule out other causes.[15] As clinically indicated, initial screening studies should include a complete blood count, com-

plete metabolic panel (hypoglycemia), coagulation panel (prothrombin time, partial thromboplastin time, and International Normalized Ratio), cardiac enzymes, an electrocardiogram to rule out an acute coronary syndrome, urine analysis, erythrocyte sedimentation rate, and a portable chest radiograph. Serum level of serotonin and urinary 5-hydroxyindole acetic acid, catecholamines, and vanillylmandelic acid are useful to rule out carcinoid syndrome. Serum and urinary histamine and serum tryptase are helpful to confirm the diagnosis of anaphylaxis after the fact. The optimal time to obtain the serum histamine level is within 1 hour and serum tryptase within 1 to 2 hours (but no longer than 6 hours) of the onset of symptoms. Samples of vomitus may be collected for the allergist to create a custom radioallergosorbent test panel for later desensitization therapy. Serial arterial blood gases may initially show hypoxemia and normocarbia, progressing into a state of hypercarbia and acidosis, reflecting clinical deterioration of the disease. Blood culture, urine culture, computed tomography of the head, lateral soft tissue of neck, and indirect and direct laryngoscopy can be considered depending on the clinical suspicions.

DIFFERENTIAL CONSIDERATIONS

The diagnosis of an anaphylactic reaction depends largely on recognizing the constellation of clinical manifestations that occur abruptly after suspected antigenic exposure. The diagnosis is easy to make in the patient who has urticaria, laryngeal edema, and circulatory collapse minutes after sustaining a bee sting. When only a portion of the full syndrome is present, it may be difficult to recognize the symptoms as an anaphylactic reaction.

Flush Syndromes and Rash

Important considerations include occult infections, carcinoid syndrome, systemic mastocytosis and urticaria pigmentosa, pheochromocytoma, hereditary angioedema, urticarial vasculitis, medullary carcinoma of the thyroid, scombroidosis, and sulfite and monosodium glutamate toxicity.

Stridor

In the absence of oropharyngeal angioedema or other clinical manifestations of anaphylaxis, the diagnosis of laryngeal edema should be confirmed by direct or indirect laryngoscopy to exclude epiglottitis and supraglottitis, retropharyngeal or peritonsillar abscess, laryngeal spasm, foreign body aspiration, or tumor.

Bronchospasm

Obstructive lung diseases such as acute asthma may be accompanied by other signs and symptoms of anaphylaxis. Patients with acute pulmonary embolism may present with shock, respiratory distress, and bronchospasm. Exercise-induced anaphylaxis should be differentiated from exercise-induced asthma because the former is usually accompanied by pruritus and other systemic manifestations.

Syncope

Vasovagal syncope is the most common differential diagnosis in the patient arriving with collapse as a result of parenteral administration of an antigen. Classically, the patient has bradycardia, hypotension, and pallor as opposed to the tachycardia, hypotension, and diaphoresis usually associated with anaphylaxis. The absence of any other clinical manifestations of anaphylaxis, along with history of stress, pain, and previous episodes of simple faints, helps point toward the diagnosis of vasovagal syncope. Other causes of syncope such as seizure, stroke, hypoglycemia, acute coronary syndrome, or cardiac dysrhythmia also need to be considered. Ordinary allergic reactions and especially anaphylaxis can precipitate an acute coronary syndrome.[72]

Shock

Clinically, anaphylactic, septic, and spinal shock may appear similarly with signs and symptoms of shock including end-organ hypoperfusion and vasodilation. Skin is usually moist and warm, suggesting a state of decreased peripheral vascular resistance. Cardiogenic, restrictive, hypovolemic, or hemorrhagic shock would more likely be seen with cold, clammy skin, suggesting a state of heightened peripheral vascular resistance. As anaphylactic shock can progress to cardiogenic shock, measurement of central venous pressures (CVPs) may be necessary.

MANAGEMENT

Prehospital

When a susceptible patient is re-exposed to an antigen to which there has been previous reaction, 50 mg of oral diphenhydramine hydrochloride should be taken if available. At the first signs of any clinical manifestations of anaphylaxis, the patient should self-administer epinephrine if available (adult dose, 0.3 mL of 1:1000 intramuscular; pediatric dose, 0.01 mL/kg of 1:1000 intramuscular). Susceptible patients may even use aerosolized epinephrine from a metered-dose inhaler to counteract the effects of laryngeal edema, bronchoconstriction, and other manifestations of anaphylaxis.[73] Multiple inhalations (e.g., 10 to 20 doses, resulting in the inhalation of 1.5 to 3 mg of epinephrine) produce therapeutic plasma levels, with the advantages of ease of administration, rapid absorption, and locally high epinephrine levels in the upper and lower airways. Epinephrine must be used with caution in elderly persons and in those with a history of cardiac or hypertensive problems.

Prehospital personnel may be required to resuscitate a moribund patient using basic life support. Their first priority should be to establish and maintain ventilation, intravenous access, cardiac monitoring, and

administration of supplemental oxygen to keep the oxygen saturation level greater than 90%.

Local measures to decrease antigen absorption from an extremity include dependent positioning of the extremity, ice to vasoconstrict locally, and application of a loose tourniquet to obstruct the venous and lymphatic circulation. The tourniquet should be released for 1 of every 10 minutes. If an insect stinger remains, the wound should not be squeezed because it may inject more venom into the patient. The stinger should be removed gently with instruments, avoiding disturbance of the venom apparatus.

Emergency Department

The goals of treatment are to slow or reverse the pathophysiologic process in order to abrogate the clinical complications of anaphylaxis. Box 117-3 summarizes the treatment options for anaphylaxis in the emergency department. Therapeutic modalities must be initiated quickly and simultaneously when possible. Because most of the morbidity and mortality associated with anaphylaxis is related to asphyxia from upper respiratory tract obstruction, acute respiratory failure from bronchospasm, or cardiovascular collapse, priority should be given to stabilizing cardiorespiratory insufficiencies.

Epinephrine and antihistamines (H_1 and H_2) should be administered early in most anaphylactic cases.[75] Patients should have supplemental oxygen administered, large-bore (e.g., 16-gauge) intravenous lines inserted to infuse crystalloid or colloid solutions, and continuous cardiac monitoring. A large volume of crystalloid fluid may be required to reverse the hypotension associated with anaphylaxis.

Upper airway obstruction from laryngeal edema or angioedema can progress rapidly. While preparing for more definitive airway management, a chin lift or jaw thrust may help obtain a patent airway. Suctioning the oropharynx of excess secretions may be necessary. A nasopharyngeal or oropharyngeal airway may aid in maintaining a patent airway at this stage. Racemic epinephrine, delivered as a 2.25% solution (0.5 mL placed in a nebulizer in 2.5 mL of normal saline), may be a temporizing measure. A laryngeal airway mask, jet ventilation, or surgical airway may be needed for difficult airways.

The success rate of intubation is improved when it is performed early and before soft tissue swelling progresses. Oral endotracheal intubation is the route of choice because significant anatomic distortion may be present as a result of edema. Sedation and paralysis should be used with caution because a distorted airway may preclude intubation after paralysis. Arterial blood gases play no role in the decision-making process for the patient in acute respiratory distress. Once a patent airway has been obtained and supplemental oxygen delivered, therapy should focus on relieving the patient's bronchospasm.

Epinephrine

Drugs used in the treatment of anaphylaxis either inhibit the release of chemical mediators or reverse the

BOX 117-3. Treatment Options for Anaphylaxis

1. Immediate general interventions
  (a) Remove any triggering agent
  (b) Place patient in the Trendelenburg position if hypotensive
  (c) Assessment of airway patency, breathing, and circulation
    (i) Hyperextension of neck, jaw thrust, chin lift
    (ii) Administer supplemental oxygen by nasal cannula or nonbreather mask
    (iii) Racemic epinephrine 0.5 mL of 2.25% in 2.5 mL of NS by nebulizer while awaiting definitive airway management
    (iv) Establish airway
      (1) Endotracheal intubation with or without RSI (rapid sequence intubation)
      (2) Adjunct airway technique (jet ventilation, LMA, surgical airway) as per local institution
    (v) Establish large bore IVs
      (1) Administer colloid/crystalloid, titrate to blood pressure
    (vi) Pulse oxymetry
    (vii) Cardiac monitoring/ECG
    (viii) Portable CXR
    (ix) Blood draw
    (x) Place a loose tourniquet proximal to the reaction site, if reaction site on extremity, place extremity in dependent position
    (xi) Inject 0.1-0.2 mL 1 : 1000 epinephrine locally to the reaction site

2. Specific measures
  (a) Epinephrine:
    (i) Intramuscular (subcutaneous route acceptable) 1 : 1000
      (1) Adult: 0.3-0.5 mL every 5 min as necessary, titrated to effects
      (2) Pediatric: 0.01 mL/kg, every 5 min as necessary, titrated to effects
      (3) Alternatively, epinephrine (EpiPen) (0.3 mL) or EpiPen Jr (0.15 mL) can be administered into anterolateral thigh. Removal of clothing is unnecessary.
    (ii) Intravenous 1 : 100,000 (0.1 mL of 1 : 1000 in 10 mL of NS)
      (1) Continuous hemodynamic monitoring required
      (2) 10 mL of 1 : 100,000 over 10 min, titrated to effects, repeat as necessary
  (b) Antihistamines:
    (i) Diphenhydramine: intravenous (or oral)
      (1) Adult: 50 mg, up to 400 mg/24 hr, titrated to effects
      (2) Pediatric: 1 mg/kg, up to 300 mg/24 hr, titrated to effects
    (ii) Ranitidine: intravenous (or oral)
      (1) Adult: 50 mg
      (2) Pediatric: 1 mg/kg
  (c) Aerosolized β-agonists and others
    (i) Adult:
      (1) Albuterol: 2.5 mg, diluted to 3 mL of NS, may be given continuously
      (2) Levalbuterol: 0.625-1.25 mg, diluted to 3 mL of NS, may be given continuously
      (3) Ipratropium: 0.5 mg in 3 mL of NS, repeat as necessary
    (ii) Pediatric:
      (1) Albuterol: 2.5 mg, diluted to 3 mL of NS, may be given continuously
      (2) Levalbuterol: 0.31-0.625 mg, diluted to 3 mL of NS, may be given continuously
      (3) Ipratropium: 0.25 mg in 3 mL of NS, repeat as necessary
  (d) Methylprednisolone:
    (i) Adult: 125-250 mg IV
    (ii) Pediatric: 40-80 mg IV

3. Special situations
  (a) Refractory hypotension:
    (i) Glucagon: 1-5 mg IV over 5 min, followed by 5-15 μg/min continuous infusion
    (ii) Consider:
      (1) Discontinue epinephrine
      (2) Dopamine, 5-20 μg/kg/min continuous infusion and/or dobutamine, 5-20 μg/kg/min continuous infusion
      (3) Norepinephrine: 8-12 μg/min (2 to 3 mL/min; 4 mg added to 1000 mL of D5W provides a concentration of 4 μg/mL)
  (b) Patients on β-blockade:
    (i) Glucagon: 1-5 mg IV over 5 min, followed by 5-15 μg/min continuous infusion
    (ii) Transcutaneous pacing for bradycardia
    (iii) Atropine for bradycardia:
      (1) Adult: 0.3-0.5 mg IV/subcutaneous, to a maximum of 3 mg
      (2) Pediatric: 0.02 mg/kg IV/subcutaneous, to a maximum of 2 mg
    (iv) Isoproterenol: 0.05 to 0.2 μg/kg/min (1 to 2 mg in 500 mL of D5W, infused at a rate of 0.5 to 2 mL/min)
  (c) Refractory bronchospasm:
    (i) Aminophylline: 5.6 mg/kg loading dose IV over 20 min, followed by 0.1-1.1 mg/kg/hr continuous infusion
  (d) Hypertensive crisis due to unopposed α-blockade:
    (i) Nitroprusside: 0.3 to 10 μg/kg/min (6 μg/kg/min, neonates) continuous infusion
    (ii) Phentolamine: 5 to 20 mg IV
  (e) Dysrhythmia:
    (i) Lidocaine 1-2 mg/kg IV bolus, followed by 2 mg/min continuous infusion

---

CXR, chest x-ray; D5W, 5% dextrose in water; ECG, electrocardiogram; LMA, laryngeal mask airway; NS, normal saline.

effects of mediators on target tissues. Epinephrine, with its combined α- and β-adrenergic agonist actions, is the first drug of choice in the treatment of anaphylaxis.[74] The α-agonist effects of epinephrine increase peripheral vascular resistance and reverse peripheral vasodilation, vascular permeability, and systemic hypotension. The β-agonist effects of epinephrine produce bronchodilation, cause positive inotropic and chronotropic cardiac activity, and result in increased production of intracellular cyclic adenosine monophosphate (cAMP). Epinephrine therefore reverses bronchospasm, stimulates increased cardiac output, and inhibits further mediator release. The α- and β-agonist actions of epinephrine can also be potentially dangerous. Excessive α-agonist activity can result in a hypertensive crisis. Excessive β-agonist activity can increase myocardial oxygen consumption through increased wall tension, contractility, and chronotropism and can result in myocardial ischemia or infarction. Increased automaticity and chronotropism can produce hemodynamically significant supraventricular and ventricular tachydysrhythmia. Epinephrine should be used with caution in elders and those with known coronary artery disease and should be avoided in patients with life-threatening tachydysrhythmia.

The route of epinephrine administration depends on the severity of the clinical presentation. Subcutaneous epinephrine is usually effective in situations in which the clinical manifestations are mild and the patient is normotensive. In the patient with diffuse, generalized urticaria, subcutaneous absorption of epinephrine may be slow and unpredictable and the intramuscular route may be more efficacious.[76]

For subcutaneous and intramuscular injections, the initial dose of epinephrine is 0.01 mL/kg of a 1:1000 solution to a maximum of 0.5 mL of 1:1000 solution (0.5 mg). A fraction of the total dose (0.1 to 0.2 mL) should be administered at the site of antigenic exposure if accessible (such as a bee sting or antigen injection in an extremity).

If the patient demonstrates severe upper airway obstruction, acute respiratory failure, or shock (systolic blood pressure less than 80 mm Hg, not associated with a ventricular tachydysrhythmia), intravenous epinephrine should be administered. The risk of supraventricular, accelerated idioventricular, and ventricular tachydysrhythmia; accelerated hypertension; and myocardial ischemia, including the stunned heart syndrome, is increased by using the intravenous route with epinephrine. Because of these risks, dilution and slow administration are recommended. The initial intravenous dose should be 10 mL of a 1:100,000 dilution of aqueous epinephrine over 10 minutes. This would be equivalent to a 100-μg bolus administered at 10 μg/min for 10 minutes. If no improvement is seen, a continuous infusion should be set up. Mixing 1 mL of a 1:1000 dilution of epinephrine in 250 mL of 5% dextrose in water (D5W) results in a concentration of 4 μg/mL. This can be started at 1 μg/min and increased to 4 μg/min if needed. In children and infants, an infusion rate of 0.1 μg/kg/min is advised, increasing in increments of 0.1 μg/kg/min to a maximum of 1.5 μg/kg/min. Continuous cardiac monitoring should be used at all times. If a percutaneous intravenous line cannot be established, alternative routes are available. In addition to the subcutaneous and intramuscular routes of administration, intraosseous or sublingual injection or endotracheal nebulization should be considered. The dosage and concentration guidelines for these routes of administration of epinephrine are the same as those for intravenous administration.

Antihistamines

In addition to epinephrine, antihistamines should be used in all cases of anaphylaxis, although their role in severe or persistent cases is limited. The antihistamines competitively block the action of circulating histamines at target tissue cell receptors but have no role in decreasing mediator release and have no effect on the leukotrienes. Seven classes of H_1 antihistamines exist, and members of the ethanolamine family, such as diphenhydramine hydrochloride, and the alkylamine family, such as chlorpheniramine maleate, are potent H_1 antagonists. Diphenhydramine hydrochloride is the most commonly used H_1 antihistamine. The typical dose is 50 mg every 4 to 6 hours in adults or 5 mg/kg/day in divided doses for the pediatric population. Diphenhydramine hydrochloride orally or by intramuscular injection may be the only medication required for mild to moderate reactions. A loading dose of 1 to 2 mg/kg intravenously (IV) to a maximum of 100 mg is recommended for severe reactions, although too large a dose or too rapid administration can result in marked sedation and hypotension. Chlorpheniramine can be administered to children by the same routes at a standard dose of 10 to 20 mg or 0.35 mg/kg/day in divided doses.

Blockade of H_2 receptors may be beneficial with simultaneous H_1 antihistamine therapy.[77] H_2 antagonists may inhibit the effect of histamine on myocardial and peripheral vascular tissue. Ranitidine (50 mg IV) or other H_2 blockers should be considered, followed by an oral course as an outpatient.

Aerosolized β-Agonists

Bronchospasm refractory to epinephrine may respond to a nebulized β-agonist such as albuterol sulfate (Ventolin, Proventil), levalbuterol (Xopenex), terbutaline (Brethaire, Brethine), bitolterol (Tornalate), pirbuterol (Maxair), and or metaproterenol (Alupent 5%). Continuous nebulization of the β-agonists may be necessary for persistent bronchospasm. The use of anticholinergic therapy with ipratropium bromide (Atrovent) is an additional option in the management of acute bronchospasm. Anticholinergic medications decrease cyclic guanosine monophosphate levels, thereby decreasing mediator release and reversing the action of mediators on target tissue cells. Nebulized ipratropium bromide is used in a dose of 0.5 mg (2.5 mL of a 0.02% solution).

As a second-line therapy for refractory bronchospasm, an aminophylline bolus (5.6 mg/kg loading dose IV over 20 minutes), followed by a maintenance infusion (0.1 to 1.1 mg/kg/hr), can also be added. Aminophylline is an old drug with a narrow therapeutic window. Its main purported action is bronchodilation, although it may also act to potentiate the action of catecholamines. Side effects include atrial fibrillation, nausea, vomiting, and abdominal pain.

Corticosteroids

Systemic corticosteroids have an onset of action of approximately 4 to 6 hours after administration and therefore are of limited benefit in the acute treatment of the anaphylactic patient.[75] They are most useful in persistent bronchospasm or hypotension and should be used to prevent the biphasic reaction of anaphylaxis. Rare cases of deterioration after corticosteroid administration may be the result of anaphylactic sensitivity to this medication. An initial intravenous loading dose of hydrocortisone (Solu-Cortef), 250 mg to 1 g, or methylprednisolone (Solu-Medrol), 125 to 250 mg, followed by oral prednisone over 7 to 10 days is an acceptable regimen after the anaphylactic episode.

Vasopressors

In patients with persistent hypotension despite administration of epinephrine and large volumes of intravenous crystalloid, the use of colloid solutions (e.g., 5% albumin) should be considered in addition to crystalloid because of increased vascular permeability in anaphylaxis. If the CVP is less than 12 mm Hg, crystalloid and colloid fluids should be administered first. If the CVP is greater than 12 mm Hg, dopamine (5 μg/kg/min) should be started and titrated to effect. Dobutamine can be added if myocardial depression is judged to be an important cause of the hypotension. Other causes of elevated filling pressures other than vascular volume or myocardial dysfunction should be considered (e.g., vasopressor administration, increased intraperitoneal and intrathoracic pressures, vasoconstriction, or pulmonary artery hypertension). If the cause of hemodynamic instability is uncertain, a pulmonary artery catheter to monitor wedge pressure and cardiac output may be required to guide the administration of fluid and vasopressor. If pulmonary hypertension exists, hyperventilation, hyperoxygenation, and large doses of steroids should be considered. The use of true pressors with primarily α-adrenergic activity, such as norepinephrine, could be considered if all of these measures fail to restore the inadequate hemodynamics.

In the rare case that the anaphylactic patient develops a hypertensive crisis secondary to unopposed α- or β-adrenergic activity from the treatment, nitroprusside drips or phentolamine should be considered. Dysrhythmias from elevated circulating catecholamines can be treated with lidocaine.[16]

Patients Receiving β-Blockade

Glucagon, with positive inotropic and chronotropic cardiac effects mediated independently of α- and β-receptors, may be helpful in patients who are receiving β-blockers and who do not respond to epinephrine and antihistamines.[78] Glucagon is thought to effect positive inotropism by augmenting cAMP synthesis through a nonadrenergic pathway. The initial dose is 1 mg for adults and 0.5 mg for children subcutaneously, intramuscularly, or intravenously, and the patient may require a glucagon infusion of 1 to 5 mg/hr to sustain its therapeutic effect. Side effects include nausea, vomiting, hypokalemia, and hyperglycemia. Atropine (0.3 to 0.5 mg IV) and isoproterenol (0.05 to 0.2 μg/kg/min; 1 to 2 mg in 500 mL of D5W, infused at a rate of 0.5 to 2 mL/min) can be tried as second-line therapy. Atropine is probably more useful for bradycardia. Isoproterenol should be used as the last resort for the rare patient who is in refractory shock after all the preceding therapy.

DISPOSITION

Most patients with anaphylaxis respond to early aggressive management and can be safely discharged to home.[5] Patients with mild to moderate anaphylaxis who respond completely to the initial treatment are appropriate for discharge after an observation period of 2 to 6 hours. An oral antihistamine, such as diphenhydramine hydrochloride 25 to 50 mg every 6 hours for 48 hours, may prevent possible relapse. These patients should be instructed to return to the emergency department if their symptoms recur. They should be warned about the sedating side effects of the antihistamines. Oral H_2 blockers for 48 hours may be useful, and patients with initially persistent bronchospasm or hypotension who required initial steroid therapy should continue oral prednisone for 7 to 10 days. Patients with initially persistent bronchospasm should continue a metered-dose β-adrenergic bronchodilator inhalant (e.g., albuterol [Ventolin], metaproterenol [Alupent]). Hospital admission should be considered for patients who have experienced hypotension, upper airway involvement, prolonged bronchospasm, or other indications of a severe reaction. Although the risk of clinical deterioration after apparently complete resolution of a severe anaphylactic reaction is minimal,[79] symptoms redevelop in a small proportion of patients 24 to 48 hours after the initial systemic reaction.[80] This may be related to the high-molecular-weight neutrophil chemotactic factor–mediated late-phase reaction of the biphasic allergic response, which peaks in 4 to 12 hours and lasts up to 48 hours. Patients taking chronic β-blocker medications may be susceptible to a similar rebound after the initial therapeutic interventions resolve. These patients may be candidates for an extended observation.

Prevention

Spending a few additional minutes with the patient before discharge, obtaining an allergy history, offering environmental modifications, and educating the patient on initiating treatment for recurrence may decrease morbidity and mortality associated with subsequent episodes of anaphylaxis (Box 117-4).[8] Avoid-

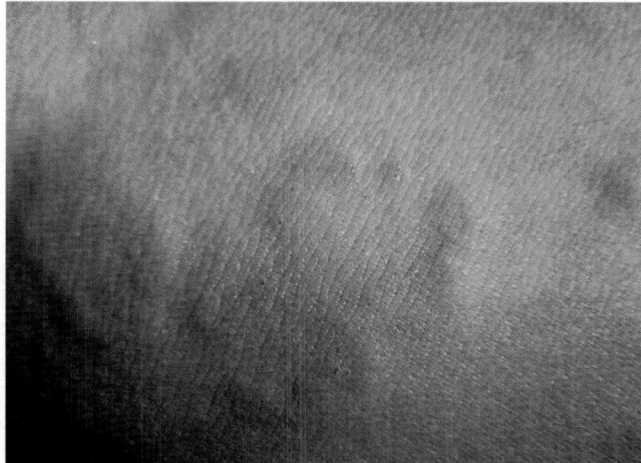

Figure 117-4. Acute urticaria. (Copyright © 2001-2003, Johns Hopkins University School of Medicine. http://dermatlas.med.jhmi.edu/derm/)

ance of antigens to which the patient is likely to be sensitive is the most important preventive measure. Obtaining a thorough personal and family drug allergy and atopic history is crucial before instituting any drug therapy, and all drugs should be correctly identified before being administered. When a drug is prescribed, a definite medical indication must be present. Whenever possible, medications should be administered orally rather than parenterally to decrease the severity of a systemic anaphylactic reaction should the patient react adversely.

Physicians who administer antigenic compounds in their medical practice must be prepared to manage an anaphylactic reaction, and resuscitation equipment should be readily available. Because most anaphylactic reactions that follow parenteral administration begin within 30 minutes, patients should be observed during this period, discharged only if completely asymptomatic, and given a warning to return for subsequent symptoms.

Human antiserum is now available for rabies, tetanus, and diphtheria; however, heterologous equine antisera is still used (e.g., for snake bites). Intradermal pretesting should be performed before treatment if time permits, as outlined in the product monographs. However, even pretesting solution can precipitate an anaphylactic reaction. Furthermore, unnecessary pretesting sensitizes predisposed patients to future hypersensitivity reactions to antiserum.

Predisposed patients who have experienced a moderate or severe anaphylactic reaction should be taught self-administration of an oral antihistamine (e.g., diphenhydramine hydrochloride) on known exposure and self-injection of epinephrine (e.g., EpiPen, Ana-Kit) at the first indication of allergic symptoms or signs. Epinephrine injection kits have a limited shelf life, which is prolonged by refrigeration. Although the true effectiveness of these kits remains unknown,[81] they should be readily available at all times, with one kit available at home, one at work or school, one in the patient's purse or briefcase, and one in the patient's automobile. Predisposed patients should be strongly encouraged to carry warning identification stating their hypersensitivity (Medic-Alert bracelet, wallet card).

Pretreatment with antihistamines and steroids significantly decreases the frequency and severity of anaphylactoid reactions in patients who have sustained a prior reaction after injection of RCM. Skin testing and hyposensitization immunotherapy by an allergist are an appropriate way to minimize the frequency and severity of subsequent anaphylactic reactions from bee stings in an appropriately sensitive population.

URTICARIA AND ANGIOEDEMA

Urticaria (hives) is a reaction that consists of papules or wheals that are nonpitting, edematous, pruritic, slightly erythematous, raised circular or annular, and range in size from millimeters to several centimeters (Figure 117-4). The centers of the wheals are usually clear and the borders can be serpiginous. The erythema is due to dilation of blood vessels in the dermal layer of the skin, and the edematous wheals are due to transudation from these blood vessels. Urticaria favors the extremities and trunk and is usually transient, with crops of hives appearing and resolving spontaneously in a matter of hours.

Angioedema is pathogenetically similar to urticaria but involves the deeper dermal and subcutaneous tissue and usually involves little pruritus. Angioedema commonly involves the face, mouth, lips, tongue, extremities, and, in men, genitalia. Recurrent episodes of angioedema and urticaria that last less than 6 weeks are considered *acute* (90%) and those that persist longer than 6 weeks are classified as *chronic* (10%). Acute urticaria tends to be associated with angioedema in about half of the cases. In about 40% of the cases, urticaria is present alone, without angioedema. In the remaining 10%, angioedema is present exclusively, without urticaria. These cases of angioedema without urticaria could be the presentation of C1 inhibitor deficiency.[82]

It should be noted that urticaria and angioedema are merely presenting symptoms and signs of potentially distinct underlying disease entities. Most of the attacks of acute urticaria and angioedema are hypersensitivity, IgE-mediated allergic reactions (similar to anaphylaxis). A variety of chemical allergens (e.g., foods, drugs, Hymenoptera venoms) and physical stimuli (e.g., dermatographism, heat, wet, cold, vibratory, exercise, solar) fit in this category. The other mechanisms include complement mediated (hereditary angioedema [HAE], serum sickness, reactions to blood products), bradykinin and substance P (angiotensin-converting enzyme [ACE] inhibitor), direct mast cell stimulation (opioids, RCM, antibiotics), and AA metabolism alteration (e.g., NSAIDS, aspirin).

HAE is an autosomal dominant condition caused by C1 esterase inhibitor deficiency or functional deficiency, which is biochemically confirmed by low levels of C4 and C1 esterase inhibitor activity. The cardinal symptoms and signs of HAE include edema of the airway, face, or extremities and abdominal pain associated with nausea, vomiting, and diarrhea. These clinical manifestations may occur singly or in combination. Trauma and stress are common precipitating factors.

The angioedema associated with ACE inhibitors has an incidence of 0.1% to 0.2% and a predilection for the tongue, lips, and laryngeal soft tissue.[83] The pathophysiology is thought to be prevention of the metabolism of bradykinin and substance P, both of which are potent mediators of tissue inflammation.[84]

The clinical evaluation of urticaria and angioedema starts with a focused search for emergency conditions, followed by a detailed history aimed at identifying the underlying cause. Life-threatening airway compromise can occur if the angioedema involves the upper airway. HAE, ACE inhibitors, thermal burn, or local allergic reaction to inhaled drugs (e.g., Quincke's disease)[85] tends to cause glossopharyngeal angioedema, resulting in upper airway obstruction or dysphagia, or both. The detailed history is aimed at eliciting exposures to foods, drugs, physical stimuli, infection (especially viral hepatitis), occupational elements, and insect stings.[82] The differential diagnosis includes evolving anaphylaxis syndrome, erythema multiforme minor, bullous pemphigoid and dermatitis herpetiformis, urticarial vasculitis, mastocytosis, HAE (C1 esterase deficiency), ACE inhibitor–associated angioedema, and serum sickness, among others. The constellation of pruritus, urticarial rash or angioedema, hypotension, and wheezing after exercise should raise the possibility of exercise-induced anaphylaxis. Angioedema of the upper extremity raises the possibility of superior vena cava syndrome. Brawny edema and shock raise the possibility of capillary leak syndrome.

Management of acute urticaria and angioedema in the emergency department is first focused on stabilizing any respiratory insufficiency and hemodynamic instability. Antihistamines (both H_1 and H_2) are the first-line therapeutic drugs. Epinephrine can be considered for moderate to severe cases but should be used with caution in patients older than 35 years to minimize the risks of precipitating an acute coronary syndrome. In the longer term, the most effective treatment of urticaria and angioedema involves removal of the etiologic factors. H_1 antihistamines such as diphenhydramine (12.5 to 100 mg per dose every 4 hours) or the nonsedating agents such as cetirizine, loratadine, or fexofenadine are the first-line drugs. Hydroxyzine (10 to 100 mg daily at bedtime) can be tried when other H_1 antihistamines are inadequate. Because 85% of histamine receptors in the skin are H_1 and 15% H_2, adding an H_2 blocker (e.g., ranitidine or cimetidine) theoretically would benefit a histamine-induced urticarial reaction.[86] Doxepin (25 to 100 mg/day) is an excellent alternative as it has both H_1 and H_2 activity. Topical steroids are of no value and systemic steroids should be reserved for pressure urticaria, vasculitis urticaria, and intractable chronic urticaria.

The treatment for HAE may require a slightly modified approach. Life-threatening acute attacks do not usually respond satisfactorily to treatment with epinephrine in normal dosage, antihistamines, or steroids. Active airway management is the mainstay of treatment. Fresh frozen plasma contains C1 inhibitor and is effective in abolishing acute attacks. High-dose epinephrine may be effective, although it should be used with caution.

MASTOCYTOSIS

Mastocytosis refers to disorders caused by too many mast cells in the body. There are two forms of mastocytosis. *Cutaneous mastocytosis*, also called urticaria pigmentosa, occurs when the mast cell hyperplasia is in the skin. Cutaneous mastocytosis is the more common form and mostly affects children. *Systemic mastocytosis* refers to the clinical syndrome caused by mast cell hyperplasia in bone marrow, gut mucosa, liver, or spleen. Pathologic fractures, osteoblastic lesions on skeletal radiographs, cutaneous pigmented lesions, abdominal pain, diarrhea, hepatosplenomegaly, lymphadenopathy, headache, flushing, anemia, and, rarely, vascular collapse (from released vasoactive substances) are some of the clinical findings in this form of mastocytosis. The diagnosis is made by a 24-hour urine collection for histamine or its metabolites or PGD_2 or serum tryptase level, supplemented by a bone scan, skeletal survey, or upper gastrointestinal workup (upper gastrointestinal series, small bowel radiograph, computed tomography scan, endoscopy). A skin or bone marrow biopsy helps confirm the diagnosis. Treatment options include steroids, interferon-α, H_1 antihistamines for pruritus and flushing (aspirin can be added if flushing is severe), H_2 blockers for dyspepsia, and tricyclics for headache.

KEY CONCEPTS

- Immune hyperreactivity is the underlying immunopathogenetic mechanism of acute allergic syndromes. Anaphylaxis is the most severe form of systemic allergic reaction in a previously sensitized individual. Foods, therapeutic agents including antibiotics, insect stings, and latex are the principal identifiable etiologic agents. Deaths from anaphylaxis most commonly result from acute respiratory failure and cardiovascular collapse.

- Rapid recognition and treatment of anaphylactic syndrome are critical to a good outcome. Although the hallmark of anaphylaxis is urticaria, acute respiratory failure and cardiovascular collapse can occur without dermatologic involvement. Mild symptoms should therefore be treated aggressively to prevent progression to more serious forms of anaphylaxis.

- Priorities should be given to airway management and stabilizing any hemodynamic instability. Epinephrine is the first drug of choice for the management of anaphylaxis. Prolonged treatment with epinephrine or glucagon may be required for patients receiving β-adrenergic blockade. Both H_1 and H_2 antihistamines should be used in all cases of anaphylaxis. Fluid, vasopressors, and inotropic agents should be instituted for refractory hypotension, guided by CVP or pulmonary catheter. Corticosteroids should be given to prevent protracted or recurrent anaphylaxis.

- Prevention of anaphylaxis by identifying and avoiding the causative agent assumes the central role in long-term management and should be discussed by the emergency physician with the patient and family before the patient's discharge.

- Urticaria and angioedema are merely presenting symptoms and signs of potentially distinct underlying disease entities. The clinical evaluation of urticaria and angioedema starts with a focused search for emergency conditions, followed by a detailed history aimed at identifying the underlying cause. Life-threatening airway compromise can occur if the angioedema involves the upper airway. Antihistamines (both H_1 and H_2) are the first-line therapeutic drugs.

REFERENCES

1. Portier P, Richet C: De l'action anaphylatique de certain venins. *C R Soc Biol* 54:170, 1902.
2. Yocum MW, et al: Epidemiology of anaphylaxis in Olmsted County: A population-based study. *J Allergy Clin Immunol* 104:452, 1999.
3. Neugut AI, Ghatak AT, Miller RL: Anaphylaxis in the United States: An investigation into its epidemiology. *Arch Intern Med* 161:15, 2001.
4. Matasar MJ, Neugut AI: Epidemiology of anaphylaxis in the United States. *Curr Allergy Asthma Rep* 3:30, 2003.
5. Yocum MW, Klein JS: Emergency room incidence of community onset anaphylaxis. *J Allergy Clin Immunol* 93:302, 1994.
6. Kemp SF, Lockey RF, Wolf BL, Lieberman P: Anaphylaxis: A review of 266 cases. *Arch Intern Med* 155:1749, 1995.
7. Barnard JH: Studies of 400 Hymenoptera sting deaths in the United States. *J Allergy Clin Immunol* 52:259, 1973.
8. Drain KL, Volcheck GW: Preventing and managing drug-induced anaphylaxis. *Drug Saf* 24:843, 2001.
9. Settipane GA, Chafee FH, Klein DE: Aspirin intolerance. II. A prospective study in an atopic and normal population. *J Allergy Clin Immunol* 53:200, 1974.
10. Hong SJ, Wong JT, Bloch KJ: Reactions to radiocontrast media. *Allergy Asthma Proc* 23:347, 2002.
11. Slater JE, Mostello LA, Shaer C, Honsinger RW: Type I hypersensitivity to rubber. *Ann Allergy* 65:411, 1990.
12. Turjanmaa K, et al: Natural rubber latex allergy. *Allergy* 51:593, 1996.
13. Liss GM, Sussman GL: Latex sensitization: Occupational versus general population prevalence rates. *Am J Ind Med* 35:196, 1999.
14. Liss GM, et al: Latex allergy: Epidemiological study of 1351 hospital workers. *Occup Environ Med* 54:335, 1997.
15. Lieberman P: Anaphylaxis and anaphylactoid reactions. In Middleton E, et al (eds): *Allergy: Clinical and Practice*. St. Louis, Mosby, 1998, pp 1079-1092.
16. Worobec AS, Metcalfe DD: Anaphylactic syndrome. In Austen KF, Frank MM, Atkinson JP, Cantor H (eds): *Samter's Immunologic Diseases*. Philadelphia, Lippincott Williams & Wilkins, 2001, pp 825-836.
17. Shearer WT, Fleisher TA: The immune system. In Middelton E, et al (eds): *Allergy: Clinical and Practice*. St. Louis, Mosby, 1998, pp 1-13.
18. Mosmann TR, et al: Two types of murine helper T cell clone. I. Definition according to profiles of lymphokine activities and secreted proteins. *J Immunol* 136:2348, 1986.
19. Umetsu DT, DeKruyff RH: Th1 and Th2 CD4+ cells in the pathogenesis of allergic diseases. *Proc Soc Exp Biol Med* 215:11, 1997.
20. Delves PJ, Roitt IM:. The immune system. First of two parts. *N Engl J Med* 343:37, 2000.
21. Sell S: Immunopathology. In Rich RR, Fleisher TA, Schwartz BD (eds): *Clinical Immunology: Principles and Practice*. St. Louis, Mosby, 1996, pp 449-477.
22. McNeil HP, Austen KF: Biology of the mast cell. In Frank MM, Austen KF, Cantor H, Atkinson JP (eds): *Samter's Immunologic Diseases*. Boston, Little Brown, 1995, pp 185-204.
23. Daeron M: Fc receptor biology. *Annu Rev Immunol* 15:203, 1997.
24. Kinet JP: The high-affinity IgE receptor (Fc epsilon RI): From physiology to pathology. *Annu Rev Immunol* 17:931, 1999.
25. Kaliner M, Shelhamer JH, Ottesen EA: Effects of infused histamine: Correlation of plasma histamine levels and symptoms. *J Allergy Clin Immunol* 69:283, 1982.
26. Morel DR, et al: Leukotrienes, thromboxane A2, and prostaglandins during systemic anaphylaxis in sheep. *Am J Physiol* 261:H782, 1991.
27. Simons FER: Antihistamines. In Middleton E, et al (eds): *Allergy: Principles and Practice*. St. Louis, Mosby, 1998, pp 612-637.
28. Felix SB, et al: Characterization of cardiovascular events mediated by platelet activating factor during systemic anaphylaxis. *J Cardiovasc Pharmacol* 15:987, 1990.
29. Lichtenstein LM: Allergy and the immune system. *Sci Am* 269(3):116, 1993.
30. Delage C, Irey NS: Anaphylactic deaths: A clinicopathologic study of 43 cases. *J Forensic Sci* 17:525, 1972.
31. Castillo R, et al: Food hypersensitivity among adult patients: Epidemiological and clinical aspects. *Allergol Immunopathol (Madr)* 24:93, 1996.
32. Wuthrich B: Adverse reactions to food additives. *Ann Allergy* 71:379, 1993.
33. Idsoe O, Guthe T, Willcox RR, Weck AD: Nature and extent of penicillin side-reactions, with particular reference to fatalities from anaphylactic shock. *Bull World Health Organ* 38:159, 1968.
34. Salkind AR, Cuddy PG, Foxworth JW: The rational clinical examination. Is this patient allergic to penicillin? An evidence-based analysis of the likelihood of penicillin allergy. *JAMA* 285:2498, 2001.

35. Alanis A, Weinstein AJ: Adverse reactions associated with the use of oral penicillins and cephalosporins. *Med Clin North Am* 67:113, 1983.

36. Patterson R, Anderson J: Allergic reactions to drugs and biologic agents. *JAMA* 248:2637, 1982.

37. Mayorga C, Torres MJ, Blanca M: Cephalosporin allergy. *N Engl J Med* 346:380, 2002.

38. Goodman EJ, et al: Cephalosporins can be given to penicillin-allergic patients who do not exhibit an anaphylactic response. *J Clin Anesth* 13:561, 2001.

39. Bernstein DI: Management of natural rubber latex allergy. *J Allergy Clin Immunol* 110(Suppl):S111, 2002.

40. McCall BP, Horwitz IB, Kammeyer-Mueller JD: Have health conditions associated with latex increased since the issuance of universal precautions? *Am J Public Health* 93:599, 2003.

41. Kim KT, Hussain H: Prevalence of food allergy in 137 latex-allergic patients. *Allergy Asthma Proc* 20:95, 1999.

42. Dibs SD, Baker MD: Anaphylaxis in children: A 5-year experience. *Pediatrics* 99:E7, 1997.

43. Patterson LJ, Milne B: Latex anaphylaxis causing heart block: Role of ranitidine. *Can J Anaesth* 46:776, 1999.

44. Agarwal S, Gawkrodger DJ: Latex allergy: A health care problem of epidemic proportions. *Eur J Dermatol* 12:311, 2002.

45. Ditto AM: Hymenoptera sensitivity: Diagnosis and treatment. *Allergy Asthma Proc* 23:381, 2002.

46. Golden DB: Stinging insect allergy. *Am Fam Physician* 67:2541, 2003.

47. Rhoades R: Stinging ants. *Curr Opin Allergy Clin Immunol* 1:343, 2001.

48. Schumacher MJ, Egen NB: Significance of Africanized bees for public health. A review. *Arch Intern Med* 155:2038, 1995.

49. Jacobs RL, Lowe RS, Lanier BQ: Adverse reactions to tetanus toxoid. *JAMA* 247:40, 1982.

50. Greineder DK: Risk management in allergen immunotherapy. *J Allergy Clin Immunol* 98:S330, 1996.

51. Butani L: Corticosteroid-induced hypersensitivity reactions. *Ann Allergy Asthma Immunol* 89:439, 2002.

52. Aldrete JA, Johnson DA: Allergy to local anesthetics. *JAMA* 207:356, 1969.

53. Glinert RJ, Zachary CB: Local anesthetic allergy. Its recognition and avoidance. *J Dermatol Surg Oncol* 17:491, 1991.

54. Kajimoto Y, et al: Anaphylactoid skin reactions after intravenous regional anaesthesia using 0.5% prilocaine with or without preservative—A double-blind study. *Acta Anaesthesiol Scand* 39:782, 1995.

55. Grammer LC: Hypersensitivity. *Nephrol Dial Transplant* 9(Suppl 2):29, 1994.

56. Shehadi WH: Adverse reactions to intravascularly administered contrast media. A comprehensive study based on a prospective survey. *Am J Roentgenol Radium Ther Nucl Med* 124:145, 1975.

57. Katayama H, et al: Adverse reactions to ionic and nonionic contrast media. A report from the Japanese Committee on the Safety of Contrast Media. *Radiology* 175:621, 1990.

58. Lieberman PL, Seigle RL: Reactions to radiocontrast material. Anaphylactoid events in radiology. *Clin Rev Allergy Immunol* 17:469, 1999.

59. Namazy JA, Simon RA: Sensitivity to nonsteroidal anti-inflammatory drugs. *Ann Allergy Asthma Immunol* 89:542, 2002.

60. Berkes EA: Anaphylactic and anaphylactoid reactions to aspirin and other NSAIDs. *Clin Rev Allergy Immunol* 24:137, 2003.

61. Simon RA: Adverse reactions to food additives. *N Engl Reg Allergy Proc* 7:533, 1986.

62. Anderson JA: Milestones marking the knowledge of adverse reactions to food in the decade of the 1980s. *Ann Allergy* 72:143, 1994.

63. Castells MC, Horan RF, Sheffer AL: Exercise-induced anaphylaxis. *Curr Allergy Asthma Rep* 3:15, 2003.

64. Castells MC, Horan RF, Sheffer AL: Exercise-induced anaphylaxis (EIA). *Clin Rev Allergy Immunol* 17:413, 1999.

65. Patterson R: Idiopathic anaphylaxis. The evolution of a disease. *Clin Rev Allergy Immunol* 17:425, 1999.

66. Patterson R, Lieberman P: Idiopathic anaphylaxis: A purely internal reaction. *Hosp Pract (Off Ed)* 31:47, 1996.

67. Fischer A, et al: Kissing and food reactions. *N Engl J Med* 347:1210, 2002.

68. Choy AC, et al: Undifferentiated somatoform idiopathic anaphylaxis: Nonorganic symptoms mimicking idiopathic anaphylaxis. *J Allergy Clin Immunol* 96:893, 1995.

69. Krasnick J, Patterson R, Harris KE: Idiopathic anaphylaxis: Long-term follow-up, cost, and outlook. *Allergy* 51:724, 1996.

70. Popa VT, Lerner SA: Biphasic systemic anaphylactic reaction: Three illustrative cases. *Ann Allergy* 53:151, 1984.

71. Viner NA, Rhamy RK: Anaphylaxis manifested by hypotension alone. *J Urol* 113:108,. 1975.

72. Constantinides P: Infiltrates of activated mast cells at the site of coronary atheromatous erosion or rupture in myocardial infarction. *Circulation* 92:1083, 1995.

73. Heilborn H, Hjemdahl P, Daleskog M, Adamsson U: Comparison of subcutaneous injection and high-dose inhalation of epinephrine—Implications for self-treatment to prevent anaphylaxis. *J Allergy Clin Immunol* 78:1174, 1986.

74. Ellis AK, Day JH: The role of epinephrine in the treatment of anaphylaxis. *Curr Allergy Asthma Rep* 3:11, 2003.

75. Ellis AK, Day JH: Diagnosis and management of anaphylaxis. *CMAJ* 169:307, 2003.

76. Simons FE, Gu X, Simons KJ: Epinephrine absorption in adults: Intramuscular versus subcutaneous injection. *J Allergy Clin Immunol* 108:871, 2001.

77. Lieberman P: The use of antihistamines in the prevention and treatment of anaphylaxis and anaphylactoid reactions. *J Allergy Clin Immunol* 86:684, 1990.

78. Javeed N, et al: Refractory anaphylactoid shock potentiated by beta-blockers. *Cathet Cardiovasc Diagn* 39:383, 1996.

79. Brady WJ Jr, et al: Multiphasic anaphylaxis: An uncommon event in the emergency department. *Acad Emerg Med* 4:193, 1997.

80. Douglas DM, Sukenick E, Andrade WP, Brown JS: Biphasic systemic anaphylaxis: An inpatient and outpatient study. *J Allergy Clin Immunol* 93:977, 1994.

81. Sicherer SH, Forman JA, Noone SA: Use assessment of self-administered epinephrine among food-allergic children and pediatricians. *Pediatrics* 105:359, 2000.

82. Joint Task Force on Practice Parameters: The diagnosis and management of urticaria: A practice parameter part I: Acute urticaria/angioedema part II: Chronic urticaria/angioedema. Joint Task Force on Practice Parameters. *Ann Allergy Asthma Immunol* 85:521, 2000.

83. Slater EE, et al: Clinical profile of angioedema associated with angiotensin converting-enzyme inhibition. *JAMA* 260:967, 1988.

84. O'Hollaren MT, Porter GA: Angiotensin converting enzyme inhibitors and the allergist. *Ann Allergy* 64:503, 1990.

85. Kestler A, Keyes L: Images in clinical medicine. Uvular angioedema (Quincke's disease). *N Engl J Med* 349:867, 2003.

86. Kaplan AP: Clinical practice. Chronic urticaria and angioedema. *N Engl J Med* 346:175, 2002.

PERSPECTIVE

Skin conditions and complaints account for an estimated 4% to 12% of all emergency department visits.[1,2] In addition to medical and family history, three factors are particularly important: onset and evolution of the skin problem, symptoms, and previous treatment. Cutaneous eruptions can be manifestations of primary dermatologic disease or can signal underlying systemic illness. Both are important because each can represent a serious threat.

For physical examination, the patient must be undressed and adequate lighting must be present. The scalp, mouth, and nails must be thoroughly examined. Although the examination depends largely on inspection, the skin should be palpated to assess the texture, consistency, and tenderness of the lesions.

Skin lesions may be divided into growths and rashes. Growths are subdivided into epidermal, pigmented, and dermal or subcutaneous proliferative processes. Rashes may be divided into two groups, depending on whether the epidermis is involved. Lesions and rashes with epidermal involvement include eczematous rashes; scaling; and vesicular, papular, pustular, and hypopigmented rashes. Rashes without epidermal involvement include erythema, purpura, and induration. The diagnosis is aided by the configuration of the lesions and their distribution on the body's surface. Occasionally, a configuration is specific for a disease; however, the morphology of the primary lesion is usually given more diagnostic weight (Table 118-1). Finally, many skin diseases have preferential areas of involvement, so the location of the eruption may aid in diagnosis.

SCALES, PLAQUES, AND PATCHES

Fungal Infection

Principles of Disease

The dermatophytoses are superficial fungal infections that are limited to the skin. A variety of lesions may occur, but the most common are scaling, erythematous papules, plaques, and patches, which often have a serpiginous or wormlike border.[3] Dermatophytes generally grow best in excessive heat and moisture and grow only in the keratin or outer layer of the skin, nails, and hair. Keratin tends to accumulate in body folds, such as between the toes and in the inguinal area, the axilla, and the inframammary areas. With the exception of

tinea capitis, dermatophyte infections are not markedly contagious.[3]

Any eruption thought to be a dermatophyte infection can be examined under the microscope in a potassium hydroxide (KOH) preparation. The specimen is examined for the characteristic branching hyphae of the dermatophytes or the short, thick hyphae and clustered spores of tinea versicolor.[4] Affected hair, nail, or scales may be cultured with Sabouraud agar incubated at room temperature for 2 to 3 weeks.[5]

Tinea Capitis

Clinical Features

Tinea capitis is a fungal infection of the scalp. Though primarily regarded as a disease of preschool children, tinea capitis is increasingly being recognized in adults, infants, and neonates. It is more common in African Americans than other racial groups, but the reasons for this predilection are unknown.[6] The current epidemic in the United States caused by *Trichophyton tonsurans* differs from the epidemic of the 1940s and 1950s caused by *Microsporum audouinii* in that many patients have seborrheic-like scaling in the absence of alopecia.[6] Clinically, "black dots" representing hair broken off near the scalp may be noted.[7,8] Hair loss occurs because hyphae grow within the shaft and render it fragile so that the hair strands break off 1 to 2 mm above the scalp. Circular patches of partial baldness may result. The disease may be transmitted by close child-to-child contact and contact with household pets, hats, combs, barber's shears, and similar items. Complications include lymphadenitis, bacterial pyoderma, tinea corporis, pigmenting pityriasis alba, "id" reaction after treatment, secondary bacterial infection, and scarring alopecia.[6]

Differential Considerations

The differential diagnosis of tinea capitis includes alopecia areata, atopic dermatitis, nummular eczema, bacterial infection, psoriasis, seborrheic dermatitis, "tinea" amiantacea, trichotillomania (hair pulling), and Langhans cell histiocytosis.

Diagnostic Strategies

A KOH preparation is not helpful in the case of kerion or if no alopecia exists, and a fungal culture should be obtained.[9] A bacterial culture should be considered in the case of kerion to exclude superinfection.[5,9] A toothbrush, Papanicolaou smear cytology brush,[10] or moistened cotton swab[11] is helpful for obtaining quick, painless sampling of large areas of the scalp.[10-12]

Table 118-1. Definitions of Skin Lesions

Lesion	Appearance
Macule	Flat; color differs from surrounding skin
Patch	A macule with surface changes (i.e., scale or wrinkling)
Papule	Elevated skin lesion <0.5 cm in diameter
Plaque	Elevated skin lesion >0.5 cm in diameter; without substantial depth
Nodule	Elevated skin lesion >0.5 cm in diameter and depth
Cyst	Nodule filled with expressible material
Vesicle	Blisters <0.5 cm in diameter filled with clear fluid
Bullae	Blisters >0.5 cm in diameter filled with clear fluid
Pustule	Vesicle filled with cloudy or purulent fluid
Crust	Liquid debris that has dried on the skin surface; usually moist and yellowish brown
Scale	Visibly thickened stratum corneum; usually white
Lichenification	Epidermal thickening characterized by visible and palpable skin thickening and accentuated skin markings
Induration	Dermal thickening that *feels* thick and firm
Wheal	Papule or plaque of dermal edema; often with central pallor and irregular borders
Erythema	Red appearance of skin caused by vasodilation of dermal blood vessels; blanchable
Purpura	Red appearance of skin caused by blood extravasated from disrupted dermal blood vessels; nonblanchable
Macular purpura	Flat, nonpalpable
Papular purpura	Elevated, palpable

Modified from Lookingbill DP, Marks JG: *Principles of Dermatology*, 3rd ed. Philadelphia, WB Saunders, 1993.

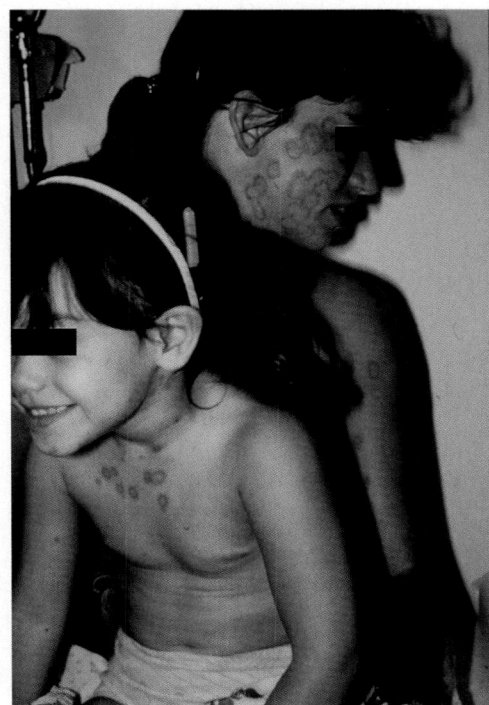

Figure 118-1. Tinea corporis. (Courtesy of David Effron, MD.)

Management

Systemic therapy is required for tinea capitis. Treatment usually begins with griseofulvin, 20 mg/kg/day, taken as a single dose with fat-containing food for a minimum of 6 weeks, or 2 weeks after clinical resolution of the inflammation.[5,9] Patients should be referred for monthly follow-up evaluation. Higher dosages may be needed. Alternative therapy includes fluconazole, 200 mg/day (adults) or 3 to 5 mg/kg/day (children), itraconazole, 200 mg daily (adults) and 3 to 5 mg/kg/day (children) for 4 to 6 weeks, oral terbinafine, 3 to 6 mg/kg/day for 4 to 6 weeks, or terbinafine cream, once a day for 8 weeks.[5,9,13,14] Selenium sulfide shampoo, 250 mg twice weekly, decreases shedding of spores.[9] Family members should be evaluated.

Kerion

A kerion is a dermatophytic infection, usually of the scalp, that appears as an indurated, boggy inflammatory plaque studded with pustules.[3] It is commonly confused with bacterial infections. Kerion should be treated as tinea capitis, with the addition of prednisone, 1 mg/kg/day for 1 to 2 weeks, to help decrease the inflammatory reaction and subsequent scarring.[6,15,16] If bacterial superinfection exists, oral

cephalexin or dicloxacillin can be added for the first week of treatment.[9]

Tinea Corporis

Clinical Features

Tinea corporis is the classic "ringworm" infection. It affects the arms, legs, and trunk and is classically a sharply marginated, annular lesion with raised or vesicular margins and central clearing (Figure 118-1). Lesions may be single or multiple, the latter occasionally being concentric. Tinea cruris, which involves the groin, is similar in appearance and may also include the perineum, thighs, and buttocks, but the scrotum is characteristically spared.

Differential Considerations

The differential diagnosis of tinea cruris includes granuloma, annular psoriasis, intertrigo with secondary candidiasis, and erythrasma.[17]

Management

Infections of the body, groin, and extremities usually respond to topical measures alone.[17] A number of effective topical antifungal agents are available, including clotrimazole (Lotrimin), haloprogin (Halotex), miconazole (Micatin), tolnaftate (Tinactin), terbinafine, naftifine, and griseofulvin 1%. Two or three daily applications of the cream form of any of these preparations results in healing of most superficial lesions in 1 to 3 weeks.[5,9,18-20] Acute inflammatory lesions displaying oozing or blisters should additionally be treated (four times a day) with open, wet compresses of Burow's solution—an aluminum acetate solution that is useful

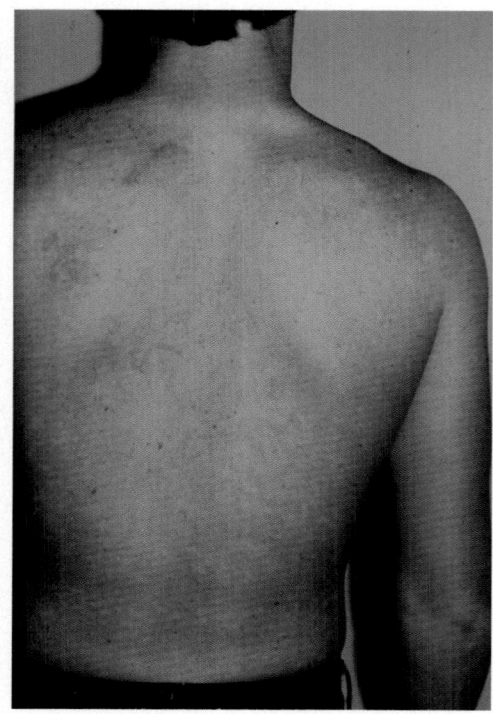

Figure 118-2. Tinea versicolor. (Courtesy of David Effron, MD.)

as a soothing wet dressing for inflammatory skin conditions. The feet and toenails are often involved.[5]

Tinea Pedis

Tinea pedis, or athlete's foot, is characterized by scaling, maceration, vesiculation, and fissuring between the toes and on the plantar surface of the foot. In extensive cases, the entire sole may be involved. A secondary bacterial infection may occur. The vesicular pustular form of tinea pedis should be considered when vesicles and pustules are noted on the instep. The differential diagnosis includes contact dermatitis and dyshidrotic eczema. A KOH preparation should help differentiate between these processes. Treatment is similar to that for tinea corporis.[21]

Tinea Versicolor

Clinical Features

Tinea versicolor is a superficial yeast infection caused by *Pityrosporum ovale*.[22] Superficial scaling patches occur mainly on the chest and trunk but may extend to the head and limbs. As the name implies, lesions can be a variety of colors, including pink, tan, or white.[3] The disease may be associated with pruritus, but medical care is often sought because the spots do not tan. On physical examination, a fine subtle scale is noted that may appear hypopigmented (Figure 118-2). Pale yellow or orange fluorescence under Wood's light is sometimes present. The differential diagnosis includes vitiligo and seborrheic dermatitis. A KOH preparation reveals short hyphae mixed with spores ("chopped spaghetti and meatballs").

Management

Tinea versicolor is treated with 2.5% selenium sulfide shampoo, imidazole cream, or oral ketoconazole as a single 400-mg dose or 200 mg daily for 3 to 5 days.[5,22-24] Recurrence rates vary from 15% to 50% and are considered the rule rather than the exception.[22] Monthly prophylaxis with propylene glycol and water, selenium shampoo, or azole creams can help prevent recurrences.[9,22] Pigmentation may not return to normal for months.

Tinea Unguium

Clinical Features

Tinea unguium results in nails that are opaque, thickened, cracked, and crumbled. Subungual debris is present, and the nail may contain yellowish longitudinal streaks. The nail of the great toe is most commonly involved. Involvement of all the nails of the hands and feet is rare.

Management

Topical therapy for the nails alone rarely results in cure because penetration into the nail keratin is poor. Fingernails typically respond more rapidly to therapy than toenails do. Oral griseofulvin and ketoconazole require prolonged courses but are associated with high relapse rates and numerous side effects.[24] Newer agents such as itraconazole, fluconazole, and terbinafine are safer and more effective. They also offer shorter treatment periods, thus improving compliance.[24] The infection may be resistant to this regimen as well, however, and surgical removal of the nail is occasionally required.[17] Recurrence is common.

Candidiasis

Perspective

Infection by *Candida albicans* can occur in infancy; old age; persons with acquired immunodeficiency syndrome (AIDS), pregnancy, obesity, malnutrition, diabetes and other endocrine imbalances, and malignancy; and those with other debilitating illnesses. Patients treated with corticosteroids, immunosuppressive agents, and antibiotics are also prone to cutaneous fungal infections.

Oral Thrush

Clinical Features

Oral thrush is the most common clinical expression of *Candida* infection.[25] Thrush occurs most commonly in newborns, with a third being affected by the first week of life. The appearance is that of patches of white or gray friable material covering an erythematous base on the buccal mucosa, gingiva, tongue, palate, or tonsils. Fissures or crust at the corners of the mouth may be present. Oral mucous membrane infection with *C. albicans* is an AIDS-defining illness.[9] Immunosuppression should be considered in the absence of dentures or antibiotic use. The differential diagnosis of oral thrush includes lichen planus, which is not as easily scraped off as *C. albicans*.

Management

Treatment of oral thrush involves painting the mouth with 1 mL of oral nystatin suspension (100,000 U/mL) four times a day for infants or 4 to 6 mL four times a day swish and swallow for older children and adults. Treatment should be continued for 5 to 7 days after the lesions disappear. Clotrimazole troches dissolved in the mouth two to five times daily is a preferable treatment option for adults.[3] If topical therapy is not effective or in patients with chronic candidiasis, oral ketoconazole, itraconazole, or fluconazole may be prescribed.[25]

Patients with oral candidiasis because of dentures should soak their dentures overnight in dilute (1:10) sodium hypochlorite solution.[3]

Cutaneous Candidiasis

Clinical Features

Cutaneous candidiasis favors the moisture and maceration of the intertriginous areas—the interdigital web spaces, groin, axilla, and intergluteal and inframammary folds. Lesions appear as moist, bright red macules rimmed with a collarette of scale, which represents the pustule roof with scalloped borders. Small satellite papules or pustules are located just peripheral to the main body of the rash. These satellite lesions are the most typical indicators of a *Candida* infection. Intertriginous lesions are prone to bacterial superinfection.

Candidal onychia and paronychia are occupational conditions in those whose hands are frequently immersed in hot water. These infections also occur with thumb sucking by children who have thrush. The paronychial area becomes red and swollen and the nails thick and brittle, with transverse ridging. Destruction of the nail plate may occur.

Differential Considerations and Diagnostic Strategies

The differential diagnosis of cutaneous candidiasis includes contact dermatitis, tinea cruris, intertrigo, malaria, and folliculitis. Candidiasis, however, is less sharply demarcated than tinea cruris and brighter red than intertrigo. A KOH preparation taken from a pustule and roof of the lesion will reveal hyphae and pseudohyphae.

Management

Treatment of intertriginous lesions requires the removal of excessive moisture and maceration. Lesions should be exposed to circulating air from a fan several times a day. Inflammatory lesions should be soaked in or covered with compresses of cool water or Burow's solution. Topical imidazole creams such as clotrimazole and miconazole should be applied sparingly to affected areas. Prescription creams such as econazole, ketoconazole, or sulconazole are also effective.

Protecting the hands from water is an integral part of the treatment of candidal paronychia. Prolonged immersion should be avoided and contact with water prevented by gloves with cotton liners. Nystatin or clotrimazole cream should be applied frequently to the nail folds for 6 to 8 weeks. A search for an underlying immunocompromising condition should begin in patients with chronic, recurrent candidiasis.

SCALY PAPULES

Fungal lesions are typically scaly, as are lesions of secondary syphilis. Additional scaly diseases are discussed next.

Pityriasis Rosea

Pityriasis rosea is a mild skin eruption predominantly found in children and young adults. The lesions are multiple pink or pigmented oval papules or plaques 1 to 2 cm in diameter on the trunk and proximal ends of the extremities. Mild scaling may be present. The lesions are parallel to the ribs and form a Christmas tree–like distribution on the trunk. Oral lesions are rare. In children, papular or vesicular variants of the disease may occur.[3]

In half the cases, the generalized eruption is preceded by a week by the appearance of a "herald patch," which is a larger lesion, 2 to 6 cm in diameter, that resembles the smaller lesions in other respects. The eruption is usually asymptomatic, although pruritus may be present.

Pityriasis rosea is self-limited and resolves in 8 to 12 weeks. Its cause is unknown, although a virus is suspected. The differential diagnosis includes tinea corporis, guttate psoriasis, lichen planus, drug eruption, and secondary syphilis. Recurrences are rare. Treatment is usually unnecessary, except for symptomatic alleviation of bothersome pruritus.

Atopic Dermatitis

Principles of Disease

Atopic dermatitis is the cutaneous manifestation of an atopic state, and although it is not in itself an allergic disorder, it is associated with allergic diseases such as asthma and allergic rhinitis. Patients with atopic dermatitis are known to have abnormalities in both humoral and cell-mediated immunity.[25] The exact mechanism is unclear, but eosinophil, mast cell, and lymphocyte activation triggered by increased production of interleukin-4 by specific T helper cells seems to be involved. Increased IgE levels are found in most, but not all patients with atopic dermatitis, but there is poor correlation between the severity of the dermatitis and the serum IgE level.[25] The course of atopic dermatitis involves remissions and exacerbations.

Clinical Features

Skin lesions appear as thickened inflammatory papular or papulovesicular lichenification and hyperpigmentation.[26,27] The skin is typically dry and may be scaly, but in the acute phase it may also be vesicular, weeping, or oozing. The distribution of lesions varies with the age of the patient. In infants, inflammatory exudative plaques are seen on the cheeks and extensor surfaces and in the diaper area. Older children and adults have lesions in the antecubital and popliteal flexion areas, neck, face, and upper part of the chest. Infantile atopic dermatitis usually begins in the fourth to sixth month of life and improves by the third to fifth year. The childhood form occurs between 3 and 6 years of age and resolves spontaneously or continues into the adult form.[26]

Intense pruritus is a hallmark of atopic dermatitis. The itching may be focal or generalized, is worse during the winter, and is triggered by increased body temperature and emotional stress. It may be particularly annoying at night. Excoriations may be prominent, and secondary bacterial infection of excoriated lesions is common. Repeated scratching and rubbing produce lichenification, a condition characterized by hyperpigmentation, thickening of the skin, and accentuation of skin furrows. Lichenification is a common feature of chronic atopic dermatitis.

Differential Considerations

The differential diagnosis of infantile atopic dermatitis includes histiocytosis X, Wiskott-Aldrich syndrome, chronic seborrheic dermatitis, phenylketonuria, Bruton's X-linked agammaglobulinemia, psoriasis, and scabies. Fixed drug eruptions and contact dermatitis round out the differential diagnosis regardless of age.[25,26] Complications of atopic dermatitis include pyogenic skin infections, otitis externa, cataracts, keratoconus, retinal detachment, and cutaneous viral infections.

Management

Treatment should be aimed at controlling inflammation, dryness, and itching. Skin dryness may be treated by the application of lubricating ointments such as Vaseline or 10% urea in Eucerin cream (not lotion). Treatment of exudative areas includes the application of wet dressings. Such dressings are useful for their moisturizing, anti-inflammatory, and antipruritic actions. Two to three layers of gauze soaked in Burow's solution should be applied for 15 to 20 minutes four times a day. Antihistamines may be helpful in reducing the pruritus and are also useful for their sedative and soporific effects.

Topical corticosteroids are the cornerstone of therapy and should be prescribed in ointment form. When the dermatitis is severe, a fluorinated corticosteroid ointment such as half-strength betamethasone valerate should be applied to affected areas of the body three times a day. Fluorinated corticosteroids should not be used on the face because they can produce permanent cutaneous atrophy. Milder corticosteroid preparations, such as 0.025% triamcinolone ointment, may be used on the face and intertriginous areas. Patients with extremely severe disease may require systemic steroids. Ultraviolet B treatment is moderately effective, although its mechanism of action is not well understood.[26]

Cyclosporine and other immunosuppressant agents are being used with some promising benefit. Further studies are needed to determine the ideal dosing and safety profiles for these agents.[26]

PUSTULES

Impetigo

Principles of Disease

Impetigo is a slowly evolving pustular eruption, most common in preschool children. Currently, *Staphylococcus aureus* is the most common pathogen, with group A streptococcus a distant second.[28] Poor health and hygiene, malnutrition, and various antecedent dermatoses, especially atopic dermatitis, predispose individuals to impetigo.

Clinical Features

Streptococcal impetigo is found most often on the face and other exposed areas. The eruption frequently begins as a single pustule but develops into multiple 1- to 2-mm vesicles with erythematous margins. When these lesions break, they leave red erosions covered with a golden yellow crust. Lesions may be pruritic but are not usually painful. Regional lymphadenopathy is commonly present. Lesions are very contagious in infants and young children and less so in older children and adults. Postpyodermal acute glomerulonephritis is a recognized complication of streptococcal impetigo.

Staphylococcal impetigo may be differentiated from streptococcal impetigo (ecthyma) by little surrounding erythema in the staphylococcal infection that is more superficial.[3] Other diagnostic considerations are herpes simplex virus (HSV) and inflammatory fungal infections. A Gram stain performed on fluid from the weepy erosion after removing the crust will reveal gram-positive cocci.

Bullous impetigo is caused by staphylococci infected by phage group 2. This form is seen primarily in infants and young children. The initial skin lesions are thin-walled, 1- to 2-cm bullae. When these bullae rupture, they leave a thin serous crust and collarette-like remnant of the blister roof at the rim of the crust. The face, neck, and extremities are most often affected. The differential diagnosis is contact dermatitis, HSV infection, superficial fungal infection, and pemphigus vulgaris. A Gram stain of the fluid from a bulla reveals gram-positive cocci. Cultures are positive 95% of the time.

Management

Both systemic therapy and topical therapy are equally successful in treating impetigo.[28-30] For more extensive lesions, systemic treatment should be used. There is no evidence, however, that systemic antibiotics prevent the development of acute glomerulonephritis.[28,31] The efficacy of topical 2% mupirocin ointment applied three times a day and oral erythromycin, 250 mg four times a day for 10 days in adults or 30 mg/kg/day in children, or cephalexin, 30 to 40 mg/kg/day three times a day for 7 to 10 days, is similar.[9,28-31]

Therapy for bullous impetigo consists of an oral penicillinase-resistant semisynthetic penicillin such as dicloxacillin, 250 mg four times a day for 5 to 7 days in adults, or erythromycin, 250 mg four times a day in adults or 30 to 50 mg/kg/day in children. If the infection is limited to a small area, 2% mupirocin ointment three times a day may be applied. Without treatment, impetigo heals within 3 to 6 weeks.[28-32]

Folliculitis

Clinical Features

Folliculitis is an inflammation in the hair follicle usually caused by *S. aureus*. It appears as a pustule with a central hair. Lesions are usually located on the buttocks and thighs, occasionally in the beard or scalp, and may cause mild discomfort. The differential diagnosis includes acne, keratosis pilaris, and fungal infection. Gram-negative folliculitis with *Pseudomonas aeruginosa* occurs with infected hot tubs and swimming pools or in individuals taking antibiotics for acne and can be differentiated from staphylococcal folliculitis by a Gram stain of the lesion.

Management

Treatment with an antiseptic cleanser such as povidone-iodine or chlorhexidine every day or every other day for several weeks is generally adequate. For patients with extensive involvement, a 10-day course of erythromycin, 250 mg four times a day, or dicloxacillin, 250 mg four times a day, may be added.[3,30,31]

Hidradenitis Suppurativa

Hidradenitis suppurativa affects the apocrine sweat glands. Recurrent abscess formation in the axillae and groin resembles localized furunculosis. The condition tends to be recurrent and may be extremely resistant to therapy. Hidradenitis suppurativa may be treated by drainage of abscesses. Antistaphylococcal antibiotics are useful if administered early and for a prolonged period.[9] Many cases do not respond, however, and eventually require local excision and skin grafting of the involved area. Antiandrogen therapy may be considered if antibiotics do not produce improvement.[9]

Carbuncle

A carbuncle is a large abscess that develops in the thick, inelastic skin of the back of the neck, back, or thighs. Carbuncles produce severe pain and fever. Septicemia may accompany the lesions. The diagnosis of skin abscess, furuncle, or carbuncle is usually made clinically.

Local heat should be applied to furuncles and carbuncles, which should be incised and drained when fluctuant. Antibiotics are unnecessary with incision and drainage unless cellulitis or septicemia is present.

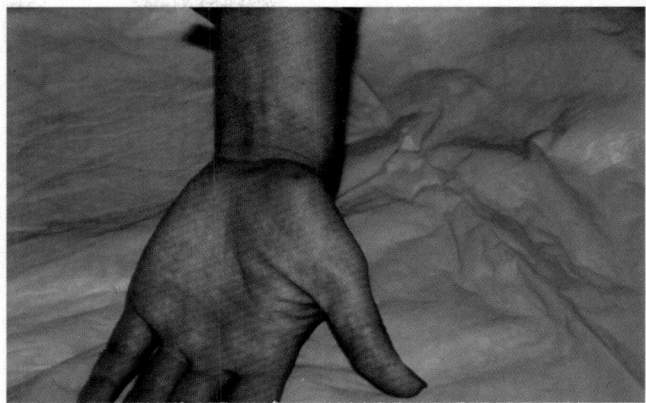

Figure 118-3. Typical skin lesions of disseminated gonococcal disease. (Courtesy of David Effron, MD.)

Gonococcal Dermatitis

Clinical Features

The arthritis-dermatitis syndrome is the most common manifestation of disseminated gonococcal disease.[33,34] It occurs in 1% to 2% of patients with gonorrhea and primarily affects women.[33] Fever and migratory polyarthralgia commonly accompany the skin lesions. The lesions are often multiple and have a predilection for the periarticular regions of the distal ends of extremities.[33]

The lesions begin as erythematous or hemorrhagic papules that evolve into pustules and vesicles with an erythematous halo (Figure 118-3). They closely resemble the lesions of meningococcemia at this stage. They are tender and may have a gray necrotic or hemorrhagic center. Healing with crust formation generally occurs within 4 to 5 days, although recurrent crops of lesions may appear even after antibiotic therapy has been started.[33]

Diagnostic Strategies

The lesions usually have a negative culture for gonococci, and Gram stain only occasionally reveals the organisms. A more reliable diagnostic technique is immunofluorescent antibody staining of direct smears from pustules.[33] This method indicates that the lesions may be the result of hematogenous dissemination of nonviable gonococci.[33]

Management

Current treatment of disseminated gonococcal infection is ceftriaxone, 1 g intramuscularly (IM) or intravenously (IV) every 24 hours, or ceftizoxime or cefotaxime, 1 g IV every 8 hours. Patients allergic to β-lactam antibiotics may be treated with spectinomycin, 2 g IM every 12 hours. A total of 7 days of antibiotic therapy is required, with the remaining course consisting of cefixime, 400 mg twice a day, cefuroxime or ciprofloxacin, 500 mg twice a day, or ofloxacin, 400 mg twice a day. Ciprofloxacin and ofloxacin are not recommended for preg-

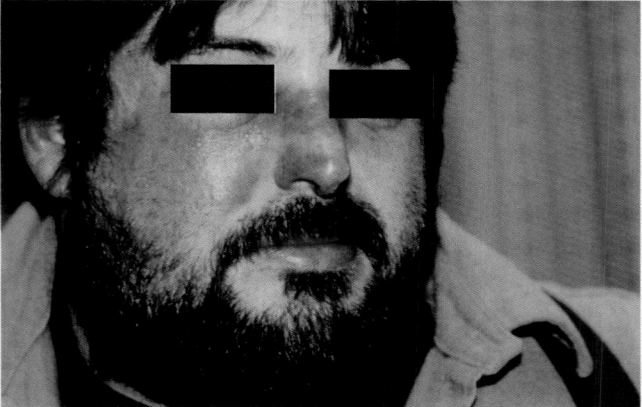

Figure 118-4. Facial cellulitis. (Courtesy of David Effron, MD.)

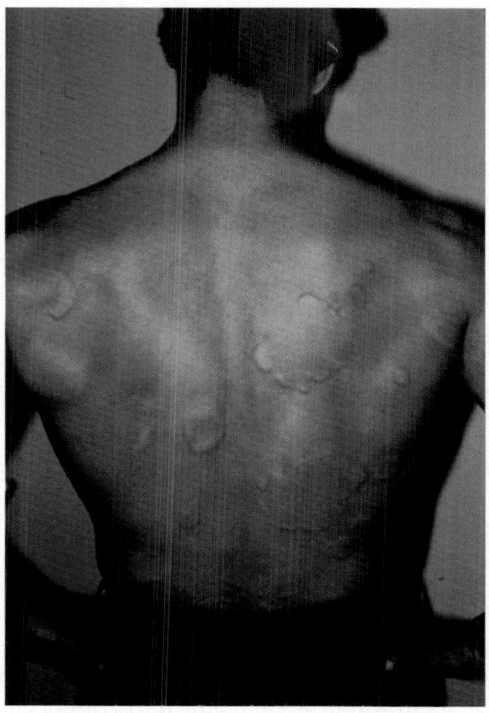

Figure 118-5. Urticaria (hives). (Courtesy of David Effron, MD.)

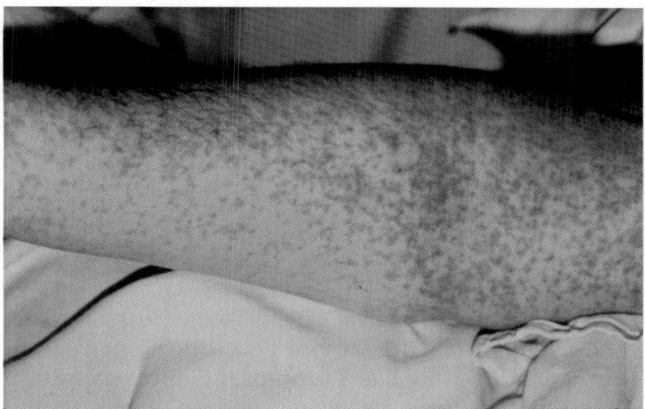

Figure 118-6. Morbilliform drug eruption. (Courtesy of David Effron, MD.)

nant women or children younger than 17 years.[33,34] Hospitalization is recommended for patients in whom the diagnosis is uncertain and for those who have septic arthritis, meningitis, or endocarditis.

ERYTHEMA

Cellulitis is an infection of the skin tissue denoted by erythema, swelling, and local tenderness (Figure 118-4).[35-39] Erysipelas is a streptococcal infection of the skin and subcutaneous tissue. The involved area is red, indurated, and edematous.[40] These disorders are covered in Chapter 131.

RED MACULES

Drug Eruption

Principles of Disease

A given drug can produce a skin eruption with a different appearance in different patients or a different appearance in the same patient on different occasions. The most common eruptions are urticaria (hives) (Figure 118-5) and, more commonly, morbilliform rashes (Figure 118-6).

Drug reactions tend to appear within a week after the drug is taken, with the exception of reactions to semisynthetic penicillins, which commonly occur later. Skin lesions may appear after use of a drug has been discontinued and may worsen if the drug or its metabolites persist in the system. Special note should be made of penicillin because it is the most frequent cause of a drug reaction. Serum sickness and urticaria are the most common manifestations of penicillin allergy. Atopic patients and those with a history of hay fever, asthma, or eczema are at special risk.

In contrast, a number of drugs in common use rarely produce eruptions. Among these medications are acetaminophen, aluminum hydroxide (Maalox), codeine, digoxin, erythromycin, ferrous sulfate, meperidine (Demerol), morphine, and prednisone.

Clinical Features

Some of the more frequent skin reactions produced by commonly used drugs are listed in Table 118-2. *Exanthematous drug eruptions* resemble the skin manifestations of various viral or bacterial infections and are usually widespread symmetrical maculopapular eruptions. Severe cases may progress to exfoliative dermatitis.

Eczematous drug rashes resemble those of contact dermatitis but are generally more extensive. They begin as erythematous or papular eruptions that may become vesicular. Previous sensitization to a topical medication is common in patients with this type of eruption.

Vasculitic lesions begin as erythematous papules or nodules but may ulcerate and become gangrenous. Purpuric drug eruptions may be the result of bone marrow

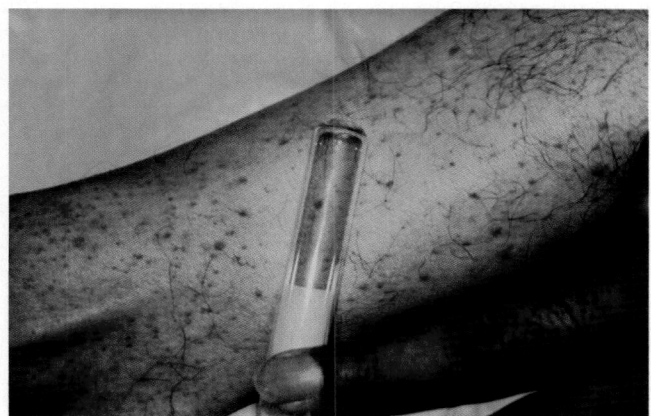

Figure 118-7. Purpuric lesions. (Courtesy of David Effron, MD.)

suppression, platelet destruction, or vasculitis (Figure 118-7). In severe cases, inpatient management with systemic corticosteroid administration, platelet transfusion, plasmapheresis, or splenectomy may be necessary.

Photosensitive drug reactions require the presence of sunlight and are seen most frequently on sun-exposed areas of skin. This class of reactions is commonly divided into phototoxic and photoallergic reactions, with phototoxic reactions occurring more frequently. Sulfonamides, sulfonylureas, thiazide diuretics, and tetracyclines are common causes (see Figure 118-7). This type of reaction does not primarily involve immunologic mechanisms and occurs in any person taking an adequate quantity of the drug and exposed to sunlight. The lesions usually have the appearance of a severe sunburn but may be bullous or papular. Pruritus is typically minimal or absent.[41]

Photoallergic reactions are precipitated by the development of antigen that results in the formation of sensitized lymphocytes. These reactions therefore represent a delayed immunologic response. A photoallergic reaction occurs only in sensitized individuals, usually 2 weeks or longer after exposure to the drug and sunlight. Its occurrence is not dose related, and the eruption usually appears eczematous and is intensely pruritic. Chlorpromazine, promethazine, and chlordiazepoxide are common sensitizers of photoallergic reactions.[41]

Inciting drugs should be withdrawn from patients with photoallergic reactions. Patients who are subject to photosensitive drug eruptions may be required to avoid prolonged sunlight exposure. Sunscreen containing 5% *p*-aminobenzoic acid should be used during any such exposure.

Fixed drug eruptions appear and recur at the same anatomic site after repeated exposure to the same drug. The lesions are usually sharply marginated and round or oval. They may be pigmented, erythematous, or violaceous. Pruritus may be prominent.

Differential Considerations

The differential diagnosis of drug eruptions includes viral exanthem, chronic exfoliative erythroderma caused by psoriasis or atopic dermatitis, malignancy, scarlet fever, staphylococcal scarlatiniform eruptions, and Kawasaki's syndrome.[9,41]

Management

Treatment of drug eruptions should begin with discontinuation of the inciting agent. Patients should be warned that drug eruptions clear *slowly* after discontinuation of the offending agent. Itching may be treated with the application of a drying antipruritic lotion such as calamine. Cool compresses, tepid water baths with colloidal oatmeal (Aveeno) emollient or cornstarch, and diphenhydramine (Benadryl), 50 mg (5 mg/kg/24 hr in children) every 6 hours, are likely to be beneficial.

Staphylococcal Scalded Skin Syndrome

Clinical Features

Staphylococcal scalded skin syndrome generally occurs in children 6 years of age or younger. It is caused by an infection with phage group 2 exotoxin-producing staphylococci. The illness begins with erythema and crusting around the mouth. The erythema then spreads down the body, followed by bulla formation and desquamation. The mucous membranes are not usually involved, but minimal involvement is occasionally seen. After desquamation occurs, the lesions dry up quickly, with clinical resolution in 3 to 7 days.

Management

Most group 2 toxin-producing organisms are penicillin resistant. Although most patients recover without antibiotic treatment, intravenous therapy with 50 to 100 mg/kg of nafcillin daily or oral cloxacillin, 50 mg/kg/day, or dicloxacillin is recommended.[9,42,43]

Toxic Epidermal Necrolysis

Principles of Disease

The main feature of non–staphylococcal-induced toxic epidermal necrolysis, or Lyell's disease, is separation of large sheets of epidermis from the underlying dermis. The full thickness of epidermis is involved. The two conditions are easily histologically distinguishable with a skin biopsy (Figure 118-8). A mortality rate of 15% to 20% is expected with this condition.[41]

Drugs, including the long-acting sulfa drugs, penicillin, aspirin, barbiturates, phenytoin, carbamazepine, allopurinol, and nonsteroidal anti-inflammatory drugs, are an important cause of toxic epidermal necrolysis. It has occurred after vaccination and immunization against poliomyelitis, measles, smallpox, diphtheria, and tetanus. It has also been found in association with lymphoma.

Clinical Features

Mucosal lesions may precede the cutaneous involvement. Patients have a positive Nikolsky sign at the site, where minor rubbing results in desquamation of the underlying skin, including the pigment. This finding is

Table 118-2. Types of Lesions Characteristically Caused by Commonly Used Drugs

Therapeutic Agents	Type of Eruption			
	Exanthematous	**Urticarial***	**Erythema Multiforme†**	**Toxic Epidermal Necrolysis**
Aminophylline				
Anovulatory drugs		X		
Barbiturates	X	X	X	X
Bromides		X	X	
Chloramphenicol		X		
Insulin	X	X		
Iodides		X	X	
Isoniazid	X	X		
Meprobamate	X	X		
Penicillin	X	X	X	X
Phenacetin				
Phenolphthalein		X	X	X
Phenothiazines	X	X	X	
Phenylbutazone	X	X		X
Quinidine	X	X	X	
Quinine	X	X		
Salicylates	X	X	X	
Sulfonamides	X	X	X	X
Tetracycline	X	X		X
Thiazides	X		X	
Others	Chloral hydrate	Opiates	Tolbutamide, phenytoin	Tolbutamide

*The most common causes of drug-induced urticaria are aspirin and penicillins.
†The long-acting sulfonamides have been linked to Stevens-Johnson syndrome.

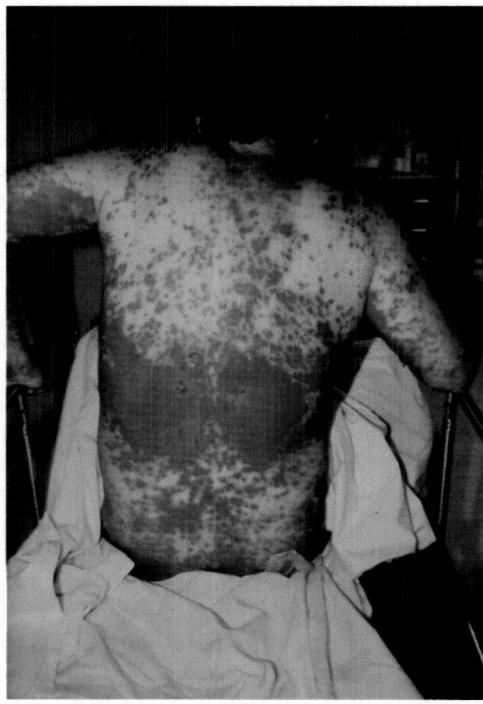

Figure 118-8. Toxic epidermal necrolysis. (Courtesy of David Effron, MD.)

contrary to staphylococcal scalded skin syndrome, in which substantial pigment remains. The onset is usually on the face, and mucous membrane involvement is the rule. Involvement of the eyes may be particularly troublesome and even result in permanent injury. The erythema usually precedes loosening of the epidermis.

Management

Treatment of toxic epidermal necrolysis includes discontinuation of the offending agent, fluid replacement, and aggressive infection control.[9,41] Administration of systemic corticosteroids is controversial.[41] They have little effect on the disease and may mask signs of impending sepsis. Plasmapheresis is considered experimental.[44] The mainstay of treatment is excellent supportive care, prevention of secondary infection, and expert wound management, which is usually best accomplished in a center with burn expertise.

Toxic Shock Syndrome

Principles of Disease

Toxic shock syndrome (TSS) is an acute febrile illness characterized by diffuse desquamating erythroderma. Classically manifested as high fever, hypotension, constitutional symptoms, multiorgan involvement, and rash, the syndrome gained notoriety in the early 1980s because of association with tampon use. However, it is also well known in men and children. Its appearance has often been linked to exotoxin-producing *S. aureus*. Most cases of nonmenstrual TSS occur in the postoperative setting. TSS has also been associated with various staphylococcal and streptococcal infections, including empyema, osteomyelitis, fasciitis, septic abortion, peritonsillar abscess, sinusitis, burns, and subcutaneous abscess.[43]

Type of Eruption					
Eczematous	Erythema Nodosum	Vasculitis	Purpura	Photosensitive	Fixed
X					
	X			X	X
	X		X		X
		X			
	X	X	X		
X			X		X
X	X	X	X		
					X
					X
X			X		X
		X	X		X
		X		X	X
	X				X
X	X	X		X	X
		X		X	X
X				X	
Diphenhydramine ephedrine, thiamine, methyldopa		Antimalarial drugs, guanethidine		Antimalarial drugs, chlordiazepoxide, reserpine	Diazepam, indomethacin

TSS is associated with severe group A beta-hemolytic streptococcal infections. It has been reported in previously healthy patients, immunocompromised patients, and elderly patients. Fatigue, localized pain, and nonspecific symptoms herald the onset of TSS, followed by septic shock and multisystem organ failure.[43,45,46]

Clinical Features

Diagnosis of TSS requires the presence of fever with a temperature of at least 38.9° C, hypotension with a systolic blood pressure of 90 mm Hg or less, rash, and involvement of at least three organ systems.[9,43] Systemic involvement may include the gastrointestinal tract, muscular system, or central nervous system (CNS) and laboratory evidence of renal, hepatic, or hematologic dysfunction. Headache, myalgia, arthralgia, alteration of consciousness, nausea, vomiting, and diarrhea may be present.

The rash is typically a diffuse, blanching macular erythroderma. Accompanying nonexudative mucous membrane inflammation is common. Pharyngitis, sometimes accompanied by a "strawberry tongue," conjunctivitis, or vaginitis, may be seen. As a rule, the rash fades within 3 days of its appearance, followed by full-thickness desquamation, most commonly involving the hands and feet.

Management

Initial treatment of TSS consists of intravenous fluid replacement, ventilatory support, pressor agents, penicillinase-resistant antibiotics, and drainage of infected sites.[43] Corticosteroids may reduce the severity of illness if initiated within 2 to 3 days after the onset of illness.[47] The routine use of corticosteroids in septic shock remains controversial.[47]

Urticaria

Principles of Disease

Approximately 15% to 20% of the population experience urticaria during their lifetime. Acute urticaria is seen in both sexes and is more likely to have an allergic cause. Chronic urticaria is more common in women in their 40s and 50s. Half of all patients with chronic urticaria have the disease for 5 years and a fourth for 20 years.[48]

Various mediators, including histamine, bradykinin, kallikrein, and acetylcholine, are thought to play a role in urticaria production. Urticaria may be initiated by immunologic or nonimmunologic mechanisms. The hives found in anaphylaxis and serum sickness represent an immunologic reaction. Nonimmunologic urticaria may be produced by degranulation of mast cells, which may be precipitated by a number of foods and drugs, including aspirin and narcotics.

Substances that can cause urticaria by contact with skin include foods, textiles, animal dander and saliva, plants, topical medications, chemicals, and cosmetics.[48,49] The role of drugs in the production of urticaria is discussed in the section on drug eruption. Almost any drug may produce urticaria, although penicillin and aspirin are the most common. Traces of penicillin may be present in dairy products, as well as in medications. The mechanism of production of urticaria by aspirin is unknown but is probably nonimmunologic, and the effects of aspirin may persist for a number of weeks after ingestion.[48,49]

A variety of food allergies, such as fish, eggs, or nuts, may result in urticaria. In addition, foods such as lobster and strawberries can release histamine through a nonimmunologic mechanism. Hereditary forms of urticaria include familial cold urticaria and hereditary angioneurotic edema.

Infections are an uncommon cause of urticaria, except in children, in whom viral infections often cause hives. Occult infections with *Candida*, the dermatophytes, bacteria, viruses, and parasites may trigger hives. Viral infections that produce urticaria include hepatitis, mononucleosis, and coxsackievirus infections.

Inhalation of pollen, mold, animal dander, dust, plant products, and aerosols may produce urticaria. Respiratory symptoms may accompany the dermatosis, and a seasonal pattern of occurrence may be noted. Stings and bites of insects, arthropods, and various marine animals may also produce an urticarial eruption.

Occasionally, an urticarial eruption develops in patients with systemic lupus erythematosus, lymphoma, carcinoma, hyperthyroidism, rheumatic fever, or juvenile rheumatoid arthritis. The association is uncommon enough that in most cases it is not necessary for an urticaria workup to include a search for malignancy.

A number of physical agents produce urticaria. Dermatographism is present when firm stroking of the skin produces an urticarial wheal within 30 minutes (Figure 118-9) and is the most common form of physical urticaria. Pressure urticaria is distinct from dermatographism in that the onset of urticaria is delayed by 4 to 8 hours after the application of physical pressure. There is no other particular significance to this form of urticaria.

Cold urticaria may be either familial or, more commonly, acquired. Cold urticaria may also be associated with underlying illness, such as cryoglobulinemia, cryofibrinogenemia, syphilis, and connective tissue disease.[48,49] Cyproheptadine, 2 to 4 mg two or three times a day, is useful for suppression of primary cold urticaria.[50] Side effects of this drug include drowsiness and an increased appetite.[50] Administration of antihistamines 30 to 60 minutes before cold exposure may be helpful. Doxepin is also useful; begin with 10 mg at bedtime and gradually increase to 10 to 25 mg three times a day.[50]

Cholinergic urticaria is induced by exercise, heat, or emotional stress. It may be associated with pruritus, nausea, abdominal pain, and headache.[48,50] The lesions of cholinergic urticaria are wheals 1 to 3 mm in diameter surrounded by extensive erythematous flares and occasionally satellite wheals. Cholinergic urticaria responds better to hydroxyzine than do other physical urticarias.[50]

Heat is a rare cause of hives. Solar urticaria, also uncommon, is confined to sun-exposed areas of the skin and clears rapidly when the light stimulus is removed. Extensive sun exposure may cause wheezing, dizziness, and syncope in a susceptible individual.[50] Sunscreens have not been proved to be effective for the prevention of solar urticaria.[50]

The cause of chronic urticaria in adults is often not determined, although the etiologic factors responsible for urticaria in children are more readily identifiable.[51]

Clinical Features

Urticaria appears as edematous plaques with pale centers and red borders and is easily recognizable (see Figure 118-5). Individual hives are transient and last less than 24 hours, although new hives may develop continuously and represent localized dermal edema produced by transvascular fluid extravasation.

Differential Considerations

The differential diagnosis of urticaria includes erythema multiforme, erythema marginatum, and juvenile rheumatoid arthritis.

Management

Treatment of urticaria involves removal of the inciting factor, when applicable, and the administration of antihistamines or other antipruritics. Hydroxyzine (Atarax, Vistaril) in a dose of 10 to 25 mg (2 mg/kg/24 hr in children) is usually effective in providing symptomatic relief. Alternatives are nonsedating antihistamines, such as terfenadine, 60 mg twice a day, astemizole, 10 mg daily, or fexofenadine, 60 mg twice a day.[52] Prednisone is also effective, but the urticaria can rebound and make cessation of prednisone therapy difficult sometimes. For chronic urticaria, long-term treatment with antihistamines may be needed.

EXANTHEMS

Principles of Disease

An exanthem is defined as a skin eruption that occurs as a symptom of a general disease. Approximately 30

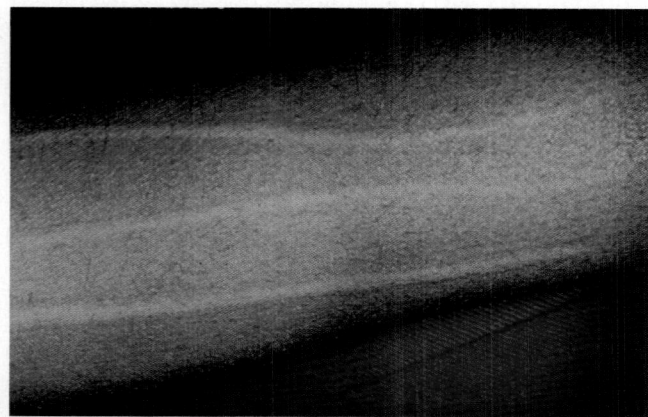

Figure 118-9. Dermatographism. (Courtesy of David Effron, MD.)

enteroviruses, predominantly the coxsackievirus and echovirus groups, and four types of adenoviruses are known to produce exanthems. Other viruses may do so as well. The exanthems of coxsackievirus and echovirus are most thoroughly documented. Most viral exanthems are maculopapular, although scarlatiniform, erythematous, vesicular, and petechial rashes are occasionally seen. The eruptions are variable in their extent, are nonpruritic, and do not desquamate. Oropharyngeal lesions may be present.

Infection with echovirus type 9 may be accompanied by meningitis and a petechial exanthem resembling meningococcemia, although the exanthem also occurs without meningeal involvement. Infections caused by echovirus type 16 (Boston exanthem) and coxsackievirus group B, type 5, may resemble roseola infantum but are more likely to occur in adults.

Infections caused by coxsackievirus group A, type 16, result in a distinctive syndrome of vesicular stomatitis and 1- to 4-mm oral vesicles involving the dorsa of the hands and lateral borders of the feet. Disease caused by coxsackievirus group A, type 9, has been the most extensively studied. It may be associated with meningoencephalitis or interstitial pneumonia. The rash is usually maculopapular, begins on the face or trunk, and spreads to the extremities. A vesicular eruption resembling varicella may occur.

The classic viral exanthems are rubeola (measles), rubella (German measles), herpesvirus 6 (roseola), parvovirus B19 (erythema infectiosum, or fifth disease), and the enteroviruses (echovirus and coxsackievirus).[3,9] Widespread immunization programs have reduced the incidence of rubeola and rubella.

Measles

Clinical Features

Measles is a highly contagious viral illness spread by contact with infectious droplets; the incubation period is 10 to 14 days. Patients are contagious from 1 to 2 days before the onset of symptoms up to 4 days after appearance of the rash.[53] Symptoms begin with fever and malaise. The fever usually increases daily in stepwise fashion until it reaches approximately 40.5° C on the fifth or sixth day of the illness. Cough, coryza, and conjunctivitis begin within 24 hours of the onset of symptoms.

On the second day of the illness, Koplik's spots, which are pathognomonic of the disease, appear on the buccal mucosa as small, irregular, bright red spots with bluish white centers. Beginning opposite the molars, Koplik's spots spread to involve a variable extent of the oropharynx.

The cutaneous eruption of measles begins on the third to fifth day of the illness. Maculopapular erythematous lesions involve the forehead and upper part of the neck and spread to involve the face, trunk, arms, and finally the legs and feet. Koplik's spots begin to disappear coincident with appearance of the rash. By the third day of its presence, the rash begins to fade, doing so in the order of its appearance, and the fever subsides.

Complications include otitis media, encephalitis, and pneumonitis. Otitis media is the most common complication. Encephalitis occurs in approximately 1 in 1000 cases of measles and carries a 15% mortality. Measles pneumonia may also be life threatening.

Management

If bacterial invasion occurs with otitis or pneumonia, the use of antibiotics is indicated; otherwise, treatment is supportive. Isolation of infected children is of limited value because exposure usually occurs before the appearance of the rash and the presence of Koplik's spots render the disease diagnosable. Measles is not contagious after the fifth day of the rash. Infection confers lifelong immunity.

The illness can be modified or prevented by the administration of human immune serum globulin in a susceptible person within 6 days of exposure. The recommended dose of immune serum globulin is 0.25 mL/kg IM in children. Live measles virus vaccine given within 72 hours of exposure may be effective in preventing measles.[53] Some authors suggest vitamin A shortly after exposure. The incidence of measles has decreased since the resurgence seen in 1989 to 1991.[54] Patterns observed during outbreaks include a shift from preschool-age children to older adults and groups who do not routinely obtain vaccination, such as immigrants.

Rocky Mountain Spotted Fever

Principles of Disease

Rocky Mountain spotted fever is caused by *Rickettsia rickettsii*, an organism harbored by a variety of ticks. The organism is transmitted to humans through tick saliva at the time of a tick bite or when the tick is crushed while in contact with the host. Though originally described in the Rocky Mountain region, this disease occurs in other portions of North, South, and Central America. Most reported cases are from the southeastern United States.

Clinical Features

Onset of the illness is usually abrupt, with headache, nausea and vomiting, myalgia, chills, and a fever spiking to 40° C. Occasionally, the onset is more gradual, with progressive anorexia, malaise, and fever. The disease may last 3 weeks and may be severe with prominent CNS, cardiac, pulmonary, gastrointestinal, renal, and other organ involvement; disseminated intravascular coagulation; or shock.

The rash develops on the second to fourth day or occasionally as late as the sixth day of the illness. It begins with erythematous macules that blanch on pressure, first appearing on the wrists and ankles. These macules spread up the extremities and to the trunk and face in a matter of hours. They may become petechial or hemorrhagic. Lesions on the palms and soles are particularly characteristic. Increased capillary fragility and splenomegaly may be present.

Diagnostic Strategies

The Weil-Felix reaction is the best known serologic diagnostic test, but the development of Weil-Felix agglutinins in patients with Rocky Mountain spotted fever is not constant, and more specific immunofluorescent procedures have been developed.[55] Treatment should not await the result of such tests, however, but should begin as soon as the disease is suspected on clinical grounds.

Management

Tetracycline (25 to 30 mg/kg/day in divided doses) is the antibiotic of choice. If the patient is unable to take oral medications, tetracycline may be administered IV, with a 15-mg/kg loading dose followed by a maintenance dosage of 15 mg/kg/day. Doxycycline may be used as well in a dosage of 4.4 mg/kg/day divided every 6 hours, followed by 1.1 mg/kg twice a day, up to 30 mg/day. Chloramphenicol may be used in patients allergic to tetracycline and in children younger than 9 years. The usual course is 6 to 10 days and should continue for 72 hours after defervescence.[55] Sulfa drugs should be avoided because they can exacerbate the illness. Rickettsiae are routinely resistant to penicillins, cephalosporins, aminoglycosides, and erythromycin.[55]

Roseola Infantum

Roseola infantum, otherwise known as *exanthem subitum* or sixth disease, is a benign illness caused by human herpesvirus 6 and characterized by fever and a skin eruption. A roseola-like illness has occasionally been associated with other illnesses.[53] Ninety-five percent of cases are seen in children 6 months to 3 years of age, and most cases occur in infants younger than 2 years. A febrile seizure may occur. The fever typically has an abrupt onset, rapidly rising to 39° C to 41° C, and is present consistently or intermittently for 3 to 4 days, at which time the temperature drops precipitously to normal.

The rash appears with defervescence. The lesions are discrete pink or rose-colored macules or maculopapules 2 to 3 mm in diameter that blanch on pressure and rarely coalesce. The trunk is involved initially, with the eruption typically spreading to the neck and extremities. Occasionally, the eruptions are limited to the trunk. The rash clears over a period of 1 to 2 days without desquamation.

Despite the presence of a high fever, the infant usually appears well. Encephalitis is a very rare complication.[53] The prognosis is excellent, and no treatment is necessary.

Rubella

Rubella, or German measles, is a viral illness characterized by fever, skin eruption, and generalized lymphadenopathy. It is spread by droplet contact, with the peak incidence occurring in the winter and early spring. The incubation period is typically 14 to 21 days, and the rash heralds the onset of the illness in children.

The maximum period of communicability encompasses the few days before and 5 to 7 days after onset of the rash.[53] Infants with congenital rubella can shed virus for more than a year.[53] In adults, a 1- to 6-day prodrome of headache, malaise, sore throat, coryza, and low-grade fever precedes the rash. These symptoms generally disappear within 24 hours after the appearance of the skin eruption.

The rash of pink to red maculopapules appears first on the face and spreads rapidly to the neck, trunk, and extremities. Those on the trunk may coalesce, but lesions on the extremities do not. The rash remains for 1 to 5 days, classically disappearing at the end of 3 days. Although clearing may be accompanied by fine desquamation, this sign is usually absent.

Lymphadenopathy may begin as early as a week before the rash. Although the lymphadenopathy is generalized, the nodes most apparent are the suboccipital, postauricular, and posterior cervical groups. Palpable adenopathy may be apparent several weeks after other signs and symptoms have subsided.

The major complications of rubella include encephalitis, arthritis, and thrombocytopenia. The most severe complication is fetal damage. Twenty-four percent of infected fetuses have a congenital defect. Maternal infection may be detected by obtaining serum for determination of hemagglutination inhibition antibody, acutely and in 2 weeks. A fourfold rise in titer is diagnostic of rubella infection. The routine use of postexposure prophylaxis for rubella in an unvaccinated woman in early pregnancy is *not* recommended.

No treatment is required in many cases of rubella. Antipyretics are usually adequate for the treatment of headache, arthralgia, and painful lymphadenopathy.

Erythema Infectiosum

Erythema infectiosum, or fifth disease, is caused by parvovirus B19 infection. It is characterized by mild systemic symptoms, fever in 10% to 15% of patients, and a distinctive rash. Arthralgia and arthritis occur commonly in adults, but rarely in children. The rash is intensely red on the face and gives a "slapped cheek" appearance with circumoral pallor. A maculopapular lacelike rash, which may be noted on the arms, moves caudally to the trunk, buttocks, and thighs. The rash may recur with changes in temperature and exposure to sunlight. The incubation period is usually between 4 and 14 days.[53,56]

Parvovirus B19 infection may also result in asymptomatic infection, upper respiratory infection, an atypical rash, and arthritis without a rash.

Rarely, it has been reported to cause hepatitis.[56] Infected immunodeficient patients may experience chronic anemia as a result of this disease. An aplastic crisis lasting 7 to 10 days may develop in patients with sickle cell disease or other hemolytic anemias.[56] Parvovirus B19 infection during pregnancy can cause fetal hydrops and death.[56] No congenital anomalies have been reported. No treatment is required.

Scarlet Fever

Clinical Features

The incidence of scarlet fever has declined in recent years. The illness has an abrupt onset with fever, chills, malaise, and sore throat, followed within 12 to 48 hours by a distinctive rash that begins on the chest and spreads rapidly, usually within 24 hours. Circumoral pallor may be noted. The skin has a rough sandpaper-like texture because of the multitude of pinhead-sized lesions. The pharynx is injected, and there may be erythematous lesions or petechiae on the palate. After resolution of the symptoms, desquamation of the involved areas occurs and is characteristic of the disease.

Complications include the development of a streptococcal infection of the lymph nodes, tonsils, middle ear, and respiratory tract. Late complications include rheumatic fever and acute glomerulonephritis (Figure 118-10).

Management

Treatment is aimed at providing adequate antistreptococcal blood antibiotic levels for at least 10 days. Oral penicillin VK is administered at a dosage of 50 mg/kg/day (40,000 to 80,000 U) in four divided doses in children or 250 mg four times a day in adults. Benzathine penicillin (given as Bicillin C-R) is administered IM. In patients weighing less than 30 lb, 300,000 U of benzathine penicillin is used; in patients weighing 31 to 60 lb, 600,000 U of benzathine is used; in patients weighing 61 to 90 lb, 900,000 U of benzathine is used; and in those weighing more than 90 lb, 1.2 million U of benzathine is used. In patients allergic to penicillin, 250 mg of erythromycin four times a day or 40 mg/kg/day should be given orally for 10 days. Other macrolides and certain other cephalosporins may also be administered.

PAPULAR LESIONS

Contact Dermatitis

Principles of Disease

Contact dermatitis is an inflammatory reaction of the skin to a chemical, physical, or biologic agent. The inducing agent acts as an irritant or allergic sensitizer. Allergic contact dermatitis is a form of delayed hypersensitivity mediated by lymphocytes sensitized by contact of the allergen with skin. It is less common than irritant contact dermatitis.[57] Caustics, industrial solvents, and detergents are common causes of irritant dermatitis. Dermatitis may result from brief contact with a potent caustic substance or from repeated or prolonged contact with milder irritants.

Clothing, jewelry, soaps, cosmetics, plants, and medications contain allergens that commonly cause allergic contact dermatitis. The most common allergens include rubber compounds, plants of the *Rhus* genus (poison ivy, oak, and sumac), nickel (often used in jewelry alloys), paraphenylenediamine (an ingredient in hair dyes and industrial chemicals), and ethylenediamine (a stabilizer in topical medications).[58] Sensitization to poison ivy results in sensitization to other plants in this family such as cashew, mango, lacquer, and ginkgo trees.[59]

Clinical Features

The primary lesions of contact dermatitis are papules, vesicles, or bullae on an erythematous bed. Of the allergens, *Rhus* species are the most likely to cause bullous eruptions. Oozing, crusting, scaling, and fissuring may be found, along with lichenification in chronic lesions. The distribution of the eruption depends on the specific contactant and may be localized, asymmetric linear, or unilateral (Figures 118-11 and 118-12). Mucous membranes are usually spared unless directly exposed to the inciting agent. A history of exposure is the most significant factor favoring the diagnosis. If doubt exists about the diagnosis, the patient should be referred for allergic patch testing.

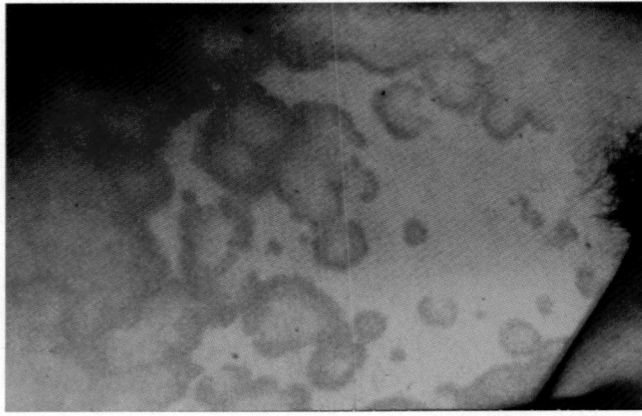

Figure 118-10. Erythema marginatum associated with rheumatic fever. (Courtesy of David Effron, MD.)

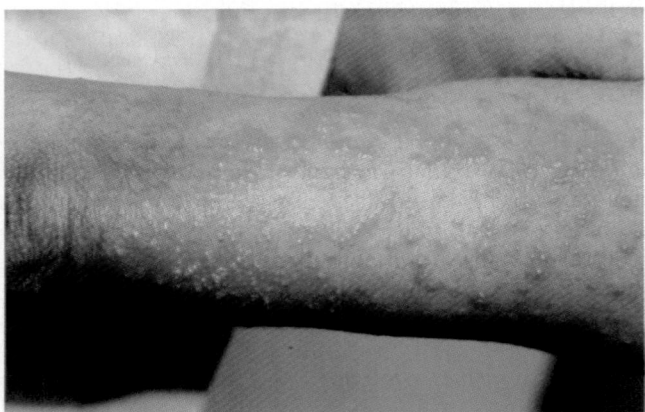

Figure 118-11. Contact dermatitis secondary to nickel. (Courtesy of David Effron, MD.)

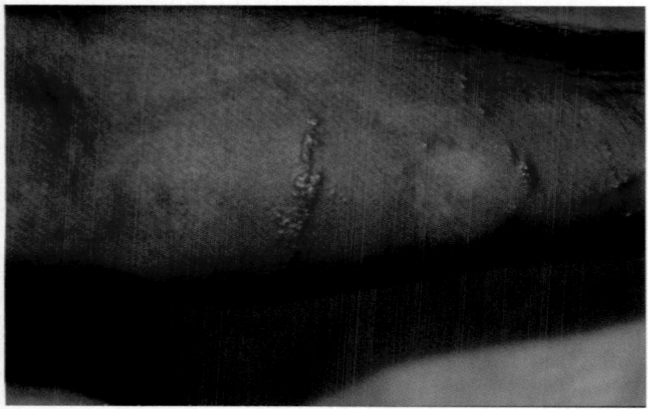

Figure 118-12. Typical linear lesions of contact dermatitis secondary to poison ivy. (Courtesy of David Effron, MD.)

Management

Treatment of contact dermatitis includes avoidance of the irritant or allergen and treatment of secondary bacterial infection. Oozing or vesiculated lesions should be treated with cool wet compresses of Burow's solution applied for 15 minutes three or four times a day. Topical baths, available over the counter, may also be comforting. A course of systemic corticosteroids is often necessary.[58] Prednisone in a dosage of 30 to 80 mg/day (depending on the severity of involvement) should be prescribed initially. It should be tapered over a period of at least 10 to 14 days and 21 days for poison ivy. The long, slow taper is needed to prevent rebound of the disease. Treatment may be discontinued when a daily dose of 10 mg is reached. Systemic antihistamines, such as hydroxyzine or diphenhydramine, may help control pruritus.[9,58,59]

The patient should also be counseled to wash all clothes that might have contacted the plant because the irritant plant oil can persist. Once the offending agent is reliably removed from skin and clothes, ongoing outbreak is attributable to the initial contact, not spread from serous fluid from the bullae. The patient is not contagious to others unless there is direct contact with the plant oil by persons who are sensitized.

Diaper Dermatitis

Clinical Features

Diaper dermatitis is a common disorder that is exacerbated by heat, moisture, friction, and the presence of urine and fecal material. Occlusive clothing in infants tends to foster all of these exacerbating factors. Lesions begin as erythematous plaques in the genital, perianal, gluteal, and inguinal areas. More severe involvement results in moist, eroded lesions that may extend beyond the primary areas of appearance.

Infection with *C. albicans* and fecal bacterial flora is an important contributory factor to the development of diaper dermatitis. Lesions infected with *Candida* are moist, red patches with well-demarcated borders. Papular or pustular satellite lesions are also present.

Diaper dermatitis may reflect the presence of atopic or seborrheic dermatitis in the infant. The occurrence of lesions elsewhere on the body, particularly on the face, in cases of atopic dermatitis or on the scalp in cases of seborrhea alerts the physician to these possibilities. Ammonia and bacterially produced putrefactive enzymes produce dermatitis as contact irritants. Such rashes are accompanied by characteristic odors. The existence of diaper dermatitis as a true allergic contact dermatitis is rare.

Management

Treatment consists primarily of altering the physical environment in which diaper dermatitis thrives. Excess clothing should be removed, and occlusive plastic or rubber diaper covers should not be used. Diapers should be changed frequently and left off for prolonged periods if possible. Sterilized cloth diapers are preferred.

If exudative lesions are present, treatment with topical cool wet compresses of saline or Burow's solution is indicated for 2 to 3 days. Continuous air exposure of the area should be attempted.[58] Zinc oxide (Desitin) may dry the area. Severe contact or seborrheic dermatitis may require short-term treatment with topical corticosteroids, such as 1% hydrocortisone in a cream base.[58] Ointment-based topical medications for the treatment of diaper dermatitis should be avoided because their occlusive nature enhances moisture retention. Nystatin cream or powder should be applied to lesions infected with *Candida*.

Erythema Multiforme

Principles of Disease

The most common precipitating factors in erythema multiforme are exposure to drugs and HSV infection. Additional causes include other viral infections, especially hepatitis and influenza A. Less common causes include fungal diseases such as dermatophytosis, histoplasmosis, and coccidioidomycosis and bacterial infections, especially streptococcal infections and tuberculosis. Various collagen vascular disorders have been known to precipitate erythema multiforme, particularly rheumatoid arthritis, systemic lupus erythematosus, dermatomyositis, and periarteritis nodosa. Pregnancy and various malignancies have also been associated with erythema multiforme. No provocative factor can be identified in approximately half of all cases. The differential diagnosis includes urticaria, scalded skin syndrome, pemphigus, and pemphigoid and viral exanthems.

Clinical Features

Erythema multiforme is an acute, usually self-limited disease precipitated by a variety of factors. It is characterized by the sudden appearance of skin lesions that are erythematous or violaceous macules, papules, vesicles, or bullae. Their distribution is often symmetrical, most commonly involving the soles and palms, the backs of the hands or feet, and the extensor surfaces of

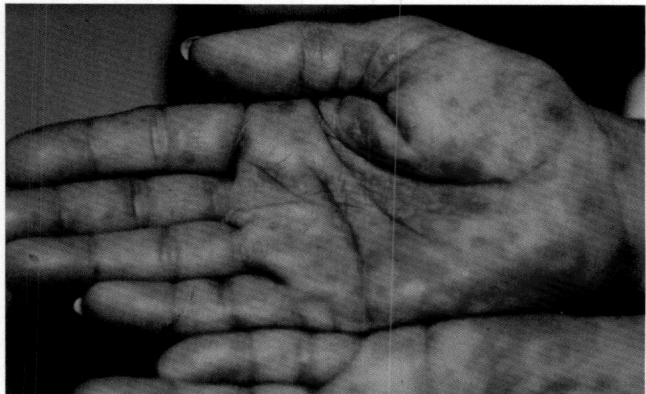

Figure 118-13. Erythema multiforme. (Courtesy of David Effron, MD.)

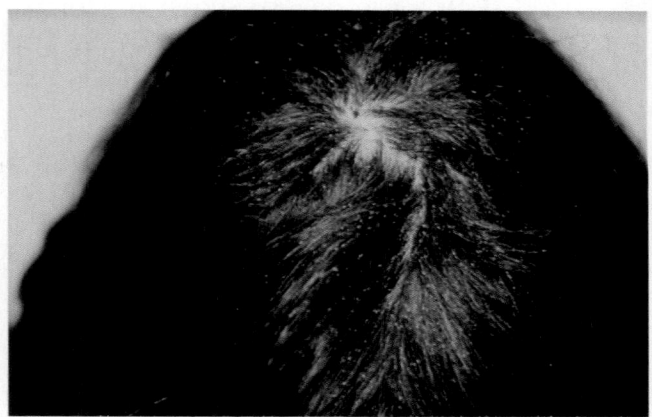

Figure 118-15. Nits as seen in head lice. (Courtesy of David Effron, MD.)

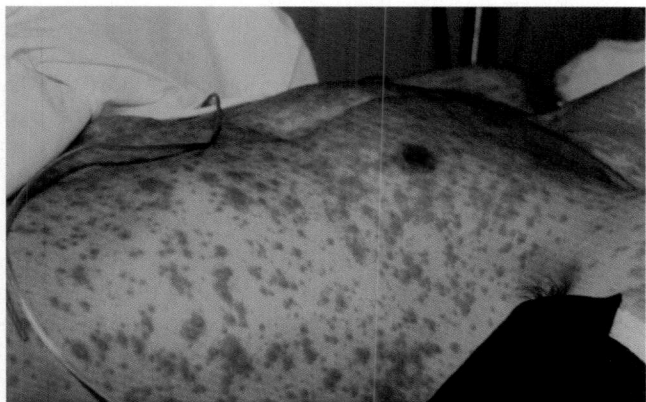

Figure 118-14. Stevens-Johnson syndrome. (Courtesy of David Effron, MD.)

the extremities. The presence of lesions on the palms and soles is particularly characteristic.[60]

The target lesion with three zones of color is the hallmark of erythema multiforme. It is a central, dark papule or vesicle that is surrounded by a pale zone, a halo of erythema (Figure 118-13), and is commonly found on the hands or wrist.

Stevens-Johnson syndrome, a severe form of erythema multiforme, is occasionally fatal. It is characterized by bullae, mucous membrane lesions, and multisystem involvement (Figure 118-14). The patient may be toxic; complain of chills, headache, and malaise; and display fever, tachycardia, and tachypnea. Systemic involvement may occur, with renal, gastrointestinal, or respiratory tract lesions resulting in hematuria, diarrhea, bronchitis, or pneumonia. Purulent conjunctivitis may be severe enough to cause the eyes to swell shut. Death results from infection and dehydration.

Management

Treatment should begin with a search for the underlying cause. Mild forms resolve spontaneously in 2 to 3 weeks. Severe cases can last up to 6 weeks and may require hospital admission for intravenous hydration, local skin care, systemic analgesia, and systemic corticosteroid therapy, which should consist of 80 to 120 mg of prednisone daily in divided doses. Bullous lesions should be treated with the application of wet compresses soaked in a 1:16,000 solution of potassium permanganate or a 0.05% silver nitrate solution several times a day. The major complications of Stevens-Johnson syndrome are infection and fluid loss. Renal involvement and pneumonia are rare. Severe conjunctivitis may result in corneal scarring and blindness. Reported mortality rates for Stevens-Johnson syndrome range from 0% to 15%.[3,15]

Pediculosis

Clinical Features

The diagnosis of pediculosis is made by identification of nits or adult lice on microscopic examination of hairs plucked from the symptomatic area. Nits are relatively more common than the adult louse form. Nits attach to the bases of hair shafts and appear as white dots (Figure 118-15). Adult forms look like blue or black grains. The patient complains of intense itching and scratching. A secondary infection may result from the latter.

The organisms causing pediculosis corporis reside in the seams of clothing and bedding materials while they feed on the human host. Except for heavily infested individuals, the parasites are absent from the body itself. Erythematous macules or wheals may be present, along with intense pruritus. Treatment consists of laundering or boiling clothing and bed linen. If nits are found in body hair, treatment with lindane lotion may be instituted, but this is not necessary in most cases (Figures 118-16 and 118-17).

Pediculosis capitis is seen more commonly in small children than in adults. Pruritus is the major symptom and may be confined to the occipital or postauricular portion of the scalp. Excoriations commonly result in secondary bacterial infection and regional lymphadenopathy.

Diagnostic Strategies

The diagnosis is made by identification of nits cemented to hairs at the hair-scalp junction (see Figure 118-15).

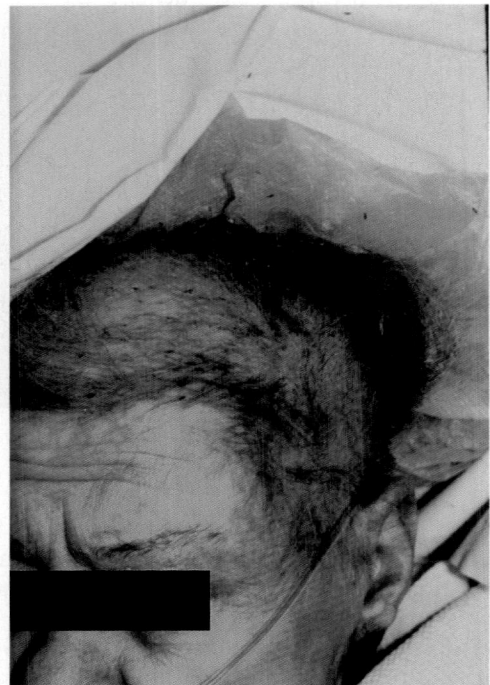

Figure 118-16. Body lice. (Courtesy of David Effron, MD.)

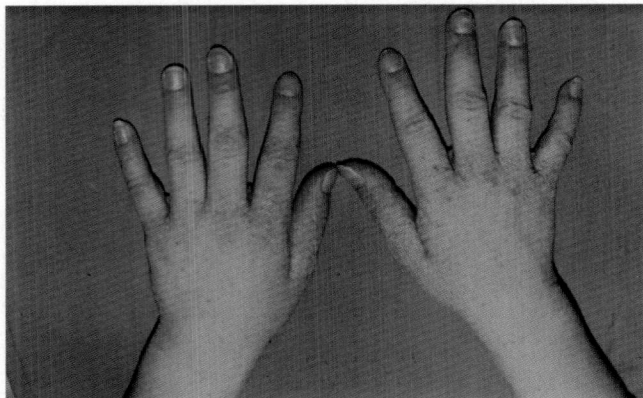

Figure 118-18. Scabies. (Courtesy of David Effron, MD.)

methrin is applied to the scalp after the hair is shampooed and dried. It is rinsed out with water after 10 minutes. It must be applied when the hair is dry because lice can close down their respiratory airways for up to 30 minutes when immersed in water.[61] Higher cure rates are achieved if the dose is repeated 1 week after the initial use.

Because the condition may be spread by sexual contact, sexual partners should also be treated. Other uninfested household members need not undergo a course of therapy. Underclothing, pajamas, and sheets and pillow cases should be machine washed (hot water) and dried, laundered and ironed, or boiled. Pruritus that persists after a course of therapy may result from irritation of the skin by the pediculicide, sensitization, or patient anxiety.

Permethrin is used to treat pediculosis capitis. A single dose of oral ivermectin, 200 µg/kg repeated in 10 days, has been shown to eradicate head lice.[61] Lindane should be reserved for treatment failures. Household contacts should be examined for involvement, but uninfected persons need not be treated.

Scabies

Clinical Features

Scabies is a mite infestation characterized by severe itching, which usually worsens at night. The areas of the body most commonly involved are the interdigital web spaces, flexion areas of the wrists, axillae, buttocks, lower part of the back, penis, scrotum, and breasts (Figure 118-18). The infestation tends to be more generalized in infants and children than in adults. The typical lesions are reddish papules or vesicles surrounded by an erythematous border and scratch marks. Scabies in infants and young children is often marked by generalized skin involvement, including the face, scalp, palms, and soles. In infants, the most common initial lesions are papules and vesiculopustules.[62]

Norwegian scabies may develop in immunosuppressed patients and is manifested by extensive hyperkeratosis and crusting of the hands, feet, and scalp. It is highly contagious because of excessive mite proliferation.[63,64] Secondary infections of these lesions are common.

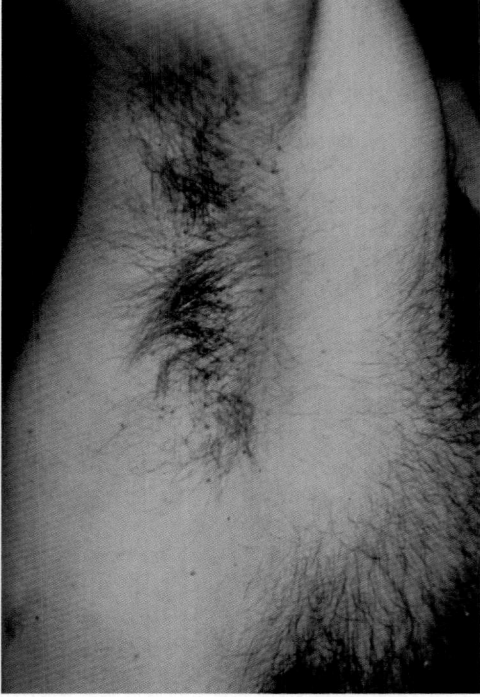

Figure 118-17. Body lice. (Courtesy of David Effron, MD.)

Management

Lindane (Kwell) lotion or cream is no longer the preferred prescription topical treatment.[61] Permethrin (Nix) is the recommended treatment. It remains active for 2 weeks. Creme rinses and conditioning shampoos should not be used during this period because they coat the hairs and protect the lice from the insecticide. Per-

Close personal contact is involved in the transmission of scabies. Multiple family members are likely to become infested. The infestation is also transmitted with sexual contact.

Management

Treatment options include crotamiton (Eurax) lotion and cream and 5% permethrin cream (Elimite). Lindane is no longer the preferred treatment. Patients in whom the former treatment fails may respond to the latter. Permethrin 5% cream (Elimite) applied overnight once weekly for 2 weeks over the entire body is the treatment of choice for infants and small children. It is more effective than crotamiton in eliminating the mite, reducing secondary bacterial infection, and decreasing pruritus. Postscabietic nodules and pruritus may persist for months, even after successful treatment.[61,62,65,66]

Treatment of Norwegian scabies may require repeated treatment with scabicides and sometimes sequential use of several agents.[66]

All family members and sexual contacts should also be treated. Intimate articles of clothing and sheets and pillow cases should be washed and dried by machine (hot water), laundered and ironed, or boiled.

It may take several weeks after therapy for the signs and symptoms to abate. A hypersensitivity state or anxiety may prolong symptoms long after the mites have been destroyed.

Syphilis

Clinical Features

Syphilis is transmitted only by direct contact with an infectious lesion. The causative organism is the spirochete *Treponema pallidum*. After an incubation period of 10 to 90 days, the primary lesion appears, lasts from 3 to 12 weeks, and heals spontaneously. In 6 weeks to 6 months after exposure, the disease enters the secondary stage, which involves a variety of mucocutaneous lesions. These lesions also heal spontaneously in 2 to 6 weeks as the disease enters the latent phase. Either a prolonged latent phase or tertiary syphilis follows. Of untreated patients, 25% display at least one relapse of mucocutaneous lesions of the oral cavity or anogenital region.

The chancre is the dermatologic manifestation of primary syphilis. Chancres usually occur as single lesions but may be multiple. They appear at the site of spirochete inoculation, usually the mucous membranes of the mouth or genitalia. The chancre begins as a papule and characteristically develops into an ulcer approximately 1 cm in diameter with a clean base and raised borders. The chancre is painless unless secondarily infected, and it may be accompanied by painless lymphadenopathy.

The secondary stage generally follows the primary stage by 6 weeks or more but rarely overlaps primary syphilis. There are a number of cutaneous manifestations of secondary syphilis. Lesions may be erythematous or pink macules or papules, usually with a

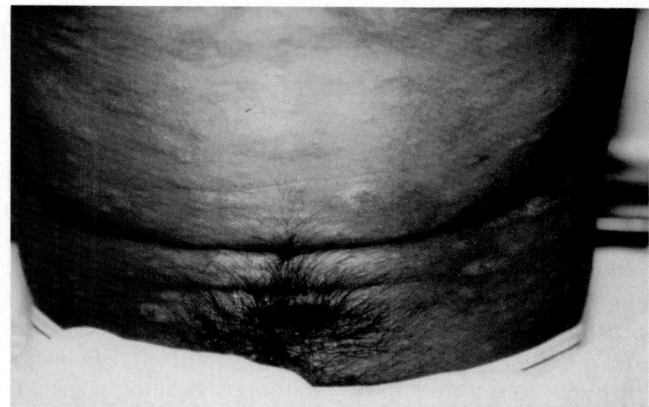

Figure 118-19. Secondary syphilis. (Courtesy of David Effron, MD.)

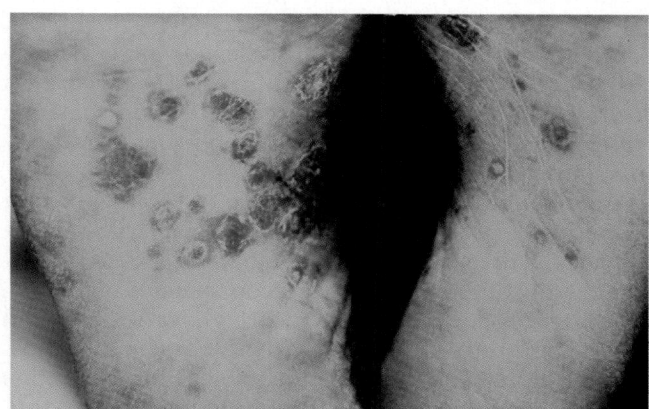

Figure 118-20. Cutaneous manifestation of secondary syphilis on the soles of the feet. (Courtesy of David Effron, MD.)

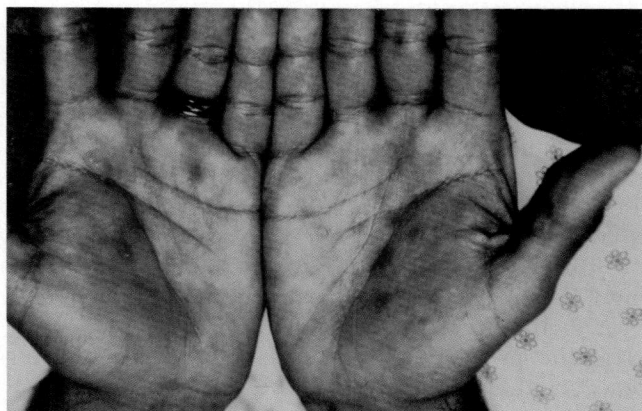

Figure 118-21. Cutaneous manifestation of secondary syphilis on the palms of the hands. (Courtesy of David Effron, MD.)

generalized symmetrical distribution (Figure 118-19). Pigmented macules and papules classically appear on the palms and soles (Figures 118-20 and 118-21). The lesions may be scaly but are rarely pruritic.

Papular, annular, and circinate lesions are more common in nonwhites. Generalized lymphadenopathy and malaise accompany the skin lesions. Irregular, patchy alopecia may be seen. Moist, flat, verrucous condylomata lata may appear in the genital area. These lesions are highly contagious.

Diagnostic Strategies

The diagnosis of primary syphilis is made primarily by the identification of spirochetes with darkfield microscopy. Because a darkfield microscope is often not available to the emergency physician, the diagnosis of primary syphilis must be suspected on clinical grounds and the patient referred to a dermatologist or appropriate public agency for diagnosis and treatment. The Venereal Disease Research Laboratory (VDRL) test, the most commonly used diagnostic serologic test, is positive in approximately three fourths of patients with primary syphilis, but the test tends to be negative early in the course of the disease.[34]

The VDRL test is invariably positive in cases of secondary syphilis, usually in titers of 1:16 or greater. Darkfield examination of moist lesions may also be positive, but the diagnosis in this stage is based on a positive serologic test. The most specific and sensitive serologic test is the fluorescent treponemal antibody absorption (FTA-ABS) test.[34]

A biologic false-positive serologic test for syphilis is defined as a positive VDRL test with a negative FTA-ABS test. This situation is seen acutely after vaccination or infections, especially mycoplasmal pneumonia, mononucleosis, hepatitis, measles, varicella, and malaria, and in pregnancy. Chronic biologic false-positive reactions (i.e., those lasting longer than 6 months) may occur with systemic lupus erythematosus, thyroiditis, lymphoma, or narcotic addiction or in elderly patients. Most false-positive reactions are in low titer ranges of 1:1 to 1:4.

Management

Incubating syphilis, the stage before the appearance of primary lesions, may be treated with 4.8 million U of procaine penicillin IM after 1 g of probenecid orally. Primary and secondary syphilis is treated with benzathine penicillin G in a dose of 2.4 million U IM. Patients allergic to penicillin should be treated for 14 days with doxycycline, 100 mg twice a day, tetracycline, 500 mg four times a day, or erythromycin, 500 mg four times a day.[34] Patients infected with human immunodeficiency virus require more intensive therapy.

Treatment may be administered in the emergency department if the diagnosis can be made on clinical, microscopic, or serologic grounds. If not possible by these means, a serologic sample should be drawn and the patient referred for treatment. The VDRL test may be expected to return to nonreactive in 6 to 12 months after the treatment of primary disease or in 1 to 1½ years after the treatment of secondary disease. Patients with tertiary syphilis who are adequately treated may nevertheless retain a positive serologic result. Within 12 hours of receiving therapy, patients may experience a febrile reaction and diffuse rash called the Jarisch-Herxheimer reaction. The reaction resolves spontaneously, usually within 24 hours.

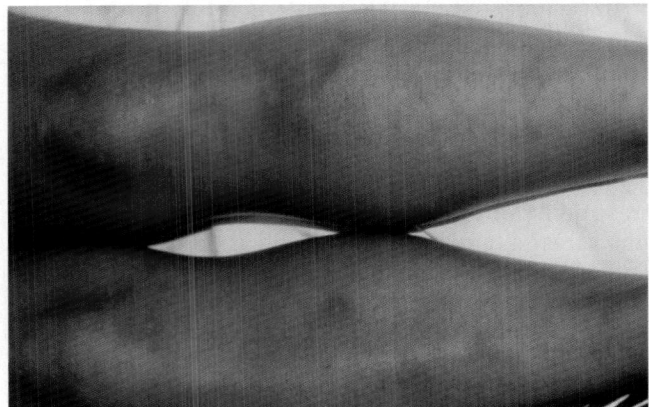

Figure 118-22. Erythema nodosum. (Courtesy of David Effron, MD.)

NODULAR LESIONS

Erythema Nodosum

Clinical Features

Erythema nodosum is an inflammatory reaction of the dermis and adipose tissue characterized by painful red to violet nodules. Nodules are elevated lesions located deep in the skin, and the skin over the nodules can be moved by palpation. These painful nodules occur most commonly over the anterior aspect of the tibia but may also be seen on the arms or body. Fever and arthralgia of the ankles and knees may precede the rash.[3,9] As the lesions evolve, they may turn yellow-purple and resemble bruises (Figure 118-22). Women are affected three times more often than men, with the highest incidence occurring in the third to fifth decades of life.[67]

A number of underlying conditions produce erythema nodosum: tuberculosis, sarcoidosis, coccidioidomycosis, histoplasmosis, ulcerative colitis, regional enteritis, pregnancy, and infection with streptococci, *Yersinia enterocolitica*, and *Chlamydia*. As with erythema multiforme, many cases of erythema nodosum are idiopathic. The relationship of drugs to erythema nodosum has been noted in the earlier section on drug eruption. Oral contraceptive agents are a leading cause of drug-induced cases. The differential diagnosis includes traumatic bruises and subcutaneous fat necrosis.

Management

When an underlying condition can be determined, it should be treated as indicated. Chest radiography may be considered to rule out sarcoidosis, tuberculosis, or deep fungal infection. Bed rest, elevation of the legs, and elastic stockings reduce pain and edema. Aspirin in a dosage of 650 mg every 4 hours or nonsteroidal anti-inflammatory agents may also afford some relief.[9,67] Erythema nodosum is a self-limited process that usually resolves in 3 to 8 weeks.[9] Patients with severe pain may be treated with 360 to 900 mg of potassium iodide daily for 3 to 4 weeks. Stopping therapy before this time may result in relapse. Potassium iodide may act through an immunosuppressive mechanism mediated via heparin release from mast cells.[9,67]

VESICULAR LESIONS

Perspective

Vesicles are elevated lesions that contain clear fluid. Vesicles larger than 1 cm are known as bullae. Vesicles may sometimes be associated with red papular lesions, as in contact dermatitis or erythema multiforme.

Pemphigus Vulgaris

Clinical Features

Pemphigus vulgaris is an uncommon, but important dermatologic disorder. The mortality rate before the use of steroids was approximately 95%. The current mortality rate of 10% to 15% is related more to steroid-induced complications than to the disease. Pemphigus is a bullous disease that affects both sexes equally, and it is most common in patients 40 to 60 years of age.[68] The typical skin lesions are small, flaccid bullae that break easily and form superficial erosions and crusted ulcerations. Any area of the body may be involved. Nikolsky's sign is present and characteristic of the disease. Blisters may be extended or new bullae may be formed by firm tangential pressure of a finger on the intact epidermis.

Mucous membrane lesions occur before the appearance of skin involvement; 50% to 60% of patients have oral lesions. The oral lesions typically antedate the cutaneous lesions by several months.[9,68] The most common site is in the mouth, especially the gums and vermilion border of the lips. Oral lesions are bullous but commonly break and leave painful, denuded areas of superficial ulceration.

The cause of pemphigus is unknown, although studies suggest an autoimmune mechanism. The development of pemphigus has been associated in a few instances with the use of medications, most notably penicillamine and captopril.[9] A positive Tzanck cytologic test suggests the diagnosis (i.e., finding acantholytic cells, or degenerated, rounded epithelial cells with amorphous nuclei). Acantholytic cells are not specific for pemphigus, however, and the diagnosis must be confirmed by serum immunofluorescence. The differential diagnosis includes bullous pemphigoid, epidermolysis, dermatitis herpetiformis, toxic epidermal necrolysis, bullous scabies, and bullous systemic lupus erythematosus (Figure 118-23).[9,68-71]

Management

Pain control and local wound care are essential components of therapy. Once the diagnosis is made, treatment with oral glucocorticoids in initial doses of 100 to 300 mg of prednisone or an equivalent drug should be instituted in conjunction with a dermatologist.

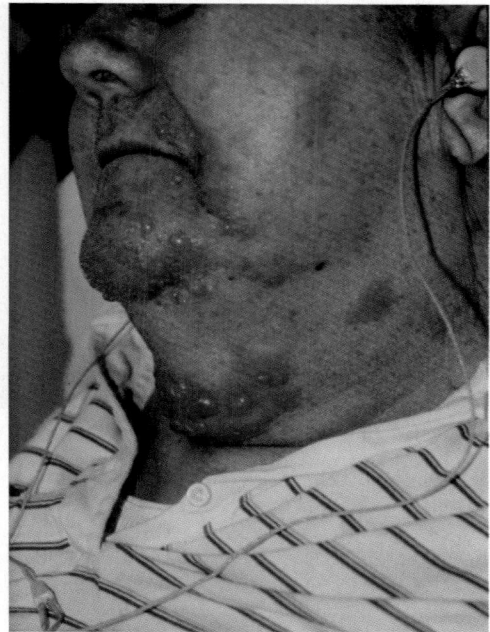

Figure 118-23. Bullous pemphigus. (Courtesy of David Effron, MD.)

Other immunosuppressant drugs may also be used. Despite the condition's localization to the skin and mucous membranes, death was the rule before treatment with steroids, and the mortality rate continues to be substantial.[9] Deaths are related to uncontrolled spread of the disease, secondary infection, dehydration, and thromboembolism. Other medical illness, as well as the side effects of high-dosage corticosteroids, also contribute to mortality.

Herpes Simplex

Perspective

Two known variants of HSV cause human infection: HSV-1 and HSV-2. The former primarily affects nongenital sites, whereas lesions caused by the latter are found predominantly in the genital area and are transmitted principally by venereal contact.

Clinical Features

The mouth is the most common site of HSV-1 infection. Children are affected more commonly than adults.[9] Small clusters of vesicles appear but are soon broken, with irregularly shaped, crusted erosions remaining. The severity of gingivostomatitis varies from the presence of small ulcers to extensive ulceration of the mouth, tongue, and gums accompanied by fever and cervical lymphadenopathy. The infection may be so severe that oral fluid intake is difficult, and dehydration may result. Healing typically occurs in 7 to 14 days unless a secondary infection with streptococci or staphylococci develops.

The hallmark of skin infection with HSV is painful, grouped vesicles on an erythematous base. Those above

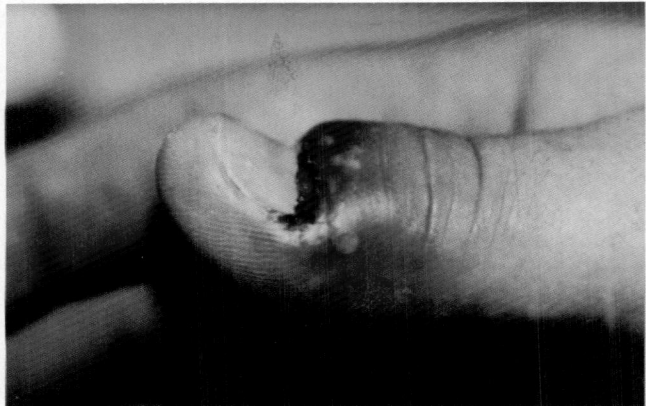
Figure 118-24. RSV-1 infection. (Courtesy of David Effron, MD.)

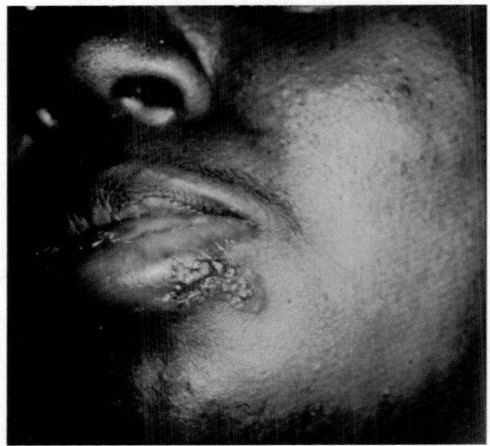
Figure 118-25. Herpetic whitlow. (Courtesy of David Effron, MD.)

the waist are usually caused by HSV-1, whereas those below the waist generally result from HSV-2 (Figures 118-24 and 118-25). The lesions are usually localized in a nondermatomal distribution. The skin distribution may become more generalized in patients with atopic eczema and other dermatoses. Adults with HSV infection should avoid contact with children with atopic dermatitis, especially in the first 3 to 5 days of infection.

HSV-2 infections in men involve either single or multiple vesicles on the shaft or glans penis. Fever, malaise, and regional adenopathy may be present.[34] A prodrome of local pain and hyperesthesia may precede the appearance of cutaneous lesions. The vesicles erode after several days, become crusted, and heal in 10 to 14 days. Infections in women involve the introitus, cervix, or vagina. Vesicles may be grouped or confluent. Herpetic cervicitis or vaginitis may be the cause of severe pelvic pain, dysuria, or vaginal discharge.[9,34] Recurrence is common, but recurrent episodes tend to be less severe. A correlation based on serologic epidemiologic data has been discovered between HSV-2 reproductive tract infections and carcinoma of the cervix.[9,34]

Management

Recommended treatment of a first clinical episode of genital herpes is acyclovir (Zovirax), 200 mg orally five times a day for 7 to 10 days, famciclovir, 125 mg twice a day, or valacyclovir, 500 mg three times a day or until clinical resolution occurs. These agents reduce the duration of viral shedding, accelerate healing, and shorten the duration of symptoms, but they have not succeeded in preventing recurrent episodes.[9] Prophylactic administration of acyclovir may be effective in ameliorating the severity of recurrent genital herpes, but the effects of long-term administration are unknown.[9] Although many episodes of recurrent herpes infection do not benefit from acyclovir therapy, 200 mg five times a day may be given orally for recurrences at the beginning of the prodrome. Famciclovir, 125 mg twice a day for 5 days, or valacyclovir, 500 mg three times a day for the same duration, are equally effective.[9]

Severe initial attacks of genital herpes have been successfully treated with an intravenous infusion of acyclovir. Admission to the hospital is required, however, because such treatment is necessary for several days, especially in immunocompromised patients. A mucocutaneous herpes infection in such patients is potentially fatal because it has a propensity for generalization and dissemination to the internal organs.

Supportive care is important and pain control is a major concern. Systemic analgesics and topical anesthetic agents may be useful. Patient education regarding prevention or spread of the disease during sexual contact and the birth process is imperative.

Varicella

Clinical Features

Varicella, or chickenpox, is an infection caused by varicella-zoster virus. After an incubation period of 14 to 21 days, the illness begins with a low-grade fever, headache, and malaise. The exanthem coincides with these symptoms in children and follows them by 1 to 2 days in adults.

The skin lesions rapidly progress from macules to papules to vesicles to crusting, sometimes within 6 to 8 hours. The vesicle of varicella is 2 to 3 mm in diameter and surrounded by an erythematous border (Figure 118-26). An unusual form of varicella consists of larger bullae (Figure 118-27). Drying of the vesicle begins centrally, with production of umbilication. The dried scabs fall off in 5 to 20 days.

Lesions appear in crops on the trunk, where they are seen in the highest concentration, and on the scalp, face, and extremities. The hallmark of varicella is the appearance of lesions in all stages of development in one region of the body. Extensive eruptions are often associated with high and prolonged fever.

Complications of chickenpox include encephalitis or meningitis, pneumonia, staphylococcal or streptococcal cellulitis, thrombocytopenia, arthritis, hepatitis, and glomerulonephritis.[53] Varicella pneumonia occurs more commonly in adults than in children.

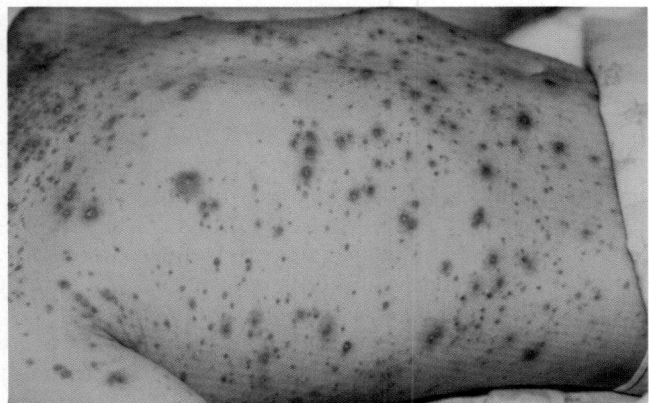

Figure 118-26. Chickenpox. (Courtesy of David Effron, MD.)

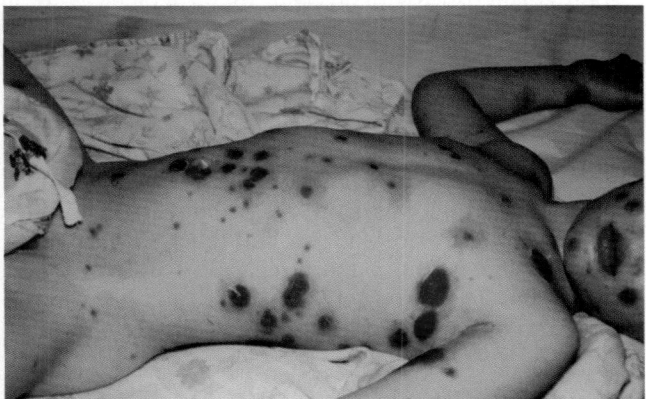

Figure 118-27. Bullous chickenpox. (Courtesy of David Effron, MD.)

Management

The illness is self-limited, and treatment is symptomatic only. Salicylates should be avoided in patients with chickenpox to minimize the risk of subsequent Reye's syndrome. Oral acyclovir may be effective if it can be started within 24 hours of the development of rash in patients with chronic respiratory or skin disease. Some studies report a diminution in the duration and magnitude of fever and the number and duration of lesions with the early use of acyclovir.[72]

Isolation of infected patients is often futile because the disease may be transmitted before the diagnosis is clinically evident. The disease has the potential to be contagious until all vesicles are crusted and dried, so infected persons should be kept at home until this stage is reached.

Varicella-zoster and varicella titers should be checked in pregnant women and immunocompromised patients who are exposed to chickenpox, and if negative, varicella-zoster immune globulin should be administered within 96 hours of exposure.[73] Fetal infection after maternal varicella in the first or early second trimester of pregnancy may result in varicella embryopathy, a condition characterized by limb atrophy, scarring on the extremities, and CNS and ocular manifestations.[53,74] Maternal varicella that occurs between 5 days before delivery and 2 days after delivery may result in disseminated herpes in the newborn.[73]

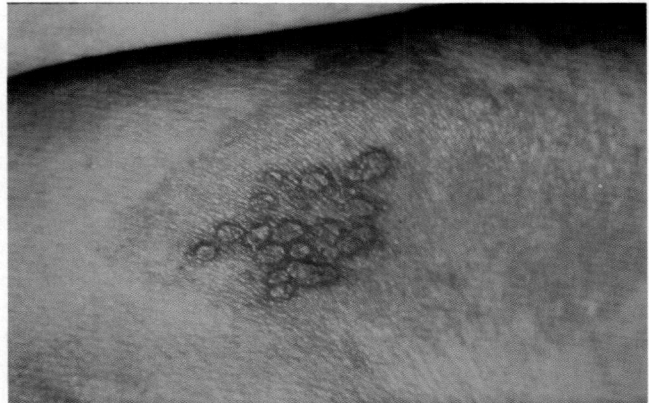

Figure 118-28. Herpes zoster. (Courtesy of David Effron, MD.)

The varicella vaccine is a live attenuated virus; it is highly efficacious and very safe.[75] A single dose is effective in children between the ages of 1 and 13 years. For older children, two doses separated by 4 to 8 weeks is recommended.[75] In addition, the incidence of zoster occurring after vaccination appears to be lower than after naturally acquired disease.[75]

Herpes Zoster

Clinical Features

Herpes zoster, or shingles, is an infection caused by varicella-zoster virus. It occurs exclusively in individuals who have previously had chickenpox. Before the rash appears, pain typically develops in a dermatomal distribution. This pain is of variable intensity; is sharp, dull, or burning in quality; and precedes the eruption by 1 to 10 days. The rash consists of grouped vesicles on an erythematous base involving one or several dermatomes. The thorax is involved in most cases, and the trigeminal distribution is the next most commonly involved region.[74]

The vesicles initially appear clear and then become cloudy and progress to scab and crust formation. This process takes 10 to 12 days, and the crusts fall off in 2 to 3 weeks (Figures 118-28 and 118-29). Herpes zoster has a peak incidence in patients 50 to 70 years old and is unusual in children. Although an association with leukemia, Hodgkin's lymphoma, and other malignancies is well known, rarely does the appearance antedate the diagnosis of such disease. Most cases of herpes zoster occur in healthy individuals.[74]

Herpes zoster may be transmitted from patients with chickenpox to susceptible individuals. Chickenpox may also be acquired by contact with shingles, although this is less common.[75] It is generally believed, however, that herpes zoster is caused by reactivation of latent varicella-zoster virus present since the initial infection with chickenpox. During the latent period between the two illnesses, the virus is thought to reside in dorsal root ganglion cells.[9,74]

Herpes zoster has a very low mortality rate and is rarely life threatening even when dissemination to visceral organs occurs. Complications include CNS involvement, ocular infection, and neuralgia. Meningoencephalitis, myelitis, and peripheral neuropathy have been reported.

Ocular complications occur in 20% to 70% of cases involving the ophthalmic division of the trigeminal nerve. The severity varies from mild conjunctivitis to panophthalmitis, which threatens the eye.[74] Eye involvement produces anterior uveitis, secondary glaucoma, and corneal scarring. There is a close correlation between eye involvement and vesicles located at the tip of the nose.

Postherpetic neuralgia, pain that persists after the lesions have healed, occurs more commonly in elderly and immunosuppressed patients.[74,76] It may last a number of months and is often resistant to treatment with standard analgesic medications.

Herpes zoster generally tends to be more severe in immunosuppressed patients, especially those with AIDS, Hodgkin's disease, or other lymphomas.[74,76] Cutaneous dissemination occurs more commonly in these patients than in the general population. Visceral and CNS dissemination is also more likely to occur in these patients, and they should therefore be considered for hospitalization.

Management

Treatment other than analgesia is rarely necessary. Compresses of Burow's solution diluted 1:20 to 1:40 in water may be applied to hasten drying. Early systemic corticosteroid therapy may shorten the duration of postherpetic neuralgia but does not lessen the severity of the pain or the rate of the healing of the lesions.[74] Antiviral chemotherapy with acyclovir, famciclovir, vidarabine, foscarnet, valacyclovir, and interferon alfa has been shown to be effective in immunocompromised patients.[74] Postherpetic neuralgia is a complicated problem with few satisfactory solutions. Capsaicin cream has met with some success but cannot be applied to inflamed or eroded skin.[9]

Intravenous acyclovir may be of some benefit in the treatment of severe ocular herpes zoster. Treatment includes mydriasis and the application of topical corticosteroids. Unlike the situation with herpes simplex conjunctivitis, eye involvement caused by herpes zoster does not appear to be exacerbated by corticosteroids.

Smallpox

The last naturally occurring case of smallpox was in Somalia in 1977. Subsequently, routine vaccination of the general public was stopped. Except for laboratory stockpiles, the variola virus had been eliminated.[77] Because of the recent concern regarding biologic agents as weapons, it is important that smallpox be differentiated from chickenpox (Table 118-3; Figure 118-30).[77]

Cutaneous Anthrax

Cutaneous anthrax begins as a pruritic pustule or vesicle that enlarges and erodes over a period of 1 to 2 days. Subsequently, a necrotic ulcer with a central black eschar is formed.[78] The lesion may be painless and may be surrounded by significant edema (Figure 118-31).

SKIN LESIONS ASSOCIATED WITH SYSTEMIC DISEASE

Numerous systemic illnesses have cutaneous manifestations (Table 118-4; Figures 118-32 to 118-39). Some of the most common illnesses include AIDS, diabetes mellitus, connective tissue diseases, and endocrine disorders.

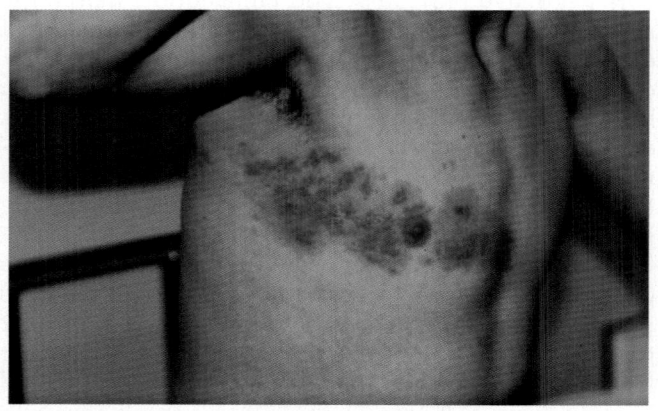

Figure 118-29. Herpes zoster infection. (Courtesy of David Effron, MD.)

Table 118-3. Differentiation of Chickenpox from Smallpox

	Chickenpox	Smallpox
Prodromal signs/symptoms	Prodromal signs/symptoms absent or mild	1-4 days of systemic signs/symptoms before onset of rash
Illness severity	Illness usually not severe unless complications/immunosuppressed	Very ill from onset, may be toxic
Lesion development	Superficial vesicles developing rapidly (1 day) and in multiple stages in each affected area	Hard, circumscribed pustules developing slowly (over days); lesions in same stage in every affected area
Lesion locations	Commonly on face and trunk, *not* palms and soles	Commonly on face and extremities, including palms and soles
Contagiousness	Contagious until all lesions crusted over	Contagious until *all* scabs have fallen off

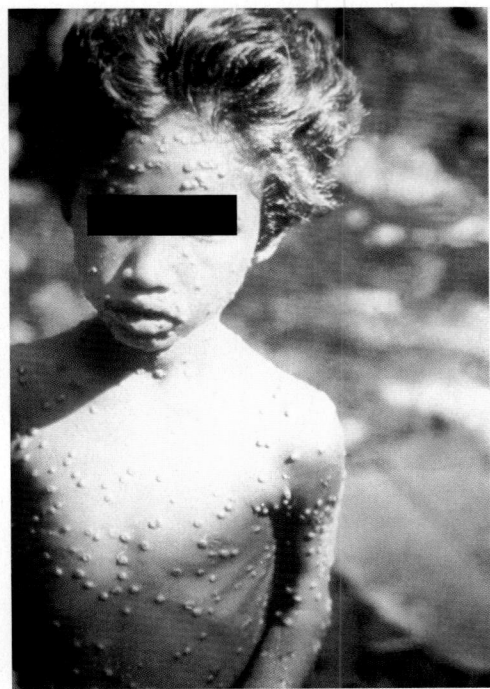

Figure 118-30. Smallpox. (From the Centers for Disease Control and Prevention (CDC) Public Health Image Library [PHIL] [http://phil.cdc.gov/phil/detail.asp?id=3277].)

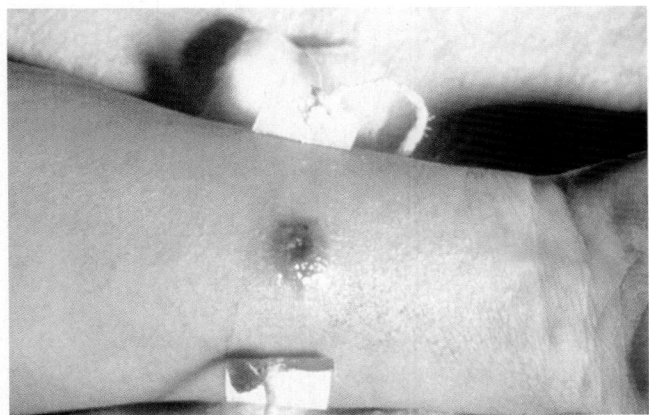

Figure 118-31. Cutaneous anthrax. (From the Centers for Disease Control and Prevention (CDC) Public Health Image Library [PHIL] [http://phil.cdc.gov/phil/detail.asp?id=1933].)

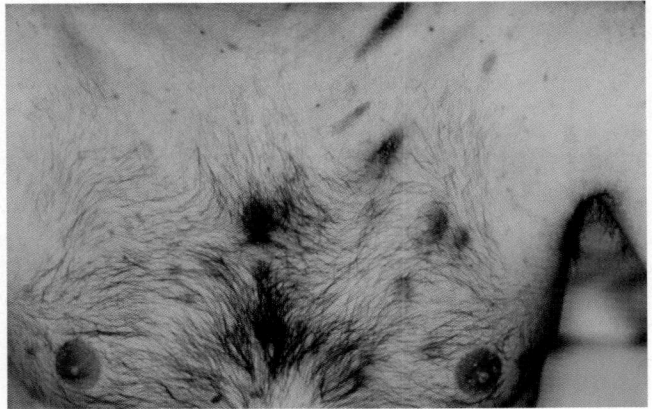

Figure 118-32. Kaposi's sarcoma associated with AIDS. (Courtesy of David Effron, MD.)

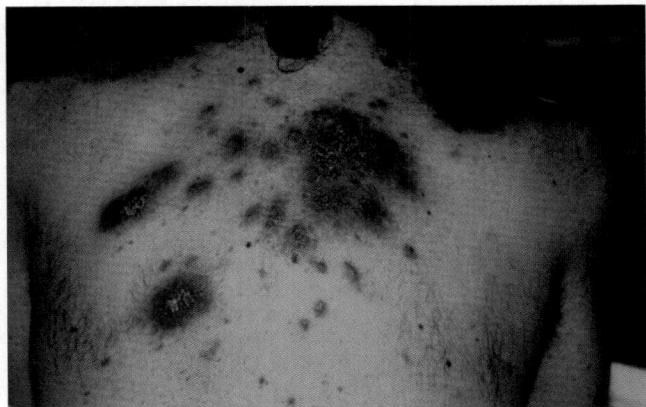

Figure 118-33. Kaposi's sarcoma in an AIDS patient. (Courtesy of David Effron, MD.)

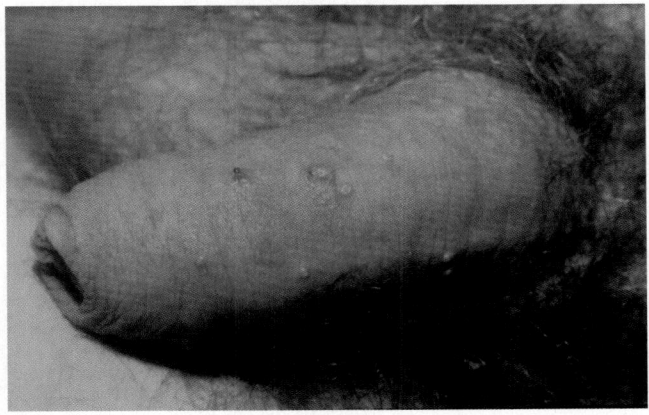

Figure 118-34. Molluscum contagiosum caused by a virus is more prevalent with AIDS. (Courtesy of David Effron, MD.)

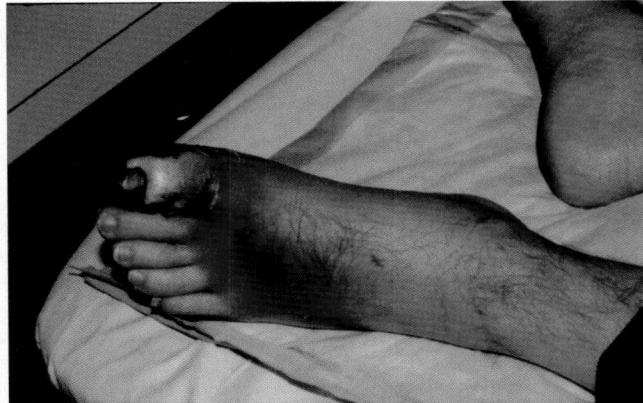

Figure 118-35. Gangrene of the toe with cellulitis in a diabetic patient. (Courtesy of David Effron, MD.)

Table 118-4. Skin Lesions Associated with Systemic Disease

Disease	Lesions	Comments
AIDS[3,9,73]	Chronic ulcerative herpes simplex	
	Kaposi's sarcoma (Figures 118-32 and 118-33)	Diagnostic for AIDS
	Severe herpes zoster	
	Oral hairy leukoplakia	
	Genital warts	
	Molluscum contagiosum (Figure 118-34)	
	Seborrheic dermatitis 2 *Pityrosporum*	
	Recurrent staphylococcal abscesses	
	Mycobacterial papules, nodules, abscesses	
	Oral and rectal squamous cell carcinoma	
	Lymphoma	
	Severe psoriasis	
	Acquired ichthyosis	
	Folliculitis	
	Human papillomavirus infection	
	Lichenoid photoeruptions	
Diabetes mellitus[67]	Diabetic dermopathy	Most common
	Necrobiosis lipoidica diabeticorum	Most characteristic
	Cellulitis (Figure 118-35)	Control of diabetes does not affect presence
	Vascular ulceration (Figure 118-36)	
	Acanthosis nigricans	
	Bullosis diabeticorum	
	Diabetic thick skin	
	Scleroderma	
Dermatomyositis[79]	Heliotrope discoloration and edema of eyelids	Skin lesions may precede muscle disease
	Scaly erythema of malar prominences	Symmetrical proximal weakness, remissions, exacerbations
	Erythematous dermatitis over joint extensor surfaces, especially hands (Figure 118-37)	Increased creatine phosphokinase aldolase with active disease
	Raynaud's phenomenon	
Systemic lupus erythematosus[80]	Discoid lesions	Patients with cutaneous discoid lupus generally have benign diseases
	Malar erythema (Figure 118-38)	
	Hypertrophic or verrucous palm and sole lesions	
	Lupus panniculitis	
	Oral ulcers	
	Raynaud's phenomenon	
Rheumatoid arthritis[81]	Rheumatoid nodules and necrobiosis	
	Vasculitic lesions	
	Pyoderma gangrenosum	
	Urticaria	Still's disease
Hyperthyroidism[67,82]	Fine, velvety, smooth skin	
	Increased sweating	
	Hyperpigmentation or hypopigmentation	
	Pretibial edema	
	Alopecia	
	Onychosis	
	Urticaria	
Hypothyroidism[67,82]	Dry, coarse skin	
	Myxedema (Figure 118-39)	
	Carotene color	
	Pruritus	
	Atopic dermatitis	
	Ichthyosis	
	Erythema nodosum	
	Easy bruising	
	Alopecia (lateral third of eyebrows)	
Ulcerative colitis[83]	Pyoderma gangrenosum	Associated with state of disease
	Erythema nodosum	
	Aphthous stomatitis	

CLINICAL FEATURES OF LESIONS ASSOCIATED WITH INTERNAL MALIGNANCY

Cutaneous lesions most directly indicative of an internal malignancy arise from extension of the tumor to the skin or by hematogenous or lymphatic metastasis. Neoplasms that most commonly produce such cutaneous extension are lymphomas, leukemias, and carcinomas of the breast, gastrointestinal tract, lung, ovary, prostate, uterus, and bladder. Skin metastases generally signify a poor prognosis.[67]

Acanthosis Nigricans

Acanthosis nigricans is associated with internal malignancy despite the fact that most patients do not have

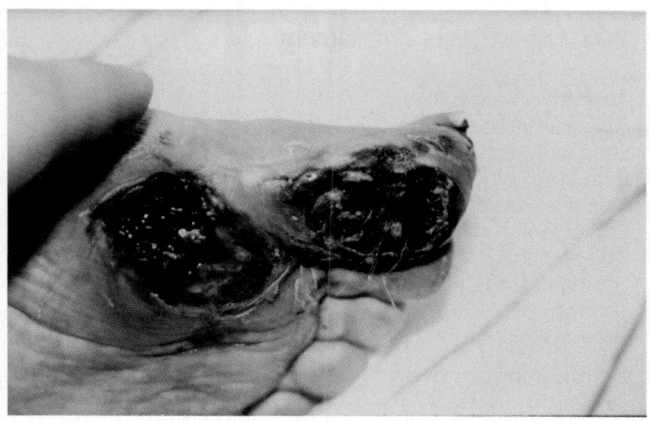

Figure 118-36. Vascular ulceration secondary to diabetes. (Courtesy of David Effron, MD.)

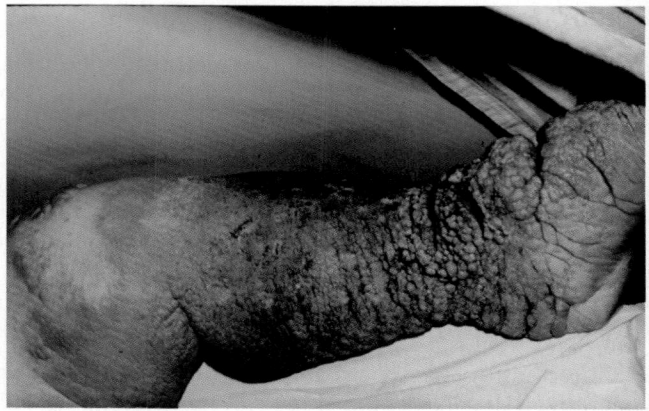

Figure 118-39. Severe myxedema in a hypothyroid patient. (Courtesy of David Effron, MD.)

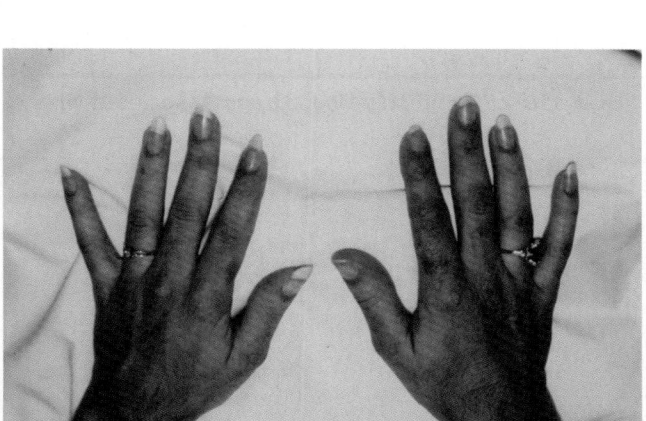

Figure 118-37. Erythematous dermatitis over the joint extensor surfaces, dermatomyositis. (Courtesy of David Effron, MD.)

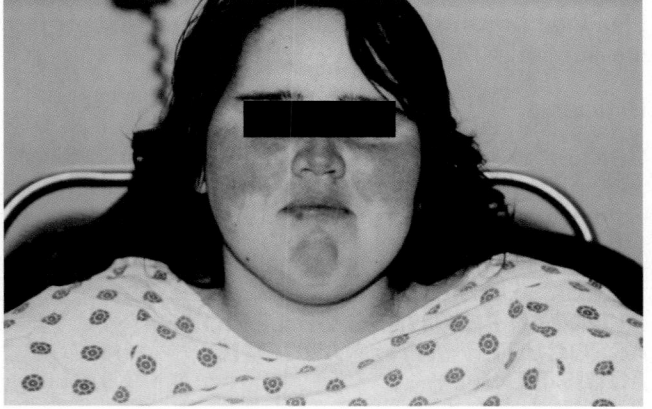

Figure 118-38. Malar erythema in a patient with systemic lupus erythematosus. (Courtesy of David Effron, MD.)

tumors.[83] Benign cases may be familial or related to endocrine disease or obesity. The term *malignant acanthosis nigricans* is used to designate the form associated with neoplastic disease. This phrasing is misleading because acanthosis nigricans is only a marker of the underlying disease and is never infiltrated with malignant cells.

The lesion appears as a hyperpigmented verrucous, velvet-like hyperplasia and hypertrophy of the skin accompanied by accentuation of the skin markings. The chief sites of involvement are the body folds, especially the axillae, antecubital fossae, neck, and groin.

More than 90% of cases of "malignant" acanthosis nigricans are associated with intra-abdominal malignancies, two thirds of which are adenocarcinomas of the stomach.[79,83] Carcinomas of the colon, ovary, pancreas, rectum, and uterus make up the majority of the rest.[83] Regardless of the tumor type, acanthosis nigricans is associated with tumors that are usually highly malignant and metastasize early.[67,79] The mechanism of this dermatosis in cases of internal malignant disease is postulated to be a result of tumor products that bind to and stimulate insulin-like growth factors in the skin.[83]

Dermatomyositis

The incidence of dermatomyositis with malignant disease ranges from 6% to 55% and is generally higher in older patients. In younger individuals, the appearance of dermatomyositis does not necessarily call for a tumor workup. Tumors commonly associated with dermatomyositis are carcinomas of the breast, ovary, and gastrointestinal and female genital tracts. Polymyositis occurring alone without the accompanying skin findings is rarely associated with malignancies.[67,84]

Erythema Multiforme

Erythema multiforme may be associated with acute forms of leukemia. It is seen with acute monocytic, lymphocytic, and granulocytic forms and is also found in chronic leukemias and Hodgkin's disease.[9,84]

Erythema Nodosum

Erythema nodosum is another reaction found in association with leukemia and Hodgkin's lymphoma, as well as with metastatic carcinoma and, as previously described, with inflammatory bowel disease.[79,85]

Erythroderma

Generalized erythroderma is almost pathognomonic for Hodgkin's disease; however, it is also a common skin manifestation of lymphocytic leukemia. Though less common, it is likewise seen with other forms of leukemia, carcinoma, and mycosis fungoides. The appearance of erythroderma may precede the diagnosis of internal malignant disease by many years. The skin eruption is invariably accompanied by intractable pruritus.[85]

Acquired Ichthyosis

Acquired ichthyosis is a skin condition manifested as generalized dryness of the skin, scaling, and superficial cracking or as hyperkeratosis of the palms and soles. Hodgkin's disease is the most common malignant disease associated with the nonfamilial form of ichthyosis. Non-Hodgkin's lymphoma and carcinomas of the breast, lung, colon, and cervix have also been associated with acquired ichthyosis.[67]

Pruritus

Itching may be an important indicator of Hodgkin's disease, leukemia, adenocarcinoma or squamous cell carcinoma of various organs, carcinoid syndrome, multiple myeloma, and polycythemia vera. It may appear years before the underlying malignancy is identified.[67,85] In cases of Hodgkin's disease, the itching is generally continuous and may be accompanied by a severe burning sensation. Though usually generalized, pruritus commonly begins in the feet and may be limited to the lower extremities. It may be intractable and associated with urticaria, erythroderma, excoriation, or lichenification.

The pruritus of leukemia and systemic carcinoma is generally less severe than that found with Hodgkin's disease. Nevertheless, itching associated with internal malignant disease may be difficult to control. Conventional anti-H_1 antihistamines, cimetidine, cholestyramine, and cyproheptadine have each been used with variable results.[85] Occasionally, only suppression of the tumor is beneficial.

Purpura

Purpura is the most common manifestation of acute granulocytic and monocytic leukemia. It may also be associated with myeloma, lymphoma, and polycythemia vera. Although the most common cause of purpura in these conditions is thrombocytopenia secondary to bone marrow infiltration, in some instances the platelet count is normal and the causative mechanism obscure.[9] Purpura is caused by vascular abnormalities, thrombocytopenia, or other coagulation defects. A variety of diseases and conditions may be the underlying cause, and treatment should be directed toward this cause whenever possible (Boxes 118-1 and 118-2).[86] Thrombocytopenic and nonthrombocytopenic forms are differentiated by the results of the patient's platelet count. Serious bleeding seldom occurs if the platelet count is greater than 50,000/mm^3. If the platelet count is less than 10,000/mm^3 or serious bleeding is

---

BOX 118-1. Causes of Purpura

Thrombocytopenic
Aplastic anemia
Drug induced
Idiopathic
Malignant disease
Sarcoidosis
Splenomegaly
Systemic lupus erythematosus
Thrombotic
Tuberculosis

Nonthrombocytopenic
Drugs
Infection (meningococcemia, Rocky Mountain spotted fever)
Qualitative platelet defect
Vasculitis

BOX 118-2. Commonly Used Drugs Associated with Purpura

Amitriptyline	Isoniazid
Aspirin	Meprobamate
Cephalothin	Methyldopa
Chloramphenicol	Penicillin
Chlorpromazine	Phenacetin
Chlorpropamide	Phenobarbital
Diazoxide	Phenylbutazone
Digitoxin	Quinidine
Furosemide	Rifampin
Hydrochlorothiazide	Sulfonamides
Indomethacin	Tolbutamide

---

encountered, platelet transfusion should be initiated. Because of the short circulating half-life of infused platelets, transfusion should be used as a short-term measure only.

Urticaria

Urticaria is occasionally found in Hodgkin's disease and more rarely in leukemia and internal carcinoma. Cold urticaria may occur with multiple myeloma (Table 118-5).

CLINICAL FEATURES OF LESIONS ASSOCIATED WITH NARCOTIC ADDICTION

Characteristic skin lesions develop in individuals who inject opiates and other drugs parenterally secondary to such use.[87] Skin lesions have been most extensively described in heroin addicts. Skin tracks, or indurated linear hyperpigmented streaks, are produced by repeated intravenous injection (Figure 118-40). They follow the course of the superficial veins used in the injection, most commonly in the antecubital fossae and dorsa of the hands.

Subcutaneous injection results in round or oval hyperpigmented atrophic depressed scars 1 to 3 cm in

Table 118-5. Common Causes of Urticaria

Cause	Common Responsible Factors
Bacterial infection	*Streptococcus*
	Staphylococcus
	Yersinia
	Mycobacterium
Viral infection	Herpes simplex virus
	Epstein-Barr virus
	Cytomegalovirus
	Hepatitis viruses (especially B)
	Many acute viral syndromes (adenovirus, enterovirus)
Other infections	Parasites
	Coccidioidomycosis
	Histoplasmosis
	Rickettsia
	Spirochete (Lyme disease)
Envenomation	Bees
	Wasps
	Scorpions
	Spiders
	Jellyfish
	Fleas
	Mites
Drugs	Penicillin
	Sulfa
	Cephalosporins
	Salicylates
	Morphine, codeine, other opioids
	Nonsteroidal anti-inflammatory drugs
	Barbiturates
	Amphetamines
	Blood and blood products
Foods	Nuts
	Shellfish
	Eggs
	Strawberries
	Tomatoes
	Milk, cheese
	Chocolate
Contacts	Chemicals
	Cosmetics
	Topical medications
	Plants
	Textiles
	Foods
Inhalants	Dust
	Pollen
	Animal dander
	Chemicals/aerosols
	Mold spores
Physical agents	Heat
	Cold
	Light
	Pressure (dermatographism)
	Water
Diseases	Collagen vascular disease
	Lupus, juvenile rheumatoid arthritis, polyarteritis nodosa, dermatomyositis, Sjögren's syndrome, rheumatic fever
	Inflammatory bowel disease
	Crohn's disease, ulcerative colitis
	Malignancy
	Carcinoma, leukemia, lymphoma
	Miscellaneous
	Serum sickness, thyroiditis, aphthous stomatitis, Behçet's disease

Data from references 9, 48, and 49.

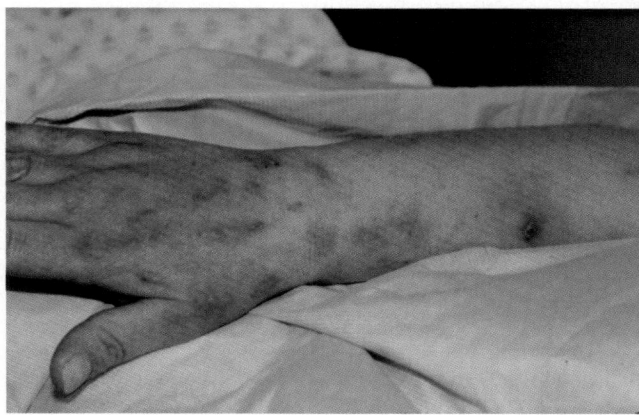

Figure 118-40. Tracks secondary to intravenous heroin abuse. (Courtesy of David Effron, MD.)

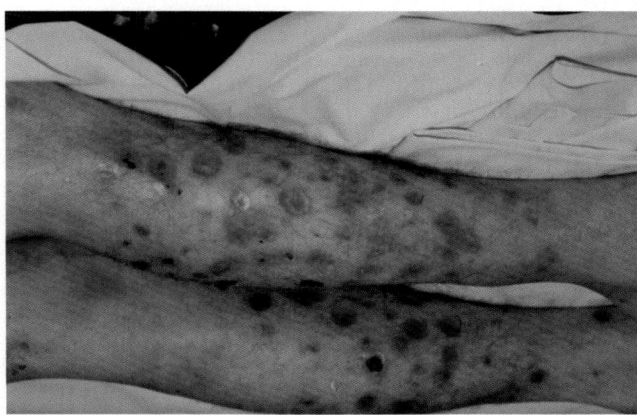

Figure 118-41. Scars from subcutaneous illicit drug injection. (Courtesy of David Effron, MD.)

diameter (Figure 118-41). Abscesses, which often require drainage, commonly precede the development of such scars. Hypertrophic scarring and keloid formation may also occur.

Increased pigmentation may occur in sun-exposed areas and at the site of tourniquet application.

KEY CONCEPTS

- Infection with *Candida albicans* can occur normally in infancy, in obese people, during pregnancy, and in old age. In other patients, the following underlying problems should be considered: AIDS and other immunodeficiency states, diabetes and other endocrine imbalances, malignancy, malnutrition, and other debilitating illnesses.

- Rashes that are associated with mucosal lesions, blisters, or desquamating skin are often caused by significant soft tissue infections, drug eruptions, or immune disorders.

- Purpura results from blood leaking from vessels into the skin and does not blanch when pressure is applied. Purpuric lesions less than 3 mm in diameter are called petechiae. Nonpalpable purpura is often caused by coagulation defects (usually platelet abnormalities), whereas palpable purpura is usually a sign of vasculitis.

- Diffuse pruritus in the absence of a rash may be a sign of underlying malignancy.

REFERENCES

1. Shivaram V, Christoph RA, Hayden GF: Skin disorders encountered in a pediatric emergency department. *Pediatr Emerg Care* 9:202, 1993.
2. Little JM, Hall MN, Pettice YJ: Teaching dermatology: Too dependent on dermatologists? *Fam Med* 25:92, 1993.
3. Lookingbill DP, Marks JG: *Principles of Dermatology*, ed 2. Philadelphia, WB Saunders, 1993.
4. Babel DE: How to identify fungi. *J Am Acad Dermatol* 6:S108, 1994.
5. Stein D: Tineas: Superficial dermatophyte infections. *Pediatr Rev* 19:368, 1998.
6. Frieden IJ, Howard R: Tinea capitis: Epidemiology, diagnosis, treatment and control. *J Am Acad Dermatol* 31:S42, 1994.
7. Stevenson L, Brooke DS: Tinea capitis. *J Pediatr Health Care* 8:189, 1994.
8. Hayes AG: Black dot tinea capitis in a man. *Int J Dermatol* 32:740, 1993.
9. Edwards L: *Dermatology in Emergency Medicine.* New York, Churchill Livingstone, 1997.
10. Hubbard TW, deTriquet JM: Brush-culture method for diagnosing tinea capitis. *Pediatrics* 90:416, 1993.
11. Friedlander S, Pickering B, Cunningham B: Use of the cotton swab method in diagnosing tinea capitis. *Pediatrics* 104:277, 1999.
12. Aly R: Ecology, epidemiology and diagnosis of tinea capitis. *Pediatr Infect Dis J* 18:180, 1999.
13. http:/www.emedicine.com/derm/topic420.
14. Maroon TS, et al: A randomized double-blind, comparative study of terbinatone vs. griseofulvin in tinea capitis. *J Dermatol Treat* 3:25, 1992.
15. Pomeranz AJ, Fairley JA: Management errors leading to unnecessary hospitalization for kerion. *Pediatrics* 93:986, 1994.
16. Honig PJ, et al: Treatment of kerions. *Pediatr Dermatol* 11:69, 1994.
17. Commens CA: Superficial mycoses: A practical approach. *Med J Aust* 158:470, 1993.
18. Aly R, et al: Topical griseofulvin in the treatment of dermatophytoses. *Clin Exp Dermatol* 19:43, 1994.
19. Smith EB: Topical antifungal drugs in the treatment of tinea pedis, tinea cruris, and tinea corporis. *J Am Acad Dermatol* 28:S24, 1993.
20. Chren MM: Costs of therapy for dermatophyte infections. *J Am Acad Dermatol* 31:S103, 1994.
21. Savin R, et al: Efficacy of terbinafine 1% cream in the treatment of moccasin-type tinea pedis: Results of placebo-controlled multicenter trials. *J Am Acad Dermatol* 30:663, 1994.
22. Assaf R, Weil M: The superficial mycoses. *Dermatol Clin* 14:57, 1996.
23. Borelli D, Jacobs PH, Nall L: Tinea versicolor: Epidemiologic, clinical, and therapeutic aspects. *J Am Acad Dermatol* 25:300, 1991.
24. Scher R: Onychomycosis: Therapeutic update. *J Am Acad Dermatol* 40:S21, 1999.
25. Hay R: Yeast infections. *Dermatol Clin* 14:113, 1996.
26. Harrigan E, Rabinowitz L: Atopic dermatitis. *Immunol Allergy Clin North Am* 19:383, 1999.
27. Berstein J, Zeiss CR: Atopic dermatitis. *Allergy Proc* 14:129, 1993.
28. Darmstadt GL, Lane AT: Impetigo: An overview. *Pediatr Dermatol* 11:293, 1994.
29. Britton JW, et al: Comparison of mupirocin and erythromycin in the treatment of impetigo. *J Pediatr* 117:827, 1990.
30. McLinn S: A bacteriologically controlled, randomized study comparing the efficacy of 2% mupirocin ointment (Bactroban) with oral erythromycin in the treatment of patients with impetigo. *J Am Acad Dermatol* 22:883, 1990.
31. Jain A, Daum R: Staphylococcal infections in children: Part 1. *Pediatr Rev* 20:186, 1999.
32. Feingold DS: Staphylococcal and streptococcal pyodermas. *Semin Dermatol* 12:331, 1993.
33. Cucurull E, Espinoza L: Gonococcal arthritis. *Rheum Dis Clin North Am* 24:305, 1998.
34. Sexually transmitted disease treatment guidelines, 2002. Centers for Disease Control and Prevention. *MMWR Recomm Rep* 51(RR-6):1, 2002.
35. Salzman M: Meningococcemia. *Infect Dis Clin North Am* 10:709, 1996.
36. Hacker SM: Common infections of the skin. *Postgrad Med* 96:43, 1994.
37. Schwartz G, Wright S: Changing bacteriology of periorbital cellulitis. *Ann Emerg Med* 28:617, 1996.
38. Sadow KB, Chamberlain JM: Blood cultures in the evaluation of children with cellulitis. *Pediatrics* 101:E4, 1998.
39. McCollough M: Progress toward eliminating *Haemophilus influenzae* type b disease among infants and children—United States 1987-1997 [commentary]. *Ann Emerg Med* 34:110, 1999.
40. Bisno AL, Stevens DL: Streptococcal infections of skin and soft tissues. *N Engl J Med* 334:240, 1996.
41. Swartz MN: Erysipelas. In Mandell GL, et al (eds): *Principles and Practice of Infectious Diseases,* 4th ed. New York, Churchill Livingstone, 1995, pp 913-914.
42. Beltrani V: Cutaneous manifestations of adverse drug reactions. *Immunol Allergy Clin North Am* 18:867, 1998.
43. Pollack S: Staphylococcal scalded skin syndrome. *Pediatr Rev* 17:18, 1996.
44. Manders S: Toxin-mediated streptococcal and staphylococcal disease. *J Am Acad Dermatol* 39:383, 1998.
45. Egan C, et al: Plasmapheresis as an adjunct in toxic epidermal necrolysis. *J Am Acad Dermatol* 40:458, 1999.
46. Cohen-Abbo A, Harper MB: Case report: Streptococcal toxic shock syndrome presenting as septic thrombophlebitis in a child with varicella. *Pediatr Infect Dis J* 12:1033, 1993.
47. Soravia C, et al: Group A beta-haemolytic streptococcus septicaemia: The toxic strep syndrome. Report of our cases developing septic shock and multiple organ failure. *Intensive Care Med* 19:53, 1993.
48. Ritacca FV, et al: Pro/con clinical debate: Are steroids useful in the management of patients with septic shock? *Crit Care* 6:113, 2002.
49. Westo WL, Badgett JT: Urticaria. *Pediatr Rev* 19:240, 1998.
50. Tharp MD: Chronic urticaria: Pathophysiology and treatment approaches. *J Allergy Clin Immunol* 98:S325, 1996.
51. Beltrani VS: Urticaria and angioedema. *Dermatol Clin* 14:171, 1996.
52. Srabani G, Kanwar AJ, Kaur S: Urticaria in children. *Pediatr Dermatol* 10:107, 1993.
53. Finn AF, et al: A double-blind, placebo-controlled trial of fexofenadine HCl in the treatment of chronic idiopathic urticaria. *J Allergy Clin Immunol* 104:1077, 1999.
54. Peter G (ed): *Red Book: Report of the Committee on Infectious Diseases.* St Louis, American Academy of Pediatrics, 1997.
55. Measles. *MMWR Morb Mortal Wkly Rep* 43:673, 1994.
56. Akinbami L, Cheng T: Rocky Mountain spotted fever. *Pediatr Rev* 19:171, 1998.
57. Resnick SD: New aspects of exanthematous diseases of childhood. *Dermatol Clin* 15:257, 1997.
58. Friedlander SF: Contact dermatitis. *Pediatr Rev* 19:166, 1998.
59. Lawrence R: Poisonous plants: When they are a threat to children. *Pediatr Rev* 18:164, 1997.
60. Dotson RL, Zurowski S, Walker KD: Erythema multiforme. *Mo Med* 90:221, 1993.

61. Burkhart CG, Burkhart CN, Burkhart KM: An assessment of topical and oral prescription and over-the-counter treatments for head lice. *J Am Acad Dermatol* 38:979, 1998.
62. Paller AS: Scabies in infants and small children. *Semin Dermatol* 12:3, 1993.
63. Duran C, et al: Scabies of the scalp mimicking seborrheic dermatitis in immunocompromised patients. *Pediatr Dermatol* 10:136, 1993.
64. Schlesinger I, Oelrich DM, Tyring SK: Crusted (Norwegian) scabies in patients with AIDS: The range of clinical presentations. *South Med J* 87:352, 1994.
65. Haag ML, Brozena SJ, Fenske NA: Attack of the scabies: What to do when an outbreak occurs? *Geriatrics* 48:45, 1993.
66. Orkin M, Maibach HI: Scabies therapy. *Semin Dermatol* 12:22, 1993.
67. Robson KJ, Piette WW: Cutaneous manifestations of systemic diseases. *Med Clin North Am* 82:P1359, 1998.
68. Scott JE, Ahmed AR: The blistering diseases. *Med Clin North Am* 82:P1239, 1998.
69. Shatley M: Bullous pemphigoid. *Mo Med* 90:274, 1993.
70. Warren SD, Lesher JL: Cicatricial pemphigoid. *South Med J* 86:461, 1993.
71. Said S, et al: Localized bullous scabies. *Am J Dermatol* 15:590, 1993.
72. Dunkle LM, et al: A controlled trial of acyclovir for chicken pox in normal children. *N Engl J Med* 325:1539, 1991.
73. Stewart M: Treatment of varicella in pregnancy. In *Critical Decisions in Emergency Medicine*, vol 9. Dallas, American College of Emergency Physicians, 1995.
74. McCrary ML, Severson J, Tyring SK: Varicella zoster virus. *J Am Acad Dermatol* 41:1, 1999.
75. Prevention of varicella. Update recommendations of the Advisory Committee on Immunization Practices. *MMWR Recomm Rep* 48(RR-6):1, 1999.
76. McCross IN, Wung D: HIV related skin disease. *Med J Aust* 158:179, 1993.
77. http://www.cdc.gov/smallpox.
78. http://www.cdc.gov/anthrax.
79. Katz SK, Gordon KH, Roenigk HH: The cutaneous manifestations of gastrointestinal disease. *Prim Care Clin Office Pract* 23:455, 1996.
80. Callen J: Lupus erythematosus in dermatological signs of internal disease. In Callen JP (ed): *Clinical Dermatology.* Philadelphia, WB Saunders, 1988.
81. Greer KE: Cutaneous disease and arthritis in dermatological signs of internal disease. In Callen JP (ed): *Clinical Dermatology.* Philadelphia, WB Saunders, 1988.
82. Greer KE: Thyroid and the skin in dermatological signs of internal disease. In Callen JP (ed): *Clinical Dermatology.* Philadelphia, WB Saunders, 1988.
83. Kim NY: Pigmentary diseases. *Med Clin North Am* 82:185, 1998.
84. Sigurgeirsson B, et al: Risk of cancer in patients with dermatomyositis or polymyositis: A population-based study. *N Engl J Med* 326:363, 1992.
85. Habif TP: Cutaneous manifestations of internal disease. In Habif TP (ed): *Clinical Dermatology,* 3rd ed. St Louis, Mosby–Year Book, 1996.
86. Macaione AS: An approach to purpura. *Cutis* 12:41, 1973.
87. Ebright JR: Skin and soft tissue infections in injection drug users. *Infect Dis Clin North Am* 16:697, 2002.

Section X **HEMATOLOGY AND ONCOLOGY**

CHAPTER
119
Anemia, Polycythemia, and White Blood Cell Disorders

Glenn C. Hamilton and Timothy G. Janz

ANEMIA

Definition

Anemia is an absolute decrease in the number of circulating red blood cells (RBCs). The diagnosis is made when laboratory measurements fall below accepted normal values (Table 119-1).

In emergency medicine, anemia may be divided into two broad categories: emergent, having immediate life-threatening complications, and nonemergent, with less imminent patient danger. Factors other than the absolute number of circulating RBCs may place the patient in one category or another (e.g., rate of onset, underlying hemodynamic reserve of the patient).[1,2] Both groups necessitate a sound diagnostic approach, but emergent anemia may require supportive therapy concomitant with or in advance of the definitive diagnosis. Although patients with nonemergent anemia are usually referred to a specialist, they are seen in the hospital often enough to make an understanding of anemia necessary for emergency physicians. The urgency of consultation depends predominantly on the patient's hemodynamic tolerance of the anemia.[1,3]

Pathophysiology

The major function of the RBC is oxygen transport from the lung to the tissue and carbon dioxide transport in the reverse direction. Oxygen transport is influenced by the amount of hemoglobin, its oxygen affinity, and blood flow. An alteration in any of the major components usually results in compensatory changes in the other two. For example, a decrease in hemoglobin from anemia is compensated by both inotropic and chronotropic cardiac changes that result in increased blood flow and decreased hemoglobin affinity at the tissue level, thereby allowing more oxygen release. These

Table 119-1. Hemogram Normal Values

Age	Hemoglobin (g/dL)	Hematocrit (mL/dL)	Red Blood Cell Count ($\times 10^6$)
3 mo	10.4-12.2	30-36	3.4-4.0
3-7 yr	11.7-13.5	34-40	4.4-5.0
Adult man	14.0-18.0	40-52	4.4-5.9
Adult woman	12.0-16.0	35-47	3.8-5.2

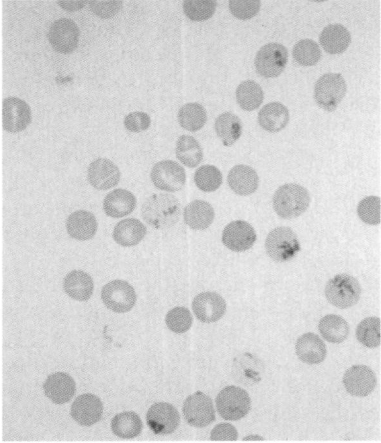

Figure 119-1. Reticulocytes with reticular material after methylene blue staining. (From Hoffbrand AV, Pettite JE: *Color Atlas of Clinical Hematology*, 3rd ed. London, Mosby, 2000, p 18.)

BOX 119-1. Causes of Rapid Intravascular Red Blood Cell Destruction

Mechanical hemolysis associated with disseminated intravascular coagulation

Massive burns

Toxins (e.g., some poisonous venoms—brown recluse spider, cobra)

Infections such as malaria or *Clostridium* sepsis

Severe glucose-6-phosphate dehydrogenase deficiency with exposure to oxidant stress

ABO incompatibility transfusion reaction

Cold agglutinin hemolysis (e.g., *Mycoplasma* organisms, infectious mononucleosis)

Paroxysmal nocturnal hemoglobinuria exacerbated by transfusion

Immune complex hemolysis (e.g., quinidine)

compensatory responses may collapse because of disease severity or underlying pathologic conditions. The result is tissue hypoxia and eventual cell death.[1,4]

Anemia often stimulates the compensatory mechanism of erythropoiesis controlled by the hormone erythropoietin. Erythropoietin is a glycoprotein produced in the kidney (90%) and the liver (10%). It regulates the production of RBCs by controlling differentiation of the committed erythroid stem cell. It is stimulated by tissue hypoxia and products of RBC destruction during hemolysis. Erythropoietin levels are elevated in many types of anemia.[5,6]

Bone marrow contains pluripotent stem cells that can differentiate into erythroid, myeloid, megakaryocytic, and lymphoid progenitors. Erythropoietin enhances the growth and differentiation of erythroid progenitors. When the late normoblast extrudes its nucleus, it still contains a ribosomal network, which identifies the reticulocyte (Figure 119-1). The reticulocyte retains its ribosomal network for about 4 days, 3 of which are spent in bone marrow and 1 in the peripheral circulation. The RBC matures as the reticulocyte loses its ribosomal network and circulates for 110 to 120 days. The erythrocyte is then removed by macrophages that detect senescent signals.

Under steady-state conditions, the rate of RBC production equals the rate of destruction. RBC mass remains constant because an equal number of reticulocytes replace the destroyed, senescent erythrocytes during the same period.[5]

Common sites of blood loss in trauma include the pleural, peritoneal, and retroperitoneal spaces. In nontraumatic circumstances, the gastrointestinal tract, uterus, and adnexa must be considered.

Causes other than blood loss may be responsible for severe anemia of rapid onset. Certain rare hemolytic conditions can cause rapid intravascular destruction of RBCs (Box 119-1). More common are patients with chronic compensated hemolytic anemia (e.g., sickle cell disease), who decompensate with an acute-onset anemia as a result of decreased erythrocyte production triggered by a viral infection.

Beyond red cell destruction, the status of hemoglobin function must be considered. Impaired hemoglobin transport of oxygen is seen in cases of carbon monoxide poisoning. Methemoglobinemia from nitrates and sulfhemoglobinemia resulting from hydrogen sulfide may severely decrease functional hemoglobin. These patients often have fatigue, altered mental status, shortness of breath, and other manifestations of hypoxia without signs of RBC loss or volume depletion.[7,8]

Diagnostic Findings in Emergent Anemia

Clinical Features

The clinical manifestation of anemia depends on the rapidity of its development and the patient's ability to compensate for and tolerate the insult. The most common cause of clinically severe anemia is blood loss.

Clinical signs and symptoms include tachycardia, decreased blood pressure, postural hypotension, increased heart rate, and increased respiratory rate. Complaints of thirst, altered mental status, and decreased urine output may accompany this picture. The patient's age, concomitant illness, and underlying hematologic, cerebral, and cardiovascular status tremendously influence the clinical findings. Infants are typically unable to communicate. Children and young adults may tolerate significant blood loss with unaltered vital signs until a precipitant hypotensive episode occurs. Elderly patients commonly have underlying disease states that compromise their ability to compensate for blood loss.[9]

Pertinent elements of the history and physical examination of patients with acute anemia are listed in Box 119-2.[10]

Ancillary Evaluation

Stabilization of emergent anemia commonly runs parallel to assessment. If the signs and symptoms suggest potential life-threatening conditions, intravenous lines are placed and samples for the following initial laboratory tests are drawn:

1. Complete blood count and peripheral smear
2. Blood sample for type and crossmatch
3. Prothrombin time
4. Partial thromboplastin time
5. Electrolyte levels
6. Glucose level
7. Creatinine level
8. Urinalysis for free hemoglobin
9. Clotting and unclotted blood samples for consultation

If possible, a blood sample is obtained for measurement of hematocrit in the emergency department. Although it may take hours before the hematocrit correctly reflects the degree of blood loss, the initial value is useful in determining the patient's baseline. Occasionally, this value reveals an underlying anemia with the acute blood loss superimposed. Depending on severity, a blood sample is sent for type and crossmatch. Peripheral smear interpretation is done on pretreatment blood samples.

Measurements of coagulation status, electrolytes, glucose, blood urea nitrogen, and creatinine are useful in the diagnosis of underlying disease processes that may relate to the patient's anemia. Values of folate, vitamin B12, iron, total iron-binding capacity, reticulocytes, and direct antiglobulin (Coombs test) are altered by transfusion. Therefore, pretreatment samples are best saved.[11,12]

Diagnostic Findings in Nonemergent Anemia

Clinical Features

Nonemergent anemias are usually seen in ambulatory patients complaining of fatigue and feeling "washed out." Other voiced complaints include irritability, headache, postural dizziness, angina, decreased exercise tolerance, shortness of breath, and decreased libido. The history and physical examination are more detailed than in a patient presenting with clinically severe anemia (Box 119-3). Most of these patients do not need immediate stabilization and can be further evaluated as outpatients.

Ancillary Evaluation

The initial laboratory evaluation includes a complete blood count with leukocyte differential, reticulocyte count, peripheral smear (Figure 119-2), and RBC indices, including mean corpuscular volume (MCV), mean corpuscular hemoglobin (MCH), and mean corpuscular hemoglobin concentration (MCHC).

Disposition

Reasonable criteria for the admission of patients with nonemergent anemia are found in Box 119-4.[12]

Differential Diagnosis

The differential diagnosis of anemia is facilitated by classifying the anemia into one of three groups: decreased RBC production, increased RBC destruction, and blood loss.[13] A complementary approach uses RBC morphology and indices.[14]

BOX 119-3. History and Physical Examination for Nonemergent Anemia

History
Symptoms of anemia
Chest pain, exercise tolerance, dyspnea
Weakness, fatigue, dizziness, syncope

Bleeding diathesis
Bleeding after trauma, injections, tooth extractions
Spontaneous bleeding, such as epistaxis, menorrhagia
Spontaneous purpura and petechiae

Sites of blood loss
Respiratory: epistaxis, hemoptysis
Gastrointestinal: hematemesis, hematochezia, melena
Genitourinary: abnormal menses, pregnancies, hematuria
Skin: petechiae, ecchymoses

Intermittent jaundice, dark urine

Dietary history
Vegetarianism
Poor nutrition

Drug use and toxin exposure, including alcohol
Racial background, family history
Underlying disease
Uremia, liver disease, hypothyroidism
Chronic disease states such as cancer, rheumatic or renal disease
Previous surgery
Miscellaneous
Previous treatment of anemia
Weight loss
Back pain

Physical Examination
Skin
Pallor
Purpura, petechiae, angiomas
Ulcerations
Eye
Conjunctival jaundice, pallor
Funduscopic hemorrhage, petechiae
Oral
Tongue atrophy, papillary soreness
Cardiopulmonary
Heart size, murmurs, extra cardiac sounds
Wheezing rales, other signs of pulmonary edema
Abdomen
Hepatomegaly, splenomegaly
Ascites
Masses
Lymph nodes
Neurologic
Altered positions or vibratory sense
Peripheral neuritis
Rectal and pelvic

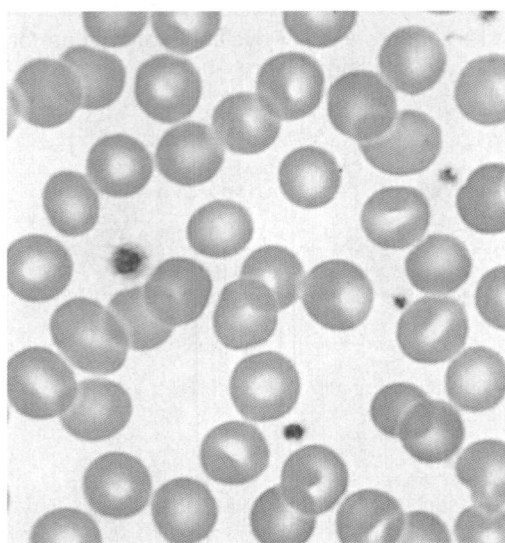

Figure 119-2. Normal smear. (From Hoffbrand AV, Pettite JE: *Color Atlas of Clinical Hematology*, 3rd ed. London, Mosby, 2000, p 22.)

BOX 119-4. Admission Criteria for Nonemergent Anemia

Developing cardiac symptoms, such as shortness of breath or chest pain, or neurologic symptoms
Initial unexplained hemoglobin value less than 8 to 10 g/dL or hematocrit less than 25% to 30%
Major difficulty in patient home-to-hospital transportation if extensive evaluation is necessary (the definition of "difficulty" may be determined by the patient, primary physician, and insurance carrier)

BOX 119-5. Differential Diagnosis of Anemias Caused by Decreased Red Blood Cell Production: Subclassification by Red Blood Cell Indices

Hypochromic Microcytic Anemias (Decreased MCV and Hemoglobin Concentration)
Iron deficiency
Thalassemia
Sideroblastic anemia or lead poisoning
Chronic disease (e.g., cancer, renal or inflammatory disease); normochromic normocytic indices are often found

Macrocytic (Elevated MCV)
Vitamin B12 deficiency
Folate deficiency
Liver disease
Hypothyroidism

Normocytic (Normal MCV and Hemoglobin Concentration)
Primary bone marrow involvement: aplastic anemia, myeloid metaplasia with myelofibrosis, myelophthisic anemia
Resulting from underlying disease: hypoendocrine state (thyroid, adrenal, pituitary), uremia, chronic inflammation, liver disease

MCV, mean corpuscular volume.

Decreased Red Blood Cell Production

Anemias caused by decreased RBC production have a natural history of insidious onset and an associated decreased reticulocyte count. A subclassification by indices of anemias caused by decreased RBC production is listed in Box 119-5. The RBC indices and morphology manifested in a peripheral smear are useful in securing the diagnosis. The definitive diagnosis is usually made outside the emergency department and may require bone marrow examination. The emergency physician rarely initiates replacement therapy, except in circumstances that require transfusion. Appropriate diagnostic tests may be initiated, but replacement of iron, vitamin B12, or folate without proof of cause is unnecessary and unwise.

RBC indices are useful in classifying anemias caused by a production deficit. Their calculation and normal ranges are provided in Table 119-2. MCV is a measure of RBC size. Decreases and increases reflect microcytosis and macrocytosis, respectively. MCH incorporates both RBC size and hemoglobin concentration. It is influenced by both and is the least helpful of the indices. The MCHC index is a measure of the concentration of hemoglobin. Low values represent hypochromia, whereas high values are noted only in patients with decreased cell membrane relative to cell volume, such as in the case of spherocytosis. An additional index is the RBC distribution width (RDW), which is a measure of the homogenicity of the RBCs measured. RDW is automatically calculated as the standard deviation of MCV divided by MCV multiplied by 100. A normal RDW is 13.5% ± 1.5%. It is useful in differentiating iron deficiency from thalassemia.[15]

Microcytic Anemias

Hypochromic microcytic anemias can be subdivided into deficiencies of the three building blocks of hemoglobin: iron (iron deficiency anemia [Figure 119-3]), globin (thalassemia), and porphyrin (sideroblastic anemia and lead poisoning). Anemia of chronic disease, a secondary iron abnormality, rounds out the differential diagnosis. Not all microcytic anemias are the result of iron deficiency, and routine iron therapy for a patient with a low MCV and MCHC is inappropriate.

Iron Deficiency Anemia. Iron deficiency is a frequent cause of chronic anemia seen in the emergency department. It is the most common anemia in women of childbearing age. In older patients, occult blood loss, especially gastrointestinal, may initially appear as iron deficiency anemia. Because changes in RBC size and hemoglobin content occur only after bone marrow and cytochrome iron stores are depleted, a patient may have early symptoms of iron deficiency (e.g., fatigue) without manifesting changes in RBC structure. Actually, a low MCV is relatively rare in iron deficiency anemia.

The diagnosis is made by laboratory evaluation of the fasting level of serum iron, serum ferritin, and total iron-binding capacity. The laboratory interpretation and pitfalls are outlined in Table 119-3. A concentrated search for occult blood loss is vital.

Therapy consists of oral iron replacement. A cost-effective form is ferrous sulfate. The dosage is 300 mg for adults (60 mg of elemental iron) or for children 3 mg/kg/day. This medication is well tolerated, although it may cause nausea, vomiting, or constipation. Patients should be warned that their stools will be blackened. In rare patients with poor oral tolerance or absorption, parenteral iron therapy may be necessary.

The patient may experience a sense of improvement in as little as 24 hours. Reticulocytosis appears over a

Table 119-2. Calculation of Red Blood Cell Indices and Normal Values

Index	Formula for Calculation	Normal Range
Mean corpuscular volume	Hematocrit (%) divided by red blood cell count ($10^6/\mu L$)	81-100 fL
Mean corpuscular hemoglobin	Hemoglobin (g/dL) divided by red blood cell count ($10^6/\mu L$)	26-34 pg
Mean corpuscular hemoglobin concentration	Hemoglobin (g/dL) divided by hematocrit (%)	31-36%

fL, femtoliter.

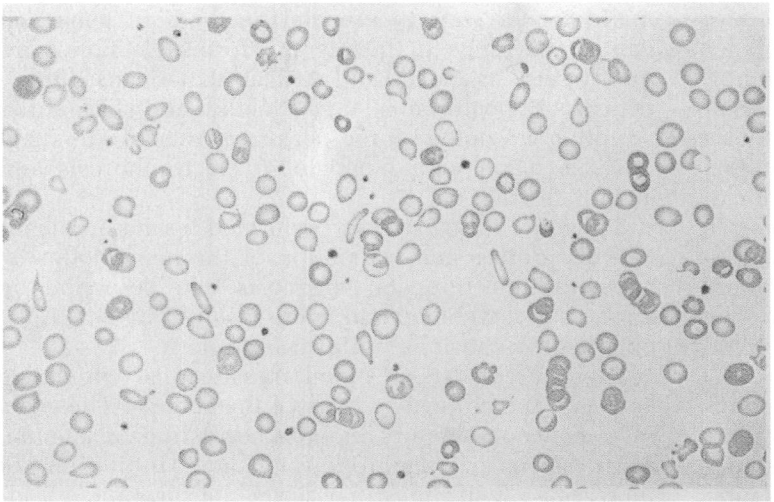

Figure 119-3. Iron deficiency anemia with hypochromic, microcytic cells and poikilocytes (abnormally shaped cells). (From Hoffbrand AV, Pettite JE: *Color Atlas of Clinical Hematology*, 3rd ed. London, Mosby, 2000, p 44.)

Table 119-3. Diagnostic Tests for Iron Deficiency Anemia

Test	Normal Result	Iron Deficiency Level	Interpretation
Fasting serum iron	60-180 µg/dL	<60 µg/dL	Diurnal variation (draw in morning); increased by hepatitis, hemochromatosis, hemolytic anemia, and aplastic anemia; decreased in infection
Total iron-binding capacity	250-400 µg/dL	>400 µg/dL	Increased in late pregnancy or hepatitis, decreased in infection
Percentage of saturation (serum iron) of total iron-binding capacity	15-45%	<15%	
Serum ferritin	10-10,000 mg/mL	<10 mg/mL	Reflects iron stores; may increase as an acute-phase reactant in infection
Bone marrow stainable iron	Hemosiderin granules in reticuloendothelial cells	Absent	Standard for assessment of iron stores

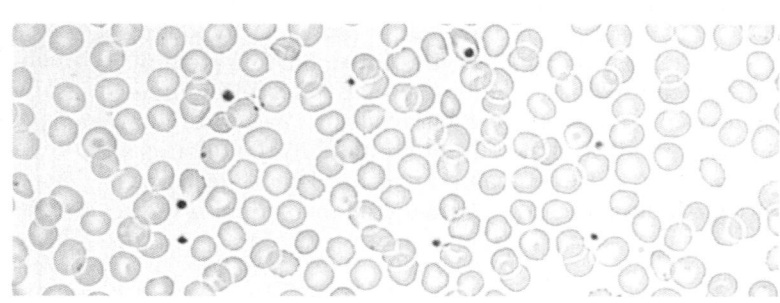

Figure 119-4. β-Thalassemia with microcytic hemochromic red cells and target cells. (From Hoffbrand AV, Pettite JE: *Color Atlas of Clinical Hematology*, 3rd ed. London, Mosby, 2000, p 96.)

3- to 4-day period in children but may take more than 1 week in adults. The hemoglobin concentration rises on a similar schedule. If such a response does not occur, the patient is noncompliant with the iron supplementation, the blood loss may exceed the replacement, the diagnosis is incorrect, or the diagnosis is partially correct with an additional process complicating the iron deficiency.[15-18]

Thalassemia. Thalassemia is a genetic autosomal defect reflected by the decreased synthesis of globin chains.[19] The globin in hemoglobin is present as two paired chains. Each type of hemoglobin is made up of different globins. For example, normal adult hemoglobin (HbA) is made up of two α chains and two β chains ($\alpha_2\beta_2$). HbA_2 is $\alpha_2\delta_2$, and fetal hemoglobin (HbF) is $\alpha_2\gamma_2$. A separate autosomal gene controls each globin chain. Deletions in this globin gene result in an absence or decreased function of the messenger RNA that codes for the creation of that globin. The various globins (α, β, δ, γ) may be affected by a number of genetic combinations. The decrease in globin production in thalassemia results in decreased hemoglobin synthesis and ineffective erythropoiesis. The latter is attributable to increased intramarrow hemolysis with destruction of RBCs before they are released. Normal erythropoiesis has a 10% to 20% incidence of ineffective release, with associated intramarrow RBC destruction. This number may double or triple in patients with thalassemia. The cause is believed to be excess chains of the uninhibited globin precipitating in RBCs.[19,20]

Although many variations in thalassemia are possible, only three are commonly considered. Homozygous β-chain thalassemia (thalassemia major) occurs predominantly in Mediterranean populations. It repre-

sents one of the most common single-gene disorders. The disease is characterized by severe anemia, hepatosplenomegaly, jaundice, abnormal development, and premature death. Patients are transfusion dependent and die of iron deposition in tissues, particularly the myocardium, or infection. Treatment is supportive and consists of transfusion and iron-chelating therapy.[21]

Heterozygous β-chain thalassemia (thalassemia minor) is manifested as a mild microcytic hypochromic anemia with target cells seen on the peripheral smear (Figure 119-4), an MCV commonly more severely lowered than with iron deficiency anemia, a normal level of serum iron, and an elevated level of HbA_2 ($\alpha_2\delta_2$) on hemoglobin electrophoresis (2% to 5%). Usually no treatment is necessary.

α-Thalassemia varies in spectrum from an asymptomatic carrier state to prenatal death. Four gene loci control this range. In the tolerated forms it is more commonly seen in Asians and African Americans. Microcytosis, hypochromia, target cells, and basophilic stippling are noted on the peripheral smear. The diagnosis is made with hemoglobin electrophoresis and genetic testing.

Screening for carriers is performed by measurement of RBC indices and estimation of the hemoglobin A_2 concentration. Prenatal diagnosis can be made by analysis of fetal blood and, more recently, by fetal DNA obtained by chorionic villus sampling.

Therapy consists of blood transfusions, which are based on the clinical severity of the anemia. The goals of transfusion therapy include correction of anemia, suppression of erythropoiesis, and inhibition of increased gastrointestinal iron absorption. Iron-

chelating therapy, most commonly deferoxamine, is often required to control excess iron stores. Bone marrow transplantation from HLA-identical donors has resulted in disease-free survival in 60% to 90% of recipients, but its role in thalassemia has yet to be determined. Although much interest centers on permanent correction of genetic deficits in thalassemia, gene therapy does not yet exist.[22]

Sideroblastic Anemia. Sideroblastic anemia involves a defect in porphyrin synthesis. The resultant impaired hemoglobin production causes excess iron to be deposited in the mitochondria of the RBC precursor, but some also circulates. The result is increased serum iron and ferritin levels, with transferrin saturation. The defective heme synthesis results in ineffective erythropoiesis, mild to moderate anemia, and a dimorphic peripheral smear with hypochromic microcytes along with normal and macrocytic cells.[23]

Sideroblastic anemia, though found in a rare sex-linked hereditary form, is more a disease of the elderly. Indeed, the idiopathic form is a common type of refractory anemia in elderly patients. Pallor and splenomegaly may be noted, and iron staining of the peripheral smear may demonstrate iron-containing Pappenheimer inclusion bodies in RBCs. Some of these patients are deficient in pyridoxine (vitamin B6) and respond to treatment with 100 mg of pyridoxine three times a day. Most remain anemic, but a 1- to 2-month pyridoxine trial is acceptable treatment. These patients may be susceptible to iron overload, particularly if long-term transfusion therapy is necessary, but they may respond to iron chelation therapy. Idiopathic sideroblastic anemia is considered a preleukemic state, and acute myelogenous leukemia develops in approximately 20% of these patients.

Secondary causes of sideroblastic anemia include toxins such as chloramphenicol, isoniazid, and cycloserine, as well as diseases such as hemolytic and megaloblastic anemia, infection, carcinoma, leukemia, and rheumatoid arthritis. The exact mechanisms of these causative agents and diseases are unknown. Lead poisoning is one reversible cause of sideroblastic anemia. It may be suggested by the appearance of RBC basophilic stippling on the peripheral smear. Elevated blood lead levels are diagnostic. Alcohol abuse may also result in disordered heme synthesis, which can be corrected by alcohol cessation or by parenteral pyridoxal phosphate in cases of continued abuse. Oral pyridoxine may be ineffective because of impaired conversion to the active form in alcoholic patients.[23]

Anemia of Chronic Disease. Anemia of chronic disease is very common. It is characterized by low serum iron levels, low total iron-binding capacity, and normal or elevated ferritin levels. The indices are commonly normocytic, normochromic. Bone marrow is normal, but staining reveals an abnormality in the mobilization of iron from reticuloendothelial cells. This anemia can be differentiated from iron deficiency by the total iron-binding capacity, the serum ferritin level, bone marrow examination, and nonresponsiveness to a trial of iron therapy. Because the hematocrit is seldom less than 25% to 30%, therapy is not usually required. A com-

plete search for occult blood loss is necessary during the evaluation of this diagnosis because iron deficiency may be superimposed. Disseminated cancer, chronic inflammation, uremia, and infection are common causes.[24-26]

Macrocytic and Megaloblastic Anemia

In terms of the potential for a therapeutic response, the most important cause of macrocytosis is megaloblastic anemia. Megaloblastic anemia is the hematologic manifestation of a total-body alteration in DNA synthesis. The defective DNA synthesis is caused by a lack of the coenzyme forms of vitamin B12 and folic acid. The deficiency appears clinically in tissues with rapid cell turnover, including hematopoietic cells and those of mucosal surfaces, particularly in the gastrointestinal tract. Hematopoietically, this deficiency is characterized by ineffective erythropoiesis and pancytopenia. Vitamin B12 and folate deficiencies have different developmental histories, but the clinical result may be similar. Differentiation of folate and vitamin B12 deficiency usually depends on measured levels in the laboratory.

Folic acid, absorbed in the duodenum and jejunum, is commonly found in green vegetables, cereals, and fruit. It may be destroyed completely by cooking. The body requires approximately 100 μg/day and usually stores 6 to 20 mg. Therefore, a 2- to 4-month supply is available before megaloblastic changes occur. Causes of folate deficiency are listed in Box 119-6. Most patients with folate deficiency have either an inadequate dietary intake, such as alcoholic patients, or increased use, as in pregnancy.

Vitamin B12 is found in foods of animal origin only and is not destroyed by cooking. It is absorbed in the ileum after binding to intrinsic factor. This glycoprotein factor is secreted by the parietal cells of the gastric mucosa and allows low levels of B12 to be actively absorbed. The adult requirement is 1 or 2 μg/day, with

---

BOX 119-6. Causes of Folate Deficiency

Inadequate Dietary Intake
Poor diet or overcooked or processed food diet
Alcoholism

Inadequate Uptake
Malabsorption with sprue and other chronic upper intestinal tract disorders, drugs such as phenytoin and barbiturates, or blind loop syndrome

Inadequate Use
Metabolic block caused by drugs such as methotrexate or trimethoprim
Enzymatic deficiency, congenital or acquired

Increased Requirement
Pregnancy
Increased RBC turnover: ineffective erythropoiesis, hemolytic anemia, chronic blood loss
Malignancy: lymphoproliferative disorders

Increased Excretion or Destruction or Dialysis

BOX 119-7. Causes of Vitamin B12 Deficiency

Inadequate Dietary Intake
Total vegetarianism: no eggs, milk, or cheese
Chronic alcoholism (rare)

Inadequate Absorption
Absent, inadequate, or abnormal intrinsic factor, as seen in patients with pernicious gastrectomy and anemia. In the latter, autoimmune antibodies act against gastric parietal cells and intrinsic factor. Abnormal ileum, as can occur in sprue and inflammatory bowel disease

Inadequate Use
Enzyme deficiency
Abnormal vitamin B12–binding protein

Increased Requirement by Increased Body Metabolism

Increased Excretion or Destruction

Table 119-4. Clinicopathologic Correlation of Manifestations of Megaloblastic Anemia

Clinical Features	Pathologic Condition
Lemon yellow skin	Combination of pallor with low-grade icterus from ineffective erythropoiesis
Petechiae, mucosal bleeding	Thrombocytopenia
Infection	Leukopenia
Fatigue, dyspnea on exertion, postural hypotension	Anemia
Sore mouth or tongue	Megaloblastosis of mucosal surfaces
Diarrhea and weight loss	Malabsorption from mucosal surface change
Paresthesias and ataxia	Related to myelin abnormality in vitamin B12 deficiency only

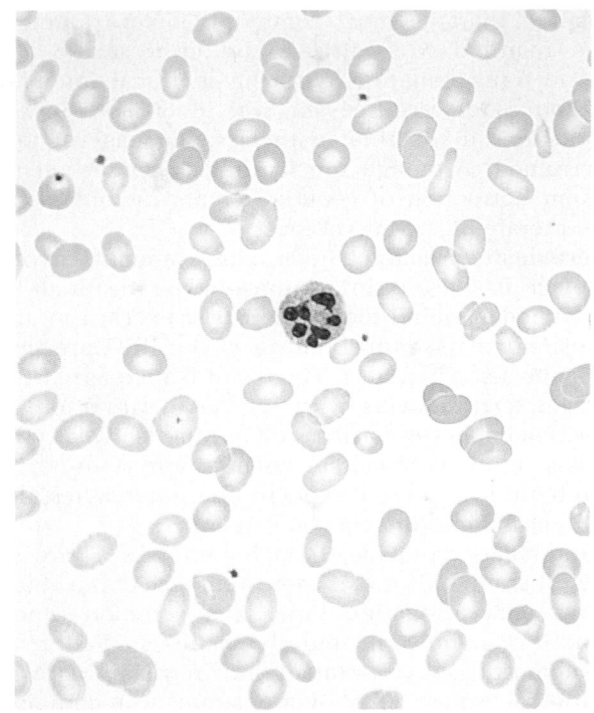

Figure 119-5. Megaloblastic anemia with macrocytic red cells and hypersegmented polymorphonuclear neutrophils. (From Hoffbrand AV, Pettite JE: *Color Atlas of Clinical Hematology*, 3rd ed. London, Mosby, 2000, p 61.)

a body store of 5 mg. Therefore, megaloblastic changes may take up to 4 years to develop after cessation of vitamin B12 uptake. The various causes of vitamin B12 deficiency are listed in Box 119-7. The most common cause is chronic malabsorption.

Megaloblastic anemia that is not responsive to folate or vitamin B12 is commonly related to antimetabolites used in chemotherapy or rare inherited disorders of DNA synthesis.

Table 119-4 lists a number of the problems associated with megaloblastic anemia and their underlying pathologic states. A unique feature of vitamin B12 deficiency is its neurologic involvement. Patients may have paresthesias in their hands and feet, decreased proprioception, or decreased vibratory sense. The insidiously developing classic neurologic complex includes loss of proprioception, weakness and spasticity of the lower extremities with altered reflexes, and variable mental changes such as depression, paranoid ideation, irritability, and forgetfulness. The latter two complaints have also been noted with folic acid deficiency. Vitamin B12 deficient patients have some of the lowest hemoglobin levels seen in any disease state.[27]

Macrocytic anemia is suggested when the MCV is greater than 100 fL^3, but other criteria must be met for megaloblastosis to be considered the cause of the macrocytic anemia. On the peripheral smear, large oval red cells (macro-ovalocytes) and hypersegmented polymorphonuclear neutrophils are believed to be diagnostic (Figure 119-5). A bone marrow aspirate may reveal morphologic changes consistent with megaloblastic erythropoiesis. Other potentially useful laboratory tests include vitamin B12 and folate levels, red cell folate, and lactate dehydrogenase (LDH). Laboratory techniques, values, and interpretations are listed in Table 119-5. Once megaloblastic anemia is diagnosed and folate or vitamin B12 deficiency determined, standard diagnostic regimens are followed to determine the precise origin of the deficiency.

Because one deficiency may cause gastrointestinal absorption changes that beget other deficiencies, the emergency physician may be forced to initiate therapy before the final diagnosis is made. However, a caution is given to obtain necessary laboratory specimens before pursuing this course. The usual dosage for patients with megaloblastic anemia secondary to folate deficiency is 1 mg of oral folic acid per day. Parenteral administration is generally unnecessary because most cases are due to dietary deficiency. In contrast, malabsorption is the most common cause of vitamin B12 deficiency, and parenteral therapy is initiated at 100 µg/day IM for the first 7 to 10 days. Thereafter, only monthly 100-µg doses are necessary. The response is often dramatic, with reticulocyte counts rising up to 30% to 50% and normalization of RBC, white blood cell

Table 119-5. Serum Tests for Diagnosis and Differentiation of Megaloblastic Anemia

Test	Technique	Value	Interpretation
Vitamin B12	Microbiologic or radioisotope	Normal: 300–900 µg/L Deficient: <200 µg/L	Although they may overlap clinically, vitamin B12 is usually normal in folate deficiency
Folate	Microbiologic or radioisotope	Deficient: <3 µg/L	Vitamin B12 deficiency may elevate folate levels by blocking transfer of serum folate to RBCs; hemolysis may elevate folate levels
Red cell folate	Calculated	Normal: 200-700 µg/L Folate deficiency: <140 µg/L	Index of tissue folate is less influenced by diet and is increased in vitamin B12 deficiency because of block
Lactate dehydrogenase	Spectrophotometric	Normal: 95-200 IU Megaloblastic anemia: 4–50 times normal	Normal in other macrocytic anemias; elevated 2 to 4 times normal in hemolytic anemias; isoenzymes may be helpful

(WBC), and platelet counts in 6 to 8 weeks. The use of vitamin B12 or folate supplements in patients with undiagnosed anemia is to be discouraged. The use of routine vitamin B12 injections in the elderly has decreased but is still a too common practice.[27,28]

Macrocytic anemias unrelated to megaloblastic changes are seen frequently. Liver disease, often associated with alcoholism, is the most common cause.[29] Macrocytic target cells may be seen on the peripheral smear in conjunction with this disorder. Hypothyroidism and hemolysis may also be manifested as macrocytic anemia. Screening tests to differentiate between megaloblastic anemia and macrocytic anemia of other causes include a peripheral smear for macroovalocytes, hypersegmented polymorphonuclear neutrophils, and the LDH level.[27,29]

Normochromic and Normocytic Anemias

The origin of normochromic and normocytic anemia secondary to decreased production is not as obvious as that of macrocytic and microcytic anemia because the latter give clues to their origin by alterations in RBC indices. One hematologic parameter that can aid in the diagnosis of normocytic anemia associated with hypoproduction is the corrected reticulocyte count. Reticulocytes reflect RBC production in bone marrow. They are RBCs released from bone marrow every 1 to 3 days and contain residual RNA that can be detected by supravital staining. Reticulocytes have an average MCV of 160 fL and in sufficient numbers can increase the MCV of the total erythrocyte count. The reticulocyte count is expressed as a percentage of the total RBC population and must be related ("corrected") to the RBC count of the patient. Thus, the corrected reticulocyte count is equal to the measured percentage of reticulocytes times the patient's hematocrit (%) divided by 45% (taken as the normal hematocrit). The normal range is 1% to 3%.

Normocytic anemia may be classified as being due to primary bone marrow involvement or a secondary marrow response to underlying disease.

Aplastic anemia is rare but may have severe manifestations. It is suspected in anemic patients with normal indices, a low reticulocyte count, and a history of exposure to certain drugs or chemicals (Table 119-6). It is related to drug or chemical exposure in 50% of cases. Viral hepatitis, radiation, and pregnancy have

Table 119-6. Aplastic Anemia Caused by Drugs or Chemicals

Cause	Relative Incidence (%)
Chloramphenicol	61
Phenylbutazone	19
Anticonvulsants	4
Insecticides	4
Solvents	4
Sulfonamides	3
Gold	3
Benzene	2

From Silver BJ, Zuckerman KS: Aplastic anemia: Recent advances in pathogenesis and treatment. *Med Clin North Am* 64.607, 1980.

been associated with aplastic anemia. Another group of patients is considered to have an "autoimmune" origin.

The aplastic state may extend to all cell lines and results from destruction by immune-stimulated lymphocytes or failure of the marrow stem cell. Occasionally, only one cell line fails, as in RBC aplasia. This condition represents injury occurring at a later stage of cellular differentiation. The precise diagnosis necessitates bone marrow examination, but the causative factor may be difficult to determine.

General treatment of aplastic anemia includes removal of suspected marrow toxins from the environment, avoidance of aspirin, oral hygiene, and suppression of menses. Transfusions are given in life-threatening circumstances only. Bone marrow or peripheral blood stem cell transplantation from a histocompatible sibling can cure the bone marrow failure, with survival rates of 77% to 90% reported. However, because just 30% of patients have suitably matched sibling donors, only a small number undergo allogeneic transplantation. Immunosuppression with antithymocyte globulin, antilymphocyte globulin, and other cytotoxic chemotherapy is used in the majority of patients who are not stem cell transplantation candidates. Unrelated donors are preferred to avoid sensitization of the patient against the non-HLA antigens that are present in bone marrow from a family donor. The disease has a wide range of severity, and the overall 5-year survival rate is 30% to 40%. Given supportive therapy, up to 80% of patients with severe aplastic anemia still die. Bone marrow transplantation before blood product

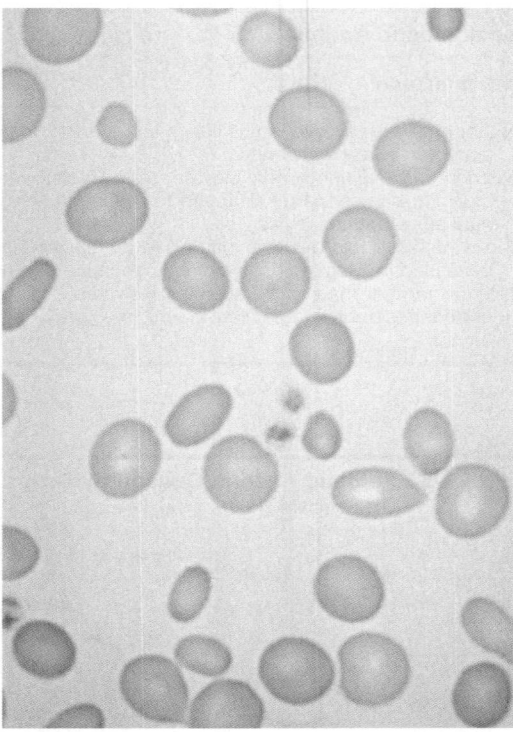

Figure 119-6. Anisocytosis and poikilocytosis. (From Hoffbrand AV, Pettite JE: *Color Atlas of Clinical Hematology*, 3rd ed. London, Mosby, 2000, p 113.)

sensitization has resulted in an 80% 5-year survival rate. This is usually combined with immunosuppressive therapy consisting of antilymphocyte globulin. Difficulty is still encountered in finding the correct immunologic match.[30,31]

Myelophthisic anemia is bone marrow failure resulting from replacement by an invading tumor, leukemia, lymphoma, or rarely, a granuloma. A more basic defect or inhibitor may complicate the problem because the degree of anemia cannot always be correlated with the extent of bone marrow invasion. Any patient with oncologic disease may be subject to the development of this type of anemia. Useful clues are signs of extramedullary hematopoiesis, such as hepatosplenomegaly and a leukoerythroblastic peripheral smear that demonstrates immature WBCs, nucleated RBCs, and poikilocytosis (teardrop-shaped red cells) (Figure 119-6). The final diagnosis is made by bone marrow examination. Therapy is directed at the underlying disorder.[30,31]

Myelofibrosis of unknown origin is the usual cause of primary bone marrow failure associated with extramedullary hematopoiesis. This myeloid metaplasia occurs in the liver and spleen and imparts a blood picture similar to that of myelophthisic anemia. The diagnosis may be made by bone marrow examination. Treatment is supportive, although splenectomy or the use of alkylating agents may be necessary to treat complications of extramedullary blood cell production, such as hepatosplenomegaly.

The hypoplastic anemias of secondary origin are commonly seen as mild chronic anemias with low reticulocyte counts. They have a normal MCV and RDW. Their diagnosis is made by exclusion. Anemia of chronic disease may have microcytic or normocytic indices. It is associated with chronic inflammation (e.g., rheumatoid arthritis, chronic infections such as tuberculosis and osteomyelitis, and malignancy). Hypoendocrinism caused by hypothyroidism, hypoadrenalism, or hypopituitarism results in a hypometabolic state in which the bone marrow responds poorly to erythropoietin. Erythropoietin levels may be low. The anemia of chronic renal failure is thought to be caused by a number of factors. Decreased erythropoietin production, hemolysis, suppression by dialyzable factors, and increased blood loss caused by platelet abnormalities combine to cause mild to moderate anemia. If necessary, it may be corrected by erythropoietin replacement therapy.[32]

Increased Red Blood Cell Destruction

The hemolytic anemias are defined by a shortened life span of the erythrocyte. In their acute form, hemolytic anemias can be devastating and require rapid diagnosis and intervention (see Box 119-1). Fortunately, they are relatively rare in comparison to the chronic hemolytic conditions. Chronic disorders may be related to primary blood disorders (e.g., sickle cell anemia) or may be a result of other disease states (e.g., chronic renal failure). These disorders may be manifested as acute hemolytic anemia if the tenuous balance between red cell production and destruction is upset. If the patient can be demonstrated to have a normal hematocrit and reticulocyte count at the same time, differentiation between acquired and inherited hemolytic anemia is possible.[33]

Clinical Features

The clinical signs and symptoms of hemolytic anemia can be categorized as being generated by intravascular or extravascular processes. Though not a precise representation of the underlying pathophysiologic condition, this division assists in the differential approach in the emergency department.

Intravascular hemolysis is usually associated with an acute process and has a dramatic appearance. Large numbers of RBCs may be lysed within the circulation. Pathologically, it primarily involves the handling of released hemoglobin and a compensatory response to an acute decrease in oxygen-carrying capability. Free hemoglobin initially binds to haptoglobin and hemopexin. This complex is transported to the liver, converted to bilirubin, conjugated, and excreted. When this binding and transport system is overwhelmed, free hemoglobin may appear in the blood. Hemoglobin is a large molecule that remains in serum and may tint it pink.

In contrast, myoglobin is a small molecule that is rapidly cleared from serum. Examination of spun whole blood demonstrates clear serum in myoglobinemia, pink serum with free hemoglobin from intravascular hemolysis, and yellow serum from extravascular hemolysis with increased bilirubin production. In

severe cases, the latter mechanism may also result in free hemoglobin.

The clinical appearance of intravascular hemolysis may vary from mild chronic anemia, as seen in cases of mechanical hemolysis, to prostration, fever, abdominal and back pain, and mental changes, as seen with transfusion reactions. Jaundice, brown to red urine, and oliguria associated with acute renal failure induced by the hemoglobin complex can also occur.

Extravascular hemolysis is more common and usually better tolerated. Splenic blood flow slows as RBCs travel in the sinusoids close to the reticuloendothelial system, the latter being uniquely designed for removing older or damaged cells. Primary splenic overactivity, antibody-mediated changes, or RBC membrane abnormalities may cause this normal splenic function to increase to a pathologic degree. Hemolysis may also occur within the bone marrow. As stated earlier, normal erythropoiesis is ineffective 10% to 20% of the time. This percentage increases when abnormal RBCs are produced, as in thalassemia, megaloblastic anemia, or some hemolytic anemias.[33,34]

After hemoglobin is disassembled in the reticuloendothelial cell, globin returns to the amino acid pool, iron is transported via transferrin to the bone marrow or iron stores, and the pyrrole ring is converted to bilirubin. The unconjugated bilirubin circulates to the liver and is transformed. It is excreted in urine as conjugated bilirubin. The clinical picture of extravascular hemolysis is usually mild to moderate anemia, mild and intermittent jaundice, and enlargement of the spleen. The signs and symptoms vary with the severity and chronicity of the hemolysis.

Ancillary Evaluation

Once hemolysis is suspected, the history and laboratory tests have diagnostic precedence over physical examination. Important historical and physical examination points are listed in Box 119-8.[33,34]

Laboratory Assessment

Important diagnostic tests for hemolysis are found in Box 119-9.

The blood smear is often more diagnostic than bone marrow examination. The typical cell seen in intravascular hemolysis is the schizocyte (Figure 119-7). The classic cell of extravascular hemolysis is the spherocyte

(Figure 119-8). It may be seen in congenital spherocytosis but more commonly indicates splenic activity against an antibody-coated RBC membrane. An increase in macrocytes reflects the presence of younger cells associated with reticulocytosis. The specific diagnosis may be made by a blood smear, as with sickled cells or Heinz bodies in glucose-6-phosphate dehydrogenase (G6PD) deficiency.[34,35]

Haptoglobin binds hemoglobin on a molecule-for-molecule basis. Its absence implies saturation and degradation after binding with hemoglobin and is an early finding in hemolysis. It has a normal range of 40 to 180 mg/mL, is decreased in hepatic failure, and

---

BOX 119-8. Pertinent Factors in the History and Physical Examination for Hemolytic Anemia

History
Alteration of color in urine or feces
    Association with drugs, cold, sleep
    Early or recent-onset anemia history with symptoms
Ethnic background
Family history of anemia or jaundice
Drug or toxic exposure
Disease states associated with hemolysis, such as systemic lupus erythematosus, renal failure, lymphoma, infectious mononucleosis, prosthetic heart valve

Physical Examination
Jaundice
Hepatosplenomegaly
Ulcerations, particularly in the lower extremities
Enlarged lymph nodes

BOX 119-9. Diagnostic Tests for Hemolysis

Peripheral blood smear
Corrected reticulocyte index or reticulocyte production index
Haptoglobin levels
Plasma free and urinary hemoglobin
Lactate dehydrogenase level
Fractionated bilirubin level
Direct and indirect Coombs' test
RBC membrane stability (osmotic fragility)

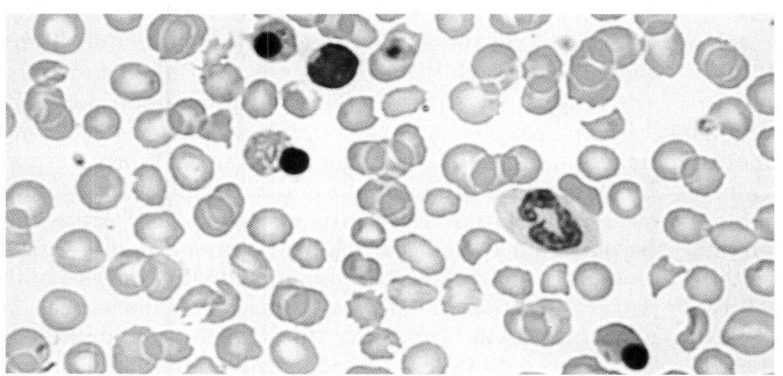

Figure 119-7. Schizocytes (fragmented cell and nucleated red cells). (From Hoffbrand AV, Pettite JE: *Color Atlas of Clinical Hematology*, 3rd ed. London, Mosby, 2000, p 115.)

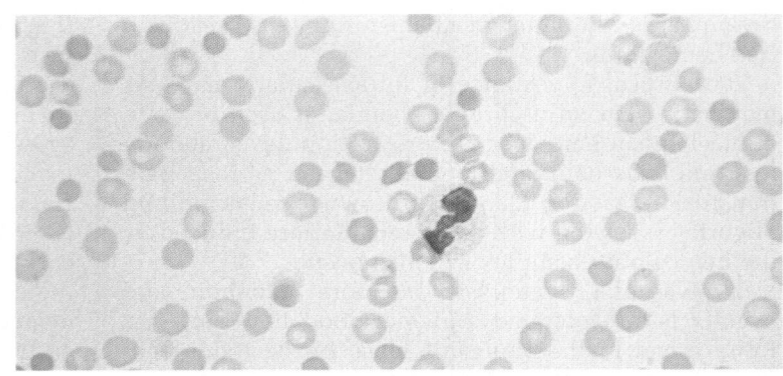

increases as an acute-phase reactant. After haptoglobin is bound, hemoglobin binds with hemopexin, transferrin, and albumin before circulating in its free form. Plasma free hemoglobin levels are determined in suspected cases of intravascular hemolysis. The result is considered positive if the level is greater than 40 to 50 mg/dL. Hemoglobin is excreted by the kidney and may be found as a smoky red pigment that is ortho-toluidine positive with no associated RBCs. Prussian blue–staining granules of hemosiderin may be found intracellularly in renal tubule cells excreted in urine during chronic hemolytic states.[35]

LDH is released when the RBC is broken down peripherally or in the marrow. It is elevated in hemolytic, thalassemic, sideroblastic, and megaloblastic anemia. It may also be seen in cases of uremia, polycythemia vera, and erythroleukemia. Normal levels of LDH range from 95 to 200 IU and may be fractionated.[34,35]

In extravascular hemolysis, bilirubin is often delivered to the liver faster than the conjugating mechanism can handle it. Normal total levels are less than 1.5 mg/dL, and the indirect component amounts to less than 0.5 mg/dL. Conjugated or indirect bilirubin may rise as high as 4 to 5 mg/dL even with normal liver function. Higher levels connote some degree of underlying hepatic insufficiency.[34,35]

The direct antiglobulin (Coombs') test detects antibody or complement on human RBC membranes. It is an essential test in the evaluation of hemolysis. Approximately 90% of patients with autoimmune hemolytic anemia have a positive direct Coombs test. The indirect test measures antibody titers in serum. The key to the direct antiglobulin test is the reagent. It contains an antihuman IgG that is produced in rabbits. This antihuman IgG in its broad-spectrum form reacts with the IgG, IgM, or C3 proteins that may coat RBCs. The reaction causes an agglutination of RBCs that is graded from 0 to 4. Agglutinating properties depend on the size of the immunoglobulin. IgM is a large antibody form that can bridge the distance between cells, cause agglutination, and fix complement. The direct antiglobulin test is limited in diagnosing IgM-mediated hemolysis. It is best in determining IgG or complement on the RBC surface. IgG is not large enough to cause agglutination, and the antihuman globulin attaches to RBC-bound IgG, which allows agglutination. C3 is detected in a similar manner. Both represent possible immunologic causes of hemolysis. This form of hemolysis is usually mediated extravascularly through the spleen because IgG is a poor initiator of the complement system. The direct antiglobulin test evaluates the RBC surface for immunologic markers. The indirect test assumes that IgG or C3 is in the serum and tests for serum antibody activity against RBCs. Positive tests for immunologic markers do not correlate agglutination activity with the severity of hemolysis.[36]

Differential Diagnosis

Hemolytic anemias may be classified as congenital or acquired, Coombs' positive or Coombs' negative, or caused by processes intrinsic or extrinsic to the cell membrane. The last method gives a useful differential classification of hemolysis (Box 119-10).

Intrinsic Enzyme Defects. Eighty-five percent to 90% of the membrane-sustaining energy production of the erythrocyte is through the anaerobic glycolytic pathway. At least eight known enzyme deficiencies are associated with this pathway. The most common is pyruvate kinase, deficiency of which is seen as hemolytic jaundice and is usually diagnosed in infancy.[37]

The remaining 10% to 15% of RBC glycolysis occurs by way of the hexose monophosphate shunt. This bypass mechanism occurs in the early stages of the glycolytic pathway and generates reduced nicotinamide adenine dinucleotide phosphate (NADPH), which is important in maintaining reduced glutathione. Glutathione is essential in the protection of hemoglobin from oxidant injury. A deficiency of the first enzyme in this pathway, G6PD, occurs in 11% of African American men. In this form the enzyme deteriorates with age, and older RBCs are subject to hemolysis by oxidant stress. G6PD deficiency is sex linked and has a wide range of severity. The most common form in African Americans is self-limited because as the bone marrow responds, younger cells with more normal levels of G6PD predominate and can handle the oxidant stress. The variants in Sicilians, Greeks, and Arabs can be particularly devastating. The clinical manifestation is usually an acute hemolytic episode that may be both intravascular and extravascular in appearance. It occurs 24 to 48 hours after the ingestion of an oxidant drug (Box 119-11) or after acute infections such as viral

BOX 119-10. Classification of Hemolytic Anemia

Intrinsic
A. Enzyme defect
  1. Pyruvate kinase deficiency
  2. Glucose-6-phosphate dehydrogenase deficiency
B. Membrane abnormality
  1. Spherocytosis
  2. Elliptostomatocytosis
  3. Paroxysmal nocturnal hemoglobinuria
  4. Spur cell anemia
C. Hemoglobin abnormality
  1. Hemoglobinopathies
  2. Thalassemias (anemias)
  3. Unstable hemoglobin
  4. Hemoglobin M

Extrinsic
A. Immunologic
  1. Alloantibodies
  2. Autoantibodies
B. Mechanical
  1. Microangiopathic hemolytic anemia
  2. Cardiovascular, such as prosthetic heart valve disease
C. Environmental
  1. Drugs
  2. Toxins
  3. Infections
  4. Thermal
D. Abnormal sequestrations, as in hypersplenism

BOX 119-11. Drugs Associated with Hemolysis in G6PD Deficiency

Analgesics and antipyretics: acetanilid, aspirin, phenacetin
Antimalarials: primaquine, quinacrine, quinine
Nitrofurans
Sulfa drugs: sulfamethoxazole, sulfacetamide, sulfones
Miscellaneous: naphthalene, fava beans, methylene blue, phenylhydrazine, nalidixic acid

G6PD, glucose-6-phosphate dehydrogenase.

hepatitis. The anemia induced by oxidant drugs is dose related. The older cells lyse at certain drug levels. The oxidant creates forms of activated oxygen, such as peroxide, that either denature the hemoglobin or destroy cell membranes. The former process produces Heinz bodies, which are clumps of denatured hemoglobin found in RBCs early during an episode. These cells are removed by the spleen. The diagnosis is made by enzymatic screening for G6PD, but this test cannot be performed immediately after the hemolytic episode. A 3-week delay avoids a false-negative result caused by a predominance of young cells. Treatment includes volume and RBC support as necessary. Avoidance of oxidant drugs is the only prevention.[38,39]

Intrinsic Membrane Abnormality. These abnormalities are manifested in a number of ways. An altered shape is the main feature of autosomal dominant hereditary spherocytosis or elliptocytosis. The spleen sequesters these abnormal cells. Clinical sequelae range from compensated asymptomatic anemia to severe life-threatening acquired aplastic crises. The diagnosis is made by reviewing the family history, blood smear, and osmotic fragility testing. Splenectomy is the treatment of choice for patients requiring therapeutic intervention.[37,40]

Paroxysmal nocturnal hemoglobinemia is a stem cell defect causing abnormal erythrocyte, neutrophil, and platelet sensitivity to complement. It is most often seen as chronic hemolysis, hemosiderinuria, leukopenia, and thrombocytopenia. The peripheral smear is normal and the direct Coombs' test is negative. Its major complication is thrombosis, with a predilection for the hepatic vein. Normal activation of complement with the use of sucrose or acid hemolysis (the Ham test) is diagnostic. Transfusion can be a life-threatening hazard in patients with this disease because RBC lysis is caused by donor complement. Because of this danger, only washed packed cells should be used.[40]

Intrinsic Hemoglobin Abnormality. More than 350 types of abnormal hemoglobin have been documented. Problems that may be seen include unstable hemoglobins that appear as Heinz body positive anemia, M hemoglobins that fix iron in its ferric or methemoglobin state, and hemoglobins with increased oxygen affinity that result in tissue hypoxia and erythrocytosis.

Sickle Cell Disease

Sickle cell disease is the most important hemoglobinopathy for the emergency physician. In hospitals serving a large African American population, it is seen on an almost daily basis. Even physicians who treat the problem are often at risk for overlooking the major complications of this disease. They may err because of complacency and the tendency to react automatically when a too well known "sickler" arrives. Physicians with less experience may fail to recognize the complexity of an unfamiliar problem.

Pathophysiology. Sickle cell disease is genetically determined. An abnormal allele at the gene loci for hemoglobin β chains produces altered messenger RNA, which in turn results in replacement of glutamic acid by valine at the sixth position from the N-terminal end of the β chain. On the molecular level, this change causes an interlocking of the affected chain with adjacent hemoglobin in the deoxygenated state. This connection causes the formation of bundles of parallel rods called tactoids. These polymers grow to form a p-crystalline gel, then a crystal. This gel formation is facilitated by low pH and reduced by the presence of other hemoglobins, such as HbF. The result is a sickled cell that is less deformable, causes an increase in the viscosity and sludging tendency of blood, and is sequestered in and destroyed by the spleen and liver. These changes may occur when smaller amounts of polymer do not result in a sickled cell and are associated with a RBC membrane leak. The clinical complex of vaso-occlusive events, chronic hemolysis, thrombosis, and organ injury is derived from this pathologic process.[41-49]

The globin in hemoglobin is made up of two pairs of identical polypeptide chains. In normal hemoglobin variants and most clinically significant hemoglobinopathies, the β chains are constant. The gene loci for β chains result in HbA (α_2, β_2). They may have a normal allelic substitution, such as δ chains, and result in HbA$_2$ (α_2, δ_2) or an abnormal substitution as noted in HbS. Each person has two non–sex-linked gene foci for β chains, one from each parent. The alleles appearing at these loci are both expressed in the formation of RBC hemoglobin. This fact explains the basis for the various HbS syndromes. In sickle cell trait (HbAS), the patient is heterozygous and only one parent contributes the abnormal S allele. In each cell, 50% of the hemoglobin is normal HbA. Sickle disease (HbSS) is homozygous, and all hemoglobin is HbS. Because a parent may contribute alleles other than S, a wide number of variants can exist. Two clinically important S variants are sickle cell–thalassemia and sickle cell–hemoglobin C disease. Therefore, all hemoglobinopathies that cause sickling are not HbS.[42,50]

In addition, HbSS is not limited to the African American population. Up to 10% of patients with various sickling disorders identify themselves as non–African American.[41-43]

Sickle cell trait is found in 8% to 10% of African Americans. It is usually asymptomatic, although it may be manifested as decreased urine-concentrating ability, spontaneous hematuria, and rare vaso-occlusive crises with an increased incidence of splenic infarction at high altitudes. No added risk occurs during general anesthesia. The diagnosis is usually made after sickle cell screening (Sickledex) and a characteristic result on hemoglobin electrophoresis. Genetic counseling is a useful service for these patients.[42,44]

Clinical Features. Sickle cell disease can be a recurrent, painful, and frustrating problem for both patients and physicians. It is estimated that less than 10% of a sickle cell population are recurrent emergency department users. The setting is usually that of a large urban hospital caring for a predominantly African American population. The patients are seen in what is considered a vaso-occlusive crisis. Preceding infection, cold exposure, and stress such as trauma are all potential precipitating factors in these crises. Many of these episodes are thought to be spontaneous in their onset. The emotional component of these crises is not well understood, but the possibility of narcotic abuse does exist. The painful crisis is believed to have its origin in tissue ischemia caused by increased viscosity, sludging, and microvascular obstruction as a result of irreversibly sickled cells. Sludging and vascular blockage cause stasis, deoxygenation, and local acidosis, which promote the vicious circle of continued sickling. The pain is commonly deep and aching and is most often found in the abdomen, chest, back, and extremities. The disease may mimic an acute abdomen (e.g., cholecystitis), pulmonary embolus, renal colic, or other painful problems. Unfortunately, HbSS may also contribute to these same problems. A directed history that relates this pain pattern to previous sickling episodes, a careful repeated physical examination, and specific organ-related laboratory tests are all the physician has to differentiate "uncomplicated" crises from a more serious pathologic condition. Children may be seen more often with skeletal crises leading to bone deformities. In these cases osteomyelitis and bone infarct must be differentiated.[44-48]

Acute chest syndrome is a leading cause of death and accounts for 25% of premature deaths associated with sickle cell disease. It is a common cause of hospitalization in sickle cell disease, second only to vaso-occlusive crisis. Patients with acute chest syndrome have fever, cough, chest pain, dyspnea, and new infiltrates on the chest radiograph. The pathophysiology of the syndrome is not well understood but suggests that it may be a specific form of acute lung injury. The injury is postulated to be related to pulmonary microvascular sludging, infarction of pulmonary parenchyma, and bone marrow fat embolization from infarcted bone. Macrovascular pulmonary embolism and infection may also have a pathogenetic role. The differential diagnosis includes pneumonia, pulmonary embolism, congestive heart failure, and adult respiratory distress syndrome. No definitive diagnosis or therapy is currently available for acute chest syndrome. Management is supportive and consists of hydration, analgesia, maintenance of adequate oxygenation and ventilation, and empirical antibiotics.[51,52]

Although most of the diagnostic and therapeutic problems of sickle cell disease are related to vaso-occlusive crises, other serious complications must be anticipated. Sickle cell disease is a chronic hemolytic state with reasonably compensated hematocrit values in the 20% to 30% range and elevated reticulocyte counts. This compensated balance may be disrupted by a rare iron deficiency or more commonly by folate deficiency. A potentially life-threatening aplastic crisis may be seen as a result of suppression of erythropoiesis by an acute postinfectious condition or folate deficiency. This aplastic condition is suspected when the hemoglobin level falls 2 g/dL or more from previous stable levels and the reticulocyte count remains low (<2%). Finally, children may have an acute splenic sequestration syndrome. This syndrome involves acute splenic enlargement from increased intrasplenic sickling and obstruction. The child may demonstrate lassitude and be in shock. Each of these conditions may result in a rapidly falling RBC count and progressive symptoms of anemia. Patients with HbSS are also subject to all other causes of anemia, such as hemolysis from G6PD deficiency.[47] An increased susceptibility to infection is a well-documented phenomenon with HbSS. In infancy, an increased incidence of sudden death may be related to pneumococcal sepsis and meningitis. A WBC count and blood cultures should be performed on all febrile children with sickle cell anemia. Those younger than 2 years with temperatures of 39.5° C or higher and WBC counts greater than 20,000/mm^3 should be given intravenous antibiotics immediately. Adults with fever require careful evaluation and laboratory assessment, including appropriate

Table 119-7. Organ Damage Seen in Sickle Cell Disease

Organ or System	Injury
Skin	Stasis ulcer
Central nervous system	Cerebrovascular accident
Eye	Retinal hemorrhage, retinopathy
Cardiac	Congestive heart failure
Pulmonary	Intrapulmonary shunting, embolism, infarct, infection
Vascular	Occlusive phenomenon at any site
Liver	Hepatic infarct, hepatitis resulting from transfusion
Gallbladder	Increased incidence of gallstones caused by bilirubin
Spleen	Acute sequestration
Urinary	Hyposthenuria, hematuria
Genital	Decreased fertility, impotence, priapism
Skeletal	Bone infarcts, osteomyelitis, aseptic necrosis
Placenta	Insufficiency with fetal wastage
Leukocytes	Relative immunodeficiency
Erythrocytes	Chronic hemolysis

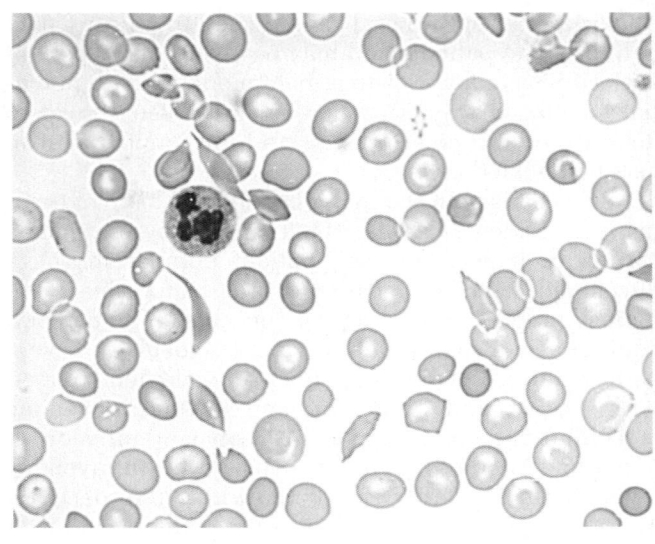

Figure 119-9. Sickle cells. (From Hoffbrand AV, Pettite JE: *Color Atlas of Clinical Hematology*, 3rd ed. London, Mosby, 2000, p 103.)

cultures. Early institution of appropriate antibiotics is necessary in patients with a discernible source of infection. In children and adults, infection with *Staphylococcus* and *Pneumococcus* species and *Haemophilus influenzae* is particularly common. An increased incidence of *Salmonella* osteomyelitis also occurs. The origin of this related immunologic deficiency is believed to be multifactorial, with functional asplenia, poorly migrating neutrophils, and decreased opsonin production being contributors.[48]

The potential for chronic organ damage in patients with sickle cell anemia is almost unlimited. A cross section of these problems is listed in Table 119-7. These associated conditions should be quickly reviewed every time a patient with sickle cell anemia enters the emergency department. The leading causes of death in HbSS patients are cardiopulmonary disease, chronic renal failure, stroke, and infection.[49]

Diagnostically, most patients with HbSS seen in the emergency department are well known with defined pain patterns. Because of a slow, but longer growth period caused by the delayed onset of puberty, adult patients with HbSS have a youthful appearance and long, thin extremities. In a patient with suspected sickle cell disease, inquiry should be made into the family history, previous pain episodes, and symptoms relative to chronic anemia, susceptibility to infection, and ischemic organ damage. Table 119-7 suggests an outline to follow for the physical examination.

All patients should have a complete blood count performed, and present blood levels should be compared with those of previous visits. A reticulocyte count should be obtained whenever the patient's hemoglobin level has decreased by 2 g/dL from baseline. In sickle cell disease the typical absolute reticulocyte count is three to four times the upper limit of normal. A reticulocyte count 3% or lower than the patient's usual

value may suggest an aplastic crisis. A reticulocyte count greater than 12%, particularly if accompanied by numerous nucleated red blood cells, may indicate rapid hemolysis. Other laboratory tests are selected on the basis of potential organ complications. Unfortunately, no test is available that detects whether a patient is in a crisis. At present, this difficult task is based on inadequate clinical grounds. In new cases, the peripheral smear may show sickled cells (Figure 119-9), and a sickle cell screening test with Sickledex may help, particularly if drug-motivated malingering is suspected. Definitive diagnosis is aided by hemoglobin electrophoresis.[42,44,49]

Management. At present, the antisickling agent hydroxyurea reduces the frequency of painful crises in adults with a history of three or more crises annually. The beneficial effects of hydroxyurea in sickle cell disease are assumed to be due to induction of hemoglobin F, but additional mechanisms may be operative. Other agents, including clotrimazole, magnesium 5-azacitidine, erythropoietin, and butyric acid, may have a future role in therapy.[53-57] Bone marrow transplantation offers the only current cure for sickle cell disease. Despite survival rates greater than 90% and disease-free survival rates of 80% to 90%, the role of bone marrow transplantation in sickle cell disease remains uncertain.[58,59]

Present therapies, including rest, adequate nutrition, hydration, oxygenation, analgesia, transfusion, and therapy for infection, are directed toward symptomatic relief and attempts to stop the cycle of deoxygenated sickling and intravascular sludging. Most patients with sickle cell anemia are mildly dehydrated because of urine-concentrating difficulty. Fluid replacement can be oral or intravenous, and the emergency physician should be aware of the potential for congestive heart failure in patients past their second decade. A satisfactory starting solution is 5% dextrose in half-normal saline begun at a rate of 150 to 200 mL/hr.[60]

Oxygen through a nasal cannula at 2 to 4 L/min may help hypoxic patients and may be given to any patient with HbSS as a low-risk treatment modality with potential benefit. Oxygenation has recently been shown to decrease erythropoietin levels and the number of irreversibly sickled cells.

Analgesia is both the major benefit and bane of treatment of sickle cell crisis. Many emergency physicians caring for large sickle cell patient populations have developed protocols for establishing better physician-patient rapport and lessening the chance of narcotic addiction and manipulation. One protocol for severe pain is the following: patients are evaluated, treated with oxygen and hydration, and given intravenous morphine sulfate, 5 mg, then a constant infusion at 5 mg/hr. Another approach consists of intravenous bolus doses of morphine sulfate (0.15 mg/kg per dose up to 10 mg per dose). At 6 hours the patient is allowed to decide whether inpatient or outpatient therapy is desired. Outpatient therapy includes 4 to 6 days of an effective oral analgesic. A 60-mg dose of oral morphine sulfate or equivalent is given 1 to 2 hours before stopping the infusion. This protocol brings uniformity to the patient's expectations for care and the physician's decisions regarding therapy and admission. Its major disadvantage has been a tendency to treat patients automatically rather than closely considering the potential acute complications of sickle cell disease. No standard pain management exists for sickle cell disease. A variety of analgesics (nonsteroidal anti-inflammatory drugs, mixed opioid agonist-antagonists, opiates), dosages, and timing intervals may be chosen. The most important aspect of pain management in these patients is a consistent, thorough, and attentive approach that offers true pain relief.

Blood transfusion has a well-accepted role in sickle cell anemia. Very selected use can decrease the chronic transfusion problems of antigen sensitization, iron overload, and hepatitis. Aplastic or splenic sequestration crises may necessitate transfusion. Serial hemoglobin values and reticulocyte counts must be obtained during hospitalization. Priapism may improve with transfusion, although urologic drainage procedures should be considered. Pharmacologic agents such as α- or β-agonists have been used in priapism with mixed success. Exchange transfusions are recommended for patients, particularly children, with cerebrovascular accidents. Acute symptoms may be reversed and the frequency of recurrence decreased with a regulated 3- to 4-week transfusion program. The goal is to suppress reticulocytosis and decrease the HbS level to less than 25%. Rarely, transfusions are given for control of bony or visceral crises. This is not an emergency department procedure and is considered only after hematologic consultation. Prophylactic transfusions to dilute HbS levels are also recommended in pregnancy and before major surgery.[61,62]

A number of other therapies are being tested for both prophylaxis and crisis management, including supplemental zinc, induced hyponatremia, gelation inhibitors, membrane-active agents, and gene manipulation. Poloxamer 188 is an artificial surfactant with hemorheologic and antithrombotic properties. Although the mechanism of action of this agent is not fully understood, it improves microvascular blood flow by reducing blood viscosity and adhesive frictional forces. In clinical trials of sickle cell patients with acute painful crisis, poloxamer reduced the total narcotic requirement, the duration of pain, and pain intensity.[63,64] Careful examination, an analgesic protocol, and compassion remain the basis for management. A reason for a painful crisis should always be sought.

The general prognosis of sickle cell patients has improved because of an improvement in their care and the rapid use of antibiotics for potential infections.

Sickle Cell–β-Thalassemia. Sickle cell–β-thalassemia disease is seen most commonly in persons of Mediterranean descent. The severity of the disease is related to the concentration of HbS in RBCs and the decrease in MCHC. It should be considered in a patient with a low MCV and a positive sickle preparation. It is generally a milder form than homozygous sickle cell disease. HbSC disease falls between HbSS and HbS-thalassemia in terms of severity. In addition to many of the complications of HbSS, HbSC disease has an increased incidence of eye hemorrhage and pregnancy complications and may cause splenomegaly. The peripheral smear demonstrates a combination of sickled cells and normocytic target cells.[42,50]

Extrinsic Alloantibodies. Alloantibodies are formed in response to foreign RBC antigens. In the case of the ABO system, these antibodies are preformed. The ABO system is one of the most important RBC wall antigens. ABO incompatibility resulting in donor cell destruction by the recipient's alloantibodies can be a life-threatening reaction. These antibodies are IgM in nature and can act as a hemolysin, both agglutinating RBCs and fixing complement and consequently causing intravascular hemolysis.

The Rh system is another set of antigens on the RBC. This system is unique in that individuals do not have antibodies that correspond to antigens in the Rh system unless they have been sensitized by previous exposure to antigens that they lack. The antibodies produced are IgG in nature, and they accelerate extravascular destruction of RBCs by the spleen and liver. Most autoimmune antibodies are directed toward antigens in the Rh system.[65]

Extrinsic Autoantibodies. Evaluation of autoimmune hemolysis is as complex as its origin. The major feature of autoimmune hemolysis is the production of an IgG or IgM antibody to an antigen present on the RBC membrane. Why the body responds in this manner is still unknown. IgM antibodies can agglutinate, fix complement, and act as intravascular hemolysins. IgG antibodies may fix complement to the cell but do not usually complete the hemolysis process. These IgG- or C3-labeled cells undergo accelerated extravascular destruction. The direct antiglobulin test is useful in revealing these labeled cells.[66]

Autoimmune hemolytic anemias are acquired disorders, with 40% to 50% being idiopathic. The remainder are associated with a number of diseases (Box 119-12). Classification of autoimmune hemolytic

BOX 119-12. Diseases Associated with Autoimmune Hemolytic Anemia

Neoplasms
Malignant: chronic lymphocytic leukemia, lymphoma, myeloma, thymoma, chronic myeloid leukemia
Benign: ovarian teratoma, dermoid cyst

Collagen Vascular Disease
Systemic lupus erythematosus
Periarteritis nodosa
Rheumatoid arthritis

Infections
Mycoplasma
Syphilis
Malaria
Bartonella
Virus: mononucleosis, hepatitis, influenza, coxsackievirus, cytomegalovirus

Miscellaneous
Thyroid disorders, ulcerative colitis
Drug immune reactions

BOX 119-13. Drugs Associated with Immune Hemolytic Anemia

Hapton type with antibodies to the drug
1. Complement-fixing antibody: quinidine, quinine, phenacetin, ethacrynic acid, *p*-aminosalicylate, sulfa drugs, oral hypoglycemic agents
2. Non–complement-fixing antibody: penicillin dosages greater than 20 million U/day
Autoimmune type with antibodies to the RBC membrane: D-Methyldopa, L-dopa, mefenamic acid, chlordiazepoxide
Cephalosporins at dosages greater than 4 g/day may cause hemolysis by direct membrane injury

anemias is based on the optimal temperature at which the antibody reacts with the RBC membrane. Therefore, there are warm-reacting (>37° C) and cold-reacting (<37° C) antibodies.[66]

Warm-reacting antibodies are characterized by a higher incidence in younger patients (30 to 60 years of age), predominance in women, variable complement fixation, and a positive direct antiglobulin test for IgG. Cold-reacting antibodies, or cold agglutinins, are seen predominantly in men and older patients (50 to 80 years of age) and with IgM complement fixation. They may also be found in patients with infectious mononucleosis and *Mycoplasma* infection, as well as lymphoma. Hemolysis may be intravascular and extravascular, and the direct antiglobulin test is positive for complement.[66]

Clinically, a patient with immune hemolytic anemia has the signs and symptoms of anemia and, often, splenomegaly. Spherocytosis and reticulocytosis are noted in the blood smear. The direct antiglobulin test is positive in 90% of cases. The strength of the direct antiglobulin test does not correlate with the severity of the hemolysis because the Coombs' reaction is a different antibody function than hemolysis or stimulation of reticuloendothelial sequestration. In patients with newly diagnosed, reticulocytopenic or severe hemolytic anemia, the emergency physician may need to institute transfusion therapy. Compatible blood may be almost impossible to find because the antibody can react with almost all donors. The most compatible donor cells in terms of the ABO and Rh systems should be transfused with the knowledge that they will be no more compatible than the patient's own blood cells. Prednisone or its equivalent in a dose of 60 to 100 mg should be given orally or intravenously. It is believed to produce an improvement in 60% of patients with warm antibody reactions. Splenectomy and immunosuppressive therapy are also effective in treating these

reactions. Cold agglutinin hemolytic anemia may be self-limited, as after infectious mononucleosis. Other forms respond well to cold avoidance, variably to immunosuppressive agents, but poorly to steroids and splenectomy. Death commonly results from uncontrolled hemolysis, the underlying primary disorder, and pulmonary embolism.[65,66]

Drug-induced hemolytic anemia may be difficult to diagnose. The emergency physician should know the drugs most often associated with this Coombs'-positive phenomenon and realize that this test is sometimes positive only in the drug's presence. Common drugs and mechanisms of action are listed in Box 119-13.[67]

Extrinsic Mechanical Causes. Hemolysis may be caused by trauma to RBCs. The peripheral smear may demonstrate schizocytes or fragmented cells, which should immediately raise the suspicion of traumatic injury (see Figure 119-7). Microangiopathic hemolytic anemia, cardiac trauma, and "march" hemoglobinemia are the most commonly encountered forms of traumatic hemolysis.

Microangiopathic hemolytic anemia is a form of microcirculatory fragmentation by threads of fibrin deposited in the arterioles. An underlying disease is inevitably present. It may be found in renal lesions such as malignant hypertension and preeclampsia, vasculitis, thrombotic thrombocytopenic purpura, disseminated intravascular coagulation, and vascular anomalies. The signs and symptoms are those of intravascular hemolysis. Treatment is directed at the causative disease.

Cardiac trauma to RBCs results from increased turbulence. It may be found in patients with prosthetic valves, traumatic arteriovenous fistula, aortic stenosis, and other left-sided heart lesions. Surgical correction may be necessary. Supportive therapy with an iron supplement is usually required.

March hemoglobinemia is a form of trauma caused by breaking of intravascular RBCs by repetitive pounding. Soldiers, marathon runners, and anyone with repetitive striking against a hard surface may incur this problem. Reassurance and a change in the patient's pattern of activity are the recommended therapy.[35,68]

Environmental Causes. Hemolysis may be seen in cases of severe burns, freshwater drowning, and hyperthermia. Toxic causes of hemolysis have been docu-

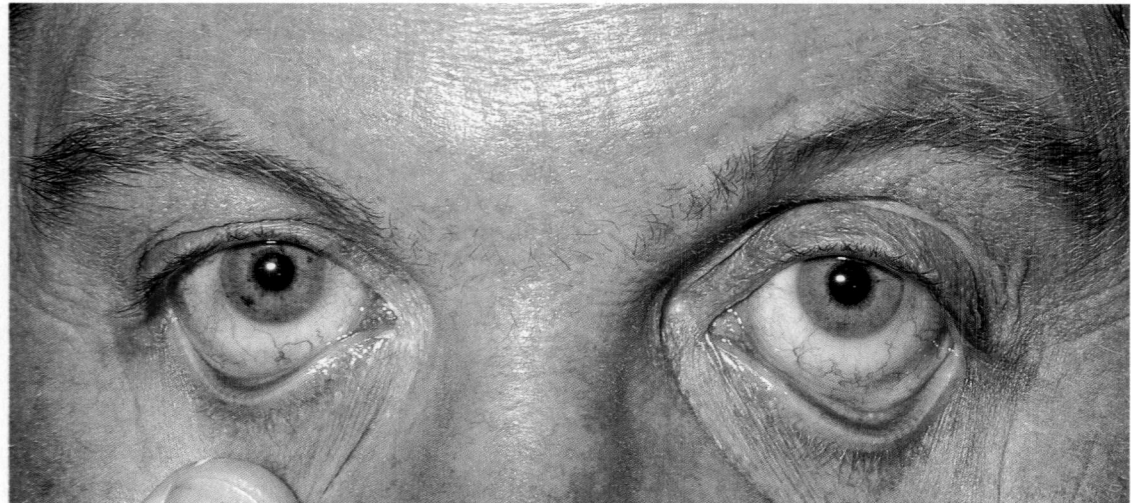

Figure 119-10. Polycythemia vera. Facial plethora and conjunctival suffusion in a 40-year-old woman (Hb, 19.5 g/dL). (From Hoffbrand AV, Pettite JE: *Color Atlas of Clinical Hematology*, 3rd ed. London, Mosby, 2000, p 248.)

mented to be of animal origin, such as brown recluse spider and some snake bites; vegetable origin, such as castor beans and certain mushrooms; and mineral origin, such as copper. Certain infections are associated with hemolytic states. Malaria, *Bartonella*, and *Clostridium* sepsis are three well-known causes.

Abnormal Sequestration. Hypersplenism may be caused by any disease that enlarges the spleen or stimulates the reticuloendothelial system. An unfortunate cycle can be set up in which the enlarged spleen traps more blood components and grows larger. It is usually seen as splenomegaly with pancytopenia and marrow hyperactivity.[51] Chromium-labeled RBCs may demonstrate increased trapping in the spleen. Therapy for symptomatic or severe disease is splenectomy. Adults usually tolerate splenectomy well, but children should be approached conservatively because the risk of postsplenectomy life-threatening sepsis is increased significantly.[69]

POLYCYTHEMIA

Definition

Polycythemia is a term commonly used for erythrocytosis (i.e., increased number of RBCs). This disorder is seen occasionally in emergency medicine but rarely in a life-threatening manner that requires emergency intervention.

Pathophysiology

Erythropoiesis is controlled by the kidney-produced glycoprotein hormone erythropoietin. It is activated in the liver and regulates the committed erythropoietic stem cell. Its major stimulant is tissue hypoxia. Neoplastic dysfunction of bone marrow may also result in an elevated absolute RBC count.

The major complication of polycythemia is related to the increase in blood viscosity associated with increased RBC numbers. As the hematocrit rises past 60%, viscosity increases in an almost exponential manner. This condition increases the possibility of reduced tissue flow, thrombosis, and hemorrhage. This hazard is usually blunted to a degree by an associated increase in blood volume and some viscosity-reducing vascular dilatation.[70,71]

Clinical Features

The history may range from only mild headaches to a full-blown syndrome of hypervolemia (vertigo, dizziness, blurred vision, headache), hyperviscosity (venous thrombosis), and platelet dysfunction (epistaxis, spontaneous bruising, and gastrointestinal bleeding).

On physical examination, the skin and mucous membrane manifestations of the elevated RBC count are often readily observed. Plethora, engorgement, and venous congestion are commonly noted (Figure 119-10). Other systems to be examined include the fundus for venous congestion, the abdomen for evidence of splenomegaly, and the cardiopulmonary system for signs of congestive heart failure. Uterine, central nervous system, renal, and hepatic tumors should be sought. All are associated with secondary polycythemia. An elevated RBC count, usually greater than the hematocrit, defines the disorder. It results in a low MCV, usually related to low serum iron and iron stores. Specific laboratory testing is discussed in the section on differential diagnosis.[71]

Differential Diagnosis

Polycythemia is classified as apparent, primary, or secondary (Box 119-14). Apparent polycythemia is a decrease in plasma volume such as found with dehydration. The RBC volume does not exceed the upper limit of normal. Although a questionable diagnostic entity, "stress" polycythemia is the tendency for an elevated hematocrit and is found in overweight, hypertensive, and overstressed middle-aged men. Increased

BOX 119-14. Classification of Polycythemia

A. Apparent polycythemia
B. Primary polycythemia vera
C. Secondary polycythemia
   1. Appropriately increased erythropoietin caused by tissue hypoxia
      a. Congenital heart disease with a right-to-left shunt
      b. Pulmonary disease (e.g., bronchial-type chronic obstructive pulmonary disease)
      c. Carboxyhemoglobinemia
      d. High-altitude acclimatization
      e. Decreased tissue oxygen release from nemoglobinopathies with high oxygen-affinity
   2. Inappropriate autonomous erythropoietin production
      a. Renal origin: carcinoma, hydronephrosis, cyst
      b. Other lesions: uterine fibroids, hepatoma of adrenal origin, cerebellar hemangioma
      c. Congenital overproduction
D. Pure or essential erythrocytosis
E. AIDS and zidovudine treatment

BOX 119-15. Diagnostic Criteria for Polycythemia Vera*

Category A
Increased RBC mass
   In men: >36 mL/kg
   In women: >32 mL/kg
Normal arterial oxygen saturation (>92%)
Splenomegaly

Category B
Thrombocytosis: platelets >400,000/mm^3
Leukocytosis: WBC count >12,000/mm^3 (with no fever or infection)
Leukocyte alkaline phosphatase score >100
Vitamin B12 >900 pg/mL, unbound vitamin B12–binding capacity <2200 pg/mL

*For polycythemia vera to be diagnosed, either all three criteria in category A or the first two criteria in category A along with any two criteria in category B must be present.

cigarette smoking with its associated increased carboxyhemoglobin level is considered to be partially responsible. The symptoms are minimal, and treatment is confined to moderation, weight loss, and blood pressure control. The risk of vascular occlusive complications is minimal. The hematocrit is usually less than 60% and RBC mass measurements are normal.[72,73]

Primary polycythemia vera is a myeloproliferative disorder found predominantly in middle-age or older patients. It may have all the clinical components of polycythemia. Initial symptoms are reported in up to 30% of patients. The most common problems are thrombotic episodes (cerebrovascular accident, myocardial infarction, deep vein thrombosis), bleeding, and bruising. Primary polycythemia vera is a disease that involves all cell lines—hematopoietic stem, erythroid, granulocytic, and megakaryocytic. The diagnostic criteria used by the Polycythemia Vera Study Group are listed in Box 119-15.

Polycythemia vera may be satisfactorily treated by phlebotomy as necessary. The reduced hematocrit improves some symptoms, but neither the leukocyte nor the platelet count is decreased. Maintaining the hematocrit at less than 55% is recommended to decrease hypervolemia and hyperviscosity. Complications necessitating additional therapy include hyperuricemia, refractory increased RBC mass, severe pruritus, excessive splenomegaly, and thrombocytosis. Additional therapy may consist of hydroxyurea, busulfan, chlorambucil, interferon alfa, anagrelide, or radioactive phosphorus (^{32}P). Recent studies suggest no improvement in long-term survival with the addition of these treatments. The natural history of the disease is that it burns out over a period of 15 to 20 years. However, myelofibrosis with myeloid metaplasia may develop. In 10% of cases, acute leukemia develops with a rapid and poorly responsive downhill course. Median survival beginning from treatment to death ranges from 9 to 14 years.[74-76] The most common causes of death are thrombosis (29%), hematologic malignancies (23%), nonhematologic malignancies (16%), hemorrhage, and myelofibrosis with myeloid metaplasia.[77]

Secondary polycythemia is classified first according to the appropriate erythropoietin response to abnormal tissue oxygen levels. This group of disorders may be ruled out by normal measured arterial oxygen saturation. Second, inappropriate autonomous erythropoietin production is considered. This condition can be assessed with an erythropoietin assay. Because of a strong association with renal pathologic conditions, intravenous pyelography or computed tomography should be to evaluate a patient with a suspected inappropriate erythropoietin response. Most patients with secondary polycythemia have no central nervous system symptoms or splenomegaly. Because erythropoietin stimulates only the red cell pathway, these patients have normal WBC and platelet counts.[78]

Management

The emergency treatment of any form of symptomatic polycythemia is phlebotomy. Usually not more than 500 mL of blood is slowly removed as the volume is replaced with a comparable amount of saline. No hemodynamic compromise should occur if this procedure is performed slowly. In true emergencies, up to 1 to 1.5 L of blood may be removed over a 24-hour period. The initial goal is to lower the hematocrit toward 60%. The final goal is a level less than 55%. Low-dose aspirin, 80 to 100 mg/day, has been shown to prevent thrombotic complications in patients with polycythemia vera and can be used in the acute and chronic treatment of this disorder.[79]

Disposition

A number of patients with known polycythemia may be managed by outpatient phlebotomies. Any newly diagnosed or symptomatic patient should be admitted to the hospital for full evaluation.

WHITE BLOOD CELL DISORDERS

The WBC count and accompanying differential are the most common laboratory tests ordered in the emergency department. It is essential that the basic physiology, pathophysiology, and clinical evaluation of WBCs be understood.

Physiology and Pathophysiology

The series has three morphologically indistinguishable cell types: B cells (humoral immunity), T cells (cellular immunity), and null cells. Because lymphocytes can freely leave and return to the circulation, the storage pools are less well defined. Only 5% of the total lymphocytes in the body are in the circulation. No marginal pool exists.[80]

Leukocytes primarily function extravascularly. The primary function of each series is closely integrated with the other. WBCs reach their site of action through the circulation. The rate that new cells enter the circulation is usually in equilibrium with the rate of loss in tissues.

Abnormal cell counts are due to changes in production, the marginal pool, or the rate of tissue destruction. Just as in anemia or platelet count abnormalities, the differential diagnosis of increased (leukocytosis) or decreased (leukopenia) WBC counts can be organized by processes altering production, destruction, loss, and sequestration. This chapter focuses primarily on quantitative rather than qualitative disorders.[80]

The granulocytic and lymphocytic series are the two cell lines of WBCs. The granulocytic series is primarily involved in phagocytic activity. Its origin is the pluripotential stem cells located in the bone marrow. A subset of these cells differentiates and matures into the phagocytic cell lines, which include neutrophils, monocytes, basophils, and eosinophils. Granulocytes are maintained in a series of developmental and storage pools. The most important is the postmitotic storage pool for neutrophils, which represents 15 to 20 times the circulating population. This pool contains metamyelocytes, band neutrophils, and mature neutrophils (polymorphonuclear neutrophils). The pool can be drawn on as a ready reserve during rapid consumption of granulocytes. Circulating neutrophils are subdivided equally into the circulating neutrophil pool and the marginal pool. The latter consists of mature cells adherent to the blood vessel walls. These cells can rapidly enter the circulating pool and cause a substantial increase, even doubling, of the WBC count. This involvement does not alter the maturity pattern of the differential count.[80] The lymphocytic series matures in lymphoid tissues located in the bone marrow, thymus, spleen, lymph nodes, and elsewhere. They are involved in the immune response against foreign substances.

Normal Values and Influences

One unique problem in WBC disorders is the wide variability in normal values and the multiple factors influencing them. WBC counts are generally performed automatically by using electrical impedance or optical diffraction techniques. Differential counts are commonly performed by direct examination of 100 to 500 cells with the oil immersion lens of the microscope. Automated techniques for all differential counts are becoming more popular, however. Normal values for the WBC count are listed in Table 119-8. The "normal" count is age dependent until childhood and may be shifted upward by exercise, gender (women), smoking, and pregnancy. Decreases in the total WBC count range of 1000 to 1200 cells/mm³ have been noted in the African American population. Laboratory errors may be due to improper sample preparation, nucleated RBCs, or platelet clumping. The blood smear differential count may also be influenced by small sample size, improper cell identification, and age group (children). Differential ranges are listed in Table 119-9. One

Table 119-8. Normal Ranges for the Blood Leukocyte Count (Cells/mm³)

Age	Average	95% Range (Average Value ± 2 SD)
1 wk	12,200	5,000-21,000
6 mo	11,900	6,000-17,500
12 mo	11,400	6,000-17,500
4 yr	9,100	5,500-15,500
8 yr	8,300	4,500-13,500
Adults	7,400	4,500-11,000

Modified from Miale JB: *Laboratory Medicine: Hematology*, 6th ed. St. Louis, CV Mosby, 1982.

Table 119-9. Normal Percentage Ranges for the Leukocyte Differential Count in Blood*

Age	Segmented Neutrophils	Band Neutrophils	Lymphocytes	Monocytes	Eosinophils	Basophils
1 wk	34 ± 15 (4100)	11.8 ± 4 (1420)	41 ± 5 (5000)	9.1 (1100)	4.1 (500)	0-4 (50)
6 mo	23 ± 10 (2710)	8.8 ± 3 (1000)	61 ± 15 (7300)	4.8 (480)	2.5 (300)	0-4 (50)
12 mo	23 ± 10 (2680)	8.1 ± 3 (990)	61 ± 15 (7000)	4.8 (550)	2.6 (300)	0-4 (50)
4 yr	34 ± 11 (3040)	8.0 ± 3 (730)	50 ± 15 (4500)	5.0 (450)	2.8 (250)	0-6 (50)
8 yr	45 ± 11 (3700)	8.0 ± 3 (660)	39 ± 15 (3300)	4.2 (350)	2.4 (200)	0-6 (50)
Adult	51 ± 15 (3800)	8.0 ± 3 (620)	34 ± 10 (2500)	4.0 (300)	2.7 (200)	0-5 (40)

*Numbers in parentheses indicate the average number of cells per cubic millimeter.
Modified from Miale JB: *Laboratory Medicine: Hematology*, 6th ed. St. Louis, CV Mosby, 1982.

BOX 119-16. Causes of Leukocytosis

Neutrophils (Absolute Count >7500 Cells/mm³)
Inflammation: rheumatoid arthritis, gout
Infection: bacterial most common
Tissue necrosis: cancer, burns, infarctions
Metabolic disorders: diabetic ketoacidosis, thyrotoxicosis, uremia
Rapid RBC turnover: hemorrhage, hemolysis
Myeloproliferative disorders: chronic myeloid leukemia, polycythemia vera
Malignancy (e.g., GI cancers)
Stress: exercise, pain, surgery, hypoxia, seizures, trauma
Drugs: epinephrine, corticosteroids, lithium, cocaine
Pregnancy
Heredity or idiopathic disease
Laboratory error: automated counters, platelet clumping, precipitated cryoglobulin

Lymphocytosis (Absolute Count >9000/mm³, Ages 1 to 6; 7000/mm³, Ages 7 to 16; 4000/mm³, Adults)
Viral infection (primary cause): mononucleosis, rubeola, rubella, varicella, toxoplasmosis
Bacterial infection: pertussis, tuberculosis, hepatitis, cytomegalovirus
Lymphoproliferative: acute or chronic lymphocytic leukemia
Immunologic response: immunization, autoimmune diseases, graft rejection
Endocrine: hypothyroidism
Relative lymphocytosis associated with granulocytopenia

Modified from Miale JB: *Laboratory Medicine: Hematology,* 6th ed. St. Louis, 1982, Mosby.

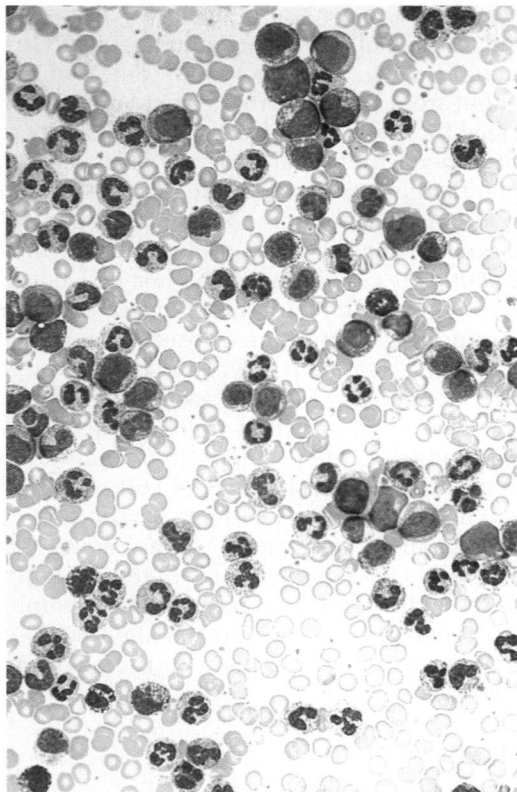

Figure 119-11. Chronic myeloid leukemia. (From Hoffbrand AV, Pettite JE: *Color Atlas of Clinical Hematology*, 3rd ed. London, Mosby, 2000, p 169.)

common but easily corrected error in laboratory reporting is giving the results in terms of the percentage of cell types. Absolute counts for each cell type are more accurate and useful in assessing the risk for infection.[81,82]

Abnormal Values

Because of the wide range of normal values, all abnormal WBC counts should be interpreted in the context of the patient's condition. A careful history and physical examination, absolute cell counts, and review of the peripheral smear differential count are the starting points for determining the origins of quantitative WBC disorders.

Leukocytosis

Most cases of leukocytosis are caused by increases in the neutrophil or lymphocyte cell lines. Neutrophil leukocytosis (neutrophilia) is an absolute neutrophil count greater than 7500 cells/mm³ and is commonly associated with infection or inflammation (Box 119-16). Because increased neutrophil destruction is associated with both these pathologic processes, bone marrow stores are drawn on, and the usual ratio of 1 band to 10 neutrophils increases. This increase is manifested as a "left shift" in the differential count and represents immature neutrophils from the postmitotic pool moving into the circulation.

WBC counts can increase without a "left shift" or an increase in band forms by demarginating neutrophils from the vessel walls. It is often seen as a response to stress, exercise, or epinephrine. Severe stress can raise the WBC count to 18,000 to 20,000 cells/mm³.[81,83,84]

Chronic Myeloid Leukemia

One of the myeloproliferative causes of neutrophilic leukocytosis is chronic myeloid leukemia (CML). Although it is the least common of the major leukemias (60% acute, 31% chronic lymphocytic leukemia, 15% CML), it must be considered in neutrophilia. Patients with CML are usually older than 40 years and have WBC counts greater than 50,000 cells/mm³. The differential count shows elevated polymorphonuclear neutrophils and metamyelocytes. Less often the basophil and eosinophil counts are increased. CML is a stem cell disorder in which the WBC count is elevated and the differential is normal. Mature and intermediate granulocytes are overproduced. Platelets may also be increased, but RBC production is down, thereby resulting in anemia. The patient often complains of fatigue, anorexia, sweating, and weight loss. Physical findings include pallor, sternal tenderness, and splenomegaly (90% of patients; Figure 119-11). In the laboratory, decreased leukocyte alkaline phosphatase and increased vitamin B12 levels are found, which helps differentiate CML from other causes of neutrophilia. The Philadelphia chromosome (Ph¹) is almost constantly associated with the disease. The chronic phase of CML is treated with an alkylating agent (e.g., busulfan) or an antimetabolite (e.g., hydroxyurea). Selected patients may benefit from bone marrow transplantation.[85,86]

The need for urgent therapy in CML is usually related to hyperuricemia and renal injury or severe anemia and subsequent angina or heart failure. Rarely, hyperleukocytosis occurs, but the more mature, "less sticky" cells in CML do not usually cause problems unless the count exceeds 500,000 cells/mm³. A higher cell count may cause leukostasis and result in deafness, visual impairment, pulmonary ventilation-perfusion abnormalities, and priapism. Treatment involves hydration, leukapheresis, transfusion as necessary, allopurinol to prevent severe hyperuricemia, and specific chemotherapy (hydroxyurea). Late problems in the natural history of CML involve progressive loss of cell differentiation and response to therapy. The term *blastic crisis* represents the sudden appearance of an acute form of leukemia, which is a rare substage of the evolving deterioration.[85-87] The condition may occur in lymphoid or myeloid forms. Blast counts greater than 50,000 cells/mm³ may predispose the patient to the complications of leukostasis.

Leukemoid Reaction

A leukemoid reaction is a nonleukemic reactive granulocytic leukocytosis that resembles CML but has no associated Ph¹ chromosome, no absolute increase in basophils and eosinophils, and an increase in leukocyte alkaline phosphatase. It is difficult to distinguish from CML in the emergency department, and both must be considered as a potential diagnosis in granulocytic leukocytosis. WBC counts are usually greater than 50,000 cells/mm³. A leukemoid reaction may be seen in tuberculosis, Hodgkin's disease, sepsis, and metastatic tumor, particularly bronchogenic, gastric, and renal carcinoma.[84]

Lymphocytic Leukocytosis

Lymphocytic leukocytosis (lymphocytosis) is an age-dependent definition: 9000 cells/mm³, ages 1 to 6; 7000 cells/mm³, ages 6 to 16; and 4000 cells/mm³, adults. It is seen in a variety of disorders, primarily infections and lymphoproliferative disease.[88]

In the past, *acute* and *chronic* were descriptive terms applied to lymphocytic neoplasms with respect to patient survival time before present therapy was available. The terms *acute* and *chronic* are currently used to describe the cell maturity, rapidity of onset, and aggressiveness of therapy.

Chronic Lymphocytic Leukemia

Chronic lymphocytic leukemia is primarily a B cell disorder and is the most common type of leukemia in the population 50 years and older. Patients initially complain of fatigue, weight loss, increased susceptibility to infection, rashes, and easy bruising. The lymph nodes are nontender and smooth and may appear in only one or two areas. Splenic and hepatic enlargement occurs in more than 50% of patients. Laboratory support of the diagnosis is an absolute lymphocyte count greater than 5000 cells/mm³ in adults. Anemia, thrombocytopenia, and neutropenia are often found. Autoimmune hemolytic anemia, a positive direct antiglobulin test, and other altered immune system problems are seen. Early therapy may be directed toward complications of anemia, thrombocytopenia, an impaired or accentuated immune response, or enlarged lymph nodes or spleen. Leukostasis is seldom seen in chronic lymphocytic leukemia, but therapy is considered when the total count rises to higher than 200,000/mm³.[89]

Acute Lymphocytic Leukemia

Acute lymphocytic leukemia is most commonly diagnosed in children younger than 10 years. It is the most frequent malignancy in children younger than 15 years. The potential for leukostasis increases in acute lymphocytic leukemia when the blast count rises above 50,000 cells/mm³. Oncologic therapy is based on clinical staging and includes chemotherapy or radiation therapy. Aggressive therapy has improved childhood survival from 1 to 15 years or more. This response to treatment has not been found to the same degree in adults.[90,91]

Leukopenia

In adults, leukopenia is defined as an absolute blood cell count less than 4000 cells/mm³. Leukopenia is commonly associated with a reduction in one cell type, the neutrophil, and this decrease has the greatest clinical significance. The absolute neutrophil count is calculated by multiplying the WBC count by the combined percentage of band and segmented neutrophils. The absolute neutrophil count can be classified as mild (1000 to 1500 cells/mm³), moderate (500 to 1000 cells/mm³), and severe (<500 cells/mm³) according to the risk for infection. The latter is a potentially life-threatening state because the patient is markedly susceptible to overwhelming infection. The physical signs of infection may be minimal in severe neutropenia because there are too few cells to generate a substantial inflammatory or purulent response. Neutropenia may be caused by decreased production, increased destruction, or movement of circulating neutrophils into marginal or tissue pools. Until recently, it was most often caused by a decrease in bone marrow production (Table 119-10). Autoimmune neutropenia is also becoming more commonly diagnosed because it is thought to have a role in acquired immunodeficiency syndrome.[84,92,93]

A thorough medication history must be taken in all patients found to have neutropenia. A previous history of neutropenia, a review of recent infection, and a family history are obtained. The review of systems focuses on bleeding problems, fatigue, sweats, weight loss, and autoimmune symptoms. The physical examination is directed toward sites of infection, lymphadenopathy, hepatosplenomegaly, and underlying disease. In patients with severe neutropenia and fever, a full radiologic and direct examination of commonly

Table 119-10. Linkage of Leukopenia to Phases of Neutrophil Maturation

Mechanism	Example
Proliferation in bone marrow	Aplastic anemia, leukemia, cancer chemotherapy (cyclophosphamide, azathioprine, methotrexate, chlorambucil)
	Drugs: phenothiazines, phenylbutazone, indomethacin, propylthiouracil, phenytoin, cimetidine, semisynthetic penicillins, sulfonamides
	Infection: viral, tuberculosis, sepsis
Maturation in bone marrow	Folate or vitamin B12 deficiency, chronic idiopathic neutropenia
	Starvation
Distribution	Hypersplenism: sarcoidosis, portal hypertension, malaria
Increased use	Infection: viral most common (mononucleosis, rubella, rubeola), *Rickettsia* organisms, overwhelming bacterial infection
	Autoimmune disease: systemic lupus erythematosus, AIDS, Felty's syndrome
Laboratory error	Leukocyte clumping, long delay in performing test

BOX 119-17. Agents and Conditions That Elevate the WBC Count

Acetylcholine	Lithium
Acidosis	Menstruation
Adrenergic drugs	Myocardial infarction
Alcohol	Neonatal asphyxia
Allergic reactions	Neoplasm
Bacterial infection	Normal pregnancy
Blood donation	Pain
Burns	Polyarteritis nodosa
Competitive running	Prednisone
Crying in infants	Pulmonary infarction
Fever	Seizures
Gout	Snake bite
Hemolysis	Supraventricular
Heparin	tachycardia
Histamine	Surgery
Hypoxia	Trauma
Iron overdose	Uremia
Juvenile rheumatoid arthritis	Viral infection
Lead and other toxins	Vomiting

involved areas, such as the chest and urine, should be performed and sputum, urine, and blood cultures obtained. Basic isolation techniques, early admission, and consultation with another specialist are recommended. Specific therapies may be started after cultures and consultation are completed. A number of empirical antibiotic regimens are recommended for febrile patients with neutropenia.[94] Human granulocyte colony-stimulating factor is often used in the setting of neutropenia, but it is best done in consultation with a hematologist.[95,96] Patients with a clear reversible source or without significant clinical findings and mild to moderate levels of neutropenia may have outpatient follow-up arranged, preferably after discussion with their physician.

RATIONALE FOR SELECTION OF WHITE BLOOD CELL AND DIFFERENTIAL COUNTS

The WBC count has not proved to be a highly sensitive or specific test for the diagnosis of a variety of disease entities.[97] However, in certain clinical situations, the WBC count may have utility. For example, recent studies evaluating the WBC count for the diagnosis of abdominal pain found it to be a useful confirming test or helpful in selecting patients for observation. In evaluating the bacterial versus viral infectious potential in febrile children, the WBC and differential counts have demonstrated limited usefulness, except in children younger than 2 years, in whom counts greater than 15,000 cells/mm^3 have an increased correlation with bacteremia.[97,98]

In addition to the nonspecificity of the WBC count, the differential count provides additional helpful information in less than 1% of cases. The absolute leukocyte count or the differential cannot reliably distinguish between viral and bacterial infection. The test should be viewed as having limited screening value in the acute care setting. Multiple agents and conditions increase the WBC count (Box 119-17), thus making the test less specific for infection than previously assumed.[99-101]

 KEY CONCEPTS

- Anemia in the elderly often occurs as an exacerbation of preexisting comorbid diseases.
- Anemia of uncertain etiology should be thoroughly evaluated. If the patient has no adverse hemodynamic consequences, the evaluation can proceed on an outpatient basis.
- One of the most important, but often overlooked studies in the evaluation of suspected hemolytic anemia is the peripheral blood smear.
- Patients with sickle cell disease who come to the emergency department are most commonly having a true crisis and are not simply exhibiting drug-seeking behavior.
- The white blood cell determination in the emergency department has poor sensitivity and specificity for disease.

REFERENCES

1. Williams MD, Wheby MS: Anemia in pregnancy. *Med Clin North Am* 76:631, 1992.
2. Izaks GJ, Westendorp RG, Knook DL: The definition of anemia in older persons. *JAMA* 281:1714, 1999.
3. Mansouri A, Lipschitz DA: Anemia in the elderly patient. *Med Clin North Am* 76:619, 1992.
4. Spivak JL, Eichner ER: *The Fundamentals of Clinical Hematology,* 3rd ed. Baltimore, Johns Hopkins University Press, 1993.
5. Hillman RS, Ault KA: Normal erythropoiesis. In Hillman RS, Ault KA (eds): *Hematology in Clinical Practice,* 3rd ed. New York, McGraw-Hill, 2002.

6. Bayless PA: Selected red cell disorders. *Emerg Med Clin North Am* 11:481, 1993.

7. Barber AE, Shires GT: Cell damage after shock. *New Horiz* 4:161, 1996.

8. Rodgers KG: Cardiovascular shock. *Emerg Med Clin North Am* 13:793, 1995.

9. Balducci L: Epidemiology of anemia in the elderly: Information on diagnostic evaluation. *J Am Geriatr Soc* 51:2, 2003.

10. Strobach RS, Anderson SK, Doll DC, Ringenberg QS: The value of the physical examination in the diagnosis of anemia. *Arch Intern Med* 148:831, 1988.

11. Jain R: Use of blood transfusion in management of anemia. *Med Clin North Am* 76:727, 1992.

12. Hillman RS, Ault KA: Clinical approach to anemia. In Hillman RS, Ault KA (eds): *Hematology in Clinical Practice,* 3rd ed. New York, McGraw-Hill, 2002.

13. Welborn JL, Meyers FJ: A three-point approach to anemia. *Postgrad Med* 89:179, 1991.

14. Bessman JD, Gilmer PR, Gardner FH: Improved classification of anemias by MCV and RDW. *Am J Clin Pathol* 80:322, 1988.

15. Fairbanks VR: Laboratory testing for iron status. *Hosp Pract* 26:17, 1991.

16. Brown RG: Determining the cause of anemia: General approach, with emphasis on microcyctic hypochromic anemias. *Postgrad Med* 89:161, 1991.

17. Andrews NC: Disorders of iron metabolism. *N Engl J Med* 341:1986, 1999.

18. Brittenham GM: Disorders of iron metabolism: Iron deficiency and overload. In Hoffman R, et al (eds): *Hematology: Basic Principles and Practice,* 2nd ed. New York, Churchill Livingstone, 1995.

19. Olivieri NF: The β-thalassemias. *N Engl J Med* 341:99, 1999.

20. Giardina PJ, Hilgartner MW: Update on thalassemia. *Pediatr Rev* 13:55, 1992.

21. Brittenham GM, et al: Efficacy of deferoxamine in preventing complications of iron overload in patients with thalassemia major. *N Engl J Med* 31:567, 1994.

22. Lucarelli G, Giardini C, Angelucci E: Bone marrow transplantation in the thalassemias. In Winter JN (ed): *Blood Stem Cell Transplantation.* Boston, Kluwer Academic, 1997.

23. Beutler E: Hereditary and acquired sideroblastic anemias. In Beutler E, et al (eds): *Williams Hematology,* 6th ed. New York, McGraw-Hill, 2001.

24. Damon LE: Anemias of chronic disease in the aged: Diagnosis and treatment. *Geriatrics* 47:47, 1992.

25. Lipschitz DA: The anemia of chronic disease. *J Am Geriatr Soc* 38:1258, 1990.

26. Means RT, Krantz SB: Progress in understanding the pathogenesis of the anemia of chronic disease. *Blood* 80:1639, 1992.

27. Hoffbrand V, Provan D: ABC of clinical haematology. Macrocytic anaemias. *BMJ* 314:430, 1997.

28. Stabler SP, Allen RH, Savage DG, Lindenbaum J: Clinical spectrum and diagnosis of cobalamin deficiency. *Blood* 76:871, 1990.

29. Babior BM: The megaloblastic anemias. In Beutler E, et al (eds): *Williams Hematology,* 6th ed. New York, McGraw-Hill, 2001.

30. Young NS: Acquired aplastic anemia. *Ann Intern Med* 136:534, 2002.

31. Young NS: Acquired aplastic anemia. *JAMA* 282:271, 1999.

32. Humphries JE: Anemia of renal failure: Use of erythropoietin. *Med Clin North Am* 76:711, 1992.

33. Santhosh-Kumar CR, Kolhouse JF: Hemolytic anemias. In Wood ME, Bunn RA (eds): *Hematology/Oncology Secrets.* Philadelphia, Hanley & Belfus, 1999.

34. Leonard KA, Klein HG: Acute hemolytic disorders. In Bell WR (ed): *Hematologic and Oncologic Emergencies.* New York, Churchill Livingstone, 1993.

35. Tabbara IA: Hemolytic anemias: Diagnosis and management. *Med Clin North Am* 76:649, 1992.

36. Nydegger UE, Kazatchkine MD, Mieschner PA: Immunopathologic and clinical features of hemolytic anemia due to cold agglutinins. *Semin Hematol* 28:66, 1991.

37. Jacobasch G, Rapoport SM: Hemolytic anemias due to erythrocyte enzyme deficiencies. *Mol Aspects Med* 17:143, 1996.

38. Valentine WN, Paglia DE: Erythroenzymopathies and hemolytic anemia. *J Lab Clin Med* 115:12, 1990.

39. Beutler E: Glucose-6-phosphate dehydrogenase deficiency. In Beutler E, et al (eds): *Williams Hematology,* 6th ed. New York, McGraw-Hill, 2001.

40. Palek J, Jarolim P: Hereditary spherocytosis, elliptocytosis, and related disorders. In Beutler E, et al (eds): *Williams Hematology,* 6th ed. New York, McGraw-Hill, 2001.

41. Bunn HF: Pathogenesis and treatment of sickle cell disease. *N Engl J Med* 337:762, 1997.

42. Embury SH: Sickle cell disease. In Hoffman R, et al (eds): *Hematology: Basic Principles and Practice,* 2nd ed. New York, Churchill Livingstone, 1995.

43. *Sickle Cell Disease: Screening Diagnosis, Management and Counseling in Newborns and Infants*, AHCPR Publication 93-0562. Rockville, Md, U.S. Department of Health and Human Services, 1993.

44. Chen H: *Resource Manual for Hemoglobinopathies.* Columbus, Division of Maternal and Child Health, Ohio Department of Health, 1992.

45. Platt OS, et al: Mortality in sickle cell disease. *N Engl J Med* 330:1639, 1994.

46. Platt OS, et al: Pain in sickle cell disease: Rates and risk factors. *N Engl J Med* 325:11, 1991.

47. Serjeant GR: *Sickle Cell Disease,* 2nd ed. Oxford, Oxford University Press, 1992.

48. Kravis E, Fleisher G, Ludwig S: Fever in children with sickle cell hemoglobinopathies. *Am J Dis Child* 16:1075, 1992.

49. Steingart R: Management of patients with sickle cell disease. *Med Clin North Am* 76:669, 1992.

50. Nagel RL, Lawrence C: The distinct pathobiology of sickle cell–hemoglobin C disease: Therapeutic implications. *Hematol Oncol Clin North Am* 5:433, 1991.

51. Hargis CA, Claster S: Acute chest syndrome in sickle cell disease. *Crit Decisions Emerg Med* 11:1, 1997.

52. Gladwin MT, Schechter AN, Shelhamer JH, Ognibene FP: The acute chest syndrome in sickle cell disease. *Am J Respir Crit Care Med* 159:1368, 1999.

53. Brugnara C, et al: Therapy with oral clotrimazole induces inhibition of the Gardos channel and reduction of erythrocyte dehydration in patients with sickle cell disease. *J Clin Invest* 97:1227, 1996.

54. de Franceschi L, et al: Oral magnesium supplements reduce erythrocyte dehydration in patients with sickle cell disease. *J Clin Invest* 100:1847, 1997.

55. Charache S, Terrin ML, Moore RD: Effect of hydroxyurea on the frequency of painful crisis in sickle cell anemia. *N Engl J Med* 332:1317, 1995.

56. Nagel RL, et al: F reticulocyte response in sickle cell anemia treated with recombinant human erythropoietin: A double-blind study. *Blood* 81:9, 1993.

57. Perrine SP, et al: Sodium butyrate enhances fetal globin gene expression in erythroid progenitors of patients with Hb SS and beta thalassemia. *Blood* 74:454, 1989.

58. Walters MC, et al: Collaborative multicenter investigation of marrow transplantation for sickle cell disease: Current results and future directions. *Biol Blood Marrow Transplant* 3:310, 1997.

59. Vermylen C, Cornu G: Hematopoietic stem cell transplantation for sickle cell anemia. *Curr Opin Hematol* 4:377, 1997.

60. Charache S, Koshy M, Milner PF: Care of patients with sickle cell anemia in the adult emergency department. In Bell WR (ed): *Hematologic and Oncologic Emergencies.* New York, Churchill Livingstone, 1993.

61. Wayne AS, Kevy SW, Nathan DG: Transfusion management of sickle cell disease. *Blood* 81:1109, 1993.

62. Vichinsky EP, et al: A comparison of conservative and aggressive transfusion regimens in the perioperative management of sickle cell disease. *N Engl J Med* 333:206, 1995.

63. Adams-Graves P, et al: RheothRx (poloxamer 188) injection for the acute painful episode of sickle cell disease: A pilot study. *Blood* 286:2099, 1997.

64. Orringer EP, et al: Purified poloxamer 188 for treatment of acute vaso-occlusive crisis of sickle cell disease: A randomized controlled trial. *JAMA* 245:2099, 2001.

65. Kickler TS, Ness PM: Blood component therapy. In Bell WR (ed): *Hematologic and Oncologic Emergencies.* New York, Churchill Livingstone, 1993.

66. Engelfriet CP, Overbeeke MA, von dem Borne AE: Autoimmune hemolytic anemia. *Semin Hematol* 29:3, 1992.

67. Salama A, Mueller-Eckardt C: Immune-mediated blood cell dyscrasias related to drugs. *Semin Hematol* 29:54, 1992.

68. Eichner ER: The anemia of athletes. *Phys Sports Med* 14:122, 1986.

69. Erslev AJ: Hypersplenism and hyposplenism. In Beutler E, et al (eds): *Williams Hematology,* 6th ed. New York, McGraw-Hill, 2001.

70. Hinshelwood S, Bench AJ, Green AR: Pathogenesis of polycythemia vera. *Blood Rev* 11:224, 1997.

71. Landaw SA: Polycythemia vera and other polycythemic states. *Clin Lab Med* 10:857, 1990.

72. Messinezy M, Pearson TC: Apparent polycythemia: Diagnosis, pathogenesis, and management. *Eur J Haematol* 51:125, 1991.

73. Djulbegovic B, Habley T, Joseph G: A new algorithm for the diagnosis of polycythemia. *Am Fam Physician* 41:113, 1991.

74. Conley CL: Polycythemia vera. *JAMA* 263:2481, 1990.

75. Beutler E: Polycythemia vera. In Beutler E, et al (eds): *Williams Hematology,* 6th ed. New York, McGraw-Hill, 2001.

76. Wehmeier A, Daum I, Jamin H, Schneider W: Incidence and clinical risk for bleeding and thrombotic complications in myeloproliferative disorders. *Ann Hematol* 63:101, 1991.

77. Berk PD, Wasserman LR, Fruchtman SM, Goldberg JD: Treatment of polycythemia vera: A summary of clinical trials conducted by the Polycythemia Vera Group. In Wasserman LR, Berk PD, Berlin NI (eds): *Polycythemia Vera and the Myeloproliferative Disorders.* Philadelphia, WB Saunders, 1995.

78. Erslen AJ: Secondary polycythemia (erythrocytosis). In Beutler E, et al (eds): *Williams Hematology,* 5th ed. New York, McGraw-Hill, 1995.

79. Landolfi R, et al: Efficacy and safety of low-dose aspirin in polycythemia vera. *N Engl J Med* 350:114, 2004.

80. Hillman RS, Ault KA: Normal myelopoiesis. In Hillman RS, Ault KA (eds): *Hematology in Clinical Practice,* 3rd ed. New York, McGraw-Hill, 2002.

81. Werman HA, Brown CG: White blood cell and differential counts. *Emerg Med Clin North Am* 4:41, 1986.

82. Shapiro MF, Greenfield S: Complete blood counts and leukocyte differential counts. *Ann Intern Med* 105:65, 1987.

83. McCarthy DA, et al: Leukocytosis induced by exercise. *BMJ* 295:636, 1987.

84. Dale DC: Neutrophilia. In Beutler E, et al (eds): *Williams Hematology,* 6th ed. New York, McGraw-Hill, 2001.

85. Faderl S, et al: The biology of chronic myeloid leukemia. *N Engl J Med* 341:164, 1999.

86. Goldman JM, Melo JV: Chronic myeloid leukemia—Advances in biology and new approaches to treatment. *N Engl J Med* 349:1451, 2003.

87. Bunin N, Pui CH: Differing complications of hyperleukocytosis in children with acute lymphoblastic or acute non-lymphoblastic leukemia. *J Clin Oncol* 3:1590, 1985.

88. Kipps TJ: Lymphocytosis and lymphocytopenia. In Beutler E, et al (eds): *Williams Hematology,* 6th ed. New York, McGraw-Hill, 2001.

89. Cheson BD, et al: National Cancer Institute–sponsored Working Group guidelines for chronic lymphocytic leukemia: Revised guidelines for diagnosis and treatment. *Blood* 87:4990, 1996.

90. Pui CH: Childhood leukemia. *N Engl J Med* 332:1618, 1995.

91. Mauer AM: Acute lymphocytic leukemia. In Beutler E, et al (eds): *Williams Hematology,* 6th ed. New York, McGraw-Hill, 2001.

92. Frontiera M, Myers AM: Peripheral blood and bone marrow abnormalities in the acquired immunodeficiency syndrome. *West J Med* 147:157, 1987.

93. Groopman JE: Management of the hemolytic complications of human immunodeficiency virus infection. *Rev Infect Dis* 12:931, 1990.

94. Hughes WT, et al: 1997 guidelines for the use of antimicrobial agents in neutropenic patients with unexplained fever. *Clin Infect Dis* 25:551, 1997.

95. Maher DW, et al: Filgrastim in patients with chemotherapy-induced febrile neutropenia: A double-blind placebo-controlled trial. *Ann Intern Med* 121:492, 1994.

96. American Society of Clinical Oncology recommendations for the use of hematopoietic colony-stimulating factors: Evidence-based clinical practice guidelines. *J Clin Oncol* 12:2471, 1994.

97. Badgett RG, Hansen CJ, Rogers CS: Clinical usage of the leukocyte count in emergency department decision making. *J Gen Intern Med* 5:198, 1990.

98. Da Silva O, Ohlsson A, Kenyon C: Accuracy of leukocyte indices and C-reactive protein for diagnosis of neonatal sepsis: Critical review. *Pedatr Infect Dis J* 14:362, 1995.

99. Callaham M: The white blood count in the emergency department. *Crit Decisions Emerg Med* 3(30):1, 1988.

100. Young GP: CBC or not CBC, that is the question. *Ann Emerg Med* 15:367, 1986.

101. Shapiro MF, Greenfield S: The complete blood count and leukocyte differential count: An approach to their rational application. *Ann Intern Med* 106:65, 1987.

Timothy G. Janz and Glenn C. Hamilton

PERSPECTIVE

Hemostasis is the process of blood clot formation and represents a coordinated response to vessel injury. It requires an orchestrated response from platelets, the clotting cascade, blood vessel endothelium, and fibrinolysis. Thrombin-stimulated clot formation and plasmin-induced clot lysis are closely related and regulated. This dynamic process is often viewed in phases: formation of a platelet plug, propagation of the coagulation cascade, formation of a clot, and fibrinolysis of the clot.

Most hemostatic abnormalities are acquired and result from drugs (e.g., aspirin or warfarin [Coumadin]), from associated disease (e.g., hepatic insufficiency), or from iatrogenic causes (e.g., multiple transfusions).

PATHOPHYSIOLOGY

Hemostasis depends on normal function and integration of the vasculature, platelets, and the coagulation pathway.

Vasculature

Vascular integrity is maintained by a lining of nonreactive overlapping endothelial cells supported by a basement membrane, connective tissue, and smooth muscle. These cells are important in maintaining a barrier to macromolecules and, when injured, in contributing to the metabolic response and local vasoconstriction. The vascular wall is an important contributor to hemostasis.[1]

The endothelium contributes to both clot formation and regulation by producing substances such as von Willebrand factor (vWF), antithrombin III, heparin sulfate, prostacyclin, nitric oxide, and tissue factor pathway inhibitor.

Platelets

Platelets have multiple and ever-expanding roles in our understanding of hemostasis. They are complex cytoplasmic fragments released from bone marrow megakaryocytes under the control of thrombopoietin. Platelets contain lysosomes, granules, a trilaminar plasma membrane, microtubules, and a canalicular system. Granules are an important component of hemostasis and contain platelet factor 4, adhesive and aggregation glycoproteins, coagulation factors, and fibrinolytic inhibitors. Each participates in the process

of coagulation. The platelet's role is termed primary hemostasis, and it serves as the initial defense against blood loss. A fibrin clot that incorporates coagulation factors usually reinforces a platelet clot. Platelet activity is summarized in Box 120-1. Any of the steps listed may be absent, altered, or inhibited by inherited or acquired disorders.[2-6]

Coagulation Pathway

The coagulation pathway is a complex system of checks and balances that results in controlled formation of a fibrin clot. Factors have been given standard Roman numerals matching their order of discovery (Box 120-2).[7]

A simplified version of the coagulation pathway is presented in Figure 120-1. The clotting cascade is traditionally depicted as consisting of intrinsic and extrinsic pathways. The intrinsic pathway is initiated by exposure of blood to a negatively charged surface, such as a glass surface in the activated partial thromboplastin clotting time. The extrinsic pathway is activated by tissue factor exposed at the site of vessel injury or thromboplastin. Both pathways converge to activate factor X, which then activates prothrombin to thrombin. The primary physiologic event that initiates clotting is exposure of tissue factor at the injured vessel site. Tissue factor is a critical cofactor that is required for activation of factor VII. Activated factor VII activates factor X directly, as well as indirectly by activating factor IX.

Because of limited amounts of tissue factor and rapid inactivation by tissue factor pathway inhibitor, the extrinsic pathway initiates the clot process. Sustained generation of thrombin and clot formation depends on the intrinsic pathway through activation of factor IX by activated factor VII, which helps explain the bleeding problems associated with hemophilia.[7,8] Intrinsic, extrinsic, and common pathways must function normally for hemostasis to occur, and each may be evaluated with laboratory tests.[1,7] The clinically important groups of coagulation factors are as follows:

1. Thrombin-sensitive factors contributing to the metabolic response and local vasoconstriction: I, V, VIII, XIII
2. Vitamin K–sensitive factors: II, VII, IX, X
3. Sites of heparin activity: IIa, IXa, Xa (major site), XIa, platelet factor 3

Thrombin-sensitive factors are activated by thrombin and may give rise to a bleeding disorder if defective synthesis occurs. Vitamin K–sensitive factors may also cause bleeding from defective synthesis, as occurs with

BOX 120-1. Role of Platelets in Hemostasis

Adhesion to subendothelial connective tissue: collagen, basement membrane, and noncollagenous microfibrils; serum factor VIII (von Willebrand) permits this function; adhesion creates the initial bleeding arrest plug

Release of adenosine diphosphate, the primary mediator and amplifier of aggregation; release of thromboxane A, another aggregator and potent vasoconstrictor; release of calcium, serotonin, epinephrine, and trace thrombin

Platelet aggregation over the area of endothelial injury

Stabilization of the hemostatic plug by interaction with the coagulation system:

  Platelet factor 3, a phospholipid that helps accelerate certain steps in the coagulation system

  Platelet factor 4, a protein that neutralizes heparin

  Pathway initiation and acceleration by thrombin production

  Possible secretion of active forms of coagulation proteins

Stimulation of limiting reactions of platelet activity

BOX 120-2. Coagulation Factors

    I. Fibrinogens
   II. Prothrombin
  III. Tissue thromboplastin
  IV. Calcium
   V. Labile factor (proaccelerin)
  VI. Not assigned
 VII. Proconvertin
VIII. Antihemophilic A factor
  IX. Antihemophilic B factor (plasma thromboplastin component, Christmas factor)
   X. Stuart-Power factor
  XI. Plasma thromboplastin antecedent
 XII. Hageman factor (contact factor)
XIII. Fibrin-stabilizing factor

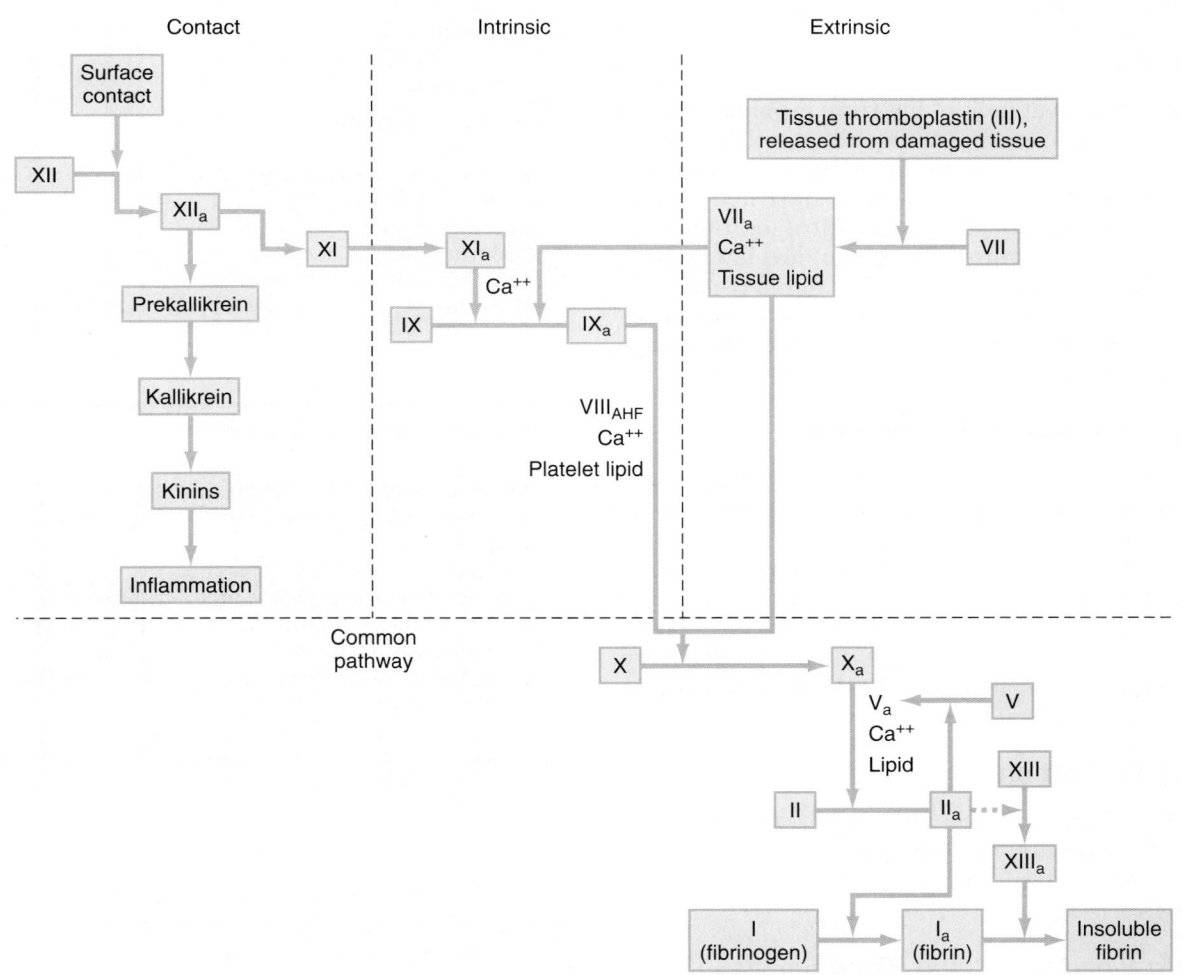

Figure 120-1. Coagulation pathway.

liver disease and warfarin anticoagulants. Heparin in combination with antithrombin III affects the coagulation pathway at multiple sites.[9-12]

Coagulation Control

All the components of the coagulation reaction are necessary to prevent excessive bleeding. Hemostasis is a balance between the excessive bleeding state and thrombosis. Once coagulation is initiated, controls are necessary to prevent local or generalized thrombosis. These controls include the following[11,13-18]:

1. Removal and dilution of activated clotting factors via blood flow, which also mechanically opposes growth of the hemostatic plug
2. Modulation of platelet activity by endothelial-generated nitric oxide and prostacyclin
3. Removal of activated coagulation components by the reticuloendothelial system
4. Regulation of the clotting cascade by antithrombin III, protein C, protein S, and tissue factor pathway inhibitor
5. Activation of the fibrinolytic system

CLINICAL FEATURES

Prehospital

The prehospital treatment of bleeding problems has no special concerns. Local pressure and volume repletion are the mainstays of therapy for blood loss. The prehospital team must be aware that inherited coagulopathies may complicate any medical or traumatic problems and that acquired forms can develop rapidly. Patients who do not respond quickly to the usual measures of hemostasis either in the field or in the emergency department should be considered to have a potential bleeding disorder.

History and Physical Examination

An outline of the history and physical examination is presented in Box 120-3. The history alone may be useful in differentiating between platelet and coagulation factor abnormalities. Platelet disorders are usually manifested as acquired petechiae, purpura, or mucosal bleeding and are more common in women. Coagulation problems are commonly congenital, are characterized by delayed deep muscle or joint bleeding, and are seen more often in men.

Ancillary Evaluation

A definitive diagnosis depends on laboratory evaluation. Tests pertinent to the emergency department are discussed in the following sections and listed in Box 120-4.

Complete Blood Count and Blood Smear

The complete blood count assesses the degree of anemia associated with the bleeding episode. Reductions in hemoglobin and hematocrit often lag behind the actual loss of red blood cells (RBCs) in acute

---

BOX 120-3. Clinical Evaluation of a Bleeding Patient

History
Nature of bleeding
 Petechiae
 Purpura
 Ecchymosis
 Significant bleeding episodes
Sites of bleeding
 Skin
 Mucosa: oral or nasal
 Muscle
 Gastrointestinal
 Genitourinary
 Joints
Patterns of bleeding
 Recent onset or lifelong
 Frequency and severity
 Spontaneous or after injury
 Challenges to hemostasis: tooth extraction, operative procedures
 Association with medication, particularly aspirin
Medications
Associated diseases
 Uremia
 Liver disease
 Infection
 Malignancy
Previous transfusion
Family history

Physical Examination
Vital signs
Skin: nature of bleeding, signs of liver disease
Mucosa: oral or nasal
Lymphadenopathy
Abdomen: liver size and shape, splenomegaly
Joints: signs of previous bleeding
Other sites of blood loss: pelvic, rectal, urinary tract

BOX 120-4. Coagulation Studies

CBC and smear (EDTA—purple top)
Platelet count (EDTA—purple top)
Bleeding time
Prothrombin time (citrate—blue top)
Partial thromboplastin time (citrate—blue top)
Other coagulation studies: fibrinogen level, thrombin time, clot solubility, factor levels, inhibitor screens
As necessary: electrolytes, glucose, BUN, creatinine, type and crossmatch

---

BUN, blood urea nitrogen; CBC, complete blood count; EDTA, ethylenediaminetetraacetic acid.

---

hemorrhage because of a slow equilibration time. The peripheral blood smear may demonstrate schistocytes or fragmented RBCs in disseminated intravascular coagulation (DIC). Teardrop-shaped or nucleated RBCs may reflect myelophthisic disease. A characteristic white blood cell morphologic condition is seen with thrombocytopenia associated with infectious mononucleosis, folate or vitamin B12 deficiency, or leukemia.[19]

Platelet Count

The platelet count may be estimated from the smear. Normally, one platelet is present per 10 to 20 RBCs. Often, the count is automated, the normal range being 150,000 to 400,000/mm³. Platelet counts less than 100,000/mm³ define thrombocytopenia. With normal function, the bleeding time increases in direct relation to a decrease in the platelet count below 100,000/mm³. Levels below 20,000/mm³ may be associated with serious spontaneous hemorrhage. However, the count gives no information about the functional capability of platelets.[20]

Bleeding Time

The bleeding time is the best test for both vascular integrity and platelet function that can be performed in the emergency department. The test is performed after making two standard incisions 1 mm deep and 1 cm long on the volar aspect of the forearm with a template while it is under 40–mm Hg pressure via a blood pressure cuff. The time is measured from the incision to the moment when the blood oozing from the wound is no longer absorbed by filter paper. A normal time is 8 minutes, a time of 8 to 10 minutes is borderline, and a time longer than 10 minutes is typically abnormal. Because of the high incidence of drug-induced platelet dysfunction, it is important to ask the patient about medications, particularly aspirin. The test is independent of the coagulation pathways.[20,21] As mentioned previously, the bleeding time is prolonged with platelet counts below 100,000/mm³, but such prolongation does not represent platelet dysfunction. However, a prolonged bleeding time associated with platelet counts greater than 100,000/mm³ suggests impaired function.

Prothrombin Time

The prothrombin time (PT) tests the factors of the extrinsic and common pathways. The patient's anticoagulated plasma is combined with calcium and tissue factor prepared from rabbit or human brain tissue. Sensitivity to factor deficiencies depends on the source of the tissue factor. The PT detects deficiencies in fibrinogen, prothrombin, factor V, factor VII, and factor X. It is typically used to test the extrinsic pathway. A normal control sample is simultaneously run, and the clotting times of both are recorded. The time in seconds is usually given over the normal control time, for example, 12.5/11.5. A PT 2 seconds or more over the control time can be considered significant. Results are usually reported as the International Normalized Ratio (INR), which compensates for differences in sensitivity of various thromboplastin reagents to the effects of warfarin. The test is helpful in monitoring the use of coumarin anticoagulants, and the time may be prolonged in patients with liver disease and other abnormalities of vitamin K–sensitive factors.[22]

Partial Thromboplastin Time

The partial thromboplastin time (PTT) tests the components of the intrinsic and common pathways, that is, essentially all factors but VII and XIII in the entire clotting cascade. In this test a phospholipid source and a contact-activating agent (kaolin) are added to anticoagulated citrate plasma. After an incubation period that allows factor XII to become activated, calcium is added and the clotting time is recorded. A normal control sample is run simultaneously. Normal ranges may vary, and each hospital laboratory should be checked. The average time is 25 to 29 seconds. The sensitivity of the test varies from factor to factor, but factor levels must usually be less than 40% before the PTT is prolonged. The test may be altered by clotting factor inhibitors of external origin (e.g., heparin) or internal origin (e.g., anti-VIII antibody). Inappropriately high values may occur if the plasma is too turbid or icteric. The activated PTT is most sensitive to abnormalities in the sequence of the coagulation cascade that precedes activation of factor X.[23-25]

Fibrinogen

Fibrinogen is present in sufficient concentration to be measured directly. Because it is the final coagulation substrate, its level reflects the balance between production and consumption. It may be decreased by hypoproduction, as in severe liver disease, or by overconsumption, as in DIC. Low levels or altered function increase the PT, PTT, and thrombin clotting time. Because fibrinogen is an acute phase reactant, certain conditions, including malignancy, sepsis, inflammation, and pregnancy, may alter interpretation of the test result.

Thrombin Time

Measurement of the thrombin clotting time bypasses the intrinsic and extrinsic pathways by directly converting fibrinogen to fibrin. It is a useful screening test for both qualitative and quantitative abnormalities of fibrinogen and inhibitors such as heparin and fibrin split products.[26]

Clot Solubility

The result of clot solubility testing may be the only abnormality in disorders involving factor XIII deficiency and some abnormal fibrinogen. A washed clot is incubated in acetic acid or urea. If the clot is not properly cross-linked, it dissolves.[12]

Factor Level Assays

Factor levels are determined either by bioassay, in which the ability of the sample of plasma to normalize controlled substrate-deficient plasma is evaluated, or by immunologic assay. Inhibitor screening tests reveal antibodies in plasma that prolong the normal plasma clotting time when mixed.[9,18,24]

DIFFERENTIAL DIAGNOSIS AND MANAGEMENT

When a bleeding disorder is diagnosed or suspected, the assessment initially includes stabilization, which

BOX 120-5. Differential Diagnosis of Vascular Disorders

Inherited
Disorders of connective tissue
    Pseudoxanthoma elasticum
    Ehlers-Danlos syndrome
    Osteogenesis imperfecta
Disorders of blood vessels
    Hemorrhagic telangiectasia

Acquired
Scurvy (vitamin C deficiency)
Simple or senile purpura
Purpura secondary to steroid use
Vascular damage
    Infection (meningococcemia)
    Azotemia (hemolytic-uremic syndrome)
    Hypoxemia
    Thrombotic thrombocytopenic purpura
    Snakebite
    Dysproteinemic purpura

BOX 120-6. Differential Diagnosis of Platelet Disorders

Thrombocytopenia
Decreased production
    Decreased megakaryocytes secondary to drugs, toxins, or infection
    Normal megakaryocytes with megaloblastic hematopoiesis or hereditary origin
Platelet pooling and splenic sequestration
Increased destruction
    Immunologic
        Related to collagen vascular disease, lymphoma, leukemia
        Drug related
        Infection
        Posttransfusion
        Idiopathic (autoimmune) thrombocytopenic purpura
    Mechanical
        Disseminated intravascular coagulation
        Thrombotic thrombocytopenic purpura
        Hemolytic-uremic syndrome
    Vasculitis
Dilutional secondary to massive blood transfusion

Thrombocytopathy
Adhesion defects such as von Willebrand's disease
Release defects: acquired and drug related
Aggregation defects such as in thrombasthenia

Thrombocytosis
Autonomous (primary thrombocythemia)
Reactive (secondary thrombocythemia)
    Iron deficiency
    Infection/inflammatory
    Trauma
    Nonhematologic malignancy
    Postsplenectomy
    Rebound from alcohol, cytotoxic drug therapy, folate/vitamin B12 deficiency

may necessitate volume, RBC, and coagulation factor replacement. If the disorder is known, clinical complications associated with its underlying pathophysiologic condition must be considered. If the disorder is unknown, a rapid differential diagnosis must be made. A clinically useful scheme approaches bleeding disorders in terms of three constituents: vascular integrity, platelets, and coagulation factors. This differential diagnostic approach can be further divided into inherited and acquired disorders.

Vascular Disorders

Vascular disorders have signs and symptoms similar to those of thrombocytopenic states. The inherited forms are rare. Acquired forms are usually associated with connective tissue changes or endothelial damage. The differential diagnosis of vascular disorders is listed in Box 120-5.[27]

Platelet Disorders

General Approach

Most platelet abnormalities occur in women and are acquired. The bleeding source is usually capillary, with resultant cutaneous and mucosal petechiae or ecchymosis. Epistaxis, menorrhagia, and gastrointestinal bleeding are common initial symptoms. The bleeding is generally mild and occurs immediately after surgery or dental extractions. Preceding trauma does not usually cause the bleeding incident. Petechiae and purpura may be noted on physical examination, and superficial ecchymoses may be found around a venipuncture site. Deep muscle hematomas and hemarthroses are not aspects of the clinical picture. The bleeding time is prolonged, and the platelet count may be low, normal, or high. The differential diagnosis of platelet disorders is listed in Box 120-6.

Thrombocytopenia

Decreased Production

Thrombocytopenia from decreased bone marrow production is usually caused by the effects of chemotherapeutic drugs, myelophthisic disease, or direct bone marrow effects of alcohol or thiazides.

Splenic Sequestration

Splenic sequestration is rare and seen primarily with hypersplenism resulting from hematologic malignancy, portal hypertension, or disorders involving increased splenic RBC destruction, such as hereditary spherocytosis or autoimmune hemolytic anemia.[28]

Increased Destruction

Immune Thrombocytopenia. Thrombocytopenia associated with increased peripheral destruction of platelets and shortened platelet survival caused by an antiplatelet antibody is seen in a number of diseases. In most cases a cause is identifiable.

Collagen vascular diseases, particularly systemic lupus erythematosus, may cause an antiplatelet antibody-related platelet decrease. Similar associations have been noted with leukemia and lymphoma, particularly lymphocytic lymphoma. All evaluations of suspected immune thrombocytopenia should include a complete blood count, peripheral smear, antinuclear antibody test, and bone marrow examination.[29] A number of drugs have been associated with thrombocytopenia of immunologic origin. Quinine and quinidine are common offenders that affect platelets through an "innocent bystander" mechanism. The platelet is coated with a drug-antibody complex, complement is fixed, and intravascular platelet lysis occurs. Because of its relatively high frequency, heparin is an important cause of drug-induced thrombocytopenia in hospitalized patients. Platelets are activated by the formation of an IgG-heparin complex.

Low molecular-weight heparin may be associated with less thrombocytopenia than standard, unfractionated heparin is; however, both forms of heparin demonstrate cross-reactivity.[30] Heparin-induced thrombocytopenia (HIT) is a serious immune-mediated side effect associated with heparin. HIT occurs in 1% to 5% of patients receiving unfractionated heparin and in less than 1% of those receiving low-molecular-weight heparin. It usually occurs within 5 to 7 days of heparin treatment. Thrombus develops in approximately half the patients with HIT. The thrombotic complications can lead to loss of a limb in up to 20% and mortality in as many as 30%. The diagnosis should be suspected in the presence of absolute thrombocytopenia or a greater than 50% reduction in platelets after the initiation of heparin. The most specific diagnostic tests for HIT are serotonin release assays, heparin-induced platelet aggregation assays, and solid-phase immunoassays. Elevated platelet-associated IgG levels are commonly present, but this finding is less specific or sensitive than the other diagnostic tests. More concerning to the emergency physician is delayed-onset HIT. This form of HIT occurs a median of 14 days after the initiation of heparin, but it has been reported to occur up to 40 days after starting heparin. Arterial or venous thrombosis typically develops in patients with HIT after receiving heparin. Treatment of thrombotic complications in these patients involves the use of direct thrombin inhibitors, such as lepirudin or argatroban.[31-33]

Digitoxin, sulfonamides, phenytoin, heparin, and aspirin are other problem drugs. The patient has usually ingested the medication within 24 hours. An idiopathic thrombocytopenic purpura (ITP) type of syndrome has been reported in intravenous cocaine users.[34] Clinical trials with platelet glycoprotein IIb-IIIa antagonists suggest that intravenous glycoprotein IIb-IIIa inhibitors may confer an increased risk for associated thrombocytopenia, independent of heparin therapy.[35] The platelet count may fall below 10,000/mm^3 and be complicated by serious bleeding. Laboratory testing may confirm the presence of antibody, especially with the use of quinine and quinidine. After stopping administration of the drug, the platelet count improves slowly over a period of 3 to 7 days. A short course of corticosteroid therapy such as prednisone in a dose of 1 mg/kg with rapid tapering may facilitate recovery.[36,37]

Postinfectious immune thrombocytopenia is usually associated with viral diseases such as rubella, rubeola, and varicella. Although many cases associated with sepsis have a mechanical origin, some immune mechanisms have been demonstrated.[36]

Posttransfusion thrombocytopenia is a rare disorder that causes a precipitous fall in platelets approximately 1 week after the transfusion. In 90% of cases, its origin is linked to the 98% of the population carrying a PLAI antigen on platelets. When transfused into a PLAI antigen–negative patient, the PLAI antibody accompanying this antigen destroys the recipient's platelets without the PLAI antigen. The platelet count often falls precipitously below 10,000/mm^3, with a significant risk for major bleeding. Intracranial hemorrhage occurs in approximately 10% of such cases. Patients are usually middle-aged women with a history of pregnancy who may have been previously sensitized to the PLAI antigen during pregnancy. Despite the fact that 2% of blood recipients are mismatched with respect to this antigen, it is fortunately a rare occurrence. Plasma exchange therapy is an effective antidote.[36,38]

Idiopathic Thrombocytopenic Purpura. Idiopathic (autoimmune) thrombocytopenic purpura should be considered after other causes have been excluded. ITP is associated with an IgG antiplatelet antibody that has proved difficult to detect. The two clinically important forms are acute and chronic.[29,39,40]

The acute form of ITP is seen most often in children 2 to 6 years of age. A viral prodrome commonly occurs within 3 weeks of its onset. The platelet count falls, usually to less than 20,000/mm^3. The course is self-limited, with a greater than 90% rate of spontaneous remission. Morbidity and mortality are low, although full recovery may take several weeks. Treatment is supportive, and steroid therapy does not alter the disease course.[36,40]

The more chronic form of ITP is primarily an adult disease found three times more often in women than men. Its onset is insidious, without a prodrome, and it is manifested as easy bruising, prolonged menses, and mucosal bleeding. The patient may have petechiae or purpura, and platelet counts between 30,000/mm^3 and 100,000/mm^3 are common. Splenomegaly is unusual in either acute or chronic ITP. Bleeding complications are of unpredictable frequency and severity, although long-term mortality is approximately 1%.[39,40] The course is one of waxing and waning severity, and spontaneous remission is rare.

Associated diseases, such as lymphoma and systemic lupus erythematosus, must be ruled out before the diagnosis can be made. Quantitative laboratory tests of antiplatelet antibody may differentiate between patients who will favorably respond to therapy and those who will not. Hospitalization is recommended during the initial evaluation because the differential diagnosis is complex and the risk of bleeding is significant. Treatment usually includes corticosteroids, splenectomy, and in refractory cases, immunosuppressive therapy such as with cyclophosphamide, azathioprine, or vincristine. Plasmapheresis, androgens, immune globulin, anti-Rh(D), danazol, and colchicine have all met with varied success. Platelet transfusions are used only to control life-threatening bleeding because of increased antiplatelet antibody titers and short-lived hemostatic effect. Though rare, life-threatening bleeding should be treated with platelet transfusions, intravenous immune globulin (1 g/kg), and methylprednisolone (30 mg/kg IV). Otherwise, care is supportive. The use of all nonessential drugs should be stopped, particularly those that might inhibit platelet function, such as aspirin.[36,39-43]

A similar pattern of thrombocytopenic purpura has been reported in sexually active homosexual men. Although the clinical findings and response to therapy mimic ITP, the mechanism is believed to be nonspecific deposition of immune complexes and complement rather than antiplatelet IgG.[44]

Nonimmune Thrombocytopenia. Nonimmune platelet destruction is usually consumptive or mechanical. Consumption occurs as part of the process of intravascular coagulation, although it may be seen at sites of significant endothelial loss. Thrombotic thrombocytopenic purpura (TTP), hemolytic-uremic syndrome, and vasculitis all initiate platelet destruction through endothelial damage.[45,46] The most striking difference between the first two is the age at onset and the prognosis.

Thrombotic Thrombocytopenic Purpura. The pathologic state of TTP is the result of subendothelial and intraluminal deposits of fibrin and platelet aggregates in capillaries and arterioles. Hemolytic-uremic syndrome is considered to be very similar to TTP; however, the former is associated with less central nervous system and more renal involvement than TTP is. Although the initiating event is unclear, prostacyclin and abnormal platelet aggregation are believed to play a central role in pathogenesis of the disease. The disease may affect patients of any age or sex, but the majority are 10 to 40 years of age and 60% of cases occur in women. Most cases of TTP are idiopathic. However, TTP can be associated with medications. Quinine is the most common drug associated with the disease. The antiplatelet drugs ticlopidine and clopidogrel, which are used in a variety of cardiovascular disorders, have also been associated with TTP. It is classically seen as the constellation of thrombocytopenic purpura, microangiopathic hemolytic anemia, fluctuating neurologic symptoms, renal disease, and fever, but only 40% of cases have the classic pentad.

The platelet count ranges from 10,000/mm³ to 50,000/mm³, and generalized purpura and bleeding complaints are common. Anemia is universal, with hematocrit levels commonly less than 20%. The hemolysis may cause jaundice or pallor, and the blood smear characteristically contains numerous schistocytes and fragmented RBCs. Neurologic symptoms include stroke, seizures, paresthesias, altered levels of consciousness, and coma, all of which characteristically fluctuate in severity. The renal component varies from hematuria and proteinuria to acute renal failure. Fever is present in 90% of patients.

Untreated, the disease follows a progressive and fatal course, with 80% mortality 1 to 3 months after diagnosis. Therapy has included corticosteroids, splenectomy, anticoagulation, exchange transfusion, and dextran. However, plasma exchange with fresh frozen plasma (plasmapheresis) is the current treatment of choice. Over the last several years, the aggressive use of plasma exchange has reduced the mortality rate from 90% to 17%. In addition to plasma exchange, initial therapy may also include steroids such as prednisone and antiplatelet agents such as aspirin and dipyridamole (Persantine). Splenectomy, immune globulin, vincristine, and other therapies may have a role in resistant cases. With the exception of life-threatening bleeding, platelet transfusion should be avoided because platelets may cause additional thrombi in the microcirculation.[45-50]

Dilutional Thrombocytopenia

Dilutional thrombocytopenia occurs in cases of massive transfusion, exchange transfusion, or extracorporeal circulation. Volume replacement with stored bank blood is platelet poor because platelets have a life span of only 9 days. The number of transfusions directly correlates with the degree of thrombocytopenia. Current transfusion practice is to monitor platelet counts for every 10 U of RBCs and transfuse once the platelet count approaches 50,000/mm³.[51]

Thrombocytopathy

Knowledge of abnormal platelet function as a clinical disorder has grown rapidly in recent years. The drug-induced form may be one of the most commonly seen causes of abnormal bleeding.[52] Defects may occur at any level of platelet function, including adhesion, release, and aggregation.

Adhesion Defects

The representative adhesion disorder is von Willebrand's disease, which is more a factor VIII problem than a platelet deficiency. Platelets are normal in terms of their morphologic condition, number, release, and aggregation. The abnormal adhesion results not from the platelet but from an endothelium-based plasma deficiency of a factor VIII component (vWF) that permits platelet adhesion.[53,54]

Release Defects

Release defects include "storage pool" syndromes in which release is normal but amounts of adenosine diphosphate, calcium, and serotonin are decreased. Release defects may be congenital or acquired, as in systemic lupus erythematosus, alcoholism, or lymphoma. Drugs induce the most common release problem. Aspirin and related drugs block the enzyme cyclooxygenase, which participates in thromboxane A_2 formation. Decreased release of thromboxane A_2 results in decreased aggregation and less local vasoconstriction. Both may contribute to an increased risk of bleeding. Testing for this risk has been suggested by development of the postaspirin bleeding time as a screening test for hemostatic disorders. Aspirin is unique in that it permanently poisons this reaction for the life of the platelet in dosages of only 300 to 600 mg. Phenylbutazone and indomethacin affect function only while measurably circulating. A similar problem may occur in patients with uremia or dysproteinemia and as a rare inherited form.[5,6,55]

Aggregation Defects

Primary aggregation defects are associated with the rare recessive trait thrombasthenia. This platelet membrane abnormality may be detected by the lack of clot retraction during a 2-hour clot retraction test.[21]

Platelet Transfusions

Most platelet function disorders are not treated by platelet transfusion because its efficacy is questionable and alloimmunization may occur. Platelet transfusions are commonly indicated for primary bone marrow disorders (e.g., aplastic anemia or acute leukemia). Assessing the risk for spontaneous bleeding by using platelet counts is an imprecise science. Less mature platelets associated with peripheral consumption or sequestration are less likely to allow spontaneous hemorrhage than are those associated with primary bone marrow involvement. An estimate of functionality is combined with the platelet count for a better predictor of primary hemostasis potential. At counts below $50,000/mm^3$, a variable degree of risk exists, especially that associated with trauma, ulcers, or invasive procedure. At counts higher than $50,000/mm^3$, hemorrhage caused by platelet deficiency is unlikely. The transfusion threshold for platelets in trauma is not well defined and may be as high as $75,000/mm^3$ to $80,000/mm^3$. Spontaneous bleeding in the absence of surgery, trauma, or other risk factors may occur in patients with platelet counts less than $10,000/mm^3$.[56]

Thrombocytosis

Thrombocytosis may be discovered in the emergency department. The reactive form is considered benign. The differential diagnosis (see Box 120-6) should be considered when confronted with a platelet count higher than 600,000 to $1,000,000/mm^3$. The primary or autonomous state may be associated with bleeding or thrombosis. It is often an associated finding in patients with polycythemia vera, myelofibrosis, or chronic myelogenous leukemia. Suspected autonomous thrombocytosis requires a full hematologic evaluation.[1,57]

Disorders of the Coagulation Pathway

The coagulation system accomplishes secondary hemostasis through a complex enzymatic cascade. The clinically significant disorders have a number of characteristic features that help differentiate them from platelet disorders, including the following[18]:

1. The bleeding source is often an intramuscular or deep soft tissue hematoma from small arterioles.

2. The congenital form of the disease occurs predominantly in men, often as a sex-linked inheritance.
3. Bleeding may occur after surgery or trauma but is delayed in onset up to 72 hours.
4. Epistaxis, menorrhagia, and gastrointestinal sources of bleeding are rare, whereas hematuria and hemarthrosis are common in severe cases.
5. The bleeding time is normal except in patients with von Willebrand's disease.

The PT and PTT are the basic laboratory diagnostic tools for the evaluation of coagulation disorders and can be used to organize the approach to their diagnosis.[18]

Abnormal Prothrombin Time and Other Tests Normal

An elevated PT reflects an extrinsic pathway abnormality mediated through deficiency of factor VII. The hereditary form is caused by a rare autosomal recessive gene. The acquired form is commonly seen as a manifestation of vitamin K deficiency, coumarin use, or liver disease. Because factor VII has the shortest half-life (3 to 5 hours) of the coagulation factors, it is the first to manifest a deficiency when its active form is underproduced. The PT is a sensitive gauge of hepatic function and the efficacy of coumarin administration. INRs calculate the prothrombin ratio raised to the power of an international sensitivity index for specific thromboplastin reagents. It is recommended with most warfarin therapy that the INR be maintained between 2.0 and 3.0.[58-60]

Abnormal Partial Thromboplastin Time and Other Tests Normal

Two groups of inherited disorders manifest an isolated elevation in the PTT. The first group consists of the contact factors (e.g., XII [Hageman factors]), prekallikrein (Fletcher factor), and high-molecular-weight kinogen. They cause a benign disorder in which the PTT is elevated but the patient has no bleeding diathesis. These deficiencies exist as isolated laboratory abnormalities, and thus they should not be invoked as a cause of the patient's bleeding problem. They may be specifically assayed when a precise diagnosis is necessary.[11,17]

The second group causes significant bleeding problems resulting from deficiencies of factors within the intrinsic coagulation system. They are the most common inherited abnormalities of the entire clotting system. Deficiencies of factors VIII, IX, and XI account for 99% of inherited bleeding disorders. Patients with active life-threatening bleeding who are suspected of having a congenital bleeding disorder can be supported with fresh frozen plasma, 15 mL/kg, while diagnostic studies are being performed. The risk of viral transmission of hepatitis B or C or human immunodeficiency virus must be considered.

In a patient with a prolonged PTT and a lifelong history of bleeding, the most important test in initiating the differential diagnosis is a factor VIII assay. This test measures the ability of the patient's plasma to correct the prolonged PTT of plasma deficient in factor VIII. This ability is compared with that of normal plasma and the result is given as a percentage of normal. The test measures the procoagulant activity of factor VIII but does not discriminate between abnormal activity resulting from abnormal factor VIII or low levels of normal factor VIII. The two forms of this deficiency are hemophilia A and von Willebrand's disease.[9,61]

Hemophilia A

Hemophilia A is caused by a variant form of factor VIII that is present in normal levels but lacks a clot-promoting property. The incidence is 60 to 80 persons per million population. Of cases, 70% have been found to have a sex-linked recessive nature; that is, the disease is carried on the X chromosome at location Xq28. Factor VIII circulates in plasma in very low concentration and is normally bound to vWF. The source of factor VIII production is uncertain, but the liver is thought to be a significant source because hemophilia A can be corrected by liver transplantation. A female carrier mating with a normal man would be predicted to pass the disease to half her sons. Likewise, a male hemophiliac would have all normal sons and all carrier daughters. The remaining 25% to 30% of cases of the disease are believed to result from a spontaneous genetic abnormality. The familial form has a remarkable consistency of severity from generation to generation, although the degree of severity has considerable variation. This severity may be directly related to the level of factor VIII coagulant (factor VIII:C) activity. Cases with less than 1% activity are severe, with a tendency toward spontaneous bleeding. Cases with 1% to 5% activity are moderate, with rare spontaneous bleeding but increased problems with surgery or trauma. Cases with 5% to 10% activity and above are considered mild, with little risk of spontaneous bleeding but still with hazards after trauma and surgery. A number of hemophiliacs may have activity above 10% but have few problems unless stressed. The PTT may lack sensitivity for this group because it is significantly prolonged only at factor VIII:C levels less than 35% to 40%.[9,62-65]

The disease is seen as a disorder of secondary hemostasis with a characteristic pattern of bleeding. Bleeding can occur anywhere, but deep muscles, joints, the urinary tract, and intracranial sites are the most common. Recurrent hemarthrosis and progressive joint destruction are major causes of morbidity in hemophilia. Intracranial bleeding is the major cause of death in all age groups of hemophiliacs. Mucosal bleeding such as epistaxis and oral bleeding or menorrhagia is rare unless the disease is associated with von Willebrand's disease or platelet inhibition, such as with aspirin use. Gastrointestinal bleeding is rare unless peptic ulcer disease is also present. Trauma is a common initiator of bleeding in all stages of severity. This potential hazard must be viewed expectantly in all hemophiliacs because late bleeding may occur, usually by 8 hours but potentially up to 1 to 3 days after trauma.[63-65]

Management of Hemophilia A

Comprehensive management of hemophilia involves a team effort of physicians, specialized nurses, physical therapists, social workers, the patient, and the patient's family. The therapeutic responsibility of the emergency physician consists of three areas: preparation for and identification of the problem, initial evaluation, and admission of new bleeders; replacement therapy for bleeding episodes; and anticipation of potential life threats and admission of known bleeders for observation in selected circumstances. At one time, treatment of hemophilia-associated bleeding was a relatively common emergency medicine activity, but since 1975, hemophilia home therapy has increasingly been instituted. Therefore, many hemophiliacs now come to the emergency department only with complicated problems or trauma-related difficulties, and most are knowledgeable about their disease.[63-66]

Preparation. In preparing for the problem, the emergency physician should have updated information covering disease processes and current therapy. A cooperative effort should be made between the emergency department and the hematology service to generate a file of known hemophiliacs in the area who are monitored at the hospital. The file should include the primary physician, diagnosis, factor VIII activity level, blood type, presence of antihemophilic factor antibodies, and time of last hospitalization. A protocol should be developed for ordering and administering factor VIII.

Replacement Therapy. The accepted therapy for hemophilia A is factor VIII replacement with cryoprecipitate or factor VIII:C concentrates. These concentrates are exposed to heat treatment or solvent-detergent mixtures to decrease transmission of hepatitis B, hepatitis C, and human immunodeficiency virus. In the past, the concentrate was made from fractionated freeze-dried antihemophilic factor and contained 250 to 1500 IU of factor VIII:C in a reconstituted volume. Factor VIII is also produced by recombinant DNA techniques and is considered by some to be the replacement product of choice. Recombinant-derived factor VIII is comparable to plasma-derived factor VIII in terms of characteristics and control of bleeding, but it has no discernible side effects. Factor VIII:C concentrates are commonly used in severe hemophilia and for home use. Cryoprecipitate is the cold precipitable protein fraction derived from fresh frozen plasma thawed at 1° C to 6° C. It was once the mainstay of hemophilia A therapy and may be used when noninfectious factor VIII concentrates are not available.[66-70]

Plasma-derived replacement therapies pose some risk for hepatitis C and hepatitis B. Persistent hepatitis B surface antigen occurs in the blood of 5% of hemophiliacs, whereas the anti-B surface antigen is found in 80%. This problem has been overshadowed by the association of acquired immunodeficiency syndrome with hemophilia. The association is related to blood product use, and although the total number is low, the incidence is high—3.6 per 1000 hemophilia A patients.[67,68]

Therapy for a bleeding episode includes a number of considerations: the circumstances in which factor VIII

Table 120-1. Recommended Factor VIII Therapy for Specific Problems in Hemophilia

Type of Bleeding	Initial Dosage	Duration	Comment
Skin			
Abrasion	None	None	Treat with local pressure and topical thrombin
Laceration	Usually none; if necessary, treat as minor	None	Local pressure and anesthetic with epinephrine may benefit; watch 4 hours after suturing, reexamine in 24 hours
Superficial			
Deep	Minor bleeding (12.5 mg/kg)	Single-dose coverage	May need hospitalization for observation; repeat may be necessary for suture removal
Nasal epistaxis			
Spontaneous	Usually none; may need to be treated as mild bleeding	None	Uncommon; consider platelet inhibition; treat in usual manner
Traumatic	Moderate bleeding (25 mg/kg)	Up to 5-7 days	Trauma-related bleeding can be significant
Oral			
Mucosa or tongue bites	Usually none; treat as minor if persists	Single dose	Commonly seen
Traumatic (laceration) or dental extraction	Moderate (25 U/kg) to severe (50 U/kg)	Single dose; may need more	Saliva rich in fibrin lytic activity; oral ε-aminocaproic acid (Amicar) may be given at 100 mg every 6 hours for 7 days to block fibrinolysis; check contraindications; hospitalize patients with severe bleeding
Soft tissue/muscle hematomas	Moderate (25 U/kg) to severe (50 U/kg)	2-5 days	May be complicated by local pressure on nerves or vessels (e.g., iliopsoas, forearm, calf)
Hemarthrosis			
Early	Mild (12.5 U/kg)	Single dose	Treat as earliest symptom (pain); knee, elbow, ankle more common
Late or unresponsive cases of early hemarthrosis	Mild to moderate (25 U/kg)	3-4 days	Arthrocentesis rarely necessary and only with 50% level coverage; immobilization is critical point of therapy
Hematuria	Mild (12.5 U/kg)	2-3 days	Urokinase, the fibrinolytic enzyme, is in urine; with persistent hematuria an organic cause should be ruled out
Major bleeding	Major bleeding (50 U/kg)	7-10 days or 3-5 days after bleeding ceases	In head trauma, therapy should be given prophylactically; early CT scan of head recommended for all
Gastrointestinal severe bleeding			
Neck/sublingual			
Retroperitoneal			
Intra-abdominal			
Major trauma			
Head injury (see text)			
Central nervous system bleeding (see text)			
Surgical procedure			

is given, the dosage, the timing of maintenance, the duration of the dosage, the presence of antibodies, and the means of gauging effectiveness. Tables 120-1 and 120-2 include guidelines for the recommended treatment in a variety of circumstances. Most important, the emergency physician should believe patients who say that they are bleeding and institute early therapy.[64,66]

The response to therapy can be monitored by clinical improvement, a decreasing PTT, and optimally, serial factor VIII:C activity levels. The infusion of 1 U of factor VIII per kilogram increases factor VIII levels by 2%. The lack of a response to factor VIII administration should raise the question of circulating antibodies. All hemophiliacs should be screened for the development of these antihemophilic factor antibodies when they are given in-hospital therapy or if they become refractory to home therapy. The 7% to 20% of patients in whom these IgG antibodies develop usually have a severe deficiency necessitating multiple factor VIII transfusions. The treatment may be complex, and

hospitalization is necessary. A variety of therapies have been considered, including "overwhelming" factor VIII doses, exchange plasmapheresis, immunosuppressive therapy, and the infusion of prothrombin complexes containing activated clotting factors. Other recommended therapies include porcine factor VIII, which has less cross-reactivity with the human product, and probably in the future, recombinant activated factor VII.[66,71-73] Acquired IgG antihemophilic factor antibodies may exist in nonhemophiliac patients. They can occur in the postpartum period, as immunologic reactions to penicillin or phenytoin, and in association with systemic lupus erythematosus, rheumatoid arthritis, or inflammatory bowel disease. The diagnosis is made by the occurrence of an acquired hemophilia-like syndrome with positive antibody titers in the appropriate setting.

The "lupus anticoagulant" is unique in that it may be associated with an increased risk for thrombosis, as well as a hemorrhagic diathesis.[64,74]

Table 120-2. Dosage of Factor VIII (Antihemophilic Factor)

Bleeding Risk	Desired Factor VIII Level (%)	Initial Dose (U/kg)
Mild	5-10	12.5
Moderate	20-30	25
Severe	50 or greater	50

Standard Calculation

1. $\left.\begin{array}{c}\text{Patient's plasma volume}\\(50 \text{ mL/kg} \times \text{weight in kg})\end{array}\right. \times \left.\begin{array}{c}\text{(Desired level of factor}\\\text{VIII [percent])}\end{array}\right. - \left.\begin{array}{c}\text{(Present level of factor}\\\text{VIII [percent])}\end{array}\right. = \left.\begin{array}{c}\text{Number of units for}\\\text{initial dose}\end{array}\right.$
2. In emergency therapy, the present level of factor VIII is assumed to be zero
3. One unit is the activity of the coagulation factor present in 1 mL of normal human plasma
4. Because the half-life of factor VIII is 8 to 12 hours, the desired level is maintained by giving half the initial dose every 8 to 12 hours
5. Cryoprecipitate is assumed to have 80 to 100 U of factor VIII:C per bag; factor VIII:C concentrates list the units per bottle on the label

Desmopressin acetate has been shown to increase levels of factors VIII:C and VIII:Ag in patients with hemophilia A and in some with von Willebrand's disease. It is given intravenously at 0.3 µg/kg per dose. Benefits are primarily noted in patients with mild to moderate disease and last for 4 to 6 hours.[75,76]

Prophylaxis. The anticipation of delayed bleeding in patients with hemophilia may necessitate admission and observation for a variety of trauma-related injuries. Candidates for prophylactic admission are patients with deep lacerations; those with soft tissue injuries in areas where the pressure from a developing hematoma could be destructive, such as in the eye, mouth, neck, back, and spinal column; and patients with a history of major trauma forces without injury. Head trauma is potentially life threatening to hemophiliacs, and central nervous system bleeding is the major cause of death for patients in all age groups. Studies find a 3% to 13% risk of intracranial hemorrhage, yet no patient given replacement therapy within 6 hours had intracranial bleeding. It is recommended that head trauma patients have factor VIII therapy initiated to a 50% activity level and be admitted, as a minimum, for 24 hours of observation. All patients with anything but the most trivial head trauma should undergo computed tomography of the head and factor VIII therapy to at least a 50% activity level. In any patient with an altered level of consciousness or focal neurologic signs, factor VIII therapy should be started immediately and a computed tomography scan performed.[77,78] Obviously, all these patients are treated in joint consultation with their primary physician and hematologist.

Gene therapy represents a potential development in the treatment of hemophilia. With cloning of the genes encoding factor VIII, the possibility exists for either a partial or complete cure of hemophilia. The goal of gene therapy is not to restore factor levels to normal but rather to convert from a severe to a mild phenotype and dramatically improve clinical outcomes. Early studies are encouraging. Although genetic testing and counseling are currently available, no genetic therapies for hemophilia A are available at present.[64,79-82]

von Willebrand's Disease

To understand von Willebrand's disease, it is helpful to review the nomenclature used to refer to factor VIII in some centers. Factor VIII has at least three activities. First is its antihemophilic, or coagulant, activity, VIII:C. All references to factor VIII in this chapter thus far have been to this activity. A second activity supports platelet adhesion and in vitro aggregation with the antibiotic ristocetin; it is called von Willebrand factor activity, or VIII/vWF. A third component reacts with rabbit antibodies to factor VIII. It is termed the factor VIII antigen, or VIII:Ag, and relates to the measured plasma level rather than the activity of factor VIII. The antigen and cofactor activity for platelet function are structurally related.[54,83] Von Willebrand's disease has both decreased factor VIII:Ag levels and decreased VIII:C activity secondary to underproduction. The patient's platelets are normal in number, morphologic condition, and other functions, but in the absence of circulating factor VIII/vWF, their adhering properties are diminished. Von Willebrand's disease is the most common hereditary bleeding disorder, with an estimated prevalence of 1%. The disease occurs in 5 to 10 persons per million population as an autosomal dominant trait with a variable penetrance pattern. A rare X-linked inheritance has been described.[54,83,84]

Manifestations of von Willebrand's disease are usually milder and less crippling than those of hemophilia. The factor VIII:C level is in the 6% to 50% range. Bleeding sites are predominantly mucosal (e.g., epistaxis) and cutaneous. Hemarthroses are rare, but menorrhagia and gastrointestinal bleeding are common. Laboratory differentiation from hemophilia A includes an abnormal bleeding time, a decreased level of factor VIII:Ag, and abnormal platelet aggregation with ristocetin.[85] In patients with severe disease, replacement therapy with factor VIII in the form of intermediate purity factor VIII concentrate is the method of choice. The initial dose is 20 to 30 IU/kg every 12 hours to keep vWF levels at 50% or to control bleeding. A unique response to the transfusion of plasma components in patients with von Willebrand's disease is the stimulation of a progressive increase in VIII:C activity that lasts 12 to 40 hours. After the initial dose, fewer units are necessary, and longer dosage schedules may be followed by a clinical response and a combination of factor VIII:C activity and serial bleeding times.

In extreme circumstances without alternatives, fresh frozen plasma may be used. A factor VIII concentrate

(Humate-P) has also demonstrated sufficient VIII/vWF to treat the disease.[56,86] Drug therapy with desmopressin is of benefit in patients with mild to moderately severe von Willebrand's disease. It is most useful in a specific type of the disease and should not be given without previous consultation with a hematologist.[75,87,88]

Hemophilia B (Christmas Disease)

Hemophilia B is a deficiency of factor IX activity. Its genetic pattern and clinical findings are indistinguishable from those of hemophilia A, but its incidence is only a fifth that of hemophilia A. Factor IX is a vitamin K–dependent glycoprotein. Its deficiency is diagnosed by a factor IX assay, usually after the factor VIII:C assay is found to be normal. The replacement schedule for factor IX is similar to that for hemophilia A, but a purified factor IX concentrate or recombinant factor IX preparation is used. The plasma prothrombin complex (factors II, VII, IX, and X) and fresh frozen plasma are also useful, but they pose a higher risk of viral transmission and venous or arterial thrombosis. The maintenance dosage schedule is increased to every 24 hours because of the longer half-life of factor IX.[66,89,90]

Similar to hemophilia A, gene testing and counseling are available. Gene therapy in animals has demonstrated promising results, and preliminary results from a human study suggest that the severity of hemophilia B can be altered and improved by gene manipulation.[79,80,91,92]

Miscellaneous Coagulation Disorders

A number of other disorders may be caused by a deficiency in the common coagulation pathway. An altered fibrinogen level or abnormal function is a relatively common cause. Patients with this deficiency also have an abnormal thrombin time. The inherited forms are rare. The acquired forms have been related to fibrin-blocking substances and hypofibrinogenemia, which are found most often in cases of DIC and dysfibrinogenemia associated with macroglobulinemia, multiple myeloma, and hepatoma. In the context of emergency medicine, fibrinogen's most important role relates to its activity in DIC.

The other components of the common pathway (factors II, V, and X) have rare inherited deficiencies. The acquired forms are far more common and relate to vitamin K deficiency (decreased factor II, VII, IX, and X activity), warfarin use (same factors as with vitamin K deficiency), hepatic insufficiency (potentially all factors except VIII), and massive transfusion of stored blood (low in factors V and VIII and platelets).

Disseminated Intravascular Coagulation

DIC is a relatively common acquired coagulopathy. Its ubiquitous nature, multiple origins, and potentially devastating sequelae, balanced by an effective mode of therapy, make early diagnosis of this hematologic process critical. It is most often encountered in the critical care setting. Hemostasis is achieved by a fine balance between procoagulants and inhibitors and thrombus formation and lysis. The balance may be disturbed by pathologic processes that result in an out-of-control coagulation and fibrinolytic cascade within the systemic circulation. The following occurs in this abnormal clotting sequence:

1. Platelets and coagulation factors are consumed, especially fibrinogen and factors V, VIII, and XIII.
2. Thrombin is formed, and it overwhelms its inhibitor system and acts to accelerate the coagulation process and directly activate fibrinogen.
3. Fibrin is deposited in small vessels in multiple organs.
4. The fibrinolytic system by means of plasmin may lyse fibrin and impair thrombin formation.
5. Fibrin degradation products are released and affect platelet function and inhibit fibrin polymerization.
6. Coagulation inhibition levels (e.g., antithrombin III, protein C, and tissue factor pathway inhibitor) are decreased.

The clinical consequence of these processes is the life-threatening combination of a bleeding diathesis from loss of platelets and clotting factors, fibrinolysis, and fibrin degradation product interference; small vessel obstruction and tissue ischemia from fibrin deposition; and RBC injury and anemia from fibrin deposition. The condition must be suspected in any patient in whom purpura, a bleeding tendency, and signs of organ injury, particularly the central nervous system and kidney, develop in the appropriate clinical setting. This broad description is further confused clinically by the variable acuteness and intensity of intravascular clotting, the effectiveness of fibrinolysis, and other systemic manifestations of the initiating disease.[93-95]

The clinical diagnosis is necessarily supported by laboratory tests. The tests recommended in Table 120-3 usually confirm the presence of DIC. Other tests (e.g., specific degradation products of fibrin and fibrinogen) can confirm the diagnosis. These tests are rarely available in the emergency department.

Two conditions that may simulate DIC are severe liver disease and primary fibrinolysis. Liver disease of this severity is usually manifested by clinical jaundice and splenomegaly. Primary fibrinolysis is a rare disorder that affects fibrinogen and fibrin but generally leaves the coagulation components (platelets, factor V, and factor VIII) in the low normal range. The paracoagulation test is negative, and the euglobulin lysis time is rapid.[95,96]

When planning therapy, the emergency physician must remember that defibrination is always secondary to a serious underlying pathologic process. Once the diagnosis is confirmed, the initial treatment is focused on reversing the triggering mechanism. Many episodes of DIC are self-limited, such as in a transfusion reaction, or compensated, such as associated with a tumor mass, and do not require intervention other than support.[93-95]

Replacement therapy is usually instituted simultaneously with attempts to control the primary process. The goal is to avoid depletion of clotting factors. Treatment is partially based on which of the two major pathologic components of DIC dominates the clinical

Table 120-3. Laboratory Diagnosis of Disseminated Intravascular Coagulation

Test	Finding	Pathophysiology
Peripheral smear	Low platelets, schistocytes, RBC fragments	RBC fragmentation on fibrin strands; schistocytes not always seen
Platelet count	Low (usually <100,000/mm^3)	Consumed in clotting; lower numbers are reflected in the bleeding time
PT	Prolonged	Factors II and IV consumed
PTT	Prolonged	Factors II, V, and VIII consumed
Thrombin time	Prolonged	Decrease in factor II and fibrin degradation products
Fibrinogen level	Low	Factor II consumed; may be difficult to interpret because it is an acute phase reactant
Fibrin degradation products	Zero to large	Dependent on the amount of secondary fibrinolysis
Serum creatinine or urinalysis	May be abnormal	Functional assessment of the organ most commonly injured by fibrin deposition

PT, prothrombin time; PTT, partial thromboplastin time; RBC, red blood cell.

picture. If active bleeding is present, replacement therapy with platelets, coagulation factors found in fresh frozen plasma or cryoprecipitate (I, V, VIII), and blood is recommended. Selective replacement therapy can be based on the laboratory and clinical response. Retardation of bleeding, a decrease in fibrin degradation products, and a rise in platelet counts and fibrinogen levels are useful monitors. Normalization of clotting times occurs too late to be of value in monitoring.[93-96]

Heparin has selective use in the treatment of DIC when fibrin deposition and thrombosis dominate the pathologic picture. Certain disease states are associated more with fibrin deposition, in which case heparin therapy should be considered. Examples include purpura fulminans, retained dead fetus before delivery, giant hemangioma, and acute promyelocytic leukemia. Heparin therapy is of little benefit in cases of meningococcemia, abruptio placentae, severe liver disease, and trauma. Low doses of heparin (300 to 500 U/hr) as a continuous infusion are currently recommended. Low-molecular-weight heparin may also be used instead of unfractionated heparin. Continuous monitoring of the clinical response, heparin levels, and bleeding status is necessary.

Other therapeutic agents such as antithrombin III and activated protein C have been evaluated. However, none have demonstrated an improved outcome in DIC, and only recombinant activated protein C (drotrecogin alfa) has been associated with improved outcomes in septic shock, regardless of whether DIC was present.[97-99]

The goals of emergency care of patients with DIC include initial suspicion, aggressive pursuit of the diagnosis, understanding of potential life-threatening complications, and only rarely, initiation of therapy.

DISPOSITION

All patients with bleeding disorders of unknown cause or of a significant degree should be admitted to the hospital for further evaluation. The circumstances in which a patient with a known bleeding disorder may be discharged for home care are discussed in earlier sections on individual disease states. Transferring these

patients may be necessary, particularly if hematologic consultation is not readily available. The standard criteria of hemodynamic stability, appropriate monitoring, and full knowledge and understanding on the part of the family and accepting physician should be met before transfer. Because of the delayed bleeding pattern in hemophiliacs, it may be especially hazardous to transfer them long distances. Therefore, the importance of advance knowledge and preparation is reemphasized. Outpatients are usually managed under the auspices of the hematologic consultant. Early notification and appropriate follow-up arrangements should be made with these specialists.

KEY CONCEPTS

- Although hemostatic disorders are confirmed by specific patterns of laboratory tests, a careful history and focused physical examination are often the key to the diagnosis of hematologic diseases.

- The frequency of hemostatic disorders seen in the emergency department is unknown; however, they are likely to be more common than thought. Although classic diseases such as hemophilia and DIC are uncommon, the use of antiplatelet and anticoagulation agents is common in other disease states such as cardiovascular diseases.

- Hemophilia patients are often highly informed about their disease. Patient input should be solicited and respected, and early consultation with the patient's hematologist is encouraged. Early treatment with replacement factor while diagnostic testing proceeds is encouraged.

- Platelet dysfunction is often equated with low platelet counts. Even though critical thrombocytopenia increases the risk of bleeding, particularly with trauma and surgery, dysfunction can occur at normal platelet counts. For example, antiplatelet therapy and renal disease can alter platelet function without reducing blood counts.

REFERENCES

1. Rogers GM: Endothelium and the regulation of hemostasis. In Greer JP, et al (eds): *Wintrobe's Clinical Hematology,* 11th ed. Baltimore, Williams & Wilkins, 2004.
2. Coughlin SR: Protease-activated receptors and platelet function. *Thromb Haemost* 82:353, 1999.

3. Sixma JJ, et al: Platelet adhesion to collagen: An update. *Thromb Haemost* 78:434, 1997.

4. Shattil SJ, Kashiwagi H, Pampori N: Integrin signaling: The platelet paradigm. *Blood* 91:2645, 1998.

5. Lefkovits J, Plow EF, Topol EJ: Platelet glycoproteins IIb/IIIa receptors in cardiovascular medicine. *N Engl J Med* 332:1553, 1995.

6. Parise LV, Boudignon-Proudhon C, Keely PJ, Naik UP: Platelets in hemostasis and thrombosis. In Greer JP, et al (eds): *Wintrobe's Clinical Hematology,* 11th ed. Baltimore, Williams & Wilkins, 2004.

7. Greenberg CS, Orthner CL: Blood coagulation and fibrinolysis. In Greer JP, et al (eds): *Wintrobe's Clinical Hematology,* 11th ed. Baltimore, Williams & Wilkins, 2004.

8. Rapaport SI, Rao LV: The tissue factor pathway. How it has become a "prima ballerina." *Thromb Haemost* 74:7, 1995.

9. Jesty J, Nemerson Y. The pathways of blood coagulation. In Beutler E, et al (eds): *Williams Hematology,* 6th ed. New York, McGraw-Hill, 2001.

10. Broze GJ: Tissue factor pathway inhibitor and the revised theory of coagulation. *Annu Rev Med* 46:103, 1995.

11. Bauer KA, Rosenberg RD: Control of coagulation reactions. In Beutler E, et al (eds): *Williams Hematology,* 6th ed. New York, McGraw-Hill, 2001.

12. Mosesson MW: The roles of fibrinogen and fibrin in hemostasis and thrombosis. *Semin Hematol* 29:177, 1992.

13. Perry DJ: Antithrombin and its inherited deficiencies. *Blood Rev* 8:37, 1994.

14. Brass LF: Thrombin and platelet activation. *Chest* 124:18S, 2003.

15. Baugh RJ, Broze, GJ, Krishnasawamy S: Regulation of extrinsic pathway factor Xa formation by tissue factor pathway inhibitor. *J Biol Chem* 273:4378, 1998.

16. Moncada S, Higgs A: The L-arginine–nitric oxide pathway. *N Engl J Med* 329:2002, 1993.

17. Rosenberg RU: Regulation of the hemostatic mechanism. In Stamatoyannopoulos G, et al (eds): *Molecular Basis of Blood Diseases,* 3rd ed. Philadelphia, WB Saunders, 2000.

18. Bennett JS: Blood coagulation and coagulation tests. *Med Clin North Am* 68:557, 1985.

19. Clodfelter RL: The peripheral smear. *Emerg Med Clin North Am* 4:59, 1986.

20. Miletich J: Bleeding time. In Beutler E, et al (eds): *Williams Hematology,* 6th ed. New York, McGraw-Hill, 2001.

21. Rodgers RPC, Levin J: A critical reappraisal of the bleeding time. *Semin Thromb Hemost* 16:1, 1990.

22. Miletich J: Prothrombin time. In Beutler E, et al (eds): *Williams Hematology,* 6th ed. New York, McGraw-Hill, 2001.

23. Angelos MA, Hamilton GC: Coagulation studies. *Emerg Med Clin North Am* 4:95, 1986.

24. Kessler CM, Bell WR: Coagulation factors. In Spivak JL, Eichner ER (eds): *The Fundamentals of Clinical Hematology,* 3rd ed. Baltimore, Johns Hopkins University Press, 1993.

25. Miletich J: Activated partial thromboplastin time. In Beutler E, et al (eds): *Williams Hematology,* 6th ed. New York, McGraw-Hill, 2001.

26. Bovill E, Tracy R: Methods for the determination of the plasma concentration of fibrinogen. In Beutler E, et al (eds): *Williams Hematology,* 6th ed. New York, McGraw-Hill, 2001.

27. Schneiderman P: The vascular purpuras. In Beutler E, et al (eds): *Williams Hematology,* 6th ed. New York, McGraw-Hill, 2001.

28. Hill-Zobel RL, et al: Organ distribution and the fate of human platelets: Studies of asplenic and splenomegalic patients. *Am J Hematol* 23:231, 1986.

29. Goebel RA: Thrombocytopenia. *Emerg Med Clin North Am* 11:445, 1993.

30. Warkentin TE, et al: Heparin-induced thrombocytopenia in patients treated with low-molecular weight or unfractionated heparin. *N Engl J Med* 332:1330, 1995.

31. Warkentin TE: Clinical presentation of heparin-induced thrombocytopenia. *Semin Thromb* 35:9, 1998.

32. Warkentin TE: Heparin-induced thrombocytopenia: A clinicopathologic syndrome. *Semin Haemost* 82:439, 1999.

33. Rice L, Attisha WK, Drexler A, Francis JL: Delayed-onset heparin-induced thrombocytopenia. *Ann Intern Med* 136:210, 2002.

34. Burdy MJ, Martin SE: Cocaine-associated thrombocytopenia. *Am J Med* 91:656, 1992.

35. Gingliano RP, Hyatt RR: Thrombocytopenia with GPIIIa/IIb inhibitors: A meta-analysis. *J Am Coll Cardiol* 31:185A, 1998.

36. Kovachy RJ: Immune thrombocytopenic purpura. In Wood ME, Bunn PA (eds): *Hematology/Oncology Secrets,* 2nd ed. Philadelphia, Hanley & Belfus, 1999.

37. Kaufman DW, et al: Acute thrombocytopenia purpura in relation to the use of drugs. *Blood* 82:2714, 1993.

38. Waters AW: Post-transfusion purpura. *Blood Rev* 3:83, 1989.

39. Nugent DJ: Immune thrombocytopenic purpura. In Bell WR (ed): *Hematologic and Oncologic Emergencies.* New York, Churchill Livingstone, 1993.

40. Cines DB, Blanchette VS: Immune thrombocytopenic purpura. *N Engl J Med* 346:995, 2002.

41. Cortelazzo, S, Finazzi G, Buelli M, et al: High risk of severe bleeding in aged patients with chronic idiopathic thrombocytopenic purpura. *Blood* 77:31, 1991.

42. Cheng Y, et al: Initial treatment of immune thrombocytopenic purpura with high-dose dexamethasone. *N Engl J Med* 349:831, 2003.

43. Law C, et al: High-dose intravenous immune globulin and the response to splenectomy in patients with idiopathic thrombocytopenic purpura. *N Engl J Med* 336:1494, 1997.

44. Walsh C, et al: Thrombocytopenia in homosexual patients. *Ann Intern Med* 103:542, 1985.

45. Hassell K: Thrombotic thrombocytopenic purpura and hemolytic uremic syndrome. In Wood ME, Bunn PA (eds): *Hematology/Oncology Secrets,* 2nd ed. Philadelphia, Hanley & Belfus, 1999.

46. George JN, El-Harake M: Thrombocytopenia due to enhanced platelet destruction by nonimmunologic mechanisms. In Beutler E, et al (eds): *Williams Hematology,* 5th ed. New York, McGraw-Hill, 1995.

47. Tsai HM: Advances in the pathogenesis, diagnosis, and treatment of thrombotic thrombocytopenic purpura. *J Am Soc Nephrol* 14:1072, 2003.

48. Ruggenenti P, Noris M, Remuzzi G: Thrombotic microangiography, hemolytic uremic syndrome, and thrombotic thrombocytopenic purpura. *Kidney Int* 60:831, 2001.

49. Medina PJ, Sipols JM, George JN: Drug-associated thrombotic thrombocytopenic purpura–hemolytic uremic syndrome. *Curr Opin Hematol* 8:286, 2001.

50. Allford SL, Hunt BJ, Rose P, Machin SJ: Guidelines on the diagnosis and management of the thrombotic microangiopathic haemolytic anaemias. *Br J Haematol* 120:556, 2003.

51. George JN: Thrombocytopenia: Pseudothrombocytopenia, hypersplenism and thrombocytopenia associated with massive transfusion. In Beutler E, et al (eds): *Williams Hematology,* 6th ed. New York, McGraw-Hill, 2001.

52. Bennett JS, Kolodzik MA: Disorders of platelet functions. *Dis Mon* 38:577, 1992.

53. Ruggeri A, Zimmerman T: Review: von Willebrand factor and von Willebrand's disease. *Blood* 70:895, 1987.

54. Bloom AL: Von Willebrand factor: Clinical features of inherited and acquired disorders. *Mayo Clin Proc* 66:743, 1991.

55. Bick RL: Acquired platelet function defects. *Hematol Oncol Clin North Am* 5:1203, 1992.

56. College of American Pathologists: Practice parameter for the use of fresh frozen plasma, cryoprecipitate, and platelets. *JAMA* 271:777, 1994.

57. Buss DH, Stuart JJ, Lipscomb GE: The incidence of thrombotic and hemorrhagic disorders in association with extreme thrombocytosis. *Am J Hematol* 20:365, 1985.

58. Hirsh J, et al: Oral anticoagulants: Mechanism of action, clinical effectiveness, and optimal therapeutic range. *Chest* 114:445S, 1998.

59. Mammen EF: Coagulation abnormalities in liver disease. *Hematol Oncol Clin North Am* 6:1287, 1992.

60. Erban SB, Kinnar JL, Schwartz SJ: Routine use of the prothrombin and partial thromboplastin times. *JAMA* 262:2428, 1989.

61. Hultin M: Coagulation factor assays. In Beutler E, et al (eds): *Williams Hematology,* 6th ed. New York, McGraw-Hill, 2001.

62. DiMichele D, Neufeld EJ: Hemophilia. A new approach to an old disease. *Hematol Oncol Clin North Am* 12:1315, 1998.

63. Bell B, Canty D, Audet M: Hemophilia: An updated review. *Pediatr Rev* 16:290, 1995.

64. Mannucci PM, Tuddenham GD: The hemophiliac—from royal genes to gene therapy. *N Engl J Med* 344:1773, 2001.

65. Cahill MR, Colvin BT: Haemophilia. *Postgrad Med J* 73:201, 1997.

66. The United States Pharmacopeial Convention, Inc: Hemophilia management. *Transfus Med Rev* 12:128, 1998.

67. Pierce GF, et al: The use of purified clotting factor concentrates in hemophilia: Influence of vial safety, cost, and supply on therapy. *JAMA* 261:3434, 1989.

68. Bray GL, et al: The Recombinate Study Group: A multicenter study of recombinant factor VIII (Recombinate): Safety, efficacy, and inhibitor risk in previously treated patients with hemophilia A. *Blood* 83:2428, 1994.

69. Serenetis S, et al: Human recombinant DNA–derived antihemophilic factor (factor VIII) in the treatment of hemophilia A: Conclusion of a 5-year study of home therapy. *Haemophilia* 5:9, 1999.

70. Berntop E: Second generation, B-domain deleted recombinant factor VIII. *Thromb Haemost* 78:256, 1997.

71. Ehrenforth S, et al: Incidence of development of factor VIII and factor IX inhibitors in haemophiliacs. *Lancet* 339:594, 1992.

72. Yee TT, et al: Factor VIII inhibitors in haemophiliacs: A single-center experience over 34 years, 1964-1997. *Br J Haematol* 104:909, 1999.

73. Hedner U, Glazer S, Falch J: Recombinant activated factor VII in the treatment of bleeding episodes in patients with inherited and acquired bleeding disorders. *Transfus Med Rev* 7:78, 1993.

74. Gastineau DA, et al: Lupus anticoagulant: An analysis of the clinical and laboratory features of 219 cases. *Am J Hematol* 19:265, 1985.

75. Rose EH, Aledort LM: Nasal spray desmopressin (DDAVP) for mild hemophilia A and von Willebrand disease. *Ann Intern Med* 114:563, 1991.

76. Nolan B, et al: Desmopressin: Therapeutic limitations in children and adults with inherited coagulation disorders. *Br J Haematol* 109:865, 2000.

77. Andes WA, Wulff K, Smith WB: Head trauma in hemophilia: A prospective study. *Arch Intern Med* 144:1981, 1984.

78. Dietrich AM, James CD, King DR, et al: Head trauma in children with congenital coagulation disorders. *J Pediatr Surg* 29:28, 1994.

79. Pasi KJ: Gene therapy for haemophilia. *Br J Haematol* 115:744, 2001.

80. Hortelano G, Chang PL: Gene therapy for hemophilia. *Artif Cells Blood Substit Immobil Biotechnol* 28:1, 2000.

81. Roth DA, Tawa NE, O'Brien JM, et al: Nonviral transfer of the gene encoding coagulation factor VIII in patients with severe hemophilia A. *N Engl J Med* 344:1735, 2001.

82. Manno CS, Chew AJ, Hutchinson S, Larson PJ: AAV-mediated factor IX transfer to skeletal muscle in patients with severe hemophilia B. *Blood* 101:2963, 2003.

83. Miller J: Von Willebrand disease. *Hematol Oncol Clin North Am* 4:107, 1990.

84. Rodeghiero F, Castaman G, Dini E: Epidemiological investigation of the prevalence of von Willebrand's disease. *Blood* 69:454, 1987.

85. Triplett DA: Laboratory diagnosis of von Willebrand disease. *Mayo Clin Proc* 66:832, 1991.

86. Berntorp E, Nilsson IM: Use of a high severity factor VIII concentrate (Humate-P) in von Willebrand disease. *Vox Sang* 56:212, 1989.

87. Mannucci PM: Treatment of von Willebrand's disease. *Haemophilia* 4:661, 1998.

88. Dunn AL, et al: Adverse events during use of intranasal desmopressin acetate for haemophilia A and von Willebrand's disease: A case report and review of 40 patients. *Haemophilia* 6:11, 2000.

89. Roberts HR, Eberst ME: Current management of hemophilia B. *Hematol Oncol Clin North Am* 7:1269, 1993.

90. Roth DA, Kessler CM, Pasi KJ, et al: Human recombinant factor IX: Safety and efficacy studies in hemophilia B patients previously treated with plasma-derived factor IX concentrates. *Blood* 98:3600, 2001.

91. Xu L, Gao C, Sands MS, et al: Neonatal or hepatocyte growth factor–potentiated adult gene therapy with a retroviral vector results in therapeutic levels of canine factor IX for hemophilia B. *Blood* 101:3924, 2003.

92. Kay MA, et al: Evidence for gene transfer and expression of factor IX in haemophilia B patients treated with an AAV vector. *Nat Genet* 24:257, 2000.

93. Seligsohn U: Disseminated intravascular coagulation. In Beutler E, et al (eds): *Williams Hematology,* 6th ed. New York, McGraw-Hill, 2001.

94. Matsuda T: Clinical aspects of DIC—disseminated intravascular coagulation. *Pol J Pharmacol* 48:73, 1996.

95. Levi M, ten Cate H: Disseminated intravascular coagulation. *N Engl J Med* 341:586, 1999.

96. Yu M, Nardell A, Pechet L: Screening tests of disseminated intravascular coagulation: Guidelines for rapid and specific laboratory diagnosis. *Crit Care Med* 28:1777, 2000.

97. Warren BL, et al: Caring for the critically ill patient. High-dose antithrombin III in severe sepsis: A randomized controlled trial. *JAMA* 286:1869, 2001.

98. Bernard GR, Vincent JL, Laterre PF, et al: Efficacy and safety of recombinant human activated protein C for severe sepsis. *N Engl J Med* 344:993, 2002.

99. Smith OP, et al: Use of protein-C concentrate, heparin, and haemodiafiltration in meningococcus-induced purpura fulminans. *Lancet* 350:1590, 1997.

Selected Oncologic Emergencies

Nnamdi Nkwuo, Neil Schamban, and Marc Borenstein

PERSPECTIVE

In 2001, cancer was the second leading cause of death in the United States. In that year alone, more than 1 million cases were diagnosed with more than 550,000 deaths.[1,2] More than 20 million patient-physician contacts occurred, ranging from routine follow-up visits to critical emergency department encounters. Oncologic emergencies include fever and neutropenia, superior vena cava syndrome (SVCS), acute tumor lysis syndrome, hyperviscosity syndrome, hyperuricemia, hypercalcemia, neoplastic cardiac tamponade, spinal cord compression, and raised intracranial pressure (ICP). The accurate diagnosis and appropriate treatment of oncologic emergencies can improve the quality of life dramatically in patients with cancer. In addition, a reversible life-threatening emergency can occur in a patient with an underlying malignancy that is otherwise highly treatable or even curable, making identification and management of the oncologic emergency a potentially lifesaving action.

There are many factors that can hinder the identification and management of oncologic emergencies in the emergency department (Box 121-1).

Changing trends in cancer that have produced an increased number of emergency department visits secondary to cancer and its complications include:

- Increased number of elderly patients receiving chemotherapy
- More aggressive chemotherapy regimens
- Broader use of chemotherapy for cancer treatment
- Increasing use of bone marrow transplantation
- More effective treatment options, increasing cure and survival rates

FEVER

Fever, a common problem in the cancer patient, can be caused by inflammation, transfusions, antineoplastics, antimicrobials, and tumor necrosis. Although fever can be secondary to malignancy with a significant tumor burden, 55% to 70% of fevers in cancer patients have an infectious etiology. *Granulocytopenia* is defined as polymorphonuclear leukocytes fewer than 500/mm³ or a count of less than 1000 cells/mm³ with a predicted decrease to less than 500/mm³. The risk of infection is increased with polymorphonuclear leukocytes less than 1000/mm³, with severe infections when counts are less than 100/mm³. In addition to the total number of polymorphonuclear leukocytes, the risk of infection is related to the duration of granulocytopenia and the rate of development.

Cancer patients with *significant fever* (defined by the Infectious Disease Society of America as a single oral temperature ≥ 38.3° C [101° F] or an elevation of 38° C [100.4° F] for at least 1 hour) and a polymorphonuclear leukocyte count less than 500/mm³ should be presumed to have an infectious etiology. Antimicrobial therapy should be started immediately after appropriate cultures have been obtained.[3]

Clinical Features

Because fever is often the first and occasionally the only sign of infection in the granulocytopenic cancer patient, the emergency physician must take a deliberate history and perform a meticulous physical examination. In the absence of granulocytes, traditional markers of inflammation such as erythema, warmth, and pyuria may be absent or minimal, making it essential to search for and not minimize subtle signs of inflammation. Fever indicates the presence of infection in more than 90% of granulocytopenic patients. There are many factors that predispose the neutropenic patient to infection and sepsis (Box 121-2). However, there is no predictable pattern, severity, or incidence of infectious complications in the neutropenic host.[4]

With the onset of granulocytopenia, the host's inflammatory response is markedly altered, impairing the ability to detect the presence of infection, and an undetected and untreated infection can be rapidly fatal in this population of patients. Infection is the number one cause of cancer death, and untreated infections are associated with 20% to 50% 48-hour mortality.[5-7] Therefore, broad-spectrum empirical antibiotic therapy should be initiated promptly in all febrile, granulocytopenic patients (Box 121-3).

Diagnostic Strategies

While antibiotics are being started, the patient should have a complete blood count (CBC), differential cell count, platelet count, prothrombin time, partial thromboplastin time, blood chemistries, urinalysis, and analysis of any accessible sites suggestive of infection. Two sets of blood culture specimens should be obtained for aerobic, anaerobic, and fungal growth. If an indwelling catheter is present, at least one set of blood culture specimens should be obtained from the device lumen as well as from a peripheral vein.[3] Obtaining a routine chest radiograph is currently the standard of care at most institutions. However, studies

BOX 121-1. Factors That Can Hinder Identification and Management of Oncologic Emergencies

- Patient or physician discomfort with the diagnosis of cancer
- A voluminous and frequently changing database with esoteric chemotherapeutic agents and complex classification systems
- Time constraints
- Lack of an established physician-patient relationship
- Inappropriate or premature labeling of the cancer patient as "terminal"
- Failure to appreciate that effective treatments are available for oncologic emergencies and many of the cancers that cause them

BOX 121-2. Factors Predisposing to Infection and Sepsis

- Clinical debilitation, prolonged bed rest
- Nutritional compromise
- Disruption of mucous membranes and skin barriers
- Indwelling catheters
- Central nervous system dysfunction secondary to cancer, sedatives, opiates, or psychotropic medications

BOX 121-3. Current Recommendations for Antimicrobial Therapy of Fever in Neutropenic Cancer Patients[2,5,10]

An antipseudomonal penicillin + an aminoglycoside
  ± vancomycin
Ceftazidime ± an aminoglycoside
Ceftazidime ± vancomycin
Cefepime ± an aminogylcoside
Cefepime ± vancomycin
Imipenem/cilastatin
Meropenem

show that a chest radiograph is not necessary in patients with no respiratory symptoms and a normal physical examination.[3,8] Urine should be sent for culture even in the absence of pyuria. However, the use of sputum culture and Gram's stain, although still recommended, has become controversial because of inconsistencies in collection and preparation that have led to false-negative and false-positive results.

Some oncologists discourage rectal temperature readings for patients with neutropenia because of the risk of tearing the rectal mucosa and establishing a potential nidus for disseminated infection. However, this has not yet become the standard of care and may vary between institutions. An indwelling nasogastric tube predisposes the neutropenic patient to sinusitis and should be used with caution. However, sinus films are difficult to interpret and when sinusitis is suspected,

computed tomography (CT) scanning is preferred. A lumbar puncture, preceded by head CT scanning, is indicated when symptoms point to the central nervous system (CNS). Some authorities have recommended surveillance cultures of the stool, nose, and throat. This recommendation is not universally accepted and is generally not indicated in patients with solid tumors. Despite an intensive and comprehensive evaluation, an infectious cause is initially substantiated in only 50% to 70% of febrile, granulocytopenic patients. Nuclear scans, gallium citrate, and indium III scans do not have a place in the emergency diagnosis and management of these patients but may be useful in the definitive evaluation.

Differential Considerations

Overall, approximately 85% of the initial pathogens are bacterial, and of these 60% to 70% are gram-positive pathogens. Gram-negative pathogens were previously the predominant pathogens. However, the administration of prophylactic antibiotics during chemotherapy and the widespread use of indwelling central venous catheters have caused an increase in gram-positive pathogens.[3,9] Fungal, viral, and parasitic infections are also important primary and secondary complications. Overall, 67% of adults and 30% of children with leukemia who are febrile and granulocytopenic from their illness or combination chemotherapy have documented bacterial infections, and approximately 8% have fungal infections.[5,6] *Staphylococcus aureus*, *Staphylococcus epidermidis*, and *Streptococcus viridans* are the predominant gram-positive pathogens. Once believed to be a contaminant, *S. epidermidis* has arisen as a major pathogen and may be resistant to antistaphylococcal penicillins and cephalosporins. *Escherichia coli*, *Pseudomonas aeruginosa*, and *Klebsiella* species remain the most common gram-negative organisms. Fungal infections, especially with *Candida albicans*, can be a major problem in granulocytopenic febrile patients treated with broad-spectrum antibiotics for protracted periods. Although significant institutional variation has been noted, *Histoplasma*, *Cryptococcus*, *Aspergillus*, and *Phycomycetes* are additional fungal pathogens encountered in the compromised host. In contrast to patients with acquired immunodeficiency syndrome (AIDS), patients with solid tumors do not commonly have parasitic infections. *Pneumocystis carinii*, however, may be seen when corticosteroid use or hematologic malignancy has resulted in lymphocyte dysfunction. Herpes simplex, herpes varicella zoster, and cytomegalovirus are common viral pathogens. The compromised host is at risk for a large number of individual pathogenic agents, further complicating the diagnosis and management of these complex patients.[2,5]

Occasionally fever is without a source and is believed to be secondary to the underlying disease. However, it is impossible to differentiate patients with bacteremia-induced fever from those with unexplained fever on the basis of clinical and demographic factors such as age, sex, underlying malignancy, or the types of therapeutic modalities or invasive diagnostic procedures they received. In addition, the absence of physical findings indicative of infection does not exclude a potentially life-threatening septic event because at least 50% of septic patients lack any distinct physical findings. Despite the potential for few physical findings, a meticulous physical examination should be conducted, including the fundi (looking for *Candida* endophthalmitis); rectum, perineum, and groin (for perirectal abscess); skin and mucous membranes (for any lesions suggesting malignancy or cellulitis); axillae; and catheters.[2,5,10]

Management

In the initial evaluation and management of the febrile cancer patient, one must take into account the particular underlying malignancy, prior use of antimicrobial therapy, and how the degree of treatment has affected the host's immunologic compromise. For example, in acute leukemia normal circulating neutrophils and monocytes are largely replaced by blast cells, which do not function well in the phagocytizing and killing of bacterial and fungal agents. Chemotherapeutic agents and irradiation exacerbate or potentiate the underlying defect in already compromised host defenses. Corticosteroids impair granulocyte and mononuclear cell mobilization in leukemic patients. The individuals who should be most urgently treated in the emergency department are those with severely compromised host defenses and in whom fever is accompanied by an increased respiratory rate, a change in mental status, agitation or apprehensiveness, and hemodynamic instability.

The optimal antimicrobial regimen should be synergistic, broad spectrum, and bactericidal with a low potential for toxicity and chosen for efficacy against the most likely causes of systemic and rapidly progressing infection: *S. aureus*, *S. epidermidis*, *E. coli*, *P. aeruginosa*, and *Klebsiella* species. A two-drug regimen is usually selected because historical studies from the 1980s disclosed a greater survival rate with gram-negative bacteremia when the isolate was sensitive to and treated with two antibiotics in a combined regimen than when the isolate was sensitive to only one of two antibiotics used in a combined regimen.

In the past 10 years there have been significant advances in the antimicrobial armamentarium with development of broad-spectrum single agents such as the carbapenems (imipenem-cilastin, meropenem) and third- to fourth-generation cephalosporins (ceftazidime, cefepime). These agents, when investigated as monotherapy for granulocytopenic, febrile patients, have been found to be as effective as a dual-drug combination of an antipseudomonal penicillin (ticarcillin, carbenicillin, or piperacillin) and an aminoglycoside (gentamycin or tobramycin) in clinical trials.[2,5,11]

Use of initial empirical vancomycin is included as first-line therapy at institutions where there has been a significant incidence of methicillin-resistant *S. aureus*. Amikacin is generally reserved as a second-line aminoglycoside for isolates that demonstrate aminoglycoside resistance.

Vancomycin should be included in the initial empirical therapy in selected patients, those with[3]:

- Clinically suspected serious catheter-related infections
- Known colonization with penicillin- and cephalosporin-resistant pneumococci or methicillin-resistant *S. aureus*
- Positive blood cultures for gram-positive bacteria before final identification and susceptibility testing
- Hypotension or other evidence of cardiovascular impairment (see Table 121-1)

Patients should be admitted to an isolation room if possible, but rapid movement out of a congested waiting room into a private space is the higher priority. Hand washing and reverse isolation techniques should be used.

SUPERIOR VENA CAVA SYNDROME

Epidemiology

SVCS is an acute or subacute process caused by the obstruction of the superior vena cava (SVC) secondary to compression, infiltration, or thrombosis. Malignancy currently accounts for 85% to 95% of SVC obstruction and is encountered as a complication in 3% to 8% of patients with cancer of the lung or lymphoma.[11,12] Small cell and squamous cell lung cancers exceed all other causes of malignant SVC obstruction and are causal in 65% of all cases. It is noteworthy, however, that breast and testicular cancers produce 10% to 15% of SVC obstruction. From 40 to 50 years ago, benign etiologies accounted for up to two thirds of SVC obstructions. Thoracic aortic aneurysm alone accounted for up to 40% of cases, mostly related to the high incidence of luetic aneurysm, which Hunter first described in 1957.[13,14] Gradually, benign causes of SVCS have decreased, constituting 10% to 25% of the reported cases. Other common nonmalignant etiologies include goiter, pericardial constriction, primary thrombosis, idiopathic sclerosing aortitis, tuberculous mediastinitis, fibrosing mediastinitis (histoplasmosis and methysergide treatment), arteriosclerotic or (rarely) luetic aneurysm, and indwelling central venous catheters.[15,16] In contrast to that in the adult population, SVCS in pediatric patients is most often iatrogenic, secondary to indwelling catheters, ventriculoperitoneal shunts, and complications of cardiovascular surgical procedures.

Clinical Features

Knowledge of the unique anatomic relationship of the SVC in the anterior superior mediastinum is crucial to understanding the clinical presentation of SVC obstruction. The SVC is easily compressed by any of its bounding contiguous structures (trachea, heart, aorta, azygos vein, and paratracheal and bronchial lymph nodes). This compression can produce a constellation of symptoms that reveal the exact site of the pathophysiologic process (Figure 121-1). The SVC arises from the innominate veins, which in turn arise from the internal

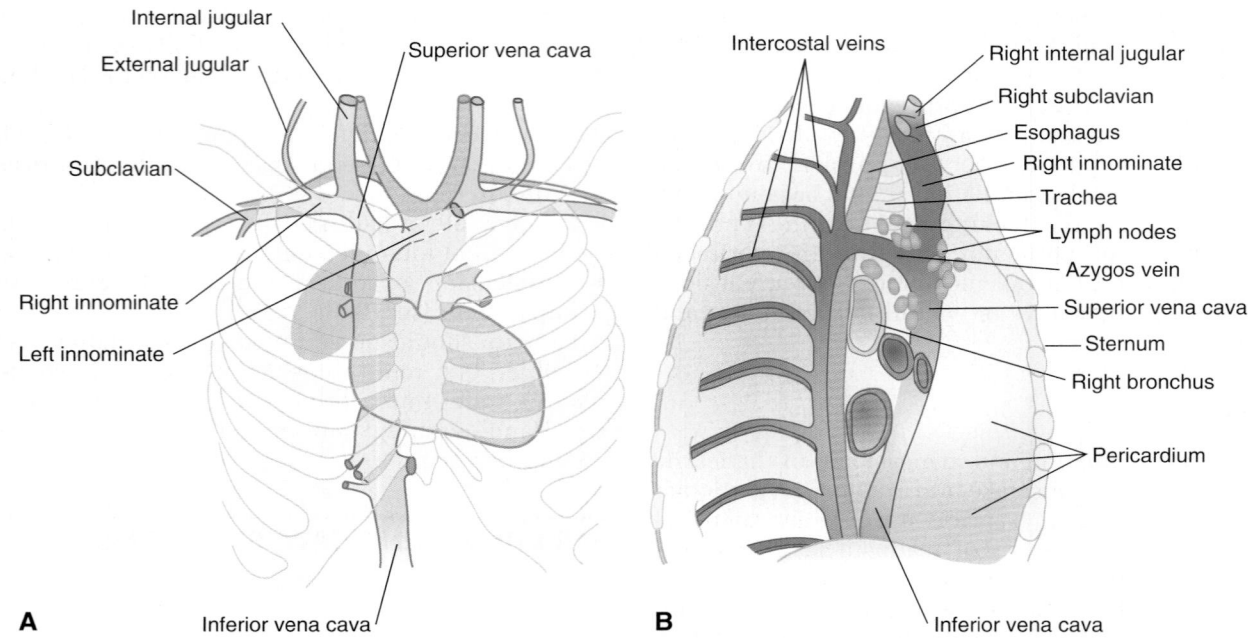

Figure 121-1. Frontal (**A**) and sagittal (**B**) sections of the thorax showing the relationship of the azygos vein to the superior vena cava (SVC), coalescence of innominates to form the SVC at the right second rib, and encasement of the SVC by nodal structures. Shaded area indicates classical site of obstruction. (From Lokich JL, Goodman R: Superior vena cava syndrome. *JAMA* 231:58, 1975.)

jugular and subclavian veins. The azygos vein, the last main auxiliary vessel of the SVC, drains blood from the chest wall. As a consequence of this anatomic relationship, if the SVC is blocked above or at the entrance of the azygos, blood may bypass and decompress the obstruction through the chest wall collateral vessels and rejoin the SVC through the azygos. If the obstruction falls below or at the entrance of the azygos, blood must traverse in a retrograde manner down the azygos and other chest wall veins to reach the drainage area of the inferior vena cava and subsequently cause more prominent symptoms and further embarrassment to the patient.[17]

Because the clinical features of the SVC are characterized by venous hypertension within the area ordinarily drained by the SVC, many of the findings are more evident in the recumbent or stooped-over position. Early signs may include periorbital edema, conjunctival suffusion, and facial swelling, which are most evident in the early morning hours and subside by midmorning. The differential diagnosis also includes the nephrotic syndrome, although a history of lower extremity–dependent edema is also elicited. In one study the most common symptom was shortness of breath (>50%), with swelling of the face, trunk, and upper extremities observed in approximately 40% of patients. Cough, dysphagia, and chest pain are less commonly reported, each occurring in approximately 20% of patients. With increasing impedance to blood flow, the full-blown syndrome begins to manifest itself with thoracic and neck vein distention (67% and 59%), facial edema (56%), tachypnea (40%), tightness of the shirt collar (the Stokes sign), plethora of the face, edema of the upper extremities, and cyanosis.[12,17] The severity of the syndrome is also related to the pace of

the obstruction; the more gradual the onset of obstruction, the longer the time for development of collateralization with less severe symptoms as a result.

Early reports of severe SVCS describe patients with increased ICP resulting in headache, blurred vision, altered mental status, coma, seizures, cerebral hemorrhage, and papilledema. In rare cases, death from cerebral edema was noted.[13] Portacaval shunts as a result of portal venous hypertension were reported to give rise to esophageal varices and tortuous collateral vessels on the chest and abdomen mimicking the caput medusae of a patient with cirrhosis, although the direction of flow is caudad (i.e., from cava to portal) in this instance. Airway obstruction and cardiac complications were reported. Without appropriate intervention, prolonged SVC obstruction was believed to lead to irreversible thrombosis and death.[13,14,18]

Important concepts have changed since these early reports. Seizures do not usually occur in the absence of intracranial metastases. Airway obstruction does not usually occur in the absence of tracheal compression by extrinsic tumor. Overall, little evidence in the current literature substantiates the notion of untreated SVC obstruction as life-threatening except when it occurs with tracheal compression.[16,17]

SVCS can occur in conjunction with spinal cord compression (the Rubin syndrome). Venous obstruction usually develops before the spinal cord compression, which is localized in most instances to the low cervical or upper thoracic spinal cord. This syndrome is most commonly found with malignancies of lymphoma and lung cancer. Patients with venous obstruction and back pain should be evaluated with magnetic resonance (MR) imaging of the vertebral spine.

Ancillary Evaluation

The clinical diagnosis of SVC obstruction should be apparent but is mimicked by a few other clinical entities—most noteworthy are pericardial tamponade and heart failure, which can usually be excluded by physical examination. Mild and early cases can be difficult to differentiate clinically. Ultrasonography can be utilized to exclude pericardial effusion. Because SVCS usually does not represent an immediately life-threatening oncologic emergency, when the clinical diagnosis is entertained, a tissue biopsy specimen should be obtained promptly. Although supportive therapy may be instituted to alleviate symptoms, definitive therapy should await the determination of histologic diagnosis because malignancy is known to be the cause of 85% to 95% of reported cases. The chest film reveals a mass in nearly 10% of patients and a superior mediastinal mass. In 75%, the superior mediastinal mass lies on the right and in approximately 50%, the masses are combined with pulmonary lesions or hilar adenopathy. Pleural effusion is an associated finding in approximately 20% to 25% of patients and is customarily found in the right hemithorax.[12,17] Morbidity secondary to excessive bleeding from puncture sites has been reported with venous access procedures, although in general they are safe. Intravenous injections may be less reliable because of slowing of drug distribution. Low flow rates may result in local irritation with thrombosis or phlebitis. Venous access is preferable on the side contralateral to the obstruction.

Venography is relatively contraindicated because of its concomitant bleeding complications. Invasive diagnostic procedures, including bronchoscopy, mediastinoscopy, scalene node biopsy, and limited thoracotomy are commonly used to establish the diagnosis and extent of the disease. When SVC obstruction is suspected, the appropriate consulting services should be notified and plans for immediate diagnosis undertaken.[11,12,16]

Management

Historically, radiation therapy has been emphasized as the primary treatment for SVC compression. Current treatment uses chemotherapy because of the increased incidence of tumor sensitivity to newer antineoplastic agents. However, temporizing measures that would alleviate symptoms related to vascular compression should be immediately instituted.

Elevation of the head of the bed has been shown to be an effective immediate measure. Diuretics have been used with transient symptomatic relief, although they must be used judiciously because overzealous administration can result in hypovolemia and further slowing of blood flow. Steroids have been shown to be of limited effectiveness but may be useful in the presence of respiratory compromise.[12] However, steroids are effective only if the tumor is steroid sensitive and usage prior to histologic identification has not yet become the standard of care. Current management approaches include percutaneous transluminal stent placement.[15,19]

The prognosis for patients treated for SVCS depends on the tumor type, with better survival with lymphoma than with bronchogenic carcinoma. The overall survival is approximately 25% at 1 year and 10% at 30 months after treatment.

ACUTE TUMOR LYSIS SYNDROME

Acute tumor lysis syndrome most commonly occurs within 1 to 5 days of instituting chemotherapy or radiation therapy of rapidly growing tumors that are extremely sensitive to antineoplastic drugs. This syndrome is most commonly seen after chemotherapy of hematologic malignancies, including acute leukemias and lymphomas, particularly Burkitt's lymphoma.[20-23] With advances in the effectiveness of chemotherapy, it has been described after treatment of solid tumors such as small cell lung carcinoma germ cell tumors treated with platinum-based chemotherapy regimens. The risk of acute tumor lysis syndrome increases with the bulk of the tumor and with the presence of hyperuricemia or renal impairment before antineoplastic therapy. A correlation between a very high blood lactate dehydrogenase level and the development of tumor lysis syndrome has been observed[20,21] (Box 121-4).

Biochemical hallmarks of this syndrome include hyperuricemia (DNA breakdown), hyperkalemia (cytosol breakdown), and hyperphosphatemia (protein breakdown). Hypocalcemia develops secondary to hyperphosphatemia. Acute renal failure, cardiac dysrhythmias, neuromuscular symptoms, and sudden death from hyperkalemia or hypocalcemia may ensue.

Clinical Features

Symptoms are related to the underlying malignancy and hyperuricemia, hyperkalemia, hyperphosphatemia, and hypocalcemia. Hyperuricemia with resultant urate nephropathy is the most commonly recognized metabolic cause of renal insufficiency.[20,21]

The kidney provides the primary mechanism for excretion of uric acid, potassium, and phosphate. Rapid proliferation of tumor cells may exceed the removal rate of the respective substances, resulting in increased levels. In fact, increased quantities of these substances have been observed in patients undergoing rapid lysis of chemosensitive tumors.

BOX 121-4. Risk Factors for Acute Tumor Lysis Syndrome

Increased lactate dehydrogenase levels (>1500 U/L)
Advanced disease with abdominal involvement
Preexisting renal dysfunction
Posttreatment renal failure
Acidic urine
Concentrated urine
Preexisting volume depletion
Young

The integrity of renal function is a critical factor in determining the degree of metabolic derangements. In patients with preexisting renal insufficiency, the metabolic derangements of acute tumor lysis are more likely to be severe. However, even when renal function appears normal at the start of treatment, the rapid lysis of certain tumors may overwhelm the excretory capacity of the kidney. Similarly to hyperuricemia, hyperphosphatemia may cause renal failure. A possible mechanism is precipitation of calcium phosphate within the kidney.[21,23]

Hyperkalemia, along with a contributing hypocalcemia, may result in life-threatening ventricular dysrhythmias. Hypocalcemia may also cause neuromuscular instability with muscle cramps and occasionally tetany. Confusion and convulsions have also been described in case reports.[21,23]

Management

Because of the life-threatening complications associated with acute tumor lysis, patients at high risk for developing the syndrome should be treated with prophylactic measures as soon as possible. Chemotherapy should be delayed, if possible, until metabolic disturbances, especially prerenal azotemia and hyperuricemia, are corrected. Initial management is aimed at the control of preexisting hyperuricemia with hydration, allopurinol, and alkalinization of the urine to a pH greater than 7. Diuretics are added if necessary, and frequent monitoring of electrolytes, calcium, and phosphorus is essential.

Most articles agree that it is wise to alkalinize the urine as a prophylactic measure against hyperuricemia, but caution is advised should hyperphosphatemia and hypocalcemia develop. Under these circumstances, alkali therapy may exacerbate manifestations of hypocalcemia such as tetany.[21,23] Although alkalinization increases the solubility of uric acid, the primary means of uric acid control is hydration and diuresis to maintain adequate urinary flow.[21,23]

If tumor lysis syndrome develops, hemodialysis should be considered as early as possible as a potentially lifesaving measure. This therapy is effective in lowering uric acid, potassium, and phosphate levels as well as in controlling uremic symptoms. See the suggested criteria for instituting hemodialysis in Box 121-5.

The prognosis is good in the absence of renal failure. If renal failure exists and hemodialysis of 5 to 7 days is necessary, the prognosis is grave. With aggressive management, the incidence of renal and metabolic complications of cytoreductive therapy may be decreased.

HYPERVISCOSITY SYNDROME

Viscosity is the resistance that a liquid exhibits to the flow of one layer over another. Excessive elevations in certain paraproteins, marked leukocytosis, or erythrocytosis can result in elevated serum viscosity and the development of significant sludging, decreased perfu-

BOX 121-5. Criteria for Instituting Hemodialysis

Serum potassium >6 mEq (6 mmol/L)
Serum uric acid >10 mg/dL (590 μmol/L)
Serum creatinine >10 mg/dL (880 μmol/L)
Serum phosphorus >10 mg/dL (phosphate >3.2 mmol/L) or rapidly rising
To reduce volume overload
Symptomatic hypocalcemia

sion of the microcirculation, and vascular stasis. The outcome of these pathophysiologic events is the development of hyperviscosity syndrome (HVS). This development deserves urgent medical therapy to forestall or reverse the effects of sludging in the microcirculation of the CNS, visual system, and cardiopulmonary system.[24]

Pathophysiology

The most common causes of HVS include the dysproteinemias. The most common is Waldenström's macroglobulinemia, which accounts for 85% to 90% of all HSV cases. Multiple myeloma, the next most common cause, is responsible for 5% to 10% of cases. Other etiologies include cryoglobulinemia, a benign hyperglobulinemia of the immunoglobulin M (IgM)-IgG type, and leukemias.[24-26]

The blastic phase of chronic myelogenous leukemia, chronic granulocytic leukemia, and the blast cell crisis of acute lymphoblastic and nonlymphoblastic leukemias also commonly cause HVS.[24,25] Other more benign causes include leukemoid reaction, polycythemia vera, and the accumulation of abnormal hemoglobins in sickle cell disease. The incidence of HVS in Waldenström's macroglobulinemia is approximately 20%, in IgG myeloma approximately 4.2%, and in IgA myeloma as high as 25%.[25]

The inherent physiochemical properties of the dysproteinemias along with extremely high concentrations of these proteins seem to predispose to the development of hyperviscosity. Paradoxically, HVS has also been reported in kappa light chain disease owing to a greater tendency to form unstable, highly polymerized circulating aggregates. The etiologic factor most responsible for HVS in the leukemias appears to be leukocytosis with white blood cell (WBC) counts in excess of 100,000, usually accompanied by blast forms exceeding 100,000 in the peripheral smear. The clinical manifestations of HVS become most apparent when the serum viscosity relative to water is greater than 4 to 5, normal serum viscosity relative to water being 1.4 to 1.8.[24-26]

Clinical Features

A symptomatic triad of bleeding, visual disturbances, and neurologic manifestations is a classical presentation of HVS. Visual disturbances, and on occasion visual loss, may occur with retinopathy characterized by venous engorgement (e.g., "sausage link" or "boxcar" segmentation), which is also seen in the bulbar conjunctiva; microaneurysms; hemorrhages; exudates; and occasionally papilledema. Persistent bleeding diatheses from mucosal surfaces, especially nasal mucosa, the gastrointestinal tract, and sites of minor surgery or trauma, even in the presence of a normal platelet count are common. Other clinical findings encompass myriad neurologic disturbances, including headache, dizziness, jacksonian and generalized seizures, somnolence, lethargy, coma, auditory disturbances (including hearing loss), and hypotension. Constitutional symptoms of fatigue, anorexia, and weight loss that are nonspecific early on are commonly associated with the underlying malignancy or with numerous electrolyte disturbances related to the underlying malignant process. Cardiopulmonary findings, including acute respiratory failure and hypoxemia, congestive heart failure, myocardial infarction, and valvular abnormalities, have all been reported. Renal insufficiency and failure may be complications of the syndrome.[24,25]

The laboratory evaluation of the patient with suspected HVS should include coagulation, renal, electrolyte, and differential white count profiles. Serum and urine protein electrophoresis should be done with all suspected dysproteinemias, with the diagnosis supported by a large spike on the serum electrophoresis. A clue to the presence of hyperviscosity may be the inability of the laboratory to perform chemical tests on the blood because of the serum stasis and increased viscosity that jams analyzers. In multiple myeloma significant hypercalcemia may also occur, and with high M protein fractions a factitious hyponatremia may be present. The diagnosis may also be entertained when a patient is brought to the emergency department in a stupor or coma and anemia and rouleaux formation are found on the peripheral smear.[27]

Because HVS is often a presenting characteristic of dysproteinemias and leukemias with blastic transformation and because a history of previously documented disease is often absent, this syndrome must be considered in patients with unexplained somnolence and coma.

Management

Emergency leukapheresis or plasmapheresis is the definitive treatment. Temporizing measures provided by the emergency physician should focus on adequate rehydration and diuresis. An immediate temporizing measure in a patient with frank coma and an established dysproteinemia is a two-unit phlebotomy with replacement of the patient's red blood cells with physiologic saline.[24-27] After plasmapheresis or leukapheresis has adequately alleviated the clinical findings, chemotherapeutic modalities can be used.

HYPERURICEMIA

Pathophysiology

Hyperuricemia, defined as a serum uric acid concentration exceeding 7 to 8 mg/dL, is a serious and well-known consequence of certain malignant disorders, which, if recognized early, can result in a significant decrease in morbidity for the cancer patient. The major source is cell breakdown, and its major excretory pathway is renal. The pathogenesis of hyperuricemia results from either increased production or decreased excretion of uric acid, or both. Increased production of uric acid commonly results from rapid dissolution of neoplastic tissues following chemotherapy or radiation therapy of undifferentiated lymphomas or lymphoblastic lymphomas and with acute lymphoblastic leukemias. In addition, hyperuricemia may be seen with multiple myeloma and occasionally with disseminated metastatic carcinoma. With massive release of precursors, uric acid levels rise precipitously and may become as high as 15 to 20 mg/dL. As a result, uric acid crystals form in the highly concentrated and acidified urine of the distal tubules. Intrarenal obstruction follows, and acute renal failure ensues.[23,28]

Chronic, moderately elevated levels of the serum uric acid may result in renal colic, obstructive uropathy, or chronic renal failure. Either uric acid renal calculi or interstitial deposits of sodium urate develop. This situation is associated with neoplastic overproduction of uric acid precursors. Polycythemia vera, myeloid metaplasia, mast cell disease, and chronic granulocytic leukemia are often associated with this type of hyperuricemia.

Decreased excretion may be a result of underlying renal insufficiency or of precipitation of urates in the renal tubules, parenchyma, or ureters with subsequent development of renal insufficiency and further reduction in excretion of uric acid. Three types of renal diseases are attributable to hyperuricemia: acute hyperuricemic nephropathy, uric acid nephrolithiasis, and gouty nephropathy.

Clinical Features

Hyperuricemia can occur with or without symptoms. Symptoms may be associated with the underlying malignancy. Hyperuricemia precipitated or worsened by therapy of these diseases may occur as an isolated metabolic disturbance or may be accompanied by other manifestations of the tumor lysis syndrome. If an underlying neoplastic disease has been diagnosed, hyperuricemia should be sought and treated before renal damage develops. In patients with urate stones and hyperuricemia, examination of the peripheral blood may provide evidence of an underlying myeloproliferative disorder. Acute oliguria after chemotherapy or radiation therapy suggests the diagnosis of hyperuricemia, and the uric acid level in the blood often far exceeds that associated with acute renal failure.

A number of benign diseases are associated with hyperuricemia that may coexist with neoplasia. These include hereditary gout, hyperparathyroidism, psoriasis, sarcoidosis, and renal failure of any cause. From a therapeutic standpoint, however, the finding of hyperuricemia obviates the importance of the primary cause; the therapy is the same. The long-term administration of certain drugs may lead to elevation of the serum uric acid level. Various diuretics, including thiazides and furosemide, are important examples.[20,23]

Management

When possible, hyperuricemia should be treated before chemotherapy or radiation therapy, especially with bulky tumors or if the serum uric acid level is borderline or increased. If a uric acid elevation of more than 9 mg/dL is found, allopurinol, fluids, and alkalinization of the urine should be initiated. If possible, this regimen should be started a day or two before the initiation of chemotherapy or radiation treatment. Patients with histories of gouty arthritis should also receive colchicine, 0.6 mg orally twice a day, to avoid the acute attacks that can be associated with allopurinol administration. Patients should be kept well hydrated. Alkalinization of the urine with oral sodium bicarbonate may help prevent nephropathy. In patients with acute distal tubular uric acid obstruction, management includes the administration of allopurinol, together with the fluid and electrolyte management used in other forms of acute renal failure.

If hyperuricemia is secondary to malignancy, cytolytic therapy should be stopped. Allopurinol in dosages of 300 to 600 mg/day usually causes a decrease in the serum uric acid level in approximately 3 days, and its administration should be started 2 or 3 days before cytolytic therapy, if time permits. Hydration is vital in maintaining a urine output above 2 L/day. Alkalinization to keep the urine pH above 7 can be accomplished by administering sodium bicarbonate, 100 mEq/day. Diuretics are to be used as needed. Acetazolamide (Diamox) in doses of 1 g/day usually alkalinizes the urine temporarily until allopurinol becomes effective. If oliguria occurs, mannitol may be started with 12.5 g of a 20% solution given intravenously over 3 minutes to keep urine output more than 250 mL/hr. The dose of mannitol is limited to 100 g per 24 hours to avoid clinical features resembling those of water intoxication. If these measures fail, peritoneal dialysis or hemodialysis or flushing the ureters through retrograde catheters may be considered.

Urate oxidase is currently being studied for treatment of hyperuricemia. Urate oxidase is a nonhuman proteolytic enzyme that catalyzes the enzymatic oxidation of uric acid into allantoin, a metabolite that is 5 to 10 times more soluble in urine than uric acid. The primary advantage of urate oxidase is its rapid onset of action. Although commercially available in Europe, urate oxidase has not yet become the standard of care in the United States. A recombinant DNA version is in clinical trials and appears to be well tolerated and a potent uricolytic agent.[21,29] Clearly, prevention of this complication is far better than treatment. The cancer patient who comes to the emergency department with renal colic warrants careful evaluation for hyperuricemia. The prognosis depends on the underlying malignancy and degree of renal failure.[21,22]

HYPERCALCEMIA

Hypercalcemia occurs in approximately 20% to 40% of cancer patients and is the most common life-threatening metabolic disorder associated with cancer.[30] It affects multiple organ systems and induces a variety of pathophysiologic events that may be more immediate threats to life than the cancer itself.

Two mechanisms have been proposed to explain the development of hypercalcemia associated with malignancy. The first mechanism affects patients with metastatic bone involvement. The hypercalcemia is most likely associated with the release of calcium and phosphate caused by associated osteolysis. The second mechanism affects patients with no bone disease. A variety of tumor-produced hormone-like substances have been associated with the development of hypercalcemia, including parathyroid hormone, prostaglandins, and peptides, all of which affect bone turnover.

Hypercalcemia is a common feature of many malignancies but most often complicates cancer of the breast, lung, head, and neck as well as multiple myeloma and leukemia. Bone metastases are not a prerequisite for hypercalcemia and, when present, do not necessarily cause hypercalcemia. Of patients who are hypercalcemic from squamous cell lung cancer, only one in six has bone metastases. In small cell lung carcinoma; hypercalcemia is almost never seen despite the presence of bone marrow metastases in 20% to 50% of cases. A complex interaction of various substances (parathyroid hormone, prostaglandins, peptides, steroids, osteoclastic factors) appears to be the result of both increased bone synthesis and degradation. The exception is multiple myeloma, in which bone destruction is accompanied by minimal bone synthesis. Other entities that cause hypercalcemia are listed in Box 121-6.[31,32]

BOX 121-6. Nonneoplastic Causes of Hypercalcemia

Hyperparathyroidism
Hyperthyroidism
Renal insufficiency (diuretic phase of acute renal failure, after transplantation, secondary hyperparathyroidism)
Drugs (thiazide diuretics, lithium, and calcium carbonate)
Hypervitaminosis (A and D)
Acute adrenal insufficiency
Immobilization (Paget's disease, fracture, paraplegia)
Acromegaly
Myxedema
Milk-alkali syndrome
Sarcoidosis
Benign monoclonal gammopathy
Rarer still are factitious hypercalcemia, idiopathic hypercalcemia of infancy (with elfin facies), familial hypocalciuric hypocalcemia, and hypercalcemia from pheochromocytoma or periostitis

Clinical Features

There is little correlation between serum calcium levels and the presence and severity of symptoms. Acute hypercalcemia results in marked CNS effects ranging from personality changes (depression, paranoia, lethargy, somnolence) to coma. With chronic hypercalcemia, symptoms include a history of anorexia, nausea, vomiting, constipation, polyuria, polydipsia, memory loss, and a shortened QT interval on the electrocardiogram. The symptoms, signs, and complications of hypercalcemia are summarized in Box 121-7.

In patients with carcinoma, any of these symptoms should suggest the diagnosis of hypercalcemia, but the emergency physician should be particularly suspicious of hypercalcemia in any cancer patient with lethargy or a change in mental status. Many may also have electrolyte abnormalities such as hypokalemia and dehydration. Thus, evaluation of serum electrolytes should accompany the measurement of serum calcium, phosphorus, albumin, and alkaline phosphate. In general, a serum calcium level above 14 mg/dL constitutes a medical emergency. In chronic hypercalcemia, one may see patients with blood calcium levels as high as 15 mg/dL with only mild symptoms. With an acute onset, one can see patients comatose at a level of only 12 to 13 mg/dL.[23,32]

Many nononcologic conditions can result in hypercalcemia. The most common are hyperparathyroidism and Paget's disease of bone (Figure 121-2). Clinical features include a long history of hypercalcemia symptoms, particularly renal stones. Chronic changes on bone films, such as subperiosteal reaction and cysts or a "ground glass" appearance of the skull, suggest hyperparathyroidism. Diagnosis of Paget's disease rests on biopsy results. Vitamin D excess, milk-alkali syndrome, and adrenal insufficiency are other common causes in the differential diagnosis of hypercalcemia.[23,32]

The acute onset of severe hypercalcemia or chronic exposure of the renal tubules to elevated calcium levels may reduce the glomerular filtration rate and renal blood flow, resulting in acute renal failure.[23]

Management

The therapeutic modalities used in the treatment of hypercalcemia are numerous, but they should always be used in conjunction with therapy of the underlying malignant disease. The exception to this is breast cancer, in which hormone therapy should be stopped until hypercalcemia is regulated.

The treatment depends on the clinical status of the patient and on the calcium level in the blood, but the general principles of treatment include treating the cancer when possible, encouraging ambulation, correcting dehydration, increasing calcium excretion, decreasing calcium removal from bone, and reducing calcium intake.

If serum calcium levels are below 14 mg/dL and the patient has normal mental status, oral rehydration and ambulation may suffice. Normal saline solution can be administered if the oral intake is not sufficient. If the serum phosphate level is not elevated, oral phosphates may be used cautiously. Monobasic and dibasic sodium phosphate (Phospho-Soda), 5 mL by mouth two or three times daily, is usually tolerated with mild to no diarrhea.

Saline rehydration and diuresis stimulates renal tubular excretion of calcium and is the most important initial component of the emergency management of hypercalcemia. Dehydration should be corrected within 1 to 2 hours with normal saline solution. When urine flow is adequate, furosemide, 40 to 60 mg intravenously (IV), may be given to increase excretion of calcium. Although the calciuric effect of furosemide is modest, it is also useful in preventing fluid overload in patients predisposed to cardiac failure. Careful attention to fluid input and output to ensure that the patient remains euvolemic is necessary. Calcitonin may be effective in doses of 4 to 8 IU/kg intramuscularly (IM). This treatment, although relatively safe when renal function is normal, is not generally part of the initial emergency management of hypercalcemia. If prostaglandin production is suspected, as in renal cancer, indomethacin or aspirin may be given, although its theoretic appeal exceeds its practical value. Fifty

---

BOX 121-7. Common Signs and Symptoms of Hypercalcemia in Malignancy

General
Itching

Neurologic
Fatigue, muscle weakness, hyporeflexia, lethargy, apathy, disturbances of perception and behavior, stupor, coma

Renal
Polyuria, polydipsia, renal insufficiency

Gastrointestinal
Anorexia, nausea, vomiting, constipation, abdominal pain

Cardiovascular
Hypertension, dysrhythmias, digitalis sensitivity

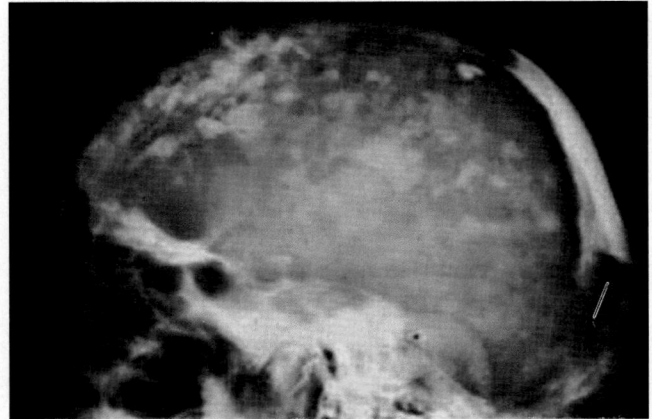

Figure 121-2. Skull radiograph showing Paget's disease of bone.

percent of hypercalcemic cancer patients also have hypokalemia. Serum potassium levels should be monitored every 4 hours and potassium chloride (20 to 40 mEq) supplemented IV or orally as necessary to prevent severe hypokalemia.[23,29,30,31]

If the serum calcium level is greater than 14 mg/dL or significant symptoms are present, more aggressive management should be undertaken. Continuous cardiac monitoring in the emergency department is necessary and central venous or pulmonary artery pressure monitoring may be required. Intravenous phosphates, although they can effectively lower the serum calcium level through precipitation of inorganic calcium phosphate salts in bone, are not recommended in view of their serious complications, which include widespread visceral calcifications, shock, and renal failure.

In the 5 years following approval by the Food and Drug Administration, bisphosphonates have become the treatment of choice for management of cancer-induced hypercalcemia, supplanting all other pharmacologic approaches except corticosteroids. Bisphosphonates are analogues of pyrophosphate and powerful inhibitors of bone resorption. Several agents are now available including clodronate, pamidronate, and ibandronate with other more potent bisphosphonates in development. Pamidronate, 90 mg, given as an infusion over 4 to 24 hours effectively and safely achieves normocalcemia within a few days (mean 4 days) in more than 90% to 95% of patients.[32-35] Zolendronate, a new third-generation bisphosphonate, appears to be more effective treatment than pamidronate in preliminary trials. It has been shown to normalize calcium faster and for longer periods of time. Zolendronate can be administered as 1- to 4-mg doses given over a few minutes IV.

Mithramycin given as 25 µg/kg IM once every 4 to 5 days is not generally part of the initial emergency management of hypercalcemia and has been supplanted in most cases by the bisphosphonates. Prednisone, 60 to 80 mg/day, or other corticosteroids may be effective within a few days to a week. Prednisone is more useful for long-term treatment than for acute control. Corticosteroids are particularly valuable in breast carcinoma, myeloma, and lymphoma. They should not be initiated without oncologic consultation because they are chemotherapeutic agents for these malignancies.

NEOPLASTIC CARDIAC TAMPONADE

Although cardiac tamponade resulting from neoplasm is rarely seen in the emergency department, it is an important clinical problem because it can occur abruptly and result in the death of a patient with a tumor that may be responsive to treatment with a resultant complete remission or significantly prolonged partial remission. The decompensated state of cardiac function comes from a marked rise in intrapericardial pressure caused by accumulation of fluid within the pericardial sac resulting from malignancy or from pericardial thickening with scar formation, which results in a thick constrictive neoplastic encasement. This condition needs to be recognized early to allow fluid decompression or pericardiectomy in order to avoid circulatory compromise and death of the patient. Signs and symptoms are partially affected by the rapidity of development. In the era prior to diagnostic ultrasonography, this medical-oncologic emergency was often unrecognized. In one early series before ultrasonography, the diagnosis was missed by the first physician in 11 of 17 patients and a number of times was missed by more than a single examiner.[36]

In most instances, pericardial effusion is accompanied by signs and symptoms that presage the development of the clinical picture of tamponade including dyspnea, apprehension, anxiety, and chest pain. In rare instances, tamponade may be the first manifestation of the malignancy, solid tumor, or leukemia. Any patient in the emergency department with a history of cancer, shortness of breath, and hypotension should be suspected of having pericardial tamponade. The diagnoses of pulmonary embolism, congestive heart failure, and anxiety can be mistakenly made in this setting.

Etiology

The most common cause of neoplastic pericardial tamponade is malignant pericardial effusion, often associated with postirradiation pericarditis, fibrosis, and effusion. Only rarely does a tumor or radiation fibrosis cause a neoplastic constrictive pericarditis with resultant tamponade. In most reported cases, cardiac tamponade represents a clinical progression of neoplastic or postirradiation pericarditis.

Neoplastic pericarditis can result from any number of benign, malignant, primary, or secondary tumors of the pericardium or mediastinum.[37-39] The most common benign tumors of the pericardium or mediastinum are fibromas, angiomas, and teratomas. Pericardial mesothelioma can have a clinical course characterized by rapid accumulation of massive quantities of bloody pericardial fluid, eventually leading to tamponade. Secondary involvement of the pericardium may result from either direct invasion from structures or metastases from a distant primary tumor. These metastases are usually multiple rather than solitary lesions. The tumors most commonly associated with pericardial involvement include those of the lung and breast, leukemia, Hodgkin's and non-Hodgkin's lymphomas, melanomas, gastrointestinal primary tumors, and sarcomas.[39,40] Clinically recognizable symptoms or signs of pericardial disease are difficult to appreciate before death. Less than 30% of patients with autopsy-proven malignant pericardial disease were diagnosed before death.[39,40]

Radiation pericarditis has been a well-known complication of radiotherapy since the introduction of modern megavoltage techniques. The cardiac effects of radiotherapy may manifest themselves immediately with acute pericarditis or be delayed for months to years, although the majority develop effusion within the first year. The acute forms are inflammatory or effusive, usually self-limited, and subside without residual constriction; the chronic effusive and constrictive types may lead to tamponade and death.[40]

Neoplastic constrictive pericarditis, although rare, may be caused by invasion of the pericardium by metastatic lesions or indirectly by the complication of radiation therapy with resultant fibrous thickening of the pericardium. Each of these entities can progress to cardiac tamponade because of thickening by tumor or radiation fibrosis, resulting in a decrease in the distensibility of the pericardium, thus reaching the critical point of cardiopulmonary decompensation earlier, despite smaller volumes of slowly accumulating effusion.

The symptoms and signs of neoplastic and radiation pericarditis mimic those of pericarditis of other causes, and because of the usual insidious onset of the effusion of fibrous pericardial thickening, the condition might be attributed to the underlying malignancy and not suspected until the full-blown picture of cardiac tamponade develops.

Pathophysiology

The severity of cardiac tamponade and eventual cardiopulmonary decompensation depend on the rate of development of pericardial fluid accumulation, the fluid volume, and the rate of compression of the heart. Clinically, the progressive elevation of intrapericardial pressure interferes with ventricular expansion and results in a decrease in the cardiac volume. There is a rapid rise of intracardiac chamber pressures with subsequent transmission of this pressure peripherally in pulmonary and vena caval beds. In an effort to maintain cardiac output, various compensatory mechanisms come into play (tachycardia, peripheral vasoconstriction, decrease in renal flow with resultant increase in blood volume by sodium and water retention), all to maintain arterial pressure and venous return. When these compensatory mechanisms fail to maintain cardiac output, ventricular end diastolic pressure increases and subsequent circulatory collapse is impending. The signs and symptoms parallel these pathophysiologic changes. The most common symptoms include extreme anxiety and apprehension, a precordial oppressive feeling, or actual retrosternal chest pain with dyspnea of varying degrees. True orthopnea and paroxysmal nocturnal dyspnea are uncommon, but when they occur the patient assumes a variety of positions to get relief from the chest pain and the dyspnea. Other prominent symptoms include cough, hoarseness, hiccups, and occasional gastrointestinal manifestations such as dysphagia, nausea, vomiting, and epigastric or right upper quadrant abdominal pain that is probably the result of visceral congestion.[12,39-42]

Clinical Features

In contrast, patients with severe tamponade are acutely ill and may appear ashen, pale, or markedly diaphoretic with an impaired consciousness ranging from mildly confused to unresponsive. Rapid, shallow, and occasionally labored breathing may be present along with peripheral cyanosis and distended jugular veins. Seizures have been reported. Striking facial plethora and a full neck secondary to edema (Stokes' collar) have also been seen in SVCS. Pulses are soft and easily compressible. The systolic blood pressure is usually low, with a decreased pulse pressure, although normal systolic, diastolic, and pulse pressures have been reported with moderate degrees of tamponade. Kussmaul's signs (quiet heart sounds, an enlarged cardiomediastinal silhouette, tachycardia, and most notably pulsus paradoxus) are extremely useful findings in the physical evaluation of tamponade. One must remember that with significant hypotension, atrial septal defect, and aortic insufficiency, pulsus paradoxus may be absent and an unreliable finding. Ascites, hepatomegaly, peripheral edema, and mottling are other findings that reflect the elevation in venous pressure and decrease in cardiac output.[16,39-43]

Diagnostic Strategies

The electrocardiogram may demonstrate low voltage and the nonspecific findings of pericardial effusion, sinus tachycardia, ST elevation, and nonspecific ST-T wave changes. Electrical alternans with 1:1 total atrial-ventricular complexes has been considered almost pathognomonic of cardiac tamponade. Approximately two thirds of patients with neoplastic pericarditis who have tamponade caused by massive pericardial effusion also exhibit pulsus alternans. The alternation customarily disappears soon after removal of a small volume of fluid, but it can also disappear spontaneously or be observed in attendance with a fluid increase.[40]

Radiographic signs of tamponade suggestive of pericardial effusion include an enlarged cardiac silhouette with clear lung fields and normal vascular pattern, although a normal chest radiograph does not exclude tamponade. The typical "water bottle" appearance of the heart on a plain radiograph is often present. Echocardiography is the simplest and most sensitive of diagnostic tests and can be done at the bedside immediately for confirmation of pericardial effusion. Therapeutic intervention with echocardiography equipment can then guide the pericardiocentesis. Thoracic CT scanning has also become an important diagnostic tool in diagnosing pericardial effusions.[40,41,44]

The diagnosis of cardiac tamponade should be suspected in any cancer patient with dyspnea. Highly suggestive symptoms include clouded sensorium, thready pulse, pulsus paradoxus exceeding 50% of the pulse pressure, low systolic pressure, engorged neck veins, a falling pulse pressure below 20 mm Hg, and electrical alternans. There is an uncommon yet pathognomonic sinusoidal variation in QRS size secondary to the pendular effect of the heart swinging in the fluid medium of the pericardial sac.[43] In this setting, sudden death may occur and pericardiocentesis should be performed as soon as possible.

Management

In the emergency department, the only lifesaving treatment for tamponade that is effective is immediate removal of the pericardial effusion by pericardiocentesis. The procedure carries some risk, including induction of cardiac dysrhythmias and hemorrhage from an injured coronary vessel. Aspiration of as little as 50 to 100 mL of fluid has been shown to alleviate the pathologic process temporarily.[16,39-41] Removal of the maximal amount of fluid is advisable, along with insertion of an indwelling catheter, during the first pericardiocentesis because fluid may reaccumulate during the first 24 hours. When the pericardial fluid has been obtained, it must be sent for biochemical and cytologic analysis. Other types of supportive therapy may be needed during the evaluation process while preparing for pericardiocentesis, such as intravenous hydration with normal saline and oxygen therapy.

When the patient has been stabilized, additional therapeutic interventions should be planned and initiated by the appropriate admitting services because reaccumulation of effusion in neoplastic tamponade is not easily managed on a short-term basis. Pericardial windows, radiotherapy, intrapericardial chemotherapy, and pericardiectomy may be justified.[16,39-41]

The prognosis of neoplastic cardiac tamponade is dependent on the underlying type and extent of cancer. The presence of total electrical alternans is an adverse prognostic sign, even when the alternans disappears with pericardiocentesis. Despite a poor prognosis for patients with cancers such as melanoma or non–small cell lung cancer, some patients with treatment-responsive lymphomas have had long-term survival after neoplastic cardiac tamponade.

NEUROLOGIC EMERGENCIES

Of all patients with cancer, 15% to 20% have neurologic complications.[45] Neurologic symptoms are occasionally the presenting complaint in patients with systemic cancer, but more often symptoms develop in patients known to have cancer. In both settings it is necessary to initiate both an appropriate workup and emergency intervention. Neurologic emergencies in cancer patients include cerebral herniation, seizures, epidural spinal cord compression, CNS infections, and reversible toxic or metabolic encephalopathies. Treatment is needed within minutes to hours after the patient arrives at the emergency department to prevent permanent neurologic dysfunction or death.

Cerebral Herniation

Pathophysiology

Cerebral herniation occurs when the ICP increases locally within the skull from an expanding mass lesion. The increase produces a shift of brain substance in the direction of least resistance caudally through the tentorial opening and the foramen magnum. Causes of cerebral herniation in cancer patients commonly include primary or metastatic brain tumors and intracerebral hemorrhage. Less common causes include subdural hematoma, brain abscess, acute hydrocephalus, and radiation-induced brain necrosis.[46] Primary brain tumors account for approximately one half of intracranial tumors. Metastatic brain tumors are seen most commonly in lung, breast, colon, kidney, and testicular cancer and in patients with choriocarcinoma and malignant melanoma.[45,47]

Clinical Features

Three distinct herniation syndromes have been described: uncal, central, and tonsillar herniation. In *uncal* herniation a lateral mass displaces the temporal lobe, which compresses the upper brainstem. A rapid loss of consciousness is seen in conjunction with unilateral pupillary dilatation and ipsilateral hemiparesis. *Central* herniation usually results from slowly expanding, multifocal lesions that cause a downward and lateral shift of the diencephalon and upper pons. A slowly decreasing level of consciousness, small reactive pupils, and Cheyne-Stokes respirations, without focal signs, are seen clinically. Central herniation is sometimes mistaken for toxic or metabolic encephalopathy because of the lack of focal signs. A history of headache or focal neurologic complaints or any lateralizing findings mandates the acquisition of a CT scan to rule out a herniating mass lesion before lumbar puncture. *Tonsillar* herniation is produced by a large posterior fossa mass that pushes the cerebellar tonsils through the foramen magnum, compressing the medulla and resulting in a rapidly decreasing level of consciousness, occipital headache, vomiting, hiccups, hypertension, meningismus, and abrupt changes in the respiratory pattern.[45-48]

Management

When the clinical diagnosis of cerebral herniation is made, emergency management is mandatory before the cause can be established. Intubation with hyperventilation to a carbon dioxide partial pressure (pCO_2) of 25 to 30 mm Hg temporarily lowers the ICP by producing cerebral vasoconstriction. This should be avoided if possible but may be necessary for brief periods in response to reversible, acute neurologic deterioration. Excessive or prolonged hyperventilation may cause paradoxical vasodilation and should be avoided. Mannitol, 1 g/kg IV, should be given and may be repeated in 4 to 6 hours. Dexamethasone, 12 to 24 mg IV, has not been shown to improve outcome or reduce ICP acutely in severe head injury[49,50] but is often administered in patients with raised ICP or impending herniation caused by CNS malignancy because of the effect of corticosteroids on reducing cerebral edema associated with the neoplastic process. A CT scan of the brain should be obtained as soon as emergency stabilization is accomplished. Epidural or subdural hematoma and hydrocephalus usually require surgery, whereas abscess and metastases are usually managed with antibiotics and antineoplastics or radiation, or both, respectively. When stabilization and an initial diagnosis have been made, neurologic or neurosurgical consultation and prompt admission to an intensive care unit are mandatory.[45,46]

Seizures

Seizures are common in patients with cancer. Their immediate management is necessary to prevent physical injury, increased ICP, and risk of aspiration. Seizures increase the brain's metabolic requirements and lead to increased cerebral blood flow. This may precipitate increased ICP in susceptible patients. Seizures may be due to brain metastases, toxic or metabolic disturbances (usually hyponatremia or uremia), vascular problems (especially intracerebral hemorrhage or subdural hematomas), and infections. Diagnostic laboratory studies should include a CBC, electrolytes, glucose level, blood urea nitrogen (BUN), calcium and magnesium levels, liver function tests, coagulation studies, and appropriate cultures. A head CT scan should be done and followed by a lumbar puncture, when indicated.[45,46]

The therapy for seizures depends on the specific cause and the patient's clinical status. For example, a single hypoglycemic or hypoxic seizure usually requires only correction of the underlying metabolic defect. Patients with a single seizure whose workup reveals a chronic problem (e.g., a cerebral metastasis) require anticonvulsants and therapy specific for the malignancy. A loading dose of phenytoin (15 to 18 mg/kg IV) may be given followed by oral maintenance. Prolonged single seizures or repetitive seizures require more aggressive treatment, including diazepam, 5 to 10 mg IV, or lorazepam, 1 to 2 mg IV, followed by IV phenytoin. Active airway and ventilatory management is essential. A bedside fingerstick glucose level should be obtained immediately. Thiamine and naloxone are not routinely indicated. In addition, when repetitive seizures have occurred, management of the underlying cause should be initiated rapidly and the patient admitted to an intensive care unit.[45,46]

Epidural Spinal Cord Compression

Principles of Disease

Epidural spinal cord compression from metastatic cancer is common, serious, and potentially treatable. It is most often caused by lymphoma or lung, breast, or prostate carcinoma. With the exception of lymphoma, which extends through the intervertebral foramina from paravertebral lymph nodes, these tumors metastasize to the vertebral body and extend into the spinal canal to compress the spinal cord. Less common causes of spinal cord compression in patients with cancer include melanoma, myeloma, renal cell carcinoma, vertebral subluxation, spinal epidural hematomas, and intramedullary metastasis. Acute myelopathy in patients with cancer may also be caused by radiation, paraneoplastic necrotizing myelitis, a ruptured intervertebral disk, and meningeal carcinomatosis with spinal cord involvement. Most cases (68%) of epidural cord compression occur in the thoracic spine, 15% occur in the cervical spine, and 19% in the lumbosacral spine.[51]

Clinical Features

Back pain, either local or radicular, is the initial symptom in 95% of patients with epidural metastasis.

It may be acute in onset or develop insidiously over weeks to months and usually predates other symptoms. The pain may increase during physical examination with spinal percussion, neck flexion, Valsalva's maneuver, or straight leg raising and is usually located at the level of the tumor.[48,52,53] Other symptoms are usually present at the time of diagnosis and may include weakness (75% of patients) and autonomic or sensory symptoms (50% of patients). Fifty percent of patients are not ambulatory at the time of diagnosis. The neurologic examination usually reveals symmetrical weakness with either flaccidity and hyporeflexia (if the diagnosis is made very early) or spasticity and hyperreflexia (if the diagnosis is made later).

Diagnostic Strategies

Plain films show evidence of tumor in the vertebral body in 70% to 90% of patients with vertebral metastases.[45,49] Immediate myelography or MR imaging is indicated if the plain films are abnormal, regardless of whether the neurologic examination is abnormal or is consistent with spinal cord compression or what the findings on plain x-ray films are. In cases with questionable findings on plain films of the spine, tomograms, coned-down views, or a CT scan may reveal bone metastases not otherwise appreciated. Myelography can demonstrate a complete or near-complete obstruction of contrast dye flow at the level of vertebral body involvement. MR imaging has emerged as the procedure of choice for intramedullary metastases and has also replaced myelography, which is associated with significant morbidity related to lumbar puncture and dye insertion at multiple levels (including cisternal puncture), to demonstrate the length of the compression or skip lesions along the spinal cord.[48,53]

Management

Because minimal weakness at the time of presentation may progress to profound, irreversible weakness over several hours, treatment should be started immediately. In the emergency department, a loading dose of dexamethasone, 10 to 100 mg IV, followed by 4 to 24 mg every 6 hours for 3 days to reduce cord edema is initiated at the time of diagnosis. Immediate oncology and radiation oncology consultations should be obtained. Although corticosteroids are routinely administered to patients with suspected spinal cord compression, high-dose corticosteroids, such as dexamethasone 100 mg, have been associated with complications and their use is controversial.[53] Radiation treatment is the usual therapy and can be initiated after steroid treatment. The prognosis depends on the radiosensitivity of the tumor, the location of the compression, the pretreatment performance status, and the rate of decompensation. Surgery is indicated only if the diagnosis is in doubt, if a tissue diagnosis is required, if the spine is unstable, or when radiation to the involved area has already been given in maximal doses.[45,47,54]

Intramedullary metastases are similar in presentation and treatment to epidural cord compression but are associated with a very poor prognosis. Epidural hematomas have been described in patients with thrombocytopenia or a coagulopathy as a complication of lumbar puncture. A rapidly progressive paraparesis and back pain are seen. MR imaging or myelography can establish the diagnosis; the treatment is surgical decompression. Platelet transfusions may limit progression in the emergency department.[45,54]

Central Nervous System Infections

Principles of Disease

Patients with cancer are susceptible to a variety of CNS infections. These patients may have impaired immune responses secondary to their underlying disease or treatment with steroids, chemotherapy, splenectomy, or irradiation. Most CNS infections occur in patients with leukemia, lymphoma, or head and neck cancer. Patients with head and neck cancer are susceptible (in addition to the reasons discussed) because of fistula formation and tumor invasion, which allows organisms access to the CNS. Important CNS infections include meningitis, brain abscess, and encephalitis. These often have similar presentations, making their differentiation in the emergency department difficult.

Clinical Features

Meningitis is characterized by fever, headache, and altered mental status. Meningismus is often absent. The diagnosis of meningitis in patients with cancer is often delayed because the manifestations of the disease are attributed to other processes: fever to systemic infection, headache to cerebral metastases, and altered mental status to a toxic or metabolic encephalopathy.

Diagnostic Strategies

All cancer patients with fever and an altered mental status require a lumbar puncture, which should be preceded by a head CT scan if cerebral metastases are suspected.[46,50] In addition, thrombocytopenia and coagulopathy should be considered and either ruled out or treated appropriately with platelet transfusions or fresh frozen plasma, respectively, before a lumbar puncture is done. Platelet transfusion is usually reserved for patients with platelet count less than 10,000/µL. The fluid obtained should be sent for a cell count and differential cell count, Gram's stain, India ink stain, protein and glucose levels, bacterial and fungal cultures, cryptococcal antigen level, and cytologic examination. The absence of WBCs in the CSF does not rule out meningitis, especially in neutropenic patients. The likely organisms responsible for meningitis vary with the underlying disease and the peripheral WBC count.

Differential Considerations

Brain abscess is usually seen in patients with leukemia or head and neck tumors and accounts for 30% of CNS infections in cancer patients.[46] Patients have symptoms of elevated ICP (headache, vomiting, and papilledema), lateralizing findings, and a source of infection.[47,50] Fever is usually present. Head CT scanning character-

istically demonstrates an ill-defined mass early in the course of an abscess, with the classical well-defined mass with a low-density center and a contrast enhancing ring seen later. Edema and mass effect are common. A lumbar puncture is not helpful in making the diagnosis and may precipitate cerebral herniation. Organisms that cause abscess include gram-negative rods, *Aspergillus* and *Phycomycetes* species, and *Toxoplasma gondii*. Emergency management includes high-dosage antibiotics. If herniation develops, immediate steps to reduce the ICP, followed by emergency surgery, are indicated.

Encephalitis is rare in patients with cancer and is most often caused by herpes zoster or *T. gondii*. The presenting complaints are usually headache, fever, and altered mental status. The CT scan is commonly normal but may show diffuse edema, whereas the lumbar puncture may show pleocytosis with an elevated protein level but no demonstrable organism. It is difficult to distinguish encephalitis from meningitis in the emergency department, but the overall clinical picture in both diseases mandates hospital admission for further evaluation.

Management

However, empirical broad spectrum antibiotic coverage should be initiated for all patients with a third-generation cephalosporin (ceftriaxone or ceftazidime) and vancomycin. Ampicillin may be added when there is suspicion of *Listeria*. Ceftazidime with or without an aminoglycoside is generally selected when the likelihood of infection with *Pseudomonas* is high. Neutropenic patients (polymorphonuclear WBC count <1000/mm³) with either leukemia or lymphoma usually have a gram-negative infection (often with *P. aeruginosa*). Patients with lymphoma and a normal WBC count are commonly infected with *Listeria monocytogenes*, *Streptococcus pneumoniae*, or *Cryptococcus neoformans*. Infections with *Haemophilus influenzae* and *Neisseria meningitidis* are uncommon. Patients with head and neck tumors may develop staphylococcal infection.[45-47]

Encephalopathy

Toxic and metabolic encephalopathy should be actively sought when patients with cancer have an acute or subacute altered mental status in the absence of fever or headache. Toxic and metabolic causes should be routinely excluded even when infection or a metastatic complication is suspected. Signs of encephalopathy include confusion, aberrant behavior, and a decreased level of consciousness. These may develop acutely or insidiously over days to weeks. Patients with cancer are particularly susceptible to toxic and metabolic encephalopathy because their disease can have multiple organ system involvement, can cause electrolyte and nutritional abnormalities, and the drugs used to treat the disease (especially chemotherapeutic agents and narcotics) can cause encephalopathy even when used in therapeutic doses.[45,47] In the emergency department, encephalopathic patients should first be evaluated carefully for a possible infection or mass lesion. The metabolic workup should include electrolytes; BUN, creatinine, glucose, and calcium levels; arterial blood gases; and liver function tests. Toxicology screens should be considered in possible ingestions and in patients who are unable to give a history. Naloxone and 50% dextrose should be given while the workup is proceeding. Specific treatment is indicated for any abnormalities found during the workup. Hospital admission is usually required unless the cause is easily and rapidly reversible and is unlikely to recur.

 KEY CONCEPTS

- Hypercalcemia secondary to malignancy is unrelated to bone metastases in 20% of patients and is associated with a poor prognosis independent of therapeutic response. Hydration and use of bisphosphonates (such as pamidronate) have become the mainstays of initial treatment.

- Spinal cord compression arises as back pain in more than 95% of patients. If ambulatory at the time of diagnosis, 80% of patients maintain the ability to ambulate. MR imaging has become the diagnostic modality of choice, and high-dose dexamethasone is given to all patients followed by radiation therapy in most cases.

- Superior vena caval obstruction is rarely life threatening and requires tissue diagnosis. Although caused by malignancy in 70% to 80% of cases, thrombosis secondary to indwelling central lines is increasing as an etiology. Stenting of the SVC has become the approach to SVC obstruction unresponsive to chemotherapy or radiation therapy, or both.

- Fever and neutropenia in the cancer patient is a true medical emergency requiring rapid diagnosis, cultures, and treatment with broad-spectrum, bactericidal, synergistic antimicrobials. An aminoglycoside plus an extended-spectrum penicillin and third-generation cephalosporin with or without vancomycin remain the standard combinations in patients without penicillin allergy.

- Neoplastic pericardial effusion can arise insidiously with symptoms such as apprehension, anxiety, dyspnea, and weakness. Bedside ultrasonography has become a rapid, safe imaging modality for establishing the diagnosis prior to the development of a critically ill patient in clinically apparent tamponade.

- Acute tumor lysis syndrome, previously limited to hematologic malignancies, is now being described in patients receiving chemotherapy for solid tumors. It can arise with dyspnea, mental status changes, cardiac dysrhythmia, or seizures. Treatment includes urinary alkalinization and emergency hemodialysis in cases complicated by acute renal failure.

REFERENCES

1. Arias E, et al: Deaths: Final Data for 2001. *Natl Vital Stat Rep* 52:3, 2003.
2. Anderson R, Smith BL: Deaths: Leading causes for 2001. *Natl Vital Stat Rep* 52:15, 2003.
3. Hughes WT, et al: 2002 guidelines for the use of antimicrobial agents in neutropenic patients with cancer: The Infectious Disease Society of America. *Clin Infect Dis* 34:730, 2003.
4. Glauser MP: Neutropenia: Clinical implications and modulation. *Intensive Care Med* 26:103, 2000.
5. Friefeld AG, Walsh TJ, Pizzo PA: Fever and neutropenia. In DeVita VT et al (eds): *Cancer: Principles and Practice of Oncology*, 5th ed. Philadelphia, Lippincott-Raven, 1997.
6. Chanock SJ, Pizzo PA: Fever in the neutropenic host. *Infect Dis Clin North Am* 10:777, 1996.
7. Pizzo PA: Management of fever in patients with cancer and treatment-induced neutropenia. *N Engl J Med* 328:1323, 1993.
8. Oude Nihhuis CSM, Gietma JA: Routine radiography does not have a role in the diagnostic evaluation of ambulatory adult febrile neutropenic cancer patients. *Eur J Cancer* 39:2495, 2003.
9. Oude Nijhuis CS, et al: Fever and neutropenia in cancer patients: The diagnostic role of cytokines in risk assessment strategies. *Crit Rev Oncol Hematol* 44:163, 2002.
10. Alexander SW, Pizzo PA: Current considerations in the management of fever and neutropenia. *Curr Clin Top Infect Dis* 19:160, 1999.
11. Kibber CC: Neutropenic infections: Strategies of empirical therapy. *J Antimicrob Chemother* 36(Suppl B):107, 1995.
12. Keefe DL: Cardiovascular emergencies in the cancer patient. *Semin Oncol* 27:244, 2000.
13. Hunter W: History of aneurysm of the aorta with some remarks on aneurysm in general. *M Obser Aug (London)* 1:323, 1957.
14. Schecter MM: The superior vena cava syndrome. *Am J Med Sci* 227:46, 1954.
15. Rowell NP, Gleeson FV: Steroids, radiotherapy, chemotherapy, and stents for superior vena caval obstruction in carcinoma of the bronchus: A systemic review. *Clin Oncol (R Coll Radiol)* 14:338, 2002.
16. Krimsky W, Behrens R, Kerkvleit G: Oncological emergencies for the internist. *Cleve Clin J Med* 69:209, 2002.
17. Yahalom Y: Superior vena caval syndrome. In DeVita VT et al (eds): *Cancer: Principles and Practice of Oncology*, 5th ed. Philadelphia, Lippincott-Raven, 1997.
18. Lokich JJ, Goodman RL: Superior vena cava syndrome. *JAMA* 231:58, 1975.
19. Jackson JE, Brooks DM: Stenting of superior vena cava obstruction. *Thorax* 50(Supp1):531, 1995.
20. Altman A: Acute tumor lysis syndrome. *Semin Oncol* 28:3, 2001.
21. Sallan S: Management of acute tumor lysis syndrome. *Semin Oncol* 28:9, 2001.
22. Kalemkerian GP, Darwish B, Varterasian ML: Tumor lysis syndrome in small cell lung carcinoma and other solid tumors. *Am J Med* 103:363, 1997.
23. Warrell RP: Metabolic emergencies. In DeVita VT et al (eds): *Cancer: Principles and Practice of Oncology*, 5th ed. Philadelphia, JB Lippincott, 1997.
24. Kwaan HC, Bongu A: The hyperviscosity syndromes. *Semin Thromb Hemost* 25:199, 1999.
25. Gertz MA, Kyle RA: Hyperviscosity syndrome. *J Intensive Care Med* 10:128, 1995.
26. Gertz MA, Fonseca R, Rajkumar SV: Waldenstrom's macroglobulinemia. *Oncologist* 5:63, 2000.
27. Anderson KC, Hamblin TJ, Traynor A: Management of multiple myeloma today. *Semin Hematol* 36(1 Suppl 3):3, 1999.
28. Flombaum CD: Metabolic emergencies in the cancer patient. *Semin Oncol* 27:322, 2000.
29. Coiffer B, Mournier N, Bologna S: Efficacy and safety of rasburicase (recombinant urate oxidase) for the prevention and treatment of hyperuricemia during induction chemotherapy of aggressive non-Hodgkin's lymphoma: Results of the GRAAL1 study. *J Clin Oncol* 21:4402, 2003.
30. Mundy GR, Guise TA: Hypercalcemia of malignancy. *Am J Med* 103:134, 1997.

31. Barri YM, Knochei JP: Hypercalcemia and electrolyte disturbances in malignancy. *Hematol Oncol Clin North Am* 10:775, 1996.
32. Davidson TG: Conventional treatment of hypercalcemia of malignancy. *Am J Health Syst Pharm* 58(Suppl 3):S8, 2001.
33. Body JJ: Current and future directions in medical therapy: Hypercalcemia. *Cancer* 88(12 Suppl):3054, 2000.
34. Nussbaum SR, et al: Single-dose intravenous therapy with pamidronate for the treatment of hypercalcemia of malignancy: Comparison of 30-, 60-, and 90-mg doses. *Am J Med* 95:297, 1993.
35. Purohit OP, et al: A randomised double-blind comparison of intravenous pamidronate and clodronate in the hypercalcemia of malignancy. *Br J Cancer* 72:1289, 1995.
36. Williams C, Soutter L: Pericardial tamponade: Diagnosis and treatment. *Arch Intern Med* 94:571, 1954.
37. Silkey S, Reyes CV: Cardiac tamponade in lung cancer. *J Surg Oncol* 28:201, 1985.
38. Fraser RS, Viloria JB, Wans NS: Cardiac tamponade as a presentation of extracardiac malignancy. *Cancer* 45:1697, 1980.
39. Helms SR, Carlson MD: Cardiovascular emergencies. *Semin Oncol* 16:463, 1989.
40. Pass HI: Malignant pleural and pericardial effusions. In DeVita VT et al (eds): *Cancer: Principles and Practice of Oncology*, 5th ed. Philadelphia, JB Lippincott, 1997.
41. Spodick D: Acute cardiac tamponade. *N Engl J Med* 349:684, 2003.
42. Vaitkus PT, Herrmann HC, LeWinteer MM: Therapy of malignant pericardial effusion. *JAMA* 272:59, 1994.
43. Maguire WM: Mechanical complications of cancer. *Emerg Med Clin North Am* 11:421, 1993.
44. Johnson FE, et al: Unsuspected malignant pericardial effusion causing cardiac tamponade: Rapid diagnosis by computed tomography. *Chest* 4:501, 1982.
45. DeAngelis LM, Posner JB: Neurologic complications. In Holland JF, et al (eds): *Cancer Medicine*, 4th ed. Baltimore, Williams & Wilkins, 1997.
46. Cascino TL: Neurologic complications of systemic cancer. *Med Clin North Am* 77:265, 1993.
47. Quinn JA, DeAngelis LM: Neurologic emergencies in the cancer patient. *Semin Oncol* 27:311, 2000.
48. Jeyapalan SA, Batchelor TT: Diagnostic evaluation of neurologic metastases. *Cancer Invest* 18:381, 2000.
49. Byrne TN: Spinal cord compression from epidural metastases. *N Engl J Med* 327:614, 1992.
50. Quadri TL, Brown AE: Infectious complications in the critically ill patient with cancer. *Semin Oncol* 27:335, 2000.
51. Rodichock LD, et al: Early diagnosis of spinal epidural metastases. *Am J Med* 70:1181, 1981.
52. Rodichock L, et al: Megadose steroids in severe head injury. *J Neurosurg* 58:326, 1983.
53. Dearden NM, et al: Effect of high-dose dexamethasone on outcome from severe head injury. *J Neurosurg* 64:81, 1986.
54. Daw HA, Markman M: Epidural spinal cord compression in cancer patients: Diagnosis and management. *Clev Clin J Med* 67:497, 2000.

Section XI **METABOLISM AND ENDOCRINOLOGY**

CHAPTER

122 Acid-Base Disorders

Jamie L. Collings

The human body must be maintained in a precise acid-base balance for healthy cellular function. This balance is maintained by the lungs, kidneys, and serum buffers, interacting and responding to physiologic changes. Physiologic insults such as vomiting, diarrhea, respiratory failure, kidney dysfunction, diabetes, toxic ingestions, and others can result in life-threatening acid-base crises. Identifying and optimally treating the underlying condition is often achieved only through the diagnostic insights gained from acid-base measurements and calculations. This chapter presents essential acid-base physiology, beginning with an overview of the principles of acid-base function. This is followed by a discussion of primary respiratory acidosis and alkalosis and then metabolic causes of acidosis and alkalosis. Finally, mixed acid-base disorders are analyzed. Clinical implications are included along with the mathematical knowledge that the emergency physician requires to expertly manage these complex and potentially life-threatening conditions.

PRINCIPLES OF DISEASE

The kidneys, lungs, and physiologic buffers normally maintain the serum pH within a narrow spectrum, between 7.36 and 7.44. Each of these three systems dynamically responds to small changes in acid-base balance. Such precise physiologic control is required for normal cellular function. Consequently, disorders of kidneys, lungs, and physiologic buffers result in acid-base abnormalities.

Blood pH is determined by the ratio of the serum bicarbonate concentration and $PaCO_2$ (partial pressure of CO_2 in arterial blood). Primary metabolic acid-base disorders and the secondary metabolic compensation for primary respiratory disturbances alter the serum HCO_3^- concentration. Primary respiratory acid-base disorders and the secondary respiratory compensation for primary metabolic disturbances alter the $PaCO_2$.

The Henderson-Hasselbalch equation relates the concentrations of the acid-base pair to the pH:

$$pH = pK_a + \log\frac{[HCO_3^-]}{[H_2CO_3]}$$

where pK_a is the carbonic acid dissociation constant.

As the pH changes, so does the concentration. Because the equation is based on the logarithm, subtle changes in the serum pH can cause large and often significant alterations in the concentration of the acid-base pair. Clinically, this equation dictates how drugs will disperse, enzymes will react, and medications will bind at a given serum pH. In humans, H^+ concentration is extremely low (approximately 4×10^{-12} mEq/L) and strictly regulated. This is vitally important because protein and enzyme systems function properly only within a narrow pH spectrum.

Normally, blood is slightly alkalemic relative to water (pH 7.0). Blood pH must be maintained within relatively narrow limits, because a pH outside the range of 6.8 to 7.8 is generally incompatible with life. *Acidemia* is defined as a serum pH of less than 7.36. Conversely, *alkalemia* is defined as a pH of greater than 7.44. *Acidosis* is defined as a pathologic process that lowers the serum bicarbonate concentration (metabolic acidosis) or raises the $PaCO_2$ (respiratory acidosis); *alkalosis* is defined as a pathologic process that raises the serum bicarbonate concentration (metabolic alkalosis) or lowers the $PaCO_2$ (respiratory alkalosis).

Physiologic Buffers

Physiologic buffers, defined as a weak acid and its salt, oppose marked changes in pH after the addition of an organic acid or a base, as follows:

$$H^+ + buffer^-\ Na^+ \leftrightarrow buffer^-\ H^+ + Na^+$$

The human body uses three important physiologic buffers to minimize surges in pH: (1) the bicarbonate–carbonic acid system (primarily located in red blood cells), (2) intracellular protein buffers, and (3) phosphate buffers located within bone. Patients with malnutrition or chronic disease, and thus low albumin and bone density, and anemic patients have an ineffective buffering capability.

Bicarbonate–Carbonic Acid Buffer System

The bicarbonate–carbonic acid buffer system is unique among physiologic buffering systems. The system is open ended; continuous removal of organic acid is made possible by the exhalation of carbon dioxide (CO_2). In equilibrium, the equation is as follows:

$$H^+ + HCO_3^- \leftrightarrow H_2CO_3 \leftrightarrow H_2O + CO_2$$

Bicarbonate is present in large quantities and can be controlled by the lungs and kidneys; thus, it serves as the major contributor to the maintenance of acid-base balance. Clinically, its importance is in the transient buffering of serum and interstitial fluid. It is the primary system to handle the acute load of organic acidemia, and its components are easily measured.

Intracellular Blood Protein Buffers

Many protein buffers in blood are effective in maintaining acid-base homeostasis. The most important blood buffer is hemoglobin, which can buffer large amounts of H^+, preventing significant changes in the pH. If hemoglobin did not exist, venous blood would be 800 times more acidic than arterial blood, circulating at a pH of 4.5 instead of the normal venous pH of 7.37.

Bone as Buffer

Bone contains a large reservoir of bicarbonate and phosphate and can buffer a significant acute acid load.

Pulmonary Compensation

The second compensatory system for pH changes involves a relationship between the peripheral chemoreceptors, located in the carotid bodies, and central chemoreceptors, located in the medulla oblongata. Both these receptors influence respiratory drive and can initiate changes in minute ventilation. A drop in pH stimulates the respiratory center, resulting in increased minute ventilation. This in turn lowers the partial pressure of arterial carbon dioxide ($PaCO_2$), driving the pH toward the normal range. Conversely, an increase in pH decreases ventilatory effort, which increases $PaCO_2$ and lowers the pH back toward normal. A diabetic patient in ketoacidosis will hyperventilate to compensate for the organic acidemia and would be expected to have a low $PaCO_2$. This compensatory response is the expected reaction to a fall in serum pH. In general, compensatory processes will return the pH toward normal but not fully normalize it.

Renal Compensation

The kidneys play little role in the acute compensation of acid-base disorders because they do not immediately respond to changes in pH. More than 6 to 12 hours of sustained acidosis will result in active excretion of H^+ (predominantly in the form of ammonium, NH_4^+) with retention of bicarbonate, HCO_3^-. Conversely, more than 6 hours of alkalemia will stimulate renal excretion of bicarbonate with retention of H^+ in the form of organic acids, resulting in near-normalization of pH.

In metabolic acidosis, there is either an excess production or an infusion of H^+ (e.g., lactic acid production, ketoacid production) or an excessive loss of anion (HCO_3^-) and accompanying sodium and potassium cations (Na^+, K^+) (e.g., diarrhea). In general, the kidney attempts to preserve Na^+ by exchanging it for excreted H^+ or K^+. The quantity of potassium excreted depends on the level of acidosis and the serum K^+ level. In the presence of an H^+ load, hydrogen ions move from the extracellular fluid (ECF) into the intracellular fluid. For this to occur, potassium moves outside the cell into the ECF to maintain electroneutrality. In cases of severe acidosis, significant overall depletion of total body K^+

stores can occur despite serum hyperkalemia. Clinically, this is the rationale for initiating intravenous potassium in the patient with diabetic ketoacidosis, despite an often elevated serum K^+ level.

In metabolic alkalosis, there is a shift of H^+ extracellularly, accompanied by an electroneutral shift of serum Na^+ and K^+ intracellularly. Renal excretion of K^+ also occurs in an attempt to preserve H^+. If the alkalosis continues, the renal compensation may be unable to keep pace, especially if hypokalemia ensues. With excessive excretion of potassium, the kidney paradoxically begins to excrete H^+ in an attempt to retain K^+; thus, an aciduria can exist with a serum alkalosis. This paradoxical aciduria is a clinical clue to the magnitude of hypokalemia and explains why renal compensation is unable to correct for alkalosis until potassium levels are restored.

Conditions that change serum potassium will also alter serum pH. Excessive diuresis, occurring without potassium supplementation, will generate a mild alkalemia, as H^+ is shifted intracellularly to support the extracellular osmotic movement of K^+. Conversely, excessive administration of potassium can cause H^+ to shift extracellularly, which may produce a mild acidosis.

DIAGNOSTIC STRATEGIES

A stepwise clinical approach to acid-base disorders starts with a well-conducted history and physical examination. Particular attention should be paid to the patient's past medical history, current medications, chance of toxic ingestion, occurrence of vomiting or diarrhea, level of consciousness on admission, respiratory rate, skin turgor, and urine output.

Evaluation progresses with analysis of serum electrolytes and pH, and calculation of any anion gap, delta gap, or base excess or deficit. These calculations will assist in determining what type of acidosis or alkalosis is present and whether a mixed condition is present. The anion gap (AG) can be calculated as follows:

$$AG = Na^+ - (Cl^- + HCO_3^-)$$

Traditionally, a normal AG has been considered 12 ± 3 mEq/L. This number can vary from one laboratory to another and the clinician should take this possibility into consideration. The "gap" provides an estimate of unmeasured anions in plasma, primarily albumin plus small amounts of sulfate, phosphate, and organic anions (e.g., citrate). If there are excess organic acids in the circulation, the organic acids dissociate and the resulting H^+ is titrated by HCO_3^-, which increases the anion gap. If the anion gap is increased, especially when it is more than 10 mEq/L above the upper limit of the reference range, the clinician should suspect an excess in organic acids or acidic substances. The concept of a "low" AG (<3 mEq/L) may be useful in the diagnosis of lithium toxicity, immunoglobulin G myelomas, and hypoalbuminemia of chronic disease.

Calculating the delta gap (ΔG = deviation of AG from normal − deviation of HCO_3^- from normal) may help resolve the possibility of a mixed acid-base disorder or further differentiate an elevated AG metabolic acidosis.[1] Mathematically refined and with normal values substituted, the equation is as follows:

$$\Delta G = (\text{calculated AG} - 12) - (24 - \text{measured } HCO_3^-)$$

Values greater than +6 equate with metabolic alkalosis or respiratory acidosis. Values less than −6 imply a greater loss of HCO_3^-, suggesting a mixed disorder.

No significant differences were found for pH, $PaCO_2$, or HCO_3^- concentrations when values obtained from intraosseous sites were compared to central venous specimens during steady and low-flow cardiac states.[2] Venous blood gas measurements, when compared to arterial specimens, accurately demonstrate the degree of acidosis in adult emergency department patients presenting with organic acidemia.[3] In infants, capillary tube blood gases are as reliable as formal arterial blood gases in determining hypercarbia or acidosis.[4]

It is also possible to utilize the acid-base calculations to predict the magnitude of shock and need for blood products. The base deficit or base excess can be a valuable indicator of shock and the efficacy of resuscitation.[5] The base excess is a calculated figure that provides an estimate of the metabolic component of the acid-base balance. The base excess is defined as the amount of H^+ ions that would be required to return the pH of blood to 7.35 if the PCO_2 were adjusted to 40. If there is a large base deficit (typically more severe than −6), it indicates that even if the patient's respiratory problems were resolved, a significant metabolic acidosis is present. The clinician should keep in mind, however, that given the dynamic condition of pH balance, the base deficit and base excess numbers could be out of synch with the real-time condition of the patient. Therefore, circumspection is required when deciding what these numbers mean to treatment.

RESPIRATORY ACIDOSIS

Respiratory acidosis is defined as decreased pH that results from pulmonary CO_2 retention. In other words, hypoventilation leads to hypercapnia. CO_2 retention results in excess H_2CO_3 production, which leads to acidemia. In the acute state, the serum HCO_3^- concentration is normal. The transition from acute to chronic respiratory acidosis is defined as the point at which renal compensation manifests as HCO_3^- retention (Figure 122-1).[6]

Clinical Features

Respiratory acidosis is caused by any disorder that results in a decrease in minute ventilation and thus CO_2 retention. Common causes include pulmonary pathologic conditions, airway obstruction, and conditions that influence respiratory drive (Box 122-1). The clinical picture depends on the severity and chronicity of the process as well as on the underlying disease. Patients with acute respiratory acidosis may have CO_2

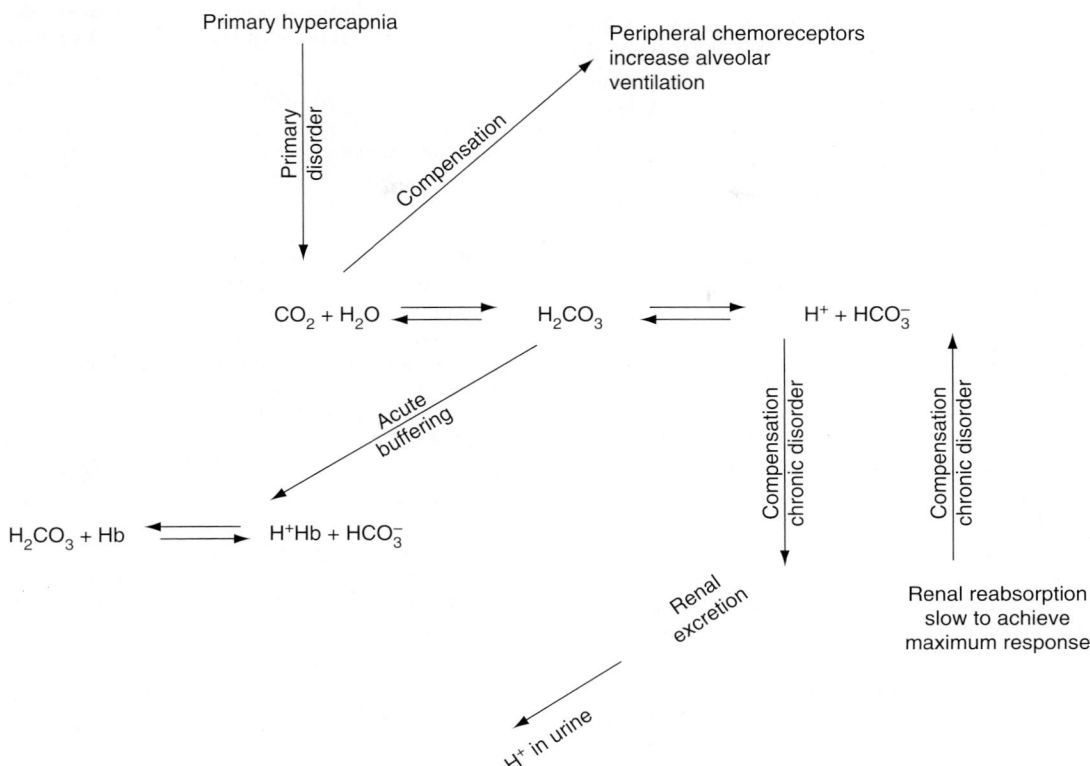

Figure 122-1. Respiratory acidosis and regulation.

In the figure:

Primary hypercapnia

Primary disorder

Compensation → Peripheral chemoreceptors increase alveolar ventilation

$$CO_2 + H_2O \rightleftharpoons H_2CO_3 \rightleftharpoons H^+ + HCO_3^-$$

Acute buffering

$$H_2CO_3 + Hb \rightleftharpoons H^+Hb + HCO_3^-$$

Compensation chronic disorder

Compensation chronic disorder

Renal excretion

Renal reabsorption slow to achieve maximum response

H^+ in urine

Acute
Airway disturbances
  Obstruction (foreign body,
    bronchospasm,
    laryngospasm)
  Aspiration
Drug-induced CNS
    depression
  Alcohol
  GHB/GABA toxicity
  Narcotics
  IV sedation
Pulmonary disease
  Pneumonia
  Edema
Thoracic cage disorders
  Pneumothorax
  Flail chest

Hypoventilation of
    muscular or CNS origin
  Myasthenia gravis
  CNS injury
  Guillain-Barré syndrome

Chronic
Lung disease
  Chronic bronchitis
  Chronic obstructive
    pulmonary disease
  Interstitial fibrosis
Neuromuscular disorders
  Myasthenia gravis
  Muscular dystrophy
Obesity with decreased
    alveolar ventilation

CNS, central nervous system; GHB/GABA, γ-hydroxybutyrate/γ-amino-butyric acid; IV, intravenous

Physiologic Compensation

In acute respiratory acidosis, the only effective buffers are the intracellular proteins. The HCO_3^- formed by intracellular buffering diffuses out of the cell into the ECF, increasing about 1 mEq/L for every 10-mm Hg rise in the $PaCO_2$. In acute situations, this HCO_3^- compensation is insignificant and has only minimal effect on the prevailing pH. Profound acidemia develops quickly if ventilation is not improved.

In chronic respiratory acidosis, such as chronic obstructive pulmonary disease, renal retention of HCO_3^- plays a significant role in acid buffering. The initial response occurs beyond the first 6 to 12 hours and takes several days to reach maximal contribution. Chloride is excreted to maintain electrical neutrality and results in the characteristic hypochloremia of a chronic respiratory acidosis. Plasma HCO_3^- concentration increases approximately 3.5 mEq/L for every 10-mm Hg increase in the $PaCO_2$. This response provides excellent compensation and normalizes the pH.

Management

Therapy of acute respiratory acidosis is directed toward correction of minute ventilation, thus returning the $PaCO_2$ to normal. This may entail establishment of a definitive airway, initiation of artificial respiration, or treatment of an underlying toxic or neurologic condition.

Likewise, improving ventilation treats chronic respiratory acidosis. Bronchodilators, postural drainage, and antibiotics for infection are used to manage the under-

narcosis, characterized by symptoms and signs such as headache, asterixis, weakness, tremors, blurred vision, confusion, or somnolence. If prolonged, signs of intracranial pressure elevation with papilledema will become manifest.

lying cause. Sensitivity of the respiratory center progressively decreases with prolonged exposure to acidosis and hypercapnia, resulting in a ventilatory drive that is dependent on relative hypoxemia. Administration of oxygen to these patients will reduce their hypoxic drive and minute ventilation, potentially creating CO_2 narcosis. Oxygen must therefore be given with caution to patients with chronic respiratory acidosis. If the patient has severe hypoxemia, however, sufficient oxygen must be administered and the physician should be prepared to actively manage airway and ventilation. If assisted ventilation is required, the $PaCO_2$ should be lowered slowly to avoid posthypercapnic metabolic alkalosis.[7]

In patients with known coronary artery disease, research suggests that acute respiratory acidosis leads to direct vasodilation of coronary vasculature. This is believed to be an instinctive attempt to maintain myocardial blood flow.[8]

RESPIRATORY ALKALOSIS

Increased minute ventilation is the primary cause of respiratory alkalosis, characterized by decreased $PaCO_2$ and increased pH. Patients with uncompensated acute respiratory alkalosis have normal plasma HCO_3^- concentration. In chronic respiratory alkalosis, eventual renal compensation results in decreased plasma HCO_3^- concentration.

Etiology

Conditions that lead to respiratory alkalosis are central nervous system (CNS) diseases, hypoxemia, anxiety, hysteria, hypermetabolic states, toxicity states, hepatic insufficiency, and assisted ventilation (Box 122-2). Alkalemia of pregnancy (pH 7.46-7.50) is primarily respiratory in origin, occurs early, and is sustained throughout the gestation. A $PaCO_2$ of 31 to 35 mm Hg is considered normal in the antepartum period. Therefore, a $PaCO_2$ of 40 mm Hg in the pregnant woman would represent hypercapnia. Renal compensation leads to an excretion of HCO_3^-, and a serum bicarbonate level between 18 and 22 mEq/L in these women is normal.[9]

Clinical Features

Symptoms vary according to the degree and chronicity of the alkalosis and the associated symptoms caused by the underlying disorder. The symptoms of alkalosis result from irritability of the central and peripheral nervous systems and from increased resistance in the cerebral vasculature. Symptoms include paresthesias of the lips and extremities, lightheadedness, dizziness, muscle cramps, and carpopedal spasms; symptoms are identical to those seen with hypocalcemia.

Physiologic Compensation

Acute Alkalosis

After the onset of respiratory alkalosis, H^+ ions are secreted from within the cell to the ECF. These H^+ ions

---

BOX 122-2. Causes of Respiratory Alkalosis

Hypoxia-mediated hyperventilation
  High altitude
  Severe anemia
  Ventilation/perfusion inequality
CNS-mediated hyperventilation
  Voluntary, psychogenic
  Cerebrovascular accident
  Increased intracranial pressure, tumor
  Trauma
Pharmacologic
  Salicylate, caffeine, or nicotine toxicity
  Progesterone
  Pressors, epinephrine
  Thyroxine
Septicemia
Pulmonary
  Pneumonia
  Pulmonary embolism
  Edema
  Mechanical hyperventilation
  Atelectasis
Hepatic
  Encephalopathy
Hyponatremia

---

reduce the plasma HCO_3^- concentration, attempting to offset the acute alkalosis. During the acute state, the plasma HCO_3^- concentration is lowered approximately 2 mEq/L for each 10-mm Hg decrease in the $PaCO_2$.

Chronic Alkalosis

With persistently low $PaCO_2$, renal H^+ secretion is decreased. Mild hypokalemia often occurs as potassium shifts into the cells while H^+ enters the ECF. Renal secretion of HCO_3^- occurs, and chloride is retained to maintain electroneutrality. This creates the hypokalemia and hyperchloremia characteristic of a chronic respiratory alkalosis. During the first 7 to 9 days, compensation is insufficient to normalize the pH, and alkalemia prevails. Beyond 2 weeks, patients with a chronic respiratory alkalosis will have a normal or near-normal pH. This is the only primary acid-base disorder in which the pH does often normalize.

Management

Treatment of respiratory alkalosis is directed toward the underlying cause. In the patient with tetany or syncope caused by psychogenic hyperventilating, a rebreathing mask or paper bag allows for CO_2 retention and acid-base normalization. This should be used cautiously and only when other serious conditions (e.g., hypoxia, salicylate or other toxic ingestion, intracranial event) have been eliminated from the differential diagnosis.

METABOLIC ACIDOSIS

Metabolic acidosis is defined as acidemia created by a primary increase in H^+ concentration or a reduction in

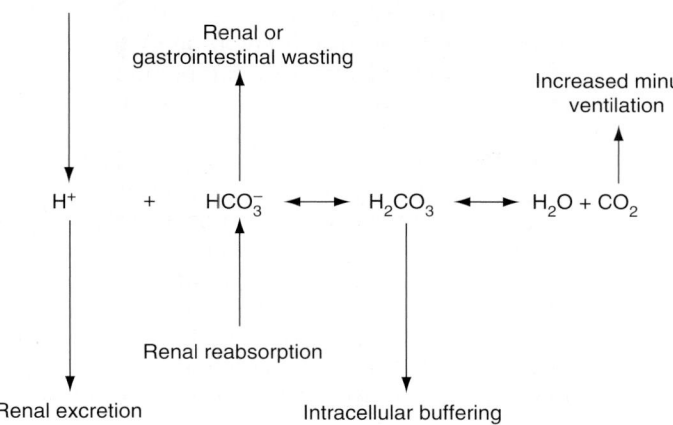

Figure 122-2. Metabolic acidosis and regulation. Hb, hemoglobin.

Acid load/introduction

Renal or gastrointestinal wasting

Increased minute ventilation

$H^+ + HCO_3^- \longleftrightarrow H_2CO_3 \longleftrightarrow H_2O + CO_2$

Renal reabsorption

Renal excretion

Intracellular buffering

BOX 122-3. Causes of Anion Gap Metabolic Acidosis

"CAT MUD PILES"
Carbon monoxide/**C**yanide exposure
Alcohol intoxication/**A**lcoholic ketoacidosis
Toluene exposure
Methanol exposure
Uremia
Diabetic ketoacidosis
Paraldehyde ingestion
Isoniazid/**I**ron intoxication
Lactic acidosis
Ethylene glycol intoxication
Salicylate intoxication

BOX 122-4. Causes of Normal Anion Gap Metabolic Acidosis

"F-USED CARS"
Fistulae (pancreatic)
Uretoenteric conduits
Saline (0.9% NaCl administration)
Endocrine (hyperparathyroidism)
Diarrhea
Carbonic anhydrase inhibitors (e.g., Diamox, Sulfamylon)
Arginine, lysine, chloride (total parenteral nutrition with excess)
Renal tubular acidosis
Spironolactone

HCO_3^- concentration. The acute state is compensated for by hyperventilation, resulting in reduction of $PaCO_2$. Chronically, renal reabsorption of HCO_3^- takes place (Figure 122-2).

Etiology

Metabolic acidosis can be caused by one of three mechanisms: (1) increased production of acids, (2) decreased renal excretion of acids, or (3) loss of alkali. The causes of metabolic acidosis can be clinically divided into those that create an elevation in AG (Box 122-3) and those that do not (Box 122-4). In the pediatric age group, dehydration from prolonged diarrhea is the most common cause of normal gap metabolic acidosis.[10]

Elevated Anion Gap

Metabolic acidosis with an elevated AG implies either the addition of exogenous acids or the creation of endogenous acids that are unable to be fully neutralized by bicarbonate. The mnemonic CAT MUD PILES (see Box 122-3) helps to apply historical and laboratory findings to the causality of acidemia.

Carbon Monoxide and Cyanide Poisoning

Elevated serum levels of carbon monoxide and cyanide have increasingly been found together in patients exposed to smoke from fires.[11] Victims of smoke inhala-

tion found unconscious and with metabolic acidosis should be considered exposed to both agents. Known as *cellular poisons,* both toxins interfere with cellular respiration at the cytochrome/electron transfer stage, resulting in anaerobic metabolism and the generation of organic acidemia.

Alcoholic Ketoacidosis

Alcoholic ketoacidosis (AKA) results from the abrupt termination of alcohol intake after a prolonged, massive ingestion of ethyl alcohol. There is a component of malnutrition and dehydration as well. Clinically, AKA manifests similarly to diabetic ketoacidosis (DKA); however, hyperglycemia and glycosuria are traditionally absent. Patients may present with AGs in the range of 30 to 35 mEq/L and hypocapnia secondary to compensatory hyperventilation. They may also have double and triple acid-base disorders due to alcohol withdrawal (respiratory alkalosis) and vomiting (metabolic alkalosis), which results in a pH that may be alkalemic. The ratio of β-hydroxybutyrate to acetoacetate is much higher in AKA (approximately 6:1) than in DKA (about 3:1).[12] This is important because there is a greater chance of missed diagnosis and inappropriate therapy in cases of AKA, since the β-hydroxybutyrate is not detected by the usual means and because during recovery, as β-hydroxybutyrate is converted to acetoacetate and acetone, this results in a paradoxical worsening of the ketoacidosis. (The usual dipstick tests have 0% sensitivity for β-hydroxybutyrate, 100% for acetoacetate, and 5% for acetone.)

Toluene Inhalation

Traditionally used as a solvent, toluene has become an inhalational agent abused for its euphoric effect. Toluene produces AG acidosis that is further complicated by distal renal tubular damage.[13] The end result is actually a mixed metabolic acidosis due to the renal tubular acidosis and bicarbonate loss.

Methanol, Ethylene Glycol, and Paraldehyde

The toxic effects of methanol (methyl or wood alcohol) result from the formation of its metabolite, formaldehyde, which is converted to formic acid, contributing to the metabolic acidosis. Ethylene glycol's toxic metabolites are oxalates, aldehydes, and lactic acid; oxalates result in significantly elevated AGs and increased mortality. Paraldehyde poisoning is rare; its use is now restricted to hospitalized patients and patients under close medical supervision. Ingestion leads to the creation of acetic and chloracetic acids.

Uremia

The acidosis in uremic patients results from a failure by the kidney to excrete acids. Hydrogen ion elimination is a direct secretory function of the renal tubules. The ability to excrete NH_4^+, HSO_4^-, and HPO_4^{-2}, however, varies directly with the glomerular filtration rate (GFR). Any pathologic process affecting the GFR will increase HSO_4^- and HPO_4^{-2}, resulting in an increased AG. In cases of pure uremia, the AG rarely exceeds 25 mEq/L. In the patient with chronic renal failure, increased AG metabolic acidosis is common. In cases of acute renal failure, however, hyperchloremic, non-AG metabolic acidosis is more common.

In pyelonephritis or obstructive uropathy, the acidosis is not related to an increased AG because tubular function is affected more than GFR. Increased AG metabolic acidosis in the patient with elevated serum blood urea nitrogen and creatinine levels suggests renocortical disease.

Diabetic Ketoacidosis

Diabetic ketoacidosis manifests clinically as a triad: hyperglycemia (usually >200 mg/dL), ketonemia (>1:2 dilutions), and acidemia (pH < 7.3). DKA can be caused by any condition that reduces insulin availability or activity or that increases glucagon. DKA occurs most often in type 1 diabetic patients with little or no endogenous insulin; however, its occurrence in patients with type 2 diabetes, particularly obese African Americans, is not as rare as once thought. DKA in these patients results from increased lipolysis, and the breakdown of free fatty acids leads to production of ketoacids. Precipitating events usually include infections, surgery, and emotional or physical stressors.

Isoniazid and Iron Toxicity

Isoniazid is a common, important, but potentially lethal medication used for the treatment of tuberculo-

sis. Clinicians must be aware that ingestions of greater than 40 to 60 mg/kg pose a danger of not only recurrent seizures but also life-threatening metabolic acidosis (as a result of the lactate-producing seizure activity). Treatment involves pyridoxine administration to control seizures and hemodialysis to reduce both intravascular drug concentration and acidemia.

Elevated AG metabolic acidosis from iron ingestion is a direct result of mitochondrial poisoning and uncoupled oxidative phosphorylation. Metabolic acidosis is typically appreciated in phase I of toxicity, usually within 6 hours of ingestion. It becomes quite apparent in phase III, signaling impending hepatic failure and shock. Effective treatment depends on early recognition and administration of deferoxamine.

Lactic Acidosis

There are two forms of lactic acid, the "L" form and the "D" form. The "L" form is most common and is the traditional form measured when obtaining serum lactate levels. A product of anaerobic metabolism, lactic acidosis develops when an imbalance exists between lactic acid production and subsequent conversion by the liver and kidney. Thus, lactic acidosis is a marker of hypoperfusion and ongoing shock as hypoperfusion, hypoxemia, hypermetabolic states or some combination of these results in an increase in serum lactate.[14]

The "D" form has recently gained attention because of an increasing number of patients with small-bowel resection or gastric bypass surgery.[15] D-Lactic acidosis is characterized by episodes of encephalopathy and acidemia. Development of short-gut syndrome requires ingestion of a large carbohydrate load, carbohydrate malabsorption with increased delivery of carbohydrates to the large bowel, prominent lactobacilli, diminished colonic motility, and impaired D-lactic acid metabolism.

Nucleoside analogue reverse transcriptase inhibitors (e.g., zidovudine and stavudine) for human immunodeficiency virus have also been shown to induce lactic acidosis. The syndrome that results from the mitochondrial toxicity of these agents can manifest with severe lactic acidosis, hepatic steatosis, and a high rate of mortality.[16]

Initial measurement of metabolic acidosis (serum lactate levels), compared with the traditional carboxyhemoglobin levels, might better indicate the severity of carboxyhemoglobin toxicity and better predict hyperbaric treatment requirements.[17]

Metformin, currently considered the initial drug of choice for overweight patients with type 2 diabetes mellitus, is a biguanide derivative that is pharmacologically related to phenformin hydrochloride, which was withdrawn from the U.S. market in 1976 (owing to a high incidence of lactic acidosis). Studies support the clinical experience of metformin-induced lactic acidosis as well.[18] Metformin is believed to induce lactic acidosis, especially in the patient with renal insufficiency, by reducing pyruvate dehydrogenase activity and enhancing anaerobic metabolism. A serum creatinine concentration greater than 1.5 mg/dL, congestive heart failure requiring medications, acute or chronic metabolic acidosis, or exposure to iodinated contrast agents within 48 hours are considered absolute contraindications to the drug.

Salicylates

Salicylates' first toxic effect on acid-base balance results from direct stimulation of the respiratory center, increasing minute ventilation and inducing hypocapnia. In the early presentation of salicylate toxicity, respiratory alkalosis is often the only acid-base disturbance appreciated. Salicylates can also cause metabolic acidosis by uncoupling oxidative phosphorylation and inhibiting the dehydrogenase enzymes of the Krebs cycle.

Normal Anion Gap Metabolic Acidosis

Metabolic acidosis with a normal AG is caused by either an excessive loss of HCO_3^- or an inability to excrete H^+ and can be remembered with the mnemonic F-USED CARS (see Box 122-4). Any condition that causes excessive loss of intestinal fluid distal to the stomach can cause a normal AG metabolic acidosis. Normal AG metabolic acidosis is primarily a bicarbonate wasting condition and in 95% of cases results from diarrhea. Other possible, although less common, causes include tube drainage and skin fistulae, with loss of HCO_3^--rich intestinal, biliary, or pancreatic fluids. Ureterosigmoidostomy (surgical insertion of ureters into the sigmoid colon) produces a hyperchloremic acidosis because of loss of HCO_3^- in exchange for the reabsorption of Cl^-.

Patients with renal failure develop an inability to excrete their dietary H^+ load; the severity is proportional to the degree of reduction in the GFR. Patients with renal tubular acidosis type 1 are unable to secrete H^+ at the distal tubule, whereas impairment of HCO_3^- reabsorption at the proximal tubule is the defect in renal tubular acidosis type 2. Calculation of the urinary anion gap ($UAG = [Na^+ + K^+] - Cl^-$) may be helpful; a negative urinary anion gap suggests gastrointestinal loss of bicarbonate, whereas a positive urinary anion gap suggests altered urinary acidification, indicating a renal tubule abnormality.

Other causes of normal AG metabolic acidosis include hyperparathyroidism, medications such as carbonic anhydrase inhibitors (e.g., acetazolamide [Diamox], mafenide acetate [Sulfamylon]) and spironolactone, and hyperalimentation with excess arginine, lysine, or chloride.

Physiologic Compensation

The body responds to acidemia by utilizing four buffering systems: (1) extracellular bicarbonate–carbonic acid system, (2) intracellular blood protein system, and (3) renal and (4) respiratory compensation systems (see Figure 122-2).

The first two processes minimize the initial H^+ concentration while the kidneys eliminate excessive H^+ in the urine, reabsorb HCO_3^-, and restore acid-base homeostasis. The CNS responds to increased H^+ concentration, through direct stimulation of the chemoreceptors

in the medulla oblongata, by stimulating the respiratory center. This results in an increase in alveolar ventilation, producing a compensatory elimination of $PaCO_2$ and elimination of excess H^+. It may take 12 to 24 hours to achieve a maximal respiratory response to a sustained metabolic acidosis. When the arterial pH is 7.10 or less, the minute ventilation can reach 30 L/min. This type of prolonged and prominent hyperventilation, *Kussmaul's respiration,* is characteristic of metabolic acidosis.

In response to metabolic acidosis, H^+ ions are excreted by the kidney while HCO_3^- is reabsorbed. The rate-limiting reaction (the synthesis of H_2CO_3 from CO_2 and H_2O) is catalyzed by carbonic anhydrase. Therefore, inhibitors of this enzyme can create a metabolic acidosis by preventing the renal excretion of H^+. The excretion of H^+ requires buffering with HPO_4^- or NH_3, with ammonium playing the largest role. This buffering is called *titratable acidity.* The kidney responds to an increased H^+ load by the augmentation of cellular NH_3 production and consequently NH_4^+ excretion.

In summary, H^+ ions are acutely buffered by extracellular and intracellular mechanisms. However, these mechanisms are not potent enough to correct acidosis sufficiently. Acidemia will stimulate the CNS ventilatory center, and the $PaCO_2$ will be reduced secondary to Kussmaul's respiration. With continued and chronic acidemia, the kidneys will secrete H^+ (as NH_4^+ and $H_2PO_4^-$) and reabsorb HCO_3^- in an attempt to neutralize the acidosis.

Management

In treating patients with metabolic acidosis, primary efforts should be directed at restoring their homeostatic mechanisms. The clinician must treat the *patient,* using laboratory markers only as a guide.

Active correction of the pH depends on the severity of the acid-base imbalance, the cause, the patient's compensatory capabilities, and the potential harm caused by therapy. Most patients with metabolic acidosis do not require aggressive attempts at pH manipulation. For many, the causality is easily discernible, and treatment involves stabilization of homeostatic mechanisms. For example, metabolic acidosis after a seizure resolves within approximately 15 minutes. Rather than administration of sodium bicarbonate ($NaHCO_3$), immediate treatment would involve termination of the seizure activity, maintenance of the airway, and provision for acid-base normalization by ventilatory loss of CO_2.

Therapy with $NaHCO_3$ has some inherent complications, and rapid $NaHCO_3$ replacement can result in paradoxical CNS intracellular acidosis, impaired oxygen delivery, hypokalemia, hypocalcemia, "overshoot" alkalosis, hypernatremia, volume overload, and hyperosmolality. Bicarbonate penetration into the CNS across the blood-brain barrier is very slow; consequently, intravenous HCO_3^- therapy alkalinizes the plasma much faster than the CNS. As the serum pH increases, the peripheral chemoreceptors will decrease minute ventilation, raising $PaCO_2$ in an attempt to normalize the serum pH. CO_2, which rapidly diffuses across the blood-brain barrier, will rise intracerebrally, and the CNS will become more acidotic despite alkalinization of the plasma. This inverse reaction is referred to as *paradoxical CNS acidosis*. Much discussion surrounds this phenomenon and intravenous bicarbonate use. Buffer therapy during out-of-hospital cardiac arrest had little to no benefit in one study, regardless of the arterial pH.[19] The only prospective, randomized, controlled study failed to demonstrate any difference between the bicarbonate and control groups.[20] Furthermore, alkali therapy can lead to ECF volume overload (especially in patients with congestive heart failure) and hypokalemia, which may lead to respiratory muscle weakness and inability to hyperventilate if it is severe. Administration of loop diuretics may prevent or treat this complication, but if adequate diuresis cannot be established, emergent dialysis may be necessary.

Because $NaHCO_3$ imparts a significant sodium load on the patient, several low-sodium buffers have been developed. Unfortunately, none have proven to be clinically more efficacious than $NaHCO_3$.[21]

Because of the inherent complications associated with bicarbonate replacement, a rule of thumb is to treat patients who have a pH less than 7.1 with $NaHCO_3$ 1 mEq/kg.[22] Another formula available to assist in determining the adequate dose is the following:

$$NaHCO_3 \text{ (mEq)} = 25 - \text{(measured } HCO_3^-) \times \text{(weight [kg]/2)}$$

Half should be replaced initially and further $NaHCO_3$ therapy should be determined by patient response and laboratory parameters. Patients with normal AG metabolic acidosis have a greater loss of HCO_3^- than those with an increased anion gap, and therefore the clinician may have a lower threshold for replacement.

METABOLIC ALKALOSIS

Metabolic alkalosis is produced by conditions that increase HCO_3^- or reduce H^+. This usually requires either the loss of H^+ or the retention of HCO_3^-. The diagnosis requires knowledge of the $PaCO_2$, because elevation of the plasma HCO_3^- may be secondary to renal compensation of a chronic respiratory acidosis.

Etiology

Metabolic alkalosis is usually caused by an increase in HCO_3^- reabsorption secondary to volume, potassium, or chloride loss (Box 122-5). Loss of H^+ and Cl^- from aggressive vomiting and nasogastric suctioning can also lead to HCO_3^- retention. Renal impairment of HCO_3^- excretion, especially in the setting of alkali therapy, can lead to a significant metabolic alkalosis.

An ECF volume reduction can increase the plasma HCO_3^- concentration when combined salt and water losses occur, typically in patients using diuretics. This state forces a contraction of the ECF around a constant

---

BOX 122-5. Causes of Metabolic Alkalosis

Volume-Contracted (Saline-Responsive)
Vomiting/gastric suction
Diuretics
Ion-deficient baby formula
Colonic adenomas

Normal Volume/Volume-Expanded (Saline-Resistant)
Primary aldosteronism
Exogenous mineralocorticoids (licorice, chewing tobacco)
Adenocarcinoma
Bartter's syndrome
Cushing's disease
Ectopic adrenocorticotropic hormone

---

plasma HCO_3^-, creating a relative excess in HCO_3^- concentration; this is known as *contraction alkalosis*.

Metabolic alkalosis can be caused by hypokalemia as H^+ is shifted intracellularly in exchange for the osmotic movement of K^+ extracellularly. There is also an increase in renal H^+ secretion and HCO_3^- reabsorption. The net effect is ECF alkalosis with paradoxical intracellular acidosis, which is easily reversed with potassium therapy.

Primary hyperaldosteronism, hyperreninism, licorice ingestion, Cushing's syndrome, and congenital adrenal hyperplasia are associated with mineralocorticoid excess. This leads to an increased Na^+ reabsorption in the distal tubule with its accompanying H^+ and K^+ secretion to maintain electroneutrality.

Physiologic Compensation

Although somewhat less predictable, acute compensation of metabolic alkalosis involves the respiratory center, and chronic compensation involves the renal system. During acute compensation, chemoreceptors controlling ventilation respond to an increased pH by inducing hypoventilation, thus increasing $PaCO_2$ and forming H^+, which lowers the pH back to normal. A $PaCO_2$ of greater than 55 mm Hg is unlikely to be caused by simple respiratory compensation of metabolic alkalosis,[23] and this value should alert the clinician to a ventilation disorder complicating the picture. Chronic compensation for metabolic acidosis results from the kidney excreting excess HCO_3^- in the urine. In patients with renal failure, impairment in renal HCO_3^- excretion results in sustained metabolic alkalosis.

Management

Clinicians can easily treat the simple loss of H^+ from aggressive vomiting or nasogastric suction. For more complicated causes, however, management can be directed by measurement of the urinary chloride, which helps classify metabolic alkalosis into saline-responsive or saline-resistant.

Saline-Responsive Alkalosis

Patients with saline-responsive alkalosis have a urinary chloride level less than 10 mEq/L. Treatment is directed toward correcting the urinary excretion of HCO_3^-. Administration of NaCl and KCl suppresses both renal acid excretion and renal HCO_3^- excretion. NaCl and KCl should be considered for patients with mild to moderate saline-responsive alkalosis. In patients who are severely volume depleted, consultation for admission and administration of intravenous mineral acids (e.g., arginine monohydrochloride) may be necessary. In edematous states for which saline therapy may be contraindicated, acetazolamide will increase the excretion of $NaHCO_3$, treating both the alkalosis and the edema. In renal failure patients, severe metabolic alkalosis should be treated with dialysis.

Saline-Resistant Alkalosis

Patients with saline-resistant alkalosis have a urinary chloride level greater than 10 mEq/L. In mineralocorticoid excess, hypokalemia and increased secretion of aldosterone lead to excessive renal excretion of H^+ and a reabsorption of HCO_3^-. Treatment can be successful with potassium replacement by reversing the intracellular shift of H^+. This reduction of cellular H^+ also enhances HCO_3^- excretion. Additional therapy can be directed toward reducing mineralocorticoid activity (e.g., administering spironolactone, an aldosterone antagonist).

MIXED ACID-BASE DISORDERS

Double and triple primary acid-base disturbances are common. Traditionally, mixed disorders have been difficult to evaluate in the emergency department.[24] However, recent literature provides some guidelines for ascertaining the mixed disorder and its causes. Clues to the presence of a mixed acid-base disturbance can either be historical (e.g., polydrug ingestion) or clinical, with varied chemistry and arterial blood gas findings that differ from those anticipated. From that point, the "three-step approach of Haber" is useful because it involves a logical, easily remembered, rules-based approach that can be applied clinically.[25]

Step 1 involves measuring the pH. It is necessary to first assess whether the patient has an acidemia (pH < 7.36) or alkalemia (pH > 7.44). The human body almost never fully compensates for any primary acid-base disturbance except for chronic respiratory alkalosis.

Step 2 requires the clinician to calculate the AG. Box 122-3 lists possible causes of an AG greater than 15 mEq/L, and Box 122-4 lists possible causes for a case in which the AG is normal but the patient has a metabolic acidosis.

Step 3 involves calculating the delta gap (ΔG = deviation of AG from normal − deviation of HCO_3^- from normal) to help resolve the possibility of a mixed acid-base disorder or further differentiate an elevated AG metabolic acidosis.

Values for the ΔG are all gaussian, and therefore the mean value should be near zero.[26] An expected normal range for the ΔG would be 0 ± 6. A positive ΔG (+6 or greater) is almost always caused by high AG acidosis

---

BOX 122-6. Relationships in Acid-Base Disturbances

Respiratory Acidosis

Acute
1. HCO_3^- increases 1 mEq/L (range, 0.25–1.75) for every 10-mm Hg increase in P_{CO_2}.
2. pH drops 0.08 for every 10-mEq/L rise in HCO_3^-.

Chronic (>5 days of hypercapnia)
HCO_3^- increases 4 mEq/L for every 10-mm Hg increase in P_{CO_2} (±4).
Limit of compensation: bicarbonate will rarely exceed 45 mEq/L.

Metabolic Acidosis
Note: It may take 12 to 24 hours for maximal respiratory response to develop.
1. $Pa_{CO_2} = (1.5 \times HCO_3^-) + 8 \pm 2$
2. Pa_{CO_2} is equivalent to last two digits of pH (i.e., if P_{CO_2} is 20, pH should be 7.20).
3. $\Delta P_{CO_2} = 1 - [1.3 \times (\Delta HCO_3^-)]$
4. For pure anion gap acidosis, the rise in anion gap should be equal to the fall in bicarbonate concentration (i.e., Δgap should equal 0).
5. For pure non–anion gap (hyperchloremic) acidosis, the fall in bicarbonate should be equal to the rise in chloride concentration (i.e., Δbicarb = $-\Delta$chloride).
Limit of compensation: Pa_{CO_2} will not fall below 10 to 15 mm Hg.

Respiratory Alkalosis

Acute
HCO_3^- drops 1 to 3.5 mEq/L for every 10-mm Hg drop in P_{CO_2}.
Limit of compensation: bicarbonate is rarely below 18 mEq/L.

Chronic (renal compensation starts within 6 hours and is usually at a steady state by 1½ to 2 days)
HCO_3^- drops 2 to 5 mEq/L for every 10-mm Hg drop in P_{CO_2}.
Limit of compensation: bicarbonate is rarely below 12 to 14 mEq/L.

Metabolic Alkalosis
1. $P_{CO_2} = 0.9 (HCO_3^-) + 9$
2. P_{CO_2} increases 0.6 mm Hg for each 1-mEq/L increase in HCO_3^-.
Limit of compensation: P_{CO_2} rarely exceeds 55 mm Hg.

---

and a primary metabolic alkalosis. DKA or AKA with severe vomiting, lactic acidosis in the setting of chronic diuretic use, and renal disease with vomiting are clinical examples.

A negative ΔG (−6 or less), on the other hand, can be of varied clinical representation. Most often there is either a mixed high AG and normal AG acidosis, or a high AG acidosis with chronic respiratory alkalosis and a compensating hyperchloremic acidosis. Clinically, these patients often have severe underlying metabolic disease with ongoing toxic ingestion (e.g., profound hypermagnesemia, hyponatremia, or hypercalcemia in patients with lithium toxicity) or chronic lung disease, acute lactic acidosis, and furosemide use. Other algorithms and relationships in these disorders can also assist in rapid interpretation of mixed acid-base disturbances (Box 122-6).

KEY CONCEPTS

- Changes in serum pH are dealt with by three compensatory systems: (1) the physiologic buffers, (2) the lungs, and (3) the kidneys.

- Bicarbonate is present in large quantities and can be controlled by the lungs and kidneys, making it the major contributor to the maintenance of acid-base balance and the primary system to handle the acute load of organic acidemia.

- Respiratory acidosis is defined as decreased pH that results from pulmonary CO_2 retention. This CO_2 retention leads to excess H_2CO_3 production and acidemia.

- Increased minute ventilation is the primary cause of respiratory alkalosis, characterized by decreased $PaCO_2$ and increased pH.

- Metabolic acidosis can be caused by one of three mechanisms: (1) increased production of acids, (2) decreased renal excretion of acids, or (3) loss of alkali. The causes of metabolic acidosis can be divided into those that create an elevation in the anion gap and those that do not.

- Metabolic alkalosis is usually caused by an increase in HCO_3^- reabsorption secondary to volume, potassium, or chloride loss.

- Contraction alkalosis can result from extracellular volume reduction, with a consequent increase in the plasma HCO_3^- concentration, when combined salt and water losses occur. This typically occurs in patients using diuretics.

- Determination of a mixed acid-base disorder requires knowledge of the pH, calculation of the AG, and calculation of the delta gap.

REFERENCES

1. Salem MM, Mujais SK: Gaps in the anion gap. *Arch Intern Med* 152:1625, 1992.
2. Kissoon N, et al: Comparison of the acid-base status of blood obtained from intraosseous and central venous sites during steady and low-flow states. *Crit Care Med* 21:1765, 1993.
3. Brandenburg MA: Comparison of arterial and venous blood gas values in the initial emergency department evaluation of patients with diabetic ketoacidosis. *Ann Emerg Med* 31:459, 1998.
4. Harrison AM, et al: Comparison of simultaneously obtained arterial and capillary blood gases in pediatric intensive care unit patients. *Crit Care Med* 25:1904, 1997.
5. Davis JW, Shackford SR, Hollbrook TL: Base deficit as a sensitive indicator of compensated shock and tissue oxygen utilization. *Surg Gynecol Obstet* 173:473, 1991.
6. Narins RG, Emmett M: Simple and mixed acid-base disorders: A practical approach. *Medicine* 59:161, 1980.
7. Kassirer JP: Serious acid-base disorders. *N Engl J Med* 291:773, 1974.
8. Kazmaier S, et al: Effects of respiratory alkalosis and acidosis on myocardial blood flow and metabolism in patients with coronary artery disease. *Anesthesiology* 89:831, 1998.
9. Landon M: Acid-base disorders during pregnancy. *Clin Obstet Gynecol* 37:16, 1994.
10. Chabli R: Diagnostic use of anion and osmolal gaps in pediatric emergency medicine. *Pediatr Emerg Care* 13:204, 1997.
11. Baud FJ, et al: Elevated blood cyanide concentrations in victims of smoke inhalation. *N Engl J Med* 325:1761, 1991.
12. McGarry JD, Foster DW: Diabetic ketoacidosis. In Rifkin H, Raskin P (eds): *Diabetes Mellitus*. American Diabetic Association, 5:185, 1981.
13. Kamijima M, et al: Metabolic acidosis and renal tubular injury due to pure toluene inhalation. *Arch Environ Health* 49:410, 1994.
14. Bernardin G, et al: Blood pressure and arterial lactate levels are early indicators of short-term survival in human septic shock. *Intensive Care Med* 22:17, 1996.
15. Uribarri J, Oh MS, Carrol HJ: D-lactic acidosis: A review of clinical presentation, biochemical features and pathophysiologic mechanisms. *Medicine* 77:73, 1998.
16. Gerard Y, et al: Symptomatic hyperlactatemia: Emerging complication of antiretroviral therapy. *AIDS* 14:2723, 2000.
17. Turner M, Esaw M, Clark RJ: Carbon monoxide poisoning treated with hyperbaric oxygen: Metabolic acidosis as a predictor of treatment requirements. *J Accid Emerg Med* 16:96, 1999.
18. Misbin RI, et al: Lactic acidosis in patients with diabetes treated with metformin. *N Engl J Med* 338:265, 1998.
19. Dybvik T, Strand T, Steen PA: Buffer therapy during out-of-hospital cardiopulmonary resuscitation. *Resuscitation* 29:89, 1995.
20. Levy MM: An evidence-based evaluation of the use of sodium bicarbonate during cardiopulmonary resuscitation. *Crit Care Clin* 14:457, 1998.
21. Offenstandt G: Alkali therapy in the treatment of acute metabolic acidosis. *Minerva Anestesiol* 65:202, 1999.
22. Cummins R, et al: *Advanced Cardiac Life Support, 1997-1999*. Dallas, Scientific Publishing, 1997.
23. Weinberger SE, Schwartzstein RM, Weiss JW: Hypercapnia. *N Engl J Med* 321:1223, 1989.
24. Schreck DM, Zacharias D, Grunau CF: Diagnosis of complex acid-base disorders: Physician performance versus the microcomputer. *Ann Emerg Med* 15:164, 1986.
25. Haber RJ: A practical approach to acid-base disorders. *West J Med* 155:146, 1991.
26. Wrenn K: The delta gap: An approach to mixed acid-base disorders. *Ann Emerg Med* 19:1310, 1990.

PERSPECTIVE

Abnormalities of serum electrolyte levels generally cannot be diagnosed by the history and physical examination alone. Severe electrolyte disturbances can be fatal, however, and some disorders may produce no symptoms or nonspecific clinical manifestations until life-threatening effects occur.

SODIUM

Normal Physiology

Water makes up approximately 60% of body weight and is distributed in three compartments: the intracellular space, the interstitial space, and the intravascular space. The intracellular space makes up approximately two thirds of total body water, with the remaining one third in the interstitial space and intravascular space. The concentration of sodium, the predominant extracellular cation, governs the movement of water among these three compartments. When the extracellular sodium concentration decreases, water shifts to the intracellular space to restore osmotic equilibrium. When the extracellular sodium concentration rises, water shifts out of the intracellular space. Under normal conditions, sodium leaks passively into cells down a concentration gradient and is transported back out of the cell by the sodium-potassium adenosine triphosphatase (Na^+,K^+-ATPase) pump.

Sodium homeostasis and water balance are under the hormonal regulation of the renin-angiotensin system and antidiuretic hormone, respectively. Renin, an enzyme produced by the kidney, is released in response to decreases in circulating intravascular volume. Renin catalyzes the production of angiotensin I, which is then converted to angiotensin II in the lung. Angiotensin II stimulates the production of aldosterone, a mineralocorticoid hormone produced by the zona glomerulosa of the adrenal glands. Aldosterone enhances sodium reabsorption and potassium excretion in the distal nephron.

Antidiuretic hormone (ADH, vasopressin, arginine vasopressin) is synthesized in the hypothalamus and secreted from the posterior pituitary. ADH is released primarily in response to rises in serum osmolality but also to decreases in intravascular volume or arterial pressure. Volume depletion is the most potent stimulus for ADH production, and with decreases in plasma volume, ADH may be secreted even in the face of hypotonicity. ADH enhances renal water reabsorption by increasing tubular water permeability. Other factors that may stimulate ADH release include angiotensin, catecholamines, opiates, caffeine, stress, hypoglycemia, and hypoxia.

Hyponatremia

Principles of Disease

Hyponatremia is defined as a serum sodium concentration of less than 135 mEq/L. Hyponatremia can be classified into three categories based on the patient's clinical volume status: (1) hypovolemic hyponatremia, (2) euvolemic hyponatremia, and (3) hypervolemic hyponatremia (Box 123-1). When assessing the patient with a low serum sodium level, it is also important to consider the possibility of sampling errors (e.g., phlebotomy from a venous site proximal to an infusion of hypotonic solution), as well as pseudohyponatremia and redistributive hyponatremia.

Pseudohyponatremia

Pseudohyponatremia refers to a falsely low serum sodium measurement in patients whose plasma contains excessive protein or lipid. The relative percentage of water in plasma is reduced. Flame photometry, which determines sodium content per unit of plasma, shows an artifactually low sodium level, although both the total sodium content and the serum osmolarity remain within the normal range. Measurement of the serum sodium by direct potentiometry avoids this problem.[1]

Redistributive Hyponatremia

Redistributive hyponatremia is caused by osmotically active solutes in the extracellular space that draw water from the cell, diluting the serum sodium concentration. Common situations causing such hyperosmolar states include hyperglycemia (e.g., diabetic ketoacidosis) and parenteral administration of mannitol or glycerol for the management of intracranial hypertension or glaucoma. The measured serum sodium in patients with hyperglycemia can be corrected by adding approximately 1.6 mEq/L for every 100-mg/dL rise in the serum glucose over 100 mg/dL.

Hypovolemic Hyponatremia

Hypovolemic hyponatremia results from the loss of water and sodium with a greater relative loss of sodium. Typical causes include vomiting, diarrhea, gastrointestinal suction or drainage tubes, fistulas, and

BOX 123-1. Causes of Hyponatremia

Sampling error
Pseudohyponatremia
  Hyperlipemia
  Hyperproteinemia
Redistributive type
  Hyperglycemia
  Mannitol
Hypovolemic type
  Renal losses
  Gastrointestinal
  Third-space losses

Excessive sweating
Addison's disease
Euvolemic type
  SIADH
  Psychogenic polydipsia
Hypervolemic type
  Congestive heart failure
  Hepatic cirrhosis
  Nephrotic syndrome

SIADH, syndrome of inappropriate secretion of antidiuretic hormone.

BOX 123-2. Causes of Syndrome of Inappropriate Secretion of Antidiuretic Hormone

CNS disease
  Brain tumor, infarction, injury, or abscess
  Meningitis
  Encephalitis
Pulmonary disease
  Pneumonia
  Tuberculosis
  Lung abscess
  Pulmonary aspergillosis
Drugs
  Exogenous vasopressin
  Diuretics
  Chlorpropamide
  Vincristine
  Thioridazine
  Cyclophosphamide

CNS, central nervous system.

"third spacing" of fluids (e.g., burns, intra-abdominal sepsis, bowel obstruction, pancreatitis). Causes specifically attributable to renal losses include diuretic use, mineralocorticoid deficiency, renal tubular acidosis, and salt-wasting nephropathy. When sodium losses are sufficient to decrease the glomerular filtration rate (GFR) significantly, the amount of filtrate delivered to the loop of Henle (where free water is generated) is decreased, and little free water appears in the urine. Also, because ADH is released in response to intravascular volume deficits despite hypotonicity, hyponatremia may be maintained even in patients whose GFR would otherwise be adequate to excrete excess free water. Hypovolemic hyponatremia can also be worsened when fluid losses are replaced with hypotonic fluids.

Euvolemic Hyponatremia

The many causes of euvolemic hyponatremia include the syndrome of inappropriate secretion of ADH (SIADH), defined as the secretion of ADH in the absence of an appropriate physiologic stimulus. Its hallmark is an inappropriately concentrated urine despite the presence of a low serum osmolality and a normal circulating blood volume. Causes of SIADH include central nervous system (CNS) disorders, pulmonary disease, drugs, stress, pain, and surgery (Box 123-2). Before the diagnosis of SIADH can be confirmed, other potential causes of euvolemic hyponatremia (e.g., hypoadrenalism, hypothyroidism, renal failure) should be ruled out. Psychogenic polydipsia is a rare cause of euvolemic hyponatremia. This is most often seen in patients with psychiatric disorders who consume large volumes of water, usually in excess of 1 L/hr, overwhelming the capacity of the kidneys to excrete free water in the urine.[2] In contrast to SIADH, the urine in patients with psychogenic polydipsia is maximally dilute.

Hypervolemic Hyponatremia

Hypervolemic hyponatremia results when sodium is retained but retention of water exceeds that of sodium. This is seen in edematous states such as congestive heart failure, hepatic cirrhosis, and renal failure. In these conditions, decreased effective renal perfusion causes the secretion of both ADH and aldosterone. This leads to increased tubular reabsorption of both sodium and water, decreased delivery of water to the distal nephron, and inability to produce hypotonic urine.

Clinical Features

The signs and symptoms of hyponatremia depend on the rapidity with which the serum sodium concentration declines, as well as on its absolute level. The acutely hyponatremic patient is almost always symptomatic when the serum sodium level falls below 120 mEq/L, whereas patients with chronic hyponatremia may tolerate much lower levels. Very young and very old patients typically develop symptoms with lesser decreases in the serum sodium level.

The primary symptoms of hyponatremia are related to the CNS, including lethargy, apathy, confusion, disorientation, agitation, depression, and psychosis. Focal neurologic deficits, ataxia, and seizures have been reported.[3] Other nonspecific signs and symptoms include muscle cramps, anorexia, nausea, and weakness.

Diagnostic Strategies

The urinary sodium concentration can be a useful tool in the assessment of the patient with hyponatremia. Patients with hypovolemic hyponatremia caused by renal sodium wasting typically have an inappropriately high urinary sodium concentration (>20 mEq/dL); those with extrarenal sodium wasting and intact renal sodium-conserving mechanisms have a low urinary sodium concentration (<10 mEq/L). Patients with euvolemic hyponatremia generally have a urinary sodium concentration greater than 20 mEq/L. Patients with hypervolemic hyponatremia caused by congestive heart failure or cirrhosis typically have a concentration below 10 mEq/L, and those with renal failure have a concentration above 20 mEq/L.[4]

Management

Because tolerance for hyponatremia is highly variable, treatment should be guided by the severity of symptoms, the estimated duration of illness, and the patient's volume status rather than by the serum level alone. Severe neurologic dysfunction and seizures are an indication for immediate treatment. Patients with signs of shock or symptomatic fluid overload also require rapid intervention. Because individuals with acute hyponatremia typically develop more prominent symptoms than those with chronic hyponatremia and are more tolerant of rapid correction of sodium deficits, aggressive treatment is a reasonable goal in these patients. In contrast, patients with chronic hyponatremia are usually less symptomatic and are more susceptible to complications when the serum sodium level is corrected rapidly, making aggressive treatment both less necessary and less desirable.

Hypovolemic Hyponatremia

Patients with hypovolemic hyponatremia should have volume deficits corrected with isotonic NaCl (0.9%). Isotonic saline is hypertonic compared with the hyponatremic patient's serum and will therefore cause a modest elevation of the serum sodium concentration.

Euvolemic Hyponatremia

Patients with hyponatremia and a normal total circulating volume can usually have free water intake restricted while the cause of the hyponatremia is determined and specific treatment for the underlying disorder is begun. Significantly, patients with SIADH who are given normal saline may actually experience a further decrease in the serum sodium as free water is retained and a hypertonic urine is excreted. Lithium and demeclocycline, which inhibits the action of ADH, can also be used in the treatment of SIADH.

Hypervolemic Hyponatremia

The cornerstone of therapy for patients with hypervolemic hyponatremia is fluid restriction, which is effective in most patients. The addition of diuretics may accelerate water excretion, although this approach should be used with caution because sodium excretion is also enhanced. Dialysis may be required to remove large amounts of water in patients with advanced renal failure.

Symptomatic Hyponatremia

Patients with severely symptomatic hyponatremia may require administration of 3% NaCl (513 mEq of Na$^+$/L). The rate of correction of hyponatremia should be dictated by the rapidity of its onset. Acute hyponatremia can be corrected at rates of up to 1 to 2 mEq/L/hr, and chronic hyponatremia should be corrected at a rate not greater than 0.5 mEq/L/hr. In general, the serum sodium level should not be corrected to above 120 mEq/L or increased by more than 10 mEq/L in a 24-hour period. Hypertonic saline should be administered through a controlled intravenous infusion, with careful attention to fluid input and output and frequent assessment of serum electrolytes. The approximate required dose of hypertonic saline can be calculated with the following formula:

$$(\text{Desired } [Na^+] - \text{measured } [Na^+]) \times (0.6) \text{ (weight in kilograms)} = mEq\ [Na^+] \text{ administered}$$

Overaggressive correction of the serum sodium level can have serious consequences. Central pontine myelinolysis, also known as *cerebral demyelination*, involves the destruction of myelin in the pons and is thought to result from rapid elevation of the serum sodium. Patients may develop cranial nerve palsies, quadriplegia, or coma. Central pontine myelinolysis is more likely to occur in patients with chronic hyponatremia than in those with acute hyponatremia. Most cases have been associated with rapid correction of serum sodium in alcoholic, malnourished, and elderly patients, although it has also been described in otherwise healthy patients.

Hypernatremia

Principles of Disease

Hypernatremia is defined as a serum sodium concentration above 145 mEq/L. Patients at the extremes of age and those with chronic disorders are particularly vulnerable.[5] Hypernatremia is most often the result of a decrease in free water because of either reduced water intake or increased water loss. Less often, hypernatremia is caused by an increase in total sodium (Box 123-3). This classification scheme helps in identifying the underlying cause and guiding therapy.

Reduced water intake may be the result of limited access, inability to tolerate oral fluids, defective thirst mechanisms, or depressed mentation.

Increased water loss can occur through several different organ systems, including the gastrointestinal tract, skin, respiratory tract, or kidney. Gastrointestinal losses can occur from protracted diarrhea, vomiting, nasogastric tube suction, or third spacing. Renal causes of water loss include osmotic diuresis (e.g., hyperglycemia, mannitol administration) and renal tubular concentrating defects. Diabetes insipidus (DI) results in the loss of large amounts of dilute urine from the loss of concentrating ability in the distal nephron. DI may be central (lack of ADH secretion from the pituitary) or nephrogenic (lack of responsiveness to circulating ADH) (Box 123-4). Central DI is seen with CNS disease or surgery involving the hypothalamus and pituitary. Common mechanisms include stroke, infection, tumor, trauma, and systemic diseases. Nephrogenic DI can be caused by congenital disease, renal failure, sickle cell anemia, hypercalcemia, hypokalemia, and certain drugs, including lithium, cisplatin, amphotericin B, aminoglycosides, and demeclocycline. With a normal thirst mechanism and access to water, DI patients are generally able to maintain near-normal serum levels.[6,7] However, they quickly become hypernatremic when removed from a water source, and any sodium-containing intravenous fluids will exacerbate the problem.

BOX 123-3. Causes of Hypernatremia

I. Reduced water intake
   A. Disorders of thirst perception
   B. Inability to obtain water
      1. Depressed mentation
      2. Intubated patient
II. Increased water loss
   A. Gastrointestinal
      1. Vomiting, diarrhea
      2. Nasogastric suctioning
      3. Third spacing
   B. Renal
      1. Tubular concentrating defects
      2. Osmotic diuresis (e.g., hyperglycemia, mannitol)
      3. Diabetes insipidus
      4. Relief of urinary obstruction
   C. Dermal
      1. Excessive sweating
      2. Severe burns
   D. Hyperventilation
III. Gain of sodium
   A. Exogenous sodium intake
      1. Salt tablets
      2. Sodium bicarbonate
      3. Hypertonic saline solutions
      4. Improper formula preparation
      5. Salt water drowning
      6. Hypertonic renal dialysate
   B. Increased sodium reabsorption
      1. Hyperaldosteronism
      2. Cushing's disease
      3. Exogenous corticosteroids
      4. Congenital adrenal hyperplasia

BOX 123-4. Causes of Diabetes Insipidus

Central
Idiopathic
Head trauma
Suprasellar/infrasellar tumors (e.g., craniopharyngioma)
Cerebral hemorrhage
CNS infections (e.g., meningitis, encephalitis)
Granulomatous disorders (e.g., tuberculosis, sarcoid, Wegener's, histiocytosis)

Nephrogenic
Congenital renal disorders
Obstructive uropathy
Renal dysplasia
Polycystic disease

Systemic Disease with Renal Involvement
Sickle cell disease
Sarcoidosis
Amyloidosis

Drugs
Amphotericin B
Phenytoin
Lithium
Aminoglycosides
Methoxyflurane

CNS, central nervous system.

Excessive sodium intake, accidentally, intentionally, or iatrogenically, can cause hypernatremia in the absence of corresponding intake of water. Because the kidney can usually excrete an increased sodium load effectively, most cases are seen in patients with renal insufficiency. Examples include hypertonic enteral or parenteral nutritional fluids, saline absorption, administration of large amounts of sodium bicarbonate, seawater drowning, and salt ingestion.[6] The administration of ticarcillin and carbenicillin, which contain large amounts of sodium chloride, is another potential cause.

Clinical Features

In cases of hypernatremia, free water is lost in excess of sodium, so patients may be significantly dehydrated before signs of volume depletion are evident. Total free water deficits are often underestimated in this setting. Common symptoms include anorexia, nausea, vomiting, fatigue, and irritability.[3] Physical findings include lethargy, confusion, stupor, coma, muscle twitching, hyperreflexia, spasticity, tremor, ataxia, or focal findings such as hemiparesis or extensor plantar reflexes.

Management

Hypovolemic Hypernatremia
The primary goals in the emergency management of hypovolemic hypernatremia are to restore volume deficits and to maintain organ perfusion. Treatment should be initiated with an infusion of isotonic saline solution (0.9% NaCl). Once the patient is hemodynamically stable, the remaining free water deficits can be replaced.

Euvolemic Hypernatremia
Euvolemic hypernatremic patients may have had either hypotonic fluid losses (e.g., with DI) or hypertonic fluid losses from increased insensible fluid loss. Patients with DI generally have a low urine specific gravity (<1.005) and low urine osmolality. The DI is usually the result of a previously recognized disorder, and patients can usually maintain their serum osmolality if they have access to water. Treatment is with oral fluids or 0.45% saline. Patients with central DI require parenteral or intranasal vasopressin. The response to vasopressin can be monitored by checking urine osmolality, urine specific gravity, and serum electrolytes.[7]

Hypervolemic Hypernatremia
The treatment of hypervolemic hypernatremia should focus on increasing renal sodium excretion while maintaining free water intake. A strategy of diuretic administration (e.g., furosemide) followed by infusion of hypotonic fluids will gradually restore the serum sodium to the normal range. Dialysis may be needed for patients with renal failure.

Symptomatic Hypernatremia
Patients with acute hypernatremia usually tolerate rapid correction of free water deficits. On the other hand, aggressive treatment of chronic hypernatremia

with hypotonic fluids may result in life-threatening complications. It is recommended that in this setting free water deficits be corrected over at least a 48-hour period. When hypernatremia develops over days, brain cells produce osmotic substances (*idiogenic osmoles*) that hold water in the cell and help maintain cellular volume and tonicity.[6] Overzealous administration of hypotonic fluids may cause rapid shifts of water into brain cells, cellular swelling, and cerebral edema.

Assuming only loss of free water, the free water deficit can be calculated as follows:

$$\text{Water deficit (L)} = \text{total body weight (kg)} \times$$
$$0.5(L^{water}/kg) \times \left(\frac{\text{plasma sodium mEq/L}}{140\ \text{mEq/L}} - 1 \right)$$

POTASSIUM

Normal Physiology

The relative concentrations of potassium in the intracellular fluid and extracellular fluid are the major determinants of the normal osmotic and electrochemical gradients of all living cells. Precisely controlled transcellular movement of potassium in excitable tissues is required for neuronal transmission, cardiac conduction, and excitation-contraction coupling. Potassium is also important for acid-base balance; the exchange of potassium ions (K^+) and hydrogen ions (H^+) across the cell membrane serves as a first-line buffering system during acute acidosis and alkalosis. Potassium is also required for intracellular glucose metabolism, oxidative phosphorylation, and protein synthesis.[8]

The adult human body contains between 2500 and 3500 mmol of potassium, 98% of which is found in the intracellular compartment. For this reason, the serum potassium level is not an accurate indicator of total potassium stores. The normal range of the serum potassium concentration is 3.5 to 5.0 mEq/L.[9]

Ingested potassium is absorbed in the small intestine through passive transport mechanisms. Renal excretion is the major route of potassium elimination; less than 8% of losses occur in the feces and sweat. In the kidneys, 90% of the filtered load of potassium is reabsorbed in the proximal tubule, and potassium balance is determined by the handling of the cation in the distal nephron. The Na$^+$,K$^+$-ATPase pump transports potassium from the serum into distal tubular cells against a concentration gradient. Potassium then moves passively into the tubular lumen in exchange for sodium and is excreted in the urine. When the serum potassium level increases, pump activity increases and renal potassium excretion increases. When the serum potassium level falls, the pump is less active and excretion decreases. Aldosterone also controls potassium homeostasis. Increased aldosterone release causes retention of sodium and excretion of potassium at the distal tubule. Decreased aldosterone release or inhibition of aldosterone (by drugs such as angiotensin-converting enzyme inhibitors or spironolactone) promotes potas-

sium retention. Acidosis and alkalosis also affect renal potassium handling. Acidosis promotes secretion of H^+ into the distal tubule, with retention of potassium, and alkalosis tends to favor renal potassium excretion.[10]

The serum potassium level depends on the distribution of potassium between the serum and cells, as well as the balance between potassium intake and excretion. Acute decreases in the plasma pH cause potassium to shift out of the cell in exchange for H^+. Conversely, alkalosis promotes movement of extracellular potassium into the cell in exchange for intracellular H^+. In general, a change of 0.1 pH unit causes an inverse change of approximately 0.6 mEq in the serum potassium. Respiratory acid-base disturbances affect serum potassium in the same manner as metabolic changes, but not as predictably. Potassium levels are also influenced by hormones and hormone receptor stimulation. Insulin increases cellular potassium uptake by means of the Na$^+$,K$^+$-ATPase pump. Insulin release is stimulated by hyperkalemia, and hypokalemia inhibits insulin release. α-Adrenergic stimulation promotes hyperkalemia, and β-stimulation causes uptake of potassium into cells.[9]

Hypokalemia

Principles of Disease

Hypokalemia is relatively common, although life-threatening hypokalemia is much less common.[10] Hypokalemia may be the result of decreased potassium intake, increased potassium excretion, or transcellular potassium shifts (Box 123-5).

Hypokalemia resulting from decreased dietary intake is rare. However, when poor intake is combined with other factors (e.g., vomiting or diarrhea, high insulin or aldosterone levels), severe hypokalemia can result. Patients suffering from prolonged starvation may become hypokalemic when they are fed because insulin secretion and increased cellular uptake cause potassium to move into cells.

Pronounced renal or gastrointestinal potassium losses can result in hypokalemia. Diuretic therapy, the most common cause of hypokalemia in clinical practice, increases sodium delivery to the distal tubule, promoting potassium excretion. Associated volume depletion and high levels of aldosterone cause K^+ and H^+ excretion and may worsen hypokalemia. In addition, alkalosis from H^+ excretion promotes cellular potassium uptake, further lowering the serum potassium level.[10]

Other disorders can cause significant renal potassium loss. These include osmotic diuresis, high mineralocorticoid states, magnesium depletion, and high urinary concentrations of anions such as penicillin. Intrinsic renal causes of potassium loss include renal tubular acidosis (RTA), chronic interstitial disease, and drugs that affect tubular potassium reabsorption. RTA type 1 is caused by a defect in H^+ secretion in the distal tubule, and RTA type 2 is associated with a similar defect in the proximal tubule. In both cases, increased potassium excretion at the distal tubule is the result. Other causes of increased renal potassium loss include hypercalcemia, toxins (e.g., cisplatin, amphotericin B,

BOX 123-5. Causes of Hypokalemia

I. Decreased intake
   A. Decreased dietary potassium
   B. Impaired absorption of potassium
   C. Clay ingestion
   D. Kayexalate
II. Increased loss
   A. Renal
      1. Hyperaldosteronism
         a. Primary
            1. Conn's syndrome
            2. Adrenal hyperplasia
         b. Secondary
            1. Congestive heart failure
            2. Cirrhosis
            3. Nephrotic syndrome
            4. Dehydration
         c. Bartter's syndrome
      2. Glycyrrhizic acid (licorice, chewing tobacco)
      3. Excessive adrenocorticosteroids
         a. Cushing's syndrome
         b. Steroid therapy
         c. Adrenogenital syndrome
      4. Renal tubular defects
         a. Renal tubular acidosis
         b. Obstructive uropathy
         c. Salt-wasting nephropathy
      5. Drugs
         a. Diuretics
         b. Aminoglycosides
         c. Mannitol
         d. Amphotericin B
         e. Cisplatin
         f. Carbenicillin
   B. Gastrointestinal
      1. Vomiting
      2. Nasogastric suction
      3. Diarrhea
      4. Malabsorption
      5. Ileostomy
      6. Villous adenoma
      7. Laxative abuse
   C. Increased losses from skin
      1. Excessive sweating
      2. Burns
III. Transcellular shifts
   A. Alkalosis
      1. Vomiting
      2. Diuretics
      3. Hyperventilation
      4. Bicarbonate therapy
   B. Insulin
      1. Exogenous
      2. Endogenous response to glucose
   C. β_2-Agonists (albuterol, terbutaline, epinephrine)
   D. Hypokalemic periodic paralysis
      1. Familial
      2. Thyrotoxic
IV. Miscellaneous
   A. Anabolic state
   B. Intravenous hyperalimentation
   C. Treatment of megaloblastic anemia
   D. Acute mountain sickness

aminoglycosides), leukemia, interstitial nephritis, and postobstructive diuresis.

Primary hyperaldosteronism (Conn's syndrome), which is typically caused by adrenal adenoma, is characterized by hypertension and hypokalemia.[11] Secondary hyperaldosteronism, due to increased renin release, causes hypokalemia in the face of volume depletion as potassium is exchanged for sodium at the distal tubule. In Bartter's syndrome, a disorder causing hyperplasia of the juxtaglomerular apparatus and hyperreninism, patients typically have weakness and hypokalemia.

Gastrointestinal losses of potassium occur in patients with protracted vomiting and diarrhea. Vomiting itself does not cause potassium loss; rather, hypokalemia results from hypovolemia, secondary hyperaldosteronism, and alkalosis. Diarrhea can cause hypokalemia from losses in the stool and secondary hyperaldosteronism. Patients with villous adenomas classically have tremendous losses of potassium from diarrheal fluid.

Loss of potassium from the skin in sufficient quantities to cause hypokalemia is unusual unless the patient has experienced extreme sweating or is a victim of extensive burns or toxic epidermal necrolysis.[10]

Hypokalemia may result from transcellular potassium shifts, most often because of alterations in acid-base balance. As mentioned, acidosis causes potassium to move out of the cell in exchange for H^+, and the reverse is true for alkalosis. Although acidosis is typically associated with hyperkalemia, acidosis may also be associated with hypokalemia in the presence of increased urinary potassium losses (e.g., diabetic ketoacidosis). β-Receptor stimulation is another common cause of hypokalemia resulting from transcellular shifts. In the emergency department, this is most likely to occur in the patient receiving large doses of β-agonists for the treatment of asthma or chronic obstructive pulmonary disease.[12,13]

The periodic paralyses are associated with varying serum potassium levels, including hypokalemia. They often are associated with thyroid disease and are distinguished by symmetric proximal weakness.[14]

Clinical Features

Hypokalemia can affect the neuromuscular, cardiovascular, gastrointestinal, and renal systems, as well as acid-base balance. Signs and symptoms of neuromuscular dysfunction usually occur when the serum potassium level is less than 2.5 mEq/L.[15] CNS signs include lethargy, depression, irritability, and confusion. Peripheral manifestations include paresthesias, depressed deep tendon reflexes, fasciculations, myalgias, and prominent muscle weakness. Muscular paralysis can occur with serum levels below 2.0 mEq/L.

Patients with severe hypokalemia may develop rhabdomyolysis because of impaired energy metabolism, membrane pump dysfunction, and local muscle ischemia.[16] Potassium is released from injured muscle, so the responsible hypokalemia may not be clinically evident, with serum levels normal or even elevated.

Cardiovascular manifestations of hypokalemia include palpitations, postural hypotension, ectopy, and dysrhythmias. First- and second-degree heart block, atrial fibrillation, paroxysmal ventricular contractions, ventricular fibrillation, and asystole have all been reported. The electrocardiogram (ECG) shows flattening of T waves, ST-segment depression, and the appearance of U waves.[16]

Hypokalemia impairs intestinal smooth muscle activity and may cause nausea, vomiting, and abdominal distention. Severe hypokalemia may produce paralytic ileus.[10] The renal manifestations of hypokalemia include polyuria, polydipsia, and impaired ability to concentrate urine or excrete an acid load.

The effect of hypokalemia on acid-base balance is to promote metabolic alkalosis. In response to a low serum potassium level, potassium moves out of the cell in exchange for H^+, causing an extracellular alkalosis and an intracellular acidosis. In response to the drop in intracellular pH, renal tubular cells excrete H^+, leading to paradoxical aciduria and exacerbating the extracellular alkalosis.

Management

Because potassium is an intracellular cation, a low serum potassium level reflects a much greater total potassium deficit. In the absence of acute shifts caused by acid-base disturbances, a decrease of the serum potassium by 1.0 mEq/L may reflect a 370-mEq deficit of total potassium. Because up to 50% of administered potassium is excreted in the urine, correction of large deficits may require several days.

Whenever possible, oral therapy is preferable to intravenous therapy because the risk of hyperkalemia is significantly less. However, patients with prominent symptoms (e.g., dysrhythmias) and those who are unable to tolerate oral supplements should receive intravenous potassium replacement. Intravenous potassium is usually given at a rate of 10 to 20 mEq/hr, but larger doses can be given to patients with severe depletion or severely symptomatic hypokalemia (e.g., respiratory muscle weakness). Doses greater than 20 mEq/hr should be given in a monitored setting through a large-bore peripheral venous catheter or a central venous access site.[17]

Burning at the infusion site is the most common side effect of intravenous potassium administration. Slowing the rate of infusion will usually decrease venous irritation. The most important potential risk of intravenous potassium administration is acute hyperkalemia, which is most likely in patients with renal insufficiency. If dysrhythmias (e.g., frequent premature ventricular contractions, heart block, tachycardia,

widening of the QRS complex) develop, the potassium infusion should be discontinued immediately.

Oral potassium is preferred for mild hypokalemia. Several oral preparations are available in liquid or tablet form. Although liquid preparations are typically better absorbed, matrix tablets are often better tolerated. Hypokalemia can be effectively corrected with oral supplements, and large amounts of oral potassium can be given to increase serum levels rapidly.

Potassium can be given as the chloride salt in most patients. Potassium phosphate, rather than potassium chloride, can be given if there is associated hypophosphatemia (e.g., in diabetic ketoacidosis). Patients with distal RTA should be treated with potassium bicarbonate, potassium citrate, or potassium gluconate, which provide both potassium and base equivalents. The hypokalemia of proximal RTA may be better treated with potassium chloride because the administered base cannot be reabsorbed well proximally and can obligate potassium loss when it reaches the distal tubule.

Hyperkalemia

Principles of Disease

Hyperkalemia may be the result of increased potassium intake, enhanced potassium absorption, impaired potassium excretion, or shifts of potassium out of cells into the serum (Box 123-6).

When faced with a report of a high serum potassium level, the emergency physician should first consider the possibility of laboratory error. Hemolysis during phlebotomy, as can occur when blood is obtained with a small needle or sampled in a high-vacuum tube, releases potassium into the sample and causes a spuriously high potassium level to be measured. Laboratory technicians usually note the presence of pink serum, indicating hemolysis. Pseudohyperkalemia can also occur when potassium is released from platelets in patients with severe thrombocytosis or from leukocytes in patients with extreme leukocytosis.[18]

Hyperkalemia rarely results from increased potassium intake. This is more common when potassium supplements are inadvertently taken by patients with renal insufficiency or in those taking a potassium-sparing diuretic or an angiotensin-converting enzyme inhibitor.[18] Parenteral medications such as penicillin and carbenicillin, as well as transfused blood, also contain significant amounts of potassium and can precipitate hyperkalemia.

Renal insufficiency (i.e., decreased GFR), defects in tubular potassium secretion, or hypoaldosteronism can cause hyperkalemia. As GFR decreases to approximately 5 to 15 mL/min, excretion of the normal daily potassium load is impaired. Defects in tubular potassium excretion are associated with a number of conditions. Hypoaldosteronism may be the result of causes as varied as RTA type 4, Addison's disease, nonsteroidal anti-inflammatory drugs, and angiotensin-converting enzyme inhibitors.

Transcellular potassium shifts (e.g., acute acidosis, β-receptor antagonism) are another major cause of hyper-

BOX 123-6. Causes of Hyperkalemia

I. Pseudohyperkalemia
   A. Hemolysis of sample
   B. Thrombocytosis
   C. Leukocytosis
   D. Laboratory error
II. Increased potassium intake and absorption
   A. Potassium supplements (oral and parenteral)
   B. Dietary (salt substitutes)
   C. Stored blood
   D. Potassium-containing medications
III. Impaired renal excretion
   A. Acute renal failure
   B. Chronic renal failure
   C. Tubular defect in potassium secretion
      1. Renal allograft
      2. Analgesic nephropathy
      3. Sickle cell disease
      4. Obstructive uropathy
      5. Interstitial nephritis
      6. Chronic pyelonephritis
      7. Potassium-sparing diuretics
      8. Miscellaneous (lead, systemic lupus erythematosus, pseudohypoaldosteronism)
   D. Hypoaldosteronism
      1. Primary (Addison's disease)
      2. Secondary
         a. Hyporeninemic hypoaldosteronism (renal tubular acidosis type 4)
         b. Congenital adrenal hyperplasia
         c. Drug induced
            i. Nonsteroidal anti-inflammatory drugs
            ii. Angiotensin-converting enzyme
            iii. Heparin
            iv. Cyclosporine
IV. Transcellular shifts
   A. Acidosis
   B. Hypertonicity
   C. Insulin deficiency
   D. Drugs
      1. β-Blockers
      2. Digitalis toxicity
      3. Succinylcholine
   E. Exercise
   F. Hyperkalemic periodic paralysis
V. Cellular injury
   A. Rhabdomyolysis
   B. Severe intravascular hemolysis
   C. Acute tumor lysis syndrome
   D. Burns and crush injuries

kalemia. Periodic paralysis is an inherited disorder characterized by hyperkalemia caused by cellular efflux of potassium associated with stressors such as exercise, infection, and diet. Drugs may also be the cause of transcellular potassium shifts. Digitalis poisons the Na^+,K^+-ATPase pump, with resultant hyperkalemia in severe cases. Succinylcholine causes transient potassium efflux because of depolarization of the muscle cell membrane. High-dose trimethoprim-sulfamethoxazole has also been implicated in hyperkalemia, especially with concomitant renal insufficiency.[19,20]

Life-threatening hyperkalemia may result when large amounts of potassium are released from damaged cells. Rhabdomyolysis, tumor cell necrosis, and hemolysis are important causes.[15] Acute renal failure that may be associated with these conditions impairs potassium excretion, further exacerbating endogenous hyperkalemia.

Clinical Features

Cardiovascular and neurologic dysfunction are the primary manifestations of hyperkalemia.[18] Patients may have a variety of dysrhythmias, including second- and third-degree heart block, wide-complex tachycardia, ventricular fibrillation, and even asystole. The ECG can provide valuable clues to the presence of hyperkalemia. As potassium levels rise, peaked T waves are the first characteristic manifestation. Further rises are associated with progressive ECG changes, including loss of P waves and widening and slurring of the QRS complex. Eventually, the tracing assumes a sine wave appearance, followed by ventricular fibrillation or asystole.

Concomitant alkalosis, hypernatremia, or hypercalcemia antagonizes the membrane effects of hyperkalemia and may delay or diminish the characteristic ECG findings.

Neuromuscular signs and symptoms of hyperkalemia include muscle cramps, weakness, paralysis, paresthesias, tetany, and focal neurologic deficits, but these are rarely specific enough to suggest the diagnosis in themselves.[15,16]

Management

The treatment of hyperkalemia includes cardiovascular monitoring, administration of calcium chloride or gluconate to treat hemodynamic instability, initiation of measures to lower serum potassium concentration, and correction of the underlying cause.

All patients with suspected hyperkalemia should be on a cardiac monitor with attention to the morphology of the T waves and QRS complex. Peaked T waves, loss of P waves, slurring of the QRS, and second- or third-degree heart block all suggest hyperkalemia and are indications for immediate therapy. Treatment of the hyperkalemic patient is directed toward antagonism of the membrane effects of hyperkalemia, promotion of transcellular potassium shifts, and removal of potassium from the body.

Calcium Chloride or Gluconate

Immediate antagonism of potassium at the cardiac membrane is achieved with intravenous administration of calcium chloride or gluconate. This is indicated in patients with unstable dysrhythmia or hypotension. Several ampules of calcium (10 mL of 10% solution) may be required.[16,18] Because of the brief duration of action (approximately 20 to 40 minutes), other measures should also be instituted promptly.[18]

Sodium Bicarbonate

Sodium bicarbonate infusion promotes a shift of potassium into cells. One ampule (44 mEq) should be given by slow intravenous push over 5 to 15 minutes. The duration of action is approximately 2 hours. Sodium bicarbonate should be used with caution when hypertonicity, volume overload, or alkalosis poses a risk to the patient. Bicarbonate therapy is less efficacious than insulin or albuterol.[21,22]

Glucose and Insulin

Cellular uptake of potassium can also be induced with a regimen of intravenous glucose and insulin. Regular insulin (10-20 U) can be given by bolus infusion. Dextrose should be administered to euglycemic and diabetic patients with a blood glucose level below 250 mg/dL to prevent hypoglycemia. This combination lasts 4 to 6 hours.[18] Rapid infusion of hypertonic glucose solution may transiently exacerbate hyperkalemia by its osmotic effect on cells.

β₂-Agonists

The known effect of β_2-agonists to cause movement of potassium into cells can be harnessed to lower the serum potassium level acutely. Treatment with nebulized albuterol (5-20 mg) lowers the serum potassium level for at least 2 hours.[22,23]

Exchange Resins

Definitive treatment for hyperkalemia remains the removal of potassium from the body. Exchange resins (e.g., sodium polystyrene sulfonate [Kayexalate]) and hemodialysis are two such options. Given orally or rectally, each gram of Kayexalate can remove approximately 1.0 mEq of potassium. An oral dose of 20 g of Kayexalate in a sorbitol produces effects in 1 to 2 hours. Rectal enemas of 50 g of Kayexalate, retained for 30 minutes, work in approximately 30 minutes. Kayexalate should be used with caution in patients with poor cardiovascular reserve because of the potential to exacerbate volume overload.

Dialysis

Hemodialysis corrects hyperkalemia rapidly, and consultation with a nephrologist is indicated in the unstable hyperkalemic patient with newly diagnosed or chronic renal failure. Hyperkalemia resulting from severe rhabdomyolysis is difficult to treat with the usual measures and also mandates consultation for emergency dialysis. Dialysis removes potassium from the blood only, and subsequent shifts of intracellular potassium may cause rebound hyperkalemia. Dialysis can be effective in treating hyperkalemia-induced cardiac arrest.[24]

Underlying Cause

Treatment of any underlying causative disorder should be initiated at the same time as therapy for hyperkalemia. This may include the treatment of rhabdomy-

olysis with fluids and bicarbonate; treatment of Addison's disease with corticosteroids, intravenous fluids, and glucose; treatment of digitalis toxicity with digoxin-binding antibodies; or discontinuation of drugs that may have precipitated hyperkalemia.

Patients with hyperkalemia should be admitted to a monitored bed, with care provided by a clinician skilled in the treatment of electrolyte disorders.

CALCIUM

Normal Physiology

Hundreds of enzymatic reactions are mediated by changes in intracellular calcium. Cellular growth and reproduction, membrane integrity, receptor activation, neurotransmission, glandular secretion, enzyme activation, muscle contraction, cardiac contractility, platelet aggregation, and immune function all depend on the precise regulation of free calcium. Evidence also indicates that cellular injury and ultimately cell death are mediated by changes in free intracellular calcium.[25]

The adult human body contains approximately 1200 g of calcium, with more than 99% in the mineral component of bone. The remaining 1% is distributed in three different plasma fractions: (1) approximately 50% is bound to serum proteins, primarily albumin; (2) 10% is complexed with serum anions (phosphate, bicarbonate, citrate, lactate); and (3) 40% is in the free ionized state. Ionized calcium is the physiologically active form, and concentrations are tightly regulated by the endocrine system.

Dietary calcium is absorbed in the proximal intestine through both active and passive processes. Absorption is enhanced by the action of vitamin D. In the kidneys, 99% of the filtered load of calcium is reabsorbed. Approximately 90% of calcium reabsorption occurs passively in the proximal tubule and loop of Henle. The remaining 10% occurs in the distal tubule under the control of *parathyroid hormone* (PTH, parathormone). A fall in free serum calcium stimulates the release of PTH, which in turn increases reabsorption. PTH also mediates the hydroxylation of vitamin D to its active form, 1,25-dihydroxycholecalciferol (1,25-DHCC).

The skeleton acts as a calcium pool that buffers acute changes in serum concentration. When the serum calcium level falls, PTH stimulates an increase in bone turnover and the release of calcium into the serum. A rise in serum calcium suppresses PTH production and causes the release of calcitonin. *Calcitonin* decreases osteoclastic activity and enhances skeletal deposition of calcium.

The serum calcium level reflects the net outcome of several processes. On one hand, intestinal absorption and bone resorption add calcium to the blood; on the other, calcium is lost from the blood by renal excretion, skeletal uptake, or abnormal deposition in soft tissues. A decrease in the serum ionized calcium activates the PTH–vitamin D system to increase the entry of calcium into the blood from the bone and gastrointestinal tract.

A rise in the serum calcium level suppresses the PTH–vitamin D system and increases the release of calcitonin, which decreases calcium entry into the blood.

Most hospital laboratories measure total serum calcium concentrations. Normal values range from 8.5 to 10.5 mg/dL. However, the total serum calcium is often a poor indicator of the ionized calcium status. Several factors influence the measurement of the total serum calcium, regardless of the ionized calcium. Alterations in serum protein concentrations (primarily albumin) affect the total calcium. A decrease in albumin concentration will lower the measured serum calcium, and an increase will raise it. Physiologically, this change is not of significance because the ionized calcium remains unchanged. A corrected serum calcium level that accounts for changes in serum albumin concentrations can be calculated as follows:

$$\text{Corrected calcium} = \text{serum calcium (mg/dL)} + 0.8[4 - \text{serum albumin (g/dL)}]$$

This formula is only an estimate, and the ionized calcium should be measured whenever hypocalcemia is suspected. Blood gas analyzers can measure ionized calcium from a sample of blood or serum. The normal range is 1.00 to 1.15 mmol/L.

Changes in acid-base status influence the ratio of bound to ionized calcium without altering the total measured calcium. Acidosis decreases calcium binding to albumin, and alkalosis increases binding. Thus, acute changes in blood pH may have important physiologic effects by changing the ionized calcium level even when the total serum calcium level remains unchanged.[25]

Hypocalcemia

Principles of Disease

The causes of ionized hypocalcemia are numerous (Box 123-7) and can be divided into disorders causing PTH insufficiency, vitamin D insufficiency, PTH resistance states, and calcium chelation.

Parathyroid Hormone Insufficiency

Parathyroid hormone insufficiency can be caused by either primary or secondary hypoparathyroidism. Primary hypoparathyroidism is rare and is usually congenital. Maternal hyperparathyroidism may result in fetal parathyroid hypoplasia and transient hypoparathyroidism.

Secondary hypoparathyroidism is more common and is most often iatrogenic, resulting from inadvertent removal of the parathyroid glands or disruption of the vascular supply during parathyroid, thyroid, or carotid surgery. Permanent hypocalcemia is the usual consequence. Excision of a functional parathyroid adenoma, leaving only the chronically suppressed but otherwise unaffected parathyroid tissue, causes hypocalcemia that usually resolves over several days. Metastatic carcinoma or infiltrative disorders (e.g., hemochromatosis, sarcoidosis, Wilson's disease) may destroy parathyroid tissue and cause hypocalcemia. Both severe hypomag-

---

BOX 123-7. Causes of Hypocalcemia

I. Parathyroid hormone insufficiency
   A. Primary hypoparathyroidism
      1. Congenital syndromes
      2. Maternal hyperparathyroidism
   B. Secondary hypoparathyroidism
      1. Neck surgery
      2. Metastatic carcinoma
      3. Infiltrative disorders
      4. Hypomagnesemia, hypermagnesemia
      5. Sepsis
      6. Pancreatitis
      7. Burns
      8. Drugs (chemotherapeutics, ethanol, cimetidine)
II. Vitamin D insufficiency
   A. Congenital rickets
   B. Malnutrition
   C. Malabsorption
   D. Liver disease
   E. Renal disease
      1. Acute and chronic renal failure
      2. Nephrotic syndrome
   F. Hypomagnesemia
   G. Sepsis
   H. Anticonvulsants (phenytoin, primidone)
III. Parathyroid hormone resistance states (pseudohypoparathyroidism)
IV. Calcium chelation
   A. Hyperphosphatemia
   B. Citrate
   C. Free fatty acids
   D. Alkalosis
   E. Fluoride poisoning

---

nesemia and severe hypermagnesemia can impair PTH release. Drugs that may suppress parathyroid function include chemotherapeutic agents, cimetidine, and ethanol.

Vitamin D Deficiency

Vitamin D deficiency can result in hypocalcemia because of decreased gastrointestinal calcium absorption. Nutritional vitamin D deficiency is rare in the United States because of the fortification of milk but can occur when exposure to sunlight is limited, especially in elderly, chronically ill, and debilitated patients. Children of mothers with vitamin D deficiency may be born with congenital rickets. Characteristic findings include hypocalcemia, hypophosphatemia, and specific radiographic findings (widening of the distal radius and ulna, craniotabes). Vitamin D insufficiency resulting from intestinal malabsorption can occur in patients with small bowel or biliary disease or pancreatic exocrine failure. Cholestyramine can also prevent adequate vitamin D absorption. Once absorbed, vitamin D is hydroxylated in the liver and kidney to its active form, 1,25-DHCC. Hepatic disease and renal disease may lead to inadequate activation of the vitamin. Hypercatabolism of vitamin D may occur in association with agents that stimulate the hepatic microsomal oxidase system, such as the anticonvulsants phenytoin and primidone.

Parathyroid Hormone Resistance States

Parathyroid hormone resistance states are termed *pseudohypoparathyroidism.* These rare familial syndromes are characterized by renal unresponsiveness to PTH and resultant parathyroid hyperplasia.[26] Differentiation from hypoparathyroidism is based on elevated PTH levels and a lack of increase in urinary cyclic adenosine monophosphate after PTH administration.

Hypocalcemia is common in patients with chronic renal failure. This results from vitamin D deficiency, impaired responsiveness to PTH, and phosphate retention. Generally, these patients are asymptomatic, possibly because of a protective effect of systemic acidosis. However, rapid correction of metabolic acidosis with exogenous sodium bicarbonate can precipitate severe hypocalcemia, often causing tetany and seizures.

Calcium Chelation

Calcium complexes with several different substances in serum, including proteins, fatty acids, and anions. Increases in the concentration of these substances may thus result in ionized hypocalcemia. Citrate is used as a blood preservative and anticoagulant. The citrate load associated with massive blood transfusion (>6 U) causes hypocalcemia in up to 94% of patients.[27] Hypocalcemia is usually short-lived, and ionized calcium levels return to normal shortly after transfusion. Because citrate is metabolized by temperature-dependent enzymes in tissues and excreted by the liver, hypothermia and hepatic failure are important risk factors for protracted hypocalcemia after blood transfusion. Citrate is also a constituent of radiocontrast material, and hypocalcemia has been associated with the administration of these agents.

Exogenous administration of phosphate and endogenous hyperphosphatemia (e.g., with acute renal failure, rhabdomyolysis, or tumor lysis syndrome) are well-known causes of hypocalcemia.[28] Exogenous bicarbonate also complexes with calcium and may cause symptomatic hypocalcemia. Alkalosis, either metabolic or respiratory, enhances the binding of calcium to serum proteins, resulting in ionized hypocalcemia. Free fatty acids liberated in various conditions (e.g., acute pancreatitis, hyperadrenergic states, acute ethanol ingestion) can chelate free calcium to form calcium soaps. Fluoride poisoning can also cause hypocalcemia. This may occur after exposure to hydrofluoric acid or ammonium bifluoride, components of many household cleaners and rust removers. These compounds release free fluoride ion, a direct cellular toxin that binds calcium, forming calcium fluoride. Numerous cases of severe hypocalcemia, cardiac dysrhythmias, and death have been reported after ingestion, inhalation, or cutaneous exposure to these products.

Clinical Features

The clinical manifestations of hypocalcemia depend not only on the serum level but also on the rapidity with which it declines. Although the signs and symptoms of hypocalcemia are numerous (Box 123-8), the effects on neuromuscular function predominate.

BOX 123-8. Clinical Features of Hypocalcemia

Neuromuscular
Paresthesias
Muscle weakness
Muscle spasm
Tetany
Chvostek's and Trousseau's signs
Hyperreflexia
Seizures

Cardiovascular
Bradycardia
Hypotension
Cardiac arrest

Digitalis insensitivity
QT prolongation

Pulmonary
Bronchospasm
Laryngeal spasm

Psychiatric
Anxiety
Depression
Irritability
Confusion
Psychosis
Dementia

A declining serum calcium level is associated with progressive neuromuscular hyperexcitability. CNS manifestations include depression, irritability, confusion, and focal or generalized seizures. Peripheral nervous system manifestations include perioral paresthesias, muscle weakness and cramps, fasciculations, and tetany.[25] Latent tetany can often be demonstrated by eliciting Chvostek's or Trousseau's sign. *Chvostek's sign* is elicited by tapping over the facial nerve and causing twitching of the ipsilateral facial muscles. *Trousseau's sign* describes carpal spasm in response to inflation of an arm blood pressure cuff to 20 mm Hg above systolic blood pressure for 3 minutes.

Severe hypocalcemia causes a decrease in myocardial contractility and, rarely, bradycardia, hypotension, and symptomatic congestive heart failure. Patients with preexisting cardiac dysfunction and those taking digoxin or diuretics are especially at risk. The ECG may demonstrate QT prolongation, and an inverse relationship exists between the serum calcium level and the QT interval. However, the ECG is a poor predictor of hypocalcemia and should not be used to rule in or rule out this disorder.

Bronchospasm and laryngeal spasm occur rarely. Symptoms and signs ranging from anxiety and depression to psychosis and dementia can be seen.

Management

In patients with suspected hypocalcemia or a documented low total serum calcium level, the first step in management should be verification of true ionized hypocalcemia. When hypocalcemia is the presumed cause of tetany, seizures, hypotension, or dysrhythmias, it may be appropriate to initiate treatment before the ionized calcium level is available. All patients with symptomatic hypocalcemia should be treated with parenteral calcium. Two different formulations are readily available in most emergency departments: (1) 10-mL ampules of 10% calcium chloride, which contain 360 mg of elemental calcium, and (2) 10-mL ampules of 10% calcium gluconate, which contain 93 mg of elemental calcium. For the adult patient, the recommended initial dose is 100 to 300 mg of elemental calcium given as calcium chloride or calcium gluconate. This dose of calcium will increase the serum ionized calcium level for only a short time (1-2 hours) and should be followed by repeated doses or an infusion at a rate of 0.5 to 2 mg/kg/hr.[25] For neonates, infants, and children, the recommended initial dose is 0.5 to 1.0 mL/kg of 10% calcium gluconate over 5 minutes.[26]

The most common side effects of intravenous calcium administration are hypertension, nausea, vomiting, and flushing. Bradycardia and heart block occur in rare cases. Patients receiving intravenous calcium should be placed on a cardiac monitor, and administration should be discontinued if bradycardia ensues. Calcium should be administered with extra caution in patients taking digoxin because it may precipitate (or exacerbate) digoxin-induced cardiotoxicity. Because calcium can cause severe tissue irritation and necrosis if it extravasates, it should always be given through a well-functioning catheter. Whenever possible, calcium chloride should be diluted in 5% dextrose in water (D5W).[25,26]

Symptoms refractory to appropriate doses of calcium may be caused by coexisting hypomagnesemia. In patients with normal renal function, administration of 2 to 4 g of 10% magnesium sulfate should be considered.

Patients with asymptomatic hypocalcemia can be treated with oral calcium supplements. Available preparations include calcium ascorbate, calcium gluconate, and calcium lactate. Most patients require 1 to 4 g of elemental calcium daily in divided doses.

Hypercalcemia

Principles of Disease

Hypercalcemia is a relatively common medical disorder. Routine laboratory screening can be expected to detect hypercalcemia in 0.1% to 1.0% of patients, depending on the population being screened.[29-31] Hypercalcemia is usually mild (<12 mg/dL) and asymptomatic and rarely requires emergency treatment. Nevertheless, hypercalcemia may be an important clue to a serious underlying medical disorder. *Hypercalcemic crisis* occurs in a subset of patients who have severe hypercalcemia (usually >14 mg/dL) and is generally associated with prominent signs and symptoms. In this situation, immediate measures to lower the serum calcium level are indicated.

Although hypercalcemia has many causes, more than 90% of cases result from primary hyperparathyroidism or malignancy (Box 123-9).[32]

Primary hyperparathyroidism is the most common cause of hypercalcemia in outpatients, accounting for 25% to 50% of cases.[33] This can result from parathyroid adenoma (80%), parathyroid hyperplasia (15%), or parathyroid carcinoma (5%).[34] Hyperparathyroidism can also occur in association with other endocrine tumors as part of one of the familial syndromes of multiple endocrine adenomatosis. In primary hyperparathyroidism, the PTH level is elevated in more than 90% of cases; the remainder of patients have high-normal PTH levels that are inappropriate for the degree of hypercalcemia. An elevated PTH level leads to increased bone resorption, a relative decrease in renal calcium excretion, and increased intestinal calcium absorption. Patients typically develop hypercalcemia, phosphaturia, hypophosphatemia, and a hyperchloremic metabolic acidosis.

Malignancy is the most common cause of hypercalcemia in hospitalized patients, and hypercalcemia is the most common paraneoplastic complication of cancer. The reported prevalence of hypercalcemia in patients with cancer ranges from 15% to 60%.[35,36] A multitude of solid tumors can cause hypercalcemia, including cancers of breast, lung, colon, stomach, cervix, uterus, ovary, kidney, bladder, and head and neck. Hypercalcemia is also seen with hematologic malignancies such as multiple myeloma and lymphoma. Hypercalcemia in patients with cancer can result from several different mechanisms, including production of PTH-related protein by the tumor.[37,38] This polypeptide is homologous to PTH in its first 13 N-terminal amino acids and binds to the PTH receptor, mimicking all the actions of the hormone. PTH-related protein is secreted by solid malignancies and their metastases and is not subject to normal feedback control mechanisms.[39] Assays for PTH-related protein are available to confirm this cause of cancer-related hypercalcemia.[40] Less often, hypercalcemia results from the production of other bone-resorbing substances by the tumor (e.g., transforming growth factor-α)

BOX 123-9. Causes of Hypercalcemia

Primary hyperparathyroidism
Malignant disease
    Parathyroid hormone–related protein
    Ectopic production of 1,25-dihydroxyvitamin D
    Other bone-resorbing substances
    Osteolytic bone metastasis
Medications
    Thiazide diuretics
    Lithium
    Estrogens
    Vitamin D toxicity
    Vitamin A toxicity
    Calcium ingestion
Granulomatous disorders
    Sarcoidosis
    Tuberculosis
    Coccidioidomycosis
    Berylliosis
    Histoplasmosis
    Leprosy
Nonparathyroid endocrine disorders
    Hyperthyroidism
    Adrenal insufficiency
    Pheochromocytoma
    Acromegaly
    Vasoactive intestinal polypeptide–producing tumor
Miscellaneous
    Milk-alkali syndrome
    Immobilization
    Idiopathic hypocalcemia of infancy
    Physiologic (in the newborn)

or the local effects of osteolytic skeletal metastasis. Virtually all patients with cancer-associated hypercalcemia have low concentrations of PTH, readily distinguishing this cause of hypercalcemia from primary hyperparathyroidism.

Thiazide diuretics are associated with up to 20% of cases of hypercalcemia. These agents can increase the reabsorption of calcium in the distal convoluted tubule by as much as 70%. Hypercalcemia is typically mild, although it may be exaggerated in patients with dehydration.

Granulomatous disorders (e.g., sarcoidosis, tuberculosis, coccidioidomycosis, histoplasmosis, leprosy) can cause hypercalcemia. In these conditions, activated macrophages convert 25-hydroxyvitamin D to its active form (1,25-DHCC), resulting in enhanced intestinal calcium absorption, hypercalcemia, and hypercalciuria.[41] Certain lymphomas cause severe hypercalcemia by a similar mechanism. Interestingly, hypercalcemia in patients with sarcoidosis occur as a seasonal event in patients who live in the Northern Hemisphere, presumably because of increased production of vitamin D in the skin during longer exposure to the summer sun.[42]

Acute vitamin A intoxication is an uncommon but well-recognized cause of hypercalcemia, resulting from an increase in osteoclastic activity. This usually occurs after an accidental massive ingestion of a preparation containing vitamin A. Chronic hypervitaminosis A can occur in patients using large doses of the vitamin for a variety of dermatologic conditions (e.g., acne vulgaris). Because vitamin A is highly lipophilic, toxicity may take several weeks to resolve after discontinuation of the vitamin. Increased exogenous vitamin D intake may also result in hypercalcemia.

Milk-alkali syndrome is caused by excessive ingestion of calcium and absorbable antacids such as milk or calcium carbonate and is characterized by hypercalcemia, alkalosis, and renal failure. The disorder is less common since nonabsorbable antacids and H_2-receptor antagonists became available for the treatment of peptic ulcer disease.

Lithium therapy for bipolar (manic-depressive) disorders can put patients at increased risk for developing hypercalcemia. Clinical and in vitro studies suggest that lithium alters the release of PTH by shifting the set point for inhibition of hormone secretion by circulating calcium.

Thyroid hormone causes hypercalcemia by increasing bone turnover through direct stimulation of osteoclastic bone resorption. In most cases, the symptoms of hyperthyroidism predominate, and hypercalcemia does not become apparent until hyperthyroidism is managed. Hypercalcemia can also be seen in patients after renal transplantation or in the early phase of acute tubular necrosis.

Clinical Features

The clinical manifestations of hypercalcemia are nonspecific and vary widely from patient to patient (Box 123-10). Severity of symptoms depends on both

BOX 123-10. Clinical Features of Hypercalcemia

Neurologic
Fatigue, weakness
Confusion, lethargy
Ataxia
Coma
Hypotonia, diminished deep tendon reflexes

Cardiovascular
Hypertension
Sinus bradycardia, atrioventricular block
ECG abnormalities (short QT, bundle branch block)
Ventricular dysrhythmias
Potentiation of digoxin toxicity

Renal
Polyuria, polydipsia
Dehydration
Loss of electrolyte
Prerenal azotemia
Nephrolithiasis
Nephrocalcinosis

Gastrointestinal
Nausea, vomiting
Anorexia
Peptic ulcer disease
Pancreatitis
Constipation, ileus

ECG, electrocardiographic.

the level of serum calcium and the rapidity of its rise.

Hypercalcemia decreases neuronal conduction and in general causes CNS depression. Symptoms range from fatigue, weakness, and difficulty concentrating to confusion, lethargy, stupor, and even coma.

Hypercalcemia has several effects on the cardiovascular system. The volume depletion with which hypercalcemia is typically associated can result in hypotension. Because hypercalcemia causes an increase in vascular tone, however, the blood pressure may be misleadingly normal. Characteristic ECG changes include shortening of the QT interval and to a lesser degree prolongation of the PR interval and QRS widening. Rarely, severe hypercalcemia causes sinus bradycardia, bundle branch block, high-degree atrioventricular block, and even cardiac arrest. Calcium potentiates the action of digoxin, and the side effects of digoxin are accentuated when hypercalcemia is present.[34]

An acute rise in the serum calcium level impairs the reabsorption of fluid and electrolytes in the renal tubule, promoting the development of dehydration, which is worsened by vomiting and poor fluid intake. This may lead to a vicious cycle of volume depletion, reduced GFR and calcium excretion, intensified hypercalcemia, and further dehydration, culminating in oliguric renal failure, coma, and death. Chronically, hypercalcemia and associated volume depletion predispose the patient to renal calculi, nephrocalcinosis, and calcium-induced interstitial nephritis.

BOX 123-11. Management of Hypercalcemia

I. Restoration of intravascular volume
    A. Correct dehydration with isotonic solution
    B. Correct associated electrolyte abnormalities
II. Enhancement of renal calcium elimination
    A. Saline diuresis
    B. Loop diuretics (e.g., furosemide)
    C. *Avoid* thiazide diuretics
III. Reduction of osteoclastic activity
    A. Bisphosphonates
        1. Etidronate, 7.5 mg/kg over 24 hr
        2. Pamidronate, 60 to 90 mg over 24 hr
    B. Plicamycin, 25 µg/kg over 4 hr
    C. Calcitonin, 4 IU/kg every 12 hr
    D. Hydrocortisone, 200 to 300 mg/day
    E. Gallium nitrate, 200 mg/m^2
IV. Treatment of primary disorder
    A. Parathyroidectomy for hyperparathyroidism
    B. Withdrawal of causative medications
    C. Treatment of nonparathyroid endocrine disorders

Anorexia, nausea, vomiting, and abdominal pain are common but nonspecific symptoms of hypercalcemia. Hypercalcemia decreases smooth muscle tone and may lead to constipation or intestinal ileus. An increased serum calcium level enhances the release of hydrochloric acid, gastrin, and pancreatic enzymes. Chronic hypercalcemia has been associated with an increased risk of peptic ulcer disease and pancreatitis.

Management

Treatment should be initiated at once in patients with evidence of significant dehydration, alteration of consciousness, or symptomatic dysrhythmias. Patients with severe hypercalcemia (>14 mg/dL) require immediate treatment regardless of symptoms. The four basic goals of therapy are (1) restoration of intravascular volume, (2) enhancement of renal calcium elimination, (3) reduction of osteoclastic activity, and (4) treatment of the primary disorder (Box 123-11). Although it may not be realistic to expect to achieve these goals in the emergency department, it is important for the emergency physician to initiate therapy and involve the appropriate consultants as early as possible.

Fluid Administration

The administration of isotonic saline is the first step in the management of severe hypercalcemia. Once the intravascular volume has been restored to normal, the serum calcium level will usually have decreased by 1.6 to 2.4 mg/dL, although hydration alone rarely leads to complete normalization. The expansion of intravascular volume increases renal calcium clearance by increasing GFR and sodium delivery to the distal tubules. The rate of fluid administration should be based on the severity of hypercalcemia, the degree of dehydration, and the patient's cardiovascular tolerance of acute volume expansion. In elderly patients and those with poor left ventricular function, central venous pressure monitoring can be used to adjust fluid administration rates. Two to 5 L per day is often required. Coexisting electrolyte deficiencies should also be corrected.

Furosemide

Loop diuretics such as furosemide inhibit the resorption of calcium in the thick ascending loop of Henle, increasing the calciuric effect of hydration. Volume expansion must precede the administration of furosemide, however, because the drug's effect depends on the delivery of calcium to the distal nephron. Intravenous doses of 10 to 40 mg every 6 to 8 hours are usually sufficient. Thiazide diuretics should not be used because they enhance distal absorption of calcium and may worsen hypercalcemia.

Osteoclast Inhibitors

Therapy for severe hypercalcemia should also include agents that reduce the mobilization of calcium from bone. Drugs that inhibit osteoclast-mediated bone resorption include the bisphosphates, plicamycin, calcitonin, glucocorticoids, and gallium nitrate.

The bisphosphonates act by inhibiting osteoclastic bone resorption and decreasing the viability of osteoclasts.[43] Etidronate and pamidronate have similar efficacy and a reasonable adverse effect profile.[44-47] Etidronate is administered at 7.5 mg/kg over 4 hours daily for 3 to 7 days. Serum calcium concentrations reach normal levels in 60% to 100% of patients. Reported side effects include transient rises in serum creatinine and serum phosphate levels. Pamidronate is administered in a single 24-hour intravenous infusion of 60 to 90 mg. Adverse effects are limited to mild hyperpyrexia, transient leukopenia, and hypophosphatemia.

Plicamycin (mithramycin) inhibits RNA synthesis in osteoclasts and is an effective agent in the treatment of hypercalcemia. It is administered intravenously over 4 hours in a dose of 25 µg/kg. Serum calcium levels decrease within 12 hours, typically reaching a nadir within 48 to 72 hours. Side effects such as phlebitis, nephrotoxicity, hepatotoxicity, and thrombocytopenia limit the use of plicamycin in the treatment of hypercalcemia.

Calcitonin is a naturally occurring hormone that lowers serum calcium when given in doses of 4 IU/kg subcutaneously every 12 hours. Among the antilcemic agents available, calcitonin has the most rapid onset of action, although it causes only a modest reduction in the serum calcium.[48] Side effects include mild nausea, abdominal cramping, flushing, and rare allergic reactions. When hypercalcemia is severe and the need to lower the serum calcium is urgent, it is reasonable to administer a dose of calcitonin in combination with a more potent agent such as a bisphosphonate.

The glucocorticoids act by inhibiting the actions of vitamin D. They may be effective calcium-lowering agents in patients with hypercalcemia caused by hematologic malignancies, granulomatous disorders, or vitamin D intoxication. Hydrocortisone 200 to 300 mg/day or the equivalent dose of another glucocorticoid is recommended.

Underlying Cause

Pharmacologic therapy does not permanently normalize the serum calcium concentration. The underlying cause of the hypercalcemia needs to be treated as well. Primary hyperparathyroidism is definitively managed by parathyroidectomy. In the hands of experienced surgeons, more than 90% of patients are cured. When hypercalcemia is caused by malignancy, treatment must be directed at the underlying tumor because normocalcemia is difficult to sustain without successful treatment of the underlying cause. Hypercalcemia caused by medication responds to discontinuation of the offending agent. Hypercalcemia caused by nonparathyroid endocrine disease responds to treatment of the underlying disorder.

MAGNESIUM

Normal Physiology

Magnesium is the second most abundant intracellular cation. It is a cofactor in hundreds of enzymatic reactions, including all those involving adenosine triphosphate (ATP). Magnesium is essential for the production and use of energy, DNA, and protein synthesis, ion channel gating, hormone receptor binding, neurotransmission, cardiac excitability, and muscle contraction.[49]

The adult human body contains approximately 2000 mEq of magnesium. One half of total magnesium is in the mineral component of bone, and 40% to 50% is found in the intracellular compartment. Only 1% to 2% of the body's magnesium is present in the extracellular fluid, so the serum magnesium level is often a poor reflection of the total magnesium content. One third of the serum magnesium is bound to albumin, with the rest in the biologically active ionized form. The normal range for serum magnesium is 1.8 to 3.0 mg/dL. A balance between gastrointestinal absorption and renal excretion maintains magnesium homeostasis.

Dietary sources of magnesium include green vegetables, meats, fish, beans, nuts, and grains. Absorption of ingested magnesium occurs in the small intestine through both active and passive transport mechanisms. In the kidney, 95% of the filtered load of magnesium is reabsorbed in the proximal tubule and loop of Henle.[50] In deficiency states, magnesium resorption is enhanced in the distal convoluted tubule under the influence of PTH. In hypermagnesemic states, renal excretion of magnesium increases.

Hypomagnesemia

Principles of Disease

Hypomagnesemia is one of the most common electrolyte deficiencies in clinical practice.[49] Approximately 10% to 20% of hospitalized patients and 50% to 60% of patients admitted to the intensive care unit are hypomagnesemic.[51] Despite the high prevalence of hypomagnesemia, several factors can make the diagnosis a challenge. First, the clinical manifestations of hypomagnesemia are nonspecific, so the disorder is often overlooked. Second, the serum magnesium level is not measured as part of the "routine" electrolyte panel.[52] Third, the serum magnesium level is an insensitive indicator of magnesium deficiency. Although a low serum magnesium level is indicative of a magnesium deficit, patients with a normal magnesium level may still have a severe deficiency. Fourth, hypomagnesemia often coexists with and may be masked by other electrolyte deficiency states.

Numerous studies have demonstrated the high prevalence of hypomagnesemia in patients with hypokalemia.[53] Because magnesium is required for the normal functioning of the Na^+,K^+-ATPase pump, hypomagnesemia can result in refractory hypokalemia that is not correctable by the administration of potassium alone. Magnesium replacement enhances potassium retention and decreases the amount of supplemental potassium required to achieve a net positive balance.[54] Magnesium is also required for the normal synthesis and release of PTH. Patients with hypomagnesemic hypocalcemia typically have inappropriately low levels of PTH and target organ resistance to the hormone, which are corrected by magnesium administration. A high prevalence of hypophosphatemia in patients who are hypomagnesemic has also been described.

Because the kidneys normally conserve magnesium efficiently, significant hypomagnesemia usually occurs only when there is renal magnesium wasting or when intestinal losses exceed dietary intake and absorption (Box 123-12). In the emergency department, hypomagnesemia is most often associated with the use of diuretics and with alcohol abuse.

Diuretics

Patients taking diuretics for the treatment of hypertension, congestive heart failure, or both are at significant risk for hypomagnesemia. Both the thiazide and the loop diuretics promote renal magnesium loss and may cause severe magnesium deficiency.[55] In one study, typical diuretic doses increased urinary magnesium excretion by 25% to 50%. Some authors recommend that all patients receiving diuretics be considered candidates for magnesium supplementation. The use of a potassium-sparing diuretic in conjunction with a conventional diuretic is less likely to cause hypomagnesemia because these agents also have a magnesium-sparing effect.

Alcoholism

The reported prevalence of hypomagnesemia in alcoholic patients varies widely, from 30% to 80%.[56,57] Hypomagnesemia in the alcoholic patient is multifactorial; potential causes include poor nutrition, increased urinary excretion, gastrointestinal losses from vomiting and diarrhea, and pancreatic insufficiency.

Renal, Gastrointestinal, and Endocrine Disorders

Hypomagnesemia can also result from renal magnesium wasting or from decreased production of (or end-

BOX 123-12. Causes of Hypomagnesemia

Alcoholic abuse
Diuretic use
Renal losses
    Acute and chronic renal failure
    Postobstructive diuresis
    Acute tubular necrosis
    Chronic glomerulonephritis
    Chronic pyelonephritis
    Interstitial nephropathy
    Renal transplantation
Gastrointestinal losses
    Chronic diarrhea
    Nasogastric suctioning
    Short-bowel syndrome
    Protein-calorie malnutrition
    Bowel fistula
    Total parenteral nutrition
    Acute pancreatitis
Endocrine disorders
    Diabetes mellitus
    Hyperaldosteronism
    Hyperthyroidism
    Hyperparathyroidism
    Acute intermittent porphyria
Pregnancy
Drugs
    Aminoglycosides
    Amphotericin
    β-Agonists
    Cisplatin
    Cyclosporine
    Diuretics
    Foscarnet
    Pentamidine
    Theophylline
Congenital disorders
    Familial hypomagnesemia
    Maternal diabetes
    Maternal hypothyroidism
    Maternal hyperparathyroidism

organ responsiveness to) PTH.[58] Magnesium wasting may be seen in some patients with postobstructive diuresis, acute tubular necrosis, chronic glomerulonephritis, chronic pyelonephritis, or interstitial nephropathy, as well as after renal transplantation. The decreased magnesium excretion typically found with acute and chronic renal failure, however, generally results in these patients tending to be hypermagnesemic.

Gastrointestinal causes of hypomagnesemia include short-bowel syndrome, protein-calorie malnutrition, bowel fistula, continuous nasogastric suctioning, chronic diarrhea, and administration of total parenteral nutrition.[58] Patients with acute pancreatitis typically have an intracellular magnesium deficiency despite normal serum concentrations. This is most likely in patients who are also hypocalcemic.

Hypomagnesemia is the most common electrolyte abnormality in ambulatory diabetic patients and is also a common finding in patients with diabetic ketoacidosis. Excessive urinary loss associated with glycosuria and transcellular shifts of the cation are the proposed mechanisms. The clinical consequences of magnesium deficiency include impairment of insulin secretion and peripheral insulin resistance. Hypomagnesemia also may play a role in the development of retinopathy, hypertension, and the abnormal platelet function often observed in diabetic patients. Other endocrine and metabolic causes of hypomagnesemia include primary and secondary aldosteronism, hyperthyroidism, primary hyperparathyroidism, and acute intermittent porphyria.

Pregnancy

Pregnancy is marked by a state of hypomagnesemia. Serum levels usually decline in the third trimester. Patients with preterm labor are more likely to have a significantly depressed serum magnesium level.[59]

Drugs

Hypomagnesemia has also been associated with a number of drugs.[60] It can result from renal magnesium wasting (e.g., aminoglycosides, amphotericin B, cisplatin, diuretics, foscarnet, pentamidine) or from transcellular magnesium shifts (e.g., β-agonists, cyclosporine, theophylline).[61]

Congenital Disorders

Congenital disorders causing hypomagnesemia include primary infantile hypomagnesemia and familial hypomagnesemia. Maternal diabetes, maternal hyperparathyroidism, and maternal hypothyroidism are also associated with hypomagnesemia in the newborn.

Clinical Features

The clinical manifestations of hypomagnesemia are nonspecific and can easily be confused with those caused by other metabolic abnormalities. Symptoms are inconsistent, variable in severity, and not well correlated with a specific serum magnesium level. However, patients are usually symptomatic at serum levels of 1.2 mg/dL or less. The clinical manifestations of hypomagnesemia most likely to be prominent in the emergency setting involve the neuromuscular and cardiovascular systems.

Neuromuscular manifestations include muscle weakness, tremor, hyperreflexia, tetany, and a positive Chvostek or Trousseau sign. CNS findings range from apathy, irritability, and dizziness to seizures, papilledema, and coma. Focal neurologic findings have also been described.

Dysrhythmia is the most common cardiovascular manifestation of hypomagnesemia. A number of studies demonstrate an increased incidence of supraventricular dysrhythmias (atrial fibrillation, multifocal atrial tachycardia, paroxysmal supraventricular tachycardia) and ventricular dysrhythmias (premature ventricular contractions, ventricular tachycardia, torsades de pointes, ventricular fibrillation) in patients who are magnesium deficient.[62] Patients taking diuretics for the treatment of congestive heart failure are particularly vulnerable. Digitalis-induced dysrhythmias are also more likely in the presence of hypomagnesemia. Because magnesium is an essential cofactor for the Na^+,K^+-ATPase pump that is inhibited by digitalis, hypomagnesemia typically worsens the manifestations of digitalis toxicity.

Hypomagnesemia has been associated with a wide range of ECG findings, including prolongation of the PR, QRS, and QT intervals; ST-T–segment abnormalities; flattening and widening of the T wave; and presence of U waves. These findings, however, are nonspecific and may be at least partly caused by associated hypokalemia. Thus, the ECG should not be used to rule out magnesium disturbances.

The relationship between hypomagnesemia and ischemic heart disease is controversial. Hypomagnesemia is common in emergency department patients with chest pain and in those admitted to the coronary care unit.[62] Patients who have a myocardial infarction are more likely to be hypomagnesemic than those who do not. This finding has been shown to be independent of concomitant diuretic use. Serum magnesium levels decline transiently after acute myocardial infarction, increasing the risk of dysrhythmia.[63,64] Proposed mechanisms include transcellular shifts of the cation and chelation with free fatty acids released after acute myocardial infarction. Although several studies demonstrate a benefit of empiric magnesium administration after acute myocardial infarction, the largest trial to date, the International Study of Infarct Survival, failed to confirm a significant benefit.[65]

Management

Because it is often an inaccurate reflection of total magnesium stores, the serum magnesium level should not be used alone to guide therapy. However, magnesium administration is appropriate in patients with a low serum level (<1.2 mg/dL), as well as in those with a normal serum magnesium level and symptoms suggestive of hypomagnesemia. For life-threatening conditions (dysrhythmias, seizures) in which hypomagnesemia is the suspected cause, parenteral magnesium should be given. In patients with normal renal function, 2 to 4 g of 50% magnesium sulfate (16.6-33.3 mEq) is a reasonable initial dose. This should be diluted in saline or dextrose and given over 30 to 60 minutes. More rapid administration may result in venous irritation and phlebitis. Bolus administration should be avoided because this may cause bradycardia and varying degrees of heart block, as well as hypotension. Magnesium should be administered with caution, if at all, in patients with atrioventricular block or renal insufficiency. Most administered magnesium is promptly excreted in the urine. Total magnesium repletion therefore requires administration of more than a single dose, generally over days.

Several different oral magnesium formulations are available. Preparations of magnesium gluconate, magnesium carbonate, magnesium oxide, and magnesium chloride each provide different doses of elemental magnesium. Large doses of magnesium salts can cause

diarrhea. Magnesium as the chloride salt or as enteric-coated tablets (e.g., Slow-Mag) is usually better tolerated.

Hypermagnesemia

Principles of Disease

Hypermagnesemia is a fairly rare disorder. Under normal circumstances, the kidneys increase magnesium excretion as the magnesium load increases. A healthy adult can excrete more than 6 g of magnesium daily. For this reason, clinically significant hypermagnesemia is encountered almost exclusively in the setting of renal insufficiency (Box 123-13). Serum magnesium levels rise as the creatinine clearance falls below 30 mL/min and typically reach approximately 2.5 mEq/L as renal function nears zero. Although severe renal failure alone can cause symptomatic hypermagnesemia, this is more likely when a patient with preexisting renal failure is challenged with an exogenous magnesium load. Clinically significant hypermagnesemia can be produced even by usual therapeutic doses of magnesium-containing preparations in patients with renal insufficiency. Elderly patients misusing over-the-counter medications are particularly at risk.

Iatrogenic hypermagnesemia can result from parenteral magnesium administration, excessive magnesium in dialysate solutions, or ingestion of magnesium-containing antacids or laxatives.[66] Severe hypermagnesemia occurs rarely in the patient with normal renal function, but only when such massive magnesium loads are administered that magnesium absorption exceeds the normal renal excretory capacity. Intravenous magnesium infusion for the treatment of preeclampsia and eclampsia is a common cause of hypermagnesemia but leads to problems only when excessive doses are given or when renal function is compromised. Another situation particularly relevant to the emergency physician is multidose administration of magnesium-containing cathartics during overdose management. Although several case reports document severe hypermagnesemia in this setting, clinically significant hypermagnesemia is rare in the absence of preexisting renal insufficiency.[67] A review of 102 patients receiving multiple doses of magnesium citrate during overdose management (mean dose, 9.22 g) reported only modest rises in serum magnesium, with no clinically significant side effects.[68]

Decreased gastrointestinal motility may cause an increase in the absorption of magnesium-containing substances and result in toxicity. This may occur after the ingestion of certain drugs (e.g., anticholinergics, narcotics) or in patients with hypomotility disorders (e.g., chronic constipation, colitis, bowel obstruction, gastric dilation). Although symptomatic hypermagnesemia is more likely in patients with preexisting renal insufficiency, it has been reported in patients with normal renal function.[69]

Other, less common causes of hypermagnesemia include rhabdomyolysis, tumor lysis syndrome, adrenal insufficiency, hyperparathyroidism, hypothyroidism, and lithium therapy.

Clinical Features

The clinical manifestations of hypermagnesemia generally correlate well with the serum level. Early signs of hypermagnesemia, including nausea, vomiting, weakness, and cutaneous flushing, usually appear at serum levels of approximately 3 mg/dL. As levels rise above 4 mg/dL, hyporeflexia is seen, and deep tendon reflexes are eventually lost. Hypotension and ECG changes (e.g., QRS widening, QT and PR prolongation, conduction abnormalities) are seen at serum levels of 5 to 6 mg/dL. Levels greater than 9 mg/dL are associated with respiratory depression, coma, and complete heart block.[70] Asystole, cardiac arrest, and death have been reported in patients with serum magnesium levels of 10 to 15 mg/dL.[71,72] Although hypermagnesemia may decrease the anion gap, numerous cases of hypermagnesemia with a normal anion gap have been reported.

Management

The first step in the management of hypermagnesemia is to discontinue all exogenous magnesium. Further treatment depends on the clinical presentation, the degree of hypermagnesemia, and the patient's underlying renal function. Patients with mild symptoms and normal renal function may require only observation. If more prominent symptoms are present, hydration with isotonic fluids and administration of intravenous furosemide can be used to accelerate magnesium elimination. If these measures are used, the serum potassium level should be closely monitored.

Patients with severe hypermagnesemia should receive intravenous calcium. Calcium directly antagonizes the membrane effects of hypermagnesemia and reverses respiratory depression, hypotension, and cardiac dysrhythmias. For life-threatening manifestations of hypermagnesemia, 100 to 200 mg of calcium, as either 10% calcium gluconate (93 mg calcium per ampule) or 10% calcium chloride (360 mg calcium per ampule), is a reasonable dose. Repeat boluses or a continuous infusion (2-4 mg/kg/hr) may be required to sustain the effect while measures to increase magnesium elimination are instituted. Dialysis should be considered in patients with coma, respiratory failure, or hemodynamic instability and in those with severe hypermagnesemia associated with renal failure.

PHOSPHORUS

Normal Physiology

Phosphorus is located primarily in the cell complexed with oxygen and hydrogen as phosphate. In this form, phosphate is an important component of nucleic acids (RNA and DNA) and of the phospholipid cell membrane. Phosphate is an essential component of ATP, the energy currency of all living cells, and of erythrocyte 2,3-diphosphoglycerate (2,3-DPG), which promotes the release of circulating oxygen at the tissue level. Phosphate also binds with calcium to form hydroxyapatite, the major salt of bone matrix.[73]

In the serum, phosphate is an important acid-base buffer. In the presence of acidosis, divalent phosphate (HPO_4^{-2}) binds excess hydrogen ion, shifting to the monovalent form ($H_2PO_4^-$). The reverse occurs when the extracellular fluid becomes alkalotic.

The normal adult human body contains approximately 700 g of phosphate, 80% of which is contained in the mineral component of bone. Phosphate balance is maintained by three different organs: intestine, kidney, and bone. PTH and vitamin D are the major hormonal regulators of plasma phosphate concentration, although these hormones are released in response to changes in ionized calcium rather than phosphate. Normal serum phosphate levels range from 3 to 4.5 mg/dL.

Dietary sources of phosphate include fruits, vegetables, meats, and dairy products. Absorption of ingested phosphate occurs through active and passive transport in the small intestine. Vitamin D enhances the absorption of both phosphate and calcium.

In the kidneys, 90% of the filtered load of phosphate is reabsorbed in the proximal tubule. Renal reabsorption increases in deficiency states. When serum phosphate levels increase, renal reabsorption decreases. PTH acts at the proximal and distal tubules to inhibit phosphate resorption. In the absence of normal renal function, PTH cannot increase phosphate excretion and may actually increase serum phosphate levels because of its effect on intestine and bone.[74] Thyroid hormone and growth hormone both increase renal phosphate resorption.

The release and uptake of phosphate by bone are primarily determined by the mechanisms governing calcium metabolism. When the serum calcium level

BOX 123-14. Causes of Hypophosphatemia

I. Renal loss
   A. Diuretic therapy
   B. Renal tubular dysfunction
   C. Hyperosmolar states
      1. Diabetic ketoacidosis
      2. Hyperosmolar hyperglycemic nonketotic coma
   D. Hyperparathyroidism
   E. Aldosteronism
   F. Glucocorticoid administration
II. Insufficient intestinal absorption
   A. Decreased dietary intake
   B. Starvation/malnutrition
   C. Phosphate-binding antacids
   D. Vitamin D deficiency
   E. Chronic diarrhea
   F. Nasogastric suctioning
III. Transcellular shift
   A. Respiratory alkalosis
      1. Sepsis
      2. Heatstroke
      3. Salicylate poisoning
      4. Neuroleptic malignant syndrome
      5. Hepatic encephalopathy
      6. Alcohol withdrawal
   B. Hyperglycemia
   C. Insulin administration

falls, both calcium and phosphate are released into the extracellular space by the action of PTH. When serum calcium levels rise, bone formation increases, and phosphate and calcium shift from the serum into bone.[73]

Hypophosphatemia

Principles of Disease

Hypophosphatemia has traditionally been classified as mild (2.5-2.8 mg/dL), moderate (1.0-2.5 mg/dL), or severe (<1.0 mg/dL). The incidence of hypophosphatemia in hospitalized patients is 2% to 3% and as high as 30% in those admitted to the intensive care unit. Severe hypophosphatemia is seen in up to 0.5% of hospitalized patients. Important risk factors include diabetic ketoacidosis, malnutrition, diuretic or antacid therapy, sepsis, and alcoholism. The many causes include (1) disorders that result in increased renal excretion, (2) disorders that are associated with decreased gastrointestinal absorption, and (3) disorders in which phosphate shifts from the serum into cells (Box 123-14).[75]

Renal phosphate loss is most often the result of diuretic therapy. The thiazides, loop diuretics, and acetazolamide promote renal phosphate wasting.[74-76] Hypophosphatemia can also be seen in patients with acute renal failure, renal transplantation, and long-term peritoneal dialysis, although renal insufficiency is typically associated with hyperphosphatemia rather than hypophosphatemia.[77] In hyperparathyroidism, high levels of circulating PTH increase renal phosphate excretion and may cause hypophosphatemia.

Diabetic ketoacidosis is an important cause of hypophosphatemia. Metabolic acidosis and insulin deficiency mobilize intracellular phosphate stores, and in the setting of an ongoing osmotic diuresis, urinary losses increase. Because of a shift of phosphate from cells to the blood, serum levels may be normal in the face of a profound total deficit. Treatment of diabetic ketoacidosis with insulin causes phosphate to move back into cells and may result in a sharp decline in the serum level.[78] The benefit of routine phosphate replacement in diabetic ketoacidosis is unproven, although patients with low serum phosphate levels in the face of acidosis should be presumed to have a severe deficiency. Because these patients are often hypokalemic, replacement with potassium phosphate salts is a reasonable approach.

Decreased phosphate intake and impaired intestinal phosphate absorption are other causes of hypophosphatemia. Up to 50% of alcoholics are hypophosphatemic. Increased renal excretion and decreased intake are the proposed mechanisms. Hypophosphatemia may be exacerbated when glucose-containing solutions are administered, because these cause phosphate to shift from the serum into cells.

Because phosphate is ubiquitous in most food sources, starvation and chronic malnutrition are relatively uncommon causes in the developed world, although low-birth-weight infants are particularly vulnerable. Decreased intestinal phosphate absorption occurs in malabsorptive syndromes, chronic diarrhea, and vitamin D deficiency. Phosphate-binding antacids (calcium carbonate, aluminum hydroxide, aluminum carbonate) prevent the absorption of dietary phosphate, and long-term therapy can lead to hypophosphatemia.

Transcellular shifts of phosphate from the extracellular space into cells is the third mechanism of hypophosphatemia. Respiratory alkalosis is a common cause of hypophosphatemia. Reduction of intracellular carbon dioxide tension increases the activity of phosphofructokinase, the rate-limiting enzyme of glycolysis, and phosphorylation of glucose precursors increases cellular uptake of serum phosphate, causing hypophosphatemia. Hyperventilation-induced hypophosphatemia may occur in the setting of sepsis, heatstroke, salicylate poisoning, neuroleptic malignant syndrome, hepatic encephalopathy, alcohol withdrawal, and acute panic disorders.

The administration of glucose-containing solutions to chronically malnourished patients can precipitate the so-called refeeding syndrome, in which insulin release increases cellular phosphate uptake, decreasing the serum concentration. This can be prevented by adding supplemental phosphate to the diet. β-Receptor agonists used in the management of acute asthma stimulate cellular uptake of phosphate and can precipitate hypophosphatemia.[79,80] Administration of catecholamines and sodium bicarbonate also shifts phosphate into the cell. Increased metabolic demands in postoperative patients increase cellular phosphate uptake and can cause a deficiency state. Certain rapidly growing malignancies (e.g., leukemia, Burkitt's lymphoma, his-

BOX 123-15. Clinical Features of Hypophosphatemia

Cardiovascular	**Hematologic**
Decreased contractility	Decreased tissue oxygen
Hypotension	delivery
Dysrhythmias	Hemolysis
Cardiomyopathy	Leukocyte dysfunction
	Platelet dysfunction
Pulmonary	
Respiratory failure	**Neurologic**
Ventilator dependence	Paresthesias
	Seizures
Skeletal Muscle	Coma
Weakness	
Myalgias	
Rhabdomyolysis	

tiocytic lymphoma) also take up enough phosphate to cause hypophosphatemia.

Clinical Features

The signs and symptoms of hypophosphatemia result from impaired production of ATP and inadequate energy metabolism. Virtually every organ system can be affected (Box 123-15). Mild or moderate hypophosphatemia is usually asymptomatic, and major clinical sequelae are usually seen only in severe hypophosphatemia.

With severe phosphate depletion, myocardial depression is seen, and hypotension, impaired pressor responsiveness, and left ventricular dysfunction have been reported.[81] Hypophosphatemia also reduces the threshold for ventricular dysrhythmias.

Respiratory insufficiency is common among severely hypophosphatemic patients. Decreased energy substrate leads to respiratory muscle weakness, depressed diaphragmatic contractility, hypoxia, and respiratory acidosis. Rapid correction of chronic respiratory acidosis with assisted ventilation may decrease the serum phosphate level further by shifting the anion into the cell. Inability to wean a ventilated patient may be an important consequence of hypophosphatemia.

The effects of hypophosphatemia on skeletal muscle are also related to depletion of intracellular ATP. Symptoms include muscle weakness, myalgias, and fatigue.[82] Hypophosphatemia can cause rhabdomyolysis. This may be asymptomatic, manifested only by increased serum muscle enzyme levels, or may cause severe muscle pain and weakness and acute renal failure. Rhabdomyolysis may be precipitated by acute alcohol withdrawal, by the treatment of diabetic ketoacidosis, and in hypophosphatemic patients by hyperalimentation. Significant rhabdomyolysis results in the release of phosphate from muscle cells, and serum phosphate levels can be normal or even high despite intracellular hypophosphatemia.

Hypophosphatemia results in impaired production of 2,3-DPG in the erythrocyte, causing a leftward shift of the oxyhemoglobin dissociation curve and decreased tissue oxygen delivery. In the absence of adequate ATP stores, the erythrocyte is unable to maintain membrane integrity and the ability to deform and alter its shape as it passes through capillaries. This may result in hemolysis and increased destruction in the spleen. Hypophosphatemia is also associated with leukocyte dysfunction with impaired chemotaxis, phagocytosis, and opsonization, increasing the susceptibility to infection.

Neurologic manifestations of severe hypophosphatemia include weakness, confusion, seizures, and coma. Peripheral neuropathy and an ascending motor paralysis resembling Guillain-Barré syndrome have been reported.

Management

The treatment of hypophosphatemia depends both on the serum level and on the severity of symptoms. Mild or moderate hypophosphatemia can usually be treated with oral supplements such as potassium phosphate. Severe hyperphosphatemia should be treated with intravenous phosphate. Two preparations are available: potassium phosphate and sodium phosphate. Because hypophosphatemia and hypokalemia can coexist in some disorders (e.g., diabetic ketoacidosis, alcoholism), replacement with the potassium salt is most appropriate.[83,84]

Complications of intravenous phosphate administration include acute hypocalcemia and hyperphosphatemia. Patients should be monitored for signs of hypocalcemia, such as tetany. Phosphate should be administered with particular caution in patients with renal dysfunction.[73,74]

Hyperphosphatemia

Principles of Disease

Hyperphosphatemia (>5.0 mg/dL) is rare in patients with normal renal function because the kidneys readily excrete an excess phosphate load. True hyperphosphatemia can result from decreased phosphate clearance, an increased endogenous phosphate load, or an increased exogenous load (Box 123-16).

Pseudohyperphosphatemia represents a spurious elevation of inorganic phosphate measurements caused by interference with analytical methods. Causes include paraproteinemia (e.g., multiple myeloma), hyperlipidemia, hemolysis, and hyperbilirubinemia.

Renal failure is the most common cause of hyperphosphatemia.[74] The serum phosphate level typically remains normal until the creatinine clearance falls below 30 mL/min.[85] Hyperphosphatemia is usually mild unless an exogenous phosphate load is given. Hyperphosphatemia may also occur in patients with normal renal function when renal phosphate resorption is increased, as occurs with PTH deficiency, and in the setting of thyrotoxicosis or excessive vitamin D administration.

Hyperphosphatemia can also occur with large endogenous phosphate loads, as with extensive cell damage, which causes phosphate to be released into the extracellular space. This may occur in the setting of

BOX 123-16. Causes of Hyperphosphatemia

I. Pseudohyperphosphatemia
   A. Paraproteinemia
   B. Hyperlipidemia
   C. Hemolysis
   D. Hyperbilirubinemia
II. Renal
   A. Acute and chronic renal failure
   B. Increased renal tubular reabsorption
     1. Hypoparathyroidism
     2. Thyrotoxicosis
     3. Excess vitamin D administration
III. Cellular injury
   A. Rhabdomyolysis
   B. Tumor lysis syndrome
   C. Hemolysis
IV. Increased intake
   A. Phosphate enemas or laxatives
   B. Intravenous or oral phosphate administration

rhabdomyolysis, tumor lysis syndrome, or hemolysis.[86] Patients with these disorders often develop renal failure, impairing phosphate excretion and further increasing serum levels.

Hypophosphatemia may also result from exogenous loads, as with intravenous, oral, or rectal phosphate administration. Infants, elderly persons, and patients with preexisting renal insufficiency are particularly vulnerable.[87-90]

Clinical Features

The clinical signs of hyperphosphatemia reflect the associated hypocalcemia that results when excess serum phosphate binds with calcium and precipitates in tissues. Signs of neuromuscular hyperexcitability (e.g., paresthesias, hyperreflexia, tetany, seizures) and myocardial depression (e.g., hypotension, bradycardia, left ventricular dysfunction) predominate. Tissue deposition of calcium phosphate may result in acute heart block and death.

Management

The emergency treatment of hyperphosphatemia involves supportive care and treatment of symptomatic hypocalcemia. In patients with normal renal function, infusion of isotonic saline increases phosphate clearance. The administration of dextrose and insulin drives phosphate into cells, temporarily lowering the serum level.

Aluminum-containing antacids are the mainstay of the prevention of hyperphosphatemia in patients with chronic renal failure.[91] Although these are usually not administered in the emergency department, their use is reasonable in the management of hyperphosphatemia after a large overdose of exogenous phosphate. When hyperphosphatemia poses a threat to life, hemodialysis or peritoneal dialysis should be considered, especially in patients with renal failure.

KEY CONCEPTS

- The primary symptoms of hyponatremia are related to the CNS, including lethargy, apathy, confusion, disorientation, agitation, depression, and psychosis.
- Treatment of hyponatremia is based on severity of symptoms, estimated duration of illness, and patient's volume status. Patients with acute hyponatremia are usually symptomatic (e.g., severe weakness, diminished consciousness, seizures) when the serum sodium level falls below 120 mEq/L, whereas patients with chronic hyponatremia can tolerate much lower levels.
- Acute hyponatremia may be corrected at rates of up to 1 to 2 mEq/L/hr, and chronic hyponatremia should be corrected at a rate not greater than 0.5 mEq/L/hr. In general, the serum sodium level should not be increased by more than 10 mEq/L in a 24-hour period.
- Oral therapy for hypokalemia is preferable to intravenous therapy because of the risk of inducing hyperkalemia through the intravenous route. However, patients with prominent symptoms (e.g., dysrhythmias) and those who are unable to tolerate oral supplements should receive intravenous potassium replacement.
- The ECG can provide valuable clues to the presence of hyperkalemia (e.g., peaked T waves, loss of P waves, QRS widening).
- Treatment of hyperkalemia includes cardiovascular monitoring, administration of calcium for hemodynamic instability, lowering of serum potassium, and correction of the underlying disorder.
- Treatment of hypercalcemia (intravenous fluids, furosemide, osteoclastic inhibitors such as bisphosphonates [etidronate, pamidronate], plicamycin, calcitonin, glucocorticoids, and gallium nitrate) should be initiated in patients with significant symptoms (e.g., severe dehydration, alteration of consciousness, dysrhythmias) or when the calcium level is above 14 mg/dL. The goals of therapy are normalization of volume status, enhancement of renal calcium elimination, diminution of osteoclastic activity, and treatment of the underlying disorder.
- In hypomagnesemia, although the serum magnesium level often inaccurately reflects total body stores, magnesium supplementation should be considered when the level is less than 1.2 mg/dL. Intravenous magnesium therapy should be instituted for patients with significant symptoms (e.g., seizures, dysrhythmias).

REFERENCES

1. Weisberg LS: Pseudohyponatremia: A reappraisal. *Am J Med* 86:315, 1989.
2. Illowsky BP, Kirch DG: Polydipsia and hyponatremia in psychiatric patients. *Am J Psychiatry* 145:675, 1988.
3. Riggs JE: Neurologic manifestations of fluid and electrolyte disturbances. *Neurol Clin* 7:509, 1989.
4. Chung SM, et al: Clinical assessment of extracellular fluid volume in hyponatremia. *Am J Med* 83:905, 1987.
5. Snyder NA, Feigal DW, Arieff AI: Hypernatremia in elderly patients: A heterogenous morbid entity. *Ann Intern Med* 107:309, 1987.
6. Conley S: Hypernatremia. *Pediatr Clin North Am* 37:365, 1990.
7. Buoncore CM, Robinson AG: The diagnosis and management of diabetes insipidus during medical emergencies, *Endocrinol Metab Clin North Am* 22:411, 1993.

8. Brown RS: Potassium homeostasis and clinical implications. *Am J Med* 77:3, 1994.

9. Brem AS: Disorders of potassium homeostasis. *Pediatr Clin North Am* 37:419, 1990.

10. Zull DN: Disorders of potassium metabolism. *Emerg Med Clin North Am* 7:771, 1989.

11. Young WF, et al: Primary aldosteronism: Diagnosis and treatment. *Mayo Clin Proc* 65:96, 1996.

12. Salmeron M, et al: Nebulized versus intravenous albuterol in hypercapnic acute asthma: A multicenter, double-blind, randomized study. *Am J Respir Crit Care Med* 149:1466, 1994.

13. Bodenhamer J, et al: Frequently nebulized β-agonists for asthma: Effects on serum electrolytes. *Ann Emerg Med* 21:1337, 1992.

14. Capobianco DJ: Hyperthyroidism and periodic paralysis. *J Fla Med Assoc* 77:884, 1990.

15. Riggs JE: Neurologic manifestations of fluid and electrolyte disturbances. *Neurol Clin* 7:509, 1989.

16. Weisberg LS, Szerlap HM, Cox M: Disorders of potassium homeostasis in critically ill patients. *Crit Care Clin* 3:835, 1987.

17. Hamill RJ, et al: Efficacy and safety of potassium infusion therapy in hypokalemic critically ill patients. *Crit Care Med* 19:694, 1991.

18. Williams ME, Rosa RM, Epstein FH: Hyperkalemia. *Adv Intern Med* 31:265, 1986.

19. Alappan R, Peerazella MA, Buller GK: Hyperkalemia in hospitalized patients treated with trimethoprim-sulfamethoxazole. *Ann Intern Med* 124:316, 1996.

20. Mimh LB, Rathburn RC, Resman-Targoff BH: Hyperkalemia associated with high dose trimethoprim-sulfamethoxazole in a patient with the acquired immunodeficiency syndrome. *Pharmacotherapy* 15:793, 1995.

21. Allon M: Hyperkalemia in end-stage renal disease: Mechanisms and management. *J Am Soc Nephrol* 6:1135, 1995.

22. Allon M, Shanklin N: Effect of bicarbonate administration in plasma potassium in dialysis patients: Interactions with insulin and albuterol. *Am J Kidney Dis* 28:508, 1996.

23. Allon M, Dunlay R, Copkney C: Nebulized albuterol for acute hyperkalemia in patients on hemodialysis. *Ann Intern Med* 110:426, 1989.

24. Lin JL, et al: Outcomes of severe hyperkalemia in cardiopulmonary resuscitation with concomitant hemodialysis. *Intensive Care Med* 20:287, 1994.

25. Reber PM, Heath H III: Hypocalcemic emergencies. *Med Clin North Am* 79:93, 1995.

26. Kainer G, Chan JCM: Hypocalcemic and hypercalcemic disorders in children. *Curr Probl Pediatr* 10:497, 1989.

27. Wilson RF, et al: Electrolyte and acid-base changes with massive blood transfusions. *Am Surg* 58:535, 1992.

28. Crain JC, Hodson EM, Martin HC: Phosphate enema poisoning in children. *Med J Aust* 160:347, 1994.

29. Potts JT: Management of asymptomatic hyperparathyroidism. *J Clin Endocrinol Metab* 70:1489, 1990.

30. NIH conference. Diagnosis and management of asymptomatic primary hyperparathyroidism: Consensus development conference statement. *Ann Intern Med* 114:593, 1991.

31. Palmer M, et al: Prevalence of hypercalcemia in a healthy survey: A 14-year follow up study of serum calcium values. *Eur J Clin Invest* 18:39, 1988.

32. Bilezikian JP: Etiologies and therapy of hypercalcemia. *Endrocrinol Metab Clin North Am* 18:389, 1989.

33. Rizzoli R, Bonjour JP: Management of disorders of calcium homeostasis. *Baillieres Clin Endocrinol Metab* 6:129, 1992.

34. Kaye TB: Hypercalcemia: How to pinpoint the cause and customize therapy. *Postgrad Med* 97:153, 1995.

35. Pimentel L: Medical complications of oncologic disease. *Emerg Med Clin North Am* 11:407, 1993.

36. Walls J, Bundred N, Howell A: Hypercalcemia and bone resorption in malignancy. *Clin Orthop* 312:51, 1995.

37. Broadus AE, et al: Humoral hypercalcemia of cancer: Identification of a novel parathyroid hormone–like peptide. *N Engl J Med* 319:556, 1988.

38. Kao PC, et al: Parathyroid hormone–related peptide in plasma of patients with hypercalcemia and malignant lesions. *Mayo Clin Proc* 65:1399, 1990.

39. Budayr AA, et al: Increased serum levels of a parathyroid hormone–like protein in malignancy-associated hypercalcemia. *Ann Intern Med* 111:807, 1989.

40. Burtis WJ, et al: Immunocytochemical characterization of circulating parathyroid hormone–related protein in patients with humoral hypercalcemia of cancer. *N Engl J Med* 322:1106, 1990.

41. Rizzato B, Fraioli P, Montemurro L: Nephrolithiasis as a presenting feature of chronic sarcoidosis. *Thorax* 50:555, 1995.

42. Connin CC, et al: Precipitation of hypercalcemia in sarcoidosis by foreign sun holidays: Report of four cases. *Postgrad Med J* 66:307, 1990.

43. Sato M, Grasser W: Effect of diphosphonates on isolated rat osteoclasts as examined by reflected light microscopy. *J Bone Miner Res* 5:31, 1991.

44. Singer FR, et al: Treatment of hypercalcemia of malignancy with intravenous etidronate: A controlled multicenter study. *Arch Intern Med* 151:471, 1991.

45. Singer FR: Role of the bisphosphonate etidronate in the therapy of cancer-related hypercalcemia. *Semin Oncol* 17:34, 1990.

46. Fitton A, McTavish D: Pamidronate: A review of its pharmacological properties and therapeutic efficacy in resortive bone disease. *Drugs* 41:289, 1991.

47. Gucalp R, et al: Comparative study of pamidronate disodium and etidronate disodium in the treatment of cancer-related hypercalcemia. *J Clin Oncol* 10:134, 1992.

48. Levine MM, Kleeman CR: Hypercalcemia: Pathophysiology and treatment. *Hosp Pract* 22:73, 1987.

49. Whang R, Ryder KW: Frequency of hypomagnesemia and hypermagnesemia. *JAMA* 263:3063, 1990.

50. Olinger ML: Disorders of calcium and magnesium metabolism. *Emerg Med Clin North Am* 7:795, 1989.

51. Martin BJ, Black J, McLelland AS: Hypomagnesemia in elderly hospital admission: A study of clinical significance. *Q J Med* 78:177, 1991.

52. Whang R, Hampton EM, Whang DD: Magnesium homeostasis and clinical disorders of magnesium deficiency. *Ann Pharmacother* 28:220, 1994.

53. Ryan MP: Interrelationship of magnesium and potassium homeostasis. *Miner Electrolyte Metab* 19:290, 1993.

54. Hamill-Ruth RJ, McGory R: Magnesium repletion and its effect on potassium homeostasis in critically ill adults: Results of a double-blind, randomized, controlled study. *Crit Care Med* 24:38, 1996.

55. Ramsey LE, Yeo WW, Jackson PR: Metabolic effects of diuretics. *Cardiology* 2:48, 1994.

56. Elisaf M, et al: Acid-base and electrolyte abnormalities in alcoholic patients. *Miner Electrolyte Metab* 20:274, 1994.

57. Ragland G: Electrolyte abnormalities in the alcoholic patient. *Emerg Med Clin North Am* 8:761, 1990.

58. Al-Ghamdi SM, Cameron EC, Sutton RA: Magnesium deficiency: Pathophysiologic and clinical overview. *Am J Kidney Dis* 24:737, 1994.

59. Kurzel RB: Serum magnesium levels in pregnancy and preterm labor. *Am J Perinatol* 8:119, 1991.

60. Cameron JD: Serum magnesium as affected by drugs. *Clin Chem* 35:506, 1989.

61. Shah GM, Kirschenbaum MA: Renal magnesium wasting associated with therapeutic agents. *Miner Electrolyte Metab* 17:58, 1991.

62. Millane TA, Ward DE, Camm AJ: Is hypomagnesemia arrhythmogenic? *Clin Cardiol* 15:103, 1992.

63. Salem M, et al: Hypomagnesemia is a frequent finding in the emergency department in patients with chest pain. *Arch Intern Med* 151:2185, 1991.

64. Rasmussen JS, et al: Magnesium deficiency in patients with ischemic heart disease with and without acute myocardial infarction uncovered by an intravenous loading test. *Arch Intern Med* 148:329, 1988.

65. ISIS-4: A randomised factorial trial assessing early oral captopril, oral mononitrate, and intravenous magnesium sulphate in 58,050 patients with suspected acute myocardial infarction. ISIS-4 (Fourth International Study of Infarct Survival) Collaborative Group. *Lancet* 345:669, 1995.

66. Quereshi TI, Melonakos TK: Acute hypermagnesemia after laxative use. *Ann Emerg Med* 28:552, 1996.

67. Gerald SK, Hernadez C, Khayam-Bashi H: Extreme hypermagnesemia caused by an overdose of magnesium-containing cathartics. *Ann Emerg Med* 17:728, 1988.

68. Woodard JA, et al: Serum magnesium concentration after repetitive magnesium cathartic administration. *Am J Med* 8:297, 1990.

69. Clark BA, Brown RS: Unsuspected morbid hypermagnesemia in elderly patients. *Am J Nephrol* 12:336, 1992.

70. Mosseri M, et al: Electrocardiographic manifestations of combined hypercalcemia and hypermagnesemia. *J Electrocardiol* 23:235, 1990.

71. Ferdinandus J, Pederson JA, Whang R: Hypermagnesemia as a cause of refractory hypotension. *Ann Intern Med* 141:669, 1991.

72. Zwerling H: Hypermagnesemia-induced hypotension and hypoventilation. *JAMA* 266:2374, 1991.

73. Yucha CB, Toto KH: Calcium and phosphorus derangements. *Crit Care Clin* 6:747, 1994.

74. Peppers MP, Gehelo M, Desai H: Hypophosphatemia and hyperphosphatemia. *Crit Care Clin* 7:201, 1991.

75. Thatte L, et al: Review of the literature: Severe hyperphosphatemia. *Am J Med Sci* 310:167, 1995.

76. Itescu S, Haskell LP, Tannenberg AM: Thiazide-induced clinically significant hypophosphatemia. *Clin Nephrol* 27:161, 1987.

77. Kurtin P, Kouba J: Profound hypophosphatemia in the course of acute renal failure. *Am J Kidney Dis* 10:346, 1987.

78. Bohannon NJ: Large phosphate shifts with treatment for hyperglycemia. *Arch Intern Med* 149:1423, 1989.

79. Brady HR, et al: Hypophosphatemia complicating bronchodilator therapy for acute severe asthma. *Arch Intern Med* 10:2367, 1989.

80. Laaban JP, et al: Hypophosphatemia complicating management of acute severe asthma. *Ann Intern Med* 112:68, 1990.

81. Davis SV, Olichwier KK, Chakko SC: Reversible depression of myocardial performance in hypophosphatemia. *Am J Med Sci* 295:183, 1988.

82. Gravelyn TR, et al: Hypophosphatemia-associated respiratory muscle weakness in a general inpatient population. *Am J Med* 84:870, 1988.

83. Lentz RD, Brown DM, Kjellstrand CM: Treatment of severe hypophosphatemia. *Ann Intern Med* 89:941, 1989.

84. Lloyd CW, Johnson CE: Management of hypophosphatemia. *Clin Pharm* 7:123, 1988.

85. Sirmon MD, Kirkpatrick WG: Acute renal failure: What to do until the nephrologist comes. *Postgrad Med* 87:55, 1990.

86. Vachvanichsanong P, et al: Severe hyperphosphatemia following acute tumor lysis syndrome. *Med Pediatr Oncol* 24:63, 1995.

87. Biarent D, et al: Acute phosphate intoxication in seven infants under parenteral nutrition. *J Parenter Enteral Nutr* 16:558, 1992.

88. Fass R, Do S, Hixson LJ: Fatal hyperphosphatemia following Fleet Phospho-Soda in a patient with colonic ileus. *Am J Gastroenterol* 88:929, 1993.

89. Korzets A, et al: Life-threatening hyperphosphatemia and hypocalcemic tetany following the use of Fleet enemas. *J Am Geriatr Soc* 40:620, 1992.

90. DiPalma JA, et al: Biochemical effects of oral sodium phosphate. *Dig Dis Sci* 41:749, 1996.

91. Ghazali A, et al: Management of hyperphosphatemia in patients with renal failure. *Curr Opin Nephrol Hypertens* 2:566, 1993.

CHAPTER

124 Diabetes Mellitus and Disorders of Glucose Homeostasis

Rita K. Cydulka and Jeffrey Pennington

PERSPECTIVE

Diabetes mellitus is the most common endocrine disease. It comprises a heterogeneous group of hyperglycemic disorders characterized by high serum glucose and disturbances of carbohydrate and lipid metabolism. Acute complications include hypoglycemia, diabetic ketoacidosis, and hyperglycemic hyperosmolar nonketotic coma. Long-term complications include disorders of blood vessels, especially the microvasculature. The cardiovascular system, eyes, kidneys, and nerves are particularly susceptible to complications. Despite the discovery of insulin more than 75 years ago by Banting and Best,[1] the incidence of severe debilitating complications, including arteriosclerosis, renal failure, retinopathy, and neuropathy, remains high. The Diabetes Control and Complications Trial proved that tight blood glucose control reduces the risk of these late sequelae.[2] Patients with diabetes mellitus incur emergency department costs three times higher and are admitted to the hospital four times more often than nondiabetic patients.

PRINCIPLES OF DISEASE

Normal Physiology

Maintenance of the plasma glucose concentration is critical to survival because plasma glucose is the predominant metabolic fuel used by the central nervous system (CNS). The CNS cannot synthesize glucose, store more than a few minutes' supply, or concentrate glucose from the circulation. Brief hypoglycemia can cause profound brain dysfunction, and prolonged severe hypoglycemia may cause cellular death. Glucose regulatory systems have evolved to prevent or correct hypoglycemia.[3]

The plasma glucose concentration is normally maintained within a relatively narrow range, between 60 and 150 mg/dL, despite wide variations in glucose that occur after meals and exercise. Glucose is derived from three sources: intestinal absorption from the diet; *glycogenolysis*, the breakdown of glycogen; and *gluconeogenesis*, the formation of glucose from precursors, including lactate, pyruvate, amino acids, and glycerol. After glucose ingestion, the plasma glucose concentration increases as a result of glucose absorption. Endogenous glucose production is suppressed. Plasma glucose then rapidly declines to a level below the baseline.

Insulin

Insulin receptors on the beta cells of the pancreas sense elevated blood glucose and trigger insulin release into the blood. For incompletely understood reasons, glucose taken by mouth evokes more insulin release than parenteral glucose. Certain amino acids induce insulin release and even cause hypoglycemia in some patients. Sulfonylurea oral hypoglycemic agents work, in part, by stimulating the release of insulin from the pancreas.

The number of receptor sites helps determine the sensitivity of the particular tissue to circulating insulin. The number and sensitivity of receptor sites are also the primary factors in the long-term efficacy of the sulfonylurea oral hypoglycemic agents. Receptor sites are increased in glucocorticoid deficiency and may be relatively decreased in obese patients.

Under normal circumstances, insulin is rapidly degraded through the liver and kidney. The half-life of insulin is 3 to 10 minutes in the circulation. Whereas insulin is the major anabolic hormone pertinent to the diabetic disorder, glucagon plays the role of the major catabolic hormone in disordered glucose homeostasis.

Although most tissues have the enzyme systems required to synthesize and hydrolyze glycogen, only the liver and kidneys contain glucose-6-phosphatase, the enzyme necessary for the release of glucose into the circulation. The liver is essentially the sole source of endogenous glucose production. Renal gluconeogenesis and glucose release contribute substantially to the systemic glucose pool only during prolonged starvation.

The hepatocyte does not require insulin for glucose to cross the cell membrane. However, insulin augments both the hepatic glucose uptake and storage needed for the process of energy generation and glycogen and fat synthesis. Insulin inhibits hepatic gluconeogenesis and glycogenolysis.[4]

Muscle can store and use glucose, primarily through glycolysis to pyruvate, which is reduced to lactate or transaminated to form alanine. Lactate released from muscle is transported to the liver, where it serves as a gluconeogenic precursor. Alanine may also flow from muscle to liver. During a fast, muscle can reduce its glucose uptake, oxidize fatty acids for its energy needs, and, through proteolysis, mobilize amino acids for transport to the liver as gluconeogenic precursors. Adipose tissue can also use glucose for fatty acid synthesis for oxidation to form triglycerides. During a fast, adipocytes can also decrease their glucose use and satisfy energy needs through the β-oxidation of fatty acids. Other tissues do not have the capacity to decrease glucose use on fasting and therefore produce lactate at relatively fixed rates.

Glucose transport across the fat cell membrane also requires insulin. A large percentage of the adipocyte glucose is metabolized to form α-glycerophosphate, required for the esterification of fatty acids to form triglycerides. Although most insulin-mediated fatty acid synthesis occurs in the liver, a very small percentage occurs in fat cells, using the acetyl coenzyme A generated by glucose metabolism. Very low levels of insulin are required to inhibit intracellular lipolysis while stimulating the extracellular lipolysis required for circulating lipids to enter the fat cell.

Glucose Regulatory Mechanisms

Maintenance of the normal plasma glucose concentration requires precise matching of glucose use and endogenous glucose production or dietary glucose delivery. The regulatory mechanisms that maintain systemic glucose balance involve hormonal, neurohumoral, and autoregulatory factors. Glucoregulatory hormones include insulin, glucagon, epinephrine, cortisol, and growth hormone. Insulin is the main glucose-lowering hormone. Insulin suppresses endogenous glucose production and stimulates glucose use. Insulin is secreted from the beta cells of the pancreatic islets into the hepatic portal circulation and has important actions on the liver and the peripheral tissues. Insulin stimulates glucose uptake, storage, and use by other insulin-sensitive tissues such as fat and muscle.[3]

Counterregulatory hormones include glucagon, epinephrine, norepinephrine, growth hormone, and cortisol. When glucose is not getting into the cells because of either a lack of food intake or lack of insulin, the body perceives a "fasting state" and releases *glucagon*, attempting to provide the glucose necessary for brain function. In contrast to the fed state, in the fasted state the body metabolizes protein and fat. Glucagon is secreted from the alpha cells of the pancreatic islets into the hepatic portal circulation. Glucagon lowers hepatic levels of fructose 2,6-biphosphate, resulting in decreased glycolysis and increased gluconeogenesis, an effect that may be enhanced by ketosis.[5] Glucagon increases the activity of adenyl cyclase in the liver, thereby increasing glycogen breakdown to glucose and further increasing hepatic gluconeogenesis. Glucagon acts to increase ketone production in the liver. Thus, whereas insulin is an anabolic agent that

BOX 124-1. Classification of Diabetes Mellitus and Other Categories of Glucose Intolerance

Diabetes Mellitus
Type 1 (or type I, formerly "insulin-dependent")
   Immune mediated
   Idiopathic
Type 2 (or type II, formerly "non–insulin-dependent")
Other specific types
   Genetic defects of beta cell function
   Genetic defects in insulin action
   Diseases of exocrine pancreas
   Endocrinopathies
   Drug or chemical induced
   Infections
   Uncommon forms of immune-mediated diabetes
   Other genetic syndromes sometimes associated with diabetes

Gestational Diabetes Mellitus

Impaired Glucose Tolerance
Impaired fasting glucose

From American Diabetes Association: Report of the Expert Committee on the Diagnosis and Classification of Diabetes Mellitus. *Diabetes Care* 20:1183, 1997.

reduces blood glucose, glucagon is a catabolic agent that increases blood glucose. Glucagon is released in response to hypoglycemia as well as to stress, trauma, infection, exercise, and starvation. It increases hepatic glucose production within minutes, although transiently.

Epinephrine both stimulates hepatic glucose production and limits glucose use through both direct and indirect actions mediated through both α- and β-adrenergic mechanisms. Epinephrine also acts directly to increase hepatic glycogenolysis and gluconeogenesis. It acts within minutes and produces a transient increase in glucose production but continues to support glucose production at approximately basal levels thereafter. Norepinephrine exerts hyperglycemic actions by mechanisms similar to those of epinephrine, except that norepinephrine is released from axon terminals of sympathetic postganglionic neurons.

Growth hormone initially has a plasma glucose–lowering effect. Its hypoglycemic effect does not appear for several hours. Thus, growth hormone release is not critical for rapid glucose counterregulation; this is also true for *cortisol*. Over the long term, both growth hormone and cortisol may also increase glucose production.

Types of Diabetes

The National Diabetes Data Group (NDDG) defines four major types of diabetes mellitus: type 1 diabetes mellitus, type 2 diabetes mellitus, gestational diabetes, and IGT/IFG (Box 124-1).[6] The 1997 NDDG report discontinued the use of the terms "insulin-dependent diabetes mellitus" and "non–insulin-dependent diabetes mellitus" because they are confusing and clinically inaccurate. The group also recommended that arabic numerals 1 and 2 be used to replace roman numerals I and II in the designation of types "one" and "two."[6]

Type 1 Diabetes Mellitus

Type 1 (or I) diabetes is characterized by abrupt failure of production of insulin with a tendency to ketosis even in the basal state. Parenteral insulin is required to sustain life. From 85% to 90% of patients with type 1 diabetes demonstrate evidence of one or more autoantibodies implicated in the cell-mediated autoimmune destruction of the beta cells of the pancreas. Strong human leukocyte antigen (HLA) associations are also found in type 1 diabetes. The autoimmune destruction has multiple genetic predispositions and may be related to undefined environmental insults.[6]

Type 2 Diabetes Mellitus

Patients with type 2 (or II) diabetes may remain asymptomatic for long periods and show low, normal, or elevated levels of insulin because of insulin resistance. Ketosis is rare in type 2. Patients have a high incidence of obesity. No association exists with viral infections, islet cell autoantibodies, or HLA expression. Hyperinsulinemia may be related to peripheral tissue resistance to insulin because of defects in the insulin receptor.[7] Defects in muscle glycogen synthesis have an important role in the insulin resistance that occurs in type 2. A subgroup of patients who develop type 2 before 25 years of age have a mutation in the glucokinase gene and on chromosome 7.[8]

Gestational Diabetes

Gestational diabetes "mellitus" is characterized by an abnormal oral glucose tolerance test (OGTT) that occurs during pregnancy and either reverts to normal during the postpartum period or remains abnormal. The clinical pathogenesis is thought to be similar to that of type 2. The clinical presentation is usually nonketotic hyperglycemia during pregnancy.

Impaired Glucose Tolerance

A fourth category is impaired glucose tolerance (IGT) and its analogue, *impaired fasting glucose* (IFG). This group is composed of persons whose plasma glucose levels are between normal and diabetic and who are at increased risk for the development of diabetes and cardiovascular disease. The pathogenesis is thought to be related to insulin resistance.[6] Presentations of IGT/IFG include nonketotic hyperglycemia, insulin resistance, hyperinsulinism, and often obesity.

IGT/IFG differs from the other classes in that it is not associated with the same degree of complications of diabetes mellitus. Many of these patients even spontaneously develop normal glucose tolerance. The emergency physician, however, should not be complacent about the patient with IGT because the decompensation of this group into the category of diabetes mellitus is 1% to 5% per year.[9,10]

Epidemiology

The prevalence of diabetes is difficult to determine because many standards have been used. The NDDG, using the 75-g OGTT as the diagnostic criterion, estimates the prevalence as 6.6%, with 11.2% of the population having IGT.[3] These figures are probably too high because most subjects diagnosed with IGT or diabetes by OGTT never develop diabetes.[3] The true prevalence of the disease is probably 6.3% of the population.[11] Approximately 5% to 10% of these patients have type 1, and 90% to 95% have type 2.[3] Some groups have a much higher rate of diabetes, such as the Pima Native Americans, who have a 40% rate of type 2; however, diabetes mellitus is significantly more prevalent in whites than in nonwhites.[12]

The peak age of onset of type 1 diabetes is 10 to 14 years. Approximately 1 of every 600 schoolchildren has this disease. In the United States the prevalence of type 1 is approximately 0.26% by age 20 years, and the lifetime prevalence approaches 0.4%. The annual incidence among persons from birth to 16 years of age in the United States is 12 to 14 per 1 million population. The incidence is age dependent, increasing from near-absence during infancy to a peak occurrence at puberty and another small peak at midlife.[13]

The morbidity in diabetes is related mostly to its vascular complications. A mortality of 36.8% has been related to cardiovascular causes, 17.5% to cerebrovascular causes, 15.5% to diabetic comas, and 12.5% to renal failure.

Pathophysiology and Etiology

Type 1 diabetes results from a chronic autoimmune process that usually exists in a preclinical state for years.[4] The classical manifestations of type 1, hyperglycemia and ketosis, occur late in the course of the disease, an overt sign of beta cell destruction.

The most striking feature of long-standing type 1 diabetes is the near-total lack of insulin-secreting beta cells and insulin, with the preservation of glucagon-secreting alpha cells, somatostatin-secreting delta cells, and pancreatic polypeptide–secreting cells.

Although the exact cause of diabetes remains unclear, research has provided many clues. Studies of the pathogenesis of diabetes mellitus have demonstrated that the cause of the disordered glucose homeostasis varies from individual to individual.[14,15] This cause may determine the presentation in each patient. Individual patients are currently not studied for the source of their disease except on an experimental basis. The goals of the work in progress, however, are to identify who is susceptible to the development of diabetes and to prevent diabetic emergencies and sequelae or to prevent expression of the disease.

A genetic basis for diabetes is suggested by the association of type 1 with certain HLA markers and by the findings of numerous twin and family studies.[4,16] Families who move from areas with a low frequency of type 1 diabetes to areas with a high frequency have an incidence of disease similar to that in the areas where they reside; this suggests an environmental basis for diabetes. An autoimmune cause has been clearly demonstrated in many type 1 diabetic patients. Islet cell amyloid has also been associated with diabetes. In both types a variety of viruses have been implicated, most notably congenital rubella, Coxsackie B virus, and cytomegalovirus.

Research has identified two groups of cellular carbohydrate transporters in cell membranes. Sodium-linked glucose transporters are found primarily in the intestine and kidney. The glucose transporter (GLUT) proteins are found throughout the body and transport glucose by facilitated diffusion down concentration gradients. The GLUT-4 transporter, found primarily in muscle, is insulin responsive, and a signaling defect in the protein may be responsible for insulin resistance in some diabetic patients.[17]

CLINICAL FEATURES

Type 1

The patient with type 1 diabetes is usually lean, younger than 40 years of age, and ketosis prone. Plasma insulin levels are absent to low; plasma glucagon levels are high but suppressible with insulin, and patients require insulin therapy when symptoms appear. Onset of symptoms may be abrupt, with polydipsia, polyuria, polyphagia, and weight loss developing rapidly. In some cases the disease is heralded by ketoacidosis.[3] A myriad of problems related to type 1 diabetes may prompt an emergency department visit, including acute metabolic complications such as diabetic ketoacidosis and late complications such as cardiovascular or circulatory abnormalities, retinopathy, nephropathy, neuropathy, foot ulcers, severe infections, and various skin lesions.

Type 2

The patient with type 2 diabetes is usually middle aged or older, overweight, with normal to high insulin levels. Insulin levels are lower than would be predicted for glucose levels, however, leading to a relative insulin deficiency, probably because of an insulin secretory defect.[3] All type 2 patients demonstrate impaired insulin function related to poor insulin production, failure of insulin to reach the site of action, or failure of end-organ response to insulin.

As with type 1 diabetes, research suggests distinct subgroups of patients under the classification of type 2 diabetes. Although most adult patients are obese, 20% are not. Nonobese patients form a subgroup with a different disease, more similar to type 1. Another subgroup comprises young persons with maturity-onset diabetes.[8] They have an autosomal dominant inheritance of their disease, are usually not obese, and have a relatively mild course of disease.

Symptoms tend to begin more gradually in type 2 diabetes than in type 1. The diagnosis of type 2 is often made because of an elevated blood glucose found on routine laboratory examination. Glucose may be controlled by dietary therapy, oral hypoglycemic agents, or insulin, depending on the individual. Decompensation of disease usually leads to hyperosmolar nonketotic coma rather than ketosis.

Type 2 diabetes is increasingly being diagnosed in children and adolescents.[18]

DIAGNOSTIC STRATEGIES

Serum Glucose

As a rule, any random plasma glucose level greater than 200 mg/dL, a fasting plasma glucose concentration greater than 140 mg/dL, or a 2-hour postload OGTT is sufficient to establish the diagnosis of diabetes. In the absence of hyperglycemia with metabolic decompensation, these criteria should be confirmed by repeated testing on a different day.[6] A value of 150 mg/dL is likely to distinguish diabetic from nondiabetic patients more accurately. Formal OGTTs are unnecessary except during pregnancy or in patients suspected of having diabetes who do not meet the criteria for a particular classification. The World Health Organization and NDDG provide protocols for performance of the OGTT.

Glycosylated Hemoglobin

Measurement of glycosylated hemoglobin (HbA$_{1c}$) is one of the most important ways to assess the level of glucose control. Elevated serum glucose binds progressively and irreversibly to the amino-terminal valine of the hemoglobin β-chain. The HbA$_{1c}$ measurement provides insight into the quality of glycemic control over time. Given the long half-life of red blood cells, the percentage of HbA$_{1c}$ is an index of glucose concentration of the preceding 6 to 8 weeks, with normal values approximately 4% to 6% of total hemoglobin, depending on the assay used.[19] Levels in poorly controlled patients may reach 10% to 12%. Measurement of glycated albumin can be used to monitor diabetic control over 1 to 2 weeks because of its short half-life but is rarely used clinically. The American Diabetes Association (ADA) recommends at least biannual measurements of HbA$_{1c}$ for the follow-up of all types of diabetes.[19] The ADA currently sets an HbA$_{1c}$ of less than 7% as a treatment goal.[20]

Urine Glucose

Urine glucose measurement methods are basically of two types: reagent tests and dipstick tests. The *reagent tests* (e.g., Clinitest) are copper reduction tests. They are somewhat more cumbersome and expensive than dipstick methods, use tablets that are very caustic and dangerous if accidentally ingested, and may be affected by many substances (Box 124-2).

Dipstick tests generally use glucose oxidase, which may also be affected by different substances (Box 124-3). Dipsticks are inexpensive and convenient but may vary in their sensitivity and strength of reaction to a given concentration of glucose. Dipstick interpretation can vary significantly, depending on the observer

---

BOX 124-2. Substances Interfering with Copper Reduction Tests (False-Positive Results)

Ascorbic acid	Levodopa
Cephaloridine	Metaxalone (Skelaxin)
Cephalothin	metabolite
Dilute urine	Methyldopa
Gentisic acid (aspirin)	Penicillin
Glucuronic acid conjugates	Probenecid
Homogentisic acid	Reducing sugars
Isoniazid	Salicylates
Lactose in pregnant women	Streptomycin

From *Contemp Pharm Pract* 3:224, 1980.

BOX 124-3. Substances Interfering with Glucose Oxidase Tests

False-Positive Results	Glutathione
Chloride glucose hypochlorite	Homogentisic acid
	Hydrogen peroxide
False-Negative Results	Peroxide
Ascorbic acid	5-Hydroxyindole acetic acid
Aspirin	5-Hydroxytryptamine
Bilirubin	5-Hydroxytryptophan
Catalase	L-Dopamine
Catechol	Levodopa
Cysteine	Meralluride injection
3,4-Dihydroxyphenylacetic acid	Methyldopa (Aldomet)
	Sodium bisulfate
Epinephrine	Tetracycline (with vitamin C)
Ferrous sulfate (Feosol)	Uric acid
Gentisic acid	

From *Contemp Pharm Pract* 3:224, 1980.

---

and the type of lighting. Both falsely high and falsely low urine glucose readings can also occur.[21] With the "plus" system, one-plus, two-plus, three-plus, and four-plus have different implications about urine glucose concentrations, depending on the brand of dipstick. Using reflectance colorimeters to read dipsticks increases accuracy. Urine glucose tests must be interpreted loosely because many factors can affect their results.

Urine Ketones

Urine ketone dipsticks use the nitroprusside reaction, which is a good test for acetoacetate but does not measure β-hydroxybutyrate. Although the usual acetoacetate/β-hydroxybutyrate ratio in diabetic ketoacidosis is 1:2.8, it may be as high as 1:30, in which case the urine dipstick does not reflect the true level of ketosis. When ketones are in the form of β-hydroxybutyrate, the urine ketone dipsticks may infrequently yield negative reactions in patients with significant ketosis.

Dipstick Blood Glucose

Dipsticks for testing blood glucose are clearly a more accurate means of monitoring blood glucose than urine dipsticks but also may be inaccurate. Hematocrits below 30% or above 55% cause unduly high or low readings, respectively, and a number of the strips specifically disclaim accuracy when used for neonates. Sensitivity of dipsticks to a variety of factors varies with the particular brand. The largest errors are in the hyperglycemic range. Dipstick readings rarely err more than 30 mg/dL when actual concentrations are below 90 mg/dL. Although specific glucose concentrations may not be accurately represented, blood glucose dipsticks are useful in estimating the general range of the glucose value.

Reflectance meters increase the accuracy of the dipstick blood glucose determination. If maximum accuracy is desired, however, the emergency physician should normally order a laboratory blood glucose determination.

Patients' subcutaneous insulin regimens must be closely managed by their primary physician or endocrinologist, tailored to achieve optimal glycemic control based on HbA$_{1c}$ measurements. Patients are also able to individualize their insulin regimen by using an insulin pump. The insulin pump requires the patient to insert a new plastic hub subcutaneously approximately every 3 days. The delivery tubing from the palm-sized pump is inserted into the hub, ensuring a reliable infusion of insulin. The pump can be dynamically programmed by the patient to deliver sufficient insulin to metabolize the carbohydrates consumed. Use of the pump obviously requires the patient to develop substantial skill.

HYPOGLYCEMIA

Hypoglycemia is a common problem in patients with type 1 diabetes, especially if tight glycemic control is practiced, and may be the most dangerous acute complication of diabetes. The estimated incidence of hypoglycemia in diabetic patients is 9 to 120 episodes per 100 patient-years.[22-24] As aggressive efforts continue to keep both fasting and postprandial glucose within the normal range, the incidence of hypoglycemia may increase. The most common cause of coma associated with diabetes is an excess of administered insulin with respect to glucose intake. Hypoglycemia may be associated with significant morbidity and mortality. Severe hypoglycemia is usually associated with a blood sugar level below 40 to 50 mg/dL and impaired cognitive function.[25]

Principles of Disease

Protection against hypoglycemia is normally provided by cessation of insulin release and mobilization of counterregulatory hormones, which increase hepatic glucose production and decrease glucose use. Diabetic patients using insulin are vulnerable to hypoglycemia because of insulin excess and failure of the counterregulatory system.[3]

BOX 124-4. Precipitants of Hypoglycemia in Diabetic Patients

Addison's disease	Oral hypoglycemics
Akee fruit	Overaggressive treatment of
Anorexia nervosa	diabetic ketoacidosis and
Antimalarials	hyperglycemic
Decrease in usual food	hyperosmolar
intake	nonketotic coma
Ethanol	Pentamidine
Factitious hypoglycemia	Phenylbutazone
Hepatic impairment	Propranolol
Hyperthyroidism	Recent change of dose or
Hypothyroidism	type of insulin or oral
Increase in usual exercise	hypoglycemic
Insulin	Salicylates
Islet cell tumors	Sepsis
Malfunctioning, improperly	Some antibacterial
adjusted, or incorrectly	sulfonylureas
used insulin pump	Worsening renal
Malnutrition	insufficiency
Old age	

Hypoglycemia may be caused by missing a meal, increasing energy output, or increasing insulin dosage. It can also occur in the absence of any precipitant (Box 124-4). Oral hypoglycemic agents have also been implicated in causing hypoglycemia, both in the course of therapy and as an agent of overdose.

Hypoglycemia without warning, or *hypoglycemia unawareness*, is a dangerous complication of type 1 diabetes probably caused by previous exposure to low blood glucose concentrations.[25] Even a single hypoglycemic episode can reduce neurohumoral counterregulatory responses to subsequent episodes.[26,27] Other factors associated with recurrent hypoglycemic attacks include overaggressive or intensified insulin therapy, longer history of diabetes, autonomic neuropathy, and decreased epinephrine secretion or sensitivity.[25]

The *Somogyi phenomenon* is a common problem associated with iatrogenic hypoglycemia in the type 1 diabetic patient. The phenomenon is initiated by an excessive insulin dosage, which results in an unrecognized hypoglycemic episode that usually occurs in the early morning while the patient is sleeping. The counterregulatory hormone response produces rebound hyperglycemia, evident when the patient awakens. Often, both the patient and the physician interpret this hyperglycemia as an indication to increase the insulin dosage, which exacerbates the problem.[28] Instead, the insulin dosage should be lowered or the timing changed.

Clinical Features

Symptomatic hypoglycemia occurs in most adults at a blood glucose level of 40 to 50 mg/dL. The rate at which glucose decreases, however, as well as the patient's age, gender, size, overall health, and previous hypoglycemic reactions, also contributes to symptoms. Signs and symptoms of hypoglycemia are caused by excessive secretion of epinephrine and CNS dysfunction and

BOX 124-5. Summary of Treatment for Hypoglycemia

1. Suspect hypoglycemia.
   Check serum glucose; obtain sample before treatment.
   If clinical suspicion of hypoglycemia is strong, proceed before laboratory results are available.
2. Correct serum glucose.
   If patient is awake and cooperative, administer sugar-containing food or beverage PO.
   If patient is unable to take PO:
     25-75 g glucose as D50W (1-3 ampules) IV
     Children: 0.5-1 g/kg glucose as D25W IV (2-4 mL/kg)
   Neonates: 0.5-1 g/kg glucose (1-2 mL/kg) as D10W
   If unable to obtain IV access:
     1-2 mg glucagon IM or SC; may repeat q20min
     Children: 0.025-0.1 mg/kg SC or IM; may repeat q20min

include sweating, nervousness, tremor, tachycardia, hunger, and neurologic symptoms ranging from bizarre behavior and confusion to seizures and coma.[22] In patients with hypoglycemia unawareness, the prodrome to marked hypoglycemia may be minimal or absent. These individuals may rapidly become unarousable without warning. They may have a seizure or show focal neurologic signs, which resolve with glucose administration.

Diagnostic Strategies

The cardinal laboratory test for hypoglycemia is blood glucose. It should be obtained, if possible, before therapy is begun. As noted, dipstick readings are very helpful in permitting rapid, reasonably accurate blood glucose estimates before therapy.

Laboratory testing should address any suspected cause of the hypoglycemia, such as ethanol or other drug ingestion. If factitious hypoglycemia is suspected, testing for insulin antibodies or low levels of C peptide may be helpful.

Management

In alert patients with mild symptoms, consumption of sugar-containing food or beverage orally is often adequate (Box 124-5). In other patients, after blood is drawn for glucose determination, one to three ampules of 50% dextrose in water (D50W) should be administered intravenously while the airway, breathing, and circulation of resuscitation are being completed. Augmentation of the blood glucose level by administering an ampule of D50W may range from less than 40 to more than 350 mg/dL.[29] These therapeutic steps are appropriately performed in the field if prehospital care is available. If alcohol abuse is suspected, thiamine should also be administered. D50W should not be used in infants or young children because venous sclerosis can lead to rebound hypoglycemia. In a child younger than 8 years it is advisable to use 25% (D25W) or even 10% dextrose (D10W). D25W may be prepared by diluting D50W 1:1 with sterile water.

The dose is 0.5 to 1 g/kg body weight or, using D25W, 2 to 4 mL/kg.

If intravenous (IV) access cannot be rapidly obtained, 1 to 2 mg of glucagon may be given intramuscularly or subcutaneously.[30] The onset of action is 10 to 20 minutes, and peak response occurs in 30 to 60 minutes. It may be repeated as needed. Glucagon may also be administered intravenously; 1 mg has an effect very similar to that of one ampule of D50W. Glucagon is ineffective in causes of hypoglycemia in which glycogen is absent, notably alcohol-induced hypoglycemia.

Families of type 1 diabetic patients are often taught to administer intramuscular glucagon at home. Of the families so instructed, only 9% to 42% actually inject the glucagon when indicated.[31] Intranasal glucagon may become more widely accepted.[32] Prehospital care providers and emergency physicians should seek a history of glucagon administration because it alters initial blood glucose readings.

All patients with severe hypoglycemic reactions require aspiration and seizure precautions. Although the response to IV glucose is generally rapid, older patients may require several days for complete recovery.

Overdoses of oral hypoglycemic agents pose special problems because the hypoglycemia induced tends to be prolonged and severe. The hypoglycemia may be delayed in onset by as much as 24 hours and may recur more than 72 hours later. Chlorpropamide is particularly troublesome in this respect. Thus, patients with overdose of oral hypoglycemic agents should have a minimum observation period of 24 hours and more if hypoglycemia is recurrent. Patients with overdose of oral hypoglycemic agents often require constant infusion of D10W to maintain a normal serum glucose.

When therapy for hypoglycemia has been given, a careful history must be taken to determine the cause.

Disposition

Type 1 diabetic patients with brief episodes of hypoglycemia uncomplicated by other disease may be discharged from the emergency department if a cause of the hypoglycemia can be found and corrected by instruction or medication. All patients should be given a meal before discharge to ensure the ability to tolerate oral feedings and to begin to replenish glycogen stores in glycogen-deficient patients. Patients who are discharged should receive short-term follow-up for ongoing evaluation. Patients with hypoglycemia caused by oral agents should be observed in the hospital because of the high likelihood of recurrent hypoglycemia.

Nondiabetic Patients

Hypoglycemia in the nondiabetic patient may be classified as postprandial or fasting (Box 124-6). The most common cause of *postprandial hypoglycemia* is alimentary hyperinsulinism, such as that seen in patients who have undergone gastrectomy, gastrojejunostomy, pyloroplasty, or vagotomy. *Fasting hypoglycemia* is caused when there is an imbalance between glucose production and use. The causes of inadequate glucose production include hormone deficiencies, enzyme defects, substrate deficiencies, severe liver disease, and drugs. Causes of overuse of glucose include the presence of an insulinoma, exogenous insulin, sulfonylureas, drugs, endotoxic shock, extrapancreatic tumors, and a variety of enzyme deficiencies.

Emergency treatment is similar to that of hypoglycemia in the diabetic patient. The determination of inpatient versus outpatient evaluation of hypoglycemia in a nondiabetic patient should be based upon the suspected cause and the nature of the episode (i.e., factors such as severity, persistence, and recurrence),

DIABETIC KETOACIDOSIS

Principles of Disease

Pathophysiology

Diabetic ketoacidosis (DKA) is a syndrome in which insulin deficiency and glucagon excess combine to produce a hyperglycemic, dehydrated, acidotic patient

---

BOX 124-6. Causes of Hypoglycemia

Postprandial
Alimentary hyperinsulinism
Fructose intolerance
Galactemia
Leucine sensitivity

Fasting
Underproduction of Glucose
Hormone deficiencies
   Hypopituitarism
   Adrenal insufficiency
   Catecholamine deficiency
   Glucagon deficiency
Enzyme defects
Substrate deficiency
   Malnutrition
   Late pregnancy
Liver disease
Drugs

Overuse of Glucose
Hyperinsulinism
   Insulinoma
   Exogenous insulin
   Sulfonylureas
   Drugs
   Shock
Tumors

---

with profound electrolyte imbalance (Figure 124-1).[33] All derangements producing DKA are interrelated and are based on insulin deficiency. DKA may be caused by cessation of insulin intake or by physical or emotional stress despite continued insulin therapy.

The effects of insulin deficiency may be mimicked in peripheral tissues by a lack of either insulin receptors or insulin sensitivity at receptor or postreceptor sites. When the hyperglycemia becomes sufficiently marked, the renal threshold is surpassed and glucose is excreted in the urine. The hyperosmolarity produced by hyperglycemia and dehydration is the most important determinant of the patient's mental status.[34]

Glucose in the renal tubules draws water, sodium, potassium, magnesium, calcium, phosphorus, and other ions from the circulation into the urine. This osmotic diuresis combined with poor intake and vomiting produces the profound dehydration and electrolyte imbalance associated with DKA (Table 124-1). Exocrine pancreatic dysfunction closely parallels endocrine beta cell dysfunction, producing malabsorption that further limits the body's intake of fluid and exacerbates electrolyte loss.

In 95% of patients with DKA, the total sodium level is normal or low. Potassium, magnesium, and phosphorus deficits are usually marked. As a result of acidosis and dehydration, however, the initial reported values for these electrolytes may be high. Hypokalemia may further inhibit insulin release.

The cells, unable to receive fuel substances from the circulation, act as they do in starvation from other causes. They decrease amino acid uptake and accelerate proteolysis such that large amounts of amino acids are released to the liver and converted to two-carbon fragments.

Adipose tissue in the patient with DKA fails to clear the circulation of lipids. Insulin deficiency results in activation of a hormone-sensitive lipase that increases circulating free fatty acid (FFA) levels. Long-chain FFAs, now circulating in abundance as a result of insulin deficiency, are partially oxidized and converted in the liver to acetoacetate and β-hydroxybutyrate. This alteration of liver metabolism to oxidize FFAs to ketones rather than the normal process of reesterification to triglycerides appears to correlate directly with the altered glucagon/insulin ratio in the portal blood. Despite the pathologic glucagon-mediated increased production of ketones, the body acts as it does in any form of starvation, to decrease the peripheral tissue's use of ketones as fuel. The combination of increased ketone production with decreased ketone use leads to ketoacidosis.

Table 124-1. Average Fluid and Electrolyte Deficits in Severe Diabetic Ketoacidosis (per Kilogram Body Weight)

Weight	Water (mL/kg)	Sodium (mEq/L)	Potassium (mEq/L)	Chloride (mEq/L)	Phosphorus (mEq/L)
<10 kg	100-120	8-10	5-7	6-8	3
10-20 kg	80-100	8-10	5-7	6-8	3
>20 kg	70-80	8-10	5-7	6-8	3

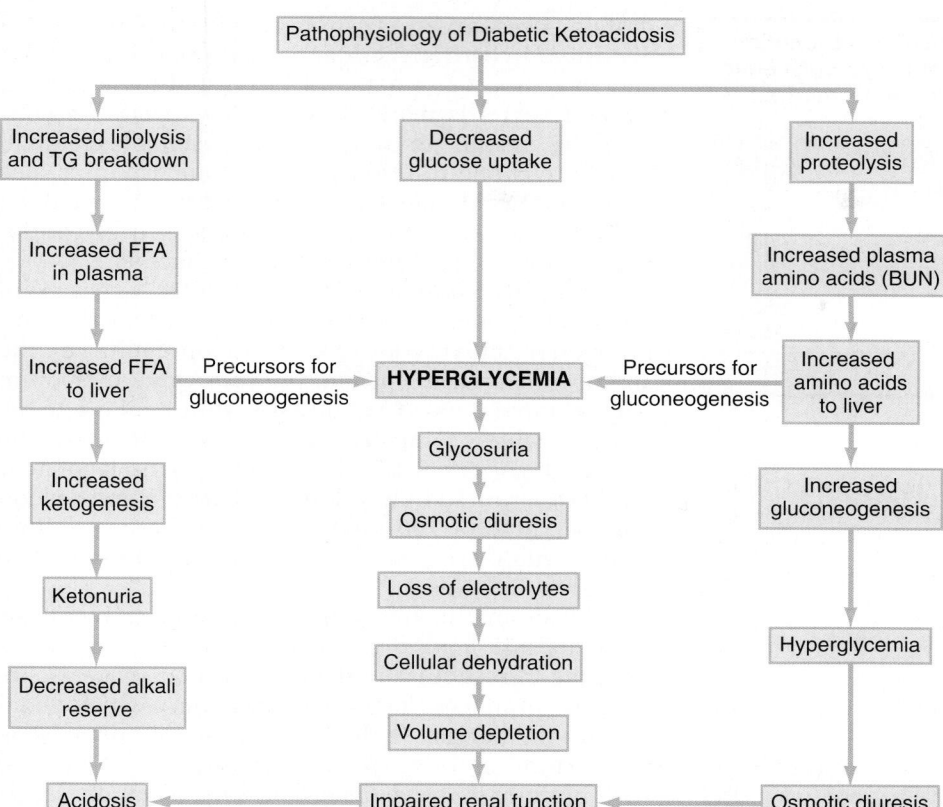

The degree of ketosis has been related to the magnitude of release of the counterregulatory hormones epinephrine, glucagon, cortisol, and somatostatin. Glucagon is elevated fourfold to fivefold in DKA and is the most influential ketogenic hormone. It is believed to affect ketogenesis by reducing the concentration of malonyl coenzyme A and by inhibiting glycolysis. Epinephrine, norepinephrine, cortisol, growth hormone, dopamine, and thyroxin have all been shown to enhance ketogenesis indirectly by stimulating lipolysis. Because propranolol and metyrapone can block the effect of counterregulatory hormones, they have been successfully used to inhibit the development of DKA in patients with frequent episodes not otherwise treatable.

Acidosis plays a prominent role in the clinical presentation of DKA. The acidotic patient attempts to increase lung ventilation and rid the body of excess acid with Kussmaul's respiration. Bicarbonate (HCO_3^-) is used up in the process. Current evidence suggests that acidosis compounds the effects of ketosis and hyperosmolality to depress mental status directly.

Acidemia is not invariably present, even with significant ketoacidosis. *Ketoalkalosis* has been reported in diabetic patients vomiting for several days and in some with severe dehydration and hyperventilation. The finding of alkalemia, however, should prompt the consideration of alcoholic ketoacidosis, in which this finding is much more common.

Etiology

Most often, DKA occurs in patients with type 1 diabetes and is associated with inadequate administration of insulin, infection, or myocardial infarction (MI). DKA can also occur in type 2 patients and may be associated with any type of stress, such as sepsis or gastrointestinal (GI) bleeding. Approximately 25% of all episodes of DKA occur in patients whose diabetes was previously undiagnosed.[5,35]

Diagnostic Strategies

History

Clinically, most patients with DKA complain of a recent history of polydipsia, polyuria, polyphagia, visual blurring, weakness, weight loss, nausea, vomiting, and abdominal pain. Approximately one half of these patients, especially children, report abdominal pain, which may mimic that in acute inflammation of the abdomen. In children this pain is usually idiopathic and probably caused by gastric distention or stretching of the liver capsule; it resolves as the metabolic abnormalities are corrected. In adults, however, abdominal pain more often signifies true abdominal disease.

Physical Examination

Physical examination may or may not demonstrate a depressed sensorium. Typical findings include tachyp-

Table 124-2. Typical Laboratory Values in Diabetic Ketoacidosis (DKA) and Hyperglycemic Hyperosmolar Nonketotic Coma (HHNC)

	DKA	HHNC
Glucose (mg/dl)	>350	>700
Sodium (mEq)	low 130s	140s
Potassium (mEq)	~4.5-6.0	~5
Bicarbonate (mEq)	<10	>15
BUN (mg/dL)	25-50	>50
Serum ketones	Present	Absent

BUN, blood urea nitrogen.

nea with Kussmaul's respiration, tachycardia, frank hypotension or orthostatic blood pressure changes, the odor of acetone on the breath, and signs of dehydration.[36] An elevated temperature is rarely caused by DKA itself and suggests the presence of sepsis.

Laboratory Tests

Initial tests allow preliminary confirmation of the diagnosis and immediate initiation of therapy (Table 124-2). Subsequent tests are made to determine more specifically the degree of dehydration, acidosis, and electrolyte imbalance and to reveal the precipitant of DKA.

On the patient's arrival at the emergency department, serum and urine glucose and ketones, electrolytes, and arterial blood gases (ABGs) should be checked. *Glucose* is usually elevated above 350 mg/dL; however, euglycemic DKA (blood glucose <300 mg/dL) has been reported in up to 18% of patients.[3] ABGs demonstrate a low pH. Venous pH is not significantly different from arterial pH in patients with DKA, and some researchers consider the use of venous blood superior to repeated arterial puncture. *Metabolic acidosis* with anion gap is secondary to elevated plasma levels of acetoacetate and β-hydroxybutyrate, although lactate, FFAs, phosphates, volume depletion, and several medications also contribute to this condition.[3] Rarely, a well-hydrated patient with DKA may have a pure hyperchloremic acidosis and no anion gap. If an immediate *potassium* level is not available through ABG, an electrocardiogram may indicate potassium levels. Despite initial potassium levels that are normal to high, a total potassium deficit of several hundred milliequivalents results from potassium and hydrogen shifts.

Other tests may include complete blood count with differential, magnesium, calcium, amylase, blood urea nitrogen (BUN), creatinine, phosphorus, ketone, and lactate level determinations. A complete urinalysis helps in assessment of infection or renal disease. Elevations of urine specific gravity, BUN, and hematocrit suggest dehydration. Appropriate cultures should be dictated by clinical findings. A patient with mild DKA or with recurrent episodes receives testing as deemed appropriate by the emergency physician.

The serum *sodium* value is often misleading in DKA. Sodium is often low in the presence of significant dehy-dration because it is strongly affected by hyperglycemia, hypertriglyceridemia, salt-poor fluid intake, and increased GI, renal, and insensible losses. When *hyperglycemia* is marked, water flows from the cells into the vessels to decrease the osmolar gradient, thereby creating dilutional hyponatremia. Lipids also dilute the blood, thereby further lowering the value of sodium. Newer autoanalyzers remove triglycerides before assay, thus eliminating this artifact.

Hypertriglyceridemia is common in DKA because of impaired lipoprotein lipase activity and hepatic over-production of very-low-density lipoprotein.[3] In the absence of marked lipemia, the true value of sodium may be approximated by adding 1.3 to 1.6 mEq/L to the sodium value on the laboratory report for every 100 mg/dL glucose over the norm. Thus, if the laboratory reports a serum sodium value of 130 mEq/L and a blood glucose value of 700 mEq/L, the total serum sodium value is more accurately assessed to be between 137.8 and 139.6 mEq/L.

Acidosis and the hyperosmolarity induced by hyperglycemia shift *potassium*, *magnesium*, and *phosphorus* from the intracellular to the extracellular space. Dehydration produces hemoconcentration, which contributes to normal or high initial serum potassium, magnesium, and phosphorus readings in DKA, even with profound total deficits. The emergency physician may correct for the effect of acidosis on the serum potassium determination by subtracting 0.6 mEq/L from the laboratory potassium value for every 0.1 decrease in pH noted in the ABG analysis.[37] Thus, if the potassium is reported as 5 mEq/L and the pH is 6.94, the corrected potassium value would be only 2 mEq/L, representing severe hypokalemia. While insulin is administered and the hydrogen ion (H^+) concentration decreases, the patient needs considerable potassium replacement. Finally, hyperglycemia and the anion gap have significant effects on the plasma potassium concentration, independent of acidosis.[34] No conversion factor has been developed for estimating true magnesium levels, although initial values may be high.

All laboratory determinations must be interpreted with caution. Serum creatinine determinations made by autoanalyzer may be falsely elevated.[33] Leukocytosis more closely reflects the degree of ketosis than the presence of infection. Only the elevation of band neutrophils has been demonstrated to indicate the presence of infection, with a sensitivity of 100% and a specificity of 80%. The diagnosis of pancreatitis is confounded by the usually elevated urine and serum amylase levels in DKA. Typically, this is salivary amylase, but most laboratories are not equipped to make this distinction. A serum lipase determination helps to distinguish pancreatitis from elevated salivary amylase levels.

Differential Considerations

Alcoholics, especially those who have recently abstained from drinking, with Kussmaul's respiration, a fruity odor to the breath, and acidotic ABG values may have *alcoholic ketoacidosis*. These patients may be euglycemic or hypoglycemic, and a large part of

BOX 124-7. Summary of Treatment for Diabetic Ketoacidosis

Identify DKA: serum glucose, electrolytes, ketones, and ABG; also draw CBC with differential; urinalysis; chest x-ray film and ECG, if indicated.

1. Supplement insulin.
   ± Bolus: 0.1 U/kg regular insulin IV
   Maintenance: 0.1 U/kg/hr regular insulin IV
   Change IV solution to D5W 0.45% normal saline when glucose ≤300 mg/dL.
2. Rehydrate.
   1–2 L normal saline IV over 1-3 hours
   Children: 20 mL/kg normal saline over first hour
   Follow with 0.45% normal saline
3. Correct electrolyte abnormalities.
   Sodium
     Correct with administration of normal saline and 0.45% normal saline.
   Potassium
     Ensure adequate renal function.
     Add 20–40 mEq KCl to each liter of fluid.
   Phosphorus
     Usually unnecessary to replenish

Magnesium
  Correct with 1–2 g $MgSO_4$ (in first 2 L if magnesium is low).
4. Correct acidosis.
   Add 44–88 mEq/L to first liter of IV fluids only if pH ≤ 7.0.
   Correct to pH 7.1.
5. Search and correct underlying precipitant.
6. Monitor progress and keep meticulous flow sheets.
   Vital signs
   Fluid intake and urine output
   Serum glucose, K^+, Cl^-, HCO_3^+, CO_2, pH
   Amount of insulin administered
7. Admit to hospital or intensive care unit.
   Consider outpatient therapy in children with reliable care-taker *and*
   Initial pH > 7.35
   Initial HCO_3^- ≥ 20 mEq/L
   Can tolerate PO fluids
   Resolution of symptoms after treatment in emergency department
   No underlying precipitant requiring hospitalization

ABG, arterial blood gas; CBC, complete blood count; DKA, diabetic ketoacidosis; ECG, electrocardiogram.

their acidosis is often caused by the unmeasured β-hydroxybutyric acid. Alcoholic ketoacidosis accounts for approximately 20% of all cases of ketoacidosis.

Ketoacidosis can also develop with fasting in the third trimester of pregnancy and in nursing mothers who do not eat.[38]

Other entities that may manifest with various combinations of altered mental status, acidosis, and abdominal pain include hypoglycemia, cerebrovascular accident (stroke), trauma, sepsis, hyperglycemic hyperosmolar nonketotic coma, postictal states, lactic acidosis, uremic acidosis, and abdominal emergencies. Intoxications by ethanol, salicylates, methanol, isopropyl alcohol, chloral hydrate, paraldehyde, ethylene glycol, and cyanide all share some features of DKA.

Management

General Measures

The approach to the patient with severe DKA is the same as that to any patient in extremis. The comatose patient, especially if vomiting, requires intubation. Once the patient is intubated, hyperventilation should be maintained to prevent worsening acidosis. The patient in hypovolemic shock requires aggressive fluid resuscitation with 0.9% saline solution rather than pressors. Other possible causes of shock (e.g., sepsis or myocardial dysfunction secondary to MI) should be considered. Close monitoring of vital signs is essential. In the patient whose therapy may precipitate fluid overload caused by cardiac compromise or renal failure, a central venous pressure line or Swan-Ganz line should be inserted.

The diagnosis of DKA is generally simple. When hyperglycemia, ketosis, and acidosis have been estab-lished, fluid, electrolyte, and insulin therapy should begin (Box 124-7).

Insulin

DKA cannot be reversed without insulin, and insulin therapy should be initiated as soon as the diagnosis is certain. In the past, very high dosages of insulin were administered to diabetic patients in DKA because they were thought to be extremely insulin resistant. However, low-dosage insulin therapy has proved as effective as high-dosage therapy.[5] The rate of decrease in blood sugar is equal or only slightly more gradual. The overall potassium requirement is less. High dosages of insulin have potentially harmful effects, including a greater incidence of iatrogenic hypoglycemia and hypokalemia.[33]

The exact amount of insulin administered varies. Many start therapy with a bolus of 10 units of regular insulin intravenously. This initial bolus may produce certain problems, however, and makes no significant difference in therapy.[39] The current therapy of choice is regular insulin infused at a rate of 0.1 U/kg/hr up to 5 to 10 U/hr, mixed with the IV fluids. Regular insulin, 10 to 20 U/hr, administered intramuscularly accomplishes similar effect but subjects the patient to repeated painful injections. In theory, intramuscular insulin may accumulate at a poorly perfused administration site, failing to enter the systemic circulation in a timely manner.

In children, the IV dosage of regular insulin may be calculated at 0.1 U/kg. Children are more likely than adults to develop cerebral edema in response to a rapid lowering of plasma osmolarity. Thus, reduction of glucose levels in children should be gradual.

Because the half-life of regular insulin is 3 to 10 minutes, IV insulin should be administered by constant infusion rather than by repeated bolus. When the blood glucose has dropped to 250 to 300 mg/dL, dextrose should be added to the IV fluids to prevent iatrogenic hypoglycemia and cerebral edema. In patients with euglycemic DKA, dextrose should be added to the IV fluids at the start of insulin therapy.

Insulin adheres to the walls of glass and polyvinyl bottles and tubing, making the exact amount of insulin being administered uncertain.[40] Running approximately 10 units of the insulin infusion through the tubing accomplishes adherence without altering the delivered concentration of the remainder of the infusate.

Insulin resistance occurs rarely in diabetic patients and requires an increase in dosage to obtain a satisfactory response. Resistance may be caused by obesity or accelerated insulin degradation.[3]

Two general categories of insulin resistance are described.[41] *Postreceptor-binding resistance* is the more common type. It is a mild to moderate resistance probably caused by defects in intracellular metabolism. It takes only a small amount of insulin to fill the receptors. When they are filled, administration of additional insulin produces no further effect. The second type, *prereceptor-receptor resistance*, is rare. This severe resistance may be caused by insulin antibodies, high concentrations of stress hormones, antireceptor antibodies, or any combination of these.[42]

Dehydration

The severely dehydrated patient is likely to have a fluid deficit of 3 to 5 L. No uniformly accepted formula exists for the administration of fluid in this disorder.

If the patient is in hypovolemic shock, normal saline (NS) should be administered as rapidly as possible in the adult, or in 20 mL/kg boluses in the child, until a systolic pressure of 80 mm Hg is obtained. In the adult who has marked dehydration in the absence of clinical shock or heart failure, 1 L of NS may be administered in the first hour. In general, 2 L of NS over the first 1 to 3 hours is followed by a slower infusion of half-NS solution. Patients with DKA without extreme volume depletion may be successfully treated with a lower volume of IV fluid replacement.[35] NS solution at 20 mL/kg over the first hour is the usual fluid resuscitation therapy for a child. Thereafter, fluid rate should be adjusted according to age, cardiac status, and degree of dehydration to achieve a urine output of 1 to 2 mL/kg/hr. Whereas some authors advocate half-NS or colloid solution, most evidence and practice favor initial resuscitation with 0.9% NS solution.

Fluid resuscitation alone may help to lower hyperglycemia. Because even in DKA a low level of circulating insulin may be present, increased perfusion may transport insulin to previously unreached receptor sites. In addition, a large volume of glucose may be cleared by the kidneys in response to improved renal perfusion. The mean plasma glucose concentration has been noted to drop 18% after administration of saline solution without insulin.[5]

Acidosis also decreases after fluid infusion alone. Increased perfusion improves tissue oxygenation, thus diminishing the formation of lactate. Increased renal perfusion promotes renal H^+ loss, and the improved action of insulin in the better-hydrated patient inhibits ketogenesis.

Some authors believe that the rapid decrease of the hyperosmolarity of DKA caused by the administration of 0.45% NS solution may precipitate cerebral edema, one of the most dangerous complications associated with the patient in DKA, especially children.[43-45]

Potassium

Potassium replacement is invariably needed in DKA. The initial potassium level is often normal or high despite a large deficit because of severe acidosis. Potassium levels often plummet with correction of acidosis and administration of insulin. Potassium should be administered with the fluids while the laboratory value is in the upper half of the normal range. Renal function should be monitored. In patients with low serum potassium at presentation, hypokalemia may become life threatening when insulin therapy is administered. IV potassium should be aggressively administered in concentrations of 20 to 40 mEq/L as required.

Some administer a portion of the potassium as the phosphate salt. In DKA, phosphate falls from a mean value of 9.2 to 2.8 mg/dL within 12 hours of therapy, reflecting an average total deficit of 0.5 to 1.5 mmol/kg.[41] This may result in a decreased level of 2,3-diphosphoglycerate (2,3-DPG) and subsequent poor oxygen delivery to red blood cells. Other problems associated with the hypophosphatemia are depressed myocardial and respiratory muscle performance, hemolysis, impaired phagocytosis, thrombocytopenia, platelet dysfunction, confusion, and disorientation.[5] The only caveat with phosphorus administration is that its magnesium- and calcium-lowering properties may induce symptomatic hypomagnesemia and hypocalcemia. Despite theoretical benefits, no clinical benefit from the routine administration of phosphorus in DKA has been shown.[5]

Magnesium

Magnesium deficiency is a common problem in patients with DKA without renal disease. Both the initial pathophysiology and the therapy for DKA induce profound magnesium diuresis. Magnesium deficiency may exacerbate vomiting and mental changes, promote hypokalemia and hypocalcemia, or induce fatal cardiac dysrhythmia. The normal person requires 0.30 to 0.35 mEq/kg/day. Thus, it is reasonable to include 0.35 mEq/kg of magnesium in the fluids of the first 3 to 4 hours, with further replacement dependent on blood levels and the clinical picture. This amounts to 1.0 to 3 g of magnesium sulfate in the 70-kg patient.

Acidosis

Bicarbonate therapy may be indicated in severely acidotic patients (pH $\leq$ 7.0).[5] The use of bicarbonate is not warranted in less ill patients for several reasons.[46,47]

1. Bicarbonate worsens the inhibition of oxygen release from red blood cells caused by the 2,3-DPG deficiency seen in phosphorus-depleted patients with DKA.

2. Overly rapid correction of acidosis is contraindicated because the blood-brain barrier (BBB) is much more permeable to carbon dioxide than to bicarbonate. Thus, the correction of intravascular acidosis terminates Kussmaul's respiration, further augmenting the blood carbon dioxide available to cross the BBB. Slowly, sufficient bicarbonate crosses the BBB to provide adequate buffering. In the short term, however, as the blood acidosis is corrected, the acidity of the fluid surrounding the brain increases, causing paradoxical cerebrospinal fluid acidosis. The clinical significance of an acid cerebrospinal fluid pH is controversial.

3. The administration of bicarbonate increases the potassium requirement, both immediately by driving potassium into the cell and more gradually by affecting the kidney, making iatrogenic hypokalemia more likely. When bicarbonate is used, serum potassium levels need to be followed even more closely.

4. The overaggressive use of bicarbonate may produce alkalosis, which induces dysrhythmias largely through its effect on the distribution of electrolytes. Alkalemia occurring late in the course of therapy is more common in patients who have received bicarbonate because ketones are metabolized to carbon dioxide, water, and bicarbonate.

5. Evidence suggests that lowered pH produces a feedback mechanism that directly inhibits ketogenesis. Bicarbonate can increase ketonuria and delay the fall in serum ketones compared with saline infusion alone.

6. Patients treated with bicarbonate fare no better and possibly fare worse than patients treated without bicarbonate. Studies indicate that bicarbonate worsens the prognosis even in patients with severe acidosis and pH values in the range 6.9 to 7.1. It is possible to manage patients who have severe DKA with fluids and insulin alone. When this is done, pH normalization is similar to that in a bicarbonate control group.

When bicarbonate therapy is deemed necessary, the pH should not be corrected above 7.1. Response to therapy should be followed initially with hourly vital signs; fluids should be administered and urine output measured; insulin should be given; and glucose, pH, and anion gap measurements should be determined. Plasma bicarbonate may remain low even while pH increases and anion gap narrows because of the hyperchloremia that develops from rapid saline infusion, loss of bicarbonate in the urine as ketones, and exchanges with intracellular buffers.

Complications

The precipitating causes of DKA may have associated morbidity and mortality equal to or worse than those of DKA itself. These include iatrogenic causes as well as infection and MI. Morbidity in DKA is largely iatrogenic: (1) hypokalemia from inadequate potassium replacement, (2) hypoglycemia from inadequate glucose monitoring and failure to replenish glucose in IV solutions when serum glucose drops below 250 to 300 mg/dL, (3) alkalosis from overaggressive bicarbonate replacement, (4) congestive heart failure from overaggressive hydration, and (5) cerebral edema probably caused by too rapid osmolal shifts. DKA is responsible for 70% of diabetes-related deaths in children. Poor prognostic signs include hypotension, azotemia, coma, and underlying illness.[48]

The mortality in treated DKA decreased from approximately 38% between 1930 and 1959 to about 5% to 7% in the 1980s. The primary causes of death remain infection (especially pneumonia), arterial thromboses, and shock. The decrease in mortality demonstrates that appropriate therapy can make a difference.

Cerebral edema should be suspected when the patient remains comatose or lapses into coma after the reversal of acidosis. It generally occurs 6 to 10 hours after the initiation of therapy. There are no warning signs, and the mortality is currently 90%. Cerebral edema has been associated with low partial pressures of arterial carbon dioxide, high BUN concentration, and the use of bicarbonate. Subclinical cerebral edema in children is probably very common. Furthermore, subclinical cerebral edema may either precede or follow the onset of therapy, raising the question of whether this entity is caused by therapy or is simply a manifestation of the basic pathophysiology of DKA.

Because clinically evident cerebral edema does not usually occur unless the blood sugar level is below 250 mg/dL and insulin is being used, insulin may directly antagonize the brain's defenses against fluid shifts while the plasma glucose level approaches normal values. Other theories attribute the formation of cerebral edema to (1) "idiogenic osmols" developed in the brain as a result of insulin therapy, (2) the rate of fluid administration, and (3) the rate of correction of the acidosis. Other less common causes have been suggested. Several authors recommend the administration of mannitol, 0.25 to 2 mg/kg, at the first sign of altered mental status in children being treated for DKA.[44] Steroids are ineffective treatment for cerebral edema secondary to DKA and may worsen DKA.

Disposition

Most patients require hospital admission, often to the intensive care unit. All pregnant diabetic patients in DKA require admission and consultation with an endocrinologist and obstetrician specializing in the care of high-risk pregnancies. Some children (initial pH > 7.35, bicarbonate ≥ 20 mEq/L) with resolution of findings who can tolerate oral fluids after 3 or 4 hours of treatment may be discharged home with a reliable caregiver.[49] Patients who have mild DKA may be treated on an outpatient basis if (1) the patient or parent is reliable, (2) the underlying causes do not require inpatient therapy, and (3) close follow-up is pursued.

HYPERGLYCEMIC HYPEROSMOLAR NONKETOTIC COMA

Hyperglycemic hyperosmolar nonketotic coma (HHNC) represents a syndrome of acute diabetic decompensation characterized by marked hyperglycemia, hyperosmolarity and dehydration, and decreased mental functioning that may progress to frank coma. Ketosis and acidosis are generally minimal or absent. Focal neurologic signs are common. DKA and HHNC may occur together; some even consider HHNC and DKA to be at two ends of a spectrum, with many patients in the middle.[5,50]

Principles of Disease

Pathophysiology

As with DKA, the pathophysiology of HHNC varies with the particular patient. Because most patients with HHNC are elderly, decreased renal clearance of glucose produced by the decline of renal function with age often contributes to the illness. As with DKA, decreased insulin action results in glycogenolysis, gluconeogenesis, and decreased peripheral uptake of glucose. The hyperglycemia pulls fluid from the intracellular space into the extracellular space, transiently maintaining adequate perfusion. Soon, however, this fluid is lost in a profound osmotic diuresis, limited finally by hypotension and a subsequent drop in the glomerular filtration rate (GFR). The urine is extremely hypotonic, with urine sodium concentration between 50 and 70 mEq/L, compared with 140 mEq/L in extracellular fluid. This hypotonic diuresis produces profound dehydration, leading to hyperglycemia, hypernatremia, and associated hypertonicity. Often the patient is prevented from taking in adequate fluids by stroke, Alzheimer's disease, or other diseases, greatly exacerbating the dehydration of renal origin.

The reason for the absence of ketoacidosis in HHNC is unknown. FFA levels are lower than in DKA, thus limiting substrates needed to form ketones. The most likely reason for the blunted counterregulatory hormone release and lack of ketosis seems to be that these patients continue to secrete the tiny amount of insulin required to block ketogenesis.[51]

Etiology

HHNC is a syndrome of severe dehydration that results from a sustained hyperglycemic diuresis under circumstances in which the patient is unable to drink sufficient fluids to offset the urinary losses. The full-blown syndrome does not usually occur until volume depletion has progressed to the point of decreased urine output.

HHNC is most common in elders with type 2 diabetes but has been reported in children with type 1 diabetes.[52] Box 124-8 lists the broad range of predisposing factors.[4] HHNC may occur in patients who are not diabetic, especially after burns, parenteral hyperalimentation, peritoneal dialysis, or hemodialysis.[53]

BOX 124-8. Precipitants of Hyperglycemic Hyperosmolar Nonketotic Coma

External Insult
Trauma
Burns
Dialysis
Hyperalimentation

Disease Process
Cushing's syndrome and other endocrinopathies
Hemorrhage
Myocardial infarction
Renal disease
Subdural hematoma
Cerebrovascular accident
Infection
Down syndrome

Drugs
Antimetabolites
L-Asparaginase
Chlorpromazine
Chlorpropamide
Cimetidine
Diazoxide
Didanosine
Ethacrynic acid
Furosemide
Glucocorticoids
Immunosuppressants
Phenytoin
Propranolol
Thiazides

Clinical Features

The prodrome for HHNC is significantly longer than that of DKA. Clinically, extreme dehydration, hyperosmolarity, volume depletion, and CNS findings predominate.[51] If awake, patients may complain of fever, thirst, polyuria, or oliguria. Approximately 20% of patients have no known history of type 2 diabetes. The most common associated diseases are chronic renal insufficiency, gram-negative pneumonia, GI bleeding, and gram-negative sepsis. Of these patients, 85% have underlying renal or cardiac impairment as a predisposing factor. Arterial and venous thromboses often complicate the picture.

The patient often exhibits orthostatic hypotension or frank hypotension, tachycardia, and fever with signs of marked dehydration. On average, the HHNC patient has a 24% fluid deficit, or 9 L in the 70-kg patient. The depression of the sensorium correlates directly with the degree and rate of development of hyperosmolarity. Some patients have normal mental status. Seizures are usually associated with neurologic findings, especially epilepsia partialis continua (continuous focal seizures) and intermittent focal motor seizures. Stroke and hemiplegia are also common. Less common neurologic findings include choreoathetosis, ballism, dysphagia, segmental myoclonus, hemiparesis, hemianopsia, central hyperpyrexia, nystagmus, visual hallucinations, and acute quadriplegia.

Diagnostic Strategies

Laboratory findings usually reveal a blood glucose level greater than 600 mg/dL and serum osmolarity greater than 350 mOsm/L. The BUN concentration is invariably elevated (see Table 124-2). Although patients with HHNC do not have a ketoacidosis caused by diabetes, they may have a metabolic acidosis secondary to some combination of lactic acidosis, starvation ketosis, and retention of inorganic acids attributable to renal hypoperfusion.

The patient with HHNC typically manifests more profound electrolyte imbalance than the patient with DKA. Levels of potassium, magnesium, and phosphorus may seem initially high, even in the presence of marked total deficit. In the absence of acidemia, however, the discrepancy between the initial electrolyte reading and body stores is less than that of DKA. Initial serum sodium readings are inaccurate because of hyperglycemia.

Differential Considerations

The differential diagnosis of HHNC is identical to that of DKA. In addition, diabetic patients receiving chlorpropamide are subject to water intoxication with dilutional hyponatremia, which may manifest as coma without acidosis that is clinically indistinguishable from HHNC. The patient with HHNC who has a sharply depressed sensorium may not be initially distinguishable from the patient with profound hypoglycemia. When blood glucose cannot be rapidly checked, the immediate administration of one ampule of D50W minimally worsens HHNC and may be lifesaving for patients with hypoglycemia.

Management

The fluid, electrolyte, and insulin regimens for the initial resuscitation in HHNC are subject to the same controversies as the therapies for DKA (Box 120-9). Whereas some physicians use half-NS solution rapidly infused, most use NS solution, switching to half-NS later in the resuscitation. Just as in DKA, overly rapid correction of serum osmolarity may predispose to the development of cerebral edema in children. There are few reports of cerebral edema complicating HHNC in adults.

Dehydration

Under central venous or pulmonary artery pressure monitoring, rapid administration of NS in a similar fashion to initial therapy for DKA is generally safe. For patients in coma or hypovolemic shock, initial IV fluid infusion should be given as rapidly as possible. If the patient does not have central monitoring and is not in coma or shock, aggressive IV fluid administration, such as 1 L/hr, is prudent and provides sufficient rehydration. In any circumstance, after 2 to 3 L of NS, 0.45% NS solution should be substituted. As the fluid deficits and hyperosmolarity are corrected, the infusion rate must be slowed and electrolytes managed. In patients with concomitant congestive heart failure, sterile water has been successfully administered by central venous line at a rate of 500 mL/hr, with no detectable hemolysis or other complications. Glucose should be added to resuscitation fluids when the blood glucose level drops below 300 mg/dL.

Electrolytes

The guidelines for the administration of potassium, magnesium, and phosphorus are similar to those for DKA.

BOX 124-9. Summary of Treatment for Hyperglycemic Hyperosmolar Nonketotic Coma

Identify HHNC, then treatment is the same as initial DKA treatment.
1. Supplement insulin.
   ± Bolus: 0.05-0.1 U/kg regular insulin IV
   Maintenance: 0.05-0.01 U/kg regular insulin IV
   Caution: serum glucose rapidly corrects with fluid administration alone; monitor glucose to avoid hypoglycemia.
   Change IV solution to D5W 0.45% normal saline when glucose ≤300 mg/dL.
2. Rehydrate.
   Rapid administration of 2-3 L normal saline over first several hours
   CVP or Swan-Ganz monitoring may be necessary in patients with history of heart disease
   Correct one half of fluid deficit in first 8 hours, remainder over 24 hours
3. Correct electrolyte abnormalities.
   Sodium
      Correct with administration of normal saline and 0.45% normal saline.
   Potassium
      First ensure adequate renal function.
      Add 20-40 mEq KCl to each liter of fluid.
   Phosphorus
      Usually unnecessary to replenish
   Magnesium
      Correct with 1–2 g $MgSO_4$ (in first 2 L if magnesium is low).
4. Correct acidosis.
   Add 44–88 mEq/L to first liter of IV fluids *only* if pH ≤ 7.0.
   Correct to pH 7.1.
5. Search and correct underlying precipitant.
6. Monitor progress and keep meticulous flow sheets.
   Vital signs
   Fluid intake and urine output
   Serum glucose, K^+, Cl^-, HCO_3^-, CO_2, pH, ketones
   Amount of insulin administered
7. Admit to hospital or intensive care unit

CVP, central venous pressure; DKA, diabetic ketoacidosis; HHNC, hyperosmolar nonketotic coma.

Insulin

Low-dosage insulin, such as that administered in the patient with DKA, is generally effective and safe when the restoration of volume has been instituted.

Other Considerations

A vigorous search for the underlying precipitant for HHNC must be pursued. Response to therapy should be followed in the manner described for patients in DKA. *Phenytoin* (Dilantin) is contraindicated for the seizures of HHNC because it is often ineffective and may impair endogenous insulin release. Phenytoin-induced HHNC even occurs in nondiabetic patients. Low-dosage subcutaneous *heparin* may be indicated to lessen the risk of thrombosis, which is increased by the volume depletion, hyperviscosity, hypotension, and inactivity associated with HHNC.

Complications

Reasons for high morbidity and mortality rates are not always clear, but many patients with HHNC are elders who have underlying cardiac and renal disease. Pediatric HHNC differs from adult HHNC in that children have a much higher incidence of fatal cerebral edema.[54] Other causes for morbidity and mortality are similar to those described for DKA. The mortality rate of treated HHNC patients has been 40% to 70% in the past but now ranges from 8% to 25%.[55]

Disposition

All patients with HHNC must be hospitalized for IV hydration, glucose control, and evaluation of precipitating and complicating conditions.

LATE COMPLICATIONS OF DIABETES

Late complications of diabetes cause significant morbidity and mortality. They develop approximately 15 to 20 years after the onset of overt hyperglycemia. The Diabetes Control and Complications Trial showed that tight glycemic control significantly reduces the risk of microvascular disease, such as microalbuminuria (the earliest sign of nephropathy), neuropathy, and retinopathy, but at the expense of greatly increasing the risk of recurrent hypoglycemia.[56-58]

Vascular Complications

Diabetes is associated with an increased risk for atherosclerosis and thromboembolic complications, which are a major cause of morbidity and premature death.[59] The cause of accelerated atherosclerosis is unknown, although it is probably related to oxidated low-density lipoprotein and increased platelet activity. Atherosclerotic lesions are widespread, causing symptoms in many organ systems. Coronary artery disease and stroke are common. Diabetic patients have an increased incidence of "silent" MI, complicated MIs, and congestive heart failure.[6,60,61] Peripheral vascular disease is noted clinically by claudication, nonhealing ulcers, gangrene, and impotence.

Diabetic Nephropathy

Renal disease is a leading cause of death and disability in diabetic patients. Approximately one half of end-stage renal disease in the United States is caused by diabetic nephropathy.[62] Diabetic nephropathy involves two pathologic patterns: diffuse and nodular. Clinical renal dysfunction does not correlate well with the histologic abnormalities. Disease usually progresses from enlarged kidneys with elevated GFR to the appearance of microalbuminuria, to macroproteinuria with hypertension, reduced GFR, and renal failure.[63] The appearance of microalbuminuria correlates with the presence of coronary artery disease and retinopathy.[64]

Azotemia generally does not begin until 10 to 15 years after the diagnosis of diabetes is made. Progression of renal disease is accelerated by hypertension.

Meticulous control of diabetes can reverse microalbuminuria and may slow the progression of nephropathy.[2,17,56-58] Hypertension should be aggressively managed. Angiotensin-converting enzyme inhibitors are effective in controlling hypertension and lowering microalbuminuria.[64,65] Chronic hemodialysis and renal transplantation are unfortunate endpoints for many diabetic patients with renal disease.

Retinopathy

Diabetes is a leading cause of adult blindness in the United States. Approximately 11% to 18% of all diabetic patients have treatable diabetic retinopathy ranging from mild to severe and manifesting in many forms. The severity of diabetic retinopathy is clearly related to the quality of glycemic control.[61]

Background (simple) *retinopathy* is found in most diabetic patients who have prolonged disease. Background retinopathy is characterized by microaneurysms, small vessel obstruction, cotton-wool spots or soft exudates (microinfarcts), hard exudates, and macular ischemia.[63] The characteristics of *proliferative retinopathy* are new vessel formation and scarring. Complications of proliferative retinopathy are vitreal hemorrhage and retinal detachment, which may ultimately cause unilateral vision loss. Treatment for diabetic retinopathy is photocoagulation.

Maculopathy is background retinopathy with macular involvement. It results primarily in a deficit of central vision. As with proliferative retinopathy, it is vital that the patient be under the care of an ophthalmologist. Laser therapy in the early stages can dramatically alter the course of this disabling disease.

The diabetic patient may enter the emergency department with complaints ranging from acute blurring of vision to sudden unilateral or even bilateral blindness. Less often, diabetic patients have more gradual vision loss caused by the common senile cataract or the "snowflake" cataract, which may disappear as hyperglycemia is corrected. The associated hyperlipidemia of diabetes may lighten the color of retinal vessels, producing lipemia retinalis. Anterior ischemic optic neuropathy has been reported.

Diabetic patients with retinopathy should be referred to an ophthalmologist. Even in those with normal vision, ophthalmologic procedures may limit visual loss or prevent crises such as neovascular glaucoma.

Neuropathy

Both autonomic and peripheral neuropathies are well-known complications of diabetes. The prevalence of peripheral neuropathy ranges from 15% to 60%.[3] The cause of the neuropathy is not clearly understood, but evidence suggests several factors in its development. Neuropathy may result from the effects of diabetic vascular disease on the vasa nervorum. Myoinositol, the polyol pathway, and nonenzymatic glycosylation of protein may have roles. All these factors are related to an elevated blood glucose level. Neurologic manifestations of diabetes may regress with improved glycemic control. Pathologically, segmental demyelinization occurs with loss of both myelinated and unmyelinated axons, particularly those affecting the distal part of the peripheral nerve.

Several distinct types of neuropathy have been recognized in diabetes. *Peripheral symmetrical neuropathy* is a slowly progressive, primary sensory disorder manifesting bilaterally with anesthesia, hyperesthesia, or pain. The pain is often severe and worse at night. It affects upper and lower extremities, although lower extremities and the most distal sections of the involved nerves are most often affected. There may be a motor deficiency as well. Pain is very difficult to control. Simple pain medications, amitriptyline, and fluphenazine are effective for some patients.[66]

Mononeuropathy, or *mononeuropathy multiplex*, affects both motor and sensory nerves, generally one nerve at a time. The onset is rapid, with wasting and tenderness of the involved muscles. Clinically, sudden onset of wristdrop, footdrop, or paralysis of cranial nerves III, IV, and VI is noted.

Diabetic truncal mononeuropathy occurs rapidly in a radicular distribution. In contrast to other mononeuropathies, it is primarily, if not exclusively, sensory. If it causes pain, it may mimic that of an MI or acute abdominal inflammation. Like diabetic mononeuropathy, it may be most bothersome at night and generally resolves in a few months. Whereas diabetic mononeuropathy is often the first clue of diabetes, truncal mononeuropathy is more often found in known diabetic patients.

Autonomic neuropathy occurs in many forms. Neuropathy of the GI tract is manifested by difficulty swallowing, delayed gastric emptying, constipation, or nocturnal diarrhea. Impotence and bladder dysfunction or paralysis may occur. Orthostatic hypotension, syncope, and even cardiac arrest have resulted from autonomic neuropathy. Diabetic diarrhea responds to diphenoxylate and atropine, loperamide, or clonidine. Orthostatic hypotension is treated by sleeping with the head of the bed elevated, avoidance of sudden standing or sitting, and the use of full-length elastic stockings.

The Diabetic Foot

Approximately 20% of hospitalizations in diabetic patients are related to foot problems. Sensory neuropathy, ischemia, and infection are the principal contributors to diabetic foot disease. Loss of sensation leads to pressure necrosis from poorly fitting footwear and small wounds going unnoticed. The most common cause of injury is pressure on plantar bony prominences. All neuropathic foot ulcers should be assessed for infection and debrided of devitalized tissue, with radiographs for the presence of foreign bodies, soft tissue gas, or bone abnormalities. Weight bearing must be eliminated by total-contact casting.[66]

Not all ulcers are infected. Infection is suggested by local inflammation or crepitation. Conversely, some uninflamed ulcers are associated with underlying osteomyelitis. Most mild infections are caused by gram-positive cocci, such as *Staphylococcus aureus* or streptococci, and may be treated with oral antibiotics, a strict non–weight-bearing regimen, meticulous wound care, and daily follow-up. This approach may not be possible when patients are deemed unreliable, do not have good home support, or do not have ready access to follow-up care.

Deeper, limb-threatening infections—as evidenced by full-thickness ulceration, cellulitis greater than 2 cm in diameter with or without lymphangitis, bone or joint involvement, or systemic toxicity—are usually polymicrobial and caused by aerobic gram-positive cocci, gram-negative bacilli, and anaerobes. These patients require hospitalization and, after culture, IV empirical antimicrobial therapy with ampicillin-sulbactam, ticarcillin-sulbactam, cefoxitin, imipenem, or a fluoroquinolone and clindamycin; strict non–weight-bearing status; tight glycemic control; early surgical intervention for debridement; drainage; and meticulous wound care.[66,67] Occult osteomyelitis should be considered in all cases of neuropathic ulceration. Up to one third of patients must undergo amputation.

Infections

Diabetic patients are more susceptible to complications of infections because of their inability to limit microbial invasion with effective polymorphonuclear leukocytes and lymphocytes.[3] They have an increased incidence of extremity infections and pyelonephritis compared with the general population. In addition, they are particularly susceptible to certain other infections such as tuberculosis, mucocutaneous candidiasis, intertrigo, mucormycosis, soft tissue infections, nonclostridial gas gangrene, osteomyelitis, and malignant *Pseudomonas* otitis externa.[3] Treatment for diabetic patients with infection includes rapid culture and antibiotics, glycemic control, and generally hospitalization.

Cutaneous Manifestations

Dermal hypersensitivity refers to pruritic, erythematous indurations that occur at insulin injection sites. The declining prevalence of this condition has paralleled the improved purification of insulin. Insulin *lipoatrophy* likewise seems to be a result of insulin impurities and is manifested as subcutaneous depressions at injection sites. Although lipoatrophy is now more common than dermal hypersensitivity, its prevalence has also declined sharply because insulin preparations have improved. Insulin *lipohypertrophy* is manifested by raised areas of subcutaneous fat deposits at insulin injection sites. These lesions generally reflect the failure of the patient to rotate injections sites adequately. They resolve spontaneously over months if insulin injection is avoided in the affected areas and sites are properly rotated.

Insulin pumps are often associated with localized skin problems, usually a reaction to the tape securing the tubing and needles. Occasionally, sensitivity to the catheters is seen. Skin infections at the site of injection are the most common complication of insulin pumps. Changing the patient to buffered pure-pork from unbuffered beef-pork insulin is the only intervention that seems to reduce the rate of infection. A few patients have been noted to develop hard nodules at the injection site. The cause of these nodules is uncertain.

Diabetic patients who use oral hypoglycemic agents may develop rashes associated with these medications. After consuming ethanol, approximately 38% of type 2 patients taking chlorpropamide exhibit a "flush" consisting of redness of the face and neck and a sense of warmness or burning. Patients may demonstrate urticaria in response to both insulin and oral hypoglycemics.

Diabetic skin conditions include fungal infections, acanthosis nigricans, necrobiosis lipoidica diabeticorum, xanthoma diabeticorum, bullosis diabeticorum, and diabetic dermopathy. *Acanthosis nigricans* is characterized by a velvety brown-black thickening of the keratin layer, most often in the flexor surfaces. It is the cutaneous marker for a group of endocrine disorders with insulin resistance.[7] *Necrobiosis lipoidica diabeticorum* begins as erythematous papular or nodular lesions, usually in the pretibial area, but in other areas as well. The early lesions may contain telangiectasias. These lesions spread and frequently form a single pigmented area of atrophic skin, often with a yellow and sometimes ulcerated center and an erythematous margin. A history of previous trauma is sometimes found.

The three forms of diabetic thick skin are (1) scleroderma-like skin changes of the fingers and dorsum of the hand associated with stiff joints and limited mobility, (2) clinically inapparent but measurable thick skin, and (3) "scleroderma adultorum," or increased dermal thickness on the back and posterior upper neck in middle-aged, overweight patients with type 2 diabetes.

Xanthoma diabeticorum is evidence of the hyperlipidemia associated with diabetes. It is similar to the xanthoma found in nondiabetic hyperlipidemic patients. Xanthomas have an erythematous base and a yellowish hue.

Bullosis diabeticorum is a rare occurrence. Bullae are usually filled with a clear fluid and are most often found on the extremities, especially the feet. The fluid is occasionally slightly hemorrhagic. The bullae usually heal spontaneously without scarring.

Diabetic dermopathy, or "skin spots," is the most common finding in diabetes. It arises as discrete, depressed, and brownish lesions generally less than 15 mm in diameter and found in the pretibial area.

Resistant, aggressive *impetigo* or *intertrigo* should suggest diabetes.

Insulin Allergy

Insulin allergy is mediated by immunoglobulin E and is manifested by local itching or pain and delayed brawny edema, urticaria, or anaphylaxis. Systemic reactions are usually seen in patients who have previously discontinued insulin and then resumed therapy. Mild reactions may be treated with antihistamines, whereas anaphylaxis must be treated with epinephrine. Patients with significant reactions must be admitted for desensitization.[3]

DIABETES IN PREGNANCY

Before the discovery of insulin in 1922, diabetes in pregnancy was associated with a fetal death rate of 60% to 72% and maternal morbidity of approximately 30%. In 1977, a linear relationship between glycemic control and perinatal mortality was discovered. Strict metabolic control is now a goal in all diabetic pregnancies.[38,54]

Pregnant patients should be watched extremely closely and aggressively treated for impending or actual DKA. For a variety of reasons, pregnant women have a special predisposition to both glucose intolerance and excess ketone production. Although uncommon, DKA may cause perinatal asphyxia and reduce fetal oxygen delivery.[38,54] Intellectual deficits in offspring have been associated with maternal ketonuria from any cause.

Pregnancy is associated with progression of *retinopathy* for unknown reasons.[68] Whether pregnancy worsens diabetic nephropathy or hastens the progression to end-stage renal disease is controversial.[69] Although *nephrotic syndrome* develops in 71% of pregnancies, blood pressure and proteinuria eventually return to first-trimester values. *Diabetic nephropathy* is associated with an increased risk of preterm labor, stillbirth, neonatal death, fetal distress, and intrauterine growth retardation; otherwise, the literature is sparse on the effect of pregnancy on diabetic neuropathy. *Autonomic neuropathy*, particularly gastroparesis, makes adequate nutrition difficult for both mother and fetus. Pregnant women should be referred for parenteral feedings if conservative therapy fails to control vomiting.[38]

Hypoglycemia is common in pregnancy in part because of intensive insulin treatment to maintain euglycemia.[70] Hypoglycemic unawareness is not uncommon. The effects of hypoglycemia on the fetus are unclear. *Ketoacidosis* is associated with a 50% to 90% fetal mortality rate.[38,71]

ORAL HYPOGLYCEMIC AGENTS

The widespread availability of a variety of oral medications for hyperglycemia, some with serious side effects, requires the emergency physician to be familiar with these drugs. *Sulfonylureas*, developed in the 1940s, continue to be the mainstay of oral diabetes treatment. These drugs increase insulin secretion by binding to specific beta cell receptors.[72] This class of drugs works best in patients with early onset of type 2 diabetes and fasting glucose less than 300 mg/dL.[73] This class of drugs is contraindicated in patients with known allergy to sulfa agents.

Metformin works by decreasing hepatic glucose output, leading to decreased insulin resistance and lower blood glucose. Used alone, metformin does not cause hypoglycemia, but it is contraindicated in patients with renal insufficiency and metabolic acidosis. Metformin should be withheld for 48 hours before or after administration of iodinated contrast media because of the risk of acidosis. Metformin must be used with caution in patients with hypoxemia, liver compromise, and alcohol abuse. These patients are at increased risk for developing lactic acidosis, which has a 50% mortality rate.[73,74]

The *thiazolidinediones* reduce insulin resistance and are especially useful in patients who require large amounts of insulin and still lack adequate glucose control. Because of a rare case of hepatic toxicity, troglitazone is now limited to use only with other agents.[74] Pioglitazone and rosiglitazone are approved for monotherapy. Liver function should be monitored for at least 1 year after the initiation of therapy with thiazolidinediones.

α-Glucosidase inhibitors delay intestinal monosaccharide absorption and prevent complex carbohydrate breakdown.[73] They must be titrated to minimize GI side effects and should not be used in patients with certain GI disorders. Liver function monitoring is required because of dose-dependent hepatotoxicity.

Repaglinide is similar to the sulfonylureas in action and mechanism. It has a more rapid onset of action, involves less risk of hypoglycemia, and is suitable for patients allergic to sulfa.[74] Care should be used in patients with renal or hepatic dysfunction.[73]

NEW-ONSET HYPERGLYCEMIA

Patients often present to the emergency department with typical diabetic symptoms such as polyuria, polydipsia, and polyphagia. Many have serum glucose greater than 200 mg/dL but are not ketotic. These patients with normal electrolytes may be treated with IV hydration alone or with insulin, often reducing the glucose to 150 mg/dL. In reliable patients whose initial glucose is greater than 400 mg/dL, initiation of oral hypoglycemic therapy may be appropriate, with lifestyle modification. An HbA_{1c} value should be obtained before initiation of therapy to help evaluate treatment. Initial therapy with sulfonylureas is appropriate; glyburide (2.5 to 5 mg once daily) or glipizide (5 mg once daily) is recommended. In obese patients or those in whom sulfonylureas are contraindicated, metformin may be an alternative. Follow-up should be stressed and warning signs of hypoglycemia discussed.

NEW TRENDS

Changes in the therapy of diabetes include greater use of human insulin, which has prevented some of the adverse reactions to beef and pork products. Unfortunately, some patients demonstrate sensitivity reactions even to subcutaneously injected human insulin.[75] More physicians are teaching their type 1 patients and families how to administer glucagon to treat severe hypoglycemia. Initiation of immunosuppressive therapy at the initial diagnosis of type 1 diabetes can prolong the patient's ability to secrete insulin. However, this beneficial effect, whether achieved by azathioprine or cyclosporine, is not usually sustainable.[76] The potential side effects of immunosuppressive agents have precluded large trials in patients early in their disease.[77] Prophylactic insulin therapy, nicotinamide, oral insulin, or glutamate decarboxylase and avoidance of cow's milk may prevent or delay the onset of type 1 diabetes in patients at risk.[4]

Glycemic control now involves improved technology and more widespread individual monitoring. More patients alter their insulin dosages daily in response to their findings. Diabetic patients with tight glycemic control benefit by limiting the progression of microvascular disease: neuropathy, renal disease, and certain types of retinopathy. However, they are more likely than other diabetic patients to experience hypoglycemic episodes.

Emergency physicians and prehospital care providers are encountering patients with insulin pumps. Many insulin pumps are available, each having a pump mechanism, a reservoir for insulin, tubing, and indwelling subcutaneous needles. They are attached, usually with tapes, to the patient's body and administer insulin at a regular adjustable rate. Most pumps also allow the patient to administer additional boluses of insulin as necessary. These pumps support tight glycemic control and are acceptable to some patients. However, motivated patients can achieve equivalent control by adjusting daily injections. Insulin pumps are associated with a variety of complications (e.g., iatrogenic hypoglycemia).

Because glucose rotates the polarization of light waves, new fiberoptic technology has been developed to determine blood glucose noninvasively. This technology may be applied to the insulin pumps in the future.

The basic concepts of the diabetic diet remain unchanged, although many studies emphasize foods and medications that alter glucose absorption. Various high-fiber diets have improved glycemic control. The mostly beneficial but occasionally deleterious effects of exercise have also been elaborated.[72]

Newer therapies include pancreatic and pancreatic beta cell transplants. Solid-organ pancreatic transplantation remains controversial among both diabetologists and transplant surgeons. Transplantation ameliorates many secondary complications of diabetes, such as nephropathy, neuropathy, gastroparesis, retinopathy, and microvascular changes. The percentage of grafts functioning after 1 year and the 1-year survival rate of patients are greater than 75% in selected medical centers. Rejection, posttransplantation pancreatitis, and graft thrombosis, as well as other vascular and immunosuppression problems, continue to plague transplant recipients.

Research into peptides involved in glucose regulation offers an additional avenue for future treatments. These peptides include glucagon-like peptide 1, amylin, and insulin-like growth factor I.[72] Advances in understanding the genetics of diabetes may allow identification of persons at risk for its development and prevention of its phenotypic expression.[4]

KEY CONCEPTS

- Hypoglycemia may be associated with significant morbidity and mortality. When the diagnosis is suspected and, if possible, confirmed by laboratory evaluation, treatment should be initiated immediately.

- Hypoglycemia caused by oral hypoglycemic agents may be prolonged. Patients should be observed for an extended period or hospitalized.

- The essentials of treatment of diabetic ketoacidosis are restoration of insulin, correction of dehydration, correction of potassium, correction of acidosis, and treatment of the underlying cause.

- Hyperglycemic hyperosmolar nonketotic coma is often associated with focal neurologic signs that resolve with treatment. The essentials of treatment are correction of profound dehydration, correction of electrolytes, and treatment of the underlying cause.

REFERENCES

1. Banting FG, Best CH: Pancreatic extracts. *J Lab Clin Med* 7:464, 1922.
2. Diabetes Control and Complications Trial Research Group: The effect of intensive treatment of diabetes on the development and progression of long-term complications in insulin-dependent diabetes mellitus. *N Engl J Med* 329:977, 1993.
3. Eisenbarth GS, Polonsky KS, Buse TB: Type 1 diabetes mellitus. In Larsen PR, Krunenberg HM (eds): *Williams Textbook of Endocrinology*, 10th ed. Philadelphia, WB Saunders, 2003, pp 1485-1504.
4. Atkinson MA, MaClaron NK: Mechanisms of disease: The pathogenesis of insulin-dependent diabetes mellitus. *N Engl J Med* 21:1428, 1994.
5. Umpierrea GE, Khajavi M, Kitabchi AE: Review: Diabetic ketoacidosis and hyperglycemic hyperosmolar nonketotic syndrome. *Am J Med Sci* 311:225, 1996.
6. American Diabetes Association: Report of the Expert Committee on the Diagnosis and Classification of Diabetes Mellitus. *Diabetes Care* 20:1183, 1997.
7. Perez MI, Kohn SR: Cutaneous manifestations of diabetes mellitus. *J Am Acad Dermatol* 30:519, 1994.
8. Froguel PH, et al: Familial hyperglycemia due to mutations in glucokinase. *N Engl J Med* 328:697, 1993.
9. Birmingham Diabetes Survey Working Party: Ten-year follow-up report on Birmingham Diabetes Survey. *Br Med J* 2:35, 1976.
10. National Diabetes Statistics. National Diabetes Information Clearinghouse (NDIC). http://diabetes.niddts.nih.gov/populations/index.htm (Accessed 2/24/05.)
11. Bingly PJ, et al: Can we really predict IDDM? *Diabetes* 42:213, 1993.
12. Knowler WC, et al: Diabetes incidence and prevalence in Pima Indians: A 19-fold greater incidence than in Rochester, Minnesota. *Am J Epidemiol* 108:497, 1978.
13. Krolewski AS, et al: Epidemiologic approach to the etiology of type I diabetes mellitus and its complications. *N Engl J Med* 317:1390, 1987.
14. MaClaren N, Schatz D, Drash A: Initial pathogenic events in IDDM. *Diabetes* 38:534, 1989.
15. Atkinson MA, et al: 64,000 Mr autoantibodies are predictive of insulin-dependent diabetes. *Lancet* 225:1357, 1990.
16. Gianani R, et al: Prognostically significant heterogeneity of cytoplasmic islet cell antibodies in relatives of patients with type I diabetes. *Diabetes* 41:347, 1992.
17. Shepherd PR, Kahn BB: Glucose transporters and insulin action. *N Engl J Med* 341:248, 1999.
18. National Diabetes Information Clearinghouse—NIH. http://diabetes.niddts.nih.gov/dm/pubs/statisting/index.htm#8 (Accessed 2/22/2005.)
19. American Diabetes Association: Clinical practice recommendations. *Diabetes Care* 16:5, 1993.
20. American Diabetes Association: Standards of medical care for patients with diabetes mellitus (position statement). *Diabetes Care* 20(Suppl 1):S5, 1997.
21. James GP, Bee DE: Glucosuria: Accuracy and precision of laboratory diagnosis by dipstick analysis. *Clin Chem* 25:966, 1979.
22. Bell DS, Cutter G: Characteristics of severe hypoglycemia in the patient with insulin-dependent diabetes. *South Med J* 87:616, 1994.
23. DCCT Research Group: Epidemiology of severe hypoglycemia in the Diabetes Control and Complications Trial. *Am J Med* 90:450, 1991.
24. Mulhausser I, Berger M, Sonnenberg G: Incidence and management of severe hypoglycemia in 434 adults with insulin-dependent diabetes mellitus. *Diabetes Care* 8:274, 1985.
25. Cranston I, et al: Restoration of hypoglycaemia awareness in patients with long-duration insulin-dependent diabetes. *Lancet* 344:283, 1994.
26. Heller SR, Cryer PE: Reduced neuroendocrine and symptomatic responses to subsequent hypoglycemia in non-diabetic humans. *Diabetes* 40:223, 1991.
27. Widom B, Simonson DC: Effect of intermittent hypoglycemia on counter regulatory hormone secretion. *Diabetologia* 33:84, 1990.
28. Bolli GB, et al: Glucose counterregulation and waning insulin in the Somogyi phenomenon (posthypoglycemic hyperglycemia). *N Engl J Med* 311:1214, 1984.
29. Adler PM: Serum glucose changes after administration of 50% dextrose solution: Pre- and in-hospital calculations. *Am J Emerg Med* 4:504, 1986.
30. Collier A, et al: Comparison of intravenous glucagon and dextrose in treatment of severe hypoglycemia in an accident and emergency department. *Diabetes Care* 10:712, 1987.
31. Daneman D, et al: Severe hypoglycemia in children with insulin-dependent diabetes mellitus: Frequency and predisposing factors. *J Pediatr* 115:681, 1989.
32. Pontiroli AE, et al: Intranasal glucagon as remedy of hypoglycemia: Studies in healthy subjects and type I diabetic patients. *Diabetes Care* 12:604, 1989.
33. Kitabchi AE, Wall BM: Diabetic ketoacidosis. *Med Clin North Am* 79:9, 1995.
34. Adrogué HJ, et al: Determinants of plasma potassium levels in diabetic ketoacidosis. *Medicine (Baltimore)* 65:163, 1986.
35. Lebovitz HE: Diabetic ketoacidosis. *Lancet* 345:767, 1995.
36. Holmes L: The patient with chronic endocrine disease. In Herr R, Cydulka RK (eds): *Emergency Care of the Compromised Patient*. Philadelphia, JB Lippincott, 1994, pp 121-126.
37. Adrogué HJ, Madias NE: Changes in plasma potassium concentration during acute acid-base disturbances. *Am J Med* 71:456, 1981.
38. Reece EA, Homko CJ: Diabetes-related complications of pregnancy. *J Natl Med Assoc* 85:537, 1993.
39. Lindsay R, Bolte RG: The use of an insulin bolus in low-dose insulin infusion for pediatric diabetic ketoacidosis. *Pediatr Emerg Care* 5:55, 1989.
40. Weisenfeld S, et al: Adsorption of insulin to infusion bottle and tubing. *Diabetes* 17:766, 1968.
41. Foster DW, McGarry JD: The metabolic derangements and treatment of diabetic ketoacidosis. *N Engl J Med* 309:159, 1983.

42. Filer JS, Kahn CR, Roth J: Receptor, antireceptor antibodies and mechanism of insulin resistance. *N Engl J Med* 300:413, 1979.

43. Duck SC, et al: Cerebral edema complicating therapy for diabetic ketoacidosis. *Diabetes* 25:111, 1976.

44. Duck SC, Wyatt DT: Factors associated with brain herniation in the treatment of diabetic ketoacidosis. *J Pediatr* 113:10, 1988.

45. Glaser N, et al: Risk factors for cerebral edema in children with diabetic ketoacidosis. *N Engl J Med* 344:264, 2001.

46. Viallon A, et al: Does bicarbonate therapy improve the management of severe diabetic ketoacidosis? *Crit Care Med* 27:2690, 1999.

47. Green SM, et al: Failure of adjuvant bicarbonate to improve outcome in severe pediatric diabetic ketoacidosis. *Ann Emerg Med* 31:41, 1998.

48. Kent LA, Grill GV, Williams G: Mortality and outcome of patients with brittle diabetes and recurrent ketoacidosis. *Lancet* 844:778, 1994.

49. Bonadio WH: Pediatric diabetic ketoacidosis: Pathophysiology and potential for outpatient management of selected children. *Pediatr Emerg Care* 8:287, 1992.

50. Cahill GF Jr: Hyperglycemic hyperosmolar coma: A syndrome almost unique to the elderly. *J Am Geriatr Soc* 31:103, 1983.

51. Siperstein MD: Diabetic ketoacidosis and hyperosmolar coma. *Endocrinol Metab Clin North Am* 21:915, 1992.

52. Vernon DD, Postellon DC: Nonketotic hyperosmolal diabetic coma in a child: Management with low-dose insulin infusion and intracranial pressure monitoring. *Pediatrics* 77:770, 1986.

53. Levine SN, Sanson TH: Treatment of hyperglycaemic hyperosmolar non-ketotic syndrome. *Drugs* 38:462, 1989.

54. Steel JM, et al: Insulin requirements during pregnancy in women with type I diabetes. *Obstet Gynecol* 83:253, 1994.

55. Wachtel TJ, Silliman RA, Lamberton P: Prognostic factors in the diabetic hyperosmolar state. *J Am Geriatr Soc* 35:737, 1987.

56. Zimmerman BR: Glycaemia control in diabetes mellitus towards the normal profile. *Drugs* 47:611, 1994.

57. Hadden DR: The Diabetes Control and Complications Trial (DCCT): What every endocrinologist needs to know. *Clin Endocrinol (Oxf)* 40:293, 1994.

58. Clarke WL: The Diabetes Control and Complications Trial: New challenges for the primary physician. *Va Med Q* 121:185, 1994.

59. Winocour PD: Platelets, vascular disease, and diabetes mellitus. *Can J Physiol Pharmacol* 72:295, 1994.

60. Brownlee M, Cahill GH: Diabetic control and vascular complications. In Paoletti R, Gotto AM (eds): *Atherosclerosis Review,* vol 4. New York, Raven Press, 1979, pp 100-105.

61. Stephenson J, Fuller JH: Microvascular and acute complications in IDDM patients: The EURODIAB IDDM complications study. *Diabetologia* 37:278, 1994.

62. Woodrow G, Brownjohn AM, Turney JH: Acute renal failure in patients with type 1 diabetes mellitus. *Postgrad Med J* 70:192, 1994.

63. Konen JC, Shihabi ZK: Microalbuminuria and diabetes mellitus. *Am Fam Physician* 48:1421, 1993.

64. Chavers BM, et al: Relationship between retinal and glomerular lesions in IDDM patients. *Diabetes* 43:441, 1994.

65. Hamet P: Hypertension and diabetes. *Clin Exp Hypertens* 15:1327, 1993.

66. Caputo GM, et al: Assessment and management of foot disease in patients with diabetes. *N Engl J Med* 330:854, 1994.

67. Pliskin MA, Todd WF, Edelson GW: Presentations of diabetic feet. *Arch Fam Med* 3:273, 1994.

68. Klein BEK, Moss SE, Klein R: Effect of pregnancy on progression of diabetic retinopathy. *Diabetes Care* 13:34, 1990.

69. Kitzmiller JL, Combs CA: Maternal and perinatal implications of diabetic nephropathy. *Clin Perinatol* 20:561, 1993.

70. Diamond MP, et al: Impairment of counter-regulatory hormone secretion in response to hypoglycemia in pregnant women with insulin dependent diabetes mellitus. *Am J Obstet Gynecol* 166:70, 1993.

71. Kitzmiller JL: Diabetic ketoacidosis and pregnancy. *Contemp Obstet Gynecol* 20:141, 1982.

72. Mahler RJ, Adler ML: Clinical review 102: Type 2 diabetes mellitus, update on diagnosis. *J Clin Endocrinol Metab* 84:1165, 1999.

73. Florence JA, Yeager BF: Treatment of type 2 diabetes mellitus. *Am Fam Physician* 59:2835, 1999.

74. Abramowicz M (ed): Rosiglitazone for type 2 diabetes mellitus. *Med Lett Drugs Ther* 41:71, 1999.

75. Grammer LC, Metzger BE, Patterson R: Cutaneous allergy to human (recombinant DNA) insulin. *JAMA* 251:1459, 1984.

76. Bougneres PF, et al: Limited duration of remission of insulin dependency in children with recent overt type I diabetes treated with low-dose cyclosporine. *Diabetes* 39:1264, 1990.

77. Fathman CG, Myers BD: Cyclosporine therapy for autoimmune disease. *N Engl J Med* 326:1693, 1992.

CHAPTER

125 Rhabdomyolysis

Laura J. Bontempo

PERSPECTIVE

Rhabdomyolysis is a clinical syndrome caused by injury to skeletal muscle that results in release of cellular contents into the extracellular fluid and the circulation. The diagnosis rests on measurement of these released substances in either plasma or urine. The injury can be reversible or irreversible, potentially leading to disability, renal failure, or death.

The earliest reference to rhabdomyolysis occurs in the Old Testament, from the Book of Numbers.[1] During the Exodus, the Israelites consumed large amounts of quail, and many became ill and died from an illness involving intense muscle pain and weakness. The quail ingested by the Israelites may have fed on hemlock seeds during their westward migration to the Sinai Peninsula. This theory is supported by reports of severe muscle pain and even muscle paralysis after consuming quail that had fed on hemlock seeds. In the late 19th century, a clinical syndrome of muscle pain, weakness, and brown urine was called "Meyer-Betz disease" in the German literature.[2]

In 1941, Bywaters and Beall[3] described the clinical course of four victims with crush injuries to the limbs after air raids during World War II. They noted the link between muscle injury and renal dysfunction in their classic monograph, as follows:

"The patient has been buried for several hours with pressure on a limb. On admission he looks in good condition except for swelling of the limb, some local anesthesia and whealing. The hemoglobin, however, is raised and a few hours later despite vasoconstriction made manifest by pallor, coldness and sweating, the blood pressure falls. This is restored to the pre-shock level by (often multiple) transfusions of serum, plasma, or occasionally, blood. Anxiety may now arise concerning the circulation in the injured limb, which may show diminution of arterial pulsation distally, accompanied by all the changes of incipient gangrene. Signs of renal damage soon appear, and progress even though the crushed limb be amputated. The urinary output, initially small, owing perhaps to the severity of the shock, diminishes further. The urine contains albumin and many dark brown or black granular casts. These later decrease in number. The patient is alternately drowsy and anxiously aware of the severity of his illness. Slight generalized edema, thirst, and incessant vomiting develop, and the blood pressure often remains slightly raised. The blood urea and potassium, raised at an early stage, become progressively higher, and death occurs comparatively suddenly, frequently within a week. Necropsy reveals necrosis of muscle and in the renal tubules, degenerative changes and casts containing brown pigment."

The relationship between traumatic muscle injury and kidney failure was aptly described and has been reviewed extensively in the past 60 years. In the mid-1970s, the first references were made to nontraumatic rhabdomyolysis.[4,5] Since then, the number of known causes for this syndrome has greatly increased.

Acute renal failure (ARF) is one of the most serious complications of rhabdomyolysis. Approximately 5% to 15% of patients hospitalized with ARF in the United States have rhabdomyolysis as the cause.[6,7] Well-designed prospective studies of rhabdomyolysis and its complications are lacking, so the true incidence of ARF in this setting is unknown but is estimated at 4% to 33%.[15]

PRINCIPLES OF DISEASE

Anatomy and Physiology

Skeletal muscle is the largest organ in the human body. The functioning of muscle cells is critically dependent on a healthy cell membrane, the sarcolemma, which maintains cellular ionic gradients and ensures proper metabolic functioning. The sarcolemma contains sodium-potassium pumps, calcium protein-carrier pumps, and other channels and structures.[8] The sodium-potassium pump moves sodium out of the cell's sarcoplasm and potassium into the sarcoplasm. More sodium is transported out than potassium is transported in, which creates a net negative charge to the interior of the cell. In addition, a concentration gradient is created between intracellular and extracellular sodium ions. Normally, the concentration of intracellular sodium ions is very low, approximately 10 mEq/L, when compared with the extracellular fluid.[8]

The calcium pumps work to maintain a low intracellular fluid calcium concentration. Located in the sarcolemma, the pumps move calcium from the sarcoplasm to the outside of the cell. Additional pumps help to move calcium into the muscle cell's internal structures, the sarcoplasmic reticulum, and the mitochondria. As sodium ions move down the electrochemical gradient (i.e., return into the cell), calcium ions are able to move out from the cell into the extracellular fluid (Figure 125-1).[8]

With the exception of the sodium-calcium exchange, all these pumps rely on active transport and use adenosine triphosphate (ATP) as their energy source.[8]

Myoglobin is also found in a cell's sarcoplasm. It is the major heme protein that supplies oxygen to skeletal and cardiac muscle. Myoglobin has a higher affinity than hemoglobin for oxygen, which causes influx of oxygen into muscle cells.[9] Cell damage results in myoglobin release, which produces the classic dark-colored urine of rhabdomyolysis.

Skeletal muscle cells contain, in their cytoplasm, proteases and other proteolytic enzymes that have low activity in the cell's normal physiologic state. These enzymes decompose myofibrillar proteins so that they can be recycled. The activity level of these enzymes appears to depend on intracellular calcium levels; the greater the concentration of calcium, the more disinhibited or active the enzymes become. With significant elevation of intracellular calcium, their activity level is raised to a point at which these enzymes become destructive to the cell.[10]

Pathophysiology

Despite the large number of specific diseases causing rhabdomyolysis, the final common pathway of injury involves damage to the sarcolemma with loss of its intrinsic functions. The damage results in an influx of calcium and a subsequent rise in the intracellular calcium concentration, as well as liberation of intracellular contents, such as myoglobin, aldolase, aspartate transaminase, lactate dehydrogenase, creatine kinase, potassium, uric acid, and phosphorus.[11]

Loss of function of the cell membrane results in loss of the ionic gradients created by the sodium-potassium pumps and the sodium-calcium channels. This causes extracellular hypocalcemia and intracellular hypercalcemia.[12] Elevated intracellular calcium leads to greater

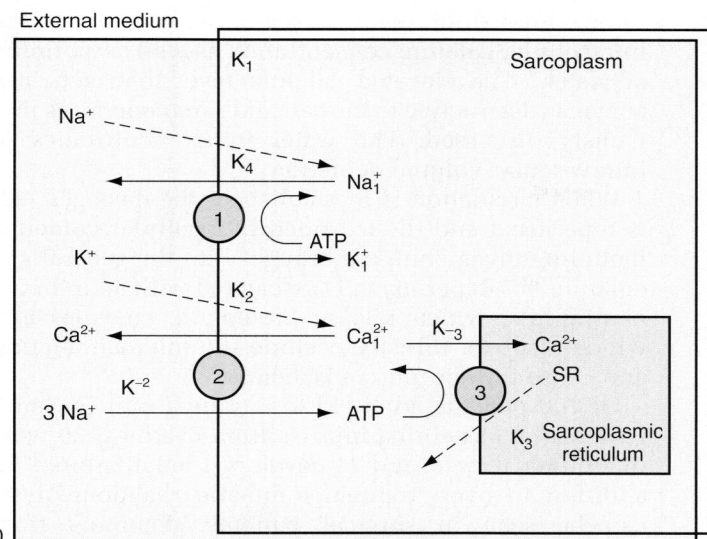

External medium

K_1

Sarcoplasm

Figure 125-1. Normal membrane ionic pump function of skeletal muscle cell. When this function is ineffective, calcium stores will increase in the cell, which may initiate a series of outputs leading to cellular injury. (Redrawn from Blaustein MP: Sodium ions, calcium ions, blood pressure regulation, and hypertension: A reassessment and a hypothesis. *Am J Physiol* 232:C165, 1977.)

activity of intracellular proteases, phospholipases, and other proteolytic enzymes. These enzymes then cause further cell damage and destruction.[9,13]

Intracellular calcium can accumulate secondary to direct cellular membrane damage (i.e., crush injury) or through ATP depletion. Membrane damage from direct trauma makes the sarcolemma more permeable to calcium, which follows the electrochemical gradient and travels into the cell.[10,14] In cases of atraumatic rhabdomyolysis, lack of adequate energy, in the form of ATP, can cause the ion pumps to stop functioning, which results in calcium accumulation in a muscle cell.[9,10] The ATP depletion can result from a mismatch between energy supply and demand (e.g., vigorous or prolonged exercise) or a defect in energy use (e.g., McArdle's syndrome, or absence of muscle phosphorylase).[9]

Once destruction of the myocyte has begun, myoglobin is released. As the levels of free plasma myoglobin increase, excess myoglobin is filtered by the kidneys and enters the urine.[15] Myoglobin accumulation, coupled with hypovolemia and acidosis, can precipitate and cause blockage to renal tubular flow.[16] Myoglobin may also be directly toxic to the renal tubular cells.[6,9,17]

The most common cause of rhabdomyolysis-induced ARF is acute intrinsic renal failure (AIRF), formerly known as acute tubular necrosis. AIRF is defined as a decrease in the glomerular filtration rate (GFR) caused by a toxic or ischemic event that is not reversed on discontinuation of the insult. AIRF is invariably associated with some degree of tubular injury and has a characteristic urine profile of low specific gravity (approximately 1.010), brown casts, and a fractional excretion of sodium greater than 1% (Box 125-1).

The role of myoglobin in the renal pathology of rhabdomyolysis has been well studied. Bywaters and Beall[3] first noticed the association of renal failure with the excretion of acid urine. They studied the effect of myoglobin infusions on renal function in the rabbit and concluded that hypovolemia and an acid urine were

---

BOX 125-1. Diagnostic Parameters in Acute Renal Failure and Acute Intrinsic Renal Failure

Odorless urine
Specific gravity <1.015
Urine sediment: "dirty" brown, granular casts
Urine osmolarity <350 mOsm/L
U/P osmolarity ratio <1.1
Urine sodium >20-40 mEq/L
U/P urea <4
U/P creatinine <20
Renal failure index: $\dfrac{U_{Na}}{U/P \text{ creatinine}} > 1\text{-}2$
Fractional excretion of filtered sodium >1-20%
Free water clearance: rising to >15 mL/hr

U/P, urinary to plasma.
Modified from McGoldrick MD: Diagnosis and management of acute renal failure: Part I. *Cardiovasc Rev Rep* 5:1031, 1984.

---

required for this substance to cause renal injury.[3,18] Myoglobin infusions in normovolemic rabbits with urine pH above 6 had no deleterious effect on kidney function.[18]

Other studies have demonstrated that myoglobin dissociates into its two components, globin and ferrihemate, at pH values of 5.6 or less.[18] Infusions of the globin component have no effect on renal function even in the presence of hypovolemia and acidic urine. Ferrihemate may be the toxic subunit of myoglobin.[19]

Tubular obstruction by myoglobin, uric acid, and other muscle breakdown products may also be causative in the development of ARF. Tubular obstruction, however, although universally present, may not be the primary event in the development of AIRF associated with rhabdomyolysis.[7]

Compartment syndromes may be a cause or a complication of rhabdomyolysis. A compartment syndrome exists when the circulation to tissues within a closed space is compromised by increased pressure within

BOX 125-2. General Causes of Rhabdomyolysis

Metabolic myopathies
Drugs and toxins
Trauma and compression
Infections
Exertion
Electrolyte abnormalities
Electrical current
Hypoxia
Hyperthermia
Idiopathic

that space.[20,21] The excessive pressure may occur as a result of a decrease in the size of the compartment, an increase in the size of the contents of the compartment, or a combination of both. Once established, a compartment syndrome tends to be self-sustaining because (1) capillaries become occluded as a result of the increased pressure; (2) venous pressure increases, further decreasing perfusion pressure; and (3) arteriolar vasospasm leads to tissue ischemia, swelling, and edema. The swelling and edema cause an increase in the compartmental pressure and the cycle continues. In 2 to 4 hours, ischemic skeletal muscle can develop functional deficits, which may become irreversible after 10 hours.[20] Within 30 minutes, nerve tissue undergoing vascular compromise exhibits reversible deficits, which may become permanent within 12 to 24 hours.[21] Therefore, it is critical that the diagnosis of rhabdomyolysis be made as early as possible.

Etiology

Exercise, alcohol, drugs, infections, trauma, compression, and seizures are the leading causes of rhabdomyolysis.[10] In many cases, the cause is multifactorial (Box 125-2).

Metabolic Myopathies

Certain genetic defects do not allow appropriate use of carbohydrates or lipids as energy substrates. These disorders include defects in glycolysis or glycogenolysis, defects of fatty acid oxidation, and dysfunction of cellular mitochondria. Each entity can cause recurrent attacks of reversible rhabdomyolysis or progressive weakness.[9] These enzyme defects are found in 23% to 47% of adult patients with rhabdomyolysis.[22,23] Such inappropriate use of carbohydrates and lipids causes an imbalance between the energy demand and supply of the muscle cell and results in ATP depletion.

Trauma and Compression

Most information regarding rhabdomyolysis from trauma and compression has been obtained from mass-casualty incidents.[24-26] Muscle injury from trauma and compression is multifaceted. Initially, there is direct mechanical injury to the sarcolemma, and its homeostatic functions are disrupted.[14] Sodium and calcium travel down their concentration gradients into the

intracellular fluid. This causes an abrupt rise in the intracellular calcium concentration as well as an influx of water.[9] The elevated calcium level then activates enzymes destructive to the cell and sarcolemma, as previously discussed. The water influx contributes to intravascular volume depletion.[10,14,27]

When circulation is reestablished, the damaged cell is reperfused and the extruded intracellular contents, including myoglobin, are brought into the general circulation.[10,28] Reperfusion is associated with an influx of neutrophils, which release proteolytic enzymes and which also can directly occlude the microcirculation and cause further muscle ischemia.[9,10]

Of 200 patients admitted to a trauma unit in South Africa after sustaining injuries from beatings, 26 were in a prerenal state, and 21 developed renal failure.[29] In addition to overt trauma, traumatic rhabdomyolysis can be seen in surgical patients stemming from improper operative positioning and in anesthetized or otherwise comatose patients who remain in one position for a prolonged time.[9,30]

Exertion

Rhabdomyolysis can result from prolonged or strenuous exercise and is seen in both trained and untrained athletes.[31-33] Eccentric exercise (work done by a muscle during lengthening) is more damaging to muscle fibers, as evidenced by higher creatine kinase levels, than concentric exercise (work done by a muscle during shortening).[11] Hot conditions contribute to the incidence of exertional rhabdomyolysis because of increased dehydration and increased activity of heat-sensitive degradative enzymes.[33,34] With prolonged exercise, the sarcolemmic ion pumps can also fail from depletion of cellular energy sources, specifically ATP.[9] These factors can lead to elevated intracellular calcium and subsequently rhabdomyolysis, which, coupled with dehydration and acidosis from lactic acid production, can cause ARF.[10,33,35]

Exertional rhabdomyolysis is not always the result of voluntary muscle exertion. The same pathophysiology is seen in patients with status epilepticus, myoclonus, dystonia, chorea, tetanus, and mania.[9,36-38]

Electrical Current

Rhabdomyolysis occurs in approximately 10% of patients who initially survive a high-voltage electrical injury or lightning strike.[39] Rhabdomyolysis from electrical current appears to be a result of both the heat generated by the electrical current and the direct effects of the current on the sarcolemma (electroporation).[40]

Heat Injury

Many disorders can raise the core body temperature and result in sarcolemma disruption. Neuroleptic malignant syndrome (fever in patients treated with phenothiazines or haloperidol), malignant hyperthermia (rapid rise in body temperature after anesthesia with halogenated hydrocarbons or succinylcholine), and both classic and exertional heat stroke are some of the most common causes.[16,41,42] In hyperpyrexic syndromes, cellular energy demands outstrip available energy supplies, causing membrane dysfunction and cellular injury.[43]

Hypothermia can also cause rhabdomyolysis, most likely through direct injury to components of the sarcolemma, which cannot maintain structural integrity below certain temperature levels.[44]

Drugs and Toxins

Drugs in almost every class of medication have been implicated as a cause of rhabdomyolysis.[9] Common offenders include ethanol, cocaine and other illicit drugs, lipid-lowering agents, carbon monoxide, and biologic toxins.

Ethanol
Ethanol is directly toxic to the skeletal muscle cell membrane, and this toxicity appears to be potentiated by starvation.[10] For this reason, ethanol-induced rhabdomyolysis is often seen in patients who are "binge drinkers." Electrolyte abnormalities also play a role. Chronic alcohol abusers often have hypokalemia, hypophosphatemia, and hypomagnesemia.[16] These deficiencies, coupled with ethanol's direct sarcolemmic toxic effects, make the ethanol abuser more susceptible to rhabdomyolysis.[10]

Ethanol is also a sedative-hypnotic, which can induce obtundation and lead to immobilization of a body part with external compression of its blood supply. In addition, excessive motor activity from seizures or delirium tremens can induce rhabdomyolysis.

Cocaine
The incidence of rhabdomyolysis in patients who use cocaine varies from 5% to 30% in published reports.[41] It is unclear why cocaine causes rhabdomyolysis. Hypotheses include cocaine-induced vasospasm with resultant muscle ischemia, excessive energy demands placed on the sarcolemma, and direct toxic effects on myocytes.[45-47] Seizures, agitation, trauma, and hyperpyrexia may also play a role.[9] In general, the severity of the rhabdomyolysis parallels the severity of the cocaine intoxication, and those patients with very high creatine kinase levels tend to have the most severe complications from this disease.[45,48] Intravenous cocaine use may be associated with a higher incidence of rhabdomyolysis-induced ARF compared with smoking cocaine.[45]

Other Illicit Drugs
Agents such as PCP (phencyclidine hydrochloride), amphetamines, and "ecstasy" (3,4-methylenedioxymethamphetamine) can also cause this syndrome.[9,49] These drugs can raise the energy demands of a normal muscle cell to a level that cannot be met by available ATP energy supplies.[50]

Lipid-Lowering Agents
The 3-hydroxy-3-methylglutaryl coenzyme A (HMG-CoA) reductase inhibitor lipid-lowering agents (e.g.,

lovastatin, simvastatin) have been associated with rhabdomyolysis, as have the branched-chain fatty esters that inhibit liver triglyceride synthesis (e.g., clofibrate, gemfibrozil).[9,51,52] The mechanisms of action are unclear. These agents can precipitate rhabdomyolysis when used alone or with other drugs. Patients with preexisting renal dysfunction may be more susceptible.[53] Rhabdomyolysis has occurred in many patients taking HMG-CoA reductase inhibitors along with gemfibrozil.[51,54,55]

Carbon Monoxide
Rhabdomyolysis is a known complication of carbon monoxide poisoning.[56,57] The pathophysiology is unknown, but hypoxia, direct muscle compression from coma, and direct myocyte toxic effects may play a role.[56]

Biologic Toxins
Some snake envenomations cause rhabdomyolysis through direct myocyte injury resulting in the release of intracellular contents to the extracellular circulation. Species known to do this include the European adder, the Australian tiger snake, the Australian king brown snake, sea snakes, North and South American rattlesnakes, and the death adder. Several myocyte toxins can be present in a single venom.[9]

Stings from Africanized bees and honeybees ("killer bees") can also cause rhabdomyolysis. This is also mediated through direct myotoxins.[9,58,59]

Infections

Bacterial, viral, and parasitic infections have been associated with rhabdomyolysis.[60] Influenza viruses A and B are the most frequently cited viral causes.[61,62] The influenza virus may be directly toxic to myocytes, but this has not been proven.[10,63] Rhabdomyolysis associated with human immunodeficiency virus (HIV) has been reported in many patients. However, the independent role of HIV in causing the disease is unclear because many of the investigated patients were also taking multiple medications and some had concurrent infections.[64,65]

Legionella is the most common known bacterial cause of rhabdomyolysis. Its myotoxic effects are mediated through an endotoxin.[10,66,67] Salmonella and Streptococcus also can induce rhabdomyolysis through both direct myocyte invasion and inhibition of glycolytic enzymes.[10,66,68]

Electrolyte Abnormalities

Hypophosphatemia is believed to cause membrane injury by severe depletion of ATP. Hypokalemia has also been shown to cause rhabdomyolysis. Potassium is a vasodilator of the microcirculation for metabolically active muscle cells when its extracellular concentration is high enough. Hypokalemia may prevent local vasodilation and lead to focal muscle ischemia.[6,10] Both hyponatremia and hypernatremia have been associated with rhabdomyolysis.[9] Case reports of the former primarily involve patients with hyponatremia induced by psychogenic polydipsia.[69]

Hypoxia

Any condition causing tissue hypoxia will promote cellular injury and may lead to this syndrome. Intrinsic vascular injury or obstruction, hypotension, or external compression of the blood supply to a muscle group can all cause tissue hypoxia and rhabdomyolysis.[7] Certain blood disorders (e.g., sickle cell anemia) may cause vascular thrombosis, resulting in tissue hypoxia and subsequent muscle injury.[12,70]

Idiopathic Cause

Some patients develop rhabdomyolysis, at times recurrently, without obvious cause. Whether such patients have a genetic defect requires further study.

CLINICAL FEATURES

Patients with rhabdomyolysis classically present with complaints of muscle weakness, swelling, and pain. The myalgias may be focal or diffuse, depending on the underlying cause of the disease. The patient may also note dark- or tea-colored urine. However, a high clinical suspicion for rhabdomyolysis must be maintained in patients at risk because up to 50% of those with serologically proven rhabdomyolysis do not report myalgias or muscle weakness.[71]

History

The history can be extremely helpful in making the diagnosis. For example, if a patient is brought to the emergency department with an overdose of a sedative-hypnotic drug, information about the patient's body position and length of time immobilized is useful. Unfortunately, many patients with rhabdomyolysis from this cause are unable to give an adequate history because of their altered mental status.

The history should include any recent trauma or compression, excessive exertion, envenomations, infections, electrical shock, or temperature extremes. Other areas of interest are the use of prescription medications, over-the-counter drugs, alcohol or illicit drugs, known medical conditions, and a family history of muscle dysfunction or disease.

Physical Examination

Physical examination may reveal motor weakness with tenderness to palpation of the affected muscle groups. The overlying skin may be discolored and there may be evidence of trauma. With trauma or compression, the affected area may have sensory and motor losses that do not follow one nerve distribution.[14] The patient may also appear clinically dehydrated from the reduced extracellular fluid volume. Unfortunately, characteristic physical signs are present in only 4% to 15% of patients.[71] Some patients with severe rhabdomyolysis show respiratory insufficiency, presumably caused by diffuse muscle injury resulting in weakened respiratory efforts. In addition, some patients develop hepatic insufficiency.

Compartment syndromes are relatively common complications of rhabdomyolysis. Therefore, the physical examination may reveal firm muscle compartments, pain with passive flexion, and neurovascular compromise of the affected extremity. Studies have reported persistent peripheral nerve deficits in 10% to 20% of patients with compartment syndrome.[72]

DIAGNOSTIC STRATEGIES

The most reliable method of diagnosing rhabdomyolysis is laboratory evaluation. Useful tests include measurements of serum and urine myoglobin, serum creatine kinase, and serum electrolyte levels.

Myoglobin

In the past, the diagnosis of rhabdomyolysis rested on the demonstration of myoglobin in the serum. Serum myoglobin, however, is an unreliable marker for rhabdomyolysis for several reasons. The half-life of myoglobin in plasma is 1 to 3 hours, and it may disappear completely from plasma within 6 hours of injury. Myoglobinuria is pathopneumonic of rhabdomyolysis. The amount of myoglobinuria depends on the plasma concentration of myoglobin, the GFR, the extent of myoglobin binding in plasma, and urine flow rate. For example, a patient with moderate muscle injury and a normal GFR who is excreting very concentrated urine may have a significant amount of myoglobin in the urine. On the other hand, a patient with a much larger amount of muscle injury but a low GFR and very dilute urine would have much less myoglobin in the urine. Normal urine myoglobin levels are less than 5 ng/mL.

Urinalysis typically shows brown urine with a large amount of blood on dipstick evaluation but few, if any, red blood cells (RBCs) on microscopic evaluation. This occurs because most dipstick tests cannot distinguish myoglobinuria from hematuria or hemoglobinuria.[73] Brown casts and renal tubular epithelial cells are also sometimes found.[9]

Methods used to measure urine myoglobin include immunodiffusion, radioimmunoassay, and specific dipstick tests. The dipstick tests involve use of reagents (e.g., guaiac, or o-toluidine) and are only slightly less sensitive than radioimmunoassay, which is the best method available.[73] Because of the rapid excretion of myoglobin from the urine, however, a significant number of patients with rhabdomyolysis have false-negative dipstick results.[71]

Creatine Kinase

Measurement of creatine kinase levels (CK; formerly CPK, creatine/creatinine phosphokinase) is a more sensitive method than myoglobin testing to detect rhabdomyolysis. CK is an excellent marker for this disease because it is easily measured, is present in the serum

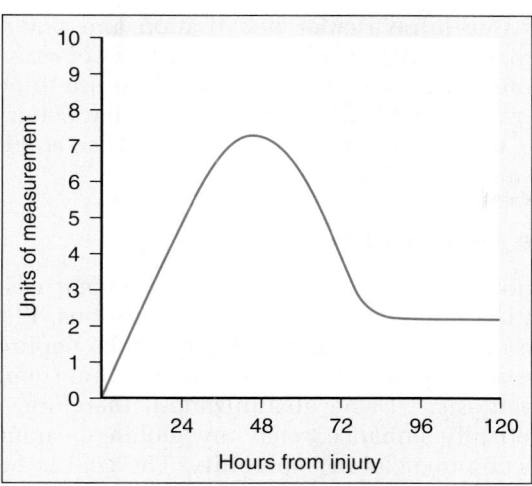

Figure 125-2. Typical creatine kinase elimination curve.

immediately after muscle injury, and is not rapidly cleared from serum. In general, peak CK levels occur within 24 to 36 hours of muscle injury and diminish by approximately 39% per day (Figure 125-2).[42] Failure of levels to decrease in this manner suggests ongoing muscle injury, possibly from an undetected compartment syndrome.

Rhabdomyolysis cannot be defined by a specific CK level. In general, however, a CK level greater than five times normal is diagnostic, and levels as high as several hundred thousand have been reported.[11,35,46,64] A clear relationship exists between CK level and the severity of disease, although patients can have significant morbidity with only moderately elevated CK levels.[46,74,75] For this reason, even modest elevations of CK level must be taken seriously, particularly early in the disease process. The CK subtype present in skeletal muscle is MM, but when considerable skeletal muscle injury occurs, a small amount of CK-MB also is present in the serum. This fraction rarely exceeds 3% to 5% of the total CK in the absence of coincident myocardial infarction.

Other Tests

Electrolyte evaluation may show hyperkalemia, hyperphosphatemia, hypocalcemia, hyperuricemia, and hypoalbuminemia. An elevated anion gap is characteristically present.[76] Hyperkalemia (>5.5 mEq/L) has been reported on initial laboratory studies in 20% to 40% of patients.[71] It is caused by a combination of intracellular potassium release from muscle necrosis and decreased renal excretion.[7] Hyperphosphatemia associated with this syndrome is caused by a leakage of phosphorus from injured muscle. Levels usually do not exceed 7 mg/dL.

Hypocalcemia is the most common metabolic abnormality and occurs early in the course of rhabdomyolysis. In one series of 76 patients, hypocalcemia was present in 63%.[77] Hypercalcemia often develops later in this syndrome, and most hypercalcemic patients also experience ARF.[71] Although the exact cause of hyper-calcemia in this setting is unknown, it is hypothesized that calcium is mobilized from damaged muscle, and parathyroid hormone and 1,25-dihydroxycholecalciferol levels are increased during recovery from rhabdomyolysis.[10]

The combination of elevated serum phosphate and calcium may result in precipitation of calcium phosphate (CaPO$_4$) in soft tissue, blood vessels, and eyes.[9]

For reasons related to increased muscle mass, hyperuricemia is particularly likely to occur in well-trained athletes with exertional rhabdomyolysis. Hypoalbuminemia may result from leakage of protein from injured vessels coupled with proteinuria.

Many patients with acute rhabdomyolysis demonstrate evidence of disseminated intravascular coagulation. Thrombocytopenia, hypofibrinogenemia, and an elevated D-dimer with prolongation of prothrombin time can be seen. The coagulopathy is a result of muscle necrosis and liberation of activating substances (e.g., thromboplastin) from injured cells.

Some patients have elevated levels of aspartate transaminase, alanine transaminase, and lactate dehydrogenase from muscle injury alone. Occasionally, a patient may be misdiagnosed as having hepatic injury when, in fact, all enzyme elevations are caused only by muscle injury.

DIFFERENTIAL CONSIDERATIONS

Findings on the history, physical examination, and laboratory evaluation of patients presenting with rhabdomyolysis are unique to this disease entity. On initial presentation, however, the patient must be fully evaluated and alternate diagnoses considered.

Pigmenturia has a variety of causes (Box 125-3). Patients with pigmenturia must be differentiated into those with myoglobinuria and those with hematuria, through microscopic identification of RBCs in the urine; patients cannot be differentiated by dipstick testing alone. Patients with hemoglobinuria will have a positive dipstick test for blood but no, or few, RBCs on microscopic analysis. Pigmenturia is differentiated from rhabdomyolysis by checking for plasma discoloration. With hemoglobinuria, but not with myoglobinuria, the plasma will also be discolored.[16] Hematuria and hemoglobinuria have lengthy differential diagnoses of their own. Hematuria can be present with rhabdomyolysis if there was associated renal trauma.

Pigmenturia can be associated with acute intermittent porphyria. Patients with this condition generally have a very different clinical presentation from those with acute rhabdomyolysis, and the urine will contain porphobilinogen.[9] Bilirubin, a degradation product of heme, will also cause pigmenturia when present in the urine. In this case, the urine will test positive for urobilinogen. Pigmenturia can also be a direct drug or food effect. In this situation, the urine should test negative for blood, and few or no RBCs are seen on microscopic evaluation.

In crush injury patients, the motor weakness and possible paralysis can mimic spinal injury.[78] All trauma patients must be treated with spinal precautions, and laboratory-proven rhabdomyolysis does not rule out concurrent spinal injury. With rhabdomyolysis, however, motor function will often improve as the disease is treated.

Myocardial infarction must be considered in patients with an elevated CK level and pain, especially if the pain is localized to the chest. Measuring serum troponin concentration will help assess for a cardiac cause of the CK elevation.

MANAGEMENT

Saline Infusion

The mainstay of therapy for rhabdomyolysis is the administration of large volumes of saline very early in the course of the disease. In patients with trauma or compression, saline resuscitation should begin in the field.[79] Early intervention has decreased the incidence of AIRF.[10] Resuscitation should be undertaken with normal saline. Potassium-containing fluids should be avoided because of the risk of rhabdomyolysis-associated hyperkalemia. High-volume infusions should be started as soon as possible and infusion rates titrated for a urine output of 200 to 300 mL/hr.[15]

Patients may require up to 20 L fluid in the first 24 hours to achieve adequate urine flow rates. Cardiac, pulmonary, and electrolyte status should be carefully monitored.

Mannitol

Mannitol may have many beneficial effects in the treatment of rhabdomyolysis. It acts as an osmotic diuretic, an intravascular volume expander, a renal vasodilator, and possibly a free radical scavenger. As a diuretic, mannitol increases urine flow, which may help prevent obstruction from myoglobin casts. Renal vasodilation increases renal blood flow and GFR and may also decrease tubular obstruction. As a volume expander, mannitol draws fluid from the interstitial space,

decreasing intravascular dehydration and potentially reducing muscular swelling.[9,16,80] In cases of early ARF, mannitol may convert oliguric renal failure to nonoliguric renal failure, which has a somewhat better prognosis.[7] Loop diuretics (e.g., furosemide) can acidify the urine and should not be used.[15]

Urine Alkalinization

Myoglobin protein binding and subsequent cast precipitation is enhanced in acidic conditions. Elevated serum myoglobin levels alone may not be nephrotoxic unless accompanied by intravascular volume depletion and acidosis.[18] Urine alkalinization, therefore, could theoretically enhance renal myoglobin clearance by increasing myoglobin's solubility. The goal is to keep the urine pH greater than 6.5. This can be accomplished by adding bicarbonate (1-2 amps, for example) to half normal saline. With 2 amps of bicarbonate in 1 L of half normal saline, the fluid becomes slightly hypertonic. Mannitol is also hyperosmolar. Therefore, if mannitol is used, it is prudent to add 1 amp of bicarbonate to 1 L of half normal saline instead of 2 amps. Although the use of large fluid volumes and bicarbonate early in the course of rhabdomyolysis seems very effective, prospective randomized studies using these agents have not been performed. Volume expansion alone may be effective therapy for these patients.

Chelation Therapy

A potential role for iron chelators, such as desferrioxamine, is under investigation. Chelation therapy reduces renal injury in animal models.[81] The theory is that iron chelation protects against exposure to free iron, which helps to protect against lipid peroxidation and therefore myocyte breakdown.

General Measures

Electrolyte Abnormalities

Concurrent with the previous treatments, electrolyte abnormalities must be monitored and managed. Hyperkalemia is a potentially life-threatening complication of rhabdomyolysis and should be treated following the usual medical regimen. Hyperkalemia coupled with hypocalcemia can predispose to malignant cardiac dysrhythmias. Intravenous calcium may be ineffective as a treatment for hyperkalemia if given to a patient with hyperphosphatemia. The calcium and phosphate can combine and precipitate.[9] Dialysis may be required.

The use of calcium for asymptomatic hypocalcemic patients should be avoided because it may raise intracellular calcium levels, promoting further muscle injury. Symptomatic hypercalcemia generally requires only volume expansion and diuretic therapy.

For patients with a rising or elevated potassium level, persistent acidosis, or oliguric renal failure with fluid overload, dialysis may be necessary.[9,10] Dialysis with supportive care should effectively limit the morbidity and mortality from ARF associated with rhabdomyolysis.

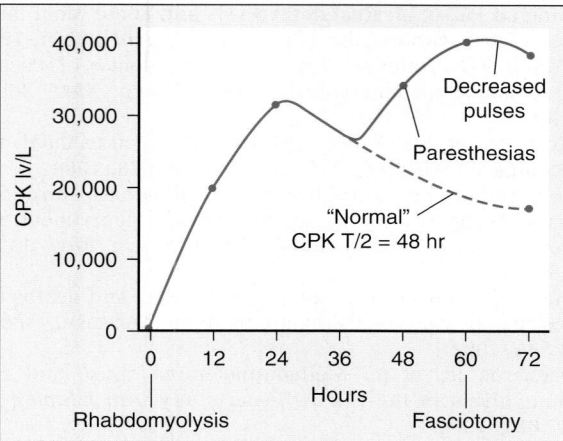

Figure 125-3. Rhabdomyolysis: second-wave phenomenon. Serum creatine kinase (CK, CPK) activity resulting from a single bout of muscle injury usually peaks at about 24 hours. Its half-life is about 48 hours. A second rise may occur if necrosis has involved a muscle in a tight fascial compartment in which sufficient edema accumulates to produce ischemia and a second wave of necrosis. (Redrawn from McGoldrick MD: Diagnosis and management of acute renal failure: Part I. *Cardiovasc Rev Rep* 5:1031, 1984.)

KEY CONCEPTS

- Rhabdomyolysis classically manifests in patients reporting muscle weakness, swelling, and pain. Because only half of patients have all these physical findings, however, the emergency physician should suspect the syndrome in all patients at risk, particularly when they present with an altered sensorium.

- In patients with rhabdomyolysis, urine dipstick testing is strongly positive for blood, with very few, or no, RBCs seen on microscopic examination. The diagnosis is confirmed by an elevated serum CK level.

- Early fluid resuscitation resulting in a urine output of 200 to 300 mL/hr is key in reducing the risk of rhabdomyolysis-induced renal failure. Intravenous fluids are the primary treatment, with mannitol and urine alkalinization as options. Loop diuretics should not be used, since they can acidify the urine.

- Hyperkalemia with hypocalcemia can precipitate malignant cardiac dysrhythmias and must be treated aggressively.

- A CK level that does not decrease appropriately or continues to rise beyond 48 hours may indicate continued muscle injury. The patient requires careful evaluation for compartment syndromes or other causes.

Coagulopathy

Therapy for the coagulopathy associated with this syndrome is directed at treatment of the underlying disease process. DIC usually resolves spontaneously after several days if the underlying cause is corrected, but if hemorrhagic complications occur, therapy with platelets, vitamin K, and fresh frozen plasma may be necessary.

Compartment Syndrome

Clinicians should monitor compartmental pressures in the patient with suspected or existing compartment syndrome. When compartmental pressure exceeds 35 mm Hg, fasciotomy should be strongly considered, although the decision to perform a fasciotomy must be decided on a case-by-case basis.[82] The failure of CK levels to decline appropriately should suggest ongoing muscle injury from a compartment syndrome (Figure 125-3).

DISPOSITION

No good prospective studies support a standardized approach to disposition of the patient with rhabdomyolysis. The high risk for renal failure, however, mandates close monitoring of renal function, electrolytes, and hydration status, which usually requires admission to the hospital. Also, if the patient is a victim of trauma, serial CK levels will need to be followed to assess for ongoing muscle injury. If the patient is not a victim of trauma or compression injury, the underlying cause of the rhabdomyolysis requires investigation to prevent recurrences.

REFERENCES

1. Book of Numbers 11:31-35.
2. Meyer-Betz F: Beobachtungen an einem eigenartigen mit Muskellah-mungen verbunden Fall von Haemoglobinurie. *Dtsch Arch Klin Med* 101:85, 1911.
3. Bywaters EGL, Beall D: Crush injuries with impairment of renal function. *BMJ* 1:427, 1941.
4. Koffler A, Friedler RM, Massry SG: Renal failure due to non-traumatic rhabdomyolysis. *Ann Intern Med* 85:23, 1976.
5. Grossman RA et al: Nontraumatic rhabdomyolysis and acute renal failure. *N Engl J Med* 291:807, 1974.
6. Zager RA: Rhabdomyolysis and myohemoglobinuric acute renal failure. *Kidney Int* 49:314, 1996.
7. McGoldrick MD: Acute renal failure following trauma. In *Anesthesiology*. Philadelphia, JB Lippincott, 1989.
8. Guyton AC: *Textbook of Medical Physiology,* 7th ed. Philadelphia, WB Saunders, 1986.
9. David WS: Myoglobinuria. *Neurol Clin* 18:215, 2000.
10. Visweswaran P, Guntupalli J: Environmental emergencies: Rhabdomyolysis. *Crit Care Clin* 15:415, 1999.
11. Hemer R: When exercise goes awry: Exertional rhabdomyolysis. *South Med J* 90:548, 1997.
12. Lopez JR, et al: Myoplasmic calcium concentration during exertional rhabdomyolysis. *Lancet* 345:424, 1995.
13. Reddy MK, et al: Removal of Z-lines and actinin from isolated myofibrils by a calcium activated neutral protease. *J Biol Chem* 250:4278, 1975.
14. Gans L, Kennedy T: Management of unique clinical entities in disaster medicine. *Emerg Med Clin North Am* 14:312, 1996.
15. Slater MS, Mullins RJ: Rhabdomyolysis and myoglobinuric renal failure in trauma and surgical patients: A review. *J Am Coll Surg* 186:693, 1998.
16. Vanholder R, et al: Rhabdomyolysis. *J Am Soc Nephrol* 11:1553, 2000.
17. Holt S, Moore K: Pathogenesis of renal failure in rhabdomyolysis: The role of myoglobin. *Exp Nephrol* 8:72, 2000.

18. Bywaters EGL, Stead JK: The production of renal failure following injection of solutions containing myohemoglobin. *Q J Exp Physiol* 33:53, 1944.

19. Braun SR, et al: Evaluation of the renal toxicity of heme proteins and their derivatives: A role in the genesis of acute tubule necrosis. *J Exp Med* 131:443, 1970.

20. Edlich RF, Edgerton MT, McLaughlin RE: Compartment syndrome. In Edlich RF, Spyker DA (eds): *Current Emergency Therapy.* Rockville, Md, Aspen, 1985.

21. Heppenstall RB, et al: The compartment syndrome: An experimental and clinical study of muscular energy metabolism using phosphorus nuclear magnetic resonance spectroscopy. *Clin Orthop* 226:138, 1988.

22. Lofberg M, et al: Metabolic causes of recurrent rhabdomyolysis. *Acta Neurol Scand* 98:268, 1998.

23. Tonin P, et al: Metabolic causes of myoglobinuria. *Ann Neurol* 27:181, 1990.

24. Collins AJ: Renal dialysis treatment for victims of the Armenian earthquake. *N Engl J Med* 320:1291, 1989.

25. Sheng ZY: Medical support in the Tangshan earthquake: A review of the management of mass casualties and certain major injuries. *J Trauma* 27:1130, 1987.

26. Shimazu T, et al: Fluid resuscitation and systemic complications in crush syndrome: 14 Hanshin-Awaji earthquake patients. *J Trauma* 42:641, 1997.

27. Poels PJE, Gabreels FJM: Rhabdomyolysis: A review of the literature. *Clin Neurol Neurosurg* 95:175, 1993.

28. Rubinstein I, et al: Involvement of nitric oxide in experimental muscle crush injury. *J Clin Invest* 101:1325, 1998.

29. Knottenbelt JD: Traumatic rhabdomyolysis from severe beating: Experience of volume diuresis in 200 patients. *J Trauma* 37:214, 1994.

30. Bildsten SA, et al: The risk of rhabdomyolysis and acute renal failure with the patient in the exaggerated lithotomy position. *J Urol* 152:1970, 1994.

31. Sinert R, et al: Exercised-induced rhabdomyolysis. *Ann Emerg Med* 23:1301, 1994.

32. Teitjen DP, Guzzi LM: Exertional rhabdomyolysis and acute renal failure following the Army Physical Fitness Test. *Mil Med* 154:23, 1989.

33. Knochel JP: Catastrophic medical events with exhaustive exercise: "White collar rhabdomyolysis." *Kidney Int* 38:700, 1990.

34. Zager RA, Aultschuld R: Body temperature: An important determinant of severity of ischemic renal injury. *Am J Physiol* 251:F87, 1986.

35. Line RL, Rust GS: Acute exertional rhabdomyolysis. *Am Fam Physician* 52:502, 1995.

36. Sato T, et al: Recurrent reversible rhabdomyolysis associated with hyperthermia and status epilepticus. *Acta Paediatr* 84:1083, 1995.

37. Manji H, et al: Status dystonicus: The syndrome and its management. *Brain* 121:243, 1998.

38. Jankovic J: Myoglobinuric renal failure in Huntington's chorea. *Neurology* 36:138, 1986.

39. Slater MS, Mullins RJ: Rhabdomyolysis and myoglobinuric renal failure in trauma and surgical patients: A review. *J Am Coll Surg* 186:693, 1998.

40. Brumback RA, Feeback DL, Leech RW: Rhabdomyolysis following electrical injury. *Semin Neurol* 15:329, 1995.

41. Abraham B, et al: Malignant hyperthermia susceptibility: Anaesthetic implications and risk stratification. *Q J Med* 90:13, 1997.

42. Winston T, et al: Rhabdomyolysis and myoglobinuric acute renal failure associated with classic heat stroke. *South Med J* 88:1065, 1995.

43. Levenson JL: Neuroleptic malignant syndrome. *N Engl J Med* 313:163, 1985.

44. Kasper DL, et al (eds): *Harrison's Principles of Internal Medicine,* 11th ed. New York, McGraw-Hill, 1987.

45. Singhal PC, et al: Rhabdomyolysis and acute renal failure associated with cocaine abuse. *Clin Toxicol* 28:321, 1990.

46. Welch RD, Todd K, Krause GS: Incidence of cocaine-associated rhabdomyolysis. *Ann Emerg Med* 20:154, 1991.

47. Roth D, et al: Acute rhabdomyolysis associated with cocaine intoxication. *N Engl J Med* 319:673, 1988.

48. Counselman FL, et al: Creatine phosphokinase elevation in patients presenting to the emergency department with cocaine-related complaints. *Am J Emerg Med* 15:221, 1997.

49. Henry JA, Jeffreys KJ, Dawling S: Toxicity and deaths from 3,4-methylenedioxymethamphetamine (ecstasy). *Lancet* 2:384, 1992.

50. Richards JR, et al: Methamphetamine abuse and rhabdomyolysis in the ED: A 5-year study. *Am J Emerg Med* 17:681, 1999.

51. Pierce LR, Wysowski DK, Gross TP: Myopathy and rhabdomyolysis associated with lovastatin-gemfibrozil combination therapy. *JAMA* 264:71, 1990.

52. Hino I, et al: Pravastatin-induced rhabdomyolysis in a patient with mixed connective tissue disease. *Arthritis Rheum* 39:1259, 1996.

53. Biesenbach G, et al: Myoglobinuric renal failure due to long-standing lovastatin therapy in a patient with pre-existing chronic renal insufficiency. *Nephrol Dial Transplant* 11:2059, 1996.

54. Duell PB, Connor WE, Illingworth DR: Rhabdomyolysis after taking atorvastatin with gemfibrozil. *Am J Cardiol* 81:368, 1998.

55. Tal A, Rajeshawari M, Isley W: Rhabdomyolysis associated with simvastatin-gemfibrozil therapy. *South Med J* 90:546, 1997.

56. Florkowski CM, et al: Rhabdomyolysis and acute renal failure following carbon monoxide poisoning: Two case reports with muscle histopathology and enzyme activities. *Clin Toxicol* 30:443, 1992.

57. Shapiro AB, et al: Carbon monoxide and myonecrosis: A prospective study. *Vet Hum Toxicol* 31:136, 1989.

58. Kolecki P: Delayed toxic reaction following massive bee envenomation. *Ann Emerg Med* 33:114, 1999.

59. Hiran S, et al: Rhabdomyolysis due to multiple honey bee stings. *Postgrad Med J* 70:937, 1994.

60. Friedman BI, Libby R: Epstein-Barr virus infection associated with rhabdomyolysis and acute renal failure. *Clin Pediatr* 25:228, 1986.

61. Goebel J, et al: Acute renal failure from rhabdomyolysis following influenza A in a child. *Clin Pediatr* 36:479, 1997.

62. Singh U, Scheld WM: Infectious etiologies of rhabdomyolysis: Three case reports and review. *Clin Infect Dis* 22:642, 1996.

63. Kagan H, et al: Formation of ion permeable channels by tumor necrosis factor-alpha. *Science* 255:1427, 1995.

64. Chariot P, et al: Acute rhabdomyolysis in patients infected by human immunodeficiency virus. *Neurology* 44:1692, 1994.

65. Del Rio C, et al: Acute human immunodeficiency virus infection temporally associated with rhabdomyolysis, acute renal failure and nephrosis. *Rev Infect Dis* 12:282, 1990.

66. Byrd RP Jr, Roy TM: Rhabdomyolysis and bacterial pneumonia. *Respir Med* 92:359, 1998.

67. Malvy D, et al: Legionnaire's disease and rhabdomyolysis. *Intensive Care Med* 18:132, 1992.

68. Abdulla AJ, Moorehead JF, Sweeny P: Acute tubular necrosis due to rhabdomyolysis and pancreatitis associated with *Salmonella enteritidis* food poisoning. *Nephrol Dial Transplant* 8:672, 1993.

69. Korzets A, et al: Severe hyponatremia after water intoxication: A potential cause of rhabdomyolysis. *Am J Med Sci* 312:92, 1996.

70. Devereuz S, Knowles SM: Rhabdomyolysis and acute renal failure in sickle cell anemia. *BMJ* 290:1707, 1985.
71. Gabow PA, Kaehny WD, Kellener SP: The spectrum of rhabdomyolysis. *Medicine* 61:141, 1982.
72. Kunkel JM: Thigh and leg compartment syndrome in the absence of lower extremity trauma following MAST application. *Am J Emerg Med* 5:2, 1987.
73. Loun B, et al: Adaptation of a quantitative immunoassay for urine myoglobin: Predictor in detecting renal dysfunction. *Clin Chem* 105:479, 1996.
74. Ward MM: Factors predictive of acute renal failure in rhabdomyolysis. *Arch Intern Med* 148:1553, 1988.
75. Brody SL, et al: Predicting the severity of cocaine-associated rhabdomyolysis. *Ann Emerg Med* 19:1137, 1990.
76. Oster JR, et al: Metabolic acidosis with extreme elevation of anion gap: Case report and literature review. *Am J Med Sci* 317:38, 1999.
77. Bank WJ, et al: A disorder of muscle lipid metabolism and myoglobinuria: Absence of carnitine palmityl transferase. *N Engl J Med* 292:443, 1975.
78. Michaelson M, et al: Crush syndrome: Experience from the Lebanon war, 1982. *Isr J Med Sci* 20:305, 1984.
79. Pretto EA, et al: An analysis of prehospital mortality in an earthquake. *Prehosp Disaster Med* 9:260, 1994.
80. Odeh M: The role of reperfusion-induced injury in the pathogenesis of the crush syndrome. *N Engl J Med* 324:1417, 1991.
81. Paller MS: Hemoglobin and myoglobin-induced renal failure in rats: Role of iron in nephrotoxicity. *Am J Physiol* 255:F539, 1988.
82. Owen CA, et al: Intramuscular pressure with limb compression: Clarification of the pathogenesis of the drug-induced compartment syndrome/crush syndrome. *N Engl J Med* 5:2, 1987.

CHAPTER

126 Thyroid and Adrenal Disorders

Jeffrey Sternlicht and John M. Wogan

The three conditions described in this chapter—hyperthyroidism, hypothyroidism, and adrenal insufficiency—are similar in several respects. They advance in a slow, insidious fashion, expressing nonspecific signs and symptoms over months to years, and then are acutely precipitated by intercurrent stress. Each is relatively uncommon. Emergency physicians may not have the clinical experience to facilitate ready diagnosis. The characteristic symptom complexes are subtle and may be difficult to recognize, especially in their early stages. All three conditions are potentially lethal if untreated, and in their extreme manifestations, these endocrine disorders may constitute medical emergencies. No confirmatory laboratory studies are immediately available. Therefore, it is often necessary to initiate treatment on the basis of clinical judgment alone.

HYPERTHYROIDISM

Perspective

Historical Background

Although Parry recognized the association of exophthalmos, goiter, and cardiovascular hyperactivity as early as 1786, Graves and von Basedow are commonly credited with the initial descriptions (in 1835 and 1840) of the diseases that bear their names.[1] Trosseau accidentally administered tincture of iodine rather than tincture of digitalis to a hyperthyroid patient and astutely recognized its therapeutic value.[2] The usefulness of sympathetic blockade was initially demonstrated when postoperative thyrotoxic patients were successfully treated with procaine spinal anesthesia.[3] Canary and Ramey and their colleagues demonstrated the efficacy of peripheral pharmacologic adrenergic block.[4,5]

The terms *hyperthyroidism, thyrotoxicosis, thyrotoxic crisis*, and *thyroid storm* do not have precise, consensual definitions. They refer to the continuum of disease that results from thyroid hyperfunction. Hyperthyroidism and thyrotoxicosis designate milder forms of disease. Thyroid storm and thyrotoxic crisis refer to the heightened and life-threatening manifestations of thyroid hyperactivity, including high fever and cardiovascular, neurologic, and gastrointestinal dysfunction.[6-8]

Whereas hyperthyroidism is common, true thyroid storm is rare. From 1% to 2% of patients with hyperthyroidism may progress to thyroid storm, which usually supervenes on a long history of uncomplicated hyperthyroidism.[6-8] Six to 8 months of symptoms are usual, and hyperthyroidism may have been present for as long as $2\frac{1}{2}$ to 5 years.[8-11]

A number of stresses may precipitate thyroid storm (Box 126-1). The transition from simple thyrotoxicosis to thyroid storm may be abrupt, coincident with the acute precipitant.[9]

Etiology

Hyperthyroidism and thyrotoxicosis have many causes (Box 126-2). Most cases of thyroid storm are secondary to *toxic diffuse goiter* (*Graves' disease*) and therefore, as with the underlying disease, occur in women in their

BOX 126-1. Precipitants of Thyroid Storm

Medical
Infection
Vascular accidents
Pulmonary embolism
Visceral infarction
Surgery
Burns
Trauma
Emotional stress

Endocrine
Hypoglycemia
Diabetic ketoacidosis
Hyperosmolar nonketotic coma

Drug Related
Iodine 131 therapy
Premature withdrawal of antithyroid therapy
Ingestion of thyroid hormone
Contrast radiographic studies
Drug reaction (thioridazine hydrochloride [Mellaril],
    iothiouracil [Itrumil])

BOX 126-2. Etiologic Factors of Thyrotoxicosis

Toxic diffuse goiter (Graves' disease)
Toxic multinodular goiter
Toxic uninodular goiter
Factitious thyrotoxicosis
T_3 toxicosis
Thyrotoxicosis associated with thyroiditis
    Hashimoto's thyroiditis
    Subacute (de Quervain's) thyroiditis
Graves' or Basedow's disease
Metastatic follicular carcinoma
Malignancies with circulating thyroid stimulators
TSH-producing pituitary tumors
Struma ovarii with hyperthyroidism
Hypothalamic hyperthyroidism

T_3, triiodothyronine; TSH, thyroid-stimulating hormone.

third and fourth decades of life. *Toxic multinodular goiter* may produce thyroid storm, usually in women in their fourth through seventh decades. Thyroid storm from *toxic uninodular goiter* is uncommon and less severe.

Factitious hyperthyroidism results from an exogenous source of thyroid hormone and may be difficult to diagnose.[12,13] It occurs most often in the settings of acute intoxication or fad dieting; full-blown thyroid storm in this setting is rare.[14]

Amiodarone, an iodine-rich antidysrhythmic indicated for the treatment of ventricular and supraventricular dysrhythmias, has complex effects on thyroid physiology. Asymptomatic changes in thyroid hormone levels are common. Clinically relevant thyrotoxicosis has been reported in 1% to 24% of patients receiving amiodarone and should be suspected when a patient who is taking amiodarone shows signs of cardiac

decompensation, tachydysrhythmias, restlessness, or weakness.[15,16] Hyperthyroidism secondary to *thyroiditis*, either Hashimoto's or subacute, rarely causes thyroid storm and is usually but not always mild.[13] Other causes of hyperthyroidism (see Box 126-2) are even less likely to cause thyroid storm.

Principles of Disease

The pathophysiologic mechanisms underlying both thyrotoxicosis and the shift from uncomplicated hyperthyroidism to thyroid storm are not entirely clear. Many of the signs and symptoms are those of adrenergic hyperactivity.[17] However, neither catecholamine sensitivity nor serum catecholamine levels appear to be elevated. The concept of catecholamine hyperfunction is useful, however, and adrenergic blockade forms the cornerstone of therapy.

Thyroid hormone has direct inotropic and chronotropic effects on the heart, but these effects do not explain the clinical spectrum of thyroid storm.[18] In addition, thyroid levels are not necessarily acutely elevated when the transition from uncomplicated thyrotoxicosis to thyroid storm occurs.[6] Thyroid storm probably reflects the addition of adrenergic hyperactivity, induced by a nonspecific stress, to the setting of untreated or undertreated hyperthyroidism.[19]

Clinical Features

Lahey[20,21] recognized that two distinct clinical presentations are possible with thyroid hyperactivity. He designated these syndromes as "activated thyroidism" and "unactivated thyroidism." The distinction proved clinically useful, and Lahey's syndromes are currently referred to as hyperthyroidism and apathetic hyperthyroidism, respectively. Hyperthyroidism occurs in younger patients, and its signs and symptoms, typically with multiple organ involvement, probably reflect the end-organ responsiveness to thyroid hormone in this group. Apathetic hyperthyroidism occurs in elders in whom end-organ responsiveness is attenuated. In younger patients the clinical picture is dominated by depressed mental function and cardiac complications.

Signs and symptoms of hyperthyroidism may be distinctive (Box 126-3). The signal symptoms of hyperthyroidism include agitation, nervousness, palpitations, and weight loss. Weight loss is common and may be dramatic.[6,8,11] For this reason, thyroid hormone is inappropriately prescribed as part of many fad diets. Between one fourth and one half of patients coming to the emergency department in thyroid storm report a weight loss of more than 40 pounds.[8,11]

Fever is often present in thyroid storm, may be quite high, and may herald the onset of thyrotoxic crisis in previously uncomplicated disease.[11] Heat intolerance is common and reflects the underlying hypermetabolic state.

Cardiovascular manifestations of thyrotoxicosis are dramatic and characterized by a hyperdynamic, electrically excitable state. Common symptoms include palpitations, dyspnea, and chest pain.[2,9,11] Enhanced contractility produces elevations in systolic blood

BOX 126-3. Signs and Symptoms of Thyrotoxicosis

Symptoms

Common
Weight loss (20 to 40+ lb)
Palpitations
Nervousness
Tremor

Less Common
Chest pain
Dyspnea
Edema
Psychosis
Disorientation
Diarrhea/hyperdefecation
Abdominal pain

Signs

Common
Fever
Tachycardia (100 to 170+ beats/min)
Wide pulse pressure (40 to 100 mm Hg)
Congestive heart failure
Thyromegaly
Tremor
Hyperhidrosis
Thyrotoxic stare/lid retraction

Less Common
Weakness
Shock
Psychosis
Somnolence/obtundation/coma
Infiltrative ophthalmopathy
Jaundice
Tender liver
Pretibial myxedema

pressure and pulse pressure, leading to a dicrotic or water-hammer pulse.[2] Unless there is underlying hypertensive heart disease, the diastolic pressure is usually not elevated.[22] A systolic flow murmur is often present, which resolves with treatment of the thyrotoxicosis.[2,23] Either sinus tachycardia or, less often, atrial tachydysrhythmia is usually present.[11,22] Sinus tachycardia is seen independent of congestive heart failure (CHF) and out of proportion to fever.[10] Hyperthyroid atrial fibrillation may occur either with or without underlying heart disease, is typically refractory to digitalis therapy, and reverts in 20% to 50% of cases after antithyroid therapy.[10,22,24] Atrial premature contractions and atrial flutter may also occur in thyrotoxicosis.[22]

For many years the existence of "thyrocardiac" disease (i.e., CHF caused by thyrotoxicosis without any concomitant heart lesion) was controversial. Most sources now agree that thyrocardiac heart failure is a real phenomenon.[10,25] Thyrocardiac disease may be accompanied by an increased sympathetic tone; it occurs primarily in elders and can usually be treated by digitalis, possibly in combination with β-blocker therapy (although β-blockers can exacerbate preexisting heart failure in rare cases); it is ameliorated by antithyroid treatment.[25,26]

When hyperthyroidism results from Graves' disease, ophthalmopathy may be seen. Indeed, eye findings may be valuable clues to the existence of underlying thyroid disease. The severity of ophthalmopathy does not necessarily parallel the magnitude of thyroid dysfunction but reflects the responsible autoimmune process.[27] The manifestations of ophthalmopathy include upper lid retraction, staring, lid lag (Graefe's sign), exophthalmos, and extraocular muscle palsies.[1,28,29]

Behavior is characterized by agitation, anxiety, and restlessness. Wide mood swings are typical. Fear and even frank paranoia occur. Careless examination may lead to incorrect emergency department triage to psychiatric evaluation rather than appreciation of the medical nature of the disease. In more severe cases, agitation may lead to seizures and even coma.

Proximal myopathy is common, particularly in elders. Thyrotoxic periodic paralysis involves paresis or plegia, which may occur in the absence of other signs or symptoms of thyrotoxicosis. Although more common in males of Asian descent, it has been reported in whites. Serum potassium may be either normal or low. Thyrotoxicosis should be considered when evaluating acutely weak individuals. Correcting electrolyte abnormalities, when present, treating the hyperthyroidism, and administering propranolol are effective in reversing weakness.[30-32] A number of nonspecific gastrointestinal disturbances are possible. Hyperphagia, diarrhea, nausea, vomiting, and abdominal pain have all been noted but are not usually signal symptoms of the disease. Hepatic dysfunction, with or without CHF, is possible.[6,9,33] When jaundice occurs as a primary hepatic sign, it is primarily unconjugated, mild, and probably from the unmasking of occult liver disease (e.g., Gilbert's disease). Treatment of the thyrotoxicosis is sufficient to resolve jaundice.[33]

With respect to dermatologic manifestations, the thyrotoxic patient is typically flushed with warm, moist skin; hair is fine and straight; and 60% to 97% of patients with underlying Graves' disease have an appreciable goiter.[34,35] Hyperpigmentation, vitiligo, or alopecia may occur, especially when an autoimmune mechanism is responsible for the disease. Pretibial myxedema may be present in 5% of cases.

Thyroid storm is a life-threatening, clinical syndrome characterized by exaggerated signs and symptoms of hyperthyroidism, including fever and altered mentation. It occurs most commonly in patients with Graves' disease and is often precipitated by a concurrent illness or injury.

Diagnostic Strategies

The clinical suggestion of thyrotoxicosis must be confirmed by laboratory studies. Pituitary and hypothalamic causes of hyperthyroidism are unusual. Primary thyroid glandular hyperfunction is the rule, and serum levels of various thyroidal hormones reflect this fact. Free thyroxine (FT_4) and free triiodothyronine (FT_3) levels are elevated, whereas the thyrotropin (thyroid-stimulating hormone [TSH]) level is depressed. Various measures are used to assess each of these hormones.

The TSH level is an excellent screening tool. Hyperthyroidism is virtually excluded if TSH is in the normal range. The only exception would be the exceedingly rare clinical entity of secondary hyperthyroidism, which is due to a TSH-producing anterior pituitary adenoma.[36] However, although a normal TSH excludes hyperthyroidism in the vast majority of cases, a low TSH by itself is not diagnostic of the syndrome. Serum TSH may be reduced as a result of chronic medical illnesses such as liver disease or renal failure.[37] In addition, various drugs such as glucocorticoids may cause a reduction in TSH.[37] Additional laboratory confirmation is necessary. The most useful tests are FT_4 and FT_3. A low TSH with an elevated FT_4 confirms thyrotoxicosis. However, a low TSH combined with a normal FT_4 and an elevated FT_3 is also diagnostic (T_3 thyrotoxicosis).[36,37] With the improved assays for FT_4 and FT_3, there is now little indication to measure total T_3 and total T_4.[36,37] If Grave's disease is suspected, thyroid antibody titers (to thyroid peroxidase or thyroglobulin) may ultimately be helpful.[37]

Electrolytes, glucose, calcium, bilirubin, hematocrit, and liver function tests should be checked in addition to thyroid function tests. Laboratory abnormalities in thyroid storm are multiple, mild, and nonspecific.

Hyperglycemia is present in 30% to 55% of patients.[9] Possible explanations for hyperglycemia include insulin resistance, decreased insulin secretion, increased glycogenolysis, and rapid intestinal absorption of glucose.[11]

Hypercalcemia is fairly common, occurring in at least 10% of cases, and is usually mild and asymptomatic. A normocytic, normochromic anemia is common, as is leukocytosis. Either *hypernatremia* or *hyponatremia* is possible but is rarely abnormal enough to cause symptoms. Depressed cholesterol levels are often noted. Minimal elevations in liver function studies, even in the absence of CHF, are seen.[9,33]

Differential Considerations

The differential diagnosis is crucial because a number of serious illnesses, including other endocrine diseases, can show similar symptoms. Differential possibilities include sepsis and intoxication with anticholinergic and adrenergic agents, notably cocaine and amphetamines. *Hypoglycemia* and several withdrawal syndromes (e.g., from ethanol, narcotics, and sedative-hypnotics) may produce a picture of adrenergic hyperfunction with altered mental status, which might be mistaken for hyperthyroidism. *Heat stroke*, with its characteristic hyperpyrexia and disturbed sensorium, may appear similar to thyrotoxicosis but is usually distinguished by its clinical setting. Patients with psychiatric illness may show signs similar to those of thyroid hyperactivity. Other endocrine abnormalities, especially hypothyroidism, may mimic some of the symptoms of apathetic hyperthyroidism.

Apathetic Hyperthyroidism

In 1931, Lahey[21] called attention to a second form of thyrotoxicosis, nonactivated or apathetic thyroidism.

Table 126-1. Comparison of Activated and Apathetic Thyrotoxicosis

Parameter	Activated	Apathetic
Age	4th decade	7th decade
Duration of symptoms	8 mo	26 mo
Weight loss	10 lb	40 lb
Thyroid weight	70 g	45 g
Eye findings	Frequent	Rare
Congestive heart failure	Common	Common
Atrial fibrillation	One third	Three fourths
Depression/apathy	Uncommon	Common

Signs and symptoms of this condition are few and subtle, and the initial appearance of disease may be single-organ failure (e.g., CHF), producing diagnostic confusion by pointing to diagnoses other than thyrotoxicosis.[38]

The cause of apathetic hyperthyroidism is usually multinodular goiter rather than Graves' disease, and the patients are therefore typically older (in their seventh or eighth decades), have small multinodular or nonpalpable goiters, and lack autoimmune ophthalmopathy.[39,40] Cardiovascular symptoms, especially CHF and atrial fibrillation, are prominent, as might be expected from the advanced age of patients. Weight loss is significant, averaging 40 pounds in one study.[40] Depressed mental function, ranging from a placid demeanor to frank coma, is common but may alternate with tremor and hyperactivity. Apathetic thyrotoxicosis usually occurs in elderly patients but has been reported in most age groups, including children (Table 126-1).[39,41]

Management

Mild hyperthyroidism does not require emergency therapy, and the hyperthyroid patient may be referred to an outpatient setting for further evaluation. Thyroid storm, on the other hand, requires immediate therapy. Treatment has five goals: (1) inhibit hormone synthesis, (2) block hormone release, (3) prevent peripheral conversion of T_4 to T_3, (4) block the peripheral effects of thyroid hormone, and (5) provide general support (Box 126-4).

Inhibition of Hormone Synthesis

Thioamides, including *propylthiouracil* (PTU) and *methimazole*, inhibit thyroidal peroxidase, thereby preventing hormone synthesis. PTU is generally preferred over methimazole because it has the additional minor effect of inhibiting peripheral conversion of T_4 to T_3. PTU is given in an initial dose of 600 to 1000 mg by mouth (PO) or by nasogastric (NG) tube, followed by 200 to 250 mg every 4 to 6 hours. Further organification of iodine is blocked within 1 hour of PTU administration, but the drug should be continued for several weeks while the hyperthyroidism is brought under control.

BOX 126-4. Treatment of Thyroid Storm

1. If the diagnosis of thyroid storm is highly likely (on the basis of clinical criteria) and the patient is toxic, immediate therapy, as below, is indicated. If immediate therapy is not needed, draw diagnostic studies and refer for further evaluation.
2. Block synthesis: PTU 150 mg PO/NG q6h
   Block release: SSKI 3–5 drops PO/NG q8h
   Block peripheral effects:
   T_4 conversion: Dexamethasone 2 mg PO/NG q6h
   β-Blockade: Propranolol 1–2 mg IV q15 min prn
   Supportive care: Treat fever with acetaminophen (Tylenol)
   Treat heart failure with digitalis and diuretics
   Identify and treat precipitating factors
   Rehydrate
   Hydrocortisone 100 mg IV q8h

IV, intravenously; NG, by nasogastric tube; PO, orally; PTU, propylthiouracil; SSKI, potassium iodide, T_4, thyroxine.

Blockage of Hormone Release

Because preformed T_4 and T_3 are stored in the thyroid colloid, release of hormone can occur for weeks despite synthesis inhibition. Thus, prevention of colloid hormone release is the second goal of therapy. Both iodine and lithium can inhibit thyroid hormone release. Lithium is not generally used because it can be difficult to titrate the dose, and toxic effects are common. Thioamides should be given at least 1 hour before iodine therapy to prevent organification of the iodine. *Lugol's iodine solution*, 30 drops per day in three or four divided doses, is administered PO or by NG tube; *potassium iodide* (saturated solution of KI), 5 drops every 6 hours PO or by NG tube, is also acceptable. Iodine is contraindicated in patients with a history of iodine anaphylaxis. In these patients lithium carbonate should be given in a dose of 300 mg every 6 hours. Lithium levels should be monitored and kept below 1 mEq/L. In addition, iodine should not be given to patients with iodine overload–induced hyperthyroidism such as those with amiodarone-induced thyrotoxicosis. These patients should be treated with potassium perchlorate, which blocks thyroid uptake of iodine. The recommended dose is 0.5 g of potassium perchlorate per day.[42]

Prevention of Peripheral Hormone Conversion

The peripheral conversion of T_4 to T_3, which is responsible for perhaps 85% of T_3 present in the circulation, may be blocked by PTU, propranolol, or dexamethasone.[43,44] For PTU and propranolol, this effect is probably not quantitatively significant. *Dexamethasone*, however, is effective through this mechanism and should be given as 2 mg intravenously (IV) every 6 hours.[45] If hydrocortisone is given, dexamethasone is probably unnecessary.

Peripheral Adrenergic Blockade

Blockade of the peripheral adrenergic hyperactivity of thyroid crisis may be the most important factor in reducing morbidity and mortality. Initial attempts at blockade were surgical.[3] β-Blockade is currently the method of choice for stanching the peripheral manifestations of thyroid storm. *Propranolol* can reduce dysrhythmias, hyperpyrexia, tremor, palpitations, restlessness, anxiety, and perhaps myopathy.[46,47] Propranolol is effective IV in slow 1- to 2-mg boluses, which may be repeated every 10 to 15 minutes until the desired effect is achieved.[48] Effective oral propranolol therapy usually begins at 20 to 120 mg per dose or 160 to 320 mg/day in divided doses.[49,50]

The contraindications to β-blockade (reactive airway disease, diabetes mellitus, CHF, pregnancy) are the same as for other medical conditions. High-output CHF and heart failure associated with tachydysrhythmias may respond to β-blocker therapy. In rare cases, β-blockers have been associated with worsening of CHF, usually in patients with preexisting, nonthyroid cardiac disease. Therefore, the clinical response to these agents should be monitored carefully. In severe asthmatics, reserpine 2.5 mg every 4 hours may be considered in lieu of β-blockade.[42] The complicated patient with both a tachydysrhythmia and CHF might be managed with a judicious combination of β-blockade and digitalis.

Supportive Care

Supportive care addresses several areas. Hyperpyrexia should be treated aggressively with acetaminophen. Aspirin should not be used because it displaces thyroid hormone from thyroglobulin, thus theoretically increasing the pool of metabolically active hormone. Ice packs and hypothermia blankets may also be used.

CHF should be managed with digitalis, diuretics, and oxygen. Dehydration is a common complication of fever, diarrhea, and vomiting and requires appropriate fluid replacement.

Corticosteroids are uniformly used (in stress dosages of 300 mg/day of hydrocortisone equivalent administered IV) for potential relative adrenal insufficiency. Glucocorticoid use in thyroid storm is associated with improved survival rates.[51] In the rare patient who has contraindications to PTU or methimazole, such as a prior severe reaction, direct removal of thyroid hormone has been described. Plasmapheresis, charcoal plasma perfusion, and peritoneal dialysis may be considered.[42]

Vigorous attempts should be made to identify and treat factors that might have precipitated thyroid storm. Precipitants are usually of a medical rather than a surgical nature (see Box 126-1).[11,19,38] In about 50% of cases, no acute precipitant is identified.[9]

With appropriate therapy, fever, tachycardias, tremor, and altered sensorium should all show improvement in the first 12 to 24 hours. Indeed, sinus tachycardia should respond within minutes of IV propranolol injection. CHF may not revert for weeks. Neuromuscular manifestations resolve slowly over weeks to months.

HYPOTHYROIDISM

Perspective

Historical Background

As early as the fourth century AD, a condition resembling myxedema was reportedly treated with ground sheep thyroid.[52] Paracelsus, in the 16th century, and Platter, in the early 17th century, called attention to the association of cretinism and endemic goiter.[1] Curling[53] described two cretins with absent thyroids. In 1873, Gull[54] recognized a syndrome that resembled childhood cretinism in adult women. Ord[55] described five more cases in 1877. He was struck by the nonpitting, gelatinous nature of the generalized edema and coined the term *myxedema*. He also correlated the thyroid atrophy found at autopsy with the clinical state of myxedema. Murray[56] described an effective treatment of myxedema in 1891 using ground sheep thyroid extract.

Epidemiology

Hypothyroidism, as with hyperthyroidism, has a broad spectrum of clinical findings. It includes subclinical presentations (detectable only by an elevated TSH level) and full-blown myxedema coma, characterized by hypothermia, mental obtundation, and myxedema.[57]

Hypothyroidism occurs 3 to 10 times more often in women than in men.[58-60] This fact reflects the increased prevalence of autoimmune thyroid disease in women. The peak incidence is in the seventh decade; however, hypothyroidism can occur at any age.[60,61] About 50% of cases of myxedema become evident after admission to a hospital.[62]

Because hypothyroidism deprives the body of calorigenic ability, patients are unable to deal with low ambient temperatures. Consequently, most cases of hypothyroidism become manifest during the winter months.[60,63]

Principles of Disease

Thyroid failure may result from disease of the thyroid (primary hypothyroidism), pituitary (secondary), or hypothalamus (tertiary). Secondary failure accounts for 4% or fewer cases.[62] Tertiary failure is even less common. The two major causes of primary hypothyroidism are autoimmune destruction of the gland and iatrogenic failure after surgical or other ablation of the gland (Box 126-5).[58,59]

The many complex effects of iodine-rich amiodarone on thyroid physiology may lead to asymptomatic abnormalities of thyroid hormone levels, including elevated TSH, as well as clinically relevant hypofunction of the thyroid gland. Hypothyroidism has been estimated to occur in 1% to 32% of patients taking amiodarone.[16]

Clinical Features

As in many other endocrine conditions, hypothyroidism usually follows an indolent course. A 4-year

---

BOX 126-5. Etiologic Factors of Hypothyroidism

Primary
Autoimmune hypothyroidism
Idiopathic
Postsurgical thyroidectomy
External radiation therapy
Radioiodine therapy
Inherited enzymatic defect
Iodine deficiency
Antithyroid drugs
Lithium, phenylbutazone

Secondary
Pituitary tumor
Infiltrative disease (sarcoid) of pituitary

BOX 126-6. Precipitants of Myxedema Coma

Exposure to cold
Infection (usually pulmonary)
Congestive heart failure
Trauma
Drugs: phenothiazines, phenobarbital, narcotics, anesthetics, benzodiazepines, lithium
Iodides
Cerebrovascular accident
Hemorrhage (especially gastrointestinal)
Hypoxia
Hypercapnia
Hyponatremia
Hypoglycemia

---

delay may occur between the appearance of symptoms and diagnosis.[58] Many hypothyroid patients consult more than one physician before their disease is discovered. Patients with mild hypothyroidism may develop dramatic clinical presentations, even myxedema coma when physiologically stressed by one of several factors (Box 126-6). Precipitating factors other than exposure to cold can be identified in less than one half of patients. In one study, fewer than 10% of patients had not been exposed to cold.[61] Infection is difficult to identify. Signs and symptoms, such as fever, tachycardia, sweating, and leukocytosis, may not develop in hypothyroid patients.[38] Prognosis and extent of intervention are determined by the severity of hypothyroidism.

As with hyperthyroidism, the diagnosis of hypothyroidism should be sought when signal symptoms and signs are present, especially in a high-risk demographic group. Typical symptoms include fatigue, cold intolerance, and paresthesias. Suggestive signs are pseudomyotonic deep tendon reflexes, hypothermia, dry skin, and depressed mental function. Elderly women are at high risk.

The signs and symptoms of hypothyroidism have varying frequencies (Table 126-2). It is often difficult to distinguish, solely on clinical grounds, primary disease

Table 126-2. Prevalence of Clinical Features of Hypothyroidism

Clinical Feature	Frequency (%)
Symptoms	
Paresthesias	92
Loss of energy	79
Intolerance to cold	51
Muscular weakness	34
Muscle and joint pain	31
Inability to concentrate	31
Drowsiness	30
Constipation	27
Forgetfulness	23
Emotional lability	15
Depressed auditory acuity	15
Headaches	14
Dysarthria	14
Blurred vision	8
Fullness in throat	81
Signs	
Pseudomyotonic reflexes	95
Change in menstrual pattern	86
Hypothermia	80
Dry scaly skin	79
Puffy eyelids	70
Hoarse voice	56
Weight gain	41
Dependent edema	30
Sparse axillary and pubic hair	30
Pallor	24
Thinness of eyebrows	24
Yellow skin	23
Loss of scalp hair	18
Abdominal distention	18
Goiter	16
Decreased sweating	10
Weight loss	6
Unsteady gait	5

From Bloomer H, Kyle LH: Myxedema: A reevaluation of clinical diagnosis based on eighty cases. *Arch Intern Med* 104:234, 1959.

BOX 126-7 Primary versus Secondary Hypothyroidism

Primary (Thyroid)
Previous thyroid surgery
Obese
Hypothermia more common
Increased serum cholesterol
Voice coarse
Pubic hair present
Sella turcica normal
Plasma cortisol normal
Skin dry and coarse
Heart increased in size
Normal menses and lactation
No response to TSH
Good response to levothyroxine without steroids
Serum TSH increased

Secondary (Pituitary)
No prior thyroid surgery
Less obese
Hypothermia less common
Normal serum cholesterol
Voice less coarse
Pubic hair absent
Sella turcica may be increased in size
Plasma cortisol decreased
Skin fine and soft
Heart usually normal
Traumatic delivery, no lactation, amenorrhea
Good response to TSH
Poor response to levothyroxine without steroids
Serum TSH decreased

TSH, thyroid-stimulating hormone.
From Senior RM. et al: The recognition and management of myxedema coma. *JAMA* 217:61, 1971.

BOX 126-8. Causes and Complications in Myxedema Coma and Hypothyroidism

Hypothyroidism
Hypercapnic narcosis
Hypoxia
Hypothermia
Hypotension
Hypoglycemia
Hyponatremia
Sepsis
Drugs: sedatives, hypnotics, anesthetics, tranquilizers
Adrenal insufficiency

from secondary disease (Box 126-7).[64] Definitive discrimination of primary failure from secondary failure is based on laboratory parameters.

The significant life threats that accompany profound hypothyroidism are respiratory insufficiency, hypotension, and coma. These elements are more characteristic of myxedema coma in its dramatic extreme than of simple hypothyroidism, but they are described first because they pose the greatest danger to the patient.

Myxedema coma is a poorly defined but readily recognizable syndrome that represents hypothyroidism in its dramatic extreme. It is coma that results from either hypothyroidism or one of the causes or complications of hypothyroidism (Box 126-8).[58,61,62,65,66] The readily treatable conditions should be considered before attributing coma solely to hypothyroidism.

Hypothyroid coma is rare and not well understood.[38] In one series, it occurred in only 0.1% of all patients with hypothyroidism. It is extremely rare in the under-50 age group. Behavioral disturbances varying from confusion to frank psychosis are usually present before coma supervenes. Milder degrees of hypothyroidism may be manifested by mental slowing, depression, dementia, or lethargy.

Drug-induced coma is particularly noteworthy. Metabolism of tranquilizers, sedatives, and anesthetics is reduced in hypothyroidism.[38] The effects of these agents are thus potentiated and prolonged. The often-cited case of myxedema coma that occurs after hospitalization or surgery is usually drug induced.

Cold intolerance is a complaint in about one half of patients.[58,61] Weight gain, seldom more than 15 pounds and usually 7 to 8 pounds, is usually not associated with increased appetite.[58] Nonspecific symptoms, including decreased energy, weakness, inability to concentrate, and poor memory, are common.[58,61] Constipation is reported in one fourth of patients.[58]

Hypothermia is present in approximately 80% of patients with myxedema.[61,62] Temperatures as low as 24° C (75.2° F) have been recorded in myxedema coma.[62] Loss of the calorigenic action of thyroid hormone may be exacerbated by the absence of shivering.[67] Hypothermia is so common in myxedema that a normal temperature, present in up to 25% of patients, should suggest an underlying infection. Hypothermia may contribute to abnormal mental function in myxedema coma. If used, mercury thermometers must be shaken down well so as not to elevate the patient's temperature falsely into the normal range. Automated hypothermia thermometers are preferable. Hypothyroid habitus, absence of shivering, and pseudomyotonic reflexes may help distinguish myxedematous from accidental hypothermia. Fewer than 15% of hypothyroid patients survive temperatures below 32.2° C (90° F).[68]

The primary pulmonary abnormality is depression in respiratory drives, both hypoxic and hypercapnic.[69,70] Hypoxia is correctable with hormone replacement, but hypercapnia is only partially correctable.[69-71] Carbon dioxide narcosis is a prime cause of altered sensorium in myxedema coma.[72] Pulmonary function studies reveal normal volumes and flow rates with disordered neuromuscular function.[73] Other respiratory problems include upper airway obstruction from glottic edema, vocal cord edema, and glossomegaly. Pleural effusions are demonstrable in one third of cases.[69-71]

The blood pressure may be elevated, normal, or low. Diastolic hypertension is described.[60] Of patients in full myxedema coma, 50% initially exhibit clinical shock, with systolic pressure less than 100 mm Hg, but another third may have a blood pressure greater than 120/80 mm Hg.[61] *Sinus bradycardia* is the most common dysrhythmia seen in myxedema. Patients receiving thyroid replacement therapy are sensitive to catecholamines, but ventricular tachycardia is an extremely rare complication of replacement therapy.[72] In myxedema the capillaries are "leaky."[74] Transudation produces pleural and pericardial effusions. These effusions characteristically accumulate slowly, are unlikely to produce tamponade, and resolve with thyroid replacement therapy in 6 months to 1 year.[75,76] Ascites is present in less than 4% of hypothyroid patients.[77] Ascitic fluid has a high protein content. The ascites resolves with thyroid replacement.[78]

Generalized nonpitting edema, particularly in a periorbital distribution, is typical. The edema is secondary to hyaluronic acid deposition and characteristically not initially found in dependent areas.[79,80] The skin is smooth, doughy, dry, and cool. It has been described as yellow or sallow, a change secondary to decreased conversion of carotene to vitamin A. The hair is dry and coarse. The eyebrows may be thinned or absent, especially in their lateral extent. Exophthalmopathy or pretibial myxedema may suggest previous Graves' disease. A goiter or thyroidectomy scar should be sought. Goiter is uncommon.[38] In most patients, no gland is appreciable on palpation.[61] The typical husky, deep voice of the hypothyroid patient is not neurologic but rather secondary to mucopolysaccharide infiltration of the vocal cords.[81]

Pseudomyotonic, or "hung up," *deep tendon reflexes* are observed in 58% to 92% of patients.[58,63] Characteristically, a prolonged relaxation phase may be discovered by testing the Achilles reflex while the patient kneels on a chair.[58] The relaxation phase of the deep tendon reflex is usually at least twice as long as the contraction phase.[82] Pseudomyotonic reflexes have also been described in other conditions, including diabetes, localized edema, hypothermia, and pernicious anemia.[59]

Paresthesias are present in 80% of cases.[59,83] The most common involvement is a mononeuropathy, particularly of the median nerve in *carpal tunnel syndrome*. Up to 5% of patients with carpal tunnel syndrome have hypothyroidism.[84,85]

Cerebellar symptoms were recognized in the original descriptions of myxedema; approximately 40% of patients described an unsteady gait.[86] A positive Romberg sign, ataxic gait, adiadochokinesia, intention tremor, and nystagmus have been described.[73,86,87] The pathophysiology of these changes, although not completely understood, may be related more to increased muscle tone and prolonged muscle contraction than to a primary cerebellar dysfunction. Resolution usually occurs after thyroid replacement therapy.[86]

Decreased auditory acuity and tinnitus may occur and resolve with thyroid replacement therapy.[58,59,63] An atypical facial neuralgia, vertigo, and a subjective report of blurred vision without objective evidence of optic neuritis or retinal involvement are possible.[63]

The initial signs of hypothyroidism may be primarily *rheumatic*.[88] Findings attributable to hypothyroidism include joint effusions, synovial and capsular swelling, generalized weakness, stiffness, arthralgias, and myalgias.[88-90] Effusions typically have a high volume, normal protein, normal cell count, and high viscosity. They are presumably transudates and resolve with thyroid replacement therapy.[88]

Chondrocalcinosis has been reported in association with hypothyroidism and offers one explanation for joint pain. A myopathy, with nonspecific electromyogram findings and occasionally elevated creatine kinase levels, may be present.[91]

Decreased peristalsis in myxedema can lead to constipation, abdominal distention, and even a clinical picture consistent with an acute abdomen.[66]

Menorrhagia and irregular menses may be seen.

Diagnostic Strategies

The most sensitive diagnostic test to detect primary hypothyroidism is the serum TSH assay. Because the signs and symptoms of hypothyroidism are initially subtle, objective measurement of thyroid function is necessary to confirm clinical observation. In addition, certain laboratory abnormalities may be associated with hypothyroidism.

In patients believed to have hypothyroidism, the relevant thyroid function studies are the TSH and FT_4, which are elevated and depressed, respectively. Early in the course of hypothyroidism, a physiologic compensatory elevation in TSH levels may maintain normal FT_4. Therefore, a high TSH level may be the only laboratory abnormality in hypothyroidism. T_4 levels may be spuriously depressed or elevated in hypothyroidism because of alterations in thyroxine-binding globulin (TBG) levels previously listed. Conditions that depress these levels are associated with a low T_4 level even if the patient has a normal FT_4 level and is clinically euthyroid. Elevated TBG levels can cause "normal" T_4 levels when clinical hypothyroidism exists.

Knowledge of the T_3 level is not very helpful because it may be normal in patients with overt hypothyroidism. In addition, a low T_3 level is not necessarily an indication of thyroid disease. Depression of T_4 5'-deiodinase activity decreases peripheral T_4 conversion to T_3 and is associated with an increase in reverse T_3 levels. These patients are physiologically euthyroid but have low T_3 levels, the so-called sick euthyroid state. Factors that decrease T_4 5'-deiodinase activity are chronic disease (cardiac, hepatic, pulmonary, renal), diabetes, malignancy, amiodarone therapy,[16] chronic articular disease, infections, myocardial infarction, acute starvation, chronic malnutrition, propranolol, iopanoic acid, other cholecystographic agents, seizures, and glucocorticoid therapy.

In secondary or tertiary hypothyroidism, both the FT_4 and TSH levels are low.

Hyponatremia occurs often and is usually mild. Levels as low as 110 mEq/dL have been seen.[68] The mechanism is thought to be a syndrome of inappropriate secretion of antidiuretic hormone (SIADH), and thyroid replacement therapy reverses the abnormality.[92-94] *Hypoglycemia* is unusual and typically mild; its correction usually does not materially affect the clinical symptoms.[60,95] The presence of hypoglycemia should suggest hypothalamic-pituitary involvement because it is more characteristic of secondary than primary hypothyroidism. *Hypercalcemia* is rare, mild when present, and of uncertain cause.[96] Cholesterol levels are typically elevated, are rarely less than 250 mg/dL, and in 86% of cases are greater than 290 mg/dL.[58] A mild normocytic, normochromic anemia without reticulocytosis may be present. Creatine kinase may be elevated if a myopathy coexists.

Arterial blood gas (ABG) measurements may reflect a respiratory acidosis secondary to hypoventilation.

A chest x-ray study may reveal an enlarged cardiac silhouette from either pericardial effusion or cardiomyopathy. Pleural effusions may also be present. Pericardial effusions demonstrated by echocardiography may be present in 30% of patients.[75] Chest x-ray studies and electrocardiograms (ECGs) are fallible techniques to establish the presence of pericardial effusion.[75,97] Chest x-ray studies have a 30% false-negative rate and a nearly 40% false-positive rate in detection of hypothyroid pericardial effusions.[75] Effusions are often present without an enlarged cardiac silhouette.[76] Conversely, a high cardiothoracic ratio may simply reflect cardiomyopathy and not effusion.[75] ECG evi-

dence of a pericardial effusion (e.g., low-voltage, diffuse ST-T changes) is present in only 50% of patients with an effusion and in as many as 20% without an effusion.[75]

Differential Considerations

The habitus of the myxedematous patient is characteristic and usually recognizable. Hypothermia and depressed mental acuity are seen in other conditions, which may be mistaken for hypothyroidism. Sepsis and accidental hypothermia, for example, may mimic hypothyroidism. Nephrotic syndrome with renal failure may initially be confused with myxedema coma.

The demeanor of a patient with either apathetic hyperthyroidism or clinical depression may be similar to that associated with hypothyroidism. Hyperglycemic states and intoxication with drugs such as sedative-hypnotics and barbiturates may be seen with acute lethargy and hypothermia.

Management

Thyroid replacement, in the form of T_4, is the cornerstone of treatment for hypothyroidism. Coma in the patient with myxedema is typically multifactorial, with inadequate ventilation especially important. Four areas should be addressed in treating myxedema: (1) immediate thyroid replacement therapy, (2) identification and treatment of precipitating factors, (3) reversal of metabolic abnormalities, and (4) general supportive care.

Thyroid Replacement

The magnitude of hypothyroidism dictates the route and dose of thyroid replacement therapy. Mild cases may be treated with oral thyroid hormone replacement, adjusting the dosage over a period of weeks. Myxedema coma should be treated much more aggressively and on clinical grounds alone because laboratory confirmation is not immediately available. The most important factor in survival may be prompt IV administration of significant doses of thyroid hormone. Because thyroid replacement therapy may lead to dysrhythmias or cardiac ischemia, the appropriate dose has been controversial.[38,65,76] Many patients with atheromatous disease have tolerated the doses of thyroid hormone needed to ensure survival. The efficacy of thyroid replacement therapy appears to be dose related.[61]

Levothyroxine (T_4) is generally preferred to T_3 because it has a more gradual onset of action.[38] The chance of cardiac complication is thus presumably reduced.[98] Even though oral and intramuscular formulations of T_4 may have erratic and unpredictable absorption, excellent clinical responses to oral doses of T_4 have been reported, even in the presence of myxedema ileus.[99] IV T_4 preparations would still ensure hormonal availability.[61] A dose of 500 µg of T_4, administered PO or IV on day 1, is followed by 100 µg/day.[99] Patients should receive cardiac monitoring and periodic ECGs. If signs of ischemia or dysrhythmias are observed, the dose of T_4 may be reduced by 25% and continued. Bradycardia generally improves in 24 to 48 hours.[99]

Precipitating Factors

An active search for precipitating factors is crucial. CHF and infection, especially pulmonary infection, are the two most common stresses.[61] Infection may be subtle in its presentation because many of the typical signs of infection are masked by the hypothyroidism.[38] Exposure to cold is almost always present (see Box 126-8).[62]

Along with diagnostic thyroid function tests (FT_4, TSH, TBG), electrolytes, glucose, calcium, and ABGs should be checked. A chest x-ray study and ECG should also be obtained.

Metabolic Abnormalities

Hypoventilation and *hypoglycemia* are the two immediately serious metabolic abnormalities of myxedema. ABGs may be the only indication that significant hypercapnia and respiratory acidosis exist. An elevated serum carbon dioxide partial pressure may be seen in nearly one third of patients with myxedema coma, and ventilator support can immediately reverse this cause of coma.[61] Serious hypoglycemia is unusual and is less characteristic of primary hypothyroidism than of secondary hypothyroidism.[60,61,95] If present, hypoglycemia can contribute to coma, although seizures may be a more likely outcome.[61,67] Patients should receive 5% dextrose in water (D5W), and serum glucose should be monitored.

Hyponatremia is usually mild and responds to water restriction.[65,72,94] Indications for hypertonic saline (sodium level < 110 to 115 mEq/L, mental status changes, seizures) are the same as in other medical conditions. *Hypercalcemia* is rarely significant.[95]

Signs of CHF, ischemia, dysrhythmias, and pleural or pericardial effusions may be sought on chest x-ray studies and ECGs. Tamponade is a rare complication of myxedematous pericardial effusion.[76,97] Thyroid replacement therapy and expectant observation are usually sufficient.[75,76]

Supportive Care

General supportive care should focus on maintenance of blood pressure, ventilatory support when necessary, and avoidance of sedatives, narcotics, and anesthetics when possible.

Hypotension, along with hypoventilation and hypothermia, is an acute, life-threatening complication of myxedema. A fluid challenge should be the first line of therapy; however, pressors are often necessary.[64] The response to vasopressor therapy is uniformly poor until thyroid therapy has begun.[95] The action of pressors is augmented by thyroid hormone.[100]

The approach to *hypothermia* is less aggressive. Active rewarming not only is unnecessary but also can theoretically be harmful.[62] Hormone replacement and blankets are usually adequate measures. There are few data on active core rewarming of extremely low

temperatures in conjunction with thyroid therapy of patients with hypothyroidism and hyperthermia.

Stress dosages of corticosteroids, such as 300 mg of hydrocortisone IV followed by 100 mg IV every 6 to 8 hours, are routinely given to patients in myxedema coma. Steroids are given because myxedema may be either a manifestation of panhypopituitarism or a co-existing condition with primary adrenal failure.

Untreated, myxedema coma is lethal. With aggressive treatment, mortality rates of 0% to approximately 50% have been reported.[61,65]

ADRENAL INSUFFICIENCY

Perspective

Adrenocortical insufficiency, first recognized by Addison in 1844, is an uncommon, potentially life-threatening, readily treatable condition. Production of glucocorticoids, primarily cortisol, inadequate to meet the metabolic requirements of the body is the hallmark of the condition. The protean clinical presentations of hypocortisolism are well described and detailed in the following section.

The clinical features of adrenal insufficiency vary according to the locus of the lesion producing the disease (primary or secondary adrenal failure) and the duration of the condition (acute or chronic adrenal insufficiency).

Principles of Disease

In primary adrenal insufficiency, or *Addison's disease*, the adrenal gland itself cannot produce cortisol, aldosterone, or both. Absence of glucocorticoids produces a compensatory elevation of adrenocorticotropic hormone (ACTH) and melanocyte-stimulating hormone. Likewise, lack of aldosterone leads to a reflex increase in renin production. In *secondary adrenal failure* the locus of failure is the hypothalamic-pituitary axis. Secondary adrenal failure is usually characterized by depressed ACTH secretion and blunted cortisol production, but aldosterone levels remain appropriate because of stimulation by both the renin-angiotensin axis and hyperkalemia.[101] A special case, often called *functional adrenal insufficiency*, occurs when administration of exogenous corticosteroids leads to depression of ACTH secretion. When exogenous steroids are discontinued, the clinical picture of secondary adrenal failure may follow (Box 126-9).

Acute Adrenal Insufficiency

Acute adrenal insufficiency is probably a rare condition. It may represent either an exacerbation of long-standing disease or a de novo case. Chronic disease is more prevalent and probably accounts for most cases of acute adrenal insufficiency seen in emergency departments.

The most common cause of adrenal insufficiency is hypothalamic-pituitary-adrenal (HPA) axis suppression from long-term exogenous glucocorticoid administration. When adrenal failure represents a rapid worsen-

BOX 126-9. Etiologic Factors of Adrenocortical Insufficiency

I. Primary adrenal failure
  A. Idiopathic
    1. Autoimmune
    2. True idiopathic
  B. Infectious
    1. Granulomatous
      a. Tuberculosis
    2. Protozoal and fungal
      a. Histoplasmosis
      b. Blastomycosis
      c. Coccidioidomycosis
      d. Candidiasis
      e. Cryptococcosis
    3. Viral
      a. Cytomegalovirus
      b. Herpes simplex
  C. Infiltration
    1. Sarcoidosis
    2. Neoplastic (metastatic)
    3. Lymphoma/leukemia
    4. Hemochromatosis
    5. Adrenoleukodystrophy
    6. Amyloidosis
    7. Iron deposition
  D. Postadrenalectomy
  E. Hemorrhage
  F. Congenital adrenal hyperplasia
  G. Congenital unresponsiveness to ACTH
II. Secondary adrenal failure
  A. Pituitary insufficiency
    1. Infarction (Sheehan's syndrome)
    2. Hemorrhage
    3. Pituitary or suprasellar tumor
    4. Isolated ACTH deficiency
    5. Infiltration disease
      a. Sarcoidosis
      b. Histiocytosis X
      c. Hemachromatosis
  B. Hypothalamic insufficiency
  C. Head trauma
III. Functional disease: glucocorticoid administration

ACTH, adrenocorticotropic hormone.

BOX 126-10. Precipitants of Acute Adrenal Insufficiency

Stimulators
Surgery
Anesthesia
Volume loss
Trauma
Asthma
Hypothermia
Alcohol
Myocardial infarction
Pyrogens
Hypoglycemia
Pain
Psychotic break
Depressive illness

Inhibitors
Morphine
Reserpine
Chlorpromazine
Barbiturates

BOX 126-11. Causes of Adrenal Hemorrhage

Overwhelming septicemia (Waterhouse-Friderichsen syndrome)
Birth trauma
During pregnancy
Idiopathic adrenal vein thrombosis
During seizures
Anticoagulant therapy
After venography
After trauma or surgery

develop.[109] Adrenal failure that does develop from adrenal hemorrhage is lethal.[110] It would be unusual to see a case of hemorrhagic adrenal failure in the emergency department. De novo cases in otherwise healthy persons are rare. The typical patient has a severe illness (e.g., myocardial infarction, systemic infection, burn) and is often receiving anticoagulant therapy.[108] Attention to the possibility of adrenal hemorrhage in a high-risk patient may lead to early diagnosis and therapy, with significant improvement in survival.[111] Adrenal hemorrhage associated with sepsis (acute fulminating meningococcemia, or Waterhouse-Friderichsen syndrome) may lead to adrenal failure that may contribute to shock and death.[110]

The most common cause of acute adrenal insufficiency is *functional*, from exogenous glucocorticoid administration. Many medical indications exist for glucocorticoid therapy (Box 126-12). The probability of HPA axis suppression depends on the frequency, strength, and schedule as well as on the duration of steroid therapy.[112-115] The degree of suppression cannot be predicted accurately even with consideration of these factors. Recovery of the HPA axis after discontinuation of therapy may take up to 1 year.[112] In addition to the oral route, glucocorticoids can produce HPA suppression when administered nasally or by inhalation.[116,117]

Functional adrenal insufficiency can also result from septic shock. Severe physiologic stressors cause activation of the HPA axis. A subset of individuals with septic shock suffer from adrenal insufficiency. More than 50% of patients with septic shock may have adrenal supression.[118,119] Patients with a random serum

ing of chronic adrenal failure, both the cause of the underlying failure and the precipitant of abrupt decompensation should be identified.

Acute precipitating stresses include surgery, anesthesia, psychological stresses, alcohol intoxication, hypothermia, myocardial infarction, diabetes mellitus, intercurrent infection, asthma, pyrogens, and hypoglycemia (Box 126-10).[102-107]

Acute adrenal insufficiency occurring in a previously normal HPA axis is unusual and is produced by either pituitary or adrenal hemorrhage or infarction.

Adrenal hemorrhage is a rare condition (Box 126-11).[108] Not all cases of adrenal hemorrhage lead to glandular failure. Only 10% of cases of adrenal hemorrhage may produce clinical insufficiency.[108] This is not surprising because more than 90% of the gland must be destroyed before signs of adrenal insufficiency

BOX 126-12. Nonendocrine Disorders with Glucocorticoid Therapy

1. Rheumatoid arthritis
2. Psoriatic arthritis
3. Gouty arthritis
4. Bursitis and tenosynovitis
5. Systemic lupus erythematosus
6. Acute rheumatic carditis
7. Pemphigus
8. Erythema multiforme
9. Exfoliative dermatitis
10. Mycosis fungoides
11. Allergic rhinitis
12. Bronchial asthma
13. Atopic dermatitis
14. Serum sickness
15. Allergic conjunctivitis
16. Uveitis
17. Retrobulbar neuritis
18. Sarcoidosis
19. Löffler's syndrome
20. Berylliosis
21. Idiopathic thrombocytopenic purpura
22. Autoimmune hemolytic anemia
23. Lymphomas
24. Immune nephritis
25. Tuberculous meningitis
26. Urticaria
27. Chronic active hepatitis
28. Ulcerative hepatitis
29. Regional enteritis
30. Nontropical sprue
31. Dental postoperative inflammation
32. Cerebral edema
33. Subacute nonsuppurative thyroiditis
34. Malignant exophthalmos
35. Hypercalcemia
36. Trichinosis
37. Myasthenia gravis
38. Organ transplantation
39. Alopecia areata

From Liddle G: In Williams R (ed): *Textbook of Endocrinology*, Philadelphia, WB Saunders, 1981.

Table 126-3. Prevalence of Clinical Features of Adrenal Insufficiency

Clinical Feature	Frequency (%)
Weakness and fatigue	99-100
Hyperpigmentation (skin)	92-97
Hyperpigmentation (mucous membranes)	71-82
Weight loss	97-100
Nausea, vomiting	56-87
Anorexia	98-100
Hypotension (110/70)	82-91
Abdominal pain	34
Salt craving	22
Diarrhea	20
Constipation	19
Syncope	12-16
Vitiligo	4-9
Musculoskeletal complaints	6
Lethargy	—
Confusion	—
Psychosis	—
Auricular calcification	—

cortisol less than 25 µg/dL may have a favorable hemodynamic response to stress dose hydrocortisone.[118]

Chronic Adrenal Insufficiency

The major cause of primary chronic adrenal insufficiency is *idiopathic*, representing 66% to 75% of cases. Idiopathic adrenal failure encompasses two distinct clinical entities: autoimmune adrenal failure and true idiopathic disease. Adrenal antibodies are found in 51% to 63% of cases of idiopathic disease. Antibodies to other organs can be demonstrated.[120] Autoimmune diseases of other organs, including diabetes mellitus, primary ovarian failure, Hashimoto's thyroiditis, Graves' disease, pernicious anemia, and hypoparathyroidism, are associated in 53% of cases.[121,122]

Metastasis from malignant carcinoma to the adrenal glands is not unusual, but adrenal insufficiency from metastatic disease is rare.[123] The usual primary malignancies are lung, gastrointestinal system, and breast.[123,124]

Tuberculous Addison's disease, once the most common cause of adrenal insufficiency in the United States, is now unusual.[125] Adrenal calcifications are a possible radiographic finding (see Box 126-10).

Clinical Features

Signal symptoms for adrenal insufficiency include weakness, fatigue, nausea, vomiting, and weight loss. Hypotension is typically present. These symptoms are obviously nonspecific and common, making diagnosis difficult. When primary adrenal glandular failure is chronic, patients have a characteristic hyperpigmented appearance.

Recognition of patients at risk for adrenal failure facilitates diagnosis. The most common cause of adrenal insufficiency in emergency department patients is suppression of the HPA axis as a result of long-term glucocorticoid therapy. An exacerbation of chronic primary glandular failure is also possible but usually is not a diagnostic dilemma. True acute, de novo adrenal insufficiency is rare.

The acute life threats in adrenal insufficiency are hypotension and hypoglycemia. Hypotension responds well to glucocorticoid replacement with IV hydration and hypoglycemia to IV administration of D5W.

The signs and symptoms of adrenal insufficiency have varying frequencies (Table 126-3). Lethargy is generalized. In severe cases, weakness can be severe enough to make talking difficult. The hyperkalemia of adrenal failure is rarely severe enough to produce frank muscular paralysis.[126]

The mortality and major morbidity produced by adrenal insufficiency are usually secondary to either hypotension or hypoglycemia.

Hypotension, with systolic blood pressures of less than 110 mm Hg, is often present. In one study only 3% of addisonian patients initially exhibited systolic pressures greater than 125 mm Hg.[125] Orthostatic symptoms are common. Several mechanisms produce hypotension. Cortisol deficiency, even in the presence of normovolemia, can lead to hypotension by directly depressing myocardial contractility.[127] Responsiveness to catecholamines is also reduced. If aldosterone deficiency coexists, sodium wasting can lead to hypovolemia. Volume deficits are greater in primary than in secondary adrenal insufficiency. Elevations in renin-angiotensin function and ADH secretion are seen and partially compensate for the relative or absolute hypovolemia present.[128,129] Adrenal insufficiency should be considered in patients with hypotension of uncertain etiology. As many as 19% of vasopressor-dependent hypotensive patients may be suffering from adrenal dysfunction.[130] Understandably, response to pressors is poor, to volume replacement better, and to volume plus corticosteroids best.[127]

Nonspecific gastrointestinal symptoms, including nausea and vomiting, are present in 56% to 87% of cases.[125,131] The patient may be in severe pain, and the clinical picture may include an acute abdomen. Anorexia is universally present and is one mechanism leading to the weight loss that always accompanies chronic adrenal insufficiency. Dehydration and sodium wasting can lead to a craving for salt.

More than three fourths of patients with Addison's disease have *mucocutaneous hyperpigmentation*.[125,131] The mechanism is compensatory ACTH and melanocyte-stimulating hormone secretion. No hyperpigmentation is seen in secondary adrenal insufficiency. The melanin deposits are usually in areas of trauma and friction (flexion creases of the palms and soles, elbows, knees, and buccal mucosa) and in old scars. Bluish black discolorations may be present on the lips and gums. Hyperpigmentation usually develops over months of relative adrenal insufficiency. Vitiligo may be present in some patients, usually when adrenal failure is autoimmune in origin.[131]

Nonspecific, diffuse musculoskeletal complaints are present in 6% of cases. Patients may have a generalized loss of body hair and hardening of the auricular cartilage.

Changes in mental functioning may occur. Lethargy and an organic brain syndrome picture may be the initial evidence of adrenal insufficiency, especially in elderly patients. Depression, manic psychosis, and generalized seizures have also been described.

Two thirds of patients with adrenal failure have associated *hypoglycemia*.[125,131] The symptoms are characteristic of hypoglycemia: perspiration, tachycardia, weakness, nausea, vomiting, headache, convulsions, and coma. The glucose levels are less than 45 mg/dL. The pathophysiology is decreased gluconeogenesis and increased peripheral glucose use secondary to lipolysis.

Electrolyte abnormalities are common. Hyponatremia is present in 88% of cases, hyperkalemia in 64%, either hyponatremia or hyperkalemia in 92%, and hypercalcemia in 6% to 33%.[125,131-133]

Hyponatremia, seldom less than 120 mEq/L, has several possible causes. Elevated ADH levels, secondary to either decreased circulating blood volume or decreased cortisol, lower serum sodium levels.[129] A decreased glomerular filtration rate causes decreased fluid to be delivered to the distal renal tubules, leading to diminished sodium reabsorption. Finally, if aldosterone deficiency coexists with hyponatremia, it can lead to urinary losses of sodium. On a high-sodium diet, aldosterone deficiency usually leads to no overt symptoms, but when salt intake is decreased, volume depletion can become clinically evident.

Hyperkalemia is usually in the 4.5 mEq/L range and seldom greater than 7.0 mEq/L.[126] Muscle paralysis, of the Landry type of ascending flaccid quadriplegia, is possible but rare.[127] Hyperkalemic dysrhythmias should also be considered but are rare.[134] Hyperkalemia in adrenal insufficiency is produced by acidosis, aldosterone deficiency, and depressed glomerular filtration rate.[126]

Hypercalcemia is relatively common.[132,133] Its pathophysiology is not entirely clear but may be related to either increased protein binding or volume depletion with associated facilitation of renal tubule reabsorption. Total calcium, but not ionized calcium, is increased.

Other metabolic abnormalities include azotemia and elevated hematocrit levels, both referable to hypovolemia. A mild metabolic acidosis may be present.

Diagnostic Strategies

The diagnosis of acute adrenal insufficiency is initially clinical, and therapy should often begin before laboratory values confirm the clinical impression. In some patients the condition is suggested by a history of chronic adrenal failure or glucocorticoid therapy. This history facilitates diagnosis, and the task is to identify the intercurrent stress that has precipitated symptomatic adrenal failure. However, the patient may be too ill to give a history of chronic adrenal insufficiency. Alternatively, the case may represent de novo acute adrenal insufficiency. Laboratory abnormalities (e.g., hyponatremia, hyperkalemia, hypoglycemia) may help confirm the clinical impression.

Adrenal failure may be considered when a patient complains of severe anorexia or weakness, especially when accompanied by weight loss. Hypotension of unclear cause may indicate adrenal insufficiency. Changes in mental status may also be signal symptoms of impending adrenal insufficiency, especially in elderly patients.

Once suggested, the diagnosis of adrenal failure should proceed concomitantly with treatment. The diagnosis is based on a failure of the adrenals to respond to exogenous ACTH with cortisol production, the *ACTH stimulation test*. Several ACTH stimulation protocols have been developed. In perhaps the simplest and quickest protocol, 0.25 mg of cosyntropin (synthetic ACTH, Cortrosyn) is administered at time zero. For cortisol determination, serum samples are drawn at time zero, 1 hour, and at 6- to 8-hour intervals thereafter. Normal adrenals respond with an increase in cortisol of at least 10 mg/dL or to three times baseline level. A 24-hour urine sample is obtained for 17-hydroxysteroid determination to confirm the diagnosis suggested by the serum cortisol levels.

A 48-hour ACTH stimulation test can confirm the diagnosis of adrenal insufficiency and differentiate primary from secondary causes. Whereas rapid ACTH stimulation tests have excellent sensitivity, they may occasionally result in an erroneous diagnosis of adrenal failure in patients with normal adrenal function.

Management

The goals in treating adrenal insufficiency are (1) glucocorticoid replacement, (2) correction of electrolyte and metabolic abnormalities as well as hypovolemia, and (3) treatment of the event precipitating abrupt decompensation.

Glucocorticoid Replacement

If the diagnosis of adrenal failure is unconfirmed, *dexamethasone phosphate*, 4 mg IV every 6 to 8 hours, is the corticosteroid replacement that should be used while an ACTH stimulation test is performed. Dexamethasone is approximately 100 times more potent than cortisol, and this amount of dexamethasone does not factitiously elevate serum cortisol determinations. Replacement with hydrocortisone could confound interpretation of serum cortisol determinations.

If the patient is known to have adrenal failure, 100 mg of *hydrocortisone hemisuccinate* IV every 6 to 8 hours should be used.[102] If IV access cannot be maintained, *cortisone acetate*, 100 mg intramuscularly every 6 to 8 hours, may be used, but its absorption is erratic and not as reliable as with the IV route. The dose of glucocorticoid is tapered over the next several days and eventually converted to an oral preparation.

Supportive Care

If salt and water replacement is adequate, mineralocorticoid replacement is usually not necessary. Subsequent to the addisonian crisis, patients may require titration with mineralocorticoid preparations such as *fludrocortisone acetate* (Florinef); 100 mg of hydrocortisone has the salt-retaining effect of 0.1 mg of Florinef. If dexamethasone is used, Florinef should be added to prevent salt loss.

Addisonian patients are often up to 20% volume depleted. Unless specifically contraindicated by the patient's cardiovascular status, correction of hypovolemia should be aggressive. One liter of normal saline may be infused over the first hour; D5W is usually added to treat accompanying hypoglycemia. Up to a total of 3 L may be required over the first 8 hours. Optimal correction of hypotension requires both glucocorticoid and volume replacement.

Treatment of hypoglycemia should be immediate. For symptomatic hypoglycemia or extremely low serum levels, IV glucose (50 to 100 mL of D50W) is preferable. If IV access is impossible, subcutaneous glucagon (1 to 2 mg) may be attempted, although a 10- to 20-minute period of latency should be anticipated.

Electrolyte abnormalities are usually corrected with saline rehydration. Special attention must be given to the potassium level. Symptomatic hyperkalemia in adrenal insufficiency should be treated with the same agents as hyperkalemia with any other medical illness (e.g., bicarbonate, insulin, calcium).

Precipitating Factors

The intercurrent stress causing abrupt loss of adrenal integrity should be identified and treated. Drug ingestion and psychiatric history should be elicited. Symptoms referable to myocardial infarction, asthma, or an infection must be noted. Appropriate cultures should be obtained, and if infection is suspected, antibiotics should be started.

KEY CONCEPTS

- Signs and symptoms of hyperthyroidism include agitation, nervousness, palpitations, weight loss, fever, tachycardia, ophthalmopathy, goiter, and heart failure.
- Severely hyperthyroid patients require emergency intervention with a β-blocker, a thioamide, iodine, and dexamethasone, as well as supportive therapy.
- Patients with mild hypothyroidism may develop dramatic clinical presentations, even myxedema coma when physiologically stressed.
- The most sensitive diagnostic test to detect primary hypothyroidism is the serum thyroid-stimulating hormone (TSH) assay.
- Signal symptoms of adrenal insufficiency include weakness, fatigue, nausea, vomiting, and weight loss. Hypotension is typically present.
- If adrenal insufficiency is unconfirmed, dexamethasone is optimal because it does not falsely elevate serum cortisol. If the patient has adrenal failure, hydrocortisone hemisuccinate is indicated.

REFERENCES

1. Major RH: *Classic Descriptions of Disease.* Springfield, Ill, Charles C Thomas, 1978.
2. Ginsburg AM: The historical development of the present conception of cardiac conditions in exophthalmic goiter. *Ann Intern Med* 5:505, 1931.
3. Knight RA: The use of spinal anesthesia to control sympathetic hyperactivity in hyperthyroidism. *Anesthesiology* 6:225, 1945.
4. Canary JJ, et al: Effects of oral and intramuscular administration of reserpine in thyrotoxicosis. *N Engl J Med* 257:435, 1957.
5. Ramey ER, Bernstein H, Goldstein MS: Effect of sympathetic blocking agents on the increased oxygen consumption following administration of thyroxine. *Fed Proc* 14:118, 1955.
6. Roizen M, Becker CE: Thyroid storm: A review of cases at University of California, San Francisco. *Calif Med* 115:5, 1971.
7. Nelson NC, Becker WF: Thyroid crisis: Diagnosis and treatment. *Ann Surg* 170:263, 1969.
8. McArthur JW, et al: Thyrotoxic crisis: An analysis of the thirty-six cases seen at the Massachusetts General Hospital during the past twenty-five years. *JAMA* 134:868, 1947.

9. Waldstein SS, et al: A clinical study of thyroid storm. *Ann Intern Med* 52:626, 1960.

10. Griswold D, Keating JH Jr: Cardiac dysfunction in hyperthyroidism. *Am Heart J* 38:813, 1949.

11. Mazzaferri EL, Skillman TG: Thyroid storm. *Arch Intern Med* 124:684, 1969.

12. Hamilton CR, Maloof F: Unusual types of hyperthyroidism. *Medicine (Baltimore)* 52:195, 1973.

13. Gorman CA, Wahner HW, Tauxe WN: Metabolic malingerers: Patients who deliberately induce or perpetuate a hypermetabolic or hypometabolic state. *Am J Med* 48:708, 1970.

14. Schottstaedt ES, Smoller M: "Thyroid storm" produced by acute thyroid hormone poisoning. *Ann Intern Med* 64:847, 1966.

15. Cardenas GA, Cabral JM, Leslie CA: Amiodarone-induced thyrotoxicosis: Diagnostic and therapeutic strategies. *Cleve Clin J Med* 70:624, 2003.

16. Harjai KJ, Licata AA: Effects of amiodarone on thyroid function. *Ann Intern Med* 126:63, 1997.

17. Levey GS: Catecholamine sensitivity, thyroid hormone and the heart. *Am J Med* 50:413, 1971.

18. Levey GS, Epstein SE: Myocardial adenyl cyclase: Activation by thyroid hormone and evidence for two adenyl cyclase systems. *J Clin Invest* 48:1163, 1969.

19. Rosenberg IN: Thyroid storm. *N Engl J Med* 283:1052, 1970.

20. Lahey FH: The crisis of exophthalmic goiter. *N Engl J Med* 199:255, 1928.

21. Lahey FH: Non-activated (apathetic) type of hyperthyroidism. *N Engl J Med* 204:747, 1931.

22. Sandler G, Wilson GM: The nature and prognosis of heart disease in thyrotoxicosis. *Q J Med* 28:347, 1959.

23. Graettinger JS, et al: A correlation of clinical and hemodynamic studies in patients with hyperthyroidism with and without congestive heart failure. *J Clin Invest* 38:1316, 1959.

24. Lawrence JR, et al: Digoxin kinetics in patients with thyroid dysfunction. *Clin Pharmacol Ther* 22:7, 1977.

25. Likoff WB, Levine SA: Thyrotoxicosis as the sole cause of heart failure. *Am J Med Sci* 206:425, 1943.

26. Ikran H: Haemodynamics of beta-adrenergic blockade in hyperthyroid patients with and without heart failure. *Br Med J* 1:1505, 1977.

27. Solomon DH, et al: Identification of subgroups of euthyroid Graves' ophthalmopathy. *N Engl J Med* 296:181, 1977.

28. Werner SC: Classification of the eye changes in Graves' disease. *Am J Ophthalmol* 68:646, 1969.

29. Werner SC: Modification of the classification of eye changes in Graves' disease. *Am J Ophthalmol* 83:725, 1977.

30. Kodali VR, Jeffcote B, Clague RB: Thyrotoxic periodic paralysis: A case report and review of the literature. *J Emerg Med* 17:43, 1998

31. Wu C, Chau T, Chang C, Lin S: An unrecognized cause of paralysis in the ED: Thyrotoxic normokalemic periodic paralysis. *Am J Emerg Med* 21:71, 2003.

32. Birkhahn RH, Gaeta TJ, Melniker L: Thyrotoxic periodic paralysis and intravenous propranolol in the emergency setting. *J Emerg Med* 18:199, 2000.

33. Greenberger NJ, et al: Jaundice and thyrotoxicosis in the absence of congestive heart failure. *Am J Med* 36:840, 1964.

34. Odell WD, et al: Symposium on hyperthyroidism. *Calif Med* 113:35, 1970.

35. Hegedus L, et al: Thyroid size and goitre frequency in hyperthyroidism. *Dan Med Bull* 34:121, 1987.

36. Gittoes NJ, Franklyn J: Hyperthyroidism. Current treatment guidelines. *Drugs* 1998 55:543, 1998.

37. Franklyn J: Thyrotoxicosis. *Clin Med* 3:11, 2003.

38. Urbanic RC, Mazzaferri EL: Thyrotoxic crisis and myxedema coma. *Heart Lung* 7:435, 1978.

39. McGee RR, Whittaker RL, Tulius IF: Apathetic thyroidism: Review of the literature and report of four cases. *Ann Intern Med* 50:1418, 1959.

40. Thomas FB, Mazzaferri EL, Skillman TG: Apathetic thyrotoxicosis: A distinctive clinical and laboratory entity. *Ann Intern Med* 72:679, 1970.

41. Grossman A, Waldstein SS: Apathetic thyroid storm in a ten year old child. *Pediatrics* 28:447, 1961.

42. Dillmann WH: Thyroid storm. *Curr Ther Endocrinol Metab* 6:81, 1997.

43. Schimmel M, Utiger RD: Thyroidal and peripheral production of thyroid hormones: Review of recent findings and their clinical importance. *Ann Intern Med* 87:760, 1977.

44. Oppenheimer JH, Schwartz HL, Jurks ML: Propylthiouracil inhibits the conversion of 1-thyroxine to 1-triiodothyronine: An explanation of the antithyroxine effects of PTU and evidence supporting the concept that T_3 is the active thyroid hormone. *J Clin Invest* 51:2493, 1972.

45. Croxson M, Hall TD, Nicoloff JJ: Combination drug therapy for treatment of hyperthyroid Graves' disease. *J Clin Endocrinol Metab* 45:623, 1977.

46. Zonazein J, et al: Propranolol therapy in thyrotoxicosis: A review of 84 patients undergoing surgery. *Am J Med* 66:411, 1979.

47. Turner P, Granville-Grossman KL, Smart JV: Effect of adrenergic receptor blockade on the tachycardia of thyrotoxicosis and anxiety state. *Lancet* 2:1316, 1965.

48. Das G, Krieger M: Treatment of thyrotoxic storm with intravenous administration of propranolol. *Ann Intern Med* 70:985, 1969.

49. Hellman R, et al: Propranolol for thyroid storm. *N Engl J Med* 297:671, 1977.

50. Mackin JF, Canary JJ, Pittman CS: Thyroid storm and its management. *N Engl J Med* 291:1396, 1974.

51. Tietgens ST, Leinung MC: Thyroid storm. *Med Clin North Am* 79:169, 1995.

52. Lewis NDG, Davies GR: Correlative study of endocrine imbalance and mental disease. *J Nerv Ment Dis* 54:385, 1921.

53. Curling TB: Two cases of absence of the thyroid bodies. *Med Chir Trans Lond* 33:303, 1850.

54. Gull WW: On a cretinoid state supervening in adult life in women. *Trans Clin Soc Lond* 7:180, 1873.

55. Ord WM: On myxedema, a term proposed to be applied to an essential condition in the "cretinoid" affection occasionally observed in middle-aged women. *Med Chir Trans Lond* 61:57, 1877.

56. Murray GR: Note on the treatment of myxedema by hypodermic injections of an extract of the thyroid gland of a sheep. *Br Med J* 2:796, 1891.

57. Mayberry WE, et al: Radioimmunoassay for human TSH: Clinical value in patients with normal and abnormal thyroid function. *Ann Intern Med* 74:471, 1971.

58. Bloomer H, Kyle LH: Myxedema: A reevaluation of clinical diagnosis based on eighty cases. *Arch Intern Med* 104:234, 1959.

59. Swanson JW, Kelly JJ, McConahey WM: Neurologic aspects of thyroid dysfunction. *Mayo Clin Proc* 56:504, 1981.

60. Nickerson JF, et al: Fatal myxedema, with and without coma. *Ann Intern Med* 53:475, 1960.

61. Forester CF: Coma in myxedema: Report of a case and review of the world literature. *Arch Intern Med* 111:734, 1963.

62. Senior RM, et al: The recognition and management of myxedema coma. *JAMA* 217:61, 1971.

63. Nickel SN, Frame B: Neurologic manifestation of myxedema. *Neurology* 8:511, 1958.

64. Curtis RH: Hyponatremia in primary myxedema. *Ann Intern Med* 44:376, 1956.
65. Nichols AB, Hunt WB: Is myxedema coma respiratory failure? *South Med J* 69:945, 1976.
66. Royce PC: Severely impaired consciousness in myxedema: A review. *Am J Med Sci* 261:46, 1971.
67. Malden M: Hypothermic coma in myxedema. *Br Med J* 2:764, 1955.
68. Hyams DE: Hypothermic myxedema coma. *Br J Clin Pract* 1:1, 1963.
69. Zwillich CW, et al: Ventilatory control in myxedema and hypothyroidism. *N Engl J Med* 292:662, 1975.
70. Massumi RA, Winnacker JL: Severe depression of the respiratory center in myxedema. *Am J Med* 36:876, 1964.
71. Wilson WR, Bedell GN: The pulmonary abnormalities in myxedema. *J Clin Invest* 39:42, 1960.
72. Winawer SJ, Rosen SM, Cohn H: Myxedema coma with ventricular tachycardia. *Arch Intern Med* 111:647, 1963.
73. Greene JA: Comparison of symptoms, physical and laboratory findings of myxedema and pernicious anemia: With a report of three cases. *Ann Intern Med* 10:622, 1936.
74. Lange K: Capillary permeability in myxedema. *Am J Med Sci* 208:5, 1944.
75. Kerber RE, Sherman B: Echocardiographic evaluation of pericardial effusion in myxedema: Incidence and biochemical and clinical correlations. *Circulation* 52:823, 1975.
76. Smolar EN, et al: Cardiac tamponade in primary myxedema and review of the literature. *Am J Med Sci* 272:345, 1976.
77. Watanakunakorn C, Hodges RE, Evans TC: Myxedema: A study of 400 cases. *Arch Intern Med* 116:183, 1965.
78. De Castro F, et al: Myxedema ascites: Report of two cases and review of the literature. *J Clin Gastroenterol* 13:411, 1991.
79. Goldberg RC, Chaikoff IL: Myxedema in the radiothyroidectomized dog. *Endocrinology* 50:115, 1952.
80. Aikawa JK: The nature of myxedema: Alterations in the serum electrolyte concentrations and radiosodium space and the exchangeable sodium and potassium content. *Ann Intern Med* 44:30, 1956.
81. Ritter FN: The effects of hypothyroidism on the ear, nose and throat: A clinical and experimental study. *Laryngoscope* 77:1427, 1967.
82. Maclean D, Taig DR, Emslie-Smith D: Achilles tendon reflex in accidental hypothermia and hypothermic myxedema. *Br Med J* 2:87, 1973.
83. Sanders V: Neurologic manifestations of myxedema. *N Engl J Med* 266:547, 1962.
84. Doyle JR, Carroll RE: The carpal tunnel syndrome: A review of 100 patients treated surgically. *Calif Med* 108:263, 1968.
85. Phalen GS: The carpal tunnel syndrome: Seventeen years experience in diagnosis and treatment of six hundred and fifty-four hands. *J Bone Joint Surg Am* 48:211, 1966.
86. Cremer GM, Goldstein NP, Paris J: Myxedema and ataxia. *Neurology* 19:37, 1969.
87. Jellinek EH, Kelly RE: Cerebellar syndrome in myxoedema. *Lancet* 2:225, 1960.
88. Bland JH, Frymoyer JW: Rheumatic syndromes of myxedema. *N Engl J Med* 282:1171, 1970.
89. Wilson J, Walton JN: Some muscular manifestations of hypothyroidism. *J Neurol Neurosurg Psychiatry* 22:320, 1959.
90. Crevasse LE, Logue RB: Peripheral neuropathy in myxedema. *Ann Intern Med* 50:1433, 1959.
91. Mace BEW, Mallya RK, Staffurth JS: Myxoedema presenting with chondrocalcinosis and polymyositis. *J R Soc Med* 73:887, 1980.
92. Holvey DN, et al: Treatment of myxedema coma with intravenous thyroxine. *Arch Intern Med* 113:89, 1964.
93. Goldberg M, Reivich M: Studies on the mechanism of hyponatremia and impaired water excretion in myxedema. *Ann Intern Med* 56:120, 1962.
94. Pettinger WA, Taylor L, Ferris TF: Inappropriate secretion of antidiuretic hormone due to myxedema. *N Engl J Med* 272:362, 1965.
95. Perlmutter M, Cohn H: Myxedema crisis of pituitary or thyroid origin. *Am J Med* 36:883, 1964.
96. Lowe CE, Bird ED, Thomas WC: Hypercalcemia in myxedema. *J Clin Invest* 39:42, 1960.
97. Kurtzman RS, Otto DL, Chepey JJ: Myxedema heart disease. *Radiology* 84:624, 1965.
98. Ibbertson K, Fraser R, Alldis D: Rapidly acting thyroid hormones and their cardiac action. *Br Med J* 2:52, 1959.
99. Arlot S, et al: Myxedema coma: Response of thyroid hormones with oral and intravenous high-dose L-thyroxine treatment. *Intensive Care Med* 17:16, 1990.
100. Brewster WR Jr, et al: The hemodynamic and metabolic interrelationships in the activity of epinephrine, norepinephrine and thyroid hormone. *Circulation* 13:1, 1956.
101. Williams GH, et al: Studies of the control of plasma aldosterone concentration in normal man. *J Clin Invest* 51:1731, 1972.
102. Ichikawa Y: Plasma corticotropin (ACTH), growth hormone (GH) and 11-OHCS (hydroxycorticosteroid) response during surgery. *J Lab Clin Med* 78:882, 1971.
103. Von Werder K, et al: Adrenal function during long-term anesthesia in man. *Proc Soc Exp Biol Med* 135:854, 1970.
104. Sachar EJ, et al: Disrupted 24-hour patterns of cortisol secretion in psychotic depression. *Arch Gen Psychiatry* 28:19, 1973.
105. Bellet S, et al: Effect of acute ethanol intake on plasma 11-hydroxy-corticosteroid levels in accidental hypothermia. *Lancet* 1:324, 1970.
106. Sprunt JG, Maclean D, Browning MCK: Plasma corticosteroid levels in accidental hypothermia. *Lancet* 1:324, 1970.
107. Jacobs HS, Nabarro JDN: Plasma 11-hydroxycorticosteroid and growth hormone levels in acute medical illnesses. *Br Med J* 2:595, 1969.
108. Xarli VP, et al: Adrenal hemorrhage in the adult. *Medicine (Baltimore)* 57:211, 1978.
109. Rosenthal FD, Davies MK, Burden AC: Malignant disease presenting as Addison's disease. *Br Med J* 1:1591, 1978.
110. Bosworth DC: Reversible adrenocortical insufficiency in fulminant meningococcemia. *Arch Intern Med* 139:823, 1979.
111. Anderson KC, Kuhajda FP, Bell WR: Diagnosis and treatment of anticoagulant-related adrenal hemorrhage. *Am J Hematol* 11:379, 1981.
112. Danowski TS, et al: Probabilities of pituitary-adrenal responsiveness after steroid therapy. *Ann Intern Med* 51:11, 1964.
113. Graber AL, et al: Natural history of pituitary-adrenal recovery following long-term suppression with corticosteroids. *J Clin Endocrinol Metab* 25:11, 1965.
114. Ackerman GL, Nolan GM: Adrenocortical responsiveness after alternate-day corticosteroid therapy. *N Engl J Med* 278:405, 1968.
115. Streck WF, Lockwood DH: Pituitary adrenal recovery following short-term suppression with corticosteroids. *Am J Med* 66:910, 1979.
116. Heroman WM, et al: Adrenal suppression and cushingoid changes secondary to dexamethasone nose drops. *J Pediatr* 96:500, 1980.
117. Vaz R, et al: Adrenal effects of beclomethasone inhalation therapy in asthmatic children. *J Pediatr* 100:660, 1982.
118. Marik PE, Zaloga GP: Adrenal insufficiency during septic shock. *Crit Care Med* 31:141, 2003.
119. Hatherill M, et al: Adrenal insufficiency in septic shock. *Arch Dis Child* 80:51, 1999.

120. Blizzard RM, Chee D, Davis W: The incidence of adrenal and other antibodies in the sera of patients with idiopathic adrenal insufficiency (Addison's disease). *Clin Exp Immunol* 2:19, 1967.

121. Blizzard RM, Kyle M: Studies of the adrenal antigens and antibodies in Addison's disease. *J Clin Invest* 42:1653, 1963.

122. Genant HK, Hoagland HC, Randall RV: Addison's disease and hypothyroidism (Schmidt's syndrome). *Metabolism* 16:189, 1967.

123. Sheeler LR, et al: Adrenal insufficiency secondary to carcinoma metastatic to the adrenal gland. *Cancer* 52:1312, 1983.

124. Glomset DA: The incidence of metastasis of malignant tumors to the adrenal. *Am J Cancer* 32:57, 1938.

125. Nerup J: Addison's disease—Clinical studies: A report of 108 cases. *Acta Endocrinol (Copenh)* 76:127, 1974.

126. Bell H, Hayes W, Vosbrugh J: Hyperkalemic paralysis due to adrenal insufficiency. *Arch Intern Med* 115:418, 1965.

127. Webb WR, et al: Cardiovascular responses in adrenal insufficiency. *Surgery* 58:273, 1965.

128. Schwartz J, et al: Role of vasopressin in blood pressure regulation during adrenal insufficiency. *Endocrinology* 112:234, 1983.

129. Ahmed ABJ, et al: Increased plasma arginine vasopressin in clinical adrenocortical insufficiency and its inhibition by glucosteroids. *J Clin Invest* 46:111, 1967.

130. Rivers EP, et al: Adrenal dysfunction in hemodynamically unstable patients in the emergency department. *Acad Emerg Med* 6:626, 1999.

131. Dunlop D: Eighty-six cases of Addison's disease. *Br Med J* 2:887, 1963.

132. Jorgensen H: Hypercalcemia in adrenocortical insufficiency. *Acta Med Scand* 193:175, 1973.

133. Walser M, Robinson BHB, Duckett JW: The hypercalcemia of adrenal insufficiency. *J Clin Invest* 42:456, 1963.

134. Somerville W, Levine HD, Thorn GW: Electrocardiogram in Addison's disease. *Medicine (Baltimore)* 30:43, 1951.

Section XII INFECTIOUS DISEASE

CHAPTER

127 Bacteria

Madonna Fernández-Frackelton

DIPHTHERIA

Perspective

History

References to the disease now known as diphtheria date back to ancient Syria and Egypt. In the fifth century BC, Hippocrates provided the first clinical description of this disease characterized by sore throat, membrane formation, and death through suffocation. Epidemics of "throat distemper" were described throughout the 16th, 18th, and 19th centuries. It was not until the 1820s that the French physician Pierre Bretonneau named the condition "diphtherite," from the Greek word for "leather," to describe the characteristic pharyngeal membrane.[1,2] Klebs observed the *Corynebacterium diphtheriae* microorganism on smears obtained from pharyngeal membranes in 1883, and 1 year later Löffler isolated *Corynebacterium* organisms in pure cultures. Löffler subsequently demonstrated that diphtheria was a localized infection and postulated that its systemic effects were caused by an elaborated toxin. In 1888 Roux and Yersin demonstrated that bacteria-free filtrates of diphtheria culture were able to kill guinea pigs.[2]

In 1890 von Behring and Kitasato first demonstrated diphtheria immunization using a heat- and formalin-treated toxin to make toxoid. One year later they administered the first dose of antitoxin to a human with diphtheria. Schick developed the skin test for diphtheria immunity in 1913. During the 1930s and 1940s, toxoid immunization was routinely used. In the 1950s Freeman found that only bacteria infected with the B phage produced toxin. Subsequent studies elucidate the toxin genome and the mechanism of toxin activity at the cellular level.[1,2]

Epidemiology

Humans are the only known reservoir for *C. diphtheriae*. Spread is primarily by person-to-person contact through respiratory droplets or by direct contact with skin lesion exudates. Transmission is associated with crowded living conditions. Individuals may spread the disease when they are actively ill, in the convalescent stage after acute illness, or as asymptomatic carriers. Fomites and foods have occasionally been implicated but do not represent a major route of transmission.[1]

Between 1991 and 1996 the first large-scale epidemic of diphtheria in an industrialized country in three decades occurred in the newly independent states of the former Soviet Union. During the peak of the epidemic more than 98,000 cases and 3,400 deaths were reported. Several factors contributed to this outbreak, including (1) decreased childhood immunity because of vaccine supply interruption and administration of adult-formulation tetanus-diphtheria toxoids (Td) to children, (2) increased adult susceptibility because of waning immunity, (3) poor socioeconomic conditions and increased population movement, and (4) resurgence of more toxigenic strains of diphtheria.[3]

Immunization against diphtheria is highly effective. Before widespread immunization programs in the United States, the incidence of diphtheria was in excess of 100 cases per 100,000 population and the disease predominantly affected children. By 1980 the Centers for Disease Control and Prevention (CDC) reported 0 to 5 cases per year nationwide. Currently, sporadic cases occur primarily in adults, many of whom are not adequately immunized.[3] Three urban outbreaks of predominantly cutaneous diphtheria occurred in Seattle between 1972 and 1982 among a population of urban alcohol abusers. Outbreaks are associated with poor hygiene, crowding, underlying skin disease, contaminated fomites, pyoderma, and the appearance of new *C. diphtheriae* strains.[1]

A substantial portion of the U.S. population is not adequately protected against diphtheria, and most recent outbreaks in the United States have occurred in unimmunized or underimmunized adults in urban and poor rural areas.[1] Even in industrialized nations in which childhood vaccination rates are high, more than 50% of adults older than 40 lack protective antibodies.[4] In the prevaccine era, 80% of people acquired natural immunity to diphtheria by age 15 and recurrent exposure to toxigenic strains of the bacteria acted as boosters. Because childhood immunization nearly eliminates these toxigenic strains in a population, adult immunity wanes. Thus, more adults in industrialized nations are susceptible to diphtheria.[4] The ease of international travel and the epidemic in eastern Europe in the 1990s underscore the importance of aggressively continuing childhood immunizations and reimmunization of adults.

Etiology

Diphtheria is caused by *C. diphtheriae*, an unencapsulated, gram-positive bacillus named for its shape ("korynee" for club) and for its characteristic clinical presentation ("diphtheria" for "leather hide," a reference to the leather-like appearance of the pharyngeal membrane). When viewed on stained smears, the bacteria look like Asian characters.[1]

Principles of Disease

Infection by *C. diphtheriae* occurs at various sites of the respiratory tract or the skin. Respiratory diphtheria includes faucial (pharyngeal or tonsillar), nasal, and laryngeal (tracheobronchial) types, named for the primary location of infection. Cutaneous diphtheria may occur as a primary skin infection or as a secondary infection of a preexisting wound.

The *C. diphtheriae* bacterium produces an exotoxin that contributes to formation of the diphtheritic membrane and is responsible for the systemic effects of infection.[5] The exotoxin is a 62,000-dalton polypeptide produced by bacterial strains lysogenized by the corynephage B Tox+.[1,5] The exotoxin inhibits cellular protein synthesis. Circulating exotoxin most profoundly affects the nervous system, heart, and kidneys.[1] The degree of local and systemic toxicity depends on the location and extent of membrane formation. Pha-

ryngeal diphtheria generally has the greatest toxicity and cutaneous diphtheria the least.

The diphtheritic membrane forms as a result of necrosis caused by the local effects of the exotoxin. The membrane is composed of leukocytes, erythrocytes, fibrin, epithelial cells, and bacteria. Initially, the pharynx appears erythematous, but as necrosis occurs, grayish-white patches appear and eventually coalesce. The membrane is accompanied by surrounding edema and cervical adenitis. The initial grayish-white, filmy appearance changes to a thick, grayish-black membrane with sharply defined borders. This membrane is adherent to the underlying tissue, and bleeding occurs if removal is attempted.[1]

Systemic effects of diphtheria infection are caused by the circulating exotoxin's action primarily on the cardiovascular and nervous systems. The exotoxin's disruption of cellular protein synthesis produces a peripheral neuropathy manifested by muscle weakness. About 20% of all patients with symptomatic respiratory infection have polyneuritis, but 75% of patients with severe disease develop some form of neuropathy.[5] The muscles of the palate are usually the first to become paralyzed. Less commonly, other cranial nerves, peripheral nerves, and the spinal cord may be affected. Degenerative lesions develop in the dorsal root and ventral horn ganglia of the spinal cord and in cranial nerve nuclei. Cortical cells are spared. Proximal muscle groups are affected first. In severe cases, paralysis may develop in the first few days of illness. Generally the paralysis does not last more than 10 days, and complete recovery over a longer period of time is the rule.[1]

The extent of cardiac problems correlates with the degree of local infection and membrane formation. Signs of myocardial dysfunction usually appear 1 to 2 weeks after the onset of illness. In more severe cases, cardiac symptoms arise earlier in the course of the illness. The exotoxin directly damages myocardial cells, producing myocarditis. Electrocardiographic (ECG) changes suggestive of myocarditis occur in up to two thirds of patients, but clinical manifestations of myocarditis are less common (10% to 25%).[1]

Clinical Features

History and Physical Examination

The average incubation period of respiratory tract diphtheria is 2 to 4 days but may range from 1 to 8 days. Signs and symptoms are often indistinguishable from those of other upper respiratory tract infections. In a series of 676 patients, fever and sore throat were the most frequent presenting complaints (79% and 69%, respectively). Weakness (42%), dysphagia (35%), headache (20%), change of voice (15%), and loss of appetite (10%) were also common. Cough, shortness of breath, nasal discharge, and neck edema occurred in less than 10% of patients. Fever, although common, is usually low grade. Cervical adenopathy is present in approximately one third of patients, and a diphtheritic membrane is observed in more than half of all patients. Of note, however, one report indicated that shortness of breath and neck edema were present in approximately 40% of patients who died of the disease.[6]

In patients with faucial diphtheria, the extent of the membrane usually parallels the clinical toxicity. If the membrane is limited to the tonsils, the disease may be mild; if the membrane covers the entire pharynx, the onset of illness is usually abrupt and the severity high. Swelling of the cervical lymph nodes and infiltration of tissues of the neck may be so extensive that the patient has a "bull-neck" appearance. Patients with this form of "malignant diphtheria" usually have high fever, severe muscle weakness, vomiting, diarrhea, restlessness, and delirium. Death occurs from respiratory tract obstruction or cardiac failure resulting from myocarditis. Nasal diphtheria arises with a unilateral or bilateral serous or serosanguineous discharge from the nose. A diphtheritic membrane may be visible. These patients do not usually develop constitutional symptoms. Treatment is important to prevent a persistent carrier state. Laryngeal (tracheobronchial) diphtheria may begin in the larynx or spread downward from a more cephalad primary site. Patients may develop respiratory tract edema with subsequent upper airway obstruction. Cutaneous diphtheria occurs primarily in temperate climates. Alcohol abusers and socioeconomically disadvantaged people are most at risk.[1] Patients with cutaneous diphtheria generally do not display systemic toxicity. The skin characteristically has an ulcer with a grayish membrane. Wounds from which *C. diphtheriae* is cultured are clinically indistinguishable from other chronic skin conditions.

Complications

The most serious complications of diphtheria are airway obstruction (resulting from membrane formation and edema), congestive heart failure, cardiac conduction disturbances, and muscle paralysis. Mortality in two large series ranged from 2.3% to 3% overall but was up to 7% in patients with myocarditis and 25.7% in patients with the malignant form of the disease (with neck swelling).[7] Although systemic infection is rare, endocarditis, mycotic aneurysms, osteomyelitis, and septic arthritis have all been described in immunocompromised hosts.[1]

Diagnostic Strategies

When *C. diphtheriae* is suspected, the laboratory should be notified because routine cultures do not identify this organism. Throat or nasopharyngeal swabs should be obtained for respiratory diphtheria, and, if it is present, membranous material should be examined. For cutaneous infections, samples should be obtained from skin lesions. Specimens should be collected before antibiotic therapy is initiated and should be transported to the laboratory immediately for rapid inoculation onto tellurite or Löffler's selective culture medium.[1,8] Immunofluorescent staining of a 4-hour culture may provide a rapid diagnosis, but direct staining is frequently unreliable. Definitive identification is made by using a combination of colony morphology, microscopic appearance, and fermentation reactions.[1]

BOX 127-1. Differential Diagnosis of Respiratory Diphtheria

Streptococcal or viral pharyngitis	Laryngitis
	Bronchitis
Tonsillitis	Tracheitis
Vincent's angina	Monilial infection
Acute epiglottitis	Rhinitis
Mononucleosis	

C. diphtheriae isolates should be tested for the production of toxin. The Elek immunoprecipitation test for toxin A is technically demanding and subject to misinterpretation by inexperienced users.[8] Polymerase chain reaction (PCR), which is more reliable but not as readily available, can be used to detect the diphtheria toxin structural gene.[8] A positive culture for group A beta-hemolytic streptococcus does not exclude diphtheria as a pathogen, as up to 30% of patients with diphtheria test positive for streptococcal coinfection.

Several laboratory abnormalities such as leukocytosis, mild thrombocytopenia, and proteinuria are common but are neither sensitive nor specific for diphtheria. ECG changes are nonspecific and include ST-T wave changes, varying degrees of atrioventricular block, and dysrhythmias. An ECG may be normal even in the presence of myocarditis. Cardiac enzymes may detect myocarditis, and serum aspartate transaminase levels correlate with the severity of myocarditis.[9]

Differential Considerations

In the absence of a diphtheritic membrane, it may be difficult to differentiate respiratory diphtheria from many other respiratory conditions, especially in the early phase of infection (Box 127-1). Generally, the diphtheritic membrane is darker, grayer, more fibrous, and more firmly attached to the underlying tissues than in other conditions that have a membrane-like appearance. Vincent's angina frequently involves the gingivae, which are unaffected in diphtheria. Acute bacterial epiglottitis generally has a much more rapid onset than diphtheria and indirect laryngoscopy reveals an erythematous, edematous epiglottis without membrane formation.[1]

Cutaneous diphtheria is difficult to differentiate from other acute and chronic ulcerative skin lesions. *C. diphtheriae* can secondarily infect any of these lesions, especially in high-risk patients such as alcoholic, socioeconomically disadvantaged, and unimmunized or underimmunized people.

Management

Patients with clinical evidence of diphtheria should be placed in respiratory isolation and treated presumptively for *C. diphtheriae*. The goals of therapy are to protect the airway, limit the effects of already produced toxin, and eliminate future toxin production by terminating the growth of *C. diphtheriae*. Although the likelihood of a patient in the United States developing airway obstruction from diphtheria is remote, the management is identical to that for other forms of airway obstruction. Bronchodilators may be useful in symptomatic patients.[9] Patients may be dehydrated from fever and decreased oral intake related to dysphagia or neurologic impairment. Fluid resuscitation should be undertaken cautiously as the toxin's effect on the myocardium may result in congestive heart failure.

Equine serum diphtheria antitoxin is the mainstay of therapy and should be administered promptly after the clinical diagnosis of respiratory diphtheria is made. The size and location of the membrane, duration of illness, and the patient's overall degree of toxicity determine the dosage of antitoxin. The Committee on Infectious Diseases of the American Academy of Pediatrics (AAP) recommends 20,000 to 40,000 units for pharyngeal or laryngeal involvement of 48 hours' duration, 40,000 to 60,000 units for nasopharyngeal lesions, and 80,000 to 120,000 units for extensive disease of 3 or more days' duration or for diffuse swelling of the neck.[9,10] After conjunctival or intradermal sensitivity skin testing, the antitoxin is administered intravenously (IV). If the patient exhibits sensitivity to the antitoxin, desensitization should be performed. Diphtheria antitoxin and consultation on its use can be obtained by calling the CDC in Atlanta at 404-639-2540.[9] Active immunization against diphtheria should also be initiated because clinical infection does not necessarily confer immunity.[10]

Antibiotics are beneficial in preventing growth and spread of the organism but are no substitute for antitoxin. Erythromycin, 40 to 50 mg/kg/day (up to 2 g) IV or orally in divided doses, intramuscular (IM) aqueous crystalline penicillin (100,000 to 150,000 units/kg/day in four divided doses), and procaine penicillin (25,000 to 50,000 units/kg/day in two divided doses) for 14 days given IM are acceptable alternatives.[9,10] Treatment failures are more common with penicillin than with erythromycin. The newer generation macrolides (azithromycin and clarithromycin) have activity similar to that of erythromycin in vitro and may result in better compliance. These agents, however, have not been adequately tested in clinical disease. An equivalent daily oral therapy may be substituted when the patient is able to swallow. Three negative cultures should be documented after treatment.[10]

Myocarditis and neuritis are treated with supportive care and careful monitoring. Patients with ECG changes of myocarditis have three to four times the mortality rate of those with normal ECGs. The mortality of patients with left bundle branch block and atrioventricular block is 60% to 90%, and serial tracings are recommended. No data support the use of steroids.[1,9]

Cutaneous lesions should be debrided of necrotic tissue and cleansed vigorously. A course of antibiotics is recommended, but the administration of antitoxin for cutaneous lesions is of questionable value. Some experts recommend 20,000 to 40,000 units of antitoxin,[10] but there are few data to support its use in this setting.[1]

Carriers of *C. diphtheriae* should receive oral penicillin G or erythromycin for 7 days or IM benzathine penicillin (600,000 units for those less than 30 kg and 1,200,000 units for those over 30 kg). Active immunization should also be provided for unimmunized and partially immunized carriers. After 2 weeks of therapy is completed, cultures should be obtained; if they are positive, erythromycin therapy should be given for 10 additional days.[10]

Individuals who have been in close contact with infected patients should have culture specimens taken, and the patient should be kept under surveillance for 7 days. Previously immunized close contacts should receive a booster of diphtheria toxoid if the last booster was more than 5 years earlier. The vaccine should be diphtheria, tetanus, and pertussis (DTP), diphtheria-tetanus (DT), or tetanus-diphtheria with a lower dose of diphtheria toxoid (Td) as appropriate for age according to the recommended immunization schedule. Close contacts who are not immunized or whose immunization status is unknown should receive the same antimicrobial therapy as carriers (as previously described), have culture specimens taken before and after therapy, and have active immunization initiated. Close contacts who cannot be kept under surveillance should receive benzathine penicillin IM to ensure compliance and a diphtheria toxoid booster (appropriate for age and immunization history). Some practitioners treat this group with 5000 to 10,000 units of antitoxin IM (at a site separate from the toxoid booster) after sensitivity testing. This is generally not recommended, however, because of the risk of horse serum allergy.[10]

A universal program of primary immunization along with regular diphtheria boosters every 10 years is the most effective method for controlling diphtheria. For this reason, emergency physicians should routinely administer diphtheria and tetanus toxoids as part of wound management.

PERTUSSIS

Perspective

History

Pertussis is an acute respiratory disease that was first described in 1578 when an epidemic swept through Paris. The name "pertussis" was first used by Sydenham in 1670 when he described the illness in infants.[11] Pertussis literally means "violent cough," which is the hallmark of the disease. In China it is known as "the cough of 100 days." It is also called *whooping cough* because the severe episodes of coughing are followed by forceful inspiration, which creates the characteristic whooping sound. The causative organism was identified in 1906 by Bordet and Gengou.[12] In the prevaccination era, pertussis was responsible for more infant deaths than measles, scarlet fever, diphtheria, and poliomyelitis combined. A vaccine was developed in the 1940s, but pertussis still remains a significant cause of morbidity and mortality in the United States and worldwide.[13]

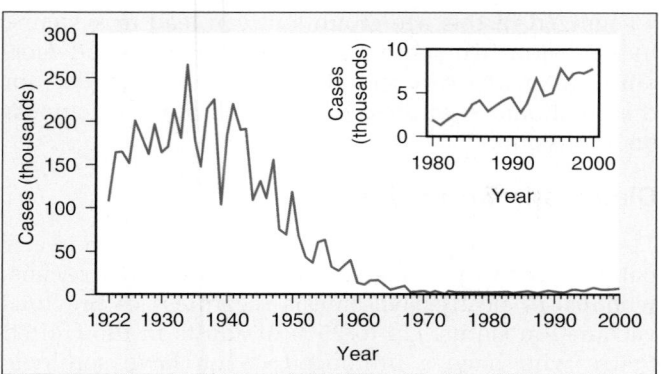

Figure 127-1. Number of reported pertussis cases in the United States by year. (From Centers for Disease Control and Prevention: Pertussis—United States, 1997-2000. *MMWR Morb Mortal Wkly Rep* 51:73, 2002.)

Epidemiology

Pertussis is a localized respiratory illness transmitted by aerosolized droplets. It is highly contagious with attack rates of 50% to 100% in susceptible individuals with a household exposure.[12] The average incubation period is 7 to 10 days but may range from less than 1 week to 3 weeks. Neither vaccination nor prior infection confers lifelong immunity, and attack rates are greater than 50% in adults exposed as long as 12 years after completion of a vaccination series.

Pertussis remains prevalent worldwide. In the United States, annual pertussis rates declined sharply after the introduction of the vaccine and reached a nadir of 1010 cases in 1976. Since 1980 there has been a steady increase in the incidence of pertussis with peaks every 3 to 4 years (Figure 127-1).[14,15] Waning immunity in the adult population and increased reporting of adult cases may be primary contributing factors. Of note, the proportion of culture-confirmed cases in infants continues to increase. A 1991 report found evidence of a causal relationship between the vaccine and acute encephalopathy, resulting in a decline in the use of the whole-cell pertussis vaccine. The acellular pertussis vaccine has been approved in the United States since 1991 for persons older than 15 months and since 1996 for infants.[15]

Although pertussis can occur at any age, it is predominantly a pediatric illness. The age-specific attack rates are highest in children younger than 1 year who have not yet received the entire vaccine series. There appears to be a seasonal variation; 50% of cases in the United States occur from June through September.

Etiology

Pertussis is caused by organisms of the *Bordetella* genus, which are small, nonmotile, gram-negative coccobacilli that occur singly or in pairs. *Bordetella pertussis* and *Bordetella parapertussis* are responsible for disease in humans. The organisms are fastidious and require nicotinamide and an optimal temperature of 35° C to 37° C to grow. *Bordetella bronchiseptica*, a flagellated, motile organism, causes illness in animals,

including kennel cough, and may rarely cause respiratory infection in immunocompromised humans.[12]

Principles of Disease

The *Bordetella* organism adheres preferentially to ciliated respiratory epithelial cells. *B. pertussis* does not invade beyond the submucosal layer in the respiratory tract and is almost never recovered in the bloodstream. The organism elaborates several toxins that act locally and systemically. These toxins include pertussis toxin, dermonecrotic toxin, adenylate cyclase toxin, and tracheal cytotoxin.[12]

Local tissue damage consists of inflammatory changes in the mucosal lining of the respiratory tract, primarily congestion and cellular infiltration with lymphocytes and granulocytes. As the infection progresses, secondary pneumonia or otitis media may occur. Systemic effects of pertussis toxin include sensitization to the lethal effects of histamine and increased secretion of insulin.[12]

Clinical Features

History and Physical Examination

Pertussis arises in three distinct sequential clinical stages: the *catarrhal phase*, the *paroxysmal phase,* and the *convalescent phase.* The catarrhal phase begins after an incubation period of approximately 7 to 10 days and lasts approximately 1 to 2 weeks. Infectivity is greatest during the catarrhal phase, when the disease is clinically indistinguishable from other upper respiratory tract infections. Signs and symptoms include rhinorrhea, low-grade fever, malaise, conjunctival injection, and anorexia. A dry cough usually begins at the end of the catarrhal phase.[12,13]

The paroxysmal phase begins as fever subsides and cough increases and lasts from 2 to 4 weeks. The paroxysms of staccato coughing occur 40 to 50 times per day. The patient coughs repeatedly in short exhalations followed by a single, sudden, forceful inhalation that produces the characteristic "whoop." Only one third of adults with pertussis develop this whoop, and it is rare in young infants, who may present with an apneic episode and no other symptoms. Paroxysms may be spontaneous, occur more frequently at night, or be precipitated by noise or cold. During the paroxysm, the patient may exhibit cyanosis, diaphoresis, protrusion of the tongue, salivation, and lacrimation. Posttussive vomiting, syncope, and brief episodes of apnea may occur. Infants may be physically exhausted after a typical paroxysm. Between episodes of coughing, patients do not appear acutely ill.[12,13]

The convalescent phase is characterized by a residual cough that lasts for several weeks to months. Paroxysms of coughing may be triggered by an unrelated upper respiratory infection or by exposure to a respiratory irritant. This recurrence of coughing does not represent recurrence of pertussis infection.

Atypical presentations may occur in young and preterm infants. Fever is usually not present in uncomplicated neonatal pertussis. Tachypnea, apnea, and cyanotic and bradycardic episodes may be the predominant symptoms.[13] Older children and adults who have partial protection from vaccination or previous illness may have a long-lasting intractable dry cough that is frequently misdiagnosed as bronchitis.[12]

Physical examination findings are nonspecific. Tachypnea is variably present and may be related to the degree of pulmonary involvement. Low-grade fever is common during the catarrhal phase, as are conjunctival injection and rhinorrhea. The presence of fever during other stages of illness suggests secondary infection. Petechiae above the nipple line, subconjunctival hemorrhages, and epistaxis may occur because of increased intrathoracic pressure during paroxysms. Chest examination may reveal rhonchi or clear lung fields; the presence of rales suggests pneumonia.[11-13]

Complications

The major complications of pertussis are superinfection causing pneumonia, central nervous system (CNS) sequelae, otitis media, and complications related to the paroxysm of coughing.[11,12,16,17] Pneumonia complicating pertussis is a leading cause of death, especially in infants and young children.[12,17] Aspiration of gastric contents and respiratory secretions may occur during the paroxysm of coughing, whooping, and vomiting. Secondary pulmonary infection may also be a consequence of decreased respiratory tract clearance related to the actions of the *Bordetella* organism and toxins on bronchial and lung mucosa. Bacterial (*Streptococcus pneumoniae*, *Streptococcus pyogenes*, *Haemophilus influenzae*, and *Staphylococcus aureus*) and viral (respiratory syncytial virus, cytomegalovirus, and adenovirus) superinfections can complicate pertussis infections. A fever during the paroxysmal phase should alert the physician to a possible superinfection.

CNS complications include seizures (3%), encephalopathy (0.9%), and intracerebral hemorrhage.[12] The causes of seizures and encephalopathy are unclear but may include hypoxia, hypoglycemia, cerebral petechia, effects of a toxin, or secondary infection by neurotropic viruses or bacteria. CNS hemorrhages may occur as a consequence of the increased cerebral vascular pressures generated during the paroxysm of coughing. Sudden increases in intrathoracic and intra-abdominal pressures can result in several other complicating conditions (Box 127-2).[12,17]

Bradycardia, hypotension, and cardiac arrest can occur in neonates and young infants with pertussis.[16] Severe pulmonary hypertension has increasingly been recognized in this age group and can lead to systemic hypotension, worsening hypoxia, and increased mortality. Intensive care monitoring is recommended for these patients, regardless of how well they may appear on admission.

Diagnostic Strategies

The diagnosis of pertussis should be entertained in any patient with prolonged cough with paroxysms, whoops, or posttussive emesis regardless of previous vaccination status. Up to 25% of adults in the United States who have a prolonged cough have serologic evidence of pertussis.[11]

Ancillary studies are of limited value in the emergency department. During the late catarrhal and early paroxysmal phases, a marked leukocytosis and a characteristic lymphocytosis are often present. The white blood cell (WBC) count of 25,000 to 50,000/mL is not uncommon and may exceed 60,000/mL in infants.[16,17] Adults with pertussis frequently do not have the characteristic leukocytosis and lymphocytosis, and some infants and immunocompromised hosts may not be able to mount this response.[16] The chest radiograph may show peribronchial thickening, atelectasis, or pulmonary consolidation.[12]

Laboratory confirmation of the diagnosis is made by nasopharyngeal culture; sputum and throat swabs are inadequate. The *Bordetella* organism is fastidious, and isolation requires a nicotinamide or Bordet-Gengou medium impregnated with antibiotics to reduce overgrowth of competing bacteria. The slow-growing hemolytic colonies of *B. pertussis* take 3 to 7 days to appear. A synthetic culture medium is also available. The sensitivity of pertussis cultures is only 20% to 40%. Direct fluorescent antibody techniques are available to identify *B. pertussis* in nasopharyngeal specimens and are a particularly useful screening tool in outbreak investigation.[12]

Adults generally come to medical attention late in the disease, at which time cultures are rarely positive (3.6%). PCR is much more likely to identify the organism (38.1% of cases) but is not widely available. Serologic testing is not widely available and requires documentation of a fourfold rise in antibody titers, making it an impractical tool in most patients.[11,18]

Differential Considerations

The differential diagnosis includes acute viral upper respiratory tract infection, pneumonia, bronchiolitis, cystic fibrosis, tuberculosis, exacerbation of chronic obstructive pulmonary disease, and foreign body aspiration. The marked leukocytosis may suggest the diagnosis of leukemia.

Management

Acute Treatment

Treatment of pertussis is primarily supportive and includes oxygen, frequent suctioning, maintenance of hydration, parenteral nutrition if necessary, and avoidance of respiratory irritants. Patients with suspected

---

BOX 127-2. Pertussis Complications

Periorbital edema	Pneumothorax
Subconjunctival hemorrhage	Pneumomediastinum
Petechiae	Diaphragmatic rupture
Epistaxis	Umbilical and inguinal
Hemoptysis	hernias
Subcutaneous emphysema	Rectal prolapse

pertussis and associated pneumonia, hypoxia, or CNS complications or those experiencing severe paroxysms should also be hospitalized. Children younger than 1 year should also be admitted because they are not yet fully immunized and have the greatest risk for morbidity and mortality.[12] Neonates with pertussis should be admitted to an intensive care unit, as apnea and significant cardiac complications can occur without warning.[16]

Antibiotic treatment does not appear to reduce significantly the severity or duration of illness when started in the paroxysmal phase and may have only a minimal effect in the catarrhal phase. The primary goal of antibiotic therapy is to decrease infectivity and carriage. Erythromycin estolate ester is the antibiotic of choice at 40 to 50 mg/kg/day (maximum 2 g/day) in two or three divided doses for 14 days.[11-13] Azithromycin (10 mg/kg on day 1 followed by 5 mg/kg on days 2 to 5), clarithromycin (15 mg/kg/day in two divided doses), and a 7-day course of erythromycin estolate ester are effective alternatives for patients who do not tolerate 14 days of erythromycin well.[11,12,19] Trimethoprim-sulfamethoxazole is an alternative for macrolide-allergic patients but may not be as effective. Although the fluoroquinolones have in vitro activity against *B. pertussis*, clinical data are lacking. Patients should be considered infectious for 3 weeks after the onset of the paroxysmal phase or until at least 5 days after antibiotics are started.[11] Strict isolation is recommended during this period.

Corticosteroids, especially in young critically ill infants, may reduce the severity and course of illness, but effectiveness is not well established. β_2-Adrenergic agonists do not reduce the frequency or severity of paroxysmal coughing episodes[16,20] but may be helpful in patients with reactive airway disease. Early clinical trials with pertussis immune globulin suggest significant improvement in lymphocytosis and paroxysmal coughing in infants, but further placebo-control trials are needed to establish efficacy.[21] Standard cough suppressants and antihistamines are ineffective.[12,20]

Postexposure prophylaxis, with erythromycin as described previously, is recommended for household contacts of patients with pertussis regardless of previous vaccination status.[11] Erythromycin should also be prescribed for any unimmunized person or partially immunized infant with a history of significant exposure to the index case.[11,12] There is no evidence to support prophylaxis for contacts other than those described previously.[22]

Vaccination

Whole-cell and acellular pertussis vaccines are distributed in combination with diphtheria and tetanus toxoids as DPT and DTaP, respectively. The acellular pertussis vaccines contain inactivated pertussis toxin and one or more other bacterial components. The acellular vaccine is as effective as the whole-cell vaccine with fewer adverse reactions reported. Most recipients develop fever, irritability, behavioral changes, and local discomfort at the site of inoculation. Moderately severe reactions are uncommon but include fever with temperature over 40° C, persistent crying, high-pitched crying, and seizures. Severe neurologic complications (prolonged seizures, encephalopathy) occur rarely but led to decreased use of the whole-cell form of the vaccine and the development of DTaP.[23] DTaP has replaced DPT for childhood immunizations, and the whole-cell pertussis vaccine is recommended for use in the United States only when the acellular vaccine is not available.[12,23]

Pertussis immunity wanes significantly 6 to 8 years after immunization and 15 years after natural infection,[24] causing an increasing incidence of the disease in people older than 15 years. The acellular pertussis vaccine is safe and effective in adolescents and adults, but routine booster immunization is not currently recommended. The vaccine may be useful for the control of pertussis during outbreaks and in patients at high risk for exposure to pertussis (parents, health care workers, and child care workers); more data are needed to define the impact of pertussis in these groups.[25]

TETANUS

Perspective

History

Tetanus is a toxin-mediated disease characterized by severe uncontrolled skeletal muscle spasms. Involvement of the muscles of respiration leads to hypoventilation, hypoxia, and death. Dramatic descriptions of this disease date back to ancient Egypt when physicians recognized a frequent relationship between tissue injury and subsequent fatal spasm.[26,27]

In 1884 Carle and Rattone produced tetanus in rabbits by injecting material from an acne pustule that came from an infected human. In the same year, Nicolaier isolated the strychnine-like toxin from anaerobic soil bacteria.[26] In 1889 Kitasato obtained pure cultures of spore-forming bacteria that caused tetanus when introduced into animals. One year later, Faber proved that tetanus was a toxin-mediated disease when he induced the illness by injecting animals with bacteria-free filtrates of *Clostridium tetani* cultures. In the 1890s von Behring and Kitasato discovered tetanus antitoxin in the serum of immune animals and demonstrated its efficacy in preventing disease. Prophylactic injection of this antitoxin provided passive immunity to wounded soldiers during World War I. It was not until the 1930s that an effective vaccine was developed. Large-scale testing during World War II indicated that the tetanus toxoid conferred a high degree of protection against disease.

Epidemiology

Despite the availability of an effective vaccine, tetanus remains endemic worldwide. It is more common in warm, damp climates and relatively rare in cold regions. The global incidence of tetanus is estimated to be between 500,000 and 1 million cases a year, with half of the cases occurring in neonates. Eighty percent of these cases occur in Africa and Southeast Asia because of low immunization rates and poor hygiene.[27]

Since the introduction of vaccination programs in the United States, the incidence of tetanus has steadily declined from 4 cases per million population in the 1940s to 0.16 cases per million population in 2000. An average of 43 cases per year was reported to the CDC between 1998 and 2000 (Figure 127-2).[28,29] The highest incidences occurred in people older than 60 years (0.35 cases per million population), Hispanic Americans (0.37 cases per million population), and diabetics (0.70 cases per million population). Fifteen percent of cases occurred in injection drug users. The overall case fatality rate was 18% but approached 50% in patients older than 70 years (Figure 127-3). Cases were reported in patients who had been fully vaccinated, but in the eight patients from 1998 to 2000, no deaths occurred [30]

Most patients with tetanus have an identifiable injury, but 7% to 27% of cases occur with no apparent source.[26,30] The most common portals of entry for the organism are puncture wounds, lacerations, and abrasions. Tetanus has also been reported in chronic wounds such as skin ulcers, abscesses, and otitis media.[27] Postoperative tetanus has been reported in patients who have undergone intestinal operations and abortions. In these cases the source of bacteria is probably endogenous, as up to 10% of humans harbor *C. tetani* in the colon.

Inadequate primary immunization and waning immunity continue to be the primary risk factors for tetanus in the United States. As tetanus vaccination of children has improved, older people have accounted for an increasing percentage of all cases.

Etiology

C. tetani is a spore-forming, motile, slender, rod-shaped, obligate anaerobic bacillus. It stains gram positive in fresh culture but has a variable staining pattern in old cultures and tissue samples. The bacillus can form a single spherical terminal endospore that swells the end of the organism to produce a characteristic drumstick appearance. *C. tetani* is ubiquitous in soil and dust and is also found in the feces of animals and humans.[27] Mature bacilli are highly susceptible to heat and other adverse environmental conditions. Spores are resistant to heating and chemical disinfectants and can survive in soil for months to years. When introduced into a wound, spores may not germinate for weeks because of unfavorable tissue conditions. When injury favors anaerobic growth, the spores germinate into mature bacilli. Only these mature bacilli produce the tetanus toxins that cause clinical disease.[29]

Principles of Disease

C. tetani is a noninvasive organism. The development of clinical tetanus requires a portal of entry for the infecting spores as well as tissue conditions that promote germination and growth in an immunologically susceptible host. Tetanus-prone wounds are those with damaged or devitalized tissue, foreign bodies, or other bacteria. Under these conditions, *C. tetani* produces the neurotoxin that causes clinical illness. Germination and replication of *C. tetani* can occur without clinical signs of a local wound infection.

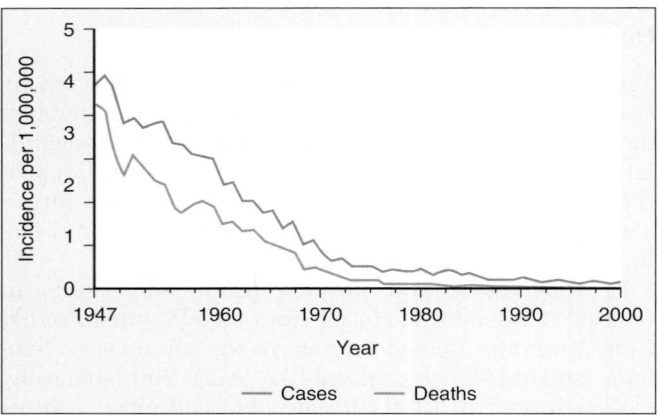
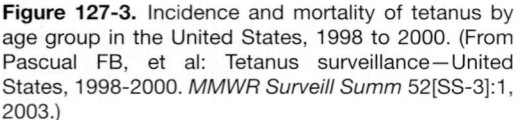

Figure 127-2. Incidence and mortality of tetanus in the United States from 1947 to 2000. (From Pascual FB, et al: Tetanus surveillance—United States, 1998-2000. *MMWR Surveill Summ* 52[SS-3]:1, 2003.)

Figure 127-3. Incidence and mortality of tetanus by age group in the United States, 1998 to 2000. (From Pascual FB, et al: Tetanus surveillance—United States, 1998-2000. *MMWR Surveill Summ* 52[SS-3]:1, 2003.)

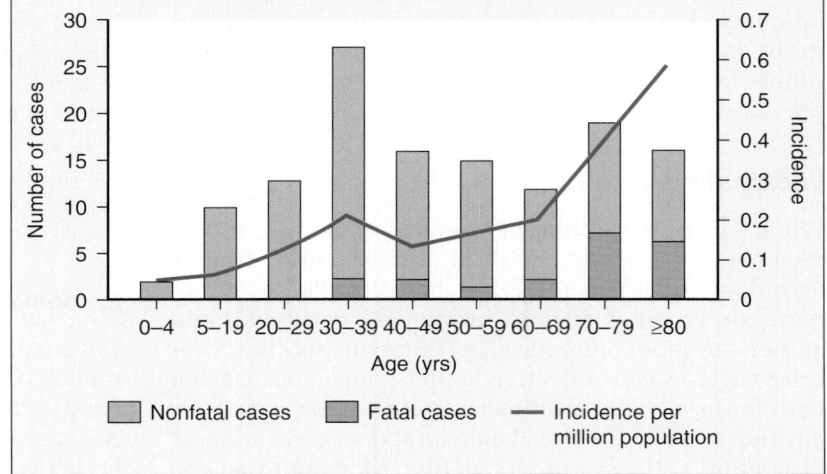

C. tetani produces the neurotoxin tetanospasmin (TS) at the site of tissue injury. TS first binds the motor nerve ending and then moves by retrograde axonal transport and transsynaptic spread to the CNS.[31] It binds preferentially to inhibitory (GABAergic and glycinergic) neurons and blocks the presynaptic release of these neurotransmitters. Interneurons afferent to alpha motor neurons are affected first.[32] Without inhibitory control, the motor neurons undergo sustained excitatory discharge, resulting in the muscle spasm characteristic of tetanus.[27,29]

TS may also affect preganglionic sympathetic neurons and parasympathetic centers, resulting in autonomic nervous system dysfunction.[32] The clinical manifestations include dysrhythmias and wide fluctuations in blood pressure. The binding of TS at the synapse is irreversible; recovery occurs only when a new axonal terminal is produced.[29]

Clinical Features

History and Physical Examination

Tetanus typically occurs as a result of a deep penetrating wound. A history of injury is present in more than 70% of patients, but the injury may be trivial in 50% of patients and unapparent in up to 27% of patients. The majority of infected individuals are inadequately immunized, but tetanus can occur even in patients who are fully vaccinated. The incubation period for tetanus ranges from 1 day to several months. A shorter incubation period portends a worse prognosis.[27] The duration of the incubation period is not useful in making the diagnosis of tetanus because many patients have no history of an antecedent wound.

Four types of clinical tetanus have been described:. *Generalized tetanus* is the most common form of the disease and results in spasms of agonist and antagonist muscle groups throughout the body. The classical initial presenting symptom of trismus ("lockjaw") caused by masseter spasm is present in 50% to 75% of patients. As the other facial muscles become involved, a characteristic sardonic smile (risus sardonicus) appears. Other early symptoms include irritability, weakness, myalgias, muscle cramps, dysphagia, hydrophobia, and drooling. As the disease progresses, generalized uncontrollable muscle spasms can occur spontaneously or as a result of minor stimuli such as touch or noise. Spasms may result in vertebral and long bone fractures and tendon rupture. Opisthotonus is a prolonged tonic contraction that closely resembles decorticate posturing. Spasms of laryngeal and respiratory muscles can lead to ventilatory failure and death. Autonomic dysfunction is the major cause of death in patients who survive the acute phase and is manifest by tachycardia, hypertension, temperature elevation, cardiac dysrhythmias, and diaphoresis. The illness is progressive, with an increase in symptoms over the first 3 days, persistence of symptoms for 5 to 7 days, and reduction of spasms after 10 days. If the patient survives, recovery is complete after 4 or more weeks. Throughout the course of this horrific illness, patients remain completely lucid unless chemically sedated.[29,32]

Localized tetanus is a form of the disease characterized by persistent muscle spasms close to the site of injury. Symptoms may be mild or severe, but mortality is greatly reduced. Although local tetanus may progress to generalized disease, most cases do not. This form of illness may be present for weeks to months before resolution.

Cephalic tetanus is a rare variant of local tetanus that results in cranial nerve palsies as well as muscle spasms. The palsies precede the spasm in 42% of cases, resulting in frequent misdiagnosis. The most commonly involved cranial nerve is the facial nerve (VII), mimicking Bell's palsy. Most of these cases occur after facial trauma or otitis media. Patients develop trismus and palsies of cranial nerve III, IV, VII, IX, X, or XII, ipsilateral to the site of local infection. The clinical course is variable. In one third of cases, resolution of symptoms is complete. Two thirds of cases progress to generalized tetanus, and the overall mortality is 15% to 30%.[29,32]

Neonatal tetanus is generalized tetanus of the newborn and occurs almost exclusively in developing countries, where maternal immunization is inadequate and contaminated material is used to cut and dress umbilical cords. Symptoms begin during the first week of life and include irritability and poor feeding. Mortality approaches 100% because of the high toxin load for body weight and inadequate medical support in developing countries.[29] The CDC reported one case of neonatal tetanus in the United States between 1998 and 2000. The infant was born at home to an unimmunized mother. The umbilical cord had been treated with bentonite clay. The child was treated and recovered after 19 days of hospitalization.[30]

Complications

Acute respiratory failure, the main cause of morbidity and mortality in tetanus, results from respiratory muscle spasms or laryngospasms and airway obstruction. If the patient survives the acute onset of illness and has adequate ventilatory support, cardiovascular complications become the leading cause of death. Autonomic instability occurs several days after the onset of generalized spasms. Disinhibition of the sympathetic nervous system predominates and causes dysrhythmias, hypertension, myocarditis, and pulmonary edema. Dysrhythmias and myocardial infarction are the most common fatal events during this phase.[29]

Forceful tetanic muscle spasms can cause vertebral subluxations and fractures, long bone fractures, and shoulder and temporomandibular joint dislocations. Rhabdomyolysis occasionally occurs and can cause acute renal failure. Renal failure may also result from dehydration and sympathetic nervous system hyperactivity. Renal vein thrombosis may cause renal failure in neonatal tetanus.

Secondary infection may occur in the initial inoculating wound or as a complication arising from invasive treatment modalities such as mechanical ventilation.[32] Hyperthermia may also result from muscle spasms and sympathetic hyperactivity. Pro-

BOX 127-3. Differential Diagnosis of Tetanus

Acute abdomen	Peritonsillar abscess
Black widow spider bite	Progressive fluctuating muscular rigidity (stiff-man syndrome)
Dental abscess	Psychogenic
Dislocated mandible	Rabies
Dystonic reaction	Sepsis
Encephalitis	Status epilepticus
Head trauma	Strychnine poisoning
Hyperventilation syndrome	Subarachnoid hemorrhage
Hypocalcemia	Temporomandibular joint syndrome
Meningitis	

longed immobility can lead to deep venous thrombosis and pulmonary embolism. Gastrointestinal complications include peptic ulcers, ileus, intestinal perforation, and constipation. The syndrome of inappropriate secretion of antidiuretic hormone occurs in a small number of patients. Hemolysis has also been reported.

Mortality is a function of the previous immunization status, incubation period, severity of illness, comorbid disease, age, and the sophistication of medical treatment available.[26,30] With appropriate intensive care treatment, elderly patients may fare as well as their middle-aged counterparts.[33] Long-term physical complications in survivors are rare. The most common persistent problem may be the psychological trauma related to the disease and its treatment.[26]

Diagnostic Strategies

The diagnosis of tetanus should be made on clinical grounds alone. Wound cultures for *C. tetani* are of little value as they are positive in only one third of cases. Even if a positive culture is obtained, it does not indicate whether the bacterium is a toxin-producing strain. There are no laboratory tests to confirm or exclude the diagnosis of tetanus.[26] In 1990 the CDC adopted a clinical case definition for the public health surveillance of generalized tetanus: "acute onset of hypertonia or painful muscular contractions (usually of the muscles of the jaw and neck) and generalized muscle spasms without other apparent medical cause (as reported by a health care professional)."[30]

Lumbar puncture may be indicated to exclude meningitis in the neonate when the diagnosis of tetanus is uncertain. A computed tomography scan is helpful in assessing for intracranial pathology. A serum calcium level is useful to exclude hypocalcemia. Electromyography (EMG) may be useful if the diagnosis of cephalic or localized tetanus is in doubt.[26,29]

Differential Considerations

Strychnine poisoning is the only clinical condition that truly mimics generalized tetanus. Strychnine, like TS, antagonizes glycine release, but unlike TS, it has no effect on γ-aminobutyric acid (GABA) release. Patients develop opisthotonus while remaining alert. The annual incidences of tetanus and strychnine poisoning are similar in the United States, and serum and urine tests for strychnine should be performed when tetanus is suspected.

In patients who present with diffuse generalized spasm, the diagnosis of tetanus is less likely to be missed, but ideally the disease should be considered and diagnosed in the early stages to minimize complications and decrease mortality. Some conditions with clinical similarities to tetanus are listed in Box 127-3. Trismus is most commonly caused by intraoral infections. These can be excluded with careful history and physical examination of the oral cavity and teeth. Mandibular dislocation can be ruled out with appropriate radiographs of the mandible and temporomandibular joints. Dystonic reactions can be differentiated from tetanus by medication history and symptoms that are alleviated by benztropine or diphenhydramine. Patients with encephalitis usually exhibit an altered mental status. Meningitis can be excluded by examining the cerebrospinal fluid (CSF). Rabies must be considered when there are symptoms of brainstem dysfunction, including dysphagia and respiratory muscle dysfunction. A history of exposure to secretions of an infected animal is the most helpful historical point. In addition, rabies does not cause trismus.

Cephalic tetanus is especially difficult to diagnose when the cranial nerve palsy precedes trismus. The differential diagnosis of cephalic tetanus also includes Bell's palsy, botulism, cranial nerve palsies, and facial cellulitis with facial nerve compression and ophthalmoplegia.

Management

Acute Treatment

There are four treatment strategies for patients with tetanus that should be undertaken simultaneously: (1) aggressive supportive care, (2) elimination of unbound TS, (3) active immunization, and (4) prevention of further toxin production.[26,29,30]

Supportive Care

Supportive care begins with control of the muscle spasms. Reflex spasms can result from stimulation of the patient, such as that caused by any movement of the patient or loud noises. Avoidance of unnecessary stimulation is recommended.[32] Benzodiazepines are the mainstay of symptomatic therapy for tetanus. These drugs are GABA agonists and indirectly antagonize many of the effects of TS. They have no effect on the inhibition of glycine release by TS. Diazepam is the most extensively studied of these agents, but lorazepam and midazolam are equally effective. Diazepam has a rapid onset of action, a wide margin of safety, and can be given orally, rectally, or IV. It is inexpensive and thus available in most parts of the world. It has a long cumulative half-life and active metabolites that can cause prolonged sedation and respiratory depression. The IV formulations of diazepam and lorazepam contain propylene glycol, which, at high doses, can produce lactic acidosis.[26] Gastrointestinal delivery of these agents is limited by motility problems associated with tetanus. Midazolam has a short half-life and does not contain propylene glycol, but it must be given by continuous infusion and is cost prohibitive in most areas of the world. Propofol infusion is effective, but it is also expensive and patients may not tolerate the lipid vehicle. Neuroleptics, barbiturates, and intrathecal baclofen have no advantage over benzodiazepines. Dantrolene is a direct muscle relaxant without CNS activity. It has been reported as an adjunctive agent for muscle spasms and may decrease the need for mechanical ventilation.[32,34] Magnesium sulfate infusion has been advocated as both adjuvant and first-line therapy for tetanus. Alone or in combination with other agents, it improves spasm control and is effective at alleviating some of the autonomic instability associated with tetanus toxicity.[29,35]

If spasm cannot be controlled with these regimens or if any signs of airway compromise develop, the patient should receive neuromuscular blockade and mechanical ventilation. Although succinylcholine can be used in the *initial* phase of the disease, the clinician must be aware of the risk of severe hyperkalemia resulting from its use in any neuromuscular disease. This effect does not begin until about 4 days after the onset of disease.[29] Long-acting nondepolarizing agents are preferred, even in the initial phase. Pancuronium has traditionally been used, but it is an inhibitor of catecholamine reuptake and may worsen autonomic instability.[27] Vecuronium and rocuronium are shorter acting and are without significant cardiovascular side effects but require continuous infusion. Whichever agent is used, adequate sedation should be provided and neuromuscular blockade should be withheld at least once a day to assess the patient's status. All intubated patients should be considered for early tracheostomy to decrease reflex spasms caused by the endotracheal tube.[27,32]

Autonomic instability requires monitoring and aggressive treatment. Sympathetic hyperactivity can be treated with combined α- and β-adrenergic antagonists such as labetalol or propranolol. The use of β-antagonists alone can lead to unopposed α-activity resulting in severe hypertension. If β-antagonists are necessary, a short-acting agent such as esmolol should be used.[27] Morphine and magnesium sulfate infusions as well as spinal anesthesia and intrathecal baclofen have all been shown to improve autonomic disfunction.[26,27] Diuretics should be avoided for blood pressure

control as volume depletion can worsen autonomic instability. Bradydysrhythmia should be treated with temporary pacing instead of atropine or sympathomimetic drugs.

Elimination of Unbound Tetanospasmin and Active Immunization

Human tetanus immunoglobulin (TIG) and tetanus toxoid should be administered as soon as possible to all patients with suspected tetanus. TIG does not neutralize toxin already present in the nervous system, nor does it treat any existing symptoms. TIG neutralizes any circulating toxin as well as toxin at the site of production and reduces mortality. TIG should be administered at a site separate from the toxoid. Dosage recommendations vary, with most authorities advising the administration of 3000 to 6000 units of TIG IM (500 units IM in infants). Some sources report equal effectiveness with doses of 500 units. If the larger doses are used, they should be given in divided doses, including administration of a portion of the TIG proximal to the site of inoculation. Local injection of TIG into the wound is of no value. Protective antibody levels are achieved 48 to 72 hours after administration of TIG. Because the half-life of TIG is 25 days, repeated doses are not needed. The preparation of TIG available in the United States is not licensed for intrathecal administration, which is of no proven benefit.[26,28,32]

Prevention of Further Toxin Production

Toxin production is eliminated by treating the *C. tetani* infection. Wound debridement and antibiotic administration can cause a transient release of TS, and the emergency physician should consider delaying these measures until after the TIG is administered. The wound should be debrided and irrigated and any foreign bodies removed. Metronidazole (500 mg orally or IV every 6 hours) is the antibiotic of choice for *C. tetani*. Pediatric doses of metronidazole depend on age and weight. (Neonates <1200 g: 7.5 mg/kg IV every 48 hours; neonates <7 days and >1200 g: 7.5-15 mg/kg/day IV divided every 12-24 hours; neonates >7 days and >1200 g: 15-30 mg/kg/day IV divided every 12 hours; Infants and children: 30 mg/kg/day IV divided every 6 hours, maximum 4 g/day.[28]) Penicillin has traditionally been used to treat tetanus and has good in vitro and in vivo activity against *C. tetani* but also has GABA antagonistic activity and may potentiate the effects of TS. Metronidazole has better penetration into devitalized tissue and abscesses than penicillin and is superior in terms of recovery time and mortality. Macrolides, doxycycline, and tetracycline are effective alternatives in metronidazole-allergic patients.[26,28,29]

Vaccination

Tetanus toxoid is an inactivated form of TS, and vaccination confers protective antibody levels in nearly 100% of people who receive three doses. Immunity wanes between 5 and 10 years after completion of the series. In high-risk patients such as elders, IV drug users, and patients with human immunodeficiency

Table 127-1. Routine Diphtheria, Tetanus, and Pertussis Vaccination Schedule for Children Younger than Seven Years—United States, 1997

Dose	Customary Age	Age/Interval	Product
Primary 1	2 mo	6 wk or older	DTaP or DTP*
Primary 2	4 mo	4-8 wk after first dose†	DTaP or DTP*
Primary 3	6 mo	4-8 wk after second dose†	DTaP or DTP*
Primary 4	15 mo	6-12 mo after third dose†	DTaP or DTP*
Booster	4-6 yr, not needed if fourth vaccination administered after birthday		DTaP or DTP*
Additional booster	Every 10 yr after last dose		Td

*DTaP is preferred; DTP is an acceptable alternative.
†Prolonging the interval does not require restarting the series.
DTaP, diphtheria, tetanus, and acellular pertussis; DTP, diphtheria, tetanus, and pertussis; Td, tetanus and diphtheria.
Modified from Recommended childhood immunization schedule—United States, 1997. *MMWR Morb Mortal Wkly Rep* 46(2):35, 1997.

Table 127-2. Routine Diphtheria and Tetanus Vaccination Schedule Summary for Persons Seven Years and Older—United States, 1991

Dose	Age/Interval	Product
Primary 1	First dose	Td
Primary 2	4-8 wk after first dose*	Td
Primary 3	6-12 mo after second dose*	Td
Booster	Every 10 yr after last dose	Td

*Prolonging the interval does not require restraint series.
Td, tetanus and diphtheria.
Modified from Diphtheria, tetanus, and pertussis: Recommendations for vaccine use and other preventive measures. Recommendations of the Immunization Practices Advisory Committee (ACIP). *MMWR Recomm Rep* 40(RR-10):1, 1991.

virus and other causes of immunocompromise, immunity wanes more quickly and the response to vaccine is less brisk.

Adults with an uncertain history of a complete primary immunization series should receive a primary series. The standard vaccination program consists of a primary series of three tetanus toxoid doses, followed by booster doses every 10 years. Age-specific guidelines for tetanus prophylaxis have been developed by the Immunization Practices Advisory Committee and published by the CDC (Tables 127-1 to 127-3).[29,36]

Tetanus vaccination should be updated for all patients who come to the emergency department for management of a wound, even if the presenting complaint is not wound related.[29] Patients with unknown or uncertain immunization status should be considered to have no previous tetanus immunization. Those younger than 7 years should receive diphtheria-tetanus or DTaP. Patients 7 years of age or older should receive Td instead of DT because adverse reactions from the larger doses of diphtheria toxoid in DT are more common in older individuals.

TIG prophylaxis (250 units IM) is recommended for unimmunized and underimmunized patients with wounds at high risk for tetanus (more than 6 hours old, greater than 1 cm deep, contaminated, stellate, denervated, ischemic, infected). When tetanus toxoid and TIG are given concurrently, separate injection sites

should be used. The only contraindication to tetanus and diphtheria toxoids is a history of a neurologic or severe hypersensitivity reaction to a previous dose. Adverse reactions to tetanus toxoid and tetanus-diphtheria toxoids occur commonly and may be the result of the preservative thiomersal. The most common side effects are minor: local swelling, pain, erythema, pruritis, fever, nausea, vomiting, malaise, and nonspecific rash. Local reactions do not preclude future use of toxoid. Serious anaphylactic reactions are rare. If a patient who requires immunoprophylaxis gives a history suggestive of a neurologic or severe anaphylactic reaction, TIG should be administered alone to protect the patient from developing tetanus as a result of the present injury. TIG does not confer active immunity, and such patients should be referred to an allergist for measurement of antibody levels, antitoxin desensitization, and immunization.[36] No evidence exists that tetanus or diphtheria toxoids are teratogenic. TIG is not contraindicated in pregnancy. For inadequately immunized patients of any age, referral should be made to ensure that the patient receives the remainder of the immunizations required.[36]

BOTULISM

Perspective

History

Botulism is a rare life-threatening paralytic illness caused by neurotoxins produced by *Clostridium botulinum*. The disease usually occurs in one of five forms: food-borne botulism, infant botulism, wound botulism, unclassified botulism, and inadvertent botulism.

In 1820, Kerner, a health officer in Germany, noted an association between sausage ingestion and a paralytic illness, and for a time botulism was known as *Kerner's disease*. The term botulism comes from the Latin *botulus*, for sausage, because of these early descriptions of the disease. Van Ermengem investigated an epidemic of botulism in a group of musicians at a funeral in Belgium in 1895. He isolated the organism from ham and demonstrated that an elaborated toxin produced illness when injected into animals. This toxin was later identified as type A toxin.[37,38]

Table 127-3. Summary Guide to Tetanus Prophylaxis in Routine Wound Management, 1991

History of Absorbed Tetanus Toxoid (Doses)	Clean, Minor Wounds		All Other Wounds*	
	Td[†]	TIG	Td[†]	TIG
Unknown or less than three	Yes	No	Yes	Yes
Three or more[‡]	No[§]	No	No[‖]	No

*Such as, but not limited to, wounds contaminated with dirt, feces, soil, and saliva; puncture wounds; avulsions; and wounds resulting from missiles, crushing, burns, and frostbite.
[†]For children <7 years old; DPT (DT, if pertussis vaccine is contraindicated) is preferred to tetanus toxoid alone. For persons ≥7 years of age, Td is preferred to tetanus toxoid alone.
[‡]If only three doses of *fluid* toxoid have been received, a fourth dose of toxoid, preferably an adsorbed toxoid, should be given.
[§]Yes, if >10 years since last dose.
[‖]Yes, if >5 years since last dose. (More frequent boosters are not needed and can accentuate side effects.)
DPT, diphtheria, pertussis, and tetanus; DT, diphtheria and tetanus; Td, tetanus and diphtheria; TIG, tetanus immune globulin.
Modified from Diphtheria, tetanus, and pertussis: Recommendations for vaccine use and other preventive measures. Recommendations of the Immunization Practices Advisory Committee (ACIP). *MMWR Recomm Rep* 40(RR-10):1, 1991.

Botulism first received attention in the United States during World War I, when housewives were encouraged to preserve fruits and vegetables. The recommended methods for home canning did not destroy the spores of *C. botulinum*. Because these foods were often not adequately heated, epidemics of botulism occurred. Meyer described the circumstances favoring toxin production and the conditions necessary to destroy spores during food processing. Wound botulism was first described in 1949. In 1950 the CDC began surveillance of this form of the disease. Infant botulism, which is now the most common form of the illness, was first described in 1976.[37,38]

Epidemiology

Seven types of toxin (A through G) are produced by *C. botulinum*, but only types A, B, E, and F cause illness in humans. *C. botulinum* spores are found throughout the United States. Type A is found more commonly in the west and type B in the east.[39] Type E is frequently associated with fish products.[37] An average of 110 cases a year are reported to the CDC; 25% are food-borne botulism, 72% are infant botulism, and the rest are wound related.[40]

Typical food-borne botulism results from the ingestion of preformed heat-labile toxin rather than ingestion of spores or live bacteria. Food-borne botulism usually results from exposure to home-canned foods that are inadequately preserved and undercooked, but occasionally large outbreaks occur after the ingestion of contaminated food at restaurants or from commercial sources. A variety of preserved foods have been implicated, and botulism has also been reported to result from ingestion of improperly prepared and stored fresh foods.[41]

Infant botulism is the most common form of the illness in the United States. It occurs in children younger than 1 year with a peak incidence at an age of 3 months. In contrast to food-borne botulism in adults, infant botulism is caused by the ingestion of spores with in vivo production of toxin. Honey and, to a lesser extent, corn syrup have been implicated as sources of *C. botulinum* spores in infant botulism. Soil and vacuum cleaner dust have also been implicated,[39] but the source of ingestion remains unknown in approximately 85% of cases.[41] Type A and B botulinum toxins have been responsible for all infant cases.

Some investigators have explored a possible relationship between infant botulism and the sudden infant death syndrome, but a 10-year prospective study of 248 infants diagnosed with sudden infant death syndrome revealed no cases attributable to *C. botulinum*.[42]

Wound botulism once accounted for approximately one botulism case per year, but the increased use of black tar heroin has resulted in a dramatic increase in cases. In 1994, 11 of the 53 adult botulism cases reported to the CDC were wound botulism. All occurred among injection drug users in California.[43] Toxin types A and B are the causative agents.

Unclassified, hidden, or adult infectious botulism is a rare illness that is analogous to infant botulism. The *Clostridium* bacterium produces its toxin in vivo. Patients with compromised gastric acidity, disturbances of gastrointestinal motility, or abnormal gastrointestinal bacterial flora may be susceptible to in vivo production of botulinum toxin. Between 1976 and 1984, 31 cases were reported to the CDC. Toxin types A, B, and F were identified in these patients. The mortality rate is highest in this form of botulism.[39-41]

Inadvertent botulism is an iatrogenic form of the disease that occurs in patients who have been treated with injections of botulinum toxin for dystonia, other movement disorders, and for cosmetic purposes. Inadvertent generalized weakness as well as unintentional focal weakness may be seen.[38]

The potential exists for botulinum toxin to be used as an offensive biologic weapon. It is highly potent and easy to produce. The Aum Shinrikyo, responsible for the 1995 sarin gas attack on the Tokyo subway, have produced and dispersed aerosols of botulinum toxin in Japan on at least three occasions between 1990 and 1995. In 1995, Iraq admitted to the United Nations that it had produced 19,000 L of concentrated botulinum toxin and loaded approximately 10,000 L into warheads. These 19,000 L are not fully accounted for and constitute three times the amount needed to kill the entire human population by inhalation.[44]

Etiology

C. botulinum is a strictly anaerobic, large gram-positive, rod-shaped organism. It forms spores that germinate under certain environmental conditions. The bacteria may then produce a potent exotoxin that is responsible for the disease. Each strain of *C. botulinum* produces a specific toxin type, either A, B, C, D, E, F, or G. Only types A, B, E, and rarely F produce disease in humans.[37] Botulinum toxins are the most potent biologic compounds known. They are 15,000 to 100,000 times more toxic than sarin, the organophosphate used in the Tokyo subway terrorist attack.[41] Doses as small as 0.05 to 0.1 μg can cause death in humans.[38] The toxins are heat labile. Heating at 100° C for 10 minutes or 80° C for 30 minutes destroys any botulism toxin. Consequently, heating toxin-contaminated food just before ingestion prevents food-borne botulism. Spores are highly heat resistant and can survive at a temperature of 100° C for several hours.[37]

Principles of Disease

Food-borne botulism results from ingesting food that contains preformed toxin. Toxin-contaminated food may have a normal appearance and taste or exhibit signs of food spoilage caused by proteolytic enzymes produced by the type A and B strains. Because of the tremendous potency of the toxin, one taste can expose a person to enough toxin to cause clinical illness. Digestive enzymes do not destroy preformed toxin. Infant and adult infectious botulism results from in vivo bacterial elaboration of toxin in the gastrointestinal tract. Achlorhydria and recent antibiotic use predispose the gastrointestinal tract to colonization with *C. botulinum*. Wound botulism results from in vivo bacterial elaboration of toxin in a wound. Inadvertent botulism results from injection of preformed toxin for medical purposes.[37,38] Primate studies indicate that aerosolized botulinum toxin can also be absorbed systemically through the respiratory tract.[41] Despite the ubiquitous nature of botulinum spores and the variety of possible routes of toxin entry, the incidence of disease is low.

The neurotoxin produced by *C. botulinum* is similar in structure and function to the TS toxin produced by *C. tetani*, but the clinical effects differ dramatically. TS targets inhibitory interneurons in the CNS causing generalized muscle spasm, whereas botulinum toxin targets peripheral neuromuscular junctions and autonomic synapses causing a flaccid paralysis.[45] When botulinum toxin is absorbed from the entry site, it circulates until it reaches the neurons. The toxin binds to the presynaptic nerve membrane, becomes internalized, and then blocks the release of acetylcholine, resulting in neuromuscular blockade. This interference with neurotransmission occurs predominantly at the cholinergic synapses of the cranial nerves, autonomic nerves, and neuromuscular junction. Clinically, this is manifested by cranial nerve palsies, parasympathetic blockade, and a descending, flaccid paralysis. Once affected, the nerve is permanently damaged and recovery requires axonal regeneration and the formation of new synapses, which may take several months.

Clinical Features

History and Physical Examination

Food-borne botulism is the prototype for understanding the clinical signs and symptoms of all forms of botulism. Symptoms begin approximately 18 to 36 hours (range, 2 hours to 14 days) after the ingestion of toxin-containing food.[38] A shorter incubation period is associated with a more severe form of illness. Early symptoms include weakness, malaise, lightheadedness, nausea, vomiting, and constipation. These symptoms are generally not severe and occur in fewer than half of the patients.

Neurologic symptoms may begin at the same time or be delayed in onset for several days. The cranial nerves are first affected. Patients experience diplopia, blurred vision, dysphonia, dysphagia, and dysarthria.[38] Vertigo is also a common symptom. Next, a symmetric descending muscular weakness occurs, involving the upper and lower extremities and the muscles of respiration.[37] Blockade of the cholinergic fibers of the autonomic nervous system leads to a variety of symptoms. Decreased salivation causes a dry mouth, which may be so severe that the patient complains of a painful tongue and sore throat. Ileus and urinary retention may also occur. In one emergency department series of patients with food-borne botulism, all had at least three of the following four symptoms: weakness, dry mouth, double vision, and difficulty speaking. This constellation of symptoms should prompt the emergency physician to inquire about the ingestion of home-canned or improperly prepared food or the presence of similar symptoms in family members or friends.

The patient with botulism is usually alert and afebrile unless secondary infection is present. Postural hypotension may be present. Ocular signs are prominent and include ptosis, extraocular palsies, and markedly dilated and fixed pupils; the absence of ocular abnormalities does not exclude the diagnosis. The oropharynx may be erythematous, with dry mucous membranes.[37] The gag reflex is depressed or absent.

Muscle weakness is usually present and varies from mild to severe. Neck muscles are often weak. Upper extremity muscles are more affected than those of the lower extremity. Proximal muscles are weaker than distal muscles. Deep tendon reflexes may be normal, symmetrically decreased, or absent. The sensory examination is normal. The abdomen may be distended with hypoactive or absent bowel sounds. Bladder distention may be apparent on examination. Respirations may be tachypneic and shallow or normal. In advanced illness, signs of respiratory failure may be present.[37]

Atypical presentations of food-borne botulism have been reported, and certain serotypes produce distinct variations in the pattern of symptoms. Type A disease may be more severe and is more commonly associated with bulbar findings and upper extremity weakness. Types A and B disease may rarely cause a decreased level of consciousness. Type E is associated with a greater incidence of gastrointestinal symptoms.[37,39]

The presentation of *infant botulism* is different from that of food-borne botulism. Constipation is a common presenting symptom, followed by several days to weeks of poor feeding, a weak cry, loss of head control, and hypotonia.[46] On physical examination, the patients have decreased muscle tone and depressed deep tendon reflexes. Cranial nerve involvement causes alterations in facial expression, ptosis, and extraocular palsies. Respiratory failure occurs in 50% of patients. Fever is absent unless secondary infection is present.

Wound botulism has some notable differences from food-borne botulism. The incubation period is longer, from 4 to 14 days, because the toxin must be produced within the wound after the spores have germinated.[37] If the wound is infected, the patient may be febrile. Gastrointestinal symptoms are notably absent in wound botulism. The clinical presentation of *unclassified (adult infectious) botulism* is similar to that of food-borne botulism, although the mortality in the former is significantly greater. Recovery from botulism is slow, and survivors are hospitalized for several weeks to months.[39]

Complications

Complications from botulism are related to respiratory failure and the problems associated with prolonged intensive care management. The major cause of death from botulism is respiratory failure resulting from weakness of the respiratory muscles. Aspiration of oral secretions and gastric contents because of loss of protective airway reflexes can occur. In the past 50 years, the overall mortality rate has decreased from 50% to less than 8% with modern intensive care.[40] In patients who recover, muscle strength and endurance may not return to normal for up to 1 year, and persistent psychological problems are common.[37]

Diagnostic Strategies

The initial diagnosis of botulism is clinical and should be suspected in any patient who presents with the constellation of gastrointestinal, autonomic, and cranial nerve dysfunction. Bilateral cranial nerve involvement and the progression of neurologic findings should increase suspicion. Routine laboratory studies are of no value in the diagnosis. If a lumbar puncture is performed, the CSF in patients with botulism is normal or may show a slight elevation of protein.[39]

The diagnosis is confirmed by detecting (1) botulinum toxin in the patient's blood; (2) botulinum toxin or *C. botulinum* in the gastric contents, stool, or wound of the patient; or (3) toxin or organisms in the suspected food source. Because most hospital laboratories are unable to process such specimens, the CDC should be notified. Serial measurements of the patient's vital capacity are helpful in recognizing deteriorating ventilatory function.

EMG can detect electrophysiologic abnormalities consistent with the diagnosis of botulism.[39] EMG may also be useful in differentiating botulism from other paralytic illnesses. The EMG signature of botulism is decreased amplitude of the compound muscle action potential in response to a supramaximal stimulus and facilitation of the muscle action potential with repetitive nerve stimulation. All motor units are affected, and normal test results do not exclude the diagnosis.[37]

Differential Considerations

The differential diagnosis of *adult botulism* includes a wide variety of illnesses.[37] Commonly, the first presenting case is misdiagnosed. Misdiagnosis occurs because early symptoms suggest diagnoses such as pharyngitis or gastroenteritis, both of which can affect several members of a single household. Only after one or more cases progress to classical botulism is the diagnosis usually suspected.

Botulism must be differentiated from other illnesses that cause paralysis. In Guillain-Barré syndrome, weakness usually starts distally and ascends, paresthesias may be present, and the CSF protein may be elevated. Tick paralysis is an ascending paralysis, notable for a lack of bulbar involvement and the presence of a tick. In myasthenia gravis, eye signs are also prominent, but pupillary response is preserved, no autonomic symptoms are present, and weakness responds to the administration of edrophonium. Of note, minimal improvement in weakness after the administration of edrophonium has been reported in botulism.[37] Poliomyelitis causes fever, asymmetric neurologic signs, and CSF abnormalities. Diphtheria can be distinguished by the prolonged interval between pharyngitis and neurologic symptoms. Eaton-Lambert syndrome does not usually involve bulbar muscles. Cerebrovascular accidents of the brainstem have an acute onset and asymmetric, neuroanatomically localizing signs and symptoms.[37-39]

Certain toxins must also be considered in the differential diagnosis of botulism. Anticholinergics (atropine, belladonna, jimson weed) cause pupillary dilation and dry, red mucous membranes but also cause delirium with alterations in mental status. Organophosphate insecticides have a characteristic odor, and poisoning causes fever and altered mental status. Dystonic reactions are self-limited and respond to diphenhydramine or benztropine. Neuromuscular blockade from the administration of aminoglycosides is distinguished by the medication history. Heavy metal poisoning produces changes in mental status. Magnesium toxicity may mimic botulism, but the history and serum magnesium levels distinguish these entities.[37,39] In paralytic shellfish poisoning, paresthesias are prominent, a history of shellfish ingestion is present, and recovery occurs within 24 hours.[41]

Infant botulism has a broader differential diagnosis. Common illnesses that mimic the presentation of infant botulism include sepsis, various viral illnesses, dehydration, encephalitis, meningitis, and failure to thrive. Neurologic illnesses such as Guillain-Barré syndrome, myasthenia gravis, and poliomyelitis should also be considered. Hypothyroidism, hypoglycemia, Reye's syndrome, diphtheria, and toxin exposures are all in the differential, as are less common conditions such as inborn errors of metabolism, congenital muscular dystrophy, and cerebral degenerative diseases.[46]

Management

The treatment of botulism consists of supportive care and specific treatment with antitoxin and other medications to block the effects of the toxin. All patients with suspected botulism should be admitted to the hospital and placed in an intensive care unit as respiratory failure may develop rapidly and insidiously. When signs of ventilatory failure develop, early endotracheal intubation should be performed. A decrease in vital capacity to less than 12 mL/kg is an appropriate criterion for intubating a patient. Ileus should be treated with nasogastric suction and urinary retention with an indwelling urinary catheter. Fortunately, the autonomic dysfunction of botulism is much less severe than that of tetanus and rarely requires any intervention.[37-39]

Saline enemas and cathartics have been recommended by some authors to cleanse the gastrointestinal tract of residual toxin. Cathartics should not be given if an ileus is present. Magnesium-containing cathartics should be avoided because elevated serum magnesium levels can exacerbate muscle weakness. Special care must be taken when using gastrointestinal clearance in infants with botulism. Because the source of toxin is outside the gastrointestinal tract in wound botulism, bowel decontamination is not indicated.[37,41]

Antitoxin should be administered as soon as possible after appropriate laboratory specimens have been obtained. Early administration prevents the progression of illness, decreases hospital length of stay, prevents respiratory failure, and shortens the duration of respiratory failure in patients with severe disease.[41,47] The antitoxin is an equine trivalent antitoxin preparation that contains antibodies to toxin types A, B, and E. It neutralizes only circulating toxin and has no effect on bound toxin. It can be obtained from the CDC. After skin testing for hypersensitivity, one 10-mL vial should be given IV. This dose results in circulating antitoxin levels capable of binding circulating toxin concentrations many times in excess of those reported in botulism patients. The serum half-life is 5 to 8 days. For these reasons, and contrary to the information in the package insert, only one vial of antitoxin is required. Repeated doses are unnecessary and may increase the risk of hypersensitivity reactions, which occur in approximately 9% of patients.[38,41]

Antitoxin is generally not recommended in infant botulism because efficacy has not been demonstrated and because of the risk of anaphylaxis to horse serum. A human botulism immunoglobulin (BIG) is available in the United States exclusively for the treatment of infant botulism under a treatment investigational new drug protocol. (The California Department of Health can be called for information on this 24 hours a day at 510-540-2646.) BIG reduces hospitalization time and intubation rate.[48]

Antibiotics are not currently recommended for food-borne botulism. Antibiotics may increase cell lysis and promote toxin release. In wound botulism, because the source of toxin is related to in vivo production within an infected wound, debridement and antibiotic administration should be considered only after antitoxin has been administered. Otherwise, the use of antibiotics should be limited to treating secondary infections (e.g., aspiration pneumonia) that may develop. Antibiotic treatment of both infant and wound botulism has no proven benefit. If an antibiotic is used for any reason in a botulism patient, all attempts should be made to avoid the aminoglycosides and tetracyclines as they can impair neuron calcium entry and worsen the effects of botulinum toxin.[37-39]

Guanidine hydrochloride may enhance the release of acetylcholine from terminal nerve fibers. For this reason, it has been recommended as an experimental component of botulism therapy.[37]

The CDC should be called for assistance in any case of suspected botulism. The CDC can be reached by calling 404-639-3311 (days) and 404-639-2540 (nights, weekends, and holidays). State and local health departments may also be helpful in investigating and preventing major epidemics. Area emergency departments should be alerted so that subsequent cases will be suspected and diagnosed.

PNEUMOCOCCEMIA

Perspective

History

More than a century after the identification of *S. pneumoniae* as a pathogen in human disease and more than 50 years after the discovery of antibiotics, pneumococcus remains a significant cause of morbidity and mortality worldwide. Pneumococcemia is defined as the presence of *S. pneumoniae* in the blood. The clinical presentation ranges from a mild illness to a fulminant, life-threatening, systemic syndrome. *S. pneumoniae* also causes myriad localized infections including otitis media, pneumonia, meningitis, and less commonly endocarditis, septic arthritis, and peritonitis.[49]

S. pneumoniae was discovered in 1881 by Sternberg in the United States and simultaneously by Pasteur in France. By the late 1880s it was referred to as "pneumococcus" because it was the most common cause of lobar pneumonia. In 1884 Friedländer described pneumococcemia. In 1902 Cole published the first case reports of pneumococcemia, including a patient who had meningitis and arthritis without pneumonia. In the early 20th century, Maynard, Lister, Wright, and others demonstrated a decreased incidence of pneumonia after inoculating miners with killed pneumococci.[49] In the 1920s, Heidelberg and Avery showed that antibodies to the surface capsular polysaccharide conferred immunity to pneumococcal disease. Two routes to bacteremia were described. Wandel described the migration of *S. pneumoniae* from the lung to the bloodstream by way of the lymphatic system. In 1964, Austrian described bacteria passing directly from the upper respiratory tract (middle ear or sinus) to the subarachnoid space, then through the arachnoid villa and into the venous sinus.[49-51]

An *S. pneumoniae* vaccine was initially developed in the 1940s but was not produced commercially because of the availability of penicillin. The first vaccine was not licensed for use in the United States until 1977. This 14-valent pneumococcal vaccine was replaced in 1983 by a 23-valent vaccine for use in people older than 2 years.[52] The heptavalent conjugate vaccine (Prevnar) is now available and licensed for use in infants younger than 2 years and for other high-risk patients.[53]

Epidemiology

S. pneumoniae remains a substantial cause of serious illness despite the availability of antibiotics and vaccine. Pneumococcal infection appears sporadically in normal individuals and in patients with impaired host defenses. Epidemics of pneumococcal infection occur rarely, although bacterial serotypes may cluster by geographic area. Most cases of pneumococcal infections are community acquired, and the peak incidence is in winter.[49]

The exact incidence of pneumococcemia is unknown because it is not a reportable disease and blood cultures are often not performed in patients with uncomplicated focal pneumococcal infections. In 1997, the CDC estimated 15 to 30 cases per 100,000 population annually in the United States for all people, 50 to 83 cases per 100,000 population annually for those older than 65 years, and 160 cases per 100,000 population annually for children younger than 2 years.[52] The introduction of the heptavalent vaccine for infants has decreased the incidence of disease by 69% in children younger than 2 years.[54] Certain populations, such as Native Alaskans and Native Americans (Apache), have a substantially higher incidence of infection. Studies demonstrate a higher incidence of pneumococcemia in men than in women. Pneumococcemia occurs in 20% to 25% of cases of pneumococcal pneumonia.[55]

People at higher risk for pneumococcemia include those with chronic respiratory or cardiovascular disease, chronic alcohol abuse, cirrhosis, diabetes mellitus, an absent or functionally impaired spleen (i.e., those with splenectomy or sickle cell disease), chronic renal failure, nephrotic syndrome, organ transplantation, lymphoma, Hodgkin's disease, multiple myeloma, and acquired immunodeficiency syndrome (AIDS).[52,55] Pneumococcus is spread from person to person by close contact, and crowded living conditions are associated with epidemics.[49]

The mortality for pneumococcemia is approximately 15% to 20% for young adults and 30% to 40% for elders, those with underlying disease, and those with localized infections such as meningitis.[52] The case fatality rate is significantly lower for children (1% to 7%).[56] The overall mortality rate from pneumococ-

cemia may increase in the future because of the increasing number of elders and AIDS patients and the emergence of antibiotic-resistant strains.

Etiology

Pneumococcemia is caused by *S. pneumoniae*, an encapsulated, gram-positive facultative anaerobic coccus that occurs in pairs and chains. Antigenic differences in the polysaccharide capsule separate *S. pneumoniae* into 90 serotypes.[49] In the United States, the seven serotypes present in Prevnar account for 80% of invasive disease in children younger than 6 years and 50% of invasive disease in people older than 6 years. Worldwide, 10 capsular types account for 62% of invasive disease.[57]

Principles of Disease

S. pneumoniae enters the blood by one of two routes: (1) It begins as a pulmonary infection and spreads to the mediastinal lymph nodes, into the thoracic duct, and then into the circulation. (2) It colonizes or causes infection in the upper respiratory tract and spreads to the subarachnoid space through the arachnoid villi to the venous sinus and into the blood (with or without meningeal involvement).

S. pneumoniae bacteremia causes a clinical picture that ranges from a minor febrile illness to life-threatening septic shock. Different capsules of *S. pneumoniae* confer varying levels of resistance to phagocytosis, resulting in a spectrum of virulence among these serotypes.

The diversity of individual clinical reactions to pneumococcemia is not well understood. Host defenses rely heavily on antibody and complement production, and people who have impaired humoral immunity are more susceptible to invasive pneumococcal disease.[49] Patients who demonstrate substantial host resistance are able to develop active immunity, and one study found that young children can recover spontaneously from blood culture–proven pneumococcemia without antibiotics.[58] In patients with pneumococcal infections, antibodies specific to the capsule serotype develop within several days of onset of infection. This response occurs approximately 30 days after a patient receives the pneumococcal vaccine.[49]

Clinical Features

History and Physical Examination

The clinical presentation of pneumococcemia ranges from mild illness to fulminant disease progressing to death within several hours. Occult bacteremia arises as a febrile illness in which the only direct indication of pneumococcemia is a positive blood culture (most often at 24 to 48 hours). Sepsis is the systemic response to infection, manifested by two or more of the following: (1) temperature greater than 38° C or less than 36° C, (2) heart rate greater than 90 beats/min, (3) respiratory rate greater than 20 breaths/min or partial pressure of carbon dioxide in arterial gas less than 32 mm Hg, and (4) WBC count greater than 12,000/mm^3, less than

4,000/mm^3, or greater than 10% immature (band) forms.[59] Patients may present with lethargy, signs of poor tissue perfusion, cyanosis, and hypoventilation or hyperventilation. Either occult bacteremia or sepsis can occur in conjunction with a localized infection.

The history should include a medical history, recent use of antibiotics, a description of symptoms, including fever, chills, cough, shortness of breath, headache, and rash, and a review of systems. The shaking chills and fever that occur with pneumococcemia are believed to be caused by a toxin. There should be an assessment of the patient's social situation, including availability of caregivers, transportation to medical care, and the ability to comply with discharge instructions.

In children, the clinical presentation of pneumococcemia is similar to that of other common febrile illnesses with the exception of a higher incidence of febrile seizures.[56] Although signs of focal infection such as pneumonia may be present, often the only indication of pneumococcemia is fever or other signs of bacterial toxicity.

Most adult patients have fever or hypothermia. Cough, rigors, pleuritic pain, and gastrointestinal symptoms occur in approximately one third of adult patients. Many patients complain of vague, nonspecific constitutional symptoms similar to those of common viral illnesses. Fever (temperature >38.5° C) occurs in 90% of younger patients but in fewer than 60% of those older than 65 years.[55] Findings on physical examination vary with the site, if any, of localized infection. Patients with signs of sepsis have an increased risk for a fulminant course with rapid deterioration.

Complications

Cardiovascular collapse can occur with fulminant pneumococcal sepsis. Patients who develop severe illness from pneumococcemia may have end-organ damage from inadequate perfusion, disseminated intravascular coagulopathy (DIC), septic emboli, and other complications. These include respiratory failure, meningitis, hypothermia, gastrointestinal bleeding, hepatic coma, renal failure, and myocardial infarction.[55]

Pneumococcemia occasionally results in hematogenous seeding, which causes peritonitis, arthritis, endocarditis, meningitis, and cellulitis.[55,56] Adults and children with functional or anatomic asplenia may develop fulminant pneumococcemia termed *overwhelming postsplenectomy infection (OPSI)*. This is characterized by septic shock, adrenal hemorrhage, and DIC.[59] Although the true incidence of OPSI is unknown, studies demonstrate that it is substantial and that the risk for it does not decrease over time after splenectomy. Most invasive pneumococcal infections occur in the first 2 years after splenectomy, and about two thirds occur between 5 and 20 years. OPSI may initially arise with symptoms indistinguishable from those of common viral illnesses.[60] The 100-fold increased incidence of pneumococcal bacteremia and meningitis in children with sickle cell disease is probably primarily due to splenic dysfunction, but complement abnormalities may also play a role.[49]

Diagnostic Strategies

The only test specific for pneumococcemia is a blood culture that grows *S. pneumoniae*. Ancillary testing of adults with suspected bacteremia should include a complete blood count with differential, blood cultures, urine culture and sensitivity, electrolytes, glucose, serum creatinine, and blood urea nitrogen. A chest radiograph may demonstrate pneumonia as the source of infection. Sputum Gram's stain, culture, and sensitivity testing, if pneumonia is suspected, are of questionable value in the emergency department, but may be useful for continued inpatient care. For sputum specimens to be of value, they should be collected before instituting antimicrobial therapy; however, therapy should not be significantly delayed for the sole purpose of obtaining sputum. Antigen testing of urine for pneumococcal polysaccharide is 86% to 90% sensitive in bacteremic pneumococcal pneumonia.[49]

If the patient appears to be toxic or has signs of respiratory compromise, an arterial blood gas and a coagulation profile should be obtained. If signs of meningitis or alterations in mental status are present, a lumbar puncture should be performed. The WBC count is usually elevated. A normal or low WBC count is suggestive of more serious disease, as are hypoxemia and hypercarbia.[55] Musher and colleagues demonstrated a higher mortality rate in patients with serum creatinine levels higher than 2.0 mg/dL, bilirubin levels higher than 1.5 mg/dL, and albumin levels less than 2.5 g/dL.[55]

Differential Considerations

Pneumococcemia in its more benign presentation must be differentiated from other febrile illnesses, such as viral infections. The combination of clinical findings and culture results enables the emergency physician to make the distinction between bacteremia and sepsis of other origins. The presence of fever and shock, with or without a distinct rash, suggests the possibility of sepsis caused by *H. influenzae*, *Neisseria meningitidis*, and other streptococcus types.

Management

Acute Treatment

Managing pneumococcemia consists of stabilizing life-threatening conditions, eradicating the infection, and treating predisposing or coexisting conditions. The decision to initiate antibiotic therapy for pneumococcemia is often made with limited objective data, which include the clinical findings, the patient's age, underlying conditions, and preliminary laboratory studies.

Elimination of the *S. pneumoniae* organism by prompt initiation of antibiotics is essential for reducing the morbidity and mortality of pneumococcal infection. Antibiotic administration should begin in the emergency department. To simplify selection of a treatment strategy, patients can be divided into three groups:

1. *Bacteremia or sepsis is suspected on the basis of clinical findings; however, the organism has not been identified.* The patient in this group is given

broad-spectrum antibiotics initially, with the selection based on factors that include the most likely organism or organisms, the patient's age (neonate, child, adult, or elder) and immune status, the presence of coexisting disorders, and local patterns of antibiotic resistance. The antibiotic regimen is changed to a narrower spectrum drug after positive identification of the organism and its sensitivities.

2. S. pneumoniae *growth is reported from cultures of blood drawn (usually 1 to 2 days) previously.* The treatment regimen for "occult bacteremia" is guided by the patient's age, history, physical examination, general appearance, and ancillary tests. Often, the antibiotic selected on the initial visit for a localized infection (e.g., amoxicillin) is sufficient to treat the pneumococcal bacteremia subsequently identified by the laboratory. The patient should be re-evaluated promptly and repeated blood cultures should be obtained. The decision to admit a child for inpatient care is based on the findings at the time of re-evaluation.

3. *Bacteremia or sepsis is suspected and* S. pneumoniae *is identified from a site of local infection, such as a Gram stain of sputum.* The antibiotic regimen is focused narrowly.

The adult patient with laboratory-proven pneumococcemia is treated with penicillin G, 6 to 12 million units/day in divided doses every 4 hours IV. If the organism is susceptible, pneumococcemia with meningitis is treated with up to 24 million units of penicillin G per day.[49] In children, the dosage for meningitis is 250,000 units/kg per 24 hours in divided doses every 4 hours IV up to a maximum of 20 million units. When meningitis is present, the drug selected must penetrate the CSF and attain acceptable concentrations.

IM ceftriaxone is commonly administered to children with suspected bacteremia who are treated as outpatients while blood culture results are pending. Ceftriaxone (initial dose of 50 to 100 mg/kg IV, followed by daily dosage of 100 mg/kg in divided doses every 12 hours, up to a maximum of 4 g) and cefotaxime (200 mg/kg/day in divided doses every 6 hours IV, up to a maximum of 12 g) offer the advantage of being excellent antibiotics for *N. meningitidis* and *H. influenzae.* Alternatives for the treatment of pneumococcemia in a penicillin-allergic patient include cefotaxime, ceftriaxone, vancomycin, and chloramphenicol. The decision to use cephalosporins or one of the other drugs is based on the type of allergic reaction to penicillin reported by the patient. Chloramphenicol has the associated risk of toxicity and interaction with anticonvulsant medications.

Penicillin-resistant *S. pneumoniae* has emerged.[49] The overall susceptibility of pneumococcus in the United States is 75%, but it varies substantially by geographic area.[49,61] Many of the penicillin-resistant strains demonstrate resistance to other antibiotics. Other antibiotics that can be used to treat pneumococcemia include ceftriaxone, cefotaxime, and vancomycin. A total of 16.4% of the isolates are resistant to one or more of the following drugs: penicillin, cephalosporins, macrolides, chloramphenicol, and trimethoprim-sulfamethoxazole. Macrolide resistance is present in 30% of *S. pneumoniae* isolates but in 67% of isolates that are highly resistant to penicillin.[61]

The recommended IV doses of penicillin and other β-lactam antibiotics generally achieve serum concentrations many times greater than the minimal inhibitory concentrations (MICs) for *S. pneumoniae* of intermediate resistance and, in some cases, even for highly resistant strains. For suspected high-level penicillin-resistant strains, it is recommended that vancomycin, imipenem, or extended-spectrum cephalosporins (with MICs < 8.0 μg/mL) be selected. Treatment of meningitis caused by penicillin-resistant *S. pneumoniae* presents a unique problem because of the high antibiotic concentration required to sterilize the CSF. Ceftriaxone and cefotaxime are preferred for empirical treatment of suspected pneumococcal meningitis; however, treatment failures have been reported. In areas where resistance to extended-spectrum cephalosporins is prevalent, empirical therapy with vancomycin plus cefuroxime or cefotaxime should be considered.[49,61] Area susceptibility patterns should guide antibiotic selection. The patient with pneumococcemia may not have an obvious response to treatment for the first 24 to 48 hours of therapy. This may be attributed to the normal course of the disease, an incorrect diagnosis, underlying illness, or an antibiotic regimen that does not treat the infection sufficiently.

Disposition of the patient depends on three factors: the patient's age, overall clinical condition, and the presence of coexisting illnesses. Toxic-appearing patients of any age should be promptly treated with antibiotics and admitted to the hospital. Patients with underlying or coexisting conditions and those with an unclear course of illness should also be admitted.

Children who are afebrile and appear well at the time of the initial examination are unlikely to have serious sequelae develop.[58] A large randomized, controlled trial involving 37,868 infants showed that invasive pneumococcal disease is rare in children who have received the heptavalent pneumococcal vaccine. Children were observed for 3 years. There was only one case of bacteremic pneumonia in a patient who had received all four doses of vaccine and two cases in children who had received one dose; one of these children had developed acute myelogenous leukemia after entering the study and was receiving immunosuppressive chemotherapy.[62] It is important to note that the heptavalent vaccine contains serotypes responsible for only 85% of pneumococcal disease in infants and children. The decision to treat a febrile child with antibiotics and discharge should be based on clinical findings, medical history, ability of the parents to follow the discharge instructions, and availability of close follow-up.

Vaccination

The pneumococcal vaccine is effective in preventing infection; the currently available 23-valent vaccine contains the purified polysaccharide antigens of the

BOX 127-4. CDC Recommendations for the Use of the 23-Valent Pneumococcal Vaccine

- Immunocompetent adults with chronic illnesses
  - Cardiovascular or pulmonary disease
  - Diabetes mellitus
  - Alcoholism or cirrhosis
  - CSF leaks
  - Those 65 years of age or older
- Immunocompromised adults including those with:
  - Splenic dysfunction or asplenia
  - Hodgkin's disease, lymphoma, or leukemia
  - Multiple myeloma
  - Chronic renal failure or nephrotic syndrome
  - Alcoholism
  - Organ transplantation associated with immunosuppression
- Adults and children older than 2 years with asymptomatic HIV infections
- Children older than 2 years with chronic illness
  - Anatomic or functional asplenia (including sickle cell disease)
  - Nephrotic syndrome
  - CSF leak
- Other conditions associated with immunosuppression
- Persons living in special environments or social settings with an identified increased risk (e.g., certain Native American populations)
- The vaccine is not indicated for children having only recurrent upper respiratory tract disease, such as otitis media and sinusitis

CDC, Centers for Disease Control and Prevention; CSF, cerebrospinal fluid; HIV, human immunodeficiency virus.

BOX 127-5. CDC and AAP Recommendations for the Use of the Seven-Valent Vaccine

- All children ages 2 to 23 months at 2, 4, 6, and 12 to 15 months.
- Children age 24 to 59 months who are at high risk of pneumococcal disease including those with:
  - Sickle cell disease
  - HIV infection
  - Other immunocompromising medical conditions
  - This should be followed by the 23-valent vaccine 2 months after the 7-valent vaccine is given.
- Consider for all children 24 to 59 months with priority given to the following:
  - Those aged 24 to 35 months
  - Alaskan natives, Native Americans, and African Americans
  - Children who attend daycare

AAP, American Academy of Pediatrics; CDC, Centers for Disease Control and Prevention; HIV, human immunodeficiency virus.

---

serotypes that cause 85% to 90% of pneumococcemia infections in the United States.[52] Although the overall protective efficacy of the vaccine is only 56% to 57%, it is safe, inexpensive, and of substantial value for well-defined groups at risk.[52] Unfortunately, the 23-valent pneumococcal vaccine has limited immunogenicity in children younger than 2 years. The seven-valent conjugate vaccine links the polysaccharide to proteins, resulting in an improved immunogenic response in children younger than 2 years.[57]

The CDC recommendations for the use of the 23-valent vaccine are given in Box 127-4.[57]

The CDC and AAP recommendations for the use of the seven-valent vaccine are listed in Box 127-5.[57]

The Immunization Practices Advisory Committee on pneumococcal vaccine recommends that revaccination be strongly considered at 6 years of age or older for people who are most likely to have a rapid decline of pneumococcal antibodies (e.g., patients with renal failure, transplant recipients, and nephrotic syndrome) and for those at risk for fatal infection (e.g., asplenic patients). Children 10 years of age or younger with nephrotic syndrome, sickle cell anemia, or asplenia should be considered for revaccination after 3 to 5 years. Patients who have received the old 14-valent vaccine should not be routinely vaccinated with the newer 23-valent vaccine. Other preventive measures for pneumococcemia include passive immunization with immunoglobulins for patients with congenital or acquired immunodeficiency diseases and daily antibiotic prophylaxis for children with functional or anatomic asplenia.[10]

MENINGOCOCCEMIA

Perspective

History

Few clinical situations in emergency medicine produce greater fear, stress, or awe than meningococcal infection. Virtually all experienced emergency physicians have had a patient who appeared relatively well on initial presentation, only to be moribund and in critical condition with fulminant infection several hours later.

"Cerebrospinal fever" was initially described in 1805 by Vieusseaux in Geneva. Weichselbaum identified the causative bacterial agent in 1887.[63] Throughout the 19th and first half of the 20th centuries, epidemics occurred periodically in most regions of the world. "Serum therapy" was introduced in France in 1907 and in the United States in 1913 as the first specific treatment of meningococcal disease. The introduction of sulfonamide therapy in 1937 replaced serotherapy and dramatically improved the outcome of meningococcal infection. Sulfonamide prophylaxis was also effective at eradicating the carrier state and was used to prevent the epidemics that occurred in military barracks. Not surprisingly, in the 1940s sulfonamide resistance began to emerge. In 1963, an outbreak of resistant meningococcal disease occurred in the United States, which spurred efforts to develop a vaccine for this devastating infection.[63] Subsequent worldwide resistance has resulted in continued efforts to develop safe and effective vaccines.

Epidemiology

In the United States, 2400 to 3000 cases of meningococcal infection are reported to the CDC annually. Of the more than 13 serogroups, groups A, B, C, Y, and W-135 cause most of the infections. More outbreaks in the United States are caused by serogroups B and C, although the incidence of outbreaks caused by group Y has increased. More than half of the cases in infants are caused by serogroup B, for which there is no effective vaccine.[64] Although grouping is important for tracking the disease, all groups are capable of causing the same spectrum of clinical disease.

The incidence of meningococcal disease peaks in the winter and falls in the summer. Superimposed on this annual variation are cyclical peaks of disease every 5 to 15 years. Approximately every 10 years massive outbreaks of serogroup A occur in sub-Saharan Africa (the "meningitis belt"). The last outbreak was in 1996 and 1997.[65] During nonepidemic periods, children younger than 5 years have the highest incidence of infection. During epidemics, the incidence increases among children ages 5 to 9, an observation that may be of value in predicting the beginning of an epidemic. Crowded living conditions increase the risk of spread of meningococcal disease. The incidence of disease and the carrier state are several times higher among military recruits in the first few weeks of service than in the general public. This is also true of college freshmen, particularly those living in dormitories or residence halls. Other risk factors for developing invasive meningococcal disease include close contact with an infected patient, complement deficiency, properdin deficiency, asplenia, chronic alcohol abuse, active and passive smoking, corticosteroid use, and recent respiratory illness.[64]

The overall mortality rate of meningococcal disease is 10% in the United States. Septicemia without meningitis carries a much higher mortality rate (20% to 60%) than meningitis alone (2% to 5%).[63,65]

Etiology

Meningococcal disease is caused by *N. meningitidis*, a fastidious, aerobic, gram-negative diplococcus. *N. meningitidis* is an encapsulated organism classified into at least 13 serogroups on the basis of the capsular polysaccharides.[63]

Principles of Disease

N. meningitidis attaches to nonciliated epithelial cells in the nasopharynx using a number of adhesion factors. Once attached, it may either remain on the epithelial surface, causing an asymptomatic carrier state, or produce mild symptoms of an upper respiratory tract infection. In certain patients the bacteria enter the bloodstream and cause symptoms and signs of localized infection, bacteremia, sepsis, or fulminant infection. The precise host and microorganism characteristics that determine whether clinical disease develops are not fully understood. Complement deficiency may play a role in a host's inability to fight this infec-

tion. The capsule is required for *N. meningitidis* to adhere to epithelium, but only unencapsulated meningococci enter epithelial cells. The release of lipooligosaccharide endotoxin by lysis of the *N. meningitidis* cell is the initial event in the development of meningococcal sepsis. The exogenous mediators appear to stimulate the release of endogenous mediators, including tumor necrosis factor, interleukin-1, and the host's complement system. All of the major pathophysiologic events of meningococcal sepsis are caused by the host's inflammatory response to disease. The complement-activating products and other chemical mediators cause functional and histologic damage to the microvasculature resulting in increased vascular permeability, pathologic vasoconstriction and vasodilation, loss of thromboresistance, DIC, and profound myocardial dysfunction.[66]

After exposure to *N. meningitidis*, protective antibodies develop. Immunity in children is conferred initially by maternal antibodies that pass through the placenta and later by the development of antibodies after exposure to the bacteria. In children, the incidence of meningococcal disease is inversely proportional to the levels of antibodies against *N. meningitidis*.[66]

Clinical Features

History and Physical Examination

The clinical presentation of meningococcemia ranges from a mild febrile illness to fulminant disease progressing to death within hours.[63] Approximately 90% of patients will have fever on presentation.[67] Other initial complaints include irritability, lethargy, myalgias, emesis, diarrhea, cough, and rhinorrhea. Only 60% of patients have the classical signs of meningococcal infection: fever and petechiae or purpura.

Occult bacteremia arises as a febrile illness in which the only direct indication of meningococcemia is a positive blood culture with results available most often 24 to 48 hours after the clinical evaluation. In its mildest form, meningococcal bacteremia cannot be readily distinguished from more benign febrile illnesses. Initial diagnoses in these patients include common childhood infections such as otitis media, acute viral upper respiratory infections, and gastroenteritis. Some patients have resolution of their illness after treatment with an oral regimen of antibiotics. In one study, three patients who were initially bacteremic had spontaneous resolution without antibiotic treatment. *N. meningitidis* accounts for 1% to 5% of occult bacteremia cases, but these patients are much more likely to develop meningitis (up to 58%) than those with *S. pneumoniae*. Also, despite the total absence of clinical clues to meningococcal infection at initial presentation, some untreated patients subsequently deteriorate rapidly.[67]

Patients with meningococcal meningitis may present in the same way as patients with meningitis of other etiologies with headache, photophobia, vomiting, fever, and signs of meningeal inflammation. This classical constellation of symptoms and signs is present in less than half of the patients. Infants and small children may present with fever, irritability, and vomiting as the only complaints. More than half of patients with meningococcal meningitis have rash on presentation and 20% present with seizures.[67,68] Patients with meningococcal meningitis have a less abrupt onset of symptoms (usually over 24 hours) and a better prognosis than those with meningococcemia without clinical signs of meningitis.

Patients with meningococcemia present with lethargy, poor tissue perfusion, cyanosis, and hypoventilation or hyperventilation. Petechiae are present in 50% to 60% of patients, but macular and maculopapular lesions also occur.[67] Petechiae generally appear first on the ankles, wrists, and axillae and may appear under pressure points such as the elastic bands of socks and underwear. They may progress to involve almost any body surface including the mucosa but typically spare the palms, soles, and head. Macular lesions may progress to purpura and ecchymoses in fulminant meningococcemia. The purpurae are not a coalescence of petechiae but a distinct entity that more specifically characterizes meningococcemia. Purpura fulminans occurs most often in children and is usually associated with DIC. This condition is characterized by rapidly spreading ecchymoses and gangrene of the extremities. Clinical signs of meningitis and CSF pleocytosis may not be present, even when diplococci are isolated from the CSF.[63] This is probably because the systemic progression of the disease is so rapid that it precludes a host meningeal inflammatory response to the organism in the CSF.

The most dreaded manifestation of the disease is fulminant meningococcemia, the Waterhouse-Friderichsen syndrome. It occurs in 10% to 20% of patients with meningococcal disease and is characterized by extreme severity of illness and rapid clinical deterioration, including vasomotor collapse and shock.[69] This dramatic example of DIC is an overwhelming disease in which the patient rapidly develops severe toxicity because of the endotoxin-mediated process. Usually a diffuse petechial and purpuric rash is present with extensive intracutaneous hemorrhage. Shock results from both intravascular volume loss and congestive heart failure, probably related to myocarditis. DIC develops with hemorrhage or thrombus formation and arterial embolization. Renal failure, coma, and bilateral adrenal hemorrhage often occur.[69]

Chronic meningococcemia is a syndrome characterized by fever, rash, and joint complaints of longer than 1 week in conjunction with a positive blood culture for *N. meningitidis*. Headache and upper respiratory symptoms are often present. This is the rarest form of meningococcal disease, accounting for 1% to 2% of cases. It may progress to meningitis, endocarditis, or fulminant meningococcemia regardless of treatment.[63,69]

Complications

The most common complication of meningococcemia is myocarditis with congestive heart failure or conduction abnormalities. Many of the inflammatory mediators released during sepsis cause myocardial dysfunction, and the severity of sepsis is related to the degree of impairment of myocardial contractility.[66] Acute respiratory failure occurs secondary to capillary leak in the patient who requires volume resuscitation. It is also likely that intrapulmonary DIC contributes to the pulmonary edema, and patients frequently require mechanical ventilation. Renal failure is common secondary to impaired renal perfusion; acute tubular necrosis may develop.[66] If meningitis accompanies meningococcemia, cranial nerve dysfunction may occur acutely, with residual effects in some cases. Children may have subdural effusions. Vasculitis in severe cases of meningococcal septicemia may result in skin lesions that necessitate plastic surgery and loss of digits or limbs resulting from gangrene.[69] Purulent arthritis may also occur.

Poor prognostic indicators in meningococcemia include seizures on presentation, hypothermia, hyperpyrexia, a total peripheral WBC count of less than 500/mm³, a platelet count of less than 100,000/mm³, the development of purpura fulminans, the onset of petechiae within 12 hours of admission, absence of meningitis, the presence of shock, a low sedimentation rate, and extremes of age.[67] In one study, all patients who developed organ system failure had one or more of the following at the time of initial presentation: circulatory insufficiency (hypotension or shock), peripheral WBC count less than 10,000 cells/mm³, or a coagulopathy.

Herpes labialis occurs in 5% to 20% of patients with meningococcal disease. Septic arthritis and immune complex–mediated arthritis may also occur, and neither typically results in permanent joint changes.[70]

Diagnostic Strategies

The tentative diagnosis of meningococcemia is based on clinical findings. The diagnosis is confirmed by the isolation of *N. meningitidis* from blood cultures or any other usually sterile site such as CSF or synovial, pleural, or pericardial fluid. Ideally, blood cultures should be obtained before the administration of antibiotics unless this unduly delays the patient's treatment. Blood cultures are positive in just over 50% of cases. The CSF shows either gram-negative diplococci on Gram's stain or a positive culture in more than 90% of cases. Even patients without clinical signs of meningitis frequently have the organism grown from the CSF, and lumbar puncture should be performed. Gram's stain of petechial scrapings may show gram-negative diplococci in up to 70% of cases, and rarely, the organism can be seen in the peripheral blood buffy coat.[67] Highly specific antigen tests for blood and CSF are available but sensitivity is low.[69] PCR of the buffy coat or CSF is more sensitive and specific than any of the preceding tests and is not affected by prior antibiotic therapy.[69]

Ancillary laboratory tests are of little value in establishing a specific diagnosis of meningococcal sepsis but may be useful in ruling out other disease, determining prognosis, and monitoring complications. The WBC count may be high, low, or normal, but a bandemia is typically present. The symptoms and signs of CNS infection may be nonspecific in the infant and child younger than 2 years. If meningitis is present, the CSF opening pressure is usually elevated, the protein level is increased, and the glucose level is decreased. Pleocytosis is usually present, with a predominance of polymorphonuclear leukocytes. Gram-negative diplococci may be seen on microscopy. Early in the disease or with fulminant disease, the CSF may be free of inflammatory cells.[63,67,69] Serologic evidence of DIC is frequently present.

Differential Considerations

It is difficult to distinguish the clinical signs of meningococcemia from those of bacteremia caused by *S. pneumoniae,* other streptococcal groups, *H. influenzae,* and *Neisseria gonorrhoeae.* The differential diagnosis of meningococcemia also includes viral exanthems, Rocky Mountain spotted fever, typhus, typhoid fever, endocarditis, vasculitis syndromes (polyarteritis nodosa and Henoch-Schönlein purpura), toxic shock syndrome, acute rheumatic fever, drug reactions, idiopathic thrombocytopenic purpura, and thrombotic thrombocytopenic purpura.[67,69]

In one study of 184 children hospitalized with fever and petechiae, 24 (11%) had proven *N. meningitidis.* The remainder had viral or other etiologies. These data were acquired prior to the initiation of a vaccination program.[71]

Management

Acute Treatment

Morbidity and mortality in meningococcemia are reduced with prompt recognition and immediate initiation of antibiotic therapy. Delays in initiating therapy for the completion of diagnostic studies or admission to an inpatient unit should be avoided. To simplify selection of a treatment strategy, patients can be divided into three general groups:

1. *Bacteremia or sepsis is suspected on the basis of clinical findings; however, the organism has not been identified.* These patients should receive broad-spectrum antibiotics, with selection based on factors that include the most likely organism or organisms, the patient's age and immune status, the presence of coexisting disorders, and local patterns of antibiotic resistance. A narrower spectrum agent is selected after positive identification of the organism and its sensitivities.
2. *N. meningitidis growth is reported from prior blood cultures.* The treatment regimen for occult bacteremia is guided by the patient's age, history, physical examination, general appearance, and ancillary tests. The antibiotic selected at the time of the initial visit may be sufficient to treat the meningococcal bacteremia subsequently identified by the labora-

tory. The decision to hospitalize the patient is based on the findings at the time of re-evaluation and the risk of sequelae. Regardless of the patient's clinical appearance, most physicians would redraw blood for cultures, consider lumbar puncture, and admit the patient to the hospital until results of repeated cultures are obtained.

3. *Bacteremia or sepsis is suspected and N. meningitidis is identified.* The antibiotic regimen is focused narrowly.

The standard antibiotic regimen for laboratory-proven meningococcemia is penicillin G, 24 million units/day in divided doses every 2 to 4 hours IV for adults, and penicillin, 250,000 to 300,000 units/kg/day in divided doses every 2 to 4 hours IV for children up to a maximum of 20 million U, or ampicillin, 200 to 400 mg/kg/day in four divided doses IV. Penicillin resistance in *N. meningitidis* remains low in the United States but has been reported in Spain and the United Kingdom.[63,72] The emergency physician should keep informed of any emerging resistance patterns in his or her practice area.

Acceptable alternatives to penicillin include cefotaxime (200 mg/kg/day IV in divided doses every 6 hours up to a maximum of 12 g) and ceftriaxone (initial dose of 100 mg/kg IV, followed by daily dosage of 100 mg/kg in divided doses every 12 hours up to a maximum of 4 g). The cephalosporins offer the advantages of safety, rapid onset of action, and excellent coverage for *S. pneumoniae* and *H. influenzae.* Chloramphenicol (75 to 100 mg/kg every 6 hours to a maximum of 4 g/day) is also acceptable.[69] Ceftriaxone IM is commonly administered to children with suspected bacteremia who are treated as outpatients while culture results are pending. Alternatives for treating meningococcemia in a penicillin-allergic patient include cefotaxime, ceftriaxone, and chloramphenicol. The decision to use cephalosporins or one of the other alternative drugs is based on the type of allergic reaction to penicillin reported by the patient.

Several reports have demonstrated the efficacy of ceftriaxone, 80 to 100 mg/kg IV in a single daily dose; however, twice-daily dosing remains the standard recommendation at this time. In addition to the obvious advantage of extended dosing intervals, ceftriaxone-treated patients have a more rapid sterilization of the CSF and a lower incidence of hearing loss than conventionally treated patients.

Patients with fulminant meningococcemia require prompt airway management, IV fluid resuscitation, and vasopressor support. Fluid requirements may be high because of third spacing of fluid, and in the setting of frequent myocardial dysfunction, intensive cardiovascular monitoring is required. Electrolyte and acid-base abnormalities should be corrected. If the patient is oliguric or anuric, hemodialysis may be necessary to correct these abnormalities. Fresh frozen plasma should be given to patients with bleeding complications.[63,67,69]

The role of steroids for the treatment of meningococcemia without meningitis remains controversial.

Although corticosteroids were once widely recommended for the treatment of the adrenal insufficiency associated with fulminant meningococcemia, more recent studies demonstrate that adrenal function is not impaired in all patients. If a patient has persistent shock despite vigorous fluid resuscitation with or without vasopressor therapy, glucocorticoid therapy should be initiated and adrenal function tested.[69]

The use of corticosteroids in patients with bacterial meningitis has been controversial. The most recent clinical data show that corticosteroid administration prior to antibiotics decreases mortality and long-term neurologic sequelae in adults and children. Dexamethasone (10 mg in adults) prior to antibiotics and every 6 hours for 4 days should be given to patients with meningitis.[63,73,74] Future therapeutic adjuncts to antibiotics may include the development of recombinant proteins that bind and neutralize either the bacteria's endotoxins or endogenous mediators.[69]

Antibiotic Prophylaxis and Vaccination

Patients with meningococcemia should be placed in respiratory isolation for at least 24 hours. Close contacts should receive antibiotic prophylaxis. Household, nursery school, and daycare center contacts should receive prophylaxis promptly. Intimate contacts and health care workers with intimate exposure (e.g., mouth-to-mouth resuscitation, intubation, or suctioning) should receive rifampin, 10 mg/kg (up to 600 mg) orally every 12 hours for four doses.[69] The dose for infants younger than 1 month is 5 mg/kg. Patients should be warned that rifampin discolors the urine, and contact lenses should be removed to avoid permanent staining. Ceftriaxone IM (125 mg for children younger than 12 years and 250 mg for those older than 12) is effective against group A strains. This is an alternative for pregnant women and for people in whom compliance with an oral regimen cannot be ensured. Ciprofloxacin (500 mg orally) is another alternative for adults.[10,64] Nasopharyngeal cultures are of no value when assessing who should receive prophylaxis.[10]

Meningococcal vaccine should be considered as an adjunct to prophylaxis in epidemics and for close contacts in sporadic cases if one of the serotypes contained in the vaccine is identified as the causative agent. The currently available vaccine is a quadrivalent vaccine containing purified capsular polysaccharides for groups A, C, Y, and W-135. Unfortunately, the polysaccharides other than A are poor immunogens for children younger than 2 years. In addition, no vaccine exists for group B, the most prevalent serogroup that causes meningococcal infection in the United States. The quadrivalent vaccine is not recommended for routine use but should be administered to children 2 years of age and older in high-risk groups, such as those with functional or anatomic asplenia and those with terminal complement deficiency.[64] The vaccine is currently administered to U.S. military recruits. Consideration should be given to vaccinating people traveling to endemic areas of the world such as sub-Saharan Africa.[69]

KAWASAKI'S DISEASE

Perspective

History

Kawasaki's disease (KD) is an acute febrile systemic vasculitis of unknown etiology. It was first described in Japan in 1967 by Tomisaku Kawasaki as *acute febrile mucocutaneous lymph node syndrome.* In 1968 Yamamoto noted that cardiac involvement was a common feature of the disease. In 1974 Kawasaki and colleagues published the first English language report of this syndrome.[75,76] In the early 1970s Melish and Hicks at the University of Hawaii independently described the same disease in children.[76] KD has now replaced acute rheumatic fever as the leading cause of acquired heart disease in children in North America and Japan. Prior to Kawasaki's clinical description, infantile periarteritis nodosa (IPN) had been described on postmortem study, and it is likely that IPN is a severe form of KD.[76,77]

The precise cause of the disease is still not well understood, and no definitive diagnostic test exists. During the 30 years that KD has been a recognized disease, myriad microorganisms and environmental conditions have been implicated as etiologic agents. Understanding of this disease is in its infancy, and current and future research is likely to bring landmark discoveries.

Epidemiology

Although possible cases of KD have been reported in adults, it is overwhelmingly a disease of young children. The peak incidence occurs at 1 to 2 years of age, and 85% of cases occur in children younger than 5 years.[76,78] Fewer than 1% of cases occur in children older than 9 years.[79]

KD is most prevalent in Asian countries and in people of Asian descent but is recognized worldwide. In the United States, whites have a lower incidence of disease than other groups. The annual incidence in Japan is 5000 to 6000 cases, or about 100 cases per 100,000 children younger than 5 years. It is estimated that there are at least 3000 cases annually in the United States, which amounts to approximately 10 cases per 100,000 children younger than 5 years. Males are affected more often than females (ratio 1.5:1) and have a greater risk of developing coronary artery aneurysms.[78-80] There is a seasonal variation of KD with a peak incidence in late winter and early spring. Despite the epidemic nature of the disease, person-to-person spread does not appear to occur.

The overall mortality in KD is less than 2.5%, and death is usually a result of cardiac complications. Of note, no deaths were reported in a 2003 review of 4248 hospitalized patients with KD over a 3-year period in the United States.[81]

Etiology

The etiology of KD is unclear despite 30 years of extensive research. An infectious agent is suggested by the following observations: KD has a seasonal peak in winter and spring; epidemics occur with a clear epicenter; the peak age group is toddlers with a few rare cases in infants, suggesting a role for transplacental antibodies in protection; the recurrence rate is low (3% in Japan and 1% in North America), suggesting acquired immunity; and KD has many clinical manifestations similar to those of known infectious diseases (e.g., scarlet fever, measles).[77,80,81] These factors, coupled with the fact that virtually all adults are immune to the disease, suggest that a ubiquitous infectious agent causes KD in genetically predisposed individuals. Residence close to a body of water appears to be a risk factor, and evidence that rainfall precedes KD clusters suggests water-related transmission.[82] A variety of other environmental exposures have been implicated, including exposure to rug shampoos, but none has yielded a consistent high-risk exposure for the disease.[77]

Principles of Disease

Regardless of the etiologic agent, KD is a systemic vasculitis that results from the host response to an as yet unidentified antigen. During the acute phase of the illness, marked immune system activation is present, with a decrease in the number of CD8 cells and an increase in the number of activated helper T cells, monocytes, and polyclonal B cells. In addition, increased levels of circulating cytokines, including tumor necrosis factor α, interleukin-1, and interferon-α, are present. The antibodies are cytotoxic to human vascular endothelial cells. The precise link between the mechanism of vascular injury and immune system activation is the subject of ongoing research. The clinical findings and laboratory abnormalities are similar to those observed in diseases caused by bacterial toxins, including streptococcal and staphylococcal toxic shock syndrome, scarlet fever, and staphylococcal scalded-skin syndrome. It is postulated that KD may be caused by a toxin acting as a "superantigen" from an as yet undefined bacterium or an aberrant host response to a common antigen.[77,82]

The vasculitis most severely affects medium-sized arteries, but autopsy findings reveal that large arteries, small arterioles, capillaries, and veins are affected to a lesser extent. In the acute phase (the first 2 weeks), the endothelial cells become edematous and degenerate. Edema and mild inflammatory changes can be seen along the adventitial layer. In severely affected vessels, inflammation affects the media with necrosis of smooth muscle. In most cases, only the inflammation in the coronary arteries is clinically significant. During this period, myocarditis is the most common cause of death. From day 11 to 30 (subacute phase), myocarditis is less pronounced, but aneurysms form with associated thrombi and stenosis of medium-sized arteries, and perivasculitis and vessel wall edema occur. In this phase, myocardial infarction, aneurysm rupture, and myocarditis are the usual causes of death. After 1 to 2 months (convalescent phase), vascular inflammation decreases and fibrous connective tissue begins to form

BOX 127-6. Case Definition of Kawasaki's Disease*

Fever for at least 5 days
Four of the following five signs:
- Bilateral conjunctival injection
- Changes of the oral mucosa
  - Erythematous dry fissured lips
  - Strawberry tongue
  - Erythematous oropharynx
- Changes of the hands and feet
  - Erythema of the palms and soles
  - Edema of the hands and feet
  - Periungual desquamation
- Rash, primarily on the trunk
- Cervical lymphadenopathy nodes >1.5 cm diameter
Illness not explained by other known process

Data from references 77 and 78.

within the vessels. Death may occur from myocardial infarction resulting from thrombosis. Coronary aneurysms regress after 1 to 2 years, but many patients still have coronary artery stenosis and consequent cardiac ischemia.[77,78]

Clinical Features

History and Physical Examination

The *acute phase* of the clinical course of KD lasts 1 to 2 weeks and is characterized by fever, myocarditis, pericardial effusion, and the other diagnostic and associated signs described in detail subsequently. The *subacute phase* lasts up to approximately 1 month after the onset of illness. During this period, the fever, rash, and lymphadenopathy resolve, but conjunctivitis, anorexia, and extreme irritability often persist. Desquamation of the fingers and toes, arthritis, arthralgias, myocardial dysfunction, and thrombocytosis most often occur in this phase. The risk of sudden death is greatest during this phase. The *convalescent phase* begins when most other clinical findings are resolved and continues until the sedimentation rate is normal, usually 6 to 8 weeks after the onset of illness.[77]

Patients with KD experience fever in association with at least four of the five features listed in Box 127-6 without another explanation for the illness. Patients with fever and fewer than four of the principal criteria can be diagnosed with KD if coronary aneurysms develop.

The fever of KD is usually high (40° C or higher) but remitting. The first day of fever marks the beginning of the illness, even if the patient develops other diagnostic criteria before fever onset. The fever generally lasts 1 to 2 weeks and resolves within 2 days on the initiation of high-dose aspirin therapy. Untreated, however, the fever may last up to 4 weeks.[77]

Bilateral nonpurulent conjunctivitis is present in 85% of patients and generally starts shortly after the fever. It involves the bulbar conjunctivae more than the palpebral conjunctivae and persists for 1 to 2 weeks if untreated. A mild uveitis is often detected by slit-lamp examination.

Cervical adenopathy is present in 50% to 75% of cases. Although it is the least common of the clinical features, it is frequently the most prominent. The nodes must be larger that 1.5 cm to meet diagnostic criteria and are frequently obvious on visual inspection alone. Nodes are firm, nonfluctuant, and tender. Patients may be misdiagnosed as having cervical adenitis and present with unresponsiveness to antibiotic therapy.[77,78]

Oral mucosal involvement is present in 90% of patients and includes diffuse oropharyngeal erythema; fissuring, cracking, and bleeding of the lips; and strawberry tongue. Oral ulceration and exudates are not present in KD.[77,78]

Changes of the hands and feet are present in 75% of patients. In the acute phase, the hands and feet are often so swollen that children refuse to hold objects and are unwilling to stand or walk because of the pain. Erythema is typically confined to the palms and soles. During the subacute phase, periungual desquamation of the fingers and toes begins. Beau's lines (transverse grooves of the nails) may appear 1 to 2 months after the onset of KD.[77,78]

The rash of KD usually appears within 5 days of the onset of fever and is present in 80% of patients. The primary lesion may include scarlatiniform erythroderma, an urticarial exanthem with large erythematous plaques, or a morbilliform maculopapular rash with or without target lesions (resembling erythema multiforme). The rash usually involves the trunk and extremities with prominence in the perineal area. Fine pustular lesions have been observed, but vesicles and bullae are not seen. Desquamation may occur in the acute phase, especially in the perineal region, and may be mistaken for candidal diaper dermatitis.[77,78]

Other signs and symptoms include arthritis and arthralgias, irritability, myositis, and myalgia. Aseptic meningitis is present in 25% of patients. Patients may have urethritis with sterile pyuria, hepatitis, diarrhea, pneumonitis, peripheral ischemia, and hydrops of the gallbladder, with or without obstructive jaundice.[78]

Although cardiac involvement is not necessary to make the diagnosis of KD, it is the hallmark of the disease. KD is the most common cause of acquired pediatric heart disease in the United States. Myocarditis occurs in the acute phase in up to 50% of patients and is manifest by tachycardia and occasionally congestive heart failure. Pericarditis and pericardial effusions occur in about 25% of patients during the acute phase, and mitral and aortic valve insufficiency has been seen in about 1% of patients. Approximately 20% of untreated patients develop coronary artery abnormalities, including aneurysms. Most fatalities occur within this period and result from myocardial infarction from thrombosis or, less commonly, coronary artery aneurysm rupture. The presenting symptoms of children with myocardial infarction related to KS are irritability, shock, vomiting, and abdominal pain. Chest pain may be a more prominent feature in older children.[77,78]

Many of the aneurysms resolve within 2 years, but arterial stenosis may remain permanently. The likelihood that an aneurysm will resolve is related to the size of the aneurysm, with the larger aneurysms having a worse prognosis. Patients with asymptomatic coronary artery stenosis may seek emergency care for cardiovascular symptoms many years later. It is important to inquire about childhood illnesses such as KD when evaluating young patients with acute cardiovascular symptoms.

Complications

The most dreaded complication of KD, coronary artery aneurysm, occurs in 20% to 25% of untreated patients and 3% to 4% of patients treated with IV immunoglobulin and aspirin (see "Management"). Myocardial infarction occurs in less than 2% of patients with KD but may result in sudden death. Approximately 39% of patients with persistent aneurysms have myocardial infarction. Congestive heart failure secondary to myocarditis or myocardial infarction is more common in patients younger than 6 months and older than 9 years. Rare complications include aneurysmal rupture with hemopericardium and distal extremity thrombosis secondary to cardiogenic shock or aneurysms in other vessels.[77,83] Patients are at long-term risk for coronary artery stenosis.

Poor prognostic indicators for KD include a low platelet count in the acute phase, fever lasting more than 16 days, recurrent fever after an afebrile period of more than 48 hours, dysrhythmias other than first-degree block, age younger than 1 year or older than 9 years, male gender, and a low hematocrit or albumin on presentation.[77]

Diagnostic Strategies

The diagnosis of KD is based on the clinical findings described in Box 127-6. These diagnostic criteria are useful in preventing overdiagnosis but may lead to misdiagnosis in atypical or incomplete KD. This is especially important in children younger than 6 months, in whom the clinical diagnosis is difficult. This younger age group is at greater risk for coronary artery aneurysms.[77]

Although no definitive test exists, the emergency physician may identify certain characteristically abnormal test results, establish a baseline for subsequent comparison, and exclude other diseases. All patients with suspected KD should have an ECG and echocardiogram performed to define baseline cardiac conduction, left ventricular function, and coronary artery anatomy. Dilation of proximal coronary arteries may be detected on the echocardiogram as early as 7 days after the onset of illness. Coronary arteriography may be indicated when persistent echocardiographic abnormalities or signs of myocardial ischemia are present.[79]

All patients should have a complete blood count, C-reactive protein, sedimentation rate, serum transaminase, and bilirubin tests. Laboratory findings in patients with KD typically include a normal or elevated leukocyte count with a left shift; a normochromic, normocytic anemia (during the acute phase); and an elevated platelet count in excess of 1,000,000/mL (which peaks in the third or fourth week of illness). A low platelet count in the acute phase is a poor prognostic sign. Serum transaminase levels may be elevated. The sedimentation rate becomes elevated during the acute phase and remains elevated after the fever resolves, a finding that may help distinguish KD from viral syndromes.[77,83]

Patients with suspected KD should also have a urinalysis, blood culture, chest radiography, antistreptolysin O titer, and throat culture for group A streptococcus (GAS) to exclude other illnesses with similar clinical findings. Because 20% to 25% of children may carry GAS in their throats, many children with KD have positive cultures. The urinalysis may show proteinuria and sterile pyuria.[79]

In difficult cases, it may be necessary to order viral cultures, Epstein-Barr viral titers, rickettsial titers, leptospirosis titers, liver function tests, rheumatoid factor, and blood and urine mercury levels. If neurologic signs suggesting meningitis are present or insufficient findings exist to explain the high fever and rash, a lumbar puncture is necessary. A slit-lamp examination to look for uveitis may be a helpful diagnostic adjunct.

Differential Considerations

The differential diagnosis of KD includes measles, toxic shock syndrome, scarlet fever, leptospirosis, Stevens-Johnson syndrome, staphylococcal scalded-skin syndrome, influenza, Rocky Mountain spotted fever, juvenile rheumatoid arthritis, drug reaction, other viral infections, and mercury toxicity. The commonly observed head and neck manifestations of KD may lead to misdiagnosis of retropharyngeal abscess or other infections of the neck, measles, and GAS infections. Patients with KD do not have Koplik's spots, exudative conjunctivitis, or severe cough, as is present in patients with measles.[79]

Management

Management of acute KD (in the first 10 days) includes the administration of high-dose aspirin and intravenous γ-globulin (IVGG). Aspirin alone at 80 to 100 mg/kg/day reduces the incidence of coronary aneurysm from 20% to 4%. The addition of IVGG not only affords a dose-dependent decrease in the incidence of coronary aneurysm but also results in rapid defervescence and normalization of acute phase reactants. Treatment should be instituted as soon as possible in the course of the illness, preferably within 10 days of the onset of fever.[78,79]

The recommended γ-globulin regimen is 2 g/kg IV as a single infusion over 8 to 12 hours. This dose may be divided for infants with cardiac compromise who cannot tolerate the fluid load. Retreatment with IVGG should be considered for patients with persistent or recurrent fever or other signs of inflammation 24 hours after the completion of therapy.[78,83]

The recommended aspirin dosage is 80 to 100 mg/kg/day in four divided doses during the acute phase of the illness until the patient is afebrile. Children with KD manifest decreased absorption and increased clearance of aspirin; most do not achieve therapeutic salicylate levels despite high-dose aspirin. For this reason, it is not necessary to monitor aspirin levels for toxicity. After the acute symptoms are controlled, aspirin is reduced to 3 to 5 mg/kg (up to 80 mg/day maximum) in a single daily dose. This is continued for 6 to 8 weeks.[79,83]

If coronary artery abnormalities exist, therapy is continued for a longer period of time. In cases judged to be at high risk for thrombosis, dipyridamole (2 to 3 mg/kg two to three times a day) may be added to the therapeutic regimen. Coumadin or heparin along with the described antiplatelet therapy may be used in some patients with severe coronary disease. Stress testing and coronary artery bypass may be necessary in these patients.[79] Other therapy should be instituted on a case-by-case basis to treat the myocarditis and related congestive heart failure (e.g., digoxin and diuretics), conduction abnormalities, dysrhythmias, or coronary artery thrombosis.

In the acute phase, patients with KD should be hospitalized to confirm the diagnosis, stabilize complications (e.g., myocarditis, pericarditis, and congestive heart failure), and initiate therapy. Hospitalization is recommended until the child is afebrile for 24 hours. Cardiac complications may necessitate admission for monitoring and treatment of congestive heart failure or management of coronary artery thrombosis with fibrinolytic therapy.[77,79,83]

TOXIC SHOCK SYNDROME

Perspective

History

Toxic shock syndrome (TSS) is a toxin-mediated systemic inflammatory response syndrome that was first described by Todd and colleagues in 1978. They reported a series of seven children ages 8 to 17 years who had high fever, rash, headache, confusion, conjunctival injection, edema, vomiting, diarrhea, renal failure, hepatic dysfunction, DIC, and shock. S. aureus was cultured from various body sites but not the blood in five of the seven cases.[84]

The disease gained notoriety in the early 1980s when many cases were reported in association with tampon use in young healthy menstruating women. The term toxic shock syndrome (TSS) was coined to describe the constellation of signs and symptoms. Investigators noted positive vaginal cultures for S. aureus, recurrence of illness during subsequent menses, and the value of antistaphylococcal antibiotics in preventing recurrences. In response to the growing concern about TSS, changes were made to reduce the absorbency and composition of tampons. Nonmenstrual cases were also recognized in both men and women as a result of a variety of predisposing conditions, and a case definition was published in 1982 (Box 127-7).[85]

BOX 127-7. Case Definition of Toxic Shock Syndrome (Revised)

Fever: temperature ≥38.9° C (102° F)

Rash: diffuse macular erythroderma

Desquamation 1 to 2 weeks after onset of illness, particularly of palms and soles

Hypotension: systolic blood pressure ≤90 mm Hg for adults or below fifth percentile by age for children less than 16 years of age, orthostatic drop in diastolic blood pressure ≥15 mm Hg from lying to sitting, orthostatic syncope, or orthostatic dizziness

Multisystem involvement—*three* or more of the following:

Gastrointestinal: vomiting or diarrhea at onset of illness

Muscular: severe myalgia or creatine phosphokinase level at least twice the upper limit of normal for laboratory

Mucous membrane: vaginal, oropharyngeal, or conjunctival hyperemia

Renal: BUN or creatinine at least twice the upper limit of normal for laboratory or urinary sediment with pyuria (≥5 leukocytes per high-power field) in the absence of urinary tract infection

Hepatic: total bilirubin, AST, ALT at least twice the upper limit of normal for laboratory

Hematologic: platelets ≤100,000/mm³

CNS: disorientation or alterations in consciousness without focal neurologic signs when fever and hypotension are absent

Negative results on the following tests, if obtained:

Blood, throat, or CSF cultures (blood culture may be positive for *Staphylococcus aureus*)

Rise in titer to Rocky Mountain spotted fever, leptospirosis, or rubeola

---

ALT, serum alanine aminotransferase; AST, serum aspartate aminotransferase; BUN, blood urea nitrogen; CNS, central nervous system; CSF, cerebrospinal fluid.

BOX 127-8. Case Definition for Streptococcal Toxic Shock Syndrome

1. Isolation of group A streptococcus from:
   A. A sterile body site
   B. A nonsterile body site
2. Clinical signs of severity
   A. Hypotension AND
   B. Clinical and laboratory abnormalities (requires two or more of the following):
      Renal impairment
      Coagulopathy
      Liver abnormalities
      Acute respiratory distress syndrome
      Extensive tissue necrosis (i.e., necrotizing fasciitis)
      Erythematous rash

Definite case: 1A + 2(A + B)
Probable case: 1B + 2(A + B)

Group A streptococcal necrotizing fasciitis
Definite:
1. Necrosis of soft tissue with involvement of fascia PLUS
2. Serious systemic disease including one or more of the following:
   A. Death
   B. Shock (systolic blood pressure <90 mm Hg)
   C. Disseminated intravascular coagulopathy
   D. Failure of organ system (respiratory failure, liver failure, renal failure) PLUS
3. Isolation of GAS from normally sterile body site
Suspected:
1 + 2 + serologic diagnosis of GAS (antistreptolysin O or DNAse B)
1 + 2 + histologic confirmation of gram-positive cocci in a necrotic soft tissue infection

---

DNAse, deoxyribonuclease; GAS, group A streptococcus.

In the late 1980s, several reports described GAS infection associated with shock and multisystem organ failure. This has been called *streptococcal toxic shock syndrome (strep TSS)* because it shares so many features with staphylococcal TSS.[86] Box 127-8 shows the case definition for strep TSS.

Epidemiology

The peak incidence of TSS occurred in 1980, with 2.4 to 16 cases per 100,000 population.[84] Since then, the reduction in cases of the menstrual form of TSS has followed an active effort to decrease certain known risk factors. Menstruation remains the most common setting for TSS, but nonmenstrual TSS accounts for just under half of the reported cases. TSS has also been reported in association with barrier contraceptives and childbirth. Nonmenstrual TSS occurs in people of all ages and in both sexes; despite the decreased incidence of menstrual cases, the incidence of nonmenstrual TSS remains constant. The CDC reported an average of about 200 cases a year (~1 case per 100,000 population) from 1994 to 2001 with a steady increase in the incidence of streptococcal TSS and a slight decrease in the incidence of staphylococcal TSS.[87] The age and sex distribution reflects the association with menses.

Nonmenstrual staphylococcal TSS is associated with superinfection of various skin lesions including burns, surgical sites, and varicella. It may also occur in association with staphylococcal respiratory infections or even with colonization by a toxigenic strain of the organism, without an obvious infectious source. Streptococcal TSS is classically associated with more severe soft tissue infections such as necrotizing fasciitis and myositis as well as pneumonia, peritonitis, myometritis, and osteomyelitis.[85,86]

The mortality rate from staphylococcal TSS has declined since the disease was first described. The case fatality rate in 1980 was 10%, and it was less than 3% in the past several years. Streptococcal TSS remains a highly fatal disease with a mortality rate of 30% to 70%.[84]

Etiology

Staphylococcal TSS is caused by colonization or infection with toxigenic strains of S. aureus. S. aureus has been detected in virtually all cases of both forms of the illness. S. aureus has been isolated from the vagina or cervix in 98% of women with menstrual TSS compared with a colonization rate of less than 10% of unaffected

BOX 127-9. Risk Factors for Toxic Shock Syndrome

Use of superabsorbent tampons
Postoperative wound infections
Postpartum period
Nasal packing
Common bacterial infections
Infection with influenza A
Infection with varicella
Diabetes mellitus
Human immunodeficiency virus infection
Chronic cardiac disease
Chronic pulmonary disease
Nonsteroidal anti-inflammatory use (may mask symptoms rather than be a risk factor)

Table 127-4. Comparison of Staphylococcal and Streptococcal Toxic Shock Syndrome

Feature	Staphylococcal	Streptococcal
Age	Primarily 15-35 yr	Primarily 20-50 yr
Sex	Greatest in women	Either
Severe pain	Rare	Common
Hypotension	100%	100%
Erythroderma rash	Very common	Less common
Renal failure	Common	Common
Bacteremia	Low	60%
Tissue necrosis	Rare	Common
Predisposing factors	Tampons, packing, NSAID use?	Cuts, burns, bruises, varicella, NSAID use?
Thrombocytopenia	Common	Common
Mortality rate	<3%	30%-70%

NSAID, nonsteroidal anti-inflammatory drug.

women. Because the organism is often not invasive, the blood cultures are often negative. Streptococcal TSS is caused by infection with toxigenic strains of GAS.[85,86]

Principles of Disease

The shock and multiorgan dysfunction associated with TSS are caused by the effects of various exotoxins produced by *S. aureus* and GAS. *S. aureus* produces toxic shock syndrome toxin (TSST-1) and enterotoxin B. TSST-1 is identified in more than 90% of menstrual cases and 60% of nonmenstrual cases. Other toxins may play a role in nonmenstrual TSS. Antibodies to these toxins are protective against disease. GAS produces streptococcal pyrogenic exotoxins A (SPEA) and B (SPEB). These exotoxins are absorbed into the bloodstream through inflamed or traumatized mucous membranes or from areas of focal infection. Absorbed toxins induce mononuclear cells to synthesize and release cytokines, tumor necrosis factor α, and interleukins, which begin the cascade of systemic vasculitis and the multisystem manifestations of the disease. Host immune factors are important in the pathogenesis of TSS. GAS is an invasive organism, and circulating GAS organisms induce tumor necrosis factor α and other cytokine production by mononuclear cells.[85,88]

Clinical Features

History and Physical Examination

The clinical presentations of streptococcal TSS and staphylococcal TSS are similar. The primary difference is that an identifiable infectious source is virtually always present with streptococcal TSS and colonization alone may be the source in staphylococcal TSS.

Patients may have fever, chills, nausea, vomiting, watery diarrhea, myalgias, and pharyngitis. An intense headache occurs in almost all cases. This prodromal illness may last for 2 to 3 days before progression to frank sepsis and organ dysfunction. Others patients may become abruptly symptomatic within hours. Rapid progression is more typical of streptococcal TSS. Patients may complain of pain at a site of infection more often with streptococcal TSS. Risk factors for TSS are listed in Box 127-9.[84-86]

The fever is usually high and abrupt in onset, although septic patients may have hypothermia on presentation. The classical rash is a nonpruritic, diffuse, blanching, macular erythroderma. It develops over the first few days of the illness and initially may be faint, evanescent, and mistaken for the flush associated with a fever. The rash is usually diffuse but may be localized to the trunk, extremities, or perineum. After about a week, a fine flaking desquamation occurs on the face, trunk, and extremities, followed by full-thickness peeling of the palms, soles, and fingers. This classical rash progression is much more common in staphylococcal TSS and is present in only 10% of patients with streptococcal TSS.[85,89]

The patient's mental status is frequently abnormal out of proportion to the degree of hypotension. Confusion, somnolence, agitation, and combativeness are present in 55% of patients with streptococcal TSS and in even more patients with staphylococcal TSS.[84,85,89]

Other findings on physical examination may include pharyngeal and conjunctival erythema, strawberry tongue, and peripheral edema. Vaginal mucosa erythema and purulent vaginal discharge may be present in menstrual TSS but are not required to make the diagnosis. As multiple organ systems become involved, a wide constellation of signs and symptoms may be seen. Gastrointestinal involvement is manifest by vomiting, diarrhea, and severe abdominal pain. Hepatomegaly may be present. Patients may become hypoxic and develop rales on pulmonary examination. Comparisons between staphylococcal and streptococcal TSS are presented in Table 127-4.

Complications

Complications of TSS include acute respiratory distress syndrome, shock, gangrene, DIC, renal failure, and a constellation of neuropsychiatric symptoms.[85,86] Less common findings in staphylococcal TSS include rhabdomyolysis, seizures, pancreatitis, pericarditis, and cardiomyopathy. Women with the menstrual form of TSS may experience one or more recurrent episodes; recurrences of the nonmenstrual form are rare. Rhabdomyolysis occurs in up to 63% of patients with strep-tococcal TSS and is usually related to the underlying soft tissue infections.[90]

Diagnostic Strategies

The case definition for TSS does not require a positive culture for *S. aureus* but does for *Streptococcus* organisms. These case definitions (see Boxes 127-7 and 127-8) are useful to the clinician, but they are not specific or foolproof. Specific tests are not required to exclude other diseases, but if such tests are obtained, the results of these studies must be negative.

There are no specific laboratory changes associated with TSS, but many abnormalities are common. Either leukocytosis or leukopenia can occur, but a marked bandemia (40% to 50%) is very common. Elevated creatinine levels and hemoglobinuria occur in most patients. Laboratory evidence of renal dysfunction occurs prior to hypotension in half of the patients. Hypoalbuminemia and life-threatening hypocalcemia are prominent initially and persist throughout the course of the disease. Other abnormalities include anemia, thrombocytopenia, hyperbilirubinemia, elevated transaminase levels, and sterile pyuria.[85,86,91]

Chest radiography may reveal evidence of acute respiratory distress syndrome or a pulmonary source of the organism. Plain radiographs of any infected skin or soft tissue site typically show only soft tissue swelling but may reveal evidence of a retained foreign body or air in the soft tissue. It is important to note that a lack of air in the soft tissue does not rule out a necrotizing soft tissue infection.

An ECG may reveal evidence of ischemia, arrhythmias, and varying degrees of atrioventricular block in association with sepsis.[84]

A lumbar puncture should be performed in febrile patients with altered mental status to evaluate for meningitis. It is prudent to wait for the results of a coagulation profile in these patients before performing the lumbar puncture as DIC may be present at presentation. The CSF is normal in patients with TSS.

Differential Considerations

The differential diagnosis includes any severe febrile illness with exanthema, associated with hypotension. Other diseases to consider include KD, staphylococcal scalded-skin syndrome, scarlet fever, drug reactions such as Stevens-Johnson syndrome, Rocky Mountain spotted fever, leptospirosis, meningococcemia, gram-negative sepsis, atypical measles, and viral illnesses.

KD occurs almost exclusively in children, usually does not progress to shock, lacks multisystem involvement, exhibits a protracted fever, and is associated with thrombocytosis later in its course. Staphylococcal scalded-skin syndrome arises with a desquamating rash acutely, whereas the desquamation of TSS occurs in the convalescent phase. Staphylococcal scalded-skin syndrome does not progress to shock, is not associated with multisystem illness, and lacks mucous membrane involvement. Scarlet fever differs in its clinical course

by lack of shock and multisystem involvement, positive cultures for GAS, and a rise in the convalescent titer. Stevens-Johnson syndrome usually occurs after drug administration, has characteristic mucous membrane lesions, and lacks desquamation. Rocky Mountain spotted fever occurs after a tick bite, does not arise with hypotension, has a distinctive rash, and is associated with a severe headache without an altered mental status. Leptospirosis occurs in endemic areas and may be distinguished by positive serologic studies and cultures. The rash of meningococcemia is characterized by petechiae and purpura occurring anywhere on the skin.[85]

Management

Patients with TSS should receive aggressive fluid resuscitation with crystalloids and may require up to 20 L/day. Supplemental oxygen should be provided to all septic patients regardless of initial pulse oxymetry. This allows maximum tissue oxygenation and reduces acidosis. Patients should be placed in a monitored setting. Hyperbaric oxygen therapy has been studied as a potential treatment for TSS but without proven benefit.[84]

The source of bacteria, such as tampons, nasal packs, and other foreign bodies, must be removed. Prompt surgical consultation should be obtained to debride wounds. If specimens are sent for culture, the laboratory should be informed of the suspected diagnosis.

Antibiotics should be initiated early in the treatment of TSS, as the clinical presentation of the disease is similar whether the source is staphylococcal or streptococcal. Antibiotics may not affect the clinical course of staphylococcal TSS but are probably beneficial if the patient has bacteremia or occult areas of infection. They are recommended in streptococcal TSS because these cases typically have an obvious source of infection. For septic patients without an identified organism, broad-spectrum antibiotics should be administered. Although the penicillinase-resistant penicillins (nafcillin, oxacillin) have been widely use in the treatment of TSS, most clinicians recommend clindamycin as a first-line agent. Clindamycin is a potent suppresser of bacterial toxin synthesis; it also facilitates phagocytosis of streptococci and has a longer postantibiotic effect than the β-lactams. The dose is 600 to 900 mg IV every 8 hours. (The pediatric dose is 20 to 40 mg/kg/day divided every 6 to 8 hours.) Clindamycin and erythromycin have also been shown to decrease monocyte synthesis of tumor necrosis factor α.[85,86,91] Patients who do not respond to fluid resuscitation require vasopressors such as dopamine, phenylephrine, norepinephrine, and epinephrine.

Patients who do not respond to massive fluid resuscitation, antibiotics, and vasopressors should be considered for IV immunoglobulin treatment, especially if pulmonary edema develops and mechanical ventilation is required. Pooled immune globulin has high titers for antibodies to TSS-1 and other exotoxins, and significant improvement has been reported with its use.[91] If used, the recommended dose is 400 mg/kg administered over several hours.[92,93]

The value of corticosteroids in TSS is still unresolved. They are not currently recommended for treating staphylococcal or streptococcal TSS but should be given to patients suspected of having adrenal insufficiency related to underlying disease or chronic steroid use.

KEY CONCEPTS

- All patients appearing septic should be treated with broad-spectrum antibiotics as soon as possible, even before a definitive diagnosis is made.

- A surgeon should be consulted immediately for patients with sepsis and a debridable source of infection.

- Immunity to diphtheria, tetanus, and pertussis wanes significantly in adults. Pertussis should always be considered as a cause of persistent cough in adults. A tetanus vaccination history should always be obtained from patients with trauma or infection. When there is doubt about the history, the age-appropriate vaccine according to CDC guidelines is administered.

- Neonates with suspected pertussis should be admitted to an intensive care setting.

- Botulism should be kept in the differential for the infant with failure to thrive, constipation, or decreased muscle tone and for the IV drug user with neurologic symptoms.

- IV γ-globulin should be administered as soon as a diagnosis of Kawasaki's syndrome is made.

REFERENCES

1. MacGregor RR: *Corynebacterium* diphtheria. In Mandell GL, Douglas RG, Bennett JE (eds): *Principles and Practice of Infectious Disease,* 5th ed. Philadelphia, Churchill Livingstone, 2000, pp 2190-2198.
2. Todar K: *Corynebacterium* diphtheria. Bacteriology at UW-Madison: Bacteriology 330 home page. http://www.bact.wisc.edu/bact330/lecturediphth, 2002.
3. Golaz A, et al: Epidemic diphtheria in the newly independent states of the former Soviet Union: Implications for diphtheria control in the United States. *J Infect Dis* 181(Suppl 1):S237, 2000.
4. Galazka A: The changing epidemiology of diphtheria in the vaccine era. *J Infect Dis* 181(Suppl 1):S2, 2000.
5. Hadfield TL, et al: The pathology of diphtheria. *J Infect Dis* 181(Suppl 1):S116, 2000.
6. Kadirova R, Kartoglu ADU, Strebel PM: Clinical characteristics and management of 676 hospitalized diphtheria cases, Kyrgyz republic, 1995. *J Infect Dis* 181(Suppl 1):S110, 2000.
7. Rakhamanova AG, et al: Diphtheria outbreak in St. Petersburg: Clinical characteristics of 1,860 adult patients. *Scand J Infect Dis* 28;37, 1996.
8. Efstratiou A, et al: Current approaches to the laboratory diagnosis of diphtheria. *J Infect Dis* 181:S138, 2000.
9. Singh MK, et al: Diphtheria. eMedicine. http://www.emedicine.com/emerg/topic138.htm, 2001.
10. American Academy of Pediatrics: *Report of the Committee on Infectious Diseases*, 23rd ed. Elk Grove Village, Ill, The Academy, 1994.
11. Wright SW: Pertussis infection in adults. *South Med J* 91:702, 1998.
12. Hewlett EL: *Bordetella* species. In Mandell GL, Douglas RG, Bennett JE (eds): *Principles and Practice of Infectious Diseases*, 5th ed. Philadelphia, Churchill Livingstone, 2000, pp 2414-2422.
13. Pasternack M: Pertussis in the 1990s: Diagnosis, treatment, and prevention. *Curr Clin Top Infect Dis* 17:24, 1997.
14. Centers for Disease Control and Prevention: Pertussis—United States, 1997-2000. *MMWR Morb Mortal Wkly Rep* 51:73, 2002.
15. Braun MM, et al: Infant immunization with acellular pertussis vaccines in the Unites States: Assessment of the first two years' data from the vaccine adverse event reporting system. *Pediatrics* 106:E51, 2000.
16. Hoppe JE: Neonatal pertussis. *Pediatr Infect Dis* 19:244, 2000.
17. Vitek CR, et al: Increase in death from pertussis among young infants in the United States in the 1990s. *Pediatr Infect Dis J* 22:628, 2003.
18. Heininger U: Pertussis: An old disease that is still with us. *Curr Opin Infect Dis* 14:329,2001.
19. Pichichiero ME, Hoeger WJ, Casey JR: Azithromycin for the treatment of pertussis. *Pediatr Infect Dis J* 22:847, 2003.
20. Pillay V, Swingler G: Symptomatic treatment of the cough in whooping cough. *Cochrane Database Syst Rev* 4:CD003257, 2003.
21. Bruss JB, et al: Treatment of severe pertussis: A study of the safety and pharmacology of intravenous pertussis immunoglobulin. *Pediatr Infect Dis* 18:505, 1999.
22. Dodhia H, Miller E: Review of the evidence for the use of erythromycin in the management of persons exposed to pertussis. *Epidemiol Infect* 120:143, 1998.
23. Decker MD, Edwards KM: Acellular pertussis vaccines. *Pediatr Clin North Am* 47:309, 2000.
24. von König CH, Halperin S, Riffelmann M, Guiso N: Pertussis of adults and infants. *Lancet Infect Dis* 2:744, 2002.
25. Keitel WA, Edwards KM: Acellular pertussis vaccines in adults. *Infect Dis Clin North Am* 13:83, 1999.
26. Bleck TP: *Clostridium tetani*. In Mandell GL, Douglas RG, Bennett JE (eds): *Principles and Practice of Infectious Diseases*, 5th ed. Philadelphia, Churchill Livingstone, 2000, pp 2537-2543.
27. Farrar JJ, et al: Tetanus. *J Neurol Neurosurg Psychiatry* 69:292, 2000.
28. Ray S, Tolan RW: Tetanus. eMedicine. http://www.emedicine.com/ped/topic3038.htm, 2004.
29. Hsu SS, Groleau G: Tetanus in the emergency department: A current review. *J Emerg Med* 20:357, 2001.
30. Pascual FB, et al: Tetanus surveillance—United States, 1998-2000. *MMWR Surveill Summ* 52(SS-3):1, 2003.
31. Humeau Y, et al: How botulinum and tetanus neurotoxins block neurotransmitter release. *Biochimie* 82:427, 2000.
32. Cook TM, Protheroe RT, Handel JM: Tetanus: A review of the literature. *Br J Anaesth* 87:477, 2001.
33. Jolliet P, et al: Aggressive intensive care treatment of very elderly patients with tetanus is justified. *Chest* 97:702, 1990.
34. Possamai C, Corbanese U, Casagrande L: Dantrolene infusion in severe tetanus. *Anaesthesia* 52:610, 1997.
35. Attygalle D, Rodrigo N: Magnesium sulphate for control of spasm in severe tetanus. *Anaesthesia* 52:956, 1997.
36. Pertussis vaccination: Use of acellular pertussis vaccines among infants and young children. Recommendations of the Advisory Committee on Immunization Practices (ACIP). *MMWR Recomm Rep* 46(RR-7):1, 1997.
37. Bleck T: *Clostridium botulinum* (botulism). In Mandell GL, Douglas RG, Bennett JE (eds): *Principles and Practice of Infectious Diseases*, 5th ed. Philadelphia, Churchill Livingstone, 2000, pp 2543-2548.
38. Cherington M: Clinical spectrum of botulism. *Muscle Nerve* 21:701, 1998.

39. Centers for Disease Control and Prevention: Botulism in the United States 1899-1996. In *Handbook for Epidemiologists, Clinicians and Laboratory Workers*. Atlanta, U.S. Department of Heath and Human Services, 1998.

40. Centers for Disease Control and Prevention: Research http://www.cdc.gov/ncidod/aid/research/bot.html.

41. Shapiro RL, Hatheway C, Swerdlow DL: Botulism in the United States: A clinical and epidemiologic review. *Ann Intern Med* 129:221, 1998.

42. Byard RW, et al: *Clostridium botulinum* and sudden infant death syndrome: A 10 year prospective study. *J Paediatr Child Health* 28:156, 1992.

43. Passaro DJ, et al: Wound botulism associated with black tar heroin injecting drug users. *JAMA* 279:859, 1998.

44. Arnon SS, et al: Botulinum toxin as a biological weapon: Medical and public health management. *JAMA* 285:1059, 2001.

45. Turtin K, Chaddock JA, Acharya KR: Botulinum and tetanus neurotoxins: Structure, function and therapeutic utility. *Trends Biochem Sci* 27:552, 2002.

46. Urdaneta-Carruyo E, Suranyi A, Milano M: Infantile botulism: Clinical and laboratory observations of a rare neuroparalytic disease. *J Paediatr Child Health* 36:193, 2000.

47. Sandrock CE, Murin S: Clinical predictors of respiratory failure and long-term outcome in black tar heroin–associated wound botulism. *Chest* 120:562, 2001.

48. Long SS: Infant botulism. *Pediatr Inf Dis J* 20:707, 2001.

49. Musher DM: *Streptococcus pneumoniae.* In Mandell GL, Douglas RG, Bennett JE (eds): *Principles and Practice of Infectious Diseases,* 5th ed. Philadelphia, Churchill Livingstone, 2000, pp 2128-2146.

50. Watson DA, et al: A brief history of the pneumococcus in biomedical research: A panoply of scientific discovery. *Clin Infect Dis* 17:913, 1993.

51. Austrian R: The pneumococcus at Hopkins: Early portents of future developments. *Johns Hopkins Med J* 144:192, 1979.

52. Prevention of pneumococcal disease: Recommendations of the Advisory Committee on Immunization Practices (ACIP). *MMWR Recomm Rep* 46(RR-8):1, 1997.

53. Abramowicz M: A pneumococcal conjugate vaccine for infants and children. *Med Lett* 42:25, 2000.

54. Whitney CG, et al: Decline in invasive pneumococcal disease after the introduction of protein-polysaccharide conjugate vaccine. *N Engl J Med* 348:1737, 2003.

55. Musher DM, et al: Bacteremic and nonbacteremic pneumococcal pneumonia. *Medicine (Baltimore)* 79:210, 2000.

56. Totapally BR, Walsh WT: Pneumococcal bacteremia in children: A 6-year experience in a community hospital. *Chest* 113:1207, 1998.

57. Preventing pneumococcal disease among infants and young children: Recommendations of the Advisory Committee on Immunization Practices (ACIP). *MMWR Recomm Rep* 49(RR-9):1, 2000.

58. Korones DN, Shapiro ED: Occult pneumococcal bacteremia: What happens to the child who appears well at reevaluation? *Pediatr Infect Dis J* 13:382, 1994.

59. Jaimes F, et al: The systemic inflammatory response syndrome (SIRS) to identify infected patients in the emergency room. *Intensive Care Med* 29:1368, 2003.

60. Kobel D-E, et al: Pneumococcal vaccine in patients with absent or dysfunctional spleen. *Mayo Clin Proc* 75:749, 2000.

61. Butler JC, Cetron MS: Pneumococcal drug resistance: The new "special enemy of old age." *Clin Infect Dis* 28:730, 1999.

62. Black S, et al: Efficacy, safety and immunogenicity of heptavalent pneumococcal conjugate vaccine in children. *Pediatr Infect Dis J* 19:187, 2000.

63. Apicella MA: *Neisseria meningitidis.* In Mandell GL, Douglas RG, Bennett J (eds): *Principles and Practice of Infectious Disease*, 5th ed. Philadelphia, Churchill Livingstone, 2000, pp 2228-2241.

64. Prevention and control of meningococcal disease: Recommendations of the Advisory Committee on Immunization Practices (ACIP). *MMWR Recomm Rep* 49(RR-7):1, 2000.

65. Booy R, Kroll JS: Bacterial meningitis and meningococcal infection. *Curr Opin Pediatr* 10:13, 1998.

66. Pathen N, Faust SN, Levin M: Pathophysiology of meningococcal meningitis and septicaemia. *Arch Dis Child* 88:601, 2003.

67. Salzman MB, Rubin LG: Meningococcemia. *Infect Dis Clin North Am* 10:709, 1996.

68. Welch SB, Nadel S: Treatment of meningococcal infection. *Arch Dis Child* 88:608, 2003.

69. Munford RS: Meningococcal infections. In Braunwald E, et al (eds): *Harrison's Principles of Internal Medicine*, 15th ed. New York, McGraw-Hill, 2001, pp 927-931.

70. Griffis JM: Meningococcal infections. In Braunwald E, et al (eds): *Harrison's Principles of Internal Medicine*, 13th ed. New York, McGraw-Hill, 1994, pp 641-644.

71. Wells LC, et al: The child with a non-blanching rash: How likely is meningococcal disease? *Arch Dis Child* 85:218, 2001.

72. Arreaza L, de la Fuenta L, Vázquez JA: Antibiotic susceptibility patterns of *Neisseria meningitidis* isolates from patients and asymptomatic carriers. *Antimicrob Agents Chemother* 44:1705, 2000.

73. van de Beck D, et al: Corticosteroids in acute bacterial meningitis. *Cochrane Database Syst Rev* CD004305, 2003.

74. de Gans J, van de Beck D: Dexamethasone in adults with bacterial meningitis. *N Engl J Med* 347:1549, 2002.

75. Kawasaki T, et al: A new infantile acute febrile mucocutaneous lymph node syndrome (MLNS) prevailing in Japan. *Pediatrics* 54:271, 1974.

76. Burns JC, Kushner HI, Bastian JF: Kawasaki disease: A brief history. *Pediatrics* 106:E27, 2000.

77. Rowley AH, Shulman ST: Kawasaki syndrome. *Clin Microbiol Rev* 11:405, 1998.

78. Saulsbury FT: Kawasaki syndrome. In Mandell GL, Douglas RG, Bennett J (eds): *Principles and Practice of Infectious Diseases*, 5th ed. Philadelphia, Churchill Livingstone, 2000, pp 2983-2986.

79. Momenah T, et al: Kawasaki disease in older children. *Pediatrics* 102:E7, 1998.

80. Freeman AF, Shulman ST: Recent developments in Kawasaki disease. *Curr Opin Infect Dis* 14:357, 2001.

81. Holman RS, et al: Kawasaki syndrome hospitalizations in the United States, 1997 and 2000. *Pediatrics* 112:495, 2003.

82. Shingadia D, Bose A, Booy R: Could a herpesvirus be the cause of Kawasaki disease? *Lancet Infect Dis* 2:310, 2002.

83. Cimaz R, Falcini F: An update on Kawasaki disease. *Autoimmun Rev* 2:258, 2003.

84. Salandy D: Toxic shock syndrome. eMedicine. http://www.emedicine.com/emerg/topic600.htm, July 2002.

85. Parsonnet J, Deresiewicz RL: Staphylococcal infections. In Braunwald E, et al (eds): *Harrison's Principles of Internal Medicine,* 15th ed. New York, McGraw-Hill, 2001, pp 889-901.

86. Wessels MR: Streptococcal and enterococcal infections. In Braunwald E, et al (eds): *Harrison's Principles of Internal Medicine*, 15th ed. New York, McGraw-Hill, 1998, pp 901-909.

87. http://www.cdc.gov/mmwr/preview/mmwrhtml/figures/m053a1t8c.gif.

88. Stevens DL: Invasive streptococcal infections. *J Infect Chemother* 7:69, 2001.

89. Hajjeh RA, et al: Toxic shock syndrome in the United States: Surveillance update, 1979-1996. CDC Emerging

Infectious Diseases 5, http://www.cdc.gov/ncidod/eid/vol5no6/hajjeh.htm, 2000.

90. Hauser AR: Another toxic shock syndrome: Streptococcal infection is even more dangerous than the staphylococcal form. *Postgrad Med* 104:31, 1998.

91. Stevens DL: The flesh-eating bacterium: What's next? *J Infect Dis* 179:S366, 1999.

92. Kaul R, et al: Intravenous immunglobulin therapy for streptococcal toxic shock syndrome. A comparative observational study. *Clin Infect Dis* 28:800, 1999.

93. Korzets A, et al: Group a streptococcal bacteraemia and necrotizing fasciitis in a renal transplant patient: A case for intravenous immunoglobulin therapy. *Nephrol Dial Transplant* 17:150, 2002.

CHAPTER 128 Viruses

Michael Alan Polis and Tenagne Haile-Mariam

PERSPECTIVE

Most viral infections manifest as benign, self-limited upper respiratory tract or gastrointestinal infections, and therapy is most often directed at control of symptoms. The exact identification of the causative virus is usually not required. For some viral diseases that have specific therapy or postexposure prophylaxis, however, recognizing the disease and promptly instituting therapy or prevention can prevent permanent sequelae or death. Examples of how prompt recognition and therapy can change the outcome of potentially fatal viral illness are the early institution of acyclovir in the treatment of herpes simplex virus (HSV) encephalitis and the appropriate use of rabies vaccine and immunoglobulin for patients exposed to rabies.

CLASSIFICATION

Viruses were first distinguished from other microorganisms by their ability to pass through filters of small pore size. Initial classifications of viruses were based on the pathologic properties (e.g., enteroviruses) or epidemiologic features (e.g., arboviruses) of the viruses. More recently, classification has been based on the genetic relationships of the viruses. The constituents of the current classification are the type and structure of the viral nucleic acid, the type of symmetry of the virus capsid, and the presence or absence of an envelope (Table 128-1).

The genetic information of viruses is encoded in either DNA or RNA, which can be either single- or double-stranded and circular (closed ended) or linear (open ended). The genomes of the smallest viruses may encode for only three or four proteins, whereas those of the largest viruses encode for several hundred proteins. A protein coat, called the *capsid,* is composed of a repeating series of protein subunits, called *capsomeres.* The viral nucleic acid and the surrounding protein coat are jointly referred to as the *nucleocapsid.* The use of repeating protein structures limits the shape of the capsid. All but the most complex viruses are either helically symmetrical or icosahedral. Finally, some virus nucleocapsids are surrounded by a lipid envelope acquired by the virus as it buds from the cell cytoplasm, nuclear membranes, or endoplasmic reticulum.

VIRAL IMMUNIZATIONS

Whereas treatment strategies against most bacterial diseases have focused on treating and eradicating bacteria from the host after disease has developed, the most successful strategies against viral diseases have concentrated on immunization. The history of immunization against viral diseases began in 1796 when Jenner injected pustular material from the lesions of cowpox into a child to prevent smallpox.[1] The term *vaccination* is derived from *vaccinia,* the virus once used as a smallpox immunization, originally meaning "inoculation to render a person immune to smallpox." Currently, the terms *vaccination* and *immunization* are used interchangeably to mean the administration of any vaccine. *Immunization* is a broader term that includes administering immunobiologics such as immunoglobulins.

Viral vaccines are suspensions of live, attenuated, or inactivated whole viruses or parts of viruses that are administered to induce immunity. Some vaccines, such as the surface antigen of hepatitis B, are highly defined; others, such as live, attenuated viruses, are complex. Immunoglobulin is an antibody preparation obtained from large pools of human blood plasma. It is given intramuscularly for passive immunization against measles and hepatitis A, and intravenously as replacement therapy for antibody-deficiency disorders. Specific immunoglobulins are preparations of monoclonal antibodies or are prepared from special donor pools preselected for high antibody titers against specific antigens such as hepatitis B, varicella-zoster, or rabies. None of the immunoglobulin preparations, when properly prepared, can transmit infectious viruses such as hepatitis B virus or human immunodeficiency virus (HIV).

Table 128-1. Classification of Viruses

Family	Example(s)	Representative Diseases, Comments
DNA viruses		
Poxviridae	Variola	Smallpox
	Orf	Contagious pustular dermatitis
Herpesviridae	HSV-1 and 2	Mucocutaneous ulcers, herpes encephalitis
	Cytomegalovirus	Pneumonitis in immunocompromised patients
	VZV	Chickenpox, shingles
	HHV-6	Roseola infantum
	EBV	Mononucleosis
	Kaposi's sarcoma herpes Virus	Kaposi's sarcoma
Adenoviridae	Adenovirus (50+ species)	Upper respiratory tract infections, diarrhea
Papillomaviridae	Papillomavirus (80+ species)	Warts (e.g., plantar, genital)
Polyomaviridae	JC virus	PML
Hepadnaviridae	Hepatitis B	Hepatitis
Parvoviridae	Parvovirus B-19	Aplastic anemia
RNA viruses		
Reoviridae	Colorado tick fever	Fever and rash
	Rotavirus	Gastroenteritis
Togaviridae	Eastern equine encephalitis	Epidemic encephalitis
	Rubella	German measles
Flaviviridae	Yellow fever	Hemorrhagic fever
	Dengue	Dengue hemorrhagic fever
	West Nile virus	West Nile encephalitis
Hepacivirus	Hepatitis C	Chronic hepatitis
Coronaviridae	Coronavirus	Upper respiratory tract infections
	SARS-CoV	Severe acute respiratory syndrome
Paramyxoviridae	Respiratory syncytial virus	Bronchiolitis
	Measles	Measles (rubeola), SSPE
	Parainfluenza	Croup
Rhabdoviridae	Rabies	Rabies
Filoviridae	Ebola	Hemorrhagic fever
Orthomyxoviridae	Influenza A, B	Influenza
Bunyaviridae	La Crosse	Encephalitis
	Hantaan	Hemorrhagic fevers, ARDS
Arenaviridae	Lassa	Hemorrhagic fever
	Lymphocytic choriomeningitis virus	Meningoencephalitis
Retroviridae	HIV	AIDS
Picornaviridae	Poliovirus	Polio
	Coxsackie B	Myocarditis
	Hepatitis A	Enteric hepatitis
	Rhinovirus (115+ species)	Upper respiratory infections
Caliciviridae	Norwalk virus	Gastroenteritis
Unclassified viruses		
	Hepatitis E	Enteric hepatitis
Subviral agents		
Satellites	Delta virus	Hepatitis
Prions		Kuru, Creutzfeldt-Jakob disease

The modern era of immunization began in 1885, when Louis Pasteur and colleagues injected the first of 14 daily doses of rabbit spinal cord suspensions containing progressively inactivated rabies virus into 9-year-old Joseph Meister, who had been bitten by a rabid dog 2 days earlier.[2] The introduction of the inactivated poliomyelitis vaccine in 1955 and the attenuated live oral polio vaccine in 1962 has virtually eliminated the threat of paralytic poliomyelitis in the United States and other developed countries.[3,4] Currently, a massive World Health Organization campaign to eradicate polio worldwide is underway. Vaccines against measles, mumps, rubella, influenza, and hepatitis B have greatly reduced morbidity and mortality associated with these diseases. The worldwide eradication of smallpox in 1977 is a testament to the advances made against viral diseases.[5]

Administration of an immunobiologic agent does not automatically confer adequate immunity. Some products require more than one dose to produce an adequate antibody response or periodic boosters to maintain protection. The simultaneous administration of immunoglobulin with a live virus vaccine may result in diminished antibody response to the vaccine. Deviation from the recommended volume or number of doses of any vaccine is strongly discouraged. Significant problems also remain in developing countries that cannot afford vaccines or have problems delivering vaccines to their at-risk populations. Table 128-2 summarizes currently available viral vaccines, their indications, and recommended uses.[6-9] Recently, a cold-adapted live intranasal vaccine has been licensed for influenza. Concerns about the precipitation of bronchospasm, transmission to contacts, and cost have limited its widespread use.[10]

Table 128-2. Viral Vaccines

Virus	Vaccine	Type	Indication	Recommended Schedule
Smallpox	Vaccinia	Live	For persons at risk or for emergency responders	Once, prior to anticipated risk of exposure
Polio	Oral polio vaccine (OPV, Sabin)	Live	During outbreaks Unvaccinated travelers	IPV preferred in almost all cases
	Inactivated polio vaccine (IPV, Salk)	Inactivated	All children	At 2, 4, and 12 to 18 months, and at 4 to 6 years
Measles	Measles, mumps, rubella (MMR)	Live	All normal children	At 12 to 15 months and 4 to 6 years
Mumps	MMR	Live	All normal children	Same as for measles
Rubella	MMR	Live	All normal children	Same as for measles
Hepatitis A	HAV vaccine	Inactivated	Persons at risk (e.g., travelers, or persons living in areas of high prevalence)	Two doses, 6 months apart Immunoglobulin should be given if travel is imminent
Hepatitis B	HBV vaccine	Inactivated or recombinant	All children Persons at risk of exposure (e.g., health care workers)	At birth, 1 to 4, and 6 to 18 months HBIG should be given in addition in case of high-risk exposure
Influenza A and B	Influenza vaccine	Inactivated	Persons at high risk for complications (e.g., elderly) or persons capable of transmitting influenza to high-risk patients (e.g., health care workers)	One dose yearly in the fall or winter
	Intranasal vaccine	Live, cold adapted	As above, for persons between 5 and 49 years old	As above
Rabies	Human diploid cell vaccine (HDCV)	Inactivated	Post-exposure prophylaxis Pre-exposure prophylaxis in high-risk groups (e.g., veterinarians)	HDCV, RVA, or PCEC 1.0 mL IM in the deltoid region on days 0, 3, 7, 14, and 28 Rabies immune globulin (RIG), 20 IU/kg should be administered around the wound site, as possible, with the remainder given IM at an anatomically distant site
	Rabies vaccine absorbed (RVA)	Inactivated		
	Purified chick embryo cell (PCEC)	Inactivated		
Yellow fever	17D virus strain	Live	Persons older than 6 months traveling to endemic areas	Boosters every 10 years
Varicella	Varicella	Live	All healthy children At-risk adults	Persons 1 to 12 years old should receive one dose Persons older than 13 should receive two doses 4 to 8 weeks apart

ANTIVIRAL CHEMOTHERAPY

Because most viral illnesses are self-limited, treatment is generally targeted at ameliorating symptoms. The revolution in molecular biology has unlocked pathophysiologic mechanisms of viral diseases and opened up the field of viral chemotherapy. The initial therapeutic armamentarium for viral diseases has been aimed at illnesses associated with significant mortality (e.g., ribavirin for Lassa fever, acyclovir for herpes simplex encephalitis) or those associated with significant end-organ damage (e.g., ganciclovir for cytomegalovirus retinitis, acyclovir for ophthalmic zoster) (Table 128-3).

Amantadine and Rimantadine

Amantadine (Symmetrel) and rimantadine (Flumadine) are effective in preventing and treating influenza A but have no activity against influenza B. They prevent or greatly reduce the uncoating of the viral RNA of influenza A after attachment and endocytosis by host cells.[11] When initiated before exposure to influenza A, amantadine, 100 mg twice a day orally, is effective in preventing illness in 50% to 90% of subjects. When begun within 2 days after the onset of symptoms of influenza A, amantadine reduces the duration of fever and systemic symptoms by 1 to 2 days. The drug is generally well tolerated, with the most common therapy-

Table 128-3. Drugs for the Treatment of Viral Illnesses

Virus	Disease	Drug of Choice	Alternate Treatment	Prophylaxis or Suppressive	Comments
Cytomegalovirus	Retinitis	Ganciclovir, 5 mg/kg IV bid for 14 to 21 days, then 5 mg/kg IV qd Valganciclovir 900 mg PO bid for 14 to 21 days, then 900 mg PO qd	Foscarnet, 90 mg/kg IV bid for 14 to 21 days, then 90 to 120 mg/kg IV qd Cidofovir, 5 mg/kg weekly IV for 2 weeks, then 5 mg/kg q2wks Ganciclovir implant Ganciclovir, foscarnet, or cidofovir intraocular injections		
	Colitis, esophagitis	Same as for retinitis, but need for maintenance not established	Foscarnet, as above		
	Pneumonitis	Ganciclovir, as above, with or without IV immunoglobulin. Need for maintenance not established			
Hepatitis B	Chronic hepatitis	Interferon alfa, 5 million units SC or IM qd or 10 million units SC or IM 3 times/wk for 16 to 24 weeks	Lamivudine 100 mg PO qd for 1 to 3 years Adefovir 10 mg PO qd	Hepatitis B immunoglobulin (HBIG)	See Chapter 89 for treatment guidelines
Hepatitis C	Chronic hepatitis	Peginterferon alfa-2b, 1 to 1.5 µg/kg SC weekly for 24 to 48 weeks *or* Peginterferon alfa-2a 180 µg SC weekly for 24 to 48 weeks *either with* Ribavirin 1000 to 1200 mg PO daily in divided doses	Interferon alfa, 3 million units SC or IM 3 times/wk with Ribavirin 1000 to 1200 mg PO daily in divided doses		See Chapter 89 for treatment guidelines
Herpes simplex virus (HSV)	Genital, primary	Acyclovir, 200 mg PO 5 times/day or 400 mg PO tid for 7 to 10 days Famciclovir, 250 PO tid for 5 to 10 days Valacyclovir, 1 g PO bid for 7 to 10 days		Acyclovir, 200 to 400 mg PO bid Valacyclovir, 500 to 1000 mg PO qd Famciclovir, 250 mg PO bid	
	Encephalitis	Acyclovir, 10 to 15 mg/kg IV q8h for 14 to 21 days			
	Mucocutaneous disease in the immunocompromised host	Acyclovir, 5 mg/kg q8h for 7 to 14 days	Foscarnet, 40 to 60 mg IV q8h (for acyclovir-resistant HSV)		
	Neonatal	Acyclovir, 20 mg/kg IV q8h for 14 to 21 days			
	Keratoconjunctivitis	Trifluridine, 1% ophthalmic solution, 1 drop topically, q2h, up to 9 drops daily for 10 days			
Human Immunodeficiency virus (HIV)		Combination therapy with: Zidovudine Didanosine Zalcitabine Lamivudine, Stavudine	See Chapter 130 for dosing and therapeutic combination therapy		See Chapter 130 for dosing and therapeutic combination therapy

Table 128-3. Drugs for the Treatment of Viral Illnesses—cont'd

Virus	Disease	Drug of Choice	Alternate Treatment	Prophylaxis or Suppressive	Comments
		Abacavir Tenofovir Emtricitabine Saquinavir Ritonavir Indinavir Nelfinavir Amprenavir Atazanavir Fosamprenavir Nevirapine Delavirdine Efavirenz Enfuvirtide, T-20			
Influenza A	Influenza A	Oseltamivir, 75 mg PO bid for 5 days Rimantadine, 100 mg PO bid for 5 days	Zanamivir, 2 inhalations bid for 5 days Amantadine, 100 mg PO bid for 5 days		
Influenza B	Influenza B	Oseltamivir, 75 mg PO bid for 5 days	Zanamivir, 2 inhalations bid for 5 days		
Lassa fever virus	Lassa Fever	Ribavirin, 1 g IV q6h for 4 days, then 500 mg IV q8h for 6 days			Treatment for Lassa fever is investigational
Papillomavirus	Condyloma accuminata	Interferon alfa-2b, 1 million units/0.1 mL intralesional injection in up to 5 warts three times weekly for 3 weeks Imiquimod 5%, topical application to warts 3 times/week			
Respiratory syncytial virus (RSV)	Severe bronchiolitis or pneumonia in infants and children	Ribavirin aerosol, 12 to 18 hours daily for 3 to 7 days with a 20 mg/mL concentration reservoir		RSV immunoglobulin can be used for prophylaxis in young children Palivizumab, a monoclonal antibody, can be given monthly to premature infants	
Varicella-Zoster virus (VZV)	Varicella (chickenpox)	Acyclovir, 20 mg/kg, up to 800 mg, PO qid for 5 days			
	Herpes zoster (shingles)	Valacyclovir, 1 g PO tid for 7 days Famciclovir, 500 mg PO tid for 7 days	Acyclovir 800 mg PO 5 times/day for 7 to 10 days		
	Varicella or zoster in an immunocompromised host	Acyclovir, 10 mg/kg IV q8h for 7 days	Foscarnet, 40 mg/kg IV q8h for 10 days (for acyclovir-resistant VZV)		

limiting toxicities being central nervous system (CNS) effects, such as nervousness, light-headedness, difficulty concentrating, insomnia, and decreased psychomotor performance. These reactions occur particularly in older patients who have impaired renal function; they should receive no more than 100 mg of amantadine daily. Rimantadine is mostly metabolized before renal excretion and has a lower incidence of CNS toxicity than amantadine. Other side effects include nausea and loss of appetite. Overdose is associated with an anticholinergic syndrome.[12]

Prophylaxis with daily amantadine or rimantadine is indicated for the duration of the influenza season in people at high risk for contracting influenza and for whom the influenza vaccine is contraindicated. When influenza A is reported in a community, appropriate management is to administer the influenza vaccine and give amantadine for 2 weeks while antibody production is induced. Adults having an acute onset of fever, cough, headache, and myalgias can be treated with 200 mg of amantadine followed by 100 mg bid for 5 to 7 days. Resistance to amantadine and rimantadine may emerge when these drugs are used to treat influenza A.

Zanamivir and Oseltamivir

Zanamivir (Relenza) and oseltamivir (Tamiflu) were approved in 1999 for the treatment of influenza A and

B. Both medications act by inhibiting the activity of neuraminidase, an enzyme involved in the release of viral progeny from infected cells.[13] They decrease the duration of moderate or severe symptoms of influenza by about 1 day. Either medication should be started within 2 days of onset of symptoms if efficacy is to be expected. These neuraminidase inhibitors are not approved for prophylactic use.[9] Zanamivir is administered by inhalation through a novel device (Diskhaler) and is approved for use in patients older than 12 years of age. The dose is two inhalations twice a day for 5 days. Most of the inhaled dose is deposited in the respiratory tract and cleared unchanged in the urine or stool. The most common side effect is bronchospasm in predisposed patients. Such patients should be given a fast-acting inhaled bronchodilator before receiving zanamivir.

Oseltamivir is an oral medication approved for patients older than 18. The dose is 75 mg twice daily for 5 days. It is cleared by renal secretion, and reduction of the dose to 75 mg daily is recommended for patients with a creatinine clearance of less than 30 mL/min.

Acyclovir

Acyclovir (Zovirax) is one of the drugs of choice for serious infections caused by HSV or varicella-zoster virus (VZV). Only 15% to 30% of the oral formulation is absorbed, so the intravenous form is required to treat HSV encephalitis, disseminated or ophthalmic zoster, or extensive HSV or VZV in the immunocompromised patient. Oral acyclovir has some use in treating primary HSV infections and in suppressing frequent HSV recurrences.[14] In general, the more immunocompromised the patient is, the higher the likelihood is that he or she will require intravenous acyclovir therapy. Acyclovir is rarely associated with gastrointestinal upset, reversible renal dysfunction, or encephalopathy. Acyclovir-resistant isolates have been found in immunocompromised patients receiving multiple courses of therapy for HSV and VZV infections. These isolates may be less virulent and may remain sensitive and respond to treatment with foscarnet.[15]

Famciclovir and Valacyclovir

Famciclovir[16] (Famvir) and valacyclovir[17] (Valtrex) are analogues of acyclovir that inhibit herpes virus DNA synthesis. They are much more bioavailable than acyclovir and can be given less frequently. Both are available only as oral formulations.

Ganciclovir

Ganciclovir (Cytovene) is used to treat life- or sight-threatening cytomegalovirus infections in immunocompromised patients.[18] Patients with acquired immunodeficiency syndrome (AIDS) and cytomegalovirus colitis or esophagitis may also improve with ganciclovir.[15] Ganciclovir is also effective against HSV, but isolates resistant to acyclovir are also resistant to ganciclovir.[16,17] Some cytomegalovirus isolates in immuno-

compromised patients have been found to be or may become resistant to ganciclovir.[19] The most common therapy-limiting toxicities of ganciclovir are granulocytopenia and thrombocytopenia, which are usually reversible when therapy ceases. Valganciclovir, the valine ester of ganciclovir, can be administered orally, producing plasma levels of ganciclovir approaching that of the intravenously administered ganciclovir.

Cidofovir

Cidofovir (Vistide) is a nucleotide agent used to treat cytomegalovirus retinitis in people with HIV infection and for acyclovir-resistant HSV infections. It is only administered parenterally but has a long half-life, making weekly or less frequent administration possible.[20] The most common toxicity is renal insufficiency, which is usually reversible with discontinuation of the drug.

Foscarnet

Foscarnet (Foscavir, trisodium phosphonoformate hexahydrate, phosphonoformic acid) is an antiviral agent with activity against the human herpesviruses and HIV-1. It has been shown to be effective against cytomegalovirus retinitis in AIDS patients and in acyclovir-resistant HSV and VZV infections.[15, 21] The main limiting toxicity of foscarnet is renal insufficiency, which is usually reversible after the drug is discontinued. Other toxicities include malaise, headache, fatigue, nausea, vomiting, anemia, hypomagnesemia, hypophosphatemia, hyperphosphatemia, and hypocalcemia.

Vidarabine

Intravenous vidarabine (Vira-A, adenine arabinoside, ara-A) can be effective for life-threatening HSV and VZV infections, but because of its toxicities, acyclovir and foscarnet have largely replaced its use.[22]

Trifluridine

Trifluridine 1% ophthalmic solution (Viroptic, trifluorothymidine) is effective for treating primary keratoconjunctivitis and recurrent epithelial keratitis caused by HSV. Treatment of ocular infections should be undertaken in consultation with an ophthalmologist. Duration of treatment depends on the lesions' response to the medication.

Interferon Alfa, Recombinant

Interferons are naturally occurring proteins with both antiviral and immunomodulating properties that are produced by host cells in response to an inducer. Injected intralesionally, interferon alfa is effective in treating refractory condyloma acuminatum but is infrequently used because of cost and toxicity.[23] High-dosage interferon alfa injected subcutaneously has induced remission in cases of Kaposi's sarcoma associated with HIV-1 infection.[24] Some patients with chronic hepatitis B have better long-term outcome with lower rates of end-stage liver disease and its complications after treatment with interferon alfa.[25] Newer treatments for hepatitis B include lamivudine and adefovir.[26] The treatment of hepatitis B is discussed in Chapter 89.

Interferon alfa-2b combined with ribavirin has been shown to induce virologic and histologic response in patients with chronic hepatitis C infection.[27] Therapy is discontinued because of side effects in about 20% of patients. The toxicities of interferon therapy include fever, malaise, headache, fatigue, alopecia, and bone marrow suppression. Use of newer pegylated interferons in combination with ribavirin is now the standard therapy for hepatitis C.[28,29]

Therapy for Human Immunodeficiency Virus Infection

There are currently four classes of 20 antiretroviral drugs available for the treatment of HIV infection. The nucleoside/nucleotide reverse transcriptase inhibitors include zidovudine, didanosine, zalcitabine, stavudine, lamivudine, tenofovir, abacavir, and emtricitabine. The nonnucleoside reverse transcriptase inhibitors include delavirdine, nevirapine, and efavirenz. The protease inhibitors include saquinavir, indinavir, ritonavir, nelfinavir, amprenavir, lopinavir, atazanavir, and fosamprenavir. A single fusion inhibitor, enfuvirtide or T-20, is available. The treatment of HIV infection is highly specialized. Treatment usually requires the administration of at least three of the antiretroviral agents. Treatment of HIV infection is covered in Chapter 130.

SPECIFIC VIRAL DISEASES

DNA VIRUSES

Poxviridae

The elimination from the natural environment of variola, the virus that causes smallpox, at one time the most devastating worldwide pestilence, is one of the great medical and public health accomplishments of this past century.[5] The elimination of smallpox from the natural environment was possible because of the lack of nonhuman reservoirs or human carriers of variola and the availability of rapid diagnostic techniques and an effective vaccine. Global eradication was certified by the World Health Organization in 1980. Other human poxvirus diseases include monkeypox, vaccinia, molluscum contagiosum, orf, and paravaccinia. The poxviruses are the largest pathogenic viruses, consisting of complex, brick-shaped capsids and double-stranded DNA.

Variola (Smallpox), Monkeypox, Vaccinia, and Cowpox Viruses

Within the Poxviridae family, the orthopoxvirus genus contains at least nine homogeneous viruses including variola, vaccinia, cowpox, and monkeypox. The last naturally acquired case of smallpox occurred in Somalia in October 1977.[5] Two cases occurred in 1978 in Birmingham, England, related to a research laboratory accident.

Principles of Disease

Recently, the possibility that military and research stores of virus might become weaponized and could be used as tools of terrorism or war has mandated that health care professionals familiarize themselves with the manifestations of smallpox, the clinical manifestations of vaccine-related illness, and the risks and benefits of the vaccine. The Centers for Disease Control and Prevention (CDC) has established extensive web-based information and training materials in preparation for the possibility of an outbreak.

Clinical Features

Smallpox is transmitted by infected droplet or close contact with a patient in any stage of illness. The most common manifestation in the unvaccinated host is variola major, which has a fatality rate of about 30%. The illness is characterized by a short prodrome of headache, backache, and fever. An ensuing enanthem progresses from small macules to papules and then vesicles over a few days. Lesions begin on the face and limbs and then spread in a centrifugal pattern. These develop into 4- to 6-mm firm, deep-seated vesicles or pustules that umbilicate, crust, and then desquamate over the next several weeks (Figure 128-1). All lesions are at the same stage of development. Modified, milder forms of smallpox can appear in previously vaccinated patients and, more rarely, in nonimmune hosts. There are also two, more rare but almost uniformly fatal forms of smallpox: a fulminant, "hemorrhagic" form and "flat type" smallpox characterized by plaquelike lesions.[30]

Major criteria for diagnosis include a prodrome of 1 to 4 days with fever greater than 38.3° C with symptoms such as headache and vomiting. Minor criteria include a centrifugal distribution of the rash, lesions on the palms and soles, a toxic patient, and a rash that develops over several days. Routine laboratory tests are not helpful in the diagnosis of smallpox. In the prodromal phase, there may be a relative granulocytopenia, but the white blood cell count is usually elevated

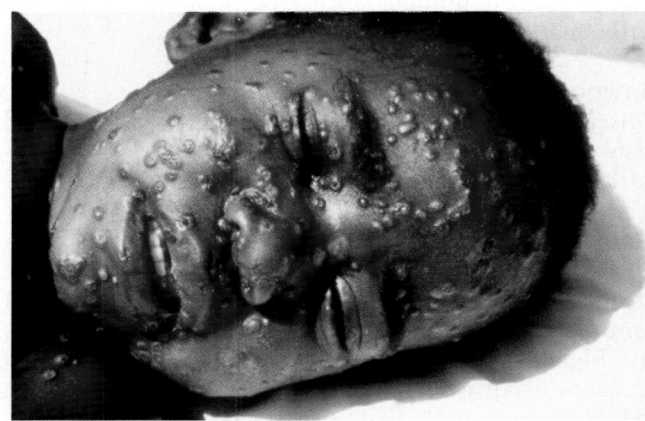

Figure 128-1. Smallpox.

in the eruptive phase. Laboratory diagnosis can be established by antibody testing, cell culture, or electron microscopy.

Differential Considerations

Smallpox has been confused with other papulovesicular eruptions, including varicella (chickenpox), measles, erythema multiforme, molluscum contagiosum, generalized vaccinia, and monkeypox. The lesions of chickenpox are generally different stages of development and healing and often spare the palms and soles.

Management and Disposition

The CDC guidelines ask physicians to classify suspected cases of smallpox into high, moderate, or low risk categories. High or moderate suspicion of smallpox by a practitioner should prompt appropriate isolation and consultation with an infectious disease specialist and/or local health care authority. Quarantine, contact tracing, and immunization efforts are a priority for public health officials, and their prompt involvement will be crucial to containment efforts in the event of an outbreak.

Immunization with vaccinia virus was the cornerstone to smallpox containment and eradication efforts. Vaccinia immunization has been associated with morbidity and mortality in vaccinated persons and their close contacts. The decision to vaccinate must balance the risk of smallpox infection against the risk of vaccine-related injury. Pre-event vaccination is contraindicated in several groups of patients, including those who are pregnant, are breast-feeding, have significant immunosuppression, or have eczema. Close household contacts of persons at risk for serious side effects from vaccine should not be vaccinated. Recent mass-vaccination campaigns have found a relatively low level of complications.[31] There are no absolute contraindications to vaccination for persons who have been exposed to smallpox.

Vaccinia Virus

The origin of the vaccinia virus is not well established. Edward Jenner, in his "An Inquiry into the Causes and Effects of the Variolae Vaccinae" in 1798, observed that the pustular material from the lesions of cowpox, when inoculated into humans, protected them from infection with smallpox.[1]

Cowpox Virus

Cowpox causes vesicular lesions on the udders and teats of cows. Human disease is manifested as vesicular lesions on the hands. Generalized infection is rare.

Monkeypox Virus

The disease of monkeypox is clinically similar to that of smallpox. Most cases have occurred in west and central Africa with a case fatality rate of 1% to 10% and higher death rates among children. An outbreak of 72 cases occurred in the Midwestern United States in the Spring of 2003 that was traced to contact with prairie dogs housed with Gambian giant rats that were imported from Ghana.[32] No deaths were associated with this outbreak.

Parapoxviruses, Molluscum Contagiosum, and Tanapox Viruses

Other viruses within the Poxviridae family that cause disease in humans include the parapoxviruses (paravaccinia and bovine pustular stomatitis virus), the molluscum contagiosum, and tanapox viruses. The milker's node virus, or paravaccinia, produces vesicular lesions on the udders or teats in cattle and is transmitted to humans by direct contact. Milker's nodules that develop on the fingers or hands are small, watery, painless nodules occasionally associated with lymphadenopathy. The lesions generally resolve completely within 3 to 8 weeks.

Bovine pustular stomatitis, ecthyma contagiosum, or orf virus causes papillomatous lesions on the mucous membranes and corneas of sheep. Single lesions generally develop in infected humans at the site of an abrasion.

Molluscum contagiosum is a generally benign human disease characterized by multiple small, painless, pearly, umbilicated nodules. They appear on epithelial surfaces, commonly in anogenital regions, and may be spread through close contact or autoinoculation. In immunocompetent people, the lesions may clear rapidly or persist for up to 18 months. The infection is often seen in people with HIV infection, in whom the lesions are often not restricted to the genital area and may increase in size and number.[33] Curettage or other forms of local ablation might be helpful in such recalcitrant cases.

Herpesviridae

There are at least eight known human herpesviruses. Herpes simplex 1 and 2 (HSV-1 and HSV-2) are the agents of herpes genitalis, labialis, and encephalitis. VZV is the agent of chickenpox and herpes zoster. Epstein-Barr virus (EBV) is the agent of infectious mononucleosis and is associated with nasopharyngeal carcinoma, Burkitt's lymphoma, and other lymphoproliferative syndromes. Cytomegalovirus is associated with heterophile-negative infectious mononucleosis and invasive disease in immunocompromised patients. Human herpesvirus-6 (HHV-6) is associated with *roseola infantum*.[34] The role of HHV-7 has not been completely elucidated. HHV-8 is associated with Kaposi's sarcoma,[35] body-cavity-based lymphomas, and multicentric Castleman's disease. In addition, a closely related monkey virus, herpesvirus simiae or herpes B virus, has been shown to cause fatal encephalitis in humans.

Herpes Simplex Virus

Principles of Disease. A localized primary lesion, latency, and a tendency for local recurrence characterize infections with HSV-1 and HSV-2 (Herpesvirus hominis). The primary lesion with HSV-1 may be mild and inapparent and may occur during childhood. Reactivation of latent HSV-1 infection usually results in herpes labialis (cold sores, fever blisters). Neurologic involvement is not uncommon with HSV-1. Although it usually occurs in association with a primary infection, neurologic signs may appear after a recrudescence and may manifest as encephalitis. Though uncommon, HSV-1 encephalitis is one of the most common causes of encephalitis in the United States, with estimates of several hundred to several thousand cases occurring yearly. HSV-2 is most commonly associated with genital herpes, although either HSV-1 or HSV-2 may infect any mucous membrane, depending on the route of inoculation. HSV-2 is commonly associated with aseptic meningitis rather than meningoencephalitis. The incubation period for primary herpes infection is 2 to 12 days.[36]

On contact with abraded skin or mucous membranes, HSV replicates locally in epithelial cells, which lyse and cause a local inflammatory response. Thin-walled vesicles on an erythematous base are the characteristic lesions of superficial HSV infection. Multinucleated giant cells with ballooning degeneration and intranuclear inclusions may be seen on a Tzanck preparation of a smear of the base of these vesicles. After primary infection, HSV can become latent within sensory nerve ganglia. Emotional stress, sunlight, fever, or local trauma can trigger reactivation of the virus. HSV encephalitis usually involves the temporal lobes, resulting in a necrotizing, hemorrhagic encephalitis.

Clinical Features. Primary HSV-1 is often asymptomatic but may appear as pharyngitis and gingivostomatitis in children younger than 5 years of age. Associated with fever, pharyngeal edema, erythema, cervical adenopathy, and multiple small vesicles that ulcerate and multiply, the disease generally lasts from 10 to 14 days. Recurrences occur in 60% to 90% of people after primary infection but are generally milder than the primary infection. Vesicles generally recur on the vermilion border, are usually small, and crust within 48 hours.

Herpes simplex infections of the eye are most often caused by HSV-1. Primary infections present as follicular conjunctivitis, blepharitis, or corneal epithelial opacities, which usually heal completely within 2 to 3 weeks. Recurrences may result in keratitis. Branching dendritic ulcers, detectable with fluorescein staining, are diagnostic and may result in diminished visual acuity. Deep stromal involvement may result in corneal scarring.

Primary herpetic finger infections, or herpetic whitlow, are generally caused by HSV-1 among medical or dental personnel and by HSV-2 among the general population. The lesions are associated with intense pain and itching but generally resolve in 2 to 3 weeks. Recurrent whitlow with severe local neuralgia may occur.

Primary genital herpes is generally seen in the sexually active population and is caused by HSV-2 in 70% to 95% of cases. The lesions usually involve the shaft or glans of the penis in men and the vulva, perineum, buttocks, cervix, and vagina in women. Primary infection may be associated with fever, malaise, anorexia, and inguinal adenopathy. Vaginal discharge is common. Urethral involvement resulting in urinary retention is not uncommon in women. Herpetic sacral radiculomyelitis is uncommon but can also lead to urinary retention, myalgias, and obstipation. The lesions can last for several weeks before completely clearing. Recurrences of genital herpes are generally shorter and milder than the primary episodes and may be preceded by a prodrome of tenderness, itching, or tingling. Healing of recurrent lesions generally is complete in 6 to 10 days.

Primary perianal and anal herpes is common among people who engage in anal intercourse and may be especially prolonged and severe among HIV-1-infected persons.

Neonatal herpes infection occurs in 7 in 100,000 births and is caused by the transmission of the virus at the time of delivery. The rate of infection is estimated to be 40% to 50% after a primary maternal infection and less than 10% after a recurrence.[37] Infection may manifest after several days to weeks with vesicles or conjunctivitis, but neurologic involvement, with seizures, cranial nerve palsies, lethargy, and coma, is common. Untreated disseminated or CNS disease is fatal in more than 70% of patients.

Encephalitis caused by HSV is uncommon, but it is the most common acute, nonepidemic encephalitis in the United States. Cases do not have a seasonal distribution. Other than in the neonate, HSV-1 is the usual pathogen. The clinical disease begins acutely, with fever and focal neurologic signs, often localized to the temporal lobe. The patient may complain of a bad odor not perceived by anyone else (temporal lobe hallucination). Headache, meningeal signs, lethargy, confusion, stupor, or coma is often present. Cerebrospinal fluid (CSF) findings are nonspecific, with a moderate mononuclear pleocytosis. Culture of the CSF is generally negative for HSV. Localization of the encephalitis within the temporal lobes via electroencephalogram, magnetic resonance imaging, or computed tomography (CT) scan increases the likelihood of a diagnosis of HSV encephalitis. The diagnosis of HSV encephalitis can be made reliably only with a biopsy of the lesion and subsequent isolation or detection of the virus by culture, direct fluorescent antibody tests, or polymerase chain reaction.[38] The mortality rate of untreated patients approaches 80%, and fewer than 10% of patients are left with no neurologic sequelae. Treatment with acyclovir appears to reduce mortality and decrease the neurologic sequelae more effectively than treatment with vidarabine.[39]

Considerations. The superficial lesions of HSV are indistinguishable from those of VZV. Pharyngitis and gingivostomatitis in children can mimic streptococcal or diphtheritic pharyngitis, herpangina, aphthous stomatitis, Stevens-Johnson syndrome, Vincent's angina, and infectious mononucleosis. Primary genital herpes can mimic the appearance of chancroid, syphilis, candidiasis, or Behçet's syndrome. In the neonate, in the absence of vesicles, congenital HSV infection can mimic disease caused by rubella, cytomegalovirus, or *Toxoplasma* organisms. Encephalitis caused by HSV may be clinically indistinguishable from other viral encephalitides, tuberculous and fungal meningitis, brain abscesses, brain tumors, and cerebrovascular accidents.

Management. Oral acyclovir (200 mg five times daily), oral valacyclovir (1 g twice daily), or intravenous acyclovir (5 mg/kg three times daily) is recommended for treating primary genital herpes or mucocutaneous herpes in the immunocompromised host, although some authorities use higher dosages in these patients.[40] Because of the safety and efficacy of oral acyclovir, there is little indication for using acyclovir ointment. In people with severe or frequent recurrences, acyclovir, 200 mg three to five times daily, can be used as an effective suppressive regimen. Both famciclovir and valacyclovir are approved for suppressive therapy and offer a more convenient dosing regimen than acyclovir.

In the immunocompromised host, acyclovir is effective in both treatment and prophylaxis of recurrent mucocutaneous herpes. Foscarnet has been shown to be effective in the host in the treatment of mucocutaneous herpes that is resistant to acyclovir.[15,22] Intravenous acyclovir, 10 mg/kg every 8 hours, is the treatment of choice for HSV encephalitis in adults and children. Vidarabine, 30 mg/kg/day IV, is also effective in neonatal encephalitis but is rarely used.[39]

Disposition. Patients with cutaneous HSV infections can generally be managed easily. The diagnosis often carries with it a great deal of stigma that must be addressed.[36] Assurance as to the generally benign nature of the infection is helpful. Counseling should include cautions about the transmissibility of the virus, even during asymptomatic periods. Women of childbearing age should discuss management of HSV during pregnancy and delivery with their obstetricians.

Encephalitis caused by HSV is a treatable medical emergency. Prompt recognition and institution of appropriate therapy in the emergency department before a definitive diagnosis has been made may decrease the high mortality rate and neurologic sequelae associated with this disease. When HSV encephalitis is suspected, empirical initiation of intravenous acyclovir is indicated in the emergency department. This approach has minimal toxicity and demonstrable efficacy.

Varicella-Zoster Virus

Varicella-zoster virus, or human (alpha) herpesvirus 3, is the agent of both chickenpox and herpes zoster, or shingles.

Clinical Features. Chickenpox is an acute, generalized viral disease with sudden onset of fever, malaise, and a skin eruption that is initially maculopapular and then vesiculated for several days before a granular scab is left (Figure 128-2). Lesions occur in crops, with several stages present at the same time. Lesions can appear anywhere on the skin and mucous membranes. There may be few lesions and mild, inapparent infections. Most cases occur in children younger than 9 years of age, but adults with the disease may have high fevers and severe constitutional symptoms. Children with acute leukemia are at increased risk of disseminated disease, which has a case fatality rate of greater than

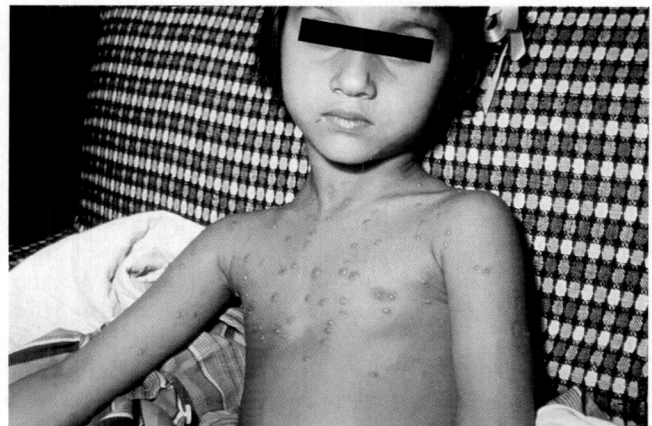

Figure 128-2. Chickenpox.

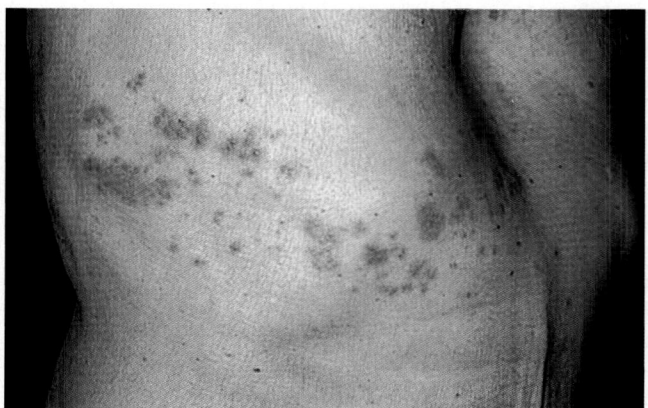

Figure 128-3. Herpes zoster.

5%. Neonates developing varicella before 10 days of age and mothers who develop the disease in the perinatal period are at increased risk for generalized disease. Fatal disease in adults, although uncommon, is usually associated with pneumonic involvement of the virus. In children, fatal disease is usually associated with septic complications and encephalitis.

Herpes zoster is a reactivation infection of VZV that has been latent in a dorsal root ganglion. Often preceded by tingling or hypesthesia, multiple vesicles on an erythematous base appear in crops along nerve pathways supplied by sensory nerves of a single or associated group of dorsal root ganglia. The distribution is usually unilateral and dermatomal (Figure 128-3). Zoster occurs predominantly in older adults but has been seen in younger people when associated with HIV infection.[41] The lesions are often extremely painful. Postherpetic neuralgia is common in elderly patients, can last for months or years, and is refractory to treatment. Involvement of the ophthalmic branch of the trigeminal nerve may lead to corneal ulceration.

Differential Considerations. The diagnoses of chickenpox and herpes zoster are clinical. Laboratory tests are generally not required. Multinucleated giant cells may be seen on Tzanck preparations from the base of a lesion, but these can also occur in herpes simplex lesions. Scrapings can also be submitted for antibody-linked fluorescent microscopy testing, which will yield rapid results and differentiate between HSV and VZV.

Management. Using acyclovir for uncomplicated chickenpox in children is safe but only modestly effective. Parents of children with chickenpox should be cautioned not to give their children aspirin or aspirin-containing compounds because of the strong association between this practice and the development of Reye's syndrome.[42] Acetaminophen can be used as an antipyretic. Adults have increased morbidity and mortality from chickenpox, so treatment of otherwise healthy adults with acyclovir, famciclovir, or valacyclovir is frequently indicated. Patients with pneumonitis or other severe illness should be treated with intravenous acyclovir. In immunocompromised patients, varicella-zoster immunoglobulin and intravenous acyclovir have been shown to decrease morbidity.

A live, attenuated vaccine has shown a high degree of protection of both normal children and children with leukemia and was licensed in the United States in 1995. It is recommended for immunocompetent people older than 12 months of age. In those older than 12 years, two doses of vaccine are to be administered 4 to 8 weeks apart. It is also recommended for use as post-exposure prophylaxis in the nonimmune host. The vaccine is most effective in preventing or attenuating illness in these circumstances if it is administered within the first 3 to 5 days after exposure.[43] The vaccine is a live attenuated virus and not recommended for immunocompromised patients.

Uncomplicated herpes zoster is generally treated with supportive measures, especially pain control, and acyclovir, famciclovir, or valacyclovir.[44] Disseminated disease and complicated zoster, involving more than one dermatome or the ophthalmic branch of the trigeminal nerve, should be treated with intravenous acyclovir. Foscarnet is useful for acyclovir-resistant VZV in immunocompromised patients.[15] Famciclovir may decrease the duration of postherpetic neuralgia. Susceptible immunocompromised patients exposed to infected individuals should receive varicella-zoster immunoglobulin within 72 hours to prevent or modify clinical illness.[43] Using corticosteroids to decrease the incidence of postherpetic neuralgia is controversial.

Disposition. Chickenpox and herpes zoster are highly contagious. Although the diseases are generally benign, patients should avoid situations that put them in contact with steroid-treated or immunocompromised persons. The incubation period is most commonly 13 to 17 days, and the period of communicability may be from 5 days before to 5 days after the appearance of the vesicles. Susceptible people should be considered potentially infectious from 10 to 21 days after exposure. Susceptible health care workers should not care for people with varicella or zoster. Health care workers without a well-documented history of chickenpox or herpes zoster should have antibody levels checked before they begin their employment to determine susceptibility to VZV, and they should strongly consider vaccination if nonimmune.

Cytomegalovirus

Principles of Disease. Cytomegalovirus, or human herpesvirus-5, is commonly associated with heterophile-negative infectious mononucleosis and is clinically and hematologically similar to EBV-associated mononucleosis. More severe infections with cytomegalovirus occur in the perinatal period and among immunocompromised patients. Severe cytomegalovirus infections are also found in transplant recipients when organs from cytomegalovirus-seropositive donors are transplanted into cytomegalovirus-seronegative recipients.

Primary infection with cytomegalovirus is often associated with a vigorous T-lymphocyte response. Cytomegalovirus persists indefinitely, probably within multiple cell types in various organs. Reactivation leading to cytomegalovirus-associated disease may occur in response to a variety of external stimulants.

Clinical Features. Cytomegalovirus infection in immunocompetent older children and adults is generally subclinical. It is characterized by fever, lymphadenopathy, exudative pharyngitis, and peripheral lymphocytosis with atypical lymphocytes present on peripheral blood smears. The acute infection resolves in 2 to 4 weeks, but malaise and viral excretion can persist for months. In the perinatal period, severe, generalized infection can occur and be associated with lethargy, convulsions, jaundice, petechiae, hepatosplenomegaly, chorioretinitis, and pulmonary infiltrates. Survivors may have varying degrees of neurologic impairment. Fetal infection can occur after primary or reactivated maternal infections, with primary infections carrying a much higher risk. Severe, generalized disease can occur in immunocompromised patients and is often associated with severe end-organ disease such as colitis, esophagitis, pneumonitis, retinitis, and adrenalitis. Retinitis caused by cytomegalovirus is the most common cause of blindness among people with AIDS.[21] Cytomegalovirus can cause a polyradiculopathy and other less common neurologic manifestations in patients with AIDS or other immunocompromised conditions. Therapy with ganciclovir and foscarnet is indicated, but treatment results may be disappointing.[45]

Differential Considerations. Mononucleosis caused by cytomegalovirus may be clinically indistinguishable from syndromes caused by EBV or toxoplasmosis. In the perinatal period, infants with generalized infections require evaluation for other common perinatal infections, such as toxoplasmosis, rubella, syphilis, and HSV. Recipients of organ transplants and other immunocompromised patients with fever and other signs and symptoms of generalized infection require intensive evaluation for bacterial and viral causes of infection. Diagnosis of cytomegalovirus infection depends on viral isolation, detection of cytomegalovirus pp65 antigen, or the demonstration of a fourfold rise in antibody to viral antigens.

Management. Only supportive care is indicated for immunocompetent adults and children. Ganciclovir, foscarnet, and cidofovir have been approved for treating cytomegalovirus retinitis in immunocompromised patients.[18,20,21] Concurrent use of intravenous immunoglobulins with ganciclovir may decrease the mortality rate associated with cytomegalovirus pneumonitis in bone marrow recipients.[46]

Immunocompetent adults and older children can be managed at home. Suspected cytomegalovirus infections in the perinatal period or in an immunocompromised patient can be life threatening and generally requires hospitalization for aggressive evaluation, monitoring, and specialized care.

Epstein-Barr Virus (Infectious Mononucleosis)

Principles of Disease. EBV, or human herpesvirus-4, is most commonly associated with infectious mononucleosis, an acute viral syndrome characterized by fever, exudative pharyngotonsillitis, lymphadenopathy, and peripheral lymphocytosis with atypical lymphocytes. EBV also has been strongly implicated in the pathogenesis of African Burkitt's lymphoma and nasopharyngeal carcinoma. Acute immunoblastic sarcoma, involving a polyclonal expansion of EBV-infected B lymphocytes, may occur in people with an X-linked immunoproliferative disorder. Hodgkin's disease and other lymphomas in immunocompromised patients, such as renal transplant recipients or people with AIDS, have also been associated with EBV infection. A chronic form of the disease has been suggested as the cause of chronic fatigue syndrome, but there are few data to support this association.[47]

Epstein-Barr virus infects and transforms B lymphocytes. Infection is common and widespread in early childhood in developing countries, where it is usually mild or asymptomatic. In developed countries, infectious mononucleosis usually presents in older children and young adults, commonly among high school and college students. It is transmitted via the oropharyngeal route, often by kissing. The incubation period may be as long as 4 to 6 weeks and pharyngeal excretion can persist for 1 year or more.

Clinical Features. The syndrome is usually mild in children, but 95% of young adults have abnormal transaminases and 4% have jaundice. Hepatosplenomegaly is common. Severe exudative pharyngitis, fevers, lymphadenopathy, and fatigue are characteristic of infectious mononucleosis. The disease generally resolves in 1 to 3 weeks, but malaise and fatigue can, rarely, persist for several months. Occasionally, tonsillar swelling causes respiratory compromise. Splenic rupture is rare, but must be considered in patients with left upper quadrant pain and a falling hematocrit. Neurologic complications, including encephalitis, aseptic meningitis, transverse myelitis, Guillain-Barré syndrome, optic neuritis, and peripheral neuropathies, occur in less than 1% of patients.

Diagnostic Strategies and Differential Considerations. Laboratory diagnosis is based on the finding of lymphocytosis greater than 50% or an elevation in heterophile antibodies (Monospot). Heterophile antibodies are sensitive and specific antibodies that usually appear early in the illness. Other virus-specific antibodies are available but are rarely needed to diagnose

mononucleosis because 90% of cases are heterophile positive.

A presumptive diagnosis can be made by the finding of significant cervical lymphadenopathy, particularly posterior cervical, and exudative pharyngitis coupled with a lymphocytosis and the presence of atypical lymphocytes on a blood smear. HHV-6, cytomegalovirus, and toxoplasmosis can cause syndromes that are clinically and hematologically similar to infectious mononucleosis.

Management. Treatment is entirely supportive, except when rare complications of organ compromise are present. The use of corticosteroids in uncomplicated illness is controversial. They are generally used for impending airway obstruction, hemolytic anemia, or severe thrombocytopenia. The infection confers a high degree of resistance to reinfection. Patients should be cautioned about potential communicability to previously uninfected people.

Human Herpesvirus-6

Principles of Disease. HHV-6 has been implicated as the agent of roseola infantum (exanthem subitum).[34]

Clinical Features. Roseola infantum is the most common exanthem of children younger than 2 years of age and occurs most often at about 1 year of age. The illness begins abruptly with the acute onset of fever, often as high as 41° C, lasting 3 to 5 days. Despite the fever, the child usually remains active and alert. A fine, evanescent, rose-colored maculopapular rash appears on the trunk after lysis of the fever and lasts for 1 to 2 days. The rash may spread to the face and extremities. Most cases are self-limited, although febrile convulsions can occur in conjunction with the fever. Although secondary cases occur with an incubation period of approximately 10 days, most cases of roseola occur without known exposure.

Differential Considerations. The disease appears similar to other childhood exanthems. The child generally looks well despite the high fever.

Management. Acetaminophen may reduce the fever. Routine supportive measures should be used if febrile seizures occur.

Human Herpesvirus-7

Human herpesvirus-7 has been associated with a clinical presentation similar to that of HHV-6, but its role in disease has not yet been fully elucidated.[48]

Human Herpesvirus-8 (Kaposi's Sarcoma–Associated Herpesvirus)

Human herpesvirus-8 has been implicated as the cause of Kaposi's sarcoma regardless of the HIV status of the affected patients.[49] Mechanisms of disease pathogenesis as well as epidemiology of transmission for this virus remain unclear and continue to be actively investigated.[48]

Herpes B Virus

Principles of Disease. Herpes B virus, or herpesvirus simiae, a close relative of human herpes simplex, is enzootic in macaques and most commonly associated with Rhesus, cynomolgus, or African green monkeys. Like human herpes simplex, herpes B virus produces mild disease in monkeys that is characterized by intermittent reactivation and shedding, particularly during times of stress, such as during handling. Among monkey handlers and those exposed to the animals' saliva or tissues, monkey B virus is a serious occupational hazard. Of 23 symptomatic human infections, 18 resulted in a progressive mucocutaneous disease and fatal encephalitis.[50]

Clinical Features. After a penetrating bite or scratch from an infected monkey, herpetiform vesicles form at the site of the injury. Giant cells can be seen on a Tzanck preparation. An acute febrile illness with headache and lymphocytosis may follow as long as 3 weeks after the injury. An ascending myelitis ensues, leading to death from respiratory paralysis or encephalomyelitis within 3 weeks of the onset of symptoms. The incidence of asymptomatic infection is unknown.

Differential Considerations. The initial skin lesions appear similar to those of herpes simplex. In the context of any exposure to monkey tissues and the appearance of a herpetiform lesion, the diagnosis of herpes B virus infection must be considered because of its high mortality rate.

Treatment. Suspected B virus infection is a medical emergency. There have been anecdotal reports of successful prevention of disease progression with intravenous acyclovir.[51] The apparent response of the infection to treatment emphasizes the need for early recognition and treatment of this disease.

Adenoviridae

Adenovirus

Principles of Disease. Adenoviruses are the most clinically important viruses because of their capacity to cause upper respiratory tract infections, conjunctivitis, and gastroenteritis. Nevertheless, no drugs or therapeutic measures are available specifically for adenoviral infections.

Clinical Features. Adenoviruses cause respiratory diseases ranging from pharyngitis and tracheitis to fulminant bronchiolitis and pneumonia. Cough, fever, sore throat, and rhinorrhea are the most common symptoms and generally last only a few days. Pneumonitis with interstitial infiltrates are occasionally seen with some strains. Upper respiratory findings may be associated with conjunctivitis (pharyngoconjunctival fever). Adenoviruses, usually types 8, 19, and 37, may cause an epidemic keratoconjunctivitis, which, in severe cases, may be associated with conjunctival scarring. Other syndromes associated with adenoviruses include hemorrhagic cystitis, infantile diarrhea, intussusception, encephalitis, and meningoencephalitis.

Differential Considerations. Other pathogens causing similar atypical pneumonia syndromes include influenza and parainfluenza viruses and *Mycoplasma pneumoniae.* Diarrheal syndromes may be similar to those caused by rotaviruses.

Management. Treatment for adenovirus infections is supportive.

Papillomaviridae

Principles of Disease. Human papillomaviruses (HPV) cause a variety of cutaneous and mucous membrane lesions, including common warts, anogenital or venereal warts (condyloma acuminatum), and respiratory or laryngeal papillomas.

More than 70 types of HPVs have been identified. Laryngeal papillomas (most commonly HPV types 6 and 11) and genital warts (most commonly HPV types 16 and 18) can undergo malignant transformation.[52,53]

Clinical Features. Common warts are generally well-circumscribed, hyperkeratotic, painless papules occurring most commonly on the extremities and transmitted by close personal contact. Plantar warts, found on the soles of the feet, may be very painful. Venereal warts, found on the internal or external genitalia or perianal region, are hyperkeratotic, exophytic papules, either sessile or pedunculated, and are sexually transmitted. Laryngeal papillomas in children are presumably acquired during passage through the birth canal. Malignant transformation can occur, particularly in patients receiving radiation therapy.

Differential Considerations. The diagnosis of warts is usually made clinically. Condyloma acuminatum must be distinguished from condyloma latum caused by syphilis. Diagnosis of cervical HPV infections can be made during colposcopy with prior application of a 3% to 5% acetic acid solution to the internal genital tract. Flat condylomata appear as shiny white patches with ill-defined borders and irregular surfaces. Acetowhitening can also reveal subclinical vulvar or penile warts.

Management. Warts generally regress spontaneously within months or years, but because of the possibility of malignant transformation of genital or laryngeal warts, they should be removed. Freezing with liquid nitrogen is effective for most accessible lesions. Salicylic acid plasters and curettage are useful for plantar warts. Podophyllin as a 10% solution in tincture of benzoin is useful for accessible genital warts. Laryngeal warts require surgery or laser therapy. Interferon alfa has been effective in the intralesional treatment of genital warts.[23] Imiquimod (Aldara) has been approved for the topical self-treatment of genital warts.[54]

All patients with genital warts should be screened for other sexually transmitted diseases. Because of the potential for malignant transformation, people with internal genital warts should be referred to a qualified specialist for treatment and follow-up care.

Polyomaviridae

Principles of Disease. JC virus and BK virus are human polyomaviruses that cause ubiquitous but asymptomatic infection in populations worldwide. Progressive multifocal leukoencephalopathy (PML) is a rare, slowly progressive, demyelinating CNS disease associated with JC virus. The demyelinated lesions of PML slowly enlarge to become large plaques, associated with progressive neurologic deterioration, dementia, and eventually death. The disease occurs mostly in severely immunocompromised patients.[55] Similarly, BK virus viruria is relatively common in immunosuppressed or pregnant people. Rare, symptomatic infection can manifest as urethral stenosis in renal transplant patients and hemorrhagic cystitis in bone marrow transplant patients.

Clinical Features. Initial presentations of PML in immunocompromised patients include paresis, personality changes, and impaired higher cortical functioning. The disease is generally rapidly progressive, usually progressing to death within 2 to 4 months of the initial neurologic symptoms. PML is commonly seen in people with advanced AIDS.[55]

Differential Considerations. The differential diagnosis includes other causes of progressive neurologic disease in immunocompromised patients, including toxoplasmic encephalitis, primary CNS lymphoma, HIV encephalopathy, tuberculous meningitis, and vascular disease. The lack of contrast enhancement on CT and magnetic resonance imaging scans is helpful in making the diagnosis. Polymerase chain reaction identification of JC virus in the appropriate clinical setting with consistent radiographic findings establishes the diagnosis.[56]

Management. No specific treatment for PML is available; the disease is generally rapidly progressive, and ultimate transfer to appropriate nursing care facilities is often necessary. Recently, there have been reports of significant improvements in persons with AIDS who have been placed on potent antiretroviral (anti-HIV) therapy.[57]

Hepadnaviridae

Hepatitis B Virus and Hepatitis Delta Virus
A description of hepatitis B and delta hepatitis can be found in Chapter 89.

Parvoviridae

Parvoviruses (Erythema Infectiosum, Aplastic Crisis)
Principles of Disease. Parvovirus B19 has been implicated as the causal agent in several epidemics of erythema infectiosum, or fifth disease. It is also associated with transient aplastic crisis in patients with chronic hemolytic disease, particularly with sickle cell disease.[58] Fetal infection also has been recognized, and infections during pregnancy have been associated with hydrops fetalis and spontaneous abortion.[59]

Clinical Features. *Erythema infectiosum* is a mild, usually nonfebrile disease of children between 4 and 10 years of age, characterized by a striking erythema of the cheeks—a "slapped-cheek" appearance (Figure 128-4). The rash usually appears after an incubation period of 4 to 14 days without a prodrome. One to 4 days later, an erythematous rash on the extremities may be seen spreading to the trunk in a lacelike pattern. The rash generally fades within a week but can persist for several weeks and may be precipitated by skin trauma or sunlight exposure. Constitutional symptoms are gen-

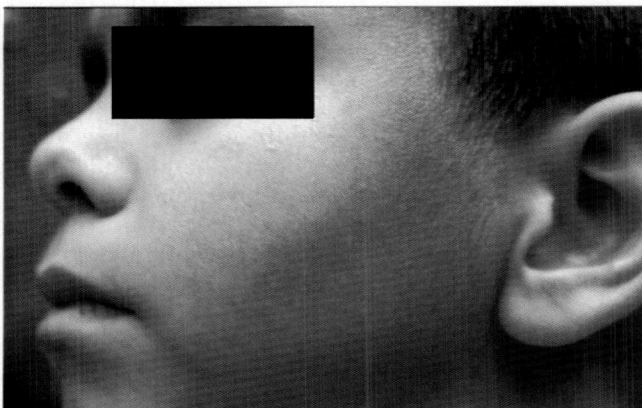

Figure 128-4. Erythema infectiosum.

erally mild in children, but adults with the disease commonly have associated arthralgias and arthritis. Rare cases of encephalitis and pneumonia have been reported.

Parvovirus B19 infects and causes a marked reduction in erythroid cell precursors and is a cause of transient *aplastic crisis* in patients with chronic hemolytic anemia. Recovery is associated with reappearance of reticulocytes in the peripheral smear 7 to 10 days after their disappearance. In patients with AIDS and other immunosuppressive illnesses, parvovirus B19 infection can manifest as chronic anemia. These patients often have persistent parvovirus infection without an appropriate immunoglobulin response.[60]

Differential Considerations. In children, erythema infectiosum resembles other viral exanthems. The "slapped-cheek" appearance of the rash is characteristic.

Management. Erythema infectiosum is generally a mild disease, and no treatment is required. Patients with parvovirus B19–associated aplastic crisis may require blood transfusions. Therapy with immunoglobulin can lessen the need for transfusions in immunosuppressed patients with chronic anemia.[61] Women who develop parvovirus infection during pregnancy should be followed closely for the development of fetal hydrops fetalis. The role of intrauterine blood transfusions in the treatment of this disorder remains controversial.[59] Although the disease is probably transmitted via respiratory secretions, patients are probably no longer infectious by the time the rash appears.[61]

RNA VIRUSES

Reoviridae

The family Reoviridae (from respiratory enteric orphans) includes four viruses causing human disease: orthoreovirus, orbivirus, coltivirus, and rotavirus. The reoviruses commonly infect humans but infrequently cause human disease. Upper respiratory infections, exanthems, pneumonia, hepatitis, encephalitis, gastroenteritis, and biliary atresia have on occasion been associated with these viruses.

Colorado Tick Fever
Principles of Disease
Colorado tick fever, or mountain fever, is caused by a coltivirus similar to the orbiviruses that are transmitted to humans through the bite of the hard-shelled wood tick *Dermacentor andersoni.* It occurs primarily in the western United States, but a serotype has been isolated from the *Ixodes ricinus* tick in Germany and the dog tick, *Dermacentor variabilis,* from Long Island, New York. Illness generally occurs in late spring through summer.

Clinical Findings and Features
The incubation period for Colorado tick fever is 3 to 6 days, and a history of tick exposure is elicited in 90% of patients. The disease generally occurs in people engaged in activities that bring them into contact with ticks. The fever is biphasic or "saddle-backed," with the patient initially acutely experiencing chills, lethargy, prostration, headache, ocular pain, photophobia, abdominal pain, and severe myalgias. The initial fever lasts 2 to 3 days, recedes for a similar period, and is then followed by a second fever lasting approximately 3 days. Rash, occasionally petechial, is an uncommon finding, occurring in 5% to 10% of patients. Meningoencephalitis is an uncommon serious complication in children.[62] Convalescence lasts 1 to 3 weeks; half of infected persons are viremic 4 weeks after the onset of illness.[62]

Differential Considerations
Colorado tick fever is commonly misdiagnosed as Rocky Mountain spotted fever. Patients with fever and rash after tick bites in endemic areas should be treated for Rocky Mountain spotted fever. Confirmation of the diagnosis of Colorado tick fever is by mouse inoculation or fluorescent staining of erythrocytes.

Management
Treatment is supportive and symptomatic.

Orbivirus

Six orbiviruses have been implicated in human disease. Changuinola virus is transmitted from *Phlebotomus* flies; Lebombo and Orungo viruses from mosquitoes; and Kemerovo, Lipovnik, and Tribec viruses from ticks. All six have been associated with febrile illnesses and, rarely, encephalitis.

Rotavirus
Principles of Disease
Rotaviruses derive their name from their wheel-like appearance when seen by transmission electron microscopy. They cause severe gastroenteritis in infants and young children, particularly between the ages of 6 months and 2 years; the gastroenteritis is manifested by severe diarrhea and vomiting, which often lead to dehydration and occasionally, death.[63] In temperate climates, illness occurs mainly in the winter, is commonly associated with nosocomial infection, and is spread primarily person to person by the fecal-oral route. The incubation period is about 2 days.

Clinical Features
Mucosal epithelial cells of the small intestine appear to be infected, selectively leading to shortening of villi and decreased absorption of salt and water. A secretory diarrhea is produced with impaired D-xylose absorption. The clinical disease ranges from asymptomatic to severe, fatal diarrhea and dehydration. The illness is abrupt in onset with nausea, vomiting, watery diarrhea, low-grade fevers, headache, and myalgias. The course of the disease is generally 3 to 5 days. Fatalities are common in developing countries but rare in the developed world. In newborns, rotavirus has been associated with neonatal necrotizing enterocolitis.[64] Infections in adults are usually asymptomatic.

Differential Considerations
Rotavirus enteritis should be suspected in any child with watery diarrhea occurring during the cooler months of the year. Fecal leukocytes and erythrocytes are not generally seen in rotaviral diarrhea. Other enteric viruses can produce a clinical syndrome similar to that of the rotavirus. Radioimmunoassays, enzyme immunoassays, and latex agglutination methods for detecting antigen are highly reliable and available at most hospital laboratories.

Management
Specific treatment for rotaviral infections is not currently available. Intravenous fluids provide effective therapy for dehydration, but if the patient tolerates oral fluids, oral rehydration using the standard World Health Organization formula of sugar and electrolytes can be used in the outpatient setting for mild to moderate dehydration.

Togaviridae

Alphavirus (Group A Arbovirus)

Principles of Disease
Arboviruses (from *ar*thropod-*bor*ne viruses) are transmitted to humans by an arthropod vector, with humans usually being an unimportant host in the reproductive cycle of the virus. Most arboviruses are mosquito borne, but ticks, sandflies, gnats, and midges serve as important vectors for some diseases. The alphaviruses and flaviviruses are the most common arboviruses causing disease in humans, but some bunyaviruses, reoviruses, rhabdoviruses, filoviruses, arenaviruses, and orthomyxoviruses also are transmitted via arboviral vectors.

The alphaviruses are transmitted by the bite of a mosquito. The three alphaviruses that cause human disease in the United States are the agents of eastern equine encephalitis, western equine encephalitis, and Venezuelan equine encephalitis. Other important alphaviruses include chikungunya (Africa, Southeast Asia, Philippines), Mayaro (South America), O'nyong-nyong (Africa), Ross River (Australia, South Pacific), and Sindbis (Africa, Asia, Soviet Union, Australia, and Scandinavia).

Clinical Features
These arboviruses can cause outbreaks of encephalitis in various parts of the United States.[65] The few cases of

eastern equine encephalitis in the United States occur predominantly near freshwater swamps of the Eastern seaboard. Although more than 95% of cases are sub-clinical, patients presenting with clinical encephalitis have a mortality rate approaching 50%. Infections occur most commonly in children younger than 10 years of age or in elderly people. The onset of symptoms is often fulminant, with headache, fevers, convulsions progressing rapidly to decreasing level of consciousness, and death. Focal neurologic symptoms may also occur. Western equine encephalitis is present throughout the United States but occurs mostly in the western and central parts of the nation. Children younger than 1 year of age and the elderly are most often affected. More than 99% of cases are inapparent, and the encephalitis is usually mild, with a mortality rate of approximately 3%. Venezuelan equine encephalitis is predominantly found in Central and South America, but the disease has been seen in Texas and Florida. Venezuelan equine encephalitis usually presents as an influenza-like illness. One third of patients have encephalitis, with a mortality rate of less than 1%, predominantly in children.

Differential Considerations

Other viral causes of encephalitis in the United States include HSV, HIV, St. Louis encephalitis (a flavivirus), California (La Crosse) encephalitis (a bunyavirus), and the recently encountered West Nile-like encephalitis (a flavivirus).[66,67] Other viruses, such as mumps, rabies, polio, and other enteroviruses, can also manifest as encephalitides. The white blood cell count in the CSF of persons with eastern equine encephalitis may be very high, and the diagnosis of meningoencephalitis must be considered. Diagnoses can be confirmed by a rise in antibody titers.

Management

Management is entirely supportive. For people with expected intensive exposure to these viruses, an investigational vaccine may be available from the U.S. Army Medical Research Institute for Infectious Diseases in Fort Detrick, Maryland.

Rubella Virus (German Measles)

Clinical Features

Rubella is a mild febrile illness associated with a diffuse maculopapular rash, fever, malaise, headache, and postauricular, occipital, and posterior cervical lymphadenopathy (Figure 128-5).

Transmission of rubella is via contact with respiratory secretions. The incubation period of rubella ranges from 12 to 23 days. Accompanied by viremia, the rash usually lasts 3 to 5 days. The disease is highly communicable from about 1 week before to 4 days after the onset of the rash. The most common complications of rubella are arthropathies, or frank arthritis, predominantly affecting the fingers, wrists, and knees; the arthropathies may persist for several months. Encephalitis and thrombocytopenia are rare complications.

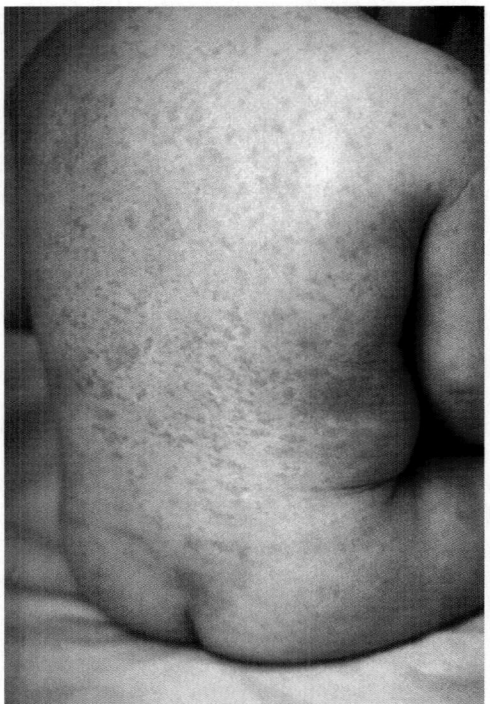

Figure 128-5. Rubella.

Although the disease is generally a mild, febrile illness in children and adults, the consequences of rubella occurring during pregnancy (congenital rubella syndrome) may be tragic. Severe consequences include fetal death, premature delivery, and a variety of congenital defects, including hearing loss, cataracts, retinopathy, mental retardation, and a variety of cardiac abnormalities. The younger the fetus is at the time of a maternal infection, the more likely it is that the fetus will be affected. During the first 2 months of pregnancy, the fetus has approximately a 90% chance of being affected. The chance of being affected is approximately 80% during the third month and 66% during the fourth month. No congenital defects were found in the 106 children born to mothers after laboratory-proven maternal infection contracted after the 17th week of pregnancy.[68]

Differential Considerations

The rash associated with rubella ("third disease") is one of the classic common exanthems of childhood. It may be similar to the rash of measles (rubeola, or "first disease"), scarlet fever ("second disease"), a variant of scarlet fever or toxin-producing staphylococcal disease ("fourth disease"), erythema infectiosum ("fifth disease"), and roseola (exanthem subitum, or "sixth disease").[69]

Management

Rubella control is required to prevent birth defects in the offspring of women who develop the disease during pregnancy. Vaccination to prevent rubella in the United States is recommended for all children at the age of 15 months. Vaccination results in a greater than 95% seroconversion rate. Because of the production of a transient viremia, pregnancy should be delayed for 3 months after a susceptible woman has been vaccinated. No cases of the congenital rubella syndrome attributable to rubella vaccine have occurred in more than 300 women inadvertently vaccinated during pregnancy who carried their infants to term.[70] There is no evidence of decreasing immunity with age. Persons with rubella should be cautioned to avoid contact with susceptible women. Because of an increasing failure to vaccinate susceptible people, a moderate resurgence of rubella and a major increase in the congenital rubella syndrome in the United States occurred in 1990.[71]

Flaviviridae

Flavivirus (Group B Arbovirus)

Principles of Disease

More than 60 flaviviruses have been identified, with more than 20 causing human disease. Three of the most common, all transmitted to humans via a mosquito vector, are the agents of yellow fever, dengue, and St. Louis encephalitis. West Nile virus is a fourth flavivirus identified as the cause of a cluster of meningoencephalitis cases in New York City in 1999 and has since reached epidemic proportions in the United States.[66] In 2003, the CDC confirmed 9858 cases and 262 deaths attributable to West Nile virus, qualifying it as the largest outbreak of arboviral meningoencephalitis recorded in the Western hemisphere.[72] The primary cycle of infection is maintained by vector mosquitoes in bird populations and the human is infected by cross-feeding mosquitoes.[67] The virus has disproportionately affected certain bird populations in the United States, resulting in bird deaths. This phenomenon led to early elucidation of the life cycle and has helped in characterization of the zoonotic activity of the virus.[67]

Non–arthropod-borne human cases from laboratory transmission and person-to-person transmission via blood transfusion, organ transplantation, maternal-fetal transmission, or breast-feeding have been documented. These modes of transmission account for a small minority of cases.[73]

Clinical Features

Yellow fever is present in tropical South America and Africa. Fever, chills, headache, nausea, and vomiting follow a 3- to 6-day incubation period.[74] The disease may be biphasic, with fever, jaundice, hemorrhage, and characteristic "black vomit" (from the coagulopathy secondary to an affected liver) occurring after a brief period of remission. The case fatality rate is 5%.

Dengue occurs in tropical areas worldwide. There are several reports of dengue transmission within the United States, but these cases have been limited to Texas.[75] Classic dengue fever (breakbone fever) is a nonfatal disease characterized by fever, headache, arthralgias, weakness, nausea, and anorexia after an incubation period of 5 to 10 days. Patients may experience severe bone pain. A generalized macular rash that occasionally desquamates may be seen. The fever

lasts 5 to 7 days, but recovery may be prolonged. Dengue hemorrhagic fever, characterized by increased vascular permeability and bleeding associated with thrombocytopenia, has a mortality rate of less than 5% in people who receive good medical care but a mortality rate of up to 50% in those left untreated.

St. Louis encephalitis occurs in the summer in most areas of the Western Hemisphere. After an incubation period of 4 to 21 days, infection with the St. Louis encephalitis virus can produce a simple fever and headache, aseptic meningitis, or encephalitis. The mortality rate associated with the encephalitis approaches 10%. The disease commonly affects elderly people.

Cases of West Nile virus have been reported from May to December.[76] The incubation period for West Nile virus appears to be 3 to 14 days. Twenty percent of infected people develop West Nile fever and 1 in 150 develops meningitis or encephalitis.[67,77] West Nile fever is usually characterized by fever, headache, myalgia, anorexia, and lymphadenopathy; half of infected patients develop a maculopapular central rash.[73] West Nile virus meningoencephalitis is characterized by fever, headache, mental status changes, and motor disturbances that range from myoclonus, tremor, and parkinsonian movement disorders to generalized weakness. A poliomyelitis-like syndrome has been described.[76] Cranial nerve and bulbar abnormalities can be seen.[78]

Laboratory abnormalities are nonspecific. CSF findings in patients with meningoencephalitis are similar to those in patients with other viral infections, with elevated protein level, normal glucose level, and a mild to moderate pleocytosis with a lymphocytic predominance.[78] Viremia usually clears by the onset of meningoencephalitis, but IgM can be detected in the CSF. IgM levels in the serum can remain elevated long after clinical illness has resolved. Imaging studies are nondiagnostic, but the magnetic resonance imaging scan can show nonspecific leptomeningeal inflammation.[78]

Disease outcome is related to patient age, and older patients are at a significantly higher risk for developing encephalitis and dying from West Nile virus infection.[78] Patients with disease severe enough to require hospitalization often have long-term sequelae.

Differential Considerations

The differential diagnosis of yellow fever is wide and includes hepatitis, malaria, typhoid, dengue, and other viral hemorrhagic fevers in endemic areas. Viral antigen detected in the blood by enzyme-linked immunoadsorbent assay provides for a rapid diagnosis. The differential diagnosis for dengue is similar to that for yellow fever. Diagnosis is made by viral isolation or serology. St. Louis encephalitis can manifest like other causes of meningoencephalitis. In elderly patients, it may be misdiagnosed as stroke. Diagnosis is made by serologic tests. West Nile virus disease is most apparent in summer and fall months and may be clinically indistinguishable from other arboviral illnesses. CSF IgM antibody testing is the best means of establishing the diagnosis but may be falsely positive after other flaviviral infections such as St. Louis encephalitis or after immunization to yellow fever.[67]

Management

Treatment for these viral diseases is supportive. The diseases are not contagious through person-to-person contact, but the virus is generally transmissible to the mosquito vector during the clinical illness. Control of epidemics is achieved by reducing the mosquito vector populations and limiting access of mosquitoes to infected hosts. Persons traveling to endemic areas should be vaccinated for yellow fever.[79]

There are currently no recommended therapies for West Nile virus. Treatment is supportive. Suspected disease should be reported to public health authorities. Control of West Nile virus infection will rest in control of vector mosquito populations. Physicians should join public health officials in aggressive efforts to educate the public on mosquito control and bite protection measures, such as the use of repellents and protective clothing.

Hepatitis C

Hepatitis C, now classified in its own genus, hepacivirus, within the flaviviridae, is an important cause of morbidity and mortality throughout the world. In the United States, hepatitis C had been associated with most cases of posttransfusion (non-A, non-B) disease. As a result of testing the blood supply, the incidence of transfusion-related hepatitis C has decreased. Yet the prevalence of infection remains high in certain populations, such as intravenous drug users. In the United States, it is estimated that 3.9 million people have hepatitis C infection.[80]

Chronic hepatitis C infection has been associated with cirrhosis and hepatocellular carcinoma. Estimates of the rate of long-term morbidity and mortality resulting from chronic hepatitis C vary. The likelihood of developing cirrhosis ranges from 5% to 25% in different studies.[81] Hepatitis C is further discussed in Chapter 89.

Coronaviridae

Coronavirus

Principles of Disease

The cause of the recently described severe acute respiratory syndrome (SARS) has been identified as a novel coronavirus (SARS-CoV).[82,83] The virus might have been transmitted to humans by handling and consumption of wild mammals, such as the civet.[84] SARS was first documented in China's Guangdong province in November 2002; by mid-February 2003, more than 300 cases of atypical pneumonia were being investigated in Vietnam, China, and Hong Kong Special Administrative Region. Before it was declared "contained" by the World Health Organization in July 2003, SARS had spread to 27 countries with more than 8000 cases and at least 774 deaths. Scattered cases have been reported in China in 2004.

As of June, 2003, there were 393 cases of SARS reported in the United States. Of these, 70 (18%) were classified as probable SARS cases based on the clinical and laboratory criteria, but no U.S. deaths were reported that were attributable to SARS.[85] Most patients had traveled to an area of documented or suspected SARS transmission.

The SARS epidemic has posed a challenge to national and international medical personnel and public health authorities. Public health measures have been implemented to contain the infection and establish sentinel systems to warn of recurrent outbreaks. Health care practitioners, especially emergency personnel, should notify local public health authorities of suspected or confirmed cases of SARS.

Clinical Features

The case definition for SARS-CoV includes the presence of two or more features: fever (>38° C), chills, rigors, myalgia, headache, diarrhea, sore throat, and rhinorrhea. Mild to moderate disease requires fever and evidence of lower respiratory illness. Severe respiratory illness is defined as patients who also exhibit radiographic evidence of pneumonia or acute respiratory distress syndrome. Laboratory criteria for the diagnosis of disease relies on SARS-CoV antibody testing, cell culture, or reverse-transcription polymerase chain reaction.[86]

Retrospective analyses of the SARS-CoV outbreak suggest an incubation period of 3 to 10 days with an ensuing viral prodrome characterized by headache, malaise, and myalgias. Fever, clinical evidence of upper and lower respiratory infection, dyspnea, and gastrointestinal disturbances are all variable. Chest radiographs are normal in up to 25% of patients with early infection despite the presence of fever and respiratory complaints.[87,88] CT scans may be more useful in identifying early pulmonary involvement. Hypoxemia, with clinical and radiographic evidence of pneumonitis, develops as the disease progresses. In a minority of patients, progressive respiratory failure and acute respiratory distress syndrome may follow. Patients older than 60 years of age and those with comorbid illness such as diabetes mellitus have worse outcomes.[87,88]

Laboratory findings are nonspecific but include lymphopenia, thrombocytopenia, elevated lactate dehydrogenase level, and prolonged activated partial thromboplastin time. Hemolytic anemia and electrolyte disturbances, such as severe hypomagnesemia with associated tetany, have been reported.[89]

Differential Considerations

The clinical features of SARS-CoV mimic those of many community and nosocomial respiratory infections, so the differential diagnosis is wide. The initial workup should include routine laboratory and radiographic evaluations as for other, more common respiratory infections. An increased level of suspicion for SARS-CoV infection should be entertained based on travel or exposure history. Specific testing for coronavirus can be conducted through the health department.

Several outbreaks of SARS-CoV occurred after exposure of patients or medical staff to a sentinel case or to a clinical specimen. Therefore, effective evaluation and management of suspected or proven cases of SARS-CoV must begin with a travel and occupational history, astute clinical observation, appropriate triaging, and patient isolation measures. Contact and airborne precautions should be instituted and protective eyewear should be considered. Detailed guidelines for the diagnosis, isolation, treatment, and disposition of patients with suspected or proven SARS-CoV infection are continuously being updated by the World Health Organization and CDC. The clinician should refer to these guidelines (www.cdc.gov; www.who.int) and contact local health officials for guidance.

Management

No therapeutic measures beyond supportive care have been shown to be clearly effective for the treatment of SARS-CoV infection.[87,89,90] Patients manifesting signs and symptoms of lower respiratory tract infection should be treated with conventional antibiotic and supportive therapy even if they are suspected of having SARS-CoV infection.

Disposition

It is not necessary to admit all patients who are suspected to have been exposed to or have a respiratory syndrome that could be attributed to SARS-CoV infection. Persons well enough to be cared for at home should be placed in home quarantine with contact and air-borne precautions. Termination of quarantine precautions for suspected SARS-CoV infection should be done in consultation with public health officials.

Other Coronaviruses

Principles of Disease

Coronaviruses are agents of the common cold in adults and of lower respiratory tract disease in children. More recently, they have been implicated in diarrheal disease in children.

Clinical Features

Coronaviruses primarily cause upper respiratory tract disease in adults. Lower respiratory tract infections caused by coronaviruses occur uncommonly in adults and more commonly in children. They appear to cause diarrheal disease in children younger than 1 year of age.

Differential Considerations

Coronaviruses probably account for 15% of adult colds. Rhinoviruses account for most of the rest, with parainfluenza viruses, influenza viruses, respiratory syncytial viruses, adenoviruses, and enteroviruses also causing upper respiratory infections and colds. Rotaviruses, Norwalk viruses, and enteroviruses cause most viral cases of gastroenteritis in children.

Management and Disposition

Treatment of most coronaviruses is entirely supportive.

Paramyxoviridae

Parainfluenza Viruses

Clinical Features

The parainfluenza viruses are the most common causes of croup in children and, along with the respiratory syncytial virus (RSV), are the most common causes of lower respiratory tract infections that require hospitalization in infants.[91]

The virus is passed via the respiratory route, and hand-to-mucous membrane transmission is likely. The incubation period is most often 1 to 4 days and results in a febrile illness lasting approximately 4 days.

Infection with the parainfluenza viruses does not confer lasting immunity. Parainfluenza virus type 1 is the predominant cause of croup, or laryngotracheobronchitis, occurring during the autumn months in children younger than 3 years of age. Parainfluenza virus type 2 is also associated with croup, causes less morbidity than type 1, and often occurs in alternate years with type 1. Parainfluenza type 3 infections occur in the spring and are associated with bronchiolitis and pneumonia in infants younger than 1 year of age, similar to RSV. Parainfluenza type 3 is also associated with croup in children younger than 3, and with tracheobronchitis in older children. Parainfluenza type 4 is recovered less often but appears to be associated with mild respiratory illness. Severe croup or bacterial superinfection of laryngotracheitis may lead to respiratory compromise.

Differential Considerations

Viruses causing upper respiratory tract infection similar to that caused by the parainfluenza viruses include adenoviruses, rhinoviruses, influenza virus, RSV, echoviruses, coxsackieviruses, and coronaviruses. Identification of parainfluenza viral infection can be made by a fourfold rise in antibody titer between acute and convalescent serum.

Management

Croup may be worse at night; mist inhalation is often helpful. Treatment with nebulized racemic epinephrine can be used to treat severe croup, but the relief it affords can be short lived, and return to pretreatment state can be seen within 2 hours of therapy. Intramuscular steroids have been shown to be helpful, and their use has been associated with a decreased requirement for hospitalization of children with croup.[91] The parainfluenza viruses can reinfect individuals within months of primary infection, so prevention of infection is unlikely.

Respiratory Syncytial Virus

Principles of Disease

Infections with RSV occur worldwide, mostly in midwinter to late spring. Infants with pneumonia show marked inflammation in the interstitial tissue and alveoli of the lungs, whereas infants with bronchiolitis show less alveolar involvement but may have marked changes in the bronchioles. Severe disease may result in obstruction of bronchioles with evidence of peripheral airway obstruction or emphysema. Transmission is via respiratory secretions and probably by hand to nose or eye droplet inoculation.

Infections caused by RSV account for the largest number of hospitalizations for respiratory infections in infants. Bronchiolitis and pneumonia, the most severe manifestations of RSV infection, commonly occur in children younger than 6 months of age. Children older than 1 year of age are less likely to have lower respiratory tract infection.[92] Older children and adults commonly have colds and cough, but older patients may have severe disease.

Clinical Features

The average incubation time of RSV infections is 2 to 8 days. The most common manifestations are bronchiolitis and pneumonia in infants; tracheobronchitis, croup, and otitis media in young children; and upper respiratory infections in older children and adults. Bronchiolitis in infancy may lead to an increased risk of asthma and the development of chronic obstructive airway disease in later life. Fatal disease can occur in immunocompromised infants.

The diagnosis of RSV infection can be made definitively by culturing the virus or detecting RSV antigens from respiratory secretions, nasal washes, or nasopharyngeal or throat swabs.

Differential Considerations

The syndromes associated with RSV infections overlap those of other upper and lower respiratory tract pathogens and include rhinovirus, parainfluenza and influenza viruses, echoviruses, coxsackieviruses, and coronaviruses. RSV can be presumptively diagnosed in an infant with pneumonia or bronchiolitis when no bacterial pathogens are noted. Noninfectious causes for hypoxemia in infants, such as foreign-body aspiration and asthma, must also be considered.

Management

Therapy of RSV is largely supportive. For infants sick enough to be hospitalized, aerosolized ribavirin has been shown to shorten the duration of illness and improve hypoxemia in normal infants.[93] Corticosteroids have not been shown to be beneficial. During the winter, high-risk infants can be protected against RSV infection with monthly infusions of human RSV immunoglobulin or with monthly intramuscular injections of a monoclonal anti-RSV antibody preparation.[93] Severe disease may occur in immunocompromised infants, and respiratory precautions are required to prevent transmission from patient to patient and staff to patient.

Mumps Virus

Principles of Disease

Mumps, or infectious parotitis, is an acute viral illness characterized by fever, swelling, and tenderness of the salivary glands, with the parotid gland most commonly involved. Mumps occurs most commonly in the winter and spring and since the advent of widespread pediatric immunization, mostly in older children. The virus is spread via the respiratory tract and by direct contact with the saliva of infected people. The incubation period is 2 to 4 weeks, and the disease is communicable from 1 week before to 9 days after the onset of parotitis, with a period of maximal infectiousness approximately 2 days before the onset of illness. One third of cases are asymptomatic.

Clinical Features

Nonsuppurative parotid swelling is the hallmark of mumps; the swelling may be unilateral. Trismus is sometimes seen. In the first 3 days, the patient's temperature may range between normal and 40° C. The most important, but less common, manifestations are epididymo-orchitis and meningitis. Orchitis occurs in 15% to 25% of postpubertal men and is usually unilateral. Although some testicular atrophy generally occurs, the incidence of sterility is very low, especially when the orchitis is unilateral.[94] More than 50% of patients with mumps have a lymphocytic pleocytosis in the CSF, and hypoglycorrhachia is common, but symptomatic meningitis occurs in fewer than 10% of cases. Encephalitis is uncommon, occurring in 1 in 6000 cases, and is the major determinant of mortality. Congenital infection is rare but may result in fetal loss if it occurs in the first trimester.[95] Rare complications of mumps include hydrocephalus, deafness, transverse myelitis, Guillain-Barré syndrome, pancreatitis, mastitis, oophoritis, myocarditis, and arthritis.

Differential Considerations

In children, the diagnosis of mumps is made by a history of infectious exposure and the presence of parotid swelling and tenderness in association with constitutional symptoms. Laboratory confirmation is generally not required. The differential diagnosis includes other viral infections and other causes of parotid swelling and tenderness, such as bacterial parotitis or sarcoidosis.

Management

Treatment is supportive and should include an analgesic and antipyretic agent. No data support the use of steroids to prevent complications of or ameliorate the symptoms of orchitis in postpubertal men.

Contacts who have had no history of mumps or of previous vaccination should be immunized. Because there is no risk in vaccinating those who are already immune, serologic screening to identify susceptible people is unnecessary. More than 95% of recipients of the vaccine develop long-lasting immunity. Previously infected people, including those with asymptomatic cases, have long-lasting, and possibly lifelong, immunity.

Measles Virus (Rubeola)

Principles of Disease

Measles is a highly communicable viral illness acquired as an infection of the respiratory tract. Generally, all susceptible people exposed to an active case will acquire infection. After multiplication in the respiratory mucosa, the virus spreads to regional lymphoid cells and then via the bloodstream to leukocytes in the reticuloendothelial system. The clinical manifestations appear after a second viremic phase.

Before the availability of an effective vaccine in 1963, measles was a ubiquitous disease. It is now uncommon in countries where routine infant vaccination is practiced but persists in epidemics in countries without such practices and accounts for 2 million deaths per year.

Clinical Features

The incubation period of measles is 10 to 14 days. Cough, coryza, conjunctivitis, and fever precede a rash by 2 to 4 days (Figure 128-6A). Pinpoint grayish spots surrounded by bright red inflammation (Koplik's spots) are characteristically found on the lateral buccal mucosa before the appearance of the rash and are considered pathognomonic for measles (Figure 128-6B). Discrete red macular and papular lesions begin on the head and progress downward over 3 days to cover the entire body. Laryngitis, tracheobronchitis, bronchiolitis, and pneumonitis may accompany the disease. Bacterial superinfections occasionally delay recovery. An acute encephalomyelitis, which has a mortality rate of 25%, can, rarely, complicate recovery. Unlike rubella, measles acquired during pregnancy is not teratogenic but may result in stillbirth or premature delivery.

Infants and malnourished children generally develop more severe illness. Deaths from pneumonia and diarrhea occur in up to 10% of cases. Measles can exacerbate vitamin A deficiency and lead to blindness.

Measles may manifest with atypical findings in people who were vaccinated with the inactivated vaccine before its removal from the market in the United States in 1968. An atypical rash, predominantly on the extremities, can accompany pneumonitis, pleural effusion, and peripheral edema. The current vaccine is a live, attenuated strain available as a single antigen or in combination with rubella vaccine or with mumps and rubella vaccines.[96]

Differential Considerations

The diagnosis is made primarily from clinical characteristics. Other viral exanthems may at times manifest with a similar rash.

Management

Treatment of the primary disease is supportive. Immunocompromised children and infants younger than 1 year of age who are susceptible and have been exposed to measles can be given passive immunization within 6 days of exposure. Healthy infants should receive 0.25 mL/kg of immunoglobulin intramuscularly, and immunocompromised children should be given 0.5 mL/kg intramuscularly, up to 15 mL.

Routine vaccination has decreased the number of cases of measles reported in the United States by more than 99%. Since 1983, there had been an increase in cases among babies younger than 15 months of age and in nonimmunized inner-city preschool-age children.[97] Outbreaks have occurred among the 2% to 5% of people who fail to seroconvert after a single dose of vaccine, notably among those living on college cam-

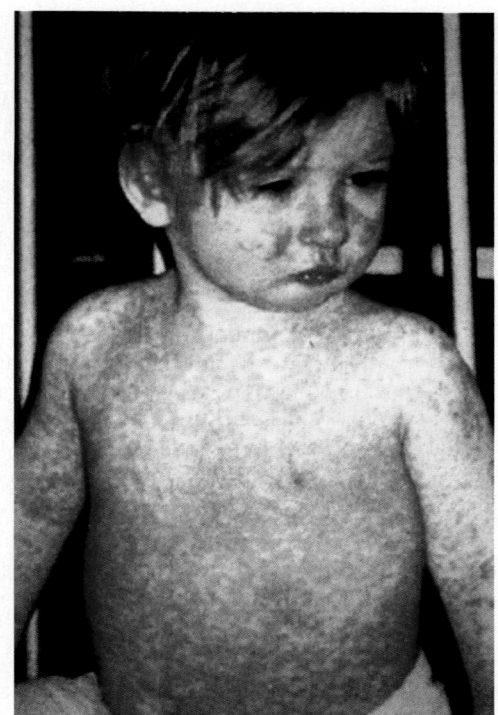

A

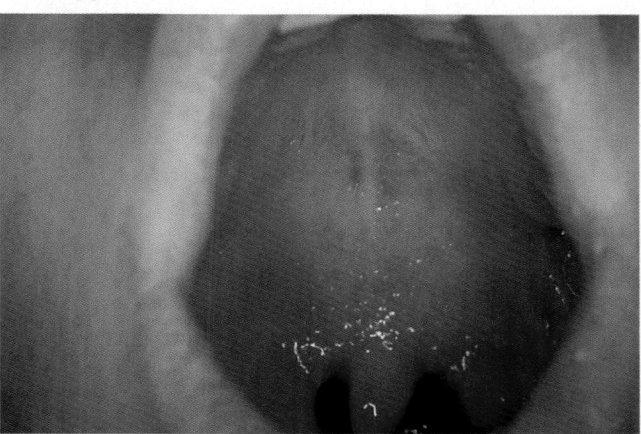

B

Figure 128-6. A, Measles. **B**, Koplik's spots due to measles.

puses.[96] Because a second dose converts 95% of initial failures, the current recommendation is for a two-dose measles vaccination program, with the first dose given at 15 months of age and the second on school entry. People should also be revaccinated if they are entering educational institutions after high school or entering hospital service and have not had either a documented case of measles or the two-dose regimen. These new recommendations have resulted in a decrease in cases of measles since the resurgence occurring from 1989 to 1991.

Measles is a reportable disease in most states, and the local health authority should be contacted. Children should be kept out of school for at least 4 days after the appearance of the rash.

Subacute Sclerosing Panencephalitis

Principles of Disease

Subacute sclerosing panencephalitis is a degenerative disease of the brain caused by measles virus or a defective variant that persists in the CNS after primary measles. Subacute sclerosing panencephalitis has virtually disappeared in the United States since the 1970s, approximately 10 years after measles vaccination began.

Clinical Features

Subacute sclerosing panencephalitis is a subacute encephalitis involving both the white and the gray matter of the cerebral hemispheres and brainstem and follows 1 in 100,000 cases of measles. It generally occurs in patients with a history of an uncomplicated case of primary measles that occurred at a younger than average age. Five to 10 years later, subacute sclerosing panencephalitis manifests with myoclonus and variable focal neurologic deficits. Progressive neurologic degeneration ensues, and death usually occurs within months to years of diagnosis.

Differential Considerations

The disease can appear like other degenerative neurologic disorders, but characteristic electroencephalographic changes and the detection of measles antibodies in the CSF and markedly elevated serum antibodies to measles confirm the diagnosis.

Management

Treatment is entirely supportive.

Rhabdoviridae

Within the Rhabdoviridae family of viruses are two genera, Lyssavirus, containing the rabies and rabies-like viruses, and Vesiculovirus, containing the vesicular stomatitis and related viruses. Lyssavirus contains six viruses, but only the rabies, Duvenhage, and Mokola viruses are known to cause disease in humans. Rabies is further discussed in Chapter 129.

Vesicular Stomatitis Virus and Related Viruses

Vesicular stomatitis virus commonly infects wild and domestic animals and occasionally infects humans. Transmission is believed to be from insect bites. Vesicular stomatitis virus New Jersey type and vesicular stomatitis virus Indiana type produce an influenza-like febrile illness 1 to 2 days after exposure that lasts 4 to 7 days. Oral vesicular lesions have occasionally been noted.[98] The disease is nonspecific. Diagnosis can be made serologically. Treatment is supportive.

Filoviridae

Marburg and Ebola Viruses

Principles of Disease

Marburg and Ebola viruses cause bleeding and shock often associated with thrombocytopenia and a systemic febrile illnesses (African hemorrhagic fever) associated with gastrointestinal bleeding and a high mortality rate. Although the viruses have infected African green monkeys and cynomolgus monkeys, respectively, the infection is fatal to the monkeys, and the natural reservoir is unknown. Monkey-to-human and human-to-human transmission via contaminated tissues or materials has been documented. Aerosol transmission has not been documented.

Clinical Features

The illness is of sudden onset 7 to 10 days after exposure to infected tissue or contact with contaminated materials. Headache, fever, myalgias, arthralgias, and lethargy are early signs. The cardinal sign of these infections is gastrointestinal bleeding. Reported cases of Marburg virus and Ebola virus disease have a mortality rate of 25% and 90%, respectively. An outbreak of Ebola viral hemorrhagic fever in Zaire in 1995 had a case fatality rate of greater than 90%.[99]

Differential Considerations

Marburg and Ebola virus diseases may appear clinically similar to other African hemorrhagic fevers, particularly Rift Valley fever, Lassa fever, and yellow fever. Diagnosis is made by isolation of the virus from blood or demonstrating rising antibody titers.

Management

No vaccine exists; treatment is supportive.[100]

Orthomyxoviridae

Influenza Virus

Principles of Disease

Influenza is generally a self-limited infection of the upper respiratory tract associated with fever, cough, coryza, sore throat, and malaise.[9] Three types of influenza are recognized. Type A has been associated with most widespread epidemics and pandemics and is associated with most mortality caused by influenza. Influenza B causes regional or widespread epidemics every 2 to 3 years. Influenza C is associated with sporadic cases.

Clinical Features

The usual clinical disease caused by influenza begins 1 to 4 days after exposure to aerosol respiratory secretions. Fevers ensue and are accompanied by myalgias, coryza, and conjunctivitis; headache; and a nonproductive cough. Patchy infiltrates can be seen on chest radiographs. Symptoms generally last only a few days, but fatigue and malaise may persist for weeks. The most common serious complications of influenza, particularly among elderly patients and people with chronic diseases, are pneumonia caused by influenza itself and pneumonia attributable to secondary bacterial infections. Rare complications of influenza infection include aseptic meningitis, pericarditis, and a postinfectious neuritis that resembles the Guillain-Barré syndrome.

Viral cultures remain the gold standard for the laboratory diagnosis of influenza, but results are often not timely enough to aid the clinician in initiating therapy. Commercially available point-of-care tests that promise results within minutes may be more relevant with the availability of the neuraminidase inhibitors.

Differential Considerations

The diagnosis of influenza is made on clinical grounds during the appropriate season. Serologic confirmation is rarely required, but definitive diagnosis can be made by serologic testing or by isolation of the virus from nasal secretions. The syndromes produced by the influenza viruses overlap with those produced by other viruses such as the parainfluenza viruses, RSV, adenoviruses, coronaviruses, and echoviruses.

Management

General supportive measures ameliorate the symptoms of influenza. The neuraminidase inhibitors zanamivir and oseltamivir have been approved for treating both influenza A and B. The dose of oseltamivir should be decreased to 75 mg qd in patients with a creatinine clearance of less than 30 mL/min. Zanamivir or oseltamivir should be administered within 2 days of the onset of symptoms if efficacy is to expected.[9] Amantadine, 100 mg twice a day, is effective in the treatment and prophylaxis of clinical disease caused by influenza A but not influenza B.[101] Confusion is a common side effect of amantadine, particularly in elderly patients, so the dosage should be decreased accordingly. Amantadine should be used with caution in patients with renal failure. Vaccination is recommended yearly for people who are at high risk of significant morbidity or mortality from influenza; these include immunosuppressed patients or those with chronic illnesses, people older than 65 years of age, and women in the second or third trimester of pregnancy. Vaccination is also recommended for service personnel, such as health care workers, police, or fire fighters, who may transmit the infection to others or who provide vital services. Aspirin and aspirin-containing products should be avoided, especially among children and adolescents, particularly during influenza epidemics because of the association between the use of aspirin during a bout of influenza and the subsequent development of Reye's syndrome.[42]

Bunyaviridae

California Encephalitis and Bunyavirus Hemorrhagic Fevers

Pathophysiology and Clinical Findings

California encephalitis viruses, including the La Crosse and Johnson Canyon viruses, are transmitted by mosquito bite, predominantly in the northern United States in the summer and fall. Approximately 100 cases are reported yearly. Infection is mostly asymptomatic, but the mortality rate of the encephalitis is approximately 1%.[102]

Hantaviruses cause a hemorrhagic fever with renal syndrome. Rodents carry the agents, and the virus is transmitted via aerosols infected from rodent urine. More than 100,000 cases occur in Asia and Europe yearly, and the mortality rate is approximately 6%.[103]

In 1994, a previously unknown hantavirus was found to cause a pulmonary syndrome associated with tachypnea, hemoconcentration, thrombocytopenia, and leukocytosis.[104] Cases occurred predominantly in the southwestern United States, were associated with a mortality rate higher than 50% and were believed to have been transmitted from the deer mouse, *Peromyscus maniculatus.* The virus has been named the *Muerto Canyon* or *Sin Nombre* virus.

Rift Valley fever virus is carried by a mosquito and generally produces a nonspecific febrile disease. Up to 100,000 cases occur yearly in Africa. Some patients develop a severe retinitis that may lead to blindness. Congo-Crimean hemorrhagic fever is a severe, rare, tick-transmitted disease that occurs in Africa and Asia and has a mortality rate approaching 50%.[100]

Management

Treatment of all these diseases is supportive. The CDC provides intravenous ribavirin for investigational use.

Arenaviridae

Lymphocytic Choriomeningitis, Lassa, and Arenaviral (Hemorrhagic Fever) Viruses

Principles of Disease

The arenaviruses are carried by parasites of rodents and probably are passed to humans from contact with infected rodent urine. Four arenaviruses are known to cause human disease: lymphocytic choriomeningitis virus causes a meningoencephalitis that may be severe but is rarely fatal; Junin and Machupo viruses, from Argentina and Bolivia, respectively, and the Lassa virus, from Africa, cause severe and often fatal hemorrhagic fevers.

Clinical Features

Lymphocytic choriomeningitis virus is commonly transmitted from person to person. Lymphocytic choriomeningitis occurs in the Americas, Europe, and Asia and is usually passed from house mice, pet hamsters, or laboratory animals.[105] Influenza-like symptoms follow a 1- to 3-week incubation period and are generally followed by complete recovery. Meningitis may ensue, but even severe cases are associated with good recovery. Orchitis and parotitis may accompany the disease. LCM still poses a hazard in research settings in the United States.[105]

Lassa fever is a highly contagious disease occurring in West Africa with a case fatality rate of 15% in hospitalized patients.[100,106] A gradual onset of fever and malaise begins after an incubation period of 7 to 18 days. Retrosternal chest pain, vomiting, and diarrhea accompany severe headache and pharyngitis. Pneumonitis and respiratory distress may develop. Early lymphopenia followed by neutrophilia and elevated transaminases are associated with a poor prognosis.

Argentine hemorrhagic fever, caused by the Junin virus, causes a skin rash and petechiae and is more likely to be hemorrhagic than Lassa fever. The disease manifests after a 7- to 10-day incubation period with fever, malaise, anorexia, and myalgias. Petechiae and gastrointestinal bleeding occur between days 4 and 6 and shock may follow. Case fatality rates range up to

30%. Bolivian hemorrhagic fever, caused by Machupo virus, is similar to Argentine hemorrhagic fever but occurs much less commonly.[107]

Differential Considerations

Lymphocytic choriomeningitis virus can resemble other viral causes of meningitis or encephalitis. The diagnosis of arenaviral infections requires a fourfold rise in antibody titer.

Management

Supportive care only is required for LCM. Ribavirin has been used effectively to treat Lassa fever and can result in a fivefold decrease in the mortality rate.[108] Argentine hemorrhagic fever and possibly Bolivian hemorrhagic fever can be successfully treated with convalescent plasma from a recovered patient. Prevention of arenaviral infections can best be accomplished by controlling the infected vectors. Special care must be taken to prevent person-to-person spread of Lassa fever.

Retroviridae

Three subfamilies are described in family Retroviridae, the type C oncoviruses (HTLV-I, HTLV-II), the lentiviruses (HIV-1, HIV-2), and the spumaviruses. Only the oncoviruses and lentiviruses have been shown to cause disease in humans.

Type C Oncoviruses

The demonstration that RNA could be transcribed into DNA by the reverse transcriptase in RNA tumor viruses laid the groundwork for the discovery of human retroviruses.[109] Human T-cell leukemia virus type 1 (HTLV-I) was isolated in 1980.[110] Approximately 1% of people infected in childhood with HTLV-I develop adult T-cell leukemia-lymphoma as adults. HTLV-I has also been associated with tropical spastic paraparesis, also known as *HTLV-I-associated myelopathy.* HTLV-II was isolated in 1982 and found to be associated with a T-cell variant of hairy cell leukemia.[111]

Human Immunodeficiency Virus

Human immunodeficiency virus is a slow virus, or lentivirus, related to animal viruses such as visna and feline leukemia virus. A full description of HIV and AIDS is found in Chapter 130.

Picornaviridae

The family Picornaviridae is derived from "pico," or very small, and "RNA," their nucleic acid type. Picornaviridae contains two viruses that infect humans, the enterovirus, containing 67 recognized species—including the polioviruses, coxsackieviruses, echoviruses, and hepatitis A virus—and the rhinovirus, with more than 100 human species.

Poliovirus

Principles of Disease

Poliomyelitis is an acute viral infection that ranges from an inapparent infection to a nonspecific febrile illness to aseptic meningitis to severe paralysis and death. Since the introduction of vaccination in the United States, only a handful of cases of paralytic poliomyelitis have been diagnosed each year, and most of these cases are either imported or vaccine associated.[112]

Poliovirus types 1, 2, and 3 can all cause paralytic poliomyelitis, with type 1 the most common isolate and type 2 the least common. Poliovirus is transmitted during close contact; transmission by both the fecal-oral route and via respiratory secretions has been documented. Susceptibility to poliovirus is universal, but paralytic infections are rare, increasing in incidence with age at the time of infection. At least 95% of infections are inapparent or asymptomatic.

Clinical Features

Paralytic poliomyelitis usually occurs after an incubation period of 7 to 14 days. The disease in children is usually biphasic, with a brief viremic phase lasting 1 ot 3 days. After recovery for 2 to 5 days, an abrupt onset of headache, fever, malaise, vomiting, and CSF pleocytosis ensues. This meningitic phase lasts for 1 to 2 days before the beginning of weakness and flaccid paralysis. Bulbar paralytic poliomyelitis involves paralysis of the muscle groups innervated by the cranial nerves. The most important complications of paralytic poliomyelitis are respiratory, especially respiratory failure caused by paralysis of the respiratory muscles, aspiration pneumonia, and pulmonary embolism. Myocarditis may rarely occur. Muscular paralysis usually extends for only 1 to 3 days after its onset. A postparalytic paralysis syndrome has been described in which neuromuscular weakness recurs several decades after the acute poliovirus infection.[113]

Differential Considerations

Paralytic poliomyelitis can usually be recognized on clinical presentation. Other enteroviruses can cause a similar syndrome. Guillain-Barré syndrome and post-encephalitic syndromes may resemble paralytic poliomyelitis. The differential diagnosis of nonparalytic poliomyelitis includes any of the causes of bacterial and viral meningitis and encephalitis. The definitive diagnosis is made by isolation of the virus from fecal material or respiratory secretions.

Management

Specific antiviral treatment for poliomyelitis is not available. Management is supportive, and reporting to local health authorities is mandatory. In the acute phase of paralytic poliomyelitis, patients require hospitalization.

Routine vaccination in the United States has dramatically reduced the number of cases of paralytic poliomyelitis. The Salk inactivated poliovirus vaccine is recommended for most indications in the United States. Inactivated poliovirus vaccine has the advantage of preventing paralytic disease, but it does not protect susceptible contacts by secondary spread. The Sabin oral polio vaccine protects susceptible contacts, but it is associated with vaccine-associated cases of paralytic disease.[114] As of January 1, 2000, the CDC recommended that all U.S. children receive four doses of inactivated poliovirus vaccine at age 2 months, 4 months, 6 to 18 months, and 4 to 6 years. Oral polio vaccine is recommended only in special situations, such as the control of an outbreak or if an unvaccinated child is to travel to an endemic region.[6]

Coxsackieviruses, Echoviruses, and Other Enteroviruses

Principles of Disease
The enteroviruses are spread from person to person via the fecal-oral route. As with poliovirus, inapparent infections greatly outnumber symptomatic cases.

All enteroviruses enter the body through the oropharynx and multiply in the tissues around the oropharynx. The viruses are stable in acid conditions and are capable of passing through the stomach to the intestines.

Clinical Features
Most enteroviral infections are inapparent. The most common clinical manifestation is that of a nonspecific febrile illness. Young children may be admitted to hospitals with enteroviral fevers that simulate bacterial sepsis. Coxsackie B virus and some of the echoviruses may cause severe perinatal infection associated with fever, meningitis, myocarditis, and hepatitis.

Febrile diseases with rashes are often associated with enteroviruses. Exanthems resembling rubella occurring during the summer months have been seen with the echoviruses and coxsackie A viruses. Vesicular lesions are seen, such as with the hand-foot-and-mouth syndrome caused by some coxsackie A and B viruses. Herpangina, a specific disease characterized by a vesicular rash on the cheeks and soft palate and associated with fever, sore throat, and severe pain on swallowing, is caused by the coxsackie A virus. Roseola-like exanthems and petechial exanthems are also associated with coxsackievirus and echovirus infections.

The enteroviruses are the most common causes of viral meningitis. The course is generally benign but often can be confused with a bacterial process, particularly in the acute phase of the infection when CSF may show a neutrophil predominance.

Coxsackie B viruses are strongly associated with myocarditis, although echoviruses and coxsackie A viruses can also cause the disease. Severe cases may lead to dysrhythmias, heart failure, or death.

Enteroviruses cause upper respiratory tract infections similar to other causes of the common cold. Interstitial pneumonias can also occur. Pleurodynia (Bornholm's disease, the devil's grip) is generally associated with the coxsackie B viruses. This disease involves the intercostal muscles and can last for several weeks.

Other proven or suggested associations with the enteroviruses and disease include enterovirus 70 and acute hemorrhagic conjunctivitis; coxsackieviruses and echoviruses with diarrhea and gastroenteritis; coxsackieviruses and echoviruses with hemolytic-uremic syndrome; and enteroviruses with acute myositis. Other possible associations include chronic cardiomyopathy, aortitis, hepatitis, pancreatitis, orchitis, diabetes mellitus, lymphadenopathy, a mononucleosis-like syndrome, and infectious lymphocytosis. A progressive,

demented, chronic meningitis associated with enteroviruses has been reported in individuals with common variable immunodeficiency syndrome.

Management
No specific treatments for the enteroviruses exist. Care is supportive. Vaccines exist for poliovirus and hepatitis A, and immune serum globulin can also prevent the acquisition of hepatitis A infection.

Hepatitis A Virus

The hepatitis A virus is now classified among the picornaviruses. Hepatitis A is discussed in Chapter 89.

Rhinovirus

Principles of Disease
Rhinoviruses are the most common cause of the common cold. More than 100 strains exist. Rhinovirus transmission generally occurs primarily via hand contact and inoculation of the eye or nasal mucosa and less commonly via aerosolization of respiratory secretion. Viral replication probably occurs on the epithelial surface of the nasal mucosa.

Clinical Features
After a 1- to 4-day incubation period, the usual symptoms of rhinoviral infection occur, including nasal obstruction, sneezing, sore throat, cough, and malaise. Severe tracheobronchitis and pneumonia may occur rarely. Fever and lower respiratory tract infections are more common in children with rhinovirus infections than in adults.

Differential Considerations
Other respiratory pathogens such as coronaviruses, RSV, parainfluenza viruses, influenza viruses, adenoviruses, and enteroviruses can produce clinical syndromes similar to those produced by the rhinoviruses. The rhinoviruses, in general, cause less morbidity than do the parainfluenza viruses and RSV. Definitive diagnosis is made by the demonstration of a rise in antibody titer.

Management
Treatment is aimed at relieving symptoms. Routine vaccination appears unlikely because of the number of serotypes. Because hand-to-face inoculation appears to be the predominant means of transmission, frequent hand-washing during epidemic periods may decrease the spread of rhinovirus infections.

Caliciviridae

Caliciviruses and Astroviruses

Principles of Disease
Caliciviruses and astroviruses are small RNA viruses implicated in outbreaks of gastroenteritis, predominantly in children. The Norwalk virus has recently been included among the caliciviruses. The Norwalk virus has been found in the stools from patients with acute gastroenteritis. These viruses have not yet been grown in vitro, but the clinical syndromes associated with them appear to be widespread.[115]

Features

The incubation period is probably 1 to 4 days, and the disease lasts from 1 to 3 days. The disease is generally mild and accompanied by low-grade fever. Vomiting appears to be less common with astroviral disease than with caliciviruses. One third of outbreaks of gastroenteritis can be attributed to a Norwalk-like agent. Diarrhea induced by these agents is associated with transient fat malabsorption. Outbreaks have occurred in schools and other institutions and through the ingestion of inadequately cooked shellfish. The mode of transmission is unknown but is probably via the fecal-oral route. Vomiting and diarrhea occur with myalgias, malaise, headache, and low-grade fever. Diarrheal stools are moderate and nonbloody.

Differential Considerations

Other causes of gastroenteritis causing a similar syndrome include adenoviruses, enteroviruses, and coronaviruses. Electron microscopy can make the definitive diagnosis.

Management

Treatment is supportive. The gastroenteritis is generally self-limited and resolves without specific treatment. Oral rehydration solutions are generally adequate; rarely, intravenous therapy is required.

Unclassified Viruses

Hepatitis E Virus

Hepatitis E virus is an RNA virus that has been identified as a cause of enterically transmitted hepatitis. It has been implicated as a cause of fulminant hepatitis in pregnant women.

Prions

Principles of Disease

Prion is the term coined from *proteinaceous infectious* particles, the transmissible agent putatively responsible for a group of chronic neurodegenerative disorders sharing certain pathologic features. Prions have not been found to contain nucleic acid.[116,117] Other terms for these agents included *unconventional virus* and *virino.* The group of diseases, also referred to as *slow virus infections* or simply *slow infections,* includes Creutzfeldt-Jakob disease (CJD), kuru, and the Gerstmann-Straussler syndrome. Bovine spongiform encephalopathy in cattle, or new-variant CJD in humans, occurred primarily in the United Kingdom in the early 1990s, probably related to a change in the practice of offal rendering.[118] By 2001, a few cases had been found elsewhere in Europe but not in the United States. Fortunately, due to changes in handling meat byproducts and cattle feed, the incidence of bovine spongiform encephalopathy appears to be decreasing.

A characteristic feature of these diseases is the lack of any inflammatory response. A reactive astrocytosis to the presence of the virus occurs in the CNS, accompanied by neuronal vacuolation resulting in spongiform encephalopathy.

Clinical Findings

Creutzfeldt-Jakob disease is a rare disease, usually manifesting in late middle age with a progressive dementia combined with ataxia and myoclonic jerking. Distribution is worldwide and sporadic. CJD has been transmitted from person to person via direct inoculation, including corneal transplants and dura mater grafts. Kuru and the Gerstmann-Straussler syndrome present as cerebellar syndromes, with dementia occurring late in the course of the disease. Kuru has been associated with cannibalism confined to a few tribes in the highlands of New Guinea.[119] Progression of CJD and kuru is rapid, with death usually occurring in less than 1 year. The Gerstmann-Straussler syndrome follows a more slowly progressive course of up to 10 years.

Differential Considerations

Creutzfeldt-Jakob disease can be confused with Alzheimer's disease or other slowly dementing diseases. Other diseases to consider in the differential diagnosis include multi-infarct dementia, nutritional deficiency syndromes, or primary brain tumors. CT and magnetic resonance imaging scans are usually nondiagnostic, but electroencephalography often shows changes characteristic of CJD.

Management

Treatment for these diseases is entirely supportive.

 KEY CONCEPTS

- The spector of smallpox has re-arisen in the context of bioterrorism. Vaccination may be necessary for some emergency health care responders. Fortunately, complications of vaccination are relatively uncommon.
- Patients who have primary genital herpes or severe or frequent recurrences of infection and patients who are immunosuppressed and have continuous infections should receive treatment with acyclovir, famciclovir, or valacyclovir. The treatment of herpes simplex encephalitis is a medical emergency requiring rapid diagnosis and treatment with intravenous acyclovir.
- Patients with herpes zoster that is disseminated or that involves more than one dermatome or the ophthalmic branch of the trigeminal nerve should be treated with intravenous acyclovir.
- West Nile virus infection affects the elderly most severely. Treatment is supportive care; control of the disease requires reporting to public health authorities and control of vector mosquito populations.
- The presentation of SARS-CoV infection mimics that of other community-acquired or nosocomial respiratory infections. Its recognition depends on obtaining a good possible contact history; its control requires prompt initiation of isolation procedures.
- People should receive an influenza vaccine annually. Patients with symptoms of influenza may have the duration of illness shortened by 1 to 2 days if treatment with amantadine, rimantadine, or neuraminidase inhibitors is initiated within 48 hours after symptom onset.

REFERENCES

1. Jenner E: *An Inquiry into the Causes and Effects of the Variolae Vaccinae.* Birmingham, Ala, The Classics of Medicine Library, 1978.

2. Centers for Disease Control: A centennial celebration: Pasteur and the modern era of immunization. *MMWR* 34:389, 1985.

3. Salk JE, et al: Studies in human subjects on active immunization against poliomyelitis. I. A preliminary report of experiments in progress. *JAMA* 151:1081, 1953.

4. Centers for Disease Control and Prevention: Poliomyelitis prevention in the United States: Updated recommendations of the Advisory Committee on Immunization Practices (ACIP). *MMWR* 49(RR-5):1, 2000.

5. Fenner F: Global eradication of smallpox. *Rev Infect Dis* 4:916, 1982.

6. Centers for Disease Control and Prevention: Recommended childhood and adolescent immunization schedule—United States, January-June 2004. *MMWR* 52:1, 2004.

7. Centers for Disease Control and Prevention: Recommended adult immunization schedule—United States, 2003-04 [Notice to readers]. *MMWR* 52:965, 2003.

8. Centers for Disease Control and Prevention: Notice to readers: FDA approval of a combined hepatitis A and hepatitis B vaccine. *MMWR* 50:806, 2001.

9. Centers for Disease Control and Prevention: Prevention and control of influenza: Recommendations of the Advisory Committee on Immunization Practices (ACIP). *MMWR* 52(RR-8):1, 2003.

10. Bergen R, et al: Safety of a cold-adapted live attenuated influenza vaccine in a large cohort of children and adolescents. *Pediatr Infect Dis J* 23:138, 2004.

11. Cox N, Subbarao K: Influenza. *Lancet* 354:1277, 1999.

12. Stiver G: The treatment of influenza with antiviral drugs. *CMAJ* 168:49, 2003.

13. Hayden FG, et al: Efficacy and safety of the neuraminidase inhibitor zanamivir in the treatment of influenza virus infections. *N Engl J Med* 337:874, 1997.

14. Whitley RJ, Gnann JW Jr: Acyclovir: A decade later. *N Engl J Med* 327:782, 1992.

15. Safrin S, et al: Foscarnet therapy in five patients with AIDS and acyclovir-resistant varicella-zoster virus infection. *Ann Intern Med* 115:19, 1991.

16. Tyring S, et al: Famciclovir for the treatment of acute herpes zoster: Effects on acute disease and postherpetic neuralgia—a randomized, double-blind, placebo-controlled trial. *Ann Intern Med* 123:89, 1995.

17. Beutner KL, et al: Valacyclovir compared with acyclovir for improved therapy for herpes zoster in immunocompetent adults. *Antimicrob Agents Chemother* 39:1546, 1995.

18. Whitley RJ, et al: Guidelines for the treatment of cytomegalovirus diseases in patients with AIDS in the era of potent antiretroviral therapy: Recommendations of an international panel. International AIDS Society-USA. *Arch Intern Med* 158:957, 1998.

19. Jabs DA, et al: Cytomegalovirus resistance to ganciclovir and clinical outcomes of patients with cytomegalovirus retinitis. *Am J Ophthalmol* 135:27, 2003.

20. Polis MA, et al: Anticytomegaloviral activity and safety of cidofovir in patients with human immunodeficiency virus infection and cytomegalovirus viruria. *Antimicrob Agents Chemother* 39:882, 1995.

21. Palestine AG, et al: A randomized, controlled trial of foscarnet in the treatment of cytomegalovirus retinitis in patients with AIDS. *Ann Intern Med* 115:665, 1991.

22. Safrin S, et al: A controlled trial comparing foscarnet with vidarabine for acyclovir-resistant, thymidine kinase deficient herpes simplex virus. *J Infect Dis* 325:551, 1991.

23. Ault KA: Human papillomavirus infections: Diagnosis, treatment, and hope for a vaccine. *Obstet Gynecol Clin North Am* 30:809, 2003.

24. Lane HC, et al: Anti-retroviral effects of interferon alfa in AIDS-associated Kaposi sarcoma. *Lancet* 2:1218, 1988.

25. Niederau C, et al: Long-term follow-up of HBeAg positive patients treated with interferon alfa for chronic hepatitis B. *N Engl J Med* 334:1422, 1996.

26. Keefe EB, et al: A treatment algorithm for the management of chronic hepatitis B virus infection in the United States. *Clin Gastroenterol Hepatol* 2:87, 2004.

27. McHutchison JG, et al: Interferon alfa-2b alone or in combination with ribavirin as initial treatment for chronic hepatitis C. *N Engl J Med* 339:1485, 1998.

28. Manns MP, et al: Peginterferon alfa-2b plus ribavirin compared with interferon alfa-2b plus ribavirin for initial treatment of chronic hepatitis C: A randomised trial. *Lancet* 358:958, 2001.

29. Fried MW, et al: Peginterferon alfa-2a plus ribavirin for chronic hepatitis C virus infection. *N Engl J Med* 347:975, 2002.

30. Breman J, Henderson D: Current Concepts: Diagnosis and management of smallpox. *N Engl J Med* 346:1300, 2002.

31. Grabenstein JD, Winkenwerder W Jr: US military smallpox vaccination program experience. *JAMA* 289:3278, 2003.

32. Reed KD, et al: The detection of monkeypox in humans in the western hemisphere. *N Engl J Med* 350:342, 2004.

33. Tyring SK: Molluscum contagiosum: The importance of early diagnosis and treatment. *Am J Obstet Gynecol* 189:S12, 2003.

34. Koch WC: Fifth (human parvovirus) and sixth (herpesvirus 6) diseases. *Curr Opin Infect Dis* 14:343, 2001.

35. Chang Y, et al: Identification of herpesvirus-like DNA sequences in AIDS-associated Kaposi's sarcoma. *Science* 266:1865, 1994.

36. Kimberlin DW, Rouse DJ: Genital herpes. *N Engl J Med* 350:1970, 2004.

37. Leung DT, Sacks SL: Current treatment options to prevent perinatal transmission of herpes simplex virus. *Expert Opin Pharmacother* (10):1809, 2003.

38. Aurelius E, et al: Rapid diagnosis of herpes simplex encephalitis by nested polymerase chain reaction assay of cerebrospinal fluid. *Lancet* 1:189, 1991.

39. Whitley R, et al: A controlled trial comparing vidarabine with acyclovir in neonatal herpes simplex virus infections. *N Engl J Med* 324:444, 1991.

40. Balfour H: Drug therapy: Antiviral drugs. *N Engl J Med* 340:1255, 1999.

41. Gnann JW Jr: Varicella-zoster virus: Atypical presentations and unusual complications. *J Infect Dis* 186:S91, 2002.

42. Hurwitz ES, et al: National surveillance for Reye's syndrome: A five-year review. *Pediatrics* 70:895, 1982.

43. Centers for Disease Control and Prevention: Prevention of varicella: Updated recommendations of the Advisory Committee on Immunization Practices (ACIP). *MMWR* 48(RR-6):1, 1999.

44. Cohen J, et al: Recent advances in varicella-zoster virus infection. *Ann Intern Med* 130:922, 1999.

45. McCutchan JA: Cytomegalovirus infections of the nervous system in patients with AIDS. *Clin Infect Dis* 20:747, 1995.

46. Emmanuel D, et al: Cytomegalovirus pneumonia after bone marrow transplantation successfully treated with the combination of ganciclovir and high-dose intravenous immune globulin. *Ann Intern Med* 109:777, 1988.

47. Fukuda K, et al: The chronic fatigue syndrome: A comprehensive approach to its definition and study. *Ann Intern Med* 121:953, 1994.

48. Levy JA: Three new human herpesviruses (HHV 6, 7, and 8). *Lancet* 349:558, 1997.

49. Moore PS, Chang Y: Detection of herpesvirus-like DNA sequences in Kaposi's sarcoma in patients with and without HIV infection. *N Engl J Med* 332:1181, 1995.
50. Palmer AE: B-virus, herpesvirus simiae: Historical perspective. *J Med Primatol* 16:99, 1987.
51. Cohen JI, et al: Recommendations for prevention of and therapy for exposure to B virus (cercopithecine herpesvirus 1). *Clin Infect Dis* 10:1191, 2002.
52. Kimberlin DW: Pharmacotherapy of recurrent respiratory papillomatosis. *Expert Opin Pharmacother* 3:1091, 2002.
53. Campion MJ, et al: Progressive potential of mild cervical atypia: Prospective cytological, colposcopic, and virological study. *Lancet* 2:237, 1986.
54. Beutner K, et al: Imiquimod, a patient-applied immune response modifier for treatment of external genital warts. *Antimicrob Agents Chemother* 42:789, 1998.
55. Berenguer J, et al: Clinical course and prognostic factors of progressive multifocal leukoencephalopathy in patients treated with highly active antiretroviral therapy. *Clin Infect Dis* 36:1047, 2003.
56. Antinori A, et al: Diagnosis of AIDS-related focal brain lesions: A decision-making analysis based on clinical and neuroradiologic characteristics combined with polymerase chain reaction assays in CSF. *Neurology* 48:687, 1997.
57. Baqi M, Kucharczyk W, Walmsley SL: Regression of progressive multifocal encephalopathy with highly active antiretroviral therapy. *AIDS* 11:1526, 1997.
58. Adler SP, et al: Risk of human parvovirus B19 infections among school and hospital employees during endemic periods. *J Infect Dis* 168:361, 1993.
59. Fairley CK, Smoleniec JS, Caul OE: Observational study of effect of intrauterine transfusions on outcome of fetal hydrops after parvovirus B19 infection. *Lancet* 346:1335, 1995.
60. Abkowitz JL, et al: Clinical relevance of parvovirus B19 as a cause of anemia in patients with human immunodeficiency virus infection. *J Infect Dis* 176:269, 1997.
61. Abkowitz JL, et al: Clinical relevance of parvovirus B19 as a cause of anemia in patients with human immunodeficiency virus infection. *J Infect Dis* 176:269, 1997.
62. Klasco R: Colorado tick fever. *Med Clin North Am* 86:435, 2002.
63. Wilhelmi I, Roman E, Sanchez-Fauquier A: Viruses causing gastroenteritis. *Clin Microbiol Infect* 9:247, 2003.
64. Sharma R, et al: Clinical manifestations of rotavirus infection in the neonatal intensive care unit. *Pediatr Infect Dis J* 21:1099, 2002.
65. Centers for Disease Control: Arbovirus disease—United States, 1993. *MMWR* 43:385, 1994.
66. Centers for Disease Control: Outbreak of West Nile-like viral encephalitis—New York 1999. *MMWR* 48:845, 1999.
67. Peterson L, Marfin A: West Nile Virus: A primer for the clinician. *Ann Intern Med* 137:173, 2002
68. Munro ND, et al: Temporal relations between maternal rubella and congenital defects. *Lancet* 2:201, 1987.
69. Shapiro L: The numbered diseases: First through sixth. *JAMA* 194:680, 1971.
70. Centers for Disease Control: Control and prevention of rubella: Evaluation and management of suspected outbreaks, rubella in pregnant women, and surveillance for congenital rubella syndrome. *MMWR Recomm Rep* 50(RR-12):1, 2001.
71. Centers for Disease Control: Increase in rubella and congenital rubella syndrome—United States, 1988-1990. *MMWR* 40:93, 1991.
72. 2003 West Nile Virus activity in the United States (reported as of April 14, 2004). Available at http://www.cdc.gov/ncidod/dvbid/westnile/surv&control.htm. Accessed May 5, 2004.
73. Sampathkumar P: West Nile Virus: Epidemiology, clinical presentation, diagnosis and prevention. *Mayo Clin Proc* 78:1137, 2003.
74. Monath TP: Yellow fever: A medically neglected disease—report on a seminar. *Rev Infect Dis* 9:165, 1987.
75. Rawlings JA, et al: Dengue surveillance in Texas, 1995. *Am J Trop Med Hyg* 59:95, 1998.
76. Peterson L, et al: West Nile Virus. *JAMA* 290:524, 2003.
77. Mostashari F, et al: Epidemic West Nile encephalitis, New York, 1999: Results of a household-based seroepidemiological survey. *Lancet* 358:261, 2001.
78. Nash D, et al: The outbreak of West Nile Virus infection in the New York City area in 1999. *N Engl J Med* 344:1807, 2001.
79. Cetron MS, et al: Yellow fever vaccine. Recommendations of the Advisory Committee on Immunization Practices (ACIP), 2002. *MMWR Recomm Rep* 51(RR-17):1, 2002.
80. Alter MJ, et al: The prevalence of hepatitis C virus infection in the United States, 1988 through 1994. *N Engl J Med* 341:556, 1999.
81. Seefe LB: Natural history of hepatitis C. *Hepatology* 26:21S, 1997.
82. Peiris JS, et al: Coronavirus as a possible cause of severe acute respiratory syndrome. *Lancet* 361:1319, 2003.
83. Rota PA, et al: Characterization of a novel coronavirus associated with severe acute respiratory syndrome. *Science* 300:1394, 2003.
84. Guan Y, et al: Isolation and characterization of viruses related to the SARS coronavirus from animals in southern China. *Science* 302:276, 2003.
85. Centers for Disease Control and Prevention: Update: Severe acute respiratory syndrome—United States, June 11, 2003. *MMWR* 52:550, 2003.
86. Public Health guidance for community-level preparedness and response to severe acute respiratory syndrome (SARS). Version 2, supplement B: SARS Surveillance. Available at http://www.cdc.gov/ncidod/sars/guidance/b/app1.htm. Accessed May 5, 2004.
87. Booth CM, et al: Clinical features and short-term outcomes of 144 patients with SARS in the greater Toronto area. *JAMA* 289:2801, 2003.
88. Lee N, et al: A major outbreak of severe acute respiratory syndrome in Hong Kong. *N Engl J Med* 348:1986, 2003.
89. Avendano M, Derkach P, Swan S: Clinical course and management of SARS in health care workers in Toronto: A case series. *CMAJ* 168:1649, 2003.
90. Wang JT, et al: Clinical manifestations, laboratory findings, and treatment outcomes of SARS patients. *Emerg Infect Dis* 10:818, 2004.
91. Johnson DA, et al: A comparison of nebulized budesonide, intramuscular dexamethasone, and placebo for moderately severe croup. *N Engl J Med* 339:498, 1998.
92. Glezen WP, et al: Risk of primary infection and reinfection with respiratory syncytial virus. *Am J Dis Child* 140:543, 1986.
93. Simoes E: Respiratory syncytial virus infection. *Lancet* 354:847, 1999.
94. Candel S: Epididymitis in mumps, including orchitis: Further clinical studies and comments, *Ann Intern Med* 34:20, 1951.
95. Siegel M, Fuerst HT, Peress NS: Comparative fetal mortality in maternal virus diseases: A prospective study on rubella, measles, mumps, chickenpox and hepatitis. *N Engl J Med* 274:768, 1966.
96. Centers for Disease Control and Prevention: Measles—United States, first 26 weeks, 1994. *MMWR* 43:673, 1994.
97. Centers for Disease Control and Prevention: Measles Outbreak—Southwestern Utah, 1996. *MMWR* 46:766, 1997.
98. Fields BN, Hawkins K: Human infection with the virus of vesicular stomatitis during an epizootic. *N Engl J Med* 277:989, 1967.

99. Centers for Disease Control and Prevention: Outbreak of Ebola viral hemorrhagic fever—Zaire, 1995. *MMWR* 44:381, 1995.
100. Borio L, et al: Hemorrhagic fever viruses as biological weapons: Medical and public health management. *JAMA* 287:2391, 2002.
101. Dolin R, et al: A controlled trial of amantadine and rimantadine in the prophylaxis of influenza A infection. *N Engl J Med* 307:580, 1982.
102. Centers for Disease Control and Prevention: La Crosse encephalitis in West Virginia. *MMWR* 37:79, 1988.
103. Chen HX, et al: Epidemiological studies on hemorrhagic fever with renal syndrome in China. *J Infect Dis* 154:394, 1986.
104. Centers for Disease Control and Prevention: Hantavirus pulmonary syndrome—Northeastern United States, 1994. *MMWR* 43:54, 1994.
105. Dykewicz CA, et al: Lymphocytic choriomeningitis outbreak associated with nude mice in a research institute. *JAMA* 267:1349, 1992.
106. McCormick JB, et al: A case-control study of the clinical diagnosis and course of Lassa fever. *J Infect Dis* 155:445, 1987.
107. MacKenzie RB: Epidemiology of Machupo virus infection. I. Pattern of human infection, San Joaquin, Bolivia, 1962-1964. *Am J Trop Med Hyg* 14:808, 1985.
108. Huggins JW, et al: Prospective, double-blind, concurrent, placebo-controlled clinical trial of intravenous ribavirin therapy of hemorrhagic fever with renal syndrome. *J Infect Dis* 164:1119, 1991.
109. Temin HM, Mizutani S: RNA-dependent DNA polymerase in virions of Rous sarcoma virus. *Nature* 226:1211, 1970.
110. Poiesz BJ, et al: Detection and isolation of type C retrovirus particles from fresh and cultured lymphocytes of a patient with cutaneous T-cell lymphoma. *Proc Natl Acad Sci U S A* 22:7415, 1980.
111. Kalyanaraman VS, et al: A new subtype of human T-cell leukemia virus (HTLV-II) associated with a T-cell variant of hairy cell leukemia. *Science* 218:571, 1982.
112. Strebel PM, et al: Epidemiology of poliomyelitis in the United States one decade after the last reported case of indigenous wild virus-associated disease. *Clin Infect Dis* 14:568, 1992.
113. Dalakas MC, et al: A long-term follow-up study of patients with post-poliomyelitis neuromuscular symptoms. *N Engl J Med* 314:959, 1986.
114. Hull HF, et al: Paralytic poliomyelitis: Seasoned strategies, disappearing disease. *Lancet* 343:1331, 1994.
115. Blacklow NR, Greenberg HB: Viral gastroenteritis. *N Engl J Med* 325:252, 1991.
116. Prusiner SB: Molecular biology of prion disease. *Science* 252:1515, 1991.
117. Johnson RT: Prion disease. *N Engl J Med* 326:486, 1992.
118. Tan L, et al: Risk of transmission of bovine spongiform encephalopathy to humans in the United States: A report of the Council on Scientific Affairs, American Medical Association. *JAMA* 281:342, 1999.
119. Gajdusek DC: Unconventional viruses and the origin and disappearance of kuru. *Science* 197:943, 1977.

SUGGESTED READINGS

Knipe DM, Howley PM: *Fields Virology*, 4th ed. Philadelphia, Lippincott Williams & Wilkins, 2001.
Mandell GL, Bennett JE, Dolin R (eds): *Principles and Practice of Infectious Diseases*, 6th ed. New York, Churchill Livingstone, 2004.

CHAPTER

129 Rabies

Ellen J. Weber

PERSPECTIVE

Rabies is arguably the oldest infection known to humankind. The term *rabies* comes from the Sanskrit "rabhas," which means "to do violence." The Eshmuna Code of Babylon, from the 23rd century BC, contains one of the earliest regulations regarding rabies: a fine of 40 shekels was issued to the owner of a dog that killed another person through a rabid bite.[1,2]

Today, rabies is a huge public health problem in the Third World; it is estimated that 40,000 to 70,000 people die from the disease each year.[3-5] In the United States, however, human rabies is extremely rare as the result of a successful vaccination program for domestic animals that began in 1947. Before that time, there were 40 human cases a year; on average, three cases per year are now reported.[6-8]

Epidemiology

Although it is believed that any mammal can contract rabies, *Carnivora* and *Chiroptera* (bat) species are considered to be the most important reservoirs for maintenance and transmission of the disease.[3,9,10] Worldwide, dogs are the most commonly infected animal and cause more transmission of rabies to humans than any other species (Figure 129-1). Dogs are the primary reservoir of rabies in Asia and in many developing countries of Africa and Latin America.[3] Until recently, dogs were also the primary reservoir for rabies in Mexico. Widespread vaccination there has resulted in a dramatic decrease in rabies in the dog population, although approximately one third of rabies in Mexico is still found in dogs.[11,12] In Europe, Canada, and the Arctic and sub-Arctic regions, the principal carrier is the fox, and in Puerto Rico, it is the mongoose. Jackals are the

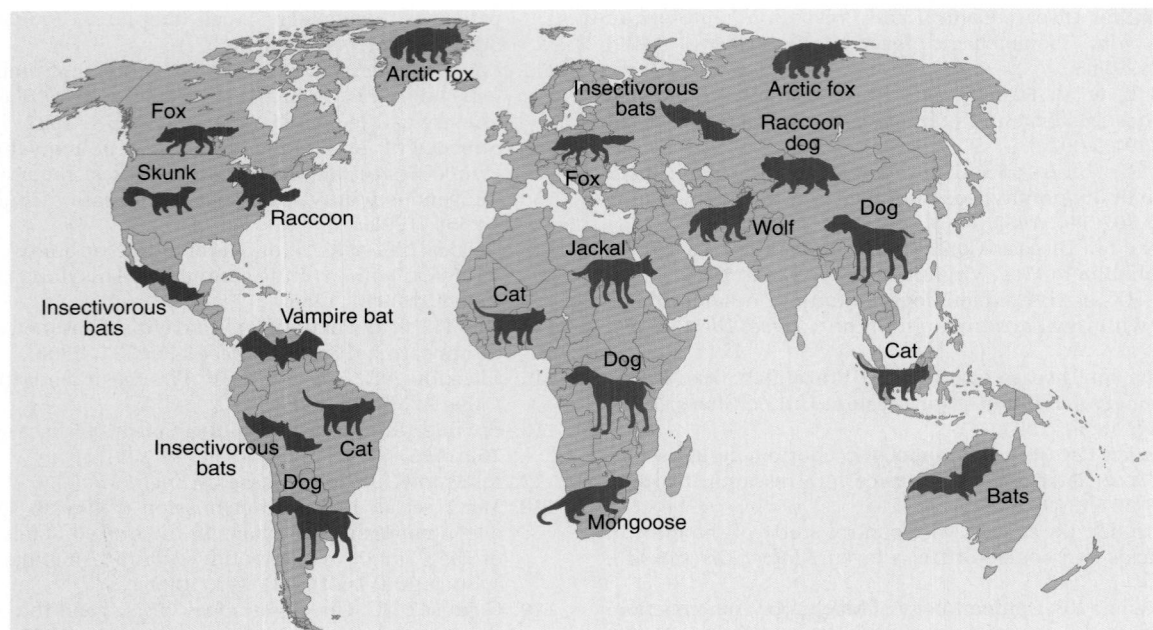

Figure 129-1. Dominant reservoirs of rabies worldwide. (Redrawn from Rupprecht CE, et al: Rabies re-examined. *Lancet Infect Dis* 2:327, 2002.)

Figure 129-2. Distribution of antigenically distinct rabies virus and their predominant terrestrial wildlife species in the United States. *The last case of rabies associated with the dog/coyote variant of the rabies virus was reported in February 2001. (Redrawn from Krebs J, et al: Rabies surveillance in the United States during 2002. *J Am Vet Med Assoc* 223:1736, 2003.)

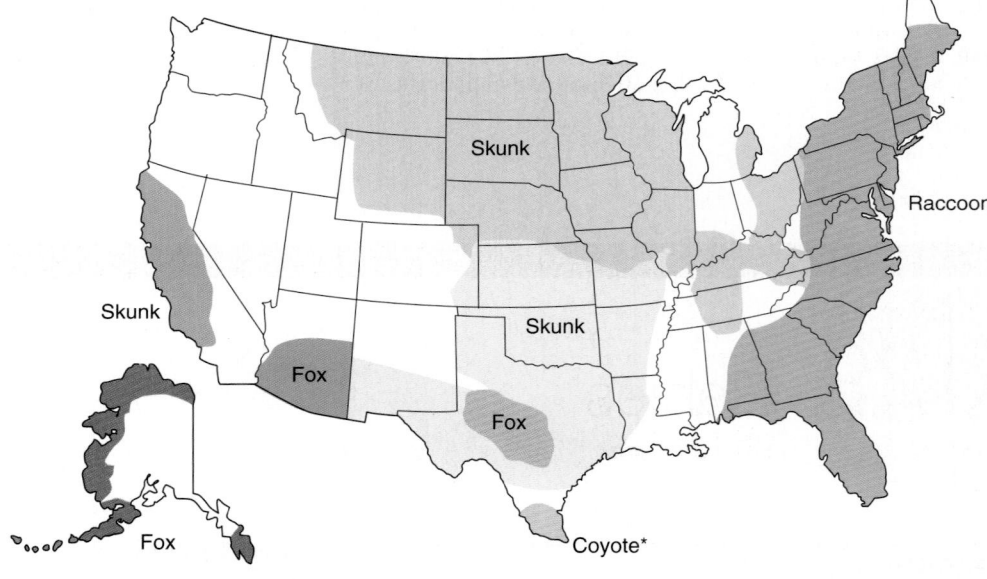

main wildlife reservoir of rabies in Africa. Bats are an important source of rabies in North and South America and Mexico. Bats carrying rabies-related lyssaviruses are also found in Africa, Europe, and Australia, and two deaths in Australia have been attributed to one such variant.[10,13]

In the United States, more than 90% of all rabies occurs in wild animals; the principal reservoirs are raccoons, skunks, foxes, and bats.[12] Rabies in terrestrial animals occurs in discrete geographic regions where the virus is primarily transmitted among members of a single species (Figure 129-2). Each species and location is associated with a unique variant of the rabies virus. Along the Eastern seaboard, rabies is endemic in rac-

coons, and they carry a unique strain of the rabies virus; a different strain of virus is carried by skunks in the North Central states, another by the skunks in the South Central states, and yet another viral strain is carried by rabid skunks endemic to California. Arctic and red foxes in Alaska carry another rabies variant; as a result of their migration across Canada, the same rabies virus variant is found in the red foxes of New England. Two additional gray fox reservoirs with unique rabies virus variants are found in Arizona and in Texas. Finally, there is a rabies virus strain associated with the dogs and coyotes of Southern Texas, the result of a longstanding interaction between unvaccinated dogs and coyotes at the Texas-Mexico border, although no cases

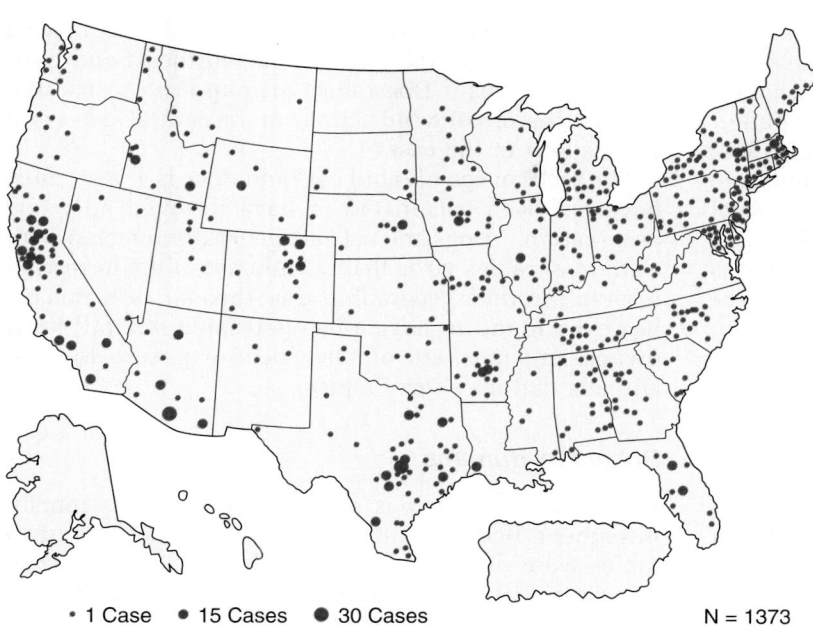

Figure 129-3. Rabid bats have been identified in all states except Hawaii, Alaska, North Dakota and Puerto Rico. (Redrawn from Krebs J, et al: Rabies surveillance in the United States during 2002. *J Am Vet Med Assoc* 223:1736, 2003.)

• 1 Case   • 15 Cases   ● 30 Cases   N = 1373

of animal rabies associated with this variant have been reported since February 2001. Rabid animals outside the United States also carry unique variants of rabies virus associated with their species and location.

In all of these areas, other wild carnivores or domestic animals may become infected by contact with the endemic species and will carry the viral variant of the endemic species (spillover). The increase in skunk rabies in New England is largely attributable to the raccoon epizootic that has occurred there, although some of the skunk rabies has resulted from spillover from foxes. Although rabies has never been transmitted from a rodent or lagomorph (rabbit/hare) to humans, these animals do contract rabies, usually from the terrestrial reservoir in their region. Most rodent cases are found in larger rodents, such as groundhogs or beavers. In the United States, infected groundhogs are generally found in the areas where raccoon rabies is endemic.[12,14,15] Rabid bats are ubiquitous throughout North America and account for 17% of all cases of rabies in U.S. animals,[12] and rabid bats constitute between 3% and 25% of bats submitted to state health departments (however, in random samples from natural populations, the prevalence of rabies is less than 1%).[8] The only U.S. state that remains rabies-free is Hawaii, where there are no rabid bats or rabid terrestrial animals.[12] Similar to terrestrial reservoirs, bats carry viral variants unique to that species but the geographic associations are less distinct, relating only to where a particular species of bats makes its home (Figure 129-3). Rabid bats are capable of infecting terrestrial animals, as well as humans, in any area of the mainland United States. However, "spillover" (in which these animals carry and transmit the bat virus variant) appears to be extremely rare.[8]

The association of a unique rabies virus variant with a particular species and locale makes it possible to determine the source of rabies in areas or species that were previously rabies-free.[16] Additionally, antigenic

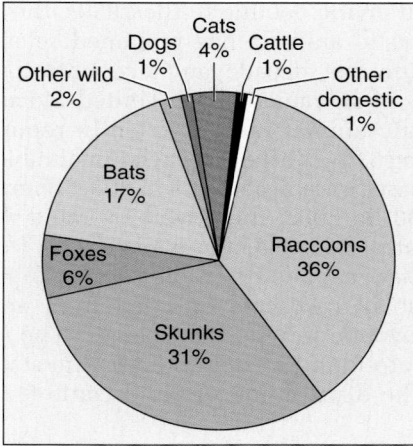

Figure 129-4. Relative proportion of cases of rabies in animals in the United States, 2002. Numbers may not add up to 100% due to rounding.

typing permits identification of the source of human infections when the animal contact is unknown.[17]

Wild and Domestic Animal Rabies

Since the 1950s, rabies in U.S. domestic animals has significantly decreased, but the population of rabid wild animals has actually increased. In 2002, rabies was found in 7967 wild animals, compared with 4742 cases in 1988.[12,18] In the 1960s and 1970s, the majority of wildlife rabies was found in skunks in the United States. However, in the late 1970s, an epizootic among raccoons began in the mid-Atlantic states and spread north and south to cover the entire Eastern seaboard; now the majority of wildlife rabies in the U.S. is attributable to raccoons (Figure 129-4). The source of this epizootic appears to be the inadvertent translocation of rabid raccoons from the southeastern states to the mid-Atlantic region by humans to stock the area for hunting, as evidenced by the fact that rabid raccoons first seen in the mid-Atlantic states, and now along the entire east coast, carry the same viral variant as those in the southeastern states.[19,20] The population spread geographically north and westward, reaching Maine in 1994, Ohio in 1996, and Tennessee in 2002. Attempts are underway to prevent spread westward by the use of animal vaccine baits, and the numbers in Ohio remain quite low.[12,21] The first rabid raccoon in Canada was found in Ontario in July 1999; 89 rabid raccoons were reported in 2001 but the number of cases declined to 26 in 2002 after wildlife control measures were instituted.[12,19] Despite the large number and widespread distribution of rabid raccoons, only one human case of rabies from a raccoon variant has ever been documented, and no history of exposure is known.[12]

Small increases in skunk rabies in the United States have been seen annually for several years and appear to be due to spillover from raccoons and foxes.[12] A smaller epizootic of coyotes began in the early 1990s in southern Texas; whereas three rabid coyotes were reported in 1990, 71 were found in 1993, but the population has since returned to low levels.[12,22,23]

After a dramatic decline in the 1950s, the number of rabid domestic animals has remained relatively constant for the last decade and accounts for approximately 7% of all rabies in the United States. Cats are the domestic animal most frequently reported rabid, representing 51% of all domestic animal rabies.[12] There were 299 cases of rabies in cats in 2002, compared with 192 in 1988. In 2002, there were 99 rabid dogs in the United States; in 1988, there were 128.[12,18] Approximately 80% of cat and dog rabies occurs in rural areas, and almost all cases are reported from areas where rabies is enzootic in wildlife species.[24] The majority of rabid cats are found in the mid-Atlantic states (Figure 129-5).[12] The distribution of rabid cattle (116 animals

in 2002) closely follows that of skunks in the central United States and raccoons in the Northeast and mid-Atlantic regions.[12] Dog rabies also appears to parallel the distribution of rabid skunks in the central states and of raccoons in the east.

The median age of rabid cats and dogs is 1 year; most have not been vaccinated or have received only one vaccination.[24] Dogs and cats are generally infected with a strain of rabies virus that is endemic in the terrestrial reservoir in their geographic area; thus far, only one cat has been found to have a bat-associated strain.[12] Most owners are unaware of their pets' exposure to wild animals that may carry rabies.

Rabies in Humans

Human cases of rabies in the United States remain infrequent. Between 1990 and 2003, 39 cases of human rabies were diagnosed in the United States and 32 of these were likely acquired within the United States.[12] Twenty-eight (88%) of these cases were associated with bats, two were associated with the dog and coyote populations of Texas, one with a raccoon in Virginia, and one with a mongoose in Puerto Rico. For most of the bat-associated cases, a history of bat contact was obtained only after the patient's death, when antigenic analysis of the rabies virus infecting the victim revealed a bat variant. In three cases, the victim was aware of a bite but did not seek rabies prophylaxis.[8,12] In approximately half of cases, the victim was known to have had contact with a bat, but no bite was thought to have occurred.[25,26] There was no history of bat exposure for the remaining victims.[8,27] Although rabies has been found in most of the bat species in the United States, the bat species most frequently identified with "cryptic" bat rabies in humans have been the silver-haired and eastern pipistrelle bats, which are solitary,

Figure 129-5. The distribution of rabies in cats in the United States in 2002 parallels that of wild animal rabies (compare with Figure 129-2). (Redrawn from Krebs J, et al: Rabies surveillance in the United States during 2002. *J Am Vet Med Assoc* 223:1736, 2003.)

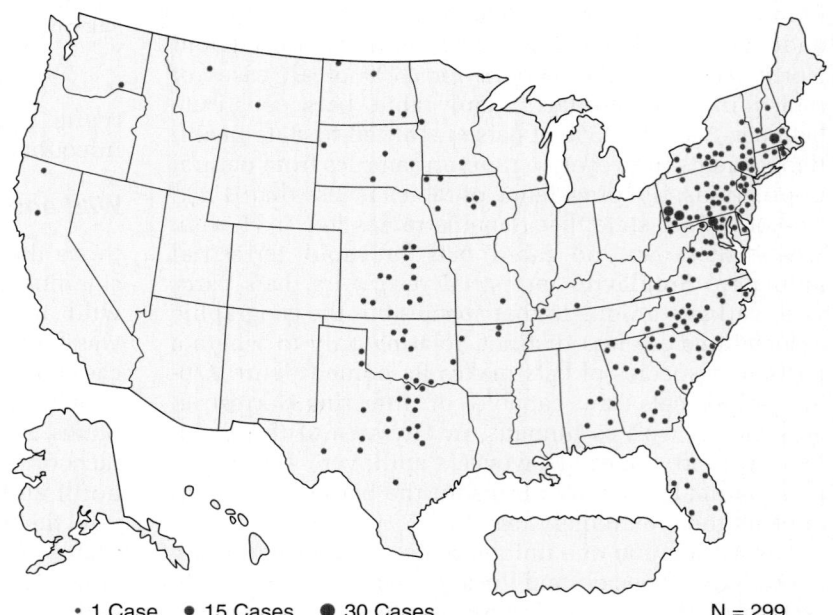

• 1 Case   ● 15 Cases   ● 30 Cases   N = 299

reclusive, tree-dwelling species that are seldom found in buildings and are thought to rarely be encountered by humans.[8,28,29] The viral strain associated with this species appears to replicate better and at lower temperatures than a canine rabies variant, suggesting that even a small, superficially administered quantity of virus is sufficient to transmit infection.[30,31]

PRINCIPLES OF DISEASE

Rabies is caused by a neurotropic rhabdovirus of the genus *Lyssavirus* (from the Greek word *lyssa,* which means "frenzy"). Rabies is not a zoonosis; animals that are infected with the virus become sick and die, usually within 3 to 9 days of the time they first begin secreting virus in their saliva.[24,32] Insectivorous bats can live 10 days; vampire bats possibly longer.[33,34] There has been some suggestion that dogs can become asymptomatic carriers, but transmission of disease from such an animal to humans has never been documented.[17,35,36] A survey of rabid dogs in the United States in 1988 found that all died within 8 days of becoming ill; the median time until death was 3 days.[24]

Animals are capable of transmitting rabies once they start secreting virus in saliva. Most animals with rabies will be sick before excretion of virus but some may not become ill for several days after virus can be found in their saliva.[32] The classic picture of a mangy dog foaming at the mouth and wildly running through town is not often seen; clinical signs are invariably present but frequently more subtle. Indeed, fewer than half of cases of rabies in domestic animals are initially recognized by veterinarians.[24] The animal may display aggressive behavior, ataxia, irritability, anorexia, lethargy, or excessive salivation; cats are more likely to demonstrate aggressive or irritable behavior than dogs. In a wild animal, however, what may be most apparent is a change in instinctive behavior: for instance, a nocturnal animal boldly walking through downtown in broad daylight.[37] An unprovoked bite from a domestic animal may be a sign of rabies; humans, especially children, often inadvertently provoke a pet by cornering it or by competing with it for its natural prey.

Rabies is transmitted when the virus is introduced into bite wounds or open cuts in skin or onto mucous membranes.[38] Almost all documented cases of rabies have been transmitted by a bite. The risk of transmission by a bite is about 50 times greater than the risk from a scratch[39]; however, one dog owner contracted rabies after his Doberman scratched him on the lip.[40] Rabies has also been contracted by recipients of transplants from infected donors.[41] Experimentally, rabies has been transmitted by aerosol to animals under extreme and artificial conditions and by ingestion; one human case may have been acquired in a laboratory. Rabies in two humans has been attributed to aerosol transmission in bat caves, but there are more plausible explanations for these cases.[6,8,9,42] In wild animals, rabies can be transmitted transplacentally.[42] Other than through transplants, human-to-human transmission has never been confirmed, although two possible cases in family members of rabies victims in Ethiopia that were not laboratory-confirmed have been described.[43] Rabies virus has never been isolated from blood.

The virus replicates in muscle cells near the site of the bite, remaining at the site of inoculation for most of the incubation period before rapidly ascending to the central nervous system along peripheral nerves. It is estimated that the virus travels along motor and sensory axons at a rate of about 12 to 100 mm/day and has a predilection for the brainstem and medulla.[44] Virus enters the salivary glands only after it has replicated in the central nervous system.[3] The incubation period from bite to disease in humans ranges from 30 to 90 days, although antigenic analysis has now confirmed latency periods of up to 7 years.[17] The risk of developing rabies after a bite ranges from 5% to 80%; the biting animal, the severity of the exposure, and the location of the bite all contribute to the ultimate mortality in unvaccinated victims.[39,45] Bites on the head and neck have a shorter incubation period (as short as 15 days) than those on the trunk or lower extremity, most likely because of the rich peripheral nerve supply in the head and neck area.[34] The mortality rate is lower in victims with lower-extremity bites.[45,46]

CLINICAL FEATURES

The prodrome of the disease in humans is nonspecific. Patients present with headache, fever, runny nose, sore throat, myalgias, and gastrointestinal symptoms. Back pain and muscle spasms are frequent.[47-49] Agitation and anxiety may result in a diagnosis of psychosis or drug intoxication.[47,48,50] Paresthesias, pain, or severe itching at the bite site may be the first neurologic symptom. Symptoms then progress over several days to a week.

Full-blown rabies occurs in two forms: the "furious" or encephalitic form is manifested by agitation, hydrophobia, and extreme irritability; periods of hyperexcitability fluctuate with lucid periods. Vital signs are often abnormal, with tachycardia, tachypnea, and fever. Hydrophobia, so named because of patients' inability to swallow, appears to result from an exaggerated respiratory tract protective reflex that results in a violent, jerky contraction of the diaphragm and accessory muscles of inspiration when the patient attempts to swallow liquids.[44] Overwhelming terror accompanies the phenomenon and may generalize to the sight of water or having water touch the face.[20] Aerophobia, an extreme fear of air in motion, can be elicited in some patients by blowing air across the face. This results in muscle spasms in the neck and pharyngeal regions.[51] Hallucinations, seizures, ataxia, focal weakness, and arrhythmias also occur. About 20% of cases present as the paralytic or "dumb" form of rabies, which resembles Guillain-Barré syndrome with prominent limb weakness; consciousness is initially spared. The two forms can overlap or progress from one to the other. In either form, patients become progressively confused

BOX 129-1. Rabies Wound Treatment

- Early treatment essential (less than 3 hours)
- Scrub wound and edges with soap and water
- If puncture, swab deeply in wound and around edges
- Follow with virucidal agent:
  1 or 2% benzalkonium chloride
     or
  povidone-iodine*
- Rinse

---

*Povidone-iodine never tested but recommended by Centers for Disease Control and Prevention.

BOX 129-2. Rabies Immunoprophylaxis

- Human rabies immunoglobulin (HRIG), 20 IU/kg. If anatomically feasible, infiltrate full dose into and around wound; remainder given IM *and*
- Human diploid cell vaccine (HDCV), 1 mL IM (deltoid) on days 0, 3, 7, 14, 28
- If previously vaccinated: no HRIG; HDCV 1 mL IM on days 0 and 3

length of the delay because evidence exists that the incubation period of rabies can be more than a year.

Wound Care

Rabies is easily killed by sunlight, soap, or drying. Experimental studies show that scrubbing and flushing the wound with benzalkonium chloride, 20% soap solution, or Ivory soap is nearly 100% protective when performed within 3 hours of inoculation of virus.[64] Povidone-iodine, which is virucidal, has not been tested. Although wound care should never be relied on as the only preventive measure, it is an *essential* part of postexposure rabies prevention, especially because there have been rare cases in which a patient developed rabies despite what was thought to be appropriate immunoprophylaxis. Furthermore, wound treatment may be the only prevention available for a victim out in the wild who is days or weeks away from medical care.

For wounds in which rabies transmission is of concern, the CDC recommends immediate and thorough washing with soap and water and a virucidal agent such as povidone-iodine (Box 129-1).[38] Wounds should be scrubbed or swabbed, not simply flushed.[65] After treatment, the wound should be thoroughly rinsed with water or saline.

Immunoprophylaxis

Rabies immunoprophylaxis requires both passive immunization with antibody (immunoglobulin) and active immunization with vaccine (Box 129-2). It is essential that both parts of this regimen be given, even when treatment is delayed. Human rabies immunoglobulin (HRIG) 20 IU/kg should be administered as soon after the bite as possible, but not longer than 7 days after tissue culture vaccine has been given. If anatomically feasible, the entire dose of HRIG should be infiltrated into and around the wound or wounds; any remaining volume should be injected intramuscularly at a site distant from the vaccine.[38]

Human diploid cell vaccine (HDCV) is the vaccine most widely available in the United States. The first dose should be administered on the day of the bite; four subsequent injections are required. The vaccine should be administered in the deltoid, rather than the gluteal region, to avoid accidental administration into fat,

which will prevent antibody formation.[53,66] HRIG and HDCV should be given in different anatomical sites and never mixed in the same syringe. All known treatment failures since 1980 have occurred after a deviation from the recommended regimen. In these cases, patients did not have their wounds cleansed with soap and water, did not receive rabies vaccine in the deltoid area, or did not receive HRIG at the wound site.[38,53,63,66,67]

Local reactions (itching, erythema, pain, or swelling) occur in 30% to 74% of PEP recipients; systemic reactions, including headache, myalgia, and nausea, occur in 5% to 40% of recipients, usually those who receive frequent vaccine boosters.[38] Anaphylaxis has occurred in 0.1% of cases; three cases of Guillain-Barré syndrome have occurred after millions of doses given.[38,68] An immune-complex type of reaction involving urticaria, arthralgia, arthritis, angioedema, nausea, and vomiting occurs in about 6% of patients who receive boosters of HDCV; it is uncommon in those receiving primary vaccination.[38] Two alternative vaccines, rabies vaccine adsorbed and purified chick embryo culture vaccine, are also available. Both appear to be associated with fewer hypersensitivity reactions in patients receiving boosters.[29,69] Although HDCV can be administered intradermally for preexposure prophylaxis, neither rabies vaccine adsorbed nor purified chick embryo culture vaccine is approved for intradermal use.

Patients requiring rabies immunoprophylaxis when outside the United States may receive a different regimen and different vaccines than those used in the United States. Some countries still use vaccines derived from nerve tissue, rather than cell culture, which are poorly immunogenic and carry the risk of more side effects. In many areas, rabies immunoglobulin may not be available.

The World Health Organization has approved several treatment regimens that reduce cost by giving fewer vaccine injections or using the intradermal route, which requires less vaccine. Additionally, the World Health Organization recommends immunoglobulin only for severe bites.[29,69] These regimens are not approved in the United States for PEP. The World Health Organization cautions that intradermal injections should be administered only by staff who have been trained in this technique.[29,69] Additionally, because chloroquine has been shown to interfere with the antibody response to vaccine given intradermally, victims of bites who are currently receiving malaria prophylaxis (with any medication) should undergo postexposure rabies prophylaxis only by the intramus-

Table 129-2. Rabies Preexposure Prophylaxis Guide

Risk Category	Nature of Risk	Typical Populations	Preexposure Recommendations
Continuous	Virus present continuously, often in high concentrations. Specific exposures likely to go unrecognized. Bite, nonbite, or aerosol exposure.	Rabies research laboratory workers;* rabies biologics production workers	Primary course. Serologic testing every 6 months; booster vaccination if antibody titer is below acceptable level.[†]
Frequent	Exposure usually episodic, with source recognized, but exposure also might be unrecognized. Bite, nonbite, or aerosol exposure.	Rabies diagnostic laboratory workers,* spelunkers, veterinarians and staff, and animal-control and wildlife workers in rabies-enzootic areas	Primary course. Serologic testing every 2 years; booster vaccination if antibody titer is below acceptable level[†]
Infrequent (greater than population at large)	Exposure nearly always episodic with source recognized. Bite or nonbite exposure.	Veterinarians and animal-control and wildlife workers in areas with low rabies rates; veterinary students; travelers visiting areas where rabies is enzootic and immediate access to appropriate medical care, including biologics, is limited	Primary course. No serologic testing or booster vaccination.
Rare (population at large)	Exposure always episodic with source recognized. Bite or nonbite exposure.	U.S. population at large, including persons in rabies-epizootic areas	No vaccination necessary.

*Judgment of relative risk and extra monitoring of vaccination status of laboratory workers is the responsibility of the laboratory supervisor.
[†]Minimum acceptable antibody level is complete virus neutralization at a 1 : 5 serum dilution by the rapid fluorescent focus inhibition test. A booster dose should be administered if the titer falls below this level.
From Human rabies prevention—United States, 1999. Recommendations of the Advisory Committee on Immunization Practices (ACIP). *MMWR Morb Mortal Wkly Rep* 48:1, 1999.

cular route.[38,69] Thus, bite victims traveling abroad may require additional treatment when they return to the United States. Public health officials should be contacted for advice.

Prophylaxis, including both passive and active immunization, given during pregnancy does not result in an increase in fetal wastage, congenital defects, or side effects and should not be withheld when indicated.[70] Corticosteroids, antimalarials, and other immunosuppressives can interfere with the development of active immunity and should be withheld during the course of treatment if possible. Patients who must receive these drugs, or those who are immunosuppressed, should receive prophylaxis via the intramuscular route and have antibody titers checked at 2 to 4 weeks after completion of the series.[38,63] Patients with histories of hypersensitivity should nevertheless be cautiously given immunoprophylaxis in a controlled setting, with antihistamines and epinephrine available.[38] Rabies developed in one patient who was sensitive to equine antirabies immunoglobulin and was not given passive immunization.[40]

Preexposure Prophylaxis

For people with frequent exposures to rabies, preexposure prophylaxis may be indicated.[38] These people include laboratory personnel working with live rabies virus, veterinarians, animal handlers, and those spending long periods in countries in which rabies is endemic and medical care difficult to obtain (Table 129-2). Preexposure prophylaxis guarantees protection for individuals who have continuous and unapparent exposures (i.e., laboratory workers); it also allows protection when postexposure therapy may be delayed

(e.g., in remote areas). After an exposure, patients who have had preexposure prophylaxis do not require HRIG; vaccine is given only on days 0 and 3 (see Box 129-2). However, travelers should be aware that chloroquine prophylaxis for malaria can interfere with antibody response to preexposure vaccination given intradermally; therefore, the vaccination regimen should be completed at least 1 month prior to starting malaria prophylaxis, or the preexposure regimen should be given intramuscularly.[7,38]

KEY CONCEPTS

- The epidemiology of rabies in the United States has undergone a major evolution, with the primary source of this disease now in wild animals, rather than in domestic animals. Despite an increase in the numbers of terrestrial wild animals with rabies, particularly raccoons, the predominant threat to humans in the United States appears to be contact with bats.

- PEP is indicated for victims of bites or significant nonbite exposures from wild carnivores in endemic areas, and in cases of bat contact in which a bite cannot be ruled out and the bat cannot be tested. In most bite cases in the United States, healthy domestic animals should be observed before starting the patient on PEP. Discussion with public health officials is highly recommended to guide decisions about PEP and to reduce the number of unnecessary treatments.

- PEP involves three important components: local wound care with soap and water and a virucidal agent, passive immunization with rabies immunoglobulin, and active immunization with vaccine. The regimen should be adhered to precisely because treatment failures can occur when it is not followed.

REFERENCES

1. Fisher DJ: Resurgence of rabies: A historical perspective on rabies in children. *Arch Pediatr Adolesc Med* 149:306, 1995.
2. Koprowski H: Visit to an ancient curse. *Scientific American: Science and Medicine* May/June:48, 1995.
3. Rupprecht CE, et al: Rabies re-examined. *Lancet Infect Dis* 2:327, 2002.
4. World Health Organization: World Survey of Rabies 34 for the year 1998. Available at: www.who.int/emc-documents/rabies/docs/wsr98/wsr98.pdf. Accessed December 30, 2003.
5. World Health Organization: Rabies. Fact Sheet No. 99. Available at: www.who.int/inf-fs/en/fact099.html. Accessed December 30, 2003.
6. Anderson L, et al: Human rabies in the U.S., 1960-79. *Ann Intern Med* 100:728, 1984.
7. Noah DL, et al: Epidemiology of human rabies in the United States, 1980 to 1996. *Ann Intern Med* 128:922, 1998.
8. Messenger SL, et al: Emerging epidemiology of bat-associated cryptic cases of rabies in humans in the United States. *Clin Infect Dis* 35:738, 2002.
9. Gibbons RV: Cryptogenic rabies, bats, and the question of aerosol transmission. *Ann Emerg Med* 39:528, 2002.
10. Woldehiwet Z: Rabies: Recent developments. *Res Vet Sci* 73:17, 2002.
11. Velasco-Villa A, et al: Antigenic diversity and distribution of rabies virus in Mexico. *J Clin Microbiol* 40:951, 2002.
12. Krebs JW: Rabies surveillance in the United States during 2002. *J Am Vet Med Assoc* 223:1736, 2003.
13. Hanna JN, et al: Australian bat lyssavirus infection: A second human case, with a long incubation period. *Med J Aust* 172:597, 2000.
14. Krebs JW, et al: Rabies surveillance in the United States during 1992. *J Am Vet Med Assoc* 203:1718, 1993. [Erratum, *J Am Vet Med Assoc* 204:423, 1994.]
15. Rabies in a beaver—Florida, 2001. *MMWR Morb Mortal Wkly Rep* 51:481, 2002.
16. Centers for Disease Control: Translocation of coyote rabies—Florida, 1994. *MMWR Morb Mortal Wkly Rep* 44:580, 1995.
17. Smith JS, et al: Unexplained rabies in three immigrants in the United States: A virologic investigation. *N Engl J Med* 324:205, 1991.
18. Eng TR, et al: Rabies surveillance, United States, 1988. *MMWR Morb Mortal Wkly Rep CDC Surveill Summ* 38:1, 1989.
19. Krebs JW, et al: Rabies surveillance in the United States during 1999. *J Am Vet Med Assoc* 217:1799, 2000.
20. Case records of the Massachusetts General Hospital. Weekly clinicopathological exercises. Case 21-1998. A 32-year-old woman with pharyngeal spasms and paresthesias after a dog bite [clinical conference]. *N Engl J Med* 339:105, 1998.
21. Centers for Disease Control: Update: Raccoon rabies epizootic—United Sates, 1996. *MMWR* 45:1117, 1997.
22. Reid-Sanden F, et al: Rabies surveillance in the United States during 1989. *J Am Vet Med Assoc* 197:1571, 1990.
23. Krebs J, et al: Rabies surveillance in the United States during 1993. *J Am Vet Assoc* 205:1695, 1994.
24. Eng T, Fishbein D: Epidemiologic factors, clinical findings, and vaccination status of rabies in cats and dogs in the United States in 1988. National Study Group on Rabies. *J Am Vet Med Assoc* 197:201, 1990.
25. Centers for Disease Control: Human rabies—California, 2002. *MMWR Morb Mortal Wkly Rep* 51:686, 2002.
26. Centers for Disease Control: Human rabies—Tennessee, 2002. *MMWR Morb Mortal Wkly Rep* 51:828, 2002.
27. Centers for Disease Control: Human rabies—Iowa, 2002. *MMWR Morb Mortal Wkly Rep* 52:47, 2003.
28. Centers for Disease Control: Human Rabies—Connecticut, 1995. *MMWR Morb Mortal Wkly Rep* 45:207, 1996.
29. Dreesen DW: A global review of rabies vaccines for human use. *Vaccine* 15(Suppl):S2, 1997.
30. Fu ZF: Rabies and rabies research: Past, present and future. *Vaccine* 15(Suppl):S20, 1997.
31. Messenger SL, et al: Emerging pattern of rabies deaths and increased viral infectivity. *Emerg Infect Dis* 9:151, 2003.
32. Sikes E: Pathogenesis of rabies in wildlife. 1. Comparative effect of varying doses of rabies virus inoculated into foxes and skunks. *Am J Vet Res* 23:1041, 1962.
33. Roine R, et al: Fatal encephalitis caused by a bat-borne rabies-related virus: Clinical findings. *Brain* 111:1505, 1988.
34. Sikes R: Rabies. In Hubbert W, McCulloch W, Schnurrenberger P (eds): *Diseases Transmitted from Animals to Man*, 6th ed. Springfield, Ill, Charles C Thomas, 1975.
35. Fishbein DB: Latent rabies [letter]. *N Engl J Med* 324:1891, 1991.
36. Hemachudha T et al: Latent rabies [letter]. *N Engl J Med* 324:1890, 1991.
37. Marin Co: Thirteenth rabid animal incident of the year. County of Marin. 1986. October 7, 1986.
38. Centers for Disease Control: Human rabies prevention—United States, 1999. Recommendations of the Advisory Committee on Immunization Practices (ACIP). *MMWR Morb Mortal Wkly Rep* 48:1, 1999.
39. Fishbein D, Robinson L: Rabies. *N Engl J Med* 329:1632, 1993.
40. Udwadia Z et al: Human rabies: Clinical features, diagnosis, complications, and management. *Crit Care Med* 17:834, 1989.
41. Centers for Disease Control: Investigation of rabies infections in organ donor and transplant recipients—Alabama, Arkansas, Oklahoma, and Texas, 2004. *MMWR Morb Mortal Wkly Rep* 53:586, 2004.
42. Afshar A: A review of non-bite transmission of rabies virus infection. *Br Vet J* 135:142, 1979.
43. Fekadu M, et al: Possible human-to-human transmission of rabies in Ethiopia. *Ethiop Med J* 34:123, 1996.
44. Jackson AC: Update on rabies. *Curr Opin Neurol* 15:327, 2002.
45. Baer G: Animal models in the pathogenesis and treatment of rabies. *Rev Inf Dis* 10:S739, 1988.
46. Shah U, Jaswal G: Victims of a rabid wolf in India: Effect of severity and location of bites on development of rabies. *J Infect Dis* 134:25, 1976.
47. Centers for Disease Control: Human rabies—California, 1987. *MMWR Morb Mortal Wkly Rep* 37:305, 1988.
48. Centers for Disease Control: Human rabies—West Virginia, 1994. *MMWR Morb Mortal Wkly Rep* 44:86, 1995.
49. Centers for Disease Control: Human rabies—Miami 1994. *MMWR Morb Mortal Wkly Rep* 43:773, 1994.
50. Centers for Disease Control: Human rabies—Texas and California, 1993. *MMWR Morb Mortal Wkly Rep* 43:93, 1994.
51. Centers for Disease Control: Human rabies—New Hampshire, 1996. *MMWR Morb Mortal Wkly Rep* 46:267, 1997.
52. Centers for Disease Control: Recovery of a patient from clinical rabies—Wisconsin, 2004. *MMWR Morb Mortal Wkly Rep* 53:1171, 2004.
53. Shill M, et al: Fatal rabies encephalitis despite appropriate post-exposure prophylaxis. *N Engl J Med* 316:1257, 1987.
54. Warrell MJ, et al: Failure of interferon alfa and tribavirin in rabies encephalitis. *BMJ* 299:830, 1989.
55. Jackson AC, et al: Management of rabies in humans. *Clin Infect Dis* 36:60, 2003.

PART THREE MEDICINE AND SURGERY • Section XII Infectious Disease

56. Smith J, et al: Case report: Rapid ante-mortem diagnosis of a human case of rabies imported into the UK from the Philippines. *J Med Virol* 69:150, 2003.
57. Mani J, et al: Magnetic resonance imaging in rabies. *Postgrad Med J* 79:352, 2003.
58. Krebs JW, et al: Causes, costs, and estimates of rabies postexposure prophylaxis treatments in the United States. *J Public Health Manag Pract* 4:56, 1998.
59. Moran GJ, et al: Appropriateness of rabies postexposure prophylaxis treatment for animal exposures. Emergency ID Net Study Group. *JAMA* 284:1001, 2000.
60. Chang HG, et al: Public health impact of reemergence of rabies, New York. *Emerg Infect Dis* 8:909, 2002.
61. Conti L, et al: Evaluation of state-provided postexposure prophylaxis against rabies in Florida. *South Med J* 95:225, 2002.
62. Kappus K: Canine rabies in the U.S. 1971-73: A study of reported cases with reference to vaccination history. *Am J Epidemiol* 103:242, 1976.
63. Wilde H, et al: Failure of rabies postexposure treatment in Thailand. *Vaccine* 7:49, 1989.
64. Dean D, et al: Studies on the local treatment of rabies-infected wounds. *Bull WHO* 28:477, 1963.
65. Kaplan M, et al: Studies on local treatment of wounds for the prevention of rabies. *Bull WHO* 26:765, 1962.
66. Lumbiganon P, et al: Human rabies despite treatment with rabies immmune globulin and human diploid cell rabies vaccine—Thailand. *JAMA* 259:25, 1988.
67. Wilde H, et al: Failure of postexposure treatment of rabies in children. *Clin Infect Dis* 22:228, 1996.
68. Knittel T, et al: Guillain-Barre syndrome and human diploid cell rabies vaccine [letter]. *Lancet* 1:1334, 1989.
69. Rabies vaccines. *Wkly Epidemiol Rec* 77:109, 2002.
70. Chutivongse S, et al: Postexposure rabies vaccination during pregnancy: Effect on 202 women and their infants. *Clin Infect Dis* 20:818, 1995.

CHAPTER

130 AIDS and HIV

Richard E. Rothman, Catherine A. Marco, Samuel Yang, and Gabor D. Kelen

PERSPECTIVE

History

The first cases of AIDS came to light in 1981, when reports of Kaposi's sarcoma (KS) and *Pneumocystis carinii* pneumonia (PCP) in previously healthy homosexual men appeared in the literature. Shortly thereafter, it was recognized that these patients shared the common characteristic of a defect in cell-mediated immunity, leading to naming the clinical disease acquired immunodeficiency syndrome, or AIDS. In 1983, a ribonucleic acid (RNA) retrovirus coined human immunodeficiency virus, or HIV, was identified as the causative agent for the syndrome. The development of an antibody assay in 1985 permitted serologic diagnosis, allowing researchers to track the HIV epidemic and identify the principal modes and risk factors for disease transmission. Significant therapeutic advances have occurred over the past two decades with institution of prophylaxis for opportunistic infections and the introduction of highly active antiretroviral therapy (HAART) for slowing progression of disease. Despite these advances, HIV continues to be a major public health threat and is responsible for a large number of acute and subacute emergency department visits each year.

Epidemiology

Most epidemiologic data regarding HIV infection are derived from patients who meet the definition of AIDS, which is a reportable disease in all states. The most up-to-date definition of AIDS, published in 1993 by the Centers for Disease Control and Prevention (CDC), is shown in Box 130-1.[1] Case definitions include either the presence of one or more AIDS indicator conditions or laboratory evidence of severe immunosuppression as evidenced by a CD4 T lymphocyte count of less than 200 cells/mm^3.

Worldwide estimates indicate that approximately 37 million adults and 2 million children were living with HIV/AIDS at the end of 2003.[2] Cumulative HIV-related deaths totaled 21.8 million. Approximately 95% of HIV-infected persons live in the developing world. Sub-Saharan Africa has the highest levels of infection, with over 25 million persons living with disease and over 3 million newly reported cases in 2003 (representing approximately 60% of all incident cases). The medical and economic impacts of HIV and AIDS continue to devastate these areas because these populations have the least access to the medical, social, and economic resources that might prevent new disease or delay the progression of HIV-related illnesses.

In developed countries, significant progress has been made in controlling the HIV epidemic. In 1996, for the first time since HIV was recognized, there was a decline in the incidence of AIDS and the number of AIDS-related deaths.[3] This trend has been attributed primarily to the availability of new antiretroviral therapies. Unfortunately, the rates of decline in AIDS cases and AIDS deaths have slowed over the past several years.[4] In North America there were an estimated 36,000 to 54,000 new cases of HIV reported in 2003 and an estimated 790,000 to 1.2 million persons living with HIV or AIDS.[2]

Within the United States, HIV-positive persons are concentrated primarily in large urban settings. Until 1987, New York, Newark, Miami, San Francisco, and Los Angeles accounted for nearly 50% of AIDS cases. Although these cities still represent high-intensity pockets of infection, significant increases have also been seen in smaller metropolitan areas. The percentage distribution of AIDS cases by area of residence in 2001 was 81% from large metropolitan areas and 7% from nonmetropolitan areas. As of December 2002, the 10 states or territories reporting the highest number of cumulative AIDS cases were New York, California, Florida, Texas, New Jersey, Illinois, Pennsylvania, Puerto Rico, Georgia, and Maryland.[4]

Approximately 80% of AIDS cases have occurred in adult men, 18% in adult women, and just over 1% in children. The proportion of adult women among those infected with HIV has increased over the past 5 years, with adult women now representing 26% of those living with HIV/AIDS.[2,4] Nearly half of all people who acquire HIV in the United States become infected before they turn 30, and the vast majority die well before their 45th birthdays. There is a disproportionate rate of infection among minority groups, with African Americans and Hispanic Americans making up an ever-increasing proportion of new HIV cases and persons living with AIDS. In 2001 more than 70% of all AIDS cases diagnosed occurred in minority racial or ethnic groups (49% African American, 19% Hispanic American).[4]

The primary risk factors associated with an increased likelihood of acquiring HIV infection include homosexuality or bisexuality, intravenous (IV) drug use, heterosexual exposure to a partner at risk, blood transfusion prior to 1985, and vertical and horizontal maternal-neonatal transmission. A greater number of risk factors are associated with a greater likelihood of infection.[5] U.S. HIV surveillance data demonstrate significant changes in the distribution of newly acquired HIV cases over the past several years. There has been a relative decrease in newly acquired HIV in homosexual and bisexual men and a relative increase in the incidence of HIV among IV drug users and heterosexual contacts. The change in the distribution of AIDS cases in adults and adolescents by mechanism of transmission since the start of the HIV epidemic is shown in Figure 130-1.

During the past several years, the greatest percentage increase in reported AIDS cases has occurred among women (attributed principally to heterosexual exposure to an infected partner), minority populations, and children. Because these populations often lack access to primary health services and are frequently underinsured, there has been a trend toward increasing use of emergency department services by patients with HIV and AIDS. Surveillance data from centers in Baltimore,

---

BOX 130-1. AIDS-Defining Illnesses*,†

CD4 cell count <200/mm³
Candidiasis, esophageal or pulmonary
Cervical cancer*
Coccidioidomycosis, extrapulmonary*
Cryptococcosis, extrapulmonary*
Cryptosporidiosis (with diarrhea for > 1 mo)
Cytomegalovirus infection (of any organ system other than liver, spleen, or lymph nodes)
Herpes simplex virus (mucocutaneous ulcer for > 1 mo, pneumonitis, or esophagitis)
HIV-associated dementia (with functional impairment)
HIV wasting syndrome
Histoplasmosis, extrapulmonary*
Isosporiasis (with diarrhea for > 1 mo)*
Kaposi's sarcoma*
Lymphoma in patients <60 yr (or >60 yr*)
Mycobacterium tuberculosis (pulmonary or disseminated)*
Pneumocystis carinii pneumonia
Progressive multifocal leukoencephalopathy
Bacterial pneumonia (recurrent)*
Progressive multifocal leukoencephalopenia
Salmonella septicemia, recurrent*
Toxoplasmosis (of internal organ)

*Requires HIV-positive serology.
†For a more comprehensive list, refer to the 1993 CDC case definition.
CDC, Centers for Disease Control and Prevention; HIV, human immunodeficiency virus.

Figure 130-1. Proportions of AIDS cases among adults and adolescents by exposure category and year of diagnosis, 1985 to 2001, United States. (From Centers for Disease Control and Prevention: http://www.cdc.gov/hiv/graphics/trends.htm.)

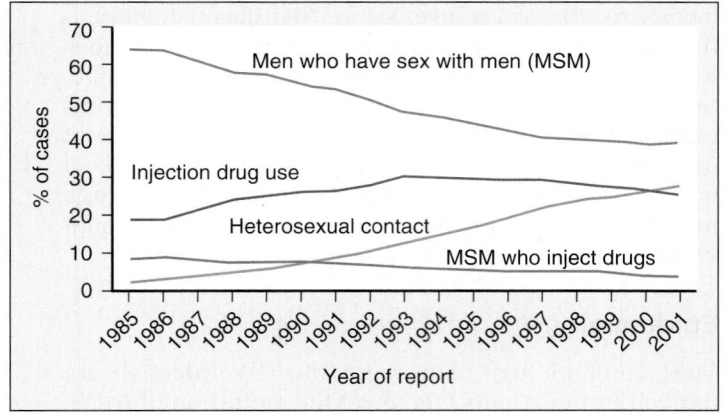

Chicago, Atlanta, and New York report HIV seroprevalence ranging from 2% to 15%.[6]

PRINCIPLES OF DISEASE

Pathophysiology

HIV is a cytopathic human retrovirus that belongs to the lentivirus subfamily. There are two major subtypes of HIV, HIV-1 and HIV-2. HIV-1 is the predominant subtype worldwide and is the cause of AIDS. HIV-2 causes a similar immune syndrome but is rarely seen in the United States; it is restricted primarily to western Africa.

The HIV virion is composed of a central single-stranded RNA molecule and the enzyme reverse transcriptase. These are surrounded by a core protein and a lipid bilayer envelope that contain virally encoded transmembrane proteins critical for recognition and attachment to target host lymphocytes (predominantly CD4 cells). HIV-1 has been isolated from a variety of body fluids including blood, serum, semen, vaginal secretions, urine, cerebrospinal fluid (CSF), tears, breast milk, bone marrow, alveolar fluid, synovial fluid, amniotic fluid, and saliva. Only a few modes of transmission have been proved: semen, vaginal secretions, blood or blood products, breast milk, and transplacental transmission in utero. There have been no instances of casual transmission, although there is one case report of possible salivary transmission. The HIV virion is extremely labile and easily neutralized by heat and common disinfecting agents such as 50% ethanol, 35% isopropyl alcohol, 0.3% hydrogen peroxide, disinfectant (Lysol), or a 1:10 solution of household bleach.

HIV selectively attacks cells within the immune system (primarily T4 helper cells, but macrophages and monocytes may also be involved), a characteristic that accounts for much of the immunodeficiency it produces in affected individuals. HIV-1 transmembrane proteins gp41 and gp120 play a critical role in recognition and attachment of HIV virions to receptors on host lymphocytes. After infection, viral RNA is reverse transcribed into deoxyribonucleic acid (DNA) by reverse transcriptase, one of the critical enzymes required for HIV replication. The viral genome thus becomes permanently integrated into the host's genome. Once integrated, retroviral DNA may lie dormant or may be actively transcribed and translated to produce virally encoded proteins and new HIV virions. HIV protease is another critical retroviral enzyme in the life cycle of the virus, responsible for activation of viral protein precursors into the functional enzymes required for virion infectivity.

Primary HIV exposure is characterized by a transient viremia and a decrease in CD4 cell counts, followed by establishment of equilibrium between virus and host immunity. A persistent latent period, during which the virus lies dormant in the host genome, can last for years. The "set point" or steady-state viral load level in the blood of the patient allows prediction of long-term clinical outcomes. Lower levels of viremia correlate with longer clinical latency periods. In the later stages of HIV, there is a sudden increase of viremia that correlates with a dramatic decrease in CD4 T lymphocytes. This increase is followed by the appearance of opportunistic infections or malignancies and ultimately death.

HIV-1 is highly heterogeneous. Multiple genetic subtypes exist in a variety of geographic and sociologic settings. Further genetic diversity exists within individual hosts because of the highly mutable character of the virus. High error rates, which occur in reverse transcription, ensure extensive viral diversity, a critical factor in the pathogenesis and ongoing emergence of drug-resistant phenotypes.[7]

Tests for HIV

HIV infection is most commonly established by HIV serology or detection of antibodies to the virus. Testing involves sequential use of an enzyme-linked immunoassay (EIA) and a Western blot (WB) assay. Criteria for positive results are a repeatedly positive EIA followed by a positive WB. EIA detects the binding of specific serum antibodies to HIV antigens that are adherent to a microtiter plate. The WB technique detects electrophoretically separated viral antigens in the patient's serum. A positive WB requires detection of two of the following: p24, gp41, and gp120/160. Final HIV serology results are reported as positive, negative, or indeterminate. Overall sensitivity and specificity of HIV serology are greater than 99.9%.

False-negative HIV tests are accounted for primarily by testing performed during the "window period" (usually the first several months) of acute infection, after viral transmission but before the appearance of antibodies. Rates of false-negative testing range from 0.3% in high-prevalence populations to less than 0.001% in low-prevalence populations. Ninety-five percent of false-negative tests become positive by 3 months and 98% by 6 months.[8] Less common explanations for false-negative results include seroreversion, which may occur in late-stage disease or in patients receiving HAART, atypical strains of HIV-1, or HIV-2 infection.[9] False-positive test results are exceedingly rare (<0.0004%); they may occur in several clinical circumstances including (1) recipients of blood transfusions containing the HIV antibody; (2) children younger than 6 months, in whom a positive test result may be caused by transplacentally acquired antibodies; (3) patients with cross-reacting antibodies (e.g., anti-hepatitis A immunoglobulin M [IgM], antihepatitis B core IgM, antinuclear, anti–smooth muscle, anti–parietal cell, and antimitochondrial antibodies); and (4) patients with cross-reactive human lymphocyte antigens from the H9 cell line or other human retroviruses. In populations with a low prevalence of true-positive results (e.g., heterosexual men or women in low-seroprevalence areas) the frequency of false-positive tests (both positive EIA and WB) is increased. This fact is often cited as one of the principal reasons for not offering indiscriminate HIV screening in the emergency department.

Indeterminate results most often occur with a positive EIA and a single band (rather than two or three) on WB. The most important factor to consider when evaluating an indeterminate WB is the patient's risk profile. Low-risk patients with indeterminate results are rarely infected with HIV-1 or HIV-2, and repeated testing usually shows persistence of one band with the cause rarely established. Referral to an infectious disease specialist and follow-up serology at 3 months are indicated. Patients in higher risk groups with indeterminate results are usually found to have definitively positive WB assays 3 or 6 months later and should thus be counseled to follow appropriate risk reduction behavior until follow-up definitive testing is completed.

Other methods for detection of HIV infection include detection of viral specific antigens and assays for HIV nucleic acid. Neither of these techniques is considered superior to routine serology in terms of accuracy, and they should be used only in patents with confusing serologic results requiring clarification. The most common situation in which emergency department physicians may consider viral detection testing is in cases of suspected acute retroviral infection. The quantitative plasma HIV RNA assay is most commonly employed and is also now used routinely for HIV staging and monitoring of response to retroviral therapy. Test results are reported as copies per milliliter, with survival time directly correlated with viral burden. Sensitivity of the various viral detection methods varies with stages of diseases but is generally greater than 99% for DNA polymerase chain reaction (PCR), 90% to 95% for quantitative HIV RNA, and 95% to 100% for viral culture of peripheral blood mononuclear cells.[10]

A variety of novel HIV tests are currently not routinely used in clinical care but are becoming increasingly relevant to emergency physicians. The single-use diagnostic system (SUDS) assay was the first rapid test to be developed and receive Food and Drug Administration (FDA) approval. The assay is analogous to EIA screening tests and can be performed in approximately 1 hour. The test is typically performed in hospital microbiology laboratories and is generally the most common method employed for the management of occupational exposures to help guide decisions in the use of postexposure prophylaxis (PEP).[11] Sensitivity is sufficient to report negative test results; positive test results should be described as "reactive" to the patient and require confirmation with routine serology. The test has also been advocated by some for routine use in inner-city emergency departments, which have high seroprevalence rates and where follow-up visits may be impractical or difficult to achieve.[12-14]

In late 2002, the FDA announced approval of the OraQuick Rapid HIV-1 Antibody Test (OraSure Technologies, Bethlehem, Pennsylvania).[15] OraQuick is a simple, easy to use, point-of-care test that can detect antibodies to HIV-1 in finger stick or whole blood specimens and provide results in as little as 20 minutes (a similar saliva-based test is also being developed but is not yet FDA approved). Sensitivity and specificity of OraQuick exceed 99%. Negative tests can be reported as negative; reactive tests require confirmatory follow-up testing with a WB. Potential advantages of the OraQuick test in addition to ease of specimen collection (i.e., finger stick) include reduced costs, rapid availability of results, and improved compliance with testing. The availability of this bedside point-of-care testing method is expected by some to revolutionize testing and awareness of HIV serostatus, as it provides the first opportunity to integrate HIV testing into routine medical care, particularly in settings that involve encounters at a single point in time, such as emergency departments.

Traditionally, it has been thought that serologic testing of patients for HIV in the emergency department is not indicated. This perception was based principally on logistic issues including difficulties with obtaining proper informed consent, providing appropriate counseling, maintaining confidentiality, ensuring appropriate follow-up for test results, and interfering with emergent diagnostic and management priorities intrinsic to emergency department practice. With the advent of rapid testing methodologies, the concept of emergency department testing for HIV is being reexamined because it is well established that early recognition of HIV (and early therapeutic intervention) can significantly delay progression of disease, reduce risk of opportunistic infections, and lead to decreased morbidity and mortality; furthermore, there is increasing recognition among HIV experts that many patients with unrecognized HIV (who represent approximately 30% of all patients infected) utilize the emergency department as their primary point of contact with the health care system. With the goal of increasing awareness of HIV serostatus in the community, the CDC is now actively advocating this approach by developing local, state, and federal programs that encourage emergency departments to offer rapid HIV testing to patients (or populations) considered at risk.

A systematic review of the evidence suggests that screening for HIV in the emergency department may be indicated under appropriate circumstances (i.e., populations in which HIV prevalence is at least 1% or emergency departments that serve patients with identifiable behavioral risk factors; sufficient resources in place to ensure appropriate pretest and posttest counseling; and the ability to make expeditious referral for patients whose test results are positive).[6] Studies conducted in the late 1990s using the SUDS test demonstrated that emergency department–based testing was feasible. Follow-up among newly tested HIV-positive patients was nearly 75%, with a cost of $40 per patient enrolled and counseled and $600 to $1100 per infection detected.[13] To ensure cost-effectiveness, however, methods for reliable identification of high-risk subgroups are required.[13,14]

More recent feasibility studies with the OraQuick test method lend further support for emergency department–based bedside HIV testing, with one busy inner-city emergency department demonstrating a 2.3% rate of new infections identified (57% of the patients had no previous test).[16] Significantly, 98% of those tested received results, and 76% entered into care. Despite the potential promise of this approach, significant obstacles for routine bedside HIV testing remain. Establishment of point-of-care HIV testing programs requires compliance with detailed local, state, and federal laboratory regulations, development of reliable reporting programs, and institution of effective quality assurance programs, all of which can add a significant burden to already overcrowded emergency departments. At present, routine HIV screening in emergency departments thus remains principally in the hands of researchers or small public health demonstration projects. For the time being, therefore, for individual patients in whom HIV is suspected on clinical grounds, emergency physicians should provide urgent referral for voluntary counseling and testing along with simple recommendations regarding risk reduction behavior.

Testing of patients for HIV in the emergency department to determine which patients require special infection control precautions is not recommended. Such practice has not been shown to alter rates of health care worker exposure to HIV-infected blood and detracts attention from other significant blood-borne infections. Furthermore, patients with undiagnosed HIV infection may have a wide range of clinical conditions and no identifiable risk factors.

CLINICAL PRESENTATIONS AND EMERGENCY DEPARTMENT MANAGEMENT

The broad spectrum of disease presentation for HIV-related disorders ranges widely from asymptomatic seropositive cases to severe, life-threatening complications of AIDS. It includes a wide variety of opportunistic infections, malignancies, and other HIV-related diseases. Nearly every organ system may be affected by HIV and related conditions. Because the differential diagnosis is so broad for many emergency department presentations, this chapter addresses clinical symptoms, signs, and some focused information on some of the common disorders. This chapter is not intended to be a decisive review of every HIV-related disorder, particularly in light of the ever-changing diagnostic and therapeutic modalities available. Appropriate updated resources and infectious disease consultants should be utilized whenever clinically indicated.

Initial Evaluation of the HIV-Infected Patient

The initial evaluation and management of the HIV-infected patient consists of rapid early assessment of stability. Airway, breathing, and circulation must be rapidly assessed and any indicated interventions performed. For unstable patients, IV access, cardiac monitoring, and administration of oxygen are typically indicated. After initial stabilization, the remainder of the history and physical examination may be conducted.

Relevant elements of the history include information pertinent to the chief complaint, including duration, location, qualities, characteristics, level of distress, and

relieving or inciting factors. Past history of similar problems should be solicited. Past medical history should be obtained, including any relevant medical problems, time of diagnosis of HIV infection, previous AIDS-defining conditions, recent hospitalizations, past surgical history, current medications, and allergies. Information regarding potential risk factors for HIV infection may be appropriate in the evaluation of many emergency department patients, particularly in endemic areas. The infection rate may be surprisingly high, even for patients with presenting complaints not associated with HIV infection.[17] Furthermore, inquiries about risk factors help in the medical evaluation, remind physicians of the potential for occupational exposure to the virus, and afford the opportunity to offer referral for testing and counseling to those who engage in high-risk behavior. Many cases of early HIV infection may not be detected during emergency department evaluation because of a low clinical suspicion of the disease, particularly in areas where AIDS is not prevalent. Although inquiries regarding risk factors may be offensive to some patients, this may often be averted by tactful inquiries about previous HIV testing or risk factors, presented as questions routinely asked to many patients.

The existence of an advance directive may be important historical information. Many HIV-infected patients have expressed opinions about the level of intervention desired in various clinical settings, particularly in critical care settings and at the end of life.

Following initial stabilization and gathering of historical information, a focused physical examination should be conducted. Elements of the examination relevant to the chief complaint should be performed, with special attention to the identification of potentially treatable disorders.

Of great importance to the emergency physician is the ability to assess the patient rapidly and effectively, identify potentially life-threatening disorders, administer urgent interventions, generate an appropriate differential diagnosis, and obtain appropriate initial therapy, consultation, and disposition.

Primary HIV Infection

Several methods of classification and staging of HIV infection have been developed. The Walter Reed classification system is based on clinical and immunologic features.[18] Other classifications are based on CD4 counts.[19] The 1993 CDC case definition of AIDS incorporated CD4 counts of less than 200 cells/mm^3. Box 130-1 illustrates selections of AIDS-defining illnesses.

Acute HIV syndrome (acute seroconversion syndrome) commonly follows primary exposure by 2 to 6 weeks and may cause nonspecific symptoms that may include fever, adenopathy, fatigue, pharyngitis, diarrhea, weight loss, and rash. Additional symptoms such as myopathy, peripheral neuropathy, or other neurologic or immunologic manifestations are less commonly present. These relatively nonspecific symptoms may be present for 1 to 3 weeks, and many patients do not seek medical attention during this phase of illness.

Predictors of Disease Progression

Although the rate of disease progression from initial HIV infection to development of AIDS-defining illnesses varies widely, the average time is 10 to 12 years. Some long-term nonprogressors have remained free of AIDS-defining conditions for over 20 years.[20] Both clinical and laboratory predictors of disease progression have been identified. Clinical predictors of more rapid development of clinically significant immunodeficiency include oral candidiasis, oral hairy leukoplakia, dermatomal varicella, lymphadenopathy, and constitutional symptoms.[21] The best predictor of immunologic susceptibility to opportunistic infection is the CD4 cell count.[22] Other laboratory markers predictive of disease progression include β_2-microglobulin levels, p24 antigenemia, neutropenia, and plasma HIV-1 RNA determinations.[23,24]

Complications

Systemic Symptoms of HIV Infection

Systemic symptoms such as fever, weight loss, and malaise are common among emergency department patients. The differential diagnosis is lengthy and includes a variety of infectious causes, malignancy, and drug reactions. Fever is a common presenting complaint in patients with AIDS. When it is caused by

Table 130-1. Chest Radiographic Abnormalities: Differential Diagnosis in the AIDS patient

Finding	Potential Etiologies
Diffuse interstitial infiltration	*Pneumocystis carinii* Cytomegalovirus *Mycobacterium tuberculosis* *Mycobacterium avium* complex Histoplasmosis Coccidioidomycosis Lymphoid interstitial pneumonitis *Mycoplasma pneumoniae*
Focal consolidation	Bacterial pneumonia *Mycoplasma pneumoniae* *Pneumocystis carinii* *Mycobacterium tuberculosis* *Mycobacterium avium* complex
Nodular lesions	Kaposi's sarcoma *Mycobacterium tuberculosis* *Mycobacterium avium* complex Fungal lesions Toxoplasmosis
Cavitary lesions	*Pneumocystis carinii* *Mycobacterium tuberculosis* Bacterial infection Fungal infection
Pleural effusion	Kaposi's sarcoma (small effusion may be associated with any infection)
Adenopathy	Kaposi's sarcoma Lymphoma *Mycobacterium tuberculosis* Cryptococcus
Pneumothorax	Kaposi's sarcoma
Normal radiograph	Histoplasmosis (40%) *Pneumocystis carinii* (20%) *Mycobacterium tuberculosis* Cryptococcosis Many other disease entities

primary HIV infection, it tends to occur in the afternoon or evening and is generally responsive to antipyretics. Evidence of an infectious cause or other reason for fever should be sought by careful history and physical examination. Laboratory investigation of fever may include a complete blood count, electrolytes, erythrocyte sedimentation rate, liver function tests, serologic test for syphilis, urinalysis and culture, blood cultures (aerobic, anaerobic, and fungal), blood tests for cryptococcal antigen, serologic tests for *Toxoplasma* and *Coccidioides,* and chest radiography. Stool culture, stool examination for ova and parasites, urine culture for fungus and mycobacteria, and sputum smear and culture for fungus and mycobacteria may yield additional important clues to diagnosis. If there are neurologic signs or symptoms or if no other source of fever is identified, lumbar puncture (LP) should be performed after a cranial computed tomography (CT) scan.

Atypical mycobacterial infection, caused by *Mycobacterium avium* complex or *M. kansasii,* causes disseminated disease in up to 50% of AIDS patients and is often associated with depressed CD4 counts.[25] It is usually associated with severe weight loss, diarrhea, and constitutional symptoms such as fever, malaise, and anorexia. It rarely causes significant pulmonary disease in patients with HIV. Ziehl-Neelsen (acid-fast) stain of stool or other body fluids commonly yields positive findings, and the organism can also be cultured from blood. Infection with *M. avium* complex may be treated with azithromycin 600 mg and ethambutol 15 mg/kg daily.[26] Clarithromycin with ethambutol may also be used. Treatment often reduces the degree of bacteremia and symptoms but does not typically eradicate the organism. Clarithromycin or azithromycin should be used as prophylaxis in patients with CD4 counts below 50 cells/mm³.

Cytomegalovirus (CMV) is a common cause of opportunistic infection. Disseminated disease is common. It is the most common cause of retinitis in HIV-infected patients. Colitis and esophagitis may also result from CMV infection. Treatment with ganciclovir or foscarnet is indicated, and oral ganciclovir may be used for prophylaxis.

Many patients with fever or other systemic symptoms may be managed as outpatients if adequate follow-up observation and home assistance are available. Indications for admission include toxic appearance, neutropenia with fever, active bleeding, or other need for urgent diagnosis and treatment.

Pulmonary Involvement

Pulmonary manifestations of HIV are among the most common reasons for emergency department visits among AIDS patients. Careful consideration is needed to establish the diagnosis and initiate early treatment.[27] The differential diagnosis of respiratory involvement is broad and includes such etiologies as bacterial infections (e.g., *Streptococcus pneumoniae, Haemophilus influenzae, Chlamydia pneumoniae, Pseudomonas aeruginosa, Staphylococcus aureus, Mycobacterium* tuberculosis, *Mycobacterium avium-intracellulare*), protozoal infections (e.g., *Pneumocystis jiroveci*, *Toxoplasma gondii*), viral infections (e.g., CMV, adenovirus), fungal infections (e.g., *Cryptococcus neoformans, Histoplasma capsulatum, Aspergillus fumigatus, Blastomyces dermatitidis*), malignancies (e.g., KS, carcinoma, lymphoma), and others (e.g., lymphocytic interstitial pneumonitis, pulmonary hypertension).

Development of pulmonary disorders is often related to CD4 counts. In patients with pulmonary involvement and CD4 counts greater than 500 cells/mm³, encapsulated bacteria, tuberculosis (TB), and malignancies are common. With lower CD4 counts, PCP, atypical mycobacteria, fungal infections, CMV, lymphoma, lymphoproliferative disorders, and KS may also be seen.[28]

Patients with fever and productive cough are likely to have a bacterial pneumonia, whereas a nonproductive cough is more likely to accompany *P. jiroveci* pneumonia (PCP; formerly known as *P. carinii* pneumonia), fungal infection, or neoplasm. Hemoptysis is often associated with pneumococcal pneumonia and TB.

Diagnostic evaluation of patients with HIV infection and pulmonary complaints may include complete blood count, chest radiography, and arterial blood gas analysis. Hypoxia may be more pronounced after exercise with *Pneumocystis* infection. Other tests may be indicated in certain situations, such as serum lactate dehydrogenase, sputum culture, Gram's stain, and special stains (Gomori, Giemsa, acid-fast). Obtaining blood cultures in the emergency department can prevent delays in initiating appropriate antimicrobial therapy.

Although radiographic findings in many pulmonary complications may be nondiagnostic, certain patterns may be suggestive of specific disorders. A focal infiltrate on plain chest radiography often suggests bacterial pneumonia.[29] A diffuse interstitial or perihilar, granular pattern on chest radiography is associated with PCP.[30,31] PCP is suggested by increased serum lactate dehydrogenase and hypoxia, which may be more severe than expected from radiographic findings. Hilar adenopathy with diffuse pulmonary infiltrates suggests cryptococcosis, histoplasmosis, mycobacterial infection, or neoplasm. Patients with KS can exhibit cough, fever, and dyspnea, and the chest radiograph may mimic that seen with PCP. Table 130-1 lists common radiographic findings and associated conditions in the HIV-infected patient.

As with all disease processes, emergency department management of pulmonary complications first includes evaluation and management of the airway, breathing, and circulation. Definitive airway management may be indicated in severe cases. Volume repletion or pressors may be indicated for hypotension. Other treatment measures should include the administration of supplemental oxygen and volume repletion if indicated. If the diagnosis can be ascertained or is strongly suspected, specific treatment can be instituted while the patient is in the emergency department, particularly if PCP is suspected. If the symptoms are of new onset or there has

been a change from previous status, admission should be considered. Decisions regarding patients with known pulmonary involvement are based on comparison with baseline status, the effectiveness of ongoing or previous treatment, and the individual's ability to obtain outpatient follow-up observation (see "Emergency Department Disposition"). Pilot studies indicate that decision guidelines used to aid in hospitalization decisions for the nonimmunosuppressed population may not apply for this population[32]; a staging system for predicting mortality from HIV-associated community pneumonia found that clinical factors associated with increased mortality include presence of neurologic symptoms, respiratory rate greater than 25 breaths/min or more, and creatinine greater than 1.2 mg/dL.[33]

Bacterial infections are the most common type of pulmonary infection among AIDS patients[34,35] and are commonly caused by *S. pneumoniae, H. influenzae, P. aeruginosa,* and numerous other organisms.[36] Presentations of bacterial pneumonia may be typical or atypical in symptoms, duration, and severity.

Pneumocystis carinii

PCP is one of the most common opportunistic infections in AIDS. More than 80% of AIDS patients acquire PCP at some time during their illness, and it is the initial opportunistic infection in many cases. PCP is caused by the organism *P. jiroveci,* formerly referred to as *P. carinii.*[37] It is still acceptable to use the acronym PCP in reference to *p*neumo*c*ystis *p*neumonia. Although *P. jiroveci* is traditionally classified as a protozoan, it has been suggested that its morphology closely resembles that of a fungus.[38] A decreased incidence of PCP has been seen since the widespread use of HAART.[39] A determined investigation of new or subtle symptoms may lead to an early diagnosis. The chest radiograph commonly shows a diffuse interstitial infiltrate but may also reveal normal findings, asymmetry, nodules, cavitation, or bullae.[40] Gallium scanning of the chest commonly yields positive findings even with negative radiographic results, but false-positive results may occur up to 50% of the time. Although bronchoscopy (bronchoalveolar lavage, brush biopsy, transbronchial biopsy) has been the mainstay of establishing the diagnosis, examination of induced sputum by indirect immunofluorescent staining using monoclonal antibodies has been shown to be an easy and effective method of diagnosing PCP.[41] The differential diagnosis includes viral, bacterial, mycobacterial, fungal, and protozoal pneumonias as well as malignancies. The more common causes to be considered in the differential diagnosis are shown in Box 130-2. Differentiation of these entities in the emergency department may be difficult if not impossible.

Establishment of a definitive diagnosis is not necessary before the initiation of treatment. Treatment should be initiated as early as possible, with 15 to 20 mg/kg/day trimethoprim and 75 to 100 mg/kg/day sulfamethoxazole (TMP-SMX), given either orally or IV for a total of 21 days[42] (e.g., two Bactrim DS tablets every 8 hours). Other therapeutic options include

BOX 130-2. Etiologies of Systemic Symptoms in HIV-Infected Patients

Infections, Including
Primary HIV infection (e.g., acute retroviral syndrome, HIV wasting syndrome)

Protozoal Infections
Pneumocystis carinii pneumonia
Toxoplasmosis
Cryptosporidiosis

Bacterial Infections
Streptococcus pneumoniae
Haemophilus influenzae
Pseudomonas aeruginosa
Salmonellosis
Bacteremia (any organism)

Atypical Bacterial Infections
Mycobacterium avium intracellulare (MAI)
Mycobacterium tuberculosis (MTB)

Fungal Infections
Histoplasmosis
Cryptococcosis
Coccidioidomycosis

Viral Infections
Herpes simplex virus
Herpes-zoster virus
Cytomegalovirus
Hepatitis viruses

Adverse Drug Reactions
Neoplasms, Including
Kaposi's sarcoma
Lymphoma
Hodgkin's disease

pentamidine isethionate, dapsone, clindamycin plus primaquine, atovaquone, and trimetrexate. In addition, steroid treatment (prednisone, 40 mg by mouth [PO] twice daily with a tapering dose over 3 weeks) is recommended for patients with a partial pressure of oxygen in arterial blood less than 70 mm Hg or an alveolar-arterial gradient greater than 35.[43] Most (60% to 80%) respond to therapy, although pneumocystis persists in the lungs of two thirds of patients. The optimal duration of therapy has not been definitively established, but 3 weeks of treatment is commonly recommended. Prophylaxis is recommended with TMP-SMX, dapsone, or aerosolized pentamidine.[44]

Adverse effects of TMP-SMX occur in up to 65% of AIDS patients and are 20 times more common than in the general population (Table 130-2); they generally become apparent after 7 to 14 days of therapy. However, 75% of patients are able to tolerate a full course of therapy. The most common adverse effects are nausea, vomiting, rash, fever, neutropenia, thrombocytopenia, hyponatremia, and hepatitis. Pentamidine can cause nausea, vomiting, diarrhea, neutropenia, hypoglycemia, hyperglycemia, renal impairment, hepatic toxicity, and orthostatic hypotension.[1] Because sterile abscesses may develop at the injection site, IV infusion is preferred. Prophylaxis against PCP may be an impor-

tant step in preventing reinfection and is recommended for patients with CD4 cell counts below 200 cells/mm^3.[45] Preferred therapeutic agents include TMP-SMX (one DS tablet, PO, once or twice daily), pentamidine, pyrimethamine plus sulfadoxine, dapsone, and pyrimethamine plus dapsone.

Mycobacterium tuberculosis

The incidence of M. tuberculosis in HIV-infected patients has increased dramatically from a low point reached in 1985, particularly in socioeconomically disadvantaged groups, including prisoners[2] and IV drug users. It is estimated that more than 10 million patients worldwide are coinfected with HIV and TB.[46] HIV-infected patients have an estimated 50- to 200-fold increased risk of acquiring TB compared with the general population.[47] The increase in TB in the HIV-infected population is thought to be secondary to a number of factors, including increased risk of reactivation of latent infection, high rates of infection after exposure, overlap in at-risk groups, and rapid progression to clinically significant disease.[48] TB may be a very early manifestation of AIDS. Common presenting symptoms include fever, cough, and hemoptysis. Radiographic abnormalities may vary considerably. Radiographic features may include alveolar infiltrates, interstitial infiltrates, cavitation, pleural effusions, mediastinal adenopathy, and alveolar opacities.[49] Although classical findings of upper lobe infiltrates and cavitation may occur in patients with CD4 counts above 200 cells/mm^3, adenopathy, atypical features, or normal radiographs are more commonly seen among patients with lower CD4 counts.[50] Extrapulmonary disease is more common among HIV-infected patients and may occur in up to 75% of cases. Central nervous system (CNS), bone, visceral, skin, pericardial, eye, pharynx, and lymph node involvement may occur.

The diagnosis of TB is based on a number of factors, including risk of infection, clinical presentation, direct examination of patients' specimens, and identification of mycobacteria from cultures. Purified protein derivative (PPD) skin testing may be unhelpful, particularly in advanced stages of immunosuppression. The use of a nucleic acid amplification test, in conjunction with clinical stratification, may have important diagnostic value.[51] Negative PPD test results are common among those infected. Attempts to diagnose M. tuberculosis by stain and culture of sputum may not be fruitful; bronchoscopy or biopsy of affected organs (e.g., lymph nodes, liver, brain) may be required.

Multidrug-resistant TB is becoming an issue of concern, particularly in the HIV-infected population. Outbreaks involving organisms resistant to multiple pharmacologic agents, including isoniazid and rifampin, have occurred.

Treatment of suspected cases should be determined in conjunction with an infectious disease specialist, taking into consideration local resistance as well as individual susceptibility tests. AIDS patients with TB should receive a four-drug regimen for 6 months with isoniazid, rifampin, pyrazinamide, and either

Table 130-2. Common Drug Reactions in HIV-Infected Persons

Drug	Fever	Rash	N/V	Diarrhea	H/A	ΔMS	Neuropathy	↑LFT	↓WBC	↓Hct	↓plt	Other
Acyclovir		×	×	×								Vertigo
Amphotericin	×		×		×				×	×	×	Nephrotoxicity
Atovaquone	×	×	×	×	×				×	×		
Azithromycin		×	×	×	×							
Clarithromycin			×	×	×							
Clindamycin		×										
Clotrimazole			×	×								
Dapsone	×	×	×		×				×	×		Hepatitis
Didanosine		×	×	×	×	×	×					Pancreatitis
Fluconazole		×	×	×	×			×				
Foscarnet	×		×	×						×		Nephrotoxicity, seizures
Ganciclovir	×		×	×					×	×		
Ibuprofen		×	×	×				×	×	×		
Indinavir		×	×		×							Nephrolithiasis
Isoniazid	×	×	×				×	×	×	×	×	Hepatitis
Itraconazole		×	×	×	×			×				
Ketoconazole			×	×				×				
Lamivudine	×		×	×	×		×					Cough
Narcotics			×			×						
Pentamidine		×							×	×		Metallic taste
Pyrimethamine									×	×		
Rifabutin		×	×					×	×		×	Skin discoloration
Ritonavir			×	×	×							Paresthesias
Saquinavir		×	×	×								
TMP-SMX	×	×	×					×	×		×	Hepatotoxicity, ↓K
Zalcitabine	×	×	×	×	×	×	×					
Zidovudine	×	×	×	×	×	×			×	×		

*This table represents only a partial list of adverse drug reactions. An authoritative source should be consulted whenever adverse drug reactions are suspected.
ΔMS, altered mental status; H/A, headache; Hct, hematocrit; HIV, human immunodeficiency virus; LFT, liver function tests; N/V, nausea vomiting; plt, platelets; TMP-SMX, trimethoprim-sulfamethoxazole; WBC, white blood cell.

ethambutol hydrochloride or streptomycin.[52] Second-line agents may include ciprofloxacin, ofloxacin, kanamycin, amikacin, capreomycin, ethionamide, cycloserine, and *para*-aminosalicylic acid. All HIV-infected patients with positive PPD findings should receive prophylaxis, with a regimen of isoniazid plus pyridoxine or rifampin plus pyrazinamide. Steps toward prevention of TB and its spread include the use of HAART, early identification of TB, early initiation of multidrug therapy, the use of respiratory isolation, and the use of personal respiratory protection devices.

Fungal pulmonary infections may be seen in AIDS patients. Etiologies may include cryptococcosis, aspergillosis, histoplasmosis, coccidioidomycosis, nocardiosis, and blastomycosis.[53] *C. neoformans* is the most common fungal pathogen and typically occurs in the stages of advanced immunosuppression, with CD4 counts less than 100 cells/mm³. Radiographic findings are often nonspecific and may include consolidation, reticulonodular infiltrates, or nodules. Aspergillus infections often arise with cavitary lesions.

Viral infections also occur in HIV-infected patients. CMV is the most common viral pulmonary pathogen and typically occurs with advanced immunosuppression. Radiographic findings may include alveolar consolidation or ground-glass opacities.

Pulmonary malignancies may include KS and others. KS is typically associated with hilar peribronchovas-cular thickening, lower lobe reticulonodular opacities, adenopathy, pleural effusion, or focal consolidation.[54] Pulmonary KS is treated with cytotoxic agents and HAART. Other malignancies, including non-Hodgkin's lymphoma, Hodgkin's disease, and bronchogenic carcinoma, may be seen and should be treated in consultation with oncologic experts.

Lymphoproliferative disorders may also cause pulmonary presentations among HIV-infected patients. Etiologies may include lymphocytic interstitial pneumonia, nonspecific interstitial pneumonia, and bronchiolitis obliterans.

Patients admitted with pulmonary involvement in whom the diagnosis cannot be determined may require bronchoscopy, bronchial lavage, and possibly biopsy. If the clinical probability of PCP is high, treatment should begin before diagnostic bronchoscopy.

Neurologic Involvement

Neurologic diseases are the initial manifestation of AIDS in 10% to 20% of patients. The frequency of neurologic complications increases over the course of HIV infection, with cross-sectional studies showing a 75% to 90% prevalence of neurologic disorders in patients with AIDS.[55] Data obtained since 1996 (since the introduction of HAART) show that the overall incidence rates of HIV-associated neurologic diseases and CNS

Figure 130-2. Advanced HIV infection plus altered mental status, new seizures, headache (severe or persistent), or focal neurologic deficits. CMV, cytomegalovirus; CSF, cerebrospinal fluid; CT, computed tomography; EBV, Epstein-Barr virus; FA, fluorescent antibody; HAART, highly active antiviral therapy; HSV, herpes simplex virus; IFN, interferon; MRI, magnetic resonance imaging; PCR, polymerase chain reaction; PML, progressive multifocal leukoencephalopathy; SV40, simian virus 40; VDRL, Venereal Disease Research Laboratory. (Modified from McArthur J, Bartlett JG: Headache in patients with AIDS. In Bartlett JG [ed]: 1999 *Medical Management of HIV Infection.* Baltimore, Port City Press, 1999, p 333.)

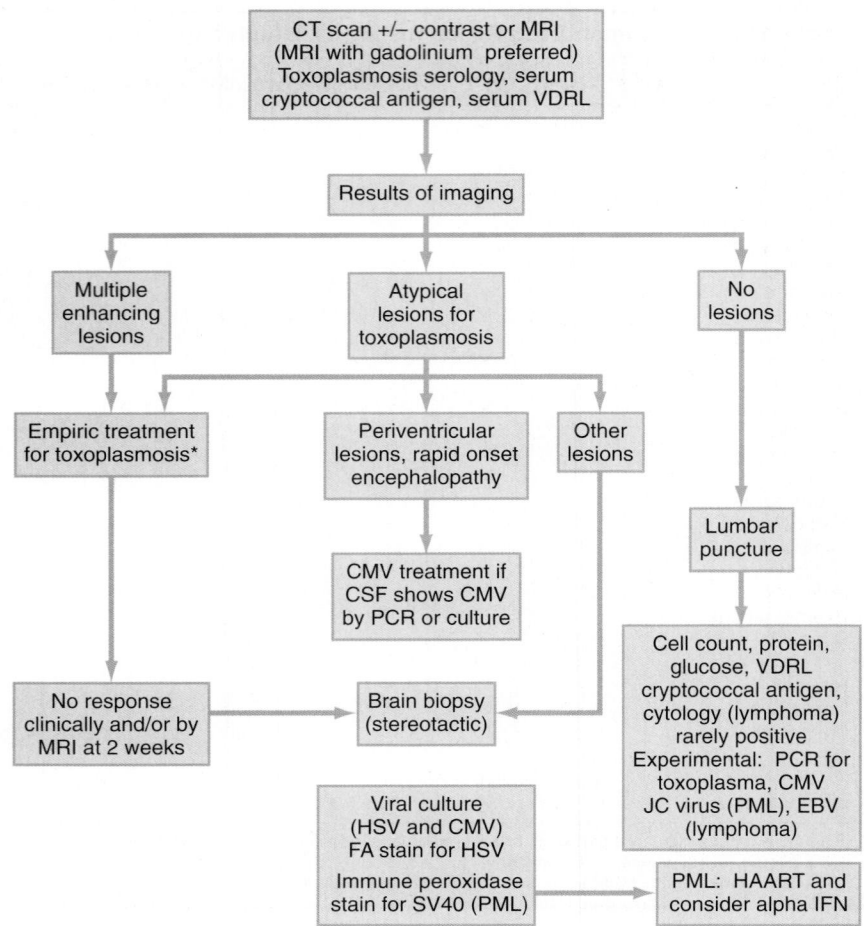

*Serology for *Toxoplasma gondii* is positive 85–90% with toxoplasmic encephalitis. Clinical response to empiric treatment is anticipated within one week. Negative serology, atypical presentation, and/or delayed clinical response should prompt early biopsy.

opportunistic infections are decreasing, although this trend is expected to change as patients develop increased resistance to antiretroviral drugs.[56]

Neurologic diseases in HIV-infected patients are generally divided into those caused by direct effects of HIV infection on the CNS and those occurring as a result of immunosuppression (i.e., opportunistic infections and neoplasms). In the early stages of HIV infection, aseptic meningitis, herpes zoster radiculitis, and inflammatory demyelinating polyneuropathy are common. Later stages of HIV are associated with cognitive dysfunction, dementia, opportunistic infections, cancers, and sensory neuropathies. The most common AIDS-defining neurologic complications are HIV encephalopathy (dementia), *C. neoformans,* toxoplasmosis, and primary CNS lymphoma.

Less common CNS infections that should be considered in the presence of neurologic symptoms include bacterial meningitis, histoplasmosis (usually disseminated), CMV, progressive multifocal leukoencephalopathy (PML), herpes simplex virus (HSV), neurosyphilis, and TB. Noninfectious CNS processes include CNS lymphoma, cerebrovascular accidents, and metabolic encephalopathies.

Clinical pictures in patients with serious neurologic complications can be nonspecific, making diagnosis

and disposition challenging. The most common symptoms indicative of CNS pathology are seizures, meningismus, focal neurologic deficits, altered mental status, and headache (new or persistent). Infection accounts for the vast majority of neurologic disorders and is most often accompanied by fever.

Patients with CD4 cell counts above 200 cells/mm^3 who present with fever and meningismus in the absence of focal neurologic deficits should have an immediate LP performed. For those with focal deficits or new seizures, immediate neuroimaging is recommended, followed by LP if neuroimaging is unrevealing. Diagnostic evaluation of patients with altered mental status or headache should proceed as in the non–HIV-infected population, with neuroimaging and LP reserved for cases in which another cause of the symptoms is not identified or with a clear indication for workup (e.g., worst headache of life).[56] For patients with CD4 cell counts less than 200 cells/mm^3 a more aggressive approach is advocated, with any of the preceding findings indicating emergent imaging, usually followed by LP (Figure 130-2).[57,58]

The choice of imaging modality in the emergency department varies. Generally, for CNS processes that require immediate identification, CT without contrast is considered adequate.[59,60] If the entire emergency department evaluation is unrevealing, more advanced diagnostic imaging should be pursued immediately, usually in an inpatient setting, if the patient's symptoms are severe or new neurologic findings are present. For all other cases, close follow-up is indicated with the patient's primary provider because it has been demonstrated that more subtle lesions may be identified by CT with contrast or magnetic resonance imaging (MRI). CSF analysis should include opening and closing pressures, cell count, glucose, protein, Gram's stain, bacterial culture, viral culture, fungal culture, toxoplasmosis and cryptococcal antigens, and coccidioidomycosis titer. It is prudent to have excess CSF held by the laboratory for further testing if the preliminary workup is unrevealing.

HIV Encephalopathy

HIV encephalopathy, or AIDS dementia complex, occurs in up to one third of patients with HIV and is the initial manifestation of AIDS in 3% of adults.[55] It is a progressive process caused by direct HIV infection and is commonly heralded by impairment of recent memory or subtle cognitive deficits, such as difficulty concentrating. Traditionally, symptoms are expected to occur in patients with CD4 counts less than 200 cells/mm^3, although since 1996 increasing numbers of cases are being seen in patients with CD4 counts greater than 200 cells/mm^3.[61] Early stages of dementia may be confused with depression, the effects of psychoactive substances, or anxiety disorders. Deficits become more debilitating in later stages of disease and can include more obvious changes in mental status, seizures, frontal release signs, and hyperactive deep tendon reflexes; in these cases physical examination usually reveals the hallmarks of advanced AIDS, including wasting, alopecia, generalized dermatitis, and lymphadenopathy.

It is important to recognize that AIDS dementia is a diagnosis of exclusion. Thus, even among patients with AIDS coming to the emergency department with an established diagnosis of dementia, the appearance of progressive signs or symptoms requires further evaluation to rule out other CNS processes. Neuroimaging findings in patients with HIV encephalopathy typically show atrophy and diffuse deep matter hyperintensities; MRI may reveal patchy punctate lesions in the white matter. LP findings are typically normal. Controlled trials in adults and children with HIV dementia have demonstrated benefit of high-dose zidovudine.[61]

Cryptococcus neoformans

C. neoformans is a fungal CNS infection that causes either focal cerebral lesions or diffuse meningoencephalitis; it occurs in up to 10% of patients with HIV, most commonly in those with CD4 counts less than 100/mm^3. The most common initial symptoms are fever and headache, often accompanied by nausea and vomiting. Less frequent are visual changes, dizziness, seizures, and cranial nerve deficits.[62] The brainstem and basal ganglia are typical locations; high intracranial pressure and sudden clinical deterioration from herniation are relatively common. Mortality is up to 30%.

Patients with C. neoformans usually have no significant findings on CT. Definitive diagnosis relies on a positive cryptococcal antigen in the CSF, which is nearly 100% sensitive and specific; other diagnostic tests include India ink staining (60% to 80% sensitive), fungal culture (95% sensitive), and serum cryptococcal antigen (95% sensitive). Additional findings associated with Cryptococcus infection include elevated opening pressure and a mononuclear pleocytosis. Treatment of cryptococcal meningitis requires admission for IV amphotericin B (0.7 mg/kg/day); 5-flucytosine (100 mg/kg/day) may be added to this regimen. The initial course of therapy lasts 8 to 10 weeks, and a response can be expected approximately 60% of the time. The most clinically significant adverse effect of treatment for cryptococcal meningitis is bone marrow suppression related to flucytosine; amphotericin B may also cause significant adverse effects, most commonly fever and renal dysfunction. Oral fluconazole (400 mg/day) is acceptable as initial therapy in patients with normal mental status. After successful treatment, chronic suppressive therapy with lower doses of oral fluconazole is indicated because of the high relapse rate (approximately 50%). This can be discontinued in those with immune reconstitution.

Toxoplasma gondii

T. gondii is the most common cause of focal intracranial mass lesions in patients with HIV infection, with an incidence of 3% to 4%.[55,61] There is an increased prevalence of this disease in areas of high toxoplasmosis seropositivity (i.e., southern Florida, Europe, and developing countries). In most cases, symptomatic disease is a result of reactivation of latent infection. Common symptoms include headache, fever, altered mental status, and seizures. Focal neurologic deficits are found in up to 80% of cases. Serologic testing is not useful in making or excluding the diagnosis because antibody to T. gondii is prevalent in the general population. The presence of antibody to T. gondii in the CSF is helpful, although there is a high rate of false-positive results. Diagnosis of toxoplasmosis is most often made by the presence of multiple subcortical lesions on CT scan (Figure 130-3). Noncontrast CT is often used as the initial study in the emergency department because addition of contrast has been shown to be of marginal value in patients with completely normal noncontrast CT scans.[60] In patients with suspicious lesions or those with a high suspicion for clinical pathology but equivocal or negative noncontrast scans, a contrast CT may be helpful. In the presence of contrast, toxoplasmosis lesions are ring enhancing with surrounding areas of edema. MRI is considered even more sensitive in detecting the number and extent of lesions but is usually not indicated in the emergency department.[63]

Clinical and radiologic features often cannot reliably distinguish CNS toxoplasmosis from a wide variety of other causes (lymphoma, cerebral TB, fungi, PML,

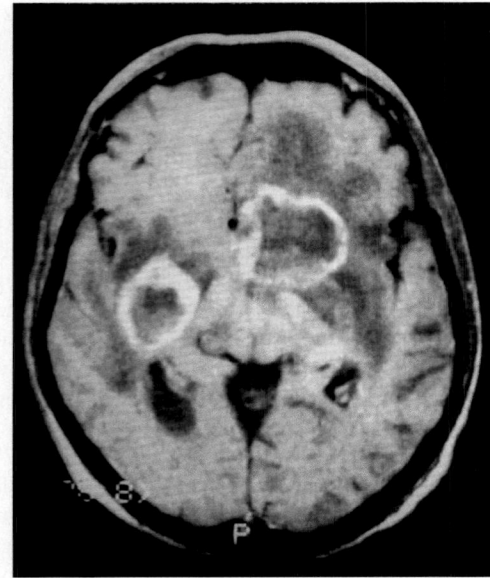

Figure 130-3. Contrast brain computed tomography scan showing typical multiple ring-enhancing lesions of brain toxoplasmosis.

CMV, KS, and hemorrhage).[63] General patterns have been described that may be helpful in determining the most likely cause. Toxoplasmosis tends to involve a greater number of lesions with a predilection for the basal ganglia and corticomedullary area, whereas lymphomas more often involve singular lesions located in the periventricular matter or corpus callosum. TB is characterized by an inflammatory appearance on CT, with a thick isodense exudate filling the basal cisterns.

Patients with suspected toxoplasmosis should be admitted and treated with pyrimethamine (100 to 200 mg PO loading dose, followed by 50 to 100 mg/day PO) plus sulfadiazine (4 to 8 g/day PO) with folinic acid (10 mg/day PO) to reduce the incidence of pancytopenia. Alternatives to sulfadiazine, include sulfisoxazole, clindamycin, azithromycin, atovaquone, and doxycycline, are often required because of the relative high frequency of side effects associated with sulfadiazine. Short courses of high-dose steroids are beneficial in cases in which significant edema or mass effect is noted; seizure prophylaxis with phenytoin may also be used in these cases.[56] Failure to respond to treatment suggests an alternative diagnosis that may require biopsy. As with cryptococcal meningitis, chronic suppressive treatment is usually indicated because of the high likelihood of relapse after successful therapy. Pyrimethamine, sulfadiazine, and folinic acid are recommended. For patients with positive toxoplasmosis serology and CD4 cell counts less than 100 cells/mm^3, prophylaxis with TMP-SMX (one DS tablet PO daily) plus folinic acid is indicated; dapsone can be substituted for TMP-SMX in patients who are intolerant of sulfa drugs.[64]

Primary Central Nervous System Lymphoma

This previously rare disorder occurs in up to 3% of patients with HIV, typically in those with CD4 cell counts less than 100/mm^3. The incidence has decreased slightly since the introduction of HAART in 1996.[61] These are polyclonal tumors originating from B cells that express Epstein-Barr virus (EBV). The most common clinical finding is a change in mental status; presentation is typical subacute. Diagnosis is usually based on CT findings, which show either hyperdense or isodense round or multiple lesions that are enhanced with contrast and have a predilection for the periventricular region; differentiation from toxoplasmosis can be challenging and is often made after failure to respond to therapy for that agent. PCR for EBV is a helpful diagnostic adjunct; definitive diagnosis, however, often requires stereotactic biopsy. Prognosis for lymphoma is poor and median survival is less than 1 month. Life expectancy may be extended to several months with whole-brain irradiation along with corticosteroids and chemotherapy (methotrexate and zidovudine).[61,65]

Progressive Multifocal Leukoencephalopathy

PML occurs in approximately 1% to 3% of patients with AIDS and is caused by reactivation of the JC virus. The most common presenting features are weakness, speech disturbances, cognitive dysfunction, and headaches. Typical CT findings are single or multiple nonenhancing white matter lesions; JC virus PCR is approximately 80% sensitive. No specific therapy exists other than immune reconstitution.

Tuberculosis Meningitis

M. avium-intracellulare infection is the most common cause of TB meningitis; it occurs in less than 1% of patients with AIDS and may be associated with intracranial abscesses or spinal cord abscesses. CT findings may be confused with those of toxoplasmosis. Because CSF may be negative, definitive diagnosis often requires brain biopsy. Three- or four-drug therapy for at least 9 months is required for cure.[61]

HIV Neuropathy

HIV infection is also associated with a variety of disorders of the peripheral nervous system. These are rarely emergent but require appropriate referral. The most common peripheral disorder to be aware of is HIV neuropathy, which occurs in up to 50% of HIV-infected patients and is characterized by painful sensory symptoms in the feet. Treatment in the emergency department should be directed toward analgesia. Ibuprofen may be used as first-line therapy, although narcotics may be required in more severe cases. Amitriptyline and phenytoin have been shown to be helpful but should be used judiciously because of their potential for causing delirium in patients with concurrent HIV dementia.

Gastrointestinal Involvement

Most AIDS patients have gastrointestinal symptoms at some time during the course of their illness. The most common symptoms are diarrhea, weight loss, malabsorption, abdominal pain, bleeding, esophageal symptoms, and hepatobiliary symptoms.[66] Nonspecific symptoms of nausea, vomiting, and abdominal pain are common adverse effects of antiretroviral therapy and may be seen with NRTIs, NNRTIs, and PIs.[67] Evaluation of specific causes is often difficult until objective studies are obtained. Often, more than one source of infection is present, and this may further complicate establishing the diagnosis. Treatment in the emergency department focuses on supportive care, fluid and electrolyte repletion, and obtaining appropriate studies for further investigation.

Oropharynx

Oral involvement is common and may include a variety of etiologies, including fungal infections (oral candidiasis, histoplasmosis, cryptococcosis, penicillinosis), viral lesions (herpes simplex, herpes zoster, CMV, hairy leukoplakia, papillomavirus), bacterial lesions (periodontal disease, necrotizing stomatitis, TB, *M. avium* complex, bacillary angiomatosis), neoplasms (KS, lymphoma, Hodgkin's lymphoma), and auto-immune or idiopathic lesions (e.g., salivary gland disease, aphthous ulcers). Oral lesions such as candidiasis and hairy leukoplakia are indicators of disease progression.[68]

Oral candidiasis affects more than 80% of AIDS patients. *Candida albicans,* the most common fungal agent in HIV-infected patients, typically involves the tongue and buccal mucosa and may be asymptomatic. Symptoms may include soreness, burning, and dysphagia. Candidiasis can be distinguished from hairy leukoplakia by its characteristic whitish lacy plaques, which are easily scraped away from an erythematous base. Three forms of candidiasis may be seen: pseudomembranous (thrush), erythematous, and angular cheilitis. Microscopic examination of the material on potassium hydroxide smear can confirm the diagnosis in the emergency department. Most oral lesions can be managed symptomatically on an outpatient basis. Clotrimazole troches (10 mg PO five times daily for 14 days) are the preferred treatment for oral candidiasis. Other treatment options include nystatin vaginal tablets, which may be dissolved slowly in the mouth four times daily, or nystatin pastilles (two pastilles dissolved in the mouth five times daily). Systemic therapy, such as ketoconazole, fluconazole, or itraconazole, may be used for resistant lesions. Nystatin suspension is not recommended because of inadequate duration of application in the oropharynx.

Hairy leukoplakia is also commonly seen and typically produces white, corrugated or filiform thickened lesions on the lateral aspects of the tongue. As it is often asymptomatic, therapy is not necessary, but, when indicated, treatment may be initiated with acyclovir, ganciclovir, foscarnet, or tretinoin (Retin-A). Lesions commonly reoccur after cessation of therapy.

Painful oral and perioral ulcerations may be caused by HSV. HSV can be diagnosed in the emergency department by the identification of multinucleated giant cells in scrapings of the lesions and can be diagnosed definitively by culture. Therapy should be initiated with acyclovir. *M. avium* complex may also cause painful oral ulcerative lesions. The diagnosis of *M. avium* complex can be established if an acid-fast stain yields positive findings.

Oral KS may appear as nontender, well-circumscribed, slightly raised, violaceous or erythematous lesions anywhere in the oropharynx. Definitive diagnosis requires biopsy. Treatment may include surgical excision, localized chemotherapy, sclerosing agents, or radiation therapy.

Periodontal disease may be seen in up to 10% of patients, including gingival erythema or necrotizing periodontal disease.[69] Outpatient treatment may be instituted, including local irrigation and mouth rinses and oral antibiotics, such as amoxicillin-clavulanate or clindamycin. Dental follow-up is essential.

Aphthous ulcerations, often painful and recurrent, have an unknown etiology but are thought to be related to immune deficiency. Other etiologies of ulcerations such as fungal or mycobacterial infection, HSV, CMV, and lymphoma should be excluded. Aphthous ulcers usually respond to topical steroids, such as 0.05% flu-ocinonide ointment, mixed 50% with an oral topical anesthetic such as benzocaine (Orabase).

Esophagus

Complaints of dysphagia, odynophagia, or chest pain may be indicative of esophageal involvement. *Candida,* HSV, and CMV infections may all cause painful esophagitis. Other etiologies may include KS, idiopathic, *M. avium* complex, or reflux esophagitis. The most cost-effective approach to the evaluation of patients with esophageal complaints is to initiate empirical therapy with oral antifungal agents for 2 weeks and proceed with endoscopy for patients who fail to improve after 2 weeks.[70] Although treatment may be initiated empirically on the basis of symptoms, endoscopy, fungal stains, viral cultures, and occasionally biopsy may be required to establish the diagnosis definitively. An air-contrast barium swallow can be obtained as part of the emergency department evaluation. An ulcerative pattern with plaques, often separated by normal mucosa, is characteristic of *Candida* esophagitis. Herpes esophagitis typically produces easily seen "punched-out" ulcerations without associated "heaped-up" plaques.

Esophageal candidiasis, the most common cause of esophageal complaints, may be treated presumptively on the basis of the symptoms and should include either fluconazole (100 to 200 mg PO daily for 2 to 3 weeks) or ketoconazole (200 to 400 mg PO daily for 2 to 3 weeks).[71] Alternative therapies may include clotrimazole or itraconazole. Relapses are common after cessation of treatment. IV amphotericin B may be used for refractory cases. Disseminated candidiasis is managed with IV amphotericin B and flucytosine. Fluconazole has been shown to be effective in prophylaxis against fungal infections in patients with a CD4 count less than 100/mm³, although survival is unaffected by prophylactic therapy[72] and any benefit gained by prophylaxis must be carefully weighed against risks of potentially significant adverse drug reaction.

Diarrhea

Diarrhea is the most common gastrointestinal complaint in AIDS patients and is estimated to occur in 50% to 90% of patients. Diarrhea can vary in severity from a few loose stools per day to massive fluid loss with prostration, fever, chills, and weight loss. Medication side effects should be considered, as antiretroviral agents are associated with a high incidence of gastrointestinal adverse effects. Potential pathogens causing diarrhea include parasites (*Cryptosporidium parvum, Enterocytozoon bieneusi, Isospora belli, Giardia lamblia, Entamoeba histolytica,* microsporidia, *Cyclospora,* and others), bacteria (*Salmonella, Shigella, Campylobacter, Helicobacter pylori, M. tuberculosis, M. avium* complex, *Clostridium difficile,* and others), viruses (CMV, herpes simplex, HIV, and others), and fungi (*H. capsulatum, C. neoformans, Coccidioides immitis,* and others). Opportunistic infections are more commonly seen among patients with CD4 cell counts less than 100 cells/mm³. Significant gastrointestinal bleeding and dehydration have been associated with many pathogens, particularly CMV. *Salmonella* infection can be of particular concern in HIV-infected patients, often producing recurrent bacteremia and other significant clinical disease. Neoplastic gastrointestinal involvement with KS or lymphoma may produce dysphagia, obstruction, intussusception, or diarrhea.

Cryptosporidium and *Isospora* infections are commonly associated with HIV infection, and both organisms may produce prolonged watery diarrhea.[73] Diagnosis may be sought using acid-fast staining of stool samples, monoclonal antibodies, or enzyme-linked immunoabsorbent assays. Treatment of these disorders is clinically variably successful. Symptoms may be treated with diet modification or loperamide. *Cryptosporidium* infections may be treated with some success with paromomycin (500 to 750 mg PO four times daily for 2 to 4 weeks) or azithromycin (2400 mg/day on day 1, followed by 1200 mg/day for 4 weeks, followed by 600 mg/day). *Isospora* infections are often successfully treated with TMP-SMX (one DS tablet, PO, three times daily for 10 days, followed by twice-weekly therapy for 3 weeks). Pyrimethamine or metronidazole may be used as alternative therapy. HAART may also reduce the duration and severity of symptoms.

Viruses causing diarrhea include CMV, adenovirus, astrovirus, rotavirus, and others.[74] Reduced incidences of viral diarrhea have been associated with HAART.

Malabsorption syndromes are relatively common. Delayed gastric emptying and intestinal infections may contribute to malabsorption and weight loss. Treatment may include nutritional counseling, parenteral nutrition, and agents such as dronabinol, megestrol acetate, and human growth hormone.[75]

Emergency department management should include repletion of fluid and electrolytes and obtaining appropriate diagnostic studies. Initial studies should include microscopic examination of stool for leukocytes and of stool samples for bacterial culture, ova, and parasites. If indicated, colonoscopy or sigmoidoscopy (with or without biopsy) may be arranged for patients who require further evaluation.[76] Often, no definitive diagnosis can be made in AIDS patients with diarrhea. Management of symptoms of severe diarrhea not requiring specific therapy may include attapulgite (Kaopectate), psyllium (Metamucil), diet modification, or diphenoxylate hydrochloride with atropine (Lomotil).

Liver

Hepatomegaly is common and occurs in up to 50% of AIDS patients. Jaundice is less common. Hepatitis B and hepatitis C are common among AIDS patients, especially among IV drug users. Previous hepatitis B virus infection may become reactivated after HIV infection or acquired with increased prevalence after HIV infection. Several opportunistic organisms, including CMV, *M. avium-intracellulare, M. tuberculosis,* and *H. capsulatum,* can produce a hepatitis-like spectrum in patients with HIV infection. Typically, the patient has an elevation in the alkaline phosphatase level that is disproportionate to other liver enzymes. Histoplasmosis may produce gastrointestinal lesions, including ulcers, nodules, hemorrhage, and obstructive lesions, as well as liver lesions.[77] Hepatotoxicity may result from a variety of medications, including indinavir.

Anorectal Disease

Complete examination of the anus and rectum is important in diagnosing such disorders. Examination for fissures, masses, infection, and inflammation should be made by inspection, palpation, digital examination, anoscopy, and, when indicated, sigmoidoscopy. Proctocolitis is common in patients with AIDS and may be caused by one or several of a long list of organisms, including *Campylobacter jejuni, Shigella* species, *Salmonella* species, *Giardia,* herpes simplex, *E. histolytica, Chlamydia,* and *Neisseria gonorrhoeae.* Diagnostic tests may include standard stool cultures; microscopic examination for leukocytes, ova, and parasites; and appropriate cultures or immunoassays for gonorrhea and chlamydial infections. The diagnosis of anal gonorrhea can be confirmed on a Gram's stain of stool by the presence of leukocytes and intracellular organisms. HSV can be diagnosed by viral cultures or by identification of multinucleated giant cells on scrapings of anal lesions.

Cutaneous Involvement

Several common cutaneous manifestations of AIDS are likely to be seen in the emergency department. Preexisting dermatologic conditions may be exacerbated by HIV infection. Common infections and conditions may arise in an atypical fashion. Generalized cutaneous complaints such as xerosis (dry skin) and pruritus are common and may be manifested before any AIDS-defining illness. Treatment of patients with these conditions is identical to that of noninfected patients. Xerosis may be treated with emollients. Pruritus may be treated with oatmeal baths and, if necessary, antihistamines.

Infections including *S. aureus* (manifest as bullous impetigo, ecthyma, or folliculitis), *P. aeruginosa* (with chronic ulcerations and macerations), herpes simplex, herpes zoster, syphilis, and scabies must always be considered and are generally treated with standard methods.

KS is the second most common manifestation of AIDS and has involved approximately 25% of the known cases to date. It is found commonly among homosexual or bisexual men. The disease is usually widely disseminated with mucous membrane involvement, although it is rarely primarily fatal. Four categories of KS exist: classical, endemic African, iatrogenic, and AIDS associated. KS typically arises in HIV-infected patients with any variation of mucocutaneous involvement, lymph node involvement, or involvement of the gastrointestinal tract or other organs. The typical appearance of cutaneous involvement is pink, red, or purple papules, plaques, nodules, and tumors. Several staging systems have been developed on the basis of cutaneous involvement, lymph node or visceral involvement, systemic signs or symptoms, and CD4 count.[78] Treatment of KS is based on sites and extent of involvement. Treatments available include cryotherapy, radiotherapy, infrared coagulation, sclerosing agents, intralesional vinblastine, and systemic chemotherapy, such as doxorubicin (Adriamycin), bleomycin, and vincristine.[79]

Varicella-zoster eruptions involving several dermatomes are commonly seen in patients with AIDS. Although seropositivity is common in all adults (90%), reactivation causing clinical disease is more common in the HIV-infected population, who are 17 times more likely to develop dermatomal zoster reactivation than the general population.[80] Recurrent episodes and multidermatomal involvement are common. In the HIV-infected patient with simple dermatomal zoster infection, outpatient management should be initiated with oral famciclovir (500 mg, twice or three times a day for 7 days), acyclovir (800 mg, five times daily), or valacyclovir (1000 mg, twice a day for 7 days).[81] Admission is warranted for any patient with systemic involvement, ophthalmic zoster, or severe dermatomal zoster. IV acyclovir is administered at a dosage of 10 mg/kg every 8 hours. Varicella immune globulin may be useful in patients with primary infection and visceral involvement.

HSV infections are prevalent among HIV-infected patients. Ninety-five percent of homosexual HIV-infected persons in the United States and Europe are seropositive for HSV-1, HSV-2, or both, and 40% to 60% of injection drug users are HSV-2 positive.[82] Both HSV-1 and HSV-2 may be seen as local infection and systemic involvement. As with many other dermatologic abnormalities, the presentation may be atypical.

HSV infections commonly arise with fever, adenopathy, malaise, and ulcerative lesions of mucosal and cutaneous sites. Common sites of involvement include oral mucosa, genital areas, and rectum. HSV and varicella-zoster virus may be difficult to distinguish clinically, and cultures may be required to differentiate the two. Reactivation is common. HSV infections respond well to standard therapies, and toxic effects are uncommon. Oral famciclovir (750 mg PO, three times daily) or acyclovir (200 mg five times daily for 10 days) is effective for mucocutaneous infection. For disseminated infection or neurologic involvement, IV acyclovir is recommended, 5 to 10 mg/mg IV every 8 hours for 7 to 21 days. Famciclovir, penciclovir, foscarnet, or valacyclovir may also be used. Suppressive therapy is effective. Patients with these viral infections should be assigned to isolation beds.

Molluscum contagiosum, arising with small flesh-colored papules with a whitish core, is commonly seen in HIV-infected individuals. Treatment may consist of cryotherapy or curettage. Therapy is recommended for symptomatic lesions only because cure is difficult.

Intertriginous infections with either *Candida* or *Trichophyton* are common and may be diagnosed by microscopic examination of scrapings in potassium hydroxide. Treatment may include topical imidazole creams (e.g., clotrimazole, miconazole, or ketoconazole).

Scabies should be considered in all HIV-infected patients, particularly those with dermatitis with excoriations or pruritus. The yield of microscopically evident mites is high. Preferred treatment is with 5% permethrin, single application. Sexual and household contacts should also be treated. Norwegian scabies is particularly difficult to treat and should be considered if lesions consistent with scabies fail to respond to traditional therapy. Treatment should be undertaken in consultation with an infectious disease specialist.

Seborrheic dermatitis is a common eruption, particularly among patients with AIDS-associated dementia. Lesions may include erythematous, hyperkeratotic scaling plaques involving the scalp, face (especially involving the nasolabial folds), ears, chest, and genitalia. Treatment with topical steroids is effective in many patients, although less successful than in the general population. Alternative therapy includes topical or oral ketoconazole.

Human papillomavirus infections occur with increased frequency in immunocompromised patients. Treatment is cosmetic or symptomatic and may include cryotherapy, topical therapy, or, in extreme cases, laser therapy.

Other dermatologic disorders occur with increased frequency in AIDS patients. Psoriasis, atopic dermatitis, and alopecia are common. Any preexisting dermatologic disorder may be exacerbated by HIV infection.

Ophthalmologic Manifestations

Ocular findings are common in the HIV-infected patient. Cotton-wool spots in the retina are the most common eye finding in AIDS patients and do not require intervention. Other common ophthalmologic manifestations of HIV include CMV retinitis and KS of eyelids or conjunctiva.

CMV retinitis occurs in 10% to 30% of HIV-infected patients and is the most common cause of blindness in AIDS patients.[83] With advances in HAART, reduced incidences of CMV retinitis have been observed, but discontinuation of HAART may result in intraocular inflammation.[84] CMV retinitis typically produces severe necrotic vasculitis and retinitis. When present, it may be asymptomatic or may arise as blurred vision, change in visual acuity, floaters, flashes of light, photophobia, scotoma, redness, or pain.[85] It is diagnosed by the characteristic appearance on indirect ophthalmoscopy of fluffy white retinal lesions, often perivascular. The differential diagnosis includes toxoplasmosis, syphilis, HSV infection, varicella-zoster virus infection, and TB. Treatment should be initiated with ganciclovir. Foscarnet may also be used. Intravitreal injections of fomivirsen may also be used for patients unresponsive to traditional therapy.[86] Similar rates of efficacy are achieved with ganciclovir and foscarnet. Ganciclovir-containing intravitreal implants are another therapeutic option that provides higher intravitreal concentrations and reduces the risk of CMV-related retinal detachment.[87] Immune recovery uveitis may occur as a complication of treatment during the recovery phase.[88] Chronic suppressive therapy with ganciclovir or foscarnet may be indicated. Patients with serum antitoxoplasma antibodies should receive prophylaxis for CD4 cell counts below 100/mm^3 with TMP-SMX.[89] Some advocate routine ophthalmologic screening of all patients with low CD4 counts.

Cardiovascular Manifestations

Clinically significant cardiac disease in the AIDS patient is relatively uncommon. Autopsy findings suggest cardiac involvement in up to 73% of deceased AIDS patients.[90] Cardiac manifestations may include pericardial effusion, cardiomyopathy, increased left ventricular mass, myocarditis, endocarditis, malignancy, and cardiotoxicity of medications.[91] The pericardium is the most common site of cardiac involvement, although many patients have clinically insignificant effusions. Pericardial effusions may be secondary to malignancies, uremia, lymphatic obstruction, or infections, such as *M. tuberculosis, S. pneumoniae, S. aureus,* or a host of other bacterial, viral, fungal, or protozoal infections. Cardiomyopathies may occur and are commonly associated with advanced HIV infection. Etiologies of cardiomyopathies may include primary HIV infection; viral, mycobacterial, fungal, or protozoal infection; drug-induced; immunologic; or ischemic. Infective endocarditis occurs commonly in HIV-infected patients with a history of injection drug use and should be considered in all IV drug users presenting with febrile illnesses. Cardiac neoplasms may also occur, typically either KS or lymphoma. Neoplasms may be clinically silent or may arise with symptoms such as congestive heart failure, tamponade, or arrhythmias.

Renal Manifestations of HIV Infection

Renal insufficiency in the AIDS patient may have a variety of etiologies. Prerenal azotemia is the most common renal abnormality, especially in conjunction with volume loss related to systemic or gastrointestinal infection. It is diagnosed and treated by evaluation and therapy of fluid status. Acute renal failure may also occur and is often secondary to drug nephrotoxicity (e.g., pentamidine, aminoglycosides, sulfa drugs, foscarnet, rifampin, dapsone, and amphotericin B). HIV-associated nephropathy (HIVAN) is typically a cause of chronic renal insufficiency in the late stages of immunosuppression but may occur earlier in disease progression.[92] Vasculitis, TB, or other systemic infections may also contribute to renal insufficiency. Postrenal azotemia may result from tubular, ureteral, or pelvic obstruction; lymphoma; stones; fungus ball; blood clot; or sloughed papilla.

Emergency department evaluation should include urinalysis, assessment of fluid status, blood urea nitrogen, and serum creatinine. If indicated, ultrasonography or intravenous pyelography may demonstrate the site and degree of obstruction. Renal biopsy may be indicated for patients with proteinuria and undiagnosed renal disease. Treatment depends on the causative agent. Therapies that have demonstrated limited benefit for HIVAN include corticosteroids, angiotensin-converting enzyme inhibitors, and dialysis and may be initiated in conjunction with a nephrologist.

Psychiatric Considerations

The diagnosis of AIDS involves complex psychological and social issues in addition to physiologic, neurologic, and psychiatric abnormalities. Interactions with family and friends may be dramatically changed, and issues of confronting chronic illness and death may prove devastating. Although psychiatric issues are common among HIV-infected patients, many do not receive optimal care.[93]

Delirium suggests the presence of a primary physiologic disease state and should be investigated as discussed previously. The differential diagnosis includes CNS, toxic, and metabolic derangements.

Depression is common among AIDS patients and is often responsive to hospitalization and psychosocial intervention. It has been estimated that 60% of HIV-infected patients experience depression during their illness.[93] Patients with a history of depression are at increased risk. Patients with depression generally have lower CD4 counts and may report more AIDS-related symptoms.[94] Depression may result in suicidal ideation and may bring the patient to the attention of the emergency department after a suicide attempt, such as a drug overdose. Antidepressant therapy may be considered if symptoms of depression continue longer than 2 weeks. Other psychiatric disorders may be seen, including personality disorders, addiction disorders, and adjustment disorders.

AIDS psychosis commonly arises with psychiatric symptoms such as hallucinations, delusions, or other abnormal behavioral changes. Treatment should be undertaken with traditional antipsychotic agents.

Sexually Transmitted Diseases

Sexually transmitted diseases may be associated with HIV infection. In addition to testing for the more common entities (e.g., gonorrhea, *Chlamydia,* and herpes infections), serologic testing for syphilis should be performed for all patients presenting with symptoms suggestive of possible sexually transmitted disease. The prevalence of syphilis in the United States has increased, and syphilis has been associated with increased susceptibility to HIV seroconversion.[95,96] Because a normal antibody response may be absent in HIV-infected individuals, care must be taken to identify potential cases of syphilis, even among those with negative serologies. Alternative means of diagnosis may include dark-field microscopy. Empirical therapy may be instituted even without laboratory proof of infection. The recommended treatment of primary or secondary syphilis of less than 12 months' duration is a single intramuscular dose of benzathine penicillin, 2.4 million units. For latent syphilis of unknown duration or secondary syphilis, three weekly injections are recommended. Patients with neurosyphilis should be treated with 12 to 24 million units of penicillin G, IV, daily for 10 to 14 days. Patients with known or suspected syphilis should be evaluated for the presence of neurosyphilis, which is increased in incidence among HIV-infected individuals.[97]

Hematologic Complications

Common hematologic complications include anemia (present in up to 80% of patients), neutropenia, and thrombocytopenia.[98] Hematopoiesis may be adversely affected by HIV infection, tumor, infection, or HIV medications.[99]

Drug Reactions

Drug reactions are extremely common among HIV-infected patients for two reasons: (1) these patients are commonly treated with a variety of drugs known to produce adverse effects in some individuals, and (2), for unclear reasons, HIV-infected individuals often have more frequent or more severe reactions to commonly used medications. Dermatologic reactions are particularly common. Antimicrobial drugs are most commonly implicated. Potential drug interactions should be considered when prescribing new medications.[100] Drug reactions should always be considered as a possible cause of new symptoms. Reactions are numerous, and current references should be consulted when drug reactions are suspected. Table 130-2 contains a brief summary of common drug reactions in the HIV-infected patient.

Table 130-3. Antiretroviral Drugs Approved by Food and Drug Administration for Human Immunodeficiency Virus

Drug Class	Generic Name	Trade Name
NRTIs*	Zidovudine (AZT, ZDV)	Retrovir
		Combivir (AZT + 3TC)
		Trizivir (AZT + 3TC + abacavir)
	Didanosine (ddI)	Videx and Videx EC
	Zalcitabine (ddC)	Hivid
	Stavudine (d4T)	Zerit
	Lamivudine (3TC)	Epivir
	Abacavir (ABC)	Ziagen
	Emtricitabine (FTCP)	Emtriva
	Tenofovir (TDF)	Viread
NNRTIs†	Nevirapine	Viramune
	Delavirdine	Rescriptor
	Efavirenz	Sustiva
PIs‡	Indinavir	Crixivan
	Ritonavir	Norvir
	Saquinavir	Invirase and Fortovase
	Nelfinavir	Viracept
	Amprenavir	Agenerase
	Atazanavir	Reyataz
	Lopinavir/ritonavir	Kaletra

*Nucleoside analogue reverse transcriptase inhibitors.
†Nonnucleoside reverse transcriptase inhibitors.
‡Protease inhibitors.

MANAGEMENT

Antiretroviral Therapy and Chemoprophylaxis

The introduction of HAART in 1996 has had dramatic effects on the clinical consequences of HIV infection in the developed world. The incidence of AIDS-defining illnesses and the death rate declined rapidly through 1998.[101] Although reports of high levels of treatment failure because of serious adverse effects, emergence of drug resistance, and difficulties in maintaining long-term adherence have raised concerns regarding the continued success of HAART, studies suggest that the reduction in morbidity and mortality associated with HAART has been sustained.[102]

Antiretroviral therapy for HIV infection is constantly evolving, and the emergency physician should have a basic understanding of the classes of drugs available, the rationale for initiating treatment, and the common adverse drug reactions. There are three classes of antiretroviral drugs: the nucleoside analogue reverse transcriptase inhibitors (NRTIs), the nonnucleoside reverse transcriptase inhibitors (NNRTIs), and the protease inhibitors (PIs) (Table 130-3). Each group of drugs independently interrupts the normal life cycle of HIV. When used with appropriate timing and in combination, these agents have been shown to delay significantly the progression of disease and prolong life.

The first drug demonstrated to have antiretroviral activity belonged to the NRTIs, which are competitive inhibitors of the viral enzyme reverse transcriptase. Several controlled trials showed that zidovudine (azidothymidine, AZT, Retrovir) decreases the number and severity of opportunistic infections.[103,104] Although zidovudine was also found to decrease the rate of AIDS progression in patients with early symptomatic HIV infection, no significant change in survival was found.[105] This finding, coupled with the recognition of the emergence of drug resistance and the appearance of significant side effects, led to the development of other NRTIs. Combination therapy, employing zidovudine and another NRTI, resulted not only in prevention of disease progression but also in decreased mortality.[106] The FDA has approved at least eight agents in this class, each with its own unique adverse effect profile. The most common side effects to be aware of include bone marrow suppression with zidovudine; distal sensory peripheral neuropathy with didanosine (Videx), stavudine (Zerit), and zalcitabine (Hivid); and pancreatitis with didanosine.[106] See Table 130-2 for a list of the more common agents and their side effects.

The NNRTIs are noncompetitive inhibitors of reverse transcriptase and block RNA-dependent and DNA-dependent DNA polymerase activity. Three NNRTIs are currently available; the most commonly used are nevirapine (Viramune) and efavirenz (Sustiva). Target organisms have a high propensity for developing resistance to these agents, which are recommended for use only as part of a three-drug (or more) regimen. Rash is the most common side effect associated with the NNRTIs, with a small minority of patients (<5%) developing Stevens-Johnson syndrome.[107]

The enzyme HIV protease activates the HIV proteins, which are required for infectivity, by cleaving the inactive viral polypeptide precursors. PIs block this step, thus preventing HIV particles from becoming infectious. Five PIs are currently approved for clinical use in the United States. Introduction of this class of drugs is believed to be responsible in large part for the marked decline in mortality rates for HIV infection, which was first realized in 1996. However, PIs are expensive and have also been associated with a high frequency of side effects. Short-term effects are principally gastrointestinal (including nausea, diarrhea, and bloating); long-term effects are metabolic, the most common of which are hyperglycemia, hyperlipidemia, and fat redistribution.[108]

In November 2003 the Department of Health and Human Services (DHHS) published updated guidelines for use of antiretroviral agents in HIV-infected adults and adolescents.[109] In general, multiple goals of antiretroviral therapy include virologic, immunologic, clinical, and therapeutic goals. Because virologic (HIV RNA levels) and immunologic (CD4 cell count) parameters are independent predictors of clinical outcomes, therapeutic recommendations are based on both of these factors. The virologic goal is to reduce viral load as much as possible, halt disease progression, and prevent development of resistant HIV variants. Immunologic goals are to achieve both quantitative (CD4 cell count) and qualitative (pathogen-specific immune response) immune reconstitution. The principal clinical goals of therapy are to prolong and improve quality of life. The therapeutic goal is to achieve the other three goals by choosing a sequence of drugs that maintains therapeutic options, minimizes side effects, and optimizes the likelihood of the patient's compliance with the chosen regimen.

Expert consensus on the timing of initiation of HAART continues to evolve. For patients who have symptoms of immunosuppression (e.g., thrush, wasting, or any opportunistic infection) treatment is mandatory, regardless of viral load or CD4 cell count. Similarly, for those with recognized primary HIV infection, antiretroviral therapy is recommended because early treatment is believed to decrease the number of infected cells, maintain or restore the immune response, and perhaps lower the viral "set point," resulting in an improved course of the disease.[106] Guidelines for asymptomatic patients are more controversial. Most experts recommend treatment for any patient with either a CD4 count less than 350 cells/mm^3 or an HIV viral load greater than 55,000 copies/mL.[108] The recommendation to treat asymptomatic patients should be individualized on the basis of the willingness and readiness of the person to begin therapy, the potential benefits and risks of initiating therapy in an asymptomatic person, and the likelihood, after counseling and education, of adherence to the prescribed treatment regimen.

Selection of an appropriate combination of drugs is also a complex issue for which no definitive recommendations exist. Twenty antiretroviral drugs are currently approved by the FDA. A complete list and up-to-date guide for their use can be found on the National Institutes of Health website (AIDSinfo.nih.gov). The current DHHS recommended first-line HAART regimens include NNRTI-based regimens (one NNRTI and two NRTIs) or PI-based regimens (one or two PIs and two NRTIs).[108] Study suggests that the specific combination of zidovudine, lamivudine, and efavirenz may be superior to the other antiretroviral regimens used as initial therapy.[120] Alternatively, triple NRTI regimens are recommended for use as second-line regimens. Again, therapy should be individualized with consideration of tolerability, comorbidities, adverse effect profile, likely drug-drug interactions, convenience, and likelihood of adherence.

Pregnancy should not preclude women from receiving optimal treatment regimens; however, issues related to prevention of mother-to-child transmission as well as maternal and fetal safety deserve special considerations. Studies have shown that HAART reduces perinatal transmission to 1% to 2%, and the rate is strongly correlated with viral load at the time of delivery.[110] On the basis of these observations, HAART should be recommended to any pregnant woman with a CD4 count less than 350 cells/mm^3 or viral load greater than 1000 copies/mL. For pregnant women with a viral load less than 1000 copies/mL and CD4 count greater than 350 cells/mm^3, acceptable options include zidovudine (AZT) monotherapy, given its proven efficacy and safety in decreasing perinatal transmission, or a standard HAART regimen.[108] Efavirenz-containing regimens should be avoided in pregnancy or women of reproductive age because of potential teratogenic effects. In addition, elective cesarean section has established merit in reducing prenatal transmission if performed at 38 weeks of gestation with a viral load greater than 1000 copies/mL.[111]

The goal of the antiretroviral therapy is to produce long-term viral suppression. Clinical situations that should prompt consideration for changing therapy include drug toxicity or intolerance, difficulty with adherence, and failure to suppress viral infection. The decision regarding alternative treatment regimens should be made in consultation with infectious disease experts to assess potential cross resistance from previously used drugs. With advances in genotypic and phenotypic analysis of HIV strains, selection of a drug regimen on the basis of drug resistance patterns will soon become an essential part of therapeutic decision making.

Chemoprophylaxis is directed toward preventing initial and subsequent episodes of certain opportunistic infections (i.e., primary and secondary prophylaxis). Emphasis on measures to prevent opportunistic infections is critical because of the inherent limitations of HAART and the recognition that these infections are a significant cause of morbidity and mortality in the HIV-positive population. CD4 cell count is the best predictor of the risk for opportunistic infections and is used most often in making decisions about initiating or maintaining antimicrobial prophylaxis. The most serious and common infections for which antimicrobial prophylaxis has been shown to be effective include PCP, toxoplasmosis, TB, and *M. avium* complex. Specific timing and choice of agents are described in the preceding clinical sections; a more comprehensive review can be found in the Public Health Service and Infectious Diseases Society revised guidelines for the prevention of opportunistic infections.[108] The emergency physician can play a critical role in recognizing the patients who require initiation of chemoprophylaxis and then should work closely with the patient's primary care doctors or an infectious disease consultant to begin therapy.

Immunizations of HIV-Infected Patients

Response to immunizations may be variable among individual HIV-infected patients. Many HIV-infected patients have an adequate antibody response to immunizations, but the immune response is not predictable.[112] Most routine immunizations are recommended unchanged in the HIV-infected population.[113] However, HIV-infected patients should not receive live virus or live bacterial vaccines. Pneumococcal vaccine is recommended for all patients older than 2 years[114]; however, the immune response may be variable and immunization is recommended early in the disease course to optimize antibody development.[115] Hepatitis B vaccine is indicated for patients at risk for exposure, although because of the variable immune response, follow-up serologic testing is indicated. Hepatitis A vaccination should also be considered because of increased risk for severe liver damage among patients previously infected with hepatitis B

or C.[116] Influenza vaccination is considered safe and is routinely recommended, although response may be variable.[117] Measles-mumps-rubella vaccine may be considered because studies have not documented an increased incidence of adverse effects. If polio vaccine is indicated, enhanced inactivated polio vaccine may be administered. Although evidence suggests that the expression of HIV may be transiently increased by the administration of tetanus toxoid,[118] the clinical significance of this is unknown; current recommendations include providing a booster every 10 years for those who have completed their primary series. Because the smallpox vaccine has not been rigorously studied in the HIV-infected population, the adverse effects and immune response are unknown, and some authors currently advise against its use.[119] The potential risks and benefits of immunization in the HIV-infected patient should be considered when making decisions regarding immunization.

EMERGENCY DEPARTMENT DISPOSITION

When there is doubt about diagnostic or management options, consultation with other specialists is appropriate. Consultations with an infectious disease specialist, neurologist, psychiatrist, AIDS specialist, and others may be indicated. Although symptomatic patients are currently predominantly cared for by AIDS specialists, the increasing numbers of symptomatic patients are shifting the focus of primary care to nonspecialists.

Disposition decisions for HIV-infected patients are based, as for any patient, on clinical condition, availability of outpatient resources, and ability to arrange adequate follow-up observation. Any patient to be discharged must demonstrate the ability for self-care or have sufficient in-home assistance available. In the AIDS population, particular attention should be given to ability to ambulate and tolerate oral intake as well as availability of timely and appropriate medical follow-up.

Although the AIDS epidemic has raised concerns regarding the economic impact of the disease, financial considerations should not be a factor in determining management or disposition. Guidelines for admission and discharge are given in Box 130-3.

ETHICAL CONSIDERATIONS

Numerous ethical issues arise in the management of HIV-infected patients. General issues relevant to many patients may include issues of confidentiality, discrimination, access to health care, justice, informed consent, respect for autonomy, and advance directives. Additional concerns specific to HIV infection may arise, such as questions related to prenatal testing, abortion, euthanasia, suicide, access to experimental therapies, and role in clinical trials. In general, commonly accepted principles of medical ethics may be applied, which include principles of beneficence, nonmaleficence, respect for autonomy, and justice. Codes of

BOX 130-3. Considerations for Disposition Decisions for HIV-Infected Patients

Conditions Suggesting Admission

New presentation of fever of unknown origin
Hypoxemia (worse than baseline) (PaO₂ < 60 mm Hg)
Suspected *Pneumocystis carinii* pneumonia
Suspected tuberculosis
New central nervous system symptoms
Intractable diarrhea
Suicidal
Suspected cytomegalovirus retinitis
Ophthalmicus zoster
Cachexia or weakness
Unable to care for self or receive adequate care
Unable to assure appropriate follow-up

Suggested Conditions for Considering Discharge

Normal or baseline vital signs
Stable medical condition
Able to take oral medications and is not orthostatic
Follow-up and referral arranged
Patient or caregiver understands instructions and is able to comply with discharge instructions
Patient, home caregiver, or hospice able to care for patient
Patient or caregiver understands warning signs that indicate need for repeat emergency department evaluation

HIV, human immunodeficiency virus; PaO₂, partial pressure of oxygen in arterial blood.

---

ethical conduct developed by the American College of Emergency Physicians and the Society for Academic Emergency Medicine may be of general guidance.[120,121]

Testing of patients to detect HIV has some controversial aspects. Routine HIV testing initiated in the emergency department is often not appropriate because of difficulties assuring appropriate pre- and posttest counseling and confidentiality. However, recommendations and referral for testing are often indicated for patients with risk factors or clinical evidence of HIV infection. Each institution should have appropriate mechanisms arranged for these referrals.

Occupational exposures to blood and body fluids may necessitate testing of patients and health care workers in the emergency department to expedite initiation of antiretroviral therapy. In such cases, institutions not only must comply with state guidelines but also should implement uniform policies and procedures for testing that ensure pretest and posttest counseling and confidentiality of results.

Confidentiality of emergency department patients' identity and diagnoses is of paramount importance, particularly for HIV-infected patients, for whom there may be numerous clinical, social, psychological, career, and insurability effects of breached confidentiality.

Public health responsibilities may at times override the duty of the physician to maintain strict confidentiality. AIDS is a reportable disease in most states, and state guidelines for reporting should be followed as a public health measure even if this breaches confidentiality, as in cases of child abuse, gunshot wounds, or other infectious diseases. In addition, the physician who is aware of potentially contagious practices of an infected individual has an obligation to counsel the individual. Infected patients should be encouraged to share their disease state with sexual or needle-sharing partners. In many states, the physician has the discretion to inform public health officials of practices to allow partners potentially at risk to be informed.[122]

The potential value of aggressive interventions in critical care settings must be determined on an individual case basis. Some clinicians believe that in the advanced stages of AIDS, resuscitative measures are not appropriate because of the uniformly poor prognosis. Many patients may agree as they approach the terminal stages of their disease. Appropriate advance directives should be completed before the resuscitation setting. However, many patients fail to complete advance directives. Decisions regarding the withholding of extraordinary resuscitation efforts may be difficult to make in the emergency department because of insufficient information about an individual patient, the patient's wishes, his or her disease state, prognosis, and the judgment and intentions of the primary care and consultant physicians. Although some ethicists argue against the excessive use of extensive resource allocation for this class of patients, decisions in the emergency department should be largely unbiased and based on the appropriate factors relevant to the individual case. As with all patients with clinical indications for invasive monitoring or interventions, decisions should be based on factors including the patient's wishes (if known) or a surrogate's assessment of the patient's wishes, expected outcome of the intervention, and potential risks of the intervention.[123] Interventions should not be withheld or discontinued merely on the basis of the disease state of AIDS.

If certain diagnostic and therapeutic interventions are withheld, particular attention should be paid to ensuring adequate control of pain and other symptoms. Psychosocial, religious, and cultural needs should also be addressed.

The courts have addressed increasing numbers and varieties of cases regarding the treatment of AIDS and HIV-related illness. The AIDS Litigation Project (a review of cases) has shown increasing cases of litigation involving areas of AIDS education, blood supply, epidemiologic surveillance, criminal law, public places, products and fraud, torts, court system, family law, confidentiality, prisons, military, fear of exposure, homelessness, and discrimination.[124]

In general, the same ethical principles of respect for autonomy, beneficence, nonmaleficence, justice, confidentiality, communication, informed consent, and research ethics should be honored when treating HIV-infected patients as with all emergency department patients.

PRECAUTIONS AND POSTEXPOSURE PROPHYLAXIS FOR HEALTH CARE WORKERS

Precautions and Exposures

Health care workers are often exposed to the blood and body secretions of HIV-infected patients or of other individuals who are at high risk for harboring HIV and other infectious pathogens. The overall risk of having any occupational blood exposure is not insignificant, with more than half of emergency physicians reporting at least one occupational exposure during a 2-year period.[125]

The overall risk of contracting HIV remains small. As of June 2000, the CDC had received reports of 57 documented cases of HIV seroconversion that were temporally associated with occupational exposure to HIV among U.S. health care workers.[126] An additional 138 infections among health care workers were considered possible cases of occupational transmission. Global surveillance data are less reliable, and the overall rates of occupational transmission are not known. The majority of cases occurred in nurses; less frequent were cases in laboratory technicians and physicians.[125] Of all transmissions, the majority were percutaneous, followed by mucocutaneous or both. There have been no confirmed seroconversions to date with exposures to a suture needle. Efficacy of transmission is estimated as 0.3% for percutaneous exposure and 0.09% for mucocutaneous exposure.[127]

The proportion of patients infected with a pathogen varies by geographic setting and practice locale. One survey conducted at a Baltimore inner-city hospital found that up to 11% of patients were infected with HIV and nearly 24% were infected with HIV or hepatitis B or C.[128] It is important to note, however, that numerous studies have demonstrated that a substantial number of patients in the emergency department have unsuspected HIV infection, and HIV seroreactivity cannot be accurately predicted even with the aid of risk factor assessment.

HIV transmission by health care workers to patients appears to be extremely rare. There have been only seven cases to date, six of which resulted from a single dentist's practice and one apparently acquired HIV during orthopedic surgery. At this time, routine screening of health care workers is not indicated.[129]

Numerous studies have demonstrated that health care workers can significantly reduce their risk of exposure to blood-borne pathogens by following universal precautions. CDC guidelines for universal precautions include the use of protective equipment (including gloves, gown, mask, and eye protection) for any situation in which the potential for exposure exists. One study showed that protective equipment is indicated for most emergency department procedures, including examination of the bleeding patient, chest tube placement, LP, and other commonly performed procedures in which contact with blood or body fluids is likely.[130] Although significant improvement has been made in emergency physicians' observance of universal precautions, studies indicate that continued education and improvements in work environments are required to ensure consistent compliance.[130,131]

Postexposure Prophylaxis

Occupational Exposures

The CDC provides explicit guidelines for PEP for occupational exposure to HIV.[121] These recommendations are based on a retrospective case-control study of needlestick injuries from an HIV-infected source to a health care worker that included 33 cases who seroconverted and 739 control subjects. AZT prophylaxis was associated with a 79% reduction in HIV transmission after controlling for other risk factors for HIV transmission among subjects.[132] This study formed the basis of preliminary guidelines recommending antiretroviral therapy first published in 1996 and then updated in 2001.[126] Other studies supporting the benefits of PEP have demonstrated decreased rates of perinatal transmission for women who were given zidovudine during pregnancy, labor, and delivery.[133]

Current guidelines advise case-by-case determination of the risk of the exposure in order to determine whether PEP should be recommended. Recommendations are based on two primary factors: (1) type of exposure and (2) HIV status of the source (or, if the source status is unknown, evaluation of risk status of the source). Higher risk percutaneous exposures associated with an increased likelihood of transmission include deep injuries, visible blood on a device, and injuries sustained when placing a catheter in a vein or artery; lower risk percutaneous exposures are superficial or involve solid needles. High-risk sources are patients with symptomatic HIV, AIDS, acute seroconversion, or high viral load; low-risk sources are patients with asymptomatic HIV or viral load less than 1500 copies/mL.[134] When the status of the source is not known (i.e., no recent positive or negative serology), rapid testing should be performed. Negative EIA (using either SUDS or OraQuick) is adequate for a decision to withhold or discontinue therapy if initiated. Some states allow testing the source without informed consent; in those that do not, informed consent is required. In unusual circumstances, in which the source has an illness consistent with acute HIV infection, testing should include HIV RNA levels.

After determining the type of exposure and HIV status of the source, practitioners should refer to the published CDC guidelines (provided in tabular form) to direct specific therapy.[126,127] Separate tables are provided by the CDC for percutaneous and mucous membrane or nonintact skin exposures. Those with exposures involving contact between intact skin and blood or other body fluids contaminated by HIV should not be offered therapy.

Current public health guidelines (http://www.cdc.gov/mmwr/preview/mmwrhtml/rr5011a1.htm) recommend a 4-week regimen of two drugs for most HIV exposures by percutaneous or mucous membrane routes. Two-drug therapy options include either zidovudine and lamivudine (first choice), lamivudine and stavudine, or didanosine and stavudine. For highest risk exposures, a three-drug regimen with the addition of either a PI (e.g., indinavir or nelfinavir), an NNRTI (e.g., efavirenz), or an NRTI (e.g., abacavir) is advised, although there is no direct evidence to support this practice and the increased risk of adverse events decreases the likelihood that treatment will be completed. When the source person is known to be infected with a resistant HIV strain, the selection of PEP drugs to which the source person's virus is unlikely to be resistant is recommended.

PEP should be initiated as soon as possible after exposure to a source person with known HIV infection. Current guidelines suggest starting treatment within 1 to 2 hours and generally restrict therapy to those who seek treatment within 36 hours of exposure. Antiretroviral therapy may be given 36 hours after exposure in particularly high-risk incidents. Duration of PEP is 4 weeks. Initial treatment should not be delayed while awaiting information regarding the final determination of overall risk of exposure, as therapy can be altered or stopped after the first dose; two-drug PEP is reasonable to start while gathering further data. Constitutional and gastrointestinal side effects may be significant and often lead to early termination of treatment. If the source person's HIV infection status is unknown at the time of exposure, use of PEP should be decided on a case-by-case basis after considering the type of exposure and the likelihood of HIV infection in the source. If these considerations suggest a possibility for HIV transmission and HIV testing of the source person is pending, a two-drug PEP regimen should be initiated until laboratory results become available. PEP should be discontinued if the source patient is determined to be HIV negative. In addition to evaluation and management of HIV exposure risk, all patients should be tested and treated for other more highly infectious agents such as hepatitis.

As early initiation of PEP is critical for efficacy, the emergency department is often the site of referral for patients because services are available at any time. Many emergency departments are developing protocols and starter treatment packets for PEP. However, if possible, the choice of intervention and regimen is usually best accomplished in consultation with an infectious disease specialist and the patient's primary physician, which allows arrangement for appropriate medical follow-up and counseling.

Nonoccupational Exposure

Interest in the use of PEP for nonoccupational exposure has emerged because the probability of HIV transmission by certain sexual or injection drug exposures is of the same order of magnitude as percutaneous exposures, for which the CDC recommends PEP.[113] The CDC has not yet issued guidelines for nonoccupational PEP, citing the lack of data regarding the efficacy of this therapy in those populations, making it an unproven clinical intervention. Other reasons cited for not routinely offering PEP for nonoccupational exposures include lack of data on the long-term effect of antiretroviral treatment (particularly in those who may seek multiple treatments), drug resistance, and a possible increase in high-risk behaviors.

In spite of the lack of definitive national guidelines for nonoccupational PEP, emergency physicians must be equipped to formulate a rational approach to evaluation and management of such cases in the emergency department, as this is the likely site at which many of these patients present. One regional study showed that of all PEP treatments provided, the vast majority (78%) were for non–health care workers, highlighting the need for a national guideline.[135] Populations of patients who may seek nonoccupational PEP include sexual assault victims and sexual partners or needle-sharing partners of sources with known or suspected HIV infection.

The approach to evaluation in the emergency department is as follows. As with occupational exposures, PEP should be considered on a case-by-case basis. A thorough history should be taken to assess the risk of the source, risk of the exposure, and the risk for ongoing high-risk exposures. Baseline HIV testing of the exposed patient and the source (when possible) should be performed. The following general principles should also be followed (as advised by the CDC and others): (1) inform patients of the lack of definitive data, (2) restrict therapy to high-risk exposures (e.g., unprotected receptive anal or vaginal intercourse with a known HIV-positive person) and those who seek care within 36 hours, (3) select antiretroviral agents carefully and monitor their side effects and toxicities closely, and (4) address patients' underlying risk reduction needs (when applicable), limiting therapy to those most likely to maintain risk reduction behavior over time.[136] Counseling should be provided regarding medication side effects, which should be carefully considered and balanced with advantages of therapy. All sexual assault victims should be counseled regarding risk and benefits of PEP treatment.

For most cases in which the individual is likely to have continuing risk for exposure, the CDC recommends providing basic risk reduction counseling and referral to risk reduction programs rather than offering PEP. Additional resources should be used whenever possible to assist with decision making and follow-up services; in-house infectious disease consultation should be sought. Other invaluable resources for information on both occupational and nonoccupational exposures include the CDC–University of California, San Francisco National Clinicians PEP Hotline, providing a 24-hour assistance (1-888-448-4911), and the University of California, Los Angeles on-line decision-making support at http://www.needlestick.mednet.ucla.edu.

KEY CONCEPTS

- The seroprevalence of HIV and AIDS among emergency department patients in large metropolitan areas is 2% to 15%. Many of these are undiagnosed cases, and compliance of emergency department staff with universal precautions is extremely important.

- Acute HIV seroconversion syndrome commonly follows exposure by 2 to 6 weeks and arises with common, nonspecific symptoms such as fever, fatigue, diarrhea, weight loss, adenopathy, and rash. Patients fitting this profile should be screened for HIV risk factors and appropriately referred for HIV testing.

- PCP is the most common opportunistic infection in AIDS patients. It often arises as progressive dyspnea on exertion associated with a nonproductive cough. The chest radiograph commonly shows a diffuse interstitial infiltrate but may be normal. Blood gas analysis usually reveals hypoxemia that is often more pronounced after exercise.

- CNS disease is common in HIV-infected patients and is caused by the disease itself, opportunistic infections, and malignancy. An approach to evaluating HIV-infected patients with severe or prolonged headache, altered mentation, new-onset seizures, or focal neurologic deficits is shown in Figure 130-2.

- The evaluation and management of HIV-infected patients with acute symptoms are often complex and best accomplished either in the hospital or in the outpatient setting with close follow-up. Conditions suggesting admission are listed in Box 130-4.

REFERENCES

1. 1993 revised classification system for HIV infection and expanded surveillance case definition for AIDS among adolescents and adults. *MMWR Recomm Rep* 41(RR-17):1, 1993.

2. Joint United Nations Programme on HIV/AIDS: AIDS epidemic update: 2003. Available at www.unaids.org. Accessed December 11, 2003.

3. Palella FJ Jr, et al: Declining morbidity and mortality among patients with advanced human immunodeficiency virus. *N Engl J Med* 338:853, 1998.

4. Centers for Disease Control and Prevention: HIV/AIDS surveillance report. Available at www.cdc.gov//hiv/stats/hasrlink.htm. Accessed December 11, 2003.

5. Centers for Disease Control and Prevention: Update: Trends in AIDS incidence, deaths, and prevalence—United States. *MMWR Morb Mortal Wkly Rep* 46:165, 1996.

6. Rothman RE, et al: Preventive care in the emergency department: Should emergency departments conduct routine HIV screening? A systematic review. *Acad Emerg Med* 10:278, 2003.

7. Carpenter CC, et al: Antiretroviral therapy in adults: Updated recommendations of the International AIDS Society—USA Panel. *JAMA* 283:381, 2000.

8. Busch MP, Satten GA: Time course of viremia and antibody seroconversion following human immunodeficiency virus exposure. *Am J Med* 102:117, 1997.

9. Koster FT: Infection in the HIV-positive patient. In Brillman JC, Quenzer RW (eds): *Infectious Diseases in Emergency Medicine*. Philadelphia, Lippincott-Raven, 1998.

10. Daar ES, et al: Diagnosis of primary HIV-1 infection. *Ann Intern Med* 134:s25, 2000.

11. Moran GJ: ED management of blood and body fluid exposures. *Ann Emerg Med* 31:47, 1997.

12. Irwin K, et al: Performance characteristics of a rapid HIV antibody assay in a hospital with a high prevalence of HIV infection. *Ann Intern Med* 125:471, 1996.

13. Kelen GD, Shahan JB, Quinn TC: ED-based HIV screening and counseling: Experience with rapid and standard serologic testing. *Ann Emerg Med* 33:147, 1999.

14. Kelen GD, et al: Feasibility of an emergency department–based risk-targeted voluntary HIV screening program. *Ann Emerg Med* 27:687, 1996.

15. Approval of a new rapid test for HIV antibody. *MMWR Morb Mortal Wkly Rep* 51:1051, 2003

16. http://www.cdc.gov/hiv/rapid_testing/materials/USCA_Branson.pdf. Accessed December 11, 2003.

17. Kelen GD, et al: Unrecognized human immunodeficiency virus (HIV) infection in general emergency patients. *N Engl J Med* 318:1645, 1988.

18. Redfield RR, Wright DC, Tramour EC: The Walter Reed staging classification for HTLV-III/LAV infection. *N Engl J Med* 314:131, 1986.

19. Stein DS, Korvick JA, Vermund SH: CD4+ lymphocyte cell enumeration for prediction of clinical course of human immunodeficiency virus disease: A review. *J Infect Dis* 165:352, 1992.

20. Pantaleo G, et al: Studies in subjects with long-term nonprogressive human immunodeficiency virus infection. *N Engl J Med* 332:209, 1995.

21. Saah AJ, et al: Predictors of the risk of development of acquired immunodeficiency syndrome within 24 months among gay men seropositive for human immunodeficiency virus type 1: A report from the Multicenter AIDS Cohort Study. *Am J Epidemiol* 135:1147, 1992.

22. Miller V, et al: Relations among CD4 lymphocyte count nadir, antiretroviral therapy, and HIV-1 disease progression: Results from the EuroSIDA study. *Ann Intern Med* 130:570, 1999.

23. Fahey JL, et al: The prognostic value of cellular and serologic markers in infection with human immunodeficiency virus type 1. *N Engl J Med* 322:166, 1990.

24. Lin HJ, et al: Multicenter evaluation of quantification methods for plasma human immunodeficiency virus type 1 RNA. *J Infect Dis* 170:553, 1994.

25. Washington L, Miller WT Jr: Mycobacterial infection in immunocompromised patients. *J Thorac Imaging* 13:271, 1998.

26. Dunne M, et al: A randomized, double-blind trial comparing azithromycin and clarithromycin in the treatment of disseminated *Mycobacterium avium* infection in patients with human immunodeficiency virus. *Clin Infect Dis* 31:1245, 2000.

27. Raoof S, Rosen MJ, Khan FA: Role of bronchoscopy in AIDS. *Clin Chest Med* 20:63, 1999.

28. Boiselle PM, Aviram G, Fishman JE: Update on lung disease in AIDS. *Semin Roentgenol* 37:54, 2002.

29. Maki DD: Pulmonary infections in HIV/AIDS. *Semin Roentgenol* 35:124, 2000.

30. Crans CA, Boiselle PM: Imaging features of *Pneumocystis carinii* pneumonia. *Crit Rev Diagn Imaging* 40:251, 1999.

31. Boiselle PM, Crans CA, Kaplan MA: The changing face of *Pneumocystis carinii* pneumonia in AIDS patients. *Am J Roentgenol* 172:1301, 1999.

32. Khalil A, et al: Community-acquired pneumonia (CAP) decision guidelines: Are the Pneumonia Patient Outcomes Research Team (PORT) guidelines a reliable tool for predicting mortality in the immunosuppressed population? *Acad Emerg Med* 10:540, 2003.

33. Arozullah AM, et al: A rapid staging system for predicting mortality from HIV-associated pneumonia. *Chest* 123:1151, 2003.

34. Hirschtick RE, et al: Bacterial pneumonia in persons infected with the human immunodeficiency virus: Pulmonary complications of HIV infection study group. *N Engl J Med* 333:845, 1995.

35. Wolff AJ, O'Donnell AE: Pulmonary manifestations of HIV infection in the era of highly active antiretroviral therapy. *Chest* 120:1888, 2001.

36. Afessa B, Green B: Bacterial pneumonia in hospitalized patients with HIV infection: The Pulmonary Complications, ICU Support and Prognostic Factors of Hospitalized Patients with HIV (PIP) Study. *Chest* 117:1017, 2000.

37. Stringer JR: *Pneumocystis. Int J Med Microbiol* 292:391, 2002.

38. Kaneshiro ES: Is *Pneumocystis* a plant? *J Eukaryot Microbiol* 49:367, 2002.

39. Wolff AJ, O'Donnell AE: HIV-related pulmonary infections: A review of the recent literature. *Curr Opin Pulm Med* 9:210, 2003.

40. Goodman PC: *Pneumocystis carinii* pneumonia. *J Thorac Imaging* 6:16, 1991.

41. Ng VL, et al: Rapid detection of *Pneumocystis carinii* using a direct fluorescent monoclonal antibody stain. *J Clin Microbiol* 128:2228, 1990.

42. Kovacs JA, et al: New insights into transmission, diagnosis, and drug treatment of *Pneumocystis carinii* pneumonia,. *JAMA* 286:2450, 2001.

43. NIH-UC Expert Panel for Corticosteroids as Adjunctive Therapy for *Pneumocystis* Pneumonia: Consensus statement for use of corticosteroids as adjunctive therapy for *Pneumocystis* pneumonia in AIDS. *N Engl J Med* 323:1500, 1990.

44. DiRienzo AG, et al: Efficacy of trimethoprim-sulfamethoxazole for the prevention of bacterial infections in a randomized prophylaxis trial of patients with advanced HIV infection. *AIDS Res Hum Retroviruses* 18:89, 2002.

45. Kovacs JA, Masur H: Prophylaxis against opportunistic infections in patients with human immunodeficiency virus infection. *N Engl J Med* 342:1416, 2000.

46. Dye C, et al: Global burden of tuberculosis. Estimated incidence, prevalence, and mortality by country. *JAMA* 282:677, 1999.

47. Markowitz N, et al: Incidence of tuberculosis in the United States among HIV-infected persons: The pulmonary complications of HIV infection study group. *Ann Intern Med* 126:123, 1997.

48. Rigsby MO, Friedland G: Tuberculosis and human immunodeficiency virus infection. In DeVita VT, Hellman S, Rosenberg SA (eds): *AIDS: Etiology, Diagnosis, Treatment and Prevention*, 4th ed. Philadelphia: Lippincott-Raven, 1997.

49. Leung AN: Pulmonary tuberculosis: The essentials. *Radiology* 210:307, 1999.

50. Perlman DC, et al: Variation of chest radiographic patterns in pulmonary tuberculosis by degree of human immunodeficiency virus–related immunosuppression. *Clin Infect Dis* 25:242, 1997.

51. Catanzaro A, et al: The role of clinical suspicion in evaluating a new diagnostic test for active tuberculosis. *JAMA* 283:639, 2000.

52. Barnes PF, Lakey DL, Burman WJ: Tuberculosis in patients with HIV infection. *Infect Dis Clin North Am* 16:107, 2002.

53. Rizzi EB, et al: Pulmonary mycosis in AIDS. *Eur J Radiol* 37:42, 2001.

54. Ruden JF, et al: AIDS-related Kaposi's sarcoma of the lung: Radiographic findings and staging system with bronchoscopic correlation. *Radiology* 195:545, 1995.

55. Lanska DJ: Epidemiology of human immunodeficiency virus infection and associated neurologic illness. *Semin Neurol* 19:105, 1999.

56. Sacktor N: The epidemiology of human immunodeficiency virus–associated neurological disease in the era of highly active antiretroviral therapy. *J Neurovirol* 21:1, 2002.

57. Rothman RE, et al: A decision guideline for emergency department utilization of noncontrast head CT in HIV-infected patients. *Acad Emerg Med* 6:1010, 1999.

58. Graham CB, et al: Screening CT determined by CD4 count in HIV-positive patients presenting with headache. *AJNR Am J Neuroradiol* 21:451, 2000.

59. Barber CJ, et al: Clinical utility of cranial CT in HIV positive and AIDS patients with neurological disease. *Clin Radiol* 42:164, 1990

60. Bernard MS, Hourihan MS, Adams H: Computed tomography of the brain: Does contrast enhancement really help? *Clin Radiol* 44:161, 1991.

61. Bensalem M, Berger J: HIV and the central nervous system. *Compr Ther* 28:22, 2002.

62. Davis LE: Fungal infections of the central nervous system. *Neurol Clin* 17:761, 1999.

63. Arendt G: Imaging methods as a diagnostic tool in neuroAIDS: A review. *Bildgebung* 62:310, 1995.

64. Murri R: A randomized trial of cotrimoxazole and dapsone-pyrimethamine for primary prophylaxis of *P. carinii* pneumonia (PCP) and toxoplasmosis encephalitis (TE). *Int Conf AIDS* 12:298, 1998.

65. Sackoff J, McFarland J, Su S, Bryan E: Prophylaxis for opportunistic infections among HIV-infected patients receiving medical care. *J Acquir Immune Defic Syndr Hum Retrovirol* 19:387, 1998.

66. Knox TA, et al: Diarrhea and abnormalities of gastrointestinal function in a cohort of men and women with HIV infection. *Am J Gastroenterol* 95:3482, 2000.

67. Lee LM, Henderson DK: Tolerability of postexposure antiretroviral prophylaxis for occupational exposures to HIV. *Drug Saf* 24:587, 2001.

68. Katz MH, et al: Progression to AIDS in HIV-infected homosexual and bisexual men with hairy leukoplakia and oral candidiasis. *AIDS* 6:95, 1992.

69. Masouredis CM, et al: Prevalence of HIV-associated periodontitis and gingivitis in HIV-infected patients attending an AIDS clinic. *J Acquir Immune Defic Syndr* 5:479, 1992.

70. Bonacini M: Medical management of benign oesophageal disease in patients with human immunodeficiency virus infection. *Dig Liver Dis* 33:294, 2001.

71. Bonacini M, Laine LA: Esophageal disease in patients with AIDS. *Gastrointest Endosc Clin North Am* 8:811, 1998.

72. Powderly WG, et al: A randomized trial comparing fluconazole with clotrimazole troches for the prevention of fungal infections in patients with advanced human immunodeficiency virus infection. *N Engl J Med* 332:700, 1995.

73. Hunter PR, Nichols G: Epidemiology and clinical features of *Cryptosporidium* infections in immunocompromised patients. *Clin Microbiol Rev* 15:145, 2002.

74. Pollok RC: Viruses causing diarrhea in AIDS. *Novartis Found Symp* 238:276, 2001.

75. Nemecheck PM, Polsky B, Gottlieb MS: Treatment guidelines for HIV-associated wasting. *Mayo Clin Proc* 75:386, 2000.

76. Cohen J, West AB, Bini EJ: Infectious diarrhea in human immunodeficiency virus. *Gastroenterol Clin North Am* 30:637, 2001.

77. Lamps LW, et al: The pathologic spectrum of gastrointestinal and hepatic histoplasmosis. *Am J Clin Pathol* 113:64, 2000.

78. Krown SE, et al: Kaposi's sarcoma in the acquired immune deficiency syndrome: A proposal for a uniform evalua-

tion, response, and staging criteria. *J Clin Oncol* 7:1201, 1989.

79. Nasti G, et al: A risk and benefit assessment of treatment for AIDS-related Kaposi's sarcoma. *Drug Saf* 20:403, 1999.

80. Buchbinder SP, et al: Herpes zoster and human immunodeficiency virus infection. *J Infect Dis* 166:1153, 1992.

81. Tyring S, et al: Famciclovir for the treatment of acute herpes zoster: Effects on acute disease and postherpetic neuralgia. A randomized, double-blind, placebo-controlled trial. Collaborative Famciclovir Herpes Zoster Study Group. *Ann Intern Med* 123:89, 1995.

82. Siegel D, et al: Prevalence and correlates of herpes simplex infections. The population-based AIDS in Multiethnic Neighborhoods Study. *JAMA* 268:1702, 1992.

83. Henderly DE, Jampol LM: Diagnosis and treatment of cytomegalovirus retinitis. *J Acquir Immune Defic Syndr* 1:S6, 1991.

84. Whitcup SM: Cytomegalovirus retinitis in the era of highly active antiretroviral therapy. *JAMA* 283:653, 2000.

85. Wei LL, Park SS, Skiest DJ: Prevalence of visual symptoms among patients with newly diagnosed cytomegalovirus retinitis. *Retina* 22:278, 2002.

86. Vitravene Study Group: Safety of intravitreous fomivirsen for treatment of cytomegalovirus retinitis in patients with AIDS. *Am J Ophthalmol* 133:484, 2002.

87. Dhillon B, Kamal A, Leen C: Intravitreal sustained-release ganciclovir implantation to control cytomegalovirus retinitis in AIDS. *Int J STD AIDS* 9:227, 1998.

88. Song MK, et al: Effect of anti-cytomegalovirus therapy on the incidence of immune recovery uveitis in AIDS patients with healed cytomegalovirus retinitis. *Am J Ophthalmol* 136:696, 2003.

89. 1999 USPHS/IDSA guidelines for the prevention of opportunistic infections in persons infected with human immunodeficiency virus: U.S. Public Health Service (USPHS) and Infectious Diseases Society of America (IDSA). *MMWR Recomm Rep* 48(RR-10):1, 1999.

90. Yunis N, Stone VE: Cardiac manifestations of HIV/AIDS: A review of disease spectrum and clinical management. *J Acquir Immune Defic Syndr Hum Retrovirol* 18:145, 1998.

91. Barbarinia G, Barbaro G: Incidence of the involvement of the cardiovascular system in HIV infection. *AIDS* 17(Suppl 1):S46. 2003.

92. Levin ML, et al: HIV-associated nephropathy occurring before HIV antibody seroconversion. *Am J Kidney Dis* 37:E39, 2001.

93. Treisman GJ, Angelino AF, Hutton HE: Psychiatric issues in the management of patients with HIV infection. *JAMA* 286:1857, 2001.

94. Lyketsos CG, et al: Depressive symptoms as predictors of medical outcomes in HIV infection. *JAMA* 270:2563, 1993.

95. Fleming DT, Wasserheit JN: From epidemiological synergy to public health policy and practice: The contribution of other sexually transmitted diseases to sexual transmission of HIV infection. *Sex Transm Infect* 75:3, 1999.

96. Golden MR, Marra CM, Holmes KK: Update of syphilis: Resurgence of an old problem. *JAMA* 290:1510, 2003.

97. Musher DM, Hamill RJ, Baughn RE: Effect of human immunodeficiency virus (HIV) infection on the course of syphilis and on the response to treatment. *Ann Intern Med* 113:872, 1990.

98. Zon LI, Groopman JE: Hematologic manifestations of the human immune deficiency virus (HIV). *Semin Hematol* 25:208, 1988.

99. Moses A, Nelson J, Bagby GC: The influence of human immunodeficiency virus-I on hematopoiesis. *Blood* 91:1479, 1998.

100. Tseng AL, Foisy M: Management of drug interactions in patients with HIV. *Ann Pharmacother* 31:1040, 1997.

101. Palella FJ, et al: Declining morbidity and mortality among patients with advanced human immunodeficiency virus infection. *N Engl J Med* 338:835, 1998.

102. Mocroft A, et al: Decline in the AIDS and death rates in the EuroSIDA study: An observational study. *Lancet* 362:22, 2003.

103. Fischl MA, et al: A randomized controlled trial of a reduced dose of zidovudine in patients with the acquired immunodeficiency syndrome. *N Engl J Med* 323:1009, 1990.

104. Volberding PA, et al: A comparison of immunity with deferred zidovudine therapy for asymptomatic HIV-infected adults with CD4 counts of 500 or more per cubic millimeter. *N Engl J Med* 333:401, 1995.

105. The Delta Coordinating Committee: Delta: A randomized control trial comparing combinations of zidovudine plus didanosine or zalcitabine with zidovudine alone in HIV-infected individuals. *Lancet* 348:283, 1996.

106. Carpenter CC, et al: Antiretroviral therapy in adults: Updated recommendations of the International AIDS Society–USA Panel. *JAMA* 283:381, 2000.

107. Warren KJ, et al: Nevirapine-associated Stevens-Johnson syndrome. *Lancet* 351:567, 1998.

108. Hovanessian HC: New developments in the treatment of HIV disease: An overview. *Ann Emerg Med* 33:546, 1999.

109. Department of Health and Human Services, Panel on Clinical Practices for Treatment of HIV Infection: Guidelines for the use of antiretroviral agents in HIV-infected adults and adolescents. Available at: www.hivatis.org.

110. Garcia PM, et al: Maternal levels of plasma human immunodeficiency virus type 1 RNA and the risk of perinatal transmission. *N Engl J Med* 341:394, 1999.

111. Landers DV, Duarte G: Mode of delivery and risk of vertical transmission of HIV-1. *N Engl J Med* 341:205, 1999.

112. Melvin AJ, Mohan KM: Response to immunization with measles, tetanus, and *Haemophilus influenzae* type b vaccines in children who have human immunodeficiency virus type 1 infection and are treated with highly active antiretroviral therapy. *Pediatrics* 111:e641, 2003.

113. Moss WF, Clements CJ, Halsey NA: Immunization of children at risk of infection with human immunodeficiency virus. *Bull World Health Organ* 81:61, 2003.

114. Prevention of pneumococcal disease: Recommendations of the Advisory Committee on Immunization Practices (ACIP). *MMWR Recomm Rep* 46(RR-8):1, 1997.

115. Rodriguez-Barradas MC, et al: Response of human immunodeficiency virus–infected patients receiving highly active antiretroviral therapy to vaccination with 23-valent pneumococcal polysaccharide vaccine. *Clin Infect Dis* 37:438, 2003.

116. Vento S, et al: Fulminant hepatitis associated with hepatitis A virus superinfection in patients with chronic hepatitis C. *N Engl J Med* 338: 286-90, 1998.

117. Sanetti AR, et al: Safety and immunogenicity of influenza vaccination in individuals infected with HIV. *Vaccine* 20(Suppl 5):B29, 2002.

118. Stanley SK, et al: Effect of immunization with a common recall antigen on viral expression in patients infected with human immunodeficiency virus type 1. *N Engl J Med* 334:1222, 1996.

119. Bartlett JG: Smallpox vaccination and patients with human immunodeficiency virus infection or acquired immunodeficiency syndrome. *Clin Infect Dis* 36:468, 2003.

120. American College of Emergency Physicians: *Code of Ethics for Emergency Physicians.* Dallas, American College of Emergency Physicians, 1997.

121. Larkin GL: A code of conduct for academic emergency medicine. *Acad Emerg Med* 6:45, 1999.

122. Lo B: Ethical dilemmas in HIV infection: What have we learned? *Law Med Health Care* 20:92, 1992.

123. Marco CA, Larkin GL, Moskop JC, Derse AR: The determination of 'futility' in emergency medicine. *Ann Emerg Med* 35:604, 2000.
124. Gostin LO: The AIDS litigation project: A national review of court and Human Rights Commission decisions I. The social impact of AIDS. *JAMA* 263:1961, 1990.
125. Ippolito G, et al: Occupational human immunodeficiency virus infection in health care workers: Worldwide cases through September 1997. *Clin Infect Dis* 28:365, 1999.
126. Gerberding JL: Occupational exposure to HIV in health care settings. *N Engl J Med* 343:826, 2003.
127. Updated US Public Health Service guidelines for the management of occupational exposures to HBV, HCV and HIV and recommendations for postexposure prophylaxis. *MMWR Recomm Rep* 50(RR-1):1, 2001.
128. Kelen GD, et al: Trends in human immunodeficiency virus (HIV) infection among a patient population in an inner-city emergency department: Implications for emergency department–based screening programs for HIV infection. *Clin Infect Dis* 21:867, 1995.
129. Phillips KA, et al: The cost-effectiveness of HIV testing of physicians and dentists in the United States. *JAMA* 271:851, 1994.
130. Kelen GD, et al: Determinants of emergency department procedure- and condition-specific universal (barrier) protection requirements for optimal provider protection. *Ann Emerg Med* 25:743, 1995.
131. Lee CH, et al: Occupational exposures to blood among emergency medicine residents. *Acad Emerg Med* 6:1036, 1999.
132. Cardo DM, et al: A case-control study of HIV seroconversion in health care workers after percutaneous exposure. Centers for Disease Control and Prevention Needlestick Surveillance Group. *N Engl J Med* 337:1485, 1997.
133. Conner EM, et al: Reduction of maternal-infant transmission of human immunodeficiency virus type 1 with zidovudine treatment. *N Engl J Med* 331:1173, 1994.
134. Moran GJ: Emergency department management of blood and body fluid exposures. *Ann Emerg Med* 35:47, 2000.
135. Merchant RC, et al: Emergency department blood or body fluid exposure evaluation and HIV postexposure prophylaxis usage. *Acad Emerg Med* 10:1345, 2003.
136. Katz MH, Gerberding JL: The care of persons with recent sexual exposure to HIV. *Ann Intern Med* 128:312, 1998.

CHAPTER

131 Parasites

Bruce M. Becker and John D. Cahill

PERSPECTIVE

Challenge

Parasitology, previously a subject of only eclectic interest to the emergency physician, has become increasingly important for practitioners in the United States. Numerous factors have contributed to this change. During the last few decades, there has been a dramatic increase in the immigration of individuals from South East Asia, Central and South America, and Africa into urban and rural regions of the United States and Europe. Many of these people have left their countries of origin under dire circumstances, fleeing civil unrest, war, famine, economic hardship, political persecution, and environmental devastation; they often lived in regions where parasitic infections are endemic. Business and adventure travel, including ecotourism, frequently transports immunologically innocent and vulnerable hosts to sites rich in parasitic disease (Figure 131-1). Patients with acquired immunodeficiency syndrome (AIDS) who travel to countries where parasitic illnesses are endemic are at higher risk of contracting these illnesses. Patients with AIDS who emigrate or travel to the United States or Europe may harbor a host of devastating parasitic illnesses. There is a significant prevalence of endemic parasitic disease in many rural areas of the Southeastern and Southwestern United States and in some parts of Europe. Often, patients with parasitic illness seek treatment initially in the emergency department.

The diagnosis and treatment of parasitic disease can be quite satisfying; correct diagnosis and chemotherapy given early in the course of illness often result in rapid recovery (Table 131-1). Mismanagement of parasitic illness can be disastrous, however. As Osler stated, "Early in the course of disease, diagnosis is difficult and treatment easy; late in the course, diagnosis is easy and treatment difficult." His wisdom applies strongly to parasitic illness, which often begins insidiously and pursues a long, chronic course resulting eventually in end-organ damage and severe morbidity and mortality in the host. To diagnose parasitic infection, the emergency physician must play detective, obtaining a thorough travel history, performing a detailed physical examination, ordering appropriate laboratory studies, and comparing these findings with a strong understanding of the basic life cycles of parasites, their usual and unusual presentations, and the intersecting geography of the organism and host. A detailed account of individual parasites can be found in Bell's *Tropical Medicine*[1] and Guerrant and colleagues' *Tropical Infectious Diseases*.[2]

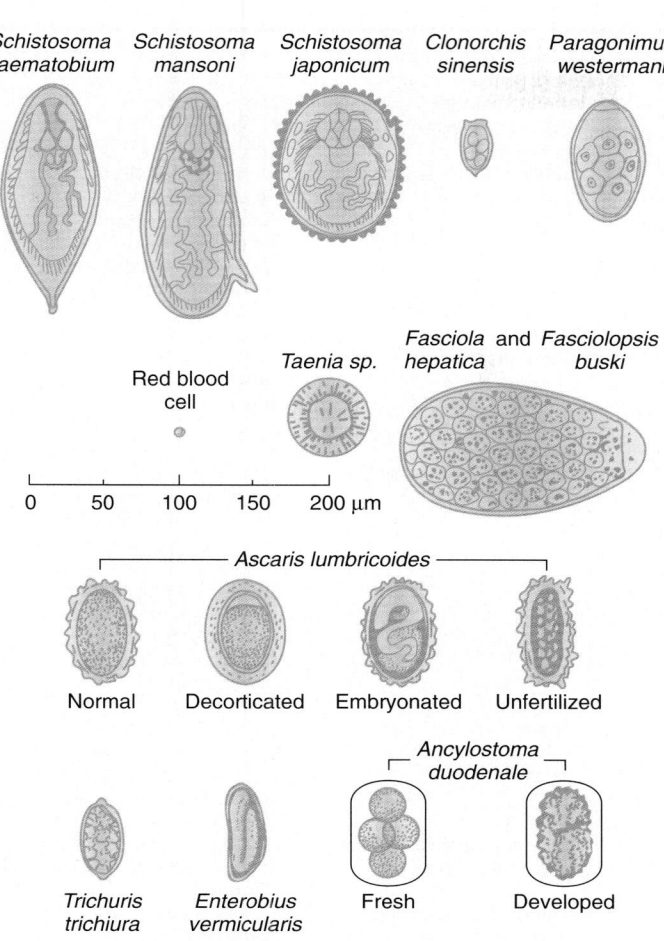

Schistosoma haematobium Schistosoma mansoni Schistosoma japonicum Clonorchis sinensis Paragonimus westermani

Red blood cell

Taenia sp.

Fasciola and Fasciolopsis
hepatica   buski

0   50   100   150   200 µm

Ascaris lumbricoides

Normal   Decorticated   Embryonated   Unfertilized

Ancylostoma duodenale

Trichuris trichiura   Enterobius vermicularis   Fresh   Developed

Figure 131-1. Eggs of major parasitic worms causing disease in humans.

Travel History

Parasitic illness should be considered in the differential diagnosis of almost every complaint imaginable, particularly in patients who recently have spent time in areas of the world with endemic parasitic illnesses (Table 131-2). As a result, a travel history should be included in the evaluation of most, if not all, emergency department patients. Important questions include the following:

1. What were the exact dates of travel?
2. What countries did the patient visit?
3. How much time was spent in each country?
4. What was the patient doing in the country, and where was he or she living?
5. Was the patient a tourist, adventure traveler, or worker?
6. Did the patient stay in cities or rural villages?
7. Was the patient sleeping in hotels or tents?
8. Did the patient engage in protected or unprotected intercourse?
9. What did the patient eat and drink?
10. What were the patient's activities (e.g., swimming in fresh water leads to schistosomiasis)?
11. Did the patient receive prophylactic immunizations before travel?
12. Did the patient take malaria chemoprophylaxis and comply with the regimen?
13. Did the patient use mosquito repellent and netting?
14. Does the patient have underlying chronic medical problems?
15. What medications does the patient take?
16. When did symptoms start, and what has been the chronology of symptoms, particularly fever and diarrhea?

For patients who recently immigrated to the United States, the following questions should be asked:

1. When did the patient arrive and from where?
2. What acute and chronic illnesses did the patient have previously while living in the country of origin?
3. What treatment did the patient receive there?
4. If a refugee, what countries did the patient pass through, and what were the living conditions (especially relevant for patients who have lived in numerous refugee camps)?
5. What was the season when the patient was in the countries (e.g., monsoon versus dry)?
6. What animal exposures and bites has the patient had?
7. Has the patient had exposure to fresh water, either in work or recreational activities?

The incubation period for the development of symptoms for parasitic diseases ranges from days (falciparum malaria) to months (vivax malaria) to years (filariasis). Uncovering parasitic illness depends heavily on Osler's principle—to *make* the diagnosis, one must first *think* of the diagnosis.

Table 131-1. Drug Classes and Modes of Action

Type of Drug	Specific Example of Drug(s)	Useful in the Treatment of	Likely Target(s) in the Parasite	Proposed Effects on Targets
Anthelmintics	Thiabendazole Mebendazole Albendazole	*Ascaris, Enterobius,* hookworm, *Strongyloides, Trichuris,* hydatid disease (long-term therapy)	Tubulin polymerization	Blocks cellular structural integrity and egg production; secondary effects on mitochondrial fumarate reductase and on glucose uptake
	Ivermectin* (Stromectol)	Many nematodes of humans (except hookworms) Filariasis Onchocerciasis	GABA-sensitive neuromuscular interface	Flaccidity or contraction (a tight-binding drug effective at low dose)
Trematodicides	Praziquantel (Biltricide)	Schistosomes Most other flukes, such as clonorchis, paragonimus, fasciolopsis (many tapeworms of humans)	Surface structure Carbohydrate metabolism	Vacuolization and surface disruption followed by immune attacks by the host; contraction of the muscles due to flooding of calcium through a permeable tegument; initial increase of glucose metabolism followed by shutdown
Antiprotozoals	Metronidazole (Flagyl) Tinidazole Niridazole	Amebiasis Balantidiasis Giardiasis *S. haematobium*	Molecular electron transport systems Acetylcholine recycling systems	Failure to sustain energy-producing systems Binds to acetylcholinesterase inactivating normal neuromuscular function
Antimalarials	Chloroquine phosphate (Aralen)	Many species of susceptible malaria	Parasite digestive vacuole hemoglobinase	Local pH is changed so that enzyme becomes inoperative
	Chloroguanide Pyrimethamine Trimethoprim and combinations of antifolate and sulfa drug (e.g., sulfadoxine/ pyrimethamine [Fansidar])	Many species of susceptible malaria Various malaria species partially or totally refractory to chloroquine	Dihydrofolate reductase step in folate synthesis or incorporation of PABA in folic acid	Blocks normal folate synthesis and eventually one-carbon metabolism

*Presently available from CDC Drug Service, Centers for Disease Control and Prevention, Atlanta, 30333, telephone: 404-639-3670 (evenings, weekends, and holidays: 404-639-2888).
GABA, γ-aminobutyric acid; PABA, *para*-aminobenzoic acid.

PRINCIPLES OF THERAPY

New and more effective antiparasitic agents are being developed continually. The list of drugs used to treat parasitic infestations is large and varied (Table 131-3; see also Table 131-1). Table 131-3 includes some of the newest pharmaceutical agents, in addition to many medications that, although still recommended, have become almost obsolete because of toxicity or mediocre efficacy.

The newer antiparasitic drugs are less toxic to the patient and more effective. Parasite biochemical pathways are sufficiently different from those of the human host to allow selective interference by relatively small doses of chemotherapeutic agents. In many instances, single-dose treatment can eradicate an entire parasite burden, and this approach has led to mass treatment programs of infected populations in endemic areas. Treatment and disposition in the emergency depart-

ment focus, however, on the individual patient and a particular disease entity. The evolutionary goal of the successful parasite is to live with and at the expense of the living host; a parasite that kills its host has no survival advantage. Most parasitic infections (with certain important exceptions, such as falciparum malaria) pursue a chronic course and are not acutely life-threatening. Alterations in host immune function can change the virulence and morbid course, however, of more benign infections (e.g., strongyloidiasis can become diffuse and fulminant in patients receiving immunosuppressive medication after organ transplant or after the initiation of long-term steroid therapy). Despite the subacute or chronic nature of most parasitic infections, when a diagnosis (or a diagnostic plan) has been made and chemotherapy instituted, the emergency physician must arrange careful follow-up and repeat laboratory examinations to ensure a cure. When the parasites are not eliminated promptly, repeat doses or alternative drugs should be considered because drug resistance is

Table 131-2. Parasites According to Geographic Location and Portal of Entry

Parasite	Geographic Distribution	Common Infective Stage and Portal of Entry
Protozoa		
Entamoeba histolytica	Cosmopolitan, especially prevalent in warm climates	Cyst via mouth
Balantidium coli	Warm climates	Cyst via mouth
Giardia lamblia	Cosmopolitan, especially prevalent in warm climates	Cyst via mouth
Trichomonas vaginalis	Cosmopolitan, United States	Trophozoite via vulva or urethra
Leishmania tropica	Mediterranean area to western India	Leptomonas via skin
Leishmania braziliensis	Mexico to northern Argentina	Leptomonas via skin
Leishmania donovani	China, India, Africa, Mediterranean area, continental Latin America	Leptomonas via skin
Trypanosoma gambiense	West and Central Africa	Trypanosome via skin
Trypanosoma rhodesiense	Central and East Africa	Trypanosome via skin
Trypanosome cruzi	Continental Latin America	Trypanosome via skin
Plasmodium vivax	Warm and cooler climates	Sporozoite via skin
Plasmodium malariae	Warm climates	Sporozoite via skin
Plasmodium falciparum	Warm climates	Sporozoite via skin
Nematodes		
Trichinella spiralis	Cosmopolitan, common in the United States	Encysted larva in pork via mouth
Trichuris trichiura	Warm, moist climates	Embryonated egg via mouth
Strongyloides stercoralis	Warm, moist climates	Filariform larva via skin
Necator americanus	Common in warm climates	Filariform larva via skin
Ancylostoma duodenale	Western South America	Filariform larva via skin
Enterobius vermicularis	Cosmopolitan, common in the United States	Embryonated egg via mouth
Ascaris lumbricoides	Cosmopolitan, common in the United States	Embryonated egg via mouth
Wuchereria bancrofti	Prevalent in warm climates	Filariform larva via skin
Brugia malayi	Asia	Filariform larva via skin
Onchocerca volvulus	Tropical Africa, Mexico, Central America, and northern South America	Filariform larva via skin
Loa loa	Tropical Africa	Filariform larva via skin
Dracunculus medinensis	Tropical Eastern Hemisphere	Larva in arthropod hose via mouth
Cestodes		
Taenia saginata	Cosmopolitan, United States	Cysticercus in beef via mouth
Taenia solium		
1. Adult worm	Cosmopolitan, United States	1. Cysticercus in pork via mouth
2. Cysticercus stage	Cosmopolitan, United States	2. Eggs human infections via mouth
Echinococcus granulosus	Cosmopolitan, United States	Eggs from canines via mouth
Echinococcus multilocularis	Central Europe, Asia, Alaska	Eggs from foxes via mouth
Hymenolepis nana	Warm climates	Eggs human infections via mouth
Hymenolepis diminuta	Warm climates	Larva in arthropod host via mouth
Diphyllobothrium latum	North Temperate Zone, Argentina, Chile, Australia	Sparganum larva fish flesh via mouth
Trematodes		
Fasciola hepatica	Sheep-raising countries	Larva on vegetation via mouth
Fasciolopsis buski	Asia	Larva encysted on water nuts
Clonorchis sinensis	Asia	Larva encysted in freshwater fish
Opisthorchis felineus	Europe, Asia	Larva encysted in freshwater fish
Opisthorchis viverrini	Thailand	Larva encysted in freshwater fish
Paragonimus westermani	Primarily oriental, also South America and Africa	Larva encysted in crabs or crayfish via mouth
Schistosoma japonicum	Asia	Cercarial larva in water via skin
Schistosoma mansoni	Africa, Latin America	Cercarial larva in water via skin
Schistosoma haematobium	Africa to India, southern Portugal	Cercarial larva in water via skin

Modified from Beaver PC, et al: *Clinical Parasitology,* 9th ed. Philadelphia, Lea & Febiger, 1984.

becoming increasingly common. Referral should be made to a geographic medicine clinic or an infectious disease clinic. Any patient who appears clinically ill or has presumptive falciparum malaria (by symptoms or travel history) should be admitted to the hospital for initial diagnosis, treatment, and observation.

FEVER

Malaria

Principles of Disease

The febrile patient with shaking chills and a time-appropriate history of travel to an endemic region

should be evaluated for malaria. *Plasmodium falciparum, Plasmodium ovale, Plasmodium vivax,* and *Plasmodium malariae* are responsible for human malaria. Greater than 41% of the world's population lives in areas where malaria is transmitted (e.g., parts of Africa, Asia, Oceania, Central America, and South America). Approximately 300 million to 500 million clinical infections occur annually, resulting in 1.5 million to 2.7 million deaths.[3] The female *Anopheles* mosquito is the arthropod vector that can transmit malaria after ingesting gametocytes from infected persons. After sexual reproduction in the gut of the mosquito, sporozoites are released from the salivary glands of the arthropod into the human host during a blood meal. Within the human host, the sporozoites

Table 131-3. Drugs for Treatment of Parasitic Infections

Infection	Drug	Adult Dosage	Pediatric Dosage
Amebiasis (*Entamoeba histolytica*)			
Asymptomatic			
Drug of choice:	Iodoquinol	650 mg tid × 20 days	30 mg/kg/day in 3 doses × 20 days
Alternative:	Diloxanide furoate	500 mg tid × 10 days	20 mg/kg/day in 3 doses × 7 days
	Paromomycin	25-30 mg/kg/day in 3 doses × 7 days	25-30 mg/kg/day in 3 doses × 7 days
Mild to Moderate Intestinal Disease			
Drug of choice:	Metronidazole	750 mg tid × 10 days	35-50 mg/kg/day in 3 doses × 10 days
Alternative:	Tinidazole	2 g/day × 3 days	50 mg/kg (maximum 2 g) qd × 3 days
Severe Intestinal Disease, Hepatic Abscess			
Drug of choice:	Metronidazole	750 mg tid × 10 days	35-50 mg/kg/day in 3 doses × 10 days
Alternative:	Tinidazole	600 mg bid or 800 mg tid × 5 days	50 mg/kg or 60 mg/kg (maximum 2 g) qd × 3 days
Amebic Meningoencephalitis, Primary (*Naegleria* spp.)			
Drug of choice:	Amphotericin B	1 mg/kg/day IV, uncertain duration	1 mg/kg/day IV, uncertain duration
Anisakiasis (Anisakis)			
Treatment of choice:	Surgical or endoscopic removal		
Ascariasis (*Ascaris lumbricoides*, roundworm)			
Drugs of choice:	Mebendazole	100 mg bid × 3 days	100 mg bid × 3 days
	Or pyrantel pamoate	11 mg/kg once (maximum 1 g)	11 mg/kg once (maximum 1 g)
Balantidiasis (*Balantidium coli*)			
Drug of choice:	Tetracycline	500 mg qid × 10 days	40 mg/kg/day in 4 doses × 10 days (maximum 2 g/day)
Alternatives:	Iodoquinol	650 mg tid × 20 days	40 mg/kg/day in 3 doses × 20 days
	Metronidazole	750 mg tid × 5 days	35-50 mg/kg/day in 3 doses × 5 days
Cutaneous Larva Migrans (Creeping Eruption)			
Drug of choice:	Thiabendazole	Topically and/or 50 mg/kg/day in 2 doses (maximum 3 g/day) × 2-5 days	Topically and/or 50 mg/kg/day in 2 doses (maximum 3 g/day) × 2-5 days
Dracunculus medinensis (Guinea Worm)			
Drug of choice:	Metronidazole	750 mg tid × 5-10 days	25 mg/kg/day (maximum 750 mg/day) in 2 doses × 10 days
Alternative:	Thiabendazole	50-75 mg/day in 2 doses × 3 days	50-75 mg/kg/day in 2 doses × 3 days
Enterobius vermicularis (Pinworm)			
Drugs of choice:	Pyrantel pamoate	11 mg/kg once (maximum 1 g); repeat after 2 wk	11 mg/kg once (maximum 1 g); repeat after 2 wk
	Mebendazole	A single dose of 100 mg; repeat after 2 wk	A single dose of 100 mg; repeat after 2 wk
Filariasis			
Wuchereria bancrofti, Brugia malayi			
Drug of choice:	Diethylcarbamazine	Day 1: 50 mg PO Day 2: 50 mg tid Day 3: 100 mg tid Days 4 through 21: 6 mg/kg/day in 3 doses	Day 1: 1 mg/kg PO Day 2: 1 mg/kg tid Day 3: 1-2 mg/kg tid Days 4 through 21: 6 mg/kg/day in 3 doses
Loa loa			
Drug of choice:	Diethylcarbamazine	Day 1: 50 mg PO Day 2: 50 mg tid Day 3: 100 mg tid Day 4 through 21: 9 mg/kg/day in 3 doses	Day 1: 1 mg/kg PO Day 2: 1 mg/kg tid Day 3: 1-2 mg/kg tid Days 4 through 21: 6 mg/kg/day in 3 doses
Onchocerca volvulus			
Drug of choice:	Ivermectin*	150 μm/kg PO once, repeated every 3-12 mo	150 μm/kg PO once, repeated every 3-12 mo
Fluke, Hermaphroditic			
Clonorchis sinensis (Chinese Liver Fluke)			
Drug of choice:	Praziquantel	75 mg/kg/day in doses × 1 day	75 mg/kg/day in 3 doses × 1 day

Table 131-3. Drugs for Treatment of Parasitic Infections—cont'd

Infection	Drug	Adult Dosage	Pediatric Dosage
Fasciola hepatica (Sheep Liver Fluke)			
Drug of choice:	Bithionol	30-50 mg/kg on alternate days × 10-15 doses	30-50 mg/kg on alternate days × 10-15 doses
Fasciolopsis buski (Intestinal Fluke)			
Drug of choice:	Praziquantel	75 mg/kg/day in 3 doses × 1 day	75 mg/kg/day in 3 doses × 1 day
Opisthorchis felineus			
Drug of choice:	Praziquantel	75 mg/kg/day in 3 doses × 1 day	75 mg/kg/day in 3 doses × 1 day
Paragonimus westermani (Lung Fluke)			
Drug of choice:	Praziquantel	75 mg/kg/day in 3 doses × 2 days	75 mg/kg/day in 3 doses × 2 days
Alternative:	Bithionol	30-50 mg/kg on alternate days × 10-15 doses	30-50 mg/kg on alternate days × 10-15 doses
Giardiasis (Giardia lamblia)			
Drug of choice:	Metronidazole	250 mg tid × 5 days	15 mg/kg/day in 3 doses × 5 days
Alternatives:	Furazolidone	100 mg qid × 7-10 days	6 mg/kg/day in 4 doses × 7-10 days
	Tinidazole	2 g as a single daily dose for 1-3 days	50 mg/kg as a single daily dose for 1-3 days
Hookworm Infection (Ancylostoma duodenale, Necator americanus)			
Drugs of choice:	Mebendazole	100 mg bid × 3 days	100 mg bid × 3 days
	Or pyrantel pamoate	11 mg/kg (maximum 1 g) × 3 days	11 mg/kg (maximum 1 g) × 3 days
Leishmaniasis			
Leishmania braziliensis, L. mexicana, L. tropica, L. donovani (Kala Azar)			
Drug of choice:	Stibogluconate sodium	20 mg/kg/day IV or IM × 20-28 days	20 mg/kg/day IV or IM × 20-28 days
Alternative:	Amphotericin B	0.25-1 mg/kg by slow infusion daily or every 2 days for 8 wk	0.25-1 mg/kg by slow infusion daily or every 2 days for 8 wk
Malaria, Treatment of (Plasmodium falciparum, P. ovale, P. vivax, and P. malariae)			
All Plasmodium except Chloroquine-Resistant P. falciparum			
Oral			
Drug of choice:	Chloroquine phosphate	600 mg base (1 g), then 300 mg base (500 mg) 6 hr later, then 300 mg base (500 mg) at 24 and 48 hr	10 mg base/kg (maximum 600 mg base), then 5 mg base/kg 6 hr later, then 5 mg base/kg at 24 and 48 hr
Parenteral			
Drugs of choice:	Quinine dihydrochloride	20 mg/kg loading dose in 10 mg/kg 5% dextrose over 4 hr followed by 10 mg/kg over 2-4 hr q8hr (maximum 1800 mg/day) until oral therapy can be started	Same as adult dose
	Or quinidine gluconate	10 mg/kg loading dose (maximum 600 mg) in normal saline slowly over 1-2 hr, followed by continuous infusion of 0.02 mg/kg/min for 3 days maximum	Same as adult dose
Alternative:	Chloroquine hydrochloride	200 mg base (250 mg) IM q6hr if oral therapy cannot be started	0.83 mg base/kg/hr × 30 hr continuous infusion or 3.5 mg base/kg q6hr IM or SC
Chloroquine-Resistant P. falciparum			
Oral			
Drugs of choice:	Quinine sulfate plus	650 mg tid × 3 days	25 mg/kg/day in 3 doses × 3-7 days
	Pyrimethamine-sulfadoxine	3 tablets at once on last day of quinine	<1 yr: ¼ tablet 1-3 yr: ½ tablet 4-8 yr: 1 tablet 9-14 yr: 2 tablets
	Or plus tetracycline	250 mg qid × 7 days	20 mg/kg/day in 4 doses × 7 days
	Or plus clindamycin	900 mg tid × 3-5 days	20-40 mg/kg/day in 3 doses × 3-5 days
Alternative:	Mefloquine	1250 mg once	25 mg/kg once (<45 kg)
Parenteral			
Drugs of choice:	Quinine dihydrochloride	Same as above	Same as above
	Quinidine gluconate	Same as above	Same as above

Continued

Table 131-3. Drugs for Treatment of Parasitic Infections—cont'd

Infection	Drug	Adult Dosage	Pediatric Dosage
Prevention of Relapses: P. vivax and P. ovale Only			
Drug of choice:	Primaquine phosphate	15 mg base (26.3 mg)/day × 14 days or 45 mg base (79 mg)/wk × 8 wk	0.3 mg base/kg/day × 14 days
Malaria, Prevention of			
Drug of choice:	Chloroquine phosphate	300 mg base (500 mg salt) PO, once a week beginning 1 wk before and continuing for 4 wk after last exposure	5 mg/kg base (8.3 mg/kg salt) once a week, up to adult dose of 300 mg base, same schedule as adult
Chloroquine-Resistant Areas			
Drug of choice:	Mefloquine	250 mg tablet PO once a week × 4 wk, then every other week continuing for 4 wk after last exposure	Same schedule as adults using the following dosing guidelines: 15-19 kg: ¼ tablet 20-30 kg: ½ tablet 31-45 kg: ¾ tablet >45 kg: 1 tablet
	or chloroquine phosphate	Same as above	Same as above
	Plus pyrimethamine-sulfadoxine for presumptive treatment	Carry a single dose (3 tablets) for self-treatment of febrile illness when medical care is not immediately available	Same single-dose approach as adults using the following dosing guidelines: <1 yr: ¼ tablet 1-3 yr: ½ tablet 4-8 yr: 1 tablet 9-14 yr: 2 tablets
	Plus proguanil (in Africa south of the Sahara)	200 mg daily starting 1-2 days before exposure and continuing for 7 days after cessation of exposure	Same schedule as adults using the following dosing guidelines: <2 yr: 50 mg daily 2-6 yr: 100 mg daily 7-10 yr: 150 mg daily >10 yr: 200 mg daily
	Or doxycycline	100 mg daily during exposure and for 4 weeks afterward	>8 yr: 2 mg/kg/day PO, up to 100 mg/ day
Schistosomiasis			
Schistosoma haematobium			
Drug of choice:	Praziquantel	40 mg/kg/day in 2 doses × 1 day	40 mg/kg/day in 2 doses × 1 day
S. japonicum			
Drug of choice:	Praziquantel	60 mg/kg/day in 3 doses × 1 day	60 mg/kg/day in 3 doses × 1 day
S. mansoni			
Drug of choice:	Praziquantel	40 mg/kg/day in 2 doses × 1 day	40 mg/kg/day in 2 doses × 1 day
Alternate:	Oxamniquine	15 mg/kg once	20 mg/kg/day in 2 doses × 1 day
S. mekongi			
Drug of choice:	Praziquantel	60 mg/kg/day in 3 doses × 1 day	60 mg/kg/day in 3 doses × 1 day
Strongyloidiasis (Strongyloides stercoralis)			
Drugs of choice:	Thiabendazole	50 mg/kg/day in 2 doses (maximum 3 g/day) × 2 days	50 mg/kg/day in 2 doses (maximum 3 g/day) × 2 days
	Or ivermectin	200 µg/kg/day × 1-2 days	200 µg/kg/day × 1-2 days
Tapeworm Infection—Adult (Intestinal Stage)			
Diphyllobothrium latum (Fish), Taenia saginata (Beef), Taenia solium (Pork), Dipylidium caninum (Dog)			
Drug of choice:	Praziquantel	5-10 mg/kg once	5-10 mg/kg once
Hymenolepis nana (Dwarf Tapeworm)			
Drug of choice:	Praziquantel	25 mg/kg once	25 mg/kg once
Larval (Tissue) Stage			
Echinococcus granulosus (Hydatid Cysts)			
Drug of choice:	Albendazole	400 mg bid × 28 days, repeated as necessary	15 mg/kg/day × 28 days, repeated as necessary
Echinococcus multilocularis			
Treatment of choice:	Surgical excision		
Cysticercus cellulose (Cysticercosis)			
Drugs of choice:	Praziquantel	50 mg/kg/day in 3 doses × 15 days	50 mg/kg/day in 3 doses × 15 days
	Or albendazole	15 mg/kg/day in 2-3 doses × 8-28 days, repeated as necessary	15 mg/kg/day in 2-3 doses × 8-28 days, repeated as necessary
Alternative:	Surgery		

Table 131-3. Drugs for Treatment of Parasitic Infections—cont'd

Infection	Drug	Adult Dosage	Pediatric Dosage
Trichinosis (*Trichinella spiralis*)			
Drugs of choice:	Steroids for severe symptoms		
	Plus mebendazole	200-400 mg tid × 3 days, then 400-500 mg tid × 10 days	Same as adult
Trichomoniasis (*Trichomonas vaginalis*)			
Drug of choice:	Metronidazole	2 g once or 250 mg tid or 375 mg bid PO × 7 days	15 mg/kg/day PO in 3 doses × 7 days
Trichuriasis (*Trichuris trichiura*, Whipworm)			
Drugs of choice:	Mebendazole	100 mg bid × 3 days	100 mg bid × 3 days
	Or albendazole	400 mg once	400 mg once
Trypanosomiasis			
***Trypanosoma cruzi* (South American Trypanosomiasis, Chagas' Disease)**			
Drug of choice:	Nifurtimox	8-10 mg/kg/day PO in 4 doses × 120 days	1-10 yr: 15-20 mg/kg/day in 4 doses × 90 days 11-16 yr: 12.5-15 mg/kg/day in 4 doses × 90 days
Alternative:	Benznidazole	5-7 mg/kg/day × 30-120 days	Same as adult
***T. brucei gambiense, T. b. rhodesiense* (African Trypanosomiasis, Sleeping Sickness) Hemolymphatic Stage**			
Drug of choice:	Suramin	100-200 mg (test done) IV, then 1 g IV on days 1, 3, 7, 14 and 21	20 mg/kg on days 1, 3, 7, 14, and 21
Alternative:	Pentamidine isethionate	4 mg/kg/day IM × 10 days	4 mg/kg/day IM × 10 days
Late Disease with Central Nervous System Involvement			
Drug of choice:	Melarsoprol	2-3.6 mg/kg/day IV × 3 days; after 1 wk 3.6 mg/kg/day IV × 3 days; repeat again after 10-21 days	18-25 mg/kg total over 1 month; initial dose of 0.36 mg/kg IV, increasing gradually to maximum 3.6 mg/kg at intervals of 1-5 days for total of 9-10 doses
Alternatives: (*T. b. gambiense* only)	Tryparsamide	One injection of 30 mg/kg (maximum 2 g) IV every 5 days to total of 12 injections; course may be repeated after 1 mo	Unknown
	Plus suramin	One injection of 10 mg/kg IV every 5 days to total of 12 injections; course may be repeated after 1 mo	Unknown
Visceral larva migrans (Toxocariasis)			
Drug of choice:	Diethylcarbamazine	6 mg/kg/day in 3 doses × 7-10 days	6 mg/kg/day in 3 doses × 7-10 days
Alternatives:	Mebendazole	100-200 mg bid × 5 days	Same as adult
	Or albendazole	400 mg bid × 3-5 days	400 mg bid × 3-5 days

*Some drugs available from CDC Drug Service, Centers for Disease Control and Prevention, Atlanta, 30333, telephone: 404-639-3670 (nights, weekends, and holidays: 404-639-2888).
Modified from Drugs for parasite infections. *Med Lett Drug Ther* 37:99, 1995.

rapidly penetrate the liver parenchymal cells. The protozoans, now termed *cryptozoites* or *exoerythrocytic schizonts,* rapidly multiply. Eventual lysis of the hepatic cells results in the release of merozoites into the bloodstream, where they invade erythrocytes. In *P. vivax* and *P. ovale* infection, a dormant hypnozoite can reside in hepatocytes, allowing for recrudescent infection many months to years later.

After invading red blood cells (RBCs), the merozoites transform into trophozoites, which feed on the cells' hemoglobin. These trophozoites mature into schizonts, which may divide asexually into additional merozoites. The RBCs undergo lysis, releasing many merozoites into the blood. Although some merozoites are destroyed by the body's immune apparatus, many enter new erythrocytes. After several repetitions of this erythrocytic cycle, the cyclic process changes, and male microgametocytes or female macrogametocytes may develop instead of merozoites. These gametes subsequently complete the reproductive cycle by fusion, sexually, within the gut of a new female *Anopheles* mosquito after she has taken a blood meal from an infected individual. A human contracts malaria from an infected vector mosquito in an endemic region. Other means of transmission have been reported, including blood transfusions, intravenous drug abuse with contaminated syringes, perinatal transmission, organ transplantation, and so-called airport malaria. *Airport malaria* refers to several reports of people acquiring malaria who have never been in an endemic area but live near or work in an international airport. The infected mosquito is transported from the endemic region and released when the plane arrives at its destination.[4-6]

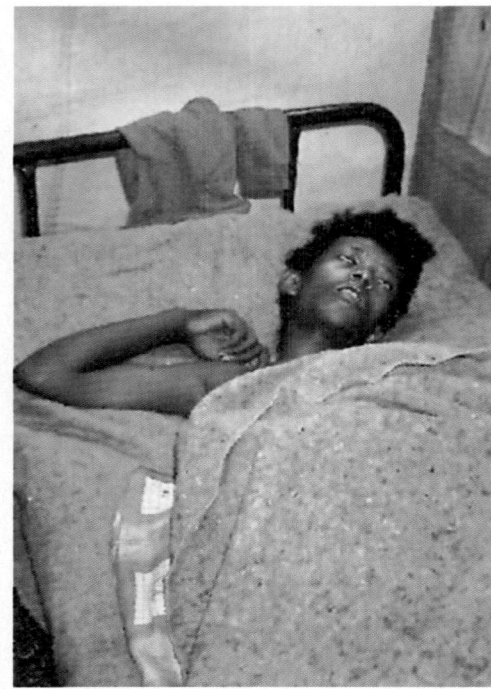

Figure 131-2. Patient with falciparum cerebral malaria and coma.

Clinical Features

The important difference between *P. falciparum* and the other species is the capacity of *P. falciparum* to cause severe and complicated disease or death. Irregular fevers are the hallmark of malaria. Other symptoms include anemia, headache, nausea, chills, lethargy, abdominal pain, and upper respiratory complaints.[7] Acute falciparum infection can have the following complications: cerebral malaria with cerebral edema and encephalopathy (Figure 131-2), hypoglycemia (especially in children), metabolic acidosis, severe anemia, renal failure, pulmonary edema, disseminated intravascular coagulation, and death.

In chronic malaria, there may be hepatosplenomegaly because of increased cellularity from the host's immune response. Within the liver, parasites and malarial pigment distend the Kupffer cells. Parasitized RBCs also adhere to the sinusoidal system of the spleen, reducing its immunologic effectiveness. Anemia results from acute and chronic hemolysis. Blackwater fever, hemoglobinuria caused by severe hemolysis, occurs in patients with chronic or acute falciparum malaria.[8]

Diagnostic Strategies

Thick and thin blood films are the gold standard for the diagnosis of malaria. Viewing several slides may be necessary if the parasite burden is not overwhelming. Giemsa and Wright stains are adequate for this purpose when used with ordinary light microscopy. The diagnosis often can be made in a simply equipped laboratory. Even if the parasite is not visualized, the physician still should treat for malaria if clinically suspected.

Management

In the past, chloroquine phosphate was the treatment of choice for acute, uncomplicated attacks of malaria. Resistance to chloroquine has been steadily increasing, and now the drug should be used only in regions of known chloroquine sensitivity, which include Haiti, Dominican Republic, Central America, and small regions of the Middle East. For uncomplicated malarial infections in patients from chloroquine-resistant regions, oral quinine and doxycycline given together may be used. Another suitable alternative is proguanil/atovaquone. For complicated *P. falciparum* (i.e., cerebral malaria, multiple organ systems involved, unable to tolerate oral medication), intravenous quinine (not available in intravenous form in the United States) or quinidine is used. Rapid infusion of intravenous quinine can cause profound hypoglycemia. Patients receiving intravenous quinine should undergo cardiac monitoring.

Although not used in the United States, the artemisinin agents are excellent antimalarials and are available in enteral and parenteral preparations. They have a rapid onset of action and are well tolerated. Primaquine is used to expunge the hepatic phases of *P. ovale* and *P. vivax,* preventing recrudescent disease. Before starting primaquine, the patient must be tested for glucose-6-phosphate dehydrogenase enzyme deficiency to avoid precipitating severe hemolysis. Prompt diagnosis and therapeutic intervention are necessary with falciparum malaria to avoid coma and death.[9,10]

Babesiosis

Babesiosis is a malaria-like illness that is becoming increasingly prevalent in the northeastern United States (*Babesia microti*), the northwestern United States (*Babesia gibsoni*), and Europe (*Babesia divergens*). The organism is a protozoan similar in structure and life cycle to the plasmodia. It is transmitted by the deer tick, *Ixodes dammini,* the same vector of Lyme disease. Several cases have been attributed to transfusion with infected blood.[11] Patients develop fatigue, anorexia, malaise, myalgia, chills, high spiking fevers, sweats, headache, emotional lability, and dark urine. They have hepatosplenomegaly, anemia, thrombocytopenia, leukopenia, elevated liver enzyme levels, and signs of hemolysis with hyperbilirubinemia and decreased haptoglobin. In a healthy host, the disease may remit spontaneously.[12] In asplenic patients, elderly patients, and immunocompromised patients (especially patients with AIDS and patients taking corticosteroids), 85% of RBCs may contain organisms. There is massive hemolysis, jaundice, renal failure, disseminated intravascular coagulation, hypotension, and adult respiratory distress syndrome.[13,14] Diagnosis rests on clinical suspicion, multiple thin and thick blood smears, and serologic testing. The treatment of choice is quinine and clindamycin. Patients infected with *B. divergens* tend to be sicker and require more supportive care. Co-infection with *Borrelia burgdorferi,* the agent that causes Lyme disease, results in more severe and prolonged illness.[15] Babesia resemble plasmodia in blood smears. The history makes the diagnosis.

Other Parasites Causing Fever

Other parasitic illnesses that commonly cause significant fever include schistosomiasis, fascioliasis, African and American trypanosomiasis, leishmaniasis, toxoplasmosis, and amebic liver abscess. Katayama fever may be the initial phase of schistosomiasis. Infected patients report brief exposures to freshwater in endemic areas. They have spiking fevers, diaphoresis, and cough. Eosinophilia is common.[16] Fascioliasis, caused by the liver fluke, *Fasciola hepatica,* is endemic throughout Asia, the former Soviet Union, southern Europe, and South America. Infection begins with the ingestion of the metacercariae. Within 6 weeks, patients manifest right upper quadrant abdominal pain, fever, and eosinophilia.[17]

American trypanosomiasis (Chagas' disease) is endemic to Central and South America. The vector, the reduviid bug, sheds the trypomastigotes in its feces proximal to the bite site, leading to local infection and subsequent systemic spread in the host. Acute Chagas' disease begins with the chagoma, the infected and swollen bite site, often periorbital, and quickly progresses to fever, malaise, facial swelling, and pedal edema. Parasitization of cardiac muscle leads to the dysrhythmias and ventricular dysfunction that are classically found in late disease (chronic Chagas' cardiopathy).[18] Leishmaniasis, spread to humans by the sandfly as vector, is found in the Middle East, in India, in East Africa, along the Mediterranean coast, and in Brazil. Although leishmaniasis can involve the skin (cutaneous) and the mucosa (mucosal), fever is seen only in visceral leishmaniasis in immunocompetent individuals. Symptoms also include massive hepatosplenomegaly, neutropenia, and weight loss.[19] Amebic liver abscesses frequently manifest with high fevers, right upper quadrant pain, and an elevated white blood cell count.[20]

NEUROLOGIC SYMPTOMS

Cerebral Malaria

Principles of Disease and Clinical Features

Cerebral malaria is a common, life-threatening complication of *P. falciparum* infection. Parasitized RBCs express malarial cell surface glycoproteins called *knobs* that are sticky. They adhere to capillary walls, causing sludging in the cerebral microvasculature, localized ischemia, capillary leak, and petechial hemorrhages. Patients have fever, altered mentation including obtundation and coma (see Figure 131-2), and occasionally seizures. A careful history and early diagnosis and therapy are essential to prevent severe morbidity and mortality.

Management

Treatment of cerebral malaria includes intravenous quinine, quinidine, or artemisinin (if available); supportive care, including mechanical ventilation for comatose patients and patients with noncardiogenic pulmonary edema; antiepileptics; and treatment of acidosis and hypoglycemia (associated with quinine use and cerebral malaria). Mortality is high, especially in children (30%), but if the patient recovers, neurologic sequelae are rare (<10%).[21,22] Corticosteroids, including dexamethasone, are not beneficial and are potentially harmful in cerebral malaria.

Cysticercosis

Principles of Disease

Cysticercosis is a disease caused by the larval form of *Taenia solium,* a common central nervous system (CNS) pathogen in many tropical areas. *T. solium* (pork tapeworm) is acquired by humans after eating pork containing the larval cysts. After ingestion of infected pork, the adult worm matures in the small intestine, whereas the larval forms may penetrate through the gut wall and end up anywhere in the body. The most common sites include the CNS, muscle, and soft tissue.[23-25]

Clinical Features

Within the brain, the larvae of *T. solium* form an expanding cyst that induces an immunologic reaction from the host, including inflammation, fibrosis, and ultimately calcification. Neurologic findings develop when the involved neural tissue cannot accommodate adequately the enlarging cyst. Seizure activity is often the first indication of cysticercosis and should be considered in any adult patient with undiagnosed seizures. The diagnosis of *T. solium* is established by finding characteristic proglottids (gravid segments) or scolices (worm heads) in stool preparations.

Diagnostic Strategies and Management

Cranial computed tomography (CT) scan with contrast enhancement may reveal an enhancing ring lesion. These lesions can appear similar to a CNS abscess, metastasis, or a primary tumor, such as glioblastoma multiforme. Praziquantel is the treatment of choice, and corticosteroids may be necessary during therapy with praziquantel, particularly if CNS cysts are present. Neurosurgical consultation should be sought when treating neurocysticercosis because acute obstructive hydrocephalus can occur.[1]

Echinococcosis

Principles of Disease and Clinical Features

Echinococcus granulosus is another tapeworm capable of causing CNS disease. Cerebral hydatid cysts are loculated structures containing *E. granulosus* scolices (heads) and remains of germinal epithelium, termed *hydatid sand.* Common types of exposure include

Figure 131-3. Hydatid cysts removed surgically.

Figure 131-4. Hydatid cysts removed surgically.

ingestion of food or water contaminated by the ova from feces of sheep or cattle infected by the adult worm or close contact with a sheepdog. Infection results in the liberation of the embryo oncosphere into the small intestine. After penetrating the intestinal wall, the larvae travel through the bloodstream to multiple sites for encystment. The liver is the target organ in nearly two thirds of cases, but the brain is involved in approximately 1 in 14 cases. In the brain, infection with *E. granulosus* is manifested by compressive effects or seizures caused by enlarging cysts.

Diagnostic Strategies and Management

The diagnosis of hydatid cyst disease is suggested by localization of the cyst on CT scan. Serologic evaluation of serum or cerebrospinal fluid (CSF) confirms the diagnosis. Aspiration of the cyst should not be attempted because widespread metastatic cysts may develop. Treatment options include using the drug albendazole and surgical resection if warranted. Resection of the cyst may cause an anaphylactoid reaction if there is spillage of hydatid sand (Figures 131-3 and 131-4).[26]

African Trypanosomiasis

Principles of Disease

African sleeping sickness is caused by *Trypanosoma brucei gambiense* and *Trypanosoma brucei rhodesiense*. The endemic region for this infection is limited to several areas of West and East Africa. These motile organisms are transmitted by the bite of the *Glossina* (tsetse) fly, which introduces the infective form of the trypanosome into the host blood. A small lesion or boil may develop and persist for several days. The flagellated organism travels throughout the bloodstream, invading the lymph nodes and spleen.

Clinical Features

Winterbottom's sign, which is posterior cervical lymphadenopathy, is usually apparent at the time treatment is sought. The patient is often febrile, and trypanosomes are visible in a thick peripheral blood smear. A maculopapular rash may be noted in fair-skinned individuals. After invasion of the CNS, severe headache may result secondary to cerebral inflammation. Some patients may manifest psychiatric symptoms, progressing eventually to extreme sleepiness and lethargy. Coma and death from starvation and trypanotoxins are inevitable in untreated patients.[27-29]

Diagnostic Strategies and Management

The diagnosis of African trypanosomiasis requires an appropriate exposure history and characteristic symptoms. Trypanosomes in peripheral blood, CSF, or lymph node and bone marrow aspirates establish the diagnosis. The presence of parasites in the CSF indicates advanced progression of the disease. Suramin sodium is the treatment of choice for early infection with *T. b. rhodesiense*. Pentamidine isethionate is the preferred treatment for early *T. b. gambiense*. Trivalent arsenicals, such as melarsoprol, which can penetrate the blood-brain barrier, are used in advanced disease with neurologic sequelae.[2]

Other Parasites Causing Neurologic Symptoms

CNS involvement with *Trichinella spiralis* has been reported in severe cases, after larval migration of this parasite into the brain and meninges. Serious consequences are meningitis, encephalitis, seizures, paresis, coma, and death. The pathophysiology may reflect obstruction of small arterioles by migrating larvae, with subsequent vasculitis or cerebral edema from immunologic reaction to the larvae or larval fragments. Therapy for trichinosis with severe muscle or CNS involvement includes mebendazole or thiabendazole coupled with steroids, which depress the host immune response to infection.[30,31]

Amebic abscess of the brain or meningoencephalitis caused by *Entamoeba histolytica* is a rare complication of infection with this intestinal parasite. Infestation occurs with ingestions of food or drink contaminated with cysts of this protozoan. Spread of amebae to the brain or meninges from the colonized large bowel wall is rare, but should be considered in any patient with

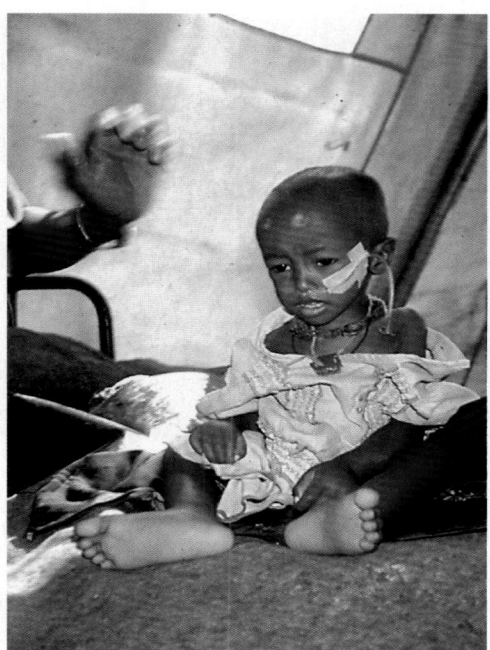

Figure 131-5. Child with severe life-threatening anemia (hematocrit 9) in association with chronic malaria.

amebiasis and subsequent neurologic impairment. The diagnosis may be made through microscopic identification of trophozoites (motile amebae) in CSF; however, biopsy of affected tissue is more specific. CNS amebiasis is treated with intravenous metronidazole.

Naegleria and *Acanthamoeba* are free-living amebae in freshwater that can be contracted while swimming and diving in ponds and lakes. The amebae are thought to invade the CNS through the olfactory neuroepithelium or cornea (violated by abrasion or associated with contact lens wear), causing an amebic meningoencephalitis. The combination of amphotericin B and miconazole is currently the treatment of choice when motile amebae are identified in CSF.[32]

Strongyloides stercoralis is a common infection in the tropics. The worm is introduced through the skin and eventually makes its way to the small bowel. Infection with *Strongyloides* is more clinically significant in an immunosuppressed patient, who may have larval dissemination throughout the body with encephalitis and pyogenic meningitis in the CNS. *Strongyloides* is treated with thiabendazole or albendazole.[33]

Granulomas may occur in the brain from egg deposition by *Schistosoma*. Generally, they do not cause major symptoms; however, several cases of transverse myelitis with paraplegia have been reported.[34]

ANEMIA

Malaria

Malaria infection often is associated with anemia. Severe anemia is seen more often in children younger than 5 years old (Figure 131-5). Anemia may develop quickly, linked to an acute infection with massive hemolysis, or it may be more insidious, developing over months. Parasitized RBCs lyse when the merozoite phase is mature. Uninfected RBCs undergo immune destruction from cell surface antibodies produced in response to parasite-associated changes in RBC surface proteins. This process of destruction is abetted by increased reticuloendothelial activity. The reticulocyte response in infected individuals is blunted by inhibition of erythropoietin secretion.[35,36] The antimalarial drug primaquine can precipitate hemolysis in patients who have glucose-6-phosphate dehydrogenase deficiency, which is common in black Africans and some Asians.

Whipworm and Hookworm

Infestation by the whipworm *Trichuris trichiura* and the two human hookworms *Necator americanus* and *Ancylostoma duodenale* may cause iron deficiency anemia. Hookworm infection has been recognized as a major cause of anemia worldwide. Adult worms penetrate into intestinal mucosa and feed, causing significant ongoing luminal blood loss. Eggs defecated in the soil mature through a rhabditiform larval form to the infective filariform larva. These larvae penetrate the human skin, usually through the feet. In trichuriasis, anemia is seen only with massive parasite infestation. Ova from the whipworm are ingested through stool-contaminated food and water. Diagnosis of these infections requires identification of characteristic ova in the stool. As with most helminthic infections, peripheral eosinophilia is common. Mebendazole or albendazole effectively controls trichuriasis and hookworm infections in adults and children. The patient also should be treated with iron if there is an intercurrent anemia.

Tapeworm

Infection with the fish tapeworm *Diphyllobothrium latum* is associated with pernicious anemia. This tapeworm competes with the human host for absorption of vitamin B_{12}. The ingestion of raw freshwater fish that contains the embryo plerocercoid larva in its muscle fibers is followed by the development of a large adult tapeworm within the human small intestine. Showing the characteristic ova in the feces secures the diagnosis. Praziquantel is the drug of choice in adults and children.

PERIPHERAL EDEMA

Elephantiasis

Principles of Disease

Elephantiasis, or filariasis, is the development of massive edema with subsequent chronic distention of the overlying skin. It is caused by infestation with the filarial worms *Wuchereria bancrofti* or *Brugia malayi*. The infection is confined to humans and is widely distributed in the warmer parts of the world, including Africa, Asia, South America, and Oceania. More than 90% of all infections are found in Asia, where the disease has reached epidemic proportions in some cities. The disease can be endemic to residents of these regions but is rare in travelers. Infected mosquitoes introduce microfilariae into the bloodstream of the human host during a blood meal. On entering the host, the worms migrate into the lymphatic system and mature into coiled, gravid adults. The presence of the adult worm within the lymphatic vessels, particularly of the lower extremities and genitalia, stimulates a profound immunologic reaction. The macrophages, lymphocytes, plasma cells, giant cells, and eosinophils congregate around the constricted lymphatic vessel. This event usually results in an erythematous, edematous, tender lymphatic tract. Its presence in patients at risk should suggest the diagnosis of filariasis.

Clinical Features

Chronic manifestations of filariasis include fibrosis of the lymphatic vessel, which sometimes encloses a dead or calcified worm. Subsequent mechanical blockage of the lymphatic system leads inevitably to severe lower extremity and genital edema accompanied by thickening of the skin. Recurrent cellulitis can be a problem in many of these patients; meticulous skin care is essential to prevent this complication.[37]

Diagnostic Strategies and Management

The adult female worm produces microfilariae, which periodically are released into the peripheral blood via the lymphatics accompanied by shaking chills and fever. Thick peripheral blood smears may show infection, particularly at night, when the release of microfilariae is most likely. Diethylcarbamazine rapidly clears the microfilariae from the peripheral blood and slowly sterilizes the gravid female nematode. Established elephantiasis of the scrotum can be successfully treated surgically. Lymphatic obstruction of the limbs rarely responds to operative intervention.[38]

DERMATOLOGIC SYMPTOMS

Cutaneous Leishmaniasis

Principles of Disease

Cutaneous leishmaniasis is among the most important causes of chronic ulcerating skin lesions in the world. *Leishmania braziliensis* and *Leishmania mexicana* are responsible for New World leishmaniasis, whereas *Leishmania tropica* causes Old World leishmaniasis. The female *Phlebotomus* sand fly transmits the promastigote form of this parasite during a blood meal. When in the human host, the leishmanial form of this parasite resides in the macrophages of the skin and subcutaneous tissue.

Clinical Features

Skin papules and nodules are seen early in leishmaniasis at the site of the insect bite. A raised macule also

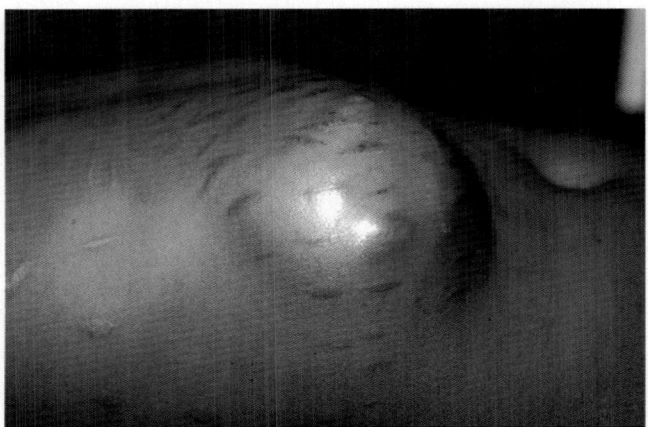

Figure 131-6. Cutaneous leishmaniasis.

can appear, which subsequently develops central ulceration and a raised border. Lymphocyte and macrophage invasion of the epidermis and dermis cause the induration that occurs at the ulcer border. Secondary bacterial infections of these ulcers increase the associated scarring. *L. braziliensis braziliensis* (subspecies of *L. braziliensis*) attacks the mucocutaneous skin borders, such as in the nose and mouth. Mutilation of the face occurs after massive tissue destruction, including nasal cartilage. The larynx and trachea also can be involved, compromising the airway. Disseminated cutaneous leishmaniasis (*L. mexicana amazonensis* in South America and *L. tropica aethiopica* in Ethiopia) is characterized by diffuse nodules and papules resembling lepromatous leprosy (Figure 131-6). Individuals with this manifestation of leishmaniasis are thought to have a defect in their cell-mediated immunity response.[39-41]

Diagnostic Strategies and Management

Definitive diagnosis of leishmaniasis is made by direct visualization of the parasite under the microscope. Diagnosis can be made by indirect fluorescent antibody test. An intradermal skin test exists (Montenegro), but it is often negative during the acute stages of the disease. Many forms of cutaneous leishmaniasis, especially *L. tropica* and *L. mexicana,* are self-limited and require no treatment, unless the wounds become secondarily infected. Treatment options include sodium stibogluconate, meglumine antimonate, and amphotericin B. These treatments rarely are initiated in the emergency department.

Dracunculiasis

Principles of Disease and Clinical Features

Dracunculus medinensis, the "fiery serpent," causes disease as the adult worm migrates through the subcutaneous tissues of the lower extremity. The head of the gravid adult female erodes through the skin of the lower extremity of the human host, and sensing immersion of the affected limb (as the human host wades in a pond or open well) releases larvae into the water. The larvae promptly infect the Cyclops water flea. Humans who drink water containing the infected crustacean complete the cycle of infection. The patient may complain of rash, intense pruritus, nausea, vomiting, dyspnea, and diarrhea before the female worm ruptures through the lower extremity skin.

Management

The typical treatment in developing countries is to wind the worm around a stick and slowly extract the parasite over the course of 1 or 2 days. If the worm breaks while being extracted in this fashion, the patient experiences an intense inflammatory reaction with cellulitis along the worm tract. Diagnosis is made when microscopic larvae are found in the fluid of the cutaneous ulcer or when the adult female worm is identified extruding from the skin. The use of metronidazole to shorten the time of extraction is controversial. The World Health Organization has set a goal of eradication of this disease through public health awareness, covered wells, filtered well water (removing the fleas), and keeping active skin lesions out of potable water (i.e., keeping the host out of potable water).

Other Parasites Causing Dermatologic Symptoms

Cutaneous larva migrans, the "creeping eruption," occurs in the host's epidermis after penetration by *Ancylostoma braziliense* (dog or cat hookworm) larvae into the skin. Exposure usually occurs after walking barefoot or lying on beaches or other warm soil contaminated by animal feces. The diagnosis is suggested by the presence of a characteristic meandering track on the skin surface caused by larval migration. Visceral larva migrans occurs in young children after ingestion of soil containing ova from the dog ascarid *Toxocara canis.* Thiabendazole, ivermectin, or albendazole is given for cutaneous larva migrans, and antipruritics give symptomatic relief. Diethylcarbamazine treats visceral larva migrans. An alternative is thiabendazole.[42]

Swimmer's itch is a dermatitis that occurs after skin penetration by the nonhuman schistosome of avians and mammals, usually from swimming in northern U.S. freshwater lakes. The infection spontaneously resolves because the nonhuman schistosome is not tolerated by the human host's immune system. Similar dermatitis also can occur after infection with human schistosomes. Treatment is symptomatic.

Strongyloides can cause a transient, pruritic rash that may appear then disappear within hours. *Taenia solium* can cause cysts in the soft tissues and muscles. These cysts often are an incidental finding. Onchocerciasis (*Onchocerca volvulus*), which is commonplace in West Africa and parts of South America, can cause severe pruritus and nodules on bony protuberances. Superficial ocular infections are serious because they lead to a sclerosing keratitis called *river blindness.*

VISUAL SYMPTOMS

Onchocerciasis

Principles of Disease

Onchocerciasis, or river blindness, is a major cause of blindness in the world. Ninety-five percent of all cases are found in Africa.[43] The parasite is found only in humans and is transmitted by the bite of the *Simulium* fly. These flies live near rivers—hence the name *river blindness.* Microfilariae of *O. volvulus* are released by adult nematodes, which coil in subcutaneous nodules in the infected host; the microfilariae then migrate through the dermis and epidermis. The presence of adult worms invokes an allergic response, including the infiltration of lymphocytes, macrophages, plasma cells, and eosinophils.

Clinical Features

The skin becomes chronically edematous and pruritic; it atrophies, resulting in loose, thin folds of skin. Patients with nodules in close proximity to the eyes are more likely to develop river blindness. When the microfilaria dies during its migration in the eye, the foreign tissue that is deposited in the iris musculature incites an immune sclerosing keratitis, often associated with iritis. This immunologic response to the dead microfilaria in the host's iris is the major cause of the ocular destruction and subsequent blindness (Figure 131-7).

Diagnostic Strategies and Management

The diagnosis of onchocerciasis requires identification of characteristic microfilariae in skin snipped from the patient. Ivermectin is the drug of choice. In many countries where the disease is endemic, the manufacturers of ivermectin have donated the drug in an attempt to eradicate the disease. Surgical excision of the subcutaneous nodules is recommended when they are located on the head.

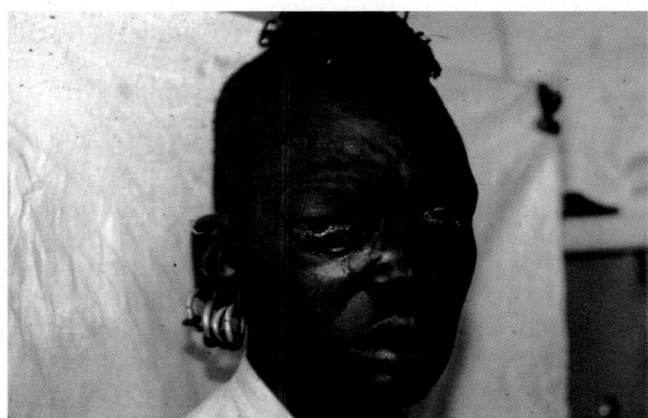

Figure 131-7. Onchocerciasis or "river blindness."

Loiasis

Principles of Disease and Clinical Features

Another filarial infection that causes ocular problems is loiasis. Loiasis is confined to forest areas in West and Central Africa. Transmission of *Loa loa* occurs through the bite of flies of the genus *Chrysops*. The edema initially associated with the migrating worm is called *Calabar swelling*. The disease is caused by a migrating adult worm in the subcutaneous tissue. The adult worm occasionally migrates through the subconjunctival tissues of the eye. This meandering worm can be surgically excised from the conjunctiva. Although upsetting to the patient, the disease often is fairly benign. The adult worm releases sheathed microfilariae into the peripheral bloodstream during the daytime.

Diagnostic Strategies and Management

Microfilariae can be detected with a thick blood smear, securing the diagnosis of loiasis. The treatment of choice for *L. loa* is diethylcarbamazine. Corticosteroids or antihistamines often must supplement specific chemotherapy because of the intense allergic reaction that occurs when the killed adult worms and microfilariae disintegrate.[44,45]

Other Parasites Causing Ocular Symptoms

T. canis has a trophism for the host's eyes. Toxocariasis is a roundworm infection often found in urban dogs. Humans ingest eggs by the fecal-oral route. The larvae migrate and often enter the retina, where they become trapped. They stimulate an immune response that culminates in granuloma formation. These granulomas can impair vision and sometimes are mistaken for retinal tumors. There is no means of direct diagnosis except tissue biopsy. Treatment is with albendazole; larvae visible in the retina can be destroyed with a laser.[1]

Toxoplasma gondii can cause vitreal inflammation with retinal hemorrhages and tears. Immunocompromised patients may develop chorioretinitis and optic neuritis with visual field defects and ocular palsies. Erythrocytes with sticky "knobs" from *P. falciparum* infection can cause retinal vascular congestion and ischemia with hemorrhage, exudate, infarction, and macular destruction. Cerebral malaria can cause cortical blindness. Mucocutaneous leishmaniasis can involve the lids, tear glands, retina, or iris and may result in total ocular destruction. *Acanthamoeba* can cause a dangerous keratitis in contact lens wearers. The patient complains of severe pain, tearing, and photophobia. Early infection may be misdiagnosed as herpetic keratitis. The infection may become chronic and require keratoplasty. Numerous worms migrate to or through the eye causing inflammation, tissue destruction, and blindness. These include *Ascaris* and hookworm. *Echinococcus* and *Cysticercus* can cause destructive cystic lesions in the eye.

PULMONARY SYMPTOMS

Patients with *P. falciparum* initially may seek treatment for fever and cough. Early in the course of treatment of severe malaria, the patient may develop noncardiogenic pulmonary edema or adult respiratory distress syndrome requiring mechanical ventilation with positive end-expiratory pressure.[46,47]

E. histolytica can cause sympathetic pleural effusions, direct pulmonary or pleural involvement by extension or rupture of an amebic liver abscess, or direct hematogenous seeding of the lungs leading to considerable additional morbidity and mortality for the patient with underlying amebic infection.[48] *Pneumocystis carinii* pneumonia is one of the most common causes of respiratory opportunistic infection in patients with human immunodeficiency virus (HIV) infections in the United States and Europe; however, it is responsible for less than 10% of pulmonary opportunistic infections in Africa and the developing world. The reason for this discrepancy is unclear. Many patients with AIDS in these countries die with CD4 cell counts that are higher than those associated with *P. carinii* pneumonia in the United States.[49]

Löffler's syndrome, characterized by persistent, nonproductive cough, substernal chest pain, wheezing, rales, pulmonary infiltrates on chest x-ray, and marked eosinophilia,[50] is often seen when larvae from the roundworm *Ascaris lumbricoides,* the hookworms *N. americanus* and *A. duodenale,* and the threadworm *S. stercoralis* transit the lungs as part of their developmental cycles. *Ascaris* larvae penetrate the small intestinal wall to gain entry into the small venules of the gastrointestinal tract, then migrate to the lungs. *Strongyloides* and the hookworm filariform larvae penetrate through the skin of the feet, entering small cutaneous venules before migration to the lungs. The pulmonary infiltrates and symptoms are transient, resolving within 2 weeks. Diagnosis depends on discovering larvae in sputum or gastric aspirates. Negative stool examinations are nondiagnostic because eggs do not appear in the stool for at least 1 month after initial infection.[51]

Patients' immune responses to the microfilariae of *W. bancrofti* and *B. malayi* cause tropical eosinophilic pneumonia.[52] These patients present with malaise, weight loss, new-onset nocturnal wheezing and asthma, shortness of breath, and chest discomfort. Chest x-rays may show nodular or interstitial infiltrates, consolidations, or cavitation. Microfilariae can be seen in lung biopsy material. Untreated infection may result in obstructive or restrictive lung disease. Patients have marked eosinophilia and elevations of serum IgE.[53]

Paragonimus westermani and echinococcal species are trophic for the lungs in their human hosts. *P. westermani* eggs are shed in stool, hatch in freshwater, and as miracidia infect a snail intermediary. After further development, cercariae are released from the snail, penetrating and encysting in freshwater crab or crayfish. After consumption by the human host, metacercariae from the crab or crayfish excyst within the duodenum, penetrating the duodenal wall into the abdominal cavity. The larvae migrate from the peritoneal cavity through the diaphragm into the pleural cavity, finally migrating to the lungs, causing hemorrhage, necrosis, and a granulomatous response. Early in the process, patients may have infiltrates and eosinophilia; later disease is marked by bronchiectasis, chronic bronchitis, fever, hemoptysis, and cachexia. Pulmonary nodules and cysts may cavitate.[54] Many of these patients may have positive purified protein derivative tests, and their symptoms and chest x-rays may mimic tuberculosis. Sputum is often blood-streaked and flecked with dark brown particles containing diagnostic ova. Radiography, stool examination, and immune testing of sputum and blood can help make the diagnosis.[55] Praziquantel is the treatment of choice.

E. granulosus causes pulmonary hydatid cyst disease that remains asymptomatic until a cyst grows large enough to cause a mass effect, becomes superinfected, or leaks cyst material, which is highly immunogenic, causing a severe anaphylactoid reaction. Pulmonary hydatid cysts also can be associated with cough, chest pain, and hemoptysis.[56] Primary hydatid disease in the liver can metastasize to the lungs or brain. A thoracic CT scan shows a unilocular lung cyst; a plain radiograph of a ruptured cyst is said to resemble a water lily and is pathognomonic. Cysts can be treated with careful surgical excision and pharmacotherapy.

Early schistosomal disease, Katayama fever, can present with fever, cough, eosinophilia, and diffuse pulmonary nodules as the schistosomula pass through the lungs. In long-standing disease, ova shed from worm pairs can lodge in the vasculature of the lungs, causing pseudotubercles, granulomatous lung disease, pulmonary hypertension, and cor pulmonale. In patients who are started on corticosteroids or immunosuppressive therapy who have long-standing, latent, and asymptomatic S. stercoralis infections, the helminth disseminates widely. Fatal, massive pulmonary infections with radiographic whiteouts and unsupportable respiratory failure have been reported in patients who have received organ transplants; this clinical disaster occurs more commonly in patients who originally came from developing countries and were never evaluated for Strongyloides infection before transplant.[57,58] Strongyloides infection can be misdiagnosed as bronchospasm and asthma, prompting the clinician to prescribe steroids, which precipitate dissemination.[59]

CARDIOVASCULAR SYMPTOMS

Chagas' Disease

Principles of Disease

T. cruzi infection causes acute and chronic myocarditis. T. cruzi is endemic in South and Central America and causes Chagas' disease. The vector is the reduviid, or "kissing bug," which inhabits the walls and roofs of thatched dwellings built adjacent to forest. Previously a disease of rural populations, urban transmigration has expanded the epidemiologic scope of Chagas' disease. The disease is not seen commonly in travelers. The reduviid's bite is no longer the only source of Chagas' disease; transfusion with blood containing live trypanosomes from infected hosts is a growing source of infection.[60,61] The reduviid bites the patient, often in the periorbital region, and excretes feces containing the trypomastigote of T. cruzi. The trypanosome enters the inflamed bite wound or other mucosal or conjunctival surfaces, causing local swelling, called a chagoma. Romaña's sign, painless unilateral periorbital edema, is pathognomonic but rarely seen. The trypomastigote migrates to trophic tissues, including smooth muscle, cardiac muscle, and autonomic ganglia in the heart, esophagus, and colon, causing local inflammation and tissue destruction.

Clinical Features

Acute infection is heralded by fever, facial and dependent extremity edema, hepatosplenomegaly, lymphadenopathy, malaise, lymphocytosis on peripheral blood smear, and elevated liver transaminases. At this stage, fatal left ventricular dysfunction and dysrhythmias are uncommon. Early illness lasts 1 to 2 months and resolves spontaneously, resulting in a latency known as the indeterminate phase, which can persist throughout the patient's lifetime. Approximately 25% of patients progress to chronic Chagas' disease, principally cardiopathy and gastrointestinal disease. Amastigotes invade cardiac muscle and the cardiac conduction system. There is chronic inflammation, mononuclear cell infiltration, and fibrosis. Patients may develop atrial bradydysrhythmias, fibrillation, right and left bundle branch blocks, complete heart block, and ventricular dysrhythmias including ventricular fibrillation. There is right and left ventricular dysfunction with dilated cardiomyopathy; cardiac muscle is replaced by fibrosis and scarring. Mural thrombi are common; thromboembolic disease manifesting as pulmonary embolism, stroke, or peripheral arterial embolism can be the first indication of long-standing asymptomatic infection. Congestive heart failure is rapidly progressive and fatal within months unless aggressively treated with pharmacologic intervention and transplantation.[62]

Diagnostic Strategies

Acute Chagas' disease can be diagnosed by the presence of motile trypomastigotes in anticoagulated blood specimens. The organism also can be cultured in special liquid media. Chronic Chagas' disease can be diagnosed using several serologic tests, including complement fixation, enzyme-linked immunosorbent assay (ELISA), or indirect immunofluorescence. The assays are nonspecific, cross-reacting with malaria, syphilis, leishmaniasis, and some collagen vascular diseases; consequently, at least two immunologic assays must be positive to confirm the presence of T. cruzi. Polymerase chain reaction technology is improving and soon will provide the gold standard for diagnosis.[63]

Management

Nifurtimox and benznidazole are used for treating *T. cruzi*. Cure rates rarely exceed 50%. The duration of treatment with nifurtimox is prolonged, and the drug causes many severe side effects. Its production has been discontinued; however, it is the only antitrypanosomal medication available in the United States today (it can be obtained from the Centers for Disease Control and Prevention). Benznidazole has fewer side effects. It is now recommended for indeterminate phase treatment. Late complications of chronic diseases are modulated by autoimmune activity and do not respond to antiparasitic pharmacotherapy. Nifurtimox and benznidazole have been associated with lymphoma in an animal model.[64,65] Chronic Chagas' disease of the heart, esophagus, or colon is treated symptomatically. Patients receiving immunosuppressive therapy to prevent rejection after cardiac transplant have shown recurrent disease in the transplanted myocardium.

Other Causes

Aberrant migration of *Ascaris* to the myocardium is well described, causing myocarditis and pericardial effusions. *E. histolytica* abscesses of the liver also may cause pericardial effusions if they erode through the diaphragm.

GASTROINTESTINAL SYMPTOMS

Diarrhea

Diarrhea is one of the most common symptoms for which travelers seek medical attention. Gorbach[66] wrote, "Travel expands the mind and loosens the bowels." Diarrhea is also the leading cause of death in children younger than 5 years old in developing countries and a major source of morbidity for older children and adults (Figure 131-8). Most diarrheal disease is viral or bacterial; however, some noteworthy parasites cause diarrhea.

Cryptosporidium parvum and *Cyclospora cayetanensis* are food-borne and water-borne coccidians that cause watery diarrhea. Both are particularly significant causes of morbidity in malnourished children and patients with AIDS. In these populations in the developing world, the prevalence may approach 50%.[67,68] Cryptosporidial oocysts can be seen in stool, and ELISA and immunofluorescent assays of stool are available. Paromomycin decreases stooling in patients with AIDS, who often have prolonged illness. Treatment is symptomatic for immunocompetent hosts.[69] *Cyclospora* oocysts can be detected in stool samples using a Ziehl-Neelsen stain. Trimethoprim-sulfamethoxazole treats the infection.[70]

E. histolytica causes an invasive or inflammatory diarrhea. Patients complain of fever, tenesmus, abdominal pain, and watery stool containing blood and mucus. Untreated disease can progress to widespread colitis and perforation of the bowel wall with peritonitis and death.[71] Stool examination reveals mobile trophozoites containing ingested RBCs. Immune assays of stool now can differentiate between *E. histolytica* and nonpathogenic ameba species. Metronidazole is the drug of choice for amebiasis. *Balantidium coli* is the other protozoan that can cause invasive diarrhea. It has trophism for the terminal ileum, sometimes appearing to be appendicitis. Tetracycline and metronidazole are active against *B. coli*.[72]

Giardia lamblia can cause persistent diarrhea, abdominal bloating, cramps, flatulence, and weight loss. The organism is ingested and reproduces exponentially in the small bowel. In severe infection, the entire jejunum becomes covered with organisms, and the patient has malabsorption with steatorrhea. The organisms are rarely seen in fresh stool preparations because they quickly break down and become indiscernible. As a result, direct immunofluorescence and ELISA of stool are used to confirm the diagnosis. *Giardia* has many animal reservoirs, including the beaver. Campers who drink unfiltered, pure mountain spring water in the United States commonly contract *Giardia*. Metronidazole and tinidazole treat the disease.

S. stercoralis, Capillaria philippinensis, T. trichiura, and *Schistosoma* all have been associated with diarrhea. Hyperinfection or dissemination of *Strongyloides* can cause persistent diarrhea, weight loss, and abdominal pain. *Trichuris* causes diarrhea when the parasite load in the intestine is high. Schistosomiasis can cause a chronic granulomatous colitis, which may resemble inflammatory bowel disease or an acute, bloody, febrile colitis associated with Katayama fever in the immunologically naive patient.

In chronic schistosomiasis, worm pairs in patients' mesenteric and portal venous systems lay eggs that become ensnared in the liver, causing intense local inflammation and scarring and the classic "pipe-stem" cirrhosis with periportal fibrosis. These patients develop portal hypertension, ascites, and esophageal varices (Figures 131-9 and 131-10). Upper gastrointestinal bleeding is not as common as in patients with alcoholic cirrhosis; however, the number of patients infected with schistosomiasis in endemic regions is great, and variceal bleeding is an important cause of gastrointestinal hemorrhage.[73,74]

Figure 131-8. Fecal-oral transmission of diarrheal agents occurring in an underdeveloped country.

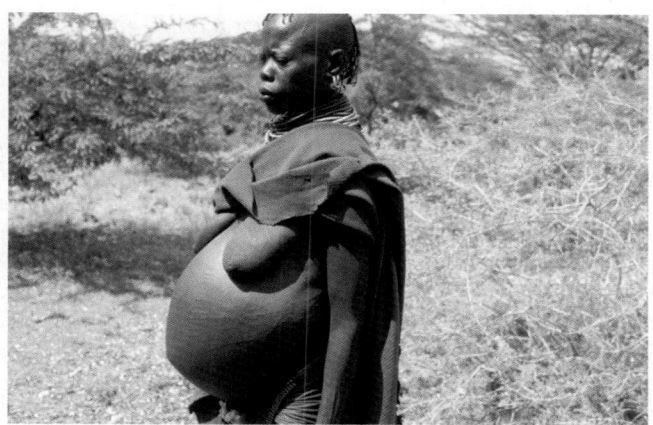

Figure 131-9. Pipe-stem cirrhosis with extensive ascites in a patient with chronic schistosomiasis.

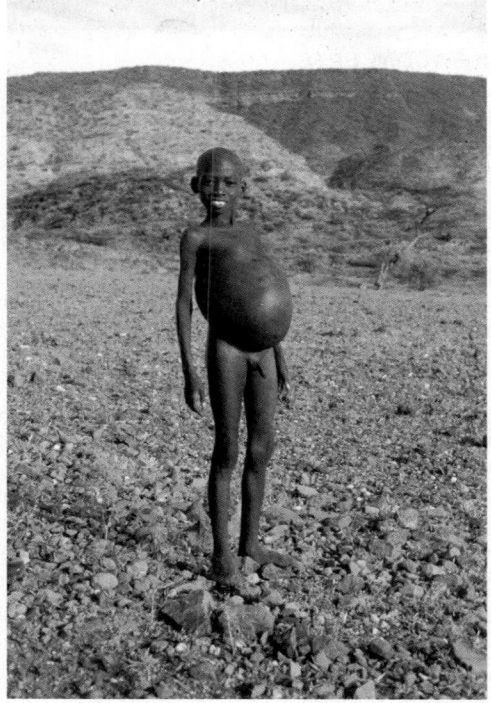

Figure 131-10. Extensive ascites in a child, which may be schistosomiasis or kala-azar (leishmaniasis).

Abdominal Pain

In an extensive review of several cases of appendicitis, parasitic infection was found to be the cause in 3%. Pathologic examination revealed enterobiasis, amebiasis, ascariasis, trichuriasis, and taeniasis.[75]

A. lumbricoides can cause significant persistent or recurrent abdominal pain in adults and partial intestinal obstruction in children with significant worm loads. Antihelminthics and conservative, supportive therapy usually eliminate the problem, avoiding surgical intervention.[76,77] The diagnosis of ascariasis is made by identifying eggs in the stool. Patients with large worm loads may excrete adult worms, especially after therapy is started. Severe intestinal amebiasis can be complicated by colonic perforation and peritonitis.

Angiostrongylus costaricensis, a nematode known as the rat lung worm, is common in Central America. Infected children may appear clinically to have Meckel's diverticula or acute appendicitis. They have nausea, vomiting, fever, abdominal pain localized to the right lower quadrant, and a tender mass. Surgical exploration may uncover abscesses, obstruction, or intestinal infarction.[78]

Anisakiasis is characterized by severe abdominal pain after eating raw fish (sushi and sashimi primarily). *Anisakis marina,* a nematode that burrows into the intestine, is responsible.[79]

The liver fluke, *F. hepatica,* causes a syndrome that mimics viral hepatitis: right upper quadrant pain, fever, nausea and vomiting, jaundice, a tender enlarged liver, and elevated transaminases. Patients also have eosinophilia and urticaria. Imaging studies, including CT, show the tracks of burrowing flukes. Serologic testing establishes the diagnosis because the patient's stool may not contain eggs for several months after ingestion.[80] As noted in the discussion of gastrointestinal bleeding, the eggs of schistosomes become trapped in the portal venules and trigger an inflammatory response, leading to granulomatous liver disease, fibrosis, and cirrhosis. Hepatic granulomas also are seen in disseminated strongyloidiasis and biliary ascariasis.

E. histolytica can cause hepatic abscesses. Patients with abscesses typically do not have amebic dysentery and do not shed *Entamoeba* in their stool. Serology is almost always positive in patients with abscesses. Patients have fever, weight loss, anorexia, and right-sided abdominal pain, but no jaundice. Treatment is with metronidazole or tinidazole and a luminal amebicide, such as iodoquinol.[81] *E. granulosus* causes hydatid cysts of the liver that, on CT, are seen as septations and so-called daughter cysts. Pharmacotherapy with albendazole and careful excision remain the treatments of choice. Leaking cyst material causes a severe anaphylactoid reaction in the host.

Jaundice may result from hemolysis secondary to direct infection of RBCs with *Plasmodium* or *Babesia* or from biliary obstruction. *Ascaris* can cause biliary colic, pyogenic cholangitis, pancreatitis, or liver abscess. Dead worms can be the nidus for gallstone formation. Biliary imaging and endoscopic retrograde cholangiopancreatography show worms in the biliary tree. Mechanical removal by endoscopy and anthelminthic therapy is curative.[82] *Clonorchis sinensis* and *F. hepatica* are trophic for the biliary tree. They can be present without symptoms for years before eventually precipitating cholecystitis, cholangitis, or cholangiocarcinoma.[83]

Pruritus Ani

Enterobius vermicularis, or pinworm, causes pruritus ani, a syndrome of intense perianal itch seen primarily in children. Autoinfection is common because children (and adults) scratch the pruritic anal area, then bite their nails or put their fingers in their mouth. The worm has a worldwide distribution. Diagnosis is clinical and is confirmed by finding the small adult worms wriggling about on the anal verge. Eggs are rarely seen in the stool but can be visualized using the tape test: transparent tape touched to the perianal region collects eggs that can be seen with light microscopy. Mebendazole is the treatment of choice.

PARASITIC CO-INFECTIONS IN PATIENTS WITH HIV AND AIDS

Perspective

HIV infection and AIDS are prevalent in the tropics of developing countries. Heterosexual and perinatal transmission are common; young children and young adults of both sexes are primarily infected. The clinician may encounter patients who are co-infected with HIV and any other infectious agent, including all of the parasites discussed in this chapter. HIV co-infection may worsen the symptoms and outcome, alter the presentation, increase the virulence, or assist the infective process.

AIDS causes abnormalities in almost every aspect of a host's immune response to infection; cell-mediated immunity (which is important in combating parasitic infection) is most affected.[84] The diagnosis and response to therapy of many parasitic infections are monitored serologically. HIV infection interferes with this response, rendering many of these tests unreliable. Therapies that are extremely effective in the normal host may be ineffective in a patient with HIV infection. Pharmacologic agents may have to be given for long periods or for the patient's entire life.

Specific Parasitic Infections

Malaria is not an opportunistic infection in patients with AIDS; however, many patients, especially children, with recurrent malaria and anemia from hemolysis, have required transfusions from blood supplies not screened for HIV and have become infected.[85] Treating febrile patients for malaria in areas where it is endemic is a common practice. Patients with AIDS have more severe allergic reactions to drugs, however, especially sulfonamides. In patients with AIDS, fever alone is not predictive of malaria; diagnosis should precede therapy. Patients with HIV infection are at greater risk for severe clinical manifestations of babesiosis.[86]

Visceral leishmaniasis is more commonly disseminated and fatal in patients with AIDS. Patients can have reactivation of latent leishmanial infections, and a prolonged febrile illness in an HIV-positive patient with a lifetime history of travel in areas of the world where leishmaniasis is endemic should prompt consideration for this co-infection.[87] Chagas' disease in the indeterminate phase can be reactivated in patients infected with HIV. These patients frequently have CNS involvement with meningoencephalitis and severe myocarditis.[88] Single-drug therapy may be insufficient; benznidazole penetration into the CSF may not be adequate. T. gondii is well recognized throughout the world as a common opportunistic infection of patients with AIDS, with a particular trophism for the CNS.

The coccidial organisms *Isospora belli, C. parvum,* and *C. cayetanensis* all have been associated with prolonged diarrhea in patients with AIDS. These organisms are difficult to treat and almost impossible to eradicate in AIDS patients. The diarrhea is extremely debilitating and can be as profuse as that seen in cholera. *E. histolytica* has a high prevalence in male homosexuals who practice unprotected anal intercourse; however, invasive amebiasis is not an opportunistic infection associated with HIV infection. Schistosomiasis enhances the pathogenesis of HIV and is more difficult to treat and eradicate in patients who are HIV-positive.[89] *S. stercoralis* is more likely to manifest as hyperinfection and disseminated disease in patients who are HIV-positive.[90] In patients who are at risk for HIV and parasitic illness, the clinician always must consider co-infection in the differential diagnosis.

KEY CONCEPTS

- Parasitic diseases may present with almost any symptom or constellation of symptoms. As a result, a travel history should be obtained in all patients with clinically significant symptoms of unclear etiology. The combination of presenting symptoms and a history of recent travel to specific geographic regions can lead to early diagnosis of most parasitic infections.
- Parasitic co-infections are particularly common in patients with HIV and AIDS.
- Acute malaria should be suspected in patients with irregular high fevers associated with headache, abdominal pain, or respiratory symptoms. Patients who are clinically ill or who are suspected of having falciparum malaria should be hospitalized for evaluation and treatment.
- Cysticercosis should be considered in the differential diagnosis of new-onset seizures.
- *Giardia* should be suspected in patients with diarrhea who recently have been camping or drinking unfiltered mountain spring water.

REFERENCES

1. Bell DR: *Tropical Medicine,* 4th ed. Oxford, Blackwell Science, 1995.
2. Guerrant RL, et al: *Tropical Infectious Diseases.* Philadelphia, Churchill Livingstone, 1999.
3. Danis M, Gentilini M: Malaria, a worldwide scourge. *Rev Prat* 48:254, 1998.
4. Isaacson M: Airport malaria: A review. *Bull World Health Organ* 67:737, 1989.
5. Van den Ende J, et al: A cluster of airport malaria in Belgium in 1995. *Acta Clin Belg* 53:259, 1998.
6. Iftikhar SA, Roistacher K: Indigenous *Plasmodium falciparum* in Queens, NY. *Arch Intern Med* 155:1099, 1995.
7. Cahill J, et al: Malaria in Rhode Island. *J Travel Med* 7:112, 2000.
8. Molyneux ME, Fox R: Diagnosis and treatment of malaria in Britain. *BMJ* 306:1175, 1993.
9. Gilles HM, Warrell DA: *Bruce-Chwatt's Essential Malariology,* 3rd ed. London, Edward Arnold, 1993.
10. Tran TH, et al: A controlled trial of artemether or quinine in Vietnamese adults with severe falciparum malaria. *N Engl J Med* 335:76, 1996.

11. Mintz ED, et al: Transfusion-transmitted babesiosis: A case report from a new endemic area. *Transfusion* 31:365, 1991.

12. Ruebush TK, et al: Human babesiosis on Nantucket Island: Evidence for self-limited and sub-clinical infections. *N Engl J Med* 297:825, 1977.

13. Golightly LM, et al: Fever and headache in a splenectomized woman. *Rev Infect Dis* 11:629, 1989.

14. Benezra D, et al: Babesiosis and infection with human immunodeficiency virus (HIV). *Ann Intern Med* 107:944, 1987.

15. Piesman J, et al: Concurrent *Borrelia burgdorferi* and *Babesia microti* infection in nymphal *Ixodes dammini*. *J Clin Microbiol* 24:446, 1986.

16. Doherty JF, et al: Katayama fever: An acute manifestation of schistosomiasis. *BMJ* 313:1071, 1996.

17. Arjona R, et al: Fascioliasis in developed countries: A review of classic and aberrant forms of the disease. *Medicine* (Baltimore) 74:13, 1995.

18. Kirchof LV: American trypanosomiasis in Central American immigrants. *Am J Med* 82:915, 1987.

19. Evans T, et al: American visceral leishmaniasis. *West J Med* 142:777, 1985.

20. Maltz G, Knauer CM: Amebic liver abscess: A 15 year experience. *Am J Gastroenterol* 86:704, 1991.

21. Van Hensbroek MB, et al: A trial of artemether or quinine in children with cerebral malaria. *N Engl J Med* 335:69, 1996.

22. Nagatake T, et al: Pathology of falciparum malaria in Vietnam. *Am J Trop Med Hyg* 47:259, 1992.

23. McCormick GF, et al: Cysticercosis cerebri. *Arch Neurol* 39:534, 1982.

24. Garcia HH, et al: Diagnosis of cysticercosis in endemic regions. *Lancet* 338:549, 1991.

25. Vaquez V, Sotelo J: The course of seizures after treatment for cerebral cysticercosis. *N Engl J Med* 327:696, 1992.

26. Morris DL, Richards KS: *Hydatid Disease, Current Medical and Surgical Management.* Oxford, Butterworth-Heinemann, 1992.

27. *Epidemiology and Control of African Trypanosomiasis.* 1986 Technical Report Series 793, Geneva, World Health Organization, 1986.

28. Ekwanzala M, et al: In the heart of darkness: Sleeping sickness in Zaire. *Lancet* 348:1427, 1996.

29. Fairlamb AH: Novel approaches to the chemotherapy of trypanosomiasis. *Trans R Soc Trop Med Hyg* 84:613, 1990.

30. Gay T, et al: Fatal CNS trichinosis. *JAMA* 247:1024, 1982.

31. Evans RW, Pattern BM: Trichinosis associated with superior sagittal sinus thrombosis. *Ann Neurol* 11:216, 1982.

32. Seidel JS, et al: Successful treatment of primary amebic meningoencephalitis. *N Engl J Med* 306:346, 1982.

33. Grove DI: *Strongyloidiasis: A Major Roundworm Infection.* London, Taylor & Francis, 1989.

34. Kirchhoff LV, Nash TE: A case of *Schistosomiasis japonica*: Resolution of CAT-scan detected cerebral abnormalities without specific therapy. *Am J Trop Med Hyg* 33:1155, 1984.

35. Burgmann H, et al: Serum levels of erythropoietin in acute *Plasmodium falciparum* malaria. *Am J Trop Med Hyg* 54:280, 1996.

36. Newton C, et al: Severe anemia in children living in a malaria endemic area of Kenya. *Trop Med Int Health* 2:165, 1997.

37. WHO Expert Committee on Filariasis Fifth Report: *Lymphatic Filariasis: The Disease and Its Control.* Technical Report Series 821. Geneva, World Health Organization, 1992.

38. Ottesen EA, et al: A controlled trial of ivermectin and diethylcarbamazine in lymphatic filariasis. *N Engl J Med* 322:1113, 1990.

39. Carvalho EM, et al: Immunologic markers of clinical evolution in children recently infected with *Leishmania donovani chagasi*. *J Infect Dis* 165:535, 1992.

40. Melby PC, et al: Cutaneous leishmaniasis: Review of 59 cases seen at the National Institutes of Health. *Clin Infect Dis* 15:924, 1992.

41. Gustafson TL, et al: Human cutaneous leishmaniasis acquired in Texas. *Am J Trop Med Hyg* 34:58, 1985.

42. Caumes E, et al: A randomized trial of ivermectin versus albendazole for the treatment of cutaneous larva migrans. *Am J Trop Med Hyg* 49:641, 1993.

43. Abiose A, et al: Reduction in incidence of optic nerve disease with annual ivermectin to control onchocerciasis. *Lancet* 341:130, 1993.

44. Natman TB, et al: Diethylcarbamazine prophylaxis for human loiasis: Results of a double-blind study. *N Engl J Med* 319:752, 1988.

45. Martin PY, et al: Tolerance and efficacy of single high dose ivermectin for the treatment of loiasis. *Am J Trop Med Hyg* 48:186, 1993.

46. Johnson S, et al: Acute tropical infections and the lung. *Thorax* 49:7214, 1994.

47. Charoenpan P, et al: Pulmonary edema in severe falciparum malaria: Hemodynamic study and clinicophysiologic correlation. *Chest* 97:1190, 1990.

48. Kubitschek KR, et al: Amebiasis presenting as pleuropulmonary disease. *West J Med* 142:203, 1985.

49. Malin AS: *Pneumocystis carinii* pneumonia in Africa. *Lancet* 347:127, 1996.

50. Löffler W: Transient lung infiltrations with blood eosinophilia. *Int Arch Allergy Immunol* 8:54, 1956.

51. Allen JN, Davis WB: Eosinophilic lung diseases. *Am J Respir Crit Care Med* 150:1423, 1994.

52. Ottesen EA, Nutman TB: Tropical pulmonary eosinophilia. *Annu Rev Med* 43:417, 1992.

53. Enzenauer RJ, et al: Tropical pulmonary eosinophilia. *South Med J* 93:69, 1990.

54. Im JG, et al: Pleuropulmonary paragonimiasis: Radiologic findings in 71 patients. *AJR Am J Roentgenol* 159:39, 1992.

55. Yee B, et al: Pulmonary paragonimiasis in Southeast Asians living in the central San Joaquin Valley. *West J Med* 156:423, 1992.

56. Jerray M, et al: Hydatid disease of the lungs: Study of 386 cases. *Am Rev Respir Dis* 146:185, 1992.

57. Morgna JS, et al: Opportunistic strongyloidiasis in renal transplant recipients. *Transplantation* 42:518, 1986.

58. Scoggin CH, Call NB: Acute respiratory failure due to disseminated strongyloidiasis in a renal transplant recipient. *Ann Intern Med* 87:456, 1977.

59. Nowokolo C, Imohiosen EAF: Strongyloidiasis of the respiratory tract presenting as asthma. *BMJ* 2:153, 1973.

60. Dunlap NE, et al: Strongyloidiasis manifested as asthma. *South Med J* 77:77, 1984.

61. Schumis GA: *Trypanosoma cruzi,* the etiologic agent of Chagas' disease: Status in the blood supply in endemic and non-endemic countries. *Transfusion* 31:547, 1991.

62. Amorim DS: Chagas' disease. *Prog Cardiol* 8:235, 1979.

63. Kirchoff LV, et al: Comparison of PCR and microscopic methods for detecting *Trypanosoma cruzi*. *J Clin Microbiol* 34:1171, 1996.

64. Teixera ARI, et al: Malignant, non-Hodgkin's lymphoma in *Trypanosoma cruzi* infected rabbits treated with nifurtimox. *J Comp Pathol* 103:37, 1990.

65. Teixera ARI, et al: Chagas' disease: Lymphoma growth in rabbits treated with benznidazole. *Am J Trop Med Hyg* 43:146, 1990.

66. Gorbach SL: Traveler's diarrhea. *N Engl J Med* 307:881, 1982.

67. Colebunders R, et al: Persistent diarrhea strongly associates with HIV infection in Kinshasha, Zaire. *Am J Gastroenterol* 82:859, 1987.

68. Molbak K, et al: Cryptosporidiosis in infancy and childhood mortality in Guinea-Bissau, West Africa. *BMJ* 307:417, 1993.

69. White AC, et al: Paromomycin for cryptosporidiosis in AIDS: A prospective, double-blind trial. *J Infect Dis* 170:419, 1994.
70. Hoge CW, et al: Placebo-controlled trial of clotrimazole for *Cyclospora* infections among travelers and foreign residents in Nepal. *Lancet* 345:691, 1995.
71. Wanke C, et al: Epidemiologic and clinical features of invasive amebiasis in Bangladesh: A case-control comparison with other diarrheal diseases and post-mortem findings. *Am J Trop Med Hyg* 38:335, 1998.
72. Garcia-Laverde A, de Bonilla L: Clinical trials with metronidazole in human balantidiasis. *Am J Trop Med Hyg* 24:781, 1975.
73. Strickland GT: Gastrointestinal manifestations of schistosomiasis. *Gut* 35:1334, 1994.
74. Saad AM, et al: Oesophageal varices in a region of the Sudan endemic for *Schistosoma mansoni*. *Br J Surg* 78:1252, 1991.
75. Gupta SC, et al: Pathology of tropical appendicitis. *J Clin Pathol* 42:1169, 1989.
76. Hamed AD, Akinola O: Intestinal ascariasis in the differential diagnosis of peptic ulcer disease. *Trop Geogr Med* 42:37, 1990.
77. Pinus J: Surgical complications of ascariasis. *Prog Pediatr Surg* 15:79, 1982.
78. Hulbert TV, et al: Abdominal angiostrongyliasis mimicking acute appendicitis and Meckel's diverticulum: Report of a case in the United States and review. *Clin Infect Dis* 14:836, 1992.
79. Kark AE, McAlpine JC: Anisakiasis as a cause of acute abdominal crisis. *Br J Clin Pract* 48:216, 1994.
80. Han JK, et al: Radiological findings in human fascioliasis. *Abdom Imaging* 18:261, 1993.
81. Barnes PF, et al: A comparison of amebic and pyogenic abscess of the liver. *Medicine* 66:472, 1987.
82. Rocha MS, et al: CT identification of *Ascaris* in the biliary tract. *Abdom Imaging* 20:317, 1995.
83. Harinasuta T, et al: Trematode infections: Opisthorchiasis, clonorchiasis, fascioliasis, and paragonimiasis. *Infect Dis Clin North Am* 7:699, 1993.
84. Morrow RH, et al: Interactions of HIV infection with endemic tropical diseases. *AIDS* 3:S79, 1989.
85. Greenburg AE, et al: The association between malaria, blood transfusions, and HIV seropositivity in a pediatric population in Kinshasa, Zaire. *JAMA* 259:545, 1988.
86. Falagas ME, Klempner MS: Babesiosis in patients with AIDS: A chronic infection presenting as fever of unknown origin. *Clin Infect Dis* 22:809, 1996.
87. Laguna F, et al: Gastrointestinal leishmaniasis in human immunodeficiency virus-infected patients: Report of five cases and review. *Clin Infect Dis* 19:48, 1994.
88. Rocha A, et al: Pathology of patients with Chagas' disease and AIDS. *Am J Trop Med Hyg* 50:261, 1994.
89. Karanja DMS, et al: Studies on schistosomiasis in Western Kenya: II. Efficacy of praziquantel on treatment of schistosomiasis in persons co-infected with human immunodeficiency virus-1. *Am J Trop Med Hyg* 59:307, 1998.
90. Newton RC, et al: *Strongyloides stercoralis* hyper-infection in a carrier of HTLV-1 virus with evidence of selective immunosuppression. *Am J Med* 92:202, 1992.

CHAPTER

132 Tick-Borne Illnesses

Edward B. Bolgiano and Joseph Sexton

PERSPECTIVE

Ticks are hematophagous parasites of humans and animals, distributed worldwide. They transmit rickettsial, bacterial, spirochetal, viral, and protozoal diseases and cause disease via their own toxins (Table 132-1). As vectors of human disease, ticks rank second in importance only to mosquitoes. Patients who travel during the summer months may return from endemic areas with tick-borne disease. In addition, recent reports of infection acquired within urban areas emphasize the need to consider tick-borne illness even in the absence of a history of travel to high-risk areas.[1] Several of the causative organisms of tick-borne diseases are now considered significant threats during biologic warfare. For this reason, research involving ticks and their diseases has become increasingly important.

Reports on ticks, their feeding habits, and their possible relation to disease can be found from early history.[2] Pliny (AD 77), in *Historia naturalis,* referred to "an animal living on blood with its head always fixed and swelling, being one of the animals which has no exit [anus] for its food, it bursts with over repletion and dies from actual nourishment." Tick-borne illness was first recognized on the North American continent by Native Americans. According to legend, Shoshone men avoided the "evil spirits" that caused illness by sending only women into certain areas of the Rocky Mountain region known to be especially hazardous. The etiologic association of the tick vector with Rocky Mountain spotted fever was noted by missionaries and by early settlers, who named the affliction "tick fever." Physicians in Idaho and Montana recorded the classic clinical descriptions of the disease in 1899.

PRINCIPLES OF DISEASE

Identification of Ticks

Ticks are arthropods but not insects. They have eight legs instead of six and generally two fusing body parts—a capitulum (head) and an opisthosoma

Table 132-1. Tick-Borne Illnesses

Type	Disease	Pathogen	Arthropod Vector	Geographic Distribution
Bacterial (including spirochetal)	Lyme disease	Borreiia burgdorferi	Ixodes scapularis I. pacificus I. ricinus	Northeastern United States Upper midwestern United States Pacific coast Europe
	Tularemia	Francisella tularensis	Dermacentor variabilis Amblyomma americanum	Southern United States
	Relapsing fever	Borrelia hermsii	Ornithodoros hemsii	Western United States
Rickettsial	Rocky Mountain spotted fever	Rickettsia rickettsii	D. andersoni D. variabilis	Predominantly southeastern United States
	Eastern spotted fever*	R. conorii R. sibirica R. australis		Eastern hemisphere
	Q fever	Coxiella burnetii	D. andersoni	Worldwide
	Ehrlichiosis	Ehrlichia canis	Rhipicephalus sanguineus	Southern and eastern United States Worldwide
Parasitic (protozoal)	Babesiosis	Babesia microti	I. scapularis	Coastal New England
Viral†	Colorado tick fever	Orbivirus	D. andersoni	Mountain areas of western United States and Canada
	Tick-borne encephalitis	Flavivirus	I. marxi I. cookei	Northern United States and Canada
Miscellaneous	Tick paralysis	Neurotoxin	D. andersoni D. variabilis A. americanum	Worldwide
	Pajaroello tick bites	Salivary toxin	O. coriaceus	Southern California and Mexico

*Several species of ixodid ticks serve as vectors for Eastern spotted fevers.
†Many other viruses are transmitted to humans by ticks. In the United States only Colorado tick fever occurs with any significant frequency.

(abdomen)—instead of three. Identification of an arthropod as a tick and subsequent categorization into family and some genera are not difficult (Figures 132-1 and 132-2). Speciation requires a trained acarologist. However, tick identification has limited importance in clinical decision making. Color, which varies seasonally, and size, which varies by amount of blood ingested at the time of presentation, are unreliable for identification purposes.

Physiology

An understanding of the physiology of feeding in arthropods is more essential than species identification in assessing the risks of transmission of diseases. Blood-sucking arthropods are divided into two groups according to their method of acquiring blood. The solenophagic feeders insert their mouthparts directly into capillaries and feed on blood alone. Telmophagic feeders insert their mouthparts indiscriminately, lyse tissue, and feed on tissue and extracellular fluids until, eventually, capillary walls are broken down and a pool of blood is produced, from which they feed. Ticks and deer flies, for example, are telmophagic feeders, whereas mosquitoes are mostly solenophagic.

Argasid (soft-bodied) ticks, specifically the vector of relapsing fever, *Ornithodoros,* are short, rapid feeders with preformed distensible endocuticles. They therefore need to feed for only minutes to hours to acquire a full meal. As a result, they tend to be found in nests and burrows where their hosts visit frequently. *Ixodes* ticks (hard-bodied) include the genera *Ixodes, Dermacentor,* and *Amblyomma,* which are those

responsible for the remainder of human tick-borne diseases. These ticks need to form a new exocuticle (phase I of feeding) and thus feed slowly during the first 12 to 24 hours. Once fully formed, the new endocuticle allows rapid feeding (phase II) and significant engorgement.

In the capitulum of ticks, the sucking structure—the chelicerae—is surrounded by a sheath from which it protrudes during feeding. Sense organs on the capitulum, or podomeres, help locate a host with chemoreceptors. Hair, or setae, on the legs act as tactile and temperature receptors. A special sensory structure, Haller's organ, is located on the first set of legs and is a humidity and olfactory receptor.[3]

When a suitable location is found, adjacent cheliceral digits incise the skin, and the chelicerae and barbed hypostome are inserted. Two mechanisms prevent the tick from being removed from the skin: the barbed hypostome and a cement-like salivary secretion composed of lipoproteins and glycoproteins from the base of the hypostome. This allows *Ixodid* ticks to attach for as long as 2 weeks. Because argasids are much faster feeders, they have no cement substance.

Trauma and salivary gland products during a bite can cause local inflammation, hyperemia, edema, hemorrhage, and skin thickening. The saliva injected during feeding contains many different substances. Both hard and soft ticks produce a histolytic secretion that liquefies tissue, which is then sucked into the gut. Eventually, the secretion breaks down the walls of the dermal blood vessels and the released blood is then ingested. To prevent hemostasis, the saliva contains a thrombokinase inhibitor, apyrase, which prevents platelet

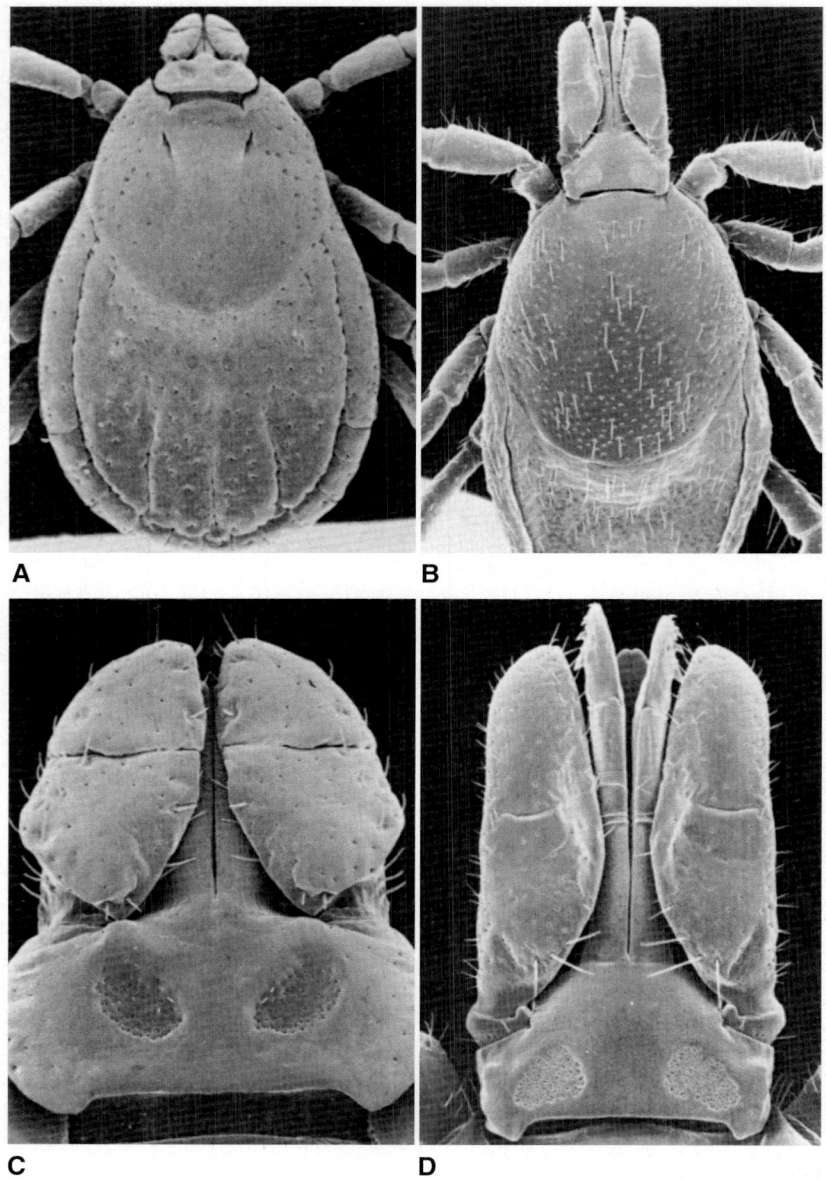

Figure 132-1. Scanning electron micrographs of two tick species. **A,** Dorsal view of adult female *Dermacentor variabilis*. **B,** Dorsal view of adult female *Ixodes scapularis*. **C** and **D,** Dorsal close-up of head. (Courtesy of Dr. J. E. Keirans, Georgia Southern University, Stateboro, Georgia.)

aggregation by depleting adenosine diphosphate, prostaglandin E_2, and prostacyclin to prevent vasoconstriction, and cytolysins. *Ixodes scapularis* has a carboxypeptidase that destroys other inflammatory mediators such as anaphylatoxins and bradykinin, as well as anticomplement C3 factor. These mediators would normally cause further inflammation, which would enhance hemostasis. All infectious agents, as well as excretory liquids from some argasids, are transmitted through this saliva. Transmission of a disease from *Ixodes* ticks is unlikely if the tick is not yet engorged with blood at the time of removal. Likewise, a tick removed within a few hours after attachment is unlikely to transmit disease. The neurotoxins responsible for tick paralysis are also found in tick saliva.

The physiologic skin changes that occur from tick feeding produce the characteristic 1 to 4 mm erythematous mark on the skin. This is common for all blood-sucking arthropods. The mark should not be confused with certain rashes associated with disease progression, for example, erythema migrans. Informing patients of this difference may be reassuring.

LYME DISEASE

Perspective

Lyme disease, the most common vector-borne disease in the United States, is a tick-borne illness caused by the spirochete *Borrelia burgdorferi*. The story of Lyme disease began in 1975, when health officials at the Connecticut State Department of Health and physicians at Yale were alerted by two skeptical mothers to an unusually large number of cases of apparent juvenile rheumatoid arthritis occurring in their small coastal community of Old Lyme, Connecticut. Investigation led to the description of a "new" entity, called Lyme arthritis.[4]

KEY TO IXODIDAE AND ARGASIDAE TICKS

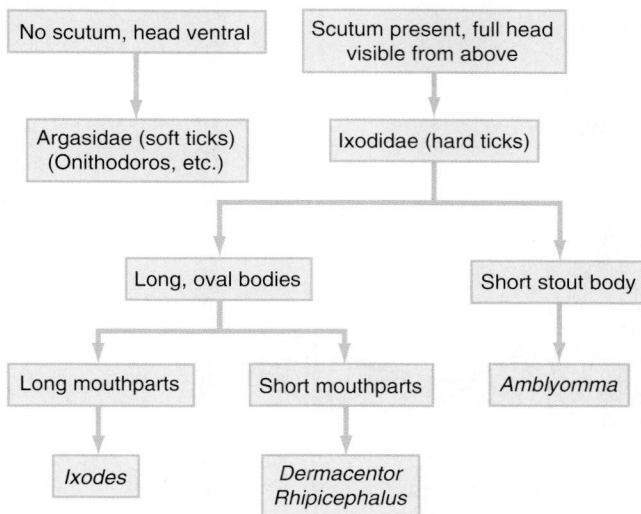

Figure 132-2. Identification scheme for genera within Ixodidae and Argasidae, the two primary disease-transmitting families of ticks.

Lyme disease occurs worldwide and has been reported on every continent except Antarctica.[5] It now accounts for more than 95% of all reported vector-borne illness in the United States.[6] The number of reported cases of Lyme disease rose from 9896 in 1992 to 17,730 in 2000 (Figure 132-3).[7] The actual overall incidence of Lyme disease is unknown, because many cases go unreported. Lyme disease occurs in people of all ages but is more common in children younger than 15 years and in adults 30 to 60 years old.[8]

Persons at greatest risk live or vacation in endemic areas. In the United States, there are three distinct endemic foci: the northeastern coastal, mid-Atlantic, and north central states. During 2000, 17,730 cases of Lyme disease were reported from 44 states and the District of Columbia. Twelve states (Connecticut, Rhode Island, New Jersey, New York, Delaware, Pennsylvania, Massachusetts, Maryland, Wisconsin, Minnesota, New Hampshire, and Vermont) accounted for 95% of cases reported in the nation.[7]

The principal tick vectors are *I. scapularis* in the Northeast and Midwest and *I. pacificus* in the West. Nymphal *Ixodes* ticks satisfy all known epidemiologic requirements for the zoonosis as it exists in nature. There is no compelling evidence for alternate arthropod vectors of infection.

The *I. scapularis* population density depends on that of its preferred hosts; the white-footed field mouse, *Peromyscus leucopus,* for the larval and nymphal forms and the white-tailed deer, *Odocoileus virginianus,* for the adult form. The white-footed mouse readily becomes infected after being bitten by infected ticks and remains highly infectious for periods of time that approach their life span in nature, thus providing an important reservoir for *B. burgdorferi.*[9] Adult *I. scapularis* ticks feed primarily on deer, which are key hosts in the tick life cycle and in whose fur the adult tick can survive the winter. The relatively recent repopulation

of several areas in the United States by white-tailed deer preceded the recent emergence of Lyme disease in those regions.[10]

Although all stages of the tick can feed on humans, the nymph is primarily responsible for the transmission of Lyme disease. It is not surprising that more than two thirds of patients with Lyme disease do not recall a tick bite, given the small size (1-2 mm) of nymphs (Figure 132-4). The nymph feeds in the spring and summer, which correlates with a peak incidence of early Lyme disease occurring between May and August. In addition, recreational and occupational exposure is greatest during this time. Later manifestations of Lyme disease may appear throughout the year.

Principles of Disease

The spirochete *B. burgdorferi* persists and multiplies in the midgut of its tick vector, *I. scapularis.* Transmission of the spirochete to humans occurs during feeding, generally about 2 days after attachment.[11] Transmission of the spirochete probably occurs via infectious saliva or, alternatively, via periodic regurgitation of gut fluids during the feeding process.[12]

After an incubation period that lasts several days to several weeks, spirochetemia develops and *Borrelia* may migrate outward via blood or lymph to virtually any site in the body. The spirochete appears to be tropic for synovial tissue, skin, and cells of the nervous system, but the mechanism of this tropism is not yet understood. Infection by the spirochete itself accounts for early clinical manifestations. It remains unclear whether late disease manifestations require the continued presence of viable spirochetes or whether an ongoing host immune response to initial infection is sufficient to cause some late disease manifestations. Although the exact roles of infecting spirochetes, spirochetal antigens, and host immune responses are unknown, it is likely that persistent live spirochetes are responsible for most later manifestations of the disease. The variable severity of Lyme disease may in part result from genetic variations in the human immune system. Patients with chronic Lyme arthritis have an increased frequency of human leukocyte antigen specificity, in particular HLA-DR4 and, less often, HLA-DR2.

Clinical Features

Lyme disease, a multisystem disorder, can be classified into three stages: early localized, early disseminated, and late disease. Virtually any clinical feature can occur alone or recur at intervals, and some patients who have no early symptoms may have late symptoms. The disorder usually begins with a rash and associated constitutional symptoms, suggesting a "viral syndrome" (early Lyme disease). Neurologic, joint, or cardiac symptoms may appear weeks to months later (early disseminated Lyme disease), and chronic arthritic and neurologic abnormalities may occur weeks to years later (late Lyme disease). The time course of the clinical features of untreated Lyme disease is illustrated in Figure 132-5.

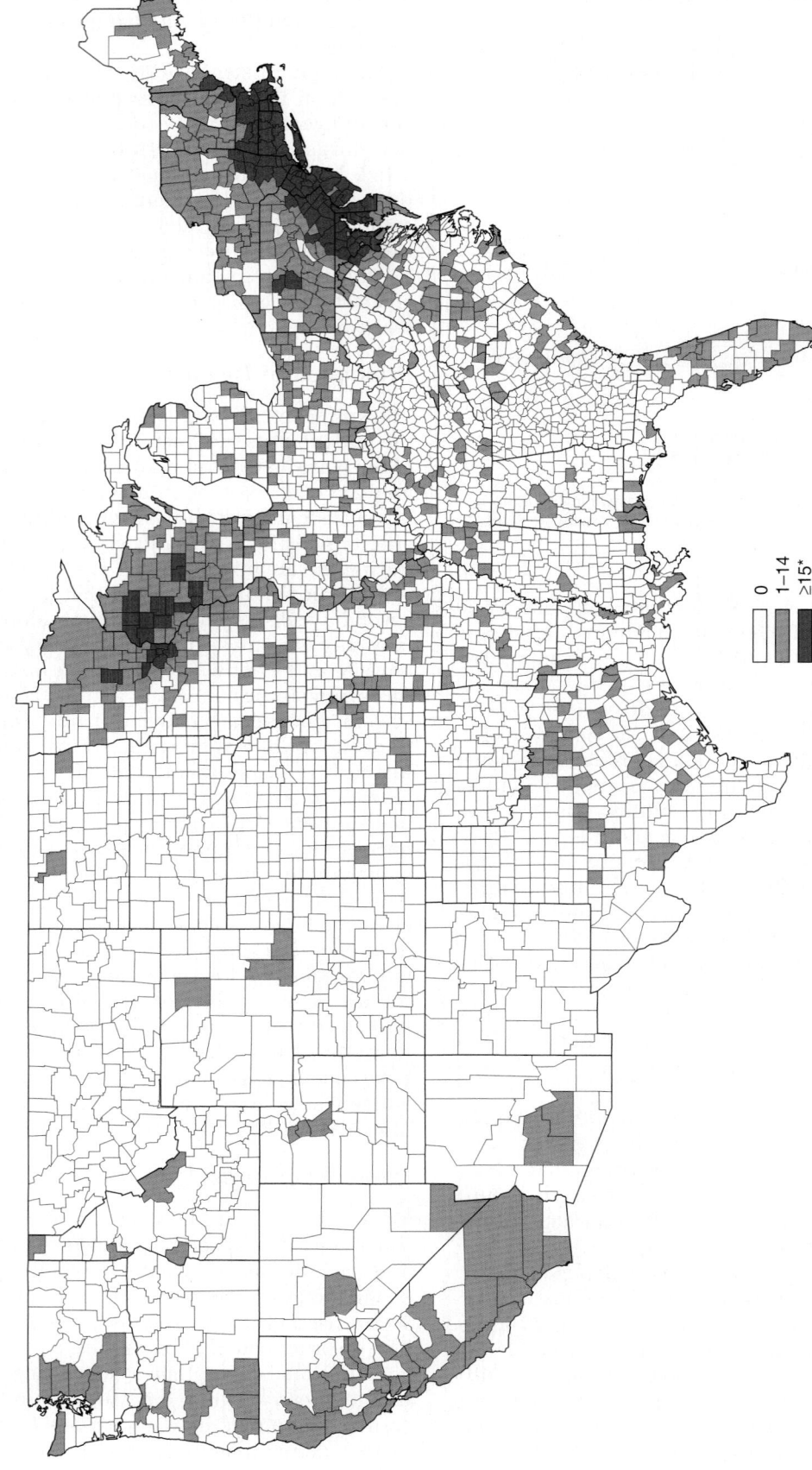

Figure 132-3. Cases of Lyme disease by county, United States, 2000. (From Centers for Disease Control and Prevention: Lyme Disease—2000. *MMWR Morb Mortal Wkly Rep* 51(2):29–31, 2002.)

0
1–14
≥15*

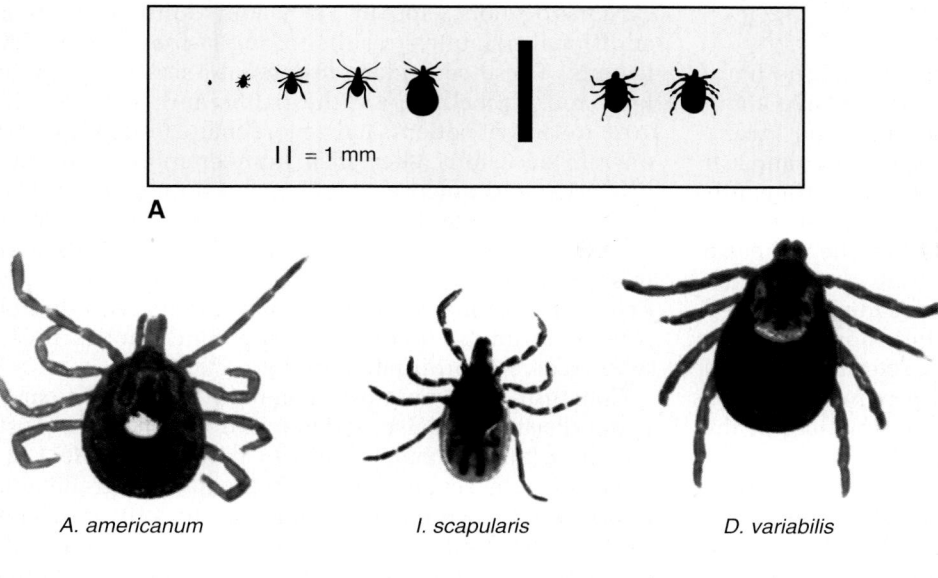

A

A. americanum   I. scapularis   D. variabilis

1 mm   Unengorged   Engorged

I. scapularis nymph

B

Figure 132-4. A, Actual size, left to right, of larva, nymph, adult male, adult female, and engorged adult female *Ixodes* sp. ticks, and adult male and female *Dermacentor* sp. ticks. **B,** Adult female *Amblyomma americanum* (lone star tick), adult female and nymphal *Ixodes scapularis* (deer tick), and adult female *Dermacentor variabilis* (dog tick). (From Hayes EB, Piesman J: How can we prevent Lyme disease? *N Engl J Med* 348:2424, 2003.)

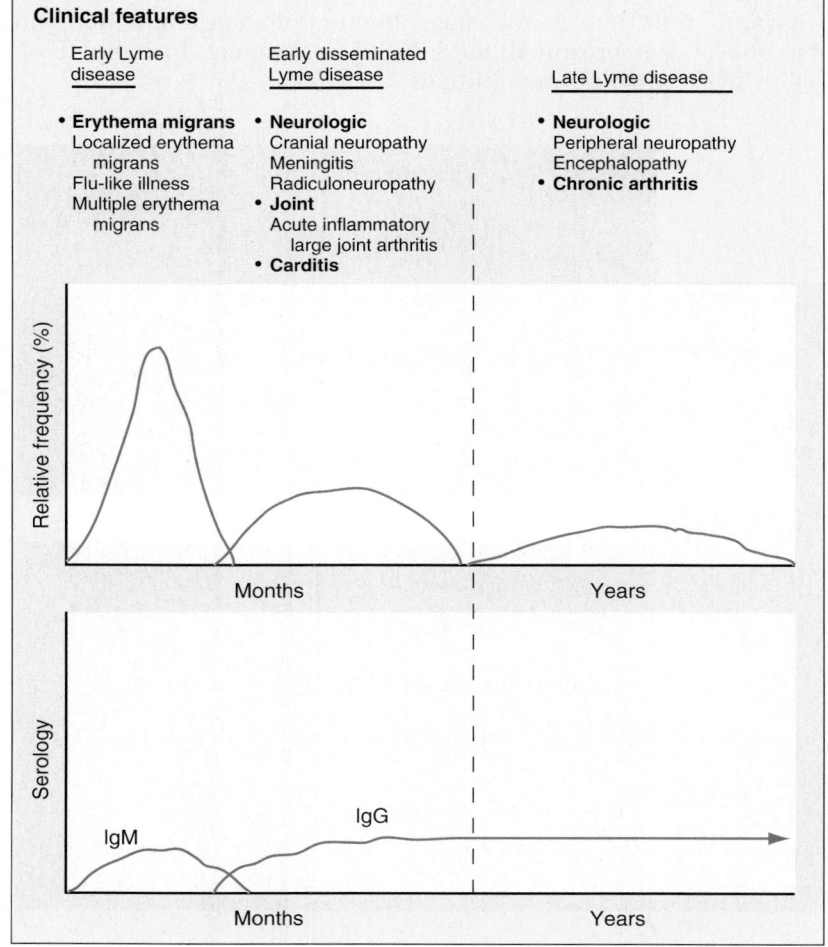

Clinical features

Early Lyme disease	Early disseminated Lyme disease	Late Lyme disease

- **Erythema migrans**
  Localized erythema
  migrans
  Flu-like illness
  Multiple erythema
  migrans

- **Neurologic**
  Cranial neuropathy
  Meningitis
  Radiculoneuropathy
- **Joint**
  Acute inflammatory
  large joint arthritis
- **Carditis**

- **Neurologic**
  Peripheral neuropathy
  Encephalopathy
- **Chronic arthritis**

Relative frequency (%)

Months   Years

Serology

IgM

IgG

Months   Years

Figure 132-5. Natural history of serologic response in untreated Lyme disease. (From Rahn DW, Evans J: *Lyme Disease.* Philadelphia, American College of Physicians, 1998.)

Early Lyme Disease

Ticks attach to human hosts at the initial point of contact (generally around ankle level) or move about until they encounter an obstruction. The groin, popliteal fossae, gluteal folds, axillary folds, and ear lobes are common sites of attachment. After transmission of *B. burgdorferi* through a tick bite, the initial site of infection is the skin at the site of the bite. After an incubation period of about 1 week (range, 1-36 days), the spirochetes cause a gradually spreading localized infection in skin and a resultant skin lesion, erythema migrans (EM). EM is the most characteristic clinical manifestation of Lyme disease, and it is recognized in 90% or more of patients. EM may go unnoticed if the entire skin surface is not examined.[13]

The rash of EM begins at the site of the tick bite with an erythematous papule or macule. The lesion expands gradually (1-2 cm/day, a rate of expansion slower than that of cellulitis). The patch of erythema may be confluent or may have bands of normal-appearing skin. Central clearing may occur but is not always present. The borders of the lesion are usually flat, but they may be raised. The lesions are generally sharply demarcated and blanch with pressure. Most EM lesions are oval or round, but triangular and elongated patches may occur. In patients presenting 1 to 7 days after the appearance of lesions, the average lesion size is approximately 8 × 10 cm (range, 2 × 3 cm to 25 × 25 cm). In some cases, the centers of some early lesions become red and indurated or vesicular and necrotic. The lesion is warm to the touch and can be described by the patient as nontender to minimally tender (Figure 132-6).[14]

Hematogenous spread of viable spirochetes (not additional tick bites) results in one or more secondary lesions. These secondary lesions are smaller, migrate less, and typically spare the palms and soles. In all, 10% to 15% of patients have more than 20 such lesions; on rare occasions, they may number more than 100. Blistering and mucosal involvement do not occur. The primary and secondary skin lesions generally fade after about 28 days (range, 1 week to 14 months) without treatment and within several days of antibiotic therapy. Recurrent lesions can develop in patients who do not receive antibiotic therapy, but apparently not in those who receive appropriate antibiotics.[14]

Constitutional symptoms commonly appear in early Lyme disease. Malaise, fatigue, and lethargy are most common (approximately 80% of patients) (Table 132-2) and may be severe. Fever is typically low grade and intermittent. Lymphadenopathy is usually regional in the distribution of EM or may be generalized; splenomegaly may occur. Musculoskeletal complaints such as arthralgias and myalgias are common and are typically short-lived and migratory, sometimes lasting only hours in one location. Frank arthritis can occur at this stage, but it is rare.

Symptoms of meningeal irritation commonly occur. Headache, the most common symptom, is usually intermittent and localized. Nausea, vomiting, and photophobia occasionally accompany the headache. Kernig's and Brudzinski's signs are usually absent, and neck stiffness usually occurs only on extreme forward flexion. At this stage, the neurologic examination and cerebrospinal fluid (CSF) assessment (usually) both yield normal findings.

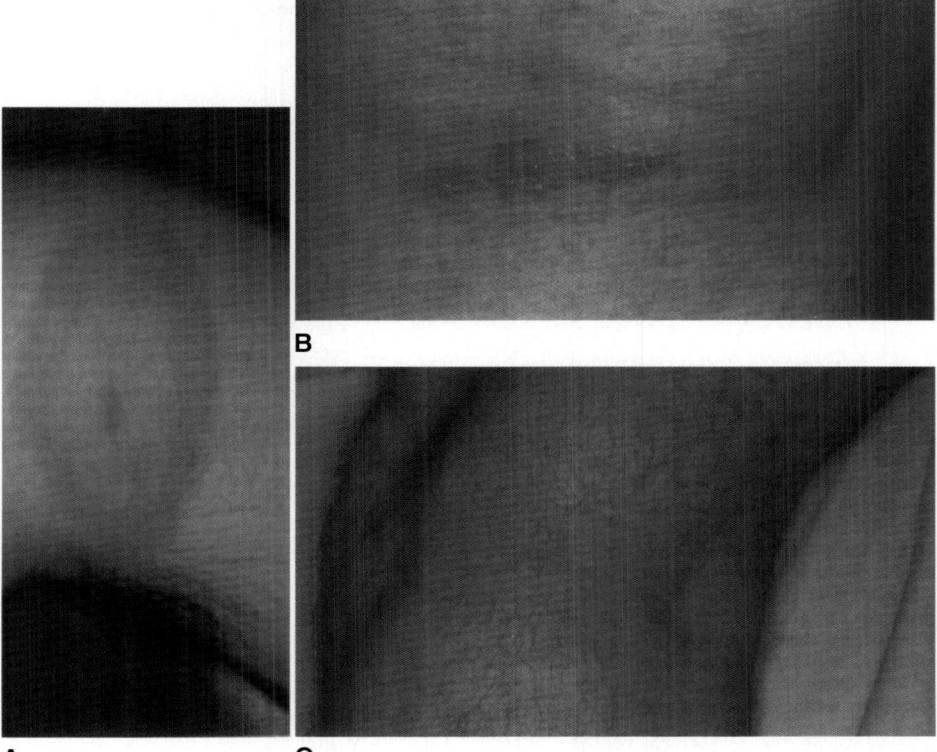

Figure 132-6. Lyme disease usually begins with a slowly expanding skin lesion, erythema migrans, which occurs at the site of the tick bite. **A,** Classic erythema migrans lesion (diameter, 9 cm) near the axilla. The lesion has partial central clearing, a bright red outer border, and a target center. **B,** A pale, homogenous erythema migrans lesion (diameter, 12 cm) on the back of a knee. **C,** An erythema migrans lesion (diameter, 10 cm) with a vesicular center on the back of a knee. In each instance, *Borrelia burgdorfi* was isolated from a skin biopsy sample of the lesion. (Courtesy Dr. Vijay K. Sikand, East Lyme, Connecticut. From Steere AC: Lyme disease. *N Engl J Med* 345:115, 2001.)

Table 132-2. Early Clinical Manifestations of Lyme Disease

	No. of Patients (N = 314)	(%)
Signs		
ECM*	314	(100)
Multiple annular lesions	150	(48)
Lymphadenopathy		
Regional	128	(41)
Generalized	63	(20)
Pain on neck flexion	52	(17)
Malar rash	41	(13)
Erythematous throat	38	(12)
Conjunctivitis	35	(11)
Symptoms		
Malaise, fatigue, lethargy	251	(80)
Headache	200	(64)
Fever and chills	185	(59)
Stiff neck	151	(48)
Arthralgias	150	(48)
Myalgias	135	(43)
Backache	81	(26)
Anorexia	73	(23)
Sore throat	53	(17)
Nausea	53	(17)
Dysesthesia	35	(11)
Vomiting	32	(10)

From Steere AC, et al: *Ann Intern Med* 99:76, 1983.
*Erythema chronicum migrans was required for inclusion in this study.

Signs and symptoms of hepatitis, including anorexia, abdominal pain, right upper quadrant tenderness, nausea, and vomiting, can occur. Mild pharyngitis may be present, but other upper respiratory symptoms such as rhinorrhea do not occur. Although the systemic symptoms of early Lyme disease are often described as *flulike*, this term can be misleading because clinically significant cough usually does not occur. Conjunctivitis develops in approximately 10% of patients.[14]

The incidence of Lyme disease without EM appears to be approximately 10%.[13] Given the variety of non-specific signs and symptoms at this stage, in the absence of the characteristic rash or a history of a tick bite, early Lyme disease can easily be confused with a viral or collagen-vascular disease. The intermittent and rapidly changing nature of the early signs and symptoms of Lyme disease may be a helpful distinguishing feature, especially in a patient from an endemic area. If untreated, early symptoms usually last for several weeks but may persist for months.

Acute Disseminated Infection

Shortly after disease onset, hematogenous spread can cause a variety of systemic symptoms and secondary sites of infection. Organ systems commonly affected are the nervous system, heart, and joints. Less commonly, eye, liver, skeletal muscle, subcutaneous tissue, and spleen are infected.

Neurologic Manifestations

A relatively symptom-free interval usually occurs between early and disseminated infection; however, neurologic signs and symptoms may be the presenting manifestations of Lyme disease or may overlap with early or late manifestations. Beginning an average of 4 weeks (range, 0-10 weeks) after the onset of EM, neurologic involvement occurs in approximately 15% of untreated patients.

The most common neurologic manifestation of Lyme disease is a fluctuating meningoencephalitis with superimposed symptoms of cranial neuropathy, peripheral neuropathy, or radiculopathy. A triad of meningitis, cranial neuropathies (usually Bell's palsy), and radiculopathy has been described, but each entity may occur alone. Headache of varying intensity is usually present; other symptoms of a mild meningoencephalitis may occur, including lethargy or irritability, sleep disturbances, poor concentration, and memory loss. Viral meningitis is often misdiagnosed. As in early disease, Kernig's and Brudzinski's signs are absent and computed tomography scan is normal. Unlike early disease, however, CSF examination findings are often abnormal, with a lymphocytic pleocytosis and elevated protein level. CSF glucose concentration is usually normal. Intrathecal *B. burgdorferi* antibody (usually IgG or IgA) is present in 80% to 90% of patients. CSF polymerase chain reaction (PCR) is positive in less than half of patients.[15]

Cranial neuropathies are common, occurring in approximately 50% of patients with Lyme meningitis; usually the seventh nerve is involved. Other cranial nerves are affected less often. Bell's palsy is bilateral in approximately one third of patients. Its duration is usually from weeks to months, and the condition generally resolves spontaneously without treatment.

Peripheral nervous system manifestations may also occur in early disseminated Lyme disease. The spinal root and plexus and the peripheral nerves may be involved in the form of thoracic sensory radiculitis, brachial plexitis, mononeuritis, and motor radiculoneuritis in the extremities. Patients often report weakness, pain, or dysesthesia. Loss of reflexes can occur. Involvement of the extremities is usually asymmetric, but cervical and thoracic dermatomes are sometimes affected. Other rare neurologic abnormalities described in association with Lyme disease include chorea, transverse myelitis, ataxia, and pseudotumor cerebri.[16] Cerebral vasculitis associated with Lyme disease has also been reported.[17]

Cardiac Manifestations

Cardiac involvement in Lyme disease is uncommon. Estimates of the incidence of carditis in untreated patients who have Lyme disease range from 4% to 10%.[18] The average time from initial illness to the development of carditis typically is 3 to 5 weeks (range, 4 days to 7 months). Direct myocardial invasion has been demonstrated with endomyocardial biopsy.[19] Electrophysiologic testing has demonstrated widespread involvement of the conduction system.[20]

The most common cardiac manifestation of Lyme disease is atrioventricular (AV) block, although conduction defects can involve any level of the conducting system. Myopericarditis, tachydysrhythmias, and ventricular impairment occur less often. In a review of 105 reported cases of Lyme carditis, 49% of cases were third-degree AV block, 16% were second-degree, and 12% were first-degree.[20] The degree of AV block demonstrated by a specific patient can fluctuate rapidly.[18]

A commonly observed feature of AV block in patients with Lyme carditis is its gradual resolution, resembling the resolution that occurs after an acute inferior wall myocardial infarction and presumably related to the resolution of inflammation. Assessment of the level of the AV block is important to determine the prognosis of a patient with Lyme carditis. In most cases, block appears to be at or above the level of the AV node; therefore, the prognosis is favorable.[21] However, infranodal AV block does occur and can be characterized by slow escape rhythms of wide QRS pattern, asystole, or fluctuating left and right bundle branch block. Other electrocardiographic findings include nonspecific ST- and T-wave abnormalities and intraventricular conduction delay.[21]

Patients with high-degree AV block are usually symptomatic. Symptoms include light-headedness, palpitations, syncope, chest pain, and dyspnea on exertion. Physical examination may reveal flow murmurs and murmurs of mild mitral regurgitation, pericardial friction rub, or evidence of congestive heart failure. Associated left ventricular dysfunction may be present and has been documented by two-dimensional echocardiography and radionuclide studies; in most reported cases, it has been mild and transient.

Arthritis

Although classically considered a sign of late Lyme disease, acute arthritis can begin during the acute disseminated stage. Weeks to months after initial illness, patients have monoarticular or oligoarticular arthritis, primarily in large joints, especially the knee. In an early study of the natural history of Lyme arthritis, about 50% of untreated patients developed one episode or multiple intermittent attacks of arthritis. Acute arthritis typically is monoarticular, with involvement of only one knee. The shoulder, elbow, temporomandibular joint, ankle, wrist, hip, and small joints of the hands and feet are involved less commonly. Episodes of arthritis typically are brief (lasting weeks to months) and separated by variable periods of remission.

Arthrocentesis generally is nondiagnostic, yielding an inflammatory synovial fluid with a mean white blood cell count of approximately 25,000 cells/mm³ (75% polymorphonuclear leukocytes). Higher white blood cell counts can occur, simulating septic arthritis.[22] The synovial glucose concentration is usually normal and protein levels are variable, ranging from 3 to 8 g/dL. Cultures of the fluid rarely identify the causative spirochete.[23] Complement level is generally greater than one third that of serum. Synovial biopsy reveals hypertrophy, vascular proliferation, and a mononuclear cell infiltrate. Findings, therefore, are similar to those in rheumatoid arthritis, except that rheumatoid factor and antinuclear antibody are negative in Lyme arthritis. Radiography may reveal nonspecific abnormalities such as juxta-articular osteoporosis, cartilage loss, cortical or marginal bone erosions, and joint effusions.

Ophthalmic Manifestations

Ocular involvement is also sometimes seen in patients with early disseminated disease, with manifestations including conjunctivitis, keratitis, choroiditis, retinal detachment, optic neuritis, and blindness.[24] These findings can also be seen in patients with late disease.

Late Lyme Disease

The chronic phase of Lyme disease is characterized by arthritic and, less commonly, neurologic symptoms. With time, there is a transition from a pattern of episodic inflammation in early disease to a more indolent persistent inflammation. The term chronic, or late, Lyme disease is used to describe continuous inflammation in an organ system for more than 1 year.[25]

A pattern of exacerbation and remission of arthritis can occur over several years, with a gradual tendency toward less frequent and less severe occurrences. The spontaneous long-term remission rate approximates 10% to 20% annually in untreated patients. However, patients commonly have episodes of periarticular involvement, arthralgias, or fatigue interspersed between attacks of frank arthritis. During the second or third year of illness, attacks of joint swelling sometimes become longer in duration, lasting months rather than weeks. About 10% of patients eventually develop chronic arthritis.[26]

Late neurologic complications include a wide variety of abnormalities of the central and peripheral nervous systems, as well as fatigue syndromes. Diagnosis may be difficult because of the large number of other neurologic conditions that Lyme disease can imitate and because late neurologic symptoms may be the first symptoms of the disease.[16] The manifestations of chronic neuroborreliosis usually appear months to years after the onset of infection.

The most common late neurologic manifestation of Lyme disease is a chronic encephalopathy that appears as a mild to moderately severe impairment of memory and learning. Hypersomnolence and mild psychiatric disturbances (depression, irritability, or paranoia) can also develop.[15]

Peripheral nervous system disease is often seen in late disease with involvement of cranial nerves, spinal roots, plexuses, and peripheral nerves. A predominantly sensory polyradiculoneuropathy that manifests as either radicular pain or distal paresthesia is common. Significant overlap occurs with early symptoms. Less commonly, a demyelinating condition resembling multiple sclerosis may appear in late disease. Symptoms are variable and, like multiple sclerosis, undergo exacerbations and remissions. Computed tomography and magnetic resonance imaging can reveal multiple white matter lesions.[16,27]

Chronic inflammation can also occur in the skin, causing a seldom-recognized late cutaneous manifestation of Lyme disease, acrodermatitis chronica atrophicans.[28] Acrodermatitis chronica atrophicans is usually found on distal extremities at the site of a tick bite. It is characterized in its initial stages by an edematous infiltration that progresses to an atrophic lesion resembling localized scleroderma in its more established form. *B. burgdorferi* has been demonstrated in the skin of patients with acrodermatitis chronica atrophicans, as well as positive results of serologic studies.

Diagnostic Strategies

The diagnosis of Lyme disease is based primarily on clinical and epidemiologic features and is difficult, especially in the early stage. A history of tick bite is elicited in only approximately one third of cases. EM is present in most patients and, in an endemic area, is considered diagnostic. However, patients sometimes have isolated late symptoms months after the initial infection and may not recall the rash. The disease should be considered in patients who live in or have visited an endemic area and who present during the summer months with nonspecific symptoms suggesting a viral illness or meningitis. In addition, the appearance of monoarticular arthritis, multiple neurologic abnormalities, or heart block in previously healthy patients should raise the suspicion of Lyme disease.

Routine laboratory studies are nonspecific and generally not helpful in diagnosing Lyme disease.[14] Abnormalities may include an elevated erythrocyte sedimentation rate, mild anemia, total white blood cell count in the normal range with a decreased absolute lymphocyte count, microhematuria, proteinuria, and increased alanine transferase level.[14,29] Culture of blood, tissue, and body fluids (including CSF and synovial fluid) for *B. burgdorferi* and direct visualization techniques are difficult and have such a low yield that they are not clinically useful.[30,31]

Serologic testing is the most practical and useful means of confirming clinical diagnoses of Lyme disease, but it is not without limitations. Results of serologic tests must be interpreted cautiously within the clinical context and should be regarded as only adjuncts in the diagnosis. Current serologic tests measure host antibody response (both immunoglobulin G [IgG] and immunoglobulin M [IgM]) to *B. burgdorferi*. Problems with the performance and interpretation of the test findings often result in diagnostic confusion. False-negative and especially false-positive results are common. The antibody response to *B. burgdorferi* develops slowly. The peak of IgM titers appears between 3 and 6 weeks after the onset of illness. Earlier in the course of the illness, IgM titers may be negative. IgM usually returns to nondiagnostic levels 4 to 6 weeks after their peak but may persist. IgG antibody may be detectable 2 months after exposure and peaks at approximately 12 months. Early antibiotic therapy may blunt or even abolish the antibody response. During the first month of illness, both IgM and IgG titers should be determined, preferably in serum samples taken during the acute and the convalescent stages. Approximately 20% to 30% of patients have a positive response in acute-stage samples, whereas even after antibiotic treatment, about 70% to 80% have a positive response in convalescent-stage samples obtained 2 to 4 weeks later. After that time, most patients have a positive IgG antibody response, and a single test is usually sufficient.

In patients with illness for longer than 1 month, a positive IgM finding alone is likely to be a false-positive result. Therefore, a positive IgM response should not be used to support the diagnosis after the first month of infection.

Testing with the enzyme-linked immunosorbent assay (ELISA) is the cornerstone of laboratory diagnosis of Lyme disease. Although ELISA alone has a sensitivity of 89% and a specificity of 72%, a positive test result in patients with a pretest probability of Lyme disease of less than 0.20 is more likely to be a false-positive than a true-positive result.[32] In patients with a positive or equivocal ELISA finding, a confirmatory Western blot test should be ordered.[33] Specimens found to be negative by ELISA are not tested further. Criteria for positive Western immunoblotting (requiring the presence of bands at particular locations) have been adopted by the Centers for Disease Control and Prevention (CDC).[33]

Immunoglobulin G antibody (and occasionally IgM antibody) can persist for several years after adequate treatment and symptom resolution. Persisting seropositivity is not diagnostic of ongoing infection. Even an IgM response cannot be interpreted as a demonstration of recent infection or reinfection unless the appropriate clinical characteristics are present. IgG antibody developed after natural infection does not always confer immunity against future infection by *B. burgdorferi*. Patients who are treated for erythema migrans may become reinfected; patients with Lyme arthritis, however, usually have high antibody titers to many spirochetal proteins and seem not to become reinfected.[34]

False-positive ELISA results are common. Serologic cross-reactivity can occur between *B. burgdorferi* and other spirochetes, most notably *Treponema pallidum*. False-positive results for Lyme disease can also occur with relapsing fever, gingivitis, leptospirosis, enteroviral and other viral illnesses, rickettsial diseases, autoimmune diseases, malaria, and subacute bacterial endocarditis.[35]

In addition, it is estimated that up to 5% of the normal population will "test positive" for Lyme disease by ELISA. Bayes' theorem states that if the pretest likelihood of the disease is low, then the positive predictive value is low: a positive test result is more likely to be a false-positive result. For this reason, screening serologic tests should not be used in the absence of objective clinical evidence of Lyme disease.[35]

Patients suspected of having acute Lyme neuroborreliosis should be evaluated with serologic tests and routine CSF examination. Paired serum and CSF samples should be obtained to evaluate for intrathecal production of antibody, although most patients with neuroborreliosis have positive results on serum serologic testing, making additional laboratory confirmation with CSF serology unnecessary.[36]

Polymerase chain reaction is superior to culture in the detection of *B. burgdorferi* in synovial fluid[37] and has a sensitivity of 73% and specificity of 99% in untreated cases of Lyme arthritis.[38]

Differential Considerations

Although Lyme disease manifests in many ways, each stage has characteristic clinical findings that are helpful in narrowing a differential diagnosis that at first may seem overwhelmingly broad. Early Lyme disease (EM and associated constitutional symptoms) is easily confused with a variety of other diseases, especially if the characteristic rash of EM is absent. A common clinical situation involves a patient presenting during the summer months with flulike symptoms, including headache, nausea, fever, chills, myalgias, arthralgias, stiff neck, and anorexia. Even in endemic areas during the summer months, most patients with such symptoms do not have Lyme disease. When headache and stiff neck are the predominant symptoms, the principal diagnostic distinction to be made is between Lyme disease and the enteroviral diseases (and other causes of aseptic meningitis). The enteroviral diseases also have their peak incidence during the summer months; however, diarrhea, commonly associated with enteroviral infection, is not a feature of Lyme disease. Abdominal pain, anorexia, and nausea suggest hepatitis; sore throat, adenopathy, and fatigue suggest mononucleosis; and myalgias and arthralgias suggest connective tissue diseases.[39]

The EM rash is characteristic, but not pathognomonic, of Lyme disease. Some patients are not aware of having had EM, and in others its appearance is atypical. Secondary lesions may be confused with the target lesions of erythema multiforme, which are generally smaller and nonexpanding. Erythema multiforme may also involve the mucous membranes, palms, and soles; EM does not. Malar rash may be present in Lyme disease and suggest systemic lupus erythematosus.[14] Erythema nodosum generally causes more painful induration than EM and has a predilection for the extensor surfaces of the legs. Erythema marginatum of acute rheumatic fever is also in the differential diagnosis of EM; the Lyme disease rash differs in having generally fewer, larger, less evanescent lesions that migrate more slowly.[40] Atypical EM appearing as an urticarial rash may suggest hepatitis B infection or serum sickness. Other cutaneous entities in the differential diagnosis of EM include cellulitis, fungal infection, fixed drug-related eruptions, plant dermatitis, and insect or spider bites. Lyme disease must be considered in a patient with any atypical rash accompanied by a "viral syndrome" or meningitis-like illness, especially during the months of peak incidence.

Acute rheumatic fever, coronary artery disease, or viral myocarditis may be suggested by the cardiac manifestations of Lyme disease. The carditis of Lyme disease, like the carditis of rheumatic fever, may follow pharyngitis and migratory polyarthritis. Erythema marginatum usually occurs with the onset of arthritis, in contrast to EM, which usually precedes the carditis. Although some patients with Lyme disease may satisfy the clinical aspects of the Jones' criteria for acute rheumatic fever, they lack evidence of a preceding streptococcal infection; in addition, valvular involvement is not a prominent feature of Lyme carditis.

The differential diagnosis of the neurologic manifestations caused by Lyme disease is extensive and includes aseptic meningitis, herpes simplex encephalitis, Bell's palsy of other causes, multiple sclerosis, Guillain-Barré syndrome, dementia, primary psychosis, cerebral vasculitis, and brain tumor. Neurologic symptoms often occur in the absence of any epidemiologic clues or preceding clinical symptoms to suggest Lyme disease, thus making the diagnosis particularly challenging.

Lyme arthritis may mimic other immune-mediated disorders. The arthritis of Lyme disease is generally asymmetric, oligoarticular, and episodic. In contrast to patients with rheumatoid arthritis, those with Lyme arthritis rarely have symmetric polyarthritis, morning stiffness, a positive test for rheumatoid factor, or subcutaneous nodules. Lyme arthritis is commonly mistaken for seronegative rheumatoid arthritis; however, Lyme arthritis is most similar to the spondyloarthropathies, particularly reactive arthritis.[41] Lyme disease and Reiter's syndrome both commonly cause huge knee effusions, but in Lyme disease, absence of the extraarticular features of Reiter's syndrome (conjunctivitis, urethritis or cervicitis, balanitis, keratosis blennorrhagica) at the time of the arthritis help distinguish it from Reiter's syndrome. In children, Lyme arthritis can mimic juvenile rheumatoid arthritis, but usually joint involvement in Lyme disease occurs in short, intermittent attacks and iridocyclitis is usually absent. Rheumatoid factor will be negative in both juvenile rheumatoid arthritis and Lyme disease. The diseases resemble one another closely enough to have been confused at the time of the initial description of Lyme disease. Other diseases in the differential diagnosis of Lyme arthritis include acute gouty arthritis, septic arthritis, gonococcal arthritis, rheumatic fever, polymyalgia rheumatica, and the temporomandibular joint syndrome.

Management

Prompt treatment of early disease can shorten the duration of symptoms and prevent progression to later stages of disease. Most of the various manifestations of Lyme disease can be treated successfully with oral antibiotic therapy, with the exception of neurologic abnormalities, which usually require intravenous therapy (Table 132-3).

Vaccination

Vaccines against infection with *B. burgdorferi* are available and should be considered for people 15 to 70 years old who live in or visit high-risk areas and are frequently exposed to ticks. Vaccination is not recommended for people who live in regions of low endemicity for the infection.[42,43] Patients who are treated for EM can become reinfected and are candidates for vaccination.[34]

The Lyme disease vaccine (LYMErix) is directed against the outer surface protein A (rOspA) of *B. burgdorferi*. LYMErix is administered by injection into the deltoid muscle, 0.5 mL (30 μg). Optimal protection is provided by three doses on a 0-, 1-, and 12-month

Table 132-3. Treatment of Lyme Disease

	Drug	Adult Dosage	Pediatric Dosage*
Early Lyme Disease	Doxycycline[†] *or*	100 mg PO bid for 21 days	
	Amoxicillin	250-500 mg PO tid for 21 days	25-50 mg/kg/day divided tid
Alternative	Cefuroxime axetil *or*	500 mg PO bid for 21 days	250 mg bid
	Erythromycin (less effective than doxycycline or amoxicillin)	250 mg PO qid for 21 days	
Neurologic Disease			
Facial nerve paralysis	For an isolated finding, oral regimens for early disease, used for at least 30 days, may suffice. For a finding associated with other neurologic manifestations, intravenous therapy is warranted (see below).		
Lyme meningitis[‡]	Ceftriaxone	2 g IV by single dose for 14-28 days	75-100 mg/kg/day IV
	Penicillin G	20 million units daily in divided doses for 14-28 days	300,000 U/kg/day IV
Alternative	Chloramphenicol	1 g IV every 6 hr for 10-21 days	
Cardiac Disease			
Mild[§]	Doxycycline[†] *or*	100 mg PO bid	
	Amoxicillin	250-500 mg PO tid	25-50 mg/kg/day divided tid
More severe	Ceftriaxone *or*	2 g IV daily by single dose for 14-21 days	75-100 mg/kg/day IV
	Penicillin G	20 million units daily in divided doses for 14-21 days	300,000 U/kg/day IV
Arthritis			
Oral	Doxycycline[†] *or*	100 mg PO bid for 30 days	
	Amoxicillin	500 mg PO tid for 30 days	50 mg/kg/day divided tid
Parenteral	Ceftriaxone *or*	2 g IV by single dose for 14-21 days	75-100 mg/kg/day IV
	Penicillin G	20 million units daily in divided doses for 14-21 days	300,000 U/kg/day IV

*Pediatric dosage should not exceed adult dosage.
[†]Tetracycline, 250 to 500 mg PO qid, may be substituted for doxycycline. Neither doxycycline nor any other tetracycline should be used for children younger than 8 years old or for pregnant or lactating women.
[‡]Regimens for radiculoneuropathy; peripheral neuropathy, and encephalitis are the same as those for meningitis.
[§]Oral regimens are reserved for mild cardiac involvement (see text).
Modified from Abramowitz M (ed): *Med Lett* 42:37, 2000; and Wormser GP, et al: *Clin Infect Dis* 31(Suppl 1):1, 2000.

schedule. Giving the third dose at 2 months provides equivalent antibody titers.[44] The third injection should be given in April to ensure sufficient antibody titers during the summer.[34] In a randomized controlled clinical trial involving more than 10,000 subjects, the vaccine efficacy was 76%.[45] Booster injections may be necessary every 1 to 3 years to maintain adequate immunity. Vaccination will cause a positive ELISA result but a negative Western blot test result.

Prophylaxis and Asymptomatic Tick Bites

Although previous expert consensus has recommended that persons bitten by deer ticks (*I. scapularis*) should not routinely receive antimicrobial chemoprophylaxis,[5] this recommendation should be modified following a recent well-designed trial, in which a single 200 mg dose of doxycycline effectively prevented Lyme disease when given within 72 hours of tick bite.[46]

The decision to administer doxycycline for a tick bite must be made on an individual basis and is warranted only in certain situations. Within 72 hours after the discovery of a deer tick that is engorged, or that was attached for more than 72 hours on an adult from an area where Lyme disease is endemic, doxycycline should be administered as a single 200 mg dose. If an attached tick is not engorged and is removed quickly (i.e., attached less than 36 hours), no other treatment is usually necessary.[47]

The efficacy of single-dose doxycycline in patients who present more than 72 hours after removing a tick is unknown. In children, dosing and efficacy of prophylactic treatment have not been evaluated. The efficacy of doxycycline in the prevention of other infections transmitted by *I. scapularis* ticks (e.g., babesiosis and human granulocytic ehrlichiosis) is unknown and should not be assumed.[46] Other antimicrobial agents that are effective for the treatment of Lyme disease (e.g., amoxicillin) and even other regimens of doxycycline (e.g., 100 mg twice daily) have unknown efficacy for Lyme disease prophylaxis.

Bites from *Dermacentor variabilis* and *Amblyomma americanum* do not require prophylactic treatment. Any patient who has been bitten by a tick should be instructed to seek medical evaluation if symptoms of tick-borne illness develop.

Early Disease

Prompt antibiotic therapy is essential in early Lyme disease because it generally shortens the duration of the rash and associated symptoms and, more important, prevents later illness in most patients. Some patients with severe early disease, however, develop later stages despite courses of antibiotics.

The drug of choice for men, nonpregnant and non-lactating women, and children older than 8 years is doxycycline, 100 mg, twice daily for 3 weeks.[5] An advantage of doxycycline is that it is also effective treatment for human granulocytic ehrlichiosis, which is transmitted by the same tick that transmits Lyme disease. Pregnant or lactating women and children younger than 8 years old should receive amoxicillin, 500 mg PO (20 to 40 mg/kg/day in three doses for children). Cefuroxime axetil is as effective as doxycycline,[48] but cephalexin is ineffective in Lyme disease.

Macrolide antibiotics are not recommended as first-line therapy for early Lyme disease.[48] They should be reserved for patients who cannot tolerate doxycycline, amoxicillin, and cefuroxime axetil. Macrolide regimens for adults include the following[5]: azithromycin, 500 mg orally daily for 7 to 10 days; erythromycin, 500 mg orally four times daily for 14 to 21 days; or clarithromycin, 500 mg orally twice daily for 14 to 21 days.

A Jarisch-Herxheimer-type reaction may occur in the first 24 hours of antibiotic treatment, consisting of fever, chills, myalgias, headache, tachycardia, increased respiratory rate, and mild leukocytosis.[49] Defervescence usually takes place within 12 to 24 hours, and the patient can be managed by bed rest and aspirin. The pathogenesis of this reaction is controversial, but it is probably caused by the killing of spirochetes with release of pyrogens. The Jarisch-Herxheimer reaction occurs more commonly with penicillin and doxycycline than with erythromycin, probably because of their superior spirocheticidal activity.

Early Disseminated Infection

Neurologic Disease
For patients with relatively mild symptoms (e.g., solitary facial nerve palsy with a normal CSF examination findings), doxycycline or amoxicillin can be used in the same dosage as for early disease, but the duration of therapy should be extended to 30 days. The use of prednisone for facial nerve palsy from Lyme disease has been suggested but is not currently recommended.

For patients with other objective neurologic abnormalities (e.g., meningitis or encephalitis, peripheral neuropathies, or cranial neuritis other than facial nerve palsy) or evidence of the spirochete in the CSF, parenteral antibiotic therapy is required. Ceftriaxone, 2 g/day IV for 14 days (75-100 mg/kg/day for pediatric patients), or penicillin G, 18 to 24 million units daily IV for 10 to 14 days, can be used.[48] Ceftriaxone may be more effective than penicillin, and many practitioners recommend longer courses (e.g., up to 4 weeks).[51] In cases of penicillin or cephalosporin allergy, oral doxycycline for 30 days can be used.

Cardiac Disease
Patients with mild cardiac conduction system involvement (first-degree AV block with a PR interval less than 0.30 seconds) and no other significant symptoms can usually be treated safely as outpatients with oral doxycycline or amoxicillin for 21 to 30 days.[48]

Patients with higher degrees of AV block, including first-degree block with a PR interval greater than 0.30 seconds or evidence of global ventricular impairment, should be hospitalized for cardiac monitoring and treated with parenteral antibiotics. Either penicillin G, 18 to 24 million units IV, or ceftriaxone, 2 g daily for 21 days (50-80 mg/kg/day for children) can be used.

The benefit of adjuvant use of aspirin or prednisone in treating patients with Lyme carditis is uncertain. Temporary cardiac pacing may be necessary in patients who have severe heart block with hemodynamic instability. The block generally resolves completely with antibiotic treatment; thus, the recognition of Lyme carditis in young patients with unexplained heart block is critical to avoid unnecessary permanent pacemaker implantation.

Late Infection

Arthritis
In cases of established Lyme arthritis, the response to antibiotic therapy may be delayed for several weeks or months.[5] Thirty-day oral regimens such as doxycycline, 100 mg PO twice daily, or amoxicillin, 500 mg three times daily, are usually effective and, for reasons of cost and convenience, may be selected as first-line therapy on an outpatient basis before parenteral antibiotic therapy is considered.[48] Persistent or recurrent joint swelling after recommended courses of antibiotic therapy can be treated with another 4-week course of oral antibiotics or with a 2- to 4-week course of intravenous ceftriaxone.[5] A small percentage of patients with Lyme arthritis, particularly those with HLA-DR4 specificity or antibody reactivity with OspA, may have persistent joint inflammation despite treatment with either oral or intravenous antibiotics.[26] Patients such as these are often resistant to any antibiotic therapy and may require arthroscopic synovectomy.

Neurologic Disease
Patients with late neurologic disease affecting the central or peripheral nervous system should be treated with ceftriaxone (2 g once a day intravenously for 2 to 4 weeks). Alternative parenteral therapy may include cefotaxime (2 g IV every 8 hours) or penicillin G (18-24 million units daily, given in divided doses every 4 hours). Response to treatment is usually slow and may be incomplete.

Lyme Disease and Pregnancy

A major concern with Lyme disease is its potential effect when contracted during pregnancy. Similar to the spirochetal agents of syphilis and relapsing fever, *B. burgdorferi* can be passed transplacentally. In rare cases, Lyme disease acquired during pregnancy leads to infection of the fetus and possibly to stillbirth, but adverse effects to the fetus have not been documented conclusively. Counseling termination of a pregnancy because of maternal Lyme disease is unwarranted.

Lyme disease contracted during pregnancy can be treated and cured. Treatment of pregnant patients can be identical to that for nonpregnant patients with the same disease manifestations, except that doxycycline should be avoided.[5] Most women give birth to normal infants despite documented Lyme borreliosis during their pregnancies.[51]

RELAPSING FEVER

Perspective

Relapsing fever is caused by bacteria of *Borrelia* species, which belong to the order Spirochaetales. Human *Borrelia* infections occur worldwide and all are associated with arthropod vectors. The epidemic (louse-borne) form of relapsing fever is caused solely by *Borrelia recurrentis.* The endemic (tick-borne) form of relapsing fever is caused by a group of closely related *Borrelia* species, their names derived from the species names of *Ornithodoros* tick vectors that carry them. The more common ones in North America are *B. hermsii, B. turicatae,* and *B. parkeri.*[52] *B. burgdorferi* has been recognized as the etiologic agent of the third and most recently described borrelial disease, Lyme disease.

Principles of Disease

Endemic (tick-borne) relapsing fever is maintained in an animal reservoir consisting primarily of wild rodents, including squirrels, mice, rats, chipmunks, and rabbits. The tick vectors are argasids belonging to several species of the genus *Ornithodoros,* which routinely reside in the nests and burrows of their mammalian hosts. Ticks acquire the infection by feeding on a spirochetemic rodent. The borreliae remain viable in the ticks for several years and can be passed transovarially to the next generation; thus, the tick is a major reservoir and vector. These soft ticks feed for brief periods (15-30 minutes), usually at night, and their painless bite generally is unnoticed by the sleeping victim. Transmission occurs by injection of infected saliva through the bite site or intact skin. Less common modes of transmission (e.g., via venipuncture equipment in intravenous drug abusers) have been reported.

In the United States, relapsing fever occurs primarily in the western mountain states. Persons who come in contact with infected ticks from wild rodents are at greatest risk. Outbreaks have been reported among groups sleeping overnight in hunting cabins inhabited by wild rodents.[52,53] A recent case study involving a rodent-infested cabin and subsequent outbreak of relapsing fever at a family outing in New Mexico clearly depicts all aspects of a typical scenario of the disease.[54]

Clinical Features

After a postbite incubation period of four to 18 days, during which time the host concentration of spirochetes increases, fever occurs abruptly and is often accompanied by shaking chills, headache, arthralgias, myalgias, nausea, and vomiting. Occasionally a pruritic eschar is present at the site of the tick bite, but this is usually absent by the onset of clinic symptoms. Consequently, the nonspecific nature of the clinical presentation often leads to the misdiagnosis of a viral illness. The temperature is high (usually 38.5° to 40°C), and generalized muscle weakness and lethargy are common. Hepatomegaly, splenomegaly, and jaundice are sometimes seen. Neurologic involvement is less common but can include delirium, nuchal rigidity, peripheral neuropathy, and pupillary abnormalities. A macular or petechial skin rash, more apparent on the trunk than on the extremities, may be present.

In tick-borne relapsing fever, the initial febrile episode lasts 3 days. This is followed by a variable asymptomatic period of approximately 7 days, during which patients generally feel better and may return to their usual daily activity levels under the assumption that they have recovered from "another viral illness." Relapse then occurs, with symptoms that mimic the original illness. With tick-borne relapsing fever, this cycle repeats itself three to five times. Each successive relapse is usually less severe.

Relapse is caused by the spirochete's ability to undergo antigenic variation within the body of the infected host. Each successive antigenic variation is cleared from the bloodstream by specific host antibodies, and a characteristic relapsing febrile course results.[52,53]

Diagnostic Strategies

The definitive diagnosis of relapsing fever depends on the demonstration of borreliae in the peripheral blood during a febrile episode. In most patients, the spirochetes are readily visible on a routine blood smear stained with Wright or Giemsa stain. Thick or thin blood smears prepared for malaria evaluation are also satisfactory. The organisms lie in the plasma spaces between blood cells or may overlie the blood cells. Several organisms per high-power field are typically visible in febrile patients with relapsing fever.[52] Smears should be obtained as the temperature curve swings up, and repeated samples may be required before obtaining a positive result. Spirochetes may also be visible in wet mounts with the use of phase contrast microscopy. Cultures, although the most sensitive test available, require a special medium and do not yield rapid results and so are not commonly performed. Serologic testing offered by the CDC can be accessed through local and state health departments. PCR is still experimental.[54]

Differential Considerations

On initial presentation, the differential diagnosis is extensive; however, it narrows with the occurrence of relapse. A history of possible tick exposure together with recurrent fever should suggest the diagnosis. Other conditions that might be initially considered include malaria, typhus, dengue, yellow fever, Colorado tick fever, and tularemia. Careful examination of blood smears, together with clinical data and other laboratory tests, will aid in making the correct diagnosis.

Management

Relapsing fever is treated effectively with tetracycline or erythromycin. Tetracycline should be avoided in children younger than 8 years and in pregnant women.

Tetracycline or erythromycin should be given in an oral dose of 500 mg for 5 to 10 days; single-dose therapy is also effective.[52] Other treatment regimens, including doxycycline, chloramphenicol, and streptomycin, have been recommended. Treatment with penicillin G has been associated with an increased rate of relapses. Success with ceftriaxone has been reported in a patient with relapsing fever who did not respond to penicillin.

As many as one third of patients experience a Jarisch-Herxheimer-type reaction after treatment with antibiotics. The reaction can be severe, especially with louse-borne relapsing fever. This phenomenon may be related to administration of cytokine intermediaries or endogenous opioids. Approximately 4 hours after antibiotic treatment and coinciding with the clearance of spirochetes from the blood, the patient usually experiences an increase in temperature, severe rigors, a drop in leukocyte and platelet counts, and hypotension. Anticipation of the reaction is crucial because intravenous volume expansion with saline solution may be required to maintain the blood pressure; the reaction can be more threatening than the disease itself. Meptazinol, an opioid antagonist with agonist properties, has been proposed for use in treatment of this reaction.

Prognosis is good in treated patients with relapsing fever, with approximately 95% achieving complete recovery. Bad prognostic signs include the presence of jaundice, high spirochete counts in the blood, and hypotension.[52] Transplacental transmission and spontaneous abortion can occur in infected pregnant women. Death is rare and is limited to infants and elderly persons.[55]

TULAREMIA

Perspective

Tularemia was first described in 1837 by Soken, who described a febrile illness with generalized lymphadenopathy in people who had eaten infected rabbit meat.[56] In 1912, McCoy first isolated *Francisella tularensis* from rodents in Tulare County, California, giving rise to the name of the disease. Francis, for whom the genus *Francisella* is named, contributed much to the understanding of the bacteriology and epidemiology.

Tularemia occurs worldwide and is endemic between 30 and 71 degrees north latitude. Ticks, lagomorphs (hares, rabbits), and rodents (mice, rats) are believed to be the most important sources of transmission to humans; however, the organism has been recovered from more than 100 animals, with significant epidemics linked to contact with a variety of them, including domestic cats.[57,58] The ticks most commonly involved in transmission in the United States are the deer tick (*I. scapularis*), the Lone Star tick (*A. americanum*), and the dog tick (*D. variabilis*). Mosquitoes are major vectors in many European countries.[59] Other insect sources such as flies and spiders may play a marginal role in transmission.

Transmission can occur by direct contact with or ingestion of infected soil, water, or fomites.[56] Inhalation of dust or water aerosol can also induce infection.

Nonimmune laboratory workers who work with *F. tularensis* can acquire the disease. Person-to-person transmission is rare. Tularemia has a bimodal prevalence in the United States, with an increased incidence in May to August associated with tick-borne transmission and a December to January peak associated with hunting and skinning of infected mammals (primarily rabbits). *Francisella tularensis* has been found to coexist in reservoir populations harboring the agent responsible for Lyme disease.[60] In the United States, tularemia has been seen in every state but is most common in the southwest central region (Arkansas, Louisiana, Oklahoma, Texas, and Mississippi). It is more common in men than in women. Individuals at increased risk for infection include hunters, trappers, butchers, agricultural workers, campers, sheepherders, mink farmers, and laboratory workers.[57] The incidence of tularemia is low; there are approximately 200 cases annually in the United States.[61] Tularemia was removed from the national list of notifiable diseases in 1995 but was reinstated recently in view of the heightened biologic weapons threat.[62] Fifty-six percent of reported cases have come collectively from Missouri, Oklahoma, South Dakota, and Arkansas.[62] Eleven cases of pneumonic tularemia proven to be from aerosolization of vegetation clippings were recently discovered in Martha's Vineyard.[63]

Worldwide, tularemia has been confirmed in 327 cases in Kosovo, through rodent contamination of food.[64] There were also 270 cases reported in an outbreak in Sweden in 2000, with the main risk factor being mosquito bites.[65]

Principles of Disease

Two types of *F. tularensis* organisms exist and can be distinguished on the basis of geographic distribution, fermentation reactions, and virulence. They are called Jellison type A and B and are serologically identical. Jellison type A (*F. tularensis* biovar *tularensis*), the predominant biovar in North America, is associated with ticks and rabbits and causes severe disease in humans. Strain B (*F. tularensis* biovar *palaeartica*) occurs in Asia, Europe, and, to a minor extent, North America; it is associated with rodents and causes milder disease in humans.

Tularemia manifests in different ways, depending on the portal of entry of the organism. The primary route of infection by *F. tularensis* is through the skin. This can occur through hair follicles or through small cuts and abrasions that may be contaminated by exposure to an infected animal; tick exposure can also introduce the bacteria.[57] Because the bacterium has not been isolated from the salivary glands of ticks, it is thought that they transmit the organism through their feces.[56] Scratching after a tick bite introduces the infected feces into the skin. Inhalation or ingestion of the organism or transmission through the conjunctivae can also cause infection. The incubation period is approximately 2 to 6 days, depending on the size of the inoculum.

After penetration of the skin or epithelial membrane, the organism usually spreads to the regional lymph nodes. An erythematous tender papule develops at the primary infection site, followed by inflammation and skin ulceration. The regional nodes enlarge, necrose, and may rupture. The necrotic, purulent, painful lymph node is termed a *bubo*. In the ulceroglandular form of the infection, the organism may not spread farther than the regional lymph nodes. If the inoculum is sufficiently large or the host defenses inadequate, bacteremia occurs with dissemination to phagocytic cells of the reticuloendothelial system.

Pulmonary tularemia may result from inhalation of small-particle aerosols containing *F. tularensis* or by hematogenous dissemination. Small areas of localized pneumonitis most commonly result; lobar consolidation or abscess formation is rare. Oculoglandular tularemia occurs when the conjunctiva becomes infected from an ulcer or contaminated finger. Typhoidal tularemia follows systemic spread of *F. tularensis* from the oropharynx and probably the gastrointestinal tract when a large inoculum is swallowed.

Clinical Features

Tularemia has six clinical presentations, depending on whether disease is localized to an entry site and its regional lymph nodes (ulceroglandular, glandular, oculoglandular, oropharyngeal) or is more invasive and generalized (typhoidal and pulmonary).

Ulceroglandular tularemia is the most common form of the disease (approximately 80% of cases). Typically, a skin lesion on an extremity at the site of primary inoculation begins as an erythematous papule, which then ulcerates 2 to 3 days later.[57] The ulcer is slow to heal and is often still present when the subsequent regional lymphadenopathy and fever develop. The distribution of the regional adenopathy reflects the primary entry site; patients with tick-borne tularemia usually have inguinal or femoral adenopathy, whereas those who acquire rabbit-associated tularemia have axillary or epitrochlear nodal involvement. Generalized lymphadenopathy may also occur. Occasionally nodes suppurate and drain.[57]

Glandular tularemia, the second most common form, is characterized by the development of lymphadenopathy (usually cervical) without an associated skin ulcer. Oculoglandular tularemia is seen in 1% to 2% of cases and is characterized by unilateral conjunctivitis with regional adenopathy involving preauricular lymph nodes. Oropharyngeal tularemia presents as severe exudative pharyngitis with associated cervical lymphadenitis. It has been known to cause acute glaucoma.[66]

Typhoidal tularemia is a systemic form of the disease in which no obvious entry site can be found; it occurs in approximately 10% of tularemia cases. Only 10 to 50 organisms are required to induce disease; incubation time is 2 to 10 days.[67] Symptoms may include fever, chills, constipation or diarrhea, abdominal pain, and weight loss.

Pulmonary tularemia is common and has symptoms similar to those of other bacterial pneumonias: fever and chills, cough (usually nonproductive), substernal burning, dyspnea, malaise, and prostration. It may result from either direct inhalation of aerosolized organisms or bacteremic spread from another site. Patchy bilateral infiltrates are usually seen on chest radiographs; consolidation and abscesses are less common. An aerosolized form of the bacterium would be the most likely delivery mechanism used in biologic warfare.[68] The disease is classified by the CDC as a Category A critical biologic agent.[69]

Uncommon complications of tularemia include pericarditis, meningitis, endocarditis, peritonitis, appendicitis, perisplenitis, and osteomyelitis.[57] Guillain-Barré syndrome associated with tularemia has been reported.[70]

Diagnostic Strategies

Diagnosis of tularemia is based on clinical findings and serologic testing. Antibody titers begin to rise approximately 7 to 10 days after exposure and peak in 3 to 4 weeks. In a patient with a clinical presentation suggesting tularemia, a single specimen with an antibody titer of 1 : 160 or greater is diagnostic. Confirmatory evidence is provided by a fourfold or greater rise in titer in a second sample obtained 2 weeks later. Rapid testing with PCR is available.[71] A rapid point-of-care test through use of an immunochromatographic approach is currently being evaluated.[72]

Aspiration of affected lymph nodes for culture is not routinely recommended because of the associated risk to laboratory personnel. If tularemia is suspected, the laboratory should be alerted so that appropriate precautions are taken in handling and so that enriched culture medium can be used.

Management

Isolation of patients with tularemia is not required. Streptomycin is the drug of choice for all forms of tularemia. When given intramuscularly in a dose of 30 to 40 mg/kg/day in two divided doses every 12 hours, streptomycin usually produces symptomatic improvement and resolution of fever in 1 to 2 days.[57] After the third treatment day, half the dose is given for a total course of 7 to 14 days.[56,57] With this regimen, relapses are unusual.

Ulcers and tender lymph nodes usually heal within 7 to 10 days; however, enlarged nodes occasionally develop into fluctuant sterile buboes, requiring incision and drainage after completion of the course of antibiotics. Gentamicin is also effective for treatment (3-5 mg/kg/day for 10 to 14 days).[67] Tetracycline and chloramphenicol are effective; however, the risk of relapse is greater than that associated with the aminoglycosides. Imipenem-cilastatin, an antibiotic without nephrotoxicity, has been used successfully to treat pulmonary tularemia in a patient with acute renal failure. Ceftriaxone is not effective against *F. tularensis* infections.[73] Prophylaxis for possible exposure requires doxycycline 100 mg twice a day for 14 days.[74] A live vaccine is available for human tularemia, but protection is not complete and the vaccine itself can induce illness.[75]

The mortality rate in untreated cases ranges from approximately 5% to 30%; the higher figure is associated with severe disease or significant pulmonic involvement. With appropriate antibiotic treatment, death is rare (less than 1%).

ROCKY MOUNTAIN SPOTTED FEVER

Perspective

Rocky Mountain spotted fever (RMSF) is an acute, febrile, systemic tick-borne illness caused by *Rickettsia rickettsii*. The clinical severity of RMSF ranges from mild or even subclinical illness to a fulminant disease with vascular collapse and death within several days of onset. It is the only rickettsiosis still associated with significant mortality, causing approximately 40 deaths in the United States each year.[76] The age-specific incidence is highest in children younger than 10 years, and case-fatality ratios are highest in persons older than 60 years.[77]

The recorded history of RMSF dates to Native American inhabitants of wooded Rocky Mountain regions who were afflicted by the disease. Early settlers named the affliction "tick fever" after missionaries noted the association of the tick vector with the disease. In 1899, RMSF was described as "an acute, endemic, noncontagious but probably infectious, febrile disease, characterized by a continuous moderately high fever, severe arthritic and muscle pains, and a profuse petechial or purpuric eruption in the skin, appearing first on the ankles, wrists, and forehead, but rapidly spreading to all parts of the body."* In 1906, the causative organism, *Rickettsia rickettsii,* was identified by Ricketts, who also described the importance of the tick vector in transmission to humans.

Although RMSF was first described in Montana and Idaho, it is now relatively rare in the Rocky Mountain states. Endemic in all 48 contiguous states except Maine, the disease continues to be most prevalent in the southeastern United States. RMSF has been reported in Canada, Central America, Mexico, and South America but never outside the Western Hemisphere. In 1987, four cases of RMSF were reported among residents of the Bronx in New York City; none of the affected individuals had recently traveled to an area known for endemic disease, thus raising the possibility that other urban foci of RMSF may exist.

Rocky Mountain spotted fever also tends to be focally endemic, with clustering of cases within a larger endemic area that may correspond to "islands" of infected ticks. These areas, ecologically distinct from surrounding areas, may be ideally suited to ticks; they usually consist of fields, deciduous forests with thick ground cover and poor water drainage, and uncultivated areas. In areas with frequent occurrence of RMSF (Oklahoma, North and South Carolina, Tennessee, and Pennsylvania), an infectivity rate of 2% to 15% of the tick population has been reported.[78]

Rickettsia rickettsii are obligate intracellular bacteria that often occur in pairs and possess a cell wall similar in structure and chemical composition to that of gram-negative bacteria.[79] *R. rickettsii* contain both RNA and DNA and, in contrast to other rickettsial organisms, can invade the nucleus as well as the cytoplasm.

The ticks feed on virtually any available warm-blooded animal, and the occurrence of *R. rickettsii* in the United States does not depend on the presence of any given order of mammal. Infected ticks feed on human beings, dogs, mice, rabbits, weasels, deer, horses, and farm animals. Domestic dogs become infected with *R. rickettsii* and can develop clinical illness similar to that in humans. Although dogs do not play an important role in the amplification cycle of RMSF, they can serve as a conduit for infected ticks, carrying them into close contact with pet owners. Dogs may serve as sentinels for RMSF in humans. Communication between physicians and veterinarians should occur when cases of zoonotic diseases are detected.[80] Humans serve only as accidental participants in the cycle of infection. A recent retrospective study revealed that none of 10 recipients of blood products found to be from donors with either confirmed or probable RMSF contracted the disease.[81]

Principles of Disease

After introduction of *R. rickettsii* into the host by the tick vector, the organisms invade and multiply in the vascular endothelial cells. They then enter deeper areas of the vessel walls and infect vascular smooth muscle. Rickettsial organisms move from cell to cell by actin-based motility.[82] Damage to endothelial cells not only exposes subendothelium but also releases tissue plasminogen activator and von Willebrand factor, thereby causing microhemorrhage, microthrombus formation, and increased vascular permeability. In addition, antibody forms with antigen activating the complement system (type III immune response) and a cellular response is recruited.

These widespread vascular lesions form the basis for most of the clinical features associated with RMSF. Hypotension, edema, and increased extravascular fluid space result from the increased small vessel permeability. The early rash results from the vasculitis and the associated changes in permeability; later petechial and hemorrhagic lesions are secondary to the vasculitis and thrombocytopenia. Microinfarcts and focal lesions occur in various organs, including the brain, heart, lungs, kidneys, adrenal glands, liver, and spleen. Rickettsial encephalitis and diffuse microinfarcts are usual features of central nervous system involvement. An interstitial pneumonitis caused by direct lung invasion by the organism may occur, and acute respiratory distress syndrome (ARDS) can ensue. Acute renal failure and hypovolemic shock, the primary causes of death, can occur as early as the second week of illness.

Clinical Features

A history of tick bite or presence in possible tick-infested areas is elicited in only 60% to 70% of patients with RMSF. The incubation period ranges from 2 to 14 days, with a mean of 7 days.[79] A short incubation period may indicate a more serious infection.

*From Maxey EE: Some observations on the so-called spotted fever of Idaho. *Med Sentinel* 7:433, 1899.

Onset of symptoms is usually abrupt but is gradual in approximately one third of patients. Early symptoms are nonspecific and similar to those of many acute infectious diseases, making early diagnosis very difficult. "Typical" patients have a sudden onset of fever, severe headache, myalgias, prostration, nausea, and vomiting. Tenderness may be present in large muscle groups (Table 132-4). As many as 80% of patients may have gastrointestinal symptoms, secondary to myositis of the abdominal wall. Fever (39° to 40°C) is nearly always present during the first 2 to 3 days of illness and may precede other signs by 1 week or more.[79,83] Occasionally, the onset of illness is mild, with lethargy, headache, anorexia, and low-grade fever; these patients may remain ambulatory. The triad of fever, rash, and tick bite occurs in only 3% of cases.[84] An extreme complication of RMSF is gangrene, which is probably induced by small-vessel occlusion.[85]

Cutaneous Manifestations

Vasculitis secondary to rickettsial invasion of vascular endothelial cells causes the rash commonly associated with RMSF; however, the rash is reportedly absent from 4% to 16% of laboratory-confirmed cases, referred to as *Rocky Mountain spotless fever*. In addition, the rash may be unnoticed in dark-skinned patients. It usually appears on the third to fifth febrile day but can emerge as early as the second and as late as the sixth day. The initial lesions are generally restricted to the ankles and wrists, spreading to the palms and soles The rash then spreads centripetally to the forearms, arms, legs, thighs, and trunk. Although usually spared, the face can be involved. Despite the common belief that the palms and soles are critical for diagnosis, they are not consistently involved (rash on the palms and soles is reported in about 50% of cases).[86] The rash of RMSF typically begins as 1 to 5 mm blanchable pink to bright red discrete macules that may be pruritic (Figure 132-7). At this initial stage, the lesions fade when pressure is applied and are not palpable. A warm compress applied to the area enhances the rash. After 6 to 12

Table 132-4. Symptoms and Signs in 262 Persons with Rocky Mountain Spotted Fever

Symptom or Sign	Present During Illness	
	Any Time (%)	*First 3 Days (%)*
Fever (37.8°-38.9° C)	99	73
Headache, mild to moderate	91	71
Fever (≥38.9° C)	90	63
Any rash	88	49
Myalgia, mild to moderate	83	57
Rash, maculopapular	82	46
Rash, palms/soles	74	28
Triad of fever/rash/history of tick exposure	67	3
Nausea/vomiting	60	38
Headache, severe	57	40
Abdominal pain	52	30
Rash, petechial and hemorrhagic	49	13
Myalgia, severe	47	25
Conjunctivitis	30	13
Lymphadenopathy	27	13
Stupor	26	6
Diarrhea	19	9
Edema	18	3
Ataxia	18	7
Meningismus	18	5

From Helmick CG, Bernard KW, D'Angelo LI: *J Infect Dis* 150:480, 1984.

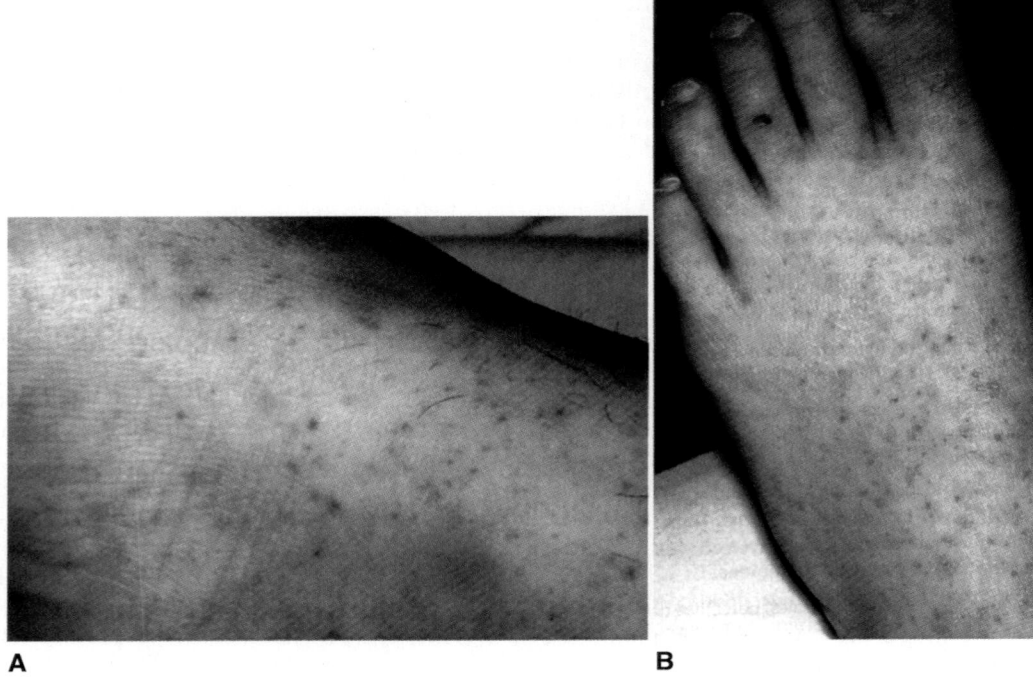

Figure 132-7. A, Exanthem of Rocky Mountain spotted fever. **B,** Exanthem of Rocky Mountain spotted fever, close up. (From McGinley-Smith DE, Tsao SS: Dermatoses from ticks. *J Am Acad Dermatol* 49:363, 2003.)

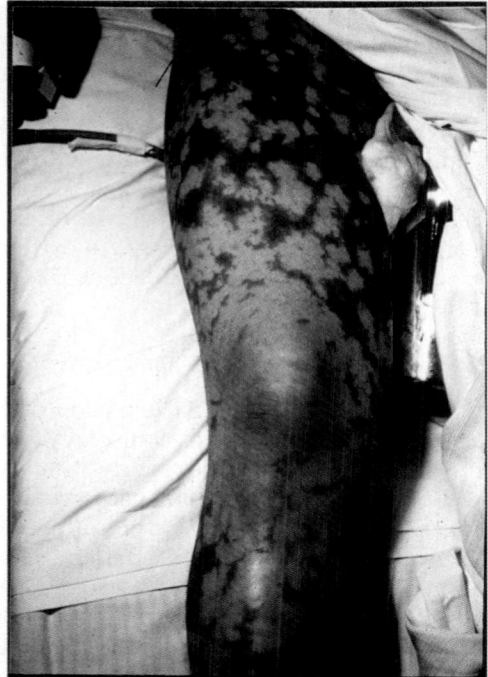

Figure 132-8. Late appearance of rash. Rocky Mountain spotted fever manifesting on lower extremity. (Courtesy Theodore Woodward, MD.)

hours, the rash spreads centripetally. After 2 to 3 days, the rash becomes maculopapular and changes to a deeper red; at this stage, the rash can be felt by light palpation. By about the fourth day, the rash becomes petechial and no longer fades with applied pressure. Applying tourniquets for several minutes or taking the blood pressure may cause additional petechiae distal to the site of occlusion (Rumpel-Leede phenomenon). Occasionally, the lesions coalesce to form large ecchymotic areas that may slough and form indolent ulcers (Figure 132-8).

Prompt institution of specific therapy can cause the initial nonfixed lesions to disappear rapidly, unlike the later fixed lesions. Patients who have had the typical rash may exhibit brownish discolorations at the site during the convalescent period.

Cardiopulmonary Manifestations

Echocardiographic evidence of decreased left ventricular contractility secondary to myocarditis commonly occurs and often is detectable even before clinical signs of RMSF appear. Clinical manifestations of left ventricular dysfunction are uncommon, however, and hypotension and pulmonary edema, when present, usually have noncardiogenic causes. Chest radiographs may demonstrate cardiac enlargement. Electrocardiographic changes include low-voltage, nonspecific ST-T changes, first-degree AV block, dysrhythmias (sinus and nodal tachycardia, paroxysmal atrial tachycardia, atrial fibrillation), and left ventricular hypertrophy. Most cardiac abnormalities are transient, but persistent echocardiographic changes have been described.

Interstitial pneumonitis and increased pulmonary capillary permeability may result from infection of the pulmonary capillaries with rickettsiae. Nonproductive cough and dyspnea secondary to pneumonitis are sometimes seen on presentation. Chest radiographic abnormalities are identified in approximately 25% of patients. These abnormalities include interstitial infiltrates, patchy alveolar infiltrates, pleural effusions, and cardiomegaly with pulmonary edema. Pulmonary consolidation is rare.[79] Severe cases can progress to noncardiogenic pulmonary edema and ARDS.

Neurologic Manifestations

Neurologic manifestations of RMSF range from mild headache and lethargy to seizures and coma. Acute disseminated encephalomyelitis has been described.[87] Headache, generally severe in nature, is common, occurring in 50% to 90% of cases. Meningismus is present in 16% to 29% of patients. The CSF may be normal or show slight protein elevation and pleocytosis of both lymphocytes and polymorphonuclear cells (usually 8 to 35 cells/mL). Glucose level and opening pressure are usually normal. Resolution of eosinophilic meningitis during RMSF after appropriate antibiotic treatment has been reported. Fewer than 40% of patients have a positive CSF finding.

Cerebral thrombovasculitis may cause focal neurologic deficits, which are usually transient. Seizures can occur, especially during the acute phase of the illness. Generalized cerebral dysfunction ranging from lethargy to coma can occur secondary to systemic toxicity (fever, hypotension, hyponatremia) or secondary to vasculitic lesions involving the central nervous system. Coma is a late finding in patients with severe disease and is seen in fewer than 10% of cases. There have been reports of patients who remain alert but are amnesic about their illness after recovery.

Other reported neurologic manifestations include transient deafness, tremor, rigidity, athetoid movements, paralysis, ataxia, opisthotonos, aphasia, and blindness. Generally, neurologic signs abate without residua; permanent neurologic deficits have been reported rarely.[79] Behavioral disturbances and learning disabilities have been reported in children who develop coma with RMSF.

Diagnostic Strategies

Most immediately available laboratory tests provide little help in diagnosing RMSF. Early in the course of the illness, the diagnosis is based primarily on clinical evidence and depends on the emergency physician's ability to correlate epidemiologic features with clinical signs and symptoms. The initial presentation of RMSF is similar to that of many acute febrile infectious diseases, and almost invariably a therapeutic decision must be made on clinical grounds alone, without the luxury of confirmatory laboratory evidence.[88] Abnormalities such as thrombocytopenia and hyponatremia may be detected by routine laboratory tests, but they are nonspecific and unhelpful diagnostically. Up to 30% of patients present with anemia.[84]

The diagnosis of RMSF requires positive results using one or more of several tests: serology, skin biopsy, or direct isolation and identification of the organism (Box 132-1).

Serology

Rickettsial infection can be confirmed by demonstrating antibody rise in paired sera. Even with the most sensitive serologic tests, however, elevations in antibody titers do not occur until approximately 5 to 7 days after the onset of initial symptoms. As a result, serodiagnosis is retrospective. It is achieved by comparing acute serum that generally yields negative findings with convalescent serum that yields positive results for antibodies. The indirect immunofluorescence assay (IFA) is generally considered the reference standard in RMSF and is the test currently used by the CDC and most state public health laboratories. IFA can be used to detect either IgG or IgM antibodies. A bedside dipstick test is available that measures both IgM and IgG antibodies by enzyme immunoassay.[89,90]

Convalescent-stage blood samples are best obtained 2 to 3 weeks after the onset of clinical illness. Antibiotic therapy does not affect the time of appearance of antibodies or their ultimate titer if such treatment is begun several days after the onset of illness. However, if antibiotic therapy is initiated early in the course of the illness, the rise in titers can be delayed for 4 weeks or more. Under these circumstances, antibody titers should be tested again at 4 to 6 weeks after the onset of illness.

Skin Biopsy

Identification by immunofluorescent assay and immunoperoxidase staining of *R. rickettsii* in biopsy specimens of the skin rash are the best rapid diagnostic tests currently available for RMSF.[91] In experienced laboratories, the diagnosis of RMSF can be confirmed as soon as 4 hours after the specimen is obtained. The organisms can be detected as early as the third day of clinical illness and as late as the 10th day. Unfortunately, this technique can be used only when a rash is visible for accurate localization of the biopsy site. Biopsy specimens are generally obtained with a 3 mm punch in the center of the skin lesion. Immunofluorescent demonstration of rickettsiae in frozen sections of skin biopsies has a sensitivity of 70%. Immunohistochemical staining of tissues at autopsy was positive in all fatal cases in one study, whereas IFA was negative in the majority of cases.[92] Failure to obtain a biopsy specimen of a rickettsial cutaneous lesion or failure to obtain sections through its center yields false-negative results. Treatment with antirickettsial drugs for 24 hours does not appreciably alter the sensitivity of the test; however, after 48 hours, rickettsiae are substantially reduced in numbers.

Isolation of Organism

For most pathogenic infections, the standard criterion of diagnosis is isolation and identification of the etiologic organism from the patient's blood or tissues. This is seldom attempted in rickettsioses, however, because the isolation procedures are time-consuming, expensive, and hazardous to laboratory personnel. In addition, primary isolation of rickettsiae by inoculation in the yolk sac of the chick embryo usually fails because of the small number of organisms in the patient's blood.

Differential Considerations

Delayed diagnosis or misdiagnosis is the principal cause of the significant mortality rate associated with RMSF. Clinical diagnosis is difficult, especially early in the course of the illness, because of the nonspecific presentation of the illness. To prevent avoidable mortality, a diagnosis of RMSF must be considered whenever a patient has an unexplained febrile illness (with or without a rash and headache), even if there is neither history of tick bite nor travel to an area known to be endemic for the disease.[93] An atypical presentation or manifestation of RMSF must also be considered during the differential diagnosis including (1) absent rash (Rocky Mountain spotless fever) or late appearance of a rash, (2) predominant gastrointestinal features or abdominal pain suggestive of an acute condition in the abdomen, (3) cough and pulmonary congestion suggestive of pneumonitis, and (4) meningismus suggestive of viral meningitis.[76] A presumed diagnosis must be made and specific therapy initiated well before specific confirmatory laboratory values are available.[76]

A wide variety of other infections with similar exanthems can be confused with RMSF.[94] The most common include meningococcal infection, measles (rubeola) and atypical measles, gonococcemia, infectious mononucleosis, toxic shock syndrome, and enteroviral infections. Less common diseases include dengue, leptospirosis, murine typhus, and epidemic typhus.

Management

Treatment of RMSF consists of antibiotic therapy, supportive care, and possibly administration of steroids. An understanding of the underlying pathophysiologic changes and an appreciation of the systemic complications that can occur in the patient afflicted with RMSF are necessary for the formulation of a balanced therapeutic regimen. The course of the disease can be complicated by circulatory collapse, coma, renal failure, and electrolyte imbalances. Although often absent from the mildly ill patient in whom antibiotic therapy alone usually suffices, these complications should be anticipated in the seriously ill patient, especially those first recognized late in the disease.[79]

The most important factor contributing to the persistent case-fatality rate of 5% is delayed administration of specific antibiotic therapy. For a select group of early-stage, mildly ill patients, outpatient therapy with oral antibiotics can be successful if the patients are reliable and close follow-up observation is arranged. More severely ill patients in whom the diagnosis is uncertain should receive hospital care with intravenous antibiotics.[79]

Antibiotics

Antibiotic therapy is most effective when initiated during the early stages of disease, coincident with the initial appearance of the rash. Although there are no data from randomized clinical trials regarding antibiotic selection for RMSF, doxycycline is widely regarded as the treatment of choice for most patients.[95] Chloramphenicol should be considered only for patients in whom the tetracyclines have caused significant adverse events and for pregnant women (except those who are near term). The recommended doses of doxycycline and chloramphenicol are summarized in Table 132-5.

Although previous treatment guidelines recommended avoiding doxycycline in children younger than 8 years, the American Academy of Pediatrics and the CDC currently recommend doxycycline therapy as the treatment of choice for RMSF in children of all ages.[93,96] The risk of cosmetically perceptible tooth staining appears to be small for a single course of treatment and is subordinate to the prospect of a potentially lethal illness.[88]

The effectiveness of therapy depends on both the duration of therapy and the interval between the onset of illness and the initiation of therapy. Treatment should begin as early as possible and continue for 7 to 10 days or until the patient is afebrile for 2 to 5 days. Patients who are clinically ill should be hospitalized for parenteral antibiotic treatment. Response to treatment, as manifested by decreased fever and improved rash, generally occurs 36 to 48 hours after beginning antibiotic therapy. Resistance to chloramphenicol or the tetracyclines has not been reported.[76] Penicillin, erythromycin, cephalosporins, aminoglycosides, clindamycin, and sulfonamides are ineffective against RMSF. In fact, empiric use of these agents for presumed bacterial infections possibly will permit progression of the illness.

If secondary bacterial infection occurs, administration of sulfonamides should be avoided because these drugs inhibit paraamino benzoic acid (an early and relatively ineffective treatment of RMSF) and may worsen the primary RMSF infection. The role of the new quinolones as potential replacements for doxycycline and chloramphenicol in the treatment of RMSF is as yet unproved.

Supportive Care

Major complications of RMSF, such as shock, congestive heart failure, disseminated intravascular coagulation, and ARDS, should be anticipated and standard supportive measures instituted when appropriate. Circulatory collapse is common in patients with severe illness and is a major cause of morbidity and mortality in RMSF. Hypotension unresponsive to fluid administration may require the use of vasopressors such as dopamine. In the critically ill patient with widespread vasculitis, however, a delicate balance exists between maintenance of effective circulating volume and excessive leakage of fluids into the tissues, including the lungs and brain. Under these circumstances, the excessive administration of intravenous fluids can be catastrophic.[76] Isolation of the patient is unnecessary, unless the diagnosis is still uncertain and other highly communicable illnesses such as meningococcemia or measles have not been excluded.

Steroids

The use of steroids in RMSF is controversial and is not routinely recommended. However, they should be used for severe cases of RMSF complicated by extensive vasculitis, encephalitis, and cerebral edema.[76] In these critically ill patients, short-term, high-dosage steroid

Table 132-5. Antibiotic Therapy of Rocky Mountain Spotted Fever

| Patient | Doxycycline* | | Chloramphenicol† | |
	Oral	Intravenous	Intravenous	Oral/Intravenous
Adult	100 mg bid	100 mg bid	Maximum 1 g/day	50 mg/kg/day
Child	2.0-2.5 mg/kg PO q12h	4.4 mg/kg initially, followed by 2.2 mg/kg q12h	10-20 mg/kg/day, maximum 1 g/day	50 mg/kg/day

*Doxycycline should not be given to pregnant women.
†Chloramphenicol should not be given to patients with thrombocytopenia.

therapy is recommended, along with concomitant specific antibiotic therapy.[79]

Q FEVER

Principles of Disease

Q fever was first described in 1937 in Australia as an occupational disease of abattoir workers and dairy farmers. Cattle, sheep, goats, and ticks are the primary reservoirs of *Coxiella burnetii,* but many other species may be infected.[97] The disease is endemic worldwide, although it is rare in Scandinavian countries. The Q fever rickettsiae are extremely resistant to desiccation and to physical and chemical agents and can survive for long periods in an inanimate environment.

Coxiella burnetii is extremely infectious for humans and animals, with a single inhaled organism sufficient to initiate infection in guinea pigs and probably in humans as well. For this reason, it has been considered as an agent of biologic warfare. This organism's infectivity and estimated casualty rate have been compared with those of anthrax.[67] Humans are most commonly infected by inhalation of aerosolized particles from contaminated environments. Q fever patients rarely have a history of tick bite.

Clinical Features

The incubation period of Q fever ranges from 14 to 39 days, with an average of 20 days. The clinical manifestations include severe retrobulbar headache, a fever to 40°C or higher, shaking chills, general malaise, myalgia, and chest pain. Although it is widely regarded as primarily a respiratory disease, the reported incidence of pulmonary involvement in patients with Q fever varies from 0% to 90%. The reasons for reported variation in the occurrence of pulmonary involvement are unclear, but explanations include geographic strain variation; plasmids that may regulate virulence; and the source, route, and dose of the agent. Hepatic involvement may be common, but liver dysfunction is usually minimal. Acute renal failure and a lymphocytic meningitis secondary to *C. burnetii* have been described.[98,99]

Q fever may also be a chronic infection, with or without an antecedent acute episode. The chronic forms of the disease include granulomatous hepatitis and culture-negative endocarditis. Endocarditis has been documented in up to 68% of patients with chronic Q fever and the mortality rate among this groups approaches 25%.[100] Most Q fever patients in whom endocarditis develops have a history of valvular heart disease, particularly affecting the aortic valve. These individuals should be especially cognizant of the potential hazards of Q fever infection and should be restricted from certain at-risk occupational settings. Patients with aneurysms and vascular grafts are also at risk. The most common presentations of patients with Q fever endocarditis are fever and congestive heart failure.[101] Human fetal demise and deaths have been attributed to *C. burnetii* infection.[102] Individuals

infected with human immunodeficiency virus are at increased risk for contracting Q fever.[103]

Diagnostic Strategies

The diagnosis of Q fever should be suspected in any patient with a severe febrile illness without obvious cause, especially someone who has had recent contact with sheep, cattle, goats, or animal byproducts. Because of the laboratory hazards associated with cultivation of Q fever rickettsiae, isolation of *C. burnetii* is not recommended for routine diagnosis. Rather, serologic studies such as IFA and ELISA are the preferred diagnostic tests, but the results are not identifiable until 2 to 3 weeks after the onset of illness.[67,104]

Coxiella burnetii displays an antigenic phase variation (phase I to phase II). In patients with acute Q fever, phase II antibodies dominate the humoral immune response and are detectable by the second week of illness, whereas phase I antibodies are prominent only in patients with chronic Q fever. The finding of "ring granulomas" on bone marrow biopsy can be characteristic of Q fever.[104]

Management

As with other rickettsial diseases, the tetracyclines and chloramphenicol are both effective in treatment of acute Q fever. In mass casualty situations, prophylaxis is accomplished with 5 to 7 days of doxycycline.[105] Most acute Q fever infections resolve without treatment, but the risk of chronic infection makes treatment advisable. The mortality rate is less than 1% in untreated patients and lower still in those treated with antibiotics. The prognosis is worse in those patients with protracted illness and hepatic involvement or endocarditis. No current therapy has been shown to completely eradicate *Coxiella* in patients with endocarditis.[103] Inactivated whole cell vaccines for Q fever have proven effective for as long as 5 years.[106] Vaccination can afford considerable protection to slaughterhouse and dairy workers and others at risk.

EHRLICHIOSIS

Perspective

There are currently two major forms of human ehrlichioses in the United States: human monocytic ehrlichiosis (HME) and human granulocytic ehrlichiosis (HGE). Before 1986, *Ehrlichia sennetsu* was the only member of the genus of these organisms thought to infect humans, having been isolated in Japan in 1954 as the causative agent of sennetsu fever, a mononucleosis-like illness. HME was discovered in 1986 and HGE in 1994. Both are identified as emerging diseases by the CDC. A third species, *E. ewingii,* has been shown to cause human disease in the United States.[107]

As of December 1999, only 18 states treat ehrlichiosis as a notifiable disease and five more routinely report it.[108] Both HME and HGE peak around June through August. High-risk populations are similar to those at high risk for Lyme disease, including those living in endemic areas or with frequent contact with wildlife or rural, wooded areas. A unique case series of ehrlichiosis in a group of golfers showed that those who spent more time in the rough and wooded areas searching lost balls were at higher risk.[109] HME has predominantly been reported in the south central and southeastern United States; HGE is mostly found in the upper Midwest and northeastern United States.[108,110] The first two reported cases of HGE in Italy have recently been described.[111]

Principles of Disease

The causative agents in the ehrlichioses are gram-negative, obligate intracellular rickettsia-like coccobacilli. Transmitted from the midguts and salivary glands of their tick vectors,[112] these organisms reside in specific circulating leukocytes in human and other mammalian hosts. Reservoirs include the white-tailed deer and the white-footed mouse. *E. canis* is the common causative agent in dogs.[113] One species, *E. equina,* has been isolated in California elk. HME, transmitted by the Lone Star tick, *Amblyomma americanum,* is caused by the organism *E. chaffeensis* (named after Fort Chaffee, Arkansas), which invades monocytes. *E. chaffeensis* has been isolated from *I. pacificus* ticks in California. Recent reclassification has placed the causative organism for HGE into the genus *Anaplasma* (*A. phagocytophilum*), closely related to the previous *Ehrlichia* genus.[113,114] These organisms invade neutrophils (granulocytes) and are transmitted by the tick *I. scapularis*. Both *I. scapularis* and *I. pacificus* (U.S. west coast counterpart of *I. scapularis*) ticks are also the vectors for Lyme disease.

Clinical Features

The clinical presentations of HME and HGE are similar, and for case management, it is not necessary to differentiate between the two illnesses. The average onset of symptoms (for HME) from time of tick discovery is 9 days but ranges from 0 to 34 days.[115] More than 90% of patients with HME report a history of tick bite or tick exposure.[116] Ehrlichiosis characteristically manifests with abrupt onset of fever, headache, myalgia, and shaking chills.[115] Other less frequently occurring symptoms include nausea, vomiting, diarrhea, abdominal pain, cough, and confusion.[115] Leukopenia, thrombocytopenia, and elevated liver function tests can be seen in 50% to 90% of patients.[117] Rashes occur in approximately one third of patients with HME but in only 2% to 11% of those with HGE. Rashes associated with Lyme disease occur in 85% of patients. Ehrlichiosis has been associated with optic neuritis.[118] Other findings such as ARDS, meningitis, pancarditis, renal failure, and disseminated intravascular coagulation have been reported.[115] The largest data pool available, from the CDC, shows case fatality ratios from 20 states to be 2.7% for HME and 0.7% for HGE.[108] Approximately 45% of HGE patients are hospitalized.

A small series of pediatric patients (average age, 7.4 years) with HME revealed a rash rate of 67%. The majority suffered permanent cognitive or other neurologic damage.[119]

Diagnostic Strategies

The initial diagnoses of HME and HGE are largely based on clinical presentation. Most tests are either retrospective or rarely available immediately. Cytopenia and abnormal liver function usually resolve after the acute phase of illness. Microscopic identification of mulberry-like clusters, called *morulae*, inside leukocytes on peripheral blood smears is helpful but is usually negative after the first week of illness with HGE, especially if the patient has been treated with doxycycline. The most common mode of diagnosis is confirmation of IgG antibodies with IFA. Unfortunately, IgM assays are not presently established. Results are therefore often retrospective. Enzyme immunoassay and confirmatory tests with Western blot have been developed.[120] PCR testing for DNA fragments, although not readily available in most hospitals, is probably most reliable in the acute phase of illness (1 week).[121] Cultures take up to 2 weeks to grow the organisms.[122] Diagnostic serologic testing is available at the CDC through state health departments.[108]

Confirmation of disease requires a fourfold rise or fall in IFA antibody titer, a positive PCR test result, or findings of morulae with a single IFA titer of greater than 63. Probable disease requires a single titer of greater than 63 or the presence of morulae within infected cells. All require compatible clinical suspicion.[108] Most patients with clinical symptoms have IFA titers between 160 and 1280 at presentation.[123]

Management

Tetracycline, which has been shown to be effective in cases of canine ehrlichiosis, is also effective in cases of human ehrlichiosis. Doxycycline and tetracycline regimens for 7 to 14 days are curative. For pediatric patients, the concern for teeth staining is obvious, although it has been argued that most of this effect is seen only with multiple dosing periods. Most patients respond rapidly after treatment is begun, and fever subsides within 24 to 48 hours. Data supporting the use of chloramphenicol are still inconclusive. Rifampin has been shown to be effective in children with human ehrlichiosis.[114] Although more than half of patients with confirmed human ehrlichiosis require hospitalization, almost all recover without residual problems.

BABESIOSIS

Perspective

Babesiosis is a tick-borne, malaria-like, acute febrile illness caused by intraerythrocytic protozoan parasites of the genus *Babesia*. Babesiosis has long been recognized as an important veterinary disease and was probably known in ancient times; in fact, it has been proposed that the fifth plague described in the Book of Exodus was actually babesiosis.

The first human cases of babesiosis were reported in Montana in 1904; investigators seeking the cause of RMSF examined blood smears from local inhabitants and described parasitic forms now known to be characteristic of *Babesia*. Since the late 1950s, several widely scattered cases (mostly in Europe) of human babesiosis have been reported in splenectomized individuals. *B. divergens,* a species primarily infecting cattle, is the most common agent reported; but other species have been implicated as well, including *B. bovis, B. equi,* and a single case of *B. caucasia* infection. Two other strains, WA-1, related to a canine pathogen *B. gibsoni,* and MO1, related to *B. divergens,* have also now been found to cause disease in humans.[112] In all these cases, the course was fulminant and usually fatal.

Since the late 1960s, more than 200 cases have been documented in the United States. Almost all of these cases were caused by *B. microti,* a rodent parasite, and almost all occurred in the coastal regions of southern New England, where *B. microti* is endemic, including Cape Cod and the offshore islands of Massachusetts (Nantucket, Martha's Vineyard) and Rhode Island (Block Island). Babesiosis has also been reported in Maryland, Virginia, Georgia, Wisconsin, Minnesota, California, and Washington. These cases differ from the European cases in that most (approximately 80%) have occurred in individuals with intact spleens. Thirty-eight percent of the counties in New Jersey have recently reported confirmed cases of babesiosis.[124] In addition, many of the patients in the United States had little morbidity despite lack of specific therapy.

Principles of Disease

Babesia microti is associated with deer and mice rather than cattle. The ecology of *B. microti* is similar to that of *Borrelia burgdorferi,* the etiologic agent of Lyme disease, with the same major vector, *Ixodes dammini,* and the same mammalian reservoirs: white-footed mice, which host the larval and nymphal stages of the tick, and white-tailed deer, which host the adult ticks.

Human babesiosis results from accidental human intrusion on the natural cycle of infection. The nymphal form of the *Ixodes* tick most commonly transmits the disease to humans, although babesiosis can also be transmitted by the adult stage. Nymphal *I. scapularis* measure only 1 to 2 mm long and thus are easily overlooked by the patient (Figure 132-9). In more than half of all cases of babesiosis, patients cannot recall tick exposure. As is true for other tick-borne illnesses, the peak incidence of babesiosis is between May and August, coinciding with the nymphal feeding period and also the time of maximal human exposure in endemic areas. Babesiosis acquired by blood transfusion has also been reported.

Clinical Features

Babesiosis has an incubation period of 1 to 4 weeks after tick exposure. Nonspecific flulike symptoms, including fever, chills, headache, fatigue, and anorexia, usually occur. Other less common symptoms are nausea, diaphoresis, depression, photophobia, myalgias, arthralgias, dark urine, emotional lability, and

Figure 132-9. The life cycle of *Ixodes scapularis*. (From Tick Information Sheet: The Deer Tick. In Hoskins JD [ed]: Tick-Transmitted Diseases. *Vet Clin North Am.* Philadelphia, Saunders, 1991.)

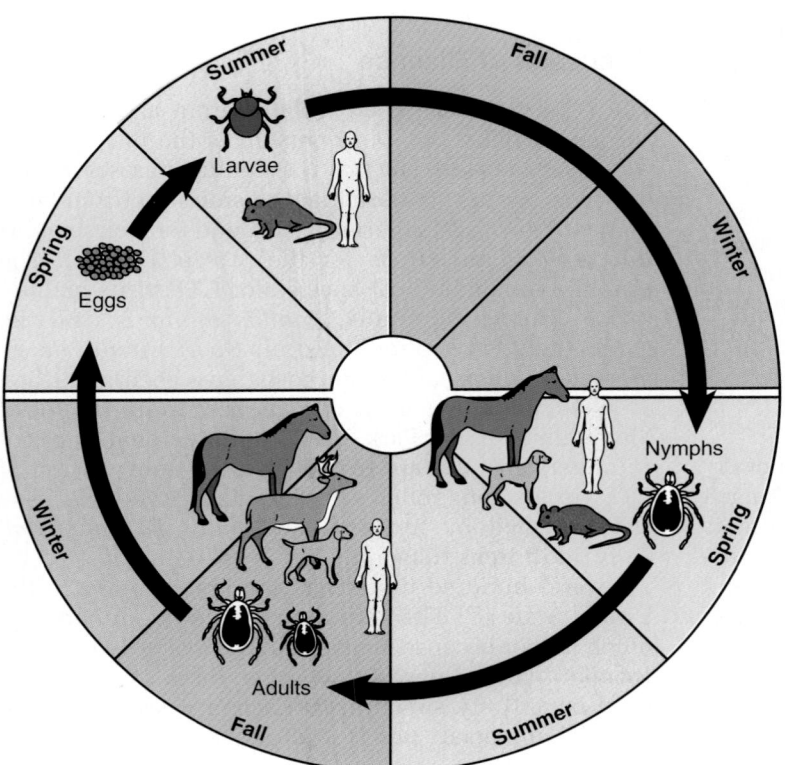

hyperesthesias. Unlike Lyme disease, rash is not a feature of the illness. Physical examination usually reveals normal findings, except for fever, which is usually present, and splenomegaly, which occurs in some patients. Meningeal signs are absent. More severe disease occurs in splenectomized patients[125]; severe hemolytic anemia, hemoglobinuria, jaundice, renal insufficiency, ARDS, and disseminated intravascular coagulation can be seen in these cases. Some patients with babesiosis are only mildly ill, and asymptomatic infection may also occur, as demonstrated by serologic surveys in endemic areas. In a review of 139 patients from New York, the mortality rate approached 6.5%.[126] The diagnosis of babesiosis should be considered in any febrile patient from an endemic area during the tick season and should be part of the differential diagnosis of posttransfusion infections.

Diagnostic Strategies

The diagnosis is established by examination of thick and thin Giemsa-stained blood smears. Characteristic intraerythrocytic forms (pyriform, ring, tetrad) may be present. Malaria can be excluded by the absence of intracellular pigment granules, schizonts, and gametocytes. The presence of parasites in budding tetrad formation, like a Maltese cross, is more suggestive of babesiosis, although this finding is uncommon. Because parasitemia may vary, in suspected cases serial smears over the course of several days may be necessary. A new immunohistochemical assay has been developed that further allows for easier differentiation between babesiosis and malarial organisms.[127]

The diagnosis can be confirmed by serologic studies. IFA antibody to *B. microti* is available through the CDC, and titers usually rise to 1:1024 or greater within the first few weeks of illness. IgM-indirect IFA is 91% sensitive and 99% specific in acute babesiosis.[128] Serologic tests for Lyme disease, which shares a common tick vector with babesiosis, should also be performed on these patients because cases of babesiosis concurrent with Lyme disease have been reported.[19] Some areas have reported that up to 10% of patients with Lyme disease are coinfected with babesial organisms. PCR is also now available and is thought to be highly sensitive and specific.[129] Other laboratory findings include mild to moderate hemolytic anemia, which is present in most patients, and resultant mild elevation in bilirubin and serum lactate dehydrogenase.

Management

Patients who have not had splenectomies generally recover without specific therapy, although prolonged malaise and fatigue are commonly seen. In patients with severe disease or in those who have had splenectomies, the combination of quinine, 650 mg orally, and clindamycin, 600 mg IV, both given every 6 hours, has been shown to be effective and is currently the treatment of choice. Antibiotic therapy is recommended only for patients with severe disease and those who have had splenectomies. Therapy should be continued for a minimum of 7 to 10 days. Other antimalarial drugs such as chloroquine and quinacrine are not effective. Another therapeutic option that may be considered under some circumstances is exchange transfusion; fulminantly ill patients with marked degrees of parasitemia and hemolysis have benefited from this treatment. Effective living vaccines have been developed for bovine babesiosis but not yet for human disease.

COLORADO TICK FEVER

Perspective

Endemic to the Rocky Mountain area, Colorado tick fever (CTF) is an acute tick-borne viral infection characterized by headache, back pain, biphasic febrile course, and leukopenia. The etiologic agent of CTF is a small RNA virus of the genus *Orbivirus*, family Reoviridae. It is one of more than 500 viruses in the heterogeneous group of arthropod-borne viruses (arboviruses).[130] CTF has a sharply defined endemic zone encompassing mountainous and highland areas, from an altitude of about 4000 to more than 10,000 feet, in the Canadian provinces of British Columbia and Alberta and in at least 11 western states (California, Colorado, Idaho, Montana, Nevada, New Mexico, Oregon, South Dakota, Utah, Washington, and Wyoming).[131] The largest number of cases has been reported in Colorado. The distribution of the virus coincides with that of its principal tick vector, *Dermacentor andersoni*. Although RMSF is transmitted by the same vector, that disease is far less common in Colorado. The cases of RMSF are outnumbered at least 20-fold by cases of CTF.

Principles of Disease

The CTF virus has been isolated from at least eight species of ticks, but *D. andersoni* is the only proven vector for humans. The tick is a significant reservoir for the virus because transstadial transmission (from larva to nymph to adult) of virus occurs, and the tick remains infected and infectious for life (up to 3 years). The primary vertebrate host species for CTF virus maintenance are the chipmunk, *Tamias minimus*, and the golden-mantled ground squirrel, *Spermophilus lateralis*; many other vertebrate hosts have been identified as well, including a species of porcupine in Rocky Mountain National Park. Larval and nymphal stages of *D. andersoni* ticks are responsible for transmission of CTF virus among rodents, and wintering of the virus is accomplished by nymphal and adult *D. andersoni*. Only adult ticks transmit CTF virus to humans.

Several hundred cases per year are reported in the United States.[131] The actual incidence is undoubtedly much higher because many cases are diagnosed as nonspecific "viral illness," and other cases may be very mild or entirely subclinical. Human susceptibility to CTF is universal, but it occurs most commonly in young men, reflecting greater occupational and recreational tick exposure.

Clinical Features

After an incubation period of approximately 3 to 5 days (range, 0-14 days), a moderate to severe flulike illness occurs abruptly, with signs and symptoms similar to those of the early stage of RMSF. Fever, chills, headache, myalgia, lethargy, anorexia, and nausea are common; vomiting and abdominal pain are occasionally reported. Early physical findings are nonspecific. A macular or maculopapular rash has been reported in 5% to 12% of patients, but unlike the rash of RMSF, the rash of CTF is not a prominent feature of the illness.

A distinct feature of the illness is a biphasic course that occurs in approximately 50% of patients, causing a characteristic "saddleback" fever curve. Initial symptoms resolve after 2 to 3 days, and the patient feels relatively well for 1 or 2 days, after which there is a return of fever, headache, and myalgias. The second phase may be more intense than the first phase and generally lasts 2 to 4 days. There may even be a third febrile period. Alternatively, a single prolonged febrile illness may occur. Recovery from CTF usually occurs within 2 weeks, but convalescence can be prolonged, especially in patients older than 30 years.

Colorado tick fever is a self-limited disease, and virtually all patients recover without sequelae. Reports of severe complications such as meningoencephalitis and hemorrhagic diathesis have been limited to children. Only a few fatalities have been recorded.[130]

Diagnostic Strategies

The peripheral leukocyte count is often depressed during the acute phase of illness to as low as 1000/mm^3 with a relative lymphocytosis. Transient thrombocytopenia can accompany the leukopenia and, less often, a mild anemia can occur. These hematologic abnormalities normalize during convalescence, but persistence of the virus in red blood cells causes a prolonged viremia even when clinical recovery is complete. Transfusion-acquired infection has been reported; it is caused by this persistent viremia in asymptomatic blood donors. No one should donate blood for at least 6 months after recovery from CTF.[130]

The diagnosis of CTF can be confirmed by serologic testing (IFA, neutralizing antibody, complement fixation, enzyme immunoassay) of acute and convalescent samples, but serologic study is of little help acutely because of the slow rise of titers.[132] The most rapid confirmation of CTF, and thus elimination of concern about possible RMSF, is provided by direct immunofluorescent staining of virus in red blood cells in peripheral blood smears. PCR testing is now available for more rapid diagnosis.[133]

Management

Treatment for CTF is entirely supportive. Most patients do not require hospitalization, but if RMSF remains a diagnostic possibility, initial treatment with tetracycline or chloramphenicol and a period of observation are necessary until the diagnosis of RMSF can be ruled out. Ribivirin has been suggested as a treatment but has not yet been tested.[133]

TICK PARALYSIS

Perspective

Tick paralysis occurs when an adult female tick attaches and releases a neurotoxin that can produce cerebellar dysfunction or an ascending paralysis. Tick paralysis was recognized as early as the beginning of the 19th century. Hovell, while traveling through Australia, wrote in 1824 of "the small insect called the tick, which buries itself in the flesh, and would in the end destroy either human or beast if not removed in time."[134]

Tick paralysis has been reported worldwide, but most cases occur in the southeastern and northwestern regions of the United States, western Canada, and Australia. Forty-three species of ticks have been found to cause tick paralysis in humans, other mammals, or birds. Most cases in North America are caused by *Dermacentor* species; in Australia, *Ixodes holocyclus* is primarily associated. Both Ixodidae (hard ticks) and Argasidae (soft ticks) have been implicated. Tick paralysis usually occurs in the spring and summer months, and most cases occur in children, primarily girls, probably because ticks are more easily concealed in longer hair. Among adults, however, more men than women acquire the disease.

Principles of Disease

Tick paralysis is thought to be caused by a toxin secreted from the salivary glands of the tick during a blood meal.[135] The mechanism of action of the toxin is poorly understood, but it appears to produce a conduction block in the peripheral branches of motor fibers, resulting in a failure of release of acetylcholine at the neuromuscular junction. Possible central sites of action of the toxin have been postulated to explain cases in which the clinical picture is dominated by cerebellar dysfunction.

Clinical Features

Onset of symptoms usually occurs from 4 to 7 days after the tick attaches. Initially, restlessness and irritability can be seen, followed by ascending flaccid paralysis, acute ataxia, or a combination of the two. Deep tendon reflexes are almost invariably lost. These symptoms can progress rapidly over a few days, with bulbar involvement, respiratory paralysis, and ultimately death, if the tick is not detected and removed.

The ascending nature of tick paralysis has been noted in most descriptions of it; however, ataxia and associated cerebellar findings in the absence of muscle weakness may occur. Thus, tick paralysis may sometimes present as "tick ataxia." Isolated facial paralysis has

BOX 132-2. Recommended Method for Tick Removal

1. Remove an embedded tick by grasping it with blunt forceps or tweezers as close to the point of attachment as possible.
2. Do not use bare fingers to remove ticks from animals or humans; when tweezers are unavailable, fingers should be shielded with a tissue, paper towel, or rubber glove.
3. Apply gentle, steady, upward traction with the forceps; do not twist or jerk the tick. Avoid squeezing or crushing the tick.
4. Do not handle the tick with bare hands. After removing the tick, thoroughly disinfect the bite site and wash hands with soap and water.
5. Dispose of ticks by placing them in a container of alcohol or flushing them down the toilet.

From Needhan GR: *Pediatrics* 75:997, 1985.

been reported in patients with ticks embedded behind the ear. Fever, other systemic symptoms, and sensory deficits are unusual.

Differential Strategies

The paralysis should be considered in the differential diagnosis of any patient thought to have Guillain-Barré syndrome, Eaton-Lambert syndrome, myasthenia gravis, poliomyelitis, botulism, diphtheritic polyneuropathy, or any disease with an ascending flaccid paralysis or acute ataxia.

Management

Treatment in the United States consists simply of removing the tick; improvement is generally seen within a few hours and complete recovery within 48 hours. The recommended procedure for the removal is summarized in Box 132-2. Supportive care, including mechanical ventilation, may be necessary. The mortality rate is approximately 10%; nearly all those who die are children.

Tick paralysis in Australia is often more devastating than in the United States. Symptoms of illness caused by the Australian tick, *I. holocyclus,* are not resolved and often worsen after tick removal. Hyperimmune serum is available in Australia and is often needed because symptoms may worsen up to 48 hours after removal.

Prophylaxis with Insect Repellents

Insect repellents have long been used to prevent mosquito bites. With recent increased public awareness and concern about tick-borne illness, especially Lyme disease, skin and clothing repellents are now also being marketed for tick protection.

The most effective topical insect repellent known is *N,N*-diethyl-*m*-toluamide, commonly called DEET. A long-acting DEET formulation (U.S. Army Extended Duration Topical Insect and Arthropod Repellent [EDTIAR]), available in the United States as Ultrathon

(3M), provides protection for 6 to 12 hours. Despite some earlier concerns, toxic and allergic reactions to DEET have been uncommon, and serious adverse effects are rare. Used as directed, concentrations up to 50% appear to be safe even in young children, although toxic encephalopathy can occur.[136]

Permethrin, actually a contact insecticide rather than a repellent, can be used as a clothing spray for protection against ticks. Applied to the clothing as an aerosol, it is nonstaining, nearly odorless, and resistant to degradation by light, heat, or immersion in water. Permethrin is toxic to the nervous system of insects, but in mammals it is poorly absorbed and rapidly inactivated. Reported adverse effects have been limited to the skin and are uncommon.

Both topical DEET and clothing impregnated with permethrin have been shown to be effective in field trials when used alone. Wearing protective clothing treated with permethrin, in addition to using DEET on exposed skin, provides the greatest degree of protection against tick bites.[136]

KEY CONCEPTS

- Tick-borne illnesses are frequently misdiagnosed as viral or bacterial infections. Early diagnosis can be facilitated by considering these diagnoses in patients who live in or have recently traveled to endemic areas and by routinely asking for a history of recent tick or insect bites in patients who present with febrile illnesses.
- Lyme disease should be suspected in patients who present with signs of a viral illness, monoarticular arthritis, meningitis, multiple neurologic abnormalities, or heart block. Diagnosis can be confirmed with serologic testing of acute and convalescent serum samples. Normal physiologic changes from bites should not be confused with erythema migrans. A significant amount of time of attachment is required for transmission of disease.
- Relapsing fever should be suspected in patients who present with recurrent viral-like illness associated with high fever. The diagnosis can be confirmed by identifying spirochetes on a blood smear obtained during a period of rising temperature.
- Ulceroglandular tularemia should be suspected in patients with slow-healing extremity ulcers associated with large regional adenopathy (buboes). The diagnosis can be confirmed with serologic testing.
- Rocky Mountain spotted fever should be considered in patients who present with an unexplained febrile illness, even in the absence of a rash or known tick exposure. Delayed diagnosis and late initiation of specific antirickettsial therapy can lead to a fatal outcome. Treatment never should be delayed pending laboratory diagnosis.

REFERENCES

1. Magnarelli LA, et al: *Borrelia burgdorferi* in an urban environment: White-tailed deer with infected ticks and antibodies. *J Clin Microbiol* 33:541, 1995.
2. Arthur DR: Ticks in Egypt in 1500 BC? *Nature* 206:1060, 1965.
3. Cupp EW: Biology of ticks. *Vet Clin North Am* 21:1, 1991.

4. Steere AC, et al: Lyme arthritis: An epidemic of oligarticular arthritis in children and adults in three Connecticut communities. *Arthritis Rheum* 20:7, 1977.

5. Wormser GP, Nadelman RB, Dattwyler RJ, et al: Practice guidelines for the treatment of Lyme disease. The Infectious Diseases Society of America. *Clin Infect Dis* 31(suppl 1):1, 2000.

6. Dennis DT: Epidemiology, ecology, and prevention of Lyme disease. In Rahn D, Evans J, editors: *Lyme Disease.* Philadelphia, American College of Physicians, 1998.

7. Centers for Disease Control: Lyme disease—2000. *MMWR* 51:29, 2002.

8. Centers for Disease Control: Lyme disease: United States, 1995. *MMWR* 45:481, 1996.

9. Donahue JG, Piesman J, Spielman A: Reservoir competence of white-footed mice for Lyme disease spirochetes. *Am J Trop Med Hyg* 36:92, 1987.

10. Steere AC, et al: Longitudinal assessment of the clinical and epidemiological features of Lyme disease in a defined population. *J Infect Dis* 154:295, 1986.

11. Spielman A, et al: Ecology of *Ixodes dammini*-borne human babesiosis and Lyme disease. *Annu Rev Entomol* 30:439, 1985.

12. Burgdorfer W, Hayes SF, Corwin D: Pathophysiology of the Lyme disease spirochete, *Borrelia burgdorferi,* in Ixodid ticks. *Rev Infect Dis* 11:S1442, 1989.

13. Nadelman RB, Wormser GP: Management of tick bites in early Lyme disease. In Rahn D, Evans J (eds): *Lyme Disease.* Philadelphia, American College of Physicians, 1998.

14. Steere AC, et al: The early clinical manifestations of Lyme disease. *Ann Intern Med* 99:76, 1983.

15. Logigian EL: Neurologic manifestations of Lyme disease. In Rahn D, Evans J (eds): *Lyme Disease.* Philadelphia, American College of Physicians, 1998.

16. Pachner AR: *Borrelia burgdorferi* in the nervous system: The new "great imitator." *Ann N Y Acad Sci* 539:56, 1988.

17. Brogan GX, Homan CS, Viccelli P: The enlarging clinical spectrum of Lyme disease: Lyme cerebral vasculitis, a new disease entity. *Ann Emerg Med* 19:572, 1990.

18. Evans J: Lyme carditis. In Rahn D, Evans J (eds): *Lyme Disease.* Philadelphia, American College of Physicians, 1998.

19. Marcus LC, et al: Fatal pancarditis in a patient with coexistent Lyme disease and babesiosis: Demonstration of spirochetes in the myocardium. *Ann Intern Med* 103:374, 1985.

20. van der Linde MR, et al: Range of atrioventricular conduction disturbances in Lyme borreliosis: A report of four cases and review of other published reports. *Br Heart J* 63:162, 1990.

21. McAlister HF, et al: Lyme carditis: An important cause of reversible heart block. *Ann Intern Med* 110:339, 1989.

22. Jacobs JC, Stevens, M, Duray PH: Lyme disease simulating septic arthritis. *JAMA* 256:1138, 1986.

23. Snydman DR, et al: *Borrelia burgdorferi* in joint fluid in chronic Lyme arthritis. *Ann Intern Med* 104:798, 1986.

24. Aaberg TM: The expanding ophthalmologic spectrum of Lyme disease. *Am J Ophthalmol* 107:77, 1989.

25. Rahn D: Natural history of Lyme disease. In Rahn D, Evans J (eds): *Lyme Disease.* Philadelphia, American College of Physicians, 1998.

26. Steere AC: Musculoskeletal features of Lyme disease. In Rahn D, Evans J (eds): *Lyme disease.* Philadelphia, American College of Physicians, 1998.

27. Ackermann R, et al: Chronic neurologic manifestations of erythema migrans borreliosis. *Ann N Y Acad Sci* 539:16, 1988.

28. Kaufman LD, et al: Late cutaneous Lyme disease: Acrodermatitis chronica atrophicans. *Am J Med* 86:828, 1989.

29. Duffy J: Lyme disease. *Infect Dis Clin North Am* 1:511, 1987.

30. Steere AC, et al: The spirochetal etiology of Lyme disease. *N Engl J Med* 308:733, 1983.

31. Shrestha M, Grodzicki RL, Steere AC: Diagnosing early Lyme disease. *Am J Med* 78:235, 1985.

32. American College of Physicians: Guidelines for laboratory evaluation in the diagnosis of Lyme disease. *Ann Intern Med* 127:1106, 1997.

33. Centers for Disease Control: Recommendations for test performance and interpretation from the Second International Conference of Serologic Diagnosis of Lyme Disease. *MMWR* 44:590, 1995.

34. Steere AC: Lyme disease. *N Engl J Med* 345:115, 2001.

35. Sigal LH: Use of the laboratory in the confirmation and management of Lyme disease. In Rahn DW, Evans J (eds): *Lyme Disease.* Philadelphia, American College of Physicians, 1998.

36. Reed KD: Laboratory testing for Lyme disease: Possibilities and practicalities. *J Clin Microbiol* 40:319, 2002.

37. Nocton JJ, et al: Detection of *Borrelia burgdorferi* DNA by polymerase chain reaction in synovial fluid from patients with Lyme arthritis. *N Engl J Med* 330:229, 1994.

38. Dumler JS: Molecular diagnosis of Lyme disease: Review and meta-analysis. *Mol Diagn* 6:1, 2001.

39. Malawista SE: Lyme disease. In Wyngaarden JB, Smith LH (eds): *Cecil Textbook of Medicine,* 18th ed. Philadelphia, WB Saunders, 1988.

40. Steere AC, et al: Erythema chronicum migrans and Lyme arthritis: The enlarging clinical spectrum. *Ann Intern Med* 86:685, 1977.

41. Steere AC, Schoen RT, Taylor E: The clinical evolution of Lyme arthritis. *Ann Intern Med* 107:725, 1987.

42. Centers for Disease Control: Recommendations for the use of Lyme disease vaccine: Recommendations of the Advisory Committee on Immunization Practices (ACIP). *MMWR* 48(RR07):1, 1999.

43. Thanassi W, Schoen RT: The Lyme disease vaccine: Conception, development, and implementation. *Ann Intern Med* 132:661, 2000.

44. Schoen RT, et al: Safety and immunogenicity profile of a recombinant outer-surface protein A Lyme disease vaccine: Clinical trial of a 3-dose schedule at 0, 1, and 2 months. *Clin Ther* 22:315, 2000.

45. Steere AC, et al: Vaccination against Lyme disease with recombinant *Borrelia burgdorferi* outer-surface lipoprotein A with adjuvant. Lyme Disease Vaccine Study Group. *N Engl J Med* 339:209, 1998.

46. Nadelman RB, et al: Prophylaxis with single-dose doxycycline for the prevention of Lyme disease after an *Ixodes scapularis* tick bite. *N Engl J Med* 345:79, 2001.

47. Hayes EB, Piesman J: How can we prevent Lyme disease? *N Engl J Med* 348:2424, 2003.

48. Abramowicz M (ed): Treatment of Lyme disease: New drugs for allergic conjunctivitis. *Med Lett* 42:37, 2000.

49. Moore JA: Jarisch-Herxheimer reaction in Lyme disease. *Cutis* 39:397, 1987.

50. Luft BJ, et al: New chemotherapeutic approaches in the treatment of Lyme borreliosis. *Ann NY Acad Sci* 539:352, 1988.

51. Maraspin V, et al: Treatment of erythema migrans, in pregnancy. *Clin Infect Dis* 22:788, 1996.

52. Butler T: Relapsing fever. In Wyngaarden JB, Smith LH (eds): *Cecil Textbook of Medicine,* 18th ed. Philadelphia, WB Saunders, 1988.

53. Perine PL: Relapsing fever. In Braunwald E, et al (eds): *Harrison's Principles of Internal Medicine,* 11th ed. New York, McGraw-Hill, 1987.

54. Centers for Disease Control and Prevention: Tickborne relapsing fever outbreak after a family gathering—New Mexico, August 2002. *MMWR* 52:809, 2003.

55. Horton JM, Blaser MJ: The spectrum of relapsing fever in the Rocky Mountains. *Arch Intern Med* 145:871, 1985.

56. Marcus LC: Wilderness-acquired zoonoses. In Auerbach PS, Gehr EC (eds): *Management of Wilderness and Environmental Emergencies,* 2nd ed. St Louis, Mosby, 1989.

57. Kaye D: Tularemia. In Braunwald E, et al (eds): *Harrison's Principles of Internal Medicine,* 11th ed. New York, McGraw-Hill, 1987.

58. Liles WC: Tularemia from domestic cats. *West J Med* 158:619, 1993.

59. Sanford JP: Tularemia. In Gorbach SL, Bartlett JG, Blacklow NR (eds): *Infectious Diseases,* 2nd ed. Philadelphia, WB Saunders, 1998, p 1564.

60. Vyrostekova V, et al. Prevalence of coinfection of *Francisella tularensis* in animal reservoir animals of *Borrelia burgdorferi* sensu lato. *Wien Klin Wochenschr* 114:482, 2002.

61. Gill V, Cunha B: Tularemia pneumonia. *Semin Respir Infect* 12:61, 1997.

62. Levy L, Chiang W: Tularemia—United States, 1990-2000, *MMWR* 51:181, 2002.

63. Feldman KA, et al: Outbreak of primary pneumonic tularemia on Martha's Vineyard. *N Engl J Med* 345:1601, 2001.

64. Reintjes R, et al: Tularemia outbreak investigation in Kosovo: Case control and environmental studies. *Emerg Infect Dis* 8:69, 2002.

65. Eliasson H, et al: The 2000 tularemia outbreak: A case-control study of risk factors in disease-endemic and emergent areas, Sweden. *Emerg Infect Dis* 8:956, 2002.

66. Parssinen O, Rummukainen M: Acute glaucoma and acute corneal oedema in association with tularemia. *Acta Ophthalmol Scand* 75:732, 1997.

67. Franz DR, et al: Clinical recognition and management of patients exposed to biological warfare agents. *JAMA* 278:399, 1997.

68. Stupak HD, et al: Tularemia of the head and neck: A possible sign of bioterrorism. *Ear Nose Throat J* 82:263, 2003.

69. Jensen WA, Kirsch CM: Tularemia. *Semin Respir Infect* 18:146, 2003.

70. Syrjala H, et al: Guillain-Barré syndrome and tularemia pleuritis with high adenosine deaminase activity in pleural fluid (case report). *Infection* 17:152, 1989.

71. Johansson A, et al: Comparative analysis of PCR versus culture for diagnosis of ulceroglandular tularemia. *J Clin Microbiol* 38:22, 2000.

72. Berdal BO, et al: Field detection of *Francisella tularensis*. *Scand J Infect Dis* 32:287, 2000.

73. Cross JT, Jacobs RF: Tularemia: Treatment failures with outpatient use of ceftriaxone. *Clin Infect Dis* 17:976, 1993.

74. Dennis DT, et al: Tularemia as a biological weapon: Medical and public health management. *JAMA* 285:2763, 2001.

75. Drabick JJ, et al: Passive protection of mice against lethal *Francisella tularensis* (live tularemia vaccine strain) infection by the sera of human recipients of the live tularemia vaccine. *Am J Med Sci* 308:83, 1994.

76. Paddock CD, et al: Assessing the magnitude of the fatal Rocky Mountain spotted fever in the United States: Comparison of two national data sources. *Am J Trop Med Hyg* 67:349, 2002.

77. Treadwell TA, et al: Rocky Mountain spotted fever in the United States, 1993-1996. *Am J Trop Med Hyg* 63:21, 2000.

78. Dalton MJ, et al: National surveillance for Rocky Mountain spotted fever, 1981-1992: Epidemiologic summary and evaluation of risk factors for fatal outcome. *Am J Trop Med Hyg* 52:405, 1995.

79. Woodward TE: Rickettsial diseases. In Braunwald E, et al (eds): *Harrison's Principles of Internal Medicine,* 11th ed. New York, McGraw-Hill, 1987.

80. Elchos BN, Goddard J: Implications of presumptive fatal Rocky Mountain spotted fever in two dogs and their owner. *J Am Vet Med Assoc* 233:1450, 2003.

81. Arguin PM, et al: An investigation into the possibility of transmission of tick-borne pathogens via blood transfusion: Transfusion-Associated Tick-Borne Illness Task Force. *Transfusion* 39:828, 1999.

82. Hackstadt T: The biology of rickettsiae. *Infect Agents Dis* 5:127, 1996.

83. Haynes RE, Sanders DY, Cramblett HG: Rocky Mountain spotted fever in children. *J Pediatr* 76:685, 1970.

84. Walker DH: Rocky Mountain spotted fever: A seasonal alert. *Clin Infect Dis* 20:111, 1995.

85. Kirkland KB, et al: Rocky Mountain spotted fever complicated by gangrene: Report of six cases and review. *Clin Infect Dis* 16:629, 1993.

86. McGinley-Smith DE, Tsao SS: Dermatoses from ticks. *J Am Acad Dermatol* 49:363, 2003.

87. Wei TY, Baumann RJ: Acute disseminated encephalomyelitis after Rocky Mountain spotted fever. *Pediatr Neurol* 21:503, 1999.

88. Masters EJ, et al: Rocky Mountain spotted fever: A clinician's dilemma. *Arch Intern Med* 163:769, 2003.

89. Hilton E, et al: Seroprevalence and seroconversion for tick-borne diseases in a high-risk population in the northeast United States. *Am J Med* 106:404, 1999.

90. PanBioInDx website. Available af www.indxdi.com/indx1110.htm. Accessed February, 2000.

91. Procop GW, et al: Immunoperoxidase and immunofluorescent staining of *Rickettsia rickettsii* in skin biopsies. *Arch Pathol Lab Med* 121:894, 1997.

92. Paddock CD, et al: Hidden mortality attributable to Rocky Mountain spotted fever: Immunohistochemical detection of fatal, serologically unconfirmed disease. *J Infect Dis* 179:1469, 1999.

93. Centers for Disease Control and Prevention: Consequences of delayed diagnosis of Rocky Mountain spotted fever in children: West Virginia, Michigan, Tennessee, and Oklahoma May–July 2000. MMWR 49:885, 2000.

94. Drage LA: Life-threatening rashes: Dermatologic signs of four infectious diseases. *Mayo Clin Proc* 74:68, 1999.

95. Donovan BJ, et al. Treatment of tick-borne diseases. *Ann Pharmacother* 36:1590, 2002.

96. Rocky Mountain spotted fever. In Pickering L (ed): *2003 Red Book: Report of the Commission on Infectious Diseases,* 26th ed. Elk Grove Village, Ill, American Academy of Pediatrics, 2003, p 533.

97. Fournier P-E, Marrie TJ, Raoult D: Minireview: Diagnosis of Q fever. *J Clin Microbiol* 36:1823, 1998.

98. Morovic M: Acute renal failure as the main complication of acute infection with *Coxiella burnetii*. *Nephron* 64:335, 1993.

99. Schattner A: Lymphocytic meningitis as the sole manifestation of Q fever. *Postgrad Med J* 69:36, 1993.

100. Brouqi P: Chronic Q fever. *Arch Intern Med* 153:642, 1993.

101. Fournier P-E, et al: *Coxiella burnetii* infection of aneurysms or vascular grafts: Report of seven cases and review. *Clin Infect Dis* 26:116, 1998.

102. Raoult D: Q fever during pregnancy: A risk for women, fetuses, and obstetricians. *N Engl J Med* 330:371, 1994.

103. Raoult D: Q fever and HIV infection. *AIDS* 7:81, 1993.

104. Yale SH: Unusual aspects of acute Q fever-associated hepatitis. *Mayo Clin Proc* 69:769, 1994.

105. Kagawa FT, Wehner JH, Mohindra V: Q fever as a biological weapon. *Semin Respir Infect* 18:183, 2003.

106. Ackland JR: Vaccine prophylaxis of Q fever. *Med J Aust* 160:704, 1994.

107. Hmiel SP, et al: Human infection with *Ehrlichia ewingii*, the agent of Ozark canine granulocytic ehrlichiosis. Proceedings of the First International Conference on Emerging Infectious Diseases; March 8-11; Atlanta, Georgia; Addendum 4 [Abstract], 1998.

108. McQuiston JH, et al: Centers for Disease Control and Prevention: The human ehrlichioses in the United States. *Emerg Infect Dis* 5:635, 1999.

109. Standaert SM, et al: Ehrlichiosis in a golf-oriented retirement community. *N Engl J Med* 333:452, 1995.

110. Centers for Disease Control and Prevention: Summary: Provisional causes of notifiable diseases, United States, cumulative, week ending January 1, 2000. *MMWR* 48:1183, 2000.

111. Ruscio M, Cinco M: Human granulocytic ehrlichiosis in Italy: First report on two confirmed cases. *Ann NY Acad Sci* 990:350, 2003.

112. Walker DH: Tick-transmitted infectious diseases in the United States. *Annu Rev Public Health* 19:237, 1998.

113. Cohn LA: Ehrlichiosis and related infections. *Vet Clin North Am Small Anim Pract* 33:863, 2003.

114. Krause PJ, Corrow L, Bakken JS: Successful treatment of human granulocytic ehrlichiosis in children using rifampin. *Pediatrics* 112:e252, 2003.

115. Fritz CL, et al: Ehrlichiosis. *Infect Dis Clin North Am* 12:123, 1998.

116. Eng TR, et al: Epidemiologic, clinical, and laboratory findings of human ehrlichiosis in the United States, 1988. *JAMA* 264:2251, 1990.

117. Olano JP, et al: Human monocytotropic ehrlichiosis, Missouri. *Emerg Infect Dis* 9:1579, 2003.

118. Lee MS, Goslee TE, Lessell S: Ehrlichiosis optic neuritis. *Am J Ophthalmol* 135:412, 2003.

119. Schutze GE, Jacobs RF: Human monocytic ehrlichiosis in children. *Pediatrics* 100:E10, 1997.

120. Ravyn MD: Immunodiagnosis of human granulocytic ehrlichiosis by using culture-derived human isolates. *J Clin Microbiol* 36:1480, 1998.

121. Comer JA, et al: Serologic testing for human granulocytic ehrlichiosis at a national referral center. *J Clin Microbiol* 37:558, 1999.

122. Chu FK: Rapid and sensitive PCR-based detection and differentiation of aetiologic agents of human granulocytotropic and monocytotropic ehrlichiosis. *Mol Cell Probes* 12:93, 1998.

123. IGeneX: Ehrlichiosis: interpretation of laboratory results for ehrlichiosis. Available at www.igenex.com/tickopt2.htm. Accessed January 3, 2000.

124. Herwaldt BL, et al: Endemic babesiosis in another eastern state: New Jersey. *Emerg Infect Dis* 9:184, 2003.

125. Meldrum SC, et al: Human babesiosis in New York State: An epidemiological description of 136 cases. *Clin Infect Dis* 15:1019, 1992.

126. White DJ, et al: Human babesiosis in New York State: Review of 139 hospitalized cases and analysis of prognostic factors. *Arch Intern Med* 158:2149, 1998.

127. Torres-Velez FJ, et al: Development of an immunohistochemical assay for the detection of babesiosis in formalin-fixed, paraffin-embedded tissue samples. *Am J Clin Pathol* 120:833, 2003.

128. Krause PJ, et al: Efficacy of immunoglobulin M serodiagnostic test for rapid diagnosis of acute babesiosis. *J Clin Microbiol* 34:2014, 1996.

129. Krause PJ, et al: Concurrent Lyme disease and babesiosis: Evidence for increased severity and duration of illness. *JAMA* 275:1657, 1996.

130. Emmons RW: Ecology of Colorado tick fever. *Annu Rev Microbiol* 42:49, 1988.

131. Bowen GS: Colorado tick fever. In Monath TP (ed): *The Epidemiology of Arthropod-Borne Viral Diseases*. Boca Raton, Fla, CRC, 1988.

132. Calisher CH, et al: Diagnosis of Colorado tick fever virus infection by enzyme immunoassays for immunoglobulin M and G antibodies. *J Clin Microbiol* 22:84, 1985.

133. Klasco R: Colorado tick fever. *Med Clin North Am* 86:435, 2002.

134. Hovell WH: Journal kept on the journey from Lake George to Port Phillip, 1824-1825. *R Aust Hist Soc* 7:358, 1921.

135. Gothe R, Kunze K, Hoogstraal H: The mechanisms of pathogenicity in the tick paralyses. *J Med Entomol* 16:357, 1979.

136. Abramowicz M (ed): Insect repellents. *Med Lett* 45:41, 2003.

CHAPTER

133 Tuberculosis

Peter E. Sokolove and Dennis Chan

PERSPECTIVE

History and Epidemiology

Tuberculosis (TB) has plagued humankind throughout recorded history. Archaeologic excavations and medical anthropologic studies document the presence of TB in ancient civilizations. Clear evidence of tuberculous lesions of bone has been found in Egyptian mummified human remains that date to 3400 BCE.[1] The presence of TB has been microscopically confirmed in the mummies of small children, one from the dynastic period of Egyptian history and one from pre-Columbian southern Peru around 700 AD.[1-3]

Hippocrates (460 to 370 BCE) is credited for providing the first accurate clinical description of TB. He coined the term *phthisis* (to melt and to waste away) to describe the wasting character of the disease, which was also associated with fever and incurable lung ulcerations.[4] Aristotle (384 to 322 BCE) accurately described the contagious nature of the disease, noticing that the phthisis-stricken patient had a "pernicious air" and that "one takes the disease because there is in this air something that is disease-producing to others in the proximity."[5]

TB did not become a major public health problem until the industrial revolution. The urbanization of European cities led to overcrowding, widespread poverty, and poor hygienic conditions that were ideal for the epidemic spread of the disease throughout western Europe from the early 1600s through the 1800s.[6] Approximately 25% of all adult deaths in Europe were caused by TB during this period, and in 1861 Oliver Wendell Holmes named it the "white plague."[1] TB gradually became a global epidemic as Europeans colonized North America and explored and colonized other parts of the world.[6] The TB epidemic peaked in western Europe in the early 1800s and by 1900 had peaked in the Americas. Globally, the disease still has not reached a peak in some developing countries in Africa and Asia.[7]

Laënnec, who invented the stethoscope in 1816, accurately described the evolution of TB from the small initial tubercle through all of its pathologic manifestations in 1819.[4] Twenty years later, Schönlein, also recognizing the tubercle as the fundamental anatomic lesion, named the disease tuberculosis.[8] Koch identified the tubercle bacillus in 1882, and Roentgen's discovery of x-rays in 1895 greatly improved the ability to diagnose TB promptly.[1,4]

The TB epidemic provided fertile ground for quackery. Treatment of TB has progressed from homemade concoctions, the royal touch of a king, bleeding, purging, sweating, and poultices to sanatoriums, artificial pneumothorax, other surgical interventions, and finally modern chemotherapy.[1]

In 1892, Biggs instituted a comprehensive program of TB control in New York City that included public education, systemic surveillance, isolation of patients, nursing follow-up, improved sanitation, and free sputum testing.[8,9] These types of programs and the subsequent introduction of the antituberculous drugs led to an impressive decline in the incidence of TB throughout the 20th century. Between 1953 and 1985, TB cases decreased by an average of 5.8% per year.[10] As recently as the 1970s, U.S. health officials believed that TB was well under control and could soon be eradicated.[11] Unfortunately, as the incidence and perceived importance of the disease decreased, so did the public health programs to control it.[12] The premature decline in government support for TB control programs made it impossible to manage the disease appropriately. The decline of the infrastructure dedicated to TB control combined with other events during the late 1980s and early 1990s (the human immunodeficiency virus [HIV]–acquired immunodeficiency syndrome [AIDS] epidemic, increasing immigration from countries with high TB prevalence, increasing occurrence of TB in institutional living settings, escalating poverty, substance abuse, homelessness, and urban overcrowding) led to a resurgence of TB in the United States from 1986 through 1992 and contributed to the emergence of drug-resistant strains of *Mycobacterium tuberculosis* (MTB).[12]

Worldwide, the disease had become so widespread that in 1993 the World Health Organization declared TB a global emergency. TB is currently the world's second leading infectious cause of death, and one third of the world's population has been infected by TB.[13,14] Each year more than 8 million people develop active TB and nearly 2 million die from the disease.[15]

Elders who currently harbor dormant infection that is reactivated are an important reservoir of MTB in the United States.[16] Debilitating disease or immunosenescence may predispose to reactivation. Nursing homes are particularly vulnerable to TB outbreaks because reactivation of disease in remotely infected individuals may be followed by epidemic spread among the many susceptible hosts living in close quarters.

Immigration from endemic countries is another major factor.[13] As of 2002, the majority of U.S. TB cases occur among foreign-born individuals.[17] The largest numbers of people with TB originate from Mexico, the Philippines, Vietnam, and India.[17] Homelessness has also contributed to the spread of TB in major urban centers. Homelessness is often associated with conditions that decrease resistance to TB, such as malnutrition, alcoholism, or substance abuse. MTB infection in the homeless population may quickly progress to active TB.[18] Last, the HIV epidemic has had the greatest impact on the reemergence of TB in the United States.[19] The pandemic of HIV-related TB has led to an increase in TB cases among non–HIV-infected people owing to the greater numbers of source cases in the community.[20] The rate of TB among patients who are HIV infected and TB skin test positive is approximately 200 to 800 times higher than the rate of TB estimated for the U.S. population overall.[21]

The reemergence of TB has also affected children. Between 1962 and the mid-1980s, the rates of childhood TB in the United States decreased an average of 6% a year.[22,23] This trend has reversed along with the young urban adult trend, and the number of cases reported in children 4 years of age or younger increased 36% from 1985 through 1992.[10] This increase reflected ongoing transmission of TB in the community because TB in young children must result from recent infection.[10]

After a 32-year decline, the number of TB cases in the United States increased 20% between 1986 and 1992. By 1992, roughly 14% more cases (26,673) were reported over the 1985 nadir. This trend, however, reversed in 1993, largely owing to the mobilization of new federal resources provided to the states for TB control and prevention.[12] The number of reported cases during 1996 decreased in each age group as well as all ethnic groups.[24] The number of reported cases in the United States during 2002 (15,075) represents a 43% decrease from 1992 and the 10th consecutive year of decline.[17] Although the rapid resurgence of TB appears to be subsiding in the United States, there is no justification for complacency. Rates of newly diagnosed TB are still significant in different regions of the country and in certain demographic groups.[17] The populations most likely to develop and transmit TB commonly are seen by emergency physicians, who necessarily play a key role in identification, prevention, and treatment.

Etiology

TB in humans is caused by one of three pathogenic mycobacteria: *Mycobacterium bovis*, *Mycobacterium africanum*, or *M. tuberculosis*. *M. bovis* is transmitted by drinking milk from diseased cows, but as it is now common to pasteurize milk, it has become a relatively rare cause of TB. *M. africanum* is also a rare cause of human TB. This mycobacterium is thought to be intermediate between *M. tuberculosis* and *M. bovis* and has been documented to cause human TB predominately in Africa.[25] Worldwide, MTB remains the major causative agent.

Humans are the sole known reservoir for MTB. This pathogen is a primarily intracellular, aerobic, nonmotile, non–spore-forming bacillus with a waxy lipid coat.[25] The coat makes MTB resistant to decolorization with acid alcohol after staining, hence the term *acid-fast bacillus* (AFB). MTB grows slowly. Its generation time is 15 to 20 hours compared with less than 1 hour for some common bacteria; cultures take 4 to 6 weeks to grow on standard solid media.[25]

MTB produces neither endotoxins nor exotoxins. Its cell components are immunoreactive; some are immunosuppressive, and others lead to granuloma formation, macrophage activation, host toxicity, and modification of the immune response.[26]

PRINCIPLES OF DISEASE

Transmission

TB is transmitted primarily by the respiratory route; other routes, such as direct inoculation, occur primarily among health care workers. Patients with active disease expel MTB in liquid droplets during coughing, sneezing, and vocalizing. A single cough or 5 minutes of talking can produce 3000 infectious droplets, and sneezing can produce an even higher number.[6] The droplets rapidly evaporate and the desiccated bacilli circulate airborne for prolonged periods. These infective particles, or droplet nuclei, measure 1 to 5 μm in diameter, contain one to three tubercle bacilli, and can travel to the distal alveoli.

The susceptible host may become infected when only a few of the droplet nuclei are inhaled. Fomites are not important in the transmission of the disease, and patients' rooms, eating utensils, and bed clothes do not require special decontamination procedures.[25] Because the infectious droplet nuclei are airborne, exchanging contaminated air is the most important environmental control. In addition, MTB is susceptible to ultraviolet radiation, and transmission rarely occurs outdoors because of the dilution of infectious particles and possible exposure to ultraviolet radiation.[27]

The risk for TB transmission increases when source patients have airway and cavitary disease. Infectivity correlates with the number of organisms seen on sputum smear, the extent of pulmonary disease, and the frequency of cough. After institution of proper chemotherapy (three or four drugs) for 2 weeks, patients with initially AFB-negative sputum smears can be considered noncontagious. However, after 2 weeks of treatment, patients who were initially smear positive may still have viable MTB detectable in their posttreatment sputum cultures, and patients with extensive disease may still have AFB detectable on their posttreatment sputum smears. The latter two groups should generally still be considered contagious.[28] There is currently no clear epidemiologic evidence to define better the contagiousness of patients after they are started with effective therapy.[28] The Centers for Disease Control and Prevention (CDC) has published guidelines requiring three negative smears on different days to remove a patient from respiratory isolation, but there is still debate regarding this recommendation.[29,30]

Extrapulmonary TB may also be infectious but only if in the oral cavity or an open skin lesion.[29] Transmission of MTB to health care workers caring for patients with skin ulcers and draining tuberculous abscesses has been reported.[31] Irrigation of the abscess may aerosolize the bacilli, forming infectious droplet nuclei.[32]

Pathogenesis

When infectious droplet nuclei are inhaled, the airflow through the bronchial tree tends to deposit them in the midlung zone on the respiratory surface of the alveoli.[25] The deposition launches a complex series of immunologic events. Dannenberg has organized the complex pathogenesis of TB into four stages.[33]

Stage 1

The first stage begins when an alveolar macrophage phagocytoses the recently inhaled bacillus. A macrophage from a resistant host can immediately destroy a less virulent bacillus. In these cases, no tuberculous infection develops and the process ends. If a virulent bacillus can overcome a macrophage's microbicidal capability, the infection may progress to the next stage.

Stage 2

When the alveolar macrophage is unable to destroy the inhaled tubercle bacilli, the bacilli replicate until the macrophage lyses. Circulating monocytes are attracted to the site of infection by the released bacilli, cellular debris, and various chemotactic factors. The monocytes differentiate into macrophages and ingest the free bacilli. Initially, these new macrophages are not activated and cannot destroy or inhibit the mycobacteria. The bacilli multiply logarithmically within macrophages and accumulate at the primary focus of infection, now called a tubercle.[34] The infected macrophages may also be transported through lymphatics to regional lymph nodes, from which they can reach the bloodstream and spread.

During this lymphohematogenous dissemination, the pathogens tend to distribute preferentially to lymph nodes, kidney, epiphyses of long bones, vertebral bodies, meningeal areas, and the apical posterior areas of the lungs.[25] These sites may be favored because of a high oxygen tension. Others believe that the lung apices are favored because of impaired clearance mechanisms from poor lymph flow.[25]

Stage 3

The third stage of TB begins 2 to 3 weeks after the initial infection, with development of the immune response that terminates the unimpeded growth of MTB.[33] Cell-mediated immunity (CMI) occurs through CD4 helper T cells.[35] When the T cell encounters mycobacterial antigens, it is activated and produces an expanded population of specific T cells. These T cells secrete cytokines (e.g., interferon-γ, tumor necrosis factor) that attract and activate monocyte/macrophages. Once activated, the macrophages, containing previously ingested mycobacteria and their progeny, kill the bacilli. The destruction of the mycobacteria is associated with the formation of epithelioid cell granulomas and clearance of the organisms.[34]

Delayed-type hypersensitivity (DTH) is mediated by cytotoxic CD8 suppressor T cells.[35] The cytotoxic cells kill nonactivated macrophages laden with mycobacteria and thus cause local tissue destruction as well. DTH results in the formation of caseating necrotic granulomas. This stops bacillary growth; mycobacteria, now extracellular, cannot multiply in this acidic, anoxic, extracellular environment.[34] Tubercle bacilli can survive, dormant, in this solid caseous material for years.[34] The host's resistance determines whether the disease remains dormant or immediately progresses to active disease.

In the immunocompetent host with strong CMI, the primary lesion is effectively walled off by epithelioid cells. Eventually, the caseous center inspissates, and the disease is arrested, often for a lifetime.[33] Similarly, at sites of lymphohematogenous spread, the mycobacteria are quickly destroyed with little caseous necrosis by a rapid CMI response.[33] The rapid destruction of the mycobacteria by CMI terminates the infectious process, and the only evidence of the infection is the conversion to a positive tuberculin (purified protein derivative [PPD]) skin test.[25]

This sequence of events from stage 1 to stage 3 represents the pathogenesis of primary TB in the immunocompetent patient.[35] In most cases, primary TB is subclinical and self-limited. In the immunocompromised host, however, clinically active primary disease may develop rapidly after the initial MTB infection.

The less resistant host with weak CMI relies more on DTH to control the infection. The primary lesion is surrounded by nonactivated macrophages, so it is not effectively walled off, and the caseous center expands, compromising more lung tissue. If these patients eventually contain the infection, it may also go unnoticed and be evident only radiographically as healed parenchymal calcifications of the primary or Ghon focus and of the regional lymph nodes.[25] If host defenses are unable to contain the primary infection, however, as can occur in infants and immunosuppressed adults, the primary focus may become an area of advancing pneumonia.[25] This process is called primary progressive TB. In addition, this host may be unable to control the infection at the sites of lymphohematogenous spread and may form multiple uncontrolled caseous tubercles and develop disseminated TB.[34] HIV-infected patients are particularly susceptible to primary progressive TB because HIV specifically targets CD4+ cells and macrophages.

Stage 4

The final stage usually occurs months to decades after an apparent recovery from the initial infection. TB may progress to stage 4 even when residing in immunocompetent hosts. Usually, host factors lead to decreased resistance and reactivation of dormant foci of MTB. The progression is due to liquefaction and cavity formation.

The liquefied tubercle serves as an excellent growth medium for the mycobacteria. The large numbers of extracellular bacilli stimulate DTH, which secondarily causes local damage. The tubercle eventually erodes through the bronchial wall and drains its contents, forming a cavity. The liquefied caseous material, teeming with mycobacteria, enters other parts of the lung and the outside environment. The spilling of this liquefied material within the lung may produce a caseous bronchopneumonia.[34]

The cavity formed at the site of the initial focus remains a significant lesion. Cavities provide optimal conditions for mycobacterial growth. The oxygen tension is increased, and the host's defenses are ineffective at interrupting the multiplication of the mycobacteria within a cavity.[34]

CLINICAL FEATURES

The initial infection with MTB is most often asymptomatic in healthy individuals. Mild fever and malaise may develop in association with the immune response at 4 to 6 weeks, but generally the primary infection is clinically insignificant.[36] Conversion to a positive PPD skin test may be the only means of diagnosing the infection. Clinically active TB develops in 8% to 10% of otherwise healthy PPD converters who do not take prophylactic agents, 3% to 5% in the first 2 years (acute primary TB) and another 5% during the remainder of life (reactivation TB).[19] In contrast, persons also infected with HIV proceed to acute primary TB at a rate of 37% within 6 months and then develop active TB at a rate of 7% to 10% per year.[19]

Reactivation of dormant foci is responsible for the major clinical manifestations of TB.[36] Exogenous reinfection of patients with well-documented prior TB infection causes clinical disease indistinguishable from reactivation TB.[37] Because it may be incorrect to label all late-onset cases as reactivation disease, *postprimary TB* is the preferred term. Postprimary TB is active or chronic disease in a patient previously infected. In the United States and other developed countries, reactivation is thought to be the primary mechanism of postprimary TB. Exogenous reinfection has played a role where contagion levels are high, as in outbreaks of TB, in developing countries, or in immunocompromised hosts.[37-39]

Patient's History

History of Present Illness

Clinically significant pulmonary TB is often indolent, and symptoms are absent or minimal until the disease advances. The patient may also have a systemic reaction to the infection. The systemic reaction, thought to be mediated by cytokines, especially tumor necrosis factor α, causes the constitutional symptoms of anorexia, weight loss, fatigue, irritability, malaise, weakness, headache, chills, and, most commonly, fever.[36,40] The fever usually develops in the afternoon, and the patient defervesces while sleeping, which causes the classical night sweats.[36]

Cough is the most common symptom of pulmonary TB. Initially it may be nonproductive, but as caseation necrosis and liquefaction develop, mucopurulent and nonspecific sputum is usually produced.[25,36,40] Hemoptysis, caused by caseous sloughing or endobronchial erosion, is usually minor but often indicates extensive lung involvement.[25] Many asymptomatic patients present for care because they are alarmed by the hemoptysis.

Patients may also complain of pleuritic chest pain, which is caused by parenchymal inflammation adjacent to the pleural surface. Dyspnea with chest pain may indicate a spontaneous pneumothorax.[41] Shortness of breath from parenchymal lung involvement is unusual, however, and if present indicates extensive parenchymal disease or tracheobronchial obstruction.[36] Table 133-1 shows the frequency of symptoms found in one study of patients with culture-proven pulmonary TB.[42] The clinical presentation of TB among emergency department patients may be especially confusing. In one study, only one third of emergency department patients with active pulmonary TB had pulmonary chief complaints, only 64% ever reported a cough, and only 8% had hemoptysis.[43]

Any vague systemic disorder or fever of unknown etiology may represent TB.[19] Atypical presentations are particularly common in infants, elders, and immunocompromised persons. Infants and young children tend to develop large hilar lymph nodes, which may compress a bronchus, leading to atelectasis and possibly obstructive pneumonia; they may have a "brassy cough." A node may also erode through the bronchial wall, causing symptomatic endobronchial disease and allowing endobronchial spread of tuberculous pneumonia to other areas of the lungs.[25] In contrast, fewer elders present with respiratory symptoms. The diagnosis may be masked by coexistent diseases and nonspecific presenting symptoms.[44] Pulmonary TB should be considered in elders with chronic cough and failure to thrive.[16]

Clinical manifestations of TB in patients co-infected with HIV are even more subtle and nonspecific, especially because these patients are vulnerable to opportunistic infections and neoplasms that can cause the same constitutional symptoms as TB. There is a synergy between the two infections (MTB and HIV) that leads to a greatly increased viral load.[20] Active TB with HIV co-infection has been associated with an increased risk for opportunistic infections and death.[21] Patients with advanced HIV infection also commonly have extrapulmonary involvement (30%) as well as combined pulmonary and extrapulmonary TB (32%).[40]

Risk Factors

All patients in the emergency department who have been coughing should be screened for the presence of TB risk factors (Box 133-1).[45] Risks for acquiring TB may also be stratified by age. Because infants and toddlers have poorly developed CMI, they have a much higher incidence of TB than adults. Children 5 to 10 years of age are relatively resistant to TB. Infants and toddlers commonly have extrapulmonary disease and acute lower and midlung bronchopneumonia that rarely progresses to cavitary disease. Young adults

Table 133-1. Frequency of Symptoms in Pulmonary Tuberculosis

Symptom	Number with Symptom	Number Evaluated	Percentage with Symptom
Cough	144	185	78
Weight loss	134	181	74
Fatigue	112	165	68
Tactile fever	109	183	60
Night sweats	98	177	55
Chills	92	180	51
Anorexia	76	167	46
Chest pain	71	179	40
Dyspnea	64	173	37
Hemoptysis	51	181	28
No respiratory symptoms	13	186	7
None of above symptoms	9	187	5

From Barnes PF, et al: Chest roentgenogram in pulmonary tuberculosis: New data on an old test. *Chest* 94:316, 1988.

BOX 133-1. Tuberculosis Risk Factors

Close contacts of known case
Persons with HIV infection
Foreign-born from Asia, Africa, Latin America
Medically underserved, low-income populations
Elderly persons
Residents of long-term care facilities (nursing homes, correctional facilities)
Injection drug users
Groups identified locally (homeless, migrant farmworkers)
Persons who have occupational exposure

HIV, human immunodeficiency virus.
From CDC: *TB Care Guide Highlights from Core Curriculum on Tuberculosis.* Atlanta. U.S. Department of Health and Human Services, 1994.

show the adult pattern of apical pulmonary disease, including cavity formation, suggesting reactivation. Because of decreased immunocompetence, elders tend to manifest the disease similarly to young children.[25] Patients with a history of PPD conversion should be asked about the presence of medical conditions that would put them at risk for developing active postprimary disease through reactivation (Box 133-2).[45]

Patients with a history of active TB should be asked about all antituberculous medications taken or currently being taken and about their compliance. Failure to improve on an appropriate regimen after 2 months may signal nonadherence to therapy or the presence of a resistant strain.[46]

BOX 133-2. Risk Factors for Developing Active Tuberculosis in the Previously Infected

HIV infection
Recent TB infection
 (within past 2 years)
Chest x-ray study suggestive
 of prior TB in a person not
 treated
Injection drug use
Diabetes mellitus
Silicosis
Prolonged corticosteroid therapy
Immunosuppressive therapy

Head or neck cancer
Hematologic and
 reticuloendothelial
 diseases
End-stage renal disease
Intestinal bypass or
 gastrectomy
Chronic malabsorption
 syndromes
Low body weight (10%
 or more below the
 ideal)

HIV, human immunodeficiency virus; TB, tuberculosis.
Modified from CDC: *TB Core Highlights from Core Curriculum on Tuberculosis.* Atlanta. U.S. Department of Health and Human Services, 1994.

Figure 133-1. Chest radiograph demonstrating cavitary tuberculosis with left-sided pneumothorax, later diagnosed as a bronchopleural fistula. (Courtesy of John Pearce, MD.)

Physical Findings

Examination of the chest is unlikely to establish the extent of disease. Over areas of infiltration, one may hear rales when the patient breathes in after a short cough (posttussive rales), and bronchial breath sounds may be present over areas of lung consolidation. Distant, hollow breath sounds that can be heard over cavities are called amphoric breath sounds.[25] One emergency department study reported abnormal physical examination findings in 80% of patients with active pulmonary TB.[43]

Erythema nodosum or phlyctenular keratoconjunctivitis (severe unilateral inflammation of an eye) may appear with the onset of tuberculin hypersensitivity. These self-limited, allergic manifestations are not common in the United States.[25] The patient's overall appearance and state of health may be the most useful indicators when evaluating for the potential presence of TB. General signs include pallor secondary to anemia, fever, and cachexia with weight loss.

Complications

Pneumothorax

Spontaneous pneumothorax is not common (less than 5% of patients with severe cavitary disease) but may occur when a tuberculous cavity ruptures and creates a bronchopleural fistula or when a bleb ruptures into the pleural space (Figure 133-1).[47] Delayed tube thoracostomy and suction result in progressive infection and fibrosis of the pleura that leads to trapping of the lung.

Empyema

TB patients with extensive, progressive parenchymal disease and cavitation may develop an empyema.

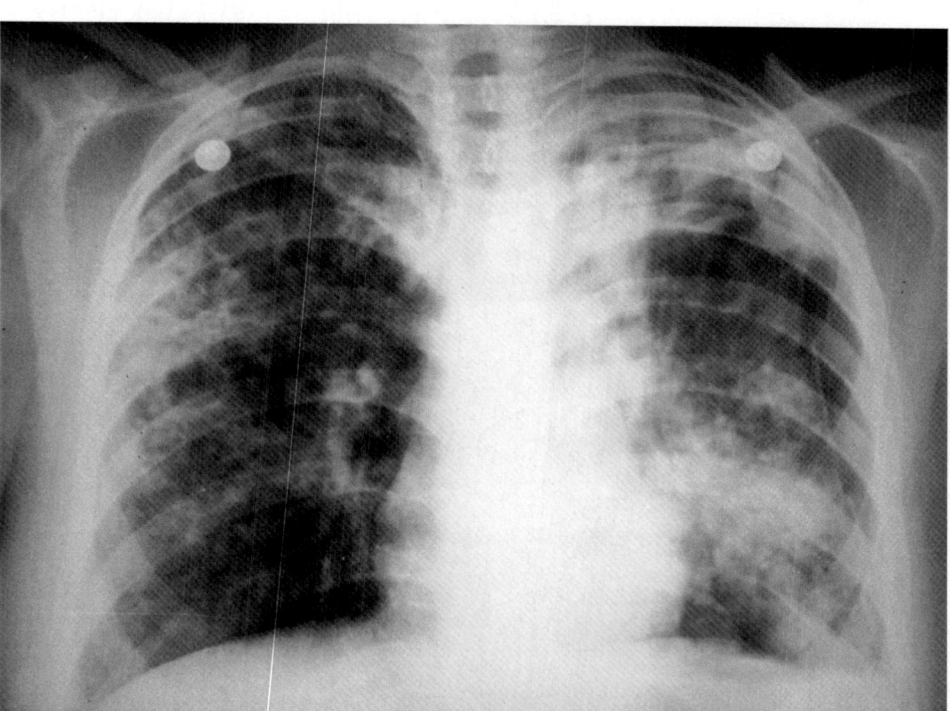

Although rare (1% to 4%), empyema is more common late in the course of the disease in debilitated patients. Rupture of a cavity into the pleural space is usually catastrophic and often associated with bronchopleural fistula formation. An untreated empyema can result in spontaneous pleurocutaneous fistula, a chest wall mass, or rib and vertebra destruction.[47]

Endobronchial Spread

Endobronchial spread is the most common complication of cavitary disease. It is manifest radiographically as 5- to 10-mm, poorly defined nodules clustered in dependent portions of the lungs. These nodules may rapidly coalesce into parenchymal consolidation, so-called galloping consumption.[47]

Airway Tuberculosis

When a cavity drains its highly infectious material into the bronchial tree, the airways not only spread the infection but also develop endobronchial TB. Bronchiectasis commonly complicates endobronchial TB. Bronchial stenosis may result from extensive damage caused by endobronchial TB or from direct extension of infection from tuberculous adenitis or from lymphatic dissemination to the airway.[25,47] Tuberculous bronchostenosis may appear radiographically as persistent segmental or lobar collapse, lobar hyperinflation, and obstructive pneumonia.[47]

Tracheal TB and laryngeal TB are less common than endobronchial TB. Laryngeal disease is the most infectious form of TB; it results from the proximal extension of lower airway disease, pooling of infected secretions in the posterior larynx, or hematogenous dissemination to the anterior larynx. Patients with laryngeal TB also usually have active pulmonary disease.[47]

Superinfection

Extensive TB infection often heals with open cavities and areas of bronchiectasis.[36] Superinfection may occur with a wide variety of organisms, including *Aspergillus fumigatus*.[48] The characteristic finding on chest radiographs is the aspergilloma or "fungus ball" (Figure 133-2). Aspergillomas are particularly significant because they may cause massive and fatal hemoptysis.[36]

Hemoptysis

Mild hemoptysis is a common complication of acute infection. TB also causes massive hemoptysis. The destruction of lung parenchyma leads to rupture of blood vessels. A tuberculous lesion or cavity may erode into a pulmonary artery, leading to pseudoaneurysm formation (Rasmussen's aneurysm) and potentially fatal hemoptysis.[47] This complication has become uncommon since the development of antituberculous medications.[25] Alternatively, superinfection of cavities by invasive organisms or tumor development in scarred lung may erode bronchial or pulmonary vessels and cause major hemorrhage. These patients often require emergency surgical resection or selective embolization.[49]

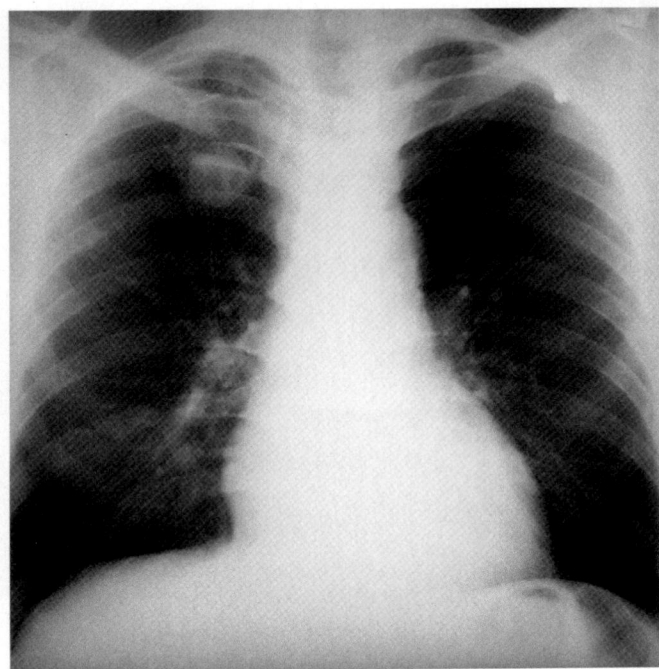

Figure 133-2. Superinfection of healed tuberculous cavity. An aspergilloma can be seen in the right upper lung. (Courtesy of John Pearce, MD.)

Primary Tuberculous Pericarditis

This complication usually results from direct extension of infection from the tracheobronchial tree, mediastinal or hilar lymph nodes, sternum, or spine. Pericardial involvement may also result from hematogenous spread secondary to acute miliary TB or from another focus elsewhere in the body.[25,50] In the United States, TB is the leading cause of pericarditis among HIV-infected individuals, with a prevalence of up to 15%.[51] The predominant symptoms are cough, chest pain, and dyspnea, and the most common signs are cardiomegaly, an audible rub, fever, and tachycardia.[52] Complications of pericardial TB include pericardial effusion, constrictive pericarditis, myocarditis, and cardiac tamponade.[50] Cardiac tamponade may result from accumulation of pericardial fluid but also may occur if enlarging lymph nodes rupture into the pericardium. Emergency echocardiography reliably confirms the presence of pericardial fluid.[53]

DIAGNOSTIC STRATEGIES

Laboratory Tests

Routine laboratory studies generally are not useful in suggesting or establishing the diagnosis.[36] Normochromic normocytic anemia, elevated erythrocyte sedimentation rate and serum globulin level, hyponatremia, and hypercalcemia can all occur in active pulmonary TB, but these tests are nonspecific.[36,48,54] Tuberculin skin testing is important epidemiologically as a modality for diagnosing MTB infection but is of limited value for detecting active clinical disease. At

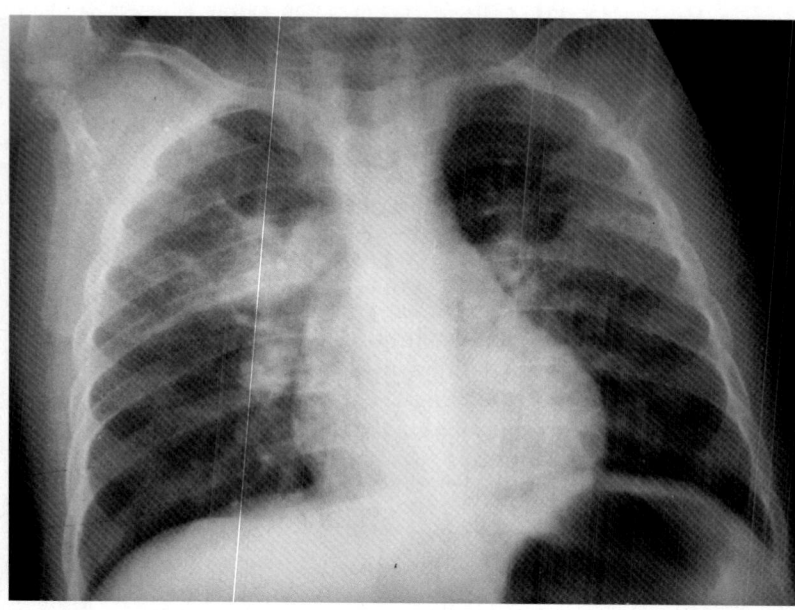

Figure 133-3. Chest radiographic findings in a child with primary tuberculosis. Note active Ghon focus with associated hilar adenopathy, bilateral infiltrates. (Courtesy of John Pearce, MD.)

least 20% of patients with active TB have false-negative tuberculin skin tests.[25]

Diagnostic Imaging

The chest radiograph is the most useful study for making a presumptive diagnosis of pulmonary TB. Chest radiographic abnormalities are not limited to the classical upper lobe cavitary infiltrates. Primary TB infection and postprimary disease each have distinctive radiographic features. A normal chest radiograph has a high negative predictive value and is therefore useful in screening emergency department patients for active pulmonary TB. However, the false-negative rate is approximately 1% in immunocompetent adults and increases to 7% to 15% in HIV-positive patients.[24] Therefore, depending on the clinical circumstances, a normal chest radiograph does not always exclude active TB, especially in patients with endobronchial disease and HIV infection.

Primary Tuberculosis

Chest radiographic manifestations of primary disease in adults are often not recognized as TB.[55,56] Primary tuberculous infiltrates can occur in any lobe.[47,57,58] For any age group, a pneumonic infiltrate with enlarged hilar or mediastinal nodes should strongly suggest the diagnosis.[57] The infiltrate is usually homogeneous and most commonly involves a single lobe. Thus, primary TB may appear radiographically identical to a bacterial pneumonia, with the associated lymphadenopathy, if present, being the only distinguishing feature.

Lymphadenopathy is considered the radiologic hallmark of primary TB in children but is seen less commonly in adults.[24,58] When present, adenopathy is usually unilateral and associated with parenchymal infiltrate (Figure 133-3). It may occur bilaterally or, more rarely, may be an isolated finding on chest radiography.[36] Massive hilar adenopathy is more common

in young children. As a result, atelectasis, resulting from airway compression by adjacent enlarged nodes, is a likely finding in children younger than 2 years but is less common in older children and adults.[47]

Other primary TB chest radiographic findings include a moderate to large pleural effusion, which is often an isolated finding whose prevalence increases with age; miliary TB (innumerable, 1- to 3-mm noncalcified nodules dispersed throughout both lungs with mild basilar predominance), which is mainly a threat to children younger than 2 years, immunocompromised patients, and elders; and tuberculomas, well-circumscribed nodular lesions of the parenchyma thought to be a result of healed primary TB.[24,47] When the healed primary focus is visible on the chest radiograph as a calcified scar, it is known as the Ghon focus. Calcified secondary foci of infection are known as Simon's foci. A Ghon focus associated with calcified hilar nodes is called a Ranke complex.[25,47] A right-sided predominance in the distribution of Ghon's foci and Ranke's complexes is well recognized and probably reflects the higher statistical probability of an airborne infection affecting the right lung.[24] Calcification seen on the chest radiograph indicates healing, but viable bacilli may still exist in a partially calcified lesion.[57]

When resolution does not occur, the result is progressive primary TB, which appears radiographically as progressive parenchymal consolidation often including secondary foci in the upper lobes.[47] In some patients the primary tuberculous pneumonia breaks down into multiple cavitary lesions or a single large abscess.[57] These chest radiographic findings may easily be confused with the findings in postprimary TB.

Postprimary Tuberculosis

Postprimary TB typically appears as an upper lung infiltrate or consolidation with or without cavitation. The lesion may be small or extensive and is usually

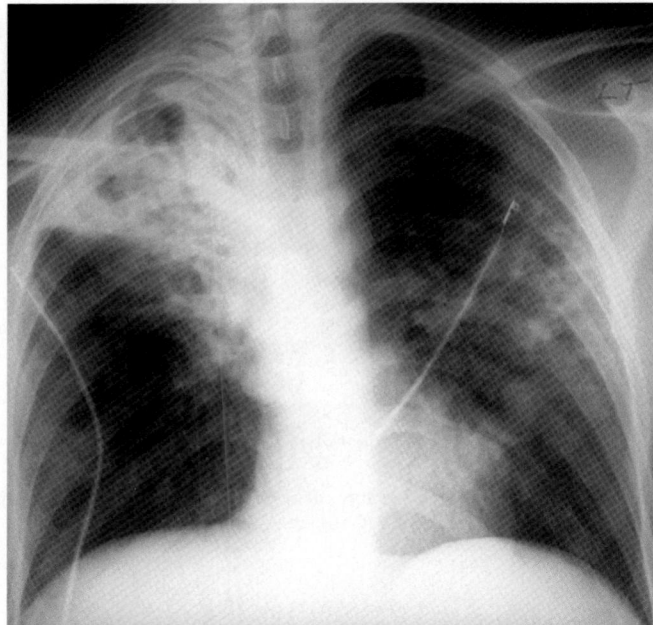

Figure 133-4. Chest radiograph shows right upper lobe cavitary disease. Also note left-sided infiltrate secondary to endobronchial spread.

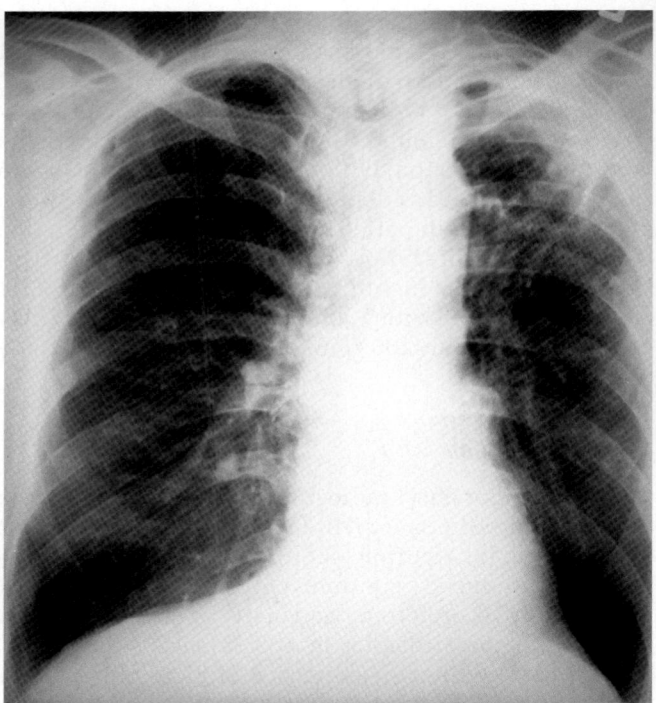

Figure 133-5. A healed, thin-walled cavity is present in the left upper lobe of this chest film. (Courtesy of John Pearce, MD.)

located in the apical or posterior segment of the upper lobe but may appear in the superior segment of the lower lobe.[59] Postprimary disease also occurs in the lower lung. In addition, bronchogenic spread can occur, leading to involvement of multiple lobes (Figure 133-4).[59] The patient with bilateral upper lobe disease is extremely likely to have TB.[57] The other important, recognizable characteristics of postprimary disease are fibrosis and cavitation.

The initial lesion of postprimary TB is a poorly defined, heterogeneous alveolar opacity called an exudative lesion.[47] These lesions are not purely exudative in that they are associated with a fibrotic pattern of nodules and a few fine, linear densities. Unchecked, the infection may rapidly progress to lobar or complete lung opacification and destruction.[47] Postprimary TB, however, usually runs a chronic course characterized by reactive fibrosis, and in most cases the initial exudative lesions are gradually replaced by more well-defined reticular and nodular opacities or "fibroproductive" lesions.[47,57]

Fibroproductive lesions are often irregular and angular in contour, have strands extending toward the hilum, and have calcification of one or more nodules. This pattern is characteristic of granulomatous disease and is rarely found in other bacterial infections.[31] As fibrosis continues, there may be distortion of normal vascular and mediastinal structures secondary to contraction and shrinkage of the scar. Severe fibrosis with upper lobe volume loss may eventually lead to retraction of the interlobar fissure and upward displacement of the hilum.[57] The chest radiographic appearance at this stage has been variably referred to as "old scarring," "no active disease," or "fibrotic, apparently wellhealed TB." Many of these patients have positive

sputum, and infectivity cannot be accurately assessed by chest radiography.[47,57] Only serial radiographs can reliably differentiate active from inactive disease. Lack of radiographic changes over a 4- to 6-month interval generally indicates "inactive" or, more precisely, "radiographically stable" disease.[24]

Cavitation should alert the emergency physician to the high infectivity of the patient and the potential for associated complications such as bronchogenic spread of TB when an area of caseous necrosis liquefies and communicates with the bronchial tree (see Figure 133-4). Cavities are usually multiple and range in diameter from a few millimeters to several centimeters.[47] The walls of the cavities initially are thick and rough and become thinner and smoother with healing (Figure 133-5). A hazy, parenchymal reaction around a cavity with an ill-defined wall strongly suggests an active lesion. Most cavities heal by obliteration and may leave a small linear or stellate scar; others remain patent and become thinwalled bullae.[57]

Although pulmonary TB usually induces chest radiographic changes, patients with sputum cultures positive for MTB may have normal chest films. In a series of 103 patients, 10 people (9.7%) with confirmed pulmonary TB had normal chest radiographs.[56] Chest radiographs may also be normal in patients with endobronchial TB.[41,60]

Chest radiographs of patients with pulmonary TB and HIV infection may be atypical in about one third of cases.[61] However, the radiographic appearance of disease is heavily influenced by the degree of immunocompromise. Patients with late HIV infection more often demonstrate mediastinal adenopathy or atypical infiltrates and less often have cavitation.[62,63] Severe immunosuppression has been reported to be associated with a miliary pattern of disease on chest radiographs.[24] Conversely, chest radiographs of patients with early HIV infection are more similar to those of patients without HIV infection, with upper lobe infiltrates, more cavitation, and less adenopathy.[64] Normal chest films are also common in patients with HIV infection. In one study, normal chest films were found in 14% of HIV-infected patients, including 21% of those with CD4 counts below 200/mm³ and 5% of those with CD4 counts greater than 200/mm³.[61]

Microbiology

Sputum Studies

If the clinical or chest radiographic findings suggest the diagnosis of pulmonary TB, mycobacteriologic studies of the patient's sputum should be ordered. Spontaneously produced sputum collected under direct supervision is preferred, and early morning samples provide the best diagnostic specimens.[25] Classically, three initial sputum specimens should be obtained on different days. A positive smear supports a presumptive diagnosis, and the number of bacilli seen correlates with infectivity. For patients who are not producing sputum, nebulized induction of sputum and gastric aspiration of swallowed respiratory secretions are the methods of choice for collecting samples.[65] Nebulizer-induced sputum samples have a higher diagnostic yield than gastric aspirates in adult TB patients, but in some patients, especially children, gastric aspirates may be the only obtainable specimens. Induction of sputum with nebulization may increase the risk of TB transmission to health care workers and should be performed only in specially ventilated rooms, preferably not in the emergency department.

When sputum is not diagnostic in adults, fiberoptic bronchoscopy with bronchial washings, brushings, and bronchoalveolar lavage or transbronchial biopsy may be necessary to establish the laboratory diagnosis of TB.[65] In children, sputum obtained by bronchoscopy has a lower culture yield, and this technique is used less often to obtain sputum from pediatric patients.[66]

Direct Microscopy

Direct microscopic examination of a stained sputum specimen for acid-fast bacilli (AFB smear) is the most rapid laboratory test widely available to support a presumptive diagnosis of TB (Figure 133-6), and results are usually available within 24 hours.[67] Although nontuberculous mycobacteria can cause pulmonary disease, they are less common than MTB and vary by geographic location and population of patients. Fluorochrome stains are more sensitive than the traditional Ziehl-Neelsen or Kinyoun methods for the detection of AFB from clinical specimens.[66,67] A negative AFB smear, however, does not rule out active pulmonary TB because microscopy is relatively insensitive when small numbers of bacilli are present. There must be at least 5000 bacilli/mL of sputum to obtain a positive result by microscopy.[67] Because cavitary disease is

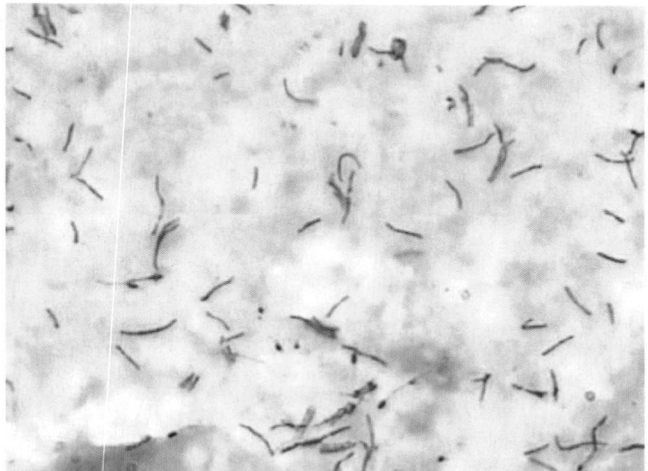

Figure 133-6. Photomicrograph of an acid-fast bacillus smear of *Mycobacterium tuberculosis*. (Courtesy of Alfredo Ponce de Leon.)

associated with great numbers of bacilli, the diagnostic yield of microscopy increases with cavitation. Concentrated smears are prepared by decontamination, liquefaction, and centrifugation of sputum, and such smears may be more sensitive than unconcentrated samples.[14] Overall, AFB smears have a sensitivity of 20% to 80% and a specificity of 90% to 100%.[67] Despite its limitations, microscopy remains an essential diagnostic test because of its ease of performance, low cost, rapid turnaround time, and reasonable diagnostic yield.

Culture

A presumptive diagnosis of TB based on a positive sputum smear is usually confirmed by isolating MTB by culture. Traditional culture methods using solid media require 3 to 8 weeks for colony formation. The development of liquid culture systems has shortened the detection time to 7 to 14 days. A number of liquid culture systems are available for detection of MTB. For example, the BACTEC method measures $^{14}CO_2$ produced by growing mycobacteria when they metabolize the ^{14}C-labeled palmitic acid contained in the system, and the mycobacteria growth indicator tube (MGIT) method measures mycobacterial oxygen consumption with a fluorescence assay.[67]

Sputum cultures are more sensitive for detecting MTB than microscopy. Liquid culture can detect 10 to 100 bacilli/mL, compared with 5000 to 10,000 bacilli/mL for AFB smear. When the presence of mycobacteria is established, the specific identification of MTB may be accomplished by subjecting the initial mycobacteria to various isolation techniques. These include the detection of pigmentation on solid culture media, various biochemical tests, high-performance liquid chromatography, and nucleic acid probes.[67]

Drug Susceptibility Testing

Because of the emergence of multidrug-resistant MTB, all initial isolates of MTB should be tested for susceptibility to isoniazid (INH), rifampin (RIF), and ethambutol (ETH).[68] Further susceptibility testing should be performed when resistance to one of the three agents is detected, if the patient has had prior TB treatment, has had exposure to a drug-resistant contact or source, or has had positive sputum cultures beyond 3 months of therapy.[68] Conventional susceptibility testing detects selective growth of drug-resistant TB on media containing antituberculous drugs. For first-line agents, this requires waiting until 4 to 7 days after the culture is positive; testing for susceptibility to other drugs may require 2 to 3 months. The BACTEC and MGIT systems can also be used for rapid drug susceptibility testing, in less than 12 days.[67] Other new approaches to susceptibility testing include flow cytometry, genotypic sequence-based methods, and bacteriophage viability testing.[67,69]

Nucleic Acid Amplification Tests

A number of nucleic acid amplification assays are available to assist in the rapid diagnosis of MTB, including polymerase chain reaction (PCR) tests, the *Mycobacterium tuberculosis* direct test (MTDT), and the ligase chain reaction.[67] These tests can be used directly on clinical specimens but are presently of limited utility in the diagnosis of MTB. Problems include their high cost and potential for suboptimal performance in clinical settings because of factors such as varying laboratory methods and the potential for specimen contamination.[14,66] Sputum smears are still needed to evaluate for infectiousness, as these tests are unable to differentiate active from treated infection. Sputum cultures are also still needed, as these tests do not assess drug susceptibility.[14] Nucleic acid amplification tests may be useful, however, when standard clinical and microbiologic tests are negative or inconclusive.

Polymerase Chain Reaction

The PCR may provide a method for confirming the diagnosis of TB within a few hours. The PCR is a DNA amplification technique that bypasses the delays inherent with mycobacterial cultures. It allows the in vitro synthesis of millions of copies of a specific MTB DNA segment.[70] The PCR amplifies the targeted DNA so that it can be detected by simple laboratory procedures. Diagnostic techniques based on PCR allow direct testing of routine clinical specimens to confirm the diagnosis of TB in hours. Test performance varies greatly, depending upon whether the sputum sample is AFB smear positive or negative. For example, for AFB smear–positive specimens, the Roche Amplicor system has a sensitivity of 95% to 96% and specificity of 100%. When it is applied to AFB smear–negative specimens, the sensitivity drops to 48% to 53%, with a specificity of 96% to 99%.[67,71]

Mycobacterium tuberculosis *Direct Test*

The MTDT enzymatically amplifies a 16S ribosomal RNA (rRNA) segment that is specific for MTB complex species. One of its advantages is that there are 2000 rRNA targets per mycobacterial cell, whereas the PCR assay has only 10 to 16 DNA targets. The amplified product is then identified by hybridization with an acridinium ester–labeled DNA probe, which is excited to produce chemiluminescence. The MTDT has shown excellent sensitivity (86% to 98%) and specificity (97% to 100%) for the rapid identification of MTB and can be performed in about 5 hours. As with PCR assays, specimen quality and the degree of AFB smear positivity affect test performance.[67,72]

Ligase Chain Reaction

This amplification assay involves repetitive cycles of high-temperature DNA denaturation, oligonucleotide annealing, and ligation. The Abbott Laboratories LCx assay has a sensitivity of 98% for AFB smear–positive specimens, 27% for AFB smear–negative specimens, and a specificity of 100% (equal to that of culture).[67] When LCx was compared with PCR and MTDT in a clinical trial, there was no significant difference in sensitivity or specificity among these three tests.[73]

Tuberculostearic Acid

Tuberculostearic acid (TSA) is a fatty acid found only in mycobacteria. It can be detected with gas chromatography–mass spectrometry in clinical specimens containing small numbers of bacilli. This test has been applied to cerebrospinal fluid (CSF), pleural and pericardial fluids, ascites, serum, and sputum. One study reported a sensitivity and specificity of 90% when it was applied to sputum samples. Sensitivity was lower when bronchial washings and pleural fluid were tested (68% and 75%).[74] TSA testing is not frequently used, as the equipment and expertise needed to run this test are not widely available outside specialized research laboratories.

Detection of Adenosine Deaminase Activity

Adenosine deaminase (ADA) is released by lymphocytes and macrophages during the cellular immune response. Increased ADA levels can be used as a diagnostic test for tuberculous pleural effusions, ascites, and pericardial effusions. Clinical studies have reported ADA sensitivity and specificity of 94% and 68% for pericardial fluid and 87% and 86% for pleural fluid.[75,76] The ADA determination is rapid and inexpensive, but because it is relatively nonspecific, it is most useful in populations with a relatively high prevalence of TB.

Interferon-γ Levels

Interferon-γ (IFN-γ) is a cytokine associated with CMI. This test can also be used as a diagnostic test for tuberculous pleural effusions, ascites, and pericardial effusions. Clinical studies have reported IFN-γ sensitivity and specificity of 100% and 100% for pericardial fluid and 78% and 97% for pleural fluid.[75,76] IFN-γ levels can be used independently, as a confirmatory test, or in combination with both ADA levels and PCR.[76]

Serology

Serodiagnosis of TB could be a minimally invasive approach to rapid diagnosis. Using an enzyme-linked immunosorbent assay (ELISA) to diagnose TB from serum would be especially useful in patients who cannot produce sputum. Although ELISA tests have been developed for several MTB antigens, in practice, no serodiagnostic approach to the diagnosis of TB is currently in widespread clinical use in the United States. Limitations of the ELISA test include inadequate accuracy and reproducibility, inability to distinguish active from latent infection, poor discrimination between MTB and other mycobacteria, and relative cost.[66,67]

Tuberculin Skin Test

While newer diagnostic tests undergo development, the tuberculin skin test remains the best tool available for detecting latent MTB infection. The tuberculin test is based on the principle that MTB infection induces sensitivity to certain antigens of the bacillus. These antigens are contained in the tuberculin preparation called PPD. The individual infected with TB usually turns PPD positive 3 to 8 weeks after the infection, when the immune response is developed.[25]

The standard 0.1-mL dose used in skin testing contains 5 tuberculin units (TU). This dose is administered intradermally with the needle bevel up, using Mantoux's technique. The properly placed test should leave a blanched, distinct wheal 6 to 10 mm in diameter.[45] An incorrectly administered test may be repeated immediately at a site several centimeters away. Various types of test kits and applicators are available (Heaf and Tine tests), but for diagnostic purposes the Mantoux test with PPD (5 TU) is preferred.[29,66,77]

Tests are read 48 to 72 hours after administration. The largest diameter of palpable induration is measured and recorded in millimeters; erythema by itself is not measured. The precise measurement that denotes a positive test depends on the patient's other clinical factors. The current CDC guidelines use 15 mm of induration as a positive test for people without TB risk factors (Table 133-2).[78]

Some individuals with prior TB infection gradually lose their hypersensitivity reaction to PPD and may react weakly or not at all. The PPD test, however, can restimulate or enhance their hypersensitivity so that a subsequent test does elicit a positive reaction. This phenomenon is called the booster effect. This boosted reaction may be mistaken for a new infection. To eliminate the booster effect as a confounding factor, a two-step testing method is recommended for persons who undergo serial PPD screening (health care workers). If the result of the first test is negative and the individual does not have a documented negative PPD during the prior 12 months, a second test is done 1 week later using the same dose. If the second test is positive, it is most likely a boosted reaction and the person should be considered previously infected. If the second test result remains negative, the person is considered uninfected and a positive reaction to a subsequent test indicates new infection.[29]

Infection with nontuberculous mycobacteria may cause a false-positive PPD result. These reactions tend to be smaller than the true-positive reaction to MTB infection. Similarly, bacille Calmette-Guérin (BCG) vaccination may produce a PPD reaction that is generally mild and deteriorates with time. A large reaction to PPD and a long time interval between BCG vaccination and the current skin test make it more likely that the reaction is due to MTB infection.[29] Because the BCG vaccine is imperfect in protecting against MTB infection and because most vaccinated individuals come from areas of high TB prevalence, the CDC recommends that tuberculin skin test results are interpreted without regard to BCG vaccination status.[79]

Table 133-2. Criteria for a Positive Tuberculin Skin Test

Size of Reaction	Persons in Whom Reaction Is Considered Positive
≥5 mm	HIV-infected persons
	Close contacts of persons with infectious tuberculosis
	Persons with an abnormal chest radiograph consistent with previous tuberculosis*
	Immunosuppressed patients receiving the equivalent of ≥15 mg of prednisone per day for ≥1 mo
≥10 mm	Foreign-born persons recently arrived (≤5 yr earlier) from a country with a high prevalence of tuberculosis
	Persons with a medical condition that increases the risk of tuberculosis†
	Injection drug users
	Members of medically underserved, low-income populations (e.g., homeless persons)
	Residents and staff members of long-term care facilities (e.g., nursing homes, correctional institutions, homeless shelters)
	Health care workers
	Children < 4yr of age
	Persons with conversion on a tuberculin skin test (increase in induration of ≥10 mm within a 2-yr period)
≥15 mm	All others‡

*An abnormal chest radiograph consistent with previous tuberculosis reveals fibrotic opacities occupying more than 2 cm² of the upper lobe; radiographs showing pleural thickening or isolated calcified granulomas are not considered to be suggestive of previous tuberculosis.
†Medical conditions that increase the risk of development of tuberculosis in the presence of latent tuberculosis infection include silicosis, end-stage renal disease, malnutrition, diabetes mellitus, carcinoma of the head and neck or lung, immunosuppressive therapy, lymphoma, leukemia, loss of more than 10% of ideal body weight, gastrectomy, and jejunoileal bypass.
‡These persons should not be screened in the absence of an indication.
HIV, human immunodeficiency virus.
From Jasmer RM, Nahid P, Hopewell PC: Latent tuberculosis infection. *N Engl J Med* 347:1860, 2002.

Many conditions can lead to false-negative reactions to PPD testing (Box 133-3). The incidence of false-negative results in one study was 25% of the 200 patients with active TB.[25] Therefore, the clinical significance of a negative PPD is best determined by considering other clinical factors.

Despite some limitations, PPD skin testing remains useful to diagnose individuals, to screen populations, and to evaluate infected persons for prophylactic treatment (Table 133-3).[78]

DIFFERENTIAL CONSIDERATIONS

Pulmonary Tuberculosis

Bacterial Pneumonia

Segmental or lobar infiltrates on chest radiographs in bacterial pneumonia may easily be confused with those in TB, especially primary disease. However, compared with TB, bacterial pneumonias usually arise with more profound symptoms of systemic toxicity, a more acute onset, and an elevated white blood cell count.[48] In pulmonary TB, there is no prompt response to antibiotics as seen in bacterial pneumonia.[25]

BOX 133-3. Factors Causing Decreased Ability to Respond to Tuberculin

Factors Related to the Person Being Tested
Infections
   Viral (measles, mumps, chickenpox)
   Bacterial (typhoid fever, brucellosis, typhus, leprosy, pertussis, overwhelming tuberculosis, tuberculosis pleurisy)
   Fungal (South American blastomycosis)
Live virus vaccinations (measles, mumps, polio)
Metabolic derangements (chronic renal failure)
Nutritional factors (severe protein depletion)
Diseases affecting lymphoid organs (Hodgkin's disease, lymphoma, chronic lymphocytic leukemia, sarcoidosis)
Drugs (corticosteroids and many other immunosuppressive agents)
Age (newborns, elderly patients with "wanes" sensitivity)
Recent or overwhelming infection with M. tuberculosis
Stress (surgery, burns, mental illness, graft-versus-host reactions)

Factors Related to the Tuberculin Used
Improper storage (exposure to light and heat)
Improper dilutions
Chemical denaturation
Contamination
Adsorption (partially controlled by adding Tween 80)

Factors Related to the Method of Administration
Injection of too little antigen
Delayed administration after drawing into syringe
Injection too close to control

Factors Related to Reading the Test and Recording Results
Inexperienced reader
Conscious or unconscious bias
Error in recording

Fungal and Nontuberculous Mycobacterial Infections

Histoplasmosis, coccidioidomycosis, and blastomycosis as well as nontuberculous mycobacterial infections (mainly *Mycobacterium avium* complex and *Mycobacterium kansasii*) may be radiologically indistinguishable from TB.[80] The incidence of these infections is influenced by geographic location.[48,81] Nontuberculous mycobacterial infection most commonly involves chronic pulmonary infection in HIV-infected individuals.[82] Immunocompetent individuals may also become infected with MTB, especially patients with chronic lung disease, such as cystic fibrosis. Other important risk factors include work in the mining industry, warm climate, advancing age, and male gender.[83]

Pneumonias in Patients with Human Immunodeficiency Virus

Bacterial pneumonias including upper lobe *Pneumocystis carinii* pneumonia and, rarely, *Nocardia* and *Rhodococcus* infections may mimic TB in patients with HIV.[54]

Cavitary Lesions

Lung abscess or cavitating pneumonia caused by *Klebsiella pneumoniae*, *Staphylococcus pyogenes*, or aspiration may appear similar to cavitary TB on chest radiographs.[48] In older patients, especially smokers, bronchogenic carcinoma may mimic TB; this is particularly true of squamous cell carcinoma, which tends to cavitate.[48] Because cancer may cause a focus of TB to spread, the two diseases may be present simultaneously.[36] Other causes of nontuberculous cavitary lesions include *M. avium* complex infection in HIV-negative hosts, pulmonary infarction secondary to pulmonary embolus, Wegener's granulomatosis, and upper lobe bullous disease secondary to emphysema and neurofibromatosis.[48,54,82]

Upper Lobe Infiltrate with and without Fibrosis

This pattern may be seen with atypical mycobacteria, ankylosing spondylitis, silicosis, collagen vascular diseases, lymphomas, and actinomycosis.[54] Upper zone fibrosis and volume loss can occur in the later stages of extrinsic alveolitis, allergic bronchopulmonary aspergillosis, and sarcoidosis. The presence of calcification suggests TB.[48]

Mediastinal Lymphadenopathy

The main differential diagnosis of adenopathy consists of lymphoma and sarcoidosis. In sarcoidosis, lymphadenopathy is usually bilateral, symmetrical, and asymptomatic. Lymphadenopathy in TB tends to be unilateral or, if bilateral, is asymmetric and associated with parenchymal lung disease. Lymphoma tends to involve very bulky mediastinal lymphadenopathy.[48]

Table 133-3. Persons at Increased Risk Who Should Be Tested for Latent Tuberculosis Infection

Risk	Examples of Persons with Risk
Increased risk of exposure to infectious cases	Persons with recent close contact with persons known to have active tuberculosis*
	Health care workers who work at facilities where patients with tuberculosis are treated
Increased risk of tuberculosis infection	Foreign-born persons from countries with a high prevalence of tuberculosis
	Homeless persons
	Persons living or working in facilities providing long-term care
Increased risk of active tuberculosis once infection has occurred	HIV-infected persons
	Persons with recent tuberculosis infection†
	Injection drug users
	Patients with end-stage renal disease
	Patients with silicosis
	Patients with diabetes mellitus
	Patients receiving immunosuppressive therapy
	Patients with hematologic cancers
	Malnourished persons or those with a recent weight loss of more than 10% of their ideal body weight
	Persons who have undergone gastrectomy or jejunoileal bypass

*We define close contact as at least 12 hours of contact with a person with infectious tuberculosis, but there are no well-established criteria for such contact.
†Persons with recent infection include children younger than 4 years and persons found to have tuberculin conversion, defined as an increase in induration of at least 10 mm on a tuberculin skin test within a 2-year period.
HIV, human immunodeficiency virus.
From Jasmer RM, Nahid, P, Hopewell PC: Latent tuberculosis infection. *N Engl J Med* 347:1860, 2002.

Extrapulmonary Tuberculosis

Tuberculous infection involving multiple sites is most commonly seen in persons less capable of containing MTB infection such as infants, elders, and immunocompromised persons.[40] Extrapulmonary TB (EPTB) accounted for roughly 15% of newly diagnosed TB cases in the United States before the HIV epidemic. As of 2002, about 21% of TB patients in the United States had extrapulmonary disease, and another 7.5% had both pulmonary and extrapulmonary infection.[17] In children younger than 4 years, about 25% of TB infections are extrapulmonary.[66] For HIV-infected individuals, EPTB infection becomes progressively more common as CD4 counts fall below 350 cells/mL.[63] One study of TB patients with advanced HIV infection reported that 38% had only pulmonary disease, 30% had EPTB alone, and 32% had both pulmonary disease and EPTB.[40]

EPTB may occur in multiple sites, with relative frequencies of lymphatic (42%), pleural (18%), bone or joint (12%), genitourinary (6%), meningeal (6%), peritoneal (5%), and other sites (11%).[17] The lymph nodes are the most common site of EPTB for both normal and HIV-infected patients. Involvement of the meninges is more common in young children than other age groups (about 4% of children with TB), and the incidence of TB in the remainder of the extrapulmonary sites increases with age.[40,66] Less commonly involved locations for EPTB include the skin, heart, pericardium, thyroid gland, mastoid cells, sclerae, and adrenal glands.

Lymphadenitis

Tuberculous lymphadenitis (scrofula) is the most common form of EPTB. Scrofula is common in children but seen most commonly in young adult women, usually of minority races.[25] The patient usually has an enlarging, painless, red, firm mass in the region of one or more lymph nodes, most commonly in the anterior or posterior cervical chain or the supraclavicular fossa. Early on, the nodes are described as discrete, rubbery masses that are freely mobile, and the overlying skin is normal. Eventually, the nodes may become matted and harder and the overlying skin inflamed. Fluctuance may be present as well as an abscess or sinus tract if a node erodes through the skin.[84] Systemic symptoms are uncommon, except in HIV-positive individuals in whom lymphadenitis is usually generalized.[40] Pulmonary infection is present in only 10% to 20% of cases.[84] The differential diagnosis includes lymphoma, metastatic cancer, fungal disease, cat-scratch disease, sarcoid, toxoplasmosis, reactive adenitis, and bacterial adenitis.

The diagnosis of scrofula is usually made by fine-needle aspiration of an affected lymph node. Although AFB smears are positive in only about 20% of cases, granulomatous inflammation may be obvious. Overall, fine-needle aspiration has a sensitivity of 77% and specificity of 93% for TB infection. First-line treatment of scrofula consists of antituberculous drugs, but surgical excision may be performed when medical therapy has failed or if the diagnosis is unclear. Incision and drainage should not be done because permanent sinuses and prolonged drainage can result.[84]

Pleural Effusion

Pleural EPTB may occur early after primary infection with MTB and arise as pleurisy with effusion, or, more rarely, it may occur late in postprimary cavitary disease and arise as an empyema.

Tuberculous pleurisy often causes no symptoms and resolves spontaneously; however, in the untreated, a 65% relapse rate has been reported with development of active pulmonary or EPTB within 5 years. Dyspnea may occur if the effusion is large, but the effusions are usually small and unilateral. Often the presentation is acute, severe, and indistinguishable from that of a bacterial pneumonia. In elderly patients, however, the onset may be more insidious and likely to be confused with congestive heart failure, cancer, or a pulmonary embolus.[25]

The diagnosis is usually confirmed by microscopic and chemical examination of pleural fluid or pleural biopsy. White blood cell counts usually range from 500 to 2500 cells/mL. The fluid is an exudate with protein usually exceeding 50% of the serum protein, and the glucose may be normal to low. Because there are few bacilli, AFB smears are rarely positive, and cultures grow MTB for only 25% to 30% of patients known to have the disease. Pleural biopsy can confirm the diagnosis in approximately 75% of patients.[25]

Bone and Joint Infection

Bone and joint TB remains a disease of older children and young adults in developing countries, and it is increasingly a disease of adults in developed countries.[25] Skeletal TB presumably develops from reactivation of dormant tubercles originally seeded during stage 2 of the primary infection or, in the case of spinal TB, from contiguous spread from paravertebral lymph nodes to the vertebrae. Generally, spinal TB (Pott's disease) accounts for 50% to 70% of the reported cases; the hip or knee is involved in 15% to 20% of cases, and the ankle, elbow, wrists, shoulders, and other bones and joints account for 15% to 20% of cases.[40] Approximately 50% of patients have a prior history or concurrent case of pulmonary TB, and the chest radiograph is normal in up to half the cases.

Patients with Pott's disease may simply complain of back pain or stiffness. Examination may show fever, point tenderness, and decreased range of motion. If the initial radiograph is normal, the diagnosis may be delayed, allowing the disease to progress. The initial lesion usually spreads to the intervertebral disk and then to the adjacent vertebrae, producing the classical radiographic appearance of anterior wedging of two involved vertebral bodies and destruction of the disk. Early changes of spinal TB can be difficult to detect on plain films and include loss of the "white stripe" of the vertebral end plate because of destruction of subchondral bone. Unfortunately, plain films are usually unable to reveal TB infection until roughly 50% of the vertebra has been destroyed.[85] Thus, computed tomography (CT) and magnetic resonance imaging (MRI) scanning should be used when the disease is suspected.[25,40]

Paraspinal "cold" abscesses develop in 50% or more of cases, with occasional formation of sinus tracts. The abscess can spread the infection up and down the spine, sometimes sparing vertebral bodies along its course, forming the so-called skip lesions.[25,85] These skip lesions can easily be missed when imaging the spine for Pott's disease. The main complication of Pott's disease is spinal cord compression.[40]

Medical management includes chemotherapy, modified bed rest, and early ambulation and results in improvement in about 90% of patients without neuro-

logic involvement.[25] Surgical treatment is usually reserved for patients with neurologic complications.

Renal Disease

The kidney is well vascularized, and hematogenous dissemination to that organ is fairly common. After the typical tuberculous lesions develop within the parenchyma, infection can spread into the calyces, renal pelvis, ureters, and bladder. As a result, tuberculous granulomas, scarring, and obstruction can occur anywhere along the urinary tract.[86]

The initial presenting symptoms of urinary involvement are nonspecific. Advanced renal disease and destruction may occur before the diagnosis is made. The urinalysis is often positive for pyuria, hematuria, and albuminuria. Sterile pyuria is classical for renal TB, but many cases with this finding have cultures positive for other urinary pathogens. The finding of pyuria in an acid urine with no organisms isolated should increase suspicion of TB.[40] In one study of the diagnosis of urinary TB, AFB stains were found to be 52% sensitive and PCR testing was 96% sensitive.[87] Both tests had excellent specificity (97% to 98%). Mycobacterial cultures should be ordered when genitourinary TB infection is suspected.

Complications of renal TB include nephrolithiasis, ureteral obstruction or reflux, recurrent bacterial infections, hypertension, papillary necrosis, renal insufficiency, autonephrectomy, and, rarely, development of transitional cell cancer.[86,87]

Male Genital Disease

Male genital TB is usually associated with coexistent renal TB. Spread of infection from the kidney involves the prostate, seminal vesicles, epididymides, and testes.[25] The patient typically has a painless or slightly painful scrotal mass and possibly symptoms of prostatitis, epididymitis, or orchitis.[40] Epididymal or prostatic calcifications may be clues to the diagnosis. TB involvement of the seminal vesicles may lead to infertility.[87]

Female Genital Disease

In women, the disease usually begins with a hematogenous focus in the fallopian tubes. The infection then spreads to the endometrium (50%), ovaries (30%), cervix (5% to 15%), and vagina (1%).[25] Women may have abdominal or pelvic pain, ascites, infertility, menstrual irregularities, and, rarely, vaginal discharge. An ulcerating mass may be present on the cervix. Genital TB may be confused with ovarian or endometrial cancer, Meigs' syndrome, vulvar or vaginal ulcer, pelvic abscess, cervicitis, or cervical carcinoma.[88] There are reports of sexual transmission of TB by individuals with active genital TB.[89] Women with genital TB who become pregnant are at risk for ectopic pregnancy.[25]

Multisystem Disease

Acute disseminated TB refers to active hematogenous spread of MTB to several organs in the body. *Miliary*

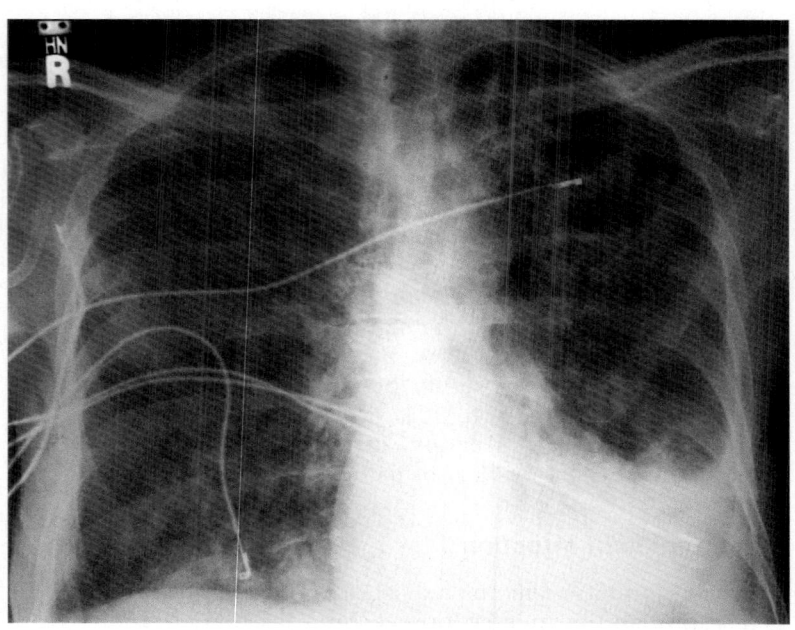

Figure 133-7. Chest radiograph demonstrates miliary pattern with left pleural effusion.

tuberculosis was first used to describe the pathologic lesions, which resemble small millet seeds. This term is now used as a clinical term referring to the massive dissemination that leads to generalized systemic illness. Miliary TB occurs when the host is unable to contain either a recently acquired or a dormant TB infection. In the past, miliary TB occurred mainly in young children after primary infection; today, it is more common in elders and in those infected with HIV.[40]

In infants and young children, the illness is generally acute and severe. In young adults, the acute illness runs a slower course and is usually less severe. Miliary TB is often a subtle disease associated with alcoholism, cirrhosis, neoplasm, pregnancy, collagen vascular disease, and use of corticosteroids or immunosuppressive medications.[25]

The clinical presentations are varied because of the multisystem nature of miliary TB. Systemic symptoms of fever, weight loss, anorexia, and weakness are generally present.[40] The choroidal tubercle (a granuloma in the choroid of the retina) may represent the only physical finding specific for disseminated TB.[40]

A presumptive diagnosis can be made rapidly if the chest radiograph shows a miliary infiltrate (Figure 133-7). Unfortunately, the classical miliary pattern is absent on radiographs in approximately 50% of cases. Routine laboratory tests are generally not helpful. Hyponatremia from the syndrome of inappropriate secretion of antidiuretic hormone (SIADH) is common and often associated with meningitis. Panculturing usually has a high yield, and HIV-infected patients may have positive blood cultures. Transbronchial biopsy can be performed to obtain tissue rapidly for analysis. Other potential biopsy sites include liver, lymph nodes, and bone marrow.[25]

Mortality for this form of EPTB is higher than for the other forms, with one case series reporting a rate of 21%.[90] The high mortality rate is often caused by delay in treatment, which should always be initiated immediately on the basis of clinical suspicion and not delayed until confirmation of the diagnosis.

A fulminant form of miliary TB may cause the adult respiratory distress syndrome and disseminated intravascular coagulation. In these cases, the addition of corticosteroids (prednisone, 60 to 80 mg/day) is indicated.[25]

Central Nervous System Disease

Approximately 6% of all cases of EPTB involve the central nervous system (CNS),[17] and CNS involvement remains a grave consequence of tuberculous infection. The peak incidence of CNS TB is in newborn to 4-year-old children.[40]

Tuberculous Meningitis

Tuberculous meningitis usually results from the rupture of a subependymal tubercle into the subarachnoid space rather than from direct hematogenous seeding of the CNS. When a complication of miliary TB, meningitis usually develops within several weeks. In children, it is an early postprimary event, usually appearing within 6 months. TB cerebral involvement is most marked at the base of the brain, and vasculitis of local arteries and veins may lead to aneurysm formation, thrombosis, and focal hemorrhagic infarction. The vessels to the basal ganglia are most commonly involved, leading to lacunar infarcts or movement disorders. Involvement of other vessels, such as the middle cerebral artery, may lead to hemiparesis or hemiplegia.[25]

Tuberculous meningitis begins with a prodrome of malaise, intermittent headache, and a low-grade fever. In 2 to 3 weeks, the patient develops a protracted headache. Vomiting, confusion, meningismus and focal neurologic signs, and coma may follow. Nuchal rigidity may be absent. Diplopia resulting from basilar exudate is present in up to 70% of patients. Hyponatremia may be present because SIADH is common. The CSF cell count usually ranges from 0 to 1500 white blood cells, with a predominance of lymphocytes; however, polymorphonuclear cells may predominate early in the course. CSF protein is usually elevated and CSF glucose is usually low, A single lumbar puncture yields a positive AFB culture in only 37% of cases, but pooled samples from multiple lumbar punctures[4] yield a positive culture in 90% of cases.[25]

The classical triad of neuroradiologic findings in patients with TB meningitis consists of basal meningeal enhancement, hydrocephalus, and cerebral or brainstem infarction. CT or MRI may also reveal rounded lesions typical of evolving parenchymal tuberculomas.[91]

Prognosis is influenced by age, duration of symptoms, and the presence of neurologic deficits. In children, the overall mortality is 13%, and about half of survivors develop permanent neurologic deficits.[66] Outcome is also closely linked to the clinical stage at which the disease arises. Complete recovery is the rule in stage 1, wherein the alert patient has no focal neurologic signs and no hydrocephalus. Stage 2 is characterized by confusion and focal neurologic changes, and patients in stage 3 present stuporous or with dense hemiplegia or paraplegia. In contrast to the excellent prognosis of stage 1 disease, about half of patients with stage 3 disease either die or are left with severe neurologic disability.[25]

Treatment starts with a four-drug regimen. INH and pyrazinamide (PZA) reach increased concentrations in the CSF in the presence of inflamed meninges. RIF also crosses the blood-brain barrier. Whereas for most other forms of EPTB 6-month regimens are used, the CDC recommends 9 to 12 months of therapy for TB meningitis.[68] Corticosteroids are also recommended by the CDC. Prednisone, 60 to 80 mg, should be given in a daily dose and tapered over 4 to 6 weeks.[25] Ventricular shunting may be needed if hydrocephalus develops.

Spinal Meningitis

Tuberculous spinal meningitis is a complication of CNS infection that usually originates by hematogenous dissemination from an outside source, although tuberculous meningitis may extend caudally and involve the spine. Local extension of bone or disk TB has also been described. Presenting symptoms result from nerve root or cord compression and may include pain, sensory changes, paralysis, or weakness of bladder or rectal sphincters.[25]

Intracranial Tuberculoma

A tuberculoma usually begins in an area of TB cerebritis as microgranulomas, which coalesce into a mature noncaseating granuloma.[91] These space-occupying lesions may cause focal or generalized symptoms, such as tonic-clonic seizures. Involvement of the CNS parenchyma may also be accompanied by meningitis. Imaging reveals either solitary or multiple tuberculomas (Figure 133-8), usually involving the frontal or parietal lobes.[91] Treatment includes chemotherapy before surgical removal. Corticosteroids may reduce

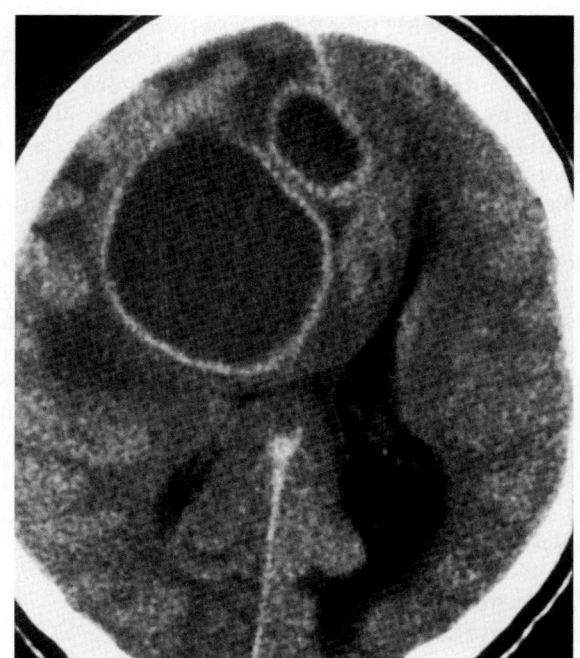

Figure 133-8. Head computed tomography scan demonstrating tuberculomas in an AIDS patient.

edema and decrease the symptoms. If MTB is discovered at the time of surgery, postoperative chemotherapy may prevent the further spread of the disease.[25]

Gastrointestinal Disease

Gastrointestinal TB infection is usually secondary to hematogenous or lymphatic spread but may also result from swallowed bronchial secretions or direct spread from local sites, such as lymph nodes or fallopian tubes.[92] TB may occur in any location from the mouth to the anus, but lesions proximal to the terminal ileum are rare. The ileocecal area is the most common site of involvement, producing symptoms of pain, anorexia, diarrhea, obstruction, hemorrhage, and often a palpable mass.

The most common symptoms of gastrointestinal TB are abdominal pain, fever, weight loss, anorexia, nausea, vomiting, and diarrhea.[92] These symptoms and physical examination findings may lead to the misdiagnosis of appendicitis, intestinal obstruction, or cancer. About 12% to 16% of cases present as an acute abdomen.[92] The signs and symptoms can be so similar to those of other diseases that the diagnosis is often made at surgery. The clinical manifestations of anal TB include fissures, fistulae, and perirectal abscesses.[40] Antimicrobial treatment of gastrointestinal TB is the same as that of pulmonary disease.[68,92]

Peritonitis

Tuberculous peritonitis may develop from local spread of MTB from a tuberculous lymph node, intestinal focus, or infected fallopian tube. In addition, peritonitis can develop from seeding of the peritoneum in miliary TB or from the reactivation of a latent focus.[25]

The patient with tuberculous peritonitis commonly has pain and abdominal swelling associated with fever, anorexia, and weight loss. Diagnosis may be confounded by the similarity of this disease to alcoholic hepatitis and by the fact that this disease often coexists with other disorders, especially cirrhosis with ascites.[40] Paracentesis is thus essential. The peritoneal fluid is exudative, with a cell count of 500 to 2000 cells. Lymphocytes usually predominate with rare exceptions early in the process, when polymorphonuclear leukocytes may predominate.[25] AFB smears of the fluid have a low diagnostic yield, with a reported sensitivity of no more than 7%, and culture is positive in only 25% of cases. Peritoneal biopsy is often necessary to confirm the diagnosis. Treatment is the same as for pulmonary TB, with a 6-month regimen.[25,68]

MANAGEMENT

Initial Emergency Department Management

The most emergent presentation of pulmonary TB is massive hemoptysis, defined as at least 600 mL of blood in 24 hours. Exsanguination rarely occurs, and the major morbidity is due to asphyxiation from aspirated blood. The airway should be secured with a large-diameter (8-mm) endotracheal tube that can accommodate fiberoptic bronchoscopy. The patient should be positioned with the bleeding lung in a dependent position. Selective main stem intubation should be considered to allow ventilation of the unaffected lung and to minimize the spread of blood from the affected lung. These patients require emergent consultations for bronchoscopy, surgical resection, or angiography with selective embolization.[49] Patients suspected of having active pulmonary TB should be immediately placed in respiratory isolation.

Medical Therapy

Patients suspected of having pulmonary TB whose sputum smears return positive for AFB can be presumptively diagnosed and treated with antituberculous therapy. In patients with negative sputum smears but clinical and radiographic findings consistent with pulmonary TB, it may also be appropriate to initiate treatment presumptively for TB.[68] A few days of antituberculous agents does not interfere with bacteriologic diagnosis, thus, severely ill patients with presumed TB should be treated immediately. Local factors, including the prevalence of TB and available resources, help determine the appropriateness of presumptive therapy.

Antituberculous Medications

Three basic therapeutic principles govern the treatment of TB: (1) any treatment regimen must contain multiple drugs to which the MTB organism is susceptible, (2) the therapeutic agents must be taken regularly, and (3), which is most problematic, the therapy must continue for a sufficient period.[46]

It is estimated that approximately 33% to 50% of patients with TB fail to follow medical recommendations. Patients at higher risk for noncompliance are those with previous treatment failures; substance abusers; patients with mental, emotional, or physical impairment; and those in whom preventive treatment has failed.[93] The most effective strategy to ensure compliance is directly observed therapy (DOT), which is now the preferred practice in the United States.

The medications used to treat MTB are generally divided into first-line and second-line agents (Tables 133-4 and 133-5).[68] Of these agents, 10 have been approved by the Food and Drug Administration (FDA) for treating MTB in the United States. The most commonly used first-line agents include INH, RIF, PZA, and ETH.[68] Agents that are used in special circumstances, but are not FDA approved, include rifabutin, levofloxacin, moxifloxacin, amikacin, and kanamycin.

First-Line Agents

INH demonstrates extremely potent early bactericidal activity and can rapidly decrease patients' infectiousness. The incidence of INH-induced hepatitis is estimated to be 0.6% when INH is given alone, 1.6% when given with other antituberculous agents (excluding RIF), and 2.7% when given with RIF. The risk increases with age and also with underlying liver disease, alcohol use, and during the postpartum period. Another adverse effect is peripheral neuropathy. This is uncommon (less than 0.2%) at standard doses and may be avoided by the administration of pyridoxine (25 mg/day). Patients who have conditions associated with neuropathy (e.g., diabetes, HIV infection, alcoholism) and pregnant or breast-feeding women are at increased risk. Supplemental pyridoxine is recommended for such patients.[68]

RIF also demonstrates strong early bactericidal activity. This agent causes orange discoloration of body fluids, including urine, tears, sweat, and sputum. Patients should be warned of this effect before administration of the medication. It is especially important to warn soft contact lens wearers, as permanent lens staining may occur. Rifapentine is a rifamycin derivative with excellent activity against MTB. Its long half-life makes it a good candidate for intermittent therapy regimens (given once weekly). Rifabutin is another rifamycin-like antibiotic that is used most often for treatment or prophylaxis of infections with *M. avium* complex; however, it is also effective against MTB. This medication is generally used for patients who do not tolerate RIF or who are taking medications that have adverse drug interactions with RIF (e.g., antiretrovirals, oral contraceptives, methadone, and warfarin).

PZA works against organisms contained in the acid environment of the macrophage. The chief side effect is hepatotoxicity, but this risk is very low at doses of 25 mg/kg/day or less. Polyarthralgias occur commonly (up to 40% of patients) but usually respond to nonsteroidal anti-inflammatory drugs or aspirin.

ETH is a first-line agent that helps prevent the emergence of RIF resistance during TB treatment. Retrobulbar neuritis can occur, resulting in decreased visual

Table 133-4. Doses of Antituberculosis Drugs for Adults and Children

| Drug | Preparation | Adults/ Children | Doses*,† | | | |
			Daily	1×/wk	2×/wk	3×/wk
First-Line Drugs						
Isoniazid	Tablets (50, 100, 300 mg); elixir (50 mg/5 mL); aqueous solution (100 mg/mL) for intravenous or intramuscular injection	Adults (max) Children (max)	5 mg/kg (300 mg) 10-15 mg/kg (300 mg)	15 mg/kg (900 mg) —	15 mg/kg (900 mg) 20-30 mg/kg (900 mg)	15 mg/kg (900 mg) —
Rifampin	Capsule (150, 300 mg); powder may be suspended for oral administration; aqueous solution for intravenous injection	Adults‡ (max) Children	10 mg/kg (600 mg) 10-20 mg/kg (600 mg)	— —	10 mg/kg (600 mg) 10-20 mg/kg (600 mg)	10 mg/kg (600 mg) —
Rifabutin	Capsule (150 mg)	Adults‡ (max) Children	5 mg/kg (300 mg) Appropriate dosing for children is unknown	— Appropriate dosing for children is unknown	5 mg/kg (300 mg) Appropriate dosing for children is unknown	5 mg/kg (300 mg) Appropriate dosing for children is unknown
Rifapentine	Tablet (150 mg, film coated)	Adults Children	— The drug is not approved for use in children	10 mg/kg (continuation phase) (600 mg) The drug is not approved for use in children	— The drug is not approved for use in children	— The drug is not approved for use in children
Pyrazinamide	Tablet (500 mg, scored)	Adults Children (max)	See Table 133-5 15-30 mg/kg (2.0 g)	— —	See Table 133-5 50 mg/kg (2 g)	See Table 133-5
Ethambutol	Tablet (100 mg, 400 mg)	Adults Children§ (max)	See Table 133-5 15-20 mg/kg daily (1.0 g)	— —	See Table 133-5 50 mg/kg (2.5 g)	See Table 133-5
Second-Line Drugs						
Cycloserine	Capsule (250 mg)	Adults (max)	10-15 mg/kg/day (1.0 g in two doses), usually 500-750 mg/day in two doses‖	There are no data to support intermittent administration	There are no data to support intermittent administration	There are no data to support intermittent administration
		Children (max)	10-15 mg/kg/day (1.0 g/day)	—	—	—
Ethionamide	Tablet (250 mg)	Adults¶ (max)	15-20 mg/kg/day (1.0 g/day), usually 500-750 mg/day in a single daily dose or two divided doses¶	There are no data to support intermittent administration	There are no data to support intermittent administration	There are no data to support intermittent administration
		Children (max)	15-20 mg/kg/day (1.0 g/day),	There are no data to support intermittent administration	There are no data to support intermittent administration	There are no data to support intermittent administration
Streptomycin	Aqueous solution (1-g vials) for intravenous or intramuscular administration	Adults (max) Children (max)	— 20-40 mg/kg/day (1 g)	— —	— 20 mg/kg	— —
Amikacin/ kanamycin	Aqueous solution (500-mg and 1-g vials) for intravenous or intramuscular administration	Adults (max) Children (max)	— 15-30 mg/kg/day (1 g) intravenous or intramuscular as a single daily dose	— —	— 15-30 mg/kg	— —
Capreomycin	Aqueous solution (1-g vials) for intravenous or intramuscular administration	Adults (max) Children (max)	— 15-30 mg/kg/day (1 g) as a single daily dose	— —	— 15-30 mg/kg	— —
p-Aminosalicylic acid (PAS)	Granules (4-g packets) can be mixed with food; tablets (500 mg) are still available in some countries but not in the United States; a solution for intravenous administration is available in Europe	Adults Children	8-12 g/day in two or three doses 200-300 mg/kg/ day in two to four divided doses (10 g)	There are no data to support intermittent administration There are no data to support intermittent administration	There are no data to support intermittent administration There are no data to support intermittent administration	There are no data to support intermittent administration There are no data to support intermittent administration

Continued

Table 133-4. Doses of Antituberculosis Drugs for Adults and Children—cont'd

Drug	Preparation	Adults/ Children	Doses*,†			
			Daily	1×/wk	2×/wk	3×/wk
Levofloxacin	Tablets (250, 500, 750 mg); aqueous solution (500-mg vials) for intravenous injection	Adults	500-1000 mg daily	There are no data to support intermittent administration	There are no data to support intermittent administration	There are no data to support intermittent administration
		Children	††	††	††	††
Moxifloxacin	Tablets (400 mg; aqueous solution (400 mg/250 mL) for intravenous injection	Adults	400 mg daily	There are no data to support intermittent administration	There are no data to support intermittent administration	There are no data to support intermittent administration
		Children	‡‡	‡‡	‡‡	‡‡
Gatifloxacin	Tablets (400 mg); aqueous solution (200 mg/20 mL, 400 mg/40 mL) for intravenous injection	Adults	400 mg daily	There are no data to support intermittent administration	There are no data to support intermittent administration	There are no data to support intermittent administration
		Children	§§	§§	§§	§§

*Dose per weight is based on ideal body weight. Children weighing more than 40 kg should be dosed as adults.
†For purposes of this document, adult dosing begins at age 15 years.
‡Dose may need to be adjusted when there is concomitant use of protease inhibitors or nonnucleoside reverse transcription inhibitors.
§The drug can likely be used safely in older children but should be used with caution in children younger than 5 years, in whom visual acuity cannot be monitored. In younger children, EMB at the dose of 15 mg/kg per day can be used if there is suspected or proven resistance to INH or RIF.
‖It should be noted that, although this is the dose recommended generally, most clinicians with experience using cycloserine indicate that it is unusual for patients to be able to tolerate this amount. Serum concentration measurements are often useful in determining the optimal dose for a given patient.
¶The single daily dose can be given at bedtime or with the main meal.
**Dose: 15 mg/kg/day (1 g) and 10 mg/kg in persons older than 59 years (750 mg). Usual dose: 750-1000 mg administered intramuscularly or intravenously, given as a single dose 5-7 days/week and reduced to two or three times per week after the first 2-4 months or after culture conversion, depending on the efficacy of the other drugs in the regimen.
††The long-term (more than several weeks) use of levofloxacin in children and adolescents has not been approved because of concerns about effects on bone and cartilage growth. However, most experts agree that the drug should be considered for children with tuberculosis caused by organisms resistant to both INH and RIF. The optimal dose is not known.
‡‡The long-term (more than several weeks) use of moxifloxacin in children and adolescents has not been approved because of concerns about effects on bone and cartilage growth. The optimal dose is not known.
§§The long-term (more than several weeks) use of gatifloxacin in children and adolescents has not been approved because of concerns about effects on bone and cartilage growth. The optimal dose is not known.
EMB, ethambutol; INH, isoniazid; RIF, rifampin.
From Centers for Disease Control: Treatment of tuberculosis. *MMWR Recomm Rep* 52 (RR-11):1, 2003.

Table 133-5. Suggested Pyrazinamide and Ethambutol Doses, Using Whole Tablets, for Adults Weighing 40-90 kg

Pyrazinamide	Weight (kg)*		
	40-55	56-75	76-90
Daily, mg (mg/kg)	1000 (18.2-25.0)	1500 (20.0-26.8)	2000† (22.2-26.3)
Thrice weekly, mg (mg/kg)	1500 (27.3-37.5)	2500 (33.3-44.6)	3000† (33.3-39.5)
Twice weekly, mg (mg/kg)	2000 (36.4-50.0)	3000 (40.0-53.6)	4000† (44.4-52.6)
Ethambutol			
Daily, mg (mg/kg)	800 (14.5-20.0)	1200 (16.0-21.4)	1600† (17.8-21.1)
Thrice weekly, mg (mg/kg)	1200 (21.8-30.0)	2000 (26.7-35.7)	2400† (26.7-31.6)
Twice weekly, mg (mg/kg)	2000 (36.4-50.0)	2800 (37.3-50.0)	4000† (44.4-52.6)

*Based on estimated lean body weight.
†Maximum dose regardless of weight.
Adapted from Centers for Disease Control: Treatment of tuberculosis. *MMWR Recomm Rep* 52(RR-11):1, 2003.

acuity or red-green color blindness. Thus, monitoring of visual symptoms is key for patients using ETH. Because of the difficulty in visual testing in small children and infants, ETH should be avoided in these populations, except in the cases of adult-type TB or INH or RIF resistance.[68]

Fixed-Dose Combination Drugs

Fixed-dose combinations are multiple antituberculous agents packaged into single tablets. They are useful to prevent monotherapy (patient selectively taking only one of prescribed drugs) and the emergence of drug resistance. Rifater contains INH, RIF, and PZA. Rifamate contains INH and RIF. These preparations are indicated when DOT is not possible.[68]

Second-Line Agents

Streptomycin was once a first-line anti-TB agent, but increasing resistance rates now limit its usefulness. Streptomycin must be given parenterally and has a peak of action 1 hour after the intramuscular dose. The chief side effects of this potentially teratogenic agent are ototoxicity and nephrotoxicity. Amikacin, kanamycin, and capreomycin are also injectable agents used for drug-resistant TB. As with streptomycin, ototoxicity and neurotoxicity are their major adverse effects. TB strains resistant to streptomycin are usually sensitive to both amikacin and kanamycin, and resistance to these two drugs is usually linked.

Cycloserine, ethionamide, and *p*-aminosalicylic acid (PAS) are oral agents used for patients with drug-

Table 133-6. Drug Regimens for Culture-Positive Pulmonary Tuberculosis Caused by Drug-Susceptible Organisms

		Initial Phase	Continuation Phase			Range of Total Doses (Minimal Duration)	Rating* (Evidence)†	
Regimen	Drugs	Interval and Doses‡ (Minimal Duration)	Regimen	Drugs	Interval and Doses‡ (Minimal Duration)		HIV⁻	HIV⁺
1	INH RIF	Seven days per week for 56 doses (8 wk) or 5 days/wk for 40 doses (8 wk)¶	1a	INH/RIF	Seven days per week for 126 doses (18 wk) or 5 days/wk for 90 doses (18 wk)¶	182-130 (26 wk)	A (I)	A (II)
	PZA		1b	INH/RIF	Twice weekly for 36 doses (18 wk)	92-76 (26 wk)	A (I)	A (II)¶
	EMB		1c**	INH/RPT	Once weekly for 18 doses (18 wk)	74-58 (26 wk)	B (I)	E (I)
2	INH	Seven days per week for 14 doses (2 wk), then twice weekly for 12 doses (6 wk) or 5 days/wk for 10 doses (2 wk),¶ then twice weekly for 12 doses (6 wk)	2a	INH/RIF	Twice weekly for 36 doses (18 wk)	62-58 (26 wk)	A (II)	B (II)¶
	RIF PZA EMB		2b**	INH/RPT	Once weekly for 18 doses (18 wk)	44-40 (26 wk)	B (I)	E (I)
3	INH RIF PZA EMB	Three times weekly for 24 doses (8 wk)	3a	INH/RIF	Three times weekly for 54 doses (18 wk)	78 (26 wk)	B (I)	B (II)
4	INH RIF	Seven days per week for 56 doses (8 wk) or 5 days/wk for 40 doses (8 wk)‖	4a	INH/RIF	Seven days per week for 217 doses (31 wk) or 5 days/wk for 155 doses (31 wk)‖	273-195 (39 wk)	C (I)	C (II)
	EMB			INH/RIF	Twice weekly for 62 doses (31 wk)	118-102 (39 wk)	C (I)	C (II)

EMB, ethambutol; INH, isoniazid; PZA, pyrazinamide; RIF, rifampin; RPT, rifapentine.
*Definitions of evidence ratings: A = preferred; B = acceptable alternative; C = offer when A and B cannot be given; E = should never be given.
†Definition of evidence ratings: I = randomized clinical trial; II = data from clinical trials that were not randomized or were conducted in other populations; III = expert opinion.
‡When directly observed therapy (DOT) is used, drugs may be given 5 days/week and the necessary number of doses adjusted accordingly. Although there are no studies that compare five with seven daily doses, extensive experience indicates this would be an effective practice.
§Patients with cavitation on initial chest radiograph and positive cultures at completion of 2 months of therapy should receive a 7-month (31 weeks; either 217 doses [daily] or 62 doses [twice weekly]) continuation phase.
‖Five-day-a-week administration is always given by DOT. Rating for 5 day/week regimens is AIII.
¶Not recommended for human immunodeficiency virus–infected patients with CD4⁺ cell counts <100 cells/μL.
**Options 1c and 2b should be used only in HIV-negative patients who have negative sputum smears at the time of completion of 2 months of therapy and who do not have cavitation on initial radiograph. For patients started on this regimen and found to have a positive culture from the 2-month specimen, treatment should be extended an extra 3 months.
From Centers for Disease Control: Treatment of tuberculosis. *MMWR Recomm Rep* 52(RR-11):1, 2003.

resistant TB when the strain is presumed or known to be sensitive to these agents. Cycloserine is also sometimes used temporarily for patients with acute hepatitis. The main adverse effect of cycloserine is psychosis or seizures (3% to 16% of patients). Ethionamide is similar to INH in both structure and toxicity. Major adverse effects of PAS include gastrointestinal distress (most commonly), hypothyroidism, and hepatitis.

Fluoroquinolones have played a more recent but limited role in the treatment of TB. They are less effective than the first-line agents and are used mainly in the treatment of drug-resistant disease. They may also be used when first-line agents are not tolerated. If they are used singly, resistance may develop quickly. The agents most active against MTB are levofloxacin, moxifloxacin, and gatifloxacin. Because there is more long-term experience regarding safety and tolerability with levofloxacin, this fluoroquinolone is preferred. The

main side effects are gastrointestinal upset, minor CNS symptoms, and photosensitivity or rash.[68]

Initial Therapy

Adults

In 2003, the American Thoracic Society, CDC, and Infectious Diseases Society of America published a joint statement providing updated evidence-based recommendations for the treatment of TB.[68] The goals of therapy are to kill rapidly large numbers of bacilli (bactericidal activity), prevent emergence of drug resistance, and prevent relapse by eliminating dormant or slowly dividing bacilli (sterilizing activity). There are four basic recommended regimens (Table 133-6).[68] These are used when the organism is known or presumed to be susceptible to INH, RIF, PZA, and EMB. All begin with a 2-month initial phase, followed by a continuation phase lasting 4 to 7 months (total treatment duration of 6 to 9 months). Therapeutic regimens of less than 6 months duration usually have an unacceptably high relapse rate. Dosing frequency varies, ranging from 1 to 7 days per week. There is also variation in the strength of evidence supporting each regimen, depending on the patient's HIV status. The regimen that is rated as preferred and supported by the strongest evidence (randomized clinical trials) consists of INH, RIF, PZA, and EMB for 8 weeks (5 to 7 days per week), followed by INH and RIF for 18 weeks (2, 5, or 7 days per week). DOT must be used whenever medications are given less than 7 days per week.[68]

HIV-Positive Individuals

Adequate treatment of active TB in patients co-infected with HIV is critical. It has been observed that immune activation from TB enhances both systemic and local HIV replication and may accelerate the natural progression of HIV infection. Active TB in HIV-infected patients has been associated with increased risk for opportunistic infections and death. TB treatment alone leads to reduction in viral load in these patients.[21] Untreated or inadequately treated TB may result in increased morbidity and mortality, not only from MTB but also from accelerated AIDS. Furthermore, TB can spread rapidly through immunocompromised populations when a source case remains contagious for a prolonged period.[94]

Current recommendations for treating MTB in HIV-infected patients are the same as those for patients who are not HIV infected, with a few important exceptions. The once-weekly INH-rifapentine dosing for the continuation phase should not be used because of a high relapse rate (17%). The twice-weekly INH-RIF dosing should also not be used in patients with CD4 counts less than 100 cells/mL because of emergence of RIF monoresistance. Treatment duration should be a minimum of 6 months. The duration should be extended to 9 months if sputum cultures remain positive after the 2-month initial phase of treatment.[68]

Significant drug interactions between rifamycins used for TB and antiretroviral drugs (protease inhibitors and nonnucleoside reverse transcriptase inhibitors [NNRTIs]) used for HIV complicate the treatment of patients with active TB who are co-infected with HIV. These drug interactions are primarily due to changes in the metabolism of the antiretrovirals and the rifamycins secondary to induction or inhibition of the hepatic cytochrome CYP450 enzyme system. The currently available rifamycins are inducers of CYP450, with RIF being the most potent, rifapentine intermediate, and rifabutin the least potent.[95] Because all of the protease inhibitors are metabolized by CYP450, coadministration of RIF and the protease inhibitors would cause a marked decrease in the blood concentration of the protease inhibitors, probably reducing their antiretroviral activity as well. When treating MTB in patients who are taking protease inhibitors, rifabutin can be used instead of the other rifamycins. Rifabutin provides good activity against MTB without substantially affecting the effectiveness of protease inhibitors.[68]

There are major differences in the actions of NNRTIs on CYP450 and the degree to which they are substrates of CYP450; therefore, their interactions with rifamycins cannot be fully summarized as a class.[95] However, RIF reduces serum concentrations of all three NNRTIs (delavirdine, nevirapine, and efavirenz). Serum concentrations of NNRTIs must be maintained at an optimal steady state to prevent resistant mutations of HIV. When RIF is used in patients taking nevirapine or efavirenz, the NNRTI dose must be increased. Alternatively, rifabutin can be substituted for RIF without NNRTI dose adjustment. Because of the dramatic reduction in serum concentration, none of the rifamycin preparations are acceptable for patients taking delavirdine.[68]

When TB treatment is initiated in HIV-positive patients, some patients develop a paradoxical reaction to medical therapy. The reaction can be manifest as development of fever, new or enlarging lymph nodes, or worsening of radiographic disease. It is more common in HIV-infected patients, occurring in 7% to 36% of cases after beginning treatment. Other causes of deterioration, such as treatment failure, must be considered when this reaction is suspected. Severe paradoxical reactions may be treated with a 2-week tapering course of prednisone or methylprednisolone.[68]

Children and Adolescents

The treatment of adolescents, children, and infants who are culture positive for MTB is in principle the same as that of adults. However, there are some important differences. Children usually develop active pulmonary TB as part of their initial infection. Their chest radiographs demonstrate hilar adenopathy and middle or lower lobe infiltrates. Less commonly, children develop "adult-type" infection, which resembles post-primary infection in adults (upper lobe infiltrates, cavitary lesions, sputum production). Because the bacillary load of primary infection is lower than with adult-type disease, the recommended regimen for children with primary TB is a three-drug regimen (INH, RIF, PZA) for the 2-month initial phase, followed by INH and RIF for a 4-month continuation phase (6 months total). For adult-type infection in children, EMB is added to the initial phase. EMB is also added if INH or RIF resistance is suspected. Because it can be difficult to isolate MTB from children, available resistance patterns of the source should be taken into consideration. Visual acuity and color discrimination should be monitored monthly for older children who are treated with EMB. Inability to monitor vision because of young age is not a contraindication to EMB use in adult-type infection or in the case of INH or RIF resistance. Some important points in treating children are shown in Box 133-4.[68]

Drug-Resistant Tuberculosis

Mycobacterial DNA undergoes spontaneous mutations, giving rise to drug-resistant strains. TB patients who are improperly treated (especially with monotherapy) or nonadherent to their treatment are likely to offer the drug-resistant strains a selective advantage. When these strains predominate, "acquired resistance" has occurred. Patients with acquired resistance can transmit drug-resistant organisms to previously uninfected (never treated) individuals, a process resulting in primary drug resistance.[96] *Multidrug-resistant TB* (MDRTB) is defined as TB with resistance to two or more first-line antituberculous agents. Multidrug resistance may occur when a single drug is added to a failing regimen, an intervention equivalent to giving monotherapy.[97]

Although all drug-resistant TB can ultimately be traced back to suboptimal treatment, it is the transmission of primary drug resistance from person to person that allows rapid dissemination of drug-resistant strains.[98,99] The spread of primary drug resistance is faster when HIV infection is highly prevalent in a population.[39,100,101] Because HIV-infected patients progress rapidly from initial TB infection to active disease, those newly infected can quickly become source cases for further transmission of the resistant bacilli.[100,101] In reports on hospital outbreaks of MDRTB, more than 90% of patients had co-infection with HIV, and case fatality rates were as high as 70% to 90%.[102-105]

However, patients without HIV infection have excellent clinical responses when treated for MDRTB.[105]

Health care workers should know the prevalence of drug resistance in their community and the risk factors (Box 133-5) for drug resistance in order to identify potential cases. Rapid identification and prompt isolation of these patients, along with other control measures, can reduce nosocomial transmission of MDRTB to patients and health care workers. Failure to control drug resistance may lead to wide dissemination of MDRTB and to a public health crisis that physicians must confront without effective medications.

Treatment of drug-resistant TB can be challenging and requires familiarity with second-line agents. For MDRTB, specialist consultation is essential. A general principle that applies to such cases is to use at least three drugs to which the organism is susceptible and that have not been used previously. In general, one of these medications should be an injectable agent. Strains that are resistant only to INH can be managed with a 6-month course of RIF, PZA, and EMB. Recommended regimens for some other resistance patterns are listed in Table 133-7.[68]

Extrapulmonary Tuberculosis

Clinical trials, including some randomized controlled trials, indicate that 6- to 9-month regimens of therapy

---

BOX 133-4. Treatment of Tuberculosis in Children

1. Infection with tuberculosis in children younger than 4 years is more likely to disseminate and therefore demands prompt recognition and aggressive management.
2. Sputum smears are a less reliable diagnostic tool. It may be more appropriate to confirm the diagnosis in a child using culture results or results from the adult source. If neither is available, early morning gastric aspirates, bronchoalveolar lavage, or tissue may be used.
3. Because of its ocular toxicity, ethambutol should be avoided in this age group. Streptomycin, kanamycin, and amikacin are alternatives.
4. The primary cause of treatment failure in this population is noncompliance. Therefore directly observed therapy is preferable, and twice-a-week regimens are an option.
5. Treat extrapulmonary tuberculosis as described above for pulmonary variety except for infections involving bones or joints, meningitis, and miliary disease, when therapy may be required for 9 to 12 months.
6. Hilar adenopathy on chest radiographs may take 2 to 3 years to resolve following treatment.

BOX 133-5. Risk Factors for Drug-Resistant Mycobacterium tuberculosis[96-99]

1. Prior unsuccessful antituberculosis treatment
2. Failure to respond or adhere to a good treatment regimen
3. Human immunodeficiency virus
4. Intravenous drug abuse
5. Close contacts of source cases
6. Recent immigration from area with a high prevalence of drug resistance
7. Cavitary lung disease
8. Homelessness
9. Imprisonment
10. Drug malabsorption due to gastrectomy or ileal bypass surgery

---

Table 133-7. Potential Regimens for the Management of Patients with Drug-Resistant Pulmonary Tuberculosis

Pattern of Drug Resistance	Suggested Regimen	Duration of Treatment (mo)
INH (±SM)	RIF, PZA, EMB (an FQN* may strengthen the regimen for patients with extensive disease)	6
INH and RIF (±SM)	FQN, PZA, EMB, IA,+ ± alternative agent‡	18-24
INH, RIF (±SM), and EMB or PZA	FQN (EMB or PZA if active), IA, and two alternative agents	24
RIF	INH, EMB, FQN, supplemented with PZA for the first 2 mo (an IA may be included for the first 2–3 mo for patients with extensive disease)	12-18

*FQN = fluoroquinolone; most experience involves ofloxacin, levofloxacin, or ciprofloxacin.
†IA = injectable agent; may include aminoglycosides (streptomycin, amikacin, or kanamycin) or the polypeptide capreomycin.
‡Alternative agents = ethionamide, cycloserine, *p*-aminosalicylic acid, clarithromycin, amoxicillin-clavulanate, linezolid.
EMB, ethambutol; FQN, fluoroquinolone; IA, injectable agent; INH, isoniazid; PZA, pyrazinamide; RIF, rifampin; SM, streptomycin.
From Centers for Disease Control: Treatment of tuberculosis. *MMWR Recomm Rep* 52(RR-11):1, 2003.

are effective treatments for EPTB. The exceptions to this are bone or joint infection and tuberculous meningitis. The CDC recommends 6 to 9 months for bone or joint infection, 9 to 12 months for meningitis, and 6 months for all other forms of EPTB.[68]

Corticosteroids

The use of corticosteroids in the treatment of EPTB is more common than in pulmonary disease. Corticosteroids may prevent constriction in tuberculous pericarditis and decrease the neurologic sequelae in all stages of tuberculous meningitis, especially if given early in the disease.[46] The CDC strongly recommends corticosteroids for MTB pericardial or CNS infections.[68] Corticosteroids may provide some benefit to children with bronchial obstruction caused by enlarged lymph nodes.[66] In addition, in patients with pulmonary TB, prednisone, 20 to 60 mg/day, may benefit those who continue to have spike temperatures and lose weight despite a good bacteriologic response to appropriate antituberculous therapy.[106]

Pregnancy

Treatment of TB during pregnancy causes little risk for the fetus, especially when compared with untreated disease. INH, RIF, and ETH cross the placenta but have no known teratogenic effects. These three drugs should be used as the initial regimen, followed by a continuation phase of INH and RIF for an additional 7 months (9 months total). Pyridoxine is recommended for pregnant women receiving INH. The use of PZA in the initial regimen is controversial, mainly because of insufficient data regarding its safety during pregnancy. When PZA is used, the total treatment duration can be reduced to 6 months. Streptomycin may cause congenital deafness and is contraindicated. Kanamycin, amikacin, and capreomycin should therefore be avoided as well. Fluoroquinolones should be avoided because of the potential for arthropathies (as demonstrated in animal models).[68] Although these chemotherapeutic agents are present in breast milk, they are not harmful to the infant and are not present in high enough concentrations (approximately 20% of the daily dose) to be therapeutic or preventive.[46,68]

Surgical Management

The most common indication for surgery is MDRTB with severe localized disease.[107] When optimal medical therapy based on drug susceptibility testing is given preoperatively and postoperatively, the outcome appears to improve.[107,108] In one study of 172 patients who underwent pulmonary resection for MDRTB, 96% of those with MTB-positive preoperative sputum samples became sputum negative for MTB after surgery.[109] The CDC recommends that surgery should be performed following several months of an intensive medication regimen.[68] Other indications for surgery may include bronchopleural fistula, massive uncontrolled hemoptysis, extensive bronchostenosis, destroyed lung, solitary nodule, trapped lung, complicated cavity, and empyema.[107,108]

Treatment of Latent *Mycobacterium tuberculosis* Infection

Following primary infection with MTB, host defenses are usually able to contain the infection within 2 to 10 weeks. This begins the latent period for MTB infection, when individuals are not contagious and do not have active disease. Preventive therapy is directed at treating MTB infection during this latent phase to prevent reactivation and development of active disease. Tuberculin skin testing for the presence of latent MTB infection should be performed in individuals who are at increased risk for either MTB infection, exposure to infectious cases, or development of active disease (see Table 133-3).[78]

Treatment of latent MTB infection is indicated for individuals who have a risk of developing active TB that outweighs the risks of the therapy itself. The risk of INH-induced hepatitis increases with age, but age older than 35 years is *not* a contraindication to INH administration. In fact, if an individual belongs to a risk group listed in Table 133-3, age is no longer a factor and treatment for latent MTB infection is warranted.[78,79] Individuals with impaired CMI, such as young children or immunocompromised patients, may not have positive tuberculin skin tests following initial infection with MTB. Thus, treatment of latent MTB infection should still be considered for such patients if they experience a recent (within 3 months) high-risk exposure to MTB.[78] Continuation of therapy in such cases should be based upon tuberculin skin test results at 3 months after the exposure. Excluding active TB with chest radiographs and clinical evaluation is a critical step before initiating therapy for latent MTB infection.

Four regimens may be used to treat latent MTB infection (Table 133-8).[79] The preferred regimen is daily INH for 9 months. The dose is 5 mg/kg in adults and 10 to 20 mg/kg for children, with a maximum of 300 mg/day for both populations. INH may also be given twice weekly by DOT. For HIV-positive patients, the recommended regimen is daily INH for 9 months or daily RIF

Table 133-8. Treatment of Latent Tuberculosis Infection

Drugs	Duration (mo)	Interval	Rating* (Evidence)† HIV⁻	HIV⁺
Isoniazid	9	Daily	A (II)	A (II)
		Twice weekly	B (II)	B (II)
Isoniazid	6	Daily	B (I)	C (I)
		Twice weekly	B (II)	C (I)
Rifampin-pyrazinamide	2	Daily	B (II)	A (I)
	2–3	Twice weekly	C (II)	C (I)
Rifampin	4	Daily	B (II)	B (II)

*A = preferred; B = acceptable alternative; C = offer when A and B cannot be given.
†I = randomized clinical trial data; II = data from clinical trials that are not randomized or were conducted in other populations; III = expert opinion.
From Centers for Disease Control: Targeted tuberculin testing and treatment of latent tuberculosis infection. *MMWR Recomm Rep* 49(RR-6):1, 2000.

and PZA for 2 months.[79] DOT is recommended for all intermittent therapy regimens and for persons at high risk for developing the disease, to decrease possible MDRTB emergence.

DISPOSITION

Most TB patients can be managed as outpatients. The ideal situation for the patient with newly diagnosed or suspected TB is to be at home, receiving antituberculosis therapy, with the patient's contacts receiving preventive treatment. The CDC strongly recommends DOT in order to maximize compliance and completion of therapy.[68] The emergency department discharge instructions should clearly emphasize the importance of adhering to the prescribed treatment regimen and home isolation procedures (avoid meeting new contacts). The patient must be immediately reported to the health department to ensure that the patient has an adequate source of TB care, that support systems and resources are available to complete the care, and that the patient's contacts are investigated and screened. Two weeks of treatment is widely accepted as the minimum time to be rendered noninfectious as long as the patient has been treated with appropriate medications (see also "Transmission").[25]

Acutely ill or elderly patients may require hospitalization during the first few days of treatment because adverse reactions are common and may occasionally be life threatening.[110] In addition, severely ill patients may require parenteral drug administration. TB patients have a high rate of HIV co-infection, and the comorbidities associated with HIV, the complex synergy between MTB and HIV, and the potentially harmful drug interactions between the antiretroviral agents and the rifamycins may favor inpatient treatment for the initial management of these complicated cases.

Hospital admission is also indicated for patients with active MDRTB. These patients commonly require observation during initiation of therapy because of the complexity of the treatment regimens, the toxicity of the drugs, and the need to monitor the patient closely for adherence with treatment and isolation measures.[97] Finally, social issues such as homelessness, households with infants or immunocompromised persons, substance abuse, and inability to care for self may necessitate hospitalization. The recalcitrant patient is a potential threat to public health and may require legal measures for involuntary hospitalization.[111]

PREVENTION OF TRANSMISSION IN THE EMERGENCY DEPARTMENT

Emergency departments often care for patients at increased risk for active pulmonary TB, such as those who are homeless, foreign born, recently incarcerated, or chronically ill. As a result, emergency department workers can be at high risk for occupational TB infection. In one county hospital in Los Angeles, 31% of emergency department workers became tuberculin skin test positive at some time during employment, including 20% of attending physicians, 32% of nurses, and 33% of residents.[112] Tuberculin skin test conversion risk was found to be 6% after 1 year of emergency department employment, 14% after 2 years, and 27% after 4 years. In addition, increased hospital occupancy and emergency department overcrowding can lead to extended waiting periods for both emergency department beds and hospital beds.[113,114] Some emergency departments may lack an adequate number of TB isolation rooms.[115] Nosocomial transmission risk in the emergency department is also increased because patients with TB often receive care before the diagnosis is suspected; this risk is particularly high with critically ill patients, who by definition require close, intense contact with multiple emergency care providers.

Early Identification

For most effective minimization of infectious exposures among health care workers and other patients, all patients with active pulmonary TB would ideally be placed in respiratory isolation when initially presenting for care. Not surprisingly, this is difficult to accomplish, and there are frequently delays in identification and respiratory isolation of such patients. In one emergency department study of patients with TB, the mean time from emergency department registration to respiratory isolation was 6.5 hours, and 46% of patients were first isolated on the hospital ward.[116] In order to improve the early identification of patients who may have TB, the CDC has recommended screening for TB at triage.[29] Triage screening protocols can detect patients with more classical presentations of TB, but reported protocols are only moderately sensitive and somewhat cumbersome.[117] Immediate respiratory isolation should be considered for patients with high-risk chief complaints, such as HIV-positive patients with cough, those with hemoptysis, or patients with a history of TB presenting with cough or fever. The best guideline is to initiate respiratory isolation as soon as TB is considered as a possible diagnosis. Masks should be placed on such patients *before* obtaining chest radiographs. In addition, the development of policies providing for expedited admission to hospital isolation beds and for improved access to local public health facilities may help decrease TB transmission at virtually no cost.[115]

Isolation and Environmental Control

In addition to triage screening, the use of proper isolation facilities and environmental control measures can help prevent TB exposures. Airflow in the emergency department plays a central role, and inadequate ventilation has been a contributing factor in many nosocomial outbreaks of TB. Ideally, there should be single-pass airflow from waiting rooms to outside the facility. Within the emergency department, air should flow from clean areas to less clean areas rather than vice versa. For emergency departments that frequently see patients with TB, at least one true respiratory isolation room should be available. The CDC recommends that respiratory isolation rooms have at least 12 air changes per hour and have "negative pressure" (air flows *into* the room from other emergency department areas). Other engineering approaches to TB infection control include the use of high-efficiency particulate air (HEPA) filters and upper room ultraviolet light irradiation.[29]

Personal Respiratory Protection

Emergency department personnel should be familiar with the appropriate use of respiratory protection against TB. Surgical masks (e.g., string-tie masks) should be placed on potentially contagious patients to decrease the production of infectious droplets into the air.[29] Air can leak around such masks, however, so they may not adequately prevent health care workers from inhaling infectious droplet nuclei.[118] Thus, surgical masks should be used only for source control, not for health care worker protection. More advanced personal respiratory protection includes N-95 particulate respirators.[119] These masks can filter 1-μm particles with at least 95% efficiency and are the preferred masks for health care workers in the emergency department. They are available in a variety of shapes and sizes and from various manufacturers. HEPA-filtered masks can also be used for health care worker respiratory protection, and these masks were used more extensively before the development of the N-95 masks. Although HEPA-filtered masks are very effective, they are more costly and can make breathing uncomfortable.[118]

Preventive Therapy after Inadvertent Exposure

Health care workers who are exposed to patients with active pulmonary TB should be referred to their primary care physicians or employee health services for follow-up testing and treatment. Tuberculin skin testing is usually performed within days after exposure to establish whether the health care worker has previously been infected with MTB. If the baseline test is negative, a follow-up skin test is performed 3 months later to determine whether tuberculin skin test conversion has occurred. Health care workers whose tuberculin skin test converts to positive (5-mm induration) after an exposure should undergo chest radiography and clinical evaluation to rule out active disease. When active TB infection is excluded, preventive therapy is recommended. The recommendations in Box 133-6 can assist physicians in deciding who should be treated after an exposure.[120] For exposures to MDRTB, expert consultation is advised for selecting an individualized regimen.

Tuberculin Skin Testing

Because all emergency department staff are potentially exposed to MTB, a skin test program is essential.[29] Skin testing at regular intervals monitors TB transmission among emergency department staff and targets staff who need prophylactic therapy or treatment. Although

---

BOX 133-6. Guidelines for Management After Accidental Exposure to Tuberculosis

1. Healthy individuals who remain PPD negative after a heavy exposure do not require chemotherapy.
2. If exposure is discovered immediately, preventive therapy should be started in particularly heavily exposed people who are known to be PPD negative. If the skin test remains negative after 3 months, therapy can be discontinued.
3. Individuals who convert to a positive PPD after the exposure should take preventive therapy regardless of age.
4. Individuals without preexposure PPD results who react positively after the exposure should be treated as convertors (see item 3 above).
5. Individuals known to be PPD positive before exposure have too slight a risk to warrant preventive therapy.
6. Individuals who are younger than 35 years, have HIV infection, are receiving cancer chemotherapy or long-term corticosteroid therapy, or are otherwise immuno-compromised should be considered for preventive therapy, regardless of the exposure.

HIV, human immunodeficiency virus; PPD, purified protein derivative. Modified from Stead WW: Management of health care workers after inadvertent exposure to tuberculosis: A guide for the use of preventive therapy. *Ann Intern Med* 122:906, 1995.

---

recommendations for various health care settings depend upon the number of TB patients encountered, most emergency department health care workers should be skin tested every 6 months.[29]

Bacille Calmette-Guérin Vaccine

Although the BCG vaccine has been used since 1921, its overall efficacy, duration of protective immunity, and optimal age for administration remain unclear. In the United States, BCG is rarely recommended because of the belief that it would undermine the epidemiologic and diagnostic value of PPD skin testing. However, tuberculin skin tests in patients given prior BCG vaccination usually demonstrate less than 10 mm of induration. Thus, prior BCG vaccination status should be ignored when interpreting skin test results.[79]

Institutional outbreaks of TB and the emergence of MDRTB are sparking reassessment of the BCG issue in the United States. Reports of BCG vaccine efficacy range from 0% to 80%. One meta-analysis reported the efficacy of BCG vaccine to be about 50%.[121] BCG is currently recommended in the United States only for tuberculin-negative infants and children who cannot take INH and have ongoing exposure to a persistently untreated or inadequately treated patient with active TB, who are continuously exposed to persons with INH- and RIF-resistant TB, or who belong to groups with rates of new MTB infection exceeding 1% per year.[121] One decision analysis suggested that BCG vaccination would be more effective than the current annual testing strategy for health care workers.[122] However, the routine use of BCG vaccine in heath care workers is still controversial. What is not controversial is that the vaccine is strongly contraindicated in individuals with HIV infection or other immunosuppressive disease. New vaccines against MTB are being researched, including those using attenuated strains of the MTB complex, recombinant mycobacteria, and subunit proteins and DNA vaccines.[123]

KEY CONCEPTS

- In the mid-1980s, there was a resurgence of TB cases in the United States. Immigration and the HIV epidemic were important contributing factors. The reemergence of TB has affected both adults and children.

- TB infection starts with primary infection, followed by a latent period in immunocompetent patients. About 10% of infected patients eventually develop reactivation of disease.

- Beyond pulmonary manifestations, a variety of extrapulmonary manifestations may occur including involvement of lymph nodes, pleura, bones or joints, CNS, and genitourinary and gastrointestinal systems.

- The clinical presentation of TB infection may be variable and more difficult to diagnose in HIV-infected or elderly patients.

- Therapy must be individualized to reflect acuity, sensitivity, system involvement, and underlying conditions. The most commonly used agents are isoniazid, rifampin, pyrazinamide, and ethambutol.

- Prevention and screening are fundamental components of any TB control strategy. Patients suspected of having active pulmonary TB should be placed into respiratory isolation as soon as possible.

REFERENCES

1. Rubin SA: Tuberculosis. Captain of all these men of death. *Radiol Clin North Am* 33:619, 1995.
2. Allison MJ, Mendoza D, Pezzia A: Documentation of a case of tuberculosis in pre-Columbian America. *Am Rev Respir Dis* 107:985, 1973.
3. Zimmerman MR: Pulmonary and osseous tuberculosis in an Egyptian mummy. *Bull NY Acad Med* 55:604, 1979.
4. Burke RM: *An Historical Chronology of Tuberculosis*, 2nd ed. Springfield, Ill, Charles C Thomas, 1955.
5. Waksman S: *The Conquest of Tuberculosis*. Berkeley, Calif, University of California Press, 1964.
6. Bates JH, Stead WW: The history of tuberculosis as a global epidemic. *Med Clin North Am* 77:1205, 1993.
7. Stead WW, Dutt AK: Epidemiology and host factors. In Schlossberg D (ed): *Tuberculosis*, 3rd ed. New York, Springer-Verlag, 1994.
8. Ayvazian FL: History of tuberculosis. In Hershfield ES (ed): *Tuberculosis: A Comprehensive International Approach*. New York, Marcel Dekker, 1993.
9. Frieden TR, et al: Tuberculosis in New York City—Turning the tide. *N Engl J Med* 333:229, 1995.
10. Cantwell MF, et al: Epidemiology of tuberculosis in the United States, 1985 through 1992. *JAMA* 272:535, 1994.
11. Bellin E: Failure of tuberculosis control. A prescription for change. *JAMA* 271:708, 1994.
12. Binkin NJ, et al: Tuberculosis prevention and control activities in the United States: An overview of the organization of tuberculosis services. *Int J Tuberc Lung Dis* 3:663, 1999.
13. Centers for Disease Control: World TB day, March 24, 2003. *MMWR Morb Mortal Wkly Rep* 52:217, 2003.
14. Frieden TR, et al: Tuberculosis. *Lancet* 362:887, 2003.
15. Corbett EL, et al: The growing burden of tuberculosis: Global trends and interactions with the HIV epidemic. *Arch Intern Med* 163:1009, 2003.
16. Dutt AK, Stead WW: Tuberculosis in the elderly. *Med Clin North Am* 77:1353, 1993.
17. Centers for Disease Control: *Reported TB in the US, 2002*. Atlanta, U.S. Department of Health and Human Services, 2003.
18. Barnes PF, et al: Transmission of tuberculosis among the urban homeless. *JAMA* 275:305, 1996.
19. Sepkowitz KA, et al: Tuberculosis in the AIDS era. *Clin Microbiol Rev* 8:180, 1995.
20. Zumla A, et al: The tuberculosis pandemic—Which way now? *J Infect* 38:74, 1999.
21. Centers for Disease Control: Prevention and treatment of tuberculosis among patients infected with human immunodeficiency virus: Principles of therapy and revised recommendations. *MMWR Recomm Rep* 47(RR-20):1, 1998.
22. Huebner RE, Castro KG: The changing face of tuberculosis. *Annu Rev Med* 46:47, 1995.
23. Jacobs RF, Starke JR: Tuberculosis in children. *Med Clin North Am* 77:1335, 1993.
24. Leung AN: Pulmonary tuberculosis: The essentials. *Radiology* 210:307, 1999.
25. Haas DW: *Mycobacterium tuberculosis*. In Mandell GL, Douglas AC, Bennet JE (eds): *Principles and Practice of Infectious Diseases*, 5th ed. Philadelphia, Churchill Livingstone, 2000, pp 2576-2607.
26. Edwards D, Kirkpatrick CH: The immunology of mycobacterial diseases. *Am Rev Respir Dis* 134:1062, 1986.
27. Nardell EA: Environmental control of tuberculosis. *Med Clin North Am* 77:1315, 1993.
28. Menzies D: Effect of treatment on contagiousness of patients with active pulmonary tuberculosis. *Infect Control Hosp Epidemiol* 18:582, 1997.
29. Centers for Disease Control: Guidelines for preventing the transmission of *Mycobacterium tuberculosis* in health-care facilities. *MMWR Recomm Rep* 43(RR-13):59, 1994.
30. Iseman MD: An unholy trinity—Three negative sputum smears and release from tuberculosis isolation. *Clin Infect Dis* 25:671, 1997.
31. Frampton MW: An outbreak of tuberculosis among hospital personnel caring for a patient with a skin ulcer. *Ann Intern Med* 117:312, 1992.
32. Hutton MD, et al: Nosocomial transmission of tuberculosis associated with a draining abscess. *J Infect Dis* 161:286, 1990.
33. Dannenberg AM Jr: Delayed-type hypersensitivity and cell-mediated immunity in the pathogenesis of tuberculosis. *Immunol Today* 12:228, 1991.
34. Dannenberg AM: Pathogenesis and immunology: Basic aspects. In Schlossberg D (ed): *Tuberculosis*, 3rd ed. New York, Springer-Verlag, 1994.
35. Nardell EA: Pathogenesis of tuberculosis. In Reichman LB, Hershfield ES (eds): *Tuberculosis: A Comprehensive International Approach*. New York, Marcel Dekker, 1993.
36. Rossman MD, Mayock RL: Pulmonary tuberculosis. In Rossman MD, MacGregor RR (eds): *Tuberculosis: Clinical Management and New Challenges*. New York, McGraw-Hill, 1995.
37. Nardell E, et al: Exogenous reinfection with tuberculosis in a shelter for the homeless. *N Engl J Med* 315:1570, 1986.
38. Van Rie A, et al: Exogenous reinfection as a cause of recurrent tuberculosis after curative treatment. *N Engl J Med* 341:1174, 1999.
39. Small PM, et al: Exogenous reinfection with multidrug-resistant *Mycobacterium tuberculosis* in patients with advanced HIV infection. *N Engl J Med* 328:1137, 1993.

40. Hopewell PC: A clinical view of tuberculosis. *Radiol Clin North Am* 33:641, 1995.

41. Hopewell PC, Bloom BR: Tuberculosis and other mycobacterial diseases. In Murray JF, Nadel JA (eds): *Textbook of Respiratory Medicine*, 2nd ed. Philadelphia, WB Saunders, 1994.

42. Barnes PF, et al: Chest roentgenogram in pulmonary tuberculosis: New data on an old test. *Chest* 94:316, 1988.

43. Sokolove PE, Rossman L, Cohen SH: The emergency department presentation of patients with active pulmonary tuberculosis. *Acad Emerg Med* 7:1056, 2000.

44. Rajagopalan S: Tuberculosis and aging: A global health problem. *Clin Infect Dis* 33:1034, 2001.

45. Centers for Disease Control: TB care guide highlights from core curriculum on tuberculosis. *MMWR Morb Mortal Wkly Rep* 43[R-10]:59, 1994.

46. American Thoracic Society: Treatment of tuberculosis and tuberculosis infection in adults and children. *Am J Respir Crit Care Med* 149:1359, 1994.

47. McAdams HP, Erasmus J, Winter JA: Radiologic manifestations of pulmonary tuberculosis. *Radiol Clin North Am* 33:655, 1995.

48. Omerod LP: Respiratory tuberculosis. In Davies PDO (ed): *Clinical Tuberculosis*. New York, Chapman & Hall Medical, 1994.

49. Jean-Baptiste E: Clinical assessment and management of massive hemoptysis. *Crit Care Med* 28:1642, 2000.

50. Fowler NO: Tuberculous pericarditis. *JAMA* 266:99, 1991.

51. Chen Y, et al: Human immunodeficiency virus–associated pericardial effusion: Report of 40 cases and review of the literature. *Am Heart J* 137:516, 1999.

52. Trautner BW, Darouiche RO: Tuberculous pericarditis: Optimal diagnosis and management. *Clin Infect Dis* 33:954, 2001.

53. Mandavia DP, et al: Bedside echocardiography by emergency physicians. *Ann Emerg Med* 38:377, 2001.

54. Friedman LN, Selwyn PA: Pulmonary tuberculosis: Primary, reactivation, HIV related, and non-HIV related. In Friedman LN (ed): *Tuberculosis: Current Concepts and Treatment*. Boca Raton, Fla, CRC Press, 1994.

55. Greenbaum M, Beyt BE Jr, Murray PR: The accuracy of diagnosing pulmonary tuberculosis at a teaching hospital. *Am Rev Respir Dis* 121:477, 1980.

56. Counsell SR, Tan JS, Dittus RS: Unsuspected pulmonary tuberculosis in a community teaching hospital. *Arch Intern Med* 149:1274, 1989.

57. Palmer PE: Pulmonary tuberculosis—Usual and unusual radiographic presentations. *Semin Roentgenol* 14:204, 1979.

58. Leung AN, et al: Primary tuberculosis in childhood: Radiographic manifestations. *Radiology* 182:87, 1992.

59. Miller WT: Tuberculosis in the 1990's. *Radiol Clin North Am* 32:649, 1994.

60. Hoheisel G, et al: Endobronchial tuberculosis: Diagnostic features and therapeutic outcome. *Respir Med* 88:593, 1994.

61. Greenberg SD, et al: Active pulmonary tuberculosis in patients with AIDS: Spectrum of radiographic findings (including a normal appearance). *Radiology* 193:115, 1994.

62. Perlman DC, et al: Variation of chest radiographic patterns in pulmonary tuberculosis by degree of human immunodeficiency virus–related immunosuppression. The Terry Beirn Community Programs for Clinical Research on AIDS (CPCRA). The AIDS Clinical Trials Group (ACTG). *Clin Infect Dis* 25:242, 1997.

63. Burman WJ, Jones BE: Clinical and radiographic features of HIV-related tuberculosis. *Semin Respir Infect* 18:263, 2003.

64. Haramati LB, Jenny-Avital ER, Alterman DD: Effect of HIV status on chest radiographic and CT findings in patients with tuberculosis. *Clin Radiol* 52:31, 1997.

65. Christie JD, Callihan DR: The laboratory diagnosis of mycobacterial diseases. Challenges and common sense. *Clin Lab Med* 15:279, 1995.

66. Shingadia D, Novelli V: Diagnosis and treatment of tuberculosis in children. *Lancet Infect Dis* 3:624, 2003.

67. Eichbaum Q, Rubin EJ: Tuberculosis. Advances in laboratory diagnosis and drug susceptibility testing. *Am J Clin Pathol* 118(Suppl):S3, 2002.

68. Centers for Disease Control: Treatment of tuberculosis. *MMWR Recomm Rep* 52(RR-11):1, 2003.

69. Kirk SM, et al: Flow cytometric testing of susceptibilities of *Mycobacterium tuberculosis* isolates to ethambutol, isoniazid, and rifampin in 24 hours. *J Clin Microbiol* 36:1568, 1998.

70. Bates JH: New diagnostic methods. In Friedman LN (ed): *Tuberculosis: Current Concepts and Treatments*. Boca Raton, Fla, CRC Press, 1994.

71. Woods GL: Molecular methods in the detection and identification of mycobacterial infections. *Arch Pathol Lab Med* 123:1002, 1999.

72. Gladwin MT, Plorde JJ, Martin TR: Clinical application of the *Mycobacterium tuberculosis* direct test: Case report, literature review, and proposed clinical algorithm. *Chest* 114:317, 1998.

73. Wang SX, Tay L: Evaluation of three nucleic acid amplification methods for direct detection of *Mycobacterium tuberculosis* complex in respiratory specimens. *J Clin Microbiol* 37:1932, 1999.

74. Muranishi H, et al: Measurement of tuberculostearic acid in sputa, pleural effusions, and bronchial washings. A clinical evaluation for diagnosis of pulmonary tuberculosis. *Diagn Microbiol Infect Dis* 13:235, 1990.

75. Burgess LJ, et al: The use of adenosine deaminase and interferon-gamma as diagnostic tools for tuberculous pericarditis. *Chest* 122:900, 2002.

76. Villegas MV, Labrada LA, Saravia NG: Evaluation of polymerase chain reaction, adenosine deaminase, and interferon-gamma in pleural fluid for the differential diagnosis of pleural tuberculosis. *Chest* 118:1355, 2000.

77. Small PM, Fujiwara PI: Management of tuberculosis in the United States. *N Engl J Med* 345:189, 2001.

78. Jasmer RM, Nahid P, Hopewell PC: Latent tuberculosis infection. *N Engl J Med* 347:1860, 2002.

79. Centers for Disease Control: Targeted tuberculin testing and treatment of latent tuberculosis infection. *MMWR Recomm Rep* 49(RR-6):1, 2000.

80. Patz EF Jr, Swensen SJ, Erasmus J: Pulmonary manifestations of nontuberculous *Mycobacterium*. *Radiol Clin North Am* 33:719, 1995.

81. Wright PW, Wallace RJ: Nontuberculous mycobacteria. In Davies PDO (ed): *Clinical Tuberculosis*. New York, Chapman & Hall Medical, 1994.

82. Brown BA, Wallace RJ: Infections due to nontuberculous mycobacteria. In Mandell GL, Douglas AC, Bennet JE (eds): *Principles and Practice of Infectious Diseases*. Philadelphia, Churchill Livingstone, 2000, pp 2630-2636.

83. Marras TK, Daley CL: Epidemiology of human pulmonary infection with nontuberculous mycobacteria. *Clin Chest Med* 23:553, 2002.

84. Munck K, Mandpe AH: Mycobacterial infections of the head and neck. *Otolaryngol Clin North Am* 36:569, 2003.

85. De Vuyst D, et al: Imaging features of musculoskeletal tuberculosis. *Eur Radiol* 13:1809, 2003.

86. Eastwood JB, Corbishley CM, Grange JM: Tuberculosis and the kidney. *J Am Soc Nephrol* 12:1307, 2001.

87. Lenk S, Schroeder J: Genitourinary tuberculosis. *Curr Opin Urol* 11:93, 2001.

88. Chow TW, Lim BK, Vallipuram S: The masquerades of female pelvic tuberculosis: Case reports and review of literature on clinical presentations and diagnosis. *J Obstet Gynaecol Res* 28:203, 2002.

89. Sutherland AM, Glen ES, MacFarlane JR: Transmission of genito-urinary tuberculosis. *Health Bull (Edinb)* 40:87, 1982.

90. Kim JH, Langston AA, Gallis HA: Miliary tuberculosis: Epidemiology, clinical manifestations, diagnosis, and outcome. *Rev Infect Dis* 12:583, 1990.

91. Bernaerts A, et al: Tuberculosis of the central nervous system: Overview of neuroradiological findings. *Eur Radiol* 13:1876, 2003.

92. Sheer TA, Coyle WJ: Gastrointestinal tuberculosis. *Curr Gastroenterol Rep* 5:273, 2003.

93. Pozsik CJ: Compliance with tuberculosis therapy. *Med Clin North Am* 77:1289, 1993.

94. Schluger NW: Issues in the treatment of active tuberculosis in human immunodeficiency virus–infected patients. *Clin Infect Dis* 28:130, 1999.

95. Burman WJ, Gallicano K, Peloquin C: Therapeutic implications of drug interactions in the treatment of human immunodeficiency virus–related tuberculosis. *Clin Infect Dis* 28:419,. 1999.

96. O'Brien RJ: Drug-resistant tuberculosis: Etiology, management and prevention. *Semin Respir Infect* 9:104, 1994.

97. Goble M: Drug resistance. In Friedman LN (ed): *Tuberculosis: Current Concepts and Treatment.* Boca Raton, Fla, CRC Press, 1994.

98. Frieden TR, et al: The emergence of drug-resistant tuberculosis in New York City. *N Engl J Med* 328:521, 1993.

99. Simone PM, Dooley SW: The phenomenon of multi-drug resistant tuberculosis. In Rossman MD, MacGregor RR (eds): *Tuberculosis: Clinical Management and New Challenges.* New York, McGraw-Hill, 1995.

100. Daley CL, et al: An outbreak of tuberculosis with accelerated progression among persons infected with the human immunodeficiency virus. An analysis using restriction-fragment-length polymorphisms. *N Engl J Med* 326:231, 1992.

101. Ellner JJ: Multidrug-resistant tuberculosis. *Adv Intern Med* 40:155, 1995.

102. Bloch AB, et al: Nationwide survey of drug-resistant tuberculosis in the United States. *JAMA* 271:665, 1994.

103. Fischl MA, et al: Clinical presentation and outcome of patients with HIV infection and tuberculosis caused by multiple-drug-resistant bacilli. *Ann Intern Med* 117:184, 1992.

104. Goble M, et al: Treatment of 171 patients with pulmonary tuberculosis resistant to isoniazid and rifampin. *N Engl J Med* 328:527, 1993.

105. Telzak EE, et al: Multidrug-resistant tuberculosis in patients without HIV infection. *N Engl J Med* 333:907, 1995.

106. Muthuswamy P, et al: Prednisone as adjunctive therapy in the management of pulmonary tuberculosis. Report of 12 cases and review of the literature. *Chest* 107:1621, 1995.

107. Pomerantz M, Brown J: The surgical management of tuberculosis. *Semin Thorac Cardiovasc Surg* 7:108, 1995.

108. Treasure RL, Seaworth BJ: Current role of surgery in *Mycobacterium tuberculosis. Ann Thorac Surg* 59:1405, 1995.

109. Pomerantz BJ, et al: Pulmonary resection for multi-drug resistant tuberculosis. *J Thorac Cardiovasc Surg* 121:448, 2001.

110. Davies PDO: Problems in the management of tuberculosis. In Davies PDO (ed): *Clinical Tuberculosis.* New York, Chapman & Hall Medical, 1994.

111. Etkind SC: The role of the public health department in tuberculosis. *Med Clin North Am* 77:1303, 1993.

112. Sokolove PE, et al: Exposure of emergency department personnel to tuberculosis: PPD testing during an epidemic in the community. *Ann Emerg Med* 24:418, 1994.

113. Forster AJ, et al: The effect of hospital occupancy on emergency department length of stay and patient disposition. *Acad Emerg Med* 10:127, 2003.

114. Liu S, Hobgood C, Brice JH: Impact of critical bed status on emergency department patient flow and overcrowding. *Acad Emerg Med* 10:382, 2003.

115. Moran GJ, et al: Tuberculosis infection-control practices in United States emergency departments. *Ann Emerg Med* 26:283, 1995.

116. Moran GJ, et al: Delayed recognition and infection control for tuberculosis patients in the emergency department. *Ann Emerg Med* 26:290, 1995.

117. Sokolove PE, et al: Implementation of an emergency department triage procedure for the detection and isolation of patients with active pulmonary tuberculosis. *Ann Emerg Med* 35:327, 2000.

118. Jarvis WR, et al: Respirators, recommendations, and regulations: The controversy surrounding protection of health care workers from tuberculosis. *Ann Intern Med* 122:142, 1995.

119. Rosenstock L: 42 CFR Part 84: Respiratory protective devices implications for tuberculosis protection. *Infect Control Hosp Epidemiol* 16:529, 1995.

120. Stead WW: Management of health care workers after inadvertent exposure to tuberculosis: A guide for the use of preventive therapy. *Ann Intern Med* 122:906, 1995.

121. Colditz GA, et al: Efficacy of BCG vaccine in the prevention of tuberculosis. Meta-analysis of the published literature. *JAMA* 271:698, 1994.

122. Marcus AM, et al: BCG vaccination to prevent tuberculosis in health care workers: A decision analysis. *Prev Med* 26:201, 1997.

123. Nor NM, Musa M: Approaches towards the development of a vaccine against tuberculosis: recombinant BCG and DNA vaccine. *Tuberculosis (Edinb)* 84:102, 2004.

134 Bone and Joint Infections

Brian J. Zink

PERSPECTIVE

Historically, bone and joint infections have been described in grim terms. *Aids to Surgery*, written in 1919, noted that "acute infective osteomyelitis . . . is a very fatal disease." With septic arthritis "the patient becomes exhausted from toxaemia or pyemia," and "ankylosis is the usual most favourable termination."[1] Advances in diagnostic methods, antibiotic therapy, and surgical techniques have resulted in much better outcomes. In the case of bone infections, the mortality rate has decreased from 15% to 25% in the preantibiotic era to less than 5% today.[2] However, with such advances come new challenges. The types of infections that are encountered today are changing, and management of bone and joint infections is becoming more complex. Emergency physicians must consider many subsets of patients who are at increased risk for infection, including intravenous (IV) drug abusers, patients with acquired immunodeficiency syndrome (AIDS), postsurgical patients, and patients with iatrogenic immune suppression.[3-6] The emphasis of modern management of bone and joint infections has shifted from preventing sepsis and death to making a prompt diagnosis, initiating treatment, and avoiding the complications and morbidity associated with chronic bone or joint infections.[7,8]

The overall occurrence of bone and joint infections appears to have remained constant over the last three decades.[4,9] The incidence of bone infections in hospitalized patients is approximately 1%. In the United States, the incidence of osteomyelitis in children younger than 13 is 1 in 5000, and that of septic arthritis ranges from 5.5 to 12 per 100,000 individuals.[10] Global epidemiologic data regarding community-acquired bone and joint infections in adults vary significantly, with an overall higher incidence in developing countries. Bone infections show a bimodal age distribution, occurring most commonly in people younger than 20 or older than 50 years. Joint infections have a similar distribution.[8,9] No known correlation exists between socioeconomic factors or race and the incidence of bone and joint infections. In children, boys have an increased susceptibility to bone infections, with most series reporting a male/female ratio of 2 to 3:1.[9] Joint infections in the pediatric age group may be slightly more common in boys. In children, bone and joint infections usually occur in previously healthy individuals. The opposite is true in adults, in whom risk factors can usually be identified that predispose to both bone and joint infection.

Infectious processes are generally designated as acute, subacute, or chronic. Orthopedic infections are also classified according to the site of involvement and include osseous (osteomyelitis), articular (septic or suppurative arthritis), bursal (septic bursitis), subcutaneous (cellulitis or abscess), muscular (infectious myositis or abscess), and tendinous (infectious tendinitis or tenosynovitis) varieties. The word *osteomyelitis* literally means inflammation of the marrow of the bone, but the term is used to refer to infection in any part of the bone. *Chronic osteomyelitis* may be defined as a bone infection lasting for more than 6 weeks. *Septic arthritis* is infection of a joint by bacterial or fungal organisms. Bacterial arthritis is sometimes called pyogenic or suppurative arthritis. Several common infectious processes can result in a sterile, secondary inflammation of joints, which is called *reactive arthritis*. Reactive arthritis is not classified as septic arthritis but is far more common than septic arthritis. It may occur after infection with human parvovirus, rubella, chickenpox, and other viruses.[11,12] Occasionally, postinfectious arthritis develops after group A streptococcal infection.

The most practical way to classify osteomyelitis for emergency medicine purposes is with the Waldvogel system. Waldvogel divides osteomyelitis into two broad categories on the basis of etiology: hematogenous osteomyelitis and osteomyelitis secondary to a contiguous focus of infection.[7,13] Osteomyelitis from a contiguous focus is further subdivided on the basis of the presence or absence of vascular insufficiency. Recognition of the etiologic mechanism of osteomyelitis may help to guide management and assist in the interpretation of diagnostic imaging examinations.

Septic arthritis usually results from hematogenous migration of bacteria into the joint. In some cases, septic arthritis may result from spread from a contiguous source of infection, direct inoculation of bacteria, or infected foreign material such as a prosthesis. Direct inoculation can result from penetrating trauma or joint aspiration. It is important to consider that septic arthritis may occur concomitantly with osteomyelitis, with infection spreading from bone to joint, and vice versa.

PRINCIPLES OF DISEASE

Bones are composed of an outer shell, or cortex, of compact bone and an inner framework of trabeculae, called cancellous, spongy, or medullary bone. On a microscopic level, compact bone comprises structural

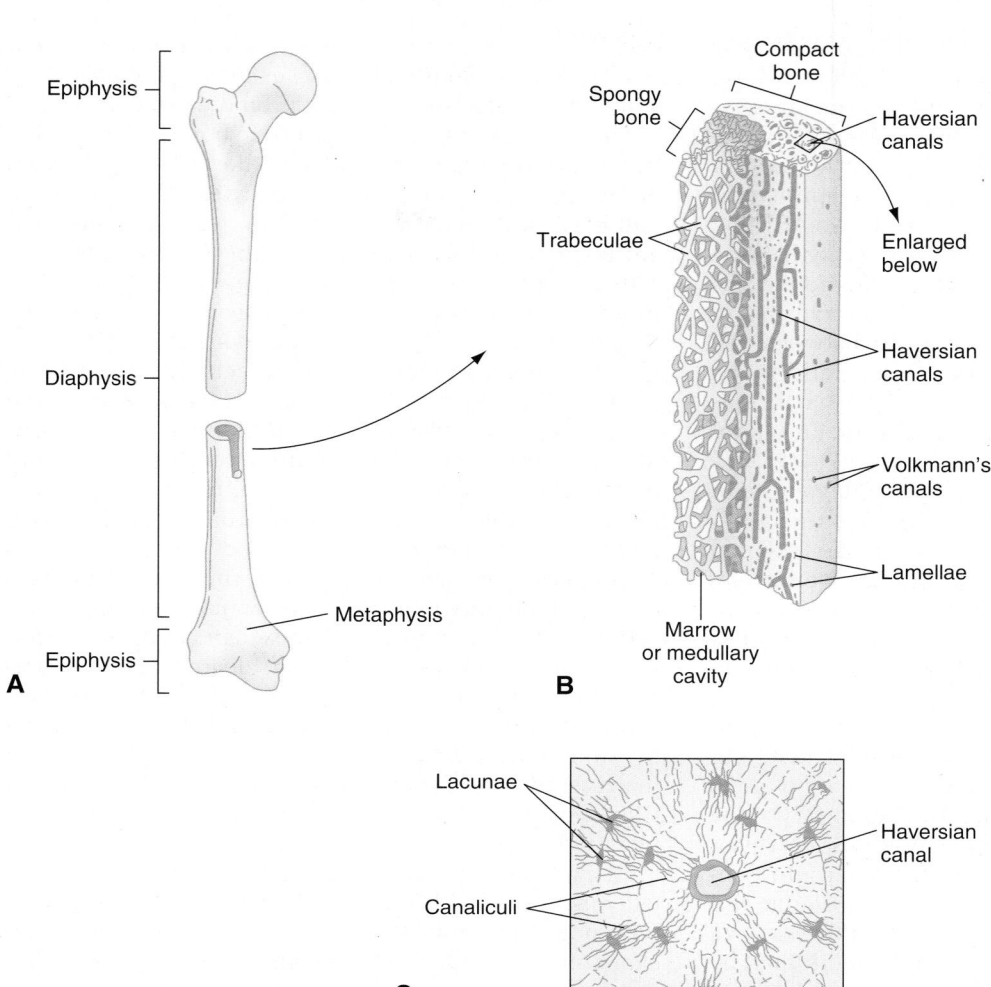

Figure 134-1. Schematic drawing of long bone. **A,** Regions of long bone. **B,** Cross-structure of long bone. **C,** Microscopic structure.

A, Regions of long bone labels:

Epiphysis

Diaphysis

Metaphysis

Epiphysis

A

B labels: Compact bone, Spongy bone, Haversian canals, Trabeculae, Enlarged below, Haversian canals, Volkmann's canals, Lamellae, Marrow or medullary cavity

C labels: Lacunae, Canaliculi, Haversian canal

units called haversian systems that are made up of concentric rings of osteocytes. Osteocytes synthesize and maintain the bone matrix. The central haversian canals run parallel to the long axis of the bone and contain the blood supply and reticular connective tissue for the haversian system. Cancellous bone consists of irregular branching trabeculae that enclose marrow cavities. Long bones consist of a diaphysis, or shaft, and two ends, called epiphyses, which communicate with other bones. The metaphysis is the region between the diaphysis and epiphysis (Figure 134-1).

Joints are enclosed within a two-layered capsule. The outer layer is dense fibrous tissue, interwoven with ligaments and the periosteum of articulating bones. The inner layer is the synovial membrane, consisting of secretory cells sitting on a loose fibrous stroma. In some joints such as the shoulder, hip, and knee, the synovial membrane extends beyond the epiphysis and attaches to the metaphysis. Because of this anatomic relationship, infection in the metaphysis of the femur or humerus may spread more easily into the joint.[13-16]

In osteomyelitis, the suppurative process extends linearly in haversian canals, and local necrosis of bone trabeculae occurs. Infection may proceed laterally through Volkmann's canals, which are small channels that run perpendicularly to the haversian canal, and reach the subperiosteal space. As edema and the infectious infiltrate occlude blood supply, larger segments of bone begin to die. In children the lateral spread of infection in the long bone results in a subperiosteal abscess. The periosteum is stimulated, and vigorous formation of new periosteum occurs. This new growth is called an *involucrum.* In adults the periosteum more firmly adheres to the underlying cortex and has less osteoblastic activity. The formation of subperiosteal abscesses and involucrum is much less common in adult osteomyelitis.[7,13] If osteomyelitis proceeds unchecked, ischemic segments of bone may disengage from surrounding bone. These separated sections are called *sequestra* and occur only in advanced or chronic osteomyelitis. Pathologic fractures may occur through these areas of devascularized bone. Unchecked chronic osteomyelitis can lead to the development of fistulae that track out to the skin.[13]

Hematogenous osteomyelitis develops when bloodborne bacteria are deposited in bone. This is most common in children and in adults with vertebral osteomyelitis. The pathologic features of hematogenous osteomyelitis differ in the infant, child, and adult. This difference is partly due to the differences in vascular anatomy as the skeleton ages. In the first year of life, arterial vessels from the metaphysis perforate the epiphyseal growth plate and terminate in the epiphysis in venous sinusoids. This communication allows osteomyelitis to advance readily from the metaphysis to the epiphysis and adjacent joint space in infants. After the first year of life there is no longer a vascular connection between the metaphyseal and epiphyseal areas. The metaphyseal arteries end in loops that abut the growth plate. The epiphyseal growth plate is avascular and inhibits the spread of infection to the epiphysis and joint. In the adult, after the closure of the epiphyseal plate, anastomoses form between the metaphyseal and epiphyseal blood vessels, and infection can once again spread from metaphysis to epiphysis and eventually into the synovium and joint space.[14,17]

A number of local and humoral factors play a role in determining whether bacteremia progresses to significant skeletal infection. Some sites in the skeletal system are more likely to become colonized by bacteria. Bones containing slow-moving venous systems or venous sinusoids, such as the metaphyses of long bones and the vertebral bodies, have increased susceptibility to hematogenous osteomyelitis. In the metaphysis, a relative lack of phagocytic cells in the venous capillaries and sinusoids may further predispose to infection. In the synovial membrane the existence of a deep venous plexus that also has sluggish blood flow may invite deposition of bacteria. The synovium, however, lacks a basement membrane, allowing bacteria to penetrate and bind to the exposed surfaces of articular cartilage, bone, and prosthetic devices. The adherence of bacteria such as *Staphylococcus aureus* is facilitated by expression of adhesins, which link to a glycoprotein called fibronectin. Fibronectin is found in bone and synovium and can coat artificial surfaces such as prostheses. *S. aureus* has been shown to produce fibronectin-binding adhesins that encourage the attachment of the bacterium. A biofilm is rapidly formed, and this promotes adherence of other bacteria and colony formation.[7,13,18]

When bacteria begin to destroy bone or the synovium, a dramatic response from local tissues occurs. The surrounding capillaries dilate and become more permeable in response to chemical signals from bacterial toxins or to the release of histamine, bradykinins, and serotonin from damaged cells. Plasma fluids, proteins, cytokines, and leukocytes pour into the area.[19,20] Complement proteins play an important role in the response to infection. The activation of complement proteins can occur directly from bacterial accumulation or through antigen-antibody complexes. Complement proteins enhance the leukocytic response through chemotaxis and opsonization of bacteria. The neutrophil and monocyte (macrophage) are the active cells in phagocytosis of bacteria. Unfortunately, leukocyte migration results in the release of neutrophil elastases, which augment the destruction of the cartilage matrix within the joint. Pressure necrosis from accumulation of purulent synovial fluid may also compromise the synovium and cartilage. Monocytes and T lymphocytes may be less numerous in the cellular response but have an important role in the production of cytokines,

such as tumor necrosis factor and interleukins 1 and 2. Cytokines modulate the sustained inflammatory response to infection and may promote osteolysis.[13,18,19]

The humoral immune response to bone or joint infection is usually well developed by the time the infection is clinically apparent. B lymphocytes sense bacterial antigens and release antibodies, and an antigen-antibody complex is formed at the site of infection. Through the complement cascade, bacteria are destroyed by neutrophils or macrophages. Bacterial toxins may be destroyed directly by bound antibody.[8,13,18,19]

Tissue injury in bone or joint infections can occur by several different mechanisms. Direct tissue destruction by invasive bacteria is the initial insult. After this, microabscesses and edema in infected tissues may lead to vascular occlusion and ischemic necrosis, which is most damaging in the venous capillaries of the metaphysis, where no collateral blood vessels exist to compensate for ischemic injury. If immune complexes become embedded in the bone or cartilage matrix, a prolonged inflammatory response can occur even after the primary infection has been cleared. This is particularly a problem in joints, where articular cartilage can be destroyed. A final type of tissue injury caused by infection is abnormal synthesis of bone or joint matrix and cells. Abnormally synthesized bone or cartilage may be structurally unsound and function poorly.[13,19]

Hematogenous spread causes almost all cases of osteomyelitis in children and in the subset of adults who have vertebral osteomyelitis. In the appendicular skeleton of adults, osteomyelitis occurs more commonly by either spread of the pathogens from a contiguous source of infection or direct implantation. The direction of contamination for contiguous focus osteomyelitis is from the soft tissues inward into the bone, and the pathogen is disseminated through haversian and Volkmann's canals to the bone marrow. This is the opposite of hematogenous osteomyelitis, in which infection starts in the medullary bone and progresses outward to involve the surrounding structures. The most common sites of contiguous focus osteomyelitis are in the foot and hand. Other common sites affected by this mechanism include the skull, maxilla, and mandible. Head and neck osteomyelitis is usually caused by sinus disease and odontogenic infections.

Most infections caused by direct implantation of bacteria into bones are caused by deep puncture wounds and tend to occur in the hands and feet. Animal bites are another cause of infections that can result in osteomyelitis. Although cats account for only 10% of animal bites, significant infection results from 20% to 50% of cat bites versus only 5% of dog bites. Most human bite injuries are related to fist fights, with contamination of the metacarpophalangeal joints and metacarpals with secondary infection. Osteomyelitis from direct implantation of pathogens is seen commonly with open fractures and can occur during surgical instrumentation. Artificial joints and other implanted surgical materials can serve as sites for colonization of bacteria.[21,22]

In septic arthritis, unless there is direct injection of bacteria into the joint, infection occurs first in the synovium and then extends into joint fluid and finally to articular cartilage. The synovial membrane responds to infection by increasing synovial fluid production, resulting in a large joint effusion. Septic arthritis is a closed-space infection, and increasing pressure in the joint contributes to a decreased rate of exchange of solutes across the synovial lining. The resultant slow diffusion of nutrients across the synovial membrane may limit the growth of bacteria and may cause bacteria to enter a dormant state. Dormant bacteria may have increased resistance to levels of antibiotics that would normally be bactericidal.[8,14,23] Even small numbers of bacteria in the joint space can elicit a profound and persistent inflammatory and immune response. Bacteria can be cleared from the joint, resulting in a sterile-appearing inflammatory response. It has been demonstrated in animal models that the injection of isolated bacterial DNA into joints can produce a marked inflammatory arthritis.[24] These types of observations have led to the hypothesis that some forms of arthritis, previously believed to be sterile or reactive, may in fact be due to an initial infection of the joint with small numbers of microorganisms followed by clearance of these microorganisms with a prolonged inflammatory response.[25]

The most important factor that determines morbidity from septic arthritis is the degree of articular cartilage destruction. Once destroyed, hyaline (articular) cartilage cannot be replaced. As part of the response to infection, synovial cells and polymorphonuclear leukocytes (PMNs) release lysosomal enzymes into joint fluid. These enzymes contain collagenase and elastase, both of which may degrade cartilage. Cytokines also seem to play a key role in the release of metalloproteinases and other harmful enzymes. Other structures that are enclosed within or adjacent to synovium, such as bursae, tendons, and bone, may become damaged in septic arthritis.[8,14,23]

ETIOLOGY AND MICROBIOLOGY OF BONE AND JOINT INFECTIONS

Certain underlying disease states predispose a patient to acquiring bone and joint infections. These conditions include diabetes mellitus, sickle cell disease, AIDS, alcoholism and IV drug abuse (IVDA), chronic corticosteroid use, preexisting joint disease, and other immunosuppressed states. Common to most of the diseases that predispose to bone and joint infections are a decreased ability to mount an inflammatory and immune response, impaired bacterial killing, and poor vasculature. Another subset of patients who are susceptible to bone and joint infections are postsurgical patients, especially those who have had prosthetic devices implanted. In children, an association may exist between prior respiratory illness or minor extremity trauma and the development of bone and joint infections.[4,15,19]

Although most serious bone and joint infections are bacterial, on rare occasions viruses, fungi, and parasites may be the responsible pathogens. The microbiology of osteomyelitis and septic arthritis is a function of several host and environmental factors. Age is an important variable in determining the type of bacteria that cause bone and joint infections. A patient's bacterial milieu has some role in determining the incidence of bone and joint infections. For example, people living in crowded conditions where tuberculosis is prevalent are at increased risk for tubercular bone and joint infections. Elderly patients in hospitals and institutions may be more susceptible to infections with gram-negative bacteria.[2,26-28]

A summary of the organisms that cause osteomyelitis and septic arthritis is given in Table 134-1. The following points deserve special mention:

1. In all age groups except neonates, *S. aureus* is the leading cause of osteomyelitis. It also accounts for more cases of septic arthritis than any other bacterium. In neonates, group B streptococci are common infecting bacteria in bone and joint infections.[20]

2. Before the introduction of the vaccine, *Haemophilus influenzae* type B caused up to 34% of septic arthritis and 13% of osteomyelitis in children younger than 2 years. However, since the introduction of the vaccine, *H. influenzae* B has essentially disappeared as a pathogen in hematogenous osteomyelitis and septic arthritis among vaccinated children.[29] Another gram-negative coccobacillus within the Neisseriaceae family, *Kingella kingae*, has become more common than *Haemophilus* in causing bone and joint infections in children.[30] *K. kingae* can be part of the normal flora of the nasopharynx and, like *H. influenzae*, can be spread hematogenously to bones and joints. It is a fastidious organism and may be mistaken for *Haemophilus* or *Neisseria* species.[2,30]

3. Gonococcal arthritis is the most common type of septic arthritis in individuals younger than 30 years.

4. In elders, gram-negative bacteria account for a higher percentage of cases of bone and joint infections than in younger people.[2]

5. Methicillin-resistant *S. aureus*, methicillin-resistant *Staphylococcus epidermidis*, and vancomycin-resistant enterococci have emerged as a significant microbiologic problem in the past decade. Multiresistant enterococci pose the greatest potential danger in that no currently available regimen is reliably bactericidal against such organisms.[26]

A typical case of hematogenous osteomyelitis or septic arthritis is caused by a single type of bacterium. In some situations polymicrobial infection is more likely to occur. These include diabetic foot osteomyelitis, posttraumatic osteomyelitis, chronic osteomyelitis, and chronic septic arthritis. Overall, polymicrobial osteomyelitis occurs in 36% to 50% of reported cases. Anaerobic bacteria can complicate polymicrobial infection and may be present in bone and joint infections more often than is commonly recognized. In chronic osteomyelitis, anaerobic bacteria may be present in up

Table 134-1. Microbiology and Initial (Empirical) Antibiotic Treatment of Bone and Joint Infection

	Septic Arthritis		Osteomyelitis	
Age Group	*Common Organisms*	*Antibiotic Regimen*	*Common Organisms*	*Antibiotic Regimen*
Neonate to <3 mo	*Staphylococcus aureus* Group B *Streptococcus* Enterobacteriaceae	PRP + Ceph 3 Alt: PRP + APAG If MRSA is prevalent, use vancomycin in place of PRP	*S. aureus* Group B *Streptococcus* Enterobacteriaceae	PRP + Ceph 3 Alt: PRP + APAG If MRSA is prevalent, use vancomycin in place of PRP
3 mo to 14 yr	*S. aureus* Group A *streptococcus* *Streptococcus pneumoniae* *Haemophilus influenzae*	PRP + Ceph 3 Alt: Vancomycin + Ceph 3	*S. aureus* Group A *Streptococcus* *H. influenzae*	PRP + Ceph 3 Alt: Vancomycin + Ceph 3, chloramphenicol
14 yr to adult	*S. aureus* Streptococcal sp Enterobacteriaceae	PRP or Ceph 3 Alt: Vancomycin + Ceph 3 or PCN + aminoglycoside or Ceph 3	*S. aureus*	PRP Alt: Vancomycin
Infection subsets				
Sexually active adolescents or adults with acute arthritis	*Neisseria gonorrhoeae*	Ceph 3 Alt: Spectinomycin or penicillin if sensitive		
Chronic osteomyelitis and diabetic foot infections			*S. aureus* Enterobacteriaceae Anaerobic bacteria	PRP + FLQ + metronidazole Alt: PRP + Ceph 3 + Clind
Infected orthopedic joint prosthesis	*S. aureus* *Staphylococcus epidermidis* *Pseudomonas aeruginosa*	Vancomycin + FLQ Alt: PRP + APAG	*S. aureus* *S. epidermidis* *P. aeruginosa*	Vancomycin + FLQ Alt: PRP + APAG
Sickle cell disease	*S. aureus* *Salmonella* sp	PRP + Ceph 3 Alt: FLQ	*S. aureus* *Salmonella* sp	PRP + Ceph 3 Alt: FLQ
Intravenous drug abuse	*P. aeruginosa, S. aureus,* Enterobacteriaceae	PRP + APAG or FLQ Alt: Vancomycin + FLQ	*S. aureus, P. aeruginosa* Enterobacteriaceae	PRP + APAG or FLQ Alt: Vancomycin + FLQ
Plantar puncture wound	*P. aeruginosa*	AP Ceph Alt: FLQ	*P. aeruginosa*	AP Ceph Alt: FLQ
Human or animal bites	*Eikenella corrodens,* *Pasteurella multocida*	Penicillin ± AC Alt: Ceph 3, TS	*E. corrodens,* *P. multocida*	Penicillin ± AC Alt: Ceph 3, TS

*Concurrent treatment for *Chlamydia trachomatis* should be given in patients with suspected *N. gonorrhoeae* septic arthritis. Bone and joint infection with *H. influenzae* is now rare in vaccinated children; however, if the Gram stain is suggestive of *H. influenzae*, empirical treatment should be started. Fluoroquinolones are not recommended for use in children.
Alt, alternative; APAG, antipseudomonal aminoglycoside; AP Ceph, antipseudomonal cephalosporin (ceftazidime or cefepime); Ceph 3, third-generation cephalosporin (e.g., ceftriaxone, cefotaxime, cefamandole, ceftizoxime, ceftazidime, moxalactam); Clind, clindamycin; FLQ, fluoroquinolone; MRSA, methicillin-resistant *S. aureus*; PRP, penicillinase-resistant penicillin (oxacillin, nafcillin, methicillin, amoxicillin-clavulanate [AC]); TS, trimethoprim-sulfamethoxazole.

to 40% of cases. Culture techniques that are inadequate for isolating anaerobic bacteria may lead to underreporting of infections caused by these agents.[2,15,16,26,31]

Pseudomonas is responsible for bone and joint infections in three main settings. The first is in puncture wounds to the foot. *Pseudomonas* does not appear to grow on puncture objects but colonizes in footwear, particularly the foam inserts in shoes. Bacteria may be inoculated into the wound and produce soft tissue infection and osteomyelitis. Patients in whom prosthetic devices are implanted during orthopedic surgery are also at risk for *Pseudomonas* bone and joint infection. IV drug users may develop hematogenous osteomyelitis, often in the spine, from *Pseudomonas* bacteria.[2,6,15,26,32]

Certain types of trauma may predispose patients to osteomyelitis by particular bacteria. Patients who are wounded or receive open fractures in fresh water are susceptible to infection with the gram-negative bacillus *Aeromonas hydrophila*.[33,34] People who are bitten by animals, particularly dogs and cats, are at risk for developing osteomyelitis from *Pasteurella multocida*.[21,35]

Tuberculosis (TB) may occur in bones and joints. The two most common forms of skeletal infection are vertebral osteomyelitis (Pott's disease) and tubercular arthritis. The spine is affected in half of cases of tubercular skeletal infection. The arthritis of TB is a chronic, low-grade inflammatory process that resembles rheumatoid arthritis more than acute septic arthritis.[27,28,36,37]

Fungal infections have become more common in hospitalized patients because of the use of broad-spectrum antibiotics, immunosuppressive medications, invasive monitoring devices, and total parenteral alimentation. Fungal organisms are responsible for less than 1% of cases of osteomyelitis, but the number of cases reported is increasing. *Candida* osteomyelitis occurs through hematogenous spread or as a postoperative wound infection. Fungal bone infection is indolent and may go through periods of activity and remission.[37-39] *Aspergillus* has been reported to cause osteomyelitis in vertebrae, hip prostheses, and ribs. In adults the infection is hematogenous. In children *Aspergillus* osteomyelitis is most common in those with prior granulomatous disease and spreads from a primary pulmonary infection. *Blastomyces* and *Cryptococcus* are two other fungi that may become disseminated and infect the skeleton.[26,39]

Patients with human immunodeficiency virus (HIV) are predisposed to a variety of common and opportunistic pathogens. Although *S. aureus* is still the most likely cause of bone and joint infections in patients with AIDS, fungal and other atypical organisms should be considered. One unusual, but particularly characteristic, form of osteomyelitis in HIV-positive patients is bacillary angiomatosis. Bacillary angiomatosis is caused by a gram-negative rickettsia-like organism that frequently leads to osteolytic bone lesions.[3,5]

CLINICAL FEATURES OF OSTEOMYELITIS

Diagnosis

History and Physical Examination

The symptoms and signs of osteomyelitis in adults are predictable, although not always present. The predominant symptom is pain over the affected bone. If the leg is involved, the patient commonly limps; children may refuse to use the limb at all. Localized warmth, swelling, and erythema may be noted by the patient. Fever is inconsistently present, although it is more common in children with osteomyelitis than in adults. Systemic complaints of headache, fatigue, malaise, and anorexia are often reported.[13,40] A careful review of the patient's past medical history is warranted in order to identify risk factors that may predispose to bone infection.

On examination, the patient usually does not appear ill. Palpation of the involved bone elicits point tenderness over the infected segment. Palpable warmth and soft tissue swelling with erythema may be present, but these findings are variable. Because osteomyelitis has a propensity to occur in the metaphyses of long bones, it is often difficult to distinguish infection in bone from infection in the neighboring joint. Adding to the confusion, a sympathetic effusion in the adjacent joint may develop in some patients with osteomyelitis who have no joint involvement. In chronic advanced osteomyelitis, the involucrum or sequestrum may be palpated, and sinus tracts that drain through the skin may be noted.

Diagnostic Strategies

Laboratory Data and Diagnostic Imaging

Laboratory data in patients with osteomyelitis are generally not helpful in establishing a diagnosis. The white blood cell (WBC) count is often, although not always, elevated. Typical values in osteomyelitis range from normal to 15,000/mm³. The erythrocyte sedimentation rate (ESR) is more helpful than the WBC count. It is a sensitive marker for bone infection; many series report elevated ESRs in more than 90% of patients who have confirmed osteomyelitis.[41] The mean ESR in one large

pediatric review was 70 mm/hr. Fewer than 8% of patients with osteomyelitis have an ESR less than 15 mm/hr. An elevated ESR in the presence of appropriate physical findings should alert the emergency physician to pursue aggressively the diagnosis of osteomyelitis, but a normal or slightly elevated ESR does not eliminate the diagnosis. Other inflammatory conditions such as cellulitis can cause an elevated ESR, although the degree of elevation of ESR is often higher with osteomyelitis. The ESR is most valuable in following response to treatment. Typically, the ESR falls steadily as osteomyelitis resolves and increases should it recur.[42,43] C-reactive protein (CRP), another nonspecific marker of inflammation, may have some use in evaluating patients with bone infections. CRP increases within the first 24 hours of infection, peaks within approximately 48 hours, and is usually normal within 1 week of therapy.[42-44]

The diagnosis of osteomyelitis in the emergency department is almost always made by skeletal imaging. Conventional radiography remains the initial imaging test of choice for suspected osteomyelitis. Radiography is readily available, relatively inexpensive, and useful in ruling out other disease entities. In addition, plain radiography is often a helpful adjunct in correctly interpreting secondary imaging studies. Unfortunately, radiography is insensitive to the detection of early osteomyelitis, limiting its utility in patients who have an acute presentation. Soft tissue edema may be present within 3 to 5 days from the onset of infection. However, fewer than one third of patients have abnormalities on plain radiographs in the first 7 to 10 days after the onset of symptoms. Before lucent areas can be detected radiographically, 30% to 50% of bone mineral must be lost. In more advanced cases, radiographs are helpful. By 28 days from the onset of disease, 90% of the plain radiographs are positive.[45-47] The characteristic early findings on the plain radiograph in osteomyelitis are lucent lytic areas of cortical bone destruction (Figure 134-2). Periosteal reaction is another early sign. It may appear as hypertrophy or elevation of the periosteum (involucrum) (Figure 134-3). These early periosteal changes are more commonly seen in children than in adults. In advanced disease the lytic lesions are surrounded by dense, sclerotic bone, and sequestra may be noted. Special attention to the radiographic appearance of the

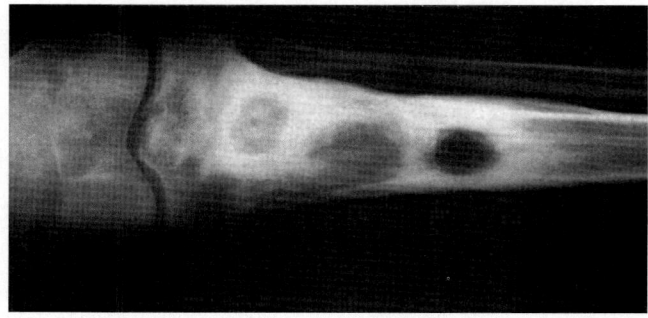

Figure 134-2. Plain radiograph of tibia. Lucent areas in metaphysis are sites of advanced osteomyelitis. (Courtesy of Department of Radiology, University of Cincinnati Medical Center.)

soft tissues is important in diagnosing osteomyelitis in its early stages. Deep soft tissue swelling, distorted fascial planes, and altered fat interfaces can be a clue to osteomyelitis in the underlying bone. Because radiographic resolution may lag behind clinical resolution, radiographs are also not helpful in tracking the course of osteomyelitis.[48]

Radionuclide skeletal scintigraphy (bone scanning) is more useful than plain radiographs in the early diag-

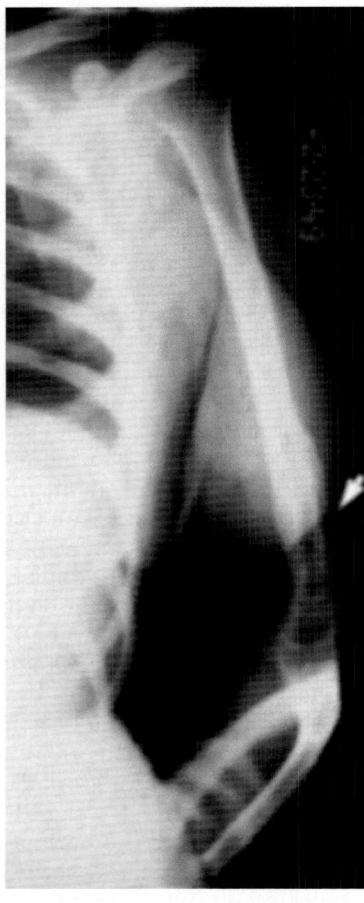

Figure 134-3. Plain radiograph of humerus. Distal portion of humerus has involucrum formation, representing advanced case of osteomyelitis. (Courtesy of Department of Radiology, University of Cincinnati Medical Center.)

nosis of osteomyelitis. Radionuclide scans can detect osteomyelitis within 48 to 72 hours after the onset of infection. A radioactive tracer is injected into the bloodstream and given time to bind or accumulate in body tissues. A γ-camera or collimator is used to sense released radioactivity, and an image is created that is evaluated for an increase or decrease in expected uptake of the radionuclide.

In the emergency department setting, the most commonly used radionuclide for skeletal scintigraphy is technetium methylene diphosphonate (^{99m}Tc MDP). Technetium-labeled diphosphonates bind to the hydroxyapatite crystals in the bone matrix. The greatest uptake is in immature bone that has increased osteoblastic activity. The standard ^{99m}Tc MDP scan is a three-phase process. After injection of the ^{99m}Tc MDP, images are obtained within 60 seconds. This "radionuclide angiogram" represents the relative blood flow to the area of concern. The second phase involves imaging of the "blood pool" of ^{99m}Tc MDP at 5 to 15 minutes after injection. The third phase is the delayed or static image that is obtained 2 to 4 hours after injection. Areas of osteomyelitis show increased uptake on all three phases of ^{99m}Tc MDP scintigraphy.[7,46,49,50] Figure 134-4 shows diagnostic categories based on ^{99m}Tc MDP three-phase scan. Figure 134-5 shows a positive ^{99m}Tc MDP scan.

The ^{99m}Tc MDP scan is a sensitive test for osteomyelitis in patients who have no existing bone abnormalities. Most series report a sensitivity of greater than 90% with the three-phase scan.. Lower sensitivities are found in cases of neonatal osteomyelitis. False-negative scans are possible if pressure and edema in an area of active osteomyelitis prevent vascular delivery of the radionuclide. The resulting "cold spot" may actually signify an area of aggressive active osteomyelitis but might be interpreted as negative. False-negative scans may also occur if the patient has been receiving antibiotic treatment before presentation. The specificity of a ^{99m}Tc MDP bone scan is not as high as its sensitivity. False-positive scans may result from trauma, surgery, tumors, or chronic soft tissue infections. Simple cellulitis does not usually produce a false-positive bone scan because the radionuclide is cleared from soft tissues before acquisition of the delayed (third phase) images. Any process that encourages inflammation and

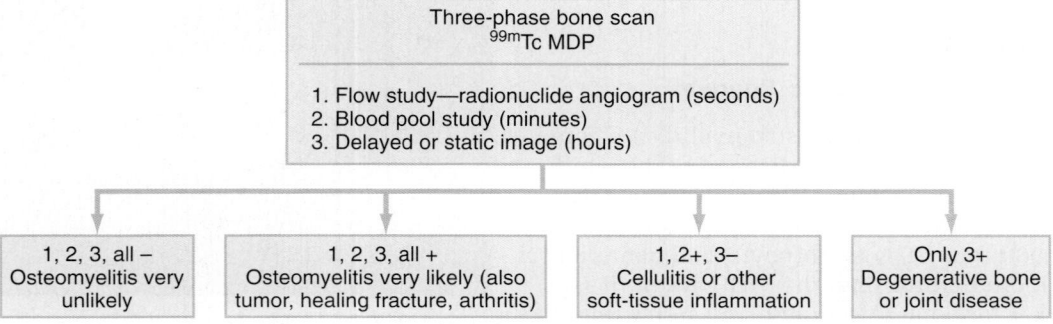

Figure 134-4. Diagnostic use of the three-phase ^{99m}Tc methylene diphosphonate (MDP) bone scan. (Modified from Demopulos GA, Bleck EE, McDougall IR: Role of radionuclide imaging in the diagnosis of acute osteomyelitis. *J Pediatr Orthop* 8:558, 1988.)

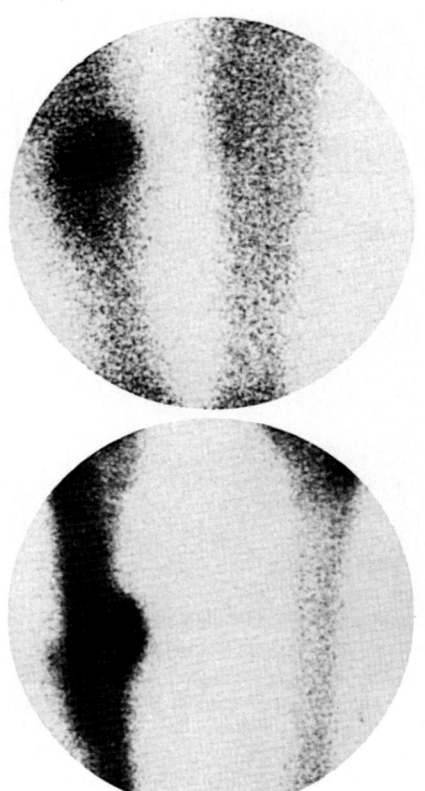

Figure 134-5. Example of gallium (top) and technetium (bottom) bone scans in advanced osteomyelitis of tibial metaphysis. Both scans show increased radionuclide uptake. (Courtesy of EB Silberstein, Department of Nuclear Medicine, University of Cincinnati.)

new bone formation can be a site of increased uptake of radionuclide. The false-positive rate has been as high as 64% in various case series.[45,47,49-51] A four-phase ^{99m}Tc MDP study with an additional image at 24 hours may further improve specificity because the amount of activity within the lesion theoretically continues to increase with time.[51]

Additional testing with other radionuclides, including gallium (^{67}Ga) citrate, indium (^{111}In) oxine, and technetium-99 hexamethylpropyleneamine oxime (HMPAO), is sometimes used to compensate for the limited specificity of the technetium-99m scans. After IV injection, ^{67}Ga accumulates in areas of acute inflammation where WBC concentrations are high. When the test is combined with technetium-99, diagnosis of osteomyelitis is considered positive if the gallium-67 uptake is greater than the technetium-99 uptake in the suspected region. Overall, the combination of gallium-67 and technetium-99 MDP for establishing a diagnosis of osteomyelitis has a sensitivity of approximately 70% and a specificity of 83% to 93%. The disadvantages of ^{67}Ga for emergency use are the 24- to 48-hour delay in obtaining a final image and the low specificity of the test (see Figure 134-5).[46,47,52]

[111]In-labeled or HMPAO WBC scans may provide added specificity to identify specific sites of infection. These studies are usually reserved for situations in which bone scan findings are equivocal or normal and

osteomyelitis is still a likely consideration. The procedure involves incubating 50 mL of whole blood with the radionuclide for 2 hours and reinjecting the labeled WBCs. Radiolabeled neutrophils then migrate to areas of infection. Images are obtained at 4 hours for the HMPAO scan and 24 hours for the indium scan. Labeled leukocytes accumulate only where there is active infection. The disadvantage for emergency use is the delay in final imaging and interpretation. Also, the large amount of blood required for labeling as well as the high radiation burden may preclude its use in infants and children. The radiation burden and half-life are significantly shorter for HMPAO than for indium-111.[47,53] Some newer techniques for bone scanning include the use of a technetium-99m–labeled murine immunoglobulin M monoclonal antigranulocyte antibody and ciprofloxacin labeled with technetium-99m, but these are still under investigation.[47]

Computed tomography (CT) and magnetic resonance imaging (MRI) may be very useful in the diagnosis of osteomyelitis. CT is most commonly used to detect and define areas of possible infection in bones with complex anatomy that is difficult to visualize on plain radiographs and bone scans. The bone cortex is particularly well seen on CT, and involucrum and sequestrum formation is easily identified. The sternum, vertebrae, pelvic bones, and calcaneus are far better imaged with a CT scan than with plain radiographs. Osteomyelitis appears as rarefaction, or lucent areas, on the CT scan images. Gas may be seen in bone abscess cavities. The limitation of CT scans for early diagnosis of osteomyelitis is the same as that for plain radiographs. The disease must be present for more than a week for changes to be apparent. An important role of a CT scan in osteomyelitis is to help localize bone lesions that have been found on bone scan. The CT scan can guide the surgeon in debridement and resection of infected bone and in choosing a site for diagnostic bone biopsy.[47,50]

A newer modality for imaging infections is fluorine-18-deoxyglucose positron emission tomography (^{18}F-FDG PET). Inflammatory cells such as leukocytes and macrophages have increased glucose metabolism and take up ^{18}F-FDG at a high rate. The ^{18}F-FDG PET scan has excellent sensitivity for identifying loci of infection and is thought to be superior to conventional radionuclide scintigraphy in its specificity and anatomic resolution. It may be especially useful in chronic osteomyelitis.[54,55]

The use of bone scans for detection of osteomyelitis in the emergency department appears to be decreasing as the availability and image quality of MRI improve and the cost decreases. The anatomic resolution of an MRI scan is far superior to that of bone scans. Soft tissue contrast is also much greater with the MRI scan than with plain radiographs or the CT scan, and cartilaginous end plates are well visualized. Even slight changes of early infection can be detected with MRI in medullary bone and the bone marrow. Unlike CT, MRI is comparable to skeletal scintigraphy in terms of detection of osteomyelitis early in its course. Osteomyelitis produces a diminished intensity of the normal marrow

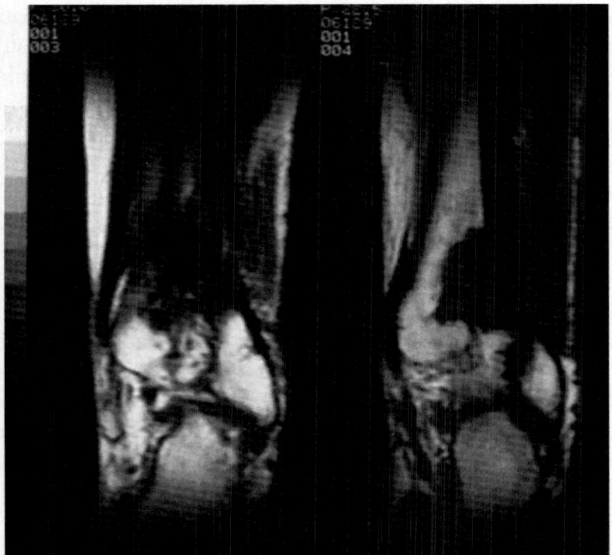

Figure 134-6. Magnetic resonance imaging scan of the lower leg in a 32-year-old man, showing altered signal in the distal tibia, consistent with osteomyelitis. (Courtesy of Department of Radiology, Albany Medical Center.)

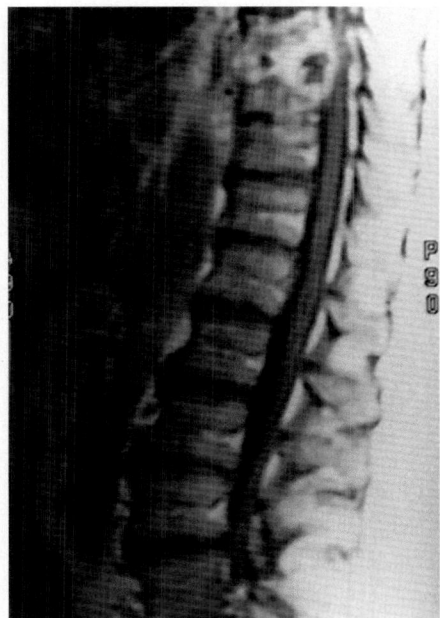

Figure 134-7. Magnetic resonance image, T$_1$-weighted with gadolinium contrast, demonstrating increased signal in the eighth and ninth thoracic vertebrae and intervertebral disk, consistent with osteomyelitis and diskitis. The patient was a 71-year-old man with back pain. Computed tomography–guided biopsy of the lesion was culture positive for *Staphylococcus aureus*. (Courtesy of Department of Radiology, University of Michigan Health System.)

signal on MRI T$_1$-weighted images and a normal or increased signal on T$_2$-weighted images. Bone cortex changes, periosteal reaction, soft tissue edema, abscesses, and sinus tracts are clearly shown on the MRI scan. Addition of the IV contrast agent gadolinium, which becomes localized in areas of increased vascularity and blood flow, helps to identify soft tissue infections such as abscesses and cellulitis and may help to differentiate bone infection from soft tissue infections. Gadolinium also helps to distinguish devitalized from normally perfused bone. Most radiologists recommend gadolinium contrast MRI when osteomyelitis is the leading suspected diagnosis. Studies suggest that for vertebral osteomyelitis, MRI with gadolinium contrast has higher sensitivity and specificity than radionuclide bone scans.[56-58] It is likely that in the next decade MRI will supplant bone scans as the preferred imaging modality for evaluating other types of osteomyelitis. In cases in which a surgical procedure will be done to obtain a microbiologic diagnosis or is needed to treat osteomyelitis, MRI has obvious advantages over a radionuclide bone scan in detailing the anatomy for the surgeon. One drawback of MRI is the presence of metal in bone, especially prosthetic joints. Metal may sometimes cause distortion of the signal in the area adjacent to a joint prosthesis, but this does not exclude MRI scanning in this group of patients (Figures 134-6 and 134-7).[7,56-59]

Microbiologic Diagnosis

The most direct and often most effective way to diagnose osteomyelitis is to obtain infected bone by needle aspiration or surgical resection. CT-guided aspiration is increasingly used for vertebral osteomyelitis. Culture results for infected bone allow specific antimicrobial therapy. Cultures of draining fistulae or sinus tracts are not an acceptable substitute because the organisms cultured from these sites are often different from those in the underlying infected bone.[7,26] Because osteomyelitis may be polymicrobial or due to unusual microorganisms, especially in immunocompromised patients, cultures for fungal and anaerobic organisms should be obtained.

Particularly in cases of hematogenous osteomyelitis, cultures of blood, urine, cerebrospinal fluid, and pus from other sites of infection can help uncover the infecting bacteria. Blood cultures in patients with acute untreated osteomyelitis are positive for the offending bacteria approximately 50% of the time.[40,59] In children with hematogenous osteomyelitis, it is not unusual to identify the infecting organism in other bodily fluid cultures in addition to blood cultures. Blood cultures are almost always negative in patients with chronic forms of osteomyelitis.[26]

The likelihood of establishing a bacteriologic diagnosis in acute osteomyelitis is 80% to 90%, but in some cases, even culturing of resected bone yields no organism. Possible reasons for this are poor culture techniques and inadequate preparation of recovered tissue for culture, previous antibiotic treatment, and culturing from necrotic ischemic regions that may be devoid of bacteria.[26,44,59]

When the emergency physician is confronted with a patient with possible osteomyelitis, the diagnostic options can seem confusing. The algorithm in Figure 134-8 provides a simplified approach to diagnostic

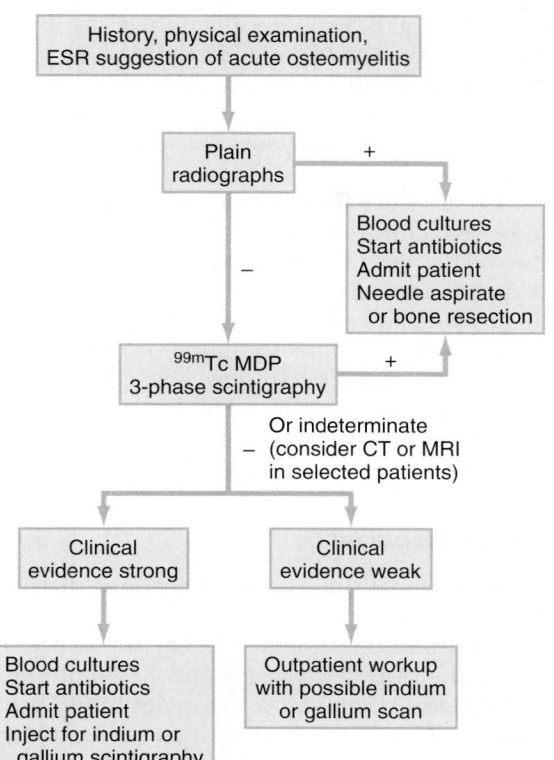

Figure 134-8. An algorithm for the use of imaging studies in emergency department diagnosis of osteomyelitis. CT, computed tomography; ESR, erythrocyte sedimentation rate; MDP, methylene diphosphonate; MRI, magnetic resonance imaging.

management of the patient with suspected osteomyelitis. A few key points should be considered when using this algorithm:

1. When there is little clinical support for a diagnosis of osteomyelitis and initial skeletal scintigraphy is negative, it is extremely unlikely that the patient has osteomyelitis.
2. In infants and children the amount of radiation exposure with imaging techniques must be considered.[60]
3. In easily accessible bones, aspiration is a low-risk procedure that often establishes a microbiologic diagnosis.
4. If the clinical presentation strongly suggests osteomyelitis, a lengthy diagnostic workup should not delay treatment. Cultures of blood, urine, and other appropriate sites should be obtained and antibiotic treatment started.[59]
5. The cost of imaging tests for osteomyelitis must be considered in deciding how to pursue the diagnosis. Expense must be weighed against the benefit of early diagnosis of osteomyelitis and the prevention of chronic osteomyelitis.

Clinical Subsets of Osteomyelitis

Acute hematogenous osteomyelitis (AHO) is the most common form of osteomyelitis, but it has different presentations, diagnosis, and treatment in adults compared with children. The other main type of osteomyelitis, arising from a contiguous focus of infection, has special diagnostic and management features. This section reviews the common clinical subsets of osteomyelitis.

Osteomyelitis in Children

Osteomyelitis in children tends to be acute and due to hematogenous spread. It can often be treated with antibiotics alone. In contrast, osteomyelitis in adults, except for vertebral osteomyelitis, is often subacute or chronic and is usually secondary to an open wound or a complication of soft tissue disease. AHO is seen in children as young as 3 months and as old as 16 years. Bacteremia is the presumed cause of bone infection. *S. aureus* is the most common infecting organism in children of all ages except neonates (see Table 134-1). As noted previously, *H. influenzae* is no longer a common cause of AHO.

AHO has a well-established male preponderance (male/female ratio of 2 to 3:1) and involves long bones approximately 80% of the time. The site of infection is usually the distal metaphysis, but up to 30% of AHO occurs in other parts of the bone. The epiphysis may be involved in a subacute type of osteomyelitis. Approximately 30% of children with AHO have antecedent minor trauma to the involved extremity or a recent upper respiratory illness (URI), although given the high incidence of minor trauma and URIs in this age range, the significance of these findings is unclear. Children with AHO may have fever, chills, vomiting, dehydration, and malaise, but they usually do not appear extremely ill. Most children have characteristic pain, limited use of, and point tenderness in the involved limb. The diagnostic evaluation for AHO is listed in Figure 134-8. Blood cultures are positive for the bacterial cause of osteomyelitis in 60% of patients with AHO. A positive blood culture and a physical examination consistent with osteomyelitis may be sufficient to make a diagnosis of AHO. Figures 134-9 and 134-10 show a typical radiograph and bone scan, respectively, of AHO.[10,40,42,46,59,60]

Neonatal osteomyelitis is increasingly reported and may be difficult to diagnose because of minimal systemic findings. Neonatal osteomyelitis is more commonly seen after abnormal pregnancies or deliveries and often accompanies other acute illnesses. Multiple sites of bone involvement are found in approximately half the reported cases. Because of the special vascular anatomy of the neonate, septic arthritis often accompanies osteomyelitis. Osteomyelitis in the neonate is more common in flat bones, such as the facial bones. Group B streptococci are becoming the leading causative bacterium in neonatal osteomyelitis, but staphylococcal species are still common. Skeletal scintigraphy is of limited value in diagnosing neonatal osteomyelitis. The reasons are an inadequate inflammatory response in the neonate, the small size of bones and joints, and active epiphyses that can concentrate the radiolabeled isotope, making it difficult to distinguish infection in the ends of bones. Plain radiographs show abnormalities within days of development of

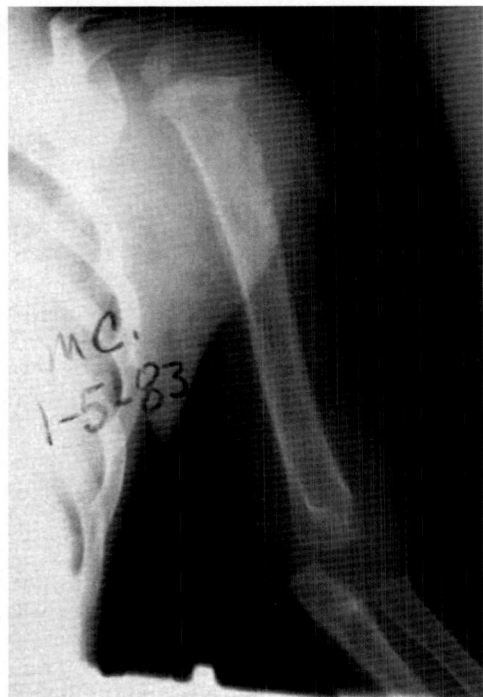

Figure 134-9. Acute hematogenous osteomyelitis in a child. Proximal humeral metaphysis is affected. (Courtesy of Department of Radiology, University of Cincinnati Medical Center.)

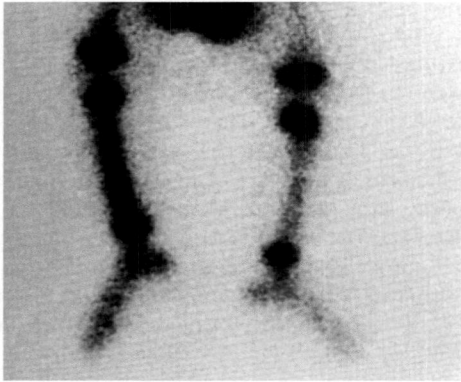

Figure 134-10. ^{99m}Tc methylene diphosphonate (MDP) bone scan in a 6-month-old girl demonstrates increased uptake in the left distal tibia, confirming the clinical diagnosis of osteomyelitis. (Courtesy of Department of Nuclear Medicine, Albany Medical Center.)

neonatal osteomyelitis and are usually positive by the time the disease is suspected.[61-63]

Two less common forms of osteomyelitis can occur in children: subacute osteomyelitis and chronic recurrent multifocal osteomyelitis (CRMO). Subacute osteomyelitis refers to a form of the disease in which clinical symptoms and signs are slow to appear, and radiographs show small areas of osteomyelitis, usually in the metaphysis of long bones. Cultures of blood and bone are negative more than 50% of the time and, when positive, usually implicate staphylococcal species. Like subacute osteomyelitis, CRMO usually affects older children (6 to 10 years) and adolescents. CRMO is char-

acterized by small foci of infection at various sites in the skeleton. The disease is defined by multiple episodes of indolent infection. Diagnosis is made by radiographs; culture of the bone sites is almost always negative. This disease may be associated with a type of psoriasis.[60,64,65]

Another subacute form of osteomyelitis that is most common in children and adolescents is *Brodie's abscess*. This is a small round cystic area of osteomyelitis that involves the femoral or tibial metaphysis around the knee. It occurs during the subacute or chronic stage of hematogenous osteomyelitis and may produce minimal symptoms. The causative organism is *S. aureus* or sometimes *Proteus* or *Pseudomonas* species. On plain radiographs the lesion is lytic, with a well-defined sclerotic margin.[48,60]

Vertebral Osteomyelitis

Vertebral osteomyelitis is a hematogenous disease that usually afflicts older adults in a manner analogous to AHO in children and appears to be increasing in frequency as the population ages and has more chronic medical diseases. The spine is susceptible to bacterial infection because the venous system surrounding vertebral bodies is valveless (permitting two-way flow of blood) and has transverse and longitudinal anastomoses. Bacteria that reach the spine and enter the venous plexus may be more likely to aggregate and cause infection in this slow-moving system. Infection can readily spread to adjacent vertebral bodies. A clear source of bacterial hematogenous seeding and positive blood cultures occurs in approximately 40% of cases of vertebral osteomyelitis. Genitourinary tract infections that seed the bloodstream are the most common precipitators of vertebral osteomyelitis. Respiratory infections, bacteremia from indwelling venous or arterial catheters, sickle cell disease, and IVDA all predispose to vertebral osteomyelitis. The causative organism is usually staphylococcal, but gram-negative bacteria are commonly isolated, often from a genitourinary tract source. Only 10% of patients appear septic or toxic; the rest have a subacute presentation. The predominant clinical findings are back pain, stiffness, and point tenderness over vertebral bodies. Neurologic deficits are reported in less than 20% of patients with vertebral osteomyelitis. On laboratory testing, the ESR is commonly elevated to greater than 50 mm/hr.[66-68]

The lumbar spine is the most common site for vertebral osteomyelitis. A progressive vertebral infection can spread through the intravertebral disk to the adjacent vertebrae. Further spread of infection from cervical spine osteomyelitis can cause a retropharyngeal abscess or with lumbar spine osteomyelitis may result in a psoas muscle abscess. When osteomyelitis affects the thoracic spine, infection can spread to the chest. Paraspinal abscesses, reactive pleural effusions, and empyema have been reported and may mislead the clinician to suspect that the primary problem is in the lungs.[66-69] The most dreaded complication of vertebral osteomyelitis is the spread of infection into the spinal canal and the development of an epidural abscess. Fortunately, this occurs in less than 15% of cases of vertebral osteomyelitis. Spinal cord compression from an epidural abscess can lead to permanent paralysis. The spinal cord may suffer ischemic injury if the vertebral infection causes septic thrombosis or compression of local blood vessels.[67,68]

The imaging strategy for diagnosis of vertebral osteomyelitis starts with plain radiographs, which may show disk space narrowing or destruction of vertebral end plates or vertebral bodies. Findings on plain radiographs are not seen until at least the second week of vertebral infection. Bone scintigraphy has been largely replaced by MRI in further imaging of suspected vertebral osteomyelitis. CT is good for defining bone destruction and is often used to assist needle aspiration of the lesion, but MRI can detect vertebral osteomyelitis at an earlier stage than CT and provides better detail and assessment of the spinal cord and adjacent structures, especially when gadolinium contrast is used (see Figure 134-7).[56,57,68] In order to avert the potentially catastrophic progression to spinal cord compression, emergency department patients who present with a clinical picture consistent with vertebral osteomyelitis should have the diagnosis rapidly confirmed either through imaging or by direct needle biopsy. Patients who are at increased risk for paralysis include elders, those with cervical spine osteomyelitis, and those with serious underlying diseases such as rheumatoid arthritis or diabetes mellitus.

A variant of vertebral osteomyelitis that must be distinguished is diskitis of childhood. This subacute disease is thought to be a low-grade infection (usually *Staphylococcus* species) within the disk, sometimes extending to the adjacent vertebral plates. The child complains of back pain and sometimes refuses to walk. Bone scintigraphy may show increased uptake in the disk space. Single-photon emission computed tomography (SPECT) imaging and pinhole collimation can accurately identify the site and extent of involvement. As in adults, MRI demonstrates the anatomy of diskitis better than bone scintigraphy. CT is used to guide aspiration. Cultures of the disk from needle aspiration are reported to be positive for bacteria 30% to 60% of the time. The disease resolves with conservative treatment.[66,67]

Posttraumatic Osteomyelitis

Posttraumatic osteomyelitis is a form of contiguous focus osteomyelitis that results from open fractures, surgery and invasive procedures, burns, bites, and puncture wounds.

At least 10% of open fractures later develop osteomyelitis, and the tibia is the most commonly affected bone. The fracture site may be directly contaminated from the environment or iatrogenically during emergency procedures or surgery. The intraoperative implantation of prosthetic devices further increases the chance of infection. Extreme damage to adjacent soft tissues may result in a necrotic nidus of infection that can spread to bone. Polymicrobial infection is more common with this type of osteomyelitis. The imaging

of posttraumatic osteomyelitis is complicated by changes induced by surgery and new bone formation in the fracture. Imaging modalities that are best in this situation are MRI, CT, and ^{18}F-FDG PET.[54,70]

Postsurgical osteomyelitis is difficult to diagnose. The sole complaint of the patient may be pain in the region of the previous surgery. The most common bacteria found in postsurgical and prosthesis-related osteomyelitis are *S. aureus* and *S. epidermidis*. Radiologic tests are less helpful because of the bone changes induced by surgery and healing bone, but CT, MRI, and ^{18}F-FDG PET are used. The most common form of postsurgical osteomyelitis is infection of a hip prosthesis, which occurs in 1% to 5% of hip replacement surgeries. It has been shown experimentally that bacteria can become immersed in an extremely adherent material called the glycocalyx, which binds to the inert substance of the prosthesis. Systemic antibiotics cannot penetrate the glycocalyx, and the only way to cure the infection may be to remove the prosthesis.[71]

Puncture wounds to the feet are associated with approximately a 2% incidence of osteomyelitis. The causative organism is usually *Pseudomonas aeruginosa* or *S. aureus*. Other puncture wounds are nosocomial—in the form of subclavian venipuncture, fetal scalp monitors, and other invasive procedures. Osteomyelitis can result from inoculation of bone with bacteria during these punctures.[22]

Diabetic Foot Osteomyelitis

The pathologic changes induced by long-standing diabetes mellitus encourage the development of osteomyelitis. Peripheral neuropathy is present in a majority of diabetic patients and leads to repetitive trauma and loss of the protective barrier of the skin and foot ulcers. When the skin has been violated and infected, the altered host defense of diabetic patients allows infection to occur and spread. The small bones and phalanges are most often affected. Infection spreads first to the periosteum and then to the cortex and may finally disrupt medullary bone. The initial phase of the pedal infection in diabetic patients may exacerbate preexisting hyperglycemia, which allows bacteria to replicate at an increased rate and causes defects in leukocyte function. These defects in infection control consist of defective chemotaxis, abnormal phagocytosis, and decreased bactericidal function.[72] Defective antibody synthesis and decreased complement levels also exacerbate osteomyelitis. The typical patient with diabetic foot osteomyelitis is older than 50 years and has advanced insulin-dependent diabetes. More than 60% of such patients have polyneuropathy, more than 50% have retinopathy, and at least 30% have concurrent cardiovascular disease.[72,73]

Local findings consist of swelling, erythema, and sometimes pain. Indolent ulcers and frank cellulitis are seen in more than 50% of cases. Because the process is often chronic, radiographic changes may have sufficient time to develop. Mottled lytic lesions are typical, and air may be present in the soft tissues. The bone scan is of limited value because of generalized poor perfusion in the area and the frequency of concurrent soft tissue infection. The only reliable way to make the bacteriologic diagnosis is by surgical culture of the bone. Diabetic foot osteomyelitis is usually polymicrobial. The most common organism is *S. aureus*. Other common organisms include streptococci, Enterobacteriaceae, and anaerobes. Surgical treatment is often required, and severe cases often lead to amputation. However, treatment with IV followed by oral antibiotics can be successful in some patients.

Osteomyelitis in Sickle Cell Disease

Patients with sickle cell disease are at increased risk for hematogenous infection, including osteomyelitis. Macrophage function is impaired in sickle cell patients, rendering them susceptible to infections with encapsulated organisms. AHO in children with sickle cell disease differs from that in otherwise healthy patients in two major ways: (1) infection in sickle cell disease is usually located in the diaphysis of long bones rather than in the metaphysis, and (2) in children with sickle cell disease who develop osteomyelitis, *Salmonella* species are the infecting organism in as many as two thirds of cases.[74] *S. aureus* remains the next most common infecting organism. Why patients with sickle cell disease are predisposed to bone infection with *Salmonella* is not completely understood, although it is postulated that microinfarcts in the bowel allow *Salmonella* bacteremia to seed the bloodstream and become hematogenous osteomyelitis.

The differentiation of bone infection from bone infarction in sickle cell patients is a challenge. Fever, a toxic appearance, and an elevated ESR are all more commonly associated with osteomyelitis than with bone infarction. Plain radiographs are not helpful in distinguishing between the two entities. Skeletal scintigraphy may help make the diagnosis. The best method appears to be ^{99m}Tc MDP followed by gallium or indium scanning. Although both infection and infarction may show increased uptake on the technetium scan, the gallium or indium scan should be "hot" with osteomyelitis but "cold" with sickle cell infarction. Another approach is to note the response to conservative therapy: Bone infarctions usually improve within 24 to 48 hours, whereas bone infection worsens.[48,74,75]

Chronic Osteomyelitis

Historically, chronic osteomyelitis usually resulted from inappropriate or inadequate treatment of AHO. However, most chronic bone infections now occur as a complication of posttraumatic infection, surgical procedures, or diabetic foot infections. A recurrent course, characterized by formation of sequestra and chronic draining tracts or fistulae, indicates that osteomyelitis has become chronic. This infection is almost always polymicrobial and commonly involves anaerobes. Bone scans are of limited use in chronic osteomyelitis; it is difficult to predict improvement or identify active foci of infection on bone scans. Cultures of sinus tracts are not a reliable method for predicting which bacteria are active in the underlying bone infection. Therefore, direct biopsy of bone is the only option for accurately diagnosing most cases of chronic osteomyelitis.[18,71,76]

Complications of Osteomyelitis

In addition to the development of chronic osteomyelitis, several other complications can arise from acute osteomyelitis. The blood may be seeded with bacteria or bacterial toxins from a focus of osteomyelitis. Sepsis may result, and toxic shock syndrome has been reported with osteomyelitis caused by *S. aureus*.[77] Depending on the location of osteomyelitis, local extension of an invasive, suppurative process can lead to brain abscess, meningitis, spinal cord compression, pneumonia, and empyema. In children, osteomyelitis damages the developing skeleton. If infection involves the epiphysis, permanent growth alteration can occur, resulting in a shorter or deformed extremity on the affected side. Pathologic fractures may occur through sites of osteomyelitis. Some cases of osteomyelitis may lead to septic arthritis.

DIFFERENTIAL CONSIDERATIONS IN OSTEOMYELITIS

Many different processes involving bone may masquerade as osteomyelitis. Bone tumors may produce local pain, radiographic changes, and even bone scan abnormalities consistent with osteomyelitis. Tumors most likely to mimic osteomyelitis are osteoid osteomas and chondroblastomas. These produce small round radiolucent lesions on radiographs. Ewing's sarcoma is a tumor of bone marrow in children that can be mistaken for osteomyelitis. Metastatic bone tumors and lymphomas should also be considered in the differential diagnosis of osteomyelitis. Trauma can produce a clinical picture similar to that of osteomyelitis. In children, when trauma is common and may be occult, the evaluation for osteomyelitis may reveal a buckle fracture.

Other inflammatory and infectious diseases that may be initially confused with osteomyelitis are myositis ossificans, erythema nodosum, cellulitis, and eosinophilic granuloma. This enlarging collection of histiocytes occurs in the marrow cavity and causes lytic destructive lesions.

MANAGEMENT OF OSTEOMYELITIS

Emergency department care of most types of osteomyelitis involves treatment of an infection that has been present for days or weeks. In the case of posttraumatic osteomyelitis, emergency care may help to prevent the disease. The proper management of open fractures in the field is to cut away surrounding clothing, pour sterile saline or water over the exposed bone, and cover the wound with moist sterile gauze bandages or a sterile sheet. Only in the case of severe vascular compromise to the distal limb should an open fracture site be manipulated or realigned because of the danger of further contaminating the wound. Because wound surface cultures in the emergency setting are not reliable in predicting future pathogens in bone infections, they need not be done as part of emergency care.[37] The early administration of prophylactic antibiotics to patients with open fractures reduces the incidence of posttraumatic osteomyelitis. First-generation cephalosporins are recommended, with the addition of gram-negative antibiotic coverage for fractures that are contaminated with soil or those occurring in water.[7]

Treatment of osteomyelitis is a combined medical and surgical approach: IV antibiotics and surgical debridement. In some cases, such as AHO of children, antibiotics alone can eradicate the infection. In other situations, such as diabetic foot osteomyelitis and chronic osteomyelitis, the use of antibiotics with surgical debridement is necessary to eradicate the infection.[2,18,73,78,79]

The ideal antibiotic for treating osteomyelitis should be bactericidal against the offending bacteria, have low toxicity, be chemically stable at the site of infection, and be relatively inexpensive. The low pH of infected bone may limit the bactericidal action of some antibiotics, particularly the aminoglycosides. Cephalosporins and penicillins are more stable in this environment. Although it is possible to measure antibiotic concentrations in bone, the clinical significance of these levels is not established. The emergency physician must usually initiate broad-spectrum treatment of suspected osteomyelitis before culture results are available.[7,18,78]

The incidence of antibiotic resistance is increasing. Resistance to both penicillinase-resistant penicillins (oxacillin and methicillin) and fluoroquinolones by staphylococci, vancomycin by enterococci, and imipenem by pseudomonads has been reported. Therefore, when the bacterium has been identified, it is important to select the most specific antimicrobial agent.[76,78,79]

The first priority remains adequately treating *Staphylococcus* species with a penicillinase-resistant penicillin such as oxacillin or nafcillin. In patients with penicillin allergy, clindamycin is a good alternative, as are the first-generation cephalosporins. Nonenterococcal streptococci are usually sensitive to antibiotics used to combat staphylococci. Gram-negative bacteria, including Enterobacteriaceae, *Escherichia coli*, *Proteus mirabilis*, and *Serratia marcescens*, are rare causes of osteomyelitis. Third-generation cephalosporins, aminoglycosides, imipenem-cilastatin, and ampicillin are the usual choices for broad gram-negative coverage. Beyond this initial broad-spectrum therapy, prophylactic treatment for anaerobic bacteria, *Pseudomonas*, and fungal organisms must be based on clinical suspicion. For fungal bone and joint infections newer azole antibiotics, such as fluconazole and itraconazole, have replaced amphotericin B as the initial antifungal agents of choice.[80]

The increase in antimicrobial resistance highlights the need for new antibiotics to expand therapeutic options. Quinupristin-dalfopristin is the first of a unique class of antibiotics called streptogramins. Clinical evidence suggests that these agents may be effective against multidrug-resistant organisms including methicillin-resistant *S. aureus* and vancomycin-resistant bacteria.[78,81] Teicoplanin, a new semisynthetic polypeptide related to vancomycin, is as effective as vancomycin against various gram-positive infections, with potentially less toxicity.[82] The development of alternative fluoroquinolones that are active against a broad spectrum of gram-positive and gram-negative organisms may improve the future treatment of osteomyelitis.[2,76,78,79,83] Table 134-1 lists common treatment regimens for the variety of bacteria that cause osteomyelitis. The standard recommendation is for a duration of therapy with IV antibiotics for osteomyelitis of 4 to 6 weeks; however, more recent studies suggest that a shorter IV course can be used followed by oral antibiotics, with no difference in outcomes.[79,83,84]

Successful treatment of osteomyelitis correlates best with serum levels of antibiotic, not the route of administration. The standard recommendation is that the antibiotic used should achieve serum levels *eight* times greater than its minimum inhibitory concentration. If the serum concentration of an antibiotic is bactericidal, bactericidal levels in bone are almost always present.[78]

In many cases of osteomyelitis, antibiotic therapy alone does not cure the infection, and surgical debridement of infected necrotic bone is necessary. This is usually true when osteomyelitis is caused by direct inoculation into bone or spreads from a contiguous focus of infection. If the area of osteomyelitis is small, aspiration or resection of the bone abscess may be both a diagnostic and therapeutic procedure.[85]

Treatment of chronic osteomyelitis is a difficult surgical problem. Instillation of antibiotic-containing beads into infected bone can help eradicate the infection so that bone grafts can be successfully used in chronic osteomyelitis.[86,87] Hyperbaric oxygen therapy is reported to be effective in treating chronic osteomyelitis in noncontrolled clinical case series and may work best in diabetic foot osteomyelitis. Further randomized clinical trials are necessary to confirm the favorable results seen in case series.[88]

DISPOSITION OF THE PATIENT WITH OSTEOMYELITIS

Several studies demonstrate that patients with osteomyelitis can be treated as outpatients with oral antibiotics. This is attempted only after a course of IV antibiotics is administered and it is documented that bactericidal levels in the serum can be achieved with oral antibiotics. IV outpatient antibiotic therapy is another option after the causative bacterium has been isolated and in-hospital bactericidal levels are demonstrated.[84,89]

CLINICAL FEATURES OF SEPTIC ARTHRITIS

Diagnosis of Septic Arthritis

Septic arthritis usually results from hematogenous migration of bacteria into a joint. In some cases, septic arthritis may result from spread from a contiguous focus of infection or direct inoculation of bacteria. Direct inoculation can result from penetrating trauma or from joint aspiration. Septic arthritis may occur concomitantly with osteomyelitis, with infection spreading from bone to joint, and vice versa. Septic arthritis occurs in all age groups but is most common in children. It is almost always a monarticular process; polyarticular involvement is present in fewer than 10% of pediatric cases and fewer than 20% of adult cases.[8,14,23,90]

Septic arthritis is most likely to occur in the joints of the lower extremity. In infants and children, the knee and hip are most often infected; in adults the knee is the site of septic arthritis 40% to 50% of the time. As noted previously, the synovial membrane extends beyond the epiphysis and attaches to the metaphysis in the knee and shoulder joints. This makes it easier for osteomyelitis in the metaphysis of the femur or humerus to spread into the joint.[14,16,90]

History and Physical Examination

The onset of septic arthritis is usually more acute than the onset of osteomyelitis. The predominant symptom of septic arthritis is joint pain, which is worse when the joint is moved. Many children who have septic arthritis do not use the involved limb at all. In patients with underlying joint disease, a careful history may help differentiate chronic joint pain from the acute pain associated with septic arthritis. Immunosuppressed patients, especially those receiving corticosteroids, may develop septic arthritis with minimal joint pain. Hip pain can be referred to the thigh or knee. A history of fever is common with septic arthritis. It is present in more than 80% of children and more than 40% of adults. Constitutional symptoms, such as weakness, malaise, anorexia, nausea, and diffuse myalgias, are inconsistently present.[4,8,15,16,90]

It is important to ascertain the presence of underlying joint disease such as osteoarthritis, gout, rheumatoid arthritis, joint surgery, and the presence of other conditions, such as IV drug use, that predispose to septic arthritis. Certain medications, such as antibiotics, anti-inflammatory agents, corticosteroids, and analgesics, can alter the course or presentation of septic arthritis.[4]

The physical examination of a patient with septic arthritis may demonstrate fever, but other vital signs are usually normal. Tachycardia and hypotension may indicate a generalized septic process. Examination of the skin, nose, ears, and pharynx may reveal a focus of infection. In the neonate or infant, there may be "pseudoparalysis" of the affected limb. In the older child and adult, signs may be more localized. The extremity is usually held motionless in the position of greatest comfort, which is slight flexion. Swelling, erythema, and warmth are commonly found in the affected joint. Palpation of the septic joint causes exquisite pain over the synovium, and both flexion and extension of the joint cause severe pain. The infected joint feels warmer than the noninvolved joint, and overlying skin may be reddened. An effusion should be evident by observation and palpation. The hip joint, with its deeper location, may not produce obvious external findings when infected. Periarticular processes such as bursitis, tendinitis, and cellulitis may produce erythema, warmth, and tenderness, but palpation of the joint line and maneuvers that stress the synovium and joint are not usually painful. Periarticular processes do not commonly produce an effusion.

One caveat with the physical examination is that an increasing number of adult patients are taking chronic immunosuppressive drugs, sometimes as a treatment for rheumatologic conditions and sometimes for organ transplants or other diseases. In these patients the classical history and examination findings with septic arthritis may be much less dramatic than in patients who are not immune suppressed.[4,14,15,90]

Diagnostic Strategies in Septic Arthritis

Joint Aspiration and Joint Fluid Analysis

The diagnosis of septic arthritis requires joint fluid for culture and analysis. It is fortunate that the knee joint is both the most likely to be infected and the easiest to aspirate. Other joints such as the hip may be more difficult to aspirate and may require orthopedic surgical consultation. Ultrasonography and fluoroscopy-guided aspiration are adjunct modalities used to obtain fluid from the joint and may be useful in detecting early, less obvious intraarticular fluid collections[91] (Figure 134-11). However, the absence of fluid by sonography by no means rules out the presence of septic arthritis. Some authors advocate injecting a small amount of contrast material into the joint during aspiration and obtaining a radiograph to confirm that the needle entered the intra-articular space.[91,92] The risk of introducing infection into a joint during intra-articular aspiration or injection is very low. Iatrogenic septic arthritis occurs in less than 1 in 10,000 joint injections or aspirations and is most likely to occur in patients with existing joint disease.[15,23]

Because joint fluid analysis is not done as often as other diagnostic tests in the emergency department, a joint fluid protocol form is useful to ensure that all necessary tests are prepared and ordered properly. Joint fluid cultures must be inoculated as soon as possible after the fluid is obtained. If significant delays occur in the processing of laboratory specimens, the physician may need to inoculate culture media in the emergency department or take the fluid directly to the microbiology laboratory. Fastidious organisms such as *Neisseria gonorrhoeae* and *H. influenzae* require plating on special media. Anaerobic and fungal media should also be inoculated.[4,23]

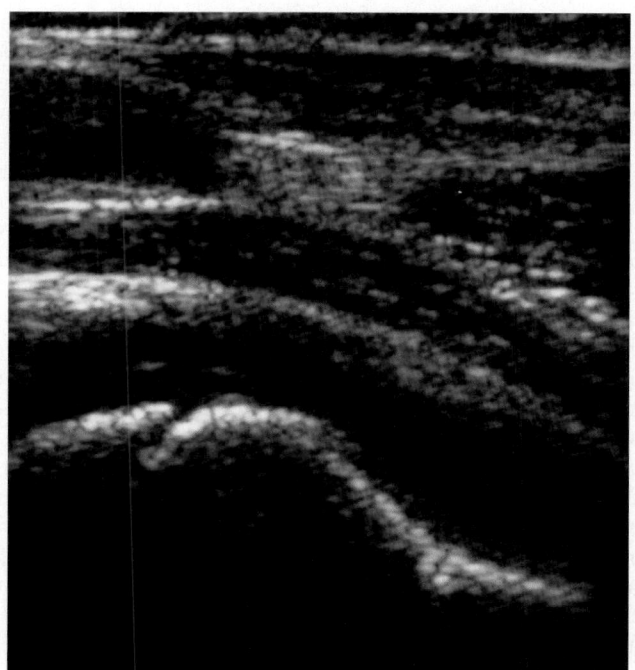

Figure 134-11. Ultrasonography of the right hip in an 8-year-old girl with septic arthritis. A significant joint effusion can be seen just superior to the round contour of the femoral head. Joint aspiration revealed purulent fluid with a white blood cell count of 71,000/mm³.

One method that may increase the yield in isolating bacteria from joint fluid is to inoculate blood culture bottles with joint fluid immediately after joint aspiration. This may allow some bacteria, which would normally die before being inoculated on culture media in the laboratory, to survive and grow in the blood culture bottle (brain-heart infusion broth).[4,16] Obtaining synovial tissue by arthroscopy for analysis may be of some benefit in diagnosing septic arthritis. Cultures of this tissue may be positive despite negative joint fluid cultures. Also, the presence of large numbers of neutrophils in the synovial tissue is much more common in infectious arthritis than in other types of joint inflammation.[4,15,16] Joint fluid culture results in clinically suspected septic arthritis are negative in 20% to 25% of cases. This negative finding may be due to an inadequate joint fluid sample, poor culturing techniques, the presence of fastidious organisms, or misdiagnosis of the joint inflammation. In addition, leukocytes may have cleared bacteria from the joint space but not the synovial membrane. If this is suspected, a synovial biopsy may reveal the organism.[4,16,25]

The definitive test to determine bacterial arthritis is joint fluid culture. Other joint fluid tests are commonly obtained, but evidence-based evaluation of their effectiveness has questioned the usefulness of most additional joint fluid tests. The primary reason for decreasing utility of the traditional joint fluid tests is the number of patients (especially adults) who have a chronically activated or suppressed immune response in the infected joint. The Gram stain, WBC count and differential, and the ratio of the joint fluid glucose to serum glucose have traditionally been used to differentiate bacterial arthritis from other joint diseases. Other tests performed on joint fluid, primarily the examination for joint fluid crystals, may be of some use in differentiating inflammatory from noninflammatory joint disease, but they are not helpful in separating infectious inflammatory joint disease from noninfectious inflammatory joint disease. The synovial fluid leukocyte count in a septic joint is often greater than 50,000 cells/mm³, with a predominance of PMNs, but other processes can give similar cell counts, and up to 30% of patients with septic arthritis have been documented to have counts less than 50,000 cells/mm³. The fasting joint fluid glucose level is often lowered in patients with septic arthritis, and the joint fluid/serum glucose ratio is less than 1:2, but this test is also not reliable in patients who have chronic joint disease or are immune suppressed. The joint fluid lactate level is often higher in infected joints than in inflamed joints, but this test does not appear to be more helpful than the glucose ratio, particularly in partially treated septic arthritis. Joint fluid WBC counts and glucose may be most helpful when the WBC count is low (less than 10,000 cells/mm³) and the glucose is normal. In this situation, septic arthritis is unlikely.[4,8,23,90,93]

When only a drop or two of synovial fluid can be recovered from a joint aspiration, the emergency physician must establish priorities for diagnostic tests. The first step is to obtain bacterial cultures. A drop of fluid is then used for a smear and Gram stain. A cell count and glucose can be obtained but are not essential.[4,14,16]

Blood tests are not consistently helpful in making a diagnosis of septic arthritis. Blood cultures reveal the infecting organism in 25% to 50% of cases, and the ESR is elevated in approximately 90% of cases of septic arthritis. The CRP level is also elevated in most cases. A WBC count greater than 10,000 cells/mm³ may suggest a systemic illness but is present in only 50% of patients with septic arthritis. Cultures of infectious foci, such as the throat and urine, may demonstrate the bacteria responsible for septic arthritis.[4,14,16,90]

Plain radiography is not an effective tool for the early evaluation of septic arthritis. Radiographs may reveal a joint effusion that displaces capsular fat planes. This is most helpful in the hip joint, where it is difficult to detect an effusion on physical examination. In most joints the small areas of attachment of the synovial membrane to bone are devoid of cartilage. These "bare areas" at the margins of the joint appear as lucencies or erosions early in the course of septic arthritis. Bone beneath the articular cartilage may start to erode 1 to 3 weeks into the disease. Radiographs provide minimal assistance in diagnosing septic arthritis in a patient with existing joint disease. Radiographs may detect osteomyelitis in bones adjacent to the joint. Air density in the joint may be a sign of infection with gas-forming organisms or may be the result of a previous joint aspiration.[45,56]

Skeletal scintigraphy has been used in the diagnosis of septic arthritis. Its main advantage is in detecting septic arthritis earlier than other imaging techniques. The specifics of technetium, gallium, and indium scanning have been previously discussed. In septic arthritis, scintigraphy shows symmetric areas of increased uptake on both sides of the joint. In a three-phase ^{99m}Tc scan, all three phases are hot with septic arthritis. It may be difficult to distinguish osteomyelitis in the metaphysis of a long bone from septic arthritis in the adjacent joint. In general, skeletal scintigraphy is used only when there is enough uncertainty about the diagnosis to warrant further investigation before proceeding with joint aspiration. This is most common in evaluating a hip for septic arthritis. In joints where aspiration is easier, skeletal scintigraphy has little role in diagnosing septic arthritis. There is some risk that the delay associated with obtaining skeletal scintigraphy may lead to further joint destruction before definitive treatment is rendered.

Ultrasonography is an important modality for detecting a joint effusion in suspected septic arthritis and in assisting in joint aspiration, particularly in the hip. Ultrasonography of suspected septic arthritis of the hip in children both permits the evaluation for effusion and helps to guide the diagnostic aspiration of the joint (see Figure 134-10).[90,92] CT provides better anatomic images of the joint and can help to assess the size of effusions. MRI is also useful in defining the anatomy of joints and determining whether septic arthritis is complicated by concurrent osteomyelitis. MRI provides a detailed image of joint structure and can detect even small effusions.[23,56,92,94]

Complications of Septic Arthritis

Septic arthritis leads to two types of serious complications: those involving the joint itself and those that are systemic. Children are at great risk for epiphyseal damage if the infection extends through subchondral bone. This can result in impaired growth and length discrepancy in the limbs. Other tissues adjacent to the joint can be invaded. Bursae, tendons, ligaments, and muscles can be destroyed by the suppurative process. Sinus tracts may lead the infection out through the skin. In the hip, the pressure and edema of a septic synovial effusion can occlude blood supply, resulting in avascular necrosis of the femoral head. Septic hip arthritis in children needs prompt diagnosis and drainage to prevent destruction of the hip joint. In other joints the end result of uncontrolled septic arthritis is ankylosis. The joint becomes stiff, fused, and devoid of articular cartilage.

In some patients with septic arthritis, the infection causes systemic sepsis. Systemic sepsis is most common in elders and immunocompromised patients.

Clinical Subsets of Septic Arthritis

Septic Arthritis in Infants and Children

Septic arthritis is more common in children than in adults, and the incidence of septic arthritis is twice that of osteomyelitis in children.[90] Of pediatric cases, two thirds occur in children younger than 2 years and boys are affected twice as often as girls.[90] The bacterial etiologic agent of septic arthritis varies with age. In neonates, group B streptococci, S. aureus, and gram-negative enteric bacilli are usual pathogens. Candida albicans must also be considered in neonates and premature infants.[27,95] Since the widespread introduction of the H. influenzae type B vaccine, S. aureus has become the most common cause of septic arthritis in children 3 months to 5 years old. In this age range concomitant respiratory infection or otitis media is often present. If the hip joint is infected, the complication rate is higher and permanent joint damage is more likely. This is especially true in infants, particularly those who have coexisting septic arthritis and osteomyelitis. Overall, S. aureus is the most common infecting organism in all pediatric age groups, followed by group A streptococci and Streptococcus pneumoniae.[10,90,96] Prior trauma or skin infection may be more common with staphylococcal septic arthritis. Even with full culturing of joint fluid and blood, a causative organism is not discovered in up to 30% of cases of septic arthritis in children. Prior antibiotic treatment in children decreases the yield of synovial fluid cultures from 80% to 38%.[10,15,23]

Gonococcal Septic Arthritis

N. gonorrhoeae is the most common cause of septic arthritis in teenagers and young adults. In the United States it is most common in those with lower socioeconomic status in urban areas. A person with gonorrhea of the urethra, cervix, rectum, or pharynx has a 0.5% to 1% chance of developing disseminated gonococcal infection (DGI). Gonococcal septic arthritis is more common in women, especially during pregnancy or after menstruation. The strains of N. gonorrhoeae that cause disseminated infection and septic arthritis have characteristics different from those of the strains that cause local infection. The strains that cause disseminated infection contain outer membrane proteins, which make them resistant to serum bactericidal activity. These strains are not more resistant to antibiotics than other types of N. gonorrhoeae; however, penicillin-resistant gonococcal infections appear to be increasing in some parts of the world. The common finding of sterile joint fluid in DGI, even when mucosal cultures are positive, suggests that the host immune response plays a significant role in the development of purulent arthritis.[14,97]

Most, but not all, patients with DGI are symptomatic with a local genital or oral infection. Symptoms are less common in women, which is probably the reason for delays in treatment and a higher incidence of the disease. The time for local infection to disseminate can vary from 1 or 2 days to weeks. Symptoms begin soon after gonococcal bacteria enter the bloodstream, and fever and chills are often present. The classical triad of DGI is migratory polyarthritis, tenosynovitis, and dermatitis. Asymmetric polyarthralgia, which may be migratory, is the most common presenting complaint, occurring in two thirds of cases; 25% of patients have monoarthralgia. Joint involvement is usually asymmetric and most frequently involves the knee, elbow, wrist, and metacarpophalangeal and ankle joints. The sacroiliac and sternoclavicular joints may be infected with gonococcal arthritis, although these sites are far less common.[97] Tenosynovitis occurs in two thirds of patients with DGI, typically occurring in the hands and fingers. Distribution is usually asymmetric and involves more than one area. Dermatitis is also present in two thirds of patients and may have a number of forms. The most common rash consists of scattered painless 0.5- to 0.75-cm hemorrhagic macules or papules distributed on the extremities and trunk. A small area of central necrosis may be present in the lesions.[14,97]

Purulent arthritis develops in approximately 40% of patients with DGI. In most cases it is monarticular, but 10% of the time it is polyarticular. Some of the strains of *N. gonorrhoeae* that produce DGI favor the development of tenosynovitis and dermatitis, whereas others favor the development of purulent arthritis. There is usually not a clear progression of the disease from polyarthralgias to tenosynovitis to purulent monarticular arthritis. Many patients are afflicted with dermatitis and tenosynovitis without developing true arthritis.[14,97]

Joint fluid analysis in gonococcal arthritis reveals some differences in comparison with other types of bacterial arthritis. The synovial fluid WBC count in gonococcal arthritis is often less than 50,000 cells/mm^3. The joint fluid glucose level is also not usually depressed. Gram stains of aspirated joint fluid are positive for bacteria only 25% of the time in gonococcal arthritis, and cultures of the joint fluid are negative in approximately 50% of cases. This may be due to poor culturing techniques or the fact that a suppurative reactive process can occur in the joint in DGIs even when bacteria are no longer present. It is important to culture the mucosal surfaces for *N. gonorrhoeae* when clinical suspicion of gonococcal arthritis is high because these may be the only places where bacteria are readily recovered. In 80% of cases, cultures of the genital tract, pharynx, or rectum are positive. Gonococcal septic arthritis responds rapidly to antibiotic treatment and, unlike other types of bacterial arthritis, rarely causes permanent damage to the joint.[14,97]

Septic Arthritis with Existing Joint Disease

Patients with underlying joint disease are more likely to develop septic arthritis. This is especially true for patients with rheumatoid arthritis and crystalline arthritis. Septic arthritis is more likely to be polyarticular and to result in complications in patients with rheumatoid arthritis.[15,23] The invasion of neutrophils that occurs in septic arthritis probably causes increased precipitation and release of crystals. The clinician who discovers crystals on joint fluid aspiration should not abandon the search for an infectious agent.

Surgical implantation of a joint prosthesis is followed by joint infection in 1% to 5% of cases. The infection is most likely to occur in the first 3 months (50% of cases) after surgery and may be due to bacterial contamination during surgery, spread from a contiguous wound infection, or spread from hematogenous seeding. The prosthesis and cement are foreign bodies and are favorite sites for bacterial colonization. The most common infectious agents are *S. epidermidis* (40% of cases), *S. aureus* (20%), and streptococcal species (20%). The predominant symptom is pain in the joint, and, unlike the pain from a loose prosthesis, it is constant and present at rest.[15,23,32,98] The clinical course is variable. With *S. epidermidis* infections, the course is usually indolent. With *S. aureus*, a more aggressive infection occurs, with more pronounced inflammation, effusion, and systemic symptoms. Radiographic changes that may signify a prosthetic joint infection include widening and lucency of the bone-cement interface to greater than 2 mm, movement of the prosthesis, periosteal reaction, and fractures through the cement. Joint aspiration reveals infection in a prosthetic joint in more than 85% of patients. Aspiration may be more difficult in this situation because of scarring and alteration of the joint space. Patients with prosthetic joints who are undergoing invasive oropharyngeal or genitourinary procedures require antibiotic prophylaxis.[15,32,98]

Fungal arthritis is uncommon, particularly in children. However, the incidence is rising, principally in hospitalized patients with immune deficiency and underlying malignancy.[27,39] The diagnosis is often delayed for months and usually made by culture and histologic examination of the synovial tissue.

Septic Arthritis in Atypical Joints

Septic arthritis can be particularly difficult to diagnose and treat if it occurs in fibrocartilaginous joints such as the sternoclavicular, acromioclavicular, and sacroiliac joints and the symphysis pubis. Cases of sternoclavicular bacterial arthritis are more commonly seen in IVDA, and *Pseudomonas* is often the infecting agent. In patients who do not have other predisposing factors, the most common bacterial causes are *S. aureus* and *S. epidermidis*. The presentation is usually pain and point tenderness over the involved joint. Fever and an elevated ESR are commonly reported, although not always present. CT or MRI may be more helpful in septic arthritis in fibrocartilaginous joints than in other joints. Bone scans are also able to detect the infected joint.[15,99,100]

DIFFERENTIAL CONSIDERATIONS IN SEPTIC ARTHRITIS

Many disease processes can be confused with septic arthritis. Osteomyelitis may mimic septic arthritis because it affects the metaphysis and the neighboring joint may develop an effusion. The two infections can be concurrent. Juvenile rheumatoid arthritis usually produces polyarticular arthritis in children younger than 16 years but may arise as a monarticular process that mimics septic arthritis. Toxic or transient synovitis is another inflammatory process in children that can be confused with septic arthritis. It occurs in the 3-month to 6-year age range, usually affects the hip, and is a self-limited disease with no long-term morbidity. It may be more common after upper respiratory infections. Children with transient synovitis do not usually appear ill and are not febrile but favor the affected leg. Diagnostic evaluation typically reveals a normal WBC count and ESR and no radiographic abnormalities. The only way to differentiate reliably between toxic synovitis and septic arthritis in the hip joint is to perform an ultrasound examination to look for effusion and a guided aspiration to obtain cultures, assess cell counts, and perform a Gram stain for bacteria.

Other diseases of the hip in children that may be mistaken for septic arthritis are Legg-Calvé-Perthes disease (avascular necrosis) and slipped capital femoral epiphysis. Rheumatic fever commonly arises with polyarthritis and may mimic gonococcal arthritis. In the adult, osteoarthritis, gout, and pseudogout may result in a joint examination similar to that in septic arthritis. Other arthropathies that must be considered in the differential diagnosis of septic arthritis are Reiter's syndrome, psoriatic arthritis, arthritis associated with inflammatory bowel disease, and ankylosing spondylitis. Collectively, these are known as the seronegative spondyloarthropathies. Trauma to the joint can produce synovitis and hemarthrosis, which may be mistaken for septic arthritis. In a patient with hemophilia, hemarthrosis causes joint inflammation and destruction and there may be superimposed infection.[8,10,14,90]

Reactive arthritis has been traditionally considered a sterile inflammatory response to a distant infection. However, data suggest that antigens from the infectious trigger are often present in the joint. Several viral and bacterial microorganisms can produce reactive arthritis. The most recognized syndrome is poststreptococcal reactive arthritis. Some other common organisms that cause reactive arthritis are *Chlamydia*, *Salmonella*, *Shigella*, *Borrelia burgdorferi* (Lyme disease), *Yersinia*, human T cell lymphotropic virus type 1 (HTLV-1), rubella virus, hepatitis B virus, adenoviruses, parvovirus, and Epstein-Barr virus. In reactive arthritis, host factors rather than microbial aggression account for most of the inflammatory process. The pathogenesis of reactive arthritis involves deposition of immune complexes in the joint, persistence of organisms in the joint, and stimulation of the immune system. Strong evidence exists to support a link between susceptibility to reactive arthritis and the HLA-B27 human leukocyte histocompatibility antigen. However, whether the presence of HLA-B27 antigen influences the disease pattern is unknown. Reactive arthritis can usually be distinguished from septic arthritis because it tends to involve multiple joints in a migratory pattern. The inflammatory process is also less severe with reactive arthritis. There is less effusion, and the joint is not as hot or tender as it is with septic arthritis. Joint fluid cell counts are usually below 50,000/mm^3, and the joint fluid glucose is not depressed.[4,11,12,25]

MANAGEMENT OF SEPTIC ARTHRITIS

Septic arthritis is an orthopedic emergency, and it is uniformly accepted that antibiotics should be promptly administered if the diagnosis is strongly suspected.

However, considerable disagreement exists regarding medical versus surgical joint decompression. Medical management consists of needle aspiration of the joint. If pus reaccumulates, repeated aspiration is performed. Surgical drainage is accomplished by arthrotomy or arthroscopy. Surgical drainage may involve placement of tubes in the joint that can be used for irrigation and drainage. The theoretical advantages of surgical drainage are that the joint can be fully cleansed of pus and debris, loculations can be broken, and irrigation and drainage tubes can keep the joint free of destructive cells and enzymes. The disadvantages are that arthrotomy usually requires general anesthesia, is a one-time procedure, and can lead to scarring and limitation of joint movement. The advantages of needle aspiration are simplicity, low morbidity, and the ease with which it can be repeated. Proponents of surgical drainage argue that needle aspiration cannot adequately drain the joint and that long-term outcome has not been adequately assessed in medical management of septic arthritis. No randomized controlled studies exist that compare these two approaches. However, there is evidence in an animal model that surgical incision and drainage protect the joint from chemical insult better than multiple aspirations.[4,8,23,98,101]

Although needle aspiration may be adequate treatment for most septic joints, surgical drainage is usually necessary in at least two settings. With septic arthritis of the hip, especially in infants and children, rapid destruction of the joint occurs if drainage is not quickly performed. Needle aspiration is often ineffective in this situation, and it is generally agreed that arthrotomy is the treatment of choice for infected hips.[90] Some experts recommend a similar approach with a septic shoulder. Infected joint prostheses are also less likely to respond to conservative therapy and often require arthrotomy and drainage.[98] The only situation in which antibiotics alone can adequately treat a septic joint is in gonococcal septic arthritis. After the diagnostic joint aspiration, almost all cases of gonococcal septic arthritis quickly resolve with antibiotics alone.[14,97]

The selection of antibiotics for the treatment of septic arthritis is outlined in Table 134-1. In most cases the emergency physician does not know the identity of the causative organism. Because the bacteria that cause septic arthritis vary with the age of the patient, treatment must be tailored to the most likely causative agents. *S. aureus* remains the predominant pathogen for all age groups, and antibiotic selection should always include an antibiotic that has excellent bactericidal activity against *S. aureus*, except when the patient has characteristic gonococcal arthritis. In young adults gonococcal septic arthritis is common. Some strains that cause gonococcal arthritis are resistant to penicillin. In regions where penicillinase-producing *N. gonorrhoeae* is prevalent, gonococcal arthritis is best treated with ceftriaxone. In elders, gram-negative septic arthritis is more common, and agents such as the third-generation cephalosporins and aminoglycosides are added to the regimen. Establishing good bactericidal serum levels of antibiotics ensures that the levels in joint fluid are also bactericidal.[4,8,14,23,97,98]

A well-designed study of IV dexamethasone for the treatment of acute hematogenous septic arthritis in children had dramatic results. Children treated with IV dexamethasone for 4 days demonstrated more rapid recovery and markedly reduced residual joint dysfunction. If these results can be confirmed and duplicated in other studies, this would represent a major advance in treatment of septic arthritis in children.[102]

DISPOSITION OF THE PATIENT WITH SEPTIC ARTHRITIS

Any patient suspected of having septic arthritis requires joint aspiration. In some cases the initial cell counts, glucose level, and Gram stain make the diagnosis of septic arthritis extremely likely. The patient should be given an initial dose of antibiotics in the emergency department and be admitted for continued management. Consultants then determine the need for further drainage procedures. In many cases, joint aspiration in the emergency department is not diagnostic, and a definitive diagnosis of septic arthritis is impossible. In this situation, if the clinical appearance strongly suggests septic arthritis, the patient should be treated with appropriate antibiotics and admitted to the hospital. If the joint fluid aspirate is not consistent with septic arthritis and clinical findings are equivocal, the patient can be discharged from the emergency department and re-evaluated in 24 hours. In some patients, septic arthritis can be difficult to detect. These include patients receiving immunosuppressive agents, those with existing joint disease, and those with prosthetic joints. A conservative approach with in-hospital observation and treatment is indicated if there is any possibility of septic arthritis in these patients.

In most cases the prognosis for the patient with septic arthritis is favorable. Two thirds of afflicted patients can expect to cover completely (i.e., full range of motion of the joint and no pain). In approximately one third of cases there is decreased mobility or ankylosis, pain on movement, chronic infection, or overwhelming sepsis and death. Despite many advances in diagnosis and treatment, the overall morbidity for patients with septic arthritis has not decreased in the last two decades. The patients most likely to do poorly include those who have a delay in diagnosis and treatment, patients with rheumatoid arthritis, those with polyarticular septic arthritis, and those who have positive blood cultures.[4] A general rule is that if the diagnosis of septic arthritis is made and treatment is initiated within 1 week of the onset of symptoms, the outcome is almost always favorable. Delays beyond 1 week are associated with worse outcomes. Diagnosis and rapid treatment of septic arthritis prove to be most elusive in two groups of patients: infants and people with existing joint disease. In infants and children early symptoms can be nonspecific and difficult to assess. Children with septic arthritis of the hip who experience a delay in diagnosis and treatment have a disappointingly high rate of complications. In patients with existing joint disease, septic arthritis may be mistaken for another flare-up of the chronic disease.[4,8,14,90]

KEY CONCEPTS

- The emergency physician should consider skeletal infection in the differential diagnosis of all patients who present with bone or joint pain. In cases in which a bone or joint infection exists, early diagnosis and treatment can have a potent impact on the long-term morbidity.
- The vascular anatomy of long bones changes throughout life. In infants and adults, vascular connections exist between the metaphysis and epiphysis, which allow extension of bone infection into the joint. In children the epiphyseal plate prevents this from happening.
- The diagnostic evaluation for septic arthritis is relatively simple. Joint aspiration is the definitive diagnostic procedure. However, culture is the only reliable joint fluid test in establishing a diagnosis. The diagnosis of osteomyelitis is more complex and usually involves a choice between bone scans and CT or MRI. Imaging tests can be time consuming and expensive and do not always demonstrate excellent sensitivity. Culture of infected bone is the most direct way to arrive at a bacteriologic diagnosis.
- Hematologic evaluation is of little value in diagnosing bone and joint infections, with the exception of the ESR, which is elevated in approximately 90% of cases of bone and joint infections.
- When clinical findings suggest the diagnosis of bone or joint infection, antibiotic treatment should not be delayed. With suspected septic arthritis, joint fluid and blood cultures are obtained as IV antibiotics are ordered. With suspected osteomyelitis, blood cultures are obtained, and IV antibiotics are administered while plans are made for further imaging studies or surgical aspiration or resection of bone.
- The most important aspect of antibiotic treatment of suspected osteomyelitis is providing potent bactericidal activity against *S. aureus*. In suspected septic arthritis, initial antibiotic treatment must be tailored to the age and clinical characteristics of the patient.

REFERENCES

1. Cunning J, Joll CE: *Aids to Surgery*, 4th ed. New York, William Wood, 1919.
2. Mader JT, et al: Bone and joint infections in the elderly: Practical treatment guidelines. *Drugs Aging* 16:67, 2000.
3. Biviji AA, Paiement GD, Steinbach LS: Musculoskeletal manifestations of human immunodeficiency virus infection. *J Am Acad Orthop Surg* 10:312, 2000.
4. Dikranian A, Weisman M: Principles of diagnosis and treatment of joint infections. In Koopman W (ed): *Arthritis and Allied Conditions: A Textbook of Rheumatology.* Philadelphia, Lippincott Williams & Wilkins, 2001, p 255.
5. Cuellar ML: HIV infection-associated inflammatory musculoskeletal disorders. *Rheum Dis Clin North Am* 24:403, 1998.
6. Kak V, Chandrasekar PH: Bone and joint infections in injection drug users. *Infect Dis Clin North Am* 16:681, 2002.
7. Lew D, Waldvogel F: Current concepts: Osteomyelitis. *N Engl J Med* 336:999, 1997.
8. Nade S: Septic arthritis. *Best Pract Res Clin Rheumatol* 17:183, 2003.

9. Gillespie W: Epidemiology in bone and joint infections. *Infect Dis Clin North Am* 4:361, 1990.

10. Sonnen G, Henry N: Pediatric bone and joint infections. *Pediatr Clin North Am* 43:933, 1996.

11. Masuko-Hongo K, Kato T, Nishioka K: Virus-associated arthritis. *Best Pract Res Clin Rheumatol* 17:309, 2003.

12. Li EK: Rheumatic disorders associated with streptococcal infections. *Best Pract Res Clin Rheumatol* 14:559, 2000.

13. Mader JT, Shirtliff ME, Calhoun JH: The host and the skeletal infection: Classification and pathogenesis of acute bacterial bone and joint sepsis. *Best Pract Res Clin Rheumatol* 13:1, 1999.

14. Shirtliff ME, Mader JT: Acute septic arthritis. *Clin Microbiol Rev* 15:527, 2002.

15. Ike RW: Bacterial arthritis. In Koopman W (ed): *Arthritis and Allied Conditions: A Textbook of Rheumatology.* Philadelphia, Lippincott Williams & Wilkins, 2001, p 2570.

16. Ike RW: Bacterial arthritis. *Curr Opin Rheumatol* 10:330, 1998.

17. Atcheson S, Ward J: Acute hematogenous osteomyelitis progressing to septic synovitis and eventual pyoarthrosis: The vascular pathway. *Arthritis Rheum* 21:968, 1978.

18. Ciampolini J, Harding KG: Pathophysiology of chronic bacterial osteomyelitis. Why do antibiotics fail so often? *Postgrad Med J* 76:479, 2000.

19. Nair S, Meghji S, Wilson M: Bacterially induced bone destruction: Mechanisms and misconceptions. *Infect Immun* 64:2371, 1996.

20. Mandal S, Berendt AR, Peacock SJ: *Staphylococcus aureus* bone and joint infection. *J Infect* 44:143, 2002.

21. Talan D, et al: Bacteriologic analysis of infected dog and cat bites. *N Engl J Med* 340:85, 1999.

22. Laughlin T, et al: Soft tissue and bone infections from puncture wounds in children. *West J Med* 166:126, 1997.

23. Carreno-Perez L: Septic arthritis. *Best Pract Res Clin Rheumatol* 13:37, 1999.

24. Krieg AM: A possible cause of joint destruction in septic arthritis. *Arthritis Res* 1:3, 1999.

25. Taylor-Robinson D, Keat A: Septic and aseptic arthritis: A continuum? *Best Pract Res Clin Rheumatol* 13:179, 1999.

26. Bouza E, Munoz P: Micro-organisms responsible for osteo-articular infections. *Best Pract Res Clin Rheumatol* 13:21, 1999.

27. Harrington JT: Mycobacterial and fungal arthritis. *Curr Opin Rheumatol* 10:335, 1998.

28. Malaviya AN, Kotwal PP: Arthritis associated with tuberculosis. *Best Pract Res Clin Rheumatol* 17:319, 2003.

29. Howard A, Viskontas D, Sabbagh C: Reduction in osteomyelitis and septic arthritis related to *Haemophilus influenzae* type b vaccination. *J Pediatr Orthop* 19:705, 1999.

30. Lundy D, Kehl D: Increasing prevalence of *Kingella kingae* in osteoarticular infections in young children. *J Pediatr Orthop* 18:262, 1998.

31. Brook I: Joint and bone infections due to anaerobic bacteria in children. *Pediatr Rehabil* 5:11, 2002.

32. Lidgren L, Knutson K, Stefansdottir A: Infection and arthritis. Infection of prosthetic joints. *Best Pract Res Clin Rheumatol* 17:209, 2003.

33. Semel J, Trenholme G: *Aeromonas hydrophila* water-associated traumatic wound infections: A review. *J Trauma* 30:324, 1990.

34. Heitmann C, et al: Musculoskeletal sepsis: Principles of treatment. *Instr Course Lect* 52:733, 2003.

35. Brook I: Microbiology and management of human and animal bite wound infections. *Prim Care* 30:25, 2003.

36. Berbari E, et al: *Mycobacterium tuberculosis*: A case series and review of the literature. *Am J Orthop* 27:219, 1998.

37. Paradisi F, Giampaolo C: Skeletal tuberculosis and other granulomatous infections. *Baillieres Clin Rheumatol* 13:163, 1999.

38. Hendrickx L, et al: Candidal vertebral osteomyelitis: Report of 6 patients, and a review. *Clin Infect Dis* 32:527, 2001.

39. Cuellar M., Silveira L, Espinoza L: Fungal arthritis. *Ann Rheum Dis* 51:690, 1992.

40. Vazquez M: Osteomyelitis in children. *Curr Opin Pediatr* 14:112, 2002.

41. Unkila-Kallio L, et al: Serum C-reactive protein, erythrocyte sedimentation rate, and white blood cell count in acute hematogenous osteomyelitis of children. *Pediatrics* 93:59, 1994.

42. Wall EJ: Childhood osteomyelitis and septic arthritis. *Curr Opin Pediatr* 10:73, 1998.

43. Roine I., Arguedas A, Faingezicht I: Early detection of sequela-prone osteomyelitis in children with use of simple clinical and laboratory criteria. *Clin Infect Dis* 24:849, 1997.

44. Gentry L: Osteomyelitis: Options of diagnosis and management. *J Antimicrob Chemother* 21:115, 1988.

45. Kothari NA, Pelchovitz DJ, Meyer JS: Imaging of musculoskeletal infections. *Radiol Clin North Am* 39:653, 2001.

46. Oudjhane K, Azouz EM: Imaging of osteomyelitis in children. *Radiol Clin North Am* 39:251, 2001.

47. Restrepo CS, Gimenez CR, McCarthy K: Imaging of osteomyelitis and musculoskeletal soft tissue infections: Current concepts. *Rheum Dis Clin North Am* 29:89, 2003.

48. Schauwecker D: The scintigraphic diagnosis of osteomyelitis. *AJR Am J Roentgenol* 158:9, 1992.

49. Holder L: Clinical radionuclide bone imaging. *Radiology* 176:607, 1990.

50. Boutin RD, et al: Update on imaging of orthopedic infections. *Orthop Clin North Am* 29:41, 1998.

51. Mandell G: Imaging in the diagnosis of musculoskeletal infections in children. *Curr Probl Pediatr* 26:218, 1996.

52. Demopulos G, Bleck E, McDougall I: Quantitative bone gallium scintigraphy in osteomyelitis. *Skeletal Radiol* 22:239, 1988.

53. Lantto E, et al: Tc-99m HMPAO labeled leukocytes superior to bone scan in detection of osteomyelitis in children. *Clin Nucl Med* 17:7, 1992

54. Gross T, et al: Current concepts in posttraumatic osteomyelitis: A diagnostic challenge with new imaging options. *J Trauma* 52:1210, 2002.

55. Zhuang H, Alavi A: 18-Fluorodeoxyglucose positron emission tomographic imaging in the detection and monitoring of infection and inflammation. *Semin Nucl Med* 32:47, 2002.

56. Kattapuram TM, Treat ME, Kattapuram SV: Magnetic resonance imaging of bone and soft tissue infections. *Curr Clin Top Infect Dis* 21:190, 2001.

57. Dagirmanjian A, Schils J, McHenry MC: MR imaging of spinal infections. *Magn Reson Imaging Clin N Am* 7:525, 1999.

58. Chung T: Magnetic resonance imaging in acute osteomyelitis in children. *Pediatr Infect Dis J* 21:869, 2002.

59. Bamberger DM: Diagnosis and treatment of osteomyelitis. *Compr Ther* 26:89, 2000.

60. Gavilan MG, Lopez JB, Artola BS: Peculiarities of osteoarticular infections in children. *Best Pract Res Clin Rheumatol* 13:77, 1999.

61. Asmar B: Osteomyelitis in the neonate. *Infect Dis Clin North Am* 6:117, 1992.

62. Baevsky RH: Neonatal group B beta-hemolytic streptococcus osteomyelitis. *Am J Emerg Med* 17:619, 1999.

63. Frederiksen B, Christiansen P, Knudsen F: Acute osteomyelitis and septic arthritis in the neonate, risk factors and outcome. *Eur J Pediatr* 152:577, 1993.

64. Ramos OM: Chronic osteomyelitis in children. *Pediatr Infect Dis J* 21:431, 2002.

65. Kleinman PK: A regional approach to osteomyelitis of the lower extremities in children. *Radiol Clin North Am* 40:1033, 2002.

66. Ta BK, Deckey J, Hu SS: Spinal infections. *J Am Acad Orthop Surg* 10:188, 2002.

67. Lehovsky J: Pyogenic vertebral osteomyelitis/disc infection. *Best Pract Res Clin Rheumatol* 13:59, 1999.

68. Huang T, Bendo JA: Vertebral osteomyelitis. *Bull Hosp Joint Dis* 59:211, 2000.

69. Bass SN, et al: Pyogenic vertebral osteomyelitis presenting as exudative pleural effusion: A series of five cases. *Chest* 114:642, 1998.

70. Tsukayama DT: Pathophysiology of posttraumatic osteomyelitis. *Clin Orthop* (360):22, 1999.

71. Munoz P, Bouza E: Acute and chronic adult osteomyelitis and prosthesis-related infections. *Best Pract Res Clin Rheumatol* 13:129, 1999.

72. Caputo G, et al: Assessment and management of foot disease in patients with diabetes. *N Engl J Med* 9:143, 1994.

73. Tan J, File TJ: Diagnosis and treatment of diabetic foot infections. *Baillieres Clin Rheumatol* 13:149, 1999.

74. Burnett M., Bass J, Cook B: Etiology of osteomyelitis complicating sickle cell disease. *Pediatrics* 101:296, 1998.

75. Wong AL, Sakamoto KM, Johnson FE: Differentiating osteomyelitis from bone infarction in sickle cell disease. *Pediatr Emerg Care* 17:60, 2001.

76. Mader JT, et al: Antimicrobial treatment of chronic osteomyelitis. *Clin Orthop* 360:47, 1999.

77. Chen S, Howes P: Purulent osteomyelitis associated with empyema and toxic shock syndrome. *J Emerg Med* 6: 285, 1988.

78. Mader JT, Wang J, Calhoun JH: Antibiotic therapy for musculoskeletal infections. *Instr Course Lect* 51:539, 2002.

79. Levy J, et al: Treatment of bone and joint infections: Recommendations of a Belgian panel. *Acta Orthop Belg* 66:127, 2000.

80. Perez-Gomez A, et al: Role of the new azoles in the treatment of fungal osteoarticular infections. *Semin Arthritis Rheum* 27:226, 1998.

81. Low D: Quinupristin/dalfopristin: Spectrum of activity, pharmacokinetics, and initial clinical experience. *Microb Drug Resist* 1:223, 1995.

82. Shea K, Cunha B: Teicoplanin. *Med Clin North Am* 79:833, 1995.

83. Lew DP, Waldvogel FA: Use of quinolones in osteomyelitis and infected orthopaedic prosthesis. *Drugs* 58(Suppl 2):85, 1999.

84. Le Saux N, et al: Shorter courses of parenteral antibiotic therapy do not appear to influence response rates for children with acute hematogenous osteomyelitis: A systematic review. *BMC Infect Dis* 2:16, 2002.

85. Tetsworth K, Cierny G III: Osteomyelitis debridement techniques. *Clin Orthop* 360:87, 1999.

86. Ostermann P, Seligson D, Henry S: Local antibiotic therapy for severe open fractures: A review of 1085 consecutive cases. *J Bone Joint Surg Br* 77:93, 1995.

87. Roeder B, Van Gils CC, Maling S: Antibiotic beads in the treatment of diabetic pedal osteomyelitis. *J Foot Ankle Surg* 39:124, 2000.

88. Wang C, et al: Hyperbaric oxygen for treating wounds: A systematic review of the literature. *Arch Surg* 138:272, 2003.

89. Tice A: Outpatient parenteral antimicrobial therapy for osteomyelitis. *Infect Dis Clin North Am* 12:903, 1998.

90. Shetty AK, Gedalia A: Septic arthritis in children. *Rheum Dis Clin North Am* 24:287, 1998.

91. Myers M, Thompson G: Imaging a child with a limp. *Pediatr Clin North Am* 44:637, 1997.

92. Craig JG: Infection: Ultrasound-guided procedures. *Radiol Clin North Am* 37:669, 1999.

93. Swan A, Amer H, Dieppe P: The value of synovial fluid assays in the diagnosis of joint disease: A literature survey. *Ann Rheum Dis* 61:493, 2002.

94. Learch TJ, Farooki S: Magnetic resonance imaging of septic arthritis. *Clin Imaging* 24:236, 2000.

95. Barson W, Marcon M: Successful therapy of *Candida albicans* arthritis with a sequential intravenous amphotericin B and oral fluconazole regimen. *Pediatr Infect Dis J* 15:1119, 1996.

96. Ross JJ, et al: Pneumococcal septic arthritis: Review of 190 cases. *Clin Infect Dis* 36:319, 2003.

97. Bardin T: Gonococcal arthritis. *Best Pract Res Clin Rheumatol* 17:201, 2003.

98. Donatto KC: Orthopedic management of pyogenic arthritis. *Compr Ther* 25:411, 1999.

99. Bar-Natan M, et al: Sternoclavicular infectious arthritis in previously healthy adults. *Semin Arthritis Rheum* 32:189, 2002.

100. Ross JJ, Hu LT: Septic arthritis of the pubic symphysis: Review of 100 cases. *Medicine (Baltimore)* 82:340, 2003.

101. Goldstein W, Gleason T, Barmada R: A comparison between arthrotomy and irrigation and multiple aspirations in the treatment of phylogenic arthritis: A histologic study in a rabbit model. *Orthopedics* 6:1309, 1983.

102. Odio CM, et al: Double blind, randomized, placebo-controlled study of dexamethasone therapy for hematogenous septic arthritis in children. *Pediatr Infect Dis J* 22:883, 2003.

CHAPTER

135 Soft Tissue Infections

Harvey W. Meislin and John A. Guisto

OVERVIEW

Soft tissue infections run the gamut from mild superficial infections that require only "tincture of time" to infections that will quickly result in death without immediate diagnosis and resuscitation. Unfortunately, the literature on soft tissue infections is often confusing with respect to definition and therapy, in part because the nomenclature has been based on individual names, anatomic areas, or events (e.g., post-surgical gangrene). The clinical characteristics of soft tissue

Table 135-1. Clinical Characteristics of Soft Tissue Infections

	Cellulitis	Necrotizing Fasciitis	Myonecrosis
Depth	Skin, subcutaneous tissue	Skin, subcutaneous tissue, fascia	Fascia, muscle
Predisposing factors	Trauma, superficial infection	Trauma, surgery, diabetes, deep soft tissue infection	Trauma, surgery, contaminated wounds
Skin	Erythema, lymphatic streaking, mildly swollen	Erythema; may have blebs, bullae, or patches of gangrene; severe swelling	Blanched with massive swelling; hemorrhagic bullae to frank necrosis to gangrene
Gas	No	Variable	Often
Pain	Mild	Moderate	Severe
System toxicity	Mild	Moderate to severe	Severe
Bacteriology	Skin flora, one or more agents	Mixed anaerobic and aerobic	Clostridia, anaerobes, aerobes
Therapy	None to local incision	Wide debridement	Radical excision
Mortality	Low	20-50%	>25%

infections often overlap (Table 135-1) as they evolve from superficial to deep. In addition, the bacteriologic spectrum can change with time, and thus the clinical manifestations, including systemic symptoms, may be altered. A patient does not strictly have to have an abscess, a cellulitis, or a fasciitis, but can have all of them at any time. A good rule of thumb is that the deeper the soft tissue infection is, the more normal the skin surface appears.

CELLULITIS

Perspective

Cellulitis is a soft tissue infection of the skin and subcutaneous tissue usually characterized by erythema, swelling, and tenderness. Cellulitis can be acute, subacute, or, on rare occasions, chronic. Trauma, or breaks in the protective cutaneous skin layer, may be a predisposing cause, but hematogenous and lymphatic dissemination can account for its sudden appearance in previously normal skin.

Principles of Disease and Clinical Features

The signs and symptoms of cellulitis are generally pain or tenderness, erythema that blanches on palpation, swelling of the involved area, and local warmth. Without therapy, it will spread in a radial fashion both distally and proximally with associated swelling. Cellulitis occurs most often in the lower extremities, then upper extremities, and the face. *Staphylococcus aureus* and *Streptococcus pyogenes* are by far the most commonly isolated organisms.[1] In children, *Haemophilus influenzae* may cause facial cellulitis, although anaerobic and oral mucosa flora play a role in facial and orbital cellulitis. Risk factors for cellulitis include lymphedema, a portal of entry, venous insufficiency, and obesity. Interestingly, diabetes mellitus, alcohol misuse, and smoking are not associated with increased risk.[2]

Ludwig's angina is a cellulitis of the submandibular spaces bilaterally. This deep soft tissue infection caused by oral flora may quickly result in respiratory distress by causing swelling and subsequent elevation of the floor of the mouth and the tongue. Odontogenic infection, especially of the second and third lower molars, is the most common origin of Ludwig's angina. Approximately 80% of patients offer a history of recent dental work or tooth pain.[3-5] Cellulitis around the perineum is often due to anaerobes or fecal flora and may spread rapidly through the soft tissues, producing a necrotizing fasciitis. In general, the bacterial cause of cellulitis is a reflection of the bacteria found on the skin or mucous membranes of the anatomic site involved.

Differential Considerations

Other conditions simulate the appearance of bacterial cellulitis, including arthropod and marine envenomation, the inflammatory response to foreign bodies, healing or postsurgical wounds, chemical or thermal burns, septic or inflammatory joints, dermatitis, and the arthritides. Differentiation, especially if the process is early and localized, may be difficult. In nonbacterial cellulitis, the inflammation tends to stay localized and is often less tender to palpation.

In bacterial cellulitis, lymphangitis and local lymphadenopathy may be seen. Fluctuance, if present, signifies abscess formation. Fever is uncommon and should prompt the physician to consider secondary bacteremia or systemic involvement. With local involvement, vital signs, other than a slight tachycardia, are usually normal. Unless there is systemic involvement, white blood cell counts are usually normal or mildly elevated with little or no shift to the left. One exception is *H. influenzae* B in children. This cellulitis is usually associated with high fever and white blood cell counts greater than 15,000/mm^3, with a left shift.[6] Fortunately, the incidence of such infections in children has decreased with the advent of an effective vaccine.

Diagnostic Strategies

Bacterial cultures of material obtained by direct needle aspiration of the area of cellulitis, either in the area of greatest erythema intensity or at the leading edge, are not helpful when no purulence is present. A recent study of needle aspiration of cellulitis indicated that only about 10% of the time is the causative bacteria identified.[7] Blood cultures of patients with cellulitis are also not helpful, except in cases of *H. influenzae* B cellulitis, which are associated with bacteremia in children more than two thirds of the time.[1,8]

Soft tissue radiographs and ultrasonograms may be useful to detect radiopaque foreign bodies, including glass. Computed tomography or magnetic resonance imaging scans are reserved for instances in which deep space infections or abscesses are suspected. For most localized infections, no radiographic procedures are indicated.

Management

The time-honored treatment for cellulitis includes immobilization, elevation, heat or warm moist packs, analgesics, and antibiotics. Studies do not document any difference in morbidity or resolution with this regimen versus the use of antibiotics alone.

When managing a patient with cellulitis, the emergency physician must attempt to identify the cause. Trauma, puncture wounds, breaks in the skin, lymphatic or venous stasis, immunodeficiency, and foreign bodies are all predisposing factors. Hematogenous or contiguous spread from nearby infected tissue is an uncommon cause. Most patients will respond to appropriate oral antimicrobial agents. Cellulitis in the area of edema from venous or lymphatic stasis is often difficult to manage and may need aggressive parenteral antibiotic therapy. Secondary bacterial overgrowth occurs commonly in these circumstances.

Disposition

Localized cellulitis of an extremity in an immunologically intact, afebrile patient can be treated on an outpatient basis with oral antibiotics. Follow-up is indicated within 24 to 48 hours if the erythematous area is not diminishing in size or if fever or systemic symptoms develop. In general, antistaphylococcal agents should be selected for outpatient management (Table 135-2), as such agents will treat the most common skin organisms that cause cellulitis. Inpatient management with parenteral antibiotics and closer observation are indicated in patients with systemic toxicity, and with severe infections involving significant portions of an extremity (particularly the hands and feet), the head and neck, or the perineum. Inpatient management is also often required for adequate treatment of significant cellulitis of the lower limb and hand. Patients whose cellulitis continues to worsen after 48 to 72 hours of appropriate outpatient therapy should be treated with parenteral antibiotics. All patients with cellulitis must be monitored closely to ensure that the process is resolving. Patients who are immunocompromised, including those who are diabetic, alcoholic, on chemotherapy or steroid therapy, asplenic, or at extremes of age require aggressive monitoring and treatment.

Patients do not have a simple cellulitis if they have a fever, hypotension, confusion, crepitus, or bullae formation of the involved soft tissues. These patients may be septic, with infectious seeding to other sites such as

Table 135-2. Oral Therapy of Superficial Soft Tissue Infections

Agent	Dose
Group A *Streptococcus*	
Penicillin V (phenoxymethylpenicillin)	250-500 mg qid
First-generation cephalosporin	250-500 mg qid
Erythromycin	250-500 mg qid
Azithromycin	500 mg × 1 dose then 250 mg qd × 4
Clarithromycin	500 mg bid
***Staphylococcus aureus* (not MRSA*)[+]**	
Dicloxacillin	125-500 mg qid
Cloxacillin	250-500 mg qid
First-generation cephalosporin	250-500 mg qid
Erythromycin (variable effectiveness)	250-500 mg qid
Azithromycin	500 mg × 1 dose then 250 mg qd × 4
Clarithromycin	500 mg bid
Clindamycin	150-450 mg qid
Amoxicillin/clavulanate	875/125 mg bid or 500/125 mg tid
Ciprofloxacin	500 mg bid
Haemophilus influenzae	
Amoxicillin/clavulanate	250-500 mg tid
Cefaclor	250-500 mg tid
Trimethoprim (TMP)/sulfamethoxazole (SMX)	160 mg TMP/800 mg SMX bid
Azithromycin	500 mg × 1 dose then 250 mg qd × 4
Clarithromycin	500 mg bid

*Methicillin-resistant *Staphlococcus aureus*.
[+]Methicillin-resistant strains require treatment with alternate antibiotics such as vancomycin, linezolid, daptomycin, and others. Combination therapies may be necessary. There is no clearly accepted therapy for vancomycin resistant strains; combinations of the above drugs with other antimicrobials may be effective. Single-drug therapy should be avoided to decrease the development of resistance.

blood, bone, lung, solid organs, or brain. They may have deep soft tissue infections necessitating aggressive surgical debridement. If an infection spreads to deeper tissues, either directly or through lymph or blood with distal seeding, the initially localized superficial infection can quickly evolve into a severe systemic illness. Patients with these symptoms should be hospitalized and evaluated for deep soft tissue infections and systemic bacteremia.[9]

SPECIAL TYPES OF CELLULITIS

Periorbital (Preseptal) and Orbital Cellulitis

Perspective

Cellulitis of the central face involving the area of the orbits must be treated aggressively. The venous drainage of that area is through communicating vessels into the brain via the cavernous sinus. Streptococcal species are currently the most common infecting organisms. The incidence of cellulitis from *H. influenzae* has decreased from previous prominence due to the advent of an effective vaccine.[10,11]

Principles of Disease and Clinical Features

Periorbital (preseptal) cellulitis is an infection lying anterior to the orbital septum. It is usually associated with swelling of the eyelid, discoloration of the orbital skin, redness, and warmth. Conjunctival ecchymosis and injection with occasional discharge, fever, and leukocytosis are present. Vision, extraocular movements, pupillary findings, and optometric examination findings are normal.

Orbital cellulitis tends to have similar but more severe symptoms than preseptal cellulitis. Patients with orbital cellulitis may have proptosis, decreased ocular mobility, ocular pain, and tenderness on eye movement. Retro-orbital gas or abscess formation increases the severity of these findings and results in decreased visual acuity; it can be detected with computed tomography or magnetic resonance imaging.

Both orbital and periorbital cellulitis tend to be associated with young age and to be unilateral. Sinusitis is the leading cause, with up to 81% of cases having co-existing sinus infections.[10] Other causes include penetrating or abrading skin trauma, facial fractures, and preexisting vascular or pustular periocular skin infections. Less common causes are chemical agents and dental infections.

Diagnostic Strategies

Differentiation of periorbital (preseptal) from orbital cellulitis is an important clinical decision that affects management and prognosis. If orbital cellulitis is suspected, a computed tomography scan of the orbit is the most useful aid to determine retro-orbital involvement.[12] Sinus and orbital x-ray films tend to be less specific.[13] Causative organisms now are predominantly streptococcus species, but S. aureus, H. influenzae, and anaerobes are also occasionally identified.[10,11] Blood cultures and lumbar punctures are indicated in those patients with high fevers or those showing signs of meningismus or sepsis.

Management

Early periorbital (preseptal) cellulitis may be followed on an outpatient basis for the first 24 to 48 hours of antibiotic therapy, with daily follow-up to determine whether resolution is occurring. A broad-spectrum antistaphylococcal agent will provide appropriate coverage. Treatment for orbital cellulitis includes hospitalization, intravenous antibiotics, and, in some cases, incision and drainage. Up to 50% of more serious infections require surgery. Indications include clinical deterioration on antibiotics, the presence of a foreign body as the cause of the infection, and the presence of an abscess.[13,14] Broad-spectrum antibiotic coverage of H. influenzae, S. aureus, S. pyogenes, and anaerobes is indicated.[4,12]

Streptococcal Cellulitis

Principles of Disease and Clinical Features

Streptococcal cellulitis, often termed *ascending cellulitis*, is usually seen after surgery or trauma but can occur with no predisposing event. The cause may be as subtle as a break in the skin around the web of the fingers or toes. Ascending cellulitis usually progresses rapidly with prominent lymphangitic streaking and a swollen extremity. Untreated patients can quickly become toxic.

Management

Treatment includes the use of an antistreptococcal agent along with elevation of the involved extremity and warm soaks.

Erysipelas

Principles of Disease and Clinical Features

Erysipelas is an acute superficial cellulitis characterized by a sharply demarcated border surrounding skin that is raised, deeply erythematous, indurated, and painful. It usually involves the dermis, lymphatics, and most of the superficial subcutaneous tissue. Erysipelas most often occurs in the very young and in 50- to 60-year-olds and is associated with small breaks in the skin, nephrotic syndrome, and postoperative wounds. Patients usually appear toxic, with a prodrome of fever, chills, and malaise preceding the eruption of a bright red cellulitis predominantly on the lower extremities or on the face. Streptococci are the predominant pathogenic organism in erysipelas, including S. pyogenes (58-67%), S. agalactiae (3-9%), and S. dysgalactiae (14-25%). Other bacteria are also found in some patients, such as S. aureus, Pseudomonas, and enterobacteria. The leg is involved in erysipelas 90% of the time, but the arm (5%), the face (2.5%), and the thigh can also be involved.[15]

Management

Treatment of erysipelas includes elevation of the infected part, treatment of the portal of entry, if any, and antibiotic therapy. Penicillin G continues to be a standard treatment, but amoxicillin can also be used for 10 to 20 days. Macrolides, cephalosporins, and fluoroquinolones have been shown to be more effective but should be reserved for complicated cases.[15]

Staphylococcal Cellulitis

Principles of Disease and Clinical Features

Staphylococcus aureus produces various toxins that result in local and systemic effects. Tissue invasion, blister formation, and inflammation are caused by toxins such as alpha toxin, hyaluronidase, fibrinolysin, various proteases, and pyrogenic toxin superantigens.[16] Staphylococcal cellulitis is usually an indolent infection. The patient often appears less toxic than with streptococcal cellulitis, and the lesions usually appear more localized and are more likely to result in the formation of an abscess.

Management

Antistaphylococcal agents are indicated, along with heat, immobilization, elevation, and incision and drainage if an abscess is present.

Staphylococcal Scalded Skin Syndrome

Principles of Disease and Clinical Features

Staphylococcal scalded skin syndrome, also called staphylococcal epidermal necrolysis, is caused by an exfoliative toxin produced by phage group II, type 71 staphylococci. This toxin acts on the zona granulosa of the skin to produce a superficial separation that results in widespread painful erythema and blistering of the skin. The syndrome usually occurs in children between the ages of 6 months and 6 years. The mortality rate is approximately 3% in children but reaches 50% in adults and up to 100% in adults with underlying systemic disease.[17,18] Mucous membranes are usually not involved. Nikolsky's sign, the easy separation of the outer portion of the epidermis from the basal layer when pressure is exerted, is often present. The skin lesion is characterized by the formation of bullae and vesicles leading to the loss of large sheets of superficial epidermis. The resultant appearance is that of scalded skin.

Differential Considerations

The primary differential diagnosis is toxic epidermal necrolysis. Toxic epidermal necrolysis is a full-thickness epidermal necrosis that starts on acral sites and involves mucous membranes. There is also usually a history of drug ingestion with toxic epidermal necrolysis, and Nikolsky's sign is positive only on the lesions. In staphylococcal scalded skin syndrome, unaffected skin also has a positive Nikolsky's sign. Staphylococcal scalded skin syndrome usually responds to antibiotics. Toxic epidermal necrolysis has no curative treatment and is associated with up to a 50% rate of mortality.[19]

Diagnostic Strategies

The diagnosis is based on clinical, histologic, and microbiologic findings, including (1) a clinical pattern of tenderness, erythema, desquamation, or bullae formation; (2) histopathologic evidence of intraepidermal cleavage through the stratum granulosum; (3) isolation of an exfoliative exotoxin producing S. aureus, and (4) the absence of pemphigus foliaceus by immunofluorescence.[19] Blister fluid and the skin are usually sterile because this syndrome is toxin generated. S. aureus may be cultured from mucous membrane sites such as the oral and nasal cavity.

Management

Treatment of staphylococcal scalded skin syndrome includes adequate hydration, management of fluid and electrolyte balance, and treatment with systemic antibiotics such as a penicillinase-resistant penicillin.[16]

Haemophilus influenzae Cellulitis

Principles of Disease and Clinical Features

Haemophilus influenzae cellulitis is usually seen in children younger than 5 years of age and occurs primarily on the face or the extremities. The skin often appears red with a violaceous tinge.[20] The patient appears acutely ill, often with a high fever, a white blood cell count greater than 15,000, and a high incidence (75-90%) of positive blood cultures. With widespread H. influenzae B immunization, there has been a dramatic decrease in the incidence of H. influenzae skin infections.

Management

Treatment is parenteral antibiotics with a second- or third-generation cephalosporin followed by ampicillin/clavulanic acid for a total of 10 to 14 days.[20]

Gram-Negative and Anaerobic Cellulitis

Gram-negative and anaerobic cellulitis usually occur in the immunocompromised patient. Cellulitis is seen most often around mucous membranes, primarily the perineum and in chronic wounds that are not kept clean and thus become superinfected. The diagnosis requires culturing the causative organism. Aggressive debridement and broad-spectrum antimicrobial coverage are indicated.

TOXIC SHOCK SYNDROME

Staphylococcal Toxic Shock Syndrome

Perspective

Toxic shock syndrome often occurs in menstruating women who use vaginal tampons. Although prevalent in the early 1980s, the incidence of toxic shock syndrome has decreased remarkably since highly absorbent tampons were withdrawn from the market. Today, toxic shock syndrome occurs in patients of both sexes who have focal soft tissue staphylococcal infections; nonmenstrual causes are more prevalent.

BOX 135-1. Toxic Shock Syndrome: Criteria for Diagnosis

Fever of 38.9° C (102° F) or higher

Rash (diffuse macular erythema) that resembles the rash of scarlet fever

Desquamation of skin 1 to 2 weeks after onset of disease

Hypotension (systolic blood pressure less than 90 mm Hg, orthostatic drop of 15 mm Hg or more, or orthostatic dizziness of syncope)

Clinical or laboratory abnormalities in at least three organ systems:

Gastrointestinal: nausea and vomiting, diarrhea

Muscular: myalgia or creatine phosphokinase at least two times normal level

Mucous membrane: vaginal, oropharyngeal, or conjunctival hyperemia

Renal: blood urea nitrogen or creatinine level at least twice normal or pyuria greater than five cells per high-power field

Hepatic: bilirubin, serum transaminases at least twice normal level

Hematologic: thrombocytopenia, <100,000/mm^3

Neurologic: disorientation or altered consciousness without focal findings

Reasonable evidence for the absence of other cause of illness

Principles of Disease and Clinical Features

In menstruating women with toxic shock syndrome, *S. aureus* is isolated more than 90% of the time. The clinical manifestations are mainly due to the exfoliative exotoxin produced by *S. aureus*. This is the same exotoxin produced in bullous impetigo, but toxic shock syndrome results from systemic circulating exotoxin, whereas the localized blistering in bullous impetigo is caused by a direct *S. aureus* inoculum. The exotoxin in both cases has exquisite specificity in causing loss of desmosome-mediated cell adhesion within the superficial epidermis only.[19] Other clinical features include fever, a "sunburn/sandpaper" rash, hypotension, and abnormalities in at least three organ systems. Mucosal inflammation, myalgia, profuse watery diarrhea, and changes in mental status are common (Box 135-1). Differential diagnosis includes Rocky Mountain spotted fever, streptococcal scarlet fever, Kawasaki syndrome, and leptospirosis.[16]

Management

Treatment includes aggressive fluid resuscitation and the use of α- and β-adrenergic vasoactive agents to maintain blood pressure and urinary output. Intravenous antibiotics that cover for penicillinase-producing staphylococci, such as nafcillin or oxacillin, should be used. However, clindamycin and vancomycin are acceptable for patients who are allergic to penicillin. Tampons and foreign bodies must be removed, focal areas of infection drained, and mucous membranes and other sources cultured for the offending pathogen.

Streptococcal Toxic Shock Syndrome

Perspective

Streptococcus has long been known to cause invasive infections. Previously, these infections occurred most commonly in patients with compromised immune systems. Since the mid-1980s, however, a streptococcal toxic shock–like syndrome has been described in otherwise healthy patients with serious soft tissue infections. Streptococcal toxic shock syndrome was first described by Cone in 1987 when he reported two cases of shock due to isolated *S. pyogenes* soft tissue infections and postulated a toxin responsible for the shock state.[21] Stevens further characterized the syndrome in 1989 as involving otherwise healthy young patients who presented in shock or progressed to a shock state within 4 hours of admission.[22] These facts seem to indicate an increased virulence of group A β-hemolytic *Streptococcus*. Also, although these cases are predominantly caused by Lancefield group A strains, other groups have also been shown to cause streptococcal toxic shock syndrome.[23]

Principles of Disease and Clinical Features

The route of pathogen entry is unknown in up to 50% of cases, with others related to surgery, minor nonpenetrating trauma resulting in hematoma or muscle strain, skin superinfection, or viral infections.[24] In children, streptococcal toxic shock syndrome most commonly follows chickenpox.[23] There is also an association with the use of nonsteroidal anti-inflammatory drugs, which may mask presenting symptoms, resulting in delayed presentation and increased severity of disease.

Patients commonly present with pain, which is severe, is abrupt in onset, and may be present prior to the onset of tenderness or other physical findings. Though usually in an extremity, the pain may mimic pelvic inflammatory disease, pneumonia, acute myocardial infarction, peritonitis, or pericarditis. A minority of patients will present with influenza-like symptoms of fever, chills, myalgias, and diarrhea.

Fever is the most common presenting physical sign. However, if shock is present, the patient may be hypothermic. Tachycardia and hypotension are also frequent signs. Most patients also have evidence of soft tissue infection: swelling, erythema, bullae, or tenderness. A scarlet fever–like rash is commonly seen (Box 135-2).[24]

These patients often have renal and respiratory failure. The hemodynamic compromise seen in affected patients suggests a cardiotoxic effect of the streptococcal toxins, resulting in normal to low cardiac output, normal systemic vascular resistance, and a reduced left ventricular stroke work index.[25] Mortality ranges from 33% to 81%.[26]

The virulence of these infections is attributed to surface proteins, toxin production, and host factors. Streptococcal strains that produce M protein seem to be associated with overwhelming infection. M protein binds to complement control factors and other host proteins to prevent activation of the alternate complement pathway and thus evade phagocytosis and killing by polymorphonuclear neutrophil leukocytes. Extracellular toxins, including superantigenic streptococcal pyrogenic exotoxins, contribute to tissue invasion and initiate the cytokine storm believed to be responsible for illnesses such as necrotizing fasciitis and the highly lethal streptococcal toxic shock syndrome.[27] The toxins act as superantigens to activate a large population of T cells, bypassing the antigen presentation phase and liberating massive amounts of cytokines, tumor necrosis factor α, interleukin-1, and interleukin-6. These cytokines induce the clinical signs of fever, hypotension, shock, rash, and ultimately multiorgan failure.[28] Lack of host antibodies to the surface proteins and toxins will predispose to infection and increased virulence.

Differential Considerations

Differential diagnosis includes staphylococcal toxic shock syndrome and gram-negative sepsis. Patients with staphylococcus infection are unlikely to show cutaneous involvement or extremity pain, may demonstrate a "strawberry tongue," rarely have soft tissue destruction, and have a lower incidence of bacteremia. Endotoxic shock is differentiated by high cardiac output with lowered systemic vascular resistance and a left ventricular stroke work index that is not reduced.

Diagnostic Strategies

A creatinine level greater than 2.5 mg/dL indicates renal involvement, which may precede hypotension. Serum creatine kinase correlates well with deep soft tissue involvement, and increasing values may indicate necrotizing fasciitis or myositis ("flesh-eating bacteria").

Other laboratory test abnormalities include hypoalbuminemia, hypocalcemia, and a sometimes mild leukocytosis with prominent "left shift." Platelets and hematocrit may be initially normal but drop within 48 hours and may be associated with disseminated intravascular coagulation. Blood cultures are positive 60% of the time, and wound cultures are positive in 95% of cases.[29]

Management

Patients with streptococcal toxic shock syndrome require hospitalization for care, usually initially into an intensive care setting. Even with appropriate antibiotic therapy and intensive supportive care, the mortality rate for this disease is 30% to 70%.

It is often difficult to determine initially whether *Streptococcus* or *Staphylococcus* is the offending bacterium, so coverage for both is necessary. Suggested regimens include penicillin plus clindamycin, erythromycin, or ceftriaxone plus clindamycin. Penicillin is only moderately effective against the large inoculum of slow-growing *Streptococcus* seen in necrotizing fasciitis or myositis. A recent retrospective study confirms that clindamycin may work better than β-lactams for streptococcal toxic shock syndrome.[30] Drugs like clindamycin seem to work by two mechanisms: (1) by more effective killing of *S. pyogenes* organisms; (2) by decreasing production of extracellular products that play a role in the pathogenesis of systemic toxicity and/or tissue destruction. Because clindamycin-resistant strains of *S. pyogenes* have been reported in some localities, the presumptive selection of a combination of clindamycin and a β-lactam antibiotic would be prudent in the initial treatment of invasive streptococcal disease.[30] Early surgical debridement may be lifesaving, and consultation is appropriate as soon as the possible need for surgical intervention is considered.

Intravenous γ-globulin remains experimental despite some reports of success. γ-Globulin preparations contain antibodies to staphylococcal toxins with some cross-reactivity to streptococcal toxins. A recent comparative observational study showed a benefit for intravenous immunoglobulin in the treatment of streptococcal toxic shock syndrome. Dosing was 2 g/kg, repeated 48 hours later if the patient was unstable.[31] A randomized controlled trial showed a trend toward decreased mortality for the arm treated with IVIG, but the study had to be stopped before significance was reached owing to slow enrollment. Dosing in that study was 1 g/kg on day 1, and 0.5 g/kg on days 2 and 3.[32]

Currently, antibiotic prophylaxis is not recommended for household contacts of patients with this disease, although contact with an infected person increases carrier rates in the young.[23,33] Elderly people are at increased risk for invasive disease after an infectious contact.[34]

IMPETIGO

Perspective

Impetigo is a superficial infection of the skin caused by group A β-hemolytic *Streptococcus* and occasionally coagulase-positive *S. aureus*. There are two distinct subtypes: impetigo contagiosa and bullous impetigo.[35,36] Impetigo is communicable and is the most common cutaneous childhood infection.[37] Most cases occur in late summer and early fall, and the incidence is higher in tropical climates.

Principles of Disease and Clinical Features

Insect bites, flies, and infected abrasions play a role in the nonbullous form of impetigo.[35] The pathogenesis and epidemiology of this infection are a mystery in that inoculation of normal skin does not produce clinical disease. During outbreaks of impetigo, streptococci usually appear on normal skin several days before spreading to the nose or throat. In contrast, *Staphylococcus* colonization of the nose and throat takes place before the development of skin lesions. Streptococci found on the skin are not the same subtype as those that infect the pharynx.[36]

The lesions of impetigo contagiosa begin as tiny papules that rapidly develop into vesicles, which quickly progress to pustules that rupture and crust over within 24 hours. The lesions are usually painless but often are pruritic and may coalesce.[35,36] The crusts are usually thick, amber colored, and crumbly. Cultures of early vesicles, pustules, or crusts usually yield β-hemolytic streptococci and occasionally *S. aureus*. After the fifth or sixth day, the crusts become thicker and reddish brown. The lesions tend to extend in size, clearing centrally. Lesions are most commonly seen on the legs, with the arms, face, and trunk less commonly affected. Regional lymphadenopathy is common, lymphadenitis is rare, and fever is not usually present.[37]

Bullous impetigo is most commonly seen in neonates. It starts as a small vesicle that quickly enlarges into a bulla, often 2 to 5 cm in diameter. When a bulla ruptures, it leaves a red base with a varnish-like thin crust and scales. Satellite lesions are frequently seen. Nikolsky's sign is not present, and the patient is not toxic.[38] Bullous impetigo occurs most commonly on the face and trunk. Regional lymphadenitis is rare. These lesions generally heal faster than those of impetigo contagiosa.

Differential Considerations

Impetigo of Bockhart is a superficial staphylococcal folliculitis consisting of clusters of small pustules surrounding hair follicles.[39]

Ecthyma is closely related to impetigo, except that the infection is usually deeper and heals with scarring. The lesions of ecthyma are usually on the legs and begin as a vesicle that ruptures to form a shallow ulcer. Causative organisms are group A β-hemolytic *Streptococcus* and rarely *S. aureus*. Treatment is 10 to 14 days of penicillin or topical mupirocin.

Diagnostic Strategies

The diagnosis is usually made clinically, since bacteria are usually not seen in the Gram stain of vesicular fluid. Certain strains of streptococci are nephritogenic. Poststreptococcal glomerulonephritis is more likely to follow streptococcal pharyngitis than impetigo. In contrast, acute rheumatic fever is not a consequence of impetigo.[36] Although serologic findings in streptococcal pyoderma may show increases in antibodies to various streptococcal antigens, primarily anti-DNAase B and antihyaluronidase, the serologic response as measured by antistreptolysin O is usually poor.[36] The streptozyme test, which measures several streptococcal antibodies, often gives false-negative results.[36]

Management

Soaks and wet dressings have not proven useful in treating impetigo. Topical antimicrobial agents such as hexachlorophene or povidone-iodine scrubs or washes are of limited usefulness and may result in the development of satellite lesions.[37] Although various topical antibiotics, including neomycin, bacitracin, polymyxin, erythromycin, and oxytetracycline, have resulted in some improvement of impetigo, topical antibiotics alone or in combination with hexachlorophene have proven ineffective in treating impetigo in military populations. Mupirocin ointment 2% is an effective alternative regimen. Other topical antibiotics may alter antibiotic resistance patterns. The addition of topical steroids to topical antibiotic agents does not improve outcome.

Systemic antibiotics are clearly superior to topical antibiotics for treating impetigo contagiosa, except for mupirocin. Oral erythromycin and phenoxymethyl penicillin are used most commonly. First-generation cephalosporins are also effective, as is clindamycin (see Table 135-2). In some studies, intramuscular benzathine penicillin G is more effective than oral phenoxymethyl penicillin or erythromycin. Although cultures of early lesions often grow only *Streptococcus*, older lesions may yield *Staphylococcus*. *Streptococcus* seems to be the prime infecting agent, with *Staphylococcus* as a secondary invader. Treatment of impetigo with systemic and topical antibiotics does not prevent poststreptococcal glomerulonephritis, although it clears lesions quickly, reduces local extension and complications such as adenitis, and prevents spread to other individuals.[35]

In cases of bullous impetigo, some topical antibiotic preparations, such as gentamicin and a mixture of polymyxin, neomycin, and bacitracin, are as effective as a combination of oral and intramuscular benzathine penicillin G. Antistaphylococcal agents such as oral cephalosporins and semisynthetic penicillins are usually very effective. In most cases, for a solitary lesion or just a few lesions, a topical antibiotic alone is reasonable therapy.[36]

ABSCESSES

Simple Cutaneous Abscesses

Perspective

A cutaneous abscess is a localized collection of pus resulting in a painful fluctuant soft tissue mass surrounded by firm granulation tissue and erythema. Abscesses occur in all areas of the body. Approximately

20% occur in the head and neck region, 25% in the axillae, 18% in the extremities, 25% in the perirectal area, and 15% in the inguinal area.[40] Most patients complain of pain and the presence of a tender fluctuant mass. Although abscesses may be associated with localized erythema and lymphangitis, the presence of fever or systemic toxicity suggest the possibility of deeper tissue involvement or systemic bacteremia.[40]

Principles of Disease and Clinical Features

The cause of localized abscesses depends on the anatomic region involved.[41] Abscesses on the extremities tend to be associated with interruptions of the integrity of the protective epithelial layer of the skin caused by minor traumas such as cuts, abrasions, or needle punctures. Abscesses of the head, neck, and perineal regions tend to be associated with obstruction of the apocrine sweat glands.[42,43] The incidence of these abscesses increases in adults because the apocrine and sebaceous glands become active after puberty. Perirectal abscesses arise from bacterial spread from the anal crypts. Vulvovaginal abscesses usually result from obstruction of the Bartholin gland duct. Pilonidal abscesses are caused by plugging of small tears in the skin, usually by hairs around the buttock crease.[44]

Although most abscesses contain bacteria, approximately 5% of abscesses, especially those associated with parenteral drug abuse, are sterile.[40] Clinically, sterile abscesses cannot be differentiated from bacterial abscesses. *Eikenella corrodens* is a microbe often seen with head and neck abscesses associated with intravenous drug abuse.[45] The bacteria in cutaneous abscesses generally reflect the skin flora of the anatomic area of the body that is involved (Table 135-3). Anaerobic bacteria, which are known to be part of the normal flora of the skin and mucous membranes, outnumber aerobes 10 to 1 in the oral cavity and 1000 to 1 in the distal colon.[46,47] Most abscesses that originate from mucous membranes (e.g., perioral, perirectal) tend to be predominately anaerobic. Bacteria from abscesses in areas more remote from the rectum are primarily constituents of the microflora of the skin. *S. aureus* is the most prevalent aerobe found in abscesses that originate from the skin, yet it is isolated in less than one third of cutaneous abscesses and one half of axillary abscesses.[48] *S. aureus* is not commonly associated with abscesses that originate from mucous membranes (i.e., perirectal, vulvovaginal).[40,48] *Bacteroides fragilis* is one of the few anaerobes resistant to penicillin.[49] Although it is the most common gram-negative anaerobic species in human feces, it is found in fewer than 50% of perineal abscesses.[40] This pathogen, which produces β-lactamase, has been associated with more than 50% of intra-abdominal infections. *Escherichia coli* and *Neisseria gonorrheae* are rarely found in cutaneous abscesses from any location.

Differential Considerations

Although the development of an abscess is usually an isolated event, recurrent abscesses in the perineal and lower abdominal area may signify the presence of inflammatory bowel disease. Recurring abscesses in the axillae and inguinal areas may represent hidradenitis suppurativa. Finally, recurring abscesses may be associated with immunocompromise such as occurs with neoplasm, corticosteroid therapy, chemotherapy, diabetes mellitus, acquired immunodeficiency syndrome, leukemia, vascular insufficiency, trauma, or thermal injury.

Diagnostic Strategies

Ultrasonography is a useful technique to localize subcutaneous and intramuscular abscesses as well as foreign bodies that are not radiopaque.[50]

The examination of Gram stain of material from cutaneous abscesses allows a quick identification of the morphotype of the offending pathogen. In general, the Gram stain shows one of three patterns: (1) white blood cells without bacteria, which indicates a sterile abscess; (2) a mixed pattern of gram-positive and gram-negative rods and cocci of varied morphotypes, which indicates

Table 135-3. Bacterial Characterization of 135 Outpatient Abscesses

Anatomic Areas	Abscesses (Number)	Percent of Total Cultures	Types of Bacterial Growth (% from Each Area)				Bacterial Species per Abscess*	
			No Growth	Aerobes Only	Anaerobes Only	Aerobes and Anaerobes	Aerobes (Average No.)	Anaerobes (Average No.)
Head and neck	25	19	4	28	20	48	1	2
Trunk	11	8	0	45	18	36	1	2
Axilla	22	16	0	55	5	41	1	1
Extremity	16	12	19	44	13	25	1	1
Hand	8	6	25	63	0	13	2	0
Inguinal	7	5	0	29	57	14	0	3
Vulvovaginal	13	10	0	15	46	38	1	3
Buttock	12	9	0	33	33	33	1	3
Perirectal	21	16	0	0	33	67	1	5

*Cultures with no growth were excluded.
From Meislin HW, et al: Cutaneous abscesses: Anaerobic and aerobic bacteriology and outpatient management. *Ann Intern Med* 87:145, 1997.

mixed aerobic and anaerobic infection; and (3) gram-positive cocci in grapelike clusters, diagnostic of *S. aureus* infection.[40]

Management

The treatment of cutaneous abscesses is incision and drainage. Several studies confirm that antibiotics are not indicated in patients with normal host defenses.[1,40,51] Thus, a Gram stain and culture are also unnecessary in these patients. In the immunosuppressed patient, Gram stain, culture, and antibiotics are indicated. The selection of antibiotics is guided by (1) the flora anticipated at the location of the abscess, (2) the Gram stain results, (3) the presence of a feculent odor that is indicative of anaerobes, and (4) culture and sensitivity findings (see Table 135-2).[40,48] Incision and drainage are generally painful because local anesthetics are less effective in inflamed acidic locations. The use of parenteral or regional analgesia may be indicated in addition to a local anesthetic agent. Nitrous oxide is an option, especially in a self-administered 50% concentration. The incision should be deep enough into the abscess cavity to ensure adequate drainage. Elliptical incisions are preferred by some to prevent premature closure of the cutaneous surface. The cavity should be gently curetted to free all loculated areas of pus, and the cavity should be irrigated. A loose packing should be removed within 48 hours or within 24 hours in cosmetically important areas such as the face. Once the packing is removed, warm soaks are recommended three or four times a day for 10 to 15 minutes for 2 to 3 days.[40,52]

Furuncle

A furuncle usually evolves from a superficial folliculitis. It is a deep inflammatory nodule surrounded by an intense local tissue reaction. The abscess tends to be very thin walled, and purulence is present. Skin flora (*S. aureus*, streptococci) are usually isolated.

Carbuncle

A carbuncle is an extensive process of interconnecting deep abscesses that extend into subcutaneous tissues. The microbes are usually aerobic; however, *Pseudomonas aeruginosa* may be present in chronic cases. Predisposing factors include folliculitis, blood dyscrasias, steroids, heavy perspiration, obesity, diabetes, and skin location, such as areas of friction (e.g., the back of the neck).

Hidradenitis Suppurativa

Perspective

Hidradenitis suppurativa is a disease consisting of chronic suppurative abscesses in the apocrine sweat glands. One in 300 adults is affected, usually after puberty and before the age of 40. It may be more common in females and blacks, and perianal occurrence is twice as common in males.[42,43] Inflammation begins deep within the acinus or convoluted tubules of the sweat glands as a result of obstruction to apocrine glandular secretions. Additional predisposing factors include obesity, poor hygiene, excessive perspiration, shaving, and irritating deodorants.[53] The axillary location is more common than inguinal and perianal.

Principles of Disease and Clinical Features

In most cases, the disease manifests as episodic occurrences of one or more painful subcutaneous nodules, associated with burning, itching, local cellulitis, swelling, and a malodorous discharge.[52] These nodules drain spontaneously or are surgically incised with drainage of scant pus. Resolution usually occurs within a few days. In some patients, however, the disease tends to be chronic and extensive, with multiple abscesses, sinus tracts, and fistulas. These often heal with hypertropic scars and may result in a tender, unsightly area.

Staphylococcus aureus, *S. viridans*, and common skin anaerobes are commonly isolated. Chronic disease often results in overgrowth with fecal flora in the perineum and *Proteus* with other mixed aerobes and anaerobes in the axilla.[52]

Differential Considerations

Hidradenitis suppurativa must be differentiated from a simple cutaneous abscess of the axillary region or perianal and perirectal abscesses. This differentiation is usually accomplished by noting the chronicity of the process, the multiplicity of abscesses, and the lack of involvement with the rectal mucosa.

Management

Although clindamycin may provide temporary recession of the disease, the almost inevitable recurrence makes surgery the definitive therapy.[53] Incision and drainage usually suffice in an acute situation. Sinus tracts and fistulas should be unroofed, all loculations excised, and all purulence and necrotic tissue evacuated. Antibiotic coverage is usually unnecessary in patients with normal host defenses and without soft tissue involvement. Chronic or extensive disease often requires extensive surgical removal of all hair-bearing skin in the apocrine gland areas. Coverage requires either primary closure, rotated skin flaps, or grafting.[53] Although rare, the most serious complication of hidradenitis suppurativa is squamous cell carcinoma, so pathologic examination of surgical specimens is recommended.[54] Routine colostomy in patients undergoing surgical treatment of perineal disease is usually not necessary, as long as aggressive wound care is instituted. Patients who might benefit from fecal diversion are those in whom proper wound care is not feasible, and those patients suffering from concomitant Crohn's disease and hidradenitis suppurativa.[42,43]

Hidradenitis suppurativa has been associated with social, personal, and vocational difficulties because of the chronic, uncomfortable, malodorous, and unsightly nature of the disease. Early referral for surgical obliter-

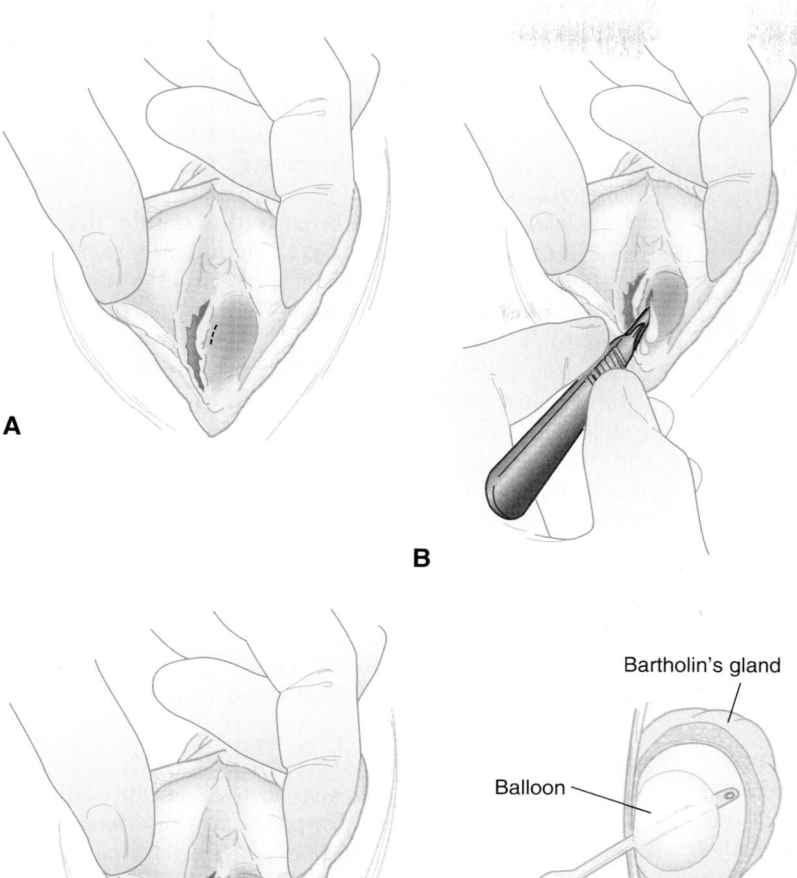

Figure 135-1. Incision and drainage of Bartholin's abscess. **A**, Local anesthetic is injected into the mucosal surface of the abscess and the mucocutaneous junction of the labia minora. **B**, A 1-cm incision is made on the mucosal surface. **C** and **D**, The Word catheter is inserted and the balloon inflated with 5 mL normal saline solution. (From Campbell CJ: Incision and drainage of Bartholin's cyst. In Rosen P, et al [eds]: *Atlas of Emergency Procedures*. St. Louis, Mosby, 2001.)

A

B

Bartholin's gland

Balloon

Cyst

Word catheter

C

D

ation of the apocrine glands should be considered in these patients.

Bartholin Cyst Abscess

Principles of Disease and Clinical Features

A Bartholin cyst abscess is caused by an obstructed Bartholin duct. The flora is usually a mixture of aerobic and anaerobic flora from the vagina, with *Chlamydia trachomatis* and *Neisseria gonorrheae* cultured approximately 10% of the time.[40,55] The patient usually has a painful cystic mass on the inferior lateral margin of the vaginal introitus. Signs and symptoms are usually localized, but septic shock can occur in rare cases.[56]

Management

Abscesses should be drained from the mucosal rather than the cutaneous surface. Simple incision and drainage carries a high risk of recurrence, so the cavity should be packed open. The Word catheter is a 10-Fr balloon catheter designed specifically for this purpose and is both convenient to use and highly successful. After incision and drainage, the catheter is inserted and

inflated with 2 to 5 mL of water or saline (Figure 135-1). The catheter should be left in place for 4 to 6 weeks so that a sinus will have time to form. Sitz baths will help keep the area clean and draining. Marsupialization is a more complex treatment option, involving incision and drainage of the cavity followed by suturing of the walls of the cyst to the skin.

Perirectal Abscess

Principles of Disease and Clinical Features

Perirectal abscesses originate in the anal crypts and extend through the ischiorectal space via fistulous tracts into nearby fatty tissue or perimuscular locations.[57,58] Often, however, the fistulous tracts that connect the abscess site to the anal crypts cannot be traced directly. Patients have pain in the anal region with a tender mass that may be indurated, fluctuant, or draining. There is usually pain on defecation or with sitting or walking.

Perirectal abscesses occur primarily in adult men, although occasionally they are found in pediatric patients. Specific causes or predisposing factors asso-

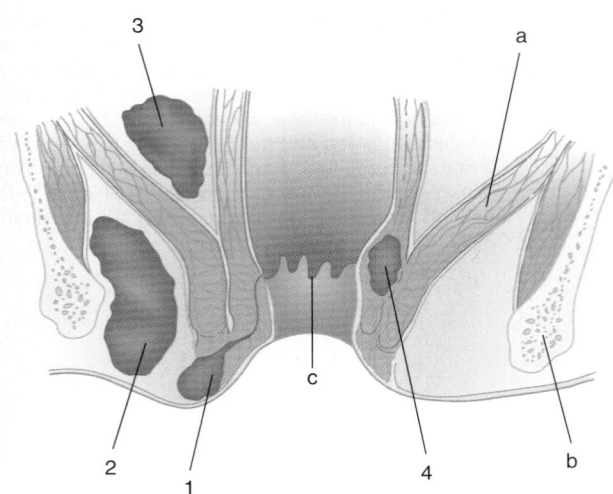

Figure 135-2. Perirectal abscesses: levator ani (a), ischial tuberosity (b), anal crypts (c), perianal abscess with anal fistula (1), ischiorectal abscess (2), supralevator ani (pelvirectal) abscess (3), intersphincteric abscess (4).

ciated with the development of anorectal abscesses include malignancy (especially hematologic malignancies), immunocompromised host, tuberculosis, actinomycosis, Crohn's disease, anal fissure, foreign body, and anorectal trauma.[57] Fecal flora are causative. The predominant anaerobe is *Bacteroides fragilis*, although most abscesses tend to have mixed anaerobic and aerobic flora.[40,48] Children, unlike adults, demonstrate *Escherichia coli* as a causative pathogen.

Management

The use of antibiotics remains controversial. When there are signs of systemic involvement, such as cellulitis, fever, or leukocytosis, antibiotics are indicated.[58] One should provide coverage for anaerobes and gram-negative fecal flora before incision and drainage to prevent bacteremia, especially in patients with a history of valvular heart disease or immunocompromise. Postoperative management includes the use of stool softeners, sitz baths, and frequent dressing changes for several days until the incision is healed. Perirectal abscesses are usually classified into four types (Figure 135-2).

Perianal Abscess

A perianal abscess is a tender swollen fluctuant mass in the superficial subcutaneous tissue just adjacent to the anus. The patient is usually afebrile, and the process is localized. The treatment is an incision made in a radial direction from the anal opening. If the abscess is extensive or a fistula is identified, the patient should be referred to have the fistulous channel excised and unroofed on an elective basis.

Ischiorectal Abscess

An ischiorectal abscess is an infection extending across the external sphincter into the ischiorectal space below

the levator ani. Infection may spread superiorly, producing a high abscess that may be difficult to diagnose even when very large, because it produces little change in the anorectal skin area. Intrarectal ultrasonography appears promising in the diagnosis of complex perirectal abscesses.[59]

Low abscesses tend to burrow down into the fatty tissue between the rectum and ischial tuberosity and produce a perirectal abscess. Perirectal abscesses produce tenderness and bulging, with shiny skin lateral to the anus.

Incision and drainage can be performed on an outpatient basis if the abscess points to the perirectal skin area and the patient is not toxic. If the abscess is large and does not point to the skin or if the patient is toxic, drainage should be performed in the operating theater. These large abscesses must be differentiated from a more extensive fasciitis. High abscesses can be drained only with an incision made deep into the ischiorectal space. Ischiorectal abscesses may burrow into the posterior rectal space, penetrating to the opposite side to form a "horseshoe abscess." These are drained in the operative setting with multiple incisions.

Pelvirectal Abscess

Pelvirectal abscesses are also known as supralevator abscesses. They form in or spread to the space above the levator ani muscle. These abscesses can result from pelvic inflammatory disease, diverticulitis, or ruptured appendicitis. They are often difficult to diagnose because clinical signs are nonspecific: rectal pain, fever, leukocytosis, and back pain.[60] Endoscopy or barium enema may reveal a bulge in the rectal mucosa. Pelvirectal abscesses are drained in the operating room through an intra-anal incision rather than through the ischiorectal space.

Intersphincteric Abscess

Intersphincteric abscesses are often seen as a tender bulge of the rectal mucosa. Incision and drainage are made through a mucosal incision in the distal rectum under general or spinal anesthesia. It may be difficult to differentiate an intersphincteric (submucous) abscess from a high ischiorectal or a supralevator abscess.

Pilonidal Abscess

Principles of Disease and Clinical Features

Pilonidal abscesses usually occur in the gluteal fold overlying the coccyx. They result from a minor disruption of the epithelium, with formation of a small pit. Squamous epithelia gradually line this cavity, which then plugs with hair or keratin, thus preventing drainage and promoting abscess formation.[44,61] These abscesses contain a combination of skin and perineal flora.[40,48] Pilonidal cysts occur more often in men and in dark-skinned or hirsute individuals.[62] Patients complain of tenderness in the gluteal fold. Inspection reveals a tender nodule that is often fluctuant. The process tends to be localized without systemic symptoms.

Management

Treatment is incision and drainage, although opinions differ regarding the advisability of a simple incision and drainage versus complete excision of the involved tissue. It is reasonable to incise and drain any pilonidal abscess that is acutely fluctuant, with subsequent referral for more definitive excision if the process tends to be deep or if sinus tracts are present. All hair or keratin plugs must be removed. Recurrence rates after simple drainage range from 10% to 90%. Recurrences take place because of remaining granulation tissue, development of new pits, or the formation of new sinuses. Chronic disease is common and often necessitates inpatient surgical removal of the cysts, sinuses, and granulation tissue. Primary closure or cryosurgery has also been advocated.[62]

Fasciitis

Principles of Disease and Clinical Features

Fasciitis is an infection of the fascia, subcutaneous tissue, and skin. Erythema, marked edema, and sometimes, areas of gangrene occur (see Table 135-1). Much confusion has surrounded the nomenclature of these necrotizing infections because they have been named for specific bacteria (e.g., hemolytic streptococcal gangrene), after individuals (e.g., Meleney's synergistic gangrene), by anatomic appearance (e.g., necrotizing fasciitis), and for specific circumstances (e.g., postoperative progressive bacterial gangrene). By definition, fasciitis does not involve muscle, but it can spread to invade underlying muscle, causing myonecrosis. Patients with fasciitis manifest moderate to severe systemic toxicity, often out of proportion to the cutaneous findings, with high fever, tachycardia, anxiety, disorientation, and often frank shock. Tissue invasion is rapid, often spreading from a cellulitis to a necrotizing fasciitis within 1 to 2 days. Massive subcutaneous edema and necrosis are common. Early on, the skin may be relatively spared, but as the disease progresses, the cutaneous tissues often demonstrate blebs, crepitus, or frank necrosis.[63] Diabetes, peripheral vascular disease, trauma, and recent surgery are predisposing factors. Pain varies because cutaneous nerve endings are quickly destroyed. Thus, the absence or cessation of pain may indicate worsening rather than improvement.[64]

Management

The initial treatment of all of these infections involves fluid resuscitation, parenteral antibiotics, and early surgical consultation for incision, drainage, and debridement. Large quantities of crystalloids are often necessary to replace fluid sequestered in the wound. Hemolysis occurs and may require the use of blood replacement products. Disseminated intravascular coagulopathy occurs in severe cases. Intravenous calcium may be necessary to reverse the hypocalcemia that results from necrosis of subcutaneous fat. The usual anaerobic infection has a foul discharge, occurs in locations near mucosal openings (perineum, oral pharynx), may manifest with tissue gas, and often has a Gram stain that shows a polymorphic array of organisms with negative aerobic cultures. The initial choice of antibiotics for necrotizing fasciitis should be guided by the Gram stain, culture, and anatomic area involved. Use of penicillin, an aminoglycoside, and clindamycin is recommended for a broad spectrum of coverage of aerobes, gram-negative enteric organisms, and anaerobes. If gram-positive organisms are expected or are seen on stain, a penicillinase-resistant penicillin should be added.[65]

NECROTIZING FASCIITIS

Principles of Disease

Necrotizing fasciitis is the preferred term for describing certain uncommon but potentially lethal infections. The condition usually occurs in men in the lower extremities and may evolve after only minimal local trauma. There are two types of necrotizing fasciitis. Type 1 is polymicrobial and involves non-group A streptococci plus anaerobes. These are typically found on the abdomen and perineum. In type 2, the pathogen is group A β-hemolytic streptococci and the infection is typically found on the extremities.[65] A substance in the cell wall of streptococci causes a separation of the dermal connective tissue, resulting in continued inflammation and necrosis. Streptococcal necrotizing fasciitis is frequently associated with streptococcal toxic shock syndrome.[66,67]

Early clinical findings are similar to those of most infected wounds, but the involved site quickly becomes erythematous, tender, and edematous; fever is usually present. Numbness or deep pain is often out of proportion to the physical findings. Early on, the skin may appear relatively benign, but necrotic patches and bullae appear between days 2 and 4, as a serosanguinous watery fluid begins to ooze. Deep structures and muscles are not involved. Hypotension, tachycardia, leukocytosis, and hypocalcemia ensue with systemic toxicity out of proportion to the clinical findings. Radiographs may reveal gas in the tissues, but tissue gas is not a universal finding.[65] The absence of gas does not exclude the diagnosis of necrotizing fasciitis. Frozen-section biopsy can be useful in diagnosis. Magnetic resonance imaging helps differentiate acute cellulitis from necrotizing fasciitis. Magnetic resonance imaging can overestimate the extent of disease due to adjacent noninfectious edema. Because of the rapidly progressive and frequently fatal outcome of this condition, delaying treatment to wait for imaging is not justified.[68,69]

Management

Treatment is surgical debridement, fluid and critical care resuscitation, and parenteral antibiotics against *S. aureus*, *Streptococcus*, gram-negative organisms, and anaerobes as directed by Gram stain and culture findings. Debridement should be aggressive and may have to be repeated. The mortality rate associated with this condition has ranged from 6% to 76%, with a cumulative mortality rate of 34%. Diabetes mellitus is the most important predictor of mortality, but advanced age, two or more associated comorbidities, and a delay before surgery of greater than 24 hours also contributed to mortality.

SPECIFIC FASCIITIS SYNDROMES

Meleney's synergistic gangrene (progressive bacterial synergistic gangrene) involves superficial and deep fascial planes with thrombosis of the subcutaneous vessels and gangrene of tissues. It is usually seen at the site of a laceration or surgical wound, but sometimes no portal of entry can be found. The skin appears erythematous and may eventually take on a bluish, gangrenous appearance. The patient is toxic, with fever and leukocytosis. Group A *Streptococcus* is found on the skin and in the blood, although *S. aureus* and gram-negative enteric organisms can also be found. Treatment is wide incision and debridement and appropriate antibiotics.[22,70,71]

Clostridial cellulitis (anaerobic cellulitis, local gas gangrene) is a gas-forming infection of the skin and subcutaneous tissue that spreads through intrafascial planes. Other bacterial flora can be seen. Healthy muscle is not involved. It results from superinfection of previously traumatized or necrotic tissue. Gas distributes in large bubbles in the fascial plane but not the muscle. Patients show signs of systemic toxicity: fever, tachycardia, edema of the affected part, and pain. Incision and debridement of involved tissue and blebs are necessary. Antibiotic treatment is penicillin or tetracycline. These patients must be hospitalized.

Nonclostridial crepitant cellulitis is similar to clostridial cellulitis except that the flora are usually polymicrobial, with aerobic and anaerobic coliforms such as *E. coli, Klebsiella, Enterobacter, Peptostreptococcus, Peptococcus,* and *B. fragilis.* These infections tend to progress from a fasciitis to a myositis. The treatment is broad-spectrum intravenous antibiotics and close observation and debridement.[72]

Fournier's syndrome is an insidious necrotizing subcutaneous infection of the perineum that occurs primarily in men, usually between 20 and 50 years of age, and usually involves the penis or scrotum. The disease occasionally occurs in women, especially in patients who are immunocompromised. Pain or itching in the genitalia is followed by fever, chills, and impressive perineal swelling, which may simulate a strangulated hernia. The inflammation may involve the entire abdomen, back, and thighs. There is frequently crepitance on palpation, indicating subcutaneous gas. Systemic symptoms include nausea and vomiting, changes in sensorium, and lethargy. Eventually, gangrenous areas demarcate and become less painful as destruction and sloughing of sensory nerves occur. The tissue breaks open, sloughs, and gives off an overwhelming feculent odor.

The most common causal factors are infection or trauma to the perianal area, including anal intercourse, scratches, chemical or thermal injury, and diabetes. Local trauma and perianal disease precede approximately one third of all cases. Cultures demonstrate bacteria of the distal colon, with a complex picture of aerobic and anaerobic bacteria. *B. fragilis* tends to be the predominant anaerobe and *E. coli* the predominant aerobe.

This bacterial invasion of the subcutaneous tissues of the perineum causes obliteration of the small branches of the pudendal arteries that supply the perineal or scrotal skin, resulting in acute dermal gangrene. This combination of erythema, edema, inflammation, and infection in a closed space stimulates anaerobic growth. Identification of the offending organism can be done with Gram stain and wound cultures. Emergency management includes antibiotic therapy against anaerobes and gram-negative enterics and wide incision and drainage of the area to remove all the necrotic tissue. The mortality rate is approximately 3% to 38%.[73]

MYOSITIS

Principles of Disease and Clinical Features

Myositis, or myonecrosis, is a deep soft tissue infection with death of muscle and a variable degree of inflammation of the overlying tissues (see Table 135-1). The skin may show minimal erythema to frank gangrene, but usually the infection is associated with massive edema. Myositis includes gas gangrene (clostridial myonecrosis), nonclostridial myonecrosis, and synergistic necrotizing cellulitis.

Clostridial myonecrosis, or gas gangrene, is a rapidly progressive muscle-necrosing infection, often with little inflammatory skin reaction but with gas formation. It is usually a result of trauma or recent surgical wounds.[74] Pathogenesis includes the elaboration of exotoxins by clostridia bacilli. Clostridia are spore-forming anaerobic gram-positive bacilli usually found in the soil and in the intestinal tracts of humans and animals. Clostridia produce a toxin that damages and kills muscle, setting up the anaerobic environment that promotes further growth of the bacilli. The incubation period is 1 to 4 days. The onset of disease can occur in 6 to 24 hours. Pain is the earliest and most important symptom. Tachycardia out of proportion to fever is noted. Temperature is not a reliable index of infection. Mentally, patients are apathetic, with varying levels of stupor and delirium. The wound appearance is striking in the later stages but does not show the usual erythema of a pyogenic cellulitis. Early on, the skin may be white, shiny, and tense, or essentially normal. Progressive swelling can produce a dusky bronze appearance of the skin, with further progression leading to formation of vesicles filled with dark-red or purplish fluid. A brown watery discharge with a peculiar, foul "mousy" odor is noted. Crepitus is not a reliable finding, owing to overlying edema. Gas alone in the tissues cannot make the diagnosis of gas gangrene.[74] The muscle appears to be cooked or dead and does not bleed when cut or retract when pinched.

Nonclostridial myonecrosis is similar to gas gangrene, except that the flora include anaerobes such as *B. fragilis* and *Peptostreptococcus* along with gram-positive aerobes such as *Staphylococcus*. The prognosis is better than that for patients with gas gangrene. Treatment is appropriate debridement and antibiotic coverage. Gas may be present.[65,74]

Synergistic necrotizing cellulitis is a rapidly progressive infection usually of the lower extremities and perineum, commonly seen in patients with diabetes or peripheral vascular disease. Systemic manifestations are variable, from minimal to frank shock. The overlying skin often has a "dishwater" discharge and may show blebs, crepitus, or necrosis. The infection often extends from skin through the muscle. Pain is usually present. The causative pathogens include aerobes, *Streptococcus*, *Staphylococcus*, *Klebsiella*, *Proteus*, *E. coli*, and anaerobes, often *Bacteroides* and *Peptostreptococcus*. Hemolysis is common and the mortality rate is high. Treatment includes aggressive fluid and blood product resuscitation, appropriate antibiotics, and rapid surgical debridement.[64,71]

Diagnostic Strategies

Gram stain smears of the area show large gram-positive rods. Radiographs may reveal gas.

Management

Treatment is wide debridement and excision of the wound. Parenteral antibiotics should be given to cover anaerobes and enterics; penicillin in large doses, a cephalosporin, or clindamycin is indicated. The mortality rate is high.[74] Hyperbaric oxygen therapy may be effective very early in this disease. Hyperbaric oxygen therapy has been advocated for deep anaerobic infections that result in necrotizing fasciitis and myonecrosis, especially by clostridia species. Hyperbaric oxygen therapy is also a consideration in cases of non-clostridial involvement and Fournier's syndrome.[75] The definitive benefit of hyperbaric oxygen therapy in necrotizing fasciitis remains unproven.[64,65] Hyperbaric oxygen therapy may provide an environment less appropriate for anaerobic growth by reducing the oxygen-reduction potential, decreasing edema via hyperoxic vasoconstriction, enhancing the ability of phagocytes to destroy bacteria, and promoting angiogenesis and subsequent granulation tissue.[75]

KEY CONCEPTS

- Soft tissue infections encountered in the emergency department vary widely in location, severity, and causative organisms.
- A working knowledge of the usual presentation of specific infections, based on the anatomic area involved and origin (mucosal or skin) of the infection will allow selection of appropriate empirical antibiotic therapy.
- Identification of the infecting organism by culture or other laboratory technique is often unnecessary in common mild to moderate infections and can usually be reserved for severe or unusual cases.
- Severe or potentially life-threatening bacterial infections mandate immediate administration of the best empirical choice of antibiotics; attempts to identify the exact organism should not delay therapy.

ACKNOWLEDGMENT

Drs. Meislin and Guisto would like to acknowledge and thank Dr. Jim Dahle for his help and assistance with the writing of this chapter.

REFERENCES

1. Bobrow BJ, et al: Incision and drainage of cutaneous abscesses is not associated with bacteremia in afebrile adults. *Ann Emerg Med* 29:404, 1997.
2. Dupuy A, et al: Risk factors for erysipelas of the leg (cellulitis): Case control study. *BMJ* 318:1591, 1999.
3. Von Ludwig FW: Medizinisches correspondenz. *Blatt Wurtemberg Arztl Ver* 6:21, 1836.
4. Grodinsky M: Ludwig's angina: An anatomical and clinical study with review of the literature. *Surgery* 5:678, 1939.
5. Spitalnic SJ, Sucov A: Ludwig's angina: Case report and review. *J Emerg Med* 13:499, 1995.
6. Fleisher G, Heeger P, Topf P: *Hemophilus influenzae* cellulitis. *Am J Emerg Med* 11:274, 1983.
7. Newell PM, Norden CW: Value of needle aspiration in bacteriologic diagnosis of cellulitis in adults. *J Clin Microbiol* 26:401, 1988.
8. Meislin HW: Pathogen identification of abscesses and cellulitis. *Ann Emerg Med* 15:329, 1986.
9. Brook I: Antimicrobial therapy of skin and soft tissue infections in children. *J Am Pod Med Assoc* 83:398, 1993.
10. Barone ST, Aiuto LT: Periorbital and orbital cellulitis in the *Haemophilus influenzae* vaccine era. *J Ped Ophthal* 34:293, 1997.
11. Donahue SP, Schwartz G: Preseptal and orbital cellulitis in childhood: A changing microbiologic spectrum. *Ophthalmology* 105:1902, 1998.
12. Skedrios DG, et al: Subperiosteal orbital abscess in children: Diagnosis, microbiology, and management. *Laryngoscope* 103:28, 1993.
13. Siddens JD, Gladstone GJ: Periorbital and orbital infections in children. *J Am Osteopath Assoc* 92:226, 1992.
14. Powell KR: Orbital and periorbital cellulitis: Epidemiology and pathogenesis of periorbital cellulitis. *Pediatr Rev* 16:163, 1995.
15. Bonnetblanc JM, et al: Erisipelas. *Am J Clin Dermatol* 4:157, 2003.
16. Lowy FD: *Staphylococcus aureus* infections. *N Engl J Med* 339:520, 1998.
17. Ladhani S, Evans RW: Staphylococcal scalded skin syndrome. *Arch Dis Childh* 78:85, 1998.

18. Farrell AM: Staphylococcal scalded-skin syndrome. *Lancet* 354:880, 1999.

19. Patel GK, et al: Staphylococcal scalded skin syndrome: Diagnosis and management. *Am J Clin Dermatol* 4:165, 2003.

20. Danik SB, Schwartz RA, Oleske JM: Cellulitis. *Cutis* 64:157, 1999.

21. Cone LA, Woodard DR, Schlievert PM, Tomory GS: Clinical and bacteriologic observations of a toxic shock-like syndrome due to *Streptococcus pyogenes. N Engl J Med* 317:146, 1987.

22. Stevens DL, et al: Severe group A streptococcal infections associated with a toxic shock-like syndrome and scarlet fever toxin A. *N Engl J Med* 321:1, 1989.

23. Schlievert PM, et al: Molecular structure of *Staphylococcus* and *Streptococcus* superantigens. *J Clin Immunol* 15:4S, 1995.

24. Stevens DL: The flesh-eating bacterium: What's next? *J Infect Dis* 179:S366, 1999.

25. Forni AL, Kaplan EL, Schlievert PM, Roberts RB: Clinical and microbiological characteristics of severe group A streptococcus infections and streptococcal toxic shock syndrome. *Clin Infect Dis* 21:333, 1995.

26. Baxter F: Severe group A streptococcal infection and streptococcal toxic shock syndrome. *Can J Anaesth* 47:1129, 2000.

27. Bisno AL, Brito MO, Collins CM: Molecular basis of group A streptococcal virulence. *Lancet Infect Dis* 3:191, 2003.

28. Manders SM: Toxin-mediated streptococcal and staphylococcal disease. *J Am Acad Dermatol* 39:383, 1998.

29. Stevens DL: Invasive group A streptococcus infections. *Clin Infect Dis* 14:2, 1992.

30. Zimbelman J, Palmer A, Todd J: Improved outcome of clindamycin compared with beta-lactam antibiotic treatment for invasive *Streptococcus pyogenes* infection. *Pediatr Infect Dis J* 18:1096, 1999.

31. Kaul R, et al: Intravenous immunoglobulin therapy for streptococcal toxic shock syndrome: A comparative observational study. The Canadian Streptococcal Study Group. *Clin Infect Dis* 28:800, 1999.

32. Darenberg J, et al: Intravenous immunoglobulin G therapy in streptococcal toxic shock syndrome: A European randomized, double-blind, placebo-controlled trial. *Clin Infect Dis* 37:333, 2003.

33. The Working Group on Severe Streptococcal Infections: Defining the group A streptococcal toxic shock syndrome. *JAMA* 269:390, 1993.

34. Davies HD, et al: Invasive group A streptococcal infections in Ontario, Canada. *N Engl J Med* 335:547, 1996.

35. Shriner DL, Schwartz RA, Janniger CK: Impetigo. *Pediatr Dermatol* 56:30, 1995.

36. Darmstadt GL, Lane AT: Impetigo: An overview. *Pediatr Dermatol* 11:293, 1994.

37. Dagan R: Impetigo in childhood: Changing epidemiology and new treatments. *Pediatr Ann* 22:235, 1993.

38. Stulberg DL, Penrod MA, Blatny RA: Common bacterial skin conditions. *Am Fam Physician* 66:119, 2002.

39. Hsu S, Halmi BH: Bockhart's impetigo: Complication of waterbed use. *Int J Dermatol* 38:769, 1999.

40. Meislin HW, et al: Cutaneous abscesses: Anaerobic and aerobic bacteriology and outpatient management. *Ann Intern Med* 87:145, 1977.

41. Brooks I, et al: Aerobic and anaerobic bacteriology of wounds and cutaneous abscesses. *Arch Surg* 125:1445, 1990.

42. Rompel R, et al: Long-term results of wide surgical excision in 106 patients with hidradenitis suppurativa. *Dermatol Surg* 26:638, 2000.

43. Mitchell KM: Hidradenitis suppurativa. *Surg Clin North Am* 82:1187, 2002.

44. Brealy R: Pilonidal sinus: A new theory of origin. *Br J Surg* 43:62, 1955.

45. Gonzales MH, et al: Abscesses of the upper extremity from drug abuse by injection. *J Hand Surg* 18A:868, 1993.

46. Vedantam G: Antibiotics and anaerobes of gut origin. *Curr Opin Microbiol* 6:457, 2003.

47. Brook I: Anaerobic bacteria in upper respiratory tract and other head and neck infections. *Ann Otol Rhinol Laryngol* 111:430, 2002.

48. Meislin HW, McGehee MD, Rosen P: Management and microbiology of cutaneous abscesses. *J Am Coll Emerg Physicians* 7:186, 1978.

49. Aldridge KE, Ashcraft D, O'Brien M, Sanders CV: Bacteremia due to *Bacteroides fragilis* group: Distribution of species, beta-lactamase production, and antimicrobial susceptibility patterns. *Antimicrob Agents Chemother* 47:148, 2003.

50. Cardinal E, et al: Ultrasound-guided interventional procedures in the musculoskeletal system. *Radiol Clin North Am* 36:597, 1998.

51. Llera TL, Levy RC: Treatment of cutaneous abscess: A double-blind clinical study. *Ann Emerg Med* 14:15, 1985.

52. Sanders AB, et al: Cutaneous infections and abscesses. *Semin Fam Med* 2:75, 1981.

53. Brown TJ, Rosen T, Orengo IF: Hidradenitis suppurativa. *Southern Med J* 91:1107, 1998.

54. Altunay IK: Hidradenitis suppurativa and squamous cell carcinoma. *Dermatol Surg* 28:88, 2002.

55. Hoosen AA, Nteta C, Moodley J, Sturm AW: Sexually transmitted diseases including HIV infection in women with Bartholin's gland abscesses. *Genitourin Med* 71:155, 1995.

56. Lopez-Zeno JA, et al: Septic shock complicating drainage of a Bartholin's gland abscess. *Obstet Gynecol* 76:915, 1990.

57. Janicke DM, Pundt MR: Anorectal disorders: Gastrointestinal emergencies, part II. *Emerg Med Clin North Am* 14:757, 1996.

58. Marcus RH, Stine RJ, Cohen MA: Perirectal abscess. *Ann Emerg Med* 25:597, 1995.

59. Cataldo PA, et al: Intrarectal ultrasound in the evaluation of perirectal abscesses. *Dis Colon Rectum* 36:554, 1993.

60. Herr CH, Williams JC: Supralevator anorectal abscess presenting as acute low back pain and sciatica. *Ann Emerg Med* 23:132, 1994.

61. Hull TL: Pilonidal disease. *Surg Clin North Am* 82:1169, 2002.

62. Allen-Mersh TG: Pilonidal sinus: Finding the right track for treatment. *Br J Surg* 77:123, 1990.

63. Goldwag DA, Purcell TB: Necrotizing fasciitis in the pediatric age group: Report of a case. *J Emerg Med* 8:299, 1990.

64. Urschel JD: Necrotizing soft tissue infections. *Postgrad Med J* 75:645, 1999.

65. Green RJ, Dafoe DC, Raffin TA: Necrotizing fasciitis. *Chest* 110:219, 1996.

66. Feingold DS, Weinberg AN: Group A streptococcal infections. *Arch Dermatol* 132:67, 1996.

67. Donaldson PM, et al: Rapidly fatal necrotizing fasciitis caused by *Streptococcus pyogenes. J Clin Pathol* 46:617, 1993.

68. Struk DW, et al: Imaging of soft tissue infections. *Radiol Clin North Am* 39:277, 2001.

69. Wong CH, et al: Necrotizing fasciitis: Clinical presentation, microbiology, and determinants of mortality. *J Bone Joint Surg Am* 85:1454, 2003.

70. Wang K, Shih C: Necrotizing fasciitis of the extremities. *J Trauma* 32:179, 1992.

71. Spach DH, Johnson RA: Cellulitis and necrotizing soft tissue infections. *Curr Pract Med* 2:545, 1999.

72. Takahira N, et al: Treatment outcome of nonclostridial gas gangrene at a Level 1 trauma center. *J Orthop Trauma* 16:12, 2002.

73. Morpurgo E, et al: Fournier's gangrene. *Surg Clin North Am* 82:1213, 2002.

74. Hoover TJ: Soft tissue complications of orthopedic emergencies. *Emerg Med Clin North Am* 18:115, 2000.

75. Riseman JA, et al: Hyperbaric oxygen therapy for necrotizing fasciitis reduces mortality and the need for debridements. *Surgery* 108:847, 1990.

136 Sepsis Syndromes

Nathan I. Shapiro, Gary D. Zimmer, and Adam Z. Barkin

PERSPECTIVE

Background

Sepsis syndrome represents the systemic inflammatory response triggered by an infection in the host and is mediated by chemical messengers. The causative agent and the host's activated inflammatory cascade cause the body's defenses and regulatory systems to become overwhelmed. Tachycardia, tachypnea, fever, and immune system activation are manifestations. If the body is unable to overcome this insult, cellular injury, tissue damage, shock, multiorgan failure, or death may ensue.

In the past, the term *sepsis* was broadly used to describe a range of disease states. A unifying effort was made in 1992 at the American College of Chest Physicians/Society of Critical Care Medicine Consensus Conference, where clear definitions of sepsis and its sequelae were delineated (Box 136-1).[1] These definitions are essential to today's current understanding of sepsis, and they have served to better focus research efforts.

The spectrum of the sepsis syndromes actually begins with the systemic inflammatory response syndrome (SIRS), "a systemic inflammatory response to a variety of clinical insults."[1] This can occur in the absence of infection. SIRS is defined by the presence of two or more of the following in the absence of known causes: tachypnea, hyperthermia or hypothermia, tachycardia, leukocytosis, or bandemia. These findings should represent a change from the baseline. This syndrome can be due to infectious insults such as bacterial and fungal infections, as well as noninfectious causes such as pancreatitis, trauma, or ischemia.[1]

Sepsis is SIRS in the setting of an infection. When sepsis progresses to a state of organ dysfunction, hypoperfusion, or hypotension, manifested by acidosis, oliguria, or acute change in mental status, severe sepsis is present. Septic shock is marked by sepsis-induced hypotension (systolic blood pressure <90 mm Hg) despite reasonable fluid resuscitation or sepsis that requires vasopressors or inotropic agents to maintain normotension. In septic shock, tissue oxygen and other nutrient demands exceed their supply, producing lactic acidosis, oliguria, and mental status changes. The ultimate endpoint is multiple organ dysfunction syndrome (MODS), defined as the "presence of altered organ function in an acutely ill patient such that homeostasis cannot be maintained without intervention."[1] MODS is the final common pathway for the critically ill.

A landmark study by Rangel-Fausto and associates[2] demonstrated this progression of disease. The authors demonstrated the clinical progression from SIRS to sepsis to severe sepsis to septic shock by showing both a stepwise progression and increased mortality rates for those patients developing the more advanced syndromes (Figures 136-1 and 136-2). There was also a direct relationship between the number of SIRS criteria initially fulfilled and an increased rate of mortality.

Bacteremia is often seen, but positive cultures are not obligatory in the diagnosis of sepsis. In recent prospective studies, only 17% to 27% of patients with sepsis, 25% to 53% of patients with severe sepsis, and 69% of patients with septic shock actually had positive blood cultures.[2-4] Culture-negative and culture-positive septic populations have similar outcomes in patients with similar severity of illness.[2,4,5]

Pneumonia, abdominal abscess with viscus perforation, and pyelonephritis are common primary causes of sepsis.[2,4,6,7] Gram-positive organisms account for 25% to 50%, gram-negative for 30% to 60%, and fungi for 2% to 10% of cases. The most common pathogens are *Escherichia coli, Staphylococcus aureus, Pseudomonas aeruginosa, Enterococcus faecalis, Streptococcus pneumoniae, Klebsiella pneumoniae, Enterobacter* species, and coagulase-negative *Staphylococcus* species.[2-4,8,9] The distribution varies with the study and, more importantly, with host factors such as the host immune system, age, recent hospitalizations, and presence of indwelling vascular catheters.

The health status of the host is a crucial risk factor in the development and progression of sepsis. Elderly patients and those with multiple comorbidities are overwhelmed more easily by systemic infection. Chemotherapy-induced neutropenia, acquired immunodeficiency syndrome, and steroid dependency increase susceptibility to sepsis. Increased use of indwelling devices such as intravascular catheters, prosthetic devices, and endotracheal tubes contribute to the risk of systemic infection and sepsis.

Epidemiology

Sepsis is now the 10th most common cause of death in the United States.[10] There are 751,000 cases of sepsis estimated per year in the United States, with approximately 215,000 deaths per year.[11] The cost of caring for septic patients is estimated to be $17 billion per year in the United States.[11] Sepsis accounts for two to 10 cases per 100 hospital admissions.[4,6,8] Mortality rates from sepsis are estimated between 20% and 50%.[2,6,7,11-16]

BOX 136-1. Definitions of Sepsis

Bacteremia (Fungemia): presence of viable bacteria (fungi) in the blood, as evidenced by positive blood cultures

Systemic Inflammatory Response Syndrome (SIRS): at least two of the following conditions:

(1) oral temperature of >38°C or <35°C, (2) respiratory rate of >20 breaths/min or $PaCO_2$ of <32 mm Hg, (3) heart rate of >90 beats/min, (4) leukocyte count of >12,000/μL or >4000/μL or >10% bands

Sepsis: SIRS that has a proven or suspected microbial source

Severe Sepsis: sepsis with one or more signs of organ dysfunction, hypoperfusion, or hypotension, such as metabolic acidosis, acute alteration in mental status, oliguria, or adult respiratory distress syndrome

Septic Shock: sepsis with hypotension that is unresponsive to fluid resuscitation plus organ dysfunction or perfusion abnormalities as listed for severe sepsis

Multiple Organ Dysfunction Syndrome (MODS): dysfunction of more than one organ, requiring intervention homeostasis

Data from Bone R, Balk R, Cerra F: Definitions for sepsis and organ failure and guidelines for the use of innovative therapies in sepsis. The APP/SCCM Consensus Conference Committee. *Chest* 101:1644, 1992.

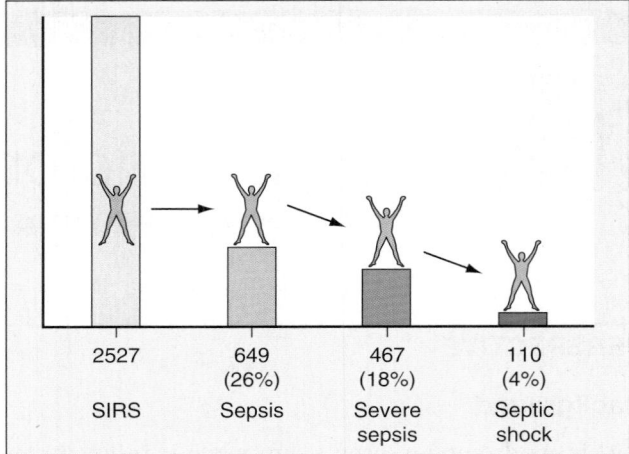

Figure 136-2. Progression of disease.

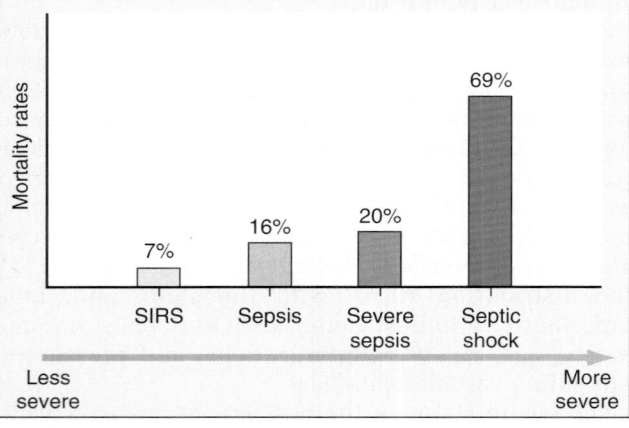

Figure 136-1. Mortality of disease state.

The incidence of sepsis is increasing as identification improves and the population ages. Estimates have suggested that the incidence will rise 1.5% per annum or more.[11,16]

PRINCIPLES OF DISEASE

Pathophysiology

Sepsis is the endpoint of a complex process that begins with an infection. The initial host response is to mobilize inflammatory cells, particularly neutrophils and macrophages, to the site of infection. These inflammatory cells then release circulating molecules, including cytokines, which trigger a cascade of other inflammatory mediators that result in a coordinated host response. Synthesis of the components of the cascade is increased at many steps along the pathway. If these mediators are not appropriately regulated, sepsis will occur. In the setting of ongoing toxin release, a persistent inflammatory response occurs with ongoing mediator activation, cellular hypoxia, tissue injury, shock, multiorgan failure, and potentially death. This interaction is complex and multifactorial, and our understanding of it continues to evolve.

A wide variety of organisms can produce sepsis. Gram-negative sepsis is best understood and is clearly initiated by endotoxin, a lipopolysaccharide component of the bacterial cell wall. This was demonstrated by Suffredini and colleagues,[17] who injected purified endotoxin into healthy human volunteers and were able to produce a transient sepsis syndrome: fever, tachycardia, and tachypnea. Kirkland and Ziegler[18] showed that pretreatment of mice with antiendotoxin antibodies prevents sepsis when they were injected with an otherwise lethal dose of endotoxin-containing bacteria. Phagocytosis of endotoxin by macrophages causes the release of cytokines to fight the infection. When sufficient numbers of macrophages are activated by this method, an excess of these inflammatory cytokines is produced and can cause sepsis.

Gram-positive organisms produce an inflammatory response through the direct action of its cell wall components and the indirect action of secreted, soluble substances. Cellular wall components such as peptidoglycan and lipoteichoic acid are thought to initiate the pathway, although the mechanism of action is unproven. Secreted, soluble substances such as exotoxins (e.g., exotoxin A from *P. aeruginosa* and TSS-1 from *S. aureus*) are substances secreted by bacteria that produce a host response through cell membrane receptors. Other extracellular enzymes such as streptokinase are secreted from many gram-positive organisms. All of these substances circulate freely in the host and can remain after an active infection has been cleared. Each of these mediators is capable of activating the inflammatory cascade and can lead to the subsequent progression of sepsis.

Mediators of Sepsis

In response to toxins, the body reacts by secreting substances such as cytokines, eicosanoids,[19] platelet activation factor,[20,21] oxygen free radicals, complement, and fibrinolysins. Cytokines are cell-signaling peptides with multiple functions. They differ from classic endocrine hormones in that several cell types, rather than a dedicated organ, produce them; they have little significance in normal homeostasis and are released in response to an exogenous stimulus. Six categories exist: interleukins, tumor necrosis factors (TNFs), interferons, colony-stimulating factors, chemotactic factors, and others; the first two have the primary role in sepsis.

Cytokines are primarily proinflammatory, anti-inflammatory, or growth promoting. The molecular mechanisms by which they are regulated are not well understood. The initial cytokine, TNF-α, is found in serum approximately 90 minutes after the administration of endotoxin to healthy volunteers.[22] Interleukin (IL)-6 and IL-8 reach peak levels at approximately 120 minutes. The main proinflammatory cytokines are IL-1, TNF, and IL-8. The primary anti-inflammatory cytokines are IL-10, IL-6, transforming growth factor β, soluble receptors to TNF, and IL-1 receptor antagonist (IL-1ra).[23-25] If the resultant inflammatory response is adequate, the infection is controlled and cleared. If the response is deficient or excessive, however, a persistent and worsening cascade is produced, ultimately leading to shock, organ failure, and potentially death.

Interleukin-1 and TNF have both been implicated as key mediators in the development of sepsis. Increasing levels of circulating IL-1 and TNF correlate with worsening clinical status.[26] At high doses, both IL-1 and TNF are lethal. They act by stimulating granulocyte-colony stimulatory factors and activating leukocytes.[27] TNF is present first in the bloodstream, and it induces the formation of IL-1.[28] Infusing either cytokine into an animal model creates a sepsis syndrome.[29] Selective blockade of either cytokine protects against sepsis in animal models.[30-33]

Anti-inflammatory regulators are released in response to rising proinflammatory mediators. IL-1ra is found in increased levels in healthy volunteers injected with endotoxin and many patients with infection.[34] IL-10 has a purely anti-inflammatory role.[35] In experimental models, it has been shown to decrease mortality in the presence of endotoxemia.

Other noncytokine molecules have been implicated in sepsis. Metabolites of the arachidonic acid pathway are involved in peripheral vasodilation, vasoconstriction, and leukocyte and platelet aggregation.[36] Prostaglandins are responsible for fever.[37] Elevated thromboxane A_2 levels are found in sepsis.[38] Little is known about the actual mechanisms by which eicosanoids participate in sepsis.

Instability in vascular tone is becoming increasingly important in our understanding of the pathophysiology of sepsis. Vasopressin, also known as antidiuretic hormone, is a naturally occurring hormone that is essential for cardiovascular stability. It is produced as a prohormone in the hypothalamus. The hormone is stored in the pituitary gland and released in response to stressors such as pain, hypoxia, hypovolemia, and hyperosmolality.[39] In severe sepsis, there is a brief rise in circulating vasopressin levels followed by a prolonged and severe suppression. This pattern of secretion is different from other forms of shock in which vasopressin levels remain elevated.[40] Vasopressin has numerous physiologic effects, including vasoconstriction of the systemic vasculature, osmoregulation, and maintenance of normovolemia.

Nitric oxide (NO) is a gas that has an important role in septic shock, regulating vascular tone[41] by an indirect effect on smooth muscle cells.[42] NO also contributes to platelet adhesion, insulin secretion, neurotransmission, tissue injury, and inflammation and cytotoxicity.[43-45] Its half-life is quite short (6-10 seconds) and it is easily diffused into cells.[42] Although its mechanisms of action are not well understood, it seems to be a key mediator of sepsis. Animal data show that nitric oxide synthase, the enzyme that produces NO, is upregulated in cases of sepsis.[46] The enhanced NO production is thought to contribute to the profound vasodilation found in patients in septic shock.

In the setting of ongoing inflammatory activation, the mediators of sepsis continue to be produced and the cascade perpetuates. Unless appropriately and rapidly controlled, the ultimate effect is a sequence of events starting with cellular dysfunction and ultimately leading to tissue damage, organ dysfunction, and death.

Organ System Dysfunction

Neurologic

Patients with sepsis often display neurologic impairment manifested by altered mental status and lethargy, commonly referred to as *septic encephalopathy*. The incidence has been reported between 10% and 70%.[47,48] The mortality rate in patients with septic encephalopathy is higher than in septic patients without significant neurologic involvement.[49] One prospective case series showed that a Glasgow Coma Scale score less than 13 correlated with an increase in mortality rate from 20% to 50%.[50] Although the pathophysiology has not been clearly defined, contributing factors include direct bacterial invasion, endotoxemia, altered cerebral perfusion or metabolism, metabolic derangements, multiorgan system failure, and iatrogenic injury. Impaired renal or hepatic function in the absence of overt organ failure has been shown to correlate with encephalopathy.[50,51]

Cardiovascular

Profound cardiovascular dysfunction is common with sepsis. Gram-negative, gram-positive, and killed organisms can cause myocardial depression.[52,53] The direct insults of the toxic mediators as well as the mobilization of host-mediators of sepsis produce a distributive shock. Early in sepsis, a hyperdynamic state characterized by increased cardiac output and decreased systemic vascular resistance develops.[54,55] Although the cardiac output is increased, it is at the expense of

---

BOX 136-2. Definition of Acute Respiratory Distress Syndrome

- Impaired oxygenation, defined as a ratio of partial pressure of arterial oxygen to fractional inspired oxygen ≤200, irrespective how much positive end-expiratory pressure is used
- Bilateral pulmonary infiltrates on frontal chest x-ray study
- Pulmonary artery occlusion pressure ≤18 mm Hg or no clinical evidence of elevated left atrial pressures

---

Data from Bernard G, et al: The American-European Consensus Conference on ARDS: Definitions, mechanisms, relevant outcomes, and clinical trial coordination. *Am J Respir Crit Care Med* 149:818, 1994.

ventricular dilation and decreased ejection fraction. Aggressive fluid resuscitation usually increases preload and, secondarily, ejection fraction, thereby improving the cardiac index, even late in shock.[56] Much of the cardiovascular compromise from septic shock is reversible and normal cardiovascular function usually returns within 10 days.[57]

Pulmonary

Pulmonary compromise is common and often lethal. The exact mechanism by which sepsis causes respiratory failure is unclear. Sepsis produces a highly catabolic state and places significant demands on the respiratory system. At the same time, airway resistance is increased and muscle function is impaired.[58] Irrespective of whether pneumonia is the cause of sepsis, the common pulmonary endpoint is acute respiratory distress syndrome (ARDS).[59] ARDS is defined clinically (Box 136-2) and correlates with the pathologic finding of diffuse alveolar damage. The development of ARDS occurs 4 to 24 hours after radiographic abnormalities develop.[60] Because of alveolar-capillary membrane damage, fluid accumulates in the alveoli. Rather than being a diffuse disease, ARDS is a heterogeneous process that results in interspersed damaged and normal alveoli. Significant right-to-left shunting, arterial hypoxemia, and intractable hypoxemia occur.

Gastrointestinal

The hollow viscus is significantly affected by the shock state. A prolonged ileus accompanies hypoperfusion and persists beyond the malperfused state. Splanchnic blood flow is dependent on mean arterial pressure because there is relatively little autoregulation. Therefore, hemodynamic dysfunction may have a profound effect on viscus metabolism.

Solid organ involvement is also common. Even in the previously normal host, elevations in aminotransferases and bilirubin are common early in sepsis, although frank hepatic failure is quite rare. The liver has also been implicated in the pathogenesis of sepsis; some of the mediators of sepsis are produced by the liver.[61]

Endocrine

The incidence of adrenocortical dysfunction in sepsis is unclear. Depending on the balance of circulating cytokines, augmentation or suppression of the hypothalamic-pituitary axis is possible. IL-1 and IL-6 both activate the hypothalamic-pituitary-adrenal axis. TNF-α and corticostatin depress pituitary function. Other factors that may contribute to adrenal insufficiency in sepsis include decreased blood flow to the adrenal cortex, decreased pituitary function, and decreased pituitary secretion of adrenocorticotropic hormone due to severe stress. As a result of these interactions, the hypothalamic thermoregulatory mechanism may be reset, and temperature lability may develop.

Hematologic

Sepsis causes abnormalities in many parts of the coagulation system. Endotoxin, TNF-α, and IL-1 are the key mediators. Pathologic activation of the extrinsic (tissue-factor dependent) pathway, protein C–protein S, and fibrinolysis lead to consumption of essential factors causing disseminated intravascular coagulation (DIC). The activation of the coagulation cascade produces fibrin deposition and microvascular thrombi. If not corrected, these depositions can compromise organ perfusion and contribute to organ failure. Tissue factor expression on monocytes is increased. This results in fibrin deposition and perhaps contributes to an increased incidence of multiorgan failure due to microvascular thrombi. In one study, the degree of tissue factor expression was found to portend a poorer prognosis.[62]

Protein C has been identified as an important modulator of both inflammation and coagulation in patients with sepsis. Impairment of the protein C–dependent anticoagulation pathway is critical to the development of the thrombotic complications of sepsis.[63] In healthy humans, protein C is activated by a combination of thrombin and thrombomodulin. The activation of protein C results in downregulation of many portions of the coagulation cascade, including release of tissue factor, inactivation of factor VIIIa and factor Va, and stimulation of fibrinolysis.[64] It is possible that protein C activation in early sepsis is impaired because of an inflammatory cytokine-mediated downregulation of thrombomodulin. As a result, a consumptive coagulopathy ensues. This leads to increased fibrin deposition and a resulting upregulation of the fibrinolytic pathway as identified by low plasma levels of the fibrinolytic proteins and increased fibrin-split products.[65] This sequence of events leads to consumption of coagulation factors and DIC. In late sepsis, the fibrinolytic system is suppressed.[66]

CLINICAL FEATURES

Symptoms and Signs

The approach to a patient with potential or presumed sepsis relies on identifying the presence of a systemically acting infection, as well as localizing the source of the initial infection. This enables appropriately aggressive and directed treatment to the infection source. Often, the source is not readily apparent, but early identification of the septic state allows implementation of broad-spectrum antibiotics that may be potentially lifesaving.

Patients with altered consciousness who are unable to protect their airway require intubation. Septic patients with severe tachypnea or hypoxia with impending or current respiratory failure also require intubation to allow positive pressure ventilation. Patients needing hemodynamic blood pressure support must be identified and rapidly and aggressively treated with fluids and vasopressor and inotropic support as needed.

The septic patient manifests signs of systemic infection through tachycardia, tachypnea, hyperthermia or hypothermia, and, if severe, hypotension. A septic patient will often have flushed skin with warm, well-perfused extremities secondary to the early vasodilation and hyperdynamic state. Alternatively, the severely hypoperfused patient with an advanced shock state may appear mottled and cyanotic. Very early in the patient's presentation, vital sign changes such as tachycardia and tachypnea may be the only early indicators of sepsis.

If the patient is in shock, the cause should be identified and differentiated from hypovolemic or cardiogenic shock. In approaching septic shock, one should remember the cause: a pathogenic insult resulting in a dysregulated inflammatory cascade with release of proinflammatory and anti-inflammatory mediators. These mediators cause vasodilation and hyperdynamic cardiovascular effects. Thus, a septic patient will classically appear flushed with warm, well-perfused extremities. This should be distinguished from patients with hypovolemic or cardiogenic shock who will appear cool, clammy, and sometimes diaphoretic with poorly perfused extremities. Neck veins will be flat and the pulse rapid and thready. A complete detailed clinical examination should allow the physician to discriminate the cause of the shock state (see Chapter 34).

Risk factors for sepsis, such as immunocompromised states (acquired immunodeficiency syndrome, malignancy, diabetes, splenectomy, and concurrent chemotherapy), elderly age, debilitation or institutionalization, and multiple comorbidities should be considered. A history of fevers or chills in the setting of intravenous drug abuse, an artificial heart valve, or mitral valve prolapse should increase the suspicion of endocarditis. The clinician should suspect endocarditis in the presence of a murmur or other stigmata of endocarditis (e.g., splinter hemorrhages, Roth's spots, Janeway lesions).

The respiratory system is the most common focus of infection in the septic patient. A history of a productive cough, fevers, chills, upper respiratory symptoms, and throat and ear pain should be sought. Both the presence of pneumonia and the findings of tachypnea or hypoxia have been found to be predictors of death in patients with sepsis; thus, particular attention should be paid to these findings.[67] Examination should also include detailed evaluation, looking for focal infection such as exudative tonsillitis, sinus tenderness, tympanic membrane injection, and crackles or dullness on lung auscultation. Also, pharyngeal thrush should be noticed as a marker of an immunocompromised state.

The gastrointestinal system is the second most common source of sepsis. A history of abdominal pain, including its description, location, timing, and palliating and aggravating factors should be sought. Further history, including last bowel movement and the presence of nausea, vomiting, and diarrhea should be noted. A careful physical examination, looking for signs of peritoneal irritation, abdominal tenderness, and hyperactive or hypoactive bowel sounds is critical in identifying the source of abdominal sepsis. Particular attention must be paid to physical findings suggestive of common sources of infection or disease: Murphy's sign indicating cholecystitis, pain at McBurney's point indicating appendicitis, left lower quadrant pain suggesting diverticulitis, or rectal examination revealing a rectal abscess or prostatitis.

The neurologic system is examined by looking for signs of meningitis, including nuchal rigidity, fevers, and change in consciousness. A detailed neurologic examination is important. Lethargy or altered mentation may indicate primary neurologic disease or may be the result of decreased brain perfusion from a shock state.

The genitourinary history includes flank pain, dysuria, polyuria, discharge, Foley catheter placement, and instrumentation. A sexual history should assess for the risk of sexually transmitted diseases. Genitalia should be evaluated for ulcers, discharge, and penile or vulvar lesions, looking specifically for the woody induration of Fournier's gangrene. A rectal examination should be performed, looking for a tender, boggy prostate consistent with prostatitis. A red and friable cervix, cervical discharge, or cervical motion tenderness is consistent with a sexually transmitted disease. Adnexal tenderness in a toxic-appearing female potentially represents a tubo-ovarian abscess.

Musculoskeletal history includes any localizing symptoms to a particular joint. Redness, swelling, and warmth over a joint, especially if there is a decreased range of motion in that joint, are of concern in that they may be signs of septic arthritis and may mandate arthrocentesis. A patient should be completely exposed and the skin examined for evidence of cellulitis, abscess, wound infection, or traumatic injury. Deep injuries, foreign bodies, and fasciitis may be difficult to identify clinically. The physician should look for crepitus representing the presence of an aggressive, gas-forming organism. Local lymphadenopathy, swelling, and streaking should also be noted as signs of an advancing infection. Petechiae and purpura may represent a *Neisseria meningitidis* infection or DIC. Generalized erythroderma and rash may represent an exotoxin from pathogens such as *S. aureus* or *Streptococcus pyogenes*.

Once patients are determined to be infected, the severity of illness that is likely to result must be deter-

Table 136-1. Mortality in Emergency Department Sepsis (MEDS) Prediction Rule

Risk Factor	Odds Ratio for Death	MEDS score
Terminal illness (death within 30 days)	6.1	6 points
Tachypnea or hypoxia	2.7	3 points
Septic shock	2.7	3 points
Platelet count <150,000/min^3	2.5	3 points
Bands >5%	2.3	3 points
Age >65 years	2.2	3 points
Pneumonia	1.9	2 points
Nursing home resident	1.9	2 points
Altered mental status	1.6	2 points

mined. Patients who are likely to become critically ill should be resuscitated in an aggressive manner in the appropriate setting. The Mortality in Emergency Department Sepsis (MEDS) score can be used to risk stratify emergency department patients with sepsis.[67] The MEDS rule is made up of the following scoring system: terminal illness with likelihood of death within 30 days from underlying disease (6 points), tachypnea or hypoxia (3 points), septic shock (3 points), platelet count less than 150,000/mm^3 (3 points), bands greater than 5% (3 points), age older than 65 years (3 points), pneumonia (2 points), nursing home residency (2 points), and altered mental status (2 points) (Table 136-1). The total score can be used to assess risk of death: very low risk (0-4 points) 1.1%, low risk (5-7 points) 4.4%, moderate risk (8-12 points) 9.3%, high risk (13-15 points) 16.1%, and very high risk (>15 points) 39%. Thus, the greater the number of risk factors, the more likely a patient is to die during the hospitalization.

DIAGNOSTIC STRATEGIES

The use of diagnostic testing in patients with sepsis syndromes or suspected syndromes serves two purposes. Diagnostic studies are used both to identify the type and location of the infecting organisms and to define the extent and severity of the infection to assist in focusing therapy. As a result, the diagnostic approach must be tailored to the particular patient.

Hematology

The white blood cell count is a marker of inflammation and activation of the inflammatory cascade. Leukocytosis is associated with infection and is incorporated in the consensus definition of sepsis; however, it is often insensitive and nonspecific, limiting its absolute utility in the emergency department. The febrile neutropenic patient has been shown to be at increased risk for severe infection. Thus a white blood cell count less than 500 cells/mm^3 should prompt admission, isolation, and empiric intravenous antibiotics in most chemotherapy patients. A bandemia (>10% bands on a peripheral smear) represents the release of immature cells from the bone marrow and is considered to be a

sign of infection and inflammation; it is part of the consensus sepsis definition. Like the white blood cell count, it is an imperfect indicator of infection. The hemoglobin and hematocrit should be obtained to ensure adequate oxygen delivery in shock. Patients should be maintained with a hematocrit greater than 30% and hemoglobin greater than 10 g/dL. Platelets are an acute-phase reactant and may be elevated in the presence of infections. Conversely, a low platelet count has been found to be a significant predictor of bacteremia in patients with shock.[9,67,68] Thrombocytopenia, elevated prothrombin time, an elevated activated partial thromboplastin time, decreased fibrinogen, and increased fibrin split products are associated with DIC and severe sepsis syndrome.

Chemistry

Electrolyte abnormalities should be identified and corrected. Low bicarbonate level suggests acidosis and inadequate perfusion. An elevated anion gap acidosis in the setting of sepsis syndrome commonly represents lactic acidosis or diabetic ketoacidosis, but other causes need to be ruled out. A high creatinine level is indicative of renal dysfunction or failure, which, if due primarily to sepsis, indicates organ failure and a worse prognosis. Calcium, magnesium, and phosphorus levels should be checked.

The presence of an elevated lactate level is associated with inadequate perfusion, shock, and a poorer prognosis.[69] The presence of lactic acidosis identifies patients who are in organ failure and could benefit from aggressive resuscitation.[70] A multicenter prospective study of intensive care unit patients showed an overall 3-day mortality rate of 59% for patients with lactic acidosis. An arterial blood gas assessment may be helpful in identifying and classifying acid-base disturbances. Metabolic acidosis suggests inadequate tissue perfusion. A low PO_2, specifically a PaO_2 less than 75 mm Hg, is part of the consensus sepsis syndrome's definition. Liver function tests can be used to identify liver failure or dysfunction. An elevated bilirubin level may suggest the gallbladder as a cause of sepsis. An elevated amylase and lipase level may represent pancreatitis as the cause of noninfectious SIRS.

Microbiology

Obtaining proper blood, sputum, urine, cerebrospinal fluid (CSF), and other tissue culture samples is important in guiding therapy. Although usually not helpful in the acute emergency department setting, culture samples should be obtained before or soon after the administration of antibiotics in the patient with sepsis syndrome. The initiation of antibiotic therapy should not be delayed while waiting for culture samples to be obtained. One well-designed prospective study suggests the following factors as predictive of a positive blood culture: fever greater than 38.3°C, the presence of a rapidly (<1 month) or ultimately (<5 years) fatal disease, shaking chills, intravenous drug abuse, acute abdomen, or major comorbidity.[3] These factors have not been validated in independent populations. The yield of all blood cultures obtained in all patients remains low (5-10%) due to a lack of reliable discriminatory guidelines for obtaining blood culture samples in the emergency department.[3,71-73] Among patients with clinical sepsis, only 30% to 60% of patients will have positive cultures.[4,6,14] Currently, all patients with suspected sepsis syndrome should have at least two sets of blood cultures sent, along with any clinically indicated sputum, urine, CSF, catheter, and wound culture samples.

A Gram stain of sputum, CSF, or abscess drainage may help in the early prediction of a suspected pathogen and guide initial antibiotic therapy. A urinalysis showing leukocytosis or bacteria is suggestive of a urinary tract infection and potential urosepsis. A lumbar puncture with CSF leukocytosis is indicative of meningitis.

Special Procedures

The comprehensive protocol of early goal-directed therapy published by Rivers and associates[70] showed that a resuscitation strategy guided by central venous pressure, an arterial line, and a central venous catheter with continuous $ScvO_2$ monitoring capability can reduce mortality in patients with sepsis. However, whether each of these components is mandatory is unclear. A central venous pressure (CVP) line may guide fluid resuscitation, with a low CVP indicating the need for continued fluid repletion. The goal CVP is 8 to 12 mm Hg in patients not on mechanical ventilation, and 12 to 16 mm Hg in patients who are ventilated. The $ScvO_2$ monitor measures venous blood saturation, which is a marker of tissue metabolism and extraction. It has been suggested that intermittent monitoring of $ScvO_2$ may suffice, although there are no firm data to support this. The goal is to ensure proper tissue oxygenation, which is routinely achieved by adjusting oxygen delivery, keeping the $ScvO_2$ greater than 70%. An arterial line can be useful for close monitoring of hypotensive patients, especially when one or more vasopressors are being titrated to maintain an adequate blood pressure. Finally, the Swan-Ganz catheter is not a mandatory part of the emergency department management, although the physiologic measurements may be useful in identifying the cause of shock and guiding fluid and inotropic therapy. Low systemic vascular resistance and high cardiac output are most commonly associated with sepsis, although this may vary with the stage of shock and the individual patient.

Radiology

A chest radiograph should be obtained in all patients with suspected sepsis syndrome, looking not only for a focal infiltrate representing pneumonia but also for the fluffy, bilateral infiltrates indicative of ARDS. An upright chest x-ray study should be obtained for suspected bowel perforation to detect free air under the diaphragm. The presence of pneumomediastinum is suggestive of esophageal perforation and current or impending mediastinitis.

Soft tissue plain radiographs of infected areas should be obtained, looking for air in the soft tissues associated with necrotizing or gas-forming infection. Periosteal thickening or bone erosion may be seen on plain radiographs of patients with osteomyelitis; a bone scan may be diagnostic. A computed tomography scan of the abdomen and pelvis may identify abdominal or pelvic pathologic lesions, provided there is no clear clinical indication for immediate operative intervention. Suspected diseases such as diverticulitis, appendicitis, necrotizing pancreatitis, microperforation of the stomach or bowel, or formation of an intra-abdominal abscess may be best diagnosed by computed tomography scan. A head computed tomography scan can identify septic emboli from endocarditis or increased intracranial pressure from a mass and should be considered before a lumbar puncture is performed. An abdominal ultrasonogram may be indicated for suspected cholecystitis, and a pelvic ultrasonogram for tubo-ovarian abscess or endometritis. A transesophageal echogram should be obtained if endocarditis is suspected to detect the presence of any valvular vegetations. A magnetic resonance imaging scan can be useful to identify soft tissue infections such as necrotizing fasciitis or epidural abscess.

DIFFERENTIAL CONSIDERATIONS

The sepsis syndromes represent a spectrum of disease and clinical presentation. SIRS is defined by hemodynamic and laboratory parameters alone, whereas sepsis must include an infectious cause. Often, noninfectious sources can cause a syndrome that mimics sepsis; thus, one must keep in mind a broad differential diagnosis when approaching these patients (Box 136-3). A detailed history and physical examination are always the first step in narrowing the differential diagnosis to identify the true source. Regardless of the source, SIRS and sepsis must be taken seriously and treated aggressively.

MANAGEMENT

Early detection and aggressive management can significantly reduce the chance of mortality from sepsis. Maintenance of adequate tissue oxygenation and perfusion remains the primary goal, but the means by which this is achieved has changed substantially in the past 5 years. With the advent of early goal-directed therapy[70] and therapy targeting the cascade leading to septic shock,[64] there is increasing evidence that the natural history of sepsis can be altered. Initial resuscitation, including appropriate airway management, intravenous access, oxygen, antibiotics, and fluid resuscitation remain the foundation on which new efforts may be applied.

In the ground-breaking study by Rivers and associates,[70] a protocol for early goal-directed therapy was used to guide resuscitation in the emergency department. This randomized, double-blind, placebo-controlled study showed a 16% mortality reduction in

BOX 136-3. Differential Considerations for Sepsis and Septic Shock

Sepsis	Septic Shock
Dehydration	Hypovolemic shock
Acute respiratory distress syndrome	Acute blood loss
Anemia	Severe dehydration
Ischemia	Cardiogenic shock
Hypoxia	Pulmonary embolus
Congestive heart failure	Myocardial infarction
Vasculitis	Pericardial tamponade
Toxicologic	Tension pneumothorax
Poisonings	Vasogenic shock
Overdose	Anaphylaxis
Drug-induced	Paralysis
Pancreatitis	
Hypothalamic injury	
Disseminated intravascular coagulation	
Anaphylaxis	
Metabolic	
Hyperthyroidism	
Diabetic ketoacidosis	
Adrenal dysfunction	
Environmental	
Burn	
Heat exhaustion/stroke	
Trauma	
Blood loss	
Cardiac contusion	
Neuroleptic malignant syndrome	

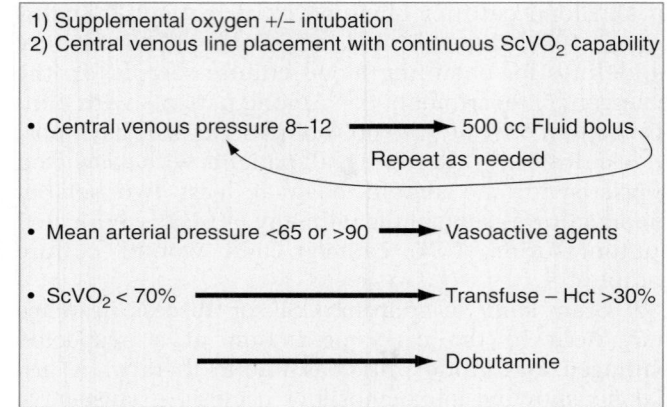

Figure 136-3. Summary of goal-directed therapy protocol.

patients with severe sepsis and septic shock. The protocol simply mandates aggressive and early fluid resuscitation, normalization of blood pressure, and adequate oxygen delivery to ensure proper tissue oxygenation. The use of this strategy has been endorsed by the Surviving Sepsis Campaign, an 11-organization international consensus panel.[74] The recommendation is for the use of goal-directed therapy on all patients who (1) have infection, (2) have two or more SIRS criteria, and (3) are in septic shock (systolic blood pressure < 90 mm Hg after 20-30 mL/kg fluid challenge) or have a lactic acid level greater than 4 mmol/dL (Figure 136-3). The theory behind the protocol is to normalize preload, pressure, and to prevent tissue hypoxia by matching oxygen delivery with consumption.

Preload

The first step in goal-directed therapy is to provide a proper filling pressure to ensure adequate cardiac preload. Patients in sepsis and septic shock are often in a state of substantial fluid deficit. Rivers and colleagues showed that patients required an average of 5 L of fluids in the first 6 hours of their resuscitation. A central venous pressure measurement should be obtained, and the patients should receive crystalloid or colloid resuscitation to keep the CVP at a level of 8 to 12 mm Hg. In intubated patients with positive pressure ventilation, the level should be 12 to 16 mm Hg.

Perfusion Pressure

The next step in goal-directed therapy is to maintain an adequate blood pressure. A mean arterial blood pressure ($^2/_3$ diastolic + $^1/_3$ systolic) should be kept between 60 and 90 mm Hg. If the mean arterial blood pressure is below 60 mm Hg in the presence of adequate preload, treatment with a vasopressor agent should be started. The choice of vasopressor is discussed elsewhere, but norepinephrine or dopamine are considered first-line agents.

Oxygen Delivery

Once preload and pressure are normalized, the next focus is on oxygen delivery. A mixed venous saturation assessment can be used to guide this part of the resuscitation. Organ hypoperfusion is a result of global and distributive changes in both systemic blood flow and the microvasculature. As a result of marrow suppression and dilution with crystalloid fluids, most patients with sepsis have a hemoglobin between 8 and 10 g/dL after initial resuscitation. A hematocrit between 27% and 30% has been reported to be most effective,[75] although other studies challenge this dogma.[76-79]

The goal is to maintain a mixed venous saturation ($ScvO_2$) greater than 70%. As oxygen demand due to sepsis increases, the $ScvO_2$ starts to fall below 70%. This must be corrected by first ensuring that preload and pressure are adequate. Next, the arterial oxygen saturation should be optimized with non-rebreather oxygen delivery or intubation, as needed. Once these are optimized, one should ensure that the patient has adequate oxygen carrying capacity by transfusing the patient to a hematocrit greater than 30%. If this is normalized, and the patient is not tachycardic, dobutamine can be added to increase cardiac contractility and increase cardiac output, resulting in an overall improved oxygen delivery. The protocol should be run continuously with an effort toward normalizing the parameters during the entire resuscitation (Table 136-2).

Respiratory Support

Altered mental status is common in patients in septic shock, and they may require rapid airway protection.

Table 136-2. Management Recommendations for Hemodynamic Support

Basic Principles
Admission to intensive care unit
Arterial cannulation in patients with shock, although insertion may not be practical in the emergency department
Resuscitation to target tissue perfusion
Central venous or pulmonary arterial catheter placement to assess cardiac filling pressures

Fluid Resuscitation
Fluids are the primary modality to resuscitation*
Colloids and crystalloids are equally effective*
Invasive monitoring for patients not responding to initial resuscitation with target pulmonary capillary wedge pressure of 12 to 15 mm Hg†
Hemoglobin concentrations should be maintained above 8 to 10 g/dL†

Vasopressor Therapy
Dopamine is the first-line agent in shock unresponsive to aggressive fluid resuscitation‡
Dopamine and norepinephrine are equally effective and can be use together†
Phenylephrine is an alternative but decreased stroke volume may be associated with worse outcome*
Epinephrine is reserved for refractory hypotension†
Routine low-dose (<5 μg/kg/min) dopamine is not recommended§
Vasopressin may be considered in refractory shock not responsive to aggressive fluid resuscitation and high-dose conventional vasopressors‡

Inotropic Therapy
Dobutamine is the first choice for patients with refractory low cardiac index‡
Dobutamine may improve cardiac index and organ perfusion, but empiric use is not recommended*
Vasopressors and inotropes can be titrated separately to maintain mean arterial pressure and cardiac output†
Epinephrine and dopamine can be used as inotropes, but splanchnic perfusion may be compromised*

---

*Supported by small, randomized trials with uncertain results.
†Supported by at least one nonrandomized, contemporaneous trial.
‡Supported by nonrandomized trials with historical controls and expert opinion or case series.[74,86]
§Supported by one randomized controlled trial with clear results.
Data from Hollenberg S, et al: Practice parameters for hemodynamic support of sepsis in adult patients with sepsis. *Crit Care Med* 27:639, 1999.

Table 136-3. Dosing of Vasoactive Therapy

Drug	Dose
Dobutamine	5-15 μg/kg/min
Dopamine	2-20 μg/kg/min
Epinephrine	5-20 μg/min
Norepinephrine	5-20 μg/min
Phenylephrine	2-20 μg/min

Patients with a respiratory rate greater than 30 breaths per minute are likely to develop respiratory collapse, irrespective of arterial oxygenation. Wheeler and coworkers[80] reported that 85% of patients with "severe sepsis" require mechanical ventilation during their hospital course. Because patients with impending respiratory failure use a disproportionately large amount of energy for the muscles of respiration, improved oxygen delivery to other organs is achieved by mechanical ventilation, sedation, and paralysis. Although there are no clear intubation guidelines, hypercapnia, persistent hypoxemia, airway compromise, and profound acidosis are valid indicators.

In addition to airway protection, intubation and mechanical ventilatory support provide positive pressure ventilation. The pattern of injury is such that normal lung parenchyma is adjacent to affected tissue. Therefore, increased airway pressures are required to maintain normal oxygen delivery. Current recommendations are to maintain transalveolar pressures (measured as plateau pressures) below 35 cm H_2O, because increased pressures are associated with ventilator-induced lung injury.[81,82] Maintaining relatively low transalveolar pressure with increasing end-expiratory pressure is an effective way to increase arterial oxygen delivery.[83]

Cardiovascular Support

Fluid Resuscitation

Patients with sepsis often require large volumes of intravenous fluid to maintain adequate perfusion.[84] The primary reasons for this intravascular hypovolemia are venodilation and diffuse capillary leak.[85] As much as 6 to 10 L of crystalloid may be required in the first 24 hours.[84] In the absence of formal early goal-directed therapy, fluid replacement should be titrated to clinical parameters such as heart rate, blood pressure, change in mental status, capillary refill, cool skin, and adequate urine output (0.5-1 mL/kg/hr). Normal (0.9%) saline and Ringer's lactate solution are equally effective and neither worsens lactic acidosis. Colloids are as effective as crystalloids, but they are far more expensive and, in the case of pooled human albumin, present an exposure risk.[84] Experience with hypertonic saline is limited, and no recommendation on its use can be made based on current literature.[86] There have been recent efforts to identify ways to measure regional perfusion more directly. In particular, direct measurement of splanchnic blood flow has been proposed. Even in the absence of global hypoxia and impaired tissue perfusion, there is evidence that regional hypoperfusion and ischemia exist.[87] Although further study is necessary, there is early evidence that therapy guided toward maintaining splanchnic perfusion can decrease the rate of mortality.[88]

Vasopressors

If appropriate fluid resuscitation has failed, vasopressor support may be required (Table 136-3). Only in cases of profound hypotension should vasopressors be started before adequate fluid resuscitation. Using mean arterial pressure alone as an indicator of overall efficacy of therapeutic intervention is not helpful.[89] A mean arterial pressure of 60 to 70 mm Hg has been recommended in otherwise healthy, normovolemic adult patients but must be correlated with other indicators of adequate perfusion, such as mental status and urine output. Patients with previously uncontrolled hypertension may require mean arterial pressures of 75 mm

Hg or even higher. Septic patients requiring vasopressors should have an arterial cannula placed as soon as possible so that blood pressure can be monitored more accurately and frequently. Placement in the emergency department should not delay rapid disposition to the intensive care unit.

Norepinephrine

Norepinephrine is a mixed α and β agonist with minimal β_2 activity. Its primary function is to increase cardiac output and systemic vascular resistance. Along with dopamine, it is considered a first-line agent. Although there are no definitive outcomes studies, it is gaining popularity as a vasopressor of choice for the treatment of septic shock. Its physiologic properties, along with some small studies using hemodynamic outcomes, make it a sensible choice. At least one controlled trial showed norepinephrine to be more effective than dopamine at reversing hypotension for at least 6 hours.[90] There was no difference between norepinephrine and dopamine in terms of adverse events. When compared with dopamine in septic patients, norepinephrine increases glomerular filtration and urine output equally well.[91-93] Norepinephrine has been studied as a rescue drug to dopamine and has produced consistent, replicated improvement in hemodynamics, although reduced mortality has not been shown. It is an important component of the therapy for septic shock, either as a sole vasopressor or in conjunction with dopamine.[86] Recommended doses are from 0.5 to 3 μg/min.

Dopamine

Dopamine is also a first-line agent used for septic shock that is unresponsive to adequate volume expansion. Dopamine is the immediate precursor of norepinephrine and epinephrine. It is primarily a β_1 and dopaminergic agonist. Although low doses alone are not effective, they may be effective in combination with other agents. "Renal-dose" dopamine has not been shown to reduce mortality or decrease dialysis dependence and should not be used.[94,95] Doses greater than 20 μg/kg/min may produce significant vasoconstriction. Persistent tachycardia, decreased PaO_2, and increased pulmonary artery occlusion pressure are common side effects of dopamine use. Dopamine has been shown to increase oxygen delivery better than other catecholamines.[96,97] Based on its mechanism of action, it is most useful in patients who have depressed cardiac output.

Phenylephrine

Phenylephrine is a selective α_1-agonist, increasing systemic vascular resistance without significant changes in cardiac output. It can produce a reflexive bradycardia or suppression in cardiac output. A single small study has shown that phenylephrine is effective in restoring perfusion in patients with septic shock refractory to dopamine or dobutamine.[98] Phenylephrine does not impair cardiac and renal function and may be a good choice when significant tachyarrhythmia limits the use of other agents.[86]

Epinephrine

Epinephrine a very potent mixed α and β agonist. Epinephrine infusion is also associated with increased oxygen consumption, increased systemic lactate concentrations, and decreased splanchnic blood flow. Studies have shown that the rise in lactate is short-term and there is no evidence regarding the long-term effects.[99,100] As a result of all of the possible adverse effects of epinephrine, it is currently recommended only for those patients who are unresponsive to other vasopressors.

Vasopressin

Vasopressin is a naturally occurring nonapeptide that is synthesized as a large prohormone in the hypothalamus. In states of septic shock, there is an early surge of vasopressin followed by a profound drop in circulating vasopressin levels.[39] This is the foundation upon which the use of vasopressin in sepsis is based. Limited outcome data are available to support the use of vasopressin, but several small published reports support the use of 0.01 to 0.04 U/min in patients with a cardiac index of 2 L/min/m^2. Doses greater than 0.04 U/min have been associated with worse outcomes.[74]

Inotropic Agents

Dobutamine

Dobutamine is a mixed α and β agonist. In dose ranges from 2 to 28 μg/kg/min, cardiac index is increased at the expense of heart rate. In addition, decreased splanchnic blood flow is common.[101] Its use should be reserved for patients with depressed cardiac index and persistent hypoperfusion in spite of adequate volume expansion and other vasopressor agents. In patients undergoing formal early goal-directed therapy, when preload, perfusion pressure, and oxygen-carrying capacity have been normalized, and a low ScvO$_2$ persists, dobutamine is used to increase cardiac output and oxygen delivery.

All of the vasopressor and inotropic agents can produce a decrease in blood flow to the splanchnic and renal vasculature. Administration should begin with a goal of improving mean arterial pressure to the lower limit of normal and then should follow other indices of adequate perfusion. The current recommendation from the Society of Critical Care Medicine is that dopamine be used as the primary vasopressor for patients with septic shock that is unresponsive to appropriate, aggressive crystalloid therapy.[86] However, norepinephrine is becoming increasingly favored, although not based on outcome data. Vasopressin has also been suggested in patients with refractory shock. Epinephrine can be used as a third-line agent for refractory hypotension. Dobutamine can be combined in the setting of persistently depressed cardiac index.

Table 136-4. Suggested Initial Antibiotic Management Pending Microbiologic Identification of Organism and Sensitivity

Infection	Modifying Factors	Antibiotic
Sepsis, unknown source	Immunocompetent	Antipseudomonal cephalosporin *plus* aminoglycoside or fluoroquinolone; *or* antipseudomonal penicillin *plus* aminoglycoside or fluoroquinolone; *or* carbapenem *plus* aminoglycoside or fluoroquinolone
	Anaerobic infection	Add metronidazole or clindamycin to above regimen
	Methicillin-resistant *Staphylococcus aureus* (MRSA)	Add vancomycin to above regimen
	Neutropenia	Antipseudomonal penicillin *plus* aminoglycoside or fluoroquinolone; *or* carbapenem *plus* aminoglycoside or fluoroquinolone
	Splenectomy	Cefotaxime *or* ceftriaxone
	HIV infection	Ticarcillin-clavulanate *plus* tobramycin
Pneumonia	Immunocompetent	Second- or third-generation cephalosporin *plus* second-generation macrolide *or* Fluoroquinolone
	Legionella suspected	Azithromycin or fluoroquinolone or high-dose erythromycin
Abdominal infection	Immunocompetent	Ampicillin *plus* aminoglycoside *plus* metronidazole
	Multidrug-resistant organism suspected	Ticarcillin/clavulanate carbapenem *or* piperacillin/tazobactam *plus* aminoglycoside
Urinary tract source		Fluoroquinolone; *or* third-generation cephalosporin; *or* ampicillin *plus* aminoglycoside
Cellulitis	Non-necrotizing fasciitis	Cefazolin *or* nafcillin
	MRSA possible	Vancomycin
Necrotizing fasciitis (surgical drainage)		Ampicillin/sulbactam; *or* Ticarcillin/clavulanate; *or* Piperacillin *plus* aminoglycoside *plus* clindamycin; *or* Carbapenem
IV catheter infection (remove catheter)	Outpatient acquired	Third-generation cephalosporin
	MRSA suspected	Add vancomycin
Fungal infection		Amphotericin B
Cerebrospinal infection	Immunocompetent	Ceftriaxone *plus* vancomycin
	Elders or immunocompromised	Add ampicillin
Intravenous drug abuse	MRSA not suspected	Nafcillin *plus* aminoglycoside
	MRSA suspected	Vancomycin *plus* aminoglycoside

Bicarbonate

Bicarbonate supplementation was previously the standard of care for patients with presumed lactic acidosis. Current consensus is that it should be reserved for severe acidemia (pH <7.0-7.2), as there may be a paradoxical decrease in intracellular pH as a result of diffusion of soluble CO_2 across the cell membrane. Alternatively, hyperventilation has been suggested to help increase systemic pH.[89]

Antibiotics

Early and appropriate antibiotic therapy should target the nidus of infection; this reduces mortality, perhaps by as much as 30% to 50%.[102-104] If the patient's condition permits, appropriate cultures should be drawn before the administration of broad-spectrum antibiotics (Table 136-4). Surgically correctable conditions, such as intra-abdominal abscesses, perforated viscus, retained products of conception, or retained foreign body (such as a tampon) should be treated concurrently.

In the absence of an obvious source of infection, the use of broad-spectrum antibiotics is recommended. The specific agent depends on many variables, including institutional preference and local resistance patterns. As results from cultures become available, therapy should be modified. There is no consensus about the need for double or triple antibiotic coverage for particular organisms, although it is common practice to double-cover virulent organisms, such as *P. aeruginosa*, as well as areas that are commonly infected with multiple organisms such as the peritoneum.

Novel Therapies

Activated Protein C

After years of unsuccessful, large-scale, multicenter trials of novel therapeutic agents for sepsis, recombinant activated protein C (APC) became the first therapy to produce a reduced mortality rate.[64] APC was shown to improve survival by 6.1% in patients with severe sepsis.[64] This benefit is realized most in patients who are more severely ill, as characterized by an APACHE II score greater than 25. The Food and Drug Administration has approved APC for use in this group only. A recent cost-benefit analysis estimated the cost per life-year saved by APC to be $27,936 in all patients. When stratified by severity of illness, the cost-benefit in patients with an APACHE II score greater than 25 is $24,484 per life-year saved; for those with an APACHE II score greater than 25, it is $575,054 per life-year saved. Although its use primarily occurs in the intensive care unit setting, patient selection can begin the emergency department setting. Additionally, as an emphasis continues to be placed on early intervention, initiation of therapy in the emergency department is likely to occur.

Steroid Therapy

It has been nearly 30 years since the first treatment attempts to block inflammation in sepsis. Because sepsis involves a systemic inflammatory response, corticosteroids are a logical treatment modality as anti-inflammatory agents. Physicians have been working for decades to prove or disprove their value. A large study in the mid-1980s conducted by the Veterans Administration Systemic Sepsis Cooperative Study Group found no reduction in mortality among patients receiving early methylprednisolone therapy.[105] Bone and associates[106] also studied the use of methylprednisolone in patients with sepsis and found increased mortality in those patients who were randomized to the steroid arm. Briegel and associates[107] showed decreased time of vasopressor therapy with stress doses of hydrocortisone but no reduction in mortality.

Recently, Annane and associates[108] performed a randomized, double-blind, placebo-controlled study of 300 patients with septic shock that demonstrated benefit when steroids (hydrocortisone 50 mg IV every 6 hours, plus fludrocortisone 50 µg each day) were given to nonresponders in a corticotropin stimulation test. Among nonresponders, those treated with steroids had a 53% mortality rate, compared to 63% in the placebo group, for a 10% absolute benefit. Steroid therapy was not beneficial to those who responded to the corticotropin stimulation test. Marik and Zaloga[109] asserted that an initial random cortisol level of less than 25 µg/dL should be used to determine adrenal insufficiency. Furthermore, there continues to be debate whether a 1 µg ACTH test should be used instead of 250 µg. In coming years, new data will emerge regarding optimal corticosteroid replacement in septic patients. At present, a random cortisol level should be measured in the emergency department to help guide inpatient therapy. If steroids are to be administered, they should be low dose (<300 mg/day of hydrocortisone).

Extracorporeal Membrane Oxygenation

There are no reports of controlled trials of the efficacy of extracorporeal membrane oxygenation circuits in adults. Its clinical use is based on several animal and small human trials. Animal models have shown promising results in that, in certain clinical settings, extracorporeal membrane oxygenation can increase hemofiltration of endotoxin and decrease serum concentrations of TNF-α, lactate, and eicosanoids.[110-112] Retrospective studies of children and neonates have shown decreased mortality in the setting of refractory septic shock, but no prospective trials have been recorded.[113-115] No adult studies have evaluated the effect of extracorporeal membrane oxygenation on mortality. Although several small studies have shown improved clearance of the mediators of septic shock, whether that will translate into a mortality benefit is unknown.[86]

Dopexamine

Dopexamine is a synthetic catecholamine that has been available in Europe for several years. It is a strong β and dopaminergic agonist but has little α-adrenergic action. It is theorized to increase hepatosplanchnic perfusion, although this benefit is at the expense of tachycardia. Hypotension has been seen as a result of its β_2 activity. There are small but promising studies that show possible benefit,[116] but based on current pooled data, it is not recommended for routine use.[86]

As our understanding of the pathogenesis of sepsis grows, future agents will likely be developed to combat specific mediators of sepsis. Given the high mortality rate from sepsis, it is clear that much work remains, and there is hope that further study will yield a drug with specific and significant value in combating sepsis-related mortality.

Disposition

Patients with sepsis syndromes should have consultation with the admitting service while in the emergency department, as dictated by their clinical presentation and course. Once the emergency department management is complete, antibiotics are given, and the need for emergency operative intervention or procedure has been excluded, patients with sepsis should be admitted to the hospital. Patients with severe sepsis and septic shock should be admitted to an intensive care unit, and those with SIRS or impending sepsis can be admitted to a monitored floor with close supervision or an intensive care unit.

 KEY CONCEPTS

- Sepsis is a progression of disease ranging from SIRS to sepsis to severe sepsis to septic shock to MODS, all of which are due to a dysregulated inflammatory cascade.
- Elderly, immunocompromised, and neutropenic patients and patients with multiple comorbidities are at increased risk for development of sepsis syndromes.
- Early administration of appropriate antibiotics is essential in the treatment of sepsis syndromes.
- Patients with septic shock should be treated with aggressive fluid resuscitation and vasopressor therapy as needed.

REFERENCES

1. Bone R: American College of Chest Physicians/Society of Critical Care Medicine Consensus Conference: Definitions for sepsis and organ failure and guidelines for the use of innovative therapies in sepsis. *Crit Care Med* 20:864, 1992.
2. Rangel-Frausto M, et al: The natural history of the systemic inflammatory response syndrome (SIRS). *JAMA* 273:117, 1995.
3. Bates D, Cook E, Goldman L, Lee T: Predicting bacteremia in hospitalized patients: A prospectively validated model. *Ann Intern Med* 113:495, 1990.
4. Brun-Buisson C, et al: Incidence, risk factors, and outcome of severe sepsis and septic shock in adults. *JAMA* 274:968, 1995.

5. Perl T, Dvorak L, Hwang T, Wenzel R: Long-term survival and function after suspected gram-negative sepsis. *JAMA* 274:338, 1995.

6. Sands K, et al: Epidemiology of sepsis syndrome in 8 academic medical centers. *JAMA* 278:234, 1997.

7. Friedman G, Silva E, Vincent J: Has the mortality of septic shock changed with time? *Crit Care Med* 26:2078, 1998.

8. Geerdes H, et al: Septicemia in 980 patients at a university hospital in Berlin: Prospective studies during 4 selected years between 1979 and 1989. *Clin Infect Dis* 15:991-1002, 1992.

9. Leibovici L, et al: Septic shock in bacteremia patients: Risk factors, features and prognosis. *Scand J Infect Dis* 29:71, 1997.

10. Kochanek K, Smith B: Deaths: Preliminary data for 2002. *Natl Vital Stat Rep* 52:1, 2004.

11. Angus D, et al: Epidemiology of severe sepsis in the United States: Analysis of incidence, outcome, and associated costs of care. *Crit Care Med* 29:1303, 2001.

12. Parrillo J: Pathogenetic mechanisms of septic shock. *N Engl J Med* 328:1471, 1993.

13. Pinner R, et al: Trends in infectious diseases mortality in the United States. *JAMA* 275:189, 1996.

14. Rangel-Frausto M: The epidemiology of bacterial sepsis. *Infect Dis Clin North Am* 13:299, 1999.

15. Sharkey R, et al: Toxic shock syndrome following influenza A infection. *Intens Care Med* 25:335, 1999.

16. Martin G, Mannino D, Eaton S, Moss M: The epidemiology of sepsis in the United States from 1979 through 2000. *N Engl J Med* 348:1546, 2003.

17. Suffredini AF, et al: The cardiovascular response of normal humans to the administration of endotoxin. *N Engl J Med* 321:280, 1989.

18. Kirkland T, Ziegler E: An immunoprotective monoclonal antibody to lipopolysaccharide. *J Immunol* 132:2590, 1984.

19. Lefer A: Significance of lipid mediators in shock states. *Circ Shock* 27:3, 1989.

20. Chang S, Feddersen C, Henson P, Voelkel N: Platelet-activating factor mediates hemodynamic changes and lung injury in endotoxin-treated rats. *J Clin Invest* 79:1498, 1987.

21. Terashita Z, Imura Y, Nishikawa K, Sumida S: Is platelet activating factor (PAF) a mediator of endotoxin shock? *Eur J Pharmacol* 109:257, 1985.

22. Deventer S, et al: Experimental endotoxemia in humans: Analysis of cytokine release and coagulation, fibrinolytic and complement pathways. *Blood* 76:2520, 1990.

23. Doughty L, Kaplan S, Carcillo J: The IL-10 response in pediatric sepsis and organ failure. *Crit Care Med* 24(suppl):A32, 1996.

24. Platzer C, et al: Upregulation of monocytic IL-10 by tumor necrosis factor-α and cAMP elevating drugs. *Int Immunol* 7:517, 1995.

25. Dinarello CA, Wolff SM: The role of interleukin-1 in disease. *N Engl J Med* 328:106, 1993. [Erratum: *N Engl J Med* 328:744, 1993.]

26. Cannon G, Tompkins R, Gelfand J: Circulating interleukin-1 and tumor necrosis factor in septic shock and experimental endotoxin fever. *J Infect Dis* 161:79, 1990.

27. Dinarello C: The proinflammatoory cytokines interleukin-1 and tumor necrosis factor and the treatment of septic shock syndrome. *J Infect Dis* 163:1177, 1991.

28. Dinarello C, et al: Tumor necrosis factor (cachectin) is an endogenous pyrogen and induces production of interleukin-1. *J Exp Med* 163:1433, 1986.

29. Okusawa S, et al: Interleukin-1 induces a shock-like state in rabbits: Synergism with tumor necrosis factor and the effect of cyclooxygenase inhibition. *J Clin Invest* 81:1162, 1988.

30. Ohlsson K, et al: Interleukin-1 receptor antagonist reduces mortality from endotoxic shock. *Nature* 348:550, 1990.

31. Tracey K, et al: Anti-cachectin/TNF monoclonal antibodies prevent septic shock during lethal bacteremia. *Nature* 330:662, 1987.

32. Meer JV, Barza M, Wolff S: A low dose of recombinant interleukin-1 protects granulocytopenic mice from lethal gram-negative infection. *Proc Nat Acad Sci U S A* 85:1620, 1988.

33. Alexander H, Sheppard B, Jense J: Treatment with recombinant human tumor necrosis factor-alpha protects rats against the lethality, hypotension and hypothermia of gram-negative sepsis. *J Clin Invest* 88:34, 1991.

34. Fischer E, Zee KV, Marano M: Interleukin-1 receptor antagonist circulates in experimental inflammation and in human disease. *Blood* 79:2196, 1992.

35. Howard M, et al: Interleukin-10 protects mice from endotoxemia. *J Exp Med* 177:1205, 1993.

36. Holtzman M: Arachidonic acid metabolism: Implications of biological chemistry for lung function and disease. *Am Rev Respir Dis* 143:188, 1991.

37. Arons M, et al: Effects of ibuprofen on the physiology and survival of hypothermic sepsis. *Crit Care Med* 27:699, 1999.

38. Bernard G, et al: Prostacyclin and thromboxane A2 formation is increased in human sepsis syndrome: Effects of cyclooxygenase inhibition. *Am Rev Respir Dis* 144:1095, 1991.

39. Holmes CL, et al: The effects of vasopressin on hemodynamics and renal function in severe septic shock: A case series. *Intens Care Med* 27:1416, 2001.

40. Reid IA: Role of vasopressin deficiency in the vasodilation of septic shock. *Circulation* 95:1108, 1997.

41. Palmer R, Ferrige A, Moncada S: Nitric oxide release accounts for the biologic activity of endothelium-derived relaxing factor. *Nature* 327:524, 1987.

42. Lowenstein C, Dinerman J, Snyder S: Nitric oxide: A physiologic messenger. *Ann Intern Med* 120:227, 1994.

43. Murad F: Signal transduction using nitric oxide and cyclic guanosine monophosphate. *JAMA* 276:1189, 1996.

44. Nguyen T, et al: DNA damage and mutation in human cells exposed to nitric oxide in vitro. *Biochemistry* 89:3030, 1992.

45. Van Dervort A, et al: Nitric oxide regulates endotoxin-induced TNF alpha production in human neutrophils. *J Immunol* 152:4102, 1994.

46. Beasley D, Schwartz J, Brenner B: Interleukin-1 induces prolonged L-arginine-dependent cyclic guanosine monophosphate and nitrite production in rat vascular smooth muscle cells. *J Clin Invest* 87:602, 1991.

47. Young G, et al: The encephalopathy associated with septic illness. *Clin Invest Med* 13:297, 1990.

48. Sprung C, et al: Impact of encephalopathy on mortality in the sepsis syndrome. *Crit Care Med* 18:801, 1990.

49. Bleck T, et al: Neurologic complications of critical medical illnesses. *Crit Care Med* 21:98, 1993.

50. Eidelman L, Putterman D, Putterman C, Sprung C: The spectrum of septic encephalopathy: Definitions, etiologies, and mortalities. *JAMA* 275:470, 1996.

51. Bowton D: Central nervous system effects of sepsis. *Crit Care Clin* 5:785, 1989.

52. Hoffman W, et al: Role of endotoxemia in cardiovascular dysfunction and lethality: Virulent and nonvirulent *Escherichia coli* challenges in a canine model of septic shock. *Infect Immunol* 64:406, 1996.

53. Natanson C, et al: Role of endotoxemia in cardiovascular dysfunction and mortality: *Escherichia coli* and *Staphylococcus aureus* challenges in a canine model of septic shock. *J Clin Invest* 83:243, 1989.

54. Gunnar R, et al: Hemodynamic measurements in bacteremia and septic shock in man. *J Infect Dis* 128(Suppl):295, 1973.

55. Hess M, Hastillo A, Greenfield L: Spectrum of cardiovascular function during gram-negative sepsis. *Prog Cardiovasc Dis* 23:279, 1981.

56. Parker M, et al: Serial cardiovascular variables in survivors and nonsurvivors of human septic shock: Heart rate as an early predictor of prognosis. *Crit Care Med* 15:923, 1987.

57. Ognibene F, et al: Depressed left ventricular performance: Response to volume infusion in patients with sepsis and septic shock. *Chest* 93:903, 1988.

58. Field S, Kelly S, Macklem P: The oxygen cost of breathing in patients with cardiorespiratory disease. *Am Rev Respir Dis* 126:9, 1982.

59. Kaplan R, Sahn S, Petty T: Incidence and outcome of the respiratory distress syndrome in gram-negative sepsis. *Arch Intern Med* 139:867, 1979.

60. Aberle D, Brown K: Radiologic considerations in the adult respiratory distress syndrome. *Clin Chest Med* 11:737, 1990.

61. Pastor C, Billiar T, Losser M, Payen D: Liver injury during sepsis. *J Crit Care* 10:183, 1995.

62. Osterud B, Flaegstad T: Increased tissue thromboplastin activity in monocytes of patients with meningococcal infections related to unfavourable prognosis. *Thromb Haemost* 49:5, 1983.

63. Faust SN, et al: Dysfunction of endothelial protein C activation in severe meningococcal sepsis. *N Engl J Med* 345:408, 2001.

64. Bernard GR, et al: Efficacy and safety of recombinant human activated protein C for severe sepsis. *N Engl J Med* 344:699, 2001.

65. Levi M, Cate H, Poll T, Deventer S: Pathogenesis of disseminated intravascular coagulation in sepsis. *JAMA* 270:975, 1993.

66. Voss R, Matthias F, Borkowski G, Reitz D: Activation and inhibition of fibrinolysis in septic patients in an internal medicine intensive care unit. *Br J Haematol* 75:99, 1990.

67. Shapiro NI, et al: Mortality in Emergency Department Sepsis (MEDS) score: A prospectively derived and validated clinical prediction rule. *Crit Care Med* 31:670, 2003.

68. Peduzzi P, Shatney C, Sheagren J, Sprung C, Group VASSCS: Predictors of bacteremia and gram-negative bacteremia in patients with sepsis. *Arch Intern Med* 152:529, 1992.

69. Stacpoole P, et al: Natural history and course of acquired lactic acidosis in adults. *Am J Med* 97:47, 1994.

70. Rivers E, et al: Early goal-directed therapy in the treatment of severe sepsis and septic shock. *N Engl J Med* 345:1368, 2001.

71. Leibovici L, et al: Bacteremia in febrile patients: A clinical model for diagnosis. *Arch Intern Med* 151:1801, 1991.

72. Bates D, et al: Predicting bacteremia in patients with sepsis syndrome. *J Infect Dis* 176:1538, 1997.

73. Makadon HJ, et al: Febrile inpatients: House officers' use of blood cultures. *J Gen Intern Med* 2:293, 1987.

74. Dellinger RP, et al: Surviving Sepsis Campaign guidelines for management of severe sepsis and septic shock. *Intensive Care Med* 30:536, 2004.

75. Czer L, Shoemaker W: Optimal hematocrit value in critically ill patients. *Surg Gynecol Obstet* 147:363, 1978.

76. Steffes C, Bender J, Levison M: Blood transfusion and oxygen consumption in surgical sepsis. *Crit Care Med* 19:512, 1991.

77. Mink R, Pollack M: Effect of blood transfusion on oxygen consumption in pediatric septic shock. *Crit Care Med* 18:1087, 1990.

78. Conrad S, Dietch K, Hebert C: Effect of red cell transfusion on oxygen consumption following fluid resuscitation in septic shock. *Circulation Shock* 31:419, 1990.

79. Hebert P, et al: A multicenter, randomized, controlled clinical trial of transfusion requirements in critical care. *N Engl J Med* 340:409, 1999.

80. Wheeler A, Gordon R: Treating patients with severe sepsis. *N Engl J Med* 340:207, 1999.

81. Hickling K, Henderson S, Jackson R: Low mortality associated with low volume pressure limited ventilation with permissive hypercapnia in severe adult respiratory distress syndrome. *Intensive Care Med* 16:372, 1990.

82. Roupie E, et al: Titration of tidal volume and induced hypercapnia in acute respiratory distress syndrome. *Am J Respir Crit Care Med* 152:121, 1995.

83. Dellinger R: Current therapy for sepsis. *Infect Dis Clin North Am* 13:495, 1999.

84. Rackow E, Falk J, Fein I: Fluid resuscitation in shock: A comparison of cardiorespiratory effects of albumin, hetastarch and saline solutions in patients with hypovolemic shock. *Crit Care Med* 11:839, 1983.

85. Rackow E, Astiz M: Mechanisms and management of septic shock. *Crit Care Clin* 9:219, 1993.

86. Hollenberg S, et al: Practice parameters for hemodynamic support of sepsis in adult patients with sepsis. *Crit Care Med* 27:639, 1999.

87. De Backer D, et al: Does hepato-splanchnic VO_2/DO_2 dependency exist in critically ill septic patients? *Am J Respir Crit Care Med* 157:1219, 1998.

88. Gutierrez G, et al: Gastric intramucosal pH as a therapeutic index of tissue oxygenation in critically ill patients. *Lancet* 339:195, 1992.

89. Shoemaker W, Kram H, Appel P: Therapy of shock based on pathophysiology, monitoring, and outcome prediction. *Crit Care Med* 18:S19, 1990.

90. Martin C, et al: Norepinephrine or dopamine for the treatment of hyperdynamic septic shock. *Chest* 103:1826, 1993.

91. Desjars P, et al: Norepinephrine therapy has no deleterious renal effects in human septic shock. *Chest* 17:426, 1989.

92. Martin C, et al: Renal effects of norepinephrine used to treat septic shock patients. *Crit Care Med* 18:282, 1990.

93. Redl-Wenzl E, et al: The effects of norepinephrine on hemodynamics and renal function in severe septic shock states. *Intensive Care Med* 19:151, 1993.

94. Kellum JA, Decker JM: Use of dopamine in acute renal failure: a meta-analysis. *Crit Care Med* 29:1526, 2001.

95. Bellomo R, et al: Low-dose dopamine in patients with early renal dysfunction: A placebo-controlled randomised trial. Australian and New Zealand Intensive Care Society (ANZICS) Clinical Trials Group. *Lancet* 356:2139, 2000.

96. Hanneman L, et al: Comparison of dopamine to dobutamine and norepinephrine for oxygen delivery and uptake in septic shock. *Crit Care Med* 23:1962, 1995.

97. Meier-Hellmann A, et al: The effects of low-dose dopamine on splanchnic blood flow and oxygen utilization in patients with septic shock. *Intensive Care Med* 23:31, 1997.

98. Gregory J, et al: Experience with phenylephrine as a component of the pharmacologic support of septic shock. *Crit Care Med* 19:1395, 1991.

99. Day N, et al: The effects of dopamine and adrenaline infusions on acid-base balance and systemic hemodynamics in severe infection. *Lancet* 348:219, 1996.

100. Wilson W, et al: Septic shock: Does adrenaline have a role as a first-line inotropic agent? *Anaesth Intensive Care* 20:470, 1992.

101. Gutierrez G, et al: Effect of dobutamine on oxygen consumption and gastric mucosal pH in septic patients. *Am J Respir Crit Care Med* 150:324, 1994.

102. Aube H, Milan C, Bletery B: Risk factors for septic shock in the early management of bacteremia. *Am J Med* 93:283, 1992.

103. Opal S, et al: Confirmatory interleukin-1 receptor antagonist trial in severe sepsis: A phase III, randomized, double-blind, placebo-controlled, multicenter trial. *Crit Care Med* 25:1115, 1997.

104. Pittet D, et al: Bedside prediction of mortality from bacteremic sepsis: A dynamic analysis of ICU patients. *Am J Respir Crit Care Med* 153:684, 1996.

105. The Veterans Administration Systemic Sepsis Cooperative Study Group: Effect of high-dose glucocorticoid therapy on mortality in patients with clinical signs of systemic sepsis. *N Engl J Med* 317:659, 1987.

106. Bone RC, et al: A controlled clinical trial of high-dose methylprednisolone in the treatment of severe sepsis and septic shock. *N Engl J Med* 317:653, 1987.

107. Briegel J, et al: Stress doses of hydrocortisone reverse hyperdynamic septic shock: a prospective, randomized, double-blind, single-center study. *Crit Care Med* 27:723, 1999.

108. Annane D, et al: Effect of treatment with low doses of hydrocortisone and fludrocortisone on mortality in patients with septic shock. *JAMA* 288:862, 2002.

109. Marik PE, Zaloga GP: Adrenal insufficiency during septic shock. *Crit Care Med* 31:141, 2003.

110. Griffen M, et al: Extracorporeal membrane oxygenation for gram-negative septic shock in the immature pig. *Circ Shock* 33:195, 1991.

111. Grootendorst A, et al: High volume hemofiltration improves right ventricular function in endotoxin-induced shock in the pig. *Intensive Care Med* 18:235, 1992.

112. Stein B, et al: Influence of continuous haemofiltration on haemodynamics and central blood volume in experimental endotoxic shock. *Intensive Care Med* 16:494, 1990.

113. Goldman A, et al: Extracorporeal support for intractable cardiorespiratory failure due to meningococcal disease. *Lancet* 349:466, 1997.

114. Beca J, Butt W: Extracorporeal membrane oxygenation for refractory septic shock in children. *Pediatrics* 93:726, 1994.

115. McCune S, et al: Extracorporeal membrane oxygenation therapy in neonates with septic shock. *J Pediatr Surg* 25:479, 1990.

116. Hannemann L, et al: Dopexamine hydrochloride in septic shock. *Chest* 109:756, 1996.

Index

Note: Page numbers followed by b, f, and t refer to boxes, figures, and tables, respectively.

Diabetic foot, 1971
  osteomyelitis in, 2185-2186
Diabetic ketoacidosis, 1928, 1962-1967
  complications of, 1967
  diagnosis of, 1963-1964
  differential considerations in, 1964-1965
  disposition in, 1967
  etiology of, 1963
  hypophosphatemia in, 1951
  in pregnancy, 1972, 2771-2772
  laboratory tests in, 1964, 1964t
  management of, 1965-1967, 1965b
  nausea and vomiting in, 205t
  pathophysiology of, 1962-1963, 1962t, 1963f
Diagnostic approach, clinical decision making
    and, 125-130, 127f, 128b, 129f
Diagnostic-therapeutic trial, in clinical decision
    making, 128
Dialysate, bloody, causes of, 1553
Dialysis
  for acute renal failure, 2650
  for acute tumor lysis syndrome, 1912, 1912b
  for barbiturate overdose, 2483
  for beta blocker overdose, 2375
  for bipyridyl compound poisoning, 2466
  for chronic heart failure, 1277
  for chronic renal failure, 1547-1554
    complications of, 1549-1554, 1550b, 1552b,
      1553t
    emergency, indications for, 1548-1549, 1548b
  for hyperkalemia, 1941
  for isopropyl alcohol poisoning, 2404
  for lithium toxicity, 2444
  for pulmonary edema in chronic renal failure,
    1546, 1548
  for rewarming in accidental hypothermia,
    2249, 2250t, 2251
  for salicylate overdose, 2342
  for toxic alcohol poisoning, 2401-2402
  for uremic pericarditis, 1282
  vascular access for, problems related to, 1364-
    1366
Dialysis disequilibrium syndrome, 1622
Diaper dermatitis, 1852
Diaphoresis
  in asthma, 1084
  in ciguatera fish poisoning, 1473
Diaphragm
  in pregnancy, 317
  injury to, laparotomy and, 504
Diaphragmatic hernia
  neonatal resuscitation in, 121
  traumatic, in children, 340, 341
Diaphyseal fracture, 2699
Diaphysis, 2175, 2175f
Diarrhea, 227-236
  acute vs. chronic, 228
  ancillary studies in, 233
  diagnostic approach to, 228-233, 230b, 231b
  differential diagnosis in, 228, 230b-231b, 234
  disposition in, 235-236
  empiric management of, 234-235, 234f, 236t
  epidemiology of, 227-228
  from abnormal motility, 228
  history in, 232
  hypokalemia from, 1938
  in Aeromonas hydrophila gastroenteritis, 1467
  in Bacillus anthracis gastroenteritis, 1469
  in Bacillus cereus food poisoning, 1471
  in Campylobacter gastroenteritis, 1460
  in ciguatera fish poisoning, 1473
  in Clostridium difficile enterocolitis, 1475
  in Clostridium perfringens food poisoning,
    1471
  in coccidial gastroenteritis, 1477, 1478
  in Escherichia coli food poisoning, 1474
  in Giardia gastroenteritis, 1479
  in hemolytic uremic syndrome, 2654
  in hemorrhagic Escherichia coli serotype
    O157:H7 gastroenteritis, 1466
  in HIV/AIDS, 1482-1484, 1482t, 1483b, 1485t,
    2084
  in inflammatory bowel disease, 1501, 2616
  in intestinal amebiasis, 1480
  in intussusception, 2610
  in parasitic infection, 2112, 2112f, 2113f
  in Plesiomonas shigelloides gastroenteritis,
    1468
  in salmonellosis, 1463

Diarrhea (Continued)
  in scombroid fish poisoning, 1472
  in shigellosis, 1464
  in staphylococcal food poisoning, 1470
  in Vibrio fish poisoning, 1472
  in Vibrio parahaemolyticus gastroenteritis,
    1466
  in viral gastroenteritis, 1476
  in Yersinia enterocolitica gastroenteritis, 1465
  infectious, 228, 230b
    pediatric, 2623-2634
    treatment of, 229t-230t, 235
  inflammatory, 228, 229t-230t
  metabolic acidosis in, 2624
  noninfectious, 228, 231b
  osmotic, 228, 2624
  pathophysiology of, 228, 229t-230t
  pediatric, 227, 2623-2634, 2628b, 2628t. See
    also Children, infectious diarrhea in.
  physical examination in, 232-233
  rapid assessment and stabilization in, 228,
    232
  secretory, 228, 2624
  severe, with blood and mucus. See Dysentery.
  traveler's, 1484-1487, 1486t, 1487b
Diastolic dysfunction
  in heart failure, 1267
  in restrictive cardiomyopathy, 1296
Diathermic rewarming, 2250
Diazepam, 2484, 2484t
  for alcohol withdrawal syndrome, 2862, 2863
  for alcohol-related seizure, 2864, 2865
  for cocaine overdose, 2389
  for febrile seizure, 2667
  for nerve agent exposure, 3030
  for psychostimulant intoxication, 2410
  for seizure, 166, 166t, 1626, 1627t
    in cancer patient, 1919
    in children, 2675t
  for status epilepticus, 2672-2673, 2672t
  for tetanus, 2011
  for vertigo, 146
  in ventilated patient, 30
  prophylactic, in severe head trauma, 361
Dichloroacetic acid, for condylomata acuminata,
    1564
Dichlorophenoxyacetic acid, 2465b
Diclofenac, 2927
Dicloxacillin
  during pregnancy and lactation, 2784
  for folliculitis, 1843
  for impetigo, 1843
  for staphylococcal scalded skin syndrome, 1845
Didanosine, 2079t
Dieffenbachia, 2473, 2473f
Diet
  BRAT, for diarrhea, 235
  diabetic, 1973
  during pregnancy, 2736
  high-fiber, for diverticular disease, 1494
  in acute pancreatitis, 1433-1434
  in burn injury, 918
Dietary guidelines
  for traveler's diarrhea prophylaxis, 1486
  of American Heart Association, 3177, 3177b
Dietary supplements, 2475-2477, 2476t
Diethylcarbamazine, for loiasis, 2110
Diethylenetriamine pentaacetic acid, for
    plutonium exposure, 3023
Difficult airway
  approach to, 8-9, 9f
  cricothyrotomy for, 22-23, 23f
  esophagotracheal combitube for, 20, 20f
  fiberoptic intubation in, 20-21, 22f
  identification of, 3-4, 3b, 4b, 5f
  in children, 2502, 2502b
  intubating laryngeal mask airway for, 19, 19f
  lighted stylet for, 19-20, 20f
  retrograde intubation of, 20
  special airway devices for, 18-23, 19f-23f
Difficult patient, 2972-2982
  as stressor for emergency physician, 3175
  behavioral classification of, 2978-2981, 2978t
  combative patient as, 2956-2969. See also
    Combative patient.
  definition of, 2972-2973
  emergency department factors in, 2973
  impaired patient-physician relationship and,
    2973, 2974f

Difficult patient (Continued)
  management of, 2973-2981
    crisis intervention in, 2976-2977, 2977b
    dealing with negative reactions in, 2975-
      2976
    general strategies in, 2973-2975, 2973b
    personality disorder classification of, 2978,
      2979b
    physician factors in, 2973
Diffuse axonal injury
  in child abuse, 971
  in head trauma, 374
Digital radiography, in fracture, 557
Digital subtraction angiography
  in peripheral vascular injury, 543
  intravenous, in aortic rupture, 480-481
Digitalis lanata, 2476
Digoxin (digitalis)
  as antidysrhythmic drug, 1211-1212, 1211t
  during pregnancy and lactation, 2787
  for acute pulmonary edema in hypotensive
    patient, 1270t, 1274
  for atrial flutter, 1229
  for chronic heart failure, 1276
  for heart failure, 2583, 2583t
  for junctional tachycardia, 1234
  hyperkalemia from, 1940
  misconceptions about, 1212
  overdose of, 2368-2373
    acute vs. chronic, 2369, 2370t
    antidotes to, 2329t
    clinical features of, 2369, 2370b
    diagnosis of, 2369-2370
    differential diagnosis in, 2370
    disposition in, 2372-2373
    dysrhythmias associated with, 2369b
    in children, 2372, 2372t
    management of, 2370-2371, 2372b
    pathophysiology of, 2368-2369, 2369b
    risk of, factors associated with, 2369b
  side effects of, 1211-1212, 1212b
Dihydrocodeine, respiratory effects of, 2453t
Dihydroergotamine, for migraine, 1633t, 1634
Dihydropyridines, 1321t
Dilated cardiomyopathy, 1293-1294
  heart failure in, 1264
  inflammatory. See Myocarditis.
  peripartum cardiomyopathy and, 1297
Dilation and curettage, after miscarriage, 2742
Dilation and evacuation, in ectopic pregnancy,
    2745
Diloxanide, for intestinal amebiasis, 1481
Diltiazem, 1211, 1321t
  during pregnancy and lactation, 2788
  for atrial flutter, 1229
  for dysphagia, 1398
  overdose of, 2376, 2377t
Dimenhydrinate, for vertigo, 146
Dilutional thrombocytopenia, 1898
Dimercaprol
  for arsenic poisoning, 2424
  for lead poisoning, 2422
2,3-Dimercaptosuccinic acid
  for arsenic poisoning, 2424
  for lead poisoning, 2422
  for mercury poisoning, 2426
Dinitrocresol, 2463, 2463b
Dinitrophenol, 2463, 2463b, 2464
Diphenhydramine
  anticholinergic toxicity of, 2345
  for acute extrapyramidal symptoms, 2449
  for anaphylactic shock, 54
  for anaphylaxis, 1831b, 1832, 2549
  for drug eruptions, 1845
  for hymenoptera stings, 904
  for local anesthesia, 847, 2931
  for OTC sleep aid overdose, 2487-2488, 2488t
  for scombroid fish poisoning, 1472
  for upper airway angioedema, 1835
  for vertigo, 146
Diphenoxylate
  for diarrhea, 236t
  overdose of, 2456
  respiratory effects of, 2453t
Diphtheria, 2001-2004, 2003b
  myocarditis in, 1291
  pharyngitis in, 1110-1111, 1113
  vaccine for, 2002, 2004, 2012, 2012t
Diphyllobothrium latum, 2102t, 2107

Nerve injury
    in electrical and lightning injuries, 2271
    in fracture, 559, 559t
    in hand trauma, 614
    in high-altitude cerebral edema, 2306
    in hip trauma, 762-763
    in neck trauma, 450
    in pelvic fracture, 719-720
    in supracondylar fracture, 2696-2697
Nerve supply
    to distal humerus and elbow, 648-649, 648f
    to face, 383-384
    to femur and hip, 737-738
    to foot, 821
    to forearm, 640t
    to hand, 586-587, 588f, 589f
    to knee, 771
    to lower leg, 797
    to shoulder, 672
    to wrist, 622, 625f
Nervous system. See Central nervous system;
    Neurologic entries; Peripheral nervous
    system.
Nesiritide, for acute pulmonary edema, 1270t,
    1272
Networks, in medical information systems, 3104
Neurapraxia, 559
Neurocysticercosis, seizure in, 1623
Neuroendocrine tumor, pancreatic, 1437
Neurofibrillary tangles, in dementia, 1657
Neurofibromatosis, vertigo in, 2683
Neurogenic bladder, in spinal cord injury, 2908
Neurogenic hypotension, secondary to spinal
    shock, 437
Neurogenic obstruction of small bowel, 1440
Neurogenic pulmonary edema
    after head trauma, 371
    after seizure, 1625
Neurohormonal alterations, in heart failure,
    1262-1263
Neuroimaging studies
    in central nervous system infection, 1719-1720
    in headache, 2679, 2680b
    in HIV/AIDS, 2079-2080, 2080f
    in minor head trauma, 364-365
    in severe head trauma, 361-362, 362t
Neuroleptic agents. See Antipsychotic agents.
Neuroleptic malignant syndrome, 2257-2258,
    2961-2962
    clinical features of, 2447, 2447t
    differential diagnosis in, 2448, 2448t
    from antipsychotic agents, 1732-1733
    management of, 2449
    serotonin syndrome vs., 2359
Neurologic abnormalities
    in acoustic neuroma, 1668-1669
    in acute renal failure, 1540
    in antidepressant overdose, 2354t, 2356
    in bacterial meningitis, 2658
    in carbon monoxide poisoning, 2439
    in central nervous system infection, 1714
    in cerebral venous thrombosis, 1670
    in cervical vascular injury, 449
    in chronic renal failure, 1542
    in ciguatera fish poisoning, 1473
    in electrical and lightning injuries, 2273-2274,
        2274
    in epidural abscess, 1684
    in epidural hematoma, 1683
    in ethylene glycol poisoning, 2399
    in head trauma, 370-371
    in headache, 172t
    in heatstroke, 2260-2261, 2262
    in hemodialysis patient, 1551-1552, 1552b
    in HIV/AIDS, 1683
    in hypothermia, 2241
    in idiopathic spastic paraparesis, 1683
    in intracerebral hemorrhage, 1611
    in ischemic stroke, 1609-1610
    in lithium toxicity, 2442
    in MAOI toxicity, 2365
    in mitral valve prolapse, 1305
    in multiple sclerosis, 1672, 1681
    in opioid overdose, 2452
    in organophosphate poisoning, 2460
    in osteogenesis imperfecta, 2700-2701
    in serotonin toxicity of, 2360
    in shigellosis, 1464
    in spinal subarachnoid hemorrhage, 1682

Neurologic abnormalities (Continued)
    in substituted phenol poisoning, 2464
    in syringomyelia, 1682-1683
    in systemic lupus erythematosus, 1807
    in transverse myelitis, 1682
    in vitamin B₁₂ deficiency, 1874
    mushrooms associated with, 2478-2479
Neurologic disorders, 1606-1723
    airway foreign body aspiration and, 866
    anxiety in, 1747-1748
    cranial nerve, 1664-1670, 1665t
    delirium in, 1645-1655
    dementia in, 1655-1662
    headache in, 1631-1643
    in botulism, 1707-1708, 2014
    in HIV/AIDS, 2079-2082, 2080f
    in Lyme disease, 2123, 2128
    in pregnancy, 2768-2771
    in Rocky Mountain spotted fever, 2134
    in spinal cord injury, 2909
    pediatric, 2657-2686
    peripheral, 1687-1701
    seizure in, 1619-1629
    spinal cord, 1675-1685
    stroke in, 1606-1617
Neurologic emergencies, in cancer patient, 1918-
    1921
Neurologic examination
    in back pain, 263
    in chest pain, 187t
    in comatose patient, 159-161, 159t
    in dyspnea, 178t
    in facial trauma, 388
    in head trauma, 356-357, 357t
    in multiple trauma, 309
    in nausea and vomiting, 202, 202t
    in seizure, 168
    in spinal injuries, 415-417
    in vertigo, 145
    of distal upper extremity, 2694t
Neuroma
    acoustic, 147t, 1668-1669
    Morton's, 837
Neuromuscular blocking agents
    competitive, for rapid sequence intubation,
        14-15, 15t
    for critically ill asthmatic patient, 1092-1093
    for intubation, 13-15
    for tetanus, 2011
    in intubated, mechanically ventilated patient,
        31
Neuromuscular disorders, 1702-1709
    clinical characteristics of, 1680t, 1703-1704,
        1703t
    diagnosis of, 1704-1705
    differential considerations in, 1703t, 1704
    history in, 1703
    in hyperkalemia, 1940
    laboratory studies in, 1704-1705
    oropharyngeal dysphagia in, 1396
    physical examination in, 1703-1704
    weakness and, 139, 139t, 140b, 1702-1709
Neuromuscular junction, 1703
Neuromuscular junction disease, 1705-1708
    clinical characteristics of, 1680t, 1703t, 1704
    in botulism, 1707-1708, 2014
    in myasthenia gravis, 1705-1707, 1706b
    in tick paralysis, 1708
Neuronal theory of headache, 2676
Neuronitis, vestibular, vertigo in, 147t
Neuronopathy
    in amyotrophic lateral sclerosis, 1700
    sensory, 1700, 1700b
Neuroophthalmologic visual loss, 1059-1061
Neuropathic pain, 1692
Neuropathy, 1687-1701. See also
    Mononeuropathy; Polyneuropathy.
    alcoholic, 1692, 2869
    anatomy in, 1688-1689, 1688f
    ancillary studies in, 1700-1701, 1701b
    asymmetric proximal and distal, 1692-1693,
        1693b
    autonomic
        diabetic, 1971
        in alcohol withdrawal syndrome, 2861
        in tetanus, 2009
    clinical features of, 1689-1700, 1703t, 1704
    cranial, 1664-1670, 1665t
        diabetic, 1669-1670

Neuropathy (Continued)
    eye movement disorders in, 1062-1063
    in ethylene glycol poisoning, 2399
    in Lyme disease, 2123
    in tetanus, 2009
    diabetic, 1669-1670, 1691-1692, 1970-1971
        in pregnancy, 1972
        lower extremity ulcers in, 1351, 1972
    epidemiology of, 1688
    in alcoholism, 1692
    in Guillain-Barré syndrome, 1690-1691
    in hip trauma, 762-763
    in HIV/AIDS, 1692, 2082
    in Lyme disease, 2124
    in plexopathies, 1692-1693, 1693b
    median nerve, 639, 639f
    metabolic, 1692
    optic
        compressive, 1060
        glaucoma as, 1055-1056, 1056f
        in ethylene glycol poisoning, 2399
        in methanol poisoning, 2395-2396
        ischemic, 1060
        toxic and metabolic, 1060
        traumatic, 1050-1051
    pathophysiology of, 1689
    patterns and prototypes of, 1690t
    peripheral vascular injury and, 539
    toxic, 1691b, 1692
Neuroprotective agents, for ischemic stroke,
    1616
Neuropsychiatric symptoms, in cocaine overdose,
    2388
Neurosis, hysterical, conversion type, 1755,
    1755b
Neurotmesis, 559
Neurotoxin
    botulinum, 2014
    tetanospasmin, 2009
Neurotransmitters
    in anxiety disorders, 1744-1745
    in delirium, 1646-1647
    in mood disorders, 1735
Neurovascular bundle, proximity wounds and,
    540, 540f
Neutron exposure, 2319-2320, 2320f
Neutropenia, 1888-1889, 1889f
    in cancer patient, 1907-1909, 1908b, 2834-
        2839, 2836t, 2838t
    in children, 2516
Neutrophil(s), 2834
    function of, 1886
    in arthritis, 1777
    in asthma, 1083
    in bacterial meningitis, 2662
    normal values for, 1886t
Neutrophilia, 1887-1888, 1887b, 1887f
Nevirapine, for HIV/AIDS, 2088
Newborn. See Neonate.
Nicardipine, 1321t
    for hypertensive emergencies, 1319
    for premature labor, 2807
    overdose of, 2377t
Nicotiana tabacum, 2474
Nicotine
    dermal exposure to, 2474
    ingestion of, 2474
    inhalation of. See Smoking.
Nicotinic acetylcholine receptors, 2345, 2347f
Nifedipine, 1321t
    during pregnancy and lactation, 2788
    for anal fissures, 1513
    for aortic dissection, 1329
    for chilblains, 2230
    for dysphagia, 1398
    for high-altitude pulmonary edema, 2304-2305
    for premature labor, 2807
    for thrombosed hemorrhoids, 1512
    overdose of, 2376, 2377t
Nifurtimox, for Chagas' disease, 2112
Night terrors, 2668
Nightstick fracture, 551t
Nikolsky's sign, in pemphigus vulgaris, 1857
Nimodipine
    for aneurysmal subarachnoid hemorrhage, 1637
    overdose of, 2377t
9-1-1 universal emergency access number, 2988
Nisoldipine, 1321t
    overdose of, 2377t

Petechiae (Continued)
  in meningococcal disease, 2022
  pediatric fever and, 2507-2508
Petroleum asphalt burns, 926-927, 937
Petroleum distillates, toxicity of, 2428, 2429t
Peyote, 2409, 2409f
Peyronie's disease, 534
pH
  in metabolic acidosis, 1929
  in metabolic alkalosis, 1930
  in mixed acid-base disorders, 1931
  in respiratory acidosis, 1925
  in respiratory alkalosis, 1926
  of blood
    changes in, compensatory responses to,
      1923-1924
    normal values for, 1923
Phagocytes, 2834
Phagocytosis, 2834
Phalangeal bones, 577-578, 579f-580f
Phalanx
  extensor tendon injury at
    distal, 605-607, 606f, 607f
    proximal, 608
  fracture of, 834
    distal, 593-594, 593f
    proximal, 594-595, 594f-596f
Phalen's sign, in carpal tunnel syndrome, 639,
  639f, 1697
Pharmacokinetics
  in children, 2935, 2952
  in elderly person, 2826
Pharyngeal pain, in pharyngitis, 1109
Pharyngitis, 274-279, 1109-1114
  ancillary studies in, 277-278, 277t
  clinical features of, 1109-1111, 1110f
  diagnosis of, 275-278, 276t, 277f, 277t, 1111-1112
  differential diagnosis in, 278, 1112
  disposition in, 1113-1114
  epidemiology of, 274
  etiology of, 1109
  high-altitude, 2304
  history in, 275-276
  in children, screening for, 2509b
  in epiglottitis, 2523
  in lingual tonsillitis, 1114
  in parapharyngeal abscess, 1122
  management of, 278-279, 278f, 1112-1113
  pathophysiology of, 274-275, 275t
  physical examination in, 276-277, 276t
  streptococcal, 274-275, 1109, 1110, 1111, 1112-
    1113, 1114
    adult epiglottitis vs., 1115
    in rheumatic fever, 1303, 1304
Pharyngoesophageal trauma, 446-447
Pharyngomaxillary space, 1121-1123, 1122f
Pharynx, foreign body in, 870-873
Phencyclidine intoxication, 2413, 2414-2415,
  2414t, 2415f, 2416, 2882b, 2891-2893
  during pregnancy, 2792
  rhabdomyolysis in, 1979
Phenelzine, overdose of, 2365
Phenobarbital
  during pregnancy and lactation, 2787
  for alcohol-related status epilepticus, 2865
  for bupropion-induced seizure, 2361
  for cyclic antidepressant poisoning, 2356
  for seizure, 166t, 167, 1627, 1627t, 1628t
    in children, 2675, 2675t
  for status epilepticus, 2672t, 2673
  overdose of, 2482, 2483
  side effects of, 1628t
Phenol and derivatives
  burn injury from, 935-936
  for wound cleansing, 848t
  ingestion of, 2384
  poisoning from, 936, 2463-2464, 2463b
Phenothiazine
  adjuvant, with opioids, 2921
  anticholinergic toxicity of, 2346b
  cardiotoxicity of, 2445
  during pregnancy and lactation, 2790
  for nausea and vomiting, 203, 208b, 208t
Phenoxybenzamine
  for hypertensive emergencies, 1319
  in frostbite, 2233
Phentolamine
  for cocaine overdose, 2390, 2391
  for hypertension, 1319, 2653

Phentolamine (Continued)
  in cocaine overdose, 2390
  in MAOI toxicity, 2365
Phenylbutazone, overdose of, 2343
Phenylephrine
  for sepsis, 2219t, 2220
  for sinusitis, 1125
  mydriasis from, 1061
Phenylephrinemethoxamine, for junctional
  tachycardia, 1234
Phenylpropanolamine, during pregnancy and
  lactation, 2790
Phenytoin, 1207
  alcohol withdrawal syndrome and, 2865-2866
  drugs affecting levels of, 1207b
  during pregnancy and lactation, 2786
  for alcohol-related status epilepticus, 2865
  for digitalis toxicity, 2371
  for seizure, 166, 166t, 1626-1627, 1627t, 1628t
    in cancer patient, 1919
    in children, 2675, 2675t
  for status epilepticus, 2672t, 2673
  gingival hyperplasia from, 1036
  hyperglycemic hyperosmolar nonketotic coma
    from, 1969
  prophylactic, in head trauma, 361, 370
  side effects of, 1628t
Pheochromocytoma
  anxiety in, 1747
  hypertension in, 1313
Phimosis, in children, 2636
Phlebotomy, for polycythemia, 1885
Phlegmasia cerulea dolens, 1352, 1370
Phlegmonous gastritis, 1390, 1391
Phobia, 1746b, 1749
Phosgene, as chemical weapon, 939, 3032
Phosphate
  for hypophosphatemia, 1952
  imbalance of. See Hyperphosphatemia;
    Hypophosphatemia.
  in diabetic ketoacidosis, 1966
  normal physiology of, 1950-1951
Phosphodiesterase inhibitors
  for beta blocker overdose, 2375
  for calcium channel blocker overdose, 2378
  for chronic heart failure, 1276
Phosphorus. See Phosphate.
Photographic documentation
  in intimate partner violence and abuse, 1001,
    1003
  in sexual assault cases, 989, 989b
Photosensitivity, drug-induced, 1845, 1847t
Phototherapy, for kernicterus prophylaxis, 2603,
  2605f
Phrenic nerve injury, 450
Phthirus pubis infestation, 1569
Physeal injuries, 2690, 2691f, 2691t, 2692, 2692f
Physical abuse
  in pregnancy, 318
  of child, 969-971, 969f, 970f, 970t, 972, 973,
    974-975
  of elder, 1009-1010
  of intimate partner, 995-996, 997. See also
    Intimate partner violence and abuse.
Physical assault
  by combative patient, 2963
  forensic aspects of, 960-963, 961b, 961f-964f
  victim identification in, 960
Physical fitness, as wellness strategy for
  emergency physicians, 3177-3178, 3177b
Physically disabled patient, 2904-2911
  abuse of, 1015
  hearing impairment in, 2904-2905
  multiple sclerosis in, 2909-2911
  pulmonary disorders in, 2907-2908
  spinal cord injury in, 2905-2909
  visual impairment in, 2905
Physician, emergency. See Emergency physician.
Physician staffing, for observation, 3062-3063
Physician-patient relationship
  and racial/ethnic disparities in health
    outcomes, 3109-3110
  pathology of, difficult patient and, 2973,
    2974f
Physiologic jaundice of the newborn, 2601-2603,
  2602t, 2603b, 2603t, 2604f-2605f
Physostigmine, for anticholinergic poisoning,
  2350
Phytobezoar, 873

Phytolacca americana, 2474-2475, 2474f
Phytophotodermatitis, 974-975
Pick's disease, dementia in, 1657, 1659
Picornavirus, 2034t, 2056-2057
Picric acid, 935
Picture Archiving and Communications Systems
  and Imaging Systems, 3101
Piece of pie sign, in lunate dislocation, 630
Piedmont fracture, 551t
Pierre Robin syndrome, neonatal resuscitation in,
  121
Pigment nephropathy, 1536, 1536b
Pigmentation changes
  in Addison's disease, 1997
  in pregnancy, 2723-2724, 2728
Pigmented gallstones, 1418, 2620
Pigmenturia, differential diagnosis in, 1981-1982,
  1981b
Pill esophagitis, 1386, 1387
Pilocarpine, for closed-angle glaucoma, 1056
Pilon fractures, 814-815, 815f
Pilonidal abscess, 2206-2207
Pilonidal disease, 1515
Pimozide, 2446t
Pinch-off syndrome, 1362, 1363
Pindolol, 1321t, 2373t, 2374
Ping-pong fracture, in head-injured child, 368
Pinguecula, 296t, 1053-1054
"Pink puffer," 1099
Pinworm, 1479-1482
  drug therapy for, 2100t
  gastroenteritis in, 1479-1482
  pruritus ani in, 2113-2114
Pipe-stem cirrhosis, in chronic schistosomiasis,
  2112, 2113f
Pirbuterol, for asthma, 2538, 2539t
Pisiform
  anatomy of, 622, 623f, 625
  fracture of, 629
Pit viper envenomation, 896-897, 897f, 898,
  900t
Pittsburgh Knee Rule, 774
Pituitary gland, in pregnancy, 2726
Pityriasis rosea, 1841
Pivot shift test, in knee trauma, 774
Placenta
  abruption of, 319-320, 2747-2748, 2809-2810
  circumvallate, 2810
  delivery of, 2804-2805
  drug transfer across, 2780-2781
  examination of, 2805
  retained, postpartum hemorrhage from, 2819
  surgical removal of, 2819
Placenta accreta, increta, and percreta, 257-258,
  257t, 2819
Placenta previa, 257, 257t, 2748, 2808-2809
Plague, 1131, 3027-3028, 3027f, 3028b
Plant poisoning, 2471-2479
  anticholinergic agents in, 2345, 2346t
  botanical identification in, 2471-2475, 2472f-
    2475f
  epidemiology of, 2471
  herbal medicines and, 2475-2477, 2476t
  mushrooms in, 2477-2479, 2478t
  unintentional childhood exposure in, 2471
Plantar fascial rupture, 836
Plantar fasciitis, 836
Plantaris strain and rupture, 804
Plaque, 1839t
  dental bacterial, 1028
  skin disorders with, 1838-1841
Plasma exchange
  for Goodpasture syndrome, 1816
  for hyperviscosity syndrome, 1913
  for myasthenia gravis, 1707
  for thrombotic thrombocytopenic purpura,
    1898
Plasmids, antibiotic resistance and, 1575
Plasmodium falciparum, 2104. See also Malaria.
Plaster cast, 571-573
Plaster splint, 569
Plastic deformation of forearm, 644, 645f
Platelet(s)
  adhesion defects of, 1898
  aggregation defects of, 1899
  in hemostasis, 1892, 1893b, 1893f
  release defects of, 1898-1899
Platelet count
  in bleeding disorders, 1895

Ranke complex, in tuberculosis, 2152
Ranson's criteria for acute pancreatitis, 1431-1432, 1432b
Rape trauma syndrome, 991-992, 991b
Rapid diagnostic tests, for viral antigens, 1135
Rapid diagnostic treatment unit. See Observation medicine.
Rapid sequence intubation, 9-12, 10b
    in asthma, 16
    in elevated intracranial pressure, 17, 18t
    in head trauma, 358-359
    in neck trauma, 444
    in shock, 51
    indications for, 7-8
    paralysis with induction phase in, 11
    pediatric, 18, 107-108, 107b, 107t
    post-intubation management in, 11-12
    prehospital, 2990, 2991
    preoxygenation in, 10, 10f
    preparations for, 9-10
    pretreatment agents for, 10, 11b
    tube placement in, 11
    vs. blind nasotracheal intubation, 12
    with competitive neuromuscular blocking agent and etomidate, 14-15, 15t
Rapid streptococcal tests, 1111
Rapid tranquilization, 2914b
    for mood disorders, 1741
    for thought disorders, 1730-1731, 1731b
    of combative patient, 2961-2963
Rash. See also Skin lesions.
    drug-induced, 1844, 1847t
    glue sniffer's, 2430
    heat, 2259
    in bacterial meningitis, 2658, 2659
    in Colorado tick fever, 2141
    in dermatomyositis, 1708
    in disseminated gonococcal infection, 1566
    in ehrlichiosis, 2138
    in erythema infectiosum, 1850
    in gonococcal arthritis, 1788
    in halothane-induced hepatitis, 1414
    in Henoch-Schönlein purpura, 1815, 2615, 2615f, 2653
    in herpes zoster, 1859, 1860f
    in Kawasaki disease, 2026, 2594, 2595f
    in Lyme disease, 2122, 2122f
    in measles, 1849, 2053, 2053f
    in Rocky Mountain spotted fever, 1849, 2133-2134, 2133f, 2134f
    in roseola infantum, 1850
    in rubella, 1850
    in scarlet fever, 1851, 1851f
    in smallpox, 2039, 2039f, 3028-3029, 3028f, 3029f
    in syphilis, 1561, 1561f
    in systemic lupus erythematosus, 1806
    in toxic shock syndrome, 1847, 2029, 2200
    oral hypoglycemic agent–induced, 1972
Rat-bite fever, 884
Rattlesnake bite, 896, 2329t
Raynaud's disease, 1347, 1357
Raynaud's phenomenon, 273, 1357
Reactionary anxiety, 1746b
Reactive arthritis, 1789-1790, 1791, 2192
Reactive hypochondriasis, 1756
Reactive oxygen species, in cerebral necrosis, 66
Reanastomosis, end-to-end, in arterial injury, 544
"Reasonable person" standard, 3166
Reassurance, in somatoform disorders, 1757-1758
Rebleeding, in traumatic hyphema, 1048-1049
Rebreathers, in diving, 2280
Recommendations for emergency medicine. See Guidelines for emergency medicine.
Rectal biopsy, in AIDS-related diarrhea, 1484
Rectal bleeding, 1508
    in Meckel's diverticulum, 2613
    with defecation, 1508
Rectal examination, 1573
    in abdominal pain, 213, 215
    in abdominal trauma, 494
    in back pain, 263
    in constipation, 239
    in diarrhea, 233
    in gastrointestinal bleeding, 222
    in genitourinary trauma, 515
    in pelvic fracture, 719
    in sexual assault victim, 988

Rectal pain, 1509
    in anal fissures, 1512-1513
    in appendicitis, 1452
    in hemorrhoids, 1510
    in levator ani syndrome, 1516
Rectal sphincter tone, in head trauma, 357
Rectal tonography, in shock, 50-51
Rectum
    disorders of. See Anorectal disorders.
    foreign bodies in, 875-877, 876f, 1521-1522, 1522f
Recurrent laryngeal nerve, injury to, 450
Red and painful eye, 283-297
    ancillary studies in, 288
    diagnostic approach to, 283-288, 284b, 285b, 287f
    differential diagnosis in, 288-290, 288f-291f
    disposition in, 293t-297t, 297
    empiric management of, 290-292, 293t-297t
    epidemiology of, 283
    history in, 285
    in infants and children, 292
    physical examination in, 285-288, 285b
    traumatic, 283, 290, 292, 297
Red blood cell casts
    in glomerulonephritis, 1534
    in urinary sediment, 1526, 1526f
Red blood cell count
    decreased. See Anemia.
    in alcoholism, 2874
    in hypothermia, 2243
    in pregnancy, 318
    increased, 273, 1884-1885, 1884f, 1885b
    normal values for, 1868t
    peritoneal lavage, 500, 500t
Red blood cell indices, normal values for, 1871t
Red blood cell mass, in thermal burns, 918
Red macules, skin disorders with, 1844-1848
Redistribution hyponatremia, 1933
Red-red tears, meniscal, 792
Reduction
    of dislocation, 565-566
        ankle, 820
        anterior elbow, 666
        carpometacarpal joint, 603
        distal interphalangeal joint, 601
        glenohumeral joint, 688-690, 689f, 690f
        hip, 757-759, 758f-759f
        hip prosthesis, 760
        inferior glenohumeral joint, 693, 694f
        metacarpophalangeal joint, 602-603, 602f
        metatarsophalangeal joint, 835
        patellar, 786
        posterior elbow, 665
        posterior glenohumeral joint, 691-692
        proximal interphalangeal joint, 602
        proximal tibiofibular joint, 803
        sternoclavicular, 684-685, 685f
        subtalar, 826
        temporomandibular joint, 1041-1042, 1041f
        tibial femoral knee, 788-789
    of femoral head fracture-dislocation, 759-760, 760f
    of fracture
        ankle, 812
        Colles', 633, 634f
        displaced supracondylar, 657, 658f
        distal femur, 776-777
        humeral shaft, 654, 654f
        intercondylar, 659-660, 659f
        intercondylar eminence, 780
        metacarpal neck, 597-598, 598f
        metatarsal shaft, 831
        phalangeal, 834
        proximal humeral epiphysis, 683
        supracondylar, 2695, 2696f
        talar, 824
    of radial head subluxation, 666, 666f, 2697-2698
Red-white tears, meniscal, 792
Reentry mechanisms, for dysrhythmias, 1204-1205, 1204f
Refeeding syndrome, hypophosphatemia in, 1951
Referral
    in elder abuse, 1013-1014
    in intimate partner violence and abuse, 1004
    in substance abuse, 2886
Referred pain
    abdominal, 212
    to back, 703, 706

Reflex(es)
    brainstem, in comatose patient, 159t, 160-161
    cremasteric, 1594
        loss of, in testicular torsion, 1595
    deep tendon
        in head trauma, 357
        in spinal injuries, 417, 417t
        pseudomyotonic, in hypothyroidism, 1992
    diving, 2312
    doll's eye, 161, 2503
    in hypothermia, 2241
    in spinal cord disorders, 1679-1680
Reflex airway closure in physically disabled patient, 2907-2908
Reflex sympathetic dystrophy, 562-563
Reflex sympathetic response to laryngoscopy, 16-17
Reflex syncope, 2685
Reflux
    gastroesophageal. See Gastroesophageal reflux.
    vesicoureteral, in urinary tract infection, 1574
Refractory periods of action potential, 1200, 1202f
Refusal of medical care
    by Jehovah's Witnesses, 3171-3172
    federal rules governing, 3170-3171
    for minors, by parent or guardian, 3171
    informed, 3169-3170
    medicolegal issues in, 3169-3172
Regional anesthesia
    in wound care, 845-846
    intravenous, 2934
Regional health information network (RHIN), 3104
Regression models, 3055
Regurgitation
    in achalasia, 1397
    in gastroesophageal reflux, 1388
Rehydralyte, for pediatric infectious diarrhea, 2630, 2630t
Reimplantation
    in hand trauma, 613, 613b
    of avulsed tooth, 1038f, 1040
    penile, 533
Reiter syndrome, arthritis in, 1789-1790
Rejection
    in heart transplant patient, 2852-2853, 2853f
    in kidney transplant patient, 2855
    in liver transplant patient, 2854
    in lung transplant patient, 2855-2856
    opportunistic infections associated with, 2848-2849, 2849f
    phases of, 2849
Relapsing fever, 2129-2130
Relative afferent pupillary defect (RAPD), in red and painful eye, 286
Relative refractory period, 1200, 1202f
Relative risk, 3059t
Relaxation, as wellness strategy for emergency physicians, 3178
Relevance of study, 3059, 3059t
Reliability, 3059, 3059t
Religious values, 3129-3130, 3130b
Remifentanil, 2922t, 2923
Renal artery
    aneurysm of, urolithiasis vs., 1591
    fibromuscular dysplasia of, hypertension in, 1311-1312
    stenosis of, hypertension in, 1312
    trauma to, 529, 530
Renal blood flow, in hypothermia, 2239
Renal cell carcinoma, urolithiasis vs., 1590
Renal colic, 1586-1593, 1586b, 1589f-1592f, 1593b, 2645-2646. See also Urolithiasis.
Renal compensation
    in acid-base disorders, 1923-1924
    in metabolic acidosis, 1923-1924
    in metabolic alkalosis, 1924
Renal dialysis. See Dialysis.
Renal disorders
    diagnosis of, 1525-1528, 1527t, 1528b
    hypermagnesemia in, 1949
    hypomagnesemia in, 1947-1948
    in acetaminophen poisoning, 2333
    in acute tumor lysis syndrome, 1911
    in diabetes mellitus, 1970
    in ethylene glycol poisoning, 2398, 2399
    in heatstroke, 2262
    in HIV/AIDS, 2086

Skin lesions *(Continued)*
  in syphilis, 1855-1856, 1855f
  in systemic lupus erythematosus, 1806, 1862t,
    1863f
  in toxic epidermal necrolysis, 1845-1846, 1846f
  in toxic shock syndrome, 1846-1847
  in ulcerative colitis, 1862t
  in urticaria, 1847-1848, 1848f
  in varicella, 1858-1859, 1859f
  malignant diseases associated with, 1862-1864
  nodular, 1856-1857
  papular, 1851-1856
  systemic diseases associated with, 1860, 1861f,
    1862t, 1863f
  vesicular, 1857-1860
Skin rash. *See also* Skin lesions.
  drug-induced, 1844, 1847t
  glue sniffer's, 2430
  heat, 2259
  in bacterial meningitis, 2658, 2659
  in Colorado tick fever, 2141
  in dermatomyositis, 1708
  in disseminated gonococcal infection, 1566
  in ehrlichiosis, 2138
  in erythema infectiosum, 1850
  in gonococcal arthritis, 1788
  in halothane-induced hepatitis, 1414
  in Henoch-Schönlein purpura, 1815, 2615,
    2615f, 2653
  in herpes zoster, 1859, 1860f
  in Kawasaki disease, 2026, 2594, 2595f
  in Lyme disease, 2122, 2122f
  in measles, 1849, 2053, 2053f
  in Rocky Mountain spotted fever, 1849, 2133-
    2134, 2133f, 2134f
  in roseola infantum, 1850
  in rubella, 1850
  in scarlet fever, 1851, 1851f
  in smallpox, 2039, 2039f, 3028-3029, 3028f,
    3029f
  in syphilis, 1561, 1561f
  in systemic lupus erythematosus, 1806
  in toxic shock syndrome, 1847, 2029, 2200
  oral hypoglycemic agent–induced, 1972
Skin tension lines, 843, 843f, 844f
Skinfold asymmetry, in developmental hip
    dysplasia, 2701
Skull
  anatomy of, 350
  fetal, 2800f
  radiography of
    in minor head trauma, 364-365
    in pediatric head trauma, 336, 368
    in severe head trauma, 362, 362t
    in skull fracture, 372
Skull fracture, 372-374
  basilar, 373
  clinical assessment and significance of, 372
  depressed, 373
  frontal, 393
  in children, 334-335, 2699
  linear, 372-373
  open, 373-374
Skull-base osteomyelitis, 1071
Skullcap, adverse effects of, 2476t
Skunk, rabies in, 2062, 2062f, 2063, 2063f, 2064
Sleep aids, OTC, overdose of, 2487-2488, 2488t
Sleep apnea, hypertension in, 1313
Sleep deprivation, from shift work, performance
    and, 3123, 3123b
Sleep disturbance
  in acute mountain sickness, 2301, 2302
  in depression, 1737
  seizures vs., 2668
Sleep talking, 2668
Sleeping, prone, sudden infant death syndrome
    and, 2715
Sleep-wake disturbances, in delirium, 1649
Sleepwalking, 2668
Sling and swathe, 569, 677, 678f
Sling immobilization
  in clavicle fracture, 677, 678f
  in scapula fracture, 680
Slipped capital femoral epiphysis, 765-767, 765f,
    766f, 2707-2709, 2708f
Slit ventricle syndrome, in developmentally
    disabled patient, 2899
Slit-lamp examination
  in corneal trauma, 1047, 1047f, 1051, 1051f

Slit-lamp examination *(Continued)*
  in red and painful eye, 287, 287f
  in traumatic hyphema, 1048, 1048f
  of ocular foreign body, 860
Slow virus infections, 1657-1658, 1659, 2058
SLUDGE mnemonic, 2328, 2459, 2459b
Small intestine
  biopsy of, in AIDS-related diarrhea, 1484
  disorders of, 1440-1449
  ischemia of, 1444-1449. *See also* Mesenteric
    ischemia.
  motility disorders of, 1440, 1441b, 1443
  obstruction of, 1440-1444, 1441b, 1443f
    adynamic ileus in, 1440, 1441b, 1443
    causes of, 1441-1442, 1441b, 1500b
    clinical features of, 1442
    complications of, 1442
    diagnosis of, 1442-1443, 1443f
    differential diagnosis in, 1443-1444
    in malrotation with midgut volvulus, 2607,
      2607f, 2608f
    management of, 1444
    mechanical vs. neurogenic, 1440
    pseudoobstruction and, 1440
  trauma to, 489, 490
  volvulus of, 1441
Smallpox, 2034t, 2039-2040, 2039f, 3028-3029,
    3028f, 3029f
  skin lesions in, 1860, 1860t, 1861f
  vaccine for, 2035t, 3029
Smith's fracture, 551t, 633-635, 635f
Smoke inhalation, 2435-2436
  airway management and respiratory care in,
    921-922
  carbon monoxide with cyanide poisoning in,
    2440-2441
  prehospital care in, 921
Smoking
  Buerger's disease and, 1351, 1352
  chronic obstructive pulmonary disease and,
    1098
Snakebite, 895-903, 897f, 897t, 900t, 1979
Sniffing position, in pediatric resuscitation, 105,
    106f
Snowbird technique for reduction of anterior
    glenohumeral joint dislocation, 689
Snowblower injuries, 609
Soap, for rabies postexposure prophylaxis, 2068
Social phobia, 1746b, 1749
Social problems, in alcoholism, 2879-2880
Social relationships, promotion of, as wellness
    strategy for emergency physicians, 3177
Social/adaptive milestones, 2495-2497, 2496t
Societal factors, in suicide, 1767-1768
Societal values, 3129, 3129b
Soda lime dust particles, in scuba diving–related
    disorders, 2283
Sodium
  dietary excess of, heart failure from, 1268
  fractional excretion of, 1527-1528, 1527t,
    1528b
  imbalance of. *See* Hypernatremia;
    Hyponatremia.
  normal physiology of, 1933
  serum
    in bacterial meningitis, 2662
    in diabetic ketoacidosis, 1964, 1964t
  skin injury from, 937
  urine, 1527-1528, 1527t, 1528b, 1934
Sodium bicarbonate
  for acute renal failure, 2650
  for cardiac arrest, 93
  for cyanide poisoning, 2437
  for cyclic antidepressant poisoning, 2355,
    2356
  for diabetic ketoacidosis, 1966-1967
  for hyperkalemia, 1941
    in acute renal failure, 1539
    in chronic renal failure, 1545, 1545t
  for hyperuricemia, 1914
  for metabolic acidosis, 1929-1930
  for pediatric asystole, 111-112
  for pediatric bradycardia, 111
  for pediatric resuscitation, 100, 101t
  for QRS prolongation in OTC sleep aid
    overdose, 2488
  for rhabdomyolysis, 1982
  for salicylate overdose, 2342
  for sepsis, 2219t, 2220

Sodium bicarbonate *(Continued)*
  for toxicant-induced metabolic acidosis, 2400-
    2401
  for ventricular fibrillation and pulseless
    ventricular tachycardia, 84
  for white phosphorus burn, 936
  topical anesthetic with, 846
Sodium channel antagonists, after cerebral
    ischemia, 71
Sodium chloride
  for hyponatremia, 1935
  hypertonic, in cyclic antidepressant poisoning,
    2356-2357
  in hydrotherapy for acid and alkali burns, 933
Sodium hydroxide, ingestion of, 2380, 2381,
    2381t
Sodium nitrite, for cyanide poisoning, 939,
    2438
Sodium phosphate
  for hypercalcemia, 1915
  for hypophosphatemia, 1952
Sodium thiosulfate
  for cyanide poisoning, 2438
  for simultaneous carbon monoxide and
    cyanide poisoning, 2440
Sodium-calcium exchanger, 1199-1200, 1200f
Sodium-potassium pump, 1200, 1200f, 1976,
    1977f
Soft tissue examination, in spinal cord injury,
    311
Soft tissue infection, 2195-2209
  clinical characteristics of, 2195-2196, 2196t
  in abscess, 2202-2207. *See also* Abscess.
  in cellulitis, 2196-2199, 2196t, 2197t
  in impetigo, 2201-2202
  in myonecrosis, 2196t, 2208-2209
  in necrotizing fasciitis, 2196t, 2207-2208
  in toxic shock syndrome, 2199-2201, 2200b,
    2201b
  superficial, antibiotics for, 2197, 2197t
Soft tissue injuries, 566-568. *See also specific
    types, e.g.,* Sprain.
  foreign body in, 878-879
  from dentoalveolar trauma, 1040
  in ankle trauma, 815-820
  in elbow and humeral trauma, 667-668
  in elderly person, 347
  in eye, 1054-1055, 1055f
  in facial trauma, 390-392
  in hand, 600
  in hip trauma, 761-763
  in lower leg trauma, 804-805
  in pelvic fracture, 719
  in shoulder, 693-699
  in wrist trauma, 639, 639f
  wound management in, 842-857
Solar urticaria, 1848
Solid-organ transplant patient. *See* Organ
    transplant patient.
Solvents, inhaled, 2428-2432, 2430f, 2886-2889,
    2887t, 2888f, 2889b
Soman, 2461, 3030-3031, 3030b, 3031b
Somatic pain, 211-212
Somatization, 1753
Somatization disorder, 1754-1755, 1754b
Somatoform disorders, 1753-1759
  clinical features of, 1753-1756, 1754b, 1755b
  diagnosis of, 1756
  differential considerations in, 1756-1757,
    1757b
  disposition in, 1759
  management of, 1757-1759
  panic attack in, 1748
  undifferentiated, 1755
Somatoform pain disorder, 1755
Somatostatin analogues, for gastrointestinal
    bleeding, 225
Somogyi phenomenon, in hypoglycemia, 1960
Sore throat. *See* Pharyngitis.
Sotalol, 1210, 2373t
Space infections of head and neck, 1027, 1028-
    1029, 1030f, 1032, 1116-1117, 1116f
  parapharyngeal, 1121-1123, 1122f
  peritonsillar, 1117-1118, 1118f
  retropharyngeal, 1120-1121, 1120f, 1121f
  submandibular, 1028, 1032, 1118-1119
Space of Poirier, 622, 624f
Spasmodic croup, 2527
Spastic paraparesis, idiopathic, 1683

Talonavicular dislocation, 825-826, 825f
Talus
 anatomy of, 808, 809f, 810f
 dislocation of, 820, 826
 fracture of, 822-824, 823f, 824f
Tamarind, drug interactions with, 2478t
Tanapox viruses, 2040
Tangential wounds, to head, 369
Tap water irrigation, for wound cleansing, 848
Tape, wound closure, 853
Tape measurement system, in pediatric
 resuscitation, 114, 114f-115f
Tapeworm infection
 anemia in, 2107
 drug therapy for, 2102t
Tar burns, 926-927, 937
Tarasoff v Regents of California, 2967-2968
Tardieu's spots, in near-hanging and
 strangulation, 451
Tardive dyskinesia, antipsychotic-induced, 1732,
 2445, 2447
Tarsal tunnel syndrome, 836-837
Tarsometatarsal joint
 anatomy of, 820, 820f
 fractures and dislocations of, 551t, 828-831,
 829f, 830f
Taser gun injuries, 2274
Taste alterations, in scombroid fish poisoning,
 1472
Tattooing
 in facial trauma, 390
 in intermediate-range handgun wounds, 956-
 957, 956f
Taxus, 2475, 2475f
Teardrop fracture, 551t
 extension, 410-411
 flexion, 401, 403f
Teardrop sign, in orbital wall fracture, 1044,
 1045f
Tears, artificial, 1063b, 1064
Technetium-99m–labeled bone scan, in
 osteomyelitis, 2180-2181, 2180f, 2181f
Teeth. *See* Tooth (teeth).
Telemedicine, 3105-3106
Telmisartan, 1322t
Temazepam, 2484, 2484t
 for sleep disturbances in demented patient,
 1662
Temperature
 altered perceptions of, in ciguatera fish
 poisoning, 1473
 body. *See* Body temperature.
 duration of exposure to, burn injury and, 915-
 916, 916f
 of material, burn injury and, 915, 915t
Temporal arteritis, 1813
 headache in, 174t
 risk factors for, 171b
 visual loss in, 1060
Temporal lobe epilepsy, 148t, 1621
Temporomandibular joint
 anatomy of, 1026, 1027f
 dislocation of, 396, 1041-1042, 1041f
 in scuba diving–related disorders, 2283
 trauma to, 395-396
Temporomandibular myofascial pain dysfunction
 syndrome, 1034-1035
Tendinitis/tendinopathy, 567-568, 1794-1801
 Achilles, 1799-1800
 bicipital, 1797
 calcific, 568, 698, 1797-1798
 common sites for, 1796f
 diagnosis of, 1800-1801
 disposition in, 1801
 history in, 1795
 management of, 1801
 of ankle, 818-820, 819f, 1799-1800
 of elbow, 1798-1799
 of foot, 838
 of hand, 604-609, 605f-607f
 of hip, 761-762
 of knee, 794, 795, 1799
 of shoulder, 1796-1798
 of wrist, 1799
 patellar, 1799
 physical examination in, 1795-1796
 rotator cuff, 1796-1797
Tenecteplase, with enoxaparin, in myocardial
 infarction, 1194-1195

Tenesmus
 in inflammatory bowel disease, 1501
 in intestinal amebiasis, 1480
 in radiation proctocolitis, 1505
Tennis elbow. *See* Epicondylitis.
Tenosynovitis
 bicipital, 697, 697f
 De Quervain's, 1799
 flexor, 616-617
 in gonococcal arthritis, 1788, 2191
 stenosing, in hand, 618
Tensilon test, in myasthenia gravis, 1705
Tension headache, 1635, 2679
Tension pneumomediastinum, 459
Tension pneumopericardium, 1288
Tension pneumothorax, 339, 462, 462f, 463f,
 464
Tenting, in dehydrated infant, 2629
Teratogen, 2779-2780, 2780b
Terazosin, 1321t
Terbinafine, for tinea capitis, 1839
Terbutaline
 for asthma, 1088, 2539t, 2541
 for premature labor, 2806-2807, 2806b
Teres minor muscle, 672, 673f
Terminal illness
 suicide in, 1770
 trajectory of dying in, 3140, 3140f
Terrorism
 role of informatics in, 3105
 weapons used in, 3021-3032. *See also*
 Weapons of mass destruction.
Terry Thomas sign, in scapholunate dissociation,
 630
Testicular appendage, torsion of, 1597, 2641
Testing requests and requirements, medicolegal
 issues in, 3158-3160
Testis
 anatomy of, 1594, 1594f
 cancer of, 1597
 in children, 2642
 superior vena cava syndrome in, 1909
 physical examination of, 1573, 1594
 torsion of, 1594-1595, 2639-2640, 2640f
 trauma to, 534-535, 535f
 tumor of, 1597
Tetanospasmin neurotoxin, 2009
Tetanus, 2007-2012, 2008f, 2010b, 2012t, 2013t
 cephalic, 2009, 2010
 neonatal, 2009
 prophylaxis against
 in burn injury, 925-926
 in human bites, 891, 891t
 in wound management, 856-857, 857b, 2012,
 2013t
Tetany, hyperventilation, heat cramps vs., 2258
Tetracaine, 846, 2931, 2931t, 2933
Tetracycline
 during pregnancy and lactation, 2784
 for ehrlichiosis, 2138
 for epididymitis, 1597t, 2639
 for Lyme disease–related myocarditis, 1292
 for periodontal abscess, 1033
 for reactive arthritis, 1790
 for relapsing fever, 2129-2130
 for Rocky Mountain spotted fever, 1850
 for syphilis, 1856
Tetrahydrocannabinol (THC), 2411
Tetralogy of Fallot, 2573, 2574f, 2579-2581,
 2579f, 2580f, 2581b
Text teletype writer (TTY), 2905
Thalassemia, 1872-1873, 1872f
Thallium ingestion, radiogardase for, 3023,
 3023t
Thenar mass or eminence, 576, 577f
Thenar muscles, 580, 581f
Thenar space infection, 617, 618
Theophylline
 during pregnancy and lactation, 2789
 for asthma, 1090, 1090t, 2542, 2543t
 for postdural puncture headache, 1641
 serum, in asthma, 1085
 sudden infant death syndrome and, 2719-2720
Thermal burn, 913-928
 airway management and respiratory care in,
 921-923
 anatomy of skin and, 914-915
 burn shock and, 918
 burn wound assessment in, 919-920, 920f

Thermal burn *(Continued)*
 burn wound care in, 924-927, 925f
 catheterization of patient in, 923
 depth of burn injury in, 918-919, 919f
 disposition in, 927, 927b
 epidemiology of, 913-914, 914f
 fluid resuscitation in, 921, 922-923
 gastrointestinal disorders in, 924
 in child abuse, 969-970, 970f, 970t
 in lightning injury, 2273
 in physical assault, 963, 964f
 metabolic response to therapy in, 919
 ocular, 1046
 pain management in, 924
 patient categorization in, 920
 pediatric considerations in, 923
 physiologic changes in, 917-918
 prehospital care in, 921
 thermodynamics of burn injury in, 915-917,
 915f, 916f, 917t
 transportation of patient in, 923-924
 white phosphorus in, 936
 zones of tissue injury in, 917, 917f
Thermal therapy, for fracture, 573-574
Thermogenesis
 decreased, hypothermia and, 2239-2240, 2240b
 increased, heat illness and, 2257
 nonshivering, in burned infant, 923
 physiology of, 2254-2255
 shivering, 2236, 2247
Thermometry
 in heatstroke, 2263
 pediatric, 2508
Thermoregulation
 hypothalamus in, 134
 impaired, hypothermia and, 2240-2241, 2240b
 mechanisms of, 2255-2256
 physiology of
 in cold exposure, 2228, 2236-2237, 2237f
 in heat exposure, 2254-2256
Thermosensors, 2255
Thiamine
 deficiency of
 in alcoholic hepatitis, 1409
 optic neuropathy from, 1060
 for alcohol intoxication, 2860
 for alcohol withdrawal syndrome, 2861, 2863
 for benzodiazepine overdose, 2326
 for toxic alcohol poisoning, 2402
 for Wernicke-Korsakoff syndrome, 2869
Thiazide diuretics
 during pregnancy and lactation, 2788
 hypercalcemia from, 1945
Thiazolidinediones, 1973
Thienopyridines, in acute coronary syndromes,
 1186-1187
Thigh
 compartments of, 737, 737t, 738f
 pain in, atraumatic, 756b
Thioamides, for thyroid storm, 1989
Thiopental
 as induction agent, 15-16
 for procedural sedation and analgesia, in
 children, 2953
Thioridazine, toxicity of, 2445, 2446t
Thiothixene, 2446t
Third stage of labor, 2804-2805
Third trimester
 complications in, 2805-2810
 fetal ultrasonography in, 2802, 2802b, 2802t
Third-degree atrioventricular block, 1220-1221,
 1221f
Third-degree burn, 919, 919f
Third-nerve palsy
 anisocoria in, 1061
 eye movement disorders in, 1062
Thompson test, in Achilles tendon rupture, 818
Thoracentesis, in pleural effusion, 1151-1152
Thoracic aorta
 aneurysm of
 chronic, 482
 superior vena cava syndrome in, 1909
 injury to, in pelvic fracture, 720
 rupture of, 476-482, 477f-479f, 481b
Thoracic duct, injury to, in neck trauma, 450
Thoracic endometriosis syndrome, 1144
Thoracic examination, in multiple trauma, 309
Thoracic lavage, for rewarming in accidental
 hypothermia, 2250

c